About the editors

David Moore - Has over twenty years experience as a wine consultant, wine buyer, writer and editorial director which has provided him with the background to co-author and edit a wine guide of such breadth and scope.

During this period he has travelled widely and been exposed to hands-on wine-making and was one of three principal judges for the New York Times "Wine Today Europe" site of the early 2000s.

Today he focuses his research on his own areas of expertise. He travels extensively to both France and Spain, taking in visits to all the major fairs and exhibitions. Visiting winemakers in their cellars though remains a cornerstone of the work on Wine behind the label. As well as extensive visits in Europe, David visits the West Coast of the United States in most years. The vast majority of the most exciting hand-made wines Stateside can only be tasted in this way. As a part of this he has been invited to key local fairs and tastings.

Neville Blech - The purchase of a run-down pub in Wales as a second home in 1971 enabled him and his wife Sonia to commercialise her abilities as an accomplished amateur cook. The pub was converted into a smart *restaurant avec chambres*, and opened in 1974, and in 1976, Sonia became the first woman chef in the UK to obtain a Michelin star.

Returning to London to open the Mijanou restaurant in 1980, which became one of the fashionable restaurants of the decade, the innovative wine list resulted in many awards, and soon he was being asked to write a wine column for a magazine called "Restaurant Business" and to help other restaurateurs with the composition of their wine lists, a function he still carries out today. In 1989, he started his own wine importing company, The Wine Treasury, which specialises in wines from California, being one of the first in the UK to realise the quality potential of Californian wines.

He continued to write occasional articles for various wine publications and broadcasted on wine for Jazz FM in London before selling The Wine Treasury and becoming co-editor of *Wine behind the label*. He has been a member of the *Grand Jury Européen* wine tasting panel and served on tasting panels for *Decanter* and other leading wine publications He is currently a member of the Circle of Wine Writers and FIJEV (*Fédération Internationale des Journalistes et Écrivans du Vin.*)

Wine behind the label

The ultimate guide to the world's leading wine producers and their wines

10th edition

Edited by David Moore and Neville Blech

'An incredibly in-depth and addictively readable survey of wines of quality from around the world
with intelligent tasting notes and informative background to the producers, plus stockists and
UK prices. For me, by far the best of the wine guides'
Steven Spurrier, Decanter Magazine

'I'm a fan.'
Hugh Johnson

'This is Robert Parker territory but succinct and cheaper'
Joanna Simon, Sunday Times

'With its championing of authenticity of origin, gifted winemakers, smaller producers, organic and biodynamicwinemaking, as
well as its wealth of detail, this could well become the annual guide by which all others are judged.'
Fine Wine Magazine

'... a guide that's immediately established itself as more or less indispensable.'
Peter McCombie MW, Restaurant Magazine

I heartily recommend this book as a thorough independent overview
of the world's best wine estates'
Tom Cannavan, wine-pages.com

'As essential to the sommelier as their corkscrew'
Paul Dwyer, BBC Radio 5 Live and BBC Radio Scotland

'If you are passionate about your wine and pay serious attention to sampling the world's finest bottles
then this book should be on your shelf... I would strongly recommend this excellent guide'
Dr Edward Fitzgerald, Oxford University Wine Society

'...a tremendously useful and comprehensive reference work...(it) is
bang up to date. Any wine nut will have a lot of fun with this book'
Jamie Goode, wineanorak.com

Wine Behind The Label Ltd
www.winebehindthelabel.org

First published in 2003
This 10th edition published in 2016
Published by Wine Behind The Label Ltd
57 Pelham St, London SW7 2NJ
Tel +44 (0)207 589 6722
E-mail: info@winebehindthelabel.com

Contributors
Jim Budd, Michael Edwards, Professor Kathleen Burk, Gary White, Ilona Thompson, Sarah Ahmed, Stuart George, & Maggie Rosen

A catalogue record for this book is available from the British Library

ISBN: 978-1-910891-13-1

Designed by Davis Wadicci

Printed by Lightning Source UK & USA

Wine behind the label

Contents

Wine behind the label

Introduction

Our concept

Wine behind the label was first conceived as an ambitious attempt to produce an authoritative single volume guide to producers of quality wines from around the world. We believe we are succeeding in what we set out to achieve but will always view it as a work in progress, continuing to respond to an ever expanding quality spectrum as well as looking for better ways to present our findings. We remain committed to providing both depth and criticism about quality wines whatever their provenance and from as many quality wine producers as possible. It is a guide for enthusiasts or would-be enthusiasts, not for those who can't detect any differences or don't care to, yet it is a reference that is accessible to the novice and learned alike. The 10th edition sees a further significant expansion in our reach, uncovering many more producers - both from the classic regions but also reflecting the quality being obtained in places that don't make the headlines. As ever, it is still far from exhaustive but hopefully there's plenty to sustain your interest.. For those new to Wine behind the label we have repeated below what you can expect to find as well as some of our thoughts about wine and winemaking.

Behind the label

The industrial mentality which has given us brilliant cars and computers doesn't have a place in high quality wine (or food) production. An essential difference between a high production brand and one produced on a more human scale is the personal effort and commitment that the family or individuals who make it have put into it. We therefore highlight individuality and character over more boring standardized production. We also attempt to bring the producer a little closer to whoever is drinking their wine so that some inkling of their philosophy and effort might enrich the enjoyment the wine brings. We lend our support particularly to small producers and talented winemakers, and wherever we see honesty and integrity but every quality wine is considered on its merits. A small producer, no matter how earnest or sincere, will not make good wine if he or she doesn't manage the vineyards well and employ sound winemaking practice. Equally, spending exorbitant sums on PR and marketing doesn't always mean the wine in the bottle is poor – though it is likely given the money spent that it could be better value.

Winemaking and a wine's origins

We've tried to provide information about where quality and character come from - the most relevant aspects of winemaking, viticulture and vineyard site that contribute to what's in your glass. There is also information on the extent of a wine's manipulation such as fining or filtration, and whether organic or biodynamic principles are employed. In recent years we have witnessed the increasing acceptance of the importance of *terroir* in tandem with a continued trend to more vineyard specific wine production. Where great wine is a combination of several small parcels it is our hope that more producers will provide details of the individual plots that contribute to the wine's character. In some cases, celebrated labels are now no longer based on the top vineyard sites that brought early acclaim (whether a Bordeaux classed growth or elsewhere in Europe or the new world). We are also keeping tabs on some of the most famous names where the pursuit of profit, lacklustre direction or a change of ownership may have compromised quality. On the other hand we point out where a new, often more highly-trained, generation has made a positive impact or where outside investment has resulted in a new lease of life.

Really useful stuff

This guide does contain a lot of information about producers and their wines. In this edition well over 3,700 producers are covered in depth. Furthermore over 19,000 wines are rated and price coded. While some of world's finest wines can be hard to get hold of in many instances there is a first point of contact that will sell direct by mail-order or over the Internet. In addtion there are a number of features that will help you find the information you want more quickly. The lists of producers by appellation or region (at the end of most section introduction's) is an excellent way to find or familiarize yourself with producers from a favourite area. Where possible there are also single page map inserts for quick reference to less well-known regions or appellations. For the many readers who only have time to dip in and out of the book we would encourage you to use the 'Author's Choice' lists at the end of each section. These contain at least one wine from most of a region's best producers and make a useful alternative starting point to discovering new wines. In particular the 'Value for money' lists highlight some of the best buys. Given that exciting new producers are emerging all the time we have included a 'Work in progress' list covering those we will be assessing in future editions.

Tasting, ratings and assessing producers

Our Quality Rating (see How to Use this guide) is intended to give a truer assessment of wine quality than a vintage dependent point score. It is nearly always based on scores from a minimum of two recent vintages. Wine shows and competitions encourage the production of wines of flattering first impressions but don't always reward those that show at their best with age. Nor do they address the implications of the vintage characteristics. Rather than a snapshot, consensual tasting mentality we believe in tasting wines again and again (both blind and non-blind) in order to gain a better understanding of a wine's style and when it should be drunk. A rating combined with an understanding of the style is the key to discovering the best wines, and that means those you will most enjoy. Before choosing a bottle for immediate consumption always ask yourself which wine works best now, reflects my mood, personality, or that of my friends or family? What flavours do I want? How much flavour? By buying wine for cellaring it will be possible to contrast different vintages of the same wine. Alternatively from a case of the same wine the gradual development and increasing maturity of a specific vintage can be assessed over a decade or more.

Conclusion

Think of this book as a catalogue to a vast array of vinous riches. Choose with the certainty of trying wines of dependable quality that our labours and experience provide through our rating system. If you haven't tasted Austrian Grüner Veltliner or Californian Syrah then try a three star example from at least two or three profiled producers. Buy the best new reds from Languedoc-Roussillon, Southern Italy, Spain or Portugal. In the past ten years Germany has made better Riesling than ever before but contrast these with those from Alsace, Austria or Australia. Discover a wealth of fine Pinot Noir from Central Otago, Victoria & Tasmania or North America. Alternatively seek out new names from the classic regions such as Burgundy, Bordeaux or the Rhône, Tuscany or Piedmont, Napa or South Australia. Most of all we implore you to sample more widely.

Wine behind the label

Winemaker awards for the 10th edition

For the 10th edition we would like to recognise some winemakers whose light has been hidden under a bushel to a greater or lesser extent. These are highly talented winemakers who have consistently been able to produce 5 and sometimes, super 5 star wines over the years, but have never, or rarely made the headlines and whose undoubted skills deserve to be better rewarded.

This list is far from comprehensive and there will surely be more to feature in future editions of the guide but these are producers of wines who have never failed to deliver and have given us such pleasurable experiences since the last edition of the guide has been published, that we felt a round of applause is appropriate as they are still consistently delivering!

In no particular order:

Jean-Paul Daumen
Dom. de la Vieille-Julienne
Châteauneuf-du-Pape
André Perret
Saint-Joseph
Wayne Dutschke
Barossa Valley
Michel Théron
Clos du Jaugueyron
Margaux & Haut-Médoc
Cristina Geminiani
Fattorina Zerbina
Romagna
Francis Egly-Ouriet
Champagne
Mark Angeli
Ferme de la Sansonnière,
Anjou
Roberto Voerzio
Barolo
Andrea Franchetti
Tenuta di Trinoro and Passopiscerio,
Tuscany & Sicily
Daniel Landi
Méntrida & Vinos de Madrid
Sandra Tavares da Silva
Wine and Soul & Quinta de Chocapalha,
Lisboa & Douro
Elias Fernandez
Shafer Vineyards
Napa Valley
Denis Bachelet
Gevrey-Chambertin
Jean-Vincent Ridon
Signal Hill Winery,
Cape Town
Stephen Hansel
Walter Hansel
Russian River Valley
Matt Trevisan
Linne Calodo
Paso Robles

Stellar Cellars 10th edition

As well as the award winning winemakers of this edition, there are many producers that stand out for the quality of their current releases. We have opted with this edition to amend our approach with many more producers awarded with rosettes to reflect the quality of their work. These are our choices of cellars that continue to produce compelling releases within their regions. From large or diverse areas we have chosen names offering contrasting styles or interpretations. Some are well-established stars, but there may be others challenging the established order or injecting new life into a region.

All Stellar Cellar award winners in this edition are evidenced by a single rosette symbol preceding their entry in the guide. These include producers who received a Stellar Cellar award in previous editions. Producers, who in our opinion, have been continuing to maintain exceptional standards or provide a regional benchmark over a number of years are evidenced by two rosettes. All make wines that should be tried at least once.

◉◉   Producers flagged up in the guide with two rosettes have been selected as a Stellar Cellar and have also been consistently exceptional performers in their regions

◉   Producers flagged up in the guide with a single rosette have been selected as a Stellar Cellar for the 10th edition and a number have been awarded in earlier editions also

Wine behind the label

How to use this guide

How to use

The major part of this guide is split into regional or country sections. Within each one you will find an Introduction including, where possible, Vintage information. This is followed by a list of the producers (by region or appellation) that have been profiled within the A-Z that makes up the bulk of the section. At the end of the A-Z of producers, other quality wines tasted from the region are included in Other wines of note. The wines listed here are only those of sufficient quality that have been tasted - in some instances other good wines from the same producer exist. Work in Progress includes (often new) estates or producers that we will be assessing for the next edition. At the very end of each section under Author's choice we have added lists of wines that are a personal selection but are also often themed by a shared style or grape variety and so should aid navigation. For Individual A-Z entries see the sample entry that follows. The use of CAPS (eg Louis JADOT) indicates the existence of a cross-referenced entry that can be found from the Index.

Vintage Charts

In those sections where vintages have the greatest significance, Vintage Charts are also provided (as is text on individual years for the classic wines of Bordeaux, Burgundy, the Rhône Valley, Piedmont, Tuscany and Port). Specific styles of wine are given an overall vintage rating between one and five stars for individual years. In some instances it is not possible to provide a balanced judgement on the vintage until nearer the wines' release (with Brunello di Montalcino for example). These have been designated NYR (not yet rated). When to drink the wines of a given vintage is a largely subjective, personal judgement and can depend as much on mood or context but the letter (A-D) following the ratings gives a general indication of their likely development:

A - wines to Anticipate, not ready for drinking
B - wines that can be Broached, but with much more to give
C - wines to Consume, at or near their best
D - wines likely to be in Decline, past their best

A-Z Order & new profiles

The order of the A-Z entries is based on the name they are most commonly referred to and they appear as they are written but with priority to surnames. 'Domaine' is ignored but 'Château', 'Castello', 'Quinta' etc are respected as is the definite article when implicitly part of the name (eg Il Poggione appears under 'I'). The only exception to these principles is in Bordeaux where the name of the château or estate takes precedent.

Where a profile is preceded by this symbol >> this indicates a new profile for the 10th edition, for example:

>> Morlet Family Vineyards (St Helena)

Visiting & Ownership

For details of visiting and ownership we have provided a comprehensive free download on our website. In this we have listed in most entries telephone and fax numbers for those readers who wish to visit producers. It is always advisable to call ahead because in many cases appointments need to be booked. It is also worth noting that many small producers are not open to visitors. Ownership is also given in the download and wherever this appears in **bold** it refers to a corporate owner rather than an individual or individuals. These corporate owners have a number of profiles that

may be crossed referenced throughout the guide. For example LVMH (LVMH Moët Hennessy · Louis Vuitton S.A.) are owners of a number of prestige wine brands including **Moët & Chandon, Veuve Cliquot, Krug** and others. Corporate owners who only appear once in the guide are not in bold. Obviously contact with a corporate owner shouldn't be assumed to be possible via the winery's address that follows it. Where the winery has a website this is included in the profile. Please visit www.winebehindthelabel.org to get the visiting and ownership details.

Ratings

★ a wine of good quality, not just sound but of good fruit and with some character.

★★ a wine with more depth, interest and concentration, usually with some aging potential

★★★ a very good, even fine, wine. In the case of many reds repaying lengthy cellaring.

★★★★ a wine of very high quality, among the very best even in a top appellation or region.

★★★★★ outstanding quality, potentially a classic.

OOOOO super 5 stars, restricted to the true classics, out-and-out world class.

☆ white stars are used to show a superior wine at a given rating

We have rated as many of a producer's wines as possible, but in some instances the wines are too new or too scarce to have yet received a rating. Such wines are covered in the text only.

Tasting notes, scores and winery database

It is not in the style of this guide to provide tasting notes for individual vintages along with their scores. However we will be featuring specific wines in our website blogs and in our new members subscription section. We have also developed a fully interactive winery and wine database which is included in the members area. (also see 'Tasting, Ratings, and assessing producers' in the Introduction)

Prices

A code is provided which represents an estimated retail price bracket and it is based on the standard 75cl bottle size. Price codes for those wines produced only in 1.5 litre (magnums), 50 cl (half litre) or 37.5 cl (half bottle) formats have been given 75cl equivalents. A half bottle costing £12.00/$15.00 for instance will have a price code of £D.

£A: less than £8 ($10)	£E: £25 - 35 ($32-$45)
£B: £8 - 12 ($10-$15)	£F: £35 - 60 ($45-$77)
£C: £12 - 18 ($15-$23)	£G: £60 - 100 ($77-$130)
£D: £18 - 25 ($23-$32)	£H: £100 or more ($130 or more)

How to use *(side tab)*

Example profiles

This is an example profile from the Burgundy Côte d'Or section of the guide.

The entries follow this simple 'all you need to know' format

Producer	Wine region	Winery website
↓	↓	↓

Dom. des Comtes Lafon (Meursault) *www.comtes-lafon.fr*
The finest domaine in Meursault and one of the very best in the Côte d'Or, with some excellent Volnay as well as outstanding Meursault. Dominique Lafon has had the mastery of this 14 ha estate for 2 decades now and in recent years has converted its viticulture to a biodynamic regime. In the Meursault premiers crus the fruit is intense, rich and pure and encased in a precise but seamless structure. An opulent Gouttes d'Or, wonderfully expressive Charmes and remarkably profound Genevrières are only surpassed by a peerless Perrières. Yet even the village wines, such as the Clos de la Barre, show good dimension and a touch of class. The fine Volnays are crowned by a rich Santenots du Milieu, with great finesse and length. The acclaim for these wines adds a premium and they need to be bought before changing hands too many times if prices are to be remotely proportionate to their quality. Most expensive, from just a few barrels, is a Montrachet of exalted reputation. A little Puligny-Montrachet Premier Cru Champ Gain is also made and some very good wines are now being produced in the Mâconnais under the Domaine des HERITIERS COMTES LAFON.

Recommended Whites: ← **Red, white or rosé wine style** ↑
Volnay 1er Cru Santenots du Milieu ★★★★☆ £F   **Individually**
Volnay 1er Cru Clos des Chênes ★★★★ £F   **researched**
Volnay 1er Cru Champans ★★★★ £F   **entry**
Volnay ★★★☆ £E
Monthelie 1er Cru Les Duresses ★★★☆ £E

Recommended Whites:
Meursault 1er Cru Perrières ✪✪✪✪✪ £G
Meursault 1er Cru Charmes ★★★★★ £G
Meursault 1er Cru Genevrières ★★★★★ £G
Meursault 1er Cru Goutte d'Or ★★★★☆ £G
Meursault Clos de la Barre ★★★★ £F
Meursault Désirée ★★★★ £F   ← **Price code**
Meursault ★★★☆ £E
         ↑
      Quality rating
       indicator

France

1	Bordeaux	8	Northern Rhône
2	Chablis	9	Southern Rhône
3	Burgundy	10	Languedoc & Roussillon
4	Beaujolais	11	Provence
5	Alsace	12	South-West France
6	Champagne	13	Jura
7	Loire Valley	14	Savoie

In order to make sense of France as a whole we have devoted a section to each of its major wine regions. As an aid to orientation, the major appellations are listed under their respective regions. More detail of each, as well as on other exciting smaller appelations, can be found at the start of the individual chapters that follow this Overview.

Bordeaux

For both quality and quantity this is France's most important wine region. Wines vary from simple everyday reds to some of the world's most expensive classic crus.

Médoc, Graves & Sauternes

The **Médoc** provides all but one of the great Cabernet based Classed-Growths of the Right Bank, the best sites at **Margaux**, **Saint-Julien**, **Pauillac** and **Saint-Estèphe** are found on superbly drained gravel soils. Good wines can also be found in the **Haut-Médoc**, **Listrac** and **Moulis** ACs but the *terroir* is less propitious. **Pessac-Léognan** is a source of not only some great reds but whites which at their best rival the great wines of the Côte de Beaune. **Graves** to the south produces some good wines without the depth or class of Pessac-Léognan. Some of the worlds greatest botryitised sweet wines are produced at **Sauternes** and **Barsac**.

St Emilion, Pomerol & other Bordeaux

Almost all the new wave of Bordeaux reds have emerged from the Right Bank. Many top Châteaux have been isolating special *crus* and bottling them separately and other small volume garage style wines have also emerged. Some are exceptional, some decidedly less so. This revolution has largely occurred in **Saint-Émilion**, rather than the much smaller **Pomerol** AC. Some of the best value has begun to emerge from the lesser and satellite appellations. The vast track of the **Entre-Deux-Mers** to the south of Saint-Émilion continues to offer good value whites.

Burgundy

This most famous wine region makes some of the finest examples of both Chardonnay and Pinot Noir. Chardonnay can achieve success almost anywhere but the tricky Pinot Noir achieves rare greatness here.

Chablis & Yonne

One of the wine world's most famous names. Located halfway between Beaune and Paris, these are distinctly cool climate Chardonnays. The white ACs include **Petit Chablis**, **Chablis**, **Chablis Premier Cru** and **Chablis Grand Cru**. The best wines have both a piercing minerality as well as a complex citrus and leesy character. Occasional fine Sauvignon is made under the **Saint-Bris** AC. Some Pinot Noir based red is also made as Irancy or under several different **Bourgogne** suffixed names.

Côte d'Or & Côte Chalonnaise

The Côte d'Or is synonymous with Burgundy and includes all its great red wines. It is comprised of two parts. The more northerly Côte de Nuits (mostly red) includes the famous villages of **Gevrey-Chambertin**, **Morey Saint-Denis** and **Vosne-Romanée**. In its southern continuation, the Côte de Beaune, some of the world's greatest dry whites are produced from **Meursault**, **Chassagne-Montrachet** and **Puligny-Montrachet** as well as some very fine reds, from the likes of **Volnay** and **Pommard**. The Côte Chalonnaise offers some wines of character and depth, both red and white With

a few exceptions the better examples from the Cote d'Or's lesser ACs tend to offer more excitement.

Mâconnais

Perhaps the most exciting of Burgundy's regions, certainly in terms of the number of emerging top quality small producers. Full-bodied minerally Chardonnay is produced from a number of appellations, pre-eminent among them being **Pouilly-Fuissé** and **Saint-Véran**. However **Viré-Clessé** and several Mâcon suffixed Villages names, such as **Mâcon-La Roche Vineuse**, are also important.

Beaujolais

The vast majority of Beaujolais is red and produced from Gamay. Generic examples come mainly from the south of the region. However it is the superior granite soils of the northern sector where the better **Beaujolais-Villages**, the *crus* **Brouilly**, **Chénas**, **Chiroubles**, **Côte de Brouilly**, **Juliénas**, **Régnié**, **Saint-Amour** together with the structured more ageworthy **Fleurie**, **Morgon** and **Moulin-à-Vent** offer wines of sometimes heady cherry, raspberry or even strawberry-scented intensity.

Alsace

One of the most northerly of France's regions in the north-east of the country. The warm, dry, sunny climate of the area, enabled through protection by the Vosges Mountains, provides uniquely rich and strikingly aromatic wines which are labelled by grape variety and classified as **Alsace** AC or **Alsace Grand Cru** AC. There is also a spakling wine classification **Crémant d'Alsace**.

Champagne

The world's greatest sparkling wine comes from this exposed marginal climate in northern France. Much of the wine is of potentially very high quality. All is produced from Chardonnay, Pinot Noir and Pinot Meunier and made by the classic Champagne method, emulated almost everywhere else for fine sparkling wines, with a secondary fermentation almost always in bottle.

Loire Valley

An extensive region which stretches from the Atlantic coast at Nantes and follows the Loire River to its source in central France. The Pays Nantais is dominated by just one wine, **Muscadet**, from a number of ACs. Anjou-Saumur is a source of the great sweet wines of the **Côteaux du Layon**, **Bonnezeaux** and **Quarts de Chaume** as well as some fine dry white from **Savennières**. Good, structured red and white are provided by **Saumur** and Cabernet based reds emanate from **Saumur-Champigny**. Touraine is home to the diverse, ageworthy Chenin Blancs of **Vouvray** and **Montlouis** as well as some fine red based on Cabernet Franc from **Bourgeuil**, **Chinon** and **Saint-Nicolas-de-Bourgeuil**. To the east are the vineyards of **Sancerre** and **Pouilly-Fumé**. Some of finest minerally, gooseberry scented Sauvignon Blanc is made here. The region also stretches south to the Auverne, where some soft easy-drinking red is made.

Jura/Savoie

The Alpine vineyards of Jura and Savoie provide some of the most unusual and strikingly flavoured whites and reds. In the Jura you will also encounter two rare and unusual specialities. *Vin jaune* (yellow wine) a dry white made aged naturally under a *flor* yeast like in fino sherry but producing very intense long-lived wines. *Vin de paille* (straw wine) is a sweet wine produced from late-harvested, dried

France

grapes. The key appellations in the Jura are **Arbois**, **L'Étoile** and the **Côtes du Jura**. In Savoie **Vin de Savoie** and **Bugey** are the ACs to note.

Rhône Valley

This huge sprawling area stretches down the narrow river valley of the Rhône towards Provence. The bulk of the regions output is generic **Côtes du Rhône**, almost exclusively from the south. There are also many high quality wines red and white produced throughout the region.

Northern Rhône

Some of the worlds finest red and white wine is produced here. Syrah is the mainstay of the reds including the great wines of **Hermitage**, **Côte-Rôtie** and **Cornas**. **Saint-Joseph** and **Crozes-Hermitage** are increasingly important. A small amount of very ageworthy white is made at Hermitage and elsewhere from mainly Marsanne and some Roussanne. The exotically peachy **Condrieu** is the ultimate expression of the aromatic Viognier.

Southern Rhône

As well as the sea of generic red produced here there are some striking and classic reds from the large AC of **Châteauneuf-du-Pape**. As elsewhere in the southern Rhône the wines are based on Grenache, and some of the finest expressions of the variety emanate from here. Its also well worth considering the reds of **Gigondas** and **Vacqueyras** as well as the reds and whites from many of the emerging **Côtes du Rhône Villages**. These are wines that currently offer exciting quality and often great value.

Languedoc-Roussillon

This vast geographical area, still the purveyor of a vast lake of bulk produced Vin de France (formerly Vin de Table) and Indication Géographique Protégée (formerly Vin de Pays), is also the source of some of the most exciting, newly-emerging wines in France.

Languedoc

Of the two sub-regions, this is much the larger. Key to quality in all the appellations are the isolation of excellent hillside *terroirs* and the planting of Rhône varieties both red and white. The Carignan variety is also proving a valueable resource old bush vines. **Languedoc** (which now covers the whole area) is by far the largest of the appellations with the smaller ACs **Faugères** and **Saint-Chinian** also providing wines of real substance. The appellations round the coast towards the Roussillon, including **Minervois** and **Corbières** tend to produce softer, lighter wines.

Roussillon

Perhaps the greatest potential in the Midi comes from the vineyards of the Roussillon. The region was best known for the quality of its splendid fortified reds, **Maury**, **Rivesaltes** and **Banyuls**. However many old vine plantings are now providing exceptional raw material for a growing number of high quality light dry reds and a few very impressive whites also. Old Grenache and Carignan are of great importance and increasing amounts of Syrah and Mourvèdre are also being planted. Some wines are classified as IGP (Indication Géographique Protégée) others are **Côtes du Roussillon** and **Côtes du Roussillon-Villages**.

Provence & Corsica

Provence is becoming justifiably better known for the quality of its reds. Rhône varieties are widely planted in the key appellations. Cabernet Sauvignon is also becoming increasingly important. The top red AC, **Bandol** provides striking, long-lived reds largely based on Mourvèdre. Corsica offers some sound reds from interesting idigenous varieties and fine sweet Muscat.

South-West France

A wide and diverse range of wines are produced in this large area. To the north **Bergerac** produces reds and whites from the Bordeaux varieties. Big structured reds are produced to the south at **Cahors**, largely from Auxerrois (Malbec) and at **Madiran** mainly from Tannat. Some exceptional white is produced at **Jurançon**, including great moelleux, and good whites also emerge from **Pacherenc du Vic-Bilh**. Some of the most unusual and diverse styles come from **Gaillac** to the north-east of Toulouse.

To most people Bordeaux is probably the most well-known of France's great wine regions. In recent years it has enjoyed bountiful harvests, the maintenance of quality – and many improvements too. The last few years have also seen dynamic changes on the Right Bank of the Gironde in Saint-Emilion, with major investment in established properties and the creation of a number of exciting new labels. The development of the so-called garage wines, produced in tiny quantities all over the Saint-Emilion appellation, has been welcome in instances where exotic and fine and ageworthy blends have been produced from isolated first-class terroirs. However, where these wines are sourced from lesser sites, they are often over-extracted, lacking in class but nevertheless still marketed and sold at high prices. Perhaps if the current trend towards more realistic pricing in general continues there will be a much-needed reality check. The lesser areas like Fronsac and particularly the Côtes de Castillon continue to forge ahead with exciting developments at prices that mere mortals can afford. It is also important not to lose sight of the fact that there are properties, particularly on the Left Bank in the Médoc, which have consistently been producing some of the world's greatest wines for decades and continue to do so.

Geography

The Bordeaux region can effectively be looked at in three parts. There are the appellations surrounding Bordeaux itself and stretching to both the north and south. These vineyards are all located on the western side of the Gironde estuary and further south the river Garonne. This is often referred to as the Left Bank. The Right Bank comprises the vineyard areas east of the Gironde and the river Dordogne, particularly the appellations of Saint-Emilion and Pomerol near Libourne. There is another vast tract of vineyard land between the Dordogne and the Garonne. This is neither Left nor Right Bank and is largely dry white wine territory, including the large Entre-Deux-Mers AC. The vast bulk of Bordeaux's commercial wine trade emanates from the city itself. Libourne, though, is also important commercially, with a number of its own *négociants*.

Generic Bordeaux

AC **Bordeaux**, the bottle you're most likely to come across, can be sourced anywhere within the large Bordeaux region, which includes the areas mentioned above and other outlying appellations. The total production is mind-boggling. Some 5.5 to 6 million hectolitres of red and nearly another million of white are produced every year. Around two-thirds of this is generic Bordeaux. This would not be such a huge problem in itself but most of the red is vinified from Merlot, the workhorse grape of the region and often grown in heavy and productive soils. This allied to over-ambitious yields is always going to present a challenge to fully ripening the crop. So much generic Bordeaux not only tastes dilute but can also have a green, vegetal component. **Bordeaux Supérieur** AC, is usually a step up from generic Bordeaux and by law cannot be sold until it has been 12 months in bottle. Ripening the white grapes here tends to be less of a problem and these wines can often be better bets.

Médoc, Graves and Sauternes

Some of the world's greatest and noblest red wines are produced here as well as benchmark sweet whites and a very small amount of immensely stylish dry white. The **Médoc** AC itself, rather than the area of the Médoc which runs from Bordeaux north to Soulac at the mouth of the Gironde, is centred around the small town of Lesparre-Médoc and is the northernmost of the Left Bank ACs. There is a higher proportion of clay in the soil rather than the fabled gravel and the wines are generally soft and forward, with a few better examples. The **Haut-Médoc** encompasses all four of the great communal appellations close to the Gironde (Saint-Estèphe, Pauillac, Saint-Julien and Margaux) as well as **Listrac** and **Moulis**. There can be a wide variation in quality in the Haut-Medoc AC but a few properties are very serious indeed, producing classic, long-lived cedary reds. Both Listrac-Médoc and Moulis are located just to the north-west of Margaux. Listrac seems to offer less potential but there are attempts here to fashion some modern garagiste-style wines and make the best of the fruit available. Moulis has greater potential, with a number of very good properties.

The northernmost of the great red wine appellations of the Médoc is **Saint-Estèphe**. There are five Classed Growths and the wines are generally the densest, sturdiest examples of the area. Modern winemaking has gone some way to address those firm youthful tannins and the wines are more approachable than they were even a decade ago and are very impressive at their best. **Pauillac** is synonymous with some of the greatest wines of the region. Châteaux Latour, Lafite-Rothschild and Mouton-Rothschild are all here. The deep gravel vineyards provide an ideal base for these strikingly rich styles laden with cassis and spice. The top wines need considerable age. To the south, the wines of **Saint-Julien** are less opulent than Pauillac, more perfumed and with intense cigar box and cedar notes. There are eleven Classed Growths and the extraordinarily refined Léoville-Las-Cases should be a First Growth in many people's books. **Margaux** is just to the north of Bordeaux and contains 21 Classed Growths. At their best these are are the most elegant and refined wines of the Médoc. For a long time Margaux has been an underperforming appellation but change is happening aplenty – new investment, a renewed commitment to quality and, in Marojallia and Clos du Jaugueyron, the first serious garagiste wines on the Left Bank. Marojallia is vinified by Jean-Luc Thunevin, owner of Valandraud, one of the first garagiste wines in Saint-Emilion.

Immediately south of Bordeaux, indeed part of the AC is in the outer suburbs of the city, are the vineyards of **Pessac-Léognan**. Originally part of the larger **Graves** appellation it was granted its own appellation status in 1987 in recognition of the superior quality of its sites. The soil is finely drained deep gravel and all of the properties in the 1959 Classification of the Graves are to be found here. Only Haut-Brion, with its First Growth status in the 1855 Classification, was absent from the list. Some splendid reds are produced here as well as a small number of dry whites. At their best these are rich, complex and very ageworthy and rival the great whites of the Côte de Beaune (see Burgundy). White winemaking in general throughout the Graves has improved immeasurably in recent years. The rest of the region stretches to the east and some way south of the Garonne. It is never as good as Pessac-Léognan but some good red and dry white are regularly produced. There are also a few sweet wines under the **Graves Supérieures** AC, but these are largely pretty dull.

Just north-west of the town of Langon are the great sweet wine appellations of Sauternes and Barsac. A third sweet wine appellation, **Cérons**, is immediately to the north but does not benefit to the same degree as the other two AC's from the remarkable geographical influence of the tiny Ciron river, which creates the conditions for the development of noble rot. Cérons and also the sweet wines from immediately across the Garonne in **Sainte-**

Bordeaux

France

Croix-du-Mont and **Loupiac** can be impressive but they never achieve the same intense botrytis quality as **Sauternes**. **Barsac** is one of the five communes of Sauternes and properties here may chose to label their wines Sauternes or Barsac. After a run of very successful vintages in the 1980s these wines are now fetching the kind of prices that make their production economic and indeed profitable. Fifteen to 20 years ago it was nigh-on impossible for producers to achieve a commercial return. Harvesting is incredibly labour intensive, with multiple *tris* (passes through the vineyard), and the yield is necessarily tiny. However, major investment has dramatically changed the area. Many wines of truly magnificent concentration and intensity are now being made. In the lesser years cryo-extraction has been used by a number of chateaux to improve quality.

Saint-Emilion, Pomerol and the Rest of Bordeaux
Saint-Emilion and Pomerol are the two great names associated with the Right Bank but there are an increasing number of well-priced, exciting wines emerging from the other ACs. It is also interesting to note that these are all red wine appellations. **Saint-Emilion** itself is the driving force in terms of volume and accounts for some 40 per cent of all wines produced here. As a result it's not surprising that there is a wide variation in quality and very diverse *terroirs*, some exceptional and some, particularly in the southern plains of the AC, distinctly ordinary, with heavy productive soils. Many of Bordeaux's major developments in vinification techniques and the influence of consultant winemakers have their origins in Saint-Emilion. Pre-fermentation cold soaking (or maceration), malolactic fermentation in barrel and micro-oxygenation are now practiced all over the world.

Saint-Emilion's Classification has been revised a number of times in recent years. There are 18 Premiers Grands Crus Classés with four A-rated properties, Ausone and Cheval-Blanc, joined by Angélus and Pavie in 2012 and 14 B-rated, including newly promoted (in 2012) La Mondotte, Canon La Gaffeliére, Valandraud, Pavie Macquin and Larcisse-Ducasse, as well as 64 properties rated Grand Cru Classé. There have been major investments in recent years in both vineyards and cellars, resulting in some highly priced wines made in very limited quantities. The most notable of these has been La Mondotte, produced at Canon-La-Gaffelière. Many other tiny-production wines or *vins des garagistes* have also emerged. Some have been very impressive, but others are over-extracted and they have generally been pretty expensive.

Pomerol, in contrast, continues to provide some impressive and startlingly opulent wines, full of dark and spicy fruit, generally supple and more approachable than many of the other top wines in Bordeaux. Inevitably there are exceptions to the rule and these tend to occur where there is a higher proportion of Cabernet Franc or Cabernet Sauvignon planted or the soil has more gravel. Pomerol's clay soils suit Merlot very well and provide this uniquely exotic style. Pomerol's wines can also be some of the priciest anywhere on the globe. There has been investment and development here but not on the scale of Saint-Emilion's. The lower tier of the appellation, though, can disappoint. The odd wine of distinction is also beginning to emerge from the lesser Saint-Emilion satellite ACs, **Lussac-Saint-Emilion, Montagne-Saint-Emilion, Puisseguin-Saint-Emilion** and **Saint-Georges-Saint-Emilion**, as well as **Lalande-de-Pomerol**.

To the north-west of Libourne are the areas of **Côtes de Bourg** and **Côtes de Blaye**. The former produces reds, some decent and some very impressive while dry whites are produced in the latter. To the immediate west of Libourne are **Fronsac** and **Canon-Fronsac**. Good, stylish, well-made dark-fruited styles have been produced here for a decade or so. To the east of Saint-Emilion are the **Côtes de Castillon** and **Bordeaux-Côtes de Francs**. Again these are areas of great potential and the best wines are still well-priced, if becoming less so.

Between the Dordogne and Garonne rivers is a substantial vineyard area comprising some nine appellations. Geographically and physically by far the most important is the **Entre-Deux-Mers**, an appellation devoted to dry whites. A number of properties here are also producing good AC Bordeaux red. The appellation is all about maximising modern white winemaking with some good results, using pre-fermentation skin contact, ageing on lees and, in the more expensive wines, limited barrel-fermentation and ageing with new wood as well. Some well-priced wines have been available for some time now. Vibrant red and rosé is made in the **Premières Côtes de Bordeaux**, just to the east across the Garonne from the city of Bordeaux, and there are good sweet wines on the eastern bank of the river at **Cadillac, Loupiac** and **Sainte-Croix-du-Mont**. In the far east is **Saint-Foy-de-Bordeaux**, where there are reds as well as dry and sweet whites.

A-Z of producers by appellation/commune

Medoc, Graves		Ch. Boyd-Cantenac	20
& Sauternes		Ch. Brane-Cantenac	20
Barsac		Ch. Cantenac-Brown	21
Ch. Climens	22	Ch. Dauzac	23
Ch. Coutet	23	Ch. Ferrière	24
Ch. Doisy-Daëne	23	Ch. Giscours	24
Ch. Doisy-Védrines	23	Ch. d'Issan	25
Ch. Nairac	30	Clos du Jaugeyron	26
Graves		Ch. Kirwan	26
Ch. de Chantegrive	21	Ch. Lascombes	27
Clos Floridène	22	Ch. Malescot-Saint-Exupéry	29
Ch. Moutin	42	Ch. Margaux	29
Vieux-Château-Gaubert	34	Marojallia	29
Ch. Villa Bel Air	35	Ch. Marquis-de-Terme	29
Haut-Médoc		Ch. Palmer	30
Ch. d'Agassac	19	Ch. Prieuré-Lichine	32
Ch. Belgrave	20	Ch. Rauzan-Ségla	32
Ch. Cambon la Pelouse	21	Ch. Siran	33
Ch. Camensac	21	Ch. du Tertre	34
Ch. Cantemerle	21	**Médoc**	
Ch. Charmail	22	Ch. Haut-Condissas	33
Ch. Cissac	22	Ch. Lanessan	27
Karolus	33	Magrez Tivoli	28
Ch. La Tour Carnet	27	Ch. Potensac	32
Ch La Lagune	26	Ch. Preuillac, Chateau	32
Ch. Peyrabon	31	Ch. Rollan-de-By	33
Ch. Sénéjac	33	Ch. Vieux Robin	35
Ch. Sociando-Mallet	34	**Moulis**	
Listrac-Médoc		Ch. Chasse-Spleen	22
Ch. Clarke	22	Ch. Poujeaux	32
Ch. Mayne-Lalande	29	**Pauillac**	
Margaux		Ch. d'Armailhac	19
Ch. d'Angludet	19	Ch. Batailley	20
Ch. Bel-Air Marquis d'Aligre	20	Ch. Clerc-Milon	22

Wine behind the label

Wine behind the label

Bordeaux

France

1 Médoc
2 Haut-Médoc
3 Saint-Estèphe
4 Pauillac
5 Saint-Julien
6 Listrac-Médoc
7 Moulis
8 Margaux
9 Pessac-Léognan
10 Graves
11 Cérons
12 Barsac
13 Sauternes
14 Premières Côtes de
   Bordeaux
15 Loupiac
16 Sainte-Croix-du-Mont
17 Entre-Deux-Mers
18 Ste-Foy-Bordeaux

19 Côtes de Castillon
20 Côtes de Franc
21 Saint-Emilion satellites
22 Saint-Emilion
23 Pomerol
24 Lalande-de-Pomerol
25 Fronsac &
   Canon-Fronsac
26 Côtes de Bourg
27 Côtes de Blaye /
   Premières
   Côtes de Blaye

Bordeaux vintages

As in other parts of France Bordeaux has been generally fairly lucky with vintages during the last six or seven years, particularly at the turn of the millenium. There haven't been the number of great years as the Rhône Valley from 1998 but after the disappointments of the early 1990s things have been decidedly better. Winemaking has evolved here and generally for the better. With the top reds, particularly, it is worth bearing in mind if you are purchasing from a fine current vintage that the approach in the cellar is different to that of 20 years ago. The wines are suppler and more approachable but it remains to be seen whether they will be as long-lived as some of their predecessors.

2015: After a mild winter and a warmer than usual April, even flowering took place in May for the first time in some years, giving hope to the growers for good yields. A much hotter than usual May, June and July with intermittent rain produced stress conditions for the vines, but an unusually wet August and a relatively cool September proved the perfect timing to recover. The turns in the weather came just at the right moment for many of the growers to experience perfect harvest conditions. This has resulted in a very even vintage where it was hard to make bad wine. Whilst perhaps not quite reaching the heights of the 2009 and 2010 vintages, it is very nearly there with perhaps only the sweet wines falling a little below expectations.

2014: A wet, warmish winter ensured that the water tables were replenished after a few years of drought. This led to an early bud burst in the middle of March, which was followed by a warm, dry April. In May the flowering took place quickly. Problems began to arrive with rot, oidium and mildew because wet conditions in May were followed by a warm, sunny June, and a severe hail storm struck the northern part of the Medoc on June 8th. A wet and cool July with hail storms in St. Emilion did not help either. Insufficient sun and heat in August and early September augured a very moderate vintage. But things began to turn around with10 consecutive days of hot, sunny weather in mid September. A little rain followed for a few days, which helped to push the harvest back with the month finishing in a blaze of sunshine to make the vintage the best since 2010. A good, but not great vintage for the reds, with the whites, both dry and sweet, showing good consistency.

2013: A cold wet early spring did not augur well for this vintage. The weather improved marginally in April, but an unusually cold and wet May put things back even further. June was also inclement and this resulted in poor fruit set and *millerandage* in many vineyards. Massive storms on July 26th and August 2nd put paid to any hope of a decent vintage which might have been saved by sunny weather in July. But heat spikes coupled with excess moisture resulted in a lot of rot. A fine August and early September saved the day for many producers, but yields were considerably down and only those producers who had the resources to buy state of the art technology had a chance to make passable wines. Some decent wines will be found in this vintage but there needs to be careful selection on behalf of the buyer. The silver lining is perhaps that the weather conditions were ideal for noble rot and some very decent sweet wines were made.

2012: With a very unusual weather and ripening process, there were bound to be large variations in the quality of the fruit: Merlot and Cabernet Franc seemed to have generally fared the best, with the Cabernet Sauvignons suffering the greatest problems of consistency. *Terroir* also played an important part in expressing quality. Those great chateaux with recognised superb *terroir* on good sites with good drainage excelled, whilst those of lower rank struggled to obtain sufficient ripeness resulting in excessive over extraction in some cases. All in all, though, this was not as bad a vintage as some tried to make out and with careful selection, one could find some excellent wines, particularly from those Châteaux with enough financial muscle to buy in the latest in technology.

2011: An early spring and a hot dry April and May with a heat spike in June left some of the wines gasping for water with some fruit affected by sunburn. July then became one of the coldest months on record, reversing growth and when the rains did come it was often too little and too late. It was also one of the earliest harvests on record and the result of all this has led to some very uneven production. A greater selection was needed to discard unripe and rotted grapes resulting in technically low yields without the necessary accompanying quality. Yes, some very fine wine were made, particularly in Pomerol and the rest of the right bank, but by and large this is not a vintage for keeping. It was however, a very fine year for the sweet wines and the dry whites were also good.

2010: Another good year for Bordeaux wines, 2010 is probably a bit more uneven than 2009, when it was so consistent that is was difficult to make bad red wine. There will probably be a bit more variations in 2010 but on the other hand there will be some exceptional winners and a number of chateaux will making 2010s that are superior to their already excellent 2009s. Wines are generally well balanced and early impressions of the reds find wines that are displaying good, dark, ripe fruit with integrated oak, soft tannins and a good degree of charm although a number of the less well made wines suffered from over extraction. Whites are more aromatic and crisper than those of the previous vintage but many of the sweet wines lack concentration and botrytis definition.

2009: This looks certain to become one of the great vintages for reds on both Right and Left Banks. It may even exceed the quality achieved in those other great recent years; 2005 and 2000. There may not be the ultimate consistency of 2005 but the best performing properties have produced stunning wines.They are showing excellent balance and were picked at otimum ripeness with thick skins and high sugar levels. Whites are good with impressive weight and concentration but not the fresh and crisp character of 2008s, 2007s and 2006s. Sauternes should turn out to be very good with wines of rich, complex botrytis character.

2008: This was another year where excellent late season weather helped the vintage. Good reds were produced throughout the region and Merlot looks to be sumptuously rich and this is likely to be a particularly good year on the Right Bank. Dry whites are good and wines of elegance and power will be produced.Sauternes will provide some good bottles but overall the levels of botrytis were less than in 2007.

2007: This proved to be a challenging year throughout region for reds. A cold wet summer was followed by a balmy September that was the saviour of the vintage. The wines though are on the leaner side and marked by higher than normal levels of acidity. Undoubtedly a year for the successful winegrower. There were fewer problems with the dry whites which should be elegant and ageworthy. Sauternes had a good year with decent levels of botrytis in both Sémillon and Sauvignon Blanc, particularly those who harvested late with as many *tris* as possible.

2006: This was a challenging vintage after the excellence throughout the region in 2005. The weather was extremely variable and growers found a lot of rot. Inevitably those with the better viticultural skills and commitment will produce the best results. Acidity levels in particular are very high and the best reds are likely to require patience. There were fewer problems with the dry whites

Wine behind the label

Bordeaux

which were be elegant and ageworthy. Some potentially excellent Sauternes looks likely with good levels of botrytis.

2005: Red wine producers on both banks hailed this as the the best vintage since 2000. The summer was hot and dry without the excesses of 2003. Some truly great reds were made throughout the Medoc and the Cabernet Sauvignon was exceptional. The best wines on the Right Bank are equally impressive although some excessively extracted, super-ripe wines also emerged. Whites were also very good with good acidity as well as considerable richness. Sauternes may prove exceptional. Not quite the concentration of 2003 but very elegant and balanced wines in general.

2004: This is a good to very good year producing good reds throughout the region. On the Left Bank in particular, the wines are powerful and initially backward. Many producers compared the wines to those of 1998. It was also an abundant year and those who thinned their crops achieved better results. The dry whites were promising whereas Sauternes was good rather than great.

2003: Marked by a very hot summer this is a year of very good Left Bank reds, in particular to the north of the Medoc. To the south Graves was more uneven. There are likely to be some exceptional examples from the Right Bank from sites with good moisture retention. Those who picked at optimum ripeness were very fine. Many though are either under or overipe. A small amount of very rich Sauternes emerged.

2002: This was a good rather than a great year for reds. The year turned out to be more successful in the Medoc, particularly Saint-Julien and to the north. It was predominantly a Cabernet Sauvignon vintage. Earlier-ripening Merlot was most hit by late September rains. Some very good whites were produced and was a good year too for Sauternes.

2001: After the magnificent 2000 red vintage this is a good, sometimes very good year for red. The style is sturdy, dense and with firm tannins and notable but not excessive acidity. These are classically structured wines. Look for good wines on both the Left and Right Banks, including some fine examples from the lesser appellations. Sauternes and sweet wines in general look to be very impressive indeed. This could be the best vintage for botrytised wines since 1990. The dry whites were also close to exceptional.

2000: A magnificent year for red Bordeaux. The crop was bountiful and the quality exceptional. The combination of a hot dry August followed by a long even and balmy ripening period throughout September provided the châteaux with perfect late-harvesting conditions. Grapes were picked full of deep colour, super-ripe, fine, supple tannins and intense and heady flavour. This is the best vintage since 1990 for reds throughout Bordeaux. While dry whites enjoyed conditions nearly as good, this was a disappointing year for Sauternes.

1999: A generally impressive year throughout the region with the largest crop of the late 1990s. The summer was good, with warm consistent weather, however early rains in September meant that there was some variation. Those châteaux who went for maximum ripeness and harvested late did well. Whites were generally good and harvested before the rain, whereas Sauternes had a successful late harvest and some splendid wines were produced.

1998: There was a lot of late September rain in the Médoc and quality was variable. To the south Graves fared a little better but it was mainly earlier-ripening Merlot on the Right Bank that did best, producing wines with suppler and riper tannins. Dry whites were good and generally harvested in ideal weather. Sauternes was also very good although the crop was tiny.

1997: A generally trying year, the one exception being Sauternes,

which produced its best vintage since 1990. Quantities, though, were small and the top châteaux, who were rigorous in their selection, produced the best results. The dry whites were generally average to good but some properties harvested grapes lacking in full flavour development and many of these wines should have been drunk.

1996: This was another year when the Bordeaux money men should have been singing the praises of the gods. It was the second very large harvest in a row, a trend that was to continue through to the millennium. It was also a year of great wines in the Médoc, particularly in the northern appellations.The Right Bank fared less well, being hit by rain just as the Merlot ripened. Late-harvested Cabernet Sauvignon was consistently more successful. Very good dry whites were produced and the best wines are drinking well now. Sauternes had its best year since 1990. The wines are rich, heady and very intense..

1995: A good, indeed very good year for both Left and Right Bank. The harvest was reasonably consistent and although there was some rain during Setember it was not heavy enough to cause real problems with ripening. The results were very good in Pauillac and Saint-Julien and the wines are not only classically structured but have rich ripe fruit as well. The lesser reds are now beginning to drink well, the top wines are now approachable. There were some good dry whites and these are now drinking well. However Sauternes was generally disappointing.

1994: Many top wines are now approaching their peak. It was a good year for dry whites and the top wines should now be drunk. Lesser white Pessac-Léognan should now have been drunk. This was a dismal year in Sauternes.

1990: The finest red wine vintage since 1982. Also impressively good for dry whites, some of the very best are still drinking well but should now be drunk up. It was exceptional for Sauternes. The weather was remarkably even up to and throughout the harvest and the wines consequently had exceptional balance. Most of the top reds are drinking now but will continue to develop.

1989: This was generally a very good year, producing excellent reds on both banks, the only question mark being excessive ripeness. Sweet wines were very good and many are now drinking well.

1988: A good rather than great year. The top wines turned out well. The reds are classically structured and restrained and in general will continue to drink well for another decade. Excellent Sauternes, which is drinking and will continue to develop harmoniously.

1986: A great vintage in the Médoc with many harmonious long-lived wines. More patchy on the Right Bank though. A very fine year for Sauternes as well.

1985: Good for both Left and Right Banks but exceeded by the quality of the 1986s.

1983: Dependable for both Banks. Some exceptional Margaux's. Very top wines will keep.

1982: This was a classic year with many superb reds being made. The Médocs look to have turned out better than those from the Right Bank. Top examples will now be excellent.

Earlier Years: For older vintages great Médocs from 1978 and 1970 are superb, the best will evolve further. A handful of 1975s have turned out very well. 1966 was good in the Médoc. 1964 might be worth a look for top Saint-Emilion or Pomerol. 1961 was a classic and many wines are still excellent. You could also consider 1959, 55, 49, 47, 45 and if you're exceptionally adventurous 35 or 28. Bear in mind that the provenance of the wine is as important as anything if you are acquiring very old vintages.

France

Bordeaux vintage chart

	Northern Médoc	Southern Médoc	Red Graves	White Graves
	inc Saint-Èstephe Paulliac	inc Margaux Saint-Julien		
2015	★★★★☆ A	★★★★☆ A	★★★★☆ A	★★★ A
2014	★★★ A	★★★ A	★★★ A	★★★ B
2013	★ B	★ B	★ B	★ B
2012	★★★ B	★★★ B	★★★ B	★★★ B
2011	★★★ B	★★★ B	★★★ B	★★★ B
2010	★★★★★ A	★★★★★ A	★★★★★ A	★★★★★ B
2009	★★★★☆ A	★★★★☆ A	★★★★☆ A	★★★★☆ B
2008	★★★★ B	★★★★ B	★★★★ B	★★★★ B
2007	★★★ B	★★★ B	★★★☆ B	★★★★ C
2006	★★★★ B	★★★★ B	★★★★ B	★★★★☆ B
2005	★★★★★ A	★★★★★ B	★★★★★ A	★★★★☆ B
2004	★★★★ B	★★★★ B	★★★☆ B	★★★★ B
2003	★★★★ C	★★★★ B	★★★★ B	★★★★ C
2002	★★★★ B	★★★☆ B	★★★☆ B	★★★★ C
2001	★★★☆ B	★★★☆ B	★★★☆ B	★★★★☆ C
2000	★★★★★ B	★★★★★ B	★★★★★ B	★★★★ C
1999	★★★☆ B	★★★☆ B	★★★☆ B	★★★★ C
1998	★★★☆ B	★★★☆ B	★★★★ B	★★★★☆ C
1996	★★★★☆ B	★★★★ B	★★★★ B	★★★★ C
1995	★★★★ C	★★★★ C	★★★☆ C	★★★☆ D
1990	★★★★★ B	★★★★★ B	★★★★ C	★★★★☆ C
1989	★★★★ C	★★★★ C	★★★★ D	★★★☆ C
1988	★★★★ C	★★★★☆ C	★★★★ C	★★★★ D
1982	★★★★★ C	★★★★☆ C	★★★★★ C	-

	Saint -Emilion	Pomerol	Sauternes
2015	★★★★☆ A	★★★★☆ A	★★★ A
2012	★★★ A	★★★ A	★★ A
2013	★ B	★ B	★★★ B
2012	★★★ B	★★★ B	★★ B
2011	★★★☆ B	★★★☆ B	★★★★ B
2010	★★★★★ A	★★★★★ A	★★★★ B
2009	★★★★★ A	★★★★★ A	★★★★ B
2008	★★★★☆ B	★★★★☆ B	★★★★ B
2007	★★★ B	★★★ B	★★★★☆ A
2006	★★★★ B	★★★★ B	★★★★ B
2005	★★★★★ A	★★★★★ A	★★★★☆ B
2004	★★★★ B	★★★★ B	★★★☆ B
2003	★★★★ B	★★★★ B	★★★★☆ B
2002	★★★☆ C	★★★☆ C	★★★★☆ B
2001	★★★★ B	★★★★★ B	★★★☆ B
2000	★★★★★ B	★★★★★ B	★★ C
1999	★★★☆ B	★★★☆ B	★★★★ B
1998	★★★★ B	★★★★☆ B	★★★★ B
1996	★★★☆ C	★★★☆ C	★★★★☆ B
1995	★★★★ C	★★★★ C	★★★☆ C
1990	★★★★★ C	★★★★★ C	★★★★ C
1989	★★★★☆ C	★★★★☆ C	★★★★ C
1988	★★★★ C	★★★★ C	★★★★★ C
1982	★★★★★ C	★★★★★ C	-

A-Z of producers - *Médoc, Graves & Sauternes*

Ch. d'Agassac (Haut-Médoc) *www.agassac.com*
Things are taking a turn for better at this medium-sized operation based in the southern part of the Haut-Médoc and owned by the insurance company Groupama. The wine is now showing good depth and some attractive dark fruit notes and harmonious tannins. A medium-weight style, better with 5 or 6 years' ageing. The rating applies to 1999 onwards. The second wine is Château Pomies d'Agassac. (DM)
Recommended Reds:
Château d'Agassac Haut-Médoc ★★☆ £D

Ch. d'Angludet (Margaux) *www.chateau-angludet.fr*
Well-established Cru Bourgeois with 30 year-old vineyards planted to Cabernet Sauvignon, Merlot and Petit Verdot, which comes from the oldest parcel of vines and adds extra character. The emphasis at the property is to achieve a natural balance in the vineyard and this shows through in the quality of the wine which is medium-weight with refinement and finesse. There is a second label, La Ferme d'Angludet, and a rosé, Clairet d'Angludet. (DM)
Recommended Reds:
Château d'Angludet Margaux ★★★☆ £D

Ch. d'Arche (Sauternes 2ème CC) *www.chateaudarche-sauternes.com*
Only around 5,000 cases a year are produced here from 29 ha. This is reasonably impressive, full and concentrated Sauternes with a generally good performance in the most favourable vintages over the 2 decades since Pierre Perromat became involved. Harvesting is as selective as necessary, and a portion of new oak is used to age the wine. Good in 2010 as well as 09, 07, 06, 05 03, 02, 01, 00; 98 and 97 are also worth seeking out. (DM)
Recommended Whites:
Château d'Arche Sauternes ★★★☆ £E

Ch. d'Armailhac (Pauillac 5ème CC) *www.chateau-darmailhac.com*
Like its prestigious neighbour MOUTON ROTHSCHILD this château is also owned by Baronne Philippine de Rothschild. At its best, in top years like 2010, 09, 06, 05, 03, 00, 99, 98 and 95, this medium-sized property is undoubtedly producing ★★★☆ Pauillac. When conditions are less favourable, though, the wine struggles a little. Grown in relatively light soils the wine is structured but not overly so, retaining some of the marked cassis and cedar notes of its big brother, and will provide good drinking at 6 or 7 years. (DM)
Recommended Reds:
Château d'Armailhac Pauillac ★★★ £E

Ch. Bastor-Lamontagne (Sauternes) *www.bastor-lamontagne.com*
A consistently fine, small to medium-sized operation which has performed admirably over a long period, providing the essence of Sauternes at an affordable price. As well as Sémillon and Sauvignon Blanc, Michel Garat has just a small amount of Muscadelle to add aroma. The wine is barrel-fermented for an extended 3–4 weeks with around 15% new oak to lend structure and shows classic honeyed, peachy botrytis character even in lesser years. Look out for recent top years. The second wine produced from young vines is Les Remparts de Bastor. (DM)
Recommended Whites:
Château Bastor-Lamontagne Sauternes ★★★☆ £E

Bordeaux /Médoc, Graves & Sauternes

France

Ch. Batailley (Pauillac 5ème CC)

A consistently reasonably priced Fifth Growth, Batailly is a wine that has performed reliably throughout the 1990s and shown further improvement in recent vintages. Good classic blackcurrant and cedar notes can be found, and the wine has sufficient oak with creamy vanilla notes and a supple texture aided by malolactic in barrel. Good, now with impressive depth and some complexity. (DM)

Recommended Reds:

Château Batailley Pauillac ★★★☆ £E

Ch. Bel Air Marquis d'Aligre (Margaux)

Cru Bourgeois property that has been performing impressively in recent years. This small château consists of just 13ha with a surprisingly high (35%) proportion of Merlot. Production is low at less than 3,000 cases a year. Low volume, a careful control of yields and meticulously tended vineyards all contribute to the consistently excellent results achieved here. The wine is a refined mediumweight, rather than blockbuster style, a proper Margaux with a real fruit intensity and stylish perfume. Good in the top years since 1990. (DM)

Recommended Reds:

Château Bel Air Marquis d'Aligre Margaux ★★★☆ £E

Ch. Belgrave (Haut-Médoc 5ème CC) *www.dourthe.com*

Purchased by Vignobles Dourthe in 1980, it was only with the 1998 vintage that this property really began to forge ahead. During the past two decades the vineyard has been replanted. Cabernet Sauvignon dominates the blend, with a tiny amount of Petit Verdot. Now that the vines are maturing, the wine is evolving from the straightforward, essentially fruit-driven style of the early to mid-1990s to one where there is real depth and refinement. It represents particularly good value for money. The current rating is for 2000 on. (DM)

Recommended Reds:

Château Belgrave Haut-Médoc ★★★☆ £D

Ch. Beychevelle (Saint-Julien 4ème CC) *www.beychevelle.com*

Beychevelle is a sizeable property with 90 ha of vineyards planted to Cabernet Sauvignon, Merlot, Cabernet Franc and a little Petit Verdot. It is a Classed Growth with a reasonable, rather than spectacular track record over recent years. At its best the wine shows real finesse, splendid purity of fruit and very subtle oak, not full and powerful but more refined and elegant. Choose your vintage with a bit of caution and avoid lesser years. Amiral de Beychevelle, the second wine, is entitled to the Saint-Julien AC, while Les Brulières-de-Beychevelle is from vineyards in the Haut-Médoc. (DM)

Recommended Reds:

Château Beychevelle Saint-Julien ★★★☆ £F

Ch. Boyd-Cantenac (Margaux 3ème CC)

This Third Growth property is turning out very good elegant Margaux. This was not always so. Boyd-Cantenac spent decades in the doldrums but should now be on anyone's shopping list since the vintages of the late 1990s, which have shown a marked turn for the better. An increasing use of new oak – up to 60% – and, since 1997, no filtration has contributed to this improvement. The wine is fragrant and supple with attractive dark berry fruit and an increasing richness. The rating applies to vintages from 2004 on. (DM)

Recommended Reds:

Château Boyd-Cantenac Margaux ★★★☆ £F

❀ Ch. Branaire (Saint-Julien 4ème CC) *www.branaire.com*

For a long time this was a seriously underachieving property. However there has been a significant turnaround here during the last 6 or 7 years. Investment in the cellar, along with a commitment to quality that avoids filtration and employs only limited egg-white fining and racking by gravity, is undoubtedly paying off. The style has moved from light to much fuller and richer. The Cabernet Sauvignon component now really shows and the wines are sturdier and denser with much greater depth and power. Almost all the vintages since 1994 have impressed. 1995, 96, 98 and 99 were all on the cusp of ★★★★ and since 2000 the property has excelled. Duluc de Branaire-Ducru is the second label. (DM)

Recommended Reds:

Château Branaire Saint-Julien ★★★★☆ £F

Ch. Brane-Cantenac (Margaux 2ème CC) *www.lucienlurton.com*

Since the late 1990s Brane-Cantenac has been showing real evidence of its status as a Second Growth. After 1996 the only vintage which has disappointed a touch has been the 97. The wine is a classic blend of Cabernet Sauvignon, Merlot and Cabernet Franc with intense, cedary Margaux perfume, subtle oak and sheer class and intensity. Domaines Lucien Lurton also own a number of other important châteaux, among them CLIMENS in Barsac, DURFORTVIVENS in Margaux and BOUSCAUT in Pessac-Léognan. The second wine, Baron de Brane, is of decent quality. (DM)

Recommended Reds:

Château Brane-Cantenac Margaux ★★★★ £F
Baron de Brane Margaux ★★☆ £D

❀ Ch. Branon (Pessac-Léognan CC)

Under the same ownership as HAUT-BERGEY, this boutique winery (4,000 cases) makes a single red wine from equal parts of Cabernet Sauvignon and Merlot. It is a wine of enormous power and concentration with intensely perfumed fruit. The 2 ha of vines lie between those of HAUT-BAILLY and MALARTIC-LAGRAVIÈRE and since 2000 Jean-Luc Thunevin of Château de VALANDRAUD has been the consultant winemaker. (NB)

Recommended Reds:

Château Branon Pessac-Léognan ★★★★★ £G

Ch. Brown (Pessac-Léognan CC) *www.chateau-brown.com*

This château has shown considerable improvements since it was purchased by Jean-Christophe Mau in 2004. Aided and abetted by consultant Stéphane Derenoncourt, it has now moved on to a different plane. There are 23.5 ha under vine for the red wine and 4.5 for the white. The white (70% Sauvignon, 30% Sémillon) shows finesse and balance, whilst the red (70% Cabernet Sauvignon, 27% Merlot and 3% Petit Verdot) shares these characteristics along with a degree more upfront fruit than one would normally expect in this appellation. (NB)

Recommended Reds:

Château Brown Pessac-Léognan ★★★ £D

Recommended Whites:

Château Brown Pessac-Léognan ★★★ £C

Ch. Caillou (Sauternes 2ème CC) *www.chateaucaillou.com*

This is one of those confusingly labelled properties which takes the Sauternes AC although it is located in Barsac. There are two cuvées of the principal wine, the regular Caillou and a barrel selection, La Private Cuvée, produced in top years. Fermentation is in a mix of new oak and inox and ageing is between 18 and 24 months with

a marked new oak component. This is an intense and heady sweet white but inevitably the regular Caillou suffers in those vintages when La Private Cuvée is released. A second wine, Les Erables, is also produced. (DM)

Recommended Whites:
Château Caillou Sauternes ★★★☆ £D

Ch. Calon-Ségur (Saint-Estèphe 2ème CC)
Like many Bordeaux properties Calon-Ségur has shown a marked upturn in quality during the late 1990s. As well as a more meticulous approach in the vineyard, which has resulted in a reduced crop, the objective in the winemaking has been to produce an altogether suppler, more harmonious style. The wine achieves this and is both opulent and modern with weight, concentration and power. It has a much more velvety texture than of old. Very good since 1996 and seemingly improving with the vintages since 2000, with excellent wines in the better vintages as well as 2000. (DM)

Recommended Reds:
Château Calon-Ségur Saint-Estèphe ★★★★ £F

Ch. Cambon-la-Pelouse (Haut-Médo) www.cambon-la-pelouse.com
Impressively structured Haut-Médoc that has been on much improved form since 1999. The property is fairly substantial with 64ha of vineyards and sur-prisingly for the Médoc the mix of varieties planted is 50% Merlot to 35% Cabernet Sauvignon, with the remaining 15% Cabernet Franc including 2% Petit Verdot. As a result, the wine tends to be full, fleshy and relatively forward. Nevertheless, it possesses well-honed tannins and an impressive depth and purity. This wine remains particularly well priced. (DM)

Recommended Reds:
Château Cambon-La-Pelouse Haut-Medoc ★★★ £C

Ch. Camensac (Haut-Médoc 5ème CC) www.chateaucamensac.com
The quality of this property has gradually improved since it was acquired in 1964 by the Forner family. Much of the vineyard has been replanted and there is now a relatively high proportion of Merlot (25%) contributing to the style, which is round, forward and accessible. The wine spends between 17 to 20 months in oak, up to 70% new oak is used, depending on the vintage, whilst the rest of the barriques are of one vintage only. The wine drinks well at 5 years or so. Just a notch up in 2005, 03 and 00, early tastings of the 2010 confirm class well above its station. (DM)

Recommended Reds:
Château Camensac Haut-Médoc ★★★☆ £D

Ch. Cantemerle (Haut-Médoc 5ème CC)
The 87 ha at Cantemerle are planted to a mix of 50% Cabernet Sauvignon and, unusually for the Left Bank, a whopping 40% Merlot, with the remaining 10% divided evenly between Cabernet Franc and Petit Verdot. Production is sizeable, with 50,000 cases produced annually. After significant replanting two decades ago the vine age is beginning to show and this together with the high proportion of Merlot provides a rich, vibrantly dark-fruited Médoc at its best. The very latest vintages are promising and 1998 and 96 are good. It has to be said, though, that the wine has not performed well in lesser years, particularly in the early 1990s, although quality seems to be consistently on the rise now and nudging ★★★☆. (DM)

Recommended Reds:
Château Cantemerle Haut-Médoc ★★★ £E

Ch. Cantenac-Brown (Margaux 3ème CC)
Purchased in 1987 by AXA Millésimes, which also owns a number of other prestigious Bordeaux properties including PICHON-LONGUEVILLE and SUDUIRAUT in Sauternes. Quality has been disappointing throughout the 1970s, 80s and, with the exception of 1990, the 90s prior to 96. The rating is for its current performance rather than earlier vintages and, given the performance of other châteaux within the AXA group, one would expect things here to continue to improve. Vintages from 2006 are a clear step up from somewhat disappointing previous vintages. (DM)

Recommended Reds:
Château Cantenac-Brown Margaux ★★★☆ £E

Ch. Carbonnieux (Pessac-Léognan) www.carbonnieux.com
Good red and particularly white Pessac-Léognans come from this property which will be run now by Philibert and Eric Perrin after the death of their father Antony in late 2008. Production is substantial for the appellation at over 30,000 cases a year. The white is good and has performed well. Some skin contact is allowed before fermentation in barrel, around half of which is new, and ageing is on lees. The red doesn't quite reach the same level but has also been consistent over recent vintages. Sound, well-crafted and approachable, it is lighter than some other Pessac-Léognan reds but displays attractive berry fruit and a fine mineral undercurrent. Both white and red will benefit from five years' bottle-ageing. Château Haut-Vigneau is another solid property producing decent red under the AC and there is a second wine, La Tour Léognan, produced in both red and white. The latter can often impress. (DM)

Recommended Reds:
Château Carbonnieux Pessac-Léognan ★★★ £E
Château Haut-Vigneau Pessac-Léognan ★★ £D
Recommended Whites:
Château Carbonnieux Pessac-Léognan ★★★☆ £E

Ch. Les Carmes Haut-Brion www.les-carmes-haut-brion.com
This a tiny property and, like HAUT-BRION, located amongst the suburbs of Bordeaux in Pessac-Léognan. Just 5 ha are under vine, with an unusually high proportion of 55% Merlot, along with 30% Cabernet Franc and 15% Cabernet Sauvignon. Dedication to quality has delivered impressive results since the late 1990s. Soil is managed organically and vinification in small vats enables plots within the vineyard to be fermented separately. Since 2012 whole berries have been fermented along with a small amount of stems. Malolactic takes place in barrel and around one half is of new wood. The wine is elegant, supple and rich, with firm but nicely rounded tannins. (DM)

Recommended Reds:
Château les Carmes Haut-Brion Pessac-Léognan ★★★★☆ £F

Ch. de Chantegrive (Graves) www.chantegrive.com
This property consists of 50 ha of red varieties and 38 ha of white, with production now quite substantial at over 40,000 cases a year. Four wines are produced. A good red with a fine balance of dark fruit, cedar and subtle oak is joined by a regular white Graves, an easy, fruit-driven style fermented at low temperatures. There is also the limited production Cuvée Caroline, barrel-fermented in a portion of new oak with regular use of bâtonnage to add weight and a rich, creamy texture. The sweet Cérons is a full, fat style with good depth and some honeyed complexity. (DM)

Recommended Reds:
Château de Chantegrive Graves ★★☆ £C

Bordeaux /Médoc, Graves & Sauternes

France

Recommended Whites:
Château de Chantegrive Graves Cuvée Caroline ★★★ £C
Château de Chantegrive Cérons ★★☆ £C
Château de Chantegrive Graves ★★☆ £B

Ch. Charmail (Haut-Médoc)
A consistent Left Bank performer for at least the last decade producing uniformly classy, cedary and structured claret from vineyards located just to the north of Saint-Estèphe. Bernard d'Halluin purchased the estate in 2008, but the previous owner, Olivier Seze, continues to manage the estate to this day. The wine, which has a high proportion of Merlot (48% of the vineyard) is modern and stylish. Neither fined nor filtered, it is marked by supple tannin and attractive, forward, dark berry fruit and hints of cassis, not least as a result of a touch of pre-fermentation maceration. There are none of the often green and herbaceous notes found in some lesser Bordeaux reds dominated by the variety.
Recommended Reds:
Château Charmail Haut-Médoc ★★★☆ £C

Ch. Chasse-Spleen (Moulis) www.chasse-spleen.com
Chasse-Spleen, along with POUJEAUX and MAUCAILLOU, is one of the only wines in the Moulis AC really to perform with any consistent class. The property is sizeable, with just under 85ha under vine. The wine is a blend of Cabernet Sauvignon, Merlot and Petit Verdot. With the odd exceptions (1997, 94 and 91) this property has fashioned a rich, concentrated and harmonious red. Wines produced since 2004 are noteworthy. It's a shame there aren't more properties turning out wines of this class in the appellation. The second wine, L'Oratoire de Chasse-Spleen, can be better than most and another wine, L'Héritage de Chasse-Spleen, is produced from some 20 ha of vines within and outside the Moulis appellation, so is classed as a Haut-Médoc is also well made. (DM)
Recommended Reds:
Château Chasse-Spleen Moulis ★★★☆ £D

Dom. de Chevalier (Pessac-Léognan) www.domainedechevalier.com
An important and sizeable producer, noted particularly for its splendid white. The production of this is very low, with just 4.5 of the 37.5 ha vineyard planted to Sauvignon Blanc and Sémillon. There is a high proportion of Sauvignon (70%) in the blend. Barrel-fermented and aged, it is a remarkably fine and elegant white capable of considerable age. The red has been less impressive than the white in the past but since consultant Stéphane Derenoncourt has been advising on the red there has been a big step up in quality and whilst the wine has consistently been of ★★★★ quality, it is certainly on the cusp of 5 stars now. (DM)
Recommended Reds:
Domaine de Chevalier Pessac-Léognan ★★★★☆ £F
Recommended Whites:
Domaine de Chevalier Pessac-Léognan ★★★★★ £G

Ch. Cissac (Haut-Médoc) www.chateau-cissac.com
Cissac is still made in a traditional, firm Médoc style but it is very fairly priced and generally well-crafted. But, although structured and austere when very young, it is increasingly rounder and suppler than of old with a little age. Wooden as well as stainless steel vats are used for fermentation and an increasing amount of new wood (30–40%) is used to age the wine. From the best vintages the wine is undoubtedly complex and harmonious but really needs cellaring for 8–10 years to show at its best. (DM)

Recommended Reds:
Château Cissac Haut-Médoc ★★★ £C

Ch. Clarke (Listrac-Médoc) www.cver.fr
Listrac, like Moulis, is quite a long way inland from the Gironde and the soil here has even less gravel than it does nearer the estuary, which will always hinder the admirable efforts made here. This property with increasingly old vines outclasses almost all of its neighbours but there remains a slightly coarse note. However, since 1995 the wine is more concentrated and harmonious, while retaining its soft and supple, earthy, dark fruit character. Clearly ★★★ now in the better years and very striking in 2005. (DM)
Recommended Reds:
Château Clarke Listrac-Médoc ★★★ £D

Ch. Clerc-Milon (Pauillac 5ème CC) www.bpdr.com
Moderate-sized property, with some 30 ha of vineyards and production running at just under 15,000 cases a year. The Cabernet Sauvignon component is quite low at less than 50% and 35% of the vineyard is planted to Merlot. As a result the style is very rounded and surprisingly approachable for Pauillac. While overshadowed by its sister château and neighbour MOUTON-ROTHSCHILD, Clerc-Milon is nevertheless an excellent, stylish source of the appellation, with a harmonious mix of dark fruits and cedar, all of which is nicely underpinned by its ripe and plummy Merlot component. At its current level since 1995. (DM)
Recommended Reds:
Château Clerc-Milon Pauillac ★★★★ £F

❀ Ch. Climens (Barsac 1er CC) www.chateau-climens.fr
Climens is an exceptional sweet wine and the leading property in the Barsac commune. It is outclassed only by Château d'YQUEM amongst the great botrytised wines of the Sauternes. Production is low at just over 3,000 cases a year and the vineyard, which is just 31ha, is planted solely to Sémillon. Despite the absence of Sauvignon Blanc the wine possesses not only intense and very concentrated honeyed fruit but a marvellously fresh acid balance as well. Best to age it for at least 5 years and it will be better with twice that time in the cellar. The wine was truly great in 2007, 05, 03, 01, 97, 90 and 89. Other very good more recent vintages include 2010, 09, 02, 00, 98, 96, 88 and 86. (DM)
Recommended Whites:
Château Climens Barsac ✪✪✪✪✪ £G

Clos Floridène (Graves) www.denisdubourdieu.fr
The main focus is on white wine, with 13 ha planted as opposed to 5.5 ha for red varieties. The white is a particularly impressive example and puts many more exalted Pessac-Léognans to shame. It is barrel-fermented and aged with *bâtonnage* to add richness but it is the citrus and mineral quality of the fruit that really marks it out. It will evolve nicely over the short to medium term. The red is sound and well-crafted but lacks the same excitement. The late Denis Dubourdieu also made the wines of Château REYNON. (DM)
Recommended Reds:
Clos Floridène Graves ★★☆ £C
Recommended Whites:
Clos Floridène Graves ★★★ £C

Ch. Clos Haut-Peyraguey (Sauternes 1er CC)
Very small Sauternes property. There are just 12 ha of vineyards, 90% of which are Sémillon, the balance Sauvignon Blanc. Quality

is good to very good but the wine just lacks the depth and intense concentration of the best of the other First Growths of the appellation. The style is more one of finesse and elegance than sheer weight and concentration. Very good in 2007, 05, 03, 01, 98, 97, 90 and 88, while other years are not quite of the same order. The second wine is Château Haut Bommes. (DM)

Recommended Whites:
Château Clos Haut-Peyraguey Sauternes ★★★★ £E

❀ Ch. Cos d'Estournel (Saint-Estèphe 2ème CC) www.estournel.com

One of the greatest wines of the Médoc and the premier château in Saint-Estèphe. Purchased from Bruno Prats by the Taillan Group, who also own GRUAUD-LAROSE, in 1998 and then by Michel Reybier in 2000, Jean-Guillaume Prats remained in charge of the property and enhanced the exceptional standards laid down by the Prats family there throughout the 1970s, 80s and 90s. After a dip in the late 1990s the wine has been right back on form. Using sophisticated vinification including must concentration, malolactic in barrel and new oak for ageing, the wine is very powerful as well as opulent. It should, however, show remarkable depth and harmony with a decade or more in the cellar. The second wine was originally called MARBUZET, which is itself a Cru Bourgeois, but is now labelled Les Pagodes de Cos. Reybier's massive investment in state-of-the-art technology has helped Prats to bring the level of this estate to new heights. However, Prats' departure at the beginning of 2013 has shown no let up in the quality of the wines produced and the new team led by Aymeric de Gironde continues where he left off. A white Cos d'Estournel has ben produced since 2005 although the quantities were so small that the wine was not sold commercially until the 2009 vintage. Made from around 80% Sauvignon Blanc and 20% Sémillon, it displays great ripeness, harmony and balance. La Goulée is a Médoc wine produced since 2003 and shows remarkable roundness of fruit for its pedigree. (NB)

Recommended Reds:
Château Cos d'Estournel Saint-Estèphe ✪✪✪✪✪ £H
Les Pagodes de Cos Saint-Estèphe ★★★☆ £F
La Goulée is a Médoc ★★★ £D

Recommended Whites:
Château Cos d'Estournel Bordeaux ★★★★ £G

Ch. Cos Labory (Saint-Estèphe 5ème CC)

Although overshadowed by its famous neighbour COS D'ESTOURNEL, this property improved greatly in the late 1980s and some of the vintages since have been impressive. 1996, 95, 90 and 88 were all a notch up on what has generally been achieved here previously. The late 1990s have somewhat disappointingly not maintained this level but the wine looks promising once more in recent vintages and since 2004 has been very consistent. At its best Cos Labory is full, marked by impressive blackcurrant fruit and underpinned by a firm, rounded, tannic structure. (DM)

Recommended Reds:
Château Cos Labory Saint-Estèphe ★★★☆ £E

Ch. Couhins-Lurton (Pessac-Léognan CC) www.andrelurton.com

André Lurton is now a major proprietor in the Graves, Entre-Deux-Mers and Margaux. At this tiny 5.5 ha Pessac property he produces less than 2,000 cases of very stylish white a year from 100% Sauvignon Blanc. No Sémillon is planted here but the wine is barrel-fermented in 50% new wood and aged with *bâtonnage* and has the structure and density to age well in bottle with a wonderfully intense mineral, gree fruit and citrus infused quality. A red is also produced

from mainly Merlot, with around a quarter Cabernet Sauvignon and is a touch less striking. (DM)

Recommended Reds:
Château Couhins-Lurton Pessac-Léognan ★★★ £E

Recommended Whites:
Château Couhins-Lurton Pessac-Léognan ★★★★ £E

Ch. Coutet (Barsac 1er CC) www.chateaucoutet.com

Very good property and near neighbour of CLIMENS, although the wine here doesn't quite reach the same heights. As well as Sémillon, which accounts for 75% of the blend, and Sauvignon Blanc, there is a little Muscadelle, just 3%. There is no doubt that there is a marked aromatic character in the wine in addition to its classic rich vanilla and peach notes. In exceptional years a special super-concentrated very limited production Cuvée Madame is released. This is certainly ✪✪✪✪. (DM)

Recommended Whites:
Château Coutet Barsac ★★★★ £F

Ch. Dauzac (Margaux 5ème CC) www.chateaudauzac.com

André Lurton had controlled this property for its insurance company owners until 2013. Now management has been taken over by Laurent Fortin who is instigating a change towards biodiversity. There are 46 ha under vine here and production is just shy of 25,000 cases, so it is a sizeable operation. The style is supple and rich with an emphasis on approachable dark fruit and well judged oak. The wine is only kept in barrel for 12 months but 50–80% is new. Quality has improved dramatically since the 1990s. (DM)

Recommended Reds:
Château Dauzac Margaux ★★★ £E

Ch. Doisy-Daëne (Barsac 2ème CC) www.denisdubourdieu.fr

This is a Barsac, until 2016 made by the late Denis Dubourdieu. It is marked by its elegance rather than its sheer weight or richness. It can be piercingly aromatic, though, and very intense. Of a completely different order – richer and fuller – is an occasional very limited *cuvée* called L'Extravagance. It is only produced in exceptional vintages, including 2010, 07, 05, 03, 01, 97 and 96. As well as the sweet wines a good dry Bordeaux Blanc is rich and fruity. (DM)

Recommended Whites:
Château Doisy-Daëne Barsac ★★★★ £E   Bordeaux ★★ £C

Ch. Doisy-Védrines (Barsac 2ème CC) www.domainedechevalier.com

This is the biggest of the three Doisy properties with 27 ha. In contrast to DOISY DAËNE and most other fine Barsacs, this property tends to produce wine with more overt luscious honeyed fruit. It is very impressive, retaining an elegant finesse in lighter years when the wine carries less sheer weight. There is 5% Muscadelle planted here, which provides an aromatic undercurrent to the wine. (DM)

Recommended Whites:
Château Doisy-Védrines Sauternes ★★★★ £D

❀ Ch. Ducru-Beaucaillou www.chateau-ducru-beaucaillou.com

One of the greatest wines of Saint-Julien. The 50 ha of 2ème CC Ducru based in the south of the appellation are planted to a mix of Cabernet Sauvignon (65%), Merlot (25%), and an equal portion of Cabernet Franc and Petit Verdot. It is a very impressive, classically structured example of the appellation: always elegant, very intense, with subtle cedar and dark fruit underpinned by finely integrated oak. It requires patience and cellaring. From the current crop of

France

excellent vintages 2010, 09, 06, 05, 03, 00, 98, 96 and 95 were exemplary but 97 was something of a disappointment. (DM)

Recommended Reds:

Château Ducru-Beaucaillou Saint-Julien ⚫⚫⚫⚫⚫ £H

Ch. Duhart-Milon (Pauillac 4ème CC) www.lafite.com

Intriguingly, this Rothschild property is also part-owned by the Chalone Wine Group from the USA (now owned by drinks giant Diageo), which established its reputation with the CHALONE winery in Monterey, California. There is no doubt that the 50 ha of vineyards have benefited greatly from the Lafite input since the property was purchased in 1962. Fermentation is modern in stainless steel and ageing taking place in barrels, 50% new, that are coopered at Lafite-Rothschild. (DM)

Recommended Reds:

Château Duhart-Milon Pauillac ★★★★ £F

Ch. de Fargues (Sauternes) www.chateau-de-fargues.com

A rare wine with a price to match. An average of only 15,000 bottles are made annually from 15 ha of vines owned by the Lur-Saluces family of YQUEM fame. The property did not produce any sweet wine until 1943 but this is one of the finest examples of Sauternes now made and one of the longest-lasting wines in the appellation. (NB)

Recommended Whites:

Château de Fargues Sauternes ★★★★★ £F

Ch. Ferrière (Margaux 3ème CC) www.ferriere.com

Small Classed Growth which has improved dramatically during the 1990s. Production is barely more than 4,000 cases a year and the dedicated commitment to quality here by Claire Villars-Lurton has ensured that this is one of the best properties in the Margaux appellation. The wine is rich, intense and concentrated and now shows great harmony and refinement. There is minimal processing with egg-white fining and malolactic in barrel. The wine comfortably absorbs the impact of 60% new oak. The property has become progressively biodynamic and received official certification in 2015.(DM)

Recommended Reds:

Château Ferrière Margaux ★★★★ £E

Ch. de Fieuzal (Pessac-Léognan CC) www.fieuzal.com

The style here, particularly with the red, is to produce opulent, richly textured, forward, modern and approachable wines, accessible very shortly after release. The white, which unlike the red is not in fact a Cru Classé, also shows rich, forward, honeyed fruit with a solid dose of new oak but with a depth and structure that ensures good, medium-term cellaring and is the more impressive of the two. These wines, particularly the whites, offer very good value. (DM)

Recommended Reds:

Château de Fieuzal Pessac-Léognan ★★★☆ £E

Recommended Whites:

Château de Fieuzal Pessac-Léognan ★★★★ £E

Château Filhot (Sauternes 2ème CC) www.filhot.com

A pretty consistent château regularly producing wines with a good balance of sweetness and acidity. It has always been a bit on the light side, probably due to the high proportion of Sauvignon Blanc, around a third, but it remains good drinking value for a classed-growth Sauternes. (DM)

Recommended Whites:

Château Filhot Sauternes ★★★☆ £E

Ch. de France (Pessac-Léognan)

Improving medium-sized Pessac property of some 35 ha. Just 3 ha of the vineyard is so far planted to white varieties, with Sauvignon accounting for 70% and the balance Sémillon. Red grapes are 60% Cabernet Sauvignon and 40% Merlot. The quality of the wines has greatly improved since the late 1990s. In part this is due to the involvement of Michel Rolland who advises on the winemaking. Vinification of the red is traditional with a fermentation temperature in the low 30s celsius and malolactic is conducted in *cuve*. Ageing is for 14–18 months in *barrique*. Medium-weight, with lightly cedary fruit the wine will add flesh with 4 or 5 years' age. The white is barrel-fermented with *bâtonnage*. (DM)

Recommended Reds:

Château de France Pessac-Léognan ★★☆ £D

Recommended Whites:

Château de France Pessac-Léognan ★★★ £C

Ch. Giscours (Margaux 2ème CC) www.chateau-giscours.com

Giscours like du TERTRE is now in the ownership of Eric Albada Jedgersma and similarly has been performing at a much improved level in recent vintages. Investment in the vineyard and cellars with reduced yields and careful vinification has produced some impressive examples. The property is sizeable and covers 85 ha of vineyards planted to Cabernet Sauvignon (55%), Merlot (40%) and Cabernet Franc. Despite the high proportion of Merlot the wine, at its recent best, is richly textured, powerful and less obviously perfumed than other examples of the appellation. Two secondary wines are produced which both offer some of the character of the *Grand Vin*. Sirene de Giscours takes the Margaux appellation and there is a budget label, Haut-Médoc de Giscours. The top wine will add increasing richness with 8–10 years' age. (DM)

Recommended Reds:

Château Giscours Margaux ★★★★ £E

Ch. Gloria (Saint-Julien) www.chateau-gloria.com

This has been a consistently sound Cru Bourgeois over the years. Gloria has performed admirably throughout the 1970s, 80s and 90s. It is a sizeable property, with widely scattered plots, with some 47 ha under vine producing around 25,000 cases a year. The wine is not immensely complex or long-lived but is full of vibrant, dark, brambly blackcurrant fruit, nicely judged oak and an elegant hint of cedar in the background. It has been of its impressive current quality since 2000. (DM)

Recommended Reds:

Château Gloria Saint-Julien ★★★☆ £E

Ch. Grand-Puy-Lacoste (Pauillac 5ème CC) www.haut-batailley.fr

Under the same ownership as HAUT-BATAILLEY, this has been an admirable and classic red Bordeaux for the past three decades and there have been many admirable vintages since World War II. This is the quintessential example of what you expect from fine Pauillac, a wine loaded with cassis and cedar, refined and elegant but with real power and density. 1990, and more recently 95, 96 and 2000 are wines of significant class. 2003, 04, 05, 06, 09 and 10 look very much of the same order. (DM)

Recommended Reds:

Château Grand-Puy-Lacoste Pauillac ★★★★ £F

Ch. Gruaud-Larose (Saint-Julien) *www.gruaud-larose.com*
Large Saint-Julien property with production approaching 40,000 cases a year, responsible for some formidable and massively structured wines during the 1980s. 1982 and 86 were without a doubt ✪✪✪✪, with a number of others on the cusp. Quality generally has remained impressive throughout the 1990s and 2000s but not at quite the same level. These are powerful, dense and tannic reds in need of at least 8–10 years' cellaring. The second wine, Sarget de Gruaud-Larose, can be good, particularly in better years. (DM)

Recommended Reds:
Château Gruaud-Larose Saint-Julien ★★★★ £F

Ch. Guiraud (Sauternes 1er CC) *www.chateauguiraud.fr*
The property was bought from the Narbys in 2006 by Robert Peugeot, a financier, Olivier Bernard, of Domaine de Chevalier, Stefan von Niepperg, of Ch. Canon-la-Gaffelière and others and Xavier Planty, who had run the estate for the Narbys since they bought it in 1981. Xavier Planty turned out impressive Sauternes in the top vintages of the 1990s. and with a consistent replanting process has much improved the ratio of Sémillon to Sauvignon Blanc and plantings of the former now account for 70% of the vineyard. Since the purchase, even greater improvements have been made and whilst the estate is still producing ripe, fat and honeyed wines, they have, in recent years, been much better balanced and less of a blockbuster. A movement towards organic farming since the purchase has resulted in the estate gainng full organic certification commencing with the 2011 vintage. Since the purchase by the partnership, the wines have been consistently good with 2009, 2010, 2011, 2013, 2014 and 2015 on the cusp of super five stars. (DM)

Recommended Whites:
Château Guiraud Sauternes ★★★★★ £E

Ch. Haut-Bailly (Pessac-Léognan CC) *www.chateau-haut-bailly.com*
A supple, elegant and consistently well-crafted red which is both approachable and refined. In contrast with most neighbouring properties, no white is made here. Haut-Bailly was purchased by Robert Wilmers, an American banker, in 1998 but the original proprietors, the Sanders family, are still involved in the direction and management. Consistent throughout the last two decades, the wine ages very well indeed. In 2012, Wilmers purchased neighbouring Château le Pape, a 7 hectare property which is undergoing substantial renonvation and upgrading by the team led by Valerie Sanders. In the meantime, he has turned it into a luxury boutique hotel which enables guests to experience a stay at a real Bordeaux château. (DM)

Recommended Reds:
Château Haut-Bailly Pessac-Léognan ★★★★ £F

Ch. Haut-Bergey *www.chateau-haut-bergey.com*
Middle-ranking Pessac-Léognan CC property with 25ha given over to red grapes (54% Cabernet Sauvignon; 46% Merlot) and only 2ha to whites (84% Sauvignon; 18% Sémillon). The white usually shows the better quality, with a great deal of finesse, whilst the red is often a bit muscular and needs time to come round. Also produces the Pessac super-*cuvée* BRANON. (DM)

Recommended Reds:
Château Haut-Bergey Pessac-Léognan ★★★ £D

Recommended Whites:
Château Haut-Bergey Pessac-Léognan ★★★☆ £E

Ch. Haut-Batailly (Pauillac 5ème CC) *www.haut-batailley.fr*
Under the same ownership as GRAND-PUY-LACOSTE. Quality here used to be somewhat variable and lesser vintages were light and lacking in substance as well as possessing a hard, at times austerely firm edge. This was surprising given the quality of the other properties owned by the Borie family but the mid-1990s saw an improvement and change in style. The wine is now less aggressive and raw and possesses a fine, more supple and even texture. It is altogether more accessible and harmonious. Significantly more impressive in 1995, 96 and 2000. Some fine examples have also followed in 2003, 04, 05, 06 and 2007 as well as 2009 and 2010. (DM)

Recommended Reds:
Château Haut-Batailley Pauillac ★★★ £E

✪✪ Ch. Haut-Brion (Pessac-Léognan 1er CC) *www.haut-brion.com*
One of the four original properties classified as a First Growth in the 1855 Classification of red Bordeaux wines. The property is under the same ownership as Châteaux la MISSION HAUT-BRION and la TOUR HAUT-BRION. The vineyards are planted in superbly drained gravel soils that provide an almost ideal supply of moisture to optimise fruit ripening. Red grapes occupy 48 ha, while less than 3 ha provides a tiny amount of exquisite, subtly barrel-fermented white from Sémillon and Sauvignon Blanc. The property, now surrounded by the ever-encroaching suburbs of Bordeaux, is small in comparison to the other First Growths, producing a total of some 12,500 cases a year. Both red and white have been magnificent through the late 1990s and into the whole decade of the 2000s, only the 1997 and 91 red dipping a little. Great older vintages include 1990, 89, 86, 82, 75 and the astonishing 61. The second wine, Le Clarence de Haut-Brion was formerly labelled Château Bahans Haut-Brion, can also be very impressive. A second white is made from both Haut-Brion and la Mission Haut-Brion, labelled La Clarté de Haut-Brion. (DM)

Recommended Reds:
Château Haut-Brion Pessac-Léognan ✪✪✪✪✪ £H
Le Clarence de Haut-Brion ★★★★ £G

Recommended Whites:
Château Haut-Brion Pessac-Léognan ✪✪✪✪✪ £H

Ch. Haut-Marbuzet (Saint-Estèphe)
Henri Duboscq produces a fleshy, powerful, very rich Saint-Estèphe marked by well-integrated spicy new oak. Not only is this an outstanding Cru Bourgeois but it is only surpassed within the appellation by COS D'ESTOURNEL and MONTROSE. Production is not inconsiderable at close to 30,000 cases a year. The wine has been impressive in recent years and has been performing comfortably out of its class. It offers very good value and there is a decent soft and forward second label, Chambert-Marbuzet. (DM)

Recommended Reds:
Château Haut-Marbuzet Saint-Estèphe ★★★★ £F

Ch. d'Issan (Margaux 3ème CC) *www.chateau-issan.com*
This property was often disappointing in the late 1980s and early 90s. However since 1995 things have been looking decidedly better and the wine is once more in the elegant, cedary and perfumed style that represents fine Margaux. Major investment in both vineyard and cellars and input on the winemaking from Jacques Boissenet (one of a number of high-profile Bordeaux consultants, who also advises André Lurton as well as the Napa Valley QUINTESSA operation) are clearly having a positive effect. (DM)

Recommended Reds:
Château d'Issan Margaux ★★★☆ £F

Bordeaux /Médoc, Graves & Sauternes

France

⚙ Clos du Jaugueyron (Margaux)

Michel Théron is a third-generation vigneron and a graduate in viticulture and oenological science. In 1993 he acquired the Clos du Jaugueyron, a 0.4 ha estate in the commune of Cantenac but only entitled to the Haut-Médoc appellation. The grapes have an average age of 50 years and are 60% Cabernet Sauvignon, 20% Merlot, 10% Petit Verdot, 5% Carmenère and 5% "others". There is remarkable quality for the price. Flushed with the success of this wine, he acquired a small parcel of adjoining vines which happened to be in the Margaux appellation. The fact that there are only a few hundred cases produced under this appellation, together with the attention given to it by certain influential North American wine writers, has probably made this the ultimate garagiste property in the Médoc. Continuing improvements over the last few years has led to even more harmonious wines in both appellations. (NB)

Recommended Reds:
Clos du Jaugueyron Margaux ★★★★★ £F
Clos du Jaugueyron Haut-Médoc ★★★★ £D

Ch. Kirwan (Margaux 3ème CC) *www.chateau-kirwan.com*

The Schÿler family, who also run the Schroder and Schÿler négociant operation in Bordeaux, had sold their interest in this small to medium-sized property in the early 1990s but promptly bought it back again a couple of years later. The result has been a real boost for the fortunes of the property and in particular the quality of the wine. Michel Rolland provided guidance on the winemaking front until 2006 and quality has been consistently good since 1996. Recently KIrwan have replaced their stainles steel tanks with concete vats and are co-inoculating bacteria with the fermenting yeast to produce simutaneous alcoholic and malolactic fermentation which should enhance the reliability of the wines further. A second wine, Les Charmes de Kirwan, is also made. (DM)

Recommended Reds:
Château Kirwan Margaux ★★★☆ £F

⚙ Ch. Lafaurie-Peyraguey *www.lafaurie-peyraguey.com*

Silvio Denz, a Swiss entrepreneur and owner of CH. FAUGÈRES and CH. PÉBY-FAUGÈRES in St. Émilion has recently (2014) purchased this Sauternes 1er CC domaine from the Cordier family. From 40 ha under vine in the commune of Bommes, with a grape mix of Sémillon (90%), Sauvignon Blanc (8%) and Muscadelle (just 2%), some of the finest Sauternes is now being made at this property. This has only been the case for the last 15 years or so. The 1970s were a disappointment but the wines are now quite exemplary. They combine the intense richness and honeyed concentration of the finest Sauternes with something of the elegance found in CLIMENS. The wines are very stylish and long-lived. The 2009, 07, 05, 03, 02, 99, 98 and 97 are all extraordinarily fine and 2011 may have the potential to be exquisite. (DM)

Recommended Whites:
Château Lafaurie-Peyraguey Sauternes ★★★★★ £F

⚙⚙ Ch. Lafite-Rothschild (Pauillac 1er CC) *www.lafite.com*

One of the world's great reds and a consistent and superlative performer throughout the mid- to late 1990s. Exceptional wines have been produced since 1996. However, all has not always been rosy here and 20 or so years ago the quality was much more uneven. The vineyard is planted to some 100 ha of Cabernet Sauvignon (75%), Merlot (20%), Cabernet Franc (4%) and Petit Verdot (a mere 1%). A minimum of 15–20 years is required to achieve a harmony between the formidable, powerful tannins and the intense and fragrantly rich cedar and cassis fruit. 1982 marked a real turning point in the quality of the wine and other years of particular note are 1986, 88, 90 and 96. The 53 and 59 were both superb but surprisingly 61 failed to achieve the high quality of that year. Latterly, 2000, 03, 05, 08, 09 and 10 have produced top quality but the chateau has been a model of consistency for the whole decade. The second wine, Les Carruades de Lafite-Rothschild, is very impressive for a second label. (DM)

Recommended Reds:
Château Lafite-Rothschild Pauillac ⚫⚫⚫⚫⚫ £H
Les Carruades de Lafite-Rothschild ★★★★ £H

Ch. Lafon-Rochet (Saint-Estèphe 4ème CC) *www.lafon-rochet.com*

Under the same ownership as PONTET-CANET, Lafon-Rochet has performed well, sometimes very well throughout the mid- to late 1990s. The vintages of the early 1990s did not achieve the same level but that is unsurprising given the difficult conditions of those years. The wine is a great deal more supple and approachable than it used to be and much of the reason has been a progressive replanting of the vineyard with a higher proportion of Merlot, now some 40%. In 2012 they hired Jean-Claude Berrouet as a consultant, who had also worked with CH. PETRUS and began replacing some of their stainless steel tanks with concrete vats. No doubt both these moves have assisted in improving quality. 2010, 09, 08, 05, 03, 01, 00, 98, 96 and 95 stand out with 2014 being one of the few successes of the vintage. (DM)

Recommended Reds:
Château Lafon-Rochet Saint-Estèphe ★★★★ £F

Ch. Lagrange (Saint-Julien 3ème CC) *www.chateau-lagrange.com*

The Japanese-owned Suntory company has pushed wine quality at this property forward dramatically since its purchase in the early 1980s and Lagrange was very well run by Marcel Ducasse until 2007 when he was succeded by his assistant of 17 years, Bruno Eynard. Lagrange is very large, even by the standards of the Médoc, with over 110 ha under vine. The wine is rich and concentrated, but in an approachable style, with supple, well-rounded tannin. Consistently good over the last 5 or 6 years, it just needs that extra dimension to take it into the top division. (DM)

Recommended Reds:
Château Lagrange Saint-Julien ★★★☆ £F

Ch. La Lagune (Haut-Médoc 3ème CC) *www.chateau-lalagune.com*

Some great reds were made at this property during the 1970s and 80s but more recently this sizeable 77-ha estate has produced some less exciting wines, although recent vintages under the current ownership, who are aslso the ownwers of the PAUL JABOULET AINE estate in the Northern Rhône have shown a marked improvement. The vineyard is mainly Cabernet Sauvignon (60%), Merlot (20%) and the balance Cabernet Franc and Petit Verdot. things appear to be taking a turn for the better. Increasingly impressive, elegant and cedary claret is being made using stainless steel temperature-controlled tanks for vinification, with ageing in an increasing amount of new oak. Since 2004, under the direction of Caroline Frey, the wines have been biodynamically produced. (DM)

Recommended Reds:
Château La Lagune Haut-Médoc ★★★☆ £F

Ch. Lamothe-Guignard *www.chateau-lamothe-guignard.fr*

This is the larger of the two Lamothe properties in Sauternes. The other Lamothe, owned by Guy Despujols, does not quite reach the

same heights. 90% of the vineyard at this Sauternes 2ème CC is planted to Sémillon along with 5% Muscadelle and 5% Sauvignon Blanc. The style is increasingly elegant with luscious botrytis character showing through in the best years. (DM)

Recommended Whites:
Château Lamothe-Guignard Sauternes ★★★ £D

Ch. Lanessan (Haut-Médoc) *www.lanessan.com*
This was a somewhat old-fashioned style of Médoc located close to Saint-Julien. Medium- rather than full-bodied or super-rich, the wine can be long-lived, elegant and intense, particularly in the best vintages when it can really ripen its at times angular tannins. With time, complex cedar and elegant, evolved tertiary characters emerge. A new direction was taken in 2012 when Paz Espejo took over as manager. Optical sorting, environmental management certification and the appointment in 2015 of Hubert de Boüard of CH. ANGELUS in a consultancy role, should see marked improvements in future vintages although good wines were made in 1996, 2000, 2005, 2009 and 2010. (DM)

Recommended Reds:
Château Lanessan Haut-Médoc ★★★ £D

Ch. Langoa-Barton (Saint-Julien 3ème CC) *www.leoville-barton.com*
Sister property to LÉOVILLE-BARTON and in the Barton family for nearly two centuries. This has always been a consistent performer, producing elegant Saint-Julien with attractive dark fruit and a rich, cedary complexity. The two châteaux are in fact vinified in the same winery facility, and are renowned for their fair prices. Both also share the same label for the second wine, Réserve de Léoville-Barton, which can also be good. 2010, 09, 06, 05, 04, 03, 01, 00 and 98 stand out among recent vintages. (DM)

Recommended Reds:
Château Langoa-Barton Saint-Julien ★★★☆ £F

Ch. Larrivet Haut-Brion (Pessac-Léognan) *www.larrivethautbrion.fr*
There are 52 ha of vines planted here, 43 ha of which account for an even split of Cabernet Sauvignon and Merlot. The white varieties are also evenly split, between Sémillon and Sauvignon Blanc. Both wines are impressive and consultancy input on the winemaking is provided by Michel Rolland. The property is worthy of being upgraded to Cru Classé status. The quality in top years since 2000 has been very good. The red is stylish, refined and approachable at a few years, while the white is an elegant and notably piercing barrel-fermented style with a harmonious mix of fresh green and citrus fruits and subtle oak. (DM)

Recommended Reds:
Château Larrivet Haut-Brion Pessac-Léognan ★★★★ £F
Recommended Whites:
Château Larrivet Haut-Brion Pessac-Léognan ★★★☆ £E

Ch. Lascombes (Margaux 2ème CC) *www.chateau-lascombes.com*
There has been a sea-change at this château since it was acquired by capital Col;ony in 2001. Since the 2000 vintage (the first vintage produced by the then new owners) consultant enologist Michel Rolland and the home team led by Dominique Befve have worked wonders. Gone are the weedy wines produced under the previous regime; in are wines of power and strength which are nevertheless underscored by Margaux finesse. The wines are full rich black fruits. Surprisingly, the largest proportion of grapes are Merlot (50%), with the balance split 45/5 between Cabernet Sauvignon and Petit Verdot.Chevalier de Lascombes is a solid second wine with a

greaster proportion of Merlot in the blend. In July 2011, the estate was sold by Capital Colony to the present owners, a French pensions group, who have promised to ensure continuity by retainiung the whole winemaking team. (NB)

Recommended Reds:
Château Lascombes Margaux ★★★☆ £F
Chevalier de Lascombes Margaux ★★☆ £D

✹✹ **Ch. Latour (Pauillac 1er CC)** *www.chateau-latour.com*
To many this is the greatest of all the great wines of the Médoc and to some the greatest in the entire region. There is no doubt that it is one of the world's most remarkable reds, which at its magnificent best is both massive and concentrated but at the same time harmonious and very refined. It requires cellaring and you should allow one or preferably two decades. While the wine performs consistently at a very high level now, a number of vintages in the early to mid-1980s were less impressive, nowhere near its current ✹✹✹✹ ranking. Fortunately, with a production of over 30,000 cases a year, the wine is not impossible to find – unlike a number of new 'super' wines being made elsewhere around the world. Recent vintages have all been very striking. Among the great earlier years 82, 71, 66, 61, 59 and 49 are all legendary. Les Forts de Latour is a very impressive second wine. (DM)

Recommended Reds:
Château Latour Pauillac ✹✹✹✹✹ £H
Les Forts de Latour ★★★★☆ £H

Ch. La Tour Carnet (Haut-Médoc) *www.cave-bernard-magrez.com*
A rich, fleshy style of Médoc which is produced from Cabernet Sauvignon (52%), Merlot (42%) and a little Cabernet Franc and Petit Verdot. Michel Rolland consults over the winemaking for which fermentation is carried out in wooden vats with malolactic typically in *barrique*. Around 70% new oak is used and all operations are now carried out by gravity. the wine is ripe and reasonably forward; 4–5 years are required to integrate the fruit and initially dominant oak. The white is a blend of mainly Sauvignon Blanc, Sémillon and a touch of Muscadelle. (DM)

Recommended Reds:
Château La Tour Carnet Haut-Médoc ★★★☆ £E
Recommended Whites:
Château La Tour Carnet Bordeaux ★★★ £E

Ch. Latour-Martillac (Pessac-Léognan) *www.latour-martillac.com*
Good white and red Pessac is produced at this property, with around threequarters of the output red. Increasing vine age is one of the reasons why quality has surged forward during the 1990s. The red varieties now average 30 years and the whites a full 40 years. The red is an approachable, supple wine with refined tannins and nicely judged oak that varies between 30 and 50% depending on the year. The white is rich and honeyed, with a real toasty, creamy character from barrel-fermentation and bâttonage underpinned by loads of character and style. Both offer good value for money. (DM)

Recommended Reds:
Château Latour-Martillac Pessac-Léognan ★★★ £D
Recommended Whites:
Château Latour-Martillac Pessac-Léognan ★★★☆ £D

✹ **Ch. Léoville-Barton** *www.leoville-barton.com*
This marvellously consistent Saint-Julien 2ème CC red has long been one of Bordeaux's great-value wines. It is produced from 48 ha of vineyards planted to a mix of Cabernet Sauvignon (70%), Merlot

Bordeaux /Médoc, Graves & Sauternes

France

(22%) and Cabernet Franc (8%). It is vinified in the same winery as the Barton families other top Saint-Julien red LANGOA-BARTON with the same attention to detail. The wine is a stylish, cedary, medium full claret with well-judged oak and a supple but youthfully firm texture that requires time to achieve balance and harmony. It is no blockbuster but very good, intense and long-lived nonetheless. It was seriously nudging ✪✪✪✪ in 1996, 2000 and 2005 as well as 2010. The 89, 86 and 82 were also very fine. (DM)

Recommended Reds:
Château Léoville-Barton Saint-Julien ★★★★★ £F

✿ Ch. Léoville-las-Cases (Saint-Julien 2ème CC)
Almost universally regarded now as the finest of the super-seconds, on many occasions this magnificent property outclasses the First Growths. Not surprisingly the wine carries a price to match this performance and has in a number of recent top vintages held up extraordinarily well on auction markets. This is also a fairly significant château, with 97 ha under vine. The high standards in place here ensure that a significant amount of the *Grand Vin* is declassified as Petit Léon de Léoville from the 2007 vintage. Clos du Marquis, which was considered as the second wine and regarded as one of the very best of the Médoc's second labels in fact comes from its own separate vineyard. With a proportion of its fruit also going into Petit Léon de Léoville expect to see further gains with Clos du Marquis. The quality here at Léoville-la-Cases has been top-notch throughout the 2000s and 1990s – only 1992 and 91 saw some ground lost, and the wine was a testament to the trying conditions of those years. The Delon family also own POTENSAC in the Médoc and NENIN at Pomerol. (DM)

Recommended Reds:
Château Léoville-las-Cases Saint-Julien ✪✪✪✪✪ £H
Clos du Marquis Saint-Julien ★★★★ £F

✿ Ch. Léoville-Poyferré *www.leoville-poyferre.fr*
The third among the great Léoville super-seconds. This was originally regarded as the first among equals and today, after a period of relative decline in the 1960s and 70s, it is once more challenging the other two Léoville properties. Poyferré, while a serious, dense and powerfully structured wine, is more approachable than the other two. It has a more vibrant, upfront, dark blackcurrant and mulberry fruit character and is an altogether more opulent style, partly achieved through a portion of the wine being put through malolactic in barrel. Nevertheless it remains very refined and elegant, an excellent expression of its *terroir*. 2000, 96 and 90 were all extremely fine examples and 2003 and 2005 look to have similar potential. This has now been confirmed by the quality of the 2009 and 2010 vintages. The second wine, Moulin Riche, is good to very good on occasion. (DM)

Recommended Reds:
Château Léoville-Poyferré Saint-Julien ★★★★★ £G

Ch. La Louvière (Pessac-Léognan) *www.andrelurton.com*
This is one of several properties in the André Lurton Graves empire. As well as the wines of La Louvière, the company owns Château DAUZAC in the Margaux appellation, Château BONNET in the Entre-Deux-Mers as well as three other Pessac-Léognan properties: Château de CRUZEAU, Château ROCHEMORIN and Château COUHINS-LURTON. The La Louvière vineyard comprises some 48 ha, of which 33 ha are planted to Cabernet Sauvignon and Merlot. The smaller white vineyard holding is dominated by Sauvignon Blanc, which accounts for around 85%, the balance being Sémillon. Both

wines are approachable and forward in style but will also age well in the medium term. The red is supple, with refined, nicely rounded tannin and the white ripe and full of citrus and subtle toasted oak. (DM)

Recommended Reds:
Château la Louvière Pessac-Léognan ★★★☆ £E
Recommended Whites:
Château la Louvière Pessac-Léognan ★★★★ £E

✿ Ch. Lynch-Bages (Pauillac 5ème CC) *www.lynchbages.com*
Regarded rightly during the 1980s as one of the great super-seconds despite its lower official classification. Talented Jean-Michel Cazes unquestionably had a vast influence on quality here during that period. During the late 1990s he has lost just a touch of the sheen. The wine at its best is still very fine, full of dark cassis and ripe stylish tannin, and is surprisingly approachable. A good straightforward lightly oaked Bordeaux Blanc is also produced, along with the second wine, Haut-Bages-Avérous. Among recent vintages the 2010, 09, 06, 05, 00, 96 and 95 were all very impressive. Among earlier years the trio of 88, 89 and 90 were very fine, as were 85, 82 and 70. (DM)

Recommended Reds:
Château Lynch-Bages Pauillac ★★★★★ £G
Recommended Whites:
Château Lynch-Bages Bordeaux ★★ £D

Ch. Lynch-Moussas (Pauillac 5ème CC) *www.lynch-moussas.com*
This château has always been considered one of the dullest in the area but recently the wine has become more vibrant and fleshed out. Although it is still a wine for relatively early drinking, it is now producing big tannins with enough fruit underneath to ensure a bit of extra longevity. 2003, 2005 , 2010 and 2015 are the best of the recent vintages. This is a much improved and improving estate and the prices are still reasonable. This château has always been considered one of the dullest in the area but recently the wine has become more vibrant and fleshed out. Although it is still a wine for relatively early drinking, it is now producing big tannins with enough fruit underneath to ensure a bit of extra longevity. 2003, 2005 , 2010 and 2015 are the best of the recent vintages. This is a much improved and improving estate and the prices are still reasonable. (NB)

Recommended Reds:
Château Lynch-Moussas Pauillac ★★★ £D

Magrez-Tivoli (Médoc) *www.bernard-magrez.com*
One of a number of wines including PASSION DU PRIEURÉ MALESAN and Gérard Depardieu's LA CROIX DE PEYROLIE that are marketed by Bernard Magrez. This comes from a tiny 2.5 ha plot planted twothirds/one-third Cabernet Sauvignon and Merlot. The vineyard is sited on classic Médoc gravel soil and is now 40 years old. Low yields, hand-harvesting, hand-sorting and vinification in small vats all contribute to the impressive quality. The wine is handled entirely by gravity and aged in oak for 22 months. It is both fleshy and concentrated with a pure cedary undercurrent to the fruit as well not inconsiderable new oak. (DM)

Recommended Reds:
Magrez-Tivoli Médoc ★★★★ £F

✿ Ch. Malartic-Lagravière *www.malartic-lagraviere.com*
This Pessac-Léognan CC property was sold by Champagne house LAURENT-PERRIER to the Bonnie family in 1997 and since then there

has been significant investment with a dramatic raising of standards. The vineyard is now tended organically with reduced yields and a massive renovation of the cellars now means that winery operations are handled where possible by gravity. Michel Rolland consults for the reds. With 20% Sémillon added to the white it offers a ripe and opulent, lightly oaked style with none of the sulphur of old, while the red is rich, ripe and approachable. Both will develop well over the medium term. The second label for both red and white, Le Réserve de Malartic, now offers very good reliable drinking and the Bonnie family also have a second property in the appellation, Gazin Rocquefort source of an additionally characterful red. A new venture in Argentina, Bodega DIAMANDES was established in 2005. (DM)

Recommended Reds:
Château Malartic-Lagravière Pessac-Léognan ★★★★☆ £E
Château Gazin Rocquencourt Pessac-Léognan ★★★☆ £E
La Réserve de Malartic Pessac-Léognan ★★★ £D

Recommended Whites:
Château Malartic-Lagravière Pessac-Léognan ★★★★☆ £E
La Réserve de Malartic Pessac-Léognan ★★☆ £D

❀ Ch. Malescot-Saint-Exupéry www.malescot.com
During the 1980s and early 90s this was a reliable if somewhat unexciting Margaux, but reasonably priced. Quality has taken a significant step up in recent vintages and the price has risen but not excessively so. As is so often the case, a new generation has meant progressive moves forward. The wine is now riper and fuller but not at all extracted, retaining a typically elegant, perfumed Margaux character. With the exception of 1997, which was a touch below par, every recent vintage looks very good with 2005, 06, 09, 10, 14 and 15 clearly putting it into the ★★★★★ bracket. (DM)

Recommended Reds:
Château Malescot-Saint-Exupéry Margaux ★★★★★ £F

Ch. de Malle (Sauternes 2ème CC) www.chateau-de-malle.fr
The Comtesse de Bournazel has been producing consistently fine and elegant Sauternes since the late 1980s from 30 ha of Sémillon, Sauvignon Blanc and Muscadelle. The château itself is registered as a national monument and is open to the public. The wine increasingly shows a rich opulent character as well as an intense fragrance. It perfectly balances weight and finesse. It has been very good since 1997. A decent white Graves, M de Malle, is also made as well as a red, Château de Cardaillan. (DM)

Recommended Whites:
Château de Malle Sauternes ★★★★ £E

❀❀ Ch. Margaux (Margaux 1er CC) www.chateau-margaux.com
Corinne Mentzelopoulos and general manager the late Paul Pontallier have crafted truly great red Bordeaux now for upwards of two decades. The wine is not only remarkably elegant, with the unmistakably intense perfume of the appellation, but also enormously rich. Loaded with dense but supple tannins, Margaux is remarkably powerful and needs a minimum of 10–12 years' ageing to begin to reveal itself. Meticulous care in the vineyard and at harvest, along with traditional vinification in wooden fermenters, defines the style and quality. The second label, Pavillon Rouge, ensures the integrity of the Grand Vin but is itself regularly very impressive. As well as the 82 ha of red varieties planted there are some 12 ha of Sauvignon Blanc, which produce an intense floral, grassy and complex white sold under the humble Bordeaux AC. Among the great years are 2009, 06, 04, 03, 01, 00, 99, 96, 95, 90,

86, 83, 82, 79 and 78, with 2005 and 2010 being the vintages of the decade. Surprisingly the wine was very uneven prior to this and the Mentzelopoulos family involvement. (DM)

Recommended Reds:
Château Margaux Margaux ⚜⚜⚜⚜⚜ £H
Pavillon Rouge de Château Margaux ★★★★☆ £G

Recommended Whites:
Pavillon Blanc de Château Margaux Bordeaux ★★★★★ £H

❀ Marojallia (Margaux) www.marojallia.com
Tiny property and vineyard with an exceptional terroir, mainly located in the commune of Arsac close to Château du TERTRE. There are now 4ha under vine on superbly drained deep gravel soils. Vineyard management includes leaf removal, green-harvesting prior to veraison and of course hand-picking and hand-sorting. The Grand Vin is aged solely in new oak and comes from a blend of Cabernet Sauvignon (55%) and Merlot (45%). Very lush and rich, with a sumptuous texture and impressive depth, the wine will drink extremely well with 5 or so years' ageing. The second wine, Clos Margalaine, is also aged in 100% new wood. It is more obviously fleshy and forward and is very impressive indeed as a second label. The consultant oenologist is Michel Rolland. (DM)

Recommended Reds:
Marojallia Margaux ★★★★★ £F Clos Margalaine Margaux ★★★★ £D

Ch. Marquis de Terme www.chateau-marquis-de-terme.com
This Margaux 4ème CC château has been in the hands of the Sénéclauze family since 1935 and tradition and loyalty are in full sway, shown by the fact that in the period of their ownership the estate has had only two managers. But a continuing programme of modernisation has ensured that the current offerings are holding their own with more overtly progressive operations. This property was in the past considered a bit too butch for the appellation, but its profile is more acceptable to modern tastes and recent vintages have certainly shown plenty of fruit beneath the tannins. Marquis de Terme has always been a slow-maturing wine and needs patient cellaring. (NB)

Recommended Reds:
Château Marquis de Terme Margaux ★★★ £D

Clos Marsalette (Pessac-Léognan CC) www.neipperg.com
Small, potentially excellent property now with involvement from Stéphan von Neipperg, who also owns CANON-LA-GAFFELIÈRE, d'AIGUILHE and La MONDOTTE. The vineyards have an excellent exposure and are planted in fine, well-drained gravel soils and are organically farmed. Just under 3,000 cases a year of red are made and less than 400 cases of a very rare white. A blend of 60% Cabernet Sauvignon, 35% Merlot and 5% Cabernet Franc aged in 50% new wood, the wine has a rich and supple texture and much finer tannins than many from this AC in the vintage. Expect this to develop very well in the medium term. (DM)

Recommended Reds:
Clos Marsalette Pessac-Léognan ★★★★ £E

Ch. Mayne Lalande www.chateau-mayne-lalande.com
Small 17 ha Listrac property producing increasingly impressive and structured examples of this lesser appellation. The vineyards are planted to a combination of Cabernet Sauvignon (45%), Merlot a whopping 45% also and 5% each of Petit Verdot and Cabernet

France

Franc. Despite this the wine is firm, sturdy and marked by an intense cedary rather than plummy character. The 2000 here was particularly good, clearly ★★★, expect recent vintages to develop well in bottle for 5–7 years. (DM)

Recommended Reds:

Château Mayne Lalande Listrac-Médoc ★★☆ £C

✿✿ Ch. La Mission Haut-Brion *www.haut-brion.com*
Like HAUT-BRION, this property is owned by the Domaine Clarence Dillon. La Mission is only surpassed among Graves reds by Haut-Brion itself. This is a massive, dense and powerful red. Dark, mineral and black fruits are underpinned by cedar and oak. While the wine perhaps lacks the absolute refinement of its illustrious stablemate, it hasn't fallen far short and is on occasion the more impressive of the two. 2010, 09, 06, 05, 03, 00, 98 and 95 are recent benchmarks with 2015 showing great powerful promise and 90, 89, 82, 78 and 75 were all of legendary quality. 2000, 2005 and 2009 are likely to be of a similar standard. The white originally produced here and labelled Laville Haut-Brion has been renamed. It is a blend of mainly Sémillon, with Sauvignon Blanc and just a hint of Muscadelle, and comes from a separate and distinct vineyard plot. The second red wine, La Chapelle de la Mission Haut-Brion, is impressive in the ripest years. A second white La Clarté de Haut-Brion, comes from fruit from both Haut-Brion and la Mission Haut-Brion. (DM)

Recommended Reds:

Château la Mission Haut-Brion Pessac-Léognan ✿✿✿✿✿ £H
Château la Chapelle de la Mission Haut-Brion Pessac-Léognan ★★★★ £F

Recommended Whites:

Château la Mission Haut-Brion Pessac-Léognan ✿✿✿✿✿ £H
La Clarté de Haut Brion Pessac-Léognan ★★★★ £G

✿ Ch. Montrose *www.chateau-montrose.com*
This 90 ha 2ème CC property, including 22 ha just added from PHELAN-SÉGUR, produces exceptional Saint-Estèphe each year. The property is second only behind fellow Second Growth COS D'ESTOURNEL in the appellation hierarchy. These are massive, powerful, brooding wines – dense, tannic and long-lived. Sometimes the fruit struggles to emerge through the iron fist in which it is enveloped. Generally though, in the last decade the wine has become suppler and possesses greater harmony and it was consistently good through the 1990s. 1990 and 95 suggest ✿✿✿✿✿ status and more recently 2010 achieves the same. 03, 05, 06, 09, 14 and 2015 should all be comparable in time. La Dame de Montrose is an impressive second wine.(DM)

Recommended Reds:

Château Montrose Saint-Estèphe ★★★★★ £G
Château Montrose La Dame de Montrose Saint-Estèphe ★★★☆ £E

✿✿ Ch. Mouton-Rothschild (Pauillac 1er CC) *www.bpdr.com*
Unique among the First Growths of Bordeaux in that the wine was elevated to its current classification only in 1973, after the successful lobbying of Baron Philippe de Rothschild. The wine is the most opulent and approachable of the top growths, full of dark cassis and cigar box aromas, supported by powerful, supple tannin. Stunning wine was produced in 1982 and 86 but there was some loss of form in the late 80s and early 90s. However, 1996, 98, 99 and 00 have all been back among the very best and 2003, 05, 06, 09, 10, 12, 14 and 15 all of a similar calibre. Overall quality continues to improve, particularly since the complete renovation of the cellars in 2013. The second wine is Le Petit Mouton, and a small amount of a premium white Aile d'Argent is also produced. There is a sizeable merchant

business producing a range of pretty ordinary generic AC labels along with the dreary Mouton Cadet. Of greater interest are the two premium partnerships of OPUS ONE with the MONDAVI winery in California, now owned by Constellation and ALMAVIVA with CONCHA Y TORO in Chile. (DM)

Recommended Reds:

Château Mouton-Rothschild Pauillac ✿✿✿✿✿ £H
Le Petit Mouton Rothschild Médoc ★★★★ £H

Recommended Whites:

L'Aile d'Argent Blanc du Mouton Rothschild Bordeaux ★★★★ £F

Ch. Nairac (Barsac 2ème CC) *www.chateau-nairac.com*
A small property of just some 17 ha with annual production of barely more than 1,000 cases. The wine often outperforms its Second Growth status. Always picked very ripe, it gains real structure from a high proportion of new oak used for ageing. At times this can seem almost overpowering in its youth but given patience the wine can show a marvellous balance of intense, peachy botrytised fruit and almost sweet vanilla oak. Definitely cellar for 6 or 7 years. (DM)

Recommended Whites:

Château Nairac Barsac ★★★★ £F

Ch. Les Ormes de Pez (Saint-Estèphe) *www.ormesdepez.com*
Les Ormes de Pez is one of the most underrated wines in the Médoc. It is a chunky, dense, plummy wine, normally showing a fair amount of upfront fruit. Jean-Michel Cazes and his team have got just about the maximum potential from this property, the price is fair and it makes solid drinking value. (NB)

Recommended Reds:

Château Les Ormes de Pez Saint-Estèphe ★★★ £D

✿✿ Ch. Palmer (Margaux 3ème CC) *www.chateau-palmer.com*
This marvellous property is often thought of as a Second Growth and for a period before the Mentzelopoulos years at Château MARGAUX it was also the benchmark for the AC. At its best the wine displays not only the perfume of the appellation but ripe, powerful, almost sumptuous dark fruit. In part this must be down to the very high proportion of Merlot planted, at 47% the same as Cabernet Sauvignon. The second wine, Alter Ego de Palmer, tends to have an even higher proportion of Merlot in the final blend and less new oak whilst ageing. 2010, 09, 06, 04, 03, 01, 00, 99, 98, 96 and 95 Palmer were of a very high standard and the most recent vintages have similar promise. 2005 looks likely to set new standards for the property. Of the great years here, 89 and 83 also stand out as do the earlier years of 70, 66 and 61. Since 2014, the vines are being farmed biodynamically with a view to receiving organic certification by 2017.(DM)

Recommended Reds:

Château Palmer Margaux ✿✿✿✿✿ £H
Alter Ego de Palmer ★★★★ £F

✿ Ch. Pape-Clément (Pessac-Léognan CC) *www.pape-clement.com*
Excellent 32.5 ha property dominated by red vine plantings and like Haut-Brion engulfed by the suburbs of Bordeaux. The white varieties account for a mere 2.5 ha with 10% of this being Muscadelle. Both wines are very rich and powerful and the red has real density and grip but remains approachable and harmonious. Best vintages are 2010, 09, 08, 05, 04, 01, 00 and 1996. 2015 looks promising, too. The tiny production of white has an elegant, intense mineral and citrus streak adding to its complexity and all nicely supported by sufficient creamy new oak. Generally very good throughout the 1990s and

particularly after 1995 and it has not lost any of its lustre since with 2007, 2011 and 2013 being the best of the recent vintages. (DM)

Recommended Reds:

Château Pape-Clément Pessac-Léognan ★★★★★ £F
Le Clémentin de Pape Clément Pessac-Léognan ★★★☆ £E

Recommended Whites:

Château Pape-Clément Pessac-Léognan ★★★★★ £G

Ch. Peyrabon (Haut-Médoc) *www.chateau-peyrabon.com*

Sizeable 57 ha property, purchased in 1998 by Millésima, Europe's leading direct mail wine retailer. Most of the vineyards consist of 50 ha in the Haut-Médoc but there is also a small holding of 7 ha in Pauillac where the vines are vinified and bottled separately under the Lafleur Peyrabon label which is AOC Pauillac. Both represent excellent-value modern, stylish, cedary claret, albeit in a full and ripe style. Both wines are blends of Cabernet Sauvignon, Merlot, Cabernet Franc and a little Petit Verdot, more so in La Fleur Peyrabon, which just has that extra dimension with hints of cassis and spice adding a little extra complexity. Recent vintages for both have been impressive. Both wines are likely to add further complexity with 5 or 6 years' cellaring, La Fleur improving for a decade or so. (DM)

Recommended Reds:

Château Peyrabon La Fleur Peyrabon Pauillac ★★★ £E
Château Peyrabon Haut Médoc ★★☆ £D

Ch. Phelan-Segur (Saint-Estèphe) *www.phelansegur.com*

One of the most consistent performers in the Médoc, this château was among only 9 upgraded in the 2004 Cru Bourgeois reclassification to Exceptionnel status. The Gardiners have worked hard to put behind them some disastrous vintages in the early 80s and now rate among the best in the bourgeois division of the Bordeaux hierarchy. The wine has softer tannins than one would expect from a Saint-Estèphe and is quite elegant if lacking a little depth and structure. (DM)

Recommended Reds:

Château Phelan-Segur Saint-Estèphe ★★★ £E

Ch. Pibran (Pauillac)

From the same stable as PICHON-LONGUEVILLE, this relatively small Pauillac Cru Bourgeois consists of 17ha and is planted to a mix of 54% Merlot, 45% Cabernet Sauvignon and just 1% Petit Verdot. Quality continues to improve as the vineyard becomes more mature – the current vine age is 30 years. Understandably, given the grape blend here, the wine is sweet-fruited and richly textured with supple, quite soft tannins, but the cassis character of the appellation still shines through. Cellaring for 5 or 6 years will provide increased complexity. (DM)

Recommended Reds:

Château Pibran Pauillac ★★★ £E

✿✿ Ch. Pichon-Longueville *www.pichonlongueville.com*

Sizeable Second Growth with some 73ha under vine, bought in 1987 by AXA Millésimes – the fine-wine arm of the AXA insurance company. Jean-Michel Cazes, who owns Château LYNCH-BAGES, took over the management of the Bordeaux AXA operation and quality quickly improved with very successful vintages in 1989 and 90. These are world-class, ✪✪✪✪✪ wines: deep, dark, powerful Pauillac but very finely balanced. Now run and managed by Christian Seely, after a dip had been suffered in the early part of the millennium, vintages in the last 10 years look to be solidly back

on form with the 2015 being one of the outstanding wines of the vintage. A massive investment in state-of-the-art technology, including optical sorting, is certainly paying off. The château effectively has two second wines - Les Tourelles de Longueville being a more traditional second wine and since 2012 Les Griffons de Pichon Baron, crafted from some of the estates oldest vines whose fruit are not going into the grand vin. As a result, this is a chunkier, bolder wine than Les Tourelles. (DM)

Recommended Reds:

Château Pichon-Longueville Pauillac ✪✪✪✪✪ £G
Les Griffons de Pichon Baron Pauillac ★★★★☆ £F
Les Tourelles de Longueville Pauillac ★★★★ £F

✿ Ch. Pichon-Longueville-Lalande *www.pichon-lalande.com*

A 2ème CC property marked by its rich, elegant, almost sumptuous style of wine. It is no surprise that there are considerable plantings of Merlot (35%). The balance was Cabernet Sauvignon (45%), Cabernet Franc (12%) and a relatively whopping 8% of very old Petit Verdot. Now the aim is to increase the proportion of Cabernet Sauvignon to 60% at the expense of the other three varietals, mainly the Cabernet Franc. Around half the vines are now being farmed organically and it is the intention to increase this percentage significantly. The vineyards border Saint-Julien and this also helps contribute to the wine's intense, fragrant and complex style. However, there have been some strange variations in quality over the last couple of decades. Vintages of the late 1990s have been disappointing, whereas 1995 and 96 were magnificent, clear ✪✪✪✪✪ wines. Since 2000 it looks to be back in the top division, although 2005 was leaner than expected. After the acquisition by the present owners in 2008, a massive renovation programme has taken place which is still ongoing. The estate is now managed by Nicolas Glumineau previously of Ch. Montrose. Other exceptional years have included 86, 83 and, of course, the legendary 82. Réserve de la Comtesse is the second wine. (DM)

Recommended Reds:

Château Pichon-Longueville-Lalande Pauillac ★★★★★ £G
Réserve de la Comtesse ★★★ £E

Ch. Pontac Monplaisir *www.pontac-monplaisir.fr*

This is a very small Pessac-Léognan CC estate producing some classy wines. It can be difficult to find but invariably gives good value for money. There are 9 ha of red grapes, planted 60% Merlot and 40% Cabernet Sauvignon, and just 2 ha of white in the same proportions respectively of Sauvignon and Sémillon. The white shows good, easy-drinking finesse with a good deal of complexity, whilst the red has good fruit and soft tannins, if perhaps lacking a little in weight. Nevertheless, both wines possess excellent balance and are fairly priced. (NB)

Recommended Reds:

Château Pontac Monplaisir Pessac-Léognan ★★★ £D

Recommended Whites:

Château Pontac Monplaisir Pessac-Léognan ★★★ £D

✿ Ch. Pontet-Canet (Pauillac 5ème CC) *www.pontet-canet.com*

This property has been in the ownership of the Tesseron Family, who also own Château LAFON-ROCHET, for over two decades. They have been responsible for bringing it up to its current level, where it has more than justified its Fifth Growth status. Produced from vineyards planted on some of the best gravel soils of the appellation, at its peak it is exactly what you think of as quintessential Pauillac – big, powerful and dense with supple, well-rounded tannin and an

Bordeaux /Médoc, Graves & Sauternes

France

intense fragrance of cassis and cedar. 1989 saw a significant upturn in quality. After the generally poor years between 1991 and 93, really only 97 has been lighter and less impressive. Alfred Tesseron and right hand man Jean-Michel Comme have been champions of non-intervention in the vineyards and the cellar and eschew sate-of-the art technology, but nevertheless are consistently producing top quality wines. Biodynamic since 2004 and certified organic in 2010 has resulted in the current run of vintages showing very impressive results.(DM)

Recommended Reds:
Château Pontet-Canet Pauillac ★★★★★ £G

Ch. Potensac (Médoc) *www.chateau-potensac.com*
Under the same ownership as LÉOVILLE-LAS-CASES, this is without doubt one of the finest property sold as Médoc AC. The now very old vines are planted on a mix of alluvial gravel and clay soils. The wine is consistently excellent: ripe but sufficiently firm, with a hint of new wood (about 20%) providing additional depth. Bottled without filtration it is better with 5 years' cellaring. Both 2000 and 96 are particularly impressive and 2010, 09, 06, 05, 04 and 01 are also very striking. 2015 should fare well. All in all this is a very good-value claret. The second wine is Chapelle de Potensac which is mainly Merlot. (DM)

Recommended Reds:
Château Potensac Médoc ★★★☆ £D

Ch. Poujeaux (Moulis) *www.chateaupoujeaux.com*
Along with CHASSE-SPLEEN, this is one of the two best wines in the Moulis AC. It has performed with an impressive consistency throughout the last 10 years and more and since the purchase in 2008 by Philippe and Mathieu Cuvelier, the owners of CLOS FOURTET, it has been enhanced by the contribution of consultant Stéphane Derenoncourt. There are 53 ha under vine here, with Cabernet Sauvignon accounting for slightly more of the vineyard than Merlot. As with most quality-conscious wine producers, there is a dedication in the vineyard and cellar which contributes to the final wine. The style is rich and sumptuous with a hint of vanilla from its 12 months of oak-ageing. Handling is kept to a minimum, with just egg-white fining and no filtration. They also produce a second wine - La Salle de Poujeaux. (DM)

Recommended Reds:
Château Poujeaux Moulis ★★★☆ £E

Ch. Preuillac (Médoc) *www.chateau-preuillac.com*
Jean-Christophe Mau bought this neglected and run-down château in 1999 and has struggled to bring it back to its former glory despite massive investment in the vineyard and the winery. The vineyard has 30 ha of vines in a single stretch, with gravelly hilltops planted to 50% Merlot, 48% Cabernet Sauvignon and 2% Cabernet Franc. The appointment of Stéphane Derenoncourt as consultant enologist in 2003 has resulted in a quantum leap in quality. The soft and silky palate now found is a result of the grapes being picked by hand and sorted in the vineyard. Each varietal and each plot is separately vinified in 180 hl temperature-controlled vats for up to 5 weeks before the wine is run off into barrels to be matured for 12 months. The special selection Emotions is richer and denser 100% malolactic in barrel providing an impressive, silky texture. The château was sold to a Chinese investment company in 2014 after two difficult vintages but Jean-Christophe agreed to stay on as manager for one year. However, the 2015 wine has turned out to be a disappointment so it is not certain in which direction this château will be going. (NB)

Recommended Reds:
Château Preuillac Emotions de Preuillac Médoc ★★★☆ £D
Château Preuillac Médoc ★★★ £C

Ch. Prieuré-Lichine (Margaux 4ème CC) *www.prieure-lichine.fr*
The Ballandes, who run the *négociant* operation the Ballande group, purchased this property from the Lichine family in 1999. Unusually there are parcels of vineyard spread throughout the appellation. The estate is managed by Justin Onclin, who is also the owner of CH. VILLEMAURINE in Saint-Émilion and there has been consultancy input from Stéphane Derenoncourt. A replanting programme began as soon as the estate was purchased and 2013 saw the completion of the modernisation of the cellars. The wine is increasingly sumptuous and supple. This is an ambitious operation and it will be interesting to see how quality develops over the next 5 years or so. (DM)

Recommended Reds:
Château Prieuré-Lichine Margaux ★★★ £E

✿ Ch. Rabaud-Promis (Sauternes 1er CC) *www.rabaud-promis.com*
After a long period in the doldrums, this 33 ha property has now been making impressive Sauternes for two decades. This is a full, rich and honeyed wine with not only impressive depth, concentration and the structure to age very well but also real balance and harmony. It can be very intense and stylish, particularly in top years. Very impressive since 1994 and prior to that 90, 89 and 88 are very good indeed as are 2001, 2003, 2007, 2009 and 2010 since the turn of the century. (DM)

Recommended Whites:
Château Rabaud-Promis Sauternes ★★★★ £F

Ch. Rauzan-Ségla (Margaux 2ème CC) *www.rauzan-segla.com*
This château was acquired by the Wertheimers, who own the Chanel perfume business, in 1994 and a large amount of investment has been put into the property since then. They also now own Château CANON in Saint-Emilion. Prior to the change of ownership the property performed remarkably well in the run of vintages from 1988 to 90 but this wasn't always so. Vinification is now very modern, using temperature-controlled stainless steel, and ageing is in 60% new oak for 18 months. The wine has a fine, elegant texture and displays a complex array of dark fruits and cedar. There is surprising tannin here, though, and the wine will improve with at least 5 or 6 years' cellaring. It has been reasonably consistent since 1995 but seems to have moved up a gear recently with the 2009 and 2010 on the cusp of ★★★★★. (DM)

Recommended Reds:
Château Rauzan-Ségla Margaux ★★★★☆ £F

Ch. Raymond-Lafon (Sauternes) *www.chateau-raymond-lafon.fr*
The production is tiny at just over 1,600 cases a year from the 18 ha of vineyard. The blend is 80% Sémillon with the balance Sauvignon Blanc and no Muscadelle. Not a Classed Growth, Raymond-Lafon is located right next to Yquem and has consistently produced wines in the great years of the last two decades which rival all but the absolute best in Sauternes. This has been achieved through a dedicated approach in the vineyard, tiny yields of just 8.5 hl/ha, careful and repeated selective harvesting (*tris*) and extensive use of new oak in the cellar. The wine is aged for up to 3 years in wood. Jeunes Pousses de Raymond-Lafon is a fine second wine. (DM)

Recommended Whites:

Château Raymond-Lafon Sauternes ★★★★★ £F

Jeunes Pousses de Raymond-Lafon Sauternes ★★★ £D

Ch. de Rayne-Vigneau (Sauternes 1er CC) *www.raynevigneau.fr*

This relatively sizeable property has some 80ha of vineyards. It is under the same ownership as Château GRAND-PUY-DUCASSE in Pauillac. The gravel soils here suggest a real potential to the *terroir* that has not yet fully been realised. However, like so many Sauternes châteaux, its reputation has improved over the last two decades. The wine is characterised by its elegant and complex botrytised fruit, with a tight, restrained structure. These are not overfull, super-weighty wines but at their best are impressively refined and intense. (DM)

Recommended Whites:

Château de Rayne-Vigneau Sauternes ★★★ £E

❂ Ch. Rieussec (Sauternes 1er CC) *www.lafite.com*

Under the same ownership as LAFITE-ROTHSCHILD, this Sauternes is generally regarded as being second only in weight and power to YQUEM. It has generally performed at that level since 1995 and particularly during the trio of great Sauternes years from 88 to 90. Aged in a high proportion of new oak it is almost always a powerful, very rich, opulent but classically structured wine in need of 8–10 years' ageing, often longer in truly great vintages. In recent vintages, apart from the 2012, when it was declassified and not made, it has consistently proved to be one of the top performers in Sauternes. (DM)

Recommended Whites:

Château Rieussec Sauternes ✪✪✪✪✪ £G

Ch. Rollan-de-By (Médoc) *www.rollandeby.com*

This 37 ha property has performed with distinction throughout the past decade and is a shining light for other producers in the outlying areas of the Médoc. The vineyard is planted with a sizeable 70% Merlot and this, allied to the judicious use of new oak, accounts for the ripe, almost lush, plump and approachable fruit style. Haut-Condissas is a premium label with more Cabernet Sauvignon in the blend. (DM)

Recommended Reds:

Château Haut-Condissas Médoc ★★★★ £F

Château Rollan-de-By Médoc ★★★☆ £D

Ch. Saint-Pierre *www.chateau-saint-pierre.com*

This Saint-Julien 2ème CC property was purchased in 1981 by the late Henri Martin (the former owner of GLORIA) and is now run by his daughter, Françoise Triaud. Although the wine has been consistently good in the 1990s, it never quite achieved the potential that its classification suggests until the last decade. The approach to vinification is always meticulous, with a rigorous selection pre-fermentation and judicious use of new oak. A complete renovation of the wine making facilities was completed in 2016 with an eye to state-of-the-art technology and whilst the wine is certainly very well above average in top recent vintages, a quantum leap in quality could be expected in the future. (DM)

Recommended Reds:

Château Saint-Pierre Saint-Julien ★★★★ £F

Ch. Sénéjac (Haut-Médoc) *www.chateau-senejac.com*

Relatively sizeable Haut-Médoc property with 39 ha under vine. The vineyard comprises Cabernet Sauvignon (48%), Merlot (37%),

Cabernet Franc (11%) and Petit Verdot (4%). The wine has been increasingly good across recent vintages and is produced in a lighter style but with impressive cedary complexity and persistence of fruit. The wine is made and the vineyards biodynamicaly farmed and managed by Alfred Tesseron's team from CH. PONTET-CANET. Karolus, a special cuvée made from 100% Cabernet Sauvignon has not been made since 2005. A second wine, Artigues de Sénéjac, is now also produced but has not been tasted. (DM)

Recommended Reds:

Château Sénéjac Karolus Haut-Médoc ★★★★ £F

Château Sénéjac Haut-Médoc ★★★☆ £C

Ch. Sigalas-Rabaud (Sauternes 1er CC)

This is the smaller part of the original Château Rabaud, which was divided nearly a century ago. The other half is RABAUD-PROMIS and both are Sauternes First Growths. The wine is very rich and gloriously honeyed and can show very marked botrytis but it is still refined and very elegant. Indeed the wine has been impressive for years and was one of the few properties to perform well in the 1960s and 70s, a period of recession in the appellation. The great vintages in these decades can at least be approached with some optimism. More recently 2010, 09, 07, 06, 03, 01, 99, 98, 97 and 96 were all on top form and are nudging ★★★★★ as are the great trio of 88, 89 and 90. (DM)

Recommended Whites:

Château Sigalas-Rabaud Sauternes ★★★★☆ £F

Ch. Siran (Margaux) *www.chateausiran.com*

The vineyard of Château Siran consists of 40 ha in all, of which 24 ha are in Margaux. A further 15ha qualify as Bordeaux Supérieur and 1ha as Haut-Médoc. It is planted to 45% Cabernet Sauvignon, 35% Merlot, 12% Petit Verdot and 8% Cabernet Franc. From 1995 until 2004 the winemaking had been guided by Michel Rolland and a fair degree of consistency had been achieved. Subsequently consultancy was provided by the late Denis Dubourdieu and from the 2015 vintage, Hubert de Boüard of CH. ANGELUS. Typically Margaux, this has never been a blockbuster wine, but one that regularly affords a good price/quality ratio. Recent vintages have shown more suppleness and finesse than previously, which augurs well for the future. The second wine, S de Siran, is made from younger Margaux vines. (NB)

Recommended Reds:

Château Siran Margaux ★★★ £D

❂ Ch. Smith Haut Lafitte *www.smith-haut-lafitte.com*

The wines here under the current ownership are now very good. Around 80% of the production is red, with a mix of 55% Cabernet Sauvignon, 34% Merlot 10% Cabernet Franc and1% Petit Verdot. The white is dominated by Sauvignon Blanc but there is a sprinkling of Sémillon and more unusually Sauvignon Gris (similar in flavour to Sauvignon Blanc but with a slight pink tinge to its skin). The red is lighter in style than some of its neighbours but now possesses impressive depth. The white is fermented relatively cool to retain a marked floral, herbal core and is aged in 50% new oak. Neither wine is filtered and both have performed admirably since 1995, with some exceptional wines over the last decade.Whilst the reds have reached incredible heights in 2009, 2010 and 2015, with big price differences for the vintages, the whites have been perhaps more consistent in quality over the past 5 years. Ratings below relate to wines produced after the 2004 vintage. (DM)

Bordeaux /Médoc, Graves & Sauternes

France

Recommended Reds:
Château Smith Haut Lafitte Pessac-Léognan ★★★★★ £G
Recommended Whites:
Château Smith Haut Lafitte Pessac-Léognan ★★★★★ £G

⊛ **Ch. Sociando-Mallet (Haut-Médoc)** *www.sociandomallet.com*
This is now undoubtedly the most impressive estate in the Haut-Médoc, a title that at one stage would almost invariably have been given to La LAGUNE. Quality here since 1995 has been good to very good. Perhaps in 97 and 98 it did not quite rate ★★★★ but the wines are impressive dark, powerful and very ageworthy all the same. The style is of a true *vin de garde*, in part due to the well-drained gravel soils, which produce supple but youthfully firm, powerful tannins. Impressive earlier vintages include 1990, 89 and the classic 82. The second wine is Demoiselle, which can be good. (DM)
Recommended Reds:
Château Sociando-Mallet Haut-Médoc ★★★★ £E

Ch. Suduiraut (Sauternes 1er CC) *www.suduiraut.com*
More care has been taken with harvesting at this property which neighbours YQUEM since its purchase by AXA in 1992. The fruit is now picked more selectively and late enough to maximise the effect of noble rot. As a result the wine has become increasingly full and rich. It is aged for 18–24 months in barrel, further adding to its impressive depth and concentration. It was very good in 1989 and 90 as well as more recently in 95, 96, 97, 01, 03, 06 and 07. THe wines from 2009 onwards, with the possible exception of 2012, have been particularly on song. The second wine, Castelnau de Suduiraut, can be of sound quality and ensures the integrity of the Grand Vin, whilst a third wine, Lions de Suduiraut, made from almost 100% Sémillon, has been produced since the 2011 vintage but has not been tasted. (DM)
Recommended Whites:
Chateau Suduiraut Crème de Tete Sauternes ★★★★★ £H
Château Suduiraut Sauternes ★★★★★ £F

Ch. Talbot (Saint-Julien 2ème CC) *www.chateau-talbot.com*
Originally a Cordier négociant property, Talbot has been retained by members of the family and the quality of the Grand Vin has remained reasonably consistent, particularly after 1995. It is now very international in styled and quite different to some of the very firm earlier examples under Cordier ownership. 1998, 00, 01, 03, 05, 06, 08, 09 and 10 were all very good and 14 and 15 look to be promising. The second wine, Connetable Talbot, has been good in the better years and there is a small amount of a white, Caillou Blanc, produced under the Bordeaux AC. This used to be variable with marked sulphur but a more modern approach to its vinification is now undertaken with better results. (DM)
Recommended Reds:
Château Talbot Saint-Julien ★★★☆ £F

⊛ **Ch. du Tertre (Margaux 5ème CC)** *www.chateaudutertre.fr*
Eric Albada Jedgersma and his wife also own the revitalised Château GISCOURS, another Classed Growth Margaux property. While not the size of its sister château, du Tertre is by no means small with 52 ha under vine, planted in sandy gravel soils in the commune of Arsac. Cabernet Sauvignon accounts for a mere 40% of the vineyard, with 35% Merlot, 20% Cabernet Franc and the balance a small amount of Petit Verdot. Its only since the 1999 vintage that the property has begun to show its true worth but du Tertre is one of the most beguiling and perfumed of all Margaux reds. Cellaring for 6 or more

years will result in further complexity. (DM)
Recommended Reds:
Château du Tertre Margaux ★★★★☆ £E

Ch. La Tour Blanche (Sauternes 1er CC) *www.tour-blanche.com*
There are a total of some 40 ha under vine at this property run by the Ministry of Agriculture and although this is also an agricultural school very high standards are maintained. The vineyards are particularly well sited and result in a big, full-bodied Sauternes produced with marked botrytis and well-judged new oak. The wines have real intensity and power 2013, 11, 09, 07, 05, 03, 02, 01, 98, 97 and 96 have all been very good and the trio of 88, 89 and 90 were also excellent. (DM)
Recommended Whites:
Château la Tour Blanche Sauternes ★★★★☆ £F

Ch. La Tour Haut Brion (Pessac-Léognan CC) *www.haut-brion.com*
Originally the second wine at LA MISSION HAUT-BRION, this property stood alone with its own identity until 2006 when it was merged back again with La Mission Haut Brion. It neighboured its former big brother and although the wines were still overshadowed by the powerful dense style of La Mission they became increasingly impressive in their own right. Some 80% of the vineyard is planted to Cabernet Sauvignon and Cabernet Franc, resulting in a very sturdy style in the wine's youth. There is still plenty of this wine available on the market (at a price) but at least you won't have to worry about drinking it too young. (DM)
Recommended Reds:
Château la Tour Haut-Brion Pessac-Léognan ★★★★☆ £H

>>**Ch. Tronquoy Lalande (Saint Estèphe)** *www.tronquoy-lalande.com*
Just up the road from CH. MONTROSE, this was purchased by the Bouygues brothers at pretty much the same time in 2006. They probably could have merged these under-performing vineyards into Montrose, but instead decided to spend the best part of 10 million euros upgrading it, which might have seemed a bit over the top considering that the wines do not sell for much money. But local wisdom dictates that Tronquoy-Lalonde is sitting on some of the best terroir in Saint-Éstéphe and it only needs a bit of TLC (plus money and expertise) to catapult it into the big time. So apart from putting in some state-of-the-art technology, they brought in the team that runs Montrose, headed by Jean Bernard Delmas, who was for many years the managing director of CH. HAUT-BRION. In 2015 the results are really beginning to show and as a result may be the outstanding price/quality ratio wine of the vintage. Only time will tell. Ratings relate only to recent vintages. (NB)
Recommended Reds:
Château Tronquoy-Lalande Saint-Estèphe ★★★★ £D

Vieux Château Gaubert (Graves)
One of the best properties in the Graves AC and a model for many less than perfect performers in the supposedly superior Pessac-Léognan. Both red and white are produced. The red is a 50/50 blend of Cabernet Sauvignon and Merlot and this is emphasised in its vibrant dark plummy fruit character. Structure and depth are lent by an extended fermentation and maceration of 15–20 days and 12 months in 40% new wood. The white, from a roughly equal blend of Sémillon and Sauvignon Blanc, is barrel-fermented in 60% new oak and aged on lees with *bâtonnage*. Nonetheless it is remarkably restrained with intense citrus and lightly grassy aromas subtly supported by sophisticated oak. It will be all the better for 2 or 3

Wine behind the label

years' ageing in bottle. (DM)
Recommended Reds:
Vieux Château Gaubert Graves ★★★ £D
Recommended Whites:
Vieux Château Gaubert Graves ★★★ £C

Ch. Vieux Robin (Médoc) *www.chateau-vieux-robin.com*
Vieux Robin is located in the north of the Médoc peninsula and
the property has now been classified as a Cru Bourgeois Supérieur.
There are 18 ha under vine and the vineyard is planted to a
combination of Cabernet Sauvignon (60%) and Merlot (35%), with
the remaining 5% split between Cabernet Franc and Petit Verdot.
The vineyard age of around 40 years is a major contributor to the
quality. The regular Médoc is straightforward, a relatively simple
fruit-driven style. The Bois de Lunier label is a notch up: the vines
are over 40 years old, the wine is aged in new oak (40%) and part
of the malolactic takes place in barrel. There is also a limited-release
Collection bottling selected from the very best plots. White Blanc
de Lunier is produced from old-vine Sauvignon Blanc vinified and
matured in 50% new wood. (DM)
Recommended Reds:
Château Vieux Robin Médoc Bois de Lunier ★★★ £D
Château Vieux Robin Médoc ★★ £C

Ch. Villa Bel Air (Graves) *www.villabelair.com*
Reliable Graves property producing around 12,000 cases each
of red and white Graves. The property was taken over by Jean-
Michel Cazes in 1990 and the cellars were modernised and the
winemaking brought up to speed. Barrel-fermentation for the white
and a red which emphasises attractive dark, black fruit in a supple,
approachable style are the keys here. (DM)
Recommended Reds:
Château Villa Bel Air Graves ★★ £C
Recommended Whites:
Château Villa Bel Air Graves ★★☆ £C

✿✿ Ch. d'Yquem (Sauternes 1er GCC) *www.yquem.fr*
Arguably the greatest sweet wine in the world. Owned by the Lur
Saluces family for more than 2 centuries, it was purchased by LVMH
in 1999. Alexandre de Lur Saluces continued to make the wine for
a while until Pierre Lurton, the director at CH. CHEVAL BLANC, took
over in 2004 . There are 103 ha under vine but the vineyards have a
superb exposure in the centre of the appellation and enjoy an ideal
mix of morning mist and warm sunshine. With a sizeable production
of around 8,000 cases a year it is certain that, while occasional TBAs
from Germany or SGNs from Alsace might rival it for sheer depth,
dimension and fruit intensity, they never will match the volume
produced at Yquem. The same remarkable level of attention is
spent producing the wine, with harvesting not so much by *tris* but
more berry by berry and at a microscopic yield. New oak is used
throughout and the wine is bottled without filtration after spending
more than 3 years in cask. These are wines of supreme quality that
will last for half a century or more, always outstanding in top years.
(DM)
Recommended Whites:
Château d'Yquem Sauternes ✿✿✿✿✿ £H

Other wines of note - *Médoc, Graves & Sauternes*

Ch. Andron Blanquet
Recommended Reds: Saint-Estèphe ★★ £C

Ch. Beaumont
Recommended Reds: Haut-Médoc ★★ £C
Ch. Bel-Air
Recommended Reds: Saint-Estèphe ★ £C
Ch. Belle Vue
Recommended Reds: Haut-Médoc ★★★ £C
Ch. Bellevue de Tayac
Recommended Reds: Margaux ★★★☆ £D
Ch. Bernadotte
Recommended Reds: Haut-Médoc ★★☆ £C
Ch. Biston-Brillette
Recommended Reds: Moulis ★★☆ £C
Ch. Bournac
Recommended Reds: Médoc ★★☆ £C
Ch. Bouscaut
Recommended Reds: Pessac-Léognan ★★☆ £E
Recommended Whites: Pessac-Léognan ★★☆ £D
Ch. La Bridane
Recommended Reds: Saint-Julien ★★☆ £C N
Ch. Cantegril
Recommended Whites: Sauternes ★★★ £E
Ch. Cantelys
Recommended Reds: Pessac-Léognan ★★ £C
Recommended Whites: Pessac-Léognan ★★ £C
Ch. Citran
Recommended Reds: Haut-Médoc ★★ £C
Ch. Clauzet
Recommended Reds: Saint-Estèphe ★★☆ £D
Ch. Clément Pichon
Recommended Reds: Haut-Médoc ★★☆ £C
Clos Dady
Recommended Whites: Sauternes ★★★ £E
Clos Le Comte
Recommended Whites: Sauternes Celine ★★★ £E
Ch. Cornélie
Recommended Reds: Haut-Médoc ★★ £C
Ch. Coufran
Recommended Reds: Haut-Médoc ★★ £C
Ch. Crabitey
Recommended Reds: Graves ★★ £C
Cru Barréjats
Recommended Whites: Sauternes ★★★ £F
Ch. de Cruzeau
Recommended Reds: Pessac-Léognan £D
Recommended Whites: Pessac-Léognan £D
Ch. Desmirail
Recommended Reds: Margaux ★★★ £E
Ch. Deyrem-Valentin
Recommended Reds: Margaux ★★ £D
Ch. Durfort-Vivens
Recommended Reds: Margaux ★★★ £E
Ch. des Eyrins
Recommended Reds: Margaux ★★☆ £C
Ch. Ferran
Recommended Reds: Pessac-Léognan ★★ £C
Recommended Whites: Pessac-Léognan ★★ £C
Ch. Fonbadet
Recommended Reds: Pauillac ★★ £D
Ch. Fonréaud
Recommended Reds: Listrac ★☆ £C

Wine behind the label

Bordeaux /Médoc, Graves & Sauternes

France

Ch. Fourcas-Dupré
Recommended Reds: Listrac ★★ £C
Ch. Fourcas-Hosten
Recommended Reds: Listrac ★ £C
Ch. La Garde
Recommended Reds: Pessac-Léognan ★ £C
Recommended Whites: Pessac-Léognan ★★ £C
Ch. de Gironville
Recommended Reds: Haut-Médoc ★★☆ £C
Ch. du Glana
Recommended Reds: Saint-Julien ★★☆ £C
Ch. Grand-Puy-Ducasse
Recommended Reds: Pauillac ★★ £E
Ch. Les Grands Chênes
Recommended Reds: Médoc ★★ £D
Ch. Greysac
Recommended Reds: Médoc ★★ £C
Ch. Haura
Recommended Reds: Graves ★★ £C
Ch. Haut-Bages-Libéral
Recommended Reds: Pauillac ★★☆ £D
Ch. Haut Beaséjour
Recommended Reds: Saint-Estèphe ★★ £C
Ch. Haut-Bergeron
Recommended Reds: Sauternes ★★☆ £E
Ch L'Inclassable
Recommended Reds: Médoc ★★ £C
Ch. Les Justices
Recommended Whites: Sauternes ★★★ £E
Ch. Labégorce-Zédé
Recommended Reds: Margaux ★★ £E
Ch. Lalande de Gravelongue
Recommended Reds: Médoc Croix de Gravelongue ★★☆ £D
Médoc ★★ £C
La Patache
Recommended Reds: Médoc ★★ £C
Ch. de Lamarque
Recommended Reds: Haut-Médoc ★ £C
Ch. La Tour de By
Recommended Reds: Médoc ★☆ £C
Ch. Lilian-Ladouys
Recommended Reds: Saint-Estèphe ★★ £D
Ch. Liot
Recommended Whites: Barsac ★★ £D
Ch. Liversan
Recommended Reds: Haut-Médoc ★★ £C
Ch. Lousteauneuf
Recommended Reds: Médoc ★★ £C
Ch. Malescasse
Recommended Reds: Haut-Médoc ★★ £C
Ch. Marbuzet
Recommended Reds: Saint-Estèphe ★★ £C
Ch. Maucaillou
Recommended Reds: Moulis ★★ £C
Ch. Maucamps
Recommended Reds: Haut-Médoc ★★ £C
Ch. Meyney
Recommended Reds: Saint-Estèphe ★★ £D
Ch. Mille-Roses
Recommended Reds: Haut-Médoc ★★☆ £C

Ch. Monbrison
Recommended Reds: Margaux ★★☆ £D
Ch Moulin de La Rose
Recommended Reds: Saint-Julien ★★ £E
Ch. du Moulin Rouge
Recommended Reds: Haut-Médoc ★ £C
Ch. de Myrat
Recommended Whites: Barsac ★★ £D
Ch. Noillac
Recommended Reds: Médoc ★★☆ £B
Ch. Olivier
Recommended Reds: Pessac-Léognan ★★ £D
Recommended Whites: Pessac-Léognan ★★ £D
Ch. Les Ormes-Sorbet
Recommended Reds: Médoc ★★ £D
Ch. Paloumey
Recommended Reds: Haut-Médoc ★★★ £C
Ch. Patache d'Aux
Recommended Reds: Médoc ★★ £D
Ch. Petit-Bocq
Recommended Reds: Saint-Estèphe ★★☆ £D
Ch. de Pez
Recommended Reds: Saint-Estèphe ★★ £D
Ch. Poumey
Recommended Reds: Pessac-Léognan ★★ £D
Ch. Rahoul
Recommended Reds: Graves ★★ £C
Recommended Whites: Graves ★★ £C
Ch. Ramage-La-Batisse
Recommended Reds: Haut-Médoc ★★ £C
Ch. Rauzan-Gassies
Recommended Reds: Margaux ★★★ £E
Ch. Respide-Médeville
Recommended Reds: Graves ★★ £D
Recommended Whites: Graves ★★ £D
Ch. de Rochemorin
Recommended Whites: Pessac-Léognan £E
Ch. Romer-du-Hayot
Recommended Whites: Sauternes ★★ £D
Ch. de Rouillac
Recommended Reds: Pessac-Léognan ★★ £D
Ch. Saint-Amand
Recommended Whites: Sauternes ★★★ £D
Ch. Saint-Robert
Recommended Reds: Graves ★★☆ £C
Ch. Ségur de Cabanac
Recommended Reds: Saint-Estèphe ★★☆ £D
Ch. Sérilhan
Recommended Reds: Saint-Estèphe ★★★ £D
Ch. Soudars
Recommended Reds: Haut-Médoc ★ £C
Ch. Suau
Recommended Whites: Barsac ★★ £E
Ch. La Tempérance
Recommended Reds: Haut-Médoc ★★ £C
Ch. Le Thil Comte Clary
Recommended Reds: Pessac-Léognan ★★☆ £C
Recommended Whites: Pessac-Léognan ★☆ £C
Ch. Tour-Haut-Caussan
Recommended Reds: Médoc ★★☆ £C

Ch. Tour-Seran
Recommended Reds: Médoc ★★☆ £C

Ch. Tour du Haut-Moulin
Recommended Reds: Haut-Médoc ★★ £C

Ch. Verdignan
Recommended Reds: Haut-Médoc ★★ £C

Work in progress!!

Producers under consideration for the next edition
Clos Dady (Sauternes)
Ch. Lamothe (Sauternes)
Ch. Lieujean (Médoc)
Ch. Saint-Amand (Sauternes)
Ch. Gilette (Sauternes)

Author's choice - *Médoc, Graves & Sauternes*

Great Cellarworthy Left Bank Reds
Ch. Cos d'Estournel Saint-Estèphe 2ème CC
Ch. Ducru-Beaucaillou Saint-Julien 2ème CC
Ch. Haut-Brion Pessac-Léognan 1 Er CC
Ch. Lafite-Rothschild Pauillac 1 Er CC
Ch. Latour Pauillac 1 Er CC
Ch. Léoville-Barton Saint-Julien 2ème CC
Ch. Léoville-Las-Cases Saint-Julien 2ème CC
Ch. Lynch-Bages Pauillac 5ème CC
Ch. Margaux Margaux 1 er CC
Ch. Montrose Saint-Estèphe 2ème CC
Ch. La Mission-Haut-Brion Pessac-Léognan CC
Ch. Mouton-Rothschild Pauillac 1 er CC
Ch. Palmer Margaux 3ème CC
Ch. Pape-Clément Pessac-Léognan CC
Ch. Pichon-Longueville Pauillac 2ème CC
Ch. Pichon-Longueville-Lalande Pauillac 2ème CC

The Best of Sauternes And Barsac
Ch. Climens Barsac 1 er CC
Ch. Coutet Barsac 1 er CC
Ch. Guiraud Sauternes 1 er CC
Ch. Lafaurie-Peyraguey Sauternes 1 er CC
Ch. Raymond-Lafon Sauternes
Ch. Rieussec Sauternes 1 er CC
Ch. Sigalas-Rabaud Sauternes 1 er CC
Ch. Suduiraut Sauternes 1 er CC
Ch. La Tour Blanche Sauternes 1 er CC
Ch. d'Yquem Sauternes 1 er GCC

Classic Dry Whites
Ch. Carbonnieux Pessac-Léognan CC
Dom. de Chevalier Pessac-Léognan CC
Clos Floridène Graves
Ch. de Fieuzal Pessac-Léognan
Ch. Haut-Brion Pessac-Léognan
Ch. Laville-Haut-Brion Pessac-Léognan CC
Ch. La Louvière Pessac-Léognan
Ch. Pape-Clément Pessac-Léognan
Pavillon Blanc de Margaux Bordeaux
Ch. Smith-Haut-Lafitte Pessac-Léognan

Good Values and Fine Lesser Growths
Reds:
Ch. Beychevelle Saint-Julien 4ème CC
Ch. Branaire Saint-Julien 4ème CC
Ch. Clerc-Milon Pauillac 5ème CC
Ch. d'Issan Margaux 3ème CC
Ch. Léoville-Poyferré Saint-Julien 2ème CC
Ch. Pontet Canet Pauillac 5ème CC
Ch. Potensac Médoc
Ch. du Tertre Margaux 5ème CC
Whites:
Vieux Ch. Gaubert Graves
Ch. Bastor-Lamontagne Sauternes

A-Z of producers - *Saint-Emilion, Pomerol & other Bordeaux*

✿ Dom. de l'A (Côtes de Castillon)
This is the tiny 4 ha home property of winemaking guru Stéphane Derenoncourt. It is planted to old-vine Merlot, Cabernet Franc and a little Cabernet Sauvignon and is farmed biodynamically. The result is remarkably dense and powerful wine from this outlying Bordeaux appellation. The wine is fermented in wood, aged on lees to add weight and texture and afterwards bottled without fining or filtration. Along with a number of other small impressive properties, this is a model for producers from the region's lesser ACs. (DM)
Recommended Reds:
Domaine de l'A Côtes de Castillon ★★★☆ £E

✿ Ch. d'Aiguilhe (Côtes de Castillon) *www.neipperg.com*
This very fine Castillon property is under of the same ownership as CANON LA GAFFELIÈRE and LA MONDOTTE. The property consists of 110 ha of which 50 are planted to vines on the upper slopes which not only have an excellent southerly exposure but also very well-drained clay/limestone soils. The wine is blended from Merlot (80%) and Cabernet Franc. Fermentation in oak vats but with temperature control has recently been augmented by the addition of cone shaped concrete vats whilst completing an overhaul of the winemaking facilities in 2014. At the same time, in common with other properties owned by von Niepperg, farming has been switched to sustainable, biodynamic and organic methods. The ageing of the wine in a very high proportion (80%) of new oak on its lees has recently been reduced to 50% to give it a rounder, suppler feel. It is neither fined nor filtered. Lushly textured, concentrated and impressively complex, it has a fine tannic structure, firm in its youth, which needs a good 5 or 6 years' ageing. In 2014 the estate produced its first white wine, d'Aiguilhe blanc from 100% Sauvignon Blanc but this has not yet been tasted. (DM)
Recommended Reds:
Château d'Aiguilhe Cotes de Castillon ★★★★ £D

✿✿ Ch. Angélus (Saint-Emilion 1er GCC "A") *www.angelus.com*
This has consistently been one of the top-performing Saint-Emilion Grands Crus Classés over the last 20 years. In 1996 the property was upgraded to Premier Grand Cru Classé and in 2012 to Premier Grand Cru Classé "A". A complete renovation of the cellars and winemaking facilities finished in 2014 will ensure continuance of the château's elevated status. These are deeply coloured, concentrated and extracted wines with deep, and dark blackcurrant and plum fruit. They are always produced with well-judged oak treatment but very finely balanced as well. 1995 and 2000 have both been outstanding vintages and there has been great consistency throughout the last

Wine behind the label

Saint-Emilion, Pomerol & other Bordeaux

decade. Hubert de Boüard de Laforest is also one of the partners in the recently established MASSAYA winery in Lebanon's Bekaa Valley. The latest project is the development of the 5.5 ha Chateau DAUGAY.(DM)

Recommended Reds:

Château Angélus Saint-Emilion Grand Cru Classé ⬤⬤⬤⬤⬤ £H

Ch. Ampélia (Côtes de Castillon)

Yet another example of why this appellation is emerging as one of the most exciting of the Right Bank satellites. The wine is big, full and fleshy but also retains a mineral purity that can now be found in many of the top examples from the AC. Very dominated by Merlot, which accounts for 95% of the vineyard, it also contains a little Cabernet Franc. Give it 3 or 4 years. (DM)

Recommended Reds:

Château Ampélia Cotes de Castillon ★★★ £C

Ch. l'Archange (Saint-Emilion GC) *www.vignobleschatonnet.com*

This is the home property of emerging consultant Pascal Chatonnet. The vineyards are located to the west of the town of Saint-Emilion in close proximity to CHEVAL BLANC, ROL VALENTIN and La DOMINIQUE. The wine is marked by its sweet, rich and opulent fruit. Velvety, supple tannins and a relatively soft structure make this a wine for drinking at 3 or 4 years.(DM)

Recommended Reds:

Château l'Archange Saint-Emilion Grand Cru ★★★ £E

⬤⬤ Ch. Ausone *www.chateau-ausone.fr*

One of the great wines of the Right Bank. 1er GCC "A" Ausone, along with CHEVAL BLANC, has always been considered to stand out and are rightly classified Premiers Grands Crus Classés A-grade properties. The wine has been consistently impressive since the mid 1990s and in the last half a dozen years has been produced in a rich, supple and immensely velvety style. Very fine and complex, it is now increasingly rich and oaky. The blend now comprises around 55% Merlot and 45% Cabernet Franc. It has been absolutely top-flight since 1995 when Alain Vauthier took over the reigns with the exception of 1997. The balance between fruit, tannins and minerality is extraordinary. Approachable at 5 or 6 years, the wine benefits from at least twice that time. The second wine, La Chapelle d'Ausone is generally made with equal proportions of Merlot and Cabernet France with up to 10% of Cabernet Sauvignon added. (NB)

Recommended Reds:

Château Ausone Saint Émilion Grand Cru Classé ⬤⬤⬤⬤⬤ £H
Chapelle d'Ausone Saint Émilion Grand Cru ★★★★ £H

Ch. Barrabaque (Fronsac) *www.chateaubarrabaque.com*

Small 9-ha property planted to Merlot (70%), Cabernet Franc (20%) and Cabernet Sauvignon (10%). The robust, densely structured, plummy Prestige comes from one of the best-exposed sites in the appellation, which stands on a mix of sandy-clay and chalky-clay soils. A straightforward Tradition bottling is also produced. The Prestige, ★★★☆ in the best recent vintages, gets an extended vatting of up to 3 weeks and is aged in new wood (40%) for up to a year. (DM)

Recommended Reds:

Château Barrabaque Canon-Fronsac Prestige ★★★ £C

❀ Ch. Beau-Séjour Bécot *www.beausejour-becot.com*

This 1er GCC "B" property has been in the hands of the Bécot family since 1929 and now Juliette Bécot has ben in charge of the

estate since 2014. A lot of changes have been experienced by this estate over the period of ownership, with its size increasing and contracting at various times. Now, with the inclusion of the vines at La Gomerire, which were separately produced and labelled until 2011, the estate extends to 22.5ha, planted as to 73% Merlot, 21% Cabernet Franc and 6% Cabernet Sauvignon. The wines are supple and silky, showing a great balance of richness and minerality. 2005, 06, 09, 10, 11, 12 and 14 are the best of the current vintages with 2015 looking like it will be the best yet.The ratings for La Gomerie are only up to 2011. (NB)

Recommended Reds:

La Gomerie Saint-Emilion Grand Cru ★★★★★ £H
Château Beau-Séjour Bécot Saint-Emilion Grand Cru Classé ★★★★ £F

Ch. Beauregard (Pomerol) *www.chateau-beauregard.com*

Recently sold to a partnership of the Moulin family, who own Galleries Lafayette and the Cathiard family of CH. SMITH HAUT LAFITTE, this is one of Pomerol's lesser-known châteaux, this 17.5 ha property has an unusually high proportion of Cabernet Franc planted, around 30%. This is in part because of a high gravel component in the soil. The wine is ripe and forward, with attractively brambly fruit and a hint of oak spice, but with less overtly fleshy, plummy Merlot fruit than some others in the appellation. Very good in 1998 and particularly 2000, 2005 and 2010, with 2015 looking promising. It is approachable and supple at 4 or 5 years. (NB)

Recommended Reds:

Château Beauregard Pomerol ★★★☆ £E

Ch. Beauséjour (Saint-Emilion 1er GCC ")

Prior to 1985 this property was a notable underperformer among the Premier Grands Crus Classés. Since then the wine has been altogether more impressive. The style is medium to full with a marked black fruit opulence but sufficiently firm tannins to provide the structure needed for real cellaring. 1990 was truly impressive and the property has been consistent throughout the 90s and 00s. Further improvements have been made with input now from consultants Stéphane Derenencourt and Nicolas Thienpont, resulting in cult wines being produced in 2009 and 2010 (with prices to match) and seamless consistency since then. The property was upgraded to Grand Cru Classé "B" in the recent reclassification and fully deserves this. (NB)

Recommended Reds:

Château Beauséjour Saint-Emilion Grand Cru Classé ★★★★ £F

Ch. Bel-Air La Royère (Blaye) *www.bel-air-la-royere.com*

Small, top-class Blaye property with a total of 13 ha of vineyards producing not only Blaye but a Premières Côtes de Blaye and a second label called L'Esprit de Bel Air la Royère. Merlot is the major variety (55%) but unusually there is 45% Malbec blended with it. The Blaye is rich, full and impressively concentrated, with a really dark, smoky character. The not inconsiderable oak needs at least 4 or 5 years to fully integrate. (NB)

Recommended Reds:

Château Bel-Air La Royère Blaye ★★★ £E

Ch. Bellevue (Saint-Emilion GCC)

This property is now under the same ownership as CH. ANGELUS and is under the direction of Hubert de Boüard de Laforest who has carried on the good work started by Nicholas Thienpont and Stéphane Derenoncourt who were instrumental in upgrading the quality of the wines from this estate since 2000. There are just 6.5

ha under vine which until 2015 was 98% Merlot and 2% Cabernet Franc. Now it is 100% Merlot. These are big, powerful and structured wines with rich, dark fruit, well-judged oak and powerful tannins in their youth, which will flesh out and become more elegant with age resulting in impressive depth, purity and impeccable balance. The wines undoubtedly needs 5 or 6 years' cellaring. (NB)

Recommended Reds:

Château Bellevue Saint-Emilion Grand Cru Classé ★★★★ £F

Ch.Bellevue-Mondotte(Saint-EmilionGC) *www.vignoblesperse.com*
A tiny-production *cuvée* from Gérard Perse, the owner of PAVIE. From a 2 ha parcel on limestone-based soils, the wine is a blend of 90% Merlot and 5% each of Cabernet Franc and Cabernet Sauvignon. Yields from the 45-years-old vineyard are in fact much lower than at Pavie or Pavie Decesse at just 15hl/ha, which contributes to the rich, concentrated, almost opulent style. This is a big, full and formidably extracted wine with lashings of new oak; very good, if just lacking the depth and purity of the truly great Right Bank reds. Give it 5 years to soften the tannin, although it is quite approachable for a wine at this level. (DM)

Recommended Reds:

Château Bellevue-Mondotte Saint-Emilion Grand Cru ★★★★ £H

Ch. Berliquet (Saint-Emilion GCC) *www.chateau-berliquet.com*
Berliquet is sited on the Saint-Emilion plateau close to CANON and has been a Grand Cru Classé since 1985. The wines are certainly very reasonably made if not yet quite matching the status of some neighbouring properties of a similar classification. Quality has been at least sound since 1998, but there was a slightly aggressive, rugged edge to the tannins, which can often be a touch dry and hard. Since 2007, consultancy by Stéphane Derenoncourt and Nicolas Thienpoint has resulted in a great deal more finesse in the wines. (NB)

Recommended Reds:

Château Berliquet Saint-Emilion Grand Cru Classé ★★★☆ £F

Ch. La Bienfaisance (Saint-Emilion GC) *www.labienfaisance.com*
Good small property located on the northern plateau of Saint-Emilion with a total of 16 ha planted in limestone, sand and clay/limestone soils across three parcels. Merlot dominates plantings at around 80% with 15% Cabernet Franc and a smattering of Cabernet Sauvignon. Vinification for La Bienfaisance is traditional with fermentation in cement and ageing in a small proportion of new oak. A richer and more opulent garage-style wine, Sanctus, is aged in 100% new oak. Produced with consultation from Stéphane Derenoncourt, it is less extracted and better balanced than many of its peers. Consistently good in a recent vintages it is a very marked step up on the regular label. (DM)

Recommended Reds:

Sanctus Saint-Emilion Grand Cru ★★★★ £E
Château La Bienfaisance Saint-Emilion Grand Cru ★★☆ £D

Ch. Le Bon Pasteur (Pomerol) *www.rollandcollection.com*
Small Pomerol property of less than 7ha which was owned by roving wine consultant Michel Rolland. The vineyards, planted to a combination of 80% Merlot plus Cabernet Franc, are rigorously maintained and yields tightly harnessed. The wine is inevitably fleshy, rich and characteristic of the Rolland style with malolactic fermentation instigated in barrel. While structured and ageworthy the wine is supple, rounded and approachable with just a few years' cellaring. In 2013 the property was sold to Sutong Pan, but the

Rollands still continue to mange the estate. (NB)

Recommended Reds:

Château Le Bon Pasteur Pomerol ★★★★ £F

Ch. Bonalgue (Pomerol) *www.jbaudy.fr*
Small Pomerol property which has been in the Bourotte family since 1926. Pierre Bourotte is also the proprietor at CLOS DU CLOCHER in Pomerol and du Courlat in Lussac-Saint-Emilion. Here at Bonalgue he has 6.5 ha and Merlot is the dominant variety, accounting for 90% of the vineyard. The balance is Cabernet Franc. The wine is a typically modern fleshy, supple example with good depth and well-honed tannins. Expect it to drink well with 4 years' age or so. (DM)

Recommended Reds:

Château Bonalgue Pomerol ★★★ £E

Ch. Bonnet (Entre-Deux-Mers) *www.andrelurton.com*
This now very substantial operation is owned by André Lurton who achieves first-class results with a number of Châteaux in the Graves and Pessac-Léognan appellations, including Château La LOUVIÈRE. This is his home base though and output is well over 100,000 cases a year and the property has over 200 ha under vine. Red, white and a Bordeaux clairet – a lightly coloured style of rosé – are all produced. The reds take the Bordeaux appellation and include a Réserve aged partly in new wood. The dry whites, a tank-fermented Classique and barrel-fermented Divinus, are sold as Entre-Deux-Mers. A fine cedary new prestige red *cuvée*, also Divinus, has been added to the range. A further Lussac Saint-Emilion property Barbe-Blanche has also been acquired. (DM)

Recommended Reds:

Château Bonnet "Divinus" Bordeaux Réserve ★★★☆ £D
Château Bonnet Bordeaux Réserve ★★☆ £B

Recommended Whites:

Château Bonnet Entre-Deux-Mers ★☆ £B

Ch. Bourgneuf (Pomerol) *www.chateaubourgneuf.com*
Another Pomerol property that offers good value for the appellation with dark and spicy wines of reasonable depth and concentration. A little more depth and refinement would lift them into the top division. The 9 ha vineyard close to TROTANOY is planted mainly to Merlot (90%) with the remainder Cabernet Franc. Increased complexity can be expected with 4 or 5 years' ageing. (DM)

Recommended Reds:

Château Bourgneuf-Vayron Pomerol ★★★ £E

Ch. Canon (Saint-Emilion 1er GCC "B") *www.chateaucanon.com*
Now under the same ownership as Château RAUZAN-SEGLA. Historically a very significant property and one that is now making a welcome return to the top division of Saint-Emilion estates. The vineyard has been extended with the purchase of Château Curé-Bon in 2001, which has been incorporated into Canon. The cellars have also been cleaned up and modernised after taint problems. The 1998 was a clear step-up in quality and 2000, 01, 03, 04 and 05 were all ★★★★ and all the subsequent vintages have maintained this trend. Prior to this you should tread with caution. At its best this is a taut, restrained style with finely structured tannin. It is elegant, medium in weight and once more very ageworthy. (DM)

Recommended Reds:

Château Canon Saint-Emilion Grand Cru Classé ★★★★ £F

✿ Ch. Canon-la-Gaffelière () *www.neipperg.com*
Canon-la-Gaffelière is now a Saint Émilion 1er GCC "B" and one

of a number of striking labels and properties run by Stéphan von Neipperg, who owns the CLOS DE L'ORATOIRE, also in Saint-Emilion, and the outperforming Château D'AIGUILHE in the Côtes de Castillon. The style here, as with all the von Neipperg wines, is opulent, rich and supple, with finely integrated oak and soft, velvety tannin. Canon-la-Gaffelière is itself surprisingly approachable at 3 or 4 years. The property is located on the lower-lying limestone slopes below the town of Saint-Emilion. Dominated by old-vine Cabernet Franc, it has been consistently good over the last 6 or 7 vintages. The super-cuvée La MONDOTTE is also now made here. Both Canon-la-Gaffelière and La Mondotte are now fully organically produced.. (NB)

Recommended Reds:

Château Canon-la-Gaffelière Saint Émilion G C Classé ★★★★☆ £F

Ch. Carignan *www.chateau-carignan.com*

This 25 ha Premières Côtes de Bordeaux property is producing very good well-priced Bordeaux from one of the outlying appellations. The vineyards are planted on well-sited south-facing slopes in clay-limestone soils covered with stony gravel, which provides excellent drainage. Wines are produced from a combination of Merlot (65%), Cabernet Sauvignon (25%) and Cabernet Franc. The splendid château here was originally built in 1452 and the origins of the property date back to the 11th century. Roughly one-third of the vineyard is now over 40 years old and where replanting takes place vine density is being increased. Consultancy advice comes from Louis Mitjaville, whose father owns TERTRE ROTEBOEUF. The richly textured, dark plum and spice Prima is one of the best examples from the lesser appellations and is aged in 100% new wood for 18 months. The regular wine is rich, berry-scented and displays very good fruit and the second wine, L'Orangerie de Carignan, ensures the integrity of the top labels. (DM)

Recommended Reds:

Château Carignan Prima Premières Côtes de Bordeaux ★★★☆ £E
Château Carignan Premières Côtes de Bordeaux ★★☆ £C

Ch. Carsin (Premières Côtes de Bordeaux) *www.carsin.com*

A good example of what many properties are now beginning to achieve in the less fashionable outlying appellations of Bordeaux. It is based in the Premières Côtes de Bordeaux and the reds are labelled as such, the whites as Bordeaux AC. The regular bottlings are sound and attractive enough, with nicely developed forward fruit, but it is the white Cuvée Prestige and red Cuvée Noire that particularly stand out here. The white has a touch of barrel-fermentation and is ripe and lightly tropical, with well-judged oak. The red is supple, soft and approachable, with just a hint of vanilla oak underpinning it. Signature l'Etiquette Gris is a limited-production white from Sauvignon Gris and there is also a sweet, moderately intense Cadillac. (DM)

Recommended Reds:

Château Carsin Cuvée Noire Premières Côtes de Bordeaux ★★★ £D

Recommended Whites:

Château Carsin Bordeaux Cuvée Prestige ★★☆ £C

Ch. Certan-de-May (Pomerol)

Very good, stylish and elegant Pomerol from a tiny holding of vineyards close to PÉTRUS. This is more classically structured than many of its peers and is tight and almost austere when young. Cabernet Franc accounts for 25% of the vineyard, along with a little Cabernet Sauvignon that lends tannin and grip. The wine in the best vintages become very harmonious with up to a decade's age

and from 2009 onwards show a marked improvement from the somewhat inconsistent results over the past two decades. (NB)

Recommended Reds:

Château Certan-de-May Pomerol ★★★★☆ £G

Ch. Chauvin (Saint-Emilion GCC) *www.chateauchauvin.com*

Sylvie Cazes, co-proprietor of Domaines Jean-Michel Cazes, has recently purchased this estate from the Ondet's whose family had been in ownership since 1891. The property has been a consistent performer through most of the mid- to late 1990s and continues to be so. Consultancy input has come from Michel Rolland and the style is full, rich and fleshy, with supple, well-rounded tannins and real complexity. Needs 5 years plus. (DM)

Recommended Reds:

Château Chauvin Saint-Emilion Grand Cru Classé ★★★★ £F

✿✿ Ch. Cheval Blanc *www.chateau-cheval-blanc.com*

One of the two great wines of Saint-Emilion and produced in much greater quantity than AUSONE – some 12,500 cases a year as against barely 2,000. It has also regularly performed at the very highest level throughout the last two decades. Cheval Blanc is located close to the appellation boundary with Pomerol. There is a high proportion of Cabernet Franc in the vineyard (over 50%), which makes the wine quite different to those of its near neighbours. Bernault Arnault and Albert Frère purchased the property in the late 1990s and no expense will be spared in attempting to establish Cheval Blanc as the greatest property on Bordeaux's Right Bank. The style is rich, concentrated and opulent, with intensely complex, dark berry fruit and spice all underpinned by a structured velvety texture. To fully appreciate it in all its glory, 10 years or more of ageing is required. A wine of truly legendary proportions (DM)

Recommended Reds:

Château Cheval Blanc Saint-Emilion Grand Cru Classé ✪✪✪✪✪ £H
Château Petit Cheval Saint-Emilion Grand Cru ★★★★ £E

Ch. La Clémence (Pomerol) *www.vignoblesdauriac.com*

The holding here is very small, just 3 ha, with 85% Merlot and the balance Cabernet Franc. The Dauriac family also own the Saint-Emilion property DESTIEUX. As well as this they are developing vineyards in South Africa with plantings of Pinotage, Shiraz, Merlot and Cabernet Sauvignon. La Clémence is marked by its opulent, upfront plummy fruit and possesses a rich, supple texture, if a little dominated by new wood. It will need time to soften. (DM)

Recommended Reds:

Château La Clémence Pomerol ★★★☆ £F

Clos du Clocher (Pomerol) *www.jbaudy.fr*

Small property with just 5.7 ha under vine, split 80/20 between Merlot and Cabernet Franc. Pierre Bourotte also owns another small Pomerol estate, Château BONALGUE. Clos du Clocher is a marginally denser and richer wine than its stablemate with generally greater concentration and a firmer, sturdier structure. It is made in a more classical style and as such will benefit from 5 or 6 years' patience. Winemaking input comes from Michel Rolland. (DM)

Recommended Reds:

Clos du Clocher Pomerol ★★★☆ £F

Ch. Clinet (Pomerol) *www.chateauclinet.com*

Michel Rolland has provided consultancy input at this property for over 10 years, first to the late Jean-Michel Arcaute and now to

Jean-Louis Laborde. The style has remained consistent throughout the period. Ripe to very ripe, full, rich and almost opulent with a supple silky texture, the wine is always bottled with neither fining nor filtration and is aged in 100% new oak. Don't be fooled, though, as there is both depth and a firm tannic structure to the young wine. Best with at least 5 years' ageing. (DM)
Recommended Reds:
Château Clinet Pomerol ★★★★ £G

Ch. Clos des Jacobins (Saint-Emilion GCC) www.closdesjacobins.com
Small Saint-Emilion property which has performed admirably in recent years. There are 8.5 ha under vine planted to a combination of Merlot (70%), Cabernet Franc (28%) and a mere 2% of Cabernet Sauvignon. Every vintage since 2000 has been on good form. The wine offers rich, dark and plummy fruit with very finely judged oak and impressive purity and intensity. Recent vintages have been on the cusp of ★★★★. Give it 4 or 5 years at least. (DM)
Recommended Reds:
Château Clos des Jacobins Saint-Emilion Grand Cru Classé ★★★☆ £E

✿ Clos L'Église (Pomerol)
There are just 6 ha of vines producing this fine and impressively dense and powerful Pomerol. The wine is lent considerable structure by the inclusion of up to 40% Cabernet Franc. Very rich and fleshy, it is loaded with dark plum and spicy vanilla oak. It has been very stylish since 1998 and will cellar well for up to a decade. There is also a good second wine, L'Esprit de l'Église and other interests now include BRANON, BARDE-HAUT in Pessac-Léognan as well as new wines from POESIA and CLOS DES ANDES in Argentina. (DM)
Recommended Reds:
Clos l'Église Pomerol ★★★★★ £H

Ch. La Conseillante (Pomerol) www.laconseillante.com
One of the great Pomerol names, La Conseillante has an excellent vineyard aspect and is located close to L'ÉVANGILE and CHEVAL BLANC across the appellation boundary. With some Cabernet Franc (20%) as well as Merlot (80%) planted in gravel and clay based soils, the wine is both rich, fleshy and full of dark fruit but also firmly structured. The best years show a remarkably complex array of dark fruits and oriental spices. The wine benefits from 6–7 years' ageing at least. 2000 was exceptional and the wine has shown consistant ★★★★★ quality throughout the current decade. Earlier classics were 90, 89, 85 and 82. (DM)
Recommended Reds:
Château La Conseillante Pomerol ★★★★★ £G

Ch. Côte de Baleau (Saint-Emilion GCC)
Under the same ownership as Les GRANDES MURAILLES and Clos SAINT MARTIN, this property has been performing well in recent vintages under the management of Sophie Fourcade. There are just under 8 ha here and the 35-year-old vineyard is a mix of Merlot (70%) and Cabernet Franc (20%) with the balance Cabernet Sauvignon. The wine offers not only exuberant fruit and some youthfully toasty notes from ageing in 100% new oak but also displays an elegant mineral purity. It is long and persistent and will be better with 5 years' age or so. (DM)
Recommended Reds:
Château Côte de Baleau Saint-Emilion Grand Cru ★★★☆ £E

Ch. La Couspaude (Saint-Emilion GCC) www.aubert-vignobles.com
This is now a very impressive property located to the east of the appellation and planted with Merlot and 15% each of Cabernet Sauvignon and Cabernet Franc in limestone soils. The property is another of many benefiting from Michel Rolland's consultancy and the style is characteristically sumptuous and fleshy, with supple, velvety tannin and a complex, dark fruit character with abundant oak spice. Half a decade or so of ageing is needed to throw off the initially firm tannic grip. (DM)
Recommended Reds:
Château La Couspaude Saint-Emilion Grand Cru Classé ★★★☆ £F

Ch. La Croix-de-Gay (Pomerol)
This is a good middle-ranking Pomerol with an attractive plump, plummy Merlot character after three or fours years of bottle-age but without any great depth or complexity. There are 10 ha planted, 90% to Merlot. What marks the property out is the quality of a superior selection coming from just 3 ha called la Fleur-de-Gay. Produced from 100% Merlot, this is dense, opulent, rich and oaky. Not surprisingly it is fairly pricey. (DM)
Recommended Reds:
La Fleur-de-Gay Pomerol ★★★★ £H
Château La Croix-de-Gay Pomerol ★★★ £E

Ch. La Croix du Casse (Pomerol) www.lacroixducasse.com
This is a dense and powerfully structured Pomerol with a marked cedary, savoury component. The vineyard has a high proportion of Cabernet Franc (some 30%) as well as Merlot and the terroir is marked by a high gravel component. The wine is firmly structured and 5 or 6 years' patience will be rewarded with greater complexity. The Château was acquired in 2005 by the Castéja family the owners of the Borie-Manoux négociant firm who also own CH. TROTTVEILLE and CH. BATAILLY among others in Bordeaux. (DM)
Recommended Reds:
Château La Croix du Casse Pomerol ★★★☆ £F

Ch. Dassault (Saint-Emilion GCC) www.chateaudassault.com
Since Laurence Brun took over the running of this property in 1995, quality has been consistently good, often very good, with significant consultancy from Michel Rolland and Louis Mitjavile. The wine offers plenty of depth, in a now very modern, fleshy, supple and oak-dominated style, although the tannin can just have a slightly hard, raw edge to it. The vineyard, planted on chalky siliceous sandy soils and located on the northern slopes of the appellation is relatively sizeable for the area at 24ha. It is planted to a 65/30/5 mix of Merlot, Cabernet Franc and Cabernet Sauvignon. Grand Cru Classé since 1969. Give it 5 years to let the woody tannins integrate. The next door property La Fleur was acquired in 2002 and is rich, plump and fleshy, a little more approachable than Dassault. (DM)
Recommended Reds:
Château Dassault Saint-Emilion Grand Cru Classé ★★★☆ £F
Château La Fleur Saint-Emilion Grand Cru Classé ★★★☆ £E

Ch. de La Dauphine (Fronsac) www.chateau-dauphine.com
Impressive estate formerly owned by the Moueix family's négociant arm. Performance here was somewhat erratic during the early 1990s but has shown a significant improvement of late. Four labels come under the La Dauphine estate banner. Both the La Croix Canon, which comes from largest vineyard (13 ha), and the La Dauphine are in a fleshy, upfront style with marked dark, spicy blackberry and plum fruit. This contrasts with the Canon-de-Brem, which is more purposefully structured with tannin that can be almost austere when the wine is young. Additional refinement is achieved through

France

limited use of new oak. All the wines have shown impressive depth since 2001 when the Halleys purchased the estate. Canon-de-Brem in particular needs 5 years' ageing. A soft, forward rosé La Dauphine is also made. (DM)

Château La Dauphine
Recommended Reds:
Château La Dauphine Fronsac ★★★ £C

Château Canon-de-Brem
Recommended Reds:
Château Canon-de-Brem Canon-Fronsac ★★★ £C

Château La Croix Canon
Recommended Reds:
Château La Croix Canon Canon-Fronsac ★★☆ £C

Ch. Dauphiné-Rondillon (Loupiac)
The Darriet family pursue a number of interests from their base in Loupiac but it is the splendid Dauphiné-Rondillon that really stands out. This is a very fine alternative to lesser Sauternes from vineyards just the other side of the river Garonne. These are planted in clay and gravel soils and hold 60–80 year old vines, a real rarity in Bordeaux. The harvest is in several *tris* and the yield is comfortably less than 20 hl/ha. Maturation is for 18 months and just 20% new wood is used. The wine is characterised by its rich, botrytised, peachy character and excellent balance. Just 3 ha of Merlot and Cabernet Sauvignon and 1ha of Sauvignon Blanc produce a pair of fine, essentially fruit-driven Graves. Premières Côtes de Bordeaux, both red and white, is also produced. (DM)

Château Dauphiné-Rondillon
Recommended Whites:
Château Dauphiné-Rondillon La Cuvee d'Or Loupiac ★★★☆ £D

Château Moutin
Recommended Reds:
Château Moutin Graves ★★ £C
Recommended Whites:
Château Moutin Graves ★★ £C

Ch. Destieux (Saint-Emilion GCC) *www.vignobles-dauriac.com*
The Dauriac family also own the small Pomerol property La CLÉMENCE. The red here offers a good deal better value both in comparison to its stablemate and when compared to a number of other Saint-Emilion Grands Crus. Quality has been at least good since 1998. The vineyard is small at just 8 ha and the planting is a mix of 70% Merlot and equal holdings of Cabernets Franc and Sauvignon. The wine is rich and supple with a forward, fleshy texture and should drink well at 3 or 4 years of age. (DM)
Recommended Reds:
Château Destieux Saint-Emilion Grand Cru Classé ★★★ £E

Ch. La Dominique (Saint-Emilion GCC)
This property, with an ideal location in very close proximity to CHEVAL BLANC, has been a reasonably consistent performer since the late 1980s. The style is not only opulent and fleshy with marked new oak and rich, concentrated, spicy, dark fruit but there is an underlying finesse and quality here. The wine is supple but well-structured and very ageworthy. 1998, 2000 and 2005 were very good and the wines have continued to impress since Jean-Luc Thunevin was taken on board as a consultant in 2007. The small-volume garage-style wine, Saint Dominique, is no longer made. (DM)
Recommended Reds:
Château La Dominique Saint-Emilion Grand Cru Classé ★★★★ £F

Dom. de L'Église (Pomerol) *www.domainedeleglise.com*
There are just over 7ha here planted mainly to Merlot (95%) with a smattering of Cabernet Franc. The Castéja family are also significant négociants and own TROTTEVIEILLE in Saint-Emilion. A rich and sumptuous example of the AC, the wine has a firm mineral structure that will ensure continued development in bottle, particularly in the classic vintages. Youthful oak means 4 or 5 years is needed to achieve real balance and harmony. (DM)
Recommended Reds:
Domaine de L'Église Pomerol ★★★★ £F

✿ Ch. L'Église-Clinet (Pomerol) *www.eglise-clinet.com*
Magnificent small Pomerol property with a holding of just 5.5 ha of Merlot and Cabernet Franc. The vineyard is very old, with some of the vines nearing 100 years. The style bears little comparison with those neighbours who opt for modern extracted wines and dollops of new oak. L'Église-Clinet is structured, dense and backward when young. Given 6 or 7 years the result is an elegant, velvety and classically proportioned example of the appellation. Exceptional in every vintage since 2004 and very impressive in other years since 1995. (DM)
Recommended Reds:
Château L'Église-Clinet Pomerol ✪✪✪✪✪ £H

Essence de Dourthe (Bordeaux) *www.dourthe.com*
This is the flagship red of the Dourthe négociant house. It is unusual for Bordeaux in being the antithesis of *terroir* driven wines, sourced from 10 ha of the best plots of the firm's leading properties throughout the region. These include Château BELGRAVE in the Haut-Médoc, La GARDE in Pessac-Léognan and MARSAU in the Côtes de Francs. A blend of Cabernet Sauvignon (55%) and Merlot, the wine is rich, full and showy. While it is impressively structured with real dimension, it just seems to be missing an element that would move it up among the region's great reds. Give it 4 or 5 years. (DM)
Recommended Reds:
Essence de Dourthe Bordeaux ★★★★ £F

✿ Château l'Évangile (Pomerol) *www.lafite.com*
This is an impressively deep, structured and powerful example of Pomerol. Like L'ÉGLISE-CLINET, it is markedly different from many of its supple, rounded, softly structured contemporaries. Owned since 1990 by the Rothschilds, the wine is traditionally vinified and possesses sturdy, dense, firm tannin when young, along with formidably concentrated levels of complex, dark, spicy fruit. There is oak evident here but its very harmoniously integrated. It has been remarkably good in the best years of the last decade or so of the 20th century; 1990 was of legendary quality – ✪✪✪✪✪ – and the wines of the first decade of the 21st century, with perhaps the exception of 2003 and 2007 are also very impressive. (DM)
Recommended Reds:
Château l'Évangile Pomerol ★★★★★ £H

Ch. Faizeau (Montagne-Saint-Emilion) *www.chateau-faizeau.com*
Good Saint-Emilion satellite made from 10 ha of Merlot planted in finely drained limestone soils. Quality is boosted by the age of the vines, which are now over 30 years old. This is a ripe, forward style with blackberry and plum fruit and impressive depth and substance. It is not over-extracted and offers firm enough tannin for short-term development in bottle. (DM)

Recommended Reds:

Château Faizeau Montagne-Saint-Emilion Vieilles Vignes ★★★ £C

Ch. Falfas (Côtes de Bourg) *www.chateaufalfas.fr*

Decent Bourg property run on biodynamic lines by John Cochran. The winemaking origins of the property go back to 1612. There are 22 ha of vines planted, 55% Merlot, 30% Cabernet Sauvignon and unusually 10% of Malbec. The balance is Cabernet Franc. There is a cold soak for 48 hours, traditional fermentation and malolactic in *cuve*, followed by ageing in 30% new wood. The wines are richly textured and full of dark plummy fruit and a marked spicy, tobacco character no doubt emphasised by the inclusion of Malbec. The top label, Le Chevalier, has an added dimension and is regularly on the edge of ★★★. (DM)

Recommended Reds:

Château Falfas Le Chevalier Côtes de Bourg ★★☆ £C

Château Falfas Côtes de Bourg ★★ £B

Ch. Faugères (Saint-Emilion GCC) *www.chateau-faugeres.com*

Major investment in both the vineyard and cellars under the current ownership has wrought major change and delivered increasingly impressive wines. The Château Faugères regular Saint-Emilion is a dense, richly concentrated and spicy Grand Cru Classé which is aged in 100% new oak and has the depth and structure to develop well over a decade or more. Since 1998 a super-rich special *cuvée*, Château Péby Faugères, has been produced which is both sumptuously fleshy and very powerful. The Cap de Faugères is a supple, rounded and forward style produced from vineyards owned in the Côtes de Castillon. (DM)

Chateau Faugères

Recommended Reds:

Péby Faugères Saint-Emilion Grand Cru Classé ★★★★☆ £G

Château Faugères Saint-Emilion Grand Cru Classé ★★★☆ £E

Chateau Cap de Faugères

Recommended Reds:

Château Cap de Faugères Cotes de Castillon ★★★☆ £C

>> Ch. Fayat (Pomerol) *www.chateau-fayat.com*

Under the same ownership as La DOMINIQUE in Saint-Emilion, this is a merger in 2009 of three Châteaux, Chateaux Commanderie de Mazeyres, Vieux Château Bourgneuf and Prieurs de la Commanderie. Château Fayat now has just over 16 ha of a diverse range of *terroir*. The combination of soil and microclimate is unique to each vineyard and each harvest is produced to a combination of Merlot and Cabernet Franc, which does vary vintage to vintage between 80/20 and 90/10. Results have been a little variable since the merger and the wine is less upfront and showy than many Pomerols. Consulting input is from Michel Rolland. About 1,000 cases of a second wine, Prieurs de la Commanderie is made but has not been tasted. (NB)

Recommended Reds:

Château Fayat Pomerol ★★★ £F

Ch. Feytit-Clinet (Pomerol)

Really characterful and impressive Pomerol is now being made at this well-sited property close to TROTANOY. Merlot is very much the dominant variety, occupying 90% of the 6 ha vineyard, and Cabernet Franc is the only other variety cultivated. The wine offers real style and substance: rich, concentrated dark-berry fruit is underpinned by lots of very well-integrated new oak. It has been good throughout the last decade. This is a supple and approachable wine, but give it 4 or 5 years for real balance and harmony. (DM)

Recommended Reds:

Château Feytit-Clinet Pomerol ★★★★ £F

Ch. Figeac (Saint-Emilion 1er GCC "B") *www.chateau-figeac.com*

The traditional qualities of this Premier Grand Cru Classé – namely refinement, elegance and a harmonious balance of subtle, dark, spicy fruit and lightly smoky oak – have been apparent in a number of recent vintages but strangely absent in others when one would expect the property to have performed well. The vineyard has an unusually high proportion of Cabernet Sauvignon and Cabernet Franc for Saint-Emilion, mainly because of the marked gravel component of the soil, with just one-third planted to Merlot. The resulting wines are inevitably powerful and structured when at their best and long-lived. Recent vintages look generally good, although 2003 and 2007 were a little disappointing. (DM)

Recommended Reds:

Château Figeac Saint-Emilion Grand Cru Classé ★★★☆ £G

Ch. La Fleur de Boüard *www.lafleurdebouard.com*

One of the benchmark properties from Lalande-de-Pomerol and, with the Le Plus *cuvée*, one that commands the highest prices. A total of 19 ha are planted to Merlot (80%), Cabernet Franc (15%) and Cabernet Sauvignon (5%). The regular label is rich, concentrated and fleshy with opulent, dark, spicy fruit. The brilliantly crafted Le Plus offers layers of flavour and complexity and has a special minerality and fine cedary structure that mark it as one of the region's great reds. The approachable La Fleur will benefit from 4 or 5 years' ageing, while Le Plus really requires 6–8 years' patience. (DM)

Recommended Reds:

Le Plus de La Fleur de Boüard Lalande-de-Pomerol ★★★★☆ £G

Château La Fleur de Boüard Lalande-de-Pomerol ★★★☆ £E

Ch. Fleur-Cardinale *www.chateau-fleurcardinale.com*

Well-priced and improving Saint-Emilion Grand Cru Classé which has shown a consistent upturn in quality since the Decosters acquired the estate in 2001. The property is situated in the north-east of the appellation and planted to 70% Merlot, the balance equal proportions of Cabernet Sauvignon and Cabernet Franc, in *argilo-calcaire* soils. The average age of the vines is now 40 years and under the insistence of consultant Jean-Luc Thunevin yields are being reduced in a consistent drive for quality. Richly textured, approachable reds are likely to be a regular occurence here. The wine will nonetheless benefit from 3 or 4 years age. (DM)

Recommended Reds:

Château Fleur-Cardinale Saint-Emilion Grand Cru ★★★☆ £D

Ch. La Fleur-Pétrus (Pomerol)

Like PÉTRUS itself this property is owned by the Moueix family. The vineyards have a higher proportion of gravel than is commonly found here and the wine is less opulent and rich than many of its neighbours. It is refined, medium, rather than full-bodied and tightly structured and restrained in its youth. With age it will become very fine and complex and is extraordinarily long-lived. 1975 still seems youthful. Somewhat erratic in the 1980s, the wine has been a model of consistency since the mid to late 90s. (DM)

Recommended Reds:

Château la Fleur-Pétrus Pomerol ★★★★☆ £G

Ch. Fombrauge (Saint-Émilion GCC) *www.fombrauge.com*

Bernard Magrez, owner of PAPE-CLEMENT in Pessac-Léognan,

purchased Fombrauge in 1999. While Fombrauge has been going from strength to strength, particularly throughout the late 1990s, it has achieved new heights under the current ownership. With over 50 ha of vineyards and located to the north-east of the appellation, away from the established grandee properties, Fombrauge is proving as elsewhere that the less-fancied plots in this sizeable appellation can provide impressive wines. A limited-production, highly priced special *cuvée*, Magrez-Fombrauge, has also now been released. Massively powerful and extracted, it remains to be seen how this wine will develop, as with other super-*cuvées* from lesser plots, but it has considerable promise. Bernard Magrez has also produced a number of small-scale garagiste-style wines of great potential from a number of properties throughout the region and has provided input to actor Gérard Depardieu and actress Carole Bouquet in similar properties in both Bordeaux and the Midi and equally excitingly Spain, Argentina, Morocco and Algeria. (DM)

Recommended Reds:
Magrez-Fombrauge Saint-Emilion Grand Cru ★★★★★ £G
Château Fombrauge Saint-Emilion Grand Cru ★★★ £D
Recommended Whites:
Château Fombrauge Bordeaux ★★★ £D

Ch. Fontenil (Fronsac) *www.rollandcollection.com*
This small Fronsac property is owned by Michel and Dany Rolland. The 9 ha are planted to 90% Merlot, the balance Cabernet Sauvignon. The wine is lushly textured, rich, supple and full of opulence, with just a hint of cassis adding depth and weight to the bramble and dark berry fruit. The new oak so apparent when the wine is young will become more balanced and harmonious with time. One of the better examples of this lesser appellation. A tiny-production mini-*cuvée*, Défi de Fontenil, is also now produced, although it is not excessively expensive. (DM)

Recommended Reds:
Château Fontenil Fronsac ★★★☆ £D

Ch. Fougas (Côtes de Bourg) *www.fougas-maldoror.com*
This is the larger of the two properties of the Béchets, who also own the tiny Saint-Emilion property RIOU DE THAILLAS. There are just 17 ha under vine here, planted to Merlot (50%) and equal proportions of Cabernet Sauvignon and Cabernet Franc. The site is surrounded by two streams which provide excellent natural drainage from its alluvial, clay, sand and gravel soils. Each parcel of vines is vinified separately after cold maceration, and the wines spend a small period on their gross lees. The special *cuvée* Maldoror is sourced from the best individual plots on the property and is aged in 100% new oak. Both wines will stand a litle age and the richly textured, dark plum and spice Maldoror demands 2–3 years to integrate the not inconsderable high-toast oak. (DM)

Recommended Reds:
Château Fougas Maldoror Côtes de Bourg ★★★☆ £D
Château Fougas Côtes de Bourg ★★ £B

Clos Fourtet (Saint-Emilion GC) *www.closfourtet.com*
Philippe Cuvelier purchased this estate from the Lurton's in 2001 and the high standards practised by them have continued, especially with input from Stéphane Derenoncourt. There are 20 ha of vineyards planted to a mix of Merlot (80%), Cabernet Sauvignon (12%) and Cabernet Franc. The resulting wines have generally been big, full and sturdy, particularly during the last decade, which has seen a consistent raising of standards. The wine is densely extracted and sees a high proportion of new oak. Recent vintages have been refined and classy with great intensity. The property should continue to move towards greater things. (DM)

Recommended Reds:
Clos Fourtet St-Émilion Grand Cru ★★★★☆ £F

Ch. Franc-Maillet (Pomerol) *www.vignobles-g-arpin.com*
Very good small producer with less than 10ha spread across two vineyards. The Lalande-de-Pomerol, Vieux Château Gachet, is impressively structured at this level and almost restrained in style. Aged in one-third new wood, it is dense and backward and will open out and offer great drinking with 5 years' ageing. The Franc-Maillet is a classically structured Pomerol with subtle cedar as well as dark berry and plum notes. Put this away for at least 5 years, and longer for the Jean Baptiste label. This comes from an older vine parcel of just 0.7 ha with 90% Merlot. Aged in 90% new oak it is not only remarkably deep and concentrated but offers a piercing minerality to its fruit and great purity. The wines are very well priced and no doubt very scarce. The Arpin family also own the Montagne-Saint-Emilion property Château GACHON. (DM)

Château Franc-Maillet
Recommended Reds:
Château Franc-Maillet Jean Baptiste Pomerol ★★★★ £E
Château Franc-Maillet Pomerol ★★★☆ £D
Vieux Château Gachet
Recommended Reds:
Vieux Château Gachet Lalande-de-Pomerol ★★★ £C

Ch. Franc-Mayne *www.chateau-francmayne.com*
Relatively tiny Grand Cru Classé property of just 7ha which has produced increasingly good wine in recent vintages. The vineyards are planted in limestone soils to the west of the town of Saint-Emilion, close to neighbouring GRAND-MAYNE. The limited *cuvée* La Gomerie from BEAU-SÉJOUR BÉCOT is also sourced from these slopes. Merlot dominates plantings at 90%; the balance is Cabernet Sauvignon. The wine is richly textured and impressively concentrated with dark spicy fruit and sufficiently supple tannin to drink well with 3 or 4 years' ageing. Michel Rolland provides the winemaking direction and the style of the wine reflects his input. Malolactic is in barrel and copious new oak is used for ageing. Total output is barely 3,000 cases and around a third of this is earmarked for the very decent second label, Les Cèdres de Franc-Mayne. (DM)

Recommended Reds:
Château Franc-Mayne Saint-Emilion Grand Cru Classé ★★★☆ £E

Ch. des Francs (Bordeaux Côtes de Francs) *www.hebrard.com*
Hubert de Boüard, owner of the benchmark Lalande-de-Pomerol property La FLEUR DE BOÜARD, also part-owns this excellent satellite property. There are 31 ha under vine and 29 of these are planted to reds – Merlot (80%), Cabernet Franc (10%) and Cabernet Sauvignon (10%). Production is currently about 11,000 cases a year. The regular bottling offers good value and accessible easy drinking. The Les Cerisiers *cuvée* is altogether more serious, offering rich, plummy varietal Merlot character and a fleshy, densely textured palate with impressive depth. It will benefit from at least 4–5 years' patience. (DM)

Recommended Reds:
Château de Francs Les Cerisiers Bordeaux Côtes de Francs ★★★ £C
Château de Francs Côtes de Francs ★★ £B

Ch. Gachon (Montagne-Saint-Emilion) *www.vignobles-g-arpin.com*
Gérard Arpin, who also owns Château FRANC-MAILLET in Pomerol,

produces one of the best wines from this Saint-Emilion satellite appellation. Part of the quality is contributed by 35-year-old vines planted on south-east facing slopes. The wine is a blend of Merlot (70%), Cabernet Franc (20%) and Cabernet Sauvignon (10%). It is rich and fleshy in a fruit-driven style with an impressively supple structure and minimal oak influence. Four years or so will see real harmony. (DM)

Recommended Reds:

Château Gachon Montage-Saint-Emilion ★★★ £C

Ch. La Gaffelière *www.chateau-la-gaffeliere.com*

After a period when this 22 ha property was relatively disappointing in the early to mid-1990s the wines appear to be consistently improving. There has been no new ownership or marked change in the style, just, it would appear, a general sharpening of the act. This is very much a classically structured Saint-Emilion: stylish, medium-rather than full-bodied with a restrained mineral character as well as subtle, smoky, dark fruit. It will add weight with 5 years' cellaring. (DM)

Recommended Reds:

Château la Gaffelière Saint-Emilion Grand Cru Classé ★★★★ £G

Ch. Gazin (Pomerol) *www.gazin.com*

This is among Pomerol's larger properties, with 23 ha under vine, the vast majority being Merlot, with small amounts of Cabernet Sauvignon and Cabernet Franc also planted. The vineyards consist of gravel/clay soils and are sited next to PETRUS and L'EVANGILE. 10,000 cases a year are produced, 8,000 of which are the *Grand Vin*, the balance being the second wine L'Hospitalet de Gazin. The wines have been cosistently good now for a decade. The 1990s have seen a transformation, with improved management and control in both vineyard and cellar. The vintages of 1998, 99, 00 and particularly 2001 were very good here. Not surprisingly 2006 and 2005 seem to be of a similar order. The style is rich, forward and opulent with ripe and plummy dark fruit, sufficiently firm and sturdy tannins and an increasing amount of new oak used. (DM)

Recommended Reds:

Château Gazin Pomerol ★★★★ £G

Ch. Le Gay (Pomerol)

This 10 ha property is now owned by Catherine Péré-Vergé, whose portfolio of interests also includes another Pomerol property, MONTVIEL, and a share in Argentina's CLOS DE LOS SIETE. Le Gay is increasingly impressive and maintaining the high standards set of late. The wine is in an opulent, modern, fleshy style laden with rich berry fruit. It has loads of concentration and oak but there is a highly impressive cedary complexity and a finely crafted structure here as well. No doubt 6 or 7 years' patience will be amply rewarded. (DM)

Recommended Reds:

Château Le Gay Pomerol ★★★★ £F

Gracia (Saint-Emilion GC)

Small garage operation with facilities in the centre of Saint-Emilion. Michel Gracia produces two wines, both aged in new French oak, and his use of wood is well judged. Les Angelots is the lighter and more accessible and comes from a separate 1.25 ha plot of 27-year-old Merlot (80%) and Cabernet Franc (20%). The Gracia label itself is richer and fleshier with loads of dark blackberry fruit and sweet oak. It offers impressive depth and is supple and well structured. The vine age now averages over 30 years and as well as Merlot and Cabernet Franc there is a smattering of Cabernet Sauvignon. (DM)

Recommended Reds:

Gracia Saint-Emilion Grand Cru ★★★★ £F
Gracia Les Angelots de Gracia Saint-Emilion Grand Cru ★★★ £E

Ch. Grand Corbin-Despagne *www.grand-corbin-despagne.com*

Moderate-sized Grand Cru Classé property with just over 26 ha under vine. The Despagne family have been producing good well-priced examples of the appellation since the 1998 vintage. As well as their *Grand Vin* they also produce a decent second label, Petit Corbin-Despagne. The vineyard, which is a mix of Merlot (75%), Cabernet Franc (24%) and a tiny amount of Cabernet Sauvignon, is planted in sandy-clay soils. The harvest is carefully sorted and with an average vine age of over 40 years the wine has no problem handling the 20–30 days of vatting and ageing in 50% new wood for up to 18 months. Rich and fleshy in style, it requires 4–5 years' cellaring to throw the aggressive character of its youthful tannin. (DM)

Recommended Reds:

Château Grand Corbin-Despagne St-Emilion Grand Cru Classé ★★★ £D
Petit Corbin-Despagne Saint-Emilion ★☆ £C

Ch. Grand-Mayne *www.grand-mayne.com*

Grand-Mayne produces impressively dark, dense and well-structured SaintÉmilions. There are some 17 ha under vine and the estate is located towards the western side of the appellation. Quality has much improved in recent vintages and the wine is suppler and has better fruit quality than of old. An increasing use of new oak is helping to underpin the character of the château. While firmly structured when young, the wine avoids austerity. (DM)

Recommended Reds:

Château Grand-Mayne Saint-Emilion Grand Cru Classé ★★★★ £F

Ch. Grand Ormeau *www.chateaugrandormeau.com*

Two *cuvées* are now made at this 11.5 ha Lalande-de-Pomerol property. The vineyards have an aspect facing north to south and are located in the highest part of the appellation. Merlot is inevitably the dominant variety at just under two-thirds of the plantings but both Cabernet Franc and Cabernet Sauvignon are significant, each covering 18% of the *vignoble*. The regular bottling is soft and approachable, while the Cabernet elements are quite apparent in the impressively structured, dark and spicy Madeleine. This in particular should be given 5 years or so to soften and open out. (DM)

Recommended Reds:

Château Grand Ormeau Madeleine Lalande-de-Pomerol ★★★☆ £E
Château Grand Ormeau Lalande-de-Pomerol ★★☆ £C

Ch. Grand-Pontet *www.chateaugrandpontet.com*

There are 14 ha of vines here, mainly Merlot with a reasonably high proportion of Cabernet Franc (15%) and Cabernet Sauvignon (10%). The clay-rich soils provide a subtle and elegant style. The wine has been at least good throughout the mid- to late 1990s and this consistency has been continued into the 2000s. Greater fruit ripeness and suppler tannins have been the keys. (DM)

Recommended Reds:

Château Grand-Pontet Saint-Emilion Grand Cru Classé ★★★☆ £E

Ch. Les Grandes Murailles *www.lesgrandesmurailles.fr*

Purchased from the Rieffers family together with Clos SAINT-MARTIN and CÔTE DE BALEAU, this property is tiny with a mere 2 ha, 95% of which is Merlot, the balance Cabernet Franc. The vineyards are

France

now on average 40 years old and this helps in providing rich, dense and concentrated fruit-driven wines. Expect the wine to drink well young although a few years' patience will be rewarded. (DM)
Recommended Reds:
Château Les Grandes Murailles St-Emilion Grand Cru Classé ★★★☆ £E

Ch. Les Gravières (Saint-Emilion GC) *www.denis-barraud.com*
Good and well-priced Saint-Emilion from a small property with barely more than 3 ha of vineyards planted on argilo-calcareous soils very close to MONBOUSQUET. Unusually, the wine is 100% Merlot and it is made in a fleshy, lightly plummy style with a hint of herb-spice in the background. Expect it to drink well at 3 or 4 years. (DM)
Recommended Reds:
Château Les Gravières Saint-Emilion Grand Cru ★★★ £E

Ch. Gree Laroque (Bordeaux Supérieur) *www.greelaroque.com*
This tiny-volume wine sourced from 1.6 ha of vineyards to the north of Libourne and Fronsac is a testament to the commitment of Benoit de Nyvenheim and the winemaking skills of consultant Stéphane Derenoncourt. The vines, a mix of Merlot (75%) and Cabernet Franc (20%) as well as a sprinkling of Cabernet Sauvignon, are planted in well-drained gravel, clay and clay/limestone soils. Of equal importance is the age of the vineyard at over 40 years, virtually unheard of in this lesser appellation. Vinification is modern and precise. The harvest is carefully sorted and malolactic takes place in barrel with the wine aged on lees for 12–18 months in one-third new oak. Bottled unfiltered, the wine is impressively deep and concentrated with dark, spicy fruit, opulent oak and just a hint of dark pepper in the background. Give it 3–4 years. (DM)
Recommended Reds:
Château Gree Laroque Bordeaux Supérieur ★★★ £D

Ch. Haut-Bertinerie *www.chateaubertinerie.com*
Sizeable Premières-Côtes-De-Blaye operation producing just over 35,000 cases a year in red, white and rosé styles. The top wines from the oldest and best-sited vines – some 30–50 years old – are labelled Haut-Bertinerie 1er Vin and Cru Reserve. There are now three properties with three selections of site. The oldest vines have a higher gravel component than normal and Cabernet Sauvignon accounts for 40% of the 43 ha of red plantings. Merlot is planted on the clay-limestone slopes. The high Cabernet Sauvignon component is reflected in the Haut-Bertinerie reds, which have a bigger, firmer structure than most from the appellation. The Château Bertinerie and a second wine of Haut-Bertinerie are softer and more approachable. Whites come from 18 ha, all of which is Sauvignon Blanc. The white Haut-Bertinerie and Bertinerie Cru Reserve are both barrelfermented with a rich, full texture on the palate and good background acidity. As well as the Bertinerie white there is also a second label from Haut-Bertinerie both of which are aged on fine lees. A straightforward red and white at a lower level are released under each Château label. These are labelled "Little HB" for Haut-Bertinerie and B de Bertinerie. (DM)
Recommended Reds:
Château Haut-Bertinerie Landreau Premières-Côtes-de-Blaye ★★★ £D
Château Haut-Bertinerie Premières-Côtes-de-Blaye ★★☆ £C
Château Bertinerie Cru Reserve Premières-Côtes-de-Blaye ★★☆ £C
Château Bertinerie Premières-Côtes-de-Blaye ★★ £B
Recommended Whites:
Château Haut-Bertinerie Premières-Côtes-de-Blaye ★★ £C
Château Bertinerie Cru Reserve Premières-Côtes-de-Blaye ★★ £C

Château Bertinerie Premières-Côtes-de-Blaye ★☆ £B

Ch. Haut-Carles (Fronsac) *www.hautcarles.com*
Small Fronsac property that has been consistently fine in recent vintages. There are just 8 ha under vine with Merlot accounting for 95% of the red plantings and the balance from Cabernet Franc. Two whites are also produced under the Bordeaux AC, including a Blanc de Renouil, and there is a simple, fruit-driven Petit Renouil red as well as a further Fronsac labelled Château du Pavillon. The Haut-Carles red is very good indeed with real style. Marvellously extracted dark, plummy fruit is balanced by subtle, lightly vanilla-scented wood. Expect the wine to continue to develop well over 4 or 5 years or more. (DM)
Recommended Reds:
Château Haut Carles Fronsac ★★★ £C

Ch. Haut-Chaigneau *www.vignobleschatonnet.com*
Haut-Chaigneau is one of the largest properties in Lalande-de-Pomerol with some 21 ha of vineyards. The Chatonnets also own a 5 ha parcel of 40-year-old vines on finely drained sandy-clay and gravel soils from which they produce La Sergue. Haut-Chaigneau is a blend of Merlot (70%) and 15% each of Cabernet Sauvignon and Cabernet Franc. It is made in a very ripe, sweet style and is supple and approachable young. The more structured and backward La Sergue, which comes from lower yields, is nevertheless rich and very ripe in the house style with more marked new wood. Give it 5 or 6 years' ageing. A second label is also produced, Château Tour Saint-André. (DM)
Chateau Haut-Chaigneau
Recommended Reds:
Château Haut-Chaigneau Lalande-de-Pomerol ★★☆ £C
Château La Sergue
Recommended Reds:
Château La Sergue Lalande-de-Pomerol ★★★ £D

Ch. Haut-Mazeris (Canon-Fronsac/Fronsac)
This 11 ha estate is half in the Canon-Fronsac appellation and half in the Fronsac appellation. The property stands on the highest slopes of the Fronsac AC. and is planted to a mix of Merlot (a mere 65%), Cabernet Sauvignon (20%) and Cabernet Franc (15%) on finely drained clay-limestone soils and the vineyard is now over 35 years of age. The Fronsac AC wine has greater structure and grip than those from most neighbouring properties, no doubt aided by the high proportion of the Cabernets in the blend. It is rich, dense and fleshy with just a hint of youthful oak apparent (50% of the barrels are new each year) and it will be better with 5 years' ageing. The Canon-Fronsac AC wines offers some of the finest red wine in this small satellite appellation. The wines are deep, dark and concentrated with a real old-vine quality to them, loaded with dark blackberry and herb-spice character. A 2 ha parcel of the oldest vines is retained to produce the richly textured Cuvée Spéciale. Both wines should be given 4 or 5 years' ageing. (DM)
Recommended Reds:
Château Haut-Mazeris Cuvée Spéciale Canon-Fronsac ★★★☆ £D
Château Haut-Mazeris Canon-Fronsac ★★★ £C
Château Haut-Mazeris Fronsac ★★★ £C

Ch. Hosanna (Pomerol) *www.moueix.com*
Small Pomerol property showing consistently high-quality over the lastdecade. Hosanna produces just over 1,500 cases a year from 4.5 ha of Merlot (70%) and Cabernet Franc (30%) with a superb

exposure close to LAFLEUR and PÉTRUS. The property was originally known as Certain-Guiraud but the name was changed by the Moueix family. This is a rich, supple and very elegant wine with a fine mineral core, no doubt helped by the sizeable proportion of Cabernet Franc. Give it at least 5 or 6 years. (DM)

Recommended Reds:
Château Hosanna Pomerol ★★★★ £G

Ch. Hostens-Picant *www.chateauhostens-picant.fr*
Absolute benchmark property for Sainte-Foy Bordeaux. The Picants have a total of 40 ha under vine, three-quarters of which are red. They also produce a decent white Cuvée des Demoiselles, with a high proportion of Sémillon. Both reds are modern and fleshy; the regular label is more fruit-driven, with the clear hand of consultant Stéphane Derenoncourt's input, with the Lucullus being is bigger and fuller with very marked dark, plummy fruit and spicy oak undertones but excellent balance too. The Lucullus in particular will evolve nicely over 4 or 5 years. (DM)

Recommended Reds:
Château Hostens-Picant Lucullus Sainte-Foy Bordeaux ★★★☆ £D
Château Hostens-Picant Sainte-Foy Bordeaux ★★☆ £C
Recommended Whites:
Château Hostens-Picant Cuvée des Demoiselles Sainte-Foy Bordeaux ★★★ £C

Ch. Joanin Bécot (Côtes de Castillon) *www.beausejour-becot.com*
This small and very fine Castillon property is owned by the Bécot family of BEAU-SÉJOUR-BÉCOT. There are just over 5ha under vine and production is tiny at a mere 2,500 cases a year. Merlot is the dominant variety but the vineyard also has a fair amount of Cabernet Franc, accounting for a quarter of the plantings. This is a rich, dense Castillon with a hint of new oak, impressive depth and a subtle mineral purity. Give it 3 or 4 years although its opulent character suggests the wine will be very attractive in its relative youth. (DM)

Recommended Reds:
Château Joanin Bécot Côtes de Castillon ★★★☆ £D

✿ Ch. Lafleur (Pomerol)
Tiny Pomerol property consisting of a mere 4.5 ha of vines, more than half surprisingly planted to Cabernet Franc. This component helps provide the considerable structure which enables the wine to age gracefully for two decades and more. In recent vintages an increasing amount of new oak has been used and the wine possesses not just a finely structured, almost mineral core but a rich, concentrated, opulence also. It has been remarkably consistent over the last 20 years. (DM)

Recommended Reds:
Château Lafleur Pomerol ✿✿✿✿✿ £H

Ch. Larcis-Ducasse *www.larcis-ducasse.com*
This Grand Cru Classé "B" property has 11 ha of Merlot, Cabernet Franc and Cabernet Sauvignon planted in south-east facing vineyards on the brilliantly exposed Côte Pavie. The estate is run by Nicolas Thienpont with consultancy input from Stéphane Derenoncourt and recent vintages have been very good. The wine is produced in a supple, accessible style with loads of dark, spicy, fleshy fruit underpinned by fairly high-toast oak. Unlike at a number of other properties the wood is well judged without excessive oak tannins. At present this wine offers great value. (DM)

Recommended Reds:
Château Larcis-Ducasse Saint-Emilion Grand Cru Classé ★★★★ £E

Ch. Laroze (Saint-Emilion GCC) *www.laroze.com*
This is another Saint-Emilion property much improved since the late 1990s. Careful grape selection prior to fermentation ensures the wine is crafted in a lush, fleshy and opulent style with supple tannins and a very appealing youthful character. Dark, spicy plummy fruit is very apparent. Part malolactic in barrel helps to underpin the wine. The 27 ha of vineyards are located on the western plateau of the appellation and are planted in sandy soils with a chalky/clay bedrock offering good drainage. The estate has been farmed biodynamically since 1991 and the vine age is gradually creeping up although it is still relatively young at 25 years. Certainly it would appear that the best is yet to emerge here. The wine is bottled unfiltered. (DM)

Recommended Reds:
Château Laroze Saint-Emilion Grand Cru Classé ★★★☆ £D

✿ La Mondotte (Saint-Emilion 1er GCC "B") *www.neipperg.com*
Along with Le DÔME, this is one of the two great garage wines to emerge in the last half decade. Produced at CANON-LA-GAFFELIÈRE, the vineyard consists of 4.5 ha planted on clay/silt soils over a rocky subsoil. It is superbly drained with an unusually steep south-facing aspect. It is this low-yielding *terroir* that is responsible for a wine of remarkable depth and concentration. Blended from 80% Merlot and 20% Cabernet Franc, it offers a truly opulent and exotic array of dark fruits and oriental spices. It is produced in the classic Derenoncourt style with ageing on lees in new oak for a year and a half and is bottled unfiltered. (DM)

Recommended Reds:
La Mondotte Saint-Emilion Grand Cru Classé ✿✿✿✿✿ £H

Ch. Latour-á-Pomerol (Pomerol) *www.moueix.com*
This is another property under the Moueix family umbrella. These are supple, ripe and at their best richly plummy examples of Pomerol, produced to showcase the more opulent character of the appellation. The wine has generally performed well during the period from 1994 onwards, with just the odd hint of aggressive tannin sometimes marring the style. It develops well with 6 or 7 years' age. (DM)

Recommended Reds:
Château Latour-á-Pomerol Pomerol ★★★☆ £G

Ch. de Laussac (Cotes de Castillon) *www.vignoblesrobin.com*
Despite the fact this property has one of the lower lying of the Castillon vineyards it is an excellent big, full-on example of the appellation. While Merlot dominates with 75% of the plantings, Cabernet Franc is also important at 25%. Dark, spicy and plummy Merlot fruit is nicely underpinned by a subtle hint of cedar with a little oak in the background. Impressively long and persistent. Best with 4 or 5 years. (DM)

Recommended Reds:
Château de Laussac Cotes de Castillon ★★★☆ £D

✿ Le Dôme (Saint-Emilion GC) *www.maltus.com*
This vies with LA MONDOTTE to be first among the garage wines of Saint-Emilion. It is produced by Jonathan Maltus at his property Château TEYSSIER, from a single parcel of 2.85 ha which neighbours Chêau ANGELUS. It has now been joined by a second single vineyard wine LES ASTÉRIES. Cabernet Franc is the main component at 70%, with the balance Merlot. The wine is modern in style with a

France

pre-fermentation maceration and both *pigeage* and pumping over are employed during fermentation. Malolactic is conducted in barrel and then 50% is drawn off and aged in a second series of brand new oak barrels. Yet while it is deep and very concentrated, the wine's fine mineral structure provides exemplary balance. It will require 7 or 8 years' patience to show at its peak. (DM)

Recommended Reds:

Le Dôme Saint-Emilion Grand Cru ★★★★★ £G

Les Asteries (Saint-Emilion GC) *www.maltus.com*
Produced, like the profound LE DÔME by Jonathan Maltus at his property Château TEYSSIER. Les Astéries comes from a single tiny parcel of just 1.1 ha. The vineyard originally formed part of Chateau Fonroque and is close to CLOS FOURTET. It is planted on clay soils with a layer of rocky limestone 'Astéries' which contributes to the elegant, minerally character of the wine, while its rich and complex dark cherry and plum fruit is defined by the considerable age of the vines, which are up to 80 years old. Vinification is typically modern with malolactic in a combination of barrel and vat and the lees fed back into the wine for six months with *bâtonnage*. Ageing is for around 12 months. More elegant and refined than many of Saint-Emilions low volume wines it is likely to improve for a decade and keep a good deal longer. (DM)

Recommended Reds:

Les Asteries Saint-Emilion Grand Cru ★★★★☆ £F

Ch. Lucie (Saint-Emilion GC)
A recently established tiny property with less than 2 ha under vine. The wines are made with consultancy advice from Stéphane Derenoncourt. The first wines were vinified here in the 1995 vintage although a sizeable proportion of the vines date back over 100 years, which contributes a great deal to the style and quality achieved. The vineyard is planted to Merlot and Cabernet Franc on a mix of sand and clay with a part on clay/limestone. L'ANGÉLUS is a neighbouring property. This is a true garage wine: the vinification takes place in the town of Saint-Emilion but in excellent underground cellar conditions with good ventilation. Malolactic in barrel and ageing in new oak for 12–15 months help create the rich, opulent style. The wine is loaded with dense, dark fruit but there is a real purity and depth often missing in other wines made in a similar style from the region. Accessible from a young age, the wine will nevertheless add further complexity with cellaring. (DM)

Recommended Reds:

Lucia Saint-Emilion Grand Cru ★★★★ £E

Clos Les Lunelles (Cotes de Castillon) *www.vignoblesperse.com*
Very impressive old-vine Castillon from the owner of Château PAVIE. The vineyard is now over 40 years of age and yields are deliberately restricted to 20 hl/ha. Merlot accounts for 80% of the vineyard with the balance Cabernet Franc and Cabernet Sauvignon. The old-vine character of the wine really shines through with complex, smoky, dark berry and cocoa spice aromas and considerable depth and concentration. Just a hint more purity and elegance would lift this to a different level. Best years are on the edge of ★★★★. (DM)

Recommended Reds:

Clos les Lunelles Cotes de Castillon ★★★☆ £E

Ch. Lusseau (Saint-Emilion GC)
This tiny Saint-Emilion property is owned by Laurent Lusseau, who is the regisseur at Château PAVIE. His holding consists of just 2 ha of Merlot (80%) and Cabernet Franc (20%), and the vineyard is now 35

years old. He keeps a tight control on his yields and a green harvest is conducted prior to *veraison* to keep the crop at around 30–35 hl/ha. This is a ripe example with piercing dark berry fruit and good depth and fruit intensity. It should drink well from 3 or 4 years. (DM)

Recommended Reds:

Château Lusseau Saint-Emilion Grand Cru ★★★☆ £E

Lynsolence (Saint-Emilion GC) *www.denis-barraud.com*
Tiny garage-style operation producing barely more than 500 cases a year from 100% Merlot. Proprietor Denis Barraud also owns the Saint-Emilion Grand Cru Les GRAVIÈRES. Yields are kept low and the vineyard is adjacent to MONBOUSQUET and VALANDRAUD in the south-east of the appellation. Fermentation takes place in small-lot 400-litre barrels and malolactic is in barrel although the wine is not kept on lees. This is very good, rich, fleshy and concentrated wine and the oak is very well judged. It is a supple, forward style with a velvety texture that will drink well with 3 or 4 years' ageing. (DM)

Recommended Reds:

Lynsolence Saint-Emilion Grand Cru ★★★★ £F

Ch. Magdelaine (Saint-Emilion GC) *www.moueix.com*
Another Moueix family property. This is an opulent, richly plummy, Merlot dominated wine crafted from older vines than is usual for the region. Supple and approachable but nevertheless possessing a fine, well-structured mineral backbone, the wine can be enjoyable with as little as 5 years' cellaring and will keep for much longer. (DM)

Recommended Reds:

Château Magdelaine Saint-Emilion Grand Cru ★★★★ £F

Ch. Marsau (Bordeaux Cotes des Francs)
Small stand-out property in this lesser-known AC, along with de FRANCS and PUYGUERAUD. The 8-ha vineyard is planted solely to Merlot and production is barely more than 2,000 cases a year. The vineyard is also one of the sources of Dourthe's top Bordeaux red ESSENCE DE DOURTHE, a blend from appellations on both Left and Right Banks. Marsau is less extracted than the wines from some neighbouring properties and is all the better for that. The wine is dominated by subtle red berry and plum fruit and offers great definition and elegance with impressive length and intensity. Give it 3 or 4 years at least. (DM)

Recommended Reds:

Château Marsau Bordeaux Cotes de Francs ★★★ £D

Ch. La Mauriane (Puissegiun-Saint-Émilion) *www.lamauriane.com*
Tiny 3.5 ha property producing just the micro-*cuvée* La Mauriane, a blend of 85/10/5 Merlot, Cabernet Franc and Cabernet Sauvignon. Output is tiny at barely more than 1,000 cases a year so you'll have to hunt around a bit for this. Pierre Taix is one of those rare producers who are beginning to show the potential of *terroirs* in Saint-Emilion's satellite appellations, particularly where the vines are of considerable age, as is the case with his 50-year-old vineyard. The wine is a modern, fleshy, dark-spiced claret with lots of extract and good depth. Drink it with 3 or 4 years' age. (DM)

Recommended Reds:

Château La Mauriane Puissegiun-Saint-Émilion ★★★ £D

Ch. Monbousquet (Saint-Emilion GC) *www.vignoblesperse.com*
A typically modern extractive style of winemaking produces a ripe and bold style of Saint-Emilion here. Michel Rolland is the consultant and his techniques of ripe, late-harvested fruit, deep colour and malolactic in barrel are all on show. The driving force behind the

renaissance of this once-mediocre property is Gérard Perse, who also owns PAVIE and PAVIE-DECESSE. Expect the wines to develop well in the medium term. (DM)

Recommended Reds:

Château Monbousquet Saint-Emilion Grand Cru ★★★★ £F

Ch. Mont Pérat (Premières Cotes de Bordeaux) *www.despagne.fr*

As well as the sizeable TOUR DE MIRAMBEAU, the Despagne family also own this much smaller 16-ha property. A typical blend of Merlot and Cabernet Sauvignon, this a dense and muscular red and a benchmark for this appellation along with Château CARIGNAN. The wine is loaded with dark berry fruit and undercurrents of smoke and vanilla. Firmly structured in its youth, it needs 5 years or so. (DM)

Recommended Reds:

Château Mont Pérat Premières Cotes de Bordeaux ★★★ £D

Ch. Montviel (Pomerol)

Catherine Péré-Vergé, who also now owns Le GAY, is continuing to produce excellent results at this 7.5 ha Pomerol château. Merlot is the dominant variety and the 20% or so of Cabernet Franc lends useful structure to the wine. It is rich and concentrated with a typically fleshy Merlot palate but stands out thanks to a real purity and a mineral quality to the fruit that is often absent in the appellation. The wine deserves 5 or 6 years' patience. (DM)

Recommended Reds:

Château Montviel Pomerol ★★★★ £E

Ch. Le Moulin (Pomerol) *www.moulin-pomerol.com*

Rich and sumptuous, if pricey, Pomerol is produced at this tiny 2.4 ha property. The vineyard is planted to a mix of 80/20 Merlot and Cabernet Franc and the wine displays loads of dark, exotic, plummy, spicy Merlot character. While supple and approachable, it also possesses a depth and persistence so often absent in other examples. Expect this wine to drink very well with mediumterm cellaring. (DM)

Recommended Reds:

Château Le Moulin Pomerol ★★★★ £G

Ch. Moulin Haut-Laroque (Fronsac) *www.moulinhautlaroque.com*

This is one of the more impressive properties in the increasingly fashionable Fronsac appellation. The 15 ha are mainly Merlot but there is a significant amount of old-vine Cabernet Franc, along with Cabernet Sauvignon and Malbec. The style is ripe and full with an element of new oak showing through and a supple, velvety structure. Recent vintages have been particularly impressive and the 2009 and 2010 are likely to be at a similarly impressive level. Better with 4–5 years' age. A solid second wine Hervé Laroque is softer and more approachable. (DM)

Recommended Reds:

Château Moulin Haut-Laroque Fronsac ★★★☆ £E
Château Hervé Laroque Fronsac ★★ £C

Ch. Moulin Pey-Labrie (Canon-Fronsac) *www.moulinpeylabrie.com*

Small property of some 6.5 ha producing modern, stylish and ripe reds with a high proportion of Merlot and increasing use of new oak. The approach mirrors that of other quality-minded properties from lesser Bordeaux appellations in emphasising forward, dark and richly plummy fruit in a soft, fleshy, textured style. The rounded, velvety tannin is assisted by completion of the malolactic fermentation in barrel. (DM)

Recommended Reds:

Château Moulin Pey-Labrie Canon-Fronsac ★★★ £D

Ch. Moulin Saint-Georges (Saint-Emilion GC)

Located in close proximity to AUSONE and in fact owned by the same family. Quality here has been consistently improving in recent vintages, and has rated ★★★★ since 1998. The 8 ha, Merlot-dominated vineyard is meticulously managed and careful vinification produces richly fruity and fleshy wines often high in alcohol with marked new oak. They will be all the better for 4 or 5 years' ageing. (DM)

Recommended Reds:

Château Moulin Saint-Georges Saint-Emilion Grand Cru ★★★★ £F

Clos de l'Oratoire (Saint-Emilion GCC) *www.neipperg.com*

Under the same ownership as CANON-LA-GAFFELIÈRE and the super-*cuvée* LA MONDOTTE. As at Stéphan von Neipperg's other properties, the style here is modern and approachable but the wine is neither overripe nor excessivelyextracted. There is a hallmark of underlying refinement and elegance. The finely crafted tannins need 5 or 6 years to achieve real harmony. Classy and ageworthy. (DM)

Recommended Reds:

Clos de l'Oratoire Saint-Emilion Grand Cru Classé ★★★★ £G

❁ Ch. Pavie (Saint-Emilion 1er GCC "A") *www.vignoblesperse.com*

This property was purchased in 1998 by Gérard Perse who also owns PAVIE DECESSE and MONBOUSQUET. Quality was formerly variable but substantial investment in the cellars is bringing greater consistency. However, the Perse wines and particularly Pavie have become the most controversial of the new wave of late-harvested and highly extracted reds which focus on opulence and concentration perhaps more than elegance or purity. Achieving a balance of the two is what marks the greatest of the new wave. Pavie is increasingly very late harvested and more akin to a full-blown Napa red than a classical Saint-Emilion of the old school. If you are a fan of rich and concentrated reds with massive extract and not inconsiderable alcohol then this will appeal, otherwise you may prefer to look elsewhere. There is no doubting the commitment to quality, with a modern and sophisticated approach to vinification and minimal handling in the cellars. Prior to 1998 the wines were adequate at best with only the earlier vintages of 1990, 89, 86 and 82 being of real note. (DM)

Recommended Reds:

Château Pavie Saint-Emilion Grand Cru Classé ★★★★★ £H

❁ Ch. Pavie-Decesse (Saint-Emilion GCC) *www.vignoblesperse.com*

Like PAVIE, owned by Gérard Perse and now producing wines of greater density and power than a few years back. The style, as at Pavie, is for rich and opulent reds but there has always been a tighter, leaner edge to Decesse when compared with its larger, more illustrious neighbour. The wine is reasonably harmonious with copious quantities of sweet, dark fruit and lots of spicy, vanilla scented oak. Since 1997 it is of a much richer style than of old. It should age reasonably well but is reasonably approachable young. (DM)

Recommended Reds:

Château Pavie-Decesse Saint-Emilion Grand Cru Classé ★★★★☆ £G

❁ Ch. Pavie-Macquin *www.nicolas-thienpont.com*

Consultancy input at this 1er Grand Cru Classé "B" property comes from Stéphane Derenoncourt and the Château is farmed

France

biodynamically. It shares the same limestone plateau as PAVIE DECESSE and has an elegant hard, tight and structured mineral edge to its character. In the cellar minimal handling is the order of the day and the results are enormously impressive. The wines are dense, powerful and structured, with seamlessly integrated dark, spicy fruit and oak as well as displaying marvellous purity. They age very well. The wines from the late 1990s on show a serious hike in quality. (DM)

Recommended Reds:
Château Pavie-Macquin Saint-Emilion Grand Cru Classé ★★★★★ £F

Ch. Petit-Village (Pomerol) *www.petit-village.com*
This property is part of AXA Millésimes and under the same ownership as PICHON-LONGUEVILLE in Pauillac. The style here has been for fairly sturdy, structured wines with reasonable depth and refinement There has been a step up in quality here since 1998 and the wines are suppler and richer in recent vintages. 2001, 00 and 99 were all reasonably dense and concentrated and 2006 and 2005 look to have decent potential. (DM)

Recommended Reds:
Château Petit-Village Pomerol ★★★☆ £G

✿✿ Ch. Pétrus (Pomerol) *www.moueix.com*
One of the most expensive wines in the world, it used to be the most expensive by a long way but has been challenged in recent years not only by near neighbours but also by limited-production special *cuvées* in California. Much depends on the vagaries of the international auction markets. There is no doubt, though, that Pétrus is one of Bordeaux's truly great reds. A very high proportion of Merlot (95%), with the balance Cabernet Franc, is planted in vineyards that sit upon a plateau of remarkably well-drained clay soils and provide a unique *terroir*. Extraordinary care is taken in both the vineyard and cellars in producing a wine that is immensely rich and concentrated with a bewildering array of dark fruits, oriental spices and seamlessly integrated oak, all supported by very fine supple tannins. It is consistently great and perhaps only struggles very slightly in lesser years, but then so does every other property in the region. (DM)

Recommended Reds:
Château Pétrus Pomerol ✪✪✪✪✪ £H

✿✿ Ch. Le Pin (Pomerol)
Production here is tiny at only around 700 cases a year and two decades ago the wine was just a hobby of owner Jacques Thienpont. However, it has become an auction favourite and, partly because of its scarcity, has on occasion fetched higher prices than PÉTRUS. The style is for ripe, opulent and approachable wines rather than ones that are overstructured and austere and the vinification reflects this approach. Malolactic is carried out in barrel and the wine sees 100% new oak which is seamlessly integrated. Undoubtedly a very fine and richly opulent example of Pomerol. 6 ha have also just been acquired in Saint-Emilion. This site is planted to Cabernet Franc and Merlot and is located close to TROPLONG-MONDOT and VALANDRAUD. (DM)

Recommended Reds:
Château Le Pin Pomerol ✪✪✪✪✪ £H

Ch. Le Pin Beausoleil *www.lepinbeausoleil.com*
Small-production, top-quality red from one of the region's humbler appellations. The property is located just the other side of the Dordogne from the Côtes de Castillon and is producing similarly impressive results to some of the better examples of that AC, thanks to consulting input from Stéphane Derenoncourt. Less than 2,000 cases a year are made from the 5 ha here. The vineyards are planted to Merlot (60%), Cabernet Franc (20%), Cabernet Sauvignon (17%) and a tiny amount of Malbec. Initially backward and firm in structure, it displays an array of dark, spicy almost exotic flavours. Give it 4 or 5 years to round out. (DM)

Recommended Reds:
Château Le Pin Beausoleil Bordeaux Supérieur ★★★ £C

Clos Puy Arnaud (Côtes de Castillon)
This is one of a handful of really impressive properties from this now excellent satellite appellation. Unlike neighbouring Château d'AIGUILHE, the vineyard area here is small at a mere 7ha. Planted to a mix of 70% Merlot, 20% Cabernet Franc and the balance Cabernet Sauvignon, its aspect is excellent with south facing slopes and the limestone-based soils provide excellent drainage. The vines are also now farmed biodynamically. Clos Puy Arnaud is dense and richly concentrated with dark berry fruit, spicy oak and supple, firmly structured tannin all in evidence. Consultant Stéphane Derenoncourt uses all his techniques during vinification: pre-fermentation maceration, malolactic in barrel and ageing on lees in 50% new oak. The wine is consistently right on the cusp of ★★★★. Pervenche Puy Arnaud is a very decent second wine. (DM)

Recommended Reds:
Clos Puy Arnaud Côtes de Castillon ★★★☆ £D
Château Pervenche Puy Arnaud Côtes de Castillon ★☆ £B

Ch. Puygueraud (Bordeaux-Côtes de Francs) *www.puygueraud.com*
There are a number of impressive producers in this small appellation north-east of Saint-Emilion but Puygueraud particularly stands out. The wine is both refined and surprisingly structured for a lesser appellation and displays an impressive array of cedar, dark fruit and oriental spices, all tightly gripped by firm youthful tannin. The wine will benefit from a few years in the cellar. A special limited production wine, Cuvée Georges, is a step up. (DM)

Recommended Reds:
Ch. Puygueraud Cuvée Georges Bordeaux-Côtes de Francs ★★★☆ £D
Château Puygueraud Bordeaux-Côtes de Francs ★★★ £C

Ch. Quinault (Saint-Emilion GCC) *www.chateau-quinault-lenclos.com*
Now owned by LMVH, although former owner Alain Raynaud remains as a consultant, this small estate produces around 5,000 cases a year, mainly from some very old Merlot and Cabernet Franc. There are a total of 15ha; Merlot accounts for 65% and Cabernet Sauvignon and Malbec just 15% between them, with the balance Cabernet Franc. Despite being only a regular Saint-Emilion Grand Cru, this is a serious enterprise and the wine bears little resemblance to many of the garagiste operations that produce barely more than a few hundred cases a year. Quality is certainly helped by a vineyard with an average age of around 50 years. The style is rich, supple and opulent and is best with 8–10 years' age. (DM)

Recommended Reds:
Chäteau Quinault L'Enclos Saint-Emilion Grand Cru Classé ★★★★ £F
Lafleur de Quinault Saint-Emilion Grand Cru ★★☆ £D

Ch. Quintas (Saint-Emilion GCC) *www.chateau-quintas.com*
In June 2011, Domaine Clarence Dillon, owners of CH. HAUT-BRION and CH. LA MISSION HAUT-BRION, acquired Ch. Tertre Daugay and re-named Château Quintus. In October 2013, Château Quintus in turn acquired its neighbouring property, Château L'Arrosée, and

these estates are now united in order to produce wines under the Ch. Quintas label from the 2013 vintage onwards. It is too early to know in what direction the estates will differ from the paths trodden by their previous, separate owners. Ratings below, therefore, relate to those previously owned estates. (NB)

Recommended Reds:
Château Tertre-Daugay Saint-Emilion Grand Cru Classé ★★★★ £E
Château l'Arrosée Saint-Emilion Grand Cru Classé ★★☆ £D

Ch. Reignac (Bordeaux-Supérieur) *www.reignac.com*
Stéphanie and Yves Vatelot produce some of the very best examples of this lesser appellation and should be a benchmarks for others. They have a sizeable holding of some 76 ha of which just 2 ha are devoted to whites, producing a good but pricey white Reignac. The red blend has a slightly higher proportion of Merlot than Cabernet Sauvignon and the wine is dense, dark and structured. It should develop very well in the medium term. There is also a special limited-release Reignac, again with a high proportion of Merlot (75%). Modern and fleshy, the wine is cold-macerated before fermentation, with malolactic on lees in barrel. The top label is the Balthus micro-*cuvée*, which bears all the hallmarks of consultant Michel Rolland. Produced from a tiny yield of 15hl/ha and from nearly 40 year old vines this 100% Merlot is extraordinarily dense and concentrated for Bordeaux. While both the Reignac red and Balthus have the depth and sufficiently finely structured tannin to support considerable development in bottle, both are supple and very approachable with 3 or 4 years. (DM)

Château Reignac
Recommended Reds:
Reignac Bordeaux Supérieur ★★★ £D
Château Reignac Bordeaux Supérieur ★★ £C
Recommended Whites:
Château Reignac Bordeaux ★★★ £D
Balthus
Recommended Reds:
Balthus Bordeaux Supérieur ★★★★ £E

Ch. Richelieu (Fronsac)
This is now one of the best names in Fronsac and an excellent source of rich, plummy and subtly spicey Merlot dominated reds. It is named after its famed original owner who acquired the property in 1632. The vineyards, which are farmed organically, have an excellent southerly exposition and are planted at a high density on mixed calcareous, blue clay and fossilised shell soils. The result is grapes of rich concentration and flavour intensity. The cellars are well-equipped and the wines vinified in thermo regulated tanks. As you would expect the top wine La Favorite, a selection of the best plots and oldest vines, spends the longest time in oak, 15 months with half new barrels whereas the Richelieu sees a little less new wood and for around a year. These are supple, fleshy and approachable reds although La Favorite will gain in depth and complexity with four or five years patience. (DM)

Recommended Reds:
Château Richelieu La Favorite de Richelieu Fronsac ★★★☆ £E
Château Richelieu Fronsac ★★★ £D

Ch. Reynon *www.denisdubourdieu.fr*
Denis Dubourdieu, the owner of CLOS FLORIDtNE in the Graves, is an extremely well-known and respected professor of enology in the region. At Château Reynon in the Premières Côtes de Bordeaux

AC, he makes some very good dry white and red, along with a little sweet Cadillac from a total of some 57ha of vineyards. The red is good and stylish in a medium-weight style; the regular white is crisp and fresh; and the Vieilles Vignes is classier and subtly barrel-fermented. Both the Vieilles Vignes white and the red will evolve nicely in the short term. (DM)

Recommended Reds:
Château Reynon Premières Côtes de Bordeaux ★★☆ £C
Recommended Whites:
Château Reynon Bordeaux Vieilles Vignes ★★★ £C

Ch. Riou de Thaillas (Saint-Emilion GC) *www.vignoblesdubech.fr*
This property is situated in the prolongation of CH. CHEVAL BLANC and CH. FIGEAC. There are a total of just 3ha of Merlot set on a hilltop with an aspect facing directly south. At present the vines are just over 35 years old, with the sandy-clay subsoil and gravelly topsoil provides good drainage. Maturation takes place *en barriques*, 50% in new oak and 50% in older wood for some 16 months which results in more supple wines from recent vintages than had hitherto been under the previous ownership. Nevertheless, the wines still require some years of cellaring before their full potential is realised.

Recommended Reds:
Château Riou deThaillas Saint-Emilion Grand Cru ★★★ £C

Ch. La Rivière (Fronsac) *www.chateau-de-la-riviere.com*
Twenty years ago this substantial Fronsac property was producing wines of somewhat variable quality. There are 59 ha under vine, mainly Merlot with Cabernet Sauvignon, Cabernet Franc and a few hectares of Malbec. During the late 1990s some of the quality achieved during the mid-1980s has been replicated, although the wines are now modern and produced in an attractively ripe, dark berry fruit style with soft velvety tannins. A special bottling, Aria, is a model of good balance, ripe fruit and integrated oak. Until the 2010 vintage, this *cuvée* was made from 100% Merlot and was rather pricey – now the owner has decided to blend in about one quarter in equal proportions of Cabernet Sauvignon and Cabernet Franc to the Merlot and reduce the price by half, which seems to be a smart move. A clairet is also made. The reds will benefit from 4 or 5 years' aging. (DM)

Recommended Reds:
Château la Rivière Aria Fronsac ★★★★ £E
Château la Rivière Fronsac ★★☆ £D

Ch. Roc de Cambes (Côtes de Bourg) *www.roc-de-cambes.com*
This property is not only a serious benchmark for the Côtes de Bourg but also for all the lesser Right Bank appellations. The property is relatively small at 10 ha and Merlot dominates the plantings, accounting for 60% of the vineyard. Always harvested as late as possible and from very low yields, the wine is typically rich and ripe, always displaying dense, dark, spicy berry fruit and a hefty dollop of well-integrated oak. It is long, complex, powerful and ageworthy. Minimal cellar handling helps to ensure consistently impressive results. (DM)

Recommended Reds:
Château Roc de Cambes Côtes de Bourg ★★★★ £F

Ch. Rol Valentin (Saint-Emilion GC) *www.vignoblesrobin.com*
Former professional footballer Eric Prisette bought Rol Valentin in 1994 and sold it to Alexandra and Nicolas Robin in 2009. Since Prisette's purchase, the wines have progressively emerged as some of the most exciting of the new wave of reds from the appellation.

Wine behind the label

Saint-Emilion, Pomerol & other Bordeaux

The property is small with just over 7.5 ha planted to Merlot, Cabernet Franc and Cabernet Sauvignon. Of this 3 ha were added by the Robins planted on clay limestone soils. Yields are much lower than elsewhere in the region and the vine age is now 35–40 years. All the modern cellar techniques are in evidence: 100% new oak, malolactic in barrel and ageing on lees with micro-oxygenation. This opulent, rich and supple wine will drink well young but has the depth and finely crafted structure to develop well for a decade or more. Eric Prisette has purchased 10 ha in the Côtes de Castillon where he is producing a red labelled Roc. Stéphane Derenencourt advises both properties. (DM)

Recommended Reds:

Château Rol Valentin Saint-Emilion Grand Cru ★★★★ £F

Ch. Rouget (Pomerol) *www.chateau-rouget.com*

Sizeable property for the appellation with some 17.5 ha, making good, well priced Pomerol from a well-sited vineyard close to l'ÉGLISE-CLINET. The vines are 85% Merlot with the balance Cabernet Franc. Consultancy input has come from Michel Rolland since 1997 and the wine is crafted in typical Rolland style – rich and plummy with concentrated dark, plummy fruit but real minerality as well. A total of 6,500 cases are produced, half of which are the *Grand Vin* and half the second wine, Vieux Château des Templiers. (DM)

Recommended Reds:

Château Rouget Pomerol ★★★ £E

Ch. La Rousselle (Fronsac)

The Davau's tiny property with just 4.6 ha under vine is one of the emerging lights of Fronsac. Wine consultant Stéphane Derenoncourt also helps by weaving his own elegant magic on the wine. The vineyard is planted to a mix of Merlot (65%), and Cabernet Franc (35%) on finely drained argilo-calcareous soils. Traditionally vinified and aged for around a year in oak, the wine shows marked Merlot character when young as well as impressive purity and depth. Rich, dark plum aromas are underpinned by a subtle leafy character and firm youthful tannin. Four or five years' ageing will provide greater richness and weight. (DM)

Recommended Reds:

Château La Rousselle Fronsac ★★★ £C

Clos Saint Martin (Saint-Emilion GCC) *www.lesgrandsmurailles.com*

This tiny 1.3 ha property, the smallest Grand Cru Classé in the appellation, is planted in finely drained clay-limestone soils and has an ideal south-facing exposure. This, along with a vine age of over 30 years, provides fruit of tremendous intensity. The wine is a blend of Merlot (70%) Cabernet Franc (20%) and Cabernet Sauvignon (10%) adding extra density and structure. It is a full, rich and concentrated red with dark, spicy-plummy fruit and a hint of vanilla and cocoa from 100% new wood. It needs at least 4–5 years, as the tannins can be a bit raw and aggressive in its youth. The estate is managed by Sophie Fourcade who also runs CH. GRANDES MURAILLES and CH. COTE DE BALEAU. (DM)

Recommended Reds:

Clos Saint Martin Saint-Emilion Grand Cru Classé ★★★★ £F

Ch. Sansonnet (Saint-Emilion GCC) *www.sansonnet.com*

Sansonnet is a small property with an ancient grand chateau situated in the north-east of the appellation. Just over 6 ha are planted to a mix of Merlot (85%) and Cabernet Franc (15%) and output is only just over 1,500 cases a year, so the wine is fairly scarce. It offers impressive depth and substance, with dark, ripe berry fruit

and marked new oak and is supple and finely structured. It will evolve well for a decade and needs half that to hit its stride. (DM)

Recommended Reds:

Château Sansonnet Saint-Emilion Grand Cru Classé ★★★☆ £E

Clos de Sarpe (Saint-Emilion GC) *www.clos-de-sarpe.com*

Barely 1,000 cases are made a year of this massive and densely textured old style Bordeaux red. A blend of Merlot and Cabernet Franc, it is sourced from argilo-calcareous soils and from vines cropped at very low yields. The wine is dark when young and marked by an intense, almost overwhelming blackberry fruit character. There is a hint of oak in the background and considerable tannin which demands 7 or 8 years' patience. The second label, Charles de Sarpe, is softer and more accessible young. (DM)

Recommended Reds:

Clos de Sarpe Saint-Emilion Grand Cru ★★★★☆ £G

Charles de Sarpe Saint-Emilion Grand Cru ★★★ £E

Ch. Taillefer (Pomerol)

This quite grand 12 ha property is to be found in the southern part of the appellation on the edge of Libourne. The vineyards are now around 30 years old and are planted to 80% Merlot with the balance Cabernet Franc. The wine is made in a fairly traditional plummy, earthy style with supple, easy tannins and gains additional depth and intensity from its aged vine fruit. It will drink well with 3 or 4 years' ageing. (DM)

Recommended Reds:

Château Taillefer Pomerol ★★★ £E

❀ Ch. Tertre-Rôteboeuf (Saint-Emilion GC)

Although this remarkable Saint-Emilion has not been elevated to Grand Cru Classé status, the property enjoys a highly propitious site for producing fine wine. Low yields, meticulous care in the vineyard and ageing in new oak for a year and a half all contribute to the very high quality of the wine, which has been exemplary for the last 15 years. It is immensely complex with a myriad of dark and spicy fruits and stylish oak. It will age gracefully and requires 6 or 7 years' patience. (DM)

Recommended Reds:

Château Tertre-Rôteboeuf Saint-Emilion Grand Cru ★★★★★ £H

❀ Ch. Teyssier (Saint-Emilion GC) *www.maltus.com*

Englishman Jonathan Maltus purchased this property in 1994 and since then has added a number of other more impressively sited vineyard holdings. Teyssier itself is a soft and attractive, relatively forward, spicy Saint-Emilion full of fleshy, dark, plummy fruit. It is sourced from the low-lying vineyards in the south of the appellation and is a testament to what can be achieved from these lesser sites. Vinification is modern, as with all the wines here, with pre-fermentation maceration, malolactic in barrel and ageing on lees for added richness. Château Laforge is produced from a number of superior Grand Cru sites, including the Le Chatelot vineyard purchased from Château CANON in 2000. The wine is rich and supple, finely structured and with impressive depth and concentration. The high Merlot content (92%) of the blend accounts for its opulent, exotic style. Le DÔME is the top red label and comes from a single parcel neighbouring Château ANGELUS. There is also an excellent barrel-fermented white, Nardian, which blends all three white Bordeaux varieties. The Muscadelle comes from vines planted in the mid-1930s. Sourced from 3 tiny, ideally exposed parcels in limestone soils just across the river Dordogne south of the Saint-

Emilion AC, this is a rich and complex, subtly oaked white. New from the 2004 vintage were LES ASTÉRIES, a super-premium low yielding *cuvée* and Château Grand Destieu. To these have been added Le Carré, a single vineyard red from a site that abuts Clos FOURTET. New from 2008 has been an additional red label, Vieus Château Mazerat, part of the original vineyard of which produced LE DÔME. Maltus also now makes wine in California at WORLD'S END WINES in the Napa Valley. The most recent development is the hiring of Jacques Lurton, who has made wine with his brother François in France, Spain and South America. Jacques will not only consult for Bordeaux whites but also a new range of wines in the Napa Valley. (DM)

Recommended Reds:
Château Laforge Saint-Emilion Grand Cru ★★★★ £F
Château Grand Destieu Saint-Emilion Grand Cru ★★★☆ £E
Château Teyssier Saint-Emilion Grand Cru ★★★ £D
Recommended Whites:
Nardian Bordeaux ★★★★ £F

Ch. Thieuley (Bordeaux) *www.thieuley.com*
This is an excellent example of what can be achieved under the humble Bordeaux AC but so very rarely is. Francis Courselle now has some 80 ha of vineyard, 45 ha of which are planted to red varieties. These go towards the crafting of stylish, straightforward, berry-fruited AC Bordeaux, impressively dense, structured Supérieur Réserve and attractively fruity clairet. A Premières Côtes de Bordeaux, Clos Sainte-Anne, is also now produced. The regular white is crisp and fresh and full of grassy green apple fruit, whereas the Cuvée Francis Courselle, which is barrel-fermented and aged with *bâtonnage*, is elegantly toasty and oaky. (DM)

Recommended Reds:
Ch. Thieuley Francis Courselle Réserve Bordeaux Supérieur ★★☆ £C
Château Thieuley Bordeaux ★☆ £B
Recommended Whites:
Château Thieuley Cuvée Francis Courselle Bordeaux ★★★ £C
Château Thieuley Bordeaux ★★ £B

Ch. Tour de Mirambeau (Entre-deux-Mers) *www.despagne.fr*
The Despagne family have a total of nearly 90 ha under vine and production is not inconsiderable at nearly 50,000 cases a year. Just over half the land is planted to red varieties and it is these that really stand out here. A decent regular white takes the Bordeaux AC as does a rosé and there is an Entre-deux-Mers white as well. Cuvée Passion white is good and the red version is one of the best wines of the Bordeaux Supérieur AC. The recently produced super-*cuvée* Girolate only takes the humble Bordeaux AC but is a wine of serious depth and structure. Produced from an extraordinarily steep 10 ha site with very low yields, this dark, spicy, almost over-extracted red sets new standards for the area. It is likely to drink well young. The family also own the Premières Côtes de Bordeaux property Château MONT PÉRAT. (DM)

Château Tour de Mirambeau
Recommended Reds:
Château Tour de Mirambeau Bordeaux Supérieur Passion ★★★ £C
Château Tour de Mirambeau Bordeaux Supérieur ★☆ £B
Recommended Whites:
Château Tour de Mirambeau Bordeaux Supérieur Passion ★★★ £C
Girolate
Recommended Reds:
Girolate Bordeaux ★★★★★ £E

Ch. La Tour Figeac (Saint-Emilion GCC)
Biodynamically tended 14.6 ha property planted to Merlot (60%) and Cabernet Franc. Low yields are maintained and consultancy comes from Christine Derenoncourt, wife of roving Bordeaux guru Stéphane. The wine is produced very much in an opulent, forward and showy style and the oak can be just a bit assertive in its youth, but it will offer good drinking within 4 or 5 years. (DM)

Recommended Reds:
Château La Tour Figeac Saint-Emilion Grand Cru Classé ★★★★ £F

Ch. Les Trois Croix (Fronsac) *www.chateaulestroiscroix.com*
The Léon family purchased this 15 ha estate in 1995. The vineyard is dominated by Merlot (90%) and the balance is Cabernet Franc, which provides a nicely lifted, leafy, cedary quality to the wine. The vineyard is also one of the highest in the appellation and this too tends to result in a lighter, more elegant style than at many neighbouring properties. The ripest vintages though always seem to result in wines of depth and intensity as well as impressively deep, dark, rich fruit. Four to five years' cellaring is advisable. (DM)

Recommended Reds:
Château Les Trois Croix Fronsac ★★★ £C

❂ Ch. Troplong-Mondot *www.chateau-troplong-mondot.com*
This has been a consistently excellent source of top Saint-Emilion over the past decade and longer and was unquestionably a justifiable candidate for elevation to Premier Grand Cru Classé "B" status. There are some 30 ha of vines, the bulk of which are Merlot. This high percentage is reflected in the wine, which is full, rich, plump and fleshy with marked new oak and considerable refinement. The initial firm tannic structure means the wine needs 6 or 7 years' cellaring. Very long and impressive and top-notch in recent vintages. Very fine since 2000, with the exception of the difficult 2002 vintage. (DM)

Recommended Reds:
Ch. Troplong-Mondot Saint-Emilion Grand Cru Classé ★★★★★ £G

Ch. Trotanoy (Pomerol) *www.moueix.com*
Typically small Pomerol property of 7 ha, which, like PÉTRUS, is owned by the Moueix family. The wine is dense and very seriously structured, with considerable grip and tannin when young. Seven or 8 years' cellaring will see the evolution of all sorts of opulent black fruit characters and oriental spices all effortlessly wrapped up in very classy new wood. On top form since 1997, although there were a number of disappointing vintages in the 1980s which you should aware of if buying older wine. (DM)

Recommended Reds:
Château Trotanoy Pomerol ★★★★★ £H

Ch. Trotte Vieille (Saint-Emilion 1er GCC "B") *www.trottevieille.com*
Since 2000 this property has reclaimed its place in the top rank of Saint-Emilion after a period in the relative doldrums in the early to mid-90s. There are a total of 10 ha here with Merlot accounting for 50% of the vineyard, Cabernet Franc a very sizeable 45% and the balance Cabernet Sauvignon. The wine is rich and plump with dark, spicy berry fruit and marked new oak. This is all underpinned by a fine mineral purity. This firm and structured wine needs at least five or six years to bring the fruit, oak and tannin fully into balance. (DM)

Recommended Reds:
Château Trotte Vieille Saint-Emilion 1er Grand Cru Classé ★★★★ £F

Saint-Emilion, Pomerol & other Bordeaux

France

❀ **Ch. de Valandraud (Saint-Emilion 1er GCC "B")** *www.thunevin.com*
This is the original garagiste wine, first made in 1991. Like most of its kind it was originally produced in limited volumes, although output is increasing following vineyard acquisitions. The property consists of various plots, some of them on the low-lying plain below the town of Saint-Emilion. New sites were added between 1997 and 1999 and Clos Badon, Virginie de Valandraud and Prieuré Lescours are now produced separately. To help ensure the integrity of the Valandraud labels a second wine, 3 de Valandraud, is also produced. Yields are restricted and the harvest is carefully sorted prior to vinification. The winemaking is modern, with a pre-fermentation cold soak and malolactic in barrel. The wines are neither fined nor filtered and, particularly in the case of Valandraud and Clos Badon, offer dense, fleshy and extracted reds of increasing depth and purity. The style is forward and accessible, yet they possess striking grip and structure. A very impressive Kosher Valandraud red is also produced, although due to the need to make it under strict conditions it doesn't have quite the level of complexity or depth of Valandraud itself. A white Bordeaux is also now being produced in tiny quantities and is labelled No. 1 Blanc de Valandraud. Jean-Luc Thunevin is involved with a number of other small-scale projects, among them GRACIA and Andréas in Saint-Emilion and MAROJALLIA in Margaux. He has also purchased the Margaux property BELLEVUE DE TAYAC which shows much promise. (DM)

Château de Valandraud
Recommended Reds:
Château de Valandraud Saint-Emilion Grand Cru Classé ★★★★★ £F
Château de Valandraud Kosher Saint-Emilion Grand Cru ★★★☆ £F

Clos Badon
Recommended Reds:
Clos Badon Saint-Emilion Grand Cru ★★★★ £F

Virginie de Valandraud
Recommended Reds:
Virginie de Valandraud Saint-Emilion Grand Cru ★★★☆ £F

Chateau Preuré Lescours
Recommended Reds:
Château Prieuré Lescours Saint-Emilion Grand Cru ★★★ £E

Ch. Veyry (Cotes de Castillon)
Tiny 4 ha property planted to Merlot (95%) and Cabernet Franc. The sole wine, a Côtes de Castillon, was first made only in 1997. It has been consistently good during the last 5 or 6 years. The wine has a lovely piercing mineral quality to its fruit, with characteristic warm, dark and spicy Merlot flavours and real depth, elegance and class for this level. Up to 5 years' ageing would not go amiss. (DM)
Recommended Reds:
Château Veyry Cotes de Castillon ★★★☆ £D

Ch. La Vieille Cure (Fronsac) *www.la-vieille-cure.com*
This is yet another of a number of outperformers in Bordeaux's lesser appellations and money has been pumped into the property to improve quality over the last 15 years. There are 18 ha under vine, 75% planted to Merlot. Michel Rolland has provided consultancy input and the wine is typically extracted, ripe and seductive in style. Only the slightest hard edge can occasionally drift into the equation. The wine is a good medium-term ageing prospect. It has been good to very good since the late 1990s. There is also now an impressive rich and fleshy second wine, Sacristie de La Vieille Cure, which other more esteemed properties from grander appellations would struggle to emulate. (DM)

Recommended Reds:
Château La Vieille Cure Fronsac ★★★ £D

❀ **Vieux-Château-Certan (Pomerol)** *www.vieuxchateaucertan.com*
Cabernet Franc and Cabernet Sauvignon account for 40% of the 14 ha of vineyard here and this is in part the reason for the surprisingly dense and powerful structure of the wine. The tannin can be very firm in the wine's youth and it really needs a decade to begin to show its true class, when it becomes very refined and harmonious. Excellent from 1998 on. (DM)
Recommended Reds:
Vieux-Château-Certan Pomerol ★★★★★ £H

Ch. Vieux Maillet (Pomerol) *www.chateauvieuxmaillet.com*
Small property with barely more than 4 ha under vine. This is dominated by Merlot (90%) with the remainder planted to Cabernet Franc. The wine is a traditional, earthy style of Pomerol with some reasonably hard tannins. It offers good depth and intensity but is made in a fairly extracted way and this can on occasion be just a touch overdone. It definitely needs 4 or 5 years' ageing. (DM)
Recommended Reds:
Château Vieux Maillet Pomerol ★★★☆ £F

Ch. Villars (Fronsac) *www.chateauvillars.com*
Decent Fronsac property that has been producing consistently good wine throughout recent vintages. The property is relatively large with just under 30 ha of vineyards planted to a mix of Merlot (73%), Cabernet Franc (18%) and Cabernet Sauvignon (9%). The wine possesses impressive depth as well as typically dark, berry-scented fruit. The inclusion of the Cabernets gives it a firm tannic grip and it needs 1 or 2 years longer than many others from this AC. (DM)
Recommended Reds:
Château Villars Fronsac ★★★ £D

Other wines of note - *Saint-Emilion, Pomerol & other Bordeaux*

Ch. d'Arvouet
Recommended Reds: Montagne-Saint-Emilion ★★★ £D
Ch. Balestard-La-Tonnelle
Recommended Reds: Saint-Emilion Grand Cru Classé ★★☆ £E
Ch. Barde-Haut
Recommended Reds: Saint-Emilion Grand Cru Classé ★★★ £E
Ch. Bauduc
Recommended Whites: Bordeaux Les Trois Hectares ★★ £C
Ch. Beaulieu
Recommended Reds: Bordeaux ★★ £C
Ch. Beauséjour
Recommended Reds: Montagne-Saint-Emilion ★★★ £D
Ch. Beau-Soleil
Recommended Reds: Pomerol ★★ £E
Ch. Bellefont-Belcier
Recommended Reds: Saint-Emilion Grand Cru Classé ★★★ £E
Ch. Bellegrave
Recommended Reds: Pomerol ★★ £E
Ch. Les Bertrands
Recommended Reds: Premières Côtes de Blaye Nectar Des Bertrands ★★★ £B
Premières Côtes De Blaye Prestige ★★☆ £B
Recommended Whites: Premières Côtes de Blaye Tradition ★★ £B

Ch. Bonnes Rives
Recommended Reds: Lalande-de-Pomerol ★★ £C

Ch. Branda
Recommended Reds: Puisseguin-Saint-Émilion ★★☆ £C

Ch. Brisson
Recommended Reds: Côtes de Castilllon ★★☆ £B

Ch. Brûlesécaille
Recommended Reds: Côtes de Bourg ★★☆ £B

Ch. Brun Despagne
Recommended Reds: Bordeaux Supérieur Quintessence ★★☆ £C
Bordeaux Supérieur ★☆ £B

Ch. Cadet Bon
Recommended Reds: Saint-Emilion Grand Cru Classé ★★ £E

Ch. Canon
Recommended Reds: Canon-Fronsac ★★ £C

Ch. Cantelauze
Recommended Reds: Pomerol ★★★ £E

Ch. Cap de Mourlin
Recommended Reds: Saint Émilion Grand Cru Classé ★★ £D

Ch. Cassagne Haut-Canon
Recommended Reds: Canon-Fronsac Truffière ★★☆ £C
Canon-Fronsac ★★ £B

Ch. de Cérons
Recommended Whites: Cérons ★★ £B

Ch. Chadenne
Recommended Reds: Fronsac ★ £B

Ch. Les Charmes Godard
Recommended Whites: Bordeaux Côtes de Francs ★★★ £C

Ch. Charron
Recommended Whites: Premières Côtes de Blaye Acacia ★★ £B

Ch. de Chelivette
Recommended Reds: Premières Côtes de Bordeaux ★★☆ £B

Ch. Clos Chaumont
Recommended Reds: Premières Côtes de Bordeaux ★★ £B

Ch. Clos De La Tour
Recommended Reds: Bordeaux Supérieur ★★ £B

Ch. La Commanderie
Recommended Reds: Saint-Emilion Grand Cru Classé ★★ £D

Ch. La Croix de L'Espérance
Recommended Reds: Lussac Saint-Émilion ★★ £D

Confiance
Recommended Reds: Premières Côtes de Blaye ★★★ £D

Ch. Corbin Michotte
Recommended Reds: Saint-Emilion Grand Cru ★★ £F

Ch. Côte Monpezat
Recommended Reds: Côtes de Castillon ★★ £C

Ch. de La Cour d'Argent
Recommended Reds: Bordeaux ★★ £D

Ch. La Couronne
Recommended Reds: Montagne-Saint-Emilion Reclos ★★ £C

Domaine de Courteillac
Recommended Reds: Bordeaux Supérieur ★★ £B
Recommended Whites: Bordeaux Supérieur ★ £B

Ch. La Croix
Recommended Reds: Pomerol ★★ £D

Ch. La Croix Bellevue
Recommended Reds: Lalande-de-Pomerol ★☆ £C

Croix de Labrie
Recommended Reds: Saint Émilion Grand Cru ★★★ £F

La Croix du Prieuré
Recommended Reds: Premières Côtes de Blaye ★★ £D

Ch. La Croix Saint-Georges
Recommended Reds: Pomerol ★★★☆ £E

Ch. La Croix Taillefer
Recommended Reds: Pomerol ★★☆ £D

Ch. du Cros
Recommended Whites: Loupiac ★★ £C

Ch. Cros Figeac
Recommended Reds: Saint-Emilion Grand Cru ★★ £E

Ch. Les Cruzelles
Recommended Reds: Lalande-de-Pomerol ★★☆ £C

Ch. Dalem
Recommended Reds: Fronsac ★★☆ £D

Ch. Daugay
Recommended Reds: Saint Émilion Grand Cru ★★★ £E

Ch. Le Doyenné
Recommended Reds: Premières Côtes de Bordeaux ★★ £C

Ch. L'Ecuyer
Recommended Reds: Pomerol ★★★ £E

L'Egrégore
Recommended Reds: Bordeaux ★★★ £D

Ch. L'Enclos
Recommended Reds: Pomerol ★★★ £E

Ch. La Fleur
Recommended Reds: Saint-Emilion Grand Cru ★★ £D

Ch. La Fleur-Mongiron
Recommended Reds: Bordeaux ★★★ £C

Ch. de Fonbel
Recommended Reds: Saint-Emilion Grand Cru ★★★ £E

Ch. Fonplégade
Recommended Reds: Saint-Emilion Grand Cru Classé ★★★ £E

Ch. Fonroque
Recommended Reds: Saint-Emilion Grand Cru Classé ★★ £E

Ch. du Gaby
Recommended Reds: Canon-Fronsac ★★ £C

Ch. Gadras
Recommended Reds: Bordeaux ★☆ £B

Ch. Garraud
Recommended Reds: Lalande-de-Pomerol ★★ £C

Ch. Gigault
Recommended Reds: Premières Côtes de Blaye ★★★ £C

Ch. Gombaude Guillot
Recommended Reds: Pomerol ★★★ £E

Ch. Les Grands Maréchaux
Recommended Reds: Premières Côtes de Blaye ★★☆ £C

Ch. La Grangere
Recommended Reds: Saint-Emilion Grand Cru ★★ £D

Ch. La Grave À Pomerol
Recommended Reds: Pomerol ★★ £E

Ch. Haut-Ballet
Recommended Reds: Fronsac ★★☆ £C

Ch. Haut-Maco
Recommended Reds: Côtes de Bourg Cuvée Jean ★☆ £C

Ch. Haut-Mouleyre
Recommended Whites: Bordeaux ★★ £C

Ch. Haut Rian
Recommended Reds: Premières Côtes de Bordeaux ★★ £B

Ch. Haut Saint Clair
Recommended Reds: Puisseguin-Saint-Emilion ★★☆ £C

Ch. Haut-Segottes
Recommended Reds: Saint-Emilion Grand Cru ★★☆ £D

Saint-Emilion, Pomerol & other Bordeaux

France

Hommage de Malesan
Recommended Reds: Bordeaux ★★★ £D

Ch. L'Isle Fort
Recommended Reds: Bordeaux Supérieur ★★☆ £C

Ch. Jean de Gué
Recommended Reds: Lalande-de-Pomerol Cuvée Prestige ★★★ £D
Lalande-de-Pomerol ★★☆ £C

Ch. Les Jonqueyres
Recommended Reds: Premières Côtes de Blaye ★★ £B

Ch. Labadie
Recommended Reds: Côtes de Bourg Vieilli En Fûts de Chêne ★☆ £C

La Croix de Peyrolie
Recommended Reds: Croix de Peyrolie Lussac-Saint-Émilion ★★★☆ £F

La Fleur d'Arthus
Recommended Reds: Saint-Emilion Grand Cru ★★★ £D

Ch. Lafleur-Gazin
Recommended Reds: Pomerol ★★ £E

Ch. Lagarosse
Recommended Reds: Premières Côtes de Bordeaux Les Comyes ★☆ £C

Ch. Lagrange
Recommended Reds: Pomerol ★★ £E

Ch. Larmande
Recommended Reds: Saint-Emilion Grand Cru Classé ★★★ £E

Ch. Lassègue
Recommended Reds: Saint-Emilion Grand Cru ★★★ £E

Ch. La Tour-du-Pin-Figeac
Recommended Reds: Saint-Emilion Grand Cru ★★ £E

Ch. Les Laudes
Recommended Reds: Saint-Emilion Grand Cru ★★☆ £C

Clos Leo
Recommended Reds: Côtes De Castillon ★★★ £C

Ch. Loubens
Recommended Whites: Sainte-Croix-du-Mont ★★ £C

Ch. du Lyonnat
Recommended Reds: Lussac-Saint-Émilion ★★ £C

Ch. Machorre
Recommended Reds: Bordeaux Supérieur ★★☆ £B

Ch. Manoir du Gravoux
Recommended Reds: Côtes De Castillon ★★ £B

Ch. Marjosse
Recommended Reds: Bordeaux ★★☆ £B

Ch. La Marzelle
Recommended Reds: Saint-Emilion Grand Cru ★★☆ £E

Ch. La Madeleine
Recommended Reds: Saint-Emilion Grand Cru ★★ £E

Ch. Mazeyres
Recommended Reds: Pomerol ★★★ £E

Ch. Mercier
Recommended Reds: Côtes de Bourg Cuvée Prestige ★★ £C

Ch. Messile Aubert
Recommended Reds: Montagne-Saint-Émilion ★★ £C

Ch. Mongiron
Recommended Reds: Bordeaux La Fleur Mongiron ★★★ £C

Ch. Nénin
Recommended Reds: Pomerol ★★★ £F

Ch. Nodoz
Recommended Reds: Côtes de Bourg ★☆ £B

Ch. Parenchère
Recommended Reds: Bordeaux Cuvée Rapahael ★★☆ £C
Bordeaux ★☆ £B

Ch. Penin
Recommended Reds: Bordeaux Supérieur Sélection ★★ £B

Ch. Petit Grave-Ainé
Recommended Reds: Saint-Emilion Grand Cru ★★★ £D

Ch. Peyroutas
Recommended Reds: Saint-Emilion Grand Cru ★★☆ £C

Ch. Pipeau
Recommended Reds: Saint-Emilion Grand Cru ★★★ £D

Ch. La Pointe
Recommended Reds: Pomerol ★★ £E

Ch. Pomeaux
Recommended Reds: Pomerol ★★★ £E

Ch. La Prade
Recommended Reds: Bordeaux Côtes de Francs ★★★ £C

Ch. de Pressac
Recommended Reds: Saint-Emilion Grand Cru Classé ★★☆ £D

Ch. La Rame
Recommended Whites: Sainte-Croix-du-Mont Réserve ★★★ £E
Sainte-Croix-du-Mont Tradition ★★ £C

Ch. Rauzan Despagne
Recommended Whites: Bordeaux Blanc Cuvée Passion ★★ £C

Reclos de La Couronne
Recommended Reds: Montagne-Saint-Emilion ★★ £C

Ch. Rempimplet
Recommended Reds: Côtes de Bourg ★☆ £B

Ch. La Reverence
Recommended Reds: Saint-Emilion Grand Cru ★★★☆ £E

Ch. Ripeau
Recommended Reds: Saint-Emilion Grand Cru Classé ★★ £E

Ch. Robin
Recommended Reds: Côtes de Castillon ★★ £C

Ch. de La Roche Beaulieu
Recommended Reds: Bordeaux Rex Bibendi ★★★ £D
Côtes de Castillon Amavinum ★★ £C

Ch. Rochebelle
Recommended Reds: Saint-Emilion Grand Cru Classé ★★ £D

Ch. Rocher Bellevue Figeac
Recommended Reds: Saint-Emilion Grand Cru ★★★ £D

Ch. Roland La Garde
Recommended Reds: Premières Côtes de Blaye Grand Vin ★★☆ £C

Romulus
Recommended Reds: Pomerol ★★★ £E

Ch. Roylland
Recommended Reds: Saint-Emilion Grand Cru ★★ £D

Clos Saint-Julien
Recommended Reds: Saint-Emilion Grand Cru ★★★☆ £E

Ch. Sainte-Colombe
Recommended Reds: Côtes de Castillon ★★ £C

Ch Sainte-Marie
Recommended Reds: Bordeaux Supérieur Alios ★★ £C
Bordeaux Supérieur ★ £B
Recommended Whites: Entre-Deux-Mers Madlys ★★ £C
Entre-Deux-Mers ★★ £B

Ch. de Sales
Recommended Reds: Pomerol ★★★ £E

Ch. Tayac
Recommended Reds: Côtes de Bourg Cuvée Prestige ★★ £C
Côtes de Bourg Cuvée Reservée ★★ £C

Ch. Tire-Pé
Recommended Reds: Bordeaux La Côte ★★☆ £C Bordeaux ★★ £B

Ch. Tournefeuille
Recommended Reds: Lalande-de-Pomerol Cuvée La Cure ★★★ £D
Lalande-de-Pomerol ★★★ £C

Ch. Trianon
Recommended Reds: Saint-Emilion Grand Cru ★★★ £E

Villa Mongiron
Recommended Reds: Bordeaux ★★ £B

Ch. Vignol
Recommended Reds: Saint-Emilion Grand Cru ★★ £D

Ch. Villhardy
Recommended Reds: Saint-Emilion Grand Cru ★★★ £E

Ch. La Voute
Recommended Reds: Saint-Emilion Grand Cru ★★★ £E

Ch. Vrai Canon Bouché
Recommended Reds: Canon-Fronsac ★★★ £C

Ch. Yon Figeac
Recommended Reds: Saint-Emilion Grand Cru Classé ★★☆ £E

Work in progress!!

Producers under consideration for the next edition
Ch. Cantelauze (Pomerol)
Ch. du Champ des Treilles (Sainte-Foy Bordeaux)
Ch. Chapelle Maracan (Bordeaux Supérieur)
Ch. La Gravière (Lalande-de-Pomerol)
Ch. La Serre (Saint-Émilion Grand Cru Classé)
Ch. Mémoires (Premières Côtes De Bordeaux)
Dom. Mondésir-Gazin (Premières Côtes De Blaye)
Vieux Ch. Champs de Mars (Côtes De Castillon)

Author's choice - *Saint-Emilion, Pomerol & other Bordeaux*

Great Cellarworthy Right Bank Reds
Ch. Ausone   Saint-Emilion 1er Grand Cru Classé
Ch. Cheval-Blanc   Saint-Emilion 1 er Grand Cru Classé
Ch. La Conseillant   Pomerol
Ch. L'Église-Clinet   Pomerol
Ch. Lafleur   Pomerol
Ch. Pavie-Decesse   Saint-Emilion Grand Cru Classé
Ch. Pétrus   Pomerol
Ch. Le Pin   Pomerol
Ch. Tertre-Rôteboeuf   Saint-Emilion Grand Cru
Ch. Troplong-Mondot   1er Saint-Emilion Grand Cru Classé
Ch. Pavie   Saint-Emilion 1er Grand Cru Classé
Ch. Canon   Saint-Emilion Grand Cru Classé
Ch. de Valandraud   Saint-Emilion Grand Cru Classé
Vieux Ch. Certan   Pomerol
Ch. Chauvin   Saint-Emilion Grand Cru Classé

New Classic Right Bank Reds
Ch. Beau-Séjour Bécot   Saint-Emilion La Gomerie Grand Cru
Ch. Beauregard   Pomerol
Ch. Faugères   Saint-Emilion Péby-Faugères Grand Cru
La Fleur du Boùard   Lalande-De-Pomerol
Ch. Fombrauge   Saint-Emilion Magrez-Fombrauge GC Classé
La Mondotte   Saint-Emilion Grand Cru Classé
Le Dôme   Saint-Emilion Grand Cru
Les Astéries   Saint-Emilion Grand Cru
Ch. Monbousquet   Saint-Emilion Grand Cru
Ch. Quinault   Saint-Emilion Quinault L'Enclos Grand Cru Classé
Ch. Gazin   Pomerol

Ch. Fombrauge   Saint-Emilion Magrez-Fombrauge Grand Cru

Emerging Right Bank reds
Dom. de L'A   Côtes de Castillon
Ch. d'Aiguihe   Côtes de Castillon
Ch. Fontenil   Fronsac
Ch. Moulin Pey-Labrie   Canon-Fronsac
Clos Puy Arnaud   Côtes de Castillon
Ch. Puygueraud   Bordeaux-Côtes des Francs
Ch. de La Rivière   Fronsac
Ch. Roc de Cambes   Côtes de Bourg
Ch. La Vieille Cure   Fronsac
Ch. Ampélia   Côtes de Castillon
Ch. Carignan   1er Côtes de Bordeaux Prima
Essence de Dourthe   Bordeaux
Ch. Moulin Haut-Laroque   Fronsac
Ch. Grand Corbin-Despagne   Saint-Emilion Grand Cru

Top Right Bank values
Reds:
Ch. Barrabaque   Fronsac
Ch. Bel-Air La Royère   Côtes de Castillon
Ch. Bonnet   Bordeaux Réserve
Ch. La Dauphine   Fronsac
Ch. Dauphiné-Rondillon   Loupiac La Cuvée d'Or
Ch. Reignac   Bordeaux Superieur
Ch. Cap de Faugères   Côtes de Castillon
Vieux Ch. Gachet   Lalande-de-Pomerol
Ch. La Mauriane   Puisseguin-Saint-Emilion
Whites:
Clos Nardian   Bordeaux
Ch. Reynon   Bordeaux Vieilles Vignes
Ch. Carsin   Bordeaux Cuvée Prestige

France

SEREIN

Auxerre

Chablis

Dijon

Marsannay

Fixin

Gevrey-Chambertin

Morey-Saint-Denis

Chambolle-Musigny

Vougeot

Vosne-Romanée

Nuits-Saint-Georges

Pernand-Vergelesses

Savigny-lès-Beaune

Aloxe-Corton

Beaune

Pommard

Volnay

Auxey-Duresses

Meursault

Puligny-Montrachet

Chassagne-Montrachet

Chagny

Santenay

Bouzeron

Rully

Mercurey

Givry

Chalon-sur-Saône

Montagny

SAÔNE

Viré

Clessé

Milly-Lamartine

La Roche Vineuse

Vergisson

Mâcon

Pouilly

Fuissé

Chaintré

1 Chablis
2 Yonne (other vineyards)
3 Côte de Nuits
4 Hautes Côtes de Nuits
5 Côtes de Beaune
6 Hautes Côtes de Beaune
7 Côte Chalonnaise
8 Mâcon, Mâcon-Villages
9 Viré-Clessé
10 Pouilly-Fuissé
11 Pouilly-Loché, Pouilly-
    Vinzelles
12 Saint-Véran

Burgundy can be considered as four distinct entities. In the north lies Chablis, at its heart is the Côte d'Or, next comes the Côte Chalonnaise then, still further south, the Mâconnais. The main appellations for each are given below, with more detail in the individual sections that follow.

Chablis & Yonne

Chablis and the surrounding Auxerrois are isolated from the heart of Burgundy - Chablis is located about 90 miles south east from Paris, halfway to the Côte d'Or. All Chablis is produced from the Chardonnay grape and is classified by vineyard site as either **Petit Chablis**, **Chablis**, **Chablis Premier Cru** or **Chablis Grand Cru**. Other than Chablis, there's distinctive Sauvignon around **Saint-Bris** and in good years pure cherryish Pinot Noir in **Irancy**, both villages with their own appellations. Pinot Noir or Chardonnay from other villages in the Yonne is suffixed **Bourgogne**.

Côte d'Or & Côte Chalonnaise

The Côte d'Or is synonymous with Burgundy and includes all its great red wines. The two parts are the more northerly Côte de Nuits (mostly reds for cellaring) and extending southwards, the Côte de Beaune (pre-eminent whites and elegant reds).

The CÔTE DE NUITS is Burgundy's most classic red wine district, based primarily on just one grape variety, Pinot Noir. The Côte runs from south of Dijon in **Marsannay** and **Fixin**, a source of ever better, gently priced wine. Then it's onto the big gun downs through the top communes of **Gevrey-Chambertin** (home of *grands crus* **Chambertin** and **Clos de Bèze**), **Morey-Saint-Denis** (cradle of *grands crus* **Clos de la Roche**, **Clos Saint-Denis**, **Clos des Lambrays** and **Clos de Tart**. In **Chambolle Musigny**, the wines attain an ethereal character in tune with a fine-boned structure, partly in **Bonnes Mares** and supremely in **Le Musigny**). Further southwards to **Vougeot** and particularly in *grand cru* **Clos de Vougeot**, the reds can assume a majestic power. Grands **Echezeaux** is the Monsieur of **Flagey-Echezeaux** and then probably the most sought after village - **Vosne-Romanée**, site of legendary *grands crus* **Richebourg**, **Romanée -Saint-Vivant**, **La Romanée**, **La Grande Rue** and the summit In **Romanée-Conti** and **La Tâche**. The Côte ends in **Nuits St Georges**, with no *grands crus* but some very fine *premier crus* from great producers.

The CÔTE DE BEAUNE is famous for great white Burgundy made from Chardonnay, although more Pinot Noir is planted. Much of both is at least potentially very high quality. In a confusion of appellations in the north, **Aloxe-Corton** with the famous *grands crus* of **Corton** (mostly red) and **Corton-Charlemagne** (white) stands out. **Beaune**, **Pernand-Vergelesses** and **Savigny-lès-Beaune** produce fine reds but some good whites too, while the celebrated **Pommard** and **Volnay** are restricted to red. **Monthélie**, and **Auxey-Duresses** provide more affordable red and a little white, while **Saint-Romain** and the often excellent **Saint-Aubin** do better with white. The big three white Burgundy appellations are **Meursault**, **Puligny-Montrachet** (including *grands crus* **Chevalier-Montrachet**, **Le Montrachet** and part of **Bâtard-Montrachet**) and **Chassagne-Montrachet**. The latter also produces red as do **Santenay** and **Maranges** in the tail of the Côte d'Or.

The CÔTE CHALONNAISE begins close to this tail. Both the wines and the countryside are distinctly different but the village appellations are again classified for wines from Chardonnay and/ or Pinot Noir – with the exception the first village, **Bouzeron**, which is classified for Aligoté. **Rully** makes more white than red, while **Mercurey** and **Givry** produce mostly red of much improved quality from new rootstock planted around 15 years ago. The southernmost appellation, **Montagny**, is for Chardonnay alone. **Crémant de Bourgogne** is for the region's sparkling wine.

Mâconnais

As in the Côte de Beaune here too there is greatness in white wine (from Chardonnay), with a new wave of excellent producers beginning to emerge. Quality wine production is focused on **Pouilly-Fuissé** (with its four communes of Chaintré, Fuissé, Solutré and Vergisson), adjoined at its eastern end by the small **Pouilly-Loché** and **Pouilly-Vinzelles** ACs. There is a move to classify these premium vineyards, especially Pouilly Fuissé as *premiers crus*. Many other vineyards north and south of Pouilly-Fuissé qualify as **Saint-Véran** which in the right hands and sites can equal Pouilly Fuissé. There is fine quality too from **Viré-Clessé** and increasingly from several of some 43 villages that can be suffixed to Mâcon (eg **Mâcon-Bussières**).

France

Chablis is one of the great white wines of the world, and partly because the cultivation of the Chardonnay grape in these cool hills is so close to the limit of where obtaining full ripeness is possible. Success rarely comes easily, fraught with an annual battle against frost and rain, demanding constant diligence. The importance of fully ripe fruit cannot be understated. The wines should be vigorous, fresh, suffused with minerality but also with generosity and length of flavour without the greenness, harshness or indeed sulphur that some disciples have been duped into believing it was authentic Chablis character.

Style

So what defines that unique Chablis character? A fine, subtle gun-flint, smoke or stony mineral character and greengage plum aromas are typical – but these must be ripe plums. Some wines are more floral or show apple, citrus or peach tones. Yet there should still be an unmistakable mineral aspect and marvellous depth, with a toasty, nutty (or honeyed) complexity with age. The vintage matters greatly; while the longevity of Chablis should never be underestimated, most wines from a weaker vintage will evolve quite quickly and the leanness, often greenness on the palate will never disappear.

Controversy

Two major areas of debate in the past two decades have been the extension of the premier cru vineyard area and the use of new oak, (now more moderate). Just as important to quality are the issues of yield (often too high) and mechanical harvesting, which is still widespread. The Union des Grands Crus in Chablis, founded by Michel Laroche in 2000, quickly banned mechanical harvesting: many premiers crus are harvested in this way, in part due to the greater ease of using this method here in contrast to the Côte d'Or, where difficulties are posed by the more fragmented ownership of vineyards. Much of the argument over expansion of the vignoble concerns soil types and whether Portlandian, Jurassic and other limestones are capable of the same quality as fossilised Kimmeridgian limestone found in the established grands and premiers crus. The second area of debate is whether to oak or not. There are now many good exponents of both schools of thought, though the style of each varies significantly. A grand cru from Domaine François Raveneau (aged in used oak) is a benchmark but most of the 1-5-year-old oak versions from Pinson or Domaine Chanson are also of very high quality and have as much validity as those from the unoaked camp. Quality is the key, the question of style is more subjective and unless the oak overwhelms the wine it is down to personal choice. That said, Chablis should always taste of its origins and not be mistaken for something from the Côte de Beaune or further afield.

Classification

Understanding the Chablis classification is straightforward. The entire *vignoble* of more than 4600 ha (currently in production) is classified as one of four levels: **Chablis Grand Cru**, **Chablis Premier Cru**, **Chablis** or **Petit Chablis**.

The seven grands crus covering 100ha of vineyards (just over 2%) are Blanchot (12.7ha), Bougros (12.6ha), Les Clos (26ha), Grenouilles (9.3ha), Preuses (11.4ha), Valmur (13.2ha) and Vaudésir (14.7ha). Unsurprisingly, given the size of each cru, there are significant differences in altitude and exposition within each. In the right hands and from the best plots all seven are capable of real class even if

there are arguably more consistently good examples of Les Clos, Valmur and Vaudésir than the others.

Such is the importance of the producer, however, premiers crus from the best estates can easily outperform weaker grand cru efforts. Almost eight times the area is designated Chablis Premier Cru, encompassing forty names. Less than half of these are in common usage as the main premier cru name is usually taken. Regrettably this precludes a better understanding of individual plots or climats within these large vineyard areas that could help in identifying both style and quality. However some producers (lately Verget but others too) are increasingly identifying a special plot by adding the *lieu-dit* name to the label - and for regular Chablis as well as premier crus. Broadly speaking, those premiers crus with the greatest potential to be fine are Fourchaume, Montée de Tonnerre and Mont de Milieu, all lying on the same side (northern, right bank) of the river Serein as the grand crus and with similar exposures. But poorer examples of these will be surpassed easily by the best versions of premiers crus from the other side of the Serein (left bank), especially Montmains, Vaillons and Côte de Léchet. The quality of regular Chablis (from more than 3000 ha) is very much dependent on the producer. Petit Chablis, once derided as generally to be avoided, can often delight, particularly if sourced from unusual sites.

Yonne - life beyond Chablis

Most of the wines made in the area surrounding Chablis are made from Chardonnay, Pinot Noir or Aligoté. If conditions are generally less favoured in terms of soil and climate than in much of Chablis, it is possible to produce wines of reasonable concentration and sufficient ripeness in both colours from villages such as Coulanges-la-Vineuse and Irancy providing there is a fastidious approach to viticulture – the wines of Anita & Jean-Pierre Colinot are proof enough. **Irancy** is an AC for red in its own right; other villages are suffixed Bourgogne (**Bourgogne Coulanges-la-Vineuse**, **Bourgogne Chitry**) for red and white. **Bourgogne Côtes d'Auxerre** covers other villages in the vicinity of Auxerre (including Pinot Noir and Chardonnay from Saint-Bris-le-Vineux).

Those from around Tonnerre, to the east of Chablis, are labelled **Bourgogne Épineuil** (for Pinot Noir) or **Bourgogne Tonnerre** (recently sanctioned for whites). Some growers are at least as successful with rosé as red. If the cultivation of Sauvignon in the Yonne seems unusual, consider that it's a relatively short hop to the Central Vineyards of the Loire Valley from here. Few examples of **Saint-Bris** (Sauvignon from around Saint-Bris, Irancy and Chitry) are better than green and edgy, despite its promotion in 2003 to appellation status. The real exceptions are those from Goisot whose brilliant wines (not to be missed) also include Chardonnay and Pinot Noir, seemingly from another planet in quality terms. Further afield, some Chablis-like white is made some 50 km to the south of Chablis and Auxerre at Vézelay (**Bourgogne Vézelay**).

Chablis vintages

No two vintages in Chablis are quite alike and even from a good producer the choice of vintage can make a significant difference to the quality in your glass. though the effects of beneficial climate change have recently eased the struggle for ripeness in cooler years. Yet the attendant problems of increased humidity, mildew and rot in wetter years still make it important to choose a vintage carefully especially if the wines are intended for cellaring. Top artisans like Raveneau and Samuel Billaud are the exceptions who make great wine in fair or unexceptional years

2015 ★★★★: The polar opposite of 2014, Chablis 2015 Is a sun-blessed vintage with one of the warmest and driest summers for many years. However, just at the start of the harvest around September 2nd, localized but destructive hail storms hit some of the Grands and Premiers Crus: Blanchots especially, part of Les Clos, Montée de Tonnerre and Montmains. The berries pulverised by hail lost their juice and did not enter the wineries of the best producers. Skins affected by hail were either removed at the cold settling of the "must" or before that on sorting tables of the grapes - a long overdue practice in the Chablisien. In other words, volume was affected, not quality. On the resumption of picking, weather conditions were excellent, sunny days with cool nights. Berries were small but healthy. A warm vintage like 2003 has been avoided by top domaines who harvested "al dente", when the grapes were pale yellow, not gold, to avoid the loss of acidity and liveliness. A little early to say whether this is a very good vintage or a truly excellent one.

2014 ★★★★: A topsy- turvy Chablis growing season, which after a lot of nail- biting ended well, even triumphantly. A mild spring and successful mid-June flowering was followed by a wet July and still wetter August. Luckily the sun returned at the end of the month, and as the result of a perfect sunny harvest under blue skies, this is a little classic, coolish year. The fruit is riper and rounder than in 2013 but with fine acidity - one for discreet connoisseurs, the Kimmeridgian mark of chiselled mineral flavours exuding class. Medium weight, the wines of Billaud -Simon, Samuel Billaud, Domaine Laroche (under a new winemaker) shine. Exquisite Mouton from Long Depaquit. Worth buying now before prices rise.

2013 ★★★☆: This year Chablis was not affected by spring frosts and hail, but the weather that followed was somewhat irregular. A cool and rainy month of May caused irregular flowering resulting in *coulure*. As a result, the fruit set was difficult and even though September was fine, it did not make up for the loss. The grapes ripened very quickly, but the hot and humid weather that followed early in October raised fears of botrytis. Stopping the rot was therefore of paramount importance. Those who harvested more speedily by machine had a big advantage over those who harvested by hand. Yields were very much down but what has been produced has good alcohol content and well-balanced with good acidity levels.

2012 ★★★★☆: Another classy year for Chablis. Despite yields being around 40% down due to frosts, hot and dry weather during the summer led to some "burnt" fruit and careful selection had to be made at harvest. However, what has been produced is generally of the highest quality with ripe fruit and reasonably good acidity.

2011 ★★★★☆: Despite frost in the spring and hail at the end of June and an exceptionally wet June and July, perfect weather in August and September produced some really balanced wines. Low yields from the top producers have ensured some classic Chablis, somewhere between the austerity of the 2010s and the fruitiness of the 2009s.

2010 ★★★☆: There was a small crop in Chablis, with healthy fruit. The wines are showing good acidity and minerality with good alcoholic strength.

2009 ★★★★☆: This is a potentially very good vintage. After an even flowering, the summer was warm with the occasional July storm followed by a balmy autumn producing healthy grapes with lots of fruit. As elsewhere in Burgundy, the wines are quite forward but retain sufficient acidity and balance to show both mineral and intense citrus and green fruit qualities.

2008 ★★★★: Shows a lot of promise despite unpredictable conditions during the summer. The vineyards experienced unsettled weather and although spared frost and hail, there was plenty of light and wind in the latter part of the summer to give the grapes enough hang time to produce wines of elegant minerality which should be good for laying down.

2007 ★★★☆: A mild warm spring was followed by a wet summer which ruined the chances of success unless strict selection procedures were employed. Good weather in the last week in August until mid September ensured those who waited produced wines of purity and minerality in contrast to the fleshier wines of 2006.

2006 ★★★★: Whether this turns out as good as 05 remains to be seen however a decidedly cool and wet August actually helped compensate for the heat of the previous 2 months. Aromatic wines with good minerality.

2005 ★★★★★: An excellent vintage. Top examples show purity allied to good concentration and structure.

2004 ★★★★: This was always going to be a cooler vintage than 2003 and due to a successful flowering it was a large crop. Despite some claims of 'quality and quantity' only where yields were kept down and the healthiest, ripest fruit used are the wines first-rate.

2003 ★★☆: A hitherto almost inconceivable vintage in Chablis, which suffered the same extreme heat as much of Europe, the like of which had never before been experienced here.

2002 ★★★★☆: This was a much more complete vintage than 2003. The wines are ripe and concentrated, although just occasionally a little broad and diffuse. From the top echelon of producers the wines are balanced and ageworthy.

2001 ★★☆: A difficult vintage: the wet and cold conditions of July and September resulted in rot and under-ripeness for many, and even where ripeness was achieved some wines lack balance.

2000 ★★★☆: Overall quality was higher than in 2001 with a warm sunny run in to another early vintage in late September. However yields were generally high (a few producers excepted) and some wines are evolving quite quickly. The best, though, are concentrated, structured and balanced.

Earlier Years: Of early vintages, the best in the 90s (1990 apart) all came from the latter half of the decade. 1995, 1996, 1997 and 1999 all produced good wines, particular the latter despite a very hot August. The frost, hail, mildew affected 1998 is generally best avoided now as are most wines from 1994, 1993, 1992, and 1991. However for a taste of how well Chablis can age consider the best from 1990 (an exceptional vintage), 1988 or even 1986.

A-Z of producers

Dom. Barat *www.domaine-barat.fr*
A small family run operation with 20 ha of vineyards, the Barat siblings, Angèle and Ludovic are now very much in charge, having launched in 2014 a new cuvée- l'Umani- based on 40-year-old vines. This is a fine range of well-made Chablis with good weight, intensity and a proper expression of its origins. There's no oak here, yet there is better concentration, definition and life than found in many more unwooded examples. Premiers Crus Vaillons, Côte de Léchet and Mont de Milieu all faithfully express of the character of their respective sites. Attractive, regular Chablis is one of the better examples with a good floral, mineral stamp. Great value.
Recommended Whites:
Chablis Premier Cru Mont de Milieu ★★★ £D
Chablis Premier Cru Vaillons ★★★ £D
Chablis Premier Cru Côte de Lechet ★★★ £D

Burgundy /Chablis & Yonne

Chablis Premier Cru Les Fourneaux ★★★ £D
Chablis l'Umani, 40-year-old vines ★★★ £D   Chablis ★★ £C

Jean-Claude Bessin

One of Chablis' best small domains. Former architects Jean-Claude Bessin and his wife Evelyne had the good fortune to inherit (from her Tremblay family) prime Chablis vineyards. Seven of their 12 ha are located in three leading crus, the premiers crus Montmains and Fourchaume, and grand cru Valmur; the Fourchaume in particular contains a wealth of fine old vines. Bessin has only been bottling his own wine since 1992 but has already produced plenty of rich, fruit-intense, unoaked Chablis notable for its ripeness. Oak is now employed for the Valmur but doesn't overwhelm its concentrated fruit, instead adding structure that should enhance its longevity. The regular Chablis can be drunk quite young, but the crus are better with 3 years' age up to a decade.. His 2014s are among the finest in Chablis -chiseled classics

Recommended Whites:
Chablis Grand Cru Valmur ★★★★☆ £E
Chablis Premier Cru Fourchaume ★★★☆ £D
Chablis Premier Cru Montmains ★★★ £D
Chablis Premier Cru La Fôret ★★★ £D
Chablis ★★ £C

>> Samuel Billaud samuel-billaud.com

In 2014 this brilliantly gifted winemaker decided to go on his own, creating a label quite separate from Billaud-Simon. At first, he didn't own the vineyards but managed them. Yet Fortune shined on his project when just before the excellent '14 vintage, Samuel succeeded in getting into his own choice premier cru vineyards that included a plot of Côte de Léchet belonging his great grandmother and a perfect slice of Mont de Milieu based on 100-year-old vines. The straight Chablis Les Grand Terroirs punches above its weight in a skilled assemblage of old-vines Les Cartes which gives flesh while Parges and Chapelot give tension, energy and a crystalline feel - as good as it gets. The Côte de Léchet, almost certainly the classiest left bank cru, is quiet and graceful at first, typically growing in weight and complexity in the glass, with the promise of a decent long life ahead. The Mont de Milieu is splendidly rounded with notes of stone-fruits like white peach and Mirabelle plum, reined by beautiful acidity. No mention of oak is claimed, which is not to deny that there may be a little in the Mont de Milieu. (ME)

Recommended Whites:
Chablis Premier Cru Côte de Léchet ★★★★ £D
Chablis Premier Cru Mont de Milieu ★★★★ £D
Chablis Premier Cru Les Fourneaux ★★★ £D
Chablis Les Grands Terroirs ★★★ £C

Billaud-Simon www.billaud-simon.com

A family domaine dating from 1815 making brilliant, predominantly unoaked Chablis, until recently under the winemaking direction of Samuel BILLAUD: Finding life under the aegis of his iconic uncle Bernard constricting, Samuel has now gone out on his own, creating further marvels. (see new entry) Billaud-Simon changed hand in 2014 and Is now owned by Faiveley, the eminent Côte d'Or house of Nuits St Georges. The Billaud wines, judged on the crystalline 2014s are as good as ever under new winemaker The estate's 20 ha include parcels of three grands crus (Les Clos, Preuses and Vaudésir) and a few ares of Blanchots, as well as significant vineyards in the premiers crus of Mont de Milieu, Montée de Tonnerre and Vaillons, plus a little Fourchaume. There is a high proportion of old vines - especially in

the superb Vielles Vignes vines bottling of Mont de Milieu, which shows a mineral-rich smoky complexity allied to optimally ripe, sometimes exotic fruit further enhanced by great definition and structure. A carefully temperature-controlled vinification in stainless steel is followed by a lengthy low-temperature débourbage (cold settling) Oak fermentation and ageing are judiciously employed for the top crus, with since 2011 some very successful use of large oak foudres, which have less woody impact than barriques on these great terroirs especially the old-vines Les Clos, Vaudésir and fragrant Les Preuses. So, overall these are quite delicious, graceful Chablis with extra distinction and depth at the premier cru level and exceptional dimension and complexity at the grand cru level. If the prices are edging upwards they still represent marvelous value vis-à-vis similar quality from the Côte de Beaune. Even the Petit Chablis is worth considering here.

Recommended Whites:
Chablis Grand Cru Vaudésir ★★★★★ £F
Chablis Grand Cru Les Clos ★★★★★ £F
Chablis Grand Cru Preuses ★★★★★ £F
Chablis Premier Cru Montée de Tonnerre ★★★★ £D
Chablis Premier Cru Mont de Milieu ★★★★ £D
Chablis Premier Cru Vaillons ★★★ £D
Chablis Premier Cru Fourchaume ★★★ £D
Chablis Tête d'Or ★★☆ £C   Chablis ★★ £C
Petit Chablis ★ £C

Dom. de Bois d'Yver www.boisdyver.com

I well remember tasting in 1990 at this now organically farmed 22 ha domaine of Georges Pico on the back roads towards the cooler slopes of Courgis: I recall a steely vivacity and generous weight that could only be Chablis. Fostered by Georges and his partner Eliana Punta that vrai Chablis style is alive and well in recent years, both the Chablis tout court and particularly at premier cru level, notably a sturdy Mortmain 2012 for long ageing; Vaillons too shows good ripeness, mineral character and a certain elegance. All the range is fermented in stainless steel, except for the Grand Cru Blanchot, which is aged at least in used -oak; the complexity and pretty elegance of Blanchot is clear, though it lacks a touch of grand dimension. Some wines come from bought-In grape and are labelled only as "mis en bouteilles par Domaine de Bois d'Yver"

Recommended Whites:
Chablis Grand Cru Blanchots ★★★ £E
Chablis Premier Cru Montmains ★★★★ £D
Chablis Premier Cru Vaillons ★★★ £D
Chablis Premier Cru Beauregard ★★ £D   Chablis ★★★ £C

A & F Boudin/Dom. de Chantemerle www.chablis-boudin.com

The redoubtable Adhémar Boudin's bijou domaine- the best of tradition- has been brilliantly run in recent years by his son Francis, who regularly makes exciting, classic Chablis based in the village of La Chapelle Vaupelteigne on the left bank of the Serein, looking up to Fourchaume on the right bank. Low yields, ripe fruit and vinification in inert vats contribute to an opulent style that is also profoundly mineral, without any oak influence. Particularly worth seeking out are naturally the two expressions of Fourchaume, which are benchmarks of this leading premier cru. The straight Fourchaume particularly good in 2014, is a scintillating dance of honeyed richness and mineral depth. The Homme Mort ('dead man') is altogether more serious and complex, its distinction shaped by the soils it shares with the next- door grands crus- for long cellaring. All the other wines can be drunk quite young but if you think their

immediacy suggests they won't keep, you are wrong. The depth, structure and concentration of fruit means they'll keep for a decade and that often includes the regular Chablis.

Recommended Whites:

Chablis Premier Cru L'Homme Mort ★★★★ £D
Chablis Premier Cru Fourchaume ★★★ £D   Chablis ★★ £C

Jean-Marc Brocard   *www.brocard.fr*

In 1974 Jean-Marc Brocard had just a single hectare of vines, now he has 135 ha (though not all of it in the Chablis AC), 40 of which are cultivated biodynamically. Based at Préhy, on the edge of the Chablis region, he has turned out reasonably consistent, lively, assertive Chablis since the early 1980s. The emphasis is on producing 'typical' Chablis that is minerally and elegant. Though for the most part from mechanically harvested grapes, these stainless steel-vinified Chablis usually deliver adequate fruit and structure, particularly with a couple of years' bottle-age, but they can sometimes be a bit lean and underripe. the most interesting character is to be found among the premiers crus and grands crus, which under son Julien Brocard are on the cusp of greatness in Grand Cru les Preuses in 2014 and are also decent value for money including Grands Crus Valmur and Bougros.. They should, however, not be drunk too young (4 years is a minimum). A series of Bourgogne Blancs produced to differentiate between different soil types in the Chablis region are of good Petit Chablis quality, while newer is a series of blended Premier Cru Chablis that go some way to live up to their names: Minéral, Extrème, Sensuel and Paradoxe (the last sees some new oak). Chablis Domaine de la Boissoneuse is a biodynamically produced example. Other Auxerrois wines include reds Bourgogne Côtes d'Auxerre and Irancy from Domaine Sainte Claire. All in all, the wines are a good bet in a fine vintage if more variable from lesser years.. (ME)

Recommended Whites:

Chablis Grand Cru Les Preuses ★★★★★ £F
Chablis Grand Cru Valmur ★★★★ £F
Chablis Grand Cru Bougros ★★★★ £F
Chablis Premier Cru Montmains Le Manant ★★★ £D
Chablis Premier Cru Beauregard ★★★ £D
Chablis Premier Cru Vaucoupin ★★★ £D
Chablis Premier Cru Côte de Jouan ★★★ £D
Chablis Vieilles Vignes Dom. Sainte-Clair ★★ £D
Chablis Dom. Sainte-Claire ★ £C
Bourgogne Blanc Kimméridgien ★ £B
Bourgogne Blanc Jurassique ★ £B
Bourgogne Blanc Portlandien ★ £B
Bourgogne Aligoté ★ £B

La Chablisienne   *www.chablisienne.com*

With 1,100 ha of vineyards, covering a third of the total appellation, La Chablisienne is the major player in Chablis and one of the most respected co-ops in France. Much Chablis under the label of the large Beaune *négociants* are sourced in volume from here. Yet for superior wines that appear under the Chablisienne banner, great strides in quality have been made, particularly at Premier and Grand Cru level, since 201o/2012 - largely thanks to supremo and brand ambassador Hervé Tucki, a vastly knowledgeable expert and scholar of fine Chablis. The careful use (and varying ages) of oak barrels now provides subtler flavours and bolstering structures to the best crus, without the mask of excessive woodiness: even at base level, a special Petit Chablis from a favoured parcel often captivates and the intense Les Vénérables Vieilles Vignes is streets ahead of

much villages Chablis. The new Chablis Dame Nature, now in its third vintage is an A-B organic cuvée: vinified in stainless stainless, this is very popular for its finesse and white-flower s elegance, yet with enough in reserve to keep well. Of the premier crus Mont de Milieu has the usual generosity of fruit in this suntrap tempered by cleansing acidity and classis tension. At the top of the Grand Cru Pyramid, Preuses has its habitual florality but something more, dense, complex, with a scintillating finish. Reputedly Chablisienne's greatest wine, the 7.2 ha Château de Grenouilles shows durable sturdiness and the capacity to age gracefully, in forward and keeper vintages alike. Prices are quite for a co-op, but for the exceptional quality offered in 2012, 2014 one hopes 20105, these wines are actually terrific value compared to the great whites of the Côte de Beaune.

Recommended Whites:

Chablis Grand Cru Château de Grenouilles ★★★★ £E
Chablis Grand Cru Preuses ★★★★ £E
Chablis Grand Cru Blanchots ★★★☆ £E
Chablis Premier Cru Mont de Milieu ★★★ £D
Chablis Premier Cru Vaulorent ★★★ £D
Chablis Les Vénérables Vieilles Vignes ★★☆ £C
Chablis Dame Nature ★★☆ £C
Petit Chablis pas si petit ★★ £B

Dom. du Chardonnay   *www.domaine-du-chardonnay.com*

Established in 1987 this 36 ha estate includes 9.5 ha of premiers crus. Very consistent quality yet with fine varied expression of the sites by winemaker Étienne Boileau including floral, mineral Vaugiraut, more structured, mineral and stony Vaillons; finely nuanced Montmains. Two more, Montée de Tonnerre and Mont de Milieu are at least in part, vinified and aged in oak. Both show more weight and fullness, the Mont de Milieu in particular adds complexity and style over the other wines. The wines are also labelled Étienne Boileau.

Recommended Whites:

Chablis Premier Cru Mont de Milieu ★★★☆ £D
Chablis Premier Cru Montée de Tonnerre ★★★☆ £D
Chablis Premier Cru Vaillons ★★★ £D
Chablis Premier Cru Vaugiraut ★★★ £D
Chablis Premier Cru Montmains ★★★ £D
Chablis ★★ £C

>> Dom. Chanson   *www.domaine-chanson.com*

Bought by the Bollinger group in 1999, this small 18th century Beaune house has been transformed by Gilles de Courcel and Jean-Pierre Confuron his exceptional winemaker who has applied his skills as much to Chablis as to the Côte d'Or. Scrupulously identifying the best organically farmed plots within the Chablisien, Jean-Pierre buys from trusted growers; the grapes are pressed in Chablis but vinified in Chanson's modern winery near Savigny in the Côte de Beaune. Everything in the Chablis range is good too excellent, as tasted in the sturdy 2012, light-framed but here successful 2013 and the true classic that is 2014, rounded yet mineral in a fragrant style. The straight Chablis is all It should be, fresh with admirable tension in tune with scented ripe fruit notes of hawthorn and *agrumes* (grapefruit). Rising to the premier cru and grand cru level, Confuron exhibits his mastery of oak in wines which are structured but expressive through aeration, to the point that you don't sense they have scarcely seen the inside of a barrel. Notable 2014 successes: mineral Montée de Tonnerre with a delicate touch of light vanilla; Preuses flowery, opulent, athletic; Valmur magical mouthfilling volume yet fine-drawn, precise and taut.

Burgundy /Chablis & Yonne

France

Recommended Whites:
Chablis Grand Cru Valmur ★★★★ £E
Chablis Grand Cru Preuses ★★★★ £E
Chablis Premier Cru Montée de Tonnerre ★★★★ £D
Chablis Premier Cru Montmains ★★★ £D
Chablis ★★ £C

Anita, Jean-Pierre & Stéphanie Colinot *www.irancy-colinot.fr*
If the pure, pristine, cherry-scented character of very cool-climate Pinot drives you to distraction then this is the place to come. Try these racy PInots, served cool with 'meaty' fish like monkfish or tuna. One or two others in Irancy can also make enticing red but their wines are let down more often by a lack of complete ripeness. From 12 ha (which, typically for this Auxerrois region, includes a little César), Jean-Pierre and recently, his charming daughter Stéphanie make supple elegant wines with good intensity of flavour and length. The César (5-10% is used) which needs lots of sun to get fully ripe can detract a little in cooler years. Of the various *cuvées*, the Côte du Moutier has good fruit intensity and depth, Palotte is supple and fruity while Les Mazelots is more complex and concentrated - rich and stylish. But the most concentrated of them all - and capable of ageing for up to 15 years, is the Très Vieilles Vignes. Unfortunately the wines have a deserved following in France and can be difficult to find but it's worth the effort, particularly from a good vintage. All will improve for at least 5 years, and the Très Vieilles Vignes for a lot longer. For other quality Auxerrois reds see Ghislaine et Jean-Hugues GOISOT.

Recommended Reds:
Irancy Très Vieilles Vignes ★★★ £C   Irancy Côte du Moutier ★★ £B
Irancy Les Mazelots ★★ £B   Irancy Palotte ★★ £B

Dom. du Colombier *www.chabliscolombier.com*
Thierry and his two brothers, Jean-Louis and Vincent, are now responsible for this 43 ha estate and are building on the reputation established by their father. All levels of Chablis are produced and all are unwooded. The style is for ripe, intense examples with good minerality and restrained lees influence. Premier crus Fourchaume and Vaucoupin are refined with good fruit and length. A richer and more concentrated Bougros is also refined with impressive underlying structure. Petit Chablis and Chablis should be drunk fairly young but both premiers crus and Bougros with at least 5 years' age.

Recommended Whites:
Chablis Grand Cru Bougros ★★★★ £E
Chablis Premier Cru Fourchaume ★★★ £D
Chablis Premier Cru Vaucoupin ★★★ £D
Chablis ★★ £C   Petit Chablis ★ £B

Daniel Dampt *www.chablis-dampt.com*
Daniel Dampt married the daughter of Jean Defaix, a highly respected vigneron who little by little reclaimed vineyards abandoned following phylloxera: his Defaix Côte de Léchet 1949 (as tasted in1990) was a legend. The Dampts now make good Chablis from 27 ha of vineyards, including 13 ha of premiers crus (predominantly Côte de Léchet and Vaillons). The wines are vinified in stainless steel, with the emphasis on a ripe fruited character but retaining very firm acidity and a mineral influence. The pride of the domaine are the Côte de Léchet vineyards, which lie close to the winery and produce arguably the most classic, mineral-rich wine, but there is good quality in all the premiers crus. There's also a good inexpensive source of Chablis that drinks well with 3 or 4 years' age but will keep for longer in the case of the premiers crus. Daniel's

sons, Vincent and Sébastien, whilst working on the family estate, have also created a merchant company producing two Grand Crus, Bougros and Les Clos, from bought in grapes. The Bougros 2014 tasted en primeur in early 2015 is excellent, broad-shouldered yet fine.

Recommended Whites:
Chablis Grand Cru Bougros ★★★★ £E
Chablis Premier Cru Côte de Léchet ★★★★ £D
Chablis Premier Cru Beauroy ★★★ £D
Chablis Premier Cru Fourchaume ★★★ £D
Chablis Premier Cru Vaillons ★★★ £D
Chablis ★★ £C

Jean & Sébastien Dauvissat *www.chablisjsdauvissat.com*
The less famous Dauvissats (cousins of those below) also make good wines. From 9 ha the small range of wines is most notable for grand cru Preuses and a Vieilles Vignes version of Vaillons (from vines of 70 years). Used oak is the choice for vinification and *élevage* but newer barrels are typically used for these two wines. The Preuses is more Côte de Beaune in style than some but makes up in concentration and character the little it loses in mineral precision. Regular Vaillons and Montmains are generally well-balanced with lots of breadth and flavour and drink well with 3-8 years. Séchet is rarely as good but the basic Chablis usually shows well with 2-5 years' age.

Recommended Whites:
Chablis Grand Cru Preuses ★★★★ £E
Chablis Premier Cru Vaillons Vieilles Vignes ★★★★ £D
Chablis Premier Cru Vaillons ★★★ £D
Chablis Premier Cru Montmains ★★★ £D
Chablis Premier Cru Séchet ★★ £D   Chablis ★ £C

❀ René & Vincent Dauvissat
The Dauvissats have deep roots in the region going back centuries. Vincent's grandfather started domaine bottling in the 1930s and his father René built up and maintains a rich viticultural resource; almost all of the 11.5 ha are either premier or grand cru. In the vineyard, a uniform high average vine age is maintained as old or weak vines are replaced individually, grafted from the best existing vines (*sélection massale*). In addition, all the grapes are manually picked, not just the leading crus – a relatively rare occurrence in Chablis. Vincent uses oak, used not new, to ferment and age most of the wines. The resulting Chablis are simply marvellous, characterised by their depth, breadth and body, filled with a gently honeyed ripeness and stylish minerality. All are fine, even the Petit Chablis, but the distinctive mineral yet contrasting premiers crus Vaillons and Forest are surpassed by the bigger, more concentrated grands crus Preuses and Les Clos. The latter need 6 or 7 years' ageing, premiers crus 4 or 5, and even the regular Chablis 3 or 4. The wines can be in short supply, having long been favoured by top Parisian restaurants.

Recommended Whites:
Chablis Grand Cru Les Clos ✪✪✪✪✪ £H
Chablis Grand Cru Preuses ★★★★ £G
Chablis Premier Cru Séchet ★★★★ £F
Chablis Premier Cru Forest ★★★★ £F
Chablis Premier Cru Vaillons ★★★★ £F
Chablis ★★★ £D   Petit Chablis ★★ £C

Dom. Bernard Defaix *www.bernard-defaix.com*
From grape-growing family tradition, Bernard Defaix set up independently in 1959. There are now 25 ha, half of it in premier cru sites, run by his sons Sylvain, responsible for the winemaking,

and Didier who takes care of the vineyards. Sustainable viticulture is practised and work to maintain and revitalise the soils is ongoing. Since 2009, the vineyards have been certified organic. All the vineyards are on the left bank of the Serein and include a large chunk of premier cru Côte de Léchet. This produces a very distinctive floral, mineral and flinty example with good weight and breadth. Other wines are good too, properly ripe with fine body in part from lees enrichment; Les Lys is more floral, Vaillons more mineral. There is some use of oak to enhance the structure, such as in a Vieille Vigne version of Côte de Lechet, one of the best wines in challenging 2013. while there is not the intensity or definition of the very best examples, these wines show good fruit with the crus bringing out the characteristics of their specific terroirs, and will keep well. Some Fourchaume and grand cru Bougros are produced from bought-in grapes and sold under the Sylvain & Didier Defaix label.

Recommended Whites:

Chablis Premier Cru Côte de Lechet ★★★ £D

Chablis Premier Cru Les Lys ★★★ £D

Chablis Premier Cru Vaillons ★★★ £D   Chablis Vieille Vigne ★★ £C

Daniel-Étienne Defaix   *www.chablisdefaix.com*

The Defaix lineage goes back centuries in the Chablis region. Even recent history relating to the domaine goes back to the 18th century. The domaine's reputation rests with three premiers crus of 4 ha each, almost half the estate's total of 26 ha. Viticulture is effectively organic, though not certified as such, vine age is high and grape selection rigorous. A sustained fermentation and long lees contact also contribute to the character of these wines. There is less of the floral, mineral and pure fruit character of other good producers but there is depth, intensity and complexity. The Les Lys has more mineral, citrus character plus honey with age; in Côte de Léchet and Vaillons there is more of a leesy influence but a little more structure too, particularly in the latter. Rarely seen is a little Bourgogne Rouge from very old vines, successful in the best vintages. A tiny amount of Grand Cru Blanchots is also made. Most of the wines can be drunk soon after their delayed release but will keep for longer.

Recommended Whites:

Chablis Premier Cru Côte de Léchet ★★★ £E

Chablis Premier Cru Les Lys ★★★ £E

Chablis Premier Cru Vaillons ★★★ £E

Chablis Vieilles Vignes ★★ £D

❀ Jean-Paul & Benoît Droin   *www.jeanpaul-droin.fr*

Jean-Paul Droin and his son Benoît draw from 20 ha of vines spread over five grands crus (with around 1ha each of Vaudésir, Valmur and Les Clos) and seven premiers crus. The range is generally of high quality. At the premiers and grands crus levels the wines are (to a greater or lesser degree) fermented and aged in oak of varying age and provenance, resulting in rich, ripe full wines. The use of oak has become gradually more refined over the past decade (save for too woody '13s); oak serves to enhance structure and cradle the ripe, minerally fruit. Nearly all the wines can be drunk with just 3 or 4 years' ageing, but will improve for as long again. Try the crus, particularly the Montée de Tonnerre, Vaudésir and Les Clos; the regular Chablis and Petit Chablis are more variable. In addition to those below, a little grand cru Blanchots and premier cru Vaucoupin are also made.

Recommended Whites:

Chablis Grand Cru Les Clos ★★★★ £E

Chablis Grand Cru Grenouilles ★★★★ £E

Chablis Grand Cru Vaudésir ★★★★ £E

Chablis Grand Cru Valmur ★★★★ £E

Chablis Premier Cru Montée de Tonnerre ★★★★ £D

Chablis Premier Cru Vaillons ★★★ £D

Chablis Premier Cru Montmains ★★★ £D

Chablis Premier Cru Côte de Léchet ★★★ £D

Chablis Premier Cru Fourchaume ★★★ £D

Chablis Premier Cru Vosgros ★★★ £D

Joseph Drouhin (Chablis)   *www.drouhin.com*

Under Robert Drouhin, the house of Joseph DROUHIN, an important high quality Beaune négociant, added Chablis vineyards to its holdings in the Côte d'Or in the late 1960s. Though the wines are vinified at the company's headquarters in Beaune, the grapes from more than 40 ha are pressed locally. The estate includes 3ha of grand cru vineyards spread over 4 climats, mostly Vaudésir and Les Clos. Low yields contribute to ripe, pure concentrated fruit and, though oak is important to the style, it is only used in the top wines and can be beautifully woven into the dense ripe fruit and fine minerality. Classy Les Clos (100% barrel-fermented and aged) is spicy and complex, if in the past sometimes likely to be mistaken for a top Côte de Beaune white. The latest welcome news is that Drouhin is now using much less new oak, clearly seen in the 2014s; applies as much to Chablis as to the Côte de Beaune whites. As well as an intense and streamlined Vaillons, fragrant and nuanced Montmains and stony Séchet, a regular Chablis Premier Cru from a blend of other sites is bottled separately. For ripe, concentrated everyday Chablis, the Domaine de Vaudon version is hard to beat.

Recommended Whites:

Chablis Grand Cru Vaudésir ★★★★ £F

Chablis Grand Cru Les Clos ★★★★ £F

Chablis Premier Cru Vaillons ★★★ £E

Chablis Premier Cru Montmains ★★★ £E

Chablis Premier Cru Séchet ★★★ £E

Chablis Domaine de Vaudon ★★★ £D

Chablis ★☆ £C

Gérard Duplessis   *www.chablis-duplessis.com*

This excellent small grower's 8 ha of vineyards are mostly in 4 of the very best premiers crus. Gérard Duplessis vinifies in stainless steel and matures in old wood for classic Chablis flavours. The wines can start out a little austere but there is that wonderful Chablis combination of underlying richness and a steely, minerally character that can provide wonderful drinking with 5 years' ageing, and is even better with another 5 or 10 in a top vintage.

Recommended Whites:

Chablis Grand Cru Les Clos ★★★★ £F

Chablis Premier Cru Fourchaume ★★★ £D

Chablis Premier Cru Montée de Tonnerre ★★★ £D

Chablis Premier Cru Montmains ★★★ £D

Chablis Premier Cru Vaillons ★★★ £D   Chablis ★★ £C

Jean Durup et Fils   *www.durup-chablis.com*

Jean Durup led the movement for expansion of the Chablis vignoble in direct opposition to William Fèvre in the 1970s and 80s. His 186 ha estate, partly resulting from the authorized expansion, is the largest in the region (much of it regular Chablis but there are also substantial holdings of premiers crus). It is very competently run and is now directed by Jean Durup's son, Jean-Paul. Jean has gradually earned greater respect for the sound quality of his wines

France

and remains a leading advocate of unoaked Chablis. The wines are generally well-balanced, with adequate ripeness, if sometimes lacking a little character and extra flair. Most of the wines drink well with 2–5 years' ageing but premiers crus can age for up to a decade. While the most important labels are Jean Durup, Domaine de l'Eglantière and Château de Maligny, the same wines are also bottled under Domaine de la Paulière and Domaine des Valéry labels for some importers. Some grand cru Vaudésir and Les Clos have also been made.

Recommended Whites:
Chablis Premier Cru L'Homme Mort ★★★ £D
Chablis Premier Cru Fourchaume ★★★ £D
Chablis Premier Cru Vau-de-Vey ★★★ £D
Chablis Premier Cru Montée de Tonnerre ★★ £D
Chablis Vigne de la Reine ★★ £D   Chablis Vieilles Vignes ★★ £C
Chablis Care de César ★★ £C   Chablis ★ £C

✿ William Fèvre   www.williamfèvre.com
Since the takeover by Joseph Henriot (also see HENRIOT Champagne and BOUCHARD PÈRE in the Côte d'Or) in 1998 the William Fèvre domaine is again one of the leaders of Chablis – combining very high quality and important volume. The Domaine comprises 47ha and includes an unrivalled collection of premiers and grands crus (12 and 15.2ha respectively). In the late 80s and early 90s William Fèvre was the staunchest and most vocal of those opposed to the expansion of the Chablis vineyards. The use of new oak became an increasing theme too, to the point of compromising the inherent fruit character of Chablis. Now, under the direction of Didier Séguier, there has been a return to manual harvesting and much more rigorous grape selection. New oak is used much less, the wines are bottled later, and so there is better concentration and something more of each wine's origin is captured and enhanced by the subtler oak. Very complex and complete is the consistently exceptional Les Clos which comes from 4ha of almost 60- year old vines in the higher part of the grand cru. Valmur is a personal favourite providing a real contrast with its soaring elegant intensity yet durable structure. Other gems are the expansive, classy Côte Bouguerots (from very steep slopes), and spicy, deep Preuses,. In addition to the Domaine wines rated below, a few including a good Mont de Milieu are made from bought-in grapes. Vintages since 1998 and older vintages are highly recommended, but those from the mid-1990s are more variable. Older wines can be labelled as Domaine de la Maladière. Perhaps a valid criticism today might be that in the search for aerien delicacy the grapes are sometimes harvested a little early, losing the added complexity that good phenolic maturity brings.

Domaine William Fèvre
Recommended Whites:
Chablis Grand Cru Les Clos ✪✪✪✪✪ £G
Chablis Grand Cru Valmur ✪✪✪✪✪ £G
Chablis Grand Cru Vaudésir ★★★★ £F
Chablis Grand Cru Bougros Côte de Bougerots ★★★★ £F
Chablis Grand Cru Preuses ★★★★ £F
Chablis Grand Cru Bougros ★★★★ £E
Chablis Premier Cru Fourchaume Vignoble de Vaulorent ★★★★ £E
Chablis Premier Cru Vaillons ★★★★ £D
Chablis Premier Cru Montée de Tonnerre ★★★★ £D
Chablis Premier Cru Montmains ★★★ £D
Chablis Premier Cru Les Lys ★★★ £D
Chablis Premier Cru Beauroy ★★ £D
Chablis ★★ £C

>> Dom. Nathalie & Gilles Fèvre   www.nathalieetgillesfevre.com
This couple are the rising stars of top level Chablis. Of their enviable 43 ha of vineyards, they sell a third of the production to the La Chablisienne (where Nathalie was the Dijon Faculty trained winemaker.) This allows them to concentrate on their best parcels in grand cru Les Preuses and premiers crus Vaulorent, Mont de Milieu and Vaulorent plus good volumes of Chablis Villages. Gilles is very much a man of the vines: like a Benedictine monk he tastes the soils to show why Vaulorent Is more mineral than Fourchaumes. That force and energy of Kimmeridgian limestone clay/marl is what drives him: it is certainly a supporting presence in their parcel of Mont de Milieu. Nathalie likes precise wines fermented mainly in stainless steel and uses oak sparingly in her genuinely great Les Preuses which in every vintage since 2012 has been exceptional: glorious perfumed floweriness - one taster thinks of magnolia - but also splendid structure, intensity, spiciness, depth, even a Burgundian sense of the forest floor. (ME)

Recommended Whites:
Chablis Grand Cru Preuses ★★★★☆ £E
Chablis Premier Cru Mont de Milieu ★★★★ £D
Chablis Premier Cru Vaulorent ★★★ £D
Chablis ★★★ £C

✿ Ghislain & Jean-Hugues Goisot   www.goisot.com
Thanks to a seemingly inexhaustible rise in quality, the Goisots have completely transformed the image of wines produced in the Yonne from outside of Chablis. Their 27 ha of Auxerrois vineyards (certified organic) lie mostly in the less than glamorous Saint-Bris, which promotes Sauvignon rather than Chardonnay. But both varieties are produced here (an extremely rare occurrence in France, in contrast to much of the New World) along with Aligoté and Pinot Noir. Through the meticulous and dedicated work of Jean-Hugues in the vineyards (now planted at a high density 10,800 plants per hectare) and lately from his son Guilhem in the cellar, all the wines are of extremely high quality yet don't command high prices thanks to their lowly appellations. A regular pure-fruited Chardonnay is sold as Bourgogne Côtes d'Auxerre while the cool, elegant Sauvignon with a floral, elderflower and gooseberry character takes the Saint-Bris appellation. The wines are ripe, concentrated and aromatic, with lovely definition and length, with added depth, breadth and complexity in the more ageworthy Corps de Garde versions. The Sauvignon under this label is brilliant; made from the Fié Gris clone, it is concentrated, classy and pure, comparable to top Pouilly-Fumé or Sancerre. Also made are single climat Côtes d'Auxerre Chardonnays: Biaumont, Gondonne and Gueule de Loup. Gondonne is very classy, pure and expressive , as well as remarkable value. Also exciting is the elegant but complete red Irancy Les Mazelots. Unquestionably, the Goisots' (winemaking) example is exemplary and serves as beacon to producers anywhere who lack the clout of an established name or appellation.

Recommended Whites:
Bourgogne Côtes d'Auxerre Gondonne ★★★★ £D
Bourgogne Côtes d'Auxerre Corps de Garde ★★★ £D
Bourgogne Côtes d'Auxerre ★★ £C
Saint-Bris Corps de Garde ★★★ £C
Saint-Bris ★★ £B   Bourgogne Aligoté ★★ £C
Recommended Reds:
Irancy Les Mazelots ★★★ £C
Bourgogne Rouge Corps de Garde ★★★ £B

Corinne & Jean-Pierre Grossot *www.chablis-grossot.com*

This is a good source for both premiers cru and regular Chablis. If initially a little austere, the wines are intensely fruity, with excellent definition, weight and fine perfumes. While the basic Chablis is machine-harvested all the better wines are now harvested manually. Though there are no grands crus, the 18 ha includes some excellent premiers crus. Stainless steel dominates their production but some oak is used for the Fourneaux and Mont de Milieu premiers crus and the village *cuvée*, 'Grossot'. Only the latter is obviously oaky, the others properly racy and minerally. While the wines are delicious with 3 or 4 years' ageing, they will keep. Solid quality and reasonable prices too.

Recommended Whites:

Chablis Premier Cru Fourchaume ★★★ £D
Chablis Premier Cru Mont de Milieu ★★★ £D
Chablis Premier Cru Fourneaux ★★ £D
Chablis Premier Cru Montmains ★★ £D
Chablis Premier Cru Vaucoupin ★★ £D
Chablis La Part des Anges ★★ £C
Chablis Grossot ★★ £C   Chablis ★★ £C

>> Dom. d'Henri *www.larochewines.com*

When Michel LAROCHE went into recent semi-retirement, having effectively merged and then sold his impressive business to JeanJean- Advini Group, a lot of people thought Michel would turn to his other great passion, sailing. He did, on one occasion traversing the Atlantic solo from the Caribbean to Brittany, the birthplace of his charming, supportive wife Gwenael. Any of us who've known Michel since the 70s knew that the Ocean would never quite enough for this guy, who combines restlessness and sanity like nobody else. In his own words, he had unfinished business in Chablis. His far-sightedness had led him in negotiations for leasing his vineyards to Advini to keep for his family the six hectares he had inherited from his father Henri, with some village Chablis and some prize Fourchames. The Phoenix quickly rose from the ashes, Domaine d'Henri was born and is now run by his daughters Cécile and Margot, and no doubt his son Romain, when he's a little older. The first vintage propitiously was 2012, which we report is potentially of very high class in the right hands. Certainly the trio of Dom Henri's Fourchaumes at various ages of the vine are classic examples of the genre, especially the vieilles vignes (40 years old vines) and the Heritage from a vineyard planted in 1937. Philippe Thieffry, the chief winemaker at Veuve Clicquot and one of the surest palates in the trade has said that these Fourchaumes were among the most impressive he had tasted in recent years. The 2014s will make a fascinating comparison.(ME)

Recommended Whites:

Chablis Premier Cru Fourchaume Heritage ★★★★☆ £E
Chablis Premier Cru Fourchaume Vieilles Vignes ★★★★ £D
Chablis Chablis ★★★ £C

Dom. Laroche *www.larochewines.com*

Laroche remains one of Chablis' major players and an innovative force in the South of France (MAS LA CHEVALIÈRE), Chile (Viña Punto Alto) and South Africa (L'AVENIR). The estate's offices are based in the Obédiencerie in the heart of Chablis, originally a monastery dating back to the ninth century. The Saint-Martin monks here established Chablis' first vines. Though the Laroche family of Maligny gradually became vignerons from 1850 the major expansion of the domaine, under Michel Laroche and his father Henri, came in the early 1970s, from 6 ha then to 130 ha today: Their largest

Grand Cru holding is Blanchots but there's also some Les Clos and a little Bouguerots (Bougros), and 29 ha of premiers crus centred on Fourchaume, Vaillons and Vau de Vey. When Michel Laroche, faced with the 2008 international financial crisis, decided to merge and eventually sell the business, jealous rivals cried crocodile tears too soon. For the new owners, the Advini group, have proved very enlightened masters. While the négoce wines under the plain Laroche label are straightforward and of good fruit, the domaine's crus are as fine as ever under gifted new winemaker Grégory Viennois. At recent en primeur tastings of the 2014 in Paris and London, Fourchaumes Vieilles Vignes shone for its strength and complexity, and. both the Blanchots and its super selection Reserve de l'Obedience were epic. If these prove too expensive go for the excellent Chablis Saint-Martin, a selection of the best regular Chablis vineyards. For quality and value, the new monoparcel village wine Chablis Vielle Voye (ancient path) is a step up with 70-year-old vines below Vaillons. Of pristine purity and elegance with fine texture and density, complexity Is added by the 25-year-old cask in which it was made and matured.

Domaine Laroche

Recommended Whites:

Chablis Grand Cru Blanchots Réserve de l'Obédience ★★★★★ £F
Chablis Grand Cru Les Clos ★★★★ £F
Chablis Grand Cru Blanchots ★★★★ £F
Chablis Premier Cru Fourchaumes Vieilles Vignes ★★★★ £D
Chablis Premier Cru Vaillons Vieilles Vignes ★★★ £D
Chablis Premier Cru Vau de Vey ★★★ £D
Chablis Premier Cru Montmains ★★★ £D
Chablis Premier Cru Beauroy ★★★ £D
Chablis Saint-Martin ★★ £C

Bernard Legland/Dom. des Marronniers

This is a good source of attractive, well-made and relatively inexpensive Chablis. Bernard Legland's 19 ha doesn't include much in the way of prime vineyards; 2.5 ha of Montmains is the most prized possession. The domaine was established in 1976 and has adhered to a principle of unoaked Chablis. Previously the premiers crus (there is also a little Côte de Jouan) were made from relatively young vines but these are now more than 20 years old, giving the wines added richness and depth.

Recommended Whites:

Chablis Premier Cru Montmains ★★★ £D
Chablis Premier Cru Côte de Jouan ★★ £D   Chablis ★☆ £C

Long-Depaquit *www.albertbichot.com*

This historic estate dates from the time of the French Revolution. There are now 65 ha but much of it has been acquired in the last 30 years or so. As well as a sprinkling of wines from premier and grand cru vineyards, the wine of the famous La Moutonne vineyard is made here. Acquired in 1791 by Simon Depaquy, it is a *monopole* of 2.35 ha that straddles part of grands crus Vaudésir and Preuses that belonged originally to the monks of the Abbey of Pontigny. Though most of the wines are both vinified and aged in stainless steel in order not to compromise the classic, flinty, minerally Chablis style, the grands crus see varying percentages of oak. Quality has been a bit uneven in the past but a new regime at BICHOT (see Côte d'Or) has ensured that since 2002 the wines are cleaner and better balanced with intensity, style and finesse. The top wines, especially La Moutonne, develop a gentle honeyed richness with age - the 2014 is sublime. The selected crus below are the most consistently fine and ageworthy, lesser wines are also recently improved.

Burgundy /Chablis & Yonne

France

Recommended Whites:
Chablis Grand Cru La Moutonne ★★★★☆ £E
Chablis Grand Cru Les Clos ★★★★ £E
Chablis Grand Cru Blanchots ★★★★ £E
Chablis Grand Cru Vaudésir ★★★★ £E
Chablis Premier Cru Montée de Tonnerre ★★★ £D
Chablis Premier Cru Vaucoupin ★★★ £D
Chablis Premier Cru Vaillons ★★★ £D

Dom. des Malandes www.domainedesmalandes.com
Established in 1986 from the family inheritance of Lyne Marchive (née Tremblay), this 27 ha estate has a strong following for unoaked Chablis of class. The reputation has been built on producing wines from low yields and fully ripe fruit and a non-interventionist winemaking philosophy, something that should be maintained as a new generation. The wines are ripe, more floral and fruit driven in the lesser cuvées but with more mineral intensity and complexity, as well as concentration, in the grands crus. Fourchaume and Montmains are perhaps the pick of the premiers crus but a fruit-emphasized Vau de Vey and very mineral, more classically austere Côte de Lechet are also very good. Both the grands crus are exceptional reflecting their respective terroir -the Vaudésir is the grand monsieur from a rare old clone of Chablis. Though most can be drunk fairly young (attractive Petit Chablis) these are the wines to keep.

Recommended Whites:
Chablis Grand Cru Vaudésir ★★★★★ £F
Chablis Grand Cru Les Clos ★★★★ £E
Chablis Premier Cru Côte de Léchet ★★★ £D
Chablis Premier Cru Montmains ★★★ £D
Chablis Premier Cru Fourchaume ★★★ £D
Chablis Premier Cru Vau de Vey ★★★ £D
Chablis Vieilles Vignes Tour du Roy ★★★ £D
Chablis ★★ £C Petit Chablis ★ £C

☙ Dom. Louis Michel et Fils www.louismicheletfils.com
Fifth-generation Jean-Loup Michel has made the wines here for some years but the 25 ha estate's international reputation was established by his father, Louis Michel, who died in 1999. Jean-Loup is being succeeded by his nephew, Guillaume Giqueau-Michel, an excellent open-minded winemaker who has improved the wines further, particularly in terms of tension, energy and harmony. Much of the production is now exported and widely available but remarkably without the high prices and compromised quality of some exporters. For its unoaked style of Chablis this is one of the most respected producers in the English-speaking world. The wines, from vines with an average age of 40 years, spend an extended period of time in stainless steel before a relatively late bottling. Austere but with an underlying mineral richness when young, the premiers crus are always better with 3–5 years' ageing, the grands crus with 5 or more. At their best these are excellent Chablis with fine terroir definition and real elegance and length on the palate if not the texture or dimension of the very best. That said these are wines to buy from the better vintages only; a cool or wet or generally more difficult vintage can reveal a lack of full ripeness as well as a tendency to age more rapidly than usual.

Recommended Whites:
Chablis Grand Cru Les Clos ★★★★☆ £E
Chablis Grand Cru Grenouilles ★★★★ £E
Chablis Grand Cru Vaudésir ★★★ £E
Chablis Premier Cru Montée de Tonnerre ★★★ £D

Chablis Premier Vaillons ★★★ £D
Chablis Premier Cru Fourchaume ★★★ £D
Chablis Premier Montmains ★★★ £D
Chablis ★★ £C Petit Chablis ★ £C

☙ Dom. Christian Moreau www.domainechristianmoreau.com
Another to benefit from the expiry of the lease of some of excellent parcels of grand cru Chablis, Christian Moreau (uncle to Louis below) has wasted no time since setting up operations in 2000 in the 17th century Grange aux Dimes in the heart of Chablis. He set his well-qualified son Fabien to work and they have been getting very good results since 2002. All the grapes are hand-picked before being subject to a further sorting prior to vinification. The regular Chablis sees only stainless steel, oak (10% new) figuring to some degree in either the vinification or ageing (or both) of premier and grand cru wines. The Cuvée Guy Moreau version of Vaillon comes from vines planted by Christian's father in 1934. It needs a little more time than the regular version (a minimum of 5 years) and can add a honeyed aspect to its fine mineral character. The grands crus are excellent including a Valmur with typical finesse and singularity, a fragrant Blanchots and a Les Clos that is classically full, complex and complete. At the top of the tree, Le Clos des Hospices is the filet mignon of Les Clos, from a perfect site on the mid-slope that shapes a powerful, majestic wine as great as any. A 5-star triumph in Fabien's hands.

Recommended Whites:
Chablis Grand Cru Les Clos Le Clos des Hospices ★★★★★ £F
Chablis Grand Cru Les Clos ★★★★☆ £F
Chablis Grand Cru Valmur ★★★★☆ £F
Chablis Grand Cru Vaudésir ★★★★ £F
Chablis Premier Cru Vaillon Cuvée Guy Moreau ★★★☆ £E
Chablis Premier Cru Vaillon ★★★☆ £E
Chablis ★★★ £C

Louis Moreau www.louismoreau.com
Louis and Anne Moreau control 120ha including the 50 ha Domaine Louis Moreau but also the the separate estates of Domaine de Biéville (65 ha) and Domaine du Cèdre Doré (5 ha). Vinified in stainless steel, without recourse to any wood, the wines are quite racy and austere when young but have great reserves of fruit underneath, particularly in the two premiers crus, Vaulignot (Vau Ligneau) and Fourneaux. The wines should not be confused with those of the négociant house, J Moreau (Boisset) from which the grands crus, made since 2002 were previously leased to. These see a little new oak and though only moderately concentrated should add richness with age. Led by a classy Vaudésir, they also include Valmur, Les Clos and, from a plot of vines within Les Clos, Clos des Hospices.

Dom. Louis Moreau
Chablis Grand Cru Valmur ★★★★ £E
Chablis Grand Cru Vaudésir ★★★★ £E
Chablis Grand Cru Les Clos des Hospices ★★★★ £E
Chablis Premier Cru Fourneaux ★★★ £D
Chablis Premier Cru Vaulignot ★★ £D Chablis ★ £C

Dom. de Biéville
Recommended Whites:
Chablis ★★ £C

Dom. du Cèdre Doré
Recommended Whites:
Chablis ★★ £C

Moreau-Naudet

Stéphane Moreau, no relation to the Moreaus above, has been running this 21 ha estate since 1999 and the wines are now very good indeed. Yields have been substantially lowered and a return to manual picking has contributed to ripe, clean wines with real fruit intensity and a classic minerally complexity. Even Petit Chablis and Chablis can be bought with confidence. Several excellent premiers crus, including a Montée de Tonnerre imbued with smoke, mineral and citrus, give good expression to their origins. Deep, minerally Valmur is long and classy, an excellent and affordable example of this often pricey grand cru.

Recommended Whites:

Chablis Grand Cru Valmur ★★★★ £E
Chablis Premier Cru Montée de Tonnerre ★★★★ £D
Chablis Premier Cru Vaillons ★★★ £D
Chablis Premier Cru Montmains ★★★ £D   Chablis ★★ £C

Didier & Pascal Picq

The small village of Chichée lies some 3 km south-east of the town of Chablis. The villas terroir is enviable, sharing the Kimmeridgian outcrops of nearby Grand Cru Blanchots. Here the Picqs have 13 ha, including Chichée's two premiers crus. Didier Picq is responsible for the winemaking, his brother Pascal maximizes grape quality. The grapes are picked as late as possible and both fermentation and ageing are in stainless steel. The wines are crisp, fresh, floral, fruity, but with excellent intensity in the Vieilles Vignes and extra character and concentration in the premiers crus. From most vintages the Vieilles Vignes should be drunk with at least 3 years' ageing, the premiers crus with 5 or more. The wines are also labelled Gilbert Picq et Fils.

Recommended Whites:

Chablis Premier Cru Vaucoupin ★★★★ £D
Chablis Premier Cru Vosgros ★★★★ £D
Chablis Vieilles Vignes ★★★ £C
Chablis ★★☆ £C

Dom. Pinson Frères   *www.domaine-pinson.com*

Very traditional, even rustic, would once have best described the atmosphere chez Pinson. However, brothers Laurent and Christophe, in charge of this small 14 ha estate since 1988, seemed set on a new image while continuing to make Chablis of real depth and character. In 2008, they were joined by Laurent's daughter Charlene, having obtained an oenology degree at Beaune, who has been instrumental in ratcheting the quality several notches higher. The parcels of vines are all of the first order, including 2.5 ha of Les Clos on the richer lower part of the hill and nearly 5 ha of Mont de Milieu. Used oak is employed in their ageing (only the regular Chablis is unoaked), which contributes to their excellent texture and breadth but only subtly influences flavour, though it is sometimes more apparent on the Montmains. The wines have been a little uneven before in terms of their ability to age but quality is often remarkably high. All the wines are better with 5 years' ageing or more, the Les Clos often with 10 or more. A little of the premiers crus Vaillons and Vaugiraut are also made.

Recommended Whites:

Chablis Grand Cru Les Clos ★★★★ £E
Chablis Premier Cru La Forêt ★★★ £D
Chablis Premier Cru Mont de Milieu ★★★ £D
Chablis Premier Cru Montmains ★★★ £D
Chablis ★★ £C

Isabelle & Denis Pommier   *www.denis-pommier.com*

Denis Pommier started out with just 2.5 ha in 1990 but now has 11 ha. He is already forging a reputation as a talented young vigneron. Though he has started fermenting and ageing his premiers crus in barrel, apart from the Beauroy; only part of the wine gets this treatment and then only a small percentage of the oak is new. Certainly the quality of the grapes is very good and the wines show concentrated ripe fruit; the mineral and citrus intensity is set against a spicy oak character and a gently buttery texture in the most recent vintages of the Côte de Léchet, their best wine. The overall balance and oak integration in the Beauroy has been less convincing but that is changing as the Pommiers' wines get better year by year. At present the small production quickly sells out. The Vieilles Vignes also shows some oak influence but the regular version sees none. A very small amount of Fourchaume is also made from relatively young vines.

Recommended Whites:

Chablis Premier Cru Côte de Léchet ★★★ £D
Chablis Premier Cru Beauroy ★★ £D   Chablis Vieilles Vignes ★★ £C
Chablis Croix aux Moines ★★ £C   Chablis ★★ £C

Denis Race   *www.chablisrace.com*

Denis Race is an exponent of unoaked Chablis. He and his wife have 15 ha of vines including 5.5 ha of premier cru Montmains. There is careful attention to the grapes prior to harvesting (and what is left ready for picking) – the key to quality when the grapes are machine-harvested as so much in Chablis now is. The Montmains appears in two bottlings, the Vieilles Vignes version from vines that are 70 years old and there is a marked difference in depth and oomph in the latter. All the wines show good *terroir* definition. A steely, mineral Mont de Milieu contrasts with a softer, more elegant Vaillon. A little grand cru Blanchot is also made.

Recommended Whites:

Chablis Premier Cru Montmains Vieilles Vignes ★★★★ £D
Chablis Premier Cru Montmains ★★★ £D
Chablis Premier Cru Mont de Milieu ★★★ £D
Chablis Premier CruVaillon ★★★ £D   Chablis ★★ £C

✿✿ Dom. Raveneau

Continuing the work of their father, François Raveneau, brothers Jean-Marie and Bernard Raveneau make superb Chablis from just 7.5 ha of premier and grand cru sites. Unquestionably the grape quality is paramount – all are handpicked and from low-yielding vines – but if anyone makes the case for the use of oak and how it should be used, surely this is the model to emulate. The wines have fabulous structure yet never taste as if they have seen the inside of a barrel. Typically pure mineral, citrus, greengage notes prevail on the nose, if occasionally more floral or with a hint of smoke, while the palate is taut, intense and steely when young but with wonderful dimension, underlying concentration and depth that builds in richness and complexity over a decade or longer. No two wines are quite the same but there is fine quality here even in weaker vintages. The domaine also has small plots in Chapelot, Forest (Forêt) and Montmains.

Recommended Whites:

Chablis Grand Cru Les Clos ✪✪✪✪ £H
Chablis Grand Cru Blanchots ★★★★★ £H
Chablis Grand Cru Valmur ★★★★★ £H
Chablis Premier Cru Butteaux ★★★★ £G
Chablis Premier Cru Vaillons ★★★★ £G
Chablis Premier Cru Montée de Tonnerre ★★★★ £G

Burgundy /Chablis & Yonne

France

Dom. Vocoret *www.vocoret.com*
This family domaine of 42 ha includes around 4 ha of grands crus (mostly Blanchots and Les Clos) and more than 15 ha of premiers crus (especially Vaillons and La Forêt). Third-generation Jérôme makes the wines while his uncle Patrice manages the vineyards. Though much of the fruit is mechanically harvested, the fruit is generally ripe and concentrated. Vinification is in stainless steel but the crus are aged in large used oak. Quality is generally very good with an intense, vibrant fruit character and reasonable depth, though the wines can miss a little extra concentration in more difficult vintages. In addition to those below, small quantities of the grands crus Valmur and Vaudésir and premier cru Mont de Milieu are also made.

Recommended Whites:
Chablis Grand Cru Les Clos ★★★ £E
Chablis Grand Cru Blanchot ★★★ £E
Chablis Premier Cru Côte de Léchet ★★ £D
Chablis Premier Cru Montmains ★★ £D
Chablis Premier Cru Montée de Tonnerre ★★ £D
Chablis Premier Cru Vaillons ★★ £D
Chablis Premier Cru La Forêt ★★ £D   Chablis ★ £C

Other wines of note (all whites)

Dom. Alain Besson
Chablis ★★ £C
Chablis Premier Cruvaillons ★★★ £C
Chablis Premier Cru Montmains ★★★ £D
Dom. de La Concièrgerie
Chablis Premier Cru Montmains ★★★ £D
Dom. Jean Collet et Fils
Chablis ★★ £C
Chablis Premier Cru Vaillons ★★★ £D
Chablis Premier Cru Montmains ★★★ £D
Chablis Grand Cruvalmur ★★★★ £E
Dom. Dauvissat-Camus
Petit Chablis ★ £C
Chablis Premier Cruvaillons ★★★ £D
Chablis Premier Cru La Forest ★★★ £D
Chablis Grand Cru Les Clos ★★★★ £F
Dom. d'Élise
Chablis ★★ £C
Dom. Alain Gautheron
Chablis Premier Cru Les Fourneaux Vieilles Vignes ★★★ £D
Dom. des Geneves
Chablis Vieille Vigne ★★ £D
Dom. Alain Geoffroy
Chablis Dom. Le Verger ★★ £C
Chablis Vieilles Vignes Dom. Le Verger ★★ £C
Chablis Premier Cru Beauroy ★★ £D
Chablis Premier Cru Fourchaume ★★★ £D
Chablis Grand Cru Les Clos ★★★★ £F
Dom. Jean Goulley et Fils
Chablis ★★ £C   Chablis Premier Cru Fourchaume ★★ £D
Chablis Premier Cru Montmains ★★★★ £D
Dom. Hamelin
Chablis Vieilles Vignes ★★ £C
Chablis Premier Cru Beauroy ★★ £D
Chablis Premier Cruvau Ligneau ★★★ £D
Louis Jadot
Chablis ★★ £C

Chablis Premier Cru Côte De Lechet ★★★ £D
Chablis Premier Cru Fourchaume ★★★ £D
Chablis Grand Cru Preuses ★★★★ £E
Dom. de La Meulière
Chablis Premier Cru Fourchaume ★★★ £C
Dom. Millet
Chablis ★★ £B
Chablis Vieilles Vignes ★★ £C
Chablis Premier Cruvaucoupin ★★★ £D
Sylvain Mosnier
Chablis ★★ £C
Chablis Vieilles Vignes ★★ £C
Chablis Premier Cru Beauroy ★★★ £D
Chablis Premier Cru Côte de Léchet ★★★ £D
Dom. Oudin
Chablis ★★ £C
Chablis Les Serres ★★ £C
Chablis Premier Cru Vaugiraut ★★★ £D
Chablis Premier Cru Vaucoupin ★★★ £D
Francine et Olivier Savary
Chablis ★★ £C
Chablis Vieilles Vignes ★★ £C
Chablis Premier Cru Fourchaume ★★★ £D
Dom. Laurent Tribut
Chablis ★ £C
Chablis Premier Cru Beauroy ★★ £D
Chablis Premier Cru Montmains ★★★ £D
Chablis Premier Cru Côte de Léchet ★★★ £D
Dom. J C & D. Tupinier
Chablis ★★ £C
Chablis Premier Cruvaillons ★★ £D
Chablis Premier Cru Montmains ★★★ £D
Chablis Premier Cru Montée De Tonnerre ★★★ £D
Dom. de Vauroux
Chablis Vieilles Vignes ★ £D
Chablis Premier Cru Montmains ★ £D
Chablis Premier Cru Montée De Tonnerre ★★ £D
Chablis Grand Cru Bougros ★★★ £E

Author's choice

A selection of classic Chablis
Billaud-Simon   Chablis Grand Cru Vaudésir
Samuel Billaud   Chablis Premier Cru Mont de Milieu
Jean-Claude Bessin   Grand Cru Valmur
Adhémar & Francis Boudin   Chablis Premier Cru L'Homme Mort
Dom. Du Colombier   Chablis Grand Cru Bougros
Jean et Sébastien Dauvissat   Chablis Grand Cru Preuses
René et Vincent Dauvissat   Chablis Grand Cru Les Clos
Dom. Bernard Defaix   Chablis Premier Cru Côte de Léchet
Jean-Paul Droin   Chablis Premier Cru Montée de Tonnerre
Joseph Drouhin   Chablis Grand Cru Vaudésir
William Févre   Chablis Premier Cru Vaulorent
Jean-Pierre Grossot   Chablis Premier Cru Mont de Milieu
Domaine d'Henri Chablis Premier Cru Fourchaumes Vieilles Vignes
Dom. Laroche   Chablis Vielle Voye (new see main entry)
Dom. des Malandes Chablis Premier Cru Côte de Léchet
Dom. Louis Michel Chablis Premier Cru Montée de Tonnerre
Christian Moreau Père et Fils   Chablis Grand Cru Valmur
Moreau-Naudet   Chablis Premier Cru Montée de Tonnerre
Dom. Pinson   Chablis Grand Cru Le Clos

Denis Race Chablis Montmains Vieilles Vignes
Dom. Raveneau   Chablis Grand Cru Blanchots

Good value Chablis & Yonne whites
Dom. Barat   Chablis
Jean-Claude Bessin   Chablis Vieilles Vignes
Billaud-Simon   Chablis Tête d'Or
Jean-Marc Brocard   Chablis Vieilles Vignes Dom. Sainte-Claire
Joseph Drouhin   Chablis Dom. de Vaudon
William Fevre   Chablis
Ghislaine et Jean-Hugues Goisot   Bourgogne Côte d'Auxerre
Ghislaine et Jean-Hugues Goisot   Saint Bris
Dom. Laroche   Chablis Saint-Martin
Dom. des Malandes   Petit Chablis
Dom. Oudin   Chablis
Didier & Pascal Picq   Chablis Vieilles Vignes
Denis Race   Chablis

Burgundy /Côte d'Or & Côte Chalonnaise

What a difference a new generation and a responsive market can make. Younger, highly-trained and talented winemakers have played their part in transforming quality in this the most complex and magical of France's wine regions. No stronger argument can be made for the validity of terroir than in Burgundy, where subtle differences of climate, soil composition and aspect identified over the course of centuries and expressed in individual climats make this region so complex and fascinating. Red Burgundy should enthrall with its perfume, complexity, finesse and textural qualities rather than power, oak and out-and-out concentration. White Burgundy should express complexity in both aroma and flavour, be it more minerally or buttery and nutty, and have a depth, structure and balance proportionate to its origins. Both should be more than just the most noble expression of two grapes, now familiar the world over, Pinot Noir and Chardonnay.

A change of direction

In the Côte d'Or, Burgundy's heart, the fragmentation of the vineyard area is extreme, and a complete contrast to Bordeaux's more coherent, larger patchwork. With a few rows here and a few there and the difficulties of vinifying such small quantities of grapes, it made sense to sell to a *négociant* as almost all growers did in the early 20th century. The cost in terms of quality has been well documented but through buying, trading and marriage a host of new independent growers have provided much of the impetus for higher quality.

Yet as recently as 20 years ago Burgundy was in dire straits. Excessive use of potassium and other chemicals on the soils (especially in the Côte de Nuits) led to reduced natural acidity levels and the dependence on pesticides, in turn leading to generally debilitated vineyard health. The resulting grapes were low in both sugar and acidity. Many producers considered it necessary to both overchaptalize and acidify, a dual-pronged desperation made illegal in 1987. Whilst one practice or the other may be employed within strict limits there is little doubt that some producers still continue to do both despite some high-profile prosecutions by the authorities. Others, though, have sought to restore the health of their vineyards and obtain grapes of high quality and a new order of producers has emerged, better qualified but more often than not getting back to basics. They have improved the soil and plant health and consequently that of the grapes and wines. A movement towards organic and biodynamic viticulture has been stronger here than probably anywhere else in the wine-producing world. Currently many top estates take the advice of soil scientist Claude Bourguignon to enhance further the quality of their soils. Another consequence of the Burgundy's weak constitution was a tendency towards excessive fining and filtration in order to ensure the wine's stability. Better fruit quality as well as widely expressed criticism of heavy reliance on these practices, mean this trend has been reversed. Lower yields have been advocated too with much debate about how they should be achieved; whether through winter pruning, increasing vine densities, the use of different rootstocks or green harvesting.

The best wines are now cleaner, riper and much more consistent even in more difficult years – though in the 1990s nature seems to have rewarded the many varied efforts – yet the wines are far from standardised. And even though there has been a general trend to ever bigger, oakier and more concentrated wines, at least some succeed admirably in retaining balance without losing the stamp of *terroir*. Where there were pockets of quality and occasional bright spots in some of the larger appellations now there are many producers turning out consistently high-quality wines. Yet from too many of the big merchants or négociants the wines continue to be very mediocre and it is why so many of them are missing from the following producer profiles. The ones included are the exception and in some instances are very good indeed. Much of the best wine comes from the smaller growers but an increasing number now also buy in some grapes.

Côte d'Or

The basic hierarchy in the Côte d'Or is of grands crus at the top, followed by premiers crus – always associated with one of 25 villages (premiers crus are often blended together due to fragmentation, so labelled simply Premier Cru) – then the level of the village itself (e.g. Gevrey-Chambertin) before the sub-regional appellations (such as Côte de Nuits-Villages) and finally the regional generics: **Bourgogne Rouge** (Pinot Noir), **Bourgogne Blanc** (Chardonnay) and **Bourgogne Aligoté**. The lowest level is not necessarily the humblest, however, as wine from any level may be sold as a generic (for instance, recently replanted vines that have only just come into production or vines that lie just outside a classified area). It is also worth noting that premier cru wine may also be included in part of a village-level bottling. This may be due to insufficient quantities for a separate bottling or a grower's decision not to compromise the integrity of his premier cru when faced with unsatisfactory quality in a difficult vintage. Also important to understanding the appellation system in Burgundy is the concept of climat or individual vineyard areas. Occasionally only part of a named area may be designated premier cru (e.g Chambolle-Musigny la Combe d'Orveaux) while within the unclassified village areas (which may be large, as in Meursault) the named vineyards (lieux-dits) may be added to the label (e.g. Meursault Tillets). The best of these will be close to premier cru level, just as several premiers crus are comparable to some of the less well-defined grands crus. Note too that the spelling of a particular vineyard can vary slightly from one producer to another. What follows is a brief breakdown of the most important villages and their most important crus.

Côte de Nuits

Production from the more northerly Côte de Nuits is almost exclusively red. **Marsannay** and **Fixin** at the north end of the Côte de Nuits, begin the band of mostly east-facing hills that stretches, with twists and breaks, until Santenay and Maranges in the tail of the Côte de Beaune. Marsannay tends to be light but scented and produces, unusually for the Côte de Nuits, a significant amount of rosé and white. Fixin in contrast, produces quite forceful, earthy Burgundy, including some powerful reds from premiers crus on slopes above the village. The wine, like that from the southern end of the Côte de Nuits, can be sold as **Côte de Nuits-Villages**. After the briefest of interludes (around Brochon) begins Burgundy's great rich seam of red.

Gevrey-Chambertin has 26 premiers crus including the outstanding Clos Saint-Jacques (grand cru in all but name) and Les Cazetiers at the centre of an arc of premiers crus on slopes to the east of the town. South of the village itself begins the great chain of grands crus that run almost to the southern edge of Vosne-Romanée. Of the nine in Gevrey, the 12.9 ha **Chambertin** and 15 ha **Clos-de-Bèze** are easily the most important. Seven

Wine behind the label

others all append the name Chambertin: **Mazis-Chambertin** and **Ruchottes-Chambertin** are arguably the next best in potential; **Griottes-Chambertin**, **Charmes-Chambertin** (under which much of **Mazoyères-Chambertin** is sold) and **Chapelle-Chambertin** are also capable of greatness; the last, **Latricières-Chambertin**, rarely reaches the quality of the best premiers crus. Gevrey at any level should be distinguished by its greater power, concentration and structure than its neighbouring communes. Despite a radical improvement, too much of it remains pretty poor. **Morey-Saint-Denis** undeservedly lacks the lustre of Gevrey and Chambolle, but can combine the muscle of the former with the elegance of the latter, though which prevails to the greater degree depends as much on the grower as the on vineyard site. A tiny amount of white is made here too. While significantly smaller than Gevrey, it still boasts 20 premiers crus and four grands crus – **Clos de la Roche** (17 ha), **Clos Saint-Denis** (6.6 ha), **Clos des Lambrays** (8.8 ha) and **Clos de Tart** (7.5 ha) – as well as a thin slice of the 15 ha **Bonnes Mares** which falls mostly in **Chambolle-Musigny**. Bonnes Mares, with its mixed soils, is of variable style but is usually sturdier when sourced from the Morey end of the vineyards. Then the chain of grands crus is broken, before continuing with **Le Musigny** (10.7 ha) at the southern end of the commune. Some fine premier cru vineyards lie between the two, including Cras, Fuées and Baudes, but closest in style and proximity to Musigny are the often superb Amoureuses and Charmes. Musigny, like no other cru, can express the sumptuous elegant beauty of red Burgundy.

The commune of **Vougeot** is dominated by the massive 50 ha grand cru of **Clos Vougeot**. Though continuous and walled-in, in its lower, flatter reaches it juts deep into what corresponds to only village-quality land in neighbouring Vosne-Romanée. Arguably it ought to be partitioned into three different levels. Without due care you may find you have paid a grand cru price for what is, in effect, only village-level wine, although your choice of grower among the 80 owners of the vineyard counts for as much as the position of the vines. At its highest it adjoins both Musigny and Grands Echezeaux and at its best it is full, rich and complex if less aristocratic than the former. Both of the grands crus **Echezeaux** and **Grands Echezeaux** (with 32 ha and 9 ha respectively in production) fall in the commune of Flagey-Echezeaux. At their best both produce sturdy, characterful Burgundy, though much of Echezeaux lacks the class expected in a grand cru. Neighbouring **Vosne-Romanée** is a commune like no other in the Côte de Nuits. Behind the village lie the great vineyards that produce Burgundy's most expensive and sought-after wines. At the heart of 27 ha of grands crus are **La Romanée** (0.85 ha) and **Romanée-Conti** (1.8 ha) with **Richebourg** (8 ha) to the north, **Romanée-Saint-Vivant** (9.4 ha) closer to the village, and **La Grande Rue** (1.65 ha) and **La Tâche** (6.1 ha) to the south. These in turn are flanked by some marvellous premiers crus including Malconsorts, Chaumes and Clos des Réas on the southern edge of the commune with Nuits-Saint-Georges; with Brûlées, Suchots and Beaux Monts on the northern side, the latter two pressing up against Echezeaux. The best of these are rich, intense and concentrated but with varying degrees of finesse, opulence or silkiness, dependent as much on producer as location. Village-level Vosne comes from east of the village.

The last major village in the Côtes de Nuits is **Nuits-Saint-Georges** though vineyards continue on south to Comblanchien. Here, the best wines offer power and intensity as well as a degree of finesse in the best of 38 premiers crus (which extend into the more southerly

commune of Prémeaux). Damodes, Boudots and Murgers are some of the best between Nuits-Saint-Georges (the town) and Vosne-Romanée; Vaucrains, Pruliers and Les Saint-Georges are the most notable to the south of Nuits. There are no grand crus. Lesser wine can be flavoursome if chunky but the worst is rough and dilute. The cooler hinterland of the Côte de Nuits contains pockets of vineyards in favourable sites which constitute the **Hautes-Côtes de Nuits**. South of the town of Beaune is the equivalent **Hautes-Côtes de Beaune**. A significant amount of the wine is made by the co-op Les Caves des Hautes-Côtes; these wines or an example from a top grower can be good in an exceptional vintage.

Côte de Beaune

The Côte de Beaune's reputation is more for white than red yet the majority of wines are in fact red. From here south the gradients are lower and the swathe of vineyards wider, occasionally receding into the hills behind the main slopes. It begins in a cluster of villages around the famous hill of Corton. The humble AC of **Ladoix** (with seven premiers crus) is not widely seen and some of thewine is sold under the sub-regional appellation of **Côte de Beaune-Villages**. Wine for the latter can also come from another 15 villages, making it much more important than the Nuits equivalent. **Aloxe-Corton** at the foot of the Corton hill includes the famous appellations of Corton and Corton-Charlemagne, though vineyards spill into adjoining Ladoix and Pernand-Vergelesses. Most of the white from Burgundy's largest grand cru is sold as **Corton-Charlemagne** (51 ha) and most of the red as **Corton** (98 ha), though there is a little white Corton too (2.5 ha). The trend to planting Chardonnay begun in the mid-19th century continues, the paler soils at the top of the hill being the best site. Great Corton-Charlemagne is full-bodied but slow-developing due to a powerful structure and requires patience. Red Corton (which oftens attaches one of several *lieu-dit* names) can be similarly austere when young but develops a richness and a distinctive minerally elegance with age. Aloxe-Corton AC, almost entirely red, includes 13 premiers crus which lie directly below the red Corton vineyards. To the west of the Aloxe-Corton commune lies **Pernand-Vergelesses**, some of it tucked into the folds in the hills. Increasingly good red and white is made under the AC. The best premier cru, Ile des Vergelesses, favours reds of finesse rather than power but they add weight with age. To the south, it adjoins **Savigny-lès-Beaune**, which extends east up a little valley to the village itself. The best vineyards lie on both sides, the more northern band of premiers crus (including Guettes, Serpentières and Lavières) are more elegant than those from the southern band (including Dominodes, Marconnets, Narbantons and Peuillets), which tend to be fuller and firmer. Importantly, this is a reasonably plentiful source of good-value Burgundy. Rarely exciting is wine from **Chorey-lès-Beaune**, from flat land to the east of the Savigny AC.

Beaune, historically and commercially, is the heart of Burgundy but it is also one of the three leading Côte de Beaune red wine villages and includes some excellent premiers crus from the gentle slopes west of the town. Due to diverse soil types, leading premiers crus vary from the full and firm to softer, more elegant wines. Marconnets, Fèves and Bressandes are of the first category, Grèves and Teurons are richer and softer, Clos des Mouches full but elegant too. Important vineyard owners such as Jadot, Albert Morot, Bouchard Père and Drouhin all provide the opportunity to compare and contrast some of the best crus from a single source. Another major vineyard owner, and one of the most important in the Côte de Beaune, is the Hospices de Beaune, their many (often

France

oaky) *cuvées* (unique blends of predominantly premiers crus named for their benefactor) are sold at the famous auction in November. The wines are then 'finished' by the purchasing négociant, a factor that has a further bearing on their (variable) quality. The rarely seen **Côte de Beaune** AC is for a few vineyards in the hills behind Beaune AC. **Pommard** is a continuation of Beaune and its reputation for sturdy, full-bodied reds is in part due to more clayey, often iron-rich, soils than its neighbours. Grands Epenots and Rugiens Bas are the finest premiers crus. In **Volnay** the soils are lighter and poorer, contributing to the wine's refinement and elegance. Most of the best premiers crus come from south of the village, including Taillepieds, Clos des Chênes, Caillerets Dessus and Santenots. Santenots actually lies within the adjacent Meursault but is generally sold as Volnay when made from Pinot Noir, and as Meursault if from Chardonnay. South and west of Volnay an ascending flank of vineyards extends into the hills and includes the villages of **Monthelie**, **Auxey-Duresses** and **Saint-Romain**. The first two can provide excellent reds from several premiers crus but also a little good village white, especially in Auxey-Duresses. Good Saint-Romain white can be better than its position in the Hautes-Côtes de Beaune hills might suggest.

Meursault is one of the three biggest communes in the Côte d'Or and is the most important white wine village. But as with Beaune or Gevrey-Chambertin, with size comes variability. At its worst it is heavy and characterless but good examples are full, ripe and fruit-rich. The finest are intense, stylish and in the case of the would-be grand cru, Perrières, minerally and refined. There are no grands crus but other fine premiers crus include the best examples of Genevrières, Charmes, Poruzots and Goutte d'Or. Village lieux-dits names of note include Chevalières, Grands Charrons, Narvaux, Tessons and Tillets. **Blagny** is a small red wine outpost nestled against Meursault and **Puligny-Montrachet**. 'Puligny' and 'world's best' often share the same sentence and with good reason. The village includes the grands crus **Chevalier-Montrachet** (7.36 ha), **Bienvenues-Bâtard-Montrachet** (3.69 ha) and half of the 8 ha **Le Montrachet** and 6 ha of the 11.87 ha **Bâtard-Montrachet**. Le Montrachet is the greatest, and most expensive, of all but is a wine capable of marvellous concentration, sublime proportions and exquisite complexity. Chevalier-Montrachet, from thinner soils above, is potentially the closest in quality but Bâtard-Montrachet, from flatter vineyards, can offer superb richness and intensity too. There are many outstanding premiers crus which also command high prices. Caillerets (including Les Demoiselles) and Pucelles, adjoining the grands crus, will surpass any grand cru not at its full potential. Clavoillon and Folatières and the more elevated Champ Gain and La Garenne can highlight the Puligny finesse and intensity as can Champ-Canet, Combettes and Referts which extend as far as Meursault's Perrières and Charmes. As well as the continuation of grands crus Le Montrachet and Bâtard-Montrachet, the village of **Chassagne-Montrachet** adds the tiny 1.57 ha grand cru of **Criots-Bâtard-Montrachet**. The wines sold under the Chassagne AC were once predominantly red but its reputation is now emphatically white. Leading premiers crus include Caillerets, Champs Gains, Embrazées, Morgeots, La Romanée and Ruchottes – mostly confined to lighter-coloured soils on the higher slopes. Reds vary from the thin and unripe to full and fleshy and can be a source of good value (they only command around half the price of a white from the same vineyard, thus the trend to white continues). La Boudriotte, Clos Saint-Jean, La Maltroie, Morgeots and Chenevottes are the most noted red premiers crus. Behind Chassagne and Puligny

lies the commune of **Saint-Aubin**. Some remarkably good white is produced by the best growers from the most worthy premier cru vineyards: La Chatenière and those that adjoin Chassagne (Le Charmois) and Puligny (En Remilly and Murgers des Dents de Chien – backing on to the Mont Rachet hill). Reds tend to be relatively light and slightly earthy.

Santenay is the Côte de Beaune's last significant commune for quality as the tail of the vineyard area swings west. From south-facing vineyards red wines dominate, the best of these are both full and stylish. These are likely to come from the premiers crus Gravières, La Comme and Clos des Tavannes that extend to the edge of Chassagne. One or two excellent whites are also being produced. While a fast improving AC with some excellent-value wines, Santenay is not so good from a weaker vintage or from a mediocre producer when the wine may be lean and stalky. To the west the vineyards adjoin **Maranges**, more earthy and robust than the best Santenay, though exceptions exist.

Côte Chalonnaise

The Chalonnaise is not a continuation of the Côte d'Or but an area of less sheltered rolling hills where the grapes ripen later and the wines are lighter. However as a source of quality and value the best growers can provide a real alternative to lesser villages of the Côte d'Or. **Bouzeron**, the first of five separate appellations is classified for Aligoté only, its Pinot Noir and Chardonnay sold as **Bourgogne Côte Chalonnaise**. **Rully** lies east and south of Bouzeron and makes more white than red – both of which can reveal ripe, attractive fruit in a top example. Less ripe Chardonnay is likely to be made into **Crémant de Bourgogne**. South of Rully is **Mercurey**, the region's most important AC. Most of the wine is a quite structured red, surprisingly rich and intense from a combination of a top year and producer, but hard and lean when not. A little good white is also produced. Slightly more supple yet stylish reds are produced in Givry, where the balance of red and white is similar to that of Mercurey. The southernmost appellation is **Montagny**, where exclusively white wine is made. The wines can be fuller if sometimes less distinguished than those from Rully.

A-Z of producers by appellation/region

Burgundy /Côte d'Or & Côte Chalonnaise

France

Henri Felettig	94
Hudelot-Noëllat	100
Jacques-Frédéric Mugnier	110
Dom. Roumier	116
Comte G de Vogüé	118
Vougeot	
Dom. Bertagna	81
Vosne-Romanee	
Arnoux-Lachaux	80
Sylvain Cathiard	85
Bruno Clavelier	88
François Confurion-Gindre	90
Confuron-Cotétidot	90
René Engel	93
Frères et Soeurs	107
Jean Grivot	98
Anne Gros	99
Michel Gros	99
Pascal Lachaux	102
François Lamarche,	103
Vicomte Liger-Belair	106
Dom. Méo-Camuzet	107
Dom. Mugneret-Gibourg	110
Michel Noellat	111
Dom. de la Romanée-Conti	115
Emmanuel Rouget	115
Nuits-Saint-Georges	
Bertrand Ambroise	78
Dom. de l'Arlot	79
Robert Chevillon	87
Jean-Jacques Confuron	89
Dom. Faiveley	94
Dom. Henri Gouges	97
Dominique Laurent	104
Chantal Lescure	106
Alain Michelot	108
Dom. des Perdrix	91
Nicolas Potel	113
Daniel Rion	114
Michele & Patrice Rion	114
Patrice Rion	115
Dom. de la Vougeraie	118
Hautes Cotes de Beaune	
Jean-Yves Devevey	91
Aloxe-Corton	
Comte Senard	116
Corton-Charlemagne	
Dom. Bonneau du Martray	83
Pernand-Vergelesses	
Dom. Rapet Père et Fils	114
Savigny-les-Beaune	
Simon Bize et Fils	81
Chandon de Briailles	86
Maurice Ecard et Fils	93
Jean-Jacques Girard	96
Dom. Antonin Guyon	99
Jean-Marc Pavelot	111
Chorey-les-Beaune	
Tollot-Beaut	117
Beaune	
Dom. de Bellene	81

Dom. Albert Bichot	81
Bouchard Père et Fils	83
Maison Champy	85
Dom. Chanson	86
Chanson Père et Fils	86
Dom. du Clos Frantin	81
Ch. de la Commaraine	101
Drouhin-Laroze	92
Joseph Drouhin	91
Dom. Gagey	101
Camille Giroud	97
Grands Vins de Bourgogne	97
AF & Parent F Gros	98
Louis Jadot	100
Marquis de Laguiche	92
Louis Latour	104
Lucien Lemoine	105
Duc de Magenta	101
Albert Morot	110
Dom. du Pavillon	81
Pommard	
Comte Armand	79
Jean-Marc Boillot	82
Dom. de Courcel	90
Volnay	
Marquis d'Angerville	79
Jean Boillot et Fils	82
Dom. Carré-Courbin	85
Micel Lafarge	102
Deux Montille	108
Hubert de Montille	108
Dom. de la Pousse d'or	113
Joseph Voillot	118
Monthelie	
Darviot-Perrin	91
Auxey-Duresses	
Dom. Leroy	105
Dom. Agnès Pacquet	111
Saint-Romain	
Dom. d'Auvenay	80
Meursault	
Michel Bouzereau	84
Dom. Boyer-Martenot	84
J-F Coche-Dury	89
Arnaud Ente	94
Jean-Philippe Fichet	95
Jean-Michel Gaunoux	95
Dom. Génot-Boulanger	96
Henri Germain et Fils	96
Albert Grivault	98
Patrick Javillier	101
Antoine Jobard	101
Remi Jobard	101
Comtes des Lafon	103
Latour-Giraud	104
Dom. Matrot	107
François Mikulski	108
Dom. Morey Blanc	109
Pierre Morey	109
Jacques Prieur	113
Dom. Roulot	115

Stephane Aladame	78
Darviot-Perrin	91
Puligny-Montrachet	
François Carillon	85
Jacques Carillon	85
Ch. de Puligny-Pontrachet	87
Alain Chavy	87
Dom. Leflaive	100
Olivier Leflaive	105
Paul Pernot et Fils	111
Etienne Sauzet	116
Chassagne-Montrachet	
Guy Amiot et Fils	78
Blain-Gagnard	82
Château de la Maltroye	86
Michel Colin-Deléger	89
Vincent Dancer	91
Richard Fontaine-Gagnard	95
Jean-Noel Gagnard	95
Vincent et François Jouard	102
Bernard Moreau et Fils	108
Michel Morey-Coffinet	110
Marc Morey	109
Thomas Morey	109
Vincent & Sophie Morey	109
Michel Niellon	111
Fernand & Laurent Pillot	112
Jean Pillot et Fils	112
Dom. Ramonet	113
Saint-Aubin	
Dom. Marc Colin et Fils	89
Hubert Lamy	103
Santenay	
Roger Belland	80

Denis et Françoise Clair	88
Vincent Girardin	96
Cote Chalonnaise	
Bouzeron	
A et P de Villaine	113
Rully	
Michel Briday	84
Vincent Dureuil-Janthial	93
Henri et Paul Jacqueson	100
Claudie Jobard	101
Mercurey	
Dom. Brintet	84
Ch. de Chamirey	91
Dom. Devillard	91
Emile Juillot	102
Michel Juillot	102
Dom. Lorenzon	106
Ch. de Mercey	115
François Raquillet	114
Antonin Rodet	115
Ch. de Rully	115
Givry	
Dom. Chofflet-Valdenaire	87
Clos Salomon	88
Dom. de La Ferte	91
Dom. Joblot	102
François Lumpp	107
Montagny	
Stéphane Aladame	78
Other	
Verget	118

Côte d'Or & Côte Chalonnaise vintages

In general terms red Burgundy doesn't offer the same potential longevity as do Bordeaux or other great Cabernet-based wines. Exceptional wines, both red and white, can, however, be very long-lived. As ageing potential is influenced by both origin and the style favoured by a given producer, the general vintage characteristics detailed below need to be considered together with remarks made in the individual producer profiles. The very best estates, aided by a generally fine run of vintages in the past decade or so, now produce consistently high quality. Yet away from the top names and most famous sites the choice of vintage remains crucial, especially at a lower level, given the struggle for ripeness in Burgundy's many more marginal vineyard sites.

2015: A long hot summer in the Côte d'Or and Chalonnais has ensured some rich wines in both colours. But as so often, when the temperature soars, a cautious approach is needed and these are early days. 2015 is undoubtedly a dramatic 'solar' year in the Côte, almost Californian in its extremes of heat in July and August. The red wines are ripe, plump and generous, with particularly good wines at regional and villages level – showing good value and a higher level of quality in this vintage. It was an excellent vintage for Côte de Beaune reds and the bigger crus of Gevrey Chambertin, Morey St Denis and Nuits St Georges are the places to look for very high quality (a brilliant Clos des Lambrays 2015 tasted sur place in June 2016). However, there is less terroir expression, as is typical

Burgundy /Côte d'Or & Côte Chalonnaise

France

in a warmer year, and some wines picked a little late lack balance especially when there is a sense of heat or alcohol on the finish. White Burgundies from 2015 are altogether more variable. The best wines were picked early and show ripe orchard stone fruits like peach and apricot, aligned with low but ripe acidity – generous, succulent, perfumed. The rest can be very ripe and broad rather than elegant. The reds' market is bullish, resulting in sharply rising prices- now that frost-afflicted 2016 looks like being the smallest vintage in Burgundy since 1974.

2014: As Burgundians ruefully remember, this was a roller coaster summer season in spades. A warm spring and successful flowering in early June had raised hopes of a ripe and generous harvest. Alas, the weather turned nasty on June 28, a serious hail storm wreaking havoc (again!) in Beaune, Pommard, Volnay and parts of Meursault. Damage was extensive but at least happened so early that it did not affect eventual quality unduly. July was pretty sunless, wet and wetter still in August. The Suzuki fruit fly hungrily piqued the grapes of Pinot Noir, particularly in the Côte de Nuits, so selection and tables de tri would be essential - vignerons were facing an unripe, rot-incipient harvest.   Thank the Lord, their prayers were answered, as the sun came out at August's end, a north wind blew and the harvest was picked under ideal warm and sunny conditions. In the end, it all ended well in a good vintage for red wines, showing fidelity of terroir(s) expression. Yet above all, 2014 is likely to be a great white Burgundy vintage in the Côte de Beaune and the Chalonnais – also, some say, the best year in the Mâconnais since 1999.

2013: Once again, yields have been substantially reduced, resulting in a small crop which will inevitably lead to higher prices. A poor, wet spring and early summer caused *millerandage* and uneven fruit setting. Worst of all, a massive hailstorm on July 23 decimated many vineyards in the Côtes de Beaune in particular. But what has been produced appears to be of good quality, with fresh, well-balanced whites and sturdy reds which will require long cellaring. With careful selection, some great wines are promised in this vintage.

2012: Cold weather, right up to the end of June, together with some hail, seriously affected the flowering and yields were dramatically reduced, with some producers making little or no wine at all. But from mid July, right up to the end of September, the weather changed for the better, saving the vintage from being an utter disaster. What has been made, however, is of excellent quality, both red and white, resulting wines of deep concentration and of lasting qualities. A difficult vintage to produce, but those who managed to see it through were well rewarded.

2011: The size of the crop came almost bang in the middle of those of 2009 and 2010 and there was more evenness of fruit. A hot spring followed by a cool June and wet July had some growers worried, but the weather picked up in August followed by some splendid harvesting conditions in September, which led to a lot of smiles all round particularly for the reds. Rully was badly hit by hail twice, but the rest of the appellations seemed to have escaped major damage. What white Rullys did escape, seem to have been made into some of the best whites of the vintage which once again produced whites which should be drunk up earlier rather than later. Reds are a different story - they are lighter than the wines of the two previous vintages, but show a great deal of finesse and purity which means that they could be approached earlier than the 2009s and 2010s, but with nevertheless enough staying power to make them cellarworthy for the medium term.

2010: Production was down on average by 25% over 2009 and the vintage was marked by colder than average temperatures until the end of June resulting in some late and irregular flowering. July was hot but was accompanied by some violent hail storms, particularly in the southern part of the area, which led to more unevenness in the crop. August was warm but a little wet, which added to the unevenness, especially in the south, but a sunny and fine September saved the day somewhat, especially for the reds in the Côte de Nuits. As a result, there are some very good reds - well worth cellaring - but the whites have less staying power and should be consumed earlier rather than later, but with careful selection one will be able to find ageworthy wines from Puligny, Chassagne and Meursault. Côte Chalonnais reds are also very sound.

2009: This almost certainly seems to be turning out to be an exceptional vintage for reds and also very promising indeed for whites. Growing conditions for both Pinot Noir and Chardonnay were good right through the summer. During ripening rainfall was lower than normal and both heat and sunshine hours were above average producing grapes with excellent flavour intensity. The reds are very flattering, forward and fleshy and while acidities are low and tannins relatively soft the wines are also very elegant. The whites are full of fresh, attractive fruit as well as excellent acidity.

2008: A difficult vintage with insufficient sunshine almost right up to the beginning of September but then once again, the north wind came to the rescue with dry sunny days for the most part from the middle of September which saved the harvest. However, rot and mildew was rife and the *vignerons* had to make careful selections at the sorting tables. The result is that quantities are down, but what has been made by those who carefully selected is clean and pure - especially the reds. This is a vintage where you really have to taste before you buy - the wines are very variable, but the best are really top quality.

2007: After some unusual and extraordinary hot weather in April, the Burgundy growers got themselves mentally ready for harvesting in August. However, the weather took a decided turn for the worse from mid May until August with cool, damp weather provoking an unusual amount of rot among the vines, leaving the *vignerons* with difficult and stressful work on their hands if they were to save anything from the vintage. Fortunately, Nature lent a hand from the last week in August until the middle of September with dry and windy weather which saved the day for the whites a little more than the predominately rot-prone Pinot Noirs. As a result, the reds are forward and light, for early drinking rather than keeping, although some of them are quite charming, whilst the better whites, with both backbone and acidity are potential classics although there is great variation in the vintage.

2006: To follow 2005 would always be difficult, especially for reds. The somewhat erratic growing season gave producers a difficult time. The cool wet August following the heat of June and July worked for some but caused problems for others. Good September weather helped too but this is another vintage where real quality, with depth and structure as well as ripeness, will only come from those producers whose skill and vineyard management ensured top quality grapes. In general terms whites edge reds for quality.

2005: Bordeaux had much of the media attention but 2005 is undoubtedly a superlative vintage in Burgundy too. Nature seems to have conspired to get everything right. A relatively dry growing season, timely rain and a warm finish and harvest resulted in very healthy, ripe fruit. Quantities are slightly below the recent average and there are many outstanding reds, particularly from the Côte de Nuits and northern Côte de Beaune but also in the Chalonnaise. Whites can be excellent but are variable (if sometimes very good) from hail-affected Puligny, Chassagne and Santenay.

2004: All change after 2003, it was cool, wet and grey, despite finishing with a decent September. Worse it was hit by hail and oidium (mildew which attacks the grapes). As in Chablis yields are very high unless the potential crop was constantly cut back in the vineyard. Whites can be very good if missing the extra depth and structure of an outstanding year. Reds are very producerdependent but can be supremely elegant and *terroir*-driven from a top grower.

2003: An extraordinarily hot year that required both intelligence and speed from growers. Quantities are small and much, often raisined, fruit had to be discarded. Ripe to very ripe reds with good substance but not refined or classically structured. Good quality can be had from lesser appellations where the grapes usually struggle to ripen. Whites are generally disappointing, but variable from grower to grower. Many have a ripe, exotic fruit appeal but are overblown and lack structure so drinking now.

2002: An exciting red wine vintage despite a warm but wet early September. Yields were low, the grapes small but high in sugar, with good colour and acidity that has ensured intense, ripe and ageworthy wines throughout the Côte d'Or. Some of the most exceptional reds have come from Volnay and Nuits-Saint-Georges. Whites are very good too (including the Chalonnaise) with concentration, structure, perfectly ripe fruit and good balance - the best cellaring prospect for white Burgundy in more than a decade.

2001: As in 2000 the Côte de Nuits did better than Côte de Beaune (in Volnay and Pommard quantities were reduced by hail). A wet year with a mostly fine finish - only the best-managed vineyards produced ripe, concentrated grapes with good acidities. Reds have improved considerably in the bottle and show good *terroir* expression. Whites were variable - some have both good acidity and concentration but others lack ripeness - not for keeping.

2000: In red this was a much better vintage in the Côte de Nuits than the Côte de Beaune. Santenay was particularly badly affected by rain. Not one to cellar but fine quality further up the hierarchy. Generally a very good vintage for whites if highish yields and slightly less consistent than 1999. Most have aged better than the disappointing evolution seen in the whites of 96, 97 and 98.

1999: A generally excellent large vintage for reds with remarkable colour, good acidity and ripe tannins. The size of the crop encouraged growers to be more rigorous in removing the less promising bunches. These reds, particularly good in the Côte de Beaune, are vigorous and intense and only the generic or more humble village appellations should have been drunk yet. Whites were plentiful too, and, though more variable than the reds, initially showed very well, especially from the top estates. While a better bet than for keeping than previous late 90s vintages here too some bottles have proved less ageworthy than expected. Some excellent reds were made in the Chalonnaise.

1998: A problematic growing season lowered expectations but this has turned out to be a vintage with more potential for reds than 1997 thanks to better acidity and more stuffing. Quantities were down due to severe Easter frosts. Though generally very good, quality is much more irregular at a lower level, with a lack of full ripeness in the tannins due in part to some very hot August days. Isolated hail hit the volume of whites, especially in Meursault, and quality was variable, some lacking concentration. Almost all have evolved quite quickly.

1997: A much smaller vintage of more forward reds than 1996 but very attractive and one that has already given much pleasure. The wines have lowish acidities but it a red vintage that can still provide good drinking now. Whites can had lowish acidities too but despite no lack of richness or intensity in the top wines many have developed very quickly.

1996: One of the finest red wine vintages of the 1990s, with both quantity and quality at the top level. Among the best growers there is excellent fruit intensity and ripeness in the tannins (although in some cases tannins have not softened) allied to good acidity that will repay further keeping. Many remain closed but more humble appellations from a good grower can be drunk now. Also exceptional for reds from the Chalonnaise, if largely of academic interest now.

1995: Not a vintage of great richness in the reds but fine nonetheless. The best have added weight with age, are ripe and structured and will still improve. An excellent vintage for whites, although some wines have suffered from the same premature ageing that beset late 90s vintages.

1994: Arguably the weakest red wine vintage in the last 15 years but there is not much between this and 1992 in quality. A better bet in the Côte de Nuits than the Côte de Beaune. Whites are merely attractive when from a good producer, others are best left for the unwary.

1993: A very fine red wine vintage with great vigour, structure and intensity. Good village-level examples or those from lesser climats should be drunk now but the best will still improve. Much weaker in the whites, though a few both concentration and structure providing rich, mature drinking now.

1992: A large red harvest, though not as much as 1990, and some of it full and charming though missing the extra concentration or structure of a really good vintage. Producers noted for their low yields are a safer bet though generally there is a lack of intensity and definition. Whites showed some delicious fruit but only in the top examples can this still be enjoyed.

1991: Many rich, concentrated and structured reds. The best still have plenty of life but some lack harmony and fully ripe tannins. Find a good bottle, though, and it's likely to be much cheaper than the 1990 of the same wine. Good drinking now, though a handful might keep a bit longer. Whites were mostly ordinary at best and should only be bought with extreme care.

1990: A superlative vintage for red wines and unequalled in recent decades for the overall quality of the vintage, though due to vinicultural improvements many individual producers have made wines of higher quality since. A very good vintage for whites too. Many fine bottles, including those from some of the lesser climats, and these will last for many years to come.

1989: A warm, plentiful vintage with relatively low acidity in the reds, though it is still good at top level. Whites had particularly good structure and have proved more long-lived than 1988, 90 or 92.

1988: A rather firm, austere vintage with high acidity and tannins in the reds. It has taken a long time to come into its own but the best examples can now revealing the underlying refinement. Some whites have aged well.

Earlier Years: At the top level 1985 can still provide good drinking, though whites are a safer bet as the once rich, ripe reds are mostly past their best due to low acidity levels. A few of the structured reds from the 1983 vintage can still be vigorous where rot was avoided. Even older vintages might only be considered for an outstanding cru from an impeccable source. Vintages from the 1970s include 78, 76 and 71 while the more successful 1960s include 69, 66, 64, 62 and 61. For these and wines from any older vintages, however, consider the advice of a trusted merchant or friend who still has other bottles of the same wine, or consult Michael Broadbent's Vintage Wine.

Burgundy /Côte d'Or & Côte Chalonnaise

France

Côte d'Or & Côte Chalonnaise vintage chart

	Côte de Nuits Red	Côte de Beaune Red	Côte Chalonnaise Red	Côte de Beaune White
2015	★★★★ A	★★★★ A	★★★★ A	★★★ A
2014	★★★★ A	★★★★ A	★★★★ A	★★★★☆ A
2013	★★★★ A	★★★★ A	★★★★ A	★★★★ B
2012	★★★★ A	★★★★ A	★★★★ A	★★★★ A
2011	★★★★ A	★★★★ B	★★★★ B	★★★★ B
2010	★★★★☆ A	★★★★ A	★★★★ A	★★★★☆ A
2009	★★★★ A	★★★★ A	★★★ B	★★★★ B
2008	★★★ B	★★★ B	★★★ B	★★★ B
2007	★★★ B	★★★★ B	★★★ B	★★★★ B
2006	★★★★ B	★★★★ B	★★★★ B	★★★★ B
2005	★★★★★ B	★★★★★ B	★★★★ B	★★★★ B
2004	★★★★ C	★★★★ C	★★★★ C	★★★★ C
2003	★★★ C	★★★ C	★★★★ C	★★★ C
2002	★★★ C	★★★ C	★★★ C	★★ C
2001	★★★★ C	★★★★ C	★★★★☆ C	★★★★ C
2000	★★★★ C	★★★★ C	★★★★ C	★★★★ C
1999	★★★★☆ C	★★★★ C	★★★★ C	★★★ C
1998	★★★★ C	★★★★ C	★★★★ C	★★★★ C
1997	★★★ C	★★★★ C	★★★ C	★★★ C
1996	★★★★ C	★★★★ C	★★★ C	★★ D
1995	★★★★ C	★★★★ C	★★★ C	★★★ C
1995	★★★★ C	★★★★ C	★★★ C	★★★ C
1993	★★★★ C	★★★★ C	★★★ C	★★ D
1991	★★★★★ C	★★★★ C	★★★★ C	★ D
1990	★★★★ D	★★★★ C	★★★★ C	★★★★ D
1989	★★★★ C	★★★★ C	★★★★ C	★★★★ D
1988	★★★★ D	★★★★ C	★★★★ D	★★★★ D

A-Z of producers

Stéphane Aladame (Montagny)   *www.aladame.fr*
The leading independent grower of Montagny earns a new set of spurs with the delightful distinctive terroirs of his 6.5 ha holdings in successful 2014. The Découverte is, as always, expressive and open, Les Vignes Derrière (aptly named) more backward but deep and satisfying. The Vielles Vignes is the show-stopper – ripe golden fruit, aromas of flowers from the Chalonnais meadows but with some exotic blooms, too. Seductive mouthfeel, richness and poise in fine harmony. (ME)

Recommended Whites:
Montagne 1er Cru Vieilles Vignes ★★★☆ £D
Montagny 1er Cru Découverte ★★★ £C
Montagny 1er Cru Les Vignes Derrières ★★★ £D

Dom. Bertrand Ambroise   *www.ambroise.com*
Smallholder vignerons in Prémeaux based in Nuits-Saint-Georges since the 18th century, the domaine was revived in 1987 by Bertrand Ambroise and now extends to 21 ha spread across several fine premiers crus in Nuits-Saint- Georges and grand cru parcels in Corton and Clos de Vougeot. In 2013, the estate was certified Agriculture Biologique by Ecocert. Ambroise's reputation and impact rests on his red wines, which are at one extreme of the Burgundian wine styles -for colour and oomph, they have few equals, but is that what great red Burgundy is all about? Bold and oaky when young,

Amboise's best red, Corton Le Rognet suits his robust style and does settle down with age. The Clos Vougeot is a meaty mouthful but lacks perhaps a full expression of this supreme terroir's mix of majestic power with finesse. The whites come as a nice surprise, rich and succulent but not too oaky, in a notable Saint-Aubin and Corton Charlemagne. Prices, for the moment, are reasonable. Buy quickly. (ME)

Recommended Reds:
Corton Le Rognet ★★★★ £F
Clos de Vougeot ★★★ £F
Nuits-Saint-Georges 1er Cru Clos des Argillières ★★★ £E
Nuits-Saint-Georges 1er Cru Rue de Chaux ★★★ £E
Nuits-Saint-Georges 1er Cru Les Vaucrains ★★★ £E
Nuits-Saint-Georges Vieilles Vignes ★★★ £E
Nuits-Saint-Georges ★★☆ £D
Vougeot 1er Cru Les Cras ★★☆ £E
Côte de Nuits-Villages ★★ £C
Recommended Whites:
Corton-Charlemagne ★★★★ £F
Chassagne-Montrachet 1er Cru Maltroie ★★★ £E
Saint-Aubin 1er Cru Murgers Dents de Chien ★★★ £D

Dom. Guy Amiot et Fils (Chassagne Montrachet)
Guy Amiot and his son Thierry make a string of white Chassagne-Montrachet crus, which have shown increasing refinement and complexity in the most recent vintages. The wines are now bottled later than previously but perhaps more importantly Thierry has made changes in the vineyard resulting in richer, riper fruit from vines with an increasingly high average age (especially Vergers and Caillerets). At least as interesting if not at the same quality level are the red wines, which have very good richness for southern Côte de Beaune reds, with added length and style in the Clos Saint-Jean bottling. All the better reds deserve at least 3 or 4 years' age. Only a very little Puligny-Montrachet Premier Cru Les Demoiselles and Montrachet are made. Lesser whites can be drunk young but the best need at least 3 or 4 years' ageing.

Recommended Reds:
Chassagne-Montrachet 1er Cru Clos Saint-Jean ★★★ £E
Chassagne-Montrachet 1er Cru La Maltroie ★★★ £E
Chassagne-Montrachet Les Chaumes ★★ £C
Chassagne-Montrachet ★☆ £C
Santenay La Comme Dessus ★☆ £D
Recommended Whites:
Puligny-Montrachet 1er Cru Les Demoiselles ★★★★ £E
Chassagne-Montrachet 1er Cru Les Caillerets ★★★★ £E
Chassagne-Montrachet 1er Cru Les Vergers ★★★★ £E
Chassagne-Montrachet 1er Cru Les Macharelles ★★★★ £E
Chassagne-Montrachet 1er Cru Clos Saint-Jean ★★★ £E
Chassagne-Montrachet 1er Cru Champgains ★★★ £E
Chassagne-Montrachet 1er Cru Les Baudines ★★★ £E
Chassagne-Montrachet ★★★ £E
Saint-Aubin 1er Cru En Remilly ★★★ £E

Amiot-Servelle (Chambolle-Musigny)   *www.amiot-servelle.com*
Christian and Elizabeth Amiot farm almost 7 ha of vines. Since 2003 the vines have been farmed organically and the estate received full organic certification in 2008. In 2006 the winery was completely modernised with the installation of stainless steel vats in order to obtain greater control over wine making procedures. The wines are sturdy, and can at times be a little too structured to let the fruit sing through. However, when it does, the wines are rich and plump.

Nevertheless these are fine, often from old vines and as always are beginning to offer more with a few years' bottle-age. As well as a concentrated Chambolle-Musigny Amoureuses, the little known premier cru Derrière la Grange (which lies below Les Fuées) can show lots of style and there's some well-sited Clos de Vougeot. Bourgogne Rouge and a little Aligoté and Chardonnay are also made.

Recommended Reds:
Clos Saint-Denis Grand Cru ★★★★ £G
Charmes-Chambertin Grand Cru ★★★★ £G
Chambolle-Musigny 1er Cru Les Amoureuses ★★★★★ £F
Chambolle-Musigny 1er Cru Les Charmes ★★★★ £F
Chambolle-Musigny 1er Cru Derrière la Grange ★★★★ £F
Chambolle-Musigny ★★★ £E

❀ Marquis d'Angerville (Volnay) *www.domainedangerville.fr*
The greatly respected Jacques d'Angerville died in 2003 but the legacy of his estate and wines seems certain to continue under Guillaume d'Angerville. These remarkable expressions of Volnay are taut and structured when tasted very young but are classy and refined with concentrated, intense fruit underneath. Production, now directed by François Duvivier comes from 13 ha and is dominated by four premiers crus, including the prize 2.4 ha *monopole* Clos des Ducs. Low yields, with rigorous selection and full destemming are part of the formula and the red-fruits intensity is always well integrated with subdued oak. The wines have been on very good form since the late 1980s. Through a string of very different vintages in the late 90s and early in the new century the wines are wonderfully consistent but in every vintage deserve to be drunk with at least 5 or 6 years' age. All crus show the elegance and refinement of Volnay. Of the four most important crus, the elegant, stylish Frémiets is complemented by a medium-full, fragrant yet quite powerful Champans. Taillepieds combines great refinement and fullness while Clos des Ducs reveals a fabulous structure and superb length and class. A powerful Meursault-Santenots white has lots of substance and fruit richness.

Recommended Reds:
Volnay 1er Cru Clos des Ducs ✪✪✪✪✪ £F
Volnay 1er Cru Taillepieds ★★★★★ £F
Volnay 1er Cru Champans ★★★★☆ £F
Volnay 1er Cru Frémiets ★★★★☆ £F

Recommended Whites:
Meursault-Santenots 1er Cru ★★★★ £F

Dom. Arlaud (Morey-Saint-Denis) *www.domainearlaud.com*
Hervé Arlaud and his next generation, Cyprien, Romain and Bertille, have over 12 ha of vineyards at their disposal from an estate put together by their paternal grandparents, farmed with sustainable farming methods. It is split between Morey, Gevrey and Chambolle and includes 2 ha of grands crus. His Clos-Saint-Denis is a fine example with old vine cherry-raspberry fruit depth. It is well-proportioned and very classy and not too bold or extracted. The Charmes-Chambertin has a similar sense of proportion together with refinement, depth and a spiced cherry intensity. In fact good definition and a fine ripe fruit intensity are characteristic of all the wines. Two of the premiers crus stand out; the Gevrey Combottes and Morey Ruchots are both excellent expressions of their respective origins - the latter with classic preserved cherry, plum and beetroot character. Village examples tend to be simpler and lighter but are well-made. The basic Bourgogne red can also be very good if somewhat vintage dependent. A little Clos de la Roche and

Bonnes Mares are also made.

Recommended Reds:
Clos Saint-Denis ★★★★★ £G
Charmes-Chambertin ★★★★☆ £F
Gevrey-Chambertin 1er Cru Aux Combottes ★★★★ £F
Morey-Saint-Denis 1er Cru Millandes ★★★☆ £F
Morey-Saint-Denis 1er Cru Ruchots ★★★☆ £F
Morey-Saint-Denis ★★★ £E
Chambolle-Musigny 1er Cru Les Noirots ★★★☆ £F
Chambolle-Musigny ★★★ £E
Bourgogne Rouge Roncievie ★★☆ £C

Dom. de L'Arlot (Nuits-Saint-Georges) *www.arlot.com*
This worthy estate, created in 1987 after the purchase of an existing domain by French insurance giant AXA Millésimes, has now had 25 years of steady direction. Some 14 ha includes 2 ha of white grapes and two substantial Nuits-Saint-Georges monopoles, the 7 ha Clos des Fôrets-Saint-Georges and 3 ha Clos de l'Arlot. Farmed organically since 2003, great care is taken in the vineyards and there is minimal interference in the vinification and only a moderate use of new oak. The whites are more consistent than the reds as they do not tend to show the leanness encountered in lighter vintages for reds. Due at least partly to a policy of not destemming, there can be a lack of both flesh and depth to the reds and at times a stemmy quality (as some of the stalks included must still retain a green aspect, despite careful selection). However, in the ripest vintages this is rarely a problem and elegance and class shine through. The wines will always put on weight with age too, losing any sturdiness of youth to become very refined and harmonious. Recent vintages have been better. A regular Nuits-Saint-Georges made from young vines in the Clos des Fôrets has been redesignated premier cru from 2000.

Recommended Reds:
Romanée-Saint-Vivant ★★★★ £G
Vosne-Romanée 1er Cru Les Suchots ★★★ £F
Nuits-Saint-Georges 1er Cru Clos de l'Arlot ★★★ £F
Nuits-Saint-Georges 1er Cru Clos des Fôrets-Saint-Georges ★★★ £F
Nuits-Saint-Georges 1er Cru ★★☆ £E
Côtes de Nuits-Villages Clos du Chapeau ★★★★ £D

Recommended Whites:
Nuits-Saint-Georges 1er Cru Clos de l'Arlot ★★★ £F
Nuits-Saint-Georges Cuvée Jeunes Vignes ★★ £E

Comte Armand (Pommard) *www.domaine-comte-armand.com*
The Comte Armand's Domaine des Epeneaux for long produced just one wine, the famous Pommard Clos des Epeneaux from a 5 ha vineyard that forms part of the premier cru Les Grands Epenots. Since 1995 red and white Auxey-Duresses have been added, as has a very good Volnay Frémiets. Yields are low and the reds are notable for their colour, structure and depth. In 1999 Benjamin Leroux took over making the wines from Pascal Marchand, who had firmly established a quality regime here from the mid-1980s. Pascal's minimal use of chemicals has been taken a stage further - production has been certified biodynamic since 2001. The Clos continues to be made from three separately vinified parcels of vines differentiated by their age. The wine is always full-bodied and powerful but balanced and complex. Village Pommard is produced from some of the younger-vine fruit not used in the Clos. A little Meursault, Meix-Chavaux has also been produced.

Recommended Reds:
Pommard 1er Cru Clos des Epeneaux ★★★★★ £F
Pommard ★★★ £E

Burgundy / Côte d'Or & Côte Chalonnaise

France

Volnay Frémiets ★★★☆ £E
Auxey Duresses 1er Cru ★★★ £E
Recommended Whites:
Bourgogne Blanc Condemaine ★★☆ £D
Auxey-Duresses ★★ £D

Dom. Arnoux-Lachaux www.arnoux-lachaux.com
Pascal Lachaux is the son-in-law of the late Robert Arnoux and he has been making better and better wines here over the past decade. The top wines, of which there are several, receive 100% new oak treatment but rarely is this obvious. The wines, neither fined nor filtered, are sturdy, structured with at times almost overwhelming intensity and power. Premiers crus such as Corvées Pagets and Suchots show their inherent class to best effect while the grands crus reveal great depth and texture but all are also very good in other recent vintages too. In 2008 the domaine purchased a holding in Latricières-Chambertin but this wine has not yet been tasted. Pascal has also been producing a range of négociant wines since 2002 under his own name (see PASCAL LACHAUX).
Recommended Reds:
Romanée-Saint-Vivant ✪✪✪✪✪ £H
Clos de Vougeot ★★★★★ £G   Echezeaux ★★★★★ £G
Vosne-Romanée 1er Cru Les Suchots ★★★★☆ £G
Vosne-Romanée 1er Cru Aux Reignots ★★★★ £F
Vosne-Romanée 1er Cru Les Chaumes ★★★★ £F
Vosne-Romanée Les Hautes-Maizières ★★★ £F
Vosne-Romanée ★★★ £F
Nuits-Saint-Georges 1er Cru Les Corvées Pagets ★★★★ £F
Nuits-Saint-Georges 1er Cru Les Procès ★★★ £F
Nuits-Saint-Georges Les Poisets ★★★ £F
Nuits-Saint-Georges ★★★ £E   Chambolle-Musigny ★★★ £E

Dom. d'Auvenay (Saint-Romain)
This is the private estate of Madame Lalou Bize and is quite distinct from both the considerably larger Domaine LEROY and the Leroy négociant business. Though there are just 3.9ha (farmed biodynamically) there are several exquisite small crus which are made to the same exacting standards as Domaine Leroy. While reds dominate the production of Domaine Leroy, apart from a little grand cru Bonnes-Mares and Mazis-Chambertin, here it is white magic that prevails. The wines are rich, pure and concentrated – even at the level of Auxey-Duresses or Bourgogne Aligoté. Prices are astoundingly high and though the same general ratings apply (★★★★★ for the grands crus, at least ★★★★ for the premiers crus and ★★★ for the other wines), I'd find the individuality and grandeur of the Domaine Leroy reds a greater temptation if I had the money to spend. The wines to look out for are: Chevalier-Montrachet, Criots-Bâtard-Montrachet, Puligny-Montrachet (La Richarde, Premier Cru Folatières), Meursault (Narvaux, Premier Cru Goutte d'Or), Auxey-Duresses (Boutonniers, Les Clous) and some Bourgogne Aligoté. A straight village Meursault is sometimes bottled separately as Chaumes de Perrières and Pré de Manche. Very fine in 2014.
Recommended Whites:
Chevalier-Montrachet ★★★★★ £H
Meursault Narvaux ★★★★ £F   Bourgogne Aligoté ★★★☆ £D

❀ Denis Bachelet (Gevrey-Chambertin)
Denis Bachelet's wines are not that widely seen, such are the small quantities he produces, but they are wines of great finesse and class with lovely fruit intensity and harmony. In fact they might almost be considered atypical for an appellation that delivers up powerful, meaty, sometimes tannic, examples of Pinot. If the rich, intense Premier Cru Les Corbeaux and complex and classy grand cru Charmes-Chambertin are hard to find, the village Gevrey-Chambertin Vieilles Vignes is a super example at this level; all three are made from old vines. There's also reasonable quantities of a Côte de Nuits-Villages and a Bourgogne Rouge that make delicious red Burgundy seem almost affordable.
Recommended Reds:
Charmes-Chambertin ★★★★★ £F
Gevrey-Chambertin 1er Cru Les Corbeaux Vieilless Vignes ★★★★ £F
Gevrey-Chambertin Vieilles Vignes ★★★★ £F
Côte de Nuits-Villages ★★☆ £D   Bourgogne Rouge ★★ £C

Ghislaine Barthod (Chambolle-Musigny)
This sought-after bijou estate.was founded by Jura-born Gaston Barthod when he married a Noellat girl. After military service he took over the domaine in the 1950s. His daughter Ghislaine who has made the wines a beacon of fine Chambolle internationally, served an apprenticeship under her father before becoming the winemaker in the 1990s. Small is very beautiful: in the 6.5 ha holdings there is a benchmark village Chambollle and seven Premier Cru climats, some of which are measured in ares rather than hectares. Working the soil is rigorous, there's minimal intervention in the winemaking and new oak is restricted to 30 percent. 1er Cru Les Fuées on old-vines close to the Morey St Denis border has strength and "shoulders" but still keeps Ghislaine's signature of elegant acidity and charm like the rest of her parcels. Les Charmes, also on old-vines, is supremely sophisticated with a silken texture. Higher altitude Véroilles close to Bonnes Mares, has a lovely weightlessness in tune with density, suiting the 2014 vintage – in some ways her most interesting wine. Les Baudes has a wild cherry appeal and a streak of tartness that delights the palate. Les Cras as always is rich and gras yet within the fine athletic Barthod style. If you're on a budget, the Bourgogne Rouge is a wine of character with grainy tannins. (ME)
Recommended Reds:
Chambolle-Musigny 1er Cru Les Véroilles ★★★★☆ £F
Chambolle-Musigny 1er Cru Les Charmes ★★★★ £F
Chambolle-Musigny 1er Cru Les Baudes ★★★★ £E
Chambolle-Musigny 1er Cru Les Fuées ★★★★ £E
Chambolle-Musigny 1er Cru Les Beaux Bruns ★★★ £E
Chambolle-Musigny ★★★ £E
Bourgogne Rouge ★★ £C

❀ Roger Belland (Santenay) www.domaine-belland-roger.com
This fine 23 ha domaine has just 4 ha in Santenay, much of the rest is in the gems of Chassagne and Puligny including the largest parcel of Criots-Batard- Montrachet, fully worth a 5-star rating. Roger Belland is a great white Burgundy maker, his wines offering good value, too. The reds have been somewhat burly in the past, but Roger's daughter Julie joined her father in 2003 and has since refined the winemaking, using less new oak and some whole grape fermentation for extra finesse.. In common with many of the great domaines, Belland is a dedicated viticulturalist and goes to great lengths in the vineyard to maximise the quality of the fruit. Whites see new oak – 90% for the grand cru Criots – but the intensity and depth of the fruit are only enhanced by it. Red Santenay includes the leading premiers crus at the northern end of this sizeable appellation; these are very good examples, full of ripe berry fruits but with good structure and length too. A source of great value Burgundy too. (ME)

Recommended Reds:

Pommard Les Cras ★★★ £F   Volnay 1er Cru Santenots ★★★ £F
Chassagne-Montrachet 1er Cru Morgeot Clos Pitois ★★★ £E
Santenay 1er Cru Commes ★★★ £D
Santenay 1er Cru Beauregard ★★★ £D
Santenay 1er Cru Gravières ★★★ £D
Santenay Charmes ★★ £D   Maranges 1er Cru La Fussière ★★ £D
Maranges ★☆ £C

Recommended Whites:

Criots-Bâtard-Montrachet ✪✪✪✪✪ £H
Puligny-Montrachet 1er Cru Les Champs Gains ★★★★★ £F
Chassagne-Montrachet 1er Cru Morgeot Clos Pitois ★★★★ £E
Santenay 1er Cru Beauregard ★★★ £D   Santenay ★★ £D

Dom. de Bellene (Beaune)   *www.domainedebellene.com*
After working with his father, the late Gèrard Potel at the DOMAINE DE LA POUSSE D'OR until 1997, Nicolas founded his eponymous négociant house NICOLAS POTEL, making superb wines from bought in grapes until he sold out to Cottin Frères in 2007. He had already started his own domaine from 2005 but after a legal wrangle with Cottin was legally unable to use his own name on wine labels and from 2008 has bottled under the name of Domaine de Bellene. He also makes some négociant wines under the name Maison Roche de Bellene. He purchased parcels of old vines ranging from 50 to 110 years old in Santenay, Saint Romain, Savigny, Volnay, Beaune, Nuits-St-Georges and Vosne-Romanée. The wines are produced biodynamically and no chemical products are used. His style of controlled elegance is apparent in the wines we have tasted although we have not tasted anything like all the range.

Recommended Reds:

Vosne-Romanée 1er Cru Les Suchots ★★★★ £G
Beaune 1er Cru Grèves ★★★ £E
Savigny-les-Beaune Vieilles Vignes ★★★ £D

Dom. Bertagna (Vougeot)   *www.domainebertagna.com*
This 30 ha estate has a wide spread of vineyards in the Côte de Nuits, having steadily acquired more parcels since it was bought in 1982 by Günter Reh (see von KESSELSTATT in Germany), father of the current director, Eva Reh- Siddle. Between 1999 and 2006 the wines were made by Claire Forrestier and the reds are vigorous, rich and structured. But the *terroir* is emphasised rather than suppressed, especially as the wines age, so there is density and muscle in wines like Vougeot Les Cras, but class and intensity in Vosne-Romanée Les Beaux-Monts and finesse in Clos Saint-Denis. Clos de la Perrière is a *monopole*. Corton Les Grandes Lolières is typically intense and concentrated as well as lightly mineral. All the best premiers crus and grands crus need 8–10 years' age. A little Chambertin is also made. Whites, Vougeot Premier Cru and Corton Charlemagne, are classsy and structured with lots of flavour and individuality and only miss the extra purity and definition for really fine.

Recommended Reds:

Clos Saint-Denis ★★★★☆ £G   Clos de Vougeot ★★★★ £G
Corton Les Grandes Lolières ★★★★ £G
Vougeot 1er Cru Clos de la Perrière ★★★★ £F
Vougeot 1er Cru Les Cras ★★★ £F
Vougeot 1er Cru Petits Vougeots ★★★ £F
Vosne-Romanée 1er Cru Beaux-Monts ★★★★ £F
Nuits-Saint-Georges 1er Cru Les Murgers ★★★★ £F
Chambolle-Musigny 1er Cru Les Plantes ★★★★ £F
Chambolle-Musigny Le Village ★★★ £E

Recommended Whites:

Corton-Charlemagne ★★★★☆ £G   Vougeot Blanc ★★★★ £F

Albert Bichot (Beaune)   *www.bourgogne-bichot.com*
A new broom here has made a world of difference. One of Burgundy's best known export labels, this long-established domaine-owning négociant (from 1831) has been determinedly re-orientated towards quality and under new direction since 1999. There are a sprinkling of merchant wines often from leading crus from Chablis in the north down through the Côte d'Or. Wines are also produced from the Mâconnais as well as the Rhône and Languedoc-Roussillon. There is also a marvellous resource in the domaine wines. The 13 ha Domaine du Clos Frantin offers top flight Côte de Nuits reds while 17 ha Dom. du Pavillon top red and white crus from the Côte de Beaune. For a wealth of riches from Chablis see Domaine LONG-DEPAQUIT (under Chablis). The new style reds are modern and fruit-rich with lots of charm if for the most part still missing the extra definition and detail of the best examples. As well as the wines rated below Clos du Frantin includes Richebourg, Romanée-Saint-Vivant, Chambertin and Gevrey-Chambertin while Domaine du Pavillon includes more Pommard, Beaune, Volnay-Santenots and Meursault-Charmes. Grands Echezeaux is particularly fine while Corton Clos des Maréchaudes has considerable potential if not quite the balance for more - the Aloxe-Corton comes from the lower part of this Clos. The more widely available basic generics are better made than previously if still not very exciting. Further wines will be added with consistent results.

Domaine du Clos Frantin

Recommended Reds:

Grands-Echezeaux ★★★★☆ £G   Clos Vougeot ★★★★ £G
Echezeaux ★★★★ £G
Vosne-Romané 1er Cru Les Malconsorts ★★★☆ £F

Domaine du Pavillon

Recommended Reds:

Corton Clos des Maréchaudes ★★★★ £F
Pommard 1er Cru Les Rugiens ★★★ £F
Aloxe-Corton Clos des Maréchaudes ★★★ £E

Recommended Whites:

Corton-Charlemagne ★★★★ £G

Dom. Simon Bize et Fils   *www.domainebize.fr*
This serious sizeable (22 ha) domaine remains the reference for Savigny despite the sudden death in 2013 of Patrick Bize, a passionate and respected grower, whose winemaking vision was for a classic style of Burgundy, unafraid of gamey notes and largely impervious to modes and trends. Patrick's sister Marielle Grivot has taken the torch, respecting the classic vision but using increasing whol grape fermentation for the reds to add allure and finesse to wines that are still bold, sturdy, and needing age to show their class -Les Serpentières Premier Cru 2013 shows exemplary refinement in a challenging cool year following the admirably now à point 2007). Les Marconnets and Les Fourneaux are fine combinations of density with delicacy. A little Latricières Chambertin toute en finesse is also made. The whites are fresh and floral, from a structured yet finely fruited Corton Charlemagne to a Bourgogne Blas which is as well made as the grander whites. (ME)

Recommended Reds:

Latricières Chambertin ★★★★ £F
Savigny-lès-Beaune 1er Cru Aux Vergelesses ★★★ £E
Savigny-lès-Beaune 1er Cru Aux Serpentières ★★★ £E
Savigny-lès-Beaune 1er Cru Marconnets ★★★ £E

Burgundy /Côte d'Or & Côte Chalonnaise

France

Savigny-lès-Beaune 1er Cru Fourneaux ★★★ £E
Recommended Whites:
Corton-Charlemagne ★★★★ £F

Blain-Gagnard (Chassagne-Montrachet)

Jean-Marc and his wife Claudine (whose father is Jacques Gagnard) have a small selection of precious sites, thanks largely to her family. The wines are handled carefully with restrained oak and not overworked, resulting in wines of good richness and structure that remain true to their origins. A ripe, minerally and well-structured regular Chassagne develops nicely with 3–4 years' age. The premiers crus add more depth and richness and, although they can be drunk fairly young, deserve 4 or 5 years' age. Considerably more expensive but a big step up in quality is a Bâtard-Montrachet made in reasonable quantities. This has the characteristic Bâtard power and terrific dimension on the palate, becoming marvellously complex with even a little age. A little Criots-Bâtard-Montrachet is also made and a tiny amount of Le Montrachet (from Jacques Gagnard) has also recently been added. Premier cru Chassagne red is delicate and fine, while Clos Saint-Jean adds a little more depth. Both, as with all the whites, are reasonably priced. Gagnard-Delagrange is Jacques Gagnard's label, which includes La Boudriotte and Morgeots and outstanding Bâtard-Montrachet and Montrachet. The Gagnard inheritance is still secure in the hands and wines of Blain- Gagnard and the Blains' son Marc- Antonin is making fine Chassagnes and very good Bâtard-Montrachet. (ME)
Recommended Reds:
Volnay 1er Cru Champans ★★★ £E   Pommard ★★ £D
Chassagne-Montrachet 1er Cru Clos Saint-Jean ★★★ £D
Recommended Whites:
Bâtard-Montrachet ★★★★★ £G
Chassagne-Montrachet 1er Cru Caillerets ★★★★ £E
Chassagne-Montrachet 1er Cru Morgeots ★★★★ £E
Chassagne-Montrachet 1er Cru La Boudriotte ★★★★ £E
Chassagne-Montrachet1er Cru Clos Saint-Jean ★★★ £E
Chassagne-Montrachet ★★★ £D   Puligny-Montrachet ★★★ £E

Dom. Jean Boillot et Fils (Volnay)

Henri Boillot, brother of Jean-Marc BOILLOT, is now making the wines on his father's domaine as well as running an expanding négociant business, Maison Henri Boillot. Though the domaine is based in Volnay, there's a decent parcel of Puligny vines, including a substantial 4ha wholly owned *lieu-dit* within Perrières, Clos de la Mouchère, as well as one or two other choice crus. The fruit is picked very late, the reds 100% destemmed and both reds and whites see a lot of new oak. The wines are rich, even opulent and consequently can be drunk quite young, though the Volnays, particularly the excellent Caillerets, deserve at least 4 or 5 years' aging. The pick of the whites, Les Pucelles, which reflects the class and finesse of that wonderful site, also demands a little patience. The négociant Henri Boillot wines includes some top-notch crus, and can be very good indeed if slightly less consistent.
Domaine Jean Boillot
Recommended Reds:
Volnay 1er Cru Caillerets ★★★★★ £G
Volnay 1er Cru Frémiets ★★★★☆ £F
Volnay 1er Cru Clos de la Rougette ★★★★☆ £F
Volnay 1er Cru Chevrets ★★★★ £F
Beaune 1er Cru Clos du Roi ★★★ £E
Beaune 1er Cru Epenottes ★★★ £E
Savigny-lès-Beaune 1er Cru Les Lavières ★★☆ £E

Recommended Whites:
Puligny-Montrachet 1er Cru Clos de la Mouchère ★★★★★ £F
Puligny-Montrachet 1er Cru Les Pucelles ★★★★ £F
Puligny-Montrachet 1er Cru Les Perrières ★★★★ £F
Puligny-Montrachet ★★★ £E
Meursault 1er Cru Les Genevrières ★★★★ £F
Savigny-lès-Beaune 1er Cru Les Vergelesses ★★★☆ £E

Jean-Marc Boillot (Pommard)   www.jeanmarc-boillot.com

Jean-Marc Boillot, grandson of Étienne Sauzet, seems equally at ease making both red and white, as indeed he needs to be with half of his 10.5 ha planted to Chardonnay. The wines have a fruit richness and depth to marry with the oak input. The reds range from a full Beaune to more structured Pommards, including a tiny amount of superb rich Rugiens, and a Volnay-like Jarolières (contiguous with Volnay Frémiets) to stylish, perfumed Volnays. Even the village examples are very good. The whites if anything are even better. A string of Puligny premiers crus (the SAUZET inheritance) all have an intense pure fruit and great class, nowhere better expressed than in Les Combettes. There is also a little Bâtard-Montrachet. Some Rully and Puligny-Montrachet Les Pucelles have recently been made from bought-in fruit. Jean-Marc Boillot is now also making wine in the Coteaux du Languedoc at Domaine La Truffière (see Languedoc-Roussillon).
Recommended Reds:
Pommard 1er Cru Rugiens ★★★★ £F
Pommard 1er Cru Jarolières ★★★ £F   Pommard ★★★ £E
Volnay 1er Cru Carelle sous la Chapelle ★★★☆ £F
Volnay 1er Cru Pitures ★★★ £F
Volnay 1er Cru Le Ronceret ★★★ £F
Volnay ★★★ £E
Beaune 1er Cru Montrevenots ★★☆ £D
Recommended Whites:
Puligny-Montrachet 1er Cru Les Referts ★★★★☆ £F
Puligny-Montrachet 1er Cru Champ Canet ★★★★☆ £F
Puligny-Montrachet 1er Cru Les Combettes ★★★★ £F
Puligny-Montrachet 1er Cru La Truffière ★★★★ £F
Puligny-Montrachet 1er Cru La Garenne ★★★☆ £F
Puligny-Montrachet ★★★☆ £E

Dom. Louis Boillot et Fils (Chambolle-Musigny)

Louis Boillot is the husband of Ghislaine BARTHOD and has split with his brother Pierre the estate of Lucien Boillot et Fils (see below) which they used to jointly run. The 7ha of vineyards stretches from Gevrey-Chambertin to Volnay. Many of the same wines are repeated under the new label of Louis Boillot et Fils. It is too soon yet to discern significant differences in quality or style between the two estates. Of four Volnays premier cru Caillerets has the greatest potential but needs 10-15 years while Les Grand Poisots is a good village -level example - dense, full, somewhat Pommard-like. Also listed here are some of the very reasonably priced wines (including good village climats from Gevrey and Morey-Saint-Denis) made under the existing négociant business of Louis Boillot.
Domaine Louis Boillot et Fils
Recommended Reds:
Volnay 1er Cru Les Caillerets ★★★★☆ £E
Volnay 1er Cru Les Angles ★★★☆ £E
Volnay 1er Cru Les Les Brouillards ★★★☆ £E
Volnay Les Grands Poisots ★★★ £E
Morey-Saint-Denis 1er Cru Aux Charmes ★★★★ £E
Morey-Saint-Denis ★★★ £E

Gevrey-Chambertin ★★★ £E   Chambolle-Musigny ★★★ £E

Maison Louis Boillot

Recommended Reds:

Gevrey-Chambertin Les Carougeots ★★★ £E

Gevrey-Chambertin ★★★ £E

Morey-Saint-Denis 1er Cru Les Sorbes ★★★★ £E

Morey-Saint-Denis Les Ruchots ★★★ £E

Morey-Saint-Denis ★★★ £E   Chambolle-Musigny ★★★ £E

Dom. Lucien Boillot (Gevrey Chambertin)

Though Gevrey-based, this domaine draws half of its grapes from original family vineyards in Volnay and Pommard. The vineyards were split in 2003 between 'fils' Louis and Pierre and the latter continues to make the wines under the Lucien Boillot label. The grapes are only partially destemmed and an extended maceration is favoured, resulting in wines with structure, breadth and flavour intensity, though not always with the concentration or fullness to match. Some wines from late 1990s can be disappointing but rmore recent vintages show good promise with plenty of intensity and extract without being overdone. For the wines of Louis Boillot, including existing négociant wines, see above.

Recommended Reds:

Gevrey-Chambertin 1er Cru Les Cherbaudes ★★★★ £E

Gevrey-Chambertin 1er Cru Les Corbeaux ★★★ £E

Gevrey-Chambertin Evocelles ★★★ £D

Gevrey-Chambertin ★★ £D

Nuits-Saint-Georges 1er Cru Les Pruliers ★★★ £E

Volnay 1er Cru Caillerets ★★★★ £E

Volnay 1er Cru Angles ★★★★ £E

Volnay 1er Cru Brouillards ★★★ £E   Volnay ★★☆ £D

Pommard 1er Cru Fremiers ★★★ £E

Pommard 1er Cru Les Croix Noires ★★ £E

Pommard ★★ £D   Beaune Epenottes ★☆ £D

✿ Dom. Bonneau du Martray   www.bonneaudumartray.com

An outstanding 11 ha domaine producing just two wines. The white Corton-Charlemagne comes from 9.5 ha of the best-sited part of the famous vineyard. The red comes from 1.5 ha at the base of the Corton hill. As good as the wines are now, the reputation of this domaine has only been fully re-established by Jean-Charles Le Bault de la Morinière, who has made tremendous progress since taking over from his father. The red, in particular, has improved; since 1995 a previously rather dilute, insubstantial wine has taken on greater flesh and extract without sacrificing its finesse. The white has long been a wine of tremendous richness and great depth and character that will keep for many years from the best vintages. It is also one of the few wines made from this large vineyard to show true grand cru class.

Recommended Reds:

Corton ★★★★ £F

Recommended Whites:

Corton-Charlemagne ✪✪✪✪✪ £F

✿ Bouchard Père et Fils (Beaune)   www.bouchard-pereetfils.com

This merchant is one of the best-known names in Burgundy, thanks in part to its substantial holdings. Domaine vineyards total 130 ha, including 12 ha of grands crus and 74 ha of premiers crus and two-thirds of the vineyards are planted to Pinot Noir. Its decline under family ownership and the scandal of its conviction for flouting legal winemaking practices have been well-documented. Yet from the time of the purchase by the much respected Champenois Joseph

Henriot (see HENRIOT) in 1995, quality has dramatically improved. Despite the poor health of the vineyards, almost immediately the reds showed greater richness and better structure and more recently have added more expression and individuality. The ongoing investment in both people and winemaking facilities is backed by a determination to maximise quality and consistency. In more difficult vintages, such as 2000 for red, Bouchard was prepared to sell off a large quantity of wine in order to maintain the progress made in re-establishing the integrity of its label. The best whites show superb fruit combined with excellent structure and concentration.. As with other leading négociants the range is quite vast. Most of the wines below are 'domaine' bottlings though one or two generics are made from purchased grapes as is the very fine Chambertin Clos-de-Bèze which shows fabulous breadth, depth and complexity. Excellent style and recent consistency here.

Recommended Reds:

La Romanée ✪✪✪✪✪ £H

Chambertin Clos-de-Bèze ✪✪✪✪✪ £H

Chambertin ★★★★★ £H   Le Corton ★★★★ £G

Gevrey-Chambertin 1er Cru Les Cazetiers ★★★★ £F

Gevrey-Chambertin ★★ £E   Chambolle-Musigny ★★★ £E

Bonnes Mares ★★★★★ £G   Clos de Vougeot ★★★★ £G

Echezeaux ★★★ £H

Vosne-Romanée 1er Cru Aux Reignots ★★★ £G

Nuits Saint-Georges 1er Cru Clos des Argillières ★★★★ £F

Nuits Saint-Georges 1er Cru Les Cailles ★★★★ £E

Nuits Saint-Georges 1er Cru Clos Saint-Marc ★★★★ £E

Nuits Saint-Georges ★★★ £E   Savigny-lès-Beaune ★★ £D

Savigny-lès-Beaune 1er Cru Les Lavières ★★ £D

Beaune 1er Cru Grèves Vigne de L'Enfant Jésus ★★★★ £F

Beaune 1er Cru Teurons ★★★ £E

Beaune 1er Cru Beaune du Château ★★★ £E

Beaune 1er Cru Clos de la Mousse ★★ £E

Pommard 1er Cru Rugiens ★★★★ £F

Pommard 1er Cru Pezerolles ★★★★ £E

Pommard 1er Cru Les Chanlins ★★★ £E   Pommard ★★★ £E

Volnay 1er Cru Caillerets Ancienne Cuvée Carnot ★★★★ £F

Volnay 1er Cru Clos des Chênes ★★★★ £F

Volnay 1er Cru Fremiets Clos de la Rougeotte ★★★ £F

Volnay 1er Cru Taillepieds ★★★ £F

Monthelie 1er Cru Clos des Champs Fuillot ★★★ £E

Monthelie 1er Cru Les Duresses ★★ £D   Monthelie ★★★ £C

Recommended Whites:

Le Montrachet ✪✪✪✪✪ £H   Chevalier-Montrachet ★★★★★ £H

Corton-Charlemagne ★★★★★ £G   Puligny-Montrachet ★★★ £E

Puligny-Montrachet 1er Cru Champs Gains ★★★★ £F

Meursault 1er Cru Perrières ★★★★★ £F

Meursault 1er Cru Genevrières ★★★★★ £F

Meursault 1er Cru Les Gouttes d'Or ★★★★ £F

Meursault 1er Cru Les Bouchères ★★★★ £F

Meursault Les Clous ★★★ £E   Meursault ★★★ £E

Beaune 1er Cru Clos Saint-Landry ★★★ £D

Beaune 1er Cru Sur Les Grèves ★★★ £D

Beaune 1er Cru Beaune du Château ★★ £D

Montagny Les Platières ★★ £D   Pouilly-Fuissé ★★ £C

Rene Bouvier (Gevrey-Chambertin)

This increasingly fine domaine based on 17 ha of vineyards has been transformed from a producer of fine Marsannay to one that includes many other fine crus from the Côtes de Nuits. Working in part in a négociant role Bernard Bouvier is expanding on his father's

Burgundy /Côte d'Or & Côte Chalonnaise

achievements. As well as good Gevrey-Chambertin recently there has been fine Chambolle-Musigny, Vosne-Romanée and even Echezeaux and Clos de Vougeot. Some of the best value is at the lower levels: some of the grands crus while good aren't up there with those from the very best growers.

Recommended Reds:
Charmes-Chambertin ★★★ £G Clos de Vougeot ★★★★ £G
Gevrey-Chambertin 1er Cru Petite Chapelle ★★★★ £F
Gevrey-Chambertin 1er Cru Cazetiers ★★★★ £F
Gevrey-Chambertin Jeunes Rois ★★★ £E
Gevrey-Chambertin Racines du Temps Très Vieilles Vignes ★★★ £E
Morey-Saint-Denis 1er Cru Genevrières ★★★ £F
Chambolle-Musigny 1er Cru Les Noirots ★★★ £F
Marsannay Longeroies ★★ £D Marsannay En Ouzeloy ★★ £D
Marsannay Champs Salomon ★★ £C
Marsannay Clos du Roy ★★ £C Fixin Crais de Chêne ★★ £D
Côtes de Nuits-Villages ★★ £D
Recommended Whites:
Marsannay Vieilles Vignes ★★ £D Marsannay Le Clos ★★ £D

Michel Bouzereau (Meursault) www.michelbouzereauetfils.fr
Devotees of white Burgundy will recognise a Michel Bouzereau label as a good bet for ripe, full yet elegant Meursault and as Michel's son Jean-Baptiste assumes responsibility it seems certain to remain that way. The domaine comprises 12 ha, more than three-quarters of it white. Stylish and pure, the whites show good definition with subtle differences between the various crus. Most outstanding are Meursault-Charmes and Meursault-Perrières. Meursault-Blagny can be the most austere but is deep and minerally, Genevrières is very suggestive of this cru, and there is plenty of style and fruit in the humbler village-level Grands Charrons, Limouzin and stylish complete Les Tessons too. Caillerets is much the better of the two Pulignys but this is reflected in the price difference. There's only a little red and if it's not at the same level as the whites it is at least reasonably priced for the quality. Good value, too, are the basic Bourgogne Rouge and Bourgogne Chardonnay.
Recommended Reds:
Pommard Les Cras ★★★ £F Volnay 1er Cru Les Aussy ★★★ £F
Beaune 1er Cru Vignes Franches ★★ £E
Recommended Whites:
Meursault 1er Cru Charmes ★★★★☆ £F
Meursault 1er Cru Perrières ★★★★☆ £F
Meursault 1er Cru Genevrières ★★★★ £E
Meursault 1er Cru Blagny ★★★★ £E
Meursault Les Tessons ★★★☆ £E Meursault Limouzin ★★★ £E
Meursault Les Grands Charrons ★★★ £E
Puligny-Montrachet 1er Cru Cailllerets ★★★★ £F
Puligny-Montrachet 1er Cru Champ Gain ★★★ £F
Bourgogne Chardonnay ★★ £C Bourgogne Aligoté ★ £C

Boyer-Martinot (Meursault) www.boyer-martenot.com
Fourth generation Vincent Boyer has been making the wines here since 2001. The union of his parents' holdings in 1983 formed the basis of the current 10 ha of vineyards. He is making classic rich, plump and full-flavoured Meursault, traditional in the best sense with a measure of restraint when young. A high average vine age is maintained as is apparent in wines with plenty of personality and depth but that are also well-balanced with good definition. Les Narvaux vies with Les Tillets as the best of the village Meursault climats while Perrières is arguably the finest premier cru Meursault, with a little extra breadth and complexity characteristic of the

vineyard. This in turn vies with an intense, refined and classy Puligny-Montrachet Le Cailleret as the top wine. All the better crus will keep for 6–8 years but can readily be drunk with just 2 or 3 years. Good Bourgogne Chardonnay can show good fruit and flavour, too, if in a simpler fashion. Vincent's sister Sylvie has started a small negociants operation and labels these wines under her own name.
Boyer-Martenot
Recommended Whites:
Meursault 1er Cru Genevrières ★★★★ £F
Meursault 1er Cru Perrières ★★★★ £F
Meursault 1er Cru Charmes ★★★★ £F
Meursault Narvaux ★★★ £E Meursault Tillets ★★★ £E
Meursault En L'Ormeaux ★★★ £D
Meursault ★★☆ £D
Puligny-Montrachet 1er Cru Le Cailleret ★★★★ £F
Puligny-Montrachet Les Reuchaux ★★★ £E
Bourgogne Blanc ★☆ £B

Dom. Michel Briday (Rully) www.domaine-michel-briday.com
Stéphane Briday is one grower determined to make the most of Rully's potential and the now 15ha estate his father Michel built up since the late 70s. Whites are the stronger suit and finesse and structure are sought with the use of just 10% new oak in the crus. Both Gresigny and La Pucelle are excellent intense, pure and well-defined whites, the latter just adding a little extra breadth and complexity. Mercurey premier cru Clos Marcilly is also made. Drink the characterful (Bouzeron) Aligoté young.
Recommended Reds:
Rully 1er Cru Champs Cloux ★★ £D Rully Quatre Vignes ★ £C
Recommended Whites:
Rully Clos de Remenot ★★★ £E Rully 1er Cru Les Cloux ★★★ £D
Rully 1er Cru La Pucelle ★★★ £D Rully 1er Cru Grésigny ★★★ £D
Rully ★★ £D Bouzeron Cuvée Axelle ★ £C

Dom. Brintet (Mercurey)
Luc Brintet's 13 ha are mostly red as would be expected in Mercurey but he makes a little white that is every bit as good. Reds are rigorously sorted and totally destemmed and a long *cuvaison* is sought with an extended period of pre-fermentation maceration. Both reds and whites are oakier than some but have ripe succulent fruit underneath and good structure and definition. The premiers crus are a definite notch up in quality and are among the best in the appellation. Whites are better with 2 or 3 years' age, reds with 3–5 years.
Recommended Reds:
Mercurey 1er Cru Levrières ★★★ £D Mercurey 1er Cru Crêts ★★☆ £D
Mercurey 1er Cru Vasées ★★☆ £D Mercurey Vieilles Vignes ★★ £C
Mercurey Charmée ★☆ £C
Recommended Whites:
Mercurey 1er Cru Crêts ★★★ £C Mercurey Vieilles Vignes ★★ £C
Mercurey ★☆ £B

Alain Burguet (Gevrey-Chambertin)
Already experienced, Alain Burguet first got a foothold of his own in Gevrey back in 1974 and has now progressed to 6 ha. His reputation is for being tough and intransigent both in personality and in his approach to winemaking. Yet there is clearly a mellowing of sorts as he has modified and refined his vinification and ageing methods in the 1990s, including complete destemming and longer oak ageing. It has taken a couple of vintages to perfect but since 1998 the wines have been more stylish and complete

though still with good richness and power. If most of the wines are only village level (there is now a little Premier Cru Champeaux), a Vieilles Vignes bottling (now labelled Mes Favorites) of great depth and richness is consistently of comparable quality to some of the best Gevrey made. All the wines show good classic Gevrey spice, strength and red and black fruit intensity. Older vintages can be slightly tougher, more rustic but can mellow and soften with age, too and are unlikely to disappoint from a good vintage. Bourgogne Rouge is decent too. In 2011, Alain's sons, Jean-Luc and Eric, who had been working with him since the late nineties, officially took over the domaine. Since then they have obtained organic certification, reduced the number of Gevrey-Chambertin *cuvées* and have begun to make wines from bought in grapes from Vosne-Romanée, Chambolle-Musigny, Pouilly-Fuissé and Meursault. A small amount of Grand Cru Chambertin Clos de Bèze is also made from a neighbour's holding. Watch this space.

Recommended Reds:
Gevrey-Chambertin Vieilles Vignes Mes Favorites ★★★★ £E
Gevrey-Chambertin 1er Cru Champeaux ★★★ £E
Gevrey-Chambertin Symphonie ★★ £E
Bourgogne Rouge Les Pince Vins ★ £C

Dom. François Carillon *www.francois-carillon.com*
The great Louis Carillon estate was divided amicably by Louis's two sons in 2010 and thus a new era begins for the Carillons. François and his family operate 6.5 ha of the old domaine, taking over the entirety of the holdings in Puligny-Montrachet at Folatières and Combottes, Chenevottes and Clos St-Jean in Chassagne, and La Combe and the red Pitangerets in St-Aubin. Puligny villages, Perrières and Champ-Canet vineyards are divided between the two brothers as is the holding at Chassagne Macherelles. He also has a small holding of Chevalier-Montrachet. It is too early at this stage to discover whether there will be a marked difference in the wines produced by each brother. For the moment, we must consider this as work in progress, but we don't doubt for a moment that there will be any diminishment in quality.

Recommended Reds:
Saint-Aubin 1er Cru Pitangerets ★★ £D
Recommended Whites:
Puligny-Montrachet 1er Cru Perrières ★★★★ £F
Puligny-Montrachet 1er Cru Combettes ★★★★ £F
Puligny-Montrachet 1er Cru Champ Canet ★★★☆ £F
Puligny-Montrachet ★★★ £E

Dom. Jacques Carillon *www.jacques-carillon.com*
As explained above, there are two Carillon domaines now and it remains to be seen which way each of them will develop. Jacques takes over the Referts vineyard and the holding in Bienvenue-Bâtard, whilst sharing the Puligny villages, Perrières and Champ-Canet vineyards as well as the holding at Chassagne Macherelles. He also makes white wine from his holding in the Mercurey Champs Martin vineyard.

Recommended Whites:
Bienvenues-Bâtard-Montrachet ✪✪✪✪✪ £H
Puligny-Montrachet 1er Cru Referts ★★★★☆ £F
Puligny-Montrachet 1er Cru Perrières ★★★★ £F
Puligny-Montrachet 1er Cru Champ Canet ★★★☆ £F
Puligny-Montrachet ★★★ £E

✪ Dom. Carré-Courbin (Volnay)
There has been a younger generation in charge here in recent

years and the structure and balance in the wines has been steadily improved. There was a tendency for the wines from just over 9 ha of vineyards to be too extracted and without a compensating fruit richness. There is classic Volnay perfume, expression and refinement allied to good grip and intensity. Premiers crus Clos de la Cave des Ducs and Taillepieds are especially fine with weight and breadth to go with the style and intensity. Pommard Grands Épenots is sturdy, powerful and requires the greatest patience. Drink village Volnay and Pommard with 5 years' or more, Volnay premiers crus with 6-10 and Grands Épenots with 10 or more. Some red and white Beaune premier cru Les Reversées is also made along with some Meursault.

Recommended Reds:
Volnay 1er Cru Taillepieds ★★★★★ £F
Volnay 1er Cru Clos de la Cave des Ducs ★★★★ £F
Volnay 1er Cru Les Lurets ★★★★ £F
Volnay 1er Cru Robardelle ★★★★ £F
Volnay Vieilles Vignes ★★★★ £E   Volnay ★★★ £E
Pommard 1er Cru Grands Epenots ★★★★ £F
Pommard ★★★ £E

✪✪ Sylvain Cathiard (Vosne-Romanée)
Sylvain Cathiard makes very refined, super stylish and harmonious wines. In the past some of the lesser wines needed a little more richness and ripeness but that's no longer the case with Sylvain's son Sébastien making the wines. In truth at Villages level, they are now excellent. All Vosne-Romanée (including an exceptional village example) show marvellous expression, purity as well as breadth, depth and intensity. The inspired grand cru Romanée-Saint-Vivant is exquisitely intense, seductive and refined. Of the Vosne premiers crus, En Orveaux (nearest to Chambolle-Musigny) is classy and fruit-rich, Aux Reignots has fabulous perfume and a veritable peacock's tail expression on the palate. Suchots and Malconsorts are a little bigger and richer - the purity and intensity of Suchots contrasts with the grand cru like breadth and depth of Malconsorts. Nuits-Saint-Georges Aux Murgers has great class, very much the essence of Nuits. A sophisticated Bourgogne Rouge and elegant Chambolle-Musigny apart, all the wines deserve to be kept for at least 5 or 6 years from the vintage date.

Recommended Reds:
Romanée-Saint-Vivant ✪✪✪✪✪ £H
Vosne-Romanée 1er Cru Les Malconsorts ✪✪✪✪✪ £F
Vosne-Romanée 1er Cru Les Suchots ★★★★★ £F
Vosne-Romanée 1er Cru En Orveaux ★★★★★ £F
Vosne-Romanée 1er Cru Aux Reignots ★★★★☆ £F
Vosne-Romanée ★★★☆ £E
Nuits-Saint-Georges 1er Cru Aux Murgers ★★★★☆ £E
Chambolle-Musigny Clos de L'Orme ★★★★ £F
Bourgogne Rouge ★★☆ £C

Maison Champy (Beaune) *www.champy.fr*
This négociant house founded in 1720 is the oldest in Burgundy. In 2012, Pierre Beuchet, the founder of Diva wine distribution took over the company from the Meurgey family who had bought the maison in 1990 and greatly improved the wines, especially since 1999 when the talented Dimitri Bazas was appointed oenologist and winemaker. He is now managing director. The heart of the business is Champy's ownership of now 25 ha in the Côte de Beaune; these vineyards are farmed in a fine mix of sustainable, agriculture biologique and biodynamic viticulture. Champy has an important presence in Pernand Vegelesses – in 2014, the Pernand Ile de Vegelesses was as good as several Corton-Charlemagne next door-

Burgundy /Côte d'Or & Côte Chalonnaise

their own Charlemagne is excellent. Others gentle buys are the Beaune 1er cru reds , which are benchmarks made by whole-grape fermentation for extra finesse (exceptional Beaune Les Cras in 2015). Good contracts in the Côte de Nuits bring fine examples of Bonnes Mares, Romanée-Saint-Vivant and Vosne Romanée Les Suchots. (ME)

Recommended Reds:

Bonnes Mares ★★★★ £G   Romanée-Saint-Vivant ★★★★ £G

Vosne Romanée Les Suchots ★★★★ £F

Beaune 1er Cru Les Cras ★★★☆ £E

Beaune 1er Cru Les Champs Pimonts ★★★ £E

Beaune 1er Cru Les Grèves ★★★ £E

Savigny -lès- Beaune Villages ★★ £D

Recommended Whites:

Corton-Charlemagne ★★★★ £F

Meursault 1er Cru Genevrières ★★★ £E

Pernand Vergelesses Ile de Vergelesses ★★★☆ £E

Chandon de Briailles   www.chandondebriailles.com

A popular and fine domaine and a leading proponent of Savigny-lès-Beaune, Pernand-Vergelesses and Corton. François de Nicolay and his sister Claude Drouhin work with their mother to produce wines from low yields that favour elegance over power. Corton Clos du Roi is the top red, the most structured and profound. Corton-Bressandes has better dimension, weight and length than Les Maréchaudes, though the latter almost matches it for finesse and style. The Pernand-Vergelesses are only medium-bodied, though the racy, slender but classy and intense Île des Vergelesses adds a little more weight with age. Both Savigny wines can be good value, with a stylish Fourneaux and slightly leaner Les Lavières. Whites are very good too, tight and minerally when very young but with real intensity and length, becoming quite rich with a little age. The Corton becomes fuller and broader than a deeper, more minerally Corton-Charlemagne. François de Nicolay also owns a vineyard in his own right, producing an aromatic, plump white Savigny.

Recommended Reds:

Corton Clos du Roi ★★★★ £F

Corton Les Bressandes ★★★★ £F

Corton Les Maréchaudes ★★★★ £F

Volnay 1er Cru Les Caillerets ★★★☆ £E

Pernand-Vergelesses 1er Cru Île des Vergelesses ★★★ £D

Pernand-Vergelesses 1er Cru Les Vergelesses ★★★ £D

Savigny-lès-Beaune 1er Cru Les Fourneaux ★★★ £D

Savigny-lès-Beaune 1er Cru Les Lavières ★★ £D

Recommended Whites:

Corton-Charlemagne ★★★★ £F   Corton Blanc ★★★★ £F

Pernand-Vergelesses 1er Cru Île des Vergelesses ★★★ £D

Savigny-lès-Beaune 1er Cru Aux Vergelesses ★★★ £D

Dom. Chanson (Beaune)   www.chanson-vins.com

Since its acquisition in 1999 by the Jacques Bollinger group, the wines of this historic Beaune House have been greatly improved. The image and core reality now focuses on the Chanson domaine (NB the name change) of 45 ha of vineyards owned exclusively in Premiers and Grands Crus of the Côte d'Or: Most particularly, Chanson is rightly considered as one of the specialists in the 10 Premiers Crus of Beaune, where value and quality happily co-exist in these still fairly reasonably priced fine Burgundies. Gilles de Courcel of the exceptional Domaine de Courcel in Pommard is in his day job managing director of Chanson, his winemaker the very talented Jean-Pierre Confuron. Of the Beaune Premiers Crus, in white the Clos des Mouches, is a suave sophisticated white burgundy punching

above its weight, the oak better integrated than in other houses' versions of this well -known vineyard. Of the reds, Beaune Greves or Fevres are usually the most complete, though in terroir-expressive 2014, Beaune Teurons stole the show for its richness and a delightful smokiness. The Chanson domaine from Santeay ranges right on through Corton to the grands crus of Gevrey Chambertin. Confuron also makes excellent Chablis from favoured growers (see Chablis entry). Perhaps the most unusual and beguiling wine is the Corton Grand Cru Vergennes Blanc: Above Aloxe, this is red wine country save that this plot has a stratum of white limestone making it the cradle of an exceptional Chardonnay for rich seafood, lobster, crab and even tuna. (ME)

Recommended Reds:

Chambertin Clos de Bèze Grand Cru ★★★★ £G

Bonnes Mares Grand Cru ★★★★ £G

Le Corton Grand Cru ★★★★ £G   Beaune 1er Cru Grèves ★★★☆ £E

Beaune 1er Cru Teurons ★★★☆ £E

Beaune 1er Cru Clos des Fèves ★★★☆ £E

Savigny-lès-Beaune 1er Cru Dominode ★★★☆ £E

Recommended Whites:

Corton Charlemagne Grand Cru ★★★★ £F

Corton Vergennes Grand Cru ★★★★ £F

Beaune 1er Cru Clos des Mouches ★★★☆ £E

Pernand-Vergelesses 1er Cru Les Caradeux ★★★☆ £E

Philippe Charlopin   www.domaine-charlopin-parizot.com

Starting from a meagre 1.8 ha of family vineyards in 1976, Philippe Charlopin's Gevrey-Chambertin based holdings have since mushroomed to more than 25 ha. To the more humble village parcels have been added small segments of several grands crus. Harvesting often very late for Burgundy, Philippe subjects his very ripe grapes to a rigorous selection. Vinification involves a long maceration followed by minimal racking (sometimes leading to a measure of reduction in the wines) and quite liberal helpings of new oak; 100% new oak in the case of the Vieilles Vignes Gevrey-Chambertin and the 7 grands crus. They are also unfined and unfiltered. The result is usually richly textured, chewy, sometimes tannic wines, a style that does work (for the most part) and the wines still reflect the general style of their appellations. The regular village wines have plenty of immediate appeal and are for relatively early drinking. The top wines will keep for at least a decade. Of the simpler reds, the Marsannay and Bourgogne Rouge can be good value while the whites, too, can offer ample fruit and character. Bonnes Mares, Clos de Vougeot and Echézeaux are the newest of the grands crus.

Recommended Reds:

Chambertin ★★★★ £H   Charmes-Chambertin ★★★★ £G

Mazis-Chambertin ★★★★ £G   Clos Saint-Denis ★★★★ £G

Bonnes Mares ★★★★ £G

Gevrey-Chambertin Vieilles Vignes ★★★ £F

Gevrey-Chambertin La Justice ★★ £F   Chambolle-Musigny ★★★ £F

Vosne-Romanée ★★★ £F   Morey-Saint-Denis ★★ £E

Marsannay En Montchenevoy ★★ £D

Fixin Clos de Fixey ★★ £D   Bourgogne Rouge ★★ £D

Recommended Whites:

Fixin Blanc ★★£D   Marsannay Blanc ★★ £D

Ch. de La Maltroye (Chassagne-Montrachet)

In a few short years the fortunes of this 15 ha Chassagne-Montrachet estate have been transformed. Jean-Pierre Cornut now makes some of the best wines in the appellation. The premier cru

whites are all consistently fine – ripe, concentrated and with terrific fruit intensity and excellent balance. Dents de Chien is arguably the best Chassagne premier cru made by the Domaine while La Romanée is minerally and elegant and Grandes Ruchottes is more powerful but also minerally. The more affordable white Santenay is a fine example of the appellation. There is a significant amount of red produced too, including that from part of the 2.5 ha Clos du Château de la Maltroye *monopole*. It has depth, intensity and real charm, becoming increasingly silky with age. A little Bâtard-Montrachet is also made.

Recommended Reds:
Chassagne-Montrachet 1er Cru Clos Château de Maltroye ★★★ £E
Chassagne-Montrachet 1er Cru Clos Saint-Jean ★★★ £E
Santenay 1er Cru Comme ★★ £D

Recommended Whites:
Chassagne-Montrachet 1er Cru Dent de Chien ★★★★ £F
Chassagne-Montrachet 1er Cru Clos Château de Maltroye ★★★☆ £F
Chassagne-Montrachet 1er Cru Grandes Ruchottes ★★★★ £F
Chassagne-Montrachet 1er Cru Morgeot Vignes Blanches ★★★★ £F
Chassagne-Montrachet 1er Cru La Romanée ★★★★ £F
Chassagne-Montrachet 1er Cru Chevenottes ★★★☆ £F
Chassagne-Montrachet ★★★☆ £E
Santenay 1er Cru Comme ★★★ £D

Ch. de Puligny-Montrachet *www.chateaudepuligny.com*
The transformation of this important domaine with 20 ha of vineyards is the work of Étienne de Montille (of Domaine de MONTILLE). From the beginning of 2002 he has reduced yields and moved to organic practices, giving whites of much better definition, depth and style. Holdings include significant amounts of Saint Aubin, Monthelie and Chassagne-Montrachet as well as premiers crus in Meursault and Puligny-Montrachet. Puligny Folatières and both Meursault Poruzots and Perrièrres combine intensity with class. Of reds tasted, Saint Aubin En Remilly is far better than Monthelie, which still lacks depth and concentration. Very small amounts of Chevalier-Montrachet and Le Montrachet are also made.

Recommended Reds:
Pommard ★★☆ £E   Saint-Aubin 1er Cru En Remilly ★★ £D
Monthelie ★☆ £D

Recommended Whites:
Puligny-Montrachet 1er Cru Les Folatières ★★★★ £F
Puligny-Montrachet ★★★ £E
Meursault 1er Cru Perrières ★★★★ £F
Meursault 1er Cru Les Poruzots ★★★★ £F
Chassagne-Montrachet ★★★ £E
Saint-Aubin 1er Cru En Remilly ★★★ £E
Monthelie ★★☆ £D   Bourgogne Blanc Clos du Château ★★☆ £D

Dom. Alain Chavy (Puligny-Montrachet)
Alain and Jean-Louis, sons of Gérard, made many changes at their family's small domaine, prior to dividing the vineyards between them after the 2004 vintage. Typical of small, well-run family domaines, there are no short cuts taken and every wine is given the same measure of respect. Bourgogne Blanc can be very good while the regular example of Puligny has some substance and style and a good example of Saint-Aubin is made too. But it is the premiers crus that are forging the reputation, including a very minerally, full Perrières and an elegant Clavoillons that contrasts with the firmer, more structured Folatières. An intense weighty Champs-Gain shows real promise too. The wines can be a bit reduced if drunk very young but the generally excellent quality is matched by good prices. Older

wines are labelled Gérard Chavy et Fils.
Recommended Whites:
Puligny-Montrachet 1er Cru Perrières ★★★★ £E
Puligny-Montrachet 1er Cru Clavoillons ★★★★ £E
Puligny-Montrachet 1er Cru Folatières ★★★★ £E
Puligny-Montrachet 1er Cru Champs-Gain ★★★★ £E
Puligny-Montrachet Charmes ★★★☆ £D
Puligny-Montrachet ★★★ £D
Saint-Aubin 1er Cru En Remilly ★★☆ £D
Bourgogne Blanc ★★ £C

Dom. Robert Chevillon *www.domainerobertchevillon.fr*
Robert Chevillon is one of the celebrated names of this appellation at the southern end of the Côte de Nuits, a village that is synonymous with red Burgundy. In 2003, Robert made way for his sons and Bertrand Chevillon now makes the wines from the vines tended by his older brother, Denis. There are no less than eight different premiers crus (six of them in the central section of Nuits, which has a higher clay content and is south of the town itself), all with a high average vine age. No two taste quite the same, each giving a different expression of its individual *terroir*. With relatively high fermentation temperatures and a small percentage of stems retained, the wines are fairly full-bodied and tannic but with the flesh, depth and fruit intensity to be very rich and satisfying with 8–10 years' age. The regular Nuits, Bousselots and to a lesser extent Chaignots (the Chevillons' two crus north of Nuits) can be a bit light in lesser vintages but the others regularly deliver the fruit to match their robust structures. The fullest and most structured are the Les Saint-Georges and Vaucrains, followed by Les Cailles. Also made is a little white Nuits-Saint-Georges with a very good reputation.

Recommended Reds:
Nuits-Saint-Georges 1er Cru Les Vaucrains ★★★★ £F
Nuits-Saint-Georges 1er Cru Les Saint-Georges ★★★★ £F
Nuits-Saint-Georges 1er Cru Les Cailles ★★★★ £F
Nuits-Saint-Georges 1er Cru Les Chaignots ★★★☆ £E
Nuits-Saint-Georges 1er Cru Les Perrières ★★★ £E
Nuits-Saint-Georges 1er Cru Les Pruliers ★★★ £E
Nuits-Saint-Georges 1er Cru Les Roncières ★★★ £E
Nuits-Saint-Georges 1er Cru Les Bousselots ★★★ £E
Nuits-Saint-Georges Vieilles Vignes ★★★ £E
Bourgogne Rouge ★★ £D

Dom. Chofflet-Valdenaire (Givry)
This 13 ha Givry estate is one of but a handful that is able to produce ripe well balanced reds in both hotter and cooler vintages. Two reds are particularly good, the premiers crus Clos de Choué and Clos Jus. Both see one-third new oak but it is rarely obvious. The stylish Clos de Choué exhibits floral and mineral nuances and ripe fruit and shows much more refinement than the basic. red. Still more classy Clos Jus adds a touch of smoke and spice and has more depth and density. There is no hurry for these, both are structured wines deserving at least 5-6 years' age. The white Givry is attractive and fruit-driven but with good substance.

Recommended Reds:
Givry 1er Cru Clos Jus ★★★ £D   Givry 1er Cru Clos de Choué ★★☆ £D
Givry ★★ £C

Recommended Whites:
Givry Les Galaffres ★★ £D

❀ Bruno Clair (Marsannay) *www.brunoclair.com*
Bruno Clair has been a style leader for nearly three decades,

France

producing the mostly northern Nuits reds of great balance, harmony and elegance. One of the beneficiaries of the noted Clair-Daü estate (many of the prime vineyards went to Louis JADOT), he now commands 23 ha, nearly 5 ha of which are planted to Chardonnay. The classics are his Gevrey premiers crus Clos Saint-Jacques and Cazetiers, and the grand cru Chambertin Clos de Bèze. These are wines with great purity, elegance and with exceptional length of flavour. Not to be overlooked are the *monopole* Clos du Fonteny, a deep, dense Savigny, La Dominode, and an increasingly classy Corton-Charlemagne. The best value lies in the three Marsannay reds (though a white can be good too), with the floral, intense Longeroies usually vying with the slightly darker-fruited Grasses Têtes as the best of these. While the reds have been generally less impressive in lighter vintages such as 1997, there are excellent 96s, 98s and 99s, and 00, 01 and 02 all look promising. All the reds can seem a little firm and austere when young and shouldn't be drunk with less than 3 or 4 years' age; 7 or 8 for the top examples - the 04s are typically backward but intense and structured. A rare Morey-Saint-Denis white is made from the same vineyard as the red, while a white Pernand-Vergelesses is a recent addition.

Recommended Reds:
Chambertin Clos de Bèze ★★★★★ £G
Gevrey-Chambertin 1er Cru Clos Saint-Jacques ★★★★★ £G
Gevrey-Chambertin 1er Cru Les Cazetiers ★★★★ £G
Gevrey-Chambertin 1er Cru Petite Chapelle ★★★★ £F
Gevrey-Chambertin 1er Cru Clos du Fonteny ★★★★ £F
Morey-Saint-Denis En La Rue de Vergy ★★★ £E
Chambolle-Musigny Véroilles ★★☆ £E
Vosne-Romanée Champs-Perdrix ★★★ £E
Savigny-lès-Beaune 1er Cru La Dominode ★★★★ £E
Fixin La Croix Blanche Domaine André Geoffroy ★★★ £E
Marsannay Grasses Têtes ★★★ £D   Marsannay Longeroies ★★★ £D
Marsannay Vaudenelles ★★☆ £D

Recommended Whites:
Corton-Charlemagne ★★★★ £G
Morey-Saint-Denis En La Rue de Vergy ★★★ £E
Pernand-Vergelesses ★★ £D   Marsannay Blanc ★★ £D

Françoise et Denis Clair (Santenay) *www.domaineclair.fr*
Denis and his son Jean-Baptiste produce some of the best examples of red Santenay but their 14 ha of vineyards also includes fine Saint-Aubin whites. Santenays range from a deep and intense village-level Clos Genet to fine premiers crus including rich and structured Clos de Tavannes and classy Clos de la Comme. While prices have risen the red are particularly good in the best vintages and provide a good alternative to village level wines from more famous appellations. In cooler or wet vintages the wines can suffer more than most. Of the Saint-Aubin whites, Murgers des Dents de Chien is particularly well-structured and Les Frionnes is intense and composed with delicious fruit. Others are En Remilly and Sur le Sentier des Cloux. Also made is some Puligny-Montrachet La Garenne.

Recommended Reds:
Santenay 1er Cru Clos de la Comme ★★★ £E
Santenay 1er Cru Beaurepaire ★★★ £E
Santenay 1er Cru Clos des Tavannes ★★★ £E
Santenay 1er Cru Clos des Mouches ★★☆ £E
Santenay Clos Genet ★★ £D

Recommended Whites:
Saint-Aubin 1er Cru Murgers des Dents de Chien ★★★ £D
Saint-Aubin 1er Cru Les Frionnes ★★★ £D

✿ Bruno Clavelier (Vosne-Romanée) *www.bruno-clavelier.com*
Bruno Clavelier is a relatively new star who took over his grandfather's vines in 1987 and started bottling wine previously sold in bulk. He has since expanded into other Côte de Nuits communes. The domaine is now fully biodynamic and there has been a steady refinement in the wines while adding greater richness and expression, particularly in the most recent vintages. The amount of new oak used is low and the average vine age very high (most are either 60 or 80 years old), giving wines with delicious fruit, ample concentration and a real sense *terroir*. Of the premiers crus, Vosne-Romanée Beaux-Monts has the greater structure, Aux Brulées a touch more refinement. The Nuits-Saint-Georges, lying close to Vosne-Romanée, tastes like a cross between the two appellations. The Chambolle-Musigny is even better, combining grace and purity with richness. From 2000 the regular Vosne-Romanée, from some of the highest slopes in the commune, has been bottled as La Combe Brulée and Les Hauts de Beaux Monts. A third of a hectare of Corton Rognets was purchased in 1999 and is also from old vines and has the potential to be the best wine of the lot.

Recommended Reds:
Vosne-Romanée 1er Cru Les Beaux Monts V V ★★★★☆ £F
Vosne-Romanée 1er Cru Aux Brulées ★★★★ £F
Vosne-Romanée La Combe Brulée V V ★★★★ £F
Vosne-Romanée Les Hauts Maizières V V ★★★☆ £F
Vosne-Romanée La Montagne ★★★☆ £E
Vosne-Romanée Les Hauts de Beaux Monts ★★★☆ £E
Chambolle-Musigny 1er Cru Combe d'Orveau V V ★★★★★ £F
Nuits-Saint-Georges 1er Cru Aux Cras ★★★★ £E
Gevrey-Chambertin 1er Cru Les Corbeaux ★★★ £F

Clos Salomon (Givry) *www.du-gardin.com/clossalomon*
This 8.5 ha estate is centred on a single vineyard, the walled Clos Salomon which dates from the middle ages. By pursuing very low yields, Ludovic du Gardin (whose family have owned the Clos since 1632) and Fabrice Perrotto produce a powerful, fleshy Burgundy full of wild red fruits. After 12 months in 30% new oak it is bottled unfined and unfiltered. While it can struggle in cooler vintages, it is ripe with real breadth and a vibrant acidity in good years. A white Montagny Le Clou (6000 bottles) was first produced in 2003 and is quite dense and flavoursome. Better is the new white Givry (less than 3000 bottles) which is intense, pure and mineral with the depth and structure to improve for at 3-5 years.

Recommended Reds:
Givry 1er Cru ★★★ £D

Recommended Whites:
Givry 1er Cru La Grande Berge ★★★☆ £D
Pernand-Vergelesses ★★☆ £C

✿ Clos de Tart (Clos de Tart) *www.clos-de-tart.com*
A former winemaker at the Hospice de Beaune and scholarly cartographer of Bourgogne Viticole, Sylvain Pitiot has in 20 years since 1996 made this famous domaine great again. Founded by the Sisters of the Abbey of Tart in the 12th Century, the 7.63 walled vineyard passed in the 1930s to the Mommessin family, who shrewdly bought it for a song. Sixty years on, they knew that the viticulture and winemaking needed improving and gave Sylvain carte blanche to restore the vineyard and the means to do it. He began a complete referencing of every part of the vineyard and its complex mix of soils, also monitoring every incidence of diseases like oidium and mildew. He says that "in my time here I feel I have got to know every one of the 80,000 vines". He also progressively

made viticulture ultra eco-friendly. Today most of the precepts of biodynamism are followed, without the constraints of certification. Yields have dropped dramatically and viti-viniculture is an intelligent mix of traditional de-stemming and whole grape fermentation. The result is that Clos de Tart has the succulence of neighbouring Clos des Lambrays but with its own style of firmer but ripe tannins in tune with Climate Change. A second wine La Forge is made in less complex vintages and is fine and elegant. Sylvain officially "retired" in autumn 2015 to spend more time with his family and books plus a new project in the Chalonnais. He is delighted that his successor at Clos de Tart is Jacques Devignes. formerly at L'Arlot. (ME)

Recommended Reds:
Clos de Tart ✪✪✪✪✪ £G
Morey-Saint-Denis 1er Cru La Forge ★★★ £E

✪✪ Jean-François Coche-Dury (Meursault)

An outstanding domaine. Jean-François's Meursaults are rivalled only by those from LAFON and perhaps one or two others. Yet apart from from a little grand cru Corton-Charlemagne and premier cru Perrières, his reputation has been established with village-level wines, an indication of his talent and dedication. There is great attention to detail in the vineyard and as at many top-quality estates vines are replaced one at time when necessary and from the best existing plant material. The approach to vinification is flexible to maximise the potential of each vintage and long fermentations are also favoured. What makes the wines so special? Well, a grace, subtlety and purity allied to a remarkably well delineated complexity. The depth, length, structure and concentration are also given. The floral, fruit and mineral components, as well as a fine grilled nuts character that comes with age, give the wines extra finesse over most other examples. Of 11ha, almost 2.5 are planted to Pinot Noir and a chance to try the Volnay Premier Cru shouldn't be passed up. A little red Auxey-Duresses and Monthelie are also made. The Meursault Vireuils is now being bottled separately as Vireuils Dessous and Vireuils Dessus. Nearly all the whites deserve 5 years' age but will keep for 10 or more. Finding any of the wines at reasonable prices will be a minor miracle.

Recommended Reds:
Volnay 1er Cru ★★★☆ £F   Bourgogne Pinot Noir ★☆ £D

Recommended Whites:
Corton-Charlemagne ✪✪✪✪✪ £H
Meursault 1er Cru Perrières ✪✪✪✪✪ £H
Meursault 1er Cru Rougeots ★★★★★ £G
Meursault Chevalières ★★★★☆ £G Meursault Caillerets ★★★★☆ £G
Meursault Vireuils ★★★★ £F   Meursault Narvaux ★★★★ £F
Puligny-Montrachet Les Enseignières ★★★★☆ £G
Bourgogne Chardonnay ★★☆ £D   Bourgogne Aligoté ★☆ £D

Dom. Marc Colin et Fils (Saint-Aubin) www.marc-colin.com

Marc Colin and his sons, Joseph, Pierre-Yves and Damien manage 20 ha and the domaine's reputation is built on its finest whites. These are rich, ripe wines with good complexity and a distinct and attractive minerality in the best examples. Several Chassagne-Montrachets, led by an intense, minerally Caillerets, are made to a high standard and there is a galaxy of really fine Saint-Aubin in both colours (more than a third of the estate is planted to Pinot Noir). A very minerally, stylish En Remilly vies with a slightly more structured La Chatenière and classy Les Charmes as the best Saint-Aubin white, though newish Sentier du Clou from old vines is very rich. For red, the Santenay Vieilles Vignes shows what is possible from that appellation, particularly when from an excellent vintage. This still-

expanding domaine also produces some négociant wines, including a Bâtard-Montrachet.

Recommended Reds:
Santenay Vieilles Vignes ★★★ £D   Chassagne-Montrachet ★★ £D
Saint-Aubin 1er Cru Frionnes ★★★ £D
Saint-Aubin 1er Cru ★★ £D   Saint-Aubin ★☆ £C

Recommended Whites:
Montrachet ★★★★★ £H
Chassagne-Montrachet 1er Cru Caillerets ★★★★ £G
Chassagne-Montrachet 1er Cru Chevenottes ★★★★ £F
Chassagne-Montrachet 1er Cru Vide Bourse ★★★★ £E
Chassagne-Montrachet 1er Cru Champ Gain ★★★★ £E
Chassagne-Montrachet Enseignières ★★★☆ £E
Puligny-Montrachet 1er Cru Garennes ★★★★ £F
Saint-Aubin 1er Cru En Remilly ★★★☆ £D
Saint-Aubin 1er Cru Les Charmes ★★★ £D
Saint-Aubin 1er Cru La Chatenière ★★★ £D
Saint-Aubin 1er Cru Sentier du Clou ★★★ £D
Saint-Aubin 1er Cru En Montceau ★★★ £D
Saint-Aubin 1er Cru Les Combes ★★☆ £D
Saint-Aubin Fontenotte ★★☆ £D   Bourgogne La Combe ★★☆ £D

Michel Colin-Deléger et Fils (Chassagne-Montrachet)

It is all change here as in 2004 most of the family's 19 ha of vineyards were divided between Michel's sons Philippe and Bruno. Starting with the 04 vintage most of the wines below appear under their respective labels. But the standard here has been very high, with intense, concentrated but beautifully balanced wines produced from low-yielding vines. En Remilly heads a raft of fine Chassagne-Montrachet premiers crus. Of the very fine Puligny-Montrachet premiers crus made in small quantities, an outstanding Les Demoiselles is tucked up against a tiny amount of grand cru Chevalier-Montrachet. The reds used to be a little tough but are now richer with riper tannins, especially from a good red wine vintage. Santenay Gravières and Chassagne-Montrachet Morgeots both stand out; Michel Colin is unusual in producing a fine example of both red and white Morgeots. The best reds, like the whites, will benefit from 5 or 6 years' age, sometimes more. If buying from 04 or 05 expect to find only Chassagne Remilly, Puligny Demoiselles and the Chevalier-Montrachet under Michel's own label.

Recommended Reds:
Chassagne-Montrachet Morgeots ★★★ £E
Chassagne-Montrachet Vieilles Vignes ★★ £D
Santenay 1er Cru Gravières ★★★ £D   Santenay ★★ £C

Recommended Whites:
Puligny-Montrachet 1er Cru Les Demoiselles ★★★★★ £G
Puligny-Montrachet 1er Cru La Truffière ★★★★ £G
Puligny-Montrachet ★★★☆ £F
Chassagne-Montrachet 1er Cru Morgeots ★★★★ £F
Chassagne-Montrachet 1er Cru En Remilly ★★★★ £F
Chassagne-Montrachet 1er Cru Les Chaumées ★★★★ £F
Chassagne-Montrachet 1er Cru Vergers ★★★★ £F
Chassagne-Montrachet 1er Cru Chevenottes ★★★ £F
Chassagne-Montrachet 1er Cru La Maltroie ★★★ £F
Chassagne-Montrachet ★★★ £E
Saint-Aubin 1er Cru Les Charmois ★★★ £D

Dom. Jean-Jacques Confuron www.jjconfuron.com

Alain Meunier and his wife Sophie make increasingly good wines from 8 ha of their own vineyards in the heart of the Côte de Nuits. By following organic principles, much has been done to restore the

France

health of the vineyard and yields are low. A cold pre-fermentation maceration is employed, with moderately high temperatures, and a lot of new oak is used in ageing the wines. Quite dense and concentrated when young, the powerful fruit unfurls with 5–10 years' age. The results can be a little uneven and the wines have occasionally suffered from a little reduction or too much oak. But if patience is needed there's great intensity and length of flavour, particularly in the premiers and grands crus. Alain Meunier also oversees production for the part-domaine, partnégociant Domaine Féry/Féry-Meunier label.

Recommended Reds:

Romanée-Saint-Vivant ★★★★★ £G Clos Vougeot ★★★★ £G
Vosne-Romanée 1er Cru Beaux Monts ★★★★ £E
Chambolle-Musigny 1er Cru ★★★★ £E
Chambolle-Musigny ★★★ £E
Nuits-Saint-Georges 1er Cru Boudots ★★★★ £E
Nuits-Saint-Georges Les Fleurières ★★★ £E
Nuits-Saint-Georges Chaboeufs ★★★ £E
Côte de Nuits-Villages Les Vignottes ★★☆ £D

Dom. Confuron-Cotétidot (Vosne-Romanée)

The next generation, Jean-Pierre and Yves now maintain this fine 11 ha. property, further building on their father Jacky's considerable achievements, particularly in the vineyards. In truth, they have done rather more than that. For both are consummate winemakers, linked to Gilles de Courcel of the historic Domaine de Courcel in Pommard: Gilles is also head of the revitalised Domaine Chanson, where Jean-Pierre has immeasurably improved its wines on the Cote de Beaune and from Chablis. All the while, Yves weaves his magical lightness of touch at De Courcel. Yves is on his home patch a master of whole grape fermentations, which has put an athletic step in the Confuron-Cotétidot reds, without sacrificing their serious grandeur. Now with finer tannins, partly as a result of climate change and a judicious touch of new oak, they are fin wines for today, where you have to be slightly less patient than before. I particularly like the Vosne Les Suchots and the Gevrey Lavaux Saint Jacques, which have freshness, elegance and precision with a discreet underlying power to remind you where they come from. A little Charmes-Chambertin and Echezeaux is also made. (ME)

Recommended Reds:

Charmes-Chambertin ★★★★ £G Echezeaux ★★★★ £G
Vosne- Romanée 1er Cru Suchots ★★★★ £F
Gevrey-Chambertin 1er Cru Lavaux-Saint-Jacques ★★★★ £F
Gevrey -Chambertin 1ere Cru Petite Chapelle ★★★★ £F
Vosne- Romanée ★★★ £E Chambolle-Musigny ★★★ £E

>> Dom. François Confuron-Gindre (VosneRomanée)

Confuron is a famous name shared by several growers in Vosne Romanée. This 10 ha. domaine of the delightful couple, François Confuron and his wife Claudine (née Gindre) may be the least known of the clan, yet their wines were a highlight of my en primeur tastings in January 2016.The 1er Crus and one Grand Cru have the density and richness of old vines, are aged in a deep cool cellar, but are available only in limited quantities: My favourites of the Vosnes in both challenging 2013 and better fruited 2014 are the aptly- named Les Brûlées, with its thick- textured vielles vignes fruit and opulent vinosity, touched with smoke- great with rib of beef; in fascinating contrast Les Beaumonts is sophisticated, aristocratic, keeping its counsel and worth cellaring. Much of this sizeable estate's production is in Bourgogne Rouge, one of the best around and going for a song- a real bargain, buy now, as Burgundy

prices rise steeply with the expected shortfall in the 2016 harvest. The Confurons' son Edouard has just finished his studies at the Lycée Viticole de Beaune and is travelling the wine world in both hemispheres before joining the domaine. (ME)

Recommended Reds:

Èchezeaux Grand Cru ★★★★ £G
Vosne Romanée I er Cru Les Brûlées ★★★★ £F
Vosne Romanée 1er Cru Les Beaumonts ★★★★ £F
Nuits St Georges ★★★ £E Bourgogne Rouge ★★☆ £D

Dom. de Courcel (Pommard)

Gilles de Courcel works with Yves Confuron (CONFURON-COTÉTIDOT), a winemaker who favours whole-bunch fermentation after having harvested late for fully ripe grapes. Yields are low and the percentage of wine bottled by the domaine has gone from around half to the lion's share of what it grows. At the heart of the estate's 8 ha is 5 ha of Grand Epenots, supplemented by sometimes brilliant Rugiens and another classy premier cru, Fremiers. There were some fine wines made prior to Yves's arrival but the standard is even higher now. Recent vintages have been vigorous, sturdy, concentrated, more oaky than previously and capable of ageing for at least a decade. Don't go near the wines with less than 8-10 years age - all show typical power and extract - but it's not just the extract but also a reductive component that impedes early enjoyment. Grand Clos des Epenots and the Rugiens need almost that long before they've even started to open up. The elegance and complexity of the Rugiens is only fully apparent with age. Consistently excellent Bourgogne Rouge deserves a couple of years' bottle-age, too. A fine village Pommard, Vaumuriens, has been made since 1999. The domaine had a very hard time in 2014 with severe hail damage. Wait for the 2015 which should be epic.

Recommended Reds:

Pommard 1er Cru Rugiens ★★★★★ £F
Pommard 1er Cru Grand Clos des Epenots ★★★★☆ £F
Pommard 1er Cru Fremiers ★★★☆ £E
Pommard Les Valmuriens ★★★☆ £E
Pommard 1er Cru Croix Noires ★★★☆ £E
Bourgogne Rouge ★★ £D

Dom. Pierre Damoy www.domaine-pierre-damoy.com

Under the direction of the young Pierre Damoy (the current generation Damoy who shares the domaine's name), this important 11 ha estate only started to realise its potential in the 1990s. A remarkable 5.3 ha are in Chambertin Clos-de-Bèze but as well as a decent chunk (2.2 ha) of Chapelle-Chambertin there's some Chambertin and a solely-owned village *lieu-dit*, Clos Tamisot from vineyards surrounding the cellar. The wines are harvested late and the yields are now low, considerably reduced from what they were prior to Pierre's stewardship. The wines are lush, powerful and concentrated, with good breadth and length, but are also oaky with a lot of tannin, particularly in a heavily structured and more austere Chambertin. There has been a lack of consistency in the 1990s but now the wines can be broached with confidence. Ripe fruity Bourgogne Blanc and a lightish Bourgogne Rouge are also made.

Recommended Reds:

Chambertin Clos-de-Bèze ★★★★☆ £H
Chambertin ★★★★ £H Chapelle-Chambertin ★★★★ £G
Gevrey-Chambertin Clos Tamisot ★★★ £F
Gevrey-Chambertin ★★☆ £E

Vincent Dancer (Chassagne-Montrachet) *www.vincentdancer.com*
Having made a big impression from the outset, Vincent Dancer had continued to the point of becoming one of Burgundy's most outstanding young *vignerons*. With only 5 ha of vineyards, half red, half white, there isn't very much of any particular wine. Quality comes from the vineyard where life is being restored to the soils and the emphasis is on restricting yields prior to flowering. The winemaking approach is one of minimal intervention using only indigenous yeasts with very long fermentations but no *bâtonnage*. What is strking about the whites is the detail, intensity and definition, as well as fabulous length. The heady, classy Meursault Perrières is destined to be a classic. The reds are not quite at the same level, partly due to mostly more modest origins. But they are properly ripe and well-balanced, avoiding the over-extraction of some in 04. Red Chassagne is atypically good for reds from this appellation. Not all the wines have been tasted (a little Chevalier-Montrachet is also made) but all seem certain to be worth buying.

Recommended Reds:
Pommard 1er Cru Les Pézerolles★★★★ £F
Pommard Les Perrières★★★ £E
Chassagne-Montrachet 1er Cru Morgeot La Grande Borne★★★☆ £E

Recommended Whites:
Meursault 1er Cru Perrières ★★★★★ £F
Meursault Grands Charrons ★★★☆ £F
Meursault Les Corbins ★★★☆ £E
Chassagne-Montrachet 1er Cru Morgeots Tête du Clos ★★★★☆ £F
Chassagne-Montrachet 1er Cru Romanée ★★★★☆ £F
Chassagne-Montrachet ★★★☆ £E

Darviot-Perrin (Monthelie)
Didier Darviot's cellar is in the quiet pretty village of Monthelie but his 9.5 ha estate includes Volnay, Meursault and Chassagne-Montrachet, much of it inherited by his wife. The wines are elegant and racy with fine pure fruit, and are increasingly generous and complex with 5 years' age. Premiers crus Charmes and Perrières are excellent examples of their noble *terroirs*. Dark, deep and intense Volnay with classic perfumes and really delicious fruit show similarly sophisticated winemaking. Though not quite at the same level, these wines are, in fact, a very credible alternative if superstars like COCHE-DURY or COMTES LAFON remain out of reach due to the demand-inflated prices. Village-level Meursaults Clos de la Velle and Tesson have only been produced separately from 2000 and an excellent Meursault Premier Cru Genevrières since 01. A little Pommard is also made.

Recommended Reds:
Volnay 1er Cru Santenots ★★★★ £E
Volnay Les Blanches ★★★ £E Volnay 1er Cru La Gigotte ★★★ £E
Chassagne-Montrachet 1er Cru Les Bondues ★★★ £E
Chassagne-Montrachet Les Chambres ★★★ £D
Monthelie ★★☆ £D

Recommended Whites:
Meursault 1er Cru Genevrières★★★★☆ £F
Meursault 1er Cru Perrières★★★★£F
Meursault 1er Cru Charmes★★★★ £F
Meursault Le Tesson★★★ £E
Meursault Clos de la Velle★★★ £E
Chassagne-Montrachet 1er Cru Blanchots-Dessus★★★★ £F
Chassagne-Montrachet La Bergerie★★★ £F
Bourgogne Blanc Vieilles Vignes★★☆ £C

Jean-Yves Devevey (Hautes-Côtes de Beaune) *www.devevey.com*
Although based in the humble Hautes Côtes, Jean-Yves Devevey is an excellent source of inexpensive red and white Burgundy. Two Hautes-Côtes de Beaune white are both fermented and aged in oak - Les Champs Perdrix is atypically full and concentrated with an unusual mix of cool and ripe fruit flavours. Les Chagnots ('XVIII lunes' for 18 months in 15% new oak) is more overly oak enriched but has lots of promise and is likely to be better than a good many basic village Meursault. Also produced are a very appealing, fruit expressive Beaune Pertuisots with good purity and length, and a village-level Chassagne-Montrachet of good depth and style.

Recommended Reds:
Beaune 1er Cru Pertuisots ★★★ £E

Recommended Whites:
Chassagne-Montrachet★★★☆ £E
Hautes-Côtes de Beaune Les Chagnots XVIII lunes ★★★ £C
Hautes-Côtes de Beaune Les Champs Perdrix ★★☆ £C
Bourgogne Aligoté★☆ £C

Domaines Devillard (Mercurey) *www.domaines-devillard.com*
Bertrand Devillard is the celebrated ex-director of RODET. Domaines Devillard comprises Bertrand Devillard's own 12 ha property in Nuits-Saint-Georges, Domaine des Perdrix as well as red and white Mercurey from Château de Chamirey from his late former wife Christine's family (the labels bear her father's name, Marquis de Jouennes d'Herville, who did much to establish the house of Rodet) and Givrys from Domaine de la Ferté (Arnold Thénard). Those already familiar with the Devillard style (seen in the Rodet wines) of ripe, concentrated fruit with depth and extract, will find the Chalonnaise wines much to their liking. They are in stark contrast to the many lean and under-ripe offerings from the region but are also slightly more forced than some, perhaps sacrificing a little elegance and expression. The intense, powerful Ruelles Mercurey tastes like a promising young red Beaune or Pommard. The Perdrix wines are rich, ample and structured even in lighter vintages and have a deserved following. The Aux Perdrix *monopole* which gives the estate its name is the top wine. (ME)

Domaine des Perdrix
Recommended Reds:
Echezeaux ★★★★ £G Vosne-Romanée ★★★☆ £E
Nuits-Saint-Georges 1er Cru Aux Perdrix ★★★★★ £F
Nuits-Saint-Georges ★★★ £E

Château de Chamirey
Recommended Reds:
Mercurey 1er Cru Les Ruelles★★★★ £D Mercurey★★☆ £D

Recommended Whites:
Mercurey 1er Cru La Mission★★★★ £D Mercurey★★ £D

Domaine de la Ferté
Recommended Reds:
Givry 1er Cru Servoisine ★★★ £D Givry ★★ £C

❋ **Joseph Drouhin (Beaune)** *www.drouhin.com*
An excellent high-profile 73 ha domaine and négociant that combines integrity and know-how. The fourth generation are now at the helm with Frédéric having assumed overall direction from his father, Robert. There are stylish reds and whites at every level but especially from the estate vineyards overseen by the towering Philippe. Striving for better balance in their their top Cote de Beaune whites and their Grands Crus Chablis the use of new oak is being reigned in. As celebrated as any of the Drouhin wines are the red and white from the Beaune premier cru Clos des Mouches. While

France

the red can be good, it can be surpassed by a Grèves bottling, but the white can be superb, with its delicate spice, flavour complexity, real presence on the palate and considerable elegance. Generally the wines are not big or overly powerful yet are dense, intense and expressive. Of the reds, the attractive Côte de Beaune (a Beaune appellation but usually including young-vine Clos des Mouches) and similarly-priced examples usually need 3 years' ageing; Vosne, Chambolle and other village-level wines and the Beaune premiers crus around 6 years; the top crus 8–10 years. Not all the grands crus are of the same standard but Drouhin's versions of Griotte-Chambertin and Grands-Echezeaux, where good examples can be hard to find, are usually excellent. In Chablis, where Drouhin is an important vineyard owner (see Joseph DROUHIN CHABLIS), there are facilities to press the grapes, though vinification takes place in Beaune. A small vineyard in Rully is a recent acquisition, promising better Chalonnaise wines. Drouhin also make the wines for the Marquis de Laguiche including the brilliant, wonderfully refined Montrachet, which comes from the appellation's largest single parcel. DOMAINE DROUHIN is the company's quality outpost in Oregon, run by Veronique (sister to Frédéric and Philippe). As well as those listed, a little of the grands crus Chambertin, Chambertin Clos de Bèze, Charmes-Chambertin, Clos Saint-Denis, Clos de la Roche, Romanée-Saint-Vivant, Corton and Bâtard-Montrachet are also made, as are generic examples of leading village appellations.

Joseph Drouhin
Recommended Reds:
Musigny ✪✪✪✪ £H Grands-Echezeaux ★★★★★ £G
Griotte-Chambertin ★★★★ £G Bonnes Mares ★★★★ £G
Clos de Vougeot ★★★★ £G Echezeaux ★★★ £G
Corton Bressandes ★★★★ £F
Morey-Saint-Denis 1er Cru Clos Sorbé ★★★ £F
Chambolle-Musigny 1er Cru Amoureuses ★★★★ £F
Chambolle-Musigny 1er Cru ★★★ £F
Chambolle-Musigny ★★ £E
Vosne-Romanée 1er Cru Petits Monts ★★★ £F
Vosne-Romanée ★★★ £E
Beaune 1er Cru Clos des Mouches ★★★ £F
Beaune 1er Cru Grèves ★★★ £E
Savigny-lès-Beaune 1er Cru Serpentières ★★ £E
Savigny-lès-Beaune ★ £D Chorey-lès-Beaune ★★ £D
Volnay 1er Cru Clos des Chênes ★★★ £F
Volnay 1er Cru Chevret ★★ £E Volnay ★★ £D
Côte de Beaune ★★ £D Côte de Beaune-Villages ★ £D
Rully ★★£D

Recommended Whites:
Corton-Charlemagne ★★★★ £G
Beaune 1er Cru Clos des Mouches ★★★★ £G
Puligny-Montrachet 1er Cru Folatières ★★★★ £F
Meursault ★★★ £E Côte de Beaune ★★ £D
Saint-Aubin ★ £D Saint-Romain ★ £D
Rully ★★ £D

Marquis de Laguiche
Recommended Whites:
Montrachet ✪✪✪✪ £H Chassagne-Montrachet★★★★ £F

Drouhin-Laroze (Beaune) www.drouhin-laroze.com
A long established but previously under-performing domaine, all changed when Philippe Drouhin (not to be confused with Philippe of Joseph DROUHIN) assumed full control with the 2001 vintage. His 11.5 ha includes six grand cru parcels which now provide tremendous value against some of the more established names.

The leap in quality comes from improvements both in the vineyard and cellar. New oak is used (100% for the grands crus) but doesn't overwhelm the rich fruit cores. Deep and complex Bonnes Mares expresses much of the essence of the vineyard but with the extract and structure deserving of at least 10 years' ageing. A wonderfully pure and intense Clos de Vougeot is excellent for this variable appellation while much has also been wrought from some of Gevrey's deservedly maligned great growths. Chapelle-Chambertin is a particularly fine example while from Clos-de-Bèze is harnessed both the structure as well as the refined spice, earth and fruit intensity that give it its magic. The premiers crus which see less new oak also show good promise. If your budget is more modest, the regular village-level Gevrey offers plenty of flavour and intensity.

Recommended Reds:
Chambertin Clos-de-Bèze ★★★★★ £G
Bonnes Mares ★★★★☆ £G
Chapelle-Chambertin ★★★★☆ £F
Latricières-Chambertin ★★★★ £F Clos de Vougeot ★★★☆ £F
Gevrey-Chambertin 1er Cru Lavaux-Saint-Jacques ★★★★ £F
Gevrey-Chambertin 1er Cru Au Closeau ★★★☆ £F
Gevrey-Chambertin 1er Cru Clos Prieur ★★★☆ £F
Gevrey-Chambertin ★★★ £E

✿ Claude Dugat (Gevrey-Chambertin)
There are similarities between Claude Dugat and his cousin Bernard (Bernard DUGAT-PY). Both have small holdings (Claude has just 4 ha) and both make very rich, concentrated wines swaddled in, but not swamped by, new oak. In addition, yields are low, occasionally very low, and there is an intuitive feel for the vine that runs back a generation or two. Unsurprisingly perhaps, Claude Dugat's wines have gone down a treat in the US and their prices have soared (at first filling the pockets of the middlemen). The wines are rich with, in some instances, old-vine succulence as well as balancing fine ripe tannins and good acidities but how many of these wines get the 6–10 years' ageing they deserve, and occasionally need, I wouldn't hazard a guess at. A tiny amount of Chapelle-Chambertin is also made. As well as the premiers crus and grands crus there's very good if no longer inexpensive village-level Gevrey and Bourgogne Rouge. Both cousins also have beautiful, restored medieval cellars.

Recommended Reds:
Charmes-Chambertin ✪✪✪✪✪ £H
Griottes-Chambertin ✪✪✪✪✪ £H
Gevrey-Chambertin 1er Cru Lavaux-Saint-Jacques ★★★★★ £G
Gevrey-Chambertin 1er Cru ★★★★ £G
Gevrey-Chambertin ★★★★ £F Bourgogne Rouge ★★ £D

✿✿ Bernard Dugat-Py (Gevrey-Chambertin) www.dugat-py.fr
Bernard Dugat has been making wine since 1975 but only bottling his own since 1989. His 7.2 ha are planted exclusively to Pinot Noir, with the domaine going totally organic in 2003. The concentrationand richness of fruit, lush oak, silky textures and fine tannins make the wines irresistible. Nearly all the wines see 100% new oak but only rarely does this or the amount of extract or tannin seem overdone. These are big, dense wines but in the best sense. The Lavaux-Saint-Jacques and the grands crus have extra class and dimension as well as concentration. The Chambertin is distinguished by very, very concentrated black fruits that make the structure difficult to assess, a testament to very low-yielding and very old, very densely planted vines. Gevrey-Chambertin Coeur de Roy also comes from a selection of very old vines. Vieilles Vignes Vosne-Romanée (from 70-year-old vines) has only been made since

1999. Only tiny amounts of Mazis-Chambertin and Chambertin are made. Since 2003, the Dugats have been acquiring vineyards in Pommard, Meursault and Chassasgne, with the latest acquisition of vines in Corton-Charlemagne and Pernand Vergelesses in 2011.

Recommended Reds:

Echezeaux ✪✪✪✪ £G

Nuits-Saint-Georges 1er Cru Aux Perdrix ★★★★★ £F

Chambertin ✪✪✪✪✪ £H   Mazis-Chambertin ✪✪✪✪✪ £H

Charmes-Chambertin ✪✪✪✪✪ £H

Gevrey-Chambertin 1er Cru Petite Chapelle ★★★★★ £G

Gevrey-Chambertin 1er Cru Lavaux-Saint-Jacques ★★★★★ £G

Gevrey-Chambertin 1er Cru ★★★★ £G

Gevrey-Chambertin Évocelles ★★★★ £F

Gevrey-Chambertin Coeur de Roy ★★★★ £F

Gevrey-Chambertin Vieilles-Vignes ★★★★ £F

Vosne-Romanée Vieilles-Vignes ★★★★ £F

● **Domaine Dujac (Morey-Saint-Denis)** *www.domainedujac.com*
Jacques Seysses is one of the best-known and most respected winemakers in Burgundy. His openness and generosity have helped many a fellow Burgundian and more than a few New World Pinot-phile winemakers along their way. Perhaps unsurprisingly the winemaking reflects modern influences as well as Burgundian traditions. There is great attention to detail, scrupulous hygiene and new oak is favoured for the top wines. A preference for clonal selection and cultured yeasts is offset by a desire for whole-bunch fermentation (no destemming). As a consequence the wines are never that deeply coloured but are intense, clean, elegant and perfumed. Now that Seysses is assisted by his son Jeremy, past criticisms of a lack of weight and occasionally too much oak have been countered with a slightly more flexible approach in recent vintages. At any rate the wines gain in richness and harmony with age, becoming ever more expressive of their *terroir*. Of the 5 grands crus, the Bonnes Mares is arguably the best, with remarkable breadth, power and flavour profile. An intense, vigorous Echezeaux and an expansive Clos de Roche are stylish examples of their respective appellations but all are fine and individual, as are the Chambolle and Gevrey premiers crus. The splendid regular Morey-Saint-Denis premier cru comes from Ruchots and some younger vines in Clos de la Roche. Some Vosne-Romanée Premier Cru Les Beaumonts is also made on a sharecropping basis. A little of the estate's 15-oddha is planted to Chardonnay for some white Morey-Saint-Denis, including some Monts Luisants since 2000. Wines made from bought-in grapes are sold under the label Dujac Fils et Père and include very good village level Gevrey-Chambertin, Morey-Saint-Denis and Chambolle-Musigny for red and Meursault and Puligny-Montrachet whites. The estate became certified organic in 2008.

Domaine Dujac

Recommended Reds:

Bonnes Mares ✪✪✪✪✪ £H   Clos de la Roche ★★★★★ £H

Echezeaux ★★★★£H   Clos Saint-Denis ★★★★★ £G

Charmes-Chambertin ★★★★ £H

Gevrey-Chambertin 1er Cru Aux Combottes ★★★★ £G

Chambolle-Musigny 1er Cru Les Gruenchers ★★★★ £G

Chambolle-Musigny ★★★ £F   Morey-Saint-Denis 1er Cru ★★★★ £F

Morey-Saint-Denis ★★★☆ £E

Recommended Whites:

Morey-Saint-Denis ★★☆ £E

Morey-Saint-Denis 1er Cru Mont Luisants ★★★☆ £F

Dujac Fils et Père

Recommended Reds:

Gevrey-Chambertin ★★★ £F

Morey-Saint-Denis ★★★ £E   Chambolle-Musigny ★★★ £E

● **Dom. Vincent Dureuil-Janthial** *www.dureuiljanthial-vins.com*
Vincent Dureuil's 17 ha estate is planted to more red than white but the whites are the better suit and among the best made by a local grower. Having established his own domaine he has been able to gradually increase its size with plots inherited from his father, Raymond, who also made attractive red and white Rully, albeit in a slightly less modern style. Greater use of new oak is apparent but whites have a depth and fullish fruit character as well as decent acidity to drink well with 2 or 3 years' ageing. The stars are premiers crus that come from low-yielding old vines. Nuits-Saint-Georges Clos des Argillières was first made in 1999 while new is Puligny-Montrachet Champs-Gain. Bourgogne Rouge is good value.

Recommended Reds:

Rully Maizières★★★ £D   Rully Vieilles Vignes ★★★ £D

Rully ★★☆ £D   Mercurey ★★ £D   Bourgogne Rouge ★ £C

Nuits-Saint-Georges 1er Cru Clos des Argillières ★★★☆ £E

Recommended Whites:

Rully 1er Cru Le Meix Cadot ★★★ £D

Rully 1er Cru Margotés ★★★ £D

Rully 1er Cru Molesme ★★☆£D   Rully ★★ £C

Maurice Écard et Fils (Savigny-lès-Beaune)

Here is a source of good-quality, full and concentrated red Burgundy at reasonable prices. Maurice and Michel Écard have around 2 ha in each of several leading Savigny-lès-Beaune premiers crus. The wines don't have quite the finesse of PAVELOT but consistently deliver plenty of fruit and style. Serpentières is the most floral, Peuillet more solid if less expressive and Narbantons has the richness and depth typical of this cru. Best is Jarrons which comes from vines over 50 years old and offers still more concentration and depth. It deserves to be kept for at least 5–6 years. A little white Savigny is also made.

Recommended Reds:

Savigny-lès-Beaune 1er Cru Jarrons ★★★ £E

Savigny-lès-Beaune 1er Cru Narbantons ★★★ £D

Savigny-lès-Beaune 1er Cru Serpentières ★★★ £D

Savigny-lès-Beaune 1er Cru Peuillets ★★★£D

Savigny-lès-Beaune ★★ £D

René Engel (Vosne-Romanée)

For more than two decades prior to his untimely death in May 2005, Philippe Engel steadily revived the estate established by his industrious and learned grandfather René. All 7 ha are in the commune of Vosne and neighbouring Flagey and Vougeot. The style is one of power, structure and richness and is achieved in part through destemming, high fermentation temperatures, long cuvaisons and a moderately high percentage of new oak. The wines are typically deep coloured, full and structured with a dark fruit richness and impressive depth and length. Older vintages had a tendency to be a bit too brutal but in the 1990s the wines gained better balance and now show more of their intrinsic quality and class, while retaining their muscular, concentrated stamp. Vosne-Romanée Les Brulées comes from very old vines and shows tremendous fruit quality and arguably represents the best value of this fabulous range. All the wines become ever richer and more luscious with age; the village Vosne-Romanée needs 5 years' ageing while the others are better with 10 years. Following Philippe's death,

Burgundy /Côte d'Or & Côte Chalonnaise

France

the estate was purchased by François Pinault, and run by Frédérick Engerer, the manager of CH. LATOUR, with the local assistance of oenologist Michel Mallard and re-named DOMAINE D'EUGENIE. The wine ratings below relate solely to the wines made by Philippe Engel.

Recommended Reds:

Grands-Echezeaux ✪✪✪✪✪ £G
Clos de Vougeot ★★★★★ £F
Vosne-Romanée 1er Cru Les Brulées ★★★★★ £F
Echezeaux ★★★★£G Vosne-Romanée ★★★ £E

Arnaud Ente (Mersault)

Arnaud Ente is a young grower able to make only a relatively small amount of wine but a lot of effort goes into each one. Yields are kept low and there is a good smattering of old vines. The wines are ripe, concentrated but not overdone with fine structures and good flavour intensity and depth. Of the two superior Meursaults, the Goutte d'Or has a more floral, exotic character in contrast to a citrusy but very concentrated Vieilles Vignes. The Puligny has a spicy intensity but less depth. Decent Bourgogne Blanc and Bourgogne Aligoté usually show good fruit too.

Recommended Whites:

Meursault 1er Cru Goutte d'Or ★★★★ £F
Meursault Vieilles Vignes ★★★★ £F Meursault★★★☆ £E
Puligny-Montrachet 1er Cru Les Referts ★★★☆ £F
Bourgogne Chardonnay ★★ £C

Frédéric Esmonin (Gevrey-Chambertin)

This small estate only started bottling its own wines in the late 1980s after Frédéric's father, André, had established a reputation as a top grower. Most of the wines here are made from leased vineyards on a sharecropping basis; in addition some of the top crus are from bought-in grapes as this estate has also established a separate small négociant operation. Most significant is 1 ha of the prized small premier cru Estournelles; the wine's concentration, depth and refinement do justice to the cru's cachet. The other estate wines show fine fruit and depth too. An intense, meaty, structured Ruchottes-Chambertin is rivalled by a very powerful, black-fruited and classy Mazis-Chambertin, made from the Esmonins' share of that which they cultivate for the Hospices de Beaune. A fine example of another grand cru, Griottes-Chambertin, was made here until 1999. Wines made to a high standard from purchased grapes (or wine) include Clos de Vougeot, Chambertin and Chambertin Clos-de-Bèze. Prices are very reasonable across the range.

Recommended Reds:

Chambertin ★★★★★ £G
Chambertin Clos-de-Béze ★★★★★ £G
Mazis-Chambertin ★★★★★ £G
Ruchottes-Chambertin ★★★★ £G
Charmes-Chambertin ★★★★ £G
Gevrey-Chambertin 1er Cru Lavaux Saint-Jacques ★★★★ £F
Gevrey-Chambertin 1er Cru Estournelles Saint-Jacques ★★★★ £F
Gevrey-Chambertin Clos Prieur ★★★☆ £E

Sylvie Esmonin (Gevrey-Chambertin)

This small 7 ha domaine, previously called Domaine Michel Esmonin et Fille (after Sylvie's father) makes some splendid Gevrey-Chambertin. Prior to 1987 most of the wine was sold to négociants but the highly trained Sylvie Esmonin has worked with her father for more than a decade and after making an immediate impact has continued to improve the wines. There is an extra vigour

and concentration in the most recent vintages but this has been added whilst retaining their silky elegance. The wines can be drunk reasonably young but the better vintages need more time.

Recommended Reds:

Gevrey-Chambertin 1er Cru Clos Saint-Jacques ★★★★☆ £F
Gevrey-Chambertin Vieilles Vignes ★★★★ £E
Gevrey-Chambertin ★★★ £E Volnay Santenots ★★★ £F
Côte de Nuits-Villages ★★☆ £D Bourgogne Rouge ★★ £C

Dom. Faiveley (Nuits-Saint-Georges) *www.domaine-faiveley.com*

Faiveley command more than 120 ha of vines in the Côte d'Or and Côte Chalonnaise. Nearly all the wines of an extensive high-quality range come from their own vineyards, either owned or leased, and quality is closely supervised by Erwan Faiveley, who took over the domaine from his father in 2007. A long *cuvaison* is favoured and temperatures are kept well below the average for the red wine fermentation. The wines typically show fine perfumes combined with lots of depth and dimension on the palate. They also add richness with age and are proven keepers at every level. The character varies enormously from appellation to appellation, from intense, raspberryish Mercureys to burly, meaty Nuits-Saint-Georges premiers crus to deep, stylish Gevrey Cazetiers to an extracted but classy, intense and very long Clos des Cortons. The wines can be a little slight in lighter years, though they will still keep well. They are superb in the best years. Nuits-Saint-Georges *monopole* Clos de la Maréchale has been relinquished (see Jacques-Frédéric MUGNIER) but newly acquired is another, Beaune Clos de L'Écu. Clos des Cortons and most of the Mercureys are also monopoles. All the leading domaine wines are listed below but there are others.

Recommended Reds:

Chambertin Clos-de-Bèze ✪✪✪✪✪ £H
Mazis-Chambertin ★★★★★£G Latricières-Chambertin ★★★★ £G
Corton Clos des Cortons ★★★★★ £G Echezeaux ★★★£G
Clos de Vougeot ★★★ £G
Gevrey-Chambertin 1er Cru Cazetiers ★★★★£F
Gevrey-Chambertin 1er Cru Combe aux Moines ★★★ £F
Gevrey-Chambertin Les Marchais ★★ £F
Chambolle-Musigny 1er Cru La Combe d'Orveau ★★★ £F
Chambolle-Musigny 1er Cru Les Fuées ★★★ £F
Nuits-Saint-Georges 1er Cru Aux Chaignots ★★★ £F
Nuits-Saint-Georges 1er Cru Damodes ★★★ £F
Nuits-Saint-Georges 1er Cru Les Saint-Georges ★★★ £F
Nuits-Saint-Georges 1er Cru Porets Saint-Georges ★★ £E
Nuits-Saint-Georges 1er Cru Vignerondes ★★ £F
Nuits-Saint-Georges 1er Cru Lavières ★★ £F
Mercurey Clos des Myglands ★★ £D Mercurey Clos du Roy ★★ £D
Mercurey La Framboisière ★★ £D
Mercurey Les Mauvarennes ★★ £D
Mercurey Domaine de la Croix Jacquelet ★★ £D

Recommended Whites:

Corton-Charlemagne ★★★★ £H Mercurey Les Mauvarennes ★£D
Mercurey Clos Rochette ★£D

>> Henri Felettig (Chambolle Musigny) *www.felletig.com*

Since 2011, this tightly knit family domaine has been transformed. A new gravity feed has been installed in the winery and of the wines tasted in London (September 2016 the trio are impeccable. A 2014 Bourgogne Rouge does show a little oak still but it shares in a minor key an impressive style of substance in tune with tension. The villages Chambolle 2013 is a model of its kind and the Nuits St Georges (again 2013) has remarkable purity, elegance and

digestibility. Modern winemaking at its best. We have yet to taste the full range but there's a lot of promise here. (ME)

Recommended Reds:
Nuits Saint Georges ★★★☆ £E
Chambolle-Musigny ★★★ £F Bourgogne Rouge★★☆ £D

Jean-Philippe Fichet *www.domaine-fichet-meursault.com*
Jean-Philippe Fichet produces ever better white wines from a range of different climats in the Côte de Beaune. Most come from vineyards managed on a sharecropping basis but he is able to supplement his production by buying back the vineyard owners' share of the crop. Meursault are village-level wines but as well as an excellent regular bottling several individual lieux-dits are made and show definite stylistic differences from a ripe, typical Meursault Gruyaches through appealingly complex Chevalières to a structured, classy and richly expressive Le Tesson. All contrast with a Puligny of real vigour and intensity. Without a superstar tag his wines are reasonably priced if made in fairly modest quantities. A little red wine is also made.

Recommended Whites:
Puligny-Montrachet 1er Cru Les Referts ★★★★☆ £F
Meursault Le Tesson ★★★★ £E
Meursault Les Chevalières ★★★☆ £E
Meursault Meix sous le Château ★★★☆ £E
Meursault Les Gruyaches ★★★☆ £E
Meursault Criots ★★★☆ £E Meursault ★★★☆ £E
Auxey-Duresses ★★☆ £C
Bourgogne Blanc Vieilles Vignes ★★☆£C

Richard Fontaine-Gagnard *www.domaine-fontaine-gagnard.com*
Richard Fontaine married one of Jacques Gagnard's daughters, Jean-Marc Blain the other (see BLAIN-GAGNARD). Both make fine wines. There are three grands crus and a host of Chassagne premiers crus made to increasingly high standards from a 9 ha estate. The wines are full and ripe, with lots of fruit, good breadth and balanced acidities, not heavy or overoaked. All the premiers crus show fine citrus and mineral intensity when young but generally drink best with between 4 and 8 years' age. The grands crus add more weight, breadth and class: the Criots has more finesse but the Bâtard more richness, while the Montrachet has both and then some. In addition to those listed, other fine premier cru Chassagne-Montrachet whites include La Grande Montagne, Les Murées, Chevenottes and Morgeots and new Clos Saint-Jean. Some Pommard is also made.

Recommended Reds:
Volnay 1er Cru Clos des Chênes★★★ £F
Chassagne-Montrachet 1er Cru Morgeots★★ £E
Chassagne-Montrachet 1er Cru Clos Saint-Jean★★ £E
Chassagne-Montrachet★ £D

Recommended Whites:
Montrachet ✪✪✪✪✪ £H Bâtard-Montrachet ★★★★★ £G
Criots-Bâtard-Montrachet ★★★★★ £G
Chassagne-Montrachet 1er Cru La Boudriotte ★★★★ £F
Chassagne-Montrachet 1er Cru La Maltroie ★★★★ £F
Chassagne-Montrachet 1er Cru Caillerets ★★★★ £F
Chassagne-Montrachet 1er Cru Vergers ★★★★ £F
Chassagne-Montrachet 1er Cru La Romanée ★★★★ £F
Chassagne-Montrachet ★★★ £E

✿ Dom. Fourrier (Gevrey-Chambertin)
Since assuming control from his father in the mid-1990s, Jean-Marie Fourrier has determinedly pursued quality. Yields are kept low and while there is nothing unusual in a cold pre-fermentation maceration, minimal or no sulphur is utilised. A steady and gentle fermentation is sought in the pursuit of finer structures that allow the fruit to shine. To the same end, a relatively low percentage of new oak is used. He certainly has a good smattering of diverse crus from which subtle differences of *terroir* may be unearthed. All the wines are deep and ripe, with increasing concentration and complexity in the top wines. The Griotte-Chambertin is outstanding, probably the best there is. There is also an excellent example of the would-be grand cru, Clos Saint-Jacques - all preserved fruit depth and finesse - and very good Combe aux Moines and persuasive Chambolle Gruenchers too. All the wines are labelled 'Vieille Vigne' (sic).

Recommended Reds:
Griotte-Chambertin ✪✪✪✪✪ £G
Gevrey-Chambertin 1er Cru Clos Saint-Jacques ★★★★★ £F
Gevrey-Chambertin 1er Cru Combe aux Moines ★★★★ £F
Gevrey-Chambertin1er Cru Cherbaudes ★★★★ £F
Gevrey-Chambertin 1er Cru Champeaux ★★★ £F
Gevrey-Chambertin 1er Cru Goulots ★★★ £E
Gevrey-Chambertin Aux Echezeaux ★★★ £E
Gevrey-Chambertin ★★★ £E
Chambolle-Musigny 1er Cru Les Gruenchers ★★★★ £F
Chambolle-Musigny ★★★ £E

Jean-Noël Gagnard *www.domaine-gagnard.com*
Caroline Lestimé has taken over the running of this domaine, one of the leading Chassagne estates, from her father, Jean-Noël Gagnard (whose brother is Jacques Gagnard – see BLAIN-GAGNARD). With a score or so vintages to her credit, the wines have gained in both richness and finesse. As well as a fine village example, Les Masures, there are several premiers crus, from the concentrated, expressive if more forward Chevenottes, through fuller Champgains, to rich, concentrated Blanchot-Dessus and Caillerets that need at least 5 or 6 years to reveal their full glory. The Bâtard-Montrachet adds more again but can usually be drunk from a similar age. The reds, including some Santenay Clos des Tavannes and Chassagnes Clos Saint-Jean and Morgeots, can be attractive but lack richness and depth, even in better years. In addition to those listed some Chaumées, La Boudriotte (recently split from Morgeots) and La Maltroie white Chassagne premiers crus are made.

Recommended Reds:
Chassagne-Montrachet L'Estimée ★★☆ £E
Recommended Whites:
Bâtard-Montrachet ★★★★★ £H
Chassagne-Montrachet 1er Cru Caillerets ★★★★☆ £F
Chassagne-Montrachet 1er Cru Champgains ★★★★ £F
Chassagne-Montrachet 1er Cru Morgeots ★★★★ £F
Chassagne-Montrachet 1er Cru Chevenottes ★★★★ £F
Chassagne-Montrachet 1er Cru Blanchots-Dessus ★★★★ £F
Chassagne-Montrachet 1er Cru Clos de la Maltroye ★★★★ £F
Chassagne-Montrachet Les Masures ★★★ £E

Jean-Michel Gaunoux (Meursault) *www.jean-michel-gaunoux.com*
Jean-Michel Gaunoux established his own label in 1990 (from his father's Domaine François Gaunoux) and produces fine examples of Meursault including very good examples of Goutte d'Or and Perrières. The Goutte d'Or is usually ripe and intense with spice and preserved citrus fruits while Perrières has much of the classic minerally complexity possible from this cru. There is also Genevrières with great intensity, structure and length (under the Gaunoux-

Burgundy /Côte d'Or & Côte Chalonnaise

Hudelot label). A little red from Pommard and Volnay also show excellent intensity and ripeness. The latter from the Clos des Chênes premier cru has impressive breadth and complexity and deserves at least 6–10 years' age.

Jean-Michel Gaunoux
Recommended Reds:
Volnay 1er Cru Clos des Chênes ★★★ £F
Recommended Whites:
Mercurey 1er Cru La Mission★★★ £D
Meursault 1er Cru Perrières ★★★★☆ £F
Meursault 1er Cru La Goutte d'Or ★★★★☆ £F
Meursault ★★★ £E
Puligny-Montrachet 1er Cru Les Folatières ★★★★ £F

Geantet-Pansiot (Gevrey-Chambertin) *www.geantet-pansiot.com*
This 13 ha estate is a fine source for intense, concentrated and well-balanced northern Côte de Nuits reds. Vincent Geantet employs long macerations, but at a low temperature, prior to fermentation and has gone to great lengths to reduce yields and ensure optimum ripeness in his grapes. The very high average vine age shows in the wines, adding a succulence and intensity to the fruit. There are no poor wines here and they increasingly show well in lighter vintages as well the best years. The Charmes-Chambertin (from almost half a hectare) is a really fine example of how good this grand cru can be. Since taking full control in 1989, Vincent Geantet has steadily built up the estate and from 1999 has had a new cellar and some new wines following the sale of the Vachet-Rousseau domaine. Gevrey-Chambertin En Champs, from a small parcel of extremely old vines, has only been made since 2000. There's good value here, too particularly in the Vieilles Vignes Gevrey.
Recommended Reds:
Charmes-Chambertin ★★★★★ £G
Gevrey-Chambertin 1er Cru Le Poissenot ★★★★ £F
Gevrey-Chambertin En Champs ★★★★ £E
Gevrey-Chambertin Vieilles Vignes ★★★★ £E
Gevrey-Chambertin Jeunes Rois ★★★ £E
Chambolle-Musigny 1er Cru ★★★★ £E
Chambolle-Musigny Vieilles Vignes ★★★☆ £E
Marsannay Champ-Perdrix ★★☆ £D

Génot-Boulanger (Meursault) *www.genot-boulanger.com*
A large domaine with important vineyards in the Côte de Beaune but also a significant holding in Mercurey. Some 17 ha of 27.5 ha in total are in fact planted to Pinot but it is the whites, led by Meursault and Puligny crus, that provide the greatest interest. There is good concentration and intensity in village-level Meursault such as Clos du Cromin or from Puligny Les Levrons. There is a step-up with premiers crus La Garenne and a very good Folatières. Those rated include several of the best wines but there are more besides worthy of investigation including some white Savigny-lès-Beaune. White Corton-Charlemagne is ripe and concentrated with typical spicy, citrusy, minerally intensity but the red (grand cru) Corton is more of decent Aloxe-Corton standard. Mercurey Les Bacs, Meursault Clos du Cromin and Puligny Les Nosroyes stand out as particularly good value in an otherwise reasonably priced range.
Recommended Reds:
Corton Les Combes ★★ £E
Recommended Whites:
Corton-Charlemagne ★★★★ £F
Puligny-Montrachet 1er Cru Folatières ★★★★ £F
Puligny-Montrachet 1er Cru La Garenne ★★★★ £F

Puligny-Montrachet Les Levrons ★★★ £E
Meursault 1er Cru Bouchères ★★★ £E
Meursault Clos du Cromin ★★★ £D
Chassagne-Montrachet 1er Cru Chevenottes ★★★★ £E
Chassagne-Montrachet 1er Cru Vergers ★★★★ £E

Dom. Henri Germain et Fils (Meursault)
Henri Germain possesses just 5 ha, 2 ha of Pinot Noir and 3 ha of Chardonnay, but his son Jean-François continues the habit of making fine wines. Even the village Meursault is of good quality and exemplifies the efforts that go into every wine; its weight, structure and balance is particularly impressive so that it tastes attractive when fairly young, with pronounced citrus, spice and floral aspects, but it also has the capacity to keep far longer than average. Much is made of the importance of a cold cellar for the *élevage* and this does seem to be borne out here. The wines' slow development makes for late bottling. Reds are subject to both a cold maceration and long cuvaisons, evident in both the fine, complex, sappy but ripe, cherry, berry aromas and the real intensity and breadth on the palate. Both reds and whites are better with a little age and promise much more with 6 years or so. Some red Chassagne-Montrachet is also made, while more Meursault (Perrières) has been added as the estate expands a little.
Recommended Reds:
Beaune 1er Cru Bressandes ★★★ £E
Recommended Whites:
Meursault 1er Cru Charmes ★★★★ £F
Meursault Chevalières ★★★ £E   Meursault Limozin ★★★ £E
Meursault ★★★ £D
Chassagne-Montrachet 1er Cru Morgeot ★★★★ £F
Bourgogne Blanc ★★ £C

Jean-Jacques Girard *www.domaine-girard.com*
Any number of good Savigny-lès-Beaune reds are made here. The wines are intense and expressive with good acidity. They are less rich, less sturdy than some and oak plays no part in the flavour profile but all will fatten up with a little age and each shows distinctive *terroir* and fruit characters. The best premiers crus include elegant complex Les Lavières and Les Serpentières which impress more when young than the more tannic and sturdy Les Fourneaux and Les Peuillets, which are more gamey with age. At least as good as the Savignys is a very intense and classy Pernand Vergelesses Les Vergelesses. Some sophisticated white Pernand-Vergelesses Les Belles Filles is also made.
Recommended Reds:
Savigny-lès-Beaune 1er Cru Serpentières ★★★ £D
Savigny-lès-Beaune 1er Cru Lavières ★★★ £D
Savigny-lès-Beaune 1er Cru Fourneaux ★★★ £D
Savigny-lès-Beaune 1er Cru Peuillets ★★★ £D
Savigny-lès-Beaune 1er Cru Rouvrettes ★★ £D
Savigny-lès-Beaune ★★ £C
Pernand-Vergelesses 1er Cru Vergelesses ★★★ £D
Bourgogne Rouge ★ £C
Recommended Whites:
Savigny-lès-Beaune ★★ £C Pernand-Vergelesses Belles Filles ★★ £D

Vincent Girardin (Santenay) *www.vincentgirardin.com*
This dynamic initially Santenay-based grower acquired a négociant's licence only in the mid-1990s but has rapidly expanded, requiring a second move to larger winemaking premises in 2002. From his own expanding estate he has made some brilliant affordable red and

white Santenay. The wines are modern, fruit-rich and clean with a healthy but rarely excessive dose of new oak. There is an energy and zip about most of the wines, a certain style and precision, yet they are still indicative of their respective appellations. In his négociant role, only grapes (rather than wine) are bought in, for while the sources are good this allows for further sorting for quality. Girardin vinifies both red and white with equal ease and is as successful in producing both more humble village wines as grands crus, though some of the top wines fail to match the very best made. There is real consistency too, important in an extensive and growing range of wines. Despite the number of wines, most are made in relatively small quantities and Girardin's total production is dwarfed by the likes of JADOT or Louis LATOUR. In September 2010, Girardin purchased the Domaine de la Tour du Bief at Chénas in Beaujolais, with vineyards in Chénas and Moulin-à-Vent. The wines listed below are most of those that are regularly made. In 2012 Vincent Girardin sold his operation to Jean-Pierre Nié, President of the Compagnie des Vins d'Autrefois in Beaune, who continues to employ the small team of 9 people, who had been faithful to the Maison for many years. Eric Germain, who worked with Vincent Girardin as winemaker for over 10 years will ensure continuity of style.

Recommended Reds:
Charmes-Chambertin ★★★★★ £G
Clos de la Roche ★★★★ £G Echezeaux ★★★★ £G
Corton Renardes ★★★★ £F
Gevrey-Chambertin Lavaux Saint-Jacques ★★★★ £F
Beaune 1er Cru Clos des Vignes Franches ★★ £D
Pommard 1er Cru Grands Epenots ★★★ £F
Pommard Les Vignots ★★★ £E
Volnay 1er Cru Santenots ★★★★ £F
Chassagne-Montrachet 1er Cru Clos de la Boudriotte ★★★ £E
Santenay 1er Cru Gravières Vieilles Vignes ★★★ £D
Santenay Clos de la Confrérie ★★☆ £C
Maranges Clos des Loyères ★★ £C Bourgogne Saint-Vincent ★☆ £C

Recommended Whites:
Bienvenue-Bâtard-Montrachet ★★★★★ £H
Bâtard-Montrachet ★★★★ £H
Corton-Charlemagne ★★★★ £F
Puligny-Montrachet 1er Cru Folatières ★★★★ £F
Puligny-Montrachet 1er Cru Les Referts ★★★★ £F
Puligny-Montrachet Enseignières ★★★★ £E
Puligny-Montrachet Vieilles Vignes ★★★ £E
Chassagne-Montrachet 1er Cru Morgeots ★★★★ £F
Meursault 1er Cru Charmes ★★★☆ £F
Meursault 1er Cru Poruzots ★★★ £E
Meursault Narvaux ★★★☆ £E
Saint-Aubin 1er Cru Murgers de Dents de Chien ★★★☆ £E
Savigny-lès-Beaune Vermots Dessus ★★ £D
Santenay 1er Cru Clos de Tavannes ★★☆ £D
Santenay 1er Cru Clos du Beauregard ★★☆ £D
Santenay 1er Cru Beaurepaire ★★☆ £C
Rully 1er Cru Rabourcée ★★☆ £D
Bourgogne Saint-Vincent ★★ £C

Dom. Camille Giroud (Beaune) *www.camillegiroud.com*
Ann Colgin (of COLGIN CELLARS) and her husband Joe Wender led a consortium of American investors to revive this old négociant house (established by Camille Giroud in 1865). Large stocks of old wines, released only when deemed ready, had stifled investment in buying in top quality fruit for new wines. The new owners have put their faith in the young winemaker David Croix whose experience

includes working with Benjamin Leroux (at Comte ARMAND) and at the American owned Domaine des Croix. Most of the grapes continue to be bought-in but some premier cru Beaune vineyards owned by the Girouds have been leased. Those below are some of the best 'new' wines tasted, others, including several whites, will be added in the future. There may be some treasures to be found amongst older wines but care needs to be taken before purchasing any significant quantity.

Recommended Reds:
Gevrey-Chambertin 1er Cru Lavaux Saint-Jacques ★★★★ £F
Gevrey-Chambertin ★★★ £E Volnay 1er Cru Carelles ★★★ £F
Beaune 1er Cru Avaux ★★★ £E
Maranges 1er Cru La Croix aux Moines ★★☆ £E

Dom. Henri Gouges (Nuits-Saint-Georges) *www.gouges.com*
This famous 14.5 ha estate is run by two cousins. Pierre takes care of the vines, Christian the winemaking, but it was their grandfather, Henri, who first established the domaine and was one of the pioneers of domaine bottling in Burgundy. He amassed a full hand of some of Nuits' best crus, including Les Saint-Georges, Vaucrains and Pruliers as well as the 3.5 ha *monopole* of Clos des Porrets-Saint-Georges. The use of grasses to counter erosion has also made it possible to move slowly towards an essentially organic operation. The grapes are fully destemmed but the use of new oak is minimal (a maximum of 20%). Christian makes powerful, structured wines with excellent definition but most of all with an intensity and a quality to the fruit (particularly in the Vaucrains and the Les Saint-Georges) that sets them apart from most other Nuits. This core of quality is evident even when young and relatively tannic. Lush, soft and easy thankfully they are not; all the wines deserve (demand) at least 6–8 years' ageing. A further premier cru, Les Chênes Carteaux is also made. The Nuits white (from a Pinot Noir mutation) is a treat with its spice, mineral and unusual exotic flavour intensity but benefits from a little age too. Prices are very good for the quality.

Recommended Reds:
Nuits-Saint-Georges 1er Cru Les Saint-Georges ★★★★★ £F
Nuits-Saint-Georges 1er Cru Les Vaucrains ★★★★★ £F
Nuits-Saint-Georges 1er Cru Les Pruliers ★★★★☆ £E
NSGs 1er Cru Clos des Porrets-Saint-Georges ★★★★☆ £E
Nuits-Saint-Georges 1er Cru Les Chaignots ★★★★ £E
Nuits-Saint-Georges ★★★ £E
Bourgogne Rouge ★☆ £C

Recommended Whites:
Nuits-Saint-Georges 1er Cru La Perrière ★★★ £E
Bourgogne Pinot Blanc ★★ £C

>> Grands Vins de Bourgogne Meurgey- Croses
Pierre Meurgey, is a pure Burgundian in his early fifties. His grandfather Ernest was a régisseur of several Côte d'Or domaines and an oenologist, his father Henri a knowledgeable, leading broker. Pierre himself in the1990s was the driving force in the renaissance of Champy, the oldest Beaune wine house and its domaine of vineyards, as well as being a director of Diva Distribution. In 2013, Pierre went his separate ways with his first vintage of wines from the Mâconnais, where his mother Marie Thérèse Croses was born in the family house at Uchizy Pierre buys his grapes from friends and neighbours of his family and to mark the link with his heritage baptised the new Mâconnais enterprise by the name of his two parents - Meurges-Croses. Pierre believes that his familial roots there helps him find quality grapes at independent wine growers. He works with a single vigneron in each appellation/ climat, and

Burgundy /Côte d'Or & Côte Chalonnaise

France

controls also the date and condition of the harvesr and its transport to the winery in Davayé in the heart of the Mâconnais. Pierre Meurgey's aim is to produce wines that simply express the terroirs from which they came. In a modern cellar environment, it's possible for him to vinify very precisely: fermentation takes place in tanks, 400 or 600 litre large tuns or in barriques of 228 litres, depending on the appellation. The Mâcon Uchizy is fermented and aged only in tanks to emphasise the fruitiness and freshness. Uchizy in the northern part of the Mâconnais is known for its aromatic, mineral expression. The Viré Clessé comes from the commune which is quite near the river Saône, affording a warm intensity of fruit from vines that have decent to excellent age, from 28 to 80 years planted on a south-east facing slope of 15 ha called Mount. The wines are vinified on site, avoiding the impact of transport and oxidation. The St Véran gets up 0f 20% oak fermentation to unleash the complexities of the Davayé soils. The Pouilly Fuissé is fully fermented in oak, of which only 20% is new- a grand vin giving the Côte de Beaune a run for its money, Under the Grands Vins de Bourgogne banner, Pierre continues to select great wines from the Côte d'Or, his skills honed in his years at Champy. (ME)

Recommended Whites:
Pouilly Fuissé ★★★★ £F Saint Véran ★★★ £E
Macon Vire-Clessé ★★★ £E Macon Uchizy ★★ £D

Dom. Albert Grivault (Meursault)
This small estate has 5 ha planted to Chardonnay and more specifically Meursault. Some of the very best plots that Meursault has to offer in fact, including Perrières but more importantly the *monopole* of Clos des Perrières of almost 1 ha (95 ares). While top houses have long enjoyed a share of these Meursault pickings, that bottled here continues to rise in quality. If the regular Perrières can be better by examples from some top growers the significantly superior Clos des Perrières with tremendous depth, style and purity is harder to surpass. Of grand cru quality it can age tremendously well, particularly from top years. A further hectare is planted to Pinot Noir, in the shape of Pommard premier cru Clos Blanc.

Recommended Whites:
Meursault 1er Cru Perrières ★★★★★ £G
Meursault 1er Cru Charmes ★★★★ £F Meursault ★★★ £E

✪✪ Dom. Jean Grivot (Vosne-Romanée) *www.domainegrivot.fr*
A brilliant 15 ha estate whose wines are much sought after. In 1987 Étienne took over the already successful family domaine built up by his grandfather, Gaston Grivot, in the first half of the 20th century. He immediately embraced some of the principles of the controversial consultant enologist Guy Accad. After a period of adjustment, the wines since the mid-1990s have been better than ever. The use of a cold pre-fermentation maceration seems to have been the main legacy of Accad's input but much thought and precision goes into every aspect of both viticulture and vinification. The wines are marvellous, combining great richness and concentration, and despite their size avoid any heaviness, with an excellent balance of acidity and fine tannins. The wines can sometimes show a reductive quality when tasted young but this doesn't persist. They all need at least 5 years' age and will be better with 10 or more. The top Vosnes and grands crus are an excellent cellaring prospect if you can afford them. Tiny amounts of Vosne premiers crus Les Chaumes and Les Reignots are also made to a very high standard.

Recommended Reds:
Richebourg ✪✪✪✪✪ £H Echezeaux ✪✪✪✪✪ £G
Clos de Vougeot ★★★★☆ £G

Vosne-Romanée 1er Cru Les Beaux Monts ✪✪✪✪✪ £F
Vosne-Romanée 1er Cru Les Suchots ★★★★★ £F
Vosne-Romanée 1er Cru Aux Brulées ★★★★★ £F
Vosne-Romanée 1er Cru Les Rouges ★★★★ £F
Vosne-Romanée Bossières ★★★ £E Vosne-Romanée ★★★ £E
Nuits-Saint-Georges 1er Cru Les Boudots ★★★★ £F
Nuits-Saint-Georges 1er Cru Les Pruliers ★★★★ £F
Nuits-Saint-Georges 1er Cru Les Roncières ★★★★ £F
Nuits-Saint-Georges Les Charmois ★★★ £E
Nuits-Saint-Georges Les Lavières ★★★ £E
Chambolle-Musigny La Combe d'Orveaux ★★★ £E
Bourgogne Pinot Noir ★★☆ £C

✪ Robert Groffier (Morey-Saint-Denis)
Since the late 1990s the wines have become very rich and concentrated, adding to their already intense and classy character. With 8 ha, Robert's son Serge and his son, Nicolas are now in charge of making a little wine across several different appellations. Most stunning are the grands crus; a small amount of Clos-de-Bèze and almost 1 ha of Bonnes Mares are owned. There is also slightly over 1ha (the largest holding) of the excellent premier cru Les Amoureuses from Chambolle-Musigny. While new oak contributes to the wines' lush texture, low yields of first-rate fruit is the underlying reason behind the quality. The whole range is impressive and only rarely is the oak excessive, with real charm and style in the Hauts Doix and Les Sentiers and greater richness, dimension and complexity in the top trio. The wines can be drunk fairly young but bring further rewards to the patient; wait 8 years for the best.

Recommended Reds:
Chambertin Clos-de-Bèze ✪✪✪✪✪ £H Bonnes Mares ✪✪✪✪✪ £G
Chambolle-Musigny 1er Cru Les Amoureuses ★★★★★ £G
Chambolle-Musigny 1er Cru Les Sentiers ★★★★ £F
Chambolle-Musigny 1er Cru Les Hauts Doix ★★★★ £F
Gevrey-Chambertin ★★★ £E Bourgogne Rouge ★★ £D

Anne-Françoise Gros & François Parent (Beaune) *www.af-gros.com*
Anne-Françoise Gros is one of many family members involved in wine. Like brother Michel GROS she also includes some Vosne-Romanée in her range of wines. The wines are made by Anne-Françoise's husband, François Parent, and share the same cellar space as his wines, in Beaune. While the wines have very good depth and breadth, they had a tendency to be somewhat alike and indistinguishable.However, since 1999 there has been more finesse and flair. The Vosne-Romanée lieux-dits are reasonably priced, the Echezeaux rich and concentrated and the Richebourg really profound, intense and very powerful and long. François Parent, in addition to existing Beaune and Pommard vineyards, acquired a further 12ha from Pommard-based Raymond Launay in 2004. Some fine solid Beaune and Pommard are made under his label.

A F Gros
Recommended Reds:
Richebourg ✪✪✪✪✪ £H Echezeaux ★★★★☆ £G
Vosne-Romanée Aux Réas ★★★★ £F
Vosne-Romanée Aux Maizières ★★★☆ £E
Vosne-Romanée Clos de la Fontaine ★★★ £E
Chambolle-Musigny ★★★☆ £E
Savigny-lès-Beaune 1er Cru Clos des Guettes ★★★ £D
Bourgogne-Hautes Côtes de Nuits ★★ £C

F Parent
Recommended Reds:
Pommard 1er Cru Les Arvelets ★★★★ £F

Beaune 1er Cru Les Boucherottes ★★★ £E

Anne Gros (Vosne-Romanée) www.anne-gros.com

Anne's 6.5 ha is the smallest of the various Gros estates but the wines are the most complete and refined of all. From Bourgogne Rouge to Richebourg, though deeply coloured with plenty of extract, there is a harmony and fruit quality that set the wines apart. A new cellar contains vats that can be adjusted in size according to the amount of wine to be vinified. Though only village level, Chambolle-Musigny and Vosne-Romanée are lovely examples of their respective appellations. The outstanding Clos de Vougeot and Richebourg absorb the high percentage of new oak used and both have a wonderful, silky texture that belies an excellent structure. Not surprisingly the small quantities of wine are keenly sought after. In addition to some Bourgogne Blanc, a little Bourgogne-Hautes Côtes de Nuits Blanc has been made since 2000. Older wines will be labelled Domaine Anne et François Gros. In 2008, Anne, together with fellow Burgundian vigneron, Jean-Paul Tollot of DOMAINE TOLLOT-BEAUT, purchased substantial parcels of vineyards at Cazelles in the Minervois where they make an excellent range at Domaine Anne GROS & JEAN-PAUL TOLLOT.

Recommended Reds:

Richebourg ✪✪✪✪✪ £H

Clos de Vougeot Grand Maupertuis ★★★★★ £G

Vosne-Romanée Les Barreaux ★★★★☆ £F

Chambolle-Musigny La Combe d'Orveau ★★★★ £E

Bourgogne Rouge ★★☆ £D

Bourgogne Hautes-Côtes de Nuits ★★ £D

Recommended Whites:

Bougogne Blanc ★★☆ £D

Bourgogne Hautes-Côtes de Nuits ★★ £D

Michel Gros (Vosne-Romanée) www.domaine-michel-gros.com

For a time Michel Gros made wines both under his own name and those of his family's domain (Domaine Jean Gros). Now the estate of Michel Gros is, like those of his brother Bernard (Gros Frère et Soeur) and sister Anne-Françoise (A F GROS), a distinct entity. Michel has nearly 18 ha but much of it lies in the Hautes-Côtes de Nuits and only a little in the top sites. The real exception is the 2.12 ha monopole Clos des Réas, a Vosne-Romanée premier cru. A dedicated and skilled vigneron, Michel avoids green-harvesting by careful pruning earlier in the growing season. Quite a lot of new oak is used, with 100% in the Clos de Vougeot. These are intense, elegant, very stylish wines, structured but not big or overpowering. Some Richebourg used to be made but this has now been relinquished. New is a Morey-Saint-Denis produced from young vines in En La Rue de Vergy. The Hautes Côtes de Nuits is a consistently good example.

Recommended Reds:

Clos de Vougeot ★★★★ £G

Vosne-Romanée 1er Cru Clos des Réas ★★★★★ £G

Vosne-Romanée 1er Cru Aux Brulées ★★★★ £F

Vosne-Romanée ★★★☆ £E

Morey-Saint-Denis En la Rue de Vergy ★★★ £E

Nuits-Saint-Georges 1er Cru ★★★☆ £F

Nuits-Saint-Georges Chaliots ★★★ £E

Nuits-Saint-Georges ★★☆ £E

Chambolle-Musigny ★★★ £E Bourgogne Rouge ★★£C

Bourgogne Hautes-Côtes de Nuits ★★ £D

Recommended Whites:

Bourgogne Hautes-Côtes de Nuits ★★ £D

>> Dom. Franck Grux (Meursault)

Respected head winemaker at Olivier LEFLAIVE, Franck Grux makes a complete Meursault of his own that has everything. It comes from his aunt's vineyard and is called Meix Chavaux (the name means "up the valley"). The vines are ideally placed on gentle south-east facing slopes, catching the early morning sun. In the 2014, shimmering green-gold, vigorous, fresh fragrant nose; intense joyful fruitiness; perfect acidity and crisp moreish aftertaste. A true classic and wonderful value. (ME)

Recommended Whites:

Meursault Meix Chavaux ★★★★☆ £E

Dom. Antonin Guyon www.guyon-bourgogne.com

Two brothers, Michel and Dominique Guyon oversee this relatively large (50 ha), predominantly red wine domaine that has only recently moved up an extra notch or two in quality. They are now producing rich, clean, concentrated wines with an immediate appeal that is only partly due to a measure of new oak. While yields are high, wines since the late 1990s have shown an extra depth and intensity. The cellars are in Savigny but the extensive range of wines includes some of the best sites from the surrounding appellations, in some instances from old vines. If not of the very highest order, there are some very good medium-long term reds and delicious whites. Of the Cortons, a more structured Bressandes needs more time (8-10 years) than a Renardes (6-8 years) with good depth and dimension. Clos du Roy isn't quite as deep or expressive but is supple and flavoursome. The Guyons' Corton-Charlemagne is a good example with typical structure and depth. In addition to the other wines rated below also made are some Charmes-Chambertin, village Gevrey-Chambertin and Chambolle-Musigny (monopole Clos du Village).

Recommended Reds:

Corton Bressandes★★★★☆ £F

Corton Renardes ★★★★ £F Corton Clos du Roy ★★★☆ £F

Volnay Clos des Chênes ★★★ £E

Pernand-Vergelesses 1er Cru Fichots ★★ £E

Pernand-Vergelesses 1er Cru Vergelesses ★★ £E

Aloxe-Corton 1er Cru Fournières ★★ £F

Aloxe-Corton 1er Cru Vercots ★★★ £F Savigny-lès-Beaune ★★ £D

Bourgogne Hautes-Côtes de Nuits Dames de Vergy ★☆ £D

Recommended Whites:

Corton-Charlemagne★★★★ £G

Meursault 1er Cru Charmes Dessus★★★ £F

Pernand-Vergelesses 1er Cru Sous Frétille★★ £D

Dom. Heresztyn www.domaine-heresztyn.com

This 11 ha Gevrey-based estate has been making steadily better wines over recent vintages. There is good ripe fruit, depth and plenty of expression, particularly with a little age. An extra harmony and finesse in the structures can be found in the better vintages. Premiers crus La Perrière and Les Goulots are perhaps less well-known but the latter in particular is deep, ripe and stylish. Les Champonnets is often the richest, fullest example. They rarely show their full potential with less than 6–8 years from the vintage. Also good are a regular Chambolle-Musigny and Morey-Saint-Denis 1er Cru Les Millandes which has a cool, refined red fruits expression and is expansive and long if more pricey. Clos Saint-Denis is a good example with lots of class, depth and length, best with 8–10 years age.

Recommended Reds:

Clos Saint-Denis ★★★★ £F Morey-Saint-Denis Millandes ★★★ £F

France

Gevrey-Chambertin 1er Cru Champonnets ★★★★ £F
Gevrey-Chambertin 1er Cru Les Goulots ★★★★ £F
Gevrey-Chambertin 1er Cru Les Corbeaux ★★★ £F
Gevrey-Chambertin 1er Cru La Perrière ★★★ £F
Gevrey-Chambertin Vieilles Vignes ★★★ £E
Chambolle-Musigny ★★★ £E

Hudelot-Noëllat (Chambolle-Musigny)
Greater consistency has been a feature of this domaine in the 1990s and the latest vintages continue to endorse this view. The estate's 10 ha is planted entirely to Pinot Noir and the constancy of the landholding makes it possible to track older vintages of many of the wines. Charles Hudelot has now taken over the running of the domaine from his grandfather Alain Hudelot-Noëllat and has been assisted by Vincent Munier who has helped to reduce yields whilst maintaining good balance in the vineyard. A light but responsive hand can be seen in the winemaking, along with an adeptness at bringing out the best in the grapes. A small proportion of the stems are usually retained and only about 50% new oak is used in the top wines. Some of the wines have a certain rigour and austerity when young but become supple, opulent, stylish wines with great depth and expression with the appropriate age; about 8 years for the Vosne premiers crus and the grands crus but closer to 5 years for the other wines. Only a little Richebourg (the top wine) and Vosne Malconsorts is made. Village wines and premiers crus are good value.

Recommended Reds:
Romanée-Saint-Vivant ★★★★★ £H
Clos de Vougeot ★★★★ £G
Vosne-Romanée 1er Cru Malconsorts ★★★★☆ £F
Vosne-Romanée 1er Cru Petits Vougeots ★★★★ £F
Vosne-Romanée 1er Cru Beaux-Monts ★★★★ £F
Vosne-Romanée 1er Cru Suchots ★★★★ £F
Vosne-Romanée ★★★ £E Vougeot 1er Cru ★★★ £F
Chambolle-Musigny 1er Cru Charmes ★★★★ £F
Chambolle-Musigny ★★★ £E
Nuits-Saint-Georges 1er Cru Murgers ★★★★ £E

Paul et Marie Jacqueson (Rully) www.domainejacquesson.fr
This small domaine run by Paul Jacqueson and his daughter Marie makes superb Rully in both colours. The 11 ha of vineyards are planted mostly to Pinot Noir and Chardonnay but also include a little Aligoté and Gamay. The wines are natural, pure and expressive, with delicious fruit. Aligoté is excellent in a Bourgogne basic, fuller but less vigorous in the Bouzeron version. Of the white Rully, a Pucelle is full and stylish, with a slightly floral, exotic character, while the Grésigny is more structured and minerally. Even better is the rich but minerally Les Margotés from vines owned by the estate's UK importers. Red Chaponnières has an enticing perfume and good depth but not the extra weight or class of Les Cloux. More basic reds include ripe, spicy Bourgogne Rouge that is more interesting than an otherwise decent Bourgogne Passetoutgrains. The wines remain reasonably priced both in the context of the Chalonnaise and against wider comparison.

Recommended Reds:
Rully 1er Cru Les Cloux ★★★ £D
Rully Chaponnières ★★ £C
Mercurey 1er Cru Les Naugues ★★ £D
Mercurey Les Vaux ★★ £C
Bourgogne Rouge ★☆ £C

Recommended Whites:
Rully 1er Cru Les Margotés ★★★☆ £D
Rully 1er Cru La Pucelle ★★★ £D Rully 1er Cru Grésigny ★★★ £D
Bouzeron Les Cordères ★★£C Bourgogne Aligoté ★★ £C

❂ Louis Jadot (Beaune) www.louisjadot.com
Under the direction of Pierre-Henry Gagey and the winemaking mastery of Jacques Lardière and Frédéric Barnier, this giant producer (by Burgundian, not international standards) has made Burgundy of the highest order. Around half of the 144 ha is in the Côte d'Or, the rest in Beaujolais (see CHÂTEAU DES JACQUES). As well as a string of grands crus, there are many of the leading premiers crus and most of the top wines come from their own vineyards, comprising five separate domaines. The Domaine des Héritiers Louis Jadot provides Corton, Corton-Charlemagne and Chevalier-Montrachet grands crus and other important Côte de Beaune premiers crus. Domaine Louis Jadot includes the superb Côte de Nuits grands crus and premiers crus, much of it from the original Clair-Däu domaine. Domaines André Gagey, Robert Tourlière and Duc de Magenta add further riches. The key is the know-how that ensures the highest possible quality from a diverse range of sources (including every village in the Côte d'Or) in every vintage, and the expert organisation of logistics. Destemming, a pre-fermentation maceration, high fermentation temperatures and long cuvaisons are important features of the red wine vinification.New oak, where it is used (up to 30%), never takes on more than a supporting role. A flexibile, responsive but generally non-interventionist approach can similarly seen in the white winemaking. Reds nearly always have good colour, excellent breadth and depth and plenty of structure but also marvellous concentration, complexity and class in the top wines. Not every bottle is a great one but most will provide a very good example of its appellation and if your only experience of Jadot is one of the humble generics then try one of the many fine domaine wines listed below. There are also several other outstanding 5-star wines from contract grown grapes, including whites Bâtard-Montrachet, (Le) Charlemagne and (Le) Montrachet.

Domaine Louis Jadot / Domaine des Héritiers Louis Jadot
Recommended Reds:
Musigny ✪✪✪✪✪£H Bonnes Mares ✪✪✪✪✪ £H
Chambertin Clos de Bèze ✪✪✪✪✪ £H
Chapelle-Chambertin ★★★★ £G
Clos Vougeot ★★★★£G Echezeaux ★★★★ £H
Gevrey-Chambertin 1er Cru Clos Saint-Jacques ★★★★★ £G
Gevrey-Chambertin 1er Cru Estournelles-Saint-Jacques ★★★★★ £G
Gevrey-Chambertin 1er Cru Lavaux-Saint-Jacques ★★★★★ £G
Gevrey-Chambertin 1er Cru Cazetiers ★★★★ £F
Chambolle-Musigny 1er Cru Les Amoureuses ★★★★ £F
Chambolle-Musigny 1er Cru Les Fuées ★★★★ £F
Chambolle-Musigny 1er Cru Les Feusselottes ★★★★ £F
Côte de Nuits-Villages Le Vaucrain ★★★ £D
Corton Pougets ★★★★ £F
Pernand-Vergelesses1erCruCaradeuxClosdelaCroixdePierre ★★★ £E
Beaune 1er Cru Vignes Franches Clos des Ursules ★★★★ £F
Beaune 1er Cru Boucherottes ★★★☆ £E
Beaune 1er Cru Clos de Couchereaux ★★☆ £E
Beaune 1er Cru Avaux ★★★ £E
Beaune 1er Cru Bressandes ★★★ £E
Beaune 1er Cru Grèves ★★★ £E
Beaune 1er Cru Chouacheux ★★★ £E
Savigny-lès-Beaune 1er Cru Les Vergelesses ★★★ £E

Pommard 1er Cru Rugiens ★★★★ £F
Santenay Clos de Malte ★★☆ £E
Recommended Whites:
Chevalier-Montrachet Les Demoiselles ✪✪✪✪✪ £H
Corton-Charlemagne ★★★★★ £G
Meursault 1er Cru Genevrières ★★★☆ £G
Puligny-Montrachet 1er Cru Les Folatières ★★★★ £G
Puligny-Montrachet 1er Cru Les Referts ★★★☆ £G
Santenay Clos de la Malte ★★☆ £E
Domaine Gagey
Recommended Reds:
Chambolle-Musigny 1er Cru Les Baudes ★★★★ £F
Nuits-Saint-Georges 1er Cru Les Boudots ★★★★ £F
Beaune 1er Cru Theurons ★★★ £E
Savigny-lès-Beaune 1er Cru Clos des Guettes ★★☆ £E
Recommended Whites:
Puligny-Montrachet 1er Cru Champ Gain ★★★★☆ £G
Beaune 1er Cru Grèves Le Clos Blanc ★★★★ £E
Savigny-lès-Beaune 1er Cru Clos des Guettes ★★★☆ £E
Domaine du Château de la Commaraine
Recommended Reds:
Pommard 1er Cru Clos de la Commaraine ★★★ £E
Duc de Magenta
Recommended Reds:
Recommended Whites:
Puligny-Montrachet 1er Cru Clos de la Garenne ★★★★☆ £G
Chassagne-Montrachet Morgeots Clos de la Chapelle ★★★★ £G

Dom. Patrick Javillier (Meursault) *www.patrickjavillier.com*
Patrick Javillier produces a range of fine village Meursaults and bottles individually several different lieux-dits. The best of these actually taste like premiers crus and certainly offer better value than a top site from an underperforming producer. The wines are rich and ripe, with surprising class and depth for their origins particularly Les Clousots, Les Tillets and Les Narvaux which almost always show a little more verve and racy minerality. Tête de Murgers is the richest, deepest and most complex of all, an exceptional example of non-premier cru Meursault. Two Bourgogne Blancs are also treated like Meursault – which the richer, more structured of the two, Cuvée Oligocène, effectively is. A village level Puligny-Montrachet, in contrast, shows more of a Puligny style, with more finesse and delineation, if less character, than the Meursaults. There's good white Savigny-lès-Beaune, too. All the whites are now being vinified in two different ways before being blended back together prior to bottling. Corton-Charlemagne has been made since the 1999 vintage and is getting better and better. A tiny amount of premier cru Meursault Charmes might also be found. A small amount of red is also made.
Recommended Whites:
Corton-Charlemagne ★★★★★ £G
Meursault Tête de Murgers ★★★★ £F
Meursault Les Tillets ★★★☆ £F   Meursault Les Clousots ★★★☆ £E
Meursault Clos du Cromin ★★★ £E
Meursault Les Narvaux ★★★ £E
Puligny-Montrachet Levrons ★★★ £F
Savigny-lès-Beaune Montchevenoy ★★★ £E
Bourgogne Blanc Cuvée Oligocène ★★★ £D
Bourgogne Blanc Cuvée des Forgets ★★ £D

Antoine Jobard (Meursault)
François Jobard retired in 2008 and his son Antoine, took over, continuing to make somewhat tighter, more traditional wines

than his cousin, Rémi JOBARD. Low yields are achieved through rigorous pruning, while vinification is a relatively hands-off affair. While favouring long oak-ageing, *bâtonnage* is avoided and the percentage of new wood is kept low. A rather old-fashioned, heavy sulphur treatment can show in the wines when tasted young but they are meant to be aged. More austere and minerally but with underlying intensity when young, a deep, ripe, leesy nuttiness and flavour complexity develops with extended cellaring. In general the Blagny is usually deep and minerally, Poruzots is also minerally but peachier, Genevrières the more honeyed and the Charmes the most refined. The Meursaults, particularly the premiers crus, deserve at least 5 years' ageing but even the Bourgogne Blanc needs 3 years or more. A little Puligny-Montrachet and some red Blagny are also made.
Recommended Whites:
Meursault 1er Cru Charmes ★★★★ £F
Meursault 1er Cru Poruzots ★★★★ £F
Meursault 1er Cru Genevrières ★★★★ £F
Meursault 1er Cru Blagny ★★★ £F
Meursault En la Barre ★★★ £E   Bourgogne Blanc ★★ £D

>> Dom. Claudie Jobard (Rully) *www.domaineclaudiejobard.fr*
Respected *pépiniériste* (nursery vine Éleveur) and oenologist, Claudie Jobard has her own domaine in Rully, probably the best Chardonnay commune of the Chalonnais. This selection is of excellent quality, all from mature vines of 40 years +. The wines are first cold settled (*débourbage à froid*) to guard against oxidation, then fermented and reared mainly in 228 litre oak barrels. Her Rully Blanc en Villerange on deeper clay to the south of the village, where the mature vines burrow deep into the soil, shaping a wine of lemon-rind acidity and substance, calling for hearty food like poularde à la crème. The Rully Blanc 1er Cru Les Cloux comes from a stony vineyard in one of the best sites east of Rully. From 50/60-year-old vines, the wine is fermented in larger 324 litre casks -the lovely 2014 is green-gold with perfumed entry, of model balance; the texture is nobly opulent, checked by a delightful saline finish. Class in a glass and a serious alternative to a pricier Côte de Beaune. The Rully Rouge La Chaume is delicious young, all cherries and raspberries, but develops spicy rich flavours with age. Claudie also makes a couple of ler Crus from Beaune and Pommard (not yet tasted). (ME)
Recommended Whites:
Rully Blanc 1er Cru Les Cloux ★★★★ £E
Rully Blanc en Villerange ★★★ £D
Recommended Reds:
Rully Rouge La Chaume ★★ £D

Rémi Jobard (Meursault)
Rémi Jobard has assumed the responsibility of running this 8 ha estate from his father, Charles (brother of François JOBARD). These are rich, ripe concentrated Meursaults with good depth and balance. The three premiers crus show more class and length but there is good style, too, in the village bottlings, even if the Sous la Velle and Chevalière tend to be broader and slightly heavy in warm years. The Charmes is consistently the finest Meursault with superb fruit, excellent balance and a long, intense finish. The most recent vintages, benefitting from later bottling after being refreshed in tank, show increasing finesse. Despite having so many different *cuvées* of Meursault, only around half the estate is planted to Chardonnay. Inexpensive Bourgogne Aligoté is regularly made and from 2.5 ha of Pinot Noir there is good Bourgogne Rouge and some Monthelie and Volnay Santenots.

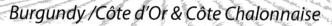

Burgundy /Côte d'Or & Côte Chalonnaise

France

Recommended Whites:
Meursault 1er Cru Charmes ★★★★ £F
Meursault 1er Cru Genevrières ★★★★ £F
Meursault 1er Cru Poruzots-Dessus ★★★★ £F
Meursault En Luraule ★★★☆ £E   Meursault Sous la Velle ★★★ £E
Meursault Chevalières ★★★ £E   Bourgogne Blanc ★★ £D

Dom. Joblot (Givry)
Jean-Marc Joblot's 13.5 ha estate is one of Givry's most important owing to a demanding approach to both viticulture and winemaking. Yields are low, reflected in reds with intense, concentrated fruit and plenty of acidity. Powerful oak-enhanced structures ensure they are approachable young but capable of at least 5–6 years' age. This applies especially to both Grand Marole and Clos de la Servosine which are particularly rich with impressive depth and length. Alternatively try the intense and fruity Pied de Chaume or stylish, complex Cellier aux Moines. Whites have good intensity and precision too. Clos de la Servoisine is richer and more oaky in style than village *cuvées* yet starts out more austere than the plump En Veau.

Recommended Reds:
Givry 1er Cru Clos de la Servoisine ★★★ £D
Givry 1er Cru Clos des Bois Chevaux ★★★ £D
Givry 1er Cru Clos Grand Marole ★★★ £D
Givry Cellier aux Moines ★★★£D   Givry Pied de Chaume ★★ £D

Recommended Whites:
Givry 1er Cru Clos de la Servoisine ★★★ £D
Givry 1er Cru En Veau ★★★£D   Givry Pied de Chaume ★★ £D

Vincent & François Jouard (Chassagne-Montrachet)
Brothers Vincent and François Jouard produce only a part of what they grow under their own label but the wines are increasingly good. There are top crus but at better prices than more established names command. La Maltroie has ripe fruit and spice and a certain elegance; Champs Gain reveals both concentration and structure; Morgeot shows depth and vibrancy; and Les Chaumées (Clos de la Truffière) has real class with lots more to come. The Bâtard-Montrachet has much of the depth and intensity expected but not quite the extra class or richness of the best examples.

Recommended Whites:
Bâtard-Montrachet★★★★★ £G
Chassagne-Montrachet 1er Cru Champ Gain★★★★ £E
Chassagne-Montrachet 1er Cru Chaumées Clos de la Truffière★★★★ £E
Chassagne-Montrachet 1 er Cru Maltroie★★★★ £E
Chassagne-Montrachet 1er Cru Morgeot Fairendes★★★★ £E

Dom. Émile Juillot (Mercurey) *www.theulotjuillot.eu*
Created by Emile Juillot this 11.5 ha family estate is today run by his daughter Nathalie and her husband Jean-Claude. Grapes are manually harvested and yields are closely controlled. Reds dominate production with more than 9 ha planted to Pinot Noir. Premier Cru La Cailloute is a *monopole* and provides an expansive structured red. Les Combins, from a south-facing site has a similar texture and mouthfeel with real potential from a good year, although needing 5 years' age or more. Les Croichots from slopes below La Cailloute is full and plummy if more earthy and less refined. Whites include premier crus La Cailloute and Champs Martin, with up to 30% new oak. Both impress for breadth and weight and have sufficient structure to improve for at least 3-4 years. Also made is another

white premier cru, Les Saumonts. Wines labelled Vignobles Theulot are from bought-in grapes and include red premier cru Les Vellées. Ratings are for best years.

Domaine Émile Juillot
Recommended Reds:
Mercurey 1er Cru Combins★★★ £D
Mercurey 1er Cru Cailloute★★☆ £D
Mercurey 1er Cru Croichots★★☆ £D
Mercurey Château Mipont★★ £C

Recommended Whites:
Mercurey 1er Cru Champs Martin ★★★ £D
Mercurey 1er Cru Cailloute ★★☆ £D

Dom. Michel Juillot (Mercurey) *www.domaine-michel-juillot.fr*
The Juillot vineyards comprise 32.5 ha in total, including 10 ha of red Mercurey, 3 ha of white Mercurey and 8.5 of red and white premiers crus. Laurent Juillot has taken over from his father and there are some very attractive whites and excellent reds, including four premiers crus culminating in the well sited Clos des Barraults. The latter is the most forbidding and structured red but all reveal good depth and richness with 3 years' age or more. Both pumping over and punching down are employed, no doubt contributing to some youthful austerity. As well as the reds listed below, some Combins and a few magnums of the highly regarded Clos du Roi (both premiers crus) are also made. Other than Mercurey, a little of the grands crus Corton Perrières (red) and Corton-Charlemagne together with some village-level Aloxe-Corton are produced.

Recommended Reds:
Mercurey 1er Cru Clos des Barraults ★★★ £D
Mercurey 1er Cru Champs-Martin ★★★ £D
Mercurey 1er Cru Clos Tonnerre ★★£D   Mercurey ★★ £C

Recommended Whites:
Mercurey 1er Cru Clos des Barraults ★★★ £D
Mercurey 1er Cru Champs-Martin ★★ £D
Mercurey 1er Cru En Sazenay ★★ £D   Mercurey ★★ £C

Pascal Lachaux (Vosne-Romanée)
These wines are Pascal's négociant wines which he makes in addition to those at Domaine Robert ARNOUX. The same winemaking care and expertise with up to 18 months in new oak and no fining or filtration has resulted in some extremely good examples of grand cru Burgundy: very classy, intense and pure with a concentrated seductive fruit quality and impeccable balance without the least excess of oak, extract or tannin. In addition to those below a Chapelle-Chambertin and Chambolle-Musigny premier cru Charmes have also been produced. Prices are reasonable in the context of what these wines now generally sell for.

Recommended Reds:
Bonnes Mares ★★★★★ £H   Chambertin-Clos de Bèze ★★★★★ £H
Clos Saint-Denis ★★★★☆ £G
Chambolle-Musigny 1er Cru Les Fuées ★★★★ £F

Michel Lafage (Volnay) *www.domainelafarge.fr*
The venerable Michel Lafarge and his son Frédéric have an excellent and deserved reputation for Volnay and are as good a source of fine Côte de Beaune reds as anybody. The domaine is now farmed biodynamically and relatively old vines that give lowish yields are picked at full physiological ripeness to provide the fine raw materials. A Lafarge bottle nearly always delivers fine quality wine that is balanced and complete and a lovely expression of where it comes from. The wines are elegant and sophisticated, with

magical aromas and superb fruit together with good structure and concentration. Most of the wines can be drunk fairly young but will only really start to open out after 5 years or more; in the case of the Clos des Chênes this is a minimum. Only 8 ha of a total of 10 is planted to Pinot Noir and some Meursault is made. There's also a little Pommard Premier Cru Pézerolles. New is a small amount of Volnay Premier Cru Caillerets, which was purchased by Frédéric. Bourgogne Rouge is usually a fine example.

Recommended Reds:
Volnay 1er Cru Clos des Chênes ★★★★★ £F
Volnay 1er Cru Clos du Château des Ducs ★★★★ £F
Volnay 1er Cru Caillerets ★★★★ £F
Volnay 1er Cru ★★★★ £F
Volnay Vendange Sélectionée ★★★☆ £E
Volnay ★★★ £E Beaune 1er Cru Grèves ★★★ £F
Bourgogne Rouge ★★☆ £C

◉◉ Dom. des Comtes Lafon (Meursault) *www.comtes-lafon.fr*
The finest domaine in Meursault and one of the very best in the Côte d'Or, with some excellent Volnay as well as outstanding Meursault. Dominique Lafon has had the mastery of this 14 ha estate for 2 decades now and in recent years has converted its viticulture to a biodynamic regime. In the Meursault premiers crus the fruit is intense, rich and pure and encased in a precise but seamless structure. An opulent Gouttes d'Or, wonderfully expressive Charmes and remarkably profound Genevrières are only surpassed by a peerless Perrières. Yet even the village wines, such as the Clos de la Barre, show good dimension and a touch of class. The fine Volnays are crowned by a rich Santenots du Milieu, with great finesse and length. The acclaim for these wines adds a premium and they need to be bought before changing hands too many times if prices are to be remotely proportionate to their quality. Most expensive, from just a few barrels, is a Montrachet of exalted reputation. A little Puligny-Montrachet Premier Cru Champ Gain is also made and some very good wines are now being produced in the Mâconnais under the Domaine des HERITIERS COMTES LAFON.

Recommended Reds:
Volnay 1er Cru Santenots du Milieu ★★★★☆ £F
Volnay 1er Cru Clos des Chênes ★★★★ £F
Volnay 1er Cru Champans ★★★★ £F
Volnay ★★★☆ £E Monthelie 1er Cru Les Duresses ★★★☆ £E

Recommended Whites:
Meursault 1er Cru Perrières ◉◉◉◉◉ £G
Meursault 1er Cru Charmes ★★★★★ £G
Meursault 1er Cru Genevrières ★★★★★ £G
Meursault 1er Cru Goutte d'Or ★★★★☆ £G
Meursault Clos de la Barre ★★★★ £F
Meursault Désirée ★★★★ £F Meursault ★★★☆ £E

◉ Dom. François Lamarche *www.domaine-lamarche.com*
Much improved since the turn of the century, this estate has some prized possessions in its patchwork of 10 ha, including all 1.65 ha of that wedge of grand cru, La Grande Rue, lying between La Tâche and La Romanée-Conti. The wines previously showed a certain finesse but missed their real potential though have become more concentrated and classy under François's direction. Yields have been reduced, the grapes are now fully destemmed and up to 60% new oak is used but the wines still start out quite tight and tannic and this noble but at times slightly austere style demands patience. La Grande Rue is not only unique but very classy with great dimension and refinement. Echezeaux is also fine with considerable elegance

and individuality. Another grand cru, Grands-Echezeaux is made too but hasn't yet been tasted. La Croix Rameau and Malconsorts are the best of the Vosne premiers crus, which is reflected in their marginally higher prices. Only the most recent vintages should be bought for cellaring.

Recommended Reds:
La Grande Rue ◉◉◉◉◉ £G Echezeaux ★★★★☆ £G
Clos de Vougeot ★★★★ £F
Vosne-Romanée 1er Cru Malconsorts ★★★★☆ £F
Vosne-Romanée 1er Cru La Croix Rameau ★★★★☆ £F
Vosne-Romanée 1er Cru Suchots ★★★★ £F
Vosne-Romanée 1er Cru Chaumes ★★★★ £F
Vosne-Romanée ★★★☆ £E

Dom. Clos des Lambrays (Morey-Saint-Denis) *www.lambrays.com*
In 2014, the LVMH Moët group made its first acquisition in Burgundy when it bought the prestigious Domaine des Lambrays for an estimated 100 million euros. Th previous owners Günter and Ruth Freund, a wealthy Burgundy-loving couple from Koblenz bought th property in 1996. They poured money into further care of the vineyard and advances in the winery. More important still, they gave Thierry Broin, one of Burgundy's finest winemakers his head - as illustrated in the fresh, ethereal 2008, the magnificent complete 2009 and the concentrated, structured 2012.The 8.84-hectare Domaine Lambrays, is the largest Grand Cru Pinot Noir vineyard in one hands in the Côte d'Or. The Clos itself is also the steepest of the Morey Grands Crus. The heart of the vineyard is the 5.72 ha Les Larrets on the mid-slope, which has the best drainage and exposure to the sun. At the top of the Clos the 2 ha Les Bouchots brings elegance, tension and energy to the wine: Cool airs from the Combe de Morey valley streams down on the vines. The red soil in this upper part of the vineyard is rather special and rich in iron oxide, thus shaping precise cooler fruit and a positive mineral imprint. The grapes are picked early about the 15th September for optimal freshness. The aromas of the wine are gorgeously heady with a distinctive sense of aromatic wild plants and fruits, even a touch of elderflower. The palate is succulent, caressing, the polar opposite of heavy- handed extraction. The Morey St Denis 1er Cru is a bright wild cherry mouthful, gentle yet with an athletic vigour within, propelling it forward. A small quantity of two very exciting Puligny Montrachet ler Crus are made. Structured and very long lived. (ME)

Recommended Reds:
Clos des Lambrays ★★★★★ £G
Morey-Saint-Denis 1er Cru Les Loups ★★★★ £F
Morey-Saint-Denis ★★★ £E
Recommended Whites:
Puligny Montrachet Clos de Caillerets ★★★★★ £G
Puligny Montrachet ler Cru La Folatières ★★★★ £F

Dom. Hubert & Olivier Lamy *www.domainehubertlamy.com*
This is another estate where the input of a new generation has had a positive impact on quality. ALready good Saint-Aubin whites have been honed into ripe, rich and stylish examples under the winemaking expertise of Hubert Lamy's son, Olivier. Only 20% of the 18.5 ha of vineyard are planted to Pinot Noir but the reds are increasingly ripe and concentrated too. This is a good source of both red and white Burgundy without silly prices. The bottling of Puligny, Les Tremblots, for instance, could pass for a premier cru wine. A very small amount of Criots-Bâtard-Montrachet is also made.

Recommended Reds:
Saint-Aubin 1er Cru Derrière Chez Edouard ★★★ £E

Burgundy /Côte d'Or & Côte Chalonnaise

France

Saint-Aubin 1er Cru Les Castets ★★☆ £D
Chassagne-Montrachet Goujonne Vieilles Vignes ★★ £D

Recommended Whites:

Chassagne-Montrachet 1er Cru Macherelles ★★★☆ £F
Puligny-Montrachet Les Tremblots ★★★☆ £E
Saint-Aubin 1er Cru Murgers Dents de Chien ★★★☆ £E
Saint-Aubin 1er Cru En Remilly ★★★ £E
Saint-Aubin 1er Cru Clos de la Chatenière ★★★ £E
Saint-Aubin 1er Cru Les Frionnes ★★★ £E
Saint-Aubin 1er Cru Clos du Meix ★★★ £E
Saint-Aubin Princée ★★☆ £D

Louis Latour (Beaune) www.louislatour.com

This historic house (founded 1797) is one of Burgundy's heavyweight négociants but is also a domaine of 50 ha including an astounding 29 ha of grands crus. Wines are made from Chablis down through the Côte d'Or to the Chalonnaise, Mâconnais and Beaujolais, as well as from the Ardèche and the Var. The continued use of flash-pasteurisation for the red wines (in order to kill bacteria) and filtration remain the most controversial aspects of their production. In addition a short *cuvaison* (8–10 days) has long been favoured – in search of greater finesse it is argued – but too often the reds lack vigour, depth and vibrancy as well as the flavour amplitude they surely otherwise have the potential for. White grapes are harvested late for optimum ripeness, yields are low and plenty of new oak is used in their *élevage*. While generally better quality and value can be found elsewhere, some of the top crus (including all six white grands crus) reveal great concentration, complexity and power. A selection of the best white wines is listed below.

Recommended Whites:

Bâtard-Montrachet ★★★★£H
Corton-Charlemagne ★★★★ £G
Chevalier-Montrachet Demoiselles ★★★★ £H
Meursault 1er Cru Goutte d'Or ★★★ £E
Meursault 1er Cru Château de Blagny ★★★ £E
Puligny-Montrachet 1er Cru Truffières ★★★ £F
Puligny-Montrachet 1er Cru Folatières ★★★ £F
Chassagne-Montrachet 1er Cru Morgeot ★★★ £E

Latour-Giraud (Meursault) www.domaine-latour-giraud.com

This previously underperforming domaine is now making whites of a quality expected of its impressive holdings. Of 10 ha, 8 ha planted to Chardonnay, arguably the most prized is that of a large, 2.4 ha section of Genevrières. Recent vintages show great class and an elegant and intense expression that is true to its origins. Both this and the tiny production of a minerally Perrières shouldn't be rushed; the depth and intensity will slowly unfurl with up to 10 years' ageing. As well as some fine Charmes, two other premiers crus, Bouchères and Poruzots, are also made but there's also fine quality in Le Limozin and Cuvée Charles Maxine, which both give classic Meursault style and richness with less age and at a more affordable price. Besides a little Puligny some red is made, mostly from Maranges.

Recommended Whites:

Meursault 1er Cru Perrières ★★★★★ £F
Meursault 1er Cru Genevrières ★★★★★ £F
Meursault 1er Cru Charmes ★★★★ £F
Meursault Charles Maxime ★★★ £E
Meursault Le Limozin ★★★ £E

Puligny-Montrachet Champs Canet ★★★★ £F

Dominique Laurent (Nuits-Saint-Georges)

Ex-pastry chef Dominique Laurent buys only the best small lots of young red wine made from old low-yielding vines, ages them himself, then sells the many individual *cuvées* for very high prices. His considerable following in both France and other premium wine markets stems in part from the support of the influential French journalist Michel Bettane. The wines are typically big, powerful and very concentrated, with lots of extract and tannin. Oak, and lots of it, was an early theme, resulting in some excessively oaky wines, though this is much less common in more recent releases. Now, in the same way that pastries can be butter-rich, many of the wines can be oak-rich (but without compromising the wine's structure with excessive oak tannins as is typical in a badly wooded wine) with the requisite balance of fruit richness and extract that is enriched and enhanced by the oak, resulting in a succulent creaminess. Quality is generally very high indeed but rare lapses can result in rather tough, chewy wines. Thanks, though, to the high prices obtained for other wines, even these can be declassified. Though all the wines are bought in, many of the exact same parcels can be acquired year after year. Some of the wines made fairly regularly include: (grands crus) Chambertin Clos de Bèze, Mazis-Chambertin, Le Musigny, Bonnes Mares, Clos de la Roche and Clos de Vougeot; (premiers crus) Vosne-Romanée Beaux Monts and Suchots, Chambolle-Musigny Charmes, Gevrey-Chambertin Clos Saint-Jacques, Nuits-Saint-Georges Les Saint-Georges, Vaucrains and Richemone, Volnay Clos des Chênes, Pommard Epenots, Beaune 1er Cru and Grèves as well as some excellent village examples designated Vieilles Vignes. If you like vibrant, rich, oaky Burgundy with often remarkable depth, length and intensity, never turn down the chance to taste any of the many varied offerings. Dominique applies some of the same methods in both the northern and southern Rhône (and beyond) where with Michel Tardieu he turns out small-volume, high-priced *cuvées* under the TARDIEU-LAURENT label.

Olivier Leflaive (Puligny-Montrachet) www.olivier-leflaive.com

Olivier Leflaive set up this merchant house in 1984 and continued to co-manage the family domaine (Domaine Leflaive) until 1994. The company now has a small 12 ha domaine of its own, though the lion's share of production (threequarters of a million bottles) is made from bought-in grapes. Franck Grux, the winemaker for more than 20 years, has provided a largely consistent and sometimes enviable range of white Burgundy. Leading premiers crus from Puligny-Montrachet, Chassagne-Montrachet and Meursault can be good if a little variable. In addition, examples of all six Côte de Beaune grands crus are made, including very fine Criots-Bâtard-Montrachet and Le Montrachet. If at a lower level the wines can be a little dull, occasionally even dilute in a lesser vintage, the Côte Chalonnaise whites, Rully and Montagny, can be also be very good. A increasing amount of fine Chablis is being made, including a range of fine premiers crus. While more than 90% of production is white, a relatively small range of reds is also made. The best, mostly Pommard and Volnays, are quite structured, with appreciable oak, but have the depth and richness to be very satisfying with 5 years' age or more. Bourgogne Blanc Les Sétilles is usually a good example of everyday white Burgundy. Listed are only some of the best wines that are regularly made. Franck GRUX also makes some good

Meursault Meix Chavaux under his own label.

Recommended Reds:

Volnay 1er Cru Champans ★★★ £F

Volnay 1er Cru Santenots ★★★ £F

Volnay 1er Cru Clos des Angles ★★★ £F

Volnay ★★ £E Pommard 1er Cru Charmots ★★★ £F

Pommard 1er Cru Rugiens ★★★ £F

Pommard ★★ £E Aloxe-Corton ★★ £E Santenay ★★ £D

Recommended Whites:

Montrachet ✪✪✪✪✪ £H

Criots-Bâtard-Montrachet ★★★★★ £G

Puligny-Montrachet 1 1er Cru Pucelles ★★★★ £F

Puligny-Montrachet 1er Cru Champ Canet ★★★ £F

Puligny-Montrachet 1er Cru Les Referts ★★★ £F

Puligny-Montrachet 1er Cru Champs Gain ★★★ £F

Chassagne-Montrachet 1er Cru Abbaye de Morgeot ★★★ £F

Chassagne-Montrachet 1er Cru Les Chaumées ★★★ £F

Chassagne-Montrachet 1er Cru Clos Saint-Marc ★★★ £F

Meursault 1er Cru Perrières ★★★★ £F

Meursault Narvaux ★★★ £E

Meursault 1er Cru Poruzots ★★★ £F

Saint-Aubin 1er Cru En Remilly ★★ £E

Saint-Aubin 1er Cru Les Perrières ★☆ £D

Rully 1er Cru Rabourcé ★★ £D Rully 1er Cru Vauvry ★★ £D

Rully 1er Cru Les Clous ★★£D Rully 1er Cru ★☆ £D

Montagny 1er Cru Bonneveaux ★★£D

Montagny 1er Cru ★☆ £C

Chablis Premier Cru Montée de Tonnerre ★★★ £D

Chablis Premier Cru Vaillons ★★★ £D

Chablis Premier Cru Fourchaumes ★★★ £D

✿ Dom. Leflaive (Puligny-Montrachet) *www.leflaive.fr*

Under the direction of Vincent Leflaive this estate gained a fabulous reputation during the 1960s and 70s, so much so that the wines have been both sought after and very expensive for as long as many wine enthusiasts can remember. Under the direction of his daughter the late Anne-Claude, who initially worked with her cousin Olivier (dedicated to his own business OLIVIER LEFLAIVE since 1984), the unsurpassed holding of prime white Burgundy vineyard has become progressively biodynamic, totally so since 1998. Of the 23.5 ha, 11.5 ha are of premiers crus, 5 ha of grands crus, including nearly 2 ha each of Chevalier-Montrachet and Bâtard-Montrachet. Pierre Morey has made the wines until his retirement in 2008 and brought to an end some of the criticism directed at wines from vintages between the mid-1980s and early 90s, when yields were high and the wines' considerable reputation for ageing was tarnished. With the balance and the health of the vineyards now paramount, wines from recent vintages look set to rival past glories, but as Anne-Claude admitted, the problem of premature oxidation still persists in Burgundy. Having changed their cork supplier in 2007, there have been fewer incidents of this for the domaine, but it may, however, be advisable to stick to the most recent vintages. No end of descriptions of flavour nuances can do them justice and when on form, the wines have wonderful purity and clarity, great concentration and intensity but almost perfect precision and poise, together with compelling complexity, dimension and length in the grands crus.

Recommended Whites:

Le Montrachet ✪✪✪✪✪ £H Chevalier-Montrachet ✪✪✪✪✪ £H

Bienvenues-Bâtard-Montrachet ✪✪✪✪✪ £H

Bâtard-Montrachet ✪✪✪✪✪ £H

Puligny-Montrachet 1er Cru Les Pucelles ★★★★★ £G

Puligny-Montrachet 1er Cru Les Combottes ★★★★★ £G

Puligny-Montrachet 1er Cru Les Folatières ★★★★ £G

Puligny-Montrachet 1er Cru Clavoillon ★★★★ £G

Puligny-Montrachet ★★★☆ £F Bourgogne Blanc ★★☆ £D

Lucien Lemoine (Beaune) *www.lucienlemoine.com*

A remarkable partnership between two people totally unconnected with the world of wine until, we suppose we could say, they were bitten by the bug. Mounir, one could say, was a Trappist monk until he discovered Chardonnay, where he learned to make it at the monastery. He then threw off his habit and having studied oenology in Montpelier, set off to work in different wineries in Burgundy, the rest of France and California. Dedicated to producing hand-crafted, quality wines, he set up in business with Rotem Brakin in 1999, by buying a small cellar in Beaune, sourcing top quality made wine from selected growers and maturing them in their cellar in accordance with their most rigorous standards to produce small quantities of Grand and Premier Cru wines under the label of Lucien Lemoine. Rotem comes from a cheese making family, studied agriculture in Dijon with a leaning towards wine, whilst assisting in many harvests in Burgundy and California. The result is a large selection of a few hundred bottles of top Burgundian Crus, which vary from year to year, depending on their view of what is good or not in any particular year. Whilst you may not find the same crus from year to year, by 2012 they had produced 42 different Burgundian Crus as well as having expanded into Châteaneuf-du-Pape with three more. Not bad for a two-man (actually, one man and one woman) band! Of course it's impossible to list all the wines that they produce in this publication (not that we have tasted them all either), but the quality of the wines we have tasted is undoubted and what we have listed below may be considered indicative. They are not cheap by a very long chalk.

Recommended Reds:

Chambertin Clos de Bèze ★★★★★ £H

Chambolle-Musigny 1er Cru Les Charmes ★★★★☆ £H

Recommended Whites:

Corton-Charlemagne Grand Cru ★★★★☆ £H

Meursault 1er Cru Genevrières ★★★★☆ £H

Dom. Leroy (Auxey-Duresses) *www.domaineleroy.com*

Madame Lalou Bize-Leroy, one of the most formidable and dynamic wine personalities on the planet, directs one of Burgundy's most prestigious domaines. Built around the former Domaine Charles Noëllat (Vosne-Romanée) purchased in 1988, it now boasts 22 ha of some of the finest crus in the Côte d'Or. Lalou Bize has championed the cause of biodynamic viticulture and has built a domaine to rival the Domaine de la ROMANÉE-CONTI, which she co-managed until 1993. In terms of out and out quality there is arguably no finer estate. Yields are tiny (20–24 hl/ha is typical), and in common with Romanée-Conti there is no destemming, long cuvaisons and more than enough new oak to keep the tonnelier (barrelmaking) firms happy. The wines are distinguished by quite staggering concentration and richness, in some instances with almost overwhelming extract and structure, as well as great intensity, depth and length. Every wine needs the best part of a decade's age and they usually have the balance to keep for much longer. Due to insufficient repeated tastings of the wines they have not been rated individually but as an indication of their ratings generally the grands crus (8 red and 1 white) are 5 stars, leading premiers crus 4 or 5 stars, and others at least 3 stars. Reds include: (grands crus) Chambertin,

Wine behind the label

Burgundy /Côte d'Or & Côte Chalonnaise

France

Latricières-Chambertin, Clos de la Roche, Musigny, Clos de Vougeot, Richebourg, Romanée-Saint-Vivant and Corton Renardes; (premiers crus) Gevrey-Chambertin Combottes, Chambolle-Musigny Charmes, Vosne-Romanée Aux Brulées and Beaux Monts, Nuits-Saint-Georges Boudots and Vignerondes, Volnay Santenots and Savigny-lès-Beaune Narbantons; (villagelevel) Chambolle-Musigny Fremières,Vosne-Romanée Genevrières, Nuits-Saint-Georges Au Bas du Combe, Aux Allots and Lavières and Pommard Les Vignots. The only white is some Corton-Charlemagne. Bize-Leroy's own domaine is Domaine D'AUVENAY, while Leroy SA is the négociant and distribution operation.

Dom. Chantal Lescure (Pommard) *www.domaine-lescure.com*
More than 18 ha of vineyard were inherited by the children of Chantal Lescure, who established this estate in 1975. Winemaker François Chavériat was brought in to lift quality and his considerable progress can be seen in recent vintages of these wines, having assumed direction of the estate in 2001. Production is now organic with no fining, filtration or acidication. Following a relatively long maceration (20-25 days), a high percentage of new oak is used for the top *cuvées* and is apparent in wines which are very seductive with rich fruit and a lush, almost creamy texture. There is also plenty of extract, depth and style in a fine fruit-rich but complete Clos de Vougeot and a deep, ripe and lush version of Les Suchots. Only a limited number of other wines have been tasted - there is good depth and fullness in the Pommards and Beaune Chouacheux - but this sweet-fruited, sumptuous style seems to be maintained throughout. If there is not the elegance or originality of some it is hard to argue against wines with consistent ripeness, richness and persuasive textures that don't leave the drinker short-changed. As well as some Volnay, Nuits-Saint-Georges and Chambolle-Musigny, two white Côte de Beaune (Le Grande Châtelaine and Clos des Topes Bizot) are also made together with a Meursault (Les Pellands) and a Nuits-St.-Georges Blanc (Creux Fraîches Eaux).
Recommended Reds:
Clos de Vougeot ★★★★☆ £G
Vosne-Romanée 1er Cru Les Suchots ★★★★ £F
Pommard 1er Cru Les Bertins ★★★☆ £F
Pommard Les Vaumuriens ☆ £E
Pommard Les Vignots ★★★ £E
Beaune 1er Cru Les Chouacheux ★★★ £E

Dom. du Comte Liger-Belair (Vosne-Romanée) *www.liger-belair.fr*
Louis-Michel Liger-Belair took over the once extensive Vosne domaine in 2000 founded by Comte Louis Liger-Belair, one of Napoleon's successful generals in 1815. The first plots Louis- Michel had title to, some 3 ha, were two parcels, of Vosne Villages and 1er Cru Les Chaumes. In 2002, he gained ownership of La Romanée grand cru. In 2006 he took over a slice of Echezeaux ,more Vosne 1er crus, and one of Nuits St Georges. He now has 9 hectares. Enlightened methods of organic and biodynamic viticulture are followed. Chemicals eliminated, the soils ploughed. The grapes are de-stemmed and placed gently into the vats. The La Romanée is an epic wine, very much up there with DRC, and with extraordinary length of flavour, particularly lovely in 2009. (ME)
Recommended Reds:
La Romanée Grand Cru ⭘⭘⭘⭘⭘ £H
Chapeaux Grand Cru ★★★★☆ £H
Vosne-Romanée 1er Chaumes ★★★★ £G
Vosne-Romanée 1er Cru Aux Reignots ★★★☆ £F

Hubert Lignier (Morey-Saint-Denis) *www.hubert-lignier.com*
Romain Lignier, Hubert's son, had gradually honed the quality of his family's wines from 1991 until his untimely death in 2004. The estate is now run by Romain's brother, Laurent. Just over 8 ha include a decent amount of Clos de la Roche and five premier cru bottlings. There is also a tiny amount of Charmes Chambertin. Moderately low yields are maintained and good extraction is favoured; Romain aided the *pigeage* by entering the vats himself and physically agitating the grapes and pulp in what seems to be a family proclivity. The wines can start off quite tight but have real depth and intensity that more than covers their fine but abundant tannin. The wines don't lack for oak, particularly the Combottes, but this is generally better integrated than previously. The premiers crus are markedly more expensive than the village wines but this is where the real quality kicks in. The excellent Morey-Saint-Denis Premier Cru Vieilles Vignes combines the crus of Faconnières and Chenevery and is a little bolder and deeper than the other two Morey premiers crus. After the death of Romain Lignier, his wife, Kellen, decided to take on the mantle of winemaker in a style largely influenced by her late husband. This did not please Hubert Lignier, who commenced legal action against Kellen in order to try and take back the vineyards that had not been fully transferred to Romain. This was only partially successful and Kellen began producing wines under the Domaine Lucie et Aguste Lignier label (the names of her two infant children) and Hubert changed the name of the original estate to that of Hubert Lignier Père et Fils. Initially the 2004s and 2005s were vinified by Hubert and bottled by Kellen, but it is now unclear what wines appear under the labels of the respective separate domaines. The wine ratings below relate only to those wines made by Romain Lignier and any subsequent bottlings by either estate must be considered as work in progress for us.
Recommended Reds:
Clos de la Roche ★★★★★ £H
Morey-Saint-Denis 1er Cru Vieilles Vignes ★★★★ £G
Morey-Saint-Denis 1er Cru La Riotte ★★★ £G
Morey-Saint-Denis 1er Cru Les Chaffots ★★★ £F
Gevrey-Chambertin 1er Cru Les Combottes ★★★ £G
Chambolle-Musigny 1er Cru Les Baudes ★★★ £F

Dom. Lorenzon (Mercurey) *www.domainelorenzon.com*
Bruno Lorenzon is one of a number of young growers in Mercurey who are maximising the potential from the appellation's best sites. He has travelled widely thanks to his ongoing work with a cooperage company and his contact with other producers of Pinot Noir has enriched his own reds. He gets fully ripe fruit and the wines have shown lots of intensity and extract in recent vintages. There is not perhaps the elegance of others but the tannins are ripe and the wines, promise much with 5 years' age. Cuvée Carline is particularly fine – suggestive of good village-level Vosne-Romanée. A small amount of white is also made from a part of the 5 ha of vineyard, both Champs Martin and another premier cru, Croichots. Both are vibrant and intense but with better breadth and style in the finely oaked Champs Martin.
Recommended Reds:
Mercurey 1er Cru Champs-Martin Cuvée Carline★★★ £E
Mercurey 1er Cru Champs-Martin★★ £D   Mercurey★★ £D
Recommended Whites:
Mercurey 1er Cru Champs Martin ★★★ £D
Mercurey 1er Cru Croichots ★★ £D

François Lumpp (Givry) *www.francoislumpp.com*
One of the best Givry producers (others include JOBLOT and CLOS SALOMON) with wines to match the best from the other Côte Chalonnaise appellations, too. From just 6.5 ha (5 Pinot Noir) François Lumpp keeps yields low and shows a light hand in the winemaking that results in supple, harmonious and balanced reds, especially with a couple of years' bottle-age. The red from Crausot is particularly impressive. Whites are fine, too, ripe but not overripe, with good intensity and balanced acidities and an elegant minerality in the Petite Marole.

Recommended Reds:
Givry 1er Cru Crausot ★★★ £D Givry 1er Cru Clos Jus ★★ £D
Givry 1er Cru Clos du Gras Long ★★ £D
Givry 1er Cru Petite Marole ★★ £D Givry Pied du Clou ★★ £D

Recommended Whites:
Givry 1er Cru Petit Marole★★★ £D
Givry 1er Cru Crausot ★★ £D
Givry Clos des Vignes Rondes ★★ £D

Frédéric Magnien (Morey-Saint-Denis) *www.frederic-magnien.com*
Frédéric Magnien works with his father to make the wines on the family domaine (DOMAINEMICHELMAGNIEN ET FILS) but also makes a large number of négociant wines under his own label. Many of these wines, in a similar style to those below are very good although can sometimes show a little bit too much oak or extract. The range is quite extensive, those listed include some of the most consistently impressive.

Recommended Reds:
Morey-Saint-Denis 1er Cru Les Ruchots ★★★★ £F
Morey-Saint-Denis 1er Cru Clos Sorbé ★★★☆ £F
Morey-Saint-Denis 1er Cru Clos Baulet ★★★☆ £F
Nuits-Saint-Georges 1er Cru Les Saint-Georges ★★★★ £F
Nuits-Saint-Georges 1er Cru Les Pruliers ★★★★ £F

Dom. Michel Magnien *www.domaine-magnien.com*
This long-established domaine, now comprising of some 19 ha, includes some excellent sites, mostly in the communes of Morey-Saint-Denis and Gevrey-Chambertin but the Magniens, father and son have only been bottling all of their production since 1994. The Magnien style, formulated by Frédéric is for richness and extract combined with lots of new oak is showing increasing refinement. The wines are succulent, dense and fruit intense, with lots of extract but ripe tannins, at least in the best years. Sometimes a lighter hand is needed. Clos de la Roche is particularly impressive. Both grands and premiers crus need time, 6-8 years' but will keep for longer. A little Charmes-Chambertin is also made. Additional vineyards in Marsannay and the Côtes de Nuits were purchased in 2008.

Recommended Reds:
Clos de la Roche★★★★★£H Clos Saint-Denis★★★★ £H
Gevrey-Chambertin 1er Cru Les Cazetiers★★★ £G
Gevrey-Chambertin Seuvrées Vieilles Vignes★★★ £F
Gevrey-Chambertin Aux Echezeaux★★★ £F
Morey-Saint-Denis 1er Cru Les Chaffots★★★★ £F
Morey-Saint-Denis 1er Cru Aux Charmes★★★☆ £F
Morey-Saint-Denis 1er Cru Les Millandes★★★☆ £F
Morey-Saint-Denis Le Très Girard★★★☆ £E
Morey-Saint-Denis Mont Luisants★★★ £E

Dom. Matrot (Meursault) *www.matrot.com*
Thierry Matrot is a devoted vigneron, bestowing great care on his vines, ensuring low yields and harvesting as late as possible. He is not a huge fan of new oak and is not an advocate of *bâtonnage* but produces rich, powerful and structured whites, sometimes with more than a hint of sulphur when young. The wines can seem a little awkward at first, but all the premiers crus should have a minimum of 5 years' age before they are ready. Amongst the reds, both Volnay Santenots and Blagny are ripe, long and quite classy. The shape of this domaine is evolving as another Matrot estate, that of Thierry's sister, comes into existence. The Domaine wines (below) now appear under any of either of two labels (Pierre Matrot or Thierry Matrot). Other wines, made from bought-in grapes are labelled as Thierry et Pascale Matrot.

Recommended Reds:
Volnay 1er Cru Santenots ★★★★ £F
Blagny 1er Cru La Pièce sous le Bois ★★★ £E

Recommended Whites:
Meursault 1er Cru Perrières ★★★★★ £F
Meursault 1er Cru Blagny ★★★★ £F
Meursault 1er Cru Charmes ★★★★ £F
Meursault Chevalière ★★★ £E Meursault ★★★ £E
Puligny-Montrachet 1er Cru Les Chalumeaux ★★★★ £F
Puligny-Montrachet 1er Cru Les Combettes ★★★★ £F

✿ **Méo-Camuzet (Vosne-Romanée)** *www.meo-camuzet.com*
One of Burgundy's great 20th-century winemakers, Henri Jayer, made the wines from this Domaine between 1945 and 1988. The rich legacy of prime vineyards that belonged to Étienne Camuzet provided Jayer with the opportunity to make some magnificient wines both for himself and others. The Méo-Camuzet label has only been around since the 1980s but most of that Camuzet legacy is now in the hands of the current generation, who have built up the holdings to 15 ha. Jean-Nicolas Méo, son of Jean Méo, continues with the Jayer method, including total destemming, cold pre-fermentation maceration and an extended *cuvaison* and 100% new oak. The new oak is nearly always in evidence but there is a polish and a completeness that is the hallmark of these wines. At a lower level there isn't always the purity or intensity of others, at least at comparable prices, but the Cros Parentoux and Richebourg and increasingly the Corton and Echezeaux are very classy, very exciting wines. The Frères et Soeurs labelled wines, for those made from bought-in grapes continues to augment.

Domaine Méo-Camuzet
Recommended Reds:
Richebourg ✿✿✿✿✿ £H Clos de Vougeot ★★★★☆ £H
Echezeaux ★★★★☆ £H Corton ★★★★☆ £H
Vosne-Romanée 1er Cru Cros Parentoux ★★★★★ £H
Vosne-Romanée 1er Cru Aux Brulées ★★★★★ £H
Vosne-Romanée 1er Cru Les Chaumes ★★★★ £G
Vosne-Romanée ★★★☆ £G
Nuits-Saint-Georges 1er Cru Aux Murgers ★★★★ £G
Nuits-Saint-Georges 1er Cru Aux Boudots ★★★★ £G
Nuits-Saint-Georges Au Bas de Combes ★★★☆ £F
Nuits-Saint-Georges ★★★ £F

Recommended Whites:
Bourgogne-Hautes Côtes de Nuits Blanc Clos Saint Philibert ★★★ £D
Frères et Soeurs
Recommended Reds:
Chambolle-Musigny 1er Cru Les Feusselottes ★★★★☆ £G
Morey-Saint-Denis ★★★☆ £F Marsannay ★★☆ £E
Fixin ★★★ £E Côtes de Nuits-Villages ★★ £E
Bourgogne Rouge ★★ £D

Burgundy /Côte d'Or & Côte Chalonnaise

France

Recommended Whites:
Bourgogne Blanc ★★☆ £C

Alain Michelot (Nuits-Saint-Georges)

Alain Michelot, now assisted by his daughter Elodie, has almost 8 ha of vineyards. This falls almost entirely in Nuits-Saint-Georges but also includes a little Morey-Saint-Denis (Les Charrières) and some Bourgogne Rouge. The wines are better defined, fuller and more expansive than previously. Yields are lower and the grapes are now 100% destemmed with a prolonged *cuvaison* of 3–5 weeks. A maximum of 30% new oak is used and the wines are bottled without filtration when possible. Most outstanding are Champs Perdrix, Les Chaignots, Les Porrets Saint-Georges and Vaucrains. All are deep with lots of dimension and intensity but need 8–10 years from the vintage to open out fully. Les Cailles and La Richemone also have plenty of depth and intensity as does a characterful, black-fruited Vieilles Vignes version. Very small quantities of Les Saint-Georges are also produced.

Recommended Reds:
Nuits-Saint-Georges 1er Cru Vaucrains ★★★★ £F
Nuits-Saint-Georges 1er Cru Champs Perdrix ★★★★ £F
Nuits-Saint-Georges 1er Cru Porrets-Saint-Georges ★★★★ £E
Nuits-Saint-Georges 1er Cru Chaignots ★★★★ £E
Nuits-Saint-Georges 1er Cru Richemone ★★★ £E
Nuits-Saint-Georges 1er Cru Cailles ★★★ £E
Nuits-Saint-Georges Vieilles Vignes ★★★ £E
Morey-Saint-Denis 1er Cru Charrières ★★★ £E

✪ François Mikulski (Meursault) *www.domainemikulski.fr*

François is one of the brightest stars of the Côte de Beaune and makes the sort of wines that get noticed. He has 8.5 ha and concentrates on Meursault. The wines, which are to all intents organically produced, if not certified, are ripe and full-bodied and develop a creamy, honeyed richness with even a little age. Most convincing and complete of five regular premiers crus is the Genevrières, which has the structure to match the concentration although the Charmes *cuvée* 1913, made from a parcel of vines planted in that year in that vineyard, takes the prize for being the nearest to grand cru status with it's weight and richness. Yet a deeply flavoured, citrusy Poruzots and a floral, exotic old-vine regular Charmes are in much the same style. The Perrières and the Goutte d'Or are perhaps a little less concentrated. A regular Meursault is rich and ripe too but if you find the Meursaults out of reach then there's ripe, fruity Bourgogne Blanc and Aligoté that don't lack for flavour or character. From 2010, vines from the Meix Chavaux vineyard have been vinified separately from the regular Meursault but this has not been tasted. Two reds, a premier cru Meursault and a Volnay, are also made and have been improving in quality over the years, whilst some Passetoutgrains and a Bourgogne have been produced from new vineyards acquired.

Recommended Reds:
Volnay 1er Cru Santenots de Milieu ★★★★ £G
Meursault 1er Cru Les Caillerets ★★★★ £F

Recommended Whites:
Meursault 1er Cru Charmes "1913" ★★★★★ £G
Meursault 1er Cru Genevrières ★★★★ £F
Meursault 1er Cru Poruzots ★★★★ £F
Meursault 1er Cru Charmes ★★★★ £F
Meursault 1er Cru Perrières ★★★ £F
Meursault 1er Cru Goutte d'Or ★★★ £F
Meursault ★★★ £E Bourgogne Blanc ★★ £C Bourgogne Aligoté ★ £C

☯ Dom. de Montille (Volnay) *www.demontille.com*

With the recent passing of Hubert de Montille, the stewardship of this excellent domaine is now firmly in the hands of son Etienne and daughter Alix. One of the leading producers of both Volnay and Pommard Hubert always favoured fermentation at high temperatures and an extended *cuvaison* followed by a low percentage of new oak. The wines? They showed great dimension and depth but also tended to have a lot of extract and tannin, only opening out with 10 years' age, but vintages since 1998 have been made by Hubert's son Étienne. The wines are now less formidable, with finer tannin yet without sacrificing their elegance and individuality. They are now also produced biodynamically. Of the Pommards, the brilliant Rugiens is the essence of Pommard but Pézerolles is scarcely any less intense and classy. Volnays are similarly fine led by a superb Taillepieds that reveals great length, breadth and finesse. Newer additions are the red Beaune premier crus and a dense, classy (potentially 5-star) Clos-Vougeot. Their expansion into the Côtes de Nuits sees acquisitions in Nuits-St-Georges, Clos-Vougeot and Vosne-Romanée making their holdings some 20 ha in all. Whilst all the reds are Domaine wines, most of the whites are made by Alix under the négociant label of Deux Montille as well as the Domaine whites themselves. These seem certain to be a better bet than wines from some of the more established négociant operations, especially if the same vineyard sites are retained and quantities are kept small.

Domaine de Montille
Recommended Reds:
Volnay 1er Cru Taillepieds ✪✪✪✪✪ £G
Volnay 1er Cru Champans ★★★★☆ £G
Volnay 1er Cru Mitans ★★★★ £F
Volnay 1er Cru Les Brouillards ★★★ £F
Pommard 1er Cru Rugiens-Bas ★★★★★ £G
Pommard 1er Cru Pézerolles ★★★★☆ £G
Pommard 1er Cru Grands Epenots ★★★★ £G
Beaune 1er Cru Perrieres ★★★ £F
Beaune 1er Cru Les Sizies ★★★ £F
Clos-Vougeot Grand Cru ★★★★☆ £G
Corton Clos du Roi Grand Cru ★★★★ £G

Recommended Whites:
Corton-Charlemagne Grand Cru ★★★★☆ £G
Puligny-Montrachet 1er Cru Cailleret ★★★★☆ £G
Meursault Les Narvaux ★★★ £E

Deux Montille
Recommended Whites:
Meursault 1er Cru Bouchères ★★★★ £F
Meursault 1er Cru Les Poruzots ★★★★ £F
Meursault Casse Tête ★★★☆ £E Meursault Les Vireuills ★★★ £F
Meursault Grands Charron ★★★ £E
Meursault 1er Cru Les Charmes ★★★★ £F
Puligny-Montrachet 1er Cru Champgains ★★★★ £F
Puligny-Montrachet 1er Cru Caillerets ★★★★ £F
Pernand-Vergelesses 1er Cru Sous Frétille ★★★ £E
Saint-Aubin 1er Cru Sur Gamay ★★★ £E Saint-Romain ★★ £E
Montagny 1er Cru Les Coères ★★ £E

Bernard Moreau et Fils (Chassagne-Montrachet)

Examples of fine white Chassagne-Montrachet are now many and here is another excellent source. As so often there is a roughly equal division between white and red; however, as far less often, the examples of red Chassagne are very good too. Quality has recently been ratcheted up as a direct result of Bernard's son Alexandre

Wine behind the label

taking on the winemaking and second son, Benoît taking on he responsibility of focussing on the vineyards. Around 25-30% new oak is used but isn't in the least intrusive. Whites are vibrant, pure and well-defined with splendid nuance and complexity in the best premier crus. In particular, Grandes Ruchottes is powerful and structured; Morgeot starts out taut, elegant and mineral, while La Maltroie is slightly showier yet intense and stylish too. Reds are ripe and intense with added finesse from the La Cardeuse *monopole*. In 2005 the family's 9 ha of vineyard was boosted to 14 ha. The lease of 5 ha includes more Chenevottes as well as village white and red.

Recommended Reds:
Chassagne-Montrachet 1er Cru Morgeot La Cardeuse ★★★ £E
Chassagne-Montrachet Vieilles Vignes ★★★ £D
Recommended Whites:
Chassagne-Montrachet 1er Cru Les Grandes Ruchottes ★★★★☆ £F
Chassagne-Montrachet 1er Cru Morgeot ★★★★☆ £F
Chassagne-Montrachet 1er Cru Chevenottes ★★★★ £F
Chassagne-Montrachet 1er Cru La Maltroie ★★★★ £F
Chassagne-Montrachet ★★★ £E
Saint-Aubin 1er Cru En Remilly ★★☆ £E

Thomas Morey *www.thomasmorey-vins.com*
When Bernard Morey retired in 2005, the estate was run by his two sons, Thomas and Vincent, but in 2007, the brothers decided to go their separate ways and split the estate to form domaines under their own, separate names. Since 2011, Thomas has been working to produce more organically, although not certified and his almost unique method of dosing sulphur in dribs and drabs throughout the year allows him to keep the *dosage* low at bottling time. Of several fine Chassagne-Montrachets, the Vide Bourse shows very ripe fruit, with lots of depth and richness if not the definition and structure of the Morgeots. A little Bâtard-Montrachet is also made.
Recommended Reds:
Chassagne-Montrachet Vieilles Vignes ★★★ £D
Recommended Whites:
Chassagne-Montrachet 1er Cru Morgeot ★★★★ £F
Chassagne-Montrachet 1er Cru Vide Bourse ★★★ £F
Chassagne-Montrachet 1er Cru Embrazées ★★★ £F
Chassagne-Montrachet 1er Cru Baudines ★★★ £F

Dom. Vincent & Sophie Morey *www.morey-vins.com*
The other half of the Bernard Morey estate is in the capable hands of Vincent Morey and his wife Sophie, already an accomplished vigneronne at the Ménager-Belland domaine at Santenay. Working with his father since 1986, Vincent believes that good wine starts with top quality fruit and meticulous attention to detail. The result is a splendid array of rich and classy whites and sound reds. Bâtard-Montrachet reaches great complexity and of several fine Chassagne-Montrachets, the Vieilles Vignes come from almost 80-year-old vines and shows very rich fruit, but the Caillerets and the Morgeots show just that bit of extra class. A rich powerful, minerally but stylish Puligny La Truffiére can be even better. The reds are less exciting but nevertheless sound.
Recommended Reds:
Chassagne-Montrachet Vieilles Vignes ★★★ £D
Santenay 1er Cru Passetemps ★★ £D
Recommended Whites:
Chassagne-Montrachet 1er Cru Morgeot ★★★★ £F
Chassagne-Montrachet 1er Cru Caillerets ★★★★ £F
Chassagne-Montrachet 1er Cru Embrazées ★★★ £F
Chassagne-Montrachet Vieilles Vignes ★★★ £E

Puligny-Montrachet 1er Cru La Truffière ★★★★ £F
Saint-Aubin 1er Cru Charmois ★★ £D

Dom. Marc Morey (Chassagne-Montrachet)
Bernard Mollard, recently joined by his daughter Sabine, makes outstanding whites from a small 9.5 ha domaine that has improved year-on-year under his direction. All the vineyards lie within or close to Chassagne-Montrachet. An excellent, minerally village-level example is structured, with good citrus intensity and can be drunk young or kept for 3 or 4 years. The premiers crus are all classy, with depth, intensity and fine structure. Les Vergers is tight and minerally in contrast to a more forward, fatter, more obvious Virondot. Cailleret and Morgeot are both rich and concentrated. The top wine is a powerful, classy and complex BČtard-Montrachet. A very respectable Bourgogne Blanc is always attractive and fruity with decent acidity. Some Saint-Aubin comes from the Les Charmois premier cru adjacent to Chassagne-Montrachet. Good Puligny-Montrachet is also made, some Pucelles and Referts. Prices are reasonable for the quality, A significant amount of red is made too. These are slightly austere when young but, while the regular version can lack for ripeness, Morgeot has attractive red fruit and good breadth.
Recommended Reds:
Chassagne-Montrachet 1er Cru Morgeot ★★ £D
Recommended Whites:
Bâtard-Montrachet ✪✪✪✪✪ £G
Chassagne-Montrachet 1er Cru Cailleret ★★★★ £F
Chassagne-Montrachet 1er Cru Morgeot ★★★★ £F
Chassagne-Montrachet 1er Cru Les Vergers ★★★★ £F
Chassagne-Montrachet 1er Cru En Virondot ★★★★ £F
Chassagne-Montrachet 1er Cru Les Chenevottes ★★★★ £F
Chassagne-Montrachet ★★★ £E
Puligny-Montrachet 1er Cru Referts ★★★★ £F
Saint-Aubin 1er Cru Charmois ★★★ £E   Bourgogne Blanc ★☆ £C

Pierre Morey / Morey Blanc (Meursault) *www.morey-meursault.fr*
Pierre Morey is one of Burgundy's most highly regarded white winemakers, making the wines for Domaine Leflaive (until 2008) as well as those of his own. He now has some 11 ha of vines - red and white - and has been farming organically since 1991, with the estate becoming 100% biodynamic in 1997. Over the last few years, his daughter, Anne, has been working with him and is now co-manager The wines build great richness and opulence with age, becoming nutty, buttery and peachy. Of his own estate wines there's intense minerally depth in the Meursault Perrières and indisputable class and complexity in the Bâtard-Montrachet. The wines can have quite a lot of sulphur and are generally quite closed when young. Buy these wines to cellar and give them at least 5–6 years from a good vintage. Good Bourgogne Blanc and Aligoté are usually better with a couple of years too. Reds include good Pommard Epenots and Monthelie. Morey Blanc is the label for the négociant wines, made to the same high standards but from bought-in grapes.
Pierre Morey
Recommended Reds:
Pommard Grands Epenots ★★★☆ £F   Monthelie ★★ £D
Recommended Whites:
Bâtard-Montrachet ✪✪✪✪✪ £H
Meursault 1er Cru Perrières ★★★★★ £F
Meursault Tessons ★★★★ £F   Meursault ★★★☆ £E
Bourgogne Blanc ★★☆ £C
Bourgogne Aligoté ★☆ £C

Morey Blanc
Recommended Whites:
Meursault 1er Cru Genevrières★★★★ £F
Meursault Navaux★★★ £E Meursault★★★ £E
Saint-Aubin 1er Cru★★ £D

Dom. Morey-Coffinet *www.domaine-morey-coffinet.com*
Michel Morey makes increasingly fine Chassagne-Montrachet whites from almost 8 ha of vineyards. Only the village-level example is a little disappointing as although it has plenty of fruit it is a little simple with modest structure. Premiers crus are of a different order with impressive intensity and concentration and are well defined with good structures. La Romanée has both class and complexity; Les Caillerets has impressive depth and richness; while En Remilly and Morgeot Fairendes are typically well balanced and refined. All deserve to be drunk with at least 5–6 years' age. Also excellent is Puligny-Montrachet Les Pucelles which has the great breadth and sheer style of this cru. Bâtard-Montrachet is big with typical richness and breadth if not the extra class and precision of the very best.

Recommended Whites:
Bâtard-Montrachet ★★★★★ £H
Chassagne-Montrachet 1er Cru En Remilly ★★★★ £F
Chassagne-Montrachet 1er Cru Romanée ★★★★ £F
Chassagne-Montrachet 1er Cru Caillerets ★★★★ £F
Chassagne-Montrachet 1er Cru Morgeot Faiendes ★★★★ £F
Chassagne-Montrachet ★★★ £E
Puligny-Montrachet 1er Cru Les Pucelles ★★★★ £F

Dom. Albert Morot (Beaune)
This 8 ha domaine, based on vineyards acquired in the 1890s, was run by Mademoiselle Choppin, whose grandfather Albert Morot ran a négociant business. From the beginnning of the new millennium her nephew, Geoffroy Choppin de Janvry, has been in charge. The domaine is unusual in that it produces almost exclusively premier cru Beaune from the heart of the richest vein of crus on the slopes behind the town. The only exception is a sturdy but concentrated premier cru Savigny, with impressive depth and length for the appellation. All the wines see a percentage of new oak after an extended maceration, resulting in wines that can be quite robust and meaty when young but with a great propensity to age, especially in top vintages. In lesser vintages the oak and extract can be a little overdone yet all of the wines are of an increasingly high standard and all deserve at least 5 years' cellaring. A concentrated and classy Teurons can be the most satisfying but is at least matched for complexity by an old-vine Bressandes. As well as three other premiers crus, a miniscule amount of Grèves is also made. Relatively new (first made in 2001) is some Beaune Les Aigrots, sited closer to Pommard than the existing premiers crus. The white version is structured and powerful.

Recommended Reds:
Beaune 1er Cru Bressandes ★★★☆ £F
Beaune 1er Cru Toussaints ★★★☆ £F
Beaune 1er Cru Teurons ★★★ £F
Beaune 1er Cru Cent Vignes ★★★ £E
Beaune 1er Cru Marconnets ★★★ £E
Beaune 1er Cru Aigrots ★★☆ £E
Savigny-les-Beaune 1er Cru Bataillère aux Vergelesses ★★★ £E

Recommended Whites:
Beaune 1er Cru Aigrots ★★★☆ £F

✿ Dom. Denis Mortet *www.domaine-denis-mortet.com*
Before his tragic recent loss to Burgundy and the wine world, Denis Mortet directed one of the truly outstanding Gevrey estates, with 11.5 ha of fine premiers crus and some of the best village lieux-dits. His work is being continued by his wife, Laurence and son, Arnaud. Denis' first vintage under his own name was in 1992, after he and his brother Thierry (who also makes fine Gevrey and Chambolle-Musigny) split up the former Domaine Charles Mortet. After a flying start the wines continued to improve with the upmost attention to each and every vin` /e. Rigorous selection, total destemming, a pre-fermentation maceration and a long *cuvaison* are important to the style, while the type and percentage of new oak is carefully adapted to each different *cuvée*. These are marvellously complete wines, full, ripe and rich and with everything in balance. The one criticism, that the oak and extraction were slightly overdone, has been countered in the most recent vintages, which show still greater refinement and harmony. Apart from the regular Gevrey-Chambertin and the Marsannay, all the wines should be drunk with 5 years' ageing or more. A little Bourgogne Blanc is also made.

Recommended Reds:
Chambertin ✪✪✪✪ £H Clos de Vougeot ★★★★☆ £H
Gevrey-Chambertin 1er Cru Lavaux Saint-Jacques ★★★★★ £G
Gevrey-Chambertin 1er Cru En Champeaux ★★★★ £G
Gevrey-Chambertin 1er Cru ★★★★ £G
Gevrey-Chambertin En Champs Vieilles Vignes ★★★★ £F
Gevrey-Chambertin En Motrot★★★☆ £F
Gevrey-Chambertin La Combe de Dessus★★★☆ £F
Gevrey-Chambertin Au Vellé★★★ £F Gevrey-Chambertin★★★ £E
Chambolle-Musigny 1er Cru Beaux Bruns★★★★☆ £F
Marsannay Les Longeroies★★☆ £E Bourgogne Rouge★★ £D

Mugneret-Gibourg/G. Mugneret *www.mugneret-gibourg.com*
Sisters Marie-Christine and Marie-Andrée, assisted by their mother, make consistently refined wines from this 8.8 ha estate. The original vineyards of the property are sold under the Mugneret-Gibourg label while those acquired by their widely respected late father, Dr Georges Mugneret, are sold under his name. Most of the vineyards are taken care of by others on a sharecropping basis. The grapes are now fully destemmed and the wine is given a maceration on the skins both before and after a fermentation at relatively high temperatures. Up to 80% new oak is used for the grands crus, each one being made in small quantities, but all the wines show a measure of oak. They also have a lovely ripe pure Pinot fruit within a firm structure and there is real class, style and definition to each. The village wines and the elegant, seductive Chambolle-Musigny need 5 years, the complex, refined Chaignots and the grands crus 8 years or more.

Recommended Reds:
Clos de Vougeot ★★★★ £F Ruchottes-Chambertin ★★★★★ £F
Echezeaux ★★★★ £F Vosne-Romanée ★★★☆ £E
Chambolle-Musigny 1er Cru Les Feusselottes ★★★★ £E
Nuits-Saint-Georges 1er Cru Les Chaignots ★★★★ £E
Nuits-Saint-Georges ★★★ £D Bourgogne Rouge ★★ £C

✿ Jacques-Frédéric Mugnier *www.mugnier.fr*
The early 18th-century Château de Chambolle-Musigny is rather at odds with the style of the wines here. For me, the architecture of the building pales beside the elegance, finesse even grandeur of these, at times, sublime wines. Since taking charge in 1984, Frédéric Mugnier has not only refined the practices on then 4 ha estate (grape quality and selection are paramount and high

fermentation temperatures are a feature of the vinification) but he has also pursued his passion for flying as a commercial airline pilot. Don't come looking for powerful blockbusters; not even the more robust Bonnes Mares, the most sturdy of these wines, offers that. And if it's masses of oak, extract and flesh you want in your glass, then again look elsewhere. Building in richness and complexity with age, these are beautiful wines true to their appellations and with wonderful finesse and harmony. The regular Chambolle-Musigny can sometimes be a little slight but there's a hint of nobility even here. 2004 saw the first releases from the 10 ha Clos de la Maréchale *monopole* that had been previously leased out to Faiveley. Mugnier's signature elegance is already apparent in both wines - the second wine being Clos des Fourches which results from a decision to vinify fruit from young vines separately.

Recommended Reds:
Musigny ✪✪✪✪✪ £H   Bonnes Mares ★★★★★ £H
Chambolle-Musigny 1er Cru Les Amoureuses ★★★★★ £G
Chambolle-Musigny 1er Cru Les Fuées ★★★★ £G
Chambolle-Musigny ★★★ £F
Nuits-Saint-Georges 1er Cru Clos de la Maréchale ★★★☆ £F
Nuits-Saint-Georges Clos des Fourches ★★★ £E

❂ Michel Niellon (Chassagne-Montrachet)
This domaine is remarkably small considering some of the plaudits it has received. The wines are made in quite a reductive manner (with minimal aeration), the oak is restrained and the wines tight and intense when young. The grands crus are usually brilliant but the premiers crus, until recently at least, have been bettered by the same crus from other top estates. There has always been depth, fine fruit concentration and good style. All the wines deserve at least 5–6 years' age.

Recommended Whites:
Chevalier-Montrachet ✪✪✪✪✪ £H
Bâtard-Montrachet ✪✪✪✪✪ £H
Chassagne-Montrachet 1er Cru Clos de la Maltroie ★★★★☆ £G
Chassagne-Montrachet Chaumées Clos de la Truffière ★★★★☆ £G
Chassagne-Montrachet 1er Cru Les Chenevottes ★★★★☆ £G
Chassagne-Montrachet 1er Cru Champs Gain ★★★★ £F
Chassagne-Montrachet 1er Cru Clos Saint-Jean ★★★ £F
Chassagne-Montrachet ★★★ £E

Dom. Michel Noëllat (Vosne-Romanée)
This 25 ha estate with significant holdings in some prime Côte de Nuits vineyards has now extended into the Côte de Beaune as far as Pommard. In the past a significant proportion of the wines were sold off to négociants but as this has decreased quality has risen. The top wines combine strength and plenty of extract with grace and style and promise much with 10 years' age. Most notable are grand crus Clos de Vougeot and Echezeaux - the latter is a particularly fine and individual interpretation. Two Vosne premier crus will also reward the patient with a good *terroir* influenced expression. More wines will be added with further tastings.

Recommended Reds:
Echezeaux★★★★☆£H   Clos de Vougeot★★★★ £G
Vosne-Romanée 1er Cru Beaux-Monts★★★★ £F
Vosne-Romanée 1er Cru Les Suchots★★★★ £F

>> Dom. Agnès Paquet (Auxey- Duresses) *www.vinpaquet.com*
After university, Agnès changed course and studied winemaking to maintain the continuity of the familyestate in the hinterland of the Côte de Beaune at Auxey-Duresses but with vines also in Saint-Aubin. The Auxey Duresses Rouge is from a soil with high limestone elements. Riper in 2014 than in the already impressive, linear 2013. Inviting purple ruby hue and open aromas. And there's an even better balance between freshness, fruit expression, structure and friendly tannins, due in part to 25% whole bunch fermentation. Terrific value. The Saint-Aubin Premier Cru Blanc is a new selection of Ier Cru sites on superb terroirs. Mineral yet creamy, with fine length and complexity – worth buying this bargain early, as Saint-Aubin is becoming more expensive. (ME)

Recommended Reds:
Auxey-Duresses Rouge ★★★ £D
Recommended Whites:
Saint-Aubin Premier Cru Blanc ★★★☆ £E

Jean-Marc & Hugues Pavelot *www.domainepavelot.com*
A superior domaine in an appellation with a reputation for providing wines with plenty of fruit and body, though they can also be a bit coarse and simple too. Not so here. The Pavelots - Jean-Marc's son, Hughes, is now taking over the winemaking - have premiers crus from Savigny's more northern band, where the wines are generally lighter and more elegant, but also in the southern group of premiers crus (nearer Beaune), where the wines are fuller but firmer. Yet all their wines have a grace and charm that sets them apart. From the northern band both a vigorous Guettes and a seductive Aux Gravains reveal delicious fruit and a stylish complexity with a little age; Narbantons and Peuillets from closer to Beaune are fuller, meatier but less stylish. La Dominode comes from very old vines and is the richest and most complete Savigny. Regular red and white Savigny have ample fruit and good structure and are great drinking with a little bottle-age. The premiers crus are capable of ageing for at least 8–10 years, though I doubt many are kept that long.

Recommended Reds:
Savigny-les-Beaune 1er Cru La Dominode ★★★☆ £E
Savigny-les-Beaune 1er Cru Narbantons ★★★ £E
Savigny-les-Beaune 1er Cru Aux Gravains ★★★ £E
Savigny-les-Beaune 1er Cru Guettes ★★★ £E
Savigny-les-Beaune 1er Cru Peuillets ★★☆ £E
Savigny-les-Beaune ★★☆ £D
Pernand-Vergelesses 1er Cru Les Vergelesses ★★☆ £D
Recommended Whites:
Savigny-les-Beaune ★★☆ £D

❂ Paul Pernot et Ses Fils (Puligny-Montrachet)
The owners of this relatively large estate of 23 ha only bottle a portion of the grapes they grow, but it is very good. The remainder must be gratefully received by the merchants. Paul Pernot is assisted by two of his sons and now a grandson and makes concentrated, powerful whites that become increasingly rich and honeyed with age. There's arguably not the definition or poise of a Domaine Leflaive equivalent but there is wonderful proportion and balance despite the wines' size, and real finesse as well as great complexity in the premiers and grands crus. Reds have good intensity if not that much refinement or depth. The grands crus, though hardly cheap, are better priced than most others and the village Puligny-Montrachet is remarkably good value.

Recommended Reds:
Volnay 1er Cru Carelles★★★ £E   Beaune 1er Cru Teurons★★ £E
Beaune 1er Cru Renversées★★ £E
Beaune Clos du Dessus des Marconnets★★ £D
Pommard Noizons★★ £E

Burgundy /Côte d'Or & Côte Chalonnaise

France

Recommended Whites:
Bâtard-Montrachet ✪✪✪✪✪ £G
Bienvenues-Bâtard-Montrachet ✪✪✪✪✪ £G
Puligny-Montrachet 1er Cru Les Pucelles ★★★★ £F
Puligny-Montrachet 1er Cru Folatières ★★★★ £F
Puligny-Montrachet ★★★ £E Bourgogne Blanc ★☆ £D

Perrot-Minot (Morey-Saint-Denis) www.perrot-minot.com
Christophe Perrot works with his father to produce wines less extracted than previously but still with impressive power and intensity. The wines can still be quite austere and firm when young but nearly always have the fruit richness underneath to reveal great style and individuality with 7 or 8 years' age or more. Though all the wines are true to the general style, they are also true to their appellations and individual *terroirs*. The Chambolle-Musigny Premier Cru La Combe d'Orveau, adjacent to Le Musigny, is arguably the most classy and complex wine of all, though the grands crus, particularly the Chambertin, contrast with greater power and structure. The standard of the range is consistently high, with good Bourgogne Rouge at a lower level. The purchase of the Pernin-Rossin domaine in Vosne-Romanée has enlarged the family's holdings to 14 ha. These exciting new wines include some old-vine Nuits-Saint-Georges La Richemone, some Vosne-Romanée Les Beaux-Monts and Gevrey-Chambertin Les Cazetiers. The first releases would seem to have already obtained the same balance, intensity and combination of elegance and vigour seen in the existing wines. Wines were at one time labelled either Henri Perrot-Minot or Christophe Perrot-Minot, but now have reverted to Domaine Perrot-Minot. Their négociant wines are simply labelled "Perrot-Minot".
Recommended Reds:
Chambertin ★★★★£H
Charmes-Chambertin ★★★★ £H
Mazoyères-Chambertin ★★★★ £H
Morey-Saint-Denis 1er Cru La Riotte Vieilles Vignes ★★★★ £H
Morey-Saint-Denis En la Rue de Vergy ★★★ £F
Chambolle-Musigny 1er Cru La Combe d'Orveau ★★★★ £G
Chambolle-Musigny 1er Cru Les Fuées ★★★★ £G
Chambolle-Musigny Vieilles Vignes ★★★ £F
Vosne-Romanée 1er Cru Les Beaux-Monts ★★★★ £G
Nuits-Saint-Georges 1er Cru La Richmone ★★★★ £G
Gevrey-Chambertin ★★★ £F Bourgogne Rouge ★★ £C

Fernand et Laurent Pillot www.vinpillot.com
This 14.5 ha estate had its beginnings in the late 19th century. Although it is Chassagne-based, the recent addition of several sites planted to Pinot Noir, mostly in Pommard, means slightly more red is now produced than white. Quality used to be a little uneven and the lesser reds in particular have struggled for ripeness and richness in cooler years. The latest releases, however, are very good. Premiers crus Les Morgeots, Vide Bourse and Grandes-Ruchottes are particularly impressive. Also very good is Meursault Caillerets. The pick of the reds are the Pommard premiers crus although the village-level Tavannes shouldn't be overlooked. The Clos des Vergers is elegant and refined while Rugiens (100% new oak) is richer, deeper and very classy.
Recommended Reds:
Pommard 1er Cru Rugiens ★★★★☆ £G
Pommard 1er Cru Clos de Vergers ★★★ £F
PommardTavannes ★★★ £E Volnay ★★★ £E
Beaune 1er Cru Les Avaux ★★★ £F

Recommended Whites:
Chassagne-Montrachet 1er Cru Grandes Ruchottes ★★★★ £F
Chassagne-Montrachet 1er Cru Morgeots ★★★★ £F
Chassagne-Montrachet 1er Cru Vide Bourse ★★★★ £F
Chassagne-Montrachet 1er Cru Vergers ★★★☆ £F
Meursault 1er Cru Caillerets ★★★★ £F
Puligny-Montrachet Noyers Brets ★★★ £E

Jean Pillot et Fils (Chassagne-Montrachet)
Jean-Marc Pillot runs this family domaine of 14 ha. The estate's reputation, like that of the commune (albeit only in modern times), is for whites, yet half the vines are Pinot Noir and this is an increasingly good source of red Chassagne. The whites have long been good but have become more consistent and richer, riper and oakier under Jean-Marc's hand. There is now marvellous concentration, breadth and depth in the top premiers crus. A bottle from a fine vintage is particularly rewarding. The reds show proper ripeness and richness too. The range is continuing to expand and, as well as very good estate wines, some very fine Puligny-Montrachet Premier Cru Les Caillerets and Chevalier-Montrachet is made from bought-in wine. Good Saint-Romain white, red Santenay and Bourgogne red and white are made in most vintages too. The wines have been labelled both as Jean Pillot et Fils and Jean-Marc Pillot.
Recommended Reds:
Chassagne-Montrachet 1er Cru Morgeots ★★★ £E
Chassagne-Montrachet 1er Cru Les Macherelles ★★☆ £E
Chassagne-Montrachet ★★£D
Santenay Champs Claude ★★ £D
Recommended Whites:
Chassagne-Montrachet 1er Cru Les Chevenottes ★★★★ £F
Chassagne-Montrachet 1er Cru Caillerets ★★★★ £F
Chassagne-Montrachet 1er Cru Morgeots ★★★★ £E
Chassagne-Montrachet 1er Cru Les Vergers ★★★★ £E
Chassagne-Montrachet 1er Cru Les Macherelles ★★★☆ £E
Chassagne-Montrachet 1er Cru Les Champs Gain ★★★☆ £F
Chassagne-Montrachet ★★★ £E
Puligny-Montrachet ★★★ £E

⊙ Dom. Ponsot (Morey-Saint-Denis) www.domaine-ponsot.com
This is a very serious traditional and historic family estate that places huge importance on *terroir* and respect for the soil and the natural order. Laurent Ponsot has gradually assumed control from his father, Jean-Marie over the past decade or so. Several decades of expertise and refinement can be seen in the wines. The Ponsots undertake to pick the grapes as late as possible from vines with an average age of 40 years, though some individual parcels are as much as twice that age. Yields are very low, and naturally so without any green harvesting, which is abhorred. The Ponsots do not have a high tolerance for new oak or sulphur either and their use is kept to a minimum. No two wines are quite alike but there is a strength underpinning the truly marvellous expression and fine, silky textures that can be spellbinding. Though a charge of inconsistency has often been levelled at the domaine's wines, there seems little evidence of this in recent vintages. The Morey-Saint-Denis white, made mostly from Aligoté in recent vintages, is very full and ripe but structured too, not remotely like most Aligoté. A very small amount of Chambertin is also made. Village Gevrey and Morey can be superb value. In 2009 the family acquired parcels of vines to produce wines from Saint Romain, Corton-Charlemagne, Corton and Chambertin Clos de Bèze.

Recommended Reds:

Clos de la Roche Vieilles Vignes ✪✪✪✪✪ £H
Clos Saint-Denis Vieilles Vignes ✪✪✪✪✪ £H
Griotte-Chambertin ✪✪✪✪ £H Chapelle-Chambertin ★★★★ £H
Morey-Saint-Denis 1er Cru Alouettes ★★★★ £F
Morey-Saint-Denis Cuvée des Grives ★★★ £G
Gevrey-Chambertin Cuvée de l'Abeille ★★★ £F
Chambolle-Musigny 1er Cru Les Charmes ★★★★ £G

Recommended Whites:

Morey-Saint-Denis Clos des Mont-Luisants ★★★ £F

Nicolas Potel (Nuits-Saint-Georges) *www.nicolas-potel.fr*

Nicolas Potel fashioned some seriously good reds with his late father, Gérard at the Domaine de la POUSSE D'OR until 1997 and since then employed his talents on an extensive range of bought-in wines. In 2004, he sold the business to Cottin Frères, who also own Laboure-Roi, and continued to work for them until 2009, when he decided to part company with them to develop his own domaine (DOMAINE DE BELLENE). Comments here relate only to when Nicolas was in charge of the business. Volnay was still a strength but he made a host of others to a generally high standard, though there was some variability, more perhaps as a result of the disparate sources than anything else. Already well-established were some stylish, fragrant Volnays, concentrated Pommards and full, quite classy Nuits-Saint-Georges. His Clos de Vougeot was a fine example of this frustratingly uneven grand cru. This was now an extensive range, though only a selection is included below. Since Nicolas's departure, the business has concentrated on generic Burgundies which have not been tasted, although we believe that they still hold stocks of wines made by him up to 2008.

Recommended Reds:

Chapelle-Chambertin ★★★★ £G
Charmes-Chambertin ★★★★★ £G
Clos de la Roche ★★★★★ £G Clos Saint-Denis ★★★★☆ £G
Bonnes-Mares ★★★★★ £H Clos de Vougeot ★★★★ £G
Grands Echezeaux ★★★★★ £H
Echezeaux ★★★★ £H
Gevrey-Chambertin 1er Cru Combe aux Moines ★★★★ £F
Chambolle-Musigny 1er Cru Les Charmes ★★★★ £F
Chambolle-Musigny 1er Cru Les Fuées ★★★★ £G
Vosne-Romanée 1er Cru Malconsorts ★★★★ £G
Vosne-Romanée 1er Cru Beaumonts ★★★★ £G
Vosne-Romanée 1er Cru Les Suchots ★★★★ £G
Nuits-Saint-Georges 1er Cru Vaucrains ★★★ £F
Nuits-Saint-Georges 1er Cru Roncières ★★★ £F
Aloxe-Corton 1er Cru Les Valozières ★★★ £F
Volnay 1er Cru Pitures ★★★★ £G
Volnay 1er Cru Santenots ★★★☆ £G
Volnay 1er Cru Champans ★★★☆ £G Volnay Vieilles Vignes ★★★ £F
Pommard 1er Cru Rugiens ★★★★£G
Pommard 1er Cru Epenots ★★★☆ £G
Pommard 1er Cru Pezerolle ★★★☆ £F
Beaune 1er Cru Epenottes ★★★£E Beaune 1er Cru Grèves ★★★ £E
Savigny-les-Beaune Vieilles Vignes ★★★ £D
Bourgogne Rouge ★★ £C

Dom. de la Pousse d'Or (Volnay) *www.lapoussedor.fr*

After an initial dip in quality following the death of Gérard Potel (and its subsequent sale in 1997) this famous estate has been gradually revitalised. The 18 ha include the premier cru Volnay monopoles of La Bousse d'Or (2.14 ha), the celebrated 2.4 ha Clos des 60 Ouvrées (in the centre of Caillerets) and Clos d'Audignac as well as new purchases of parcels in Corton of Bressandes and Clos du Roi. New owner Patrick Landanger has overseen many changes including a further reduction in yields, extended maceration times and an increased percentage of new oak. Also made is a very good Santenay from a leading site, Clos Tavannes, Pommard Jarollières, Clos de la Roche, several vineyards in Chambolle-Musigny and a single white Puligny-Montrachet 1er cru le Cailleret.

Recommended Reds:

Volnay 1er Cru Clos de la Bousse d'Or ★★★★☆ £G
Volnay 1er Cru Clos des 60 Ouvrées ★★★★☆ £G
Volnay 1er Cru En Caillerets ★★★★☆ £F
Santenay 1er Cru Clos Tavannes ★★★ £E

Dom. Jacques Prieur (Meursault) *www.prieur.com*

This prestigious estate is owned by the Labruyère family and run by Martin Prieur. There are 21 ha, two-thirds to Pinot Noir, one-third to Chardonnay including some of the finest premier and grand cru vineyards of the Côte d'Or. The Jacques Prieur whites are rich, ripe and powerful though sometimes at the expense of expression and finesse and include grands crus Le Montrachet, Chevalier-Montrachet and Corton-Charlemagne, and premiers crus Meursault PerriZres and Puligny-Montrachet Les Combettes. Reds include grands crus Musigny, Echezeaux, Chambertin, Clos de Vougeot and Corton Bressandes; and premiers crus from Volnay (Santenots and *monopole* Clos des Santenots) and Beaune (Grives, Champs Pimont and *monopole* Clos de la Féguine). Further wines will be rated with more consistent notes.

Recommended Reds:

Clos de Vougeot ★★★★☆ £H
Echezeaux ★★★★ £H Corton Bressandes ★★★★ £H
Beaune 1er Cru Grèves ★★★★ £G
Beaune 1er Cru Champs Pimont ★★★ £F
Beaune 1er Cru Clos de la Féguine ★★★ £F
Volnay 1er Cru Clos des Santenots ★★★ £G

Recommended Whites:

Corton-Charlemagne ★★★★★ £H
Meursault 1er Cru Perrières ★★★★ £G
Puligny-Montrachet Les Combettes ★★★ £G
Beaune 1er Cru Clos de la Féguine ★★★ £F

❀ Ramonet (Chassagne-Montrachet)

Ramonet is another of the great white Burgundy estates. There is a division of responsibilities between brothers Jean-Claude and Noël Ramonet but it is Noël who makes the wines. There are 17 ha of mostly first-rate Chassagne-Montrachet vineyard plus a little of three grands crus in Puligny, which makes for a fantastic array of wines. The winemaking is somewhat intuitive and responsive to the vintage conditions but usually results in wines that have an explosive concentration and breadth within a powerful structure. Only occasionally has anything less than very good wine been produced in the last couple of decades but there is some variability, with a tendency to be almost too structured and slightly hard in some instances. Others have lacked balance, with excess alcohol for the fruit concentration, and there can be a reductive quality in others. However these are the exceptions and can be avoided by taking the precaution of tasting and/or comparing notes of a specific wine and vintage before adding one or more of these great wines to a cellar (an approach advisable not just here but anywhere that involves the kind of sums the world's best wines now command). Reds play second fiddle to the whites but have been

Burgundy /Côte d'Or & Côte Chalonnaise

France

very good in recent good vintages including some Chassagne-Montrachet Premier Cru La Boudriotte (owned by Noël Ramonet and sold under his own label). A little Montrachet is made, as is some Puligny-Montrachet Premier Cru Champ Canet, while some Chevalier-Montrachet is produced from bought-in wine.

Recommended Reds:
Chassagne-Montrachet 1er Cru Clos de la Boudriotte ★★★ £F
Chassagne-Montrachet 1er Cru Morgeots ★★★ £F
Chassagne-Montrachet 1er Cru Clos Saint-Jean ★★★ £F

Recommended Whites:
Bâtard-Montrachet ✪✪✪✪ £H
Bienvenues-Bâtard-Montrachet ★★★★★ £H
Chassagne-Montrachet 1er Cru Grandes Ruchottes ★★★★★ £G
Chassagne-Montrachet 1er Cru Caillerets ★★★★ £G
Chassagne-Montrachet 1er Cru Morgeots ★★★★ £G
Chassagne-Montrachet1er Cru Boudriottes ★★★★ £G
Chassagne-Montrachet 1er Cru Les Vergers ★★★☆ £G
Chassagne-Montrachet 1er Cru Les Chaumées ★★★☆ £G
Chassagne-Montrachet ★★★ £F
Saint-Aubin 1er Cru Le Charmois ★★☆ £E

Dom. Rapet Père et Fils *www.domaine-rapet.com*
The input of Vincent Rapet over recent vintages has given a considerable boost to this long-established domaine. Though some two-thirds of the 18 ha are planted to Pinot Noir, the reputation rests as much with the whites as reds. The core of the production is very good Pernand-Vergelesses but fine examples of Corton and Corton-Charlemagne are also made. There is now better grape selection, the whites have longer lees-contact than previously and show good depth, richness and restrained oak. Reds can be sturdy, occasionally with slightly coarse tannins, but generally show more refinement and depth in the most recent vintages, particularly in the very stylish Pernand-Vergelesses. All the better reds should be drunk with 5 years' or more, but whites can be drunk younger. From the 2000 vintage white Pernand-Vergelesses is now being bottled as separate specified premiers crus (including Le Clos du Village, En Caradeux and Sous Frétille) following the promotion of some village land.

Recommended Reds:
Corton ★★★★ £G   Corton Pougets ★★★★ £F
Pernand-Vergelesses 1er Cru Île de Vergelesses ★★★ £F
Pernand-Vergelesses 1er Cru Les Vergelesses ★★☆ £E
Beaune 1er Cru Grèves ★★★ £E
Beaune 1er Cru Clos du Roi ★★★★ £E
Aloxe-Corton ★★☆ £E

Recommended Whites:
Corton-Charlemagne ★★★★ £G
Pernand-Vergelesses 1er Cru Sous Frétille ★★★ £E
Pernand-Vergelesses 1er Cru En Caradeux ★★☆ £E
Pernand-Vergelesses 1er Cru Clos du Village ★★☆ £E

François Raquillet (Mercurey) *www.domaine-raquillet.com*
François Raquillet is a young vigneron who is turning his family's 11 ha of vineyards into some of the most prized in Mercurey. A series of premiers crus reds benefit from being part aged in new oak resulting in wines of good colour, intensity but also accessibility. The purity of fruit is retained but the firmness of some Mercurey is usually avoided. Naugues is the most sophisticated but there is good intensity and character in all the reds. In 2010 a special *cuvée* from 100 year old vines from the Veleys vineyard was produced after spending 18 months en futs (two-thirds new and one-third one year old) without fining or filtration. We haven;t tasted this yet - but are

looking forward to it!

Recommended Reds:
Mercurey 1er Cru Le Clos l'Eveque ★★★ £D
Mercurey 1er Cru Naugues ★★★ £D
Mercurey 1er Cru Puillets ★★★ £D
Mercurey 1er Cru Vasées ★★★ £D   Mercurey 1er Cru Veleys ★★ £D
Mercurey Vieilles Vignes ★★ £D

Recommended Whites:
Mercurey 1er Cru Veleys ★★ £D

Dom. Louis Rémy *www.domaine-chantal-remy.com*
This is a very small Morey-Saint-Denis based domaine with just 3 ha of vineyards but includes three grands crus. There is little to choose between them in quality terms but direction from Chantal Remy has ensured greater consistency. The style is a little tight, intense and fall just short of classic expressions of the different terroirs. Nonetheless the combination of fruit intensity, acidity, extract and tannin promises a fine return for those prepared to cellar the grands crus for a decade or even longer. What's more they are significantly cheaper than those from more famous names.

Recommended Reds:
Clos de la Roche ★★★★ £G   Chambertin ★★★★£G
Latricières-Chambertin ★★★★ £G

Daniel Rion (Nuits-Saint-Georges) *www.domaine-daniel-rion.com*
Christophe and Olivier are now making the wines here on their own after the departure of their brother, Patrice (Michèle & Patrice RION), following the 2000 vintage. Over the course of two decades Patrice had established a solid reputation for this estate created by his father. The 18 ha is based primarily on Nuits-Saint-Georges and Vosne vineyards and includes some Chardonnay and Aligoté as well as Pinot Noir. The wines have long been characterised by their strength and a certain firmness allied to depth and intensity. In recent years there has been a gradual shift to finer tannins and more immediate richness and the wines are particularly successful in the best years, if sometimes a little harsh or tough in lighter vintages. Beaumonts, in particular is a classic old vine expression of Vosne-Romanée. Produced since the 1998 vintage are an Echezeaux as well as Clos de Vougeot from a different source to that previously made. The reds shouldn't be rushed, in fact they can be transformed with a little extra bottle age. The rich creamy white Nuits is produced from Pinot Blanc.

Recommended Reds:
Clos de Vougeot ★★★★★ £H
Vosne-Romanée 1er Cru Beaux-Monts ★★★★★ £G
Vosne-Romanée 1er Cru Chaumes ★★★★ £F
Vosne-Romanée ★★★ £E
Nuits-Saint-Georges 1er Cru Vignes Rondes ★★★★ £F
Nuits-Saint-Georges Grandes Vignes ★★★ £E
Nuits-Saint-Georges Lavières ★★☆ £D
Côte de Nuits-Villages Le Vaucrain★★ £C

Recommended Whites:
Nuits-Saint-Georges 1er Cru Terres Blanches ★★★ £E

✿ Michèle & Patrice Rion *www.patricerion.com*
Some very good wine was made by Patrice Rion for his own label even before he handed over the winemaking reins at the family domaine (Daniel RION ET FILS) to his two brothers. From 2000 the range here has been greatly expanded to include bought-in wines but these are labelled as simply Patrice Rion. Given an insistence on high-quality fruit, this promises to be a good quality range of

négociant wines. The estate range has been expanded too with recent additions including an intense, full Chambolle-Musigny Les Charmes and very classy Nuits-Saint-Georges Clos des ArgilliŽres. Since 2005 there has been a really super new white Nuits (premier cru Les Terres Blanches) from 80% Chardonnay and 20% Pinot Blanc.

Domaine Michèle & Patrice Rion

Recommended Reds:

Chambolle-Musigny 1er Cru Charmes ★★★★☆ £G
Chambolle-Musigny Les Cras ★★★★ £F
Nuits-Saint-Georges 1er Cru Clos des Argillières ★★★★ £G
Bourgogne Rouge Bons Batons ★★☆ £D

Patrice Rion

Recommended Reds:

Gevrey-Chambertin Clos Prieur ★★★☆ £F
Nuits-Saint-Georges Vieilles Vignes ★★★☆ £F

Antonin Rodet (Mercurey) www.rodet.com

This is a négociant house with substantial holdings (160 ha) in both the Côte d'Or and Côte Chalonnaise. Estates either owned, partly owned or made and distributed by Antonin Rodet include: Château de Rully (Rully) and Château de Mercey (Maranges-based for Hautes Côtes de Beaune red and white, and Mercurey). The wines are made by Anne-Laure Hernette. The best of those under the Antonin Rodet label (many of them designated Cave Privée) are consistently very good indeed, at times quite oaky but rich and ripe, with great depth and complexity. Those listed include some of the best wines made on a regular basis. Of the consistently good Côte Chalonnaise wines the wholly owned premier cru Clos La Bressande is a powerful example of oak-aged white Rully while the ageworthy reds impress too. In addition, as well as a range of Vin de Pays d'Oc varietals Antonin Rodet also owns the Domaine de l'AIGLE in Limoux, Languedoc-Roussillon. For the bold, confident wines of Château de Chamirey (Mercurey) and Domaine des Perdrix see Domaines DEVILLARD.

Antonin Rodet

Recommended Reds:

Charmes-Chambertin ★★★★ £G
Clos de Vougeot ★★★★ £G
Gevrey-Chambertin 1er Cru Estournelles ★★★★ £F
Nuits-Saint-Georges 1er Cru Porêts-Saint-Georges ★★★★ £F
Nuits-Saint-Georges 1er Cru Les Saint-Georges ★★★ £F

Recommended Whites:

Meursault 1er Cru Perrières ★★★★ £F
Bourgogne Blanc Vieilles Vignes ★★ £D

Château de Mercey

Recommended Reds:

Mercurey 1er Cru En Sazenay ★★☆ £D
Bourgogne Hautes-Côtes de Beaune ★☆ £C

Recommended Whites:

Mercurey ★★ £D   Bourgogne Hautes-Côtes de Beaune ★☆ £C

Château de Rully

Recommended Reds:

Rully 1er Cru Molesme ★★★ £D   Rully ★★£D

Recommended Whites:

Rully 1er Cru Clos La Bressande ★★★ £D   Rully ★★ £D

Dom. de La Romanée-Conti www.romanee-conti.com

DRC, as it referred to by both devotees and novices alike, is considered by many to be Burgundy's greatest domaine. The history and nobility of these famous grand cru vineyards make this a difficult assertion to refute, though over the past decade this

domaine has been seriously challenged by part-owner Lalou Bize-Leroy's own estate, Domaine LEROY. Any serious text on Burgundy will provide background on both the estate and individual wines. Currently yields are lower than previously, the average vine age is now high across all the wines and the viticulture is now essentially biodynamic (in practice if not in name), making for healthier soils than previously. The most distinctive features of the vinification are that there is little or no destemming and automatic punching down is carried out. All the wines see 100% new oak. Individual wines seem to have had slight ups and downs but when on form they all rate 5 stars. Montrachet apart, all are made in decent quantities by Burgundian standards, assuming, that is, you can afford them. The holdings are: La Romanée Conti (1.81 ha), La Tâche (6.06 ha), Richebourg (3.51 ha), Romanée-Saint-Vivant (5.28 ha), Echezeaux (4.67 ha), Grands-Echezeaux (3.53 ha) and the solitary white, Le Montrachet (0.68 ha). All the wines are £H. The first two are monopoles and are considered the brightest stars in the firmament, while the other reds account for a substantial proportion of the vineyard area of their respective appellations. A second selection, Cuvée Duvault-Blochet, sold as Vosne Romanée Premier Cru, has been produced in most years since 1999

Rossignol-Trapet (Gevrey-Chambertin) www.rossignol-trapet.com

This the other half of the original Louis Trapet estate has made great strides under Nicolas and David Rossignol, making it now probably the more interesting part of the Trapet Estate. Organic and biodynamic farming is maintained in the vineyards Organic and biodynamic farming is maintained in the vineyards. For some years, the most graceful and feminine wine has been the Latricières-Chambertin. There is also more elegance in the Petite Chapelle and greater class in Le Chambertin. The Beaune Les Teurons is a fine buy and good value. (ME)

Recommended Reds:

Le Chambertin ★★★★ £H   Latricières- Chambertin ★★★★ £H
Gevrey-Chambertin 1er Cru La Petite Chapelle ★★★★ £G
Beaune 1er Cru les Teurons ★★★ £E

Emmanuel Rouget (Vosne-Romanée)

Emmanuel Rouget is the nephew of Henri Jayer and has retained a portion of the vineyards that Jayer, one of the great 20th-century figures in Burgundy, made famous. Jayer's use of a cold pre-fermentation maceration, 100% destemming, plenty of new oak, no filtration and rigorous attention to hygiene transformed the face of Burgundy as many others followed in his footsteps. Rouget's early efforts looked promising but some of the wines from vintages in the late 1990s and more recently seem to have lost a bit of the vigour and concentration of old. Yet quality is still good with no lack of style or class. Prices however are very high.

Recommended Reds:

Echezeaux★★★★ £H
Vosne-Romanée 1er Cru Cros Parentoux★★★★ £H
Vosne-Romanée 1er Cru Les Beaumonts★★★☆ £H
Vosne-Romanée★★★£G   Nuits-Saint-Georges★★★ £G

Dom. Roulot (Meursault)

Since 1989 Jean-Marc Roulot has run this highly respected domaine with a hatful of Meursault crus, built up by his father Guy some 30 years earlier. The wines show something of a leesy character and and some new oak influence but neither dominate and the percentage of new oak is sometimes less than 20%. The premiers crus Charmes, Perrières (and more recently, Bouchères) are the

top wines, the Perrières easily the most complex and complete of the three, but this is reflected in their prices. The most significant proportion of the estate's 12 ha comes from vineyards lying on higher slopes running towards Auxey-Duresses. Les Tessons and Les Tillets (from vines with a high average age) are arguably the pick of these and offer relatively good value for Meursault. Though majoring on Meursault, Roulot also produces an intense, vibrant, minerally Monthelie premier cru that adds richness with 2 or 3 years' age. Bourgogne Aligoté and a flavoursome, scented Bourgogne Blanc are more than dependable.

Recommended Whites:
Meursault 1er Cru Perrières ★★★★★ £G
Meursault 1er Cru Charmes ★★★★★ £G
Meursault 1er Cru Bouchères ★★★★☆ £G
Meursault Les Tessons ★★★★ £F
Meursault Les Tillets ★★★★ £E
Meursault Les Luchets ★★★ £E   Meursault Les Vireuils ★★★ £E
Meursault Meix Chavaux ★★★ £E
Monthelie 1er Cru Champs Fulliot ★★★ £E
Bourgogne Blanc ★★★☆£D   Bourgogne Aligoté ★☆ £C

●● Dom. Roumier (Chambolle-Musigny) *www.roumier.com*
A fabulous domaine whose wines express the essence of Chambolle-Musigny. Christophe Roumier has now had three decades of input, achieving ever better balance in his vineyards and maximising the potential of each site. The vines are of a high average age and low-yielding, but naturally so without the need for the excessive pruning or green harvesting required elsewhere. Quality is consistently high but that is not to say the wines are the same year in, year out; rather each expresses something of the vintage without its defects. What is most impressive is the structure of the wines; always there's a dimension and depth without a trace of hardness, allied to harmony and persistence. The Chambolles, in particular, are fragrant and elegant with more power, depth and concentration in the premiers crus. In the grands crus the power and elegance of Le Musigny contrasts with the muscle, intensity and grip of Bonnes Mares. From outside Chambolle-Musigny, the 2.5 ha *monopole* Clos de la Bussière in Morey-Saint-Denis produces a firmer, tighter wine, now showing more refinement and class than previously, and it can be very good value. Tiny amounts of very high quality Ruchottes-Chambertin and Charmes-Chambertin are also made, as is a little Corton-Charlemagne.

Recommended Reds:
Le Musigny ✪✪✪✪✪ £H   Bonnes Mares ✪✪✪✪✪ £H
Chambolle-Musigny 1er Cru Les Amoureuses ✪✪✪✪✪ £H
Chambolle-Musigny 1er Cru Les Cras ★★★★★ £G
Chambolle-Musigny ★★★ £E
Morey-Saint-Denis 1er Cru Clos de la Bussière ★★★★ £F
Bourgogne Rouge ★★ £C

●● Dom. A. Rousseau *www.domaine-rousseau.com*
Eric Rousseau and his sister Brigitte gradually assumed control of this the most famous Gevrey-Chambertin domaine that has been directed by their father, Charles Rousseau, for more than 40 years until Brigitte retired in 2012. Her place has now been taken on by Eric's daughter, Cyrielle. The estate was built up in the early part of the 20th century by their grandfather Armand but was further enlarged by Charles. A remarkable 8ha of the 14 ha planted exclusively to Pinot Noir are grands crus. Only a small percentage of the stems are retained to assist a moderately long vinification complete with automatic *pigeage*. The top wines, Chambertin and

Chambertin Clos-de-Béze, show all the class and breed of great grand cru Burgundy, with a breadth and presence in the mouth that even the very best premiers crus lack. These and the Clos Saint-Jacques receive 100% new oak but the oak treatment is rarely, if ever, excessive, though shows more in the Clos-de-Béze than the Chambertin. Other crus receive at most 30% new oak. In the Charmes-Chambertin and Mazy-Chambertin finesse and elegance are emphasised yet there is a vigour and intensity about all the wines. The textures of all the Rousseau wines are very impressive too, even if other wines may provide greater richness and extract. All the wines need 5 years, the top wines 10 or more. The Premier Cru Lavaux Saint-Jacques, previously part of the regular Gevrey, has been bottled separately since 1999.

Recommended Reds:
Chambertin ✪✪✪✪✪ £H   Chambertin Clos-de-Béze ✪✪✪✪✪ £H
Ruchottes-Chambertin Clos des Ruchottes ✪✪✪✪✪ £H
Mazy-Chambertin ★★★★★ £G   Clos de la Roche ★★★★★ £G
Charmes-Chambertin ★★★★☆ £G
Gevrey-Chambertin 1er Cru Clos Saint-Jacques ✪✪✪✪✪ £G
Gevrey-Chambertin 1er Cru Les Cazetiers ★★★★★ £F
Gevrey-Chambertin 1er Cru Lavaux-Saint-Jacques ★★★★ £F
Gevrey-Chambertin ★★★☆ £E

● Etienne Sauzet (Puligny-Montrachet) *www.etiennesauzet.com*
This estate has a fabulous reputation and highly respected winemaker in Gérard Boudot. However it is now significantly smaller than it once was. Gérard's wife, Jeanine Boudot, grand daughter of Étienne Sauzet, has retained only a third of the vines, though their company has another third under contract for some time to come (the rest of the legacy has gone to brother Jean-Marc BOILLOT). There are now 8ha (but much boosted by bought-in grapes) with small amounts of four grands crus (Bâtard-Montrachet, Bienvenues-Bâtard-Montrachet, Le Montrachet and Chevalier-Montrachet) and more significant mounts of some of Puligny's best premiers crus. Form in the 1990s was irregular, the wine sometimes lean and slightly undistinguished - missing some of the class and finesse for which they are famous. Nor have they always aged as well as previously. High demand has of course contributed to high prices but some caution should be taken before investing heavily. Since 2006 the estate has practiced organic farming and from 2010 has switched to biodynamic cultivation. The use of Sardinian corks which are denser than the Portuguese ones have appeared to have overcome the oxidation problems which occurred in the '90s and the early part of the 21st century and here has ben more consistency in the wines over the past 5 years.

Recommended Whites:
Le Montrachet ★★★★★£H   Bâtard-Montrachet ★★★★ £H
Chevalier-Montrachet ★★★★★ £H
Bienvenue-Bâtard-Montrachet ★★★★★ £H
Puligny-Montrachet 1er Cru La Garenne ★★★★☆ £G
Puligny-Montrachet 1er Cru Champ-Canet ★★★★ £G
Puligny-Montrachet 1er Cru Les Perrières ★★★★ £G
Puligny-Montrachet 1er Cru Les Referts ★★★★ £G
Puligny-Montrachet 1er Cru Les Combettes ★★★★ £G
Puligny-Montrachet 1er Cru Les Folatières ★★★★ £G
Puligny-Montrachet ★★★ £F

Comte Senard (Aloxe-Corton) *www.domainesenard.com*
Philippe Senard was one of those to work with the controversial consultant Guy Accad in the early 1990s, aiming for more colour and greater aroma and fruit intensity, in part from an extended cold

maceration on skins prior to fermentation. Like other producers advised by Accad, he gradually incorporated the best of his advice to make stylish, aromatic and intensely fruity red Burgundies. More recently his daughter, Lorraine has assumed responsibility for the winemaking. Some of the lesser wines can struggle for full ripeness but typically there is a cool, pure vibrant fruit intensity to which is added more breadth, length and elegance in the various Cortons. This is a good cellar from which to compare several different Cortons including gentle but broad framed *monopole* Clos des Meix with deep, intense Bressandes, and refined and harmonious Clos du Roi. En Charlemagne has cool, classy fruit but the least of these. All deserve at least 5 years' age. Good whites are also made, including an Aloxe-Corton from old-vine Pinot Gris, while a Corton Blanc is gaining in richness and complexity. A tiny amount of Corton-Charlemagne is also made. (Around 450 bottles). Other reds include a Chorey-les-Beaune and a premier cru Beaune. Ratings apply only to top years. The Senards also make the wines of Domaine des TERREGELESSES.

Recommended Reds:
Corton Bressandes★★★★ £F   Corton Clos du Roi★★★★ £G
Corton Clos des Meix★★★★ £F
Corton En Charlemagne★★★☆ £F
Aloxe-Corton 1er Cru Les Valozières★★☆ £E
Aloxe-Corton★☆ £E

Recommended Whites:
Corton Blanc★★★★ £G   Aloxe-Corton★★ £E

Serafin Père et Fils (Gevrey-Chambertin)
Christian Sérafin has been quietly working away on his family's small 5 ha estate, gradually refining his winemaking practices and producing ever more satisfying and consistently good wines. His signature is the power that might be expected from Gevrey together with plenty of oak and spice that embellish wines that are lush and fruit-rich, with lots of obvious appeal. The top crus add more class and breadth. The best wine made in any real quantity is the Vieilles Vignes bottling, which is meaty and full of ripe fruit, with plenty of depth. All the wines show very well with just 5 years' age. A tiny amount of top-quality Charmes-Chambertin is also made but is likely to be hard to find. Winemaking has recently been taken over by Christian's niece, Frederique Bachotet, and with the management of the estates in the hands of his daughter, Christian is beginning to take a back seat knowing that the future of the estate will remain in family hands.

Recommended Reds:
Gevrey-Chambertin 1er Cru Les Cazetiers ★★★★★ £G
Gevrey-Chambertin 1er Cru Les Corbeaux ★★★★ £G
Gevrey-Chambertin 1er Cru Fontenys ★★★★ £G
Gevrey-Chambertin Vieilles Vignes ★★★★ £F
Gevrey-Chambertin ★★★ £E
Chambolle-Musigny 1er Cru Les Baudes ★★★★ £G
Morey-Saint-Denis 1er Cru Les Millandes ★★★★ £G

Tollot-Beaut (Chorey-lès-Beaune)
Tollot-Beaut's 24 ha estate includes some of the northern Côte de Beaune's lesser but better-value appellations. With lots of new oak and ripe, forward fruit, the wines have had plenty of appeal in the past but lacked structure despite some firm tannins and some aged quite quickly. However it has always been a team effort and the current members in charge, Nathalie, Jean-Paul and Olivier have improved the wines 1999. Yields have been lowered, though they were never high and the wines have shown better definition and

balance and have much more to offer with 4 or 5 years' age than previously. That said, there is a tendency still to too much oak and extract for the quality of the fruit, especially in lighter vintages. Chorey-les-Beaune from the *monopole* of La Pièce du Chapitre is usually an atypically good example of the appellation. Only a little white is made but includes some Corton-Charlemagne. Ratings apply to the most recent vintages only.

Recommended Reds:
Corton ★★★★£G   Corton Bressandes ★★★★ £G
Aloxe-Corton 1er Cru Fournières ★★★ £F
Aloxe-Corton 1er Cru Vercots ★★★ £F
Aloxe-Corton ★★ £E   Beaune 1er Cru Clos du Roi ★★★ £F
Beaune 1er Cru Grèves ★★★ £F
Chorey-les-Beaune Pièce du Chapitre ★★★ £D
Chorey-les-Beaune ★★★ £D
Savigny-les-Beaune 1er Cru Lavières ★★☆ £E
Savigny-les-Beaune 1er Cru Champs Chevrey ★★ £E

Dom. Tortochot (Gevrey-Chambertin)   www.tortochot.com
Recently much improved Gevrey-Chambertin estate. After taking over from her father, Chantal Tortochot has produced wines with better restraint, balance and expression. The wines still have impressive colour and intensity with plenty of extract and will be very good if given sufficient time. Village Gevrey lieuxdits need 5 years; a classy, pure but powerful Premier Cru Lavaux-Saint-Jacques needs 6–8 years; while grands crus Charmes-Chambertin (with impressive breadth and extract to match) and Mazy-Chambertin (powerful, concentrated and black-fruited) deserve a full 10 years' ageing. Regular Morey-Saint-Denis is also well made with lots of extract, character and ripe tannins. Also made are a tiny amount of Chambertin and some Gevrey-Chambertin Premier Cru Les Champeaux. Since 2008 the wines have been produced organically.

Recommended Reds:
Mazy-Chamberlain ★★★★★ £G   Charmes-Chambertin ★★★★ £G
Gevrey-Chambertin 1er Cru Lavaux-Saint-Jacques ★★★★ £G
Gevrey-Chambertin Les Corvées ★★★ £F
Gevrey-Chambertin Champerrier Vieilles Vignes ★★★ £F
Gevrey-Chambertin Jeunes Rois ★★ £E   Morey-Saint-Denis ★★★ £E

Dom. Trapet Pere et Fils   www.domaine-trapet.com
The original Domaine Louis Trapet (source of some famous bottles from the 1950s and 60s) was built up from the late 19th century before being divided in 1990 between Jean and his sister (ROSSIGNOL-TRAPET). Jean's son, Jean-Louis, has revived their venerable vineyards, which include nearly 2 ha ofChambertin and decent segments of Chapelle-Chambertin and Latricières-Chambertin. The raw material is now of much higher quality than previously, with reduced yields from higher than typical vine densities under a regime that became progressively more biodynamic in the late 1990s. The 13 ha also includes some excellent Premier Cru Petite Chapelle and Clos Prieur as well as village Gevrey-Chambertin and Marsannay. There is a measured use of new oak but the accent is on the quality of the fruit and producing wines of finesse and real class. There is great depth and dimension as well as a particular strength and definition characteristic to the wines, which require patience. Five years' is needed for Gevrey, 5–10 for the premiers crus, and a minimum of 10 for Chambertin. Given time these wines are some of the very best from Gevrey and are reasonably priced in that context.

Recommended Reds:
Chambertin★★★★★ £H

Burgundy /Côte d'Or & Côte Chalonnaise

France

Latricières-Chambertin ★★★★ £H
Gevrey-Chambertin 1er Cru Clos Prieur ★★★★ £G
Gevrey-Chambertin 1er Cru Petite Chapelle ★★★★ £G
Gevrey-Chambertin ★★★ £E   Marsannay ★★ £D

Verget   www.verget-sa.com

Since 1990 Jean-Marie Guffens has constructed a merchant house of remarkable constitution. It is not built around the great crus of the Côte de Beaune, though there are some of those, but rather the less hallowed vineyards of the Mâconnais and increasingly Chablis (see VERGET CHABLIS). The Mâconnais wines (including Pouilly-Fuissé, Saint-Veran and various Mâcon-Villages) are covered, together with the wines of his own private estate, GUFFENS-HEYNEN in the Mâconnais section. The wines from the Côte d'Or are true to the Verget style, which is one of great extract, concentration and richness, made from fully ripe grapes sourced from low-yielding vineyards. There is not always continuity of production from particular appellations, but almost all of the Verget wines can be broached fairly young but should keep for a decade. CHÂTEAU DES TOURETTES in the Côtes du Luberon (see Southern Rhône) also belongs to Guffens-Heynen.

Recommended Whites:
Bâtard-Montrachet ★★★★★ £H
Corton-Charlemagne ★★★★★ £G
Meursault Tillets ★★★★ £F Meursault Rougeots ★★★☆ £F
Puligny-Montrachet 1er Cru Sous le Puits ★★★★ £F
Puligny-Montrachet Enseignières ★★★★ £F
Chassagne-Montrachet Franchemont ★★★ £F

✿ A et P de Villaine (Bouzeron)   www.de-villaine.com

Aubert de Villaine, co-director of the Côte d'Or's most prestigious estate (Domaine de la ROMANÉE-CONTI), and his wife Pamela continue to improve on their pure, natural expressions of the Côte Chalonnaise. The wines are organically produced and grapes are manually harvested from the 21 ha of estate vineyards. More than half is planted to Aligoté (the grape which dominates the appellation) and a fine characterful (Bouzeron) example - as good as any produced - is made along with stylish Bourgogne reds and white. Wines in both colours are elegant and harmonious with definition and vibrancy. Also made is a refined, structured Rully, complemented by a beautifully expressive Mercurey Montots which is quite extraordinary for a village wine. All are better with 2 or 3 years' age (including the Aligoté) while the Montots might be kept for 5 or 6 years.

Recommended Reds:
Mercurey Les Montots ★★★☆ £D
Bourgogne Côte Chalonnaise La Digoine ★★★ £C
Bourgogne Côte Chalonnaise La Fortune ★★☆ £C
Recommended Whites:
Rully Les Saint-Jacques ★★★ £D
Bourgogne Côte Chalonnaise Les Cloux ★★★ £C
Bouzeron ★★☆ £C

✿✿ Dom. Comte Georges de Vogüé (Musigny)

This estate is known for one of the single greatest red Burgundies made. The Musigny has an exalted reputation based in part on the on-going quality of the wine but also on some legendary old vintages (including 1945, 47, 59, 69 and 72). The domaine owns 7.2 ha of the 10.7 ha grand cru, though this includes 0.5 ha of Musigny Blanc (recently sold as Bourgogne Blanc), the only place in the

commune of Chambolle-Musigny where Chardonnay is permitted to be grown. François Millet has made the wines here since the Comte died in 1986 and his daughter took over the running of the estate. Vine age is high and yields vary but are kept low; adjustments are made where necessary in response to vintage conditions. The approach to vinification is also vintage-responsive, with individual parcels of vineyard treated in different ways, though a long *cuvaison* is favoured. Since 1990 few if any expert tasters have been left in any doubt about the true greatness of the Musigny Vieilles Vignes after some leaner offerings in the 1970s and 80s. The wine is now more deeply coloured than previously and its extraordinary aromatics, with preserved fruits and floral notes, precede a considerable structure that underpins the silky texture, wonderful definition and mouthfilling dimension on the palate that becomes increasingly opulent with age, the intense flavours being sustained long on the finish. Its remarkable longevity from top vintages make it a cellaring must for the few who can afford it. There is wonderful class, intensity and concentration in the Amoureuses too; and a rich, sturdy, darker fruit density to the Bonnes Mares.

Recommended Reds:
Musigny Vieilles Vignes ✪✪✪✪ £H   Bonnes Mares ★★★★★ £H
Chambolle-Musigny 1er Cru Les Amoureuses ★★★★★ £H
Chambolle-Musigny ★★★ £G

Dom. Joseph Voillot (Volnay)   www.joseph-voillot.com

Since taking over in 1995 Jean-Pierre Charlot, son-in-law of Joseph Voillot, has gradually wrought finer and finer examples of Volnay and Pommard from this 10 ha family estate. Pruning and de-budding are used to keep yields low and the grapes are completely destemmed prior to a pre-fermentation maceration. 25% new oak is used for ageing following a moderately long *cuvaison*. The resulting wines are expressive, classy with plenty of extract and nearly all need at least 6-8 years' age. Prices are very reasonable from the sytlish Bourgogne to premiers crus. In addition to those listed below are premiers crus Volnay Brouillards and Pommard Clos Micault.

Recommended Reds:
Volnay 1er Cru Les Caillerets ★★★★☆ £F
Volnay 1er Cru Les Champans ★★★★ £F
Volnay 1er Cru Les Fremiets ★★★★ £F
Volnay Vieilles Vignes ★★★☆ £E
Pommard 1er Cru Les Rugiens ★★★★☆ £F
Pommard 1er Cru Les Epenots ★★★★ £F
Pommard 1er Cru Pézerolles ★★★★ £F
Bourgogne Pinot Noir Vieilles Vignes ★★☆ £D

Dom. de La Vougeraie   www.domainedelavougeraie.com

Now a respected southern Côte de Nuits-based estate comprising all of Boisset's (Burgundy's single biggest producer) own vineyards. Boisset recruited Pascal Marchand, the very highly regarded winemaker of the Clos des Epeneaux (Comte ARMAND) in Pommard, to direct operations. He had full responsibility for both viticulture and winemaking from 2000 to 2006. His successor, Pierre Vincent comes from within the Boisset group. The vineyards total an impressive 37ha, which are certified organic and now treated biodynamically, predominantly planted to Pinot Noir and much of it in the Côte de Nuits. Yields are low (less than 30 hl/ha in the reds), which is immediately apparent in wines of richness, depth and class. Gevrey-Chambertin and Nuits-Saint-Georges feature, including some premier cru sites, while grands crus run to Corton Clos du Roi, Clos de Vougeot, Bonnes Mares, Charmes-Chambertin and a third of a hectare of Musigny. Nearly all the wines are proving to be, at the

very least, good examples of their respective appellations. Corton-Charlemagne and the solely-owned Vougeot cru are already very good whites. Some recent releases have been slightly marked by a cellar taint problem including Vougeot white.

Recommended Reds:

Clos de Vougeot ★★★★ £G

Charmes-Chambertin ★★★★ £G

Vougeot 1er Cru Les Cras ★★★ £F

Vougeot Clos du Prieuré ★★★ £F

Chambolle-Musigny ★★★ £E

Gevrey-Chambertin Les Evocelles ★★★★ £F

Corton Clos du Roi ★★★☆ £G

Pommard Les Petit Noizons ★★★ £F

Côtes de Beaune Les Pierres Blanches ★★ £D

Bourgogne Rouge Terres de Famille ★★ £C

Recommended Whites:

Vougeot 1er Cru Clos Blanc de Vougeot ★★★★ £G

Corton-Charlemagne ★★★★ £G

Other wines of note

This list includes notable wines from a range of producers but is not intended to be a comprehensive list of a given producer's wines; just those that we have encountered. In some instances there may be several more good wines.

Robert Ampeau

Recommended Whites: Meursault ★★★ £G

Meursault 1er Cru Perrières ★★★★ £G

Meursault 1er Cru Pièce Sous Le Bois ★★★ £G

Puligny-Montrachet 1er Cru Combettes ★★★★ £G

Auxey-Duresses 1er Cru Ecusseaux ★★★ £E

Recommended Reds: Volnay 1er Cru Santenots ★★★ £G

Savigny-Les-Beaune 1er Cru Lavières ★★ £E

Dom. d'Ardhuy

Recommended Whites: Corton-Charlemagne ★★★ £G

Meursault Les Pellans ★★★ £F   Savigny-Les-Beaune ★★ £E

Arnoux Père et Fils

Recommended Reds: Corton Rognets ★★☆ £G

Beaune 1er Cru Cent Vignes ★★☆ £E

Savigny-Les-Beaune 1er Cru Vergelesses ★★☆ £E

Savigny-Les-Beaune ★★ £D   Chorey-Les-Beaune Confrelins ★★ £D

Jean-Claude Bachelet

Recommended Whites: Puligny-Montrachet ★★★ £F

Puligny-Montrachet 1er Cru Sous Le Puits ★★★ £F

Saint-Aubin 1er Cru Les Champlots ★★ £E

Bachelet-Ramonet

Recommended Whites: Chassagne-Montrachet ★★★ £E

Chassagne-Montrachet 1er Cru Caillerets ★★★★ £F

Chassagne-Montrachet 1er Cru Grande Montagne ★★★ £F

Recommended Reds:

Chassagne-Montrachet 1er Cru Clos Saint-Jean ★★ £E

Ballot-Millot

Recommended Whites: Meursault Les Narvaux ★★★☆ £F

Meursault 1er Cru Genevrières ★★★★ £G

Meursault 1er Cru Perrières ★★★★☆ £G

Chassagne-Montrachet 1er Cru Morgeot ★★★★ £G

Pierre Bertheau

Recommended Reds: Chambolle-Musigny 1er Cru ★★★ £F

Chambolle-Musigny 1er Cru Charmes ★★★★ £G

Guillemette & Xavier Besson

Recommended Whites: Givry Le Haut Colombier ★★ £C

Recommended Reds: Givry Le Haut Colombier ★£C

Givry Les Grands Prétans ★★ £D

Billard-Gonnet

Recommended Reds: Pommard ★★★ £E

Pommard 1er Cru Rugiens ★★★★ £G

Pommard 1er Cru Pezerolles ★★★★ £F

Pommard 1er Cru Chaponnières ★★★ £F

Dom. Bizot

Recommended Reds: Echezeaux ★★★ £F

Vosne-Romanée Les Jachées ★★☆ £F

Jean-Marc Bouley

Recommended Reds: Volnay 1er Cru Les Carelles ★★★★ £F

Volnay 1er Cru Clos Des Chênes ★★★☆ £F

Volnay 1er Cru Caillerets ★★★ £F   Volnay Clos de La Cave ★★☆ £E

Volnay Vieilles Vignes ★★★ £E   Pommard 1er Cru Frémiets ★★★ £F

Pommard 1er Cru Rugiens ★★★ £F

Bourgogne-Hautes Côtes de Beaune ★☆ £D

Recommended Whites:

Bourgogne-Hautes Côtes de Beaune ★★ £D

René Bourgeon

Recommended Reds: Givry ★ £C   Givry Baraude ★★ £D

Recommended Whites: Givry Clos de La Brulée ★★ £C

Denis Boussey

Recommended Whites: Meursault 1er Cru Charmes ★★★★ £F

Meursault Clos Du Pré de Manche ★★★ £F

Meursault Vieilles Vignes ★★★ £E   Monthelie ★★ £D

Jean-Claude Brelière

Recommended Whites: Rully 1er Cru Margotée ★★ £D

Recommended Reds: Rully 1er Cru Préaux ★★ £D

Rully 1er Cru Montpalais ★★ £D

Dom. Philippe Brenot

Recommended Whites: Bâtard-Montrachet ★★★★☆ £H

Puligny-Montrachet Les Enseignières ★★★ £F

Chassagne-Montrachet En L'ormeau ★★★ £F

Santenay Le Clos Genet ★★ £D

Cave des Vignerons de Buxy

Recommended Whites:

Montagny Domaine Des Pierres Blanches ★★ £D

Montagny 1er Cru Cuvée Speciale ★ £D

Montagny 1er Cru Chaignots ★★ £D

Jacques Cacheux

Recommended Reds: Echezeaux ★★★★ £G

Vosne-Romanée 1er Cru Les Suchots ★★★ £G

Lucien Camus-Bruchon

Recommended Reds: Pommard 1er Cru Arvelets ★★★ £E

Savigny-Lès-Beaune Liards Vieilles Vignes ★★ £D

Savigny-Lès-Beaune 1er Cru Lavières ★★ £E

Beaune 1er Cru Clos Du Roi ★★★ £E

Recommended Whites: Savigny-Lès-Beaune Goudelettes ★★ £E

Capitain-Gagnerot/Dom. Francois Capitain

Recommended Whites: Corton-Charlemagne ★★★★☆ £G

Recommended Reds: Corton Les Grandes Lolières ★★★☆ £G

Chartron & Trébuchet

Recommended Whites: Bourgogne Blanc ★ £D

Puligny-Montrachet 1er Cru Clos Des Caillerets ★★★ £G

Saint-Aubin 1er Cru Murgers Des Dents de Chien ★★ £D

Saint-Aubin 1er Cru Châtenière ★★ £D

Dom. du Château de Chorey

Recommended Whites: Pernand-Vergelesses ★★ £D

Recommended Reds: Beaune 1er Cru Vignes Franches ★★ £E

Beaune 1er Cru Cras ★★ £E   Beaune 1er Cru Teurons ★★ £F

Burgundy /Côte d'Or & Côte Chalonnaise

France

Chorey-Lès-Beaune ★ £D

Château de La Saule
Recommended Whites: Montagny 1er Cru ★★☆ £D
Montagny 1er Cru Fût-En-Chêne ★★★ £D

Jean Chauvenet
Recommended Reds: Nuits-Saint-Georges ★★★ £E
Nuits-Saint-Georges 1er Cru Damodes ★★★ £F
Nuits-Saint-Georges 1er Cru Bousselots ★★★ £F
Nuits-Saint-Georges 1er Cru Vaucrains ★★★★ £F

Hubert Chauvenet-Chopin
Recommended Reds: Nuits-Saint-Georges ★★★ £E
Nuits-Saint-Georges 1er Cru Murgers ★★★★ £F
Côte de Nuits-Villages ★★ £D

Dom. Chevalier Père et Fils
Recommended Whites: Corton-Charlemagne ★★★☆ £G
Ladoix 1er Cru Les Gréchons ★★ £D

Domaine des Clos
Recommended Reds: Beaune 1er Cru Les Avaux ★★★ £E
Nuits-Saint-Georges Les Crots ★★★ £E

Dom. Alain Coche-Bizouard
Recommended Whites: Meursault Luchets ★★ £E
Meursault 1er Cru Gouttes D'or ★★★ £F
Meursault 1er Cru Charmes ★★★ £F

Marius Delarche
Recommended Whites: Corton-Charlemagne ★★★ £G
Recommended Reds: Corton Renardes ★★☆ £G

Digioia-Royer
Recommended Reds:
Chambolle-Musigny Vieilles Vignes ★★★☆ £F
Chambolle-Musigny 1er Cru Groseilles ★★★☆ £F
Chambolle-Musigny 1er Cru Gruenchers ★★★☆ £F

David Duband
Recommended Reds:
Bourgogne-Hautes Côtes de Nuits Louis Auguste ★★☆ £C
Gevrey-Chambertin Les Evocelles ★★★☆ £F
Chambolle-Musigny ★★★ £F Morey-Saint-Denis ★★★☆ £F
Morey-Saint-Denis 1er Cru Clos Sorbe ★★★★ £F
Nuits-Saint-Georges ★★★ £E
Nuits-Saint-Georges 1er Cru Procès ★★★★ £F
Nuits-Saint-Georges 1er Cru Pruliers ★★★★ £F
Vosne-Romanée ★★★☆ £F
Echezeaux ★★★★☆ £G

Dublere
Recommended Whites: Corton-Charlemagne ★★★★ £F
Chassagne-Montrachet 1er Cru Les Chaumes ★★★★☆ £F

Benoit Ente
Recommended Whites:
Puligny-Montrachet 1er Cru Les Folatières ★★★★ £G
Puligny-Montrachet 1er Cru Champ-Gain ★★★★ £G
Puligny-Montrachet 1er Cru Les Referts ★★★★ £G
Puligny-Montrachet ★★★ £F

Follin-Arbelet
Recommended Whites: Corton-Charlemagne ★★★★ £G
Recommended Reds:
Corton Bressandes ★★★★ £G Romanée Saint-Vivant ★★★★☆ £H
Aloxe-Corton 1er Cru Clos Du Chapitre ★★☆ £F

Dom. Forey Père et Fils
Recommended Reds: Echezeaux ★★★★ £G
Vosne-Romanée 1er Cru Gaudichots ★★★★ £G
Vosne-Romanée 1er Cru Les Petit Monts ★★★★ £G
Vosne-Romanée ★★★ £F

Fougeray de Beauclair
Recommended Whites: Marsannay Saint Jacques ★★★ £E
Recommended Reds: Marsannay Saint Jacques ★★ £E
Marsannay Les Favières ★★ £D
Côtes de Nuits-Villages ★★☆ £D Fixin Clos Marion ★★★ £E
Bonnes Mares ★★★★ £G

Dominique Gallois
Recommended Reds: Gevrey-Chambertin ★★★ £F
Gevrey-Chambertin 1er Cru Combe Aux Moines ★★★★ £F

Alex Gambal
Recommended Whites: Meursault Clos Du Cromin ★★★ £F
Chassagne-Montrachet 1er Cru La Maltroie ★★★★ £G
Bourgogne Chardonnay ★★ £D Fixin Blanc ★★ £D
Recommended Reds: Gevrey-Chambertin Vieilles Vignes ★★★ £F
Vosne-Romanée ★★ £F Bourgogne Les Deux Papis ★ £D

Paul Garaudet
Recommended Reds: Monthelie 1er Cru Duresses ★★★ £E
Monthelie ★★ £D Monthelie 1er Cru Clos Gauthey ★★ £D
Volnay ★★★ £E

Michel Gay et Fils
Recommended Reds: Corton Renardes ★★★★ £G

Emmanuel Giboulot (Biodynamic)
Recommended Whites:
Bourgogne-Hautes Côtes de Nuits ★★☆ £D
Côte de Beaune La Grande Chatelaine ★★★☆ £D
Côte de Beaune La Combe D'eve ★★★☆ £D

Gros Frère et Soeur
Recommended Reds: Clos de Vougeot Musigni ★★★★ £G
Vosne-Romanée★★★ £F Bourgogne-Hautes Côtes de Nuits ★★ £C

Franck Grux
Recommended Whites: Bourgogne Les Grandes Coutures ★★ £D
Meursault Les Meix Chavaux ★★★☆ £F

Harmand-Geoffroy
Recommended Reds: Mazis-Chambertin ★★★★ £G
Gevrey-Chambertin 1er Cru Lavaux Saint-Jacques ★★★☆ £F
Gevrey-Chambertin 1er Cru La Bossière★★★ £F
Gevrey-Chambertin Clos Prieur ★★☆ £F

Humbert Frères
Recommended Reds: Charmes-Chambertin ★★★★ £G
Gevrey-Chambertin★★★ £E
Gevrey-Chambertin 1er Cru Poissenots ★★★★ £F

Dom. Lucien Jacob
Recommended Reds: Savigny-Lès-Beaune ★★ £D
Recommended Whites:
Savigny-Lès-Beaune 1er Cru Les Vergelesses★★★ £E
Savigny-Lès-Beaune ★★ £D

Dom. Jayer-Gilles
Recommended Reds: Echezeaux ★★★★ £H
Côte de Nuits-Villages★★★ £D
Bourgogne-Hautes Côtes de Nuits ★★☆ £D
Bourgogne-Hautes Côtes de Beaune ★★☆ £D
Recommended Whites:
Bourgogne-Hautes Côtes de Beaune ★★☆ £D

Alain Jeanniard
Recommended Reds:
Morey-Saint-Denis Vieilles Vignes★★★ £F
Morey-Saint-Denis 1er Cru Les Chenevery ★★★☆ £F

Dom. Jeannin-Naltet
Recommended Reds:
Mercurey Clos des Grands Voyens ★★★ £D

Dom. Jobard-Morey
Recommended Whites: Meursault Les Tillets ★★★ £E
Meursault 1er Cru Poruzot ★★★☆ £F
Meursault 1er Cru Charmes ★★★★ £F

Gilles Jourdan
Recommended Reds: Côtes de Nuits-Villages ★★★ £D

Dom. Lamy-Pillot
Recommended Whites: Chassagne-Montrachet ★★★ £E
Chassagne-Montrachet 1er Cru Morgeots ★★★ £F
Chassagne-Montrachet 1er Cru Caillerets ★★★★ £F
Recommended Reds:
Chassagne-Montrachet 1er Cru Clos Saint-Jean ★★ £E
Chassagne-Montrachet 1er Cru Morgeots ★★ £E

Dom. Larue
Recommended Whites:
Saint-Aubin 1er Cru En Remilly ★★☆ £D
Saint-Aubin 1er Cru Vieilles Vignes ★★☆ £D
Saint-Aubin 1er Cru Murgers des Dents de Chien ★★★ £D
Puligny-Montrachet 1er Cru La Garenne ★★★★ £F
Chassagne-Montrachet ★★ £E

Dom. Aleth Le Royer-Girardin
Recommended Reds: Pommard ★★ £E
Pommard 1er Cru Charmots ★★ £F
Pommard 1er Cru Rugiens-Bas ★★★ £F
Beaune Clos Des Mouches ★★ £E

Philippe et Vincent Lechenaut
Recommended Reds: Morey-Saint-Denis ★★★☆ £E
Morey-Saint-Denis Clos Des Ormes ★★★☆ £F
Nuits-Saint-Georges 1er Cru Pruliers ★★★★ £F
Nuits-Saint-Georges ★★★ £E   Vosne-Romanée ★★★☆ £E

Thibault Liger-Belair
Recommended Reds: Richebourg ★★★★ £H
Clos Vougeot ★★★☆ £H
Nuits-Saint-Georges 1er Cru Les Saint-Georges ★★★★ £F
Vosne-Romanée Aux Reas ★★★☆ £F
Bourgogne Les Grands Chaillots ★★★ £D

Lignier-Michelot
Recommended Reds: Clos de La Roche ★★★★ £G
Morey-Saint-Denis 1er Cru Aux Charmes ★★★☆ £F
Morey-Saint-Denis 1er Cru Les Faconnières ★★★ £F
Morey-Saint-Denis En La Rue de Vergy ★★★ £F
Morey-Saint-Denis Vieilles Vignes ★★★ £F
Chambolle-Musigny ★★★ £E

Jean-Paul Magnien
Recommended Reds: Clos Saint-Denis ★★★★☆ £G
Morey-Saint-Denis 1er Cru Les Faconnières ★★★★ £F
Morey-Saint-Denis ★★★☆ £F

Maroslavac-Leger
Recommended Whites:
Puligny-Montrachet 1er Cru Champgains ★★★★ £F
Puligny-Montrachet 1er Cru Combettes ★★★★ £F
Saint-Aubin 1er Cru Murgers Des Dents de Chien ★★★ £D

Bertrand Maume
Recommended Reds: Gevrey-Chambertin 1er Cru ★★★ £E
Gevrey-Chambertin 1er Cru Champeaux ★★★ £F
Gevrey-Chambertin 1er Cru Lavaux Saint-Jacques ★★★★ £F

Dom. du Meix Foulot
Recommended Whites: Mercurey 1er Cru ★★ £D

Didier Meuneveaux
Recommended Reds: Corton Perrières ★★★☆ £G
Corton Bressandes ★★★☆ £G

Thierry Mortet
Recommended Reds: Gevrey Chambertin ★★ £E
Gevrey Chambertin 1er Cru Clos Prieur ★★★ £F
Chambolle-Musigny 1er Cru Beaux Bruns ★★★ £F
Chambolle-Musigny ★★ £E

Gérard Mouton
Recommended Reds: Givry 1er Cru Clos Jus ★★ £D
Givry 1er Cru Clos Charlé ★★☆ £D

Gérard Mugneret
Recommended Reds: Vosne-Romanée ★★★ £E
Nuits-Saint-Georges 1er Cru Boudots ★★★★ £E
Bourgogne Rouge ★★ £C

Dom. Lucien Muzard et Fils
Recommended Reds: Santenay 1er Cru Beauregard ★★ £D
Santenay 1er Cru Clos Faubard ★★ £D
Santenay 1er Cru Clos des Tavannes ★★★ £D

Philippe Naddef
Recommended Reds: Gevrey-Chambertin Vieilles Vignes ★★★ £F
Gevrey-Chambertin 1er Cru Cazetiers ★★★★ £F

Claude Nouveau
Recommended Whites: Santenay ★★☆ £D
Bourgogne-Hautes Côtes de Beaune ★★☆ £D

Dom. Jean et Annick Parent
Recommended Reds: Monthelie 1er Cru Duresses ★★ £D
Pommard 1er Cru Rugiens ★★★ £F

Dom. Parize Père et Fils
Recommended Reds: Givry 1er Cru Grandes Vignes ★★ £D
Recommended Whites: Givry 1er Cru Grandes Vignes ★★ £D

Paul Pillot
Recommended Whites:
Chassagne-Montrachet 1er Cru Caillerets ★★★ £F
Chassagne-Montrachet 1er Cru Clos Saint-Jean ★★★ £F
Saint-Aubin 1er Cru Charmois ★★ £D

Henri Prudhon
Recommended Whites:
Puligny-Montrachet Les Enseignières ★★★ £F
Saint-Aubin Murgers Dents de Chien ★★ £D

Michel Prunier
Recommended Whites:
Auxey-Duresses Vieilles Vignes ★★ £D

Dom. Ragot
Recommended Reds: Givry 1er Cru Grande Berge ★★ £D

Henri et Gilles Remoriquet
Recommended Reds: Nuits-Saint-Georges Allots ★★ £E
Nuits-Saint-Georges 1er Cru Damodes ★★★ £F
Nuits-Saint-Georges 1er Cru Les Saint-Georges ★★★★ £F

Dom. Roblet-Monnot
Recommended Reds: Volnay Saint-François ★★★☆ £E
Volnay 1er Cru L'ormeau ★★★☆ £F
Volnay 1er Cru Taillepieds ★★★☆ £F

Remi Rollin Pere et Fils
Recommended Whites:
Pernand-Vergelesses 1er Cru Sous Frétille ★★★ £D
Corton-Charlemagne ★★★★ £F
Recommended Reds:
Pernand-Vergelesses 1er Cru Ille de Vergelesses ★★★ £D

Nicolas Rossignol
Recommended Reds: Volnay 1er Cru Chevret ★★★★ £F
Volnay 1er Cru Cailleret ★★★★ £F
Volnay 1er Cru Santenots ★★★★ £F
Volnay 1er Cru Ronceret ★★★★ £F

Burgundy /Côte d'Or & Côte Chalonnaise

France

Joseph Roty
Recommended Reds:
Charmes-Chambertin Tres Vieilles Vignes ★★★★★ £H
Gevrey-Chambertin 1er Cru Fontenys ★★★★ £G

Laurent Roumier
Recommended Reds: Bonnes Mares ★★★★☆ £H
Clos Vougeot ★★★★ £G Chambolle-Musigny ★★★★ £E

Roux Pere et Fils
Recommended Whites: Saint-Aubin La Pucelle ★★ £D
Saint-Aubin 1er Cru Les Cortons ★★★ £E
Corton-Charlemagne ★★★☆ £G

Marc Roy
Recommended Reds: Gevrey-Chambertin Clos Prieur ★★★☆ £F

Dom. Michel Sarrazin et Fils
Recommended Whites: Givry Grognots ★ £D
Recommended Reds: Givry 1er Cru Grands Pretants ★★ £D
Givry Vieilles Vignes ★☆ £D

Dom. de Suremain
Recommended Reds: Rully 1er Cru Préaux ★★ £D
Monthelie Ch. de Monthelie ★★ £D
Monthelie 1er Cru Sur La Velle ★★★ £E

H et Y de Suremain
Recommended Reds: Mercurey 1er Cru En Sazenay ★★ £D

Dom. Jean Tardy et Fils
Recommended Reds: Clos de Vougeot ★★★☆ £H
Echezeaux ★★★ £G Vosne-Romanée Vigneux ★★☆ £F
Vosne-Romanée 1er Cru Les Chaumes ★★★ £F

Dom. des Terregelesses
Recommended Whites: Corton-Charlemagne ★★★☆ £G

Dom. Charles Thomas
Recommended Reds: Romanée-Saint-Vivant ★★★★☆ £H
Chambertin Clos-de-Bèze ★★★★☆ £H
Vosne-Romanée 1er Cru Les Malconsorts ★★★★ £G
Nuits-Saint-Georges 1er Cru Clos de Thorey ★★★☆ £F

Gérard Thomas
Recommended Whites: Saint-Aubin ★★ £C
Saint-Aubin 1er Cru Murgers Des Dents de Chien ★★☆ £D

Cecile Tremblay
Recommended Reds: Echezeaux ★★★★ £G
Vosne-Romanée Vieilles Vignes ★★★☆ £F

Author's choice

30 classic red Burgundies
Marquis d'Angerville   Volnay 1er Cru Clos des Ducs
Dom. de L'Arlot   Nuits-St-Georges 1er Cru Clos des Forêts-St-Georges
Comte Armand   Pommard 1er Cru Clos des Epeneaux
Dom. Robert Arnoux   Vosne-Romanée 1er Cru Les Suchots
Ghislaine Barthod   Chambolle-Musigny 1er Cru Les Charmes
Bouchard Père et Fils   Pommard 1er Cru Rugiens
Sylvain Cathiard   Romanée-Saint-Vivant
Robert Chevillon   Nuits-Saint-Georges 1er Cru Les Saint-Georges
Bruno Clair   Gevrey-Chambertin 1er Cru Les Cazetiers
Clos de Tart   Clos de Tart
Dom. de Courcel   Pommard 1er Cru Grand Clos des Epenots
Dom. Dujac   Clos de La Roche
Dom. René Engel   Clos de Vougeot
Dom. Faiveley   Chambertin Clos-de-Bèze
Geantet-Pansiot   Charmes-Chambertin
Dom. Henri Gouges   Nuits-Saint-Georges 1er Cru Les Vaucrains
Dom. Jean Grivot   Vosne-Romanée 1er Cru Les Beaux Monts
Anne Gros   Richebourg

Louis Jadot   Gevrey-Chambertin 1er Cru Clos Saint-Jacques
Michel Lafarge   Volnay 1er Cru Clos des Chênes
Dom. des Lambrays   Clos des Lambrays
Méo-Camuzet   Vosne-Romanée 1er Cru Cros Parentoux
Hubert de Montille   Volnay 1er Cru Taillepieds
Denis Mortet   Gevrey-Chambertin 1er Cru Lavaux Saint-Jacques
Jacques-Frédéric Mugnier   Musigny
Dom. Ponsot   Griotte-Chambertin
Dom. Roumier   Bonnes Mares
Dom. Armand Rousseau   Chambertin
Dom. Trapet   Gevrey-Chambertin 1er Cru Petite Chapelle
Dom. Comtes Georges de Vogüé   Musigny Vieilles Vignes

Consistently Fine Côte de Beaune Whites
Guy Amiot et Fils   Chassagne-Montrachet 1er Cru Les Caillerets
Roger Belland   Chassagne-Montrachet 1er Cru Morgeot Clos Pitois
Dom. Bonneau du Martray   Corton-Charlemagne
Michel Bouzereau et Fils   Meursault 1er Cru Genevrières
Louis Carillon   Puligny-Montrachet 1er Cru Perrières
Gérard Chavy et Fils   Puligny-Montrachet 1er Cru Folatières
Jean-François Coche-Dury   Meursault 1er Cru Perrières
Michel Colin-Deléger   Puligny-Montrachet 1er Cru Les Demoiselles
Jean-Philippe Fichet   Meursault Tessons
Vincent Girardin   Chassagne-Montrachet 1er Cru Morgeot
Patrick Javillier   Meursault Les Tillets
Dom. des Comtes Lafon   Meursault 1er Cru Charmes
Dom. Leflaive   Puligny-Montrachet 1er Cru Les Pucelles
Dom. Roulot   Meursault 1er Cru Perrières

Value for money red Burgundy
Denis Bachelet   Côtes de Nuits-Villages
Roger Belland   Santenay 1er Cru Beauregard
Dom. Carré-Courbin   Volnay Vieilles Vignes
Sylvain Cathiard   Bourgogne Rouge
Jean-Jacques Confuron   Côtes de Nuits-Villages Les Vignottes
Geantet-Pansiot   Gevrey-Chambertin Vieilles Vignes
Dom. des Comtes Lafon   Monthelie 1er Cru Les Duresses
Philippe et Vincent Lechenaut   Morey-Saint-Denis
Jean-Marc Pavelot   Savigny-Lès-Beaune 1er Cru La Dominode
François Raquillet   Mercurey 1er Cru Les Naugues
Michele & Patrice Rion   Bourgogne Rouge Bons Bâtons
Dom. Roblet-Monnot   Volnay Saint-François
Tollot-Beaut   Chorey-Lès-Beaune Pièce du Chapitre
A & P de Villaine   Bourgogne Côte Chalonnaise Digoine
Dom. Joseph Voillot   Bourgogne Pinot Noir Vieilles Vignes

Value for money white Burgundy
Roger Belland   Santenay 1er Cru Beauregard
Bouchard Pere et Fils   Beaune 1er Cru Clos Saint-Landry
Dom. Michel Briday   Rully 1er Cru La Pucelle
Champy   Pernand-Vergelesses
Michel Colin-Deléger   Chassagne-Montrachet
J-Y. Devevey   Hautes-Côtes de Beaune Les Chagnots XVIII Lunes
Vincent Dureuil-Janthial   Rully 1er Cru Les Margotés
Jean-Jacques Girard   Pernand-Vergelesses Les Belles Filles
Henri et Paul Jacqueson   Rully 1er Cru La Pucelle
Patrick Javillier   Bourgogne Cuvée Oligocène
Dom. Joblot   Givry 1er cru Les Clos de La Servoisine
Dom. Michel Juillot   Mercurey 1er Cru Clos des Barraults
Hubert Lamy   Bourgogne Blanc
Olivier Leflaive   Rully 1er Cru Vauvry
François Lumpp   Givry 1er Cru Petite Marole

The Mâconnais is Burgundy's frontier region where the full potential of the Chardonnay grape is only just beginning to be realised. Thanks in part to a new wave of producers Pouilly-Fuissé is now at an unprecedented level of quality, increasingly expressed in individual climats that make this region so complex and fascinating. Not only has there been a strong movement away from previously overblown high-octane examples but a handful of growers are also revitalising the soils of exceptional vineyard plots scattered wide across the Mâconnais.

Village secrets

The Mâconnais produces as much wine as the Côte d'Or and Côte Chalonnaise combined, though much of it is pretty ordinary. Red under the **Mâcon** and **Mâcon Supérieur** ACs is usually poor and Gamay-based; any better reds are likely to be sold as Bourgogne Rouge. Limestone soils are important to the increasing percentage of Chardonnay planted in the region and much of what is produced is sold as **Mâcon-Villages** or hyphenated with the name of the individual village (such as Uchizy or Chardonnay). This is increasingly a source of good-quality, and often relatively inexpensive, white Burgundy. Many of the best examples come from producers based in Pouilly-Fuissé or Saint-Véran (see below). Of these, Jean Rijckaert has been a leader in realising the untapped potential here. Other good examples are coming from growers based in one of the many communes spread across the rolling countryside who have been brave enough to go it alone instead of selling to the dominant co-ops. Try the wines from Fichet or Maillet. Since 1998, **Viré-Clessé** has been a separate appellation for a stretch of vineyards near the eastern edge of the Mâcon centred on the villages of Viré and Clessé.

Heart of the Mâconnais

For long the greatest interest has been centred on **Pouilly-Fuissé** in the very south of the Mâconnais. This large appellation has a little over twice the vineyard area of Meursault and there are considerable differences in both quality and style across the four communes of Chaintré, Fuissé, Solutré and Vergisson - the latter two being famous for the rock bluffs that proved useful in prehistoric times for herding and killing wild animals. Now, these slopes that run down from the foot of the cliffs are some of the best in the region for producing rich, ripe, full-bodied whites. There are still some heavy, alcoholic whites but radical improvement over the last decade or so has seen the emergence of wines to rival all but the most elegant, refined and complete premier and grand cru Côte de Beaune whites. In contrast to Chablis many more growers harvest all their grapes manually and there is better identification of individual climats. As well as displaying increasing balance and harmony there is definite refinement and elegance from the top sites. At a lower level the wines are more immediate and obvious than something from the Côte de Beaune.

North of Chaintré at the eastern limit of these hills are the separate villages of **Pouilly-Loché** and **Pouilly-Vinzelles**. Quality here has been mixed at best but there has been improvement - the Bret Brothers/La Soufrandière have shown what is possible. **Saint-Véran** encompasses Chardonnay vineyards from villages to the north and south of Pouilly-Fuissé. Although quality is very producerdependent, ranging from the lean and angular to intense, ripe and minerally wines (usually at lower prices than Pouilly), there has generally been an enormous improvement over the last 5-10 years. From the best plots some growers are actually able to make better Saint-Véran

than they do Pouilly-Fuissé. Still more potential is being realised from other sites further along a north-west axis from Pouilly-Fuissé, including Merlin at La Roche Vineuse, Guffens-Heynen/Verget at Sologny and Héritiers du Comte Lafon at Milly Lamartine.

Mâconnais vintages

The ageing potential of the finest white Burgundy from the Mâconnais varies greatly, even within Pouilly-Fuissé. More everyday examples will only improve for 2 or 3 years' from the vintage date while vineyard-designated or special *cuvées* might improve for 5 to 10 years. Quality varies from producer to producer and longevity is dependent on the structure, concentration and depth that owe as much to the health of the vineyard and winemaking techniques as vintage conditions. While it is difficult to generalise about ageing potential for an indication of the style and structure each producer achieves look at the A-Z profiles below.

2015 NYR A little too early to judge 2015, one of the warmest and driest in southern Burgundy. This far south we need to be cautious – there are likely to some magical wines and other serious disappointments. Watch this space after Autumn tastings in 2016.

2014 ★★★★☆ After two short vintages in a row, the Mâconnais was back to normal with a classic balanced vintage of normal size. It is of excellent quality with proper levels of ripeness, for it was sensibly warmer here than in the Cote d'Or without being too hot. Dominique Lafon thinks it is the best vintage since he started in 1999. Impressively, there is a freshness and elegant acidity which is not always the case. Even the wines from warmest southern part around Chaintré have a sprightliness in tune with golden fruit.

2013 ★★★★ As in the rest of Burgundy, yields have been substantially reduced, resulting in a small crop. A poor, wet spring and early summer caused *millerandage* and uneven fruit setting. But what has been produced appears to be of good quality, with fresh, well-balanced whites and sturdy reds.

2012 ★★★★ Frost and rain in the spring did not auger well for this vintage but some remarkably fine summer weather allowed the harvest to commence around September 15th. Again, careful selection was needed to avoid fruit affected by rot and many producers made some very fine wines.

2011 ★★★★ A warm spring resulted in early flowering and continuing good weather in June and July was only spoilt by a wet August. But fine weather in September ensured that the best growers were able to produce rich and fruity wines perhaps lacking a little in finesse.

2010 ★★★☆ Hail on July 10th affected quality, but those growers who managed to sort carefully have managed to produce well-balanced wines with good combinations of fruit and acidity for early drinking.

2009 ★★★★☆ There was some hail (the same storms that hit parts of the Northern Beaujolais) in July and August 2009. Because of this some growers experienced reduced yields. The best growers will produce some excellent wines.

2008 ★★★★ Difficult summer weather conditions not dissimilar to 2007 reduced quantity but generally fruit of a high standard. By mid September, ideal conditions prevailed allowing both whites and reds to obtain higher acidity levels than usual thus ensuring some longevity for the wines.

2007 ★★★ A hot April gave way to a miserably cold and wet, hail-infected summer retarding growth and encouraging rot. By the end of August, the weather took a turn for the better and some producers, particularly those who picked late, made some decent wines. However, it will be necessary to cherry-pick as there are great

France

inconsistencies in the vintage.

2006 ★★★☆ Another satisfactory vintage in southern Burgundy. The pattern of a hot summer tempered a cool wet August then followed by a mostly dry fine September was repeated here although the wines seem unlikely to have the structure of a great year and there was some incidence of grey rot. Consider drinking them up.

2005 ★★★★☆ A vintage described by one grower as a cross between 03 and 04, combining richness and ripeness with good definition and structure. The wines are now fully mature.

2004 ★★★★ An excellent year with good freshness, intensity and purity of fruit. All but the very best should now be drunk up.

2002 ★★★★☆ A year when healthy grapes were harvested with excellent balance between ripeness and acidity despite variable weather conditions. There are many good wines, vibrant with marvellous fruit and style. The best are now at optimum maturity.

2001 ★★★ An unsettled growing season meant a struggle to achieve ripeness but also to avoid rot due to damp, warm conditions. Despite this the best 01s, if sometimes leaner, have shown good minerality and ripe fruit, although only the very best should have been drunk by now.

2000 ★★★★ In most instances a better bet than 2001 with plenty of excellent wine due to a favourable growing season and harvest. The very best are fully mature.

Older vintages

These should only be considered from a top producer but any of the vintages of the late 90s might be considered. Occasionally it is possible to find bottles with as much as 10 or even 15 years' age still in exceptional condition and a great pleasure to drink.

A-Z of producers

Auvigue (Pouilly-Fuissé) *www.auvigue.fr*
Based outside Pouilly-Fuissé at Charnay-les-Mâcon, Auvigue produces less than 20,000 cases of a range of Mâcon whites. Top wines show particularly good structure. All the grapes are hand-harvested, with the estate vineyards supplemented by bought-in grapes for the lesser *cuvées*. Mâcon-Fuissé is a good example of round, plump, fruity white Burgundy, while the Les Chênes version of Saint-Véran has well-integrated oak with its lemony fruit. Cru Pouilly-Fuissé show good restraint if not the concentration of some examples but the most remarkable wines are the Vieilles Vignes and Hors Classé versions. The Vieilles Vignes adds much more depth and intensity and a structure that calls for at least 4 or 5 years' age. The Hors Classé is only made when conditions are right, and is late-picked – while in the rich blockbuster style, it is balanced by excellent strucure.

Pouilly-Fuissé Hors Classé ★★★★ £E
Pouilly-Fuissé Vieilles Vignes ★★★☆ £E
Pouilly-Fuissé La Frairie ★★☆ £D
Pouilly-Fuissé Les Chailloux ★★☆ £D
Saint-Véran Les Chênes ★★☆ £C
Saint-Véran Moulin du Pont ★★☆ £C
Mâcon-Fuissé Moulin du Pont ★★ £C
Mâcon-Solutré Moulin du Pont ★★ £C

Daniel Barraud (Pouilly-Fuissé) *www.domainebarraud.com*
Daniel Barraud, now working with his son Julien, was a leader in differentiating and better defining the various *terroirs* of Pouilly-Fuissé. Most of their 7 ha of vines are on the higher slopes of Vergisson, beneath the dramatic rock itself, where the grapes generally ripen a little later than in lower-lying vineyards. While new oak is employed, it is usually well-judged. Wines from vineyards with an average vine age in excess of 40 years are designated Vieilles Vignes. En Buland equates to a grand cru for Pouilly-Fuissé and is the richest and most powerful example with compelling texture and breadth. La Verchère, from 50-year-old vines, has classic flavour and depth while Les Crays with good freshness comes from higher slopes. En France is from more clayey soils giving a characteristic peachy richness to the wine. Alliance is a blend of 3-4 different parcels, depending on the vintage. Of two Saint-Vérans, the lighter En Crèches is more expressive a dense, weighty Les Pommards from 40-year-old vines. The Mâcon-Vergisson also comes from Vergisson vineyards but from just outside the Pouilly-Fuissé boundaries. Recent vintages maintain the high standards although there is not quite the definition and energy seen in the past.

Recommended Whites:
Pouilly-Fuissé En Bulands Vieilles Vignes ★★★★ £E
Pouilly-Fuissé La Verchère Vieilles Vignes ★★★☆ £D
Pouilly-Fuissé Les Crays Vieilles Vignes ★★★ £D
Pouilly-Fuissé En France ★★★ £D   Pouilly-Fuissé Alliance ★★★ £D
Saint-Véran Les Pommards ★★★ £D   Saint-Véran En Crèches ★★☆ £C
Mâcon-Vergisson La Roche ★★☆ £B

Denis Barraud/Dom. des Nembrets *www.denis-barraud.com*
Denis Barraud in Pouilly-Fuissé is less well-known than his brother Daniel yet around half of his wine is exported. Quantities however are very small, rising to just 12,000 bottles in the 2004 vintage. The style is contrasting too, with the wines being made in a more austere, understated style. Two-thirds of production is of Pouilly-Fuissé. Les Chataigniers comes from predominantly calcareous soils and is cool, minerally and citrusy, needing a couple of years to fill out. There is more spiced apple and peach in Les Folles Vieilles Vignes which is from clayey soils. It is restrained when young but has good structure and will show well with 3-4 years' age. Only *barriques* are used for his refined, classy and expressive La Roche but this is used oak from a combination of barrels of one, two and three years age. The elegance and subtle complexity is very much the epitome of the style here. While it can be drunk fairly young, it should be given at least 3-4 years. Also made are an intense and characterful Saint-Véran and a couple of thousand bottles of Mâcon-Vergisson.

Recommended Whites:
Pouilly-Fuissé La Roche Vieilles Vignes ★★★☆ £D
Pouilly-Fuissé Les Folles Vieilles Vignes ★★★ £D
Pouilly-Fuissé Les Chataigniers ★★☆ £D   Saint-Véran ★★ £B

André Bonhomme (Viré-Clessé) *www.vireclessebonhomme.fr*
Founded in 1956 by André Bonhomme with just 4 ha., André has been a pioneer of domaine-bottling of fine sites in Vire-Clessé in the later half of 20th century. The torch has now passed to his daughter Jacqueline, son-in-law Eric Pathey; their grandson Aurélien is a gifted oenologist.. His 9 ha are manually harvested and there has always been a willingness to wait until the grapes are fully ripe. This domaine has been the one of the few steady alternatives to the lean, acidic wines that are still too prevalent in the wider Mâconnais. The regular *cuvée*, from younger vines, is vinified solely in vats but oak is used in part for the Cuvée Speciale and Vieilles Vignes, around a quarter new for the latter. Older wines (they can keep for up to 5 years) made before the new Viré-Clessé appellation came into being, are labelled as Mâcon-Viré.

Recommended Whites:
Viré-Clessé Vieilles Vignes ★★★ £C

Viré-Clessé Cuvée Spéciale ★★★ £C   Viré-Clessé ★★★ £C

Ch. de Beauregard/ Joseph Burrier *www.joseph-burrier.com*
The Burriers have lived in Southern Burgundy since the early 14th century and owned the Château de Beauregard since 1883. The family are a major force in the southern Mâconnais with 43 ha. in Pouilly Fuisse, St-Véran, and named Mâcon villages. Included in this total, the estate alsoo 10 ha in the top Beaujolais crus, where exceptional Moulin-à-Vent and Fleurie are being made. (See Beaujolais section.) It's clear that passion and commitment have been striking since Frédéric- Marc Burrier of the current generation, in the last 15 years, has tapped into the exceptional potential for Pouilly Fuissé's finest climats and single-site bottlings. He is also a guardian of quality as head of the consortium delineating the putative premier crus of the region, lobbying the INAO to turn this ambition into the achieved goal of new legislation, in an extension of the current appellations. Watch this space. Beauregard itself is enviably situated on the road out of Fuissé with beautiful vistas north-east up to the rock of Vergisson. Frédéric's favourite climat is Pouilly Fuissé Vers Cras, which surrounds the Château. Especially fine in both 2013 and 2014, the wine is a bridge between the mineral detail and energy of Vergisson and the richer expansiveness of both Fuissé and Pouilly. Two to three years on, it's still a baby: fine-limbed and precise, it will develop poised richness with patient ageing in bottle, after having been fermented and matured in oak (of various ages) for 10 -11 months. How memorable it can be, as one of the very best wines of the appellation was obvious in the honeyed yet fresh 1971 tasted at the château in 2007. The Pouill Fuissé Vers Pouilly is opulent and seductive but needs natural acidity of a good year (2014) to be good for 10 years ageing. The Vignes Blanches is altogether a delightful wine to be drunk fairly young to catch its freshness, scents of white flowers and juicy refreshing flavours . The 4 ha domaine of Georges Burrier is a good source of well-made fairly priced wine, notably the high altitude La Côte. What value the whole range has -not lost on growers in the Cote d'Or who continue to buy land and plant vines here in the Mâconnais. (ME)
Ch. de Beauregard
Recommended Whites:
Pouilly-Fuissé Les Cras ★★★★☆ £E
Pouilly Fuissé Vignes Blanches ★★★ £D
Pouilly Fuissé Vers Pouilly ★★★ £D   Pouilly-Fuissé ★★☆ £D
Dom. Georges Burrier
Recommended Whites:
Pouilly-Fuissé La Côte ★★★ £D   Pouilly-Fuissé ★★☆ £D

Ch. de Fuissé (Pouilly-Fuissé) *www.chateau-fuisse.fr*
Under the ownership of the gifted Vincent family since the 19th century, this is the best- known large estate in Pouilly Fuissé, for decades making among, is not the, best wines in the appellation. That its pre-eminence has been challenged in our 21st century, is owing to are several top estates knocking at the door (CH. DE BEAUREGARD, Daniel BARRAUD, Domaine Cornier). Some critics say the wines are overoaked – that may be true of the St-Véran, but hardly accurate of the top wines of the château. Antoine Vincent, who took over as general manager and winemaker in 2003, has steadily reduced the impact of new oak for better harmony in the range overall. The heart of the estate Le Clos still has claim to be the greatest wine in Pouilly Fuisse. There are now 30 ha, mostly in the commune of Fuissé from which a number of different Pouilly-Fuissé *cuvées* are made, including three separate climats (Le Clos, Les Brêles, Les Combettes). All are vinified in oak followed by 9

months' ageing in barrel. At their best, the top wines combine a ripe fruit intensity with excellent structure and depth and usually come into their own with at least 5 years' age. Recent tastings reveal a slight lack of intensity, even hollowness, with the Vieilles Vignes easily the most convincing wine. Saint-Véran, Mâcon-Villages and Mâcon-Fuissé are also made under the Château-Fuissé label. A second range of wines is made under the Vincent label, in part from family domaines and in part from bought-in grapes. These include Pouilly-Fuissé, Saint-Véran (Domaine des Morats), Mâcon-Villages, Mâcon-Fuissé and two Beaujolais, Morgon Les Charmes and Juliénas Domaine le Cotoyon.
Recommended Whites:
Pouilly Fuissé Le Clos★★★★☆ £F
Pouilly Fuissé Vieilles Vignes ★★★★ £F
Pouilly Fuissé Les Brulées (misspelt in last edition) ★★★☆ £E
Pouilly Fuissé Les Combettes ★★★ £E
Pouilly Fuissé ★★★ £E   St-Véran ★★ £D
Recommended Reds:
Juliénas ★★★ £E

Ch. des Rontets (Pouilly-Fuissé) *www.chateaurontets.com*
Claire Gazeau and her Italian husband, Fabio Montrasi, have transformed the wines from this old family property since the mid-1990s. There are just 6 ha but all are planted to Chardonnay. Being well-established, the average vine age is high (50 years in the Clos Varambon, over 70 in Les Birbettes). The Clos Varambon a 4.5 ha site, pebbles over Bathonian limestone, 50-year-old vines, lovely fresh, athletic citrus fruit, made complex by mineral undertow. Aged 12 months on old oak. Pierrefolle from more granitic soils also offers depth, a rich mouthfeel and a spicy component which derives in part from a small percentage of new oak. The top *cuvée*, Les Birbettes, from more clayey soils has really superb fruit which easily takes up the new oak (30%) as well as excellent depth and complexity. One of the most stylish examples of Pouilly-Fuissé, it is comparable to good premier cru Chassagne or Puligny-Montrachet. A very pure, seductive Saint-Amour is also now made.
Recommended Whites:
Pouilly-Fuissé Les Birbettes ★★★★ £D
Pouilly-Fuissé Clos Varambon ★★★★ £D
Pouilly-Fuissé Pierrefolle ★★★☆ £D
Recommended Reds:
Saint-Amour ★★☆ £C

>> Dom. Sophie Cinier *www.domaine-sophiecinier.fr*
This bijou Fuissé domaine with 2.5 ha of old vines inherited from her grandfather and mother, Sophie Cinier is a vigneronne independente to watch. Her production is entirely manual, there's no tractor. Mineral treatments of the vine and 99% fermentation in oak are the simple, classic order of the day. The results are exemplary wines in a compact range for every pocket from Mâcon Blancs that punch above their weight to a trio of Pouilly Fuissés that can hold their own – blind- with the famed whites of the Côte de Beaune. In late-harvested warmer 2014, Mâcon Viré-Clessé, the Indian summer captured spice, citrus and honeyed yellow fruits (peach and apricot). The Pouilly-Fuissé Collection that year is actually from one favourite vineyard La Dame: With its tiny berries and old vines, it has an impressive intensity and vinosity, flesh and freshness in complete harmony. Pouilly Fuissé Vers Cras is more delicate and of admirable definition. I have not yet tasted the St- Véran à la Côte, a south-facing high-altitude vineyard, now covering nearly one hectare, partly of bought-in grapes from trusted growers, as Sophie does a

Burgundy /Mâconnais

little négoce work to meet demand and her reputation grows. She is a member of the Les Vigneronnes de Bourgogne, an association of leading women wine growers. (ME)

Recommended Whites:
Pouilly-Fuissé La Dame Collection ★★★★ £F
Pouilly -Fuissé Vers Cras ★★★☆ £E
St-Véran a la Côte ★★★ £E   Macon Vire-Clessé ★★★ £E
Macon Les Amandiers ★★☆ £D

Dom. de La Collonge/ Gilles Noblet *www.gillesnoblet.com*
Gilles Noblet, a fourth generation Pouilly-Fuissé grower, gets a particular intensity to his wines from relatively straightforward yet minerally Mâcon-Fuissé to the structured, dense and flavoursome Les Champs Pouilly-Fuissé from old vines. The average vine age generally, is high across 9 ha of vineyard where what are are essentially organic practices are employed. Large oak is used for fementation and ageing but in conjunction with *barriques* (a small percentage new) for Les Champs. The oak serves only to enhance structure, letting the ripe fruit deliver the flavour. A lively Saint-Véran is more singular than the Mâcon if missing the extra breadth of Pouilly-Fuissé.

Recommended Whites:
Pouilly-Fuissé Vieilles Vignes Les Champs ★★★☆ £D
Pouilly-Fuissé Tradition ★★★ £D   Saint-Véran ★★ £C
Mâcon-Fuissé ★☆ £C

✿ **Dom. Cordier (Pouilly-Fuissé)** *www.domainecordier.com*
Since Christophe Cordier joined his father Roger, this estate's inherent potential has been further realised. Their 30 ha of vineyards are based in the commune of Fuissé but also includes some Saint-Véran and Mâcon-Villages. In addition some wine, including Viré-Clessé, Mâcon Milly Lamartine and Pouilly-Fuissé, is made from bought-in grapes and sold under the Christophe Cordier label. Domaine wines are very powerful, many of them high in alcohol – being made from very ripe, low-yielding fruit – but are still remarkably well-balanced. There is progressively more concentration and depth, as well as power, in the top *cuvées*. An intense minerality complements a preserved citrus character and oak derived spiciness in many of the wines. Prices are now high, even in the context of the prices Pouilly-Fuissé now commands, but so is the quality. Most of the wines can be drunk young for their dramatic, exuberant richness, though the more structured and profound Vers Cras and Vers Pouilly, will be better with 4 or 5 years' age.

Recommended Whites:
Pouilly-Fuissé Jean-Gustave ★★★★ £E
Pouilly-Fuissé Fine Joséphine ★★★★ £E
Pouilly-Fuissé Juliette La Grande ★★★★ £E
Pouilly-Fuissé Vers Cras ★★★★ £E
Saint-Véran Les Crais ★★★★ £D
Saint-Véran Clos à la Côte ★★★ £D
Saint-Véran En Faux ★★ £C   Pouilly-Loché ★★★ £D
Mâcon-Milly Clos du Four ★★★☆ £E
Mâcon Viré-Clessé Vieilles Vignes ★★★☆ £D
Mâcon-Fuissé ★★ £C   Mâcon Blanc ★★ £B

Corsin (Pouilly-Fuissé) *www.domaine-corsin.com*
Gilles and Jean-Jacques Corsin are the current generation making the wines at this long-established Pouilly-Fuissé estate. The 12 ha are split between Pouilly-Fuissé and Saint-Véran. The wines are fermented and aged both partly in vats and partly in oak, and typically show moderately concentrated ripe fruit and a some oak

character. Saint-Véran and Mâcon can provide relatively inexpensive drinking with 2 or 3 years' age. A Tirage Précoce bottling of Saint-Véran from younger vines, is bottled sooner and can be drunk earlier. Pouilly-Fuissé is a step-up in quality - fuller and more concentrated with added succulence and flavour in Aux Chailloux, albeit without the vibrancy and expression of the best. Both can be drunk young or with 5 years' age or more.

Recommended Whites:
Pouilly-Fuissé Aux Chailloux ★★★ £D
Pouilly-Fuissé ★★★ £D   Saint-Véran Tirage Précoce ★★ £C
Saint-Véran ★★ £C   Mâcon-Villages ★☆ £C

Dom. de la Croix Senaillet *www.domainecroixsenaillet.com*
The Martin brothers, with their 22 ha very largely in Davayé, are masters of Saint-Véran, as it should taste, full of fruit and delicacy. The Mâcon-Davayé is a steal, unoaked and captivating, the perfect bistrot white burgundy or as an aperitif at home. Of the two St-Vérans, Les Rochats is the more structured and worth cellaring for a couple of; The En Pommard is all about intense pleasure , rich, ripe a fine match for salmon with a sorrel sauce or poulet de Bresse à la crème aux morilles. They also make Pouilly Fuissé from their vines in Vergisson. (ME)

Recommended Whites:
Saint-Véran Les Rochats ★★★☆ £D
Saint-Véran En Pommard ★★★☆ £D
Pouilly-Fuissé ★★★ £D
Mâcon Davayé ★★☆ £C

>> A & A Devillard (Pouilly-Fuissé) *www.domaines-devillard.com*
The children of Bertrand Devillard of Domaines DEVILLARD (qv) are now responsible for this historic Chalonnais estate's holdings in the Mâconnais. The 2014s are exceptional, as in the classy Pouilly Fuissé Le Renard: vital lemon hue, Welsh gold lights; aristocratic scents, clear, tense, precise, with a certain restraint; weightless silken-textured mouthfeel, also energetic and beautifully defined; long and detailed finale. The Mâcon Bussière Domaine de la Garenne from the same stable has an exotic nose of Asian spices (star-anise) enhancing notes of nutty, honeyed ampleness and wood smoke. In the mouth, there's much vigour and dynamic drive. Punches well above the appellation. (ME)

Recommended Whites:
Pouilly-Fuissé Le Renard ★★★☆ £E
Macon-Bussières Domaine de la Garenne ★★★ £D

Dom. des Deux Roches (Saint-Véran) *www.collovrayterrier.com*
While a number of Pouilly-Fuissé estates make fine Saint-Véran in addition to their top whites, the 36 ha Deux Roches majors on Saint-Véran. As well as attractive, fruity regular *cuvées*, a percentage of new oak is used for fermenting and ageing the top wines. Generally there is good ripeness as well as a mineral aspect to most of the wines. Terres Noires and Rives de Longsault have classic fruit/mineral intensity and vitality, Vieilles Vignes reveals added flavour and length while deep, classy Les Cras is reminiscent of fine Saint-Aubin or Puligny. If not at the same level, a decent standard is maintained in the Collovray & Terrier wines made from bought-in grapes including a Vieilles Vignes Pouilly-Fuissé drawn from several small parcels, and an oakier Plenitude de Bonté. Owners Christian Collovray and Jean-Luc Terrier also produce some very good wines from Chardonnay at Domaine d'ANTUGNAC in the Limoux AC in the Languedoc-Roussillon.

Dom. des Deux Roches
Recommended Whites:
Saint-Véran Les Cras ★★★☆ £D
Saint-Véran Rives de Longsault ★★★ £C
Saint-VéranTerres Noires ★★★ £C
Saint-Véran Vieilles Vignes ★★★ £D Saint-Véran ★★ £C

Collovray & Terrier
Recommended Whites:
Pouilly-Fuissé Vieilles Vignes ★★★ £D
Pouilly-Fuissé Plenitude de Bonté ★★☆ £D
Saint-VéranTradition ★☆ £C
Mâcon-Villages ★☆ £B

Dom. Thierry Drouin (Pouilly-Fuissé) *www.domaine-drouin.com*
The Drouin's have 7.5 ha in the southern Mâconnais, including 4.5 ha in Pouilly-Fuissé. A lot of work goes into improving the quality of the fruit and each parcel is picked by hand before being vinified separately. Unusual is La Vieille Vigne du Bois D'Ayer (previously Vieilles Vignes) with very ripe exotic preserved peach, even guava and overripe quince and some residual sweetness which sometimes lacks a corresponding structure. More convincing is a concentrated, minerally Mâcon-Vergisson La Roche. Also made is Mâcon Rouge in a fruity, juicy Beaujolais style for everyday drinking.
Recommended Whites:
Mâcon-Vergisson La Roche ★★★ £C
Mâcon-Bussières Dom. du Vieux Puits ★★ £C
Pouilly-FuisséTerres de Vergisson ★★ £D
Pouilly-Fuissé Métertière ★★ £D
Pouilly-Fuissé La Vieille Vigne du Bois d'Ayer ★★ £D

Dom. J A Ferret (Pouilly-Fuissé) *www.louisjadot.com*
This domaine has been bottling its own wine for over 60 years, though it had its beginnings more than two decades before the French Revolution. Colette Ferret's Pouilly-Fuissés, made famous by her mother before she died in 1993, have been compared not just to premier cru but also grand cru Côte de Beaune whites. Colette herself died in 2007 and having already established a working arrangement with Maison LOUIS JADOT, it naturally followed that Jadot acquired the domaine in 2008. Not wanting to change the distinctive style and operation of the estate, Jadot kept on the whole of the production team, now ably led by Audrey Braccini. The wines are certainly very full-bodied with remarkable concentration and extract and with added finesse and purity in the best examples. As might be expected, yields are low, the average vine age high and the grapes are manually harvested. The wines are barrel-fermented and aged with extended lees-contact for maximum enrichment. From 15 ha are fashioned four great crus: Le Clos, Les Ménétrières, Les Perrières and Tournant de Pouilly. These are given the greatest amount of new oak and the longest period of ageing. Other bottlings are also made including 3 other crus, Les Sceles, Les Vernays and Les Moulins, which are sold only in the US. Rich and honeyed, the wines also display fine floral, mineral aspects as well as a classic grilled nuts character. The Hors Classé designation applies only to a selection of old vines in the best years and these wines are slightly more expensive than the Tête de Cru bottlings.
Recommended Whites:
Pouilly-Fuissé Ménétrières Hors Classé ★★★★ £E
Pouilly-Fuissé Tournant de Pouilly Hors Classé ★★★★ £E
Pouilly-Fuissé Le Clos Tête de Cru ★★★ £E
Pouilly-Fuissé Perrières Tête de Cru ★★★ £E

Dom. Fichet (Mâcon-Igé) *www.domaine-fichet.com*
Here is a family-run 19 ha domaine showing what is possible from supposedly less prepossessing vineyards on rolling hills in the wider reaches of the Mâconnais. Pierre-Yves and Olivier Fichet are building on their father's work following his decision to withdraw from the co-op back in 1976. The wines are now made by Olivier but quality is based in the vineyards (overseen by Pierre-Yves). Only whites have been tasted but they offer good fruit and definition even in the more everyday *cuvées*. Really worthwhile but still reasonably priced is the Vieilles Vignes *cuvée* which adds intensity and density. The oak is slightly overdone in the rich and succulent Terroir de La Cra *cuvée* but the potential exists for a great wine. Other wines include Bourgogne Rouge, Crémant de Bourgogne and a Chardonnay from botrytis grapes, Quintessence du Chardonnay which will be rated in the future.
Recommended Whites:
Mâcon-Igé Terroir de Burgy ★★★ £D
Mâcon-Igé Cuvée Vieilles Vignes ★★★ £C
Mâcon-Igé Terroir de La Cra ★★☆ £D
Mâcon-Igé Château London ★★ £C Mâcon-Igé La Crépillonne ★☆ £C

❀ **Eric Forest (Pouilly-Fuissé)** *www.ericforest.fr*
Eric Forest is an exciting young grower with a cellar in Vergisson and 5 ha of some of the excellent crus beneath the rock itself. He took over the vineyards planted by his grandfather Henri in the 1960s and under whose label they appeared until 2000 and has now, since 2010, combined this with his father, Michel's vineyards, who has now retired. Following Montpellier training and a stint with Jean-Marie Guffens (GUFFENS-HEYNEN), he has already shown considerable competence in producing wines that combine splendid fruit with restrained oak (averaging a 15% renewal each year) and impeccable structure. Since 2008 he has reduced the number of *cuvées* he produces from 6 to 4 by combining 'Les Tillets' (for finesse) and 'La Côte' (for exuberant power) under the name 'L'Ame de Foret' to produce a wine of stunning equilibrium and by combining 'Les Crays' with the tiny 'Haut de Crays' vineyard, situated on the south side of the rock of Vergisson, well protected from the north winds, producing wines of both opulence and minerality with citrus aromas. Even the Mâcon-Vergisson is fruit-filled with a mineral component of great precision. Finally, there is a small parcel of vines at Saint-Véran - 'Le Paradis', which has not been tasted. The wines are neither fined nor filtered.
Recommended Whites:
Pouilly-Fuissé Les Crays ★★★★ £D
Pouilly-Fuissé L'ame Foret ★★★★ £D
Mâcon-Vergisson Sur La Roche ★★☆ £C

Dom. des Gerbeaux (Pouilly-Fuissé)
The husband-and-wife team of Beatrice and Jean-Michel Drouin make excellent examples of Mâcon, Saint-Véran and Pouilly-Fuissé whites which are not that widely seen on account of the production always selling out. The wines show excellent intensity, texture and structure and have balanced alcohol. There is attractive minerality even in Mâcon-Solutré, a lively intensity to ripe Saint-Véran and more depth and richness in Pouilly-Fuissé. The wines are also very reasonably priced without the premiums that the wines of more high-profile producers have acquired. All the wines can be drunk fairly young but the Pouilly-Fuissé in particular will also repay keeping. Two other special *cuvées* of Pouilly-Fuissé are also made, En Champs Roux and Jacques Charvet, which express even greater weight and intensity.

Burgundy /Mâconnais

Recommended Whites:
Pouilly-Fuissé Jacques Charvet ★★★★ £D
Pouilly-Fuissé En Champs Roux ★★★★ £D
Pouilly-Fuissé Terroir de Solutré Vieilles Vignes ★★★ £D
Saint-Véran ★★ £C   Mâcon-Solutré Le Clos ★★ £C
Mâcon-Chaintré ★★ £B

Dom. Guffens-Heynen/Verget (Pouilly-Fuissé) www.verget-sa.com
Jean-Marie Guffens is one of the wine world's larger-than-life
characters but also one of its most exciting winemakers. Both
through the substantial negociant VERGET operation and a small
number of wines made at this, his own private 3 ha estate, he
has made a significant impact on the fine wine scene. The grapes
are picked very ripe from low-yielding vines that have been
meticulously cared for, before being pressed very slowly in an old-
fashioned vertical press. A mix of oak, both new and used, small
and large, is used in their fermentation and ageing. Not only do
the wines have fantastic richness, depth and substance but they
also show finesse and elegance. They are not as consistent as some
but neither is there uniformity; when these wines are particularly
successful they will provide memorable drinking for up to a decade.
Guffens-Heynen cru bottlings of Pouilly-Fuissé have included Les
Croux, Roche and Hauts de Vignes. The Verget Mâconnais wines are
included below, for others see the Côte d'Or section.

Guffens-Heynen
Recommended Whites:
Pouilly-Fuissé ★★★★ £E   Mâcon-Pierreclos Le Chavigne ★★★★ £D
Mâcon-Pierreclos ★★★ £C

Verget
Recommended Whites:
Pouilly-Fuissé Terroir de Vergisson ★★★ £E
Saint-Véran Terres Noires ★★★ £D
Saint-Véran Vignes de Saint-Claude ★★★ £D
Saint-Véran Terroirs de Davayé ★★ £C
Mâcon-Burgy En Chatelaine ★★★ £C
Mâcon-Burgy Les Prusettes Cuvée Levroutée ★★ £C
Mâcon-Bussières Vieilles Vignes de Montbrison ★★★ £C
Mâcon-Vergisson La Roche ★★★ £C
Mâcon-Charnay Clos Saint-Pierre ★★ £C
Pouilly-Vinzelles Les Quarts ★★ £C

Héritiers du Comte Lafon (Macon-Villages)
Dominique Lafon's arrival in the Mâcon may not have aroused
much interest amongst those who regularly jostle for his marvellous
Meursaults (see Domaine des Comtes LAFON) but taste these
wines and you'll see there is much more to this than a source of
(somewhat) cheaper, more everyday white Burgundy. The wines
have already improved considerably since the debut 1999s and now
the potential quality that is possible in the Mâcon is increasingly
apparent. The Mâcon-Milly-Lamartine shows a pure elegant
minerally fruit and is very stylish and expressive. Clos du Four has
more of everything – more depth, more mineral, more structure –
and consequently needs more time. Mâcon-Bussières Le Monsard
starts out austere but has real intensity of ripe citrus with a stony
aspect, best with 4 or 5 years' age. New vineyards from the villages
of Chardonnay and Uchizy have recently augmented production.
The citrusy Clos de la Crochette is again in a refined style but is a
little fuller textured than that from Milly-Lamartine. new Saint-Véran
from a vineyard called Montchanin, made a brilliant debut in 2014.

Recommended Whites:
Mâcon-Milly-Lamartine Clos du Four ★★★☆ £D

Mâcon-Milly-Lamartine ★★★ £C
Mâcon-Bussières Le Monsard ★★★☆ £D
Mâcon-Chardonnay Clos de la Crochette ★★★ £D
Mâcon-Uchizy Les Maranches ★★ £C
Mâcon Villages ★★ £C   Saint-Véran Montchanin ★★★☆ £D

>> Denis Jeandeau (Pouilly-Fuissé) www.denisjeandeau.com
Born in 1977, Denis Jeandeau has quickly made his mark as a rising
star. After taking his BTS degree in oenology and wine making, he
looked to broad horizons in the New World beyond his roots in
Saône et Loire, his family having been vignerons in the Mâconnais
for five generations. Returning home, Denis set up his domaine in
2006 with good holdings in Pouilly Fuissé around Vergisson, also
Pouilly itself, as well as St-Véran and Mâcon-Viré. After 10 years, his
southern white Burgundies grace the tables of some of the world's
great restaurants from Trois Gros and Lameloise locally onto Arpège
and Ambroisie in Paris and Manhattan's Restaurant Jean- Georges.
Denis' approach to viticulture and winemaking embraces the best
modern precepts without religious extremes. With a proper respect
for the environment, he works his soils to encourage microbiological
diversity, ploughs with a horse so that the earth does not become
compacted. He is largely organic, favours indigenous yeasts and
whole bunch fermentations, avoiding fertilizers and chemicals. The
Pouilly Fuisse Minéral from Solutré/Vergisson- at 450 metres above
sea- level - has remarkable finesse; that from the village of Pouilly
itself is different, very rich and salty. His St-Véran is a model of its
kind from a south and south-east facing vineyard over limestone
and clay, close to his tasting room in Davayé. His Macon-Viré clings
to a close hillside with south west aspect that encourages later
picking and optimal maturity. Exciting stuff. (ME)
Recommended Whites:
Pouilly Fuissé 'Minérale' ★★★★ £D   Saint-Véran ★★★☆ £D
Pouilly Fuissé vers Pouilly ★★★ £D   Mâcon-Viré ★★★ £C

Dom. Roger Lassarat (Pouilly-Fuissé) www.roger-lassarat.com
Roger Lassarat was inspired by quality pioneers CHÂTEAU DE FUISSÉ
and J A FERRET and set out to emulate them as he established his
own estate more t han 30 years ago. Here as at so many of the best
Pouilly-Fuissé estates the secret to the quality of the fruit is manual
picking of carefully maintained, low yielding old vines. The grapes
receive a gentle pressing and partial barrel-fermentation with
prolonged lees-enrichment in barrel before the wines are bottled
unfiltered. The wines are ripe and richly textured, with increasing
definition and better balance and structure in the most recent
vintages. The range of wines has been expanded to single out more
individual climats. Rich, concentrated Saint Véran Le Cras (Puligny
or Meursault premier cru level) and classy, elegant Les Mûres are
of even better quality than the Pouilly-Fuissés which include a
seductive, stylish if forward Cuvée des Murgers and more expansive,
structured Clos de France.
Recommended Whites:
Saint-Véran Le Cras ★★★★ £D   Saint-Véran Les Mûres ★★★☆ £D
Saint-Véran Cuvée Prestige ★★☆ £D
Saint-Véran Fournaise ★★ £D   Saint-Véran Cuvée Plaisir ★★ £C
Pouilly-Fuissé Clos de France ★★★☆ £D
Pouilly-Fuissé Cuvée des Murgers ★★★ £D
Pouilly-Fuissé Cuvée Prestige ★★★ £D
Mâcon-Vergisson La Roche ★★ £C

● Nicolas Maillet (Mâcon-Verzé) www.vins-nicolas-maillet.com
Nicolas Maillet has 6 ha in Verzé (some way north of La Roche

Vineuse) in the west of the southern Mâconnais. From vineyards which include a little Gamay, Aligoté and Pinot Noir he makes excellent, inexpensive wines without any oak. The wines have excellent fruit and purity, great character and expression with fine minerality in Mâcon-Verzé. Even better, with more structure, depth and intensity, is a Le Chemin Blanc version. Of other wines, well-made Bourgogne Aligoté and Crémant de Bourgogne show good fruit but better is a stylish Bourgogne Rouge with pure cherry and cassis fruit, a subtle minerality and fine tannins. Mâcon-Verzé Rouge (100% Gamay) can show a green edge but is sound, everyday drinking. Now if only there were more like him throughout the scattered villages of the Mâconnais!

Recommended Whites:
Mâcon-Verzé Le Chemin Blanc ★★★ £C
Mâcon-Verzé ★★ £C   Bourgogne Aligoté ★☆ £B
Crémant de Bourgogne ★☆ £C
Recommended Reds:
Bourgogne Rouge ★★ £C

Manciat-Poncet (Pouilly-Fuissé)
Claude Manciat and his wife Simone recently ceded control of the 12 ha domaine they formed back in 79. Their daughter Marie-Pierre and her husband Olivier Larochette now make the wines, making the best of the high quality fruit. As well as an excellent characterful Mâcon-Charnay for everyday drinking there are two fine Pouilly-Fuissé lieu-dits. The high altitude La Roche has the typical elegance and style of this site, almost understated but long and intense, opening out with a little age. The Les Crays, from vines more than 50 years old is another great example of this vineyard (see Daniel BARRAUD, both FORESTS and Michel REY). Riper than La Roche it has surprising delicacy with a floral, herbal inflection to spiced white peach/peach fruit.

Recommended Whites:
Pouilly-Fuissé Les Crays Vieilles Vignes ★★★☆ £D
Pouilly-Fuissé La Roche Vieilles Vignes ★★★ £D
Mâcon-Charnay Les Chênes ★★ £C

Olivier Merlin (Mâcon-Villages) www.merlin-vins.com
A graduate of the Lycée Viticole de Beaune, Olivier worked as a winemaker at a cooperative in the Jura, then moved the United States for a stint in California before returning to southern Burgundy establishing the Domaine du Vieux Saint Sorlin as one of the most reliable and exciting wines of the Mâconnais from the late 1980s. These are fine wines of great character with the structure, complexity and length of flavour to rival the best Côte de Beaune whites. His Mâcon La Roche Vineuse is better than most Pouilly Fuissés. He is also involved in a venture at Clos des Quarts at Pouilly-Fuissé Clos des Quarts with Dominique LAFON. (ME)

Recommended Whites:
Pouilly-Fuissé Terroir de Vergisson ★★★★ £E
Pouilly-Fuissé Clos des Quarts ★★★ £E
Pouilly-Fuissé Terroir de Fuissé ★★★☆ £D
Pouilly-Fuissé Terroir de Chaintré ★★★ £D
Mâcon-La Roche Vineuse Les Cras ★★★☆ £C
Mâcon-La Roche Vineuse Vieilles Vignes ★★★☆ £C
Mâcon-La Roche Vineuse ★★☆ £C
Recommended Reds:
Moulin-à-Vent ★★☆ £C

Cave de Prissé-Sologny-Verzé www.terres-secretes.com
Aptly re-named Cave de Prissé-Sologny-Verzé Les terres secretes

(in translation) the lands of secrets, this is an important, quality-conscious group of three co-ops composed of 40o growers across 1,000 hectares of the Mâconnais, which include some exceptional hillsides sites including the great rock of Vergisson. The standard of winemaking, led by the example of the fine team at Prissé, is widely admired for its purity and precision at very keen prices, which should give some New World Chardonnay producers pause for thought. From the excellent 2014 vintage, some say the best since 1999 (warmer here than in the Côte d'Or) two St-Vérans stand out: the privileged south-east facing Croix de Monceaux on some of the finest limestone in the southern Mâconnais, giving beautiful fruit enhanced by the stones; and the Pierres Blanches a great success, combining a very ripe harvest, incisive, mineral, white-pebble terroir and freshness thanks to attentive non- oxidative winemaking. That precision and brisk impact is also there in Macon La Roche Vineuse and Pouilly Fuissé Terre de Vergisson. By contrast, The Pouilly Fuissé Terroir de Chaintré is a sunny opulent mouthful for Coulibiac of Salmon or soft -shell crabs. (ME)

Recommended Whites:
St-Véran Croix de Monceaux ★★★☆ £E
St-Véran Pierre Blanches ★★★ £E
Pouilly Fuissé Terroir de Vergisson ★★★☆ £E
Pouilly Fuissé Terroir de Chaintré ★★★ £E
Clos des Quartz ★★★ £E   Mâcon La Roche Vineuse ★★☆ £D

Michel Rey (Pouilly-Fuissé)
Michel and Eve Rey have 6 ha in Vergission and a further hectare in Juliénas. Pouilly-Fuissé is produced in a ripe, rich oak-influenced style yet they are also elegant and intense and not overblown. Both Les Crays and Les Charmes come from vineyards planted more than 50 years ago. Les Crays is classy and Puligny-like while the elegant, complex Les Charmes is of similar quality. La Maréchaude with mineral, floral nuances and a very long finish is arguably more singular, if less complete. A very small quantity of a special *cuvée*, Harmonie is made each year. A blend of three parcels it spends 18 months in *barrique* resulting in a big but well-balanced, rich and concentrated style. There is impressive texture, breadth and a lingering fruit-filled (crushed peach) finish. Two Saint-Véran (Les Champs de Perdrix, A Lessard) are also made but like the Juliénas (Les Pacquelets), haven't yet been tasted.

Recommended Whites:
Pouilly-Fuissé Harmonie ★★★☆ £E
Pouilly-Fuissé Terroir de Vergisson ★★★ £D
Pouilly-Fuissé Les Crays ★★★ £D
Pouilly-Fuissé Les Charmes ★★★ £D
Pouilly-Fuissé La Maréchaude ★★★ £D

❁ Dom. Rijckaert (Viré-Clessé) www.rijckaert.fr
Jean Rijckaert is one of the Mâconnais' most exciting producers. He used to work with Jean-Marie Guffens (GUFFENS-HEYNEN) but he is now giving the Mâconnais a further boost with his own range of wines. Having helped mould the VERGET style, it is no surprise that the same principles of slow pressings, enhanced lees-enrichment and intelligent oak-ageing, are being continued here. Rijckaert also believes passionately in restoring life to the soils and the importance of promoting deep roots in the vines. He makes more than two dozen individual *cuvées*, mostly from 35–40-year-old vines, both from his own 4 ha of vineyards and for other small growers. He seeks precision and minerality in his wines and achieves it with some superb aromatic, concentrated wines that show excellent definition and purity. Rarely is there any need to hurry to drink these wines, as

Burgundy /Mâconnais

most will be better with 3 or 4 years' age. A brown label indicate a grower's wine (and also includes their name), while a green label is used for the domaine wines. Only a selection are listed below. Jean has no heirs and he has groomed his protégé the very talented Florent Rouve to take over and he has made the wines since 2013. Also see Domaine RIJCKAERT (JURA) in the Jura section.

Recommended Whites:

Pouilly-Fuissé Les Bouthières Vieilles Vignes ★★★☆ £E
Pouilly-Fuissé Vers Chânes Vieilles Vignes ★★★ £D
Saint-Véran En Faux Vieilles Vignes ★★★ £C
Saint-Véran En Avonne ★★ £C   Saint-Véran L'Epinet ★★ £C
Viré-Clessé Les Vercherres Vieilles Vignes ★★★☆ £C
Viré-Clessé En Thurissey Vieilles Vignes ★★★ £C
Viré-Clessé Le Mont Chatelaine ★★ £C
Saint-Aubin En Monceau ★★★ £D
Mâcon-Lugny Terroirs de Bissy Les Crays vers Vaux VV ★★★ £C
Mâcon Montbellet En Pottes ★★☆ £C   Mâcon-Villages ★★ £B

❀ Robert-Denogent (Pouilly-Fuissé) *www.robert-denogent.com*
Jean- Jacques Robert took over his grandfather's vines in 1988. Much of the fruit of the holdings used to go to the cooperative, but Jean-Jacques retained five hectares of the best parcels in special terroirs, for they had a rich resource of old vines planted in an interesting variety of soil- types. With his son Nicolas joining him in 2007, quality has rapidly increased to a point where the wines have an intensity and complexity akin to the whites of the Côte de Beaune but with a real sense of their Mâconnais roots. Yields are low, pruning rigorous; some new oak is used but a common thread throughout is a lovely fruit intensity with a fine undertow of minerals. The Mâconnais Solutré exudes a stony character and class, way above its Appellation. The Pouilly Fuissé Les Carrons from 92 years old vines over strong clay soils with weathered limestone is very powerful and complex. The Pouilly-Fuissê La Croix over blue schist is maybe the most harmonious wine of all. (ME)

Recommended Whites:

Pouilly-Fuissé Les Carrons ★★★★ £E
Pouilly-Fuissé Cuvée Claude Denogent ★★★★ £D
Pouilly-Fuissé La Croix Vieilles Vignes ★★★☆ £D
Mâcon- Solutré Clos des Bertillons ★★★ £C

Jacques & Nathalie Saumaize *www.saumaize.com*
A welcoming couple, the Pouilly-Fuissé based Saumaizes are both from the Mâconnais; they're very passionate about their land and the potential of the soils around the rocks of Solutré and Vergisson. They have been making wine here for over 20 years in their near eight hectares of Pouilly- Fuissé, St-Véran and a small half hectare of Mâcon-Bussière which is just outside the PF appellation north of Vergisson- the Bussière, no surprise, provides classy mineral flavours at a gentle price. The Pouilly-Fuissé Sur La Roche from the upper slopes of the Vergisson bluff is showing extremely well in its second outing in 2006 – viewed by several authorities as one of the best vintages since 1999. The Pouilly-Fuissé Vieilles Vignes, is a superior assemblage of mature fruit from Solutré and Vergisson. There's a fine variety of excellent St-Véran – the Poncetys, planted in 1944, has the richness of 70-year-old vines, though a favourite is the stainless-steel fermented, fresh regular en Crèches version. The Saumaizes are members of Les Artisans Vignerons du Sud de Bourgogne along with stars like Lafon and Barraud. (ME)

Recommended Whites:

Pouilly-Fuissé Sur La Roche ★★★★ £D
Pouilly-Fuissé Vieilles Vignes ★★★☆ £D
Pouilly-Fuissé Les Courtelonges ★★★ £D
Saint Véran Poncetys ★★★ £D   Saint Véran en Crêche ★★☆ £D
Mâcon-Bussières Montbrison ★★☆ £B

Dom. Saumaize-Michelin *www.domaine-saumaize-michelin.com*
Roger Saumaize is one of the stars of Vergisson. The family estate, run biodynamically since 2005, extends to 9.5 ha and as well as several different *cuvées* of Pouilly-Fuissé, some fine Saint-Véran and Mâcon-Villages are made. There is the utmost attention to detail and hygiene and the resulting consistency, both from year to year and across the range, is very impressive. The wines see some oak. They can be quite firm and steely when very young but they have good definition and added richness with age. Pentracrine is detailed and mineral but the best Pouilly-Fuissé *cuvées* come from old vines. The well-defined Vignes Blanches reveals a floral, blossom mineral and spice complexity. Minerally, old-vine Clos sur la Roche has the class and depth of premier cru Chassagne-Montrachet. The excellent new Le Haut des Crays has lovely depth and a plump fullness within a vibrant structure (contrast this with Eric FOREST's version). The top wine, Ampelopsis, a sort of super *cuvée*, is remarkably concentrated and proportioned. As well as two good Saint-Véran a well-structured and good value Mâcon-Villages is made.

Recommended Whites:

Pouilly-Fuissé Ampelopsis ★★★★ £D
Pouilly-Fuissé Le Haut des Crays ★★★☆ £D
Pouilly-Fuissé Ronchevats ★★★☆ £D
Pouilly-Fuissé Clos sur la Roche ★★★☆ £D
Pouilly-Fuissé Vignes Blanches ★★★☆ £D
Pouilly-Fuissé Pentacrine ★★★ £D
Saint-Véran Vieilles Vignes ★★★ £C
Saint-Véran Les Crêches ★★☆ £C
Mâcon-Villages Les Sertaux ★★☆ £B

La Soufrandière/Bret Brothers *www.bretbrothers.com*
These two young vigneron brothers have made the finest wines ever under the small Pouilly-Vinzelles AC, which together with the contiguous Pouilly-Loché AC has less than 100 ha of vines. The Brets have little more than 5 ha but their rich, ripe, structured wines have finally shown that these separate zones at the south-eastern end of Pouilly-Fuissé have similar exciting potential to that being realised elsewhere in the region. The estate is now biodynamic and all the grapes are picked by hand. The wines are ripe and concentrated, verging on being overdone in both the regular bottling and Les Quarts, which comes from older vines. The top *cuvée* Millerandée show tremendous richness, coming from very small (millerandé) grapes from 70-year-old vines. While there is not the finesse of a top Côte de Beaune white it is well-proportioned and deserves to be drunk with 5 years' age. The Bret Brothers label covers an expanding range of wines from bought-in grapes and includes Mâcon-Cruzille as well as examples of Viré-Clessé, Saint-Véran, Pouilly-Loché and Pouilly-Fuissé. In addition to their own holdings in Vinzelles, is the best part of a hectare in Beaujolais-Leynes.

Dom. La Soufrandière
Recommended Whites:

Pouilly-Vinzelles Les Quarts Millerandée ★★★★ £E
Pouilly-Vinzelles Les Quarts ★★★☆ £D
Pouilly-Vinzelles Les Longeays ★★★ £D
Mâcon-Vinzelles Le Clos de Grand-Père ★★☆ £C

Bret Brothers
Recommended Whites:

Pouilly-Fuissé En Carementrant ★★★☆ £E

Saint-Véran En Combe ★★☆ £D
Mâcon-Cruzille Clos des Vignes du Mayne ★★☆ £C

Dom. La Soufrandise (Pouilly-Fuissé) *www.soufrandise.ex-flash.com*
Nicolas Melin has a very fragmented patchwork of plots that total 6 ha of vineyard. From it he produces three different *cuvées* of Pouilly-Fuissé in addition to a Mâcon-Fuissé. Full ripeness is vigorously pursued and there is also an emphasis on promoting health in the vineyard and environment. Mâcon is bright and ripe, a quaffer with character while the Clos Marie Pouilly which has been isolated from vines next to the winery, is in a similar direct style but has more weight and structure as well as a refined minerally streak. The classic *cuvée* is the Vieilles Vignes; richer, deeper and able to improve for at least 3-5 years. The Levrouté is a late-harvested style, not dissimilar to others in this vein (if not of the Thévenet standard) being rich and exotic with some initial sweetness yet reasonably well-balanced and finishing essentially dry.

Recommended Whites:
Pouilly-Fuissé Levrouté ★★★ £D
Pouilly-Fuissé Vieilles Vignes ★★★ £D
Pouilly-Fuissé Clos Marie ★★☆ £D
Mâcon-Fuissé Le Ronté ★★ £B

Domaine Thévenet/de la Bon Grain *www.bongran.com*
"The terroir is the composer of the music, the vigneron is just the conductor of the orchestra", so says Jean Thévenet, whose wines are like nobody else's. His home hamlet of Quintaine is close to the river Saône, the closeness of water offering some shelter from spring frosts. The river also brings autumn mists after a warm summer that can encourage overripe grapes as in his Cuvée Levrouté, suffused as it is with scents of truffles; in humid late harvest, a little noble rot is made in the BonGran Cuvée botrytis, which still has freshness structure and capacity to age gracefully. There are two domaines here, Dom. De la Bon Gran and Domaine Emilian Gillet, which has been managed by his son Gautier for several years but who since 2013 has taken charge of the winemaking in both domains. Gautier also makes a fine Mâcon villages at his Domaine de Roally. Emilian Gillet tends to be more floral than BonGran but both are great wines which have skirmished with the appellation authorities who have decreed that, owing to their high levels of residual sugar they can now only be called Mâcon-Villages. (ME)
Dom. Emilian Gillet
Recommended Whites:
Mâcon-Villages Quintaine ★★★★ £G
Dom. de la Bongran
Recommended Whites:
Mâcon-Villages Cuvée Tradition Botrytis EJ Thévenet ★★★★ £E
Mâcon-Villages Cuvée Tradition Sélection EJ Thévenet ★★★★ £D
Dom. de Roally
Recommended Whites:
Mâcon-Montbellet Tradition ★★★ £E

Dom. Thibert Père et Fils (Pouilly-Fuissé) *www.domaine-thibert.com*
Christophe Thibert and his wife Catherine run this 16 ha estate, which has around half its vineyards in Pouilly-Fuissé. The wines show more finesse and less upfront richness than some but combine a minerally intensity with good concentration in the best years. Oak is used to enhance structure and is considerably less overt in most of the wines than in many a Pouilly-Fuissé. Though less immediate, the wines have excellent ageing potential, especially the top *cuvées*. Premium Vignes de la Côte is usually matched by the slightly

cheaper Vieilles Vignes version. Ripe, peachy Pouilly-Vinzelles is also made. Recent releases have been a little uneven but always elegant.
Recommended Whites:
Pouilly-Fuissé Vieilles Vignes ★★★ £D
Pouilly-Fuissé Vignes Blanches ★★★ £D
Pouilly-Fuissé Vignes de la Côte ★★★ £D
Pouilly-Fuissé ★★ £C   Pouilly-Vinzelles Longeays ★★ £C
Mâcon-Prissé En Chailloux ★☆ £C   Mâcon-Fuissé ★☆ £C

Dom. Valette (Pouilly-Fuissé)
Baptiste and Philippe Valette have now taken over the running of this famous domaine from their father Gérard what is effectively an organic estate of 17 ha. Although more than half of it is in Mâcon-Chaintré, the rest is in Pouilly-Fuissé, producing full-bodied, very ripe-fruited blockbusters. The grapes are harvested very late from often very low-yielding old vines and a percentage of new oak is used for fermenting the two Réserve *cuvées*, resulting in very powerful, rich wines. The style is also influenced by location. Chaintré is warmer and farther south than any other communes in Pouilly Fuissé. They also have the courage to do their utmost in the cellar to age their wines on lees to achieve the maximum depth and character and be *à point* on release at a date sometimes later their neighbours: the wines rich and voluptuous but well defined and balanced. In the meantime you can enjoy the fresh, fruit-filled Mâcon-Chaintré made for relatively early drinking. A little Pouilly-Vinzelles is also made. (ME)
Recommended Whites:
Pouilly-Fuissé Clos de Monsieur Noly V V Réserve ★★★★☆ £F
Pouilly-Fuissé Clos Reyssie Réserve ★★★★ £E
Pouilly-Fuissé Tradition ★★★☆ £E
Mâcon-Chaintré Vieilles Vignes ★★★ £C

Dom. Pierre Vessigaud (Pouilly-Fuissé) *www.vinspierrevessigaud.fr*
Living in the hamlet of Pouilly, Pierre Vessigaud is one of the talented newly prominent producers, farming 11 hectares in the Pouilly Fuissé and named Macon villages appellations. The fifth generation of a family of vignerons, Pierre is committed to ecological viticulture that is largely organic; he uses only sulphur as a necessary treatment of his grapes which are hand-picked and whole bunch pressed. The wines are barrel-fermented without added yeasts or temperature control and judiciously aged in barrel on lees for 12 months. Particularly fine are his single-climat Pouilly Fuissés, each individual, all easy to compare with a Côte de Beaune white Burgundy. The Vers Pouilly is rich and dense reflecting the marly soils of this village. The Vers Asnières is very pure and elegant. Macon-Fuissé Les Tâches is a very good bottle for little outlay. (ME)
Recommended Whites:
Pouilly Fuissé Vers Pouilly ★★★☆ £D
Pouilly Fuissé Vers Asnières ★★★ £D
Pouilly Fuissé Vieilles Vignes ★★★ £D
Mâcon-Fuissé Les Tâches ★★☆ £C

Other wines of note - *Mâconnais*

Dom. de La Chapelle
Recommended Whites:
Pouilly-Fuissé ★★★ £D
Dom. Chataigneraie Laborier
Recommended Whites:
Pouilly-Fuissé ★★ £C
Pouilly-Fuissé Bélemnites ★★☆ £C

Burgundy /Mâconnais

France

Pouilly-Fuissé La Roche ★★★ £D
Michel Chavet et Fils
Recommended Whites:
Saint-Véran ★★☆ £C
Michel Cheveau
Recommended Whites:
Pouilly-Fuissé Les Trois Terroirs ★★ £D
Joseph Drouhin
Recommended Whites:
Mâcon-Villages ★★ £B
Saint-Véran ★★ £C
Pouilly-Fuissé ★★ £D
Dom. Eloy
Recommended Whites:
Mâcon-Villages ★☆ £B
Mâcon-Fuissé ★★ £C
Pouilly-Fuissé Vieilles Vignes ★★☆ £D
Recommended Reds:
Bourgogne Rouge Cuvée Prestige ★☆ £B
Dom. David Fagot
Recommended Whites:
Pouilly-Fuissé ★★☆ £C
Dom. de Fussiacus
Recommended Whites:
Mâcon-Fuissé ★☆ £B
Saint-Véran ★★ £B
Pouilly-Vinzelles ★★ £C
Pouilly-Fuissé Dom. Les Vieux Murs ★★ £D
Pouilly-Fuissé Vieilles Vignes ★★★ £D
Pierette et Marc Guillemot-Michel
Recommended Whites:
Mâcon-Villages Quintaine ★★☆ £C
Maurice Lapalus et Fils
Recommended Whites:
Mâcon Pierreclos ★★ £B
Recommended Reds:
Mâcon Pierreclos Rouge ★☆ £B
Mâcon Pierreclos Sélection Vieilles Vignes ★★☆ £C
Jean Manciat
Recommended Whites:
Mâcon-Charnay ★★ £B
Dom. Alain Normand
Recommended Whites:
Mâcon La Roche Vineuse ★★★ £C
Mâcon La Roche Vineuse Vieilles Vignes ★★★ £C
Pouilly-Fuissé ★★★☆ £D
Recommended Reds:
Mâcon La Roche Vineuse Rouge ★☆ £C
Dom. Gérald et Philibert Talmard
Recommended Whites:
Mâcon-Uchizy ★☆ £B
Mâcon-Chardonnay ★☆ £C
Dom. Paul et Mallory Talmard
Recommended Whites:
Mâcon-Uchizy ★☆ £B
Dom. Vervier et Fils
Recommended Whites:
Pouilly-Fuissé ★★ £C
Dom. des Vieilles Pierres / Jean-Jacques Litaud
Recommended Whites:
Saint-Véran Les Pommards ★★ £C

Pouilly-Fuissé La Roche Vieilles Vignes ★★★ £D
Pouilly-Fuissé Les Crays Vieilles Vignes ★★★☆ £D
Dom. des Vignes du Maynes / Julien Guillot (Biodynamic)
Recommended Whites:
Mâcon-Cruzille Clos Des Vignes Du Maynes ★☆ £C
Mâcon-Cruzille Clos Des Vignes Du Maynes Aragonite ★★★ £C
Recommended Reds:
Mâcon-Cruzille Clos Des Vignes Du Maynes Les Rosiers ★★☆ £C

Author's choice

20 Great Mâcon Whites
Daniel Barraud   Pouilly-Fuissé en Buland Vieilles Vignes
Dom. Georges Burrier   Pouilly-Fuissé Les Champs
Ch. des Rontets   Pouilly-Fuissé Les Birbettes
Dom. Cordier Père et Fils   Pouilly-Fuissé Vignes Blanches
Héritiers du Comte Lafon   Mâcon Milly Lamartine Clos du Four
Dom. des Deux Roches   Saint-Véran Les Cras
Dom. J A Ferret   Pouilly-Fuissé Ménétrières Hors Classé
Eric Forest   Pouilly-Fuissé Haut de Crays
Dom. Guffens-Heynen   Pouilly-Fuissé
Roger Lassarat   Saint-Véran Le Cras
Olivier Merlin   Pouilly-Fuissé Terroir de Vergisson
Michel Rey   Pouilly-Fuissé Les Charmes
Dom. Rijckaert   Viré-Clessé En Thurissey Vieilles Vignes
Dom. Robert-Denogent   Pouilly-Fuissé Cuvée Claude Denogent
Jacques & Nathalie Saumaize   Pouilly-Fuissé Les Courtelongs
Dom. Saumaize-Michelin   Pouilly-Fuissé Ampelopsis
La Soufrandière   Pouilly-Vinzelles Les Quarts Millerandée
Jean Thévenet   Mâcon-Villages Quintaine Domaine Emilian Gillet
Dom. Valette   Pouilly-Fuissé Clos de M Noly Vieilles Vignes Réserve
Dom. Vessigaud   Pouilly-Fuissé Vers Pouilly

Value for money Mâcon whites
Auvigue   Mâcon-Fuissé Moulin Du Pont
André Bonhomme   Viré-Clessé Cuvée Speciale
Dom. de La Croix Senaillet   Saint-Véran
Dom. Fichet   Mâcon-Igé Vieilles Vignes
Dom. des Gerbeaux   Saint-Véran
Maurice Lapalus & Fils   Mâcon Pierreclos
Roger Lassarat   Saint-Véran Cuvée Prestige
Nicolas Maillet   Mâcon-Verzé
Olivier Merlin   Mâcon-La Roche Vineuse Vieilles Vignes
Alain Normand   Mâcon-La Roche Vineuse
Dom. Robert-Denogent   Pouilly-Fuissé La Croix Vieilles Vignes
Jacques & Nathalie Saumaize   Saint-Véran En Creches
Saumaize-Michelin   Mâcon-Villages Les Sertaux
Verget   Mâcon-Charnay Clos Saint-Pierre

Now that the cheap trick that was Beaujolais Nouveau seems pretty much played out the world over, more seems set to be made of the region's real strengths. Its crus, the Gamay grape, the old vines, its granite, schist and sandy soils, its many small estates and some dedicated vignerons are the fundamentals. Add improved vinification, breathe life back into the soils and promote a willingness to explore different interpretations of just what Beaujolais can be (both a quaffer and something more serious) and more wine lovers should be adding it to their shopping lists.

Beaujolais by village

Burgundy's Mâconnais melts into Beaujolais where a few Chardonnay vines qualify to be sold as Beaujolais Blanc. But the real story concerns the Gamay grape and its predisposition for a radically different growing environment as granite, schist (and in places sand or clay) soils take over from the limestone based soils of Burgundy proper. In these soils old vines seem to count for more than low yields and grapes must be hand-picked as they are subject (in most instances) to a vinification that involves semi-carbonic maceration of whole bunches of grapes. The quality of the fruit can leave much to be desired and too much Beaujolais finishes abruptly with a hard, green edge. Better examples are richly fruity but relatively short-lived with little real structure but easy drinkability. Different interpretations of style do exist however, and some producers get more structure into the wines without losing too much of their charm and quaffability. Jadot and one or two others make the wines in the style of red Burgundy with a similar vinification and oak-ageing as for Pinot Noir-based reds. Though it may not seem worth the effort the difference a dedicated progressive grower can make to the quality of Beaujolais can be a revelation.

The best Beaujolais comes from the northern or Haut-Beaujolais, with purer soils and better slopes. It is sold as Beaujolais-Villages or better still as one of ten recognised crus from within this area. There is a trend to increasing identification of individual climats within the crus. The vineyards of **Saint-Amour**, where Beaujolais takes over from Mâconnais, are on rather mixed soils and are generally a little unexciting. **Juliénas** in contrast, from well-positioned slopes and a significant clay component in its soils, is a consistent provider of wines with better depth and intensity than most. Lighter **Chénas** occupies higher ground than the adjoining **Moulin-à-Vent** and it is the latter that has the most strength, structure and longevity of all the *crus*. There are an increasing number of different interpretations from fruit-rich Château de Beauregard examples to the more expressive and burgundian special *cuvées* of Château des Jacques. The prices are matched only by **Fleurie**, the best examples of which are perfumed but also often unequalled for their density of fruit and lush texture. Be sure to taste those from Clos de la Roilette, Michel Chignard and Domaine de la Madone.

Chiroubles has some of the most elevated vineyards in the region; the best wines are light but as refined as they get. At the heart of **Morgon** is the Côte de Py with its distinctive roches pourries soils of friable schist, the wines are dense and intensely cherryish. Compare and contrast those from Jean Foillard, Jadot's Château des Lumières, Piron and Louis-Claude Desvignes. **Régnié** is the most recent *cru* and rarely exciting (try from Christian Ducroux). The large **Brouilly** *cru* surrounds the hill of Mont Brouilly whose slopes provide **Côte de Brouilly**. The best Brouilly (such as from Château des Tours) can have attractive fruit but much of it is poor, however an increasing number of good examples of Côte de Brouilly are now being made;

those from Château Thivin and Nicole Chanrion can be excellent.

Beaujolais vintages

Do vintages in Beaujolais matter with most of the wines being drunk so young? As some of the better quality cru Beaujolais need at least 2 or 3 years' to open out, for these choosing one vintage over another can make a big difference to what's in your glass.

2015 ★★★☆: The great heat of the long summer has evoked some superlatives. Some thoughtful observers though remind us that when temperatures rise, there are inevitably winners and losers. The higher vineyards coped better with the heat. .

2014 ★★★★: As in Burgundy, so in Beaujolais after a cold summer when morale was low, the vintage was saved by a brilliant sunny September. Less mineral but riper and more abundant than 2013, the profile of violet scents, expressive woodland red fruits (especially fraises de bois in tune with fine acidity) makes 2014 a winner for professionals and amateurs alike the slopes of Fleurie la Madone, Morgon Côte de Py and Côte de Brouilly produced classic Beaujolais crus worth ageing into 2017/18.

2013 ★★★★☆: A late harvest – due to *coulure* and widespread *millerandage* which affected flowering, has reduced crop size, but on the other side of the coin, because the Gamay grapes received the highest amount of sunlight for many years, they were ripe and in great condition, with more concentrated juice, promising vibrant and exciting wines. .

2012 ★★: Adverse weather conditions throughout the growing season resulted in a crop loss of some 50% in the region, with some producers on the verge of bankruptcy. Careful selection was needed to counteract the effect of frost, hail and rain with generally smaller berries at the time of harvest. This has led to some over concentrated wines lacking freshness, but as usual the best producers have managed to make something decent.

2011 ★★★☆: In contrast to the two previous years, this year had a warm spring and early summer followed by a rather damp August. As a result the wines produced in the Beaujolais show a little less elegance, but with good weight. Maconnais wines lack structure but are supple and aromatic suitable for early drinking.

2010 ★★★★: After a cold winter and an unsettled early part of the summer, good weather from mid August onwards led to fine aromatic wines from a small crop in the Beaujolais. A hailstorm on the 10th July led to further crop reduction in the Maconnais, but on the whole the wines show a good balance between the fruit and the acidity.

2009 ★★★★: is likely to see some ripe and forward wines emerging with attractive dark berry fruit and although lower in acidity than other recent vintages the wines will drink very well in the short to medium term. Some late summer hail did present growers with some unexpected challenges, so be a little selective.

2008 ★★★: A mild winter resulted in early flowering of the vines. Early summer was cool, but July and the beginning of August saw the return of hot weather. Late summer hail in the north of the appellation resulted in drastic yields for those crus. The weather cooled again in later August, but the sun returned in September. Again, careful selection is needed, but those who worked hard and conscientiously produced good results.

2007 ★★☆: A difficult growing season with a hot April followed by a cool summer inhibiting ripeness. The best showed good raspberry fruit character, coupled with a little spiciness. The lesser wines, however, are rather astrigent and one-dimensional and should now be avoided.

2006 ★★★☆: Despite talk of a more difficult vintage in (after 05)

France

many wines have shown full ripeness, good substance and acidity. A more demanding growing season has translated into a less uniformly high quality vintage but some excellent wines emerged from top growers (especially those profiled below).

2005 ★★★★☆: An exciting vintage with a combination of ripeness, balance and good acidity. There are plenty of vibrant and expressive wines which will be drinking well now.

Earlier Years: 2004 and 2003 were both decent years and the best crus will still offer good drinking.

A-Z of producers

Jean-Marc Burgaud (Morgon)   *www.jean-marc-burgaud.com*
Some of the best parcels of Morgon make up the greater part of this estate of 14 ha; the 10 ha of Morgon are supplemented by 3 ha of Beaujolais-Villages (Château de Thulon) and 1ha of Régnié (Vallières). Young Jean-Marc Burgaud practices a fairly standard vinification but gets good differentiation between a lush, fruit-filled old vine Les Charmes and more minerally and firmly structured Côte du Py that is subject to a more lengthy maceration. Balance can be more difficult to achieve in the latter but seems most successful in warmer years It is also produced in a Vieilles Vignes version and a more ambitious oak-aged Réserve which will be rated with further tastings. Château de Thulon has good up-front fruit for everyday drinking. A new *cuvée* of Beaujolais Blanc was produced in 2012 from Chardonnay vines plated in 2010

Recommended Reds:
Morgon Les Charmes ★★★ £C   Morgon Côte du Py ★★☆ £C
Beaujolais-Villages Château de Thulon ★☆ £B

❂ **Dom. Calot (Morgon)**   *www.domaine-calot.com*
This 12 ha estate has long been an excellent source of ripe, concentrated and characterful Morgon. There are several *cuvées*, from a supple, fruity regular Cuvée Tradition to a deep, intense Vieilles Vignes that needs 3 years or so in order to soften a little. Vinification is traditional and not the semi-carbonic maceration favoured by most. An old-fashioned vertical press is employed and both small and large oak are used for ageing. A small amount of Tête de Cuvée and an intense, complex Cuvée Jeanne have also been made in recent vintages. All are very reasonably and honestly priced for the quality – there has been no attempt to sell any of the wines at a premium to enhance the domaine's status or cash flow as some growers in the region have done.

Recommended Reds:
Morgon Cuvée Jeanne ★★★ £C   MorgonTête de Cuvée ★★★ £C
Morgon Vieilles Vignes ★★★ £C   Morgon Tradition ★★☆ £B

Nicole Chanrion / La Voûte des Crozes (Côte de Brouilly)
This small estate produces one of the best examples of Côte de Brouilly from 6 ha of well-established vines. It is consistently expressive and fruit-rich with plenty of intensity and depth and a profusion of mineral, raspberry and cherry is framed by good acidity and soft tannins. It can be drunk young or with 3–5 years' age. Recent vintages confirm the step up in quality that Nicole Chanrion has consistently achieved over the years ever since she took over the domaine in the 1970s.

Recommended Reds:
Côte de Brouilly ★★★☆ £C

Dom. de La Chaponne (Morgon)   *www.laurent-guillet.com*
If you like soft, fruit-driven Beaujolais for immediate consumption

then this is not the producer for you. From 11 ha and some very old vines – up to 90 years old – come powerful, structured examples of Morgon that need to be drunk with some age. There is great intensity and fruit depth but sometimes the wines can be a little too extracted. The mineral, cherry and raspberry of good Morgon is always there but so too is the structure and strength. Cuvée Joseph, the oak-aged version, adds oak spice to a deep plum, cherry and mineral intensity and needs at least 5 years of cellaring before it should be approached.

Recommended Reds:
Morgon Cuvée Joseph Vieilles Vignes Fûts de Chêne ★★★ £C
MorgonVieilles Vignes ★★ £B

Ch. de Beauregard / Joseph Burrier   *www.joseph-burrier.com*
Château de Beauregard is more likely to be encountered in the shape of fine Pouilly-Fuissé or other Mâconnais whites (see Mâconnais section) but the family also have 10 ha in Beaujolais, including 6ha in Fleurie and 3 ha in Moulin-à-Vent. No *macération carbonique* is employed and for the crus around 50% of the fruit is destemmed before 10–15 days fermentation with *pigeage*. The wines can show a touch of reduction when young but are full and supple, with real density and flesh in Moulin-à-Vent. A Clos de Pérelles (25% new oak for 8 months) has rich, mineral-imbued fruit and both depth and breadth. With plenty of extract and fine, ripe tannins, it needs 4–5 years' age and is both complex and classy. As well as another Moulin-à-Vent, La Salomine, a special version of Fleurie, Les Colonies de Rochgrès, is also produced.

Recommended Reds:
Moulin-à-Vent Clos de Pérelles ★★★ £D
Moulin-à-Vent ★★★ £C   Fleurie ★★ £C

>> Ch. de Moulin -à-Vent   *www.chateaudumoulinavent.com*
An historic leading property dating from 1737 in Moulin à Vent, which was one of the first renowned southern Burgundy communes to gain appellation contrôlée status in 1936. In the early 2000s, the estate was bought by the Parinet family who have invested a lot in improving everything in the vineyards (37 hectares) and winery. The real assets which rises markedly above the level of the simple, clean and well-made entry-level wines, are selected parcels which are serious terroirs with the potential to make fine wine. Two climats deserve special mention: Le Croix des Vérillats with an easterly aspect at the top of the hill has sandy, granite soil, so the instant attractions are aromatic scents of violets and a delicately filigreed texture in the mouth, which is slightly deceptive, for the wine also has good length of black fruits flavours and a driving energy. The Champ de Coeur by comparison is all harmony and completeness, which comes from old vines in a very privileged site. We haven't yet tasted the latest release La Rochelle from the top of the vineyard, reported to be dark in colour, seamless, opulent, with the driving energy of a high site. This property goes from strength to strength. (ME)

Recommended Reds:
Moulin -à- Vent Croix des Vérillats ★★★☆ £E
Moulin -à- Vent Champ de Cour ★★★☆ £D   Moulin -a -Vent ★★☆ £D

Ch. Thivin (Côte de Brouilly)   *www.chateau-thivin.com*
Château Thivin is renowned for its Côte de Brouilly and is one of Beaujolais' historic properties, with medieval origins. The top *cuvée*, Zaccharie Geoffray, is named for one of Claude Geoffray's ancestors who purchased the property in 1877. The 24 ha include a second domaine, Manoir du Pavé (from his wife's family), which is the

source of a good Beaujolais-Villages. While ripe and supple with fine structures, the wines show real individual expression and distinctive fruit, with a mineral, floral and herbal quality that is unique to the local soils. Other *cuvées* now bottled separately and made to the same standards, include Clos Bertrand and La Croix Dessaigne. Prices are reasonable for the quality.

Recommended Reds:

Côte de Brouilly La Chapelle ★★★ £C
Côte de Brouilly Zaccharie Geoffray ★★★ £C
Côte de Brouilly ★★ £B   Brouilly ★ £B
Beaujolais-Villages Manoir du Pavé ★ £B

✿ Dom. Chignard (Fleurie)

There probably isn't any better Fleurie than that from this domaine. Under the wing of father Michel for the last few years, son Cédric has now assumed full responsibility. Their wines manage to be ripe, full and intense with rich textures that offer some immediate gratification but have the structure and substance to improve for several years. Moriers is one of the best parts of Fleurie, close to both La Roilette and some of the best climats in Moulin-à-Vent, but the very composed and refined nature of the wines is also proof of a high degree of care and skill on the part of the producer. A bonus for the Chignons is that they have managed to buy the Moriers vineyard in 2011, where they have been tenants for the last four generations. Most vintages will improve for at least 6–8 years' but it isn't necessary to wait.

Recommended Reds:

Fleurie Spéciale Vieilles Vignes ★★★☆ £D
Fleurie Les Moriers ★★★☆ £C

Clos de la Roilette / Coudert (Fleurie) *www.clos-de-la-roilette.com*

Within their 9.5 ha of vineyard, the Couderts possess the best part of La Roilette, the finest climat in Fleurie. The site gives Fleurie of more body, depth and complexity than is typical and theirs is a parcel of very old vines. The grapes are harvested very ripe and in the small amount of a special bottling called Cuvée Tardive there is more intensity and richness. The wines are sleek and supple, with a black fruit character and a subtle mineral streak. Both are consistently fine yet reasonably priced Beaujolais that drink well with anything from 1 –3 years' age, and the Tardive sometimes considerably more. The newish Cuvée Christal is even more accessible with soft silky tannins.

Recommended Reds:

Fleurie Clos de la Roilette ★★★ £C
Fleurie Cuvée Tardive ★★★ £C   Fleurie Cuvée Christal ★★ £C

Dom. de Colonat (Morgon) *www.domaine-de-colonat.fr*

The Collonges have 12 ha of vines and make Chiroubles, Régnié and Beaujolais-Villages but their prized possession is in Les Charmes in Morgon. The soils include friable schist and decomposed rock with typical dense planting of 10,000 vines per hectare. The wines are not of the pristine, fruit-driven style but more traditional in structure. The regular *cuvée* is aged in used wood and is quite closed when young, without any immediate fruit richness, and needs 3–4 years to unfurl. Cuvée Prestige comes from vines more than 50 years old and is aged in *barriques* but again starts out tight and closed. Yet there is real breadth with fruit intensity and depth underneath and with 5 years' age or more it begins to develop a Pinot-like complexity.

Recommended Reds:

Morgon Les Charmes Prestige ★★★ £C
Morgon Les Charmes Tradition ★★ £B

Dom. Louis-Claude Desvignes *www.louis-claude-desvignes.com*

Louis-Claude Desvignes was one of the first in Beaujolais to produce separate *cuvées* from the best parcels in his Morgon estate. From 1.5 ha of Côte de Py and 2 ha of Javernières (from different soils within the Côte de Py) are regularly produced two rich vibrant, aromatic and distinctly different Morgons that bear little resemblance to most of what comes out of the Beaujolais region. There is undoubted skill and care in their production; low yields and a cold pre-fermentation maceration are just two contributing factors. Though there are now several other versions of Côte de Py (including Jean FOILLARD'S), few rival this one and none at the price, which remains low. These are wines to drink with at least 3 or 4 years' age if their full potential is to be realised.

Recommended Reds:

Morgon Côte de Py ★★★ £C   Morgon La Voûte Saint-Vincent ★★ £C
Morgon Javernières ★★ £C

Georges Duboeuf (Beaujolais) *www.duboeuf.com*

For many around the world Duboeuf represents Beaujolais, or at least the decent stuff. A production of 30 million bottles is one of the reasons why it can be found in local wine shops and supermarkets almost everywhere. Duboeuf has been admirably consistent despite the phenomenal growth over more than 3 decades. Many small domaines, including some in every cru, come under the Duboeuf umbrella and are marketed and bottled accordingly. Though some of the *cuvées*, especially the generic crus, are simple and rather short and firm on the finish, others show more expression, and more succulence and finesse in their structures. The individual *cuvées* (most from single domaines) are nearly always worth the small premium they command, particularly those from Moulin-à-Vent and Fleurie, when compared to regular examples of the more southerly Beaujolais crus, Brouilly or Régnié. Individual crus can be drunk with a couple of years' ageing but don't need it. Prices of fine wines around the globe may have escalated but those of most of these Beaujolais, like their quality, have remained steady. Some fresh, attractive whites with good substance are also made, as are many Rhône wines and vins de pays from the Languedoc-Roussillon. Below are some of the very best of Duboeuf's Beaujolais/Mâconnais wines.

Recommended Reds:

Moulin-à-Vent Prestige ★★★ £C
Moulin-à-Vent Domaine de la Tour de Bief ★★★ £C
Moulin-à-Vent Domaine des Rosiers ★★ £C
Moulin-à-Vent Fût de Chêne ★★ £C
Moulin-à-Vent ★★ £B   Morgon Prestige ★★★ £C
Morgon Domaine Jean Descombes ★★ £C
Morgon ★ £B   Fleurie La Madone ★★ £C
Fleurie Domaine des Quatre Vents ★★ £C
Fleurie Château des Bachelards ★ £C
Fleurie Château des Déduits ★ £C   Fleurie ★ £B
Chiroubles Domaine des Tilleuls ★★ £C
Saint-Amour Domaine du Paradis ★★ £C
Saint-Amour Domaine des Sablons ★ £C
Beaujolais-Villages Château de Varennes ★★ £B
Juliénas Domaine de la Seigneurie ★ £C
Brouilly Domaine de Combillaty ★ £C

Recommended Whites:

Pouilly-Fuissé Prestige ★★ £C
Pouilly-Fuissé Fût de Chêne ★☆ £C
Saint-Véran Domaine Saint-Martin ★ £B
Mâcon-Villages Prestige ★ £B

Beaujolais

Christian Ducroux (Régnié)

Christian Ducroux makes the best Régnié I've ever tasted and by some distance. That's hardly makes it a big deal but his family's meagre 4 ha are typically densely planted and cultivated biodynamically (Demeter certified) and it is evident that the life being restored to the soils is having an impact on the fruit quality. Vinification is the usual semi-carbonic maceration yet there is lovely purity and expression. A more richly textured Vieilli en fût de Chêne version is complex and structured but only likely to be at its best with 6 years' age.

Recommended Reds:

Régnié Vieilli en fût de Chênes ★★★ £C Régnié ★★☆ £B

Henry Fessy (Beaujolais) www.henryfessy.com

Since the purchase of this domaine by Maison Loius Latour in 2008, wine production has been completely re-vamped and the Henry Fessy label now relates to mainly generic Beaujolais and Crus from every village in the region as well as some wines in the Maconnais. Two single estates, Château des Reyssiers in Regnie and Château des Labourons in Fleurie complete the range of this now 70ha négociant-domaine. Previous wine labels from the Fessys have now been abandoned and incorporated into the new regime. The wines listed below relate to those made by the Fessys up to 2009 and the wines bottled under the Latour regime must be considered as work in progress at the moment.

Recommended Reds:

Brouilly Cuvée Georges Fessy ★★ £C
Brouilly Domaine du Plateau de Bel Air ★★ £B
Brouilly Pur Sang ★★ £C Fleurie La Roilette ★★ £C
Fleurie Mauriers ★★ £C Morgon Cuvée Luquet ★★ £B

Jean Foillard (Morgon)

Jean Foillard is a disciple of Jules Chauvet, a noted enologist who believed in fashioning Beaujolais in an altogether different way from the modern standard of semi-carbonic maceration. Foillard's 8 ha (cultivated organically though not certified) include one of the best sites in the whole Beaujolais region, Morgon's Côte du Py. Important to the style are low yields and very ripe grapes, which are subject to a long cool vinification, practically zero use of sulphur and minimal or no filtration. It's not what you would normally associate with Beaujolais; an intense, spice- and mineral-rich structured wine that needs 5 years or more before it is ready. Light years away from simple, fruity quaffing Beaujolais, it does achieve real harmony in the best years.

Recommended Reds:

Morgon Côte du Py ★★★ £C Morgon Première ★★☆ £B

❂ Louis Jadot (Beaujolais) www.louis-jadot.com

Long before its purchase by Louis JADOT, Château des Jacques was the leading estate in the Beaujolais region. Singular in its approach to vinification, with a Pinot-like destemming followed by fermentation in open tanks and *pigeage*, the wines have been richer and fuller with none of the woodiness or greeness that the whole-bunch fermentation practised by others can bring. Following the arrival of Jadot's Jacques Lardière, (now succeeded by Frédéric Barnier) maceration times have been extended and there is some use of automatic *pigeage*. In addition, 5 separate sites have been isolated from within the estate's 27 ha of Gamay vines and each of these is aged in new oak (Clos du Grand Carquelin, Grand Clos de Rochegrès, Champ de Cour, La Roche and Clos des Thorins). So the Côte d'Or has come to Beaujolais and with some clout, in order to promote further efforts towards higher quality (and higher prices). The wines show a previously unseen sumptuous, velvety quality and in the case of the Grand Carquelin and the Rochegrès at least also show promising complexity and structure, while Champ de Cour is arguably the most refined. Wines must be kept a minimum of 5 years. There are also 9ha of Chardonnay from which the white Beaujolais (stainless steel-vinified) and Bourgogne Blanc (barrel-fermented and aged) are made. Combe aux Jacques is a separate facility dedicated to producing high-quality Beaujolais-Villages in conjunction with local growers. In 2001 Jadot added Château Bellevue, one of Morgon's most prized estates, where a fine Morgon Côte du Py under the name Château des Lumières is at least the equal of the best from Château des Jacques. This is a wine with remarkable purity, fruit depth and intensity within a powerful but fine structure - keep it for at least 5-6 years.

Château des Jacques

Recommended Reds:

Moulin-à-Vent Grand Clos des Rochegrès ★★★☆ £D
Moulin-à-Vent Clos du Grand Carquelin ★★★ £D
Moulin-à-Vent Champ de Cour ★★★ £D
Moulin-à-Vent La Roche ★★★ £D Moulin-à-Vent ★★ £C

Recommended Whites:

Beaujolais-Villages Chardonnay ★★ £B
Bourgogne Blanc Clos de Loyse ★★ £B

Château des Lumières

Recommended Reds:

Morgon Côte du Py ★★★☆ £D Morgon ★★☆ £C

Dom. Paul & Eric Janin www.domaine-paul-janin.fr

Eric Janin makes excellent Moulin-à-Vent to a biodynamic recipe. The domaine of 10 ha of old vines are carefully nurtured by father and son and the result is a marvellous fruit quality and good concentration and depth in the wines. Occasionally the tannins can be a little firm in the finish but the Clos du Tremblay (which is a selection of the very best old vines) in particular benefits from a couple of years' age. Two-thirds of production is Moulin-à-Vent, the rest Beaujolais-Villages from the smaller Domaine des Vignes des Jumeaux. Recently, there is another *cuvée* of Moulin-à-Vent, Vieilles Vignes des Greneriers a rustic blockbuster from vines planted in 1914. Prices, as so often from those most dedicated to the land, are very reasonable.

Recommended Reds:

Moulin-à-Vent Clos du Tremblay ★★★ £C
Moulin-à-Vent Vieilles Vignes des Greneriers ★★☆ £C
Moulin-à-Vent Vignes du Tremblay ★★ £C
Beaujolais-Villages Domaine des Vignes du Jumeaux ★☆ £B

Jacky Janodet / Dom. Les Fine Graves (Moulin-à-Vent)

Jacky Janodet is one of the best-known growers based in Moulin-à-Vent. He has just over 10 ha, of which 6.5 ha are in Moulin-à-Vent itself and much is planted to very old vines. The wine is classically powerful with good depth, its concentration, structure and texture owed in part to ageing in small barrels. Some Beaujolais-Villages and a tiny amount of white is also made.

Recommended Reds:

Moulin-à-Vent Vieilles Vignes ★★★ £C Chénas ★★☆ £B

Hubert Lapierre (Chénas) www.domaine-lapierre.com

Chénas is not the most exciting cru in Beaujolais but those from Hubert Lapierre can show good weight and ripe raspberryish fruit. As well as a Vieilles Vignes version a small amount is aged in mostly

used *barriques* for 10 months, enriching both texture and flavour. The 7.5 ha of vineyards also includes more ample, riper, darker-fruited Moulin-à-Vent with good acidity that is better with 2–3 years and in the case of the Vieilles Vignes version usually keeps 5–6 years. The wines show exceptionally well from warm vintages.

Recommended Reds:
Moulin-à-Vent Vieilles Vignes ★★★ £C
Moulin-à-Vent Tradition ★★ £B
Chénas Fût de Chêne ★★☆ £C   Chénas Vieilles Vignes ★★ £B

Matthieu Lapierre (Morgon) *www.marcel-lapierre.com*
Marcel Lapierre, Beaujolais' most fastidious vigneron, was joined by his son, Matthieu in 2005 and sadly passed away at the end of the 2010 harvest. His son now runs the 13 ha family estate known as Domaine des Chênes following the methods laid down by his father. Vines, cultivated organically, average 60 years and include 2 ha on the famed Côte du Py. A rigorous selection follows manual harvesting with no added yeasts or sulphur. Marcel, who took over from his father, was another influenced by Jules Chauvet (see Jean Foillard) but he does begin fermentation with the usual semi-carbonic maceration following a period of cold maceration. Press wine is added back and the wines are aged in used barrels for around 9 months. At their best the wines are very pure with intense old viney cherry fruit and minerality. Building in richness with age the wines deserve at least 5 years' age where for once the old maxim about tasting like classed growth Burgundy does often hold true. A newer wine is the Raisins Gaulois, a racy quaffer made from younger vines comprised mainly from vines planted in the Morgan AOC and a little bit outside the appellation, but only entitled to the designation Vin de France.

Recommended Reds:
Morgon ★★★☆ £C   Raisins Gaulois ★★☆ £B

Dom. de La Madone (Fleurie) *www.domaine-de-la-madone.com*
Jean-Marc Despres and his son Arnaud consistently produce benchmark Fleurie from almost 9 ha of vines on south-west facing slopes. The regular *cuvée* is supple and smooth with raspberry, cherry and refined floral characters. There is no hardness or greenness even in a poor vintage, and there is depth and breadth without being overdone. The Vieilles Vignes offers more complexity, refinement and density. This ability to respond to the vintage conditions marks these wines out; too many others are over extracted and unbalanced in all but the best years. Another *cuvée* of old vines, Grille Midi, comes from a particularly warm part of the vineyards and can be more fleshy, more structured but displays a fine minerality. Also made since 2005, is a Fleurie Domaine de Niagra, made from vines, some of which are more than 80 years old, previously owned by Arnaud's great grandfather.

Recommended Reds:
Fleurie Vieilles Vignes Cuvée Speciale ★★★☆ £D
Fleurie Grille Midi Vieilles Vignes ★★★ £C   Fleurie ★★☆ £B

Bernard Métrat (Fleurie) *www.domainemetrat.fr*
This is a typical small Beaujolais estate but with 6.5 ha in Chiroubles and Fleurie Bernard Métrat ensures that his are no run-of-the-mill examples. A very perfumed, floral, berry-fruited Chiroubles has very good fruit intensity if not the greatest depth, as is typical of the cru. Yet there is good structure to it and it will flesh out nicely with at least 2–3 years' age so don't hurry to drink it. The Fleurie vines in highly regarded La Roilette, contiguous with some of the best lieux-dits in Moulin-à-Vent, produce even better wine – supple and

exceptionally smooth with real breadth and elegance. It wil benefit from at least 2–3 years' age in warmer vintages.

Recommended Reds:
Fleurie La Roilette Vieilles Vignes ★★★ £C
Fleurie La Roilette Tradition ★★ £B   Chiroubles ★★★ £B

Domaines Piron (Morgon) *www.domaines-piron.fr*
Descended from a long line of grape growers stretching back to the mid-17th century, Dominique Piron has put much effort into improving viticulture and the quality of his grapes. His 22 ha of vineyard with an average vine age of 40 years are composed of the 17 ha Domaine de la Chanaise and 5ha Domaine de Combiaty. The best wines can show a minerality that, given the soils, ought to be seen in more Beaujolais – yet most simply exhibit attractive fruit and floral characters. This is most evident in the Morgon Côte de Py, the only one of six climats bottled separately by daughter Anne-Marie. Given a relatively long maceration, this is usually the top wine but Brouilly can also be very good, although quality of the sometimes complex Moulin-à-Vent is a little more irregular. Good Beaujolais-Villages and a little Beaujolais Blanc (from Chardonnay) are also made. As well as the Domaines Piron wines, Dominique Piron acts as a négociant producing wines under his own name and own-label Beaujolais for Fortnum & Mason in London.

Recommended Reds:
Morgon Côte du Py ★★★ £C   Morgon ★★ £B
Moulin-à-Vent Les Vignes du Vieux Bourg ★★★ £C
Brouilly Château du Prieuré ★ £B   Régnié ★ £B
Beaujolais-Villages Les Vignes de Pierreux ★ £B

Dom. des Terres Doreés (Beaujolais)
Jean-Paul Brun's domaine is situated in the south of the Beaujolais region, known as the Pierres Doreés. His wines are the exception in what is otherwise a sea of inferior plonk (most of which appears under a simple 'Beaujolais' label). Soils in these parts are predominantly limestone, and that part of Brun's 30 ha of vineyards with calcareous soils is planted not to Gamay but instead to Chardonnay and Pinot Noir. Therefore as well as producing pure, intense Beaujolais that really tastes of its origins there's both a light Bourgogne Grand Ordinaire (Pinot Noir) and Beaujolais Blanc (En Fût is a *barrique*-fermented version) that are intense and original. Late-harvested wines are also produced including Labeur d'Octobre and 'E sens de chardon né', from botrytis-affected Chardonnay grapes. Good Côte de Brouilly and Moulin-à-Vent are also made.

Recommended Reds:
Côte de Brouilly ★★ £C   Moulin-à-Vent ★★ £C
Beaujolais Cuvée à l'Ancienne ★★ £B Bourgogne Grande Ordinaire ★ £B
Recommended Whites:
Beaujolais Blanc ★ £B

Michel Tête / Dom. Clos du Fief (Juliénas) *www.micheltete.com*
Michel Tête has 13 ha of vineyard from which he produces a rare good example of Saint-Amour and two versions of Juliénas. Saint-Amour is silky, refined and harmonious particularly in good warm vintages. Regular Juliénas is full and chewy with good structure while a Prestige version from lower-yielding old vines is oak-aged. The latter is lush with better depth and breadth but can be kept at least 4–5 years, becoming more seductive and complex.

Recommended Reds:
Juliénas Cuvée Prestige ★★★ £C   Juliénas ★★ £B
Saint-Amour Les Capitans ★★★ £B   Beaujolais-Villages ★☆ £B

Beaujolais

France

Dom. du Vissoux (Beaujolais) *www.chermette.fr*
The wines from this 30 ha estate continue to improve and include excellent examples of both Fleurie and Moulin-à-Vent. Fleurie has lovely style and intensity, the Garants showing the lusher texture of the two bottlings. Moulin-à-Vent, both Rochegrès and slightly superior Rochelle, are now combined with wines from Rochenoire to produce a single *cuvée*, showing more spice, minerality and breadth. The regular Beaujolais Traditionelle, sourced from the southern Beaujolais, is not of the same ilk. A recent purchase has been a plot of vines at the foot of Mount Brouilly at Pierreux but the wine has not yet been tasted.

Recommended Reds:
Fleurie Les Garants ★★★ £C   Fleurie Poncié ★★ £C
Moulin-à-Vent Les Trois Roches ★★★ £C

Other wines of note (all reds)

Dom. Régis Champier
Brouilly Extrait de Terroir ★★★ £B
Gérard Charvet
Moulin-à-Vent Vieilles Vignes ★★ £C
Moulin-à-Vent La Réserve d'Amelie ★★☆ £C
Ch. du Basty
Beaujolais-Villages ★☆ £B   Régnié ★★ £B
Ch. de La Chaize
Brouilly ★☆ £B
Ch. de Pierreux
Brouilly ★★★ £C   Brouilly La Réserve du Château ★★★ £C
Ch. des Tours
Brouilly ★★☆ £C
Dom. Émile Cheysson
Chiroubles ★★☆ £B   Chiroubles Prestige ★★☆ £B
André Colonge et Fils
Beaujolais-Villages ★☆ £B   Fleurie ★★☆ £C
Georges Descombes
Brouilly ★★ £B   Morgon ★★★ £B
Joelle et Gérard Descombes
Beaujolais-Villages ★☆ £B
Juliénas - Dom. Les Côtes de La Roche ★★☆ £C
Georges Despres
Beaujolais-Villages ★☆ £B
Beaujolais-Villages Cuvée Joseph Vieilles Vignes ★★ £B
Dom. Diochon
Moulin-à-Vent Vieilles Vignes ★★ £C
Dom. Dubost
Brouilly La Bruyère Vieilles Vignes ★★ £B
Cave Coopérative de Fleurie
Fleurie Cuvée Millésimé ★★ £B
Dom. Maurice Gaget
Morgon Côte Du Py ★★★ £C
Jacky Gauthier
Régnié Domaine de Colette ★☆ £B
Dom. Gay-Coperet
Moulin-à-Vent Réserve Vieilles Vignes ★★ £C
Moulin-à-Vent Cuvée Prestige ★★ £C
Dom. de La Grand Cour
Fleurie Clos De La Grand Cour ★★ £B
Fleurie Fût De Chêne V V ★★★ £C
Pascal Granger
Chénas ★ £B   Juliénas Cuvée Speciale ★★ £B
Dom. de Gry-Sablon

Fleurie ★★ £C   Morgon ★★ £B
Marcel Jonchet/Dom. des Roches Du Py
Morgon Côte Du Py ★★★ £C
Alain Margerand
Moulin-à-Vent Rochegrès ★★ £C
Jean-Pierre Margerand
Juliénas ★★ £B
Laurent Martray
Brouilly Vieilles Vignes ★★ £B
Alain Michaud
Brouilly ★★ £B   Morgon ★★ £B
Monmessin
Beaujolais-Villages Vieilles Vignes ★ £B   Morgon Les Griottes ★★ £B
Fleurie La Cerisaie ★★ £C
Albert Morel
Fleurie ★★ £B
Christophe Pacalet
Chiroubles ★☆ £B   Chénas ★★☆ £B
Côte De Brouilly ★★ £B
Alain Passot/Dom. de La Grosse Pierre
Chiroubles ★★ £B
Dom. des Pins/Jean-Francois Echallier
Saint-Amour ★★☆ £B
Jean-Charles Pivot
Beaujolais-Villages ★★ £B   Côte De Brouilly ★★ £B
Potel-Aviron
Morgon Côte du Py Vieilles Vignes ★★★ £C
Fleurie Vieilles Vignes ★★★ £C
Moulin-à-Vent Vieilles Vignes ★★★ £C
Dom. Les Roches Bleues
Côte De Brouilly ★★ £B
Bernard Santé
Chénas ★★ £B   Juliénas ★★ £B
Dom. des Vieilles Caves
Chénas Vieilles Vignes ★★ £B   Moulin-à-Vent Vieilles Vignes ★★★ £C
Dom. Georges Viornery
Côte De Brouilly ★★ £B

Author's choice

Some favourite Beaujolais
Dom. Calot   Morgon Tête de Cuvée
Nicole Chanrion/La Voute des Crozes   Côte de Brouilly
Ch. de Beauregard   Moulin-à-Vent Clos des Pérelles
Ch. des Jacques   Moulin-à-Vent Clos du Grand Carquelin
Ch. des Jacques   Moulin-à-Vent Clos des Rochegrès
Ch. des Lumieres   Morgon Côte du Py
Ch. de Pierreux   Brouilly
Michel Chignard   Fleurie Les Moriers
Clos de La Roilette/Coudert   Fleurie Clos de La Roilette
Dom. de Colonat   Morgon Les Charmes Marguerite Montchanay
Georges Duboeuf   Moulin-à-Vent Prestige
Christian Ducroux   Régnié Vieilli En Fût de Chênes
Dom. Paul et Eric Janin   Moulin-à-Vent Clos du Tremblay
Marcel Lapierre   Morgon
Dom. de La Madone   Fleurie Vieilles Vignes Cuvée Speciale
Michel Tete/Dom. Clos du Fief   Saint-Amour

This is one of France's most unusual and exciting regions. Culturally it is as much German as it is French and twice during the last 140 years or so has been a part of the former. It is one of France's most spectacular regions to visit, with the splendour of the Vosges mountains complemented by the medieval architecture of many towns and villages. Unlike in other regions, the grape varietal plays a key element in wine labelling. The wines themselves can be piercingly aromatic and are quite unique in style. Although there are some substantial merchant operations and large co-ops the area is not a purveyor of bulk wine. However there is still a wide variation in quality and yields generally throughout the region are too high, with most wine still coming from over-productive sites on the plains. As elsewhere, who produced the wine is the key

Geography

The region of Alsace is a narrow stretch of vineyards running north-south at the base of and nestled into the eastern foothills of the Vosges mountains. These, along with the Rhine just to the east of the *vignoble*, provide the region with an impressively favourable climate for such a northerly latitude. Sunshine hours are high during the growing season and rainfall low. The vineyard area stretches from just west of Strasbourg in the north to Mulhouse in the south, with the heart of the region centred around the town of Colmar. This is where the greatest concentration of top villages and vineyard sites, particularly grands crus, is to be found. These southern stretches are known as the **Haut Rhin**; the northern part is the **Bas Rhin**. There are fewer great sites in the Bas Rhin but some very fine wine is produced nonetheless. In some respects the region resembles the Côte d'Or. The finest sites are inevitably on the slopes of the Vosges, with well-drained, meagre soils. By contrast those vineyards planted on the fertile, heavy alluvial soils on the plains towards the Rhine are far less propitious for quality wine production.

Wine Styles

The generic appellation of the region is simply **Alsace** AC. The vast majority of wine is labelled by its grape variety. There is an ongoing debate in the region about the importance of the varieties themselves, as opposed to site and *terroir*, in determining style. There is just one permitted red grape, Pinot Noir, which can be good but is often light and insubstantial, needing a good vintage. The white varietals are the fairly neutral Pinot Blanc and Sylvaner (although there are some impressive old-vine examples) and the more aromatic Riesling, Muscat, Pinot Gris (formerly Pinot Gris) and Gewürztraminer. There is some Chasselas producing the odd varietal wine, as well as Auxerrois, but both will generally be used with Sylvaner and Pinot Blanc in generic blends. These are covered by the Alsace AC and are labelled either Edelzwicker or Gentil. An unusual rarity in the higher reaches of the Bas Rhin is the Klevner de Heiligenstein. No wines of real note have been produced from it. Confusingly, Auxerrois is often referred to as Klevner.

The 50 grands crus here were established in 1983. Wines produced from these are classified **Alsace Grand Cru** AC. The majority of these sites can be found in the heart of the Haut Rhin and were created to pinpoint the best vineyards. Much work still needs to be done with the region's labelling system and although there is talk of it, there is no further official classification. Many wines make reference to their *lieux-dits* in order to emphasise potential quality. A number of these sites produce wines that are comfortably a match for many *grands crus*. The vineyards of the latter must be planted to Gewürztraminer, Muscat, Riesling or Pinot Gris. Almost all wines are varietal but there are experiments, particularly those by Jean-Michel Deiss, in establishing field blends.

Some of the region's greatest wines are the late-harvested wines, **Vendange Tardive** (VT) and **Sélection de Grains Nobles** (SGN). Being made from late-harvested grapes, these are generally sweet styles. Noble rot may occur, particularly in the SGNs, but not always. However, the classification is based on grape ripeness at harvest and some Vendange Tardive wines can be surprisingly dry. Indeed the whole question of levels of residual sugar can be confusing. Some producers tend towards a very steely, dry style, while others prefer to let nature take its course, with fermentation stopping naturally. The results in the latter case are wines with often surprising levels of sugar and extract. The best, though, are very well balanced with sometimes remarkable depth. In order to help with this confusion a scale has been established, indicating on the back label the degree of sweetness. The final style is **Crémant d'Alsace** AC. These are made by the traditional method and are mostly produced from Pinot Blanc and Riesling, although Auxerrois, Pinot Noir and Pinot Gris are also permitted. The best examples have reasonable depth and structure, often with marked acidity.

Alsace vintages

The region is sunny and warm and, like many areas of France, governed by a marginal climate. While this is important in the development of great wines, there will inevitably be some vintage variation. Lesser whites should be drunk young and certainly by the time they have had four or five years' ageing. Riesling is better in slightly cooler years, Gewürztraminer and Pinot Gris add dimension in warmer years. The chart below will provide a reliable guide as to to expect. The very best grand cru and late-harvest styles are remarkably ageworthy. Of the great earlier years to consider are 1990, 1989, 1988, 1985, 1983, 1976 and for very top wines 1971.

Alsace vintage chart

	Riesling	Pinot Gris	Gewürz-traminer	Late Harvest
	Grand or Top Cru	Grand or Top Cru	Grand or Top Cru	VT or SGN
2015	★★★ A	★★★☆ A	★★★☆ A	★★★☆ A
2014	★★★★ A	★★★★ A	★★★★ A	★★★A
2013	★★★ A	★★★ A	★★★ A	★★★ A
2012	★★★★ A	★★★★☆ A	★★★ A	★★★★A
2011	★★★★ A	★★★★ A	★★★★ A	★★★★ A
2010	★★★★☆ A	★★★★☆ A	★★★★☆ A	★★★★☆ A
2009	★★★★☆ A	★★★★☆ A	★★★★☆ A	★★★★☆ A
2008	★★★★☆ A	★★★★ B	★★★★ B	★★★★☆ A
2007	★★★★ B	★★★★ B	★★★★ B	★★★★☆ B
2006	★★★☆ B	★★★☆ B	★★★☆ B	★★★★ B
2005	★★★★ B	★★★★ B	★★★★ B	★★★★ B
2004	★★★☆ B	★★★☆ B	★★★☆ B	★★★ B
2003	★★★★ B	★★★★ B	★★★★ B	★★★☆ B
2002	★★★★ C	★★★★☆ C	★★★★☆ C	★★★★ C
2001	★★★★ C	★★★★ C	★★★★ C	★★★★ C
2000	★★★★ C	★★★★ C	★★★★ C	★★★★ C
1999	★★★★ C	★★★☆ C	★★★☆ C	★★★★ C
1998	★★★★☆ C	★★★★ D	★★★★ D	★★★★☆ C
1997	★★★★ D	★★★★☆ D	★★★★☆ D	★★★★☆ D
1996	★★★★☆ D	★★★★☆ D	★★★★ D	★★★★☆ D
1995	★★★★☆ D	★★★★☆ D	★★★★ D	★★★★☆ D

Alsace

France

A-Z of producers

Jean-Baptiste Adam (Ammerschwihr) *www.jb-adam.com*
A long-established Alsace producer, founded in 1614 and now with fifteen generations of the family involved. There are just 15 ha of biodynamic vineyards and certified Demeter. Fruit is also bought in to produce no fewer than 100,000 cases a year, making this one of the larger operations in the region. The generic Tradition and Réserve wines offer reliable drinking the Jean-Baptiste labels a touch more depth, including decent Pinot Noir in warmer years. There is also a small range of fine biodynamic wines labeled Les Natures. The heart of the Adam estate is based on the *lieu-dit* Letzenberg and Grand Cru Kaefferkopf. Letzenberg is just 3 ha of mass-selected Riesling and Pinot Gris grown on mainly clay soils. The top site, the Kaefferkopf, has been cultivated by the Adam family since the early 1800s. Finely drained granite soils produce excellent Riesling and Gewürztraminer as well as the Traditional Kaefferkopf Cuvée, a blend of both varieties. Occasional Vendange Tardive and SGN bottlings are released as well as some sound Crémant d'Alsace Les Natures Brut. (DM)

Recommended Whites:
Gewürztraminer SGN ★★★☆ £F
Gewürztraminer Vendange Tardive ★★★★ £F
Gewürztraminer Kaefferkopf G C V V de J-B Adam ★★★★ £E
Gewürztraminer Les Natures ★★ £C
Riesling Vendange Tardive ★★★☆ £F
Riesling Kaefferkopf G C V V de J-B Adam ★★★★ £E
Riesling Winneck-Sclossberg G C de J-B Adam ★★★ £E
Riesling Letzenberg de Jean-Baptiste Adam ★★ £C
Riesling Les Natures ★★ £C
Pinot Gris Letzenberg de Jean-Baptiste Adam ★★★ £D
Pinot Gris Les Natures ★★ £C Muscat Réserve ★☆ £C
Auxerrois Vieilles Vignes ★★ £C
Crémant d'Alsace Les Natures ★★ £C
Pinot Noir Les Natures ★★ £C

Dom. Lucien Albrecht (Orschwihr) *www.lucien-albrecht.fr*
There are just over 30 ha of vineyards at this property. The regular wines are simple, straightforward and emphasise their varietal character well. The best wines are from Grand Cru Pfingstberg, particularly the special bottlings labelled Cuvée A de Albrecht. Vendange Tardive and SGN can be impressive as well. Top Pinot Gris and Gewürztraminer are quite opulent and reasonably approachable; Riesling is in a tighter, more structured mould – citrusy and intense with some age but relatively austere when young. Prices are very reasonable. (DM)

Recommended Whites:
Gewürztraminer Pfingstberg GC Cuvée A de Albrecht ★★★ £D
Gewürztraminer Cuvée Martine Albrecht ★★★ £C
Riesling Vendange Tardive ★★★☆ E
Riesling Pfingstberg GC Cuvée A de Albrecht ★★★ £D
Pinot Gris Vendange Tardive ★★★★ £F
Pinot Gris GC Pfingstberg ★★★ £D
Muscat Bollenberg ★★ £C

Dom. Jean Becker (Zellenberg) *www.vinsbecker.com*
Fine old family domaine established in 1610, which now has 30 ha of vineyards in the villages of Zellenberg, Riquewihr, Beblenheim and Ribeauvillé. Farming is increasingly moving towards both organic and biodynamic practices. Of these, 4 ha are grand cru and a small amount of fruit is bought in from other growers around

Zellenberg. Among the grands crus, floral, elegant Riesling, Pinot Gris, Muscat and Gewürztraminer come from Froehn. Riesling and Gewürztraminer from the marl soils of Schoenenbourg can produce excellent late-harvest wines. Gewürztraminer is also grown at the Sporen, Sonnenglanz and Praelatenberg sites, while minerally Riesling comes from the Grand Cru Schlossberg. Among the lieux-dits, fresh fruity Riesling comes from Hagenschlauf and Pinot Gris and Gewürztraminer, often produced as Vendange Tardive and occasionally as SGN, from Rimelsberg. Good fruit-driven Pinot Blanc and regular Pinot Gris are produced organically. The style of the wines is traditional but they all show good fruit intensity. The top crus have a fine mineral complexity to them and expect them to age well. (DM)

Recommended Whites:
Gewürztraminer Grand Cru Sonnenglanz SGN ★★★★ £F
Gewürztraminer Vendange Tardive ★★★★ £E
Gewürztraminer Grand Cru Sonnenglanz ★★★☆ £D
Gewürztraminer Grand Cru Froehn ★★★☆ £D
Riesling Grand Cru Schlossburg ★★★ £D
Riesling Grand Cru Froehn ★★★ £D
Riesling Hagenschlauf ★★☆ £C
Pinot Gris Grand Cru Froehn Vendange Tardive ★★★★ £E
Pinot Gris Grand Cru Froehn ★★★☆ £D
Pinot Gris Rimelsberg ★★★ £D Pinot Gris ★★ £C
Muscat Grand Cru Froehn ★★★ £D
Crémant d'Alsace B de Becker ★☆ £C
Pinot Blanc ★☆ £B Gentil ★☆ £B

Recommended Reds:
Rouge F de Zellenberg ★★ £C

Dom. Jean-Marc Bernhard (Katzenthal) *www.jeanmarcbernard.fr*
This family domaine has been running since 1802 at Katzenthal to the west of Colmar in the more southerly reaches of the region. The wines, to some degree, reflect this and are in a full, rich and concentrated style, often with noticeable residual sugar.; the late-harvest wines being very opulent. At the top end they also offer very good value as well. Gewürztraminer is full of classic lychee spice, the Rieslings are firmly structured and with a nice underlying minerality in the Grand Cru bottlings. Perhaps the most exciting of the wines is the Pinot Gris SGN, full of citrus, spice and an alluring toasty quality. The Riesling SGN offers great intensity and a fine underlying mineral structure. There are just over 9 ha planted and an extensive range of wines at all levels are produced. As well as the Rieslings from Winneck Schlossberg and Schlossberg, Pinot Gris comes from the Grand Cru Furstentum and there is a Hinterburg Vendanges Tardives. Grand Crus Kaefferkopf, Florimont and Mambourg are all sources of fine and spicy Gewürztraminer and there are *barrique* bottlings of both Pinot Blanc and Pinot Noir. Expect the top wines to continue to evolve well in bottle for up to a decade. (DM)

Recommended Whites:
Gewürztraminer SGN ★★★★☆ £F
Gewürztraminer Vendange Tardives ★★★★ £E
Gewürztraminer GC Kaefferkopf ★★★☆ £D
Gewürztraminer GC Mambourg ★★★☆ £D
Gewürztraminer GC Florimont ★★★☆ £D
Riesling SGN ★★★★☆ £F
Riesling VT Le Jus de Jules ★★★☆ £E
Riesling GC Winneck Schlossberg ★★★☆ £D
Riesling GC Schlossberg ★★★☆ £D
Pinot Gris SGN ★★★★☆ £F
Pinot Gris Vendange Tardives Elixir d'Elena ★★★★ £E

Pinot Gris GC Kaefferkopf ★★★☆ £D
Muscat d'Alsace Vendange Tardives ★★★★ £D

Domaine Bernhard & Reibel www.domaine-bernhard-reibel.fr
Small to medium-sized producer based in the village of Châtenois
with an output of around 8–9,000 cases a year from 17 ha of
vineyards planted to Riesling, Pinot Gris, Gewürztraminer, Pinot
Blanc and a little Sylvaner planted in well-drained granite soils. The
domaine, is unusually run by mother Cécile and son Pierre. There are
no grand cru vineyards but they have small holdings in the lieux-dits
Weingarten, Hahnenberg and Rittesberg. The Rieslings are the best
bets, very pure with classic varietal character, while the Pinot Gris are
rich and weighty wines that go through malolactic fermentation.
Vendanges Tardives are produced from Riesling, Gewürztraminer
and Pinot Gris. Prices are very reasonable. (DM)
Recommended Whites:
Riesling Weingarten ★★★ £D   Riesling Vieilles Vignes ★★☆ £C
Pinot Gris Hahnenberg ★★★ £D
Pinot GrisTradition ★★ £C   Pinot Blanc ★☆ £B

Léon Beyer (Eguisheim) www.leonbeyer.fr
This is quite a substantial property producing wines from its own
vineyards and also buying in grapes for its négociant wines. Vineyard
holdings include the Grands Crus Eichberg and Pfersigberg but
as at HUGEL no wines are released as such. As one would expect,
the generic bottlings do not set the world on fire but are generally
well crafted and offer a particularly dry, almost austere style. They
will develop well in bottle. Better are the Grandes Cuvées Comtes
d'Eguisheim labels, which are rich and reasonably concentrated.
Riesling Ecaillers and Gewürztraminer Réserve also stand out.
Vendange Tardive Gewürztraminer is good but just lacks some of
the weight one might hope for. Sélection de Grains Nobles from the
same variety is very impressive. The Pinot Gris SGN is remarkable:
structured, rich and very ageworthy and a tiny volume Quintessence
is also made. (DM)
Recommended Whites:
Gewürztraminer SGN ★★★★ £G   Gewürztraminer VT ★★★☆ £E
Gewürztraminer Comtes d'Eguisheim ★★☆ £D
Riesling Comtes d'Eguisheim ★★☆ £D
Riesling Ecaillers ★★ £D   Pinot Gris SGN ★★★★★ £G

⚜ Dom. Paul Blanck (Kientzheim) www.blanck.com
Medium-sized family producer with an output approaching 20,000
cases a year. Quality is generally good to very good across the board
and the wines tend to be made in an opulent, rich vein. Often quite
marked levels of residual sugar can be found in the drier styles.
Generic labels including Riesling and Pinot Blanc are sound but can
be a little simple. Very good is an intense, green apple Sylvaner from
old vines. There are a range of vieilles vignes, grand cru, VT and SGN
bottlings. You can expect almost all grand cru bottles to be at least
★★★. Very good examples are produced from the Grands Crus
Furstentum, Sommerberg and Schlossberg and there are fine wines
produced from other lieux-dits as well. Fine VT is almost invariably
★★★★ and there is an explosively rich and opulent Pinot Gris SGN.
Make sure you get the right address; there is more than one Blanck
in Kientzheim. (DM)
Recommended Whites:
Gewürztraminer Furstentum GC VT ★★★★☆ £F
Gewürztraminer Furstentum GC Vieilles Vignes ★★★★ £E
Riesling Furstentum GC ★★★★ £E
Riesling Schlossberg GC ★★★★ £E

Riesling Patergarten ★★★ £D   Riesling Rosenbourg ★★☆ £C
Pinot Gris SGN ✪✪✪✪ £G
Pinot Gris Furstentum GC ★★★★ £E
Pinot Gris Patergarten ★★★ £D
Pinot Auxerrois ★☆ £C

⚜ Dom. Léon Boesch (Westhalten) www.domaine-boesch.fr
This small family owned domaine is producing wines that now rival
some of the best names in the region. Run by Gérard Boesch, the
family have an impressive holding on the Zinnkoepflé Grand Cru a
source of some exceptional Gewürztraminer, Pinot Gris and Riesling.
The *lieu-dit* of Breitenberg is also an additionally fine resource for
both Gewürztraminer and Riesling. The total vineyard holding is
13 or so ha and an average age now over 25 years aids the quality
and richness of the wines. They are made in a very minimalist way
and this often means leaving a degree or two of residual sugar.
Nature and the indigenous yeast population rule here rather than
man. The Pinot Blanc Klevner is a very good example of its type,
ripe nutty, green apple fruit and impressive structure will ensure
it benefits from a little age. Pinot Gris Tradition is ripe and full, the
Grand Cru Zinnkoepflé opulent but finely structured. Riesling Luss
and Breitenberg Vallée Noble are minerally, citrusy and packed
with youthful green fruits and offer real weight and dimension.
The Gewürztraminer and Pinot Gris Grand Cru Zinnkoepflé both
have real depth with a mineral edge adding further complexity.
The Vendanges Tardive and SGN Gewürztraminer bottlings are
particularly opulent and possess a firm acidity that the variety so
often fails to exhibit. Look for gloriously complex citrus fruit with
undercurrents of apricot, peach and spice. The Grand Cru wines will
age very well. (DM)
Recommended Whites:
Gewürztraminer Zinnkoepflé GC SGN ✪✪✪✪✪ £G
Gewürztraminer Zinnkoepflé GC VT ★★★★★ £F
Gewürztraminer Zinnkoepflé GC ★★★★ £E
Riesling Breitenberg VT ★★★★☆ £F
Riesling Zinnkoepflé GC ★★★☆ £E
Riesling Luss Vallee Noble ★★★☆ £D
Riesling Breitenberg Vallee Noble ★★★☆ £D
Pinot Gris Zinnkoepflé GC ★★★★ £E
Pinot Gris Clos Zwingel ★★★ £D
Pinot GrisTradition ★★☆ £C
Pinot Blanc Klevner ★★ £B
Recommended Reds:
Pinot Noir Tradition ★★ £C

⚜ Dom. Bott-Geyl (Beblenheim) www.bott-geyl.com
Impressive small family domaine that has some 14 ha of estate
vineyards producing close to 8,000 cases a year. The quality is
nearly always very sound right across the range. The style is almost
explosively rich and the wines will often have marked residual sugar.
Harvesting as ripe as possible and letting nature and indigenous
yeasts run their natural course produces such results. Good generic
Pinot d'Alsace Métiss and Pinot Gris, Gewürztraminer as well as
Muscat both under the Éléments brand offer very good value. There
are also considerable grand cru holdings. Gewürztraminer and Pinot
Gris from Grands Crus Furstentum and Sonnenglanz are always
★★★, often better, and also come from the excellent *lieu-dit* of
Schlosselreben. Riesling comes from Mandelberg, Schoenenbourg
and Grafenreben. The Mandelberg tends to be fullest – rich
and weighty with a marvellously pure mineral core. While the
Gewürztraminer VT is quite tight and restrained in style, the Pinot

France

Gris SGN from Sonnenglanz can be explosive, rich and sumptuous but with a marvellous fresh, structured backbone. The top wines will inevitably age extraordinarily well. Most offer very good value. (DM)

Recommended Whites:
Riesling Mandelberg GC ★★★★ £E
Gewürztraminer Sonnenglanz GC VT ★★★★★ £F
Gewürztraminer Sonnenglanz GC Vieilles Vignes ★★★★ £E
Gewürztraminer Furstentum Grand Cru★★★☆ £E
Pinot Gris SGN ❺❺❺❺ £G
Pinot Gris Sonnenglanz GC VT ★★★★★ £F
Pinot Gris Furstentum GC ★★★★ £E
Pinot Gris Éléments ★★★ £C
Muscat Éléments ★★ £C
Pinot d'Alsace Métiss ★☆ £B

Albert Boxler (Niedermorschwihr)

Jean-Marc Boxler's small domaine, nearly 14 ha, produces just over 4,000 cases across a small but well-made range. Generics including Riesling and Pinot Blanc are very good, but Gewürztraminer can occasionally disappoint. Top Gewürztraminer and Pinot Gris comes from the Brand vineyard, Riesling from Brand and Sommerberg. The Rieslings particularly stand out. The style is for very dry, almost austere wines with a restrained, youthful, green-apple and markedly mineral character. Pinot Gris and Gewürztraminer, even at grand cru level, do not have the formidable structure and depth of the Rieslings. They tend more towards a simpler, riper if more opulent style. Riesling VT and SGN can be stunning as can a very impressive Pinot Gris – all are ★★★★, often ★★★★★ or occasionally ❺❺❺❺. The top Rieslings will age magnificently and should not be broached without 6 or 7 years' ageing. (DM)

Recommended Whites:
Riesling Sommerberg GC ★★★★ £E
Riesling Brand GC ★★★☆ £E   Riesling ★★☆ £C
Gewürztraminer Brand GC ★★★☆ £E
Pinot Gris ★★☆ £C   Pinot Blanc ★★ £B

Ernest Burn (Gueberschwihr) www.domaine-burn.fr

This is a very impressive small, traditional domaine with a holding of just 10 ha. The wholly owned *monopole* Clos Saint Imer is part of the Grand Cru Goldert and this accounts for over half the vineyard holdings. A fine Pinot Blanc is joined by some very well-crafted rich and stylish Muscat, Pinot Gris, Gewürztraminer and Riesling. The style of the grand cru wines is for rich, very late-harvested fruit with real density and immense depth. They can almost seem overblown but always retain a fine, structured undercurrent. Riesling can be a touch overwhelmed in this style when the vintage produces very ripe, soft wines and tends to be at its best in the cooler years. Some very fine, sumptuous and honeyed VT is made from Gewürztraminer and Pinot Gris. (DM)

Recommended Whites:
Gewürztraminer Goldert GC Cuvée de la Chapelle ★★★★ £E
Riesling Goldert GC Cuvée de la Chapelle ★★★☆ £E
Pinot Gris Goldert GC Cuvée de la Chapelle ★★★★ £E
Pinot Gris ★★☆ £C
Pinot Blanc ★★ £B

Cave de Cleebourg (Cleebourg) www.cave-cleebourg.com

An extensive range is made at this sizeable co-op established in 1946. There are 192 member growers with a total of 180 ha of vineyard holdings in the extreme north of the Alsace region. The vineyard area was destroyed during the Second World War but has been progressively built up since and some of the plantings are now of considerable age. Some excellent, pure and intense single vineyard Gewürztraminer, Riesling and Pinot Gris are produced as well as good examples of Muscat and Pinot Auxerrois and a clean, fresh Crémant d'Alsace. Vendanges Tardives and SGN are released occasionally. They are sound but do not offer the same value as the other wines. (DM)

Recommended Whites:
Riesling Hannesacker ★★★ £C   Gewürztraminer ★☆ £B
Gewürztraminer Reiffenberg ★★☆ £C
Pinot Gris Vieilles Vignes ★★ £C
Pinot Gris Karchweg ★★ £C
Muscat Sigille ★☆ £B
Pinot Blanc/Auxerrois ★☆ £B
Cremant d'Alsace Symphonie en Clerostein ★☆ £C

✿✿ Marcel Deiss (Bergheim) www.marceldeiss.com

The Deiss family has been producing wines here for well over 50 years. Jean-Michel Deiss is in charge of the property and runs the domaine along biodynamic lines. He is unquestionably now one of the three or four best producers in the entire region. An exemplary range of wines is made from very low yields from a range of sites including grand cru holdings at Altenberg, Mambourg and Schoenenbourg. A very good generic Pinot Blanc is made, as well as a Rouge from Saint-Hippolyte, Pinot Gris, Riesling and Gewürztraminer. The grands crus are very fine. Riesling comes from Altenberg and Schoenenbourg, Gewürztraminer and Pinot Gris from Altenberg. Deiss also produces three remarkable and very rich grands crus from Altenberg, Mambourg and Schoenenbourg that are field blends of the noble varieties. As well as these, there are now a range of blends from a number of sites including Burg, Engelgarten, Grasberg and Gruenspiel. The intention is to increase the complexity of the wines and emphasise their *terroir* rather than their varietal character. The approach throughout is to achieve very ripe fruit and the wines regularly have very marked sugar levels. Occasional super-rich VT and SGN are made. (DM)

Recommended Whites:
Mambourg GC ❺❺❺❺❺ £G   Schonenbourg GC ❺❺❺❺❺ £G
Altenberg GC ❺❺❺❺❺ £G   Gewürztraminer ★★★☆ £D
Pinot Gris ★★★☆ £D   Pinot Blanc ★★★ £C

✿ Dirler-Cadé (Bergholz) www.dirler-cade.com

The Dirlers produce an excellent range of traditionally made wines from all the major Alsace varieties. The property was founded in 1871 and there are some 16 ha of producing vineyards, which since 1998 have been farmed biodynamically. Over 40% of the family holding is grand cru with vines planted in the Saering, Spiegel, Kessler and Kitterlé sites. The Dirlers also have holdings in the lieux-dits Schwarzberg, Bux, Bollenberg, Schimberg and Belzbrunnen. While the wines are traditional in style, dry and tightly structured with a real mineral component running through them, vinification benefits from modern equipment, with temperature control for fermentation in *inox* as well as wood. Muscat in particular is very striking here and the Grand Cru Spiegel bottling is one of the very finest in the appellation. Some truly excellent grand cru Riesling and Gewürztraminer are produced as well as rich and pure VT and an exquisite Gewürztraminer Spiegel SGN. Expect the wines to develop very well in bottle, particularly the top crus. (DM)

Recommended Whites:
Gewürztraminer GC Spiegel SGN ★★★★★ £G
Gewürztraminer GC Kessler Vendanges Tardives ★★★★☆ £E

Gewürztraminer GC Kessler ★★★★ £D
Gewürztraminer GC Spiegel ★★★★ £D
Gewürztraminer Bux ★★★☆ £D
Riesling GC Kessler Vendanges Tardives ★★★★☆ £E
Riesling GC Spiegel ★★★★ £D
Riesling GC Saering ★★★★ £D
Riesling GC Kessler ★★★☆ £D
Pinot Gris Schwarzberg Vendanges Tardives ★★★★☆ £F
Pinot Gris GC Kessler ★★★★ £D
Pinot Gris Reserve ★★★ £C
Muscat GC Spiegel ★★★★ £D   Muscat ★★☆ £C
Sylvaner Vieilles Vignes ★★ £C   Crémant d'Alsace Brut ★★ £C

Fernand Engel (Rorschwihr) *www.fernand-engel.fr*

This third-generation family-run domaine has 41ha of vineyards spread across 150 parcels and and 6 villages. As a result a vast array of soils, subsoils, vineyard sites and mesoclimates make up the varied terroirs of the wines. Output is over 30,000 cases a year although grand cru, late-harvested and selected-grape bottlings account for less than 1,000 cases of this total. The vineyards are cultivated organically and all harvesting is done by hand. The wines are all vinified in stainless steel with temperature control and some micro-oxygenation is used. The regular white Alsace bottlings are labelled Réserves and will have a little residual sugar. The Cuvée Engel wines get a little more ageing on fine lees. The best wines are the Vins de Terroir, including the Clos des Anges bottlings and the late-harvest wines. The Clos des Anges site has deep marly, limey soils with a clay subsoil. The wines have impressive depth and intensity, particularly a steely Riesling and toasty, nutty Pinot Gris. Oak aged Pinot Noir impresses more than most. Of the late-harvest wines, there is a splendid and very concentrated full-blown Muscat SGN and best of all a superbly intense and pure Gewürztraminer SGN. These top whites will age well in bottle. (DM)

Recommended Whites:

Gewürztraminer GC Altenberg de Bergheim VT ★★★★ £E
Gewürztraminer GC Altenberg de Bergheim ★★★☆ £D
Gewürztraminer Clos des Anges ★★☆ £C
Riesling SGN ★★★★ £F
Riesling GC Praelatenberg de Kintzheim ★★★ £C
Riesling Clos des Anges ★★★ £C
Riesling Cuvée Engel ★☆ £B
Pinot Gris SGN ★★★★ £E
Pinot Gris Clos des Anges ★★★☆ £D
Muscat SGN ★★★★ £E   Muscat Vendanges Tardive ★★★ £D
Cremant d'Alsace Brut Chardonnay ★★ £C

Recommended Reds:

Pinot Noir Eleve en Futs de Chene ★★☆ £D
Pinot Noir ★☆ £B

Pierre Frick (Pfaffenheim) *www.pierrefrick.com*

An impressive and diverse range is produced by the Fricks at their biodynamically farmed 12 ha property, which they inevitably harvest solely by hand. In the winery chaptalisation is strictly avoided and fermentation is carried out naturally without interference. Ageing takes place in large cask. The resulting wines often have some degree of residual sugar but are rich, opulent and, crucially, always balanced. There is a range of good generic Cuvées de Création but it is the single-vineyard and grand cru wines which really stand out here. The domaine possesses holdings in the lieux-dits Bergweingarten, Bihl, Carrière, Rot Murlé and Strangenberg as well as Grands Crus Steinert, Vorbourg and Eichberg. Both Vendange

Tardive and SGN wines are released in propitious vintages. All the top wines here will develop very well in bottle. (DM)

Recommended Whites:

Gewürztraminer GC Steinert ★★★★ £E
Riesling GC Vorbourg VT ★★★★ £E
Pinot Gris Rot Murlé ★★★☆ £D
Auxerrois Carriere ★★☆ £C
Sylvaner Bergweingarten Vin Moelleux ★★★ £D

Recommended Reds:

Pinot Noir Rot Murlé ★★★☆ £D

Dom. Paul Ginglinger (Eguisheim) *www.paul-ginglinger.fr*

This ancient domaine dates back to 1636. Paul Ginglinger, who heads the latest generation, now possesses some 12 ha, 1.5 ha being Pinot Noir, although it is his excellent whites that stand out. Decent enough Muscat and a Clevner are released but it is the classic Alsace varieties of Riesling, Gewürztraminer and Pinot Gris that impress most as well as a very good, piercing, finely structured, appley Pinot Blanc. Vinification is strictly non-interventionist and the wines often have a touch of residual sugar. The Rieslings have a penetrating mineral quality and demand cellaring, particularly the grand cru bottlings which come from Eichberg as well as Pfersigberg. Both the Pinot Gris and Gewürztraminer tend towards the opulent, again with that degree of residual sugar often apparent, but the Pinot Gris in particular is also tight and structured when young, with a marked mineral quality. The Gewürztraminer, notably the Pfersigberg, is opulent and classically full of lychee and spice – full, deep and very pure. Expect to age the top wines here for at least 5 or 6 years. (DM)

Recommended Whites:

Gewürztraminer GC Pfersigberg ★★★★ £E
Gewürztraminer Wahlenbourg ★★★ £C
Riesling GC Pfersigberg ★★★☆ £E
Riesling Cuvée Drei Exa ★★★ £C
Pinot Gris GC Eichberg ★★★☆ £E   Pinot Blanc ★★ £B

⚫ Dom. Gresser (Andlau) *www.gresser.fr*

Rémy Gresser produces an exemplary small range of wines, almost exclusively sourced from grand cru and *lieu-dit* sites. The Gresser domaine is one of a number of ancient Alsace properties, dating from 1667, and now has a holding of just over 10 ha. Almost all is white but there is 0.65 ha of Pinot Noir as well. The vineyard is currently being converted to biodynamic farming. Andlau is in the centre of the Bas-Rhin, so is cooler than most areas in the region and as such strongly favours the production of tight, minerally, pure Rieslings of classic structure and dimension. Inevitably they are relatively austere when young. The Grand Cru Kastelberg is notable for its slatey, schistous soils, which encourage late-season ripening. Riesling also comes from the Grand Cru Moenchberg, with warmer years often producing wines of Vendange Tardive ripeness. Gewürztraminer and Pinot Gris will evolve well in bottle for at least 6 or 7 years, the Rieslings often longer. Sylvaner, Pinot Blanc and Muscat are more approachable but still stand out examples for those varieties. (DM)

Recommended Whites:

Riesling GC Moenchberg SGN ★★★★★ £G
Riesling GC Webelsberg SGN ★★★★★ £G
Riesling GC Wiebelsberg Vendange Tardives ★★★★☆ £F
Riesling GC Moenchberg ★★★★ £E
Riesling GC Kastelberg Vieilles Vignes ★★★★ £E
Riesling GC Kastelberg ★★★☆ £E

Alsace

Riesling GC Webelsberg ★★★☆ £E
Riesling Duttenberg ★★★ £C
Gewürztraminer Andlau ★★★☆ £D
Gewürztraminer Duttenberg Vieilles Vignes ★★★☆ £D
Gewürztraminer Kritt ★★★ £C
Pinot Gris Brandhof Vieilles Vignes ★★★☆ £D
Muscat Brandhof ★★★ £C   Sylvaner Duttenberg ★★★ £C
Pinot Blanc Saint-André ★★☆ £B
Pinot Blanc Kritt ★★☆ £B

✿ Hugel et Fils (Riquewihr)   www.hugel.fr

Along with TRIMBACH, this is one of the best-known names in the region. As well as being a substantial merchant operation Hugel also has extensive vineyard holdings – some 127 ha. The top wines here are good to exceptional and are excellent, structured examples of the region. The Tradition and Classic generic wines have improved markedly in recent releases. Gewürztraminer, Pinot Blanc, Riesling and Pinot Gris are very sound with good varietal character and produced in a completely dry style. A number of Estate labels have also recently been released which are sourced from specific parcels around Riquewihr. These will be farmed organically. As well as excellent Riesling, Gewürztraminer is also made. The Jubilee wines and the VT and SGN cuvées are of a very good class. Riesling Jubilee is taut and intense, minerally with great structure; Pinot Gris is powerful with subtle, honeyed notes; the Jubilee Gewürztraminer floral and spicy with classic but youthfully restrained lychee character. These are wines that should be cellared for at least 4 or 5 years as they will continue to develop very well in bottle. VTs are very intense. The style tends towards the drier end of the spectrum but they have remarkable depth. Both Pinot Gris and Riesling SGN are quite splendid wines with remarkable depth and complexity. The Riesling is perhaps the finest, with astonishing toasty, citrus and mineral character. (DM)

Recommended Whites:

Riesling SGN ✪✪✪✪✪ £H   Riesling V T ★★★★★ £F
Riesling Jubilee ★★★☆ £D   Riesling Estate ★★★ £C
Riesling Tradition★★☆ £C   Pinot Gris SGN ✪✪✪✪✪ £H
Pinot Gris Vendange Tardive ★★★★☆ £F
Pinot Gris Jubilee ★★★☆ £D
Pinot Gris Tradition ★★ £C
Gewürztraminer Vendange Tardive ★★★★☆ £F
Gewürztraminer Jubilee ★★★☆ £D
Gewürztraminer Tradition ★★☆ £C
Pinot Blanc Blanc de Blancs Tradition ★★ £B
Muscat Tradition ★☆ £B   Gentil ★ £B

Josmeyer (Wintzenheim)   www.josmeyer.com

A long-established top-quality producer whose origins date back to 1854. Output is sizeable for the region but dwarfed by some of the larger merchant houses. The Meyer family possesses some 31 ha of vineyard which form the base for an extensive collection of 6 small ranges. The Classic labels are straightforward and easy drinking, the Artist Label series a step up, of which the Riesling Kottabe, Pinot Gris Fromenteau and Gewürztraminer Folastries stand out. Muscat, Riesling and Pinot Noir are all produced from the Herrenweg site, the Riesling labelled Dragon. Of particular interest, though, are the prestige selections, which include not only fine, pure Pinot Gris Foundation 1854 and opulent, spice-strewn Gewürztraminer Archenets but also very intense Pinot Blanc Les Lutins. Grand cru holdings include plots on both Brand and Hengst. Vendanges Tardives are produced from Pinot Gris and Riesling, SGN from Pinot

Gris and Gewürztraminer. Particularly rare and unusual is the late-harvest Pinot Blanc Derrière La Chapelle, probably the best example of the variety in the region. All the top wines are very ageworthy. (DM)

Recommended Whites:

Gewürztraminer GC Hengst ★★★★ £F
Gewürztraminer Les Archenets ★★★★ £E
Gewürztraminer Les Folastries ★★★ £D
Pinot Blanc Les Lutins ★★★ £D
Riesling GC Hengst ★★★★ £E
Riesling Le Kottabe ★★ £C
Pinot Gris Foundation 1854 ★★★★ £E
Pinot Gris Le Fromenteau ★★★ £D
Pinot Auxerrois Vieilles Vignes ★★★ £D

André Kientzler (Ribeauvillé)   www.vinskientzler.com

André Kientzler makes a small but very impressive range of wines. They are marked by their purity of fruit and elegant structure at all levels. The top grand cru bottles are very ageworthy and require cellaring. No varieties stand out but the Rieslings, particularly from the Grands Crus Geisberg and Osterberg, are truly profound. On occasion Geisberg produces a Riesling VT and SGN. These are wines of remarkable complexity: the latter is astonishingly rich while the former is very structured, almost dry. You can expect them to be ★★★★, often ★★★★★ or ✪✪✪✪✪. Very good Muscat and Pinot Gris is made from Kirchberg. Gewürztraminer is not grand cru but there are occasional bottles of VT and SGN. Even the lesser Pinot Blanc, Auxerrois and Chasselas offer excellent quality and value. (DM)

Recommended Whites:

Gewürztraminer VT ★★★★ £F   Gewürztraminer ★★☆ £C
Riesling Geisberg GC ★★★★ £E   Riesling ★★★ £C
Pinot Gris Kirchberg GC ★★★★ £E
Pinot Gris ★★☆ £C   Auxerrois ★★ £B
Pinot Blanc ★★ £B   Chasselas★☆ £B

Marc Kreydenweiss (Andlau)   www.kreydenweiss.com

Marc Kreydenweiss's 12 ha domaine is in the north of the region in the Bas Rhin. He produces wines using biodynamic principles in the vineyard. In addition to the Alsace property, Marc and his wife Emmanuelle own the Costières de Nîmes property Domaine des PERRIÈRES (see Languedoc-Roussillon & Provence). The approach at both properties is the same: to achieve elegance and refinement rather than weight and power. The wines here are marked most by their intense fruit purity. Taut and with an almost gripping structure the top wines should be cellared for 6 or 7 years, sometimes more. Marc produces an unusual blend of mainly Riesling and some Pinot Gris labelled Le Clos du Val d'Eléon, which technically is an Edelzwicker but is unlike almost all you're likely to encounter elsewhere. Plots are farmed in a considerable number of sites, both lieux-dits and grands crus. Supreme examples include Pinot Gris from Moenchberg, and Riesling from Kastelberg and Wiebelsberg. Among the great lieux-dits are Gewürztraminer from Kritt and Pinot Gris from both Rebberg and Lerchenberg. Fine Muscat Clos Rebgarten is intense, floral and musky and there is also a most unusual, very impressive Klevner from the Kritt site. Very stylish VT and SGN are produced from Gewürztraminer and VT Riesling comes from Kastelberg. (DM)

Recommended Whites:

Riesling Kastelberg GC ★★★★ £E
Riesling Wiebelsberg GC ★★★☆ £E

Pinot Gris Moenchberg GC ★★★★ £E
Pinot Gris Rebberg ★★★ £D
Pinot Gris Lerchenberg ★★★ £D
Gewürztraminer Kritt ★★★ £D
Le Clos du Val d'Eléon ★★★ £D
Klevner Kritt ★★★ £C

Kuentz-Bas (Husseren-les-Châteaux) www.kuentz-bas.fr
Solidly established old merchant business now owned by Jean-Baptiste ADAM. There are 11 ha of owned vineyards including plots in the Grands Crus Eichberg and Pfersigberg. As well as this a considerable volume of grapes are also bought in. Quality, particularly when contrasted with other négociants, is very good across the board, the best wines being rich, full and long-lived. The style can vary: some bottlings are relatively dry, while others can have a touch of residual sugar. The regular varietal bottlings are labelled Tradition, of which the Pinot Gris stands out. The Collection wines are a step up and made from a number of vineyard sites. The Muscat and Gewürztraminer have impressive depth and substance. A number of organic wines are also released under the Trois Châteaux label and the firm's own sites. A range of first-class wines is produced from the Eichberg and Pfersigberg vineyards. Riesling is minerally and finely structured, Pinot Gris more opulent. Very good Gewürztraminer, Riesling and Pinot Gris Cuvée Caroline Vendange Tardive is produced. Quite exceptional is the rich, fine and intense Cuvée Jérémy Pinot Gris. All the top wines will age well, the late-harvest bottlings for up to a couple of decades. (DM)

Recommended Whites:
Gewürztraminer Cuvée Caroline VT ★★★★ £F
Gewürztraminer GC Pfersigberg Trois Chateaux ★★★☆
Gewürztraminer Collection ★★☆ £C
Gewürztraminer Tradition ★☆ £B
Riesling Cuvée Caroline VT ★★★★☆ £F
Riesling GC Pfersigberg Trois Chateaux ★★★☆ £E
Riesling GC Eichberg Trois Chateaux ★★★☆ £F
Riesling Collection ★★ £C   Riesling Tradition ★☆ £B
Pinot Gris Cuvée Jérémy SGN ★★★★★ £G
Pinot Gris Cuvée Caroline VT ★★★★ £F
Pinot Gris GC Florimont Trois Chateaux ★★★★ £E
Pinot Gris GC Eichberg Trois Chateaux ★★★☆ £E
Pinot Gris Tradition ★☆ £B   Muscat Collection ★★ £B
Pinot Blanc Tradition ★☆ £B

❀ Dom. Seppi Landmann (Soultzmatt) www.seppi-landmann.fr
With vineyard holdings of just 8.5 ha, Seppi Landmann produces a bewildering array of wines of exemplary quality. Good examples are made from lowly varieties such as Sylvaner and Pinot Blanc and a range of Crémant d'Alsace is produced, the Brut Réserve being the top label. Sylvaner Z comes from the Grand Cru Zinnekoepflé like the best of Landmann's wines but this variety is not allowed cru status. The regular wines are labelled Vallée Noble and these range from good to very fine in the case of the Gewürztraminer Vendange Tardive. A number of special selections are released as Hospices de Strasbourg, where the wines are matured. Gewürztraminer, Riesling and Pinot Gris are produced from the Zinnekoepflé site and occasional Vendange Tardive and SGN are released. A real purity and character can be found in all the wines and you can expect the top examples to age very well. (DM)

Recommended Whites:
Gewürztraminer GC Zinnekoepflé SGN ★★★★★ £G
Gewürztraminer GC Zinnekoepflé VT ★★★★★ £F

Gewürztraminer Vallée Noble VT ★★★★ £E
Gewürztraminer GC Zinnekoepflé ★★★★ £E
Gewürztraminer Vallée NobleSigilé ★★★ £C
Riesling GC Zinnekoepflé ★★★☆ £E
Riesling Vallée Noble Sigilé ★★☆ £C
Pinot Gris GC Zinnekoepflé SGN ★★★★★ £G
Pinot Gris GC Zinnekoepflé ★★★★ £E
Pinot Gris Hospices de Strasbourg ★★★ £D
Pinot GrisVallée Noble Sigilé ★★☆ £C
Sylvaner Cuvée Z ★★★☆ £D
Pinot BlancVallée Noble ★★ £B
Cremant d'Alsace Brut Réserve ★★ £C
Cremant d'Alsace Brut de Brut ★☆ £C

Dom. Francois Lichtlé www.domaine-lichtle.com
Hervé Lichtlé has progressively improved quality at this small family domaine at Husseren-les-Châteaux and it is a property to watch. There are currently 6 ha of vineyards spread across 33 separate plots. Sylvaner, Pinot Blanc, Gewürztraminer and Pinot Noir are grown in the *lieu-dit* of Horain and are some of the oldest vines of the property. There is a small holding of Riesling in the Grand Cru Pfersigberg as well as a little Chardonnay which is used in the Crémant d'Alsace. The wines all display pure varietal characters with good depth and intensity, particularly in the Réserve and Vieilles Vignes bottlings. Pinot Gris Leo is rich and pungent, in marked contrast to the fine, minerally, steely Riesling Pfersigberg. Good to very good examples of both Vendange Tardive and SGN are produced from Gewürztraminer and Pinot Gris and there is a fine, elegant and intense Riesling SGN too. Expect the top wines here to develop well in bottle over the medium term. Prices are very reasonable. (DM)

Recommended Whites:
Gewürztraminer Vieilles Vignes ★★★☆ £E
Gewürztraminer Réserve ★★★ £D
Gewürztraminer ★★ £B
Riesling SGN ★★★★☆ £F
Riesling GC Pfersigberg ★★★☆ £E
Riesling ★★ £B   Pinot Gris Cuvée Leo ★★★★ £E
Pinot Gris Réserve ★★☆ £D
Pinot Gris ★★ £B   Pinot Blanc ★☆ £B

Dom. Etienne Loew (Westhoffen) www.domaineloew.fr
A small range of good to very good wines are made at this domaine. Six ha is planted in the vast majority to white varieties, less than half a hectare is Pinot Noir. These are rich almost unctuous wines often with a touch of residual sugar, although an edgy mineral quality and decent acidity is also apparent. The vineyards are in fact in the north of the region, which no doubt contributes to the underlying style. As with so many modern domains in the area some indication of the level of sweetness would undobtedly be of help on the label. Etienne has holdings in the Grand Crus of Altenberg de Bergbieton and Engelberg as well as in a number of lieux-dits, with the wines from Bruderbach being particularly striking. All the wines are excellent value for money and well worth considering. (DM)

Recommended Whites:
Gewürztraminer Grand Cru Altenberg de Bergbieton SGN ★★★★☆ £F
Gewürztraminer Grand Cru Altenberg de Bergbieton ★★★★ £E
Gewürztraminer Ostenberg ★★☆ £C
Gewürztraminer Cormier ★★☆ £C
Gewürztraminer Westhoffen ★★☆ £C
Riesling Grand Cru Altenberg de Bergbieton ★★★☆ £E

Alsace

Riesling Bruderbach Clos des Frères ★★★ £D
Riesling Ostenberg ★★☆ £C
Pinot Gris Bruderbach Clos Marienberg ★★★ £D
Muscate Les Marnes Vertes ★★☆ £C

❀ **Dom. Albert Mann (Wettolsheim)** *www.albertmann.com*
Very fine producer with a bewildering array of wines from 21ha
of vineyards, which are now, like so many others, being tended
organically. The style is for very ripe, full-bodied, traditional wines.
Generics can be very good: Pinot Blanc/Auxerrois is one of the best
in the region. Gewürztraminer at the generic level also impresses.
Rieslings have considerable weight and depth – more so than
most – and they work best in a cooler vintage. The great Grand
Cru Furstentum is a source not only of Riesling but of very rich and
concentrated Gewürztraminer too, full of lychee and spice. Pinot
Gris is very important and there is an excellent regular cuvée from
old vines as well as first-class bottles from Altenbourg, Furstentum
and Hengst. VT can be stunning and both the Grand Cru Hengst
and Furstentum SGNs are remarkable wines, immensely rich and
concentrated with substantial toffee, honey and peach. The style
throughout is rich, opulent, almost extracted and the wines can be
approached quite young, though the top examples age very well
indeed. Prices are very fair. (DM)
Recommended Whites:
Pinot Gris Hengst GC SGN ⚫⚫⚫⚫⚫ £G
Pinot Gris SGN ⚫⚫⚫⚫⚫ £F
Pinot Gris Altenbourg VT ★★★★★ £F
Pinot Gris Hengst GC ★★★★ £E
Pinot Gris Furstentum GC ★★★☆ £E
Pinot Gris Vieilles Vignes ★★★ £C
Gewürztraminer Furstentum GC Vieilles Vignes ★★★★☆ £E
Gewürztraminer Steingrubler GC ★★★★ £E
Gewürztraminer ★★★☆ £C
Riesling Pfleck VT ★★★★ £F
Riesling Furstentum Grand Cru ★★★☆ £E
Riesling Schlossberg GC ★★★☆ £E
Pinot Blanc /Auxerrois Vieilles Vignes ★★☆ £C
Muscat ★★ £B
Recommended Reds:
Pinot Noir Vieilles Vignes ★★☆ £D

❀ **Mittnacht Frères (Hunawihr)**
This excellent domaine based in the village of Hunawihr in the
heart of the region to the north of Colmar is now farmed on 100%
biodynamic lines by cousins Christophe and Marc Mittnacht.
Their small holding totals just over 18 ha and includes Grand Crus
Rosacker, Osterberg and most recently adding vines at Mandelberg
to their holding. Quality is underpinned by holdings at the excellent
lieux-dits of Muehlforst and Clos Wilhelmine. Pinot Blanc/Auxerrois
is one of the better examples from the region. Riesling is steely and
very mineral but offering impressive ripeness too. Pinot Gris and
Gewürztraminer are also rich and concentrated while offering the
same underlying mineral structure. Pinot Noir is considerably more
successful than at many other domaines, particularly the old-vine
bottling, the wines standing out in warmer vintages. Sylvaner
and Muscat are also produced and a Crémant d'Alsace is regularly
released. (DM)
Recommended Whites:
Gewürztraminer 'Procyon'Vendanges Tardives ★★★★☆ £F
Gewürztraminer Rosacker GC ★★★★ £E
Gewürztraminer Osterberg GC ★★★☆ £E

Gewürztraminer ★★☆ £C   Riesling Mandelberg GC ★★★★ £E
Riesling Osterberg GC ★★★★ £E
Riesling Rosacker GC ★★★☆ £E
Riesling Muhlforst ★★★ £D   Riesling ★★☆ £C
Pinot Gris Muhlforst ★★★☆ £D
Pinot Gris ★★☆ £C   Pinot Blanc/Auxerrois ★★ £B
Recommended Reds:
Pinot Noir Vieilles Vignes ★★★ £E
Pinot Noir ★★ £C

René Muré (Rouffach) *www.mure.com*
René Muré's total production is not vast but sizeable for the area.
There are two distinct sides to the operation here. Domaine wines
are labelled Clos Saint-Landelin and produced from 20 ha of estate
vineyards at the Grand Cru Vorbourg and a number of neighbouring
sites. The Muré family solely own the Clos Saint-Landelin vineyard,
a *monopole* within the Vorbourg. The quality and prices of the
wines are substantially above those of the négociant wines under
the René Muré label. These are a range of generics which generally
offer good value along with a decent Crémant d'Alsace. Superior
bottlings of varieties go under the Côte de Rouffach label. Among
the Domaine wines there is impressively steely Sylvaner from the
clos which is full of ripe, green fruits and minerals and one of the
finest examples in the region. Intense, long-lived Riesling comes
from Vorbourg and Clos Saint-Landelin, as does rich, spicy and
opulent Gewürztraminer and Pinot Gris coming from Lutzeltal
as well as the clos. Some better-than-average Pinot Noir is also
produced, plus some very fine Muscat, as both VT and SGN,
along with Riesling, Gewürztraminer and Pinot Gris. Clos Saint-
Landelin is favoured by the regular occurrence of noble rot. The
Gewürztraminer and Pinot Gris are more approachable than the
Rieslings, which really will benefit from 6 or 7 years in bottle. The
generic René Muré labels will be enjoyable on release, the Côte de
Rouffach wines will be better for 2 or 3 years' ageing. (DM)
Domaine du Clos Saint-Landelin
Recommended Whites:
Gewürztraminer Clos Saint Landelin Vorbourg GC VT ★★★★☆ £F
Gewürztraminer Vorbourg GC ★★★☆ £E
Riesling Clos Saint Landelin Vorbourg GC ★★★★ £F
Riesling Vorbourg GC ★★★☆ £E
Pinot Gris Clos Saint Landelin Vorbourg GC ★★★★ £E
Pinot Gris Lutzeltal ★★☆ £D
Sylvaner Cuvée Oscar ★★ £C
Recommended Reds:
Pinot Noir V ★★☆ £D
René Muré
Recommended Whites:
Gewürztraminer Côte de Rouffach ★★☆ £D
Gewürztraminer ★☆ £B   Riesling Côte de Rouffach ★★ £C
Pinot Gris Côte de Rouffach ★★☆ £D
Muscat Côte de Rouffach ★★ £C
Crémant d'Alsace ★★ £C
Recommended Reds:
Pinot Noir Côte de Rouffach ★★ £D

Gérard Neumeyer (Molsheim) *www.gerardneumeyer.fr*
This fine, small Molsheim domaine has 16ha of vineyards and an
output of less than 10,000 cases a year. The vines are all cultivated
organically and the core of the holding is on the Grand Cru
Bruderthal. The regular labels are good and very well crafted with
impressive varietal purity. The Pinot Gris here is particularly good,

both the Coteau de Chartreux and the splendidly structured and intense Bruderthal. Expect the top wines to develop very well with 4–5 years cellaring. As well as the wines rated here it would be well worth looking out for the Vendange Tardive and SGN bottlings of Gewürztraminer. (DM)

Recommended Whites:

Gewürztraminer Bruderthal GC ★★★☆ £E
Gewürztraminer les deux M ★★☆ £C
Pinot Gris Bruderthal GC ★★★★ £E
Pinot Gris Coteau des Chartreux ★★★ £C
Riesling Bruderthal GC ★★★☆ £D
Pinot Blanc la Tulipe ★★☆ £B

❂ Ostertag (Epfig) *www.domaine-ostertag.fr*

For more than 10 years André Ostertag has taken a radical approach to winemaking in the region. The vineyards are now farmed biodynamically but of greater significance has been the creation of wines that are given *barrique* treatment, including Pinot Blanc, Pinot Gris and Pinot Noir. Some of his experiments have brought him into open conflict with the appellation bureaucrats in the past. The generic labels he classifies as *vins du fruit*, the lieux-dits as *vins de pierre*, grands crus as *vins du terroir*, and his late-harvest bottlings are *vins du temps*. In general the oak-handled wines work well. He also makes very good Rieslings with no recourse to wood, most notably from the Grand Cru Muenchberg, and some very fine Gewürztraminer. Ostertag favours producing a dry style but the Gewürztraminer will often have a touch of residual sugar for balance. Sylvaner from very old vines is arguably the best example in the region. Top wines are not only very ageworthy but require 5 or 6 years' cellaring at a minimum. (DM)

Recommended Whites:

Gewürztraminer Fronholz VT ★★★★☆ £F
Gewürztraminer d'Epfig ★★★☆ £D
Riesling Muenchberg GC VT ★★★★☆ £F
Riesling Muenchberg GC ★★★★ £E   Riesling Fronholz ★★★ £D
Pinot Gris Muenchberg GC ★★★★ £F
Pinot Gris Zellberg ★★★☆ £E
Pinot Gris Barriques ★★☆ £C
Sylvaner Vieilles Vignes ★★☆ £C
Pinot Blanc Barriques ★★ £C

Cave de Ribeauvillé (Ribeauvillé) *www.cave-ribeauville.com*

Founded in 1895, this is the oldest wine co-operative in France. Its 110 members provide up to 265 ha of vineyards and output is sizeable for the region at upwards of 200,000 cases a year. As well as a good range of generic varietal wines the Ribeauville co-op has just released a series of exciting bio-dynamically producers wines which are quality benchmarks for large producers throughout the region. An extensive range of well-priced grand cru wines is available: Gewürztraminer comes from Gloekelberg and Osterberg, Pinot Gris from Gloekelberg and Riesling from Altenberg de Bergheim, Kirchberg, Osterberg and Rosacker. A range of wines is also released under the Collection d'Artistes label which supports local arts and culture, notably for blind people. The wines will develop well in the short to medium term, the grand cru labels keeping longer. (DM)

Recommended Whites:

Gewürztraminer Collection d'Artistes ★★ £C
Gewürztraminer ★★ £C
Riesling Mühlforst ★★★ £C
Riesling Collection d'Artistes ★★☆ £C
Riesling ★★ £C   Pinot Gris Schoffweg ★★★ £C

Tokay Pinot Collection d'Artistes ★★☆ £C
Pinot Gris ★★ £C
Pinot Blanc Old Vines ★★ £B
Pinot Blanc Collection d'Artistes ★★ £B

Dom. Rieflé (Pfaffenheim) *www.riefle.com*

The Rieflé estate has been handed down from father to son since the 15th century and Jean-Claude Rieflé is currently at the helm. The dry meso-climate of the family's vineyards helps to increase the concentration of fruit without making the wines too alcoholic. The generic bottlings represent good value for money, whilst the special cuvées and single-vineyard wines show just how high a standard can be attained without going overboard on price. Pinot Gris has powerful fruit aromas reflected in intense autumnal flavours. The Gewürztraminer eschews the lychee for a touch of tamarind and is spicy and refreshing. The late-harvest wines are only made in exceptional years. (NB)

Late harvest range

Recommended Whites:

Gewürztraminer SGN ★★★★ £F
Gewürztraminer VT ★★★★ £F
Pinot Gris SGN ★★★★☆ £F
Pinot Gris Vendange Tardive ★★★★☆ £F

Grand Cru Steinert

Recommended Whites:

Gewürztraminer ★★★ £E   Riesling ★★★ £E
Pinot Gris ★★★☆ £E

Côtes du Rouffach range

Recommended Whites:

Gewürztraminer Côtes du Rouffach ★★★☆ £D
Riesling Côtes du Rouffach ★★★ £D
Pinot Gris Côtes du Rouffach ★★★☆ £D
Muscat Côtes du Rouffach ★★★ £D

Generic range

Recommended Whites:

Gewürztraminer ★★ £C   Riesling ★★ £C
Pinot Gris ★★ £C   Muscat ★★ £B   Pinot Blanc ★★ £B
Silvaner ★ £B   Cremant d'Alsace ★★ £C

Rolly-Gassmann (Rorschwihr)

An extensive range of very good, traditionally produced wines emerges from this family domaine. There are a number of wines from some excellent lieux dits. As well as the varietal and vineyard-labelled wines, including a good Edelzwicker, there are some particularly fine Vendange Tardive and SGN bottlings. The Muscat, Pinot Gris and Gewürztraminer are marked by pungent and concentrated varietal character. Riesling is intense and lightly mineral in style but with a piercing citrus character regularly showing through. The top wines need some cellaring to show at their best. Release dates can be confusing with a number of bottlings held back in the cellar and released with several years' age. This is however a rare source for purchasing top wines approaching their peak and as a result prices tend to reflect this. (DM)

Recommended Whites:

Gewürztraminer SGN ★★★★☆ £F
Riesling Kappelweg VT ★★★★ £F
Riesling Kappelweg ★★★☆ £E
Riesling Pflaenzereben ★★★☆ £E
Riesling Réserve ★★★ £D   Pinot Gris ★★☆ £C
Muscat Moenchreben VT ★★★★ £F

Alsace

France

Muscat Moenchreben ★★★ £D
Pinot Blanc Auxerrois Moenchreben ★★ £C

Dom. Schlumberger (Guebviller) *www.domaines-schlumberger.com*
This is the largest domaine in the region in terms of vineyard holdings, which at some 140 ha rival some of the larger co-ops. Of particular significant are the terroirs of the various plots spread across a 5km stretch of the southern Vosges. The vineyards are planted in sandstone at an altitude of 250–380m with a south-easterly aspect. Amongst the plots are holdings in the Grands Crus Kitterle, Kessler, Saering and Spiegel. Rich, perfumed and opulent Gewürztraminer and Pinot Gris from these sites are especially good. Riesling tends to impress less in this southerly location and among the regular Les Princes Abbés labels it is the Gewürztraminer which stands out. Some very fine late-harvest wines are also produced. In addition to the Cuvée Christine Vendange Tardive Gewürztraminer, SGNs Cuvée Anne (Gewürztraminer), Cuvée Clarisse (Pinot Gris) and Cuvée Ernest (Riesling) are also produced in exceptional vintages, generally only once or twice a decade. The top wines are firmly structured and require at least 5 or 6 years' cellaring. (DM)
Recommended Whites:
Gewürztraminer Cuvée Christine VT ★★★★ £F
Gewürztraminer GC Kitterelé ★★★★ £E
Gewürztraminer GC Kessler ★★★☆ £E
Gewürztraminer GC Saering ★★★☆ £E
Gewürztraminer Les Princes Abbés ★★★ £C
Riesling GC Saering ★★★ £D
Riesling GC Kitterelé ★★☆ £E
Riesling Les Princes Abbés ★☆ £C
Pinot Gris Cuvée Clarisse SGN ★★★★★ £F
Pinot Gris GC Spiegel ★★★ £E
Pinot Gris GC Kitterelé ★★★ £E
Pinot Gris Les Princes Abbés ★☆ £C

✿ Dom. Schoffit (Colmar)
There are some 16 ha planted at this brilliant domaine based in Colmar, with production now running at around 8,000 cases a year. The regular bottlings are all very good. Pinot Blanc and particularly the humble Chasselas produced from venerable vines really stand out. A significant part of the Schoffits' vineyard holding is in lesser sites but quality is still admirable. The focal point of the domaine, though, is the fine volcanic soil of the Clos Saint-Théobald in the Grand Cru Rangen, which yields wines that are structured but with a remarkable array of exotic fruit aromas and always a pure mineral undercurrent. VT and SGN are very fine to exceptional. Given the extraordinary quality, the entire range represents excellent value for money. (DM)
Recommended Whites:
Gewürztraminer Clos Saint-Théobald Rangen GC VT ★★★★★ £G
Gewürztraminer Clos Saint-Théobald Rangen GC ★★★★ £E
Gewürztraminer Harth Cuvée Alexandre Vieilles Vignes ★★★☆ £D
Riesling Clos Saint-Théobald Rangen GC VT ❁❁❁❁❁ £G
Riesling Clos Saint-Théobald Rangen GC ★★★★ £E
Riesling Harth Cuvée Alexandre ★★★ £D
Pinot Gris Clos Saint-Théobald Rangen GC SGN ❁❁❁❁❁ £G
Pinot Gris Clos Saint-Théobald Rangen GC ★★★★★ £E
Pinot Gris Cuvée Alexandre Vieilles Vignes ★★★☆ £D
Chasselas Vieilles Vignes ★★★☆ £C
Pinot Blanc Vieilles Vignes ★★☆ £C
Muscat Tradition ★★ £C

✿ Dom. Bruno Sorg (Eguisheim) *www.domaine-bruno-sorg.com*
Very fine small grower, based just to the south of Colmar with 10 ha of well sited vineyards which include holdings in the Grands Crus Eichberg, Florimont and Pfersigberg. François Sorg is one of the best producers of Muscat in Alsace. The wines are always pure, musky and complex and the dry Pfersigberg is a benchmark example. Riesling is steely and minerally with a real intensity, particularly the finely structured and very ageworthy Vieilles Vignes. Pinot Gris and Gewürztraminer are richly textured and opulent, the latter full of concentrated lychee and tropical spices, but the wines always have great varietal purity and are impeccably balanced. Some very fine to exceptional Vendanges Tardives and SGN are also produced. The regular and old-vine bottlings will drink well with 2 or 3 years' age but will keep very well. It's best to leave the grands crus for 5 or 6 years, particularly the Rieslings. (DM)
Recommended Whites:
Gewürztraminer Vendanges Tardives ★★★★☆ £F
Gewürztraminer GC Eichberg ★★★★ £E
Gewürztraminer GC Pfersigberg ★★★★ £D
Gewürztraminer Vieilles Vignes ★★★☆ £D
Riesling GC Pfersigberg Vieilles Vignes ★★★★ £E
Riesling GC Pfersigberg ★★★☆ £D   Riesling ★★☆ £C
Pinot Gris GC Florimont ★★★★ £E
Pinot Gris Vieilles Vignes ★★★☆ £D   Pinot Gris ★★☆ £C
Muscat GC Pfersigberg ★★★ £D
Muscat ★★ £C

Dom. Vincent Stoeffler (Barr) *www.vins-stoeffler.com*
This ever improving small domaine has vineyard holdings not only around the village of Barr but also to the south in the heart of the region around Ribeauvillé. The 13 ha are now farmed organically. The key gem is the holding on the Grand Cru Kirchberg de Barr. Lieux-dits at Kronenbourg and Rotenberg are also important. Very good AC Alsace wines come from a range of sites and terroirs including vines planted in both limestone and granite soils. Vinification is traditional and the whites are aged in large *foudres*, while the ripe and gamey Pinot Noir Rotenberg is aged in *barriques*. All the wines impress although the Grand Crus are of a different order. Tight, structured and very mineral, the brilliant Gewürztraminer Kirchberg de Barr SGN is ripe and opulent with intense citrus and spicy fruit and subtle underlying botrytis. A brilliant persistent mineral acidity adds intensity and real depth. Expect the top wines to keep very well. (DM)
Recommended Whites:
Gewürztraminer GC Kirchberg de Barr SGN ★★★★★ £F
Riesling GC Kirchberg de Barr ★★★★ £E
Riesling Kronenbourg ★★★☆ £D
Pinot Gris Vendanges Tardives ★★★★ £E
Pinot Gris ★★☆ £C
Recommended Reds:
Pinot Noir Rotenberg ★★★ £D

✿ Dom. Marc Tempé (Zellenberg) *www.marctempe.fr*
In recent vintages Marc Tempé has emerged as one of the new stars of the region. He has a reasonable holding on the Maimbourg Grand Cru and the Zellenberg and Rodelsberg sites are also important sources for him. That latter is a *lieu-dit* from which he produces an excellent field blend of Gewürztraminer and Pinot Gris. Alliance is his entry-level field blend from a range of grapes. His is also one of the best examples of Auxerrois in the appellation, firm, structured and intense it shows lots of old vine complexity. Riesling is steely

and minerally with real depth. Look out also for bottlings from Saint-Hippolyte and Zellenberg as well as of course Maimbourg. The two Gewürztraminers from this vineyard are truly great with excellent varietal character and purity. The Grand Cru offering is a wine of superb concentration and opulence. The SGN is rich and sweet but with great definition and a piercing minerality. Pinot Gris from Rodelsberg as well as Pinot Blanc from Priegel and Zellenberg should also be considered. (DM)

Recommended Whites:

Gewürztraminer Maimbourg GC SGN ✪✪✪✪✪ £G
Gewürztraminer Maimbourg GC ★★★★☆ £F
Gewürztraminer Zellenberg ★★★★ £E
Riesling Burgreben ★★★★ £E
Pinot Gris Zellenberg ★★★★ £E
Auxerrois Vieille Vignes ★★★ £E
Rodelsberg ★★★☆ £D   Alliance ★★☆ £C

>> Dom. Trapet Alsace (Riquewhir) *www.domaine-trapet.fr*
Jean-Louis Trapet and his wife Andrée are best known for their domaine in Gevrey-Chambertin. However they make a small range of very fine wines in Alsace where, like in Burgundy they follow biodynamic farming processes. To look after two properties with this kind of dedicated farming is no easy task. They have a small Grand Cru holding of just over 2 ha in Schoenenourg, Schlossberg, Sporen and Sonnenglanz. The other varietal wines are labelled after the villages of Beblenheim and Riquewihr. The style is elegant and refined, Gewürztraminer is perfumed rather than overwhelmed with lychee fruit aromas. The Rieslings are floral and characterful. The Schlossberg Grand Cru has intensity and a fine steely minerality. The Trapet Ox should not be overlooked either. It is a very well-priced Auxerrois with persistent and rich green fruit qualities. (DM)

Recommended Whites:

Gewürztraminer Beblenheim ★★★☆ £C
Riesling Schlossberg ★★★★ £E   Riesling Beblenheim ★★★☆ £C
Riesling Riquewihr ★★★☆ £C   Trapet Ox ★★☆ £B

✿ Trimbach (Ribeauvillé) *www.maison-trimbach.fr*
Large well-established merchant house producing close to 100,000 cases a year. As at HUGEL, the top wines are very impressive, although perhaps of not quite the same dimension. This is with the exception of the remarkable Riesling Clos Sainte-Hune, arguably the greatest dry expression of the variety in the region and one of the greatest anywhere in the world. Indeed, the Rieslings are the most successful of the varietals. They are structured, very dry in style and have a pure and intense mineral depth. They age remarkably well. The Gewürztraminer Seigneurs de Ribeaupierre is in a similarly dry, structured style. Rich, aromatic, lychee notes and an increasingly honeyed character will emerge with 5 or 6 years' cellaring. VT and SGN bottlings are certainly impressive. They are structured and rich, just a little way short of the very best. The generics are less exciting than many equivalents you may find from smaller domaines and the prices for these are quite steep. (DM)

Recommended Whites:

Gewürztraminer VT ★★★★☆ £F
Gewürztraminer Seigneurs de Ribeaupierre ★★★☆ £E
Gewürztraminer ★★ £C
Riesling Clos Sainte-Hune ✪✪✪✪✪ £H
Riesling Cuvée Frédéric Émile ★★★★☆ £F
Riesling Réserve ★★★ £C   Riesling ★★ £C
Pinot Gris SGN ★★★★☆ £G
Pinot Gris Réserve Personnelle ★★★☆ £E

Pinot Gris Réserve ★★☆ £C   Muscat Réserve ★★☆ £C

Cave de Turckheim (Turckheim) *www.cave-turckheim.com*
This is another fine co-op in a region that features an impressive number of such quality-conscious operations. Turckheim's co-op is one of the more recently established, dating from 1956. The Cave can call on 310 ha of vineyards owned by its members and output is sizeable, approaching 300,000 cases annually. There are some sound generic wines under the Tradition label, in particular Gewürztraminer and Pinot Gris. The Réserves are a step up. The best part of the operation is a solid range of single-vineyard and grand cru wines along with some excellent Vendange Tardive bottlings, particularly the Gewürztraminer. Both Pinot Gris and Gewürztraminer from the great Hengst and Brand sites stand out. Gewürztraminer is opulent and spicy with real depth, the Hengst offering a subtle extra dimension, while Pinot Gris is rich and honeyed with a fine mineral structure. Riesling tends to pale by comparison and lacks the depth and intensity of the other varieties. The Brand bottling is sound but you feel there should be more. Top Pinot Gris and Gewürztraminer will develop very well in bottle. (DM)

Recommended Whites:

Gewürztraminer VT ★★★★☆ £F
Gewürztraminer GC Hengst ★★★★ £E
Gewürztraminer GC Brand ★★★☆ £E
Gewürztraminer Reserve ★★★☆ £C
Gewürztraminer Tradition ★☆ £B   Riesling GC Brand ★★☆ £E
Pinot Gris VT ★★★★ £F   Pinot Gris GC Hengst ★★★☆ £E
Pinot Gris Reserve ★★☆ £C
Pinot Gris Tradition ★☆ £B
Cremant d'Alsace Mayerling ★☆ £C

✿✿ Dom. Weinbach (Kaysersberg) *www.domaineweinbach.com*
Weinbach is one of the great names of Alsace. The Faller family run an impressive 26 ha estate partly converted to biodynamic cultivation since 1998. The wines are rich, powerful and complex, particularly concentrated and impressive in the top cuvées, and they are rarely disappointing. The richest styles can be magnificent. The most important holdings are those of the 5 ha walled Clos des Capucins and 10 ha in the Grand Cru Schlossberg, but outstanding wines are also made from *lieu-dit* Altenbourg. The number of bottlings is extensive and somewhat complicated with special cuvées named after family members. Cuvée Theo Gewürztraminer and Riesling come only from the Clos. Cuvée Sainte-Catherine is a rich Riesling from the lower part of Schlossberg, usually harvested in late November, but a more select bottling is additionally labelled Grand Cru Schlossberg while L'Inédit represents the very best selection of this vineyard. Regular Cuvée Laurence Pinot Gris and Gewürztraminer comes from the foot of Altenbourg, while those additionally labelled Altenbourg come from the vineyard itself. A small amount of Gewürztraminer also comes from the Grand Cru Furstentum. VT and SGN styles add more sweetness to the usual Weinbach concentration and depth whilst retaining good balance. Cuvée d'Or Quintessence SGN is reserved for formidable rich and sweet cuvées made when conditions allow it, such as an intensely sweet and spicy botrytised Gewürztraminer. A scented, stylish Muscat Réserve is also very good if drunk fairly young. (DM)

Recommended Whites:

Gewürztraminer Cuvée d'Or Quintessence SGN ✪✪✪✪✪ £H
Gewürztraminer Furstentum VT ✪✪✪✪✪ £F
Gewürztraminer Altenbourg Cuvée Laurence ★★★★☆ £F
Gewürztraminer Cuvée Theo ★★★☆ £E

Alsace

Riesling Schlossberg GC VT ★★★★★ £G
Riesling Schlossberg GC Cuvée Sainte-Catherine l'Inédit ★★★★★ £F
Riesling Schlossberg GC Cuvée Sainte-Catherine ★★★★★ £F
Riesling Cuvée Theo ★★★☆ £E
Pinot Gris Cuvée Sainte-Catherine ★★★★☆ £E
Muscat Réserve ★★★ £D   Pinot Blanc Réserve ★★★ £D

✪✪ Dom. Zind-Humbrecht (Turckheim) *www.zind-humbrecht.fr*
It is very easy to eulogise both the wines and the winemaking ethos of Olivier Humbrecht. The family's 40ha of vineyards cultivated by Olivier's father Léonard (and biodynamic since 1997) offer an enviable resource from which individual terroirs have been given expression. In fact, from a combination of several different grape varieties and many excellent sites, one of France's, indeed the world's great white wine producers has created a miniature vinous wonderland. More than 30 wines are produced in every vintage – multiply that by the different vintage permutations that a non-interventionist winemaking approach emphasises and you might not ever find time to drink anything else. The wines, made only from fully ripe grapes, are full, concentrated and intense, each expressing something of the essence of their origins. A number of Zind-Humbrecht's crus are also produced in late-harvested styles and although even regular versions can vary in the degree of residual sugar there is almost always the necessary balance between sweetness and acidity. If the range and variable levels of sweetness can make it difficult to choose an individual bottle, a scale of sweetness on each label between Indice 1 and 5 (1 being dry) will help make it less bewildering. Some of the very dry styles can seem almost extreme with a deep colour, underlying acidity and not inconsiderable alcohol sometimes over 15%. Highlights include a fascinating array of fine Riesling: Clos Saint-Urbain combines breadth and a fine minerality; Brand has great structure and power that unfurls slowly with age and the late-harvested examples are of stunning qualty. Clos Windsbuhl shows an intense fruit depth; while Clos Hauserer can be more classically crisp and stimulating. Fine Pinot Gris include a very rich, creamy Vieilles Vignes example, potent Rotenberg, vibrant and deeply fruity Clos Windsbuhl and the smoky, minerally and at times almost austerely dry but exhilarating Clos Saint-Urbain, all of which are surpassed by the Clos Jebsal for sheer richness and substance, the VT being one of the greatest examples of the variety in the region. Impressively rich and aromatic Gewürztraminers include fine, minerally Wintzerheim, broad and powerful Herrenweg, rich, almost overwhelming Heimbourg, exotic Goldert and marvelously deep and concentrated Clos Windsbuhl. Perhaps the best comes from the great Hengst vineyard. There is also a very small amount of Grand Cru Rangen Clos Saint-Urbain. Fine Muscat is also made, both deeply grapey Herrenweg and a more expressive, floral Goldert. Muscat excepted, almost all the wines need a decent amount of bottle-age to show at their best. Regular bottlings should have at least 2 or 3 years' ageing; most lieu-dits or grands crus (whether in regular versions or either VT or SGN styles) deserve at least 5 or 6 years and the wines will keep very well indeed. Recently added is a Vin de France Zind which is an interesting and unusual blend of Chardonnay and Auxerrois. The list below includes most but not all of the extensive range. (DM)
Recommended Whites:
Gewürztraminer Hengst GC VT ✪✪✪✪✪ £G
Gewürztraminer Goldert GC VT ★★★★★ £F
Gewürztraminer Hengst GC ★★★★★ £F
Gewürztraminer Clos Windsbuhl ★★★★★ £F
Gewürztraminer Goldert GC ★★★★ £F

Gewürztraminer Heimbourg ★★★★ £E
Gewürztraminer Herrenweg ★★★☆ £E
Gewürztraminer Wintzenheim ★★★☆ £D
Riesling Brand GC SGN ✪✪✪✪✪ £H
Riesling Brand GC VT ✪✪✪✪✪ £G
Riesling Brand GC ✪✪✪✪✪ £G
Riesling Rangen de Thann GC Clos Saint-Urbain ✪✪✪✪✪ £G
Riesling Clos Windsbuhl ★★★★ £F
Riesling Clos Hauserer ★★★★ £E
Riesling Heimbourg ★★★★ £E   Riesling Turckheim ★★ £C
Pinot Gris Clos Jebsal VT ✪✪✪✪✪ £F
Pinot Gris Rangen de Thann GC Clos Saint-Urbain ★★★★★ £F
Pinot Gris Clos Windsbuhl ★★★★★ £F
Pinot Gris Clos Jebsal ★★★★☆ £F
Pinot Gris Heimbourg ★★★★ £F
Pinot Gris Rotenberg ★★★★ £F
Pinot Gris Vieilles Vignes ★★★☆ £E
Muscat Goldert GC ★★★★ £E   Muscat Herrenweg ★★★☆ £D
Pinot d'Alsace ★★☆ £C   Vin de France Zind ★★★ £C

Other wines of note

Allimant-Laugner
Recommended Whites: Muscat ★ £B   Riesling ★★ £B
Gewürztraminer ★★ £B
Dom. Auther
Recommended Whites: Muscat ★ £B   Riesling ★★ £C
Riesling GC Winzerberg ★★★ £D
Dom. Barmes-Buecher
Recommended Whites: Gewürztraminer Wintzenheim ★★ £D
Gewürztraminer GC Hengst ★★★ £E
Jean-Pierre Bechtold
Recommended Whites: Gewürztraminer Silberberg ★★☆ £D
Riesling Engelberg GC ★★★ £D
Joseph & Christian Binner
Recommended Whites: Gewürztraminer Beatrice ★★★☆ £D
Gewürztraminer Kaefferkopff ★★★ £D
Gewürztraminer VT ★★★ £E   Pinot Gris VT ★★★ £E
Riesling De Katzenthal ★★☆ £C
Dom. François Braun
Recommended Whites: Riesling GC Pfingtsberg ★★★ £D
Dopff & Irion
Recommended Whites: Pinot Gris Maquisards ★☆ £C
Pinot Gris Vorbourg GC ★★☆ £D
Dopff Au Moulin
Recommended Whites: Gewürztraminer Brand GC ★★ £D
Dom. Jean-Marie Haag
Recommended Whites: Pinot Gris Vallee Noble ★★ £C
Cave de Hunawihr
Recommended Whites: Muscat Réserve ★ £B
Gewürztraminer Rosacker GC ★★ £C
Riesling Rosacker GC ★★ £C   Pinot Gris Réserve ★★ £B
Pinot Gris Rosacker GC ★★★ £D
Dom. Roger Jung
Recommended Whites: Riesling Vieilles Vignes ★★ £C
Riesling Schoenenbourg GC ★★★☆ £C
Pinot Gris Schoenenbourg GC ★★★☆ £D
Dom. Clement Klur
Recommended Whites: Cremant d'Alsace ★ £B
Pinot Blanc Grain D'or ★☆ £B   Pinot Gris Vieilles Vignes ★★☆ £C
Riesling Sommerberg GC ★★★ £D

Gewürztraminer Sclossberg GC ★★★ £D
Jean-Luc Mader
Recommended Whites: Pinot Blanc ★ £B
Gewürztraminer ★★ £C
Gewürztraminer Rosacker GC ★★★ £D
Pinot Gris ★★ £C   Riesling ★★ £B
Dom. Jean-Louis & Fabienne Mann
Recommended Whites: Sylvaner Vieilles Vignes ★ £B
Gewürztraminer Steinweg ★★★ £C
Gewürztraminer Pfersigberg GC ★★★ £D
Dom. des Marronniers
Recommended Whites: Riesling Moenchberg GC ★★★ £D
Riesling Kastelberg GC ★★★ £D
Dom. Materne-Haegelin
Recommended Whites: Gewürztraminer★☆ £B
Riesling Bollenberg ★★ £C
Jean-Luc Meyer
Recommended Whites: Edelzwicker ★ £B   Pinot Blanc ★ £B
Gewürztraminer Vieilles Vignes ★★★ £C
Meyer-Fonné
Recommended Whites: Riesling Katzenthal ★★ £C
Riesling Winneck-Schlossberg GC ★★★ £D
Gewürztraminer Winneck-Schlossberg GC ★★★ £D
Dom. Mittnacht-Klack
Recommended Whites: Riesling Muhlforst ★★☆ £C
Riesling Schoenenbourg GC ★★★ £D
Gewürztraminer Schoenenbourg GC ★★★ £D
Cave de Pfaffenheim
Recommended Whites: Riesling Goldert GC ★★ £C
Riesling Zinnkoepflé GC ★★ £C
Domaine Martin Schaetzel
Recommended Whites: Pinot Blanc Réserve ★★ £B
Riesling Réserve ★★ £C   Riesling Ammerschwihr ★★★ £C
Riesling Kaefferkopf Nicolas ★★★★ £D
Pinot Gris Réserve ★★ £C
Pinot Gris Oberberg ★★★☆ £C
Gewürztraminer Kaefferkopf Cathérine ★★★☆ £D
André Scherer
Recommended Whites: Riesling Pfersigberg GC ★★★ £D
Dom. Charles Schleret
Recommended Whites: Sylvaner ★☆ £B
Riesling Herrenweg ★★★☆ £C
Pinot Gris Herrenweg ★★★☆ £C
Roland Schmitt
Recommended Whites:
Riesling Altenberg De Bergheim Gc Roland ★★★ £C
Gérard Schueller
Recommended Whites: Muscat Reserve ★★ £B
Pinot Gris Reserve ★★ £C
Dom. Jean Sipp
Recommended Whites: Gewürztraminer Vieilles Vignes ★★★ £C
Pinot Gris Trottacker ★★☆ £C
Louis Sipp
Recommended Whites: Gewürztraminer GC Osterberg ★★★ £C
Pinot Gris Réserve Personelle ★★☆ £C
Pierre Sparr
Recommended Whites: Gewürztraminer Gc Mambourg ★★ £C
Pinot Gris Réserve ★★ £C
Dom. Sylvie Spielmann
Recommended Whites:
Gewürztraminer Blosenberg Bergheim ★★ £C

Gewürztraminer GC Altenberg De Bergheim ★★★ £D
Paul Zinck
Recommended Whites: Riesling Prestige ★★ £B
Riesling Rangen GC ★★★ £C
Pinot Gris Prestige ★★ £C
Gewürztraminer Prestige ★★ £C
Gewürztraminer Eichberg GC ★★★ £D
Valentin Zusslin
Recommended Whites: Riesling GC Pfingstberg ★★★ £D
Riesling Clos Liebenberg ★★★ £D
Pinot Gris Clos Liebenberg ★★★ £D
Gewürztraminer Bollenberg La Chapelle ★★★☆ £D
Recommended Reds: Pinot Noir Bollenberg Harmonie ★★☆ £C

Work in progress!!

Producers under consideration for the next edition
Laurent Barthe
Agathe Bursin
Frédéric Geschickt
Christian & Véronique Hebinger
Dom. Pierre Hering
Robert Faller
Huber & Bléger
Dom. Otter
Dom. Lucas & André Rieffel
Dom. Eric Rominger
Ziegler-Mauler

Author's choice

12 Alsace value whites
Dom. Bott-Geyl   Muscat Riquewihr
Ernest Burn   Pinot Blanc
Dirler-Cadé   Riesling Saering GC
Marc Kreydenweiss   Klevner Kritt
Dom. Albert Mann   Pinot Blanc/Auxerrois Vieilles Vignes
Ostertag   Sylvaner Vieilles Vignes
Dom. Rieflé   Gewürztraminer Côtes du Rouffach
Dom. Schoffit   Riesling Harth Cuvée Alexandre
Andre Kientzler   Gewürztraminer
Dom. Weinbach   Riesling Cuvée Theo
Zind-Humbrecht   Pinot Gris Vieilles Vignes
Pierre Frick   Pinot Blanc Précieuse
Cave de Turkheim   Pinot Gris Réserve

15 striking dry whites
Dom. Bott-Geyl   Riesling Mandelburg GC
Ernest Burn   Pinot Gris Goldert GC Cuvée de La Chapelle
Marcel Deiss   Altenberg GC
Dom. Albert Mann   Pinot Blanc/Auxerrois Vieilles Vignes
René Muré   Riesling Clos Saint Landelin Vorbourg GC
Seppi Landmann   Gewürztraminer Zinnkoepflé GC
Dom. Schoffit   Gewürztraminer Harth Cuvée Alexandre VV
Trimbach   Riesling Clos Sainte-Hune
Dom. Weinbach   Muscat Réserve Personelle
Dirler-Cadé   Gewürztraminer Kessler GC
A & R Gresser   Riesling Kastelberg GC
Bruno Sorg   Pinot Gris GC Florimont
Dom. Rieflé   Pinot Gris GC Steinert
Gérard Neumayer   Pinot Gris GC Bruderthal

Alsace

France

Zind-Humbrecht   Riesling Brand GC

An exciting selection of Late Harvest whites
Dom. Jean Becker   Gewürztraminer Schoenenbourg GC SGN
Dom. Léon Beyer   Pinot Gris SGN
Dom. Bott-Geyl   Pinot Gris Sonnenglanz GC SGN
Hugel et Fils   Riesling SGN
André Kientzler   Gewürztraminer VT
Dom. Albert Mann   Pinot Gris Hengst GC SGN
Ostertag   Gewürztraminer Fronholz Vendange Tardive
Rolly-Gassmann   Muscat Moenchreben Vendange Tardive
Dom. Schoffit   Riesling Clos Saint Théobald Rangen GC VT
Dom. Weinbach   Gewürztraminer Cuvée D'or Quintessence SGN
Dom. Schlumberger   Gewürztraminer Christine VT
Kuentz-Bas   Riesling Caroline Vendange Tardive
Cave de Turkheim   Pinot Gris Vendange Tardive
Dom. Rieflé   Pinot Gris SGN
François Lichtlé   Riesling SGN

Champagne carries almost mystical properties for a vast number of people. However, there are a bewildering number of Champagne houses, co-operatives and growers bottling wine under their own labels and a further huge own-label business with wines of immensely variable quality all being bottled under the auspices of just one appellation. The great Champagne houses virtually invented the concept of the brand in winemaking and in most cases they do a very acceptable job. Nonetheless, in the absence of a better classification system the area remains a minefield for consumers. At the last count, there were some 33,000 plus ha. under vine with many of the 19,000 growers cultivating no more than a hectare or two. Both in the cellars of the region and in the vineyards there are inevitably substantial variations in quality. Things however are changing. Though accounting for only a very small percentage of exports, 30 or so top independent Champagne domaines are make a big impact visually out of all proportion to their size in the smart streets and restaurants of cities worldwide. Window shop down New York's Fifth Avenue or London's St James and you are as likely to see a bottle of Selosse or Jacquesson as a flagon of Krug or Cristal. The same holds true for Milan, Melbourne, Singapore and Tokyo. The boutique ethos has had as much qualitative effect on Champagne as in Haute Couture.

The appellation and its districts

Making sparkling wine is realistically the only consistent vinegrowing activity that can be undertaken here, among the windswept rolling hills of the most northerly of France's wine regions. Alsace may be on a not dissimilar latitude but crucially it is protected by the Vosges Mountains. Ripening the three varieties, Pinot Noir, Meunier and Chardonnay is by no means easy. Pinot Noir and Chardonnay are at their optimum in the production of the great wines of the Côte d'Or some 240 km (150 miles) to the south. The vital requirement here is to provide grapes that are physiologically ripe and of sufficient intensity to produce good wine. That means controlling yields and harvesting properly ripened fruit, which remains a problem. By contrast, Champagne has been lucky to have had a run of good to excellent vintages since the millenium -only 2001 was really poor. The risk of unripe fruit (as happened unexpectedly in 2011) is generally now less acute as a result of discernible warming since the late 1980s. But challenges are still very real on the negative side of climate change: the chaotic distribution of summer rainfall, destructive hail storms and devastating spring frosts- the Aube lost at least 80% of production in spring 2016.

Within the appellation the communes have been classified as Grand Cru, Premier Cru or Deuxième Cru. This does not however give an indication of quality or the potential of a given *terroir* as it does in Burgundy but works more as a means by which to establish the price a grower gets for his harvest. You may have an outstanding performer in a second-classed village and a moderate grower in a grand cru.

The appellation falls into five main districts, which account for some two-thirds of the working vineyard area. These five districts may yet become their own sub-appellations in a desired move to establish better regional identity within this geographically extensive AC. The rest of the appellation is spread across a vast area. Indeed, the idea that all Champagne comes from fabled chalk soils is not the case. Much of the vignoble is clay and sandstone. In the classic zone of Champagne, the **Montagne de Reims** is just to the south of that Cathedral city. The north-facing slopes of the Montagne at Verzenay, Verzy and Beaumont sur Veille are home to Pinots of majesty and tension, capable of long life. The aspect of the vineyards affords warmer temperature as the Montagne extends southwards. Pinot Noir and Meunier are the predominant varieties here and are famed for producing rich, full-bodied Champagnes. The village of **Bouzy** is as well known for producing the best still Côteaux Champenois reds as it is sparkling wines. Other villages nearer the river making excellent Côteaux Champenois Pinot Noir are south-facing Äy and Cumières, particularly in 2015, one of the warmest dry summers for many years.

The **Vallée de la Marne** to the north-west of the Montagne de Reims stretches east along the River Marne. The centre of the district is the town of Épernay and the best vineyard sites are to the east, particularlry in Äy itself and its neighbour Mareuil -sur-Äy. Red grapes are predominant here and the wines tend to be a touch lighter than those from the Montagne de Reims, with more elegance and refinement. The **Côte des Blancs** is, as the name suggests, white wine territory. Chardonnay is virtually the exclusive grape here with very few red plantings. The vineyards are largely sited with an easterly aspect. The great Chardonnay villages of Cramant, Avize, Le Mesnil-sur-Oger and Vertus are found here.

In the far south west of the main Champagne area, north of Troyes, is the **Côte de Sézanne**, with the small town of the same name at its heart. The vineyards are dominated by Chardonnay, which accounts for some seven out of every 10 vines. As in the Côte des Blancs there is extensive chalk in the soil but not to the same degree. Way to the south of Troyes and away from the main Champagne appellation boundaries is the **Aube.** The main vineyards in the district, now known as the Côte des Bar are one hundred miles from Reims. The soil is different, there is little chalk but more of the Kimmeridgian clay and limestone soils of Sancerre and Chablis. The latter is in fact a good deal closer to the Aube than any of the other Champagne vineyards.

At present the Aube is largely planted to Pinot Noir. There is a case for a considerable increase in Chardonnay. The area could potentially make extremely rich and powerful Blanc de Blancs.

The styles

The range of different styles available takes in sparkling white and rosé along with the still red wines which use the Côteaux Champenois appellation. While the role of the master blender in Champagne remains as significant as ever, the development of wines that come from single terroirs or from the same, very specific sources when vintage conditions favour – like the great Salon wines – seems likely to accelerate as time goes on. The sheer quality of many of the emerging small growers is a signal of things to come.

The styles and method outlined below should only be used as a very general guide; there can be significant variation within these. It is quite possible to find deluxe super-premium cuvées that are non-vintage (NV), Blanc de Blancs that may be from a single vineyard or a blend of many, or Blanc de Noirs in vintage and NV versions.

Most common and providing the bulk of the output of the great Champagne houses are the regular **NV** blends. The use of reserve wine stocks is an undoubted asset, but a huge variation in quality exists. Available vineyard resources (and consequent fruit quality)

France

and the length of time on lees in bottle are just two of the factors that affect the style of these wines. You should expect **Vintage** cuvées to be a significant step up. They should be denser and richer with significantly greater structure. Inevitably there will be more variation in style with these as they reflect the nature of the year. Generally they should only be released after good harvests.

Blanc de Blancs is produced solely from Chardonnay while **Blanc de Noirs** is produced from Pinot Noir and/or Meunier, to the complete exclusion of Chardonnay. Blanc de Blancs is more refined and elegant and often has a tighter structure when young, whereas a Blanc de Noirs is fuller, with richer, more opulent flavours. The pink **Rosés** can be made either by blending in a little red wine (the only AC where this is permitted) or, and generally with better results, by the normal manner of a short maceration on skins. The best rosé generally comes from pure Pinot Noir.

The most expensive Champagnes are the Deluxe bottlings or Luxury Cuvées. There is a wide range of styles but the best are among the finest white or rosé wines in the world. One of the most distinctive of these is the great Dom Ruinart vintage Rosé made from 80% Chardonnay with 20% of the best still Pinot Noir

Champagne vintages

Because of the variable and challenging climate there is much vintage variation. Vintage wines are only produced when conditions permit. 2015 had one of the warmest and driest seasons on record - but the heatwave extremes of 2003 were avoided, thanks to needed rain in late August. The great Marne producers who picked fairly early in September have certainly made great Pinot Noirs: some fine mineral Chardonnays also In vigilantly tended vineyards and well-equipped wineries deploying cold settling of the "must". However, it was generally too hot for the great white grape farther south the Aube. Early days, for sure, many producers will make a vintage but will it be great but more likely selectively very good? 2014 is very variable, from commune to commune: Some fine tension in the whites of the Cote des Blancs but the two Pinots are tainted by the attacks of the Suzuki fruit fly, as In Burgundy. Vintage bottlings may be rare.

2013 is reputed to be one of the best vintages especially for Chardonnay since 1996. Despite losing some of the crop due to millerandage, the small harvest that remained is of excellent quality. 2012 was a welcome return to quality (some great Pinot Noir) after two poor harvests, with low yields enhancing the prospect of good vintage Champagnes. 2011 was marked by difficult growing conditions and vintage Champagnes for this year will be few and far between. 2010 also was a year where the skills of the winemaker will be paramount. It remains to be seen how many vintage wines will be made. 2009 produced a generally good yield of top quality fruit. As a result, excellent, harmonious vintage wines are beginning to emerge. 2008 provided challenging growing conditions but the late season weather looks certain to see some very fine wines for the patient. 2007 was a low-yielding year of variable quality (actually showing better in maturity) that nevertheless put pressure on prices. 2006 is already showing very well in charming, fresh, elegant vintage wines after a seesaw summer but a warm, sunny harvest. 2005 is mixed: there are some opulent Cote des Blancs Chardonnays but Pinot Noirs can be clumsy, ill-balanced and affected by humidity and incipient rot.

2004 produced a bumper crop and some very fine-drawn wines despite the record volume. 2003 in maturity has also produced some surprisingly elegant vintage bottles despite the heat. Volume too was very low. 2002 was exceptional. 2001, though, was a disaster with unprecedented rainfall. From 1995 to 2000 the Champenois were very lucky, having a string of good to very good vintages. Argument rages over which Is the best of the two important vintages, 1995 or 1996. For several of the top chefs de caves (and this reviewer) 1995 is the most even and balanced vintage of the decade after a perfect warm summer season: the wines, moreover, were not distorted by intense heart. In maturity (2016/17)

1995 shows better than 1996, which in fairness has some assertive great champagnes but quite a few others which disappoint because of the disjoint of overripe aromas and still eye-wateringly acidic flavours - a year for the master winemakers at Roederer, Billecart-Salmon, Bollinger and Pol Roger. The subsequent 1998 is the joker in the pack, which showed some variation in adolescence but the best vintage cuvées are now very stylish gems, which you can drink now: especially the sublime Dom Pérignon Plénitude 2.

Immediately prior to 1995 the only really half-decent year was 1993. 1992 received a savage press for some green and hard wines. However, against the trend, there are some classy Chardonnay-led cuvées, which shouldn't be a surprise as '92 was a great vintage for white burgundy. 1990 is regarded as a classic but if one may suggest It, likely to be more oxidative in maturity than 1989, which though with only moderate acidity, the wines can be marvels of freshness and future life after 27 years - Veuve Clicquot and Charles Heidsieck are wonderful.

There are fine wines on release now, like the Bollinger RD 1995 and 1988 which are still very good. 1985, 1983 and 1982 are all great earlier years and top wines encountered from these will be worth considering, although 1985 needs drinking. Some very astute tasters prefer 1983 to the highly praised 1982. In Spring 2016, 1983 Charles Heidsieck was approaching the apex of glorious maturity; in 2014 the Salon 1983 was perfection.

A-Z of producers

✿ **Agrapart**   *www.champagne-agrapart.com*
One of the two best domaines at Avize, an exceptional small family-owned producer run by brothers Pascal and Fabrice with 9.6 ha of vineyards on the Côte des Blancs, almost half of which are at Avize. Other plots are mostly in the grand cru villages of Oger, Cramant (notably in Bionnes) and Oiry. The Agraparts' holdings are exclusively Chardonnay, traditionally established by massal selection and crucially the vines are of significant age: the oldest parcels around 65 years. This is clearly perceptible in the wines which have great purity and intensity. The NV Brut 7 Crus and Terroirs are both typically low dosage, partly oak-aged, with at least four years on its lees. The Brut Minéral is vinified in demi-muid casks and comes from calcareous soils at Avize and argilo-calcareous soils at Cramant (Les Bionnes). Both richness and complexity are gained from six years on lees. The top wine, the marvellously intense, citrus and mineral-laden L'Avizoise gets a similar period of lees-ageing and comes from the oldest vines. It will age very well in bottle. (DM)

Recommended Whites:
L'Avizoise Brut Grand Cru Vintage ★★★★★ £G
Brut Minéral Grand Cru Vintage ★★★★ £F

Wine behind the label

Champagne

France

Brut Terroirs Grand Crus NV ★★★☆ £E
Brut 7 Crus NV ★★★ £D

Ayala www.champagne-ayala.fr

After a quiet, declining period in the '90s and into our new century, Ayala was bought in 2005 by Bollinger, whose president Ghislain de Montgolfier saw a lot of potential in resuscitating the very dry style of Ayala in its 1930s heyday, when it was the favourite Champagne of King George V1. Montgolfier set about a complete overall of the range. As a result of Ghislain's efforts a decade ago, the well- known Brut Majeur, once a foursquare, even rustic wine has since become much more stylish and refined with a 40/40/20 mix of Pinot Noir/Chardonnay/Meunier, crucially with a lowered dosage of 7g/l. The most radical new cuvée Brut Nature has zero dosage, is bone-dry but no asperity having spent four years on lees; it's selected from the ripest grapes in preferably warmer years. Caroline Latrine the new chef de caves since 2013 continues the focus on freshness and elegance. The Vintage Brut is a good decent wine but outclassed by the Vintage Blanc de Blancs, which is made in small quantities. Aged on lees for at least six years, it has real structure and surprising opulence. There is also a light, fruit-driven rosé. The pride of the cellar is the vintage Perla d'Ayala, a true work of craftsmanship made only in outstanding vintages, using traditional local techniques. Chardonnay makes up 80% of the cuvée, rounded out with 20% Pinot Noir - dosage 6 g/l. Ample and silky, it's a gastronomic wine for the greatest ocean fish. Quite exceptional in 2002 and 2008, soon to be released. (ME)

Recommended Whites:
Cuvée Perle d'Ayala Vintage ★★★★★ £G
Brut Blanc de Blancs Vintage ★★★★ £F
Brut Vintage ★★★ £F
Brut Majeur NV ★★★ £E
Recommended Rosés:
Brut Majeur NV ★★ £E

Paul Bara www.champagnepaulbara.com

This is an excellent traditional domaine, founded in 1833, with vineyard holdings of 11 ha, all within the Grand Cru commune of Bouzy. Chantale Bara has taken over the reins from her legendary father Paul, a legion in these parts and the point of reference for the best Coteaux Champenois red wine in the village. The Brut Réserve Grand Cru NV is an exceptional wine for quality and value. The high level of Pinot Noir (80%) accounts for richness and structure yet remarkably the wine is forward, attractively aromatic with notes of nectarine and mirabelle; opulent in the mouth with a lifting spiciness. The Grand Cru Vintage is quite stolid, yet with a fine balance of pure evolving fruit and autolytic hints of baked bread; the Special Club shows extra depth and there is a very impressive, intense rosé. The Comtesse Marie de France is lighter and more elegant. The Bara Bouzy Rouges (Coteaux Champenois) are as good as it gets, especially in warm even years like 2009. (ME)

Recommended Whites:
Brut Grand Cru Comtesse Marie de France Vintage ★★★★ £F
Grand Cru Special Club Vintage ★★★★ £F
Brut Grand Cru Vintage ★★★ £E
Recommended Rosés:
Brut Grand Cru Grand Rosé de Bouzy ★★★★ £E
Recommended Reds:
Bouzy Rouge Coteaux Champenois ★★★★ £E

Edmond Barnaut www.champagne-barnaut.com

The 14 ha of vineyards are, like those of the Bara family, planted around the village of Bouzy. Unlike the Bara vineyards, though, they contain a high proportion of Chardonnay. This gives an added finesse and grip although the wines are of an impressively weighty, substantial style. There are two fine NV wines: the Sélection-Extra and Grand Réserve. The former has a higher proportion of Pinot Noir which is evident, as it is in a rich, bready Blanc de Noirs. The Authentique Rosé gains its colour from the Pinot Noir skins rather than from blending with red base wine. There is also a Grand Cru vintage bottling and a limited-production special Cuvée Edmond Brut, a Cuvée Douceur Sec and a fruity Bouzy Rouge. (DM)

Recommended Whites:
Brut Sélection-Extra NV ★★★★ £E
Grand Réserve NV ★★★ £E
Blanc de Noirs NV ★★★ £E
Recommended Rosés:
Brut Authentique NV ★★★ £E

Beaumont des Crayeres www.champagne-beaumont.com

This bijou, tightly managed co-op at Mardeuil, 8 kms from Epernay, has just 200 growers who between them farm 90 ha of vineyards. Output for a co-op is also deliberately controlled at just 700,000+ bottles in the interests of optimal quality, for the soils in this best part of the Marne valley are still rich in chalk (hence the brand's name Crayères) before it burrows underground as the Marne then flows west in the direction of Paris and the soils become progressively heavier with clay. Mardeuil is thus a dream spot for a specially elegant strain of Meunier, more refined and racy than the earthy image of the variety would have you believe. The notable Grande Réserve NV is Meunier -led at 60%, its softness and generosity of yellow stone fruits tinged with a creamy touch of patisserie reined by a mineral frame and spiciness that makes it a digestible and fresh champagne at any time of the day or night. The vintage Fleur de Prestige is particularly good value, with 60 per cent Chardonnay adding intensity and elegance. There's a new more intense Cuvée Fleur de Meunier, excellent since 2008.The top cuvée, Nostalgie, follows the classic mix of 60 per cent Chardonnay and 40 per cent Pinot Noir but is richer and fuller with surprising opulence for such a blend. The 1996 was highly successful round and softly structured. Well distributed in the UK and Japan. (ME)

Recommended Whites:
Nostalgie Vintage ★★★★☆ £F
Fleur de Prestige Vintage ★★★★ £E
Fleur de Meunier ★★★★ £E
Brut Grande Réserve NV ★★★☆ £D
Brut Grand Prestige NV ★★★ £D

◉ Billecart-Salmon www.champagne-billecart.fr

A medium-sized, outstanding house, largely family-owned but with extra horsepower supplied by a financial partner, Billecart-Salmon now produce 1.2 million bottles. As his son Nicolas joins the business, President François Billecart says unsentimentally "tradition means little, without the injection of new blood and ideas." The family was first in Champagne to introduce the technology of cold settling of the "must" for clarifying the wines and protecting them from oxidation. An historic maison founded in 1818, Billecart is now in the vanguard of new or resuscitated ideas from the best of the old. The Brut Réserve NV is classy stuff at this level and the top wines are very intense and marvellously refined. A sizeable proportion of Chardonnay is used and this helps the wines' balance

155

France

and classic Champagne structure. The elegant NV Blanc de Blancs is sourced mainly from Le Mesnil-sur-Oger and is normally a blend of two vintages. At vintage level, some fermentation in oak has been re- introduced, exemplified in the prestige Cuvée Nicolas-François Billecart : the great 2002 is a very complex and elegant blend of 40 per cent Chardonnay and 60 per cent Pinot Noir of the highest class. A vintage Blanc de Blancs is also produced. Sadly, the Grande Cuvée (N.F. Billecart with extra lees ageing) Is no longer offered: the 1996 is magnificent, if you ever see it auction. There is also a tiny amount of exquisite prestige rosé Cuvée Elisabeth Salmon and a new prestige bottling from a single walled 1ha vineyard, Clos Saint-Hilaire, which is seriously pricey but its pure 100% PInot Noir flavours, substantial yet elegant, are life-enhancing. (ME)

Recommended Whites:
Brut Cuvée Nicolas-François Billecart Vintage ✪✪✪✪✪ £H
Clos St Hilaire Vintage Pinot Noir ★★★★★ £H
Blancs de Blancs Grand Cru NV ★★★★ £F
Brut Réserve NV ★★★★ £E
Demi-Sec NV ★★★ £E

Recommended Rosés:
Prestige Rose Elizabeth Salmon Vintage ★★★★★ £H
Brut Rosé NV ★★★★ £F

>> Boizel www.boizel.com

This is a now long established small family owned house, established in 1834. It is one of seven producers within the independent Lanson-BCC group where houses work together to improve development, sustainability and distribution. A fine and well-priced range is made. There are extensive arrangements with growers and grapes are sourced from the Côte des Blancs, the Montagne de Reims, the Vallée de la Marne and the Aube. Vinification is separate for both grape varieties and villages and modern stainless steel is employed with careful control of primary fermentations. In the cellar during maturation there is a tendency to opt for a lower dosage. Among a range of 10 Champagnes, there is a fine non-vintaged Brut Réserve, a blend of all three of the regions grapes, biscuity complexity emerging with three years on lees and a really stylish Blanc de Blancs. Brut Grand Vintage gets significant bottle age, the current vintage is 2004, Chardonnay is half the blend and ageing on lees is from seven up to 10 years. The two top wines are the prestige white and rosé Joyau de France. The white is richly textured, offering a biscuity, buttery complexity. It is a Champagne with real character from a blend of roughly one-third/two-thirds Chardonnay and Pinot Noir, the wine is aged on lees for 12 years. The rosé offers delicate and intense strawberry fruits and comes from a similar blend to the white although 10% of the fruit is vinified as a red wine. Again extended lees ageing of up to ten years adds further depth and dimension. (DM)

Recommended Whites:
Joyau de France Vintage ★★★★ £G
Brut Grand Vintage ★★★ £E
Blanc de Blancs NV ★★★ £D
Brut Réserve NV ★★★ £D
Brut Ultime (Zero) ★★ £E
Demi-Sec NV ★★ £D

Recommended Rosés:
Joyau de France Rosé ★★★★ £G
Brut Rosé NV ★★ £D

✪✪ Bollinger www.champagne-bollinger.fr
One of the greatest names in sparkling wine production. Bollinger

produces around 2 million bottles a year. It is one of just a handful of producers here to still ferment base wines in used oak, exclusively so for Its renowned vintage wines. A high proportion of Pinot Noir is used and the NV Special Cuvée, always full and rich, is now on a roll, with an extra dimension of tension and finesse. The vintage Grande Année can almost take on a hint of Burgundian gaminess with age, as can the remarkable RD (récemment dégorgé). That wine is kept in bottle on its yeast sediment for up to 10 years and possesses a rich toastiness; it is both concentrated and exceptionally well balanced- the epic 2002 is the current release. A tiny amount of a 100 per cent Pinot Noir cuvée, Vieilles Vignes, is made from ungrafted, very low-yielding old vines and there is an excellent Côteaux Champenois red, Côte aux Enfants, notably in the very warm, complex 2015 vintage (DM)

Recommended Whites:
RD ✪✪✪✪✪ £H
Brut Vieilles Vignes Vintage ★★★★★ £H
Brut Grande Année Vintage ★★★★★ £G
Brut Spécial Cuvée NV ★★★★ £F

Recommended Rosés:
Brut Grande Année Rosé Vintage ★★★★ £G
Brut Rosé NV ★★★ £F

Recommended Reds:
Côte aux Enfants Vintage ★★★★ £G

>> Francis Boulard & Fille www.francis-boulard.com
Francis Boulard and his daughter Delphine (the winemaker) now run this small domaine mainly in the hills of Saint Thierry north west of Reims, also in spots along the Marne valley and at a prize parcel of Grand Cru Mailly on the Montagne de Reims. The average age of the vines is a very respectable 30 years +: they are cultivated organically, with more than a nod to biodynamism. The Les Murgiers Brut Reserve NV is a ripe and forward expression of Meunier essentially. And like the whole Boulard range is offered either as a Brut Nature (zero dosage) or as an Extra Brut with less than 6 grams of sugar per litre.The vintage Brut Millésime Les Rachais bottling offers a rich biscuity texture and real depth and intensity. The Blanc de Blancs is tighter and more restrained, as one would expect, and gains added depth from old vines. The splendidly rich and opulent Petraea comes from a perpetual reserve, similar to a solera system, going back to 1997; It is bottled unfined and unfiltered. A rosé is also made. (ME)

Recommended Whites:
Petraea Brut NV ★★★★☆ £F
Brut Millésimé Les Rachais Vintage ★★★★ £F
Grand Cru Mailly Vintage ★★★☆ £F
Blanc de Blancs Brut NV ★★★ £E
Les Murgiers Brut Réserve NV ★★★ £E

Cattier www.cattier.com
This relatively small house, production just over 50,000 cases a year, has been in the hands of the Cattier family since 1763 when they started cultivating their first vineyards. All of their wines are produced from Premier Cru sites on the Montagne de Reims. They own 20 ha themselves, 15 ha of which are planted to red varieties. In addition to the wines profiled here it is worth looking out for the vintage Cuvée Renaissance, a NV Blanc de Blancs and a superior white NV the Brut Antique. The Brut Premier Cru NV is a blend of mainly Pinot Noir and Meunier with around a quarter Chardonnay. It is soft, rounded and forward with simple green apple fruit and a slight hint of yeastiness. The vintage Brut Vinothèque is more

seriously structured and offers a rich, bready and biscuity character to its fruit and steely acidity. The Glamour Rosé is soft and forward in a demi-sec style with light red berry fruit and moderate depth, while the demi-sec Glamour Blanc is fresh and attractive with better grip and structure than other examples of the style. Pride of place though goes to the top wine Clos du Moulin which is from a 2.2 ha single vineyard. It is a 50/50 blend of Chardonnay and Pinot Noir and shows a rich citrus and evolved autolytic character reined by fine measured acidity. It is always blended from three separate vintages. (DM)

Recommended Whites:
Clos du Moulin NV ★★★★ £G
Brut Vinothèque Vintage ★★★ £E
Brut Premier Cru NV ★★ £E
Glamour NV ★☆ £D

Recommended Rosés:
Glamour NV ★★ £D

Dehours www.champagne-dehours.fr
Interesting independent Marne valley producer in the tiny village of Ceseuil once famous for its cherries, but now home to a subtle style of champagne, all mineral precision and energy owing to its location near Mareuil le Port on the south bank of the river with some slopes facing Châtillons sur Marne on the sunny other side. Jerome Déhours and his family own a useful 14 ha planted mostly to Meunier with some Chardonnay and a little Pinot Noir. Extra-Brut bottlings are a particular speciality here and they're very impressive. Under the Collection label wines are sourced from individual sites as well as from small blends of a few. In addition to Les Genevraux rated below, there is a Blanc de Pinot Noir (Mareuil Le Port Vieilles Vignes) and an additional lieu-dit bottling Brisefer. The single vineyard sites being identified for their soil, drainage and exposition. Les Genevraux offers pure, mineral and piercingly citrus scented fruit with a subtle 'salted-biscuits' undertone. Of the regular bottlings there is an Extra-Brut Grande Réserve as well as the full, fruit driven and light yeasty Brut Grande Réserve. Two rosés are produced, a Brut and a superior Confidentielle. The vintage Brut is produced from all three authorised varieties. Finally, there is a rich and finely structured Cuvée Trio S which is an intricate estate blend made from a separate solera begun in 1998 and held in tank and barrel, blending all three grape varieties. The Trio bottling in each year is entirely from this solera; it is replenished each year to its ageing volume with the new season's wine accounting for 30%. An intriguing fine wine which completes the first fermentation in wood. These are interesting and characterful wines that are well worth searching out. (DM)

Recommended Whites:
Extra Brut Lieu-dit Les Genevraux Vintage ★★★★ £F
Extra Brut Cuvée Trio S NV ★★★★ £E
Brut Grande Réserve NV ★★★ £D
Extra Brut Grande Réserve NV ★★★ £D

Deutz www.champagne-deutz.com
Now owned by Louis ROEDERER, Deutz has also had a successful sparkling wine partnership in New Zealand with BRANCOTT. By comparison with many great houses the annual production here used be relatively modest but has increased from 96,000 bottles in 1995 to three million today. Quality remains generally good to very good, touching the exceptional at the top of the range. The NV Brut Classic has been greatly improved by cellar master Michel Davesne since 2003: now It's a well-structured, dry and complete entry champagne, very different from the sharp, acidic wine that

made you want grip the table in the early '90s. Desvesne can also be credited with a mini-renaissance of the prestigious Cuvée William Deutz in shepherding the golden elegant 2002 to full maturity, now deliciously à point. Amour de Deutz is the other luxury cuvée, first released as an aristocratic Blanc de Blancs from Grand Cru grapes in Le Mesnil, Avize and Cramant: it is particularly fine in exceptional Chardonnay years like 1995 and 2004; it is now joined by the stylishly succulent new Amour de Deutz Rosé 2006. The straight Brut Vintage the Blanc de Blancs are good solid wines, released carefully in decent years worthy of the name. (ME)

Recommended Whites:
William Deutz Vintage ★★★★★ £H
Amour de Deutz Vintage Blanc de Blancs ★★★★ £H
Brut Vintage ★★★★☆ £G
Blanc de Blancs Vintage ★★★ £G
Brut Classic NV ★★★ £F

Recommended Rosés:
Amour de Deutz Vintage Rosé ★★★★ £H
Brut Rosé Vintage ★★★ £F

>> Drappier www.champagne-drappier.com
The leading independent merchant and domaine proprietor of Aubois Champagne, Michel Drappier, now with his son Hugo, is a driving force for innovative excellence and is a beacon of quality in the south of Champagne. The family are as Champenois as it gets, having started their house and vineyards in 1807 at Urville, 15 minutes' drive from Bar-sur-Aube. Their domaine now extends to 50+ hectares of beautiful Pinot Noir, 15 ha. of which are in organic certified conversion since 2014. This would have pleased his grandfather (on his mother's side) who was the first grower in the 1930s to rip out the inferior Gamay vines and replace them with Pinot. For nearly 30 years now, Drappier has thought a lot about a more ecological approach to his vines and winemaking. The result now is the complete elimination of chemicals in the fields; the soils are regularly ploughed by a horse, largely replacing tractors etc so that the earth should not be compacted. Drappier's boldest conviction early on has been his awareness of the need to radically reduce the amount of sulphur in his champagnes. The Brut Zéro and particularly the Brut Zéro Sans Souffre (no sulphur) have been a great success in Paris and are holding up quite well. The Brut Nature Rosé NV, made by the saignée method, is both floral and mineral. The Cuvée Quattuor is a celebration of old Champenois cépages, the grape mix 25% each of Pinot Blanc, Arbanne and Petit Meslier joining 25% Chardonnay, on a 2010 base (a good year in the Aube). The Brut Millésime d'Exception is the most traditional of the vintage wines, with an enviable reputation for excellence and long life. Bottles and magnums from the 1970s are still alive and vital in the Cistercian cellar beneath the Urville house. Grande Sendrée Vintage is one of Champagne's best prestige cuvées, the Pinot Noir (55%) coming from this prize lieu-dit at the top of the Urville slope. It hasn't always been a single vineyard bottling, as until quite recently it used to have also a dollop of Grand Cru Chardonnay from Cramant. Go for the Grande Sendrée 2002 and the 1996, if you see them at auctions. (ME)

Recommended Whites:
Prestige Cuvée Grande Sendrée Vintage ★★★★☆ £H
Millésime d'Exception Vintage ★★★★ £G
Cuvée Quattuoir NV ★★★ £F
Brut Nature Zéro Dosage NV ★★★ £F
Brut Nature Zéro Sans Souffre NV ★★★ £F
Brut Carte d'Or NV ★★☆ £E

Champagne

Recommended Rosés:
Brut Nature Rosé ★★★ £F
Rosé des Desmoiselles NV ★★★ £E

Duval-Leroy *www.duval-leroy.com*

This sizeable house is one of a few rare examples nowadays where the company is headed by a woman, the formidable Carol Duval-Leroy. Under her direction a range of increasingly impressive Champagnes are being produced. A much larger than normal vineyard holding is one of the keys to quality here. 170 ha of owned vines, account for around 25% of the company's annual requirements. The bulk of the range goes under the Traditional banner. There is a striking and expressively aromatic Brut Fleur de Champagne majoring in Chardonnay, while a Demi-Sec has more depth than most, as does the Brut Rosé which gets a period on skins for colour by the saignée method. The Extra Brut is typically incisive, coming solely from Chardonnay and has a well-judged array of citrus fruit and rich biscuity notes. There are a range of special bottlings. The cuvées Authentis Trépail and Cumières are both lieu-dit (named- site) wines with lots of character. Design Paris is a special release bottle with a painted bottle signed by artist LeRoy Neiman. Finally, the well-distributed and pricey Femme de Champagne is a rich and toasty super-cuvée produced from almost all Chardonnay with a little Pinot Noir from 4 grand cru vineyards. Quite outstanding in 1996, it is aged on lees for nine years. (DM)

Recommended Whites:
Femme de Champagne Vintage ★★★★★ £H
Authentis Cumières Vintage ★★★★ £G
Authentis Trépail Vintage ★★★★ £G
Extra Brut NV ★★★ £E
Fleur de Champagne ★★☆ £D
Demi-Sec NV ★★ £E
Recommended Rosés:
Brut Rosé NV ★★ £E

❀ Egly-Ouriet

Very impressive, exceptional family-run property with some 9 ha of Grand Cru Pinot Noir & Chardonnay at Ambonnay, Bouzy and Verzenay plus a tiny holding of Meunier in Vrigny on the western Montagne. Quality is high, with well-aged vineyards that are well over 30 years old. Owner Francis Egly is an original, his brusque aversion to journalists is due to shyness which masks a warm heart and passion for the vigneron's craft. Wisely, he stoutly maintains that acidity is not fundamental, and almost always sufficient, while bitterness Is almost always fatal. The high natural ripeness of his wines is amplified by green harvesting in July and shaped in a stunning mineral frame. Egly's work in the vines is rigorously sustainable: he eschews chemical insecticides, uses only organic fertilizers and ploughs his vineyards as his grandfather had done. The excellent Tradition Brut Grand Cru Ambonnay NV, 70/30 Pinot Noir & Chardonnay is fermented using natural yeasts and unusually aged on lees for a full 12 months before bottling without fining or filtration. Francis' most admired Champagne is his Blanc de (Pinot) Noirs Vieilles Vignes which are up to 100 years old. Though labelled NV, it's often from a single year: even in the weak 2001 vintage the wine was a triumph. Across the whole range, the results are wonderfully pure, full-bodied wines of great character. A beautiful Côteaux Champenois rouge is also produced but available only in very limited quantities. (ME)

Recommended Whites:
Grand Cru Vintage ★★★★★ £G

Blanc de Noirs Vieilles Vignes NV ★★★★★ £F
Brut Tradition NV ★★★★ £E
Recommended Rosés:
Brut Rosé NV ★★★ £E
Recommended Reds:
Coteaux Champenois ★★★★ £F

>> Fleury Père et Fils *www.champagne-fleury.fr*

Jean-Pierre Fleury, now in his early 70s, says proudly, "We are a family of pioneers." For the Fleurys had been grape farmers in Courteron, in the far south of the Barséquenais, bordering Burgundy since the 1890s. But it was Robert Fleury who, in 1930, decided to make and sell his own champagnes, as the way to escape from the deprivations and hardships that the Aubois vignerons endured during the Great Depression. Jean-Pierre his grandson was certainly a pioneer for ecologically sensitive tending of the vines in the early 1980s after some very costly trials and errors with organic methods more suitable to Provence than Champagne. Yet with true grit J-P became the father of biodynamic viticulture in the Côte des Bar, having treated his vineyards according to the strict principles of Rudolf Steiner from 1989. Today, Jean-Pierre and his sons Sébastien and Benoît, have 20 ha., the health of their soils and vines being widely admired and emulated in the wine community. What's more, the wines though fermented in oak retain a floral expression and precision that naturally balance the rich vinous flavours shaped by the local limestone, clay and silt soils. The Fleury Brut Tradition is typically Aubois champagne driven by ripe succulent Pinot Noir – it is quite a strong evolved yellow, has peachy flavours on both nose and palate – a good straightforward champagne for colder nights. Notes Blanches Vintage, as its name implies, is made from 100% Pinot Blanc, still found in the Aube -a racy aromatic champagne of tension and poise, which recalls Alsace a little. Sonate nos 9 /10 vintage is more sérieux from the Val Prune Vineyard; it marvellously expresses the depth and character Pinot Noir can achieve in Courteron. The Sonate Rosé, especially in 2009, is a fine instance of why Aubois rosé can be among the best in Champagne. (ME)

Recommended Whites:
Sonate Brut Vintage no 10 ★★★★ £F
Notes Blanches Vintage no 10 ★★★ £D
Brut Tradition NV ★★☆ £E
Recommended Rosés:
Sonate Brut Vintage no 09 ★★★★ £F

René Geoffroy *www.champagne-geoffroy.com*

Fine owner-grower family (récoltant-manipulant) dating from the 17th century in Cumières. The dynamic and committed Jean-Baptiste Geoffroy (son of René) recently moved to his redesigned gravity-fed winery in Äy. He has14 ha, 12 of which are planted to Pinot Noir and Meunier. The entry-level Expression Brut Premier Cru faithfully reflects the vineyards of Cumières, probably the sunniest village in the Marne. A classic 50/40/10 mix of Meunier, Pinot Noir and Chardonnay, this wine is all about ripe Pinot black fruits, leavened by a lightly spiced Meunier softness- very digestible! The vintage Extra Brut dominated by 70 % Chardonnay is a winner, particularly in 2004 all elegance, and successfully opulent in 2005, despite the mixed reputation of the vintage: but then non-malolactic fermentation and a minimal dosage of 2 g/l, ensures fine energy in tune with the richness of old vines. The Volupté made up of two thirds Chardonnay gets decent 4 years+ yeast aging. It is rich and full with real biscuity depth and is impressively structured. The Rosé de Saignée is bankably excellent, never more so than in

exceptional, warm 2015. (ME)

Recommended Whites:

Extra Brut Premier Cru Vintage ★★★★ £F

Premier Cru Empreinte Cuvée Volupté NV ★★★★ £E

Expression Premier Cru NV ★★★☆ £E

Elixir Demi-Sec Premier Cru NV ★★ £E

Recommended Rosés:

Rosé de Saignée Premier Cru NV ★★★★ £D

Pierre Gimonnet et Fils *www.champagne-gimmonet.com*

Leading family domaine run by brothers Didier and Olivier Gimonnet. The estate now extends to nearly 29 ha, which includes for the first time one hectare of Grand Cru Oger, bringing a further repertoire of delicate fin flavours to the estate's arsenal. The main vineyards since the 1930s are enviably situated in the best Chardonnay villages of the Northern Côte des Blancs. These are always elegant wines, revealing purity of taste, a pervasive mineral imprint and subtle complexities, due in part to the considerable age of the vines. Part of the vineyard holding is Premier Cru, Cuis especially, and part Grand Cru in Chouilly, Cramant and a little Avize. This provides the property with a superb resource of base wine material. The style of the house is well expressed in fresh, taut and lightly toasty Cuis Premier Cru which is admirably balanced by regular use of reserve wines. The richer Fleuron and Club Premier Cru vintages are excellent choices for fine cuisine, particularly roast Turbot. The Extra Brut Oenophile, bottled without dosage, is superbly revealed in all its racy delicacy in the great 2008, a reference year for the domaine. There is also a new Rosé de Blancs made with 88% Chardonnay and 12% of red wine from Bouzy added and a single village Oger cuvée. Didier Gimonnet's strength as a winemaker is his cool assessment of what works best for his panoply of great vineyards. He farms sustainably, but as an empirical observer he is doubtful about fashionable 'isms, doesn't use oak and stays with malolactic fermentation for added complexities and balance. What's more, with the exception of the single village Oger, he prefers a careful use of assemblage (blending) for the greater benefit of all his cuvées. Gimonnet is certainly blue-chip, surely among the 25 best producers in Champagne. (ME)

Recommended Whites:

Extra-Brut Oenophile Vintage ★★★★★ £F

Brut Special Club Premier Cru Vintage ★★★★ £F

Brut Fleuron Premier Cru Vintage ★★★☆ £F

Brut Gastronome Vintage ★★★ £E

Blanc de Blancs Cuis Premier Cru NV ★★★ £E

❀ Henri Giraud *www.champagne-giraud.com*

This is a very fine small family operated Champagne house. With an address in the same village AS BOLLINGER it is no surprise that the wines here are of a very high standard. The origins of the maison date back to 1625 and it is still the oldest in the hands of the founding family. Yet before the new century it was extremely difficult to find the wines because they were only sold to a small group of private clients. So, Claude Giraud, who combines the mind of an academic with the nous of a businessman, a few years ago made the decision to extend the distribution of his wines in a careful and limited manner. What wonderful raw material to play with! The family now owns 35 different parcels of vines in Äy, pre-eminently in the finest sites of Pinot Noir, such as the superb south-facing lieu-dit of Les Valnots -but with a good holding of Chardonnay, too. Giraud is one of the few Champagne producers to conduct the ferment the majority of the wines in oak. But oak with a difference, for it comes

on Claude's sole initiative from the local forest of Argonne south east of Chalons en Champagne, near Sainte Ménehould. Argonne oak has always been gentle and flattering, historically a natural nursery for the delicate wines of Champagne until the vast expansion of Champagne exports post 1945 and the shift to inert enamel-lined and stainless steel cuves. Never the dogmatist, Claude still ferments in stainless steel thermo-regulated cuves for the Esprit de Giraud blanc & rosé NV; at this level both are an impressive standard and made roughly with two thirds Pinot Noir. A Blanc de Blancs Esprit is also produced. The François Hémart Hommage is richer and fuller in blends 70% Pinot Noir and 30% Chardonnay. The top wine used to be Fût de Chêne, which as Its name implies is vinified and aged in small oak before bottling. Now though the vintage leader is called Argonne after the forest, and with all winemakers on a learning curve like Claude's son in law Sébastien the use of oak has become subtler, particularly in the elegant 2004 vintage. Two other wines, Code Noir and Code Noir Rosé are special Blanc de Pinot Noir bottlings raised in oak specifically from the forest of Argonne. A Coteaux Champenois Blanc is also made. Claude has also called publicly for other houses to support local Champenois oak. (ME)

Recommended Whites:

Brut Grand Cru Argonne Vintage ★★★★★ £H

Code Noir Blanc de Noirs Vintage ★★★★ £G

Brut Grand Cru Hommage François Hémart NV ★★★★ £F

Brut Esprit de Giraud NV ★★★☆ £F

Recommended Rosés:

Code Noir Rose ★★★★ £G

Brut Esprit de Giraud NV ★★★☆ £E

Gosset *www.champagne-gosset.com*

This is probably the oldest-known wine producing house in Champagne, dating from 1584, well before the wines started to sparkle. The regular NV Excellence was a fresh and inviting newcomer in the 1990s and is now very consistent. The Grande Réserve and especially Grand Rosé, both NV, are richer champagnes for the table and the vintage offerings here can be a step up. The style is one of weight and a rich toastiness in the top wines but unfortunately a lack of elegance can creep in as well. Celebris is clearly a cut above the rest. (DM)

Recommended Whites:

Celebris Vintage ★★★★★ £G

Grande Millésime Vintage ★★★☆ £G

Grande Réserve NV ★★★ £F

Brut Excellence NV ★★★ £E

Recommended Rosés:

Grand Rosé NV ★★★★ £F

Alfred Gratien *www.alfredgratien.com*

Excellent, bijou traditional house founded in Epernay in 1867 by Alfred Gratien, who also established Gratien & Meyer in Saumur. The Epernay chefs de caves have been in the same Jaeger family for three generations- young Nicolas the current incumbent stays true to the classical style of fermenting in oak. This is all the more remarkable when you remember that in 2004, the family house was bought by Henkell, the leading Sekt producer. Big changes were expected, but the directors of the German giant knew that they had a little gem in Epernay and have left Jaeger a free rein to make the wines as his father and grandfather had done. Factually, there is a new range of separately labelled champagnes for mainly the cost conscious German market. But a decade on, connoisseurs can rest easy for the true Gratien twines are as fine and traditional

France

as ever. The well-known Brut Réserve NV, the house Champagne at England's Wine Society for 100 years, is still vinified in 228-litre oak barrels; the wine Is full bodied, Pinot-rich but more refined now, thanks to less taille (second pressings) in the blend. The marvellous Prestige Cuvée Paradis, though labelled NV is often from a single year, as in 2002. Dominated by Chardonnay from the best sites, it also has the palate filling spiciness of Meunier and a little classy touch of Pinot Noir. The wine has a lovely buttercup hue, its maturity of flavours frequently deserving 20 years of bottle age. The very beautiful Paradis Rosé is made in tiny qualities. The vintage bottlings Include a delightful à point 1998, all grilled bread and brioche aromas, then a precise yet ample mouthfeel. The 'malo' is usually blocked for freshness and long life across the Gratien range. (ME) (DM)

Recommended Whites:
Paradis NV ★★★★★ £F
Brut Vintage ★★★★ £F
Brut Réserve NV ★★★ £F
Recommended Rosés:
Brut Rosé Paradis NV ★★★★★ £G

⚘ Charles Heidsieck *www.charlesheidsieck.com*
Under the ownership of Remy-Cointreau and now a very wealthy private owner in luxury goods, the quality of the wine at this house over the past 20 years has probably never been surpassed. The non-vintage Brut Réserve, the1990s creation of the legendary Daniel Thibault, is a widely admired non vintage, its harmony and aromatic subtlety shaped by as much as 40% reserve wines in the blend. The house Is likely to go to greater heights still with the 2015 appointment of Cyril Brun as chef de caves. He won golden opinions in his 15 years at Veuve Clicquot, being particularly involved in the red wine making of La Grande Dame Rosé. For Cyril Brun, great wine is as much about emotion as numbers, a conviction that sits well with the Charles philosophy. There are two first-class white vintage reserves: the elegant, superbly-crafted Blanc des Millénaires 100% Grand Cru Chardonnay and the Pinot-dominated Brut Millésime, a powerful, concentrated, weighty but very refined wine. The vintage rosé is one of the best examples in the region. There are plans to revive the Prestige Champagne Charlie, and a new release, the 2004, for the Blanc des Millénaires as a burgeoning sequel to the very great 1995. (ME)

Recommended Whites:
Blanc des Millénaires Vintage ✪✪✪✪ £G
Brut Millésime Charlie Vintage ★★★★★ £G
Brut Réserve NV ★★★★ £F
Recommended Rosés:
Brut Rosé Vintage ★★★★ £G

Henriot *www.champagne-henriot.com*
Medium-sized producer accounting for 96,000 bottles a year of fairly priced and meticulously crafted Champagne. Essentially this maison is greatly admired by insiders but is not as revered as it should be, even by connoisseurs. The straight Brut Vintage has always been a bargain, especially successful 1996 and the Prestige Cuvée des Enchanteleurs 1988 one of the greatest vintages here since 1945. Even at the entry level of the range, the new chef de caves has made the Brut Souverain less burly and more elegant and the Blanc de Blancs NV is excellen.t (ME)

Recommended Whites:
Cuvée des Enchanteleurs ★★★★★ £G
Brut Vintage ★★★★ £F

Brut Souverain NV ★★★ £E
Blanc de Blancs NV ★★★ £E
Recommended Rosés:
Brut Rosé Vintage ★★★★ £F

⚘ Jacquesson *www.champagnejacquesson.com*
This is an excellent little family operation, officially a négociant-eleveur but in reality closer to a domaine, run by two passionate brothers, Jean-Hervé and Laurent Chiquet, who really think of themselves more as growers. From the year 2000, their most original creation has been the Cuvée 700 series of the Dry Brut Champagne, seeking to prize excellence over consistency by crafting a wine that reflected the main vintage in the assemblage, rather than the replicated flavours of traditional NV blends. The new aim is to give each wine its own distinctive personality, reflecting the character of the dominant vintage. First off, Cuvée 728 was so numbered being the 728th cuvée since the house's foundation. As the numbered 700 series has progressed over the last decade, it's arresting to see the ever increasing quality and individuality of successive harvests: No surprise that 730 (2002 base) 734 (2004) 738 (2008) and 739 (2009) are particularly fine but all rivetingly different. The quality of grapes for these is very high, coming from the family's Grand and Premier Cru vineyards. There are also pricey bottlings of several single site champagnes, especially the pre-eminent Chardonnay Grand Cru Avize Champ Caïn and the Pinot Noir Grand Cru Äy Vauzelle Terme. There are from time to time late releases of these gems called Dégorgement Tardif (DT) from longer lees aging., and DT of the Cuvée 728 first of the numbered series, is soon to be released. These are of very high quality. The base wine for all the range is fermented in large oak foudres (ME)

Recommended Whites:
Avize Grand Cru Dégorgement Tardif Vintage ★★★★★ £G
Ay Grand Cru Vauxelle Terme ★★★★☆ £G
Cuvee 700 series NV (especially 730 738 and 739) ★★★★ £F

⚘⚘ Krug *www.kruglovers.com*
Now managed with flair by Margaret Henriques, the enlightened LVMH Director and Olivier Krug as reassuring brand ambassador, this is still the most iconic grande maison in Champagne. Production has been kept deliberating small, currently less than 400,000 bottles, in order to maintain the highest standards of quality. There is no danger that volume will be increased in the foreseeable future. These are quite remarkably impressive and structured wines. Tight and very restrained, perhaps more so than all other Champagnes, they demand cellaring. Even the multi-vintage Grande Cuvée, a wine often on the cusp of a super-five rating, will benefit from at least five to seven years ageing after release. Check the bottling date with your smart phone on the interactive back label! The Clos du Mesnil is that rare breed in this appellation, a single walled vineyard of Grand Cru Chardonnay, epic in sunny years like 2000 and of remarkable freshness in the torrid heat of 2003. Quality is impressive in its Pinot Noir brother, the tiny Clos d'Ambonnay, but it's strictly for those with fat wallets. The range is completed by the tiny production of an undoubtedly very fine NV Rosé. (DM)

Recommended Whites:
Clos du Mesnil Vintage ✪✪✪✪ £H
Vintage ★★★★★ £H
Grande Cuvée Multi Vintage ★★★★★ £H
Clos d'Ambonnay ★★★★ £H
Recommended Rosés:
Rosé Brut NV ★★★★ £H

>> Lancelot-Pienne   www.champagne-lancelot-pienne.fr

This 8.5 ha. family estate atop the hill of Cramant has some of the finest vineyards in the first commune of the Côte des Blancs to have been rightly made a Grand Cru after the Great War. Gilles Lancelot took over the reins of the long established domaine from his father in 2008. Although he is a fine oenologist, Gilles knows that great Chardonnay wine is about much more than numbers and he's extremely proud of his mid-slope lieux-dits of Les Bourons, Les Busons and Goûtte d'Or. These form the heart of his superb top vintage Blancs de Blancs Marie Lancelot named for his physician daughter, Dr. Marie. In a great vintage like 2008, and scarcely less so in riper 2009, this wine is on the cusp of a 5-star rating. Another boon is the excellent quality of the little wines. The Brut non-vintage is very superior, driven by a particular strain of fine yet succulent Meunier from across the valley in a sector called Côte d'Epernay Sud- such great value. Don't forget the Cuvée Perceval, composed of dominant Pinot Noir from Boursault in the Marne valley, balanced by the refinement of Cramant Grand Cru Chardonnay. None of these beguiling wines see oak, all go through the malolactic fermentation for balance and extra complexity. There is now a new Table Ronde Extra Brut NV. Total production of the range is a controlled 70,000 bottles a year, 60% exported. A real discovery. (ME)

Recommended Whites:
Cuvée Marie Lancelot Vintage Brut ★★★★★ £G
Cuvée Perceval Vintage Brut ★★★★ £F
Brut NV ★★★☆ £E
Table Ronde Extra Brut NV ★★★☆ £D

Lanson   www.lanson.com

Production here is vast at close to some 7.2 million bottles a year. In the light of that, quality has been at least solid. The Black Label Brut is probably the best known Champagne brand after the MOËT & CHANDON Brut Impérial; recent releases have shown a sound upturn in form – by no means where it could be, but a marked improvement. A dramatic step up Is the luxury Prestige NV Cuvée Lanson Père et fils, from longer lees ageing and doubtless better rated grapes. As well as the big brand a NV rosé is fairly unexciting but there is a stylish Blanc de Blancs vintage and a decent enough Ivory Label Demi-Sec. The Brut Gold Label vintage was good rather than spectacular in 1995 but the quality of the current wines does seem to indicate real progress. The Noble Cuvée is a seriously structured and impressive Champagne. But don't fprget the Gold Label straight vintages, quite exceptional in 1996 and 2002, and very good value. There are also extra- aged non-vintage cuvées based on an assemblage of three good years. The walled Clos Lanson next to the house in Central Reims is a promising newcomer. Experienced, adept new cellarmaster is introducing some non-malo fermentations for a rounder style. (DM)

Recommended Whites:
Noble Cuvée Vintage ★★★★ £G
Gold Label Vintage ★★★★ £F
Blanc de Blancs Vintage ★★★★ £F
Prestige Lanson Père et Fils NV ★★★★ £F
Clos Lanson ★★★ £G
Brut Black Label NV ★★ £D

❀ Larmandier-Bernier   www.larmandier.fr

Small, top-class grower based in Vertus on the Côte des Blancs, also some prize Grand Cru Cramant with old vines. Like most really quality-conscious winemakers around the world, Pierre Larmandier keeps the human input to a minimum: in his case, his higher education was in business school rather than oenology which maybe explains his instinctive talent for winemaking. The style is for very structured, mineral- intense Champagnes, which have been given extra weight and depth through cask-ageing (no éhere) with the Né d'un Terre de Vertus being bone dry. The wines have the depth and texture to support the style but will reward cellaring, the vintage wines for many years. Sometimes, under pressure of demand the vintage cuvees are released a touch too early. A very small amount of red Côteaux Champenois is also produced and is among the very best examples of the style. The fact that the wines are excellent value is another plus. (DM)

Recommended Whites:
Extra Brut Vieille Vignes de Cramant Vintage ★★★★★ £F
Né d'Un Terre de Vertus Non Dosé NV ★★★★ £F
Extra Brut Tradition NV ★★★ £E
Blanc de Blancs NV ★★★ £E

Recommended Rosés:
Extra Brut Rosé de Saignée NV ★★★ £E

Laurent-Perrier   www.laurent-perrier.co.uk

There is a family ethos here, ever since the late Bernard de Nonancourt rescued this ailing house in 1948 and made it into one of the major forces in Champagne, with interests in other houses such as DE CASTELLANE, DELAMOTTE, the prestige SALON and IRON HORSE in California. The great wines traditionally are the Grand Siècle labels, at their best very refined, even If recently the multi-vintage Blanc may have lost a little of its élan. The Vintage Grand' Siècle Cuvée Alexandra is still tops, named for Nonancourt's daughter, who is still active in the business. The regular Brut NV is much improved in recent tastings with a Chablis-like dash and tension from a high proportion of Chardonnay. The non-vintage rosé, made by the saignée method is stylish and fresh, a great commercial success. The Ultra Brut is a bit in the doldrums - where is that piercing intensity and pureness of flavour created by de Nonancourt and Alain Terrier, his masterly chef de caves, who retired in 2004? The vintage bottlings can still be excellent in that Chablis-like style and released only in vintages worthy of the name. (ME)

Recommended Whites:
Grand Siècle La Cuvée NV ★★★★ £H
Vintage ★★★★ £F
Brut LP NV ★★★ £E
Ultra Brut NV ★★ £F

Recommended Rosés:
Grand Siècle Alexandra Rosé Vintage ★★★★★ £H
Brut Rosé NV ★★★ £G

A R Lenoble   www.champagne-lenoble.com

This *bijou* house in a fine period property off Damery's main square was founded in 1920 by Armand Raphael Graser, an Alsacien who, after the First War preferred to call his estate by a French name AR Lenoble. His great grandchilden, sister and brother Anne and Antoine Malassagne took over in 1995 and have transformed this country affair into one of the jewels of Champagne. A & A are fiercely independent, answerable only to each other, happy to wait patiently for their wines to mature properly before releasing them. Their confidence is based on the excellent worth of their vineyards, some 18 ha, spanning the Grand Cru Chardonnay territory of Chouilly, closest to Epernay; the premier cru Pinot Noir of Bisseul, near Ay where the Marne valley meets the Montagne de Reims; and the best parcels of Damery Menier by the Marne river, home to an

France

ideal amalgam of chalk, limestone and clay. All these are the major resource that Antoine and his team of a dozen work with, plus a few parcels of top parcels from trusted growers who are old friends. Output is currently just under 36,000 bottles a year. There is a fresh and tightly structured Brut Intense NV showing the flowery scents and verve of this Chardonnay- dominant cuvée. The vintage Blanc de Noirs 100% Pinot Noir and combines gras ampleness with sturdy backbone. The latest vintage Rosé is rather special, subtly made from about 85% Chardonnay and 15% de-stemmed Pinot Noir from Busseuil- a pink of real persistence, particularly in 2012. The real excitement here though are the Chardonnay wines from six Grand Cru villages on the Côte des Blancs. The NV gets around 25% reserve wine and is nicely structured. The Gentilhomme vintage is tighter with a purer mineral structure and impressive depth. Particularly striking is the luxury cuvée Les Aventures which comes from the terroir of the same name in the village of Chouilly. Some of the base wine is barrel-fermented to lend extra structure and the wine has a slightly lower dosage than the other bottlings. Give it two or three years after release. (DM)

Recommended Whites:
Cuvée Les Aventure Grand Cru Blanc de Blancs Vintage ★★★★ £G
Blanc de Blancs Gentilhomme Grand Cru Vintage ★★★★ £F
Blancs de Noirs Premier Cru Bisseul Vintage ★★★★ £F
Blanc de Blancs Grand Cru NV ★★★ £E
Brut Intense NV ★★ £D
Recommended Rosés:
Brut Rosé Terroirs NV ★★★☆ £D

>> **Nicolas Maillart** *www.champagne-maillart.fr*
The ninth generation of a family of wine-growers dating back to 1753 in neighbouring Chamery, Nicolas Maillart is the rising star of the Petite Montagne, the land of sandstone, which has a very distinctive terroir yielding very aromatic Pinot Noir especially in Ecueil, which is famous for the great black grape. After graduating in oenology and agronomy, Nicolas in 2008 took charge of the holdings that include Ecueil and Villers Allerand, both Premiers Crus plus a slice of Grand Cru Bouzy, giving a vineyard resource of great potential and variety. In The Platine Extra Brut Platine Pinot Noir is dominant, with a nice balance of Chardonnay. The high percentage of reserve wines (30 – 40%) ensures high consistency and regularity; only Grand and Premier Cru grapes in the Montagne de Reims go into the assemblage. The dosage is just 3 grams per litre (g/l): Superior stuff, with notes of stone red fruits, a whiff of hazelnut, a slight toastiness. By contrast, Les Chaillons Gillis Premier Cru is from old-vines Chardonnay produced only in great years. A hand-made approach from grape to glass, vinified and long-aged in oak and then rested for three months before sale. Very delicate and lightly toasted. Dosage 2g/l. a fine wine for fish gastronomy. The Brut Grand Cru Rosé NV (70% Pinot Noir 30% Chardonnay) is macerated on the Pinot skins for 52 hours -admirably fresh yet vinous rosé with a finale of terrific finesse.The pre-eminent Les Francs de Pied Premier Cru is from one parcel of Ecueil, from old ungrafted Pinot Noir vines on sandy soils (the phylloxera aphid historically hates sand!) As much a great wine as a Champagne, in 2005 and 2008 it is a riveting, fascinating creation- intense yet delicate, ethereal but durable, it deserves to be decanted before what is a rare emotional experience in the presence of greatness. (ME)

Recommended Whites:
Les Francs de Pied Premier Cru ★★★★★ £G
Les Chaillons Gillis Premier Cru Vintage ★★★★ £F
Platine Extra Brut NV ★★★☆ £E

Recommended Rosés:
Brut Rosé Grand Cru NV ★★★★ £G

Mailly Grand Cru *www.champagne-mailly.com*
Among the leading co-ops this one could claim to be the first among equals in Champagne, based in the Grand Cru village of Mailly on the Montagne de Reims. Indeed, the house is the only one in the region to produce wines solely from Grand Cru sources in Pinot Noir and Chardonnay exclusively Vineyards face all points of the compass, catching the sun at some point in the day. Their open Northerly location also favours a subtle spicy style of Champagne that needs time. Of the dominant Pint Noir sites, two of the finest lieux dits are westerly Les Poules and Les Hautes Cotes, near Verzenay A total of 13 wines are made from growers with holdings exclusively within the Grand Cru appellation across 480 plots.. Vinification is very assured under a new chef de cave, modern with a gravity-feeding winemaking facility. The three Classic cuvées all impress, the Brut Millésimé just having an extra dimension with a marked mineral imprint. The elegant Extra Brut is restrained and elegant with a citrus quality running through: It has zero dosage and is a very fine example of the style. The Délice offers a mix of citrus, subtle green fruits and a bready hint, a demi-sec with real elegance and a subtle caramel quality. The luxury cuvees offer real class. There is a very finely structured and elegant rosé L'Intemporelle which has a sizeable proportion of Chardonnay (40%) very well balanced with Pinot Noir from 40 plus year-old vines. The white L'Intemporelle is similarly elegant with great carry and intesnsity being vinified from a similar blend and some of the finest plots. The Échansons is a fuller style, marked by a higher proportion of Pinot Noir (75%). It is made only in the finest years. An additional prestige cuvée, Exception Blanche is a Blanc de Blancs from a combination of vineyards in Mailly and the Côte des Blancs. Restrained and very elegant it has a subtle creamy, citrus edge. (DM)

Recommended Whites:
Échansons Grand Cru Milésimé ★★★★ £G
L'Intemporelle Grand Cru Milésimé ★★★★ £G
Exception Blanche Blanc de Blancs Grand Cru Milésimé ★★★ £F
Brut Grand Cru Milésimé ★★★ £E
Extra Brut Grand Cru NV ★★★ £E
Brut Grand Cru Réserve NV ★★★ £D
Délice Grand Cru NV ★★ £D
Recommended Rosés:
L'Intemporelle Grand Cru Milésimé ★★★★ £G
Brut Grand Cru NV ★★★ £E

❀ **Serge Mathieu** *www.champagne-serge-mathieu.fr*
A small but very good property based in the Aube. Pinot Noir is the key component here and the wines certainly display a real weight and concentration. However, what marks them out is their elegance and refinement, something that a great many of the family's near neighbours struggle to achieve. The vintage Brut is impressively concentrated, rich, bready and toasty but with a fine mineral backbone. The Select is subtler, more refined, with a higher proportion of Chardonnay and a shorter period on lees. Both are ageworthy. (DM)

Recommended Whites:
Brut Millésime Vintage ★★★★ £F
Select NV ★★★★ £E
Brut Prestige NV ★★★ £E
Brut Tradition NV ★★★ £D
Demi-Sec NV ★★ £D

Recommended Rosés:
Brut Rosé NV ★★★ £E

Moët et Chandon   www.moet.com
Of all the Champagne houses this is the one that most readily comes to most consumers' minds. The tendency among the majority of occasional wine drinkers is to think of Moët as a brand rather than understanding it as a great Champagne house. Production is considerable, around 30 million bottles a year. Brut Impérial can be a lot more impressive than it is often given credit for. The White Star is marketed in the US and contains a higher dosage. The vintage Brut is well made with reasonable yeasty complexity and will age well over the medium term. Like the house itself, Dom Pérignon is the most established of the region's luxury cuvées and production is not small (rumoured to be about 5 million bottles). The wine is excellent and consistent, becoming increasingly complex and harmonious with age. There is a fine vintage rosé and a very small amount of the Dom Pérignon Rosé, every bit as impressive as the white. There is also a super-premium Oenothèque which is given 13 years on its lees, six more than the regular Dom Pérignon and an extraordinarily rare rosé. The new Plenitude concept (P1, P2, P3) highlights this great champagne at various ages of maturity, on release at about 7 years, at more than 15 years, at 30 years +. The Dom Pérignon 1998 P2 is a magnificent nectar to drink in 2017. (DM)
Recommended Whites:
Dom Pérignon Vintage ✪✪✪✪✪ £H
Brut Grand Vintage ★★★☆ £F
Brut Impérial NV ★★★ £E
Brut White Star NV 1922 ★★ £E
Recommended Rosés:
Dom Pérignon Rosé Vintage ★★★★★ £H
Brut Rosé Grand Vintage ★★★ £G

Pierre Moncuit   www.pierre-moncuit.fr
The Moncuits produce three very fine Blanc de Blancs at their 20 ha property at Le Mesnil-sur-Oger. The Grand Cru Vintage bottling is superbly crafted, intense and refined with not a hint of austerity, rather a rich, biscuity approachability. The Vieilles Vignes is a very fine expression of Champagne hand-crafted from Chardonnay – intense, refined and very ageworthy. Sadly very little is made. What makes these wines all the more remarkable is the reasonable prices. (DM)
Recommended Whites:
Blanc de Blancs Nicole Moncuit Vieilles Vignes Vintage ★★★★ £F
Blanc de Blancs Grand Cru Vintage ★★★★ £E
Blanc de Blancs Grand Cru NV ★★★ £E

Montaudon
Small and reasonably long-established Champagne house originally founded in 1891 and with a sizeable vineyard holding of some 45 ha. The wines are all very well crafted in a showy and opulent style. The NV Reserve is tight and citrussy, with a nice mineral undercurrent and fine biscuity persistence. The vintage is richer and fuller with surprising flesh and mid palate weight. The elegant Classe M is the house's luxury cuvée and offers real breadth as well as persistence with very complex candied, citrus and toasted aromas opening out on the palate. The wines all drink very well on release. (DM)
Recommended Whites:
Millésimé Vintage ★★★★☆ £F
Classe M NV ★★★★ £F

Réserve Première NV ★★★ £E

G H Mumm   www.mumm.com
Pernod Ricard purchased this old house in 2001 and it now joins PERRIER JOUËT in the same stable. The main brand, Cordon Rouge, was for a long time a serious underperformer. However, particularly since 2006 the quality has been much sounder thanks to a radical overhaul of sources by talented cellarmaster Didier Mariotti. The wine is not complex but has a good core of appley fruit and Pinotish body; the dosage is a little more moderate. The Cordon Rouge Vintage Is much better since 2006, Didier's first solo vintage. There is also a fine Blanc de Noirs NV (Pure Verzenay) a new non-vintage assemblage Grand Cru, a decent Brut Rosé and of course the very good prestige, René Lalou, back on form in 1999 and excellent in 2002. On the way upwards in quality. (DM)
Recommended Whites:
René Lalou Vintage ★★★★ £H
Grand Cru Vintage ★★★ £F
Cordon Rouge Vintage ★★★ £F
Cordon Rouge NV ★★ £E
Recommended Rosés:
Brut Rosé NV ★★ £E

Bruno Paillard   www.champagnebrunopaillard.com
With his exhaustive knowledge of Champagne learned as a broker and his fine business brain, Bruno Paillard is one of the most influential men in the community, guardian of the Champagne appellation and the grand chef with Philippe Baijot of the Lanson-Boizel-Chanoine French group of quality conscious houses. In his own perfectionist maison, founded In 1982, Bruno and his daughter Alice run a modern, intelligently organized cellar producing a controlled 550,000 bottles a year. The style is unfailing for fine very dry champagnes of low dosage, as shown in his exemplary Brut Premiere Cuvee NV which achieves the difficult balancing act of being fresh and incisively mineral while showing lovely fruit and vinosity. It's cleverly vinified mainly in stainless steel but also 20% oak fermentation to aerate the cuvée and give it a touch of real class. The prestige NPU (Nec Plus Ultra) is undoubtedly a serious, multi-flavoured leader of the range , very pricey, but always blue-chip in great and difficult vintages (a remarkably successful 2003). For quality and value, the vintage Blanc de Blancs is on the cusp of a five-star rating especially in great Chardonnay years like 1995 and 2004.The wines are labelled with a date of disgorging which gives a clear idea about when to drink the wines. (ME)
Recommended Whites:
Nec Plus Ultra Vintage ★★★★★ £H
Vintage Brut Blanc de Blancs ★★★★☆ £F
Brut Millésime Vintage ★★★★ £F
Brut Première Cuvée NV ★★★ £E
Recommended Rosés:
Brut Rosé Première Cuvée NV ★★★ £E

✿ Joseph Perrier   www.josephperrier.com
Relatively small among the big Champagne houses, Joseph Perrier is noted for traditional, medium- to full-bodied wines with some exceptional vintage bottles. The Brut Royale NV has roughly equal proportions of Chardonnay, Meunier and Pinot Noir in the blend, resulting in a full, fruity style, nicely tempered now with a moderate dosage (7g/l) There is a striking, intensely individual Blanc de Blancs, while the vintage Royale is rich and complex, again with reduced dosage.. Two very good wines released to celebrate 185

France

years of the house. A very fine, structured and piercing Blanc de Blancs has a touch more depth and carry than a nevertheless very impressive rosé coming from Pinot Noir, Chardonnay and Meunier. The Joséphine vintage is now one of the finest of all the luxury cuvées. The concentrated Pinot fruit is beautifully balanced by a refined, nutty quality with its Chardonnay component providing finesse and a real depth and mineral purity. This will cellar very well. Approachable, well made non-vintage demi-sec and rosé are also produced under the Cuvée Royale label. (DM)

Recommended Whites:
Brut Joséphine Vintage ★★★★★ £H
Cuvée Brut Blanc de Blancs Vintage ★★★★ £F
Cuvée Royale Brut Vintage ★★★★ £F
Cuvée Royale Brut Blanc de Blancs NV ★★★ £E
Cuvée Royale Brut NV ★★★ £E
Cuvée Royale Demi-Sec NV ★★★ £E

Recommended Rosés:
Cuvée Brut Rosé Vintage ★★★★ £F
Brut Royale NV ★★★ £E

Perrier-Jouët   www.perrier-jouet.com
Like G H MUMM this house, nearly 200 years old, is now under the Pernod Ricard banner. The wines have a relatively high proportion of Chardonnay but at the lower level they struggle to offer a great deal. The basic NV Brut is a straightforward and simple offering with more green apple than complex, yeast-developed flavours. The Brut Rosé is a touch more impressive and there is a NV Blason white which provides a hint of bready complexity with a little time in bottle. The Blason Rosé, has very simple and straightforward fruit. The vintage Brut has better depth than the regular and a hint of toastiness but there should be greater dimension. The prestige cuvée La Belle Époque has a stylish bottle design and impressively tight, Chardonnay-based fruit. It achieves good to very good complex characters with age. There's a very good Belle Époque rosé as well. (DM)

Recommended Whites:
La Belle Époque Vintage ★★★★ £H
Grand Brut Vintage ★★ £F
Brut Blason de France NV ★★ £E

Recommended Rosés:
Grand Brut NV ★★ £E

>> Pierre Péters   www.champagne-peters.com
This 17.5 ha estate of the Péters family, originally from Luxembourg, is home to one of the best producers in the top sites of the Côte des Blancs at Avize, Oger and particularly Le Mesnil, where the family's parcel of Les Chétillons is one of the finest bits of earth in Champagne. Just how fine this and other vineyards was revealed in a visit of February 2008 to taste the new wines of 2007, which suffered a lot of pre-harvest rain and an August that felt like November. After a winter in the vats, the wines were amazingly good, a classic example of the greatness of these terroirs defying whatever the heavens might throw at them. The Musette vineyard in Mesnil was supple and round, whereas La Fosse in the lower clay-rich soils of Avize was much more powerful, even burly. Then the coup de grace Les Chétillons at four months quite typically had bracing acidity and a mineral force that needed a lot of time: Nine years on, the 2007 is a delight of minerality and grace. The name of the vineyard was originally never mentioned, just called Cuvée Spéciale. Now Rodolphe Péters has printed Chétillons on the label for all to see. If you like Champagne with a bit of age, the 2000

Chétillons is exceptional. There is a fine, always appreciated Brut Cuvée de Réserve NV with aged classy notes of hazelnuts and confit of apricot – also a good, balanced Extra-Brut and an intriguing Rosé d'Albane, a blend of Chardonnay blended with a Rosé de Saignée. (ME)

Recommended Whites:
Le Mesnil Grand Cru Les Chétillons Vintage ★★★★★ £G
Extra Brut NV ★★★ £F
Cuvée de Réserve Brut NV ★★☆ £E

Recommended Rosés:
Rosé d'Albane Brut NV ★★ £E

✿ Philipponnat   www.champagnephilipponnat.com
This is a relatively small négociant-manipulant with an output of just 600,00 bottles a year that has been making an excellent small range over the past decade or so under the management of Charles Philipponnat. Among the wines a good, attractive, strawberry-fruited rosé is joined by the Royale Réserve, which has good depth and a light nutty, biscuit character. The Non Dosé example is tight and structured with a fine mineral character. The vintage is a step up, more complete and complex, while the impressive Grand Blanc is a complex Blanc de Blancs that needs time. Impressive also are the vintaged Brut 1522 wines, both a Premier Cru rosé and a Grand Cru Brut with both wines dominated by Pinot Noir. The top wine is the great prestige cuvée Brut Clos de Goisses, a wine of really impressive depth and finesse. There is also a subtle classy blanc de noirs (100% Pinot Noir) the Vintage Les Cintres Extra Brut (a creditable 1996 in a patchy vintage). This wine, the 1522 labels and particularly Clos des Goisses will benefit from additional cellaring – up to five years' ageing after release. (DM)(DM)

Recommended Whites:
Clos des Goisses Vintage ★★★★★ £H
Extra Brut Blanc de Noirs Les Cintres Vintage ★★★★ £H
1522 Grand Cru Brut Vintage ★★★★ £G
Grand Blanc Brut Vintage ★★★★ £F
Réserve Millésimé Brut Vintage ★★★ £F
Royale Réserve Non Dosé Brut NV ★★★ £E
Royale Réserve Brut NV ★★ £E

Recommended Rosés:
1522 Premier Cru Brut Vintage ★★★★ £G
Réserve Rosé NV ★★ £E

Piper-Heidsieck   www.piper-heidsieck.com
Under the same new ownership as Charles HEIDSIECK, the Champagne house, a favourite of Hollywood stars is into a new lease of life. The NV Brut is much Improved, its fruit purer with a crisper texture and linear carry. The Brut Rosé is simple, with attractive berry fruit. The Brut vintage is a definite level up – the wine has structure and depth with some complex toasty notes. The Cuvée Sublime demi-sec is opulent but does not cloy. The Piper Rare Vintage is very special, made in challenging vintages that were turned into triumphs (eg 1988 and 1999) The 2002 is on the cusp of a 5-star rating. (ME)

Recommended Whites:
Rare Vintage ★★★★★ £G
Brut Vintage ★★★★ £F
Brut NV ★★★ £E
Sublime Demi-Sec NV ★★★ £E

✿ Pol Roger   www.polroger.co.uk
Family-owned, medium sized house, much loved in Britain, with

production approaching some 1.8 million bottles a year. The NV Réserve (formerly White Foil) is always excellent with real depth and refined secondary flavours but, like all the wines here, elegance and intensity is displayed more than weight. The Brut Pure is bone-dry without dosage, great with oysters. The vintage is just that bit more complex and structured, very fine and intense in both colours. There is a first class Blanc de Blancs Chardonnay vintage which is lighter still in style but impeccably balanced. Sir Winston Churchill is a very impressive prestige cuvée, which demands to be cellared; the 1996 has years of life still (DM)

Recommended Whites:
Sir Winston Churchill Vintage ✪✪✪✪✪ £H
Brut Chardonnay Vintage ★★★★★ £F
Brut Vintage ★★★★ £F
Brut Réserve NV ★★★★ £E
Brut Pure NV ★★★ £E

Recommended Rosés:
Brut Vintage ★★★ £F

Pommery *www.pommery.com*
Production is considerable at this large house. However, the LMVH group has sold its interest to Vranken who, while commercially successful throughout the appellation, have not so far established themselves as a beacon of top quality. Under LMVH ownership the quality throughout the range has been at least sound. There is now an improved NV Brut Royal – biscuity with none of that raw edge of old – a decent NV Apanage and a sound rosé. The vintage Grand Cru is refined and very well balanced in the best years, not overly weighty but long and intense. The Cuvée Louise is very impressive, not a full style but very long, harmonious and ageworthy. There is also a very fine Louise Rosé. Time will tell how the style and quality of the house will develop as a part of the Vranken empire. (DM)

Recommended Whites:
Louise Vintage ★★★★ £H
Brut Grand Cru Vintage ★★★ £F
Brut Royal NV ★★★ £E
Brut Apanage NV ★★ £E

Recommended Rosés:
Brut NV ★ £E

✪✪ Louis Roederer *www.champagne-roederer.com*
This has long been established as one of the great Champagne houses. It is still family-owned and the company has invested heavily in other projects. As well as the ROEDERER ESTATE venture in California's Anderson Valley (see California North Coast), much closer to home it has acquired DEUTZ, along with Château PICHON LALANDE (Comtesse), Château de PEZ in the Médoc and in Portugal the Port house RAMOS PINTO. The style of the brilliant Brut Premier NV is Pinot Noir driven, with a finesse and seamless complexity unmatched save for one or two other greats. The Blanc de Blancs Vintage is a model of restraint, its malolactic avoided for freshness and to achieve balance and harmony. Cristal is one of the greatest and most refined sparkling wines in the world. It needs time. There is fine new Brut Nature without dosage made only in warm ripe years - so far 2006 & 2009. The peerless quality of the whole range is enhanced by biodynamic farming in 40% of Roederer great estate of vineyards, the biodynamic project the largest of its kind in Champagne. (DM)

Recommended Whites:
Cristal Vintage ✪✪✪✪✪ £H
Blanc de Blancs Vintage ★★★★ £G

Brut Nature Vintage ★★★★ £G
Brut Vintage ★★★★ £F
Brut Premier NV ★★★★ £F

Recommended Rosés:
Cristal Vintage ✪✪✪✪✪ £H
Brut Vintage ★★★★ £G

✿ Ruinart *www.ruinart.com*
Founded In 1729 Ruinart is a house steeped in history, its Roman chalk cellars - les Crayères- are now classified as a Unesco World Heritage Site. Although production is a respectable 1.7 million bottles, the house has maintained a relatively low profile in recent years under the same ownership as MOËT & CHANDON. That is changing with *chef de cave* and roving brand ambassador Frederick Panaiotis, one of the best and most articulate winemakers who speaks five languages. The wines are good to very good, indeed the Blanc de Blancs Dom Ruinart and the DR Rosé are worthy of a super-five rating on occasion. Chardonnay is an important part of the blending equation here and the wines are both refined and powerful because the Chardonnays come from both the Montagne de Reims and the Côte de Blancs, aided by extensive ageing of the base wines. The NV Brut is consistently one of the soundest of its kind. The Blanc de Blancs NV is much improved especially in magnums and a rare Jéroboam tasted recently though not carrying a vintage label was a pure great 2008 - added value! One hears less of the luxury blend of six grands crus and five vintages all from Chardonnay, the rare and pricey l'Exclusive de Ruinart. (ME)

Recommended Whites:
Dom Ruinart Vintage ★★★★★ £H
Brut R de Ruinart Vintage ★★★★ £G
Blanc de Blancs NV ★★★★ £F
Brut R de Ruinart NV ★★★ £E

Recommended Rosés:
Dom Ruinart Vintage ★★★★★ £H
Brut R de Ruinart NV ★★★ £F

✪✪ Salon
Now owned by Laurent-Perrier, just one exceptional wine is produced here: a Blanc de Blancs, in fact the first created, sourced entirely from selected vineyard plots in the village of Le Mesnil. Only bottled in the very best vintage years (the average through the last century was just over one year in four), an exceptional 1997 is surprisingly rich and intense, but of course as well structured as one would expect, the wine should be cellared for at least a decade after release. 2002 is the current release, about which "the experts" are divided. Some applaud its supremacy: others are a little disappointed, expecting more. Of older vintage, the 1983 is wonderful still, overtaking the highly vaunted 1982 which is starting to tire. DELAMOTTE, Salon's sister house from the same cellars can be remarkable value. (DM)

Recommended Whites:
Salon Vintage ★★★★★ £H

François Secondé *www.champagnefrancoisseconde.com*
Based in the Marne village of Sillery, François Secondé produces very well priced and finely structured Champagne from just 5 ha. Around three-quarters of the vineyard is planted to Pinot Noir with the balance Chardonnay, but the style is for tight, restrained, wines which need a little time to show at their best. The vineyards are farmed organically and the vines are approaching 40 years, all

France

of which helps in providing excellent raw material. The wines are traditionally made with manual remuage. They offer very good value. (DM)

Recommended Whites:
Brut NV ★★★ £E
Brut Clavier NV ★★★ £E

Recommended Rosés:
Brut Rosé NV ★★ £E

☉ Jacques Selosse

This is a remarkable small producer. Anselme Selosse bottles less than 60,000 bottles of very impressive Champagne every year. The approach in the vineyard was once biodynamic, now more sustainable ("I believe in science" says Anselme now) and yields are severely restricted to provide the purest, greatest intensity of fruit possible. What has made the approach here radical is the use of new as well as old oak to barrel-ferment the base wine. Extensively aged prior to release, these are strong and powerful wines for Champagne but no less impressive for that. On occasions, some adamant critics have said that the oak overwhelms the sense of terroir particularly in young or newly released wines: If that was ever true, it isn't any longer. With his son Guillaume helping Papa make the wines, the wood is better Integrated - Anselme has found the harmony he has always wanted. These are distinctive, important wines like no other. The Selosses own the luxury but very relaxed hotel Les Avises on this site. (DM)

Recommended Whites:
Les Carelles Extra Brut NV ★★★★★ £H
Originale Extra-Brut NV ★★★★★ £H
Brut Initial NV ★★★★ £H

☉ De Sousa   www.champagnedesousa.com

This excellent small Champagne house makes a small range of very structured and intense wines. The top wines coming from Chardonnay can be very restrained on release and deserve at least a couple of years to show at their best. They are though extremely complex and characterful. Wines are released under both the De Sousa and Zoémie de Sousa, of which the Brut Merveille is widely available. It comes from a similar blend of the red grapes as well as Chardonnay to the Brut Tradition. It is the Blanc de Blancs cuvées though, that stand out here. Much of the key to these remarkable wines is the holding of very old Chardonnay vines. Viticulture is organic, with some plots farmed biodynamically and the wines are produced with minimal intervention and no filtration. The Réserve is a blend of two or three different years with quite a bit of reserve wine, the Caudalies NV, like the vintage bottling has the base wine vinified in small oak. Both are intensely complex and finely structured and demand cellaring. (DM)

Recommended Whites:
Blanc de Blancs Cuvée des Caudalies Millésime ★★★★★ £G
Blanc de Blancs Cuvée des Caudalies NV ★★★★ £F
Blanc de Blancs Réserve NV ★★★ £F
Brut Tradition NV ★★★ £E

☉ Taittinger   www.taittinger.com

A large house producing around 5 million bottles a year of reliable NV Brut Réserve., which combines Chardonnay with the two Pinots. There are also some really very fine vintage wines and an exceptional prestige Cuvée Comtes de Champagne, matched by an equally exquisite and very rare rosé. New is the single-vineyard Les Folies de la Marquetterie which is a blend of Chardonnay

and Pinot Noir and offers a rich and full style of Champagne with impressive original flavours, a riot of cherries and mango, as distinctive as any vigneron's champagne Also produced are Prelude, a non-vintaged wine solely from Grand Cru fruit and the low-dosage Nocturne Sec. Taittinger also has an investment in Domaine CARNEROS in California. (DM)

Recommended Whites:
Blanc de Blanc Comtes de Champagne Vintage ★★★★★ £H
Les Folies de la Marquetterie NV ★★★★ £F
Brut Millésime Vintage ★★★★ £F
Brut Réserve NV ★★★ £E

Recommended Rosés:
Comtes de Champagne Vintage ★★★★★ £H
Brut Prestige NV ★★ £F

Tarlant   www.tarlant.com

This small house produces an excellent small range of wines with some striking dry examples. The Tarrant family have been cultivating vineyards in the region since 1687 and the current generation now farm 13 ha across 4 different crus on the Vallée de la Marne. The terroirs of the vineyards is varied and soils range from chalk, clay-limestone, sand and limestone to small pebbles. Although Pinot Noir and Meunier dominate plantings, there is a significant holding of Chardonnay, just under 4 ha. In the winery two new Coquart presses ensure juice of the highest quality and the primary fermentation is done plot by plot and in a combination of small oak and stainless steel. The Réserve wines are a blend of all the varieties and from a range of *terroirs*. The same is the case with the impressively intense Brut Zero, which is bottled as the label suggests with zero *dosage*. The Prestige vintage bottlings also offer excellent value for the quality. The white is dominated by Chardonnay and offers a subtle elegant toasty complexity. The fine rosé, surprisingly has an even higher proportion of Chardonnay, 85% is blended with Pinot Noir. The Cuvée Louis is rich and toasty, a barrel-fermented blend of three older vintages and a mix of 50/50 Chardonnay and Pinot Noir from 60-year-old vines. The most complete champagne here. Then here is the excellent Vigne d'Antan (meaning Vines of Yesteryear) which comes from ungrafted Chardonnay. It has a very intense mineral and steely quality with a nutty, toasty character. It is an Extra-Brut style and gets a minimal *dosage*. (DM)(DM)

Recommended Whites:
Extra Brut La Vigne d'Antan NV ★★★★☆ £F
Extra Brut Cuvée Louis NV ★★★★☆ £F
Extra Brut La Vigne d'Antan NV ★★★★ £F
Extra Brut Prestige Vintage ★★★★ £F
Brut Zero NV ★★★ £E
Brut Réserve NV ★★★ £D
Demi-Sec Réserve NV ★★ £D

Recommended Rosés:
Brut Prestige Vintage ★★★ £E

De Venoge   www.champagnedevenoge.com

The Swiss de Venoge family originally founded this house in 1837 and it remained in the hands of the family until the 1950s. Much investment has since gone into the brand and one of the keys to quality here is that only the wine from the first pressing is used. The second pressing is always sold off. Brut Rosé is soft and round and marked by lifted red berry fruit and should be drunk soon after purchase. The Cordon Bleu NV bottling is a clean, fresh and fruit driven style dominated by red grapes. Blanc de Noirs is a

touch fuller, 80% Pinot Noir, the balance Meunier. There is a good vintage bottling which includes 70% Pinot Noir and 15% each of Chardonnay and Meunier. It requires a little patience for its green apple and berry fruit to develop a richer biscuity character but has good depth and persistence. Tighter, more citrussy is the Blanc de Blancs vintage. The top wine the Grand Vin de Princes is rich, toasty and biscuity on release. 100% Chardonnay it is produced solely from Grand Cru sites on the Côte des Blancs and will develop for a decade after release. (DM)

Recommended Whites:
Brut Grand Vin des Princes Vintage ★★★★ £G
Brut Blanc de Blancs Vintage ★★★ £F
Brut Millésimé Vintage ★★★ £F
Brut Blanc de Noirs NV ★★ £E
Extra Brut Cordon Sélect Bleu NV ★★ £E
Recommended Rosés:
Brut NV ★ £F

❂ Veuve Clicquot *www.veuve-clicquot.fr*

This house is second to MOËT & CHANDON in the LVMH hierarchy in terms of volume but most certainly ahead in terms of quality. Throughout the last five or six years the quality here has always been good, even for the regular Carte Jaune (Yellow Label) which gets better year or year, now it has a 5% spell in large oak foudres. The vintage wines have weight and structure and are full of rich, toasty character also helped on by a soupçon of. La Grande Dame is an exceptional wine, both the more easily available white and the scarce rosé. Both are rich, increasingly elegant blends of Pinot Noir and Chardonnay. A number of prestige wineries around the world originally purchased by Veuve Clicquot now fall within the LVMH banner. These include CLOUDY BAY in New Zealand, CAPE MENTELLE in Western Australia and NEWTON in the Napa Valley. The house of Canard-Duchêne, was for long under the Clicquot wing but is now owned (and improved) by Alain Thiénot. The Clicquot Cave Privée Collection of venerable vintages include some fabulous years such as the white and rosé in 1989, certainly worth a super 5-star ratings. (DM)

Recommended Whites:
La Grande Dame Vintage ★★★★★ £H
Cave Privée Vintage Collection ★★★★★ £H
Vintage Réserve ★★★★ £F
Brut Carte Jaune NV ★★★ £F
Recommended Rosés:
Rosé Réserve Vintage ★★★★ £G

>> Veuve Fourny & Fils *www.champagne-veuve-fourny.com*

If you are looking for great Chardonnay champagne of crystalline purity, this medium-sized domaine might be your first port of call for top quality and value. Brothers Charles- Henri and Emmanuel ('Manu') Fourny manage the 14 ha of their Premier Cru vineyards with perfectionist care. Unusually, every one of their wines comes from within the family's home commune of Vertus but pre-eminently in the top eastern part on the hilly slopes called Monts Ferrés. Just over the hill to the north is famed Le Mesnil; even the Fourny's postal address is route du Mesnil, giving you an idea of the delights to expect. Manu the winemaker has all the right credentials, a graduate of Reims prestigious oenology faculty he's also an intuitive artisan who has done stages in Gevrey Chambertin, so he is not afraid of oak but uses it with a Champenois precision for his delicate wines. The brothers are specialists in Extra Brut and Brut Nature champagnes of low

dosage or none: Manu makes them more assuredly than other makers because he insists these bone-dry wines come from great terroirs and old vines to prevent any sense of rasping aggressive flavours. The Grande Reserve Premier Cru NV is a fine, rounded NV (from 40-year-old vines). It used to have a touch of Pinot Noir but is now all Chardonnay like the rest of the white range. Cuvée "R" has a feisty strong character in memory of the late Roger Fourny. A favourite always is the vintage Monts Ferrés of lovely tension and refined richness, as much in saline keeper 2008 as in more exuberant 2009s. There are two fine rosés, especially Les Rougemonts its south facing exposure giving an extra surge of strawberry fruit within a good structure from clay elements in the soil. The single vineyard within the walled Clos du Faubourg Notre Dame is a real gem, the 60-year-old vines above a deep sub-soil of finest chalk and limestone, and the warm walled microclimate. It ages wonderfully, especially in ripe but not too extracted vintages like 1999 and 2006. The Fournys now have a dining room for invited guests at lunch or dinner. (ME)

Recommended Whites:
Cuvee du Clos de Notre Dame Vintage ★★★★☆ £G
Les Monts Ferrés Vintage Brut Premier Cru ★★★★ £G
Brut Nature NV ★★★★ £F
Cuvee "R" NV ★★★ £F
Cuvee Grande Reserve NV ★★★ £E
Recommended Rosés:
Premier Cru Vintage "Les Rougemonts" ★★★ £F

>> Vilmart & Cie *www.champagnevilmart.fr*

The Champs family of Vilmart were one of the first Champagne growers to employ sustainable viticulture and a return to oak fermentation in the late 1980s. Père Rene Champs was a carpenter cum winemaker (now retired). His son Laurent has always been a conscientious vigneron in the vines, tilling them by hand and reducing the use of chemical treatments. On a first visit in 1992, it was even more obvious that here was a thoughtful, talented winemaker: returning most recently in 2016 it is so gratifying to see that he goes from strength to strength. Laurent's vineyards (11 ha +) are all in Premier Cru Rilly la Montagne, a solid enough village, but in his hands the wines have risen to a whole new level of excellence, particularly in the finer Cellier and Cellier d'Or upwards. For optimal finesse, these cuvées major in Chardonnay, minimum 70%, in balance with 30% Pinot Noir and are vinified in large oak foudres. The Cellier d'Or has greater intensity and depth but at a Champagne masterclass in London in June 2016, the plain Cellier won everyone's hearts for the freshness, precision and sheer pleasure it gave. The top the range Coeur de Cuvée the heart of the first pressings, is one of Champagne's great wines, vinified in 222 litre barriques: where once the taste of oak intruded, now it's seamlessly integrated in the wine and showing beautifully in 2006 and 2008, two very different vintages. (ME)

Recommended Whites:
Coeur de Cuvée Vintage ★★★★☆ £G
Cellier d'Or Brut Vintage ★★★★ £G
Cellier Brut NV ★★★☆ £F
Grande Réserve NV ★★ £E
Recommended Rosés:
Cuvée Rubis ★★ £E

Champagne

Other wines of note

Michel Arnould
Recommended Whites:
Carte d'Or Grand Cru NV ★★★ £E
Grande Cuvée Brut Vintage ★★★☆ £E
Mémoires des Vignes Blanc de Noirs Vintage ★★★★ £F

Benoit Lahaye
Recommended Whites:
Vintage ★★★★ £F
Brut Essentiel NV ★★★★ £E
Blanc de Noirs NV ★★★ £E

Bérèche et Fils
Recommended Whites:
Solera Reflet d'Antan ★★★★ £F
1er Cru Vintage ★★★☆ £E
Extra Brut Rive Gauche NV ★★★ £E
Recommended Rosés:
Extra Brut Rosé Campania Remensis NV ★★★☆ £E

H. Billiot et Fils
Recommended Whites:
Cuvée Laetitia Prestige ★★★★ £F
Vintage Brut ★★★ £E
Cuvée de Julie Vintage ★★★ £E
Cuvée de Reserve ★★★ £E

H Blin
Recommended Whites:
Brut Vintage ★★ £E

Alexandre Bonnet
Recommended Whites:
Blanc de Blancs Vintage ★★★ £F
Blanc de Noirs NV ★★★ £E
Grande Réserve Brut NV ★★ £D

Cédric Bouchard
Recommended Whites:
Val Vilaine Brut NV ★★★☆ £E;
Vintage Les Ursules ★★★☆ £E

Philippe Brugnon
Recommended Whites:
Brut Premier Cru Vintage ★★★ £D
Brut Premier Cru NV ★★ £D
Demi-Sec Cuvée Elégance NV ★★ £D
Recommended Rosés:
Brut Rosé NV ★ £D

Roger Brun
Recommended Whites:
Brut Réserve NV ★★ £D
Brut Réserve Grand Cru NV ★★★ £D
Cuvée des Sires Grand Cru NV ★★★ £E
La Pelle Grand Cru Äy Vintage ★★★★ £G

Guy Cadel
Recommended Whites:
Carte-Blanche NV ★★ £D
Brut Vintage ★★★ £E
Recommended Rosés:
Brut Rosé NV ★★ £D

Guy Charlemagne
Recommended Whites:
Blanc de Blancs Grand Cru Vintage ★★★☆ £E

Jacky Charpentier
Recommended Whites:
Brut Prestige NV ★★ £E
Brut Vintage ★★★ £E
Recommended Rosés:
Brut Rosé NV ★★ £E

Chartogne- Taillet
Recommended Whites:
Cuvée Ste Anne NV ★★★★ £E
Extra Brut Mont Redon non dosé ★★★☆ £E
Lettre de mon Meunier NV ★★★ £E

Colin Vertus
Recommended Whites:
Blanc de Blancs NV ★★★ £E
Blanc de Blanc Vintage Paranthèse ★★★☆ £F

Ullyse Collin
Recommended Whites:
Blanc de Noirs NV ★★★ £E

Marie Courtin
Recommended Whites:
Vintage ★★★ £E

Delamotte
Recommended Whites:
Brut NV ★★☆ £E
Brut Vintage ★★★ £E
Blanc de Blancs Vintage ★★★★ £F

Paul Déthune
Recommended Whites:
Grand Cru NV ★★★ £D
Grand Cru Vintage ★★★ £E
Princesse Déthune Prestige NV ★★★★ £F

Devaux
Recommended Whites:
D de Devaux Vintage ★★★★ £G
D de Devaux NV ★★★ £F
Recommended Rosés:
Brut NV ★★☆£E

J. Dumangin
Recommended Whites:
Brut Grande Réserve NV ★★ £E
Brut Vintage ★★★ £F
Extra Brut NV ★★★ £E
Recommended Rosés:
Brut Rosé de Saignée NV ★★ £E

Gallimard
Recommended Whites:
Cuvée Réserve NV ★★☆ £E
Cuvée de Prestige Vintage ★★★ £F

Gatinois
Recommended Whites:
Grand Cru Vintage ★★★ £F
Réserve Grand Cru NV ★★★ £E
Grand Cru NV ★★☆ £E
Recommended Reds:
Coteaux Champenois Pinot Noir ★★★★ £F

Pierre Gerbais
Recommended Whites:
Brut Prestige NV ★★ £E

Michel Gonet
Brut Réserve NV ★★ £D
Cuvée Prestige Vintage ★★ £E

Blanc de Blancs Grand Cru Vintage ★★★ £F
Recommended Rosés:
Brut Rosé NV ★★ £E
Henri Goutorbe
Recommended Whites:
Brut Cuvée Tradition NV ★★★ £E
Jacquart
Recommended Whites:
Blanc de Blancs Mosaïque Vintage ★★★ £E
A. Jacquart
Recommended Whites:
Blanc de Blancs Vintage ★★★ £E
Jean-Luc Lallement
Recommended Whites:
Brut Réserve NV ★★★ £E
Grand Cru Vintage ★★★★ £F
J. Lassalle
Recommended Whites:
Cuvée Imperial Préférence NV ★★ £E
Cuvée Special Club Vintage ★★★ £E
Recommended Rosés:
Premier Cru NV ★★ £E
Champagne Le Mesnil (co-op)
Recommended Whites:
Blanc de Blancs Grand Cru NV ★★★ £E
Blanc de Blancs Grand Cru Vintage ★★★ £E
Cuvée Sublime Grand Cru Vintage ★★★★ £E
Cuvée Prestige Grand Cru Vintage ★★★★ £F
Marie-Noëlle Ledru
Recommended Whites:
Cuvee du Goulté Vintage ★★★★☆ £F
Lilbert
Recommended Whites:
Blanc de Blancs Grand Cru Cramant NV ★★★ £E
Grand Cru Cramant Vintage ★★★★☆ £F
A. Margaine
Recommended Whites:
Brut Premier Cru NV ★★★ £D
Special Cuvée Club Blanc de Blancs Vintage ★★★★ £E
Demi-Sec NV ★★ £D
Recommended Rosés:
Brut NV ★★★ £D
Henri Mandois
Recommended Whites:
Brut NV ★★☆ £D
Blanc de Blancs Vintage ★★★ £E
Brut Cuvée Victor Vieilles Vignes Vintage ★★★☆ £F
Demi-Sec NV ★☆ £E
Recommended Rosés:
Brut Premier Cru NV ★☆ £D
Moutard
Recommended Whites:
Cuvée 6 Cépages Vintage ★★★ £E
Chardonnay Champ Persin NV ★★★ £E
Pnot Noir Vigne Beugneux NV ★★★ £E
Cuvée Prestige NV ★★★ £E
Recommended Rosés:
Cuvée Prestige NV ★★★ £E
Jean Moutardier
Recommended Whites:
Brut Carte D'or NV ★★ £D

Brut Selection NV ★★ £E
Brut Vintage ★★★ £E
Nicolas Feuillatte
Recommended Whites:
Brut Réserve Particulière NV ★★ £E
Brut Premier Cru Vintage ★★☆ £E
Cuvée Spéciale Vintage ★★★★ £F
Demi-Sec NV ★ £D
Recommended Rosés:
Brut Rosé Premier Cru NV ★★ £D
Pannier
Recommended Whites:
Brut Sélection NV ★★ £D
Brut Vintage ★★★ £E
Blanc de Noirs Vintage ★★★ £E
Egérie Extra Brut Vintage ★★★★ £F
Recommended Rosés:
Egérie Rosé de Saignée NV ★★★ £E
Roger Pouillon
Recommended Whites:
Brut Réserve NV ★★★ £D
Fleur de Mareuil NV ★★★☆ £E
J.P. Robert
Recommended Whites:
Cuvée Réserve NV ★★ £D
Jérôme Prévost
Recommended Whites:
Meunier Vintage ★★★★ £F
Sadi Malot
Recommended Whites:
Brut NV ★★★ £E
Saint-Gall
Recommended Whites:
Cuvée Orpale Blanc de Blancs Vintage ★★★★ £F
J.P. Secondé
Recommended Whites:
Brut Grand Cru NV ★★☆ £D
Brut Vintage ★★★ £E
Recommended Rosés:
Brut Rosé NV ★★ £D
Soutiran-Pelletier
Recommended Whites:
Blanc de Blancs Grand Cru NV ★★★ £E
Pierre Vaudon
Recommended Whites:
Brut Premier Cru NV ★★★ £D
Brut Premier Cru Vintage ★★★ £E
Recommended Rosés:
Brut Premier Cru NV ★★ £D
Jean Vesselle
Recommended Whites:
Brut Réserve NV ★★★ £D
Grand Cru Vintage ★★★ £E
Dom. de Vouette & Sorbée
Recommended Whites:
Cuvée Fidèle Vintage ★★★ £E
Waris Larmandier
Recommended Whites:
Blanc de Blancs Cuvée Empreinte Vintage ★★★ £E

Champagne

France

Good value Champagnes
Benoit Lahaye   Brut Essentiel NV
Boizel   Blanc de Blancs NV
François Secondé   Brut Clavier NV
Joseph Perrier   Cuvée Royale Brut NV
Lancelot Pienne   Brut Tradition NV
Veuve Fourny   Brut Nature NV
Agrapart   Grand Cru Minéral Extra Brut Vintage See
Beaumont de Crayères   Fleur de Prestige Vintage
Delamotte   Blanc de Blancs Vintage
A. Margaine   Special Club Vintage
Serge Mathieu   Brut Select Tête de Cuvée Vintage
J-P Vergnon   Grand Cru Le Mesnil Cuvée Confidence Vintage

A selection of lesser known fine Champagnes
Paul Bara   Brut Grand Cru Vintage
Philiponat   Clos des Goisses Vintage
Egly-Ouriet   Brut Tradition NV
Pierre Gimonnet et Fils   Blanc de Blancs Cuis Premier Cru NV
Alfred Gratien   Paradis NV
Larmandier-Bernier   Extra Brut Vieille Vignes de Cramant Vintage
Serge Mathieu   Brut Millésime Vintage
Gosset   Celebris Vintage
Bruno Paillard Nec Plus Ultra Vintage

Pick of the luxury cuvée's
Billecart-Salmon   Brut Cuvée Nicolas-François Billecart Vintage
Bollinger   RD Vintage
Charles Heidsieck   Blanc des Millénaires Vintage
Krug   Clos du Mesnil Vintage
Laurent-Perrier   Grand Siécle Cuvée Alexandra Rosé Vintage
Moët et Chandon   Dom Pérignon Vintage & Vintage Rosé
Pol Roger   Sir Winston Churchill Vintage
Louis Roederer   Cristal Vintage & Vintage Rosé
Salon   Salon Vintage
Veuve Clicquot   La Grande Dame Vintage & Vintage Rosé

The Loire is perhaps the most diverse and certainly geographically the most extensive of all France's classic wine regions. Inevitably there is a vast difference in styles from Nantes on the Atlantic coast to the heart of the Auvergne. The Loire drains tow thirds of France and its source is only around 100 kilometres north of the Mediterranean. The Loire's most southerly vineyards in the Côtes de Forez are on the same latitude as Côte Rotie to the south of Lyon. Much of the region is steeped in tradition but, while you won't find the wave of new developments that is happening in the Midi for instance, there are new high-quality producers emerging in almost all appellations. A number of them are committed to either organic farming practices or indeed biodynamic viticulture. Applying these principles in this northerly climate is a far taller order than in, say, dry and sunny Provence. The Loire is prone to spring frosts usually in April – sometimes with devastating consequences. The worst in recent memory was in 1991 when production overall was just a third of normal. Other years with significant frost damage include 1994, 2008, 2012 and 2016.

Pays Nantais

The Pays Nantais generally means just one wine to the majority of people: Muscadet, which was hugely popular in the UK until the devastating 1991 April frost. This coincided with the arrival of the influx wines from the southern hemisphere, in particular Australia. Inevitably Muscadet has never recovered the market share it enjoyed in the 1980s and the region has been through tough times. There has been a substantial reduction in the area planted with Melon de Bourgogne – over 13,000 hectares at its height but now down to around 9000 hectares. This is still a big area and one of France's largest appellations.

Although there were always quality producers like Domaine de l'Ecu, Louis Métaireau, Château de Cléray and Domaine Luneau-Papin, the overall standard has improved greatly and now some of the best value French whites come from here. The new *crus communaux*, with their long lees aging, are particularly exciting offering new levels of complexity.

It is worth paying a little extra for a zonal Muscadet. Easily the largest AOP is **Muscadet de Sèvre-et-Maine** with the best wines bottled sur lie. This means the wine spends a period of time on its lees for added richness. There are two other superior ACs, **Muscadet-Côteaux de la Loire** and **Muscadet Côtes de Grandlieu**. Good Muscadet can be crisp, minerally and with a real green-fruited depth, not dissimilar to sound village Chablis. Good Muscadet also has the potential to age for several decades. Covering the same area is the **Gros Plant AOP**, producing simple, quite austere wines that are a perfect match for oysters.

The Pays Nantais is also a good source for **IGP Val de Loire** – in particular Chardonnay. Also noteworthy is the Fie Gris (Sauvignon Rose) from Eric Chevalier (Domaine d'l'Aujardière). To the south is the **Fiefs Vendéens** – you are most likely to encounter these on holiday in the area. However, there are a few exciting, high quality producers here – Domaine St Nicolas, Mourat and Prieurie de Chaume. The range of grape varieties used includes Chenin Blanc, Chardonnay, Cabernet Franc, Pinot Noir and a curiosity – Negrette otherwise found much further south in France in Fronton.

Anjou

The **Anjou** appellation includes red, rosé and white wines. Theoretically it covers a large area mainly to the south of the River Loire, from the west of Angers east to beyond Saumur and the boundary with Touraine. In practice producers in the Saumur region uses Saumur appellations rather than Anjou.

There is a considerable range of quality, although fortunately the leading *négociant* companies like Ackerman and Les Grands Chais de France have upped their game. Increasingly they take responsibility for vinifying their wines giving them greater control over quality.

There are some stylish barrel-fermented whites from the major white variety of the region, Chenin Blanc. Some appear under the rather discredited **Anjou Blanc** appellation, while others from producers like Richard Leroy and Mark Angeli opt for the simple **Vin de France** category. There is a move to try to create a **Chaume** appellation for dry whites to give dry whites from this part of the Layon increased credibility.

The great white wines here, though, are the steely, intense dry whites of **Savennières** and the sweet botrytised wines of the **Côteaux du Layon**. Within the Côteaux du Layon are the ACs of **Quarts de Chaume** – now the Loire's first Grand Cru – and **Bonnezeaux** along with a number of communes, which may append their names at the Côteaux du Layon. These sweet wines tend to be traditional, quite restrained and very ageworthy. Those from the **Côteaux de l'Aubance** tend to be a little less rich at the top end. There are, however, some good examples, which like those from the Layon have the potential to age for several decades and more .

Rosé is an important category here. There are three types – **Rosé de Loire** (dry), **Rosé d'Anjou** (medium dry- medium sweet) and **Cabernet d'Anjou** (sweet). The permitted grape varieties for Rosé de Loire are Cabernet Franc, Cabernet Sauvignon, Grolleau, Pineau d'Aunis, Gamay et Côt (Malbec). This rosé can be made throughout Anjou-Saumur and Touraine. In practice, however, most is made in Anjou often using a majority blend of Grolleau and Gamay.. These days the oft-reviled Rosé d'Anjou, with a required majority of Grolleau, is often well made – it does what it says on tin even if it isn't to everyone's taste. In the past Cabernet d'Anjou was an ageworthy rosé with still drinkable examples dating from vintages like 1945, 47 and 49. Nowadays Cabernet d'Anjou is made for pleasant, early drinking with an emphasis on red fruits.

Reds from Anjou tend to be more tannic from the schist and slate soils here than those from the limestone vineyards of Saumur and Western Touraine. Careful use of extraction and tannic management is essential if these reds if mouth-puckering tannins and sharp acidity are too be avoided. It is not unknown here for the most rigorous growers to pick selectively going through their vineyards twice to pick only properly ripe grapes. **Anjou Rouge** should be for easy and early drinking with an emphasis on the fruit. Cabernet Franc, Cabernet Sauvignon, Gamay and Pineau d'Aunis are the permitted grape varieties.

Anjou-Villages should be more structured with only Cabernet Franc and Cabernet Sauvignon allowed. It is not allowed to bottle this red early and can only be bottled after the 1st September following the vintage. The Anjou Villages Brissac appellation is restricted to the ten communes around and including Brissac-Quincé. It covers the same area as for the Coteaux de l'Aubance.

It is only in Anjou that Cabernet Sauvignon can be successfully ripened and then only in particularly good parcels. The best known nearly pure Cabernet Sauvignon is Croix de la Mission from Domaine des Rochelles. It includes 10% Cabernet Franc and

Loire Valley

can age very well. Although there are some good and ageworthy examples of Anjou Villages and Anjou Villages Brissac it is rare for the reds of Anjou to have the finesse of those from Saumur and Western Touraine.

There is also a separate appellation for **Anjou Gamay**. Production is small with most of it is sold in the local market as Primeur in mid-November at the same time as Beaujolais Nouveau. It is worth looking out for juicy, black-fruited Grolleau, from producers like Château de Breuil and Topette from Domaine de Bablut (includes some Cabernet Franc) sold as **IGP Val de Loire**.

Saumur

Between Anjou and Saumur there is an important change of rock type. For much of the Pays Nantais and Anjou it is the hard, impervious rock of Brittany – granite, slate and schist. This gives way to the clay and porous limestone of the Paris basin that stretches from Saumur right through to Pouilly-sur-Loire. In Anjou underground cellars are few and far between because it is difficult and expensive to excavate the hard rock, whereas from Saumur eastwards there are hundreds of kilometres of underground cellars along with troglodyte houses built into the rock a feature of valley landscapes. The change of rock makes a difference to the wine – whites from the clay limestone tend to be a little more acidic, while reds usually have softer, less marked tannins.

Saumur is the centre of the Loire's sparkling wine industry with several well-known houses such as Ackerman, Bouvet Ladubay, Gratien et Meyer (owned by Henkell) and Langlois Chateau (owned by Bollinger). For years **Saumur Mousseux** was the main appellation but **Crémant de Loire** (created in 1975) has gradually become increasingly important until the production of Crémant now just exceeds that of Saumur. Annual production of Saumur Mousseux is around 11.25 million bottles, while Crémant is now about 12.1 million bottles. However, although the majority of Crémant is made in the Saumur region the Crémant de Loire appellation covers not only Saumur but also Anjou and Touraine.

Apart from the bubbles Saumur is now best known for its reds from Cabernet Franc. It is the western part of the Kingdom of Cabernet Franc that includes Bourgueil, Saint-Nicolas-de-Bourgueil and Chinon in nearby Touraine. This is the world's largest concentration of quality Cabernet Franc. **Saumur-Champigny** is the best-known appellation here – ranging from young easy drinking cuvées to more structured wines that can age beautifully for several decades.

There are also some very good whites (**Saumur Blanc**) made from Chenin Blanc with some of the best coming from the communes close to the Loire, like Souzay-Champigny and Parnay, along with the hillside vineyards of Brézé to the south east of Saumur. Top Saumur Blanc from producers like Château de Villeneuve and Château de Targé along with Domaine St Just and Domaine du Collier can age beautifully and are great value for their quality. There is also an agreeable summer rosé – Cabernet de Saumur

Over the past 25 years there has been a revival of interest in and the production **Coteaux de Saumur** – a sweet, late harvest wine made from Chenin Blanc. It tends to be lighter than those of the Coteaux du Layon with attractive citric notes. Like other sweet Loire wines it has an excellent capacity to age.

Touraine

As in Anjou there is a catch all **Touraine** AC that encompasses most of the region and covers all styles of wine including sparkling.

However, quality minded producers here often opt to make Crémant de Loire because of its its stricter regulations and more up-market image.

Sauvignon Blanc is the important variety for whites here, especially east of Tours. The Touraine appellation stretches from Candes Saint-Martin in the west to Soings-en-Sologne in the east. The Cher Valley to the east of Tours is the most important area.

Traditionally Touraine has been a melting pot for grape varieties with a wide range planted – the crossroads between those of the western Loire – principally Cabernet Franc and Chenin Blanc – and those of the east – Sauvignon Blanc, Gamay, Pinot Noir and Côt (Malbec). Unfortunately recent reform to AC Touraine has attempted to restrict producers' level of choice. This has mainly been determined by the varieties that dominate in the eastern part of the appellation.

Under the reforms 100% Cabernet Franc and 100% Chenin Blanc are no longer allowed. This ignores the reality in the western part of the appellation around Chinon where Chenin and Cabernet Franc are the principal varieties. AC Touraine white can only be made from Sauvignon Blanc or a blend of Sauvignon Blanc and Sauvignon Rose (locally called Fie Gris). Previously 100% Fie Gris was allowed – rightly as plantings of this variety in Touraine predates Sauvignon Blanc. Touraine Rosé is supposed to be made from at least three varieties where previously peppery Pineau d'Aunis has been a popular and attractive choice. This idiotic reform, however, has yet to be implemented. Initially it was due to come into force in 2016 but it has been deferred.

There are several Touraine 'villages' appellations. These wines are not necessarily better than the best of straight appellation Touraine. **Touraine Mesland** has all three colours: red – Cabernet, Côt, Gamay; rosé – Gamay; white – Chenin Blanc. **Touraine Amboise** is again red rosé, white with a similar palette of varieties. Whites are exclusively from Chenin Blanc while Gamay, Cabernet and Côt are for rosé and red.

Touraine Noble-Joué and **Touraine Azay-le-Rideau** (white – Chenin Blanc, rosé – mainly Grolleau plus Cabernet, Côt and Gamay). Noble-Joué is an interesting rosé made from three Pinots – Gris, Meunier and Noir. Touraine-Amboise is expected to be promoted to **Amboise** in 2017 for white (Chenin Blanc) and red (Côt). There are two recent 'villages' creations: **Touraine-Oisly** (white – exclusively Sauvignon Blanc, **Touraine Chenonceaux** (white – exclusively Sauvignon Blanc; red – Côt, Cabernet Franc).

In the far west of the region are the red wine appellations of **Bourgueil** and **Saint- Nicolas-de-Bourgueil** north of the river Loire and **Chinon** just to the south mainly in the valley of the Vienne. Cabernet Franc is the chief grape variety. There is also a small amount of white Chinon made exclusively from Chenin Blanc.

The style of these wines very much depends on whether the vines are planted on sand, gravel or the limestone coteaux. Wines from sandy vineyards are the lightest, those from the gravel of medium weight while those from the limestone coteaux are the most structured and remarkably ageworthy. Hidden away in some growers' cellars there are still a few rare and drinkable bottles from 19th Century!

The best of these wines are very good indeed with many of the top wines matured in oak often using barrels between 400-600 litre to avoid over-oaking. Bourgueil tends to be the most full bodied, while Saint-Nicolas can show show greater elegance and Chinon

grown on the limestone côteaux is equally refined. In practice the differences between the soils and the quality of the producers is more often marked than the appellations.

Just to the east of the city of Tours are the vineyards of **Vouvray** and **Montlouis** using Chenin Blanc. Vouvray allows 10% Menu Pineau but it is rarely used. Vouvray is on the north of the Loire, Montlouis just to the south between the Loire and the Cher. Depending on the vintage conditions – dry, demi-sec and moelleux styles are all made. The latter can be some of the greatest and longest-lived sweet wines in the world. Green and minerally in their youth, the dry and medium styles become increasingly rich and honeyed with age. The dry styles can be very austere when young and the searing acidity can be almost overwhelming. This can be the same with the moelleux wines – it's just better disguised by the residual sugar. Like many of the sweet wines along the valley the dependence on liberal sulphur additions has been waning and you don't need to wait 20 years now for it to dissipate.

Around 60% of the production of Montlouis and Vouvray is bottle fermented sparkling wine. The difference – 65 hl/ha for sparkling against 52 hl/ha between the yields allowed for sparkling wine and still is a strong incentive to make fizz. However, it is also true that some of the best Loire sparkling wines are made here. Both appellations make fully sparkling as well as pétillant, which has up to 2.5 bars of pressure. Montlouis/Vouvray Pétillant is often finer than the fully sparkling version. Since 2007 Montlouis also has pétillant originel with only one fermentation allowed plus a ban on the use of enzymes, chaptalisation and added yeasts.

To the north of Tours and the Touraine appellation are the regions of the **Côteaux du Loir** and its sub-region of **Jasnières**, which is exclusively Chenin Blanc. The climate here is extremely marginal and now apart from a small vineyard near Caen, France's most northerly vine growing area in Western France. The best wines – dry and late-havested Chenin Blancs – are Jasnières from vines planted on south-facing aspects with a protected mesoclimate. Pineau d'Aunis plays an important part in the red Côteaux du Loir. Although a small area, there are now some dynamic producers here making some very good wines. A little further east in the valley of Le Loir is **Coteaux de Vendômois** making wine in all three colours.

To the south of Blois are the regions of **Cheverny** and **Cour-Cheverny**. The permitted red/rosé varieties are Gamay, Pinot Noir, Cabernet Franc and Pineau d'Aunis, while Chardonnay, Chenin Blanc and Sauvignon Blanc are the white varieties. Cheverny has to be a blend. In white Sauvignon Blanc is the predominant variety complered by Chardonnay. Cour-Cheverny is a white-only appellation centred on the town of Cheverny and is exclusively for the unusual Romorantin grape. Romorantin gains considerable complexity with three or four years and more in bottle.

The small appellation of **Valençay** adjoins the eastern extremity of generic Touraine. Although all three colours are made, red is dominant and can be made from Côt, Cabernet Franc, Cabernet Sauvignon, Gamay and Pinot Noir. For rosé Pineau d'Aunis is also permitted. The whites are mainly Sauvignon Blanc with Chardonnay and Arbois also allowed. The wines are pleasant but not memorable.

A little under 100-kilometres south of Tours and just to the north of Poitiers is the appellation of **Haut-Poitou**, where there are some interesting whites and reds in vineyards to the north of the town of Poitiers around the small town of Neuville de Poitou. Production used to be dominated by the Cave Cooperative of Haut-Poitou, However, that is now bankrupt and the largest producer is the

organic Ampelidae.

Central Vineyards

The Central Vineyards are undoubtedly France's and perhaps the world's Kingdom of Sauvignon Blanc. Although there are now some very good reds being made here, from Pinot Noir, Sauvignon Blanc is the dominant variety and has been since the recovery from phylloxera early in the 20th century. Prior to that Sancerre predominantly produced red wine, especially from Pinot Noir and Gamay.

Sancerre is the largest, best known and scenically the most spectacular appellation. Around 80% is planted with Sauvignon Blanc and 20% Pinot Noir for red and rosé. There are three types of soil: caillottes (limestone), terres blanches (clay limestone) and silex (flit). Early drinking wines tend to come from caillottes and the longest-lived from terres blanches, often steep slopes.

There are some disappointing Sancerres, partly due to being bottled too soon after vintage, the leading producers are admirably keen to continue to improve their wines. Top white Sancerre, whether made in stainless steel or fermented and aged in wood has the capacity to age well – certainly 10 to 15 years or more. Over the last 20 years the quality of the reds has improved greatly as yields have been cut and growers have become more ambitious.

The small town of Pouilly-sur-Loire, on the east bank of the Loire, is administratively in Burgundy. It is also the midway point of the Loire's 1000 kilometre (600 mile) journey. The **Pouilly-Fumé** appellation (100% Sauvignon Blanc) is about half the size of Sancerre, while AOP **Pouilly-sur-Loire** is for Chasselas. In 19th Century Pouilly was famous for supplying Chasselas to Paris as an eating grape. Only about 30 hectares remain – a pleasant curiosity. Top Pouilly-Fumé is on a par with Sancerre, while tending to be a little softer and rounder with the potential to age well.

Côtes de la Charité is a small IGP area south east of Pouilly-sur-Loire and east of la Charité. It is mainly planted with Chardonnay and Pinot Noir producing good quality wines. The most significant owners come from Pouilly-sur-Loire and Sancerre.

The small and scatter appellation **Coteaux du Giennois** extends to the north of Pouilly-Fumé producing fresh, citric Sauvignon Blanc and mainly light reds. The reds are hobbled by the INAO by having to be a blend of Gamay and Pinot Noir rather than pure Pinot Noir

There are two very small appellations around Orléans – **Orléans** and **Orléans-Clery**. Orléans-Clery is reserved for reds from Cabernet Franc. It is quite ambitious to hope to always ripen Cabernet Franc this far east. Orléans white is mainly Chardonnay with some Pinot Gris also allowed. The rosé is mainly Pinot Meunier with Pinot Gris and Pinot Noir also permitted. Red is again mainly Pinot Meunier with some Pinot Noir allowed.

Menetou-Salon is contiguous with the western extremity of Sancerre. Just over 450 hectares the vineyards (Sauvignon Blanc and Pinot Noir) are more scattered mainly around the small towns of Morogues and Menetou-Salon. There are a number of high quality producers here.

Quincy and **Reuilly** are two small appellations in the Cher Valley close to Vierzon, a railway and motorway junction town. Both appellations virtually disappeared during the 1960s/70s but started to revive from the 1980s. Only Sauvignon Blanc is permitted in Quincy producing some attractive citric wines from gravel soils but rarely with complexity of top Sancerres. Reuilly makes wine in three

Loire Valley

France

colours: Sauvignon Blanc, Pinot Gris for rosé and Pinot Noir mainly red. There are some good quality producers here.

The Upper Loire

Although Pouilly-Fumé is the end (or the beginning depending how you look at it) the internationally known Loire vineyards, there are a number of scattered appellations in the Upper Loire producing some increasingly good wines. Gamay and Pinot Noir are for red and rosé. As in a number of other Loire appellations 100% Pinot Noir has not been permitted since Châteaumeillant became an appellation controlee in 2009.

Châteaumeillant is very close to the centre of France and makes red and rosé from Gamay with some Pinot Noir allowed. Undergoing a renaissance with Quincy producers buying vines here.

Saint-Pourçain, to the north of Vichy, has wines in all three colours. Grapes for the white are the local Tressalier and Chardonnay with Sauvignon Blanc also permitted.

To the south is the Auvergne. There are now some very good red wines coming from both the **Côte Roannaise**, to the west of Roanne, and a little further south in the **Côtes du Forez**. Gamay is the variety here. Not surprising as the Beaujolais is not far to the east. There are also some excellent IGP whites from producers in the Roannaise and Forez using a range of grapes including Roussanne, Viognier and Aligoté. The choice of Roussanne and Viognier may appear surprising but Forez is south of Lyon and on a line with the northernmost vineyards of the Northern Rhône.

To the west are the scattered vineyards of the Côtes d'Auvergne to the north and south of Clermont-Ferrand. Prior to the arrival of phylloxera in the second half of the 19th century, the Auvergne was France's third largest vineyard – 45,000 hectares in 1890. The grape varieties used are Chardonnay, Gamay and Pinot Noir. Under appellation rules 100% Pinot Noir is not permitted, which is unfortunate as some Pinot Noirs I have tasted suggests that these could potentially be among the best reds of the appellation.

A-Z of producers by appellation/region

Anjou
Ch. la Varière	181
La Ferme de la Sansonnière	188
Rene Mosse	192
Dom. Ogereau	193
Dom. des Rochelles	194

Anjou-Saumur
Dom. des Baumard	178

Bonnezeaux
Ch. de Fesles	180

Bourgueil
Yannick Amirault	177
Dom. Breton	179
Dom. de la Butte	180
Dom. de la Chevalerie	182
Pierre-Jacques Druet	185
Dom. Guion	187
Dom. des Ouches	193

Chinon
Philippe Alliet	177
Bernard Baudry	178
Ch. de Coulaine	180
Couly-Dutheil	184
Dom. Dozon	185
Dom. Charles Joguet	188
Logis de la Bouchardiere	190
Dom. de La Noblaie,	192
Dom. de Pallus	193

Côteaux du Layon
Patrick Baudouin	178
Ch. de la Genaiserie	181
Ch. Pierre-Bise	181
Philippe Delesvaux	185
Dom. FL	186
Dom. des Forges	186
Dom. de Juchepie	188
Dom. Richard Leroy	190

Côteaux du Loir
Dom. de Bellivière	178

Fiefs-Vendéens
Dom. Saint-Nicolas	195

Jasnières
Joël et Ludovic Gigou	187

Montlouis
Francois Chidaine	182
Benoit Mérias	191
Taille aux Loups	196

Menetou-Salon
Dom. Mincin	191
Henry Pellé	193

Muscadet Sèvre-Et-Maine
Dom. de l'Écu	186
Dom. Haute-Fevrie	188
Pierre Luneau-Papin	190

Pouilly-Fumé
Alain Cailbourdin	180
Ch. de Tracy	181
Jean-Claude Chatelain	182
Didier Dagueneau	184
Masson-Blondelet	191
Dom. de Thibault	185
Dom. Michel Redde	194

Saint-Nicolas-de-Bourgeuil
Dom de la Cotellerie	184
Dom. Sébastien David	185
Dom. Frédéric Mabileau	190
Taluau & Foltzenlogel	196

Sancerre
Dom. Jean-Paul Balland	177
Dom. Henri Bourgeois	179
Hubert Brochard	179
Daniel Chotard	183
Pascal Cotat	184
François Crochet	184
Lucien Crochet	184
André Dézat	185
Vincent Gaudry	187
Dom. Gitton	187
Alphonse Mellot	191
Mollet-Maudry	192
Gerard Morin	192
Dom. Henry Natter	192
Vincent Pinard	193
Dom. P & N Reverdy	194
Dom. Claude Riffault	194
Dom. Sébastien Riffault	194
Jean-Max Roger	195
Dom. Christian Salmon	196
Dom. Vacheron	196

Saumur
Ch. de Fosse-Seche	181
Ch. Yvonne	182
Dom. Guiberteau,	187
Langlois-Château	189
Dom. de Saint-Just	195

Saumur-Champigny
Dom. de la Bonnelière,	178
Ch. de Villeneuve	182
Ch. du Hureau	181
Clos Rougeard	183
René-Noel Legrand	189
Dom. des Roches Neuves	195
Dom. Saint-Vincent	196
Dom. des Varinelles	196

Savennières
Ch. d'Epiré	180
Coulée de Serrant	183
Dom. du Closel	183
Dom. Laureau,	189
Dom. aux Moines,	191
Eric Morgat	192

Touraine
Dom. La Grange Tiphaine	189
Henry Marionnet	190

IGP Val de Loire
Ampelidæ	197

Vouvray
Dom. des Aubuisières	177
Dom. Bourillon-Dorléans	179
Didier Champalou,	180
Dom. du Clos Naudin	183
Huet l'Echansonne	188
Dom. Vigneau-Chevreau	197

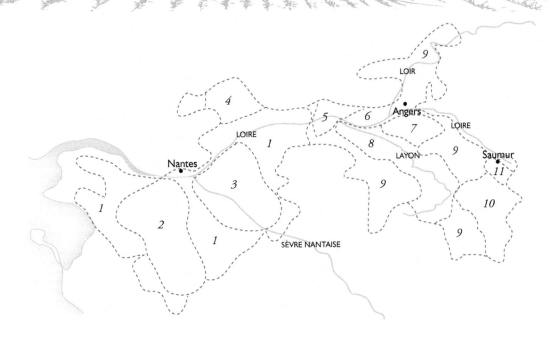

1 Muscadet
2 Muscadet Côtes de Grand Lieu
3 Muscadet de Sèvre-et-Maine
4 Muscadet des Côteaux de la Loire
5 Anjou Côteaux de la Loire
6 Savennières
7 Côteaux de l'Aubance
8 Côteaux du Layon
9 Anjou
10 Saumur
11 Saumur-Champigny
12 Jasnières

13 Côteaux du Loir
14 Saint-Nicolas-de-Bourgeuil
15 Bourgeuil
16 Chinon
17 Vouvray
18 Montlouis
19 Touraine
20 Cheverny, Cour Cheverny
21 Reuilly
22 Quincy
23 Menetou-Salon
24 Sancerre
25 Pouilly-Fumé

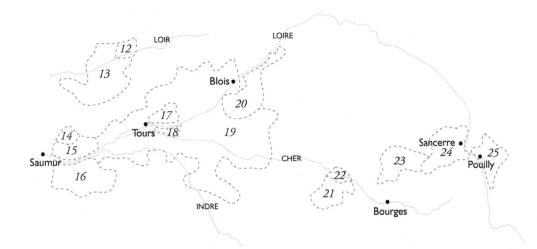

Loire Valley

Loire Valley vintages

With an area as geographically extensive and as diverse in climate as the Loire it is difficult to generalise about its wines or individual years. Cooler conditions in a given year may favour dry whites, while sweet whites and reds need warm vintages.

2016: By early July the omens were already not good. A very mild winter was followed by a cold March and April. Then in the second half of April there were a series of frosts with that of the early morning of 27th April being the most severe. By the end of April around 30% of the crop had been lost. The cool weather continued into May with very heavy rain and floods at the end of the month. With all this humidity the threat of mildew became very significant with all the wet weather making it difficult to get into the vineyards to treat the vines. It was also far from ideal for some of the flowering in June due to cool and wet conditions.

2015: After a hot, dry summer there was heavy rain in late August and mid-September. Picking started quite early. 2015 is certainly a good vintage but is it a very good one or is 2014 better. 2015 is a very approachable, friendly, charming vintage? Did the heavy rain of late August and mid-September dilute the grapes a little? There is no doubt that by early August there was a need for some rain but nothing like the amounts that fell in parts of Touraine - over 100 mm. Promising sweet wines. Increasingly I think 2014 will prove to be the better vintage

2014: This is a very fine vintage made by a dry and warm September with a drying wind from the east that followed a poor, cool summer. The wines have a lovely balance of fruit and acidity. The Reds, in particular, have rich fruit balanced by acidity and structure. Many are delicious drinking. Some very fine sweet wines, especially from the Layon.

2013: this was a very difficult vintage with a very cold March, April, May and into June. There was some frost at the end of April but less severe and extensive than in 2012. Flowering didn't start until late June. Fortunately summer arrived at the beginning of July. The race was on to find a sufficient amount of ripe enough fruit before the rot. Some producers did better than others in this respect, so careful selection is necessary this year. Dry whites have generally fared best although they are on the light side. The little sweet wine that was made had good concentration but not a lot of structure. Reds were also pretty rather than ugly. All in all a vintage for early drinking.

2012 was a difficult growing year but sustained sunshine in September saved the day, particularly for the dry whites. Conditions for the sweet whites were dreadful with over 200mm of rain in the Layon during October. Many producers made either no sweet wine or very little. Treat any prestige sweet wine cuvées with due suspicion. Reds are softer and more supple than in the previous two vintages and are not for long keeping. **2011** looks good for Anjou and Saumur and for late-harvested Vouvray and Montlouis but was less good for Muscadet and the Central Vineyards. In 2010 it was a growers year in Touraine and the Central Vineyards, those who restricted yields had good results. The reds in Touraine though show much promise while for later harvested Vouvray it was a more difficult year than in Anjou, which was splendid. **2009** was very good right across the Loire, although there were some crop losses with hail damage especially severe in Menetou-Salon and parts of Sancerre. Decent late season weather in both **2008** and **2007** followed some difficult growing conditions but some good reds and dry whites in 2008, while sweet Anjou are exceptional with brilliant balance. **2006** was potentially good complicated by rot at vintage time. Full-bodied whites and reds for medium term keeping.

Cabernet Franc reds are currently drinking well. **2005** – long hot summer and autumn allowed relaxed growers to pick at optimum moment. Powerful dry whites and reds and good sweet wines from Anjou and Vouvray. **2004** was a bountiful vintage with fine weather in September. Rigorous producers made good wines but vintage has been overshadowed by 2005.

The heat of **2003** produced some exceptional sweet whites and good reds, although Sancerre and Pouilly Fumé will be fully evolved now, even in the best cases. **2002** turned out to be very good across the region.

A huge amount of the general output of the region is best drunk young. You will, though, find the top Muscadet, which will age for several decades, especially the new crus communaux. The best red and white wines will age very well. They have great structure and the intense acidity that is characteristic of such a marginal climate. The reds are more marked by their acidity than their tannin. The great dry whites of Savennières and top demi-secs from Vouvray and Montlouis are capable of being held in your cellar for well over three decades. They will generally need at least six to seven years before they show their more exotic honeyed characters, though increasing use of oak, new and old, and macération pellicullaire are providing more accessible styles. Top Sancerre and Pouilly-Fumé, particularly those wines that are barrel-fermented, are surprisingly ageworthy and a far cry from the kind of tropical, gooseberry-laden examples of Sauvignon Blanc from the southern hemisphere that will barely make it past their first birthday.

Of the great earlier vintages Savennières was particularly impressive in 1985, 1983, 1982, 1978 and 1976. The great sweet wine vintages to consider were 1997, 1996, 1990, 1989, 1985, 1983, 1982, 1976, 1971, 1959, 1949, 1947 and 1921. Top reds were made in 1996, 1995, 1990, 1989, 1986, 1985, 1983, 1982, 1978 and 1976. If you find a Chinon from 1964 go for it!

Loire Valley vintage chart

	Anjou & Touraine Top Dry Whites	Anjou & Touraine Sweet Whites	Saumur & Touraine Top Reds	Sancerre & Pouilly-Fume Whites
2015	★★★☆ A	★★★★ A	★★★☆ A	★★★☆ A
2014	★★★★ A	★★★★☆ A	★★★★☆ A	★★★★ A
2013	★★★ A	★★☆ A	★★☆ A	★★★☆ A
2012	★★★ A	★ A	★★★ A	★★★ A
2011	★★★★ A	★★★★☆ A	★★★★ B	★★★☆ B
2010	★★★★ B	★★★★☆ B	★★★★☆ B	★★★☆ B
2009	★★★★☆ B	★★★★☆ B	★★★★☆ B	★★★★☆ C
2008	★★★☆ B	★★★☆ B	★★★☆ B	★★★★ C
2007	★★★☆ B	★★★★ B	★★★ B	★★★☆ C
2006	★★★☆ B	★★★ B	★★★☆ C	★★★★ C
2005	★★★★☆ B	★★★★☆ B	★★★★☆ B	★★★★ C
2004	★★★★ C	★★★★ C	★★★★ C	★★★★ C
2003	★★★★☆ C	★★★★☆ C	★★★★☆ C	★★★ B
2002	★★★★ C	★★★★ C	★★★☆ C	★★★★☆ C
2001	★★★ C	★★★ C	★★★☆ D	★★★ D
2000	★★★☆ D	★★★☆ C	★★★ C	★★★★☆ D
1999	★★★ D	★★★ C	★★★ D	★★★★☆ D
1998	★★★ D	★★★ C	★★★ D	★★★★☆ D
1997	★★★★☆ D	★★★★☆ C	★★★★ D	
1996	★★★★☆ C	★★★★☆ C	★★★★☆ D	
1995	★★★★ D	★★★★ D	★★★★☆ D	
1990	★★★★☆ D	★★★★☆ D	★★★★☆ D	

A-Z of producers

✿ Philippe Alliet (Chinon)
One of the very best producers in Chinon with 17 ha of Cabernet Franc planted on both gravel in Cravant-les-Coteaux and on the Coteau de Noire in Chinon. Philippe and his wife Claude took over the domaine in 1978 expanding the domaine and establishing a high reputation. In the vineyard Alliet severely restricts his yields and looks to produce a full, powerful style with an extended fermentation and maceration. No weedkillers or chemical fertilisers are used. The resulting wines possess marvellously pure blackcurrant and cedar fruit all underpinned by supple, velvety tannins. New oak is avoided as are fining and filtration. The top wines possess additional depth and weight. The Coteau de Noiré, a further red L'Huisserie (also on the Coteau) and Vieilles Vignes (on gravel) are the sturdiest and longest-lived. Alliet also makes a small amount of white Chinon (100% Chenin Blanc) (DM/JB)

Recommended Reds:
Chinon Coteau de Noiré ★★★★ £E
Chinon Vieilles Vignes ★★★☆ £D
Chinon ★★☆ £C

✿ Yannick Amirault (Bourgueil) *www.yannickamirault.fr*
The Amirault family domaine possesses 19 ha of vines spread throughout both Bourgueil (13 ha) and Saint-Nicolas-de-Bourgueil (6 ha). The wines are among the very best produced in either appellation. Yannick took over the domaine in 1977 with just 3.40 hectares of vines. His son, Benoît joined in 2003. The domaine in now organic – the conversion started in 2009. The Bourgueils are marginally deeper, more brawny wines, the Saint-Nicolas bottlings a touch more elegant and tightly structured. La Petite Cave is a splendid, dark and complex wine produced from old vines. Malgagnes is the denser, more tannic of the Saint-Nicolas-de-Bourgueils. Young-vine cuvées of both are also produced as well as a further complex Bourgueil, Le Grand Clos. The top wines are very ageworthy and will improve in bottle for 15 years or more. (DM/JB)

Recommended Reds:
Saint Nicolas-de-Bourgueil Malgagnes ★★★★ £E
Saint Nicolas-de-Bourgueil La Source ★★★☆ £D
Bourgueil La Petite Cave ★★★★ £E
Bourgueil Le Grand Clos ★★★☆ £E
Bourgueil Quartiers ★★★☆ £D
Bourgueil La Coudraye ★★★☆ £D

Ampelidæ (IGP Val de Loire) *www.ampelidae.com*
This is an increasing important operation run by the dynamic and energetic Frédéric Brochet based in Haut-Poitou with the majority of wines sold as IGP. The top of the range wines are made at Château des Roches, Marigny-Brizay, while the cheaper wines are made at nearby Neuville de Poitou in the premises of the now bankrupt the Cave de Neuville de Poitou – the local cooperative that went bust in 2013. Ampelidæ took over the Coop's premises in April 2014 retaining the vines of many of the co-op's members. In 2016 Brochet and his partners Benji and Kate Meuli (Château des Roches) took over the vines and winery of Pierre-Jacques Druet, who went bankrupt in March 2016. Ampelidae has also taken over the vines of bankrupt Clos du Porteau – Touraine and Montlouis. Brochet also makes the wines for the Levin winery near Montrichard, Touraine that is owned by restaurateur David Levin. There are three main categories of wines: Marigny-Neuf for fruit driven varietals, Brochet – the middle range, and Ampelidae for the 'Grand Vins'. In addition there is Blanc d'Hiver is a Sauvignon Blanc vin nouveau released soon after the vintage, sparkling Armance B (Chardonnay) and alias – wines with no sulphur. The Ampelidae range includes Le S, a barrel vinified Sauvignon Blanc of some depth and concentration, fatter and fuller than most Touraine examples from further north. Le C is an old-vine Chardonnay with impressive weight and a quite marked toasty, nutty, barrel-ferment character. Two reds are also produced under this label. Le K is produced from old-vine Cabernet Sauvignon and aged in small oak, some new, and is rich, cedary and impressively concentrated for the region. The main range is completed by a finely textured Pinot Noir PN 1328, which is sourced from a specific numbered limestone-based parcel. There are also 11 single plot Sauvignon Blancs – 'Crus de la Vienne'. These are sold at auction. (DM/JB)

Recommended Reds:
IGP Val de Loire PN 1328 ★★★ £D
IGP Val de Loire Le K ★★☆ £D

Recommended Whites:
IGP Val de Loire Le C ★★★ £C
IGP Val de Loire Le S ★★☆ £C

Dom. des Aubuisières (Vouvray)
Bernard Fouquet makes very good Vouvray from bone dry to lusciously sweet at this 30-ha domaine. The 2-hectare Petit Clos, acquired in 2013, is the latest addition. Production is relatively small and an extensive range is produced when conditions are favourable. Silex is dry, almost austere and very pure, while the stylish Marigny Sec is barrel-fermented. The Girardières shows a sweet citrus and mineral style and is refined and well balanced. For sweet moelleux, when the right conditions do occur, the magnificent top bottling is the Cuvée Alexandre. All of the wines will age very well – the 1989 Le Marigny Moelleux is still very youthful. (DM/JB)

Recommended Whites:
Vouvray Girardières Demi-Sec ★★★ £C
Vouvray Marigny Sec ★★★ £C
Vouvray Silex Sec ★★☆ £C
Vouvray Brut ★★ £C

Dom. Jean-Paul Balland (Sancerre) *www.balland.com*
Very good, small family domaine producing typically ripe and expressive whites from a total of 22ha of limestone and chalk based vineyards around the village of Bué - in particular from the Grand Chemarin and Chêne Marchand sites. Jean-Paul is now assisted by his Burgundy trained oenologist daughter Isabelle, while Élise, his other daughter handles the commercial side. The wines are increasingly impressive. Both whites are cool fermented at a low temperature, which emphasises their ripe and rich character. Fining is avoided and there is only a very light filtration. The Grand Cuvée is amongst the best examples of the appellation. It is rich opulent and with the structure to facilitate additional complexity with age. It is sourced from the domaine's oldest vines, now upwards of 40 years, and is aged in used demi-muids. The red is sound enough although as with many other examples it definitely benefits from a warm vintage. A fresh, fruity rosé is also produced. (DM/JB)

Recommended Reds:
Sancerre ★★ £C

Recommended Whites:
Sancerre Grand Cuvée ★★★★ £D
Sancerre ★★★ £C

Loire Valley

France

❀ **Patrick Baudouin (Côteaux du Layon)** *www.patrick-baudouin.com*
During the 1990s along with Jo Pithon Baudouin was one of the Layon's 'sugar hunters', which was an important stage in the renaissance of sweet wines from the Coteaux du Layon after decline during the 1970s and early 1980s. Baudouin and Pithon showed what was possible in Anjou with Chenin Blanc. Times have moved on. The style here is rich, heady and unctuously sweet. What impresses, though, is the balance and elegance achieved at the same time. He also produces decent reds and a number of Anjou whites including a Savennières. The Anjou Rouge is solely from Cabernet Franc and displays some attractive berry and leafy notes. The Anjou-Villages is more serious and structured; a blend of both Cabernets, it is part oak-aged. Neither is filtered. Of the great sweet wines the regular Bruandières is intense and honeyed and it just needs a little extra dimension for true class. The Grains Nobles and Quarts de Chaume Maria Juby are seriously impressive. Both are honeyed with marked botrytis and the Maria Juby has a marvellously fresh mineral balance. Expect the sweet whites to age well but are surprisingly approachable when young. (DM)
Recommended Reds:
Anjou-Villages ★★☆ £C
Anjou ★★ £C
Recommended Whites:
Quarts de Chaume Maria Juby ★★★★★ £F
Côteaux du Layon Grains Nobles ★★★★☆ £F
Côteaux du Layon Les Bruandières ★★★☆ £E

Bernard Baudry (Chinon) *www.bernardbaudry.com*
Trained in Beaune Bernard started the domaine in 1975 with just 2 hectares. Matthieu, his son, joined in 2000 and has now Matthieu Baudry has now taken over the running of this domaine in Cravant-les-Coteaux from his father. Now they have 32-ha divided between the communes of Chinon and Cravant-les-Coteaux. They have vines both on the gravel terraces of the River Vienne and the limestone Coteaux. 90% is planted with Cabernet Franc and 10% with Chenin Blanc from which he makes an impressive white Chinon Croix Boisée. Good regular red Chinon is marked by approachable leafy, berry fruit and a hint of spiciness. Les Granges is soft, vibrant and forward. Of the three top cuvées that stand out, Clos Guillot is sturdy and dense, Grézeaux deep and extracted but supple and sufficiently soft too. The top red Croix Boisée is dark, dense and complex and needs 3 to 4 years' ageing. (DM/JB)
Recommended Reds:
Chinon Croix Boisée ★★★★ £E
Chinon Grézeaux ★★★ £C
Chinon Clos Guillot ★★★ £C
Chinon Les Granges ★★☆ £C
Chinon ★★ £C

❀ **Dom. des Baumard (Anjou-Saumur)** *www.baumard.fr*
Although the history of this 40 ha domaine based in Rochefort-sur-Loire dates back to 1634, it was the arrival of Jean Baumard in 1955 who enlarged and created the Baumards' reputation. In 1957 Jean Baumard acquired five hectares in the Quarts de Chaume and in 1968 15 hectares in Savennières. In 1968 Jean Baumard explored the possibility of Quarts de Chaume becoming a Grand Cru but nothing came of this initiative. Jean's son, Florent, joined the domaine in 1987 and is now in charge. Unfortunately around 1989 the Baumards discovered cryoextraction and were seduced by the facility and reduction of risk in the making of sweet wines that this process offered. Cryoextraction has allowed Florent Baumard to pick

his Chenin Blanc for their Quarts de Chaume without waiting for full ripeness and with generous yields. In the very difficult 2012 vintage the Baumards made a remarkable quantity of Quarts de Chaume despite more than 200mm of rain in October. It is not known whether Baumard uses cryoextraction for other wines in their portfolio. The Baumards opposed the new more rigorous Quarts de Chaume appellation and its creation as the Loire's first Grand Cru in 2011. They took a legal challenge to France's Supreme Court and lost comprehensively. Baumard's Quarts de Chaume is made in the winery not in the vineyard. While Domaine des Baumard remains an important domaine in Anjou WBTL is unable to recommend their wines. (JB)

❀ **Dom. de Bellivière (Côteaux du Loir)** *www.belliviere.com*
Brilliantly styled, mineral whites are made at this 15 ha domaine across five communes in the valley of Le Loir. Reds from the Côteaux du Loir are also worth looking at. Very intense red berry fruit can be found in the Rouge Gorge, which comes from Pineau d'Aunis. Gamay and Cabernet Franc red is also made in lighter styles. The acidity and tight structure of Rouge Gorge requires at least 4 or 5 years patience and it is not easy young, but expect an increased smoky complexity with time. A special, very old-vine red cuvée, Hommage à Louis Derré, is also made in great years. The main focus here, though, is on steely, piercingly mineral dry whites from the 7ha or so of Chenin Blanc. The Côteaux du Loir L'Effraie comes from younger vines, which here means less than 50 years of age. It has marvellous poise and intensity. The old-vine Eparses comes from vines of 50 to 80 years of age and is a wine of marvellous depth and persistence. Subtle honeyed notes will emerge in time. A relatively young-vine cuvée, Haute-Rasné, is made from a late-harvested lieu-dit that regularly develops noble rot. The Jasnières Prémices comes from young vines, Les Rosiers from a mix of older vines but under 50 years of age. It is very tight, intensely mineral and backward when young. Its intense, peachy and honeyed fruit is more immediately apparent in opulent years. A wine of serious depth and class, it will develop well with a decade or more of age. An old-vine cuvée Calligramme is also produced as well as two late-harvest wines, Discours de Tuf and a vin liquoreux Elixir de Tuf. These will undoubtedly be very well worth considering. (DM/JB)
Recommended Reds:
Côteaux du Loir La Rouge-Gorge ★★★ £C
Recommended Whites:
Côteaux du Loir Eparses Vieilles Vignes ★★★★☆ £F
Jasnières Les Rosiers ★★★★ £E
Jasnières Prémices ★★★☆ £E
Côteaux du Loir L'Effraie ★★★☆ £E

>> **Dom. de La Bonnelière** *www.labonneliere.com*
High quality 37-hectare Saumur-Champigny family domaine but not one of the most fashionable names. Based in Varrains the domaine was founded in 1972 by André Bonneau and now run by Anthony and Cédric Bonneau. New winery functional winery built in 2010, barrel aging in traditional limestone cellar. André Bonneau was one of the first to introduce machine harvesting in Saumur-Champigny. Poor and rotten grapes are cut off prior to harvest. 35 ha of Cabernet – 34 ha Franc, 0.5ha Cabernet Sauvignon, 2ha Chenin Blanc. The Bonneaus stress the importance of site rather than vine age. They have 3ha in heart of Les Poyeux, a famous Saumur-Champigny 15ha vineyard producing their best red, which is only released in good vintages. At just 8€ this is remarkable value as is their Saumur-Champigny Tradition. The Tradition and Les Poyeux are softly fruited

Wine behind the label

Loire Valley

France

but with structure with Les Poyeux, in particular having a good potential to age. Prices kept low for their loyal clients who buy direct. The Bonneaus also make several very small volume cuvées – one with 15% Pineau d'Aunis another with 15% Cabernet Sauvignon plus Franc – 100% Cabernet Franc with 36 months in barrique. Two Saumur Blancs (100% Chenin) – crisp, easy drinking Tradition and the more structured Les Perruchers – vinified in stainless steel aged 8 months in *barrique*. (JB)

Recommended Reds:
Saumur Champigny Les Poyeux ★★★★ £C
Saumur Champigny Tradition ★★★ £B
Recommended Whites:
Saumur Blanc Les Perruchers★★★ £C
Saumur Blanc Tradition ★★ £B
Recommended Rosés:
Cabernet de Saumur Tradition ★★ £A

❂ **Dom. Henri Bourgeois (Sancerre))** *www2.henribourgeois.com*
This is a substantial and very impressively dynamic Sancerre family producer and négociant based in Chavignol. The Bourgeois vinify in a modern and very well equipped winery in Chavignol from140 hectares of vines – half from their own vineyards and half bought in. The domaine covers a total of some 72 ha with 50 ha planted to Sauvignon Blanc, the balance Pinot Noir. Les Baronnes is the regular cuvée of Sancerre, while the MD de Bourgeois (named after the local Monts Damnés slopes) and Bourgeoise are a level up. There are good Pouilly-Fumés as well, especially La Demoiselle de Bourgeois. Among the top cuvées d'Antan is very concentrated, made from 65-year-old vines, while Jadis is intense and minerally from vines planted in Kimmeridgian marl. The top wine, produced in extremely small quantities, is the very intense, flinty and lightly nutty Étienne Henri, vinified in oak for 12 months on fine lees. The top white wines need two or three years in bottle to show their best and will happily age for at least 10 to 15 years. The red Sancerre Bourgeoise is increasingly good, especially with the benefit of a warm, sunny vintage. When conditions permit they also make a small amount of late harvest Sauvignon – Vendanges de la Saint Charles. On the négociant side they offer the full range of wines from the Central Loire appellations plus Le Petit Bourgeois IGP – white (Sauvignon Blanc), rosé (Pinot Noir) and red (Cabernet Franc). In 2000 they founded CLOS HENRI in Marlborough making Sauvignon Blanc and Pinot Noir – a New Zealand *terroir* with a French accent. (DM/JB)

Recommended Reds:
Sancerre Bourgeoise ★★ £D
Recommended Whites:
Sancerre d'Antan ★★★★ £E
Sancerre Jadis ★★★★ £E
Sancerre Bourgeoise ★★★ £D
Sancerre La Côte des Monts Damnés ★★★ £D
Pouilly Fumé Demoiselle de Bourgeoise ★★★ £D
Sancerre Les Baronnes ★★☆ £C
Pouilly Fumé ★★ £C

Dom. Bourillon-Dorléans (Vouvray) *www.bourillon.com*
Founded in 1921 there are some 26ha at this Vouvray property, based in Rochecorbon, where the emphasis is on dry and demi-sec Chenin wines. Moelleux La Coulée d'Or is made when the vintage conditions allow. The range is also buoyed up by a regularly produced sparkling Brut. The dry styles are very tight and minerally in their youth with piercing green-apple aromas. The Coulée d'Argent gets a touch more oak during vinification, some of it new.

The Demi-Sec is minerally and honeyed; it will become rich and profound with age. Handling is kept to a minimum and there is just a light filtration prior to bottling. (DM/JB)
Recommended Whites:
Vouvray Cuvée Gaston Dorléans Demi-Sec ★★★ £D
Vouvray Coulée d'Argent Sec ★★★ £D
Vouvray Indigène Sec ★★☆ £C

Dom. Breton (Bourgueil) *www.domainebreton.net*
The Breton's farm 17ha of biodynamically farmed vineyards mainly in Bourgueil (10 ha) with 6 ha in Chinon and Vouvray (1 ha), where at the latter a dry sparkling white and a dry white is made. The reds though are the heart of this domaine and all come from Cabernet Franc. The three most approachable of the reds are La Dilettante with a high proportion of carbonic maceration and Nuits d'ivresse, which comes from a selection of old vines planted in argilo-calcaire soils. A touch more sructured, although from young 15 year old vines is the Trinch! Similar depth and concentration can also be found in the Bourgueil Les Galichets and the Chinon Beaumont. The top three wines are from the lowest yielding vines and demand a period of cellaring, at least three to four years. The dense and structured Les Perrières comes from 70-year old vines, while the intense and refined Chinon Les Picasses comes from a very fine argilo-calcaire terroir, arguably the best wine of the range. (DM/JB)
Recommended Reds:
Chinon Les Picasses ★★★☆ £D
Bourgueil Les Perrières ★★★☆ £D
Bourgueil Clos Sénéchal ★★★☆ £D
Bourgueil Les Galichets ★★★ £D
Bourgueil Nuits d'ivresse ★★★ £D
Chinon Beaumont ★★★ £C
Bourgueil Trinch! ★★☆ £C
Bourgueil La Dilettante ★★ £C

Dom. Hubert Brochard (Sancerre) *www.hubert-brochard.fr*
Based in the village of Chavignol, the Brochards produce white, red and rosé Sancerre as well as a sound, raw blackcurrant scented Pouilly-Fumé from old vines. The reds are two of the better examples of the appellation, if fairly pricey. The village wine is fermented at moderate temperature to lift its fruit and is aged in older oak. It is good in ripe and warm vintages and edging towards ★★★. The Vieilles Vignes is aged in a mix of new and older oak and this quite apparent when young. Offering good depth and dimension, it can be just a touch over-extracted in leaner vintages but rich and concentrated in warmer years. The regular white Sancerre comes from a range of terroirs and villages, including the home vineyards around Chavignol and from *argilo-calcaire* and *silex* soils. It is forward and fruit driven with a subtle mineral undercurrent. The Silex Sancerre, coming exclusively from these soils, is the most youthfully austere of the wines. The Aujord'hui Comme Autrefois is rare for Sancerre in that it is vinified completely naturally and bottled unfiltered. Like the village wine it is sourced from a range of sites and has a real depth and purity. The Vieilles Vignes bottling comes from mainly argillaceous soils and is aged in one year old *demi-muids*. While offering good weight and a hint of minerality, it lacks the purity and intensity of some of the other wines. La Côte des Monts Damnés comes exclusively from the Brochard's vineyards at Chavignol. Long and pure, this wine will develop well over 4 or 5 years. (DM)
Recommended Reds:
Sancerre Vieilles Vignes ★★☆ £D

Loire Valley

France

Sancerre ★☆ £C
Recommended Whites:
Sancerre La Côte des Monts Damnés ★★★ £E
Sancerre Vieilles Vignes ★★★ £D
Sancerre Aujord'hui Comme Autrefois ★★☆ £C
Sancerre Silex ★★☆ £C
Pouilly-Fumé Vieilles Vignes ★★☆ £D
Sancerre ★★ £C

❀ Dom. de La Butte (Bourgueil) *www.jackyblot.fr*
Montlouis and, more recently, Vouvray, Jacky Blot bought this fine 16-ha Bourgueil domaine in 2002 from which he is producing some of the best reds of the appellation. The property is solely planted to Cabernet Franc almost entirely on south facing slopes on the coteaux. The vineyard is divided into parcels in a Burgundian style. The Pied de la Butte comes from the base of the slope and is aged in inox, is good if a touch light and leafy. Perrières is aged in foudres and offers impressive depth and concentration; it is a clear step up. The Haute de la Butte is rich, dense and full of dark, cedary fruit. It is partly aged in new oak, which is seamlessly handled. Top cuvée Mi-Pente comes from the middle of the slope, which enjoys the best exposure and protection from north winds. It is rich dense and very ripe, opulent in top years and among the Loire's top Cabernet Francs. It needs three or four years in bottle as in youth it is firm with powerful tannins, especially from good vintages, to show its best. Mi-Pente ages extremely well – potentially at least 15-20 years. (DM/JB)
Recommended Reds:
Bourgueil Mi-Pente ★★★★ £E
Bourgueil Le Haut de la Butte ★★★☆ £C
Bourgueil Perrières ★★★ £C
Le Pied de la Butte ★★ £C

Dom. Alain Cailbourdin *www.domaine-cailbourdin.com*
Alain Cailbourdin has 16 ha under vine at Pouilly Fumé The vineyards, some up to 65 years old, are tended as naturally as possible and there are varied soils including limestone and flint. Temperature control is used during fermentation and the wines are very lightly filtered before bottling. The Cuvée de Boisfleury is the lightest and most floral of the 3 bottlings; Les Cris is fuller and more structured, becoming lightly tropical and richer with 2 or 3 years' age. Les Cornets, grown in clay-limestone is the sturdiest and most backward when young. (DM)
Recommended Whites:
Pouilly Fumé Cuvée de Boisfleury ★★★☆ £D
Pouilly Fumé Les Cris ★★★ £C
Pouilly Fumé Les Cornets ★★★ £C

Didier Champalou (Vouvray) *www.champalou.com*
Founded in 1983 Didier and Catherine Champalou run a model Vouvray property with 21ha of vineyards. In 2006 their daughter, Céline, started working with them after gaining experience around the world including spells in New Zealand, South Africa, Canada and Corsica. Total output is around 8,000 to 8,500 cases a year. The regular Vouvray and the Fondraux are vinified in stainless steel and aged in old wooden casks. They are generally sec in style but can have a fair level of residual sugar depending on the nature and conditions of the vintage. In cooler years a stylish sparkling Brut is produced and in great years for sweet wines, a moelleux style labelled La Moelleuse is made. Very occasionally a very sweet and late-harvested Trie de Vendange is released. Both of these sweet wines are rich, honeyed and extremely long-lived. (DM/JB)
Recommended Whites:
Vouvray Fondraux ★★★ £C
Vouvray ★★ £C

Ch. de Coulaine (Chinon)
A number of good wines are now being made by the Bonnaventures. They have a holding of 14 ha, just 0.5 ha of which is Chenin Blanc from which a little white Chinon is made. They also have a few parcels in Bourgueil from which they produce a single cuvée Bonnaventure which, like the Chinon reds, is marked by its elegant, stylish fruit and well-defined supple tannic structure. Fuller than the Chinon of the same label, this is less extracted than a number of other Bourgueils. The regular Chinon is produced from young vines and is more obviously fruit-driven with a hint of leafiness but good brambly upfront fruit dominating. The three top cuvées are more structured wines of some dimension and depth. The Diablesses is tighter and a touch more intense than the Clos de Turpenay, while Les Picasses is more recently added. (DM/JB)
Recommended Reds:
Chinon La Diablesse ★★★ £D
Chinon Les Picasses ★★☆ £D
Chinon Clos de Turpenay ★★☆ £C
Chinon Bonnaventure ★★☆ £C
Chinon ★★☆ £C
Bourgueil Bonnaventure ★★☆ £C

Ch. d'Epiré (Savennières) *www.chateau-epire.com*
Luc Bizard produces Savennières as well as a red Anjou, Clos de la Cerisaie, from his 11ha of vineyards. Viticulture is traditional and the harvest is handpicked with up to three tries. The wines are vinified in *inox* and aged on lees in barrel. A small-production bottling, Hu-Boyau, is sourced from the oldest parcel in the vineyard and is barrel-aged for 9 months. Cuvée Spéciale is usually just 15% of the harvest and is generally sourced from parcels that are closest to COULÉE DE SERRANT. These are tightly structured, minerally examples and all show good depth and intensity. They are also well priced. (DM)
Recommended Whites:
Savennières Cuvée Spéciale ★★★ £D
Savennières Moëlleux ★★★ £D
Savennières ★★☆ £C

Ch. de Fesles (Bonnezeaux) *www.fesles.com*
This famous Bonnezeaux landmark has had a number of recent owners. Bordeaux producer Bernard Germain who owns YON-FIGEAC purchased Château de Fesles in 1996 and sold it again to Grand Chais de France, a substantial négociant firm, in 2008. At the time Germain purchased the property it had been through a period of serious decline. In the 1970s and 1980s the top Bonnezeaux had been labelled La Chapelle and if you encounter any old vintages prior to 1985 they can be superb., be sure of their provenance though. The Bonnezeaux is now just labelled as such and has been very good in more recent top vintages for sweet wines here. The best examples possess a mineral intensity and firm structure as well as a piercingly subtle botrytis character rarely found even in the most exalted of its neighbours. The rating applies to examples made under the stewardship of Bernard Germain. There are also some decent reds from Anjou, particularly the dense and chunky Anjou-Villages. (DM)

Recommended Reds:
Anjou-Villages ★★☆ £C
Anjou Vieilles Vignes ★★ £C
Recommended Whites:
Bonnezeaux ★★★★★ £F

❀ **Ch. de Fosse-Sèche (Saumur)** *www.chateaudefosseseche.fr*
This small, Swiss-owned property has 16 ha under vine planted in *argile-siliceous* soils. Both reds and whites of impressive depth come from 17 ha of 30 to over 50-year-old vines picked as ripe as possible. The regular white Saumur is vinified in stainless steel to emphasise its rich, forward, honeyed fruit but it has good acidity to maintain balance as well. The Tris de La Chapelle is sourced from very late harvested fruit, often picked as late as November, and is vinified in small oak, a proportion of which is new. On occasion the fruit has 100% botrytis resulting in an extraordinarily low yield of just 8–10 hl/ha yet the wine is fermented fully dry. These are impressively ripe and concentrated wines but they will not be to all tastes. The cedary and elegant regular red Saumur is two thirds Cabernet Franc, the balance Sauvignon. The Clef de Voûte is a similar blend although deeper and fuller and aged in used small oak. The top red, the Réserve de Pigeonnier, is one of the best examples in the region. Rich and very concentrated, with lovely dark, smoky, cedary fruit, it is a vineyard selection from yields of barely more than 20hl/ha. The wine is aged in 50/50 new and 1-year-old oak. Minimal handling is employed throughout and the wines are bottled unfined and unfiltered. (DM)
Recommended Reds:
Saumur Réserve de Pigeonnier ★★★★ £E
Saumur La Clef de Voûte ★★★ £D
Saumur Eolith ★★☆ £C
Recommended Whites:
Saumur Les Tris de La Chapelle ★★★★ £E
Saumur Arcane ★★★ £C

Ch. de La Genaiserie (Côteaux du Layon) *www.genaiserie.com*
In 2003 Frédéric Julia bought this property from Yves Soulez, who had run into financial difficulties. Very good, stylish and refined Côteaux du Layon and Chaume in a more restrained style than most is made here. The wines are quite different from the new wave of super-ripe and unctuous styles achieved elsewhere. They are tight and often quite backward when young but have a real intensity and finesse also. There are three very fine special cuvées in addition to the regular bottling. Les Simonelles is elegant and minerally with subtle botrytis and comes from vines grown on volcanic, schistous soils. La Roche is from a vineyard with a high charcoal content and is very restrained. Les Tétuères is the fullest and most obviously honeyed of the three and generally has more marked botrytis character. There is also good Anjou-Villages red from Cabernets Franc and Sauvignon as well as a range of fruity, fresh wines under the Lys du Château label. These include a medium-sweet Cabernet d'Anjou; a revelation in comparison with so many wines sold under this label and a juicy Anjou Gamay. (DM)
Recommended Reds:
Anjou-Villages ★★ £C
Anjou Lys du Château Gamay ★☆ £B
Recommended Whites:
Chaume Les Tétuères ★★★★ £F
Côteaux du Layon-Saint-Aubin La Roche ★★★★ £F
Côteaux du Layon-Saint-Aubin Les Simonelles ★★★☆ £E

Ch. du Hureau (Saumur-Champigny) *www.domaine-hureau.fr*
Philippe Vatan produces excellent Saumur Blanc and sumptuous and supple Saumur-Champigny. He possesses 21 ha planted in tufa/limestone soils, which are particularly suitable for producing first-rate Cabernet Franc. As well as the regular red cuvée and a further well priced example, Fours à Chaux there are two very fine wines produced from old vines. Cuvée des Fevettes gets new wood treatment, whereas the Lisgathe has more exuberant, fleshy dark berry fruit and is aged in old barrels. The white is everything that good dry Chenin Blanc should be. Minerals, citrus and honey are all in evidence. These are approachable but ageworthy wines, keeping well for 10 years and more in the best vintages. (DM)
Recommended Reds:
Saumur-Champigny Lisgathe ★★★☆ £C
Saumur-Champigny Fevettes ★★★ £C
Saumur-Champigny Tuffe ★★☆ £B
Recommended Whites:
Saumur ★★★ £C

❀ **Ch. Pierre-Bise (Côteaux du Layon)**
Based in sleepy Beaulieu-sur-Layon, the Papin family possess 54 ha of vines spread across the Anjou-Villages, Côteaux du Layon and Savennières appellations. They are one of the best-established quality producers in the region with the management of the domaine having passed from Claude to his sons Christophe and René Papin. The wines are well crafted and offer great value for money. The reds are full of rich blackberry and mulberry fruit and are aged in a small proportion of new oak. The Côteaux du Layon cuvées are marked by qualities of peach, honey and nutmeg in the best years and are always well structured, refined and ageworthy. The Quarts de Chaume is richer still, with formidable depth. The intense, ageworthy, Clos de Coulaine Savennières is not only very well-priced but has a piercing citrus and mineral character. It will be all the better with 5 or 6 years' cellaring. (DM)
Recommended Reds:
Anjou-Villages Sur Spilite ★★★ £C
Anjou-Villages Clos de Coulaine ★★☆ £C
Recommended Whites:
Quarts de Chaume ★★★★★ £F
Côteaux du Layon-Rochefort Rayelles ★★★★ £E
Côteaux du Layon-Beaulieu Rouannières ★★★★ £E
Savennières Clos de Coulaine ★★★☆ £C
Anjou Haut de la Garde ★★ £B

Ch. de Tracy (Pouilly-Fumé) *www.chateau-de-tracy.com*
This is an historic property with a Renaissance château whose origins date back to 1396. There are approximately 31 ha under vine, all of which are Sauvignon Blanc. A small range is made and output is by no means small, approaching 20,000 cases a year. As well as the appellation label a couple of premium wines are also released; 101 Rangs and Haute Densité, which are pricier. A cheaper label Mademoiselle de T (£C) is also made. The Pouilly-Fumé has been consistently good in recent vintages. It is a steely, flinty style with surprisingly exotic fruit emerging with age. Structured and refined it needs at least a year or two in your cellar. (DM)
Recommended Whites:
Pouilly-Fumé ★★★☆ £D

Ch. La Varière (Anjou) *www.chateaulavariere.com*
Good-quality Anjou, both red and white, is made at this sizeable 160ha property, which can trace its vine growing origins back

France

to the 15th Century. In 2015 the Beaujeau family sold to Loire négociant Ackerman. This included their Domaine de la Perruche in Saumur-Champigny. The various red cuvées from Brissac stand out among the dry wines and red plantings account for around three-quarters of the domaine. The top red cuvée is the Grande Chevalerie, an impressively dense example dominated by Cabernet Sauvignon. Other red labels include J. Beaujeau and Prestige. The really striking wines, though, are the late-harvest whites, which are some of the best of the region, particularly in great vintages. Various parcels are held in the Côteaux du Layon, Bonnezeaux and Quarts de Chaume. The Bonnezeaux Melleresses has an intensely honeyed, peachy concentration but with a citrus undercurrent that gives it exceptional balance. Best of all, the Quarts de Chaume Les Guerches offers similar depth with a piercing undercurrent of quince. These wines offer more structure and grip than other 'sugar-hunter' examples and should age very well. (DM/JB)

Recommended Reds:
Anjou-Villages Brissac La Grande Chevalerie ★★★ £D
Recommended Whites:
Quarts de Chaume Les Guerches ★★★★★ £F
Bonnezeaux Melleresses ★★★★ £F
Anjou ★★ £C

Ch. de Villeneuve *www.chateau-de-villeneuve.com*
Very good property producing red and white from the Saumur-Champigny and Saumur ACs. The vineyards are run organically and partly on biodynamic principles. The focus here is the quality of the fruit, its intensity and concentration achieved through careful viticulture, a tight control on yields and minimal handling in the cellar. The white Cormiers is subtly oaked and barrel-fermented with a period on lees. The reds are concentrated, dark and spicy examples of the very best Loire Cabernet Franc. A special cuvée, Grand Clos, is a super-rich special bottling made in the greatest years only. These are all very ageworthy, improving in bottle for 5 to 10 years. (DM)

Recommended Reds:
Saumur-Champigny Le Grand Clos ★★★☆ £E
Saumur-Champigny Vieille Vignes ★★★ £C
Saumur-Champigny ★★☆ £C
Recommended Whites:
Saumur Cormiers ★★★☆ £D
Saumur ★★★ £C

⚫ Ch. Yvonne (Saumur)
Brilliant domaine making stunning white Saumur and some of the best red in the Saumur-Champigny appellation. The property was only founded in 1996. It is now owned and run by Mathieu Vallée, who took over in 2007. It is run biodynamically and consists of 11 ha – 8 hectares of Cabernet Franc and 3 Chenin Blanc. The vineyard is sited solely on argillaceous and calcareous soils and the oldest vines now exceed 80 years. A fierce commitment to respecting the natural characteristics of their terroir, some very old vines and the consequent low yields all contribute to the quality of the wines. The harvest is carried out manually and in the winery, filtration and fining are eschewed for both wines. The Saumur white is 100% barrel fermented and offers a subtle and piercing intensity of citrus fruits underpinned by a beguiling minerality and subtle creaminess from ageing on lees. The wine should develop very well for a decade or so although it offers less of the austerity to be found further east in Vouvray and Montlouis. The Saumur-Champigny has become increasingly impressive under Mathieu Vallée. It comes solely from Cabernet Franc of between 35 and over 50 years of age. The intense

and subtle red berry fruit matched by a classic leafy Cabernet Franc character and an impressive persistence of fruit. It will undoubtedly benefit from 4 or 5 years ageing and continue to drink well for at least another decade. (DM/JB)

Recommended Reds:
Saumur-Champigny ★★★☆ £D
Recommended Whites:
Saumur ★★★★ £D

Dom. Jean-Claude Chatelain *www.domaine-chatelain.fr*
Father and son Jean-Claude and Vincent have 20 ha of vines in the Pouilly-Fumé AC and act as small-scale négociants, buying in fruit to supplement their needs. They are now producing a regular Sancerre as well as the Pouilly and if anything it's the better of the two. Les Charmes is a level up, richer and with a hint of oak (10% is barrel-fermented), while the top cuvée, the Prestige, from old vines is tight and structured and very classy. It is vinified in stainless steel but gets 6 to 7 months on lees. Pilou, an unusual and concentrated barrel-fermented style, is occasionally produced from late-harvest dried grapes if vintage conditions permit. (DM)

Recommended Whites:
Pouilly Fumé Préstige ★★★★ £E
Pouilly Fumé Les Charmes ★★★ £C
Pouilly Fumé Harmonie ★★☆ £C
Sancerre Sélection ★★☆ £C

Dom. de La Chevalerie (Bourgueil) *www.domainedelachevalerie.fr*
The Caslot family has been cultivating vines in this appellation for three centuries. Their 38 ha of vineyards are mainly planted around the family domaine on alluvial terraces with a south to south-west exposure. Produced from Cabernet Franc, they are classic examples of the appellation, deeply coloured reds with weight and some structure. There is a soft forward red Diptique, the other wines coming from specific *lieu-dits*. Le Peu Muleau is the lightest of the seven wines and is aged in *foudres*. Although only partly aged in *foudres* Les Galichets is fuller and firmer but with an underlying soft fruit driven character. La Chevalerie comes from older vines and is richer and offers greater depth and weight. Les Busardières comes from clay and limestone soils. It is a tighter, more elegant wine than the opulent La Chevalerie and will need a couple of years longer to open out. Bretêche is a relatively big, firm style coming, like Busardières and a further *cru* La Grand Mont, from somewhat younger vines planted in clay and limestone. Expect all the wines to develop very well in bottle. (DM)

Recommended Reds:
Bourgueil Busardières ★★★ £D
Bourgueil Bretêche ★★★ £C
Bourgueil La Chevalerie Vieille Vignes ★★★ £C
Bourgueil Les Galichets ★★☆ £C
Bourgueil Le Peu Muleau ★★☆ £C

⚫ Dom. François Chidaine (Montlouis) *www.francois-chidaine.com*
This domaine is now one of the very finest in the appellation, producing wines of real class and finesse. There are currently 20 ha in Montlouis and a further 10 ha in Vouvray as well as 7 hectares of vines in the Cher Valley near to Montrichard in the Tourainbe appellation. An extensive range includes a number of single-plot wines as well as cuvées at different sweetness levels and in 2003 exceptional wines were made across the board. In addition to Vouvray and Montlouis, a straightforward, clean and varietally pure Sauvignon de Touraine and a Crémant de Loire are regularly

produced. Among the dry bottlings, Vouvray Les Argiles is very tight and stuctured while Vouvray Clos Baudoin and Montlouis Clos du Breuil carry a little more residual sugar, with a hint of new oak in the latter. The Montlouis Clos Habert and Les Tuffeaux are both demi-sec, the latter tighter and more mineral. Good moelleux bottlings are produced in both appellations. The Vouvray Le Bouchet, offers exemplary depth and concentration. The top of the tree here is the exceptional Le Lys, a vin liquoreux produced only in exceptional years and with naturally very high sugar and marked botrytis. All the Vouvrays and Montlouis bottlings will age gloriously. As is often the case, the sec wines will be the most austere in their youth. Since 2014 Chidaine's Vouvrays have to be labeled Vin de France due to local idiocy probably based on a misinterpretation of wine laws. The Chidaine family also have an investment in a small red wine project in Bullas, in south-eastern Spain, TRES P. (DM/JB)

Recommended Whites:
Montlouis Le Lys ★★★★★ £F
Montlouis Moelleux ★★★★ £E
Montlouis Les Tuffeaux ★★★★ £D
Montlouis Clos Habert ★★★☆ £D
Montlouis Clos des Breuil ★★★ £C
Vouvray Le Bouchet ★★★★ £E
Vouvray Moelleux ★★★☆ £D
Vouvray Clos Baudoin ★★★ £C
Vouvray Les Argiles ★★☆ £C
Touraine Sauvignon ★☆ £B
Cremant de Loire ★☆ £C

Daniel Chotard (Sancerre)   *www.chotard-sancerre.com*
The Chotard family has been *vignerons* in the appellation here since the time of the Revolution. There are 14 ha of vines, which are planted on limestone soils in the south west of the region on a sloping south to south east aspect. 80% of the holding is Sauvignon, the balance Pinot Noir. An organic approach is taken in the vineyard and grass grown between the vine rows. De-budding and green harvesting are both practiced to optimise quality. Daniel has invested in his winemaking but aims to make wines that very much reflect his *terroir*. The approach to vinification of his floral, green-fruited and mineral laden Sancerre Blanc includes a cold maceration and settling for three days before a temperature controlled cool fermentation in stainless steel tanks. There is no malolactic and the wine is aged in tank for six to eight months. The Sancerre Rosé is fuller and richer than most and full of attractive red berry fruit. Like the white there is a period of cold maceration to gain colour and a little structure, it is cool fermented and then given a short tank ageing before spending eight months in bottle prior to release. As with most rosés it should be enjoyed young. Daniel also makes a rouge as well as two special cuvées, the white Marcel Henri and the red Champ de l'Archer. (DM)

Recommended Whites:
Sancerre Sec ★★★ £C
Recommended Rosés:
Sancerre Sec ★★ £C

❀❀ Clos de La Coulée de Serrant   *www.coulee-de-serrant.com*
Nicolas Joly has 14.5 ha of Chenin Blanc which is tended biodynamically. Indeed, Joly is one of the most outspoken proponents of this concept of farming and has gradually been joined by a vast number of like minded producers over recent years. These are some of the finest expressions of dry Chenin to be found anywhere. The supremely structured and refined Coulée de Serrant

is loaded with subtle citrus, mineral and flint. This is a very fine wine with a remarkable capacity to age: it is not really ready for 10 years and will keep with ease for more than twice that time. The Clos de la Bergerie is also impressive and more accessible although it still ages very well. The Vieux Clos offers relatively good value. When vintage conditions allow, there is a small amount of Moelleux. (DM)

Recommended Whites:
Savennières Coulée de Serrant ❀❀❀❀❀ £F
Savennières Roches aux Moines Clos de la Bergerie ★★★★☆ £F
Savennières Vieux Clos ★★★☆ £E

Dom. du Clos Naudin (Vouvray)
Philippe Foreau is a marvellous traditional producer of the some of the greatest Vouvrays made in recent decades. Intense and very well crafted *sec* and *demi-sec* wines are tight, very minerally and finely structured. They need time to emerge from their shell and will age for decades. A very good sparkling Méthode Traditionelle Brut is also made. When the gods are favourable in this most marginal of climates for great sweet wines, Foreau produces precisely that: magnificent Moelleux and Moelleux Réserve. (DM)

Recommended Whites:
Vouvray Demi-Sec ★★★☆ £D
Vouvray Sec ★★★ £C
Vouvray Méthode Traditionelle Brut ★★★ £C

❀ Clos Rougeard (Saumur-Champigny)
Over the past 25 years this small domaine in Chacé under the tutelage of brothers – Jean-Louis (Charly) and Bernard (Nady) Foucault has become one of the most famous in the Loire. Charly, the elder brother died at the end of 2015. There are 10 ha under vine and just one of those is planted with Chenin Blanc, the balance being Cabernet Franc. Inevitably the impressive Saumur Blanc Brezé is very rarely encountered. It is a subtly barrel-fermented style and strikingly intense. There is a very good regular Saumur-Champigny with ripe, dark fruit and soft and supple tannins. The two superior cuvées, Bourg and Poyeux, are equally velvety in texture but with greater depth and power. Le Bourg offers slightly darker and more overt notes of cassis while the Poyeux is the more elegant with classic leafy, Loire spice. Because of the wines rarity and classic status they are becoming increasingly expensive particularly when sold via brokers. (DM/JB)

Recommended Reds:
Saumur-Champigny Bourg ★★★★★ £F
Saumur-Champigny Poyeux ★★★★ £E
Saumur-Champigny ★★★ £C

❀ Dom. du Closel (Savennières)   *www.savennieres-closel.com*
This excellent domaine now run with considerable style by Evelyne de Pontbriand (born De Jessey) has been owned by her family for many generations. Now fully organically certified, it is one of the very finest sources of steely, intense Savennières. Also made is some very decent fruit driven Anjou and better, denser and more concentrated lightly cedary Anjou Villages red. The top white is the rich, and mineral-laden Savennières Clos du Papillon, one of the benchmarks of the appellation. It is intense and minerally but with a remarkable depth of citrus and rich honeyed aromas emerging with age. Two further *cuvées* are also made from the appellation. Les Caillardières which is sourced from sandy soils has impressive density and generally released with a small touch of residual sugar. The third Savennières, La Jalousie is a softer more overtly fruity style with very attractive youthful green apple fruit apparent in

France

the wines youth. Sparkling wine is also important and both white and rosé Crémant de Loire are made. The Brut Sauvage is one of the area's better examples. Particularly characterful and rare for the region is a Vin de France white, Eau de Pluie which is intense, lightly aromatic with citrusy, honeyed aromas with a touch of sweetness and is vinified from the Madeira grape Verdelho. The Savennières are cellarworthy, particularly the Clos du Papillon. A Clos du Papillon *moëlleux* style Cuvée Spéciale is occasionally released in the best years. (DM)

Recommended Reds:

Anjou-Villages ★★☆ £C

Anjou ★☆ £B

Recommended Whites:

Savennières Clos du Papillon ★★★★☆ £E

Savennières Caillardières ★★★☆ £D

Savennières La Jalouisie ★★★ £C

Vin de France Eau de Pluie ★★★ £D

Crémant de Loire Brut Sauvage ★★ £C

✿ Pascal Cotat (Sancerre)

The Cotats – cousins François and Pascal – make some of the very individual Sancerres. Their parents worked together but the domaine has now been divided between François and Pascal. Production is very small with minimal intervention in both vineyard and cellar. Their sites are superb and naturally low yielding and all that is required is to ensure that the vines stay in balance. The wine is fermented naturally and no fining or filtration is undertaken. These are rich, explosive Sauvignon Blancs, which need at least 3-4 years' to show at their best. (DM/JB)

Recommended Whites:

Sancerre Chavignol La Grande Côte ★★★★ £F

Sancerre Chavignol Mont Damnés ★★★★ £F

Dom. de La Cotellerie www.domaine-cotelleraie.fr

This fine Saint-Nicolas property now has 27 ha of vineyards producing an impressive small range of reds. The vineyard area is dominated by Cabernet Franc, which accounts for 98% of the planting. The balancing 2% is Cabernet Sauvignon. Vinification for all the wines is modern with stainless steel vats used to keep temperatures under control and ageing in small oak barrels. Les Perruches is the lightest of the wines, with attractive, bright, red-berry fruit and soft, easy tannins. The fine Cuvée Domaine is sourced from throughout the Vallées' holding. It is soft, forward and vibrant with impressive intensity. Le Vau Jaumier comes from a sloping southerly aspect on clay and limestone soils and is thicker, sturdier and aged in used oak. The L'Envolée is rich, full and very intense and offers real grip and structure. The L'Envolée and Vau Jaumier will both develop with a little bottle age. (DM)

Recommended Reds:

Saint-Nicolas-de-Bourgueil L'Envolée ★★★☆ £D

Saint-Nicolas-de-Bourgueil Le Vau Jaumier ★★★☆ £D

Saint-Nicolas-de-Bourgueil Cuvée Domaine ★★★ £C

Saint-Nicolas-de-Bourgueil Les Perruches ★★★ £C

Couly-Dutheil (Chinon) www.coulydutheil-chinon.com

Sizeable and impressive long established Chinon based producer with origins going back to 1921. Unfortunately there has been a bitter family feud with the late Jacques Couly (died 2016) and his son Arnaud keeping control of the company while Pierre and Bertrand Couly have set up their own eponymous domaine. ¬ Recent vintages have been increasingly good here, particularly

the lower level fruit driven wines, red, white and rosé. The vineyard holding is substantial and now stretches to close to 90 ha of Cabernet Franc and a further smal holding for whites. The house is also able to draw on a total of 130 ha including their own holdings. Much of their terroir consists of poor chalk, clay and limestone soils, excellent for high quality wine grapes. Among the upper echelon wines, Les Chanteaux is barrel- fermented and aged with bâtonnage for four to five months. Of the top three reds, Clos de l'Olive and Crescendo are both aged in small oak, the Clos de l'Echo in cuve. All three are kept on skins during vinification for up to a month. (DM/JB)

Recommended Reds:

Chinon Clos de l'Echo Crescendo ★★★☆ £E

Chinon Clos de l'Echo ★★★ £D

Chinon Clos de l'Olive ★★☆ £C

Chinon Domaine René Couly ★★☆ £C

Chinon La Diligence ★★ £C

Chinon Les Gravières ★☆ £C

Recommended Rosés:

Chinon Coeur de Franc ★☆ £B

François Crochet (Sancerre)

This domaine surprisingly has a larger holding of Pinot Noir than Sauvignon Blanc. Pinot accounting for 7 ha of the 10.5 ha planted in different parcels in four communes Bué, Sancerre, Crézancy and Thauvenay. The appellation wines red and white are a blend of all the different terroirs. They just lack a little of the depth and intensity of the other wines. The unfined white Les Amoureuses comes from various parcels grown in *argilo-calcaire* soils and offers a very fine restrained mineral character. Le Chêne Marchand is similarly unfined and comes from a number of sites. It is more opulent with citrus as well as mineral characters. La Réserve de Marcigoué red is a blend of some of the domaine's best Pinot vines, particularly those cultivated in calcareous soils. A regular Sancerre rosé is also made. (DM)

Recommended Reds:

Sancerre Réserve de Marcigoué ★★★ £E

Sancerre ★★ £C

Recommended Whites:

Sancerre Le Chêne Marchand ★★★☆ £E

Sancerre Les Amoreuses ★★★ £D

Sancerre ★★☆ £C

Lucien Crochet (Sancerre) www.lucien-crochet.fr

The Crochets have 35 ha of their own vineyards in Sancerre and also act as négociants. Inevitably the best wines here are from their own vineyards. As well as the white Sancerre, which is vinified without new oak, the reds are also noteworthy. So often Pinot Noir fails to perform in this climate and red Sancerre is frequently light and insubstantial, but not here. Late harvesting and ripe fruit is always the key to quality. The Cuvée Prestige white and red are both old-vine bottlings and most impressive. The white Le Chêne Marchand is lighter but very intense and minerally. The Prestige labels will be better given 4 or 5 years' ageing. (DM)

Recommended Reds:

Sancerre Cuvée Prestige ★★★ £E   Sancerre Le Croix du Roy ★★ £C

Recommended Whites:

Sancerre Cuvée Prestige ★★★☆ £E

Sancerre Le Chêne Marchand ★★★ £C

✿✿ Dom. Didier Dagueneau (Pouilly-Fumé)

The late Didier Dagueneau was the finest producer in Pouilly Fumé

and while he had a few rivals in Sancerre he stood out as the region's standard-bearer for magnificent, complex and very ageworthy Sauvignon Blanc. The family also have a now well established joint venture in Jurançon at Les Jardins de Babylone with dry and late harvested wines made. The Dagueneau Pouilly wines remain light years away from the simple gooseberry and tropical flavours many associate with the variety. The keys have always been immense care in the vineyard, yields kept low, harvesting only at peak maturity with several passes through the vines and handling in the cellar kept to an absolute minimum. Buisson Renard, Pur-Sang and the magnificent Silex are all barrel-fermented but in no way does the oak become intrusive. What you are left with is an intense and very complex mix of green fruits and minerals. Superbly structured, these are wines that demand cellaring for half a dozen years or more. His children continue his work. (DM)

Recommended Whites:
Pouilly-Fumé Silex ✪✪✪✪✪ £G
Pouilly-Fumé Pur-Sang ✪✪✪✪✪ £G
Pouilly-Fumé Buisson Renard ★★★★★ £G
Pouilly-Fumé Blanc Fumé de Pouilly ★★★★☆ £F

Dom. Sébastien David www.stnicolasdebourgueil.fr
Sébastien David has emerged as one of the new dynamic talents of Saint-Nicolas de Bourgueil. He also, like an increasing number of his fellow *vignerons* from the region, follows biodynamic farming practices on his eight or so hectares. His *terroir* includes a mix of clay, limestone and gravel soils. The wines are macerated at relatively low temperatures to get a balanced extraction with some whole bunch fermentation and the grapes trodden by foot. L'Hurluberlo, which means "crazy boy" is a bright, exuberant and approachable red made with a proportion of pure carbonic maceration. In Vivo and Vin d'une Oreille, which comes from 80 year-old vines, get the malolactic completed in barrel. No sulphites are used and Sébastien believes that the oxygen present in the skins and the wines lees provide a natural equilibrium and balance. These are richly textured modern reds with approachable fruit and real complexity in the case of the Vin d'une Oreille. Two further labels are also now offered, Kézako Roll and Roc and Ni Dieu Ni Maître. (DM)

Recommended Reds:
Saint-Nicolas de Bourgueil Le Vin d'une Oreille ★★★☆ £E
Saint-Nicolas de Bourgueil In Vivo ★★★ £D
Saint-Nicolas de Bourgueil L'Hurluberlo ★★☆ £C

✪ Philippe Delesvaux (Côteaux du Layon)
Philippe Delesvaux is one of a small new group of dedicated and quality-conscious wine producers in the sleepy Côteaux du Layon. Delesvaux handcrafts intense, stylish examples. The Anjou reds are deeper and with better grip and structure than most. The Anjou bottling is Cabernet Franc; the more substantial Anjou-Villages is Cabernet Sauvignon. Both are vinified in *inox*. In whites there is a very stylish barrel-fermented Anjou Blanc as well as the sweet Layons. What marks these wines out is not just their rich, honeyed botrytised character but their intensity, refinement and balance. While the SGN stands out as a classic wine of the appellation, the Authentique is unique and very rare, coming from ungrafted vines. It is a wonderfully taught and structured wine, the Delesvaux's simply wish to see the difference in their *terroir* of the wines from the 19th century. They are fully aware that the life of the vineyard is likely to be no more than 15 years or so. (DM)

Recommended Reds:
Anjou La Montée de l'Épine ★★ £B

Anjou Le Roc ★★ £B
Recommended Whites:
Côteaux du Layon SGN ★★★★★ £F
Côteaux du Layon-Saint-Aubin Clos de la Guiberderie ★★★★ £E
Côteaux du Layon-Saint-Aubin ★★★☆ £E
Anjou Authentique ★★★☆ £E   Anjou Feuille d'Or ★★★ £C

Dom. André Dezat (Sancerre) www.dezat-sancerre.com
Impressive Sancerre small domaine now run by brothers Louis and Simon Dezat. The family has long been a benchmark for very classy white Sancerre from their 20 ha spread across the appellation but in recent years they have also purchased Domaine de Thibault in Pouilly-Fumé. The backbone of the property is a site close to CHÂTEAU DE TRACY and further plots have been added. It is a piercing, intense mineral style with lovely fresh fruit from fermentation in stainless steel. Vinification is similar for the Sancerre, which offers not only ripe blackcurrant fruit but also a marked steely minerality. The Sancerre rosé is a good example of the style and should be drunk young. Reds offer more depth and structure than most from the region, particularly in warmer vintages. The regular bottling comes from 25 year-old vines and is aged in small used barrels, the Cuvée Prestige by contrast sees 9 months in new oak. Rich, dense and finely structured it needs at least 3 to 4 years to knit the oak with the fruit. (DM)

Domaine André Dezat
Recommended Reds:
Sancerre Cuvée Prestige ★★★ £E
Sancerre ★★☆ £D
Recommended Whites:
Sancerre ★★★☆ £D
Recommended Rosés:
Sancerre ★☆ £C
Domaine de Thibault
Recommended Whites:
Pouilly-Fumé ★★★☆ £D

Dom. Dozon (Chinon) www.domaine-dozon.fr
Good quality small Chinon domaine in Ligré with 14 ha of vineyards, which changed hands in autumn 2013 with Eric Santier taking over from the Dozon family. The vines are cultivated on a mixture of argilo-siliceux and argilo-calcaire soils. 97% of the domaine is planted with Chenin Bl;anc with just 3% with Chenin Blanc. The reds are all made from 100% Cabernet Franc and there is a little white Chinon and rosé produced. The simplest of the reds, C du Plaisir is sourced from younger vines from different terroirs. Light and elegant with subtle leafy fruit, the wine is traditionally aged en cuve. Coming from vines over 40 years old the Clos du Saut au Loup is also aged in cuve although for up to 16 months and offers fuller, richer fruit and a greater pure blackcurrant character. Laure et Le Loup is from the oldest vines on the property and offers a rich and concentrated black fruit style. A portion of the Clos du Saut au Loup, L'Exception, is also aged in barriques, which are 1 and 2 years old. The top three wines will all stand a little cellaring. (DM/JB)

Recommended Reds:
Chinon L'Exception ★★★ £D
Chinon Laure et Le Loup ★★★ £C
Chinon Clos du Saut au Loup ★★☆ £C
Chinon C du Plaisir ★★ £B

✪ Dom. Pierre-Jacques Druet (Bourgueil)
This was once a brilliant source of top Cabernet Franc from 13

Loire Valley

ha of domaine vineyards. Although Pierre Jacques Druet was an exceptional winemaker, he was a poor businessman, which latterly was exacerbated by personal problems. In March 2016 he filed for bankruptcy. The vineyards have been taken over by Frédéric Brochet's AMPLEDIAE, who will be making the 2016 vintage. A series of Druet's Bourgueils recently tasted were disappointing and not of the same standard as before. The 2010 Vaumoreau, which was only very recently bottled, lacked fruit in the finish. Due to Druet's financial problems I suspect that this Vaumoreau lost some of its fruit from being bottled almost six years after the vintage. Brochet aims to restore this domaine's high reputation. **Historic assessment:** 'The Bourgueil rosé is delicious and fruity, far better than most of its kind. There are three cuvées of Bourgueil as well as the marvellously elegant and pure Chinon Clos de Danzay, which is aged in demi-muids. The Bourgueil Cent Boisselées is handled entirely in stainless steel and displays classic blackcurrant fruit and just a subtle hint of leafiness. The Grand Mont is refined and elegant with hints of cassis and cedar. Produced from chalk vineyards the tannin is supple and well balanced. The top red Vaumoreau comes from 100-year-old vines. It is an unfiltered, dense, very powerful and concentrated red, full of ripe intense cassis and cedar. A wine of immense class and finesse, it is only produced in top years.' (DM/JB)

Recommended Reds:

Bourgueil Vaumoreau ★★★★ £E
Chinon Clos de Danzay ★★★☆ £D
Bourgueil Grand Mont ★★★ £C
Bourgueil Cent Boisselées ★★☆ £C

Recommended Rosés:

Sancerre ★★ £B

✿ **Dom. de L'Ecu (Muscadet Sèvre-et-Maine)** *www.domaine-ecu.com*
This 20.5 ha domaine produces some of the finest of all Muscadet. The domaine's reputation was established by Guy Bossard, who has now retired. Bossard started to covert the domaine to organic viticulture in 1972 moving to biodynamics in 1978. Fred Niger Van Herck took over from Bossard in 2013 greatly expanding the range of wines made. Van Herck is a big fan of amphores and may well have the largest park of amphores in the Loire. The age of the vines for the top wines varies between 40 and 50 years and the three special *terroir* cuvées are all sourced from different soils and making strikingly different wines. A regular bottling is also produced "Classique" which while it doesn't have quite the piercing mineral depth of the terroir wines is impressively intense and smoky. The three *terroir* labels are, as one would expect from Melon de Bourgogne, relatively austere in style but each has a rich, deep mineral character and an intensity lacking in most Chablis. The most austerely mineral and stony is the Gneiss. The Granit, perhaps the best of the three has a citrus and melon undercurrent to its stony fruit. All possess impressive weight and substance. The domaine also make a number of very limited premium release wines. Taurus is a remarkable example of what Muscadet can produce. It offers intense restrained mineral and citrus qualities and is neither fined nor filtered. A small number of wines are also made under the Vin de France banner but are far from ordinary. The white Carpe Diem is vinified from Melon de Bourgogne but is unusually aged in amphora for 15 months. The red Mephisto comes from a small 0.8 ha plot of Cabernet Franc grown in granite. It offers an impressive concentration of cool climate red fruit aromas. Expect the terroir Muscadets and the top labels to develop well in bottle for at least 5 to 7 years. A very presentable Gros Plant is made as well as a traditional method sparkler and a further premium release Faust.

(DM/JB)

Recommended Reds:

Vin de France Mephisto ★★★☆ £D

Recommended Whites:

Vin de France Carpe Diem ★★★★ £E
Muscadet Sèvre-et-Maine Taurus ★★★☆ £D
Muscadet Sèvre-et-Maine Granit ★★★ £C
Muscadet Sèvre-et-Maine Orthogneiss ★★★ £C
Muscadet Sèvre-et-Maine Gneiss ★★★ £C
Muscadet Sèvre-et-Maine Cuvée Classique ★★ £B
Gros Plant du Pays Nantais Gros Pet' ★☆ £B

✿ **Dom. FL (Côteaux du Layon)** *www.domainefl.com*
This operation brought together the former domaines of Jo Pithon and Château de Chamboureau and including all the two original domaines terroirs. Domaine FL is owned by local telecoms businessman, Philip Fournier, and is run by his son Julien. A large modern winery has been built at Rochefort-sur-Loire. Consultancy input now comes from Kyriakos Kynigopoulos, who is based in Beaune. Previously Stéphane Derenencourt from Bordeaux was the consultant. Jo Pithon himself has left the project to establish a new label, Pithon-Paillé. As well as the sweet whites here there are some very well crafted dry Chenins. There are two Savennières, the complex Chamboureau and oaky Roche-aux- Moines. Of the Anjou bottlings, Les Bergères sees a little new wood and shows subtle barrel-ferment character. The regular Côteaux du Layon comes from plots in four different villages. It is relatively lightly influenced by botrytis, just 50% of the fruit, and is elegant and finely structured with a marked mineral component providing backbone. The Quarts de Chaume comes from 100% botrytised fruit, with striking aromas of nutmeg and honey as well as a peachy, citrus character. The wines will all drink well with 2 or 3 years' ageing and the opulent sweeties will keep in the medium term. An Anjou red, Le Cochet, is also made. (DM)

Recommended Whites:

Quarts de Chaume ★★★★☆ £F
Côteaux du Layon Les 4 Villages ★★★★ £E
Savennières Roche aux Moines ★★★☆ £D
Anjou Les Bergères ★★★☆ £C
Savennières Chamboureau ★★★☆ £C

✿ **Dom. des Forges (Côteaux du Layon)** *www.domainedesforges.net*
Family estate now run by Stéphane and Séverine Branchereau. Stéphane is the fifth generation of the family domaine, which was established in 1890. A wide range of Anjou wines are made at this increasingly reputed property with 47 hectares of vines: good straightforward Sauvignon Blanc and Chardonnay IGP Val de Loire along with supple, fruity Anjou reds and some decent Anjou white. However best of all are the impressive sweet whites – stylish, rich but restrained Côteaux du Layon and Quarts de Chaume. The top wines are the Quarts de Chaume and Côteaux du Layon 1er Cru Chaume. There is also good well-crafted Savennières, which is tight and flinty. (DM/JB)

Recommended Whites:

Quarts de Chaume ★★★★☆ £F
Côteaux du Layon 1er Cru Chaume ★★★★ £E
Côteaux du Layon-Saint-Aubin ★★★☆ £D
Côteaux du Layon ★★★ £C
Savennières Clos du Papillon ★★☆ £C

Vincent Gaudry (Sancerre) *www.vincent-gaudry.com*

This small biodynamically farmed operation just outside the town of Sancerre has a small holding of 8 ha, 90% of which is planted to Sauvignon Blanc. From less than 1 ha Vincent produces his humorously named red Pinot Noir Sancerre. Yields are carefully checked and the wine has a lengthy vatting of 28 days or so. Ageing in small oak is for anything between 12 and 24 months depending on the nature and structure of the vintage. Like others, the wine benefits from a warm year. It is bottled unfiltered and unfined. Le Tournebride is the most accessible and fruit driven of the white Sancerre bottlings with grassy, fresh gooseberry fruit and a hint of citrus. A Mi-Chemin is altogether more serious and impressively structured for Sancerre. Coming from a yield of barely 20 hl/ha the wine is vinified and aged in used small oak. An old-vine bottling Mélodie de Vieilles Vignes is also produced. (DM)

Recommended Reds:

Sancerre Vincengétorix ★★☆ £C

Recommended Whites:

Sancerre A Mi-Chemin ★★★ £C

Sancerre Le Tournebride ★★☆ £C

❀ Dom. de La Charrière (Jasnières) *www.gigou-jasnieres.com*

The Gigou family are immensely dedicated growers in this most marginal and extreme of Loire Valley climates. The vineyard is close to organic, yields are kept in check and balanced vines mean no vendange vert. There are two intense and almost austere dry whites. A real mineral backbone runs through the wines and they have piercing acidity but are very ageworthy. The Clos Saint-Jacques will take on a marvellously rich citrus and honeyed character with age. Also produced is a very fine late-harvest white, which is far removed from a Bonnezeaux or a Quarts de Chaume. The wine is tightly structured, lightly honeyed but very long and intense. It is extraordinarily long-lived. The Gigous also make several reds, including a pure Pineau d'Aunis. They also use Pineau d'Aunis to make a sparkling – La Bulle Sarthoise. (DM/JB)

Recommended Whites:

Jasnières Sélection Raisons Nobles ★★★★☆ £E

Jasnières Cuvée Clos Saint-Jacques Vieilles-Vignes ★★★☆ £C

Jasnières Jus de Terre ★★☆ £B

Vignobles Gitton (Sancerre) *www.gitton.fr*

Pascal Gitton's family-owned domaine covers some 36 ha with vineyard parcels spread across various sites (26 ha in Sancerre, 7.5 ha in Pouilly-Fumé and 2.5 ha in Giennois). All the wines are from separate vineyards and display the characteristics of their individual terroirs. The Pouilly-Fumé Clos Joanne d'Orion like the Sancerres is vinified as a separate parcel. It is certainly very good, if perhaps lacking the outright depth and definition of the best Sancerre bottlings. Rosé comes from Les Romains and is lighter in style than most but offers good depth and grip. Red also comes from the same site as well as a subtle minerally white of impressive intensity. Both the softer fruit-driven Montachins and the more structured and mineral older-vine L'Amiral come from chalky soils. Les Belles Dames is from *silex* (flint) soils and is classically mineral in style. Les Herses, also from flinty soils, is even more ferociously mineral. A selection from Les Herses, Herses d'Or, is barrel-fermented in a proportion of new oak and a slight citrus element creeps in as well as smoky, toasty notes. La Vigne du Larrey is the family's oldest vineyard holding, planted in 1953 from a mass selection. The wine is vinified in used 600-litre barrels and has a rich and concentrated texture and real depth. Galinot is vinified in new oak, again of 600-litre size and

3,000 litre *foudre*, and is more obviously citrusy and opulent. The top wines here should develop very well in bottle for 4 or 5 years. A range of wines are also produced in the Côtes de Duras in South-West France and a mousseux sparkler Saint Agouant comes from 100% Sémillon. (DM)

Recommended Whites:

Sancerre Galinot ★★★ £D

Sancerre Vigne du Larrey ★★★ £D

Sancerre Les Herses d'Or ★★★ £D

Sancerre Les Belles Dames ★★☆ £D

Pouilly Fumé Clos Joanne d'Orion ★★☆ £C

Sancerre L'Amiral ★★ £C

Sancerre Les Herses ★★ £C

Sancerre Les Romains ★★ £C

Sancerre Les Montachins ★★ £C

Recommended Rosés:

Sancerre Les Romains ★☆ £B

Dom. Guiberteau (Saumur) *www.domaineguiberteau.fr*

Roman Guiberteau established this excellent small domaine just over a decade ago. The 14.5 hectare property is planted with both Cabernet Franc and Chenin Blanc with a significant proportion planted at Brezé. Output is small but quality is very impressive. The low-yielding vineyards are now handled organically and great pains are taken to work the soil effectively to ensure deep-rooting vines and top-quality fruit, even in difficult years. In the winery minimal handling is the order of the day, although some micro-oxygenation is used to help ensure rich, supple wines. The regular red Saumur is elegant and intense with classic Cabernet Franc fruit. The Motelles is aged in used wood for up to 30 months and has that extra dimension with piercingly intense red berry fruit and the firm structure to develop very well in bottle for 6 or 7 years. The top red, Les Arbois, is similarly given long oak-ageing in one-third new wood. It is rich and really intense. Two whites are now produced and both are vinified and aged in barriques. The Saumur is lightly opulent with a real citrus undercurrent. Les Clos de Guichaux, a cru, is really intense and offers great fruit persistence with honey and citrus notes as well as a hint of toastiness from one-third new oak. These wines will all develop very well in the medium term. An additional top red and white are now also made. Brézé rouge comes from a clos of over 50-year old vines and the younger vine Chenin from the Clos des Carmes. (DM)

Recommended Reds:

Saumur Les Arboises ★★★★ £F

Saumur Motelles ★★★ £E

Saumur ★★☆ £C

Recommended Whites:

Saumur Le Clos de Guichaux ★★★☆ £E

Saumur ★★☆ £C

Dom. Guion (Bourgueil)

This small Bourgueil domaine is producing modest volumes of well made, characterful and very well priced red as well as a small amount of rosé. The vineyards are farmed organically and the vines range from just over 10 to 80 years. In no small measure does this account for the really impressive intensity and persistence of the Cuvée Prestige. The Domaine wine is certainly the lighter of the two reds but has a fragrance and depth of fruit that matches the finer examples from other top producers. Vatting is carefully judged for the style with a maceration of 8 to 10 days and the wine has sufficient acidity to enable it to develop well in bottle for five years

and more. The Prestige is bigger, firmer and offers greater depth and concentration. While elegant and reserved in style the wine provides real intensity from older vines planted on the appellation's limestone Côteaux. Macerated for up to three weeks and aged in small wood for 12 months the wine will continue to develop for at least a decade. (DM)

Recommended Reds:

Bourgueil Cuvée Prestige ★★★ £C
Bourgueil Cuvée Domaine ★★☆ £B

Dom. La Haut-Févrie www.lahautefevrie.com

Claude Branger is a further example of the potential this appellation can achieve where so many of its *vignerons* so markedly fail to so do. His estate dates back to 1915 and there have now been three generations of vinegrowers. The property is to the south east of Nantes and has a favourable exposition overlooking the Sèvre. There are a total of 21 ha and the vineyards are farmed as naturally as possible, avoiding the use of chemical fertilizers. The grapes are all hand picked. The regular bottling is crisp and immediately approachable. The Excellence and Gras Moutons require a little patience. The latter shows a real mineral intensity and impressive persistence. (DM)

Recommended Whites:

Muscadet Sèvre-et-Maine Les Gras Moutons ★★☆ £C
Muscadet Sèvre-et-Maine Excellence Vieilles Vignes ★★☆ £B
Muscadet Sèvre-et-Maine ★★ £B

✪✪ Huet L'Echansonne (Vouvray) www.huet-echansonne.com

There may be a rising tide of new quality-conscious producers in Vouvray but this biodynamically farmed domaine remains the standard-bearer for the appellation. It was Gaston Huet, whose first vintage was 1928, and then Noël Pinguet, his son-in-law, who made Domaine Huet's reputation. On Huet's death in 2002, the property was sold to Anthony Hwang. Noël Pinguet left the domaine in 2012 in acrimonious circumstances. The domaine is now managed by Hugo and Susan Hwang, Anthony's children with the wine made by Jean-Bernard Berthomé and assisted by Benjamin Joliveau. The property has a total of 30 ha and sources its fruit from three different sites; Clos du Bourg, Haut-Lieu and Le Mont. The wines are made as sec, demi-sec and when conditions allow, some magnificent moelleux including the extraordinary Cuvée Constance. The dry wines are intense, minerally and very backward when young. They will, though, evolve into superb, complex, honeyed masterpieces with time, but you have to be patient. The Demi-Sec and Moelleux are more immediately approachable, drinking with 3 or 4 years' ageing but very fine indeed. (DM)

Recommended Whites:

Vouvray Cuvée Constance ✪✪✪✪✪ £G
Vouvray Le Mont Moelleux ★★★★★ £F
Vouvray Haut-Lieu Moelleux ★★★★★ £F
Vouvray Clos du Bourg Moelleux ★★★★★ £F
Vouvray Haut-Lieu Demi-Sec ★★★★ £E
Vouvray Haut-Lieu Sec ★★★☆ £D
Vouvray Clos du Bourg Demi-Sec ★★★☆ £E
Vouvray Clos du Bourg Sec ★★★☆ £E
Vouvray Le Mont Sec Demi-Sec ★★★☆ £E
Vouvray Le Mont Sec ★★★☆ £D

Dom. Charles Joguet (Chinon) www.charlesjoguet.com

The Joguet domaine is mainly planted to Cabernet Franc with just a small holding of Chenin Blanc. Jacques Genet now owns the estate.

He is ably assisted by his winemaker, Kevin Fontaine. Up to nine different cuvées are made and these are based on both vine age and soil type. The Terroir and Clos de la Cure bottlings are relatively soft and forward, the most approachable of these most traditional of Chinons. The Varennes du Grand Clos is grown in limestone soils and produced from a yield of 40 hl/ha. The top two wines the Clos du Chene Vert and Clos de la Dioterie come from lower-yielding plots, barely 30 hl/ha. The wines are marked by their traditional vinification with fermentation being instigated in the high 30s celsius, and are correspondingly backward when young. Even the lesser cuvées can seem angular and awkward before gaining richness with age. Chenin Blanc was planted in the early to mid-1990s and now makes a decent Touraine white Clos de la Plante Martin. (DM)

Recommended Reds:

Chinon Clos du Chêne Vert ★★★☆ £E
Chinon Clos de la Dioterie ★★★☆ £E
Chinon Les Varennes du Grand Clos ★★★ £D
Chinon Clos de la Cure ★★☆ £C
Chinon Terroir ★★☆ £C

✪ Dom. de Juchepie (Côteaux du Layon) www.juchepie.fr

Eddy Oosterlinck's tiny Layon property is making some increasingly good dry and late-harvested whites. He currently has 7 ha under vine and his output is a mere 1,200 or so cases a year so the wines won't be that easy to find. However, they are good value for money and will be worth the hunt. The vineyard faces south to south-west and there are two parcels – Les Churelles, with carboniferous soils, and Les Quarts, which has slatey soils on a clay bedrock. The vines average 40 years and the oldest are over 100 years. The sweet Layons are harvested in 6–8 tries and yields are low at 30 hl/ha for the dry Anjou and just 10 hl/ha for the Layons. The two Anjou whites, vinified in used oak, have a pronounced citrus character and gain weight from ageing on fine lees. The Quarts as well as the Quintessence, are both marked by their rich, unctuously sweet fruit. The wines have good grip and sufficient acidity but will drink well young. Expect them to develop nicely over the medium term. (DM)

Recommended Whites:

Côteaux du Layon La Quintessence de Juchepie ★★★★☆ £F
Côteaux du Layon Les Quarts de Juchepie ★★★☆ £E
Anjou Le Clos de Juchepie ★★★☆ £D
Anjou Les Monts de Juchepie ★★★ £C

✪✪ La Ferme de La Sansonnière (Anjou)

Marc Angeli and his Martial farm 7 ha biodynamically and they make some of the very finest examples of the humble Anjou AC. In order to maximise his own flexibility and as a protest against appellation rules the wines are released as Vin de France rather than as AC. As well as from Anjou vineyards he has also produced tiny amounts (from less than a hectare) of exquisite Bonnezeaux released as Le Coteau du Houet in a super rich passerillé style. The largest volume here is saved for his Anjou La Lune, which accounts for nearly half his holding at 3.1 ha. The wine is produced from low yields and is vinified in 400- to 600-litre barrels. It is remarkably pure with an intense mineral quality amidst complex, very subtly tropical fruit. It is occasionally bottled with just a hint of residual sugar. Les Fouchardes and the pricier Vieilles Vignes des Blanderies are produced from much smaller holdings and are hard to find. The range is completed by a Cabernet Sauvignon Les Jeunes Vignes des Gélinettes and a Rosé d'Anjou, Rosé d'Un Jour. (DM/JB)

Recommended Reds:

Vin de France Le Jeunes Vignes des Gélinettes ★★★ £D

Wine behind the label

Recommended Whites:
Bonnezeaux ✪✪✪✪ £G
Vin de France Les Vieilles Vignes des Blanderies ★★★★★ £F
Vin de France Les Fouchardes ★★★★☆ £E
Vin de France La Lune ★★★★ £E
Recommended Rosés:
Vin de France Rosé d'Un Jour ★★☆ £C

Dom. La Grange Tiphaine *www.lagrangetiphaine.com*
Damien Delecheneau is producing some of the best examples not just of the Touraine Amboise appellation where he is based but the whole Touraine AC. Add to this some fine Montlouis white and this is one of the most exciting emerging domains in the Loire. The property has been handed down from father to son for more than a century. A combination of some very old vineyards and *argilo-calcaire* soils in Amboise help considerably with the quality of the wines. As well as the reds there is a fruit-driven attractive rosé from a blend of red varieties and a fine dry white Bel Air and occasional *demi-sec* Bel Air from 70-year old Chenin vines. Of the reds both Les Cassiers and Ad Libitum come from marginally younger vines, although up to 45 years in the case of Ad Libitum. The old vine Côt is very characterful and complex at this level, no doubt aided by vineyards averaging no less than 115 years of age. The Bécarre is unusually from 100% Cabernet Franc and offers a firm structure and balanced cedary fruit. The top red Clef de Sol is from 60-year old Cabernet Franc and Côt planted in clay and limestone soils. The Montlouis Bulles sparkler is fresh and clean, the dry Clef de Sol piercing and intense. As well as the *demi-sec* Grenouillères, a sweet Buisson Viau and unctuously sweet liquoureux style Equilibriste are also produced in the ripest vintages. (DM)
Recommended Reds:
Touraine Amboise Clef de Sol ★★★ £C
Touraine Amboise Bécarre ★★★ £C
Touraine Amboise La Cuvée Côt Vieilles Vignes ★★★ £C
Touraine Amboise Ad Libitum ★★☆ £B
Touraine Amboise Les Cassiers ★★ £B
Recommended Whites:
Montlouis Les Grenouillères ★★★☆ £D
Montlouis Clef de Sol ★★★ £C
Montlouis Les Bulles ★★☆ £C
Touraine Amboise Bel Air Sec ★★ £B
Recommended Rosés:
Touraine Riage tournant ★★ £B

Langlois-Château (Saumur) *www.langlois-chateau.fr*
This sizeable Saumur producer, with an output of close to 50,000 cases a year, established its reputation with good quality and value sparklers and now has input from Champagne house BOLLINGER. The range though also covers the other red and white Saumur appellations and Sancerre and Muscadet are additionally produced. There are a total of 73 ha and the vineyards are cultivated organically. White and rosé Crémant de Loire are clean and fresh styles, getting respectively 24 and 18 months ageing on their fine lees, providing additional weight and depth. Altogether more serious is the Quadrille, comprising Chenin Blanc, Chardonnay and a little of both Cabernets. Sourced from some of the firms best parcels on chalk, clay and silica soils the wine has a subtle biscuit complexity and fresh character with 4 years lees ageing. It is a standard bearer for the appellation. The Cabernet de Saumur from 100% Cabernet Franc gets 12 to 24 hours skin contact, it is fresh and lightly fruity with a subtle intensity of light red berry fruit. Chateau

de Fontaine-Audon comprises 10 ha in Sancerre grown on silex soils. It is a lightly mineral and gooseberry scented example fermented cool in stainless steel and gaining from a short period on lees. There are two very good white Saumur bottlings. The regular is finely structured and with a real purity of fruit. The Vieilles Vignes comes from vines over 35 years of age and is fatter and fuller with barrel-fermentation and ageing on lees with bâtonnage. The wine though does not go through malolactic and this gives it a really piercing fresh mineral intensity. Both the reds are solely from Cabernet Franc. The regular Saumur is much the softer and fruitier of the two, the Vieilles Vignes is from lower yields and gets both more skin contact during and after fermentation and is aged in 500 litre casks around a third new. Both Vieilles Vignes wines will continue to improve over four to five years with the white good for at least 10 years. Drink the other still wines on purchase, while Crémants can gain with two or three years in bottle depending on the style preferred. (DM/JB)
Recommended Reds:
Saumur-Champigny Vieilles Vignes ★★★ £D
Saumur ★★ £C
Recommended Whites:
Saumur Vieilles Vignes ★★★ £D
Crémant de Loire Quadrille ★★★ £D
Sancerre Château de Fontaine-Audon ★★☆ £C
Saumur ★★ £B
Touraine Amboise Bel Air Sec ★★ £B
Crémant de Loire Brut ★☆ £C
Recommended Rosés:
Crémant de Loire Brut ★☆ £B
Cabernet de Saumur ★ £B

Dom. Laureau (Savennières) *www.damien-laureau.fr*
In just over 15 years Damien Laureau has established a reputation for making top quality Savennières is from this organic domaine since he took over the reins in 1999. The current dry whites are now among the best of either appellation and the domaine is relatively small at just 7.1 ha in total. The Savennières vineyards have an excellent south-west exposition and the wines will continue to improve in bottle for a decade or more. Les Genêts is traditionally aged in foudres and offers tighter mineral fruit. The Bel Ouvrage is barrel-fermented and aged and is the more opulent and approachable of the two. A somewhat pricier Roche-aux-Moines is also made. (DM/JB)
Recommended Whites:
Savennières Bel Ouvrage ★★★☆ £D
Savennières Les Genets ★★★ £D

Dom. René-Noël Legrand *www.domaine-legrand.fr*
Legrand is a well-established and very impressive Saumur-Champigny family producer, established in the 17th Century. Since 2013 René-Noël has been joined by Clotilde, his daughter. The domaine has 15 ha and produces around 5,000 cases a year. The reds are very traditional but have a great purity and real style. He has just 1ha of Chenin Blanc from which he produces a very acceptable, ripe and full Saumur white from fruit harvested late – sometimes, almost overly so. Four reds are produced. Les Lizières is the softest and most accesible of the wines. Les Terrages is denser and fuller with ageing in cuve. La Chaintre is aged in foudres and offers altogether more complexity and intensity. Les Togelins, the top label, is aged in part new oak, which is in no way overdone as the depth and purity of fruit comfortably absorbs the new wood. Give the top 2 wines at least 3 or 4 years to fully unfurl. (DM/JB)

Loire Valley

France

Recommended Reds:

Saumur-Champigny Les Rogelins ★★★☆ £C
Saumur-Champigny La Chaintre ★★★ £C
Saumur-Champigny Les Terrages ★★☆ £C
Saumur-Champigny Les Lizières ★★ £B

Recommended Whites:

Saumur ★★ £B

Dom. Richard Leroy (Vin de France/Anjou)

Based in Rablay-sur-Layon since 1996 Richard Leroy possesses two excellent sites in the Côteaux du Layon with a holding of just 2.7 ha cultivated organically. Originally released as Anjou, Leroy now labels his wines as Vin de France. The majority of his holding, some 2 ha at Les Noëls de Montbenault, is comprised of 50 year-old vines planted in finely drained volcanic soils. The wines are a touch more mineral and structured than those from Clos des Rouliers, where the vines are younger at around 15 years although the vineyard with a southerly exposition is planted on propitious schist soils. (DM/JB)

Recommended Whites:

Anjou Noëls de Montbenault ★★★★ £E
Anjou Clos des Rouliers ★★★☆ £E

Logis de La Bouchardiere (Chinon) www.sergeetbrunosourdais.com

The Sourdais family produces fine, traditional and firmly structured Chinon reds, all of which offer excellent value. Their origins in the appellation go back a considerable way, the property having been passed down from father to son since 1850. It is now run by Serge and his son Bruno. Their holdings are not inconsiderable with 55 ha, planted mainly to Cabernet Franc, producing up to 20,000 cases a year. In 2006 they took over Le Haut Olive vineyard in Chinon. The wines may be traditional but the Sourdais have stainless steel vats with temperature control to aid vinification. The Sourdais-Taveau Chinon comes from young vines and has a light, green pepper character and soft berry fruit. La Bouchardière is less obviously fruit driven and comes from older vines of over 25 years. The impressively concentrated Le Chêne Vert is from an individual south west facing clos and is aged in barriques. Le Clos by contrast is traditionally aged and offers greater elegance and intensity in a firm vin de garde style. Richest and fleshiest is the top wine of the domaine, Les Cornuelles. This comes from vines grown in argilo-calcaire and silex soils that are now well over 60 years and a rich and complex old-vine character really shows through in the wine. Ageing is in a mix of mainly foudres and a small amount of new oak. With the exception of the Sourdais-Taveau, which should be enjoyed young, the wines will cellar well, in particular Les Cornuelles. (DM/JB)

Recommended Reds:

Chinon Les Cornuelles ★★★☆ £D
Chinon Le Clos ★★★ £C
Chinon Le Chêne Vert ★★★ £C
Chinon La Bouchardière ★★★ £C
Chinon Cuvée Sourdais-Taveau ★★ £C

Dom. Luneau-Papin www.domaineluneaupapin.com

This has long been one of the very best sources of top Muscadet, light years away from the dull lifeless wine that most people associated with the name before the overall standard improved considerably. The domaine's current reputation was established by Pierre Luneau, the seventh generation of vignerons of his family in the region, and his wife Monique. Pierre is now semi-retired. Pierre-Marie, his son and his wife, Marie, are now in charge. There are 49 ha spread across a range of terroirs. Rich and full with a real

old-vine depth is the Clos des Allées, from the schists of the village of Landreau and from vines around 40 years old. A maceration pelliculaire is used and the wine spends seven months on lees. Le L d'Or is vinified in a similar manner and now comes from over 40 year old vines in granite soils. Some very old bottles are available as the domaine's top wines age brilliantly – examples of Le L d'Or de Pierre Luneau for the 1970s are still remarkably youthful. Pierre and Pierre-Marie are among a number of vignerons here who are keen to establish the best sites for the appellation and create Grand Cru Muscadet. Excelsior comes from a single vineyard comprising schist soils and planted to very old vines, around 75 years old. The wine has a wonderful citrus and mineral intensity and ageing for 30 months on lees with bâtonnage adds an additional weight and dimension to the wine. Pueri Solis from a vineyard planted on schist that in part overlooks the Marais de Goulaine with Nantes in the distance. Some of the vines were planted in 1947. This cuvee also spends a long time on its lees – 30 months and more depending on the vintage. Their Gros Plant is delicious with good depth and shows what can be done with this variety. (DM/JB)

Recommended Whites:

Muscadet Sèvre-et-Maine Excelsior Cru Communal Goulaine ★★★ £D
Muscadet Sèvre-et-Maine Clos des Allées Vieilles Vignes ★★★ £C
Muscadet Sèvre-et-Maine Le L d'Or de Pierre Luneau ★★☆ £C

Dom. Frédéric Mabileau www.fredericmabileau.com

Frédéric Mabileau has been running his small domaine with his wife Nathalie since the early 1990s. He now has a total of 27 ha under vine and produces wines in the Bourgueil, Anjou and Saumur appellations as well as in Saint-Nicolas-de-Bourgueil. There is a softly fruity Cabernet Sauvignon Anjou made from younger vines and a Bourgueil, Les Racines. Two whites are also now made, a Saumur Chenin Blanc and a white Anjou, Chenin de Rouillères as well as a Rosé de Loire, Osez. Saint-Nicolas-de-Bourgueil stands out and there are three good to very good and pure bottlings, marked more by their elegance and refinement than by their weight. The Mabileaus possess plots across the AC in a range of terroirs. Les Rouillères is the softest of the trio, sourced from sandy/gravel soils where the vines are relatively young. Les Coutures is fuller and firmer, sourced from older vines (over 40 years) grown in gravel. The wine gets a brief cold soak, 20 day maceration and is aged for 12 months in oak. The brilliant, piercingly intense top wine, Éclipse, comes from the lowest-yielding plots of clay/gravel over limestone. The wine gets 12 months in oak, a proportion new, and malolactic takes place in barrel. The top two wines in particular will benefit from 5 or 6 years' ageing. (DM)

Recommended Reds:

Saint-Nicolas-de-Bourgueil Éclipse ★★★☆ £D
Saint-Nicolas-de-Bourgueil Les Coutures ★★★ £C
Saint-Nicolas-de-Bourgueil Rouillères ★★☆ £C

Dom. Henry Marionnet (Touraine) www.henry-marionnet.com

This substantial operation has long been regarded as a benchmark for Touraine AC wines and still continues to be so, although quality is now rivalled by some smaller domaines. The two key varieties here are Gamay and Sauvignon. There is also a little Cot, Chenin Blanc and Romorantin planted. Of the whites, the regular Touraine Sauvignon is fresh and grassy with reasonable varietal character. The Vinifera bottling, like all those under this label, is produced from ungrafted vines and is a clear step up with greater depth, structure and intensity. Other bottlings include M de Marionnet and a special IGP bottling from very old vines, Provinage. Of the reds, the Touraine

Gamay is soft and forward while the Première Vendange, from Gamay plots of over 45 years of age, is vibrant and deeper with great fruit intensity. The IGP Cépages Oubliés is a rarity, from an almost obsolete clone of the Gamay, de Bouze, which is darker in colour and surprisingly firm in structure. The Vinifera Gamay is subtler and lighter but offers impressive intensity. Best of the Vinifera bottlings is the Cot. Full of dark berries and spices, it has impressive depth and concentration. A further rarity is the La Pucelle de Romorantin. It comes from the variety of the same name, of which there are very limited plantings and some of the vines date back to 1860. All will drink well with a couple of years of age except the regular Touraines which should be drunk young. (DM)

Recommended Reds:
Touraine Cot Vinifera ★★★ £C
Touraine Gamay Vinifera ★★☆ £C
IGP Gamay Cépages Oubliés ★★☆ £C
Touraine 1ère Vendange ★★ £B
Touraine Gamay ★ £B

Recommended Whites:
IGP Val de Loire Provignage ★★★★ £E
IGP Val de Loire La Pucelle de Romorantin ★★★ £D
Touraine Sauvignon Vinifera ★★☆ £C
Touraine Sauvignon ★☆ £B

❂ **Masson-Blondelet (Pouilly-Fumé)** *www.masson-blondelet.com*
One of the most respected names in Pouilly-sur-Loire, Jean-Michel Masson and his son Pierre-François and daughter Mélanie have some 21 ha, almost all of it planted to Sauvignon Blanc. As well as excellent Pouilly-Fumé, red and white Sancerre is also released under the Thauvenay label. Les Angelots is the basic label grown on chalky soils and accounting for around a third of the domaine's output. It offers the steely character of the appellation, although from young vines it lacks the intensity of the other two cuvées. By contrast Villa Paulus, grown in kimmeridgian clay soils is richer and fuller offering more depth and concentration. At a similar level, Les Pierres de Pierre comes from a mix of argile and silex soils and a Sancerre Thauvenay is also now made. The top wine, Tradition Cullus, is similarly grown in kimmeridgian soils and the vines are old, between 40 and 70 years. The wine is barrel-fermented in demi-muids and then aged for up to six months on lees, adding further complexity. This is undoubtedly one of the top wines of the appellation. Since 1998 they have Château de Tersac in the Corbières (DM/JB)

Recommended Whites:
Pouilly-Fumé Tradition Cullus ★★★★ £E
Pouilly-Fumé Villa Paulus ★★★☆ £D
Pouilly-Fumé Les Angelots ★★☆ £C

❂ **Alphonse Mellot (Sancerre)** *www.mellot.com*
Mellot is one of the leading producers in Sancerre. There are négociant wines including good Menetou-Salon and Pouilly-Fumé but the domaine wines are of a different order, particularly the top cuvées. The white Edmond and Génération XIX, made from very old vines and vinified in oak, are wines of real dimension, the latter often on the cusp of ★★★★★. The Pinot Noirs are increasingly impressive, displaying considerable depth and a round, supple texture, especially the brilliant, subtly oaked Génération XIX. The top wines will undoubtedly develop very well in bottle. (DM)

Recommended Reds:
Sancerre Génération XIX ★★★★ £F

Recommended Whites:
Sancerre Génération XIX ★★★★☆ £F
Sancerre Edmond ★★★★ £F
Sancerre La Moussière ★★★☆ £E

Benoît Mérias (Montlouis) *www.benoitmerias.fr*
The vineyards here have been farmed since 1996. Holdings stretch to 6 ha of which the great majority are planted to very old vines ranging from 40 to over 80 years of age. This priceless raw material allied to low yields of less than 35 hl/ha is resulting in some of the finest wines of the Mountlouis appellation. Les Maisonnettes is a tight, steely dry style with classic Chenin Blanc varietal character. The La Vallée is *demi-sec* but the piercing fruit and high acidity tend to mask the sweetness. Backward and restrained, the wine ideally needs 6 or 7 years to add some flesh; expect it to become increasingly honeyed with time. In the cellar SO2 additions are kept to a minimum and the wines are never chaptalised. Two further *sec* styles are made, the good value Les Quartes and the rarer and pricier La Loge which is barrel fermented. Two sparkling wines, La Méthode (brut and *demi-sec*) and Récréation, a brut nature, are also produced. (DM)

Recommended Whites:
Montlouis La Vallée ★★★ £C
Montlouis Les Maisonnettes ★★☆ £C

Dom. Minchin (Menetou-Salon)
Fast emerging as one of the very leading lights in Menetou-Salon, the Minchin family also produces excellent Valençay, Clos Delorme and good Touraine red from Cot and Cabernet Franc and white from Sauvignon. There is also a very decent Sauvignon from the IGP Val de Loire. In Menetou-Salon at La Tour Saint-Martin, Bertrand Minchin only makes reds and whites. He has a total of some 15ha and the vineyards all have a south to south east exposure and the soils are a mix of *argile*, limestone and Kimmeridgian marl. The wines are modern, stylish, vibrant and essentially fruit-driven. The Morogues white is vinified in *inox*, the red a mix of *cuve* and *inox*. The red Celestin gets 12 months ageing in a mix of *barriques* and tonneaux and is rich and savoury with a hint of new oak. The Honorine is aged on fine lees with *bâtonnage* and offers greater depth and intensity than the Morogues. All the wines drink well young although the reds will benefit from a couple of years' patience. (DM)

Recommended Reds:
Menetou-Salon La Tour Saint-Martin Celestin ★★☆ £E
Touraine Franc du Cot Lie ★★☆ £C
Menetou-Salon La Tour Saint-Martin Morogues ★★ £C
Valençay Clos Delorme ★★ £C

Recommended Whites:
Menetou-Salon La Tour Saint-Martin Honorine ★★★☆ £E
Menetou-Salon La Tour Saint-Martin Morogues ★★★☆ £C
Valençay Clos Delorme ★★☆ £C
Touraine Hortense ★★ £B

Dom. Aux Moines (Savennières) *www.domaine-aux-moines.com*
Decent Savennières is produced at this small 8 ha domaine. The vineyards have an excellent exposure at the summit of the coteau overlooking the Loire at La-Roche-aux-Moines. Monique Laroche and her daughter Tessa have invested in stainless steel vats for fermentation and a modern pneumatic press so there is nothing rustic about these wines. The dry Savennières is barrel-fermented and aged and offers pure and complex Chenin fruit with hints of acacia and a fine background minerality. It will develop very well

with half a dozen years' ageing. On occasion late-harvest *moelleux* and *doux* bottlings, Cuvée du Nonnes are produced as well as a little Anjou-Villages red. Particularly unusual here are the plethora of older vintages that can be purchased going back over a dozen years. (DM)

Recommended Whites:
Savennières Roche-aux-Moines ★★★ £D

Mollet-Maudry (Sancerre)
Now that Florian has taken over the reins from his father Jean-Paul he is the 10th generation of his family at the long-established Mollet domaine. Between the two sides of his family he nows looks after holdings in both Sancerre and Pouilly-sur-Loire. The regular Sancerre and Pouilly-Fumé are good, rather than spectacular. The vine age of 40 odd years enables a fairly sound commercial yield of 60 hl/ha. The Sancerre is more marked by citrus and has a fuller, fleshier texture. A clear level up are the Pouilly-Fumé Les Sables and Sancerre Roc de l'Abbaye from older vines, around 45 years old. Les Sables comes from Kimmeridgian marl soils and displays raw gooseberry and blackcurrant aromas. Roc de L'Abbaye, in marked contrast, is from *silex* (flint) soils and is much less obviously fruity, tighter and more piercingly mineral in style. L'Antique is the top label. Again the Pouilly-Fumé comes from Kimmeridgian marl and is fuller and more opulent in style than the Sancerre from a combination of limestone and clay. These are the oldest vines of the domaine, around 60 years, and the depth and intensity of the wines is apparent. The top labels will develop very well for 5 to 7 years. There is also a wood-aged Sancerre but this lacks the piercingly mineral quality of L'Antique. (DM)

Recommended Whites:
Sancerre L'Antique ★★★ £D
Pouilly Fume L'Antique ★★★ £D
Sancerre Roc de L'Abbaye ★★★ £C
Sancerre Futs de Chene ★★☆ £D
Pouilly Fume Les Sables ★★☆ £C
Sancerre ★★ £C
Pouilly Fume ★★ £C

Dom. Eric Morgat (Savennières)
Eric Morgat at Domaine de la Monnaie is a very good source of dry white wine from this small appellation. He currently cultivates just 7 ha, which provides at present, no more than around 1,000 cases a year. He is though adding to this with a half hectare of La Roche aux Moines and he has also purchased a Clos "La Possonière" which has planting rights under the appellation regulations. His plans don't just include Savennières but also Côteaux du Layon where he now has a plot next to Château du Breuil, recently purchased by a wealthy car salesman, where he has been retained as consultant. His wines are in stark contrast to the traditional view of Savennières. They are rich, almost opulent and approachable within two or three years, although with a subtle mineral quality. (DM)

Recommended Whites:
Savennières L'Enclos ★★★☆ £D

Gérard Morin (Sancerre)
Gérard Morin epitomises the image of a French vigneron who holds sway in his candlelit cave. His domaine is based in the commune of Bué, a hamlet just 3km from Sancerre, which has a reputation for making the fullest and fattest wines of the appellation. His son Pierre, who developed his winemaking craft in Australia, has been taking on more and more responsibility and is now making the wine. The white is typically fat and richly aromatic. The red is a little

less consistent, being more subject to the vagaries of the climate, but in a good vintage the depth and colour can reach Burgundian proportions. (NB)

Recommended Reds:
Sancerre ★★ £D

Recommended Whites:
Sancerre Cuvée François de La Grange ★★★☆ £E
Sancerre ★★★ £D

Dom. René Mosse (Anjou) www.domaine-mosse.com
The Mosse domaine consists of 13 ha planted to Chenin Blanc, Chardonnay, Cabernets Sauvignon and Franc, Gamay and Grolleau. There is a soft, easy, fruit-driven Rosé d'Anjou, which is made using pressurage direct and a more serious red Anjou, a good example of the style aged in oak for 12 months with malolactic in barrel. All the Anjou dry whites are vinified and aged in oak for a year. The special bottlings, Rouchefer and Bonnes Blanches, offer more depth and intensity. Both wines offer subtle use of oak and a lightly honeyed and citrus character with great purity. A bottling from over 60-year-old vines, Marie-Besnard, is also produced. The top wine is the Côteaux du Layon Le Champ Boucault, made in the best vintages. The Anjou whites and red will develop well in the medium term; the Côteaux du Layon is finely structured and will develop well over a decade. (DM)

Recommended Reds:
Anjou ★★☆ £C

Recommended Whites:
Côteaux du Layon Le Champ Boucault ★★★★ £F
Anjou Rouchefer ★★★☆ £E
Anjou Les Bonnes Blanches ★★★☆ £E
Anjou ★★☆ £C

Dom. Henry Natter (Sancerre) www.henrynatter.com
Established in 1974, this domaine based in the top village of Montigny is now one of the best for fine-quality white Sancerre. As well as the regular white there is a small-volume special bottling, Cuvée François de la Grange de Montigny, a fruity red and rosé and L'Expression Cécile red and white from a selection of parcels. Vinification of the whites is traditional with fermentation in large oak vats. The regular version is then aged in stainless steel, while François de la Grange de Montigny sees 12 months in oak. The wines have been consistently good in recent years and will develop well with short bottle age. (DM)

Recommended Whites:
Sancerre Cuvée François de La Grange ★★★☆ £E
Sancerre ★★★ £D

Dom. de La Noblaie (Chinon) www.lanoblaie.fr
This is a long established family domaine now run with considerable expertise by Jérôme Billard who makes not only red Chinon but also a much rarer white example of the appellation. The vineyards are all now farmed on organic principles and have been bio certified (ECOCERT) since 2011. Cabernet Franc dominates vine plantings with 19 ha but Chenin Blanc also accounts for a further 3 ha. As well as the wines rated below a Chinon rosé and a Touraine Petillant sparkler are also made. Two additional red Chinons are also made. Les Blancs Manteaux comes from a limestone based parcel of 60 year old vines, while Pierre de Tuf comes from vines grown in *silex* soils and is unusually vinified in an earth vat in the cellar. Both are aged in 500 litre barrels with minimal oak influence. A second white Chinon, La Part des Anges is dry but includes some botrytised fruit.

It spends two years in barrel. The Chinon La Noblaie Chenin Blanc is fresh and vibrant but with a fine structure. Vinification is in *inox* with ageing on fine lees for four months and then the malolactic fermentation is avoided. The red La Noblaie is vinified and aged in tank providing a more obviously fruit lifted example. Les Chiens-Chiens comes from a *lieu-dit* of the same name and is raised in 400 litre oak for 18 months. Both elegant and impressively concentrated the wine retains the characteristic leafy complexity of Cabernet Franc. (DM)

Recommended Reds:
Chinon Les Chiens-Chiens ★★★☆ £D
Chinon La Noblaie Cabernet Franc ★★★ £C
Recommended Whites:
Chinon La Noblaie Chenin Blanc ★★★ £D

Dom. Ogereau (Anjou) *www.domaineogereau.com*
Vincent Ogereau produces very good Anjou-Villages reds, decent minerally dry white Anjou and rich, well-crafted Côteaux du Layon. The regular Anjou-Villages is a blend of Cabernet Franc and Cabernet Sauvignon, whereas the Côte de la Houssaye is a dense and powerful, brambly Cabernet Sauvignon. Both will be the better for 5 years' ageing. The Côteaux du Layon is powerful, sweet and unctuous and achieves a really intense botrytised peachy character in the very best years. A special selection, Clos de Bonnes Blanches, is also produced. (DM)

Recommended Reds:
Anjou-Villages Côte de la Houssaye ★★★ £C
Anjou-Villages ★★☆ £C
Anjou ★★ £B
Recommended Whites:
Côteaux du Layon-Saint-Lambert ★★★★ £E
Anjou Prestige Sec ★★☆ £C

Dom. des Ouches (Bourgueil) *www.domainedesouches.com*
First class Bourgueil producer offering classic, restrained and ageworthy examples of the appellation at very keen prices indeed. The style is tighter and more backward than many, even from this cool-climate region. All the wines have an angular character in their youth, as much from their high acidity as from their tannin, and require a few years' ageing to add flesh. The top two cuvées in particular should be cellared for at least 4 to 5 years. Cabernet Franc is the main variety but there is a little (10%), Cabernet Sauvignon in the Grande Réserve. Some of the vines are remarkably old here, up to 100 years, and this undoubtedly contributes to quality. With the exception of the Grande Réserve, which is aged in new oak (50%) with malolactic in barrel, as well as the barrel aged Coteau des Ouches the other wines are traditionally vinified and the Ignoranda aged in *foudres*. (DM)

Recommended Reds:
Bourgueil Grande Réserve ★★★☆ £D
Bourgueil Coteau des Ouches ★★★ £C
Bourgueil Ignoranda ★★☆ £C
Bourgueil 20 ★★ £B

Dom. de Pallus (Chinon) *www.lespenseesdepallus.info*
This is a Chinon property with tremendous potential. It is the family domaine of Bertrand Sourdais who is a winemaker in Spain's Ribera del Duero region. Two wines are made, the very well priced Les Pensées de Pallus and the much pricier Pallus. However given the potential showed in the main wine this is a domaine that really deserves profiling. Pallus, which is made only in the finest years and

in tiny quantities is much the pricier of the two wines and comes from four separate old-vine parcels. The average age of the *vignoble* for Les Pensées is hardly young either, the vines average over 35 years. The estate has 30 small parcels, which are planted on a mix of limestone-rich clay and sand, offering a wide range of potential fruit characters. In the winery there is a long and slow *cuvaison*, over 30 days and Les Pensées is aged in used barrels from Château HAUT-BRION for up to 18 months. This is a beguiling and characterful example of the appellation with cedar and subtle red berry fruit with just the slightest leafy backdrop. As with all great wines a pure mineral note underpins the wine. (DM)

Recommended Reds:
Chinon Grand Vin de Pallus ★★★★ £E
Chinon Les Pensées de Pallus ★★★ £C

Dom. Henry Pellé (Menetou-Salon) *www.henry-pelle.com*
This is one of the leading estates in Menetou-Salon and a producer of Sancerre as well. The domaine is based in Morogues at the east of the Menetou-Salon appellation, although they also have vines in Menetou-Salon itself. The domaine is run by Anne Pellé and her son, Paul-Henry. There are 41 ha under vine and these split roughly two-thirds to one-third Sauvignon Blanc to Pinot Noir. The vineyards in Menetou-Salon are planted on Kimmeridgian clay and tended organically, and green harvesting is practised. Straightforward Menetou-Salon and Sancerre white and red now come from a mix of estate and bought-in grapes. Of the estate- grown wines, the white Menetou-Salon tends to impress more than the Sancerre, the vineyards of which are younger, although the Sancerre is increasingly improving as the vines mature. White Vignes de Ratier is from a single parcel as is the rich and intense Les Blanchais, which is from the domaine's oldest vines and posseses an impressive depth of ripe gooseberry fruit and a fine, mineral structure. The reds, especially Les Cris, are increasing impressive. It will be interesting to see how a new and pricey red cuvée, Coeur de Cris fares. (DM/JB)

Recommended Reds:
Menetou-Salon Les Cris ★★★ £C
Sancerre La Croix au Garde ★☆ £D
Recommended Whites:
Menetou-Salon Les Blanchais ★★★ £D
Menetou-Salon Vignes de Ratier ★★☆ £C
Menetou-Salon Morogues ★★☆ £C
Sancerre La Croix au Garde ★★ £C

Vincent Pinard (Sancerre) *www.domaine-pinard.com*
There are some 15 ha at this model Sancerre domaine, based in Bué, where Florent and Clément Pinard, who have taken over from their father Vincent, produce good to very good white and red Sancerre. The two brothers are constantly seeking to improve their already impressive wines refusing to sit on their laurels. This is an admirable attitude shared by the leaders of the new generation of Sancerre producers. The regular red is good, light but exuberantly fruity with attractive berry fruit. Charlouise is denser, richer. A third red, the impressive Vendanges Entières is also made. These are good examples of how the quality of the best red Sancerres has been transformed over the past 20 years or so. Of the whites the Cuvée Florès emphasises ripe classic gooseberry fruit. The top whites are fuller and more complex, and both are vinified in wood. Harmonie in particular is spicy and toasty in its youth, needing 3 or 4 years to achieve a balance of fruit and oak. (DM/JB)

Recommended Reds:
Sancerre Vendanges Entières ★★★★ £E

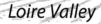

Loire Valley

France

Sancerre Charlouise ★★★ £E
Sancerre ★★ £D
Recommended Whites:
Sancerre Harmonie ★★★☆ £E
Sancerre Nuance ★★★ £D
Sancerre Cuvée Florés ★★☆ £C

Dom. Michel Redde (Pouilly-Fumé) *www.michel-redde.com*
Thierry Redde is the 6th generation of his family at this medium sized domaine of which he took over the reins in 1997. The family now have a holding of 40 ha, the vast majority of which is planted to Sauvignon Blanc with just a little Chasselas. As well as their Pouilly wines a red and white Sancerre Les Tuilières are also made. The Gustave Daudin is a very good example of Pouilly-sur-Loire, flinty and characterful gaining weight from a year on lees. Petit Fumé is a fruit driven selection from young vines, La Moynerie the main cuvée of the property is aged for a year in *inox*. It comes from a range of the family's holdings. More complex and similarly raised in stainless steel for just under a year are three single vineyard wines, coming from different villages and soils with vines ranging from 30 to 40 years of age. The top wine, the ageworthy Majorum is a selection of the very oldest vines. Again the wine is aged is stainless steel and kept on its fine lees for up to 18 months, adding weight and dimension to its intense mineral and citrus scented fruit. (DM)
Recommended Whites:
Pouilly-Fumé Majorum ★★★☆ £E
Pouilly-Fumé Les Bois de Saint-Andelain ★★★ £E
Pouilly-Fumé Les Champs des Billons ★★★ £E
Pouilly-Fumé La Moynerie ★★★ £D
Pouilly-Fumé Petit Fumé ★★ £C
Pouilly-sur-Loire Gustave Daudin ★★ £C

Dom. P & N Reverdy (Sancerre)
This relatively small domaine based in the northern stretches of Sancerre in the hamlet of Maimbury in the commune of Sury-en-Vaux, labels its generic wines after the hamlet "Terre de Maimbury". A rosé as well as the red and the white is also produced. The Reverdy family own 14 ha, of which 11 ha are planted to Sauvignon Blanc. Sadly Pascal's brother Nicolas was killed in a vineyard accident in 2007 while felling a tree, although the domaine name remains the same. A committed approach is maintained to ensure the best quality wines. Vineyard plots are vinified separately and of course yields kept under control. The vineyards themselves are planted on steeply sloping argilo-calcaire soils. The top red and white are strikingly good, the red particularly in warmer vintages. Formerly labelled Evolution this is now Hommage à Nicolas. It comes from calcareous soils between Sancerre and Bué, is aged in a mix of new oak and demi-muids and bottled unfined and unfiltered. Les Angelots gets 10 months ageing in wooden cuve and is also bottled unfiltered. (DM/JB)
Recommended Reds:
Sancerre Rouge Hommage à Nicolas ★★★ £D
Sancerre Terre de Maimbray ★★ £C
Recommended Whites:
Sancerre Les Angelots Vieilles Vignes ★★★☆ £D
Sancerre Terre de Maimbray ★★★ £C

Dom. Claude Riffault (Sancerre) *www.clauderiffault.com*
The wines here are in marked contrast to those produced by Sébastien RIFFAULT. They are though very good and classically styled and structured examples of Sancerre. There are 13.5 ha

planted across four separate villages and including no fewer than 33 different parcels. The wines are named after specific vineyards and plots. Of the three whites, perhaps the most striking is the citrus and mineral scented Les Denisottes which comes from Terre Blanche soils. Les Boucauds and particularly Les Chasseignes are a touch more austere and backward. Two further whites are now made, Les Chailloux and Les Desmallets. Two reds are now made, both fresh elegant examples of the appellation. As well as the white, there is a red from Les Chailloux. La Noue comes from a small site with vines ranging from just under 10 to almost 60 years of age adding complexity in the wine. In the context of the appellation, the wines offer good value. (DM)
Recommended Reds:
Sancerre La Noue ★★ £C
Recommended Whites:
Sancerre Les Denisottes ★★★ £D
Sancerre Les Chasseignes ★★★ £C
Sancerre Les Boucauds ★★☆ £C

Dom. Sébastien Riffault (Sancerre)
Sébastien Riffault produces some striking and some would say extreme examples of Sancerre from around 2 ha of his own vineyards as well as vinifying the far more conventional wines of his father Etienne at the family property, Domaine des Quarterons which are quite typical of the appellation. Well made and structured with a lightly mineral white and a red berry scented red. All the wines are made with a minimal dependence on sulphur though to achieve as pure a fruit character as possible, Sébastien's wines see no sulphur at all except a tiny amount at bottling. His own cuvées also come from a yield barely half that of the Domaine des Quarterons wines, typically around 20 as opposed to 40 hl/ha. They are marked with a rich, opulent and very lightly oxidative character. Both whites unusually go through the malolactic fermentation and the Akmeniné is a touch more mineral than the more citrus laden Skeveldra from *silex* soils. Both whites are kept in cask on lees and are not fined. The Pinot Noir is raised in barrel for around a year and everything is handled by gravity wherever possible. To a certain extent with Sébastien's wines its a case of *caveat emptor*, they are not what you might generally be expecting from the AC but are also to be commended for really pushing the quality winemaking envelope in a region full of annual pitfalls. They are well worth seeking out. (DM)
Recommended Reds:
Sancerre Raudonas ★★★☆ £E
Sancerre Domaine des Quarterons ★★ £D
Recommended Whites:
Sancerre Skeveldra ★★★☆ £D
Sancerre Akmeniné ★★★ £D
Sancerre Domaine des Quarterons ★★☆ £D

Dom. des Rochelles (Anjou) *www.domaine-des-rochelles.com*
These wines may sometimes be found on merchant lists as J.-Y. A. Lebreton rather than by their domaine name. Excellent Anjou white as well as Anjou-Village reds from the village of Brissac are made. The sweet Côteaux de l'Aubance whites are among the very best of the appellation. The domaine has been in the family for four generations and is now run by Jean-Hubert Lebreton. There are just over 50 ha planted in finely drained slate soils, with 36 ha accounted for by Cabernet Franc and Cabernet Sauvignon. The reds have impressive depth and are finely structured. The village wine being softer and more obviously fruit driven with a higher

proportion of Cabernet Franc. Les Millerits is firmer and will evolve well for up to a decade, it needs time to integrate marked new oak when young. La Croix de Mission is more opulent and open in its youth. Both are first class reds. In top years the Côteaux de l'Aubance whites stand comparison with some of the best bottles in the neighbouring Côteaux du Layon. In a top vintage the Ambre des Roches des Rochelles offers explosively rich botrytis character and is underpinned by a steely minerality. Rosé de Loire, Cabernet d'Anjou and an IGP Sauvignon Blanc are also produced. (DM)

Recommended Reds:
Anjou-Villages Brissac Les Millerits ★★★☆ £D
Anjou-Villages Brissac Croix de Mission ★★★ £C
Anjou-Villages Brissac ★★☆ £C

Recommended Whites:
Côteaux de l'Aubance Ambre des Roches des Rochelles ★★★★ £E
Côteaux de l'Aubance ★★★ £C
Anjou Roches des Rochelles ★★☆ £C

❀ Dom. des Roches Neuves *www.rochesneuves.com*

Thierry Germain based in Saumur-Champigny produces opulent, powerful, ripely extracted reds from Cabernet Franc. The wines are deeply coloured, dense and oaky. Vinification is aimed at maximum extraction, with the fruit getting a pre-fermentation cold soak and the wine staying on its skins in order to achieve rounded, supple tannins. He notably succeeds in reducing some of the austere youthful characteristics that can often show in other Loire Cabernets. He also makes a very good barrel-fermented white Saumur, which is stylish and refined with a nice balance of toasty, citrus fruit and a fresh mineral structure. The Terres Chaudes and the Marginale are the two top reds. The latter is marked by new oak in its youth and needs time. (DM)

Recommended Reds:
Saumur-Champigny Marginale ★★★☆ £E
Saumur-Champigny Terres Chaudes ★★★ £D
Saumur-Champigny ★★☆ £C

Recommended Whites:
Saumur Insolite ★★★ £D

Dom. Jean-Max Roger (Sancerre) *www.jean-max-roger.fr*

Sancerre and Menetou-Salon red and white are made at this domaine along with a Pouilly-Fumé. The whites understandably dominate the production and account for the bulk of the vineyard. The Sancerre holdings are based around the village of Bué and the style is for rich, full almost tropical wines with a subtle mineral elegance. Vinification reflects this, fermentation in stainless steel is cool, around 16 to 17C followed by short ageing on lees and bottling at around six months. Although all the vines are now over 25 years of age, a Vieilles Vignes from the oldest plots over 45 years is also produced and this gets a touch longer on lees. The Menetou-Salon is a little lighter than the Sancerres, however all are best-enjoyed young or with a couple of years' cellaring. (DM)

Recommended Whites:
Sancerre Cuvée GC ★★★ £D
Sancerre Les Caillottes ★★★ £D
Menetou-Salon Morogues Le Petit Clos ★★☆ £C

Dom. Saint-Just (Saumur) *www.st-just.net*

Although Although only recently established in 1996 former financier the late Yves Lambert's 40 ha of vineyards, now run by son Arnaud, are the source of some impressive red Saumur-Champigny and white Saumur. Three decent sparklers are also produced. Of the

reds, all grown in clay/limestone soils. Les Terres Rouges is aged in tank, the other two wines in cask. Le Clos Moleton is impressively rich. Macerated for 30 days, the dark berry complexity from 55 to 65 year old vines is very apparent. The white Saumur Les Perrières is fermented in stainless steel and offers attractive forward citrus fruit. The Coulée de Saint-Cyr is tighter more, structured with a mineral purity underpinning subtle tropical notes. Barrel-fermented and aged it will develop well over five to ten years, as will the best reds. The Crémant is fresh and clean, the rosé a soft, fruity blend of both Cabernets. Both are easy summer quaffers. Most interesting of the sparklers, however, is the red Saumur Mousseux. Again a blend of the Cabernets an extended period on lees adds to the richness of its berry and blackcurrant fruit. An additional range of Saumur wines is also made at Château de Brézé, including a number of single Clos wines which should be well worth searching out. (DM)

Recommended Reds:
Saumur-Champigny Le Clos Moleton ★★★ £D
Saumur-Champigny La Montée des Roches ★★☆ £C
Saumur-Champigny Les Terres Rouges ★★☆ £C
Saumur-Mousseux L'Ardoisier ★★ £C

Recommended Whites:
Saumur La Coulée de Saint-Cyr ★★☆ £C
Saumur Les Perrières ★★ £C
Crémant de Loire Tradition ★★ £C

Recommended Rosés:
Crémant de Loire Tradition ★★ £C

Dom. Saint Nicolas (Fiefs Vendéens) *www.domainesaintnicolas.com*

This property is a real benchmark for this unheralded region on the Atlantic coast south of Nantes. The domaine has been run on biodynamic lines since 1995 and the vineyard holding now covers 40 ha. Chenin, Chardonnay and a little Groslot are planted for whites and Gamay and Pinot Noir are the dominant red grapes with a smattering of Cabernet Franc and Négrette. Of the whites, Les Clous is a full, fat and lightly mineral blend of Chenin Blanc and Chardonnay. Le Haut de Clous is solely Chenin Blanc from lower yields on argile and schist soils. It is very intense and a subtle lees and barrel-ferment character shows through. The Soleil de Chine cuvée is again 100% Chenin from old vines and a yield of just 15–20 hl/ha. It has a touch of residual sugar adding a little sweetness to its rich texture. There is a good, light Reflets rosé from Pinot Noir and a red from mainly Pinot Noir with a little Gamay. Softer and less structured is the ripe and strawberry-fruited Gamay Gammes en May. The Cuvée Jacques is the top Pinot Noir bottling. It offers subtle, finely structured fruit and quite a marked youthful oak character. The fascinating Le Poiré is produced solely from the smallholding of Negrette, a grape variety found in the South-West but only in this part of the Loire. It has an intensely piercing, bright cool-climate berry character as well as impressive depth. The top wines will evolve well with a little age. (DM/JB)

Recommended Reds:
Fiefs Vendeens Le Poiré ★★★ £E
Fiefs Vendeens Cuvée Jacques ★★★ £E
Fiefs Vendeens Reflets ★★☆ £C
Fiefs Vendeens Gammes en May ★☆ £B

Recommended Whites:
Vin de France Cuvée Soleil de Chine ★★★ £E
Fiefs Vendeens Le Haut des Clous ★★★ £E
Fiefs Vendeens Les Clous ★★☆ £C

Recommended Rosés:
Fiefs Vendeens Reflets ★☆ £B

Loire Valley

Dom. Saint-Vincent (Saumur-Champigny) *www.st-vincent.com*
The 35 ha of vineyards here were originally planted in the 15th century. They are cultivated in clay and limestone and the local tuffeau sub-soil. A cover crop of grass is grown between the vine rows to opmtimise mineral nutrition and aid ripening. Les Trezellières, like all the reds produced solely from Cabernet Franc, is the mainstay accounting for 80% of the Saumur-Champigny output. It comes from the youngest vines, although some of these are up to 30 years old. The wine offers attractive brambly fruit and impressive richness. More seriously structured are the top two cuvées. Les Adrialys is aged part in tank and part in cask whereas the more opulent and fleshy, as well as somewhat oaky, Lea is raised purely in *barriques*. These two will evolve well for up to a decade. There are only 3ha planted to Chenin Blanc but the wines are good. La Papareille, arguably the best wine at the domaine, is serious and requires a little time to show at its best. (DM)

Recommended Reds:
Saumur-Champigny Léa ★★★ £D
Saumur-Champigny Les Adrialys ★★★ £D
Saumur-Champigny Les Trézellières ★★☆ £C

Recommended Whites:
Saumur La Papareille ★★★ £D

Dom. Christian Salmon (Sancerre) *www.sancerre-salmon.com*
Armand Salmon's small family domaine is based in Bué. Very much in the style of this village his Sancerre is full, fat and rich. It offers impressive depth and concentration, gaining additional complexity from old vines. Expect the wine to drink well young although there is a fine mineral undercurrent which adds a further dimension. A well-priced Pouilly-Fumé, Clos des Criots, is also produced, as well as a Chêne Marchand and a red and rosé Sancerre. (DM)

Recommended Whites:
Sancerre ★★★☆ £D

✿ Taille Aux Loups (Montlouis) *www.jackyblot.fr*
Originally a *négociant* Jacky Blot and Joëlle, his wife, started their Montllouis adventure in in 1988. Over the ensuing nearly 30 years the Blots have becoming amongst the Loire's leading and model producers. Despite other business commitments the Blots are very hands-on. They started in Montlouis with a handful of hectares and now have some 70 hectares – around 50 ha in Montlouis, 5 in Vouvray and 16 in Bourgueil – Domaine de la BUTTE. The Blots along with FRANÇOIS CHIDAINE are now undoubtedly the leading estates in Montlouis. Between them they have been the impetus to transform Montlouis' reputation. Most A varying small range of sec, demi-sec and sweet wines are made both in Montlouis and Vouvray. Recent vintages have seen the production of mainly dry and medium styles along with good sparkling wines including Brut Tradition and a very dry Pétillant, although some brilliant late- harvest wines have emerged in good years. The Montlouis Remus sec is barrel-fermented in new oak and aged on lees with bâtonnage. The impressive demi-sec is not oversweet and when nature is kind moelleux are very impressive indeed. The Montlouis Cuvée des Loups and particularly Montlouis Cuvée Romulus in ripe vintages can be explosively rich. Vouvray is also now produced from Clos de Venise as well as some fine bottlings of Bourgueil at Domaine de la BUTTE. (DM/JB)

Recommended Whites:
Montlouis Cuvée des Loups ★★★★ £F
Vouvray Clos de Venise Sec ★★★☆ £E
Montlouis Moelleux ★★★☆ £E

Montlouis Pétillant Triple Zéro ★★★ £C
Montlouis Demi-Sec ★★★ £C
Montlouis Sec Rémus ★★☆ £C
Montlouis Brut Tradition ★★ £C

Taluau & Foltzenlogel *www.vins-taluau-foltzenlogel.com*
This is one of the best addresses in Saint-Nicolas-de-Bourgueil. Its reputation was established by the late Joël Taluau, who died in 2013 and was one of the leaders of the appellation. His son-in-law Thierry Foltzenlogel and Clarisse, his wife, now have 30 hectares of vines – 25 in Saint-Nicolas and 5 in Bourgueil on the argile and calcareous soils of the Côteaux at Bourgueil. These are all classic, traditional Touraine reds. Firm and sturdy tannins, underlying acidity and an impressive purity of fruit are apparent in all. None of the vineyards here are particularly young, even the Jeunes Vignes cuvée is crafted from vines close to 20 years of age. The Vau Jaumier comes from a single plot of just over 5 ha, the densely structured Vieilles Vignes from vines over four decades old. The top red L'Insoumise, like many of their neighbours, is a touch more modern in style with 40% being aged in new barriques for 18 months. The balance is aged traditionally. Expect the older vine cuvées to require 4 or 5 years' ageing. The Jeunes Vignes by contrast is immediately approachable. (DM/JB)

Recommended Reds:
Saint-Nicolas-de-Bourgueil L'Insoumise ★★★☆ £D
Saint-Nicolas-de-Bourgueil Vieilles Vignes ★★★ £C
Saint-Nicolas-de-Bourgueil Vau Jaumier ★★☆ £C
Bourgueil ★★ £B

Dom. Vacheron (Sancerre)
The Vacherons have 47 ha under vine – 35.5 ha Sauvignon Blanc and with no less than 11.5 ha Pinot Noir. This family domaine based the old streets of Sancerre is now run by Vacheron cousins Jean-Dominique and Jean-Laurent and the domaine is certified biodynamic. They have been amongst the leaders of the younger generation to work on improving very considerably the quality of red Sancerre. There are regular red and white Sancerres and two very impressive reserve cuvées; the white Les Romains and the dense and surprisingly powerfully structured red Belle Dame. Good rosé is also produced. The white Sancerre has fine grass and mineral notes and the Romains an impressive depth with subtle, nutty, oak-derived notes and real finesse. The top wines have the structure to develop well with 5 years' cellaring or more. Recently they have released further single vineyard/terroir white Sancerres to complement the existing Les Romains. These include Chambrates, Guigne-Chèvres and Le Paradis. (DM/JB)

Recommended Reds:
Sancerre Belle Dame ★★★ £E
Sancerre ★★☆ £D

Recommended Whites:
Sancerre Romains ★★★☆ £E
Sancerre ★★★ £D

Dom. des Varinelles (Saumur-Champigny) *www.daheuiller.com*
Good quality red and white is made at this 42 ha domaine with vineyards spread across both Saumur appellations. The fruit is all harvested manually and undoubtedly the piercing quality of the Cabernet Franc reds is aided by sizeable plots of very old vines, a few being over 100 years old. The white L'Ingénue has a marked mineral quality and gains weight and texture from ageing on lees. The regular Saumur-Champigny is soft and forward with bright berry

fruit and just a hint of leafiness. The Vieilles Vignes has greater depth and dimension, coming from vines up to 70 years old. The Larivale and Larentiale both offer impressive concentration. Larivale is aged for 12 months in oak, some new with bâtonnage. Laurentiale is perhaps the best wine here and dominated by the sheer quality of the fruit. The top three reds will all develop very well over five years or so. They also make a white and a rosé Crémant de Loire from Chardonnay and Pinot Noir. DM/JB)

Recommended Reds:
Saumur-Champigny Laurentiale ★★★ £D
Saumur-Champigny Larivale ★★★ £C
Saumur-Champigny Vieilles Vignes ★★☆ £C
Saumur-Champigny ★★ £C
Recommended Whites:
Saumur L'Ingénue ★★☆ £D

Dom. Vigneau-Chevreau (Vouvray) *www.vigneau-chevreau.com*
Fine Vouvray is made at this 33 ha biodynamically cultivated domaine, first established in 1875. It was the late Jean-Michel Vigneau, who converted the domaine to organic viticulture in the 1990s receiving certification in 1999. Jean-Michel's sons, Christophe and Stéphane, now run the domaine. Where, conditions permit, they make a full range of Vouvray's styles under the appellation including sec, demi-sec and moelleux. A well-priced Pétillant Brut sparkler is also produced. The regular dry white is released every year and is grown in some of the domaine's heavier clay soils. The piercingly mineral and citrus scented Clos de Rougement comes from a monopole planted on finely drained limestone. The demi-sec and sweet wines come from the oldest vines of the domaine, now over 65 years. Noble-rot is always present when the fruit is picked, with the moelleux wines often harvested as late as early November. Expect all to age very well. (DM/JB)

Recommended Whites:
Vouvray Moelleux Chateau Gaillard ★★★☆ £E
Vouvray Moelleux Clos Baglin ★★★☆ £E
Vouvray Moelleux ★★★ £D
Vouvray Sec Clos de Rougemont ★★★ £C
Vouvray Demi-Sec ★★☆ £C
Vouvray Sec ★★☆ £C

Other wines of note

Pays Nantais
Serge Batard
Recommended Whites: Muscadet Les Hautes Noëlles ★ £B
Muscadet Côtes de Grandlieu Sur Lie ★☆ £B
Muscadet Côtes de Grandlieu Sur Lie Les Granges ★★ £B
Ch. La Ragotière
Recommended Whites:
Muscadet-de-Sèvre-Et-Maine Clos Petit Chateau ★☆ £B
Muscadet-de-Sèvre-Et-Maine Collection Privée M ★★ £B
Chéreau-Carré
Recommended Whites:
Muscadet-de-Sèvre-Et-Maine Chateau Chasseloir ★☆ £B
Bruno Cormerais
Recommended Whites:
Muscadet-de-Sèvre-Et-Maine Sur Lie ★☆ £B
Michel David
Recommended Whites:
Muscadet-de-Sèvre-Et-Maine Sur Lie Clos du Ferré ★ £B

Dom des Dorices
Recommended Whites:
Muscadet-de-Sèvre-Et-Maine Sur Lie ★☆ £B
Dom. Gadais
Recommended Whites:
Muscadet-de-Sèvre-Et-Maine La Grande Reseve du Moulin ★ £B
Muscadet-de-Sèvre-Et-Maine Vieilles Vignes ★★ £B
Dom. Guindon
Recommended Whites:
Muscadet-Côteaux de La Loire Sur Lie Tradition ★★ £B
Muscadet-Côteaux de La Loire Prestige ★★ £C
Dom. des Hautes Pemions
Recommended Whites: Muscadet-de-Sèvre-Et-Maine ★ £B
Dom. La Roche Renard
Recommended Whites:
Muscadet-de-Sèvre-Et-Maine ★ £B
Dom. de La Louvetrie
Recommended Whites: Muscadet-de-Sèvre-Et-Maine ★★ £B
Muscadet-de-Sèvre-Et-Maine Clos de La Cazière ★★ £B
Muscadet-de-Sèvre-Et-Maine Amphibolite Nature ★★ £C
Muscadet-de-Sèvre-Et-Maine La Fief du Breuil ★★★ £C
Vin de France Melonix ★★★ £C
Louis Métaireau
Recommended Whites:
Muscadet-de -Sèvre-Et-Maine Cuvée LM ★★ £B

Anjou
Pierre Aguilas
Recommended Whites: Côteaux du Layon Cuvée Claire ★★★ £D
Dom. de Bablut
Recommended Reds: Anjou-Villages-Brissac Rocca Nigra ★★☆ £C
Recommended Whites: Côteaux de L'Aubance Sélection ★★★ £D
Côteaux de L'Aubance Grand Pierre ★★★★ £E
Côteaux de L'Aubance Vin Noble ★★★★ £E
Dom. de La Bergerie
Recommended Whites: Chaume 1ere Cru ★★★ £E
Dom. Michel Blouin
Recommended Whites: Chaume 1ere Cru ★★★ £E
Dom. Cady
Recommended Whites:
Côteaux-du-Layon Saint-Aubin Cuvée Voluptué ★★★ £E
Ch. de Brossay
Recommended Whites:
Côteaux-du-Layon Vieilles-Vignes Eparses ★★★☆ £E
Ch. de La Guimonière
Recommended Reds: Anjou ★☆ £B
Recommended Whites:
Côteaux du Layon Chaume Julines ★★★ £E
Ch. des Noyers
Recommended Whites: Anjou-Villages ★★ £C
Côteaux-du-Layon Réserve Vieilles Vignes ★★★★ £C
Ch. de Passavant
Recommended Whites: Anjou-Villages ★★ £C
Côteaux-du-Layon Les Greffiers ★★★ £D
Ch. Prince
Recommended Whites:
Côteaux de L'Aubance ★★★ £C
Ch. de La Roulerie
Recommended Reds: Anjou ★★ £B
Recommended Whites:
Côteaux du Layon Chaume Aunis ★★★★ £E

Loire Valley

France

Ch. de Soucherie
Recommended Whites: Savennières Cuvée Anais ★★ £C
Côteaux du Layon-Beaulieu ★★★ £E

Ch. de Suronde
Recommended Whites: Quarts de Chaume ★★★★ £E

Ch. de Tigné
Recommended Reds: Anjou-Villages Mozart ★★★ £D
Anjou-Villages Cyrano ★★★ £D

Ch. de Varenne
Recommended Whites: Savennières ★★ £C

Dom. des Chesnaies
Recommended Reds: Anjou-Villages La Musse ★★ £C

Clos de Varennes
Recommended Whites: Savennières ★★★ £D

Dom. de Haute Perche
Recommended Whites:
Côteaux de L'Aubance Les Fontanelles ★★★ £D

Dom. Les Grandes Vignes
Recommended Reds: Anjou-Villages L'Ancraie ★★ £C
Anjou-Villages Cocainelles ★★☆ £C
Recommended Whites: Anjou Varenne de Combre ★★★ £C
Côteaux de Layon ★★★ £D
Côteaux de Layon Noble Selection ★★★☆ £D
Bonnezeaux ★★★ £D
Bonnezeaux Noble Selection ★★★★ £E

Dom. de Montgilet
Recommended Whites: Côteaux de L'Aubance ★★ £C
Côteaux de L'Aubance Les Trois Schistes ★★★ £D
Côteaux de L'Aubance Le Tertereaux ★★★★ £E
Côteaux de L'Aubance Clos de s Huittières ★★★★ £E

Dom. du Petit Metris
Recommended Whites: Côteaux du Layon Chaume ★★★ £D
Côteaux du Layon Chaume Les Tetuères ★★★☆ £E
Quarts de Chaume ★★★★ £E
Savennières Clos de La Marche ★★☆ £C

Dom. du Petit Val
Recommended Whites:
Côteaux du Layon Cuvée Simon ★★★☆ £D
Bonnezeaux La Montagne ★★★★ £E

Dom. des Petits Quarts
Recommended Whites: Bonnezeaux ★★★☆ £D
Bonnezeaux Malabé ★★★★☆ £E

Dom. des Quarres
Recommended Reds: Anjou-Villages Les Métifs ★ £B
Recommended Whites:
Côteaux de Layon-Faye Le Magdelaine Prestige ★★★ £D

Dom. Roy René
Recommended Whites:
Côteaux du Layon-Lambert Le Cormier ★★★ £D

Dom. Richou
Recommended Whites: Anjou Chaviné ★★ £B
Côteaux de L'Aubance Cuvée Les Trois de smoiselles ★★★ £C

Dom. de Richambeau
Recommended Whites: Côteaux du L'Aubance ★★★ £C

Dom. des Sablonnettes
Recommended Reds: Anjou Les Copines Aussi ★★ £B
Anjou Les Grands Chênes ★★☆ £C
Anjou Les Pivoines ★★☆ £C
Recommended Whites: Anjou Petit Blanc ★★ £B
Anjou Genêts ★★★ £C
Côteaux du Layon Champ du Cygne ★★★★ £E

Saumur

Bouvet-Ladubay
Recommended Reds: Saumur Mousseux Brut Rubis ★★ £C
Recommended Whites:
Saumur Mousseux Crémant Excellence ★★ £C
Saumur Mousseux Brut Saphir Vintage ★☆ £C
Saumur Mousseux Brut Trésor ★★ £C

Chapin & Landais
Recommended Whites:
Saumur Mousseux Brut Le Grand Saumur Vintage ★☆ £B

Dom. de Ch. Gaillard
Recommended Reds: Saumur ★★★ £C

Ch. de Targé
Recommended Reds: Saumur-Champigny Traditionelle ★★ £B
Saumur-Champigny Cuvée Ferry ★★ £C
Recommended Whites: Saumur Les Fresnelles ★★ £C

Filliatreau
Recommended Reds: Saumur-Champigny ★☆ £B
Saumur-Champigny Vieilles-Vignes ★★★☆ £C

Dom. La Perruche
Recommended Reds:
Saumur-Champigny Clos de Chaumont Prestige ★★ £C
Recommended Whites: Côteaux de Saumur ★★ £C

Dom. du Petit Saint-Vincent
Recommended Reds: Saumur-Champigny ★★ £B
Saumur-Champigny Pélo ★★☆ £C

Dom. de Nerleux
Recommended Reds: Saumur-Champigny ★★ £B
Recommended Whites: Saumur ★☆ £B

Touraine

Thierry Amirault
Recommended Reds: Saint-Nicolas-de-Bourgueil ★ £B

Dom. de L'Aumonier
Recommended Whites: Touraine Sauvignon ★ £B

Dom. Baudry-Dutour
Recommended Reds: Chinon Clos de s Marroniers ★★☆ £B

Dom. de Beauséjour
Recommended Reds: Chinon ★★ £B Chinon L'Ancelot ★★☆ £C

Dom. Brisebarre
Recommended Whites: Vouvray Cuvée Amédée ★★ £B
Vouvray Réserve Personnelle ★★ £B Vouvray Moelleux ★★★ £C

Ch. de L'Aulée
Recommended Reds: Chinon Cèdre ★★ £B

Ch. Gaillard
Recommended Whites: Touraine-Mesland ★★ £B

Ch. Gaudrelle
Recommended Whites: Vouvray ★★ £C
Vouvray Réserve Spéciale ★★★ £C

Clos Baudoin
Recommended Whites: Vouvray Aigle Sec ★★ £B

Clos de La Briderie
Recommended Whites: Touraine-Meslands Vieilles-Vignes ★★ £B

Clos Roche Blanche
Recommended Reds: Touraine Côt ★★☆ £B
Touraine Gamay ★★ £B
Recommended Whites: Touraine Sauvignon No 5 ★★ £B

Dom. du Clos Roussely
Recommended Whites: Touraine Le Clos ★☆ £B

Max Cognard
Recommended Reds: Bourgueil Les Tuffes ★★ £C

Saint-Nicolas-de -Bourgueil Estelle ★★ £C
Saint-Nicolas-de -Bourgueil Malgagnes ★★ £C
Dom. de Corbillères
Recommended Whites: Touraine Sauvignon ★★ £B
Dom. Delaunay
Recommended Reds: Bourgueil Prestige ★☆ £B
Joel Delaunay
Recommended Whites: Touraine Sauvignon ★☆ £B
Benoit Gautier
Recommended Whites: Vouvray Argiles ★★ £B
Dom. de La Haute Borne
Recommended Whites: Vouvray Sec ★★ £B
Vouvray Tendre ★★★ £C
Vouvray Moelleux ★★★☆ £D
Dom. des Huards
Recommended Reds: Cour-Cheverny ★★ £B
Recommended Whites:
Cour-Cheverny Cuvée François 1er ★★☆ £C
Pascal Lambert
Recommended Reds: Chinon Tradition Graves ★★☆ £C
Chinon Danaé ★★☆ £C   Chinon Marie ★★☆ £C
Lamé Delisle Boucard
Recommended Reds: Bourgueil Chesnaies ★★ £B
Bourgueil Vieilles Vignes ★★★ £C
Dom. des Liards
Recommended Whites: Montlouis Demi-Sec Vieilles-Vignes ★★ £C
Alain Marcadet
Recommended Whites: Touraine Sauvignon ★☆ £B
Philippe Pichard
Recommended Reds: Chinon L'Ancestral ★ £B
Dom. Pichot
Recommended Whites: Vouvray Sec Coteau de La Biche ★★ £B
Vouvray Demi-Sec Peu de La Moriette ★★ £C
Dom. de La Presle
Recommended Whites: Touraine Sauvignon Blanc ★☆ £B
Dom. des Raguenières
Recommended Reds: Bourgueil ★☆ £B
Bourgueil Les Haies ★☆ £B
Dom. Raifault
Recommended Reds: Chinon ★★ £B
Chinon Allets ★★☆ £C
Dom. Ricard
Recommended Whites: Touraine Le Petiot ★★ £B
Touraine Trois Chênes ★★☆ £C
Touraine ★★★☆ £E
Touraine L'Effrontée ★★★☆ £D
Dom. du Roncée
Recommended Reds: Chinon Clos des Marronniers ★★ £C
Dom. Wilfrid Rousse
Recommended Reds: Chinon Cuvée Terroir ★★ £B
Chinon Vieilles Vignes ★★☆ £C
Dom. La Sauvete
Recommended Reds: Touraine ★☆ £B
Recommended Whites: Touraine Sauvignon ★☆ £B

Central Vineyards
Dom. Michel Bailly
Recommended Reds: Coteau de Giennois ★☆ £B
Recommended Whites: Pouilly-Fumé Les Vallons ★★☆ £C
Balland-Chapuis
Recommended Whites:

Sancerre Le Chêne Marchand ★★ £C
Dom. Francis Blanchet
Recommended Whites: Pouilly-Fumé Les Pernets ★★ £C
Pouilly-Fumé Cuvée Silice ★★★ £C
Dom. des Caves
Recommended Whites: Quincy ★★ £B
Dom. Champault
Recommended Reds: Sancerre Les Pierris ★★ £C
Recommended Whites: Sancerre Clos du Roy ★★★ £C
Dom. de Chatenoy
Recommended Reds: Menetou-Salon ★★ £C
Recommended Whites: Menetou-Salon ★★☆ £C
Dom. Chavet
Recommended Whites: Menetou-Salon ★★☆ £C
Paul Cherrier
Recommended Whites: Sancerre Vieilles-Vignes ★★ £C
Dom. de Chevilly
Recommended Whites: Quincy ★★ £B
Dom. de La Commanderie
Recommended Whites: Quincy ★ £B ////
Jean-Claude Dagueneau
Recommended Whites: Pouilly-Fumé ★★★ £C
Serge Dagueneau
Recommended Whites: Pouilly-Fumé ★★☆ £C
Vincent Delaporte
Recommended Whites: Sancerre ★★★ £D
Pierre et Alain Dézat
Recommended Whites: Sancerre ★★★ £C
Recommended Rosés: Sancerre ★★ £C
Dom. Fournier
Recommended Whites: Menetou-Salon ★☆ £C
Pierre Girault
Recommended Whites: Sancerre Chêne du Roy ★★ £C
Dom. Jean-Claude Guyot
Recommended Whites: Pouilly-Fumé Les Loges ★★ £C
Hippolyte-Reverdy
Recommended Whites: Sancerre ★★★ £D
De Ladoucette
Recommended Whites: Pouilly-Fumé ★★ £D
Pouilly-Fumé Baron de L ★★★ £E
Serge Laloue
Recommended Reds: Sancerre ★★ £C
Recommended Whites: Sancerre ★★ £C
Dom. Laporte
Recommended Whites: Sancerre Le Grand Rochoy ★★★☆ £D
Sancerre La Rochoy ★★★ £C
Sancerre La Rochoy ★★★☆ £D
Pouilly-Fumé La Vigne de Beaussoppet ★★★☆ £D
Dom. Mardon
Recommended Reds: Reuilly ★ £B
Recommended Whites: Reuilly ★★ £B
Dom. Martin
Recommended Reds: Sancerre Chavignol ★★☆ £C
Recommended Whites: Sancerre Chavignol ★★☆ £C
Sancerre L'Indigène ★★★ £D
Recommended Rosés: Sancerre Chavignol ★☆ £C
Dom. Merlin Cherrier
Recommended Whites: Sancerre ★★ £C
Roger Neveu
Recommended Whites: Sancerre ★★☆ £C
Dom. Jean Pabiot

Loire Valley

France

Recommended Whites: Pouilly-Fumé ★★☆ £C
Dom. Philippe Portier
Recommended Whites: Quincy ★★ £B
Dom. Paul Prieur
Recommended Reds: Sancerre ★☆ £C
Recommended Whites: Sancerre ★★ £C
Matthias Roblin
Recommended Reds: Sancerre ★☆ £C
Recommended Whites: Sancerre ★★ £C
Dom. de La Rossignol
Recommended Whites: Sancerre ★★☆ £C
Dom. Sautereau
Recommended Whites: Sancerre Vieilles Vignes ★★ £C
Dom. Hervé Seguin
Recommended Whites: Pouilly-Fumé Cuvée Prestige ★★ £C
Dom. Annick Tinel
Recommended Whites: Pouilly-Fumé ★★ £C
Dom. Andre Vatan
Recommended Whites: Sancerre Saint-François ★☆ £C

Work in progress!!

Producers under consideration for the next edition
Dom. Patrice Colin (Côteaux du Vendômois)
Dom. du Collier (Saumur)
Dom de La Garrelière (Touraine)
Dom. des Griottes (Anjou)
Les Rocher des Violettes (Montlouis)
Pithon-Paille (Anjou)
Jean-Pierre Robinot (Jasnières)
Franz Saumon (Montlouis)

Author's choice

A Diverse Selection of Sweet Whites
Patrick Baudouin   Quarts de Chaume Maria Juby
Dom. des Baumard   Quarts de Chaume
Ch. de Fesles   Bonnezeaux
Dom. du Clos Naudin   Vouvray Moelleux
Philippe Delesvaux   Côteaux du Layon Grains Nobles
Joël Gigou   Jasnières Sélection de Grains Nobles
Huet L'Echansonne   Vouvray Haut-Lieu Moelleux
Taille Aux Loups   Montlouis Cuvée Romulus
Dom. des Forges   Quarts de Chaume
Ch. La Varière   Quarts de Chaume Les Querches
René Mossé   Côteaux du Layon-Saint-Lambert Bonnes Blanches
Dom. François Chidaine   Montlouis Le Lys

A Choice of Individual Dry Whites
Dom. Henri Bourgeois   Sancerre La Bourgeoise
Dom. du Closel   Savennières Clos du Papillon
Ch. de Villeneuve   Saumur Cormiers
Jean-Claude Chatelaine   Pouilly Fumé Prestige
Clos de La Coulée de Serrant   Savennières Coulée de Serrant
Pascal Cotat   Sancerre Monts Damnés
Didier Dagueneau   Pouilly Fumé Silex
Henry Pellé   Menetou-Salon Clos des Blanchais
Dom. de La Sansonnière   Anjou La Lune
Dom. de Bellivière   Côteaux du Loir Eparses Vieilles Vignes
Dom. Saint-Nicolas   Fiefs Vendéens Le Haut des Clous

The Best of the Reds
Philippe Alliet   Chinon Vieilles-Vignes
Yannick Amirault   Saint-Nicolas-de-Bourgueil Malgagnes
Bernard Baudry   Chinon Croix Boisée
Ch. du Hureau   Saumur-Champigny Lisgathe
Clos Rougeard   Saumur-Champigny Poyeux
Pierre-Jacques Druet   Bourgueil Vaumoreau
Dom. Ogereau   Anjou-Villages Côte de La Houssaye
Dom. des Ouches   Bourgueil Grande Réserve
Dom. des Roches Neuves   Saumur-Champigny Marginale
Dom. de La Cotelleraie   Saint-Nicolas-de-Bourgueil L'Envol
Dom. de La Noblaie   Chinon Les Chiens-Chiens
Dom. Frédéric Mabileau   Saint-Nicolas-de-Bourgueil Éclipse

A selection of Great Loire Values
Reds:
Dom. René-Noel Legrand   Saumur La Chaintre
Dom. de La Butte   Bourgueil Perrières

Whites:
Alain Cailbourdin   Pouilly Fumé Les Cris
Ch. de Villeneuve   Saumur
Dom. François Chidaine   Montlouis Clos des Breuil
Dom. Benoît Mérias   Montlouis La Vallée
Dom. du Clos Naudin   Vouvray Sec
Dom. du Closel   Savennières Caillardières
Dom de L'Ecu   Muscadet Sèvre-Et-Maine Expression de Granit
Dom. Guiberteau   Saumur Le Clos
Dom. La Tour Saint Martin   Menetou-Salon Morogues
Dom. Gérard Morin   Sancerre PMG

The vineyards of the Jura in particular and Savoie produce some of the most strikingly original wines in France. They are steeped in tradition and relatively unknown outside of their homeland but some fine and very diverse styles are produced. The Jura is more marked by rolling hills than high mountains. The Savoie by contrast offers a magnificent backdrop with the Alps in the background. With the proximity of the ski fields and their thirsty winter tourists, much of what Savoie produces is disappointingly light and dilute. As in all regions though there are instances of really characterful wines being made. To enjoy the best both regions have to offer you are likely to have to visit in person.

Jura

Located to the west of Burgundy's Côte d'Or, the vineyard area is situated at altitude on the western slopes of the Jura mountains. There are a number of appellations here. The **Côtes du Jura** AC encompasses the whole region and produces red, rosé and white wine. Reds and rosés are produced from the local Poulsard and Trousseau as well as Pinot Noir. Those produced from Pinot and the sturdy and structured Trousseau are the best bets. Among the whites, Chardonnay is good and can be very elegant and structured with great fruit purity. Equally interesting are the nutty, characterful Savagnin-based wines. Some oak is used but it tends to be subtle and restrained. The speciality of the region is *vin jaune*. This is not dissimilar to fino sherry in character as it is aged under a yeast film, yet it remains unfortified. Many regular Savagnin wines are also produced in a similar style but generally spend less time under the *flor* yeast. Vin Jaune is remarkably ageworthy.

There are also three smaller ACs. **Arbois** produces good red and white (from the same varieties as in the Côte du Jura), Vin de Paille and sparkling wines are also produced. At **L'Étoile** dry whites from Chardonnay and Savagnin and some moderate sparkling wine are produced as well as *vin jaune*. The spectacularly sited vineyards of **Château Chalon** are solely for the production of *vin jaune*. Another speciality found throughout the region is the rare *vin de paille*. It is, like examples in the northern Rhône, a late-harvested sweet white with a hint of nutty oxidation. Both whote and red varieties are used and some examples can be very sweet indeed. Most sparkling wine is made by the traditional method and is labelled as **Crémant de Jura**. There is the odd decent example. Most growers also offer **Macvin du Jura**, a *vin de liqueur* which has *marc* added to fermenting grape juice. There are some characterfully nutty examples, which are quite unique in style

Savoie

This high alpine vineyard area is located to the south-west of Geneva and covers a large area. The backdrop of the Alps provdes for some of the most spectularly sited vineyards in France. The regional AC is **Vin de Savoie**. There are some good whites from the Altesse and Bergeron (Roussanne) grapes, which are fresh and floral and reds mainly from Pinot Noir and Mondeuse. The latter particularly are worth considering. The wines at best are sturdy, structured and very characterful. Altesse is also known as Roussette and has its own AC, **Roussette de Savoie**. Good light, fresh, dry whites from Altesse and sparkling wines from Molette (with some Altesse) are produced under the **Seyssel** AC. The Chasselas-based whites at **Crepy** AC are generally unexciting.

Jura & Savoie vintages

With the large variation in styles throughout the two regions providing detailed vintage assessments is nigh on impossible. Most Savoie whites and reds should be drunk young and fresh. Mondeuse will though stand a little age. Of recent available vintages, 2015 and 2014 are considered average to above average in quality. Good ripe and attractive wines have also emerged in 2013, 2012, 2011, 2010 and 2009, while 2008, 2007, 2006, 2005 and 2004 offer some good well structured wines, whereas 2003 was marked as elsewhere by the summer heat and very big sturdy wines have been produced. In the Jura Trousseau and Pinot Noir will both develop with 3- 4 years cellaring, as will the structured, minerally, Chardonnay. Savagnin is very ageworthy particularly Vin Jaune which will keep for decades.

A-Z of producers - *Jura*

Paul Benoit (Arbois-Pupillin) *www.paulbenoitetfils-pupillin.com* This is among the very best of the small producers based in the sleepy little village of Pupillin to the south of Arbois. Paul Benoit has a number of very well sited vineyard holdings in some of the best terroirs in the appellation. He has a total of some 13 ha under vine and makes a full range of reds and whites as well as some intriguing Macvin, both white and, more unusually, rosé. Chardonnay is crisp and fresh in style and is vinified in *inox*. La Loge is a Savagnin vinified in oak with *bâtonnage*. It offers very impressive depth and intensity. The Savagnin is more traditional and vinified in the same oxidative manner as the vin jaune, which itself has really piercing citrus and lightly nutty fruit underpinned by a marked *flor* character. The reds don't quite have the same substance. The Ploussard (the local synonym for Poulsard) is soft and fruit-driven and typically light in colour. Pinot Noir offers a little more depth and structure. The Trousseau from Arbois vineyards is firm and needs time. The top red, La Grande Chenevrière is solely Pinot Noir. Subtle and elegant, it offers really good depth and intensity. The vin de paille is a blend of Savagnin, Chardonnay and Poulsard which offers better acidity and structure than many of the style as well as unctuously sweet fruit. The range is completed by a fresh and well made Crémant du Jura. (DM)

Recommended Reds:
Arbois-Pupillin La Grande Chenevrière ★★☆ £D
ArboisTrousseau ★★☆ £D
Arbois-Pupillin Ploussard ★★ £C
Arbois-Pupillin Pinot Noir ★★ £C

Recommended Whites:
Arbois-Pupillin Vin de Paille ★★★★ £F
Arbois-Pupillin Vin Jaune ★★★★ £F
Arbois-Pupillin La Loge ★★★☆ £E
Arbois-Pupillin Savagnin ★★★ £D
Arbois-Pupillin Chardonnay ★★☆ £C
Crémant du Jura ★☆ £C

Dom. Berthet-Bondet (Château-Chalon) *www.berthet-bondet.net* First-class traditional Jura producer, making top-quality whites from Chardonnay and the local white Savagnin. Three Côtes du Jura dry whites are made, a Chardonnay, the more complex and structured Tradition from a blend of Savagnin and Chardonnay and Naturé, a Savagnin. These offer marvelously pure and intense mineral and light citrus fruit characters. In the Tradition an almost salty tang underpins the wine. The Château-Chalon, a vin jaune, is not dissimilar to a top level Fino sherry and has an earthy, salty character derived from the layer of *flor* yeast under which it is aged in cask. Unlike Fino, these wines have a piercing acidity, lending them the structure for very long ageing. The wines require time to show at

France

their best. (DM)

Recommended Whites:
Château-Chalon ★★★★ £F
Côtes du Jura Tradition ★★★☆ £D
Côtes du Jura Chardonnay ★★★ £C

Ch. d' Arlay (Côtes du Jura) *www.arlay.com*

This château and historic monument dates back to the 1700s. The vineyards are planted to a mix of 17 ha of red varieties and just 10 ha of Chardonnay and Savagnin. Annual output is around 10,000 cases a year. The unusual red Cuvée Corail is a blend of all five red and white Jura varieties. Maceration is around one and a half weeks and the wine is in a light style, very pale in colour, but offers good intensity nonetheless. The Vin Rouge is solely from Pinot Noir and is structured and quite backward for the variety. It should add more flesh with age. Chardonnay is aged for three years on lees and is likewise very traditional in style. It will open out splendidly with time. The Blanc Tradition is richer and fuller. A blend of Savagnin and two-thirds Chardonnay there is just a hint of oxidation from the Savagnin. The vin jaune is marked by a piercing citrus and peat quality and quite different to the wines of nearby Château-Chalon. Like the Corail, the vin de paille is characterised by the number of varieties in the blend, four in this case. The residual sugar varies considerably from year to year from quite sweet to surprisingly dry. These are good, traditional and initially austere wines which need time. Good red and white Macvin and a Vieille Fine Réserve Marc are worth considering. (DM)

Recommended Reds:
Côtes du Jura Le Vin Rouge ★★ £C
Côtes du Jura Cuvée Corail ★★ £C

Recommended Whites:
Côtes du Jura Le Vin de Paille ★★★★ £F
Côtes du Jura Le Vin Jaune de Garde ★★★☆ £F
Côtes du Jura Tradition ★★★ £C
Côtes du Jura Chardonnay a la Reine ★★ £C

Dom. Ganevat (Côtes du Jura)

Good white and red are made here. Jean François Ganevat worked for René Monnier in Burgundy and this influence comes through in his wines. As well as a lightly citrusy and nutty Chardonnay there is a fine old-vine bottling and a dry Savagnin with the white range completed by a Vin Jaune. These are good, if somewhat traditional and austere wines which need time. The red Poulsard is light but exuberant and has impressive intensity. The Trousseau is big, firm and structured; it demands five years' cellaring at least. Pinot Noir of subtle but piercing depth is found in the Cuvée Julien. Low yields are key and the Pinot crops at barely more than 20 hl/ha. The Poulsard will drink well young; the other wines will improve with age and will keep for a decade. (DM)

Recommended Reds:
Côtes du JuraTrousseau Plein Sud ★★★☆ £D
Côtes du Jura Pinot Noir Cuvée Julienne ★★★ £D
Côtes du Jura Poulsard Vieilles Vignes L'Enfant Terrible ★★☆ £C

Recommended Whites:
Côtes du Jura Chardonnay Les Grands Teppes Vieilles Vignes ★★★☆ £D
Côtes du Jura Chardonnay Cuvée Florine Ganevat ★★★ £C

❀ Emmanuel Houillon (Arbois Pupillon)

Emmanuel Houillon took over the running of this excellent small Jura domaine in 2001 from Pierre Overnoy having been a long-term apprentice of his mentor. There are now just over 6 ha of

Chardonnay, Savagnin and Ploussard. Overnoy himself was one of those brave early individuals to avoid the use of sulphur in his vineyards and winemaking. Emmanuel Houillon continues this tradition and the whites are very much in the rarer non-oxidative spectrum that you can find in the region with the barrels always topped up. The wines are made very carefully with extensive use of protective carbon dioxide and ageing on lees provides further antioxidation. The whites are very striking, mineral and intense but the red Ploussard should not be overlooked either. This is the local Pupillon synonym for Poulsard. Intense and very characterful red cherry fruit abounds on the palate and the wine offers really impressive depth and persistence of flavour. With their nervy and impressive acidity expect all the wines to age very well, although the Ploussard should drunk up a little earlier. (DM)

Recommended Reds:
Arbois Pupillon Ploussard ★★★ £D

Recommended Whites:
Arbois Pupillon Savagnin-Chardonnay ★★★★ £E
Arbois Pupillon Savagnin Ouille ★★★★ £E

❀ Dom. Labet (Côtes du Jura)

The Labet family possess 12 ha of vineyards in the southern Côtes du Jura from where they make an extensive range of wines both from different sites and from specific lieu-dits. They do not fall into the oxidised or non-oxidised camps, producing wines of both styles. Much of the character and quality here can be attributed to the considerable age of the vineyards. The Fleurs cuvée is produced from the youngest Chardonnay vines across their holdings and is bright and subtly melon scented with a soft easy structure. The Fleur de Chardonnay also comes from Les Varrons from 50 year old vines planted by mass selection. A *lieu-dit* bottling Les Varrons from older 65 year old vines is also produced from the same site. The wines labelled Fleur de Marne are generally from vines over 50 years old and planted on *argile* soils. Finely structured, rich and full La Bardette is produced from 65 year old vines, the tighter and more mineral En Billat is sourced from a holding of 105 year old vines planted at a higher altititude of some 305 metres. The Chardonnay/Savagnin and Savagnin bottlings are produced in the oxidative style where the barrels are not topped and the wine sits under a *flor* yeast. The Chardonnay/Savagnin is aged for 24 to 36 months, the richer and more characterful Savagnin for 36 to 72 months and giving something of the citrussy, salty character of the domaine's Vin Jaune. The red Poulsard is from old vines and typically light in colour with persistent red cherry fruit and marked acidity. As with most Jura reds you should taste a few to get the hang of them because they are by no means everyone's cup of tea. A Pinot Noir is also made. A fine and comprehensive range is completed by a very fine Vin de Paille which is rich, unctuous and very characterful, a blend of Chardonnay, Savagnin and Poulsard all of which are left on straw mats for 4 to 5 months. The top Chardonnays and the oxidised styles will age very well. (DM)

Recommended Reds:
Côtes du Jura Poulsard Vieilles Vignes ★★★ £C

Recommended Whites:
Côtes du Jura Vin de Paille ★★★★★ £F
Côtes du Jura Savagnin ★★★★ £D
Côtes du Jura Chardonnay/Savagnin ★★★★ £D
Côtes du Jura Fleur de Marne En Billat ★★★☆ £C
Côtes du Jura Fleur de Marne La Bardette ★★★ £C
Côtes du Jura Fleur de Chardonnay ★★★ £C
Côtes du Jura Fleurs ★★☆ £B

Dom. Rijckaert (Arbois) *www.rijckaert.fr*

Jean Rijckaert now owns his own small domaine in Arbois as well as his property in Viré-Clessé (see Burgundy/Mâconnais) where he weaves his particular magic, not only with Chardonnay but also the indigenous Savagnin. As with his Burgundies a mineral purity can be found in all these bottles. Rijckaert avoids the more traditional oxidative style of winemaking and even with his Savagnin the barrels are always topped up. He possesses just 5 ha of his own and also buys in fruit. A brown label indicates a grower's wine (and also includes their name), while a green label is used for the domaine wines, as is the case with all those assessed here. Expect all of these to develop well in bottle the Chardonnays requiring at least 3 or 4 years, the Savagnin a little longer. (DM)

Recommended Whites:
Arbois Chardonnay En Paradis Vieilles Vignes ★★★☆ £D
Arbois Chardonnay En Chantemerle ★★★☆ £D
Côtes de Jura Savagnin Les Sarres ★★★☆ £D
Côtes de Jura Chardonnay Vignes des Voises Vieilles Vignes ★★★☆ £D
Côtes de Jura Chardonnay Les Sarres ★★★ £C

❀ Dom. Rolet (Arbois) *www.rolet-arbois.com*

This is a sizeable producer for the region but also one of the very best. The Rolets now have a total vineyard holding of 61 ha: 36 ha in Arbois, 21 ha in the Côtes du Jura and the remaining 4 ha in L'Étoile. The Poulsard Vieilles Vignes is soft and fruit-driven albeit with the complexity of old vines and the natural acidity found in all the region's wines. Trousseau is firm and structured but possesses an elegance and subtlety not found elsewhere. Pinot Noir is strawberry scented, light and elegant with good intensity. It too is edging ★★★. The top red, Memorial, is a very impressive 80/20 blend of Trousseau and Pinot Noir. Aged in oak for 15–18 months, this not only has depth and intensely striking red berry fruit but a richer texture than many other reds from the region. There are three fine Chardonnays, of which the Arbois is a little more tropical than the others and the L'Étoile is the most mineral and structured. All are barrel fermented in one-third new wood. The Côtes du Jura white comes from vineyards very close to Château-Chalon. It is a rich and concentrated blend of 50/50 Chardonnay and Savagnin from untopped barrels and consequently has a light *flor* character. The Arbois Tradition is a similar blend and aged in wood for 30–36 months. It offers a little more structure and intensity. The vin jaune is one of the very best in the region with a very subtle yeast character and intensely nutty, citrusy fruit and superb length. Vin de paille is rich and intense although not as sweet as some. It is a very fine, piercing blend of Poulsard, Savagnin and Chardonnay full of dried-fruit character. The Crémant du Jura is clean and fresh with a little complexity from 21 months on lees. (DM)

Recommended Reds:
Arbois Memorial ★★★ £C
Arbois Trousseau ★★★ £C
Arbois Pinot Noir ★★☆ £C
Arbois Poulsard Vieilles Vignes ★★ £B

Recommended Whites:
Arbois Vin de Paille ★★★★★ £F
Arbois Vin Jaune ★★★★★ £F
Arbois Tradition ★★★ £D
Arbois Chardonnay ★★★ £C
Côtes du Jura Expression de Terroir ★★★ £C
Côtes du Jura Chardonnay ★★★ £C
Crémant du Jura ★★★ £C

❀ André & Mireille Tissot (Arbois) *www.stephane-tissot.com*

Like the Quénards in the Savoie, there are a number of Tissots in the Jura so take care to avoid confusion. These Tissots produce some of the most outstanding wines in the region and in a very pure, fruit-driven style quite unlike many of their neighbours. This is in no small part down to son Stéphane who has had experience in Australia and South Africa and now handles all the winemaking. There are three very good and well priced Chardonnays, all striking, intense and pure wines vinified in one-third new oak, as well as a special cru from a small parcel, Le Clos de la Tour de Curon. Les Bruyères is the tightest and most mineral, Les Graviers the most opulent. The fascinating Sélection is a nutty, citrusy blend of 70% Chardonnay with Savagnin, and it's the latter that really drives the wine. The varietal Savagnin is in a reductive style – the casks are kept filled and *flor* is not allowed to develop. Rich and pure, it offers great concentration with ripe lemon and grilled nut character. The Vin jaune wines are of course traditional and lightly citrusy with subtler yeast character than others as well as marvelous piercing depth and intensity of flavour. The most extraordinary wines are the *vin de pailles*, although because of their residual sugar they are not classified as appellation wines. The brilliant Spirale is now joined by a very pricey PMG. Reds are good, although not quite of the same order. Poulsard is bright with strawberry fruit, Trousseau impressively structured without hard or dried tannins. The unfiltered Pinot Noir en Barberon comes from Côtes du Jura vineyards yielding barely 20hl/ha and is aged in 60% new wood. (DM)

Recommended Reds:
Arbois Trousseau ★★★ £D
Arbois Poulsard Vieilles Vignes ★★ £C
Côtes du Jura Pinot Noir En Barberan ★★★ £D

Recommended Whites:
Spirale Passerillé ★★★★★ £F
Château-Chalon ★★★★★ £F
Arbois Vin Jaune ★★★★☆ £F
Arbois Sélection ★★★☆ £E
Arbois Savagnin ★★★☆ £D
Arbois Chardonnay la Mailloche ★★★☆ £D
Arbois Chardonnay les Bruyères ★★★☆ £D
Arbois Chardonnay les Graviers ★★★☆ £D

Dom. Jacques Tissot (Arbois)

Jacques Tissot has been running his family domaine just outside Arbois since 1962. He has a total of 32 ha spread across the Arbois, Arbois-Pupillin and Côtes du Jura ACs. An extensive range is made including dry white and red, vin jaune, vin de paille, some Crémant du Jura and characterful local Macvin. There is a good fresh, forward Chardonnay as well as a richer Grande Réserve. The Arbois Nature from young-vine Savagnin is young and fresh with some depth and intensity and a nice citrus undercurrent. The Blanc-Typé is a more seriously structured blend of Savagnin and Chardonnay. The varietal Arbois Savagnin is regularly topped up in barrel, resulting in a rich and characterful style with loads of nutty, citrus character. The splendid Arbois vin jaune stands out. It has a marvellous citrus depth to its fruit and magnificent intensity. Of the reds, the Poulsard is soft and approachable, as is the Tradition, which blends in a little Pinot Noir. The very good and well-structured Trousseau Grande Réserve is a real *vin de garde* that needs time to shed a touch of youthfully hard tannin. The Côtes du Jura Pinot En Barberon is bright and elegant with a firm and fresh undercurrent and should develop well with 5 years' age. The top whites all demand up to 10 years'

Jura & Savoie

France

patience and the vin jaune labels will keep for decades. (DM)

Recommended Reds:
Arbois Trousseau Grande Reserve ★★★ £C
ArboisTradition ★★ £C
Côtes du Jura Pinot Noir En Barberon ★★★ £C
Arbois-Pupillin Poulsard ★★ £C

Recommended Whites:
Arbois Vin Jaune ★★★★☆ £F
Arbois Savagnin ★★★☆ £D
Arbois Blanc-Typé ★★★ £C
Arbois Naturé ★★☆ £C
Arbois Chardonnay ★★ £C

A-Z of producers - *Savoie*

Dom. Belluard (Vin de Savoie) *www.domainebelluard.fr*
This 11 ha domaine south of Crépy in the Haute-Savoie is run organically and is in the process of being converted to full biodynamic cultivation. The *terroir* has real potential with vineyards planted at a significant altitude of some 450 metres on slopes with well-drained glacial soils and a southerly aspect. As elsewhere, these Alpine vineyards benefit from warm summer days and cool nights, which ensure good acidity and structure in the fruit. The Gringet white is a piercing, fruit-driven style, which is not put through malolactic, fresh acidity being the key to its style. The variety, is thought to be related to the Jura's Savagnin and although it is less obviously weighty it shares some of the characteristic citrus and lightly peachy character found in that variety. The Mondeuse is darkly coloured with a classic dark cherry twist to its fruit and is well structured with youthfully firm but supple tannins. It will benefit from 3 or 4 years' patience. A good Ayze Mousseux is also produced. (DM)

Recommended Reds:
Vin de Savoie Mondeuse Amphore ★★☆ £C

Recommended Whites:
Vin de Savoie Gringet Le Feu ★★☆ £C

Dom. G & G Bouvet (Vin de Savoie) *www.domaine-bouvet.com*
An extensive range of both red and white is made at this 13 ha domaine just to the east of Chignin. These are spectacularly sited vineyards, sloping down from the rock wall behind the village, the Massif des Bauges. *Argilo-calcaire* soils and a south-south-east exposure provide an excellent *terroir*, where those international favourites Chardonnay and Cabernet Sauvignon are planted as well as the more established local varieties. There is a soft, forward, fruit-driven Roussette de Savoie. Chardonnay is in a quite cool-climate style with some oak. Chignin-Bergeron is from Roussanne and is lightly floral with a subtle nutty undercurrent. The white Grand Savoie is a blend of Chardonnay, Jacquère and Altesse (Roussette) also aged in oak, but it doesn't quite have the same depth and fruit definition. Reds are the main focus here. The Mondeuse La Persanne offers both depth of both flavour and colour. The L de Bouvet Mondeuse Prestige is fuller and richer as a result of a longer *cuvaison* and ageing for 3–6 months in oak. The Grand Savoie red is a blend of Mondeuse, Pinot Noir and Gamay. Round and supple with good berry fruit, this is a little softer than the Mondeuse Prestige. The top Mondeuse Cuée Guillaume Charles is one of the best examples of the variety in the region. The concentrated dark cherry and bramble fruit comfortably absorbs the oak, some of it new. The top red in particular will benefit from 4 or 5 years' ageing. (DM)

Recommended Reds:
Vin de Savoie Cuvée Guillaume Charles Mondeuse ★★★ £D
Vin de Savoie Grand Savoie ★★ £C
Vin de Savoie Mondeuse Sainte Barbe ★★ £C
Vin de Savoie Mondeuse La Persanne ★ £B

Recommended Whites:
Vin de Savoie Chardonnay Saint Antoine ★★ £C
Vin de Savoie Grand Savoie ★★ £C
Vin de Savoie Chignin-Bergeron ★★ £C
Roussette de Savoie ★★ £B

Dom. André & Michel Quénard (Vin de Savoie)
Perhaps the best known of the various branches of the Quénards in Chignin. There are 23 ha of vineyards and whites are the main plantings with 17 ha of Jacquère, Bergeron and Altesse. The regular Vin de Savoie and Roussette de Savoie whites are floral and fruit-driven, while the Chignin has a touch of minerality. The Chignin-Bergeron Les Terasses is honeyed, nutty and intensely mineral in character. A fine old-vine Chignin is also made. Among reds from the small holding of Gamay, Mondeuse and Pinot Noir the Chignin Mondeuse Vieilles Vignes is particularly striking, with concentrated black cherry fruit and a real old-vine quality. It will benefit from 5 or so years of ageing. (DM)

Recommended Reds:
Vin de Savoie Chignin Mondeuse Vieilles Vignes ★★ £C

Recommended Whites:
Vin de Savoie Chignin-Bergeron Les Terrasses ★★★ £C
Roussette de Savoie ★★ £B
Vin de Savoie Chignin ★☆ £B

Dom. J-P & J-F Quénard (Vin de Savoie) *www.jf-quenard.com*
This domaine is quite a bit larger than very near neighbour and namesake Le Fils de René QUÉNARD but quality is similarly impressive. Gamay is simple and straightforward. Mondeuse is altogether more serious. The regular bottling is deep and spicy, full of dark berry fruit and spices with not inconsiderable tannin. The Sélection de Terroir is a vineyard selection aged in used oak, which gives the wine extra weight and dimension on the palate. Both will benefit from 5 years' ageing. Of two Chignin whites made from Jacquère, the Anne de la Biguerne comes from 65 to 70-year-old vines and is richer and more intense. The Chignin-Bergeron Les Demoiselles comes from a 3-ha south-west-facing plot grown on calcareous soils and is cool-fermented to emphasise its floral, lightly tropical and minerally fruit. All three should be drunk young. An old-vine bottling, Tradition, is produced from a specific 0.6-ha plot. This is made from Roussanne and vinification and ageing are in used small oak. It comes from the last pass through the vineyard and should develop well with 2 or 3 years. (DM)

Recommended Reds:
Vin de Savoie Mondeuse Cuvée Séléction de Terroir ★★★ £C
Vin de Savoie Mondeuse ★★☆ £C
Vin de Savoie Gamay ★☆ £B

Recommended Whites:
Vin de Savoie Cepage Tradition ★★★ £C
Vin de Savoie Chignin-Bergeron Les Demoiselles ★★☆ £C
Vin de Savoie Chignin Anne de la Biguerne ★★ £C
Vin de Savoie Chignin ★★ £B

Le Fils de René Quénard (Vin de Savoie)
Jacky and Georges Quenard have now taken over this domaine from their father Raymond. It consists of close to 20 ha in the village of

Chignin. The larger part of Raymond's domaine was recently handed over to his son Pascal who now makes his own wine separately. The whites are evenly split between Jacquère and Bergeron, while the red plantings comprise Gamay and Mondeuse. The Gamay is a good example – full, fruit-driven and plush, to be drunk young. The structured but sufficiently supple Mondeuse is more serious, full of dark berry, spice and cherry fruit. It is almost rustic but in the best sense. The Chignin Cépage Jacquère is made from very old vines. Vinified in *inox* with no malolactic, it is very pure, deep and minerally with great intensity. The Chignin-Bergeron (100% Roussanne) is fuller and more opulent in style with a touch of oak. Old vines again contribute to the style and quality. A late-harvest Chignin-Bergeron is also produced. (DM)

Recommended Reds:
Vin de Savoie Mondeuse ★★☆ £C
Vin de Savoie Gamay ★☆ £B
Recommended Whites:
Vin de Savoie Chignin La Cigale ★★★ £C
Vin de Savoie Chignin-Bergeron ★☆ £B

Other wines of note - *Jura*

Fruitière Vinicole d'Arbois
Recommended Whites: Arbois Chardonnay ★☆ £B
Arbois Cuvée Bethanie ★★ £C
Arbois Savagnin Grand Sélection ★★★ £C
Arbois Vin Jaune ★★★☆ £E
Dom. Jean Macle
Recommended Whites: Côtes du Jura ★★★ £C
Château-Chalon ★★★★ £F
Dom. Jacques Puffeney
Recommended Whites: Arbois Chardonnay ★★★ £C
Caves de La Reine Jeanne
Recommended Whites: Côtes du Jura Chardonnay ★★ £B
Arbois Trousseau ★★ £B
Dom. de La Tournelle
Recommended Whites:
Arbois Chardonnay Terre de Gryphées ★★★ £D
Arbois Fleur de Savagnin ★★★ £D
Arbois Vin de Paille ★★★★ £F
Arbois Vin Jaune ★★★★ £F
Recommended Reds:
Arbois Poulsard L'Uva Arbosiana ★★☆ £C
Arbois Trousseau Les Corvées ★★☆ £C

Other wines of note - *Savoie*

Pierre Boniface
Recommended Whites: Vin de Savoie Jacquère ★☆ £B
Patrick Charlin
Recommended Whites: Bugey Montagnieu Altesse ★★ £B
Ch. de Ripaille
Recommended Whites: Vin de Savoie ★★ £B £C
Dom. Michel Grisard
Recommended Whites: Roussette de Savoie ★★ £B
Dom. Edmond Jacquin
Recommended Whites: Vin de Savoie Chardonnay ★★ £C
Roussette de Savoie ★★ £B
Dom. Bruno Lupin
Recommended Whites: Roussette de Savoie Frangy ★★ £B

Dom. Louis Magnin
Recommended Whites: Roussette de Savoie ★★ £B
Recommended Reds:
Vin de Savoie Mondeuse Vieilles Vignes ★★★ £C
Dom. Vullien
Recommended Whites: Roussette de Savoie ★★ £B

Work in progress!!

Producers under consideration for the next edition
Lucien Aviet (Côtes du Jura)
Caves de La Reine Jeanne (Arbois)
Dom. Dupasquier (Vin de Savoie)
Dom. Durand-Perron (Chateau-Chalon)
Dom. Ligier (Arbois)
Dom. Frédéric Lornet (Arbois)
Dom. de La Pinte (Arbois)
Dom. Saint-Germain (Vin de Savoie)
Dom. Charles Trosset (Vin de Savoie)

Author's choice

A dozen good value reds and whites
Reds:
Dom. Paul Benoit Arbois-Pupillin Ploussard
Dom. Belluard Vin de Savoie Mondeuse
Whites:
Dom. Berthet-Bondet Côtes du Jura Alliance
Ch. d'Arlay Côtes du Jura Chardonnay A La Reine
Dom. Ganevat Côtes du Jura Cuvée Florine Ganevat
Dom. Rijckaert Côtes de Jura Chardonnay Les Sarres
Dom. Rolet Abois Chardonnay
Andre & Mirille Tissot Arbois Sélection
Jacques Tissot Arbos Chardonnay
André & Michel Quénard Roussette de Savoie
Le Fils de René Quénard Vin de Savoie Chignin-Bergeron
Dom. J-P & J-F Quénard Vin de Savoie Chignin

A selection of classics from the Jura
Reds:
Dom. Ganevat Côtes De Jura Julienne Ganevat
Dom. Paul Benoit Arbois-Pupillin La Loge

Whites:
Dom. Berthet-Bondet Château-Chalon
Ch. d'Arlay Côtes du Jura Tradition
Dom. Rolet Arbois Tradition
Dom. Rolet Arbois Vin Jaune
Andre & Mireille Tissot Arbois Savagnin
Andre & Mireille Tissot Spirale IGP
Jacques Tissot Arbois Savagnin
Jacques Puffeney Arbois Chardonnay

Some of the best of Savoie
Reds:
G & G Bouvet Vin de Savoie Amariva
Dom. J-P & J-F Quénard Vin de Savoie Mondeuse Sélection Terroir
Le Fils de René Quénard Vin de Savoie Mondeuse
Dom. Louis Magnin Vin de Savoie Mondeuse Vieilles Vignes

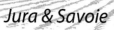

Jura & Savoie

France

Whites:
Dom. Belluard   Vin de Savoie Gringet
Bruno Lupin   Roussette de Savoie Frangy
Michel Grisard   Roussette de Savoie
A & M Quénard   Vin de Savoie Chignin-Bergeron Les Terrasses

No longer undiscovered gems of French wine, the top vineyards of the Rhône are producing increasingly widely distributed wines of world class. The established and increasing number of Rhône super-cuvées are now some of the most exciting as well as expensive wines in the world. However, there remains a vast sea of simple, sometimes disappointingly poor wine at the bottom end of the market. Two-thirds of all wine made throughout the Rhône Valley is generic AC Côtes du Rhône, although the region is improving fast and smart and slick generic marketing is being allied to generally higher quality standards. It is worth seeking out the ever-increasing number of young growers, mainly in the south, who are endeavouring to produce wines of quality and style at still very fair prices, rather than selling to the co-ops or large négociants.

Northern Rhône

The northern and southern parts of the valley are very different geographically. The Northern Rhône stretches south down the narrow valley of the River Rhône, from Vienne in the north to Valence in the south. The vineyards of Côte-Rôtie are on steep, precipitous terraces and provide some of the world's most challenging viticultural conditions. The name Côte-Rôtie means 'roasted slope'. This may be the most northerly of the Rhône appellations, but the vineyards have a superb aspect facing south-east and the soils are ideal for viticulture – high in minerals, relatively infertile and very well drained.

There are only some 200 ha under vine, with a number of cru sections identified. The best quality wine comes from the centre of the appellation. Côte Brune to the north of Ampuis produces wines of fuller body, the Côte Blonde to the south lighter more elegant wines often with Viognier blended in, which is permitted here. The style of Côte-Rôtie is perhaps less overtly muscular than the wines of Hermitage and Cornas and its climate can be very marginal in achieving full ripeness. In great years, when everything comes together at vintage these wines at their best are quite sublime.

Immediately south of Côte-Rôtie, the vineyards of **Condrieu** continue on the western bank of the river. They are planted on granite and sandstone rather than on the schistous soils to the north. The slope becomes less precipitous and the conditions are more suitable for that uniquely perfumed, aromatic variety Viognier. Widely planted now further afield, from the Languedoc to California, the variety has only come into vogue in the last decade or so. While the weight and aromatic power of **the** wines can be almost overwhelming, Viognier is a difficult variety to grow and Condrieu lacks the structure of other great French whites. The majority are best drunk in their first two or three years. An increasing number are now barrel-fermented on lees with *bâtonnage* and a few more are produced as late-harvest and very occasionally botrytis affected wines. The best of these can be stunning.

The most extensive appellation in the north is **Saint-Joseph**. It encompasses the southern part of Condrieu and runs right down the western bank of the river to the borders of Cornas, just to the north of Valence. The reds are produced from Syrah, while the whites are a blend of Marsanne and Roussanne. The best wines are produced from the gravel-based soils close to the river. An impressive number of very good wines, both red and white, have been made in recent years and prices are rising. The best sites have real potential.

The great hill of **Hermitage** and its wines, dark, brooding and powerful, are perhaps the quintessential expression of classic northern Rhône reds. There are many fewer producers here than at Côte-Rôtie and a mere 131 ha of vineyards. The hill is split up into seven different crus or lieux-dits with varying soil types. One grower, Jean-Louis Chave, is able to draw on all seven in blending his reds. The Syrah is joined by whites based on Marsanne with some Roussanne. These can be remarkably long lived, often more so than the reds. New oak and destemming in the cellar are playing an increasing role and the whites often see barrel-fermentation. More often than not here though, the oak is used rather than new. Red Hermitage should be cellared, as it is slow-developing. The white, too, needs years to show at its best. It can be approachable for a couple of years and then mysteriously close up, so if you plan to drink it young, do so within a year or two or else you will be very disappointed.

Surrounding the hill of Hermitage are the vineyards of **Crozes-Hermitage**. The same grapes are used but the vineyard area is much larger and encompasses some 1,238 ha of vines. The better wines are made on isolated outcrops of granite and there can be a wide variation in quality. The best are very good and generally well-priced and there are an increasing number of relatively highly priced special cuvées.

To the south and on the west bank of the river opposite Valence, are the appellations of **Cornas**, which borders southern Saint-Joseph, and immediately to its south **Saint-Péray**. Cornas is dense and muscular Syrah. It shares more in common with Hermitage than Côte-Rôtie, which is not surprising given its near proximity. A wide range of styles are produced, from the modern oak-influenced wines of Jean-Luc Colombo to the fiercely traditional style of Auguste and Pierre-Marie Clape. At their finest, these are dark-fruited, intense and splendidly long-lived expressions of Syrah.

Many of the Cornas growers also produce the still and sparkling wines of Saint-Péray; the still having greater potential on the whole. They are blended from Marsanne and Roussanne, like their white counterparts to the north. A further sparkling wine comes from a little further south-east under the **Clairette de Die AC**, which produces lighter semi-sweet sparkling Muscats. **Crémant de Die** is now the AC for dry sparklers from Clairette. At best they are crisp and fresh. There also some dry white still wines produced under the **Châtillon-en-Diois** appellation, from cool-planted Chardonnay and Aligoté in the same area.

Southern Rhône

While the north meanders down a narrow river valley, giving it its unique viticultural environment, the southern Rhône covers a much greater area, and is extensively planted with vines. The total vineyard area planted in the north is just under 2,700 ha, whereas the total for the whole region is some 75,000 ha and nearly 42,000 ha of that Côtes du Rhône. The climate is altogether warmer in the south and Grenache is the mainstay variety. There can be a significant influence on the region from the cold Mistral wind, which blows down out of the Alps. While it has some influence in the north, it can cause devastation in the south, with not only physical damage to vineyards but stressing of the vines, causing them to shut down. The same Mistral can on occasion help in ripening fruit close to vendange and keeping cellars free of humidity. The most important quality region in the south is **Châteauneuf-du-Pape**. This is a

France

sizeable appellation with some 3,084 ha of vineyards. Quality has soared in recent very good vintages and an increasing number of growers are now bottling their own wine. The main Châteauneuf variety is Grenache, but there are 13 permitted varieties in the red blend, a number of them white. Syrah and Mourvèdre are also very important in lending structure and grip. The Châteauneuf soils are varied with clay, gravel and stone all playing a role. The larger *galets roulés*, the famous round stones that store up heat and reflect it onto the vines at night are not universally found throughout the appellation and many consider the clay to be the key component in controlling moisture supply.

Among current trends an increasing number of growers are making limited production special cuvées from old vines. While some of these are very splendid wines, there is some question as to whether the quality of the regular bottlings suffers as a consequence. The best red Châteauneuf is rich, heady, almost exotic and very ageworthy. The best will easily continue to improve for a decade or more. The white can be good, floral and nutty and there are some more serious structured wines as well, with oak playing a limited role. In general the whites should be drunk young.

To the north and west of Châteauneuf-du-Pape and the ancient Roman town of Orange are the **Côtes du Rhône-Villages** and the separate appellations of **Gigondas** and **Vacqueyras**. The best vineyards of Gigondas are planted on the slopes of the Dentelles de Montmirail, the small range that merges into the hills of the Vaucluse. The wines are dense, massive and brooding. They tend to lack the refinement of the very greatest Châteauneufs, but they can offer not only excellent quality but also value for money. Like Gigondas, Grenache is the most important variety in Vacqueyras, which was awarded its own AC in 1990. The wines are generally lighter than Gigondas and an increasing amount of Syrah is now being used. There are even some varietal wines being produced. The best have an intoxicating combination of ripe dark berry fruit and a marked *garrigue* character. Three further villages have been upgraded to full appellation status. These are **Beaumes de Venise**, **Vinsobres** and **Rasteau**.

There are now 17 villages which can append their names after the Côtes du Rhône-Villages name. Among these are **Cairanne** and **Sablet** to the south and **Valréas** and **Saint-Maurice** further north where, unsurprisingly, the Syrah is planted with greater success. It is the southern villages, though, and particularly Cairanne, which are producing the greatest number of stylish wines. At their best these express vibrant and complex dark fruit and subtle herbal notes. Those wines produced from old vines can be both excellent value and remarkably impressive. Outside these 16 villages there are several thousand hectares of vines producing straight Côtes du Rhône-Villages. A number of very good wines under both this appellation and the humble **Côtes du Rhône** label are now being produced. The latter tend to emphasise their forward fruit, but there are also some very serious and ageworthy wines being produced. Some of the better Rhône-Villages domaines may also have vineyards outside the appellation boundaries, or may chose to label younger-vine *cuvées* as Côtes du Rhône.

There are also two regional specialities, which have their own appellations. **Muscat de Beaumes de Venise** is a floral, grapey fortified Muscat. It is not late harvested and tends to lack the quality found in the Muscat de Rivesaltes wines of the Roussillon. **Rasteau**

Vin Doux Naturel (VDN) is a fortified red *vin doux naturel* produced from Grenache that can develop marked *rancio* notes with cask age. This AC should not be confused with Rasteau, where some of the best modern southern reds are being made.

To the west of Châteauneuf-du-Pape are the appellations of **Lirac** and **Tavel**. The latter is for rosé only, Lirac for both rosé and, of greater importance from a quality point of view, some very good Grenache-based reds planted in the limestone-rich soils. The rosé can often be excessively high in alcohol and dull.

Towards the outer extremities of the Rhône are four other appellations. To the north of the Côtes du Rhône-Villages sector, west and east respectively of the River Rhône, are the **Côtes du Vivarais** and the Côteaux du Tricastin, which since 2010 is known as **Grignan-les-Adhémar**. To the south in the Vaucluse are the vineyards of the **Ventoux**, where encouraging progress is being made by a number of domaines and reds of some substance are being produced. Immediately south again, on the borders of Provence, is the **Lubéron**. The odd exciting red is beginning to emerge and there are some stylish whites as well. To the far east towards the Alpes some good reds and whites are also emerging from the **Côteaux de Pierrevert**.

There are a number of IGP, now known as IGP (Indication Géographique Protégée) classifications. In the northern Rhône the important one is the **IGP des Collines Rhodaniennes**, under which some impressive red and white is produced. Two important southern vins de pays offering wines largely based on Grenache (but also Cabernet Sauvignon in the case of the former) are the **IGP de la Principauté d'Orange** and further south the **IGP de Vaucluse**.

Just to the west of the River Rhône is the emerging region of the **Costières de Nîmes**. Not surprisingly the wine here has more in common with the blends of the southern Rhône than the rest of the Languedoc and for this reason is covered here. Intense, strawberry-scented, Grenache-based reds are being produced by a number of good domaines and increasing use is being made of Mourvèdre. Many of these properties are also making rich, stylish blends of Cabernet Sauvignon and Syrah, generally labelled as **IGP du Gard**.

A-Z of producers by appellation/commune

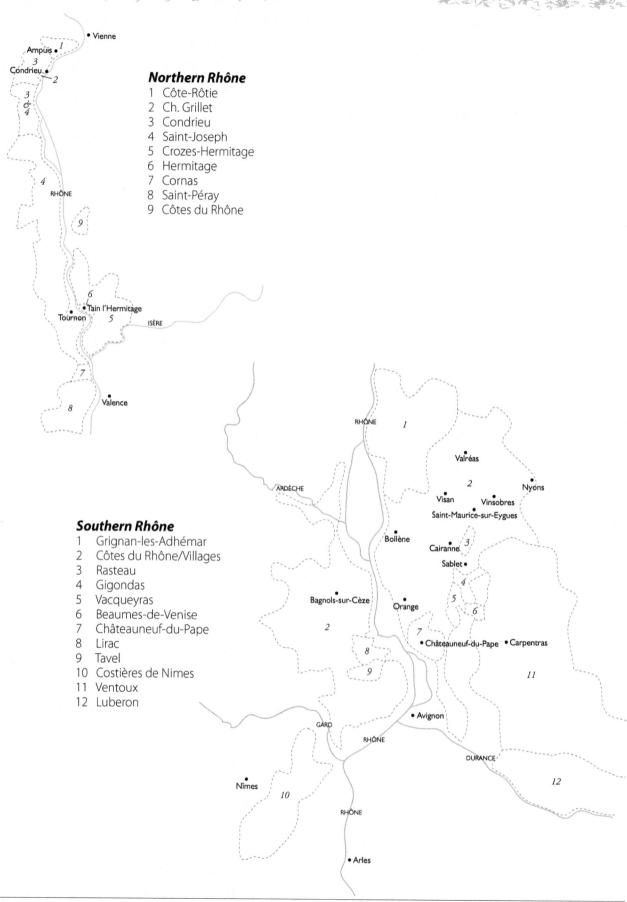

Rhône Valley

France

Northern Rhône
1. Côte-Rôtie
2. Ch. Grillet
3. Condrieu
4. Saint-Joseph
5. Crozes-Hermitage
6. Hermitage
7. Cornas
8. Saint-Péray
9. Côtes du Rhône

Southern Rhône
1. Grignan-les-Adhémar
2. Côtes du Rhône/Villages
3. Rasteau
4. Gigondas
5. Vacqueyras
6. Beaumes-de-Venise
7. Châteauneuf-du-Pape
8. Lirac
9. Tavel
10. Costières de Nîmes
11. Ventoux
12. Luberon

Wine behind the label

Rhône Valley vintages

From 2004 throughout the Rhône Valley there have been some very successful vintages in both the north and south. Over the same period, the lesser Rhône-Villages wines have performed in a similarly impressive manner to those at Châteauneuf-du-Pape. The top wines in top appellations will keep very well, 10 even 20 years in the best examples. The lesser wines from recent years will last comfortably for five years or more.

2015: This was a significant step up on the previous year. In the north there were warm growing conditions through the summer and the diurnal variation was sufficient to ensure acidity in the grapes and balance in the resulting wines. In the south there is real potential but some fruit ripened with less than ideal acidity. It will though likely be a good year for top reds.

2014: This was a challenging vintage throughout the region, north and south. Yields were good but late season and harvest rains, more so in the south, mean this will be a lighter year for early drinking among the reds. There was also a big negative influence from fruit flies in the north, causing growers further problems. The whites look to have a little more promise and the best have decent structure and fresh acidity.

2013: Like many other areas in France the vintage was marked by late flowering due to cold weather in the spring resulting in a low yielding harvest. Careful selection had to be made to ensure that there was sufficient ripeness in the fruit to make palatable wines. All-in-all, what was produced seems to be of good quality thus extending the remarkable run of good vintages in the Rhône Valley.

2012: Did better generally than the rest of France. Not easy growing conditions but everything seems to have fallen nicely into place to produce well-balanced wines at reasonable levels of alcohol. The result is a quantum leap in quality which will go down as one of the best vintages in recent years.

2011: Another fine year throughout the region. There was a very early budbreak and the vintage might have been early and with very ripe wines as a result of a hot August. There was though a balmy long late summer and the harvest was later than expected with well balanced tannins being produced after an even ripening period. The reds are supple and opulent without the nervy character of the 2010s. The whites too are very good with great intensity.

2010: A very good year indeed following on from 2009. The wines are not just marked by an impressive concentration in reds and whites throughout the region but also by a freshness and nervy acidity. Issues during flowering have influenced yields and while the crop was reduced flavour intensity in the fruit benefitted, particularly in the south.

2009: This was a great year in both the north and south of the region. The north had a very hot late summer with low rainfall. However the cold wet winter provided sufficient nourishment for the vines to sustain them and fine well balanced wines have resulted. In the south the warm summer resulted in slightly lower than normal yields but quality is very fine. The wines will perhaps be more structured, fresh and ageworthy than the 2007s.

2008: There were trying growing conditions in both the north and the south. In the north rain in early September was followed by late harvest sunshine and a drying out of the crop from the Mistral. Those who were careful in their selection made some good wine. In the south the run of excellent vinatges came to an end. However the best wines have excellent acidity and good elegant reds were made by many quality concious growers.

2007: This was a decent, if not great year in the north with temperamental growing season weather but a good end to the cycle with sunny conditions at harvest and for those growers who harvested as late as possible the wines are elegant and intense with good concentration. In the south it was yet another fine year and the wines are more opulent and approachable than those from the previous vintage. They are likely to reach full maturity somewhat earlier.

2006: Once again the whole of the Rhône Valley was blessed with excellent growing and ripening conditions. The problems that plagued a number of other regions further north were absent here. The late summer was relatively cool and there was just sufficient rain in early September to nourish the vineyards. In both the north and the south growers were delighted that they achieved excellent phenolic ripeness as well as a healthy yield.

2005: This has turned out to be a very good vintage in both the northern and southern areas. The harvest was low and unlike the sapping heat of 2003 the weather was cooler and the wines will have good natural acidities and in the reds better more refined tannins. The acidity levels also look likely to provide fresher better balanced whites than might have been feared in the drought conditions. Reds look like they will be at least as good as in 2004.

2004: A much easier year for growers in both the north and south of the region. The best reds look like they have good depth with deep colours and form and in the main well ripened tannins. Likely to be of a similar level to 2001 in the north and 1999 in the south.

2003: The super warm summer of resulted in some good wines from this vintage in the north. The key was who had harnessed the ripening of their grape tannins best, a difficult feat. Potentially good in the south, some wines are very alcoholic though and achieving balance with Grenache was the key.

2002: After the previous four bountiful vintages this was a disappointment. There was very heavy rain in the north requiring extreme care and selectivity by growers to achieve any real quality. In the south it was a similar tale of woe with heavy flooding. The top wines are at optimum maturity now.

2001: This was very good throughout the valley, if not quite hitting the heights of 1999 for the northern appellations or 2000 for the south. Nevertheless these are impressive and cellarworthy examples, a smaller than normal yield helping to ensure this. White Hermitage is very ageworthy.

2000: A generally very good year, particularly in the south with good crop levels and some very rich, profound and complex wines being made. The best are ripe, very full and approachable. Not quite the same quality in the north, but good and very ageworthy wines were produced. Côte-Rôtie was the most successful among the reds.

1999: A very good year throughout the north, with well-structured, opulent and heady wines being produced in all the major appellations. Conditions were excellent with a balmy and dry summer and adequate rainfall. The wines are surprisingly forward and approachable but should be long-lived. The south was good to very good but lacked the sheer quality of 1998 and 2000.

1998: The northern appellations fared well, producing very good results. The wines are generally sizeable and and masculine in structure. They have been very good cellaring prospects but without the opulence or elegance of 1999. In the south the vintage was spectacularly good. They were excellent in their relative youth but the best remain good cellaring prospects.

1995: Generally the best year since 1990 for reds with the exception of the magnificent 1991 Côte-Rôties. Whites were somewhat less impressive and will be surprisingly short-lived. They should have been drunk except for the best white Hermitage.

Northern Rhône

France

1991: This was a good to very good year in the northern Rhône and in Côte-Rôtie in particular. There was quite marked variation particularly in Cornas and Hermitage. The south was disappointing and the wines should by now have been drunk.

1990: A superb year for great long-lived Hermitage. These will need more time to achieve their full potential. Côte-Rôtie did not quite match the superb 91s. Cornas and Côte-Rôtie are both drinking well now, as are some of the excellent wines produced at Châteauneuf-du-Pape.

Earlier Years: Very opulent reds were made in 1989. 1988 was a classic year for northern reds. 1985 was good throughout. 1983 produced some excellent long-lived Hermitage. Châteauneuf-du-Pape in 1981 is worth considering from very top producers. A few good 1979s from both north and south are still drinking well. 1978 was a truly great year in the north, with some very fine Châteauneuf also. Other very good earlier years for the north were 1971, 1970, 1969, 1966, 1964 and 1961.

Rhône Valley vintage chart

	Côte-Rôtie	Red Hermitage	White Hermitage	Châteauneuf-du-Pape
2015	NYR	NYR	NYR	NYR
2014	★★★ A	★★★ A	★★★☆ A	★★☆ A
2013	★★★★ A	★★★★ A	★★★★ A	★★★★ A
2012	★★★★★ A	★★★★★ A	★★★★☆ A	★★★★☆ A
2011	★★★★☆ A	★★★★☆ A	★★★★☆ A	★★★★☆ A
2010	★★★★☆ A	★★★★☆ A	★★★★☆ A	★★★★☆ A
2009	★★★★☆ A	★★★★☆ A	★★★★☆ A	★★★★☆ A
2008	★★★☆ A	★★★☆ A	★★★☆ A	★★★☆ B
2007	★★★☆ A	★★★☆ A	★★★☆ A	★★★★☆ B
2006	★★★★☆ B	★★★★☆ B	★★★★☆ B	★★★★☆ B
2005	★★★★☆ B	★★★★☆ B	★★★★☆ B	★★★★☆ B
2004	★★★★ B	★★★★ B	★★★★ B	★★★★ B
2003	★★★☆ B	★★★☆ B	★★★★ B	★★★☆ B
2002	★★ C	★★ C	★★★ C	★★ C
2001	★★★★ B	★★★★ B	★★★★☆ B	★★★★ C
2003	★★★☆ B	★★★☆ B	★★★★ B	★★★☆ B
2002	★★ C	★★ C	★★★ C	★★ C
2001	★★★★ C	★★★★ B	★★★★☆ C	★★★★ C
2000	★★★★☆ C	★★★★ C	★★★★ C	★★★★☆ C
1999	★★★★☆ C	★★★★☆ C	★★★★☆ C	★★★★ D
1998	★★★★ C	★★★★ C	★★★★ C	★★★★★ C
1995	★★★★ D	★★★★ D	★★★☆ D	★★★★ D
1991	★★★★★ C	★★★★ D	★★★★ D	★☆ D
1990	★★★★ D	★★★★★ C	★★★★☆ D	★★★★☆ D
1989	★★★★ D	★★★★☆ D	★★★★ D	★★★★☆ D
1988	★★★★ D	★★★★ D	★★★★☆ D	★★★★ D

A-Z of producers - *Northern Rhône*

✿ Thierry Allemand (Cornas)

Small Cornas domaine producing two rich, sturdy and powerful Syrah wines. Total production is tiny but the quality is exceptional and among the best in the appellation. Vinification is traditional with a long *cuvaison* at high temperatures to extract both flavour and supple, well-rounded tannins. New wood is avoided here and the resulting wines are impressive, concentrated and very elegant. They are both bottled unfiltered. Reynard, made from vines that are over 80 years old, is very ageworthy and will continue to improve for up to a decade, sometimes longer in the best years. (DM)

Recommended Reds:
Cornas Reynard ★★★★★ £G
Cornas Chaillot ★★★★☆ £F

Dom. Balthazar (Cornas)

Franck Balthazar produces traditionally vinified and aged Cornas that is generally very good. He took over from his father in 2002 and since then added half a hectare giving him 2 ha of between 50 and nearly 100 years of age. Recent vintages are all ripe and structured, with the depth and complexity of dark berry fruit that can only be coaxed from a vineyard planted with very old vines. Aged in large old wood the wine is nevertheless surprisingly ripe, forward and approachable with just 4 or 5 years' ageing. Like many producers in this village Balthazar offers very good value. (DM)

Recommended Reds:
Cornas ★★★★ £E

Gilles Barge (Côte-Rôtie) www.domainebarge.com

Gilles Barge took over from his father Pierre in the mid-1990s and is now producing three excellent examples of Côte-Rôtie, if not in the absolute top flight. He has not only reduced yields from his holdings of around 7ha but has refined the approach in the cellar as well. The wines are still vinified with stems but the tannins are riper and suppler. They are characterised by elegance and finesse rather than by raw power and are bottled unfiltered. The Cuvée du Plessy is the lightest, Le Colombard a touch more structured with the Côte Brune showing both depth and complexity. All three are impressively ageworthy and will improve in bottle for 7–10 years. The red Saint-Joseph is spicy, berry-fruited and approachable, while you should enjoy the peachy Condrieu and Saint-Joseph whites young. (DM)

Recommended Reds:
Côte-Rôtie Côte-Brune ★★★★ £F
Côte-Rôtie Le Colombard ★★★☆ £F
Côte-Rôtie Cuvée du Plessy ★★★ £E
Saint-Joseph Clos des Martinets ★★★ £D

Recommended Whites:
Condrieu La Solarie ★★★ £F

Dom. Belle (Hermitage) www.domainebelle.com

This young domaine which has been producing good red and white for upwards of a decade. Total vineyard holdings are now close to 19 ha, almost all in Crozes-Hermitage. Reds are made traditionally and de-stemming is avoided. Good, structured, ageworthy wines result in the best years and the key is to get the stems as well as the fruit fully ripe at harvest. The whites are partly aged in oak and the Hermitage is fat and toasty with real depth and concentration. The top wines will be all the better for 5 or 6 years' cellaring. (DM)

Recommended Reds:
Hermitage ★★★☆ £F
Crozes-Hermitage Cuvée Louis Belle ★★★ £D
Crozes-Hermitage Les Pierelles ★★☆ £C

Recommended Whites:
Hermitage ★★★☆ £E
Crozes-Hermitage Les Terres Blanches ★★ £C

✿ Dom. Bonnefond (Côte-Rôtie)

From their small holding of 6 ha, the Bonnefond brothers produce

very good Condrieu and – in their top bottling, Les Rochains – one of the finest of all Côte-Rôties. The style of the reds is modern, with destemming and new oak in the top cuvée, and a really elegant spicy, mineral character shows through in all the wines. The Colline de Couzou is a little lighter than the Côte Rozier and Les Rochains but is nonetheless ripe and well-structured. Côte Rozier, with 10% Viognier has a characteristic floral undercurrent but with depth and real dimension. Les Rochains is rich, opulent and firmly structured, needing 2–3 years longer in bottle than the other reds, and should not be broached without 5 or 6 years' ageing. Condrieu is opulent, peachy and immediately accessible. (DM)

Recommended Reds:
Côte-Rôtie Les Rochains ★★★★★ £F
Côte-Rôtie Côte Rozier ★★★★☆ £F
Côte-Rôtie Colline du Couzou ★★★☆ £E
Recommended Whites:
Condrieu ★★★☆ £F

Dom. de Bonserine (Côte-Rôtie) *www.domainedebonserine.com*
This is a large property for the appellation, which has been developed with considerable outside investment and is now owned by GUIGAL. It is also the second-largest vineyard owner after its parent with a total of just under 10ha of Syrah (97%) and Viognier (3%) spread across 17 different parcels. Vinification is modern and the fruit is all destemmed before ageing in barrel. The regular cuvée, La Sarrasine, has 5% Viognier blended in whereas the two top wines, La Viallière and La Garde, are both 100% Syrah and are aged in new oak for 24 months, which tends to show through when the wine is very young. These are impressive, modern and opulent examples of the appellation which should be aged for 5, even as much as 7, years. A Condrieu is also made. (DM)

Recommended Reds:
Côte-Rôtie La Garde ★★★★ £F
Côte-Rôtie Les Moutonnes La Viallière ★★★☆ £F
Côte-Rôtie La Sarrasine ★★★☆ £E

❀ Bernard Burgaud (Côte-Rôtie)
Just one wine is produced here but it is among the better examples in the appellation. It is made from a number of different sites that are always vinified separately to maximise the wine's complexity. Bernard Burgaud maintains strict control of yields, and a portion of the harvest is regularly sold off after careful sorting. Finally a saignée of up to 20% of the juice prior to fermentation results in a wine that is both concentrated and full of character, and which benefits from 4–5 years' ageing. It always offers good value. (DM)

Recommended Reds:
Côte-Rôtie ★★★★★ £F

Dom. de Champal (Saint-Joseph) *www.domaine-champal.com*
Eric Rocher has 26ha of vines planted, mainly red grapes in Saint-Joseph and Crozes-Hermitage as well as white varieties, mostly Viognier in Condrieu along with a little Roussanne and Marsanne. He produces a IGP Viognier as well as a decent Condrieu but it is the reds that offer the greatest interest and value. The Crozes-Hermitage, from the northern stretches of the appellation, is marked by firm tannin and fresh acidity and delivers more poise and balance than many. The Terroir de Champal is now emerging as one of the best Saint-Joseph reds, with great purity of fruit and just a hint of new oak. It has been onthe cusp of ★★★★, in recent vintages, and will develop very well over six or seven years. (DM)

Recommended Reds:
Saint-Joseph Terroir de Champal ★★★☆ £D
Crozes-Hermitage Chaubayou ★★★ £C
Recommended Whites:
Condrieu La Coste ★★★ £E
Saint-Joseph Mayanne ★★★ £D

❀❀ M. Chapoutier (Hermitage) *www.chapoutier.com*
One of the most important négociants in the northern Rhône, with the largest vineyard holding on the great Hermitage hill. Interests are not restricted to the Rhône and include Domaine TOURNON in Victoria, a project in Alsace, Schieferkopf and a couple of Touriga based reds are made in Portugal. Fine, rich Banyuls, and a Rivesaltes come from the Roussillon. Côtes du Roussillon is also the source of new reds and a white from Domaine de Bila Haut as the Chapoutiers were not slow to realise the potential of the Agly Valley. Three further wines have been added, L'Esquerda, Agly Brothers and the pricey V.I.T. Amidst the vast array of Rhône labels the top wines are superbly crafted examples of their appellations. New benchmarks have been set in both Crozes-Hermitage – with the dense, muscular and very concentrated Les Varonniers – and Saint-Joseph, with both red and white Les Granits. These are not cheap but have established new standards that others are following. Côte-Rôtie La Mordorée is a magnificent example of the appellation; even though not quite of the order of the three GUIGAL super-cuvées it is still very impressive. Hermitage red and white now comes in a number of guises. Pavillon and L'Ermite are perhaps the finest among the reds and the former is the weightiest and most powerful with a fourth label, Les Greffieux now added. Of the whites Cuvée de l'Orée is now joined by Le Méal and L'Ermite. There is no doubting the supreme quality at this level. The wines are remarkably plush, even when relatively young, and very different to a Jean-Louis CHAVE Hermitage. The regular Hermitage Monier de la Sizeranne and Chante Alouette white pale a little in comparison, but at least won't break the bank. In the south, Châteauneuf-du-Pape is good to very good and Barbe Rac is 100% Grenache. New is the Côteaux du Tricastin Château des Estubiers,with a very good red example of that appellation as well as a rosé. At a lower level the wines from lesser appellations can be a touch disappointing. The generic Côtes du Rhône Belleruche labels are relatively light. The top Hermitage and Crozes-Hermitage wines are labelled with the traditional spelling, Ermitage. (DM)

Northern Rhône
Recommended Reds:
Côte-Rôtie La Mordorée ✪✪✪✪✪ £H
Côte-Rôtie Les Bécasses ★★★☆ £F
Hermitage 'Ermitage' Le Meal ✪✪✪✪✪ £H
Hermitage 'Ermitage' L'Ermite ✪✪✪✪✪ £H
Hermitage 'Ermitage' Le Pavillon ✪✪✪✪✪ £H
Hermitage Monier de la Sizeranne ★★★★ £F
Saint-Joseph Les Granits ★★★★ £F
Saint-Joseph Deschants ★★☆ £C
Crozes-Hermitage 'Crozes-Ermitage' Les Varonniers ★★★★ £F
Crozes-Hermitage Les Meysonniers ★★★ £C
Crozes-Hermitage La Petite-Ruche ★★☆ £C
Cornas Les Arènes ★★★☆ £E
Recommended Whites:
Condrieu Invitare ★★★☆ £E
Hermitage Vin de Paille ✪✪✪✪✪ £H
Hermitage Le Meal ✪✪✪✪✪ £H
Hermitage Cuvée de l'Orée ✪✪✪✪✪ £H

Wine behind the label

Northern Rhône

France

Hermitage Chante Alouette ★★★★ £F
Saint-Joseph Les Granits ★★★★ £F
Saint-Joseph Deschants ★★ £D
Crozes-Hermitage Les Meysonniers ★★ £C
Crozes-Hermitage La Petite-Ruche ★☆ £C

Southern Rhône
Recommended Reds:
Châteauneuf-du-Pâpe Barbe Rac ★★★★★ £H
Châteauneuf-du-Pâpe Croix de Bois ★★★★☆ £G
Châteauneuf-du-Pâpe La Bernadine ★★★☆ £E
Côteaux du Tricastin Ch. des Estubiers ★★ £B
Rasteau ★★ £C
Côtes-du-Rhône Villages Signargues ★☆ £B
Recommended Whites:
Châteauneuf-du-Pâpe La Bernadine ★★★ £E
Muscat de Beaumes-de-Venise ★★ £C

Roussillon
Recommended Reds:
Banyuls Terra Vinya ★★★★ £E
Banyuls ★★★ £D
Côtes du Roussillon-Villages
Dom. de Bila-Haut Occultum Lapidem ★★★☆ £D
Côtes du Roussillon-Villages
Dom. de Bila-Haut Les Vignes de Bila-Haut ★★☆ £B

❀❀ Ch. d'Ampuis (Côte-Rôtie) www.guigal.com
Guigal is rightly famed for the resurrection of the wines of Côte-Rôtie during the 1970s and 80s. His top three red cuvees from the AC, La Mouline, La Landonne and La Turque, are now sold under the Château d'Ampuis rather than E. GUIGAL label. Super-rich, very extracted and with loads of new oak, they are produced in very limited quantities and not surprisingly sell for stratospheric prices. However, their balance and extraordinary finesse is more important still. All three are truly profound wines with that extra dimension and depth found in only a handful of truly great wines. Perhaps La Turque is the finest. The vinification of each is quite unique. The Côte-Rôtie Château d'Ampuis and Condrieu La Doriane are very good but not of the same order. Very pricy red and white Hermitage, labelled Ex-Voto, are also now offered both at a similar level to the top Côte-Rôtie wines. In 2001 Marcel Guigal purchased the domaine and vineyards of Jean-Louis Grippat, embellishing his estate with top-class sites in both Saint-Joseph and Hermitage. These wines are now labelled Lieu-Dit Saint Joseph and are released under the d'Ampuis label. The Vignes de l'Hospice red remains particularly striking under the Guigal ownership. (DM)
Recommended Reds:
Côte-Rôtie La Turque ✪✪✪✪✪ £H
Côte-Rôtie La Landonne ✪✪✪✪✪ £H
Côte-Rôtie La Mouline ✪✪✪✪✪ £H
Côte-Rôtie Ch. d'Ampuis ★★★★★ £H
Saint-Joseph Vignes de L'Hospice ★★★★ £F
Saint-Joseph Lieu-dit Saint-Joseph ★★★☆ £E
Recommended Whites:
Condrieu La Doriane ★★★★★ £G
Saint-Joseph Lieu-dit Saint-Joseph ★★★☆ £E

Ch. Grillet (Château Grillet) www.chateau-grillet.com
This is in fact a tiny appellation as well as a single estate and one of the smallest in France at around 3 ha. Like Condrieu the wine is produced solely from Viognier and has always been vinified in barrel on its lees. Unlike many Viogniers, at its best this wine can be aged.

After a period in the doldrums the quality at Grillet has improved significantly. There is still a little way to go before the wine offers the same quality and dimension of the best examples in Condrieu. To further aid the *grand vin* a selection is also released as a Côtes du Rhône, Pontcin. (DM)
Recommended Whites:
Château Grillet ★★★★ £F

❀❀ Dom. Jean-Louis Chave (Hermitage)
Utterly splendid ancient domaine, perhaps the finest in the northern Rhône and among the best in France. The Chave family own plots in all 7 lieux-dits on the Hermitage hill, which contributes to the marvellous complexity and finesse of their wines. Any of the components felt to be below standard will be sold off in order to protect the integrity of the wine. In this respect Jean Louis Chave has also established a small merchant label "Selection Jean-Louis Chave" producing Côtes du Rhône 'Mon Couer', as well as red Hermitage 'Farconnet' and white Hermitage 'Blanche'. These will give you a very good idea of what the Domaine wines offer at a much lower price. Cuvée Cathelin is a special red selection which sees more new wood and is produced only in top years. Both red and white Domaine Hermitage are extraordinarily ageworthy and are not wines to approach in their youth. Also produced are a very good Saint-Joseph and an extraordinary vin de paille, the latter only in tiny quantities. (DM)
Recommended Reds:
Hermitage Ermitage Cuvée Cathelin ✪✪✪✪✪ £H
Hermitage ✪✪✪✪✪ £H
Saint-Joseph ★★★☆ £E
Recommended Whites:
Hermitage ✪✪✪✪ £H

Dom. Yann Chave (Crozes-Hermitage) www.yannchave.com
Fine, improving small domaine with around 19 ha (18 ha in Crozes-Hermitage) of Syrah and a tiny amount of Marsanne and Roussanne producing increasingly impressive supple and structured red wines. Vinification is modern and more new wood is being used both for red and white. These are now wines of finesse and depth and the top reds need cellaring. The red Crozes-Hermitage Le Rouvre and Hermitage will improve in bottle for up to 10 years, the latter for even longer in great years. (DM)
Recommended Reds:
Hermitage ★★★★ £F
Crozes-Hermitage Le Rouvre ★★★☆ £D
Crozes-Hermitage ★★☆ £C
Recommended Whites:
Crozes-Hermitage ★★☆ £C

Dom. du Chêne (St-Joseph) www.domaineduchenerouviere.com
Marc Rouvière makes small but impressive quantities of both red and white Saint-Joseph, as well as a striking and intensely peachy, honeyed Condrieu. Medium- rather than full-bodied, with a fine lightly mineral structure, this will drink well over 3–4 years. A late harvest Condrieu, Julien is also made. In addition to the regular Saint-Joseph bottlings – a good fruit-driven white produced from Marsanne and a medium-weight, spicy, strawberry-scented red – there is a much deeper special Cuvée Anais. Firm and structured in its youth, with rich, dark berry fruit and spicy oak, it should be aged for 3 or 4 years to show at its best. (DM)
Recommended Reds:
Saint Joseph Anais ★★★☆ £E

Saint Joseph ★★☆ £C
Recommended Whites:
Condrieu Volan ★★★★ £E
Saint Joseph ★★☆ £C

Dom. Louis Chèze (Condrieu) *www.domainecheze.com*

Louis Chèze has gradually built up a small domaine of some 37 ha, with the largest plots planted to Syrah in Saint-Joseph. His holding of Viognier in Condrieu is mainly young vines but the wines are stylish and well-crafted with good, nicely integrated oak. The Coteau de Brèze in particular is very fine with rich, peachy, opulent fruit. The white Saint-Joseph emphasises Marsanne's broad, nutty character. Côte-Rôtie is also now made, Belle Demoiselle and four characterful IGP "Les Vignobles de Seyssuel", two reds, a white and a rosé. The top reds are supple and sufficiently structured to provide excellent drinking with a few years' cellaring. (DM)
Recommended Reds:
Saint-Joseph Cuvée des Anges ★★★☆ £E
Saint-Joseph Caroline ★★★ £D
Saint-Joseph Ro-Rée ★★☆ £D
Recommended Whites:
Condrieu Coteau de Brèze ★★★★ £F
Condrieu Pagus Luminis ★★★ £E
Saint-Joseph Ro-Rée ★★☆ £D

❀ Auguste Clape (Cornas)

Pierre-Marie now makes the wine at this domaine, an established leader in the appellation. The winemaking is fiercely traditional and no new wood is used whatsoever. However, any stems retained during vinification are always fully ripened and the the wines are supple with harmonious tannin and fruit, balanced and very refined. Vines that date from the 1890s contribute to the impressive quality. Cuvée Renaissance is a second wine, although made to help maintain the quality of the Cornas, it is very impressive also. Inevitably from younger vines, it lacks the weight and power of the *grand vin*. Both the spicy Côtes du Rhône red and Saint-Péray offer good value and there is also a IGP Syrah, Le Vin des Amis. (DM)
Recommended Reds:
Cornas ✪✪✪✪✪ £F
Cornas Cuvée Renaissance ★★★★☆ £F
Côtes du Rhône ★★★ £C
Recommended Whites:
Saint-Péray ★★★ £C

❀ Clusel-Roch (Côte-Rôtie) *www.domaine-clusel-roch.fr*

Among the leading handful of small domaines in Côte-Rôtie, this tiny operation possesses just 8ha of Syrah, Viognier and now Gamay from which three wines, two reds and a rosé are made in the AOC Côteaux du Lyonnais. The top Côte-Rôties are powerful and structured for the long haul, particularly Les Grandes Places, made from old vines and occasionally ✪✪✪✪✪. There is also a Classique and a small amount of La Viallière as well as a young vine La Petite Feuille. The Condrieu is good, with attractive peachy Viognier fruit, but lacks the intensity and depth of the reds. (DM)
Recommended Reds:
Côte-Rôtie Les Grandes Places ★★★★★ £G
Côte-Rôtie ★★★★ £F
Recommended Whites:
Condrieu ★★★☆ £F

Dom. du Colombier (Hermitage)

Another small, improving northern Rhône domaine. The Viale family own just over 15ha of vineyards, some with very old vines on the Hermitage hill. They produce a small range including a cool-fermented white Crozes-Hermitage, vinified with a touch of oak, a white Hermitage and 3 stylish, complex reds. The Crozes-Hermitage Cuvée Gaby and in particular the Hermitage are powerful, structured reds that benefit from 5 or 6 years' cellaring. The Hermitage keeps extremely well. (DM)
Recommended Reds:
Hermitage ★★★★ £G
Crozes-Hermitage Cuvée Gaby ★★★☆ £E
Crozes-Hermitage ★★★ £D
Recommended Whites:
Crozes-Hermitage ★★☆ £C

❀ Jean-Luc Colombo (Cornas) *www.vinscolombo.fr*

This operation was originally marketed under three labels. However every wine is now released under the Jean-Luc Colombo brand. Wines are produced from vineyards in and around Cornas and Saint-Péray, and from further afield for an extensive range of négociant wines. The vast majority of the range comes from Rhône Valley sources with a Muscat and a Rivesaltes coming from the Roussillon as well as good fruit driven IGP d'Oc Syrah and Viognier. Reds and rosés are also now produced from vineyards in Provence's Côteaux d'Aix-en-Provence. The rosé Les Pins Couchés is IGP, the red and white are both produced under the Côteaux d'Aix-en-Provence appellation. Of the extensive range of Rhône négociant wines, which range from sound to very good. Top Cornas cuvées Les Ruchets and La Louvée are most impressive and a further super premium example Le Vallon de l'Aigle is also offered. Aged in new oak, the wines are always well-balanced and are some of the best in the appellation. (DM)
Recommended Reds:
Cornas La Louvée ★★★★☆ £G
Cornas Les Ruchets ★★★★☆ £G
Cornas Terres Brûlées ★★★☆ £F
Hermitage Le Rouet ★★★☆ £F
Côte Rôtie La Divine ★★★☆ £F
Saint-Joseph Les Lauves ★★★ £E
Saint-Joseph Le Prieuré ★★☆ £D
Crozes-Hermitage Les Fées Brunes ★★☆ £D
Crozes-Hermitage La Tuilière ★★ £C
Châteauneuf-du-Pape Les Bartavelles ★★★★ £F
Vinsobres Au pied de la terre ★★☆ £C
Côtes du Rhône Les Forots Syrah ★★ £C
Côtes du Rhône Abeilles ★★ £B
IGP des Collines Rhodaniennes Collines de Laure Syrah ★☆ £B
IGP d'Oc Syrah La Violette ★★ £B
Recommended Whites:
Hermitage Le Louet ★★★☆ £F
Condrieu Amour de Dieu ★★★ £F
Muscat de Rivesaltes Les Saintes ★★★ £D
IGP d'Oc Viognier La Violette ★☆ £B
Recommended Rosés:
IGP de la Méditerranée Les Pins Couchées ★☆ £B

Dom. Combier (Crozes-Hermitage) *www.domaine-combier.com*

Good stylish and concentrated wines are made at this domaine. The regular red and white wines are well crafted and see some new

France

wood during maturation. There is also now a second tier Cuvée Laurent Combier label for both red and white Crozes. The Clos des Grives are altogether more serious and amongst the best in the appellation. The red, which is macerated for around 30 days on skins, is dense and muscular, with refined fruit and supple, balanced tannins. The wine is aged in new oak and requires a little patience before it is ready. The white is mainly Roussanne, barrel-fermented and kept on lees with *bâtonnage*. Marsanne dominates the other whites. Both the top two reds will develop well in the medium term. The Combier family are also involved in the TRIO INFERNAL project in Spain's Priorat region. (DM)

Recommended Reds:
Crozes-Hermitage Clos des Grives ★★★☆ £E
Crozes-Hermitage Laurent Combier ★★★ £D
Crozes-Hermitage ★★☆ £C
Saint-Joseph ★★★ £D

Recommended Whites:
Crozes-Hermitage Clos des Grives ★★★ £E
Crozes-Hermitage Laurent Combier ★★☆ £D
Crozes-Hermitage ★★ £C

✿ **Dom. de Coulet (Cornas)** *www.domaineducoulet.com*
This Domaine was established in 1998, with 10.1 ha in Cornas and a further 3 ha classified as Côtes du Rhône. Mathieu Baret's vineyards are biodynamic with cover crops grown. He uses no pumps in the winery and an absolute minimum of sulphur dioxide. Output at present is just over 2,000 cases a year. As well as the Cornas reds, three Côtes du Rhônes are made in small quantities as well as a Crozes Hermitage from the 2011 vintage. The Côtes du Rhône Carignache is a blend of roughly two-thirds Carignan and the balance from Grenache. The Côtes du Rhône Petit Ours Brun and No Man's Land are both 100% Syrah, the latter from plots between the Saint Joseph and Cornas appellations. The vines are over 40 years old planted on clay-calcareous and silty soils and the yield tiny at less than 10 hl/ha. Four Cornas reds are produced from vines planted in a mix of granite, silt and clay and with the exception of the more approachable Brise Cailloux which comes from younger vines and lower lying old vines, they will benefit from at least 5 years' ageing. Les Terrasses du Serre is a touch softer and more accessible than the top wine Billes Noires which is just that bit deeper and more structured, made with fruit from higher-altitude vineyards and from vines with an average of 55 years of age. It is a wine of tremendous potential. A fourth label, Gore, is bottled solely in magnums. The wines are all bottled unfined and unfiltered. (DM)

Recommended Reds:
Cornas Les Billes Noires ★★★★☆ £G
Cornas Les Terrasses du Serre ★★★★ £F

Dom. Courbis (Saint-Joseph) *www.vins-courbis-Rhône.com*
The bulk of this estate's 33 ha is in Saint-Joseph, with 5 ha planted to white varieties. The average vine age is fairly young. This is to some extent illustrated in the wines, which as yet do not have quite the density or complexity of the best in the appellation. The Cornas bottlings, though, are of a different order. Les Eygats and La Sabarotte are wines of dense muscular power. The latter comes from old vine plantings and is very ageworthy. It is close to ★★★★★ in top years. Both top Cornas will improve for up to a decade with ease. A fresh, approachable IGP Syrah is also made. (DM)

Recommended Reds:
Cornas La Sabarotte ★★★★☆ £F
Cornas Les Eygats ★★★★ £E

Cornas Champelrose ★★★☆ £E
Saint-Joseph Domaine Les Royes ★★★ £D
Saint-Joseph ★★☆ £C

Recommended Whites:
Saint-Joseph ★★ £C

Dom. Pierre Coursodon (Saint-Joseph)
During the early to mid-1990s the Coursodon wines were sound enough but often possessed a raw, harsh undercurrent. Destemming was not practised and old *foudres* were the order of the day. Jérôme Coursodon has now taken over the winemaking and the results currently have been impressive, particularly with the top red cuvées. The wines have concentrated dark fruit but are more refined and better balanced than of old. The very fine bottling of La Sensonne is produced in association with Patrick LESEC. (DM)

Recommended Reds:
Saint-Joseph La Sensonne ★★★★☆ £F
Saint-Joseph Le Paradis St-Pierre ★★★★ £F
Saint-Joseph L'Olivaie ★★★☆ £E
Saint-Joseph Silice ★★★ £D

Recommended Whites:
Saint-Joseph Le Paradis St-Pierre ★★★ £E
Saint-Joseph Silice ★★☆ £D

✿ **Yves Cuilleron (Condrieu)** *www.cuilleron.com*
One of the superstars of the northern Rhône, Cuilleron has established his reputation on some superb Condrieu made in a number of guises including Les Ayguets, a very intense and distinctive botrytised example that spends 8 months in wood and Les Chaillets from old vines. There are two further cuvées; Vertige is from a single parcel and La Petite Côte is sourced from all the domains parcels. The wines are barrel-fermented and aged on lees. He also produces a small range of first-class Saint-Joseph, both red and white. The whites are barrel-fermented and aged and the reds macerated for 3–4 weeks and aged in oak. He is also working with François VILLARD and Pierre GAILLARD in the small-scale négociant venture, Les VINS DE VIENNE. An additional Côte-Rôtie, Madinière and a small range of Vins de Pays and Vins de France are the latest additions and among these is a striking new Syrah, Ripa Sinistra from the Côteaux de Seyssuel. The wines offer generally good value. (DM)

Recommended Reds:
Côte-Rôtie Terres Sombres ★★★★★ £G
Côte-Rôtie Coteau de Bassenon ★★★★☆ £F
Saint-Joseph Les Serines ★★★★ £F
Saint-Joseph L'Amarybelle ★★★☆ £E
Saint-Joseph Les Pierres Sèches ★★★ £E
Vin de France Syrah Signé ★★★ £D
Vin de France Syrah Les Candives ★★☆ £C

Recommended Whites:
Condrieu Les Ayguets ✪✪✪✪✪ £G
Condrieu Vertige ★★★★★ £F
Condrieu Les Chaillets Vieilles Vignes ★★★★★ £F
Condrieu La Petite Côte ★★★★ £F
Saint-Joseph Le Lombard ★★★☆ £E
Saint-Joseph Côteaux Saint-Pierre ★★★ £E
Saint-Joseph Lyseras ★★★ £E
IGP Marsanne Les Vignes d'à Côté ★★☆ £C

✿ **Delas Frères (Hermitage)** *www.delas.com*
Once one of the northern Rhône's under-performers, Delas is

Wine behind the label

now a serious player among the top Rhône négociants. While the extensive spread of wines from the northern appellations is particularly impressive, the south of the regions is also well represented. The range is comprehensive and even the humbler wines are now sound and well-crafted. Far better fruit quality and well-handled new oak in the better wines are just two of the keys here to the transformation in fortune and quality. Star turns are the top cuvées, which are densely textured and explosively rich and concentrated. The outstanding Hermitage Les Bessards and Côte-Rôtie La Landonne are remarkably ageworthy propositions now, demanding at least 6–7 years' cellaring. The other top reds and white Hermitage also deserve cellaring. (DM)

Northern Rhône
Recommended Reds:
Côte-Rôtie La Landonne ★★★★★ £G
Côte-Rôtie Seigneur de Maugiron ★★★★ £F
Hermitage Les Bessards ✪✪✪✪ £H
Hermitage Domaine des Tourettes ★★★★☆ £F
Saint-Joseph Sainte-Épine ★★★☆ £E
Saint-Joseph François de Tournon ★★★☆ £E
Saint-Joseph Les Challeys ★★★ £D
Crozes-Hermitage Le Clos ★★★★ £F
Domaine des Grands Chemins ★★★ £D
Crozes-Hermitage Les Launes ★★ £C
Cornas Chante Perdrix ★★★ £F

Recommended Whites:
Condrieu Clos Boucher ★★★★☆ £F
Condrieu Galopine ★★★★ £F
Hermitage Domaine des Tourettes ★★★★ £F
Saint-Joseph Les Challeys ★★★ £D
Crozes-Hermitage Les Launes ★★ £C

Southern Rhône
Recommended Reds:
Châteauneuf-du-Pâpe ★★★ £D
Gigondas ★★★ £D
Vacqueyras Domaine des Genêts ★★ £C
Côtes du Ventoux ★☆ £B
Côtes du Rhône Saint-Esprit ★☆ £B
Recommended Whites:
Côtes du Rhône Saint-Esprit ★☆ £B

Dom. Duclaux (Côte-Rôtie) *www.coterotie-duclaux.com*
This fine small domaine of just 5.5 ha now produces two examples of the appellation. The property was founded in 1928 and has remained in the family since. The vineyards, all planted by mass-selection, are found in the southern sector of the appellation where a combination of a steep south to south-eastern exposition and granite soils provide a dense and finely structured red, La Germine with impressive dark, spicy berry fruit and a piercing mineral undercurrent. The supple, roundly textured character of the wine is aided by full de-stemming a lengthy vatting of three to four weeks and up to 24 months in oak. The blend includes around 5% of Viognier. Ageing from five to seven years will no doubt add greater complexity. The second wine, Maison Rouge comes from Syrah the vines being around 50 years old. (DM)
Recommended Reds:
Côte-Rôtie La Germine ★★★★ £F

Dom. Dumazet (Condrieu)
Somewhat controversial among Condrieu producers, Domaine Dumazet produces wines which are rich, dense and full of classic

Viognier dried peaches, spices and minerals. Don't expect modern squeaky-clean fruit-driven wines here. The IGP offers a similar style at a lower level than the Condrieus. Old-fashioned and quite heavily oaked, the Condrieus are at times almost rustic. However they are also characterful, powerful and structured. This is an excellent source of traditional wines from the appellation. (DM)
Recommended Whites:
Condrieu Côte de Fournet ★★★★☆ £F
Condrieu Rouelle Midi ★★★★ £F
IGP Viognier ★★☆ £D

Eric & Joël Durand (Cornas)
Just five reds are made here from a small holding of some 12ha. They are traditionally vinified and are bottled unfiltered. Ageing at present is in older barrels and, while the wines are dense and impressively concentrated, they are not quite in the first division. However, the vineyard is still relatively young and the best has probably yet to emerge. The wines are firmly structured and will age well for a number of years. An additional Cornas, Confidence and a Saint-Joseph, Lautaret have been added to the small range. The Cornas bottlings require 4–5 years at a minimum. (DM)
Recommended Reds:
Cornas Empreintes ★★★☆ £E
Cornas Prémices ★★★ £E
Saint-Joseph Les Côteaux ★★★ £D

Dom. des Entrefaux (Crozes-Hermitage)
The Tardys are now very well established in the appellation and make an exemplary range of both red and white wines. They possess a total of 22 ha of Syrah and a further 6 ha of white varieties, mainly Marsanne with a little Roussanne. Both the regular red and white are sound. The white is vinified solely in *inox* to emphasise its fruit while the red is aged in *cuve* and used small wood. Under the Coteau des Pends label the white is a blend of Marsanne and Roussanne (which adds a floral fragrance) vinified in small oak, while the red, which also sees some oak during ageing, is rich and reasonably concentrated with good varietal fruit and a hint of oak spice. The Cuvée des Machonnières is sourced from a selection of *terroirs* characterised by their *argilo-calcaire* soils and, while certainly oaky, this has great fruit substance and class. By contrast the Cuvée des Champs Fournée, from a single parcel of vines, is marked by its fruit but also an impressive purity and depth. (DM)
Recommended Reds:
Crozes-Hermitage La Cuvée des Champs Fournée ★★★ £D
Crozes-Hermitage La Cuvée des Machonnières ★★★ £C
Crozes-Hermitage Coteau des Pends ★★☆ £C
Crozes-Hermitage ★★ £C
Recommended Whites:
Crozes-Hermitage Coteau des Pends ★★ £C
Crozes-Hermitage ★☆ £C

Bernard Faurie (Hermitage)
Producer of old-style Hermitage and Saint-Joseph from a tiny holding of just 3.5 ha of vines. The wines are at their best in great years, when they are both ripe and powerful. In lesser vintages the odd green note can creep in. The Hermitage Bessard/Méal packs a real punch of complex old-vine fruit. They demand cellaring for 10 years or more. (DM)
Recommended Reds:
Hermitage Le Bessard/Méal ★★★★ £F
Hermitage ★★★★ £F

Northern Rhône

France

Saint-Joseph Cuvée Vieilles-Vignes ★★★☆ £E
Saint-Joseph ★★☆ £D
Recommended Whites:
Hermitage ★★★☆ £F

Philippe Faury (Condrieu) *www.domaine-faury.fr*
Philippe Faury farms 17 ha across three appellations producing increasingly impressive reds and whites. The Saint-Joseph white offers a subtle nutty Marsanne character, while both the Condrieu bottlings understandably offer quite a bit more. The Viognier fruit in both is not overstated with an underlying mineral component clearly evident with both wines aged on lees for just under a year. La Berne has a richer, fuller texture, coming from older vines and has a touch more new oak. Among the striking reds the regular Saint-Joseph is dark, spicy and berry laden, the old vine La Gloriette clearly more intense and firmly structured. Give it three or four years in your cellar. The wine is aged in a combination of larger *demi-muids* and smaller oak, a small portion of which is new. The Côte-Rôtie has a high proportion (10%) of Viognier adding a classic spicy edge to the wine. One-third new oak is very well integrated and the wine will gain further intensity with five or six years age. (DM)
Recommended Reds:
Côte-Rôtie Réviniscence ★★★★ £F
Saint-Joseph Vieilles-Vignes La Gloriette ★★★☆ £E
Saint-Joseph Hedonism ★★★ £D
Recommended Whites:
Condrieu La Berne ★★★★ £F   Condrieu ★★★☆ £E
Saint-Joseph ★★☆ £C

Dom. Fauterie (Cornas)
This is a recently established domaine but assuredly traditional in its approach to viticulture. Sylvain Bernard trained with Jean-Louis CHAVE before establishing his own small holding of vineyards in Saint-Peray, Saint-Joseph and now of most interest in Cornas. The vines in the latter, which are leased, are around 100 years old. They are grown in ideal sandy, granite soils with an exceptional and very sunny mesoclimate. The result is a wine with considerable depth, complexity and some power. It will be all the better for 5 years' ageing. Top recent vintages are particularly impressive. (DM)
Recommended Reds:
Cornas ★★★★ £E
Saint-Joseph Les Combaud ★★★☆ £E
Saint-Joseph ★★★ £D
Recommended Whites:
Saint-Péray Les Hauts de Fauterie ★★☆ £D

✿ Pierre Gaillard (St-Joseph) *www.domainespierregaillard.com*
A diverse range of wines from a scattered 25 ha in Saint-Joseph, Côte-Rôtie, Cornas, Crozes Hermitage and Condrieu. Gaillard also runs to a good Côtes du Rhône Viognier, Les Gendrines and, when conditions permit, an excellent late-harvest Condrieu and a rare *vin de paille* Jeanne-Elise. Though small, this is an expanding domaine and the wines are modern and stylish. New oak is present but not overdone in the best reds. The regular Côte-Rôtie is lighter and more elegant, with the inclusion of Viognier. It like the Saint-Joseph Les Pierres and Clos du Cuminaille is a good medium term cellaring prospect. The Rose Pourpre is altogether denser and more firmly structured. It requires 5 or 6 years' cellaring at a minimum. A further IGP Syrah red, Asiaticus comes vineyards in Seyssuel on the eastern banks of the Rhône. Among other projects Gaillard is also the inspiration and one of the partners behind the excellent range at

LES VINS DE VIENNE. He also makes a range of Collioure and Banyuls wines at Domaine de MADELOC and four Faugères under his own Cottebrune label. A number of IGP varietal wines are additionally made under the Jeanne Gaillard banner. (DM)
Domaine Pierre Gaillard
Recommended Reds:
Côte-Rôtie Rose Pourpre ★★★★★ £G
Côte-Rôtie ★★★★ £E
Saint-Joseph Clos du Cuminaille ★★★★ £D
Saint-Joseph Les Pierres ★★★☆ £D
Saint-Joseph ★★★ £D
Recommended Whites:
Condrieu Fleur d'Automne ✪✪✪✪ £G
Condrieu ★★★★ £F   Saint-Joseph ★★★ £E
Côtes du Rhône Les Gendrines ★★★ £D
Domaine Cottebrune
Recommended Whites:
Faugères Caïrn ★★★ £D
Domaine de Madeloc
Recommended Reds:
Banyuls Cirera ★★★☆ £E
Collioure Magenca ★★★ £D
Collioure Serral ★★★ £D
Recommended Whites:
Collioure Tremadoc ★★★ £D

✿ Dom. Yves Gangloff (Condrieu)
Yves Gangloff has been established here for nearly 20 years and has gradually built up a small holding in the same way as many of his neighbours. He now has 3.5 ha. The rich and opulent Condrieu is sourced from 2 separate parcels, La Bonnette and Chéry, adding to the wine's complexity. For Viognier it is finely structured with sufficient grip to develop well over 4 or 5 years. There are two Côte-Rôties, Barbarine, which is blended with a little Viognier and produced from younger vines, and the sturdier Sereine Noir, which is partly aged in new wood. Both are very impressive, with the Sereine Noir requiring 5 years or so to show at its best. (DM)
Recommended Reds:
Côte-Rôtie Sereine Noir ★★★★★ £G
Côte-Rôtie Barbarine ★★★★☆ £F
Recommended Whites:
Condrieu ★★★★☆ £G

✿ Jean-Michel Gerin (Condrieu) *www.domaine-gerin.fr*
Jean-Michel Gerin's 9 ha are the source of some fine rich and modern Côte-Rôtie, wines with an emphasis on dark, brambly and chocolaty fruit. New oak is not used sparingly either. Champin Le Seigneur is in a lighter style whereas La Landonne and Les Grandes Places, which is produced from vines that are close to 90 years old, are very good indeed. A fourth example, La Vialliere is also made. Modern and oaky they may be but the wines are superbly crafted and display a fine balance of complex fruit and firm but supple rounded tannins. These top cuvées need 5 years or so of ageing at a minimum and will keep much longer. Peachy Condrieu offers good value for the AC and IGP Syrah and Viognier are also made. Gerin is also one of the three partners involved in the TRIO INFERNAL Priorat project in north eastern Spain. (DM)
Recommended Reds:
Côte-Rôtie La Landonne ★★★★★ £H
Côte-Rôtie Les Grandes Places ★★★★★ £G
Côte-Rôtie Champin Le Seigneur ★★★★ £F

Recommended Whites:
Condrieu Coteau de la Loye ★★★ £E

Dom. Pierre Gonon (Saint-Joseph)
Pierre and Jean Gonon are now producing some of the best reds in the Saint- Joseph appellation. They have 7.5 ha of Syrah and a couple of Roussanne and Marsanne. The white is produced in a very firm, structured style but nevertheless offers good fruit and real intensity. The red is full, savoury and concentrated with dark, blackberry and black pepper spices. It is vinified and aged traditionally in *foudre* and will be all the better for 5 years' ageing. (DM)
Recommended Reds:
Saint-Joseph ★★★ £E
Recommended Whites:
Saint-Joseph Les Oliviers ★★★ £E

Alain Graillot (Crozes-Hermitage)
In barely three decades Alain Graillot has become a benchmark, if not the benchmark, producer of Crozes-Hermitage, both white and red. His son Maxime is also now involved with him as well as producing wines at his own separate property Domaine des Lises. Others domains are now emerging and new special bottlings from the likes of CHAPOUTIER may challenge him but he has been the inspiration for an appellation that for too long represented mediocrity. Yields are kept in check but green harvesting is not practised. Graillot considers winter pruning sufficient to set the yield for the year, the productivity of his vineyard being fully in balance. The white is vinified in wood and *inox* and kept on lees and the reds given an extended maceration of up to 21 days. The special cuvée La Guiraude is a very impressive barrel selection. The reds, particularly La Guiraude, will age very well. Graillot also makes a Syrah, Tandem from Morocco. (DM)
Recommended Reds:
Crozes-Hermitage La Guiraude ★★★★ £E
Crozes-Hermitage ★★★ £D   Saint-Joseph ★★★ £D
Recommended Whites:
Crozes-Hermitage ★★☆ £C

Bernard Gripa (Saint-Joseph)
Long-established grower and a real benchmark for characterful white Saint-Peray, arguably the best producer of the appellation. Fine Saint-Joseph, both red and white, is also produced from a total of a mere 12ha of vineyards. The regular Saint-Joseph labels are good and characterful but it is the Les Berceau bottlings that stand out. The regular white Saint-Peray is rich and characterful, showing Marsanne at its best, while the densely textured Les Figuières is surely the best wine here – long, persistent and ageworthy. (DM)
Recommended Reds:
Saint-Joseph Les Berceau ★★★☆ £E   Saint-Joseph ★★★ £D
Recommended Whites:
Saint-Joseph Les Berceau ★★★ £E   Saint-Joseph ★★☆ £D
Saint-Peray Les Figuières ★★★☆ £E
Saint-Peray Les Pins ★★★ £C

E Guigal (Côte-Rôtie)   www.guigal.com
The E. Guigal label covers an extensive range produced from the length and breadth of the Rhône Valley. The firm is far and away the largest producer of Côte-Rôtie and also owns Domaine de BONSERINE, Domaine de VALLOUIT as well as the merchant house of VIDAL FLEURY. The vibrant red Côtes du Rhône, if not quite of the quality of a decade ago, remains a model of consistency. The Côte-Rôtie Brune et Blonde, which is sourced mainly from bought-in fruit, is good rather than great. More impressive is the Hermitage, which is dense and concentrated. It generally offers very fair value for the appellation. The southern Rhône wines in general lack the quality and refinement of their northern counterparts. The top Guigal wines appear under the separate CHÂTEAU D'AMPUIS label. (DM)
Recommended Reds:
Hermitage ★★★☆ £F   Côte-Rôtie Brune et Blonde ★★★ £E
Châteauneuf-du-Pape ★★★ £D   Gigondas ★★ £C
Côtes du Rhône ★☆ £B
Recommended Whites:
Condrieu ★★★ £E   Hermitage ★★★ £E
Côtes du Rhône ★ £B

✿ Paul Jaboulet-Aine (Hermitage)   www.jaboulet.com
A Large *négociant* operation with some 100 ha of their own vineyards, 84 ha of which are planted to Syrah. The firm has the largest holding of vineyards producing under their own label of the big Rhône merchant houses. An extensive range is produced but the main focus is the northern Rhône appellations. The Jaboulet name is most famous for one massive and very ageworthy cuvée of red Hermitage, La Chapelle. With dense and dark fruit, the wine is more approachable than, say, a Jean-Louis CHAVE but not as modern and opulent as a top CHAPOUTIER. There is also a much lighter second red Hermitage, Le Pied de la Côte, produced from younger vines. A white La Chapelle is also now being made. During the 1990s the Raymond Roure property was added to the portfolio and with the dense and chocolaty Thalabert offers good to very good quality in Crozes-Hermitage. Domaine de Saint-Pierre Cornas is powerful and tannic in its youth and the Châteauneuf-du-Pape Les Cèdres has been better of late. Top wines are ageworthy but the lesser appellations should be approached young. (DM)
Northern Rhône
Recommended Reds:
Hermitage La Chapelle ✪✪✪✪✪ £H
Crozes-Hermitage Thalabert ★★★☆ £E
Crozes-Hermitage Raymond Roure ★★★☆ £E
Crozes-Hermitage Les Jalets ★★ £C
Cornas Domaine de St Pierre ★★★☆ £F
Cornas Les Grandes Terrasses ★★★ £E
Côte-Rôtie Domaine des Pierrelles ★★★★ £F
Saint-Joseph La Grand Pompée ★★☆ £C
Recommended Whites:
Hermitage Chevalier de Sterimberg ★★★★★ £F
Crozes-Hermitage Mule Blanche ★★★ £D
Crozes-Hermitage Raymond Roure ★★★ £D
Crozes-Hermitage Les Jalets ★☆ £C
Condrieu Domaine des Grands Amandiers ★★★☆ £F
Saint-Joseph La Grand Pompée ★★☆ £C
Southern Rhône
Recommended Reds:
Châteauneuf-du-Pape Les Cèdres ★★★ £E
Gigondas Pierre Aiguille ★★ £D   Vacqueyras Les Cyprès ★★ £C
Recommended Whites:
Muscat de Beaumes-de-Venise Le Chant des Griolles ★★★ £C

✿ Dom. Jamet (Côte-Rôtie)
Brothers Jean-Luc and Jean-Paul Jamet own 6.5ha of Syrah and a tiny amount of Viognier. They make a sumptuous, almost opulent

France

Côte-Rôtie which has marvellous balance and poise. The oak is seamlessly handled and the wine is bottled unfiltered. Top years are almost always at ✪✪✪✪✪ level. An attractive light and vibrant Côtes du Rhône Syrah is also produced from young vines. Given the splendid quality here prices are never unreasonable, certainly from the domaine. (DM)

Recommended Reds:
Côte-Rôtie ★★★★★ £G

Dom. Jasmin (Côte-Rôtie)

Patrick Jasmin took over the running of this fine, traditional domaine after his late father Robert's early death. Patrick continues to make the wines in a traditional and elegant style. However destemming is now employed, which helps in lesser years, and the wine is aged for around two years in mainly old wood. Never a blockbuster, there is always great purity of fruit and impressive intensity and depth. Top years require 7 to 10 years' ageing. A Syrah IGP is also made from young vines. (DM)

Recommended Reds:
Côte-Rôtie ★★★★ £F

>> Dom. Johann Michel (Cornas)

Johann Michel began making his own wines in 1997 and from just over 4 ha now produces benchmark Cornas as well as a white Saint-Péray and a further red Syrah, Grain Noir. The vineyards are cultivated, as you would expect with low yields and with sustainable farming practices, the fruit coming from four separate lieux-dits in sand, granite and limestone soils. The result is two Cornas reds of really impressive style and dimension full of earthy, concentrated black fruit and black pepper. The Cornas is marginally the more approachable of the two. Full de-stemming takes place before a three-week vatting and ageing for a year to a year and a half in used 600 litre barrels. The Cuvée Jana approach is slightly different. Vinification is solely with whole bunches and ageing is in new 600 litre vessels. Expect the wines to age and evolve very well for a decade and more, although they are more immediately approachable than many other examples from the appellation. (DM)

Reds: Cornas Cuvée Jana ★★★★☆ £F
Cornas ★★★★ £E

❁ Dom. du Monteillet (Condrieu) *www.montez.fr*

Stéphane Montez runs this small family domaine in Condrieu. The property consists of some 7ha in Condrieu, Côte-Rôtie and Saint-Joseph. Vinification is modern and plenty of new oak is used in the top cuvées. The Condrieu is rich and peachy but has a fine minerally backbone. The top cuvée Les Grandes Chaillées is particularly impressive. Both should develop well over 3 or 4 years. A late-harvest label, Tries Grains de Folie, is also produced when conditions permit. The reds are ripe and spicy; both the Cuvée Papy and Côte-Rôtie are wines of considerable dimension and should be cellared for a good 4 or 5 years. (DM)

Recommended Reds:
Côte-Rôtie Fortis ★★★★ £F
Saint-Joseph Cuvée Papy ★★★☆ £E
Saint-Joseph ★★★ £D

Recommended Whites:
Condrieu Tries Grains de Folie ★★★★★ £F
Condrieu Les Grands Chaillees ★★★★★ £F
Condrieu Chanson ★★★★ £E
Saint-Joseph ★★★ £D

Dom. du Murinais *www.domainedumurinais.com*

This is an impressive producer of well priced Crozes-Hermitage with 12.5 ha of Syrah and a mere 0.5 ha planted to Marsanne. The Tardys produce a little under 4,000 cases a year. The white is good and lightly nutty with moderate depth and intensity. The reds are a step up, particularly the densely structured Vieilles Vignes bottling from vines that are over 30 years old. A special selection Caprice de Valentin is also now produced in exceptional years.(DM)

Recommended Reds:
Crozes-Hermitage Caprice de Valentin ★★★☆ £E
Crozes-Hermitage Vieilles Vignes ★★★ £D
Crozes-Hermitage Cuvée Amandier ★★☆ £C

Recommended Whites:
Crozes-Hermitage Cuvée Marine ★★ £C

❁ Dom. Niero (Condrieu) *www.vins-niero.com*

Robert Niero has been in charge of this fine domaine since the 1980s. The vineyard holding is typically small, with some 3ha in Condrieu and a small parcel within Les Viaillères in Côte-Rôtie. Insecticides are never used and the vines tended as naturally as possible. Les Ravines is part vinified in *inox* and part in old wood and is elegant and lightly mineral with less overt peachy, honeyed character than others. The Chéry comes from old vines, some approaching 60 years, and the wine is fuller and more opulent with an added dimension and greater weight and concentration. A third special selection Condrieu, Héritage is also made. The Côte-Rôtie is lighter than some of his neighbours' examples but very elegant, not least because of the 10% Viognier in the blend. Both Condrieus should be drunk young but the Côte-Rôtie will benefit from 5 years' cellaring. (DM)

Recommended Reds:
Côte-Rôtie Eminence ★★★★ £F

Recommended Whites:
Condrieu Chéry ★★★★★ £F
Condrieu Les Ravines ★★★★ £F

❁ Dom. Michel Ogier (Côte-Rôtie)

Some exceptional Côte-Rôtie is made at this 3.5ha property as well as very good IGP La Rosine from vineyards just to the south of Ampuis towards Condrieu. Winemaking is modern and the fruit is always destemmed prior to fermentation. New oak is used both for the regular Côte-Rôtie as well as for the limited-release special bottlings, Belle Hélène, Les Embruns and Lancement. The wines are supple and velvety, with a real dimension to the fruit. The Belle Hélène has become established as one of the super-cuvées of the appellation and as such is very pricey. An IGP Viognier Rosine is also made now along with a well-priced red Saint-Joseph and a red from the increasingly trendy Seyssuel vineyard area. (DM)

Recommended Reds:
Côte-Rôtie Belle Hélène ✪✪✪✪✪ £H
Côte-Rôtie Embruns ★★★★★ £H
Côte-Rôtie Lancement ★★★★★ £H
Côte-Rôtie ★★★★ £F
IGP des Collines Rhodaniennes La Rosine ★★★ £D

Dom. Alain Paret (Saint-Joseph) *www.maison-alain-paret.fr*

Some excellent Condrieu and very good Saint-Joseph red are made here. As well as this, Alain Paret makes an extensive range of red and white vins de pays. The white Saint-Joseph Larmes du Père is a typically full, fat Marsanne with reasonable depth and a touch of Roussanne blended in. Of the reds, the Larmes du Père is the softest

with bright, forward berry fruit and a hint of new oak. The top red is the 420 Nuits, which is aged in 100% new wood and offers really formidable depth and intensity. Ceps du Nebadon is the lighter and less intense of two Condrieu bottlings, although showing a fimer edge than many from the AC. The Lys de Volan is more seriously structured with hints of both minerals and rich apricot and peach – a wine with real style and class. (DM)

Recommended Reds:
Saint-Joseph 420 Nuits ★★★☆ £E
Saint-Joseph Larmes du Père ★★★ £D
Saint-Joseph ★★★ £D
Recommended Whites:
Condrieu Lys de Volan ★★★★ £F
Condrieu Ceps du Nebadon ★★★☆ £F
Saint-Joseph Larmes du Père ★★☆ £D

Vincent Paris (Cornas)

One of the undoubted bright new stars, not only of Cornas but also the Northern Rhône. Both these Cornas bottlings are ripe, spicy and full of classic varietal Syrah fruit. They offer not only impresssive depth and concentration but elegance and finesse as well, qualities that can often be lacking in this appellation. Granit 60 (which refers to the angle of the vineyard slope and the soil) comes from the highest plots whereas the Granit 30 is sourced from Vincent's lower lying and younger vines. Ageing is in used *barriques* for the Granit 60 and a combination of both small wood and *cuve* for the Granit 30. Both are bottled unfined and unfiltered and will develop very well in bottle for five years and more for the 60. A third slightly pricier Cornas La Geynale is also made and aged in *barrique*. (DM)

Recommended Reds:
Cornas Granit 60 ★★★★☆ £F
Cornas Granit 30 ★★★★ £E

❊ André Perret (Condrieu)   *www.andreperret.com*

André Perret took over the family domaine in 1982 and now has some 13 ha of vines from which he produces Condrieu, Saint-Joseph, Côtes du Rhône and varietals. The Condrieus are some of the finest of the AC. These and the white Saint-Joseph are vinified in a combination of *inox* and oak, some of it new and kept on lees. The reds are fully destemmed and spend 2–3 weeks on their skins. Some late-harvest grapes are also included in the blend, adding greater complexity. Les Grissières is dense and dark with ripe, black pepper notes. It will age well. Varietal Syrah and Marsanne are produced as vins de pays and offer attractive early drinking. (DM)

Recommended Reds:
Saint-Joseph Les Grissières ★★★★ £D
Saint-Joseph ★★★☆ £D
Recommended Whites:
Condrieu Coteau du Chéry ★★★★★ £F
Condrieu Clos Chanson ★★★★☆ £F
Condrieu ★★★★ £E   Saint-Joseph ★★★☆ £D

Dom. Étienne Pochon (Crozes-Hermitage)

Étienne Pochon makes straightforward, attractively fruity regular red and white Crozes-Hermitage and a special Château de Curson bottling of each. These are vinified using more oak and are a significant step up in quality. The property consists of a total of 15.6ha with 11.6 planted to Syrah plus around 4ha of Roussanne and Marsanne. The Curson white is dominated by Roussanne and is enticingly floral as well as lightly toasty and spicy. The red Curson is weighty but supple and will benefit from 2 or 3 years' cellaring. (DM)

Recommended Reds:
Crozes-Hermitage Château de Curson ★★★ £C
Crozes-Hermitage ★★ £C
Recommended Whites:
Crozes-Hermitage Château de Curson ★★★ £C
Crozes-Hermitage ★☆ £C

Dom. des Remizières   *www.domaineremizieres.com*

This 27-ha Crozes Hermitage property has greatly improved in recent vintages. At best the wines used to be no more than middle-ranking examples of their appellations. The reds are now deep and intense. The Hermitage Émilie is powerful and structured with considerable grip but there is also real concentration and old-vine complexity here. Patrick LESEC also produces his own cuvée of the same wine in association with Philippe Desmeure. The Cuvée Christophe red is ripe and full of dark fruit and further pricier red Crozes and Hermitage, Autrement have been added, while the whites display all the nutty, pure character of Marsanne at its best. The wines also represent very good value. (DM)

Recommended Reds:
Hermitage Cuvée Émilie ★★★★☆ £F   Saint-Joseph ★★★ £D
Crozes-Hermitage Cuvée Christophe ★★★ £D
Recommended Whites:
Hermitage Cuvée Émilie ★★★★ £F
Crozes-Hermitage Cuvée Christophe ★★★ £D

Gilles Robin (Crozes-Hermitage)   *www.gillesrobin.com*

Gilles Robin has emerged as one of the leading lights among red Crozes producers during the last 5 years. His wines have a depth and purity of Syrah fruit rarely found among his neighbours. He now has 12 ha under vine and his output has reached between 4,500 and 5,000 cases a year. The regular Crozes, Papillon, has impressive and very pure varietal fruit while the Albéric Bouchet shows real depth, structure and character. Both wines will develop well and the Bouchet needs 5 years to achieve perfect harmony. A red Hermitage, a Saint-Joseph, Andre Péalat, have now been added to this small range as well as 1920 a special plot selection red Crozes and a white Les Marelles. (DM)

Recommended Reds:
Crozes-Hermitage Albéric Bouchet ★★★☆ £D
Crozes-Hermitage Cuvée Papillon ★★☆ £C

❊ Rene Rostaing (Côte-Rôtie)   *www.domainerostaing.com*

Rostaing is now one of the very best producers of great Côte-Rôtie. He is continually seeking to keep yields in check, to harvest at optimum ripeness and to minimize handling in the cellar. The wines are uniformly bottled without filtration. He has tremendous vineyards to draw upon, having taken over the running of those of Albert Dervieux-Thaize as well as Marius Gentaz-Dervieux. The wines are deep and extracted but always refined and with supple, finely crafted, velvety tannins. The top cuvées are very ageworthy. They will improve in bottle for a decade or more. La Landonne is dense, massive in its youth, while the Côte Blonde is lighter and typically more elegant as one might expect from vines planted in these soils. The Condrieu is marked by glorious ripe, peachy varietal fruit and should be drunk young. A red and white Languedoc, Puech Noble, are also now being made. (DM)

Recommended Reds:
Côte-Rôtie Côte Blonde ✪✪✪✪✪ £G
Côte-Rôtie La Landonne ★★★★★ £G
Côte-Rôtie Classique ★★★★ £F

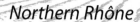

Northern Rhône

France

Recommended Whites:
Condrieu La Bonnette ★★★★ £F

Marc Sorrel (Hermitage) *www.marcsorrel.fr*
The top *cuvées*, both red and white, are some of the finest expressions of the great wines of the Hermitage hill. The regular bottlings, in particular the red, don't have the same depth and substance. They can shine in years like 2008 when Le Gréal wasn't made. The red Crozes-Hermitage is a reasonable example with moderately intense, dark berry fruit in a lighter style than some but stylish for what it is. What marks out Le Gréal is its powerful, dense and complex fruit and backward structure. If you give it 7 or 8 years at least you'll be rewarded with a great example of the appellation. In exceptional years this can be legendary. Les Rocoules is an equally fine, but equally backward example of great Marsanne. Honeyed, nutty and complex with age, this really needs at least 10 years. (DM)
Recommended Reds:
Hermitage Le Gréal ★★★★★ £H
Hermitage ★★★★ £F Crozes-Hermitage ★★☆ £C
Recommended Whites:
Hermitage Les Rocoules ★★★★★ £H
Hermitage ★★★★ £F Crozes-Hermitage ★★ £C

Cave de Tain l'Hermitage (Hermitage) *www.cavedetain.fr*
The growers belonging to this co-operative have a considerable holding, in total some 1,000ha, planted throughout the region and production is around 500,000 cases a year. The range is fairly extensive and there are varietal IGP as well as AC bottlings. These are impressive wines within most appellations. These are labelled both Classique as well as after specific parcels, which are a clear step up in quality. Occasionally a little vin de paille is also produced, which is rich, intense and nutty. A number of Organic reds have also been added to the extensive range. (DM)
Recommended Reds:
Hermitage Epsilon ★★★★☆ £G
Hermitage Gambert de Loche ★★★★ £F
Hermitage Classique ★★★ £E Cornas Classique ★★★ £D
Crozes-Hermitage Les Hauts du Fief ★★☆ £C
Crozes-Hermitage Classique ★☆ £B
Saint-Joseph Esprit de Granit ★★☆ £C
Saint-Joseph Classique ★☆ £C
Recommended Whites:
Hermitage Vin de Paille ★★★★☆ £G
Hermitage Classique ★★★ £E
Crozes-Hermitage Classique ★☆ £B

Dom. du Tunnel (Saint-Péray)
Very good Saint-Péray as well as Cornas are made at this property which was established as recently as 1994. A total of 7.5 ha are worked with. The Saint-Péray is fresh, forward, richly textured and attractively nutty, unusually from 100% Roussanne. There are three Cornas reds made from ancient vineyard plantings and as well as the village label and Vin Noir there is a tiny amount of a pricier Pur Noir. The wines are dense, sumptuous and full of classic dark fruit, spice and black pepper, the Vin Noir characterised by complex old-viney fruit. A small amount of well-crafted Saint-Joseph is also made, along with a second Saint-Péray. (DM)
Recommended Reds:
Cornas Vin Noir ★★★★☆ £F
Cornas ★★★★ £F Saint-Joseph ★★★☆ £E

Recommended Whites:
Saint-Péray Roussanne ★★★☆ £E

❀ **Dom. Georges Vernay (Condrieu)** *www.georges-vernay.fr*
Vernay is one of the great Condrieu producers. His daughter Christine now runs the domaine with her husband Paul Amsellem and they possess some 9 ha of Viognier and a further 7 ha of Syrah from which they are making increasingly impressive Côte-Rôtie, an appellation they used to struggle with. There has been some consultancy for the reds from Jean-Luc COLOMBO. Other reds are a simple red IGP, a sound fruit-driven Côtes du Rhône and stylish Saint-Joseph. Good white IGP Viognier is made from the youngest vines but it is the three Condrieus that are the main focus here. Terasses de l'Empire, the regular bottling, is well-crafted but lacks a little depth. The other two wines are part barrel-fermented and of serious depth and weight; Chaillées de L'Enfer is just a little more opulent and heady. Both will develop well in the short term. (DM)
Recommended Reds:
Côte-Rôtie Cuvée Maison Rouge ★★★★☆ £F
Côte-Rôtie Blonde du Seigneur ★★★★ £F
Saint-Joseph La Dame Brune ★★★★ £E
Saint-Joseph Terres d'Encre ★★★☆ £D
Recommended Whites:
Condrieu Coteau du Vernon ★★★★★ £G
Condrieu Les Chaillées de L'Enfer ★★★★☆ £F
Condrieu Les Terrasses de L'Empire ★★★★ £F
IGP Collines Rhodaniennes Viognier Le Pied de Samson ★★★ £D

❀ **François Villard (Condrieu)** *www.domainevillard.com*
There are now 25 ha of vineyards, 10 ha being planted to white varieties from which benchmark Condrieu is produced. These wines are vinified in new oak on their lees with careful bâtonnage, they have considerable depth and structure for Viognier and age uncharacteristically well. A sweet Vin de France, Quintessence, is also made as are very good Côte-Rôtie and red and white Saint-Joseph along with Saint-Péray. The range is completed by a number of other Vin de France bottlings of impressive quality. François is also involved with Pierre GAILLARD and Yves CUILLERON in Les VINS DE VIENNE. (DM)
Recommended Reds:
Côte-Rôtie Galet Blanc ★★★★★ £F
Saint-Joseph Reflet ★★★★☆ £E Saint-Joseph Mairlant ★★★★ £E
Saint-Joseph Poivre et Sol ★★★☆ £D
Vin de France Syrah l'Appel des Sereines ★★★☆ £C
Recommended Whites:
Vin de France Quintessence ✪✪✪✪☆ £G
Condrieu de Poncins ★★★★☆ £F
Condrieu Les Terrasses du Palat ★★★★☆ £F
Condrieu Grand Vallon ★★★★☆ £F
Saint-Joseph Mairlant ★★★★ £E
Vin de France Viognier Contours de Deponcins ★★★☆ £E

❀ **Vins de Vienne (Côte-Rôtie)** *www.vinsdevienne.com*
This is a moderately sized operation that is part domaine and part négociant. The partners were pioneers in re-establishing the pre-phylloxera vineyards of the Côteaux du Seyssuel to the west of Vienne. This once famous area, known to Pliny and Plutarch, produces a red Sotanum, a wine of real potential, a partially barrel-aged Viognier, Taburnum as well as a second red. The vines are as yet still relatively young and the wines are likely to improve further as the vineyards age. The négociant offerings range from good to

exciting. New oak is evident in all the wines but is well handled. One criticism might be that the character of the individual appellations can sometimes struggle to show through. The Côte-Rôtie Les Essartailles and Condrieu La Chambée particularly stand out. The best are undoubtedly very ageworthy. (DM)

Northern Rhône
Recommended Reds:
Côte-Rôtie Les Essartailles ★★★★☆ £F
IGP des Collines Rhodaniennes Sotanum ★★★★ £E
Hermitage Les Chirats de Saint-Christophe ★★★★ £F
Cornas Les Barcillants ★★★☆ £E
Crozes-Hermitage Palignons ★★☆ £C   Saint-Joseph ★★ £C
Recommended Whites:
Condrieu La Chambée ★★★★ £E
IGP des Collines Rhodaniennes Taburnum ★★★★ £E
Saint-Péray Les Bialères ★★★ £C   Saint-Joseph L'Elouède ★★☆ £C

Southern Rhône
Recommended Reds:
Châteauneuf du Pape Les Oteliées ★★★☆ £E
Gigondas Les Pimpignoles ★★★ £D
Côtes du Rhône-Villages Visan La Tine ★★★ £C
Cairanne La Perpendaille ★★★ £C   Vacqueyras La Sillote ★★☆ £C
Côtes du Rhône Les Cranilles ★★ £B
Recommended Whites:
Côtes du Rhône Les Laurelles ★★ £B

⚜ **Alain Voge (Cornas)** *www.alain-voge.com*
As well as his very powerful and muscular Cornas, Alain Voge also produces some of the best Saint-Péray, both dry and sparkling. The Harmonie is unoaked and marked by impressive nutty Marsanne fruit, while the Terres Boisée sees some new oak. The top Fleur du Crussol is amongst the very finest in the appellation. His Cornas vineyards are of increasingly venerable age and this is showing through in the wines with immensely complex smoky dark fruits and black spices emerging in the Vieilles Vignes and Vieille Fontaines bottlings. A very small amount of new oak is used to barrelage the wines, which you should expect to cellar for 5 years or more. A little Saint-Joseph and Côtes du Rhône red is also made. (DM)
Recommended Reds:
Cornas Vieilles Fontaines ★★★★★ £F
Cornas Vieilles Vignes ★★★★☆ £F   Cornas Les Chailles ★★★★ £E
Recommended Whites:
Saint-Péray Fleur du Crussol ★★★☆ £E
Saint-Péray Terres Boisée ★★★ £C
Saint-Péray Cuvée Harmonie ★★★ £C
Saint-Péray Brut Les Bulles d'Alain ★★☆ £C

Other wines of note - *Northern Rhône*

Dom. Guy Bernard
Recommended Reds: Côte-Rôtie ★★★ £F
Recommended Whites: Condrieu ★★★ £F
Dom. Betton
Recommended Reds: Crozes-Hermitage Caprice ★★☆ £C
Dom. de Biguet
Recommended Reds: Cornas ★★★ £E
Recommended Whites: Saint-Péray ★★ £C
Dom. Boisseyt-Chol
Recommended Reds: Côte-Rôtie Côte Blonde ★★★ £F

Dom. Frédéric Boissonet
Recommended Whites: Condrieu Les Rochains ★★★ £F
Condrieu ★★☆ £F
Dom. Stéphane Chaboud
Recommended Reds: Cornas ★★★ £E
Recommended Whites: Saint-Péray ★★ £C
Joel Champet
Recommended Reds: Côte-Rôtie ★★★ £F
Dom. Champal-Rocher
Recommended Reds: Saint-Joseph ★★★ £D
Ch. Montlys
Recommended Reds: Côte-Rôtie ★★★☆ £F
Caves des Clairmonts
Recommended Reds: Crozes-Hermitage ★☆ £B
Recommended Whites: Crozes-Hermitage ★☆ £B
Dom. de La Côte Sainte-Epine
Recommended Reds: Saint-Joseph ★★★☆ £E
Dom. Curtat
Recommended Reds:
Crozes-Hermitage Fées des Champs ★★★☆ £D
Emmanuel Darnaud
Recommended Reds: Crozes-Hermitage Mise en Bouch ★★☆ £C
Crozes-Hermitage Les Trois Chênes ★★★☆ £D
Martin Daubrée
Recommended Reds: Côte-Rôtie Paradis ★★★ £F
Olivier Dumaine
Recommended Reds: Crozes-Hermitage La Croix du Verre ★★☆ £C
Recommended Whites: Crozes-Hermitage ★★☆ £C
Dom. Dumien-Surette
Recommended Reds: Cornas Patou ★★★ £E
Christian Facchin
Recommended Whites: Condrieu Les Grands-Maison ★★★ £F
Dom. Farjon
Recommended Reds: Saint-Joseph ★★☆ £C
Saint-Joseph Ma Sélection ★★★ £D
Recommended Whites: Condrieu ★★★☆ £E   Condrieu Les Grains Dorée ★★★★ £F
Saint-Joseph ★★☆ £C
Cave Fayolle
Recommended Reds: Crozes-Hermitage Les Pontaix ★★★ £C
Crozes-Hermitage Sens ★★★ £C
Crozes-Hermitage Clos Les Corniretes Vieille Vignes ★★★ £C
Hermitage ★★★☆ £F
Recommended Whites: Hermitage ★★★☆ £F
Dom. Ferraton
Recommended Reds: Ermitage Le Méal ★★★★☆ £F
Ermitage Les Dionnières ★★★★ £F
Hermitage Les Miaux ★★★☆ £F   Cornas Patou ★★★★ £E
Cornas Les Eygats ★★★☆ £E
Crozes-Hermitage La Matinière ★★★☆ £D
Recommended Whites: Ermitage Le Reverdy ★★★★☆ £G
Saint-Joseph La Source ★★★☆ £D
Gilles Flacher
Recommended Reds: Saint-Joseph Terra Louis ★★★☆ £D
Recommended Whites: Condrieu Les Rouelles ★★★☆ £F
Dom. Gallet
Recommended Reds: Côte-Rôtie ★★★☆ £F
Dom. Garon
Recommended Reds: Côte-Rôtie La Sybarine ★★★☆ £E   Côte-Rôtie Les Triotes ★★★★ £F

France

Maxime Graillot
Recommended Reds: Crozes-Hermitage Equinoxe ★★★ £C

Dom. des Hauts Chassis
Recommended Reds: Crozes-Hermitage Esquisses ★★ £C
Crozes-Hermitage Les Galets ★★☆ £C
Crozes-Hermitage Les Chassis ★★☆ £C

Dom. Philippe & Vincent Jaboulet
Recommended Reds: Cornas ★★★★ £E
Crozes Hermitage Cuvée Nouvelière ★★★☆ £E

Dom. Yves Lafoy
Recommended Reds: Côte-Rôtie ★★★ £F
Recommended Whites: Condrieu Moelleux ★★★ £F

Jacques Lemencier
Recommended Reds: Cornas ★★★☆ £E

Dom. Les Bruyères
Recommended Reds: Crozes-Hermitage ★★☆ £C

Bernard Levet
Recommended Reds: Côte-Rôtie Les Journaries ★★★☆ £E
Côte-Rôtie La Chavaroche ★★★★ £F

Dom. des Martinelles
Recommended Reds: Hermitage ★★★ £F
Crozes-Hermitage ★★ £C
Recommended Whites: Crozes-Hermitage ★☆ £C

Dom. François Merlin
Recommended Whites: Condrieu ★★★ £E
Condrieu Cuvée Jeancaude ★★★☆ £F

Dom. Michelas Saint Jemms
Recommended Reds: Cornas Les Murettes ★★★★ £E
Crozes Hermitage La Chasselière ★★★☆ £D
Crozes Hermitage Signature ★★☆ £C

Dom. Monier Perreol
Recommended Reds: Saint-Joseph Terres Blanches ★★★☆ £D

Dom. Didier Morion
Recommended Whites: Condrieu ★★★ £F

Dom. Mouton
Recommended Reds: Côte-Rôtie ★★★☆ £E
Recommended Whites: Condrieu Côte Bonnette ★★★ £E
Condrieu Côte Chatillon ★★★☆ £F

Dom. Mucyn
Recommended Reds: Crozes Hermitage les Entrecoeurs ★★☆ £C
Recommended Whites: Crozes-Hermitage Les Charmeuses ★★☆ £C

Dom. Pichat
Recommended Reds: Côte-Rôtie Löss ★★★★ £F
Côte-Rôtie Champon's ★★★★☆ £F

Christophe Pichon
Recommended Reds: Côte-Rôtie La Comtesse ★★★★ £F
Saint-Joseph ★★★ £C
Recommended Whites: Condrieu ★★★☆ £E

Cave de Saint-Désirat
Recommended Reds: Saint-Joseph ★★★ £C

Jean-Michel Stéphan
Recommended Reds:
Côte-Rôtie Vieilles Vignes En Coteau ★★★☆ £F
Côte-Rôtie Coteau de Tupin ★★★ £E Côte-Rôtie ★★★ £E

Daniel, Rolande & Gisèle Vernay
Recommended Reds: Côte-Rôtie ★★★ £E

Vidal Fleury
Recommended Reds: Côte-Rôtie La Chatillon ★★★☆ £F
Côte-Rôtie Brune et Blonde ★★★☆ £F
Saint-Joseph ★★ £C
Recommended Whites: Condrieu ★★★☆ £E

Author's choice - *Northern Rhône*

10 of the Northern Rhône's most distinguished reds
Thierry Allemand Cornas Reynard
M. Chapoutier Ermitage Le Pavillon
Ch. d'Ampuis Côte-Rôtie La Turque
Jean-Louis Chave Hermitage Ermitage Cuvée Cathelin
Auguste Clape Cornas
Clusel Roch Côte-Rôtie Les Grandes Places
Paul Jaboulet Ainé Hermitage La Chapelle
Dom. Jamet Côte-Rôtie
René Rostaing Côte-Rôtie Côte Blonde
Marc Sorrel Hermitage Le Gréal

A choice of opulent dry whites
M. Chapoutier Hermitage Cuveé de l'Orée
Jean-Louis Chave Hermitage
Dom. du Chene Condrieu
Yves Cuilleron Condrieu Chaillets Vieilles Vignes
Dom. Yves Gangloff Condrieu
Dom. du Murinais Crozes Hermitage Vieilles Vignes
André Perret Condrieu Côteaux du Chéry
Georges Vernay Condrieu Les Chaillées de L'Enfer
François Villard Saint-Joseph Côtes de Mairlant
Alain Voge Saint-Péray Cuvée Fleur du Crussol

A selection of up and coming reds and whites
Reds:
Albert Belle Crozes-Hermitage Cuvée Louis Belle
M. Chapoutier Saint-Joseph Les Granits
Yann Chave Crozes-Hermitage Le Rouvre
Delas Frères Crozes-Hermitage Le Clos
Dom. Michel Ogier IGP des Collines Rhodaniennes La Rosine
Whites:
Jean-Luc Colombo Hermitage Le Louet
Dom. Combier Crozes-Hermitage Clos des Grives
Yves Cuilleron Saint-Joseph Le Lombard
Pierre Gaillard Côtes du Rhône Viognier
Dom. du Tunnel Saint-Péray Prestige

A-Z of producers - *Southern Rhône*

⚜ **Daniel & Denis Alary (Cairanne)** *www.domaine-alary.fr*
A comprehensive and impressive range of Côtes du Rhône and
Cairanne village wines are made here from the Alarys' 29ha. Just
over 90% of the vineyard is planted to red varieties, with some of
the plantings now of notable age. The floral, forward white Côtes du
Rhône La Chevre d'Or blends Clairette with Roussanne, Viognier and
Bourboulenc. The L'Estevenas white is a step up, a rich, nutty and
complex blend of Clairette and Roussanne. The reds are unfiltered,
full of dense and aromatic garrigue scents and complex, heady,
berry fruit. The L'Estevenas and Jean de Verde are among the best
expressions of old-vine Grenache outside Châteauneuf-du-Pape. The
former usually has a proportion of Syrah, whereas La Jean de Verde
is mainly Grenache and a smattering of Carignan. The overall quality
across all the wines is very good indeed as are the prices. The top
two reds will age well. (DM)
Recommended Reds:
Côtes du Rhône-Villages Cairanne L'Estevenas ★★★★ £D
Côtes du Rhône-Villages Cairanne La Jean de Verde ★★★★ £D

Côtes du Rhône-Villages Cairanne La Brunote ★★★☆ £C
Côtes du Rhône-Villages Cairanne ★★★ £C
Côtes du Rhône La Gerbaude ★★☆ £B
Recommended Whites:
Côtes du Rhône-Villages Cairanne L'Estevenas ★★★ £C
Côtes du Rhône La Chevre d'Or ★★ £B
Recommended Rosés:
Côtes du Rhône ★☆ £B

Dom. des Amadieu (Cairanne) www.domainedesamadieu.com
Small 7 ha domaine purchased in 2007 by Yves Jean Houser,
producing some excellent-value Cairanne. The property is planted
to mostly red Grenache, Syrah and Mourvèdre and the Grenache
vines now average over 50 years of age. Yields are restricted to an
average of 35 hl/ha and pigéage is employed during vinification.
With output a mere 1,500 cases or so the wines will not be the
easiest to find. The small range now consists of six wines, the four
reds, a white Haut de Beauregard and a rosé. Of the reds there is a
regular Côtes du Rhône-Villages, and three Cairanne wines which
are labelled Garrigues, Vieilles Vignes and Le Haut de Beauregard.
Garrigues and the village wine are dominated by Grenache and
are softer, more vibrantly fruit-driven examples but with a fine
underlying structure also. The Vieilles Vignes comes from a blend of
roughly 45/30/25 Grenache, Mourvèdre and Syrah. A proportion is
aged in barriques, and the wine is denser and firmer and will age
well for four or five years. The top wine, Le Haut de Beauregard will
develop for close to a decade and comprises a varied blend of the
best old vine lots from the year and aged in French oak for up to
two years. (DM)
Recommended Reds:
Côtes du Rhône-Villages Cairanne Le Haut de Beauregard ★★★☆ £D
Côtes du Rhône-Villages Cairanne Vieilles Vignes ★★★ £D
Côtes du Rhône-Villages Cairanne Cuvée des Garrigues ★★★ £C
Côtes du Rhône-Villages ★★ £C

Dom. Amido (Tavel) www.domaineamido.fr
This is the most significant domaine in Tavel from a quality point
of view, producing one of the best examples of the appellation.
The wine undergoes a 36 hour pre-fermentation maceration and is
fermented cool to preserve its attractive fresh berry fruit, something
many in the appellation fail to achieve. More important from a
quality perspective are a fine Côtes du Rhône-Villages blended from
Grenache (70%) and Syrah (30%) and a benchmark red Lirac. This is
produced from 50-year-old Grenache (just over 50%) plus Syrah and
Mourvèdre. It is aged first in cement tanks and then transferred to
used oak. The wine shows rich dark berry fruit and classic southern
herbal spice and will benefit from a year or two of bottle age. (DM)
Recommended Reds:
Lirac ★★★ £C Côtes du Rhône-Villages ★★☆ £C
Recommended Rosés:
Tavel Les Amandines ★★☆ £C

Dom. des Amouriers (Vacqueyras)
First-class operation run by Patrick Gras, producing very stylish,
balanced wines. There are 25 ha all planted to reds, half Grenache
with the balance a mix of Mourvèdre, Syrah, Carignan and other
grapes used in the IGP labelled wines. Up until the mid-1990s the
estate fruit was sold on but in only a few years this has become
one of the finest sources in the Vacqueyras AC. These are wines
of depth and rich savoury fruit and considerable structure, with
new oak playing a part in the style. Top vintages of Genestes are

benchmarks for the appellation and will age very well. The top labels
are ageworthy, Les Genestes rising ★★★★ in recent vintages. (DM)
Recommended Reds:
Vacqueyras Les Genestes ★★★☆ £D
Vacqueyras Truffières ★★★☆ £D Vacqueyras Signature ★★★ £C
Vacqueyras ★★☆ £C Côtes du Rhône ★☆ £B
IGP du Vaucluse Les Hautes Terrasses ★★★☆ £E
IGP du Vaucluse Suzanne ★☆ £B

Dom. Paul Autard (Châteauneuf-du-Pape) www.paulautard.com
A small but impressive range of wines is made by Jean-Paul Autard
at his 12 ha family domaine. The winemaking style has become
more modern over the last decade: the fruit is not only carefully
sorted at harvested but the reds are now fully destemmed as well.
The good, sound, forward Côtes du Rhône red blended from Syrah
and Counoise should be drunk young. More serious are the red
Châteauneuf-du-Papes. The regular cuvée blends 70% Grenache
with Syrah, Counoise and Mourvèdre and is aged in a mix of foudres
and barriques. It is marked by its peppery, herbal garrigue notes
and approachable berry fruit. The Côte Ronde is considerably
fuller and richer with a firmer structure. It demands 5 years' ageing,
particularly in top years. A blend of Grenache and Syrah, it is aged
in part new and part used barriques for up to 18 months. The
nicely concentrated, nutty and toasty barrel-fermented white
Châteauneuf-du-Pape comes from Grenache Blanc, Clairette and
Roussanne. A further premium red Châteauneuf, Juline, blending
Grenache and Syrah is also made. (DM)
Recommended Reds:
Châteauneuf du Pape La Côte Ronde ★★★★ £F
Châteauneuf du Pape ★★★☆ £E
Recommended Whites:
Châteauneuf du Pape ★★★ £E

Dom. Elodie Balme (Rasteau)
This is an excellent new small domaine with great potential. Elodie
Balme began her wine education with the great Marcel RICHAUD
at his Cairanne domaine. She has now taken control of growing a
part of her family's 28 ha of vineyards. She is currently producing
her wines from 14 ha and has now added a further holding of IGP
and also produces a Côtes du Rhône-Villages Roaix from Grenache,
Syrah and Mourvèdre. The first harvest was in 2006 and she has
now moved into a new winery with the 2009 vintage. The more
approachable, spicey and wonderfully vibrant Côtes du Rhône
bottling blends Grenache, Syrah and Carignan while the more
seriously structured Rasteau blend has a touch more Syrah. A
domaine to follow with interest. (DM)
Recommended Reds:
Rasteau ★★★☆ £D Côtes du Rhône ★★★ £C

Dom. Lucien Barrot (Châteauneuf-du-Pape)
This is a small family-run operation with 16 ha of vineyards spread
across the Châteauneuf-du-Pape appellation. The Barrots have
been established as winemakers here since the late 17th century.
The vines are old, averaging 50 years, planted on limestones soils
with a galets roués stone topsoil. The resulting wine is dense,
complex and stylish and possesses a classic rich, savoury, garrigue
scented character. It is blended from Grenache, Syrah, Mourvèdre
and Cinsault and vinification is traditional: the grapes are not
destemmed and maceration lasts up to 4 weeks in top years.
The wine is then aged in foudres for around 18 months. Firmly
structured when young, it will drink well at 5 years or so. Excellent

Southern Rhône

value for the appellation. (DM)
Recommended Reds:
Châteauneuf du Pape ★★★☆ £D

◉ Dom de Beau Mistral (Rasteau)

This has emerged as one of the flagship domaines in the village of Rasteau. Red, white and rosé are all produced as well as Rasteau VDN both red and white. Jean-Marc Brun now has 25 ha under vine planted in clay-limestone soils and just under 20 ha are found in the new Rasteau appellation. The light wines were originally just entitled to the Côtes du Rhône-Villages Rasteau classification which has changed for 2010 and you will find earlier vintages with this label. The white nutty, ripe and peachy Rasteau comes from a blend of Viognier, Marsanne, Roussanne as well as a small proportion of Clairette and Grenache Blanc. There is a period of up to 24 hours on skins and then fermentation follows in vat with a small portion in barrel with *bâtonnage*. Bottling is after 6 to 8 months. The reds are all de-stemmed and temperature is controlled during fermentation and then maceration for a balanced extraction. The Côtes du Rhône blending Grenache with Syrah, Cinsault and Mouvèdre, is soft ripe and berry laden for consumption young. The Rasteau reds are progressively more serious. The rich and ripe dark-fruited Cuvée Séduction is from a similar blend and is aged in vat. The complex, dark and beguiling Vieilles-Vignes is Grenache, Mouvèdre and Syrah and has a small portion aged in small barrels. The Cuvée Saint-Martin has recently been added to the range and is a blend of Grenache, Syrah and Mourvèdre with some vines up to 100 years old. The top red is the splendidly dense and concentrated Florianaëlle. This comes from the best steeply aspected south-facing plots and comes from roughly 70% very low-yielding Grenache, 20% old-vine Mourvèdre and 10% of Syrah. The wine is aged in barrel and on fine lees. It will develop very well over a decade. (DM)
Recommended Reds:
Rasteau Florianaëlle ★★★★ £D
Rasteau Saint Martin ★★★★ £D
Rasteau Vieilles Vignes ★★★☆ £C
Rasteau Séduction ★★★ £C   Côtes du Rhône ★★☆ £B
Recommended Whites:
Rasteau Elégance ★★★ £C

Dom. de Beaurenard (Châteauneuf-du-Pape)   *www.beaurenard.fr*

The Coulon family make an impressive range of stylish reds and whites in modern, well-equipped cellars. The lighter reds and white Châteauneuf-du-Pape are forward and full of fruit, the latter enjoying some lees-enrichment. The Rasteau has 20% Syrah blended into the Grenache, to add to the wine's structure. A limited cuvée Rasteau, Argiles Bleues is also now made from a similar blend. The regular Châteauneuf-du-Pape red is supple, rich and forward, whereas the Boisrenard is a dense, powerful wine produced from very low yields of 15–20 hl/ha. It requires 6 or 7 years' ageing in the best years. The fortified Rasteau is one of the better examples. (DM)
Recommended Reds:
Châteauneuf du Pape Boisrenard ★★★★☆ £F
Châteauneuf du Pape ★★★☆ £E
Rasteau ★★☆ £C Côtes du Rhône ★★ £B
Rasteau VDN ★★ £C
Recommended Whites:
Châteauneuf du Pape ★★★ £E

Dom. de Bérane (Ventoux)   *www.domainedeberane.com*

Although this 12 ha Ventoux property is recently established, the

vines are very old, particularly the Grenache that makes up 80% of the holding, and the terroir is excellent, south-east facing with a combination of finely drained argile and schist soils. Three cuvées of red are now currently produced including a marginally pricier (£C) Crescendo. Les Agapes is a blend of 80/20 Grenache and Syrah, while Les Blaques is Syrah-dominated (80%). Care is taken not to over-extract the wines. The wines are aged in cuve for 6 months and are marked by the quality and purity of fruit. Les Blaques will stand a bit of bottle-ageing, although the wines will be attractive young. Its also worth looking out for Le Rosé and Le Dit Vin, a light red style. (DM)
Recommended Reds:
Côtes du Ventoux Les Blaques ★★★ £C
Côtes du Ventoux Les Agapes ★★☆ £B

Dom. Berthet-Rayne   *www.berthet-rayne.fr*

The Berthet-Rayne family produce a small range of good middle-grade Châteauneuf-du-Pape and sound red and white Côtes du Rhône from their property in the north of the appellation, where the limestone soils are covered by the famous galet stones. Of the Rhônes, the white offers straightforward light, nutty fruit, while the red is more intense, a blend dominated by Grenache and sourced from vineyards just on the Châteauneuf appellation boundary. Among the Châteauneuf labels, the white is in a clean fresh, fruit driven style and should be drunk within a couple of years of release. The regular red is in a modern, fleshy mould with bright berry fruit and soft, easy tannins. It will drink well young. Vieilli en Fûts de Chêne is only released in good vintages and blends Grenache with Mourvèdre and Syrah. Cadiac is the most structured and dense of the wines, rich and impressively concentrated. Produced from equal proportions of Grenache and Mourvèdre it is relatively backward and firm young and will benefit from 4 or 5 years' cellaring. (DM)
Recommended Reds:
Châteauneuf du Pape Cuvée Cadiac ★★★★ £F
Châteauneuf du Pape Vieilli en Fûts de Chêne ★★★☆ £E
Châteauneuf du Pape ★★★ £E
Côtes du Rhône Vieilles Vignes ★☆ £B
Recommended Whites:
Châteauneuf du Pape ★★☆ £E

◉ Bois de Boursan (Châteauneuf-du-Pape)

Small, extremely quality-conscious Châteauneuf producer, located just on the edge of the village itself, with around 16 ha planted mainly to Grenache, Syrah and Mourvèdre. The white is relatively unexciting but both the reds are dense, powerful wines needing time to soften their youthful tannins and fiery character. Both are bottled without filtration. The Cuvée Felix is aged in part in smaller oak and offers more opulent and exotic characters. Both wines are finely structured and notably ageworthy. (DM)
Recommended Reds:
Châteauneuf du Pape Cuvée des Felix ★★★★★ £F
Châteauneuf du Pape ★★★★ £E

◉ Henri Bonneau (Châteauneuf-du-Pape)

A somewhat controversial producer, M. Bonneau is, as was the late Jacques Reynaud at CH. RAYAS, one of Châteauneufs more interesting characters. The two special cuvées, which are produced from a high proportion of Grenache, are generally only bottled if the vintage justifies it – otherwise a regular Châteauneuf-du-Pape is produced – and he sells to *négociants* to maintain quality. Both the Marie Beurrier and Réserve des Célestins wines will improve with a

decade or more in bottle. (DM)
Recommended Reds:
Châteauneuf du Pape Réserve des Célestins ✪✪✪✪✪ £H
Châteauneuf du Pape Marie Beurrier ★★★★★ £G
Châteauneuf du Pape ★★★ £E

⚫ **Bosquets des Papes** *www.bosquetdespapes.com*
The Boiron family own 8 ha of vineyards but also lease from other properties, working with close to 30 ha in total. The average vine age is around 50 years and over 3 ha is now up to 100 years old providing fruit with tremendous potential. There is an improving white as well as four potentially classic dense and rich reds from Chateauneuf. La Folie blended from old Grenache and Mourvèdre was added with the 2007 vintage. Vinification is traditional and the fruit is not destemmed. They have been some of the most impressive traditional Châteauneufs, particularly the old-vine Cuvée Chantemerle. Bottling was carried out according to demand, however winemaker Philippe Cambie (Domaine CALENDAL) is now consulting here so a more modern approach is taken. (DM)
Recommended Reds:
Châteauneuf-du-Pape Cuvée Chantemerle ★★★★★ £F
Châteauneuf-du-Pape A la Gloire de Mon Grand-Père ★★★★ £F
Châteauneuf du Pape ★★★☆ £E

Dom. Bressy Masson (Rasteau) *www.domaine-bressy-masson.com*
First class Rasteau-based property with 30 ha of vineyards. Although Viognier and Clairette are planted it is the red Côtes du Rhône Rasteau bottlings that stand out here. The regular red is a soft, brambly and immediately approachable blend of Grenache, Syrah, Mourvèdre and Cinsault. The Cuvée Paul Emile is fuller and richer and gets the benefit of some Grenache from vines that are over 80 years old. It is aged in small oak Expect to age the top red for at least 4–5 years. Also produced is a classic rancio Rasteau made in the traditional manner. (DM)
Recommended Reds:
Rasteau Cuvée Paul Emile ★★★ £C   Rasteau ★★☆ £C

Dom. Brusset (Cairanne) *www.domainebrusset.fr*
The Brusset family make an excellent range of wines, producing some 30,000 cases annually from a sizeable vineyard holding of 84 ha. The top wines are modern in style with pre-fermentation maceration, ageing on lees and no filtration. They are marked by rich, concentrated fruit and ripe but powerful tannins; they need to be cellared to show of their best but are less backward than some, particularly in Gigondas. Les Hauts de Montmirail is a magnificent, complex old-vine cuvée mainly from Grenache. In contrast lesser cuvées exhibit vibrant juicy fruit and are great youthful gluggers. (DM)
Recommended Reds:
Gigondas Les Hauts de Montmirail ★★★★ £E
Gigondas Le Grand Montmirail ★★★☆ £D
Côtes du Rhône-Villages Cairanne Vendange Chabrille ★★★☆ £D
Côtes du Rhône-Villages Cairanne Travers ★★☆ £C
Côtes du Rhône Laurent Brusset ★☆ £B
Côtes du Ventoux La Boudalles ★☆ £B
Recommended Whites:
Côtes du Rhône Viognier Les Clavelles ★★☆ £C
Côtes du Rhône-Villages Cairanne Travers ★★ £B

Dom. de Cabasse (Seguret) *www.cabasse.fr*
An impressive small range of Rhône wines are made here. In the

southern Rhône a total of 20 ha are spread across Séguret, Sablet and Gigondas with white varieties accounting for just 2.3 hectares. A fine, juicy rosé is made by the saignée method and a white Séguret, Les Primevères, comes from Viognier, Grenache Blanc and a little Clairette, cool-fermented to emphasise its fresh floral fruit. Among the reds, Les Deux Anges comes from Sablet and is the most obviously fruit-driven; Grenache dominates, with a little Syrah and Carignan added. The Cuvée Garnacho, not surprisingly dominated by Grenache but with a little Carignan, Counoise and Syrah, is richer and more complex with a marked old vine character showing through. The dense and structured Casa Bassa, a blend of Grenache and Syrah, is aged in barriques for 12 months and comes from vines up to 50 years old. It has perhaps more overt muscle than the piercingly intense Gigondas, which is aged in foudres. A Côtes du Rhône red, Marguerite, which is from young plantings of Grenache is also made. (DM)
Recommended Reds:
Gigondas Cuvée Jucunditas ★★★ £D
Côtes du Rhône-Villages Seguret Cuvée de La Casa Bassa ★★★ £D
Côtes du Rhône-Villages Seguret Cuvée Garnacho ★★★ £C
Côtes du Rhône-Villages Sablet Les Deux Anges ★★☆ £C
Recommended Whites:
Côtes du Rhône-Villages Seguret Les Primevères ★★ £B
Recommended Rosés:
Côtes du Rhône-Villages Seguret Le Rosé de Cabasse ★★ £B

Maison Camille Cayron (Cairanne) *www.maisoncamillecayran.com*
Formerly known as the Cave de Cairanne this is a good modern co-op producing an extensive range of wines from this important southern Rhône village as well as decent straightforward Côtes du Rhône. The basic cuvées represent good value with attractive berry fruit and are best drunk young, while the top wines are a notch up in quality. Les Voconces is made from over 40-year-old vines, while the red Camille Cayran Antique is quite firmly structured and will benefit from 3 or 4 years of ageing. Under the label a Rasteau, a Rasteau VDN and a Gigondas. The top reds are bottled unfiltered and represent very fair value for money. (DM)
Recommended Reds:
Côtes du Rhône-Villages Cairanne Camille Cayran Antique ★★☆ £C
Côtes du Rhône-Villages Cairanne Les Voconces ★★ £B
Côtes du Rhône-Villages Cairanne La Réserve ★☆ £B
Recommended Whites:
Côtes du Rhône-Villages Cairanne Les Voconces ★★ £B

Dom. Calendal (Côtes du Rhône-Villages)
The Just one single wine is made here, a red of real depth and density. It is a partnership between the influential consultant oenologue Philippe Cambie and the Ferrand family from Domaine des ESCARAVAILLES in Rasteau. Cambie is a controversial individual in a number of quarters, with an argument that he promotes wines with over developed fruit flavours that lose the typicité of the local appellation, in particular in Châteauneuf du Pape, where he consults widely. As ever opinions can be polarised. Experience of wines produced under his guidance in Châteauneuf in recent vintages suggests some examples of real depth and concentration and in the best cases impressive finesse as well. This red may not hit the stellar heights of the top wines from some of his clients but it is a brilliant buy for Côtes du Rhône-Villages. Currently sourced from 4.5 ha although this is may increase. The blend itself is unusual 50/50 Mourvèdre and Grenache. It will surely continue to develop for five years and more. Cambie also makes a small range from a number of

France

Rhône appellations under a second label Halos de Jupiter. (DM)
Recommended Reds:
Côtes du Rhône-Villages Plan de Dieu ★★★★ £E

Dom. de Cassan (Beaumes de Venise) *www.domainedecassan.fr*
This fine Beaumes-de-Venise property was equally well known for the quality of its fine, sturdy, classic Gigondas. The vineyards for this have been sold but up to the 2009 vintage this will be worth looking for. This is a dark, structured wine of great depth and persistence. The Beaumes-de- Venise bottles are really no less impressive. The regular red is soft and lightly structured but with sufficient depth to stand a little age. The Saint-Christophe benefits from some of the domaine's older vineyard holdings, some up to 45 years, which add greater depth and complexity. Expect both this and the Gigondas to evolve for 8–10 years. Further wines are also now made from Ventoux and the Côtes du Rhône. (DM)
Recommended Reds:
Beaumes-de-Venise Cuvée Saint-Christophe ★★★ £C
Beaumes-de-Venise ★★☆ £B   Gigondas ★★★ £D

Dom. du Cayron (Gigondas)
Just 1 wine is made at this traditional estate, and very good it is in most years. The vineyard holding is not small at 15ha, split between Grenache (70%) and an equal amount of Cinsault and Syrah, and yields around 5,000 cases a year. With vines over 50 years old and very well-drained stony soils producing fruit of exceptional quality, this is one of the best estates in the appellation. Occasional years can be a bit disappointing, but most recent vintages have been on good form. (DM)
Recommended Reds:
Gigondas ★★★☆ £D

Dom. de La Charbonnière *www.domainedelacharbonniere.com*
Good and consistent Vacqueyras and Châteauneuf-du-Pape. The wines are produced from a total of 21 ha of vines. Michel Maret avoids filtration and in the best years the results are very impressive. The Mourre de Perdrix is partially aged in new wood, but it is the impressively concentrated Haut Brusquières (blending a proportion of Syrah with Grenache) and Vieilles Vignes bottlings that really stand out. The Vacqueyras is a good chunky, earthy example and represents good value for money. A further red Châteauneuf has been added, L'Envol which is dominated by Mourvèdre. (DM)
Recommended Reds:
Châteauneuf-du-Pape Vieilles Vignes ★★★★ £F
Châteauneuf-du-Pape Haut Brusquières ★★★★ £F
Châteauneuf-du-Pape Mourre des Perdrix ★★★★ £F
Châteauneuf-du-Pape ★★★☆ £E
Vacqueyras ★★☆ £C
Recommended Whites:
Châteauneuf-du-Pape ★★★ £D

Gérard Charvin (Châteauneuf-du-Pape)
Small, high-quality domaine now run by Laurent Charvin, producing full blown, rich spicy reds. Both the Côtes du Rhône and the Châteauneuf-du-Pape offer quality and value. The latter is a blend of Grenache with a little Syrah, Mourvèdre and Vaccarese adding both definition and a firm youthful structure. The wine has been particularly impressive in the current run of fine vintages – a real blockbuster style, it will age very well. (DM)
Recommended Reds:
Châteauneuf-du-Pape ★★★★ £F   Côtes du Rhône ★★ £B

Ch. Beaubois (Costières de Nîmes) *www.chateau-beaubois.com*
A small range of well made and well-priced reds, whites and a good fruity rosé are made at this not inconsiderable 105ha property by Jacqueline and Fanny Boyer. Vineyards account for 60 ha of the family holdings and the wines are very much in the style of the appellation with Syrah playing a significant role with the reds and accounting for 40% of the domaines planting. The regular red and white Costières bottlings are more immediately approachable in style, the white lightly nutty and the red showing bright red berry fruit. The Elégance wines are quite a significant level up, particularly the white, which is dominated by Roussanne at 90%, the balance Viognier. Rich, nutty, herb scented, floral southern fruit is emphasised through cool fermentation and ageing for a short time on lees gives some definition and structure to the palate. Whites and the rosé though should all be enjoyed young. The Elégance red is dominated by Syrah, with something of a ripe Crozes character about it. Aged traditionally in tank for 6 months it will gain a little extra depth and complexity with two or three years cellaring. A pricier, albeit not expensive, red Confidence of impressive quality and red Harmonie are also produced. (DM)
Recommended Reds:
Costières de Nîmes Confidence ★★★☆ £D
Costières de Nîmes Elégance ★★★ £C
Costières de Nîmes Expression ★★ £B
Recommended Whites:
Costières de Nîmes Elégance ★★☆ £C
Costières de Nîmes Expression ★☆ £B
Recommended Rosés:
Costières de Nîmes Elégance ★★☆ £C
Costières de Nîmes Expression ★☆ £B

✿✿Ch. de Beaucastel (Châteauneuf-du-Pape) *www.beaucastel.com*
Among the very top echelon of producers in the southern Rhône. Notable for the organic approach in their 131ha estate vineyards, where all 13 permitted varieties are planted, the Perrins also employ a process called *vinification à chaud* for their red Châteauneuf, which extracts good colour and fruit and guards against bacteria and oxidation. The very finest quality is achieved in both red and white, the former unusually dominated by Mourvèdre and Syrah, and there is a good second label Coudoulet de Beaucastel. The red is not filtered but is given a light fining to help soften the very firm structure of the wine in its youth. Also produced are a range of négociant wines under the Domaines PERRIN label, while the Côtes du Rhône property Château du Grand Prebois is a recent acquisition. Further afield the Perrins have a partnership in the Californian Paso Robles winery TABLAS CREEK. Both the Châteauneuf red and white must be cellared, up to 8–10 years in top vintages. (DM)
Recommended Reds:
Châteauneuf du Pape Homage à Jacques Perrin ✪✪✪✪✪ £H
Châteauneuf du Pape ★★★★★ £G
Côtes du Rhône Coudoulet du Beaucastel ★★★ £D
Recommended Whites:
Châteauneuf-du-Pape Vieilles Vignes ✪✪✪✪✪ £H
Châteauneuf-du-Pape ★★★★★ £G
Côtes du Rhône Coudoulet du Beaucastel ★★★ £D

Ch. Beauchêne (Châteauneuf-du-Pape) *www.chateaubeauchene.fr*
This relatively sizeable domaine of some 80 ha produces not only fine, modern fruit driven Châteauneuf-du-Pape but also a number of Côtes du Rhônes from a range of sites and properties mainly to the north and south of Orange. As well as the wines profiled here

other wines include Côtes du Rhônes red and white Le Pavillon du Château Beauchêne from relatively young vines, albeit over 25 years, a varietal Viognier Grande Réserve, as well as Château Souffles de Costerelle. There are two Côtes du Rhônes-Villages, Château Beauchêne Les Charmes and Vignoble de la Vialle. A *barrique* aged Les Sens de Syrah is also made as well as white Châteauneuf-du-Pape The family have been based at the property since the middle of the 17th century and Michel Bernard has headed the current generation since 1971 ably assisted now by his wife Dominique and daughter Amandine. Immediately approachable is the fat, rounded, nutty cool-fermented white Grande Réserve white Côtes du Rhône. The intense fruit driven red bottling comes from vines up to 50 years old. Firmer and more structured is the impressive Premier Terroir, blending around a third Syrah and Mourvèdre with Grenache that ranges from 40 to 100 years. It is fully de-stemmed and vatted for up to three weeks. The darkly pepper spiced varietal Les Sens de Syrah is again de-stemmed and finely structured enough to age for five years or so. Of the two Châteauneuf reds, the Vignobles de la Serrière is softer more obviously fruit driven but with a good underlying depth from some older vines. The Grande Réserve is altogether richer and fuller, albeit in a modern style with immediately apparent and approachable fruit. It comes from 100 year old Grenache which adds real complexity, along with 15% of Syrah and 5% Mourvèdre. Expect it to continue to evolve well for at least six or seven years. (DM)

Recommended Reds:
Châteauneuf-du-Pape Grande Réserve ★★★★ £F
Châteauneuf-du-Pape Vignobles de La Serrière ★★★☆ £D
Côtes du Rhône Premier Terroir ★★☆ £C
Côtes du Rhône Le Sens de Syrah ★★ £B
Côtes du Rhône Grande Réserve ★★ £B

Recommended Whites:
Châteauneuf-du-Pape Vignobles de La Serrière ★★★☆ £D
Côtes du Rhône Grande Réserve ★★ £B

Ch. du Campuget (Costières de Nîmes) *www.campuget.com*
Sizeable Nîmes property with 160 ha under vine. As well as producing a range of Costières de Nîmes under the Campuget label, the Dalle family also own Château de l'AMARINE. A good nutty white blend from Grenache Blanc and Roussanne, a Vin du Pays du Gard Viognier and a rosé from Grenache and Syrah are produced in addition to the reds. Vineyard age now averages around 30 years. The soft, forward and lightly herb-scented Invitation red is a blend of Syrah and Grenache. The 1753 Syrah offers more depth and concentration and is a very modern, vibrant and fleshy style. A 1753 Grenache is also made. La Sommelière, the top wine is a Syrah dominated blend with real potential. (DM)

Recommended Reds:
Costières de Nîmes La Sommelière ★★★ £C
Costières de Nîmes Invitation ★★☆ £C
Costières de Nîmes 1753 ★★☆ £C

❀ Ch. de Fonsalette (Côtes du Rhône) *www.chateaurayas.fr*
Benchmark 11 ha Côtes du Rhône property owned by the Reynaud family of CHÂTEAU RAYAS. Emmanuel Reynaud now also undertakes vinification here as well as at Rayas and his own Vacqueyras property, CHÂTEAU DES TOURS. The regular bottling is a blend of Grenache with a sizeable dollop of Cinsault. These fine, intense and firmly structured wines are long-lived albeit expensive examples of the AC. (DM)

Recommended Reds:
Côtes du Rhône ★★★★☆ £F
Recommended Whites:
Côtes du Rhône ★★★☆ £E

Ch. de Fontsegugne (Côtes du Rhône)
Impressive, small Côtes du Rhône property which produced its own wines for the first time in 2000. The vineyard, planted on well-drained gravel-pebble soils, is tended with minimal use of fertilisers and the resulting wines are all bottled unfiltered. Three cuvées are produced. The Tradition, from over 30-year-old vines, is a blend of Grenache, Syrah, Mourvèdre, Cinsault and Carignan, while Santo Estello comes from 50-year-old vines and is a blend of Grenache and Syrah with a touch of Mourvèdre. It is aged for 10 months in 500-litre tonneaux. All the wines are marked by impressive fruit purity and the will develop well with 3 to 5 years' ageing. (DM)

Recommended Reds:
Côtes du Rhône Santo Estello ★★★ £C
Côtes du Rhône Tradition ★★☆ £B

Ch. Fortia (Châteauneuf-du-Pape) *www.vin-chateauneufdupape.fr*
The former owner of Château Fortia, Baron Pierre le Roy de Boiseaumarie was instrumental in setting down a set of rules for making the wines of Châteauneuf-du-Pape. These are maintained today and have been a key factor in ensuring the quality of the appellation and have been widely adopted elsewhere. His proposals included specified borders, grape varieties and viticultural practices among others. Appellations all over the world have since emulated these concepts. Fortia comprises some 30 ha of which less than 3 ha are planted to white varieties. At a time when the appellation is becoming as much known for rich, ripe and sometimes overripe blockbusters, the wines here are a welcome reminder of a more traditional style. They are structured and well made but may be approached with just two or three years bottle ageing and tend to offer the most in the great years. The white is a blend of Roussanne, Clairette and Grenache Blanc and the herb-scented, lightly honeyed elements of the Roussanne are immediately apparent. The Tradition red has more Grenache in its blend than the Baron, while the Reserve, the most recently established cuvée, has a greater amount of Syrah but still offers classic aromas of dark-berry fruits, herb-spice and *garrigue*. (DM)

Recommended Reds:
Châteauneuf-du-Pape Reserve ★★★★ £F
Châteauneuf-du-Pape Cuvée du Baron ★★★☆ £E
Châteauneuf-du-Pape Tradition ★★★ £D
Recommended Whites:
Châteauneuf-du-Pape Tradition ★★★ £D

❀ Ch. La Gardine (Châteauneuf-du-Pape) *www.gardine.com*
A modern approach to vinification here allied to a dedication to *terroir* results in an impressive range of wines. The reds are dense and deeply coloured when young but supple and impeccably balanced. In their youth they are sturdy and firm and they require several years' ageing. Temperature control is used in producing fruity, gloriously nutty whites, with new oak in abundance in the top wines. At La Gardine a new super *cuvée* L'Immortelle has now been added from very old vines, very fine although twice the price of the Gaston Philippe. The Brunels purchased the Lirac property Château Saint-Roch in 1998 and have brought about considerable improvements. The reds in particular have a fine, subtle *garrigue*-laden intensity. A small range of *négociant* wines are also made and

France

labelled Brunel de la Gardine. (DM)

Château La Gardine
Recommended Reds:
Châteauneuf-du-Pape Cuvée L'Immortelle ★★★★★ £G
Châteauneuf-du-Pape Générations Gaston Philippe ★★★★☆ £F
Châteauneuf-du-Pape Peur Bleue ★★★★ £F
Châteauneuf-du-Pape Tradition ★★★★ £E
Rasteau ★★☆ £C
Recommended Whites:
Châteauneuf-du-Pape Generations Marie-Léoncie ★★★★ £F
Châteauneuf-du-Pape Tradition ★★★ £E

Château Saint Roch
Recommended Reds:
Collioure ★★★ £D
Lirac Cuvée Confidentielle ★★★ £D
Lirac Cuvée Palmes ★★★ £D
Lirac Tradition ★★☆ £C
Recommended Whites:
Lirac Tradition ★★ £C

Brunel de La Gardine
Recommended Reds:
Côte-Rôtie ★★★ £E   Gigondas ★★★☆ £C

● **Ch. La Nerthe (Châteauneuf-du-Pape)** *www.chateaulanerthe.fr*
This large (for Châteauneuf) property has been performing at a
high level since the mid-1980s. Annual production is now around
25,000 cases. There tends to be less Grenache in the reds here than
elsewhere. The Cadettes, a sturdy blend of 100-year-old Grenache
and Mourvèdre, is right on the edge of ★★★★★ in top years.
Throughout the small range a modern, sophisticated approach to
vinification has produced excellent results, with destemming and
extended vatting for reds and increasing use of *barriques* for both
reds and whites. (DM)
Recommended Reds:
Châteauneuf-du-Pape Cuvée des Cadettes ★★★★★ £G
Châteauneuf-du-Pape ★★★★ £E
Recommended Whites:
Châteauneuf-du-Pape Clos de Beauvenir ★★★★☆ £F
Châteauneuf-du-Pape ★★★☆ £E

● **Ch. Mas Neuf (Costières de Nîmes)** *www.chateaumasneuf.com*
Luc Baudet has a sizeable property of 60 ha, 53 ha of which are
planted to red varieties. A fruit driven range of three wines are
produced, labelled IGP Conviviales, a red from Cabernet Sauvignon,
a white from Chardonnay and a rosé from Cinsault. A white Costières
de Nîmes Rhône Paradox is ripe and fruity with some nutty, spicy
tones blending Grenache Blanc and Roussanne. Richer and fuller is
the Compostelle Blanc, a blend of Roussanne and Viognier which is
lent some additional depth from ageing in oak. The red Costières de
Nîmes Rhône Paradox is a sturdy, forward blend of Syrah, Grenache
and Mourvèdre with a hint of Carignan adding some herbal spice
notes. The Compostelle red, a blend of Syrah, Mourvèdre and
Grenache is a serious step up. An additional red Château François
de Pasquières is elegant and spicy. Also now released under the
Rhône Paradox banner are premium Châteauneuf-du-Pape, Côte
Rôtie and Condrieu as well as a Crozes Hermitage. There are also
three very good IGP reds; Avec des Si is 100% Syrah, La Mourvache
a 50/50 blend of Mourvèdre and Grenache. There is also a limited-
production red super-cuvée, Armonio, made in association with
Louis Mitjavile of CH.TERTRE-RÔTEBOEUF in Saint-Emilion, which
is a thoroughly modern blend of Grenache, Merlot and Cabernet

Sauvignon. None of the top wines is either fined or filtered after a
long 30-day maceration and ageing is in *barriques* for 8–12 months,
in the case of the Armonio 20 months and in 100% new wood.
These wines will benefit from at least 2 or 3 years' further cellaring
after release. (DM)
Recommended Reds:
IGP d'Oc Armonio ★★★★☆ £E
IGP d'Oc Avec des Si ★★★★ £E
IGP d'Oc La Mourvache ★★★★ £E
Costières de Nîmes Compostelle ★★★ £C
Costières de Nîmes Château François de Pasquières ★★☆ £B
Costières de Nîmes Rhône Paradox ★★☆ £B
Recommended Whites:
Costières de Nîmes Compostelle ★★★ £C
Costières de Nîmes Rhône Paradox ★★ £B

Ch. Mont-Redon *www.chateaumontredon.fr*
By the standards of the appellation this is a large property
producing good to very good rather than exceptional wines and
with an output now approaching 70,000 cases a year. Vinification is
modern, using a mix of *inox* and some *barriques* for the Châteauneuf
bottlings. A Lirac property, Château Cantegril, was recently
purchased and these wines are now marketed under the Mont-
Redon label. Expect quality at the Cantegril property to improve.
The red Châteauneuf ages well over the medium term, acquiring
additional depth and finesse. These are well priced wines. (DM)
Recommended Reds:
Châteauneuf-du-Pape ★★★☆ £E
Lirac ★★☆ £C   Côtes du Rhône ★★ £C
Recommended Whites:
Châteauneuf-du-Pape ★★★ £E
Lirac ★★ £C   Côtes du Rhône ★☆ £B

Ch. Mourgues du Grès *www.mourguesdugres.com*
Some 30,000 cases of red, white and rosé are now made here
each year. As one would expect the majority of the planting is to
red varieties, which make up 51 ha of the 65 ha. Of these, Syrah
accounts for 70%, the balance being mainly Grenache with a small
amount of Carignan and Mourvèdre. Whites consist of Grenache
(40%), Roussanne (40%) and Viognier. Galets is the label for the
basic red, white and rosé and these are straightforward wines
characterised by their approachable, forward fruit. The second
tier Terre d'Argence and Cuvée 46 wines are more serious. There
is a nutty, floral white dominated by Roussanne and two dense,
powerful reds. The top wine is Capitelles des Mourgues, which
spends a year in barrel. There is also a premium rosé under the same
label. The top reds will improve with short ageing. (DM)
Recommended Reds:
Costières de Nîmes Capitelles des Mourgues ★★★☆ £D
Costières de Nîmes Terre d'Argence ★★★ £C
Costières de Nîmes Cuvée 46 ★★★ £C
Costières de Nîmes Galets Rouge ★★☆ £B
Recommended Whites:
Costières de Nîmes Terre d'Argence ★★☆ £C

Ch. d'Or et de Gueules *www.chateau-or-et-gueules.com*
This Costières de Nîmes based property was recently established in
1998. The vineyards have an excellent south to south-east exposure
and its large pebbles and stones retain heat well, aiding ripening. A
couple of rosés are produced including a Cuvée Trassegum which
is part barrel-fermented. The Cep de Diane Chardonnay is full, rich

and toasty, with an almost toffeed character. It is vinified in barrel on lees. A barrel-fermented Trassegum and fruit driven Cimels white are also made. Among the Costières de Nîmes reds, Cimel is a blend of Syrah, Carignan and Grenache. Some of the Carignan is very old and adds dark and spicy complexity. The wine is full of old-viney character. A level up are the Cuvée Trassegum red and La Bolida. Trassegum, blending Syrah with a little Carignan is not over oaked and is the better for it. La Bolida is a blend of 90% very old Mourvèdre and 10% Grenache. Rich and supple it is a wine of great potential. Two further Costières de Nîmes reds are made. Castel Noù is a blend of Grenache and Mourvèdre which is aged in barrel for a year and Qu'es Aquo is made from over 80 year old Carignan. Also recently added is an IGP d'Oc Syrah, La Charlotte. (DM)

Recommended Reds:
Costières de Nîmes La Bolida ★★★☆ £E
Costières de Nîmes Cuvée Trassegum ★★★ £C
Costières de Nîmes Cimel ★★ £C
Recommended Whites:
IGP d'Oc Le Ceps de Diane ★★☆ £D

⚫ Ch. Pesquié (Ventoux) *www.chateaupesquie.com*
Medium-sized property with 100 ha of vineyards producing close to 50,000 cases a year. Quality is generally good across the board, with attractive forward, fruit-driven white IGP bottlings and a ripe and crunchy fresh rosé. The well priced Le Paradou labels are full of fresh, vibrant fruit. Under the Terrasses label a serious rosé, a white (Viognier, Roussanne and Clairette) and a fine red are produced, the latter from Grenache and Syrah. The very well-crafted Quintessence white is a recent addition to the Chardonnay labels. The two stand out wines here though are the red Quintessence and benchmark Artemia. They are both richly concentrated and finely structured, among the best examples of an increasingly exciting appellation. Quintessence is 80% Syrah but the small proportion of Grenache over 70 years old. It is aged in small barrels, around 30–35% new. The top wine now is the Artemia a dense, powerful and superripe example of old vine 80 year old Grenache blended with an equal part of the oldest and lowest yielding Syrah on the property. The altitude of the vineyards at around 300 metres just adds that touch of acidity for balance and the rounded open texture on the palate is aided by malolactic in barrel. Expect the top two reds to continue to evolve for up to a decade, Artemia potentially for a little longer.(DM)

Recommended Reds:
Ventoux Artemia ★★★★ £E
Ventoux Quintessence ★★★☆ £D
Ventoux Les Terrasses ★★★ £C
IGP d'Oc Le Paradou ★★ £B
Recommended Whites:
Ventoux Quintessence ★★★☆ £D
IGP Les Terrasses ★★☆ £C
IGP Chardonnay du Pesquié ★★ £B
IGO d'Oc Le Paradou Viognier ★☆ £B
Recommended Rosés:
Ventoux Les Terrasses ★★☆ £C

⚫⚫ Ch. Rayas (Châteauneuf-du-Pape) *www.chateaurayas.fr*
Legendary estate, which produced stunning red and white Châteauneuf for decades under the late Jacques Reynaud. The second label, Pignan, is also very impressive and comes from a separate plot rather than a selection. The property consists of just under 14 ha with old vines planted on sand and clay/limestone soils, rather than on galets roulés. The red is made solely from Grenache

while an even split of Clairette and Grenache Blanc contribute to the very ageworthy white. The wines are now vinified by Jacques' nephew, Emmanuel Reynaud of CHATEAU DES TOURS, who also produces the wines at the Rayas sister property CHATEAU DE FONSALETTE. A Côtes du Rhône, Pialade is also made which blends mainly Grenache, Cinsault and a little Syrah. (DM)

Recommended Reds:
Châteauneuf-du-Pape ✪✪✪✪ £H
Châteauneuf-du-Pape Pignan ★★★★★ £G
Recommended Whites:
Châteauneuf-du-Pape ★★★★★ £G

Ch. Redortier (Gigondas) *www.chateauredortier.canalblog.com*
Although a little white is produced it is the reds that show real refinement and class at this excellent property. As yet the overall vine age, at around 25 years, is younger than at some other estates, so there should be more to to look forward to. The blend for the Gigondas is dominated by Grenache but there is a hefty dollop of Syrah as well. The wine is firmer and more structured than some of its neighbours. It undergoes extended cask-ageing and requires a few years of patience. The Beaumes-de-Venise Cuvée Monsieur le Comte is an undoubted star of that village. (DM)

Recommended Reds:
Gigondas ★★★☆ £D
Beaumes-de-Venise Cuvée Monsieur le Comte ★★★ £C
Beaumes-de-Venise ★★☆ £C
Côtes du Rhône ★☆ £B

⚫ Ch. Saint-Cosme (Gigondas) *www.saintcosme.com*
Louis Barruol owns vines only in Gigondas but in recent years he has made an excellent small range of négociant wines as well which are labelled Saint-Cosme. The Côtes du Rhône offerings represent excellent value, notably the reds, whereas the Gigondas limited release Valbelle, Le Claux, Le Poste and Hominis Fidis as well as the Châteauneuf-du-Pape and Côte-Rôtie are all impressively concentrated and ageworthy. The Gigondas bottlings are dense and powerful and with richly textured fruit and well judged new oak. They are among the finest in the appellation, both intense and very complex. There is also increasingly good Condrieu and the potential here is exciting. Red and white approachable, easy drink styles are also released under the Little James label. (DM)

Château de Saint-Cosme
Recommended Reds:
Gigondas Hominis Fides ★★★★★ £F
Gigondas Le Poste ★★★★★ £F
Gigondas Le Claux ★★★★★ £F
Gigondas Valbelle ★★★★ £F
Gigondas ★★★☆ £E Côtes du Rhône Les Deux Albion ★★★ £C
Saint-Cosme
Recommended Reds:
Côte-Rôtie ★★★★ £F
Châteauneuf-du-Pape ★★★☆ £F
Saint-Joseph ★★★ £E Côtes du Rhône ★★ £B
Recommended Whites:
Condrieu ★★★★ £F Côtes du Rhône ★★ £B

Ch. Saint-Estève d'Uchaux *www.vins-saint-esteve.com*
Some very good reds and whites are made at this sizeable 60-ha property in the northern Vaucluse, at the southern limit of the Côtes du Rhône-Villages appellation. There are three regular reds and the same number of whites. The straightforward white Côtes du

Rhône is a blend of mainly Grenache Blanc and Roussanne. There are also two fine Viognier-based whites, one from young vines which is blended with a little Grenache Blanc and a very striking top cuvée, Dionysos, which is 100% varietal. In reds, there is a good straightforward fruit driven Côtes du Rhône as well as two more serious Côtes du Rhône-Villages. Grande Réserve is 60% Grenache and 40% Syrah whereas the dense and impressively structured Vieilles Vignes is the reverse blend. The range is completed by a straightforward juicy rosé and a Méthode Traditionelle Blanc de Blancs sparkler. There is also a very limited production pricey oak-aged Viognier Cuvée Thérèse. Top reds will benefit from 2 or 3 years' ageing. (DM)

Recommended Reds:
Côtes du Rhône-Villages Vieilles Vignes ★★★ £D
Côtes du Rhône-Villages Grande Réserve ★★☆ £C
Côtes du Rhône Tradition ★☆ £B
Recommended Whites:
Côtes du Rhône-Villages Dionysos ★★★ £C
Côtes du Rhône Viognier ★★ £B
Côtes du Rhône ★☆ £B

Ch. Simian (Châteauneuf-du-Pape) *www.chateau-simian.fr*
This small biodynamically farmed Châteauneuf domaine has been producing some very good wines in recent vintages. The vineyard holdings are spread throughout the appellation. The property has been owned since the early 1980s by Jean-Pierre Serguier. As well as the Châteauneuf bottlings there are also several Côtes du Rhônes. A white Jocundaz is 100% Viognier, a red Jocundaz label is Côtes du Rhône Villages Massif d'Uchaux, a blend of Grenache and around a third Syrah as well as a Côtes du Rhône red. There are two white Châteauneuf cuvées, a village wine and a more expensive label, La Font d'Hippolyte which is unusually 65% Clairette with Grenache Blanc and Roussanne. The regular red Châteauneuf is opulent and approachable, full of dark fruits and with an underlying scent of herbs. The top wine though is undoubtedly the red Les Grandes Grenachières. A wine of dimension and depth , it is 95% old-vine Grenache Noir (with vines up to around 130 years old) along with other unspecified varieties. (DM)

Recommended Reds:
Châteauneuf-du-Pape Les Grandes Grenachières ★★★★☆ £F
Châteauneuf-du-Pape Le Traversier ★★★☆ £E
Côtes du Rhône-Villages Massif d'Uchaux Jocundaz ★★☆ £C
Recommended Whites:
Châteauneuf-du-Pape La Font d'Hippolyte ★★★☆ £E
Châteauneuf-du-Pape Le Traversier ★★★ £E
Côtes du Rhône Jocundaz ★★ £C

Ch. Sixteen (Châteauneuf-du-Pape) *www.chateau-sixteen.com*
Originally going solely under the Cuvée du Vatican label this property is now known as Château Sixteen. There are a total of 23 ha under vine and just 2 ha of the vines are white. These are planted to Clairette, Grenache, Roussanne and a little Bourboulenc which successfully adds acidity and grip to the lightly floral wine. The regular Cuvée du Vatican red Châteauneuf is an impressively dense, powerful and structured example that offers more depth than most of the so-called classique offerings from others in the AC. A Côtes du Rhône-Villages Vatican is also made. The dark and smoky Château Sixteen is one of the great wines of the appellation, a blend of old Grenache, Syrah and Mourvèdre partially aged in small oak and partially in *foudres*. Formidable depth and concentration are allied to great complexity. A second label Manus dei du Château Sixteen is

also made. Both Châteauneuf reds should be cellared for 6 or 7 years and upwards. (DM)
Recommended Reds:
Châteauneuf-du-Pape Château Sixteen ★★★★☆ £F
Châteauneuf-du-Pape Cuvée du Vatican ★★★★ £E
Recommended Whites:
Châteauneuf-du-Pape Château Sixteen ★★★☆ £E

Ch. des Tours (Vacqueyras) *www.chateaurayas.fr*
As well as owning this excellent 40 ha property, Emmanuel Reynaud, the nephew of the late Jacques Reynaud, is now vinifying the wines at Château RAYAS and Château de FONSALETTE. His Vacqueyras has long been a yardstick example for the AC and is produced from mainly Grenache from very low-yielding old vines. Always emphasising classic *garrigue* aromas, these are complex, even refined wines, in marked contrast to some of the more extracted examples of some of his neighbours. A ripe and fruit-laden red and nutty white IGP complete the small range. (DM)
Recommended Reds:
Vacqueyras ★★★☆ £E   Côtes du Rhône ★★☆ £C
Recommended Whites:
Côtes du Rhône ★★ £C

Ch. Val Joanis (Luberon) *www.val-joanis.com*
The Chancel family acquired this property in the 1970s and have since invested heavily in both the Château as well as the winery and vineyards. There are 186 ha under vine planted in calcareous soils, all farmed sustainably, of which 60 ha take the Côtes du Luberon appellation. The climate in the Luberon is mixed with the continental influence of the Alps meeting the maritime influence of the Mediterranean. The Côtes du Luberon labels are all three marked by a clean, fresh and vibrant fruit character. The strawberry scented rosé comes from Syrah and Grenache as does the spicy red which is matured for two years in older barrels. The white is a nutty, citrus scented blend of Grenache Blanc, Roussanne and Ugni Blanc. A reserve white, Les Aubépines, blends mainly Grenache Blanc, of some age now, over 40 years, as well as Roussanne. There is a limited skin contact at very low temperature followed by a cool fermentation and ageing on lees adding a rich creamy texture. The red Réserve Les Griottes is also a blend of Syrah and Grenache. Yields for both reserve wines are low barely 30 hl/ha and the rouge comes from three separate parcels on some of the estates highest sited vineyards. Dark and spicy with black pepper notes the wine is aged in one-third new Aller oak for between 6 and 12 months. It is bottled without fining or filtration. An additional reserve white Les Agasses comes from Viognier and there is a premium, low volume red Vigne du Chanoine Trouillet (£E). (DM)
Recommended Reds:
Luberon Réserve Les Griottes ★★★ £D
Luberon ★★ £C
Recommended Whites:
Luberon Réserve Les Aubépines ★★☆ £D
Luberon ★★ £C
Recommended Rosés:
Luberon ★☆ £C

Dom. Chaume-Arnaud (Vinsobres)
This is a good source of well-priced southern Rhône red and white. The domaine is small with 13.5 ha situated around the lesser-known appellation and village of Vinsobres. Reds are dominated by Grenache and Syrah and there is a little Viognier and Marsanne

for the white. Quality is key, yields are kept low and no artificial fertilizers are used on the soil. The property also benefits from some very old vines. The small amount of Carignan used in the Vinsobres red is now over 60 years old. Both the Vinsobres reds will develop well in bottle with 3 or 4 years' age. (DM)

Recommended Reds:

Vinsobres La Cadene ★★★ £C

Vinsobres ★★☆ £C   Côtes du Rhône★★ £B

Recommended Whites:

Côtes du Rhône La Cadene ★★☆ £C

>> Chêne Bleue (Ventoux) *www.chenebleu.com*

This small and very fine domaine is based in the Ventoux appellation and makes wines under both that classification as well as IGP Vaucluse. The property is high up in the Dentelles de Montmirail close to Gigondas and organic and biodynamic farming is practiced. The 35 ha of vineyards are planted in a mix of clay and limestone at considerable altitude, around 550 metres with a south, to southeast exposition and are ringed and protected by pine and oak forests. The Rolet family have a number of talented people who provide input to the domaine including winemaking consultants Zelma Long (who makes VILAFONTÉ in South Africa) and Philippe Cambie who has a long roll call of top Rhône Valley clients. While there is a traditional approach to winegrowing, the best modern techniques are employed and the winery is gravity fed. Yields are kept low in the range of 14 to 25 hl/ha and the harvest is hand picked. The rosé is a serious example and capable of short ageing. Coming from a blend of Grenache, Syrah and Cinsault it is fresh and zesty with delicate red fruits and restrained minerality. The complex Aliot white with hints of toasted nuts, citrus and an edgy minerality comes from Roussanne, Grenache Blanc, Marsanne and a tiny proportion of Viognier. The rich rounded texture is helped by nine months in small French oak. Astralabe is the most approachable of the three reds. Marked by rich black fruits and a hint of pepper spice it is a 75/25% blend of Grenache and Syrah raised for six months in *foudres*. The top two reds are benchmarks for the area. Abélard is dominated by over 40 year old Grenache with a hint of Syrah. The wine offers great intensity with complex red and black fruits, herb and oriental spices. Héloïse is equally fine, comprising mainly Syrah with a third Grenache and a touch of Viognier. More obviously black fruited with black pepper and liquorice aromas all apparent. Both wines are aged for 18 months in French oak and will evolve further over a decade from release. (DM)

Recommended Reds:

IGP Vaucluse Héloïse ★★★★★ £F

Ventoux Abélard ★★★★★ £F

Ventoux Astralabe ★★★☆ £D

Recommended Whites:

IGP Vaucluse Aliot ★★★★ £E

Recommended Rosés:

IGP Vaucluse ★★★☆ £D

Dom. de La Citadelle (Luberon) *www.domaine-citadelle.com*

Among the absolute top flight of producers in the Lubéron appellation. The Rousset-Rouards have 44 ha of vineyards spread across no fewer than 65 separate parcels. The soils are highly varied and they possess some very fine terroirs. The winery is completely gravity-fed and stainless steel, temperature control and new oak are all used. Of the IGP wines, Le Cabernet (Cabernet Sauvignon) is sound if a touch leafy, Le Viognier more interesting with some vibrant honey and peach character. A Chardonnay dominated

white, Court Métrage is also made. La Châtaignier is the basic Lubéron label and red, white and rosé are all produced. The red is soft and berry-laden, immediately drinkable but with real character. Les Artèmes white is an enticing floral, nutty blend of Roussanne, Clairette, Grenache Blanc, and a smattering of Marsanne which is aged in inox on fine lees. The red Les Artèmes comes from Syrah and Grenache with the remainder Carignan. Ageing is for 12 months in a mix of barriques and foudres. The top label red is Gouverneur Saint Auban which is an impressively dense and concentrated blend of Syrah and Grenache. Ageing for this is 12 months in small oak, 20% new. A Gouverneur Saint Auban white is also made from Viognier, Roussane, Grenache, Chardonnay and Vermentino. (DM)

Recommended Reds:

Côtes du Luberon Gouverneur Saint-Auban ★★★☆ £D

Côtes du Luberon Les Artèmes ★★★ £C

Côtes du Luberon La Châtaignier ★★☆ £B

IGP de Vaucluse Le Cabernet ★☆ £B

Recommended Whites:

Côtes du Luberon Les Artèmes ★★ £C

IGP de Vaucluse Le Viognier ★☆ £B

✹ Clos du Caillou (Châteauneuf-du-Pape) *www.closducaillou.com*

Jean-Denis Vacheron (related to the VACHERONS of Sancerre) has been in charge of the winemaking at this domaine since the late 1990s and quality has gone from strength to strength. Careful vineyard management, modern vinification with some malolactic in cask and a tight control of yields are producing excellent results. Les Quartz is tight and firmly structured, the Réserve bottling richer and more opulent with added dimension from a large dollop of Mourvèdre. The top two cuvées will age very well. (DM)

Recommended Reds:

Châteauneuf-du-Pape Réserve Clos du Caillou ✹✹✹✹✹ £G

Châteauneuf-du-Pape Les Quartz ★★★★☆ £F

Châteauneuf-du-Pape Les Safres ★★★★ £E

Côtes du Rhône Réserve ★★★★ £E

Côtes du Rhône Les Quartz ★★★ £C

Côtes du Rhône Bouquet des Garrigues ★★☆ £C

Recommended Whites:

Châteauneuf-du-Pape Les Safres ★★★☆ £E

Clos du Caveau (Vacqueyras) *www.closducaveau.com*

This small estate has been run with great skill in recent years. Indeed the Lao Muse is one of the signature wines of the appellation. The 12 ha vineyard consists of a single plot on the slopes of the Dentelles de Montmirail. With organically tended vineyards planted at some altititude on excellent limestone subsoils the potential for high quality is there and yields from Grenache, Syrah, Cinsault and Mourvèdre are also restricted to a maximum of 35 hl/ha. The Côtes du Rhône is soft, juicy and forward and the regular Vacqueyras is produced in a similarly fruit-driven style but offers a fim grip and structure. The Lao Muse is deeper with darker spicy berry fruit and a real old-vine quality and depth. The oldest vines here are now around 70 years. The Vacqueyras needs a little age, the Lao Muse ideally 5 years or so. (DM)

Recommended Reds:

Vacqueyras Lao Muse ★★★☆ £D

Vacqueyras Carmin Brillant ★★★ £C

Côtes du Rhône ★★☆ £C

Recommended Whites:

Vacqueyras Carmin Brillant ★★★ £C

Southern Rhône

France

Clos des Cazaux (Vacqueyras) *www.closdescazaux.fr*
The Archimbaud-Vache family make a surprisingly diverse range of wines from their holdings in Vacqueyras and Gigondas. There is a very good nutty white Vacqueyras, a blend of Clairette, Roussane and Grenache Blanc which is aged in *cuve* to emphasise its fruit. A very small amount of a 100% Grenache Blanc Quintessence is also made, along with a Vieilles Vignes bottling. The red Cuvée Saint Roch is mainly Grenache with some Syrah and Mourvèdre. The Templiers is dominated by Syrah. Green harvesting is practised and there is minimal intervention in the cellar. Particularly unusual and generally successful is a late-harvest Vacqueyras, Grénat Noble, produced from Grenache infected by noble rot. It has great depth and intensity. La Tour Sarrazin Gigondas is dominated by Grenache with a little Syrah and Mourvèdre both lending structure. A second Gigondas Prestige is also made. Expect the reds to develop well in the medium term. (DM)
Recommended Reds:
Vacqueyras Grénat Noble ★★★☆ £E
Vacqueyras Cuvée des Templiers ★★★ £C
Vacqueyras Cuvée Saint Roch ★★★ £C
Gigondas La Tour Sarrazine ★★★ £D
Recommended Whites:
Vacqueyras Cuvée des Clefs d'Or ★★ £C

Clos du Joncuas (Vacqueyras) *www.closdujoncuas.fr*
The Chastan's produce a number of very characterful, traditionally styled reds which can be purchased with significant bottle age approaching a decade from the vintage. Also made is a white Séguret from Clairette, Roussanne and Marsanne as well as a Gigondas rosé vinified from Grenache, Cinsault and Syrah. The vineyards, which are up to 90 years old, are spread across 30 ha and as well as being certified organic in 1989 (ECOCERT) they are also now farmed biodynamically. Vinification for the reds is traditional. Fermentation and maceration is in cement *tuns* and the Gigondas aged in *foudres* for 12 months, the Vacqueyras and Séguret in tank. The dense and powerful Gigondas offers rich fruit with a hint of earthiness and comes from mainly Grenache with a little Mourvèdre, Syrah and Cinsault. The Vacqueyras and Séguret are a touch lighter, with the Vacqueyras blended from Grenache and Syrah adding some additional substance, while the more spiced Séguret is comprised of mainly Grenache with Carignan, Mourvèdre and a number of other undisclosed varieties. A further Gigondas, Esprit de Grenache is also made and comes from the oldest Grenache and is aged in *demi-muids* as well as in *foudres*. (DM)
Recommended Reds:
Gigondas Esprit de Grenache ★★★★ £E
Gigondas Clos du Joncuas ★★★☆ £D
Vacqueyras La Font de Papier ★★★ £D
Côtes du Rhône-Villages Séguret Domaine La Garancière ★★☆ £C

Clos du Mont Olivet *www.clos-montolivet.fr*
These wines remain very traditional, old fashioned examples of the appellation, and in the best sense. However, an increasing number of moves towards modernity are having a striking effect on the quality and approachability of the wines and most important the quality and consistency of their fruit. Prior to fermentation partial de-stemming is now practiced and perhaps most important of all the wine is bottled (if not in one go for all the cuvées) after cask ageing, then very shortly thereafter. The wines, since 2000, are consistently showing better fruit and balance but also retaining the style and character of the domaine. The regular bottling is a touch

overshadowed by the top wine but offers dark and meaty fruit with subtle herbal scents and reasonable depth. The Cuvée du Papet is altogether bigger and fuller and loaded with old vine character. Dense and very concentrated, impressive complexity will be added to the wine with 10 to 15 years cellaring. A fruit driven lighter style, Le Petit Mont is also now made along with a number of Côtes du Rhônes. (DM)
Recommended Reds:
Châteauneuf-du-Pape Cuvée du Papet ★★★★☆ £F
Châteauneuf-du-Pape ★★★☆ £E
Recommended Whites:
Châteauneuf-du-Pape ★★★☆ £E

✿✿ Clos des Papes (Châteauneuf-du-Pape) *www.clos-des-papes.fr*
One of the great benchmark names in Châteauneuf-du-Pape, producing just 1 white and 1 red. The Avrils have 34ha of which 31ha are planted to reds. Considerable investment in the cellar during the 1990s has enabled the property to go from strength to strength. The red is a very structured, ageworthy example of the AC. It is always destemmed and the different varieties are fermented together, which the Avrils feel adds complexity. The red needs 5 or 6 years' patience and the white will also age well, which is unusual for a white Châteauneuf. Vincent has now taken over the winemaking from his father Paul. (DM)
Recommended Reds:
Châteauneuf-du-Pape ✪✪✪✪✪ £G
Recommended Whites:
Châteauneuf-du-Pape ★★★★★ £F

Clos Petite Bellane (Valréas) *www.clos-petite-bellane.com*
Impressive property producing modern, stylish wines with classic Rhône fruit. The vineyard covers an area of 44 ha and some of the vines, particularly the Grenache, are up to around 65 years old. The white Côtes du Rhône is half Roussanne and half Viognier and like all the whites is given a period of *macération pelliculaire*. The white Les Echalas is finer and purer, produced from 100% Roussanne. The red Côtes du Rhône is ripe, forward and brambly, the Valréas bottlings fuller and more concentrated they are both now blends of Grenache and Syrah. The top reds have real depth and concentration. Les Echalas is fine and complex, full of old-viney character and spicy, herbal scents. A Côtes du Rhône Village Valreas rosé, Altitude is also made. (DM)
Recommended Reds:
Côtes du Rhône Valréas Les Echalas ★★★☆ £D
Côtes du Rhône Valréas ★★☆ £C   Côtes du Rhône ★★ £B
Recommended Whites:
Côtes du Rhône Valréas Les Echalas ★★★ £D
Côtes du Rhône ★★ £B

✿ Clos Saint Jean (Châteauneuf-du-Pape) *www.closstjean.fr*
In recent vintages the wines at this property, located close to VIEUX TÉLÉGRAPHE, have been transformed from somewhat rustic and old-fashioned to dense, rich complex and very well made. Some of this is certainly down to consultancy from southern Rhône and Languedoc *oenologue* Philippe Cambie but also a commitment to lifting quality from the family. There are 41 ha with over half planted in a mix of *argilo-calcaire* and *galet roulés* top soils. nutty, stylish Clos Saint Jean blanc comes from an equal blend of Grenache, Clairette and Roussanne and vinified in small oak, a proportion new. The reds are all dominated by Grenache. The dark, spicy regular red comes from a yield of just 25 hl/ha, the top reds even less. La Combe des

Fous has a big dollop of old-vine Grenache, the Deus ex-Machina, the very oldest Grenache along with 40% of Mourvèdre adding a formidable underlying structure to the wine. All the reds will develop well for at least six or seven years, the Deux-ex-Machina potentially twice that. A further very limited release, Sanctus Sanctorum is also now made and comes from over 100 year old Grenache. The domaine also makes a further Châteauneuf-du-Pape red, Chimère, in partnership with Manfred Krankl of SINE QUA NON in California. (DM)

Recommended Reds:
Châteauneuf-du-Pape Deus ex-Machina ✪✪✪✪✪ £H
Châteauneuf-du-Pape La Combe des Fous ★★★★★ £G
Châteauneuf-du-Pape ★★★★☆ £E
Recommended Whites:
Châteauneuf-du-Pape ★★★★ £E

Dom. Coste Chaude (Visan) *www.domaine-coste-chaude.com*

Small hillside estate with 21 ha under vine. The vineyards are planted on a mix of gravel and clay soils with a large pebble topsoil providing excellent drainage – ideal conditions for producing excellent fruit. Grenache, Syrah, Mourvèdre and Carignan are all planted. The Côtes du Rhône and Côtes du Rhône-Villages are both soft, forward and brambly. The Rocaille and l'Argentière bottlings are altogether more serious and sourced from the plots at higher altitude. Rocaille is vinified from Grenache and Syrah and aged in *cuve*, offering an impressive depth of dark, spicy, lightly plummy fruit. L'Argentière by contrast is aged in small oak for 12 months, which is well integrated and complements the sweet and spicy berry-fruit character of the wine. (DM)

Recommended Reds:
Côtes du Rhône-Villages Visan L'Argentière ★★★ £C
Côtes du Rhône Visan-Villages Rocaille ★★☆ £C
Côtes du Rhône-Villages Cuvée Madrigal ★★ £C
Côtes du Rhône Cuvée Florilege ★☆ £B

Dom. Côteaux du Travers (Rasteau) *www.coteaux-des-travers.com*

Robert Charavin produces some of the best examples from this Rhône village, which now has its own appellation for dry red wines as well as for the fortifieds that the Rasteau AOC covers. He has 20 ha under vine, including a sizeable planting of old vines, and produces around 5,000 cases a year. In the vineyard everything is as natural as possible and no fertilizers are used on the soil. There is a good, nutty white, which blends equal parts of Marsanne and Roussanne. The soft, forward red Côtes du Rhône is produced from young vines and is Grenache and Carignan with some Syrah. More serious are the Rasteau reds. La Mondona is made from old vines, a blend of Grenache, Syrah, old Carignan and Mourvèdre which gets 12 months in wood and concrete. The complex, structured Cuvée Paul, is full of old-vine character and very ageworthy. Produced from 50- to 100-year-old vines it blends Grenache and Syrah with a little Mourvèdre. It needs a year or 2 of bottle-ageing to integrate the 18 months spent in oak. A Cairanne red and a Rasteau VDN are also made as well as two new Rasteau reds with the 2015 vintage, Les Travès and Lou Montel. (DM)

Recommended Reds:
Rasteau Cuvée Paul ★★★ £D
Rasteau La Mondona ★★☆ £C
Rasteau Labartalas ★★ £C
Côtes du Rhône Char à Vin ★☆ £B
Recommended Whites:
Côtes du Rhône-Villages Cuvée Marine ★★ £D

❀ Dom. de Cristia (Châteauneuf-du-Pape) *www.cristia.com*

Baptiste Grangeon makes very good red Côtes du Rhône and Châteauneuf-du-Pape in a modern accessible style. The Côtes du Rhône is aged in cuve and is light, soft and fruit-driven, whereas the Côtes du Rhône Villages is richer and sturdier. A blend of mainly Grenache with 20% Syrah, it is aged in a combination of cuve and used barrels. The white Châteauneuf-du-Pape is a blend of Roussanne, Clairette and Bourboulenc. Vinified in stainless steel it possesses very fresh fruit, full of citrus, nutmeg and herbs. Drink it young. A Vieilles Vignes example is also made. The regular red Châteauneuf is mainly Grenache but has a good proportion of Syrah and Mourvèdre blended in. Finely crafted, with attractive bright berry fruit, it has a firm but supple structure which will enable it to develop well over 5–7 years and to keep for longer. Like the white, a red Vieilles Vignes is also made which comes solely from 85 year old Grenache. The top wine, Cuvée Renaissance, is mainly sourced from a 100-year-old vineyard of Grenache with a small amount of 50 year old Mourvèdre added. Aged in old oak to preserve the remarkable intensity and character of the fruit it needs a minimum of 8–10 years to show at its best. Baptiste Grangeon's most recent venture is to make a number of other wines which are labelled Cristia Collection. These include a Gigondas, a Vacqueyras, a Rasteau, a Ventoux red as well as a Muscat de Beaumes de Venise and a Cotes de Provence rosé. (DM)

Recommended Reds:
Châteauneuf-du-Pape Cuvée Renaissance ★★★★★ £F
Châteauneuf-du-Pape ★★★★ £E
Côtes du Rhône-Villages ★★★ £C
Côtes du Rhône ★★ £B
Recommended Whites:
Châteauneuf-du-Pape ★★★☆ £E

Cros de la Mûre (Côtes du Rhône) *www.crosdelamure.sitew.com*

Small estate making stylish, elegant Côtes du Rhône, Côtes du Rhône-Villages and denser fuller Gigondas. A Châteauneuf-du-Pape has also been added. These wines are not blockbusters but display very good classic *garrigue*-scented red berry fruit. The Côtes du Rhône has a high proportion of old-vine Grenache and will drink well in the short to medium term. The Villages bottling has a higher proportion of Syrah and a touch more density and structure. The Gigondas is the sturdiest of the wines and will benefit from tucking away for 4 or 5 years. All the wines offer good value. (DM)

Recommended Reds:
Gigondas ★★★ £D
Côtes du Rhône-Villages Massif d'Uchaux ★★★ £C
Côtes du Rhône ★★☆ £C

Dom. de Deurre (Vinsobres)

Hubert Valayer's property is relatively newly established but the results are very promising and the wines have shown increasing potential. The vintages over the last decade have all been very impressive. The Saint-Maurice is supple and well-structured, with around 30% Syrah in the blend, and the Vinsobres richer, more savoury, with a touch of Mourvèdre. Both are edging towards ★★★. There are two fine varietal wines. Les Oliviers is 100% Syrah and the brilliant Les Rabasses 100% Grenache. Newly added Cuvée J.M. Valayer, which is aged in used *barriques*, resembles a very good Châteauneuf-du-Pape. (DM)

Recommended Reds:
Vinsobres Cuvée J.M. Valayer ★★★☆ £D
Vinsobres Les Rabasses ★★★☆ £D

Southern Rhône

Vinsobres Les Oliviers ★★★ £D
Vinsobres ★★☆ £C
Côtes du Rhône-Villages Saint-Maurice ★★☆ £C
Côtes du Rhône ★★ £B

Dom. Durban (Beaumes-de-Venise) *www.domainedurban.com*
The Beaumes de Venise Vieilles Vignes at this sizeable 57 ha property is a good, spicy, nicely intense red dominated by Grenache, with some Syrah and Mourvèdre. Made from 50-year-old vines, it is traditionally vinified and aged in *cuve*. A Gigondas and Prestige label red Beaumes de Venise are also made. However, it is the fortified Muscat de Beaumes-de-Venise that marks out this estate. One of the very best examples made, it is richly intense and gloriously honeyed but has a real finesse and elegance very rarely encountered in these wines. It should, though, in the style of the appellation, be drunk young and fresh. (DM)
Recommended Reds:
Beaumes-de-Venise Vieille Vignes ★★☆ £C
Recommended Whites:
Muscat de Beaumes-de-Venise ★★★☆ £D

❀ Dom. des Escaravailles (Rasteau) *www.domaine-escaravailles.com*
Now one of the finest addresses in Rasteau. Current owner Gilles Ferran, who took over the running of the property in 1999 is the third generation of his family here. The holding is quite extensive and stretches to 40 ha planted on the Rasteau Côteaux in *argilo-calcaire* soils as well as a further 25 ha, including plots in Cairanne and Roaix. Gilles Ferran has retained Philippe Cambie for guidance on vinification and between the two of them they also produce the splendid Côtes du Rhône CALENDAL. The Escaravailles range is fairly extensive. There are two well made whites, La Ponce is a Côtes du Rhône blend of Roussanne, Marsanne, Grenache Blanc and Clairette while the more serious Rasteau, Galopine is a rich and concentrated blend of Roussanne, Marsanne and Viognier. A fresh fruited strawberry scented rosé Les Antimagnes blends Cinsault and Grenache. There are a number of very well made red cuvées. The Classique Rasteau is an approachable and vibrant blend of Grenache, Syrah and Carignan, while La Ponce is a touch more structured and dense, a blend of very old Grenache and around 20% of Syrah. Les Antimagnes rouge is an impressive Grenache and Syrah from mainly Rasteau plots. The black-fruited, spicy Cairanne La Ventabren comes from south to south-east facing slopes of chalk and clay and includes a little old Carignan as well as Grenache and Syrah. The really concentrated blackberry and dark pepper scented Les Hautes Granges from Roaix comes from naturally low-yielding clay soils and blends 90% Syrah with Grenache. Perhaps the finest of the reds is the Héritage 1924 Rasteau which is made from the oldest Grenache plots. Full of very complex dark berry fruit the is a real old-vine quality. Three good examples of Rasteau Vin Doux Naturel are also made. A nutty white from Grenache Blanc, A rosé from Grenache Noir and a rich and characterful red also from Grenache. (DM)
Recommended Reds:
Rasteau Héritage 1924 ★★★★ £E
Côtes du Rhône-Villages Roaix Les Hautes Granges ★★★☆ £C
Côtes du Rhône-Villages Cairanne La Ventebren ★★★☆ £C
Côtes du Rhône Les Antimagnes ★★★☆ £C
Rasteau La Ponce ★★★☆ £C   Rasteau Classique ★★★ £C
Rasteau Vin Doux Naturel ★★★ £D
Recommended Whites:
Rasteau Vin Doux Naturel ★★★ £D

Rasteau La Galopine ★★★ £C
Côtes du Rhône La Ponce ★☆ £B
Recommended Rosés:
Rasteau Vin Doux Naturel ★★☆ £C
Côtes du Rhône Les Antimagnes ★☆ £B

Dom. des Espiers (Vacqueyras)
With cellars based in the village of Vacqueyras, Philippe Cartoux crafts his excellent wines from parcels totalling some 10 ha around Gigondas and Sablet. A little white and rosé Côtes du Rhône is produced but it is the top reds that particularly impress. The Cuvée des Blâches is wonderfully dense and gamey with some attractive herbal garrigue notes. It is produced from 35-year-old vines. Both Gigondas cuvées will be the better for 4 or 5 years' cellaring; the Sablet too will benefit from short ageing. Philippe is married to Cécile Dusserre at Domainde de MONTVAC and looks after the vineyards at both properties. (DM)
Recommended Reds:
Gigondas Cuvée des Blâches ★★★★ £D
Gigondas ★★★☆ £C
Côtes du Rhône-Villages Sablet ★★☆ £C
Côtes du Rhône ★☆ £B

Dom. de l'Espigouette (Côtes du Rhône) *www.espigouette.com*
An excellent source of both Côtes du Rhône as well as top notch Vacqueyras. Rasteau and Gigondas are also made. Bernard Latour maintains high viticultural standards with yields regularly below 30 hl/ha. This coupled with vines averaging over 40 years provides fruit of great intensity and potential. Manual harvesting is followed by a careful selection and vinification in traditional cement as well as stainless steel. A high proportion of the wines are then aged in *foudres* without recourse to fining and only a very light filtration is employed. The Côtes du Rhône is the most obviously forward berry-fruited of the wines, with a really dark-fruited spicy dimension in top years. The Plan de Dieu is tighter and more structured with a lovely old-vine quality. The Vacqueyras is a touch more complex with a dark, smoky and spicy edge and slightly firmer, chunkier tannins. Both the top wines will age nicely for three or four years adding a further depth and dimension. (DM)
Recommended Reds:
Vacqueyras ★★★ £D
Côtes du Rhône-Villages Plan de Dieu ★★★ £C
Côtes du Rhône ★★ £B

Caves Estezargues (Côtes du Rhône)
This small Côtes du Rhône-Villages co-op was established in 1965 and is quite different to many others. There are just over 20 growers with very small vineyard holdings and a handful with larger areas under vine. The larger growers now have individual wines produced for them and are of impressive quality. A range of other wines are also made under IGP, Côtes du Rhône and Côtes du Rhône-Villages banners. The approach to vinification is traditional but using the latest equipment with minimal handling. Reds are fermented at low temperature, around 20º Celsius to emphasise their fruit and vatting can last up to 4 weeks and there is no pumping over. The wines are neither fined nor filtered before bottling. La Granacha is sourced from a number of different growers and is 100% Grenache and full of ripe spicy berry fruit. The other wines profiled here are all Côtes du Rhône-Villages Signargues with the exception of the Domaine Pierredon, which is a Côtes du Rhône. Owners Miriam and Christophe Granier also have a Signargues bottling under their label

as well. Dark and peppery Domaine d'Andezon owned by Thierry Lampietro and Serge Paneboeuf blends 80% Syrah with the balance roughly equal proportions of Grenache, Mourvèdre and Carignan. Domaine des Bacchantes from Didier Kupke is dominated by Syrah and also includes Grenache and Mourvèdre and is typically dark and peppery. The elegant red berry fruited Domaine Gres Saint Vincent owned by Patrick Vincent is dominated by Grenache (60%) which is blended with Syrah, Mourvèdre and just a touch of Carignan. Domaine de la Montagnette from Jean-Marie Granier is also mainly Grenache (70%) and is blended with the same varieties as Gres Saint Vincent. Michel Trebillon at Domaine Les Genestas offers a touch more structure from his blend of Grenache 50%, Syrah 30% and Mourvèdre 20%. Away from the Côtes du Rhône, a Costières de Nîmes, Domaine de Perillière is also made. The wines all offer excellent value. (DM)

Recommended Reds:
Côtes du Rhône-Villages Signargues La Granacha ★★☆ £B
Côtes du Rhône-Villages Signargues Domaine d'Andezon ★★☆ £B
Côtes du Rhône-Villages Signargues Dom. des Bacchantes ★★☆ £B
Côtes du Rhône-Villages Signargues Dom. Gres Saint Vincent ★★☆ £B
Côtes du Rhône-Villages Signargues Dom. La Montagnette ★★☆ £B
Côtes du Rhône-Villages Signargues Dom. Les Genestas ★★☆ £B
Côtes du Rhône Domaine Pierredon ★★ £B
Costières de Nîmes Domaine de Perillière ★★ £B

Feraud-Brunel (Châteauneuf-du-Pape)

Fine quality small négociant operation run by Laurence Feraud of Domaine du PEGAÜ and André Brunel of LES CAILLOUX in Châteauneuf-du-Pape. The traditional-style wines are vinified by the Brunel oenologue, Philippe Cambie, in a manner similar to that at Pegaü and Les Cailloux. Results here are impressive across the board offering wines of real depth and concentration and showing true characteristics of their appellations. The Vin de France, Images du Sud, is an attractive, spicy, forward red blend. All represent good value. Laurence Feraud also makes a small range under her own Selection Laurence Feraud label. (DM)

Recommended Reds:
Châteauneuf-du-Pape ★★★☆ £E
Côtes du Rhône-Villages Cairanne ★★★ £C
Côtes du Rhône-Villages ★★☆ £C   Rasteau ★★☆ £C
Vin de France Image du Sud ★★ £B

Dom. Fond-Croze www.domaine-fondcroze.com

There are 70 ha now farmed biodynamically at this long-established Côtes du Rhône-Villages property. Father Raymond and sons Daniel, who tends the vineyards, and Bruno, who runs the cellar, have between them moved the quality at this estate to a new level in recent vintages. A fairly extensive range includes IGP Merlot and Chardonnay as well as straightforward Côtes du Rhône white and rosé. The white Cuvée Analys, a Viognier from very low-yielding, late-harvested vines, is of a different order. The spicy, berry-fruited regular red Côtes du Rhône blends Grenache (70%) with Syrah. The warmly spicy Côtes du Rhône-Villages Vincent de Catari is mainly Grenache with Carignan and just a smattering of Syrah and Mourvèdre. The top labels now also come under the Côtes du Rhône umbrella. The Romanaise, originally a blend of Grenache and Syrah, is now solely Grenache. Ageing is in 400-litre used barriques and there is now a real depth and style to the fruit. The Cuvée Fond Croze is dominated by Syrah with just a small proportion of Viognier. Again new oak is avoided and the wine is aged in used tonneaux. Rich and concentrated, this in particular will age well for up to a

decade. Added in 2004 was an impressively dark and spicy Cuvée Shyros and a Rasteau from Syrah, Mourvèdre and Grenache is also made. (DM)

Recommended Reds:
Côtes du Rhône Cuvée Shyros ★★★ £C
Côtes du Rhône Cuvée Fond Croze ★★★ £C
Côtes du Rhône Cuvée Saint-Romanaise ★★★ £C
Côtes du Rhône-Villages Cuvée Vincent de Catari ★★ £C
Côtes du Rhône Cuvée Confidence ★★ £B

Recommended Whites:
Côtes du Rhône Cuvée Analys ★★ £B

Dom. de Fondreche (Ventoux) www.fondreche.com

With their 30-odd ha Sébastien and Nanou Barthélémy are making benchmark wines for the appellation. Careful viticulture with increasingly old vines (now averaging over 40 years) and minimal interference throughout vinification and élévage is paying off with an impressive range. The rosé is a fresh blend of Grenache, Syrah and Cinsault. The regular red, blended from Grenache, Syrah and Mourvèdre, is silky and forward. Nadal is roughly equal proportions of Syrah and Grenache, a blockbuster style often marked by alcohol but generally well-balanced. A number of single varietal bottlings of reds have also been produced in recent vintages. Roussanne is an important component of the two whites. The regular bottling blends in some Clairette, Grenache Blanc and Rolle as well, whereas the Persia is almost exclusively Rousanne aged in barrel on its lees. The wines are well worth seeking out and very good value. (DM)

Recommended Reds:
Ventoux Cuvée Persia ★★★☆ £D
Ventoux Cuvée Nadal ★★★☆ £C
Ventoux ★★☆ £C

Recommended Whites:
Ventoux Cuvée Persia ★★★ £C
Ventoux ★★☆ £C

Recommended Rosés:
Ventoux ★★ £B

Font de Michelle www.font-de-michelle.com

Quality at this domaine has been impressive throughout the past decade, not least because of considerable investment in the cellar. The Côtes du Rhône and Rhône-Villages Signargues reds are fruity and approachable. Les Promesses is dominated by Grenache with some Syrah, Carignan and Cinsault, while Notre Passion blends Syrah and Grenache in equal parts. It is understandably denser and fuller but ripe and forward too. Both are 80% destemmed and get a two week maceration. A small portion Notre Passion is aged in oak. The white Viognier is 100% varietal, cool-fermented and marked by clean, lightly perfumed peach fruit. It should be drunk young and fresh. It is now released with a small number of more approachable reds under the Gonnet Pères et Fils label. White Châteauneuf-du-Pape is also for early drinking, although the stylish Cuvée Etienne Gonnet, vinified with a high proportion of Roussanne, will develop well over the short term. The regular red Châteauneuf used to lack real depth and substance, with part being vinified by carbonic maceration. The style now, though, is for sturdier, longer-lived wines and the Gonnets have produced serious wines in recent vintages. Part of the key is some very old Grenache: over 50-year-old vines go into the regular wine and 90-year-old vines into the barrique-aged (part new) Etienne Gonnet, which is now very cellarworthy and will improve for a decade or more. A further very limited production red, Elégance de Jeanne is also produced in exceptional years. (DM)

Southern Rhône

France

Recommended Reds:
Châteauneuf-du-Pape Cuvée Etienne Gonnet ★★★★☆ £F
Châteauneuf-du-Pape ★★★☆ £E
Côtes du Rhône La Font du Vent Les Promesses ★★ £C
Recommended Whites:
Châteauneuf-du-Pape Cuvée Etienne Gonnet ★★★★ £E
Châteauneuf-du-Pape ★★★ £D
Côtes du Rhône Viognier ★★ £C

Dom. de Font-Sane (Gigondas) *www.font-sane.com*
First-class producer of both Gigondas and Ventoux with 14 ha
of very low-yielding vineyards. The Ventoux is among the better
examples in that AC and excellent value for money. The vineyards
are planted on the lower slopes of the Dentelles and the climate
is warmer than most in the appellation. The regular Gigondas is a
spicy herb-laden blend of Grenache, Syrah, Mourvèdre and Cinsault,
while the oak-aged barrel selection Terrasses des Dentelles is dense,
powerful and very ageworthy. It is generally made from the oldest
vines on the property and requires 5 years' patience to show at its
best. (DM)
Recommended Reds:
Gigondas Terrasses des Dentelles ★★★☆ £D
Gigondas ★★★ £C   Ventoux ★★ £B

Dom. La Garrigue (Vacqueyras) *www.domaine-la-garrigue.fr*
Very good traditional domaine with 65 ha of vineyard spread across
Vacqueyras and Gigondas with additional holdings in Beaumes
de Venise and Côtes du Rhône. Clairette and Grenache Blanc
make up the blend of the white Vacqueyras but the main focus of
the property is on red Vacqueyras and Gigondas from plantings
dominated by Grenache with a smattering of Syrah, Mourvèdre
and Cinsault. Vinification is traditional, with no destemming and no
fining or filtration. There is a 20 day *cuvaison* and the resulting wines
are sturdy and powerful. The Cuvée de Hostellerie is particularly fine
and often close to ★★★★. (DM)
Recommended Reds:
Vacqueyras Cuvée de Hostellerie ★★★☆ £D
Vacqueyras ★★★ £C
Gigondas ★★★ £D

❀ Dom. Giraud (Châteauneuf-du-Pape) *www.domainegiraud.fr*
Brother and sister François and Marie Giraud are the latest
generation to run this increasingly fine small Châteauneuf property.
They now have 19 ha spread widely across the whole appellation
with holdings in no fewer than 64 different parcels of vineyards. The
white, which blends Grenache, Clairette, Bourboulenc and Roussane
is harvested fresh in the early morning and fermented in a mix of
demi-muids and stainless steel. The reds are generally destemmed,
although this depends on the vintage. Most of the wine is aged
for around 18 months in large cement vats with just the Syrah
components of the Tradition and Gallimardes seeing small oak to
reduce the reductive nature of the variety. Les Grenaches des Pierres
is 100% varietal and from the family's oldest vines. The Gallimardes
white is not only rich and intense but has excellent balanced acidity,
the Tradition is approachable but complex, the Gallimardes red a
touch more backward. The rich, dark-fruited and smoky Grenaches
des Pierres comes from century old vines planted in sandy soils in
the Crau area close to Château RAYAS. (DM)
Recommended Reds:
Châteauneuf-du-Pape Les Grenaches des Pierres ★★★★★ £G
Châteauneuf-du-Pape Gallimardes ★★★★☆ £F

Châteauneuf-du-Pape Tradition ★★★★ £E
Recommended Whites:
Châteauneuf-du-Pape Gallimardes ★★★★ £E

Gour de Chaulé (Gigondas) *www.gourdechaule.com*
Aline Bonfils is the latest generation of her family to run this fine
small Gigondas based domaine, founded in 1900 and now farmed
with organic methods. She is assisted by her daughter Stephanie
Fumose who will continue the tradition of women running the
property. The fruit was sold off until the 1970s and even today
only half the crop is retained for the domaine wines. The bulk of
the holding is in Gigondas although parcels are also owned in
Vacqueyras and Côtes du Rhône vineyards. Much of the vineyard
was replanted immediately after the great winter freeze of 1956.
Some parcels though are up to 100 years old and undoubtedly
contribute to the depth and gamey, dark fruited complexity of
the Tradition cuvée. The majority of the *vignoble*, around 85%
is planted to Grenache with the balance comprising Syrah,
Mourvèdre and a little Cinsault. Vinification for the red, which has
no Cinsault, is traditional. The fruit is not destemmed, there is a
three week maceration on skins and the wine is aged for up to 24
months in large *foudres*. It is bottled without fining or filtration.
The winemaking may offer little in the way of modern techniques
but in recent vintages the Tradition has shown real class with
depth, intensity and an impressive fruit purity. The rosé, an unusual
example for Gigondas, is fruit driven and immediately appealing. It
includes 40% each of both Grenache and Cinsault with around 20%
Mourvèdre, which gives it enough structure to work well with food.
A small amount of red Côtes du Rhône is also made. (DM)
Recommended Reds:
GigondasTradition ★★★★ £D
Recommended Rosés:
Gigondas Amour de Rosé ★★ £B

❀ Gourt de Mautens (IGP de Vaucluse) *www.gourtdemautens.com*
Enormously impressive producer now classified as organic
(ECOCERT) and biodynamic (DEMETER). Because of Jérôme Bressy's
desire to make traditional and natural wines the domaine no
longer takes the Rasteau appellation. with some 13 ha planted
almost exclusively to red varieties: Grenache, Carignan, Syrah,
Mourvèdre and a few others. The rich, dense and ageworthy red
is produced from vines that are up to 100 years old. The Bressy
style is to create wines with considerable depth, offering not only
impressive concentration but with a really complex, dark and spicy
quality. In recent vintages it has been quite as good as many a top
Châteauneuf. The white, a blend of Bourboulenc and Grenache
Blanc, doesn't quite hit the same stellar heights but is still among
the most interesting and structured examples of the area. In
addition a third wine an unusual and partially oak aged rosé offers
additional complexity with cellaring. In keeping with the approach,
the wines are bottled unfiltered. (DM)
Recommended Reds:
IGP de Vaucluse ★★★★★ £F
Recommended Whites:
IGP de Vaucluse ★★★★ £E

❀ Dom. Gramenon (Côtes du Rhône) *www.domaine-gramenon.fr*
Long established as one of the great producers in the lesser area
of the Côtes du Rhône. Michèle Aubéry-Laurent continues to run
this family domaine with great skill. The 26ha of vineyard is planted
to Grenache and Syrah with a little Cinsault and Carignan for the

reds and a little Clairette and Viognier for the whites. Yields are very low and minimal handling and an absence of filtration in the cellar produces wines of density, concentration and finesse. The remarkable Ceps Centenaires Cuvée Mémé, produced from very old vines, is as fine as the very best from the southern Rhône. Prices are very reasonable as well. (DM)

Recommended Reds:
Côtes du Rhône Ceps Centenaires La Mémé ★★★★ £E
Côtes du Rhône-Villages Les Laurentides ★★★☆ £D
Côtes du Rhône La Sagesse ★★★☆ £D
Côtes du Rhône Sierra du Sud ★★☆ £C
Recommended Whites:
Côtes du Rhône Vie on y est ★★★ £D

Dom. de Grand Tinel *www.domainegrandtinel.com*
Fine, traditional old Châteauneuf property producing earthy, robust reds, albeit without the power of their counterparts a decade and more ago. Alexis Establet is produced from the family's parcels of particularly old vines and shows greater complexity. Three other wines are also made. A white Châteauneuf is mainly vinified in stainless steel, a fairly serious red Côtes du Rhône comes from mainly older Grenache and a 100% old vine Grenache Châteauneuf red, Cuvée Héres, complete the small portfolio. (DM)

Recommended Reds:
Châteauneuf-du-Pape Cuvée Alexis Establet ★★★★☆ £F
Châteauneuf-du-Pape ★★★☆ £E

Dom. Grand Veneur *www.domaine-grand-veneur.com*
Grand Veneur is a part of Vignobles Alain Jaume & Fils. The Jaume family produce a small range of négociant wines from throughout the southern Rhône and also own the Lirac property Clos de Sixte and some of the merchant wines are indeed very good. It is the Grand Veneur wines here though which are the benchmarks. As well as the Châteauneuf bottlings there is a Côtes du Rhône white from Viognier and a red Côtes du Rhône-Villages "Les Champauvins". The domaine is planted to 16 ha and is located in the north of the AC, close to Orange. The majority of the vineyard is dominated by the classic stone soils of the appellation and a proportion of the vines are now up to 90 years of age. The red and white bottlings of Châteauneuf are very good well made examples of the appellation. The white Miocène in particular should be drunk young. La Fontaine and particularly Les Origines offer greater depth and complexity. A small amount of a new cuvée Vieilles-Vignes is also now made. (DM)

Domaine Grand Veneur
Recommended Reds:
Châteauneuf-du-Pape Vieilles Vignes ★★★★★ £F
Châteauneuf-du-Pape Les Origines ★★★★☆ £F
Châteauneuf-du-Pape Le Miocène ★★★☆ £E
Lirac Clos de Sixte ★★★☆ £D
Côtes du Rhône-Villages Les Champauvins ★★★ £C
Recommended Whites:
Châteauneuf-du-Pape La Fontaine ★★★★ £E
Châteauneuf-du-Pape Le Miocène ★★★☆ £E
Alain Jaume & Fils
Recommended Reds:
Châteauneuf-du-Pape Vieux Terron ★★★ £E
Vacqueyras Grande Garrigue ★★ £C

Dom. du Grapillon d'Or *www.domainedugrapillondor.com*
Bernard Chauvet produces good traditional wines from around 15 ha in Gigondas, including several different parcels, and a further 9

ha in Vacqueyras. Plantings are dominated by Grenache but also include Syrah and Cinsault and, as is the practice in a number of properties, they are vinified together. The fruit is not destemmed and there is a long *cuvaison* of up to 20 days for the Gigondas. The Vacqueyras is the lighter of the wines and will drink well with 2 or 3 years age, while the Gigondas is sturdy and masculine, and will add increasing complexity with up to 10 years' age. The wines are bottled without filtration after ageing in old *foudres*. A second Gigondas, Excellence is dominated by old Grenache. (DM)

Recommended Reds:
Gigondas En Foudres ★★★☆ £D
Vacqueyras ★★☆ £C

❀ **Dom. Olivier Hillaire (Châteauneuf-du-Pape)**
The vineyards of this domaine were owned by the Boiron family and you will find earlier vintages under the domaine name of des RELAGNES. The family had been established in the appellation since 1716 and had a holding of vines averaging over 60 years of age. Henri Boirons son-in-law Olivier Hillaire purchased a part of the property in 2006 and retained just 8 ha of the holding. Château CALISSANNE in Provence purchased the other vineyards and release Domaine des Relagnes wines under the Clef de Saint-Thomas and Pierre Troupel labels. The Hillaire Côtes du Rhône Vieilles Vignes is a rich, spicy forward style and should be drunk young, as should the white Châteauneuf. The red Châteauneuf is a blend of Grenache, Syrah, Mourvèdre and Cinsault and shares the rich and ripe almost opulent style that Hillaire is producing his wines now. The Petits Pieds d'Armande comes mainly from a century-old plot of Grenache in the La Crau sector of the appellation with the vines planted in sandy soils. This is aged in a mix of small and larger oak as well as tank and is very rich and concentrated with intense sweet dark fruit. It is radically different from the traditional style of the appellation and will not please all palates. (DM)

Recommended Reds:
Châteauneuf-du-Pape Les Petits Pieds d'Armand ★★★★★ £F
Châteauneuf-du-Pape ★★★★ £E
Côtes du Rhône Vieilles Vignes ★★★ £C
Recommended Whites:
Châteauneuf-du-Pape ★★★☆ £E

❀❀ **Dom. de La Janasse (Châteauneuf-du-Pape)** *www.lajanasse.com*
Splendid, medium-sized domaine producing good to excellent wines across the board from 50 ha of vines. Les Garrigues comes from very old Grenache, Terre d'Argile from an equal blend of Grenache, Syrah and Mourvdre. The Châteauneuf vines are planted on ideal, free-draining stony soils and this, together with a vine age averaging over 60 years, results in lovely supple, dense and powerful wines. Vinification is a good deal more modern than at some properties in the region. Jean-Luc COLOMBO has consulted here and part of the red crop is always destemmed. Ageing is in an assortment of vessels with some new oak being used for the red and white Châteauneuf-du-Pape. The Chaupin and Vieilles-Vignes reds develop very well in bottle and should be given at least 4 or 5 years. (DM)

Recommended Reds:
Châteauneuf-du-Pape Vieilles Vignes ✿✿✿✿✿ £G
Châteauneuf-du-Pape Cuvée Chaupin ★★★★★ £F
Châteauneuf-du-Pape ★★★★ £E
Côtes du Rhône-Villages Terre d'Argile ★★★ £C
Côtes du Rhône-Villages Les Garrigues ★★☆ £C
Côtes du Rhône Tradition ★★☆ £B

Southern Rhône

IGP de la Principaute d'Orange Terre de Buissiere ★★ £B
Recommended Whites:
Châteauneuf-du-Pape Prestige ★★★★☆ £F
Châteauneuf-du-Pape Tradition ★★★ £D
Côtes du Rhône ★☆ £B
IGP de la Principaute d'Orange Viognier ★★ £B

⊛ Dom. La Barroche www.domainelabarroche.com
This small domaine has been in the same family since the 17th century, however it is far more recently in 2003 that wines have been made at the property rather than the harvest being sold off. Julien Barrot took over the full-time running of the domaine in 2006. He is the first of his family to be formerly trained in winemaking at the University of Montpelier. The vineyard is planted to a range of varieties and with an average age of over 60 years. In the winery most processes can be handled by gravity and the wines are richly textured, very complex, although modern and approachable. They get a cold maceration prior to fermentation which aids the style. The Domaine Signature bottling is a blend of Grenache, Mourvèdre, Syrah and Cinsault. The Fiancée is a 50/50 *assemblage* of 100 year old Grenache and Syrah, while the brilliant Pure is a 100% Grenache from the oldest vines planted close to Rayas. There is also a fourth cuvée, Terroir which comes from mainly younger Grenache. (DM)
Recommended Reds:
Châteauneuf-du-Pape Pure ★★★★★ £G
Châteauneuf-du-Pape Fiancée ★★★★★ £F
Châteauneuf-du-Pape Signature ★★★★ £E

La Bastide Saint Dominique www.bastide-st-dominique.com
Eric Bonnet has now taken over the reins at his family domaine where he makes a small range of Châteauneuf-du-Pape, Côtes du Rhône as well as red white and rosé IGP. The results are impressive with increasingly persuasive examples being made. The domaine consists of just over 30 ha with around a third planted in Châteauneuf-du-Pape. Regular red and white Côtes du Rhône are attractive and approachable. The red has a little Syrah adding extra substance to the Grenache majority, while the white has a substabntial proportion of Viognier emphasising the wines bright peachy fruit. The characterful Côtes du Rhône-Villages comprises Grenache, Syrah, Mourvèdre and Carignan while the Côtes du Rhône Jules Rochebonne is dominated by Syrah which is aged in smaller oak with a dark, spicy black fruit quality. The white Châteauneuf-du-Pape is blended from roughly one-third each of Clairette rosé, Roussanne and Grenache and from vines ranging from 25 to 50 years old adding further complexity. All the red Châteauneuf-du-Pape are stylish and modern, not a hint of rusticity. The village wine offers good depth and substance as well as attractive dark berry fruit. A combination dominated by Grenache with Syrah, Mourvèdre and Cinsault, the wine is aged for up to 18 months in tank. The top two cuvées are both very impressive and ageworthy. Les Hespérides is rich, dark fruited and concentrated, it comes from half Grenache with equal proportions of Syrah and Mourvèdre both of which are aged in small oak for a year and a half. Secrets de Pignan is intense and very complex vinified from nearly 100 year old Grenache planted in the *lieu-dit* of Pignan and just a small proportion of Mourvèdre adding additional structure. (DM)
Recommended Reds:
Châteauneuf-du-Pape Secret de Pignan ★★★★★ £F
Châteauneuf-du-Pape Les Hespérides ★★★★☆ £F
Châteauneuf-du-Pape ★★★☆ £E
Côtes du Rhône-Villages ★★☆ £C

Côtes du Rhône Jules Rochebonne ★★★ £C
Côtes du Rhône ★★ £B
Recommended Whites:
Châteauneuf-du-Pape ★★★☆ £D
Côtes du Rhône ★★ £B

Dom. La Blaque (Côteaux de Pierrevert) www.domainelablaque.fr
As well as being the leading property in size at 62 ha, Domaine la Blaque is also the beacon for quality in this small (450 ha), little-known but potentially fine appellation. A range of AC wines are joined by a couple of IGP labels, a fresh fragrant Viognier and a Pinot Noir. The vineyards are planted at altitude, 450–550m up in the Alpes de Haute Provence, and the Alps proper can be seen in the distance from the vineyards. The climate, though, is very benign for wine-growing. There are up 320 sunny days a year and during the summer the diurnal swing in temperature between day and night ensures good acidity in the fruit. The regular AC labels are vinified to emphasise their fruit, although the red has the structure to stand a little age. Both the red and white Reserves will develop well in bottle. The white, a blend of Grenache Blanc, Vermentino and Roussanne is barrel-fermented with rich, concentrated honey, citrus and nutmeg aromas and impressive structure. It will develop well over 5 years or so. The dense and structured Reserve red is mainly Syrah with carefully selected Grenache. Aged in oak for 12 months, it is dense and structured, full of black pepper and rich blackberry fruit and just a hint of herb spice. The top wine, Cuvée Collection, is dominated by old-vine Syrah. Vinified with whole bunches and macerated for 4 weeks before ageing in new oak, it is rich, pure and ageworthy. (DM)
Recommended Reds:
Côteaux de Pierrevert Reserve ★★★ £D
Côteaux de Pierrevert ★★☆ £C
Recommended Whites:
Côteaux de Pierrevert Reserve ★★★ £D
Côteaux de Pierrevert ★★☆ £C
Recommended Rosés:
Côteaux de Pierrevert ★☆ £B

Dom. La Bouissiere (Gigondas)
The Faravels make particularly striking and intense Gigondas from a small holding of just 8ha. The regular red is a blend of Grenache (70%) and Syrah. Ageing is in a mix of barrels and *cuve*, with all the oak having been used previously. Old vines of close to 40 years and no fining or filtration all contribute to the quality. The rich, and dense Font de Tonin is from even older vines and gets around one-third new wood. The blend here is roughly half Grenache and a quarter each of Mourvèdre and Syrah. Although high in potential alcohol the wines retain reasonable balance. (DM)
Recommended Reds:
Gigondas La Font de Tonin ★★★☆ £E
Gigondas Traditionelle ★★★ £D

Dom. Lafond Roc-Epine (Tavel) www.roc-epine.com
Excellent-value wines produced from Lirac, Châteauneuf-du-Pape and the Côtes du Rhône as well as one of the better Tavels, which shows some vibrant fresh fruit. The Lirac and Châteauneuf-du-Pape are blended from a mix of Grenache, Syrah and Mourvèdre, while the Côtes du Rhône is just Grenache and Syrah. Vinification of the reds is modern with fermentation in stainless steel before ageing in a mix of large and small oak. In addition, the Lafonds produce a straightforward, pleasant white Lirac from a blend of Grenache

Blanc, Viognier and Roussanne and a sumptuously rich special cuvée La Ferme Romaine, which is aged in small oak for a year. The Liracs and Châteauneuf-du-Pape will evolve well in the medium term. (DM)

Recommended Reds:

Châteauneuf-du-Pape ★★★★ £E
Lirac La Ferme Romaine ★★★☆ £D
Lirac ★★★ £C Côtes du Rhône ★★ £B

Recommended Whites:

Lirac ★★★ £C

Dom. La Guintrandy (Visan) *www.vins-cuilleras.com*

Olivier Cuilleras is emerging as one of the new stars of the southern Rhône. His family possesses 28ha of vineyards, all but 1ha being planted to reds, and produces 4–5,000 cases a year. The domaine is characterised by the extent of its old-vine plantings, which contribute greatly to the quality of the wines. As well as the 3 fine bottlings from Visan there is an improving Côtes du Rhône, which includes 70 % of 30-year-old Grenache and some very old Carignan. The IGP red, generally 50/50 Grenache and Syrah, is produced from some of the youngest vines on the property. The Visan Vieilles Vignes is a blend of mainly 50-year-old Grenache with a little Carignan and Syrah. The Cuvée Les Devès and top Cuvée Louise Amelie are both aged in oak, the Louise Amelie seeing some new wood. These wines are marked out by pure, rich and complex old-vine character. Expect all the Visan bottlings to develop well over 5 years or more. An old vine Cairanne is also now made. (DM)

Recommended Reds:

Côtes du Rhône-Villages Visan Louise Amelie ★★★☆ £D
Côtes du Rhône-Villages Visan Vieilles Vignes ★★★ £D
Côtes du Rhône-Villages Visan Les Devès ★★☆ £C
Côtes du Rhône ★★ £B
IGP de Comté de Grignan ★☆ £B

Dom. La Roquète (Châteauneuf-du-Pape) *www.vignoblesbrunier.fr*

While this property is owned by the Bruniers it is quite separate from VIEUX TÉLÉGRAPHE. Produced from vineyard parcels spread throughout the appellation, these are unfiltered modern wines of some class and finesse, the white coming solely from the *lieu-dit* of the same name. The average vine age of the red is now 45 years and this undoubtedly helps quality. The white should be broached young, the red with a little age. It is marked particularly by its vibrant, attractive, dark, spicy fruit character, supple velvety tannin and approachable style. A second fruit emphasised red Châteauneuf-du-Pape Piedlong is also now made as well as a red Ventoux, Mégaphone. (DM)

Recommended Reds:

Châteauneuf-du-Pape Domaine La Roquète ★★★☆ £E

Recommended Whites:

Châteauneuf-du-Pape Clos La Roquète ★★★ £E

⚙ Dom. La Soumade (Rasteau) *www.domainelasoumade.fr*

A great range of wines, especially the impressive red Côtes du Rhône, Rasteau and Gigondas. These are vinified as true vins de garde. Now with input from Bordeaux guru Stéphane Derenencourt, Romero goes for maximum extraction but the results are almost always very good indeed and the wines possess a marvellous balance and poise. Even the lesser wines have an abundance of vibrant, crunchy fruit. With the best cuvées the lengthy vatting, allied to extensive parcels of old vines (some over 100 years), provides for dense, chewy, powerful reds in need of 5 years'

cellaring. Romero also produces fine *vins doux naturels* under the Rasteau AC. (DM)

Recommended Reds:

Rasteau Fleur de Confiance ★★★★★ £F
Rasteau Confiance ★★★★☆ £E
Rasteau Prestige ★★★☆ £D Gigondas ★★★★ £D
Côtes du Rhône Les Violettes ★★★★ £D
Rasteau VDN ★★ £C
IGP de la Principauté d'Orange Prestige ★★ £B
IGP de la Principauté d'Orange Cabernet Sauvignon ★☆ £B

Dom. Le Couroulu (Vacqueyras)

A consistently fine Vacqueyras producer across recent years, now crafting wines of an additional depth and dimension. In part this may be down to son Guy taking over the reins of the domaine. The Ricard family can call on a total of 19 ha of vineyard resources planted in a mix of limestone, gravel and the classic galet roules of the area, most famous in Châteauneuf-du-Pape. Grenache dominates the holding with just around a third of the vineyard also planted to Syrah and Mourvèdre. Manual harvesting is followed by a careful selection and whole bunch vinification resulting in wines of an impressively rich concentration and spicy, herb-scented undertone. The old-vine bottling in particular adds a complex dimension rarely encountered here. It will undoubtedly benefit from five years ageing. Small quantities of a white Vacqueras Laura are made as well as a Côtes du Rhône red. (DM)

Recommended Reds:

Vacqueyras Vieilles Vignes ★★★ £D
Vacqueyras Cuvée Classique ★★☆ £C

Le Vieux Donjon (Châteauneuf-du-Pape)

The first wines emerged from the Michel family at this domaine in the mid 1960s. The current releases have been of a consistently impressive standard. There are 14 ha under vine with just one hectare planted to white varieties. A single white is made in very small quantities. Similarly to the red at CLOS DES PAPES there are no old-vine cuvées here and the resulting wine is rich and concentrated as well as impressively structured with real depth and character. Blended from Grenache, Syrah, Mourvèdre and Cinsault; strictly old-fashioned wine making techniques are employed but in no way is there any hint of rusticity. The wine is aged in a mix of cement tanks and *foudres* for up to 18 months. Give it at least four or five years to begin to show its potential. (DM)

Recommended Reds:

Châteauneuf-du-Pape ★★★★☆ £F

⚙ Dom. Les Aphillanthes (Travaillan)

This is one of the new rising stars of the southern Rhône based in the village of Travaillan. Les Galets, which is mainly Grenache, is open and approachable. The more seriously structured Trois Cepages blends Grenache, Syrah and Mourvèdre. The Cuvée du Cros is produced solely from Syrah, while the Vieilles Vignes is made from very old Grenache with around 20% Mourvèdre. Bottled with neither fining nor filtration all the wines show real depth and impressive concentration and will develop very well in bottle. A Côtes du Rhône made from pure low-yielding Mourvèdre is also now produced as is a Cairanne, L'Ancestrale de Puits, as well as a Rasteau 1921 from vines planted in that year. (DM)

Recommended Reds:

Côtes du Rhône-Villages Vieilles Vignes ★★★☆ £E
Côtes du Rhône-Villages Trois Cépages ★★★☆ £D

Southern Rhône

France

Côtes du Rhône-Villages Cuvée du Cros ★★★ £D
Côtes du Rhône-Villages Plan de Dieu Les Galets ★★★ £C
Côtes du Rhône Mourvèdre ★★★☆ £E
Côtes du Rhône ★★☆ £C

☸ Les Cailloux www.domaine-les-cailloux.fr
Very fine traditional producer of Côtes du Rhône and Châteauneuf-du-Pape. The Côtes du Rhônes are produced at the Brunel family property Domaine de l'Enclos. The profound Cuvée Centenaire produced from 100-year-old vines is one of the great wines of the appellation, while the regular red Châteauneuf is dense and powerful and lacks just a little of the depth of the centenarian. The Brunel family are also involved with the Feraud family of Domaine du PEGAÜ in an excellent small-scale négociant venture, FERAUD-BRUNEL. (DM)
Recommended Reds:
Châteauneuf-du-Pape Cuvée Centenaire ✪✪✪✪ £G
Châteauneuf-du-Pape ★★★★ £E
Côtes du Rhône Cuvée Sommelongue ★★★ £C
Côtes du Rhône Est Ouest ★★☆ £B

Dom. Les Grands Bois www.grands-bois.com
The Besnardeau family have a vineyard holding of 46 ha spread across seven communes, among them Rasteau and Cairanne. The majority of their vines now have considerable age with the oldest now over 70 years. The white Les Trois Soeurs is a cool-fermented fruit-driven blend of Viognier and Marsanne. There is also an attractive berry-scented rosé, Les Trois Soeurs, and a more serious spicy red version. The Villages wines, Gabrielle and Philippine, come from a number of sources and include fruit from some of the oldest vines. Both are aged in oak for 6 months, with the Philippine more berry scented, the Gabrielle more overtly oaky in its youth. The three Cairanne cuvées come from vines that range from 10–50 years and all are a blend of Grenache (55%), Mourvèdre (35%), and 5% each of Syrah and Carignan. The Maximilien is perhaps the most exciting with minimal oak influence – only the Mourvèdre sees any wood – providing a style of rich, spicy fruit and impressive complexity. The Eloise and Mireille bottlings both see up to 6 months oak ageing but it is very well handled. The Mireille is a touch more elegant, the Eloise denser and fuller. Expect all the Villages wines to develop well with 5 years' age or more. (DM)
Recommended Reds:
Côtes du Rhône-Villages Cairanne Cuvée Maximilien ★★★☆ £D
Côtes du Rhône-Villages Cairanne Cuvée Eloise ★★★ £D
Côtes du Rhône-Villages Cairanne Cuvée Mireille ★★★ £D
Côtes du Rhône-Villages Cuvée Gabrielle ★★☆ £C
Côtes du Rhône-Villages Cuvée Philippine ★★☆ £C
Côtes du Rhône Les Trois Soeurs ★★ £B
Recommended Whites:
Côtes du Rhône Les Trois Soeurs ★★ £B
Recommended Rosés:
Côtes du Rhône Les Trois Soeurs ★☆ £B

☸ Patric Lesec Selections www.chemindesvins.com
As well as a portfolio that now covers Alsace, Bordeaux, Burgundy, the Loire, the South-West and Languedoc and Roussillon, wine broker Patrick Lesec also works in association with fine quality-conscious domaines in the Rhône Valley to produce wines which are released under his own label. As a part of his portfolio he produces top cuvées from a number of properties, such as Dom. des REMIZIÈRES with their Cuvée Emilie and Dom. COURSODON with

the La Sensonne. He has now added a further Châteauneuf du Pape Bargeton which is fairly pricey, however expect it to be top notch. His approach is to vary the wines he makes with these domaines slightly to match his own style of ripe, elegant and above all approachable wines. Some of the Rhône cuvées are very, very good indeed and there is real potential here at all levels. The Languedoc wines are certainly impressive but have understandably not yet reached the level of the Rhônes. (DM)
Recommended Reds:
Hermitage Domaine des Remizières Cuvée Émilie ★★★★★ £G
Saint-Joseph Domaine Coursodon La Sensonne ★★★★ £E
Châteauneuf-du-Pape Les Galets Blonds ★★★★★ £F
Châteauneuf-du-Pape Chasse-Temps ★★★★ £E
Gigondas Les Espalines Cuvée Romaine ★★★☆ £D
Rasteau Vieilles Vignes ★★☆ £C
Côtes du Rhône Bouquet ★★ £B
Côteaux du Languedoc Château Roumanières Tonneaux ★★☆ £C
Faugères J.C. Estève Tonneaux ★★☆ £C
Saint-Chinian Domaine Rouanet Tonneaux ★★☆ £C

Dom. Les Goubert (Gigondas) www.lesgoubert.fr
An extensive range of Côtes du Rhône and Rhône-Villages wines is made by this domaine and the quality is generally good, sometimes very good. There are 23ha under vine, of which 20 or so are red, with the majority Grenache but a decent planting of Syrah as well. Barrel-fermentation is used to produce the Viognier, which has real depth and some gloriously ripe, peachy fruit. It is best drunk young. Vinification of the reds is modern without a hint of rusticity emerging in the wines and new oak is used to age the Gigondas Cuvée Florence. Both Gigondas wines are good cellaring prospects. (DM)
Recommended Reds:
Gigondas Cuvée Florence ★★★☆ £E
Gigondas ★★★ £D
Côtes du Rhône-Villages Sablet ★★☆ £C
Beaumes de Venise ★★☆ £C
Côtes du Rhône ★☆ £B
Recommended Whites:
Côtes du Rhône Viognier Cuvée de V ★★☆ £C
Côtes du Rhône-Villages Sablet ★☆ £C
Côtes du Rhône ★ £B

Les Pallières (Gigondas) www.vignoblesbrunier.fr
Now owned as a joint venture between the Bruniers of VIEUX-TÉLÉGRAPHE and US wine merchant Kermit Lynch. The potential of the *terroir* is beginning to be fully explored – the 25 ha of vineyards are ideally located in limestone soils on the precipitous slopes of the Dentelles de Montmirail. The over 50-year-old vines produce wines which are now less rustic and increasingly impressive. Some destemming has been introduced and there is careful control in the cellar. The wines are bottled without filtration after 15 months in *cuve* and *foudres*. Two additional red Gigondas, Terrasse du Diable and Les Racines as well as a rosé, Au Petit Bonheur are also now made. (DM)
Recommended Reds:
Gigondas ★★★★ £E

Dom. Maby (Tavel) www.domainemaby.fr
Richard Maby is the third generation of his family at this fine 64 ha Tavel based property. He is now producing some excellent reds and whites at Lirac as well as a fine and rich, weighty Tavel rosé

Prima Donna, a blend of Grenache and Cinsault which offers more fresh acidity than the style normally does and is a great food wine. The family holding also spreads out into the Côtes du Rhône also, from where an attractive spicy red, Variations, is made. The *terroir* at both Lirac and Tavel is similar to that at nearby Châteauneuf-du-Pape with soils that have a substantial element of *galets roulés* in the top soil on a base of clay and limestone. It is no surprise that the wines share some of the flavour character that can be found in their neighbouring appellation. Great care is taken at the harvest to ensure that all the fruit achieves full phenolic ripeness. The regular white and red Liracs both take the La Fermade label. The rich, subtly nutty white is a blend of Grenache Blanc, Clairette, Picpoul and Ugni Blanc while the berry fruited, herb scented red includes Grenache Noir, Syrah and Mourvèdre. Ageing for both is in *inox*. The Casta Diva is the top white Lirac with rich and concentrated fruit but good underlying acidity and a mineral edge. It blends Grenache Blanc with Viognier, Clairette and Picpoul. Vinification is modern with barrel-fermentation in new wood followed by lees stirring and the malolactic is blocked. The red Nessun Dorma is again very modern in style a blend dominated by Mourvèdre with additional Grenache and Syrah. A pre-fermentation maceration and three week vatting is followed by ageing in a mix of new oak and *inox*. It needs at least two or three years cellaring.(DM)

Recommended Reds:

Lirac Nessun Dorma ★★★☆ £E
Lirac La Fermade ★★★ £D
Côtes du Rhône Variations ★☆ £B
IGP Coteaux du Pont du Gard Baroques ★☆ £B

Recommended Whites:

Lirac Casta Diva ★★★☆ £D
Lirac La Fermade ★★★ £C

Recommended Rosés:

Tavel Prima Donna ★★☆ £C
Tavel Libiano ★★☆ £C
Tavel La Forcadière ★★☆ £C
Lirac La Fermade ★★☆ £C

⚙ Dom. de Marcoux *www.domainedemarcoux.fr*

Model 24 ha property run on biodynamic lines since 1990. There are 16 ha of red grapes planted and just 1ha of Roussanne and Bourboulenc, which adds a refreshing grip to the white Châteauneuf. The main purpose of the viticultural approach is to optimise the fruit quality of the late-ripening Grenache and Mourvèdre in particular. There can be no question about the results. Vieilles Vignes has for a decade been one of the benchmark wines of the appellation: very ageworthy and extraordinarily complex. A fine Lirac red is also made, which blends Grenache with Syrah and Mourvèdre. (DM)

Recommended Reds:

Châteauneuf-du-Pape Vieilles Vignes ✪✪✪✪✪ £H
Châteauneuf-du-Pape ★★★★ £F
Lirac La Lorentine ★★★☆ £D

Recommended Whites:

Châteauneuf-du-Pape ★★★☆ £E

Mas de Boislauzon (Châteauneuf-du-Pape)

Good small producer with 25 ha for red and white Châteauneuf and a little Côtes du Rhône-Villages. The vineyards are planted in *argile* and calcareous soils and have the famous galets roulés stony topsoil. The red Châteauneuf vineyard is planted to a mix of 70% Grenache and 15% each of Syrah and Mourvèdre. The white is equal parts of Grenache, Clairette, Roussanne and Bourboulenc. The red Châteauneuf is classically berry scented with an intense, herby character but is not a bit rustic. It will drink well at 4 or 5 years. A limited-production Cuvée du Quet is made from a selection of the oldest vines on the property as well as Le Tintot which comes from Mourvèdre. (DM)

Recommended Reds:

Châteauneuf-du-Pape Vieilles Vignes ★★★★ £E

Mas de Libian (Côtes du Rhône) *www.masdelibian.com*

A fine, small biodynamically farmed domaine from the western stretches of the southern Rhône and one of those high quality properties with a considerable input from the women of the family. Jean-Pierre and Jacqueline Thibon's daughter Hélène is the public face of the domaine and her two sisters are also in the wine business, Cécile also here at the family property. The wines have been going from strength to strength in recent vintages as the vineyard, now averaging 30 years, ages. The domaine holdings run to 19 ha, most planted to red grapes. The majority of the vines have a south to south-east exposition although the Syrah is planted to a more northerly aspect. The Côtes du Rhône labelled wines are planted in a mix of clay/limestone and pebble soils whereas the Côtes du Rhône-Villages come from solely one metre deep pebbled soils with excellent drainage. The white Cave Vinum is fermented relatively cool and aged for a short period on lees with a proportion of the wine in *demi-muids*, adding some structure. It is a blend of Clairette, Roussanne and just a touch of Viognier typically herb-spiced with a subtle citrus undercurrent. The Vin de Pétanque is a soft, brambly, immediately approachable style blending Grenache with around a quarter of Syrah lending a little structure. The Bout d'Zan comes from a similar blend but has more depth and grip. Khayyâm, named after the famed Persian poet who wrote many texts celebrating women and wine, is a step up. Dark-fruited and spicy, it blends again Grenache and Syrah and there is a little Mourvèdre as well. 10 months in *foudres* aids the underlying structure. The top red La Calade is more *vin de garde* in style and is dominated by meaty, tannic and structured Mourvèdre with just a little Grenache adding a ripe dark-berry fruit component. Expect the wine to develop very nicely over five to 10 years. (DM)

Recommended Reds:

Côtes du Rhône-Villages La Calade ★★★★ £E
Côtes du Rhône-Villages Khayyâm ★★★☆ £C
Côtes du Rhône Bout d'Zhan ★★★ £B
IGP Côteaux de l'Ardeche Vin de Pétanque ★★ £B

Recommended Whites:

Côtes du Rhône Cave Vinum ★★☆ £C

Dom. Mathieu (Châteauneuf-du-Pape) *www.domainemathieu.fr*

Good, small, family-run domaine with 22 ha divided into no fewer than 50 separate plots. Of these, 4ha are in the Côtes du Rhône appellation. The reds here are traditionally vinified and are not destemmed. The white, by contrast, is vinified cool at 16–17°C to emphasise its bright, nutty, floral fruit and should be drunk young. The regular red is dominated by Grenache and offers bright berry fruit with a slight herbal edge. The rich and well-structured Vin de Felibre is dominated by Mourvèdre (80%) and is aged in 60% new oak which needs a year or two to integrate. The top wine, Marquis Anselme Mathieu, comes from some of the oldest Grenache on the property, from a vineyard originally planted in 1890. Dense and complex with a real old-vine fruit quality, this impressively structured red needs at least 6 or 7 years. (DM)

Southern Rhône

France

Recommended Reds:
Châteauneuf-du-Pape Marquis Anselme Mathieu ★★★★ £F
Châteauneuf-du-Pape Vin de Felibre ★★★☆ £E
Châteauneuf-du-Pape ★★★ £E
Recommended Whites:
Châteauneuf-du-Pape ★★ £E

Vignobles Mayard www.vignobles-mayard.fr
Relatively traditional but very well made wines are crafted by the Mayard family from their 43 ha of vineyards in the heart of the Châteauneuf-du- Pape appellation. The firm is run by three siblings; Françoise, (who works with winemaker Philippe Cambie), Didier and Béatrice who are the fifth generation of *vignerons* here at this domaine. They have three separate Châteauneuf labels; Domaine du Père Pape, Clos du Calvaire and Crau de Ma Mère. The family also produce a Côtes du Rhône red Confidence from land bordering the Châteauneuf appellation as well as a juicy fruit driven rosé La Vie en Rose. Both the Domaine du Père Pape and the Clos du Calvaire are traditionally made with ageing in *foudres* and coming from vineyards up to 50 years old. Both have impressive depth and concentration, with classic aromas of dark berry fruits and herb spices. The Clos du Calvaire is a touch more opulent in style. The Crau de Ma Mère cuvée is a step up in quality, being sourced from very old vines in the Crau vineyard in the far northeast of the appellation, which is classic Grenache territory. This is 70% Grenache, 20% Mourvèdre and 10% Syrah. An attractive and nutty white Crau de Ma Mère is also produced which is full of zesty citrus fruit and typically full-bodied. A Côtes du Rhône, Confidence is also made. (DM)
Recommended Reds:
Châteauneuf-du-Pape Crau de Ma Mère ★★★★☆ £F
Châteauneuf-du-Pape Clos du Calvaire ★★★★ £E
Châteauneuf-du-Pape Domaine du Pere Pape ★★★☆ £E

Dom. La Millière (Châteauneuf-du-Pape) www.la-milliere.com
The Arnauds possess some 27ha in Châteauneuf-du-Pape as well as the Côtes du Rhône. Their vineyards vary from 30 years to over 100 years of age. This gives them tremendous raw material which, combined with organic farming and a general minimalist approach, results in some excellent wines. The Côtes du Rhône Vieilles Vignes bottling offers both grip and structure and has very impressive depth. The Côtes du Rhône-Villages, from Grenache, Cinsault and Mourvèdre, is from vines very close to the Châteauneuf border and has a real old-vine complexity. The Châteauneuf Vieilles Vignes is a blend of Grenache, Mourvèdre, Syrah, Cinsault and Counoise. Firm and structured in its youth, it needs 5 or 6 years to express its subtle violet and herb-scented aromas to the full. It is loaded with chewy, opulent old-vine character. (DM)
Recommended Reds:
Châteauneuf-du-Pape Vieilles-Vignes ★★★★ £F
Côtes du Rhône-Villages Vieilles-Vignes ★★★ £D
Côtes du Rhône Vieilles Vignes ★★★ £C

Dom. de La Monardière (Vacqueyras) www.monardiere.fr
A good, small range of wines is produced by Christian Vache at this well-established Vacqueyras property. Volume is accounted for by the reds but a small amount of a fairly pricey and oaky white Vacqueyras Galéjade is produced from less than 1ha of Grenache Blanc, Roussanne and Viognier. The regular red, Les Calades, is soft, forward and approachable, whereas the Reserve des Deux Monardes and in particular the dense and complex Vieilles Vignes are wines of greater depth, substance and structure. The Monardes is full of dark cherry character and hints of *garrigue*; the Vieilles Vignes, dense and more imposingly structured, is a wine of real depth and intensity. Both the top reds will benefit from 4 or 5 years' patience. (DM)
Recommended Reds:
Vacqueyras Vieilles Vignes ★★★ £D
Vacqueyras Réserve Les Deux Monardes ★★★ £D
Vacqueyras Calades ★★☆ £C
Recommended Whites:
Vacqueyras Galéjade ★★☆ £C

❀ **Montirius (Vacqueyras)** www.montirius.com
One of the best properties in Vacqueyras, Montirius has been run on biodynamic lines since the 1999 vintage. The Saurels have 58 ha of vineyard spread across 38 separate parcels. The white Vacqueyras Minéral blends Grenache Blanc, Roussanne and Bourboulenc, which adds a refreshing acidity, and should be drunk within a year or two. The Côtes du Rhône labelled Jardin Secret is sourced from vineyards just outside the village of Sablet. Soft and accesible it too should be broached when young and full of fruit as should the newly added Syrah based Sérine. The Gigondas Terre des Aînés comes from a 16-ha plot of which 10 ha date from 1925 and which is planted in five different soil types. Rich and complex at best, the wine has impressive substance. The Gigondas Confidentiel adds further weight, depth and impressive concentration. A third wine comes from the appellation and younger vines, La Tour. Of the red Vacqueyras, the Garrigues bottling comes from vines of around 65 years. It is a blend of 70% Grenache and 30% Syrah. The Clos Montirius comes from a particular 8.5ha sector of the Vacqueyras vineyard which enjoys a very localised drier mesoclimate and is planted in red clay Montmorillonite soils. From a blend of 50/50 Grenache and Syrah it undoubtably has an extra level of depth and complexity. A third example, Le Village comes from 25 year old vines. Two IGP de Vaucluse reds are also made. (DM)
Recommended Reds:
Gigondas Confidentiel ★★★★☆ £E
Gigondas Terre des Aînés ★★★★ £E
Vacqueyras Clos Montirius ★★★☆ £D
Vacqueyras Montirius Garrigues ★★★ £D
Vacqueyras Montirius ★★★ £C
Côtes du Rhône Jardin Secret ★★☆ £B
Côtes du Rhône Sérine ★★☆ £B
Recommended Whites:
Vacqueyras Minéral ★★☆ £C

Dom. de Montpertuis www.vignobles-paul-jeune.com
Paul Jeune produces impressively deep and concentrated red Châteauneuf-du-Pape, which is occasionally labelled Domaine de Croze. The wine, a blend of Grenache, Mourvèdre, Syrah and Cinsault, is a powerful, structured example with intense dark berry fruit and spicy, herbal *garrigue* scents. A white Châteauneuf produced from Clairette, Bourboulenc, Grenache Blanc and Roussanne is full, weighty and soft. It should be drunk relatively young. Forward, fruit-driven Côtes du Rhône and IGPs are also produced. Paul Jeune now has an interest in the Côtes du Ventoux property Château de Valcombe, where some increasingly impressive dense and structured examples of this lesser appellation are being made. The Cuvée Genevrière is very good. (DM)

Domaine de Montpertuis
Recommended Reds:

Châteauneuf-du-Pape Tradition ★★★☆ £E

Côtes du Rhône Cuvée La Ramière ★★ £C

IGP du Gard Cuvée La Counoise de Jeune ★☆ £B

Recommended Whites:

Châteauneuf-du-Pape ★★★ £D

Côtes du Rhône ★☆ £B

Château de Valcombe
Recommended Reds:

Côtes du Ventoux Cuvée Genevrière ★★☆ £C

Côtes du Ventoux Signature ★★ £B

Dom. de Montvac (Vacqueyras) *www.domainedemontvac.fr*

Jean Dussere and his daughter Cecile produce a fine, small range of Vacqueyras, a little Gigondas as well as a Côtes du Rhône red and rosé. Their vineyard holding is dominated by reds, they have 24 ha planted and less than a hectare of white grapes, Clairette, Roussanne and Bourboulenc. The approach in the vineyard is as natural as possible and the fruit always picked at otimum ripeness. There is a relatively cool and extended fermentation for the reds and the Vacqueyras cuvées are typically spicy and *garrigue* scented. The Gigondas is a touch more structured than the dark black fruited Variation and Vincila. The Variation is the ripest of the wines, with loads of rich, licoricey, almost jammy fruit. The white sees six to eight months in Burgundy barrels and has an elegant balance and intensity from the Bourboulenc in its blend. (DM)

Recommended Reds:

Gigondas Adage ★★★☆ £D

Vacqueyras Variation ★★★☆ £C

Vacqueyras Vincila ★★★ £C

Vacqueyras Arabesque ★★☆ £C

Recommended Whites:

Vacqueyras Mélodine ★★☆ £C

✿ Dom. de La Mordorée (Tavel) *www.domaine-mordoree.com*

Christophe Delorme produces an extensive and impressive range of wines from his fully biodynamic domaine in Tavel. A total of over 55 ha spread across Lirac, Tavel and Châteauneuf-du-Pape yields an excellent range of wines. An impressive number of varieties are planted, particularly white. The Tavel is a benchmark wine, arguably the best of the appellation, and the various Reine des Bois cuvées are very refined and characterful and will improve in bottle for 5–10 years, the Châteauneuf certainly longer. A superb source of very well-priced wines, although some recent very high scores from a well-known American wine journal keep inflationery pressure on them. Indeed the limited production special cuvée Plume du Peintre is very pricey. (DM)

Recommended Reds:

Châteauneuf-du-Pape Reine des Bois ★★★★★ £G

Châteauneuf-du-Pape ★★★★ £F Lirac Reine des Bois ★★★★ £E

Lirac La Dame Rousse ★★★☆ £C

Côtes du Rhône La Dame Rousse ★★☆ £C

Recommended Whites:

Lirac Reine des Bois ★★★☆ £D

Recommended Rosés:

Tavel La Dame Rousse ★★ £C

Moulin de La Gardette (Tavel) *www.moulindelagardette.com*

These are powerful, traditionally slightly rustic styles of Gigondas. Grenache (90%) and Mourvèdre comprise the blend of the regular cuvée, whereas Syrah is blended with Grenache and Cinsault in the Ventabren, which is also aged in *barrique* rather than the larger vats used for the regular bottling. Only a relatively small proportion is new and the wine is not overwhelmed by the wood, although some vintages need time for the fruit to show through. There is a general dedication to quality – the wines are neither fined nor filtered and are produced from vines that are over 50 years old. Fine and very intense, they drink very well over the medium term. (DM)

Recommended Reds:

Gigondas Cuvée Ventabren ★★★☆ £E

Gigondas ★★☆ £D

Dom. de Mourchon (Seguret) *www.domainedemourchon.com*

This property was purchased by Scotsman Walter McKinlay in 1998 and quality is moving forward very impressively. He has 24ha and an imposing mas, or farmhouse. The soft, fruity, easygoing rosé, Pié Loubié, blends Cinsault, Grenache and Syrah from 40-year-old vines but it is the Séguret reds which have marked this property out among the better producers in the region. The Tradition is a blend of Grenache (60%), Syrah (25%), Cinsault (10%) and Carignan. The vineyard is 40 years old and the wine is aged in *cuve* to emphasise its vibrant dark, spicy fruit. The Grande Réserve, a blend of Grenache in the main with 35% Syrah, is dense, powerful and concentrated with a marvellous old-vine purity. The 60-year-old vines are no doubt a major contributing element. Both wines will evolve well over several years. Marginally pricier Family Reserve Syrah and Grenache labels are also now produced and a red Châteauneuf has also been added to an evolving range. (DM)

Recommended Reds:

Côtes du Rhône-Villages Seguret Grande Reserve ★★★★ £D

Côtes du Rhône-Villages Seguret Tradition ★★★ £C

Recommended Rosés:

Côtes du Rhône Pié Loubié ★☆ £B

>> Dom. de Nalys *www.domainedenalys.com*

This significant domaine is situated in the east of the Châteauneuf-du-Pape appellation and on three soil types. It has a substantial holding of 50 ha including all 13 authorised varieties and unusually makes a substantial amount of white wine, albeit a lot less than red. There are two whites and three reds. The regular white is dominated by Grenache Blanc, whereas the Eicelenci has a substantial proportion of Roussanne which gives it substantially more depth, flavour and dimension. The classic white is mostly fermented stainless steel with the exception of the small proportion of Roussanne and Picardan both barrel fermented, whereas the Eicelenci sees much more wood for ageing as well with the wines kept on fine lees. It offers intense wite fruits with just a hint of citrus. The classic red Châteauneuf is in an approachable forward style with bright berry fruit and a hint of spice. The denser, more structured Le Châtaignier comes from a blend of mainly Grenache with Mourvèdre grown in pebble soils. The wine nevertheless offers copious ripe dark berry fruits with a classic herb edge. La Réserve again offers dark, spicy fruits, hints of black pepper although there is a richer, more exotic savoury quality as well. Syrah is the kep component blended with Grenache and Mourvèdre. The top two reds will develop well for over a decade. (DM)

Recommended Reds:

Châteauneuf-du-Pape La Réserve ★★★★ £F

Châteauneuf-du-Pape Le Châtaignier ★★★★ £E

Châteauneuf-du-Pape ★★★ £E

Southern Rhône

France

Recommended Whites:
Châteauneuf-du-Pape Eicelenci ★★★★ £F
Châteauneuf-du-Pape ★★★ £D

❀ **Dom. de l'Oratoire Saint-Martin** *www.oratoiresaintmartin.fr*
Frédéric and François are cousins of Daniel and Denis ALARY and produce equally exciting results in this outperforming Rhône village. The main Rhône varieties are planted and there are various blends. All the Cairanne bottlings are very impressive. The white Haut Coustias is a rich, nutty, almost honeyed blend of Marsanne, Roussanne and Viognier. The lesser reds have a high proportion of Grenache but are intense and heady. The Haut Coustias red is lent considerable depth and structure by its large Mourvèdre/Syrah component (60 and 20% respectively). It can hold its own against top-quality Châteauneuf-du-Pape and is rich, concentrated, powerful and very ageworthy. (DM)
Recommended Reds:
Côtes du Rhône-Villages Cairanne Haut Coustias ★★★★ £D
Côtes du Rhône-Villages Cairanne Réserve des Seigneurs ★★★☆ £D
Côtes du Rhône-Villages Cairanne Prestige ★★★ £C
Côtes du Rhône ★★☆ £B
Recommended Whites:
Côtes du Rhône-Villages Cairanne Haut Coustias ★★★☆ £C
Côtes du Rhône Seraphine ★★☆ £C

Dom. d'Ourea (Vacqueyras) *www.domainedourea.fr*
Adrien Roustan is fast establishing himself as one of the benchmarks in the appellations in which he farms his vineyards biodynamically. The domaine is very recently established with a first vintage in 2010 and vines spread across 18 ha. The Gigondas comes from the *lieu-dit* of Le Grand Montmirail and vineyards planted at between 400 and 520 metres providing a fresh edge to the wine. A combination of mainly Grenache with a little Syrah adding extra structure and depth the wine is an impressively dense and powerful red with rich black fruits and a herb-spiced edge. The Vacqueyras like the Gigondas is aged in *béton cuves*, it comes from old Grenache vines, the vineyard being planted in 1950. While it doesn't have the raw power of the Gigondas there is a real intensity and depth of old vine character. The Côtes du Rhône comes from younger vines with an age of around 15 years. There is an elegant, lighter berried fruit character but impressive carry and intensity too. Also made is a fascinating Vin de France which combines Grenache with Carignan, Aramon, Œillade and Syrah and is full of approachable forward dark fruits. Expect both the Gigondas and Vacqueyras to add further complexity and depth with five years ageing. (DM)
Recommended Reds:
Gigondas ★★★★ £E Vacqueyras ★★★★ £E
Côtes du Rhône ★★☆ £C
Vin de France Tire Bouchon ★★☆ £C

Dom. de Panisse *www.domainedepanisse.com*
Jean-Marie purchased this property in the early 1990s and is making increasingly persuasive examples of the appellation. Only reds are currently produced and there is a total of 18 ha planted with a third of this in the Châteauneuf-du-Pape appellation. The remaining vineyards are either Côtes du Rhône, the wines including the red Murmure des Vignes, or IGP. The dense and structured Confidence Vigneronne is largely Grenache and demands four or five years cellaring as does the Noble Revelation which offers a darker character to its fruit, with a higher proportion of Mourvèdre and Syrah and a sweet edge from ageing in *barriques*. (DM)

Recommended Reds:
Châteauneuf-du-Pape Noble Revelation ★★★★☆ £F
Châteauneuf-du-Pape Confidence Vigneron ★★★★ £E

❀❀ **Dom. du Pegaü (Châteauneuf-du-Pape)** *www.pegau.com*
Very fine traditional domaine run by Laurence Feraud. The Vin de France Plan Pegaü is good and in the traditional style of the property and is released along with a number of Côtes du Rhônes under the Château Pegaü label. The white Châteauneuf-du-Pape is honeyed, nutty and concentrated. The reds are classic, formidably structured wines. Cuvée Réservée is in fact the regular red bottling but is full of impressive super-ripe, dark berry Grenache character and loaded with muscular tannin in its youth. The Cuvée Laurence, which is from the same *assemblage*, gets a touch longer in cask. The immensely concentrated Cuvée da Capo has emerged as one of the Rhône Valley's great reds –dense, massively powerful but refined and very pure as well. A second premium red is also now released, Inspiration. The Ferauds are also involved with André Brunel of LES CAILLOUX in a fine *négociant* venture (FERAUD-BRUNEL) and Laurence Feraud makes her own small Selection Laurence Feraud range. (DM)
Recommended Reds:
Châteauneuf-du-Pape Cuvée da Capo ✪✪✪✪ £H
Châteauneuf-du-Pape Cuvée Laurence ★★★★★ £F
Châteauneuf-du-Pape Cuvée Réservée ★★★★☆ £F
Vin de France Plan Pegau Non-Filtré ★★ £B
Recommended Whites:
Châteauneuf-du-Pape Cuvée Réservée ★★★☆ £E

Dom. des Perrières (Costières de Nîmes) *www.kreydenweiss.com*
Marc KREYDENWEISS and his wife Emmanuelle are better known for their stylish Alsace domaine but here in the Costières de Nîmes they produce a number of good to very good elegant reds in quite marked contrast to many of their neighbours. The approach is one of refinement not muscle. Marc Kreydenweiss feels some of the Mediterranean reds are over-extracted and alcoholic. How will they age? The Domaine Les Grimaud bottling is Emmanuelle's baby and comes from its own 7 ha vineyard. Blended from Carignan, Cinsault and Grenache, it is full of upfront brambly fruit. Domaine des Perrières is a refined and harmonious blend of Carignan, Syrah and Grenache with vines ranging from 35–75 years. It has more depth and a firmer structure and will age well for 5 or 6 years. A Grenache dominated blend, Barbabelle is also now vinified as well as a rich and structured IGP, Ansata. A Châteauneuf-du-Pape red and a varietal old vine Carignan, KA from Costières de Nîmes are also made as well as a white Ansata. (DM)
Recommended Reds:
Costières de Nîmes Domaine des Perrières ★★★ £D
Costières de Nîmes Domaine Les Grimaud ★★ £C

Dom. Perrin (Côtes du Rhône) *www.perrin-et-fils.com*
This is the négociant arm of the Perrin brothers of CHÂTEAU DE BEAUCASTEL. Production is now considerable at over 300,000 cases a year. Most famous among the wines is the long-established brand, La Vieille Ferme, an original trendsetter for quality in the Côtes du Ventoux, although other producers have now taken quality there to higher levels. They also now produce reliable to very good examples from a number of southern Rhône ACs. The wines offer an attractive, approachable style with forward, juicy fruit. The stand out wine is the old-vine Grenache dominated Gigondas, Domaine du Clos des Tourelles coming from a small 9 ha vineyard planted on

limestone and sandy soils. The most recent development is a joint venture with Nicolas Jaboulet, formerly a director of JABOULET AÎNÉ, in producing a small range of wines from a number of northern Rhône appellations. The wines are labelled "Maison Nicolas Perrin". Hermitage, Côte-Rôtie, Saint Joseph, Condrieu, Cornas and Crozes Hermitage are all made. In Provence the Perrins are also involved with Brad Pitt and Anjelina Jolie at MIRAVAL. (DM)

Recommended Reds:
Gigondas Domaine du Clos des Tourelles ★★★★ £E
Châteauneuf-du-Pape ★★★ £E
Gigondas La Gille ★★★ £D
Vacqueyras Les Christins ★★☆ £C
Vinsobres Les Cornuds ★★ £C
Côtes du Rhône Réserve ★☆ £B
Côtes du Ventoux La Vieille Ferme ★☆ £B
Recommended Whites:
Côtes du Rhône Réserve ★☆ £B

❋ **Dom. de Piaugier (Sablet)** *www.domainedepiaugier.com*
Jean-Marc Autran possesses some 30ha of vineyards in Sablet and Gigondas, almost all of which are planted to red varieties. A very small amount of very good, nutty and lightly herbal white Sablet is made from Grenache Blanc, Roussanne, Viognier and Clairette, which lends a fresh grip to the wine. Among the reds the real star turns are the special cuvées from Sablet. All of these are dense, rich, powerful and very impressive for the appellation. Ténébi is an unusual 100% Counoise, Réserve de Maude 100% Syrah. The other Sablets blend Grenache with Mourvèdre. The approach to vinification is traditional and the fruit is not de-stemmed. The result, though, is never rustic. In the lesser regular Sablet, Côtes du Rhône and even the Gigondas – which are all lighter – a herb-scented undercurrent is often apparent. The top Sablet reds and the Gigondas all improve with 3 or 4 years' ageing. A further Sablet is also made, Le Rêve de Marine, along with an IGP red Les Ramières and a second Côtes du Rhône, Un Air de Famille (DM)

Recommended Reds:
Côtes du Rhône-Vill Sablet Réserve Alphonse Vautour ★★★★☆ £E
Côtes du Rhône-Villages Sablet Réserve de Maude ★★★★ £E
Côtes du Rhône-Villages Sablet Les Briquières ★★★☆ £D
Côtes du Rhône-Villages Sablet Ténébi ★★★☆ £D
Côtes du Rhône-Villages Sablet Montmartel ★★★☆ £D
Gigondas ★★★ £D
Côtes du Rhône-Villages Sablet ★★ £C
Côtes du Rhône La Grange de Piaugier ★☆ £B
Recommended Whites:
Côtes du Rhône-Villages Sablet ★★ £C

Dom. Rabasse-Charavin (Cairanne)
A good small range here with fairly extensive vineyards (over 65 ha) and a surprisingly large annual production of around 15,000 cases. All but 2 ha are planted to red varieties. The range is now extensive with a sizeable number of small volume wines made with examples from Rasteau and Plan de Dieu as well as Cairanne. The average vine age is over 50 years, which no doubt ably assists in maintaining wine quality. The approach to vinifying the reds is traditional, with no destemming and ageing in vat. The wines are well made, with good dark berry fruit and a typically intense herbal component. Cuvée Estevenas has impressive depth and firm tannin in its youth. It is mainly old Grenache with Syrah. Three other red Estevenas wines are also made, the Syrah being replaced by Mourvèdre in two, the third solely coming from Grenache. The white Estevenas is mainly

Roussanne. (DM)
Recommended Reds:
Côtes du Rhône-Villages Cairanne Estevenas ★★★ £D
Côtes du Rhône-Villages Cairanne ★★☆ £C
Rasteau ★★☆ £C
Recommended Whites:
Côtes du Rhône-Villages Cairanne ★★ £C

Dom. Raspail-Ay (Gigondas)
Dominique Ay produces just two wines from his 18 ha in Gigondas. There is a little rosé but the real interest here is the burly, powerful but elegant and very ageworthy Gigondas. The fruit is all de-stemmed and the result is not at all rustic. The wine is aged in large vats rather than in *barrique* but is none the worse for that. On occasion in earlier years the wine has lacked the intensity and power of the very best. Recent vintages have been very good though. (DM)
Recommended Reds:
Gigondas ★★★☆ £D

Dom. Réméjeanne *www.domainelaremejeanne.com*
A real benchmark for Côtes du Rhône, this medium-sized domaine makes some 12,500 cases annually, 90% of it red, from 38 ha of vineyards. Les Arbousiers red and white are classic southern Rhône blends – the red is vibrant and spicy, the white subtly nutty. Les Chevrefeuilles adds Carignan and Counoise from old vines to Grenache, Syrah, Mouvèdre and Cinsault. The top two cuvées are Les Églantiers Syrah, Grenache and Mouvèdre and Les Génevriers, a blend of Grenache and Syrah. Vinification is high-tech and modern and micro-oygenation is used during *élevage*. The top wines are rich, concentrated and develop well in bottle after 3–5 years' ageing. A powerful white Les Eglantiers, blending Roussanne, Viognier and Clairette has recently been added. (DM)
Recommended Reds:
Côtes du Rhône-Villages Les Génevriers ★★★☆ £D
Côtes du Rhône Les Églantiers ★★★☆ £D
Côtes du Rhône Les Chèvrefeuilles ★★★ £C
Côtes du Rhône Les Arbousiers ★★ £B
Recommended Whites:
Côtes du Rhône Les Arbousiers ★☆ £B

Dom. de Renjarde (Côtes du Rhône) *www.renjarde.fr*
Good, well-priced reds. There are 50 ha under vine so this is quite a substantial operation with an annual output of around 20,000 cases in all. The vineyard is planted to a blend of Grenache, Syrah, Cinsault, Carignan and Mourvèdre. Alain Dugas, the director of CH. LA NERTHE until 2008, also guides operations here. Unlike at La Nerthe, vinfication of each variety is separate, emphasising the quality of the fruit, with *assemblage* prior to bottling. Undoubtedly the quality stamp of Alain Dugas shows through, with a good, mediumweight, attractive fruit-driven Côtes du Rhône of some style and the Réserve de Cassagne, which is a particularly well-priced concentrated and structured red.(DM)
Recommended Reds:
Côtes du Rhône-Villages Massif d'Uchaux Réserve Cassagne ★★★ £C
Côtes du Rhône ★★ £B

Domaines Renouard (Costières de Nîmes) *www.scamandre.com*
This domaine is now one of the best in the Costières de Nîmes. Acquired by the Renouards in 2002 there are 20 ha planted in a mix of gravel and *argile* soils and an average age of 50 years adds further to the potential as does a moderate overall yield of just over

Southern Rhône

France

30 hl/ha. The wines are, as one would expect made with classic hand-made artisan methods. The fresh and lightly mineral rosé comes from Grenache, while the Costières de Nîmes La Scamandre Renouard is a blend of Syrah, Carignan, Mourvèdre and Grenache. It is the mainstay of the domaine and is aged in oak, one-third new, for around 12 months. Rich and characterful with spicy dark-berry fruit and really smoky oak that demands three or for years ageing to fully integrate. Much lower in volume are the top red Scamandre 1409 and Scamandre, the first vinified from Petit Verdot and the other from Carignan, Mourvèdre and Grenache. These are a touch richer, denser and more concentrated and need at least two to three years to shed some youthful oak influence, particularly the Petit Verdot. The vines are farmed biodymamically with the help of a horse and plough. There is also an opulent Vendange Tardives. (DM)

Recommended Reds:
IGP Côteaux Flavens Scamandre 1409 ★★★☆ £E
IGP Côteaux Flavens Scamandre ★★★ £D
Costières de Nîmes Scamandre Renouard ★★★ £D
Recommended Whites:
Vin de France Vendange Tardives ★★★☆ £E
Recommended Rosés:
IGP du Gard Cuvée L'Instant ★★ £B

❂ Marcel Richaud (Cairanne)

Marcel Richaud is one of a number of excellent producers from this top-performing village. He has a reasonably sizeable vineyard holding of over 40 ha, some of which dates back over 100 years, so the potential of his raw material is remarkable and this shows through in his wines. All have impressive, spicy berry fruit with intense notes of thyme and the classic scent of *garrigues* from a range offering very fair prices. The top 2 cuvées are impressively structured; the Estrambords is aged in *barriques*, while the Côtes du Rhône Les Garrigues is particularly good value. (DM)

Recommended Reds:
Côtes du Rhône-Villages Cairanne Les Estrambords ★★★★ £D
Côtes du Rhône-Villages Cairanne L'Ebrescade ★★★★ £D
Côtes du Rhône-Villages Cairanne ★★★ £C
Côtes du Rhône Les Garrigues ★★★ £C
Côtes du Rhône Terres d'Aigues ★★☆ £C
Côtes du Rhône ★★ £B
Recommended Whites:
Côtes du Rhône-Villages Cairanne ★★☆ £C
Côtes du Rhône ★☆ £B

Dom. Roche-Audran (Côtes du Rhône) *www.roche-audran.com*

Some extraordinary and very complex Côtes du Rhône red is now made at this small domaine. The white is a blend of Grenache and Viognier and is fermented in barrel with *bâtonnage*. Subtle and nutty, it shows only minimal oak character. More complexity and depth is found in the characterful César Blanc, which is dominated by white Grenache. The regular Côtes du Rhône is bright and forward: berry fruit and a supple style is the approach. The Visan red is a clear step up. Deeply coloured, dark and structured, it blends Grenache and Syrah. However the brilliant wines here are the three Côtes du Rhône cuvées, sourced from a range of terroirs, some with vines older than 100 years. Père Mayeaux is a blend of Syrah and Grenache and is aged in new oak, which is very well judged. Smoky black fruits and a hint of *garrigue* are the prominent characters. The richly-textured and very concentrated César is Grenache, Syrah and a tiny hint of Mourvèdre showing great depth and fruit purity. Also made is Le Caillou, a late harvested Grenache from very old vines as

well as a red Chateauneuf-du-Pape, again just Grenache and from the 2009 vintage on. (DM)

Recommended Reds:
Côtes du Rhône César ★★★☆ £D
Côtes du Rhône Père Mayeaux ★★★ £C
Côtes du Rhône-Villages Visan ★★★ £C
Côtes du Rhône ★★☆ £C
Recommended Whites:
Côtes du Rhône César ★★★ £C
Côtes du Rhône ★★☆ £B

Dom. Rouge Garance *www.rougegarance.com*

This is a small 5ha estate run by the Cortellini family and jointly owned with the French comedy film actor Jean-Louis Trintignant. They own a total of 28 ha spread across various vineyards in the communes of Castillon du Gard and Saint-Hilaire d'Ozilhan. Feuille de Garance is from young vines of Grenache, Syrah and Cinsault. Garances comes from mainly old vine Carignan. Only a relatively small part of the harvest each year is vinified as Rouge Garance, a blend of 70/20/10 Syrah, Grenache and Mourvèdre. The top red is the splendid Les Saintpierre from the oldest and lowest yielding Syrah vines and aged for 18 months in cask. The top reds will age well over 5 to 8 years. There is also a ripe and spicy fruit-driven Côtes du Rhône rosé and a well-priced nutty and forward easy-drinking white. (DM)

Recommended Reds:
Côtes du Rhône-Villages Les Saintpierre ★★★★ £D
Côtes du Rhône-Villages Rouge Garance ★★★ £C
Côtes du Rhône-Villages Garances ★★★ £C
Côtes du Rhône Feuille de Garance ★★☆ £B
Recommended Whites:
Côtes du Rhône Blanc de Garance ★★☆ £B
Recommended Rosés:
Côtes du Rhône Rosée de Garance ★★ £B

Dom. Roucas Toumba (Vacqueyras)

Eric Bouletins small domaine consists of just 3 ha of almost exclusively red varieties with just a smattering of white grapes planted. His family have owned the land here since the early 1700s but have only become winemakers in the last decade. Before this, like so many other small growers the harvest was sold to the local co-op. The rich and concentrated Vacqueyras is the key wine, although a IGP Pichot Roucas red and a Vin de France from de-classified Vacqueyras fruit, which helps in ensuring the integrity of the *grand vin*, are also made. A white, Blanc Les Prémisis is a blend of Grenache Blanc, Clairette, Marsanne, Roussanne and Bourboulenc. Les Restanques is dominated by over 80 year old Grenache, blended with just less than a third of Syrah, 10% Mourvèdre and a tiny amount of white fruit. The wine is aged in *demi-muids* with the exception of the Syrah which sees 18 months in small oak, lending a sumptuous almost international undercurrent to the dark and herb spiced fruit. There is a depth, structure and purity that is rarely encountered in Vacqueyras reds. (DM)

Recommended Reds:
Vacqueyras Les Restanques de Cabassole ★★★★ £D

Dom. Jean Royer *www.domainejeanroyer.fr*

Very good, traditionally made Châteauneuf is produced by Jean Royer. As well as producing his own labels he is also a source for TARDIEU-LAURENT. The wines all get a lengthy vatting and are in a dense, full-bodied style. The regular Tradition red is a touch less

muscular than the other two cuvées, a blend of Grenache and Syrah that will drink well with 4 or 5 years' ageing. The Prestige is blended from Grenache, Syrah and Mourvèdre and is a selection of older vines. It is impressively deep and structured. Give it at least 6 or 7 years. The chewy, complex Les Sables de la Crau comes from 100% old Grenache as does the top wine, made only in great vintages, Hommage à Mon Père. Dense and powerful with formidable depth, it demands 7 or 8 years and will keep well for a decade and beyond. A small amount of white Châteauneuf is produced along with a limited release 100% Syrah from 45 to 50 year old vines, Sola Syrah Regalis and a Vin de France red, Le Petit Roy. (DM)

Recommended Reds:

Châteauneuf-du-Pape Hommage à Mon Père ★★★★☆ £F
Châteauneuf-du-Pape Les Sables de La Crau ★★★★ £F
Châteauneuf-du-Pape Prestige ★★★☆ £E
Châteauneuf-du-Pape Tradition ★★★ £E

✺ Dom. Roger Sabon (Châteauneuf-du-Pape)

While there is good to very good regular Lirac and Châteauneuf-du-Pape here it is the marvellous old-vine Cuvée Prestige and Le Secret de Sabon that show real intensity and sheer class. They are produced from very low-yielding, superbly sited, venerable vines. The latter is one of the great wines of the appellation and now commands a very steep price accordingly. The wines are all bottled without filtration. (DM)

Recommended Reds:

Châteauneuf-du-Pape Le Secret de Sabon ★★★★★ £H
Châteauneuf-du-Pape Cuvée Prestige ★★★★★ £F
Châteauneuf-du-Pape Cuvée Réserve ★★★★ £E
Châteauneuf-du-Pape Les Olivets ★★★☆ £D
Lirac Chapelle de Maillac ★★★ £C
Côtes du Rhône ★★ £B

Saint Jean de Barroux (Ventoux) *www.saintjeandubarroux.fr*

This small property has become one of the shining lights in this aspiring appellation. Winemaker Philippe Gimel is widely experienced, having worked with such luminaries as PIERRE-BISE in the Loire and more locally BEAUCASTEL and JANASSE. There are 12 ha here planted at an altitude of 300–400m and a total of 7 varieties are being cultivated. The rich and nutty white is a blend of Grenache Blanc with Clairette and Bourboulenc adding structure and backbone, aged in old wood. The dense and very concentrated La Source red is a blend of Grenache, Carignan and Cinsault, again vinified in *cuve*. The very impressive La Pierre Noire, which is berry selected, blends Grenache and Syrah. It is traditionally aged in cement. A further red L'Argile is also made as well as a rosé, Le Rosé. (DM)

Recommended Reds:

Côtes du Ventoux La Pierre Noire ★★★★ £E
Côtes du Ventoux La Source ★★★☆ £D

Recommended Whites:

Côtes du Ventoux La Montagne ★★★☆ £E

>> Dom. Saint Préfert (Châteauneuf-du-Pape) *www.st-prefert.fr*

A small range of excellent wines is made at this domaine, which has been run by Isabel Ferrando since 2003. She has enjoyed input from enologist Philippe Cambie and the vineyards are now fully certified organic. All 13 authorised varieties are planted and the vines average around 60 years of age resulting in naturally low yields and impressive flavour and concentration in the grapes. Grenache is the most important variety numerically although Mourvèdre is also key

to quality with some vines approaching 100 years of age. Replanting where necessary is done by mass selection. The white Châteauneuf-du-Pape is full of character. Coming from mainly Clairette and Roussanne the wine is aged in a mix of one-third new wood and older barrels for just six months giving a rich and approachable style. The Cuvée Spéciale Vieilles Clairettes is one of the finest whites of the appellation. The old Clairette vines are dry-farmed and give a yield of just 15 hl/ha. Very intense, rich and opulent, the wine is aged for two years and bottled unfiltered. The red Cuvée Classique is ripe and approachable with attractive black fruits and spices. Grenache dominates the blend. The other two red Saint-Préfert Châteauneuf-du-Papes are a clear step up. The Auguste Favier is dominated by Grenache and also includes old Cinsault. It is aged in a mix of concrete and older hogsheads to emphasise the dark, smoky exotic fruit. The immensely complex and concentrated Collection Charles Giraud is like all the reds vinified with stems and comes from a mix of very old Grenache (80 years), Mourvèdre (60 years) and Syrah (60 years of age). Ageing is in used 600 litre hogsheads to emphasise the quality and character of the wine. The red Colombis comes from a separate domaine holding planted with very old Grenache, at least 60 years of age. Ageing is in used wood and offering intense Grenache berry fruits and spicy garrigue scents. The top reds are impressively ageworthy. (DM)

Domaine de Saint-Préfert

Recommended Reds:

Châteauneuf-du-Pape Collection Charles Giraud ★★★★★ £G
Châteauneuf-du-Pape Reserve Auguste Favier ★★★★☆ £F
Châteauneuf-du-Pape Cuvée Classique ★★★☆ £E

Recommended Whites:

Châteauneuf-du-Pape Cuvée Spéciale Vieilles Clairettes ★★★★☆ £F
Châteauneuf-du-Pape ★★★★ £E

Domaine Isabel Ferrando

Recommended   **Reds:**

Châteauneuf-du-Pape Colombis ★★★★☆ £F

Sang des Cailloux (Vacqueyras) *www.sangdescailloux.com*

The performance at this estate represents one of the region's notable turnarounds in recent years. Quality in the early to mid-1990s was acceptable but only just. The wines were light, lacked dimension and appeared heavily processed. Now, though, they have minimal manipulation and are all the better for it. A barrel-fermented white, Un Sang Blanc, is made from Grenache Blanc, Bourboulenc, Clairette and Roussanne but in tiny quantities, fewer than 200 cases a year. It is the two excellent-value reds which demand attention, particularly for their availability. They are now rich, dense and loaded with black fruit and spicy *garrigue* scents. The Classique has been variously named Doucinello, Azalais and Floureto over recent vintages. It is blended from Grenache, Syrah, Mourvèdre and Cinsault and is the mainstay of the domaine. The Cuvée Lopy is produced from the oldest vines of Grenache (75 years) and Syrah. It is firmly structured and requires 3 or 4 years. Both reds keep very well. (DM)

Recommended Reds:

Vacqueyras Cuvée Lopy Vieilles Vignes ★★★★ £E
Vacqueyras Traditionelle ★★★ £D

Recommended Whites:

Vacqueyras Un Sang ★★★ £E

✺ Dom. Santa Duc (Gigondas) *www.santaduc.fr*

For the past two decades Santa Duc has been one of the finest and most reliable names in Gigondas. Even in lesser vintages the wines

Southern Rhône

show impressively well. Just over half of Yves Gras's holding is in Gigondas and of other wines there is red IGP and Côtes du Rhône which is lighter than some but has intensity and a marked scent of *garrigues*. The wines are given a cold soak prior to fermentation and are bottled unfined and unfiltered after being aged on lees. In Gigondas there is a solid and approachable example La Garancières, but it is the other two wines covered below which really stand out. The Aux Lieux Dits *cuvée* is the softer, more forward of the two, coming from a number of sites, with the more structured and very, very fine Prestige des Hautes Garrigues seeing around one-third new oak. The balance is aged in *foudres*. A small range of other wines from the southern Rhône is also now being offered. These include wines from Rasteau, Roaix and Châteauneuf-du-Pape. Two further Gigondas reds are also made. Grand Grenache 66 which is a selection of exceptional old Grenache and Santa Roc which is an old vine *cuvée* made in association with Rémy Pédréno who makes wine in the IGP du Gard at ROC D'ANGLADE. (DM)

Recommended Reds:
Gigondas Les Hautes Garrigues ★★★★☆ £E
Gigondas Aux Lieux Dits ★★★☆ £D
Gigondas La Garancières ★★★ £C
Côtes du Rhône Les Quatre Terres ★★☆ £B
Recommended Whites:
Côtes du Rhône-Villages Sablet Le Fournas ★★★ £C

Dom. Sainte-Anne (Côtes du Rhône)
Quality has been of a high order here throughout the 1990s but the wines still remain very good value. There are some 35 ha under vine and Syrah and Mourvèdre as well as Grenache are important in shaping the style of the reds. These are full-bodied and dense; the top three cuvées in particular will benefit from medium-term ageing. The Viognier is important here and is one of the better southern Rhône examples. It should always be enjoyed young and fresh, when it will be both exotic and peachy.(DM)

Recommended Reds:
Côtes du Rhône-Villages Cuvée St Gervais Les Mourillons ★★★ £E
Côtes du Rhône-Villages Cuvée St Gervais ★★★ £D
Côtes du Rhône-Villages Cuvée Notre-Dame des Celettes ★★★ £C
Côtes du Rhône-Villages ★★☆ £C
Recommended Whites:
Côtes du Rhône Viognier ★★ £D

❀ Dom. Saint Damien (Gigondas) www.domainesaintdamien.com
With vineyards located in one of the warmest sectors of the appellation and galets roulés stony soils, Joel Saurel produces very full, rich and concentrated Gigondas. He is helped in this endeavour by vines which are in some cases over 100 years old. Even the vines for the subtle, berry-scented Classique are on average over 70 years old. No new oak is used and the wines are all bottled without fining or filtration. Les Souteyrades is much more backward, darkly spicy and mineral in character. The *terroir* is largely limestone and the wine has a very fine piercing intensity. La Louisiane comes from pure *garrigue*. Mourvèdre is blended with Grenache: there is no Syrah. Rich, heady and full, this like the Souteyrades demands 5 or 6 years' patience. A few hectares are also owned in the Côtes du Rhône from which an excellent old vine red dominated by Grenache is produced as well as a further wine La Bouveau which includes younger vine Syrah as well as much older Grenache and Cinsault. (DM)

Recommended Reds:
Gigondas Les Souteyrades ★★★★ £E
Gigondas La Louisiane ★★★★ £E

Gigondas Classique Vieille Vignes ★★★☆ £D
Côtes du Rhône Vieilles Vignes ★★★ £C

❀ Dom. de La Solitude www.domaine-solitude.com
Decent red and white Côtes du Rhône as well as some impressive Châteauneuf-du-Pape are made at this ancient estate. Indeed one of the family ancestors, Maffeo Barberini, became Pope Urbain VIII in the early 1600s. There are a total of 38ha planted in Châteauneuf-du-Pape of which 30ha are red varieties and a further 48ha are covered by the Côtes du Rhône AC. The richly juicy Côtes du Rhône red comes from two separate low-yielding vineyards where just 30 hl/ha are cropped. Two modern style white Châteauneufs see the Roussanne component barrel fermented. Ageing on lees produces a nutty, floral, almost mineral character and in the case of the Barberini great intensity. The spicy, berry-fruited Tradition red is a blend of Grenache, Syrah, Mourvèdre and a little Cinsault. The richer, fuller and denser Barberini is a mix of 40/30/30 Grenache, Syrah and Mourvèdre aged in 60% new small oak. The top wines are the remarkably complex, richly textured Réserve Secret, aged in 80% new oak and most recently a new label Cornelia Constanza which is fully old-vine Grenache. Expect the Tradition to evolve well for up to a decade, the top two reds for twice that. (DM)

Recommended Reds:
Châteauneuf-du-Pape Réserve Secret ★★★★★ £G
Châteauneuf-du-Pape Cuvée Barbarini ★★★★☆ £F
Châteauneuf-du-Pape Tradition ★★★★ £E
Côtes du Rhône ★★★ £C
Recommended Whites:
Châteauneuf-du-Pape Cuvée Barbarini ★★★★ £F
Châteauneuf-du-PapeTradition ★★★☆ £D
Côtes du Rhône ★★☆ £B

❀ Tardieu-Laurent (Côtes du Rhône) www.tardieu-laurent.fr
An exceptional range of wines from throughout the Rhône Valley is produced by the partnership of Michel Tardieu and Dominique LAURENT of Burgundy. Along with wines from the Rhône there have been selected bottlings from the Costières de Nîmes, Provence and the Languedoc. Almost everything is of at least ★★ or ★★★ quality. Top wines from Hermitage, Côte-Rôtie and Cornas in the north and Châteauneuf-du-Pape, Gigondas and Vacqueyras in the south invariably rate at least ★★★ and often ★★★ or more. (DM)

Recommended Reds:
Hermitage ★★★★★ £G
Cornas Vieilles Vignes ★★★★☆ £F
Saint-Joseph Vieilles Vignes Les Roches ★★★☆ £E
Châteauneuf-du-Pape Cuvée Spéciale ★★★★★ £G
Châteauneuf-du-Pape Vieilles Vignes ★★★★☆ £F
Rasteau Vieilles-Vignes ★★★ £D
Côtes du Rhône Cuvée Spéciale ★★★ £D
Recommended Whites:
Hermitage ★★★★★ £G

Dom. de La Tourade (Gigondas)
This 20 ha property is now responsible for some of the more exciting Gigondas. Also produced is a little spicy, forward Côtes du Rhône and two Vacqueyras, of which the old-vine Cuvée de l'Euse is much the more serious. The regular Gigondas bottling is full of characterful dark, spicy Grenache fruit. The Font des Aieux is fuller and more structured and shows real old-vine complexity. The top wine, Cuvée Morgan, blends some Syrah and Mourvèdre with Grenache and is aged in *barrique* for 12 months. One-third is new

and the wood is fairly prominent in the wine's youth. Ageing for 4 or 5 years should ensure greater harmony. (DM)

Recommended Reds:

Gigondas Cuvée Morgan ★★★☆ £E
Gigondas Font des Aieux ★★★☆ £E
Gigondas Traditionelle ★★★ £D
Vacqueyras Cuvée de l'Euse ★★★ £C
Vacqueyras ★★☆ £C

Dom. du Trapadis (Rasteau) *www.domainedutrapadis.com*

Helen Durand has been in charge here since 1994 and the estate is now run with minimal interference in vineyard or cellar. Les Adrès is a classic, Grenache based southern Rhône blend while Harys is produced from Syrah. Traditional vinification (no destemming) produces wines which are both rich and structured. Even the Côtes du Rhône will benefit from short cellaring. In short these are powerful and complex wines. A Cairanne red, a white Côtes du Rhône and a very late harvested Grenache Vendange Tradive are also made. (DM)

Recommended Reds:

Rasteau Harys ★★★☆ £D   Rasteau Les Adrès ★★★☆ £D
Rasteau ★★☆ £C   Côtes du Rhône ★★ £B

Pierre Usseglio *www.domainepierreusseglio.fr*

Jean-Pierre and Thierry are now running their father's property of some 24 ha. The white Châteauneuf is sound but it is the reds which excel. They also make a Côtes du Rhône red, a Lirac red and a fruit driven red Vin de France which is mainly Merlot. The range includes very good regular red Châteauneuf as well as the super-dense and rich old-vine Mon Aïeul and an exceptional Réserve des Deux-Frères, a very expensive special bottling that combines very old Grenache with Syrah. It is available in very small quantities. Even rarer is Not for You, aged for 36 months, it is a single barrel of very old Grenache. (DM)

Recommended Reds:

Châteauneuf-du-Pape Cuvée de Mon Aïeul ★★★★☆ £F
Châteauneuf-du-Pape Tradition ★★★☆ £E

Recommended Whites:

Châteauneuf-du-Pape Tradition ★★☆ £E

Raymond Usseglio *www.domaine-usseglio.fr*

The Usseglios' Châteauneuf vineyard is planted to 15 ha of Grenache, Syrah, Mourvèdre, Cinsault and Counoise, while there is also just 1.5 ha of the white varieties Clairette, Bourboulenc, Roussanne and Grenache Blanc. There is also 5 ha classified as Côtes du Rhône. The white is produced in an approachable forward style with attractive floral, citrus and nutty fruit. Drink it young. A reserve Roussanne is also made. The reds are sturdy and traditional. The Tradition is firmly structured in its youth while the Impériale, sourced from a plot planted in 1902, understandably offers greater depth and complexity and is a wine of real substance and power. A Mouvèdre dominated red, La Part des Anges was released with the 2007 vintage and a 100% Roussanne is also made. The reds are bottled unfiltered and offer good value. A Côtes du Rhône red is also produced. (DM)

Recommended Reds:

Châteauneuf-du-Pape Cuvée Impériale ★★★★ £F
Châteauneuf-du-Pape ★★★☆ £E

Recommended Whites:

Châteauneuf-du-Pape ★★★ £E

✿ Dom. de La Vieille-Julienne *www.vieillejulienne.com*

The wines here are now of a different order to those of a few years back. The IGP is still from reasonably young vines but for the Côtes du Rhône and Châteauneuf-du-Pape bottlings the vines are old to very old. The Vieilles Vignes Côtes du Rhône Clavin is produced from over 60-year-old plantings and is a blend of Grenache, Syrah and Mourvèdre. It is very intense and complex. The regular Châteauneuf-du-Pape is sweet, spicy and intense, full of *garrigue* and super-ripe dark berry fruit. The top two cuvées are remarkable. The Vieilles Vignes is immensely powerful and structured and it needs time. The Vieilles Vignes Réservé is extraordinary – 95% Grenache, heady and super-rich, it's the more open and approachable of the two but immensely ageworthy. (DM)

Recommended Reds:

Châteauneuf-du-Pape Vieilles Vignes Réservé ✪✪✪✪ £H
Châteauneuf-du-Pape Vieilles Vignes ★★★★★ £G
Châteauneuf-du-Pape ★★★★ £E
Côtes du Rhône Clavin ★★★ £D
Côtes du Rhône ★★ £B
IGP de la Principauté d'Orange ★☆ £B

✿✿ Dom. de Vieux-Télégraphe *www.vieuxtelegraphe.com*

The Bruniers have been benchmark producers here for two decades. They now own the Domaine LA ROQUETTE also in Châteauneuf, and have an interest in the revitalised LES PALLIÈRES in Gigondas. The 70-ha estate is planted largely to reds, understandably, with a little Clairette, Grenache Blanc, Bourboulenc and Roussanne, which are used to produce a spicy, intensely nutty and surprisingly refined white Châteauneuf. The Châteauneuf-du-Pape red is now denser and more powerful than of old but with marvellous depth and refinement. There have been significant improvements at many properties throughout the appellation in recent years but few of these wines can achieve the balance and harmony of those of the Bruniers. An additional Châteauneuf-du-Pape red Télégramme is also made as well as IGP Vaucluse red and white. The Bruniers also have an interest in Château MASSAYA in the Lebanon. (DM)

Recommended Reds:

Châteauneuf-du-Pape ✪✪✪✪ £G
IGP de Vaucluse Le Pigeoulet ★★☆ £C

Recommended Whites:

Châteauneuf-du-Pape ★★★★ £F

Dom. de Villeneuve *www.domaine-de-villeneuve.fr*

There are just 8.5 ha of red varieties planted here and output is small at around 3,000 cases a year. The vineyards are all now farmed biodynamically. The red Vieilles Vignes bottling is one of the best-value wines in the appellation, a blend of Grenache, Syrah, Mourvèdre and Cinsault with dark, peppery, spicy fruit, a hint of *garrigue* scent and real persistence on the palate. It offers loads of ripe, concentrated fruit along with firm youthful tannin and real old vine complexity and ageing for 5 or 6 years is advisable. A Côtes du Rhône red, La Griffe is also made. (DM)

Recommended Reds:

Châteauneuf-du-Pape Vieilles Vignes ★★★★ £E

✿ Dom. Vindemio (Ventoux) *www.vindemio.com*

This is the new domaine of Jean Marot who used to make some brilliant Ventoux examples at Domain LE MURMURIUM. The current owners of Le Murmurium are only selling on their fruit but you may encounter some of M. Marots earlier successes up to the 2005

France

vintage and as such these wines have been moved to the Other Wines of Note at the end of the section. Jean is now in partnership with his sommelier son Guillaume in their new project and there are a number of other investors. The Vindemio wines are no less impressive than the Murmuriums and have quickly become clear benchmarks for this often over achieving appellation. The wines are sourced from 13 ha and are very much traditional in style with no small oak but very vibrant and pure. The vineyards have been tended organically since 2007 and the intention is for them to be fully converted to biodynamic farming. Four cuvées are produced, one white and three reds. The Regain Blanc is a blend of 80/20% Cairette and Grenache Blanc, it is full of rich, nutty southern fruit character. The Regain Rouge is the most approachable of the three reds and is a blend of Grenache, Syrah and a little Carignan. It is supple, vibrant and full of bright fruit and soft tannins. Imagine is a 50/50 blend of Grenache and Syrah, it is denser and fuller with the dark, licoricey, black pepper notes of Syrah more apparent. The top wine Amadeus is a splendid blend of 80% Grenache and 20% Syrah. It is considerably more powerful and structured and will develop well for a decade plus. There are dark fruits and spicy herbs in abundance and a very fine, complex mineral edge. The wines are all relative bargains. (DM)

Recommended Reds:
Côtes du Ventoux Amadeus ★★★★ £D
Côtes du Ventoux Imagine ★★★☆ £C
Côtes du Ventoux Regain ★★★ £B
Recommended Whites:
Côtes du Ventoux Regain ★★☆ £B

❄ **Dom. Viret (Côtes du Rhône-Villages)** *www.domaine-viret.com*
Very impressive 30 ha domaine planted almost exclusively to red varieties. Just 1.5 ha are accounted for by whites and the main focus of these is the Coudée d'Or. There are good IGP white, red and rosé labelled Solstice and a superior red IGP Energie. Added to these are the La Trilogie reds, T is varietal Mourvèdre, L is Syrah, and G is Grenache. The estate is particularly noteworthy for its dedication to organic farming and what the Virets refer to as their 'cosmoculture'. Sharing some of the principles of biodynamics, cosmoculture is based on farming principles dating back to the Mayan and Inca civilisations, avoiding any unnatural practices affecting growing conditions in the vineyards. The reds are particularly striking: all come from low yields, are vinified without recourse to sulphur dioxide and are bottled without filtration. The softer and vibrant Renaissance blends Grenache, Syrah and Mourvèdre and is aged in cement. More structured are Les Colonnades, which includes Carignan rather than Syrah and is aged for 24 months with the Mourvèdre in *barrique*. The Emergence, a blend of Grenache, Syrah and Carignan, is similarly aged for 24 months but in a mix of *barriques* and vat. The densely structured and very characterful top wines will undoubtedly benefit from 5 years' ageing. (DM)

Recommended Reds:
Côtes du Rhône-Villages Saint-Maurice T ★★★★ £E
Côtes du Rhône-Villages Saint-Maurice L ★★★★ £E
Côtes du Rhône-Villages Saint-Maurice G ★★★★ £E
Côtes du Rhône-Villages Saint-Maurice Emergence ★★★★ £E
Côtes du Rhône-Villages Saint-Maurice Les Colonnades ★★★☆ £D
Côtes du Rhône-Villages Saint-Maurice Renaissance ★★★ £C
Recommended Whites:
Côtes du Rhône La Coudée d'Or ★★★ £D

Other wines of note - *Southern Rhône*

Dom. d'Aéria
Recommended Reds: Rasteau ★★☆ £C
Côtes du Rhône-Villages Cairanne Prestige ★★☆ £C
Côtes du Rhône-Villages Cairanne Tradition ★★ £C
Côtes du Rhône ★☆ £B
Dom. Pierre Amadieu
Recommended Reds: Gigondas Grand Reserve ★★★ £D
Côtes du Rhône Grand Reserve ★☆ £B
Dom. de L'Ameillaud
Recommended Reds: Côtes du Rhône-Villages Cairanne ★★☆ £C
Côtes du Rhône ★☆ £B
Dom. des Anges
Recommended Reds: Ventoux Archange ★★★☆ £D
Ventoux ★ ★★☆ £B
Recommended Whites: Ventoux Archange ★★★ £C
Ventoux ★★ £B
Recommended Rosés: Ventoux ★☆ £B
Dom. Armand
Recommended Reds: Rasteau ★★☆ £C
Maison Arnoux
Recommended Reds: Vacqueyras 1717 ★★★☆ £E
Gigondas Seigneur de Lauris ★★★ £D
Gigondas Vieux Clocher ★★☆ £C
Vacqueyras Seigneur de Lauris ★★☆ £C
Beaumes-de-Venise Vieux Clocher ★★ £C
Côtes du Rhône Seigneur de Lauris ★☆ £B
Recommended Whites: Vacqueyras Seigneur de Lauris ★★ £C
Ventoux Vieux Clocher ★☆ £B
Les Domaines Bernard
Recommended Reds: Châteauneuf-du-Pape Louis Bernard ★★ £D
Dom. des Bernardins
Recommended Reds: Beaumes-de-Venise ★★☆ £C
Côtes du Rhône Les Balmes ★★ £B
Recommended Whites: Muscat de Beaumes-de-Venise ★★★ £D
Bois Dauphin
Recommended Reds: Châteauneuf-du-Pape ★★★ £D
Dom. des Bosquets
Recommended Reds: Gigondas ★★★☆ £D
Dom. Bouchassy
Recommended Reds: Lirac ★☆ £C
Dom. de La Brunely
Recommended Reds: Châteauneuf-du-Pape ★★★☆ £E
Vacqueyras ★★★ £C Ventoux ★☆ £B
Dom. des Buisserons
Recommended Reds: Côtes du Rhône-Villages Cairanne ★★☆ £C
Dom. Chamfort
Recommended Reds: Vacqueyras ★★★☆ £D
Dom. de Chanabas
Recommended Reds: Châteauneuf-du-Pape ★★ £D
Dom. de Chanssaud
Recommended Reds: Châteauneuf-du-Pape ★★★ £E
Chante Perdrix
Recommended Reds: Châteauneuf-du-Pape ★★☆ £E
Dom. Chapoton
Recommended Reds:
Côtes du Rhône-Villages Rochegude Géodaisia ★★★☆ £C
Côtes du Rhône-Villages Rochegude ★★★☆ £C
Côtes du Rhône ★★ £B
Recommended Whites: Côtes du Rhône Géodaisia ★★ £C

Didier Charavin
Recommended Reds: Rasteau Prestige ★★☆ £C
Ch. d'Aqueria
Recommended Reds: Lirac ★★☆ £C
Côtes du Rhône ★★ £B
Recommended Whites: Lirac ★★☆ £C
Recommended Rosés: Lirac ★★ £C Tavel ★☆ £C
Ch. de L'Amarine
Recommended Reds: Costières de Nîmes Cuvée de Bernis ★★ £B
Ch. Cabrières
Recommended Reds: Châteauneuf-du-Pape Prestige ★★★☆ £E
Châteauneuf-du-Pape ★★★ £D
Ch. de Clapier
Recommended Reds: Luberon Cuvée Soprano ★★★ £C
Luberon ★★ £B
Recommended Whites: Luberon Cuvée Soprano ★★☆ £C
Luberon Cuvée Classique ★★ £B
Recommended Rosés: Luberon Cuvée Classique ★★ £B
Ch. des Fines Roches
Recommended Reds: Châteauneuf-du-Pape ★★★ £E
Recommended Whites: Châteauneuf-du-Pape ★★★ £D
Ch. de La Font du Loup
Recommended Reds: Châteauneuf-du-Pape ★★★★ £E
Recommended Whites: Châteauneuf-du-Pape ★★★☆ £D
Ch. Gigognan
Recommended Reds: Châteauneuf-du-Pape Clos du Roi ★★★☆ £E
Châteauneuf-du-Pape Cardinalice ★★★☆ £E
Recommended Whites:
Châteauneuf-du-Pape Clos du Roi ★★★☆ £E
Ch. du Grand Moulas
Recommended Reds: Côtes du Rhône-Villages ★★☆ £C
Côtes du Rhône ★★ £B
Ch. Grande-Cassagne
Recommended Reds: Costières de Nîmes Hippolyte ★★☆ £C
Costières de Nîmes La Civette ★★ £B
Costières de Nîmes Les Rameaux ★★ £B
Costières de Nîmes Tradition ★☆ £B
Recommended Whites: Costières de Nîmes Hippolyte ★★ £C
Costières de Nîmes Tradition ★☆ £B
Ch. Haut Musiel
Recommended Reds:
Côtes du Rhône-Villages SignardeTralamont ★★★ £C
Côtes du Rhône-Villages Signarde Roussignac ★★★ £C
Côtes du Rhône-Villages Roussignac ★★☆ £C
Recommended Whites: Côtes du Rhône-Villages ★★☆ £C
Ch. Jas de Bressy
Recommended Reds: Châteauneuf-du-Pape ★★★☆ £E
Ch. La Canorgue
Recommended Reds: Côtes du Rhône-Villages Laudun ★★☆ £C
Côtes du Rhône ★★ £B
Luberon ★★ £B
Ch. La Decelle
Recommended Reds: Côtes du Rhône-Villages Valréas ★★☆ £C
Grignan-les-Adhémar ★☆ £B
Ch. La Tuilerie
Recommended Reds: Costières de Nîmes Cuvée Eole ★★☆ £D
Costières de Nîmes Cuvée Vieilles Vignes ★★ £C
Recommended Whites:
Costières de Nîmes Cuvée Vieilles Vignes ★★ £B
Ch. Le Devoy Martine
Recommended Reds: Lirac Cuvée Circius ★★★☆ £C

Côtes du Rhône ★★ £B
Recommended Whites: Lirac Cuvée Circius ★★★☆ £C
Ch. Maucoil
Recommended Reds: Châteauneuf-du-Pape Privilège ★★★★ £E
Châteauneuf-du-Pape ★★★☆ £E
Châteauneuf-du-Pape Fontaines des Papes ★★☆ £D
Recommended Whites: Châteauneuf-du-Pape ★★★ £D
Ch. de Marjolet
Recommended Reds: Côtes du Rhône-Villages Laudun ★★★ £C
Côtes du Rhône-Villages ★★☆ £C Côtes du Rhône ★★ £B
Recommended Whites: Côtes du Rhône ★★ £B
Recommended Rosés: Côtes du Rhône ★★ £B
Ch. de Montmirail
Recommended Reds: Gigondas Beauchamp ★★★ £D
Vacqueyras l'Ermite ★★★ £C Vacqueyras Saint Papes ★★☆ £C
Ch. Mont Thabor
Recommended Reds: Châteauneuf-du-Pape ★★★ £E
Ch. de Nages
Recommended Reds: Costières de Nîmes JT ★★★☆ £D
Costières de Nîmes Vieilles Vignes ★★☆ £C
Costières de Nîmes ★☆ £B
Recommended Whites: Costières de Nîmes Vieilles Vignes ★★ £C
Ch. de Rouanne
Recommended Reds: Vinsobres ★★ £C
Ch. des Roques
Recommended Reds: Vacqueyras Cuvée du Château ★★★ £C
Recommended Whites: Vacqueyras Cuvée Blanche ★★★ £C
Ch. Saint Louis la Perdrix
Recommended Reds: Costières de Nîmes Cuvée Marianne ★★ £B
IGP du Gard Cabernet/Carignan ★☆ £B
Ch. de Segries
Recommended Reds:
Côtes du Rhône Clos de l'Hermitage ★★★☆ £D
Lirac Cuvée Reservée ★★★ £D
Recommended Whites: Lirac ★★ £C
Ch. Signac
Recommended Reds: Côtes du Rhône-Villages Terra Amata ★★★ £C
Côtes du Rhône-Villages Combe d'Enfer ★★☆ £C
Côtes du Rhône-Villages ★★☆ £C
Ch. du Trignon
Recommended Reds: Gigondas ★★★ £D
Côtes du Rhône-Villages Sablet ★★☆ £C
Ch. Trinquevedel
Recommended Rosés: Tavel Cuvée Traditionnelle ★★☆ £B
Tavel Autrementavel ★★ £B
Ch. de Valcombe
Recommended Reds: Costières de Nîmes Garance ★★★ £C
Costières de Nîmes Prestige ★★☆ £C
Costières de Nîmes Tradition ★★ £B
Ch. de Vaudieu
Recommended Reds: Châteauneuf-du-Pape Amiral G ★★★★☆ £F
Châteauneuf-du-Pape Val de Dieu ★★★★ £F
Châteauneuf-du-Pape ★★★☆ £E
Recommended Whites: Châteauneuf-du-Pape ★★★☆ £E
Ch. Vessière
Recommended Whites: Costières de Nîmes ★★ £B
Ch. Virgile
Recommended Reds: Costières de Nîmes ★★ £B
Clos de l'Oratoire des Papes
Recommended Reds: Châteauneuf-du-Pape ★★★ £E

Southern Rhône

France

Clos Saint-Michel
Recommended Reds:
Châteauneuf-du-Pape Cuvée Réservée ★★★ £E
Châteauneuf-du-Pape ★★☆ £D
Dom. de La Colline Saint Jean
Recommended Reds: Gigondas ★★★☆ £D Vacqueyras ★★★☆ £C
Beaumes-de-Venise ★★★ £C
Dom. Constant-Duquesnoy
Recommended Reds: Côtes du Rhône-Villages Cairanne Terra
Rhona ★★★☆ £C Vinsobres ★★★☆ £C
Côtes du Rhône Lou Cambaou ★★★ £C
Dom. des Coriancon
Recommended Reds: Vinsobres Les Hauts de Côtes ★★ £C
Vinsobres Cuvée Claude Vallot ★★ £C Vinsobres ★☆ £C
Dom. du Corne-Loup
Recommended Reds: Lirac ★★☆ £B
Recommended Rosés: Lirac ★★☆ £B
Dom. de la Côte de l'Ange
Recommended Reds: Châteauneuf-du-Pape ★★★☆ £E
Recommended Whites: Châteauneuf-du-Pape ★★★ £D
Dom. Coudoulis
Recommended Reds: Lirac Cuvée Hommage ★★★☆ £C
Lirac ★★☆ £B
Dom. Dauvergne-Ranvier
Recommended Reds: Gigondas Vin Rare ★★★☆ £D
Recommended Whites: Châteauneuf-du-Pape ★★★☆ £D
Dom. de La Daysse
Recommended Reds: Gigondas ★★☆ £C
Dom. Bruno Delubac
Recommended Reds:
Côtes du Rhône-Villages Cairanne L'Authentique ★★★ £C
Côtes du Rhône-Villages Cairanne Les Bruneau ★★☆ £C
Recommended Whites: Côtes du Rhône ★★ £B
Dom. Duclaux
Recommended Reds: Châteauneuf-du-Pape ★★★ £E
Dom. Durieu
Recommended Reds: Châteauneuf-du-Pape L'éperdu ★★★★☆ £F
Châteauneuf-du-Pape Lucile Avril ★★★★ £E
Châteauneuf-du-Pape ★★★☆ £E
Recommended Whites: Châteauneuf-du-Pape ★★★☆ £D
Dom. de Fenouillet
Recommended Reds: Beaumes-de-Venise Terres Blanches ★★☆ £C
Dom. de Ferrand
Recommended Reds: Châteauneuf-du-Pape ★★★☆ £E
Dom. de Fontaine du Clos
Recommended Reds: Vacqueyras Reflets de l'Âme ★★★☆ £D
Dom. de Fontavin
Recommended Reds:
Châteauneuf-du-Pape David & Goliath ★★★☆ £F
Châteauneuf-du-Pape Terre d'Ancêtres ★★★ £E
Gigondas Cuvee Combe Sauvage ★★★★ £E Vacqueyras ★★★☆ £C
Recommended Whites: Châteauneuf-du-Pape ★★★ £E
Dom. de Fontbonau
Recommended Reds: Côtes du Rhône ★★★☆ £C
Dom. de Fontenille
Recommended Reds: Luberon Prestige ★★★ £C
Luberon Vieilles Vignes ★★★ £C Luberon ★★☆ £B
Dom. Font-Sarade
Recommended Reds: Gigondas Les Pigières ★★★☆ £D
Vacqueyras Les Hautes de La Ponche ★★★☆ £D
Ventoux ★★★ £C

Recommended Whites: Châteauneuf-du-Pape ★★★ £E
Dom. Lou Frejau
Recommended Reds: Châteauneuf-du-Pape ★★★ £E
Galet des Papes
Recommended Reds:
Châteauneuf-du-Pape Vieilles Vignes ★★★☆ £E
Châteauneuf-du-Pape ★★★ £D
Recommended Whites: Châteauneuf-du-Pape ★★☆ £D
Dom. Galevan
Recommended Reds: Châteauneuf-du-Pape ★★★☆ £E
Dom. des Garances
Recommended Reds: Beaumes de Venise La Blache ★★☆ £C
Beaumes de Venise La Treille ★★☆ £C Ventoux ★☆ £B
Dom. du Grand Bourjassot
Recommended Reds: Gigondas Cecilie ★★★☆ £D
Côtes du Rhône-Villages Sablet ★★☆ £C
Dom. des Grand Devers
Recommended Reds: Côtes du Rhône-Villages Visan ★★☆ £C
Côtes du Rhône-Villages Valréas ★★☆ £C
Côtes du Rhône La Syrah ★★☆ £C
Côtes du Rhône Enclave des Papes ★☆ £B
Recommended Whites: Côtes du Rhône-Villages Visan ★☆ £C
Dom. de Grangeneuve
Recommended Reds: Grignan-les-Adhémar Terre d'Epices ★★☆ £C
Grignan-les-Adhémar La Truffière ★★☆ £C
Grignan-les-Adhémar Vieilles Vignes ★★ £B
Recommended Whites:
Grignan-les-Adhémar Les Dames Blanches du Sud ★★ £B
Dom. Albin Jacumin
Recommended Reds:
Châteauneuf-du-Pape La Begude des Papes ★★★☆ £E
Recommended Whites:
Châteauneuf-du-Pape La Begude des Papes ★★★ £E
Dom. Jaume
Recommended Reds: Vinsobres Altitude 420 ★★★ £C
Dom. du Joncier
Recommended Reds: Lirac ★★☆ £C
Dom. La Bastide Saint Vincent
Recommended Reds: Gigondas ★★★☆ £D
Vacqueyras La Pavane ★★★☆ £D
Côtes du Rhône-Villages Plan de Dieu ★★★ £C
Côtes du Rhône ★★☆ £B
Dom. La Consonnière
Recommended Reds: Châteauneuf-du-Pape ★★★ £E
Lirac ★★☆ £C
Dom. La Fourmone
Recommended Reds: Gigondas l'Oustau Fauquet ★★★ £D
Vacqueyras ★★☆ £C
Domaine La Manarine
Recommended Reds: Côtes du Rhône Tradition ★★★ £C
Dom. La Mavette
Recommended Reds: Gigondas ★★★☆ £D
Côtes du Rhône ★★☆ £C
Dom. La Rocalière
Recommended Reds: Lirac ★★★☆ £D
Laudun Chusclans Vignerons
Recommended Reds: La Dolia Côtes du Rhône-Villages ★★☆ £B
Esprit du Rhône Côtes du Rhône ★★ £B
Recommended Whites: Esprit du Rhône Côtes du Rhône ★☆ £B
Recommended Rosés: Esprit du Rhône Côtes du Rhône ★★ £B

Dom. Le Colombier
Recommended Reds: Vacqueyras Cuvée G ★★★ £C
Ventoux ★★ £B

Le Mas de Flauzières
Recommended Reds: Gigondas Terra Rosso ★★★★ £E
Gigondas Grande Réserve ★★★☆ £D
Gigondas Four Danuga ★★★ £D   Vacqueyras Le Pilon ★★★ £D
Côtes du Rhône-Villages Seguret Julien ★★☆ £C
Côtes du Rhône-Villages Le Laurias ★★ £C
Ventoux La Réserve du Pereyras ★★☆ £B

Dom. Les Hautes Cances
Recommended Reds:
Côtes du Rhône-Villages Cairanne Col du Débat ★★★ £C
Côtes du Rhône-Villages Cairanne Vieilles Vignes ★★★ £C
Côtes du Rhône-Villages Cairanne ★★☆ £C   Côtes du Rhône ★☆ £B
Recommended Whites: Côtes du Rhône-Villages Cairanne ★★ £C

Dom. Les 3 Cellier
Recommended Reds: Châteauneuf-du-Pape Eternelle ★★★★ £F
Châteauneuf-du-Pape Alchimie ★★★ £D
Recommended Whites: Châteauneuf-du-Pape Insolente ★★★☆ £D

Dom. de La Ligière
Recommended Reds: Vacqueyras ★★★ £C

Dom. Longue Toque
Recommended Reds: Gigondas ★★★☆ £D

Dom. L'Or de Line
Recommended Reds: Châteauneuf-du-Pape Paule Courtil ★★★ £E

Dom. Marrenon
Recommended Reds: Luberon Grand Marrenon ★★☆ £C

Dom. Martinelle
Recommended Reds: Beaumes-de-Venise ★★★ £C
Ventoux ★★☆ £B

Mas des Aveylans
Recommended Reds: IGP d'Oc Syrah Cuvée Prestige ★★ £B

Mas des Bressades
Recommended Reds: Costières de Nîmes Excéllence ★★★ £C
IGP du gard Cabernet/Syrah ★★☆ £C
Costières de Nîmes Tradition ★★ £B
Recommended Whites: Costières de Nîmes Excéllence ★★ £C
Costières de Nîmes Tradition ★☆ £B
Recommended Rosés: Costières de Nîmes Tradition ★☆ £B

Dom. du Mas Carlot
Recommended Reds: Costières de Nîmes Tradition ★★ £B
Recommended Whites: Costières de Nîmes Tradition ★☆ £B

Mas de Guiot
Recommended Reds: Costières de Nîmes Numa ★★☆ £C
IGP du Gard Cabernet/Syrah ★★ £B

Dom. Julien Masquin
Recommended Reds: Châteauneuf-du-Pape Montplaisir ★★★☆ £E
Châteauneuf-du-Pape Mémora ★★★☆ £E
Recommended Whites:
Châteauneuf-du-Pape Montplaisir ★★★☆ £D

Dom. Moulin-Tacussel
Recommended Reds:
Châteauneuf-du-Pape Hommage a Henri Tacussel ★★★★☆ £F
Châteauneuf-du-Pape ★★★☆ £E
Recommended Whites: Châteauneuf-du-Pape ★★★☆ £D

Notre Dame des Pallieres
Recommended Reds: Gigondas ★★★☆ £D
Rasteau ★★★ £C

Dom. de L'Olivier
Recommended Reds:
Côtes du Rhône-Villages L'Oree du Bois ★★★☆ £C
Côtes du Rhône-Villages ★★★ £C
Recommended Whites: Côtes du Rhône ★★☆ £C

Dom. des Pasquiers
Recommended Reds: Gigondas ★★★☆ £D
Côtes du Rhône-Villages Sablet ★★★ £C
Côtes du Rhône-Villages Plan de Dieu ★★★ £C

Dom. Pélaquié
Recommended Reds: Lirac ★★★☆ £C
Côtes du Rhône-Villages Laudun ★★ £C
Recommended Whites: Côtes du Rhône-Villages Laudun ★☆ £C

Dom. L'Oustau Fauquet
Recommended Reds: Gigondas ★★★ £D

Dom. Père Caboche
Recommended Reds: Châteauneuf-du-Pape Cuvée Elisabeth
Chambellan ★★★☆ £E
Châteauneuf-du-Pape Réserve ★★★ £D
Recommended Whites: Châteauneuf-du-Pape ★★★ £D

Dom. des Pères de L'Eglise
Recommended Reds: Châteauneuf-du-Pape Héritage ★★★★ £F
Châteauneuf-du-Pape La Calice de Saint-Pierre ★★★☆ £E
Recommended Whites:
Châteauneuf-du-Pape La Calice de Saint-Pierre ★★★ £D

Roger Perrin
Recommended Reds:
Châteauneuf-du-Pape Réserve Vieilles Vignes ★★★★☆ £G
Châteauneuf-du-Pape ★★★☆ £E
Côtes du Rhône Prestige ★★☆ £C   Côtes du Rhône ★★ £B
Recommended Whites: Châteauneuf-du-Pape ★★★ £D

Dom. Pesquier
Recommended Reds: Gigondas ★★★☆ £D

Dom. de La Pigeade
Recommended Reds: Vacqueyras ★★★☆ £D

Dom. de La Présidente
Recommended Reds:
Châteauneuf-du-Pape Grands Classique ★★★☆ £E
Côtes du Rhône-Villages Cairanne Grands Classique ★★☆ £C

Dom. Prieuré de Montezargues
Recommended Rosés: Tavel ★★☆ £C

Dom. des Relagnes
Recommended Reds:
Châteauneuf-du-Pape La Clef de St. Thomas ★★★ £E
Recommended Whites:
Châteauneuf-du-Pape La Clef de St. Thomas ★★☆ £D

Dom. Rigot
Recommended Reds:
Côtes du Rhône Prestige des Garrigues ★★☆ £C
Côtes du Rhône ★★ £B

Dom. Roche
Recommended Reds: Côtes du Rhône-Villages Cairanne ★★★ £C
Côtes du Rhône ★★ £B

Dom. de La Roncière
Recommended Reds:
Châteauneuf-du-Pape Flor de Ronce ★★★☆ £E
Châteauneuf-du-Pape ★★★ £E
Recommended Whites: Châteauneuf-du-Pape ★★★ £D

Dom. Saint-Amant
Recommended Reds: Beaumes-de-Venise Grangeneuve ★★★ £C
Côtes du Rhône Les Clapas ★★ £B

Southern Rhône

France

Recommended Whites:
Beaumes-de-Venise La Tabardonne ★★☆ £C
Côtes du Rhône La Borry ★★ £B
Dom. Saint-Gayan
Recommended Reds: Gigondas Fontmaria ★★★☆ £E
Gigondas ★★★ £D   Rasteau ★★★ £C
Dom. de Saint Paul
Recommended Reds:
Châteauneuf-du-Pape Cuvée Jumille ★★★☆ £E
Châteauneuf-du-Pape ★★★ £E
Recommended Whites: Châteauneuf-du-Pape ★★★ £D
Dom. Saint-Pierre
Recommended Reds: Vacqueyras ★★★☆ £C
Côtes du Rhône-Villages Plan de Dieu ★★★ £B
Côtes du Rhône ★★☆ £B
Dom. de Saint-Siffrein
Recommended Reds: Châteauneuf-du-Pape ★★★★ £E
Côtes du Rhône-Villages ★★☆ £C
Dom. des Sénéchaux
Recommended Reds: Châteauneuf-du-Pape ★★★★ £E
Recommended Whites: Châteauneuf-du-Pape ★★★☆ £D
Dom. des Soeurs Durma
Recommended Reds: Côtes du Rhône Cuvée Galance ★★☆ £C
Côtes du Rhône Brigand ★★☆ £C
Dom. de Tara
Recommended Reds: Ventoux Hautes Pierres ★★☆ £C
Ventoux Terres d'Ocres ★★ £B
Recommended Whites: Ventoux Hautes Pierres ★★ £C
Dom. du Terme
Recommended Reds: Gigondas ★★★ £D
Eric Texier
Recommended Reds: Côtes du Rhône-Villages Saint-Gervais
Vieilles Vignes ★★★ £C
Côtes du Rhône-Villages Seguret Vieilles Vignes ★★★ £B
Côtes du Rhône ★★☆ £B
Dom. Les Teyssoniers
Recommended Reds: Gigondas Cuvée Alexandre ★★★ £D
Gigondas ★★★ £D
Dom. Tour Saint-Michel
Recommended Reds:
Châteauneuf-du-Pape Feminessence ★★★★☆ £F
Châteauneuf-du-Pape Cuvée du Lion ★★★★ £E
Châteauneuf-du-Pape Cuvée des deux Soeurs ★★★★ £E
Recommended Whites:
Châteauneuf-du-Pape Cuvée des deux Soeurs ★★★ £D
Dom. de Verquière
Recommended Reds: Côtes du Rhône-Villages Sablet ★★☆ £C
Dom. du Vieux Lazaret
Recommended Reds: Châteauneuf-du-Pape ★★★ £E
Recommended Whites: Châteauneuf-du-Pape ★★☆ £D
Vins Stehelin
Recommended Reds: Gigondas Paillère & Pied-Gu ★★★★ £E
Gigondas Bertrand Stehelin ★★★☆ £D
Dom. Saint-Francois Xavier
Recommended Reds: Gigondas Prestige des Dentelles ★★★☆ £D
Xavier Vins
Recommended Reds: Vin de France Xavier Vignon SM ★★★★ £D

Author's choice - *Southern Rhône*

12 Benchmark Chateauneuf-du-Pape reds
Dom. de Beaurenard Châteauneuf-du-Pape Boisrenard
M. Chapoutier   Châteauneuf du Pape Barbe Rac
Ch. de Beaucastel   Hommage à Jacques`Perrin
Ch. La Nerthe   Châteauneuf du Pape Cuvée des Cadettes
Ch. Rayas   Châteauneuf du Pape
Clos des Caillou   Châteauneuf du Pape Réserve
Clos des Papes   Châteauneuf du Pape
Dom. de La Janasse   Châteauneuf du Pape Vieilles Vignes
Dom de Marcoux   Châteauneuf du Pape Vieilles Vignes
Dom. de La Mordorée   Châteauneuf du Pape Reine des Bois
Dom. de La Vieille-Julienne   Vieilles Vignes Réservé
Dom. du Vieux Télégraphe   Châteauneuf du Pape

A diverse selection of a dozen emerging reds
Daniel & Denis Alary   Cairanne La Font d'Estevenas
Dom. Brusset   Gigondas Les Hauts de Montmirail
Clos des Cazaux   Vacqueyras Grénat Noble
Clos Petite Bellane   Côtes du Rhône Valréas Vieilles Vignes
Dom. de Deurre   Côtes du Rhône Les Rabasses
Gourt de Mautens   IGP de Vaucluse
Dom. La Soumade   Rasteau Fleur de Confiance
Dom. Les Aphillanthes   Côtes du Rhône-Villages Vieilles Vignes
Dom. de L'Oratoire Saint-Martin   Cairanne Haut Coustias
Dom. de Piaugier   Sablet Réserve Alphonse Vautour
Marcel Richaud   Cairanne Les Estrambords
Dom. Santa-Duc   Gigondas Les Hautes Garrigues

A selection of good value reds and whites
Reds:
Ch. Saint-Cosme   Côtes du Rhône Les Deux Albions
Cros de La Mûre   Côtes du Rhône-Villages
Dom. de Fondrèche   Ventoux Cuvée Persia
Dom. La Garrigue   Vacqueyras
Dom. Grapillon d'Or   Gigondas
Dom. Rabasse-Charavin   Cairanne Estevenas
Dom. Réméjeanne   Côtes du Rhône Les Génevriers
Sang des Cailloux   Vacqueyras Classique
Whites:
Dom. Chaume-Arnaud   Côtes du Rhône-Villages Vinsobres
Dom. des Escaravailles   Rasteau La Galopine
Dom. Gramenon   Côtes du Rhône Vie on y est
Dom. Sainte-Anne   Côtes du Rhône Viognier

The focus here is on established pioneers, as well as the many new small domaines now placing Languedoc-Roussillon solidly on the country's quality wine map. Although many appellations here are of long standing only recently have widespread improvements been made in the standard of the wines. While many high quality domaines are emerging, in the Languedoc in particular many of the wines are over-extracted. There are fewer new names in the Roussillon but these have been producing wines of a uniformly impressive quality. Many vineyards originally used for fortifieds are now providing some great reds in particular. While prices generally remain very fair some are creeping up significantly. The transformation here is unique in France.

Languedoc

Some truly great wine is now being made in the Languedoc. Most but by no means all of this is produced under a number of different appellations. For reasons of practicality and location a number of splendid new-wave wines, particularly red, are being produced as IGP. A number are **IGP d'Oc** but **IGP de l'Hérault** also features, including two of the greatest properties in the Languedoc, Mas de Daumas Gassac and Domaine de La Grange des Pères.

To the west of the Costières de Nîmes (see Rhône Valley) is the giant spread of the **Languedoc** AC. This was formerly known as the Côteaux du Languedoc and the appellation umbrella also now includes appellation vineyards in the Roussillon as well. Vast and sprawling, it stretches from Nîmes in the east around the coastline south now to the Roussillon. In general though most wines which took the Côteaux du Languedoc classification will now be Languedoc. There are fourteen communes which are allowed to add their village names as crus and these include **La Clape**, **Pézenas**, **Cabrières**, **Montpeyroux**, **Pic-Saint-Loup** and **Saint-Drézéry**. At best there are some splendid wines, generally blends of Syrah, Grenache and Mourvèdre for the reds with whites from a host of varieties including Roussanne, Grenache Blanc and Clairette. Sadly, you are also likely to encounter a great many moderate to average bottles, so always try to buy from a good source.

Just to the north of Béziers and to the west of the old Languedoc are the small appellations of **Faugères** and **Saint-Chinian**. Some very fine small properties are now producing great reds, the most important variety being Syrah (which performs superbly in the schistous soils of Faugères) although Grenache, Mourvèdre and old-vine Carignan all play an important role in the local viticulture. There are a number of Muscat-based *vins doux naturels* as well but few are comparable to their peers from Muscat de Rivesaltes in the Roussillon. They include **Muscat de Frontignan**, **Muscat de Mireval** and **Muscat de Lunel**. To the west of Béziers, just inland from the coast, crisp and economically priced whites are made at **Picpoul de Pinet**.

South of Narbonne and stretching down to the hills of the Roussillon are a number of key appellations. **Minervois**, **Corbières** and **Fitou** had for a long time been regarded as little more than Midi workhorse wines, vinified by unambitious local co-ops or volume négociants. This has to a large extent changed for the better. The wines of Minervois have shown the most potential and within that appellation is the new cru sub-zone of **La Livinière**, the source of generally the densest and most substantial wines of the AC. Old-vine Carignan plays an important role here although plantings of the Rhône *cépages améliorateurs* continue apace with some

vineyards now possessing some increasingly old Syrah, Grenache and Mourvèdre. Carbonic maceration is widely used for Carignan, particularly in Corbières.

To the west of Minervois, the smaller new AC of **Cabardès** has real potential and the Bordeaux varieties Cabernet Sauvignon, Merlot and Cabernet Franc are important here. The biggest disappointment over recent decades has been the performance of Fitou, one of the first ACs established in the region. The co-op at Mont-Tauch has always been a solid source but other promising new producers are emerging.

To the west of Fitou, in the hills around the town of **Limoux**, cool hillside vineyards are planted to Chenin Blanc, Chardonnay and Mauzac. Good sparkling wine is made here, both **Blanquette de Limoux** and **Crémant de Limoux**, but it is the barrel-fermented Chardonnays that have come to prominence in recent years that impress most.

Roussillon

Until recently the vineyards in the Pyrenées-Orientales département were best known in quality wine terms for the production of fine *vins doux naturels*. This situation is changing apace though, and there seems perhaps even more potential here than in the Languedoc. Some stunning reds have appeared over the past decade and the emergence of exciting new small producers continues unabated. One of the region's great strengths is the extensive hillside vineyards planted to both old-vine Carignan and equally importantly Grenache. This is because of the traditional importance of fortified Rivesaltes and Maury, from north of Perpignan, and of Banyuls-sur-Mer, another fortified wine further south on the coast.

Exciting wines are being made throughout the **Côtes du Roussillon** and the **Côtes du Roussillon-Villages** ACs, particularly in the Agly Valley in the north western stretches of the Côtes du Roussillon-Villages appellation. As well as Grenache, the other Rhône varieties are important too, and a number of top cuvées vinified largely from Syrah and aged in high-quality new oak are also emerging, along with the occasional exceptional blend dominated by Mourvèdre. On the coast around the village of Banyuls-sur-Mer the **Collioure** appellation shares the same vineyard area as **Banyuls**. Syrah, Carignan, Mourvèdre and Cinsault are all cultivated here but interestingly it is Mourvèdre planted in close proximity to the sea that has performed particularly well, as it does in Bandol. The **IGP des Côtes Catalanes** is also increasingly important for red blends and these include Cabernet Sauvignon and Merlot. Some exceptional light style wines are again made in the Agly Valley. There is a tremendous resource of old vine Grenache and Carignan. Many top producers have emerged, although not all use the IGP classification.

The great traditional wines of the Roussillon are the fortified **Maury**, **Rivesaltes** and **Banyuls**, which in their most exquisite and aged manifestations are characterised by an intense baked, raisiny, *rancio* character. A whole range of styles are produced, with small differences between the appellations. Almost all these wines depend on Grenache as the backbone of the blend; indeed, many are produced solely from the variety. There are youthful, fruit-driven styles that spend only a limited time in cask, wines that are aged for an extended time and wines that are made from a blend of

Languedoc & Roussillon

France

vintages very much in a *solera*-style system. The wines of Maury tend to be more overtly tannic when young and those earlier-released vintages will need more cellaring. Most wines are aged in cool cellars but in Rivesaltes they are also left out for a period in the summer sun in large glass containers – *bonbonnes* – to encourage the development of those complex *rancio* aromas.

As well as the Grenache-based wines there is some very impressive **Muscat de Rivesaltes**, which is markedly different in style. At their best these wines emphasise Muscat's rich grapy character, and are heady and impressively perfumed. Indeed, the best examples are better generally than their equivalents in the Languedoc and the Rhône Valley at Beaumes-de-Venise.

A-Z of producers by appellation/region

1   Muscat de Lunel
2   Languedoc
3   Languedoc Pic Saint-Loup
4   Languedoc Montpeyroux
5   Muscat de Mireval
6   Muscat de Frontignan
7   Picpoul de Pinet
8   Faugères
9   Saint-Chinian
10 Muscat de Saint-Jean de Minervois
11 Minervois
12 Languedoc La Clape
13. Cabardès
14 Malepère
15 Limoux
16 Corbières
17 Fitou
18 Maury
19 Côtes du Roussillon-Villages
20 Côtes du Roussillon
21 Rivesaltes, Muscat de Rivesaltes
22 Banyuls, Collioure

France

Languedoc & Roussillon vintages

It is extremely difficult in a vast region such as this to make specific vintage assessments. Also much of the development that has been made in recent years makes a longer term assessment of the wines more erratic. However, there have been significant changes in vintage conditions from one year to another throughout the region. These variations are more pronounced as you move further inland. Vineyards nearer the coast benefit from a benign maritime climate and are more consistent. The further south you move towards the Roussillon there is also the influence of the Pyrenees and their cooling down draughts which effects local mesoclimates. In terms of the wines, the best red examples from year to year have the potential to age. Some red Languedoc wines have shown a recent tendency to fade prematurely, particularly those from the Languedoc. As producers become more successful in unleashing the best character from their grapes this is sure to improve. The *cépages améliorateurs* varieties planted in the Languedoc are also generally still young and the wines made from them can easily be over-extracted. There is no question that as these vines age and the Midi's keen young producers develop their craft the wines will become increasingly refined and cellarworthy. The Roussillon benefits from a very substantial planting of old vine Grenache as well as Carignan and this provides wines with a greater propensity for ageing.

Languedoc & Roussillon vintage chart

	Corbières & Minervois	Languedoc	Côtes du Roussillon-Villages incl Collioure
2015	★★★★ A	★★★★ A	★★★★ A
2014	★☆ A	★☆ A	★★★☆ A
2013	★★★★ A	★★★★ A	★★★★ A
2012	★★ A	★★ A	★★☆ A
2011	★★★★ A	★★★★ A	★★★★☆ A
2010	★★★★ B	★★★★ A	★★★★ A
2009	★★★★ B	★★★★☆ B	★★★★ A
2008	★★★★ B	★★★★ B	★★★★ B
2007	★★★★☆ C	★★★★☆ B	★★★★☆ B
2006	★★★★ C	★★★★ B	★★★★ B
2005	★★★★ C	★★★★ C	★★★★ B
2004	★★★★ C	★★★★ C	★★★★ C
2003	★★★☆ D	★★★☆ C	★★★★ C
2002	★★★ D	★★★ C	★★★☆ C
2001	★★★★☆ D	★★★★☆ D	★★★★☆ C
2000	★★★★☆ D	★★★★☆ D	★★★★ D
1999	★★★☆ D	★★★☆ D	★★★★ D
1998	★★★★☆ D	★★★★☆ D	★★★★☆ D
1995		★★★★ D	★★★★ D

A-Z of producers - *Languedoc*

Jean-Michel Alquier (Faugères)

Long-established quality producer in this appellation. These are impressive wines, almost rustic in the case of the reds – but in the best sense. There are some 12ha under vine with the vast majority of this planted to red varieties. Syrah accounts for 40% of the *vignoble* and does very well in the meagre, well drained, soils.

The average vine age of the *cépages ameliorateurs* is increasing and this along with a healthy planting of very old Carignan provides tremendous raw material. The regular red Faugères Les Premières, a blend of Syrah, Grenache and Carignan, is good if austere when very young, while there is an extra dimension in the two top reds. La Réserve La Maison Jaune is a mix of Syrah and Mourvèdre whereas Les Bastides is aged in some new oak and has a smattering of Grenache adding a touch of red-berry character. These two wines will age well over 6 or 7 years. The basic white IGP Roussanne/Marsanne is attractively fruity while Les Vignes du Puits is a gloriously nutty and complex southern-style white. (DM)

Recommended Reds:
Faugères Les Bastides ★★★ £D
Faugères La Réserve La Maison Jaune ★★★ £C
Faugères Les Premières ★★ £B
Recommended Whites:
IGP de l'Hérault Les Vignes du Puits ★★★ £C
IGP de l'Hérault Roussanne/Marsanne ★☆ £B

⚙ Dom. de l'Aiguelière (Languedoc Montpeyroux)

One of the finest properties in the Languedoc, producing top class reds of impressive depth and raw power. Even in the tricky 2002 vintage the wines are of very sound quality. There are 25ha planted, nearly 90% being Syrah. A small parcel of Viognier and Sauvignon Blanc results in a fresh, fruit driven white Sarments, produced for the first time in 1999. Fermented and vinified in tank, the wine is best enjoyed within a couple of years of the vintage. Tradition, which blends around 40% Grenache with Syrah, is aged in *cuve* and offers ripe, vibrant upfront dark berry fruit supported by soft youthfully accesible tannins. The tqo 100% Syrah cuvées are of an entirely different order, dense and powerful, with an underlying elegance and refinement often missing in the region. Produced from yields of barely 20hl/ha the opulent Côte Dorée comes from gravel soils, the more structured and backward Côte Rousse from limestone. Both will benefit from 5 years' ageing. (DM)

Recommended Reds:
Coteeaux du Languedoc Montpeyroux Côte Rousse ★★★★☆ £E
Coteeaux du Languedoc Montpeyroux Côte Dorée ★★★★ £E
Coteeaux du Languedoc Montpeyroux Tradition ★★☆ £B
Recommended Whites:
IGP d'Oc Sarments ★★ £B

Dom. des Aires Hautes (Minervois)

This property stands out in an appellation that often disappoints more than it should. Gilles Chabbert produces just over 12,000 cases a year from his organically farmed vines, the vast majority of which are planted to red varieties. As well as the regular forward, fruit-driven Minervois Tradition there is a spicy IGP d'Oc Malbec, a Sauvignon Blanc and a little Chardonnay. The top two reds are from the sub-appellation of La Livinière and both are blended from Syrah, Grenache and Carignan. Vinification is traditional with an extended *cuvaison* and for the Carignan carbonic maceration is employed to emphasise the fruit. The La Livinière is aged partly in used oak and partly in *cuve*; the Clos de l'Escandil sees around one-third new wood. These are impressive and finely structured examples. The l'Escandil in particular will be all the better for 3 or 4 years' cellaring. (DM)

Recommended Reds:
Minervois La Livinière Clos de l'Escandil ★★★ £C
Minervois La Livinière ★★☆ £C   Minervois Tradition ★★ £B

Dom. d'Antugnac (Limoux) *www.collovrayterrier.com*
Jean-Luc Terrier and Christian Collovray also own the Mâconnais property DOMAINE DES DEUX ROCHES and Chardonnay is their most successful variety at Limoux. They have a substantial holding of 72 ha, half of which is planted to Chardonnay, Mauzac, Sauvignon and Chenin among white varieties and half to Pinot Noir, Merlot, Cabernet Franc, Syrah, Cabernet Sauvignon and a smattering of lesser-known red grapes. The vineyard is planted at altitude and warm summer days and cool nights contribute to the fresh style. There is a decent vibrant, fruit-driven Merlot, a light and relatively simple Pinot Noir but the whites, particularly the Limoux bottlings, are the wines to go for. Rich and very Burgundian in style, they are traditionally vinified, offering opulent citrus and nutmeg character with subtle creamy vanilla oak in the background. The Gravas bottling is a step up from the standard wine but both will develop well in the short term. (DM)

Recommended Reds:
IGP de la Haute Vallée de l'Aude Pinot Noir ★☆ £C
IGP d'Oc Merlot ★ £B
Recommended Whites:
Limoux Gravas ★★★ £C
Limoux Terres Amoreuses ★★☆ £C
IGP de la Hautée Vallée de l'Aude Chardonnay ★☆ £B
IGP de la Hautée Vallée de l'Aude Les Grands Penchants ★☆ £B

⚫ Dom. d'Aupilhac (Languedoc)
This domaine is now firmly established as one of the best properties in the Languedoc. Sylvain Fadat possesses 25 ha of vineyards almost all planted to reds and covering a broad range of varietals. The top Languedoc bottlings take the Montpeyroux cru label. The rosé is fresh and clean, with fine light and spicy berry fruit from a short maceration on skins. Both whites are vinified without recourse to malolactic and retain refreshing acidity. The IGP bottling is forward and lightly nutty, a blend of Ugni Blanc, Grenache Blanc and Chardonnay. Les Cocalières is altogether richer, subtler and more complex. It blends Vermentino, Rolle and Grenache Blanc. Both whites come from north facing slopes and are aged in *cuve*. The Lou Maset red is bright and forward, mainly Grenache and dominated by dark berry fruit rather than spice. Les Services comes from 100-year-old Cinsault and shows the potential possible from the variety. Le Carignan is 100% varietal and the vines are now around 70 years old. Ageing is in *foudres* and the wine invariably offers impressively dark, brambly old-vine complexity. Carignan is also the key component in the supple, spicy Languedoc Montpeyroux. The blend also comprises Mourvèdre, Grenache and Syrah. Best of the lot though are the top Languedoc reds. Les Cocalières comprises Syrah and some old-vine Mourvèdre., while La Boda is a blend of Mourvèdre, Syrah, Carignan and Grenache. Both are backward and structured young and demand some patience. Rich and densely textured dark fruit is underpinned by marked but very supple tannin. Expect both to develop very well for up to a decade. (DM)

Recommended Reds:
Languedoc Montpeyroux La Boda ★★★★ £E
Languedoc Montpeyroux Les Cocalières ★★★★ £E
Languedoc Le Clôs ★★★★ £E
IGP du Mont Baudille Le Carignan ★★★☆ £E
IGP de l'Hérault Les Servières ★★★ £D
Languedoc Montpeyroux ★★★ £C
Languedoc Lou Maset ★★☆ £B
Recommended Whites:
Languedoc Montpeyroux Les Cocalières ★★★☆ £D

IGP de l'Hérault ★★ £B
Recommended Rosés:
Languedoc ★★ £B

Dom. Les Aurelles (Languedoc) *www.les-aurelles.com*
Although this property was only established in 1994 some of the vines are over 70 years old. The vines are planted in ancient sand and gravel terraces providing for a meagre yield of around 25 hl/ha. The owner was classically trained in Bordeaux and this seems to come through in wines which are tight, well-structured and elegant. Varieties are vinified separately and the vatting for the reds lasts between 3 and 5 weeks. They get a light egg-white fining but filtration is avoided. The Deella, a blend of Carignan, Grenache, Mourvèdre, Syrah and Carignan is soft, forward and fruit-driven. Solen and Aurel are much more seriously structured and will develop well over 5 or more years. Solen is 65% Carignan with the balance Grenache, rich and full with complex old-vine character. Aurel is a blend of Mourvèdre, Syrah and Grenache. Very fine, elegant and pure, it is tight and closed in its youth and will open up and add real complexity and depth with age. The Aurel Blanc, which is 100% Roussanne, is barrel-fermented but not in new wood and is loaded with subtle, complex spicy, nutty southern fruit. Drink it young or with a little age. (DM)

Recommended Reds:
Languedoc Aurel ★★★★ £F   Languedoc Solen ★★★ £D
Languedoc Déella ★★☆ £C
Recommended Whites:
Languedoc Aurel ★★★☆ £E

Dom. de Baron'Arques (Limoux)
Now well established joint venture producing one red wine and a white from Chardonnay from vineyards planted in the Limoux region. Early releases were labelled IGP until Limoux gained its own red wine appellation in 2003. Currently produced from just under 35 ha of vineyard the partnership has identified 150 ha which should be suitable for producing top-quality red wine. Baron'Arques is a blend of 60–70% Bordeaux varieties Merlot, Cabernets Sauvignon and Franc and 30–40% Grenache, Syrah and Malbec. The wine currently shows much more in common with Bordeaux than with other Languedoc reds. The first vintage was 1998 and subsequent vintages have shown good promise. Cellaring for 5 or more years will add weight and complexity. (DM)

Recommended Reds:
Limoux Baron'arques ★★★☆ £E

⚫ Dom. Leon Barral (Faugères) *www.domaineleonbarral.com*
Impressive, small Faugères domaine producing red wines with all the raw, spicy, meaty character of the appellation. The regular bottling is a blend of mainly Carignan along with Grenache and Cinsault. The Cuvée Jadis is a step up in quality and is a supple, structured and enticingly perfumed blend of Carignan (50%), Syrah (40%) and a smattering of Grenache. Barral's top red Valinière is a heady, rich, ripe and powerful blend of 80% of Mourvèdre plus Syrah, it is by no means cheap. A low yielding, unfiltered IGP de l'Hérault white from a blend of Terret Gris and Blanc along with Viognier and Roussanne is also made. The wines are structured and ageworthy. (DM)

Recommended Reds:
Faugères Valinière ★★★★ £F   Faugères Cuvée Jadis ★★★☆ £D
Faugères ★★★ £C

Languedoc

France

Dom. de Barroubio (Minervois) *www.barroubio.fr*

This 60 ha property has been farmed by the Miquel family since the 15th century. There are 27 ha of vineyards and just 7ha are planted to red varieties. Muscat, in both dry and sweet wines styles, is the main variety, giving some of the best examples in the region. The property is located on the borders of the Parc Régional du Haut Languedoc, one of the most striking and scenic of all France's vineyard areas. The red varietes are planted in a mix of clay and chalk, the Muscat in chalky soils and on the higher slopes of the property. With vineyards at an altitude of 200 to 300 metres above sea level, the key to the quality and finesse of the Muscats is the fresh undercurrent of acidity. For the reds both carbonic maceration and traditional vinification are employed. The regular Minervois is a blend of Syrah Carignan and Grenache. It is soft, supple and approachable. Jean Miquel is a splendidly dark and intense mix of old vine Carignan and Grenache. The former variety is now over 100 years old and provides fruit of glorious smoky, spicy complexity. Cuvée Marie-Therese is more typical of modern Minervois reds, Mainly Syrah with the balance Grenache and aged in new oak and one year old barrels. Loads of dark, spicy, chocolatey fruit is underpinned by sweet vanilla oak. The Muscat sec has to take a IGP classification because of the style. The Classique Muscat is rich, sweet and concentrated. It is cool fermented before fortification and retains an elegant freshness. The Cuvée Bleue is similarly vinified however up to one year on fine lees adds extra weight and depth. Dieuvaille is a special vineyard selection including a portion of late harvested fruit. Rich, fresh and intense with really marked musky Muscat character. The Cuvée Nicolas comes from very late harvested grapes, some as late as December, from the oldest parcel of Muscat on the property. Rich, luscious and nutty, it has a piercing citrus and orange peel character. (DM)

Recommended Reds:

Minervois Cuvée Jean Miquel ★★★☆ £D
Minervois Cuvée Marie-Thérèse ★★★ £D
Minervois ★★ £B

Recommended Whites:

Muscat de Saint-Jean de Minervois Cuvée Nicolas ★★★★ £E
Muscat de Saint-Jean de Minervois Dieuvaille ★★★☆ £D
Muscat de Saint-Jean de Minervois Cuvée Bleue ★★★☆ £D
Muscat de Saint-Jean de Minervois Classique ★★★ £C
IGP d'Oc Muscat Sec ★★ £B

✿ Dom. Bertrand-Bergé (Fitou)

Some of the best examples of Fitou are made here at this family owned domaine, which has been passed down through six generations. There are around 30 ha planted to reds, with Carignan and Grenache the important varieties. Jérôme Bertrand also makes a little Muscat de Rivesaltes and Rivesaltes from a further 3.5ha of Muscats à Petits Grains and Maccabeu he has planted. As elsewhere one of the keys to quality is a holding of very old vines, some parcels of the Bertrand vineyard are now 60 to 70 years old. The Tradition is the softest and most immediately accessible of the reds; a blend of Carignan and Grenache aged in *cuve*, it is spicy and characterful. Also aged in *cuve* and one of the best examples in the Languedoc is the old-vine Mégalithes from Carignan. There is a real dimension and sheer class to its dark berried fruit rarely encountered elsewhere. The Ancestrale is a blend of Carignan, Grenache and Syrah, the latter component being aged small oak. Fatter and fuller than the Mégalithes with grip and persistence, it doesn't quite possess the same fruit intensity. Top of the tree though in price as well as quality is the Cuvée Jean Sirven. A blend of both Carignan and Syrah this

is given 100% new oak. The yield is tiny, less than 20hl/ha and the quality and depth are immediately evident. Very classy indeed, the oak is very apparent in the wines youth but there is easily the depth of fruit to bring the wine into splendid balance with 4 or 5 years' ageing. (DM)

Recommended Reds:

Fitou Jean Sirven ★★★★ £E   Fitou Mégalithes ★★★☆ £D
Fitou Ancestrale ★★★☆ £D   Fitou Tradition ★★☆ £C

>> Dom. de La Borie Blanche (Minervois) *www.lorgerilwine.com*

This Minervois property is one of a number of single estate owned by the Lorgeril family company, including CH. DE CIFFRE in Saint-Chinian and CH. DE PENNAUTIER in Cabardes. Wines are made both from the Minervois AOP as well as Minervois La Livinière. The Lorgeril project was originally established in Cabardes but they have invested extensively elsewhere in Languedoc-Roussillon and now have a number of single estates. They purchased Borie Blanche in 1999 and have added to the vineyard holding. There are now 29 ha under vine here with vineyards planted at an altitude of 210 to as much as 350 metres above sea level. The varieties cultivated are traditionally southern, Carignan, Grenache, Syrah, Cinsault and Mourvèdre among reds as well as Marsanne and Roussanne. They also have 1 ha of Merlot. The vibrant dark fruited and approachable Le Classique comes from a blend of Syrah, Grenache and Carignan with a proportion vinified by carbonic maceration. Ageing is traditional in vats. Both Le Terroir d'Altitude and the top Grand Vin come from vineyards in La Livinière. Le Terroir d'Altitude combines Syrah, Grenache and Mourvèdre, with the Syrah vinified with carbonic maceration. Ageing is in a mix of small oak and vat and the wine offers spices, ripe dark berry fruits and a complex herb scented edge. The top red the Grand Vin is of a diffefferent dimension. Impressively dense and structured with black fruits and spicy black pepper it is a concentrated blend of Syrah and Grenache. (DM)

Recommended Reds:

Minervois La Livinière Grand Vin ★★★☆ £D
Minervois La Livinière Le Terroir d'Altitude ★★★ £C
Minervois Le Classique ★★☆ £C

Dom. Borie de Maurel (Minervois) *www.boriedemaurel.fr*

Sizeable Minervois property with 30 ha under vine with just 2 ha planted to whites Marsanne and Muscat à Petits Grains. The white Belle Aude is broad and fat with rich nutty fruit. Esprit d'Automne is a straightforward fruit-driven blend of Grenache, Syrah and Carignan, whereas Belle de Nuit is solely Grenache, which should also be enjoyed young for its vibrant fruit but has added weight and concentration. More seriously structured is the La Livinière bottling, La Féline. Spicy dark berry fruit and a dense, rich texture are provided from 70% Syrah. The Cuvée Léopold is 100% Cabernet Sauvignon. Ripe and elegant it avoids some of the green notes found in other Languedoc examples. Of the top 2 Minervois reds, Maxim is 100% Mourvèdre, Sylla 100% Syrah. Both are finely structured and will develop well with 4 or 5 years in bottle. Exclusive to the UK is a varietal Carignan, La Rêve de Carignan, dark, dense and with an attractive spicy edge to the fruit. (DM)

Recommended Reds:

Minervois Cuvée Sylla ★★★★ £E
Minervois Cuvée Maxime ★★★☆ £D
Minervois Belle de Nuit ★★★ £D
Minervois La Livinière La Féline ★★★ £C
IGP d'Oc Cuvée Léopold ★★★ £C
Minervois La Rêve de Carignan ★★☆ £C

Recommended Whites:
Minervois La Belle Aude ★★ £B

⚫ **Dom. Borie La Vitarèle (Saint-Chinian)** *www.borielavitarele.fr*
Cathy Izarn has some 19 ha under vine now, of which a mere 2.5 ha are planted with white varieties. Most are in Saint-Chinian but some extend into the Languedoc and are farmed organically and biodynamically. Powerful, dense and muscular reds are the order of the day, achieved through controlling yields, which rarely exceed 30 hl/ha. A new white has been added which is a nutty and fresh combination of Clairette, Vermentino and Bourboulenc. The IGP Cigales is a soft and vibrant, forward red combining Merlot and Grenache. Of the Saint-Chinians Les Terres Blanches is supple, approachable and full of spicy dark fruit, Les Schistes, mainly Grenache with Syrah and a touch of Carignan, has depth and a firm structure. Give it 2 or 3 years. Les Crès is named after the soil in which the vines are grown; in this case it is formed of the galet type stones found at Châteauneuf-du-Pape. The wine is a blend of Syrah, Grenache and Mourvèdre and comes from vines yielding less than 20 hl/ha. No new wood is used and it is all the better for it, emphasising its dark, brooding, spicy fruit character. The top wine is now the Midi Rouge which is a dense and very characterful mix of Syrah and Carignan produced from tiny yields and vines grown at an altitude of around 400 metres. It is fermented in new oak casks of 600 litres. There is real depth and concentration in the top two wines with the structure to ensure ageing for up to a decade or more. (DM)

Recommended Reds:
Saint-Chinian Midi Rouge ★★★★ £E
Saint-Chinian Les Crès ★★★☆ £D
Saint-Chinian Les Schistes ★★★ £C
Saint-Chinian Les Terres Blanches ★★☆ £C
IGP Côteaux de Murviel Cigales ★☆ £B

Recommended Whites:
Languedoc La Grand Mayol ★★☆ £C

Dom. Canet Valette (Saint-Chinian) *www.canetvalette.com*
There are 18 ha under vine here, all of it planted to red varieties. Along with BORIE LA VITARÈLE this is a benchmark for Saint-Chinian and the top red here, Le Vin Maghani, is arguably the finest in the AC. Minimal handling in the cellar with neither fining nor filtration helps to achieve this. No new oak is used and as a result the character of the impressively intense fruit really shines through in the wines. Une et Mille Nuits is a blend of Grenache, Mourvèdre, Syrah, Carignan and Cinsault. Aged in a mix of *inox* and older oak it is vibrant and approachable, but with sufficient structure to develop well over 4 or 5 years. Le Vin Maghani is more serious; dense, rich and very complex, the wine is full of dark fruits, spice and black pepper. Cellaring for 5 years is a must to enjoy this at its best. Two more approachable reds, Antonyme and Ivresses are also made and both are Saint-Chinians. (DM)

Recommended Reds:
Saint-Chinian Le Vin Maghani ★★★☆ £E
Saint-Chinian Une et Mille Nuits ★★★ £D

Dom. Causse d'Arboras (Languedoc) *www.causse-arboras.com*
A newly established and fine small Languedoc property in the Terrasses de Larzac area, notable for its two reds. The vineyards lie at an altitude of around 350 metres above sea level and are planted in a protected site on free-draining, sparse, lime-based soils which provides an ideal growing environment. The approach in the vineyard is as natural as possible and sustainable farming is practiced. Low yields ensure the quality of the fruit and to this end green harvesting is undertaken during the growing season. Recent plantings of Syrah and Mourvèdre are also at a far higher density which should improve flavour intensity still further. A well equipped modern winery includes manual sorting tables and vinification is carried out in small concrete tanks that have temperature control during a cold maceration and fermentation. The wine is then transferred to an underground ageing cellar with temperature and humidity control. The resulting wines are thoroughly modern and well-made but full of character as well. Les Cazes is very soft, supple and approachable wherereas Les 3J is much more complex and structured and needs a year or two of patience but will certainly drink very well young. (DM)

Recommended Reds:
Languedoc Les 3 J ★★★☆ £D
Languedoc Les Cazes ★★☆ £B

⚫ **Dom. Alain Chabanon (Languedoc)** *www.alainchabanon.com*
From his small Montpeyroux property, Alain Chabanon produces six very good reds, a rosé and a tiny amount of two whites. The dry Trelans comes from Chenin Blanc and Vermentino, the sweet white Le Villard emanating from100% Chenin Blanc and classified as Vin de France. The top reds are vinified with long macerations, often over a month. The Languedoc Campredon is mainly Syrah with Mourvèdre, Grenache and Carignan and is fleshy and approachable. The IGP d'Oc Petit Merle aux Alouettes is a vibrant Merlot. The more structured Le Merle aux Alouettes is also a Merlot loaded with ripe plum and blackberry fruit, nicely supported by fine, supple, well-rounded tannins. The powerful and structured Les Boissières is produced from Grenache with a sprinkling of Mourvèdre and Carignan. It is ripe and bold with an impressive depth of fruit. L'Esprit de Font Caude is generally produced from a blend of Syrah and Mourvèdre and is a marvellously rich, dense red, full of smoky dark berry fruit and just a subtle hint of oak. In some vintages the wine has had more Mourvèdre than Syrah, when it tends to show more elegance and less overt concentration and extract. Also now made is Saut de Côte a Languedoc dominated by Mourvèdre. (DM)

Recommended Reds:
Languedoc Montpeyroux Les Boissières ★★★★ £E
Languedoc Montpeyroux L'Esprit de Font Caude ★★★★ £E
IGP d'Oc Petit Merle aux Alouettes ★★★☆ £E

>> **Ch. d'Agel (Minervois)** *www.chateaudagel.fr*
An excellent small range of Minervois as well as an exceptional Vin de France red, are all made at this domaine. There is a mix of soil types and the climate is typically Mediterranean with warm dry summers. The most approachable wines are the three Les Bonnes labels. The white is a fresh and zesty cool fermented blend of Maccabeu, Roussanne, Grenache Blanc and Vermentino. The rosé combines Cinsault, Syrah and Grenache, is direct pressed and cool fermented. Drink it as young and fresh as possible. The red is a blend of Syrah, Grenache and Mourvèdre as well as old Carignan, which adds a further dimension to the wine. It is traditionally vinified and aged in concrete offering attractive black, pepper spiced fruit flavours. The Caudios red is by contrast a blend of Syrah and Pinot Noir cultivated in limestone soils. After vinification the wine is raised in older small oak. Grenu is a characterful southern Rhône style mix of Grenache and Syrah with dark berry fruits and herb spices. It is vinified in cement and aged in *inox* in a very pure style. The Château d'Agel Minervois is of a different dimension with depth

and some structure from very low yields of between 15 and 20 hl/ha. Coming from a combination of mainly Syrah and Grenache everything is done by hand and both vinification and ageing is in 400 litre barrels which are first fill to emphasise the quality and character of the fruit. In Extremis also blends Syrah with Grenache. The approach is a little different and the style a touch more opulent and exotic. After a vatting of up to a month the wine is aged in new *barriques* for around 12 months to balance fruit and oak. Opulent black fruits, oriental spices and a hint of vanilla are all apparent. It will develop nicely for up to a decade. Topping the tree here though is the Venustas, made solely from Syrah and so only entitled to Vin de France status. It is selected from the best parcels of the domaines limestone plots with selection by grape bunch. Vinification is in 400 litre barrels and skin contact maintained for over two months. Ageing is then for 8 months again in 400 litre barrels and bottling at a year. It is in fact very similar to the northern Rhône in that respect. It is one of the great reds of the Languedoc. (DM)

Recommended Reds:
Vin de France Venustas ★★★★☆ £F
Minervois In Extremis ★★★★ £E
Minervois ★★★☆ £D
Minervois Grenu ★★☆ £C
Minervois Caudios ★★☆ £C
Minervois Les Bonnes ★★ £B

Recommended Whites:
Minervois Les Bonnes ★★ £B

Recommended Rosés:
Minervois Les Bonnes ★☆ £B

Ch. d'Angles (Languedoc) *www.chateaudangles.com*

Eric Fabre and his wife Christine moved here from the Médoc where he had established an enviable record which, among other roles, included 8 years as technical director at LAFITE-ROTHSCHILD. They wanted their own domaine though and in 2001 identified the potential of the *terroir* here in the La Clape sub-region of the Languedoc with slopes running down towards the Mediterranean just south of Narbonne. The vineyards are all farmed using sustainable practices and benefit from over 300 days of sunshine a year. There are 36 ha under vine with a third planted to white varieties. Bourboulenc is particularly important here and provides the backbone for the two white cuvées. The Classique includes 50% of the variety and is blended with Grenache Blanc and just a little Roussanne and Marsanne. The Grand Vin includes a touch less Bourboulenc but this is from the oldest vines, now around 70 years old. This is blended with equal proportions of Grenache Blanc, Roussanne and Marsanne. The key to the quality of the Bourboulenc here is harvesting late, almost in November and retaining the firm acidity the variety can offer as well as achieving a rich texture in the resulting wines. This is certainly achieved and both gain further depth from stirring on their fine lees for several months after fermentation. Reds are equally impressive. The Classique is, as one would expect a more fruit forward style and comprises Syrah, Grenache and a little Mourvèdre. The Grand Vin has a higher proportion of Mourvèdre in the blend and there is a small amount of Carignan as well. While the Classique gains depth and a supple structure from a four week vatting, the Grand Vin is a real *vin de garde* and is macerated on skins for up to 50 days. While not unapproachable young you can expect it to develop for a decade or more. The rosé Classique is one of the better examples in the region and has sufficient structure to enable it to work very well with food. Unusually it includes 80% of Mourvèdre which is blended with a little each of Syrah and Grenache. (DM)

Recommended Reds:
Languedoc Grand Vin ★★★★ £E   Languedoc Classique ★★★ £C

Recommended Whites:
Languedoc Grand Vin ★★★☆ £D   Languedoc Classique ★★☆ £C

Recommended Rosés:
Languedoc Classique ★★☆ £B

Ch. Capion (Languedoc) *www.chateaucapion.com*

The Buhrer family also own the excellent SAXENBURG wine farm in Stellenbosch in South Africa's Cape winelands. The traditional Languedoc grapes are complimented here by a range of varieties providing the base for two whites, a red and a rosé, all of which take the IGP de l'Hérault regional classification. The vineyards are on an exposed west to northwest aspect which helps to moderate the summer heat to some degree and the vines are planted in well-drained limestone soils. This helps in providing good fruit ripening for flavour intensity with deliberately restricted yields and helps promote good levels of acidity in the resulting wines. The Château Capion red is the stand out wine and very modern and international in style. Syrah dominates the blend with the balancing 30% comprising Grenache and Mourvèdre. The wine comes from the oldest vines on the property which are now over 30 years. Fermentation is relatively cool, around 26 celsius with the objective of retaining the wines fruit and ensuring well rounded supple and approachable tannins. The wine is vatted for up to a month and then ageing is in a significant proportion of new French oak for over a year. The second red Le Juge is more traditionally vinified with less Syrah in the blend and a warmer fermentation after a cold soak to gain additional colour. The subtle nutty, citrus scented Le Colombier has 50% of Chardonnay with Roussanne and a bit less Viognier in its blend. Fermented at a relatively cool temperature to emphasise its fruit in barrel, adding depth, a richer texture and more complexity. There are three more obviously fruit-driven styles released as Fiona. They are all IGP. The red is Cabernet Sauvignon, Merlot and Syrah, the white a blend of Chardonnay and Roussanne, while the rosé is a more obviously southern blend of 80% Cinsault blended with Mourvèdre. Expect the top two reds to develop well for five or six years. (DM)

Recommended Reds:
Languedoc Chateau Capion ★★★☆ £E
Languedoc Le Juge ★★★ £E
IGP de l'Hérault Fiona ★★ £C

Recommended Whites:
IGP de l'Hérault Le Colombier ★★☆ £D
IGP de l'Hérault Fiona ★☆ £C

Recommended Rosés:
IGP de l'Hérault Fiona ★☆ £B

Ch. Capitoul (Languedoc) *www.chateau-capitoul.com*

The bulk of the production at this organically farmed 65-ha property is red and white Languedoc La Clape, with some rosé produced as well under the same appellation. The Lavandine white blends Marsanne with a little Viognier and Roussanne, while the more complex barrel-aged Rocaille adds Marsanne, to mostly Roussanne. The Lavandine red is Syrah, Grenache and Carignan whereas the striking and good-value Rocailles is Grenache and Syrah with some Carignan adding some peppery spice. Richly concentrated, the wine is given a a vatting on skins for up to 25 days and is aged in *cuve* using micro-oxygenation rather than racking during *élevage*. A small-volume red, Maelma, is produced from mainly Mourvèdre and

Carignan. (DM)
Recommended Reds:
Languedoc Pic Saint-Loup Rocaille ★★★ £D
Languedoc Pic Saint-Loup Lavandines ★★☆ £C
Recommended Whites:
Languedoc Pic Saint-Loup Rocaille ★★☆ £C

Ch. de Cazeneuve (Languedoc) *www.cazeneuve.net*
First class Languedoc Pic Saint Loup property with some 20 ha under vine. Since acquiring Cazeneuve in the late 1980s André Leenhardt has been actively planting the top red Rhône varieties which are now dominated by Syrah. Output is still low for the area. His reds come in a number of guises. Syrah features strongly in the blend of Les Calcaires and the oak-aged Le Roc des Mates. Le Sang du Calcaire, now the top red, is an individual selection of the best the harvest has to offer. It too is aged in oak. The white is a stylish, nutty barrel-fermented blend of Roussanne, Grenache Blanc and Viognier. Top reds are ageworthy. (DM)
Recommended Reds:
Languedoc Pic Saint-Loup Sang du Calvaire ★★★★ £F
Languedoc Pic Saint-Loup Roc des Mates ★★★☆ £D
Languedoc Pic Saint-Loup Les Calcaires ★★★ £C
Languedoc Pic Saint-Loup Les Terres Rouges ★★☆ £C
Recommended Whites:
Languedoc Pic Saint-Loup ★★★ £D

Ch. de Ciffre (Saint-Chinian) *www.lorgeril.com*
Small to medium-sized estate now owned by Lorgeril with 70 ha across a number of appellations. The vineyards are dominated by red varieties with just 2 ha planted to Viognier. Reds are produced under three appellations, Languedoc, Saint-Chinian and Faugères. The oak aged Terroirs d'Altitude Saint-Chinian and Faugères cuvées have a round, supple character, while the Grand Vin is a step up. Firmly structured when young, this blend of Syrah, Grenache and Mourvèdre from the best parcels the estate has in the AC is aged for 12 months in a mix of new and old *barriques*. The wines offer good value and the Grand Vin will develop well with 3–5 years' ageing. (DM)
Recommended Reds:
Faugères Grand Vin ★★★☆ £D
Faugères Terroirs d'Altitude ★★☆ £D
Saint-Chinian Terroirs d'Altitude ★★☆ £D
Saint-Chinian Classique ★★ £C

Ch. Coupe Roses (Minervois) *www.coupe-roses.com*
A quite extensive range is made at this fine Minervois producer, beginning with a simple fruit-driven white IGP from Grenache Blanc, Marsanne and Muscat. Better is the IGP Viognier, which is floral and lightly peachy, gaining weight from ageing on lees in tank. The white Minervois, wholly produced from Roussanne has a floral, nutty complexity and impressive intensity with 20% aged in small oak. The rosé is soft and fruit-driven for early drinking. La Bastide is the softest and most approachable of the Minervois reds, a 50/50 blend of Grenache and Carignan, the latter vinified by macération-carbonique. Les Plots offers considerably more depth and concentration. This is 60% Syrah blended with Grenache and Carignan aged in tank and regularly on the cusp of ★★★. The top two reds are among the best examples in the appellation. Richly textured and impressively concentrated Orience is 90% Syrah with a little Grenache; 50% is aged in new oak and 50% in 1-year-old barrels and the oak in no way intrudes on the dark, smoky fruit. The smoky, herb/spice-edged Granaxa is largely old-vine Grenache aged in small oak with around 10% Syrah blended in before bottling. The fascinating Rancio is a blend of Viognier, Grenache Blanc and Roussanne aged in barrel for between 10 and 14 years. Great intensity and rich, nutty, citrus intensity are apparent. The top two reds will benefit from 5 years' ageing. (DM)
Recommended Reds:
Minervois Granaxa ★★★☆ £E   Vin de France Rancio ★★★ £E
Minervois Cuvée Orience ★★★ £D
Minervois Les Plots ★★☆ £C
Minervois La Bastide ★★ £B
Recommended Whites:
IGP d'Oc Viognier ★★ £C   Minervois ★★ £B
Recommended Rosés:
Minervois ★☆ £B

Ch. des Crès Ricards (Languedoc)
Syrah is the important variety at this small 28 ha domaine, now owned by Jean-Paul Mas, in the Terrasses de Larzac. The summers are particularly hot and arid and the winters cold here and the wines are marked by a ripe, smoky, warm-climate character but nevertheless possess a fine, elegant backbone, no doubt aided by cooler ripening conditions and the excellent drainage afforded by the Villafranchien stony soils. A range of wines are made both blended as well as varietal and IGP and Vin de France as well as Languedoc. The Stécia is an obviously fruit-driven wine, a blend of around 60% Syrah with Grenache and Carignan aged in tank for around a year. The Oenothera combines Syrah with just Grenache. Les Hauts de Milesi is richer and fuller with more meaty concentration and just a hint of black pepper underpinning the fruit. Expect the wines to evolve well for 3 or 4 years or so. (DM)
Recommended Reds:
Languedoc Les Hauts de Milesi ★★★ £C
Languedoc Cuvée Stecia ★★☆ £C
Languedoc Oenothera ★★☆ £C

Ch. de l'Engarran (Languedoc) *www.chateau-engarran.com*
This 18th-century château has been in the Grill family since 1923. Most of the output from their 55 ha under vine is red; rosé accounts for 20% and white just 10%. The estate is run by sisters Diane and Constance and the wines have an elegance and subtly that isn't always apparent in the area. The IGP d'Oc red La Lionne is soft, straightforward and fruit-driven. The key wines here are the Languedoc reds and the Domaine de l'Engarran Adelys white. It is a ripe, tropical, piercing varietal Sauvignon Blanc, barrel-fermented for 9 months in oak that has been seasoned unusually by steam rather than the normal flame-charring, emphasising the fruit character in the wine. The Languedoc Cuvée Sainte-Cécile is soft and berry-laden with supple and approachable tannin. The Grés de Montpelier comes solely from this Languedoc cru and possesses a real *garrigue* quality. Grenat Majeure is full of Grenache character, dense, dark berry fruit and a herb spiced edge. The top red is the Cuvée Quetton Saint-Georges, coming from the Saint-Georges-d'Orques cru it is a blend of Syrah, Grenache and old vine Carignan aged in small French oak and larger vats for up to 16 months. A further Saint-Georges-d'Orques example, Le Parc is also made, as well as a rosé but these have not yet been tasted. (DM)
Recommended Reds:
Languedoc St-Georges-d'Orques Querton St-Georges ★★★☆ £D
Languedoc Grenat Majeure ★★★☆ £C
Languedoc Cuvée Sainte-Cécile ★★☆ £C

Languedoc

France

Languedoc Grés de Montpelier ★★☆ £C
IGP d'Oc La Lionne ★☆ £B
Recommended Whites:
IGP d'Oc Adelys ★★☆ £C

Ch. des Erles (Fitou) www.francoislurton.com

These are the leading reds produced in the Midi by 90s "flying winemaker" François Lurton. He now has extensive interests not only in the Midi but also now in Spain from Toro (with EL ALBAR) and Rueda, Chile and Argentina. Château des Erles comprises 89 ha, of which currently 74 ha are in current production. The vineyards, at an altitude of around 200 metres above sea level, are in the north of Fitou. Much of the key to the quality of the wines are the well-drained schist, slate and sandy soils. Rosé des Erles is a soft, vibrant pink and there is a second label Fitou, Cuvée des Abrigans, which helps ensure the quality of the top label. Château des Erles Cuvée des Ardoises is barrel-aged and is sourced from the better plots and oldest vines in the vineyard. It is a Syrah/Grenache/Carignan combination and is well structured with supple tannins and a good depth and persistence of herb-scented berry fruit. As with many of the wines from the area there is a marked minerality which may in part be down to the soils. It is lightly fined and bottled unfiltered. A number of other domaine labels are also produced including the striking Roussillons from MAS JANEIL. François Lurton also produces a number of varietal wines under the brands Fumées Blanches and Les Salices and a Saint-Chinian from Domaine du du Ministre. A Sauvignon Blanc, Fumées Blanches is crisp and zesty. (DM)

Recommended Reds:
Fitou Cuvée des Ardoises ★★★ £D
Recommended Whites:
IGP d'Oc Fumées Blanches ★☆ £B

Ch. des Estanilles (Faugères) www.chateau-estanilles.com

Julien Seydoux, who took over from Michel Louison has now fully revised his range and brands offered at this small to medium sized property. Output is around 8,000 cases a year, so a reasonably sizeable production for a high-quality Midi property. Syrah dominates the plantings in the well-drained schist soils and typically for the appellation is notably successful here. Grenache and Mourvèdre are also important among the reds and the white is a blend of Marsanne, Roussanne and Viognier. The rosé L'Impertinent is a fresh, vibrant blend of Cinsault, Grenache and Mourvèdre and a second more structured example, Rosé M, which is mainly Mourvèdre is also made. The L'Impertinent rouge is the mainstay of the domaine and is a mixed blend of Syrah, Grenache, Mourvèdre, Carignan and Cinsault which is aged in tank. The top three reds all see around a year in a combination of *barriques*, *demi-muids* and vats. Inverso is made in reasonable volume and combines Mourvèdre, Syrah and Grenache. The other two are made in much smaller volume, the dense and structured Raison d'Etre is dominated by Syrah with around a half Mourvèdre and Grenache and a mainly Syrah, Clos du Fou, is also made. The property is now certified organic. (DM)

Recommended Reds:
Faugères Raison d'Etre ★★★☆ £E   Faugères Inverso ★★★ £D
Faugères L'Impertinent ★★★ £C
Recommended Whites:
Faugères L'Impertinent ★★☆ £C
Recommended Rosés:
Faugères L'Impertinent ★★ £B

Ch L'Euzière (Languedoc Pic Saint-Loup)

The Causse siblings are, in fact, the fourth generation of vinegrowers at this impressive Languedoc property but it is only much more recently that they have established themselves as quality wine producers. They have some 22 ha under vine. A good nutty, lightly floral white, Grains de Lune, is an unusual blend of Roussanne, Vermentino, Rolle and Grenache Blanc produced from young vines. After *macération pelliculaire* it is cool-fermented with limited lees-ageing. Of the the reds, Cuvée Tourmaline is a blend of Syrah and Grenache, where-as the more serious and structured Cuvées l'Almandin and Les Escarboules are neither fined nor filtered and have a small dollop of Mourvèdre. They are both marvellously expressive with a fine balance of herb, spice and complex berry fruits and each will benefit from 3 or 4 years' ageing. (DM)

Recommended Reds:
Languedoc Pic Saint-Loup Cuvée Les Escarboules ★★★☆ £D
Languedoc Pic Saint-Loup Cuvée l'Almandin ★★★ £C
Languedoc La Tourmaline ★★☆ £B
Recommended Whites:
Languedoc Grains de Lune ★★☆ £B

Ch Grès Saint-Paul (Languedoc) www.gres-saint-paul.com

Small to medium-sized property with 24 ha of vineyards farmed along organic lines. An extensive range of wines is produced including some straightforward well-priced, fruit-driven IGP Chardonnay, Sauvignon Blanc and Merlot. It is the red Languedoc wines that are most important though from a quality point of view. Of the cuvées Romanis is dominated by Syrah with Grenache and Mourvèdre. Aged for 12 months in *cuve*, it is dense and structured. The excellent-value Antonin is mostly Syrah, the balance Grenache and Mourvèdre, produced from yields of 25–30 hl/ha. It is dark, concentrated and spicy with subtle hints of black pepper and just a touch of oak spice from the 16 months spent in one-third new barrels. The top Languedoc wine is the impressive Syrhus, a varietal Syrah produced from a yield of less than 20 hl/ha. It needs 2 or 3 years' cellaring to integrate the 100% new oak. A Vin de France varietal Merlot, Côté Sud is also made along three fruit driven reds under the Grange Philippe brand. Of the sweet white Muscats the Bohémienne has moderate depth, the Sévillane greater weight and intensity. These are well made but lack the depth of a good Muscat de Rivesaltes. (DM)

Recommended Reds:
Languedoc Syrhus ★★★☆ £E
Languedoc Antonin ★★★ £C
Languedoc Romanis ★★☆ £C
Recommended Whites:
Muscat de Lunel Sévillane ★★ £C
Muscat Moelleux Bohémienne ★☆ £C

Ch de Jonquières (Languedoc) www.chateau-jonquieres.com

This 23 ha property located in the foothills of the Plateau de Gassac now has 19 ha planted to vines. The small range includes a good straightforward white, which is barrel-fermented and aged with *bâtonnage* and has the malolactic blocked to preserve freshness. It is a blend of Grenache Blanc, Chenin Blanc, Roussanne and Viognier. its red partner is a juicy, soft, easygoing IGP de l'Hérault red Domaine de Jonquières dominated by Cinsault and Carignan. More serious is the red Languedoc which blends Syrah, Grenache, Mourvèdre and Carignan. It is dark, powerful and supple with a sufficiently firm structure and depth to ensure limited bottle-development with age, while at the same time retaining its core vibrant fruit quality. (DM)

Recommended Reds:
Languedoc La Baronnie ★★★ £D
IGP de l'Hérault Domaine de Jonquières ★★☆ £C
Recommended Whites:
IGP de l'Hérault Domaine de Jonquières ★★☆ £C

Ch. La Baronne (Corbières) *www.chateaulabaronne.com*
A source of good well-priced Corbières, this 80-ha domaine is in the Montagne d'Alaric sub-zone, arguably the best in this sizeable AC. The fine, ripe and supple Corbières Alaric is produced from a blend of Carignan, Syrah and Mourvèdre. Low yields of 12–20 hl/ha and vineyards planted at an altitude of 150 metres help to contribute to quality. A number of other Corbieres reds are also released as well as fruit driven wines under the IGP Hauterive classification. (DM)
Recommended Reds:
Corbières Alaric ★★☆ £C

Ch. La Dournie (Saint-Chinian) *www.chateauladournie.com*
Fine small Saint-Chinian property where daughter Valérie is now in charge of the winemaking and quality has been consistently good across the last 5 years or so. She is producing wines, which reflect the *terroir* and character of the appellation but also with a great exuberance of fruit. There is a soft, vibrant and easygoing rosé and a fresh IGP white but it is the reds, which stand out. The regular bottling, a blend of Syrah, Grenache and Carignan, is ripe, forward and brambly with a fine mineral undercurrent to its fruit. The more seriously structured and denser Elise is just Syrah and Grenache. Complex and offering great fruit purity this should continue to develop well for 4 or 5 years. (DM)
Recommended Reds:
Saint-Chinian Cuveé Elise ★★★☆ £C   Saint-Chinian ★★☆ £C
Recommended Whites:
IGP d'Oc Le Blanc de La Dournie ★★ £B
Recommended Rosés:
Saint-Chinian ★★ £B

Ch. La Liquière (Languedoc) *www.chateaulaliquiere.com*
This sizeable domaine with 55 ha of red varieties and 7 ha of whites under vine produces good quality in both the Languedoc and Faugères. The vineyard holding is largely at altitude and planted in the schistous soils prevalent in the best terroirs of Faugères. The white Cistus is a barrel-fermented blend of Roussanne, Grenache Blanc, Vermentino and Bourboulenc offering hints of oak and lightly nutty tropical fruit. Aged on fine lees, which add weight and a richer texture, it will nevertheless drink well young. Of the red bottlings from Faugères, the Vieilles Vignes comes from 40–100-year-old plots. It is a blend of Carignan, Grenache and small proportions of Syrah and Mourvèdre. Its dark, peppery character partly comes from carbonic maceration, by which over half the fruit is vinified. The Cistus is quite a step up in quality and as elsewhere in the appellation Syrah is very important, with the balance made up of Grenache, Mourvèdre and Syrah. This richly textured, dark, spicy red is aged in oak for 12 months and needs 4 or 5 years to show at its best. A pricy premium red Tucade, dominated by Mourvèdre, has also been added to the small range. (DM)
Recommended Reds:
Faugères Cistus ★★★ £D
Faugères Vieilles Vignes ★★☆ £C
Recommended Whites:
Faugères Cistus ★★★ £D

⊛ **Ch. de Lascaux (Languedoc)** *www.chateau-lascaux.com*
Jean-Benoit Cavalier established his Languedoc domaine located between Montpellier and Nîmes as long ago as 1984. The vineyards are planted at an altitude of 150 metres on a mix of gravel and limestone, ensuring some excellent growing conditions for the nearly 85 ha now under vine. Syrah dominates the red plantings. Whites consist of Vermentino, Roussanne, Marsanne, Viognier and Rolle and most tend to be cropped at a lower yield of 25–30 hl/ha. A good regular white Languedoc blended from Vermentino, Roussanne, Marsanne and Viognier is joined by a stylish, subtly oaked, nutty white Pierres d'Argent which has more Roussanne and Marsanne with a small proportion of Vermentino. Both should be enjoyed young. The Languedoc Garrigue red is a soft approachable blend of Syrah, Grenache and Mourvèdre, while the top reds are largely Syrah and aged in oak. All of the wines offer a marked *garrigue* character that underpins their dark berry fruit. The richly sumptuous Les Secrets reds from selected parcels and the leaner Nobles Pierres will benefit from 3 or 4 years' age. A Carra rouge and rosé, both Syrah/Grenache blends are also now made. (DM)
Recommended Reds:
Languedoc Les Secrets Madeleine ★★★★ £E
Languedoc Les Secrets Bois de Tourtourel ★★★★ £E
Languedoc Les Secrets Patus de Mussen ★★★★ £E
Languedoc Nobles Pierres ★★★ £C
Languedoc Garrigue ★★☆ £C
Recommended Whites:
Languedoc Pierres d'Argent ★★☆ £C
Languedoc Garrigue ★☆ £B
IGP Saint Guilhem le Désert Domaine Cavalier ★☆ £B
Recommended Rosés:
Languedoc Garrigue ★☆ £B

Ch. La Voulte Gasparets (Corbières) *www.lavoultegasparets.com*
One of the longer-established quality producers in Corbières, whose wine is distributed and marketed by VAL D'ORBIEU. There are 42ha under vine and decent regular red, rosé and white are produced along with two special cuvées, Réservée and Romain Pauc. The Réservée is good, stylish and shows some class and refinement but the Romain Pauc is clearly the benchmark wine here. Quality is helped by some very old vines, and the wine displays a rich, savoury concentration with marked vanilla oak and real complexity: a powerful spicy red that will age well in the medium term. (DM)
Recommended Reds:
Corbières Cuvée Romain Pauc ★★★ £C
Corbières Cuvée Réservée ★★ £B

Ch. Le Thou (Languedoc) *www.chateaulethou.com*
This estate with 17 ha under vine on the outskirts of Béziers is planted largely to Syrah. Significant improvements have been seen in the wines since the turn of the century, particularly the top cuvée Georges et Clem. Blended from Syrah (at least 70%) with the balance Grenache, the wine is rich, fleshy and opulent. Ageing takes place in both *barrique* and tank after a rigorous selection in both vineyard and winery. The supple, approachable Collection is again Syrah and Grenache and a Collection white and rosé are also made. (DM)
Recommended Reds:
Languedoc Georges et Clem ★★★ £D
Languedoc Collection ★★ £C

France

Ch. Mansenoble (Corbières) *www.mansenoble.com*
Fine, modern Corbières property with just over 22 ha planted to Carignan, Grenache, Syrah and a small amount of Mourvèdre as well as Merlot and Cabernet for IGP des Côteaux de Miramont. Three red Corbières are produced. In addition to those rated below a small amount of a special limited cuvée Marie-Annick (named after one of the owners, Marie-Annick de Witte) is produced. The Montagne d'Alaric bottling is ripe, spicy and forward. The Reserve is rich and opulent, with creamy new oak underpinning the wine's dark and spicy berry fruit. Both wines are approachable on release although the Reserve has a sufficiently firm structure to enable short-term ageing. (DM)
Recommended Reds:
Corbières Réserve ★★★ £C
Corbières Montagne d'Alaric ★★ £B

Ch. Maris (Minervois La Livinière) *www.mariswine.com*
Englishman Robert Eden owns some 40 ha in this sub region of the Minervois which is planted to mainly Syrah with some old vine Grenache and Carignan. The property is farmed biodynamically and everything is done as naturally as possible. Minimal interference carries over into the wines which are bottled unfined and unfiltered. As well as Maris he also produces a number of wines under the Rainforest label, with a portion of the revenue allocated to the Rainforest Foundation. The old vine bottlings of both Syrah and Grenache are impressively concentrated. Syrah is dark, smoky and a touch peppery, the Grenache full of dark barry fruit with a very subtle herb scented finish. An old vine Carignan is also produced. A second lighter Syrah with a little Grenache, La Touge is bright and forward with lots of blackberry fruit character but lacks the fine, structured definition of the old vine bottling. (DM)
Recommended Reds:
Minervois La Livinière Les Planels Syrah ★★★ £D
Minervois La Livinière Las Combes Grenache ★★★ £D
Minervois La Livinière La Touge ★★☆ £C

Ch. Massamier La Mignard *www.massamier-la-mignarde.com*
This relatively sizeable Minervois property with 70 ha under vine produces wines from both the Minervois and Minervois La Livinière ACs as well as under various IGP labels. The basic wines are labelled Cuvée des Oliviers. The red includes Cabernet Sauvignon along with southern varieties and there is also a rosé and a Sauvignon-dominated white. The Tradition reds are all Minervois AC, including a Cuvée Aubin. There are two wines under the Expression label, a Cinsault and a particularly striking varietal Carignan from very old vines. Vinified traditionally with no carbonic maceration, it is a wine of real density and dark-fruited spicy concentration. The top wines are the Minervois La Livinière, a dense and impressively structured Domus Maximus (80/20 Syrah and Grenache) and Tenement des Garouilas, a limited-production cuvée blended from Syrah, Grenache and Carignan. Both are aged in new oak and the Garouilas bottling is very modern with malolactic in barrel. These top wines will develop well with 4 or 5 years' age. (DM)
Recommended Reds:
Minervois La Livinière Domus Maximus ★★★ £D
IGP des Côteaux de Peyriac Expression de Carignan ★★★ £C
IGP des Côteaux de Peyriac Cuvée des Oliviers ★☆ £B

Ch. de Montpezat (Languedoc) *www.chateau-montpezat.com*
Vineyards have been planted at this estate to the west of Montpellier for over 100 years. The stone and clay/limestone soils provide the successful growing conditions for both AC Languedoc as well as IGP reds and some Sauvignon Blanc. Future plans include a vineyard Les Epines from which a traditional Carignan/Grenache red blend and a white mix of Grenache Blanc and Marsanne will be produced. The Domaine de Montpezat-labelled IGP bottles are as striking as their Languedoc stablemates. Les Enclos is a soft, vibrant lightly plummy blend of mainly Merlot with some Cabernet Sauvignon, which gets 12 months in cask. The Cuvée Prestige is bigger, and considerably more concentrated. Blending Cabernet Sauvignon (60%) with Syrah, the wine posseses both depth and surprising finesse. The Palombières is an approachable blend of Grenache and Mourvèdre. Pharaonne is big, firm and impressively structured. A mix of Mourvèdre and Grenache, it needs 4 or 5 years to bring out all its rich brambly fruit potential. The top wines get a light fining but are not filtered. (DM)
Recommended Reds:
Languedoc La Pharaonne ★★★☆ £D
Languedoc Les Palombières ★★☆ £C
IGP d'Oc Domaine de Montpezat Cuvée Prestige ★★★☆ £D
IGP d'Oc Domaine de Montpezat Les Enclos ★★☆ £C

✿ Ch. de La Negly (Languedoc La Clape) *www.lanegly.fr*
Medium-sized but consistently excellent Languedoc domaine producing sound quality at all price levels. Since taking over the family property in 1992 Jean Paux-Rosset has single-mindedly dedicated himself to producing wines of interest and excitement. He is aided by consultant Claude Gros and produces the super-cuvée Clos du Truffière from a small plot of exceptional Syrah near Pezenas, which is part owned by Bordeaux wine merchant Jeffrey Davies. The white Brise Marine blends Bourboulenc with Marsanne and Roussanne and has a fresh cutting edge to its nutty fruit. Les Embruns is ripe and full flavoured with hints of strawberry and spice, Palazy, a IGP, is the lighter of the two rosés. Two wines are released under the Domaine de Boède label. Le Pavillon is a soft fruit-driven blend of Carignan and Grenache, whereas Le Grès is a firmer richer blend of Syrah and Grenache. It gets a 45-day vatting and is aged in cuve for 14 months. La Côte is mainly Carignan. It has a fine, spicy, dark-berried character and drinks well young. La Falaise is sourced from southeast limestone slopes on the Massif de la Clape. A blend of Syrah, Grenache and Mourvèdre, it is aged in a mix of new and 1-year-old oak and needs a year or two to find its equilibrium. All of these wines are excellent value. Less so, perhaps understandably given their small production and meagre yields, are the top 3 reds. L'Ancely is a rich, powerful and highly characterful blend of 95% Mourvèdre with Grenache. You'll struggle to find a Bandol sold at this price but similarly it is rare to find wines of this quality in that appellation. Finally there are two remarkably pure, powerful and very intense 100% Syrahs. Porte au Ciel is marked by its density and sheer power. The Clos du Truffière is finer, with greater elegance and sheer harmony. It vies for the title of finest red in the Languedoc. Both require cellaring for upwards of 6 or 7 years and will age gracefully. All the reds here are bottled unfined and unfiltered. (DM)
Recommended Reds:
Languedoc Clos du Truffière ★★★★★ £G
Languedoc Porte au Ciel ★★★★★ £G
Languedoc L'Ancely ★★★★☆ £F
Languedoc La Falaise ★★★ £D
Languedoc Domaine de Boède Le Grès ★★★ £D
Languedoc La Côte ★★ £C
IGP des Côtes de Perpignan Domaine de Boède Le Pavillon ★☆ £C

Recommended Whites:
Languedoc La Brise Marine ★☆ £B
Recommended Rosés:
Languedoc Les Embruns ★★ £C

>> Ch. de Pennautier (Cabardes) *www.lorgeril.com*
This is one of the benchmark properties in the tiny appellation of Cabardes. As well as the Terroirs d'Altitude labels reviewed here, a Grand Vin L'Esprit de Pennautier red is also made (dominated by Syrah) as well as a moelleux Chardonnay Le Rêve de Pennautier, "Vendanges d'Après". Fruit driven reds, whites and rosés are also released under the Classique and Collection Fruitée labels. The estate has a substantial vineyard holding including 78 ha in the AOP and a further 82 ha which are classified IGP. A wide range of grapes is planted, both Atlantic and Mediterranean. Indeed the appellation being located some distance inland from the Med produces reds with a unique character. The Cabardes Terroirs d'Altitude is an interesting blend of Cabernet Franc, Merlot, Cot (Malbec), Syrah, Cabernet Sauvignon and Grenache. It offers an array of black fruits, both blackberry and blackcurrant with a hint of plum and black pepper spice. It gains structure from 14 months in French oak with a creamy character from just over a third of new barrels. The Marquis de Pennautier is solely from Chardonnay. The fruit comes from vines grown at an altitude of 360 metres so providing a nice fresh edge in the wine. Vinification is classic Chardonnay, barrel fermentation and tank fermentation, lees stirring and ageing for 10 months. Opulent tropical fruit underpinned by hints of vanilla oak. Drink young, the red with a couple of year's age. (DM)
Recommended Reds:
Cabardes Terroirs d'Altitude ★★★ £D
Recommended Whites:
IGP d'Oc Marquis de Pennautier Terroirs d'Altitude ★★☆ £C

Ch. Puech-Haut (Languedoc) *www.puech-haut.fr*
Substantial Languedoc property making particularly good earthy, characterful reds. Rosés tends to be light with simple berry fruit in Complice and Loup du Pic bottlings. Both are made by direct pressing rather than a period of skin contact. More serious with a little structure as well as fruit is the Languedoc Prestige from Cinsault and Grenache. Three whites are made. Complices is a soft nutty cool fermented blend of Marsanne, Roussanne and Grenache Blanc. The more serious Prestige is just Roussanne and Marsanne but much the best of the three is the Tête de Belier a blend of Roussanne (60%), Marsanne (30%) and Grenache (10%). The wine is barrel-fermented on lees with *bâtonnage* and the malolactic is blocked for freshness; the wine offering fat, full nutty southern fruit and good depth. There are five reds. Both the Complices and Loup du Pic are soft fruit-driven blends of Syrah and Grenache, the latter showing some dark smoky, peppery fruit. The Languedoc Prestige is a significant step up and a traditional earthy, almost rustic but characterful blend - again from Syrah and Grenache. The Tête de Belier is Syrah, Grenache, Mourvèdre and Carignan. Ageing is for 18 months in oak, a third of which is new. It has impressive depth and a spicy character to its dark fruit with supple well rounded tannins. Top of the tree is the serious and characterful Clos du Pic from Pic Saint-Loup. A blend of Syrah and Mourvèdre with rich, almost chocolaty fruit and a characterful underlying spiciness, it has real dimension on the palate. Expect the top reds to continue to improve over five or six years, the Clos du Pic a touch longer. (DM)
Recommended Reds:
Languedoc Pic Saint-Loup Clos du Pic ★★★★ £E

Languedoc Tête de Belier ★★★☆ £D
Languedoc Prestige ★★★☆ £D
Languedoc Pic Saint-Loup Loup du Pic ★★ £C
Recommended Whites:
Languedoc Tête de Belier ★★★☆ £D
Languedoc Prestige ★★★ £C
Languedoc Complices ★★ £C
Recommended Rosés:
Languedoc Prestige ★★☆ £C

Ch Rives-Blanques (Limoux) *www.rives-blanques.com*
This is a fine new name in the small Limoux appellation. Both still and sparkling wines are made and Chardonnay, Chenin Blanc, Mauzac and Sauvignon Blanc are all planted for whites. Pinot Noir is also included in a Vintage Rosé Crémant de Limoux. There are currently approximately 21.5 ha under vine all white varieties and yields vary between 35 and 45 hl/ha, so not high at all on a 350 metre high plateau. Output is currently about 100,000 bottles a year. In the vineyards farming is by organic methods and this ecological approach has enabled local wildlife to live amongst the vines. Considerable investment has gone into the winery includes state of the art stainless steel vats, temperature controls and up to 300 oak barrels. The still whites are all well made. Of the wines Odyssée is a Chardonnay, barrel-fermented and aged for 6 months in 1/3 new wood with *bâtonnage*. Dédicace is a characterful Chenin Blanc, coming from 30 year old vines and although fermented and matured for a similar period in wood only a very small proportion is new emphasising the quality and character of the fruit. The Occitania Mauzac is unusual, difficult to vinify as a varietal it is planted in the most exposed sites in the vineyard and shares a similar vinification to the Chardonnay with six months lees enrichment adding to the textural qualities of the wine. There are two white sparklers including a Blanquette de Limoux which blends 90% Mauzac with 10% Chardonnay and Chenin Blanc and the secondary fermentation is in bottle in the classic method. A Blanc de Blancs is also made and this is similarly vinified and aged and blends Chardonnay with Chenin Blanc. (DM)
Recommended Whites:
Limoux La Trilogie ★★★☆ £C
Limoux L'Odyssée ★★★☆ £C
Crémant de Limoux Blancs de Blancs ★★★ £C
Limoux Dédicace ★★★ £C
Blanquette de Limoux ★★☆ £B
Limoux Occitania ★★☆ £B
Recommended Rosés:
Crémant de Limoux Vintage ★★ £C

Ch. St-Jacques d'Albas (Minervois) *www.chateaustjacques.com*
The harvest at this small Minervois domaine used to be sold to the co-op before 2001. However, new owner Graham Nutter is now releasing four impressive examples of the appellation and a good IGP series (red). Winemaking expertise is provided by Australian Richard Osborne and the wines clearly have real potential. The Domaine red is a blend of Syrah with older vines Grenache and Mouvèdre since 2010 (Carignan). The grapes are all de-stemmed and carbonic maceration is not employed but the must gets a short cold soak prior to fermentation to ensure some attractive bright dark-fruit character. The Château is now Syrah and Grenache, part of which is vinified without a pre-fermentation maceration. Sturdier, deeper and more firmly structured, the Syrah component is aged for around a year in French oak, around 20% being new. Added since

Languedoc

2003 is 'La Chapelle', named after an 11th century church on the property. Almost all Syrah and from the best *lieu-dit* on the property, it demands five years cellaring to fully bring the fruit and oak into perfect balance. A fine, juicy rosé is also made, a blend of Syrah and Grenache, a white from Vermentino, Viognier and Rousanne, as well as a Grenache and Cabernet Sauvignon-based red for a trio of IGP d'Oc. Great value wines here. (DM)

Recommended Reds:
Minervois La Chapelle Chàteau Saint-Jacques d'Albas ★★★☆ £D
Minervois Chàteau Saint-Jacques d'Albas ★★★ £C
Minervois Domaine Saint-Jacques d'Albas ★★☆ £C
IGP d'Oc Le Petit Saint-Jacques ★☆ £B
Recommended Whites:
IGP d'Oc Le Petit Saint-Jacques ★☆ £B
Recommended Rosés:
IGP d'Oc Le Petit Saint-Jacques ★☆ £B

Ch. Sainte Eulalie (Minervois) *www.chateausainteeulalie.com*
Impressive Minervois operation producing a small range of red, white and rosé, not all from Minervois. The white is a 100% Sauvignon Blanc and comes from the Limoux region. There are a total of 34 ha under vine with the Minervois vineyards planted on a *terroir* consisting of pebble top soil over a clay, chalk and manganese subsoil. Of the Minervois wines there is a rosé, Printemps d'Eulalie and a Cuvée Prestige Minervois red is also produced. The Plaisir d'Eulalie is one of the best value fruit driven examples of the appellation you are likely to find, a blend of mainly Grenache and Carignan with a little Syrah aged in tank for 15 to 18 months to round the wine out. La Cantilène is altogether more serious. It is mainly Syrah with Grenache and just a little Carignan. The wine is given an extensive vatting of 15 to 20 days and is aged in small oak (40% new) for 12 months and micro-oxygenation is used. Cellaring for five years or so is recommended. (DM)
Recommended Reds:
Minervois La Livinière La Cantilène ★★★ £D
Minervois Plaisir de Eulalie ★★☆ £B
Recommended Whites:
IGP d'Oc Le Blanc de Eulalie ★★☆ £B

Chevalier Vins (Faugères) *www.chevaliervins.fr*
For 10 years Brigitte Chevalier was the export manager for Jean-Luc Thunevin of Ch. VALANDRAUD in Saint-Emilion, but in 2003 she established her own small négociant operation producing wines from her native Languedoc. Until 2007 she owned no vineyards and sources fruit from properties where the domaine owners have allowed her to select from the best parcels and to vinify and age the wines in their cellars. A maximum of 500 cases of each wine are produced and then only in the best vintages. The Laure Saint-Martin is a super-ripe, almost jammy Minervois, mainly Grenache, with a little Syrah. Finer, more structured and elegant is the Clos du Causse Minervois La Livinière which is mainly Syrah with a little Grenache, while the organic Saint-Chinian, Château La Bousquette, is from Syrah and Grenache and is more peppery and mineral. The IGP Lo Bosc comes from very old Mouvèdre grown on limestone soils in the Haut-Languedoc, it has a really smoky, damson laden old-vine complexity and a finely-chiselled tannic structure. The Minervois Concertino, a combination of Grenache and Syrah, is full of black, herb scented fruit and richer and fuller than might be expected from the blend. Corbières Concertino is full of dark, spicy brambly fruit, a blend of Mourvèdre (around 80%) and Syrah. Faugères can also be found under the Concertino label. A new Faugères, Domaine

Saint-Martin d'Agel has also been added, a characterful and mineral, dark fruited blend of Syrah, Grenache, Mouvèdre and Carignan. Additionally, Brigitte has produced a string of single-varietal entry-level wines under the Stricto Senso label at very low prices for the quality. A simple, fresh and forward fruit driven red from Grenache, Syrah and Merlot comes under a further label Avant! from 25 year old vines. Brigitte now has her own property, Domaine de Cébène in Faugères where she owns selected parcels. Les Bancèls is a blend of one-third each of Syrah, Mourvèdre and Grenache. Another Faugères, Felgaria and a IGP, Ex Arena (mainly Grenache) are also made. Across the board the wines offer great value. (DM)
Chevalier Vins
Recommended Reds:
IGP d'Oc Lo Bosc ★★★☆ £D
Minervois La Livinière Clos du Causse ★★★ £D
Faugères Saint-Martin d'Agel ★★★ £D
Saint Chinian Chateau La Bousquette ★★★ £D
Minervois Laure Saint-Martin ★★★ £C
Minervois Concertino ★★☆ £B
Corbières Concertino ★★☆ £B
Domaine de Cébène
Recommended Reds:
Faugères Felgaria ★★★★ £D
IGP d'Oc Ex Arena ★★★☆ £D
Faugères Les Bancèls ★★★☆ £D
Stricto Senso
Recommended Reds:
IGP d'Oc Syrah ★★ £B
Recommended Whites:
IGP d'Oc Chardonnay ★★☆ £B
Avant!
Recommended Reds:
IGP d'Oc ★☆ £B

Dom. Clavel (Languedoc) *www.vins-clavel.fr*
This property is situated just beyond the suburbs of the city of Montpellier. Some 33 ha are planted to Syrah, Grenache, Mourvèdre and Carignan among the reds, along with white varieties Roussanne, Grenache Blanc, Marsanne, Rolle, Viognier, Carignan Blanc, Marsanne, Clairette and Muscat à Petits Grains. The latter are blended into a lightly herb-scented, nutty, rich fruit-driven white, Cascaille. A fresh rosé, Mescladis is kept on its lees for six months adding a little structure. It is the reds, though, that are the mainstay here. Both Le Mas and Les Garrigues are ripe and sturdy with well-integrated, dark blackberry and herb spiced fruit and supple tannins, while the old-vine Copa Santa, regularly on the cusp of ★★★★, is a splendid ageworthy blend of Syrah and Grenache. The fine mineral, dark and spiced Bonne Pioche also has a little Mourvèdre in its *assemblage*. (DM)
Recommended Reds:
Languedoc La Méjanelle Copa Santa ★★★☆ £D
Languedoc Pic Saint Loup Bonne Pioche ★★★☆ £D
Languedoc Les Garrigues ★★★ £C
Languedoc Grès de Montpellier Le Mas ★★☆ £C
Recommended Whites:
Languedoc Cascaille ★★★ £C
Recommended Rosés:
Languedoc Pic St Loup Mescladis ★☆ £B

Clos de l'Anhel (Corbieres) *www.anhel.fr*
Small 7 ha property making some of the very best wine in Corbières.

Planted at an altitude of over 200 metres the vineyard comprises 2ha each of Carignan and Grenache planted in clay/limestone soils and small 0.4ha plots of both Syrah and Cinsault planted in a more gravelly/limestone soil which provides good water retention for the Syrah. Cultivation follows organic principles and harvesting is by hand. Characterful, supple, spicy and approachable red Les Terrassettes blends 60-year-old Carignan with Grenache, Syrah and Cinsault and is aged in cask with micro-oxygenation employed prior to the malolactic. Les Dimanches is a serious and more backward blend of just Carignan and Grenache. It gets a vatting of up to 3 weeks and is aged in a portion of new wood, again with micro-oxygenation rather than racking employed during *élevage*. Rich and concentrated with dark fruit and black pepper notes, it will benefit from 4 or 5 years' patience. There are two entry level wines, Le Lolo and Les Autres and a pricier top cuvée, Envie . (DM)

Recommended Reds:
Corbières Les Dimanches ★★★ £D
Corbières Les Terrassettes ★★☆ £C

Clos Bagatelle (Saint-Chinian) www.closbagatelle.com
With over 50 ha, the Simons are one of the larger Saint-Chinian growers but also one of the best. 47 ha is planted to Carignan, Grenache, Mourvèdre and Cinsault. For white they have a small holding of just 7 ha of Muscat. Production is now around 20,000 cases a year. There are four straightforward fruit-driven IGP d'Oc bottlings: a Sauvignon and a Chardonnay along with a red blend La Tuilière and a Merlot. It is though the Saint-Chinians that mark out this estate. A characterful rosé, Donnadieu Camille et Juliette, is produced from young vines and there are no fewer than five red labels as well as a white. The Tradition is crafted from some of the younger Carignan vines along with Grenache, Syrah and Cinsault. No carbonic maceration is used and the wine shows some really attractive and vibrant spicy, brambly fruit. The Donnadieu labels are sourced from some of the higher-altitude plots and are harvested a little later. Camille et Juliette is 50% Carignan put through carbonic maceration, with Grenache, Syrah and a further small proportion of Carignan vinified traditionally. Vibrant and powerful but with a firm structure, it should develop well in the short term. In the Marie et Mathieu, a small (15%) portion of Syrah goes through *macération carbonique*, with the balancing Syrah, Grenache and Mourvèdre vinified traditionally. Yields of less than 30 hl/ha ensure a rich, stylish but accessible red. The Veillée d'Automne and premium cuvée La Terre de Mon Père are more seriously structured and ageworthy examples. Both blend Mourvèdre, Syrah and Grenache, the Mourvèdre being the more important component of La Terre de Mon Père. The former is refined, well structured and intense with hint of new oak showing through; the latter is richer, purer and finer and is very intense and complex. The top red 'Je me Souviens' is only made in exceptional vintages for the domaine. It is a blend of Mouvedre (over 80%) and Grenache. It is full of intense, dark, spicy black fruits and comfortably absorbs 24 months in new oak. An excellent range is completed by a honeyed and grapey sweet Muscat of impressive poise and class. (DM)

Recommended Reds:
Saint-Chinian Je Me Souviens ★★★★ £F
Saint-Chinian La Terre de Mon Père ★★★☆ £E
Saint-Chinian Veillée d'Automne ★★★ £C
Saint-Chinian Donnadieu Camille et Juliette ★★☆ £C
Saint-Chinian Donnadieu Mathieu et Marie ★★☆ £C
Saint-Chinian Tradition ★★ £B

Recommended Whites:
Saint-Chinian ★★☆ £C Muscat de Saint-Jean de Minervois ★★ £C
Recommended Rosés:
Saint-Chinian Donnadiieu Camille et Juliette ★☆ £B

Clos du Camuzeilles (Fitou)
Fitou was the first of the Languedoc appellations to gain full AC status way back in 1948. It has however produced fewer domaines of real style than many neighbouring ACs. Laurent Tibes' Clos des Camuzeilles is very much an exception to this rule with very fine reds as well as a dry white and a Muscat de Rivesaltes as well. He only took over his family's vines in 1998 but the quality here is immediately apparent. From finely drained schistous soils he produces a very fine varietal old Carignan, which is aged in *cuve* and shows great intensity of fruit and a well defined mineral edge. La Grangette Fitou is dominated by 80 year old Carignan with a touch of close to 40 year old Grenache. Aged in one-third new oak *demi-muids*, the wine is richer and fuller than the varietal Carignan with marked oak and dark, spicy berry fruit offering real depth and purity. Expect both wines to develop well with a little age, particularly the Grangette. (DM)

Recommended Reds:
Fitou La Grangette ★★★☆ £D
IGP de La Vallée du Paradis Carignan ★★★ £C

Clos Centeilles (Minervois) www.closcenteilles.com
Stylish Minervois has been produced at this property for a decade and Patricia Domergue has been established considerably longer than some of her competitors who opt, not often wisely, for a much fuller and more extracted style. There is a minimum of new wood here and the wines are restrained, intentionally so, but are good and well crafted, with elegant fruit and well-honed, ripened tannins. A number of cuvées are produced. Carignanissime is made from 100% old-vine Carignan vinified in part by *macération carbonique*. It shows just what old-vine Carignan properly ripened can achieve. Capitelle de Centeilles is a juicy, vibrant 100% Cinsault that, like Carignanissime, is aged for a couple of years in *cuve* before bottling. Campagne de Centeilles is a straightforward soft, fruit-driven blend of Cinsault and a little Syrah. The top wine is the Minervois La Livinière which is structured and refined and needs 3–4 years. The Guigniers de Centeilles Pinot Noir doesn't quite have the same depth, possessing relatively simple red-berry fruit. (DM)

Recommended Reds:
Minervois La Livinière ★★★☆ £E
Minervois Capitelle de Centeilles ★★★ £C
Minervois Carignanissime ★★☆ £C
Minervois Campagne de Centeilles ★☆ £B

❀ Clos Marie (Languedoc Pic Saint-Loup)
Some of the best and priciest wines in the Languedoc are now emerging from this 17 ha property, which has 15.5 ha planted to mainly Grenache and Mourvèdre with some Carignan and a little Syrah. There is also a small white holding of Grenache, Roussanne and Clairette, which is used to produce a fine nutty white Manon. The four reds take pride of place and all are serious, dense and powerful examples. Vinification is traditional, with no carbonic maceration and only a small amount of new oak in the top wines. L'Olivette is ripe and forward, Simon and Métairie du Clos more structured and firm. The top label Les Glorieuses is rich and concentrated but like all the wines refined with an elegance and purity rarely encountered in the Languedoc. L'Olivette will drink well

young but the other cuvées, particularly Les Glorieuses, should be given 5 years or so of ageing. (DM)

Recommended Reds:
Languedoc Pic Saint-Loup Glorieuses ★★★★☆ £F
Languedoc Pic Saint-Loup Métairie du Clos ★★★★ £E
Languedoc Pic Saint-Loup Simon ★★★★ £E
Languedoc Pic Saint-Loup L'Olivette ★★★☆ £C

Dom. de Courbissac (Minervois) www.courbissac.com
The domaine is planted to 30 ha in marl and chalk soils and the vineyards are farmed biodynamically with Mourvèdre, Syrah, Carignan, Grenache, Roussane and Marsanne all grown. Yields are purposely restricted and new vine planting is done at high density, 8,000 vines per hectare. In the winery the fruit is rigorously sorted prior to vinification and then de-stemmed before a lengthy one month maceration. The regular Minervois is aged for 12 months in cement vat whereas the top two wines are aged for longer, 18 months in barrels of varying size, 225 to 600 litres and on the fine lees. The Minevois offers dark, herb spiced black fruits and comes from a traditional blend of Carignan, Grenache and Syrah. Pandora is a combination of Syrah and Grenache. Dark fruited and chunky it is released with some age and offers impressive depth. The Orphée is rich and concentrated with a mineral edge and a dark, smoky almost meaty and savoury character. Underpinned by firm tannin with a rich spiciness. The wines are bottled unfined and unfiltered. It should be noted that the wine brands have now changed although the wines rated should still be available in the market place. We will be seeking to bring you an update with the next edition. (DM)

Recommended Reds:
Minervois La Livinière Orphée ★★★★ £E
Minervois Pandora ★★★★ £D
Minervois ★★★☆ £C

Dom. de La Croix-Belle www.croix-belle.com
The fairly extensive range of wines made at this IGP des Côtes de Thongue property all offer good value for money. The mix of clay, limestone, silt and gravel soils have excellent drainage and assist in keeping yields down to around 45 hl/ha, helped by a green harvest. Although most of the vineyard is machine-harvested this is generally done at night to keep the fruit, particularly from the white varieties, as fresh as possible and always in a single pass or *tri*. Sulphur additions are also kept to a minimum. The straightforward varietal wines are soft and fruity but it is the Champs, No 7 and Cascaillou wines that stand out here. Les Champs are fruit-driven styles, which see no wood. Les Champ du Lys is blended from Grenache, Viognier and Sauvignon Blanc and is aged on lees for 6 months to add weight to its spicy, floral fruit. The red Champ du Coq combines Syrah, Grenache and Merlot and works better than Calades, which is Syrah, Mourvèdre and Carignan aged in oak for a year. The No 7 red and white are a clear step up, the former an unusual barrel-fermented blend of Viognier, Chardonnay, Grenache Blanc, Sauvignon Blanc, Carignan Blanc and Muscat à Petits Grains; the latter, comprising a varied mix of Syrah, Grenache, Mourvèdre, Cinsault, Merlot and Cabernet Sauvignon, is bottled unfiltered after 12 months in oak. Top of the range Cascaillou, produced from a yield of barely more than 20hl/ha is an elegant blend of Grenache, Syrah and Mourvèdre, bottled after just 8 months in *cuve* in order to emphasise the quality and intensity of its fruit. (DM)

Recommended Reds:
IGP des Côtes de Thongue Cascaillou ★★★ £D
IGP des Côtes de Thongue no 7 ★★☆ £C

IGP des Côtes de Thongue Le Champ du Coq ★★ £B
IGP des Côtes de Thongue Le Champ des Calades ★☆ £B
IGP des Côtes de Thongue Caringole ★☆ £B

Recommended Whites:
IGP des Côtes de Thongue no 7 ★★☆ £C
IGP des Côtes de Thongue Les Champ des Lys ★★ £B
IGP des Côtes de Thongue Chardonnay ★☆ £C
IGP des Côtes de Thongue Caringole ★☆ £B

Dom. Jean-Louis Denois (Limoux) www.jldenois.com
Jean-Louis Denois cultivates 38 ha of red and white varieties from which he produces an extensive range of red, white and sparkling wines from the Limoux and the Fenouillèdes of good to excellent quality from vineyards that are cultivated organically and in part biodynamically. The Limoux Grande Cuvée, an appellation benchmark is a finely structured, supple, lightly cedary blend comprising Merlot, Cabernet Franc, Cabernet Sauvignon and Malbec which will benefit from 3 or 4 years' patience. A touch richer and fuller is the cuvée Chloé, a full-blown Merlot, from old vines and aged in oak for 12 to 18 months, with occasionally a touch of Cabernet Franc included. Taut and firmly structured when young but with impressive weight and concentration it will benefit from 5 years' ageing. Neither of the wines is fined or filtered. He also makes an impressive range of sparkling wines which includes a fine white Tradition Brut. Fermented in small oak, it is a blend of Pinot Noir and Chardonnay and rivals any of the current offerings from Limoux as well as many lesser Champagnes. Of perhaps greatest interest though is the excellent barrel-fermented Sainte-Marie an elegant and finely structured Chardonnay. It possesses a piercing intensity, rare in this southerly region. Expect them to evolve well with 3 or 4 years' age. (DM)

Recommended Reds:
IGP Chloé ★★★☆ £D   Limoux Grande Cuvée ★★★ £C

Recommended Whites:
Limoux Sainte Marie ★★★☆ £D
Crémant de Limoux Tradition Brut ★★★ £C

Ermitage du Pic Saint Loup (Languedoc) www.ermitagepic.fr
This domaine is run by three brothers, Xavier, Pierre, and Jean-Marc and the Ravaille family has origins in the region going back a great many generations. They have been long term proponents of biodynamic farming since 1999 and are now fully certified. They believe this will produce the best quality fruit from their diverse *terroir*, including limestone and dolomite, red and white clay, sand, schist, and round *galets* soils on the higher slopes of the Pic Saint Loup *cru*. In the cellar the approach is one of minimal intervention. The rosé combines Syrah, Grenache, Mourvèdre and a little Cinsault and is direct pressed providing a fresh fruited style with a light salmon colour and a subtle mineral hint. The white Cuvée Sainte Agnès is marked by white fruits, a hint of peach and subtle herb spiciness. Vinified from a blend Clairette, Roussanne, Marsanne and Grenache Blanc it is fermented and aged in varying sized oak barrels. Tour de Pierres is the softest of the red trio, marked by a berry fruitiness and a peppery backbone. Syrah and Grenache are the dominant grapes with a little Mourvèdre and Carignan included. The Cuvée Sainte Agnès is denser and more concentrated, with a more intense, mineral edge to its fruit. The blend is similar but the vines are older and grown on limestone, rather than clay dominated soils. The top red is from a 50/50 blend of Syrah and venerable 85 year old Grenache providing a wine of rich concentration and impressive depth as well as a complex meaty, savoury quality to its fruit. Five

years cellaring will add further depth. (DM)

Recommended Reds:
Languedoc Pic Saint Loup Guilhem Gaucelm ★★★☆ £D
Languedoc Pic Saint Loup Cuvée Sainte Agnès ★★★ £C
Languedoc Pic Saint Loup Tour de Pierres ★★☆ £C
Recommended Whites:
Languedoc Cuvée Sainte Agnès ★★ £B
Recommended Rosés:
Languedoc Pic Saint Loup ★☆ £B

❀ Dom. de La Garance (IGP de l'Hérault)

This 11 ha property is the source of a number of fine, very traditional wines. Key here are some very old plantings of Carignan as well as the lowly Ugni Blanc allied to very low yields of around 15–20 hl/ha, not to mention an excellent *terroir* just to the north of Pézenas with vines planted in a mix of limestone, basalt and clay soils. Les Armières, old-vine Carignan and a little Syrah, is given a very long *cuvaison* of up to a month and demands 4 or 5 years to shed its early mineral austerity. It offers great depth and purity, though. The white Les Claviers blends Ugni Blanc, Grenache Gris and Clairette. It is a ripe, full and nutty wine, which will evolve well over 5 years or so. The Bruixas is made from Grenache. Fermentation is halted at around 13 degrees by fortification to leave a lightly sweet, fascinatingly pruney and figgy late-harvest red. (DM)

Recommended Reds:
Bruixas Vin de Liqueur ★★★★ £E
IGP de l'Hérault Les Armières ★★★★ £E
Recommended Whites:
IGP de l'Hérault Les Claviers ★★★★ £E

Dom. du Grand Arc (Corbieres) *www.grand-arc.fr*

Fine quality red emerges from this small domaine in the Hautes Corbières with 13.5 ha of vineyard planted on south-facing slopes on clay-limestone soils close to the famous Cathar castle of Peyrepertuse. The vines are tended as naturally as possible with minimal use of fertilisers and yields are restricted to between 35 and 45hl/ha to maximise quality. There is a good, richly berry-fruited rosé but it is the reds that stand out. The Réserve is approximately two-thirds Carignan and one-third Grenache with the merest hint of Mourvèdre. It is pure, minerally and very elegant for the AC. Fuller and more opulent, with a hint of toasty, almost chocolaty oak, the Cuvée de Quarante is a combination of Carignan, Grenache and Syrah. This wine is on the edge of ★★★ and excellent value for money. Two slightly pricier wines are also produced, Aux Temps d'Histoire and En Sol Majeur. The reds will drink well with a year or two in bottle but have the depth and supple structure to develop well in the medium term. (DM)

Recommended Reds:
Corbières Cuvée de Quarante ★★☆ £C Corbières Réserve ★★ £B
Recommended Rosés:
Corbières ★☆ £B

❀ Dom. de La Grange des Pères (IGP de l'Hérault)

The wine here now rivals the long-established leader among Languedoc-Roussillon producers, MAS DE DAUMAS GASSAC. There is no doubt that Grange des Pères is every bit as impressive as its near neighbour. The production is much smaller, though, and Laurent Vaillé has just 10ha under vine, the majority planted to Mourvèdre, Syrah and Cabernet Sauvignon farmed to almost organic standards. The wine is surprisingly approachable in its youth but has all the density, velvety tannin and class to age gracefully.

Although matured in 100% new oak this is very well integrated and the wine is, of course, bottled without fining or filtration. There is a tiny amount of a very fine Roussanne-based white with equally deftly handled oak. (DM)

Recommended Reds:
IGP de l'Hérault ★★★★★ £G

Dom. Anne Gros/Jean-Paul Tollot *www.anne-gros.com*

This partnership of two winemaking stars from Burgundy, Anne GROS and Jean-Paul Tollot of TOLLOT-BEAUT is a new source of some of the best reds from the southern stretches of the Languedoc in the Haut-Minervois around the village of Cazelles. Six wines are now made with the three Minervois and the LO de La Vie coming from individual *terroirs* and they possess a total of six different sites covering 17 ha. The three Vin de France wines are sourced from AOC vineyards but the blending options mean they have to take this classification. La Cinso is not surprisingly a varietal Cinsault, full of berry fruit and charm, the key is the age of the vines at 50 years old. La 50/50 comes from a mix of Grenache, Syrah and Carignan, again a fruit driven style it is aged in stainless steel. L'O de La Vie is from a single vineyard of young Syrah. It offers classic aromas of dark fruits, liquorice and pepper. Les Fontanilles is the most approachable of the three Minervois. A characterful blend of Syrah, Grenache, Carignan and Cinsault. Vibrant and intense the vines range from just over 20 to 50 years old adding a hint of complexity. La Ciaude is rich, intense and with a real old vine complexity too. The vineyards range from young (13 years) to very old (108 years). It is a blend of Carignan, Syrah and Grenache with 80% aged in barrel. The top wine Les Carrétals comes from a site planted in 1909 to Carignan and Grenache. Elegant, complex and very intense it is aged in stainless steel to preserve the character and quality of its fruit. It is one of the great wines of the region. (DM)

Recommended Reds:
Minervois Les Carrétals ★★★★ £E
Minervois La Ciaude ★★★☆ £D
Minervois Les Fontanilles ★★★☆ £D
Vin de France LO de La Vie ★★★ £C
Vin de France La 50/50 ★★★ £B
Vin de France La Cinso ★★☆ £B

Dom. de L'Hortus (Languedoc) *www.vignobles-orliac.com*

Jean Orliac established this 60 ha property in the late 1970s but only began producing wine himself in 1990. This is now one of the benchmark producers for Pic Saint-Loup, an appellation with a depressingly large number of average wines that should be better. The red Grande Cuvée, blended mainly from Syrah and Mourvèdre, is aged in two-thirds new wood but is surprisingly tight and restrained in its youth. The Grande Cuvée white is ripe, almost tropical and produced from barrel-fermented and aged Chardonnay, Viognier and Petit Manseng. There is a second label, Bergerie de l'Hortus which offers decent value with approachable, straightforward red, rosé and white. A further red Clos du Prieur comes from a Languedoc single vineyard of the same name. (DM)

Recommended Reds:
Languedoc Pic Saint-Loup Grande Cuvée ★★★☆ £E
Recommended Whites:
IGP Val de Montferrand Grande Cuvée ★★★ £C
IGP Val de Montferrand Bergerie de L'Hortus ★★ £C
Recommended Rosés:
Languedoc Bergerie de L'Hortus ★☆ £B

Languedoc

France

Dom. Virgile Joly (Languedoc) *www.domainevirgilejoly.com*
This recently established domaine, started in 2000, has around 10
ha under vine spread across a number of plots in the communes of
Jonquières and Saint Saturnin. The *terroir* is excellent, with meagre
argile-calcareous and gravel soils providing naturally moderate
yields of a mere 20hl/ha or so. Three reds are produced and the
vinification is traditional with four to five weeks maceration on skins
and hand plunging for the top two wines The Saturne is a blend
of Carignan, Cinsault, Syrah and Grenache. Full of impressive dark,
spicy fruit with a subtle mineral edge it will evolve well with 4–5
years' ageing. The Virgile bottling is denser and fuller. The texture is
rich and concentrated but the tannin is sufficiently firm to demand
at least 5 years' patience. The blend is Carignan (30%) and Grenache
(40%) with a further 30% of Syrah adding a darker, richer character.
Le Joly Rouge is a vibrant approachable style coming from a blend
of Syrah, Grenache, Cinsault and Carignan. The white Languedoc
Virgile is 100% Grenache Blanc. Barrel-fermented and aged for
9 months in 500-litre oak to minimise the wood influence, it is
gloriously rich and full with nutty, lightly citrus-edged fruit and a rich
texture on the palate. It will drink very well with 3 or 4 years' age. A
vin de liqueur, Carthagene, is an unusual blend of Chasselas, Servan
and Syrah. (DM)
Recommended Reds:
Languedoc Virgile ★★★☆ £E
Languedoc Saturne ★★★ £D
Languedoc Joly ★★☆ £D
Recommended Whites:
Languedoc Virgile ★★★ £D

Dom. des Jougla (Saint-Chinian) *www.domainedesjougla.com*
Alain Jougla has a holding of 40 ha from which he produces
good earthy examples of Saint-Chinian. The vineyards are partly
comprised of clay/limestone soils and partly more schistous. The
Initiale is the regular bottling, a blend of Syrah, Grenache, Carignan
and Mourvèdre. It is soft, supple and immediately approachable,
with aromas of dark fruits and spicy herbs. Ancestrale is Mourvèdre,
Syrah and Grenache. It is a clear step up in quality, with an almost
sauvage quality with a mineral undercurrent and firmly structured,
well-rounded tannins. Best of the three is the oak aged Cuvée
Signée which has a rich and concentrated old-vine character. It
is produced from Syrah, Grenache and Carignan grown on some
the property's higher schistous slopes. A IGP dry Viognier, a late
harvested Viognier Vendanges Passerillees and white Languedoc are
also produced along with a rosé and a further red Saint-Chinian Viels
Arrasics which is also aged in barrel. All of the wines offer very good
value. (DM)
Recommended Reds:
Saint-Chinian Cuvée Signéep ★★★ £C
Saint-Chinian Ancestrale ★★★ £C Saint-Chinian Initiale ★★ £B

Dom. Lacoste *www.domaine-le-clos-de-bellevue.com*
This domaine in the Muscat de Lunel appellation is very unusual in
being planted to a majority of Muscat à Petits Grains. Red varieties
have also now been planted and red Languedoc and IGP de
l'Hérault as well as rosé are also made. Sweet and late-harvest wines
are the speciality here although a dry IGP d'Oc Muscat is produced
from the estate's youger vines and cool-fermented for immediate
appeal. Of the two Muscat de Lunel bottlings, the Lacoste is forward
and richly grapey, full of simple luscious fruit but with a finesse often
absent in such wines. Yields of less than 30 hl/ha no doubt help in
achieving this. The Clos Bellevue is rich and very intense with great

poise and refinement. Produced from a yield of less than 20 hl/ha
and from some of the estate's oldest vines it is a beguiling example
of sweet fortified Muscat. A small quantity of a very late-harvested
white is also produced. This Muscat Passerillé Vendange d'Octobre
is simply labelled Vin de France. Produced from a microscopic yield
of barely 6 hl/ha from both botrytis-affected and very late-harvested
grapes it is aged solely in new oak. (DM)
Recommended Whites:
Muscat de Lunel Clos Bellevue ★★★☆ £D
Muscat de Lunel Lacoste ★★☆ £C

Dom. Lacroix Vanel (Languedoc)
Fine, newly established small domaine with just over 8 ha of
Grenache, Syrah, Carignan and Cinsault and a tiny holding of
Grenache Blanc near Pezenas. Two reds are produced at present. The
Clos Fine Amor is soft, round and forward: an immediately appealing
red. The Clos Melanie is fuller, richer and more opulent. Principally
from Syrah, with Grenache and old-vine Carignan, the wine is a
full, rich, fleshy and quite extracted style with sufficiently firm and
supple tannins to develop in the short term. Both wines will drink
well young. (DM)
Recommended Reds:
Languedoc Clos Mélanie ★★★ £D
Languedoc Clos Fine Amor ★★☆ £C

>> Dom. La Grange (Languedoc) *www.domaine-lagrange.com*
The cru village of Pézenas has fast established itself as one of the
better areas of the Languedoc with a number of very good terroirs.
Rolf and Renate Freund purchased Domaine La Grange in 2007 and
in a short period they are now producing classy, well-made wines
that nevertheless have a real sense of place. The Mediterranean
climate is moderated by fresh breezes from the Cévennes and
garrigue bushes run alongside the vineyard. There are three small
ranges produced. Castalides is the label for the top three reds. A
Réserve and Icône are also made. Édition comes from Syrah and
Grenache. Warm rich and spicy with a ripe, dark fruited Syrah
character and a hint of herb spice. Enjoy this over the next five years
or so. (DM)
Recommended Reds:
Laguedoc-Pézenas Castalides Édition ★★★★ £E

La Grange de Quatre Sous (IGP d'Oc)
The first vineyards at this property were established in the early
1980s and the age of the vines is beginning to show through in
the quality of the wines. The holding is small with 6ha of red and
just 2ha of white varieties. The viticultural approach is essentially
organic and no herbicides are used. As well as the Jeu du Mail, a
little Chardonnay is also made. Jeu du Mail is an aromatic blend of
Viognier and Marsanne, lent additional structure from ageing in oak.
Les Serrottes is a southern-style blend of Syrah and Malbec, whereas
the Lo Molin is a fine and elegant Bordeaux blend of Cabernet
Sauvignon and Cabernet Franc. Both reds will evolve well with 3 or 4
years' age. (DM)
Recommended Reds:
IGP d'Oc Lo Molin ★★★ £C IGP d'Oc Les Serrottes ★★★ £C
IGP d'Oc Jeu du Mail ★★ £B

Dom. La Madura (Saint-Chinian) *www.lamadura.com*
The Bourgnes come from Bordeaux and some of the characteristics
of the modern new wave styles from there are apparent in their
Saint Chinian reds. As well as the reds profiled here they also

produce two white IGP wines both from Sauvignon Blanc. There is a tank fermented Classic and barrel fermented and aged Grand Vin. Both are likely to be well worth searching out. Red though is the mainstay. Of the 14 ha or so they now possess, just over 13 ha is AOC Saint-Chinian. The vineyards are spread across a number of plots and in a mix of schist and clay/limestone soils. They are planted at altitudes ranging from 150 to 300 metres, aiding the development of acidity in the grapes during the warm summers. Both reds are blends of Mourvèdre, Syrah, Carignan and Grenache with a higher proportion of the first two in the Grand Vin. The Classic is more obviously fruit driven in style but possesses the classic spicy, mineral character of the appellation. The Grand Vin is richer and fatter, being aged in oak, some new and with malolactic in barrel and micro-oxygenation used to soften the wine's tannins. Both are bottled unfined and unfiltered and while they will drink well young, they will also benefit from four or five years ageing. (DM)

Recommended Reds:
Saint-Chinian Grand Vin ★★★☆ £D
Saint-Chinian Classic ★★★ £C

Dom. La Maurerie (Saint-Chinian) *www.maurerie.com*
The Depaule family have been *vignerons* at Saint-Chinian for around 200 years. As well as their excellent-value AC red they also make a soft and juicy bag-in-box wine, which is an excellent alternative to many of the often depressingly flavourless, slightly sweet and confected offerings from the big brands. The Esprit du Terroir is a blend of Syrah, Grenache and Carignan. The wine is aged for one year in used small oak and is soft, vibrant and immediately accessible. Dark red berry fruit, spicy undertones and the characteristic minerality of the appellation are all apparent. An old vines bottling is a blend of Syrah and Grenache. (DM)

Recommended Reds:
Saint-Chinian Esprit du Terroir ★★☆ £B

✿ La Pèira (Languedoc) *www.la-peira.com*
This is a significant new name, founded in 2004, for really top quality Languedoc reds. The domaine vineyards are located in the Terrasses du Larzac sub-region and are planted on gravely, limestone free-draining soils at the foot of the Larzac plateau. The approach to viticulture and vinification respectively is rigorous control of yields and non-intervention. As well as the magnificent La Pèira En Damaisela red covered below, the domaine also produces two other reds; a second wine Las Flors de la Pèira, a blend of Syrah, Grenache and Mourvèdre aged in small oak as well as the much cheaper (well relatively) Les Obriers de la Pèira. This is an unusual blend of just Carignan and Cinsault. The sole white, Deusyls de la Pèira comes from a blend of roughly two-thirds, one third Viognier and Roussanne. It is aged for up to two years in oak on lees. The crowning glory though is the top red which is also one of the most expensive from the Midi, La Pèira En Damaisela. Perhaps its no surprise that MAS DE DAUMAS GASSAC and GRANGES DES PÈRES are nearby. This is an immensely rich and extracted red but with a fine balance as well. The wine is fermented at medium/high temperature 28-30º C and is macerated on skins for anything from six to eight weeks. Individual plots are separately vinified and additional extraction is kept to a minimum with limited *pigéage*. As you would expect the wine is bottled unfiltered and unfined. (DM)

Recommended Reds:
Languedoc Terrasses du Larzac La Pèira ✪✪✪✪✪ £G
Languedoc Terrasses du Larzac Obriers de la Pèira ★★★★ £F
Languedoc Terrasses du Larzac Las Flors de la Pèira ★★★★ £E

Recommended Whites:
Languedoc Terrasses du Larzac La Pèira ★★★★★ £F
IGP de L'Herault Deusylys ★★★★ £F

La Regalona (Cabardès)
This tiny new operation of just 2 ha was established in 1999, the same year the region of Cabardès itself became AC. The two partners have plantings of Syrah, Merlot and Cabernet Sauvignon. Yields are kept below 30hl/ha, which is helped by carrying out a green harvest. Winemaking is modern with pre-fermentation cold maceration of the fruit to extract colour. The fruit is all destemmed and the varieties are vinified and aged separately. Both *pigéage* and *remontage* are employed during a 30-day vatting. Malolactic is carried out in barrel, new and one-year-old, and the wine is aged in wood for 15–18 months. (DM)

Recommended Reds:
Cabardès La Regalona ★★★☆ £D

La Sauvageonne (Languedoc) *www.gerard-bertrand.com*
This property is situated in the heart of the Terrasses du Larzac in the Languedoc with vineyards planted at an altitude of 150 to 400m above sea level, the higher slopes on very well drained schist. It is now a part of the Gerard Bertrand group. Minimal intervention is the approach here, with the wines moved as much as possible by gravity. The Grand Vin white gets a period in small barrels to add substance to the blend of Grenache blanc, Vermentino and Viognier. The rosé GMW is loaded with bright strawberry fruit. The reds all combine Syrah and Grenache. The fresh, attractive and lightly mineral Les Ruffes is the softest of the trio. This is fermented cool to lift its bright fruit. More serious is the finely structured Pica Broca. It is aged predominantly in oak with the balance in tank. The top red Le Grand Vin is impressively structured with supple well-honed tannins. The wine is vinified with part whole bunches and ageing is for 12 months in small barrels. Rich, full and concentrated with impressively dense blackberry fruit, expect this to benefit from 5 years' ageing. (DM)

Recommended Reds:
Languedoc Terrasses du Larzac Grand Vin ★★★☆ £E
Languedoc Pica Broca ★★★ £C
Languedoc Les Ruffes ★★☆ £C
Recommended Whites:
Languedoc Grand Vin ★★★☆ £D
Recommended Rosés:
Languedoc GMW ★★ £B

✿ Dom. La Terrasse d'Elise (IGP de l'Hérault)
Xavier Braucol established his small domaine in 1998 and although most of his vineyards are within the Languedoc appellation they are all classified as IGP. He feels this enables him to best express the character of his *terroir* in his chosen blends. His approach in both vineyard and cellar is as natural as possible. Pesticides are avoided and vine and soil treatments kept to a minimum. Re-planting is always by *sélection massale* and yields are typically kept to 25 hl/ha or lower. Sulphur is used sparingly during vinification and fining and filtration eschewed. The white Le Puech is one of the best Chardonnays in the Midi, barrel-fermented and aged it is richly textured with impressive depth and a creamy complexity. The dark, spicy and very characterful Le Pigeonnier is mainly Carignan, gaining weight from ageing in older oak. La Pradel is a real rarity, a 100% Cinsault; it is barrel-aged and offers a marvellously complex strawberry fruited intensity. Best of the southern styled wines is the

Languedoc

Cuvée Elise from Syrah with around a third Mourvèdre. Rich and impressively concentrated this is again aged in used oak but for longer (24 months). The Mas de Blanc doesn't quite hit the heights of the other reds. Solely from Merlot, its dark earthy, plummy fruit nevertheless outshines many an offering from Bordeaux's Right Bank. (DM)

Recommended Reds:

IGP de l'Hérault Cuvée Elise ★★★★ £E

IGP de l'Hérault La Pradel ★★★★ £E

IGP de l'Hérault Mas de Blanc ★★★☆ £E

IGP de l'Hérault Le Pigeonnier ★★★☆ £D

Recommended Whites:

IGP de l'Hérault Le Puech ★★★☆ £E

Dom. La Tour Boisée (Minervois) www.domainelatourboisee.com

This is among the very best estates in Minervois, producing wines of density and real class. Production is sizeable for the appellation at 40,000 cases a year from 80ha of estate vineyards. In addition to the top Minervois labels there is some decent regular white and rosé Minervois as well as Merlot, Cabernet Sauvignon and Chardonnay IGP d'Oc and a straightforward range of wines under the Domaine de Subremont label. The white Minervois Marie-Claude is dominated by Marsanne, with some Maccabeo and a little Muscat adding a touch of perfume to the wine's youthful oak. The regular red Minervois is a blend of Carignan, Grenache, Syrah and Cinsault. Fully destemmed prior to fermentation it is soft and rounded with lively blackberry fruit. The top Minervois cuvées are more seriously structured. Marie-Claude blends Syrah with Grenache and Carignan; Marielle et Frédérique adds in some Mourvèdre. Marie-Claude is a little firmer with some press wine and a touch of oak. The top wine Jardin Secret is an opulently rich Grenache aged in new oak. Expect all the top reds to develop well with short to mid-term ageing. The range is now completed by the 1905, which is produced from some of the very oldest vines in the appellation. (DM)

Recommended Reds:

Minervois Jardin Secret ★★★☆ £E

Minervois Marielle et Frédérique ★★★ £D

Minervois La Marie-Claude ★★★ £C

Minervois La Marie-Claude ★★ £B

Recommended Whites:

Minervois La Marie-Claude ★★☆ £C

✿ Dom. Le Conte de Floris www.domainelecontedesfloris.com

Fewer than 2,000 cases are made at this tiny Languedoc domaine with a total of just 7.5 ha under vine. However, this is one of the most exciting sources you will find from this often overlooked region. Red inevitably is king here with over 5 ha planted to those varieties and there are three cuvées: Six Rats, Villafranchien and the top wine Carbonifère, all taking the Languedoc appellation. Six Rats is a blend of Syrah, Grenache and Carignan. Villafranchien by contrast is dominated by Grenache, with a smattering of Syrah and Carignan adding a little structure. The Carbonifère is mainly Syrah, with a touch of Grenache and Carignan. While new small oak is avoided here, the preference being for one to two year old *barriques*, Carbonifère is part aged in larger new *demi-muids* adding to the richness of the wines texture and softening the Syrah. While the reds are themselves regional benchmarks, it is perhaps the whites that stand out most. The rich but approachable Arès is mainly Marsanne. Immensely characterful, both the top two wines are dominated by the rare Carignan Blanc and Daniel is a champion of both red and white versions of the variety. Lune Blanche includes a small

pot-pourri of additional varieties, among them Grenache Blanc, Roussanne and Marsanne as does Lune Rousse. Both wines are barrel-fermented, Lune Rousse seeing just a touch more new wood, albeit not a lot. The small range is rounded out with two excellent late-harvest wines. Unusually they blend both red and white grapes with the Cartagene Rouge spending four years in cask as opposed to two for the Noire. Expect all the wines to benefit from a little age, Carbonifère will improve for a decade and more. (DM)

Recommended Reds:

Languedoc Carbonifère ★★★★ £E

Languedoc Villafranchien ★★★☆ £E

Cartagène Noire ★★★☆ £E

Cartagène Rouge ★★★☆ £E

Recommended Whites:

Languedoc Lune Blanche ★★★★ £E

Languedoc Lune Rousse ★★★★ £E

Languedoc Arès ★★★☆ £D

✿ Les Clos Perdus (Corbières) www.lesclosperdus.com

This is a small Corbières property recently established by Englishmen Hugo Stewart and Paul Old. They now produce five very characterful reds with a very pure mineral intensity. Yields are carefully kept in check and leaf thinning is practiced throughout the growing season. The softest of the wines is the approachable Le Rouge, a blend of Mourvèdre and Grenache. A touch more concentrated is the Prioundo from stony soils, a blend of Grenache, Cinsault and Mourvèdre. The wine is given a three day cold soak and then fermentation and maceration on skins for up to three weeks. Ageing is in stainless steel vats, it is supple, finely structured and full of dark, spicy berry fruit. The Cuvée which is renumbered each vintage, is a variable blend with Mourvèdre, Grenache and Carignan and is richer and fuller than the Prioundo, with very good ripe fruit. The Mire La Mer is a more structured red although from the same grapes as the top red L'Extreme. This comes very low yielding vines planted on well-drained schistous soils near Maury. Grenache is blended with Syrah and Mourvèdre. To emphasise the rich, dark-berry fruit the wine gets a 6-day cold maceration before fermentation. Half the wine is fermented in small new oak on skins and half conventionally in stainless steel vats. Rich, gamey and impressively complex with a marked old-vine character and a hint of youthful oak, this is sufficiently supple and opulent to drink well with 2-3 years' ageing. Le Rosé has a big proportion of Mourvèdre and should work well with food. There is a characterful white Le Blanc from 60 year old Macabeo adding to the wine's depth as well as a tiny amount of a white L'Extreme is also being made from over 100 year old Grenache Gris and Blanc vines close to Maury. (DM)

Recommended Reds:

IGP des Côtes Catalanes L'Extreme ★★★★☆ £E

Corbières Mire La Mer ★★★★ £D   Corbières Cuvée ★★★ £C

Corbières Prioundo ★★★ £C   Corbières Le Rouge ★★☆ £B

Recommended Whites:

IGP des Côtes Catalanes L'Extreme ★★★★ £E

IGP des Côtes Catalanes Le Blanc ★★☆ £B

Recommended Rosés:

Corbières Le Rosé ★★☆ £B

Dom. Les Creisses (IGP de l'Hérault) www.les-creisses.com

Recently established domaine just outside the village of Valros, inland to the north-east of Béziers. Just two reds are produced here. The regular Domaine Les Creisses bottling is a blend of Syrah, Grenache and Cabernet Sauvignon. Produced from grapes grown in

calcareous soils, the wine has excellent definition and structure with just a slight raw edge to its youthful tannin. It will be better with 2 or 3 years' ageing. Les Brunes is a step up in quality and has a price tag to match. This richly textured dense, and cedary blend of Cabernet Sauvignon, Mourvèdre and Syrah should age well. Great potential here. (DM)

Recommended Reds:
IGP d'Oc Les Brunes ★★★☆ £E IGP d'Oc Les Creisses ★★★ £D

Dom. Les Grandes Costes (Languedoc) *www.grandes-costes.com*
Jean-Christophe Graniers small 15 ha property is based at Vacquières to the north-east of Pic Saint-Loup on the northern slopes of the vast Languedoc AOC. The vineyards are planted to red and white varieties and he produces some serious examples of the appellation as well as soft fruit-driven red and rosé Musardises. Two approachable and forward styles are also made under the IGP Saint-Guilhem-Le-Désert Mas Canail banner, in both red and white. Although the property has been family owned since 1868, Jean-Christophe only began winegrowing in 2000. *Argile* and calcareous soils provide an excellent base for cultivating naturally low-yielding Syrah, Grenache, Cinsault and Carignan. The climate is both Mediterranean and sufficiently inland to have a slightly continental influence. Jean-Christophe feels this provides just the right conditions to enable perfect phenolic maturity in his grapes. His top reds are indeed all impressive examples of the appellation. Vinification is traditional, although the grapes are all fully de-stemmed. *Remontage, délestage* and *pigéage* are all employed to optimise extraction during fermentation. Sarabande blends roughly equal amounts of Cinsault, Grenache, Carignan and Syrah. Aged in *cuve* for six months this is softly structured with a sufficiently firm backbone to enable its bright dark-berry and herb-scented fruit to gain additional complexity with 3 or 4 years' ageing. Les Grandes Costes is AOC Pic Saint Loup, a blend of Syrah, Grenache and Cinsault. Low yields of between 25 and 30hl/ha and ageing in 50% new French oak provides a smoky, dark berry laden red of impressive depth and substance. Particularly characterful is the top wine Les Sept Rangées which is dominated by old-vine Grenache with the balance from Syrah. A combination of a yield of less than 20hl/ha, 48 hours cold soaking prior to fermentation, and ageing in 100% new French oak serve to further enhance the wine's old-vine complexity. It is likely to continue to improve for up to a decade and demands cellaring for three or four years to pull the oak fully into balance. (DM)

Recommended Reds:
Languedoc Les Sept Rangées ★★★☆ £E
Languedoc Pic Saint Loup Les Grandes Costes ★★★ £C
Languedoc Sarabande ★★☆ £C Languedoc Musardises ★★ £B
Recommended Rosés:
Languedoc Pic Saint Loup Musardises ★☆ £B

✿ Dom. de La Marfée (Languedoc) *www.la-marfee.com*
Very small new property: the first vintage was in 1997, with just 6 ha of vines. The wines are sturdy, powerful and extracted but balanced in style, with a really characterful, almost earthy component. There is no doubt that there is real depth and power and an absolute commitment to quality here and the tannin now plays a less significant role than a few years ago. Les Champs Murmurés is a southern Rhône-style blend comprising roughly equal proportions of Syrah and Mourvèdre and from a yield of just 20hl/ha. Les Vignes qu'on Abat is not produced every year and is a striking example of the potential quality of very low yielding old Carignan.

Della Francesca, by contrast, is a red dominated by Mourvèdre. A wonderfully rich, complex white is also now offered, Frisson d'Ombelles, which comes from a similarly meagre yield to Les Champs Murmurés. A blend of 70/30 Roussanne and Chardonnay this is fermented and raised in *barriques* for 18 months with 50% new wood all seamlessly integrated. Les Gamines is a more immediately accessible fruit driven style, which blends Mourvèdre with Syrah and a little Grenache. (DM)

Recommended Reds:
Languedoc Les Champs Murmurés ★★★★ £E
Languedoc Della Francesca ★★★★ £E
Languedoc Les Vignes qu'on Abat ★★★☆ £D
Languedoc Les Gamines ★★★ £C
Recommended Whites:
IGP de l'Hérault Frissons d'Ombelles ★★★★ £E

Dom. Maria Fita (Fitou) *www.mariafita.com*
The Schmitts produce one of the finest examples of the Languedoc's oldest established appellation, along with an exuberant younger vine IGP and a very good white from low yields. The latter is classified only as Vin de France and comes from Grenache Gris, Grenache Blanc and a little Maccabeu. The vines are now over 35 years old and planted in calcareous and schistous soils. From a yield of just 20 hl/ha the wine is part barrel-fermented and aged on lees and is bottled without fining or filtration. Rich, nutty and spicy the Grenache fruit character is not unlike a good white Châteauneuf-du-Pape, with sufficient refreshing acidity in the background. The IGP Le Schmitou comes from young vines. A blend of Grenache, Cinsault, Syrah and Carignan it is partly vinified by carbonic maceration and aged in *cuve*. As with all the wines here it is bottled without fining or filtration. The dense and concentrated Fitou bottling comes from a similar yield, just 25hl/ha and also gets some carbonic maceration as well. The vines though, which are between 25 and 100 years of age, together with ageing in a mix of *cuve* and old as well as new small oak, gives the wine altogether greater density and structure. Expect it to continue to improve over 5 years or more. (DM)

Recommended Reds:
Fitou ★★★☆ £E
IGP de la Vallee du Paradis Le Schmitou ★★☆ £C
Recommended Whites:
Vin de France ★★★ £D

Mas des Brousses (Languedoc)
This couple make a Languedoc red of impressive potential and real style. Xavier, who looks after the winemaking, is the grandson of Lucien Peyraud of the Peyraud family of Domaine TEMPIER in Bandol (see Provence and Corsica). The vineyards are tended organically and an absolute minimum of sulphur dioxide is employed during vinification. As well as the impressively dense and concentrated Languedoc a IGP d'Oc red is also produced from Merlot, Grenache and a little Cinsault. (DM)

Recommended Reds:
Languedoc ★★★ £D

Mas Bruguière (Languedoc) *www.mas-bruguiere.com*
Guilhem Bruguière is one of the best producers in the Pic Saint-Loup subregion. This is a small property of around 20 ha spread across three separate vineyards. Syrah, Grenache and Mourvèdre are grown, along with Roussanne for the white Les Muriers; a nutty, floral, medium-weight spicy white. The basic Cuvée Calcadiz is well

France

priced but can be raw with some aggressive green notes creeping through. L'Arbouse though is round, suppler and fuller while the flagship La Grenadière is a blockbuster red: spicy and dense, with a solid chunk of vanilla oak. The top wine will keep well over 5 or 6 years. (DM)

Recommended Reds:
Languedoc Pic Saint-Loup La Grenadière ★★★☆ £D
Languedoc Pic Saint-Loup L'Arbouse ★★☆ £C
Languedoc Pic Saint-Loup Cuvée Calcadiz ★★☆ £C
Languedoc Pic Saint -Loup Les Mûriers ★★☆ £C

Mas Cal Demoura (Languedoc) www.caldemoura.com
Three good to very good reds and a simple, vibrant, berry-fruited rosé are produced here from red varieties. New is a white IGP bottling, L'Etincelle, which comes from Chenin Blanc, Grenache Blanc, Roussanne, Viognier, Muscat and Petit Manseng. It is the cuvée L'Infidèle, though, that is the serious business, a blend of Syrah, Mourvèdre, Grenache, Cinsault and Carignan, of which the Syrah, Grenache and Mourvèdre see some new oak during the 12 months of ageing. The wine is full and rich with supple tannins and real depth. Les Combariolles also impresses it is a spicy, complex blend of Syrah, Grenache and Mourvèdre, while a further red Feu Sacré is dominated by Grenache. (DM)

Recommended Reds:
Languedoc L'Infidèle ★★★☆ £E
Languedoc Les Combariolles ★★★ £C

Recommended Whites:
IGP de l'Herault L'Etincelle ★★☆ £C

Recommended Rosés:
Languedoc Qu'es Aquo ★★ £B

Mas Champart (Saint-Chinian)
There are now 16 ha planted at this fine Saint-Chinian property where the Champarts produce a fruity rosé and a rich, lightly oaked white from Roussanne, Marsanne, Viognier, Bourboulenc and Grenache, as well as four reds. Up until 1988 they sold their crop to the local co-op and a small proportion of the harvest is still sold on. The reds are blends of different terroirs across the property. The wines are only lightly fined with egg whites and the top two labels are bottled without filtration. The IGP d'Oc is an unusual blend of largely Cabernet Franc with the balance Syrah. It is lightly leafy with attractive ripe berry fruit. The brambly, forward Côte d'Arbo comprises Syrah, old vine Carignan, young Grenache and a tiny amount of Graciano. The leading two wines are more serious and firmly structured. Causse du Bouquet blends Syrah with Mourvèdre, Grenache and, in certain vintages, some Carignan. It is aged for a year in barrel and then 6 months in vat. The impressively dense and concentrated Clos de la Simonette is mainly Mourvèdre with some Grenache. It is aged in oak, some new, for around 18 months. Clos de la Simonette and Causse Bousque will both develop well for up to a decade. (DM)

Recommended Reds:
Saint-Chinian Clos de La Simonette ★★★☆ £D
Saint-Chinian Causse de Bousque ★★★ £C
Saint-Chinian Côte d'Arbo ★★☆ £C   IGP d'Oc ★☆ £C

Mas Conscience (Languedoc)
This is a very impressive new source of top class Languedoc red. 10 ha is planted in calcareous soils to mainly Carignan and lesser amounts of Grenache and Syrah. The domaine also has one and half hectares of white Rolle, Roussanne and Viognier planted, which

goes towards a floral, honeyed and lightly mineral white, L'In. The domaine is situated in the Terrasses de Larzac just over 30 km northwest of Montpelier. The vines are of some age, up to 55 years and the vineyard tended naturally and the Vidals are considering converting to biodynamic farming practices. Le Cas is from 100% old Carignan, which is why it is IGP. It is really dark, spicy and characterful. L'As is a modern Languedoc style, a blend of Syrah and Grenache, with just a touch of Carignan. It offers better elegance and balance than many other examples of the appellation and is not overblown with new oak. (DM)

Recommended Reds:
Languedoc L'As ★★★☆ £D
IGP de l'Hérault Le Cas ★★★ £C

Recommended Whites:
IGP de l'Hérault L'In ★★☆ £C

Mas de Cynanque (Saint-Chinian) www.masdecynanque.com
This small domaine has 12 ha under vine, just 1 hectare of which is planted to white varieties, Roussanne, Grenache and Vermentino. The sustainably farmed vineyards are in the heart of the visually stunning Saint-Chinian appellation and planted on a south-facing hillside on clay-limestone soils. There are three very good Saint-Chinian reds and a vibrant approachable rosé, Fleur de Cynanque. Whites include an excellent Saint-Chinian, Althea which offers intense hints of grapefruits with a pronounced mineral backbone, and a IGP doux style, Hespérides. The reds though are the core of the domaine. The Fleur de Cynanque is the softest and most approachable, a blend dominated by dark-fruited nicely ripe Carignan and a little Syrah and Grenache. Plein Gres is firmer and more structured, a blend of Syrah, Carignan and Grenache with some 100-year old Carignan, the wine is aged in vats. The Acutum is from a similar blend, although around 20% Mourvèdre is included and it is a touch more opulent and expressive, right on the cusp of ★★★★ in top years. Nominaris is a sturdy vin de garde of impressive depth and dominated by Syrah. Yields are very low at 20 hl/ha and the wine is nicely balanced with just a part being aged in smaller barrels. The top reds get at least three weeks maceration on skins but a gentle extraction of fruit and tannin is achieved with pigéage rather than pumping over. The resulting wines are full of character and have a classic underlying mineral intensity. (DM)

Recommended Reds:
Saint Chinian Nominaris ★★★☆ £D
Saint Chinian Acutum ★★★ £C
Saint Chinian Plein Grès ★★★ £C
Saint Chinian Fleur de Cynanque ★★☆ £B

Recommended Whites:
Saint Chinian Althea ★★★ £C

Recommended Rosés:
Saint Chinian Fleur de Cynanque ★★ £B

❀ Mas de Daumas Gassac www.daumas-gassac.com
Undoubtedly the most famous property in the Midi and the inspiration for the many high-quality winemakers now spread throughout Languedoc and Roussillon. Based in the IGP de l'Hérault there are some 37 ha of red varieties and 13 ha of white. The vineyard potential here in the upper Gassac Valley was discovered in 1970. The key is soil that is mineral-rich, superbly drained and that stresses the vines just sufficiently to produce grapes of remarkable flavour, the key to all great wine. The red is a dense and immensely powerful but refined blend of mainly Cabernet Sauvignon blended with a plethora of other varieties. Very backward and even austere

when young this is best left for a decade or more. The white is an intense, nutty, complex blend dominated by Viognier, Petit Manseng and Chardonnay. Finely structured with a piercing mineral core the wine needs 3 or 4 years and will keep comfortably for a great deal longer. A small amount of a limited red cuvée Exception is also made. Aimé Guibert also produces an additional and now extensive range of wines under the Moulin de Gassac label. The Cuvée Elise is a structured and firm blend of Syrah and Merlot, the Eraus is a crisp and fresh Sauvignon Blanc. (DM)

Recommended Reds:
IGP de l'Hérault Mas de Daumas Gassac ★★★★☆ £F
IGP de l'Hérault Moulin de Gassac Elise ★★★ £C

Recommended Whites:
IGP de l'Hérault Mas de Daumas Gassac ★★★★★ £F
IGP de l'Hérault Moulin de Gassac Eraus ★★ £B

Mas d'Espanet (IGP d'Oc) *www.masdespanet.com*

The 20 ha Armand property is located just inland between Picpoul de Pinet and Nîmes. Production is spread across two reds, three whites and a rosé, all of which take the IGP d'Oc classification. The white Eolienne is a barrel-fermented blend of Grenache Blanc, Picpoul and Viognier. The vines are grown in calcareous soils and from a yield of just 25 hl/ha the wine has a fine nutty intensity and is best enjoyed quite young. Freesia is an exuberant, fruit-driven blend of Cinsault and Grenache. It displays a marvellous pure strawberry character and will drink well over 3–4 years. The top red, Eolienne, is an oak-aged red. The blend includes Grenache, Syrah and Carignan providing a real black pepper and spice character. It is an impressive wine with complexity, a fine balance of dark berry fruit and herbs, subtly oaked with a supple tannic structure. The Carignan adds a greater depth to the wine. (DM)

Recommended Reds:
IGP d'Oc Eolienne ★★★ £D   IGP d'Oc Freesia ★★ £C

Recommended Whites:
IGP d'Oc Eolienne ★★☆ £C

❀ Mas de L'Ecriture (Languedoc) *www.masdelecriture.fr*

This exceptional domaine is located in the commune of Jonquières, the vineyards are planted on elevated limestone and gravel terraces providing the property with an excellent *terroir*. Yields are purposely restricted below 20 hl/ha and both leaf thinning and a limited green harvest are carried out to optimise the balance of the vineyard. Three wines are now produced. A soft, supple altogether more fruit driven style than its stablemates, Emotion Occitane blends Carignan, Grenache, Cinsaut and Syrah. Les Pensées is the more approachable and forward of the other two reds. It is a blend of Grenache, with smaller proportions of, Syrah, Cinsault and Carignan. L'Ecriture is a denser, firmer blend of mainly Syrah with some Grenache and Mourvèdre. Both the top wines are given a lengthy vatting and aged in new and one-year old oak of differing sizes for up to 12 months. The wines complete their *élevage* in *cuve* for a further 3 months before final blending. Fining and filtration is avoided. Both Les Pensees and L'Ecriture will age well, the latter gaining further complexity for up to a decade. (DM)

Recommended Reds:
Languedoc L'Ecriture ★★★★ £E
Languedoc Les Pensées ★★★☆ £E
Languedoc Emotion Occitane ★★☆ £C

Mas Foulaquier (Languedoc) *www.masfoulaquier.com*

Another top-quality small Languedoc producer with 8ha planted

to Syrah, Carignan and Grenache. The operation is very new with the first vintage emerging in 1999. Swiss winemaker Pierre Jequier makes wines, which are richly concentrated and well crafted with great fruit definition and purity. They are marked by the composition of their blends. L'Orphée is approachable and is a 50/50 Syrah/Grenache blend, with powerful scents of ripe berries and spice. Le Rollier is dominated by Grenache and is full of licorice and dark cherry character. Les Calades is mainly Syrah with a touch of oak ageing, it is the most firmly structured of this trio, it needs a minimum of 4–5 years to evolve. The wine has a marvellous mineral purity. Handling is kept to a minimum and inevitably filtration avoided. Among four additional reds Gran'T is a blend of Grenache and Carignan, Les Tonillières Syrah and Carignan, Le Petit Duc is 100% Grenache and Le Violetta is a Vin de France blend of the three estate red grapes. A rosé, Le Rosé, which comes from Grenache, is also made. (DM)

Recommended Reds:
Languedoc Pic Saint-Loup Les Calades ★★★★ £E
Languedoc Pic Saint-Loup Le Rollier ★★★ £D
Languedoc Pic Saint-Loup L'Orphée ★★★ £C

Mas de Fournel (Languedoc Pic Saint-Loup)

The wines have only been bottled here since 1997 but are among the more striking examples in Pic Saint-Loup. The soils are a combination of gravel/pebbles and some clay/limestone particularly suitable for Syrah. There are just 8 ha and only 3 ha of Syrah and some old Grenache vines are currently in production, with 5 ha having recently been replanted with Syrah and Grenache as well as Mourvèdre. Harvesting is by parcel rather than by variety to ensure maximum ripeness and all the fruit is destemmed before fermentation. The Pic Saint-Loup is 70% Syrah and 30% Grenache, ripe and supple with richly concentrated dark berry, mint, herb and spice-scented fruit and a sufficiently firm structure to suggest further development with 4 or 5 years in bottle. The Cuvée Pierre is a post-fermentation vat selection aged in small oak, a proportion of it new, and adds some rich creamy vanilla notes to the excellent fruit of the regular bottling. A third red, Nombre d'Argent, comes from Mourvèdre. (DM)

Recommended Reds:
Languedoc Pierre ★★★ £D   Languedoc ★★☆ £C

>> Mas Gabinèle (Faugères) *www.masgabinele.com*

This is a small Faugères domaine. Owner Thierry Rodriguez makes an excellent range of modern reds and whites. He has 18 hectares of vines planted in schistous soils producing reds from the appellation. He also makes a very attractive IGP de l'Hérault Tradition from 50-year-old Grenache Gris, full of nutty, citrus herb scented fruit with a rich, viscous texture. It is vinified in a mix of *inox* and new wood. The reds are manually harvested over a period of two to three weeks with several *tris*. The Tradition is full of character, black fruits and pepper as well as a herb spiced undercurrent coming from a blend of Syrah, Grenache and Carignan. After an extended vatting of up to a month the wine is aged in barrel, around a quarter new to balance fruit and oak. Of the top two reds the Faugères Inaccessible is by far the most expensive wine. Coming from a blend dominated by Mourvèdre, the wine, aged in new barrels for 16 months, reflects its name and is as yet very young and needs at least three years further cellaring after release. For early drinking the Faugères Rarissime is the more enjoyable and approachable wine, coming from a blend of Syrah, Grenache and a little Mourvèdre. It has attractive dark, spicy fruits and a supple structure with well-balanced tannins. Two

further ranges (not tasted) are made under the Prieuré Saint Server banner, Cuvées Terroir, sourced as the label states from specific *terroirs* and Cuvées Famille, which are IGP d'Oc from Syrah, Merlot, Cabernet Sauvignon and Chardonnay. (DM)

Recommended Reds:

Faugères Inaccessible ★★★★ £G
Faugères Rarissime ★★★★ £E
Faugères Tradition ★★★☆ £D

Recommended Whites:

IGP de l'Hérault Grenache Gris ★★★ £C

Mas Haut Buis (Languedoc) *www.mashautbuis.com*
The production at Olivier Jeantet's property is small and the domaine consists of 11 ha planted mainly to red varieties ranging from around 40 to over 100 year old Carignan some pre-phylloxera. The top red Costa Caoude is a blend of Grenache and Carignan, partly aged in *demi-muids* and partly in *foudres* for up to 24 months. Deep, dense and powerful but with well-judged oak and supple, well-rounded tannins, this is balanced and impressively refined. Two more approachable reds are also now made. Carlines blends Grenache, Carignan and Syrah, while Gloglou is a varietal Syrah. A white, Agrunelles is a combination of barrel aged Chardonnay and Roussanne. (DM)

Recommended Reds:

Languedoc Costa Caoude ★★★☆ £E

❀ Mas Jullien (Languedoc)
Olivier Jullien is now long established in the Languedoc. The wine style and indeed the labels have changed over the years. His vineyards are now farmed biodynamically and the oldest vines are over 50 years of age, which will improve his potential further. Two reds and a floral white IGP de l'Hérault are produced and the approach is one of restraint, in quite marked contrast to some of the extracted wines of his neighbours. The top Languedoc is tight and restrained, with a refined, intense mineral quality, whereas the États d'Âme is in a supple and forward more fruit-driven style. The reds, particularly the Languedoc, should age very well. (DM)

Recommended Reds:

Languedoc ★★★★ £E   Languedoc États d'Âme ★★★☆ £E

Recommended Whites:

IGP de l'Hérault ★★★★ £E

Mas Lumen (Languedoc)
A relatively newly established 6 ha domaine planted mainly to Syrah, Carignan and Grenache. There is also half a hectare planted to the white Terret variety, which provides a Vin de France, Orphée. Three reds are now produced, the first vintage being in 2001. The organically handled *terroir* appears to be potentially exceptional and Pascal Perret also believes in minimal handling in the cellar. The wines are rich, concentrated and very pure. Although possessing immediate appeal, the exceptional La Sylve is firm but supple and will develop greater complexity with 5 years or so of cellaring. (DM)

Recommended Reds:

Languedoc La Sylve ★★★☆ £E   Languedoc Orphée ★★★ £C
Languedoc Prelude ★★★ £C

Mas de Mortiès (Languedoc) *www.morties.com*
This is a very good property with some 25 ha under vine in the southern sector of the Pic Saint-Loup sub-region. The estate has been continually improved over recent years with a careful replanting programme to improve quality in the vineyard. A number

of good white as well as vibrant dark and chunky Languedoc reds are produced with a total of 10 wines now offered. Jamais Content is a rich, spicy peppery blend of Syrah and Grenache. The Syrah, Que Sera Sera is bigger and fuller and is first class. A further top flight Syrah, L'opportuniste has been available since 2006. (DM)

Recommended Reds:

Languedoc Pic Saint-Loup Que Sera Sera ★★★☆ £E
Languedoc Pic Saint-Loup Jamais Content ★★★ £D

Mas Mouries (Languedoc) *www.mas-mouries.com*
Fine new property located 25 km north west of Nîmes with organically tended vineyards planted in well-drained calcareous soils. Two red wines are produced, along with a white and a rosé. Mas Mouries Languedoc is a blend of Syrah and Grenache. The varieties are vinified separately before blending and ageing in *cuve*. The fruit is forward and accessible. The top cuvée Les Myrthes, which is aged in part new wood, is again a blend of Syrah and Grenache, with a little Cinsault but at a marginally lower yield – some 25 hl/ha rather than 30. The wine displays excellent black fruits with nicely handled vanilla oak; in short plenty of depth and class. (DM)

Recommended Reds:

Languedoc Les Myrthes ★★★ £D
Languedoc Pic Saint-Loup Jamais Content ★★☆ £C

❀ Mas du Soleilla (Languedoc) *www.mas-du-soleilla.com*
This 22 ha La Clape domaine is mainly planted to red wine grapes with just 3.5 ha of the white grapes Bourboulenc and Roussanne. The vineyard benefits from the moderation of local coastal breezes and is planted on clay, marl and limestone soils which yield a moderate 25 hl/ha on average. Quality is key and all the harvesting is done by hand and the grapes are meticulously sorted prior to vinification. As well as Languedoc red and white, a red IGP "Terre du Vent" comes from a blend of Merlot and Cab Franc. The white Reserve is rich, nutty and full with a hint of oak and well structured with good acidity from a third Bourboulenc in its blend. A second white La Rupture combines a majority of Bourboulenc with Roussanne. Of the reds, Les Chailles is supple and approachable with ripe and spicy dark berry fruit from mainly Grenache, with Syrah adding a little grip. L'Intrus is a characterful blend of old Carignan with Grenache and Syrah. Les Bartelles is firmer and more structured with Syrah the dominant grape with a hint of oak showing through. There is also a small volume of a pricier Languedoc red, the impressive and stylish Clot de l'Armandier which combines Syrah with old Grenache and the malolactic fermentation in new oak. A further red La Clape Réserve is given a similar cellar regime. Chambres d'Hôtes are also available here and the vineyards provide an ideal backdrop for a visit. (DM)

Recommended Reds:

Languedoc La Clape Clot de l'Armandier ★★★★ £E
Languedoc La Clape Les Bartelles ★★★☆ £D
IGP Côteaux Narbonne Terre du Vent ★★★☆ £D
Languedoc La Clape L'Intrus ★★★ £D
Languedoc La Clape Réserve ★★★ £C
Languedoc La Clape Les Chailles ★★☆ £C

Recommended Whites:

Languedoc La Clape Réserve ★★★ £C

Dom. du Méteore (Faugères)
Fine Faugères white as well as red is produced at this small domaine, and a good-quality Viognier is made here too. Three red cuvées are

produced. The Tradition is unoaked, a very classic blend of Syrah, Grenache, Mourvèdre and Carignan. Full of a
dark berry and mineral notes this offers great character and style. Deeper and fuller is the oak aged Les Orionides. Blended from Syrah, Grenache and Mourvèdre, it is more obviously modern and fleshy in style but offers great depth of fruit and perfectly judged spicy, smoky oak. The top red is the ripe, sweet fruited darkly brooding Les Perséides a blend of Strah and Mourvèdre. Both will drink well with 2 or 3 years' age. (DM)

Recommended Reds:
Faugères Les Perséides ★★★☆ £D
Faugères Les Orionides ★★★ £C   Faugères Tradition ★★☆ £C
Recommended Whites:
Faugères Tradition Les Léonides ★★☆ £C

Laurent Miquel (Saint Chinian) *www.laurent-miquel.com*
Large Saint-Chinian based operation producing sturdily traditional Saint-Chinian under the Château Cazal Viel label and a range of mainly varietal IGP d'Oc under the Laurent Miquel label. Of the latter look out for simple, attractively fruity and well-priced Nord Sud Syrah, as well as a Chardonnay/Viognier Père et Fils. Under the Nord Sud brand a Viognier, Syrah Viognier and Syrah Grenache Saint-Chinian are also produced. You can also find Père et Fils Syrah Grenache and Cabernet Syrah reds as well as a rosé Cinsault Syrah. Of a completely different order though is a fine, opulently rich, fleshy and spicy Saint-Chinian, Bardou, sourced from a single block of the finest Syrah on the Cazal Viel estate. This is also joined by IGP Viognier, Verite a selection from the best barrels and one of the better examples outside the Rhône Valley. Bardou is aged in new and one year-old oak, all seamlessly integrated, the wine offers both density and finesse. A Faugères, Saga Pegot is also now made. The Château Cazal Viel Saint-Chinians are more traditional in style, although Syrah is an important component at 65% of the estate vineyards. An old vine rosé and a white Finesse are also made. The Larmes des Fées is dense, structured and capable of developing well in bottle with 5 or more years of age. The best examples of this are right on the cusp of ★★★★. (DM)

Château Cazal Viel
Recommended Reds:
Saint-Chinian Larmes des Fées ★★★☆ £E
Saint-Chinian Cuvée des Fées ★★★ £C
Saint-Chinian Vielles Vignes ★★☆ £C
Recommended Rosés:
Saint Chinian ★★ £B
Laurent Miquel
Recommended Reds:
Saint-Chinian Bardou ★★★☆ £E
IGP d'Oc Syrah Nord Sud ★★ £B
Recommended Whites:
IGP d'Oc Viognier Verite ★★★ £D
IGP d'Oc Chardonnay/Viognier Père et Fils ★☆ £B

✿ Dom. du Montcalmès (Languedoc)
This very impressive new Languedoc red by Frederic Poutalie is produced from a mere 2.8ha. The vineyards are now established by mass-selection and exceptionally well-drained calcareous topsoils with galets roulés provide the base for raw material of outstanding quality. Green harvesting is practiced and yields are resticted to barely more than 20 hl/ha. Two wines are made. A tiny amount of white comes from Marsanne and Roussanne. The red is a dense, fleshy modern blend of Syrah, Grenache and Mourvèdre. In the

winery all operations are carried out by gravity and individual plots are vinified separately. The wine possesses real depth and intensity as well as a piercing mineral purity to its fruit. There is a balance and harmony here so often lacking in the appellation. Deep and concentrated dark berry fruit is subtly underpinned by a grip of creamy new wood and supple, well-rounded tannins. There is no doubt that 5 or so years' patience will provide both weight and additional complexity. (DM)

Recommended Reds:
Languedoc ★★★★ £E

Dom. Guy Moulinier (Saint-Chinian)
Among a wave of new domaines being established, the Moulinier family continue to produce some of the better wines in this potentially great appellation at their new winery completed in 1999. Their 24 ha of vineyards are spread across 3 communes and planted on a mix of clay/limestone, schist and sandstone soils to provide a diverse array of raw material. The bulk of the vineyards are planted at altitudes of 100–200 metres and low yields of 15–25 hl/ha are easy to achieve. The white Viognier is peachy and approachable and a stylish rosé, Saint-Chinian is made from Syrah. Stéphane Moulinier also makes a small range under his own name, including a red Cotes du Rhone. The Tradition, a blend of Grenache, Syrah and Mourvèdre aged in *cuve* is the most accessible of the wines, fruit-driven but traditionally firm. Les Sigillaires, an unusual blend of 70% Mourvèdre with Syrah aged in used barrels, is rich and full of dark, spicy herb-strewn fruit. The top wine Les Terrasses Grillées gets full oak ageing (40% new). A blend of mainly Syrah and a tiny proportion of Grenache and Mourvèdre, it positively demands 5 or so years to pull it all into balance. (DM)

Recommended Reds:
Saint-Chinian Les Terrasses Grillées ★★★☆ £E
Saint-Chinian Les Sigillaires ★★★ £C
Saint-Chinian Tradition ★★☆ £C
Recommended Whites:
IGP Pays d'Oc Viognier ★★ £B
Recommended Rosés:
Saint Chinian ★★ £B

Dom. Thierry Navarre (Saint-Chinian) *www.thierrynavarre.com*
Thierry Navarre took over from his father in the late 1980s and now has 12 ha of biodynamically farmed vines from which he produces two fine Saint-Chinians and a straightforward third wine, a Vin de France called OEillades. His *terroir* is excellent with deep, very well-drained schist soils providing an ideally stressed environment during ripening. A white is also made from Terret Gris as well as a late harvested Grenache and Muscat. The Saint-Chinians are among the more striking wines of the appellation. Le Lazouil is aged in large old vats and is dominated by Carignan with a further 30% of Grenache and 10% of Syrah and others. It is sturdy and characterful with dark and spicy fruit and a hint of minerality. The Olivier, blended from roughly equal parts of Grenache, Syrah and Carignan, is by contrast aged in some new small wood and is rounder and fleshier with impressive depth and intensity. It should develop very well with 3 or 4 years' age. (DM)

Recommended Reds:
Saint-Chinian Olivier ★★★ £C   Saint-Chinian Le Laouzil ★★☆ £C

Dom. de Nizas (Languedoc) *www.domainedenizas.com*
This well-equipped, modern domaine now has over 60 ha under vine. The style is very modern and approachable with temperature

Languedoc

control in the cellars and new-wave techniques including micro-oxygenation used to maximise the fruit-driven character of the wines. The vineyards are run on a sustainable agricultural basis to maximise the potential of the *terroir*. A number of wines are produced. There is a crisp, ripely tropical and nutty white as well as a characterful red IGP old-vine Carignan, the vines for which are over 40 years old. It is particularly fine with rich brambly, mineral fruit. The densely textured Languedoc is not only excellent value but very sound too. It blends Syrah, Mourvèdre and a little Grenache. The intense and characterful top red La Réserve blends Mourvèdre, Grenache and a little Syrah. A Languedoc rosé is soft, forward and fruity and a premium Réserve comes from Pézenas. (DM)

Recommended Reds:
Languedoc-Pézenas La Réserve ★★★☆ £D
IGP Pays de Caux Carignan Vieilles Vignes ★★★ £C
Languedoc ★★★ £C
Recommended Whites:
Languedoc Les Terres Noires ★★ £C
Recommended Rosés:
Languedoc Les Pierres Blanches ★★ £C

◉ Dom. de L'Oustal Blanc (Minervois) *www.oustal-blanc.com*
A range of reds and whites that really extend the benchmarks from this appellation. Because of the vagaries of the AC restrictions three of the wines are simply labelled Vin de France. Most of the 11 odd ha here are spread across Minervois and Minervois La Livinière. There is also just over 1ha in Saint-Chinian. Viticulture is essentially organic, and with vines over 100 years of age in some parcels the potential is immense. Overall yields are very low across the range, barely more than 20hl/ha and a hi-tech approach ensures the fruit is kept very fresh immediately after the harvest. As well as the wines tasted and rated here, there is a fresh fruity rosé Minervois, which is dominated by Carignan and vinified in barrels previously used for the white Naïck. This itself is a richly concentrated full-blown, nutty blend dominated by Grenache Gris, with just 5% of Macabeo to add balance. The reds are variously macerated on skins for between 35 and 60 days. The Cuvée K is a dark, fresh fruity style, a 100% old-vine Carignan. Two-thirds is aged in *cuve*, the balance in used oak giving a little extra structure and depth. The red Naïck is Vin de France due to the Saint-Chinian component. Supple and loaded with bright and spicy fruit the wine is a blend of Cinsault, Carignan, Syrah with the balance Grenache. Not as dark and smoky as the Naïck but offering greater depth and intensity, the Minervois Giocoso is dominated by Grenache with a little Carignan and Syrah. All the vines are old, the Carignan is over 100 years, the Grenache over 70 years, and even the Syrah now 40 years old. Intense, smoky dark fruit is underpinned by a concentrated chocolatey backbone and a firm supple tannic structure. The Syrah and Carignan is aged in new and used small oak. The La Livinière comes from mainly 80 year-old Grenache and a little 100 year-old Carignan. Aged in 500 and 600 litre barrels the wine has marvellous depth and persistence, in part due to a yield of barely 15hl/ha. The Maestoso, originally Vin de France, has taken the Minervois appellation in recent vintages. It comes from a very-low yielding equal blend of Grenache, Syrah and Carignan. Heady, rich, powerful and concentrated, it is aged in small oak. As fewer than 90 cases are produced, it will be difficult to find but as a benchmark for the appellation it will be well worth the search. The top two reds in particular will continue to improve for 12 to 15 years. (DM)

Recommended Reds:
Minervois La Livinière Prima Donna ★★★★ £E
Minervois Maestoso ★★★★ £E   Minervois Giocoso ★★★☆ £D

Vin de France Naïck ★★★ £C   Vin de France K ★★☆ £C
Recommended Whites:
Vin de France Naïck ★★★☆ £D

◉ Dom. de Peyre Rose *www.domaine-peyresroses.com*
This 25 ha property is responsible for two of the most renowned reds in the Languedoc and they certainly have a price tag to match their reputation. The vineyard is planted in ideal sparse, rocky soils and there is a commitment to low-yielding fruit of the highest quality. Of the two reds Clos des Cistes has a hint of Grenache and is the more forward of the two. It is supple and full of piercing spicy, black fruit. Clos Syrah Léone is the more structured, denser, darker and on occasion shows real animal aromas. The wines are certainly very impressive in their youth, although marked by oak and in a full throttle style. A stylish, nutty white is also now produced from Rolle, Roussanne and Viognier. (DM)

Recommended Reds:
Languedoc Clos Syrah Léone ★★★★★ £F
Languedoc Clos de Cistes ★★★★☆ £F

Plan de L'Homme (Languedoc) *www.plandelhomme.fr*
This property, originally called Mas Plan de L'Om was purchased by Rémi Duchemin in mid 2009. Rémi was previously the owner and producer of some very characterful wines at MAS DE MORTIÈS. The property in the Terrasses du Larzac is at the foot of the Larzac plateau with an excellent *terroir* consisting of sandstone, shale and pebble soils. A small range of wines is made using biodynamic farming across three classifications with some increasingly aged vineyards. Syrah is now over 20 years old, Grenache and Carignan over 40 years and Cinsault 50 years. The whites comprise an approachable fruit driven blend dominated by Roussanne with Grenache Blanc, Florès, and a more structured Alpha which is from the same varieties, barrel fermented and aged on lees with the malolactic fermentation blocked for freshness. A Florès red is also made which combines Cinsualt, Grenache and Syrah. A vibrant juicy dark fruited and characterful Carignan was recently added to the range. Both the Terrasses du Larzac reds offer impressive depth. Habilis comes from a blend of Grenache, Syrah and Carignan and is aged in *cuve* for up to 18 months. The top wine, Sapiens is darker fruited and with a touch more concentration. From a combination of Syrah, Grenache and Carignan it is raised in a mix of small barrels (not new) for 12 months and then a further 6 months in *cuve*. Both will continue to develop well over two to three years in bottle. (DM)

Recommended Reds:
Languedoc Terrasses du Larzac Sapiens ★★★☆ £D
Languedoc Terrasses du Larzac Habilis ★★★ £C
Languedoc Florès ★★☆ £B
Vin de France Carignan ★★☆ £B
Recommended Whites:
Languedoc Alpha ★★★ £C
Languedoc Florès ★★ £B

Dom. du Poujol (Languedoc) *www.domainedupoujol.com*
This small domaine situated in the Languedoc was set up in 1994 by Englishman Robert Cripps and his American wife Kim. Prior to establishing their domaine Robert spent five years winemaking in California, culminating as assistant winemaker at the prestigious Sonoma based Peter MICHAEL winery. Kim spent 10 years in winery managementfor the likes of BERINGER and CLOS DU BOIS. They now have a more artisanal existence producing very characterful reds and whites from 10 ha of Languedoc vineyards and a further

8 ha of IGP. They also vinify a dry white Muscat for Mas de Jacquet owner Vincent Salive. Unusually this musky, characterful white was put through its malolactic fermentation, almost unheard of for dry examples of the variety. With a period of pre-fermentation skin contact this provides a wine of good mid-palate weight and attractive forward fruit. A similar approach is made with the Cripps own Pico white which is based on Carignan Blanc and Vermentino. It is also cool-fermented and aged on lees for 5 months with the Vermentino adding a refreshing acidity. The top white, Teras is also dominated by low yielding Vermentino (Rolle) and is blended with Roussanne and old-vine white Carignan. Barrel-fermented and aged, it is full, weighty and nutty with a refreshing citrus and mineral undercurrent. The rosé blends Cinsault, Grenache, Carignan and a tiny amount of Syrah. A small portion is barrel-fermented which adds some weight. Of the reds the softest is the Jazz IGP which blends Grenache, Cinsault and others. More seriously structured are the Podio Alto (Syrah, Mourvèdre, Grenache and Cinsault), La Bête Noir which is a smoky and characterful Bordeaux influenced red with Cabernet Sauvignon blended with Carignan and a small amount of Cinsault. The top red is Grès de Montpellier, a dark smoky, blackberry and spice-scented blend comprised almost entirely of Syrah with just a touch of Grenache. (DM)

Domaine du Poujol
Recommended Reds:
Languedoc Grès de Montpellier ★★★★ £E
Languedoc Grès de Montpellier Podio Alto ★★★ £C
IGP Val de Montferrand La Bête Noir ★★★ £C
IGP de l'Hérault Jazz ★★ £B
Recommended Whites:
IGP de l'Hérault Teras ★★★ £C   IGP de l'Hérault Pico ★★ £B
Recommended Rosés:
IGP de l'Hérault ★☆ £B

Mas de Jacquet
Recommended Whites:
IGP de L'Hérault Muscat ★★☆ £B

● Prieuré de Saint-Jean-de-Bébian www.bebian.com
This has long been one of the esteemed names of the Languedoc but it was only in the past decade or so, under the stewardship of Chantal Lecouty and Jean-Claude Lebrun, that quality was back to where it was in the glory days of the mid- to late 1980s. They have now sold the property but Australian trained winemaker Karen Turner remains. The current bottlings of both red from Syrah, Grenache and Mourvèdre and white from mainly Roussanne are very rich and stylish, the white being a stand out for the area. Chapelle de Bébian, the second wine is lighter but at its best is a classically mineral styled example of the appellation. A particularly fine white in addition to rosé Chapelle bottlings are also now being made as well as a further premium red blend, 1152, which is dominated by Syrah. The small range is completed by a Bordeaux styled red L'Autre Versant and a fruit driven red and white labelled La Croix de Bébian. (DM)

Recommended Reds:
Languedoc ★★★★ £E
Languedoc Chapelle de Bébian ★★★ £D
Recommended Whites:
Languedoc ★★★★ £E   Languedoc Chapelle de Bébian ★★★ £D

● Dom. de Ravanes www.ravanes.com
This small family domaine with 32 ha cultivated is based to the north-west of Béziers in the IGP des Côteaux de Murviel. Unusually they have a substantial focus on the Bordeaux varieties and their *terroir* supports this with a mix of *argile*-calcareous and gravel soils. There are approachable examples of a Petit Verdot and a Merlot-Cabernet Sauvignon blend as well as a fresh crisp rosé, Guêpier, a blend of old Cinsaut and Merlot. The Diogène blend though is serious and structured. It blends mainly Petit Verdot (60%) with 30% Merlot and some Cabernet Sauvignon. Les Gravières du Taurou is a richly textured Merlot and Petit Verdot blend which is lent additional structure from 24 months in small new and used oak. The splendid Le Prime Verd completes the reds, a pure Petit Verdot of great intensity and depth. Dark, spicy and tarry, this should develop very well with 5 or 6 years' ageing. The top two reds are both bottled unfined and unfiltered. The Cuvée Qvinteszencia de l'Ille is a very sweet, richly textured Ugni Blanc with marked botrytis, harvested in November and December. From microscopic yields of less than 10hl/ha, this is not dissimilar to good Sauternes and also has a subtle floral quality. Le Renard Blanc was added with the 2003 vintage, a blend of Grenache Gris and Maccabeu. It offers a fine persistent mineral quality with nutty herb spiced fruit. Le Reynard Omega is again Grenache Gris but 100% varietal. Barrel fermented and aged in new oak but larger 400 litre barrels for balance, it has a tremedous depth of citrus fruit, great intensity and a rich, sumptuous texture. (DM)

Recommended Reds:
IGP des Côteaux de Murviel Prime Verd ★★★★☆ £F
IGP des Côteaux de Murviel Les Gravières du Taurou ★★★★ £E
IGP des Côteaux de Murviel Cuvée Diogène ★★★ £D
IGP des Côteaux de Murviel Petit Verdot ★★☆ £C
IGP des Côteaux de Murviel Merlot-Cabernet ★★ £B
Recommended Whites:
IGP des Côteaux de Murviel Qvinteszencia de L'Ille ★★★★★ £G
IGP des Côteaux de Murviel Le Reynard Oméga ★★★★☆ £F
IGP des Côteaux de Murviel Le Reynard Blanc ★★★☆ £D
Recommended Rosés:
IGP des Côteaux de Murviel Guêpier ★★ £B

Dom. Rimbert (Saint-Chinian) www.domainerimbert.com
Jean-Marie Rimbert's domaine was only established in 1997 but he is proving to be one of the really exciting producers of the appellation. He now has 20ha under vine and is producing between 7,000 and 8,000 cases per year. He has some very well sited vineyards with impoverished schistous soils planted to Carignan, Syrah, Grenache, Cinsault and Mourvèdre. Most of the vines are over 40 years old and some Carignan is extremely venerable. A number of wines are made. The Saint-Chinian Les Travers de Marceau is blended from Carignan, Cinsault and Syrah. It is a finely structured, elegant example, not at all over-extracted and with a pure mineral undercurrent running through it. Two further red Saint-Chinians are also made. There are additionally some very fine pure Carignan wines which are simply labelled as Vin de France. Le Chant de Marjolaine comes from old vines in some of the best parcels, whereas the extraordinary Carignator, blended from two vintages, is sourced from 50 to 70-year-old vines and fermented in *barriques*. Heady and exotic, it is one of the most characterful wines of the region. Two further Carignan varietal wines are also produced as well as a number of Vin de France labelled reds and a Saint-Chinian white and rosé. (DM)

Recommended Reds:
Vin de France Carignator ★★★★ £E
Vin de France Le Chant de Marjolaine ★★★☆ £D

Languedoc

Saint Chinian Les Travers de Marceau ★★☆ £C

❀ Roc d'Anglade (Languedoc)

One of the finest reds in the Languedoc is produced at this small domaine. The property is 10 km to the west of Nîmes and planted on limestone-based soils. This IGP is dominated by Carignan wirh the balance Syrah and Grenache. Yields are kept very low, generally below 25 hl/ha, and the wines are traditionally vinified with no destemming and a lengthy vatting of around three weeks. It is dark, spicy and very intense with sumptuous tannin and an elegant hint of black pepper and herbs in the background. Expect it to develop very well in bottle with 5 or more years' age. A fine apple and citrus scented barrel-fermented white from Chenin Blanc and Grenache Blanc is also produced along with a rosé. (DM)

Recommended Reds:
IGP du Gard ★★★★ £E
Recommended Whites:
IGP du Gard ★★★☆ £E

Dom. Sainte Croix (Corbieres) www.saintecroixvins.com

The Bowens established their small estate recently in 2004, however they have quickly created a small range of wines of impressive quality and character. They now have 15 ha in the Hautes Corbières and focus on classic Languedoc varieties. Their holding is split across 26 separate parcels and one of the great assets here is a substantial holding of over 100 year old Carignan. They, like other winemakers have realised that if restricted in yield and therefore allowed to achieve optimum phenolic ripeness these old holdings provide wonderfully complex and characterful wine. Needless to say everything is done by hand and the vineyards farmed as naturally as possible without herbicides. The fragrant, spicy, bright dark berry-scented Le Fournas is blended from roughly equal proportions of Syrah, Grenache and old-vine Carignan with just a touch of Mourvèdre. Ageing is in tank and the wine is kept on its lees. Quite a bit more serious and more structured is the Magneric, a blend of old-vine Grenache and Carignan with just a little young vine Syrah. A lengthy vatting, ageing in small oak and bottling without fining or filtration provide a wine of impressive depth and dimension. The white La Serre is produced from low-yielding Grenache Blanc and Gris. It has citrus, nutty fruit intensity with a proportion vinified in small oak adding weight and texture. The rosé is in a very forward fruit-driven style. Direct pressed and dominated by young Syrah it is understandably deep coloured and vibrant. Drink it as young as possible. Three additional dry reds and a late harvest style are also now made. (DM)

Recommended Reds:
Corbières Magneric ★★★☆ £D
Corbières Le Fournas ★★★ £C
Recommended Whites:
Vin de France Sainte Croix La Serre ★★★ £C
Recommended Rosés:
Vin de France Sainte Croix Rosace des Vents ★★☆ £B

Dom. J.B. Senat (Minervois) www.domaine-jeanbaptistesenat.fr

This is one of the best domaines in Minervois producing interesting, unusual and characterful reds. Jean-Baptiste Senat possesses 16 ha. As well as the traditional Rhône style varieties he also has Merlot and Pinot Noir planted. The Mais ou est donc Ornicar is the softest of the four reds here if not the cheapest. Ripe and berry-laden it contains a large proportion of Mourvèdre. The unusual Les Arpettes is a blend of Merlot and old vine Carignan. Rich old-vine fruit and a hint of prune are apparent, along with firm tannins on the finish. Give it a year or two. The Minervois La Nine is dominated by Grenache and also blended with Mourvèdre, Cinsault, Syrah and Carignan. Big, dense and impressively concentrated, it will benefit from 3 or 4 years' cellaring. The top wine Le Bois de Merveilles is one of the very best from this AC. Produced from a blend of Carignan, Grenache and Mourvèdre, the Grenache now up to 100 years old, this is firm, structured and impressively long and intense with subtle, complex dark, spicy fruit. A minimum of 5 years is required. As a range the wines offer excellent value. (DM)

Recommended Reds:
Minervois Le Bois de Merveilles ★★★☆ £D
Minervois La Nine ★★★ £C
IGP des Côteaux de Peyriac Les Arpettes ★★☆ £C
Vin de France Mais ou est donc Ornicar ★★ £B

Sieur d'Arques (Limoux) www.sieurdarques.com

A very sizeable but well-organized co-op that produces close to a million cases a year. Its membership controls around 3,000 ha of vineyards, the vast majority of the whole Limoux appellation. Good, well made Blanquette de Limoux is produced as well as Crémant de Limoux. There is a good lightly oaked regular Chardonnay but the top wines are four well-crafted Toques et Clochers bottlings, which are barrel-fermented and aged partly in new wood, on lees and with *bâtonnage*. With a number of decidedly cool mesoclimates within the AC these are surprisingly elegant and tight, with a fine piercing mineral undercurrent to the fruit. (DM)

Recommended Whites:
Limoux Chardonnay Terroir Océanique ★★★ £C
Limoux Chardonnay Terroir Méditerranéen ★★★ £C
Limoux Chardonnay Terroir Haute Vallée ★★★ £C
Limoux Chardonnay Terroir d'Autan ★★☆ £C
Crémant de Limoux Edition Limité ★★☆ £C
Blanquette de Limoux Première Bulle ★★ £C
Blanquette de Limoux Le Propriétaire ★☆ £B
Recommended Rosés:
Crémant de de Limoux Première Bulle ★☆ £C

Dom. de Tabatau (Saint-Chinian)

The Gracia brothers have a small holding of just over 10 ha of vineyards, the majority of which are planted to Syrah, Grenache and Carignan with a little Mourvèdre and Aramon. There is also around 1 ha of Chardonnay, Roussanne and Clairette. At present four reds, a rosé and a IGP Cuvée Geneviève from the white holdings are produced. The Camprigou is soft, vibrant and accessible, being aged in *cuve* for 10 months without any recourse to new oak. The more sturdy Lo Tabataire is aged for just over a year and in a mix of *demi-muids* and *barriques*. New oak is avoided because the brothers wish to emphasise the quality and character of their old vines. An additional premium Saint-Chian red Les Titous (£E) comes from Grenache and Syrah and there is an unusual Vin de France, Las Costas from a blend of Carignan and Aramon. Bottling is without filtration. (DM)

Recommended Reds:
Saint-Chinian Lo Tabataire ★★★☆ £D
Saint-Chinian Camprigou ★★★ £C
Recommended Whites:
IGP Cuvée Geneviève ★★☆ £C

❀ Dom. Terre Inconnue (Gard)

Robert Creus is based in the eastern borders of the Languedoc but

has little interest in the bureaucracy of appellation regulations. As a result his garage-style wines are simply labelled as Vin de France. His production is still very small and he now has 4 ha of vines and these are handled as naturally as possible. The wines are vinified with a minimum of sulphur and aged in *barriques* for 16–18 months. Handling is by gravity, fining is avoided and the wines are bottled without filtration. There are three main cuvées as well as a second wine, Les Bruyères, for lots which are not felt to be up to scratch. Léonie is an astonishingly heady and rich 100% Carignan, in many ways the most exciting and shocking of Creus's wines. Los Abuelos is 100% Grenache, rich and characterful, always super-ripe. Alcohol levels for any of the top cuvées can easily be 15% or more but balance and purity are always maintained. The Sylvie is dominated by Syrah, and has Grenache as well as Carignan included in its blend. More opulent than the wines of the northern Rhône and loaded with super-ripe fruit, perhaps a slightly firmer structure would add a further dimension. (DM)

Recommended Reds:
Vin de France Léonie ★★★★★ £F
Vin de France Sylvie ★★★★★ £F
Vin de France Los Abuelos ★★★★☆ £F

Val d'Orbieu (Narbonne) *www.val-orbieu.com*
This vast organisation has among its membership many of the major co-ops of the Midi as well as a number of individual growers. In 2012 it amalgamated with another substantial organisation, the UCCOAR group of *vignerons*. Interests spread as far as Bordeaux, where Val d'Orbieu now owns GRAND-PUY-DUCASSE and RAYNE VIGNEAU among others. It is responsible as well for the marketing and distribution of a number of small quality domaines. These include the CH. DE JAU in the Roussillon, and fine Corbières produced at CH. LA VOULTE GASPARETS. The prestige Val d'Orbieu label is the Cuvée Mythique, a red blend from varying sources and varieties. It is inevitably labelled as IGP d'Oc. Good stylish and moderately fleshy, it has reasonable depth for drinking over the short to medium term. (DM)

Recommended Reds:
IGP d'Oc Cuvée Mythique ★★ £C
Recommended Whites:
IGP d'Oc Chardonnay Réserve Saint-Martin ★☆ £B

Also see the following Rhône *négociants* with an entry in the section Rhône Valley:

M Chapoutier
Jean-Luc Colombo
Tardieu-Laurent

Other wines of note - *Languedoc*

Abbaye de Sylva Plana
Recommended Reds:
Faugères La Closeraie ★★☆ £C
Faugères Le Songe de L'abbé ★★★ £C
Abbaye de Tholomies
Recommended Reds:
Minervois ★ £B
Minervois La Livinière ★☆ £C
Abbotts & Delaunay
Recommended Reds:
Minervois Cumulo Nimbus ★★★ £D

Côtes du Roussillon Réserve ★★ £B
Recommended Whites:
Limoux Zephyr ★★★ £D
Languedoc Eurus ★★ £C
Dom. de L'Aigle
Recommended Whites:
Limoux Les Aigles ★★ £C
Anne de Joyeuse
Recommended Reds:
Limoux Rencontre ★★★☆ £D
Limoux La Butinière ★★★ £C
IGP Pays d'Oc Malbec Original ★☆ £B
Recommended Whites:
Limoux La Butinière ★★☆ £C
Recommended Rosés:
IGP Pays d'Oc Happy Day ★★ £B
Dom. de L'Ancienne-Mercerie
Recommended Reds:
Faugères Cuvée Couture ★★★ £D
Antech
Recommended Whites:
Crémant de de Limoux Héritage ★★☆ £C
Blanquette de Limoux Réserve ★★ £C
Recommended Rosés:
Crémant de de Limoux Emotion ★☆ £C
Dom. d'Archimbaud
Recommended Reds:
Languedoc Terrasses du Larzac L'Enfant Terrible ★★★ £D
Languedoc Saint Saturnin La Robe du Pourpre ★★★ £D
Dom. de L'Arjolle
Recommended Reds:
IGP Côtes de Thongue Paradoxe ★★★ £D
IGP Côtes de Thongue Synthèse ★★ £C
IGP Côtes de Thongue Cabernet ★★ £C
Recommended Whites:
IGP Côtes de Thongue Equinoxe ★★ £C
IGP Côtes de Thongue Equilibre ★★ £B
IGP Côtes de Thongue Sauvignon ★☆ £B
Ch. d'Aussières
Recommended Reds:
Corbières ★★☆ £C
Dom. de Bachellery
Recommended Reds:
IGP d'Oc Elevé en Fûts de Chêne ★★ £C
Dom. de Baruel
Recommended Reds:
IGP des Cevennes Syrah/Cabernet ★★ £C
Dom. Bégude
Recommended Whites:
Limoux L'Étoile ★★★ £C
Limoux Chardonnay Classique ★★ £C
IGP d'Oc Chardonnay La Bel Ange ★★ £B
Dom. Belles Pierres
Recommended Reds:
Languedoc Saint Georges d'Orques Les Clauzes de Jo ★★★ £C
Bergerie du Capucin
Recommended Reds:
Languedoc Pic Saint-Loup Larmanela ★★★☆ £D
Languedoc Pic Saint-Loup Dame Jeanne ★★★ £C
Recommended Whites:
IGP Saint Guilhem le Désert Dame Jeanne ★★ £B

Languedoc

France

Gérard Bertrand
Recommended Reds:
Corbieres Boutenac La Forge ★★★★ £F
Corbières Boutenac Château de Villemajou Grand Vin ★★★☆ £E
IGP d'Oc Cigalus ★★★ £E
IGP d'Oc Naturalys Syrah ★★ £B
Tautavel Réserve ★★★ £C
Grand Terroir Tautavel ★★☆ £C
Recommended Whites:
IGP d'Oc Cigalus ★★★☆ £E
La Clape Château l'Hospitalet Grand Vin ★★★☆ £E

Dom. Jean-Marc Boillot
Recommended Reds:
IGP d'Oc Domaine de La Truffière ★★☆ £C
IGP d'Oc Les Roques ★★ £C
Recommended Whites:
IGP d'Oc Domaine de La Truffière ★★ £C

Dom. de La Borie Blanche
Recommended Reds:
Minervois La Livinière Terroirs d'Altitude ★★★ £D
Minervois Classique ★★ £B

By Jeff Carrel
Recommended Reds:
Languedoc Les Darons ★★★☆ £C
Fitou La Tire ★★★ £C
Recommended Whites:
IGP Aude Morillon Blanc ★☆ £B

Dom. de Cabrol
Recommended Reds:
Cabardès Vent d'Est ★★ £C
Cabardès Vent d'Ouest ★★ £C

Calmel & Joseph
Recommended Reds:
Caramany ★★★ £C
Minervois ★★ £B
Recommended Whites:
IGP Pays d'Oc Villa Blanche ★★ £B

Dom. de Cambis
Recommended Reds:
Saint-Chinian Cuvée Caudomato ★★ £C
Saint-Chinian Carnet de Voyage ★★ £C

Caves de Castelmaure
Recommended Reds:
Corbières Cuvée No 3 ★★★ £D

Dom. de Causse Noir
Recommended Reds:
Faugeres Caius ★★ £C ?
Faugeres Mathias ★★ £C ?
Faugeres 3.14 ★★ £C ?

Ch. des Adouzes
Recommended Reds:
Faugères Plo de Figues ★★★☆ £D
Faugères Cuvée Elégance ★★★ £D
Faugères Elevé et Vieilli en Fut de Chêne ★★★ £C
Faugères Cuvée Tradition ★★☆ £B

Ch. Beauregard Mirouzes
Recommended Reds:
Corbières Fiaire Red ★★★☆ £D
Corbières Sol ★★★☆ £D
Corbières Lauzina ★★★☆ £C
Corbières Campana ★★☆ £B

Recommended Whites:
Recommended Rosés:
Ch. Bonhomme
Recommended Reds:
Minervois Les Amandiers ★☆ £B
Minervois Les Oliviers ★★ £C

Ch. Bouisset
Recommended Reds:
Languedoc La Clape Eugénie ★☆ £C

Ch. Cabezac
Recommended Reds:
Minervois Roc de Bô ★★★☆ £D
Minervois Belvèze Grand Cuvée ★★★☆ £D
Minervois Arthur Cuvée ★★★☆ £D
Recommended Whites:
Minervois Les Capitelles ★★★ £C

Ch. Camplazens
Recommended Reds:
Languedoc La Clape Premium ★★★ £D
Languedoc La Clape La Reserve ★★☆ £C
Languedoc La Clape La Garrigue ★★ £B

Ch. de Caraguilhes
Recommended Reds:
Corbières L'Echappée Belle ★★★★ £E
Corbières Solus ★★★★ £E
Corbières Classique ★★☆ £B
Recommended Whites:
Corbières Solus ★★★☆ £D
Recommended Rosés:
Corbières ★★☆ £B

Ch. Cascadais
Recommended Reds:
Corbières ★ £B

Ch. Cesseras
Recommended Reds:
Minervois La Livinière ★★ £C

Ch. Champs-des-Soeurs
Recommended Reds:
Fitou La Tina ★★★☆ £D
Fitou Bel Amant ★★★ £C
Fitou ★★☆ £B

Ch. de Combebelle
Recommended Reds:
Saint-Chinian ★☆ £C
Saint-Chinian Orion ★★☆ £C

Ch. Condamine Bertrand
Recommended Reds:
Languedoc Heritage ★★☆ £D
Languedoc Pézenas ★★ £C
IGP d'Oc Elixir ★★ £C

Ch. du Donjon
Recommended Reds:
Minervois Cuvée Prestige ★☆ £C

Ch. Etang des Colombes
Recommended Reds:
Corbières Bois des Dames ★★★ £D
Corbières Bicentenaire Vielles Vignes ★★☆ £C
Corbières Tradition ★★ £B
Recommended Whites:
Corbières ★★ £B

Ch. d'Exindre
Recommended Reds:
Languedoc Magdalia ★★ £C
Languedoc Amelius ★★☆ £C
Ch. de Flaugergues
Recommended Reds:
Languedoc Cuvée Colbert ★★★ £D
Languedoc Cuvée Sommelière ★★★ £C
Languedoc ★★ £B
Ch. de Fontenelles
Recommended Reds:
Corbières Renaissance ★★★ £C
Corbières Notre Dame ★★☆ £C
Ch. Gléon Montanie
Recommended Reds:
Corbières Gaston Bonnes ★★ £C
Corbières Combe de Berre ★★ £C
Ch. de Gourgazaud
Recommended Reds:
Minervois Quintus MMI ★★★ £C
Minervois La Livinière Réserve ★★☆ £C
Recommended Whites:
IGP d'Oc La Vigne de ma Mère ★★★ £C
Ch. Grand Moulin
Recommended Reds:
Corbières Boutenac ★★★ £D
Corbières Vieilles Vignes ★★☆ £C
Corbières Terres Rouges ★★ £B
Ch. Grézan
Recommended Reds:
Faugères Cuvée Arnaud Lubac ★★ £C
Ch. Guery
Recommended Reds:
Minervois Les Eolides ★★★ £C
Recommended Whites:
IGP d'Oc La Sagesse ★☆ £B
Ch. Haut-Gléon
Recommended Reds:
Corbières ★★ £C
Recommended Whites:
Corbières ★★ £B
Ch. Haut-Lignières
Recommended Reds:
Faugères Sur Le Fil ★★☆ £B
Ch. de L'Herbe-Sainte
Recommended Reds:
IGP d'Oc Artemisia ★★☆ £C
Minervois Prestige ★★☆ £C
IGP d'Oc Syrah ★★ £B
IGP d'Oc Cabernet Sauvignon ★★ £B
Recommended Whites:
IGP d'Oc Sauvignon Blanc ★☆ £B
IGP d'Oc Chardonnay Fut ★☆ £B
Ch. des Karantes
Recommended Reds:
Languedoc La Clape ★★★ £D
Languedoc Bergerie ★★☆ £B
Languedoc Terres des Karantes ★★ £B
Recommended Whites:
Languedoc ★★☆ £C

Ch. La Bastide
Recommended Reds:
Corbières Optimé ★★ £C
Ch. La Clotte Fontaine
Recommended Reds:
Languedoc Mathiérou ★★★ £D
Languedoc ★★ £C
Ch. La Grave
Recommended Reds:
Minervois Privilege ★★ £B
Ch. de Lancyre
Recommended Reds:
Languedoc Clos des Combes ★★★ £D
Languedoc Vieilles Vignes ★★★ £C
Languedoc Grande Cuvée ★★★ £C
Languedoc La Coste D'aleyrac ★★ £B
Recommended Whites:
Languedoc La Rouvière ★★★ £D
Languedoc Grande Cuvée ★★☆ £C
Recommended Rosés:
Languedoc Pic St Loup ★★☆ £C
Ch. La Roque
Recommended Reds:
Languedoc Pic Saint-Loup Cupa Numismae ★★★ £D
Languedoc Pic Saint-Loup ★★☆ £C
Languedoc Cuvée Mourvèdre ★★☆ £C
Recommended Rosés:
Languedoc Pic Saint-Loup Découverte Rosé ★★ £C
Ch. de Lastours
Recommended Reds:
Corbières La Grande Réserve ★★★ £D
Corbières Cuvée Simon Descamps ★★☆ £C
Corbières Arnaud de Berre ★★ £B
Recommended Rosés:
Corbières ★☆ £B
Ch. La Villatade
Recommended Reds:
Minervois Sanguine ★★ £B
Ch. Le Bouïs
Recommended Reds:
Corbières Cuvée Romeo ★★☆ £C
Ch. Les Palais
Recommended Reds:
Corbières Randolin Vieille Vignes ★★☆ £C
Corbières Tradition ★★ £B
Corbières Ludivine ★☆ £B
Ch. Montfin
Recommended Reds:
Corbières Cuvée Pauline ★★★ £C
Corbières Carignena ★★ £B
Recommended Whites:
Corbières Domaine de Montfin ★★ £B
Recommended Rosés:
Ch. de Nouvelles
Recommended Reds:
Fitou Gabrielle ★★★ £D
Fitou Vieilles Vignes ★★★ £C
Fitou Augusta ★★☆ £B
IGP Vallée du Torgan Terres de Nouvelles Marselan ★★☆ £B

Languedoc

France

Ch. Ollieux Romanis
Recommended Reds:
Corbières Cuvée d'Or ★★★☆ £D
Corbières-Boutinac Cuvée Atal Sia ★★★☆ £D
Corbières Cuvée Prestige ★★★☆ £C
Corbières Cuvée Classique ★★★ £C
Corbières Lo Petit Fantet d'Hippolyte ★★☆ £B
Recommended Whites:
Corbières Cuvée Prestige ★★★☆ £D
Recommended Rosés:
Corbières Cuvée Classique ★★☆ £C
Ch. d'Oupia
Recommended Reds:
Minervois ★☆ £B
Minervois Les Barons ★★ £C
Ch. Pech-Celeyran
Recommended Reds:
Languedoc La Clape Réserve ★★ £C
Ch. Pech-Latt
Recommended Reds:
Corbières Cuvée Tamanova ★★★ £D
Corbières Cuvée Vieille Vignes ★★☆ £C
Corbières Tradition ★★ £B
Ch. de Pennautier
Recommended Reds:
Cabardes Terroirs d'Altitude ★★★ £D
Ch. des Peyregrandes
Recommended Reds:
Faugères ★★☆ £B
Ch. du Prieuré des Mourgues
Recommended Reds:
Saint-Chinian Grande Réserve ★★★ £C
Ch. Ricardelle
Recommended Reds:
Languedoc La Clape Vendredi XIII ★★★ £D
Languedoc La Clape Cuvée Juliette ★★★ £D
Languedoc La Clape Blason de Ricardelle ★★★ £C
Ch. de Rieux
Recommended Reds:
Minervois ★★ £B
Ch. du Roc
Recommended Reds:
Corbières Excelsius ★★☆ £C
Corbières La Fleur ★★ £B
Ch. Romilhac
Recommended Reds:
Corbières Rapsodie ★★☆ £C
Ch. Roumanières
Recommended Reds:
Languedoc Garrics ★★ £C
Languedoc Le Chant des Pierres ★★ £C
Languedoc L'Instant ★☆ £B
Ch. Saint-Martin des Champs
Recommended Reds:
Saint-Chinian Cuvée Vieilles Vignes ★★★ £C
Ch. Saint-Auriol
Recommended Reds:
Corbières Les Terrassettes ★ £B
Ch. de Valflaunes
Recommended Reds:
Languedoc Pic Saint-Loup T'Em T'Em ★★☆ £D

Ch. Veyran
Recommended Reds:
Saint-Chinian Cuvée Henri ★★ £C
Saint-Chinian Cuvée Clos de L'Olivette ★★ £C
Ch. Villerambert-Julien
Recommended Reds:
Minervois ★★☆ £C
Minervois L'Opéra ★★ £C
Recommended Whites:
Minervois ★☆ £B
Ch. Viranel
Recommended Reds:
Saint-Chinian V de Viranel ★★★☆ £D
Saint-Chinian Cuvée Tradition ★★★ £C
IGP de Cessenon Arômes sauvages ★★★ £C
Recommended Whites:
Languedoc Cuvée Tradition ★★ £D
Recommended Rosés:
Saint-Chinian Cuvée Tradition ★★ £C
Ch. Wiala
Recommended Reds:
Fitou Harmonie ★★☆ £C
Chemin des Rêves
Recommended Reds:
Languedoc Pic St Loup La Soie ★★★☆ £D
Languedoc Pic St Loup Gueule de Loup ★★★ £C
Languedoc Grés de Montpellier L'Exubérant ★★★ £C
Recommended Whites:
Languedoc La Soie Blanche ★★★ £D
Dom. Cinq Vents
Recommended Reds:
Languedoc Montpeyroux ★★★ £C
Clos de l'Amandaie
Recommended Reds:
Languedoc Grés de Montpeller Huis Clos ★★★☆ £D
Languedoc ★★★ £D
Recommended Whites:
Languedoc ★★☆ £C
Clos des Augustins
Recommended Reds:
Languedoc Pic St Loup L'Aîné ★★★☆ £E
Languedoc Pic St Loup Sourire d'Odile ★★★ £D
Languedoc Pic St Loup Les Bambins ★★☆ £B
Clos du Gravillas
Recommended Reds:
IGP d'Oc Le Rendez-Vous du Soleil ★★★ £C
IGP d'Oc Lo Viehl ★★★ £C
Recommended Whites:
Minervois L'Inattendu ★★★ £C
Clos des Nines
Recommended Reds:
Languedoc L'Orée ★★★ £D
IGP Pays d'Hérault Pulp ★★ £B
Recommended Whites:
Languedoc Obladie ★★★ £D
Clos Ventas
Recommended Reds:
Languedoc Terrasses de Larzac ★★★ £D
Dom. de Clovallon
Recommended Reds:
IGP d'Oc Mas d'Alezon ★★★ £D

IGP d'Oc Pinot Noir ★★ £C
Recommended Whites:
IGP d'Oc Viognier ★★ £C
Dom. de La Combe-Blanche
Recommended Reds:
Minervois La Chandelière ★★☆ £C
IGP d'Oc Le Dessous de L'Enfer ★★ £B
Dom. Costes-Cirgues
Recommended Reds:
Languedoc Château Costes-Cirgues ★★★★ £E
Languedoc Bois du Roi ★★★☆ £D
IGP Pays d'Oc Saint Cyr ★★★ £C
Dom. Coston
Recommended Reds:
Languedoc Les Garigoles ★★★☆ £D
Dom. Cour Saint Vincent
Recommended Reds:
Languedoc Clos du Prieur ★★☆ £C
Dom. de Courtilles
Recommended Reds:
Corbières ★★☆ £C
Corbières Côte 125 ★☆ £B
Dom. des Creyssels
Recommended Whites:
Picpoul de Pinet ★☆ £B
Dom. Gavin Crisfield
Recommended Reds:
Languedoc Terrasses du Larzac La Traversée ★★★☆ £D
Dom. de La Croix Ronde
Recommended Reds:
IGP de La Haute-Vallée de L'Orb Tourmaline ★★ £B
Recommended Whites:
IGP de La Haute-Vallée de L'Orb Topaze ★★ £B
IGP de La Haute-Vallée de L'Orb Jade ★★ £B
Dom. Cros
Recommended Reds:
Minervois ★★ £B
Minervois Vieilles Vignes ★★☆ £C
En Silence
Recommended Reds:
Saint-Chinian ★★☆ £C
Dom. de L'Escattes
Recommended Reds:
Languedoc Tradition ★★★ £C
Dom. de Familongue
Recommended Reds:
Languedoc Terrasses du Larzac Pierre et Bastien ★★★ £D
Languedoc Terrasses du Larzac 3 Naissances ★★★ £C
Languedoc L'Ame de Familongue ★★★☆ £C
IGP de L'Hérault Le Carignan ★★ £B
Félines-Jourdan
Recommended Whites:
Languedoc ★☆ £B
Picpoul de Pinet ★☆ £B
Dom. Fons Sanatis
Recommended Reds:
Vin de France Senescal ★★★ £D
Dom. Font de L'Olivier
Recommended Reds:
IGP Côtes de Thongue Carignan Vieilles Vignes ★★★☆ £D

Dom. Fontedicto
Recommended Reds:
Languedoc Promise ★★★☆ £E
Languedoc Coulisses ★★★☆ £C
Dom. de Fontenelles
Recommended Reds:
Corbières Renaissance ★★★ £C
Corbières Notre Dame ★★★☆ £C
IGP Aude Poete Renaissance ★★ £B
Corbières Tenue de Soirée ★☆ £B
Dom. Jean-Marie Fourrier
Recommended Reds:
Faugères Élegance ★★☆ £C
Faugères Finesse ★★☆ £C
Dom. Gayda
Recommended Reds:
IGP d'Oc Chemin du Moscou ★★★☆ £D
IGP d'Oc Figure libre freestyle ★★★ £C
Recommended Whites:
IGP d'Oc Figure Libre Freestyle Blanc ★★★ £C
IGP d'Oc Flying Solo ★☆ £B
IGP d'Oc Viognier ★☆ £B
Dom. de Gournier
Recommended Reds:
IGP des Cévennes Cuvée Templière ★★ £B
IGP des Cévennes Grenache Les Hauts Calcaires ★★ £B
Recommended Whites:
IGP des Cévennes Cuvée Templière ★★ £B
IGP des Cévennes Sauvignon Les Vieilles Vignes ★★ £B
IGP des Cévennes Chardonnay ★☆ £B
IGP des Cévennes Viognier ★☆ £B
Recommended Rosés:
IGP des Cévennes ★ £B
Dom. du Grand Crès
Recommended Reds:
Corbières Majeure ★★★ £C
Corbières ★★ £B
Dom. de Granoupiac
Recommended Reds:
Languedoc ★★ £C
Languedoc Les Cresses ★★☆ £C
Dom. des Grecaux
Recommended Reds:
Languedoc Hemera ★★ £D
Maison Guinot
Recommended Whites:
Blanquette de Limoux Cuvée Réservée ★★ £C
Dom. Haut-Blanville
Recommended Reds:
Languedoc Grés de Montpelier Clos des Légende ★★★☆ £E
Languedoc Grés de Montpelier Clos de La Plénitude ★★★ £D
Languedoc Grand Réserve ★★★ £C
Languedoc Peyral ★★ £B
Dom. Haut-Lirou
Recommended Reds:
Languedoc Pic Saint-Loup L'Esprit du Haut-Lirou ★★★☆ £D
Languedoc Pic Saint-Loup Mas des Costes ★★★ £C
Languedoc Pic Saint-Loup ★★☆ £B
Recommended Whites:
IGP d'Oc ★☆ £B

Languedoc

France

Recommended Rosés:

Languedoc Pic Saint-Loup ★☆ £B

Hecht & Bannier

Recommended Reds:

Languedoc ★★★ £C

Hegarty Chamans

Recommended Reds:

Minervois No 2 ★★★☆ £D

Minervois No 1 ★★★☆ £D

Dom. Henry

Recommended Reds:

Languedoc Les Chailles ★★☆ £D

Jeanjean

Recommended Reds:

Faugères Domaine de Fenouillet ★★ £C

Dom. La Bouysse

Recommended Reds:

Corbières-Boutenac Mazerac ★★★ £C

Corbières Valensol ★★ £B

Recommended Whites:

IGP Aude Hauterive Viognier ★☆ £B

Recommended Rosés:

Corbières Floreal ★☆ £B

La Jasse Castel

Recommended Reds:

Languedoc ★★ £C

Dom. La Linquière

Recommended Reds:

Saint-Chinian Sentenelle 310 ★★★ £D

Saint-Chinian Le Chant des Cigales ★★★ £D

Saint-Chinian Tradition ★★ £B

Dom. La Rouviole

Recommended Reds:

IGP de L'Hérault ★★ £B

Minervois Classique ★★☆ £C

Minervois Coup de Theatre ★★★ £C

Minervois La Livinière ★★★ £D

Dom. La Tour Penedesses

Recommended Reds:

Faugeres Montagne Noire ★★★ £C

Faugeres Les Raisins de Colère ★★★ £C

Dom. de Lavabre

Recommended Reds:

Languedoc Pic Saint-Loup ★★ £B

Le Bien Décidé

Recommended Reds:

Languedoc ★★★☆ £E

Dom. Le Clos du Serres

Recommended Reds:

Languedoc Terrasses du Larzac La Blaca ★★★☆ £D

Languedoc Terrasses du Larzac Les Maros ★★★☆ £D

Languedoc Le Clos ★★★☆ £C

Recommended Whites:

Languedoc Le Saut du Poisson ★★★☆ £C

Le Domaine de La Tranquillitè

Recommended Reds:

IGP d'Oc ★★☆ £C

Les Fusionels

Recommended Reds:

Faugères Re-Naissance ★★★ £D

Faugères In Tempus ★★★ £C

Faugères Le Reve ★★☆ £B

Les Vignerons de Fontès - Fontesole

Recommended Reds:

Languedoc Pezenas Latude ★★☆ £C

Dom. Lerys

Recommended Reds:

Fitou Cuvée Prestige ★★☆ £C

Fitou Cuvée Tradition ★☆ £B

Dom. Lignères-Lathenay

Recommended Reds:

Minervois La Livinière Marcelin ★★★ £D

Minervois Cuvée Emma ★★☆ £C

Minervois Cuvée l'air de rien ★★☆ £C

Lorgeril

Recommended Reds:

Minervois L'Amourier ★★ £C

Dom. Luc Lapeyre

Recommended Reds:

Minervois L'Amourier ★★ £C

Ma Reference

Recommended Reds:

IGP d'Oc ★★★ £D

Dom. Magellan

Recommended Reds:

IGP des Côtes de Thongue Vieilles Vignes ★★☆ £C

Mas d'Aimé

Recommended Reds:

La Doyenne Vin de France ★★★ £C

Mas d'Amile

Recommended Reds:

IGP Saint Guilhem Vieux Carignan ★★☆ £C

Mas d'Auzières

Recommended Reds:

Languedoc Sympathie pour les Stones ★★★☆ £C

Languedoc Les Eclats ★★★ £C

Mas de La Barben

Recommended Reds:

Languedoc Calice ★★★☆ £D

Languedoc Les Sabines ★★★ £C

Mas des Cabres

Recommended Reds:

Languedoc Sommières Cuvée La Draille ★★★☆ £C

Languedoc Cuvée Terres d'Aspres ★★★ £B

Mas des Capitelles

Recommended Reds:

Faugères Collection No 2 ★★★☆ £E

Mas des Chimères

Recommended Reds:

IGP du Salagou Oeillades ★★ £C

IGP du Salagou Marie Et Joseph ★★ £C

Mas Fabregous

Recommended Reds:

Languedoc Sentier Botanique ★★★ £C

Recommended Whites:

Languedoc Sentier Botanique ★★★ £C

Mas Gabriel

Recommended Reds:

Languedoc-Pézenas Clos des Lièvres ★★★☆ £D

Recommended Whites:

IGP de L'Hérault Clos des Papillon ★★★ £C

IGP de L'Hérault Les Trois Terrasses ★★☆ £C

Mas Granier
Recommended Reds:
Languedoc Camp de l'Oste ★★★ £C
Languedoc Les Gres ★★ £C
Mas La Chevalière
Recommended Reds:
IGP d'Oc ★★ £C
Mas Laval
Recommended Reds:
IGP de L'Hérault Grande Cuvée ★★★☆ £D
IGP de L'Hérault Les Pampres Rouge ★★★ £C
Recommended Whites:
IGP de L'Hérault Les Pampres Blanc ★★☆ £B
Mas de Martin
Recommended Reds:
Languedoc Grés de Montpellier Ecce Vino ★★★☆ £D
Languedoc Grès de Montpellier Ultreia ★★★ £C
Languedoc Grés de Montpellier Cinarca ★★☆ £C
Mas de L'Oncle
Recommended Reds:
Languedoc Pic Saint-Loup Selection ★★ £C
Mas Onèsime
Recommended Reds:
Faugères Paradis Caché ★★☆ £C
Maurel-Vedeau
Recommended Reds:
Languedoc Clos de Fontedit ★★ £C
Dom. de Mont d'Hortes
Recommended Reds:
IGP d'Oc Cabernet Sauvignon ★★ £B
Recommended Whites:
IGP d'Oc Chardonnay ★★ £B
IGP d'Oc Viognier ★☆ £B
IGP d'Oc Sauvignon Blanc ★☆ £B
Caves Mont Tauch
Recommended Reds:
Fitou Hommage Cuvée Centenaire ★★★☆ £C
Fitou Ch. de Montmal vin biologique ★★★ £C
Fitou Ch. de Seguré Cuvée Olivier de Termes ★★★ £C
Fitou Les Quatre ★★☆ £C
Fitou Vieilles Vignes Terroir d'Altitude ★★ £B
Fitou Fitou Tradition Fruité et Velouté ★☆ £B
Corbières L'Enclos des Roses ★★ £B
Corbières L'Ancien Comté ★☆ £B
Dom. Ollier-Taillefer
Recommended Reds:
Faugères Castel Fossibus ★★★ £D
Faugères Grande Réserve ★★★ £C
Recommended Whites:
Faugères Allegro ★★☆ £C
Les Domaines Paul Mas
Recommended Reds:
Languedoc Pezenas Cote Mas
Languedoc Ch. Paul Mas Clos de Savignac ★★★☆ £D
Languedoc Ch. Paul Mas Les Faïsses ★★★ £D
Languedoc Dom. du Silène Silène des Peyrals ★★★ £D
Saint Chinian Mas de Mas ★★ £B
IGP d'Oc La Forge Merlot ★☆ £B
IGP d'Oc La Forge Cabernet Sauvignon ★☆ £B
Recommended Whites:
IGP d'Oc Paul Mas Viognier ★☆ £B

IGP d'Oc La Forge Chardonnay ★★ £B
Dom Perdiguier
Recommended Reds:
IGP des Côteaux d'Ensérune Oeillades ★★ £B
IGP des Côteaux d'Ensérune Marie Et Joseph ★★ £B
Dom. Piccinini
Recommended Reds:
Minervois ★★ £B
Minervois La Livinière Line Et Laetitia ★★★ £D
Dom. de La Prose
Recommended Reds:
Languedoc Grande Cuvée ★★★ £D
Languedoc Les Embruns ★★☆ £C
Languedoc Cadières ★★ £C
Recommended Whites:
Languedoc Les Embruns ★★ £C
Dom. Pujol-Izard
Recommended Reds:
Minervois Cuvée Saint-Fructueux ★★ £C
Dom. Raissac
Recommended Reds:
Languedoc Terra Incognita ★★★ £D
IGP d'Oc Gustave Fayet ★★☆ £C
IGP d'Oc Les Lions ★☆ £C
Recommended Whites:
IGP d'Oc Le Puech ★☆ £B
IGP d'Oc Ostrea ★☆ £B
Dom. de La Réserve d'O
Recommended Reds:
IGP Saint Guilhem le Désert Mello Roc ★★★ £C
Dom. de La Rochelière
Recommended Reds:
Fitou Tradition ★★☆ £B
Dom. Roque Sestière
Recommended Whites:
Corbières Vieilles Vignes ★★☆ £C
Dom. de Roudene
Recommended Reds:
Fitou Vieilles Vignes ★★☆ £C
Dom Saint-André
Recommended Whites:
IGP d'Oc Folie d'Inès ★★☆ £C
Dom Saint-Andrieu
Recommended Reds:
Languedoc Noel ★★★ £C
Languedoc Les Roches Blanches ★★ £C
Dom Saint-Antonin
Recommended Reds:
Faugères Cuvée Magnoux ★★☆ £C
Faugères Tradition ★★ £C
Dom. Saint-Hilaire
Recommended Reds:
IGP d'Oc "Silk" Syrah ★★★ £C
IGP d'Oc "Silk" Cabernet/Merlot ★★★ £C
IGP d'Oc "Advocate" Syrah ★★☆ £C
IGP d'Oc "Advocate" Cabernet/Merlot ★★☆ £C
Recommended Whites:
IGP d'Oc "Advocate" Chardonnay ★★☆ £C
IGP d'Oc "Advocate" Viognier ★★ £C
IGP d'Oc Chardonnay ★☆ £B
IGP d'Oc Sauvignon Blanc ★☆ £B

Languedoc

IGP d'Oc Vermentino ★☆ £B
Recommended Rosés:
IGP d'Oc "Advocate" Serpentine ★★ £C
IGP d'Oc ★☆ £B
Dom. Saint Jean de Noviciat
Recommended Reds:
Languedoc Grés de Montpelier Novi ★★★ £E
Languedoc Grés de Montpelier Prestigi ★★☆ £C
Recommended Whites:
IGP d'Oc Chardonnay ★★★ £D
Dom. St-Martin La Garrigue
Recommended Reds:
Languedoc St-Martin ★★★ £C
Languedoc Bronzinelle ★★☆ £C
Recommended Whites:
Languedoc ★★ £C
Picpoul de Pinet ★★ £B
Dom. Saint-Sylvestre
Recommended Reds:
Languedoc Terrasses du Larzac ★★★☆ £D
Cave de Saint-Saturnin
Recommended Reds:
Languedoc Lucian ★☆ £B
Languedoc Seigneur des deux Vierges ★★ £C
Dom Sainte Cécile du Parc
Recommended Reds:
IGP Pays d'Hérault Mouton Bertoli ★★★ £E
Languedoc Pézenas Sonatina ★★★ £C
IGP Pays d'Hérault Notes d'Orphee ★★☆ £C
IGP Pays d'Hérault Notes Franches ★★☆ £C
Recommended Rosés:
IGP Pays d'Hérault Notes Frivoles ★☆ £B
Dom. de Saumarez
Recommended Reds:
Languedoc Aalenien ★★★☆ £C
Languedoc S de Saumarez ★★☆ £C
Recommended Whites:
Languedoc ★★ £B
Recommended Rosés:
Languedoc ★☆ £B
Dom. Serres Mazard
Recommended Reds:
Corbières Cuvée Henri Serres ★★☆ £C
Dom. du Silène des Peyrals
Recommended Reds:
Languedoc ★★ £C
Skalli-Fortant de France
Recommended Reds:
Cabernet Sauvignon Édition Limité F ★★ £C
Dom. Stella Nova
Recommended Reds:
Languedoc-Pézenas Mira Ceti ★★★☆ £D
Dom. des Terre Megere
Recommended Reds:
Languedoc Dolomies ★★ £B
Dom. des Terres Falmet
Recommended Reds:
Saint-Chinian L'Ivresse des Cimes ★★☆ £C
Dom. Terres Georges
Recommended Reds:
Minervois Quintessence ★★☆ £C

Villa Symposia
Recommended Reds:
Languedoc L'Equilibrium ★★★ £C
IGP d'Oc Merlot ★★ £B
Villa Tempora
Recommended Reds:
Languedoc-Pézenas ★★☆ £C
Languedoc-Pézenas L'Ange vin ★★☆ £C
Dom. Zumbaum-Tomasi
Recommended Reds:
Languedoc Clos Maginiai ★★☆ £C

Work in progress!! - *Languedoc*

Producers under consideration for the next edition
Ch. Rouquette Sur Mer (Languedoc)
Domaine de La Coste Moynier (Languedoc)
Lauraire de Lys (Minervois)
Maxime Magnon (Corbières)
Mas Ventenac (Cabardes)
Dom. Le Pas de L'Escalette (Languedoc)
Dom. de Mouscaillo (Limoux)
Yannick Pelletier (Saint-Chinian)
Ch. Puech-Noble (Languedoc)
Zélige Caravent (Languedoc)

Author's choice - *Languedoc*

Fine Languedoc whites
Dom. Les Aurelles   Languedoc Aurel
Stricto Senso   IGP d'Oc Chardonnay
Dom. Jean-Louis Denois   Limoux Sainte Marie
Dom. Virgile Joly   Languedoc Virgile
Dom. Lacoste   Muscat de Lunel Clos Bellevue
Dom. Le Conte de Floris   Languedoc Lune Blanche
Dom. de L'Hortus   IGP Val de Montferrand Grande Cuvée
Mas Jullien   IGP de L'Hérault
Mas de Daumas Gassac   IGP de L'Hérault
Prieuré de Saint-Jean-de-Bébian   Languedoc
Dom. de La Garance   IGP de L'Hérault Les Claviers

15 top Languedoc reds
Dom. Canet-Valette   Saint-Chinian Le Vin Maghani
La Peira En Damaisela   Languedoc Terrasses du Larzac
Dom. de La Marfée   Languedoc Les Champs Murmurés
Mas de L'Ecriture   Languedoc L'Ecriture
Dom. Clavel   Languedoc Copa Santa
Alain Chabanon   Languedoc Montpeyroux L'Esprit de Font Caude
Dom. de La Grange des Pères   IGP de L'Hérault
Ch. de La Négly   Languedoc Clos du Truffière
Mas Champart   Saint-Chinian Clos de La Simonette
Mas de Daumas Gassac   IGP de L'Hérault
Prieuré de Saint-Jean-de-Bébian   Languedoc
Dom. Rimbert   Carignator
Dom. Terre Inconnue   Sylvie
Dom. Borie La Vitarèle   Saint-Chinian Midi Rouge
Ch. de Cazeneuve   Languedoc Le Sang du Calvaire

Great Languedoc values
Reds:

Dom. d'Aupilhac   Languedoc Montpeyroux

Ch. des Estanilles   Faugères L'Impertinent

Ch. de Jonquieres   Languedoc

Clos Bagatelle   Saint-Chinian La Gloire de Mon Père

Ch. Cazal Viel   Saint-Chinian Cuvée des Fées

Ch. de L'Engarran   Languedoc Grenat Majeure

Guy Moulinier   Saint-Chinian Les Terasses Grillées

Ch. Saint-Jacques d'Albas   Minervois Château Saint-Jacques d'Albas

Clos des Camuzeilles   IGP de L'Aude Carignan

Dom. La Maurerie   Saint-Chinian Esprit du Terroir

La Regalona   Cabardès La Regalona

Mas de Fournel   Languedoc Pierre

Whites:

Ch. Capitoul   Languedoc Les Rocailles

Ch. d'Angles   Languedoc Classique

A-Z of producers - *Roussillon*

Cave de L'Abbe Rous (Banyuls & Collioure) *www.abberous.com*
This tremendous co-operative makes wines from both the Banyuls and Collioure appellations and represents 750 wine growers who grow vines on no less than 1,150 ha of vineyard. Much of the key to the quality of the wines is the absence of machinery in the vineyards and widespread poor quality schist soils which in particular favour the cultivation of top quality Grenache. In addition to the wines profiled here a range of approachable wines is made under the Cuvée des Peintres label, red, white and rosé and there is also a more serious rosé, Cornet & Cie. A white and traditional Banyuls are also made as well as a number of special Banyuls Grand Cru bottlings. Among the Collioure wines the Cornet & Cie white is a blend of Grenache Blanc and Gris with a little Roussanne, Marsanne and Vermentino. In Fine is richer, more complex and just Grenache Gris and 10% Grenache Blanc. There are three fine reds, including an approachable Cornet & Cie from Grenache, Carignan, Mourvèdre and Syrah. In Fine is 90% Grenache with a little Carignan, more dark, smoky and characterful while there is a limited release red cuvée of impressive density and a little youthful oak, Cyrcée which is made with consultancy input from the Bordeaux enologist, Dr Alain Raynaud. It comes from very old Grenache as well as Syrah and Mourvèdre. There are two Cornet & Cie Banyuls. A Rimage is bottled young after just over a year with topped up barrels and there is also a Late Bottled example. Particularly impressive is the Hélyos, which comes from very low-yielding old Grenache and is bottled after around a year and given extended bottle ageing before release. (DM)

Recommended Reds:

Banyuls Hélyos ★★★☆ £D

Banyuls Cornet et Cie ★★★ £C

Collioure Cyrcée ★★★☆ £D

Collioure In Fine ★★★ £D

Collioure Cornet et Cie ★★☆ £C

Recommended Whites:

Collioure In Fine ★★★ £D

Collioure Cornet et Cie ★★☆ £C

Arcadie (Côtes du Roussillon) *www.vinarcadie.com*
This small operation is run by Agnes Graugnard who comes from a wine family in the Rhône Valley and now works with a small number of local winegrowers both in their vineyards and initially in their cellars. Once the wines have completed fermentation they are transferred to Agnes' base where they complete maturation and are bottled. She works with growers from both on the schistous soils of Montner and the limestone soils of Tautavel. The white Alba comes from Grenache Gris with the balance from Grenache Blanc. Many of the vines are over 60 years old and naturally low yielding, producing a crop of barely 20hl/ha. Harvesting of the fruit, as for all the wines, is determined by phenolic (physiological) maturity and the must is cool fermented and aged in barrel on lees for 10 months. Rich, full and nutty with a hint of toasty spice the wine goes through full malolactic but nevertheless retains sufficiently fresh acidity. The red Byzance is a mix of Lladoner Pelut, Syrah, Grenache and Mourvèdre. Fully destemmed, the wine is vatted for 2 to 3 weeks and malolactic is in barrel for the Syrah and Mourvèdre. Full and rich with marked dark-berried, spicy fruit there is a subtle mineral backbone adding a further dimension. The white will drink well young, the red with a little age. A second lighter red TP 3 is also made from a blend of Lladoner Pelut, Grenache Noir and Syrah as well as a sparkling white Brut from Maccabeu. The wines represent very good value . (DM)

Recommended Reds:

Côtes du Roussillon-Villages Byzance ★★★★ £E

Côtes du Roussillon-Villages TP3 ★★★ £C

Recommended Whites:

Côtes du Roussillon Alba ★★★★ £E

Dom. d'Arfeuille *www.domainedarfeuille.com*
Stéphane d'Arfeuille is another Bordelais to see the tremendous potential in this part of France. He has 7.5 ha planted in mainly schist soils and many vines over 50 years of age. Carignan, Grenache and Syrah are all cultivated. The vineyard is meticulously managed and everything done by hand. The canopy is thinned in the late season and an extensive sorting is carried out at harvest. The reds are given a long maceration, four to five weeks and ageing is in oak. All the reds, are marked by a dark, brooding fruit with a mineral undertone from the soil. Interestingly the top two wines are IGP, and include no Syrah in the blend. Les Gabax is Carignan and Grenache, the dense and concentrated Vieilles Vignes bottling solely Grenache. The one Roussillon white is also impressive, a 100% Macabeu from 100 year old vines. A Bordeaux Blanc, Les Matines is also made as well as a direct pressed Roussillon rosé, L'Essentiel. (DM)

Recommended Reds:

IGP des Côtes Catalanes Grenache Vieilles Vignes ★★★★ £E

IGP des Côtes Catalanes Côtes Catalanes Les Gabax ★★★☆ £D

Côtes du Roussillon-Villages L'Originelle ★★★ £C

Recommended Whites:

IGP des Côtes Catalanes Côtes Catalanes L'Originelle ★★★ £C

Dom. Arguti (IGP des Côtes Catalanes) *www.domainearguti.fr*
Two fine light wines are made at this small Roussillon property as well as a Maury red. The Argutis have just over 4ha planted at an altitude of around 300 metres, which contributes to the tightly structured and elegant style of the wines. The grapes planted are Grenache, Carignan and a little Syrah for the red, and solely Grenache Gris for the white. The vineyards are farmed as naturally as possible and finely drained schist soils provide grapes of great potential intensity, purity and minerality. While everything is handled as naturally as possible the cellar includes modern temperature controlled vats to ensure the best possible results during vinification. The red is currently a blend of just Grenache, which is the dominant variety as well as Syrah and Carignan. The average age of the vines is over 40 years and this coupled

Roussillon

France

with a pre-fermentation cold soak, a 4 to 5 week maceration and malolactic in barrel (a small proportion new) results in a wine that is ripe, full and spicy but with a mineral elegance and purity indicative of its high altitude *terroir*. The white, like the red, comes from a tiny yield of barely 20hl/ha and is fermented and matured in new oak and then aged on its fine lees. Offering lovely subtle nutty, citrus and spicy fruit, this, like the red, offers a level of elegance and sophistication often missing in other wines from the region.(DM)

Recommended Reds:
Côtes du Roussillon-Villages Ugo ★★★☆ £D

Recommended Whites:
IGP des Côtes Catalanes Côtes Catalanes Ugo ★★★☆ £D

Dom. de L'Ausseil *www.lausseil.com*
The Chancels established their Côtes du Roussillon-Villages domaine in 2001 and have 12 ha planted around the top village of Latour de France. The vineyards are planted to very ancient Carignan (over 100 years old), Grenache as well as some Syrah. In addition to five reds they produce two whites, one a fruit driven Vin de France from Macabeu and Muscat which is labelled P'tit Piaf, another, Ou Papillon ?, from Grenache Gris and Macabeu, together with a Muscat de Rivesaltes. Ou Papillon ? is more refined and complex and barrel fermented and aged on lees for six months. It is neither fined nor filtered prior to bottling. La Capitelle is soft, forward and full of spicy berry fruit but with an impressive underlying structure which will enable it age well in the short term. It is dominated by over 70 year old Carignan. Les Trois Pierres from Carignan, Syrah and Grenache is denser and more structured with supple and well-rounded tannins and a characterful minerality to its dark-berry fruit. An old vine Carignan red, Du Vent dans Les Plumes as well as a fruit driven Merlot, P'tit Piaf and a further Côtes du Roussillon-Villages, the Grenache dominated Prise de Bec, complete the reds. A Rivesaltes and a Rivesaltes Ambre are also made. (DM)

Recommended Reds:
Côtes du Roussillon-Villages Les Trois Pierres ★★★ £D
Côtes du Roussillon-Villages La Capitelle ★★☆ £C

Recommended Whites:
IGP des Côtes Catalanes Ou Papillon ? ★★★☆ £D
Vin de France P'tit Piaf ★★ £B

Dom. of the Bee *www.domaineofthebee.com*
This small domaine in the Agly Valley is owned by Arcadian Wines belonging to three partners; English wine buyer Justin Howard-Sneyd MW and his wife Amanda and Philippe Sacerdot. Between them they run the domaine in their spare time and do a remarkable job producing an excellent and very well-priced red from vineyards around Maury. Their richly textured, full bodied red is a blend of old-vine Grenache Noir and Carignan. There are a total of 3.6 ha spread across three terroirs and the vines range from roughly 40 to 80 years of age. There is a temperature-controlled fermentation and maceration on skins follows for up to four weeks. The resulting wine is softly basket-pressed and aged for just over a year in a mix of 225 and 500 litre barrels, of which a third are new for just over a year. For the quality, this wine is tremendous value. It is available for purchase online and can be supplied in the UK, USA and France. Full details are on the winery website. Please also note that the address listed is for correspondence only. A single vineyard, Les Genoux is also now made as well as a Roussillon white, Field of the Bee. Most recently added is an English sparkling white, Hart of Gold from the three Champagne grapes and vinified at RIDGEVIEW. (DM)

Recommended Reds:
Côtes du Roussillon-Villages ★★★★ £E

Camp del Roc (Côtes du Roussillon-Villages)
This small domaine in the Fenouillèdes has vineyards planted in granite soils at an altitude of between 430 and 485 metres above sea level, helping the natural acidity and balance of the wines. As well as the French Mediterranean varieties, there is a small planting of Ull de Llébre, better known in Spain as Tempranillo. The wines are impressively balanced, dense and concentrated with real character. The Erant Olim is from a field blend of old mixed varieties and is aged in older *demi-muids*. Gôme is comprised of Grenache, Mourvèdre and Carignan, with a hint of oak apparent in the wine's youth. The Vinum Patris is more obviously fruit driven but still possesses a fine mineral core in the wine's fruit. A white, Singularis from Carignan Blanc, a rosé, a third red blend, Roc Petit, as well as a Syrah, La Frontera are also made. (DM)

Recommended Reds:
IGP des Côtes Catalanes Erant Olim ★★★☆ £E
Côtes du Roussillon-Villages Gôme ★★★ £E
Côtes du Roussillon-Villages Vinum Patris ★★☆ £C

Dom. de Casenove (Côtes du Roussillon)
This is an ancient estate, which unlike many in the Midi, has been in the same family for generations. However, impressive modern fruit-driven wines are now being made at this fine property, where owner Etienne Montes has enjoyed consultancy input from Jean-Luc COLOMBO. A total of some 50 ha of vines are planted, including 16ha of whites comprising Grenache Blanc, Maccabeo, Muscat and the rare Torbat. Rich, honeyed Muscat de Rivesaltes and raisiny Rivesaltes are produced as well as a number of whites. The red Commandant François Jaubert, produced from mainly Syrah and partly aged in new oak, is powerful, dense and smoky. The Garrigue bottling is spicy and approachable. Newly added are a rich and spicy red Torrespeyes and a very limited production super-cuvée Pla del Rei, which is extremely expensive. (DM)

Recommended Reds:
Côtes du Roussillon Commandant François Jaubert ★★★☆ £E
Côtes du Roussillon Garrigue ★★☆ £C

Dom. Cazes (Rivesaltes) *www.cazes-rivesaltes.com*
In a region marked by new arrivals and vinegrowers becoming winemakers, this venerable and substantial property with some 220 ha of organic and biodynamically farmed vineyards producing a sizeable volume of both table and fortified wines a year and has done so consistently for decades. An extensive range is produced here including good red Côtes du Roussillons, red Côtes du Roussillon-Villages and Muscat de Rivesaltes, with some splendid aged examples, along with very good Rivesaltes. Le Credo is a very characterful blend of Grenache, Mourvèdre and Syrah. The Rivesaltes have an intense nutty complexity and will keep very well. There are also some remarkable and expensive limited-release old vintages available, which should unquestionably be considered and these come under the Aimé Cazes label. A recent addition to the operation is the Collioure vineyard Les Clos de Paulilles. There are 65 ha of vineyards planted in slate soils with the climate moderated by regular sea breezes. Both Collioure and Banyuls are produced. Among the Collioures there is a barrel fermented white from Grenache Blanc and Grenache Gris and a premium Cap Bear from Grenache Gris. The red is one of the better examples of the appellation. It is dominated by Mourvèdre with the balance Syrah

and Grenache. Fermentation and maceration is lengthy at three weeks before ageing is in stainless steel for 15 months. Dense and finely structured, it will develop further with 4 or 5 years' age. Two Banyuls are produced, the Rimage coming solely from Grenache while the Traditionnel gets a small proportion of Grenache Gris and gets up to 30 months' ageing to add structure and depth. (DM)

Domaine Cazes
Recommended Reds:

Rivesaltes Tuilé ★★★☆ £E   Rivesaltes Ambré ★★★ £D
Côtes du Roussillon-Villages Le Credo ★★★ £D
Côtes du Roussillon-Villages Ego ★★☆ £C
Côtes du Roussillon-Villages Alter ★★☆ £C

Recommended Whites:

Muscat de Rivesaltes ★★☆ £D

Les Clos de Paulilles
Recommended Reds:

Banyuls Traditionnel ★★★☆ £E   Banyuls Rimage ★★★ £E
Collioure ★★★ £D

Celliers des Templiers (Banyuls & Collioure)   www.banyuls.com

This is the largest co-operative in the Banyuls and Collioure regions, producing traditional Collioure and some impressive fortifieds. The ownership consists of over 750 growers who between them farm close to 900 ha in Banyuls and Collioure, producing wines under both appellations along with a IGP white. The majority of the fortified production is relatively ordinary and the Collioure bottlings are sound rather than really inspiring, although the domaine wines are altogether more serious. The top Banyuls Grand Cru cuvées, though, are a big step up in quality and are labelled Cuvées de Prestige. These are wines with a real nutty complexity and often marked by a dry tangy finish. The Henri Caris is a *demi-sec* style. (DM)

Recommended Reds:

Banyuls Grand Cru Henri Vidal ★★★★ £F
Banyuls Grand Cru Vivianne Leroy ★★★☆ £F
Collioure Château des Abelles ★★☆ £D
Collioure Les Schistes de Valbonne ★★☆ £D

Ch. de Caladroy   www.caladroy.com

Sizeable and well-established Roussillon property with a fine range of dry reds, a Muscat de Rivesaltes, a relatively light red Rivesaltes and a barrel-fermented white dominated by Chardonnay. It is an IGP and has a balance of Maccabeu and Muscat in the blend. Indeed there is a surprisingly forceful floral, grapey character to the wine. The reds are particularly impressive and well priced. Les Schistes, the lightest and softest is a blend of Syrah, Carignan, Mourvèdre and Grenache. Eclat de Schistes has no Carignan. Les Grenats is more densely structured, a blend of mainly Syrah with Mourvèdre and Grenache. La Juliane is of a similar blend with just a small proportion of Carignan as well and adding flesh through maturation in *barrique*. Particularly dark, spicy and characterful is the Cour Carrée, which is a roughly equal blend of Carignan (its dark, peppery character very evident), Syrah, Mourvèdre and Grenache. Also oak aged is the Rouge Emotion which combines mainly Syrah with Grenache. There is also a small quantity of a Mourvèdre dominant cru, Cuvée Saint Michel as well as Pierre Droite which is also mainly Mourvèdre. With the exception of the forward Les Schistes the reds will all benefit from a short period of cellaring. (DM)

Recommended Reds:

Côtes du Roussillon-Villages Saint-Michel ★★★☆ £D
Côtes du Roussillon-Villages Rouge Emotion ★★★☆ £D
Côtes du Roussillon-Villages La Juliane ★★★ £D
Côtes du Roussillon-Villages Pierre Droite ★★★ £D
Côtes du Roussillon-Villages Les Grenats ★★★ £C
Côtes du Roussillon-Villages La Cour Carrée ★★★ £C
Côtes du Roussillon-Villages Eclat de Schistes ★★★ £C
Côtes du Roussillon-Villages Les Schistes ★★☆ £C
Rivesaltes Tuilé ★★☆ £C

Recommended Whites:

IGP des Côtes Catalanes Expression de Caladroy ★★☆ £C
Muscat de Rivesaltes ★★☆ £C

Ch. de Jau (Côtes du Roussillon-Villages)

This is one of the largest properties in the Roussillon, just to the south of Corbières in the increasingly important Agly Valley. The origins of the château, date back to the 12th century. One of the original towers remains today. The estate covers a massive 500 ha of *garrigue*-strewn landscape with 100 ha planted to vines in clay/limestone, marl and schistous soils. Production is considerable for the area and to some extent this is reflected in the regular red Tradition bottling which although relatively characterful is lighter than many other examples from the region. JauJau 1er, though, is a serious step up in quality, full of black fruits, licorice and dark tar flavours. Blended mainly from Syrah, along with Mourvèdre and Grenache it is dense, rich and very powerful. It should continue to develop well in bottle for 4 or 5 years. A white Côtes du Roussillon is also produced along with Muscat de Rivesaltes and Rivesaltes. The vineyards at their Mas Cristine property are now leased to the COUME DEL MAS Tramontane Wines project. (DM)

Recommended Reds:

Côtes du Roussillon-Villages JauJau 1er ★★★ £D
Côtes du Roussillon-Villages Tradition ★★ £B

Dom. des Chênes (Côtes du Roussillon-Villages)

The 38 ha under vine here is fairly evenly divided between red and white varieties. Sturdy Côtes du Roussillon-Villages red Alzines is a blend of varieties, Grands Mères is vinified from mainly Carignan and the rich and spicy Tautavel La Mascarou is Syrah, Carignan and Grenache. A limited-release Lo Carissa is produced from Grenache, Syrah, Carignan and Mourvèdre. There is a stylish, barrel-fermented white Sorbiers as well as an impressive white Côtes du Roussillon, Magdaleniens. The range is completed by a Muscat and two well-priced Rivesaltes fortifieds. (DM)

Recommended Reds:

Côtes du Roussillon-Villages Tautavel Lo Carissa ★★★☆ £E
Rivesaltes Tuilé ★★★ £D
Côtes du Roussillon-Villages Tautavel La Mascarou ★★★ £C
Côtes du Roussillon-Villages Alzines ★★☆ £C
Rivesaltes Ambré ★★☆ £C
Côtes du Roussillon-Villages Grands Mères ★★ £C

Recommended Whites:

Muscat de Rivesaltes ★★★ £C
Côtes du Roussillon Sorbiers ★★☆ £C
Côtes du Roussillon Les Magdaléniens ★★☆ £C

❀ Clos del Rey (Maury)

The first vintage at this excellent Agly Valley domaine was only in 2001. However quality has been consistently exciting and Clos del Rey is among the finest producers in the Roussillon. There are a total of 34 ha now although only a small proportion of the harvest goes into the estate wines. The vineyards are planted to Grenache and Carignan from old vines as well as Syrah. The Mas del Rey IGP bottling is from a blend of equal parts of Grenache and Carignan.

Roussillon

Dark, spicy fruit and an almost ferocious minerality underpin the wine. Long, intense and fine, it needs at least 5 years. More edgy, nervy and intense in style is the brilliant Clos del Rey Côtes du Roussillon. Produced from mainly Carignan grown on schist soils, along with a little Grenache this has superb depth and intensity. A second Côtes du Roussillon, La Sabina, from Grenache and Syrah completes the small range. (DM)

Recommended Reds:

Côtes du Roussillon-Villages Clos del Rey ★★★★☆ £F
IGP d'Oc Mas del Rey ★★★★ £E

✺✺ Dom. Le Clos des Fées www.closdesfees.com

Very impressive domaine producing good to stunning red Roussillons from 11 ha of Carignan, Grenache, Syrah, Mourvèdre and Lladoner Pelud; the latter is not exactly a regular point of discussion around most dinner tables. Even the entry level Domaine de La Chique is full of dark, spicy bramble and herbs. Les Sorcières is more structured but with a vibrant fruit quality, approachable and supple, it is mainly aged in *cuve* with a small portion put in new oak. The Vieilles Vignes, a blend produced from very old vines, many 50–100 years old, is not racked; instead micro-oxygenation is used, as it is with Le Clos des Fées, the domaine's flagship wine. The latter is a blend of Syrah, Mourvèdre, Grenache and Carignan aged in oak for 18 months. A tiny amount of a remarkable 100% Grenache, La Petite Sibérie, is also produced. Very intense and concentrated, it displays more piercing pure berry-fruit intensity than a top Châteauneuf-du-Pape but is softer and more approachable and is very stylish indeed. The vineyard plot of some 1ha and 17 ares yields a mere 175 cases of this wine a year. Not surprisingly the price has now gone through the roof. A white is also now produced from old vine Grenache Blanc. Recent additions include Un faune avec son fifre a fascinating mainly Cabernet Franc, which seems to be endorsing the potential in the Roussillon for the variety, Images Derisoires which comes from an unusual blend of Tempranillo and Carignan as well as De battre mon coeur s'est arête, which is a pure Syrah. (DM)

Recommended Reds:

Côtes du Roussillon-Villages La Petite Sibérie ✺✺✺✺✺ £H
Côtes du Roussillon-Villages Clos des Fées ★★★★☆ £F
Côtes du Roussillon-Villages Vieilles Vignes ★★★★ £E
Côtes du Roussillon-Villages Les Sorcières ★★★☆ £C
Côtes du Roussillon-Villages Domaine de la Chique ★★☆ £C

Recommended Whites:

IGP Côtes Catalanes Vieilles Vignes ★★★☆ £E

✺ Clot de L'Oum www.clotdeloum.com

This is among the new wave in the Agly Valley. The original vineyard owners here, like many before, were happy to sell the fruit from their overcropped vines to the local co-op, unaware of the tremendous potential of the area. The three reds now produced at Clot de l'Oum are wines of great finesse and real style and purity, not in any way over-extracted or overdone. The high altitude vineyards are planted at between 200 and 500 metres on a mix of granite, gneiss and schistous soils. Drainage is excellent and the potential of the *terroir* is now being handled entirely naturally with no recourse to chemicals or fertilizers. The excellent-value La Compagnie des Papillons is produced from Grenache and Carignan with some of the vines up to 50 years old, the fruit vinified by the parcel. This ensures maximum ripeness and ageing is in used oak. The Saint-Bart Vieilles Vignes is produced from equal proportions Syrah (known here as Shiraz), Grenache Velu (known as Lladoner Pelut and closely related to Grenache Noir) and Carignan from the highest parcels on the

property. The wine is given a cold-maceration prior to fermentation resulting in a dense and opulent red that nevertheless retains a fine, elegant mineral core to its fruit. Numero Uno is named after the famous Berlin restaurant. Dominated by Syrah it is also blended with the best barrel of Carignan. Once again used oak is preferred to age the wine for 15 months and there is a remarkable depth, purity and complexity. All the wines have the structure and refinement to evolve very well in bottle. Numero Uno particularly will reward the patient. (DM)

Recommended Reds:

Côtes du Roussillon-Villages Numero Uno ★★★★ £E
Côtes du Roussillon-Villages Saint-Bart Vieilles Vignes ★★★★ £E
Côtes du Roussillon-Villages Las Compagnie des Papillons ★★★☆ £D

✺ Coume del Mas/Tramontane Wines www.coumedelmas.com

The 10 ha Coume del Mas domaine of Philippe Gard is fast emerging as one of the leading lights of both the Banyuls and Collioure appellations. The majority of the vineyard holding is in the site of Coume del Mas, with south-facing slopes and deep, well-drained clay soils with sufficient water to provide a perfect equilibrium during the hot summer months. A number of cuvées are produced from both appellations. The Folio Collioure Blanc is 90% Grenache Gris, the balance Grenache Blanc and Vermentino. Barrel-femented in new oak, this has real style from fruit grown on schist soils. A yield of just 20hl/ha ensures a wine of impressive nutty, citrus concentration. The red Schistes is in a more fruit-driven style. Produced solely from Grenache, it is aged in *cuve*. The top red Collioure, Quadratur, is a blend 50% Grenache with Mourvèdre and Carignan. Aged in one-third new oak for 12 months on lees, this is dense and characterful. The Banyuls Galateo is a blend of Grenache Noir, Gris and Blanc and like all the fortifieds here is made in a non-oxidative style. The top Banyuls, the Quintessence, is solely Grenache Noir and is given a long maceration and aged on lees in new oak. Coming from the oldest Grenache vines, it offers very impressive depth and concentration in an off-dry style. Philippe Gard is also involved with Andy Cook in their Tramontane Wines project producing excellent wines under the Mas Cristine, Tramontane Wines and Consolation labels as well as Collioure from Terrimbo which is also partly owned by Jacky Loos. The Tramontane label includes fine Banyuls and a red IGP Grenache red. A white IGP Macabeu, IGP Viognier and a Côtes du Roussillon rosé are also made. The Mas Cristine red and white Roussillon wines offer opulent, exciting fruit and good value. A red Collioure is made at Terrimbo, a blend of Grenache and Syrah, polished and stylish it is traditionally vinified in stainless steel and aged in small oak for 12 months. A Terrimbo rosé is also made from a reverse dominated blend of Syrah and Grenache. Under the Consolation banner Philippe and Andy make a number of low volume *micro-cuvées* of striking quality. Among these the Dog Strangler is a 100% Mourvedre of really impressive depth and structure and the Wild Boar an IGP Syrah. The range also includes a vintage Rivesaltes Antic, a white Rock N'Rolle from Vermentino and Petit Gris from a combination of Grenache Gris and Carignan Gris. The wines of Vial-Magnères are also distributed. (DM)

Coume del Mas

Recommended Reds:

Banyuls Quintessence ★★★★☆ £F
Collioure Quadratur ★★★★ £E
Collioure Schistes ★★★☆ £E
Banyuls Galateo ★★★★ £D

Recommended Whites:

Collioure Folio ★★★☆ £D

Mas Cristine

Recommended Reds:

Côtes du Roussillon ★★★ £C

Recommended Whites:

Côtes du Roussillon ★★★ £C

Consolation

Recommended Reds:

Collioure Dog Strangler ★★★★ £E

IGP Côtes Catalanes Wild Boar ★★★ £D

Tramontane

Recommended Reds:

Banyuls Tradition ★★★★ £D

IGP Côtes Catalanes Grenache ★★★☆ £D

Terrimbo

Recommended Reds:

Collioure ★★★☆ £E

Dom. Vial-Magnères

Recommended Reds:

Banyuls Vintage ★★★☆ £E

Dom. Depeyre (Côtes du Roussillon)

Small emerging Roussillon property with 7ha under vine, 6ha of which are red. The first vineyard was purchased in 1997 and Serge Depeyre has used his winemaking experience gained at first MAS AMIEL and then CLOS DES FÉES to very good effect. The white IGP is a blend of both Grenache Gris and Blanc as well as Muscat à Petits Grains. It is barrel-fermented and aged in oak, a small portion of which is new, and the wine absorbs it easily. Both reds are traditionally vinified getting a maceration of up to a month. The regular Roussillon is dominated by Carignan, with a little Syrah and Grenache whereas the Sainte-Colombe is mainly Grenache and aged in a combination of *cuve* and small oak. Although both will cellar well, the Sainte-Colombe just has that extra dimension. A marginally pricier Rubia Tinctoria red is also made. (DM)

Recommended Reds:

Côtes du Roussillon-Villages Sainte-Colombe ★★★☆ £D

Côtes du Roussillon-Villages ★★★ £C

Recommended Whites:

IGP Côtes Catalanes Eleve en Fûts de Chêne ★★☆ £C

❀ Dom. de L'Edre (Côtes du Roussillon-Villages) *www.edre.fr*

Small, newly established domaine producing two reds of real character and interest. Sourced from vineyards planted in poor and well-drained *argilo-calcaire* soils, a combination of old vine Grenache and Carignan and extremely low yields of 20 hl/ha both contribute to the quality and character of the wines. The vineyards are cultivated organically and leaf-thinning and green work is carried out extensively during the growing season. The wines are vinified parcel by parcel and *pigéage* and *remontage* are used to optimise extraction and skin contact during and after fermentation, which lasts between 25 and 28 days. For L'Aibre around a third is aged in *barriques* on lees while L'Edre is aged entirely in *barriques* for up to 12 months. Both wines are bottled without fining or filtration. (DM)

Recommended Reds:

Côtes du Roussillon-Villages L'Edre ★★★★☆ £F

Côtes du Roussillon-Villages L'Aibre ★★★★ £E

Dom. des Enfants *www.domaine-des-enfants.com*

This small Swiss owned domaine, founded in 2006, is in the Agly Valley, which itself is in the heart of the best stretches of the Côtes du Roussillon. The domaine takes the IGP de de Côtes Catalanes for its wines because of the makeup of the blends and the vineyards are all sustainably farmed with hand tilling and weeding and ploughing done with a horse. There are a wide diversity of soils types and the 23 ha were mostly planted prior to the Second World War with a number of vines now over 100 years old. The quality, character and structure of the wines shows this old vine complexity. The most approachable and fruit driven of the wines is l'enfant perdu. It is sourced from a number of sites and generally the younger vines, anywhere from 10 to over 60 years of age. The blend is made up of Grenache Noir, Carignan, Lladoner Pelut (Tempranillo) and Syrah. The dark berry fruit notes are underpinned by a combination of ageing in larger barrels and concrete tanks. Suis l'etoile is a touch more complex, it is dominated by old vine Grenache and Carignan and blended with Syrah and later with Mouvèdre. La larme de l'âme is the domains top priced red with a higher proportion of Syrah blended with old Grenache and Carignan. Ageing in 600 litre barrels achieves a harmonious balance of dark blackberry, spicy fruits and a firm underlying structure. Tabula Rasa is a characterful peachy, floral subtly citrus scented blend of Grenache Blanc, Macabeu and Carignan Blanc. It is barrel fermented and aged on lees for a year. A small amount of white Maury again labelled Tabula Rasa is also made. (DM)

Recommended Reds:

IGP des Côtes Catalanes la larme de l'âme ★★★★ £E

IGP des Côtes Catalanes suis l'etoile ★★★★ £E

IGP des Côtes Catalanes l'enfant perdu ★★★☆ £D

Recommended Whites:

IGP des Côtes Catalanes Tabula Rasa ★★★☆ £D

Maury Tabula Rasa ★★★☆ £D

Dom. Ferrer-Ribière *www.vinsferrerribiere.com*

A good small to medium sized producer based in the Côtes du Roussillon with 44 ha under vine of which close to half are accounted for by white varieties. Much of the vineyard is planted at altitudes of up to 200 metres and the slopes face south east close to the Mediterranean and so benefit from a cooling maritime influence. Basic IGP bottlings of both red and white now go under the brand Le F. Particularly interesting among the whites are the IGP bottlings of Grenache Gris and Grenache Blanc which both come from very old vines grown on well-drained clay and gravel soils. Yields for both are around 35hl/ha and they offer characterful nutty old-vine richness. The Grenache Gris is cool-fermented and should be drunk young to ensure its freshness. The Grenache Blanc is aged for a period on its lees and this shows through in the wine, which is subtler, more restrained and elegant than its stablemate. There is a fine range of red table styles. Characterful spicy, darkfruited old-vine Carignan goes under the Empreinte du Temps label and a varietal Syrah, Syrahnosaurus Rex has recently been added. There is also a good spicy Côtes du Roussillon, Tradition and a more serious structured bottling Memoire des Temps which has more Syrah and more aggressive tannins. The top two reds take the Côtes du Roussillon AC. Cana is a blend of Grenache, Mourvèdre and Syrah. The yield is low, particularly for the latter two varieties (which have been planted more recently) at just 20hl/la. It is a big, muscular red which is vatted for between 40 and 60 days and aged in oak (one-third new) for a year including a period on lees which adds structure. Selenae comes from tiny yields, just 15hl/ha, and is a

Roussillon

blend of Grenache, Carignan and Syrah. It gets a lengthy vatting and is then aged in oak for up to 15 months. It has a minerality and quality to its fruit that is missing from Cana. Both require medium term cellaring for six or seven years. The range is completed by a fresh, grapy Muscat de Rivesaltes. (DM)

Recommended Reds:

Côtes du Roussillon Selenae ★★★☆ £E

Côtes du Roussillon Cana ★★★ £D

Côtes du Roussillon Mémoire des Temps ★★☆ £C

Côtes du RoussillonTradition ★★☆ £C

Recommended Whites:

IGP Côtes Catalanes Empreinte du Grenache Blanc ★★☆ £C

IGP Côtes Catalanes Empreinte du Grenache Gris ★★☆ £C

Muscat de Rivesaltes ★★ £C

Dom. Fontanel *www.domainefontanel.fr*

A good small range of wine is produced in the commune of Tautavel in the Côtes du Roussillon-Villages by the Fontanels, who have a total of some 35ha from which they produce approaching 15,000 cases a year. Rich and heady fortifieds are fine examples and good value for money, as are the three Roussillon reds. The regular Roussillon is soft, forward and juicy, while Cistes is rich and opulent with upfront, nicely ripe brambly, spicy fruit. The Prieuré is denser and more powerful, a real medium term cellaring prospect. However it shows remarkably well in its youth, with opulent dark-berry fruit and a velvety, rounded, supple texture. (DM)

Recommended Reds:

Côtes du Roussillon-Villages Prieuré ★★★☆ £D

Côtes du Roussillon-Villages Cistes ★★★ £C

Côtes du Roussillon-Villages ★★☆ £C

Rivesaltes ★★★☆ £D

Recommended Whites:

Muscat de Rivesaltes ★★★ £C

✿ Dom. Gardies *www.domaine-gardies.fr*

A really first-class Côtes du Roussillon-Villages property among a seemingly ever increasing number in this exciting appellation. Some good Muscat de Rivesaltes is produced here, along with an exceptional Rivesaltes and now two excellent dry whites from the 10 ha of Grenache Blanc and Gris and a little Roussanne. It is however the reds that are particularly noteworthy. There are 25 ha of Grenache, Syrah, Mourvèdre and Carignan and the property has superbly drained limestone and schistous soils and these provide ideal growing conditions. The Millères, a blend of all 4 red varieties, is vibrant and approachable. The Clos des Vignes has a high proportion of Grenache from old vines while La Torre is a massive and dense dark, brooding mix of Mourvèdre, Grenache and Carignan. The most expensive wine, La Falaise is an extremely ageworthy and powerful expression of Syrah, with Grenache and Carignan. A further red Mataro is 100% Mourvèdre. (DM)

Recommended Reds:

Côtes du Roussillon-Villages Falaises ★★★★★ £F

Côtes du Roussillon-Villages La Torre ★★★★ £F

Côtes du Roussillon-Villages Clos des Vignes ★★★☆ £E

Côtes du Roussillon-Villages Millères ★★★ £D

Rivesaltes ★★★★★ £G

Recommended Whites:

Côtes du Roussillon-Villages Clos des Vignes ★★★☆ £E

Côtes du Roussillon Glacières ★★★ £D

✿✿ Dom. Gauby *www.domainegauby.fr*

Gérard Gauby produces a stunning range of reds and whites from his Côtes du Roussillon-Villages base. He is also now involved with the equally thrilling wines of Domaine LE SOULA in the high-altitude vineyards of the Agly Valley and are a source of inspiration for the remarkable new domaines emerging from those vineyards. The white Gauby Vieilles Vignes is a powerful nutty blend of southern varieties including Grenache Blanc, Maccabeo and Viognier, a wine of depth and great value for money. The top white Coume Gineste is sourced from a single vineyard and is produced from Grenache Blanc. Among the reds Les Calcinaires is a juicy, vibrant red made from Grenache, Syrah and Carignan and laden with sumptuous raspberry fruit, while the marvellous Vieilles Vignes is a structured, dense, powerful expression of intensely complex old-vine Grenache and Carignan with a smattering of Syrah, Mourvèdre and Cinsault. The top red, and among the most expensive wines in the South of France, is the magnificent Muntada. This is a superbly crafted Syrah, very rich, concentrated and powerful but increasingly refined and no doubt very long lived. Three further very impressive reds are made, Coume Gineste, La Foun and La Foque. Like Muntada they are very expensive. (DM)

Recommended Reds:

Côtes du Roussillon-Villages Muntada ✪✪✪✪✪ £F

Côtes du Roussillon-Villages Vieilles Vignes ★★★★★ £F

Côtes du Roussillon Les Calcinaires ★★★☆ £E

Recommended Whites:

IGP de Côtes Catalanes Coume Gineste ★★★★★ £G

IGP de Côtes Catalanes Vieille Vignes ★★★☆ £E

Dom. de L'Horizon *www.domaine-horizon.com*

Thomas Teibert has not been running his small operation long but has rapidly built up an enthusiastic and justified following for his wines. He is based in the same village, Calce, as Tom Lubbe at Domaine MATASSA and has a very similar outlook on winegrowing. He works with extremely old vines, follows biodynamic viticultural practices and ages his wines in larger barrels to emphasise their fruit qualities. This is another domaine where considerable thought has been extended towards achieving balance and elegance. Many modern Roussillon wines are big fruit monsters with high alcohol levels and can certainly struggle for balance. Altitude undoubtedly helps but Thomas is also concerned with harvesting at an equilibrium of fruit maturity and acidity. Astonishingly his 2008 white came in at a pH of less than 3.0 (thats in the Mosel scheme of things!), his red at less than 3.3. The resulting wines are very good, nervy and edgey styles, which require some patience. Both however are beguiling and intensely characterful. They should also be brilliant food wines. (DM)

Recommended Reds:

IGP des Côtes Catalanes ★★★★ £F

Recommended Whites:

IGP des Côtes Catalanes ★★★★ £F

Dom. Jones *www.domainejones.com*

Katie Jones established this small Côtes du Roussillon-Villages domaine recently. She was the export manager for the Mont-Tauch co-op until 2009 when she undertook her first vintage from her holding of 80 plus year-old vines. These are planted on black slate soils, which retain heat and reflect it back at night helping to ripen the fruit. Her vineyards overlook the Maury Valley with the spectacular backdrop of the Castle of Queribus (regarded by many as the last stronghold of the Cathars). She currently produces a small

number of wines, including a dry white and red as well as a sweet Muscat, which is fresh and unfortified and a very characterful deep and spicy Fitou red. The red, and white from her Grenache Gris are both excellent approachable fruit driven examples of the area, each though possessing a classic mineral backbone. Her 12 ha of vines are planted to Grenache Noir and Gris, Carignan and Muscat. The vines are venerable, around 75 years old and with the sparse rocky soils provide a meagre yield but intense and flavourful grapes. The vineyards elevation also adds a fresh edge to the wines. The Fitou is produced from Carignan, Grenache and Syrah. The wines can be purchased direct via her website and are being distributed in the UK. A wine club offers exclusively small volumes of a couple of reds and whites, labelled Les Perles and two single vineyard wines, a Syrah and a Grenache Gris which are labelled La Perle Rare. The wines represent great value. (DM)

Recommended Reds:
IGP des Côtes Catalanes ★★★☆ £D
Fitou ★★★☆ £D
Recommended Whites:
IGP des Côtes Catalanes ★★★☆ £C

Dom. Laguerre (Côtes du Roussillon) *www.domainelaguerre.com*
Eric Laguerre, the former head of the Saint-Martin de Fenouillet co-op, was also involved with Gérard GAUBY at DOM. LE SOULA but has his own now 50 ha domaine with high-altitude biodynamically farmed vineyards where he produces both red and white Côtes du Roussillon. The dark and spicy red has real potential as does the richly complex, nutty, mineral-scented white. The style here is influenced not only by the 600m vineyards but also by vines that range from 20–50 years of age and the well-drained granite soils. The white Le Ciste blends Marsanne, Roussanne, Rolle, Grenache Blanc and Maccabeu; the red is Grenache, Syrah, Carignan and Mourvèdre. The wines offer both excellent quality and very good value for money. A second label for each, EOS is also made as well as a rosé. The small range is completed with a Cabernet Sauvignon IGP, Altitude, a Carignan dominated Côtes du Roussillon, Le Passage, a blend of Cabernet, Carignan and Grenache labelled Le Col des Buis as well as Oxy, a rancio style white from Grenache Blanc. (DM)

Recommended Reds:
Côtes du Roussillon Le Ciste ★★★ £D
Recommended Whites:
Côtes du Roussillon Le Ciste ★★★ £D

La Passion d'Un Vie *www.bernard-magrez.com*
First class Côtes du Roussillon-Villages property owned by Henri Despeaux and Bernard Magrez in Bordeaux, the owner of PAPE-CLEMENT and much else besides. With consultancy advice from Michel Rolland this is a rich, opulent, fruit-driven red but of impressive grip and structure also. The vineyards are planted at an altitude of 180–250 metres above sea level on free-draining shale slopes. With an average vine age of over 30 years and some vines up to 100 years there is great potential here. Yields are naturally low, barely more than 20 hl/ha and a green harvest is also practised. In the winery everything is handled by gravity with a traditional vinification and ageing in 400-litre casks. Expect to be able to age the wine for 5 or more years and gain additional complexity. (DM)

Recommended Reds:
Côtes du Roussillon-Villages ★★★★ £F

✿ Dom. Le Soula (IGP des Côtes Catalanes) *www.le-soula.com*
The white and the red here are labelled under the IGP Côtes

Catalanes classification and the vineyards based in the Agly Valley. Both wines are excellent and are indicative of the long-term potential of the high-altitude vineyards from the area. The property was established in 2001 and has been developed by Gérard GAUBY and UK wine importer Mark Walford. The key to quality is the 600m elevation of the vines, at the limit of ripening but where the south-facing aspects create a sun trap. 22 ha are cultivated, 10 ha of which are planted to white varieties in a mix of granite and black schist soils. The red Le Soula is dominated by Carignan, now well over 60 years old, and the wine is extraordinarily dense, very backward young but with the potential to add layers of complex dark mineral fruit with age. Ageing is in a mix of tank, vat and 500 litre barrels for 21 months. The brilliantly intense, mineral and citrus scented white is a benchmark. There are small amounts of Chardonnay, Vermentino, Malvoisie du Roussillon, Grenache Gris, Vermentino, Marsanne and Roussane included in the blend. The wine is fermented and raised in 500 litre *demi-muids*, of which just over a third are new, on fine lees for 18 months. A second label of both the red and white is made and labeled Trigone. The vineyards are all farmed biodynamically. (DM)

Recommended Reds:
IGP des Côtes Catalanes Le Soula ★★★★☆ £F
Recommended Whites:
IGP des Côtes Catalanes Le Soula ★★★★☆ £F

Dom. La Tour Vieille (Banyuls & Collioure) *www.latourvieille.com*
Well-established producer of both Collioure and Banyuls, the quality of which is consistently good. There is an extensive range in both appellations. The nutty honeyed white Collioure, Les Canadells, is blended from Grenache Gris and Blanc as well as Roussanne, Maccabeo and Vermentino. The red La Pinède, from Grenache, Carignan and Mourvèdre is a full, dense, spicy black-fruit style, while the Puig Oriol, which is Grenache and Syrah, is more fragrant with a marvellous *garrigue* scent to the deep berry fruit, the Grenache very prominent. A further red Collioure, Puig Ambeille has recently been added. Good Banyuls comes in a number of guises: the Reserva is serious with sophisticated nutty *rancio* characters from extended time in cask and there is also a white, as well as two Rimage reds and an old *solera* Vin de Méditation bottling. (DM)

Recommended Reds:
Collioure Puig Oriol ★★★☆ £E
Collioure La Pinède ★★☆ £C
Banyuls Reserva ★★★☆ £E
Recommended Whites:
Collioure Les Canadells ★★★ £D

✿ Le Roc des Anges *www.rocdesanges.com*
Some of the finest expressions of Carignan are produced at this small domaine in the Agly valley, inland from Perpignan. Established very recently in 2001 there are 20 ha planted in a mix of schist and quartz soils, spread across 43 tiny parcels. Most of the slopes face north, stretching the ripening period and providing wines with a piercing nervy minerality and real style. As elsewhere in the region much of the character of the wines is derived from the age of the vines. In fact the average age is 65 years, with a quarter of the holding over 90 years. Quality is maintained by replanting at high densities, using *sélection massale*. The approach in the vineyard is organic while in the winery everything is handled as naturally as possible and an old vertical basket press ensures very clear juice. The Vieilles Vignes white is a blend of Grenache Gris and Maccabeu, fermented half and half in cement and small oak.

Roussillon

It is nutty, stylish and has a nice mineral undercurrent. Of the reds Segna de Cor is from younger vine Grenache and Syrah together with older vine Carignan, and offers not only ripe brambly dark berry fruit but impressive structure as well. The red Vieilles Vignes is old vine Carignan and old vine Grenache with the balance from Syrah. Impressively deep and concentrated, there is a pure minerality and intensity running through the wine. Most exciting is a varietal Carignan, 1903, which emanates from 3.5ha planted in that year. Aged in a mix of new (low toast) and used small oak the wine is a brilliant expression of the grape. It is dark and spicy and with marvellous intensity and purity. Expect all the reds but the 1903 in particular, to develop very well in bottle. The small range is completed by a late-harvested white which due to being made from almost fully Maccabeu, is only entitled to Vin de France status. Fermentation stops naturally during the winter leaving a sweet wine of rich, nutty intensity and fine balancing acidity. The Gallets also make fine Maury at a domaine they recently purchased, Les Terres de Fagayra. (DM)

Les Terres de Fagayra
Recommended Reds:
Maury Les Terres de Fagayra ★★★★ £E

Le Roc des Anges
Recommended Reds:
IGP des Pyrénées-Orientales Carignan 1903 ★★★★☆ £F
Côtes du Roussillon-Villages Vieilles-Vignes ★★★★ £E
Côtes du Roussillon-Villages Segna de Cor ★★★☆ £C

Recommended Whites:
Vin de France Passerilé ★★★☆ £E
IGP des Pyrénées-Orientales Vieilles-Vignes ★★★ £D

❀ **Mas Amiel (Maury)** *www.masamiel.fr*
This is an historic 155 ha property, best known for its remarkable range of Maury *vins doux naturels*. Two stylish and impressive red Côtes du Roussillons are also produced here in addition to a number of well-priced, vibrant IGP, Plaisir, and a white Côtes du Roussillon. The two Roussillon reds are impressively large, structured wines. The range of fortified Maury is extensive, from young minimally aged current vintages through to splendid old vintage bottles. The top cuvées are Réserve, Privilège and the immensely rich Charles Dupuy along with some splendid old vintage wines. The wines show a marked by classic burnt raisiny, toffeed *rancio* character. The top examples are extraordinarily intense. Olivier Decelle now has a number of interests in Bordeaux. (DM)

Recommended Reds:
Côtes du Roussillon-Villages Carrerades ★★★☆ £E
Côtes du Roussillon Notre Terre ★★☆ £C
IGP des Côtes Catalanes Plaisir ★★ £B
Maury Millésime 1980 ★★★★★ £F
Maury Charles Dupuy ★★★★☆ £F
Maury Privilège ★★★★ £E
Maury 15 Ans d'Age ★★★★ £E
Maury 10 Ans d'Age ★★★☆ £D
Maury Vintage Réserve ★★★ £D
Maury Vintage ★★☆ £C

Recommended Whites:
Côtes du Roussillon Altaïr ★★☆ £C
Muscat de Rivesaltes ★★☆ £C

Mas des Baux (Côtes du Roussillon) *www.mas-baux.com*
Small Côtes du Roussillon property producing a comprehensive range of IGP red, white and rosé as well as a fine, pure and complex Côtes du Roussillon red. There are just over 12 ha under vine and the first vendange was only in 1999. There is a minimalist approach in the best sense: all vineyard work is carried out as naturally as possible and handling is kept to a minimum in the cellar. Growing conditions are ideal, with sunny days, just sufficient rainfall and superbly drained soils with a layer of galets roulés helping to check yields on average at 25–35 hl/ha. Fermentation is traditional and the reds are fully destemmed. The white Baux Blond, from Muscat à Petit Grains, is cool-fermented and aged for four months in *inox* with *bâtonnage*. Like the rosé Rouge à Levres it should be drunk young and fresh. The red Velours Rouge is the softest and most immediately accessible of the reds. A blend of Grenache and Syrah, it gets a short ageing in *inox* and because of this is bottled after a light fining and earth filtration. Rouge Gorge blends Syrah and Mourvèdre with some old Grenache (over 35 years) and is aged in old oak for 12 months. The IGP Rouge Baux is a rich and opulent blend, which adds Cabernet Sauvignon to the Rhône red varietals and gets 12 months in new oak. The Côtes du Roussillon Soleil Rouge is tighter, more restrained and elegant. Low-yielding younger Syrah and Mourvèdre are blended with some of the oldest Grenache. It is aged in a combination of *inox* and older oak. A reserve red Alexandre is quite a bit pricier (£E). The top reds will comfortably improve for 5 years or more. (DM)

Recommended Reds:
Côtes du Roussillon Soleil Rouge ★★★☆ £D
IGP des Côtes Catalanes Rouge Baux ★★★☆ £D
IGP des Côtes Catalanes Rouge Gorge ★★★ £C
IGP des Côtes Catalanes Velours Rouge ★★☆ £C
Côtes du Roussillon Grand Rouge ★★ £B

Recommended Whites:
IGP des Côtes Catalanes Baux Blond ★★ £B

Recommended Rosés:
IGP des Côtes Catalanes Rouge à lèvres ★★ £B

❀ **Dom. du Mas Blanc** *www.domaine-du-mas-blanc.com*
Splendid 21 ha Banyuls and Collioure property developed by the late Dr André Parcé and now run by his son Jean-Michel. There is an extensive range from both Collioure and Banyuls. The Collioure La Llose is the regular bottling while there are several very fine single-vineyard wines. Cosprons Levant is an old-vine blend of Mourvèdre, Syrah and Counoise, Clos du Moulin is produced from Mourvèdre and Counoise and Les Junquets is from Syrah with a hint of Roussanne and Marsanne for fragrance. Production of these is small but they are very impressive, refined reds. Some of the very best Banyuls is also created here. There are two Rimage bottlings that have spent less time in cask, the sumptuous Cuvée de la Saint-Martin, which has intense, nutty, *rancio* notes and the Hors d'Age de Solera, resembling a great old Oloroso. Both these are expensive. (DM)

Recommended Reds:
Collioure Les Junquets ★★★★ £E
Collioure Cosprons Levant ★★★☆ £D
Collioure Clos du Moulin ★★★☆ £D   Collioure La Llose ★★★ £C
Banyuls Rimage La Coume ★★★★☆ £F
Banyuls Rimage ★★★★ £E

Mas de La Devèze *www.masdeladeveze.fr*
This is a recently established property in the Roussillon village of Tautavel producing both red and white. The Hughes purchased the domaine in 2012 and like others have realised the great potential

of the Agly Valley for making light as well as fortified wines of considerable flair and intensity. The former owners installed a brand new winery. The 22 ha of vineyards are planted in a mix of limestone, clay and schistous marl, providing excellent drainage to optimise the intensity of the fruit and provide good mineral nourishment. The red Roussillon-Villages is a blend of Mourvèdre and Grenache and is concentrated, dark fruited and minerally. A proportion of the wine is aged in oak with the malolactic fermentation in both tank and barrel. The very characterful, nutty white is solely from Maccabeu. There are also red and white Maury fortifieds and a Maury Sec which blends Grenache, Syrah and Mourvèdre, a Côtes du Roussillon-Villages Tautavel which combines Mourvèdre, Syrah, Grenache as well as Carignan. in addition a number of well priced wines are also made under the Malice label. (DM)

Recommended Reds:
Maury Sec ★★★☆ £D
Côtes du Roussillon-Villages Tautavel ★★★☆ £D
Côtes du Roussillon-Villages ★★★☆ £D
Recommended Whites:
IGP des Côtes Catalanes Blanc ★★★ £C

Mas Janeil www.francoislurton.com
This property is another around the village of Maury displaying the potential of these vineyards to produce really fine light wines as well as fortifieds. Owned by François Lurton of CHÂTEAU DES ERLES, Mas Janeil is the other jewel in his crown of small Languedoc-Roussillon domaines. Schist and slate soils help to impart the classic minerality that is found in many examples from the region which together with the altitude and down-drafts from the Pyrenees helps to ensure the wines always have fresh, almost nervy acidity as well as highish alcohol. In addition to the premium wines rated below fresh and forward red, white and rosé are released under the Hauts de Janeil and MJ Janeil banners. Four reds are produced under the Mas Janeil label as well as a stylish white, Le Traou de l'Ouille from a blend of Grenache Blanc, Genache Gris and Macabeu. Le Petit Pas is vibrant and forward coming from blended from Monastrell, Grenache, Carignan and Syrah. Grenache is the dominant variety in the regular red, which is blended with Syrah. Even for this bottling grapes come from vines that are very old, some well over 60 years and the wine offers impressive complexity. Sans Soufre is made without sulphur and offers a little more depth. Le Tiradou comes from some of the oldest vines on the best plot on the estate. It is nearly 100% Grenache and has altogether greater depth and structure being both very fine and very mineral in style. Pas de la Mule is sourced from particularly rocky soils and very old Grenache. Expect all to develop well over five or six years, the top two wines longer. (DM)

Recommended Reds:
Côtes du Roussillon-Villages Le Tiradou ★★★★ £E
Côtes du Roussillon-Villages Pas de la Mule ★★★☆ £E
Côtes du Roussillon-Villages Sans Soufre ★★★☆ £D
Côtes du Roussillon-Villages ★★★ £D
Côtes du Roussillon Le Petit Pas ★★☆ £C
Recommended Whites:
Côtes du Roussillon-Villages Le Traou de l'Ouille ★★★ £D

✿ Mas Karolina www.mas-karolina.com
Now well established domaine adding further evidence of the splendid potential of the wines of the Agly Valley. The vineyards are spread across a number of plots with soils that include black marls,

granite and schist. Vinification is modern with a pre-fermentation cold soak for the reds, vatting of 3–4 weeks and malolactic in new oak for the Syrah components. The white is fermented relatively cool at less than 20°C and both reds and whites are aged on fine lees. The white comes from over 50-year-old Grenache Gris and Maccabeu and from yields of no more than 20hl/ha. Rich, tropical and lightly oaky, it should drink well young. The IGP des Côtes Catalanes red is a blend of Carignan (65%) and Grenache from the black marls of Maury. Ripe and forward, the wine is full of dark, spicy and brambly fruit. The more backward and seriously structured Côtes du Roussillon-Villages is a blend of Syrah, Carignan and Grenache. The old-vine character of the fruit really shines through here, with a powerful mineral undercurrent and a hint of the new wood in which the Syrah is aged. Pride of place now though goes to a stunning IGP red, Cuvée l'Enverre which is a blend of very old Grenache and Carignan from a yield of just 15 hl/ha. There is a tremendous mineral intensity with well-judged ageing in new 300 litre barrels and a rounded palate as a result of malolactic in barrel. An excellent well priced small range. (DM)

Recommended Reds:
IGP des Côtes Catalanes Cuvée l'Enverre ★★★★☆ £E
Côtes du Roussillon-Villages ★★★★ £E
IGP des Côtes Catalanes ★★★☆ £D
Recommended Whites:
IGP des Côtes Catalanes ★★★☆ £D

Mas Mudigliza www.masmudigliza.fr
Young domaine based in the Côtes du Roussillon-Villages producing some very well-crafted and elegant fruit driven wines. Winemaker Dimitri Glipa moved from Bordeaux in time for the 2006 vintage here. Mudigliza has 10 ha under vine with an average age of over 60 years. The 350 metre altitude is also important in ensuring sufficient acidity in the fruit. The CaudaLouis comes from less than a ha of Grenache Gris. It is part vinified in oak and part in inox. The red Carminé is dominated by old vine Grenache and differs from the barrel aged Cariño in that it is cellared en cuve to emphasise the fruit and help in protecting the grape, which can be prone to oxidation. In 2007 a fine Côtes du Roussillon was also produced in partnership with his former boss Christian Veyry at Château VEYRY in Bordeaux's Côtes de Castillon. (DM)

Recommended Reds:
Maury ★★★★ £E   Côtes du Roussillon-Villages Cariño ★★★☆ £D
Côtes du Roussillon Carminé ★★★☆ £D
Recommended Whites:
IGP des Côtes Catalanes CaudaLouis ★★★☆ £D

✿ Dom. Maestrio www.domaine-mastrio.com
This is the small Côtes du Roussillon-Villages property of Michael Paetzold, a specialist in advanced filtration technology who works in Bordeaux for many leading Chateaux. When he decided to set up his own domaine as a sideline he was hugely impressed with the potential of this region. His vineyards are at significant altitude, around 300 to 450 metres above sea level and produce much more piercing, mineral laden wines than those for example around Maury. The minerality of the wines is emphasised by the granite in the soils. The vines are old, around 70 years and this helps keep yields low and fruit quality high. Vinification at present is extremely unusual. Michael has a number of specially converted portable cabins with on-site chilling facilities to ensure an efficient vinification. The reds here are very fine indeed. Dynamique is the most approachable, a blend of Grenache, Carignan and Syrah. The vine age ranges from 10

Roussillon

France

to 60 years and the wine is aged in *cuve* for six months to emphasise its fruit. Généreux is as the name suggests, perhaps his most opulent red. It is a blend of Grenache, Syrah and a little Carignan from 30 to 80 year old vines grown on granite soils and aged in oak for around 16 months. Most exciting is Elégant. This is an extraordinary old vine Carignan coming from vines ranging from 50 to 120 years old. The yield is barely 20 hl/ha and the wines is full of beguiling black fruits, pepper spice and just a hint of *garrigue*. Although approachable with a year or two in bottle expect the top two reds will develop well for a decade or more. A further red is made from Syrah and aged in *cuve*, A L'Abri du Vent. Carignan and Carignan Blanc are respectively used to craft an IGP white and rosé. (DM)

Recommended Reds:
IGP des Côtes Catalanes Elégant ★★★★☆ £E
Côtes du Roussillon-Villages Généraux ★★★★ £E
Côtes du Roussillon-Villages Dynamique ★★★☆ £D

✿ Dom. Matassa

Just a few hundred cases are made a year at this excellent high altitude property near the village of Calce in the Agly Valley. A white and four reds are produced. Much care is lavished on the vineyards and teas are used to treat the soil helping guard against fungal disease and aid full early ripening. The Matassa wines are marked by their surprisingly firm, gripping acidity and should develop well in bottle. The white is dominated by Grenache Gris and is barrel-fermented and aged for around nine months but without *bâtonnage*. The Matassa red is dominated by characterful very old vine Carignan, full of dark pepper and herbal spices. Unusually there is around 5% of Grenache Noir, Blanc and Gris interspersed in the vineyard. A wonderfully dense and concentrated special cuvée red Romanissa is also being made. This is mainly Grenache as well as Carignan and Mourvèdre. Reserved and youthfully tight the red requires 3 or 4 years at a minimum. Tom produces two other premium reds, El Sarrat (Syrah and Mourvèdre) and L'Estanya (Carignan and Mourvèdre). (DM)

Recommended Reds:
IGP des Côtes Catalanes Romanissa ★★★★☆ £F
IGP des Côtes Catalanes Matassa ★★★★ £E
Recommended Whites:
IGP des Côtes Catalanes Matassa ★★★★ £E

✿ Dom. Pertuisane *www.pertuisane.com*

Richard Case and his wife Sarah were amongst of the pioneers of a new wave of wines from this small and exceptional area of southern France. The emergence of really fine light wine styles from ancient vines in the Agly Valley in the Côtes du Roussillon-Villages is a relatively new development. A number of fine older domaines have been producing good wines for decades but much of the best fruit from old Grenache in particular, went into the region's fortified wines. The Cases initially started with just 2 ha, although this has mushroomed since. The schist-based vines are extremely low yielding and generally very old. Most of the holding is over 50 years and some vines are 100 years old. Depending on the growing conditions of the year, yields can be lower than 10 hl/ha. There is a minimal approach during vinification and the wines are basket-pressed and aged in a mix of new and used oak. Le Nain Violet is a fruit-forward and very approachable Grenache sourced from the domaine's youngest vines. La Pertuisane is much more serious coming from old-vine Grenache and Carignan. It has a really classic mineral Maury undercurrent from the schist. A new white The Guardian produced from Grenache Gris has lots of potential. (DM)

Recommended Reds:
Côtes du Roussillon-Villages Le Pertuisane ★★★★☆ £F
IGP des Côtes Catalanes La Nain Violet ★★★☆ £D
Recommended Whites:
IGP des Côtes Catalanes The Guardian ★★★☆ £D

Dom. Piétri-Géraud *www.domaine-pietri-geraud.com*

This is a very fine mother-and-daughter domaine producing benchmark Collioure and Banyuls as well as straightforward fruit driven IGP red, white and rosé labelled Fuego. As well as some excellent Collioure, a small range of Banyuls both red and a white are produced. The vineyards are planted on steep terraced, schistous slopes, to a combination of old Grenache and Carignan (the vines are generally well above 50 years of age) and younger Syrah and Mourvèdre. Yields are naturally low, barely 30 hl/ha, and the wines are generally marked by their style and refinement. In the Collioure Sine Nomine, a blend of Grenache with Syrah and Mourvèdre is used and filtration is avoided. The Banyuls Blanc gets a year in large vats, while the Cuvée Joseph Geraud sees an extended ageing period in *solera* to bring out more complex, smoky *rancio* characters. The red Collioure will benefit from 4 or 5 years' of cellaring. (DM)

Recommended Reds:
Collioure Sine Nomine ★★★☆ £E
Banyuls Joseph Géraud ★★★★ £E
Recommended Whites:
Banyuls ★★★ £D

Olivier Pithon *www.domaineolivierpithon.com*

The Pithons have 9 ha of organically tended Côtes du Roussillon-Villages vineyards spread around the village of Calce, close to Gérard GAUBY. From these they produce 4 reds and 3 whites of impressive style and intensity. Olivier is the brother of Jo Pithon, who is producing similarly exciting results with very different wines in the Côteaux du Layon. Both white and red entry level, fruit driven wines are made and labelled, P'tit Pithon. More serious, the white Lais is a blend of Maccabeu as well as Grenache Blanc and Gris. The D18 differs, being just the two Grenache varieties. Both are vinified and aged in a mix of new and used oak from very low yields of barely more than 15hl/ha. The D18 has greater depth and intensity but both offer tremendously stylish nutty southern fruit and impressive structure. The intensely dark and spicy red Lais blends old-vine Carignan and Grenache along with Syrah and Mourvèdre. It is vinified traditionally with a long 25–30 day maceration and ageing in a mix of small oak and *foudres*. Two further reds are made, Le Pilou is a 100% Carignan and the pricey Le Clot is a selection of Grenache grown in schist soils. All the wines will evolve well for 4 or 5 years, the red Lais a little longer. (DM)

Recommended Reds:
Côtes du Roussillon Cuvée Lais ★★★★ £E
Recommended Whites:
Côtes du Roussillon Cuvée D18 ★★★★ £E
Côtes du Roussillon Cuvée Lais ★★★☆ £D

Dom. Pouderoux (Maury) *www.domainepouderoux.fr*

Splendid producer, with a range of not only excellent Côtes du Roussillon reds but some very fine fortified wines as well. Although among the finest of the new wave of red wine producers in the Roussillon, the Poudereaux domaine is no flash in the pan. The family have been involved in Maury viticulture since 1826. Indeed it is this continuity across the last century in particular

that is responsible for the splendid raw material available to Robert Poudereaux. His vineyards are planted to Grenache, Syrah, Mourvèdre and Carignan grown on finely drained soils of black and white schist and limestone. There is a first-class barrel-fermented white, Roc de Plane, of real density produced from Grenache Blanc, Grenache Gris and Macabeu. Among the dry reds Latour de Grès is dense and powerful, marked by the characteristic dark berry and spice complexity of old-vine Carignan, which originates from 1901. Terre Brune blends Grenache, Syrah and Mourvèdre and gets an extra week of vatting to add depth. Like Latour de Grès it is aged in older barrels. The premium, richly opulent and complex Mouriane also blends Grenache, Syrah and Mourvèdre. Macerated on its skins for a month or more and aged in new oak for a year, it demands five years' patience. There is a splendid range of Maury all produced solely from Grenache Noir. Vendange is aged in a combination of *cuve* and bottle until release, The Mise Tardive gets three years in barrel, which adds complexity and more tertiary aromas. The top two wines are a serious step up. The Hors d'Age gets twelve years in small oak, the Grande Reserve four years in a combination of *foudres* and *bonbonnes*. There is also an excellent fortified Muscat, grown on schistous soils. Rich and opulent it is in complete contrast to the Maury reds with ripe, fresh grapey character. (DM)

Recommended Reds:
Côtes du Roussillon-Villages Mouriane ★★★★ £E
Côtes du Roussillon Terre Brune ★★★★ £E
Côtes du Roussillon Latour de Grès ★★★☆ £D
Maury Grande Reserve ★★★★ £E
Maury Hors d'Age ★★★★ £E
Maury Vendange ★★★☆ £D
Maury Mise Tardive ★★★☆ £D
Recommended Whites:
Côtes du Roussillon-Villages ★★★ £C
Muscat de Rivesaltes ★★★ £D

❋ **Dom. Puig-Parahÿ (Côtes du Roussillon)** *www.puig-parahy.fr*
Georges Puig-Parahÿ's domaine is sizeable in comparison to those of his likeminded, quality-conscious neighbours. This however is relative, certainly in comparison to the New World because Georges produces a vast total of some 8,000–9,000 cases a year! The Puig family have been involved in Roussillon viticulture since the phylloxera crisis in France in 1878 and as a result possess some remarkable old-vine holdings. Grenache is up to 80 years old, Carignan as much as 130. Syrah and Mourvèdre are also now planted to produce modern-style wines. There is a good, clean and fresh, impressively grapey Muscat IGP but more serious are the Sant Lluc and Miserys whites blended from Grenache Blanc and Gris. The former is vinified *en cuve*; the latter in a combination of tank and new oak. With low yields in well-drained *argilo-calcaire* soils the 3 Côtes du Roussillon reds are of good to very good quality. Mes Amis is mainly Carignan and Grenache but has marvellous old-vine character – not complex but exciting. Georges is similarly aged in *cuve* but is more serious and structured, containing Grenache, Syrah and Mourvèdre as well as Carignan. The top two cuvées, Le Fort de Saint-Pierre and Ballides, are both ageworthy. The former is aged in *cuve*, the latter in *barrique*. The Saint-Pierre is the better balanced, its beguiling fruit offering great class and purity. A range of exciting fortifieds is available to taste at the domaine and the Rivesaltes 1930 recently tasted for this guide is wonderfully nutty, intense and complex. (DM)

Recommended Reds:
Rivesaltes 1930 ★★★★★ £F

Côtes du Roussillon Ballides ★★★★ £E
Côtes du Roussillon Le Fort Saint-Pierre ★★★☆ £D
Côtes du Roussillon Georges ★★★ £C
Côtes du Roussillon Mes Amis ★★★ £C
Recommended Whites:
IGP des Côtes Catalanes Sant Lluc ★★★ £C
IGP des Côtes Catalanes Miserys ★★★ £C
IGP des Côtes Catalanes Muscat Sec ★★★ £C

Dom. de La Rectorie (Banyuls & Collioure) *www.la-rectorie.com*
One of the finest producers of Collioure and Banyuls, the Parcé brothers also produce the wines of LA PRÉCEPTORIE DE CENTERNACH. For La Rectorie, there are three cuvées of red Collioure and a presentable rosé. Of the reds L'Oriental is the lightest and made from 100% Grenache, whereas the denser and more structured Côte Mer is a blend of Grenache, Syrah and Carignan. The sturdiest of the three, Côte Montagne is produced from a blend of Grenache, Carignan, Mourvèdre, Counoise and Syrah. Even the latter two are not in any way overblown; they are more wines of refinement and elegance. These are complemented by a Collioure, L'Argile, a powerfully oaked Grenache Gris. Very good Banyuls includes two regular cuvées – the best is Cuvée Léon Parcé, which is aged for around a year in cask and an altogether different, less evolved style to that found at Mas Blanc – and an aged wine, L'Oublée, which is understandably pricey. (DM)

Recommended Reds:
Collioure Côte Montagne ★★★☆ £E
Collioure Côte Mer ★★★☆ £D
Collioure L'Oriental ★★★ £C
Banyuls Cuvée Léon Parcé ★★★☆ £E
Recommended Whites:
Collioure L'Argile ★★★ £C

Dom. des Schistes *www.domaine-des-schistes.com*
A small, first-class range of both table and fortified wines is produced at this property. Including AOC Côtes du Roussillon-Villages and IGP wines. The reds are characterised by the old-vine quality of the fruit, which adds an extra dimension. Indeed some of the oldest vines are over 80 years old. Tradition is a forward, fruit-driven style blended from Syrah, Grenache and Carignan and vinified both traditionally and with some carbonic maceration. Les Terrasses is produced from the same varieties but with a higher proportion of Syrah aged in 1-year-old oak, the balance in *cuve*. Stylish and intense, there is a real mineral quality running through the wine. La Coumeille, the top red, is 100% Syrah, aged in oak of which only a small portion is new and the wine is very fine with a really spicy, dark, intense fruit quality. There's a lovely nutty and raisiny Maury and a very good floral yet powerful and concentrated Muscat de Rivesaltes. (DM)

Recommended Reds:
Côtes du Roussillon-Villages La Coumeille ★★★☆ £E
Côtes du Roussillon-Villages Tautavel Les Terrasses ★★★ £D
Côtes du Roussillon-Villages Tradition ★★☆ £C
Maury La Cerisaie ★★★☆ £D
Recommended Whites:
Muscat de Rivesaltes ★★★ £C

Dom. Sarda Mallet (Côtes du Roussillon)
Based in the Côtes du Roussillon just to the south of Perpignan, this is a far longer established domaine than many of its Roussillon neighbours. Jerôme Malet now runs the family property and

Roussillon

France

Sarda-Malet are making some of the best wines of the region. There are some 37 ha planted on finely drained southwest facing clay-limestone slopes of which just over 10 ha are planted to white varieties. The traditional grapes of the area are of considerable age, mostly over 50 years, while Syrah and Mourvèdre were planted nearly 30 years ago. Le Sarda is the label for the regular Côtes du Roussillons. The fresh, nutty white is a blend of Grenache Blanc, Grenache Gris, Malvoisie and Macabeo. The juicy, spicy and lightly mineral red blends Grenache, Syrah, Mourvèdre and unusually a touch of Macebeo. The Réserve red is a dense and supple, characterful blend of Grenache, Carignan, Syrah and Mourvèdre. Yields are restricted to 25 hl/ha and the wine is ripe and spicy. The red *Terroir* Mailloles comes from Syrah and Mourvdere. Again very low yielding at just 20 hl/ha this is tight and impressively structured. Aged in one year-old barrels it is marked by its dark, pure fruit with an underlying minerality. The richly nutty, spicy white Terroir Mailloles comes from Roussanne, Marsanne and Grenache Gris and Blanc. The Roussanne and Marsanne coming from mass selected vines yield less than 15 hl/ha. It is part barrel-fermented. The brilliant L'Insouciant is an intense 100% Grenache made from vines planted between 1915 and 1940. Of the two fortified Rivesaltes, the Serrat comes from a parcel of Grenache Blanc and Gris planted in 1959. It is full of rich, nutty orange fruit peel notes and shows impressive complexity. The Carbase is a darkly rich and spicy fortified red Grenache coming from vines planted in 1945. Maceration lasts for up to five weeks and the wine is aged for less than 2 years in *cuve* to emphasise its brilliant fruit. Jerôme Malet is also involved in a joint venture, Marius producing an IGP Cabernet Sauvignon red from local vines with Frédéric Engerer, the president of Château LATOUR. (DM)

Recommended Reds:

Vin de France L'Insouciant ★★★★ £E

Rivesaltes La Carbase ★★★★ £E

Côtes du Roussillon Terroirs Mailloles ★★★★ £E

Côtes du Roussillon Réserve ★★★ £D

Côtes du Roussillon Le Sarda-Malet ★★☆ £C

Recommended Whites:

Côtes du Roussillon Terroirs Mailloles ★★★☆ £D

Rivesaltes Les Serrat ★★★ £D

Côtes du Roussillon Le Sarda-Malet ★★ £B

Dom. Seguela

Production is small at this dedicated Côtes du Roussillon-Villages producer. Yields are kept very low, fruit is carefully sorted prior to vinification and in the cellar filtration is avoided. What marks these wines out is the depth and purity of their fruit. Increasingly they are matching the structure of the very best. Les Candalières is a blend mainly of Carignan but with some Syrah and Grenache also. Soft easy tannins and spicy brambly fruit mark the style of the wine, which is excellent value. Cuvée Jean-Julien is a dense old-vine blend of Syrah and Carignan partly aged in new oak (but this is seamlessly handled), while the Planète-Seguela is an astonishingly low-yielding (as low as 12 hl/ha) *assemblage* of Carignan, Syrah, Grenache and Cinsault and is refined, long and well-structured. (DM)

Recommended Reds:

Côtes du Roussillon-Villages Planète-Seguela ★★★★ £F

Côtes du Roussillon-Villages Cuvée Jean-Julien ★★★☆ £E

Côtes du Roussillon-Villages Les Candelières ★★★ £C

❀ Dom. Serrelongue (Maury)

Tiny domaine producing exquisite wines from a small vineyard holding of just 6 ha. The plots are planted to a combination of Mourvèdre, Syrah, Carignan and Grenache and vine age ranges from 25–125 years. This combined with high altitude vineyards and a committed approach to reducing yields results in wines of remarkable depth and purity. Do not expect fruit bombs, the overriding character here is minerality, with subtle deeply spicy black fruits and intensity rarely found in the Midi. The Extrait de Passion blends Mourvèdre, Grenache with Syrah and is aged in *demi-muids*. The more approachable saveur de Vigne is dominated by old vine Grenache. A characterful IGP white is also made from old Grenache Gris and Carignan Blanc along with an approachable well priced Carignan dominated red, Carigno and red and white Maury. (DM)

Recommended Reds:

Côtes du Roussillon-Villages Extrait de Passion ★★★★☆ £E

Côtes du Roussillon-Villages Saveur de Vigne ★★★☆ £D

Recommended Whites:

IGP des Côtes Catalanes Envie de Blanc ★★★☆ £D

Dom. des Soulanes (Maury) *www.domaine-soulanes.com*

This is another recently established operation in the vineyards of the Roussillon. Based at Tautavel in the heart of Côtes du Roussillon, two of the the wines here take the IGP des Côtes Catalanes classification. They also produce Côtes du Roussillon-Villages and Maury fortifieds. The Laffites have just over 17 hectares spread across 18 diverse parcels with their Grenache and Carignan planted in a mix of schistous soils. The red Jean Pull is a soft, ripe and brambly style with Carignan as well as Grenache. A rich opulent character to the fruit is ensured through low yields and old vines. The Cuvée Bastoul-Laffite is sturdier, firmer and will develop extremely well in bottle. The spicy and exotic Sarrat del Mas is aged in new oak. Yields here are barely 20 hl/ha and the wines are bottled unfiltered. The Maury is one of the best in the AC. (DM)

Recommended Reds:

Côtes du Roussillon-Villages Cuvée Sarrat del Mas ★★★★ £E

IGP des Côtes Catalanes Cuvée Bastoul-Laffite ★★★☆ £D

IGP des Côtes Catalanes Cuvée Jean Pull ★★★ £C

❀ Dom. Thunevin-Calvet *www.thunevin-calvet.fr*

This partnership, Jean-Luc Thunevin is the owner of Château de VALANDRAUD in Saint-Emilion, purchased their small property in Maury in 2000 and the first vintages were 2001. The *terroir* is ideal for producing red wines of the highest calibre from the naturally low yielding vines. Early yields from the vineyards were less than 20 hl/ha. The soils are very finely drained black schist which produces a really piercing minerality. You are struck, as with some top Priorats, by this characteristic of the wines rather than by their fruit. Constance is a blend of Grenache and Carignan aged in *cuve*. The Côtes du Roussillon-Villages Les Dentelles blends Carignan with Grenache and Syrah; whereas the Hugo is Grenache, Syrah and the balance Carignan. Both are aged in new wood. Hugo in particular offers an extraordinarily complex character to its fruit. The most expensive of the wines by a considerable distance in the small range is the newly added, rich and structured Les Trois Marie, a 100% Grenache from a yield of barely more than 12 hl/ha. These are wines that will evolve very well with 5 or 6 years cellaring. (DM)

Recommended Reds:

Côtes du Roussillon-Villages Les Trois Marie ★★★★★ £H

Côtes du Roussillon-Villages Hugo ★★★★☆ £F

Côtes du Roussillon-Villages Les Dentelles ★★★★ £E
IGP des Côtes Catalanes Constance ★★★ £C

Dom. du Traginer (Banyuls & Collioure) *www.traginer.fr*

A fine range of Banyuls and improving Collioures are produced at this small 9 ha property. Red varieties Mourvèdre, Syrah, Grenache and Carignan are planted along with Grenache Blanc and Gris as well as Muscat. The vineyards are planted on schistous soils and since 1997 have been farmed organically. Jean-François Deu is the only remaining Banyuls grower to plough his vineyards by mule; indeed his name means mule driver in Catalan. There is a very good white Collioure, which is fermented relatively cool and aged in *cuve*, with piercing spicy, citrus fruit. The red Collioures are traditionally vinified with a maceration on the skins of 25 days. The Traditionelle is aged in *foudre*, Al Riberal in 1- to 5-year-old *barriques* and the Octobre and the top label Cuvée du Capitas in new and 1-year-old barrels. Full of dark spicy fruit the Octobre and Cuvée du Capatas are impressively structured and ageworthy. Like PIÉTRI-GÉRAUD, Traginer is one of the few remaining producers of a Banyuls Blanc. Blended from Grenache Blanc, Grenache Gris and Muscat à Petit Blancs, the wine has a marked floral as well as grapey character with considerably more intensity than you would generally find in white Port. Of the red Banyuls the Rimage is marked by its fresh berry fruit and is bottled after 7 months. Mise Tardive is aged in *foudre* for 30 months and has a notably evolved nutty character. Best of all though, the Grand Cru Hors d'Age is aged for at least 10 years in demi-muid. It is rich and toffeed with real depth and intensity. (DM)

Recommended Reds:

Collioure Octobre ★★★★ £E
Collioure Cuvée du Capatas ★★★★ £E
Collioure Al Riberal ★★★★ £E
Collioure Traditionelle ★★★☆ £D
Banyuls Grand Cru Hors d'Age ★★★★ £E
Banyuls Mise Tardive ★★★☆ £D
Banyuls Rimage ★★★☆ £D

Recommended Whites:

Collioure ★★★ £D
Banyuls Mise Tardive ★★★ £D

Dom. Jean-Louis Tribouley (Côtes du Roussillon-Villages)

Jean-Louis Tribouley produces a very good and extremely well priced range of Roussillon wines. Like many in the area the domaine is new, established in 2002. Tribouley farms just over 10 ha of organically certified vineyard, with vines ranging from 30 to 70 years of age. Yields are deliberately kept down, barely 15 hl/ha and there is a rigorous fruit selection at harvest. The white is dominated by Macabeu and given short ageing in a mix of oak and *cuve*. Of the reds, Les Copines is dominated by Carignan, L'Alba mainly Carignan and the balance Syrah and Grenache, while the top label Les Trois Lunes is equal parts of Grenache, Syrah and Carignan and aged partly in oak and partly *en cuve*. Two additional reds are also worth looking at, Orchis and the old-vine Les Bacs. (DM)

Recommended Reds:

Côtes du Roussillon-Villages Les Trois Lunes ★★★★ £E
Côtes du Roussillon L'Alba ★★★☆ £D
Côtes du Roussillon Les Copines ★★★ £C

Recommended Whites:

IGP des Côtes Catalanes ★★★ £C

Dom. Vaquer (IGP des Côtes Catalanes)

Some fine traditional wines, often radically different from many of

the region's new wave wines, are made at this long-established domaine, including outstanding Rivesaltes. Vinification is traditional and the red wines are aged in *cuve* with no use of new oak. Of the whites the Esquisse is an attractively floral, lightly nutty 100% Roussanne. More serious is the white l'Exception, a blend of Grenache Blanc and Maccabeu, just over a third of which is vinified in new oak. The oak is just a touch raw in the wine's youth, so give it a couple of years. The rosé L'Éphimère is a blend of Carignan and Syrah. Fuller and richer than most of its kind, it is marked by concentrated bright crushed berries. Of the reds the Cuvée Bernard Vaquer is the softest, a supple and forward Carignan dominated wine. The denser, more structured Exigence is 100% Grenache. Arguably the most characterful of the reds is L'Expression, a Carignan from old vines of very impressive density and structure. It smacks of rich, dark, spicy, minerally varietal fruit with great complexity. The L'Exception red is Grenache and Syrah blend. While rich and reasonably concentrated it lacks the sheer character of the L'Expression. Of the fortifieds there is a fine Muscat de Rivesaltes as well as two fine Rivesaltes. L'Extrait is the more fruit forward, while the Tuilé Post Scriptum is aged for around 6 years in *cuve* and has a classic nutty *rancio* character. A Vieux Rivesaltes is also produced in very limited quantities. (DM)

Recommended Reds:

IGP des Côtes Catalanes L'Expression ★★★☆ £E
IGP des Côtes Catalanes L'Exception ★★★☆ £E
IGP des Côtes Catalanes Exigence ★★★ £D
IGP des Côtes Catalanes Bernard Vaquer ★★☆ £C
Rivesaltes Tuilé Post Scriptum ★★★ £E
Rivesaltes L'Extrait ★★☆ £D

Recommended Whites:

IGP des Côtes Catalanes L'Exception ★★★ £D
IGP des Côtes Catalanes Esquisse ★★☆ £C

Recommended Rosés:

IGP des Côtes Catalanes L'Éphimère ★★ £C

Other wines of note - *Roussillon*

Dom. de l'Architecte
Recommended Reds:
Côtes du Roussillon Aux Figuiers ★★★ £C
Côtes du Roussillon Aux Amandiers ★★★ £C

Dom. Boucabeille
Recommended Reds:
Côtes du Roussillon-Villages Les Orris ★★★★ £E
Côtes du Roussillon-Villages Monte Nero ★★★ £C

Dom. Boudau
Recommended Reds:
Côtes du Roussillon-Villages Patrimoine ★★★☆ £D
Côtes du Roussillon-Villages Padri ★★★ £C
Côtes du Roussillon-Villages Henri Boudau ★★★ £C
Côtes du Roussillon Le Clos ★★☆ £B

Recommended Whites:
Côtes du Roussillon Le Clos Blanc ★★ £B
IGP des Côtes Catalanes Muscat sec ★★ £B

Dom. Brial
Recommended Reds:
Côtes du Roussillon-Villages Corpus ★★★ £E

Ch. Aymerich
Recommended Reds:
Côtes du Roussillon Jean Aymerich ★★ £C
Côtes du Roussillon Général Aymerich ★★ £C

Roussillon

Côtes du Roussillon Estang Poulée ★★ £C
Côtes du Roussillon Tradition ★★ £B
Recommended Whites:
Muscat de Rivesaltes ★★ £C
Ch. Montana
Recommended Reds:
IGP Côtes Catalanes Secret de Schistes ★★★★ £E
IGP Côtes Catalanes Infiniment de L'Ou ★★★☆ £D
Côtes du Roussillon ★★★ £C
Recommended Whites:
IGP Côtes Catalanes L'Astre Blanc ★★☆ £C
Ch. de L'Ou
Recommended Reds:
IGP Côtes Catalanes Secret de Schistes ★★★★ £E
IGP Côtes Catalanes Infiniment de L'Ou ★★★☆ £D
Côtes du Roussillon ★★★ £C
Recommended Whites:
Côtes du Roussillon ★★☆ £C
Ch. Planères
Recommended Reds:
Côtes du Roussillon ★★ £C
Ch. de Rey
Recommended Reds:
Côtes du Roussillon Les Galets Roulés ★★★ £D
Ch. du Rombeau
Recommended Reds:
Côtes du Roussillon-Villages Cuvée Elise ★★★ £C
Côtes du Roussillon Château Rombeau ★★ £C
Recommended Whites:
Côtes du Roussillon ★★ £C
Clos des Vins d'Amour
Recommended Reds:
Maury Sec Un Baiser ★★★☆ £D
Maury Alcôve ★★★ £C
IGP Côtes Catalanes Carignan en Famille ★★☆ £B
Recommended Whites:
Côtes du Roussillon Idylle ★★☆ £C
En Roussillon
Recommended Reds:
Côtes du Roussillon ★★★★ £E
Dom. Eternel
Recommended Reds:
Côtes du Roussillon-Villages Domaine Eternel ★★★★ £E
Côtes du Roussillon-Villages Elsa ★★★☆ £D
Recommended Whites:
IGP Côtes Catalanes Confidence ★★★☆ £E
Dom. Força-Real
Recommended Reds:
Côtes du Roussillon-Villages ★★★ £C
Côtes du Roussillon Les Hauts de Forca-Real ★★☆ £C
Rivesaltes Hors d'Âge ★★★ £C
Dom. Grier
Recommended Reds:
Côtes du Roussillon-Villages Olympus ★★★☆ £D
Côtes du Roussillon-Villages Galamus ★★★ £C
Côtes du Roussillon-Villages Odyssea ★★☆ £C
Dom. Joliette
Recommended Reds:
Côtes du Roussillon-Villages André Mercier ★★☆ £C

Dom. La Borde Vieille
Recommended Reds:
Côtes du Roussillon-Villages ★★★☆ £E
Dom. La Coume du Roy
Recommended Reds:
Maury Vintage ★★★☆ £E
Maury ★★★ £D
Maury Sec Le Désir ★★☆ £B
Recommended Whites:
Muscat de Rivesaltes ★★☆ £C
Dom. Lafage
Recommended Reds:
Côtes du Roussillon Onze Terrasses ★★★★☆ £G
Côtes du Roussillon Le Vignon ★★★★ £E
Côtes du Roussillon Cuvée Léa ★★★☆ £D
Dom. Laporte
Recommended Reds:
Côtes du Roussillon Sumeria ★★★ £C
Côtes du Roussillon Domitia ★★☆ £C
La Préceptorie de Centernach
Recommended Reds:
IGP Terre Promise ★★ £B
Côtes du Roussillon Coume Marie ★★★ £C
Maury Aurélie Pereira de Abreu ★★★ £D
Recommended Whites:
Côtes du Roussillon Coume Marie Côtes Catalans ★★ £B
Dom. La Toupie
Recommended Reds:
Maury Sec ★★★ £C
Côtes du Roussillon-Villages Volte Face ★★★ £C
Côtes du Roussillon-Villages Quatuor ★★★ £C
IGP Côtes Catalanes ★★ £B
L'Etoile
Recommended Reds:
Banyuls Extra Vieux ★★★ £E
L'Excellence de Mon Terroir
Recommended Reds:
Collioure ★★★ £E
Le Signal d'Agly
Recommended Reds:
Vin de France Vendange des Foins ★★ £B
Recommended Reds:
Côtes du Roussillon Vieilles Vignes ★★★☆ £D
Les Terres de Mallyce
Recommended Reds:
Côtes du Roussillon Villages Les Huit ★★☆ £C
IGP Côtes Catalanes Pierres de Lune ★★☆ £C
Dom. L'Héritier
Recommended Reds:
Côtes du Roussillon Romani ★★★ £D
Dom Marcevol
Recommended Reds:
Côtes du Roussillon Prestige ★★★ £D
Côtes du Roussillon ★★☆ £C
Mas Crémat
Recommended Reds:
Côtes du Roussillon Dédicace ★★★ £D
Côtes du Roussillon Bastien ★★☆ £C
Côtes du Roussillon L'Envie ★★ £B
Recommended Whites:
IGP des Côtes Catalanes ★★ £B

Mas de Lavail
Recommended Reds:
Maury Sec Initiale ★★★★ £E
Dom. Modat
Recommended Reds:
Côtes du Roussillon-Villages Caramany Sans plus attendre ★★★☆ £D
Côtes du Roussillon-Villages Caramany Comme Avant ★★★☆ £D
Recommended Whites:
Côtes du Roussillon De-ci de-là ★★★ £C
Dom. de La Perdrix
Recommended Reds:
Côtes du Roussillon Cuvée JS Pons ★★★ £C
IGP des Côtes Catalanes Corto ★★☆ £B
Dom. Piquemal
Recommended Reds:
Côtes du Roussillon-Villages Galatée ★★★☆ £D
Côtes du Roussillon-Villages Pygmalion ★★★☆ £D
Côtes du Roussillon Villages Les Terres Grillées ★★★ £C
Côtes du Roussillon Villages Tradition ★★☆ £B
Recommended Whites:
Côtes du Roussillon Les Terres Grillées ★★★ £C
Dom. Rière Cadène
Recommended Reds:
Côtes du Roussillon Fernand Cadène ★★★☆ £D
Côtes du Roussillon Cuvée Jean Rière ★★★ £C
IGP Côtes Catalanes La Tour de Schiste ★★★ £C
Recommended Whites:
IGP Côtes Catalanes J'ai rendez-vous avec vous ★★ £B
Recommended Rosés:
IGP Côtes Catalanes J'ai rendez-vous avec vous ★★ £B
Dom. Rivaton
Recommended Reds:
Côtes du Roussillon-Villages Gribouille ★★★☆ £D
Recommended Whites:
Côtes du Roussillon-Villages Blanc Bec ★★★☆ £D
Dom. de La Serre
Recommended Reds:
Côtes du Roussillon-Villages Hypogee ★★★★ £F
Côtes du Roussillon-Villages Serre Longue ★★★☆ £E
Serre Romani
Recommended Reds:
IGP des Côtes Catalanes Vallée de l'Aigle ★★★★ £E
Côtes du Roussillon-Villages Schistes ★★★☆ £D
IGP des Côtes Catalanes Providence ★★★☆ £D
Maury ★★★ £C
Recommended Whites:
IGP des Côtes Catalanes Vallée de l'Aigle ★★★★ £E
IGP des Côtes Catalanes Macabeu ★★ £B
Si Mon Père Sauvait
Recommended Reds:
Côtes du Roussillon ★★☆ £C
Dom. Singla
Recommended Reds:
Côtes du Roussillon-Villages Castell Vell ★★★☆ £D
Côtes du Roussillon-Villages Passe Temps ★★★☆ £C
Dom. Treloar
Recommended Reds:
Côtes du Roussillon Tahi ★★★☆ £D
Côtes du Roussillon Motus ★★★ £C
Côtes du Roussillon Le Secret ★★★ £C
Côtes du Roussillon Three Peaks ★★☆ £C

Côtes du Roussillon One Block Grenache ★★★☆ £C
Recommended Whites:
IGP des Côtes Catalanes La Terre Promise ★★★ £C
Dom. de Venus
Recommended Reds:
Côtes du Roussillon-Villages ★★★☆ £D
Côtes du Roussillon Vieilles Vignes ★★★☆ £C
IGP des Côtes Catalanes ★★★ £C
Recommended Whites:
IGP des Côtes Catalanes L'effrontée ★★★ £C

Work in progress!!

Producers under consideration for the next edition
Agly Brothers (Côtes du Roussillon)
Dom. Cabirau (Maury)
Dom. Chemin Faisant (Côtes du Roussillon)
Mas Becha (Côtes du Roussillon)
Mas de L'Avail (Côtes du Roussillon)
Dom. Gilles Troullier (IGP des Côtes Catalanes)

Author's choice - *Roussillon*

A selection of fortifieds
Reds:
Cellier des Templiers   Banyuls Grand Cru Henri Vidal
Dom. Cazes   Rivesaltes Ambré
Coume del Mas   Banyuls Quintessence
Dom. Puig-Parahÿ   Rivesaltes 1930
Dom. Fontanel   Rivesaltes
Dom. La Tour Vieille   Banyuls Reserva
Mas Amiel   Maury Charles Dupuy
Dom. du Mas Blanc   Banyuls Rimage La Coume
Mas Mudigliza   Maury
Roc des Anges   Maury Les Terres de Fagayra
Whites:
Dom. Piétri-Géraud   Banyuls Blanc
Dom. des Schistes   Muscat de Rivesaltes
Dom. du Traginer   Banyuls Mise Tardive

Classic Rousillon reds
Dom. de Casenove   Côtes du Roussillon François Jaubert
Clos del Rey   Côtes du Roussillon-Villages Clos del Rey
Dom. du Clos des Fées   La Petite Sibérie
Consolation   Collioure Dog Strangler
Dom. de L'Edre   Côtes du Roussillon-Villages L'Edre
Dom. Fontanel   Côtes du Roussillon-Villages Prieuré
Dom. Gardies   Côtes du Roussillon-Villages Falaises
Dom. Gauby   Côtes du Roussillon-Villages Muntada
Dom. La Tour Vieille   Collioure Puig Oriol
Clot de L'Oum   Côtes du Roussillon-Villages Numero Uno
Dom. Depeyre   Côtes du Roussillon-Villages Sainte-Colombe
Dom. de La Rectorie   Collioure La Coume Pascole
Dom. Le Soula   IGP des Côtes Catalanes Le Soula
Dom. Matassa   IGP des Côtes Catalanes Romanissa
Dom. Maestrio   IGP des Côtes Catalanes Elégant
Dom. Pertuisane   Côtes du Roussillon-Villages Le Pertuisane
Dom. Pouderoux   Côtes du Roussillon-Villages Mouriane
Roc des Anges   IGP des Pyrénées-Orientales Carignan 1903
Dom. Thunevin-Calvet   Côtes du Roussillon-Villages Les Trois Marie

Roussillon

France

A value for money red selection

Cave de L'Abbe Rous   Collioure Cornet et Cie
Dom. d'Arfeuille   Côtes du Roussillon-Villages L'Originelle
Ch. de Caladroy   Côtes du Roussillon-Villages La Cour Carrée
Clos del Rey   IGP d'Oc Mas del Tey
Dom des Enfants   IGP des Côtes Catalanes l'enfant perdu
Dom. Fontanel   Côtes du Roussillon-Villages Cistes
Les Clos de Paulilles   Côllioure
Dom. Jones   IGP des Côtes Catalanes
Dom. La Tour Vieille   Collioure Puig Oriol
Dom. Laguerre   Côtes du Roussillon Le Ciste
Mas des Baux   IGP des Côtes Catalanes Rouge Gorge
Mas Cristine   Côtes du Roussillon
Mas Janeil   Côtes du Roussillon-Villages
Dom. Piétri-Géraud   Collioure
Mas Karolina   IGP des Côtes Catalanes

Provence has emerged in recent years with a number of exciting high quality small domaines from most of her appellations. The change has been less dramatic than in the Midi, but here too many quality-minded individuals are bringing a new focus to viticulture and expressing the potential of their terroirs. The role of Provence as a purveyor of easy drinking pink plonk to sun-seeking tourists is gradually changing and indeed many of the examples are much improved. Some interesting wines and fortified styles are emerging from Corsica although the wines remain hard to find outside France. In the main they continue to be traditional, the best offering real character.

Provence

While rosé remains the mainstay of Provençal wine production, exciting reds and some very well-made whites have emerged over the last fifteen years or so. In the foothills of the Alpes-Maritimes inland of Nice the tiny appellation of **Bellet**, with a total of a mere 39 ha under vine, offers some unusual albeit pricey, well-structured reds and lightly floral nutty whites and fruity rosés. The proximity of neighbouring Italy shows itself with the Braquet (Brachetto) among the varieties that make up the permitted red blend, along with Folle Noir and the more usual Grenache and Cinsault. The vineyards are planted at altitude of some 300m, moderating the climate. This provides an unusual opportunity in ripening Chardonnay in such a southerly maritime climate, which in the whites is blended with Rolle.

The vast bulk of central Provence is covered by the appellations of **Côtes de Provence** and **Côteaux Varois en Provence**. While both produce vast amounts of rosé, some very fine nowadays, impressive reds are being produced from blends of Rhône varieties, occasionally with the addition of Cabernet Sauvignon. There also now four sub appellations of Côtes de Provence: **Sainte-Victoire**, **Fréjus**, **La Londe** and **Pierrefeu**. The **Côteaux d'Aix en Provence** and the spectacularly sited vineyards of **Les Baux de Provence** produce similar wines. Domaine de Trevallon, now forced to label its wine as **IGP des Bouches du Rhône**, set the trend with a stunning blend of Cabernet and Syrah. There are a number of other such blends now; some like Trevallon use more traditional ageing in large vats while others are seduced by new oak. Whatever the approach an exciting array of different styles is emerging.

Palette is another tiny AC of just 40ha for both red and white and with only a handful of established producers, although more are emerging. An extensive number of varieties can be planted but increasingly replanting is concentrated on Syrah, Grenache and Mourvèdre.

The two coastal appellations of **Cassis** and **Bandol** between Marseilles and Toulon are sources of red, white and rosé. Generally Cassis tends to be pretty dull fare but there is the odd impressive white. The best whites and rosés from Bandol are certainly very good but it is the reds that you should look out for. The appellation is situated in the foothills just inland of the port of Bandol in a natural coastal amphitheatre. The vineyards stretch from La Ciotat in the east to Sanary-sur-Mer in the west and enjoy a unique warm, dry maritime climate. The style of the wine itself varies surprisingly due to differing calcareous, gravel and clay soils and varying levels of Mourvèdre, the main grape variety. Established Bandol leaders Domaine Tempier and Château Pibarnon are now being joined by a new wave of small, high-quality growers. This is an exciting area to

follow. Remember, though, that these wines need cellaring, often for up to a decade.

Corsica

There are three main appellations on the island of Corsica; **Vin de Corse, Patrimonio and Ajaccio.** Almost all viticulture is carried out around the coast. The forested, mountainous interior is far too extreme for viticulture. There are also a number of crus within the Vin de Corse appellation: **Calvi, Sartène, Figari, Porto-Vecchio and Côteaux du Cap Corse.**

Both Côteaux du Cap Corse and Patrimonio are entitled to the **Muscat du Cap Corse** appellation and it is some of these good to very good rich fortified Muscats which offer the greatest excitement here. Some good reds are also produced from the native Nielluccio along with Grenache, Carignan and Cinsault.

A-Z of producers by appellation

Bandol
Dom. de la Bégude	310
Domaines Bunan	311
Ch. de la Rouvière	311
Ch. de Pibarnon	312
Ch. Jean-Pierre Gaussen	312
Ch. Pradeaux	312
Ch. Vannières	314
Dom. du Gros Noré	315
Dom. La Bastide Blanche	316
Dom. La Suffrene	316
Dom. Lafran Veyrolles	316
Dom. de la Laidière	316
Mas de la Rouvière	311
Moulin des Costes	311
Luc Sorin	318
Dom. Tempier	319
Dom. de Terrebrune	319
Dom. de la Tour du Bon	319

Bellet
Ch. de Bellet	311

Côteaux d'Aix-en-Provence
Dom. de Béates	310
Ch. Bas	311
Ch. de Beaupré	311
Ch. Revelette	312
Ch. Vignelaure	314

Côteaux Varois
Ch. Routas	313

Côtes de Provence
Ch. de Roquefort	313
Ch. du Rouet	313
Ch. Les Valentines	312
Dom. du Clos Alari	314
Dom. du Clos de la Procure	315
Dom. de la Courtade	314
Dupere Barrera	314
Dom. du Grand Cros	315
La Badiane	315
Mas de Cadenet	317
Mirabeau en Provence	317

Ott Domaines	317
Ch. de Selle	317
Ch. Romassan	317
Clos Mireille	318
Dom. Richeaume	318
Dom. Rimauresq	318
Dom. St-André de Figuière	318
Dom. St-Andrieu	318

Les Baux-de-Provence
Ch. Romanin	312
Dom. Hauvette	315
Dom. de Lauzières	316
Mas de la Dame	317
Dom. de Trevallon	319

Palette
Ch. Simone	314

Patrimonio
Antoine Arena	310

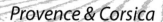

Provence & Corsica

France

1 Les Baux de Provence
2 Côteaux d'Aix en Provence
3 Palette
4 Côtes de Provence
5 Côteaux Varois
6 Cassis
7 Bandol
8 Bellet

Provence vintage chart

	Bandol	Côtes de Provence Top reds	Les Baux de Provence Top reds
2015	★★★★☆ A	★★★★☆ A	★★★★☆ A
2014	★★★☆ A	★★★ A	★★★ A
2013	★★★★ A	★★★★ A	★★★★ A
2012	★★★☆ A	★★★ A	★★★ A
2011	★★★★☆ A	★★★★☆ A	★★★★☆ A
2010	★★★★☆ A	★★★★☆ A	★★★★☆ A
2009	★★★★ A	★★★★ B	★★★★☆ A
2008	★★★★ B	★★★★ B	★★★★ B
2007	★★★★☆ B	★★★★☆ B	★★★★☆ B
2006	★★★★☆ B	★★★★☆ C	★★★★☆ B
2005	★★★★☆ B	★★★★☆ C	★★★★☆ C
2004	★★★★ C	★★★★ C	★★★★ C
2003	★★★★ C	★★★☆ C	★★★☆ C
2002	★★★ C	★★★ D	★★★ C
2001	★★★★ C	★★★★ D	★★★★ D
2000	★★★★☆ C	★★★★☆ D	★★★★☆ C
1999	★★★★ D	★★★★ D	★★★★ D
1998	★★★★☆ C	★★★★☆ D	★★★★☆ D

A-Z of producers

❀ Dom. Antoine Arena (Patrimonio)

This is one of Corsica's benchmark domaines and arguably the leading quality orientated producer on the island. All the wines are characterful and very well made with a real stamp of *terroir* and possess a classic mineral depth. Like other quality concious producers in other regions the Vin de France labelled wines have on different occasions taken the Patrimonio as well as IGP classification. The Arena family possess some 14 ha of vineyards on ideally sited south-easterley slopes and whites are the dominant plantings. Vermentino and Muscat are important, as is the red Niellucio (Sangiovese). The reds Grotte de Sole and Carco, both named after vineyard parcels are based on this variety. The Grotte di Sole is the more firm and structured of the two, the Carco more obviously fruit

driven. The white Bianco Gentile is vinified from a local variety of the same name, while the Grotte di Sole is a rich and luscious example of Vermentino. The unctuous and concentrated Muscat du Cap Corse is one of the better examples of the style. A Carco white from Vermentino is also produced along with another red Morta Maïo, which is also from Niellucio. (DM)

Recommended Reds:
Vin de France Grotte di Sole ★★★★ £E
Patrimonio Carco ★★★☆ £E
Recommended Whites:
Vin de France Bianco Gentile ★★★☆ £E
Patrimonio Grotte di Sole ★★★☆ £E
Muscat du Cap Corse ★★★☆ £E

Dom. des Béates   www.lesbeates.com

This Côteaux d'Aix-en-Provence based biodynamic operation attracted the interest of Michel CHAPOUTIER of the Rhône Valley in the late 1990s, although that interest has now been sold. No fewer than four labels are now produced with a red, white and rosé produced under each of the Bébé de Béates, Les Béatines and the superior Béates brand. The Béates red is structured, dense and powerful but with supple, well-rounded, ripe tannins. It is a blend of Syrah, Cabernet Sauvignon, and Grenache. The white is a combination of Rolle and Ugni Blanc and is barrel fermented in 500 litre barrels with lees stirring. The fine and mineral and dark fruit scented rosé comes from Syrah and a little Cabernet Sauvignon. The harvest from the oldest vines, which are over 50 years old, is reserved for the top cru, Terra d'Or, which is a serious step up. Vinified and aged in new oak, it is surprisingly approachable but rich and concentrated with a velvety texture. Complex dark berry fruit, herbal spice and subtle oak are all seamlessly integrated. This has now been joined by a Terra d'Or white made from Sauvignon Blanc and a rosé which is 100% Syrah. (DM)

Recommended Reds:
Côteaux d'Aix-en-Provence Terra d'Or ★★★★ £F
Côteaux d'Aix-en-Provence Béates ★★★ £C
Côteaux d'Aix-en-Provence Les Béatines ★★ £B

Dom. de La Bégude (Bandol)   www.lesbeates.com

This dramatically improving Bandol domaine is now producing some of the more exciting wines in the appellation. It is ideally situated at the highest point of the AC at an altitude of 430 metres. The estate itself is substantial but a mere 16 ha are planted to vines

as olive groves are also an important constituent. The vineyard is now around 30 years of age and this helps in keeping yields naturally down to 30 hl/ha or less. A red, a white and a rosé are produced. The rosé is a blend of all the red varieties here, namely Mourvèdre, Cinsault, Grenache and Carignan. It is one of the very best examples of the style and has the structure to develop well for two or three years. Quality has improved dramatically over the last three years. The white Bandol is a barrel-fermented blend of Clairette, Ugni Blanc and Rolle. The red is dominated by Mourvèdre (90%), with the balance Grenache. The wine is now less extracted during maceration and the fruit is increasingly stylish and well defined. It is bottled unfiltered and will evolve well for 7–10 years. A small volume of a limited production red Cuvée de la Brulade has also been added. (DM)

Recommended Reds:
Bandol ★★★★ £E
Recommended Whites:
Bandol ★★★ £D
Recommended Rosés:
Bandol ★★★ £D

✸ **Domaines Bunan (Bandol)** *www.bunan.com*
One of the longest-established producers in the appellation, the Bunan family arrived in Bandol in 1961. This is a family business run by Paul Bunan along with his son Laurent. Laurent has gained an international perspective having worked in California. The focal point of production here is Bandol from 3 estates. Along with the reds, both white and rosé are produced at all 3 estates and these are sound examples of the appellation, the whites fermented cool in stainless steel to emphasise their fruit. In addition to this there is a Côtes de Provence property, Domaine Belouve, producing solid red, white and rosé. Three generic Bandols are produced under the Domaines Bunan label but it is the estate reds that are the real excitement. The Mas de La Rouvière and Moulin des Costes regular bottling are the lighter wines. Moulin des Costes gets a slightly longer vatting and has Grenache as well as Mourvèdre, Cinsault and Syrah, which comprise the Mas de La Rouvière blend. The Moulin des Costes offers slightly more spicy, peppery characters but both will develop well with 5 years' ageing. The Chateau de la Rouvière is richer, more complete, sourced from a single plot of just over 2.5ha. Dense, spicy dark fruit and truffles are defined in its impressive fruit. Firmly tannic in its youth, it demands 6 or 7 years' patience. The top wine, Cuvée Charriage, is the richest and lushest of the wines. Vinified with cold maceration and extended maceration of up to a month, it is structured but supple and should be very fine with 8–10 years' cellaring. (DM)

Château de La Rouvière
Recommended Reds:
Bandol ★★★★ £E
Moulin des Costes
Recommended Reds:
Bandol Cuvée Charriage ★★★★ £F   Bandol ★★★ £D
Mas de la Rouvière
Recommended Reds:
Bandol ★★★☆ £E

Ch. Bas (Côteaux d'Aix-en-Provence) *www.chateaubas.com*
This is a sizeable property producing sound to very good red, white and rosé under the Côteaux d'Aix-en-Provence appellation. There are 72 ha of vines on the estate with 64ha planted to reds and

production is now over 30,000 cases a year. Three separate ranges, L'Alvernègue, Pierre du Sud and Cuvée du Temple, all include a red, a white and a rosé. The L'Alvernègue wines are soft, forward and fruit-driven. The red offers a little structure and grip, although it should be drunk young. The Pierre du Sud wines are a step up in quality, with well defined fruit character, and are also for drinking young – although the red will stand short ageing. The Cuvée du Temple wines are of a different order. The rosé is part barrel-fermented and has surprising depth and structure for the style. The red, a blend of Syrah, Cabernet Sauvignon and Grenache, has impressive depth. Richly texured with subtle spicy undertones, it should be aged for 3 or 4 years at least. Perhaps the standout wine here is the barrel-fermented white, blended from Sauvignon Blanc, Rolle and Grenache Blanc. Oak is subtly used and this is complimented with very pure citrus and herb spiced fruit with a rich creamy finish. While the wine drinks very well young it will also stand a little age. (DM)

Recommended Reds:
Côteaux d'Aix-en-Provence Cuvée du Temple ★★★ £C
Côteaux d'Aix-en-Provence Pierre du Sud ★★☆ £C
Côteaux d'Aix-en-Provence L'Alvernègue ★☆ £B
Recommended Whites:
Côteaux d'Aix-en-Provence Cuvée du Temple ★★★ £C
Côteaux d'Aix-en-Provence Pierre du Sud ★★ £B
Côteaux d'Aix-en-Provence L'Alvernègue ★☆ £B
Recommended Rosés:
Côteaux d'Aix-en-Provence Cuvée du Temple ★★ £C
Côteaux d'Aix-en-Provence Pierre du Sud ★☆ £B

Ch. de Beaupré (Côteaux d'Aix-en-Provence) *www.beaupre.fr*
This property has been in the same family for four generations. Vineyards were first planted by Baron Emile Double in 1892. There are now 42 ha under vine, with the vast majority accounted for by red varieties including Cabernet Sauvignon, Syrah and Grenache. White varieties include Rolle, Grenache Blanc Sauvignon and Sémillon. The top red is the impressive Collection which is a blend of 90% Cabernet Sauvignon and 10% Syrah and comes from the best plots of red plantings, around 25 years of age grown in *argilo-calcaire* soils and accounting for just 2.5 ha of the *vignoble*. Finely structured with subtle red cherry and restrained blackcurrant fruit with background herb and *garrigue* scents, the wine will develop well for four or five years. A top white Collection is also produced from Sémillon and Sauvignon as well as red, white and rosé under the regular Château de Beaupré label. Baies de Beaupré are straightforward fruit driven styles taking the Côteaux d'Aix-en-Provence appellation and the range is completed by a couple of IGP varietals from Merlot and Syrah. (DM)

Recommended Reds:
Côteaux d'Aix-en-Provence Collection du Château ★★★ £D

Ch. de Bellet (Bellet) *www.chateaudebellet.com*
This is one of a handful of properties in the tiny appellation of Bellet in the Provençal hills inland of Nice. As at neighbouring CHÂTEAU DE CRÉMAT, a red, white and rosé are produced. Because the vineyards are in a protected mesoclimate and planted at altitude, they are cooler than their southerly location would suggest. This enables Chardonnay to ripen successfully as well as the local Rolle that completes the white blend. The red and rosé are produced from Folle Noire, Bracquet, Cinsault and Grenache. The Bracquet variety can also be found further east in Piedmont in Italy, where it is known as Brachetto. The wines are good; the red perfumed, supple and approachable and the white lightly floral and aromatic with an

Provence & Corsica

underlying nutty character. They may be approached young but will benefit from a year or two in the cellar. The rosé should be drunk young. (DM)

Recommended Reds:
Bellet Baron G ★★★☆ £F
Recommended Whites:
Bellet Baron G ★★★ £E
Recommended Rosés:
Bellet ★★☆ £D

Ch. Jean-Pierre Gaussen (Bandol)

Very good traditional, earthy Bandol is made at this 14 ha property. A tiny amount of Ugni Blanc and Clairette is planted but the key to these wines is the dominant planting of Mourvèdre which accounts for all the red vines bar a tiny holding of Grenache and Cinsault. Output is in line with other small producers in the appellation at around 6,000 cases a year, so readers should be able to find these wines without too much trouble. The soils are *argile* and calcareous and provide an excellent growing environment. The Tradition bottling is softer and more youthfully supple, with a lower proportion of Mourvèdre. The Longue Garde is sturdier with a blend that is close to 100% Mourvèdre and darker and firmer in style. This is classically backward, minerally reserved Bandol that demands at least five or six years cellaring. A small amount of a soft, spicy rosé is made from Grenache, Cinsault and Mourvèdre. (DM)

Recommended Reds:
Bandol Longue Garde ★★★☆ £E   Bandol Tradition ★★★☆ £E
Recommended Rosés:
Bandol ★★☆ £C

Ch. Les Valentines (Côtes de Provence) www.lesvalentines.com

From just over 20 ha of biodynamically farmed vineyards, Les Valentines, like a number of other Côtes de Provence properties, is showing what this appellation is capable of achieving. As well as the Côtes de Provence bottlings, soft, easy-drinking red, white and rosé are produced under the Caprice de Clementine label. The rosé Les Valentines blends Cinsault with Grenache, Syrah, Mourvèdre and Tibouren. It has better definition and intensity than most Provençale examples. In addition to this a superior cuvée, Huit La Lande is also now made. Les Valentines Blanc is dominated by very old Ugni Blanc and is vinified from a combination of fruit picked early for freshness and late for increased richness, which adds both weight and complexity. Of the reds, Les Valentines is vibrant, pure and accessible young, a blend of Mourvèdre, Grenache, Syrah as well as a little Cabernet Sauvignon and Carignan. Particularly impressive is the small-production Cuvée Bagnard, which is sourced from the best parcels of Syrah, Mourvèdre and Cabernet Sauvignon and aged for 12 months in demi-muids. Richly textured, with hints of dark berry fruit, oriental spice and mocha, it will add further complexity with 5 or so years of cellaring. Two additional premium reds are also made. La Gourmande is dominated by old Syrah, La Punition is solely old Carignan. (DM)

Recommended Reds:
Côtes de Provence Bagnard ★★★☆ £E
Recommended Whites:
Côtes de Provence ★★★ £D
Recommended Rosés:
Côtes de Provence ★★☆ £C

❀ Ch. Pibarnon (Bandol) www.pibarnon.com

Pibarnon is one of the best and most established properties in the appellation. The red here is powerful and structured, very backward in its youth, requiring up to a decade to fully develop. A very large proportion of Mourvèdre (90–95%) accounts for the dark, brambly and mineral style of its wine, dense but very refined as well. The *terroir* is ideal for ripening the variety: well-drained limestone-based soils and vineyards that are cooled by elevation as well as being very sunny ensure fruit loaded with intense flavour and fine, well-ripened but sturdy tannins. Recent vintages have all shown much promise. To help underpin the quality of the *grand vin*, a supple and much more approachable second wine, Restanques de Pibarnon is also being made. While many domains regard their white and rosé as a bit of a sideline there are refreshing indications here that this is not the case. The white is a blend of Clairette, Bourboulenc (adding vital acidity), along with Roussanne and a touch of Viognier and Marsanne. The rosé is an equal blend of Mourvèdre and Cinsault, cool fermented but with sufficient structure to make it an excellent food wine. (DM)

Recommended Reds:
Bandol ★★★★☆ £E   Bandol Restanques de Pibarnon ★★★ £C
Recommended Whites:
Bandol ★★★☆ £D
Recommended Rosés:
Bandol ★★★ £D

Ch. Pradeaux (Bandol) www.chateau-pradeaux.com

Just over 4,000 cases of red are made here from 20 ha of prime Bandol vineyard that is permanently being encroached upon by urban planners. A small amount of rosé is also produced, as well as a second red Le Lys. The Pradeaux red blend is almost exclusively Mourvèdre with a little Grenache. Traditionally vinified, the fruit is not destemmed, and the wine is aged in large wooden *foudres* for over 3 years which helps in softening its raw youthful tannic edge. It is a wine that demands a minimum of 6–7 years in the cellar. Anything less would be to miss the point of it. (DM)

Recommended Reds:
Bandol ★★★☆ £E

Ch. Revelette (Côteaux d'Aix-en-Provence) www.revelette.fr

This 25 ha domaine produces a very good IGP Chardonnay, Le Grand Blanc and one of the very best reds in the region. The vineyards, located inland of the Mont Saint-Victoire, are some of the highest in the Côteaux d'Aix-en-Provence at around 400 metres. This is reflected in the style and elegance of the wines. The regular red, white and rosé Côteaux d'Aix-en-Provence are well-priced examples of the appellation. The red Grand Rouge is a blend dominated by Syrah and Cabernet Sauvignon. It is given a long vatting and aged in small oak. Very finely crafted and with great purity of fruit, it requires a minimum of 5–6 years to reveal its full complexity and rich intensity. Peter Fischer is also a partner in the Priorat operation TRIO INFERNAL. (DM)

Recommended Reds:
Côteaux d'Aix-en-Provence Le Grand Rouge ★★★★ £E
Côteaux d'Aix-en-Provence ★★★ £D
Recommended Whites:
IGP des Bouches-du-Rhône Le Grand Blanc ★★★☆ £E
Côteaux d'Aix-en-Provence ★★☆ £C
Recommended Rosés:
Côteaux d'Aix-en-Provence ★★☆ £C

Ch. Romanin (Les Baux) www.romanin.com

Sizeable, biodynamically farmed property of 250 ha. Currently 58 ha

are planted to vines with the older vines in sandy, loamy, calcareous soils whereas the newer plantings are in calcareous, stony soils. The climate is not only warm, dry and sunny but during the growing season there is sufficient wind to help rather than hinder balanced growth. Production is gradually increasing 80% of which is red. The rosé Les Baux is soft and easy drinking, the white more serious with pronounced fresh, lightly herbal fruit character and good intensity, in part achieved through blocking the malolactic. It is a blend of Rolle, Ugni Blanc and Bourboulenc. Jean le Troubador is a light, easy-drinking red made from the youngest vines, which are just over 10 years old. La Chapelle de Romanin is in effect the second wine of the property, made from an extensive blend of young-vine Syrah, Grenache, Cabernet Sauvignon and Mourvèdre along with older Carignan, Cinsault and Counoise. Lightly spicy and herbal with ripe berry fruit, the wine is aged for around a year in *inox* and cement. The Romanin red blends Grenache, Syrah, Cabernet Sauvignon and Mourvèdre. As yet although good it lacks the weight and depth of the best examples of the region, in part because the Syrah and Mourvèdre are still young. The top wine, Le Coeur de Romanin is sourced from Syrah, Mourvèdre, Cabernet Sauvignon and Grenache from the best site on the property. Vine age ranges from 8–40 years so the best should be yet to come. Finely structured with medium weight, it has a nice balance of dark fruits, cedar and herb spice, with subtle and well-judged oak. Top years are right on the edge of ★★★★. (DM)

Recommended Reds:
Les Baux-de-Provence Le Coeur de Romanin ★★★☆ £E
Les Baux-de-Provence ★★★ £D
Les Baux-de-Provence La Chapelle de Romanin ★★ £C

Recommended Whites:
Les Baux-de-Provence ★★☆ £C

Ch. de Roquefort (Côtes de Provence) www.deroquefort.com
Raimond de Villeneuve now runs one of the most exciting domaines in Provence, with a firm emphasis on high quality. The property is just inland of the Bandol appellation and has vineyards planted at an altitude of over 300 metres. The first vintage to be bottled here was as recent as 1995; prior to this the fruit was sold off in bulk. The estate is farmed on biodynamic principles, not because it's trendy but because de Villeneuve believes this approach will provide the best balance for his vineyard. There are two fruit driven wines a red and a rosé, which are labelled Grêle. Of the whites Petit Salé is a straightforward IGP produced from Clairette and is joined by the more serious, minerally Genêts, which also has Rolle in the blend and is partially barrel-fermented. The Corail rosé is elegant and intense. It is, though, the reds that stand out here. The very well priced Les Mûres blends Grenache, Syrah, Carignan, Cinsault and Cabernet Sauvignon. Pure, elegant and intense, it will keep well. The Rubrum is rich, dense and powerful. Loaded with dark old-vine character, it blends Grenache, Mourvèdre and Carignan. In exceptional years Raimond also produces a similarly dense blend of Syrah, Mourvèdre and Carignan called La Pourpre. A further red Momentum blends Grenache with Syrah and Cinsault and is aged in *foudres* for 18 months, while the Gueul de Loup combines Grenache with the Bordeaux grapes Cabernet Sauvignon and Merlot. The top reds here should be given 5–7 years. (DM)

Recommended Reds:
Côtes de Provence Rubrum ★★★★ £E
Côtes de Provence Les Mûres ★★★☆ £D

Recommended Whites:
Côtes de Provence Genêts ★★☆ £C

Recommended Rosés:
Côtes de Provence Corail ★★☆ £C

Ch. de Rouet (Côtes de Provence) www.chateau-du-rouet.com
The Savatier family have been at this property close to Fréjus in the foothills of the Estérel range since the 19th century. Rosé, white and red Côtes de Provence are produced under three labels. The l'Estérel wines are the softest and fruitiest; the 1840 range, marketed in traditional Provençale bottles, are sturdier and more structured; the Belle Pouelle label wines offering a little more depth. Small amounts of a red and rosé are also now released under the Fréjus label. Rosé is made by cold maceration and the l'Estérel is soft and straightfoward, the 1840 fuller, with a little structure from Grenache, Cinsault and Tibourenc. The Belle Pouelle is from Grenache and Syrah and made solely from first run juice. The white 1840 is cold-fermented after a period of skin maceration. It is aged on lees for 2–3 months and is a nutty, spicy blend dominated by Rolle with Ugni Blanc. The Belle Pouelle white is fully Rolle and is fermented and aged in barrel with lees-stirring providing a richer, creamier texture. The l'Estérel red is soft and vibrant, blending Carignan vinified by carbonic maceration with Grenache and Syrah. The 1840 is a traditionally vinified blend of Grenache, Syrah and Mourvèdre. It is aged for 3–4 months in *foudres* and is marked by its elegant berry and spice fruit. The Belle Pouelle is Grenache, Syrah and just a little Cabernet Sauvignon. This is firmer and more structured and needs 3 or 4 years' patience at least. The Savatiers also have a small holding of very old Alicante Bouschet from which they make a splendidly dense and characterful varietal *vin de garde*, Severac. Rich, dark and smoky, it is aged in 500-litre barrels to emphasise its splendid fruit. Just 500 cases or so are produced each year and you'll probably have to visit to get this one, but there are gîtes available so it shouldn't be a hardship. (DM)

Recommended Reds:
IGP Severac ★★★☆ £E   Côtes de Provence Belle Pouelle ★★★ £D
Côtes de Provence 1840 ★★☆ £C
Côtes de Provence Cuvée de l'Estérel ★★ £C

Recommended Whites:
Côtes de Provence Belle Pouelle ★★☆ £C
Côtes de Provence 1840 ★★ £C
Côtes de Provence Cuvée de l'Estérel ★☆ £B

Recommended Rosés:
Côtes de Provence Belle Pouelle ★★☆ £C
Côtes de Provence 1840 ★★ £C
Côtes de Provence Cuvée de l'Estérel ★☆ £B

Ch. Routas (Côteaux Varois) www.chateauroutas.com
Established for upwards of a decade, Routas is located in the wild inland Provençale hills of the Côteaux Varois and has vineyards that are just that bit cooler than its neighbours'. Former owner Philippe Bieler invested considerably in both the vineyard and the cellar, with state-of-the-art vinification equipment. Production runs at around 20,000 cases and the wines, particularly the top reds and the white Coquelicot, are good to very good. The reds, fashioned in a full but approachable style, will nevertheless improve with some cellar time. Infernet is a blend of Grenache and Syrah and the Wild Boar red a blend of Cabernet Sauvignon and Syrah. There is an easy-drinking white blend of southern French grapes, the Wild Boar white. The two best wines truly stand out: Cyrano, a spicy, smoky 100% Syrah, and Viognier, a nutty, subtly oaked, herb-scented blend of Viognier and Chardonnay. (DM)

Provence & Corsica

France

Recommended Reds:
IGP du Var Cyrano ★★★☆ £D   IGP du Var Wild Boar Red ★★ £B
Recommended Whites:
IGP du Var Cuvée Viognier ★★★ £D

❀ **Ch. Simone (Palette)**   *www.chateau-simone.fr*
This is a benchmark property in the tiny appellation of Palette just
outside Aix-en-Provence. The property has around 17 ha of vineyard
and there are a bewildering number of permitted red varieties
under the appellation regulations. Small quantities of some of
the rarer ones are still planted but the emphasis is increasingly on
Grenache, Mourvèdre and Syrah. White varieties are dominated by
Clairette and it is the white which is the most exciting of the wines.
Full, rich and decidedly old fashioned, it nevertheless possesses
some marvellous nutty, spicy and honeyed notes which increase
with age. The red is also very good. There's a small amount of decent
but pricy rosé and a more fruit driven white and rosé both labelled
Grands Carmes. (DM)
Recommended Reds:
Palette ★★★★ £E
Recommended Whites:
Palette ★★★★ £E

Ch. Vannières (Bandol)   *www.chateauvannieres.com*
This is one of the best of the current generation of Bandol
producers. Along with the likes of CHÂTEAU PRADEAUX and
Domaine du GROS NORÉ this is a property that's knocking on the
door of PIBARNON and TEMPIER. The wine is a powerful but stylish
example of the appellation. All its intense, dark-berry Mourvèdre
character and intense herbal, *garrigue* scents will shine through
when the tannin has had time to soften and the wine achieves
real balance and harmony. Good floral white Bandol is produced
along with a good rosé and recently a red Côtes de Provence, an
increasingly impressive junior version of the *grand vin*. (DM)
Recommended Reds:
Bandol ★★★★ £E

Ch. Vignelaure   *www.vignelaure.com*
Côteaux d'Aix-en-Provence based Vignelaure was purchased by
Bengt Sundstrom in early 2008. It was one of the early benchmark
properties of the AC in the 1980s and former owners the O'Briens
returned it to Provence's first division. Work in the vineyard is key,
with canopy management and a tight control on yields ensuring
top-quality fruit from well-drained limestone, gravel and clay soils.
The estate is solely planted to red varieties and there are some 60 ha
under vine. Investment and modernisation in the cellar is ongoing
and vinification is now very modern with malolactic carried out in
barrel. There are two lower priced ranges La Source de Vignelaure
and Le Page de Vignelaure, both providing very sound quality in
both red and rosé. The more expressive La Source labels are made
from a mix of the domaines grape varieties, whereas Le Page wines
are blends of Cabernet Sauvignon and Merlot. The Vignelaure rosé
is more serious and mineral, a good food wine with a little structure
and grip. It will keep a year or two. The Côteaux d'Aix-en-Provence
red rarely comes from a yield much above 30 hl/ha and is a blend
of Cabernet Sauvignon and Syrah. Ageing is in one-third new oak
for 18 months and the wine is a fine mix of elegant cedar and spicy
herb *garrigue* scents. Unfined and bottled with minimal filtration, it
will certainly benefit from 4 or 5 years' patience. (DM)
Recommended Reds:
Côteaux d'Aix-en-Provence Château Vignelaure ★★★☆ £D

Côteaux d'Aix-en-Provence La Source de Vignelaure ★★☆ £C
Côteaux d'Aix-en-Provence Le Page de Vignelaure ★★ £B
Recommended Rosés:
Côteaux d'Aix-en-Provence Château Vignelaure ★★☆ £C
Côteaux d'Aix-en-Provence La Source de Vignelaure ★☆ £B

Dom. du Clos d'Alari (Côtes de Provence)   *www.lesbeates.com*
Clos d'Alari is a small 20-ha estate with just 8ha under vine. Olives are
also grown. The vineyard comprises 6 ha of Côtes de Provence and a
further 2 ha are IGP. A minimalist approach is taken in both vineyard
and cellar, although a *vendange vert* is practiced to control crop
yields. Harvesting is by hand and vinification is traditional. There are
two rosés, the fresh and lightly herb-scented Grand Clos offers more
depth and structure the fresh and bright La p'tite Nine is marked by
its fruit and should be drunk as young as possible. The IGP Syrah and
Merlot blend is soft and fruit-driven and there is also a fine regular
Côtes de Provence red blending Syrah, Grenache, Carignan and
Cabernet. Pride of place goes to the prestige red which has taken a
number of names in recent vintages. Sourced from a particular plot
of less than 1ha it comes from a similar blend and is aged in a mix of
small oak, a quarter new. As with the other wines here, it is marked
by its elegance as well as a supple texture and great depth and
persistence of flavour. It will develop very well for 4 or 5 years. (DM)
Recommended Reds:
Côtes de Provence Cuvée Prestige ★★★ £D
Côtes de Provence Grand Clos ★★★ £C
IGP du Var Syrah/Merlot ★☆ £B
Recommended Rosés:
Côtes de Provence Grand Clos ★★ £B
IGP du Var La p'tite Nine ★☆ £B

Dom. de La Courtade (Côtes de Provence)
The Ile-de-Porquerolles is best known as a secluded destination for
holidaying Mediterranean yachtsmen. The island lies off the coast of
Provence between Bandol and Saint-Tropez. There are some 30 ha of
vines, 13 ha of them the white Rolle. This is used exclusively to vinify
the white Côtes de Provence, which is lightly oaked and displays
some ripe tropical notes as well as a more typically southern nutty
character. The rosé is an elegant blend of Grenache and Mourvèdre.
These two will stand a little age as will the red Alycastre, which is
the second wine here, produced to ensure the integrity of the top
red. Fresh forward examples of white and rosé are also made under
the Alycastre label. The *grand vin* is a rich, brambly, spicy blend of
Mourvèdre, Grenache and Syrah and is impressive, concentrated
and worth seeking out. (DM)
Recommended Reds:
Côtes de Provence ★★★☆ £E
Côtes de Provence Alycastre ★★☆ £C
Recommended Whites:
Côtes de Provence ★★★☆ £E
Recommended Rosés:
Côtes de Provence ★★☆ £C

❀ **Dupéré Barrera (Côtes de Provence)**   *www.duperebarrera.com*
This small operation with a total output of less than 6,000 cases
a year is part micro-négociant and part producer. Red and a tiny
amount of white Côtes de Provence come from the Barreras' own
Domaine du Clos de la Procure vineyard, which was purchased
in 2003. As well as this they have also produced so far Côtes du
Rhône-Villages, Côteaux du Languedoc, Costières de Nîmes and
Rivesaltes as well as Côtes de Provence from bought-in fruit. Their

most established label, and one of the most opulent and stylish of the appellation, is the Bandol India. This rich, concentrated, dark and smoky red is sourced from an *argile*-calcareous *terroir*, 90% of the grapes are destemmed and the wine is vatted for as much as 4–6 weeks. Ageing in the cellar is in a combination of *foudres* and small oak. Nowat is a sturdy, muscular blend of Syrah and Cabernet Sauvignon. TLM combines Grenache and Mourvèdre which is given extended vatting resulting in a dense, dark-berry laden, herb-spiced red of impressive dimension. A Nowat white is also made, a combination of Vermentino, Rolle, Sémillon and Ugni Blanc it has a typically nutty, spiced southern fruit character and a rich, rounded texture. The Clos de la Procure wines both come from old vines. The vineyard is at the limit of the Mediterranean influence on the local climate and the *argile*-calcareous soils are ideally water-stressed during ripening. La Procure red blends Grenache and Mourvèdre, while the white is dominated by Ugni Blanc. Handling for all the wines is kept to a minimum and they are bottled unfined and unfiltered. (DM)

Domaine du Clos de la Procure
Recommended Reds:
Côtes de Provence La Procure ★★★☆ £D
Recommended Whites:
Côtes de Provence La Procure ★★★ £D

Dupéré-Barrera
Recommended Reds:
Bandol India ★★★★ £E
Côtes de Provence TLM ★★★★☆ £F
Côtes de Provence Nowat ★★★☆ £E
Recommended Whites:
Côtes de Provence Nowat ★★★ £D

Dom. du Grand Cros (Côtes de Provence) www.grandcros.fr
A fairly extensive range of red, white and rosé is made at this 22 ha property situated in the foothills of the Massif des Maures in the centre of the Var. Vineyard development here is ongoing and new planting is at a density of 4–5,000 vines per hectare with a cover crop of grass to stress the vines sufficiently and optimise fruit ripening. Farming is as natural as possible with minimal use of pesticides and fungicides. Fruit-driven, forward wines are released under the Jules label and a characterful red particularly stands out. The regular Côtes de Provence wines are labelled L'Esprit de Provence and include a red blended from Cabernet Sauvignon and Syrah and a soft, forward rosé produced from Grenache and Cinsault along with a little Syrah and Rolle to add depth. The two Nectar wines account for just 5% of the domaine output. The white is a barrel-fermented Sémillon, whereas the red is a rich, powerful and impressively concentrated Cabernet Sauvignon, with just a touch of Syrah and Grenache, produced from yields of just 20 hl/ha. A 48-hour cold soak is undertaken prior to a temperature-controlled vinification which emphasises the dark, cedary fruit. Ageing is for 12 months in small oak with micro-oxygenation rather than conventional racking. In general the wines should be drunk young but the Nectar red will develop very well in bottle for 5 years or more. The Domaine range is completed by a fine juicy sparkling rosé, La Maitresse. (DM)

Recommended Reds:
Côtes de Provence Nectar ★★★ £D
Côtes de Provence L'Esprit de Provence ★★☆ £C
Côtes de Provence "Jules" Reserve ★★☆ £C
Côtes de Provence "Jules" ★★ £B
Recommended Whites:

Côtes de Provence Nectar ★★★ £D
IGP des Maures L'Esprit de Provence ★★☆ £C
IGP des Maures Jules Chardonnay-Vermentino ★☆ £B
Recommended Rosés:
Côtes de Provence Nectar ★★☆ £C
Côtes de Provence L'Esprit de Provence ★★ £C
Côtes de Provence "Jules" ★☆ £B

✿ Dom. du Gros Noré (Bandol) www.gros-nore.com
The first vintage at this newly established Bandol producer was as recent as 1997, but it was still one of real class and style. Almost all of the 11.5 ha are planted to red varieties but a small amount of white is also produced – a typically fat wine with broad, warm, nutty fruit – as well as a reasonable rosé. The important wine is the red Bandol, a big, brooding unfiltered blend of Mourvèdre, Grenache and Cinsault full of dark, savoury, roasted aromas with real intensity and purity. A complex, spicy, herbal undercurrent adds interest to the beefy fruit. Backward in its youth it needs time. It is very characterful and likely to improve in bottle for up to a decade or more. A Bandol rosé is also made as well as a second red Antoinette. (DM)

Recommended Reds:
Bandol ★★★★☆ £E
Recommended Whites:
Bandol ★★★ £D

✿ Dom. Hauvette (Les Baux)
Dominique Hauvette's small 13 ha property is fast emerging as one of the finest, not only in Les Baux but in Provence. A small range of three reds and one white of uniformly excellent quality is produced. The white Blanc de Blancs – a blend of Marsanne, Roussanne and Clairette, and as such labelled as IGP – is part barrel-fermented and aged on lees with *bâtonnage*. There is a piercing, nutty, citrus intensity here with finely judged oak and a rich creamy texture. It should develop very nicely in the medium term. The red Amethyste is based unusually around Cinsault, with varying amounts of Carignan, Grenache, Syrah and occasionally Cabernet Sauvignon. It is the softest, lushest of the Hauvette reds but there is sufficient structure, elegance and refinement to enable short-term development. The Cornaline is bigger, with a raw almost *sauvage* character from a blend dominated by Carignan with equal proportions of Cinsault and Grenache. Domaine Hauvette, the top red blends Grenache with Syrah and a balance of Cabernet Sauvignon. Two years in *foudres* and small oak are comfortably absorbed. The wine is rich, powerful and seriously structured. Expect to age it for at least 5–7 years to get the best out of it. (DM)

Recommended Reds:
Les Baux-de-Provence ★★★★ £E
Côteaux d'Aix-en-Provence Cornaline ★★★☆ £E
Côteaux d'Aix-en-Provence Améthyste ★★★☆ £E
Recommended Whites:
IGP des des Alpilles Dolia ★★★☆ £E

✿ La Badiane (Côtes de Provence) www.labadiane.fr
Jean-Luc Poinsot works with a number of small growers across Provences appellations producing a range of very well made and crafted wines. He selects individual terroirs that will he feels perfectly demonstrate the character and potential of a region. Red, white and rosé are all produced. Of the reds the Côteaux Varois San Bigues is the most approachable, with ripe, succulent red berry fruit and a scent of *garrigues* in the background. It is an unfiltered blend of Grenache and Carignan. Bouisson, Côtes

Provence & Corsica

France

de Provence blends Mourvèdre and Syrah, it is ripe, supple and approachable. Both Bandols are splendid, the Terres Noires is the lighter more elegant of the two and comes from black, marly clay soils. The fuller and more sturdy Mourvégué comes from red sandy soil with marked traces of pebbles. It is a true *vin de garde* and demands six or seven years ageing. Among the whites, opulent, nutty and immediately approachable is the Cassis Les deux Soeurs, the vineyard characterised by its striking twin background peaks. It is a blend of Clairette, Ugni Blanc and Bouboulenc the latter variety providing sufficient acidity to give the wine definition and structure. San Bigues is also the site for a good nutty, citrusy white from a blend of Sémillon and Rolle as well as a fresh approachable rosé from Grenache and Carignan. Best of the rosés is the softly structured Mourvégué Bandol. The Antiboul is a very characterful wine produced from the Tibouren grape. Rarely does it give enough colour for a red so Jean-Luc produces a rosé. This is sturdy and structured though, coming from old vines of over 50 years and the malolactic taking place in used casks. It is an excellent food wine. (DM)

Recommended Reds:
Bandol Mourvégué ★★★★ £E   Bandol Terres Noires ★★★★ £E
Côtes de Provence Bouisson ★★★☆ £C
Côteaux Varois San Bigues ★★★ £C

Recommended Whites:
Cassis Les deux Souers ★★★☆ £D
Côteaux Varois San Bigues ★★☆ £C

Recommended Rosés:
Bandol Mourvégué ★★☆ £C   Côtes de Provence Antiboul ★★☆ £C
Côteaux Varois San Bigues ★★ £C

Dom. La Bastide Blanche (Bandol)   *www.bastide-blanche.fr*
Red, white and rosé are produced under the Bandol AC at this 28 ha property, established by the Bronzo family over 30 years ago. The vineyards are cultivated largely organically and great care is taken at harvest to select the best fruit. The 3 reds here inevitably stand out. The sturdy Bastide Blanche is Mourvèdre, Grenache with the balance Cinsault. Both the Fontanéou and Estagnol are Mourvèdre bottlings. These last two wines are produced from vines grown on different soils. The reds will all develop very well for a decade or longer and require cellaring for at least 4–5 years. (DM)

Recommended Reds:
Bandol Fontanéou ★★★★ £E   Bandol Estagnol ★★★★ £E
Bandol ★★★ £D

Recommended Rosés:
Bandol ★★☆ £C

✿ **Dom. Lafran Veyrolles (Bandol)**   *www.lafran-veyrolles.com*
Very impressive red Bandol is now being made at this 10-ha property. Mourvèdre dominates the red plantings, while the whites are a mix of Clairette and Ugni Blanc. The vineyards are farmed organically and the argilo-calcareous soils provide an excellent base for growing fruit of the highest quality. The white is one of the better examples produced in the appellation, as is the softly strawberry-scented rosé. The two reds with their sizeable Mourvèdre component stand out. Both are dense, powerful and finely structured. Firm youthful tannin will be seamlessly integrated with 5 or 6 years' ageing. (DM)

Recommended Reds:
Bandol Spéciale ★★★★☆ £E   Bandol Tradition ★★★★ £E

Recommended Rosés:
Bandol ★★★ £D

Dom. de La Laidière (Bandol)   *www.laidiere.com*
Well-crafted and good-value red, white and rosé and in top years a Cuvée Spéciale red are produced at this Bandol property of some 24 ha. The bulk of the vineyard is planted to red varieties, with 60% Mourvèdre and 20% each of Cinsault and Grenache. The rosé is ripe and forward, while the white, from a blend of Clairette and Ugni Blanc, has a light nutty elegance and a hint of herb spice. The red, as is the case at most Bandol properties, is the key wine. Firmly structured in its youth with a savoury, almost meaty character to its fruit it will gain an extra dimension with 5 years' age. (DM)

Recommended Reds:
Bandol ★★★☆ £D

✿ **Dom. La Suffrene (Bandol)**   *www.domaine-la-suffrene.com*
Up until the 1996 vintage Cédric Gravier sold his harvest to the co-op. His welcome decision to vinify under his own label has resulted in some of the best wines to emerge from what is arguably the top Provençale appellation. A fresh IGP red and soft, easy rosé are produced but it is the Bandols that stand out. There is a sound rosé produced from Mourvèdre, Cinsault, Grenache and Carignan and a superior Sainte Catherine, which is Mourvèdre and Carignan and should work well with food. The white blends Clairette with Ugni Blanc. Vinified and aged in *inox* it has impressive depth and intensity, with a mix of floral, spice and citrus aromas. The regular Bandol is a blend of Mourvèdre, Grenache, Cinsault and just a little Carignan. Sturdy and structured with traditional, dark berry fruit and meaty characters, it shows all the potential to improve with 5 or 6 years' cellaring. The very rich, supple and concentrated top wine, Cuvée des Lauves, is dominated by Mourvèdre with just a smattering of old Carignan adding dark pepper notes to the sumptuous dark fruit. (DM)

Recommended Reds:
Bandol Cuvée des Lauves ★★★★☆ £E   Bandol ★★★☆ £D

Recommended Whites:
Bandol ★★★ £C

Recommended Rosés:
Bandol Cuvée Sainte Catherine ★★★ £C   Bandol ★★☆ £C

Dom. de Lauzières (Les Baux)   *www.domainedelauzieres.com*
Jean-Daniel Schlaepfer discovered this superbly located property at the heart of the Baux-de-Provence appellation in 1992. The vineyards are planted to a varied mix of Grenache, Syrah, Mourvèdre, Carignan, Cinsault and Petit Verdot among the reds and Grenache Blanc with a tiny amount of Clairette for the whites. Two very fair reds are produced as Baux-de-Provence, the lighter Equinoxe and the denser and more structured Solstice, but the owners believe that the conventional varieties authorised by the appellation authorities here are not capable of expressing the greatest potential of the estate and the top red is labelled as Vin de France. The white Sine Nomine is a pure and very intense barrel-fermented blend of Grenache Blanc and Clairette. The oak is superbly handled with the piercing citrus and creamy, nutty fruit dominating the wine. The red Sine Nomine very unusually blends mainly Petit Verdot with the balance Grenache. Rich, powerful and very concentrated, this muscular red needs at least 5 or 6 years. (DM)

Recommended Reds:
Vin de France Sine Nomine ★★★★ £E
Les Baux-de-Provence Solstice ★★★ £D

Recommended Whites:
Les Baux-de-Provence Sine Nomine ★★★★ £E

Mas de Cadenet (Côtes de Provence) *www.masdecadenet.fr*
This estate with vineyards only a few miles as the crow flies from Palette has been in the Négrel family since 1813. It is now entitled (since 2004) to add the Sainte-Victoire sub appellation to the AC name for its reds. There are 40 ha, most planted to red varieties, and the *terroir* consists of well-drained gravel, clay and sand. Yields are purposely restricted. The range consists of three main labels, red white and rosé Côtes de Provence are also now produced under a third label Arbaude and a sweet Vin cuit is made from pre-fermentation heated juice. The top brands are Mas de Cadenet and the more serious Mas Négrel. The Mas de Cadenet rosé and white are soft, forward and attractively fruit-driven. The red is a blend of Syrah, Grenache and Cabernet Sauvignon aged in *foudres* for 6-8 months and offers some depth and substance. The Mas Négrel Prestige is the top white, made from 100% Rolle. Aged in wood for 6–8 months on fine lees, it is nutty and characterful. The Mas Négrel Cadenet rosé is more structured than most, being aged in oak. The Mas Négrel Cadenet red is a blend of Grenache, Syrah and Cabernet Sauvignon, vatted for over 20 days to add extract and flesh and aged in oak for 12–15 months. Dark, spicy and concentrated, it requires 4 years at a minimum. (DM)

Recommended Reds:
Côtes de Provence Sainte-Victoire Mas Négrel Cadenet ★★★ £D
Côtes de Provence Sainte-Victoire Mas de Cadenet ★★☆ £C

Recommended Whites:
Côtes de Provence Mas Négrel Cadenet ★★★ £C
Côtes de Provence Mas de Cadenet ★★ £C

Recommended Rosés:
Côtes de Provence Sainte-Victoire Mas Négrel Cadenet ★★☆ £C
Côtes de Provence Sainte-Victoire Mas de Cadenet ★☆ £B

Mas de La Dame (Les Baux) *www.masdeladame.com*
A good quality producer from Les Baux-de-Provence with 57 ha of vineyards. The property was immortalised by Vincent Van Gogh when he painted it in 1889. As one would expect the great majority of vines are red varieties but there are 5 ha of whites including some Sémillon. Very good olive oils are also produced from the estate's 25 ha of olive groves. A relatively extensive range of wines is made here with consultancy provided by Jean-Luc COLOMBO. The red Réserve and white Cuvée de la Stèle offer reasonable value and straightforward drinking. The Coin Caché white is very stylish, floral, nutty and perfumed, the Cuvée de la Stèle red rich and chunky with hints of *garrigue* and smoke. The Vallon des Amants a spicy blend dominated by Mourvèdre. The Coin Caché red is a supple, smoky, powerful, old-vine blend of Grenache and Syrah. (DM)

Recommended Reds:
Les Baux-de-Provence Coin Caché ★★★☆ £E
Les Baux-de-Provence Vallon des Amants ★★★☆ £E
Les Baux-de-Provence Cuvée de la Stèle ★★★ £D
Les Baux-de-Provence Réserve ★★☆ £C

Recommended Whites:
Les Baux-de-Provence Coin Caché ★★★ £E

Recommended Rosés:
Côteaux d'Aix-en-Provence Cuvée de la Stèle ★★☆ £C

>> Mirabeau en Provence *www.mirabeauwine.com*
This excellent small artisan Côtes de Provence based operation was founded in 2009. Stephen Cronk refers to them as a *négociant* but this is a small, dedicated producer, sourcing fruit from a number of good local growers and then completing the vinification of their three wines themselves. Winemaking input comes from Jo

Ahearne MW, Bruno Siviragol and Nathalie Longefay. Both roses are marked by elegance and intensity and there is an edgy mineral quality, which adds an extra dimension. They are night harvested preserving a vital fresh edge. The Classic is a blend with a higher proportion of Syrah than Grenache. From marginally lower lying vineyards it is rounder more fruit driven in style. The Pure (Grenache and a touch less Syrah) is more restrained and comes from higher altitude sites. Both get a short maceration on skins before pressing and a cool fermentation follows. The red Falaise is only available in France currently with volume being very small. However it will be of interest to those visiting the area or scouring good French restaurant wine lists. Dominated by Grenache and Syrah, there are smaller proportions of Cabernet Sauvignon and Merlot (both successful in Provence) as well as intriguingly a touch of Tempranillo. Round and supple with good concentration, the wine possesses a typically herb spiced edge and a combination of dark berry and blackcurrant fruits. The varieties are vinified separately before completing the malolactic fermentation in barrels, which are used rather than new. Wines to look out for. (DM)

Recommended Reds:
IGP Méditerranée La Falaise ★★★ £D

Recommended Rosés:
Côtes de Provence Pure ★★★☆ £C
Côtes de Provence Classic ★★★☆ £C

Domaines Ott (Côtes de Provence) *www.domaines-ott.com*
This is perhaps the most established name in Provence and the one that will most readily come to mind when readers associate with wines from the region. Output across the three separately owned domaines is considerable for the Provence. An extensive range is produced. In addition to the wines covered below two other whites are produced at Clos Mireille, Blanc de Côte and a limited release L'Insolent. At the Château de Romassan a total of three rosés are produced as well as a limited release red Longue Garde, which is aged in oak. At Château de Selle there is a second red Comtes de Provence as well as a white which is dominated by Sémillon. There are also three easy drinking wines which go under the brand Les Domaniers. Château de Selle is the most northerly of the three near Draguignan. There are 48 ha of mainly Cabernet Sauvignon and Sémillon. Couer de Grain is light, fresh and nicely structured while the firmer Longue Garde is dominated by Cabernet and is aged in oak for 18 months. Clos Mireille is located near the coast to the east of Toulon. This is white wine territory and the schist soils are planted to 47 ha of Sémillon and Ugni Blanc. The Blanc de Blancs is floral, nutty and lightly citrus scented. The Bandol property is to the west of Toulon at Le Castellet where there are 60ha. Mourvèdre dominates but Grenache, Cinsault and some Sauvignon Blanc are also cultivated. The Bandol Couer de Grain rosé is full and well structured, a good food wine, while the Bandol red offers classic dark berry Mourvèdre character in a firm and more elegant example than many from the appellation. Expect the reds and the Bandol in particular to develop well with a little age. The other wines should be enjoyed young. (DM)

Château Romassan
Recommended Reds:
Bandol ★★★☆ £E   Bandol Couer de Grain ★★☆ £D

Château de Selle
Recommended Reds:
Côtes de Provence Longue Garde ★★★☆ £E

Recommended Rosés:
Côtes de Provence Couer de Grain ★★☆ £D

Provence & Corsica

France

Clos Mireille
Recommended Whites:
Côtes de Provence Blanc de Blancs ★★★ £D

Dom. Richeaume www.domaine-richeaume.com
Richeaume has been producing consistently excellent wine under the Côtes de Provence appellation for years. The property consists of some 25 ha planted largely to Cabernet Sauvignon, Syrah, Grenache and Merlot. There is also a small holding of white varieties. The Tradition includes all four red varieties, complemented by fine varietal Cabernet and Syrah bottlings and a splendid *grand vin*, Cuvée Columelle. This massive, dense and very concentrated wine is one of the best reds in Provence. A flagship Syrah is also now made as as a number of whites and a rosé. (DM)

Recommended Reds:
Côtes de Provence Cuvée Columelle ★★★★ £E
Côtes de Provence Tradition ★★★ £D

Dom. Rimauresq (Côtes de Provence) www.rimauresq.fr
This fine 36 ha Scottish-owned property is notable for making some of the best examples of rosé in the Côtes de Provence. They are fine and pure with subtle, elegant red berry fruit and like all the wines here have a persistent mineral character which lends a tight, firm structure. This is particularly notable in the reds and in part may be attributable to the soils which are crystalline rock with sandstone and gravel. Average vine age is now 40 years and some are up to 70 years. Replacement planting is now ensuring an increased vine density of up to 5,000 vines per hectare in an on going drive to improve quality. A superior range labelled Cuvée R has been introduced for red, white and rosé. The red R blends solely Syrah and Cabernet Savignon, whereas the regular red is mainly Cabernet with much smaller proportions of Syrah, Mourvèdre and Carignan. Both whites are blended from Ugni Blanc and Rolle and ageing is in *demi-muids*. The Cuvée R rosé is produced from older plantings of Cinsault, Grenache and Mourvèdre, which gives it extra depth and that piercing mineral and red berry fruit intensity. Both the reds are firmly structured with a herb spice character, the Cuvée R being fuller and deeper but with a background touch of austerity in its youth. Give it 5 years or so to soften. A new flagship red Quintessence has also been added. (DM)

Recommended Reds:
Côtes de Provence Cuvée R ★★★ £E
Côtes de Provence ★★☆ £D

Recommended Rosés:
Côtes de Provence Cuvée R ★★☆ £C
Côtes de Provence ★★ £C

Dom. Saint-André de Figuière www.figuiere-provence.com
This 45 ha Côtes de Provence property located just inland between Toulon and Saint-Tropez, with the Massif des Maures immediately to the north, benefits from a benign, sunny maritime climate. As a result the Combards tend to enjoy better growing conditions than other Provençale properties in difficult years. Quality is characterised here by a range of excellent old-vine and reserve cuvées. As well as the premium estate wines there are both a red, white and rosé released as Vin du Pays du Var and a regular Signature bottling of red, white and rosé, respectively labelled cuvées François, Magali and Valérie, all of which offer good everyday drinking. The estate Côtes de Provence wines are a step up. The rosé Vieilles Vignes is blended from Mourvèdre, Cinsault and Grenache, a wine of impressive intensity for the style. The white Vieilles Vignes is a cool-fermented blend of Rolle, Sémillon and Ugni Blanc, whereas the splendidly pure and intense Confidentielle is barrel-fermented and aged on lees. It is 100% Rolle. The two top reds are impressively structured with real depth and concentration. The Vieilles Vignes is blended from Mourvèdre, Carignan and Syrah. The Confidentielle is a very low yielding blend of Mourvèdre and Syrah. Both get an extended maceration of 1 month before ageing for up to a year in used oak. Cellaring for 5 years or so will bring added complexity in both wines. A Confidentielle rosé is also released as well as a sparkling Traditional Method Extra Brut rosé, Atmosphere. (DM)

Recommended Reds:
Côtes de Provence Confidentielle ★★★☆ £E
Côtes de Provence Vieilles Vignes ★★★ £D

Recommended Whites:
Côtes de Provence Confidentielle ★★★ £D
Côtes de Provence Vieilles Vignes ★★☆ £C

Recommended Rosés:
Côtes de Provence Vieilles Vignes ★★☆ £C

Dom. Saint-Andrieu www.domaine-saint-andrieu.com
This picturesque Côtes de Provence based property has been owned by the Bignon family who own Château TALBOT in Saint Julien in Bordeaux since 2003, and is distributed by the Chancel family of CHÂTEAU VAL JOANIS in the Côtes du Luberon. As well as the slightly higher priced Côtes de Provence wines a red and rosé are also produced under the Côteaux Varois appellation. The vineyards are planted in the inland hills of Provence near the small town of Brignoles. The vineyard stretches to 26 ha which is planted on a mix of hillside clay and limestone soils. With the considerable knowledge and expertise available from Bordeaux the winery and vineyards have been completely refurbished and renovated. The rosé comes from a classic blend of Mourvèdre, Grenache, Syrah and Cinsault and the fermentation is at a low to moderate temperature to provide a little structure in the wine. The white is 100% Rolle, the wine benefits from a short *macération pelliculaire* and is then pressed and fermented, again at a moderate rather than cool temperature. The red is a typically Provençale herb scented, elegant and finely structured blend of roughly two-thirds Syrah and one-third Mouvèdre. It is traditionally vinified and 40% is aged in barrels for 9 months prior to bottling. (DM)

Recommended Reds:
Côtes de Provence ★★★ £D
Recommended Whites:
Côtes de Provence ★★☆ £C
Recommended Rosés:
Côtes de Provence ★★☆ £C

Dom. Sorin (Bandol) www.chateau-du-rouet.com
The Burgundian Luc Sorin took over this small Bandol property in 1994 after having been the winemaker at CHÂTEAU ROUTAS in the Côteaux Varois. He has plots in the Côtes de Provence AC as well as Bandol and produces red and rosé wines as well as now a white Côtes de Provence of impressive density and depth. In addition to the the Tradition rouge a limited Côtes de Provence Cuvée Prestige is also produced which has 70% Syrah. The Côtes de Provence Terra Amata rosé is soft and fruit-driven and will drink well young or with a very little age. The reds are de-stemmed then fermented and macerated in large rotating oak vats, which provide an even plunging process for the fermenting skins. Newly added is a IGP du Var bottling Terres Rouges a blend of Cinsault, Grenache and Carignan. The wines certainly have a soft, supple texture and in the

Bandol real density and persistence. (DM)
Recommended Reds:
Bandol Longue Garde ★★★☆ £E
Côtes de Provence Prestige ★★★ £D
Côtes de Provence Tradition ★★☆ £C
Recommended Rosés:
Côtes de Provence Terra Amata ★★ £C

✿ Dom. Tempier (Bandol) *www.domainetempier.com*
This is one of the great Bandol producers and has remained so for
the past two decades despite the emergence of newer names such
as PIBARNON and more recently GROS NORÉ. More than anything
these wines are characterised by their elegance and refinement as
opposed to the sheer power and density often achieved elsewhere.
There are around 38 ha planted to red varieties but a mere 1ha to
produce a small amount of white. Along with the four reds there
is also a very decent rosé. The regular cuvée produced from the
youngest vines on the property is well crafted and offers impressive
depth and intensity. It is, though, the three single vineyard wines,
La Tourtine, Migoua and Cabassou, that stand out. The latter, with
the highest proportion of Mourvèdre, is the sturdiest of the trio, the
Migoua the most stylish and elegant. All will age gracefully for well
over a decade. (DM)
Recommended Reds:
Bandol Cabassou ★★★★☆ £F Bandol Migoua ★★★★ £E
Bandol La Tourtine ★★★★ £E Bandol Cuvée Classique ★★★☆ £E
Recommended Rosés:
Bandol ★★★ £D

Dom. de Terrebrune (Bandol) *www.terrebrune.fr*
The red Bandol produced by Georges Delille from his 25 ha vineyard
is a massive, muscular and brooding example of the appellation.
The vineyards have an ideal aspect with finely drained calcareous
soils and the average vine age is now over 30 years, adding intensity,
depth and character to the fruit. This is a true *vin de garde*: a dense
smoky, spicy Mourvèdre requiring 7 or 8 years at a minimum to
achieve true balance and harmony. The small amount of rosé and
white produced is of a good quality, the latter capable of some age.
(DM)
Recommended Reds:
Bandol ★★★★ £E
Recommended Whites:
Bandol ★★★ £D
Recommended Rosés:
Bandol ★★☆ £D

Dom. de La Tour du Bon (Bandol) *www.tourdubon.com*
A small property with just 12 ha planted to vines. Production is small
but the quality of the red Bandols are very good indeed. These are
stylish, supple and very well crafted and the Saint-Ferréol is finely
structured, refined and very long-lived – a wine of not only weight
and concentration but wonderful herbal intensity. As with so many
properties in the appellation, though, the rosé and white are decent
and well enough made but lack the interest of the reds. (DM)
Recommended Reds:
Bandol Saint-Ferréol ★★★★ £F Bandol ★★★☆ £E
Recommended Whites:
Bandol ★★★ £D

✿✿ Dom. de Trevallon (Les Baux) *www.domainedetrevallon.com*
It remains one of the ludicrous features of the appellation contrôlée

regulations that this benchmark Provençale red is now only entitled
to IGP status. Theoretically there should be some Grenache planted
but the vineyard with north-facing calcareous slopes will not ripen
the variety adequately. The mesoclimate here is remarkably cool,
much more so than one would imagine. The resulting red blend of
Cabernet and Syrah and the tiny amount of white produced (barely
more than a couple of barrels) are very impressive and remarkably
refined wines. Cask aging of the red is in large older wood and it
needs at least 5 years to unfurl. The wine is a classic Provençale
example of the blend with floral *garrigue* scents underpinning the
concentrated, dark, cedary fruit. The white is a barrel-fermented
blend of Marsanne, Roussanne and Chardonnay, very fine and
intense with concentrated, lightly floral, nutty fruit. (DM)
Recommended Reds:
IGP des Bouches-du-Rhône ★★★★★ £G
Recommended Whites:
IGP des Bouches-du-Rhône ★★★★★ £G

Also see the following Rhône *négociant* with an entry in the section
Rhône Valley:
Jean-Luc Colombo

Other wines of note

Provence
Dom des Alysses
Recommended Reds:
Côteaux Varois ★★ £C
Dom de l'Angueiroun
Recommended Rosés:
Côtes de Provence La Londe Prestige ★★★ £C
Côtes de Provence Réserve Cuvée Virginie ★★☆ £B
Ch. Barbanau
Recommended Reds:
Côtes de Provence L'Instant ★★ £C
Recommended Rosés:
Côtes de Provence Et Cae Terra ★★☆ £C
Côtes de Provence L'Instant ★★ £B
Ch. de Berne
Recommended Reds:
Côtes de Provence ★★★☆ £E
Recommended Whites:
Côtes de Provence ★★★ £D
Recommended Rosés:
Côtes de Provence ★★★ £D
Côtes de Provence Terre de Berne ★★ £C
Ch. des Bertrands
Recommended Rosés:
Côtes de Provence ★★☆ £C
Ch. Henri Bonnaud
Recommended Reds:
Palette Quintessence ★★★★ £E
Palette ★★★☆ £D
Recommended Whites:
Palette Quintessence ★★★★ £E
Palette ★★★☆ £D
IGP Mediterranée Terre Promis ★★☆ £C
Recommended Rosés:
Palette ★★★ £D
Côtes de Provence Sainte Victoire ★★☆ £C

Provence & Corsica

France

Ch. de Brégançon
Recommended Reds:
Côtes de Provence Prestige ★★★☆ £E
Recommended Rosés:
Côtes de Provence Isaure ★★★ £D
Côtes de Provence Prestige La Londe ★★☆ £D
Côtes de Provence Réserve du Château ★★ £C

Ch. Calissanne
Recommended Reds:
Côteaux d'Aix-En-Provence Clos Victoire ★★★☆ £D
Recommended Whites:
Côteaux d'Aix-En-Provence Clos Victoire ★★★ £D
Recommended Rosés:
Côteaux d'Aix-En-Provence Calisson de Calissanne ★★★ £D
Côteaux d'Aix-En-Provence ★★ £B

Ch. Coussin (Sumeire)
Recommended Rosés:
Côtes de Provence Sainte-Victoire ★★☆ £C

Ch. Crémade
Recommended Reds:
Palette ★★★★ £E
Recommended Whites:
Palette ★★★☆ £E
Recommended Rosés:
Palette ★★★ £D

Ch. des Demoiselles
Recommended Rosés:
Côtes de Provence ★★ £C

Ch. d'Esclans
Recommended Reds:
IGP du Var Déesse ★★★★ £E
Recommended Rosés:
Côtes de Provence Garrus ★★★★☆ £G
Côtes de Provence Les Clans ★★★★ £F
Côtes de Provence ★★★☆ £D
Côtes de Provence Whispering Angel ★★★ £C

Ch. du Galoupet
Recommended Reds:
Côtes de Provence ★★ £C
Recommended Whites:
Côtes de Provence ★☆ £B
Recommended Rosés:
Côtes de Provence ★★ £B

Ch. Gassier
Recommended Rosés:
Côtes de Provence Sainte-Victoire Le Pas du Moine ★★★ £C

Ch. Grand Boise
Recommended Rosés:
Côtes de Provence ★★☆ £C

Ch. Hermitage Saint-Martin
Recommended Rosés:
Côtes de Provence Ikon ★★★ £D

Ch. de Jasson
Recommended Rosés:
Côtes de Provence Cuvée Eléonore ★★★ £C

Ch. La Calisse
Recommended Reds:
Côteaux Varois Patricia Ortelli ★★★ £D
Recommended Rosés:
Côteaux Varois Patricia Ortelli ★★☆ £C

Ch. La Coste
Recommended Rosés:
Côtes de Provence Cuvée Bellugue ★★☆ £C

Ch. L'Afrique (Sumeire)
Recommended Rosés:
Côtes de Provence ★★ £C

Ch. Les Crostes
Recommended Whites:
Côtes de Provence Cuvée Prestige ★★★ £D
Recommended Rosés:
Côtes de Provence Cuvée Château ★★☆ £C
Côtes de Provence Clos Les Crostes ★★ £C

Ch. La Mascaronne
Recommended Reds:
Côtes de Provence Fazioli ★★★ £D
Recommended Rosés:
Côtes de Provence Quat'saison ★★★ £C

Ch. La Tour de l'Évêque (Sumeire?)
Recommended Rosés:
Côtes de Provence Chateau Barbeyrolles Pétale de Rose ★★★☆ £C
Côtes de Provence Pétale de Rose ★★★ £C
Côtes de Provence ★★ £B

Ch. Léoube
Recommended Rosés:
Côtes de Provence ★★☆ £D

Ch. Malherbe
Recommended Reds:
Côtes de Provence Malherbe ★★★☆ £D
Recommended Rosés:
Côtes de Provence ★★★ £C
Côtes de Provence Pointe du Diable ★★☆ £C

Ch. Maupague (Sumeire)
Recommended Reds:
Côtes de Provence ★★☆ £C

Ch. Mentone
Recommended Rosés:
Côtes de Provence ★★★ £C
Côtes de Provence Cuvée Emotion ★★☆ £B

Ch. Minuty
Recommended Reds:
Côtes de Provence Prestige ★★★ £C
Recommended Rosés:
Côtes de Provence Cuvée Prestige ★★★ £C

Ch. d'Ollières
Recommended Rosés:
Coteaux Varois Prestige ★★☆ £C

Ch. Paradis
Recommended Reds:
Côteaux d'Aix-En-Provence Terre des Anges ★★★☆ £D
Côteaux d'Aix-En-Provence ★★★ £D
Recommended Rosés:
Côteaux d'Aix-En-Provence Coup de Coeur ★★★ £D
Côteaux d'Aix-En-Provence ★★★ £C

Ch. Real Martin
Recommended Reds:
Côtes de Provence Optimum ★★★ £D
Côtes de Provence ★★ £C

Ch. Roubine
Recommended Reds:
Côtes de Provence Inspire ★★★☆ £D

Recommended Rosés:
Côtes de Provence Inspire ★★★ £D
Côtes de Provence La Vie en Rose ★★☆ £C
Ch. Saint Anne
Recommended Reds:
Bandol ★★★ £D
Ch. Sainte-Marguerite
Recommended Rosés:
Côtes de Provence Symphonie ★★★☆ £D
Ch. Sainte-Roseline
Recommended Reds:
Côtes de Provence Prieuré ★★★☆ £D
Recommended Rosés:
Côtes de Provence Lampe de Méduse ★★★☆ £D
Ch. Salettes
Recommended Reds:
Bandol ★★★☆ £D
Recommended Whites:
Bandol ★★★☆ £D
Recommended Rosés:
Bandol ★★★ £D
Ch. des Sarrins
Recommended Reds:
Côtes de Provence ★★ £C
Ch. Tour Saint Honoré
Recommended Rosés:
Côtes de Provence Cuvée Sixtine ★★★ £C
Clos Cibonne
Recommended Rosés:
Côtes de Provence Cuvée Caroline ★★★☆ £D
Clos Sainte-Magdeleine
Recommended Whites:
Cassis ★★★ £E
Commanderie de La Bargemone
Recommended Rosés:
Côteaux d'Aix-en-Provence ★★★ £C
Commanderie de Peyrassol
Recommended Reds:
Côtes de Provence Château Peyrassol ★★☆ £D
Recommended Whites:
Côtes de Provence Château Peyrassol ★★ £C
Recommended Rosés:
Côtes de Provence Château Peyrassol ★★☆ £C
Dom de La Croix
Recommended Rosés:
Côtes de Provence Domaine de La Croix Eloge ★★☆ £C
Côtes de Provence Domaine de La Bastide Blanche Two B ★★☆ £C
Dom du Deffends
Recommended Reds:
Côteaux Varois Champs de La Truffière ★★★ £C
Côteaux Varois Marie Liesse ★★☆ £C
Dom d'Éole
Recommended Reds:
Côteaux d'Aix-en-Provence Léa ★★★ £D
Côteaux d'Aix-en-Provence ★★ £C
Recommended Rosés:
Côteaux d'Aix-en-Provence Caprice ★★★ £C
Côteaux d'Aix-en-Provence ★★ £B
Dom de La Frégate
Recommended Reds:
Bandol ★★ £C

Dom de L'Hermitage
Recommended Reds:
Bandol ★★★☆ £D
Dom de Jale
Recommended Reds:
Côtes de Provence La Nible ★★★ £D
Côtes de Provence La Bouisse ★★ £C
Recommended Whites:
Côtes de Provence La Garde ★★★☆ £D
Recommended Rosés:
Côtes de Provence La Garde ★★ £C
Dom du Jas d'Esclans
Recommended Rosés:
Côtes de Provence Cuvée du Loup ★★★ £D
Côtes de Provence ★★☆ £C
La Ferme Blanche
Recommended Whites:
Cassis ★★★ £E
Dom Le Galantin
Recommended Reds:
Bandol ★★★☆ £D
Recommended Rosés:
Bandol ★★☆ £C
Dom Gavoty
Recommended Reds:
Côtes de Provence Cuvée Clarendon ★★★☆ £D
Recommended Whites:
Côtes de Provence Cuvée Clarendon ★★★ £D
Recommended Rosés:
Côtes de Provence Cuvée Clarendon ★★★ £D
Maîtres Vigneronnes de Saint-Tropez
Recommended Reds:
Bandol La Roque ★★★ £D
Recommended Rosés:
Côtes de Provence Château de Pampelonne ★★ £C
Mas de Gourgonnier
Recommended Reds:
Les Baux-de-Provence Réserve ★★ £D
Mas Sainte-Berthe
Recommended Reds:
Les Baux-de-Provence Louis David ★★ £C
MIraval
Recommended Whites:
Coteaux Varois ★★★ £C
Recommended Rosés:
Côtes de Provence ★★★ £C
Moulin de La Roque
Recommended Reds:
Bandol Sables Rouge ★★★☆ £D
Bandol Grande Reserve ★★★ £C
Dom Rabiega
Recommended Reds:
Côtes de Provence Clos Dière I ★★★★ £E
Maison Saint Aix
Recommended Rosés:
Côteaux d'aix-En-Provence Aix ★★ £B
Dom Saint-Estève
Recommended Reds:
Côteaux d'aix-En-Provence ★☆ £B

Provence & Corsica

France

Dom Saint Mitre
Recommended Rosés:
Côteaux Varois Clos Madon ★★★ £C
Côteaux Varois Cuvée M ★★☆ £C
Dom Souviou
Recommended Reds:
Bandol ★★★ £C
Dom de Triennes
Recommended Reds:
IGP des Var Les Auréliens ★★ £B
Villa Minna Vineyard
Recommended Reds:
IGP Bouches du Rhône Minna Vineyard ★★★☆ £D
IGP Bouches du Rhône Villa Minna ★★★ £C
Recommended Whites:
IGP Bouches du Rhône Minna Vineyard ★★★☆ £D

Corsica
Dom Comte Abbatucci
Recommended Reds:
Ajaccio Faustine ★★☆ £C
Recommended Whites:
Vin de France Cuvée Collection ★★★ £C
Ajaccio Faustine ★★★ £C
Recommended Rosés:
Ajaccio Faustine ★★ £C
Clos Alivu
Recommended Reds:
Patrimonio ★★★ £C
Recommended Whites:
Patrimonio ★★★ £C
Recommended Rosés:
Patrimonio ★★☆ £C
Dom d'Alzipratu
Recommended Reds:
Vin de Corse-Calvi ★★☆ £C
Recommended Whites:
Vin de Corse-Calvi ★★☆ £C
Clos Canarelli
Recommended Reds:
Vin de Corse-Figari ★★★ £C
Recommended Whites:
Vin de Corse-Figari ★★☆ £C
Dom Clos Capitoro
Recommended Reds:
Ajaccio ★★☆ £C
Clos Culombu
Recommended Reds:
Vin de Corse-Calvi Riberosse ★★★ £D
Vin de Corse-Calvi Prestige ★★☆ £C
Recommended Whites:
Vin de Corse-Calvi Riberosse ★★★ £D
Vin de Corse-Calvi Prestige ★★ £C
Clos Poggiale
Recommended Reds:
Corse Clos Poggiale ★★★ £C
Corse Terra Vecchia ★★☆ £C
Recommended Whites:
Corse Clos Poggiale ★★★ £C
Corse Terra Vecchia ★★ £C

Clos Teddi
Recommended Reds:
Patrimonio Grand Cuvée ★★★☆ £D
Patrimonio ★★★ £C
Recommended Whites:
Patrimonio ★★★ £C
Recommended Rosés:
Patrimonio Grand Cuvée ★★☆ £C
Patrimonio ★☆ £B
Dom. Gentile
Recommended Reds:
Patrimonio Grande Expression ★★★ £D
Patrimonio ★★ £C
Recommended Whites:
Vindimia d'Oro Vin de France ★★★★ £E
Rappu Vin de France ★★★☆ £D
Muscat du Cap Corse ★★★ £C
Patrimonio Grande Expression ★★☆ £C
Patrimonio ★★ £B
Muscat Tradition Vin de France ★★ £B
Muscat Vin de France ★☆ £B
Recommended Rosés:
Patrimonio ★☆ £B
Dom. Giacometti
Recommended Reds:
Patrimonio Cuvée Sarah ★★★ £C
Patrimonio Cru des Agriates ★★☆ £C
Dom. de Granajolo
Recommended Reds:
Corse Porto-Vecchio Granajolo ★★★ £C
Recommended Whites:
Corse Porto-Vecchio Granajolo ★★★ £C
Recommended Rosés:
Corse Porto-Vecchio Granajolo ★★☆ £C
Vignerons de l'île de Beaute - Réserve du Président
Recommended Reds:
Corse Prestige du Président ★★★☆ £C
Corse Domaine Petroni ★★★ £C
Recommended Whites:
Corse Prestige du Président ★★★ £C
Corse Domaine Petroni ★★☆ £C
Dom. Leccia
Recommended Reds:
Patrimonio ★★☆ £C
Patrimonio Petra Bianca ★★★☆ £D
Recommended Whites:
Patrimonio ★★☆ £C
Yves Leccia/Dom d'E Croce
Recommended Reds:
Patrimonio ★★★☆ £D
IGP ★★ £B
Recommended Whites:
Patrimonio ★★★ £C
IGP ★★☆ £B
Recommended Rosés:
Patrimonio ★★☆ £C
Dom. Maestracci
Recommended Reds:
Vin de Corse-Calvi Clos Reginu ★★★☆ £D
Vin de Corse-Calvi E Prove ★★★ £C

Recommended Whites:
Vin de Corse-Calvi E Prove ★★★ £C
Recommended Rosés:
Vin de Corse-Calvi E Prove ★★☆ £C
Orenga de Gaffory
Recommended Reds:
Patrimonio ★★☆ £C
Recommended Whites:
Muscat du Cap Corse ★★★☆ £E
Clos d'Orléa
Recommended Reds:
Corse Signature ★★☆ £C
Domaine Pratavone
Recommended Reds:
Patrimonio Guillaume Pratavone ★★★ £C
Recommended Whites:
Patrimonio Guillaume Pratavone ★★☆ £C
Dom. de La Punta
Recommended Whites:
Vin de Corse Bianco Gentile ★★☆ £C
Dom. Sant'Armettu
Recommended Reds:
Vin de Corse Sartène ★★★ £C
Recommended Whites:
Vin de Corse Sartène ★★★ £C
Recommended Rosés:
Vin de Corse Sartène Rosumarinu ★★★ £C
Dom. de Tanella
Recommended Reds:
Vin de Corse-Figari ★★ £C
Dom. de Torraccia
Recommended Reds:
Vin de Corse Porto-Vecchio Oriu ★★★ £D
Vin de Corse Porto-Vecchio ★★☆ £C
Recommended Whites:
Vin de Corse Porto-Vecchio Oriu ★★★ £C
Dom. Vecchio
Recommended Reds:
Corse Mélusine ★★★☆ £D
IGP Ile de Beaute Tradition ★★☆ £C

Work in progress!!

Producers under consideration for the next edition
Dom de L'Abbaye de Lérins (IGP Alpes-Maritimes)
Dom Castell-Reynoard (Bandol)
Ch. Roche Redonne (Bandol)
Clos de Bernardi (Patrimonio)
Clos Saint-Vincent (Bellet)
Dom Cordoliani (Patrimonio)
Dom Dupuy de Lôme (Bandol)
Dom La Source (Bellet)
Dom de L'Olivette (Bandol)
Dom des Peirecèdes (Côtes de Provence)
Dom Signadore (Vin de Corse Sartène)

Author's choice - *Provence & Corsica*

15 Emerging classics from Provence
Reds:
Dom Richeaume   Côtes de Provence Cuvée Columelle
Dom Tempier   Bandol Cabassou
Dom de Trevallon   IGP des Bouches-du-Rhône
Ch. de Roquefort   Côtes de Provence Rubrum Obscurum
Dom Hauvette   Les Baux de Provence
Dom de Lauzières   Sine Nomine
Dom de La Tour du Bon   Bandol
Dom du Gros Noré   Bandol
Dom Lafran-Veyrolles   Bandol Tradition
Dom Rabiega   Côtes de Provence Clos Dière I
Dom des Béates   Côteaux d'Aix-en-Provence Terra d'Or
Ch. de Pibarnon   Bandol
Ch. Pradeaux   Bandol
Whites:
Ch. Routas   IGP du Var Cuvée Coquelicot
Ch. Simone   Palette

Some great value choices from Provence and Corsica
Reds:
Ch. Vignelaure   Côteaux d'Aix-en-Provence
Dupéré Barrera   Bandol India
Dom des Béates   Côteaux d'Aix-en-Provence Béates
Dom Sorin   Bandol
Dom Rimauresq   Côtes de Provence
Dom de La Courtade   Côtes de Provence
Ch. Bas   Côteaux d'Aix-en-Provence Cuvée du Temple
Ch. du Rouet   Côtes de Provence 1840
Dom du Grand Cros   Côtes de Provence Nectar
Dom Leccia   Patrimonio
Dom de Torraccia   Vin de Corse Porto-Vecchio Oriu
Whites:
Dom Culombu   Calvi
Dom. de Granajolo   Corse Porto-Vecchio Granajolo

South-West France

France

This section of the guide covers south-western France. A number of the regions in the south-west are close neighbours of Bordeaux and the style inevitably mirrors that of the Bordelais. Further south, both in the Lot Valley at Cahors and south towards the Pyrenees at Madiran and Jurançon, first-class dry and sweet whites and rich, stylish reds are becoming justifiably known to a wider audience.

South-West France

Immediately to the east of Bordeaux on the river Dordogne is Bergerac. There are a number of ACs north and south of the river, but the large, generic **Bergerac AC** encompasses all the smaller sub-regions. Red, white and rosé are produced from the Bordeaux varieties. Quality is fairly pedestrian with high yields and widespread mechanical harvesting. The number of good reds and whites being produced here is, however, increasing. Lees-enrichment and *bâtonnage* are now being used for whites and new oak is increasingly common for both reds and whites.

The **Côtes de Bergerac** and **Pécharmant** are immediately to the north of the town of Bergerac. The former is a source of some good reds and sweet whites (labelled as **Côtes de Bergerac Moelleux**). Pécharmant should do better than it does with its well-drained sandy, limestone soils. To the south of the river are the sweet-white ACs of **Monbazillac** and **Saussignac**. The former is worth considering as an alternative to Sauternes. The wines can be remarkably rich and complex with heady levels of botrytis. Be aware though that they are becoming more established and prices are rising. Both ACs are a blend of Sémillon and Sauvignon Blanc. Some good red and dry white is made at **Montravel** in vineyards bordering the Côtes de Castillon in Bordeaux. Sweet styles are also produced here and in the small ACs of **Côtes de Montravel** and **Haut-Montravel**. Thus far they lack the richness and depth found in Monbazillac.

South of Bergerac are the appellations of the **Côtes de Duras**, **Côtes du Marmandais** and **Buzet**. Both red and white are produced in the vineyards around Duras, with an occasional late-harvest white. As at Bergerac, Bordeaux varieties are planted. The reds tend towards a vegetal character and the whites are at best fresh and grassy. More new oak is being used, with varying success. Marmandais and Buzet appellations are red only, with more interest in the Côtes du Marmandais, where as well as Bordeaux grapes some indigenous south-western varieties are also permitted. To the south-east of Bergerac along a 30-mile stretch of the river Lot are the vineyards of **Cahors**. Some of the finest red wines of the south-west are now produced here. Auxerrois (Malbec) dominates plantings, with some Merlot and Tannat. Expect anything from light, plummy, easy-drinking wines (occasionally with a green vegetal note) to serious and very structured ageworthy reds. Prices of the best examples seem to be surging upwards.

West of Cahors the AC of **Marcillac** produces spicy reds from Fer-Servadou, while to the south the AC of the **Côteaux du Quercy** produces reds of some potential. Further south, towards Toulouse, are the appellations of **Côtes du Brulhois** as well as **Lavilledieu**; and **Fronton**. The latter has turned out a number of interesting reds based on the Negrette grape. The wines are both perfumed and spicy, the best impressively structured.

To the north-east of Toulouse, **Gaillac AC** offers some unusual and diverse styles; Mauzac is the key white variety, although Muscadelle

is also important. Good dry and sweet wines are produced along with perlé (a lightly sparkling white) and Gaillac Mousseux, produced by the *méthode rural*. The majority of the red is light although there are significant examples.

To the south are the great red and white wines of Gascony. This is also bulk white **IGP des Côtes de Gasgogne** country. The **Madiran** and **Pacherenc du Vic-Bilh** ACs share the same geographical area and many growers produce both. Pacherenc can be dry or sweet and is produced from Gros and Petit Manseng, Petit Courbu and Arrufiac, with the odd touch of Sémillon and Sauvignon Blanc (for *moelleux*) blended in. The best are very good. Madiran itself produces powerful, dense and ageworthy reds based on Tannat and often blended with a bit of Cabernets Franc and Sauvignon and Fer-Servadou. It was here that the technique of micro-oxygenation was developed to harness and soften the Tannat's often aggressive and sturdy tannins. Some of the wines are world-class and provide very good value. **Jurançon** is without doubt the finest white-wine appellation of the south-west. Gros and Petit Manseng as well as Petit Courbu are planted. The wines can be sublime, particularly the sweet styles. Yields are low and inevitably prices are rising. The reds of **Béarn** are generally light and insubstantial. To the south-west of Jurançon, nestled into the foothills of the Pyrenees, **Irouléguy** provides good reds and whites from the same varieties as Madiran and Jurançon.

South-West France vintages

In general most red and white should be drunk young and only a number of appellations provide wines with the substance for real ageing. Top Cahors needs several years in bottle and evolves well. Jurançon, both dry and sweet, will improve over half a decade or more and keep much longer. Top examples of Madiran, while more approachable than in the past, need five years at least, particularly the top cuvées. Good potential with 2015 and prior to a tricky 2014 and 2013 throughout the south-west 2012, 2011, 2010, 2009, 2008, 2007, 2006, 2005, 2004, 2003, 2002, 2001, 2000, 1999, 1998, 1996 and 1995 were good to very good. 1993, 1990 and 1988 are worth considering for top Jurançon and the trio of 1990, 1989 and 1988 for top Madiran.

A-Z of producers by appellation/commune

Bergerac		Le Clos d'Un Jour	330
Dom. de l' Ancienne Cure	326	Primo Palatum	331
Ch. Tour des Gendres	329	**Fronton**	
Vignobles des Verdots	330	Dom. Le Roc	330
Monbazillac		**Gaillac**	
Ch.Tirecul-la-Gravière	328	Dom. d'Escausses	330
Montravel		Plageoles Dom Robert	331
Ch. Jonc Blanc	328	Dom. Rotier	331
Ch. Masburel	328	**Madiran**	
Côtes du Marmandais		Dom. Berthoumieu	326
Ch. Beaulieu	327	Alain Brumont	326
Cahors		Chapelle l'Enclos	327
Ch. du Cèdre	327	Ch. Barréjat	327
Ch. Lagrezette	328	Ch. Bouscassé	326
Ch. Lamartine	328	Ch. d'Aydie	327
Clos La Coutale	329	Ch. Laffitte-Teston	328
Clos Triguedina	329	Ch. Montus	326
Dom. Cosse Maisonneuve	330	Ch. Viella	329

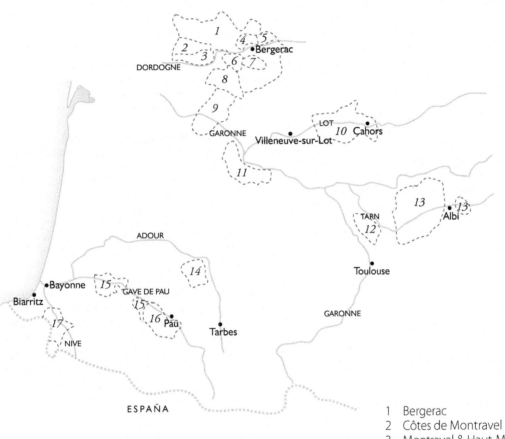

1 Bergerac
2 Côtes de Montravel
3 Montravel & Haut-Montravel
4 Rosette
5 Pécharmant
6 Saussignac
7 Monbazillac
8 Côtes de Duras
9 Côtes de Marmandais
10 Cahors
11 Buzet
12 Fronton
13 Gaillac
14 Madiran
15 Béarn
16 Jurançon
17 Irouléguy

South-West France

A-Z of producers

Dom. de L'Ancienne Cure *www.domaine-anciennecure.fr*
Christian Roche possesses 45 ha in the Bergerac, Côtes de Bergerac, Pécharmant and Monbazillac appellations with 31 ha planted to white varieties. He produces wine under three main labels, Jour de Fruit, which are soft, open and forward, L'Abbaye wines which are more complex and aged in some new and used wood and the top wines which go under the label L'Extase and are some of the best examples of their appellations. In Pécharmant, as well as a Jour de Fruit red there is also a pricier Collection brand. The L'Abbaye white is a typical blend of white Bordeaux varieties including some Sauvignon Gris aged in 30% new wood. The L'Extase has greater weight, depth and substance and is a variable blend including Sauvignon Blanc and Muscadelle as well as Sémillon. It is barrel-fermented and aged in 60% new wood for 18 months. Of the various Monbazillac bottlings, the Jour de Fruit is lightly tropical and peachy, the L'Abbaye offers more richness and botrytis influence. The L'Extase is very good indeed. Marked botrytis with rich peachy, honeyed fruit and a piercing citrus complexity mark the wine. L'Abbaye rouge is a blend of Merlot, Malbec and Cabernet Sauvignon. Bright and fleshy it is given some micro-oxygenation during ageing. The top red, L'Extase is denser, fuller and more concentrated. It is dominated by Cabernet Sauvignon with some Merlot and Malbec, and has a firmer mineral structure and a fine cedary character. Coming from *argile* and limestone soils the wine is aged in *barrique* for up to 24 months and will develop well for up to a decade. (DM)

Recommended Reds:
Côtes de Bergerac L'Extase ★★★☆ £E
Bergerac L'Abbaye ★★★ £D
Côtes de Bergerac Jour de Fruit ★☆ £B
Recommended Whites:
Monbazillac L'Extase ★★★★ £F   Bergerac L'Extase ★★★☆ £E
Monbazillac L'Abbaye ★★★ £E   Monbazillac Jour de Fruit ★★☆ £C
Bergerac L'Abbaye ★★ £C

Dom. Berthoumieu (Madiran) *www.domaine-berthoumieu.com*
Impressive 25-ha Madiran property producing around 15,000 cases a year. The main focus of the property and, it has to be said, the best wines are the two Madiran cuvées. Vinification is traditional and the wines have considerable extract and youthful tannin after a maceration of 3 weeks or so. The Tradition is spicy, dense and structured with an earthy, mineral core. A blend of Tannat, Cabernet Sauvignon, Cabernet Franc and Fer-Servadou, it is aged partly in wood and partly in *cuve*. The old-vine Charles de Batz is a rich, brooding wine with sweet, chocolaty notes. It sees a large portion of new oak. The wines here are extensively racked as opposed to using micro-oxygenation to minimise those burly, aggressive Tannat tannins. The result is uniformly ripe and supple. The Pacherenc Sec is crisp and fresh, while the sweet Symphonie d'Automne is weighty, rich and more aromatic. (DM)

Recommended Reds:
Madiran Charles de Batz ★★★☆ £E   Madiran Tradition ★★☆ £C
Recommended Whites:
Pacherenc de Vic-Bilh Cuvée Symphonie d'Automne Doux ★★★ £D
Pacherenc de Vic-Bilh Sec Vieilles Vignes ★★ £C

Dom. Bru-Baché (Jurançon)
This 10 ha domaine produces a small range of wines both dry and sweet. Claude Loustalot took over the property in 1994 and

like many other *vignerons* committed to quality his vineyards are tended alomg organic principles. The vines, planted on *argilo-limoneux* soils, now range from under 10 years of age up to well over 60 years in his most propitious plots. His approach is one of minimal intervention. Helping to ensure the quality of the sweet wines is a vineyard holding which consists of 75% of the superior Petit Manseng. In the cellar oak is widely used for both fermentation and ageing and the wines are as notable for their weight and texture as for for their floral, aromatic qualities. The subtly aromatic Casterrasses comes from Gros Manseng the palate gaining weight and texture from ageing in older barrels. The richly-textured and peachy, Quintessence is vinified and then aged for up to 18 months in *barriques*. A late-harvest Casterrasses is also made along with very small amounts of a pricier sweeet Petit manseng, L'Eminence. (DM)

Recommended Whites:
Jurançon Quintessence ★★★☆ £E
Jurançon Sec Casterrasses ★★☆ £C

✿ **Alain Brumont (Madiran)** *www.brumont.fr*
With a large vineyard holding of some 270 ha and a total production of 65,000 to 70,000 cases, Alain Brumont makes impressively structured, rich and very concentrated Madiran under the Montus and Bouscassé labels as well as a softer, more immediately appealing example labelled Torus. He also produces good dry Pacherenc de Vic Bilh under the Montus label. Mainly Petit Courbu, the wine is barrel-fermented and aged and is rich, nutty and intensely honeyed in character. There is also a Bouscassé white that is not vinified in oak and is understandably more aromatic in nature. A number of very good late-harvest Pacherencs are produced as well. Bouscassé is the secondary property, producing a well-priced regular Madiran, a superior bottling, Tour Bouscassé and a dense and powerful Vieilles Vignes. The approach to vinification emphasises power and extraction. Maceration lasts for over 4 weeks and no micro-oxygentation is employed during maturation.The regular Château Montus is full of firm, darkfruited Tannat character. The Cuvée Prestige is pricey but a serious step up. Very, powerful and structured, it demands 7 or 8 years' ageing to achieve a harmonious balance of fruit and tannin. It will show great refinement with time. There is also a very rich and opulent special cuvée La Tyre which demands up to a decades cellaring to soften its formidable structure. It has extraordinary depth and concentration but at a very heavy price. An additional top red XL is also made. (DM)

Alain Brumont
Recommended Reds:
Madiran Torus ★★☆ £C
Château Montus
Recommended Reds:
Madiran La Tyre ★★★★★ £G
Madiran Cuvée Prestige ★★★★ £F   Madiran ★★★ £D
Recommended Whites:
Pacherenc de Vic-Bilh ★★★ £D
Château Bouscassé
Recommended Reds:
Madiran Vieilles Vignes ★★★☆ £E
Madiran Argile ★★★ £D   Madiran ★★☆ £C
Recommended Whites:
Pacherenc de Vic-Bilh ★★ £C

Camin Larredya (Jurançon) *www.caminlarredya.fr*
Larredya is a small domaine producing just 4 wines from 11 ha

of vineyards. Output is currently around 3,500 cases a year and the wines are very favourably priced. The vineyards are cultivated along organic principles and Jean-Marc follows an approach of minimal intervention. There is a crisp, well-crafted dry Jurançon La Part Davan, mainly from Gros Manseng, which is floral and lightly aromatic with fine persistence and good fresh acidity lending grip. A second sec style, La Virada is a little pricier. A later-harvested *doux* is also produced, Costat Darrèr. The top wines are the two Petit Manseng-based sweet wines, Au Capcéu and A Sólhevat. Both will age very well and the Sólhevat in particular will continue to develop over 10 years or more. (DM)

Recommended Whites:
Jurançon A Sólhevat ★★★★ £F   Jurançon Au Capcéu ★★★☆ £E
Jurançon Sec La Part Davan ★★☆ £C

✿ Dom. Cauhapé (Jurançon) *www.jurancon-cauhape.com*
Henri Ramonteu's domaine is sizeable for the region at some 40ha but he is one of the finest exponents of the appellation. He makes an extensive range with 2 dry and 4 sweet wines from very low-yielding vineyards. The sweet wines are classified according the harvesting date of the grapes. The dry styles are produced mainly from Gros Manseng and vinified with some skin contact, with the Sève d'Automne being barrel-fermented, and all the wines are kept on their lees. The sweet wines, with a high proportion of Petit Manseng are increasingly luscious and richly concentrated but with a fine, fresh backbone of acidity. They are structured and very ageworthy. Rare and only produced when conditions favour it from Petit Manseng are two great sweet whites. Fruit is harvested close to the year's end for Quintessence and after the new year for Folie de Janvier and these are are among the great wines, not only of Jurançon but of France as well. (DM)

Recommended Whites:
Jurançon Quintessence ★★★★★ £H
Jurançon Noblesse du Temps ★★★★ £F
Jurançon Symphonie de Novembre ★★★☆ £E
Jurançon Sève d'Automne ★★★★ £D
Jurançon Ballet d'Octobre ★★★ £C
Jurançon Chant des Vignes ★★☆ £C

Chapelle Lenclos (Madiran) *www.famillelaplace.com*
Patrick Ducournau, in partnership with his cousins the Laplace family of CH. D'AYDIE who supervise the property, has 15ha of Madiran and there are two wines here. The Domaine Mouréou, which is also the name of the estate, is supple and surprisingly approachable for the appellation. The wine is mainly aged on fine lees in tank and requires a little time to take the hard edge off its tannins. La Chapelle Lenclos is denser and more structured; it will be better with 4 or 5 years' ageing. The wine is partly aged in *cuve* and partly in large 400-litre barrels for up to 20 months. The winemaking here emphasises fruit underplays the oak influence that is increasingly evident in some neighbouring wines. Much of the wines style is achieved through the process of micro-oxygenation. This was developed by Ducournau. (DM)

Recommended Reds:
Madiran la Chapelle Lenclos ★★★ £D
Madiran Domaine Mouréou ★★☆ £C

Ch. d'Aydie (Madiran) *www.famillelaplace.com*
A small but fine range of Madirans and Pacherenc de Vic-Bilhs is produced at this sizeable property. There are 35 ha of vineyards of which the majority are devoted to producing Madiran. Decent,

straightforward red Madiran is released as Fleury-Laplace, which is produced from bought-in fruit and offers a soft, accessible example of the appellation. Odé d'Aydie is the second label and is reasonably dense and powerful. The Château d'Aydie is a serious step up, full of dark fruit, well-judged oak and firm, youthful tannin – 5 or 6 years' ageing is needed. The wine is kept on its lees in barrel and micro-oxygenation is employed. Pacherenc is produced in a dry style under the Laplace label. This is both aromatic and intense, with piercing green, nettley fruit. Rich and impressively concentrated *moelleux* is also made. (DM)

Recommended Reds:
Madiran Château d'Aydie ★★★ £D   Madiran Odé d'Aydie ★★☆ £C
Recommended Whites:
Pacherenc de Vic-Bilh Laplace ★★ £C

Ch. Barrejat (Madiran)
Some good to very good Madiran is made by Denis Capmartin at his 22 ha domaine. One of the important keys to quality here is the impressive age of some of the vineyards, which are farmed along organic principles. For the remarkable top label, Vieux Ceps, some of the vines are an astounding 200 years of age. The regular Madiran Tradition is as forward as Madiran manages to be but it still needs a year or 2 to soften its hard youthful edge, which is promoted by a lengthy 21-day *cuvaison* and ageing in *cuve*. Richer and lusher in texture is the Séduction, a blend of 60% Tannat and 40% Cabernets Sauvignon and Franc. Aged in small oak *barriques*, a small proportion new, it is ripe and full of deep, dark, cedary fruit and subtle spicy oak. The Vieux Ceps has just 20% of the Cabernets blended with Tannat. It is both rich and understandably very complex. The top 2 wines will benefit from at leasts 5 years, ageing. (DM)

Recommended Reds:
Madiran Vieux Ceps ★★★☆ £D
Madiran Séduction ★★★ £C   Madiran Tradition ★★☆ £C

Ch. Beaulieu (Côtes du Marmandais) *www.chateaudebeaulieu.net*
Robert Schulte is among a small handful of producers independently striving for fine quality in this lesser-known appellation. Most of his neighbours choose to sell to the local co-op. Beaulieu's 26.5ha of vineyards have great potential and are planted on a mix of gravel and calcareous soils. The vineyard is also being replanted to achieve a density of up to 6,000 vines per hectare, which will improve quality further. A number of reds are made here and the style is traditional, particularly for the Côtes du Marmandais and top Cuvée de l'Oratoire. You need to give them at least 4 or 5 years' ageing to soften their firm youthful edge. These latter two wines are about structure rather than fruit. The Galapian de Beaulieu, produced from young vines, is softer and more obviously fruit driven. The Cuvée de l'Oratoire comes from vines up to 40 years old and is produced from a yield of just 18 to 20 hl/ha. It is impressively dense, rich and concentrated. (DM)

Recommended Reds:
Côtes du Marmandais l'Oratoire ★★★ £C
Côtes du Marmandais ★★☆ £C
Côtes du Marmandais Galapian de Beaulieu ★☆ £B

✿ Ch. du Cèdre (Cahors) *www.chateauducedre.com*
The Verhaegue family possess some 25ha of vineyards and produce a number of good to very good reds. The regular Cahors Héritage is made from younger vines. It is a ripe, brambly, forward style for drinking young. The Cahors cuvée is a touch sturdier and denser.

France

Of the top wines, Le Cèdre, is now fairly pricey, particularly for the appellation. Produced entirely from old Malbec vines and aged in 100% new oak, it is powerful, structured and very ageworthy – best with 5 years in the cellar or more. A recent addition is a new label GC, which is a good deal pricier. There are also ongoing experiments here with lees-ageing for reds and the use of micro-oxygenation. Pascal is also involved with the Roussillon property Domaine de MARCEVOL. Two white IGP labels are also made as well a rosé and in interesting late harvested fortified red, Malbec Vintage. (DM)

Recommended Reds:

Cahors Le Cèdre ★★★★ £E   Cahors ★★★ £C
Cahors Héritage ★★☆ £C

Ch. Jonc Blanc (Montravel)

Montravel property producing wines of real style and substance from just over 16 ha of vineyards run on organic principles and planted solely to a mix of varieties which now includes a little Sauvignon Blanc and Muscadelle as well as Cabernet, Merlot and Malbec. As well as the reds there is a straightforward, bright, fresh, fruit-driven IGP rosé, L'Heure Osée, as well as a couple of white Vins de France labels. The vineyards are planted on *argile*-calcareous soils with a very high gravel component in the topsoil which provides an ideal base for the wines. The regular bottling, the Les Sens du Fruit is traditionally vinified without recourse to new oak. The Bergerac and Class IK are both fuller and denser and see a touch of small oak. These are good, well-priced examples from an appellation that is showing increasing promise. (DM)

Recommended Reds:

Bergerac ★★★ £C   Bergerac Class IK ★★☆ £C
Vin de France Les Sens du Fruit ★★ £B

Ch. Laffitte-Teston (Madiran) *www.chateau-laffitte-teston.com*

Jean-Marc Laffitte produces not only good Madiran but also some of the most striking examples of Pacherenc du Vic-Bilh. His output of over 20,000 cases is not inconsiderable for the region but fine quality is maintained throughout. He has just over 34 ha of red varieties, 70% of which are Tannat, as well 5.5ha of white Petit and Gros Manseng and a smattering of Courbu. The stylish Ericka is barrel-fermented, with a fair proportion of new wood being used, and offers impressively piercing floral, nutty, spicy fruit. The Moelleux Rêve d'Automne is opulent and richly textured. Both will evolve well in the short term. The Madiran Reflet de Terroir is good if a touch angular in its youth, while the Vieilles Vignes is altogether rounder and fuller and is capable of adding real complexity with 6 or 7 years' ageing. (DM)

Recommended Reds:

Madiran Vieilles Vignes ★★★ £D   Madiran Reflet de Terroir ★★☆ £C

Recommended Whites:

Pacherenc du Vic-Bilh Moelleux Rêve d'Automne ★★★ £D
Pacherenc du Vic-Bilh Ericka ★★★ £C

❀ Ch. Lagrezette (Cahors) *www.chateau-lagrezette.com*

Another top-quality performer in Cahors, Alain-Dominique Perrin is a wealthy entrepreneur whose portfolio includes prestige jewellery operation Cartier. No expense is spared at this 65-ha property and roving consultant Michel Rolland provides guidance over vinification. Classic Rolland techniques are all evident including pre-fermentation maceration, extended vatting, malolactic in barrel and judicious use of new oak. A number of soft fruity négociant wines are made and the range numbers over a dozen wines in total and includes white IGP, rosé as well as red labels. The rich and

impressively concentrated Château Lagrezette is a regular Cahors given an extended maceration of up to 4 weeks. The two prestige cuvées, Dame Honneur and the very pricey Pigeonnier, are a step up, particularly the deep and saturated Pigeonnier. It is 100% Malbec sourced from the property's oldest vines and produced from a yield of barely more than 15 hl/ha. The Dame Honneur will benefit from 5 years or so, the Pigeonnier a year or two longer. (DM)

Recommended Reds:

Cahors Pigeonnier ★★★★★ £H
Cahors Lagrezette Dame Honneur ★★★★ £F
Cahors Lagrezette ★★★ £D   Cahors Chevaliers ★★☆ £C

Ch. Lamartine (Cahors) *www.cahorslamartine.com*

This is emerging as a consistently good source of Cahors. The property is relatively sizeable with 32 ha under vine. Auxerrois (Malbec) is much the most important variety, accounting for 90% of the land under cultivation. Much of the quality here is down to the aspect of the vineyards and the *terroir*, with south-facing slopes on the calcareous soils of the Cahors Côteaux. The regular bottling is sound and characterful with some spicy tobacco as well as dark fruit notes. The Cuvée Particulière comes from older vines; it is denser and fuller and is lent weight from ageing in oak. The L'Expression is one of the appellation's new wave wines, produced solely from old-vine Auxerrois and aged for 20 months in new *barriques*. Rich, dense and very serious, this requires 5 years' patience. (DM)

Recommended Reds:

Cahors L'Expression ★★★ £D   Cahors Cuvée Particulière ★★☆ £C
Cahors ★★ £C

❀ Ch. Masburel (Montravel) *www.chateau-masburel.com*

The Château here has produced wine from its vineyards since 1740. The previous owners the Donnans restored the property to its former glory in 1997 before selling it to Julian Robbins. The property is now the source of a very exciting range of reds and whites from the Côtes de Bergerac and Montravel appellations. The fruit is sourced from range of terroirs with soils varying from clay and chalk to sand and gravel providing whites with both balance and finesse and reds with rich textures and supple powerful tannins. Yields here are very low, generally between 20 and 30 hl/ha and this regime is maintained with the Lady Masburel red label. Of the top wines the Château Masburel white is dominated by Sauvignon Blanc but adds a wonderful citrus complexity and waxy texture from around one-fifth Sémillon. The top two reds are among the best examples in the region. Both get a very lengthy vatting and are aged in new barrels for around a year and a half. Mon Ravel Bolero generally has a touch more Merlot and offers a marginally richer, riper style. Expect both the top reds to develop well for a decade. (DM)

Recommended Reds:

Montravel Mon Ravel Bolero ★★★★ £E
Côtes de Bergerac ★★★☆ £E
Côtes de Bergerac Lady Masburel ★★☆ £C

Recommended Whites:

Montravel ★★★☆ £D

❀ Ch. Tirecul La Graviere (Monbazillac) *www.vinibilancini.com*

This is arguably the top property for sweet Monbazillac. The Billancinis have just 6 ha or so planted and produce a tiny amount – some 1,500 cases in total every year. The style is radically different from their neighbours' with intensely honeyed wines full of rich fruit, quince, toast and very marked botrytis. They achieve this by controlling yields and conducting a succession of *tries* as

extensive as any top Sauternes property. The regular bottling is very impressive with rich fruit and spicy, vanilla notes from new oak. There is also a tiny volume of the special and very pricey Cuvée Madame. The wines may be enjoyed young but will keep very well. (DM)

Recommended Whites:
Monbazillac Cuvée Madame ★★★★☆ £G   Monbazillac ★★★★ £E

✿ **Ch. TourdesGendres (Bergerac)** *www.chateautourdesgendres.com*
Very impressive Bergerac property with a range of reds and whites produced as Bergerac as well as a red Côtes de Bergerac, the stylish and concentrated Gloire de Mon Père. There are a total of some 52 ha of vineyards with more than half planted to red varieties. Production is now over 25,000 cases a year, which is in no way detrimental to quality. White planting is typically Bordelais, mainly Sémillon with Sauvignon Blanc and around 10% Muscadelle; reds are dominated by Merlot and full of rich, plummy fruit. The top cuvées have real dimension and class. The Anthologia bottlings are as impressive as anything yet produced from the region, the red adding a round, supple character through partial barrel-fermentation. The white is marvellously intense and pure with beautifully balanced oak. Some of the vineyards are now being farmed biodynamically. (DM)

Recommended Reds:
Bergerac Cuvée Anthologia ★★★★ £E
Bergerac Moulin des Dames ★★★☆ £D
Côtes de Bergerac Gloire de Mon Père ★★★★ £C
Bergerac ★★ £B

Recommended Whites:
Bergerac Cuvée Anthologia ★★★★ £E
Bergerac Moulin des Dames ★★★ £D
Bergerac Cuvée des Conti ★★☆ £C

Recommended Rosés:
Bergerac ★☆ £B

Ch. Viella (Madiran) *www.chateauviella.com*
The Bortolussi family is in the course of renovating the splendid old château at this property. They make a simple, very straightforward Bearn rosé but of more importance is a good barrel-fermented dry Pacherenc du Vic-Bilh from mainly Arrufiac, as well as a little Gros and Petit Manseng, and a very fine late-harvest Pacherenc which is 100% Petit Manseng. The latter is luscious but very finely structured, with a glorious ripe citrus and mineral character. The good regular Madiran is aged in *cuve* with 40% Cabernets Franc and Sauvignon blended with Tannat. It needs a year or two to add some flesh. The Cuvée Prestige is rich, dense and powerfully structured. It is 100% Tannat and aged in new wood. A minimum of 4 to 5 years is needed to achieve an equilibrium of fruit and oak. The wines are all very fairly priced. (DM)

Recommended Reds:
Madiran Cuvée Prestige ★★★ £C   Madiran ★★ £B

Recommended Whites:
Pacherenc du Vic-Bilh Moelleux ★★★ £C
Pacherenc du Vic-Bilh ★★ £B

Clos La Coutale (Cahors) *www.closlacoutale.com*
Philippe Bernède is the current winemaker at this long-established family property. His top wine, Clos la Coutale, is a little more easygoing than the traditional 'black wine' of Cahors but a long way from a fruit-forward modern style. It has beautiful floral and spice characters on the nose with hints of tobacco and oak on the palate

and a firm, long finish. The composition of the wine is generally 70% Malbec, 15% Merlot and 15% Tannat. As well as the Clos La Coutale a limited release low-yielding red is also made, Grand Coutrale. (NB)

Recommended Reds:
Cahors ★★ £C

Clos Lapeyre (Jurançon) *www.jurancon-lapeyre.fr*
There are 17 ha under vine here and both dry and sweet styles are produced. The regular Jurançon Sec is fermented in stainless steel and kept on its lees for added depth. The old-vine Vitatge Vielh is barrel-fermented, which gives greater weight. In 2006 a special sec style, Mantoulan was also added to the small range. Three sweet wines are made. The regular Moelleux is full and spicy with nicely balanced acidity; the barrel-fermented La Magendia is richer and more intensely citrusy with subtle oak in the background. The top late-harvested wine, Vent Balaguer, is produced solely from Petit Manseng grapes that are marked by *passerillage*. Remarkably rich and concentrated, it is only produced in the most exceptional years. (DM)

Recommended Whites:
Jurançon La Magendia ★★★ £E   Jurançon Moelleux ★★☆ £D
Jurançon Vitatge Vielh ★★☆ £D   Jurançon Sec ★★ £C

✿ **Clos Triguedina (Cahors)** *www.jbaldes.com*
The Baldés family have been in the region for nearly two centuries and in the Probus cuvée they established one of the benchmark wines of the appellation long before some of the more recently famous names. To this they have added a massive, dark new cuvée, New Black Wine, named after the fabled Cahors of old. There are 58 ha of reds and just over 4 ha of whites. From the latter they produce a good barrel-fermented IGP white Le Sec du Clos, blended from Chardonnay and Viognier and a small amount of late-harvest Chenin Blanc, Le Moelleux du Clos. Some rosé is also produced but it is the red Cahors which defines quality here. In order to maintain the standard of the top wines, a forward and fruit-driven secondary label, Le Petit Clos is also released. This is a blend of mainly Malbec with a smattering of Merlot. The Clos Triguedina estate red is a structured and impressively ageworthy example of the appellation. Aged in used oak, it is full of spicy tobacco and red berry fruit. Probus is fuller and darker with a marked vanilla undercurrent from new wood. The dark, spicy and concentrated New Black Wine comes from the very oldest vines. The top two reds are aged in new oak for 18 months. (DM)

Recommended Reds:
Cahors New Black Wine ★★★★ £F
Cahors Prince Probus ★★★☆ £E   Cahors ★★☆ £C

Clos Uroulat (Jurançon) *www.uroulat.com*
The Hours family possess a small holding of some 16 ha with the bulk planted to Petit Manseng and Gros Manseng with a bit of Petit Courbu. The wines produced here are not only very good but attractively priced too. Both are barrel-fermented. The dry Cuvée Marie is full of intense, citrus character and subtle, vanilla oak. The sweet Clos Uroulat is unctuous and rich with a few years in bottle but has marvellously fresh acidity cutting through it. Both will develop well with time. There are also a couple of fruit driven whites, both are labelled Happy Hours. (DM)

Recommended Whites:
Jurançon Clos Uroulat ★★★ £D
Jurançon Cuvée Marie ★★☆ £C

France

✿ Dom. Cosse Maisonneuve (Cahors)

An excellent newly established Cahors domaine, founded in 1999, producing a total of six wines from a range of different sites. Their vineyards are all farmed organically and yields are kept to a minimum. As well as the wines covered here a good soft supple red, Solis is aged in cement for 12 months. Le Combal is a step up and comes from quartz and *argile* soils, and is aged in used *barriques* for 14 months. Both La Fage and Le Petit Sid are very well priced. Le Petit Sid is 100% Malbec aged in used *barriques* and has a marvellous piercing mineral purity to its tobacco scented fruit. La Fage also aged in used oak, although just one fill barrels, is again all Malbec sourced from south facing *argile*-gravel slopes and is a riper, fuller fleshier style. Of the top two wines Le Sid comes from 30 year-old vines grown in red *argile* soils with a high limestone content. It is a blend of 90% malbec, 7% Merlot and the balance Tannat. The wine is given 14 to 18 months in new and one year old oak and and is a rich, dark, spicy and impressively concentrated and fleshy example of the AC. The top wine Les Laquets comes solely from limestone soils and over 40 year old vines and is 100% Malbec. Aged for 18 to 22 months in new and one year old *barriques* the wine is big, full and very structured with a pure mineral core. It demands cellaring for half a decade. A brilliant new source for the AC. (DM)

Recommended Reds:
Cahors Les Laquets ★★★★ £F Cahors Le Sid ★★★★ £E
Cahors La Fage ★★★☆ £D Cahors Le Petit Sid ★★★☆ £D
Cahors Le Combal ★★☆ £C

Dom. d'Escausses (Gaillac) *www.domainedescausses.com*

Denis Balaran produces a fine range of both red and white Gaillac from his 34 ha of vineyards. Around two-thirds of his holding is planted to red varieties and output is now upwards of 12,500 cases a year. There are three vibrant light berry scented reds all of which offer supple, soft tannins, good fresh acidity and impressive intensity in particular the top La Petite Croix which incorporates 35% Syrah and 30% Cabernet Sauvignon in addition to the local Fer Servadou providing extra weight and a black pepper spice character. Of the whites the vines are a little older and these wines are the quality benchmarks here. The fresh, green fruited La Vigne de l'Oubli is dominated by Sauvignon Blanc at 50% of the blend with equal parts of Mauzac and Muscadelle. Fuller and richer with a fresh minerally, herb-spiced backbone is the L'Ingénue which features 40% each of the indigenous Loin de l'oeil and Mauzac with the balance Sauvignon Blanc. The yield is lower and the wine is aged for 6 months in barrel. A fine range is completed by an impressive richly perfumed sweet late harvest white Les Vendanges Dorées. It comes from Mauzac, Loin de l'oeil and Ondenc and is fermented and aged in 20% new wood. It should develop nicely over four or five years. (DM)

Recommended Reds:
Gaillac Cuvée des Drilles ★★☆ £C
Gaillac La Vigne Blanche ★★☆ £B Gaillac La Croix Petite ★★☆ £B
Recommended Whites:
Gaillac Les Vendanges Dorées ★★★☆ £D
Gaillac L'Ingénue ★★☆ £C Gaillac La Vigne de l'Obli ★★☆ £C

Le Clos d'Un Jour (Cahors) *www.leclosdunjour.fr*

Excellent and well-priced Cahors is emerging from this small 6.5 ha domaine. These are supple and approachable reds but with real depth and a complexity to the dark core of fruit each wine has. As well as the two wines profiled here there is a Cahors bottling which is barely half the price certainly worth a look at. The vineyards are planted on well-sited clay-chalk soils and are tended as naturally as possible. No fertilizers and just sulphur and zinc sprays. Leaf thinning and canopy light exposure are regularly carried out and yields kept to a paltry 20 hl/ha. Harvesting is of course by hand and there is a careful selection. Winery operations are carried out as much as possible by gravity and the wines get a cold soak prior to a long fermentation on skins for up to a month. The wines are aged for 18 to 22 months with Un Jour seeing small oak, the Un Jour Sur Terre more unusually being aged in clay/earth jars. The wines are bottled unfined and unfiltered. (DM)

Recommended Reds:
Cahors Un Jour ★★★☆ £D Cahors Un Jour Sur Terre ★★★☆ £D

Dom. Le Roc (Fronton) *www.leroc-fronton.com*

This is the benchmark property in the small appellation of Fronton just to the north of Toulouse. As one would expect the wines are dominated by the local Negrette grape, with examples that are both poised and spicy. There is a fresh and fruit driven rosé with fine small berry fruit aromas. The regular red Classique is a spicy, herb scented example, quite lean and angular in style, it blends 70% Negrette with 20% Syrah and 10% Cabernet Sauvignon adding a touch of minty structure. Vibrant dark and spicy is the 100% Negrette La Folle Noir d'Ambat which is traditionally aged in *foudres*. Of the top two wines the Reservée is fleshier and rounder with a little new oak used for ageing and a higher proportion of Cabernet Sauvignon and Syrah, 25% of each. Most characterful though is the Don Quichotte. Dominated by Negrette (60%) with the balance all Syrah. Ageing is in a mix of larger *foudres* and 400 litre *barriques*. Neither fined nor filtered, the wine has a lovely dark spicy, elegant intensity and impressive depth. (DM)

Recommended Reds:
Fronton Don Quichotte ★★★ £C Fronton Cuvée Reservee ★★☆ £C
Fronton La Folle Noir d'Ambat ★★ £B Fronton La Classique ★★ £B
Recommended Rosés:
Fronton La Saignee ★☆ £B

✿ Vignobles des Verdots (Bergerac) *www.verdots.com*

David Foutout produces a small and impressive range of Bergerac from a number of the areas ACs. He currently has 22 ha of red varieties under vine along with 13 ha of whites. The wines are split into 3 different brands, Clos des Verdots for the wineries softest, most approachable wines, Château Tour des Verdots, which are a step up and the top selections, which are released under the Les Verdots Grand Vin label. Rosé is soft and easy drinking with no residual sugar. Of the reds the Clos des Verdots is lightly berry scented with soft, supple tannins. The Tours des Verdots is richer and fuller, a blend of older vine Merlot and Cabernet Sauvignon aged in used small oak. The top red, the big rich and structured Les Verdots Grand Vin is dominated by Merlot and gets 21 months in oak a substantial portion new. A considerable number of whites both dry and sweet are produced. Among the dry wines the fresh grassy Clos des Verdots takes the Bergerac AC, it has 80% Sémillon, the balance Sauvignon Blamc and Muscadelle. Les Tour des Verdots is more citrusy and mineral with a little Sauvignon Gris as well. Les Verdots Grand Vin comes from yields of just 20 hl/ha and is rich and concentrated with grassy, citrus fruit and underlying oak, it is barrel-fermented and aged on lees. Particularly characterful is Le Vin a blend of very old Muscadelle (50%), 20% each of Sauvignon Blanc and Gris and the balance Sémillon. Very subtle fruit and a background nutty oak character with a structured mineral core will

enable this to develop well in bottle. There are two good sweet Côtes de Bergeracs, Les Verdots Grand Vin showing greater levels of botrytis. A level up and less obviously peachy and more mineral is a very good Monbazillac Les Verdots. Best of all the sweeties is the Monbazillac Les Verdots Grand Vin. The yield is tiny, less than 10 hl/ha typically, it is barrel-fermented and spends three years in new oak. It is very rich, unctuous and concentrated. (DM)

Recommended Reds:
Côtes de Bergerac Les Verdots Grand Vin ★★★★ £E
Côtes de Bergerac Les Tours des Verdots ★★★ £C
Bergerac Clos des Verdots ★★☆ £B

Recommended Whites:
Monbazillac Les Verdots Le Vin ★★★★☆ £F
Côtes de Bergerac Les Verdots Le Vin ★★★★ £E
Côtes de Bergerac Les Verdots Grand Vin ★★★☆ £E
Monbazillac Les Tours des Verdots ★★★☆ £E
Côtes de Bergerac Moelleux Les Verdots Grand Vin ★★★ £C
Côtes de Bergerac Les Tours des Verdots ★★★ £C
Côtes de Bergerac Moelleux Clos des Verdots ★★☆ £C
Bergerac Clos des Verdots ★☆ £B

Recommended Rosés:
Bergerac Clos des Verdots ★☆ £B

Robert Plageoles (Gaillac) *www.vins-plageoles.com*
The Plageoles produce some of the most striking and original of all Gaillac with a firm commitment to the region's indigenous varieties. Syrah is the most obvious interloper and there is a little Muscadelle as well. There are a total of 22 ha under vine with 16 ha accounted for by white varieties. The reds are very much in a traditional style. No oak is used and they emphasise fruit and are pure and well crafted. They are generally light in colour and extract, particularly the Mauzac Noir, and the Syrah is the darkest of the trio with a hint of black pepper. It is the whites which are particularly important. The Mauzac Nature is a light, fresh sparkler and the Mauzac Vert is a dry style marked by a fascinating array of green fruits. The Mauzac Doux by contrast is a late-harvest white with hints of peach and a slight undercurrent of white pepper and mineral. The Plageoles also make their own version of a vin jaune, Vin de Voile, which is also from Mauzac. The dry Ondenc is rich and impressively concentrated with hints of honey, peach and quince just underpinned by a subtle green fruit character. The great wine here and surely the finest white in Gaillac is the superbly rich and concentrated Vin d'Autan, produced from Ondenc. The vines are pinched to encourage dehydration of the fruit by the Autan wind and the grapes are then further dried after harvesting in the manner of a vin de paille. The yield is microscopic barely 10 hl/ha. (DM)

Recommended Reds:
Gaillac Braucol ★★☆ £C Gaillac Syrah ★★☆ £B
IGP des Côtes du Tarn Mauzac Noir ★★ £B

Recommended Whites:
Gaillac Doux Vin d'Autan ★★★★★ £F
Gaillac Doux Mauzac Roux ★★★ £C
Gaillac Ondenc ★★★ £C Gaillac Mauzac Vert ★★ £B
Gaillac Mousseux Naturel Mauzac Nature ★★ £C

Primo Palatum (Cahors) *www.primo-palatum.com*
Xavier Copel has now established himself as a very successful small-scale merchant and négociant, specialising in limited-production bottlings from the important South West appellations as well as as in Languedoc and Roussillon. He sources fruit from some of the best growers in each of the appellations he works in. Overall production

is less than 6,000 cases a year and some wines are barely more than micro-cuvées. Apart from the wines rated below, his considerable range includes bottlings from Bordeaux, Graves, Sauternes and in the Midi, Minervois and the Côtes du Roussillon. The regular or lesser bottlings are labelled Classica and the top cuvées within an appellation are usually labelled Mythologia. The wines are very impressive: modern and stylish, with an emphasis on *terroir*, and always impeccably made in the various growers' own cellars. (DM)

Recommended Reds:
Cahors Mythologia ★★★☆ £E Cahors Classica ★★★ £C
IGP d'Oc Mythologia ★★★ £C IGP d'Oc Classica ★★ £C

Recommended Whites:
Jurançon Mythologia ★★★★ £E Jurançon Classica ★★★ £D
Limoux Mythologia ★★★ £D

Dom. Rotier (Gaillac) *www.domaine-rotier.com*
Rotier is a good-quality small Gaillac grower with an output of around 15,000 cases a year. Alain Rotier has been vinifying his own wines since 1985 and has now been joined by his brother-in-law Francis Marre. They farm 35ha of vines, 70% of which are red. The vines are now approaching an average age of 35 years and in an ongoing drive to improve quality vine density is being increased from 4,000 to over 6,000 vines per hectare. Regular red, white and rosé are labelled Initiales. More significant wines appear under the Gravels and Renaissance labels and the reds all stand out. The impressively stylish and concentrated L'Âme is a stand out example for the appellation. The Renaissance is also structured and dense and shows impressive dark fruit and cedary complexity. The dry whites don't have quite the same depth but are good examples nonetheless. The sweet white Renaissance Doux shows good, rich peachy fruit with a fine, piercing citrus structure. Most of the wines are forward and approachable but expect the Renaissance wines to develop well in the medium term, particularly the sweet white and the red. (DM)

Recommended Reds:
Gaillac L'Âme ★★★☆ £E Gaillac Renaissance ★★★ £C
Gaillac Gravels ★★☆ £C

Recommended Whites:
Gaillac Renaissance Doux ★★★☆ £D
Gaillac Renaissance ★★☆ £C Gaillac Gravels ★★ £C

❀ Dom. de Souch (Jurançon)
Yvonne Hegoburu makes some of the very finest wines of this special appellation. She possesses just 6.5 ha of vineyard which is farmed biodynamically and she makes barely more than a couple of thousand cases a year. The conversion to biodynamics though is no flash in the pan, this farming approach has been followed since 1994. The Sec is subtle, aromatic and posses a real mineral purity. The Moelleux, by contrast with the Sec, is dominated by Petit Manseng and has a balance of Gros Manseng. The wine is traditionally vinified and aged in *cuve* and again has that subtle, floral and mineral undercurrent. The top Marie Kattalin has marvellous depth and intensity with a peachy richness and a structured but rich texture. Vinification and ageing is in oak but two and three year old barrels to avoid any oak flavours impinging on the quality of the fruit. (DM)

Recommended Whites:
Jurançon Marie Kattalin ★★★★☆ £F
Jurançon Moelleux ★★★☆ £E Jurançon Sec ★★★☆ £E

South-West France

France

Other wines of note

Dom. Abotia
Recommended Reds: Irouléguy ★★ £B

Dom. Arretxia
Recommended Reds: Irouléguy ★★ £B Irouléguy Haitza ★★★ £C

Dom. Bellegarde
Recommended Whites: Jurançon ★★ £C
Jurançon Cuvée Thibaut ★★★ £C

Dom. Brana
Recommended Reds: Irouléguy ★★ £C
Irouléguy Harri Gorri ★★☆ £C

Dom. Bru-Baché
Recommended Whites: Jurançon Casterrasses ★★ £C
Jurançon Quintessence ★★★ £D

Dom. Guy Capmartin
Recommended Reds:
Madiran Tradition ★★ £B Madiran Cuvée De Couvent ★★☆ £C

Dom. Castera
Recommended Whites: Jurançon ★★☆ £C

Dom. de Causse-Marines
Recommended Whites: Gaillac Greilles ★★☆ £C
Gaillac Délires d'Automne ★★★☆ £D

Ch. Baudare
Recommended Reds: Fronton Tradition ★☆ £B
Fronton Prestige ★★ £B

Ch. Beauportail
Recommended Reds: Pécharmant Fûts De Chêne ★★ £C

Ch. Bélingard
Recommended Whites: Bergerac Blanche de Bosredon ★☆ £B
Monbazillac Blanche de Bosredon ★★★ £D

Ch. Bellevue-La-Forêt
Recommended Reds: Fronton ★☆ £B Fronton Préstige ★★ £B
Fronton Optimum ★★☆ £C

Ch. Bellevue sur Vallée
Recommended Reds: Bergerac Le Vin du Bob ★★☆ £C
Recommended Whites: Saussignac Le Vin du Bob ★★★ £D
Bergerac Le Vin du Bob Sauvignon Blanc ★☆ £B

Ch. Bouissel
Recommended Reds:
Fronton ★☆ £B Fronton Cuvée d'Or ★★ £C
Fronton Cuvée Sélection ★★ £C

Ch. Candastre
Recommended Reds: Gaillac ★★★ £C

Ch. Clement Termes
Recommended Whites: Gaillac Sec ★★ £B

Ch. Haut-Monplaisir
Recommended Reds: Cahors ★★ £B Cahors Prestige ★★ £B
Cahors Pur Plaisir ★★★ £C

Ch. Haut Perthus
Recommended Reds: Bergerac ★★ £B

Ch. Jolys
Recommended Whites: Jurançon ★★ £B
Jurançon Cuvée Jean ★★★ £C

Ch. La Caminade
Recommended Reds: Cahors ★★ £B Cahors Esprit ★★★ £C

Ch. La Croix du Mayne
Recommended Reds: Cahors ★★★ £C
Cahors Excellence ★★★☆ £E

Ch. Les Hauts d'Aglan
Recommended Reds: Cahors ★☆ £B Cahors Cuvée A ★★ £C

Ch. Miaudoux
Recommended Reds: Bergerac ★★ £B
Recommended Whites: Bergerac ★★ £B
Saussignac Réserve ★★★ £D

Ch. Monestier La Tour
Recommended Reds: Côtes de Bergerac Emily ★★★ £C
Bergerac ★★☆ £C
Recommended Whites: Bergerac ★★ £B
Bergerac Tour de Monestier ★★☆ £C

Ch. Montauriol
Recommended Reds: Fronton Elevé En Futs ★★ £B

Ch. Moulin Caresse
Recommended Reds: Côtes de Bergerac Prestige ★★☆ £C
Montravel Cent Pour 100 ★★★ £D
Recommended Whites: Montravel Cent Pour 100 ★★☆ £C

Ch. Peyros
Recommended Reds: Madiran ★★ £B
Madiran Greenwich 43 N ★★ £C

Ch. Plaisance
Recommended Reds: Fronton ★☆ £B
Fronton Cuvée Thibaut ★★ £B

Ch. Les Rigalets
Recommended Reds: Cahors Cuvée Prestige ★☆ £B
Cahors Cuvée Quintessence ★★☆ £C

Ch. Thénac
Recommended Reds: Côtes de Bergerac ★★★ £C
Bergerac Fleur du Thénac ★★ £B
Recommended Whites: Bergerac ★★★ £C
Bergerac Fleur du Thénac ★★ £B

Ch. Theulet
Recommended Reds: Bergerac ★★ £B
Recommended Whites: Monbazillac ★★★ £C

Ch. de Tiregand
Recommended Reds: Pécharmant ★★ £C

Clos de Gamot
Recommended Reds: Cahors ★★ £C

Clos Thou
Recommended Whites: Jurançon Guilhouret Sec ★★ £C

Clos d'Yvigne
Recommended Whites: Saussignac ★★★ £D

Cave de Cocumont
Recommended Reds: Côtes du Marmandais Béroy ★☆ £B

Dom. du Crampilh
Recommended Reds: Madiran Vieilles Vignes ★★ £B
Madiran Cuvée Baron ★★★ £D

Cave de Crouseilles
Recommended Reds: Madiran ★ £B

Dom. Etxegaraya
Recommended Reds: Irouléguy ★☆ £B

Dom. de Gineste
Recommended Reds: Gaillac Grande Cuvée ★★ £C
Recommended Whites: Gaillac Grande Cuvée ★☆ £C

Dom. du Haut-Montlong
Recommended Reds: Côtes de Bergerac Vents d'Anges ★★ £C

Dom. Ilarria
Recommended Reds: Irouléguy ★★ £B

Dom. Labranche-Laffont
Recommended Reds: Madiran Tradition ★★ £B
Madiran Vieilles Vignes ★★☆ £C

Dom. Laffont
Recommended Reds: Madiran Cuvée Erigone ★★☆ £C

Madiran Cuvée Hecaté ★★★ £D
Dom. de Laulan
Recommended Whites: Côtes de Duras ★ £B
Dom. Montauriol
Recommended Reds: Fronton Tradition ★ £B
Fronton Mons Aureolus ★★ £B
Dom. Pineraie
Recommended Reds: Cahors Château Pineraie ★★ £C
Dom. de La Métairie
Recommended Reds: Pécharmant ★★ £C
Producteurs Plaimont
Recommended Reds: Côtes de Saint-Mont Ch. De Sabazan ★★ £B
Dom. de San Guilhem
Recommended Whites: IGP de Côtes de Gascogne ★★ £B

Work in progress!!

Producers under consideration for the next edition
Ch. du Bloy (Monbazillac)
Ch. de Cabidos (IGP de Comté Tolosan)
Ch. La Reyne (Cahors)
Ch. La Robertie (Bergerac)
Ch. Les Marnières (Bergerac)
Clos Basté (Madiran)
Clos Guirouilh (Jurançon)
Dom. Elian da Ros (Côtes Du Marmandais)
Les Jardins de Babylone (Jurançon)

Author's choice

A selection of up and coming reds and whites
Reds:
Dom. Berthoumieu   Madiran Tradition
Alain Brumont   Madiran Torus
Chapelle Lenclos   Madiran Domaine Mouréou
Ch. du Cèdre   Cahors Prestige
Ch. Jonc Blanc   Bergerac Class K
Ch. Viella   Madiran
Dom. Le Roc   Fronton Don Quichotte
Whites:
Clos Uroulat   Jurançon Cuvée Marie
Robert Plageoles   Gaillac Ondenc
Camin Larredya   Jurançon Sec
Dom. Cauhapé   Jurançon Chant des Vignes
Ch. d'Aydie   Pacherenc De Vic-Bilh Frédéric Laplace
Ch. Tour des Gendres   Bergerac Cuvée des Conti

Cellarworthy South West reds

Dom. Berthoumieu   Madiran Charles de Batz
Alain Brumont   Madiran Château Montus Cuvée Prestige
Chapelle Lenclos   Madiran La Chapelle Lenclos
Ch. d'Aydie   Madiran Château d'Aydie
Ch. Barrejat   Madiran Vieux Ceps
Ch. Beaulieu   Côtes du Marmandais L'Oratoire
Ch. du Cèdre   Cahors Le Cèdre
Ch. Lagrezette   Cahors Pigeonnier
Ch. Tour des Gendres   Bergerac Cuvée Anthologia
Ch. Viella   Madiran Cuvée Prestige
Clos Triguedina   Cahors New Black Wine
Dom. Cosse Maisonneuve   Cahors Les Laquets
Primo Palatum   Cahors Mythologia

Dom. Rotier   Gaillac L'Âme

Diverse regional whites
Dom. de L'Ancienne-Cure   Monbazillac L'Extase
Clos Uroulat   Jurançon Clos Uroulat
Camin Larredya   Jurançon Cuvée Simon
Dom. Cauhapé   Jurançon Noblesse du Temps
Ch. Bellevue Sur Vallee   Bergerac Le Vin du Bob Sauvignon
Ch. Laffitte-Teston   Pacherenc du Vic-Bilh Ericka
Ch. Tirecul-La-Gravière   Monbazillac Cuvée Madame
Ch. Tour des Gendres   Bergerac Cuvée Anthologia
Ch. Viella   Pacherenc du Vic-Bilh Moelleux
Robert Plageoles   Jurançon Noblesse Du Temps
Primo Palatum   Jurançon Mythologia
Dom. Rotier   Gaillac Renaissance Doux
Vignobles des Verdots   Monbazillac Les Verdots Le Vin

Italy /Overview

In order to give some coherence to Italy's plethora of wine regions and appellations we have divided it into five major sections: Piedmont & North-West Italy, North-East Italy, Tuscany, Central Italy, and Southern Italy & Islands. As an aid to orientation, all of Italy's 20 regions are included within one of the sections below and all of the most important DOCs and DOCGs are summarised. They are covered in greater detail in the individual chapters that follow.

Piedmont & North-West Italy
The wines of North-West Italy are numerous and diverse. Many of the top reds come from the Langhe hills in Piedmont. These are produced in small quantities as nearly all of the top sites are divided between several growers, in a similar manner to Burgundy. They also command high prices.

Valle d'Aosta
A wide range of wines from diverse (mostly French) grape varieties come from a handful of good producers, most if not all under the **Valle d'Aosta** DOC. The wines are little seen beyond the borders of this mountain enclave.

Piedmont (Piemonte)
The noble Nebbiolo grape provides majestic **Barolo** and **Barbaresco** from the Langhe hills but also fine reds in **Roero** and, rarely, in **Ghemme** and **Gattinara**. All are DOCG, including Roero from 2004. Numerous fine examples of Barbera – albeit in diverse styles – emanate from the DOCs of **Barbera d'Alba** and DOGCs of **Barbera d'Asti**. Blended Barbera and Nebbiolo appear as **Langhe** or **Monferrato** DOC sometimes blended with a proportion of French varieties. Intense Dolcetto appears under the DOGCs of **Dolcetto di Dogliani** and **Dolcetto d'Ovada** as well as **Dolcetto di Diano d'Alba**, and of more varied style and in greater quantities in **Dolcetto d'Alba** DOC. Among the many other wines, Arneis appears as dry white **Roero Arneis**, **Gavi** is another dry white, made from the Cortese grape, and **Moscato d'Asti** is a fine sweet Muscat.

Lombardy (Lombardia)
While there's no fine wine to be had from anywhere close to Milan there is fine sparkling DOCG **Franciacorta** from the edge of Lake Iseo. Elegant reds based on Chiavennasca (Nebbiolo) come from close to Switzerland in the Alps as DOCG **Valtellina Superiore**. An intense, powerful version produced from dried grapes, **Valtellina Sforzato**, is also DOCG. In the south of Lombardy in an extension to the Colli Piacentini (see Emilia-Romagna) diverse everyday reds and whites are produced under the **Oltrepò Pavese** and **Valcalepio** DOCs. (For Lugana whites see Veneto)

Liguria
Liguria is known for some occasionally well-made if not widely exported wines, mostly lighter-style reds and whites. DOCs include **Cinqueterre** (white only), **Colli di Luni**, **Riviera Ligure di Ponente**, **Golfo di Tigullo** and **Rossese di Dolceaqua** (red only).

North-East Italy
This region is at last beginning to receive greater international recognition for both quality and diversity in both colours and from native grapes as well as international varieties.

Trentino-Alto Adige
The few excellent producers in Trentino make both varietal and blended reds and whites from international varieties, some as **Trentino** DOC, others IGT. Native varieties include the white Nosiola and the potentially exciting smoky, black-fruited red, Teroldego (as **Teroldego Rotaliano**). Decent sparkling wine appears as **Trento**. Much of the quality from the German-speaking South Tirol takes the form of familiar varietals under the **Alto Adige** DOC, including Chardonnay, Sauvignon, Gewürztraminer, Pinot Bianco, Pinot Grigio, Pinot Nero, Cabernet Sauvignon and Merlot, as well as a recent blaze of quality from the native Lagrein. High altitude and sometimes seemingly impossibly sited vineyards increasingly give high quality and expressive interpretations that are not emulated anywhere else.

Veneto
Valpolicella and **Amarone/Recioto di Valpolicella** are the stars of the Veneto, with very good examples now proliferating. **Soave** (now DOCG for **Superiore**) from a top producer is of a different order too. With better purity and concentration there are now many mineral and herb infused examples that illustrate the potential of the native Garganega grapes from volcanic derived soils. Fine sweet **Recioto di Soave** DOCG can now be sleek and fruit intense in contrast to the once commonplace more raisined efforts. **Bardolino** was always overrated (despite being DOCG for **Superiore**) but there are outcrops of good quality, both red and white, in **Breganze**, **Colli Berici** and **Colli Euganei** DOCs as well as some attractive fizz in **Prosecco**. (Now DOCG for **Colli Euganei Fior d'Arancia** and **Asolo Prosecco**). White **Lugana** and decent red and white **Garda** DOC wines come from vineyards close by Lake Garda.

Friuli-Venezia Giulia
More of Italy's fine whites come from Friuli than anywhere else but there are increasing amounts of fine reds too. Whether varietal or blended most quality wines will bear one of three DOCs: **Collio**, **Colli Orientali del Friuli** or **Friuli Isonzo**. Of the international varieties, Chardonnay, Sauvignon, Pinot Grigio, Pinot Bianco, Cabernet Sauvignon and Merlot predominate. Native whites, Tocai Friulano, Ribolla Gialla, Malvasia can be very good while the best native reds, Schioppettino and Pignolo, must be tried. Wines from the DOCs of **Friuli Grave**, **Friuli Latisana** or **Friuli Aquileia** are typically more everyday. The province of Udine now boasts of three DOGCs, **Ramandolo**, **Picolit** and **Rosazzo**.

Tuscany (Toscana)
The sheer volume of fine wine from Tuscany is remarkable. Much of it derives from Sangiovese, though the extent of its Tuscan character can sometimes be enhanced by the inclusion of other natives such as Canaiolo or Colorino or (in some instances only) compromised by Merlot, Cabernet Sauvignon, Syrah and other interlopers. These international varieties are very successful in their own right, often as varietal examples.

The classic appellations (all DOCG) include **Carmignano**, **Chianti** (often appended with a sub-zone name such as **Colli Fiorentini** or **Colli Senesi** – the best being **Rufina**), **Chianti Classico** (Tuscany's heart), **Brunello di Montalcino** (for the biggest, most powerful pure Sangiovese) and **Vino Nobile di Montepulciano**. The best-known white appellation is **Vernaccia di San Gimignano**.

DOGCs, (**Montecucco**, **Suvereto**, **Val di Cornia** and **Morellino di Scansano**) as well as DOCs or sub-zones (**Montecarlo**, **Colline Lucchesi**, **Colline Pisane**, **Montescudaio**, and **Bolgheri**) are found close to the Tuscan coast and southern Maremma. Like in the classic

appellations, many fine wines are sold as simply IGT Toscana.

Central Italy
Too often ignored by the wine drinker only familiar with Tuscany and Piedmont. Shame! because there's a mushrooming number of good producers and some real originals.

Emilia-Romagna
Viticulturally, there are two halves to this region too. By far the best reds are Sangiovese from the new (since 2010) **Romagna** DOC appellation – a very serious alternative to Sangiovese from Tuscany – or IGT equivalents from the best producers and the local white, **Albana di Romagna**, has just been granted DOGC status in all aspects from dry to liqueureux. To be sure, Emilia has fabulous ham, cheese and other food products but generally only adequate whites and reds from hillside slopes (colli), most notably in the **Colli Piacentini** DOCs and **Colli Bolognesi** DOGCs. Bologna's hills latter can provide good Barbera and Cabernet Sauvignon especially from dedicated small growers. In Piacenza's hills Barbera is combined with Bonarda in Gutturnio which can be characterful and ageworthy. Emilia is also home of the 'dreaded' Lambrusco but a few worthy exceptions to the bulk of industrial swill do exist.

Marche
Marche is for dry white Verdicchio (either **Verdicchio dei Castelli di Jesi** or **Verdicchio di Matelica** DOGCs), some of it very good, but also for other more everyday dry whites such as **Falerio dei Colli Ascolani** DOC. Here as in Abruzzo well-structured whites from the native Pecorino are also gaining ground. The best reds are based on Montepulciano and have improved hugely in the past decade. Many of the best are now sold as IGTs, sometimes including a significant percentage of other varieties. **Rosso Conero** DOC (Riservas are DOGC) is still the best known name for Montepulciano-based reds but at least as many good examples of **Rosso Piceno Superiore** DOC are now made from a delimited southern zone. Straight Rosso Piceno will, however, usually turn out to be a cheap, simple quaffer at best. Other IGT reds based on Sangiovese or imported varieties can also offer both quality and value.

Umbria
There are lots of interesting reds and whites to be found in Umbria. Good **Montefalco Rosso** should be tried as should the more demanding **Montefalco Sagrantino** DOCG. A new wave of better balanced examples of this powerful, spicy red are now emerging. A raft of other excellent reds, sold as IGT Umbria, are usually based on Cabernet Sauvignon, Merlot or Sangiovese. Some are very good indeed. **Orvieto** (a DOC which also covers part of Lazio) when made by a good producer offers personality without heaviness.

Lazio
Lazio has football and **Frascati**. I'd argue that more of the latter is now clean and characterful. Some other good dry whites are made too as are much improved reds, even if many of them come from Merlot, Cabernet or Syrah. However there is more! Seek out the best of a wave of new varietal **Cesanese** (**del Piglio**) DOGC reds and you will be tasting the first examples of a potentially high quality and original Lazio wine.

Abruzzo & Molise
Source of many of the best examples of the Montepulciano grape, especially as **Montepulciano d'Abruzzo** DOC (DOCG in the Colline Teramane). Cheaper versions are good gutsy quaffers but an increasing number of good producers make examples that are powerful, fleshy, flavoursome and ageworthy. The very best are world class. The main white appellation is **Trebbiano d'Abruzzo** DOC. While most wines based on the Trebbiano grape are dull, from a handful of producers the local clones can given remarkably complex, richly textured whites. Some adequate examples of Chardonnay are produced as IGTs.

Southern Italy & Islands
Increasingly a cornucopia of vinous delights, especially for reds and whites but also for sweet and fortified wines.

Campania
Aglianico is the star, as **Taurasi** DOCG but also in **Aglianico del Taburno**, **Falerno del Massico**, **Sannio** DOCs and various IGTs. Excellent, mostly dry whites come from native grapes Greco, Fiano and Falanghina as **Greco di Tufo**, **Fiano di Avellino** (both DOCG) and Sannio and **Taburno** DOCs for Falanghina.

Basilicata and Calabria
Basilicata has more fine Aglianico, nearly all of it labelled **Aglianico del Vulture** DOC. (Superiore is DOGC.) Once rustic and firm there are now many good examples both in more forward supple styles and concentrated and complex versions for keeping that again show the nobility of Aglianico. Calabria too has some exciting reds produced by a mere handful of quality producers. Most derive much of their character and quality from the native Gaiioppo grape.

Puglia
Negroamaro and Primitivo provide many of the best Puglian reds, many of them sold as IGTs but **Salice Salentino**, **Brindisi** and **Primitivo di Manduria** are leading DOCs, with **Primitiva di Manduria Dolce Naturale** classified as DOGC. Further reds come from Montepulciano and Uva di Troia, some under **Castel del Monte** DOGC, where elevation can add more than a touch of elegance. There are also decent scented dry whites, including some unexpectedly good Chardonnay and some of the best rosés in Italy - again much is sold as IGT.

Sicily (Sicilia)
Ever-burgeoning quantities of quality reds and whites are nearly all sold as IGT Sicilia, but there are now a few more DOCs of note. Leading native varieties Nero d'Avola and Nerello Mascalese compete with imports such as Cabernet Sauvignon, Merlot and Syrah. Most significant is the only DOGC, **Cerasuolo di Vittoria** and the DOC **Etna** for reds, and **Moscato di Pantelleria** and **Passito di Pantelleria** for often delicious sweet Muscat.

Sardinia (Sardegna)
The true potential of Sardinia remains largely untapped but there are already good dry whites from Vermentino, as **Vermentino di Sardegna** DOC and **Vermentino di Gallura** DOCG. Increasingly fine reds are from Cannonau or Carignano, as **Cannonau di Sardegna** and **Carignano del Sulcis** DOCs respectively or from several IGTs.

1   Valle d'Aosta
2   Piedmont (Piemonte)
3   Lombardy (Lombardia)
4   Liguria
5   Trentino-Alto Adige
6   Veneto
7   Friuli-Venezia Giulia

8   Tuscany (Toscana)
9   Emilia-Romagna
10 Marche
11 Umbria
12 Lazio
13 Abruzzo
14 Molise
15 Campania
16 Puglia
17 Basilicata
18 Calabria
19 Sicily (Sicilia)
20 Sardinia (Sardegna)

'Ricchezza terriera'

Piedmont has made progress like almost no other wine region over the past 30 years. While radically different approaches to winemaking have accentuated the stylistic differences possible from the noble Nebbiolo grape, there are now many outstanding varied examples. High quality is also achieved across a wide range of styles made from the classic Barbera and Dolcetto grapes while superb, exuberant Moscato and enticing dry whites remain under-appreciated. There also a host of lesser known varieties which with improved winemaking now provide more than a passing interest. But what's really special about Piedmont is man's connection with the land and the importance of the link between fine wine, the physical environment and the human endeavour therein. It is illustrated as well here as in any wine region in the world.

Valle d'Aosta

Italy's smallest region has a distinct French flavour and a wide range of varieties include those of French, Italian and Swiss origins. Nearly all the wines are sold as Valle d'Aosta (or more usually in French as Vallée d'Aoste). Interesting whites include Petite Arvine, Pinot Gris (or Nus Malvoisie) and Chardonnay while reds from Torrette, Fumin and Syrah should be tried. Good examples of all are made by the region's leading producer Constantino Charrère's Les Crêtes estate. Late picked or dried moscato grapes can produce a fine sweet wine either as Chambave Moscato Passito (Muscat Fletri) or as a vino da tavola in the case of Les Crêtes.

Piedmont (Piemonte)
Reds

At the heart of Piedmont viticulture are the Langhe hills. The finest grape is Nebbiolo. The two great wines are **Barolo** and **Barbaresco**, both DOCG, though some of the best wines from these zones are now sold under the **Langhe** DOC. One of the region's greatest strengths derives from its peasant landholding heritage. While *commerciante* or large *négociant* houses flogged the grapes of any number of small growers under generic labels in the 1950s and 60s, the subsequent success and leadership of Angelo Gaja and others paved the way for small growers to do likewise – a trend that really gained momentum in the 80s and 90s. Outside money tends to be the exception in Piedmont yet some producers have been highly receptive to new ideas. Both Barolo (a little over 1,500ha) and Barbaresco (just over 600ha) are fairly small wine regions and it is common for growers here to have just one or two hectares of this or that cru. Barolo is spread for the most part over five communes: La Morra, Barolo, Castiglione Falletto, Monforte d'Alba and Serralunga. Verduno is the most significant of six other communes that encroach on the DOCG. The southern part of Monforte and Serralunga (in the east) have mostly the older Helvetian soils, said to favour strength and structure. La Morra soils are predominantly on younger Tortonian soils, a chalky marl giving greater perfume and a less rigorous structure. Between the two there tends to be a mix of the two with varying amounts of sand and clay. More clay can help in very hot years but a higher sand component can improve drainage in cool, wet years.

Barbaresco is almost exclusively restricted to just three communes. Almost half of it comes from the commune of Barbaresco, where 60 per cent of the vineyard area is is given over to Barbaresco production, compared to only a little over 20 per cent of the vineyard area in neighbouring Neive and Treiso. Barbaresco generally is slightly less powerful than Barolo, more perfumed and ready to drink a little sooner, but producer and site are the real

determinants of style and character. The wines are required to have a minimum of nine months' wood-ageing and are released a year earlier than Barolo (which must have two years in wood). In both zones much is made of a modern versus traditional approach to winemaking yet the reality is less distinct, with a range of different approaches to vinification and winemaking. The important differences centre around the length of maceration; the type and use of oak (size, age and origin); temperature and style of fermentation; and the type of fermentation vessel – we have tried to highlight some of these differences within the individual producer profiles. Of course these differences apply as much in Burgundy but in this relatively isolated, conservative area the differences of opinion have taken on an extra intensity. There are many outstanding wines across the spectrum.

Nebbiolo under other guises includes **Carema**, **Gattinara**, **Ghemme** and **Roero**. The last, lying on sandier soils across the Tanarò river from Bra and Alba has made great strides during the last decade and can provide stylish complex examples of Nebbiolo at more affordable prices.

Piedmont's second great grape is Barbera, which can take on a number of guises. The leading two appellations are **Barbera d'Alba** and **Barbera d'Asti**. The Superiore version of the latter is now redefined by three subzones: Colli Astiani, Nizza and Tinella. Barbera has a great affinity with new oak and many of the top examples have spent around 12 months in *barriques*. Barbera also combines well with Nebbiolo and there are many good oak-aged, deeply fruity, lush examples (typically Langhe DOC) that can be drunk quite young or kept. The more northerly hills of the Asti and Alessandria provinces include similar interesting blends under the **Monferrato** DOC. Dolcetto doesn't quite make the cut in fine wine terms, although Dolcetto di Dogliani and Dolcetto di Ovada have been granted DOCG status. It does, however, make both wonderfully fruity everyday wine or something more intense and concentrated and often better with a year or two of bottle-age, depending on its maker. There are three leading manifestations: **Dolcetto d'Alba**, the small **Dolcetto di Diano d'Alba** and **Dolcetto di Dogliani**. Dolcetto is also included in the Monferrato DOC, while **Dolcetto di Ovada** is mostly of the fruity, juicy type. What else is there? Other natives varieties include Freisa and Grignolino, both sold under most of the regional DOCs, but exciting examples are few. There's also sparkling red fizz, actually DOCG in **Brachetto d'Acqui** (from Brachetto) and **Malvasia di Castelnuovo Don Bosco** from Malvasia Nera. How significant are the French imports? Not very, but Cabernet Sauvignon features in many a Langhe or Monferrato blend (see above), Merlot to a lesser extent. Pinot Nero (Pinot Noir) has yet to really impress, while plantings of Syrah remain small.
Whites

For whites, most emblematic are the perfumed and characterful Arneis (frequently as **Roero Arneis**) and relatively high acid Cortese (the best examples sold as **Gavi del Comune di Gavi** – those at the heart of a wider zone) are the leading native whites. Recently the previously obscure Timorasso grape has been transformed into a characterful white with a lush texture and a ripe peach and tropical fruit intensiy. Other natives include Favorita, a distinctive herb scented wine, and Erbaluce as **Erbaluce di Caluso** DOGC or the better sweet version from dried grapes, **Caluso Passito**. Yet the most important white grape in Piedmont is Moscato Bianco. This, the 'good' Muscat DOGC (Muscat Blanc à Petits Grains), is very widely planted in the Asti and Alba hills. Good Asti is a well made, sweet party fizz and much better than some of the nasty acidic and green branded stuff made in Germany, France and elsewhere. But

Piedmont & North-West Italy

Italy

Moscato d'Asti, made on a different scale, can be incomparably better. Delightfully perfumed and low in alcohol, it is excellent with fresh fruit. A very small amount of passito-style Muscat is made in an Asti enclave called **Loazzolo**. Of imports, Chardonnay is the leading variety, usually appearing as **Langhe** Chardonnay but occasionally under the region-wide **Piemonte** DOC. Really top examples are relatively few but there is potential here. There are small amounts of Sauvignon, even less Riesling, Viognier and other imports.

Liguria
Ligurian reds are rarely seen outside the region but include **Rossese di Dolceaqua** DOC from the Rossese grape grown behind Ventimiglia near the border with France and Ormeasco (Dolcetto) grapes under the guise of **Rivera Liguria di Ponente** from the long strip between France and Genova. Some growers are now producing the likes of Merlot and Syrah for potentially better wines. Most important for whites are Pigato and Vermentino as Rivera Ligure di Ponente varietals, but the latter also in **Colli di Luni** and **Cinqueterre** DOCs (from vineyards close to north-west Tuscany and Biachetta Genovese in the **Golfo di Tigullo** just east of Genoa. **Cinqueterre Schiacchetrà** DOC is a sweet version made from semi-dried grapes.

Lombardy (Lombardia)
Valtellina Superiore (DOCG) is Lombardy's most renown red wine appellation. Made almost entirely from Nebbiolo (Chiavennasca) the wines tend to be lighter and more austere than those from the Langhe but the very best examples are stylishly perfumed and well-balanced. The wines may also be identified by one of four subzones: Grumello, Inferno, Sassella or Valgella. Often better are the higher alcohol **Valtellina Sforzato** (Sfursat), a version made from partially dried grapes. Top examples are powerful and structured with intense sweet fruit that becomes impressively complex with age.

The closest Italy has to top Champagne in quality is **Franciacorta**. Here, near Lake Iseo in Lombardy, Chardonnay, Pinot Bianco and Pinot Nero grapes are combined in serious metodo classico sparkling wines. Satèn is a softer, creamier, low-pressure version. Sometimes very good **Terre di Franciacorta** reds are made from Cabernet Franc (or, as likely, Carmenère), Merlot, Cabernet Sauvignon and Pinot Nero. Still whites from Franciacorta include high quality Chardonnay. In the east of Lombardy some attractive dry white **Lugana** is made from Trebbiano di Lugana (see North-East Italy).

Although rarely other than ordinary **Oltrepò Pavese** counts as Lombady's third significant wine region. The best reds tend to come from Barbera, Bonarda and Cabernet Sauvignon. There is also much Pinot Nero, most of which goes into sparkling metodo classico Talento wines. Decent whites are usually from Riesling, Sauvignon, Chardonnay or Pinot Gris.

Leading Barolo crus
La Morra: Arborina, Brunate, Cerequio, Conca di Annunziata, Fossati, Gattera, Giachini, La Serra, Rocche di Annunziata
Barolo: Brunate, Cerequio, Fossati (all three are shared with La Morra) Bricco Viole, Cannubi, Cannubi Boschis, Le Coste, Sarmassa
Castiglione Falletto: Bricco Boschis, Fiasco, Monprivato, Villero, Rocche
Monforte d'Alba: Bussia Soprana, Bricco Cicala, Colonnello, Gavarini, Ginestra, Mosconi, Pianpolvere

Serralunga d'Alba: Cerretta, Falletto, Francia, Lazzarito, Marenca-Rivette, Parafada, Prapò, Vigna Rionda

Leading Barbaresco crus
Barbaresco: Asili, Martinenga, Montefico, Montestefano, Ovello, Pajé, Pora, Rabajà, Rio Sordo, Roncagliette, Secondine
Neive: Bricco, Gallina, Marcorino, Messoirano, Santo Stefano, Serraboella and Starderi
Treiso: Pajoré, Valeirano

A-Z of producers by appellation/region

Appellations
1 Valle d'Aosta
2 Carema
3 Gattinara
4 Ghemme
5 Valtellina Superiore
6 Franciacorta
7 Erbaluce di Caluso, Caluso Passito
8 Barbera d'Asti, Moscato d'Asti
9 Langhe
10 Roero, Roero Arneis
11 Barbaresco
12 Dolcetto di Diano d'Alba
13 Barolo
14 Dolcetto di Dogliani
15 Gavi
16 Oltrepò Pavese
17 Rossese di Dolceaqua
18 Riviera Ligure di Ponente
19 Cinqueterre
20 Colli di Luni

Regions
A Valle d'Aosta
B Piedmont (Piemonte)
C Liguria
D Lombardy (Lombardia)

Piedmont & North-West Italy

Italy

Piedmont vintages

There's a wide choice of top Piedmont wines for cellaring. Not just great Barolo and Barbaresco for the medium- and long-term (8–30 years) but much excellent Langhe and Barbera for the short- and medium-term (4–12 years). When to drink depends on a producer's own style but also on your own preference, whether for the fruit intensity and boldness of youth or the more mellow complexity that comes with age.

2015 A very cold winter and wet spring kept the water tables high to cope with the hottest July for over 100 years. It was also very windy during July and August which did temper the excessive heat. An even ripening of the grapes in all areas has led to some wines being made of exceptional quality, the only caveat being perhaps a lowering of acidity but not as much as in the 2003 vintage. The result is a classy crop of wines with good fruit underneath the tannins and powerful longevity.

2014 A mild winter and a cool wet summer coupled with hail in some areas brought challenging conditions to Piedmont's wine producers. Asti had most of the good weather and sunshine but Alba suffered, so it looks as if the Barberas from Asti will be the superior wine. The main Dolcetto growing areas really suffered with the hail but those who managed to avoid it have made reasonable quality wine. Late ripening Nebbiolo probably did best where producers were not affected by the hail with Barbaresco faring better than the Barolos. Not a vintage for long keeping although as usual, the best producers have made perfectly good, if not great wine. This is a vintage where it is important to follow the producer rather than the appellation.

2013 A long cool spring and heat spikes in July had the growers a little worried as to when the harvest might commence, but continued fine weather right through to the beginning of October (when rain came just at the right time to put some more juice into the fruit) allayed the fears. This augers well for well-balanced and classic wines.

2012 Uneven weather again, with an intensely cold February, followed by cool weather right up to the end of May. A long dry spell with some heat spikes in August was followed by rain at the end of the month and into September. This allowed even quality in the maturation of the grapes, resulting in wines that should be structured and well balanced without perhaps the ripeness of the 2011s

2011 Climatic conditions were uneven throughout the vintage, which led to a lowering of yields. A wet March, hot April, cool June and July and a very hot August affected the quantity of grapes. Rain in the first week in September helped the balance of the phenolic content of the fruit allowing even ripening. The combination of low yields and good tannins auger well for wines of great structure, ripeness, balance and power.

2010 The season started late with snow falling until mid March which delayed the bud break. A cool spring and low temperatures persisted until the end of June when the temperature became extremely hot and dry until the middle of August. A sudden drop in temperature with humid conditions caused anxiety over rot but this was saved by cool nights and dry hot days right up to the end of September, with the exception of three isolated wet days. The vintage, therefore, is a little uneven, with some under-ripe fruit, but on the whole, wines should be well balanced with medium weight.

2009 Producers were worried that the extremely hot weather in late summer would result in many jammy wines, but the large amount of snow from November to March and the rainfall that followed in April and May ensured there was enough moisture and balance in

the soil to cope with the extreme summer heat. Fine, sunny days and cooling winds during harvest produced balanced, harmonious wines with high sugar and ripe (not overripe) fruit. Barbera and Dolcetto fared better than in 2008 and the overall opinion is that the vintage ranks with the best of the decade.

2008: This was a good, if not great, vintage, although some producers have no doubt produced some excellent results. Heavy rain in the spring and early summer gave cause for concern, but a long spell of fine weather afterwards ensured the continued run of good vintages since 2003. Nebbiolo has done exceptionally well, especially by those producers who managed to control their yields, whilst there is more concern for the earlier ripening varieties.

2007: Due to fine, dry conditions, harvesting was around two weeks earlier than usual. Despite some hard rainfall at the beginning of the harvest, all the varietals were picked in fine weather and were ready for crush by the end of September. Whilst in 2003 the early harvest was necessary because the grapes were drying out, in 2007, the Nebbiolo was showing good fruit, structure and balance despite the severe hailstorm at the end of May. The combination of hail and the dry conditions caused a natural reduction in yield, but the resultant quality was very good.

2006: Although 05 and 04 are showing increasing promise along comes another vintage to test the growers. Together the excessive heat of July, the cool, damp August conditions and a patchy September tested both the grower and the health of the vineyards. Results are likely to be variable yet potential first rate from the top names.

2005: Not the vintage hoped for with conditions ranging from drought to cooler conditions and rain as well as isolated hail. However while most growers had to work especially hard for quality there is growing optimism for balanced and well-structured wines more in the mould of 01, 99 or 96 - without the excessive heat and high alcohol seen in some 03s, 00s and 97s.

2004: Semi-normality (and good quantities) after the extremes of recent years. Cool nights and a dry, late finish to the season (end October) with plenty of wind ensured healthy grapes. A more classic vintage with bright, perfumed whites and pure, ripe, well-structured, if less rich reds than recently.

2003: After too much rain in 2002, it was too hot and dry with some vines suffering heat stress. Very promising Dolcetto, and some top Barbera, but much more difficult for Nebbiolo.

2002: A poor summer, atypically wet and cool with rot problems. Hail also dented quantities for some. Worst for earlier ripening Dolcetto and Barbera, better for Nebbiolo as the sun eventually emerged but sound wines at best.

2001: The last in the great run of vintages since 95. High quality owed much to a hot summer followed a wet spring although intermittent rain and hail in September reduced quality for some.

2000: Initially over-hyped yet exceptional Barolo/Barbaresco from select few. A very hot August after a cool July led to rapid ripening and many wines show over-ripe fruit and under-ripe tannins. Better in Serralunga than La Morra.

1999: This generally excellent vintage combines the fruit richness and ripeness of 97 with more of the structure of 96. Very good for Barbera, Dolcetto and Nebbiolo, with many ageworthy exciting wines.

1998: A smallish crop from a hot dry summer that concluded with some rain. Colours are more evolved, more typical for the Nebbiolo-based wines; many are full, ripe and balanced. A fine vintage for medium- to long-term cellaring.

1997: In two words: Hot and dry. The very ripe, even overripe fruit

resulted in wines with a sweet, lush fruit character and relatively low acidities. Generally tannins are good and ripe but sometimes are quite marked due to a lack of full physiological ripeness. Many wines are best drunk now; keep only top names.

1996: Cool and classic, with gradual even ripening. Many growers picked very late to produce wines that are fully ripe but powerfully structured. Cellar for another 10 years from more traditional producers. Quantities of some wines were down due to hail.

1995: The first of an unprecedented run of good to great vintages. Although it's not at the same level as 1996 - 2001, attractive, well-structured if slightly leaner Barolo and Barbaresco was produced. The best are now showing well.

1994: Generally weak, with a lack of real fruit concentration, some Nebbiolo based wines provided attractive, early drinking. Usually best avoided now.

1993: The best vintage between 90 and 95. Consider only the most consistent growers (including Riservas) - many have proved too firmly structured.

1992: Wet, depressing – the poorest vintage of the 90s. No longer one to take a chance on (if you ever could) –yet there were rare successes from Barolo.

1991: A lack of balance was typical of 91, the first weak vintage in a gloomy spell for Piedmont. Usually poorly balanced wines from a wet vintage.

1990: The last outstanding vintage prior to 1996. Sustained hot weather gave rise to rich, ripe wines. The first wave of exciting new producers (Clerico, Sandrone, R Voerzio et al) became well-established stars. A good vintage to discover how great Barolo/Barbaresco begins to evolve.

1989: Another classic year with powerful, structured wines. Most can still be kept but it depends on the signature of the grower or producer.

1988: Some Nebbiolo was compromised by rain but the best are dense sturdy wines that have aged well. Many will still keep.

Earlier years: 1986 ★★★ provided some very attractive Barolo and Barbaresco – but stick with the top wines now, others are past it. **1985** ★★★☆ and **1982** ★★★★ were excellent vintages but there were nothing like the number of top examples now being made. Beware of many of the négociant labels; seek out a classic from a small grower instead. **1979** ★★★ provided some refined wines but most of the rare remaining bottles are past their best. Though long-lived, both **1978** ★★★ and **1974** ★★★ can be rather tough and old-fashioned – taste before buying any quantity and be sure of its provenance. Well-stored examples from **1971** can still be classic while **1970**, **67**, **64** and **61** might tempt the intrepid.

Piedmont vintage chart

	Barolo	Barbaresco	Barbera (premium)
2015	NYR	NYR	NYR
2014	NYR	NYR	NYR
2013	NYR	NYR	NYR
2012	★★★★☆ A	★★★★☆ A	★★★★ A
2011	★★★ A	★★★ A	★★★ A
2010	★★★ B	★★★ B	★★★ B
2009	★★★★☆ A	★★★★☆ A	★★★★☆ B
2008	★★★★ B	★★★★ B	★★★ B
2007	★★★★☆ B	★★★★☆ B	★★★★☆ B
2006	★★★★☆ B	★★★★☆ B	★★★★ B
2005	★★★★☆ B	★★★★ B	★★★★ B
2004	★★★★ B	★★★☆ B	★★★☆ B
2003	★★/★★★★ C	★★/★★★★ C	★★★☆ C
2002	★/★★★ D	★/★★★ D	★☆ D
2001	★★★★☆ C	★★★★☆ C	★★★★ B
2000	★★★/★★★★☆ C	★★★/★★★★☆ C	★★★★☆ C
1999	★★★★☆ C	★★★★☆ C	★★★☆ C
1998	★★★★ C	★★★★ C	★★★★ C
1997	★★★★☆ C	★★★★☆ C	★★★★☆ C
1996	★★★★☆ B	★★★★☆ B	★★★☆ C
1995	★★★☆ C	★★★☆ C	★★★☆ C
1993	★★★ C	★★★ C	★★★ C
1990	★★★★☆ C	★★★★☆ C	★★★★☆ D
1989	★★★★☆ C	★★★★☆ C	★★★★☆ D
1988	★★★☆ C	★★★★☆ C	★★★☆ D

A-Z of producers - *Valle d'Aosta*

Les Crêtes/Constantino Charrière *www.lescretesvins.it*
Constantino Charrère has long been regarded as the single important force for quality wine in the Valle d'Aosta. Under the Les Crêtes label he makes the best dry whites and reds of the valley (mostly varietal) from both local and imported varieties. He used to have his own label for a small range of blended reds and whites produced only from varieties considered native to the region, but now bottles a single white and a single red blend under the Les Crêtes label, Mon Blanc and Mon Rouge. The whites show a floral, and sometimes, spicy aspect and excellent structure and fruit defintion. In Chardonnay there is a mineral vein, as well as grapefruit and lemon, in the regular version, and, added breadth, vibrancy and well-judged oak in the Cuvée Bois version. The red Torrette, based on Petit Rouge, tastes like mountain Beaujolais with good flavour and soft, subtle tannins, whilst the Syrah, from the La Tour vineyard, exudes typical varietal spiciness and smokiness. Also from the same vineyard, a Pinot Noir is made, but this has not been tasted. At the top level, Fumin (from the eponymous grape variety) tastes like a rich, vibrant Echezeaux with its deep, flavoursome smoke, berry/bramble and plum character. A fine sweet Moscato Passito, Les Abeilles, made from Muscat à Petit Grains is also made. The wine is vinified without oak and is released after 6 months in bottle. The family, since 2007, has been producing a Monferrato Rosso blend in Piedmont, but this has not been tasted. None of wines represent stunning value but neither are they overpriced, and are most rewarding. If you've been skiing locally you probably deserve it.

Italy

Recommended Reds:
Valle d'Aosta DOC Fumin Vigne La Tour ★★★☆ £E
Valle d'Aosta DOC Syrah ★★★ £D
Valle d'Aosta DOP Torrette ★★☆ £C
Recommended Whites:
Valle d'Aosta DOP Chardonnay Cuvée Bois★★★☆ £E
Valle d'Aosta DOP Les Abeilles Moscato Passito ★★★ £E
Valle d'Aosta DOP Petite Arvine ★★★ £D
Valle d'Aosta DOP Chardonnay ★★★ £D

A-Z of producers - *Piedmont*

Anna Maria Abbona *www.annamariaabbona.it*
The historic zone of Dogliani has undergone a considerable
resurgence in the past decade. It's easy to be dismissive about a
zone dedicated to Dolcetto, but the best are very good indeed.
Anna Maria's Maioli is made from vines planted in 1935; rich, almost
velvety with lovely fruit, but powerful too with a refined structure.
An oak-aged Superiore adds smoke and spice and is equally good,
though it benefits from an extra one or two years' age. An attractive
fleshy Barbera, Cadò, which doesn't qualify as Barbera d'Alba due
to the location, includes 10% Dolcetto. Recently a small amount of
Langhe Nebbiolo has been produced, but this has not been tasted.
Recommended Reds:
Dolcetto di Dogliani Superiore ★★★ £C
Dolcetto di Dogliani Maioli ★★★ £C
Dolcetto di Dogliani Sorì dij But ★★ £C
Langhe Rosso Cadò ★★ £D   Langhe Dolcetto ★ £B

M & E Abbona (Dolcetto di Dogliani) *www.abbona.com*
Marziano Abbona is one of the stars of Dogliani, but with ever
expanding vineyard holdings also produces fine Barolo and
Barbaresco. All three crus are aged partly in *barrique* and partly in
large oak casks and combine strength with a certain finesse. Of
the Barolos, the Terlo Ravera is from Novello, the more powerful
Pressenda from Monforte d'Alba. A third Barolo, Cerviano, also from
Novello, is only produced in good years. Some Nebbiolo d'Alba is
also produced from Pressenda. In the Dogliani zone, where half the
vineyards are, old vines in Doriolo are source for (unoaked) Dolcetto
Papà Celso which shows a breadth uncommon to most examples
of the variety. I Due Ricu combines Cabernet, Sangiovese and Petit
Verdot. Also made is a white, Cinerino Bianco, from Viognier a Roero
Arneis and a Favorita from the Valle del Olmo (since 2008). Now
Marziano has turned his hand to producing sparkling wines from
Pinot and Chardonnay in the San Luigi vineyard in Dogliani, starting
with an extra brut rosé in 2007 and a white in 2008 (both dégorgé
in December 2010), followed by a brut and a brut rosé in 2012. We
haven't tasted these yet, but it also appears to be work in progress
for the producer as well.
Recommended Reds:
Barolo Pressenda★★★★ £F   Barolo Terlo Ravera★★★ £F
Barbaresco ★★★ £E
Dolcetto di Dogliani Papà Celso★★★ £C
Dolcetto di Dogliani San Luigi★★ £C
Barbera d'Alba Rinaldi★★ £D   Langhe Rosso I Due Ricu★★ £D

Orlando Abrigo (Barbaresco) *www.orlandoabrigo.it*
Giovanni Abrigo started working with his father Orlando in the
late 80s. He now makes very creditable Dolcetto, Barbera and
Barbaresco from 11 ha of vineyards. There is a relatively limited use
of small new oak, primarily for the Barbera d'Alba Mervisano and the

three Barolo crus, Vigna Rocche Meruzzano, Vigna Montersino and
Vigna Rongallo. Montersino, from 43-year-old vines, is aged only
in *barrique* (one-third new) and starts out structured and oaky but
develops well. The others are only part *barrique*-aged (one-third)
with the rest going into large Slavonian oak but are both elegant,
classy examples. Barbera d'Alba Vigna Roreto is in a similar mould,
eschewing new oak to emphasise only the ripe, intense fruit. Also
made are Merlot (Livraie), a Nebbiolo d'Alba Valmaggiore (also
farmed by LUCIANO SANDRONE) and a Langhe Nebbiolo - Settevie
and a little Chardonnay (Très). In addition to producing his own
wines, Giovanni works with his wife Virna, also a trained winemaker,
on her family's 8 ha estate (Virna Borgogno) in the Barolo
commune.
Recommended Reds:
Barbaresco Vigna Rongallo★★★★ £E
Barbaresco Rocche Meruzzano★★★ £E
Barbaresco Vigna Montersino★★★ £E
Barbera d'Alba Vigna Roreto★★ £C
Barbera d'Alba Mervisano★★ £C
Dolcetto d'Alba Vigna dell' Erto★ £B

✿ **Claudio Alario (Dolcetto di Diano d'Alba)** *www.alarioclaudio.it*
This estate and BRICCO MAIOLICA are champions of the small
Dolcetto zone that lies between Barolo and Barbaresco yet both
are as notable for their Nebbiolo as for Dolcetto. Here both the
Nebbiolo d'Alba and Barolo are perfumed, balanced and ageworthy.
Consistently well-made Barolo Riva from the commune of Verduno
has excellent texture, breadth and length. A new Barolo cru (Sorano)
in the Serralunga locality was acquired in 2004 and is producing
wine of similar texture to the Riva. Of the Dolcetto, Costa Fiore is the
more concentrated but backward version and is best with an extra
year or two. A new Dolcetto cru, Pradurent, is a superiore, made
from young vines, spending some 10 months in 3 year old *barriques*
giving it an extra richness and fullness in the mouth. Claudio Alario
is also a good reasonably priced source of Barbera d'Alba and
Nebbiolo d'Alba.
Recommended Reds:
Barolo Riva ★★★★ £E   Barolo Sorano ★★★★ £E
Barbera d'Alba Valletta ★★★ £C
Nebbiolo d'Alba Cascinotto ★★★ £C
Dolcetto di Diano d'Alba Superiore Pradurent ★★★ £C
Dolcetto di Diano d'Alba Costa Fiore ★★★ £B
Dolcetto di Diano d'Alba Montegrillo ★★ £B

Gianfranco Alessandria (Barolo) *www.gianfrancoalessandria.com*
Gianfranco Alessandria is an inspired young grower with a range
of ripe, full and stylish reds. From 5.5 ha of vineyards at Monforte,
(plus 1.5 ha rented) the top wines all show a measure of new oak
but it is never obvious or allowed to dominate. An intense Barbera
Vittoria from over 65-year-old vines, and beautifully balanced Barolo
San Giovanni (a special selection rather than vineyard-specific)
are particularly worthy but all of the wines deliver good fruit in
a modern accessible style. Gianfranco's version of Insieme (see
ALTARE), 45% Nebbiolo, 40% Barbera and 15% Dolcetto, is one of the
best.
Recommended Reds:
Barolo San Giovanni ★★★★☆ £F
Barolo ★★★☆ £E
Insieme ★★★★ £F   Barbera d'Alba Vittoria ★★★☆ £C
Barbera d'Alba ★★☆ £C   Langhe Nebbiolo ★★ £C
Dolcetto d'Alba ★★ £B

Elio Altare (Barolo) *www.elioaltare.com*

Elio Altare is La Morra's and Barolo's great moderniser as well as mentor to a group of other small growers – ALESSANDRIA, CORINO, Silvio GRASSO, MOLINO, REVELLO and VEGLIO. Radically low yields, short maceration times and rows of *barriques* are now common to all but nobody else quite manages to get the extra depth and concentration of Altare. It is not a purist's Barolo that emerges yet one of terrific concentration and balance that still conveys something of its origins. Super-Langhes Arborina (Nebbiolo), Larigi (Barbera) and La Villa (Nebbiolo/Barbera) take the new oak theme to its logical (or illogical, depending on your viewpoint) conclusion. There is good regular Barbera and Dolcetto too, the latter typically very composed and finely structured with 3 years' age. Altare was also the proponent behind Insieme. The band of 7 producers share winemaking resources and expertise to produce delicious, concentrated modern oak-aged blends – variations on a Nebbiolo, Barbera, Cabernet and/or Merlot theme – a percentage of the proceeds go to local cultural and artisanal causes. 1997 Barolos and 98 Langhe reds were withheld due to cork contimination problems but since then, wines across the board are a testament to Elio Altare's resolve and the maintenance of his very high standards. Since 2005, Elio has been involved with a winery in Cinqueterre, CAMPOGRANDE, producing high quality wines in small quantities.

Recommended Reds:

Barolo Brunate★★★★ £G

Barolo Arborina★★★★ £G

Barolo★★★ £E   Langhe Larigi★★★★ £G

Langhe La Villa★★★★ £G

Langhe Arborina ★★★ £F

Insieme ★★★★ £G   Barbera d'Alba ★★★ £D

Dolcetto d'Alba ★★★ £C

Antichi Vigneti di Cantalupo (Ghemme) *www.cantalupo.net*

Ghemme's one producer that gives real credibility to the zone's DOCG status. Input from top enologist Donato Lanati helps even if in the main the wines follow a fairly traditional, unadventurous vinification. Typically rather austere and firm when young, the wines mellow with age and their already enticing perfumes become ever more complex. While the regular Ghemme includes a little Vespolina and Uva Rara, special bottlings are pure Nebbiolo. Carellae and Breclemae are vineyard-specific, while Signore di Bayard is a special selection which is aged in French *barriques* (a third new). The latter is often the most flattering when young but also has the greatest dimension, intensity and sheer style. Colline Novaresi wines, Agamium (Nebbiolo) and Primigenia (Nebbiolo/Uva Rara/Vespolina), are characterful but not at the same level. Unoaked white Carolus combines Arneis, Greco and Chardonnay. There is much quality Ghemme from recent good vintages.

Recommended Reds:

Ghemme Collis Breclamae ★★★ £E

Ghemme Signore di Bayard ★★★ £E

Ghemme Collis Carellae ★★ £E   Ghemme ★£D

Araldica Vini Piemontesi (Barbera d'Asti) *www.araldicavini.com*

Araldica is a large co-op with 300 members and 900 ha of vineyard. Under the direction of Claudio Manera it has become synonymous with approachable soundly made Piemontese reds and whites. Acquisitions in recent years, including Il Cascinone in the Monferrato hills (where the vineyards have been restored) and La Battistina in Gavi, are now providing grapes of superior origins from which to fashion some high-quality wines too. D'Annona Barbera from

Il Cascinone, for instance, shows lots of promise. Also under the Poderi Alasia label (a series of premium wines based on individual vineyards) are Barbera d'Asti Rive, Roero Arneis Solaria, Langhe Nebbiolo Castellero and Sauvignon Camillona while an increasingly good Monferrato blend, Luce Monaca combines Barbera with Merlot and Cabernet Sauvignon. *Barrique*-fermented Chardonnay (Roleto) and oak-aged Pinot Nero (Re Nero) are also produced. More widely seen are the Alasia varietals which include bright, clean fruity Barbera, Dolcetto, Chardonnay and Cortese. Promising are Barbaresco (Corsini) and Barolo (Revello), the latter in particular has lots of character and is excellent value.

Araldica

Recommended Reds:

Barolo Revello ★★★ £D

Barbaresco Corsini ★★ £D

Barbera d'Asti Vigneti Croja ★★ £C

Barbera d'Asti Ceppi Storici ★ £B

Recommended Whites:

Gavi Madonnina ★★ £B

Poderi Alasia

Recommended Reds:

Barbera d'Asti Superiore D'Annona ★★★ £C

Barbera d'Asti Rive ★★ £C

Nebbiolo d'Alba Castellero ★ £C

Recommended Whites:

Roero Arneis Sorilaria ★★ £C

Monferrato Camillona ★★ £C

Ascheri (Barolo) *www.ascherivini.com*

Matteo Ascheri has an energy to match his bear-like stature. A list of his accomplishments includes planting Viognier and Syrah at Bra (outside the Barolo zone), creating the Osteria Murivecchi in the family's old cellars, promoting the Langhe at home and abroad – yet all the while maintaining realistic prices and good quality. Matteo believes strongly in natural winemaking, and recent vintages show improvement from the regeneration of the family's vineyards, with wines of bright, pure varietal character. Of two cru Barolos, Vigna dei Pola comes from the Pisapolla cru in the Verduno vineyards that lie south of Ascheri's base in Bra. The more traditional (moderately long fermentation, ageing in mostly old wood) Sorano comes from Serralunga and has more depth, grip and class. From 1999 fruit from the best vines within Sorano was vinified separately to produce Coste & Bricco which offers yet more style and expression.

Recommended Reds:

Barolo Sorano Coste & Bricco ★★★★ £F

Barolo Vigna dei Pola ★★★ £E

Barolo Sorano ★★★ £E

Montalupa Syrah ★★ £D

Nebbiolo d'Alba Bricco San Giacomo ★★ £D

Barbera d'Alba Vigna Fontanelle ★★ £C

Dolcetto d'Alba Vigna Nirane ★★ £C

Recommended Whites:

Montalupa Viognier ★★ £D

Langhe Arneis Cristina Ascheri ★ £C

❂ **Azelia (Barolo)** *www.azelia.it*

Less well-known than Enrico Scavino, Luigi similarly owns a decent chunk of the excellently positioned Fiasco vineyard, which has certain similarities to the nearby Monprivato and Villero crus. The regular Barolo, made from younger vines, sees mostly large wood (botte grande) but the two crus Bricco Fiasco and San Rocco (the

Piedmont

Italy

latter from Serralunga) both receive 50% new oak. There is evident structure but the wines are balanced with good weight, depth and dimension and definite class. Barolos are consistently fine in successive top vintages from 95 onwards. Additionally, the Barolo Riserva Voghera Brea is produced only in exceptional years from 75 year old vines and is not released until after 6 years. It has deep concentration with great fruit intensity. All need at least 6–8 years' age. Barbera d'Alba which also sees some new oak is toasty, spicy and deep-fruited and best with at least 3–4years' agee. Dolcetto is sometimes slightly too extracted yet soft and ripe, whilst the Langhe Nebbiolo, which sees no oak, is supple, ripe and juicy.

Recommended Reds:
Barolo Riserva Voghera Brea ★★★★★ £G
Barolo Bricco Fiasco ★★★★ £F
Barolo San Rocco ★★★★ £F
Barolo ★★★ £F Langhe Nebbiolo ★★★ £E
Barbera d'Alba Vigneto Punta ★★★ £D
Dolcetto d'Alba Bricco dell'Oriolo ★★ £C

Produttori del Barbaresco *www.produttori-barbaresco.it*
This super co-op manages around a sixth (100 ha) of Barbaresco's relatively tiny vineyard area. It is democratically run and winemaker Gianni Testa adheres to traditional lines with lengthy maceration and ageing in large *botti*. But what perfume, grace and charm they achieve in the top crus in a good vintage! These wines are a purist's delight, capturing much of the essence of Nebbiolo and a splendid expression of the grape in some of the most hallowed patches of soil in Barbaresco. What's more, the single-vineyard Riservas sell for less than many other producers' regular Barbaresco. All will keep for, and sometimes need, a decade or more.

Recommended Reds:
Barbaresco Riserva Asili ★★★★ £E
Barbaresco Riserva Moccagatta ★★★★ £E
Barbaresco Riserva Montefico ★★★★ £E
Barbaresco Riserva Montestefano ★★★★ £E
Barbaresco Riserva Rabajà ★★★★ £E
Barbaresco Riserva Ovello ★★★ £E
Barbaresco Riserva Pajé ★★★ £E
Barbaresco Riserva Pora ★★★ £E
Barbaresco Riserva Rio Sordo ★★★ £E
Barbaresco ★★ £D Langhe Nebbiolo ★ £C

Luigi Baudana (Barolo) *www.luigibaudana.it*
Luigi and Francesca Baudana spent a long time mulling over who was to succeed them in taking over the reins of their historic vineyards. Fortunately for them, through their long time friend, Aldo Vajra, of G D VAJRA, Aldo's son, Guiseppe stepped into the breach and since the 2008 vintage has been organically producing the wines. The vineyard area is now reduced to 4ha, given over only to three Barolo crus and a little Chardonnay, Barbera and Dolcetto is no longer made. A solid regular Barolo is surpassed by Cerretta Piani, which has the extract and power associated with Serralunga but also a certain elegance. A Baudana cru made since 99, is deep and stylish and very composed. The varietal Chardonnay delivers good fruit and intensity for the price.

Recommended Reds:
Barolo Baudana ★★★★☆ £F Barolo Cerretta Piani ★★★★ £F
Barolo ★★★ £E
Recommended Whites:
Langhe Chardonnay ★★ £C

Bava (Barbera d'Asti) *www.bava.com*
Advertising and marketing have given this medium-sized producer a higher profile than many in Piedmont, despite its being closer to Torino than any of the leading wine towns. However there is also serious intent here from the Bava brothers with several good ageworthy Barbera the main quality focus. The two top examples, Pianoalto and Stradivario are particularly impressive. The latter is rich and oaky with a deep smoky, plummy complexity with 6-8 years' age. Cheaper Arbest and Libera are also good at a lower level. Other wines, including Moscato d'Asti, are less exciting yet lively and fruity. The sweet, fragrant, frizzante red Malvasia di Castelnuovo Don Bosco is fun if drunk very young. Barolo is also made.

Recommended Reds:
Barbera d'Asti Superiore Nizza Pianoalto ★★★ £D
Barbera d'Asti Superiore Stradivario ★★★ £D
Barbera d'Asti Libera ★★ £C
Barbera d'Asti Arbest ★★ £C
Malvasia di Castelnuovo Don Bosco ★ £B
Recommended Whites:
Monferrato Alteserre ★★ £C
Moscato d'Asti Bass Tuba ★★ £C
Gavi di Gavi Cor di Chasse ★ £C

Vittorio Bera Figli (Barbera d'Asti)
Vittorio Bera's small organic estate with 10ha of vines on the rolling hills of Canelli is a typical hands-on family concern. Brother and sister, Gianluigi and Alessandria now run the estate. Although only certified as organic since 2001 they have been working this way since first bottling their own wine in the sixties. Moscato, Dolcetto and Barbera are made, as is typical for the region but these are very pure, natural unmanipulated examples giving a good expression of *terroir*. Moscato is a very sweet, intense, very delicately sparkling and low alcohol example yet is fresh and refined if drunk from the most recent vintage. Arcene is a zesty dry white, unusually from Cortese, Arneis and Favorita with well harmonized flavours. There is no filtration and only indigenous yeasts are used for the reds that include a slightly grippy, dense Dolcetto that needs a little time and a fruit-driven example of the lightly fizzy Barbera del Monferrato style (given its spritz from malo in bottle). No oak is used for Barbera d'Asti Ronco Malo which is dense and concentrated, needing 3-5 years to show at its best.

Recommended Reds:
Barbera d'Asti Ronco Malo ★★★ £D
Monferrato Dolcetto Bricco della Serra ★★ £C
Barbera del Monferrato Le Verrane ★★ £C
Recommended Whites:
Moscato d'Asti Canelli ★★☆£C Arcese ★★☆ £B

Bertelli (Barbera d'Asti) *www.bertelli-wine.it*
Aldo and his son Alberto make intense powerful often oaky wines, mostly from either Barbera or French varieties, which can be very impressive with age but occasionally struggle for balance. Deep, rich and characterful Chardonnay is very powerful if sometimes at the expense of definition and expression. Barberas are often rich, very ripe and always oaky, but in San Antonio Vieilles Vignes the marvellous old vine fruit depth easily contains the oak with a resultant complexity, seamless structure and a very long finish. A more affordable example, Nabiss was first produced in 02. Red I Fossaretti is a big, extracted Cabernet that usually harmonizes with age, while the white Fossaretti from Sauvignon Blanc is similarly in an outsized Bordeaux mould. St. Marsan is the label for a Rhône pair,

the red a very intense Hermitage-like Syrah of marginal balance. Mon Mayor is usually a well-oaked but fruit-intense Nebbiolo/ Cabernet. Also made is Plissé from Gewürztraminer. The wines are now subject to a delayed release and the range is currently being gently revamped.

Recommended Reds:

Barbera d'Asti San Antonio Vieilles Vignes ★★★★ £E

Barbera d'Asti Giarone ★★★ £E

Barbera d'Asti Montetusa ★★★ £E

Monferrato I Fossaretti ★★★ £E

Monferrato Mon Mayor ★★★ £E

St Marsan ★★★ £E

Recommended Whites:

Piemonte Chardonnay Giarone ★★★★ £E

St Marsan ★★★ £E   Monferrato I Fossaretti ★★ £E

✿ Enzo Boglietti (Barolo)   *www.enzoboglietti.com*

A young grower who started off with only a modest patchwork of vines in 1991 which have now increased to 21 ha but those sites include Brunate, Case Nere, Arione and Fossati (noted for Barbera as much as Nebbiolo). Full of fruit, oak-enriched, and with relatively soft but abundant tannin, these are good examples of the modern style – perhaps why the old-vine Barbera Vigna dei Romani (from Fossati) can impress almost as much as the Barolos. Fossati and Case Nere see a lot of new oak (50 and 80% respectively) and the structure can suffer a little from the treatment, though there is better harmony with age. The classy Brunate, subject to only a small percentage of new oak but a longer maceration, is intense and compact when young but the most expressive and stylish of the three. Recently a Riserva has been added which is given to great complexity. All need 8–10 years' age. Ripe, potent Dolcetto Tiglineri oozes delicious old-vine fruit but needs a couple of years' age. Langhe Buio, Nebbiolo with Barbera (80/20) aged in mostly new *barriques* but has real charm and style, especially with 3 or 4 years' age. A Cabernet and a Merlot have been added to the Langhe range from vines grown at Roddino. Neither of them are released commercially for 4 years (as in the case of the Barolos) and have high alcoholic content. These have not been tasted at the time of writing.

Recommended Reds:

Barolo Brunate ★★★★★ £F

Barolo Case Nere ★★★★ £F

Barolo Fossati ★★★★ £F

Barbera d'Alba Vigna dei Romani ★★★ £E

Barbera d'Alba Roscaleto ★★★ £E

Barbera d'Alba ★★ £C

Dolcetto d'Alba Tiglineri ★★★ £C

Dolcetto d'Alba ★ £C

Langhe Buio ★★★ £D   Langhe Nebbiolo ★★★ £D

Bongiovanni (Barolo)

Davide Mozzoni is not afraid to experiment and takes diverse approaches to making each of his Barolos. The regular version (from three different plots), subject to cold maceration and a short fermentation, is relatively light but modern with some charm. With Pernanno the total maceration is longer and the temperature allowed to rise to the mid-30s as the fermentation reaches completion. The extract, weight and richness evident on the palate is reinforced by ageing in (60%) new *barriques*. Micro-oxygenation is employed for the two fruity Dolcettos; the more compact, structured Diano d'Alba deserves to be drunk with an extra year or

two's age. Faletto (Cabernet, Merlot and Barbera) is fruit-rich and oaky. While these moderately priced wines are good rather than exciting, it will be interesting to see how the styles evolve.

Recommended Reds:

Barolo Pernanno ★★★★ £F   Barolo ★★★ £E

Langhe Faletto ★★★ £D   Barbera d'Alba ★★ £C

Dolcetto di Diano d'Alba ★★ £C

Dolcetto d'Alba ★★ £B

Boroli (Barolo)   *www.boroli.it*

The Borolis are gaining an excellent reputation for deep, evocative Barolo of classic depth and stature. Villero is their magic cru from which an intensity and depth is harnessed that suggests there is always more to come, even after 10 years'. Regular Barolo, also from Castiglione Falletto vineyards, is very good too (50% in large casks, 50% in used *barriques*). Barbera takes two forms, complex and composed in Bricco dei Fagiani, more direct yet fruit-rich in Quattro Fratelli. The Borolis' Dolcetto has real style too, both supple and expressive with classic bright fruit and a seamless structure. Inexpensive Langhe Rosso, Anna is a Nebbiolo/Barbera blend while Langhe Chardonnay, Bel Amì is also produced.

Recommended Reds:

Barolo Villero ★★★★☆ £F   Barolo ★★★★ £E

Barbera d'Alba Bricco dei Fagiani ★★★☆ £D

Barbera d'Alba Superiore Bricco Quattro Fratelli ★★☆ £D

Dolcetto d'Alba Madonna di Como ★★☆ £C

Recommended Whites:

Moscato d'Asti Aureum ★★☆ £B

Braida (Barbera d'Asti)   *www.braida.it*

Plenty has been written about Giacomo Bologna, who was one of Piedmont's great characters as well as innovators. Bricco dell'Uccellone, first made in 1982, is the original oak-aged Barbera of outsized proportions. Bricco della Bigotta can often match it, while Ai Suma, which incorporates late-harvested grapes, can be even richer and more powerful. All should but don't always improve for a decade and my feeling is they are often best after 6–8 years. There seems to be a real return to form from the late nineties but stick to the top vintages. Il Bacialé adds Pinot Nero to Barbera. The serious stuff aside, Barbera La Monella, Brachetto and Moscato are great examples of their effervescent type but the latter two (as ever with these styles) are best within 6 months of the vintage.

Recommended Reds:

Barbera d'Asti Ai Suma ★★★★ £F

Barbera d'Asti Bricco della Bigotta ★★★☆ £E

Barbera d'Asti Bricco dell' Uccellone ★★★☆ £E

Monferrato Rosso Il Bacialé ★★ £C   Brachetto d'Acqui ★★ £B

Barbera del Monferrato La Monella ★ £B

Recommended Whites:

Moscato d'Asti Vigna Senza Nome ★ £B

Bricco Maiolica (Dolcetto di Diano d'Alba)   *www.briccomaiolica.it*

Beppe Accomo's 24 ha estate is arguably the best in this zone, rivalled only by that of Claudio ALARIO. Nebbiolo, like CORREGGIA'S or CASCINA CHICCO'S (both in Roero), is one of the few in the Langhe outside Barolo and Barbaresco to be taken seriously. Then there are really good examples of Barbera and Dolcetto too. The oak in the best wines is taken up by decent ripe, intense fruit and consistently so. The regular Barbera in fact doesn't see any wood, while the Vigna Vigia receives 50% new, 50% used and Il Cumot Nebbiolo is put in 'second use' *barriques*. There is splendid fruit

Piedmont

in both Dolcettos; the cru has a little more amplitude and some gentle spice from 6 months in used wood. The oak-influenced white Langhe Rolando combines Chardonnay and Sauvignon, wile the red Langhe Perlet is one of the best Piedmont Pinots made. First made in 2001. More recently, a straight unoaked Sauvignon Blanc, Casa Castella,and a straight Chardonny, Pensiero Infinito, in *barriques* for 30 months have been produced but these have not been tasted.

Recommended Reds:
Nebbiolo d'Alba Il Cumot ★★★ £D
Barbera d'Alba Vigna Vigia ★★★ £D
Barbera d'Alba Briccolero ★★ £B
Langhe Perlet ★★ £D
Dolcetto di Diano d'Alba Sorì Bricco Maiolica ★★ £C
Dolcetto di Diano d'Alba ★ £B
Recommended Whites:
Langhe Rolando ★★ £C

Brovia (Barolo) *www.brovia.net*
Sisters Elena and Cristina Brovia, aided by their father Giacinto, regularly produce full, muscular but ageworthy Barolo from local plots and another (Cà Mia) in Serralunga, all without the aid of small new oak barrels. Instead, large 3,000-litre French oak is used following a relatively long maceration of around 20 days. The elegance of Rocche (di Castiglione) may be contrasted with the intensity of Villero or the build of Ca' Mia. *Barriques* are reserved for Dolcetto, especially the remarkable Solatio. Late-harvested, this purple, high-ethanol monster is typically deep, smooth and balanced. Scarce it is, but like those from other champions of intense Dolcetto (CA'VIOLA, MARCARINI, G MASCARELLO, VAJRA et al) it deserves to be tasted. Barberas are good too. Through the efforts of Elena's husband, Alex Sanchez, who hails from Cataluna, this fine range should become more widely seen.

Recommended Reds:
Barolo Ca' Mia ★★★★ £F   Barolo Rocche dei Brovia ★★★★ £F
Barolo Villero ★★★★ £F   Barbera d'Alba Brea ★★★ £E
Barbera d'Alba Sorì del Drago ★★ £D
Dolcetto d'Alba Solatio ★★★ £E
Dolcetto d'Alba Vignavillej ★★ £C

Bussia Soprana (Barolo) *www.bussiasoprana.it*
Silvano Casiraghi has a minority stake in some of the crus made famous by ALDO CONTERNO. Excellent Barolos are produced from part of 22 ha of vineyards. The wines have been particularly good since the mid-nineties. Lesser-known Mosconi, from the south of the commune, is in a more rugged, powerful style that provides an interesting contrast with the more mellow Bussia and refined Colonello.

Recommended Reds:
Barolo Bussia ★★★ £F   Barolo Mosconi ★★★ £F
Barolo Vigna Colonello ★★★★ £F
Barbera d'Alba Vin del Ross ★★ £D
Barbera d'Alba ★ £C   Dolcetto d'Alba ★ £C

Piero Busso (Barbaresco) *www.bussopiero.com*
Piero Busso controls 10 ha from the heart of the Neive commune and believes in a natural expression of each variety and the importance of place (or tipicità). He has little time for technology but there is some use of *barriques*. There are now 4 Barbaresco crus following the addition of Gallina in 1999 and San Stefanetto in 2001. All the wines have classic perfumes and structure typical to their variety and add richness and complexity with age. At least 6–8

years' is needed for the Barbarescos. The Langhe white is a blend of Chardonnay and Sauvignon Blanc, the Chardonnay component fermented and aged in *barrique*; while not special it will keep at least 3–4 years. A Langhe Arneis is also produced.

Recommended Reds:
Barbaresco San Stunet, San Stefanetto ★★★★ £E
Barbaresco Gallina ★★★☆ £E
Barbaresco Vigna Borgese ★★★☆ £E
Barbaresco Bricco Mondino ★★★ £E
Barbera d'Alba San Stefanetto ★★★ £D
Barbera d'Alba Majano ★★ £D
Langhe Nebbiolo ★★☆ £D
Dolcetto d'Alba Majano ★ £B
Recommended Whites:
Langhe Bianco di Busso ★☆ £C

Ca' Viola (Dolcetto d'Alba) *www.caviola.com*
Beppe Caviola has given many a small Piemontesi grower the technical help to produce wines of the standard to ensure they are in demand both in Italy and abroad. More recently his expertise has also been sought throughout Italy including by UMANI RONCHI in the Marche. Though a modernist, he earns respect particularly because he doesn't impose a formula but adapts his expertise to the philosophy of the individual producer. Ca'Viola is his own range of wines. Though now based in Dogliani most of his grapes are sourced from Montelupo Albese (between Barolo and Barbaresco). The wines are ripe, lush and fruit-rich, very easy to drink but with good structure and depth. Foremost is the excellent Bric du Luv, a consistently fine *barrique*-aged Barbera, but fine Dolcetto is also made in two versions. Barturot is the best selection from old vines, subtly enhanced by oak, and shows great depth and intensity, while Vilot is in a fruity, quaffing style. Graduating on to Nebbiolo, firstly at Sotto Castello in Novello to produce a Langhe Nebbiolo with silky tannins and racy upfront fruit in 2006 and then on to a Barolo from the same vineyard, with Beppe's trademark subtlty embracing the earthy, sikly characteristics of the wine. Both are produced from relatively young vines (around 10 years at present)and the wines can only further increase in complexity and finesse as the vines mature.

Recommended Reds:
Barolo Sottocastello ★★★★ £G
Langhe Bric du Luv ★★★★ £E
Langhe Nebbiolo ★★★ £E
Barbera d'Alba Brichet ★★☆ £C
Dolcetto d'Alba Barturot ★★☆ £C
Dolcetto d'Alba Vilot ★★ £C

Cantina del Pino (Barbaresco) *www.cantinadelpino.com*
Up to and including the 96 vintage Renato Vacca's family sold their grapes to the Produttori del BARBARESCO. Given the general high quality of the latter's releases it should not come as any great surprise that some of their growers have the potential for very good Barbaresco indeed. In the case of Cantina del Pino they also have in Renato the bonus of a gifted young winemaker. 50-70 year old vines with a south-west exposure in the Ovello cru provide the pinnacle of quality, a Barbaresco that is pure and expressive. From 2005 Renato has been making a Barbaresco Riserva from the Albanesi vineyard on the Santo Stefano hill, showing even greater intensity and power, coupled with ripe tannins and dark fruits. Regular Barbaresco and Barbera d'Alba (from vines over 50 years old and aged in new oak) are stylish and elegant too while well-typed Freisa and Dolcetto add further to the integrity of this fine small cellar.

Recommended Reds:
Barbaresco Albanesi Riserva ★★★★★ £G
Barbaresco Ovello ★★★★☆ £F
Barbaresco ★★★☆ £E
Barbera d'Alba ★★★ £E   Langhe Freisa ★★ £C
Dolcetto d'Alba ★★ £C

Cappellano (Barolo)

Teobaldo Cappellano, who passed away in February 2009, was one of the great traditionalists of Barolo and his wines are held in high regard by Barolo aficionados. From 3 ha of Gabutti in Serralunga are produced Piè Rupestris (from 60-year-old vines) and Franco (from entirely ungrafted vines). From limited tastings it is apparent that both are powerful, structured Barolos that are complex and harmonious even when relatively young but can age impressively. Also produced is a Nebbiolo d'Alba with stylish complexity and plenty of extract, suggestive of Barolo without the extra depth or dimension. A regular Barbera d'Alba sees 4 years in large oak. Made in a perfumed, medium-bodied style, this is not a fruit-driven wine but has a fine savoury complexity and good texture by the time it is released. The estate also produces a Barolo Chinato from an old family recipe with the wine enhanced by quinnine, herbs and spices. The estate is now in the hands opf Theobaldo's son, Augusto, who is carrying on his father's philosophy to the letter.

Recommended Reds:
Barolo ★★★★☆ £F   Barbera d'Alba ★★★ £C
Nebbiolo d'Alba ★★☆ £D

Cascina Chicco (Roero)   www.cascinachicco.com

The Faccenda brothers, Enrico and Marco, have 20 ha from which a broad range of good-quality Langhe wines are produced. An excellent Barbera is usually better than anything else – a suave, spicy and scented Bric Loira that is aged in *barriques*. However in the best years for Nebbiolo this is rivalled by a fine Roero Valmaggiore that once again shows the refinement and expression possible from this appellation. Nebbiolo d'Alba Mompissano can show similar flair when the conditions are right. Roero Arneis can be good too while Arcass is an attractive, aromatic sweet version of Arneis.

Recommended Reds:
Barbera d'Alba Bric Loira ★★★ £D
Barbera d'Alba Granera Alta ★★ £C
Barbera d'Alba ★★ £B   Roero Valmaggiore ★★★ £D
Roero Mulino della Costa ★★ £C
Nebbiolo d'Alba Mompissano ★★ £D

Recommended Whites:
Roero Arneis Anterisio ★ £B

Cascina Morassino (Barbaresco)

This 4.5 ha Barbaresco estate run by Roberto Bianco has recently produced much improved wines. Barbarescos Morassino and Ovello are soft, round and seductive, in a modern style. There is richer texture, better breadth and lots of extract in Ovello, in part due to *barrique*-ageing, but the oak is not intrusive. More overtly oaky is spicy, soft, red- and black-fruited Langhe Rosso which justs lacks a little depth. Dolcetto is a good, well-defined fruit-driven style if nothing more. Very small amounts of Barbera d'Alba (Vignot) are also made.

Recommended Reds:
Barbaresco Ovello ★★★★ £F
Barbaresco Morassino ★★★ £E
Langhe Rosso Vigna del Merlo ★★ £D

Dolcetto d'Alba ★★ £C

Cascina Val del Prete (Roero)   www.valdelprete.com

Mario Roagna has transformed the grapes from 8 ha of family vineyards into a small fine range of wines in recent years, maximising the potential from a natural amphitheatre of vines first worked, then purchased back in 1977, by his late father, Lino (Bartolomeo). Over the years, farming has been organic and fermentation is only with natural yeasts. A delightful fruit-driven, unoaked regular Barbera contrasts with Carolina (named for his mother) which comes from a single parcel of vines and is aged for 16 months in new *barriques*. The oak is evident but there is fabulous style to its smoke and plum richness too. New from 2003 is another Barbera, Serra de' Gatti from recently planted vines. A small amount of Roero is made though its oak/fruit balance is more marginal. Better is the Nebbiolo expression in Vigna di Lino; good vintages will be super with 5 years' age or more. Arneis has more weight and structure than usual and will keep a year or two. Quantities are small, even the bigger-volume Arneis and Barbera normale don't much exceed 1,000 cases each.

Recommended Reds:
Nebbiolo d'Alba Vigna di Lino ★★★ £D
Barbera d'Alba Superiore Carolina ★★★ £C
Barbera d'Alba ★★ £C   Roero ★★ £C

Recommended Whites:
Roero Arneis Luèt ★★ £B

Castellari Bergaglio (Gavi)   www.castellaribergaglio.it

Really decent Gavi is a relatively rare entity but Mario Bergaglio and his wife Vanda produce not just one but four fine examples from more than 10 ha of vineyards. The wines are perfumed with lots of fruit intensity and real depth and penetration on the palate. The wines are balanced too and underpinned by good acidity. Rolona, from older vines, has more depth and intensity than the floral, herbal Fornaci from vineyards at Tassarolo. Rovereto is produced from the oldest vineyards surrounding the winery and can be richer and more minerally. More unusual is Pilìn, produced from a selection of the healthiest fruit suitable for drying. After 30–40 days, the grapes are then fermented and aged in *barriques*. Only recently has it qualified as Gavi due to more relaxed ageing requirements but it adds breadth and texture if at the expense of purity and intensity. All have sufficient structure to keep for at least 3–4 years.

Recommended Whites:
Gavi Pilìn ★★★ £D
Gavi del Comune di Gavi Rolona ★★★ £C
Gavi del Comune di Gavi Rovereto Vigna Vecchia ★★★ £C
Gavi del Comune di Tassarolo Fornaci ★★ £C

Castello di Calosso (Barbera d'Asti)

What do you do if you have at most a few hectares and produce high quality Barbera d'Asti but need a stronger identity while still making your wine? The 10 growers of the Castello di Calosso all have a small parcel of old-vine Barbera (ranging from 40–70 years old) but share the same label under which they promote their own bottlings. The standard is high but not uniform and stylistically there are important differences too. While one or two struggle for balance nearly all are concentrated with a measure of oak and have a rich, ripe fruit intensity as well as impressive breadth and length. The growers (or estates) followed by their single-vineyard Barberas are: Livio Sorin and Giorgio Pavia's Due Colline (Rodotiglia), Maurizio Domanda (Crevacuore), Fabio Fidanza (Sterlino), Giorgio Fogliati (La

Wine behind the label

Piedmont

Italy

Cascinetta), Mauro Grasso (Sant' Anna), Renzo Grasso (Camp Maìna), Aldo and Giuseppe Bussi's La Badia (Belletta), Ignazio Giovine's L'ARMANGIA (Vignali), Roberto Paschina (Musiano) and TENUTA DEI FIORI (Rusticardi). Some of these make other wines of a standard to be worthy of a separate entry in the future.

Recommended Reds:
Barbera d'Asti La Cascinetta Giorgio Fogliati ★★★★ £E
Barbera d'Asti Musiano Roberto Paschina ★★★ £E
Barbera d'Asti Sant' Anna Mauro Grasso ★★★ £E
Barbera d'Asti Camp Maìna Renzo Grasso ★★★ £E
Barbera d'Asti Rodotiglia Due Colline ★★★ £E
Barbera d'Asti Sterlino Fidanza ★★★ £E
Barbera d'Asti Crevacuore Domanda ★★★ £E
Barbera d'Asti Belletta La Badia ★★★ £E
Barbera d'Asti Vignali L'Armangia ★★★ £E
Barbera d'Asti Rusticardi Tenuta dei Fiori ★★★ £E

Caudrina (Moscato d'Asti) www.caudrina.it
Moscato d'Asti may not age but Romano Dogliotti has been making some of the finest examples for over 20 years. He applied new technologies to grapes (off steep slopes to the east of Barbaresco) first vinified by his father. La Caudrina is light, floral and grapy with a certain elegance. The intense and tangy La Galeisa is wonderfully fragrant with apple, citrus, grape and musk scents with more of a ripe nectarine and apricot fruit in warmer vintages. La Selvatica, more usually made as a very good fully sparkling Asti, is very concentrated, intense and ripe. Still sweeter and richer is Redento in a passito style with dried nectarine and honeycomb and an explosive intensity in the mouth. Less overtly grapy than the Moscato d'Astis, it is not obviously Muscat but very long with a rich, dried fruit quality without being raisiny. Barbera d'Asti is increasingly good too. La Solista is unoaked while the more complex Montevenere is barrique-aged and needs a minimum 5-6 years' age. Partly barriqued Chardonnay Mej has the very spiced, dried citrus character of many Piemonte examples but not the nuance or style for more while Dolcetto is soft, spicy with plum and cherry fruit.

Recommended Reds:
Barbera d'Asti Superiore Montevenere ★★★ £D
Dolcetto d'Alba Campo Rosso ★ £C
Barbera d'Asti La Solista ★ £C
Recommended Whites:
Piemonte Moscato Passito Redento ★★★★ £E
Moscato d'Asti La Galeisa ★★★ £C
Moscato d'Asti La Selvatica ★★★ £C
Moscato d'Asti La Caudrina ★★ £B
Asti La Selvatica ★★ £C
Piemonte Chardonnay Mej ★★ £C

Cavallotto (Barolo) www.cavallotto.com
Cavallotto's 23 ha of vineyard constitute the Bricco Boschis estate. In the past Cavallotto's wines have tended to lack excitement but the input of a new generation of three brothers are having an impact and the most recent releases have made the most of nature's beneficence. A traditionally minded producer, Cavallotto ages the wines in large Slavonian oak casks. The money saved by not buying new oak seems to have been invested instead in more care in the vineyard (which includes the 2.5 ha solely owned Vigna San Giuseppe) and winery. Barolos recommended from top vintages since 1997.

Recommended Reds:
Barolo Riserva Bricco Boschis Vigna San Giuseppe ★★★★ £F

Barolo Bricco Boschis ★★★ £E Barolo Riserva Vignolo ★★★ £F
Barbera d'Alba Vigna del Cucolo ★★ £D
Dolcetto d'Alba Vigna Melera ★★ £C
Dolcetto d'Alba Vigna Scot ★★ £B
Langhe Nebbiolo ★★ £D
Langhe Freisa ★ £C

Ceretto (Barolo) www.ceretto.com
In the 1970s Ceretto evolved from an old-style merchant house into a modern one owning most of its grape sources. Of the many fabulous sites, the most famous perhaps is the Bricco Asili cru, (confusingly nearly all the Barbarescos produced carry this name) but it is in Barolo's Bricco Rocche (which adjoins Villero in Castiglione Falletto), Prapò and Brunate that the brothers Ceretto usually have their top wines. Each property is overseen from the impressive headquarters at the La Bernadina estate where Riesling (Arbarei), is vinified. New oak is used in all the top wines, which when on form are supple, intense and characterful.

Recommended Reds:
Barolo Bricco Rocche ★★★★ £H
Barolo Brunate ★★★★ £G
Barolo Prapò ★★★★ £F Barolo Zonchera ★★ £F
Barbaresco Bricco Asili ★★★★ £H
Barbaresco Bernadot ★★★ £G
Langhe Monsordo ★★ £E
Barbera d'Alba Piana ★★ £D
Nebbiolo d'Alba Bernardina ★★ £D
Dolcetto d'Alba Rossana ★ £C
Recommended Whites:
Langhe Arneis Blangé ★ £C

Michele Chiarlo (Barolo) www.michelechiarlo.it
With 110ha, Chiarlo is one of the most substantial vineyard owners in Piedmont. A major part of this is for Barbera d'Asti production but it also includes some top crus for Nebbiolo and a chunk of Gavi. While the wines are competently made it is often the Barberas (particularly the consistently fine La Court) that impress as much as the Barbaresco and Barolos. The latter despite their origins, can seem a little inelegant when tasted alongside their peers. Of recent releases the Cerequio shows the most purity and style, as well as balance. Barbaresco Asili shows fine quality too but is deceptive in its accessibility, and like the Barolos needs time for the tannic backbone to soften.

Recommended Reds:
Barolo Cerequio ★★★★ £F
Barolo Cannubi ★★★ £F Barbaresco Asili ★★★ £F
Barbera d'Asti Nizza Superiore La Court ★★★ £D
Barbera d'Asti Superiore Le Orme ★★ £C
Barbera d'Asti Superiore Cipressi della Court ★★ £C
Recommended Whites:
Moscato d'Asti Nivole ★★ £C
Gavi del Comune del Gavi Fornaci di Tassarolo ★ £C

Quinto Chionetti (Dolcetto di Dogliani) www.chionettiquinto.com
The benchmark producer in Dogliani now has plenty of competition (Anna Maria ABBONA, M&E ABBONA, Luigi EINAUDI, PECCHENINO and others). Of some 14 ha, six are designated Briccolero, but these are often given a close run by the rest, sold as San Luigi. Both are delicious, perfumed, full of fruit and best with 1–2 years' age.

Recommended Reds:
Dolcetto di Dogliani Briccolero ★★★ £C

Dolcetto di Dogliani San Luigi ★★★ £C

Ciabot Berton (Barolo) *www.ciabotberton.it*
The ciabot (shelter) refers to a ruin in the midst of the 7 ha Roggeri cru where the fireworks produced by a certain Signor Berton blew the roof off. Now 4 ha of these south-east facing slopes are cultivated by Marco Oberto for another fine interpretation of Nebbiolo in La Morra. The hard argillaceous soils retain water even in hot vintages so the vines don't shut down helping ensure full, even ripening. Vinification and ageing are largely traditional with a relatively long maceration, including pumping over followed by capello sommerso (submerged cap). The wine is given 12-15 months in used French oak before completing its ageing in large Slavonian oak. The result is impressive depth, density with abundant but fine tannins. Richness and complexity build with age. Amply proportioned regular Barolo Rocchettevino sees only the large used oak, while other parts of the 12 ha estate also provide Barbera and Dolcetto of a good standard, particularly the single vineyard selections.
Recommended Reds:
Barolo Roggeri ★★★★ £F
Barolo Rocchettevino ★★★☆ £F
Barbera d'Alba Bricco San Biagio ★★★ £D
Dolcetto d'Alba Rutuin ★★ £C

Fratelli Cigliuti (Barbaresco) *www.cigliuti.it*
The cru of Serraboella occupies slopes south-east of, and across from the town of Neive. It is shared between Cigliuti and PAITIN. Of Renato Cigliuti's 6 ha, 2.5 with a south-west aspect are planted to Nebbiolo. The resultant Barbaresco shows the craft of a dedicated grower. Concentrated, it shows some oak influence and quite powerful but ripe tannnins which enable it to improve for a decade or more. Briccoserra, a Barbera/Nebbiolo blend sourced mostly from the nearby Bricco vineyards, has unexpected breadth and intensity while Dolcetto and Barbera rarely disappoint. A small part of Serraboella's Barbera fruit has been bottled as Campass since 2000. BarbarescoVigna Erte is another good example but without the extra depth and refinement of Serraboella.
Recommended Reds:
Barbaresco Serraboella ★★★★ £E   Barbaresco Vigne Erte ★★★ £E
Barbera d'Alba Campass ★★★ £D   Barbera d'Alba Serraboella ★★ £D
Langhe Briccoserra ★★★ £D   Dolcetto d'Alba Serraboella ★★ £C

⚙ Domenico Clerico (Barolo) *www.domenicoclerico.it*
Domenico Clerico shot to prominence in the 1980s and has been one of Barolo's most consistent superstars ever since. Even from the miserable early 90s, the wines stand out. Maceration times are relatively short and most of the small oak is new but the wines don't lack for stuffing or structure. Clerico has built up 21 ha, more than 40% of it for three fabulous Barolos. The Ginestra cru provides both classy Ciabot Mentin Ginestra and more international Pajana; Mosconi, a stone's throw to the south, the rich, fleshy Per Cristina. Also very worthy, in descending order of value for money, are Barbera, Dolcetto and Arte (*barrique*-aged, 90% Nebbiolo topped up with Barbera and sometimes Cabernet too). In 2006, Domenico ventured out of the area of Monforte, renting vineyards in Serralunga and Bussia. The Serralunga Barolo, labelled as "Aeroplanservaj" after Domenico's own nickname, produces intense fruit, stemming form a long maceration. Around 6500 bottles are produced. Since 2008, some of the Nebbiolo from the vineyard in Bussia, Bricotto, which had previously gone into the Arte blend, has now been vinified separetely and are sold only in magnums and are built for long keeping.
Recommended Reds:
Barolo Bricotto ★★★★★ £G
Barolo Riserva Per Cristina ★★★★★ £F
Barolo Ciabot Mentin Ginestra ★★★★★ £F
Barolo Pajana ★★★★★ £F
Barolo Aeroplanservaj ★★★★★ £F
Langhe Arte ★★★★ £E
Barbera d'Alba Trevigne ★★★ £D
Langhe Dolcetto Visadì ★★ £C

Elvio Cogno (Barolo) *www.elviocogno.com*
Wedged against the Monforte and Barolo communes in the south-west of the Barolo zone is a decent chunk of the Novello commune. It's sole significant and historic cru, Ravera, is given expression by both Cogno and M&E ABBONA. From their 9 ha of vineyard, Nadia Cogno's husband, Walter Fissore, makes robustly flavoured wines with an extra intensity to the fruit than most. All are deep, well-balanced and benefit from a little extra bottle-age. Ravera, with a muted *barrique* influence, assumes an earthy, truffly, savoury complexity with even a little age. Rich, powerful Barolo Vigna Elena, first made in 1997, is unusual in being produced solely from the Rosé clone of Nebbiolo. Montegrilli is a *barrique*-aged blend, half Nebbiolo and half Barbera. Anas-cëtta, sold as a Vino da Tavola, is from the obscure local grape Nas-cëtta. A portion of the grapes are *barrique*-fermented and aged contributing to its creamy, almost oily texture without dumbing down the distinctive wild herb and grapefruit character.
Recommended Reds:
Barolo Ravera ★★★★ £F
Barolo Vigna Elena ★★★★ £F
Langhe Montegrilli ★★☆ £D
Barbera d'Alba Bricco dei Merli ★★☆ £C
Dolcetto d'Alba Vigna del Mandorlo ★★ £B
Recommended Whites:
Anas-cëtta ★★ £C

◉◉ Aldo Conterno (Barolo) *www.poderialdoconterno.com*
It is over 40 years since the late Aldo Conterno set out on his own (leaving the family estate of Giacomo Conterno to his brother Giovanni in 1969) but even by the late 1980s he had already established a house of formidable reputation (and inspiration). The style of Barolo is considered traditional because they are aged in large Slavonian oak but aspects of their vinification are more modern. Even before his death in 2012, the wines from 25 ha of estate vineyards were made by sons Franco, Giacomo and Stefano. All, but particularly Cicala, Colonello and Granbussia (a Riserva selection of all plots), show lovely style and dimension on the palate, and the ensuing complexity and nuance most other examples miss. *Barriques* come into play for Barbera, Chardonnay Bussiador and Langhe blend Il Favot (Nebbiolo).
Recommended Reds:
Barolo Riserva Granbussia ◉◉◉◉◉ £H
Barolo Cicala ◉◉◉◉◉ £G
Barolo Colonello ◉◉◉◉◉ £G
Barolo Bussia Soprana ★★★★ £F
Langhe Il Favot ★★★☆ £E   Barbera d'Alba Conca Tre Pile ★★★ £D
Recommended Whites:
Langhe Bussiador ★★★ £D

Piedmont

❀ Giacomo Conterno (Barolo)

Giovanni Conterno, whose signature was the legendary Monfortino Barolo Riserva, died early in 2004. Younger son Roberto now continues the 'traditional' work made famous by his father. Long maceration times (5–6 weeks) and extended ageing (6–7 years) in large, old oak barrels are two essential elements, producing a wine of sometimes unequalled intensity, power and longevity. Cascina Francia, a little easier to obtain, is also a great wine. Though there has been some moderation in the winemaking, the wines still show great breadth, intensity and persistence in a robust and tannic style: macho Barolo, and Barbera are true to the house style. In 2008 Roberto bought 3 ha of the prime Ceretta vineyard in Serralunga comprising of 2 ha of Nebbiolo and 1 ha of Barbera. A Langhe Nebbiolo and a Barbera d'Alba has been produced from this vineyard with a Barolo Ceretta to come.

Recommended Reds:
Barolo Riserva Monfortino ✪✪✪✪✪ £H
Barolo Cascina Francia ★★★★★ £G
Langhe Nebbiolo Ceretta ★★★★ £F
Barbera d'Alba ★★ £D

❀ Conterno-Fantino (Barolo) *www.conternofantino.it*

A partnership that serves as a beacon to others determined to producer flawless, modern-style Barolos. The rich and complete Sorì Ginestra is a great wine if not quite among Barolo's élite - cellar recent top vintages for 10-15 years. Vigna del Gris is almost at the same level and can show a more floral, exquisite perfume but just misses the extra depth and structure of Sorì Ginestra. Mosconi, opposite Ginestra, at a higher altitude shows great structure and substance with intense forest fruits. Monprà (Nebbiolo/Barbera/Cabernet) is a consistently good example of the *barrique*-aged Langhe blend, while the *barrique*-fermented and aged Chardonnay has a typical spicy oak and Piedmontese fruit expression.

Recommended Reds:
Barolo Sorì Ginestra ★★★★★ £F   Barolo Vigna Mosconi ★★★★★ £F
Barolo Vigna del Gris ★★★★ £F   Langhe Monprà ★★★ £E
Barbera d'Alba Vignota ★★ £C   Dolcetto d'Alba Bricco Bastía ★★ £B
Recommended Whites:
Langhe Chardonnay Bastía ★★★ £D

❀ Contratto (Asti) *www.contratto.it*

A producer of Asti in the 19th century Contratto has now achieved is second rejuvination in 20 years following its purchase in 2011 by the Rivetti family of LA SPINETTA fame. The production of a vineyard-specific Asti (De Miranda) made by a variation on the traditional or Champagne method was revived by Giancarlo Scaglione (FORTETO DELLA LUJA) for Carlo Bocchino, who purchased the estate in 1993 and subsequently sold it to the Rivettis. This elegant, wonderfully perfumed sparkler would actually keep a year or two. What had not been realised is that for four years prior to their acquisition, Giorgio Rivetti had ben acting as a consultant to the Contratto winery and has succeeded in producing elegant and complex sparkling wines from Pinot Noir and Chardonnay from vineyards located in Oltrepo Pavese and Costiglione. With the facility now completely in the hands of the Rivetti family, one can now expect a further upturn in quality from this famous and prestigious estate.

Recommended Whites:
Novecento Brut Contratto ★★★★ £E
Brut Riserva Millesimato Giuseppe Contratto ★★★★ £E
Millesimato Contratto ★★★ £D
For England Pas Dose Blanc de Noirs ★★★ £D

For England Brut Rosé ★★★ £D
Blanc de Blanc Brut Contratto ★★★ £D
Brut Bacco D'Oro Contratto ★★★ £D
Asti de Miranda Metodo Classico ★★★★ £C
Asti de Miranda ★★★ £C
Recommended Rosés:
For England Brut Rosé ★★★ £D

Luigi Coppo & Figli (Barbera d'Asti) *www.coppo.it*

Brilliant Barberas have been made here for a number of years. Pomorosso is a deep, rich and complex example and often among the best made, it shows what a match good Barbera fruit is for new oak. Other Barbera can be good but are not of the same order but Alterego (Cabernet/Barbera) adds more richness in late 90s vintages and Mondaccione is one of the few serious still, dry Freisas (see also VAJRA). Also notable are one of the best oak-fermented and aged Piedmont Chardonnays (Monteriolo) and ripe fizz. Pricey but impressive Riserva della Famiglia Barbera d'Asti is released with a little more age (as is a Chardonnay equivalent).

Recommended Reds:
Barbera d'Asti Pomorosso ★★★★ £E
Barbera d'Asti Camp du Rouss ★★ £D
Barbera d'Asti L'Avvocata ★★ £C
Monferrato Alterego ★★★ £D
Langhe Mondaccione ★★ £D
Recommended Whites:
Piemonte Chardonnay Monteriolo ★★★ £D
Piemonte Chardonnay Costebianche ★ £C
Riserva Brut Coppo ★★ £D

Cordero di Montezemolo (Barolo) *www.corderodimontezemolo.it*

Well-directed estate with modern, pristine cellars, drawing on 29 ha of vineyard (much of it owned) centred on the spur of Monfalletto in Annunziata. The property has been transformed over two decades and the wines since 1995 are impressive. Maceration times are now very short and there is much experimentation with different types of new oak but the approach remains flexible. It remains to be seen how well the current crop of fine vintages will age. Enrico VI shows the class of the Villero cru in Castiglione Falletto, while a promising Bricco Gattera from the Lebanese cedar-topped knoll of Monfalletto has been made since 1997. Barbera Funtanì is very good *barrique*-aged example while Curdè is an estate blended red from Pinot Nero, Barbera and Nebbiolo. New is a Barolo Riserva Gorette, a limited edition bottling of 1,000 magnums in years in which the harvest is considered ecellent. It is only available for purchase to visitors to the estate.

Recommended Reds:
Barolo Bricco Gattera ★★★★ £F
Barolo Enrico VI ★★★★ £F
Barolo Monfalletto ★★★ £E
Barbera d'Alba Superiore Funtanì ★★★ £D
Barbera d'Alba ★ £C   Dolcetto d'Alba ★ £B
Recommended Whites:
Langhe Arneis ★ £B
Langhe Chardonnay Elioro ★ £C

Giovanni Corino (Barolo) *Barolo www.corino.it*

Another producer of the Annunziata sub-zone in La Morra making modernstyled, fruit-rich Barolo. Giuliano Corino recently split the estate with his brother Renato (see below) retaining 7 ha but the wines under this label have a fine track record - highlighting the

quality inherent in Giachini, a small 3.5 ha cru, immediately east of Rocche dell'Annunziata. As well as several other Barolo crus made in small quantities, Vecchie Vigne is a superior selection made since 1997 and is deep and powerful with great cellaring potential. Regular Barolo can age impressively too and shouldn't be ignored. Dolcetto is a pure, classic example - brilliant with 3-4 years' age from a top vintage. Insieme is pretty good here too (see ALTARE), this one mostly Nebbiolo and Barbera with a little Cabernet and Merlot.

Recommended Reds:

Barolo Arborina ★★★★☆ £G
BaroloVecchie Vigne ★★★★ £H
Barolo Giachini ★★★★ £F Barolo ★★★☆ £E
Insieme ★★★☆ £F Barbera d'Alba ★★★ £C
Dolcetto d'Alba ★★★ £B Langhe Nebbiolo ★★☆ £D

Renato Corino (Barolo) *www.renatocorino.it*

Renato Corino and his brother Giuliano decided on an amicable division of their family estate in 2006 and it will be interesting to see what stylistic differences emerge between them in the coming years. Renato has 5 ha but retained Rocche dell' Annunziata and Roncaglie as well as a share of Arborina and part of an old vines parcel for a fine Vecchie Vigne bottling. Also made is another Barolo, Roncaglie with the first vintages under the Giovanni Corino label as is the case for the excellent modern-styled Barbera Pozzo.

Recommended Reds:

Barolo Arborina ★★★★☆ £G
Barolo Riserva Vecchie Vigne ★★★★ £H
Barolo Rocche dell'Annunziata ★★★★ £F
Barolo Roncaglie ★★★ £E
Barbera d'Alba Pozzo★★★☆ £E
Barbera d'Alba★★★☆ £C Nebbiolo d'Alba ★★ £D
Dolcetto d'Alba ★★ £C

Matteo Correggia (Roero) *www.matteocorreggia.com*

Roero's inspirational grower died tragically in June 2001. His legacy from 14 years of undinting effort is Nebbiolo and Barbera of unprecedented quality from the 'other' (northern) side of the River Tanaro. Ornella Correggia is now assisted by Luca Rostagno in her efforts to maintain quality. Both Nebbiolo and Barbera undergo a relatively short maceration before being aged in new oak. Like others of modernist leanings who have really succeeded, there is a density and quality to the fruit that ensure the wines have real character, structure and aroma. The dense, powerful cru Roero red, made since 1996, is consistently very impressive while a new Langhe blend, Le Marne Grigie was released from the 2000 vintage. It is made only from French varieties (Cabernet Sauvignon, Merlot and Syrah but also Cabernet Franc and Petit Verdot) vinified together. Whites include lively Roero Arneis and ripe, Bordeaux style oak-aged Sauvignon Langhe Bianco. Also made is Anthos, a dry version of Brachetto - much better is a small quantity of a enchanting Brachetto Passito (dried for 2 months) is occasionally made.

Recommended Reds:

Roero Ròche d'Ampsèj ★★★★ £F Roero ★★ £C
Nebbiolo d'Alba La Val di Preti ★★★ £D
Langhe Le Marne Grigio ★★★ £E
Barbera d'Alba Marun ★★★ £D
Brachetto Passito ★★★ £E Brachetto Secco Anthos ★ £B

Recommended Whites:

Langhe Bianco ★★ £D Roero Arneis ★★ £B

Damilano (Barolo) *www.cantinedamilano.it*

This is a historic Barolo producer recently revived by a younger generation with help from Giuseppe Caviola. Over the past few years, vineyard holdings (owned or rented) have grown from 5 ha to 73 ha and the number of Barolo crus has now increased from two to four, plus their entry level Barolo, Lecinquevigne, blended from vineyards in five different locations in the Langhe. Cannubi has arguably the greater elegance and depth, and unfurls slowly with age. In Liste the oak can be more apparent, but is also dense and extracted with considerable structure. Cerequio has elegance and persistence, whilst Brunate displays all the characteristics of this vineyard forging a good balance between fruit, structure and acidity. Regular Lecinquevigne Barolo is excellent with plenty of Nebbiolo perfume and nuance if not the class or elegance of the crus. It similarly has lots of extract and intensity and deserves to be drunk with 8–10 years' age. Dolcetto is very bright and appealing, Barbera is similarly cool and expressive and the herb-scented Nebbiolo has a red-fruits intensity.

Recommended Reds:

Barolo Cannubi ★★★★☆ £F
Barolo Cerequio ★★★★☆ £F
Barolo Brunate ★★★★☆ £F
Barolo Liste ★★★★ £F
Barolo ★★★☆ £E
Barbera d'Alba Lablu ★★☆ £C
Langhe Nebbiolo Marghe ★★ £C
Dolcetto d'Alba ★★ £B

Luigi Einaudi (Dolcetto di Dogliani) *www.poderieinaudi.com*

This estate was made famous by the first president of the Italian republic, but has been recently reinvigorated by Paola Einaudi and her husband Giorgio Ruffo. Though Dogliani-based, with 30 ha of Dolcetto vineyards, other plots provide grapes for top-flight Barolo. Costa Grimaldi is a very complete and harmonious Barolo with great intensity and a match for that from the recently acquired Cannubi vines. Both show real class and have excellent cellaring potential. Dense, intense Dolcetto needs a year or two but the crus are consistently among the best of the zone. The fruit-rich, oak-aged Langhe Luigi Einaudi blends Cabernet, Nebbiolo, Barbera and Merlot.

Recommended Reds:

Barolo Costa Grimaldi ★★★★ £E
Barolo Nei Cannubi ★★★★ £F
Barolo ★★★ £E Langhe Luigi Einaudi ★★★ £E
Langhe Nebbiolo ★★ £D
Piemonte Barbera ★★★ £C
Dolcetto di Doglianil Filari ★★★ £C
Dolcetto di Dogliani Vigna Tecc ★★★ £C
Dolcetto di Dogliani ★ £B

Fontanafredda (Barolo) *www.fontanafredda.it*

Directed by Giovanni Minetti, Fontanafredda is one of the heavyweights of the Barolo region. Tenementi Fontanafredda refers specifically to the premium wines, now being bottled with new labels in heavy bottles. Many vineyards are owned, particularly in Serralunga where the massive winery complex is found, but much is bought in too. Some poor past performances seem to have been put behind them as the whole range of wines has been recently much improved. Since 1997 the Barolos are significantly different, much more modern and expressive in style. The most perfumed, La Villa, is from the Barolo commune, while deeper La Rosa and

Piedmont

Italy

more structured Lazzarito are from Serralunga. The latter has been combined with La Delizia from 99. Barbera Papagena and Dolcetto di Diano d'Alba are the best-value wines, but Barolo Serralunga is reasonably priced too. Decent metodo classico sparklers are rather better than the ubiquitous Asti and there is a vast amount of typical Langhe blends (red and white) produced from their 85 ha of holdings for easy drinking. Moscato d'Asti, Moncucco is also very good, with classic intensity and exotic grapiness. A Roero Arneis, Pradalupo and a Riesling and Nascetta blend, Marin are also produced but have not been tasted.

Recommended Reds:
Barolo Vigna La Rosa ★★★★ £F
Barolo Lazzarito Vigna La Delizia ★★★★ £F
Barolo Vigna La Villa ★★★☆ £F
Barolo Vigna La Delizia ★★★☆ £F
Barolo Serralunga d'Alba ★★★ £E
Barbaresco Coste Rubin ★★★☆ £E
Barbera d'Alba Papagena ★★ £C
Dolcetto di Diano d'Alba Vigna La Lepre ★★ £B
Langhe Eremo ★ £B
Recommended Whites:
Moscato d'Asti Moncucco ★★ £B

Forteto della Luja (Loazzolo) *www.fortetodellaluja.it*
Giancarlo Scaglione now concentrating on his own estate, has put more than a few producers on the map. One wine, a late-harvest (Vendemmia Tardiva) Muscat (with its distinctive 'wound ribbon' label) was until recently what both this tiny DOC and its producer were all about. Production is now in the hands of son Gianni. Half the grapes are dried and half are late-harvested and botrytis-affected. A slow, very extended fermentation adds an oxidative component and honey, nuts and dried figs complement a rich fruit core. Other unusual but good-quality wines include an elegant, perfumed late-harvest Brachetto and a partly *barrique*-aged blend of (mostly) Barbera and Pinot Nero, Le Grive that is cool but pure. A 100% Barbera, Monros, is also produced.
Recommended Reds:
Piemonte Brachetto Forteto Pian dei Sogni ★★★☆ £E
Monferrato Rosso Le Grive ★★☆ £D
Recommended Whites:
Loazzolo Vendemmia Tardiva ★★★★ £E
Moscato d'Asti Piasa San Maurizio ★★ £D

☺☺ Gaja (Barbaresco) *www.gajawines.com*
Piedmont's numero uno, Gaja has been a veritable phenomenon in the pursuit of quality and the promotion of his native region. Consumption of the the often stupendous single-vineyard wines, especially the trio from Barbaresco vineyards but also Sperss, is pretty much restricted to the wealthy. The first to be made (from 1967) was Sorì San Lorenzo; the most austere in its youth, it is based on the Secondine cru. Both Sorì Tildin (made from 1970, the year winemaker Giudo Rivella arrived), often the richest and deepest, and the more forward Costa Russi (1978) derive from the Roncagliette cru. Sperss, the ex-Barolo, is sourced from the Marenca and Rivette crus in Serralunga. All these former Barbaresco and Barolo crus may now include a very small percentage of Barbera. The only official Barolo Cru in the range is called Da Gromis from vineyards in Serralunga and la Morra purchased from Gromis family in 1995. The most notable other wine is the Gaia e Rey Chardonnay, rich and expressive without mimicking the classic Burgundian style. Interestingly it is fermented in stainless steel before being aged for

6–8 months in oak *barriques* of mixed European origin. Darmagi is pure Cabernet while Sito Rey is from Barbera. Sito Moresco combines Nebbiolo, Merlot and Barbera. This trio of reds are also of good quality if missing the hallmarks of greatness. Gaja, it would seem, only needs time before reaching the peak of whichever vinous summit he attempts. Brunello (PIEVE SANTA RESTITUTA) is now (since 1995) showing the Gaja stamp of elegance together with characteristic breadth and structure. CA' MARCANDA will shift the spotlight to Bolgheri. Quantities of the top wines remains small and the prices necessarily high.
Recommended Reds:
Barbaresco ☺☺☺☺☺ £H
Langhe Nebbiolo Sorì Tildin ☺☺☺☺☺ £H
Langhe Nebbiolo Sorì San Lorenzo ☺☺☺☺☺ £H
Langhe Nebbiolo Sperss ☺☺☺☺☺ £H
Langhe Nebbiolo Costa Russi ★★★★★ £H
Langhe Nebbiolo Conteisa ★★★★★ £H
Langhe Rosso Darmagi ★★★★ £H
Langhe Rosso Sito Rey ★★★★ £G
Langhe Rosso Sito Moresco ★★★ £E
Barolo Da Gromis ★★★★★ £H
Recommended Whites:
Langhe Chardonnay Gaia e Rey ★★★★ £G
Langhe Chardonnay Rossj-Bass ★★★ £F

Filippo Gallino (Roero) *www.filippogallino.com*
Production here is confined to red and white Roero and Barbera but quality has shot up and like CORREGGIA, CASCINA CHICCO or MALVIRÀ shows what's possible from the best of Roero's soils. The Gallino family now have 15ha of vineyards and production of around 8,000 cases has increased much from the early 2000s. Both Barbera and Nebbiolo are strengths, the Superiore versions, in particular, are increasingly full but well-structured with fine tannins.
Recommended Reds:
Barbera d'Alba Superiore ★★★ £D
Barbera d'Alba ★ £C
Roero Superiore ★★★ £C Roero ★ £C
Recommended Whites:
Roero Arneis 4 Luglio ★★ £D
Roero Arneis ★ £C

Ettore Germano (Barolo) *www.germanoettore.com*
Compared to La Morra, Serralunga is somewhat bereft of top-flight small growers but Sergio Germano, who has relatively recently assumed control and ownership from his father Ettore, is certainly one. Renovation and expansion have aided the emergence of dense but well-structured Barolos. Of the two crus Prapò shows more refinement and style than the regular example, while Cerretta, which has up to two years in *barriques* (around a quarter new), is more powerful and complex. Small oak is also used for an intense Barbera, Vigne della Madre, and Langhe Balau, now 100% Merlot. Langhe Nebbiolo shows good character while a Langhe Bianco, Binel, is also unusual in combining Chardonnay and Riesling. Both Prapò and Cerretta should be drunk with at least 8–10 years' age. The estate has now expanded to 10 ha in Serralunga and 5 ha in Ciglie, where the white wines are cultivated. There is an Alta Langa Spumante made from 80% Pinot Noir and 20% Chardonnay, a Langhe Chardonnay, a Chardonnay-Riesling (Binel), a minerally Riesling Renano (Herzu) and a herby and aromatic indigenous Nascetta.

Recommended Reds:
Barolo Cerretta ★★★★ £F
Barolo Prapò ★★★ £F
Barolo ★★★ £E   Barbera d'Alba Vigna della Madre ★★★ £D
Langhe Balau ★★ £D
Dolcetto d'Alba Pradone ★★ £C
Dolcetto d'Alba Lorenzino ★ £B
Recommended Whites:
Langhe Binel ★★ £D   Langhe Bianco Nascetta ★★ £B
Herzu Riesling ★★ £B

Attilio Ghisolfi (Barolo) *www.ghisolfi.com*
Gian Marco is one of a number of talented young Piedmont winemakers able to harness the fruit potential that results from his father's viticultural expertise. The Barolo vines are located in the lesser known Visette cru (a sub-cru of Bussia) and the wine shows lovely weight and richness with deep, intense fruit. Though it can be drunk reasonably young, it should improve for a decade. A new, well-crafted Barolo Bussia has been produced from young vines since 2005 is even more approachable. A rich and complex Barolo Riserva cru, Fantini, has appeared from the 2000 vintage showing great depth and concentration. *Barriques* are used for two Langhe reds. The rich, expansive Alta Bussia is 80% Barbera, 20% Nebbiolo, whilst the straight Nebbiolo is savoury and intense. Barbera Vigna Lisi comes from old vines, receives 50% new oak and is sleek and stylish with 3 or 4 years' age. All show a similarly deft winemaking touch and fine fruit. Pinay is a Pinot Nero of some promise, though the vines are still young.
Recommended Reds:
Barolo Fantini ★★★★★ £G
Barolo Bricco Visette ★★★★ £F
Barolo Bussia ★★★★ £F
 Langhe Rosso Alta Bussia ★★★ £E
Langhe Nebbiolo ★★ £D   Langhe Rosso Pinay ★★ £D
Barbera d'Alba Vigna Lisi ★★★ £D
Barbera d'Alba Maggiore ★ £C

✿ Bruno Giacosa /Az. Ag. Falletto *www.brunogiacosa.it*
Bruno Giacosa has made many of the great bottles of Barolo and Barbaresco over the last 40 years. Much of his reputation rests on buying the best grapes from an intimate knowledge of the best vineyards. The renown of Barbaresco crus Asili, Rabajà, Santo Stefano and Barolo crus Vigna Rionda, Falletto and Villero owes much to Giacosa's supremely complex and harmonious renditions of Nebbiolo. With so many growers now making their own wines, Giacosa has also acquired vineyards of his own – some of the best sites, namely Asili in Barbaresco and Falletto in Serralunga. Riservas made from both sites are released after 5 years instead of the usual 4. (Riserva bottles have a red label rather than the usual white). Winemaker Dante Scaglione still employs a fairly traditional winemaking practice but the maceration times are now only moderately long and he uses large French oak rather than the once much favoured Slavonian casks. These are not wines for drinking young, though they might show well with 6 or 7 years. Keep all the cru Barbaresco and Barolo for a decade from the vintage date – only then will it be possible to see if current releases stack up against some of the legendary older bottlings. The prices they obtain tends to reflect their sought-after status. Barbera, Dolcetto and Roero Arneis are consistently good among several other wines made. Recent marketing policy has divided the wines made from estate owned fruit which are marketed under the label "Azienda Agricola Falletto" and bought in fruit marketed as "Casa Vinicola Bruno Giacosa".

Azienda Agricola Falletto
Recommended Reds:
Barolo Rocche del Falletto di Serralunga ✪✪✪✪✪ £H
Barolo Falletto di Serralunga ★★★★★ £H
Barbaresco Asili ★★★★★ £G
Barbaresco Rabajà ★★★★ £G
Barbera d'Alba Falletto di Serralunga ★★★ £C
Dolcetto d Alba Falletto di Serralunga ★ £C
Casa Vinicola Bruno Giacosa
Recommended Reds:
Barbaresco Santo Stefano di Neive ★★★★★ £H
Nebbiolo d'Alba Valmaggiore ★★ £D
Recommended Whites:
Roero Arneis ★★ £C

✿ Elio Grasso (Barolo) *www.eliograsso.it*
Elio Grasso has some prized steep hillside vineyards in the east of the Monforte commune. He has spent more than 20 years working his historic family vineyards and has recently relinquished the winemaking responsibility to his son Gianluca. An exisiting pair of refined, scented Barolos have been complemented by a *barrique*-aged Barolo from the replanted Runcot, a superior plot within Gavarini. As with other top *barrique*-aged examples from this area (CLERICO or CONTERNO-FANTINO) there is an inherent richness and structure from the fruit to marry with that from the oak. Maceration times are longer than for his neighbours' wines and Runcot, already impressive, seems certain to achieve greatness as the vines age. Barbera, Dolcetto and a little Chardonnay are very worthy too. No single vineyard Barolos in 2002.
Recommended Reds:
Barolo Ginestra Casa Matè ★★★★★ £G
Barolo Gavarini Vigna Chiniera ★★★★★ £G
Barolo Runcot ★★★★ £F   B
arbera d'Alba Vigna Martina ★★★ £D
Dolcetto d'Alba Vigna dei Grassi ★★ £C
Recommended Whites:
Langhe Chardonnay Educato ★ £C

Silvio Grasso (Barolo) *www.silviograsso.com*
This modern estate run by Federico Grasso can be relied on for very well-made Barolos. Both the Luciani and Manzoni crus lie near the eastern periphery of La Morra at slightly lower altitudes than some of the more celebrated crus in the zone. Though of the modern type, both show full, ripe fruit and excellent balance with well-integrated oak on the palate. Of the two, Ciabot Manzoni sometimes has the edge but it depends on the vintage. Both are best with 5–10 years' age. Federico's Insieme (see ALTARE) is a blend of almost half Nebbiolo with roughly equal parts of Barbera, Cabernet and Merlot – aged entirely in new oak. Barolos, Giachini and Pì Vigne are new from 99 and Vigna Plicotti from 2000.
Recommended Reds:
Barolo Bricco Luciani ★★★★ £G
Barolo Ciabot Manzoni ★★★★ £G
Barolo Pì Vigne ★★★ £F   Barolo Giachini ★★★ £F
Insieme ★★★ £F   Langhe Nebbiolo Peirass ★★ £D
Barbera d'Alba ★★£C
Barbera d'Alba Vigna Fontanile ★★ £C
Dolcetto d'Alba ★★ £B

Piedmont

Italy

Icardi (Barbera d'Asti) www.icardipierino.it

This sizeable estate to the east of Barbaresco is run by Claudio Icardi and makes an extraordinary plethora of pleasurable wines, most in small quantities. The wines often combine remarkable drinkability and good varietal character with a succulent fruit richness, though occasionally at the cost of character. Yet quality is high and the wines' opulence and vinosity could be suited to palates that find most Piemonte wines too demanding. Barolo Parej shows increasing depth and structure. Barbaresco Montubert is a fine fruit-rich expression of Nebbiolo as is Langhe Pafoj. Bricco del Sole combines Barbera, Nebbiolo and Cabernet. Langhe Nej is 100% Pinot Nero, while the stylish white Pafoj is partially barriqued Chardonnay/Sauvignon. Moscato and Brachetto are light and moderately sweet – fresh and splendidly scented if drunk young. Grignolino (Bric du Su) and Cortese (Balera) are also produced.

Recommended Reds:

Barolo Parej ★★★★ £F Barbaresco Montubert ★★★ £E

Langhe Pafoj ★★★ £E Langhe Nej ★★ £D

Langhe Nebbiolo Surisjvan ★★ £D

Monferrato Cascina Bricco del Sole ★★★ £E

Barbera d'Asti Nuj Suj ★★★ £D

Barbera d'Asti Tabarin ★★ £C

Barbera d'Alba Surì di Mù ★★ £D

Dolcetto d'Alba Rousori ★★ £B

Piemonte Brachetto Surì Vigin ★★ £B

Recommended Whites:

Monferrato Pafoj ★★ £D

Moscato d'Asti La Rosa Selvatica ★★ £B

Piemonte Cortese Balera ★ £B

La Barbatella (Barbera d'Asti) www.labarbatella.com

Giuliano Noè, a top consultant enologist, is the winemaker here. What he has done with a few well-situated hectares showcases his skills. One of the most celebrated Barbera d'Asti together with Sonvico, the Barbera/Cabernet blend for long known as La Vigna di Sonvico, have earned this estate an enviable celebrity in the heart of Asti's hills. The wines have proven ageing potential and possess power and concentration but without excess. Mystère, made since 1999, is another pricey but increasingly fine red that adds Pinot Nero to Barbera and Cabernet Sauvignon. White Noè combines Cortese with Sauvignon.

Recommended Reds:

Monferrato Sonvico ★★★★ £F

Monferrato Mystère ★★★ £E

Barbera d'Asti Nizza Superiore Vigna dell'Angelo ★★★ £E

Barbera d'Asti ★★ £C

Recommended Whites:

Monferrato Noè ★★ £D

La Giustiniana (Gavi) www.lagiustiniana.it

Few Gavi producers are worth making a fuss about. La Giustiniana is one of the few exceptions. Enrico Tomalino with help from Donato Lanati is now producing consistently full, concentrated unwooded Gavi from this 30 ha estate. Lugarara is the mainstay; better, though, is slightly minerally, appley Montessora, with more intensity and persistence. A special selection, Just (sold outside the DOCG), in which a relatively small percentage of the wine goes into barrique, is full, creamy and that much better again. Made since 1998 is a red version of Just – barrique-aged, ripe and balanced, and predominantly from Barbera. Whites are best within a couple of years of the vintage. Since the 2001 vintage a lees-enriched version

of Gavi called 'Il Nostro Gavi' is being made. For immediate drinking there's some very good fizzy Brachetto d'Acqui and Moscato d'Asti from the 11 ha Contero estate at Strevi that is also owned by the Lombardini family.

La Giustiniana

Recommended Reds:

Monferrato Rosso Just ★★ £D

Recommended Whites:

Just ★★★ £E

Gavi del Comune di Gavi Montessora ★★★ £D

Gavi del Comune di Gavi Lugarara ★★ £C

Contero

Recommended Reds:

Brachetto d'Acqui ★★ £B

Recommended Whites:

Moscato d'Asti di Strevi ★★ £B

✪✪ La Spinetta (Barbaresco) www.la-spinetta.com

Giorgio Rivetti has become one of Italy's most talked-about winemakers. He runs La Spinetta, based just north of the Barbaresco zone, with brothers Bruno and Carlo. Early recognition resulted from excellent Moscato, Barbera and a stylish red blend called Pin, a tribute to their father Giuseppe who established the estate in 1977. But the creation of new Barbaresco wines from the crus Gallina and Starderi (in Neive) and Valeirano (in Treiso) rocketed the Rivetti name to fame. The wines are unequivocally modern whilst expressing the fusion between grape and site. All the reds see the inside of a barrique, but they are profound with super fruit. Of the Barbarescos, Starderi is seductive, dense and very complete, Valeirano perhaps shows the most finesse, while Gallina can be backward and extracted when young but with great potential if kept for 15 years or more. Riservas of each were made in 2001 with outstanding potential - should you be lucky enough to get any, lock them away in your cellar for a decade or two. A new Barbaresco cru - Bordini - is produced from the 2006 vintage. The wines from this vineyard were hitherto blended into 'Pin' or part of the Nebbiolo Langhe wine, as the wine from this vineyard was considerably lighter than the other Barbaresco crus. However, a decision was made to produce this as a cheaper Barbaresco in the range, maturing in 50% new oak instead of 100% for the other crus. The first release - the 2006 vintage - sold out very quickly since it was priced at around half of the others, whilst displaying a great deal of elegance and earlier drinking possibilities. Barbera take three forms. Barbera d'Asti Superiore (now labelled Bionzo) has outstanding fruit quality and richness but the less showy Gallina with preserved black fruits has excellent breadth and depth while Ca' di Pian is expressive and more affordable. The long-standing Pin (currently Nebbiolo/Barbera - 65/35) is consistently full and characterful. Whites other than Moscato are Sauvignon sold under the Langhe Bianco DOC and barrique-aged Piemonte Chardonnay. Newish sweet wine, Passito Oro is produced from dried Moscato grapes. From the separate winery of Campè della Spinetta comes Barolo Campe' (from 2000 or 2001, also an exuberant 2000 Riserva) from 7 ha of established vines. From 2006, Campe's "little brother" Barolo Garetti has been produced with lighter, juicier fruit, but nevertheless capable of long ageing. Gallina and supple, accessible Langhe Nebbiolo are also made here. Since 2010, the Rivettis have expanded into sparkling wine production by the acquisition of the CONTRATTO estate at Canelli. Beyond Piemonte, down in the coastal hills of Tuscany, Giorgio Rivetti is developing exciting interpretations of Sangiovese at the CASANOVA DELLA SPINETTA winery (see Tuscany).

La Spinetta
Recommended Reds:
Barbaresco Vigneto Gallina ✪✪✪✪✪ £H
Barbaresco Vigneto Starderi ✪✪✪✪✪ £H
Barbaresco Vigneto Valeirano ✪✪✪✪✪ £H
Barbaresco Vigneto Bordini ★★★★☆ £F
Barbera d'Asti Superiore Bionzo ★★★★☆ £F
Barbera d'Asti Ca' di Pian ★★★ £D   Monferrato Pin ★★★★ £F
Recommended Whites:
Piemonte Moscato Passito Oro ★★★ £F
Piemonte Chardonnay Lidia ★★ £E
Moscato d'Asti Bricco Quaglia ★★★ £C
Moscato d'Asti Biancospino ★★★ £B   Langhe Bianco ★★ £E

Campè della Spinetta
Recommended Reds:
Barolo Campè ✪✪✪✪✪ £H
Barolo Vigneto Garetti ★★★★☆ £F
Barbera d'Alba Gallina ★★★★ £F
Langhe Nebbiolo Vigneto Starderi ★★☆ £D

Tenuta La Tenaglia (Barbera d'Asti) *www.latenaglia.com*
La Tenaglia rosé to prominence in the 1980s on the basis of very good Barbera, championing the Monferrato hills not far south of the River Po. 18 ha of a 33 ha estate are planted to vines at an altitude of 450m. The pursuit of quality is reinforced with the use of outside expertise, including the services of eminent Tuscan enologist Attilio Pagli. Barbera is still the top wine, particularly the sumptuous, complex *barrique*-aged Emozioni from a single vineyard of 70-year-old vines. Giorgio Tenaglia comes from a selection of the best vines and is leaner but stylish, needing a year or two to soften. A third, the Monferrato Barbera, is firmly textured (if sometimes a little overoaked). Crea is a simpler, unoaked Barbera d'Asti. Half a hectare is dedicated to Syrah and the resulting Paradiso is peppery and black-fruited. Chardonnay (Oltre) is not unlike a good Pouilly-Fuissé but only a little is made. Regular unoaked Piemonte Chardonnay is adequate but no more, as is Grignolino and a Chiaretto made with 70% Barbera and 30% Grignolino.
Recommended Reds:
Barbera d'Asti Emozioni ★★★ £D
Barbera d'Asti Giorgio Tenaglia ★★ £C
Barbera del Monferrato Superiore Tenaglia è ★★ £C
Paradiso ★★ £D
Recommended Whites:
Piemonte Chardonnay Oltre ★★ £E

Malvirà (Roero) *www.malvira.com*
Brothers Roberto and Massimo consistently produce Arneis that is as good as any. Renesio is an unwooded version, while Trinità sees some oak and Saglietto is oak-fermented and aged. All three can show real personality and style. Reds too, are of a very good standard, making the most of the recent string of fine vintages. The Roero Riserva has been bottled as two separate crus from the 1999 vintage and both combine intensity with real elegance and should be drunk with five years' age. The remaining Nebbiolo is sold as Langhe Nebbiolo. San Guglielmo is an unwooded, perfumed and reasonably priced example of the Langhe Barbera/Nebbiolo blend. The oak-aged Tre uve combines Sauvignon and Chardonnay with Arneis, whilst Renesium is a botrytised late harvested Arneis (90%) fermented in French oak with a honeyed, apricot and tropical fruit flavour from the Trinità vineyard.

Recommended Reds:
Roero Riserva Mombeltramo ★★★ £D
Roero Riserva Trinità ★★★ £D
Langhe San Guglielmo ★★ £D
Langhe Nebbiolo ★ £C
Barbera d'Alba San Michele ★★ £C
Barbera d'Alba ★ £C
Recommended Whites:
Renesium ★★★ £D   Roero Arneis Renesio ★★ £C
Roero Arneis Trinità ★★ £C
Roero Arneis Saglietto ★★ £C
Langhe Tre uve ★★ £C

Giovanni Manzone (Barolo) *www.manzonegiovanni.com*
Giovanni & Mauro Manzone's 7.6 ha centre is on the cru Gramolere in the Castelletto part of the Monforte commune and the wines are made on organic principles, with minimum intervention. A special part of it is bottled as Bricat and a Riserva is also made in the best years. There is partial use of French tonneaux (new and used) but maceration times are moderately long and Giovanni is avowedly not in the modern camp. A distinctive wild mint and woodsmoke character seems typical of Gramolere (rather than a lack of ripeness as some have suggested), with extra intensity and dimension in Bricat. A concentrated old-vine Barbera La Serra is the pick of the rest. An interesting white, Rosserto, is made from Rossese Bianco and is unique in Piedmont.
Recommended Reds:
Barolo Gramolere ★★★★☆ £F
Barolo Bricat ★★★★☆ £F
Barolo Riserva ★★★★ £F
Barbera d'Alba La Serra ★★★ £D
Barbera d'Alba ★☆ £C
Dolcetto d'Alba La Serra ★★ £B
Recommended Whites:
Rosserto ★★ £C

Marcarini (Barolo) *www.marcarini.it*
The Barolo here is traditionally styled, with no new oak. Though a little firm and unexpressive when young, the wines can often age impressively from a good vintage. Though the inherent quality of the crus is apparent, these very structured if fruit-intense versions contrast with more lush, forward examples. Much attention is also paid to the Dolcettos, especially the rich Boschi di Berri made from vines over a 100 years old grown on their own roots – a factor which may account for the distinctive almondy, slightly earthy streak running through the intense berry fruit flavours. One to try at least once. Langhe Nebbiolo Roero Arneis and Moscato d'Asti are also made.
Recommended Reds:
Barolo Brunate ★★★★ £F   Barolo La Serra ★★★★ £F
Dolcetto d'Alba Boschi di Berri ★★★ £C
Dolcetto d'Alba Fontanazza ★ £B
Barbera d'Alba Ciabot Camerano ★★ £D

Marchesi di Grésy (Barbaresco) *www.marchesidigresy.com*
The Tenute Cisa Asinari actually comprises three estates but the centrepiece is the famous Martinenga cru. Though not ultra-consistent, the tight, dense, compact impression that the individual plots – Camp Gros (adjoining Rabajà) and Gaiun (an extension of Asili) – give when young can lead to splendid graceful and complex drinking after a decade or more. There is some use of

Piedmont

barriques, though more for Virtus (Barbera/Cabernet) and Villa Martis (Nebbiolo/Barbera) than for the Barbarescos. A Merlot from the Monte Colombo and La Serra vineyards is generous and plummy. Other wines, sourced from Monte Aribaldo at Treiso, include two Chardonnays and one of Piedmont's best Sauvignons. Both a Moscato d'Asti and a Moscato Passito (L'Altro) are produced from the third estate, La Serra.

Recommended Reds:
Barbaresco Camp Gros ★★★★☆ £G
Barbaresco Gaiun ★★★★☆ £F
Barbaresco Martinenga ★★☆ £F
Langhe Virtus ★★ £E
Langhe Villa Martis ★★ £E Monferrato Merlot da Solo ★★ £E
Dolcetto d'Alba Monte Aribaldo ★ £B
Recommended Whites:
Langhe Sauvignon ★★ £C Langhe Chardonnay ★ £C
Langhe Chardonnay Grésy ★ £E

Franco M Martinetti (Barbera d'Asti) *www.francomartinetti.it*
A string of good vintages of Barbera (Montruc) and Barbera/ Cabernet (Sul Bric) have been made. These are powerful, concentrated reds with breadth and refinement. They are characterised by the seamless quality of their tannins whilst capable of ageing for a decade or more from top vintages. Whites are impressive too. Minaia, once again being sold as Gavi, is very classy for this generally overrated appellation; Martin, from the obscure local variety Timorasso, offers ripe pear, quince, citrus peel and exotic fruits – both are *barrique*-aged, ripe, concentrated and sophisticated. Marasco (named for the Marasco cherry), a Barolo blended from the sites in the Barolo commune, has been made since 1997 and is very modern and seductive yet not superficial. The appealing fruity Banditi Barbera is one for everyday. Recent additions include fine, modern examples of Croatina (Georgette) and Freisa (Lauren) as well as ripe-fruited, toasty metodo classico sparkling wine, Quarantatre from Chardonnay and Pinot Nero. New Langhe Nebbiolo (Siccis Omnia Dura Deus Proposuit) and a late harvest Timorasso (Alcedo) complete the range.
Recommended Reds:
Barolo Marasco ★★★★ £F
Barbera d'Asti Superiore Montruc ★★★★ £E
Barbera d'Asti Bric dei Banditi ★☆ £C
Monferrato Sulbric ★★★★ £E
Colli Tortonesi Georgette ★★☆ £E
Colli Tortonesi Lauren ★★☆ £E
Recommended Whites:
Colli Tortonesi Martin ★★★☆ £E
Gavi Minaia ★★★ £D

Bartolo Mascarello (Barolo)
Bartolo Mascarello died in March 2005, one of the great stalwarts of classic traditionally styled Barolo, he made wines without concession to the modernists. Recent vintages have increasingly been made by Bartolo's daughter, Maria Teresa. Not for wimps, these are always powerful, broad and firmly tannic yet harmonious and superbly expressive wines with age. Don't even think about drinking it young or indeed at all if only the modern style appeals. 10–15 years' age is usually a minimum. Barbera and Dolcetto are also sturdy but balanced and *terroir*-derived. Bartolo's 1996 Barolo featured the controversial 'No Barrique No Berlusconi' label that is now a collector's item worldwide. 97, 98 and 2000 should just be approachable now.

Recommended Reds:
Barolo ★★★★★ £F Barbera d'Alba Vigna San Lorenzo ★★ £D
Dolcetto d'Alba Monrobiolo e Rué ★★ £C

✿ **Giuseppe Mascarello & Figlio (Barolo)** *www.mascarello1881.com*
Monprivato is one of the great crus of Castiglione Falletto and the entire Barolo zone. Superbly situated, its 6 ha face south-west at around 280m. The wines in the best years combine superb fruit quality with an effortless structure and balance. A Riserva Ca' d' Morissio, first produced in 1993, is made only from the Michet subvariety of Nebbiolo and undergoes longer ageing in large oak. Mauro, now aided by his son Giuseppe (first names are passed from grandfather to grandson in Piedmont) also makes very small amounts of Barolo from nearby Bricco and Villero as well as Santo Stefano di Perno. Barbera and Dolcetto show great character and extract and benefit from bottle-age. Barbera Codamonte (from the Codana vineyard, which adjoins Monprivato) is from old vines, as is Scudetto, a selection from Santo Stefano di Perno. Langhe Status is Nebbiolo with a little Barbera and Freisa added in. Langhe Freisa can show all the style and intensity possible from this variety if braced by abundant fine tannin.
Recommended Reds:
Barolo Monprivato ★★★★★ £G
Barolo Riserva Ca' d' Morissio ★★★★★ £G
Barolo Villero ★★★★ £F
Barolo Bricco ★★★ £F
Barolo Santo Stefano di Perno ★★★ £E
Barbera d'Alba Scudetto ★★★ £D
Barbera d'Alba Codamonte ★★★ £D
Barbera d'Alba Santo Stefano di Perno ★★ £D
Langhe Status ★★ £C Langhe Freisa Toetto ★★ £C
Langhe Nebbiolo ★ £C
Dolcetto d'Alba Bricco ★★ £C
Dolcetto d'Alba Santo Stefano di Perno ★★ £C

✿ **Massolino (Barolo)** *www.massolino.it*
One of Langhe's best traditional producers, based around one of her top crus – Vigna Rionda. Barolos tend to show a more typical Nebbiolo colour than from those who use lots of new oak and can be deceptive and difficult to assess in their youth. Plump and flattering they are not, but the breadth and length is apparent even when young and the tight, intense core builds with age to give fullness and a marvellous complexity after a decade or so. Margheria is intense and tannic, with a certain elegance. Parafada, a more modern style with a short but high-temperature maceration and partial *barrique*-ageing, adds more breadth and weight allied to great length. Vigna Rionda Riserva, subject to a 3-week maceration, can show still more fullness, depth and complexity. More recently acqired Parussi vineyard in Castiglione Falletto, completes the Barolo range, but this has not been tasted. *Barriques* are also used for Barbera and Chardonnay. These are good examples of their type, particularly the Barbera d'Alba Gisep.
Recommended Reds:
Barolo Riserva Vigna Rionda ✪✪✪✪✪ £G
Barolo Margheria ★★★★★ £F
Barolo Parafada ★★★★★ £F
Barolo ★★★★ £E Barbera d'Alba Gisep ★★★ £D
Dolcetto d'Alba Barilot ★★ £C
Langhe Piria ★★ £E
Langhe Nebbiolo ★ £C

Recommended Whites:
Langhe Chardonnay ★★ £C

Moccagatta (Barbaresco) *www.moccagatta.eu*
The Minuto brothers are a reliable source for good modern-style wines. From 12 ha of vineyards, Barbarescos are ripe and intense but with a certain style and elegance too. Cole shows the most structure and dimension, while Balin is the most supple but there is little to choose between them. All deserve to be kept for 5–10 years. Dolcetto is more of a quaffing wine but the *barrique*-fermented and aged version of Chardonnay is increasingly good and will keep a year or two.
Recommended Reds:
Barbaresco Basarin ★★★ £F
Barbaresco Bric Balin ★★★ £E
Barbaresco Cole ★★★ £E   Barbera d'Alba ★ £C
Dolcetto d'Alba ★ £B
Recommended Whites:
Langhe Chardonnay Buschet ★★ £D   Langhe Chardonnay ★ £B

Mauro Molino (Barolo) *www.mauromolino.com*
Though based in the Annunziata part of La Morra, Mauro Molino, recently assisted by his son, Matteo, also has a few rows of vines in Monforte. As with other Altare disciples, short maceration times and *barrique*-aging are employed but the fruit quality he gets after more than a decade of being at it full-time makes for good Barolo. Of the three crus, it is considered that the higher calcareous content of Gancia gives rise to its firmer tannic structure and Conca shows real weight and complexity in addition to fine aromatic character. Galinotto, from the western side of the hill, displays more subtlety and finesse, but woiuld still need at least 6 years cellaring. He is also not alone in planting Chardonnay where the Piedmontese red grapes simply don't work. Accanzio is mostly Barbera and Nebbiolo.
Recommended Reds:
Barolo Vigna Conca ★★★★ £F
Barolo Gancia ★★★★ £F
Barolo Galinotto ★★★★ £F
Barolo ★★★ £E
Barbera d'AlbaGattere ★★★ £D
Barbera d'Alba ★ £C
Langhe Accanzio ★★ £D
Dolcetto d'Alba ★★ £B
Recommended Whites:
Langhe Chardonnay Livrot ★★ £C

Monti (Barolo) *www.paolomonti.it*
Pier Paolo Monti is an emerging grower in Monforte d'Alba, having established a patchwork of vineyards as recently as 1996. 1999 was the first vintage of Barolo Bussia and a second Barolo (from Le Coste) has been made from 2006. After a relatively short fermentation Bussia spends 1 year in *barrique* (50% new) and another in *botti* grandi. The resulting wine is lush yet powerful, missing the extra depth and dimension possible from this site but with a certain style and promise. Barbera is formulated from two different vineyards, one with 40-year-old vines. The 16 ha of vineyards also include plantings of Merlot and Cabernet Sauvignon which are combined with 20% Nebbiolo in a *barrique*-aged Langhe red, Dossi Rossi, which promises individuality and complexity. A Langhe Merlot and a Nebbiolo d'Alba is also produced. In the white, L'Aura, 30% Riesling is added to Chardonnay fermented and aged in *barrique*. While unusual it is fresh and flavoursome with ripe peach/nectarine fruit

and reasonable structure if modest depth.
Recommended Reds:
Barolo Bussia ★★★★ £F
Barolo ★★★ £E
Barbera d'Alba ★★ £D   Langhe Rosso Dossi Rossi ★★ £D
Recommended Whites:
Langhe Bianco L'Aura ★★ £C

Morgassi Superiori (Gavi) *www.morgassisuperiore.it*
If you're desperate to drink Gavi here is another good source. New to wine, Marino Piacitelli and his daughter only set themselves up here in 1991. While Gavi has been the main thrust of production from what is now 20 ha of vineyards, small quantities of other interesting whites and reds are also made. The regular Gavi has plenty of direct spicy pear and herb fruit while the Etichetta Oro (gold label) shows an oak influence and is lightly creamy but well-balanced. Also good is Timorgasso (from Timorasso) with intense ripe fruit including guava, and lovely breadth and depth seemingly typical of the lightly exotic quality of this variety. Other wines, identified by vineyard source (several were named for characters from Mozart's operas) include Cherubino (Viognier) and reds, Tamino (Syrah) and Sarastro (Barbera, Cabernet Sauvignon) that do best in top vintages.
Recommended Reds:
Tamino ★★ £D   Monferrato Rosso Sarastro ★★ £C
Recommended Whites:
Gavi di Gavi Etichetta Oro ★★★ £C
Gavi di Gavi ★★☆ £C
Monferrato Timorgasso ★★★ £C

Fiorenzo Nada (Barbaresco) *www.nada.it*
Bruno Nada (Fiorenzo's son) runs a small operation from just 7 ha. The fruit quality and intensity resulting from much diligence in the vineyard is, with some assistance from Giuseppe Caviola (CA'VIOLA), harnessed into fine, elegant yet structured reds that add richness with age. Rombone, a potentially great cru, faces south-west; the Nadas' superior selection from these slopes is aged in *barriques* but evolves into a very refined classy example with 5–10 years' age. Seifile, a Barbera/ Nebbiolo blend also gets the small oak treatment and is characterised by its complexity and fruit intensity. Dolcetto and Barbera, the latter of which sees some oak, are ripe-fruited but could sometimes use a little more weight. An estate that deserves to be better known.
Recommended Reds:
Barbaresco Rombone ★★★★ £F
Barbaresco ★★★ £E   Langhe Seifile ★★★ £F
Barbera d'Alba ★☆ £D
Dolcetto d'Alba ★☆ £C

Angelo Negro & Figli (Roero) *www.negroangelo.it*
Giovanni Negro's Roero estate is one of the appellation's leaders. While half of the 50 odd ha are planted to Arneis, it is the Barbera and Nebbiolo that have really forged a reputation for this family. The top wine, Sudisfà, is deep and powerful with ripe, smooth tannins but there is good quality throughout the reds. Good examples of Arneis are also produced, a fresh slightly spicy regular version contrasts with fuller more characterful single-vineyard Gianat and Perdaudin examples. A small amount of grapes for the latter are dried for a sweet version. In addition to those below, Birbet (Brachetto), and Favorita are also made. Bric Millon is a promising new red based on Croatina but includes some Barbera and Cabernet Sauvignon.

Piedmont

Italy

Recommended Reds:

Roero Sudisfà ★★★ £D   Roero ★★ £C

Roero Prachiosso ★★ £C   Barbera d'Alba Bric Bertu ★★★ £C

Barbera d'Alba Nicolon ★★ £C

Recommended Whites:

Perdaudin Passito ★★★ £D   Roero Arneis ★★ £C

Roero Arneis Gianat ★★ £C

Roero Arneis Perdaudin ★★ £C

Andrea Oberto (Barolo) *www.andreaoberto.com*

The father and son team of Andrea and Fabio Oberto make excellent examples of Barbera, Dolcetto and Barolo. Previously operating from rather cramped cellars they moved into new winery premises in 2003. Rotofermenters have been used since 2000 but maceration times are moderate rather than short. Andrea Oberto initially made his name with Barbera, especially for the very rich, ripe *barrique*-aged Giada (from 60–70-year-old vines), though even the regular version is based on relatively old vines and is decidedly good value. New oak is used for all the Barolos as well as Fabio, a 60/40 Nebbiolo/Barbera blend. Barolo Rocche, from a parcel directly below SCAVINO's, is a lovely example of the cru, with its unique perfumed, floral character around a deep fruit core. Delicious cru Dolcetto will keep a year or two.

Recommended Reds:

Barolo Vigneto Albarella ★★★★ £F

Barolo Rocche ★★★★ £F

Barolo Brunate ★★★★ £F   Barolo ★★★ £E

Langhe Rosso Fabio ★★★ £D

Barbera d'Alba Giada ★★★ £D

Barbera d'Alba ★★ £C   Dolcetto d'Alba Vantrino Albarella ★★ £C

Dolcetto d'Alba ★ £B

Oddero (Barolo) *www.oddero.it*

The Odderos are long-time vineyard owners, and the very significant 60 ha, a proportion of it in some of Barolo's most notable crus, run for some years by brothers Giacomo and Luigi Oddero, was split in 2006, with Luigi moving out to establish VIGNETI LUIGI ODDERO E FIGLI just down the road. Since Luigi's passing in 2009, the estate has been run by his widow, Lena. The two wines we have tasted from this estate are listed in the "other wines of note" section and will be more fully reviewed in the future. Giacomo has retained the original label, and now aided by his daughters, Mariecristina and Mariavittoria, are continuing to enhance the reputastion of the estate. (Mondoca di) Bussia Soprana (from Monforte) and Vigna Rionda (Serralunga) are now starting to realise their true potential – they had a tendency to be rather rustic and rugged in the past. Some input from leading consultant Donato Lanati has helped. Vineyards less suited to Nebbiolo have been planted to Barbera, Dolcetto and even Cabernet (Furesté is 100% Cabernet from La Morra vineyards) and Chardonnay (Collaretto). If the wines remain reasonably priced, this promises to be a good label for characterful, structured, and widely available, Barolo – but stick to the crus as regular bottlings are a bit dull.

Recommended Reds:

Barolo Mondoca di Bussia Soprana ★★★ £E

Barolo Rocche di Castiglione ★★★ £E

Barolo Vigna Rionda ★★★ £E

Langhe Furesté ★★ £D

Recommended Whites:

Langhe Chardonnay Collaretto ★ £C

Orsolani (Erbaluce di Caluso) *www.orsolani.it*

Orsolani has become the main proponent of the Erbaluce grape and the small zone created for it north of Torino. Around half of 15 ha on glacial morraine are owned and in recent vintages the wines have shown greater consistency and quality. La Rustìa is now the name for a tangy dry version with a lightly herbal spice and dried peach character. Vignot Sant'Antonio is more concentrated with some *barrique* influence. The top wine though is Sulé (since 1995; previously sold as La Rustìa), a rich, sweet, honeyed version of Erbaluce made from dried grapes and fermented in *barriques* before spending three years in barrels. Carema (from Nebbiolo), while relatively light, shows some promise. There's also vintage-dated metodo classico sparkling wine from Erbaluce that is perfumed, intense and off-dry with lively acidity.

Recommended Reds:

Carema Le Tabbie ★ £D

Recommended Whites:

Caluso Passito Sulé ★★★ £E

Caluso Spumante Brut Cuvée Tradionale ★★☆ £D

Erbaluce di Caluso Vignot Sant' Antonio ★★ £C

Erbaluce di Caluso La Rustìa ★★ £B

Paitin (Barbaresco) *www.paitin.it*

The Pasquero-Elia have 17 ha of vineyards incorporating part of the cru of Serraboella (next to CIGLIUTI). There was acclaim for their Barbaresco back in the 1980s and after the difficult early 90s, quality has taken another step forward. Dense and firm when young, though increasingly accessible too, it promises a lovely style and complexity with 8–10 years' age. Other wines are made to high standards too: in the Langhe red, Paitin, a little Cabernet and Syrah are now added to Barbera and Nebbiolo in a sleek *barrique*-aged blend. Barbera, especially Campolive, and Dolcetto show a touch of class too. A white Campolive is from Sauvignon and Chardonnay while Roero Arneis (Vigna Elisa) is also made.

Recommended Reds:

Barbaresco Sorì Paitin ★★★★ £E

Langhe Paitin ★★★ £D

Barbera d'Alba Campolive ★★★ £D

Barbera d'Alba Serra Boella ★★ £D

Dolcetto d'Alba Sorì Paitin ★★ £C

Nebbiolo d'Alba Ca'Veja ★ £C

✿ Parusso (Barolo) *www.parusso.com*

From 20 ha of vineyards Marco Parusso fashions a high-quality range of wines that continues to improve. Vinification and ageing are modern: 24 months in new French *barriques* for the Barolos (30 months for the riserve), though oak rarely dominates the top examples. Barolo Bussia, is now a blend of Vigna Munie, Vigna Rocche and Vigna Fiurin. The two riserva wines, Oro and Argento, spend an extra 6 months in *barrique* and 6 months in bottle and are only produced in the best vintage years. Le Coste Mosconi, first released in 2003, is dark, brooding and muscular. There is a weight and depth to go with their evident style, complexity and length on the palate. They are a step up from the less expensive but perfumed, occasionally oaky but classy Mariondino and supple, very attractive fruit-filled Barolo DOGC produced from vineyards in the Monforte d'Alba and Castiglione Fallertto villages. Other wines include excellent Barberas (the superior Superiore is from old vines) and a Langhe Nebbiolo, usually one of the very best examples of elegant, accessible Nebbiolo. For white, two versions of Sauvignon are produced, a nettly unoaked example and the riper, richer Bricco

Rovella which is *barrique*-aged.

Recommended Reds:

Barolo Riserva Oro ★★★★★ £G

Barolo Riserva Argento ★★★★★ £G

Barolo Bussia ★★★★★ £F   Barolo Mariondino ★★★★ £F

Barolo Le Coste Mosconi ★★★★ £F

Barolo ★★★ £E

Barbera d'Alba Superiore ★★★★ £E

Barbera d'Alba Ornati ★★★ £C

Langhe Nebbiolo ★★ £C

Dolcetto d'Alba Piani Noce ★★ £B

Recommended Whites:

Langhe Bianco Bricco Rovella ★★ £D   Langhe Bianco ★★ £C

Agostino Pavia (Barbera d'Asti) *www.agostinopavia.it*

There are many good sources of Barbera d'Asti from the hills south of Asti, but this grower from Agliano Terme (west of Nizza Monferrato) offers real value too. Giuseppe and Mauro Pavia work with their father on 8.5 ha of established vineyard (most vines are over 60 years) to give stylish, ripe fruited Barberas that have plenty of substance and excellent balance. All are very reasonably priced from unwooded Bricco Blina that opens out nicely with 2-4 years' age, through Moliss (mostly aged in large oak), with more depth and substance, to an ambitious *barrique*-aged La Marescialla version with good harmony, richness and ageing potential. There's not much other than Barbera but what there is includes Grignolino d'Asti.

Recommended Reds:

Barbera d'Asti Superiore La Marescialla ★★★☆ £C

Barbera d'Asti Superiore Moliss ★★★ £C

Barbera d'Asti Bricco Blina ★★☆ £B

Pecchenino (Dolcetto di Dogliani) *www.pecchenino.com*

Brothers Orlando and Attilio go to great lengths in order to make making better and better Dolcetto at this 25 ha estate. This means not just powerful concentrated examples but increasingly, with the aid of micro-oxygenation, Dolcetto with finer textures and less obtrusive structures. Of the dense yet succulent Dolcettos, fruit-rich San Luigi is unoaked, the classy Sirì d'Jermu sees some used oak and half the Bricco *Botti* is aged in new oak. The *barrique*-aged Langhe red, La Castella is based on Barbera but includes 30% Nebbiolo. There is also Quass, a lush, toasty oaky but well-balanced varietal Barbera, as well as vineyard holdings in Monforte d'Alba, where Barolo Le Coste is produced at San Guiseppe and in Bussia, where the Bussia Corsin cru will be released. A solitary white, Vigna Maestro is Chardonnay-based. Prices are proportionate

Recommended Reds:

Dolcetto di Dogliani Superiore Bricco Botti ★★★☆ £D

Dolcetto di Dogliani Siri d'Jermu ★★★☆ £C

Dolcetto di Dogliani San Luigi ★★☆ £C

Piemonte Barbera Quass ★★★ £C

Langhe Nebbiolo Vigna Botti ★ £D

Recommended Whites:

Langhe Vigna Maestro ★ £C

Pelissero (Barbaresco) *www.pelissero.com*

Under Giorgio Pelissero, quality at this 38-ha estate has soared dramatically in recent years. At its heart is Vanotu, a vineyard at the intersection of Barbaresco's three main communes and the source of an increasingly complex and stylish Barbaresco. It spends 18 months in mostly new oak but this is increasingly well-integrated into a rich, ripe fruit core. In 2004 a Riserva was produced from this vineyard to celebrate the first 50 years of the activity of the estate. It has not subsequently been produced. Another Barbaresco, from the Tulin vineyard, has been produced since 2001 as a separate cru from that which went into thr regular Barbaresco beforehand. Wine from the remaining plots are now bottled under the label Nubiola which is attractive with good substance and reasonable depth. There's plenty of fruit in Dolcetto too, especially Augenta – a vibrant, perfumed and expressive example of the grape. Barbera is ripe and long while Langhe Nebbiolo shows a fine preserved raspberry fruit intensity. Barbera and Nebbiolo are harmoniously combined in 'Long Now' – named for the Long Now Foundation clock (www.longnow.org) – a modern, oaky example of this blend. A reserve Barbera, from the Tulin vineyard was first produced in 2009 from vines planted in 2004. Freisa (a lightly fizzy style), and two Moscatos, (one a DOGC and a lighter one named "Mosto Parzialmente Fermentato" are also made together with a racy blend of Nebbiolo, Barbera and Dolcetto called "La Nature Vino Rosso Barlet" for easy drinking.

Recommended Reds:

Barbaresco Vanotu ★★★★ £F

Barbaresco Tulin ★★★★ £F

Barbaresco Nubiola ★★★ £E

Langhe Long Now★★★ £D

Langhe Nebbiolo ★★ £C

Barbera d'Alba Piani★★ £D

Barbera d'Alba Tulin★★ £D

Dolcetto d'Alba Munfrina★★ £C

Dolcetto d'Alba Augenta★★ £C

Elio Perrone (Moscato d'Asti) *www.elioperrone.it*

Stefano Perrone has long produced two of the finest examples of Moscato d'Asti going. But thanks to the acquisition of small plots of Barbera vines in the late 90s, recently there has been much more, particularly in the shape of an outstanding Barbera d'Asti from 70 year old vines. Around 5000 bottles are made of Mongovone, a brilliant Barbera with marvellous fruit quality and richness allied to freshness and balance. From another plot of vines is produced another fine Barbera, Grivò which is considerably cheaper yet with good substance and structure too. At a simpler level is a new Barbera d'Asti Tasmorcan that is cool and expressive. The Moscatos continue to scintillate. Both Clarté and Sourgal (made in the greater volumes) are a joy to drink with all the delicacy, balance and fusion of floral and yellow stone fruit characters that can make this such a marvellous light sweet wine for immediate consumption (as always, drink from the most recent vintage). The unusual Bigarò combines Brachetto and Moscato with similar skill and is intense and expressive with a red rosé and red fruits interplay. All are wines not to be missed.

Recommended Reds:

Barbera d'Asti Superiore Mongovone ★★★★ £D

Barbera d'Asti Grivò ★★★ £C

Barbera d'Asti Tasmorcan ★★ £C

Bigarò ★★☆ £C   Dolcetto d'Alba Giuljin ★★ £B

Recommended Whites:

Moscato d'Asti Clarté ★★★ £B

Moscato d'Asti Sourgal ★★★ £B

Pio Cesare (Barolo) *www.piocesare.it*

Cesare Pio established this house in the 19th century and its success as a commerciante or négociant make it a well-known name. Direction now comes from Pio Boffa whose recent vineyard

Piedmont

Italy

acquisitions bring the estate holdings to over 50 ha but has long included the prized Il Bricco and Ornato crus. The two wines produced from these sites, Barbaresco and Barolo respectively, can show real depth and a certain stylishness together with the propensity to age. Regular Barbaresco is increasingly good too. Barbera Fides and Chardonnay Piodilei absorb a good measure of oak but consistently show depth and character too. On the downside Dolcetto, regular Barbera, Nebbiolo and Arneis, and even the house Barolo could still be better.

Recommended Reds:

Barolo Ornato ★★★★ £G   Barolo ★★ £F
Barbaresco Il Bricco ★★★★ £F   Barbaresco ★★★ £E
Barbera d'Alba Fides ★★ £D

Recommended Whites:

Langhe Chardonnay Piodilei ★★ £D
Piemonte Chardonnay L'Altro ★ £C

E Pira & Figli (Barolo) *www.pira-chiaraboschis.com*

Chiara Boschis assumed control of this old Barolo producer in 1990. The prize here is 2.5 ha of Cannubi and recent efforts display tremendous class. There is impressive complexity and considerable elegance and purity that reflect its origins. The wines build in richness and depth with age and despite the use of new oak there is an underlying structure that demands cellaring. Recent vintages have been very good and suggest an even higher rating in the future. From a further 0.5 ha is a second Barolo, Via Nuova (also in the Barolo commune) which shows similar dimension if not the class or complexity of Cannubi. Barbera shows increasing style and purity and is best with three years' age or more. In 2009 Chiara acquired a further 4 ha vineyard, Conterni, at Monforte d'Alba. producing a Nebbiolo d'Alba wine and a new Barolo cru, Mosconi, from it.

Recommended Reds:

Barolo Cannubi ★★★★★ £G   Barolo Via Nuova ★★★★ £F
Barbera d'Alba ★★ £D   Dolcetto d'Alba ★ £C

⚫ **Luigi Pira (Barolo)** *www.piraluigi.it*

Giampaolo Pira, lately working with Giuseppe Caviola has quickly established his family's Serralunga estate as one of the very best in the whole region. He together with his brother, Romolo, and father, Luigi, have just 12 ha of vineyard. Since 1995 he has further underlined the potential of Serralunga with excellent wines from the Marenca, Margheria and (since 1997) Vigna Rionda crus. Having cut yields and modified the vinification, he is now producing dense, structured Barolos that are extremely concentrated and powerful with great cellaring potential. A mix of *barriques*, tonneaux (both new and used) and large wood is used; Vigneto Margheria sees 60% new oak, while the minute quantities of Vigna Rionda receive 100% new oak. Both deserve 10 years' cellaring. A tiny amount of Langhe Nebbiolo is also made, with a seductive fruit and texture that more examples should show. Unoaked Dolcetto is good too.

Recommended Reds:

Barolo Vigna Rionda ★★★★★ £G
Barolo Margheria ★★★★☆ £F
Barolo Marenca ★★★★☆ £F
Barolo Serralunga ★★★★ £F
Langhe Nebbiolo ★★★ £E   Dolcetto d'Alba ★★ £C

Ferdinando Principiano (Barolo) *www.ferdinandopricipiano.it*

Thanks to his dad, young Ferdinando has 10 ha of well-tended, mostly old vines in the south-eastern corner of the Barolo zone

to work with. With some help from Giuseppe Caviola, the wines from the most recent vintages are really starting to shine. The main Barolo is the Boscareto cru, adjacent to Cascina Francia of GIACOMO CONTERNO in the south of the Serralunga commune. This can be a wine of great character, complexity (including woodsmoke and truffles) and structure too. The same cru also provides half the Barbera for La Romualda – the rest coming from the celebrated Barbera vineyard Pian Romualdo (see PRUNOTTO). Rich, ripe and lush with old-vine blackberry fruit, it is best with at least two or three years' age. A previously designated Barolo, Le Coste (from Monforte d'Alba), has now been declassified to produce a Langhe Nebbiolo with a small percentage of grapes coming from Boscareto as well. Two other Barolos are now produced, the entry level Serralunga, though less powerful than Boscareto shows good balance and intensity and Ravera, from the old Michet clone on 50 year old vines, with more intensity and grip, aged for 24 months in 400 litre barrels. A second Barbewra d'Alba, "Laura," a Langhe Freisa "Chila" and a tiny amount of Late Harvest Moscato, "Leo" is also made.

Recommended Reds:

Barolo Boscareto ★★★★☆ £F   Barolo Ravera ★★★★ £F
Barolo Serralunga ★★★☆ £F   Langhe Nebbiolo Coste ★★★☆ £E
Barbera d'Alba La Romualda ★★★ £D
Dolcetto d'Alba Sant'Anna ★ £B

Prunotto (Barolo) *www.prunotto.it*

One of the best known names from the Langhe – and that was before ANTINORI (see Tuscany) took over. Once a traditional commerciante, Prunotto now owns an increasing percentage of the vineyard sources and there is some use of 500-litre French oak. Yet stylistically Antinori seem to be building on the legacy of the celebrated Beppe Colla rather than imposing a new order. A consistent and not excessively priced range is headed by the crus Barolo Bussia and Cannubi. At least something of the harmony and balance, if not the concentration or size of these Barolos can be seen in nearly all the wines. Noted Barbera d'Alba Pian Romualdo has recently been surpassed by the super Barbera d'Asti Costamiole, albeit with a considerable price differential. A Monferrato Rosso "Mompertone" made from 60% Barbera and 40% Syrah is also made but not tasted.

Recommended Reds:

Barolo Bussia ★★★★☆ £F
Barolo Cannubi ★★★★☆ £F
Barbaresco Bric Turot ★★★☆ £F
Barolo ★★★☆ £E
Barbaresco ★★☆ £E   Barbera d'Asti Costamiole ★★★★ £E
Barbera d'Asti Fiulot ★★ £C
Barbera d'Alba Pian Romualdo ★★★☆ £C
Barbera d'Alba ★☆ £B   Nebbiolo d'Alba Occhetti ★★☆ £C
Dolcetto d'Alba Mosesco ★★ £B
Dolcetto d'Alba ★☆ £B

Recommended Whites:

Moscato d'Asti ★☆ £B   Roero Arneis ★☆ £B

Renato Ratti (Barolo) *www.renatoratti.com*

Renato Ratti was one of the key modernisers in Barolo in the 80s. Now under the direction of Pietro Ratti a new cellar has been built and some outside consultancy sought to give a renewed boost to quality. There are now 35 ha of vines include the 'Marcenasco' vineyards in La Morra and vineyards in the Asti and Monferrato hills. Barolos can at times lack a little weight and richness yet have an understated charm and personality. Production of Conca was only

resumed in 98, after replanting. Villa Pattono, a blend of Barbera (at least half) with Cabernet and Merlot is much more showy, with a succulent, almost creamy, ripe red and black fruit character. Barbera d'Alba and other wines including a Sauvignon Blanc "I Cedri" show good intense fruit and sound structure. Since 2009 a new Barbera d'Asti has been produced showing the hallmark richness of the wines from this estate.

Recommended Reds:

Barolo Conca Marcenasco ★★★☆ £F
Barolo Rocche Marcenasco ★★★☆ £F
Barolo Marcenasco ★★★ £F   Monferrato Villa Pattono ★★★ £D
Barbera d'Alba ★★ £C   Barbera d'Asti ★★ £C
Dolcetto d'Alba Colombè ★★ £B

Fratelli Revello (Barolo)   *www.revellofratelli.com*

Revello, with 11 ha of vineyards, represents a softer face to Barolo with almost unbelievably short maceration times (albeit in rotofermenters) and plenty of new oak. There's no denying the wines' accessibility and upfront fruit appeal when very young but there's not the depth or structure of the very best despite some firm tannins beneath the fruit. It is possible that they age quite well but not much gets the chance given the fruit charm and lush immediacy of the wines. It does feel slightly as if we've been given the icing minus the cake yet despite these reservations the wines broaden Nebbiolo's appeal. However there is more depth and substance in recent vintages. Regular Barbera and Dolcetto are aged in stainless steel but the small quantities of an explosively fruity Barbera d'Alba Ciabot du Re (from 25-year-old vines) spend 16 months in *barrique*. The Revellos' Insieme (see ALTARE) now includes a little Petit Verdot along with the Nebbiolo, Barbera and Cabernet Sauvignon. A further Barolo, from the Gattera cru, was first produced in 1999.

Recommended Reds:

Barolo Vigna Giachini ★★★☆ £F
Barolo Rocche dell'Annunziata ★★★☆ £F
Barolo Vigna Gattera ★★★☆ £F
Barolo Vigna Conca ★★★☆ £F
Barolo ★★ £F   Insieme ★★★ £F
Barbera d'Alba Ciabot du Re ★★★ £E
Barbera d'Alba ★ £C   Dolcetto d'Alba ★ £B

✿ Giuseppe Rinaldi (Barolo)

Giuseppe Rinaldi took up the reins here in 1992 and has continued a staunchly traditional approach to winemaking. This means open-topped fermenters, punching down by hand, long macerations and 3 years or more in *botti* grandi. The resulting wines stand in stark contrast to the modern style of Barolo, being not in the least bit immediate or fruit-rich. Nor are they meant to be drunk young but rather with the splendid complexity that comes with at least 15 years' age. However, if you do taste them young they can still be splendidly perfumed with superb texture, dimension and class, especially the more widely seen Brunate-Le Coste (an equal blend of the two sites). All top vintages represent a fine candidates for cellaring. The second Barolo, from a parcel within Cannubi called San Lorenzo combined with fruit from Ravera, is likely to be more austere but has similar ageing potential. Barbera and Dolcetto are also made but just a few hundred cases of each.

Recommended Reds:

Barolo Brunate-Le Coste ★★★★★ £G
Barolo Cannubi San Lorenzo-Ravera ★★★★☆ £F

Albino Rocca (Barbaresco)   *www.albinorocca.com*

Angelo Rocca died in a plane crash in 2012, but his daughters, Daniela, Monica and Paola with son-in-law Carlo, has continued to tend the 23 ha estate, making two contrasting and very good Barbarescos. The richer, more lush but also more structured Brich Ronchi, made in greater quantities, receives the new *barrique* treatment, while Loreto, aged only in large oak, is a more pure, elegant expression of Nebbiolo. A Ronchi Riserva aged for 46 months in large 20 hl German oak casks is occasionally made s well. Barbera is also first class here; in the modern *barrique*-aged mould it shows better depth and balance than most. The white Piemonte, La Rocca is a *barrique*-aged Cortese and is better than most Gavi while a Chardonnay shows the gently spicy ripe fruit characteristic of many Piedmont Chardonnay if not much more. All are reasonably priced.

Recommended Reds:

Barbaresco Vigneto Brich Ronchi ★★★★ £F
Barbaresco Vigneto Loreto ★★★★ £E
Barbera d'Alba Gèpin ★★★ £D
Dolcetto d'Alba Vignalunga ★★ £C

Recommended Whites:

Piemonte Cortese La Rocca ★★ £D
Langhe Chardonnay Da Bertü ★ £B

✿ Bruno Rocca (Barbaresco)   *www.brunorocca.it*

The name Rabajà, one of Barbaresco's leading crus, derives from Bruno Rocca's original family estate and accounts for 5ha of vineyards. From it Bruno Rocca makes an excellent modern interpretation. His Barbaresco Rabajà is ripe, concentrated with impressive breadth as well as a more restrained oak character and better depth over the last decade. A second Barbaresco, called Coparossa and made since 1995, includes grapes from the Fausoni and Pajorè crus and is increasingly good too if not quite at the level of Rabajà. There's fine quality from both these Barbaresco's, already anticipated in the more fruit-driven Langhe red Rabajolo (from Cabernet, Barbera and Nebbiolo). Of an expanding estate (now 15 ha in total), 3 ha in the highly rated Currà cru have recently been added and a third, straight Barbaresco has been produced since 2001. A fourth Barbaresco, is a Riserva "Maria Adelaide" made fromn a selection of the best grapes on the estate. Barbera, (d'Alba as well as d'Asti), Dolcetto and a Chardonnay are also very competently made.

Recommended Reds:

Barbaresco Coparossa ★★★★☆ £F
Barbaresco Rabajà ★★★★★ £G
Langhe Rabajolo ★★★ £E   Barbera d'Alba ★★★ £D
Dolcetto d'Alba Vigna Trifolè ★★ £B

Recommended Whites:

Langhe Chardonnay Cadet ★★ £C

Rocche Costamagna (Barolo)   *www.roccheco stamagna.it*

A solid and reasonably priced source of Langhe reds, the 15 ha Rocche Costamagna provides increasingly perfumed, fruit-driven and accessible examples of Nebbiolo, Barbera and Dolcetto. Alessandro Locatelli favours relatively short maceration times for most of the wines and now prefers a lowish fermentation temperature. The use of French *barriques* is restricted to Barbera production, new in the case of lush, vanilla infused Rocche delle Rocche, although a small part of the Langhe Nebbiolo also goes into *barriques*. Barolos get 2 years in Slavonian oak and are solid but bright and perfumed, best with at least 6-8 years' age.

Piedmont

Italy

Bricco Francesco, a superior selection, is now being produced every year and comes from the highest part of the large Rocche dell'Annunziata cru. As well as being picked later, a longer maceration is preferred as well resulting in more depth and extract. Langhe Arneis and a sparkling Nebbio are also made.

Recommended Reds:
Barolo Bricco Francesco ★★★★ £F
Barolo Rocche dell'Annunziata ★★★☆ £F
Barbera d'Alba Rocche delle Rocche ★★☆ £D
Barbera d'Alba Annunziata ★★ £C
Langhe Nebbiolo Roccardo ★★ £E
Dolcetto d'Alba Rubis ★★ £C
Dolcetto d'Alba Murrae ★☆ £C

Rocche dei Manzoni (Barolo) *www.roccheimanzoni.it*
Production here, from in excess of 40 ha spread over four separate estates, is quite substantial by the usual standard for a Piedmont grower. The imposing and well-financed cellar turns out modern, bold and oaky wines that are good examples of their type. Of an ever-expanding range of Barolos, Cappella di Santo Stefano (made since 1996) is emerging with the most class and depth. Barolo Vigna Madonna Assunta La Villa is a reserve wine released only 10 years after the vintage thus the first release (1999 vintage) was only put onto the market in 2009. The relatively forward Bricco Manzoni combines Nebbiolo with Barbera while Quatr Nas is composed of Nebbiolo, Cabernet Sauvignon, Merlot and Pinot Nero, with its complex black fruits character and deceptively supple texture and plenty of underlying substance. Pinònero is pure Pinot Nero. Chardonnay is oaky but distinctly Piemontese.

Recommended Reds:
Barolo Vigna d'la Roul ★★★★ £G
Barolo Cappella di Santo Stefano ★★★★ £F
Barolo Vigna Big 'de Big ★★★☆ £F   Barolo Rocche ★★★ £F
Langhe Rosso Quatr Nas ★★★★ £E
Langhe Rosso Bricco Manzoni ★★ £E
Langhe Rosso Pinònero ★ £E
Barbera d'Alba La Cresta ★★ £E
Barbera d'Alba Sorito Mosconi ★★ £D
Recommended Whites:
Langhe Chardonnay L'Angelica ★★ £E
Valentino Brut Riserva Elena ★ £E

✿ **Sandrone (Barolo)** *www.sandroneluciano.com*
Luciano Sandrone remains as progressive and open-minded as ever yet continues to bring out greatness of both place and grape. The vines are tended by Luciano's brother Luca. Barolos are always super with splendid complexity and terrific breadth on the palate but also balanced and harmonious, with great length and a fine tannic backbone. Maceration times are quite lengthy and 600-litre oak is favoured. More or less equal amounts are made of both the famous cru Cannubi Boschis and sometimes equally fine Le Vigne (blended from the Brunate, Bussia, Cerretta and Vignane crus). The wines generally are also expressive of the vintage, unlike others that are forced into the same mould each year. Sandrone's 16 ha also provide good fruit-rich expressions of Barbera and Dolcetto while Nebbiolo d'Alba is one of a relatively few decent examples of this appellation.

Recommended Reds:
Barolo Cannubi Boschis ✪✪✪✪✪ £H
Barolo Le Vigne ★★★★★ £H
Barbera d'Alba ★★★ £D
Nebbiolo d'Alba Valmaggiore ★★☆ £E

Dolcetto d'Alba ★★☆ £C

San Fereolo (Dolcetto di Dogliani) *www.sanfereolo.com*
As with most Dogliani producers the focus here is Dolcetto. The estate's 10 ha covers several different sites within the Valdibà subzone which is the name given to what has become the regular Dolcetto. The most important Dolcetto is the San Fereolo version now designated superiore. This consistently deep, dense Dolcetto, among the best of the zone or anywhere for that matter, seems to improve with every vintage. A small part of it is aged in new oak the rest in large Slavonian casks. Also made is a little of '1593' which sees 50% new oak - an attempt at producing a long-lived style. The vineyards also provide a rich, intense Barbera that is aged partly in new oak; until recently sold under the Langhe DOC as Brumaio but since 01 as Austri. Both *barriques* and the larger tonneaux are used. A few hundred bottles of a Langhe white, Coste del Riavolo from Gewürztraminer and Riesling are also made.

Recommended Reds:
Langhe Austri ★★★☆ £D
Dolcetto di Dogliani Superiore San Fereolo ★★★ £D
Dolcetto di Dogliani Valdibà ★★☆ £C

San Romano (Dolcetto di Dogliani) *www.sanromano.com*
Giuseppe Caviola makes excellent examples of Dolcetto di Dogliani by concentrating on low yields and top-quality fruit, also utilising a pre-fermentation maceration to bring more out of the fruit. The range is now just limited to two wines, a lightish example from the Bricco delle Lepre vineyard, which is surpassed by that sourced from Vigna del Pilone which is soft but with very good breadth and depth as well as plenty of extract, requiring a further 2 or 3 years' bottle-age.

Recommended Reds:
Dolcetto di Dogliani Vigna del Pilone ★★★ £C
Dolcetto di Dogliani Bricco delle Lepre ★★ £B

Saracco (Moscato d'Asti) *www.paolosaracco.it*
One of several producers making exquisite Moscato d'Asti (CAUDRINA, LA MORANDINA, LA SPINETTA and Elio PERRONE are others) that deserves to be better known in English-speaking countries. The superior bottling is the Moscato d'Autunno, a sweet concentrated example with a delightful fusion of floral and fruity scents, reflected to some extent in the lighter yet intense regular version. Saracco also make a good unoaked Chardonnay, Prasuè, ready to drink young. A Monferrato Bianco, Graffagno made from 100% Riesling, is minerally with good body. The only red coming from this estate is a silky Pinot Nero of medium intensity from the Bricco Quaglia vineyard, vinified in stainless steel, and then kept in large barrels for some 12-14 months, giving it some degree of complexity.

Recommended Reds:
Pinot Nero DOP ★★★ £C
Recommended Whites:
Piemonte Moscato d'Autunno ★★★ £B
Moscato d'Asti ★★ £B
Langhe Graffagno ★ £C
Langhe Chardonnay Prasuè ★ £B

✿ **Paolo Scavino (Barolo)** *www.paoloscavino.com*
Enrico Scavino, like CLERICO, SANDRONE and others who shot to prominence in the 1980s, has proved to be very successful and the premium prices are a reflection of the continued high

demand for his wines. He makes arguably the definitive example of Barolo Rocche dell'Annunziata, adding power and breadth to the cru's classic perfume. Also often superb, Cannubi and Bric del Fiasc show a little more of the structure indicative of their origins. Vineyard acquisitions on the slopes of Roddi in the very north of the Barolo zone has now led to a new Cru, Bricco Ambrogio, with vines planted over a period from 1965 to 2008, displaying a softness and suppleness combined with intensity of flavour. Another new cru, from 2007, previoiusly blended into the regular Barolo, is the Monvigliero, one of the top vineyards in Verduno, which shows elegance and class over power and intensity. Scavino, who works with his daughters Enrica and Elisa , has been a keen proponent of the use of new oak for ageing Nebbiolo though this includes both *barriques* and larger wood. Occasionally the wines have suffered from an excess of oak but recently there has been good balance. The Barbera now has many rivals but still rewards cellaring of at least 5–6 years. The Langhe Nebbiolo is vinified from two vineyards in La Morra which could be used for Barolo, but Scavino's decision to bottle early and create a wine for early drinking with nevertheless fine ageing potential with a good balance between fruit and acidity could put many a Barolo to shame. The white equivalent is Sorriso, from Chardonnay and Sauvignon.

Recommended Reds:
Barolo Riserva Rocche dell'Annunziata ★★★★★ £H
Barolo Bric del Fiasc ★★★★★ £G
Barolo Cannubi ★★★★☆ £G
Barolo Carobric ★★★★☆ £G
Barolo Bricco Ambrogio ★★★★☆ £G
Barolo Monvigliero ★★★★☆ £G   Barolo ★★★★ £F
Barbera d'Alba Affinato in Carati ★★★★ £E
Langhe Nebbiolo ★★★★ £E
Dolcetto d'Alba ★★ £C

Seghesio (Barolo) *www.fratelliseghesio.com*
Riccardo Seghesio is now at the helm, following brother Aldo's untimely death in 2010, but Aldo's two sons, Sandro and Marco, and his daughter Michaela, are now working full time with Riccardo. They make seductive, showy and accessible Barolo in the modern style, which somewhat belies their location in the Castelletto subzone of Monforte where the wines more often are noted for their structure and rigour. Perhaps there could be more in terms of stuffing yet apart from the slightly excessive oak it does have obvious appeal. An oaky but rich, deep Barbera works better and is similarly remarkably approachable. Bouquet, a blend of Nebbiolo, Cabernet and Merlot, is much in the same mould while ripe, fruity unoaked Barbera and Dolcetto are also made.

Recommended Reds:
Barolo Vigneto La Villa ★★★★ £F
Barbera d'Alba Vigneto della Chiesa ★★★ £D
Langhe Bouquet ★★ £D   Barbera d'Alba ★★ £C
Dolcetto d'Alba Vigneto della Chiesa ★★ £C

Sottimano (Barbaresco) *www.sottimano.it*
Sottimano is a still expanding estate with additional recent vineyard acquisitions of Barbaresco vineyards. Direction comes from Rino Sottimano but he is assisted by his son Andrea and the rest of his family. Significant improvements in quality continue to accrue from the recent run of top vintages. Small amounts (only a few thousand bottles of each) of ripe *barrique*-aged Barbaresco are made from the Cottà, Currà, Fausoni and Pajoré crus. All are well-structured with generally well-balanced tannins and alcohol and show good

complexity with 5 or 6 years' age or more and quality continues to improve. From a recently acquired vineyard, Basarin, in Nieve, they produce a Langhe Nebbiolo from young vines with the hope of upgrading to a Barbaresco cru as the vines mature. Barbera and Dolcetto also reflect the new standards being attained here. Maté is a dry, fruity Brachetto.

Recommended Reds:
Barbaresco Currà ★★★★ £F
Barbaresco Pajoré ★★★★ £F
Barbaresco Cottà ★★★ £F
Barbaresco Fausoni ★★★ £F
Barbera d'Alba Pairolero ★★★ £D
Dolcetto d'Alba Bric del Salto ★★ £C

⚜ G D Vajra (Barolo) *www.gdvajra.it*
A first-rate producer of the highest integrity based in the Vergne sub-zone of the Barolo commune. Those of Aldo Vaira's vines grown locally are at an altitude atypically high for Barolo. The protected, south-facing Bricco delle Viole ripens Nebbiolo with a distinctive floral, plum and cherry fruit character but equally a superiore Barbera of great vigour and intensity. This altitude suits Dolcetto too and the best grapes from two nearby plots, Coste di Vergne and Fossati, have long produced a magnificent spicy, earthy Dolcetto with intense black plum fruit. Wait at least 5 years for this or keep as long again – it will outlive many Barberas and a few Barolos too. Kyé is a wonderfully expressive and increasingly refined, powerful dry Freisa. Wood is used for ageing most wines, but almost exclusively large Slavonian oak. As a result the wines are not lush or soft but have both a varietal fruit intensity and a *terroir*-derived character. Great care goes into all wines with regular Dolcetto, Barbera and Nebbiolo lately showing better definition, intensity and style than many of the more pricey cru versions from other producers. A new wine is a Pinot Nero, Langhe DOC Rosso from vineyards considered too high for Nebbiolo. Whites are excellent too, Aldo's Langhe Riesling Petracine is a very pure perfumed Riesling, tinged with lime, while finely balanced Moscato thrills with delightful fruit nuances.

Recommended Reds:
Barolo Bricco delle Viole ★★★★☆ £F
Barolo Albe ★★★☆ £F
Dolcetto d'Alba Coste & Fossati ★★★★ £E
Dolcetto d'Alba ★★ £C   Barbera d'Alba Superiore ★★★ £D
Barbera d'Alba ★★☆ £C   Langhe Freisa Kyé ★★★ £D
Langhe Nebbiolo ★★☆ £C
Recommended Whites:
Moscato d'Asti ★★★ £C
Langhe Riesling Petracine ★★☆ £D

Mauro Veglio (Barolo) *www.mauroveglio.com*
ELIO ALTARE'S neighbour, the serious, dedicated Mauro Veglio might just be his truest disciple. The 12 ha combine plots from both Mauro's and his wife Daniela's families. Barolos which have recently benefitted from further input from consultant Giuseppe Caviola are *barrique*-aged (60% new). Castelletto, from Monforte vineyards, is the most fleshy and perhaps most characterful. Arborina is sourced from outside the winery doors. These are made in the greatest quantities. Gattera shows increasing richness and depth but is well-balanced too while a tiny amount of floral, elegant and cherry-flavoured Rocche is also made. In general they have been very good over the recent string of good vintages. Cascina Nuova Barbera is aged only in *barriques* and is best with at least 3–4 years' age. Good regular Barbera and Dolcetto can be drunk very young. Langhe

Piedmont

Nebbiolo (dedicated to Mauro's father) comes from a mix of sites and offers a very appealing lighter expression of Nebbiolo. Insieme (now Langhe DOC) is Nebbiolo, Barbera and Cabernet.

Recommended Reds:
Barolo Gattera ★★★★☆ £F
Barolo Rocche ★★★★ £F
Barolo Arborina ★★★★ £F
Barolo Castelletto ★★★★ £F
Langhe Insieme ★★★☆ £F
Langhe Nebbiolo Angelo ★★★ £D
Barbera d'Alba Cascina Nuova ★★★☆ £D
Barbera d'Alba ★★☆ £C
Dolcetto d'Alba ★★ £B

Vietti (Barolo) *www.vietti.com*
Established for more than a century this house came to prominence under the direction of Alfredo Currado. 32 ha of vineyards have gradually been acquired and the majority of the wines are now produced from estate vineyards. Single vineyard Barolos are sourced from top crus. While traditionally vinified, most are now partly *barrique*-aged and Lazzarito in particular can show more than a hint of oak when young. Yet there is a big difference between these and some of the more forward, easy, modern examples from other producers. They add real weight and richness with cellaring. Rocche is the most traditionally styled and often the most classic but it is worth waiting at least 7 years before drinking any of them. A small amount of Barolo Riserva Villero is made only in exceptional years. Often superb, Barbera d'Alba Scarrone Vigna Vecchia usually repays similar ageing. Barbera d'Asti La Crena is a notable single-vineyard example while other wines are soundly made.

Recommended Reds:
Barolo Lazzarito ★★★★☆ £F   Barolo Rocche ★★★★☆ £F
Barolo Brunate ★★★★☆ £F   Barolo Castiglione ★★★☆ £E
Barbaresco Masseria ★★★ £E
Barbera d'Alba Scarrone Vigna Vecchia ★★★☆ £E
Barbera d'Alba Scarrone ★★ £D   Barbera d'Asti La Crena ★★★ £E
Barbera d'Asti Tre Vigne ★☆ £C   Dolcetto d'Alba Tre Vigne ★☆ £B
Dolcetto d'Alba Sant'Anna ★☆ £B

Recommended Whites:
Moscato d'Asti Cascinetta ★★ £B   Roero Arneis ★☆ £B

Vignaioli Elvio Pertinace (Barbaresco) *www.pertinace.com*
Named for a Roman emperor (Pertinax) of very brief reign, this co-op established in the 1970s controls some 80 ha of vineyards. Cesare Barbero supervises the making of a very reasonably priced Barbaresco and three relatively inexpensive crus. The use of some new oak complements the natural density and structure in the wines which are bold and full-blown. In particularly hot vintages there is a danger of a lack of definition and excessively high in alcohol. Of the crus, Marcarini shows a little more class and depth than Nervo. A Barolo sourced from several vineyards in the appellation is also made and small quantities of Barbera from both Alba and Asti feature. This being a Treiso-based operation, Dolcetto also features prominently and can be similarly broad and flavoursome although recent examples lack fruit intensity and definition. Langhe Nebbiolo is also made while a typical Langhe blend, Pertinace has been produced from Nebbiolo, Barbera and Cabernet Sauvignon. Whites include two Langhe Chardonnays, a Roero Arneis and a Moscato d'Asti

Recommended Reds:
Barbaresco Vigneto Marcarini ★★★ £E

Barbaresco Vigneto Nervo ★★★ £E
Barbaresco ★★ £D
Dolcetto d'Alba Vigneto Nervo ★ £B
Barbera d'Alba ★ £B

Gianni Voerzio (Barolo)
Gianni Voerzio doesn't make the blockbuster, super-concentrated wines of his brother, ROBERTO VOERZIO, but from 12.5 ha he does produce a consistent and diverse range of very fine, even elegant wines. All have great vigour, deep fruit and good balance. Arneis and Dolcetto are excellent examples, both alive and intense. The Arneis is one of the very best made, detailed and structured and capable of a little age. Dolcetto has splendid definition and uncommon style for this grape. Barbera and the Nebbiolo/Barbera blend, Serrapiù, show the most marked oak influence but this melts into the rich pure fruit with a little age. The beautifully detailed Barolo La Serra is dense and intriguing when young, inviting at least 8–10 years' cellaring. Prices are on the high side but not out of step with quality.

Recommended Reds:
Barolo La Serra ★★★★★ £G
Langhe Serrapiù ★★★☆ £E
Barbera d'Alba Ciabot della Luna ★★★ £D
Dolcetto d'Alba Rochettevino ★★★ £C
Langhe Freisa Sotto I Bastioni ★★ £D
Langhe Nebbiolo Ciabot della Luna ★★ £D

Recommended Whites:
Roero Arneis Bricco Cappellina ★★★ £D
Moscato d'Asti Vignasergente ★☆ £C

✪✪ Roberto Voerzio (Barolo) *www.voerzioroberto.it*
Voerzio's prices have inevitably risen in line with his seeming unending ascent of the Piedmont hierarchy. In fact he took a little longer to achieve greatness in his wines than other stars. Relentless in his pusuit of extra-low yields and very concentrated fruit anod unwavering in his use of new oak, he now achieves balance and harmony in all wines that earlier vintages sometimes lacked. A visit to his vineyards in July may show more fruit lying on the ground than on the vine! From 1998, there is a bottling (in magnums only), of the cru Sarmassa, which lies immediately below Cerequio and therefore in the Barolo commune. Another recent Barolo addition is based in part on Rocche dell'Annunziata, where a tiny amount of an outstanding Riserva, Vecchie Viti dei Capalot e delle Brunate, is bottled only in magnums. Voerzio's mega-Barbera (again only sold in magnums), is the most powerful and concentrated made anywhere. Vignaserra is Nebbiolo with Cabernet Sauvignon (and/or Barbera) and was regularly among the best of its type but was produced for the last time in 2000. Since then Voerzio has created a Langhe Nebbiolo, from an area outside the Barolo DOCG, at a more reasonable price than his Barolos, but nevertheless of a quality expected from such a fine producer. He is also making a Langhe Merlot, in tiny quantities, available only at the cellar door, if you are lucky. It is of a quality and price to match the best in the world.

Recommended Reds:
Barolo Brunate ✪✪✪✪✪ £H
Barolo Cerequio ✪✪✪✪✪ £H
Barolo Rocche dell' Annunziata Torriglione ✪✪✪✪✪ £H
Barolo Riserva Vecchie Viti dei Capalot e delle Brunate ✪✪✪✪✪ £H
Barolo La Serra ★★★★★ £H
Barolo Sarmassa ★★★★★ £H
Barbera d'Alba Riserva Vigneto Pozzo dell Annunziata ✪✪✪✪✪ £H
Barbera d'Alba Vigneti Cerreto ★★★★ £D

Langhe da Uva Merlot Fontanazza - Pissotta ⬢⬢⬢⬢⬢ £H
Langhe Nebbiolo Vigneti S Francesco Fontanazza ★★★★ £E
Dolcetto d'Alba Priavino ★★ £B

A-Z of producers - *Liguria*

Baia del Sole (Colli di Luni) *www.cantinefederici.com*
The Baia del Sole estate at Luni di Ortonovo – La Spezia, is situated
on the Ligurian/Tuscan border, where its 11 hectare estate has
been producing wine since 1985. Apart from the autochthonous
grape varietals of Vermentino, Albarolo, Canaiolo and Cilegiolo,
plantings of international grapes such as Sangiovese, Malvasia,
Merlot, Cabernet and Syrah have also been made. There is a deep
respect for the environment and vineyard and pest management
is achieved by natural rather than chemical controls. Additional
wine production is made through grapes bought in from carefully
selected local growers. His entry level Vermentino is quite aromatic
and fresh, with a hint of Granny Smith apple. A reserve selection,
Vermentino Selection "Oro d'Isèe" has obviously more body and
length with good finesse, but his top white, Vermentino "Sarticolo" is
a single vineyard wine with even more finesse and elegance. Of the
reds produced, "Eutichiano" is a blend of Merlot, Syrah and Cilegiolo
- this is quite cherry-like on the palate, fruity but a bit on the light
side, whilst the "Forlino", a blend of Sangiovese, Merlot and Syrah, is
disappointingly a little rustic – 6 months in oak, but perhaps not yet
integrated at the time I tasted it. (NB)
Recommended Reds:
Colli di Luni Rosso Eutichiano ★☆ £C
Golfo dei Poeti IGT Forlino ★ £D
Recommended Whites:
Colli di Luni Vermentino Sarticolo ★★★☆ £D
Colli di Luni Vermentino Selection Oro d' Isèe ★★☆ £C
Colli di Luni Vermentino ★★ £B

Bisson (Golfo del Tigullio) *www.bissonvini.it*
Bisson wines were started in 1978 by Pierluigi Lugano, a master
sommelier, who realised that the potential of Ligurian grapes grown
by local farmers were not being converted into first class wines.
Starting with the acquisition of small parcels of grapes from local
farmers, he built a winery where he could vinify these grapes with
modern equipment and the facility to experiment and improve
results as the years went by. Excellent results enabled him to revive
some wine varietals that had practically disappeared, such as
Bianchetta Genovese and Ciliegiolo. After some years of vinifying
bought in grapes, he decided to plant his own vines in order to
achieve better control of the qualitative process of the wines. In
his vineyards at Trigoso (Sestri Levante) and Campegli (Castiglione
Chiavarese), the typical vines of Liguria are grown – Vermentino,
Bianchetta and Ciliegiolo. A red wine, "Musaico" is also produced
from bought in Dolcetto and Barbera. At Riomaggiore, grown
on the terraces overhanging the sea are Bosco, Vermentino and
Albarola grapes which make a typical Cinqueterre wine called
"Marea". Minimum chemical intervention ensures natural quality
of the grapes produced on their 10 ha of vines. Vermentino "Vigna
Intrigoso", is quite perfumed and with a little more weight than the
Parma wines. Bianchetta Genovese "U Pastine" has nice weight and
perfume with good aromacy on the palate; this is a more settled
wine with softness and roundness in the mouth. Their top table
wine, "Marea" (60% Bosco, the balance a mixture of Vermentino and
Alberola), is very aromatic with a good explosive attack of fruit on
the middle palate. A late harvest Bianchetto Genovese, Caratello

Passito Vino da Tavola Bianca, is made from selected grapes that are
then de-stemmed manually, crushed and left to ferment for up to 36
months in old wooden kegs. It has an old gold colour with intense
flavours of candied fruit and an unctuous feel on the palate. (NB)
Recommended Whites:
Vino da Tavola Bianchetto Genovese Passito Caratello ★★★☆ £E
Cinqueterre Marea ★★★ £D
Golfo del Tigullio Bianchetta Genuvese U Pastine ★★☆ £C
Golfo del Tigullio Vermentino Vigna Intrigoso ★★ £C

Bio Vio (Riviera Liguria di Ponente) *www.biovio.it*
Vio Giobatta's ancestors have been growing grapes for other
wine producers in the Albenga hinterland for as long as anyone
can remember, but in 2000 he decided to make his own wine.
The difference here, though, was that he decided to make his
production totally organic, without the use of pesticides, herbicides
or fertilizers. In order to conform with his organic principles, he built
a winery which enabled him to achieve his certification. The 14
ha estate also produces olive oil and a number of different herbs
which are also sold commercially. Pigato "Ma Rene" is quite lively
and aromatic – very clean and very pure. Vermentino "Aimone" has
good citrus tones but a little less body than the Pigato. Pigato "Bon
in da Bon" is a late harvest version, coming from a single 1 hectare
vineyard and has more grip, weight and length than the regular
Pigato. The extra year in bottle adds to its smoothness as well.
The estate produces two reds - Rossese "U Bastio" - a light, cherry-
flavoured wine with good finesse and complexity and Rosso "Bacilò",
80% Rossese, 20% Grenache, which has a little more depth than "U
Bastio" and more weight. (NB)
Recommended Reds:
Colline Savonese IGT Rosso Bacilò ★★☆ £C
Riviera Ligure di Ponente Rossese U Bastio ★☆ £C
Recommended Whites:
Riviera Ligure di Ponente Pigato Bon in da Bon ★★★ £E
Riviera Ligure di Ponente Pigato Ma Rene ★★☆ £C
Riviera Ligure di Ponente Vermentino Aimone ★★ £C

Buranco (Cinqueterre) *www.burancocinqueterre.it*
If ever a great wine estate has been hiding its light under a
bushel, Buranco at Monterosso al Mare, La Spezia, must be one
of them. Nestling in a valley high above the Cinqueterre village
of Montessoro al Mare, with stunning views over the dry stone
terraces and the sea, it enjoys a unique microclimate that enables
it to produce wines that are simply outstanding for the area.
What makes the wines stand out is the sheer lusciousness that is
achieved, bringing the wines on to a much higher plane than most
of its neighbours for many miles around. The estate is now run by
Luigi Grillo, who took it over from the original German proprietors,
Sonja and Kurt Wachter, who set the parameters of standards for
this unique estate. The Cinqueterre is a trying place to cultivate; the
man-made steep terraces, inaccessible to modern machinery, will
only sustain the fruits of human effort and the dryness of the land
extracts the maximum stress out of the vines that grow there, but
the fact that so much concentration of flavour has been achieved
brings home the dedication to quality that this estate stands for.
Cinqueterre DOC, is a blend of 60% Bosco (hardly ever found
outside the Cinqueterre area) 20% Vermentino and 20% Albarola;
this has weight, lusciousness and complexity on the finish. "Magoa"
is the same blend but this is a "cru" of selected grapes which drives
the finesse just a little further than the regular wine. Rosso Buranco
Vino da Tavola (aren't some of the best Italian wines just "Vino da

Liguria

Italy

Tavola"?) - Cabernet Sauvignon (50%), Syrah (30%) and Merlot (20%) – well matured, deep and unctuous – a far cry from some of the weedy reds that you find in the area. Mind you, these are not local grapes, but they stand on a par with some of best reds of this type that Italy can produce. Finally, Buranco Sciacchetrá DOC Cinqueterre - an extraordinary amber coloured Passito, 5 months in oak and 15 months in steel, with a real intensity of flavour. Made from Bosco (80%), Vermentino (15%) and Albarola (5%), there are nuances of apricot, banana and candied fruits with a luscious and long finish. Only 1000 half bottles of this wine were produced, so it has scarcity value, too. Sumptuous! A slight caveat on compiling our 2014 update. We have found that the dry whites have tended to oxydise after 2 or 3 years, which has caused us to downgrade the ratings a notch for these wines. No problem with the red and the Schiacchetrá, though! (NB)

Recommended Reds:

Vino da Tavola Rosso Buranco ★★★★☆ £E

Recommended Whites:

Cinqueterre Buranco Passito Schiacchetrá ★★★★☆ £F

Cinqueterre Buranco Magoa ★★★☆ £E

Cinqueterre Buranco ★★★ £D

Azienda Vinicola G.B. Parma (Golfo del Tigullio)

Situated at Ne, a few kilometres inland from Chiavari on the Gulf of Tigullio, G. B. Parma have been bottling wine since 1980. They own no vineyards themselves, but buy in the best quality grapes they can find from local farmers. The worry at the time was that these local wines were beginning to disappear from lack of markets and outlets and Parma's goal was to stop these wines from sinking into oblivion. The majority of the vines consist of Vermentino, Cilegiolo and the autochthonic Bianchetta Genovese. Most have been replanted under G.B. Parma's supervision. The Golfo di Tigullio DOC was granted in 1997 in recognition of the tipicity and excellence of the fruit, planted with great effort on steep terraces. The wines are generally made for early drinking using a Vaslin press at a pressure of not more than 4 atmospheres in order to gently run off the juice from the pips and the skins. The must is then transferred into temperature-controlled vats where it is inoculated with selected yeasts and after 7 to 10 days of fermentation it is transferred again to eliminate the lees. After a further 15 days the wine is fined and filtered and is ready for bottling. The philosophy of the winery is to make as little chemical intervention as possible; the only chemical used is sulphur for stabilising the wine and usually at the level of 70/90 mg/l instead of the maximum of 200 mg/l allowed by the law. Giancu du Nostru - Vino da tavolo bianco, is an interesting blend of Vermentino and Bianchetta Genovese – crisp and easy quaffing stuff. Their straight Vermentino DOC Golfo del Tigullio is crisp and aromatic with hints of quince on the palate, whilst their Bianchetta Genovese is more aromatic than the Vermentino, biscuity on the palate and not dissimilar to a Pinot Bianco. (NB)

Recommended Whites:

Golfo del Tigullio Vermentino Giancu du Nostru ★★☆ £C

Golfo del Tigullio Bianchetta Giancu du Nostru ★★☆ £C

Vino da Tavola Giancu du Nostru ★★ £B

Giacomelli (Colli di Luni)

Roberto Petacchi founded the winery in 1993 and has continued to build a reputation for being one of the best producers in the area, in America as well as locally. His Vermentino DOC Colli di Luni, is very clean, fresh and aromatic. The usual hints of citrus with good length. Vermentino "Boboli" is a single vineyard version, much longer, smoother and more refined, whilst the Vermentino "Pinacci" is another single vineyard wine from a hillside vineyard some 250 metres above Boboli. Even more refined with a very persistent finish. (NB)

Recommended Whites:

Colli di Luni Vermentino Pinacci ★★★☆ £D

Colli di Luni Vermentino Boboli ★★★ £C

Colli di Luni Vermentino ★★ £B

Le Rocche del Gatto *www.lerocchedelgatto.it*

Since the 2002 harvest, the association between Fausto De Andreis and Gigi and Chiara Crosa di Vergagni has led to a new partnership in the world of Ligurian wine called Le Rocche del Gatto situated at Albenga (Savona) in Riviera Ligure di Ponente. De Andreis was already famous for his own unique wine, Spigàu Crocciata, and the new company, benefiting from the contribution of vineyards belonging to Crosa di Vergagni and some leased ones, produces wines only from Ligurian grapes, carefully worked to preserve the varietal characteristics of the *terroir*, using modern techniques to ensure the best results both in the vineyard and in the cellar. The vineyards stand on the plain of Albenga and produce wine from 7 ha. The composition of land is on red clay, well exposed to the sun and a constant breeze creates an ideal climate for the cultivation of the vines. Their entry level Vermentino is a little bit on the dull side, although it has reasonable length, but their Pigato is more perfumed and aromatic, with more complexity. The red Rossese/Grenache is very light but fruit riven and quite complex. A reserve Vermentino, "Init" is unoaked, but very full in the mouth with intense flavours of quince and lemon. The Azienda's most famous and most sought-after wine is Fausto De Andreis's "Spigàu Crociata", - 100% Pigato from selected grapes which are then left to mature for up to two years in bottle before being released for sale. The result is a wine of extraordinary finesse, but with enough weight to be able to accompany white meats, truffles and cheese as well as seafood and other delicate fish. A recent vertical tasting of several vintages of "Spigàu Crociata", confirms the producer's opinion that the wine reaches its best after 5 years. Certainly, the 2001 was of 5 star quality. (NB)

Recommended Reds:

Riviera Ligure di Ponente Rossese/Grenache ★★★ £D

Recommended Whites:

Riviera Ligure di Ponente Pigato Spigàu Crociata ★★★★☆ £F

Riviera Ligure di Ponente Vermentino Riserva Init ★★★ £D

Riviera Ligure di Ponente Pigato ★★ £C

Riviera Ligure di Ponente Vermentino ★ £C

Cantine Lunae (Colli di Luni) *www.cantinelunae.it*

There are good wines to be had from Liguria but few producers who seem ready to let the world know. That's what makes this operation different. The Bosoni family draw from 60 ha of vineyard in the Colli di Luna DOC, just beyond the furtherest reaches of north-west Tuscany. The number of wines may verge on the bewildering but quality is promising. Of the dry Vermentinos, the Etichetta Nera (black label) adds concentration and ripeness over a good regular Etichetta Grigia (grey label) version - both are stainless steel vinified - while a third vineyard specific example, Cavagino, is partly barrel-fermented. The latter adds a little breadth but is less vibrant. In both Fior di Luna and (more concentrated) Onda di Luna, Albarola, Greco and/or Malvasia are added to Vermentino. Both show less zip and finesse with more wild flowers, wild herbs in aroma and flavour. Reds include Niccolò V that is Sangiovese based with Merlot and

Pollera Nera making up the balance. Cool, lean and pure, there is more density and extract in a sleek, lithe Riserva. More unusual is Horae (sold as Golfo dei Poeti IGT) comprising 50% Massareta with the balance from Merlot and Pollera Nera. Although slightly firm in structure with highish acidity, it is characterful with black cherry and plum fruit. Several other wines include a late harvest white (Satiro) and sparkling styles, both frizzante and fully sparkling. There's also extra virgin olive oil.

Recommended Reds:
Colli di Luni Riserva Niccolò V ★★☆ £D   Horae ★★ £D
Colli di Luni Niccolò V ★★ £C

Recommended Whites:
Colli di Luni Vermentino Cavagino ★★★ £D
Colli di Luni Vermentino Etichetta Nera ★★★ £C
Colli di Luni Onda di Luna ★★☆ £D   Colli di Luni Fior di Luna ★★ £C
Colli di Luni Vermentino Etichetta Grigia ★★ £B

A-Z of producers - *Lombardy (Lombardia)*

Bellavista (Franciacorta)   www.bellavistawine.it
Under the direction of Vittorio Moretti and winemaker Mattia Vezzola, Bellavista make brilliant, refined yet full-flavoured sparkling wines that deservedly sell for the same prices as good non-vintage Champagne. Most include at least a component of barrel-fermentation to add further complexity. The non-vintage Brut Cuvée (predominantly Chardonnay with a little Pinot Noir and Pinot Blanc) is the most affordable, and made in by far the greatest quantities, of the DOCG Franciacorta. Gran Cuvée Brut is a step up, 3 parts Chardonnay to one of Pinot Noir. The Rosé is a sheer delight (60/40 Pinot Noir and Chardonnay) while the soft, creamy and delicately sparkling non-vintage Satèn is a lovely example of this low-pressure style. Pas Operé has no final addition of sugar, making it the driest of the range. A Riserva named after the owner has extended ageing on its lees (around 6 years). The still wines are sold under the Terre di Franciacorta DOC. The best of these is the rich, complex Convento della Santissima Annunciata, now produced only from 100% Chardonnay in this single vineyard. Curtefranca Bianco is a blend of Chardonnay and Pinot Bianco and another varietal Chardonnay, Uccellanda is rich and oaky. None of the still wines offers particularly good value for money but try the very classy fizz at least.

Recommended Whites:
Franciacorta Gran Cuvée Satèn Brut ★★★ £F
Franciacorta Gran Cuvée Pas Operé ★★★☆ £E
Franciacorta Gran Cuvée Brut ★★★ £E
Franciacorta Brut Cuvée ★★☆ £D
Terre di Franciacorta Convento della Santissima Annunciata ★★★☆ £E
Terre di Franciacorta Uccellanda ★★☆ £E

Recommended Rosés:
Franciacorta Gran Cuvée Brut Rosé ★★★ £E

✿ Ca' del Bosco (Franciacorta)   www.cadelbosco.com
Maurizio Zanella was one of Italy's modern pioneers for quality wine and was already receiving wide acclaim by the early 1980s. The wines continue to be of high quality with fine Franciacorta sparkling wines complemented by the region's best still wines. Pinèro (Pinot Nero or Pinot Noir), the Bordeaux blend, Maurizio Zanella, and Chardonnay have more competition than a decade ago but remain among the best Italian examples. The most recent innovation is Carmenero, a varietal Carmenère and a first for Italy (though it seems likely that, as in Chile, there could be a good deal of this variety planted, particularly in the North-East). Red and white Curtefranca

(previously Terre di Franciacorta) are also good. All the grapes are estate-grown from some 140 ha of vineyard. For the sparklers, fermentation of the base wine is finished in *barrique* following by some ageing before the second fermentation. The vintage Brut combines Chardonnay, Pinot Blanc and a little Pinot Noir, while the Rosé is more Pinot Noir-based. There's also a very fine Satèn but the finest sparkler is the rich, complex, mouthfilling Cuvée Annamaria Clementi. Since 2007, a Cuvée Prestige has been produced from 75% Chardonnay, 15% Pinot Nero and 10% Pinot Bianco which has spent 28 months on its lees and blended with 20% of reserves from the best vintages.

Recommended Reds:
Maurizio Zanella ★★★★ £F   Carmenero ★★★ £F
Pinero ★★★ £F   Curtefranca Rosso ★★ £C

Recommended Whites:
Franciacorta Cuvée Annamaria Clementi ★★★★ £F
Franciacorta Dosage Zero ★★★ £F
Franciacorta Satèn ★★★ £F
Franciacorta Brut Vintage ★★☆ £E
Terre di Franciacorta Chardonnay ★★★★ £F
Curtefranca Bianco ★★ £C

Recommended Rosés:
Franciacorta Rosé ★★ £F

>> Caven (Valtellina Superiore)   www.neravini.com
The Nera family also own this small estate where wine is made only from their own vines with no bought in fruit. The wines are not released until some considerable ageing (around five years after the harvest) even though legally the requirement is to age in barrel for a minimum of two years. The area designated wines (Sassella and Inferno) are smooth with good fruit and length, whilst the Late Harvest wine, "Giupa", from vineyards within the general appellation is more concentrated with a slightly bitter finish, but around the same alcoholic content. The Sforzato, as expected, is a big wine, reaching nearly 15% abv with a perfume of violets on the nose and a slight sweetness on the finish, reminiscent of a Recioto from the Veneto. (NB)

Recommended Reds:
Valtellina Sforzato Messere★★★★☆ £E
Valtellina Superiore Late Harvest Giupa ★★★★ £D
Valtellina Superiore Sassella La Priora★★★☆ £C
Valtellina Superiore Inferno Al Carmine★★★☆ £C

Il Mosnel (Franciacorta)   www.ilmosnel.com
This is an impressive and much improved producer of DOGC Franciacorta sparkling wines The regular Brut is a blend of 30% Chardonnay fermented in small *barriques*, 30% Chardonnay of previous vintages vinified in stainless steel, 30% Pinot Bianco and 10% Pinot Nero, both fermented in stainless steel. The bottles are left for over 2 years under the *méthode champenoise* before release, resulting in a crisp, biscuity flavoured wine. The Pas Dosé (same blend) finishes up with less than 3 grams of sugar per litre (as opposed to 8 grams in the regular wine) and is matured for an additional 12 months before release. Here we have an exceptionally dry finish. Unusually, they also produce a very pale pink vintage Pas Dosé Rosé, 70% Pinot Nero and 30% Chardonnay, again kept for 3 years before degorging, displaying great elegance and finesse. The Brut Saten vintage Chardonnay (fermented 60% in stainless steel and 40% in small oak *barriques*, mellows beautifully with age, whilst the Riserva Brut vintage "Emanuela Barboglio", (100% oak fermented) named in honour of the estate's founder, has intense vanilla flavours

Italy

with great length and complexity, but needs some years to realise its full potential. There is also a regular sparkling rosé and some still red and white wines but these have not yet been tasted. (NB)

Recommended Whites:
Franciacorta Brut Emanuela Barbiglio Vintage ★★★★ £F
Franciacorta Brut Satèn vintage ★★★☆ £F
Franciacorta Brut ★★★ £E Franciacorta Pas Dosé ★★★ £E
Recommended Rosés:
Franciacorta Rosé ★★★★ £F

Nino Negri (Valtellina Superiore) *www.ninonegri.net*
Nino Negri is owned by Italy's largest wine group – GIV or Gruppo Italiano Vini – and is directed by the respected enologist Casimiro Maule. There are good examples of all 4 Valtellina Superiore DOCG sub-zones: Grumello, Inferno, Sassella and Valgella. Though traditionally vinified, most are partly aged in *barrique*; of light to medium body, at their best they are intense, perfumed and elegant. Sfursat or Sforzato is a high-alcohol version (typically 14.5°) made from semi-dried grapes; in the top wine, Sfursat 5 Stelle, the grapes spend 24 days on their skins prior to ageing exclusively in new *barriques*. Drunk young it can be a bit overwhelming, with its sweet, intense fruit and evident tannin and acidity, yet it is enticingly perfumed with floral and preserved raspberry and cherry aromas. The oak-aged, perfumed white Ca' Brione is based on Nebbiolo vinified as a white wine and can show unusual structure and weight.
Recommended Reds:
Valtellina Sfursat 5 Stelle ★★★★ £F Valtellina Sfursat ★★★ £E
Valtellina Superiore Vigneto Fracia ★★★ £E
Valtellina Superiore Grumello Vigna Sassorosso ★★ £D
Valtellina Superiore Inferno Mazér ★★ £D
Valtellina Superiore Sassella Le Tense ★★ £D
Recommended Whites:
Ca' Brione ★★ £C

Pietro Nera (Valtellina Superiore) *www.neravini.com*
The Nera family have held sway here since the 1940s and own about 30 ha. of vineyards held in the classic DOGC areas of Sassello, Inferno, Valgella and Grumello. Wines produced from the Nebbiolo grape (known locally as Chiavennasca) are the mainstay of their production but they also produce some interesting whites from Nebbiolo vinified in Bianca. "La Novella" is a blend of Nebbiolo with 20% Chardonnay vinified separately, expressing freshness and fruitiness, whilst "Rezio" is a similar blend but here the grapes are partially dried to give a greater intensity of fruit and then the wine is fermented in small oak barrels and matured for around eight months. DOGC wines from all the areas show finesse with the riservas having added value complexity as well as much longer time in barrel – sometimes up to four years and in both instances the alcohol rarely exceeds 13%. Regular Valtellina Superiore wines spend at least 12 months in barrel and a further 12 months in bottle before being commercially released. For those needing a bit more of a kick from their wines, the Sforzato wines, produced from grapes dried on mats until they reach a sufficient concentration, raises the alcohol to 15% or more. Nevertheless, the drying of the grapes induces lower acidity so whilst it is intense and alcoholic, it is nevertheless softer on the palate. (NB)
Recommended Reds:
Valtellina Sforzato ★★★★ £E
Valtellina Superiore Grumello Riserva ★★★★ £D
Valtellina Superiore Sassella Riserva ★★★☆ £D
Valtellina Superiore Inferno Riserva ★★★☆ £D

Valtellina Superiore Grumello Tirso ★★★ £C
Valtellina Superiore Sassella Alisio ★★☆ £C
Valtellina Superiore Inferno Efesto ★★ £C
Recommended Whites:
Bianco IGT La Novella ★★☆ £B Bianco IGT Rezio ★★☆ £B

Aldo Rainoldi (Valtellina Superiore) *www.rainoldi.com*
The wines have been improved and modernised here to the extent that this narrow alpine valley might yet receive more attention. The length and flavour intensity in the top wines is striking. The *barrique*-aged Il Crespino (from 100% Nebbiolo) is but one of several Valtellina Superiore. As well as an Inferno *Barrique* (aged in the same) there are versions of Grumello and Sassella; the Sasella Riserva delivers a lovely savoury complexity with age. As at NINO NEGRI it is the Sfursat (Valtellina Sforzato DOCG) that shows the most power and concentration. The Fruttaio Ca' Rizzieri is similarly aged in *barriques* and is dense and powerful with excellent depth and intensity. More unusual is a very attractive white, Zapel, made from Nebbiolo (vinified as a white) and 30% Sauvignon. Though of only moderate structure the Sauvignon isn't allowed to dominate and it shows enticing ripe fruit. Ghebellino, on the other hand, is a straight Sauvignoin Blanc, fresh and fragrant having spent just 5 months on its lees before bottling.
Recommended Reds:
Vatellina Sfursat Fruttaio Ca' Rizzieri ★★★★ £E
Valtellina Sfursat ★★ £D
Valtellina Superiore Inferno Riserva Barrique ★★★ £D
Valtellina Superiore Sassella Riserva ★★★ £D
Valtellina Superiore Il Crespino ★★ £C
Recommended Whites:
Zapel ★★ £C Ghebellino ★★ £C

Triacca (Valtellina Superiore) *www.triacca.com*
Domenico Triacca is one of a few who show what Valtellina is capable of As much work is going into improving the vineyards as the cellar, reducing yields and improving the canopy to obtain better light penetration and subsequently better, riper Nebbiolo fruit. Typically it is the Sfursat/Sforzato that is one of the best wines, but the *barrique*-aged Prestigio is of comparable quality. Del Frate, a herbal, minerally Sauvignon, shows there's potential for this grape here too. Also under the same ownership are Tuscan estates La Madonnina (Chianti Classico) and Santavenere (Vino Nobile).
Recommended Reds:
Valtellina Sforzato San Domenico ★★★☆ £E
Valtellina Superiore Prestigio ★★★☆ £E
Valtellina Superiore Riserva La Gatta ★★ £D
Recommended Whites:
Del Frate ★★ £C

Other wines of note

Valle d'Aosta
Cantina di Barro
Recommended Reds:
Valle d'Aosta Mayolet Clos de Chateau Feuillet ★★ £C
Valle d'Aosta Torrette Superieur ★★★ £D
La Crotta di Vegneron
Recommended Whites:
Valle d'Aosta Chambave Moscato Passito ★★★☆ £E
Cave du Vin Blanc de Morgex et de La Salle
Recommended Whites: Valle d'Aosta Vini Estremi ★★☆ £C

Piedmont (Piemonte)

G Accornero & Figli
Recommended Reds:
Barbera del Monferrato Superiore Bricco Bastista ★★★ £E
Barbera del Monferrato Superiore Riserva Cima ★★★ £E
Monferrato Centenario (Cabt Sauv/Barbera) ★★★ £E

Giovanni Almondo
Recommended Reds: Roero Bric Valdiana ★★ £C
Barbera d'Alba Valbianchera ★★ £C

Famiglia Anselma
Recommended Reds: Barolo ★★★ £E Barolo Adasi ★★★★ £F

Batasiolo
Recommended Reds: Barolo Cerequio ★★ £F
Barolo Corda Della Briccolina ★★★ £F

Carlo Benotto
Recommended Reds: Barbera d'Asti Superiore Balau ★★ £B
Barbera d'Asti Superiore Vigneto Casot ★★ £B
Barbera d'Asti Superiore Rupestris ★★ £C

Nicola Bergaglio
Recommended Whites: Gavi del Comune di Gavi La Minaia ★★ £C

Bersano
Recommended Reds: Barbera d'Asti Superiore Nizza ★★ £C
Barbera d'Asti Superiore Generala ★★ £D

Guido Berta
Recommended Reds: Barbera d'Asti Superiore Canto di Luna ★★ £C

Franco Boasso Gabutti
Recommended Reds: Barolo Gabutti ★★★ £F

Eugenio Bocchino
Recommended Reds: Barolo ★★★ £F
Nebbiolo d'Alba La Perucca ★★☆ £D
Langhe Suo di Giacomo (Nebbiolo/Barbera) ★★ £D

Francesco Boschis
Recommended Reds:
Dolcetto di Dogliani Sorì San Martino ★★★ £B
Dolcetto di Dogliani Vigna Dei Prey ★★★ £C

Bovio
Recommended Reds: Barbera d'Alba Regia Veja ★★ £C
Barolo Arborina ★★★ £F Barolo Gattera ★★★ £F
Barolo Rocchettevino ★★★ £E

Giacomo Brezza
Recommended Reds: Barolo Bricco Sarmassa ★★★ £F
Barolo Cannubi ★★★ £F

Bricco Mondalino
Recommended Reds:
Barbera del Monferrato Gaudium Magnum ★★★ £D
Barbera d'Asti Il Bergantino ★★ £B

Gian Piero Broglia - La Meirana
Recommended Reds:
Monferrato Bruno Broglia (Barbera/Merlot/Cab Sauv) ★★ £C
Recommended Whites: Gavi Bruno Broglia ★★★ £C

Tenuta Carretta
Recommended Reds: Barbaresco Cascina Bordino ★★★ £E
Barolo Cannubi ★★★ £F

Carussin
Recommended Reds:
Barbera d'Asti Superiore Nizza Ferro Carlo ★★★ £C
Barbera d'Asti La Tranquilla ★★☆ £B Barbera d'Asti Lia Vì ★★ £B
Respizo di Vigna Vigna Tardiva Da Uve Barbera (Mod.Sweet) ★★★★ £D
Recommended Whites: Moscato d'Asti Filari Corti ★★☆ £B

Cascina Adelaide
Recommended Reds: Barbera d'Alba Superiore Vigna Preda ★★★ £D

Barbera d'Alba Superiore Amabilin ★★★☆ £D
Langhe Nebbiolo ★★★★ £D Barolo Cannubi ★★★★☆ £F
Barolo Riserva Per Elen ★★★★☆ £F

Cascina Ca' Rossa
Recommended Reds: Roero Audinaggio ★★★ £D
Roero Mompissano ★★★ £D
Barbera d'Alba ★★£C Barbera d'Alba Mulassa ★★★ £D
Langhe Nebbiolo ★★ £C

Cascina Castlèt
Recommended Reds: Barbera d'Asti Superiore Litina ★★ £D
Barbera d'Asti Passum ★★ £D
Monferrato Policalpo (Barbera/Cab Sauv) ★★ £C
Recommended Whites: Piemonte Moscato Passito Avié ★★ £E

Cascina Cucco
Recommended Reds: Barolo Vigna Cucco ★★★ £E

Cascina Fonda
Recommended Whites: Moscato d'Asti ★★ £B
Moscato Spumantetardivo ★★ £C
Vendemmia Tardiva (Moscato) ★★ £D

Cascina Garitina
Recommended Reds: Barbera d'Asti Bricco Garitta ★★ £B

Cascina La Ghersa
Recommended Reds: Barbera d'Asti Superiore Camparò ★★ £C
Barbera d'Asti Nizza La Vignassa ★★ £D

Cascina Luisin
Recommended Reds: Barbaresco Rabajà ★★★★ £F
Barbaresco Sorì Paolin ★★★ £F
Barbera d'Alba Maggiur ★★ £C Barbera d'Alba Asili ★★ £D

Cascina Monreale
Recommended Reds: Barbera d'Asti Superiore Valentina ★★ £C

Cascina Degli Ulivi
Recommended Whites: Gavi Filagnotti ★★☆ £C

Poderi Colla
Recommended Reds: Barolo Bussia Dardi Le Rose ★★★ £F
Barbaresco Roncaglia ★★★ £F

Paolo Conterno
Recommended Reds: Barolo Ginestra ★★★ £F
Barolo Riserva Ginestra ★★★ £G
Barbera d'Alba Ginestra ★★ £D Dolcetto d'Alba Ginestra ★ £B

Giuseppe Cortese
Recommended Reds: Barbaresco Rabajà ★★★ £F

Deltetto
Recommended Reds: Roero Braja ★★ £C
Barbera d'Alba Superiore Bramé ★★ £C
Recommended Whites:
Roero Arneis San Michele ★★☆ £C Langhe Favorita Sarvai ★★ £C

Alessandro & Gian Natale Fantino
Recommended Reds: Barolo Vigna Dei Dardi ★★★ £E

Benito Favaro
Recommended Whites: Erbaluce di Caluso Le Chiusure ★★ £C

Giacomo Fenocchio
Recommended Reds
Barbera d'Alba ★★☆ £C
Barolo ★★★☆ £D
Barolo Villero ★★★☆ £E
Recommended Whites:
Roero Arneis ★★ £C
Recommended Reds
Barbera d'Alba 2.5 stars £C
Barolo 3.5 stars £D
Barolo Villero 3.5 stars £E

Piedmont & North-West Italy

Italy

Ferrando
Recommended Reds: Carema Etichetta Nera ★★ £E
Recommended Whites:
Erbaluce di Caluso Cariola Etichetta Nera ★★ £C
Caluso Passito Vigneto Cariola ★★★ £F
Fontanabianca
Recommended Reds: Barbaresco Sorì Burdin ★★★ £E
Funtanin
Recommended Reds: Barbera d'Alba Ciabot Perin ★★ £C
Roero ★★ £C Roero Superiore Bricco Barbisa ★★ £D
Recommended Whites: Langhe Favorita ★ £B
Roero Arneis Vigna Pierin di Soc ★★ £C
Tenuta Garetto
Recommended Reds: Barbera d'Asti Superiore In Pectore ★★ £B
Barbera d'Asti Superiore Favà ★★ £C
Fratelli Giacosa
Recommended Reds: Barbaresco Rio Sordo ★★★ £E
Barolo Vigna Mandorlo ★★★ £E
Barbera d'Alba Maria Gioana ★★ £B
Gillardi
Recommended Reds: Harys (Syrah) ★★★☆ £E
Langhe Rossoyeta (Dolcetto/Cab Sauv) ★★★ £E
Dolcetto di Dogliani Cursalet ★★☆ £C
Dolcetto di Dogliani Vigneto Maestra ★★ £B
Giacomo Grimaldi
Recommended Reds: Barolo Le Coste ★★★ £E
Hilberg - Pasquero
Recommended Reds: Barbera d'Alba Superiore ★★★ £E
Nebbiolo d'Alba ★★★ £D
Isabella
Recommended Reds: Barbera d'Asti Superiore Bric Stupui ★★ £C
La Morandina
Recommended Reds: Barbera d'Asti ★★ £C
Barbera d'Asti Varmat ★★★ £C
Recommended Whites: Moscato d'Asti ★★★☆ £C
Iuli (Cantina del Monferrato)
Recommended Reds:
Barbera del Monferrato Superiore Umberta ★☆ £B
Barbera del Monferrato Superiore Rossore ★★☆ £C
Barbera del Monferrato Superiore Barabba ★★★ £E
Monferrato Nino (Pinot Nero) ★★ £D
Monferrato Malidea (Barbera/Nebbiolo) ★★☆ £D
La Scolca
Recommended Whites: Gavi Etichetta Nera ★★ £E
Gavi Spumante Brut Soldati ★★☆ £C
Gavi Spumante Pas Dosé ★☆ £C
Soldati La Scolca Brut Millesimato ★★☆ £C
La Volta - Cabutto
Recommended Reds: Barolo Vigna La Volta ★★★ £E
La Zerba
Recommended Whites:
Gavi Del Comune di Tassarolo Terrarossa ★★ £C
Gianluigi Lano
Recommended Reds: Barbaresco ★★★ £E
Barbera d'Alba Fondo Prà ★★ £C
L'Armangia (also see Castello di Calosso)
Recommended Whites: Piemonte Chardonnay Robi E Robi ★★ £C
Le Piane
Recommended Reds: Colline Novaresi La Maggiorina ★★ £B
Colline Novaresi Le Piane (Croatina/Nebbiolo) ★★★☆ £D
Boca (Nebbiolo/Vespolina) ★★★☆ £E

Marchesi Alfieri
Recommended Reds: Barbera d'Asti La Tota ★★ £B
Barbera d'Asti Superiore Alfiera ★★★ £D
Monferrato San Germano (Pinot Nero) ★★ £D
Monferrato Rosso Dei Marchesi (Barbera/Pinot Nero) ★★ £B
Marchesi di Barolo
Recommended Reds: Barolo Sarmassa ★★★★ £E
Barolo Cannubi ★★★ £E
Mario Marengo
Recommended Reds: Barolo Brunate ★★★ £E
Vigneti Massa
Recommended Reds: Colli Tortonesi Barbera Sentieri ★★☆ £C
Recommended Whites: Timorasso Derthona ★★☆ £C
Monchiero Carbone
Recommended Reds: Roero Printi ★★★ £D Roero Srü ★★ £C
Barbera d'Alba Mon Birone ★★ £B
Recommended Whites: Roero Arneis Re Cit ★ £B
Montaribaldi
Recommended Reds: Barbaresco Sorì Montaribaldi ★★★ £E
Barbera d'Alba Dü Gir ★★ £B Dolcetto d'Alba Niccolini ★★ £B
Fratelli Mossio
Recommended Reds: Dolcetto d'Alba Bricco Caramelli ★★★ £C
Dolcetto d'Alba Piano Delli Perdoni ★★ £C
Langhe Rosso (Nebbiolo/Barbera) ★★★ £D
Tenute Neirano
Recommended Reds: Barbera d'Asti Superiore Le Croci ★★ £C
Vigneti Luigi Oddero E Figli
Recommended Reds: Barolo Rocche Dei Rivera ★★★ £E Barolo
Vigna Rionda ★★★ £E
Tenuta Olim Bauda
Recommended Reds: Barbera d'Asti ★★ £C
Barbera d'Asti Superiore ★★ £D
Barbera d'Asti Superiore Nizza ★★★ £E
Palladino
Recommended Reds: Barolo San Bernardo ★★★ £E
Barolo Vigna Broglio ★★★ £E
Pira
Recommended Reds:
Dolcetto di Dogliani Vigna Bricco Dei Botti ★★ £B
Dolcetto di Dogliani Vigna Landes ★★ £B
Dolcetto d'Alba Vigna Fornaci ★★ £B
Piemonte Barbera Briccobotti ★★ £C
Punset
Recommended Reds: Barbaresco Campo Quadro ★★★ £E
Reverdito
Recommended Reds: Barolo ★★★ £E Barolo Moncucco ★★★ £E
Barolo Bricco Cogni ★★★★ £F Barbera d'Alba Butti ★★ £C
Dolcetto d'Alba Formica ★ £B Langhe Nebbiolo Simane ★★ £C
Ricchino
Recommended Reds: Dolcetto Diano d'Alba Rizieri ★★ £B
Cantine Sant' Agata
Recommended Reds: Barbera d'Asti Superiore Cavalé ★★ £C
Cantine Sant' Evasio
Recommended Reds: Barbera d'Asti Superiore Nizza ★★★ £C
Scagliola
Recommended Reds: Barbera d'Asti Sansì ★★★ £D
Barbera d'Asti Selezione ★★★ £E
Recommended Whites: Moscato d'Asti Volo di Farfalle ★★★ £C
Giorgio Scarzello e Figli
Recommended Reds: Barolo Vigna Merenda ★★★ £F
Barbera d'Alba Superiore ★★ £C

F & M Scrimaglio
Recommended Reds: Barbera d'Asti Superiore Acsé ★★☆ £D
Barbera d'Asti Superiore Bricco Sant'ippolito ★★☆ £D
Barbera d'Asti Superiore Roccanivo ★★ £C
Recommended Whites: Moscato d'Asti Grani di Sole ★★☆ £B
Gavi Del Comune di Gavi San Pietro ★★ £C

Mauro Sebaste
Recommended Reds: Barolo Monvigliero ★★★ £E
Barolo Prapò ★★★ £E

Sella
Recommended Reds: Lessona ★★ £D
Lessona San Sebastiano Allo Zoppo ★★★ £E

Proprieta Sperino
Recommended Reds:
Coste Della Sesia Uvaggio (Nebbiolo/Vespolino/Croatina) ★★★☆ £E
Recommended Rosés: Coste Della Sesia Rosato ★★ £C

Michele Taliano
Recommended Reds: Barbaresco Ad Altiora ★★★ £E
Roero Ròche Dra Bòssora ★★★ £D   Barbera d'Alba Laboriosa ★★ £C

Tenuta dei Fiori
Recommended Reds:
Monferrato Rosso Cinquefile (Barbera/Cab Sauv) ★★ £C

Terre da Vino
Recommended Reds: Barolo Paesi Tuoi ★★★ £E
Barolo Essenze ★★★★ £E   Barbera d'Asti La Luna E I Falò ★★ £C

Trinchero
Recommended Reds: Barbera d'Asti Superiore ★★★ £C
Barbera d'Asti Superiore Vigna Del Noce ★★★★ £D

Varaldo
Recommended Reds: Barbaresco Bricco Libero ★★ £E
Barbaresco Sorì Loreto ★★ £E   Barbaresco Vigne di Aldo ★★ £F
Barbera d'Alba ★★ £C   Langhe Nebbiolo ★★ £D
Langhe Rosso Fantasia 4.20 ★★ £D

Eraldo Viberti
Recommended Reds: Barolo ★★★ £E
Barbera d'Alba Vigna Clara ★★ £C

Villa Sparina
Recommended Reds: Monferrato Rivalta (Barbera) ★★ £D
Recommended Whites: Gavi Monte Rotondo ★★ £D

Cantine Vinchio Vaglia Serra
Recommended Reds: Barbera d'Asti Superiore ★ £B
Barbera d'Asti Superiore Nizza Bricco Laudana ★★ £D
Barbera d'Asti Superiore Vigne Vecchie ★★★ £D

Liguria
Bruna
Recommended Whites:
Riviera Ligure di Ponente Pigato U Bacan ★★ £C
Riviera Ligure di Ponente Le Russeghine ★★ £B

Walter de Batté
Recommended Whites: Cinque Terre ★★ £C
Cinque Terre Sciacchetrà ★★ £D

Ottaviano Lambruschi
Recommended Whites: Colli di Luna Vermentino Colle Marina ★★ £C
Colli di Luna Vermentinosarticola ★★ £C

Terre Rosse
Recommended Reds: Solitario (Rossese/Grenache/Barbera) ★★ £E
Recommended Whites: Rivera delle Ligure Ponente Pigato ★ £B
Apogèo (Pigato) ★★ £C
Rivera delle Ligure Ponentevermentino ★ £B

Lombardy (Lombardia)
Cavalleri
Recommended Whites: Franciacorta Brut Collezione Brut ★★★
£D   Franciacorta Satèn ★★★ £D

La Montina
Recommended Whites: Franciacorta Extra Brut ★★ £D
Franciacorta Brut Millesimato ★★★ £D

Monte Rossa
Recommended Whites: Franciacorta Brut Cabochon ★★★ £E
Franciacorta Brut Satèn ★★ £E

Mamete Prevostini
Recommended Reds: Valtellina Superiore Corte Di Cama ★★ £E
Valtellina Superiore Sassella Sommarovina ★★ £D
Valtellina Sforzato Albareda ★★★ £E

Ricci Curbastro
Recommended Whites: Franciacorta Satèn Brut ★★ £D
Franciacorta Extra Brut ★★ £D

Sertolis Salis
Recommended Reds: Valtellina Sforzato Canua ★★★★ £F
Valtellina Superiore Grumello ★★ £D
Valtellina Superiore Sassella ★★ £D

Uberti
Recommended Whites: Franciacorta Brut Francesco I ★★ £D
Franciacorta Brut Magnificentia ★★★ £E
Franciacorta Extra Brut Comarì Del Salem ★★★ £E

Author's choice

Outstanding Barolo
Azelia   Barolo San Rocco
Enzo Boglietti   Barolo Brunate
Boroli   Barolo Villero
Brovia   Barolo Rocche Dei Brovia
Cappellano   Barolo Piè Rupestris
Elvio Cogno   Barolo Vigna Elena
Domenico Clerico   Barolo Ciabot Mentin Ginestra
Aldo Conterno   Barolo Colonello
Giacomo Conterno   Barolo Riserva Monfortino
Conterno-Fantino   Barolo Sorì Ginestra
Cordero di Montezemolo   Barolo Bricco Gattera
Luigi Einaudi   Barolo Nei Cannubi
Ettore Germano   Barolo Cerretta
Attilio Ghisolfi   Barolo Bricco Visette
Bruno Giacosa   Barolo Rocche del Falletto di Serralunga
Elio Grasso   Barolo Ginestra Casa Matè
Bartolo Mascarello   Barolo
Giuseppe Mascarello & Figlio   Barolo Monprivato
Armando Parusso   Barolo Bussia Vigne Rocche
E Pira & Figli   Barolo Cannubi
Luigi Pira   Barolo Margheria
Giuseppe Rinaldi   Barolo Brunate-Le Coste
Luciano Sandrone   Barolo Le Vigne
Paolo Scavino   Barolo Bric del Fiasc
Vigna Rionda - Massolino   Barolo Parafada
Gianni Voerzio   Barolo La Serra
Roberto Voerzio   Barolo Brunate

12 Exciting Barbaresco
Produttori del Barbaresco   Barbaresco Riserva Montefico
Piero Busso   Barbaresco Vigna Borghese

Piedmont & North-West Italy

Italy

Ceretto   Barbaresco Bricco Asili
Gaja   Barbaresco
Bruno Giacosa   Barbaresco Santo Stefano di Neive
La Spinetta   Barbaresco Vigneto Starderi
Marchesi di Gresy   Barbaresco Martinenga Camp Gros
Moccagatta   Barbaresco Bric Balin
Paitin   Barbaresco Sorì Paitin
Pelissero   Barbaresco Vanotu
Albino Rocca   Barbaresco Brich Ronchi
Bruno Rocca   Barbaresco Rabajà

Other Special North-West Reds
Antichi Vigneti di Cantalupo   Ghemme Signore di Bayard
Matteo Correggia   Nebbiolo d'Alba La Val di Preti
Elio Altare   Insieme
Bricco Maiolica   Nebbiolo d'Alba Il Cumot
Ca' del Bosco   Maurizio Zanella
La Spinetta   Monferrato Rosso Pin
Les Cretes   Valle d'Aosta Fumin Vigne La Tour
Malvirà   Roero Superiore Mombeltramo
Nino Negri   Valtellina Sfursat 5 Stelle
Angelo Negro & Figli   Roero Sudisfà
Aldo Rainoldi   Valtellina Sfursat Fruttaio Ca' Rizzieri

Super Barbera
Gianfranco Alessandria   Barbera d'Alba Vittoria
Bertelli   Barbera d'Asti San Antonio Vieilles Vignes
Braida   Barbera d'Asti Ai Suma
Cascina Val del Prete   Barbera d'Alba Superiore Carolina
Castello di Calosso/Mauro Grasso   Barbera d'Asti Rodotiglia
Luigi Coppo & Figli   Barbera d'Asti Pomorosso
La Barbatella   Barbera d'Asti Superiore Vigna dell'angelo
La Spinetta   Barbera d'Asti Superiore
Tenuta La Tenaglia   Barbera d'Asti Emozioni
Franco M Martinetti   Barbera d'Asti Superiore Montruc
Andrea Oberto   Barbera d'Alba Giada
Elio Perrone   Barbera d'Asti Mongovone
Ferdinando Principiano   Barbera d'Alba La Romualda
Vietti   Barbera d'Alba Scarrone Vigna Vecchia
Roberto Voerzio   Barbera d'Alba Riserva Vigneto Pozzo
dell'Annunziata

Diverse Dolcetto
Anna Maria Abbona   Dolcetto di Dogliani Maioli
Claudio Alario   Dolcetto di Diano d'Alba Costa Fiore
Enzo Boglietti   Dolcetto d'Alba Tiglineri
Brovia   Dolcetto d'Alba Solatio
Ca'Viola   Dolcetto d'Alba Barturot
Corino   Dolcetto d'Alba
Luigi Einaudi   Dolcetto di Dogliani I Filari
Marcarini   Dolcetto d'Alba Boschi di Berri
San Fereolo   Dolcetto di Dogliani San Fereolo
G D Vajra   Dolcetto d'Alba Coste & Fossati
Gianni Voerzio   Dolcetto d'Alba Rochettevino

Piedmont Value
Reds:
Araldica   Barolo Revello
Ascheri   Dolcetto d'Alba Nirane
Produttori del Barbaresco   Barbaresco Riserva Rabajà
Enzo Boglietti   Langhe Nebbiolo

Luigi Baudana   Langhe Lorenso
Corino   Dolcetto d'Alba
Icardi   Barbera d'Asti Tabarin
Andrea Oberto   Barbera d'Alba
San Romano   Dolcetto di Doglianii
Whites:
Caudrina   Moscato d'Asti La Caudrina
Malvira   Roero Arneis Renesio

'Bianchi, rossi e altro'

If Italy contained only the viticultural resources of Piedmont and Tuscany, that would be wealth enough, but there is much, much more even if a large part of it is too often ignored by an increasingly homogenised wider world. In North-East Italy fine, elegant whites are produced in the Alto Adige and fuller, more concentrated examples in Friuli-Venezia Giulia, from a mix of both local and international varieties. Some of Italy's finest sweet wines also come from the North-East while all three provinces now also provide high quality reds. While some come from the like of Cabernet Sauvignon, Merlot or even Pinot Nero, more and more outstanding original reds result from a realisation of the true potential of the native grapes: not just Corvina in the Veneto for Valpolicella and powerful Amarone but also Lagrein and Teroldego in Trentino-Alto Adige and even the previously obscure Pignolo and Schioppettino in Friuli.

Alto Adige (Südtirol)

The German-speaking South Tyrol has become a dependable source of elegant, perfumed dry white wines and cool, refined reds. Most of the wines are are labelled as **Alto Adige** DOC with a varietal name and many of the grapes are familar to wine drinkers. The best examples of Chardonnay, Sauvignon, Gewürztraminer, Pinot Bianco and Pinot Grigio combine concentration with elegance and are complemented by fine reds from Lagrein, Cabernet Sauvignon and Merlot as well as some genuinely good examples of Pinot Nero. The native Lagrein has emerged over the past decade as a superior grape variety and most of the top producers now offer a premium oak-aged version, often in addition to simpler, supple, spicy, brambly examples. These have powered past existing styles such as Lago di Caldaro/Kalterersee produced from the Schiava grape. At its best it is a light but attractive perfumed red (Scelto, or Auslese indicates a higher degree of ripeness). Santa Maddalena/St. Magdalener is a similar offering from a smaller zone further north, close to Bolzano. Producers fall roughly into one of three categories. First is the significant and high quality output from prestigious family concerns (not least Lageder, Hofstätter and lately Manincor). Second are the increasingly high profile large co-ops. If quality tended to be consistent but unexciting in the past, many have taken a massive leap forward in the last decade (Colterenzio, San Michele Appiano, Terlano and several others). But try too the wines of a small band of star growers, each with just a few hectares of vines (the brilliant Ignaz Niedrist, Peter Pliger - Kuenhof or Franz Pratzner - Falkenstein, to name but a few).

Trentino

As in the Alto Adige, the regional **Trentino** DOC covers a wide range of varietals and though the standard is generally lower than in the Alto Adige several small producers signal the quality possible (Cesconi, Pojer & Sandri and San Leonardo shouldn't be missed). The greatest originality comes in the shape of an excellent red in **Teroldego Rotaliano** (from the Teroldego grape). Regrettably there are not that many examples yet but the superb wines of Foradori show what is possible with higher-density planting and low yields. The potential of another native variety, Marzemino, remains unrealised but some attractively floral, plummy examples do exist. Though Trentino is a major producer of sparkling wine, few examples of **Trento** have the quality to compete with the best fizz from around the world (Ferrari's top cuvée is an exception).

Veneto

The Adige river swings out of Trentino-Alto Adige and turns more easterly as it runs through Verona. On the lowest reaches of the Lessini Mountains to the north are the hills of Valpolicella, merging with Soave to the east. A number of producers have turned their backs on these classic appellations (using instead a regional IGT) as they believe they have failed to shed an image of cheap, simple plonk. In terms of quality wine the international reputation of this noble Italian province has come to depend chiefly on **Amarone della Valpolicella**. From a still relatively small number of producers, top examples of this powerful red, made from partially-dried grapes, are among Italy's finest reds. When not fully fermented to dryness this results in the sweeter **Recioto della Valpolicella**, while amandorlato is sometimes used to describe an in-between style. The biggest challenge for producers of Amarone is to retain some of the typicity of the style while losing the rusticity that has plagued its image. The excessively raisiny character and high levels of volatile acidity have become less apparent as cellar hygiene has improved and more care has gone into eliminating grapes affected by rot. Many are now aged in new oak but whether more modern or traditional in style, Amarone's strength and character doesn't give it the greatest versatility. Fortunately, despite the trend to increased quantities of Amarone, a few producers have radically improved the quality of **Valpolicella**. Modern producers have thrown out the lesser of the traditional grapes, concentrating on Corvina, but are also introducing small percentages of other grapes – such as Syrah in the case of Allegrini. Most of the best examples have benefited from some sort of enrichment. The technique known as *ripasso* (the name is exclusive to Masi) involves passing the finished wine over fermented Amarone skins, improving both the texture and character of the wine. Many a producer's premium version of Valpolicella (sometimes from a single vineyard and usually as Valpolicella Classico Superiore) benefits from it but not all – others directly incorporate a percentage of dried grapes at some point during the fermentation, producing a sort of hybrid Valpolicella/Amarone. The best Amarone need at least 5-6 years' age and will keep for 10 to 15. Recioto is often better drunk younger but top examples will keep as long. Top examples of Valpolicella generally drink well with 3-5 years' age but exceptionally will keep for more than a decade. The best recent vintages are 2009, 06, 04 01, 00, 97, 95, 93, 90, 88 and 85 but from a top producer wines from most other years are also very good.

A decade ago finding an example of **Soave** (DOCG in Superiore) that was more than an anonymous dry white lead to just a handful of producers led by Anselmi and Pieropan. Now excellent examples abound and it can be seen for what it is – a brilliant 21st century white. Lean, lithe yet intense and pure with a herb and mineral-infused singularity, it is also capable of some age in the more structured single vineyard examples. Look for the new breed (mostly 100% Garganega) from Cantina del Castello, Filippi, Gini, Inama, Nardello, Prà, Suavia or Tamellini. **Recioto di Soave** (also DOCG), the version from dried grapes, although of variable style, from oxidised and raisiny to sleek and fruit-filled, can be an excellent sweet white.

Gambellara abuts Soave to the east and is currently most notable for the wines of La Biancara. **Bianco di Custoza** and **Bardolino** to the west of Soave, on the eastern and southern fringes of Lake Garda, are sometimes cited as substitutes for Soave and Valpolicella but usually only compare with basic examples of each. From the western shores of Lake Garda one or two producers make quite concentrated, stylish **Lugana** as well as other blends (that incorporate Chardonnay and Sauvignon in the case of Ca' dei Frati).

North-East Italy

North of historic Vicenza is **Breganze**, which owes its reputation to one producer, Maculan. As well as splendid sweet whites from the native white Vespaiolo, good quality has been realised from Cabernet Sauvignon and Merlot. Vignalta in the **Colli Euganei**, found south of Padova (Padua), has also been successful with both Merlot and Cabernet but makes good dry whites too. **Prosecco** is the region's fizz and from a good producer can be fresh and attractive if drunk young (Adami, Bellenda and Bisol are amongst those recently tasted that offer a bit more).

Friuli-Venezia Giulia
Friuli's production (like that of Trentino-Alto Adige) is dwarfed by that of the Veneto but there are at least as many top-quality producers. French varieties have been planted for many years in the hilly **COF** (Colli Orientali del Friuli) and **Collio** DOCs and DOCGs, but despite the quality of the wines produced from them they fail to give the region a distinctive stamp. Yet beyond Chardonnay, Sauvignon Blanc, Pinot Grigio and Pinot Bianco there are ever-better examples of Friulano (known as Tocai Friulano until 2006), Ribolla Gialla and Malvasia Istriana: wines of distinctive character – and high quality from a top producer. While a good number of the whites are made in the prevalent unoaked fashion, an increasing number of the best wines have added structure from some use of oak. Top Collio names include Borgo del Tiglio, Jermann, Edi Keber, Russiz Superiore, Schiopetto, Villa Russiz, Zuani as well as the extraordinary wines of Gravner. Amongst those from Colli Orientali are Dal Fari, Dorigo, Livio Felluga, Miani, Moschioni, Paolo Rodaro, Ronchi di Manzano or Le Vigne di Zamè. The flatter **Friuli Isonzo** (or Isonzo del Friuli) has emerged over the past decade as the third major quality zone, led by a young generation of growers making some of the most concentrated and structured whites anywhere in the region. Taste these from Borgo San Daniele, Mauro Drius, Lis Neris, Pierpaolo Pecorari, Ronco del Gelso or the brilliant Vie di Romans.

Red wines are increasingly important and with better training, higher-density planting and lower yields the grassy character once common to so many of the reds from Cabernet Sauvignon, Cabernet Franc and Merlot has been replaced by a lush, ripe berry fruit richness in best examples. Also showing much promise in the most recent vintages are some intense and concentrated examples of native varieties, Pignolo, Refosco and Schioppettino (Moschioni is the star). Fine sweet whites are made by several producers from the native grapes Picolit and Verduzzo. **COF Picolit** is now DOCG (from 2006), complementing the existing **Ramandolo** DOCG from Verduzzo grapes from the small zone around the village of the same name (try from Dario Coos or Giovanni Dri - Il Roncat).

Good wines can also be found beyond the big three of Collio, Colli Orientali and Friuli Isonzo. **Carso** DOC covers wines produced along the thin strip of Italy between Gorizia and Trieste. Known as Karst or Kras it is a continuation of the limestone plateau of south-western Slovenia. In addition to the usual Friuli varietals most producers also make the unusual (white) Vitovska and (red) Refosco-based Terrano/Teran (try from Castelvecchio, Kante, Skerk or Zidarich). Soundly made if only rarely exciting whites and reds are produced in the large, mostly flat zone of **Friuli Grave** (Russolo) or even the smaller southern zones of **Friuli Aquileia** (Foffani) or **Friuli Latisana**.

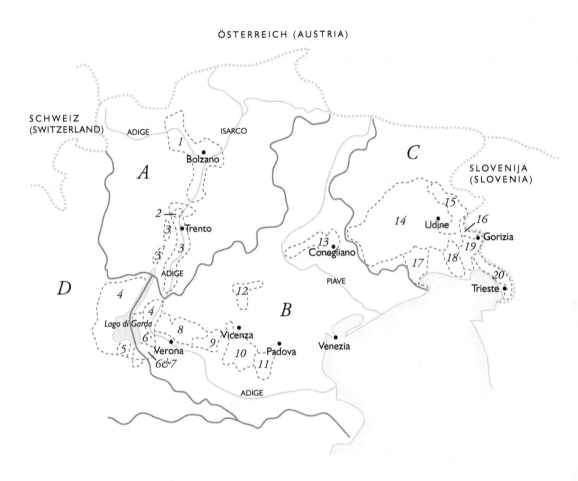

Regions
A   Trentino – Alto Adige
B   Veneto
C   Friuli-Venezia Giulia
D   Lombardy (Lombardia)

Appellations
1   Alto Adige
2   Teroldego Rotaliano
3   Trentino
4   Garda
5   Lugana
6   Bardolino
7   Bianco di Custoza
8   Valpolicella
9   Soave
10 Colli Berici
11 Colli Euganei
12 Breganze
13 Prosecco di Conegliano-Valdobiadene
14 Friuli Grave
15 Colli Orientali del Friuli
16 Collio
17 Friuli Latisana
18 Friuli Aquileia
19 Friuli Isonzo
20 Carso

Abbazia di Novacella (Alto Adige) www.abbazianovacella.it
This northern abbey, high in the Valle Isarco (well north of Bolzano where the Isarco feeds into the Adige) was founded in 1142. It is sustained by its ability to produce high-quality wines under Celestino Lucin. The usual wide range of varietals are clean, sound and attractive. What puts production amongst the best of the south Tyrol however are the Praepositus versions of the leading varieties. Especially distinctive is the Kerner with ripe fruits, herb and mineral in a full, pronounced and intense style. Its appeal may be limited but it is an intriguing, serious white. In the same way Gewürztraminer is fuller, more mineral and complex over a perfumed, floral regular example. In the blended white Praepositus, the Pinot Grigio/ Chardonnay component (the other half is Sylvaner) is fermented and aged in *barrique*. At its best it has a certain elegance and Burgundian complexity. In both Praepositus reds there is also good complexity, intense vibrant fruit and well-integrated oak, while the perfumed Moscato Rosa (Rosenmuskateller) has exceptional balance and length.

Recommended Reds:
Alto Adige Lagrein Riserva Praepositus ★★★ £E
Alto Adige Pinot Nero Praepositus ★★ £E

Recommended Whites:
Alto Adige Kerner Praepositus ★★★ £D   Alto Adige Kerner ★★ £C
Alto Adige Gewürztraminer Praepositus ★★★ £D
Alto Adige Gewürztraminer ★☆ £C
Praepositus Bianco ★★★ £D
Alto Adige Sylvaner ★★ £C

Recommended Rosés:
Alto Adige Moscato Rosa ★★★ £E

Colterenzio (Alto Adige) www.colterenzio.it
The Cantina Produttori Colterenzio, a co-op formed by 28 grape growers, is amongst the finest of the Alto Adige's many good co-ops, though has rivals in the like of SAN MICHELE APPIANO and TERLANO. Under the direction of Luis Raifer, the image and profile of Colterenzio has been transformed and investment has been realised. The improved fruit from the 320 ha of vineyards is now utilised by his son Wolfgang, now the CEO of the co-operative. There is sound quality at a regular 'classic' varietal level, though the wines can be a little simple and sometimes lacking concentration. A step up are the 'vineyard series' Praedium-labelled wines which bridge the gap between the 'classic' wines and the premium Cornell label. Cornell wines, though more pricey, are consistently impressive and show the influence of expert enologist Donato Lanati. Chardonnay Cornell in particular stands out for its excellent concentration, depth and balance over a string of recent vintages. Sauvignon Lafoa is partially *barrique*-fermented and aged and can show excellent intensity and complexity but is occasionally a little overdone. Also good are the top reds, both the blended Cornelius (Cabernet/ Merlot) and a powerful but less harmonious Cabernet Sauvignon Lafoa. Concentrated but refined Lagrein Cornell has arguably the most character, highlighting smoky, spice, clove and bramble qualities this grape can produce. In fact even the 'classic' Lagrein is most attractive. Other Cornell wines are Pinot Nero (Schwarzhaus) and Moscato Rosa. Varietal Merlot (Riserva Siebeneich) is also made.

Recommended Reds:
Alto Adige Cabernet Sauvignon Lafoa ★★★ £F
Alto Adige Cornelius Cornell ★★★ £E
Alto Adige Lagrein Cornell ★★★ £E

Alto Adige Lagrein Grieser ★★ £D

Recommended Whites:
Alto Adige Chardonnay Cornell ★★★ £E
Alto Adige Sauvignon Lafoa ★★★ £E
Alto Adige Sauvignon Prail ★★ £D
Alto Adige Pinot Bianco Weisshaus ★★ £D
Alto Adige Gewürztraminer Cornell ★★ £D
Alto Adige Gewürztraminer ★ £C

Falkenstein (Alto Adige) www.falkenstein.bz
The Vinschgau (Val Venosta) is a splendid valley channelling the upper reaches of the Etsch (Adige) river which continues west from Merano almost as far as Switzerland. If you're lucky enough to find yourself in this part of the world then look for these wines in a local wine bar or restaurant. Franz Pratzner's small range from 4ha vineyards reflect their mountain origins. With high sunshine hours alcohol levels are high but the wines are well-balanced. His varietals compare well with fine Austrian or German examples, or indeed the best from the Alto Adige. Most striking is a Riesling of great class and purity with a very refined minerally, citrusy elegance but Weissburgunder (Pinot Bianco) too has a mineral component and no lack of style or complexity. The expressive Blauburgunder (Pinot Nero) is harmonious, intense and long. Fine cherry, spice and floral aromas distinguish it from so many riper, coarser examples from both north and south of the Alps. The Sauvignon Blanc is quite grassy but not very intense, with nevertheless a nice long finish. Also made but not tasted are a regular and a late-harvest Gewürztraminer. (NB)

Recommended Reds:
Alto Adige Val Venosta Pinot Nero ★★★ £D

Recommended Whites:
Alto Adige Val Venosta Riesling ★★★☆ £C
Alto Adige Val Venosta Pinot Bianco ★★★ £C
Alto Adige Val Venosta Sauvignon ★★★ £C

Franz Gojer - Glögglhof (Alto Adige) www.gojer.it
Like Franz Pratzner (above), Franz Gojer is a grower with a very small but high quality production. Being from Santa Maddalena the local Vernatsch (Schiava) and Lagrein grapes hold sway. Both versions of Santa Maddalena (St. Magdalener) are mostly Schiava topped up with a little Lagrein. There is the typical light, supple, floral and wild cherry charm of this style but with better intensity than most. The Rondell version with a touch more Lagrein (7%) is more perfumed and expressive with slightly better structure. Lagrein, as always is a much more substantial beast and a quite structured, dense example from the Furggl vineyard needs at least 3-4 years' age. A Riserva is still more with a classic spicy, brambly, plummy profile, and a touch of vanilla from 12 months in *barriques*. With more breadth and power there is also a mineral, carob streak in its compact structure that needs 5 years' to soft and open out. At 600mts., the Karneid vineyard is at the upper limit for growing Vernatsch, but the low yielding old vines here produce a racy, minerally wine. The karneid vineyard is also planted to three white varietals, Sauvignon, Weissburgunder (Pinot Bianco) and Kerner each displaying freshness and minerality and all vinified dry to enhance their crispness.

Recommended Reds:
Alto Adige Lagrein Riserva ★★★☆ £D
Alto Adige Lagrein Furggl ★★ £C
Alto Adige Santa Maddalena Rondell ★★ £C
Alto Adige Santa Maddalena Classico ★☆ £B
Alto Adige Vernatsch Alte Reben ★★ £C

Recommended Whites:

Alto Adige Pinot Bianco (Weissburgunder) Karneid ★★ £C

Alto Adige Sauvignon Karneid ★★ £C

Alto Adige Kerner Karneid ★★ £C

Bruno Gottardi (Alto Adige) www.gottardi-mazzon.com

Despite the odd success elsewhere Italy's hopes with Pinot Noir rest with the South Tyrol. Gottardi's best efforts (labelled Blauburgunder) are up there with the established names like HOFSTÄTTER and LAGEDER. It is the focus of his production and the results can be excellent. Concentrated, ripe and savoury there is considerable dimension and depth with flavours somewhere between Burgundy and a more Germanic style. The Riserva promises even more including a lusher oak-influenced palate. In addition there is also a very small amount of Gewürztraminer made.

Recommended Reds:

Alto Adige Pinot Nero Riserva ★★★★ £E

Alto Adige Pinot Nero Mazzon ★★★☆ £D

Franz Haas (Alto Adige) www.franz-haas.it

This 55 ha estate has become one of the most consistent in the South Tyrol, producing good reds as well as whites nearly every year. The quality of the fruit and the harmony in the wines give them an extra edge over other good examples. Wines labelled Schweizer or Cru indicate a superior bottling. New vineyards are being planted at ever higher altitudes to combat climate change, with the latest planting of Pinot Noir at an altitude of 1,150 mts., the highest vineyard in the Alto Adige. The excel lent Manna, a beautifully composed blend of Riesling, Chardonnay, Traminer Aromatico (or Gewürztraminer) and Sauvignon, shows a marvellous aromatic fruit quality with a Chardonnay-like weight in the mouth yet is intense and vibrant. There's good depth and flavour in the varietals too. Istante is a structured but distinctive red from Cabernet Franc, Cabernet Sauvignon and Merlot, ripe and stylish in recent vintages, with enticing ripe Cabernet Franc aromatics. Adequate sappy Pinot Nero is also made, but much better is a more concentrated and complex Schweizer version. The moderately sweet Moscato Rosa is a fine, perfumed, delicious and generally well-balanced example of its type. Lagrein Scuro (or Dunkel) can also be good.

Recommended Reds:

Istante ★★★ £D Alto Adige Merlot Schweizer ★★ £D

Alto Adige Pinot Nero Schweizer ★★ £D Alto Adige Pinot Nero ★ £D

Recommended Whites:

Manna Schweizer ★★★ £D Alto Adige Traminer Aromatico ★★ £D

Alto Adige Pinot Bianco ★ £C

Recommended Rosés:

Alto Adige Moscato Rosa ★★★ £F

Hofstätter (Alto Adige) www.hofstatter.com

Hofstätter produces both the best Pinot Noir and one of the best Gewürztraminers in Italy. Though not a world-beater, the top Pinot Noir, from Vigna Sant'Urbano on high slopes at Mazon, shows a depth and texture uncommon to Italian examples and is increasingly successful even in more difficult vintages. Martin Foradori, who has assumed the direction of the estate from his father, has the fortune to have one or two particularly favoured sites among the estate's 50 ha of vineyards and the training is gradually being switched from pergola to the Guyot system. Site-specific reds include Yngram, at its best a concentrated expressive blend from mostly Cabernet Sauvignon and Petit Verdot, and the barrique-aged Lagrein, Steinraffler. For whites, the Kolbenhof Gewürztraminer from the village of Söll shows a depth and richness not found in many

Alto Adige examples (the poorest of which are based on ordinary Traminer). Bianco Vigna San Michele, a blend of Pinot Bianco, Chardonnay and Riesling partly aged in barriques, shows similar weight and style and a subtle oak influence. De Vite, from Pinot Bianco, Müller-Thurgau and Sauvignon is very drinkable, if more everyday. There is also a late-harvested Gewürztraminer, showing intense, exotic fruit flavours.

Recommended Reds:

Alto Adige Pinot Nero Barthenau Vigna Sant'Urbano ★★★☆ £E

Alto Adige Pinot Nero Riserva Mazzon ★★☆ £D

Alto Adige Lagrein Steinraffler ★★★ £E Yngram ★★★ £E

Recommended Whites:

Alto Adige Gewürztraminer ★★★ £E

Alto Adige Gewürztraminer Kolbenhof Söll ★★★ £D

Alto Adige Gewürztraminer ★★ £C

Alto Adige Bianco Barthenau Vigna San Michele ★★ £D

Alto Adige Pinot Bianco ★★ £C Alto Adige De Vite ★★ £C

Kuenhof - Peter Kliger (Alto Adige)

This small 4 ha of vineyard on Eisack (Isarco) river are part of the northernmost vineyard area in Italy. Being only nominally Italian the grape varieties are those you'd expect in Austria and very fine examples they are too. Only stainless steel and large used oak casks are used. Grüner Veltliner is powerful and intense with the structure to improve for at least 3-5 years. Sylvaner is made in the largest volumes (just 10,000 bottles) and has good intensity and purity and would make for interesting comparison with the best from Germany's Franken region. But the star is the Riesling Kaiton with a soaring elegance and finesse and quite remarkable length of flavour that would leave many top German examples in the shade. The quality continues with the pure refined Gewürztraminer (an Alsace Grand Cru equivalent) with rosewater, floral and mineral nuances - only the alcohol level gives any cause for concern. Although labelled in German, the wines are rated below with the Italian version to aid comparison with other wines from the region.

Recommended Whites:

Alto Adige Valle Isarco Riesling Kaiton ★★★★ £D

Alto Adige Valle Isarco Gewürztraminer ★★★☆ £D

Alto Adige Valle Isarco Sylvaner ★★★ £D

Alto Adige Valle Isarco Veltliner ★★★ £D

Alois Lageder (Alto Adige) www.aloislageder.eu

Lageder is the Alto Adige's leading private estate, driven on to exacting standards by the dynamic 'current' Alois Lageder (fifth generation). Though owning a relatively small percentage of their own vineyards, through close links with growers they are converting from pergola-trained vines to spalliera training on an increasingly organic basis. The family owned vineyards are now totally biodynamic and have been certified by the international Demeter organisation. Wines have been divided into two labels - one set under the Tenutae Lagader label, including those from the Cason Hirschprunn estate which Lageder purchased in 1991, and the other, for wines mainly from bought in fruit from trusted long time growers as well as from some estate owned vineyards, which are marketed under the Alois Lageder label While the wines can be a little simple and dilute at the varietal level, there are some fine examples of single-vineyard wines (especially Sauvignon Lehen, Pinot Bianco Haberle and excellent Pinot Grigio Porer) and the estate premium varietals and blends. The elegant, perfumed whites show real style with 3 years' bottle age or more. Cor Römingberg is the top red from a high-density, Guyot-trained vineyard – a rich,

Italy

ripe and concentrated Cabernet Sauvignon (with 3% Petit Verdot) with a fine minerally depth and class that has few rivals in North-East Italy. Though from older vines and of some style and intensity, the Cabernet Sauvignon blend, Löwengang (including 15% each of Cabernet Franc and Merlot) rather pales beside it. Much better is the white equivalent, a marvellously rich, deep, tightly structured and ageworthy Chardonnay. Also emerging with some promise are Pinot Noir, especially Krafuss (not Burgundian but intense and stylish), Lagrein (Lindenburg) and a rich Chardonnay and Sauvignon blend, Tannhammer. There is also a premium varietal Merlot (labelled with the vintage in Roman numerals).

Tenutae Lageder
Recommended Reds:

Alto Adige Cabernet Sauvignon Cor Römigberg ★★★★ £E
Alto Adige Cabernet Löwengang ★★ £E
Alto Adige Pinot Nero Krafuss ★★★ £E
Alto Adige Lagrein Lindenburg ★★ £D

Recommended Whites:

Alto Adige Chardonnay Löwengang ★★★ £E
Alto Adige Pinot Grigio Porer ★★★ £D
Alto Adige Gewürztraminer Am Sand ★★ £D

Alois Lageder
Recommended Whites:

Alto Adige Sauvignon Lehen ★★★ £D
Alto Adige Sauvignon Terlaner ★ £C
Alto Adige Pinot Bianco Haberle ★★ £C
Alto Adige Chardonnay Sauvignon Tannhammer ★★ £C
Alto Adige Chardonnay ★ £C   Alto Adige Gewürztraminer ★ £C

Laimburg (Alto Adige) www.laimburg.bz.it

When the province of Alto Adige opened the Laimburg Research Centre in 1975, it seized the opportunity to create the fusion of research and entrepreneurship in public administration. At the same time the Laimburg Province Winery was also established. Operated as part of the centre's estate management activities, it is the province's official winery, assigned with the task of carrying out research in both viticulture and vinification for the betterment of South Tyrol's wine industry. The winery produces some 2,500 hl of wine each year from some 50 hectares of vines, for which the grapes are taken from various vineyards throughout the province, each with a different microclimate. Along with a number of experimental varietals, fifteen typical South Tyrolean grape varietals are planted at the province's estate vineyards and are trained using either the pergola or guyot suspension system, depending on varietal and the incline of the vineyard itself. 70% of the wines are vinified in stainless steel tanks and those varietals that need extensive cellaring (up to 20 months depending on the varietal) are kept in barriques in an extraordinary red porphyry-walled cellar blasted out of the mountainside of the Monte di Mezzo with a naturally constant ambient temperature. 22 different wines are produced at Laimburg, mostly from autochthonous grapes (Schiava, Lagrein) but a number of interesting blends are also made. (NB)

Recommended Reds:

Alto Adige Lagrein/Petit Verdot/Tannat Col de Rèy ★★★ £D
Alto Adige Lagrein Riserva Barbagòl ★★★ £D
Alto Adige Pinot Nero Riserva Selyèt ★★★ £D
Alto Adige Estate Pinot Nero ★★★ £D
Alto Adige Cabernet Sauvignon Riserva Sass Roà ★★☆ £D
Alto Adige Estate Schiava Ölleiten ★★ £C

Recommended Whites:

Alto Adige Pinot Bianco Rayèt ★★★ £C

Alto Adige Sauvignon Blanc Oyèll ★★☆ £C
Alto Adige Gewürztraminer Elyònd ★★ £C

Recommended Rosés:

Alto Adige Moscato Rosa ★☆ £C

Loacker (Alto Adige) www.loacker.net

Since his acquisition of the Schwarhof wine estate situated on the south-facing mountainside overlooking Bolzano in 1978, Rainer Loacker has sought to produce wines in an organic-biodynamic way with considerable success. Now ably assisted by his wife, Christine and sons, Hayo and Franz-Josef, they continue to make wine according to their principals of biodynamics and homeopathy. Coupled with remedies designed to reduce the use of copper, their goal of healthy grapes and quality wines has been achieved over the 30 year life of the estate. A further innovation is the use of "Vinlok" glass stoppers as closures instead of cork for the entire range. The Loackers have subsequently expanded their operations to estates in Tuscany, Valdifalco at Maremma and Corte Pavone at Montalcino. The varietal range of wines produced at Schwarhof is typical of the area, Sylvaner, Müller-Thurgau, Sauvignon Blanc, Chardonnay, Gewürztraminer and Goldmuskateller in white and Schiava (Vernatsch), Lagrein, Cabernet, Merlot and Pinot Nero in red. All the whites are bottled as single varietals with the Sauvignon Blanc and the Chardonnay showing the most richness on the palate whilst the Gewürztraminer is quite dry and light and perhaps lacking in sufficient aromacy although there is a good balance between the fruit and the acidity. There is an entry level Schiava and also a Schiava which is DOC St. Magdelener, a tiny appellation within the bounds of the Alto Adige, which, with the permitted addition of up to 10% Lagrein, gives more depth and colour to the wine than pure Schiava, which is basically the local quaffing wine. Another mainly Schiava wine (80%) is complemented by the inclusion of 10% Merlot, 5% Lagrein and 5% Cabernet Sauvignon which brings it up a notch in balance, complexity and length ("Jus Osculi"). Pinot Nero, aged in old barriques, has the typical savouriness of Italian Pinot Noir but with enough fruit on the finish and their Lagrein is deep and unctuous with nuances of sour cherries and bitter chocolate. Their top wine is a blend of Cabernet Sauvignon (55%), Lagrein (40%) and Merlot (5%) called "Kastlett" – dark and juicy with a fine, complex finish. (NB)

Recommended Reds:

Alto Adige Kastlett ★★★★ £E   Alto Adige Lagrein ★★★☆ £E
Alto Adige Pinot Nero Norital ★★☆ £D
Alto Adige Jus Osculi ★★☆ £C
Alto Adige Sankt Magdalener Morit ★★ £C

Recommended Whites:

Alto Adige Chardonnay Ateyon ★★★ £D
Alto Adige Gewürztraminer Atagis ★★☆ £E
Alto Adige Sauvignon Blanc Tasnim ★★☆ £D

✿ Manincor (Alto Adige) www.manincor.com

The count, Michael and his wife Sophie have a first class operation that can only add further to the prestige of the region. Grapes come only from a diverse patchwork of 45 ha of estate vineyards in the vicinity of Kaltern (Caldaro) and Terlan (Terlano). From a new underground winery beneath slopes above the Kalterer See (Lago di Caldaro) winemaker Andreas Prast makes a range of wines (biodynamic from 2006) showing a good match between variety and site. Whites include an exquisite example of Moscato Giallo with uncommon purity and lightness of touch while Réserve della Contessa combines Pinot Bianco with Chardonnay and Sauvignon

without any coarseness or heavyness. More stylish is Sophie (mostly Chardonnay and Sauvignon) with an inviting herbal, acacia character. The premium white, Lieben Aich is a barrel-fermented and aged Sauvignon comparable to elegant white Bordeaux or oaked Sancerre/Pouilly Fumé. Reds impress too. Those based on Bordeaux varieties include the reasonably priced Réserve del Conte, more oaky, concentrated and characterful Cassiano, and very stylish Castel Campan (predominantly Merlot, given two years in *barriques*). The latter two should be given a minimum of five years' ageing. A medium-bodied Pinot Noir comes from Mazzon vineyards and is cool and pure (Mason di Mason is a more oak-influenced premium selection) while a promising varietal Lagrein Rubatsch was first made in 2004. Good rosé (La Rose) is also made but more orginal are all too scarce quantities of Le Petit Manincor made from 100% Petit Manseng (very late-harvested without botrytis) with all the exotic elegant sweetness of this variety. Non-DOC wines are sold as Vigneti delle Dolomiti IGT.

Recommended Reds:
Castel Campan ★★★★ £E
Alto Adige Pinot Noir Mason diMason ★★★☆ £F
Alto Adige Pinot Noir Mason ★★☆ £E
Cassiano ★★★☆ £E   Alto Adige Lagrein Rubatsch ★★☆ £D
Réserve del Conte ★★☆ £C
Alto Adige Lago di Caldaro Classico Superiore ★☆ £B
Recommended Whites:
Lieben Aich ★★★★ £E   Le Petit Manincor ★★★☆ £E
Sophie ★★★ £D   Alto Adige Moscato Giallo ★★☆ £C
Alto Adige Terlano Réserve della Contessa ★★ £C

Josef Niedermayr (Alto Adige) *www.niedermayr.it*
This long-established producer achieves quality across a large range, from top reds to simple but soundly made basic varietals with good flavour intensity. The leading whites are the premium examples of Gewürztraminer and Sauvignon with excellent structures and distinctive, penetrating aromas. Less successful are Terlano Hof Zu Pramol and Perelle (Pinot Grigio and Chardonnay) which though flavoursome and characterful show a touch of coarseness too and seem a bit overdone (though they may appeal to some palates). Better is a very well-made sparkling Talento Comitissa Brut Riserva (Pinot Bianco and Chardonnay) made by Niedermayr's enologist Lorenz Martini. Here the flavours are kept more in check, while the structure and length underscore its quality. An intense passito-style Aureus, a blend of mostly Chardonnay and Sauvignon, shows delicious ripe fruit and good balance. All of Niedermayr's versions of Lagrein are good. An excellent Lagrein Riserva (give it 6-8 years) is more composed than Euforius, which adds Merlot and Cabernet Sauvignon to Lagrein. Nevertheless the latter is dense and extracted with a wild black fruits and cedary complexity. Pinot Nero Riserva (Blauburgunder) is well-structured and flavoursome but lacks the fruit finesse of the best in the region.

Josef Niedermayr
Recommended Reds:
Alto Adige Lagrein Aus Gries Riserva ★★★☆ £D
Alto Adige Lagrein Aus Gries Blacedelle ★★ £C
Alto Adige Lagrein Aus Gries ★ £C   Euforius ★★★ £D
Alto Adige Pinot Nero Riserva ★★ £E
Recommended Whites:
Aureus ★★★ £F
Alto Adige Gewürztraminer Doss ★★★ £D
Alto Adige Sauvignon Allure ★★☆ £D
Alto Adige Sauvignon Naun ★★ £D

Perelle ★★ £C   Alto Adige Sylvaner ★ £C
Alto Adige Terlano Hof Zu Pramol ★ £C
Lorenz Martini
Recommended Whites:
Alto Adige Talento Comitissa Brut Riserva Vintage ★★ £D
Ignaz Niedrist (Alto Adige)
If you are looking for the Alto Adige's top small grower then read on. All the wines from 9ha of vineyards have a pure, handmade quality. Four whites are complemented by two reds. Pinot Bianco which includes a little Pinot Grigio and Chardonnay is partly aged in acacia wood as is a 100% Sauvignon. The latter is almost as a refined expression of Sauvignon as one could wish for with a cool herbal, mineral and elderflower poise. The Trias Mitterberg Weiss, an intriguing blend of 80% Chardonnay, 10% Petit Manseng, 5% Viognier and 5% Manzoni is a creamy, peachy, spicy wine fermented in stainless steel and new oak for 10 weeks before bottling. The same class, expression and elegance can be found in the cool pure Riesling. Reds are at a similar level from the brambly, minerally, intensely fruited and *terroir*-influenced Lagrein to expansive Pinot Nero. Perhaps only the last misses the essence of the variety and location. All should be given a little age, the Lagrein at least 5-6 years'.

Recommended Reds:
Alto Adige Lagrein Gries Berger Gei ★★★☆ £E
Alto Adige Merlot Mühlweg ★★★☆ £E
Alto Adige Pinot Nero ★★★ £E
Recommended Whites:
Alto Adige Terlano Sauvignon ★★★☆ £D
Alto Adige Riesling Berg ★★★☆ £D
Trias Mitterberg Weiss IGP ★★★☆ £D
Alto Adige Terlano Pinot Bianco ★★★ £D

Radoar (Alto Adige)
Ten years of organic viticulture at this tiny property (1.5 ha) in the Valle Isarco has certainly added something to wines of intensity and character from other-wise underwhelming grape varieties. Etza is a fascinating mountain white from Müller-Thurgau vines grown at 800m. The spicy floral, herbal complexity has unexpected intensity and there is depth and character not typical of the variety, especially from a good vintage (compare it with Tiefenbrunner's Feldmarschall). Kerner (as Radoy) is a classic example, light yet intense and without coarseness. For red there's Loach from Zweigelt vines of 20-25 years' age. As well as spicy, plummy, bramble fruit there is a certain lift and freshness many Austrian examples miss. It retains the supple texture of the variety but has good length and fine tannins and could be drunk young or with a little age.
Recommended Reds:
Loach ★★☆ £D
Recommended Whites:
Etza ★★★ £D   Radoy ★★★ £D

Produttori San Michele Appiano (Alto Adige) *www.stmichael.it*
The wines of St Michael Eppan, the more usually seen form of the name, are made under the direction of one of Italy's great white winemakers, Hans Terzer. Drawing on 300 ha of vineyards, all the whites show good fruit and the mid-range varietals are defined by the vineyard area from which they are sourced. At the premium level the wines from the prized Sanct Valentin vineyards show greater aromatic complexity as well as an extra precision and refinement that put them ahead of most other Alto Adige examples. Gewürztraminer and Sauvignon are particularly stylish but quality

North-East Italy /Alto Adige

Italy

of all the varietals is exemplary. An exquisite sweet white, Passito Comtess', from dried Gewürztraminer, Riesling, Sauvignon and Pinot Bianco grapes, is wonderfully perfumed but finely balanced and concentrated too. Reds can be very good as well, ripe with good expression and supple textures after at least two or three years' ageing. Most exciting of the reds are very promising Sanct Valentin Lagrein (made since 2000) and a classy, seductive Sanct Valentin Pinot Nero.

Recommended Reds:

Alto Adige Pinot Nero Sanct Valentin ★★★ £E
Alto Adige Pinot Nero Riserva ★★ £D
Alto Adige Lagrein Sanct Valentin ★★★ £E
Alto Adige Cabernet Sanct Valentin ★★ £E

Recommended Whites:

Alto Adige Bianco Passito Comtess' Sanct Valentin ★★★★ £E
Alto Adige Chardonnay Sanct Valentin ★★★ £D
Alto Adige Chardonnay Merol ★★ £D
Alto Adige Sauvignon Sanct Valentin ★★★ £D
Alto Adige Gewürztraminer Sanct Valentin ★★★ £D
Alto Adige Sauvignon Lahn ★★ £D
Alto Adige Pinot Bianco Schulthauser ★★ £D
Alto Adige Pinot Grigio Sanct Valentin ★★ £D
Alto Adige Riesling Montiggl ★★ £C

Cantina Terlano (Alto Adige) *www.cantina-terlano.com*

The Terlan or Terlano cooperative is another of the Alto Adige's dynamic coops. The wines have been made by Rudi Kofler since 2002 but the bold and flavoursome style was established by Hartmann Donà. Above a regular (Classico) series of varietals are an extensive range of vineyard designated varietals and four premium releases with prices to match. While oak can be a little too intrusive in these top cuvées, it does further enhance their structure, and one-off releases of Terlano and Sauvignon with more than a decade's age give an indication of their sometimes exceptional ageing potential. Both the Terlano Classico and the premium Nova Domus achieve good harmony between Pinot Bianco, Sauvignon and Chardonnay. The best of the reds are two versions of Lagrein both which need a minimum 3–5 years age open up fully, especially Porphyr which comes from 70 year old vines. Also made are Merlot (Riserva Siebeneich), Pinot Nero (Riserva Montigl), Cabernet (Riserva Siemegg) and other native varieties. "Rarities" is a special reserve Chardonnay from selected grapes, aged on the lees for 12 months in large wooden barrels and then further aged on the lees for a minimum of 10 years in stainless steel before bottling. The result is an intense but remarkably fresh tasting wine with deep flavours and complexity.

Recommended Reds:

Alto Adige Lagrein Riserva Porphyr ★★★ £D
Alto Adige Lagrein Riserva Gries ★★ £D

Recommended Whites:

Alto Adige Rareties Chardonnay ★★★★ £F
Alto Adige Terlano Nova Domus ★★★ £D
Alto Adige Terlano Classico ★★ £C
Alto Adige Sauvignon Quarz ★★★ £D
Alto Adige Gewürztraminer Lunare ★★ £D
Alto Adige Pinot Bianco Vorberg ★★ £C

Tiefenbrunner (Alto Adige) *www.tiefenbrunner.com*

Tiefenbrunner, one of the Alto Adige's best known estates for much of the latter part of the 20th century, has undergone a gradual transition from Herbert Tiefenbrunner to his son Christof who has

expanded and modernised the range. If others stole a march on Tiefenbrunner in the 90s recent quality is now closer to where it should be, especially amongst the premium wines. Basic white varietals are sound and flavoursome if simple and lacking structure. Gewürztraminer (Castel Turmhof) and Sauvignon (Kirchleiten) show great elegance. Chardonnay is increasingly sophisticated and better balanced with fine aromatics married to structure and better use of oak, particularly in the rich Linticlarus version. However the single most famous wine is Feldmarschall from the humble Müller-Thurgau grape. The Hofstatt vineyard at 1000m was the summer residence of Field Marshall von Fenner zu Fennberg who adorns the label. A return to something approaching the form of the brilliant vintages of the late 80s has only been achieved very recently following replanting in the early 90s. Its elegant, refined floral, spice and herb complexity is matched by impressive flavour intensity and not even a hint of the coarseness on the finish that characterises most Müller-Thurgau. Of the reds, Lagrein is increasingly assured and better than the Cabernet/Merlotbased Linticlarus Cuvée. There is good purity and density in the Castel Turmhof version and more concentration, minerality, oak spice and richness in Riserva Linticlarus.

Recommended Reds:

Alto Adige Lagrein Riserva Linticlarus ★★★☆ £E
Alto Adige Lagrein Castel Turmhof ★★☆ £D
Alto Adige Linticlarus Cuvée ★★ £D

Recommended Whites:

Feldmarschall von Fenner zu Fennberg ★★★☆ £D
Alto Adige Gewürztraminer Castel Turmhof ★★★ £D
Alto Adige Chardonnay Linticlarus ★★★ £D
Alto Adige Chardonnay Castel Turmhof ★★ £D
Alto Adige Sauvignon Kirchleiten ★★☆ £D

✿ Weingut Unterortl (Alto Adige) *www.unterortl.it*

Famed mountaineer Reinhold Messner, the first man to climb all the highest peaks in the Himalayas without oxygen, owns this vineyard, perched high in the hills and on the steepest of slopes in the Val Venosta region of the Alto Adige. But the day to day running – and the winemaking, is left in the more than capable hands of Martin Aurich. With vines being grown up to 1200 metres above sea level and the precipitousness of the slopes, it's a tricky operation which Aurich copes with admirably. On the plus side, there is a constant wind which blows at this height which keeps everything clean and dry thus enhancing the minerality of the wines. As a result of the climatic conditions and the altitude, Aurich generally harvests about two weeks later than his colleagues further down the valley, the longer hang time thus enabling him to achieve a good degree of ripeness in the fruit. He is also one of the few producers in the area to use Stelvin closures. Riesling, Pinot Bianco and Pinot Nero are his main grape varieties in his 4 hectares of vines, with an overall production of around 30,000 bottles a year, but he also has small holdings of Müller-Thurgau, Blatterle, and Frauler (white) and Zweigelt, St. Laurant, Garanoir and Gamaret (red) which he blends to make his entry level wines. But his pride and joy is his Pinot Nero, picked for optimum ripeness and then matured for a year in 25% new oak *barriques* and the rest in old 1,000 and 1,200 litre casks producing a good balance of fruit and acidity with harmonious elegance. His Pinot Bianco – good, biscuity stuff with tones of green apple, typically combines minerality with a glycerinous finish and his Rieslings, both dry and late harvest, both display richness on the palate (and in the case of the late harvest, just the right balance of botrytis) with some acidic backbone. The estate also boasts a distillery where full-frontal Grappe and fruit Aquavite are produced.

Wine behind the label

(NB)
Recommended Reds:
Alto Adige Val Venosta Pinot Nero Castel Juval ★★★☆ £D
Recommended Whites:
Alto Adige Val Venosta Riesling Spielerei Castel Juval ★★★☆ £E
Alto Adige Val Venosta Riesling Castel Juval ★★★ £D
Alto Adige Val Venosta Pinot Bianco Castel Juval ★★★☆ £D

Elena Walch (Alto Adige) www.elenawalch.com
Elena Walch's 30 ha of vineyards are comprised mostly of Castel Ringberg & Kastelaz with most of the varietals still labelled for one site or the other. The Ringberg slopes overlook the Kalterer See (Lago di Caldaro) but more dramatic are the steep terraces of Kastelaz above Tramin (Termeno). Aptly, it is this latter site which does so well with the variety named for the town (Traminer or Gewürztraminer). A deep and distinctive example with a preserved citrus intensity it typically retains good balance despite its richness. An adequate Merlot Riserva also comes from Kastelaz but is surpassed by the Lagrein Riserva which is arguably the best wine from Castel Ringberg with a dense fruit succulence balanced by abundant ripe tannins while a similarly modern styled Chardonnay Riserva is rich, ripe and plump only missing a little more nuance for fine. However this can be found in the flagship white, Beyond the Clouds which adds in small amounts of the more aromatic varieties. A red equivalent, Kermesse is also made as are Pinot Nero, Cabernet Sauvignon and a Moscato Rosa. Very small quantities of an intense, perfumed sweet wine, Cashmere are produced from dried Gewürztraminer and Sauvignon grapes. Regular 'Elena Walch' varietals reveal ripe round fruit if more modest structure and definition. Wines sourced from other vineyards include Chardonnay from Cardellino and Cabernet from Istrice.
Recommended Reds:
Alto Adige Lagrein Riserva Castel Ringberg ★★★☆ £E
Alto Adige Merlot Riserva Kastelaz ★★☆ £E
Recommended Whites:
Alto Adige Bianco Beyond the Clouds ★★★★ £F
Alto Adige Chardonnay Riserva Castel Ringberg ★★★☆ £E
Alto Adige Gewürztraminer Kastelaz ★★★☆ £D
Alto Adige Bianco Passito Cashmere ★★★ £F
Alto Adige Pinot Bianco Kastelaz ★★☆ £D
Alto Adige Pinot Grigio Castel Ringberg ★★ £D

A-Z of producers - *Trentino*

Cesconi (Trentino) www.cesconi.it
The Cesconi family have been grape growers for generations but it is the current generation of four young brothers, Alessandro, Franco, Lorenzo and Roberto, that have transformed this small 12 ha estate. Having switched the vines to Guyot training they produce wines of an atypical ripeness and richness, and have risen quickly to be one of Trentino-Alto Adige's best estates. All the wines, mostly sold under the Vigneti delle Dolomiti IGT, show good depth and intensity with good varietal definition as well as a certain flair and excellent balance. Oak is employed with restraint in an intense, pure Chardonnay while an unoaked Traminer is poised and expressive. Cesconi's Nosiola should also be tasted, now an atypically refined, stylish example of the variety. Olivar, a blend of Pinot Bianco, Pinot Grigio and Chardonnay can be the most complete and complex white. There are also two excellent IGT reds. The expressive and harmonious Moratel is based on Merlot but adds in Cabernet Sauvignon, Teroldego and Lagrein. For a significant step up, try Pivier, a Riserva Merlot which is deep and classy; the best years clearly 4 stars.
Recommended Reds:
Pivier ★★★☆ £D
Moratel ★★☆ £D
Recommended Whites:
Olivar ★★★ £D   Chardonnay ★★★ £D
Traminer Aromatico ★★★ £D   Nosiola ★★☆ £D
Pinot Grigio ★★☆ £C

Ferrari (Trentino) www.ferraritrento.it
Started by Giulio Ferrari in 1902 and taken up by Bruno Lunelli in 1952, Ferrari emerged as Trento's most notable sparkling wine producer in the latter part of the 20th century. Volume is centred on Trento Brut (more than 3 million bottles) while the quality focus has long been the vintage-dated Riserva del Fondatore (less than 40,000 bottles). A Blanc de Blancs Chardonnay, it gets the full metodo classico treatment and spends 8 years on its lees. As its consistency and reputation precede it, the opportunity to enjoy its full, round texture and distinctive matured honeyed finesse comes at a price (one that many Champenois would baulk at). Any vintage back to 1988 is worth a try if the wine has been well-stored. The best of cheaper, if still pricey alternatives are the vintage-dated Brut Perlé, non-vintaged Brut Maximum and Brut Perlé Rosé. The family's interests also extend to water, grappa and still wine production. The latter, from estate vineyards are produced under the Lunelli label and include good unoaked Sauvignon and decent if not great value Pinot Nero.
Ferrari
Recommended Whites:
Trento Brut Giulio Ferrari Riserva del Fondatore ★★★☆ £G
Trento Brut Perlé ★★☆ £E   Trento Brut Maximum ★★ £E
Recommended Rosés:
Trento Brut Perlé Rosé ★★☆ £F
Lunelli
Recommended Reds:
Trentino Pinot Nero Maso Montalto ★★ £E
Recommended Whites:
Trentino Sauvignon Villa San Nicolò ★★ £C

✿ Foradori (Teroldego Rotaliano) www.elisabettaforadori.com
Foradori is one of the top estates in all of Italy yet comes from a zone that is little known outside the country. Elisabetta Foradori is something of a celebrity in Italy for her renditions of Teroldego Rotaliano. Two single-vineyard versions (Vigneto Sgarzon, Vigneto Morei) have once again, been bottled separately (since 2009), surpassed only by Granato, the top selection, a wine of great style and class, which has added tobacco, spice and cedar, beautifully harmonised oak, and dense but fine, ripe tannins that ensure long ageing. The regular Teroldego, Foradori, now shows real poise and persistence allied to a deep, smoky, bramble and mineral character. Two interesting whites are also produced, the Fontanasanta Nosiola, an autochthonal grape varietal found only in the Valle dei Laghi and the hills above Trento and Pressano, fermented and aged for 8 months in clay amphorae to give it great complexity, and a Manzoni Bianco, a cross between Riesling and Pinot Bianco, aged in accacia casks for 12 months and probably needing another two or three years to develop its full potential. Both are classified as Vigneti delle Dolomiti IGT. Wines have been produced biodynamically since 2002. Prices are reasonable for the quality.

North-East Italy /Lombardy /Veneto

Italy

Recommended Reds:
Granato ★★★★☆ £F Teroldego Morel ★★★☆ £E
Teroldego Sgarzon ★★★☆ £E Foradori ★★☆ £D
Recommended Whites:
Fontanasanta Nosiola ★★★☆ £D
Fontanasanta Manzoni Bianco ★★★☆ £D

❀ **Pojer & Sandri (Trentino)** www.pojeresandri.it
Mario Pojer and Fiorentino Sandri make wines as refined as any in
North-East Italy and have been quietly maintaining high standards
for close on four decades. For something unusual, the attractive
unoaked varietals include a floral and herb-scented Nosiola
but even Müller Thurgau is good in the context of the variety.
Whites culminate in Faye, Chardonnay with 10% Pinot Bianco. It is
elegant and classy with a lovely fruit expression, building gently
in texture and complexity with age. The red version of Faye is not
a blockbuster but a very stylish, beautifully textured wine from
Cabernet Sauvignon, Cabernet Franc, Merlot and Lagrein. A stylish
Pinot Nero is in the cool, elegant spectrum and has good substance
but misses the depth of top examples. Maso Besler is a project in
the Cembra Valley where production is focused on just a single
white blend and a single red blend from 4.5 ha of vineyards. The
barrique-aged white is super with mesmerizing aromas, breadth,
purity and intensity from a mix of Pinot Bianco, Sauvignon, Riesling,
Incrocio Manzoni and Kerner. Pojer & Sandri's long-established,
often exquisite sweet wine, Essenzia, typically includes Chardonnay,
Sauvignon, Riesling, Gewürztraminer and Kerner. Sparkling Brut
Cuvée and Brut Rosé also made, from Chardonnay and Pinot Nero.
Most of the wines are sold under the Vigneti delle Dolomiti IGT. If
you're a grappa fan make for the distillery.
Pojer & Sandri
Recommended Whites:
Chardonnay ★★ £C Faye ★★★★ £D Essenzia ★★★☆ £E
Traminer Aromatico ★★★ £C Sauvignon ★★☆ £C
Nosiola ★★ £C Müller Thurgau Palai ★☆ £B
Recommended Reds:
Rosso Faye ★★★☆ £D Pinot Nero ★★☆ £D
Maso Besler
Recommended Whites:
Besler Bianck ★★★☆ £E

San Leonardo (Trentino) www.sanleonardo.it
There are only 18 ha of vineyards but this large estate of 300
ha dates back to the Middle Ages, being originally the site of a
monastery. It is held in high regard for a single red wine that has
been developed by the current owner with help from the enologist
Giacomo Tachis. Improvements to both the vineyard and vinification
have been ongoing and in a good year can result in a complex,
refined yet rich, full expression of a cooler-climate blend of Cabernet
Sauvignon, Cabernet Franc and Merlot (60/30/10). With deep
blackcurrant, spice, plum and subtle herbal character it adds further
complexity and fullness with another 3 or 4 years' cellaring after its
release (8-10 years total). In some years it is not made at all and it
has occasionally been disappointing but there have been recent
good vintages. A varietal Carmenère also needs lengthy cellaring
being built to last having spent 2 years in barrique and a further 3
years in bottle before being commercially released. Another red,
the barrique-aged Villa Gresti is Merlot-based but also includes
10% Carmenère. There is also a basic Bordeaux blend Terre di San
Leonardo, 80% aged in large Slavonian Oak barrels and 20% in

French oak but this has not been tasted.
Recommended Reds:
San Leonardo ★★★★ £E
Carmanere di San Leonardo ★★★ £D
Recommended Whites:
Sauvignon Blanc Vette di San Lorenzo ★★☆ £C

A-Z of producers - *(Eastern) Lombardy*

Ca' dei Frati (Lombardia/Lugana) www.cadeifrati.it
Ca' dei Frati have set high standards for Lugana in the same way
that Anselmi and Pieropan have done for Soave. Wines range
from a consistently stylish and characterful Lugana I Frati through
Brolettino, which is distinguished by its elegance and texture, to
Pratto, an IGT white blend of Lugana, Chardonnay and Sauvignon,
which is lush and exotic with great length of flavour. A small amount
of a concentrated Grande Annata Brolettino is also produced. Aside
from the excellent whites the quality of a red, Ronchedone, is also
improving. First produced from the two Cabernets and Merlot, it is
now made mainly from Marzemino and Sangiovese with just 10%
Cabernet. An Amarone, Pietro dal Cero is also made.
Recommended Whites:
Pratto ★★★ £D Lugana Brolettino Grande Annata ★★★ £D
Lugana Brolettino ★★★ £D
Lugana I Frati ★★☆ £C

A-Z of producers - *Veneto*

Stefano Accordini (Veneto/Valpolicella) www.accordinistefano.it
This small family estate has sourced grapes both from its own
vineyards in Negrar and those under lease but also has new
vineyards at Fumane coming on stream. Brothers Tiziano and
Daniele, the winemaker, continue to make improvements to their
rich but elegant and expressive examples of Valpolicella, Recioto
and Amarone. Valpolicella Acinatico is an intense, very ripe, berryish
ripasso version but like the Amarone and Recioto can vary in
richness and balance according to the vintage. A single-vineyard
version of Amarone, Fornetto, has also been made, but only in the
best vintages. More unusual is Paxxo, also made from dried grapes,
but adding Cabernet Sauvignon and Merlot (together 30%) to the
more usual Corvina and Rondinella.
Recommended Reds:
Amarone della Valpolicella Classico Acinatico ★★★★ £E
Recioto della Valpolicella Classico Acinatico ★★★ £E
Valpolicella Classico Superiore Acinatico ★★ £C

❀ **Allegrini (Veneto/Valpolicella)** www.allegrini.it
The 70 ha Allegrini estate is Valpolicella's leading producer of
modern-style reds. The wines have excellent fruit, balance, depth
and intensity and develop marvellously smooth velvety textures
with age. While a good regular Valpolicella is based on the three
traditional grapes, two single-vineyard reds, previously Valpolicella
crus but now sold as Veronese IGT, continue to evolve. Both are
based on Corvina (70 percent) and Rondinella, but La Grola also
includes Syrah and Oselata. Palazzo della Torre, a ripasso-style
version (but enriched by dried grapes rather than Amarone lees)
also includes a Sangiovese component. Oak is also a feature of
the best wines, including the Amarone, which shows marvellous
richness and concentration in the most recent releases. La Poja is a
pure Corvina made from late-harvested grapes grown on the top of
the La Grola hill and is a wine of striking intensity and depth, now

with a long-established record of production. Villa Giona is separate property in the Classico zone but with 5ha planted exclusively to Cabernet Sauvignon, Merlot and Syrah. The sweet Recioto, Giovanni Allegrini, is dedicated to the memory of the Allegrinis' father, who founded the company. Amarone, La Grola and Palazzo della Torre are all made in significant quantities and should be easy to obtain. New POGGIO AL TESORO wines from Tuscany are very promising.

Recommended Reds:
Amarone della Valpolicella Classico ★★★★★ £F
La Poja ★★★★★ £F
Recioto della Valpolicella Classico Giovanni Allegrini ★★★★ £F
La Grola ★★★ £D   Palazzo della Torre ★★★ £D

Anselmi (Veneto/Soave)   *www.anselmi.eu*
Roberto Anselmi used to make Soave. 'Used to' because all the wines are now Veneto IGT as one of the Veneto's, indeed Italy's pioneers for quality continues the pursuit of excellence beyond the restraints of the appellation. Only the regular bottling of San Vincenzo is made in substantial quantities but quality is consistently high. Two former crus offer a marked contrast in style with two or three years' age: Capitel Foscarino offers a lovely pure citrus and yellow plum fruit, while Capitel Croce divides opinion somewhat with its slightly exaggerated oak-influenced style with some spice, even coconut character. Foscarino and includes a little Chardonnay, whilst San Vincenzo has up to 30% Chardonnay and Sauvignon Blanc. The star, though, is the wonderfully elegant, pure-fruited and classy sweet wine, I Capitelli. The red, Realda shows concentrated blackcurrant fruit and a leafy influence.

Recommended Reds:
Cabernet Sauvignon Realda ★★ £D
Recommended Whites:
I Capitelli ★★★★ £E   Capitel Foscarino ★★★ £D
Capitel Croce ★★☆ £C   San Vincenzo ★☆ £C

Bisol (Veneto/Prosecco)   *www.bisol.it*
One of the leading lights in Prosecco, Bisol have been established here since the 16th century and it remains very much a family business. The wines are characterised by good balance with regular Prosecco is everything it should be while a lot of effort goes into more serious sparklers. Non-vintaged Garnei Brut is a good fresh, floral, bright and uncomplicated example which, with around 10g of residual sugar, is slightly off-dry. Crede, one of several site specific versions, comes from clayey soils reflected in richer fruit and a little more texture. Other Prosecco include a still Tranquillo version and a more ambitious Cartizze Superiore version (from the designated subzone) with surprising richness and complexity that has been consistently impressive in recent vintages and might reasonably be considered as an interesting alternative to decent Champagne. Talento Metodo Classico sparkling wines from Chardonnay, Pinot Nero and Pinot Bianco are also made as is Duca di Dolle, an idiosyncratic sweet white from dried Prosecco grapes. Currently a blend of 14 vintages, it is only vaguely reminiscent of good Vin Santo despite a mix of sweet unctuous honeyed raisin fruit and more caramel and gently oxidised flavours on a drier finish; the balance and a certain vitality underpin its drinkability.

Recommended Whites:
Passito di Prosecco Duca di Dolle ★★★☆ £F
Prosecco di Valdobbiadene Cartizze Superiore ★★★ £D
Prosecco di Valdobbiadene Brut Crede ★★☆ £C
Prosecco di Valdobbiadene Brut Garnei ★★ £B

⚙ Buglioni (Veneto/Valpolicella)   *www.buglioni.com*
Behind the slick presentation is a project of real substance delivering focussed elegant red wines that take Valpolicella truely into the 21st century. The first wines were only made in 2000 from vineyards bought in 1993. Diego Bertoni is the winemaker who has created both fine basics and textured, vibrant premium reds that represent a distinct departure from the coarser more raisiny styles that too many drinkers still associate with the region. The estate's 20 ha of vines are in part planted to higher density. There is excellent fruit purity as well as vitality in all the wines affording great drinkability but also fine structures that will ensure excellent medium-term drinking. Compare the regular Valpolicella with others at the same level and be very surprised or Il Ruffiano with premium versions from better known names. Amarone and Riserva are already very good but with further refinements kicking in expect even more with successive releases. The dry white, Il Clandestino is 100% Garganega, as is the passito, Il Monello.

Recommended Reds:
Amarone della Valpolicella Classico Riserva ★★★★★ £F
Amarone della Valpolicella Classico ★★★★☆ £E
Recioto della Valpolicella Il Recioto ★★★★ £E
Valpolicella Classico Superiore Ripasso Il Bugiardo ★★★☆ £D
Valpolicella Classico Superiore Il Ruffiano ★★★ £D
Valpolicella Classico ★★☆ £C   Bardolino Il Bardolino ★★ £C
Recommended Whites:
Il Clandestino ★☆ £B
Recommended Rosés:
Bardolino Chiaretto Il Balordo ★ £B

⚙ Tommaso Bussola (Veneto/Valpolicella)   *www.bussolavini.com*
A brilliant and dedicated young grower with 9.5 ha of vineyards, Tommaso Bussola only started on his own in the early 1990s yet is now one of the stars of Valpolicella. As well as a regular bottling (BG – named for his uncle, Giuseppe Bussola with whom he started out) of each wine, there are premium wines labelled TB made from the finest fruit and aged in new oak. Amarone Vigneto Alto vies with the moderately sweet Recioto TB as the best of the lot. The wines are wonderfully perfumed with ever more depth and concentration in the most recent releases. While production is small and prices very high for the TB wines, the BG versions (with more average prices) show fine fruit and intensity and are better than many bigger-volume examples. Older vintages, while good, are not at the same level as that seen since 1997. A single vineyard Valpolicella Classico Superiore Ca' del Laito and a Merlot (80%) and Cabernet blend, L'Errante, are also produced.

Recommended Reds:
Amarone della Valpolicella Classico TB Vigneto Alto ★★★★★ £G
Amarone della Valpolicella Classico TB ★★★★★ £G
Amarone della Valpolicella Classico BG ★★★ £F
Recioto della Valpolicella ClassicoTB ★★★★★ £F
Recioto della Valpolicella Classico BG ★★★ £E
Valpolicella Classico Superiore TB ★★★☆ £D
Valpolicella Classico BG ★★ £C

Cantino del Castello (Veneto/Soave)   *www.cantinacastello.it*
This small producer has turned into a really good source of consistently characterful and well-made Soave. The cellars are located in a 13th-century palazzo below Castello Scaligero, the landmark fortress of Soave, but draw on 13 ha of vineyards within the Classico zone. The regular bottling is 90% Garganega vinified in stainless steel and is very fresh, citrusy and pure when young.

North-East Italy /Veneto

Italy

Two crus are based on 80% Garganega – that from the Pressoni vineyard is more expressive than the basic wine, with a floral and spice intensity, while Carniga (given much longer contact with lees) is more minerally and salty but also fuller and more concentrated – a stylishly individual expression. Acini Soavi is produced only from late-harvested Garganega grapes from Pressoni and spends a year in 15-hl oak. Rich and lush but well structured, it has an array of citrus and stone fruits as well as a floral component. Very small amounts of Recioto di Soave Cortepittora and another sweet white from dried grapes, Acini Dolci, are also produced as is a little sparkling wine.

Recommended Whites:

Recioto di Soave Cortepittora ★★★ £E

Soave Classico Acini Soavi ★★★ £D Soave Classico Carniga ★★★ £D

Soave Classico Pressoni ★★☆ £C Soave Classico Castello ★☆ £C

✿ Corte Sant' Alba (Veneto/Valpolicella) *www.cortesantalda.it*
For those who insist that only a handful of really good producers make Valpolicella and Amarone, Corte Sant'Alda is likely to be one of several they have missed. Much of the 15 ha of vineyard has been newly replanted employing single-Guyot training (rather than the traditional pergola system) for better quality fruit. In addition oak vats are now being used for fermentation in a multi-faceted approach to further improving quality. Since the late 1990s these sleek, elegant wines have been of indisputably good quality, with excellent expression but no lack of intensity or concentration either. In fact for composed, balanced examples of Valpolicella, Amarone and Recioto this is as good a producer as any. Even the regular Valpolicella, Ca' Fiui is good – one of the best non-ripasso examples made. Minute quantities of Amarone were also produced in a Mithas version in 1997. A dry white, Retratto, is made from Sauvignon complemented by Chardonnay and Garganega, while some Soave (Vigne di Mezzane) is also made from an additional 2 ha.

Recommended Reds:

Amarone della Valpolicella ★★★★ £E

Recioto della Valpolicella ★★★★ £E

Valpolicella Superiore Ripasso Campi Magri ★★★ £D

Valpolicella Superiore Mithas ★★★ £C Valpolicella Ca'Fiui ★★ £C

✿✿ Romano dal Forno (Valpolicella) *www.dalfornoromano.it*
Valpolicella's most sought-after producer doesn't even hail from the Classico hills north-west of Verona but from slopes further to the east. It is not yet clear how his own site compares to the best slopes in the Classico zone but a radical retraining of the vines (trained low at very high densities) in order to obtain fully ripe, concentrated fruit and the use of new oak set his wines apart from the rest. The Valpolicella shows an extract and concentration missing in most Amarone and bears no resemblance to much of what shares the name. The quality is stunning and not simply showy and fruit-rich but deep and structured, with remarkable character and complexity. Most recently it has been produced only from grapes with a short amount of drying of around six weeks. One has to bear in mind, too, that the wine spends 36 months in new *barriques* and then a further 24 months in bottle before being commercially released. Extraordinary Amarone and Recioto of unprecedented breadth and depth set the standard for others to emulate with only 15 litres of Amarone produced from each 100kg. of grapes. Quantities are very small, reflected in their 'cult status' prices.

Recommended Reds:

Amarone della Valpolicella Vigneto di Monte Lodoletta ✪✪✪✪✪ £H

Recioto della Valpolicella Vigna Sere ✪✪✪✪✪ £H

Valpolicella Superiore ★★★★ £E

Filippi (Veneto/Soave) *www.cantinafilippi.it*
The promising young organic enterprise that is Visco & Filippi relies on the expertise of Alessandro (winemaker) and Filippo (in the vineyard). Taking charge (from 2003) of their own 20 ha of mostly old vine Garganega and Trebbiano on elevated hillside sites (320-400m), much effort has gone into enhancing the tipicità of the wines. Current releases are characterised by an elegance and intensity as well as impressive length of flavour. Dry Soaves are 100% Garganega and reflect different soils and expositions. Vigne della Brà from partly volcanic soils reveals an elegant, smoky, floral, herbal minerality while Monteseroni from old vines in calcareous soils is classy and intense and very long on the palate. A late-harvested version is essentially dry with a leesy, dried fruit skins character. Caprea, the Recioto spends 12 months in used *barriques* and is dense and sweet with dried stone fruits on a lingering finish. Amarone Castalberti comes from Colle Masua (in the Marano area) and is in a much more accessible style than most. From old vines in a vineyard of mixed varieties it has a pure, intense, almost racy style.

Recommended Reds:

Amarone della Valpolicella Castalberti ★★★★ £E

Recommended Whites:

Recioto di Soave Calprea ★★★★ £E

Soave Superiore Monteseroni ★★★ £C

Soave Classico Vigne della Brà ★★☆ £C Soave Classico ★★ £C

Gini (Veneto/Soave) *www.ginivini.com*
Brothers Sandro and Claudio are the current generation to run this 25 ha estate, the family having owned vines here for around 300 years. The quality of Soave is excellent, including the regular Classico which is produced in the largest quantities. Old vines give real character and concentration, even more so in two fine crus of equal quality, La Froscà (50-year-old vines) and Contrada Salvarenza (80-year-old vines). Both are *barrique*-aged to give lusher, fuller textures without overwhelming the fruit in the least. Recioto Col Foscarin shows good balance and intensity of preserved citrus fruits. Also made in relatively small volumes but not tasted are Sauvignon, Chardonnay and Pinot Nero.

Recommended Whites:

Recioto di Soave Col Foscarin ★★★ £E

Soave Classico Superiore Contrada Salvarenza Vecchie Vigne ★★★ £D

Soave Classico La Froscà ★★★ £C Soave Classico ★★ £C

Inama (Veneto/Soave) *www.inamaaziendaagricola.it*
Stefano Inama assumed control of the winemaking here in the early 1990s and the wines have attracted plenty of attention ever since. Two single-vineyard Soaves are *barrique*-fermented and aged. While characterful and well-made they miss the purity and *terroir* expression of the new breed of Soave seen better in an unoaked regular Vin Soave version with citrusy, grapefruit notes, fine balance and subtle leesy and minerally hints. The championing of Chardonnay and Sauvignon in the Soave district has attracted a fair amount of controversy. The Sauvignon is produced in oaked and unoaked versions, whilst the Chardonnay is fresh and unoaked.. The Sauvignons in particular have made great progress whether the expressive and elegant Vulcaia version or a fuller yet still stylish (oaked) Vulcaia Fume. Stefano Inama also makes Bradisismo, a blend of 70% Cabernet Sauvignon and 30% Carmenère from the Colli Berici. Now a top flight Veneto red, it displays intense wild plum and bramble fruit and sometimes a touch of austerity and leafy

herbaceousness but this contributes to its complexity with age. Also from the Colli Berici estate is a single-vineyard varietal Cabernet Sauvignon and a Carmenere Piu, made with 70% Carmanere and 30% Merlot. Binomio Montepulciano d'Abruzzo is produced in conjunction with LA VALENTINA (see Central Italy).

Recommended Reds:

Bradisismo ★★★★ £E

Recommended Whites:

Vulcaia Après ★★★☆ £E   Vulcaia Fumé ★★★ £D
Vulcaia Sauvignon ★★☆ £C
Soave Classico Superiore Vigneto du Lot ★★☆ £D
Soave Classico Superiore Vigneti di Foscarino ★★☆ £C
Soave Classico Superiore Vin Soave ★★☆ £C
Chardonnay Campo dei Tovi ★★ £D   Chardonnay ★★ £C

La Biancara (Veneto/Gambellara) www.angiolinomaule.com
Angiolino Maule runs his estate along biodynamic principles and is one of Italy's leading advocates of practices that claim to harness terrestial and cosmic energy forces. But Gambellara? Well this is a bit tacked on the eastern edge of Soave. Angiolino owns 9ha with a further 5ha leased. Whites are 100% Garganega and reflect both *terroir* and a very natural, non-interventionist approach to winemaking - including spontaneous fermentations, no fining and no filtration. Quality can be very high even if the style is unlikely to ever command a broad consensus amongst wine drinkers. Try at least the basic white, Masieri to give you an indication - a ripe, pure and intense expression of Garganega. Sassaia brings a more floral, skin contacted exoticism while Pico, from soils of volcanic origin, is intensely spicy and mineral with piercing, pure old-fashioned peach flavours, as well as being impressively long and refined. Recioto with lively acidity has an intense, sweet dried fruits character but is not in an oxidative style and should keep for an age. Reds include a Grenache (Tocai Rosso) So San, which needs at least 5-6 years' age and a more forward Rosso Masieri, half Merlot and Cabernet Sauvignon that is brighter and more distinct. A straight Merlot is also produced as well as Talbane, a botrytised Garganega, made only in those years which are conducive to producing noble rot.

Recommended Reds:

So San ★★★ £C   Rosso Masieri ★★☆ £C

Recommended Whites:

Pico ★★★★ £D   Recioto di Gambellara ★★★☆ £E
Sassaia ★★☆ £C   Gambellara Classico Masieri ★★ £C

Le Salette (Veneto/Valpolicella) www.lesalette.it
Franco Scamperle makes consistent, stylish and very drinkable Valpolicella and Amarone. Apart from regular Valpolicella Classico all the wines are vineyard specific. Of two single-vineyard Valpolicellas, Ca' Carnocchio is produced solely from dried grapes and combines the supple texture of a good Valpolicella with more of the flavour depth associated with Amarone. There are also two versions of both Amarone and Recioto. The intense but only moderately concentrated La Marega Amarone is aged only partly in *barrique* while the Pergole Vece version (made only in the best years) is aged entirely in *barriques*. Both Amarone and Recioto wines have significantly more depth and complexity in the Pergole Vece versions. A sweet white, Cesare Passito, is made from dried Garganega, Malvasia and Moscato grapes.

Recommended Reds:

Amarone della Valpolicella Classico Pergole Vece ★★★★ £F
Amarone della Valpolicella Classico La Marega ★★★ £E
Recioto della Valpolicella Classico Pergole Vece ★★★ £F
Recioto della Valpolicella Classico Le Traversagne ★★ £E
Valpolicella Classico Superiore Ca' Carnocchio ★★★ £D
Valpolicella Classico Superiore I Progni ★★ £C

Maculan (Veneto/Breganze) www.maculan.net
Fausto Maculan has been the driving force in this internationally renowned estate with 40 ha of vineyards (either owned or leased) - for long the only producer of real note in the Breganze zone some way north of Vicenza. He also works with other growers producing wine from another 50 ha in the Breganze DOC appellation. Famed for his production of some of Italy's finest sweet wines, he also makes very good reds, initially as Cabernet Sauvignon Ferrata but more recently as simply Fratta, the premium blend of Cabernet Sauvignon and Merlot. Other premium reds include Brentino, a fruit-driven Merlot/Cabernet blend, a varietal Merlot, Crosara, and a Cabernet Sauvignon, Palazzotto. There are also entry level, unoaked, reds - Salgarone (100% Merlot) Cornorotto (Marzemino), a Pinot Nero and a Cabernet blend (80% Sauvignon and 20% Franc). Dry whites are improving with more subtle oak treatment, Chardonnay and Sauvignon are now sold separately under the Ferrata label. Unoaked wines include Bidibi, a blend of Tai and Sauvignon, a 100% Vespaiolo and Pino & Toi, a blend of Pinot Bianco, Pinot Grigio and Tocai. Sweet whites include the grapy, aromatic Dindarella from a strain of Moscato, Fior d'Arancio, while Torcolato is made from dried Vespaiola grapes. Only the botrytis-affected grapes are selected for Acininobili which is aged (but not fermented) in new French oak *barriques*. There is an extra intensity to its sweet dried-fruit richness, well checked by acidity, but it is made in much smaller quantities than a similarly impressive Torcolato. Madoro is a sweet wine made from dried Marzemina grapes (80%) and Cabernet Sauvignon (20%).

Recommended Reds:

Fratta ★★★ £F   Breganze Rosso Crosara ★★ £D
Breganze Cabernet Sauvignon Palazzotto ★★ £D
Brentino ★ £C

Recommended Whites:

Acininobili ★★★★ £G   Breganze Torcolato ★★★★ £E
Dindarello ★★★ £D   Ferrata Sauvignon ★★ £D
Ferrata Chardonnay ★★ £D
Breganze Bianco Breganze di Breganze ★ £B

Marion (Veneto/Valpolicella) www.marionvini.it
The Campedelli family bought this property centred on a fine 15th-century villa in a valley east of Verona in 1988 but only initiated wine production in 1994, with own-label production since the late-90s. Stefano Campedelli, his wife and brother are assisted by Celestino Gaspari (Zymé) and have achieved consistently impressive results both with Valpolicella and Cabernet Sauvignon, and more recently Teroldego and Amarone. All are subject, at least in part, to some drying of the grapes, resulting in ripe, concentrated and vigorous reds with good ageing potential. Valpolicella includes 10% Teroldego along with Corvina and Rondinella. The Teroldego is a rare example to be produced outside Trentino and is intense, ripe and concentrated with earthy, spicy tones. Cabernet has intriguing overripe and preserved-fruit characters while Amarone has classic raisin, plum and black cherry fruit if not yet the extra dimension or complexity of the best. Also made is a sweet white from dried Garganega and Trebbiano grapes.

Recommended Reds:

Amarone della Valpolicella ★★★☆ £F
Valpolicella Superiore ★★★ £D
Cabernet Sauvignon ★★★ £E   Teroldego ★★★ £D

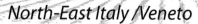

Wine behind the label

North-East Italy /Veneto

Masi (Veneto/Valpolicella) *www.masi.it*
This large family firm is synonymous with Valpolicella and Amarone and has been a leader in experimentation and innovation in the Valpolicella zone. Firsts include the bottling of single-vineyard Amarone and Recioto (Campolongo di Torbe, Mazzano and Mezzanella), the re-introduction of the ripasso method in Campofiorin (and for which they have the registered trademark) and the revised dried-grape variation for enrichment (a refermentation) in Brolo di Campofiorin from a special parcel of the same vineyard. Then there are the new wines from 'rescued' grape varieties, the best of which is Osar, based on Oseleta (80% – though complemented by the main Valpolicella grape, Corvina). Toar from Corvina and Rondinella also includes some Oseleta. Both wines show some new-oak influence. However, as impressive as early releases of many of the wines have been, down the years there has been a tendency for quality to gradually slip away and at times the wines have also been characterised by a somewhat high-toned character, leading sometimes to excessive levels of volatile acidity as the wines have aged. At a lower level there is better value to be had elsewhere and on occasion some of the well-established premium wines can lack depth and richness when tasted against some of the zone's leading wines. Production is large from a total of 400 ha of vineyards; as well as 160 ha in the Veneto, there are significant holdings in western Friuli. Grandarella, a newish red from dried grapes, is of Friuli origins; a blend of Refosco (75%) complemented by Carmenère and Corvina, it has powerful, intense fruit if not the concentration or dimension of top Amarone. The range also includes the wines of the Serègo Alighieri estate. Best is the Amarone, Vaio Armaron, while Possessioni red and white are modest. Three wines have also been produced from Argentina's Tupungato Valley in Mendoza. Corbec Appassimento from semi-dried Corvina and Malbec grapes (70/30), Passo Doble, essentially reverse proportions using a dried-grape component for enrichment and a Paso Doble Bianco from Torrontes and a little Pinot Grigio. Since 2007, the Bossi Fedrigotti estate have been working with Masi, producing not only a Bordeaux blend, Fojaneghe, but also varietals, Gewürztraminer, Marzemino, Teroldego and Pinot Grigio and more recently, a sparkling Chardonnay/Pinot Nero, Conte Federico Brut Millesimato.

Masi
Recommended Reds:
Amarone della Valpolicella Mazzano ★★★ £F
Amarone della Valpolicella Costasera ★★★ £E
Amarone della Valpolicella Campolongo di Torbe ★★ £E
Recioto della Valpolicella Classico Amandorlato Mezzanella ★★ £E
Osar ★★★ £E   Grandarella ★★★ £D   Brolo di Campofiorin ★★ £D
Toar ★★ £B   Campofiorin ★☆ £C
Recommended Whites:
Soave Classico Colbaraca ★★ £C

Serègo Alighieri
Recommended Reds:
Amarone della ValpolicellaVaio Armaron ★★★ £E
Recioto della Valpolicella Casal dei Ronchi ★★ £E

Nardello (Veneto/Soave) *www.nardellovini.it*
Nardello are yet more proof of a revitalised Soave region. This 14 ha family estate has only been producing wine under its own label since 2001 but the vines are well established (40–50 years old) and split between Monte Zoppega and Monte Tondo in the very south of the Classico zone. The family have a committed and recently trained winemaker in Daniele Nardello, who produces a striking,

assertive and flavoursome example in Meridies. After fermentation in stainless steel it spends 5–6 months on the lees – an influence which complements the white flower, herb and apple scents. A combination of 100% Garganega and the clay and volcanic soils seems to contribute to its singular character. In contrast, Recioto is refined with grapefruit, honey and gentle spice, and a lingering finish. Between the two, an off-dry Soave Vigna Turbian blends late harvest Garganegha (70%) with Trebbiano di Soave to produce a fruity, floral wine with good balance between the fruit and the acidity. Also made but not tasted is a Monte Zoppega version of Soave and a Veneto IGT Blanc de Fe made from equal proportions of Garganega, Trebbiano di Soave and Chardonnay.
Recommended Whites:
Recioto di Soave Suavissimus ★★★☆ £E
Soave Vigna Turbian ★★★ £D   Soave Classico Meridies ★★☆ £C

Angelo Nicolis & Figli (Veneto/Valpolicella) *www.vininicolis.com*
Of the three Nicolis brothers who continue the business started by their father Angelo in 1951, it is Giuseppe who is responsible for the winemaking and Giancarlo who takes care of the vines. Their partnership is an increasingly successful one with fine quality Valpolicella and, especially, Amarone from their best sites. Seccal Valpolicella is a classic ripasso style with lots of flavour intensity but the best efforts are reserved for Amarone. The regular example, a blend from 3 sites that is aged only in large oak, is intense, finely textured and well balanced. However the Ambrosan - aged in part in *barriques* and with 20% Rondinella and 10% Croatina complementing the Corvina - adds another level of depth and complexity. Extra virgin olive oil isn't bad either if you're not looking for the intensity or pungency of a Tuscan example.
Recommended Reds:
Amarone della Valpolicella Classico Ambrosan ★★★★☆ £F
Amarone della Valpolicella Classico ★★★★ £E
Recioto della Valpolicella Classico ★★★ £E
Valpolicella Classico Superiore Seccal ★★☆ £C
Valpolicella Classico Superiore ★★ £C

Pieropan (Veneto/Soave) *www.pieropan.it*
The Pieropan Soaves are made in the vineyard, in the sense that the greatest efforts have gone into producing ever better-quality grapes from this 30 ha estate. Both a reliably good Soave Classico and single-vineyard Calvarino are unoaked and based on Garganega complemented by a superior type of Trebbiano, Trebbiano di Soave. In recent years La Rocca, made solely from Garganega from a 5.5 ha slope, has been fermented and aged in double-sized *barriques* and has added more richness to its pure-fruited expression. Both this and Calvarino may be drunk young but typically keep for at least five years. The range of dry whites is complemented by a fine Recioto di Soave Le Colombare, for which the ripest Garganega grapes are dried for several months to produce a rich, ripe and delicately nutty sweet wine after two years in large wood. Passito della Rocca, in contrast, is based on Sauvignon and Riesling grapes (with smaller percentages of Trebbiano di Soave and Garganega) and aged in *barriques* to produce a more intense, exotic fruit and honeyed richness. A little of another sweet wine, Santa Lucia, is made when conditions allow for late-harvested botrytis-affected Garganega grapes. In 1999 the Pieropan family bought a previously uncultivated property in Cellore d'Illasi, in the heart of the Valpolicella and Amarone production zone and planted it with Corvina, Corvinone, Rondinella and Croatina Veronese. Ruberpan is a Valpolicella Superiore with balanced red fruit flavours, whilst the

Amarone is fresh and powerful with black fruit flavours. The vines are still relatively young (planted in 2000) and the complexity of the wines will undoubtedly increase as the vines age. An extra dry sparkling rosé is also made from Corvina grapes but this has not been tasted.

Recommended Reds:
Amarone della Valpolicella ★★★☆ £F
Valpolicella Superiore Ruberpan ★★☆ £C

Recommended Whites:
Recioto di Soave Le Colombare ★★★★ £E
Soave Classico Vigneto La Rocca ★★★☆ £D
Soave Classico Vigneto Calvarino ★★★☆ £C
Soave Classico ★★☆ £C   Passito della Rocca ★★★ £F

✿ Quintarelli (Veneto/Valpolicella)

Giuseppe Quintarelli was Valpolicella's greatest advocate of artisanal winemaking. Since his death in January 2012, the estate has continued to be run by his daughter, Fiorenza and her husband Gianpaolo with his grandsons, Francesco and Lorenzo. The wines, still bottled and labelled by hand, are based on the three classic grapes of Valpolicella but with a few interlopers. They have great power, extract and intensity, needing long barrel-ageing to evolve into something complex yet demanding. A certain variability in quality (but often great) can prove frustrating. Nonetheless, the wines will always attract those in search of sheer intensity, extract and complexity even if the balance and texture are occasionally found wanting. The remarkable Alzero with mineral, black fruits, herb, chocolate, spices and a cigar-like complexity with 10 years age, is made from partially dried Cabernet Franc and Cabernet Sauvignon grapes. Something of this complexity is also seen in Primofiore which meshes an Amarone component with Cabernet Franc grapes and is designed to be consumed much earlier, being released only two years after the vintage, rather than the 10 years for the other reds. A very small amount of a white from dried grapes is also made. Prices reflect the wines' cult status.

Recommended Reds:
Amarone della Valpolicella Classico Monte Ca' Paletta ★★★★★ £H
Recioto della Valpolicella Classico Monte Ca' Paletta ★★★★★ £H
Alzero ★★★★★ £H
Valpolicella Classico Superiore Monte Ca' Paletta ★★★★ £F
Primofiore ★★★☆ £E

Recommended Whites:
Bianco Secco ★★☆ £E

Roccolo Grassi (Veneto/Valpolicella) www.roccolograssi.it

Marco Sartori is a rapidly rising star of Valpolicella even if his10 ha of Valpolicella vineyard, Roccolo Grassi lie well to the east of the Classico zone (and north-east of Verona – DAL FORNO is in the adjacent valley to the east). There is a real focus on quality in the vineyard, in pursuing low yields per vine and in obtaining fully ripe fruit. A rigorous selection is apparent in the wines which are clean, modern and very fruit-driven yet with classic flavours. The tannins are ripe and there is good balancing acidity. In Amarone there is real richness and depth and it is almost overwhelming in its intensity if drunk young. The sheer impact of the fruit to some extent obscures any elegance the wines might otherwise show but the real test will be to see how recent releases mature. Marco also has 4 ha of Vigneto La Broia for the production of Soave and Recioto di Soave. The latter is almost decadent in its ripe and overripe exotic fruit characters. There is guava, quince, overripe apple and pear, preserved citrus and muscovado sugar but it avoids being raisiny.

Note that this has not been made since 2009. The wines previously appeared under the name Bruno Sartori, which could easily have been confused with the large commercial operation of Sartori.

Recommended Reds:
Amarone della Valpolicella ★★★ £E
Recioto della Valpolicella ★★★ £E
Valpolicella Superiore Roccolo Grassi ★★★ £D

Recommended Whites:
Recioto di Soave La Broia ★★★ £E   Soave Superiore La Broia ★ £C

Serafini & Vidotto (Veneto)

From close to the River Piave north of Treviso, this estate would seem to be well off the beaten track for quality yet the wines from Francesco Serafini and Antonello Vidotto suggest otherwise. These reds perhaps owe more to dedicated work in the vineyards (some 18 ha) and careful selection rather than to site but are of commendable quality. The top wine, Rosso dell'Abbazia, is a blend of the two Cabernets (80%) with 10% each of Merlot and Pinot Nero and is aged in new barriques. Cool but ripe-fruited with real intensity and extract, it also shows considerable complexity and a Bordeaux-like refinement. The struggle for ripeness is more evident in lesser vintages yet the wines can still show well with age (7 or 8 years). Pinot Nero can also be most enchanting with smoke, floral, herb, berry, cherry, even redcurrant aromas, if missing the texture or breadth of fine Burgundy. More moderately priced is the medium-bodied Phigaia After the Red, based on Cabernet Franc and Merlot. Though more likely to show a hint of greeness, it is sound, flavoursome and can be drunk quite young. A white, Il Bianco dell'Abazia, is a Sauvignon/Chardonnay blend but it has not been tasted. A new range of entry level varietals under the I Vitigni label (since 2008) is subject to work in progress.

Recommended Reds:
Rosso dell' Abazia ★★★★ £E   Pinot Nero ★★★ £E
Phigaia After The Red ★★ £D

Suavia (Veneto/Soave) www.suavia.it

Suavia has been making wine under its own label for more than 20 years and refined, classy Soave it is too. The young Tessari sisters are now having an impact on the winemaking, particularly Valentina. All the Soave wines except the flavoursome, characterful regular Soave Classico are 100% Garganega. The Monte Carbonare cru is vinified in stainless steel and offers an array of refined spiced fruits in contrast with the richer textured and complex, minerally Le Rive. Both have the structure to improve for at least 3–4 years. Acinatum is medium-bodied, pure and intense – not big but poised, refined and long. Massifitti, produced since 2008, is a 100% Trebbiano di Soave, spending 15 months in stainless steel on its lees, followed by 15 months in bottle before release. It's minerally and smokey with tones of dried herbs and fresh acidity. Suavia's olive oil is good too, with a spicy, herbaceous intensity.

Recommended Whites:
Recioto di Soave Classico Acinatum ★★★ £F
Soave Classico Superiore Le Rive ★★★ £D
Soave Classico Monte Carbonare ★★★ £C
Soave Classico ★★ £C   Massifitti Trebbiano di Soave ★★ £C

Tamellini (Veneto/Soave)

The Tamellini brothers are yet another helping to bring a quiet revolution to the wines of Soave. Dedication and hard work on 15ha of vineyard is enhanced by consultancy from Paolo Caciorgna (wines) and Federico Curtaz (vines) and can be seen in wines of

depth and density. Single vineyard Le Bine is more detailed and drinks well with three years' age. Another version, Anguane has also been produced but this has not been tasted recently. Recioto is super, one of the top examples produced. The crushed fruit essence of preserved peach and nectarine is given lift and expression by a fine streak of acidity. Well balanced, pure, dense but not heavy, it makes for a great dessert wine.

Recommended Whites:

Recioto di Soave Classico Vigna Marogne ★★★★ £E

SoaveClassico Le Bine ★★★ £D   Soave ★★☆ £C

Tedeschi (Veneto/Valpolicella) www.tedeschiwines.com

The fifth generation of Tedeschis to be involved in making wine here in the heart of the Valpolicella zone is now in charge. They control 67 ha of vineyards, 22 ha of which are owned. Of a substantial range, the best wines are the premium Amarone and Recioto which show classic vigour, flavour intensity and power. More occasionally made is a Fabriseria Amarone Classico, effectively a Riserva. The modern, barrique-aged Rosso La Fabriseria adds a small amount of Cabernet Sauvignon to Corvina, Corvinone, Rondinella and Dindarella. Also made are a sweet white from Garganega and Soarin grapes, Vin de la Fabriseria, a ripasso red, Capitel San Rocco, of variable quality and basic generics of Valpolicella, Bardolino, Soave, etc.

Recommended Reds:

Amarone della Valpolicella Classico Capitel Monte Olmi ★★★★ £F

Amarone della Valpolicella Classico La Fabriseria ★★★★ £E

Amarone della Valpolicella Classico ★★ £E

Recioto della Valpolicella Classico Capitel Monte Fontana ★★★ £E

Rosso La Fabriseria ★★★ £D

Valpolicella Classico Superiore Capitel dei Nicolò ★★ £C

Terre di Leone (Veneto/Valpolicella) www.terredileone.it

Terre di Leone is a young estate situated in the heart of the classic Valpolicella appellation. It now extends to 10 ha on non-irrigated volcanic soil. The vines are planted at a density of around 7,000 per hectare, thus limiting the yield of each vine in order to extract the maximum expression of the terroir. Yields are further limited by a strict selection of the grapes at harvest time with hang time being extended as far as possible. After the fermentation has finished, a further selection of the wine with the best tannins are then matured in various sizes of French oak barrels of different ages, to complete the vinification. The result is a series of very smooth wines with plenty of fruit beneath the tannins. "Dedicatum" is their entry level wine, just classfied as IGT Rosso Veronese, which is soft and smooth, although quite intense. Valpolicella Classico Superiore has notes of black cherry and is soft to the palate. Their Ripasso, passed over the skins of the current year's Amarone to give it some enrichment and then matured in French oak for 20 months, is very smooth and intense, whilst the Amarone itself is intense, complex and persistent on the finish. Since 2009, an unoaked Valpolicella Classico, Re Pazzo, also made without the use of dried grapes, has been produced, displaying fresh racy fruitiness, but with enough structure to give it a reasonable amount of complexity. (NB)

Recommended Reds:

Amarone della Valpolicella Classico ★★★★☆ £F

Valpolicella Ripasso ★★★☆ £E

Valpolicella Classico Superiore ★★★ £D

Valpolicella Classico Re Pazzo ★★★ £D

IGT Rosso Veronese Dedicatum ★★☆ £D

Vignalta (Veneto/Colli Euganei) www.vignalta.it

Many wine lovers would have trouble locating Valpolicella in the Veneto so what chance has Colli Euganei? The hills south-west of Padova don't in fact have much of a reputation yet for more than a decade Vignalta has produced fine reds and interesting whites. The top red is Gemola, 70% Merlot complemented by Cabernet Franc, a cool but ripe, elegant Bordeaux-like red that ages gracefully. A Rosso Riserva from a similar blend hasn't the same depth or concentration but is typically supple and expressive. A small volume of an unusual blend of Petite Sirah, Primitivo and Barbera called Agno Tinto was first made in 1998. As the list of varieties might suggest, this is a deep-coloured, robust, earthy but characterful red; just a little more concentration and it could be very good indeed. Of the whites the Chardonnay comes from a 30-year-old vineyard and is barrique-fermented and aged, but the best is the refined sweet Moscato, Fior d'Arancio Alpinae.

Recommended Reds:

Colli Euganei Rosso Gemola ★★★ £D

Colli Euganei Rosso Riserva ★★ £D   Agno Tinto ★★ £D

Recommended Whites:

Colli Euganei Fior d'Arancio Alpinae ★★★ £E

Colli Euganei Pinot Bianco ★★ £D

Colli Euganei Pinot Bianco Agno Casto ★★ £D

Colli Euganei Chardonnay ★★ £D   Moscato Sirio ★ £C

>> Villa Sandi (Veneto/Prosecco) www.villasandi.it

Villa Sandi is located in the heart of the Prosecco growing region, producing wines in both the DOC area of Prosecco and the DOCG area of Prosecco di Valdobbiadene. The estate has a bewildering number of different cuvees of Prosecco and other sparkling and semi-sparkling wines, but all display a great deal of finesse and balance. One of the entry level Proseccos, "Il Fresco" Brut DOC displays typical fruity flavours with a fair amount of residual sugar, but on the palate it is light and definitely non cloying which you can find in a number of Proseccos elsewhere. The DOCG Valdobbiadende Millesimato Brut has a good dry finish, but on the middle palate there is still plenty of fruity and flowery flavours. Cuvée Oris is their top cuvee from Valdobbiandende, very elegant with a good deal of finesse but once again showing residual sugar on the finish. There is a large range of sparkling wines from the extra dry to the sweet – mainly Prosecco, but there is also a range of classic Champagne grapes – Chardonnay and Pinot Noir under the Opere label. These are just listed as Veneto wines but Opere Serenissima is produced in the new Serenissima DOC created in 2011. The estate also produces a number of still red wines but these have not been tasted. (NB)

Recommended Whites:

Opera Serenissima ★★★ £C

Prosecco di Valdobbiadene Milesimato ★★★ £B

Prosecco di Valdobbiadene Superiore Cuvée Oris ★★★ £B

Prosecco di Treviso ★★ £A

Viviani (Veneto/Valpolicella) www.cantinaviviani.com

Viviani have emerged as one of the new quality pacesetters in the Valpolicella region thanks to a series of fine Amarone and Recioto released here in recent years. Parcels of well-established vines in the hills of the Classico zone (at 350-450m) provide two exceptional cru Amarone: pure and richly textured Casa dei Bepi and dense and marvellously complex Tulipano Nero. Yet regular Amarone is impressively pure and elegant too. It might be argued that some, in the pursuit of prized Amarone, neglect the more versatile, food

friendly Valpolicella but that is not the case here. Viviani's examples are first-rate led by a very classy single vineyard Campo Morar. A Ripasso version is intense but not heavy, balanced and with a certain finesse. Even regular Valpolicella Classico is fresh and perfumed and much better than most at this level. Recioto too is of a very high standard; vibrant, pure and expressive.

Recommended Reds:
Amarone della Valpolicella Classico Casa dei Bepi ★★★★☆ £F
Amarone della Valpolicella Classico Tulipano Nero ★★★★☆ £F
Amarone della Valpolicella Classico ★★★★ £E
Recioto della Valpolicella Classico ★★★★ £E
Valpolicella Classico Superiore Campo Morar ★★★☆ £C
Valpolicella Classico Superiore Ripasso ★★★ £C

Zenato (Veneto/Lugana & Valpolicella) www.zenato.it
Sergio Zenato established this well-known house in 1960 which though Lugana-based also includes a significant production from Valpolicella. Whilst the regular cuvées only rarely offer much excitement, the special bottlings can be very good indeed. As well as vibrant, chewy Valpolicella Ripassa there are the 'signature' Riserva wines – powerful Amarone and a concentrated Lugana. New is a barrique-fermented and aged Chardonnay Riserva. There is also Cresasso, an IGT red from 100% Corvina given 18 months in French oak; a dense, chewy style, it's likely to need plenty of bottle age. La Sansonina is an estate owned by Carla Prospero, the wife of Sergio Zenato. The existing Merlot vines were supplemented by further plantings and adds Cabernet Sauvignon to Merlot. This stylish red is fully ripe and shows a chocolaty, cedary complexity with five years' age or more.

Zenato
Recommended Reds:
Amarone della Valpolicella Classico Riserva Sergio Zenato ★★★ £F
Amarone della Valpolicella Classico ★ £E
Valpolicella Superiore Ripassa ★★ £C
Valpolicella Classico Superiore ★ £C
Recommended Whites:
Lugana Riserva Sergio Zenato ★★ £C

La Sansonina
Recommended Reds:
Sansonina ★★★ £E

A-Z of producers - Friuli-Venezia Giulia

Bastianich (Friuli-Venezia Giulia/COF) www.bastianich.com
Restauranteur, wine importer and winemaker Joe Bastianich is well-known in American wine and food circles (if less so than his famous mother, Lidia). On his 14 ha estate in the Colli Orientali zone he employs the best advice for big, ripe interpretations of Friulano, a blended white and two reds. Having started in the late 90s he now has a succession of vintages under his belt and mostly succeeds in achieving balance in the wines, with the alcohol levels checked by rich fruit and adequate acidity. For starters there is good freshness, minerality and lots of character in regular Friulano. Much smaller quantities are made of the fuller, riper Friulano Plus, a selection from old vines with the best exposure, part is late-harvested. The blended white is Vespa Bianco, a blend of Chardonnay and Sauvignon with 10% Picolit. Partly aged in small oak, its powerful, succulent palate is filled with concentrated peach, pear and spice flavours. Single varietal wines of Sauvignon, Ribolla Gialla, Pinot Grigio and Refosco are also made. Both reds, Vespa Rosso (Merlot, Refosco, Cabernet

Franc) and Calabrone (additionally with some Pignolo) are barrique-aged. Both are ageworthy with fine tannic structures - Calabrone is particularly fine with a smoke, herb and cigar-like complexity running through dense ripe fruit. An investment in Tuscany's Maremma has already yielded an example of Morellino di Scansano.

Recommended Reds:
Calabrone Rosso ★★★☆ £F   Vespa Rosso ★★☆ £D
Recommended Whites:
COF Friulano Plus ★★★ £D   COF Tocai Friulano ★★☆ £C
Vespa Bianco ★★★ £D

Blason (Friuli-Venezia Giulia/Isonzo) www.vinidocisonzo.it
While there are many good Friuli whites it can be more difficult finding those with a good quality/price ratio. The varietals from Giovanni Blason however certainly fit the bill. His modest production from 17 ha is dominated by Pinot Grigio (20,000 bottles), a good, lively characterful example that drinks well with 2-3 years' age. Much smaller quantities of Friulano, Chardonnay and Malvasia Istriana are similarly bright, direct with a good Friulian expression of each varietal. This is also true of the reds especially unoaked Cabernet Franc (Loire like) and Merlot which are supple and expressive with light but sufficiently ripe structures. New blends, under the label Bruma Rosso (since 2009) 70% Cabernet Sauvignon and 30% Merlot, spends 18 months in barriques and has good complexity with some body and Bruma Bianco (since 2010) 70% Malvasia Istriana and 30% Tocai Friulano spends 12 months in oak in new tonneaux and two year old barriques and has good vanilla flavours with a hint of artichoke. (NB)

Recommended Reds:
Fruili Isonzo Bruma Rosso ★★★★ £E
Friuli Isonzo Cabernet Franc ★★ £C
Friuli Isonzo Merlot ★★ £C
Recommended Whites:
Fruili Isonzo Bruma Bianco ★★★★ £E
Fruili Isonzo Pinot Grigio ★★ £C
Fruili Isonzo Tocai Friulano ★★ £C
Fruili Isonzo Chardonnay ★★ £C
IGT Venezia Giuliana Malvasia Istriano ★★☆ £C

Borgo del Tiglio (Collio) www.borgodeltiglio.it
Nicola Manferrari has nearly 17 ha of vines spread across three distinct vineyard sites. The cooler sites are planted to Riesling, Sauvignon and Chardonnay while those warmed by the Adriatic include the red grape varieties. Whites in particular are made to a high standard with good ripeness and intensity as well as the capacity to age. In addition to regular varietal examples of good varietal character, superior versions are also made. Friulano, for instance, in Ronco della Chiesa shows more oak influence and much better structure, while Chardonnay Selezione adds more depth, complexity and richness, over the standard bottling. In Studio di Bianco, Friulano, Sauvignon and Riesling are deftly combined in a stylish, ripe white with both depth and intensity. Reds are more variable, sometimes not quite achieving full ripeness in both fruit and tannins yet when they do there is good supple plummy, berry fruit depth. Rosso della Centa is a pure Merlot while Collio Rosso Riserva adds 25–30% Cabernet Sauvignon to Merlot. Nicola is also the proprietor of the CONTRADA TENNA estate in the Marche, producing wines from Montepulciano and Sangiovese.

Recommended Reds:
Collio Rosso della Centa ★★ £E
Collio Rosso Riserva ★★ £E

North-East Italy /Friuli-Venezia Giulia

Italy

Recommended Whites:
Collio Chardonnay Selezione ★★★ £E Collio Chardonnay ★★ £D
Collio Friulano Ronco della Chiesa ★★★ £E
Collio Friulano ★★ £D Collio Bianco Studio di Bianco ★★★ £E

Borgo San Daniele (Isonzo) *www.borgosandaniele.it*
Mauro Mauri and his sister Alessandra make a small but uniformly
high-quality range of wines from 19 ha of vineyards. They undertake
staggered picking to produce whites that impress both for their
individuality and structure. Most singular is a smoky, scented
Friulano fermented and aged in *botti* grandi that combines citrus
with exotic flavours. Both Pinot Grigio and Arbis Blanc (Chardonnay,
Sauvignon, Pinot Bianco and Friulano) have a measure of *barrique*
influence and show a little more breadth. Arbis Blanc in particular
impresses for its fruit richness and texture. A little red, Arbis Ròs,
is now made from 100% Pignolo. With very cool but intense
redcurrant, red cherry fruit and a hint of carob, it will turn chocolaty
but can be let down by a slightly green edge. New, is Gortmarin,
a blend of Cabernet Sauvignon, Cabernet Franc and Merlot (the
former two having been previously blended with the Pignolo in
Arbis Ròs).
Recommended Reds:
Arbis Ròs ★★ £D
Recommended Whites:
Fruili Isonzo Tocai ★★★ £D Fruili Isonzo Bianco Arbis Blanc ★★★ £D
Fruili Isonzo Pinot Grigio ★★☆ £D

Dario Coos (Friuli-Venezia Giulia/Ramandolo) *www.dariocoos.it*
Production has recently been revitalised here following new
investment in the long established family estate of Dario Coos (5th
generation). What is unusual is that there are 14 different wines
produced from 7 ha of vineyards which are predominantly from
the Verduzzo grape. Most exciting are the sweet wines but the dry
Vindos Bianco is stylish and individual with delicious ripe fruit. There
are three levels of sweet Verduzzos which relate to their successively
later harvesting times. Il Longhino is produced without oak and
is pure and intense but there's more depth and concentration in
the Ramandolo which is partly barrique aged. Still sweeter and
more concentrated is Romandus. A fine example of a sweet Picolit
provides a fascinating contrast while an excellent (red) Refosco is
also made. For this, half the grapes are dried for 2-3 months on trays.
The result is an enhanced silky texture and an exquisite cherry and
small berry fruit lushness. The Pignolo spends 24 months in new
oak and is very deep and unctuous with a nice long finish and good
ageing potential. The Schioppettino Has spice on the nose and also
on the finish, but drinks elegantly. Ribolla Gialla displays ripe melon
on the nose but can be a little short on the finish. Malvasia has a
floral nose but quite mineral in the mouth – bone dry – almost
sherry-like. Pinot Grigio is zingy and full of explosive fruit. All in all
this an estate producing fine, value for money wines. (NB)
Recommended Reds:
COF Refosco dal Peduncolo Rosso ★★★☆ £D
Pignolo IGT Venezia Giulia ★★★☆ £D
Schioppettino IGT Venezia Giulia ★★★ £C
Recommended Whites:
COF Picolit ★★★☆ £F
Ramandolo DOCG Fruili-Venezia Giulia ★★★☆ £E
COF Verduzzo Friulano Il Longhino ★★☆ £C
Princic Bianco Pinot Grigio IGT Venezia Giulia ★★★☆ £E
Malvasia IGT Venezia Giulia ★★★ £C
Vindos Bianco IGT Venezia Giulia ★★☆ £C

Ribolla Gialla IGT Venezia Giulia ★★☆ £B

Dal Fari (Friuli-Venezia Giulia/COF)
Laura Largajolli should be very satisfied with the quality of her
current releases made by Valentino Giuriato (with consultancy from
Fabio Coser) from 14 ha of vineyards. Whites are concentrated and
stylish, true both to variety and to Colli Orientali del Friuli. Tocai
Friulano is an excellent example while Bianco delle Grazie (60/20
Chardonnay and Sauvignon with 10% each of Friulano and Riesling)
has very good breadth and length in addition to ripe, finely spiced
fruit intensity. In somewhat exaggerated style, Chardonnay Oro
has impressive flavour and depth. Reds such as Cabernet (50/50
Cabernet Sauvignon and Cabernet Franc) can also shine. Rosso
d'Orsone is also cool and complex but shows well with 5–6 years'
age. The component parts (60/20 Cabernet Sauvignon and Merlot
plus 10% each of Schioppettino and Cabernet Franc) are vinified
and aged separately in *barrique* for a year before being combined
in large oak for a further year. Rutilum (100% Schioppettino) is cool
with crushed berry, herbs and green pepper, yet supple, seductive
and long with a fine structure. Given the quality and fair prices, Dal
Fari certainly deserves to be better known.
Recommended Reds:
COF Schioppettino Rutilum ★★★ £E COF Cabernet ★★★ £D
COF Rosso d'Orsone ★★★ £D
Recommended Whites:
COF Bianco delle Grazie ★★★ £D COF Tocai Friulano ★★★ £C
COF Chardonnay Oro ★★★ £C COF Sauvignon ★★ £C
COF Pinot Grigio ★★ £C

Alessio Dorigo (Friuli-Venezia Giulia/COF) *www.dorigowines.com*
Girolomo Dorigo retired in 2012 and his son, Alessio, who was
already assuming greater responsibility for a range encompassing
international as well as several local varieties has not only taken over
full control, but also moved the operation some 15 minutes down
the road into a new, modern winery. Chardonnay has a definite
oak accent but delicious fruit, balance and refinement and there's
a good Bordeaux-style single vineyard Sauvignon, Ronc di Juri,
fermented in 60% new oak. Yet it is for reds as much as whites that
these wines should be tried. Successful examples of Refosco and
Tazzelenghe have great fruit expression and relatively harmonious
structures for these difficult grapes and if you can't afford
MOSCHIONI's Schioppettino, Dorigo's appealing example shows
a lovely peppery varietal expression. A little powerful, extracted
Pignolo is also made. The top red, however, is the Bordeaux blend
labelled simply Montsclapade, a very composed example with
cedary crushed berry fruit that oozes style. Dorigo's Picolit is one of
the best examples of this elegant sweet white, though the honeyed
Verduzzo isn't far behind. Sparkling wine from Chardonnay and
Pinot Nero is also made.
Recommended Reds:
COF Rosso Montsclapade ★★★ £E COF Tazzelenghe ★★ £D
COF Schioppettino ★★ £C COF Refosco del Peduncolo Rosso ★★ £C
Recommended Whites:
COF Picolit ★★★ £F COF Chardonnay ★★★ £D
COF Verduzzo ★★ £F COF Sauvignon Ronc di Juri ★★ £D

✿ Mauro Drius (Friuli-Venezia Giulia/Isonzo) *www.driusmario.it*
Mauro Drius is a committed winegrower who makes consistently
good varietals from 12 ha of vineyards. His most recent efforts are
a further notch up on those of 5 or 6 years ago. Pinot Grigio has
an elegance and intensity that put it among the best from Friuli,

while Sauvignon has classic herb and mineral complexity. The two Friulani are also very impressive; the more classic and distinctive Collio example arguably has the edge over the stylish, zesty Isonzo. Blended white Vignis di Sìris (half Friulano, half Sauvignon and Pinot Bianco) is partly wooded and makes a good substitute for decent Meursault with its fine spice and ripe citrus character. Reds are more successful in riper vintages yet Merlot especially can be cool and elegant with sufficiently ripe tannins even in more challenging years.

Recommended Reds:
Friuli Isonzo Cabernet ★★★ £C   Friuli Isonzo Merlot ★★★ £C
Recommended Whites:
Friuli Isonzo Pinot Grigio ★★★ £C   Friuli Isonzo Vignis di Sìris ★★★ £C
Collio Sauvignon ★★ £C   Collio Friulano ★★ £C
Friuli Isonzo Friulano ★★ £C   Friuli Isonzo Pinot Bianco ★★ £C
Friuli Isonzo Malvasia ★ £C

Livio Felluga (Friuli-Venezia Giulia/COF) *www.liviofelluga.it*
This is one of the grand estates of Friuli, having been established by Livio Felluga in the 1950s. It is now being taken to new heights by his offspring, who have 135 ha to manage but with the expertise of consultant Stefano Chioccioli to assist them. Until recently the most widely acclaimed white, Terre Alte, a blend of Friulani, Pinot Bianco and Sauvignon Blanc, was wine of exquisite balance and elegance rather than concentration. Previously unoaked, a portion of the wine now receives some time in *barriques* which can be a little overdone. Since 2009, however, a new super *cuvée*, Abbazia di Rosazzo, a blend of the best Friulano, Pinot Bianco, Sauvignon, Malvasia and Ribolla Gialla on the estate, matured on its lees for 8 months in *botti* di revere, results in an ample mouthfeel of dried fruits and nuts with good complexity and length on the dry finish. An otherwise stylish and intense Illivio, an oak-aged Pinot Bianco, could also use a little more restraint. At a lower level is a well-concentrated, aromatic and characterful blend of Chardonnay and Ribolla Gialla, Shàrjs. Unoaked varietals are also of a high standard. The Picolit is an exceptionally fine if pricey, example of the grape. It is medium-sweet with honeyed vanilla, wild flowers and dried fruit characters – both long and refined and not in the least bit coarse or heavy. Reds include an attractive Merlot/Cabernet Sauvignon, Vertigo, and a deep, polished, lushly berry-fruited Merlot, Sossò. More characterful but less refined in flavour is an excellent example of Refosco.

Recommended Reds:
COF Merlot Riserva Sossò ★★★ £F
COF Refosco dal Peduncolo Rosso ★★★ £F   Vertigo ★★ £D
Recommended Whites:
COF Picolit Riserva ★★★★ £G   COF Abbazia di Rosazzo ★★★★ £G
COF Rosazzo Bianco Terre Alte ★★★ £E
COF Pinot Bianco Illivio ★★★ £C   Sharjs ★★ £C
COF Pinot Grigio ★★ £C   COF Sauvignon ★★ £C
COF Friulano ★★ £C

Adriano Gigante (COF) *www.adrianogigante.it*
Adriano Gigante together with his wife Giuliana and cousin Ariedo Gigante makes wines from 20 ha of vineyards - some 50 years after his grandfather first produced a special bottle of Tocai. That Tocai (now Friulano, of course), Vigneto Storico as it is now labelled, is still the most exciting wine made but there is both quality and value in several other whites too. Regular Friulano has good depth, flavour and intensity but Vigneto Storico is much more: full and long with a distinctive mineral, smoke and dried herb character. Sauvignon also impresses for its ripe fruit and lingering finish. Pinot Grigio is more

individual than many and decent examples of moderately sweet (and inexpensive) Verduzzo and a refined Picolit are worth trying. Reds include Schioppettino with good varietal character while Merlot needs more substance and ripeness although soundly made. North-East Italy /Friuli-Venezia Giulia Chardonnay is also produced.

Recommended Reds:
COF Schioppettino ★★ £C   COF Merlot ★★ £C
Recommended Whites:
COF Picolit ★★★☆ £E   COF Tocai Friulano Vigneto Storico ★★★☆ £C
COF Tocai Friulano ★★ £C   COF Verduzzo Friulano ★★★ £C
COF Sauvignon ★★☆ £C   COF Pinot Grigio ★★ £C

✿ Josko Gravner (Friuli-Venezia Giulia) *www.gravner.it*
Josko Gravner has gone where no-one else had previously dared in his pursuit of excellence. Not satisfied with the quality of his whites in the mid-90s, which included very complete, complex Sauvignon and Chardonnay, he went still further in experiments with both viticulture and vinification. No chemicals are used and vines are planted at very high densities and give very low yields. The two whites are now fermented with their skins in large amphorae (from Georgia) without any recourse to sulphur or temperature control. This may last 6–7 months before ageing in large oak (*botti* grandi) for 30 months. Many scoffed at such madness but recent results have been extraordinary. Breg, from Sauvignon, Chardonnay, Pinot Grigio and Riesling Italico, is deeply coloured and marvellously complex with very ripe preserved fruits and formidable texture and length. Ribolla is marginally less complex but at least as powerful and extracted with a similar light astringency on a very long finish. A slow burner, put it away for another 5-10 years from either vintage. Both whites are unfiltered and unfined.It may take some time to appreciate the style of these wines as they are not modern or immediate but they are stimulating with remarkable structure. Damijan PODVERSIC, with Kaplija, is just one of several others following a similar path. Very small amounts are also made of a red, Rosso Gravner, from Merlot and Cabernet Sauvignon as well as another example, Rujno, (100% Merlot) released from the 1994 vintage, but these have not been tasted.

Recommended Whites:
Bianco Breg ★★★★☆ £F   Ribolla ★★★★☆ £F

Il Carpino (Friuli-Venezia Giulia/Collio) *www.ilcarpino.com*
Il Carpino was established in 1987 but has only become one of the best estates in Friuli in the past 6 or 7 years. Excellent white and red wines, predominantly varietal, show a combination of superb fruit and fine balance. A fine gentle, stylish Chardonnay is complemented by a partially oaked Sauvignon which has excellent definition, rich, ripe fruit and a lingering finish. Bianco Carpino is an equal blend of both with good harmony. A fine citrusy, herbal Ribolla Gialla is also produced as is some Malvasia. Red wines are based on Merlot. A plush brambly Rosso Carpino includes 20% Cabernet Sauvignon and shows lots of promise. Even better is Rubrum (potentially 4 stars), a sumptuous, black plum fruited Merlot that tastes not unlike a young Pomerol. Both reds show good ageing potential. While all the Il Carpino wines see some French oak, Vigna Runc, a promising second label, is for unoaked varietals. Whites include Chardonnay, Pinot Grigio, Ribolla Gialla and an aromatic, floral, gooseberryish and concentrated Sauvignon Blanc. Merlot is also produced under this label. Occasionally the wines show some reduction.

Il Carpino
Recommended Reds:
Rubrum ★★★☆ £D   Rosso Carpino ★★ £C

North-East Italy /Friuli-Venezia Giulia

Italy

Recommended Whites:

Collio Sauvignon ★★★ £D Collio Chardonnay ★★★ £D
Collio Pinot Grigio ★★ £D Collio Ribolla Gialla ★★ £C
Bianco Carpino ★★ £C

Vigna Runc
Recommended Whites:

Collio Sauvignon ★★ £B Collio Pinot Grigio ★ £B
Collio Ribolla Gialla ★ £B

✿ I Clivi (Friuli-Venezia Giulia/COF) *www.clivi.it*

An excellent pair of white wines is made here by Ferdinando Zanusso. There is Goriziano DOC real craft and complexity to these old vine Friulano gems. Both wines, which come from old vines, are fermented only with indigenous yeasts and are bottled unfiltered. Galea might be expected to the finer of the two as it comes from the COF appellation from 70 year old vines, but it is Brazan, planted with 80 year old vines, coming from the slightly lesser regarded appellation of the Collio DOC thatshows slightly more finesse and detail. Both are now made with 100% Friulano. The subtle spice and minerality of Brazan contrasts with the white flower, dried peach and herb character of Galea. Both wines are excellent examples of the refinement and complexity possible from Friuli and only miss a little extra depth and richness to stand comparison with top whites from Burgundy or elsewhere. As the wines are only released with a minimum of three years' age don't expect to find either wine from the most recent vintages. Both will keep at least as long again. Prices are very fair for the quality. A range of single varietals are also made. Ribolla Gialla has ripe fruit on the nose but drinks bone dry with some elegance. Friulano has similar characteristics but is a cut above the Ribolla, whilst the unoaked Malvasia has hints of sticky toffee fruit with a bone dry finish. (NB)

Recommended Whites:

Collio Brazan ★★★★☆ £E
Collio Malvasia ★★★ £D
COF Galea ★★★★ £D
COF Fruilano ★★★ £D
Ribolla Gialla IGT Venezia ★★☆ £C

Vinnaioli Jermann (Friuli-Venezia Giulia) *www.jermann.it*

Silvio Jermann is the long-time champion of Friuli, having produced excellent whites for an age. These are not just wines of good concentration and ripe fruit but ones with good definition and character and with an added elegance and refinement in the top examples that other powerful examples lack. The prices have always been a little ahead of others but when Jermann is on form, which is most of the time, they deserve to be. Vinnae, the least expensive of the blended whites, combines Ribolla Gialla, Friulano and Riesling and is balanced and characterful. Capo Martino, which adds a lot more richness, is mainly Friulano. Better though and often the top wine is Vintage Tunina (Sauvignon, Chardonnay, Ribolla Gialla, Malvasia and Picolit), which shows intense stylish fruit, wonderful elegance and refinement, and superb length of flavour. Though it might be drunk young it is best with 5 years' age. Dreams ('Were Dreams, now it is just wine!' – to give it its full name – and originally sold as 'Where the Dreams have no end', in homage to U2's Bono) is a Chardonnay with rich oak spice and ripe fruit that can show real precision and lovely harmony on the palate and is a rare Italian example that can stand comparison with a fine Burgundian white. As well as those varietals below, other whites include a basic Chardonnay and Sauvignon. For red, a little intense Pinot Nero, Red Angel, and Pignolo, Pignacolusse are produced. In the latter, there is a seductive fullness to match the extract, and is long with fine tannins. There is also Blau & Blau – a blend of Pinot Nero (Blauburgunder) and Blaufrankisch.

Recommended Reds:

Pignacolusse ★★★ £E Red Angel ★★ £D

Recommended Whites:

Vintage Tunina ★★★★ £E Dreams ★★★★ £E
Capo Martino ★★★ £E Pinot Grigio ★★★ £D
Vinnae ★★ £D Pinot Bianco ★★ £D Traminer Aromatico ★★ £D
Riesling Afix ★★ £D

La Tunella (Friuli-Venezia Giulia/COF) *www.latunella.it*

A rising star in the Friuli-Venezia Giulia firmament, La Tunella draws on 79 ha of vineyards, mostly in the Colli Orientali for intense, concentrated wines. Winemaker Luigino Zamparo has made the most of the efforts made in the vineyards for better quality fruit and reduced yields. Broad but impressivelyflavoured Pinot Grigio and Chardonnay have both weight and persistence while an excellent Sauvignon has an elderberry, mineral, wild herb and lupin intensity and the structure to improve for 3-4 years'. Natives Ribolla Gialla and Friulano are also fine, exuding both intensity and style. Biancosesto (from 04) blends the two together. In Lalinda they are also combined but additionally with Malvasia Istriana and fermented in 500 litre tonneaux for a rich, exotic, powerful yet well-balanced white. Reds are well-made too including a rare decent Pinot Nero for the region that is not unlike a lesser village Burgundy. Only very small quantities (4000 bottles) are made of L'Arcionewhich can be a composed and complex blend of Pignolio and Schioppettino. Both are also bottled separately as single varietal wines as is Refosco del Peduncolo. Not to be overlooked is Cabernet Franc which is expressive, pure and well-defined. The sweet offering, Noans (not tasted) is from Riesling, Gewürztraminer and Sauvignon and there are also a Picolit and a Verduzzo Friulano.

Recommended Reds:

COF Rosso L'Arcione ★★★ £D COF Pinot Nero ★★☆ £C
COF Cabernet Franc ★★☆ £C COF Merlot ★★ £C

Recommended Whites:

COF Lalinda ★★★☆ £C COF Sauvignon ★★★ £C
COF Chardonnay ★★☆ £C COF Friulano ★★☆ £C
COF Ribolla Gialla ★★☆ £C COF Pinot Grigio ★★ £C

✿ Le Due Terre (Friuli-Venezia Giulia/COF)

Here's another small estate in the mould of Miani. Few wines, low yields and an even smaller output (just a few thousand bottles of each wine) but similar very high quality. Complexity, intensity of flavour and refined structures distinguish all four wines. Red and white Sacrisassi are classic Friulian blends, the white from Friulano and Ribolla Gialla and the red from Refosco and Schioppettino. The Bianco with grapefruit, citrus, peach and herbal nuances, has excellent dimension and depth. The Rosso is more classy and complete with spice, carob, vanilla, plum and herb complexity; intense and profound with a fine tannic structure. A varietal Merlot is more dense and concentrated with high acidity but with a cool climate sophistication. Pinot Nero also impresses for intensity and similarly well-judged use of oak but the flavour profile lacks the thrill and refinement of the best from Burgundy or elsewhere - perhaps indicative of its origins. The balance in all is such that they can be drunk fairly young but 5-10 years' is needed to do full justice to the reds.

Recommended Reds:

COF Sacrisassi ★★★★ £E COF Merlot ★★★★ £E

COF Pinot Nero ★★★ £E
Recommended Whites:
COF Sacrisassi ★★★☆ £D

Lis Neris (Friuli-Venezia Giulia/Isonzo) *www.lisneris.it*
Alvaro Pecorari's Lis Neris has become one of Friuli's leading estates thanks to ongoing improvements over the past decade or so. With 40 ha of vineyard, production is moderately large. Unoaked varietals such as Pinot Grigio, Friulano (Fiore di Campo) and Sauvignon are ripe with good varietal intensity. Sauvignon (Picol), Pinot Grigio (Gris) and Chardonnay (Jurosa) are also produced in partly barrel-fermented versions (60% for the latter two) that usually show more restraint and elegance than those from many producers. There are also two very good blended whites of contrasting character. Lis (Pinot Grigio, Chardonnay and Sauvignon) is full and Burgundian with good breadth and concentration, while the late-harvested Confini (Pinot Grigio, Traminer and 10% Riesling) is Alsace-like with floral, rosé, spice and grapey scents and an intense, ripe, lush and off-dry palate with good structure and length. Even better if very expensive is Tal Lùc, a passito-style sweet white from Verduzzo grapes (and 5% Riesling) that are dried for up to 12 weeks. It is *barrique*-fermented and very lush with the ripest peach fruit, lovely purity and finesse – a classic expression in a dried-fruit style. For red there's the spicy, berry-fruited estate red, Lis Neris. Primarily from Merlot (with just 5–10% Cabernet Sauvignon), it is particularly stylish and composed in good vintages.
Recommended Reds:
Friuli Isonzo Lis Neris ★★★ £E
Recommended Whites:
Tal Lùc ★★★★ £G   Confini ★★★ £E   Lis ★★★ £D
Friuli Isonzo Sauvignon ★★★ £C
Friuli Isonzo Picol Sauvignon ★★★ £C
Friuli Isonzo Gris Pinot Grigio ★★★ £C
Friuli Isonzo Pinot Grigio ★★ £C
Friuli Isonzo Jurosa Chardonnay ★★★ £C
Fiore di Campo ★★ £C

Luisa (Friuli-Venezia Giulia/Isonzo) *www.tenutaluisa.com*
As a source of typical, quality white varietals from Friuli at reasonable prices this is a name that shouldn't be ignored. Brothers Michele (winemaker) and Davide (in the vineyard) work with their father Eddi. From 60 ha Pinot Grigio and Sauvignon are produced in the greatest quantities with good varietal character and ripe, lightly mineral fruit and good length. Friulano is a little more nuanced, ripe and intense, an excellent example at the price. Chardonnay and Pinot Bianco are also made but haven't been tasted. Reds are more a work in progress, specifically the I Ferretti oak-aged versions which are overdone. However unwooded Cabernet Franc and Refosco can be a delight - exuberant, flavoursome and fruit-filled.
Recommended Reds:
Friuli Isonzo Cabernet Franc ★★☆ £C
Friuli Isonzo Refosco dal Peduncolo Rosso ★★☆ £C
Recommended Whites:
Friuli Isonzo Pinot Grigio Rive Alte ★★★ £C
Friuli Isonzo Friulano ★★★ £C   Friuli Isonzo Sauvignon ★★☆ £C

Davino Meroi (Friuli-Venezia Giulia/COF) *www.meroidavino.com*
Although producing a significant range of wines, Paolo Meroi makes only very small quantities of each from a few hundred bottles to around 3000 maximum. But they are worth seeking out, particularly if visiting the region. Dry whites are in a concentrated,

oak-enhanced (but not oaky) varietally expressive, full-bodied style usually with the depth and intensity to match, if sometimes lacking balance. Very stylish, pure, lightly mineral Chardonnay and rich Friulano are particularly striking. Reds, at least when tasted young can be a bit daunting. Their potential complexity and intense, concentrated flavours are checked by at times structures that are too aggressive with high acidiies and insufficiently ripe tannins. Ros di Buri is a Merlot, Nèstri Merlot/Cabernet Franc while Dominin is a blend of Merlot and Refosco and has great promise. Tiny quantities of sweet wines, Verduzzo and Picolit are made. The honey and spice Verduzzo is intense, moderately sweet and long but surpassed by a splendid pure Picolit that is sweeter and more concentrated. Both deserve another 3-5 years' before drinking.
Recommended Reds:
COF Ros di Buri ★★★ £E
Recommended Whites:
COF Picolit ★★★★ £F   COF Verduzzo Friulano ★★★☆ £E
COF Chardonnay ★★★☆ £D   COF Tocai Friulano ★★★ £D
COF Pinot Grigio ★★ £D   COF Sauvignon ★★ £D

⚫ Miani (Friuli-Venezia Giulia/COF)
Enzo Pontoni's meagre output is some of the most-sought after wine in northern Italy. His vineyards total 18ha, and while most, but not all, of the vines are in production, quantities are extremely modest due to low yields and severe selection. The wines are beautifully crafted, expressive, detailed and very classy, nearly perfectly balanced. The Sauvignon is barrel-fermented but far finer and more complex than most made in this style. Separate bottlings have been made since 04, a more mineral Saurint superior to a broader, more floral Banel. Refined Friulano (from 60-year old vines) captures the essence of the grape, while Merlot, a combination of two different parcels, comes in part from 40-year-old vines. It is aged in new oak but is pure with the enticing berries and plum expression too rarely seen in Merlot from around the world and manages to avoid underripeness even in cooler vintages. A Piede Franco Rosso reveals an arresting pre-phylloxera mineral and earth infused cool fruits complexity yet a refined structure. Also made are Ribolla Gialla, Chardonnay and a few hundred bottles of an exceptional and sought-after Refosco (Calvari). Try them if you get the chance.
Recommended Reds:
COF Merlot ★★★★ £E
Recommended Whites:
COF Tocai Friulano ★★★★ £E   COF Sauvignon ★★★★ £E

⚫ Moschioni (Friuli-Venezia Giulia/COF) *www.michelemoschioni.it*
To see just what is possible without compromise and by producing wine as naturally as possible try the wines from Michele Moschioni. Also seek them out to discover the potential of hitherto obscure local red varieties in Fruili. From 11 ha of vines grapes are late-harvested or in some instances the fruit is partially dried (for 10 days) for added concentration (though now less so than in the first blockbuster releases of these wines). The top wines (all potentially 5 stars) see 100% new oak for anything up to two years but this is easily absorbed by the concentrated fruit. The basic Rosso is from young-vine Merlot and Cabernet with a little of the native varieties. Refosco, aged in 50% new oak has excellent concentration and texture and the wild plum and brambly fruit of the variety. Celtico Rosso (around half-and-half Cabernet Sauvignon and Merlot) has terrific intensity and concentration, with dried fruits and fig aromas giving way to blackberry and black plum flavours. Despite the

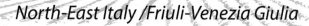

Italy

extract and richness, this is much more approachable than most
Amarone but deserves 10 years' age or more. Of at least comparable
quality are Moschioni's two brilliant creations from local varieties.
There is a marvellous contrast between the pure, seductive
elegance of the Schioppettino with floral and spicy sweet cherry-
fruited intensity and the wildness, mineral, carob and black-fruited
muscularity of Pignolo. The extract and tannin in the latter needs
8–10 years to mellow, while Schioppettino, though concentrated
and powerful, could be drunk much sooner.

Recommended Reds:

COF Pignolo ★★★★★ £F   COF Schioppettino ★★★★ £E
COF Refosco dal Peduncolo Rosso ★★★ £D
COF Celtico Rosso ★★★★ £E   COF Rosso Moschioni ★★ £D

Nec-Otium (Friuli-Venezia Giulia)   *www.necotium.it*
Christian Patat consults for several growers in Friuli producing ripe-
fruited generous styles of the classic varieties. The Nec-Otium wines,
effectively his own négociant label, are produced from special
parcels within the vineyards of growers that he works with - often
from old vines and relatively low yields. Soft, rich, ripe wines with an
oak-influence are what to expect. A very ripe, spicy, richly-textured
Sauvignon from Edi Simcic's Goriska Brda vineyards in Slovenia or an
unusually rich, powerful Malvasia are good examples as is a Collio
Bianco blend from a mixed vineyard of old vine Tocai and Ribolla
Gialla. A Rosso blends Refosco, Schioppettino and Merlot. Another
label, Cru Chale, is produced jointly with SIRCH and has included
flavoursome, intense Chardonnay and Friulano. A Prepotto cru of the
latter based on late-harvested fruit from very old vines has also been
made. Changing vineyard sources makes it difficult to rate the wines
but if you like the style remember the names.

Pierpaolo Pecorari (Isonzo)   *www.pierpaolopecorari.it*
Pierpaolo and his son Alessandro have 28 ha of vineyards spread
across the plains of Friuli Isonzo, strewn with coarse river gravels.
The accumulative benefits of continued restructuring with higher
planting densities (5500 vines per ha) are immediately apparent
in the wines. The greatest quantities come in the shape of intense,
tangy regular varietals led by Pinot Grigio and Sauvignon but also
includes Chardonnay, Malvasia, Friulano, and reds, Merlot and (gutsy,
characterful) Refosco. The excellent Altis whites are distinguished
by a pre-fermentation maceration and a period of 12 months on
their lees. They are particularly structured, concentrated examples
including an intense chiselled Sauvignon and a deep yet refined
Pinot Bianco. Premium varietal bottlings are labelled for the zones
from which they are produced. Sauvignon (Kolaus), Chardonnay
(Soris) and Pinot Grigio (Olivers) are treated similarly to the Altis
version but differ in spending 12 months in oak barrels. Coming
from still lower yielding vines (1kg per vine) of a higher average age
there is impressive flavour and concentration if not always more
personality or refinement - Sauvignon, however, is a consistently
fine oak influenced style. The red equivalents, Merlot (Baolar) and
Refosco (Tao), receive two years in *barriques* following a moderately
long maceration. Both are extracted, structured and powerful but
usually characterful and expressive especially if given 8-10 years' age
from a good vintage. Most wines are sold as Venezia Giulia IGT.

Recommended Reds:

Refosdo Tao ★★★☆ £F   Refosco dal Peduncolo Rosso ★★☆ £C
Merlot Baolar ★★★ £E

Recommended Whites:

Sauvignon Kolaus ★★★☆ £D   Sauvignon Altis ★★★ £D
Sauvignon ★★ £B   Pinot Grigio Olivers ★★★ £D

Pinot Grigio ★★☆ £C   Chardonnay Soris ★★★ £D
Pinot Bianco Altis ★★☆ £D   Friulano ★★☆ £C

Damijan Podversic (Collio)   *www.damijanpodversic.com*
Damijan Podversic is one of the most extreme of the alternative
school of winemaking now flourishing in Friuli. Rejecting all modern
winemaking devices and additions, the whites, Kaplija Bianco
(Chardonnay, Friulano and Malvasia Friulano) and Ribolla Gialla, are
subject to around 16 days maceration on the skins and fermentation
in open wood fermenters without temperature control. A response
to the stress Damijan places on the importance of the phenolics
and not just juice in making great wine. There are no corrections or
filtrations. Kaplija is complex, concentrated, deep and honeyed and
not overtly fruity, very long with evident structure. A little less rich
but perhaps more individual, his wild herb scented Ribolla Gialla is
altogether different from more conventionally made examples. To
date the red (Merlot/Cabernet Sauvignon) has been less impressive,
just missing a little ripeness and richness.

Recommended Reds:

Collio Rosso Prelit ★★ £E

Recommended Whites:

Collio Bianco Kaplija ★★★☆ £E   Ribolla Gialla ★★★ £E

Primosic (Friuli-Venezia Giulia/Collio)   *www.primosic.com*
The Primosic family have been bottling their own wines for 50 years.
Brothers Boris and Marko have gradually assumed control from
their father and in recent vintages the wines have been labelled
to reflect the particular hilly slopes around Oslavia, in the very
southeast of the Collio zone, from which they come. Beyond good
basics, Sauvignon Gmajne stands out for its refined expressive Friuli
style while Pinot Grigio Murno (a small percentage aged in oak) is
also one of the better examples going. The most outstanding wine
is the Collio Bianco Riserva Klin, now amongst the region's very
best blended dry whites in a modern oak-aged style. Sauvignon,
Friulano, Chardonnay and Ribolla Gialla grapes all make a significant
contribution to its dense, concentrated rich fruit (including pear,
spice and kiwi) and oak-fermented character. Chardonnay and
Malvasia Istriana are also produced but hasn't been tasted. Reds
include a Merlot (Murno) and Collio Riserva Metamorfosis which
adds in the two Cabernets. The latter has lots of character and dense
chocolaty fruit if in a cool spectrum.

Recommended Reds:

Collio Rosso Riserva Metamorfosis ★★★ £D

Recommended Whites:

Collio Bianco Riserva Klin ★★★☆ £D
Collio Sauvignon Gmajne ★★★ £C
Collio Pinot Grigio Murno ★★☆ £C
Collio Ribolla Gialla ★★ £C   Collio Friulano Belvedere ★★ £C

Dario Princic (Friuli-Venezia Giulia)
Dario Princic is just one of several growers in Friuli with a serious
commitment to making wines of the greatest authenticity and
expression possible. Like minded individuals include Stanislao
(Stanko) Radikon and Nico Bensa (La Castellada), who will be
profiled in future editions but also DAMIJAN PODVERSIC, Josko
GRAVNER and others. Princic harvests the grapes as ripe as possible
prior to fermentation in open fermenters. The fact that the whites
which include Sauvignon, Chardonnay, Ribolla Gialla and blended
Trebez from Pinot Grigio, Chardonnay and Ribolla Gialla have
undergone a lengthy skin maceration is immediately apparent
in their deep amber-gold colours. Of those tasted, Sauvignon is

particularly impressive, not conventional of course but with great depth, breadth and intensely flavoured with yellow stone fruits, quince and dried peach. Bianco Trebez is very long and intense but if anything more structured with a light astringency on the finish. A cedary Cabernet Sauvignon is pure, ripe and concentrated with good freshness and not overoaked. More wines will be rated with further tastings.

Recommended Whites:
Sauvignon ★★★☆ £D Bianco Trebez ★★★ £D

Paolo Rodaro (Friuli-Venezia Giulia/COF) *www.rodaropaolo.it*
From 40 ha of vineyard Paolo Rodaro produces not just well-made white varietals including Sauvignon, Friulano and Ribolla Gialla but also small volumes of very good sweet whites. A dense, concentrated Verduzzo is bettered by Picolit with a vibrant, pure stone fruit core and all the balance and quality of a lighter-style Sauternes. Also produced is a stylish example of Schioppettino, in part from dried grapes. It is medium-bodied but deep, cool and pure with soft red fruits, needing 5-6 years to open up fully. Merlot, Cabernet Sauvignon, Pignolo and Refosco are also made.

Recommended Reds:
COF Schioppettino Romain ★★ £D

Recommended Whites:
COF Picolit ★★★★ £F COF Verduzzo Friulano Pra Zenar ★★★ £E
COF Friulano ★★ £C COF Ribolla Gialla ★★ £C
COF Sauvignon ★★ £C

Ronchi di Manzano (COF) *www.ronchidimanzano.com*
This 60 ha estate in the Colli Orientali del Friuli zone produces a wide range of whites and reds, for the most part reasonably priced and well-defined examples of their type. Varietal whites are most impressive: vigorous, expressive and fruit-centred. All are aged intelligently (whether in stainless steel, large wood or *barrique* or some combination of these) according to the grape's character. The Ellegri white blends Sauvignon, Chardonnay, Friulano and Picolit in a ripe, stylish, vibrant, harmonious whole that can be drunk young or kept for 3 or 4 years. Among the reds, regular varietal examples of Cabernet Sauvignon, Cabernet Franc and Merlot could use more richness and ripeness. However, a very promising young-vine Ronc di Subule from new vineyards planted at much higher densities (8,000 vines/ha) shows opulent pure fruit, well-integrated with new oak. Le Zuccule, a blend of Cabernet Sauvignon and Merlot, and the Brauros red, which adds Refosco to the blend, show good fruit intensity and lush textures but are not overwhelmed by oak. A varietal Refosco is more robust and earthy but also more characterful than the blends. Two sweet whites are good examples of Verduzzo and Picolit respectively, the former slightly more perfumed and refined, the latter more raisiny.

Recommended Reds:
COF Merlot Ronc di Subule ★★★ £D Le Zuccule ★★ £D
COF Refosco dal Peduncolo Rosso ★★ £C
COF Rosazzo Rosso Brauros ★★ £C

Recommended Whites:
COF Picolit ★★★ £E COF Verduzzo Friulano ★★★ £E
COF Rosazzo Bianco Ellegri ★★★ £C COF Friulano ★★ £B
COF Pinot Grigio ★★ £C COF Chardonnay ★★ £B
COF Sauvignon ★★ £C

Ronco del Gelso (Isonzo) *www.roncodelgelso.com*
Giorgio Badin has done much down the years to improve quality on his family's estate. He makes mostly unoaked whites with good

purity and intensity from 20 ha of vines. Most of the varietals can be a little reticent when first bottled and need at least two years' age to show at their best. The Pinot Bianco and Latimis, a blend of Friulano, Pinot Bianco and Riesling, can be drunk soonest. Giorgio Badin believes Pinot Grigio can lack for aromatic complexity and as a consequence his Sot Lis Rivis benefits from small oak and shows real weight and a stylish complexity. There are two reds, a 60% Merlot and 40% Pignolo blend, Rosso Sintesi dei Capitoli, also benefits from oak ageing and though it can start out a little cool and angular, it is usually soft and plummy with a little age. A new winery should give quality a further boost.

Recommended Reds:
Friuli Isonzo Merlot ★★☆ £C

Recommended Whites:
Friuli Isonzo Chardonnay Siet Vignis ★★★☆ £C
Friuli Isonzo Sauvignon Sottomonte ★★★ £C
Friuli Isonzo Bianco Latimis ★★☆ £C
Friuli Isonzo Pinot Bianco ★★☆ £C
Friuli Isonzo Friulano Toc Bas ★★☆ £C
Friuli Isonzo Riesling ★★☆ £C
Friuli Isonzo Pinot Grigio Sot Lis Rivis ★★★ £C

Ronco del Gnemiz (COF) *www.roncodelgnemiz.com*
Quality has previously been good if variable at this 17 ha estate. Lately there has been much improvement among several of the varietal whites. Although consultancy has come from Roberto Cipresso, the greater consistency seems to have coincided with young Andrea Pittana assuming responsibility for both viticulture and winemaking (Andrea also makes the promising wines from BRAGATO). Sauvignon (half in tank, half in oak) is now better defined with intense mineral, herb, grass and gooseberry fruit, while Pinot Grigio shows better purity and intensity. Chardonnay has long been one of the best wines – rich, ripe and flavoursome with good structur. Bianco di Jacopo is a zesty, scented blend from younger vines. Rosso del Gnemiz (70% Merlot, 30% Cabernet Sauvignon) is the estate red. Also made is a little of special-selection Schioppettino, Merlot Sol, Malvasia Sol, Chardonnay Sol and Sauvignon Sol.

Recommended Reds:
COF Rosso del Gnemiz ★★★☆ £E COF Rosso di Jacopo ★★★ £D

Recommended Whites:
COF Chardonnay ★★★ £E COF Pinot Grigio ★★ £C
COF Sauvignon ★★ £C COF Friulano Bianco San Zuan ★★ £C
COF Bianco di Jacopo ★★ £C

Russiz Superiore (Collio) *www.marcofelluga.it*
Russiz Superiore is the leading estate of the Marco Felluga family. Like his older brother (Livio FELLUGA), Marco Felluga has Friulian viticulture in his blood and has similarly made an important contribution to establishing the region as Italy's leading area for white wines. His son Roberto and daughter Alessandra continue to expand the family's influence and holdings (and another daughter, Patrizia, is behind the promising estate of ZUANI).The wine that has done the most for the reputation of Russiz Superiore is the red Riserva degli Orzoni, Cabernet Sauvignon complemented by Cabernet Franc and Merlot. Rich and structured, it has good depth and ripeness but impresses most in top vintages. As well as some consistently fine varietals, a blended white, Russiz Disôre, is made from from Pinot Bianco, Friulano, Sauvignon and Ribolla Gialla. The leading wines from the 130-ha Marco Felluga estate are Carantan, a stylish plummy red from Cabernet Franc, Cabernet

North-East Italy /Friuli-Venezia Giulia

Sauvignon and Merlot, and Molamotta, a blend of Pinot Bianco, Friulano and Ribolla Gialla. Good varietals include Chardonnay, Sauvignon, Friulano, Refosco and unusually (for Friuli), Moscato Rosa. Since 1994, the historic Castello di Buttrio, with 20ha of vineyards, has been developed under the direction of Marco's daughter, Alessandria, but these wines have not been tasted. The family has also acquired an estate on the western fringe of Chianti Classico, San Niccolò a Pisignano, which is the source of a new red, Sorripa, from Sangiovese, Cabernet Sauvignon and Merlot.

Russiz Superiore
Recommended Reds:
Collio Rosso Riserva degli Orzoni ★★★ £E
Collio Cabernet Franc ★★ £D   Collio Merlot ★★ £D
Recommended Whites:
Collio Bianco Russiz Disôre ★★★ £E Collio Pinot Grigio ★★ £C
Collio Sauvignon ★★ £C

Marco Felluga
Recommended Reds:
Carantan ★★★ £E
Refosco dal Peduncolo Rosso Ronco dei Moreri ★★ £C
Recommended Whites:
Collio Bianco Molamotta ★★ £C Collio Friulano ★★ £C
Collio Sauvignon ★★ £C Collio Chardonnay ★★ £C

Russolo (Friuli-Venezia Giulia) *www.russolo.it*
Russolo is proof of what is possible from the flat alluvial soils north of Pordenone in Friuli (Friuli Grave). There are 20 ha of vineyards managed by Iginio and Rino Russolo. The wines are bright, open and fruity with plenty of varietal character. Ribolla Gialla and Müller-Thurgau stand out as particularly good with decent concentration and more refinement than is often is associated with these varieties. Also surprisingly good is a *barrique*-aged Pinot Nero with slightly smoky, toasty cherry/berry fruit and good texture. Borgo di Peuma is another good red, this time based on 90% Merlot with the balance from dried Cabernet Franc grapes and Refosco. Although cool and herbal, it has good texture and a savoury complexity with five years' age. Doi Raps is a sweet wine, mostly Pinot Grigio, Pinot Bianco and Sauvignon with a little Moscato Giallo. A late-harvested style, it has exotic and ripe stone fruits, a voluptous texture and a fruit-filled finish.
Recommended Reds:
Pinot Nero Grifo Nero ★★ £C   Borgo di Peuma ★★ £C
Recommended Whites:
Doi Raps ★★★ £C   Ribolla Gialla Zui ★★ £C
Müller-Thurgau Musignaz ★★ £C Pinot Grigio Ronco Calaj ★★ £C
Tocai Friulano Jacot Ronco Calaj ★★ £C

Schiopetto (Friuli-Venezia Giulia/Collio) *www.schiopetto.it*
Mario Schiopetto was one of the great figures of Friulian viticulture. Up until his death in 2003 he continued to work with his family and winemaker Stefano Menotti to make some of Friuli's best unoaked white varietals, something he had done since the 1970s. Now his children, Maria Angela, Carlo and Giorgio carry on the family tradition. Pinot Bianco, Pinot Grigio, Malvasia, Sauvignon and Friulano in particular show the intense, clear-fruited expressions that have earned such respect. The small estate of Podere dei Blumeri was added in 1996, to make a total of 30ha of vineyards. Here Sauvignon, Chardonnay and Pinot Grigio have been made with a similar intensity, excellent concentration and individual expression. Also made is an impressive, harmonious, unoaked blended white,

Blanc des Rosis, from Pinot Grigio, Friulano, Sauvignon, Ribolla Gialla and Malvasia, while the red Rivarossa is a blend of Merlot and Cabernet Sauvignon. First made in 2002 is a refined almost Burgundian blend (partly oak fermented and aged) of Chardonnay and Friulano (65/35) called simply Mario Schiopetto. A new red, Podere dei Blumeri Rosso is Merlot-based but includes Cabernet Sauvignon and Refosco.
Recommended Reds:
Rivarossa ★★ £C
Recommended Whites:
Mario Schiopetto ★★★★ £E   Blanc des Rosis ★★★☆ £E
Collio Pinot Bianco ★★★ £C   Collio Friulano ★★ £C
Collio Sauvignon ★★ £C   Collio Pinot Grigio ★★ £C

Matijaz Tercic (Friuli-Venezia Giulia/Collio) *www.tercic.com*
This is an increasingly good and reasonably priced source of Fruili wines with a perceptible increase in quality year on year. To impressive intensity and concentration have been added more expression and better balance. The best wine is the Collio Bianco Planta, 100% Chardonnay. This combines a gently creamy texture with good complexity and has the structure to improve for at least four or five years. Vino degli Orti is produced from 50% Friulano and 50% Malvasia which manages to be delightfully aromatic but concentrated too. This, like all the ripe, intense and stylish, white varietals is vinified and aged in stainless steel. Merlot is usually cool with a touch of herbaceous green pepper character to its smoky, plummy fruit yet is characterful and well made. A varietal Ribolla Gialla and a Friulano are also made.
Recommended Reds:
Collio Merlot ★★ £C
Recommended Whites:
Collio Bianco Planta ★★★ £C   Vino degli Orti ★★ £C
Collio Pinot Grigio ★★ £C   Collio Sauvignon ★★ £C
Collio Chardonnay ★★ £C

Franco Terpin (Friuli-Venezia Giulia/Collio) *www.francoterpin.it*
Franco Terpin and his family produce small quantities of wine from 10 ha of vineyard. Organically made, the wines, three whites and a solitary red, are firmly structured, powerful and assertive with lots of expression. All are bottled without stablization or filtration. Ribolla Gialla can be disappointing, coarse and simple but Collio Bianco is usually powerful and expansive with stylish peach, pear and spice fruit, coming from an equal blend of Sauvignon, Friulano, Pinot Grigio and Chardonnay. Although the fermentation is finished in *barriques* followed by 12 months ageing in the same, the oak serves only to enhance the structure. The high alcohol is more evident in the very powerful Pinot Grigio Sialis; fermentation with the skins contributes to the intense flavours that avoid any coarseness. Both food and some age (preferably both) will enhance the drinking experience. The blended red is wrought from Merlot and Cabernet Sauvignon grapes that vary in proportion from year to year. There is oak, extract and powerful dark plummy ripe fruit in abundance. A bit of a monster in its youth it promises much with 8-10 years' age. A Sialis Bianco is also produced, an equal blend of Sauvignon and Chardonnay, with 10% Pinot Grigio, but this has not been tasted.
Recommended Reds:
Collio Rosso Stamas ★★★☆ £D
Recommended Whites:
Collio Bianco Stamas ★★★☆ £D
Sialis ★★★☆ £E

✿ Vie di Romans (Isonzo) *www.viediromans.it*

Those who dismiss the quality of Chardonnay and Sauvignon produced in Friuli need to taste the wines of Gianfranco Gallo. From 50 ha of vines the grapes are turned into wines with a richness, intensity – but even more importantly a breadth and a structure – that few other examples approach. There are two Chardonnays: Ciampagnis Vieris is the unoaked version, with a tangy, pure fruit intensity; the richer, more complex and structured Vie di Romans spends 12 months in French oak. Piere is the unoaked Sauvignon, concentrated and intense with good grip if less flattering than the delicately creamy, ripe and harmonious Vieris. Flor di Uis is a very flavoursome and characterful blend of Malvasia, Friulano and Riesling, (each vinified separately). A *barrique*-aged and fermented Pinot Grigio, Dessimis, is rich and creamy with a lot of depth but is arguably the least refined of the whites. The Merlot-based red Maurus also shows real depth and intensity and an almost velvety texture with several years' age. There are other single varietals made, (Malvasia, Friulano and Riesling) but these have not been tasted.

Recommended Reds:
Friuli Isonzo Maurus ★★★ £E

Recommended Whites:
Friuli Isonzo Chardonnay Vie di Romans ★★★★ £E
Friuli Isonzo Chardonnay Ciampagnis Vieris ★★★ £D
Friuli Isonzo Sauvignon Piere ★★★☆ £E
Friuli Isonzo Sauvignon Vieris ★★★☆ £E
Friuli Isonzo Pinot Grigio Dessimis ★★★☆ £E
Friuli Isonzo Bianco Flor di Uis ★★★☆ £E

Villa Russiz (Friuli-Venezia Giulia/Collio) *www.villarussiz.it*

The dynamic Gianni Menotti directs this very professionally run estate and winery for the charitable institute Adele Cerruti. Whilst there is excellent intensity and varietal expression in the regular bottlings, it is only in the special versions that an extra depth and structure is truly evident. All the varietal-labelled whites are vinified in stainless steel and don't see any oak. Regular Sauvignon is particularly good – long and tangy, intense and aromatic – while Sauvignon de la Tour adds more breadth and structure from 10 months on its lees. Oak is employed for a very small production of Gräfin de la Tour, a Chardonnay which spends 12 months in *barriques*. Similarly small quantities are made of the red Graf de la Tour from 100% Merlot and the Defi de la Tour from 100% Cabernet Sauvignon. With two to three years in *barrique* they typically show a richness and ripeness, as well as a touch of class, that can be missing in the regular Merlot and Cabernet Sauvignon. Other varietals usually made to a high standard are Riesling, Malvasia and Ribolla Gialla.

Recommended Reds:
Collio Merlot Graf de la Tour ★★★ £E
Collio Cabernet Sauvignon Defi de la Tour ★★★ £E

Recommended Whites:
Collio Chardonnay Gräfin de la Tour ★★★ £D
Collio Sauvignon de la Tour ★★★ £D   Collio Sauvignon ★★ £C
Collio Tocai Friulano ★★ £C   Collio Pinot Bianco ★★ £C
Collio Pinot Grigio ★★ £C

Le Vigne di Zamò (COF) *www.levignedizamo.com*

The Zamò family commenced wine production in the late 1970s but their roots in the Friuli hills stretch back to 1924. Their now sizeable operation has undergone many changes over the past decade, with a transformation in vineyard resources that now total 55 ha, either owned or leased, from the zones around Rocca Bernarda, Buttrio and Rosazzo. A modern winery with a battery of stainless steel tanks underpins the cleanliness and freshness of regular varietals, while oak is employed for the premium Pinot Bianco, Tullio Zamò (named after the family patriarch), and Ronco delle Acacie, from Chardonnay and Friulano. Both can show impressive texture and complexity if missing the balance and elegance for more. Friulano is nearly always good, whether in the regular version or the old-vine Cinquant'Anni. 40% of the vineyard is planted to red grapes and the quality of the special bottlings no doubt owes something to consultancy from top enologist Franco Bernabei, better known for his Tuscan endeavours. The characterful Ronco dei Roseti is mostly from Merlot and the two Cabernets with 5% Pignolo. This and Refosco have a tendency to show too much oak, particularly the latter which has a double passage in new oak. The best red is usually the richly textured and concentrated Merlot Cinquant' Anni, which has the structure to improve for 5–10 years. Tiny amounts of Pinot Nero, Pignolo and Schioppettino are also made. Since 2003 a good, well-balanced if unexceptional sweet wine, Vola Vola is made, an equal blend of Verduzzo and Sauvignon with 20% Picolit.

Recommended Reds:
COF Rosso Ronco dei Roseti ★★★ £E
COF Merlot Vigne Cinquant' Anni ★★★ £E   COF Refosco ★★☆ £D

Recommended Whites:
COF Bianco Ronco delle Acacie ★★★☆ £D   Vola Vola ★★★ £E
COFTocai Friulano Vigne Cinquant' Anni ★★★ £D
COFTocai Friulano ★★☆ £C   COF Pinot Grigio ★★☆ £C
COF Sauvignon ★★ £C   COF Pinot Bianco Tullio Zamò ★★ £C

Zuani (Friuli-Venezia Giulia/Collio) *www.zuanivini.it*

Patrizia Felluga, one of the daughters of Marco Felluga (RUSSIZ SUPERIORE), and her son Antonio Zanon produce two marvellous white wines. Their stated goal is to make whites that are a typical expression of a specific vineyard site rather than producing varietals or a blend of varietals from different sites (as most do in Friuli). Both wines, currently drawn from 7.5 ha, are a blend of Friulano, Pinot Grigio, Chardonnay and Sauvignon Blanc. Zuani Vigne is an unoaked version that is full, ripe and expressive with excellent flavour, freshness and depth. The wine labelled simply Zuani Collio Bianco is from fruit that is harvested a little later and is a more ambitious oak-aged version, spending 8–9 months in *barrique*. This has greater breadth and complexity, the citrus and mineral fruit meshed with leesy and oak-given characters, but successive releases show great style and balance. While this 7 ha estate is expanding, volumes are currently small.

Recommended Whites:
Collio Bianco Zuani ★★★★ £D Collio Bianco Zuani Vigne ★★★☆ £C

Other wines of note

Alto Adige
Cantina Andriano
Recommended Reds:
Alto Adige Merlot Riserva Tor di Lupo ★★☆ £E
Alto Adige Lagrein Tor di Lupo ★★★ £E
Recommended Whites:
Alto Adige Gewürztraminer Tor di Lupo ★★☆ £D
Alto Adige Sauvignon Terlaner Tor di Lupo ★★☆ £D
Alto Adige Chardonnay Tor di Lupo ★★★ £D
Cantina Bolzano/Kellerei Bozen
Recommended Reds: Alto Adige Lagrein Riserva Taber ★★★ £E
Recommended Whites: Alto Adige Sauvignon Mock ★★★ £C

North-East Italy

Alto Adige Pinot Bianco KG Gries ★★☆ £C
Alto Adige Chardonnay Kleinstein ★★☆ £C
Viticoltori Caldaro
Recommended Whites:
Alto Adige Gewürztraminer Campaner ★★★ £D
Peter Dipoli
Recommended Whites: Alto Adige Sauvignon Voglar ★★★ £D
Erste & Neue – Prima & Nuova
Recommended Whites: Alto Adige Gewürztraminer Puntay ★★★ £D
Kofererhof
Recommended Whites:
Alto Adige Valle Isarco Gewürztraminer Brixner ★★☆ £C
Muri-Gries
Recommended Reds: Alto Adige Pinot Nero Riserva Abtei Muri ★☆ £D
Alto Adige Lagrein Riserva Abtei Muri ★★☆ £D
Recommended Whites: Alto Adige Pinot Bianco ★★ £C
Alto Adige Chardonnay ★★ £C
Cantina Nals Magreid
Recommended Reds: Alto Adige Pinot Nero Mazzon ★★☆ £C
Alto Adige Anticus Baron Salvadori (Merlot/Cab Sauv) ★★☆ £C
Recommended Whites: Alto Adige Moscato Giallo ★★ £C
Alto Adige Pinot Grigio ★★ £C Alto Adige Pinot Bianco ★★ £C
Alto Adige Pinot Grigio Punggl ★★★ £C
Alto Adige Pinot Bianco Sirmian ★★★ £C
Alto Adige Sauvignon Mantele ★★☆ £C
Weingut Niklas
Recommended Reds: Alto Adige Lagrein ★★☆ £C
Nusserhof
Recommended Reds: Alto Adige Lagrein Riserva ★★☆ £C
Recommended Whites: Blaterle ★ £B
Recommended Rosés: Alto Adige Lagrein Kretzer ★★ £C
Cantina Produttori Termeno
Recommended Reds: Alto Adige Lagrein Urban ★★ £D
Alto Adige Pinot Nero ★★ £C
Recommended Whites: Alto Adige Gewürztraminer Maratsch ★★ £C
Alto Adige Gewürztraminer Nussbaumer ★★★☆ £D
Alto Adige Pinot Grigio Unterebner ★★ £C
Alto Adige Sauvignon ★★ £C
Cantina Produttori Valle Isarco
Recommended Whites: Alto Adige Valle Isarco Sylvaner ★☆ £B
Alto Adige Valle Isarco Müller-Thurgau ★☆ £B
Alto Adige Valle Isarco Veltliner ★★☆ £B
Alto Adige Valle Isarco Kerner ★★☆ £C
Alto Adige Valle Isarco Gewürztraminer ★★☆ £C
Baron Widmann
Recommended Reds:
Alto Adige Rot (Cab Franc/Cab Sauv/Merlot) ★★☆ £C
Alto Adige Vernatsch ★☆ £B
Recommended Whites: Alto Adige Sauvignon ★★☆ £C
Alto Adige Gewürztraminer ★★★ £C
Alto Adige Weiss (Chardonnay/Pinot Bianco) ★★ £C
Peter Zemmer
Recommended Reds:
Cortinie Rosso (Lagrein/Merlot/Cab Sauv/Cab Franc) ★★★ £D
Recommended Whites:
Cortinie Bianco (Chard/P.Grigio/Sauvignon/Gewürztraminer) ★★★ £C

Trentino
Vallarom
Recommended Whites:
Trentino Chardonnay Riserva Vigna Brioni ★★ £C

(Eastern) Lombardy
Costaripa
Recommended Reds: Garda Classico Maim (Groppello) ★★ £C
Provenza
Recommended Reds: Garda Classico Negresco ★★ £C
Garda Classico Rosso Selezione Fabio Contato ★★★ £E
Recommended Whites: Lugana Ca' Maiol ★ £B
Lugana Superiore Molin ★★ £C

Veneto
Igino Accordini
Recommended Reds:
Amarone della Valpolicella Classico Le Bessole ★★★ £E
Adami
Recommended Whites: Prosecco Bosco di Gica Brut ★★ £C
Prosecco Vigneto Giardino ★★ £C
Balestri Valda
Recommended Whites: Soave Classico ★★ £B Soave Classico
Vigneto Sengialta ★★★ £C
Bertani
Recommended Reds: Amarone della Valpolicella Classico ★★★ £F
Carlo Bogoni
Recommended Whites: Soave Classico Superiore La Ponsara ★★ £B
Bottega
Recommended Whites:
Gold Prosecco ★★★☆ £D
Brigaldara
Recommended Reds: Amarone della Valpolicella Classico ★★★ £E
Amarone della Valpolicella Classico Case Vecie ★★★★ £E
Recioto della Valpolicella Classico ★★★☆ £E
Recommended Whites: Brigaldara Passito ★★☆ £D
Ca' Lustra/Villa Alessi
Recommended Reds: Colli Euganei Rosso ★★ £C
Sassonero Villa Alessi (Merlot) ★★★ £C
Recommended Whites: Colli Euganei Pinot Bianco ★ £B
Manzoni Bianco Villa Alessi ★ £C
A Cengia Villa Alessi (Moscato Bianco/Moscato Giallo) ★★ £C
Moscato La Betia Villa Alessi (sweet) ★★★ £C
Ca' Rugate
Recommended Whites: Soave Classico Superiore Monte Alto ★★ £C
Soave Classico Superiore Monte Fiorentine ★★ £B
Bucciato (Garganega) ★★ £C
Michele Castellani & Figli
Recommended Reds: Valpolicella Classico Superiore I Castei ★★ £C
Amarone della Valpolicella Classico I Castei Campo Casalin ★★★ £E
Amarone della Valpolicella Le Vigne Ca' del Pipa ★★★ £E
Recioto della Valpolicella I Castei Campo Casalin ★★★ £E
Collalto
Recommended Whites: Prosecco di Valdobbiadene ★★ £B
Corteforte
Recommended Reds: Amarone della Valpolicella ★★ £E
Recioto della Valpolicella Amandorlato ★★ £E
Tenuta Faltracco
Recommended Whites: Soave Classico Monte Carsarsa ★★ £C
Recioto di Soave ★★★ £E
Gino Fasoli
Recommended Reds: Valpolicella Classico La Corte del Pozzo ★ £B
Recommended Whites: Liber (Garganega) ★★ £B
Nino Franco
Recommended Whites: Prosecco di Valdobbiadene Brut ★ £C
Proseco di Valdobbiadene Rive di San Floriano ★★ £C

Frassinelli
Recommended Whites: Prosecco di Valdobbiadene ★★ £B
Guerrieri Rizzardi
Recommended Reds: Amarone della Valpolicella Calcarole ★★★ £E
La Cappuccina
Recommended Whites: Soave Superiore Fontégo ★★ £C
Soave Superiore San Brizio ★★★ £C
Le Ragose
Recommended Reds: Valpolicella Classico Superiore Le Sassine ★★ £C
Amarone della Valpolicella ★★★ £E
Recioto della Valpolicella ★★★ £E
Le Vigne di San Pietro
Recommended Reds: Cabernet Sauvignon Refolà ★★★ £E
Recommended Whites: Bianco di Custoza San Pietro ★★ £C
Due Cuori (sweet – Moscato Giallo) ★★★ £F
Loredan Gasparini
Recommended Reds:
Capo di Stato (Cabernets/Merlot/Malbec) ★★★ £E
Giovanni Menti
(all 100% Garganega)
Recommended Whites: Gambellara Classico Paiele ★☆ £B
Gambellara Classico Riva Arsiglia ★★☆ £C
Recioto di Gambellara Classico Albina ★★★☆ £D
Musella
Recommended Reds:
Valpolicella Amarone ★★★★ £G
Valpolicella Superiore Vigne Nuove ★☆ £B
Monte del Drago ★★☆ £E
Recommended Whites:
Bianco del Drago ★ £C
Prà
Recommended Whites: Soave Classico Superiore ★★ £C
Soave Classico Monte Grande ★★★ £C
Soave Classico Staforte ★★★ £C
Soave Classico Colle Sant'Antonio ★★★ £C
Recioto di Soave Classico Recioto delle Fontane ★★★☆ £D
Recchia
Recommended Reds: Valpolicella Classico Superiore ★★ £C
Valpolicella Classico Superiore Le Muraie ★★☆ £C
Amarone della Valpolicella Classico ★★★ £D
Amarone della Valpolicella Classico Ca'Bertoldi ★★★★ £D
Ruggeri
Recommended Whites: Prosecco Riserva Giustino Bisol ★★ £C
Tenuta Sant' Antonio
Recommended Reds:
Amarone della Valpolicella Campo dei Gigli ★★★ £F
Valpolicella Superiore La Bandina ★★ £C
Speri
Recommended Reds:
Valpolicella Classico Vigneto Monte Sant'Urbano ★★ £E
Amarone della Valpolicella Vigneto Monte Sant'Urbano ★★★★ £F
Recioto della Valpolicella La Roggia ★★★ £E
Trabucchi
Recommended Reds: Valpolicella Superiore Terre del Cereolo ★ £C
Valpolicella Superiore Terre di San Colombano ★ £C
Amarone della Valpolicella ★★★☆ £E
Recioto della Valpolicella ★★★☆ £E
Cantina Valpantena
Recommended Reds: Valpolicella Valpantena Ripasso ★★ £B
Amarone della Valpolicella Falasco ★★★ £D
Recioto della Valpolicella Tesauro ★★★ £D

C. S. Valpolicella
Recommended Reds:
Amarone della Valpolicella Domini Veneti ★★★ £D
Recioto della Valpolicella Domini Veneti ★★ £D
Recioto della Valpolicella Vigneti di Moron ★★★ £E
Villa Monteleone
Recommended Reds: Amarone della Valpolicella Classico ★★ £E
Friuli-Venezia Giulia
Antico Broilo
Recommended Reds: COF Cabernet Franc ★★★ £C
COF Merlot ★★ £C   COF Schioppettino ★★★ £C
COF Refosco dal Peduncolo Rosso ★★★☆ £C
Recommended Whites: COF Ribolla Gialla ★★☆ £C
COF Tocai Friulano ★★★ £C
Borc Dodon
Recommended Reds: Uis Néris (Merlot/Cab Franc/Cab Sauv) ★★★ £D
Bragato
Recommended Reds:
COF Riserva Sanzuan (Merlot/Cabernet Franc) ★★★☆ £E
Recommended Whites: COF Ribolla Gialla ★★☆ £C
COF Tocai Friulano ★★★ £C   COF Sauvignon Serena ★★★ £C
Bressan
Recommended Reds: Schioppettino ★★★ £C
Recommended Whites: Verduzzo Friulano (Dry) ★ £C
Casa Zuliani
Recommended Reds: Collio Merlot ★★ £C
Collio Rosso Winter (Merlot/Cab Sauv/Cab Franc) ★★★ £D
Recommended Whites: Collio Pinot Grigio ★★ £C
Collio Malvasia ★★ £C   Collio Tocai Friulano ★★ £C
Collio Sauvignon ★★☆ £C   Chardonnay Winter ★★★ £C
Collavini
Recommended Whites:
Collio Bray Bianco ★★★☆ £E
Di Lenardo
Recommended Reds:
Friuli Grave Refosco Vigne da Lis Maris ★★ £C
Friuli Grave Cabernet Vigne da Lis Maris ★★ £C
Recommended Whites:
Fruili Grave Toh! (Tocai Friulano) ★★ £C
Fruili Grave Chardonnay Vigne da Lis Maris ★★ £C
Pass the Cookies (sweet - Verduzzo) ★★★ £D
Ermacora
Recommended Reds: COF Refosco dal Peduncolo Rosso ★★☆ £C
COF Riul (Merlot/Cabernet Sauvignon/Refosco) ★★★☆ £E
Recommended Whites: COF Pinot Grigio ★★★ £C
COF Pinot Bianco ★★★ £C   COF Tocai Friulano ★★☆ £C
COF Sauvignon ★★☆ £C   COF Picolit ★★★ £D
Foffani
Recommended Reds:
Friuli Aquileia Rosso (Merlot/Refosco/Cab Franc) ★★☆ £C
Friuli Aquileia Refosco dal Peduncolo Rosso ★★☆ £C
Recommended Whites: Friuli Aquileia Pinot Grigio ★★ £C
Ter Vinum Bianco (Pinot Grigiio/Chardonnay/Merlot) ★★ £C
Daniele Grion
Recommended Whites: Collio Tocai Friulano ★★☆ £C
Il Roncat - Giovanni Dri
Recommended Whites: Ramandolo ★★★ £E
Edi Kante
Recommended Whites: Carso Malvasia ★★ £C
Carso Vitovska ★★★ £C Carso Chardonnay ★★★ £C
Carso Sauvignon ★★★ £C

North-East Italy

Italy

La Castellada
Recommended Whites: Collio Chardonnay ★★★ £C
Collio Sauvignon ★★★ £C Collio Ribolla Gialla ★★ £C
Collio Bianco Bianco della Castellada (Sauvignon & others) ★★★ £D
Livon
Recommended Reds: Tiareblù (Merlot/Cabernets) ★★★ £D
Recommended Whites: Collio Chardonnay Braide Mate ★★ £C
Collio Pinot Grigio Braide Grande ★★ £C
Braide Alte (Chardonnay/Sauvignon/Moscato Giallo/Picolit) ★★ £C
Lorenzon/I Feudi Di Romans
Recommended Reds: Friuli Isonzo Merlot ★☆ £B
Recommended Whites: Friuli Isonzo Sauvignon Blanc ★★ £C
Friuli Isonzo Pinot Grigio ★★ £C
Midolini
Recommended Reds:
Rosacroce Rosso (Refosco/Cabernets/Merlot) ★★ £C
Recommended Whites:
Rosacroce Bianco (Chardonnay/Sauvignon/Tocai) ★★ £C
Ornella Molon Traverso
Recommended Reds: Piave Merlot ★★ £C
Vite Rossa (Merlot/Cabernets) ★★ £C
Riserva Rosso di Villa (Merlot/Cab Sauv) ★★ £D
Recommended Whites: Sauvignon ★★ £C Traminer ★ £C
Puiatti
Recommended Reds: Collio Pinot Nero I Ruttars ★★ £D
Recommended Whites: Collio Sauvignon I Ruttars ★★ £C
Collio Pinot Grigio I Ruttars ★★ £C
Dario Raccaro
Recommended Whites: CollioTocai Friulano ★★ £C
Stanislao Radikon
Recommended Reds: Merlot ★★★ £D
Recommended Whites: Ribolla Gialla ★★★ £C
Oslavje (Pinot Grigio/Chardonnay/Sauvignon) ★★★★ £E
Oslavje Riserva ★★★★☆ £E
Ronc di Vico
Recommended Reds:
COF Vicorosso (Merlot/Cabernet Franc/Refosco) ★★★☆ £D
COF Titut Ros (Refosco/Merlot) ★★★★ £E
Recommended Whites: Matec (Verduzzo) ★★★☆ £C
COF Titut Blanc (Tocai Friulano) ★★★☆ £C
Ronco delle Betulle
Recommended Whites: COF Sauvignon ★★ £C
COF Tocai Friulano ★★ £C COF Pinot Grigio ★★ £C
Roncus
Recommended Whites: Pinot Bianco ★★ £C
CollioTocai Friulano ★★ £C
Roncús Bianco Vecchie Vigne (Malvasia/Tocai/Ribolla Gialla) ★★★ £D
Sdricca
Recommended Reds:
Schioppettino ★★★☆ £B
Sirch
Recommended Whites:
Sirch (Tocai Friulano/Ribolla Gialla/Sauvignon) ★★☆ £C
COF Tocai Friulano ★★ £C COF Pinot Grigio ★☆ £C
COF Tocai Friulano Mis Mas ★★☆ £C COF Ribolla Gialla ★★ £C
Skerk
Recommended Whites: Carso Vitovska ★★☆ £C
Specogna
Recommended Reds: Collio Pignolo ★★ £D
Recommended Whites: COF Tocai ★★ £C COF Pinot Grigio ★★ £C

Oscar Sturm
Recommended Whites: Collio Ribolla Gialla ★★ £B
Collio Pinot Grigio ★★★ £B Collio Tocai Friulano ★★☆ £B
Collio Sauvignon ★★☆ £C Chardonnay Andritz ★★☆ £C
Franco Toros
Recommended Reds: Collio Merlot ★★☆ £D
Recommended Whites: Collio Pinot Bianco ★★☆ £C
Collio Pinot Grigio ★★★ £B Collio Tocai Friulano ★★★ £C
Collio Sauvignon ★★★ £C Collio Chardonnay ★★★ £C
Valle
Recommended Whites: COF Pinot Grigio Araldica ★☆ £B
COF Sauvignon Araldica ★★ £C
COF Tocai Friulano San Blàs ★★ £B COF Ribolla Gialla San Blàs ★★ £B
Villanova
Recommended Whites: Collio Pinot Grigio ★★ £B
Friuli Isonzo Malvasia ★★ £B Collio Tocai Friulano ★☆ £B
Friuli Isonzo Chardonnay ★★ £B
Collio Sauvignon Ronco Cucco ★★☆ £C
Visintini
Recommended Whites: COF Ribolla Gialla ★★ £C
COF Pinot Grigio (Ramato) ★★★ £C
Vistorta
Recommended Reds: Merlot ★★ £C
Vodopivec
Recommended Whites: Vitovska ★★★☆ £D
Zidarich
Recommended Reds: Teran ★★★☆ £D
Recommended Whites: Carso Vitovska ★★★☆ £D

Author's choice

Diverse premium reds
Allegrini La Poja
Girolamo Dorigo COF Rosso Montscalapade
Livio Felluga COF Merlot Riserva Sossò
Foradori Teroldego Rotaliano Granato
Hofstätter Alto Adige Pinot Nero Barthenau Vigna Sant'urbano
Inama Bradisismo
Alois Lageder Alto Adige Cabernet Sauvignon Cor Römigberg
Manincor Castel Campan
Miani COF Merlot
Moschioni COF Celtico Rosso
Josef Niedermayr Alto Adige Lagrein Aus Gries Riserva
Russiz Superiore Collio Rosso Riserva Degli Orzoni
San Leonardo San Leonardo
Vignalta Gemola
Elena Walch Alto Adige Lagrein Riserva Castel Ringberg

Superior Valpolicella (or equivalent)
Allegrini La Grola
Buglioni Valpolicella Classico Superiore Il Ruffiano
Tommaso Bussola Valpolicella Classico Superiore TB
Corte Sant'alda Valpolicella Superiore Mithas
Romano dal Forno Valpolicella Superiore
Le Salette Valpolicella Classico Superiore Ca' Carnocchio
Marion Valpolicella Superiore
Quintarelli Valpolicella Classico Superiore Monte Ca' Paletta
Roccolo Grassi Valpolicella Superiore Roccolo Grassi
Viviani Valpolicella Classico Superiore Campo Morar

Other Special North-West Reds

Antichi Vigneti di Cantalupo Ghemme Signore di Bayard
Matteo Correggia Nebbiolo d'Alba La Val di Preti
Elio Altare Insieme
Bricco Maiolica Nebbiolo d'Alba Il Cumot
Ca' del Bosco Maurizio Zanella
La Spinetta Monferrato Rosso Pin
Les Cretes Valle d'Aosta Fumin Vigne La Tour
Malvirà Roero Superiore Mombeltramo
Nino Negri Valtellina Sfursat 5 Stelle
Angelo Negro & Figli Roero Sudisfà
Aldo Rainoldi Valtellina Sfursat Fruttaio Ca' Rizzieri

Reds for meditation

Allegrini Amarone della Valpolicella Classico
Tommaso Bussola Recioto della Valpolicella Classico TB
Corte Sant'alda Recioto della Valpolicella
Le Salette Amarone della Valpolicella Classico Pergole Vece
Moschioni COF Pignolo
Nicolis Amarone della Valpolicella Classico Ambrosan
Quintarelli Amarone della Valpolicella Classico Monte Ca' Paletta
Speri Amarone della Valpolicella Classico Vigneto Monte Sant'Urbano
Tenuta Sant' Antonio Amarone della Valpolicella Campo dei Gigli
Tedeschi Amarone della Valpolicella Classico Capitel Monte Olmi
Viviani Amarone della Valpolicella Classico Casa dei Bepi
Zenato Amarone della Valpolicella Classico Riserva Sergio Zenato

20 first class whites

Borgo del Tiglio Collio Bianco Studio di Bianco
Ca' dei Frati Pratto
Cesconi Trentino Chardonnay
Colterenzio Alto Adige Chardonnay Cornell
Livio Felluga COF Rosazzo Bianco Terre Alte
Franz Haas Manna
Hofstätter Alto Adige Gewürztraminer Kolbenhof Söll
Il Carpino Collio Chardonnay
Vinnaioli Jermann Vintage Tunina
Pieropan Soave Classico Superiore La Rocca
Pojer & Sandri Faye
Ronchi Di Manzano COF Rosazzo Bianco Ellegri
Russiz Superiore Collio Bianco Russiz Disôre
San Michele Appiano Alto Adige Gewürztraminer Sanct Valentin
Schiopetto Collio Pinot Bianco
Cantina Terlano Alto Adige Sauvignon Quarz
Vie di Romans Friuli Isonzo Chardonnay Vie di Romans
Villa Russiz Collio Sauvignon de La Tour
Le Vigne di Zamò COF Friulano Vigne Cinquant'anni
Zuani Collio Bianco

...and some fine sweet whites

Anselmi I Capitelli
Girolamo Dorigo COF Picolit Vigneto Montscalapade
Maculan Breganze Torcolato
Pieropan Passito della Rocca
Pojer & Sandri Essenzia
Paolo Rodaro COF Picolit
Ronchi di Manzano COF Verduzzo Friulano
San Michele Appiano Alto Adige Bianco Passito Comtess'Sanct Valentin

Wine behind the label

Tuscany

'Paradiso terrestre'

There's little excuse for ignorance of Tuscany's great wines as the region is awash with fine quality at all levels. But avoid the most strongly branded names and seek out smaller or newer producers. Tuscany's wine renaissance or rinascimento had its beginnings more than 30 years ago. Its artists include both individual producers and highly trained and experienced enologists that increasingly respond to what is required from both producer and site rather than imposing a uniform style. Outside investment and talent, including Swiss, English and American winemakers and entrepreneurs, also play a part. Since the turn of the century we are seeing more emphasis placed on native grape varieties, new or revived wine growing areas and the importance of expressing something of the wine's origins or tipicità (typicality). As well as unprecedented quality from Sangiovese (topped up with Canaiolo, Colorino etc), and very good Cabernet Sauvignon, Merlot and Syrah, more can now be detected of the different permutations of place, soil and climate. There is also better balance and less oak, allied to greater finesse and elegance.

Red wines
Central Tuscany and the classic appellations

The heart of Tuscany is **Chianti Classico**, its most historic and still its most important wine zone. The blunder of massive replanting in the 1960s with productive but poor-quality clones has started to be atoned for by recent replantings that have benefited from the research project known as Chianti Classico 2000. While the Chianti Classico DOCG now permits increasing amounts of other, foreign varieties (in many instances still at the expense of natives such as Canaiolo and Colorino), it is still based for the most part on Sangiovese (with pure examples possible since 1996). The leading communes are Greve in Chianti, Barberino Val d'Elsa, Castellina in Chianti, Radda in Chianti, Gaiole in Chianti and Castelnuovo Berardenga. Part of the communes of Tavarnelle Val di Pesa and San Casciano Val di Pesa are also included. While there are some discernible differences between each, as important are elevation, specific mesoclimates and soil types (there is much variation within each commune), better identified in sub-zones such as Monti (Gaiole) and Panzano (Greve). Interestingly, in a 'Chianti Classico 2000' tasting demonstrating the characteristics of different trialled clones there was as much affinity between wines from different clones grown in the same location, as those from the same clones but different sites. But arguably still more important is the style of winemaking. The use of new oak and variations in fermentation length, type, temperature, etc. all play a significant part in emphasising or smothering differences in *terroir*. Regular or normale Chianti Classico can be sold with a year's age, whereas Riservas, which are more likely to have been *barrique*-aged, are only released from the beginning of the third year after the vintage (i.e. the 2003s from January 2006). While there is a trend to re-establishing Chianti Classico as their leading wine, some producers continue to promote a so-called Super-Tuscan, first created as a vino da tavola when the laws were more restrictive and now often sold under the Toscana IGT. These include varietal Cabernet Sauvignon and Merlot, blends of the two together and blends of each with Sangiovese. There is also varietal Syrah and even Pinot Nero. This profusion of wine types is repeated in almost every important wine zone in Tuscany.

Chianti Classico is surrounded by several viticultural zones of differing size and importance. Immediately north in the hills closest to Florence, is **Chianti Colli Fiorentini**. Regular examples are often relatively light but can be characterful and perfumed, in part because they are much more likely to include small percentage of native varieties than Chianti Classico equivalents. North-east of Florence, from hills on either side of the river Sieve (but pressing up against the Apennines) is the small zone of **Chianti Rufina** where a small number of producers make a soaring, elegant expression of Sangiovese. Intruding into Rufina's eastern flank is the high-altitude **Pomino**, notable for its historical inclusion of French varieties and its domination by Frescobaldi. From the other side of Florence are another minor Chianti zone, **Chianti Montalbano**, and the small but high-quality zone of **Carmignano**. Though revived only since the 1970s there are historical references both to its quality and to the planting of Cabernet Sauvignon, of which 20 per cent may be added to Sangiovese. South of Carmignano and west of Colli Fiorentini is a further small Chianti zone, **Chianti Montespertoli**. West of Chianti Classico are the medieval towers of San Gimignano. Limited success with the white Vernaccia (see below) has resulted in increased planting of red varieties. Some fine blends, mostly Sangiovese, Cabernet Sauvignon or Merlot, or a combination of these, are sold mainly as Toscana IGT in preference to a newish **San Gimignano** DOC. Lesser examples of Sangiovese tend to be sold as **Chianti Colli Senesi**. This zone extends from here south around the lower reaches of Chianti Classico and also surrounds the Brunello and Vino Nobile zones – often giving the fullest and meatiest non-Classico Chianti.

Brunello di Montalcino DOCG is a wine like no other in Tuscany. Here it is hotter and drier than in any other major zone and the bigger, more muscular wines offered by an ever growing number of producers (out of almost 200 in total) have maintained high prices thanks in part to a more singular, focused image that has been effectively promoted both locally and on foreign markets. Yet the quality of these pure Sangiovese (locally called Brunello) wines varies greatly. Excessive wood-ageing requirements (in large oak casks) were blamed for the wines drying out, especially in lighter years when there is insufficient fruit to support it. However, though the wines are only available from the fifth year after the vintage (the 2010s in 2015) there is now much greater flexibility about the type of wood used to age the wines and some styles are characterised by their use of new oak. The introduction of **Rosso di Montalcino** DOC, effectively a second wine, has helped cash flow. Its more accessible, fruit-driven style also means these wines can be drunk much younger, though some examples have better structure and depth than lighter, more forward Brunello and need at least 3–5 years' age. Some of the most structured and ageworthy Brunello come from the higher ridges (400–500m) but many individual subzones are beginning to emerge – the hill of Montosoli (350m) is the best known. Sant'Antimo DOC covers examples of blends of Sangiovese and other (foreign) varieties as well as varietal examples from other grapes grown in the zone. Between Montalcino and Montepulciano lies the large newish DOC of Orcia centred on the Orcia River valley. Podere Forte gives a startling indication of what is possible from high hillside vineyards. On the south-eastern edge of this zone, near the Umbrian border, is Sarteano, notable for the wines of Tenuta di Trinoro.

Vino Nobile di Montepulciano DOCG lies to the east of Montalcino around its own small historic town. Unlike Brunello, pure Sangiovese (here called Prugnolo Gentile) was not permitted until very recently and many examples contain a percentage of Canaiolo and sometimes Mammolo. Vino Nobile has had difficulty

reclaiming its historic status but there are an increasing number of good producers and most examples are very competitively priced. Lesser vineyards are assigned as Rosso di Montepulciano which is not the same concept as **Rosso di Montalcino** and most examples are much more modestly structured and for drinking within a couple of years of the vintage. Further east in the Val di Chiana a new **Cortona** DOC has been created with provision for varietal Merlot and Syrah (and Chardonnay – see below) among other varieties, and is already being utilised by Antinori, Avignonesi and Tenementi D'Alessandro. Further north in the Valdarno (and east of Chianti Classico) is another minor Chianti zone, **Chianti Colli Aretini**, currently being rescued from its former obscurity by Petrolo and others, though the best wines are sold as Toscana IGT.

Many of Tuscany's new stars come from within the areas discussed above but increasingly important are the mostly unexploited western and southern areas of viticulture first highlighted by Sassicaia but developed at an accelerating pace over the past couple of decades.

The Tuscan coast and southern Maremma
The most northern of the Tuscan coastal zones is the **Colline Lucchesi** for wines from slopes on either side of the historic and beautiful town of Lucca. As in the east at Rufina, the vineyards lie close to the Apennines and there is a growing number of progressive producers. Plantings in the more restrictive zone around the town of **Montecarlo** include several French varieties and many of the best wines from both DOCs are sold as Toscana IGT. Some way south and east of Pisa the hills are demarcated as **Terre di Pisa** for another of the minor Chianti zones but Sangiovese, Cabernet Sauvignon and Merlot blends of high quality are made. Similarly promising wines are being produced from within the **Montescudaio** DOC which has recently made more provision for non native varieties, though again some of these and many of the Pisane wines are sold as Toscana IGT. From Castello del Terriccio, located on the periphery of these zones but one of the most high-profile producers in the area, it is but a short distance south to the famous zone of Bolgheri.

Bolgheri (and the commune of Castagneto Carducci) is where the narrow strip of the coastal Maremma might be said to start properly. Cabernet Sauvignon and Merlot dominate but Sangiovese is not completely ignored and the DOC (which includes a single-wine sub-zone for Sassicaia) covers blends that include any (or all) of the three varieties. There is a mix of both smaller producers, such as Enrico Santini, Michele Satta and Le Macchiole, and big powerful names including Antinori (Guado al Tasso), Gaja (Ca' Marcanda), Frescobaldi (Ornellaia) and A & G Folonari (Campo del Mare). Upcoming are the wines of a joint venture between Delia Viader of the Napa in California and Piemonte producer Stefano Gagliardo. There is still more potential to the south of Bolgheri. One such hotspot is **Suvereto**, where Cabernet and Merlot again are favoured and the wines of Tua Rita, Montepeloso and Gualdo del Re have incited others such as Vittorio Moretti of Bellavista (Petra) to join the action. The wider, encompassing DOCG of **Val di Cornia** adjoins Bolgheri in the north but also contains a southern outcrop north of Piombino on the coast.

The next step south on an emerging coastal patchwork is Massa Marittima which opens out into the southern Maremma. Of emerging importance, it has its own extensive DOC: **Monteregio**

di Massa Marittima. South of Grosseto is **Morellino di Scansano** DOCG, the most important appellation in the southern Maremma for Sangiovese-based reds (led by Le Pupille). Cabernet Sauvignon and Merlot are also important here, though only given IGT status. The area between them is also demarcated, as **Montecucco** DOCG, and connects up with Brunello. Other southern appellations include **Parrina**, overlooking the coast at Orbetello and centred on the vineyards of a single producer, La Parrina. **Sovana** DOC extends to the border with Lazio and makes provision not only for Sangiovese-based reds but also varietal Sangiovese, Cabernet Sauvignon and Merlot.

White wines
Most of Italy's best and most original dry whites can be found under the North-East, Central and Southern Italy sections. In Tuscany there is generally less excitement even if there are reasonable quantities of attractive everyday whites. The problem for long has been the dominance of the humdrum Trebbiano grape. Deciding what to replace it with is rarely a priority for producers in this red-oriented region. Many have worked with Chardonnay (and the new **Cortona** DOC embraces it) but while a small number of examples are very good, most lack the elegance or class that might inspire greater dedication and even better results. Equally only a handful of examples have emerged with the structure that would guarantee greater longevity. Best known is **Vernaccia di San Gimignano** which can be reasonably characterful if most examples lack the depth or style that it's DOCG status implies. Several of the coastal appellations offer whites, including Colline Lucchesi and Montecarlo whose grapes include Sémillon and Roussanne. From Montescudaio, Trebbiano is complemented by Sauvignon Blanc and Vermentino, the latter two also showing good style in Bolgheri. Val di Cornia sanctions Vermentino with Trebbiano and from further south in the Maremma good Vermentino can also be found. **Bianco di Pitigliano**, which overlaps with the most southern red DOC, Sovana, is a dedicated white wine zone for occasionally characterful Procanico/Greco/Malvasia blends.

Tuscany's best and most individual wine from white grapes has to be **Vin Santo** though it varies enormously in quality, style and sweetness. Made from dried grapes, usually hung from rafters, the best examples tend to be predominantly Malvasia rather than Trebbiano. They range from dry to rich, concentrated and sweet, and from the gently oxidised and fruit-rich (with preserved fruits and citrus peel) to more old-fashioned, more overtly nutty oxidised examples. Like the best extra virgin olive oils, few taste alike. As exciting as it can be, price and quality are often a reflection of the efforts that have gone into its production. Vin Santo del Chianti, Vin Santo del Chianti Classico and Vin Santo di Montepulciano have all obtained DOC status. The one or two good examples of the sweet wine **Moscadello di Montalcino** DOC (from Moscato Bianco grapes grown in the Brunello zone) are also worth a try.

Tuscany

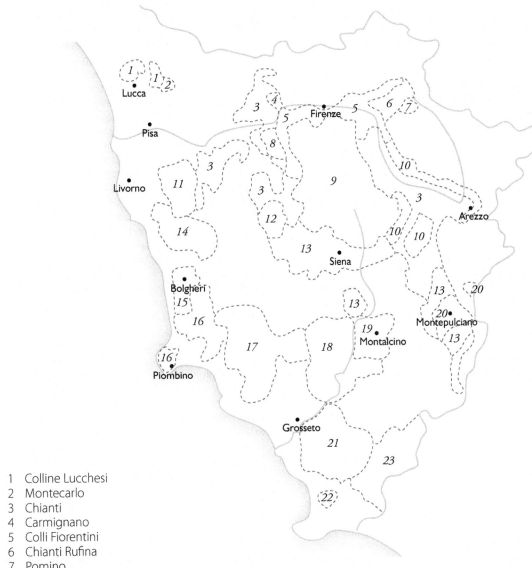

1   Colline Lucchesi
2   Montecarlo
3   Chianti
4   Carmignano
5   Colli Fiorentini
6   Chianti Rufina
7   Pomino
8   Chianti Montespertoli
9   Chianti Classico
10 Colli Aretini
11 Colline Pisane
12 San Gimignano
13 Chianti Colli Senesi
14 Montescudaio
15 Bolgheri
16 Val di Cornia
17 Monteregio di Massa Marittima
18 Montecucco
19 Brunello di Montalcino
20 Vino Nobile di Montepulciano
21 Morellino di Scansano
22 Parrina
23 Sovana

Tuscany

Tuscany vintages

Tuscany produces plenty of red wine for short and medium-term cellaring but to date not that much that has provided real pleasure for a 15- or 20-year celebration. Many of the best reds, be it Chianti Classico Riserva, the best Vino Nobile, reds from the Tuscan coast or other blends including Cabernet or Merlot, are at or near their best with 5–10 years' age, the very best after 10–15 years. Certainly some of the most sought-after labels will last longer but how much they will continue to improve is more debatable. Brunello from 1990, 93, 95, 97, 99, 01, 04, 07 and 08 should go the distance of 2 decades though most also have the balance to be ready to drink at half that age. A good Rosso di Montalcino will age better than a weaker, more forward Brunello and give a lot more satisfaction. The style of any producer's wines is as important as location or the primary grape variety so where possible the comments should be considered together.

2015: Inclement weather in the spring and early summer was counterbalanced by a perfect August and September before October rains spoiled the quality of the vintage somewhat. This will go down as a good but not great vintage, with wines from the coastal regions of Bolgheri and the Maremma showing more concentration and structure that the wines from Chianti and Brunello, which may turn out to have more elegance than power.

2014: For the second year in a row, yields were down considerably, not only by a very dry summer and an extremely cold snap in February but this time by untimely rain in May which led to uneven flowering and by consequence, uneven ripeness at harvest. Rain at the end of August did re-introduce some moistness into the vines and the wines have more structure than those of the previous vintage. Nevertheless, good wines have generally been produced in Chianti, Montelcino and Montepolciano, with the coastal vineyards faring less well.

2013: Inclement weather in the spring and early summer was counterbalanced by a perfect August and September before October rains spoiled the quality of the vintage somewhat. This will go down as a good but not great vintage, with wines from the coastal regions of Bolgheri and the Maremma showing more concentration and structure that the wines from Chianti and Brunello, which may turn out to have more elegance than power.

2012: For the second year in a row, yields were down considerably, not only by a very dry summer and an extremely cold snap in February but this time by untimely rain in May which led to uneven flowering and by consequence, uneven ripeness at harvest. Rain at the end of August did re-introduce some moistness into the vines and the wines have more structure than those of the previous vintage. Nevertheless, good wines have generally been produced in Chianti, Montelcino and Montepolciano, with the coastal vineyards faring less well.

2011: A warm dry winter and a hot dry summer brought on an early harvest, with yields down, mainly through dehydration. Except in the Maremma area, where the climate is generally hotter and dryer than in central Tuscany, there are inconsistencies with a tendency towards over ripeness and lack of structure. Producers who made intelligent adjustments to their blends came off best in combatting the heat

2010: The cooler than usual growing season allowed for even ripening, and spells of fine sunshine interspersed with showers were instrumental in balanced wines being produced all round. This is a classic, high quality vintage, from the whole of the region, with wines from Montalcino and Bolgheri being particularly fine. That doesn't mean to say that wines from the Chianti Classico and the Super Tuscans from other regions are that much behind and even the entry level wines show a good deal of finesse.

2009: Extreme heat in August and deluges of rain in September made for tricky conditions - those estates that were not effected by rain had grapes that were shriveling up and those that were too much effected by rain had problems of dilution. Nevertheless, the best producers, aided by improvements in technique, have made some excellent, well-balanced wines, particularly in the cooler areas of Chianti. In the warmer areas, particularly in the Maremma and to a lesser extent in Bolgheri, there were problems of dehydration, but there were still some excellent results from there as well as in Montalcino, with the best said to be almost on a par with the excellent wines of 2004. Expect to see some wide variations in quality this vintage.

2008: Heavy rain in the spring was followed by drought conditions which caused considerable strees among the vines. The vintage was saved by rain in September in most of the region just at the right time to produce balanced ripeness in the fruit. Sangiovese and Cabernet Sauvignon and Sangiovese did particularly well, but earlier ripening Merlot was caught by the summer drought. Wines produced have soft tannins but are sufficiently structured to give a good balance of fruit and acidity.

2007: Early budding in the spring, a dry summer and fine conditions during September and October allowed extra hanging time on the vine and as a result there is high hopes for this vintage. Those who waited longest to harvest achieved grapes of balanced ripeness which will produce wines of good acidity and that extra degree of alcohol, allowing the wines to age well. There is also quantity as well as quality this year which should make most producers very happy.

2006: Following another cold winter and a cold start, 06 proved to be an uneven growing season, characterized by spells of very hot then cool weather with a lot of rain in early August. A hot dry finish resulted in very high sugar concentrations making for difficult fermentations. However, with exceptional colour, high alcohol but also ample acidity and extract there is considerable potential, providing the requisite balance is achieved.

2005: Not remotely of the order seen in Bordeaux or Burgundy. Following a late start to the growing season (preceded by a cold winter with late snowfalls), a successful flowering and good June weather were undone by continual spells of rain from late July and throughout August. However most Sangiovese was harvested in October following improved autumn weather and there are now some attractive wines in bottle, albeit in most cases missing the concentration and structure necessary for long-term cellaring.

2004: Normal service resumed - at least in the sense that the demanding weather conditions of the previous four vintages were avoided. In fact there are all the prerequisites for a classic vintage. A long ripening season without extreme temperatures, and with measured and timely spells of rain. Certainly the best producers have realised the potential for balanced, complex, long-lived wines.

2003: In Tuscany as elsewhere, Europe's scorching summer mean't extreme heat. Yields were down due to April frost but it was all about coping with the blistering conditions. From the earliest vintage in half a century, well-established vineyards produced rich, ripe Sangiovese. Fruit from less good vineyards and other grapes, particularly Merlot is often raisined and are comparable to the poorer 2000s. So variable quality but highs as well as lows.

2002: As for most but not all of Italy this was a difficult vintage in Tuscany. However, despite being plagued by rain and cool temperatures it's a mixed picture with some pockets of quality –

especially the Maremma and southern zones. Top producers have made good wine though many of the region's top reds weren't made. Sometimes this translates to good value at lower levels as the best fruit cascades down but *caveat emptor* for, as in 92, a little good fruit can too easily be wasted if blended into vats of poor, dilute and unripe wine.

2001: Like 2000 this was another vintage affected by heat stress due to a very hot, dry summer. Quantities are down on average and quality is mostly very good with fully ripe, very concentrated reds. Late rains were, in some instances, detrimental but not for producers who had their vineyards in good shape. The best 2001 Brunello are rich and meaty.

2000: Not of the order of 99 or 97, with the characteristics typical of lack of full physiological ripeness resulting in part from a very hot August. Many Chianti Classico and Vino Nobile show an over-ripe fruit character, highish alcohol, a slight hollowness and a lack of complete ripeness in the tannins. The best however avoid these defects and have good richness and ripeness. Brunello can be impressive if lacking the vitality and richness of a top year.

1999: A very fine vintage if not quite of the standard of 1997. There is now excellent drinking in Chianti Classico Riserva or Vino Nobile but further ageing potential due to good acidities, ripe tannins and ample fruit densities. Fine Rosso di Montalcino prefigured some excellent Brunello, not as rich as 1997 but nonetheless full yet elegant and ageworthy.

1998: After 97, another highly successful but much more variable vintage. Good Vino Nobile but only from the best producers and if anything more uneven in Chianti Classico. A vintage of greater elegance than is typical with real style and complexity where there was full ripeness. 98 Brunello is generally very good; certainly much richer and more consistent than 96.

1997: An outstanding vintage, and the best of the 20th century in terms of the amount of high quality red wine produced. Though most of the best Chianti Classico normale have been consumed with gusto there remains much that should be cellared including both regular and Riserva Brunello (very rich, powerful and tannic) but also other premium examples from all over Tuscany. The top wines have excellent ageing potential - many can be drunk or kept.

1996: A good if generally overrated Tuscan vintage with some surprisingly weak, relatively forward wines in most zones. The best producers, however, did very well, the greatest consistency coming from Bolgheri. The greatest disappointments are in Brunello, where apart from Siro Pacenti and a handful of others, this is a decidedly poor vintage. The majority are fast-evolving wines that lack substance and balance and will need to be drunk now or soon.

1995: A poor growing season but saved by fine October weather. Elegant, stylish Chianti Classico and fine quality in the premium blends or Super-Tuscans. Many Chianti Classico Riserva or their equivalents are now emerging with considerable charm and style where they previously appeared a bit slight. Brunello, if occasionally too structured, has classic keeping qualities and the best will still improve.

1994: Rain-affected growing season, though picked in mostly dry conditions; the reds are generally lighter than 1993 though there is often more elegance. Never the most concentrated, most wines from Chianti Classico and the surrounding areas are already at or near their best. A reasonable vintage in Brunello, too, with more weight and richness than the 96s but a lack of complete ripeness in fruit and tannins takes the edge off some. Not one to pay over the odds for.

1993: Though poorly received, 1993 has proved to be the source of rich, gutsy if slightly rough-hewn reds. The best have good richness and are capable of further development. Some solid powerful Brunello too, a few still need more time to soften and add further complexity. 1992: The worst vintage of the last decade or so in Tuscany though some of the lesser wines were better than expected as some producers opted not to produce their Super-Tuscan blends. A vintage for drinking up, if at all.

1991: An uneven vintage with many wines characterised by a lack of balance. Only the best have aged with style, most should have been drunk up.

1990: A great year – but only in the context of the period. There are many more fine wines from 1997, the next great year, due to more widespread winemaking know-how and viticultural improvements. Nonetheless many of the celebrated properties produced marvellous wines with fabulous ripeness and balance. All the top wines may be drunk now but some bottles ought to be kept in order to see what is possible with further age.

1989: A surprisingly light and forward vintage in Tuscany (best for Brunello), not matching the high quality seen in other leading European wine regions in 89. The best provided attractive early drinking but little was worth keeping.

1988: Always a firm, relatively austere vintage and there are still a fair number of top wines that have mellowed with age, allowing an intense ripe fruit to emerge more fully with age. Some fine Super-Tuscans and Brunello, in particular, still drinking and a few might keep a little longer.

Earlier years: For earlier vintages the picture is decidedly bleak. Much of what was very good is now past its best. This is true of 1986 which with a decade's age provided some excellent Chianti Classico Riservas and Super-Tuscan blends. 1985 was a generally outstanding vintage with very ripe, flamboyant wines but only a handful of classics are likely to drink well or improve further. 1983 and 1982 were also very good vintages yet, other than the occasional Brunello, few had the stuffing or structure for two decades' ageing. Of still older vintages only 75, 71 or 70 are remotely worth taking a chance on.

Wine behind the label

Tuscany

Italy

Tuscany vintage chart

	Chianti Classico (Riserva)	Vino Nobile di Monte-pulciano	Brunello di Montalcino	Bolgheri/ Suvereto
2015	NYR	NYR	NYR	NYR
2014	NYR	NYR	NYR	NYR
2013	★★★☆ A	★★★☆ C	NYR	★★★★ A
2012	★★★★☆ A	★★★★☆ A	NYR	★★★★ A
2011	★★★★ A	★★★★ B	★★★★ A	★★★★ A
2010	★★★★☆ A	★★★★ B	★★★★☆ A	★★★★☆ A
2009	★★★★ A	★★★★ B	★★★★ A	★★★★ A
2008	★★★★ B	★★★★ B	★★★★★ A	★★★★ B
2007	★★★★☆ B	★★★★ B	★★★★☆ B	★★★★☆ B
2006	★★★★ B	★★★★ B	★★★☆ B	★★★★ A
2005	★★★ C	★★★☆ C	★★★ C	★★★☆ C
2004	★★★★☆ B	★★★★☆ C	★★★★☆ B	★★★★☆ B
2003	★★★☆ C	★★★☆ C	★★★☆ B	★★★☆ C
2002	★★ D	★☆ D	★★ D	★★ D
2001	★★★★ B	★★★☆ C	★★★★☆ B	★★★★ B
2000	★★★☆ C	★★★ C	★★★ C	★★★★ C
1999	★★★★☆ C	★★★★☆ C	★★★★☆ C	★★★★☆ C
1998	★★★ D	★★★☆ D	★★★☆ C	★★★☆ C
1997	★★★★★ C	★★★★★ C	★★★★★ C	★★★★☆ C
1996	★★★ C	★★★ D	★★ D	★★★★ C
1995	★★★★ C	★★★☆ C	★★★★ C	★★★☆ D
1994	★★★ C	★★★ D	★★★ C	★★★ C
1993	★★★☆ D	★★★ D	★★★★ D	★★★☆ D
1991	★★★ D	★★★ D	★★★☆ D	★★★ D
1990	★★★★☆ D	★★★★☆ D	★★★★☆ D	★★★★☆ D
1988	★★★★ D	★★★★ D	★★★★ D	★★★★ D

A-Z of producers

Altesino (Montalcino) *www.altesino.it*
As well as Sangiovese, Cabernet Sauvignon and Merlot also form part of the estate's 30 ha but, thoughthe resulting wines are often attactive and well made, they rarely challenge a *barrique*-aged Sangiovese, Palazzo d'Altesi, is a 100% Sangiovese wine devised when the mandatory ageing for Brunello was too long. Partially fermented by carbonic maceration, it spends a year in *barriques* and released after a further 3 months in bottle. Alte di Altesi is a blend of Sangiovese, Merlot and Cabernet in equal proportions, Of regular Brunello, they are typically full, ripe and meaty, approachable soon after release but best with 7–10 years' age. Although recent form has been uneven, in certain years, however both a powerful Riserva and Montosoli have been produced. The latter comes from a particularly favoured sub-zone in the northern part of Brunello. Made only in top years it adds both concentration, depth and finesse. Rosso IGT, an inexpensive blend of Sangiovese, Merlot and Cabernet, should not be confused with the (mostly dependable) fruit-driven Rosso di Montalcino.

Recommended Reds:
Brunello di Montalcino Montosoli ★★★★★ £F
Brunello di Montalcino Riserva ★★★★ £F
Brunello di Montalcino ★★★ £E
Palazzo d'Altesi ★★★ £E
Alte d'Altesi ★★ £E   Rosso di Montalcino ★ £C

Recommended Whites:
Vin Santo ★★ £E

Ambra (Carmignano) *www.fattoriaambra.it*
Beppe Rigoli has steadily raised quality from his small estate and provides three consistently good examples. Santa Cristina in Pili is a fine, plummy, herb10al, lightly cedary, somewhat Bordeaux-like example, usually supple and cool but properly ripe, for drinking with 5 years' age or more. More time is needed for the more oaky Riserva Elzana which has plenty of depth and complexity while the Riserva Le Vigne Alte Montalbiolo comes from one of the finest sites within the DOCG zone. Dense and compressed when young with evident oak it is nevertheless very well balanced with great dimension, class and length. It needs a minimum of 8-10 years to unfurl and show its full potential. Less consistent is another Carmignano, Montefortini. Barco Reale di Carmignano is their entry level wine just aged for around 8 months, whilst inexpensive varietal Trebbiano and Vin Ruspo (rosato) are also made. Prices are now very reasonable for the quality.

Recommended Reds:
Carmignano Riserva Le Vigne Alte Montalbiolo ★★★★☆ £E
Carmignano Riserva Elzana ★★★☆ £D
Carmignano Vigna Santa Cristina in Pilli ★★★ £C

✿ Antinori *www.antinori.it*
It's been said many times that no one has done more for Tuscan wine than Piero Antinori and this is well borne out in the radical innovation and experimentation as well as expansion he has brought about. He and his daughters continue to promote quality and to enlarge the empire which spans some 1,400 ha of vineyards. The Tuscan estates are covered below but see also PRUNOTTO (Piedmont & NW Italy), CASTELLO DELLA SALA (Central Italy) and TORMARESCA (Southern Italy). In common with many large producers, quality at the lower levels is not very exciting. Most famous are the wines of the Santa Cristina estate, Tignanello and Solaia. Tignanello, for many the original Super-Tuscan, was first made in 1971 and has been a blend of Sangiovese and Cabernet Sauvignon since 1975 (typically 80/20 but 5% of the 20 is sometimes Cabernet Franc). Not every vintage has qualified as great but it's still a very good wine. Solaia is Antinori's flagship and usually a very worthy one at that with added breadth and class; it is primarily Cabernet Sauvignon with support from Sangiovese and Cabernet Franc. As well as estates in Bolgheri (GUADO AL TASSO), Montalcino (PIAN DELLE VIGNE) and Montepulciano (LA BRACCESCA), there are also other properties scattered about Tuscany for whites and lesser reds including vineyards in the fashionable Maremma (Aldobrandesca for a varietal Aleatico). Antinori's interests also extend abroad, into Hungary, California and most recently Chile, where it is undertaking a joint venture with Haras de Pirque called Albis. Also made is Sauvignon Blanc from Marlborough in New Zealand.

Recommended Reds:
Solaia ✪✪✪✪✪ £H   Tignanello ★★★★ £G
Chianti Classico Riserva Marchese Antinori ★★ £D
Chianti Classico Riserva Badia a Passignano ★★ £C

Recommended Whites:
Vin Santo del Chianti Classico Marchese Antinori ★★ £E

Argiano (Montalcino) *www.argiano.net*
This large historic estate with 48 ha of vineyards has enjoyed a sustained revival since coming being bought by Contessa Noemi

Marone Cinzano in 1992. Improvements overseen by Giacomo Tachis (instrumental in the success of SASSICAIA) during the 1990s continue to accrue. At the beginning of 2013, the estate was sold to a group of Brazilian businessmen who we hope will continue to have the estate run in the same vein. The Brunello is structured and powerful, with considerably more depth and dimension than most. The *barrique*-aged Solengo, a blend of Cabernet Sauvignon, Syrah and Merlot (and previously Sangiovese), has been consistently rich and stylish since first created from the 1995 vintage. Vinding-Diers was also instrumental in the creation of a special *barrique*-aged cuvée of the oldest vines of Sangiovese. First produced in the 2000 vintage, Suolo is refined, intense and classy though less characterful than Solengo.

Recommended Reds:
Brunello di Montalcino ★★★★ £F
Solengo ★★★★ £F Rosso di Montalcino ★★ £C

● Avignonesi (Montepulciano) *www.avignonesi.it*

Since Virginie Saverys, of the millionaire Belgian shipping family, bought the estate in 2008, Avignonesi has been moving in a different direction. A programme of conversion to organic viticulture and the implementation of biodynamic agricultural practices has put Avignonesi on the way to obtaining organic certification. A complete rebranding has also been undertaken and new labels and logos have started to appear as from the 2010 vintage. With now 140 ha spread over four estates, Avignonesi continue to be the most important producer in Montepulciano. At one point it was as well known for production of non-indigenous varieties as for Vino Nobile but in recent years it has been experimenting with local varieties and gradually improving the quality of the Prugnolo (Sangiovese) in its vineyards. The other varieties in the classic Vino Nobile blend have also been retained. The result is a regular Vino Nobile of increasing consistency, purity and real class. Some of the austerity of past vintages has gone but there is still a structure that ensures fine drinking with five years' age or more. Riserva Grandi Annate applies only to the best years and usually adds considerable depth and dimension. Though one of the estates is planted to international varieties they are now given less prominence in the range of wines, although Grifi, a famous Sangiovese/Cabernet blend, which was discontinued after the 1996 vintage, has now been resurrected as a 60/40 blend. The '50 & 50' Merlot/Sangiovese produced jointly with CAPANNELLE continues. International and native varieties are also combined in a more everyday Avignonesi Rosso (equal parts Sangiovese, Cabernet Sauvignon and Merlot). Desiderio, previously a varietal Merlot, now includes 15% Cabernet can be rich and black-fruited with a mineral edge. Il Marzocco is a bold, powerful, toasty Chardonnay. Production of Vin Santo, one from Malvasia, Trebbiano and Grechetto grapes and Occhio di Pernice from Prugnolo (Sangiovese), is tiny (around 3,000 half-bottles of the first, 1,000 of the latter), but the richness, texture and complexity in these wines is incomparable. They ferment and age over 8 and 10 years respectively so the latest releases are from vintages more than a decade ago. Light, fresh cherryish Rosso di Montepulciano is also made. For 50 & 50 see Capannelle.

Recommended Reds:
Vin Santo Occhio di Pernice ⚫⚫⚫⚫⚫ £H
Vino Nobile di Montepulciano Riserva Grandi Annate ★★★★★ £E
Vino Nobile di Montepulciano ★★★ £D Cortona Desiderio ★★★★ £F
Avignonesi Rosso ★★ £B Rosso di Montepulciano ★★ £B
Recommended Whites:
Vin Santo ⚫⚫⚫⚫⚫ £H Cortona Chardonnay Il Marzocco ★★★ £D

Banfi (Montalcino) *www.castellobanfi.com*

No one has made an impact on Montalcino and Tuscan viticulture like Banfi. Millions of American dollars have been poured in to reshape the entire southwestern corner of the Brunello zone. There are 800 ha planted to vines and superb facilities for making great wine. However the inherent potential (or lack of it) of some of these vineyards and the varieties to which they have been planted has caused the greatest contention. What does work with increasing consistency is Sangiovese for Brunello, which despite the volumes – more than 40,000 cases of the regular example – is rich, ripe and well-balanced if missing the extra depth and breadth of the best examples. The excellent Riserva Poggio all'Oro is more complex, structured and elegant. An utterly distinctive single vineyard example, Poggio alle Mura (named for the estate's historic castle) resulted from lengthy trials with different clones and has been made only since 1997 showing a classy mineral, violet and black plum depth and great length. Rosso di Montalcino can show good Brunello-like breadth and depth in the best years, while Florus is a flavoursome, well-balanced example of Moscadello di Montalcino. Of the international wines, the premium blends are the most successful. Summus combines Sangiovese, Cabernet Sauvignon and Syrah, while Excelsus is composed of roughly equal amounts of Cabernet and Merlot. More modestly priced but succulent and fruit-driven Cum Laude, made since 99, is comprised of Sangiovese, Cabernet Sauvignon, Merlot and Syrah. As varietals, Cabernet Sauvignon Tavernelle shows good richness if not the greatest refinement, Syrah Colvecchio is typically ripe and black-fruited. Chardonnay Fontanelle can show real richness and depth but seems most successful (with better strucure) in the less good years for reds. Lesser whites and reds are well-made but only occasionally have sufficient quality to their fruit. Centine is an adequate blend of Sangiovese (60%), Cabernet Sauvignon and Merlot, Col di Sasso just Sangiovese and Cabernet.

Recommended Reds:
Brunello di Montalcino Riserva Poggio all'Oro ★★★★☆ £G
Brunello di Montalcino Poggio alle Mura ★★★★☆ £F
Brunello di Montalcino ★★★☆ £E
Rosso di Montalcino ★★☆ £C Excelsus ★★★★ £F
Summus ★★★★ £E
Sant'Antimo Cabernet Sauvignon Tavernelle ★★★ £E
Sant'Antimo Cum Laude ★★☆ £D
Sant'Antimo Syrah Colvecchio ★★ £D
Recommended Whites:
Sant'Antimo Chardonnay Fontanelle ★★ £D
Moscadello di Montalcino Florus ★★ £D

Erik Banti (Morellino di Scansano) *www.erikbanti.com*

Erik Banti, a pioneer of viticulture in the southern Maremma, makes good Morellino di Scansano from 55 ha of vineyards. Moderately long maceration, 15 days for the Riserva, and the use of Slavonian oak are favoured. Carato, previously IGT, is particularly good value and includes 15% of other varieties to complement the Sangiovese. The Riserva, a pure Sangiovese, comes from the Ciabatta vineyard and is intense and extracted, with the herb scents and fruit quality typical of the Maremma. Colle Diana is a blend of 70% Sangiovese and 30% Cabernet Sauvignon, Merlot and Syrah from outside the Morellino appellation spending 8 months in stainless steel followed by a further 10 months in *barriques*. A white, Il Vermentino is also made as are a range of food products under the Erik Banti label.

Tuscany

Recommended Reds:
Morellino di Scansano Riserva Ciabatta★★★☆ £E
Morellino di Scansano Carato★★★ £C Morellino di Scansano★★ £B

Baricci (Montalcino) www.baricci1955.com
If you have no time for the modern, fruit-accentuated, oak-accented Brunello then Baricci is for you. This is a fine example of authentic Sangiovese from Montalcino made in a traditional style – complex, savoury Brunello with real breadth and class. It is old-fashioned with a more evolved colour but there is almost always impressive depth and length. Consistently strong vintages have appeared since the mid 90s although in lighter years some fine fine wine has been made with atypical elegance for Brunello. Rosso has been tasted less often but showes good style.

Recommended Reds:
Brunello di Montalcino ★★★★ £F Rosso di Montalcino ★★ £C

Fattoria di Basciano (Chianti Rufina) www.renzomasibasciano.it
Paolo Masi (son of Renzo) made major improvements to the estate's viticulture and winemaking from the early 1990s and the quality has been evident since the late 90s. High-quality fruit and careful handling as well as long macerations and malolactic fermentation in barrique for the top wines are key components. While the major part of 30 ha is planted to Sangiovese, there is also some Cabernet Sauvignon, and Merlot and Syrah coming on stream. The regular Chianti Rufina shows ripe, lively fruit with a couple of years' age, without being overly austere, and is a good example of the zone. Chianti Rufina Riserva and two special cuvées are better still, with added richness and style; Vigna II Corto and I Pini are currently blends of Sangiovese and Cabernet (90/10 and 50/50 respectively). Perhaps reflecting the predisposition of these soils (and climate) for Sangiovese, I Pini is the least vibrant and individual of the three top wines. While not yet challenging the supremacy of SELVAPIANA or Nipozzana's best (see FRESCOBALDI), Basciano delivers both fine quality and value. A good source for Vin Santo too. Wines sold under the Renzo Masi label are made from bought-in grapes and if not generally of the same standard can provide good-value drinking, particularly the Sangiovese/Cabernet blend, Erta & China.

Fattoria di Basciano
Recommended Reds:
Chianti Rufina Riserva ★★★☆ £D
Chianti Rufina ★★☆ £B
Vigna II Corto ★★★ £C I Pini ★★★ £C
Recommended Whites:
Vin Santo ★★ £C
Renzo Masi
Recommended Reds:
Erta e China ★★ £B

Tenuta Belguardo (Morellino di Scansano) www.mazzei.it
In next to no time, having only acquired the land in 1997, the Mazzei family have turned the Belguardo estate (with 32 ha of vines) in the southern Maremma into one of the region's best. The recent acqisition of another 40 ha will result in another 30 ha of vines and the building of a new wine cellar. As well as ever better Morellino di Scansano, a premium estate wine (Tenuta Belguardo) based on Cabernet Sauvignon with 10% Cabernet Franc, has been made since the 2000 vintage. Given 18 months in French barriques, it shows the depth and intensity common to top Cabernet-based wines in the southern Maremma. In the scented and characterful Serrata di Belguardo Sangiovese is combined with 20% Alicante in a modern,

supple style. However for the most authentic expression of the Maremma stick with the Morellino. Based on the Bronzone vineyard it has classic Maremma herbs and intense cherry fruit. Additional land and been acquired and a new winery is planned for the near future.

Recommended Reds:
Tenuta di Belguardo ★★★★ £F
Morellino di Scansano Riserva Bronzone ★★★ £D
Serrata di Belguardo ★★☆ £C

Tenuta di Bibbiano (Chianti Classico) www.tenutadibibbiano.com
There is a distinctive style to these very well-made, well-balanced wines. Small wonder they're good given that the venerable Giulio Gambelli and Stefano Porcinai (ex-Consorzio Chianti Classico) are the consultants of choice. The emphasis is on Sangiovese and tradition with relatively long macerations and the use of large Slavonian oak resulting in characterful wines with slightly old fashioned plum, cherry and raisin fruit and good concentration and depth. The Riserva (100% Sangiovese) comes from a more exposed, south-facing site and spends some time in barrique. It is richer in both texture and fruit and needs 6–8 years' age. Montornello, the regular Chianti Classico, should be drunk with 3 years' age or more. Also made is Bibbiano, which includes 5% Canaiolo. Merlot, previously included in the Chianti Classico, has been taken out entirely and since 2007 an 80% Merlot, 20% Sangiovese wine, Domino has been produced.

Recommended Reds:
Chianti Classico Riserva Vigna del Capannino ★★★ £D
Chianti Classico Bibbiano ★★ £C
Chianti ClassicoMontornello ★★ £C

Biondi-Santi (Montalcino) www.biondisanti.it
This is still Montalcino's most famous estate, even if the wines are no longer the most expensive (see SOLDERA). Franco Biondi-Santi continues to make the wines from 19 ha with a traditional, non interventionist approach and without any outside assistance. The wines don't lack for power or depth or indeed complexity but can be quite forbidding when young, with a structure that makes you wonder if there's enough stuffing to match. Certainly in top vintages it would seem that there isbut patience is required. Rosso di Montalcino comes in two bottlings, a white label from young-vine fruit, and a red stripe from fruit not used for Brunello. Franco's son Jacopo has overseen the wines' distribution along with those of his own estate in the Maremma, Castello di Montepò. Schidione is Sangiovese with some Cabernet Sauvignon and Merlot, while Sassoalloro, produced in much greater quantities, is pure Sangiovese. Rich and oak-influenced, the best examples of both also have considerable structure and ageing potential. A third, Montepaone is a varietal Cabernet Sauvignon. Additional wines are being produced at Castello di Montepo but have not been tasted yet.

Tenuta Greppo
Recommended Reds:
Brunello di Montalcino Riserva ★★★★ £H
Brunello di Montalcino ★★★☆ £H
Castello di Montepò
Recommended Reds:
Schidione ★★★☆ £E Sassoalloro ★★★ £D

Boscarelli (Montepulciano) www.poderiboscarelli.com
Luca and Niccolò work with their mother and long-time consultant

Maurizio Castelli to keep this small estate (now with 18 ha of vineyards) at the top of the Montepulciano hierarchy. The wines here provide not only extra richness and depth but also better proportions and greater refinement. There is an ongoing commitment to quality, with increased planting densities and improvements to vinification. Regular Vino Nobile (aged only in large wood) and single-vineyard Nocio dei Boscarelli (previously Vigna del Nocio) from a 3.2 ha site, have the typical Sangiovese base with a little Canaiolo and Mammolo but can also include a little Cabernet Sauvignon and Merlot. In the *barrique*-aged Boscarelli dei Boscarelli Sangiovese is complemented by Cabernet Sauvignon and Merlot. There has generally been great consistency and a structured Vino Nobile Riserva with impressive breadth and length is a recent addition. Lately too, Rosso di Montepulciano has been revived to complement the existing everyday De Ferrari red (Sangiovese with 5% Canaiolo and 5% Merlot).

Recommended Reds:
Vino Nobile di Montepulciano Nocio dei Boscarelli ★★★★☆ £F
Vino Nobile di Montepulciano Riserva ★★★★ £E
Vino Nobile di Montepulciano ★★★☆ £D
Boscarelli dei Boscarelli ★★★★ £E Rosso di Montepulciano ★★ £C
De Ferrari ★☆ £B

Fattoria del Buonamico (Montecarlo) *www.buonamico.it*
Acquired by father and son, Dino and Eugenio Fontana in 2008, Buonamico continues to be one of the leaders of the relatively unsung DOC of Montecarlo, which has been growing both Tuscan and French grape varieties for several hundred years. 24 ha of the 37 ha estate are planted to vines which include Sémillon, Sauvignon Blanc, Pinot Bianco, Cabernet Sauvignon, Syrah and Merlot as well as Sangiovese, Canaiolo and Trebbiano. The Montecarlo red and white are the well-made basic wines, while Il Fortino is produced from 80-year-old Syrah vines and shows marvellous fruit intensity in a medium-bodied style that will keep for up to a decade. Cercatoja Rosso combines Sangiovese, Cabernet Sauvignon, Merlot and Syrah and is aged in small French oak; if missing some richness at first, it opens out with a little age. Vasario Bianco, based on Pinot Bianco, is *barrique*-fermented and aged. It also shows plenty of flavour intensity and has the structure to improve for at least two or three years. A little Cercatoja Rosato, based on Sangiovese, is also made.

Recommended Reds:
Il Fortino ★★★ £E Cercatoja Rosso ★★ £D
Recommended Whites:
Vasario Bianco★★ £C

Ca' Marcanda (Bolgheri) *www.terlatowines.com*
The style and shape of the wines from Angelo Gaja's lavish new Bolgheri estate are beginning to emerge. Young vines it would seem might limit the potential here for a bit but given the Gaja pedigree fabulous wines can't be too far off. This is even illustrated by Promis, the most affordable wine thus far. It is a blend of Merlot, Syrah and Sangiovese and is surprisingly complex and classy. Magari, the estate's second wine is produced from Merlot, Cabernet Sauvignon and Cabernet Franc. The top wine, labelled simply Camarcanda is made from the same grapes and shows lots of promise. From the outset we have been promised much greater quantities and more moderate prices than seen from Gaja's other operations but don't hold your breath waiting for a bargain. A new white wine, Vista Mare, a blend of Vermentino and Viognier is also made.
Recommended Reds:
Bolgheri Camarcanda ★★★★☆ £G Magari ★★★☆ £E

Promis ★★★ £D

Caiarossa *www.caiarossa.com*
Apart from owning CH. GISCOURS and CH. DE TERTRE, in Margaux, Eric Jelgersma, a Dutch entrepreneur, has ventured into Tuscany with some first rate wines. The estate goes under the name of Caiarossa, which means "red gravel" and produces four biodynamically made wines. The flagship wine is simply called "Caiarossa" the first vintage of which was produced in 2003. The wine is a blend of Merlot, Petit Verdot, Cabernet Franc, and Cabernet Sauvignon, with small quantities of Sangiovese, Alicante, Syrah, and Mourvèdre. The proportions will vary from year to year, but this wine is made from the best grapes of the year. Pergolaia, is more traditionally Tuscan, being 90% Sangiovese with the balance made up with Merlot and Cabernet Franc. Nevertheless, like the Caiarossa, it is only designated as IGT (Indicazione Geografica Tipica which denotes wine from a more specific region within Italy) but in Italy - who cares? It is very smooth and well made with soft tannins and good complexity but doesn't finish as long as one might wish. A white wine, Caiarossa Bianco, an exciting blend of Chardonnay and Viognier in equal proportions, is nicely aromatic, smooth and balanced and like the others, produced biodynamically. They also produce a dessert wine, Oro di Caiarossa, but this has not been tasted. (NB).
Recommended Reds:
Caiarossa ★★★★ £F Pergolaia ★★★☆ £E
Recommended Whites:
Caiarossa Bianca ★★★☆ £C

Camigliano (Montalcino) *www.camigliano.it*
Rapid strides have been made at this large estate and the investment is ongoing. As significant is the competence of the winemaking, now guided by Lorenzo Landi. The wines are fruit rich, expressive and well balanced. Gualto is a lush, modern, *barrique*-influenced style but shows good complexity and doesn't lack for concentration. Made as a Riserva in some vintages it is rich and chewy but would need another 5 years or more. The regular example is also very well made if more superficial but has taken a big step forward with recent vintages and is now a fine, modern yet characterful example. Rosso is fruit-driven and already approachable if better with another year or two. Poderuccio is an attractive and affordable blend of Sangiovese and Cabernet Sauvignon. Also made is Sant'Antimo Cabernet Sauvignon which is a powerful, gutsy example with the typical rich fruit of the Camigliano wines. It is also less coarse than some Sant'Antimo Cabernets. Newer vineyards are planted at higher densities and there is little doubt that the wines will continue to improve. Ratings apply to the most recent vintages. A Chianti Colli Senese made from 100% Sangiovese is produced for early drinking and entry level red Borgone (around 75% Sangiovese 25% Merlot, varying slightly from vintage to vintage) and Vermentino Gamal is also made as well as tiny quantities of a botrytis affected Moscadello, L'Aurora.
Recommended Reds:
Brunello di Montalcino Gualto ★★★★☆ £F
Brunello di Montalcino ★★★☆ £E Rosso di Montalcino ★★☆ £C
Sant'Antimo Cabernet Sauvignon ★★★☆ £D
Poderuccio ★★ £C

Camposilio
Beginning in 1994 as no more than a hobby, a fine IGT red is made here from vineyards well away from any of the classic zones, just

Tuscany

some 8 km north of the centre of Florence. The estate red has evolved into a deep, concentrated and complex *barrique*-aged blend of Sangiovese, Cabernet Sauvignon and Merlot and with the recent arrival of Lorenzo Landi as enologist, quality continues to improve. It deserves to be drunk with 6–8 years' age. I Venti di Camposilio is a second wine from 100% Sangiovese aged partly in stainless steel and partly in *barrique* and there is vibrancy and potential. Complex, spicy, grassy olive oil and fine grappa are also produced.

Recommended Reds:
Camposilio ★★★★ £E I Venti di Camposilio ★★★ £D

Canneto (Montepulciano) *www.canneto.com*
This Montepulciano estate with 20 ha of vineyards is owned by a group of Swiss investors and wine enthusiasts. It has taken on a new lease of life since 1999 – such are the rewards of working with enologist Carlo Ferrini. Regular Vino Nobile is extracted and powerful but balanced, needing 6 years' age or more. The Riserva is more complex and profound, potentially 4-star, while Rosso is intense and fruity. Vendemmia Tardiva, from Moscato and Malvasia, is no run-of-the-mill Tuscan sweet white, exuding honey, spice and preserved citrus fruits. Prices are good for the quality. Since 2007 a Supertuscan, Filippone, (50% Sangiovese, 50% Merlot) has been produced but not tasted.

Recommended Reds:
Vino Nobile di Montepulciano Riserva ★★★ £E
Vino Nobile di Montepulciano ★★★ £C
Rosso di Montepulciano ★★ £C
Recommended Whites:
Vendemmia Tardiva ★★★ £D

Capannelle (Chianti Classico) *www.capannelle.it*
This estate with 15 ha of vineyards achieved a high profile under Raffaele Rossetti during Tuscany's wine revolution. Since coming under the ownership of American James Sherwood since 1997, the wines have continued to be very good but Capannelle, one of the most prominent vini da tavola, is no longer made. The grapes now form part of a Chianti Classico Riserva thus marking a return to the once (and arguably rightly) vilified DOCG. The style has always been for very ripe fruit and lots of oak, at times to excess. However all the wines have terrific flavour complexity and style particularly when given the 8–10 years' age they deserve. The best wine is the rich, complex '50 & 50', a collaboration with AVIGNONESI, which provides the Merlot component to complement Capannelle's Sangiovese. Solare, with a significant percentage of Malvasia Nera, is a bold innovation. Chardonnay is also made.

Recommended Reds:
50 & 50 ★★★★ £E Solare ★★★☆ £F
Chianti Classico Riserva ★★★ £E

Caparsa (Chianti Classico) *www.caparsa.it*
Paolo Cianferoni describes himself as an independent organic winegrower. Working with Cristiano Castagno only 35% of production from 11.5 ha is bottled and vinification and ageing are to some extent vintage dependent. A mixture of *barriques* and tonneaux of varying ages are used and the wines are bottled unfiltered. The only wine tasted across a string of vintages is the Doccia a Matteo Chianti Classico (designated Riserva), made almost entirely from Sangiovese but with dollop of Colorino. When young the wines have remarkable colour and intense pure black fruits, herbs and spice, and are concentrated with lots of extract and

acidity. The only doubts concern the balance of the wines; some stylish wines in lighter vintages appear to be over-extracted while in more powerful vintages they seem to need another 3-5 years. Also made from 2003 was Vendemmia Tardiva, a blend of Malvasia and Trebbiano from botrytis affected grapes. Quantities are tiny as they are for the estate's extra virgin olive oil.

Recommended Reds:
Chianti Classico Riserva Doccia a Matteo ★★★ £D

❀ **Tenuta Caparzo (Montalcino)** *www.caparzo.it*
Almost half of this 180 ha estate is planted to vines, making Caparzo one of Brunello's more significant producers. Quality has been high, sometimes very high indeed, as in certain vintages of Vigna La Casa which can be remarkably concentrated, deep and powerful with very ripe, fine tannins in the best years. Wines of the mid and late-1990s (96 excepted) maintained the reputation (for which they are rated below) although there has sometimes been a question mark over their balance and stability. Since the turn od the century there have been inconsistencies but perhaps this represents a period of transition under the new ownership which has invested heavily in the winery and vineyards. Formerly vini da tavola, now Sant'Antimo DOC red and white, Ca' del Pazzo (Sangiovese/Cabernet Sauvignon) and Le Grance (mostly Chardonnay but also Sauvignon and Gewürztraminer) still show good fruit and the intelligent use of new oak. Caparzo also owns the Chianti Classico estate of Borgo Scopeto (a very large estate including 67 ha of vines) in Castelnuovo Berardenga. Improvements made are beginning to show in the wines. Borgonero is from Sangiovese, Syrah and Cabernet Sauvignon. There is also a Morellino di Scansano from a property near Istia d'Ombrone with 20 ha of vines.

Tenuta Caparzo
Recommended Reds:
Brunello di Montalcino Vigna La Casa ★★★★☆ £G
Brunello di Montalcino Riserva ★★★★ £F
Brunello di Montalcino ★★★ £E
Rosso di Montalcino Vigna La Caduta ★★★ £D
Rosso di Montalcino ★★ £C Sant'Antimo Ca' del Pazzo ★★★ £D
Rosso Caparzo Sangiovese ★★ £B
Recommended Whites:
Sant'Antimo Le Grance ★★ £C
Moscadello di Montalcino Vendemmia Tardiva ★ £E
Borgo Scopeto
Recommended Reds:
Borgonero ★★★ £E Chianti Classico Riserva Misciano ★★ £D
Chianti Classico Riserva ★★ £C Chianti Classico ★ £C
La Doga
Recommended Reds:
Morellino di Scansano ★★ £C

Capezzana (Carmignano) *www.capezzana.it*
Thanks to the direction of Count Ugo Contini Bonacossi, Capezzana has long been the foremost estate in the small Carmignano zone west of Florence. There's now a younger generation taking charge and Stefano Chioccioli has been recruited as a consultant. While there's no longer a Riserva, the Carmignano (around 20% Cabernet Sauvignon and 10% Canaiolo in addition to Sangiovese) has a refined structure, lovely depth and a touch of class missing in many other Tuscan reds. Ghiaie della Furba, originally a sort of Tuscan Bordeaux blend, now adds a little Syrah to Cabernet Sauvignon and Merlot and is a wine of persuasive style. Both benefit from 5 years' ageing. Barco Reale, a lighter style based on Sangiovese and

pioneered by Capezzana, can have delicious forward fruit but is best with just a couple of years' age. Capezzana's Vin Santo is elegant and refined with a classic, aged, gently oxidised character, though not the richness of some. Vin Ruspo is a relatively rare Rosato from this part of Italy and Chardonnay is also made. Non-wine products include impressive grappa and extra virgin olive oil. On occasion no Carmignano is made to the benefit of the Barco Reale.

Recommended Reds:
Ghiaie della Furba ★★★☆ £E
Carmignano Villa di Capezzana ★★★☆ £D
Barco Reale di Capezzana ★★☆ £C
Recommended Whites:
Carmignano Vin Santo ★★★ £E

Carobbio (Chianti Classico) *www.tenutacarobbio.com*
The first wines were produced here in 1993 and for a time fell short of their full potential if hinting at their very favourable (Panzano) origins. Just four wines are made from the 9ha of vines. The family currently employ Lorenzo Landi and Remigio Bordini, a combination that is something of a 'dream team' for serious quality estates. Chianti Classico is mostly Sangiovese with 5% from old Canaiolo, Colorino and Malvasia Nera vines. The Riserva is deeply flavoursome, characterful and chewy but balanced and long - best with 5-10 years. The two super-Tuscans are made. Leone, 100% Sangiovese, is full with lots of depth and extract but is complete and harmonious. At a similar level is the Cabernet Sauvignon, Pietraforte with great breadth, power, flavour and substance.

Recommended Reds:
Leone ★★★★ £E   Pietraforte ★★★★ £E
Chianti Classico Riserva ★★★ £D   Chianti Classico ★★ £C

Carpineto (Chianti Classico & Vino Nobile) *www.carpineto.com*
Established in 1967, Carpineto is based at Dudda in the northern part of Greve. However, while Chianti Classico production is important it is better known for two IGT reds as much of 121 ha of vineyards are located further afield, including a 73 ha estate, with winery, in the Montepulciano area. Dogajolo from Sangiovese and Cabernet Sauvignon is made in bigger quantities than Chianti Classico normale and is typically supple and scented with reasonable intensity and depth. The premium Farnito is a cedary, intensely blackcurrant Cabernet Sauvignon that is deep and chewy but cellarworthy, needing 10 years' ageing from a good vintage. Regular Chianti Classico is usually sound if unexciting but a ripe, intense Riserva gives much more, albeit in an oaky style. Vino Nobile Riserva is a significant focus of production and can be impressively long-lived, whilst their Brunello has suppleness with all the attributes of the complexity one expects from the appellation. Oak, intensity and extract also feature prominently in a series of 'Appodiati' single-vineyard wines. Poggio Sant'Enrico is 100% Sangiovese from a Vino Nobile plot while Sillano which comes from a Valdarno estate, adds 40% Cabernet Sauvignon to Sangiovese. Molin Vecchio, from another Vino Nobile vineyard, includes Syrah (20%) as well as Cabernet Sauvignon (10%). All are neither fined nor filtered and need at least 10-15 years' age. Arguably all could use a slightly lighter touch, more refined structures and greater expression, yet time may be all they need. Indeed, to assist the drinkability of the Appodiati wines, the 2004 vintage wines have only been commercially released in 2013. As the estate has grown, (in 2003 Carpineto bought a large estate in a part of the Maremma covered by the Monteregio di Massa Marittima DOC with the intention of establishing vineyards there,) so a branding selection

has grown. Dogajolo now includes a white and a rosé, whilst Farnito, still bottling the original blend, has expanded as a brand to include Chardonnay, Camponibbio (a blend of Sangiovese, Cabernet and Merlot), Vinsanto del Chianti Classico, a sparkling brut made from 100% Chardonay grapes and even an Aquavit made from Sauvignon Blanc. The Maremma wines, branded as Valcolomba, are from Vermentino in white and Merlot in red and in addition there is Spolverino, a juicy blend of at least 80% Sangiovese topped up with Canaiolo and other red grapes and Novello, Carpineto's answer to Beaujolais Nouveau, Canaiolo and Sangiovese again, vinified with 100% carbonic maceration - both IGT Toscana wines. Three fine, single vineyard olive oils are also made.

Recommended Reds:
Brunello di Montepulciano ★★★★ £F   Farnito ★★★ £E
Chianti Classico Riserva ★★★ £D   Chianti Classico ★☆ £C
Vino Nobile di Montepulciano Riserva ★★ £D
Dogajolo ★☆ £B
Recommended Whites:
Vin Santo ★★★☆ £E

Casa di Terra (Bolgheri) *www.fattoriacasaditerra.com*
The Frollani brothers produced the first wines from their family property in 2002. The land comprises two estates – Tenuta Casa di Terra is the Bolgheri property while Tenuta Ladronaia covers vineyards near Cecina. Emiliano Falsini now makes the wines – his first vintage being 2003 – and they show great promise. The style is for very ripe fruit, 3–4-week macerations and ageing in French *barriques*. The top selection is Maronea (85% Cabernet sauvignon, 15% Cabernet Franc). This is a mineral-imbued, rich, plummy and concentrated wine with balanced oak. Almost as good is Mosaico which is 50% Merlot, 35% Cabernet and 15% Petit Verdot. Moreccio is 40% Cabernet Sauvignon, 30% Merlot and 30% Syrah and it delivers lots of berryish, herbtinged fruit. Poggio Querceto is a special selection from Ladronaia (85% Syrah and 15% Cabernet Sauvignon). Also made is a fresh, tangy example of Tuscan Vermentino.

Recommended Reds:
Bolgheri Rosso Maronea ★★★★ £E   Bolgheri Rosso Mosaico ★★★ £D
Bolgheri Rosso Moreccio ★★ £B   Poggio Querciolo ★★★ £D

Casadei (Suvereto) *www.tenutacasadei.it*
There is serious intent in this promising 15ha estate. The introductory red, Armonia is based on Sangiovese with a little Syrah and Alicante. Juicy and fruit-intense it needs 3-4 years to soften up a little. Premium reds are given at least 12 months in French *barriques* (80% new). Sogno Mediterraneo is also a blend, adding the Bordeaux varieties to those used in Armonia but is much more powerful and concentrated, with a plum, smoke, spice and mineral complexity. Only very small quantities are made of single varietals Cabernet Franc, Filare 18, Syrah, Filare 22 and Petit Verdot, Filare 41. The wines can be a little tight and a touch over-extracted with high acidity but have strength, density and purity. While not wines for drinking young despite the flattering fruit qualities, all have the potential to be intense, classy reds with 7-10 years' age and will be rated after further tastings.

Recommended Reds:
Sogno Mediterraneo ★★★☆ £E   Armonia ★★☆ £C

Casaloste (Chianti Classico) *www.casaloste.it*
A small 10.5 ha organic estate in Panzano that has recently turned out a string of fine Chianti with greater depth, weight and interest

Tuscany

than many better known estates. The efforts and commitment of Giovanni Battista d'Orsi and the results of his collaboration with consultant Gabriella Tani (whose efforts have produced fine Chianti at nearby CAROBBIO as well) deserve a wider reputation. Chianti Classico normale benefits from a little age and has the potential to improve for five years or so. Two Riservas are even better but must be given at least 3–5 years' ageing. More affordable is Rosso Maniero, a supple, fruit-driven IGT Sangiovese that includes some Merlot and Canaiolo. Since 2007, the estate has produced a 90% Merlot and 10% Sangiovese blend called Inversus, which mirrors the usual percentages of grape varieties found in wines from the Chianti Classico region.

Recommended Reds:
Chianti Classico Riserva Don VincEnzo ★★★☆ £E
Chianti Classico Riserva ★★★ £D   Chianti Classico ★★★ £C
Rosso Maniero ★★ £B

☸ Casanova di Neri (Montalcino)   *www.casanovadineri.it*
Another of Brunello's new breed of stars. Giacomo Neri works with the widely consulted Carlo Ferrini to produce increasingly rich, stylish meaty Brunello even in more difficult vintages. There is some use of new wood as well as the traditional large *botti* but this only enhances the structure not the flavours. The original 27 ha were not confined to one site, which made it possible to produce both Tenuta Nuova and Riserva Cerretalto as well as a regular Brunello. The wines just get better and better. Brunello and Tenuta Nuova showcase the best of the modern style. Rosso is full and stylish, better than much commercial Brunello, and should be drunk with 3–5 years' age. Pietradomice is a deep, brash, Brunello-like Cabernet Sauvignon that wants for a little more refinement. The vineyard holdings have now expanded to 63 ha in sites around Montalcino which now enables them to produce a Brunello Selection from them, as well as an entry level blend of Vermentino and Grechetto called IB Bianco which compliments the already produced IR Rosso, made from Sangiovese and Colorino for immediate drinking.

Recommended Reds:
Brunello di Montalcino Riserva Cerretalto 🟌🟌🟌🟌🟌 £G
Brunello di Montalcino Tenuta Nuova ★★★★★ £F
Brunello di Montalcino ★★★★☆ £E   Rosso di Montalcino ★★☆ £C
Pietradomice ★★★ £E

☸ Casanova della Spinetta (Terre di Pisa)   *www.la-spinetta.com*
Giorgio Rivetti (LA SPINETTA, Piedmont) has a small 8.5 ha estate at Terricciola in the Pisa hills, not far to the north and east of CASTELLO DEL TERRICCIO. Unlike Angelo Gaja who opted for Bolgheri and Bordeaux varieties, he has chosen instead to apply his artistry to Sangiovese. There are now six reds, three of which are a blend of 95% Sangiovese and 5% Colorino - one 100% Colorino, one 100% Sangiovese and one 100% Prugnolo Gentile. The blended Sassontino and Il Nero di Casanova both come from Casanova fruit, the latter from young vines. Sezzana is said to be sourced from Casciana Terme, a neighbouring commune. The first commercial release of Sezzana was 2001 (but also made to a high standard in 2000) and it is a beautifully crafted wine with a splendid purity to its crushed cherry fruit. Sassontino 2003 and 2004 are the only vintages released so far and then withdrawn. Sezzana needs 10 years, Sassontino up to 25 years. Both Sezzana and Sassontino 2004 will be re-released in 2014, it now being company policy to release them only 10 years after the vintage, with a new label "and when people now buy and drink them, they can finally understand the potential of these Sangiovese wines, as they are still all fruit driven

and young." Il Nero is no simple quaffer but is racy, elegant and pure, comparable to fine Chianti Classico normale and should be given 3-5 years. The quality and style already augur well for the future. Chianti Riserva, made since 2007 from 100% Sangiovese, exudes round summer fruits, but with such a backbone that several years' cellaring is needed to realise the full potential of this wine. Finally, Giorgio has produced a Vermentino di Toscana from the 2009 vintage - as far away as you can get from some of the weedy examples we have tasted from other producers - this is rich, fruity, floral, full and aromatic with a long, crisp, mineral finish.

Recommended Reds:
Sezzana ★★★★☆ £F   Sassontino ★★★★☆ £F
Il Colorino di Casanova ★★★☆ £D
Il Gentile di Casanova★★★☆ £D
Il Nero di Casanova★★★ £D   Chianti Riserva★★★☆ £D
Recommended Whites:
Toscana Vermentino ★★★ £C

Casanuova delle Cerbaie   *www.casanuovadellecerbaie.com*
Under the ownership of New Yorker Roy Welland since 2008, this Montalcino estate also benefits from consultancy from Paolo Vagaggini. Vineyards are located both on the hill of Montosoli and in the south-east of the appellation at Castelnuovo dell'Abate. This favours the production of rich, lush, complex and powerful Brunello. The wines also have a lot of extract and sometimes slightly intrusive oak and as yet do not show the breadth or definition to be really fine. Nonetheless, progress is apparent and this appears to be a producer to follow for big, opulent Brunello. Give the Riserva at least 10–12 years. The spiced blackberrry and herb-scented Cerbaione from Sangiovese and Merlot is lush and intense but deserves 5-6 years.

Recommended Reds:
Brunello di Montalcino Riserva ★★★★ £F
Brunello di Montalcino ★★★ £E   Rosso di Montalcino ★★ £C
Sant'Antimo Cerbaione ★★★☆ £E

Castel Ruggero (Chianti Classico)   *www.castelruggero.it*
High-profile enologist Nicolò d'Afflitto has spent several years restructuring and replanting 12 ha of vineyard on his family's historic property. Only two wines are made and both are unequivocally modern but produced from very low yields. Chianti Classico includes 15% Merlot and 5% Cabernet Franc and is plummy and berryish – as much Bordeaux as Tuscany, yet very appealing and well-made. The estate wine is from Merlot, Cabernet Franc and Syrah and is very pure and stylish with floral, berry, plum, spice, cinnamon and toast aromas and lots of extract despite a lush, supple texture. Best only with 6–8 years' age.

Recommended Reds:
Castel Ruggero ★★★★ £E   Chianti Classico ★★ £C

Castellare di Castellina (Chianti Classico)   *www.castellare.it*
Directed by Paolo Panerai, Castellare first became well known for one of Tuscany's most innovative Super-Tuscans, I Sodi di San Niccolò, and for the elegant labels that feature a different bird with each vintage. The 33 ha of vineyards are well sited and both renewed investment and the retention of Maurizio Castelli as consultant should ensure continued success. However the wines can be a bit uneven, even if very satisfying with considerable finesse and elegance when they are on song. Regular Chianti Classico is typically bright and attractive but has been a little lean of late, despite some excellent vintages. The regular Riserva has only been

at the level of a decent normale, though a single-vineyard version, Il Poggiale, is considerably better. It is the distinctive, perfumed and complex I Sodi that still provides the greatest interest; its balance, depth and style make it a worthy flagship wine. Versions of international varieties are also made but only in very small quantities. These include Sauvignon Blanc (Spartito di Castellare), Chardonnay (Canonico di Castellare) and Cabernet Sauvignon (Coniale di Castellare) but only the latter is regularly convincing. The best wines are no longer cheap, particularly I Sodi and a more variable Merlot, Poggio ai Merli (made since 1999).

Recommended Reds:

I Sodi di San Niccolò ★★★★ £F Coniale di Castellare ★★ £E
Chianti Classico Riserva Vigna Il Poggiale ★★★ £E
Chianti Classico Riserva ★★ £D

Fattoria Castellina (Chianti) *www.fattoriacastellina.com*

Here is an interesting new source of biodynamic Tuscan wines. Located in the Chianti Montalbano zone, the estate (10 ha of vines) includes a recently revived terraced vineyard planted to Sangiovese at high densities (8,300 vines/ha) with alberello training - unusual in Tuscany. Now biodynamic under the direction of specialist agronomist Leonello Anello, there is a reflection of the health of the vineyards in the wines. Besides a juicy, supple Chianti that is best with a couple of years' age, there is the varietal Sangiovese, Terra e Cielo, a scented but dense and characterful example, a single vineyard version, Cru Albarello, Geos, a 100% Syrah produced since 2006 and a pure Merlot, Daino Bianco (in reference to the white deer once seen in the Medici hunting grounds, not some weird interpretation of the grape!). In fact this is a fine example of Tuscan Merlot, not coarse as some can be but instead plump and lush, and infused with mineral and dark raspberry fruit. Several single varietal olive oils are made but haven't been tried.

Recommended Reds:

Daino Bianco ★★★★ £F Terra e Cielo Albarello ★★★☆ £F
Terra e Cielo ★★★ £E Chianti Montalbano ★ £B

✿ Castello di Ama (Chianti Classico) *www.castellodiama.com*

During the explosion of Super-Tuscans in the 1980s, Castello di Ama instead chose to emphasise Chianti Classico, producing four single-vineyard versions that were the equal of the best vini da tavola. Winemaker Marco Pallanti, the new head of the Chianti Classico consorzio, has been involved with Ama for over 20 years and is married to director Lorenza Sebasti. He still makes two single-vineyard versions but now only in small quantities and only in the best years. Both Bellavista (which includes a percentage of Malvasia Nera) and La Casuccia (Merlot complements the Sangiovese) combine intensity with nuance and elegance but the latter is the richer of the two. Ama's original Chianti Classico is now re-classified as a Riserva, it starts out quite firm but with good intensity and depth as well as a certain class others lack. Given the vineyards' elevation (450–480m), more difficult vintages can be a little lean but the wines gain richness with age, improving for at least five years. With continuous replanting, a new Chianti Classico, Ama, is now made (since 2010) from the youngest vineyards in the Classico DOCG and has been created to avoid changing the character of the Riserva. Tuscany's first great Merlot, L'Apparita, was produced here and it continues to be one of the very best. Relatively high fermentation temperatures and a long maceration precede ageing in 100% new Allier oak. This now sizeable (90 ha) estate also provides an attractive, well-balanced Chardonnay, Al Poggio, capable of a little age, and some Pinot Nero, Il Chiuso, which, since

2009 has been blended with young vine Sangiovese in varying proportions to reflect the character of the Ama *terroir*. Also in 2009, the first vintage of Haiku, a blend of 50% Sangiovese, 25% Cabernet Franc and 25% Merlot was produced as a *vin de garde*. A tangy rosato made from 100% Sangiovese and a Vin Santo completes the range, or you may prefer Ama's very distinctive extra virgin olive oil with a lovely creamy complexity.

Recommended Reds:

Chianti Classico Vigneto Bellavista ★★★★ £E
Chianti Classico Vigneto La Casuccia ★★★★ £E
Chianti Classico Riserva ★★★☆ £C L'Apparita ★★★★ £F

Recommended Whites:

Al Poggio ★★ £C

Recommended Rosés:

Rosato ★☆ £B

Castello di Bossi (Chianti Classico) *www.castellodibossi.it*

This is a well-established and very substantial estate (650 ha) in the south of the Chianti Classico zone with 124 ha planted to vines. What's more, operations have recently expanded, taking in Montalcino (28ha of vineyard) and the southern Maremma (30 ha). Consultancy now comes from Alberto Antonini and the powerful, characterful Bossi wines are showing better balance, finer structures and greater consistency. Chianti Classico is full and meaty with a character typical of the south of the zone around Castelnuovo Berardenga. Riserva, with 15% Merlot, adds depth and concentration. Premium reds are Girolamo (40-year-old Merlot), which oozes a ripe, smoke-and-earth plumminess, and Corbaia (70/30 Sangiovese and Cabernet Sauvignon), which has similar depth and great flavour complexity. Classic and elegant they are not but neither are you short-changed – give both at least 6–8 years'. The Terre di Talamo Morellino is stylish and promising and white Vento is a ripe Vermentino. From 2006, a new blend of 50% Sangiovese, 25% Cabernet Sauvignon and 25% Merlot called In Vetro has been produced but not yet tasted. The first Brunello from Renieri were the 03s (released 08) and there is already a good Rosso and two other promising, bold and slightly coarse reds. The black-fruited 'queen' Regina is 100% Syrah, while the powerful, full flavoured 'king' Re blends Cabernet, Merlot and Petit Verdot (30/50/20); both require another 3-4 years' ageing. Ratings for Terre di Talamo and Renieri are based on initial releases only.

Castello di Bossi

Recommended Reds:

Girolamo ★★★★ £E Corbaia ★★★★ £E
Chianti Classico Riserva Berardo ★★★ £D Chianti Classico ★★ £B

Terre di Talamo

Recommended Reds:

Morellino di Scansano Tempo ★★ £C

Recommended Whites:

Vento ★ £B

Renieri:

Recommended Reds:

Re di Renieri ★★★ £D Regina di Renieri ★★★ £D
Rosso di Montalcino ★★ £C

Castello di Cacchiano (Chianti Classico) *www.castellodicacchiano.it*

These 30 ha of vineyard are some of the best in the subzone of Monti in Chianti at around 400m altitude. The owner is one of the descendants of Chianti's most famous historical figure, Barone Bettino Ricasoli (twice Italy's prime minister, first as successor to Cavour following unification) who advocated the use of Sangiovese

Italy

and Canaiolo. Although some Merlot was used here for a time, as with the adjacent ROCCA DI MONTEGROSSI of Giovanni's brother, Marco, there is now a strong belief in maintaining the typicality or tipicité of Chianti Classico. The focus of production was changed to making just a single Chianti Classico wine each year - in the best years it qualifies as Riserva and may be labelled Millennio (in reference to the estate's long history). Production prior to the mid-nineties (of normale, Riserva, and a super-Tuscan, RF) resulted in somewhat inelegant wines. The anticipated improvement, with the possible exception of the 97 Millennio, has, however, been very slow in coming. But a real sustained upswing in quality resulting from changes to viticulture can take several years to feed through and happily the most recent vintages show plenty of promise. With fine fruit, purity and intensity, these might now be wines to follow. An IGT Rosso mops up lesser quality and Vin Santo is also made.

Recommended Reds:

Chianti Classico ★★★ £C

Castello di Fonterutoli (Chianti Classico) *www.fonterutoli.com*

This historic estate, boasting an impressive new cellar from 2006, dates from 1435. One of Chianti Classico's finest, it is directed by brothers Filippo and Francesco Mazzei. For nearly two decades (from the 1995 vintage) it has taken the lead in attempting to elevate the reputation of Chianti Classico - a wellestablished Super-Tuscan, Concerto (Sangiovese/Cabernet) and Riserva Ser Lapo were sacrificised to this end. The wines from 79 ha of vines, spread across four sites, are made by Luca Biffi in collaboration with on-going consultancy from Carlo Ferrini. The same winemaking team is also employed at Tenuta BELGUARDO in the southern Maremma, and at ZISOLA, a new enterprise in south-east Sicily. (see Southern Italy). The focus here is the Castello di Fonterutoli Chianti Classico which although Sangiovese-based, includes 10-20% Cabernet Sauvignon. *Barrique*-aged, it is a rich, ripe modern example with excellent intensity and depth if at the cost of greater tipicité. A second selection (but with 90-100% Sangiovese) labelled simply Fonterutoli, is of similar quality to much good Chianti Classico. The one Super-Tuscan still made is Siepi, a wonderfully rich, enticing blend of equal parts of Sangiovese and Merlot from the Siepi vineyard. For more everyday drinking there's supple, attractive Poggio alla Badiola, now also a Sangiovese/Merlot blend (75/25). Be sure and try too Fonterutoli's superb olive oil, something likely to be found in the new Osteria di Fonterutoli - which adds to the range of eating options available to those touring the Chianti Classico vineyards.

Recommended Reds:

Chianti Classico Castello di Fonterutoli ★★★★☆ £F
Chianti Classico Fonterutoli ★★★ £C   Siepi ★★★★ £F
Poggio alla Badiola ★★ £B

Castello La Leccia (Chianti Classico) *www.castellolaleccia.com*

This 180 ha estate has only 13 ha of vines in production for Chianti Classico (out of a total of 20 ha) but a further 3 ha are coming on stream. Quality is underpinned by new clones and lower yields as well as a desire to produce a refined style of Classico. The regular version adds 10% Canaiolo to Sangiovese and is stylish and expressive but the selection Bruciagna is really something. 100% Sangiovese and *barrique*-aged, it has great class and excellent texture and is deep, powerful and long and needs another 5-6 years of cellaring. The Chianti Classico is for more immediate drinking.

Recommended Reds:

Chianti Classico Bruciagna ★★★★ £E   Chianti Classico ★★ £C

❂ Castello di Monsanto *www.castellodimonsanto.it*

Fabrizio Bianchi bought this estate in 1961 and the focus on producing a great Chianti Classico in the years that followed created an illustrious reputation. For a long time that wine, Il Poggio was made by eschewing the new oak path taken by others. This resulted in a lighter, more evolved colour that precedes a palate of good breadth and excellent flavour depth (try 90s vintages). Good as the wine could be there has recently been a switch to 50% new oak and 50% second use. Now richer and more lush, it has lost nothing of its elegance and finesse. Based on a 5.5 ha vineyard, it is also a true Chianti Classico in the sense that it is mostly Sangiovese with some Canaiolo and a little Colorino and it will evolve slowly for many years. The old ageing regime of 50% large oak and 50% used *barriques* is now employed for the normale. From the rest of the estate's 72 ha come a regular Riserva (which now sees 25% new oak and is deep and dense - keep for 10 years) and three other premium reds. Fabrizio Bianchi lends his name to both a pure Sangiovese and a recently improved Chardonnay. A Chianti from the Colli Senesi, Monrosso, is also made. Vinified in stainless steel, with around two weeks of maceration, it ages in Slavonian oak for 12 months before being commercially released. The 20-odd percent of the estate not planted to Sangiovese also provides Nemo. This Cabernet Sauvignon is sourced from Vigneto Il Mulino and gives a very distinctive cedary, but also Tuscan-scented example with intense sweet fruit within a muscular frame. But first and foremost be sure and try the Chiantis.

Recommended Reds:

Chianti Classico Riserva Il Poggio ★★★★ £F
Chianti Classico Riserva ★★★☆ £D   Chianti Classico ★★★ £D
Nemo Vigneto Il Mulino ★★★☆ £E

Recommended Whites:

Fabrizio Bianchi Chardonnay ★★☆ £C

Castello della Paneretta (Chianti Classico) *www.paneretta.it*

Located in the very west of Chianti Classico, this historic estate produces a range of wines often notable for the quality of the old-vine fruit. The vines are planted on fine galestro-alberese soils, pockets of which are found in other estates in Barberino Val d'Elsa. All the wines have good concentration and ripe, intense fruit, though can lack a little for structure, especially in weaker vintages – a problem likely to be solved by the recent recruitment of consultant Niccolò d'Aflitto. Chianti Classico Riservas include both a regular Riserva and a single vineyard wine, Torre a Destra, both which typically show plump, rich fruit. Terrine is unusual in consisting of equal parts Canaiolo and Sangiovese and shows a fine fusion of floral, black fruit and oak-given characters. Quattrocentenario by contrast is 100% Sangiovese from the estate's best old vine fruit. Vin Santo is also made.

Recommended Reds:

Quattrocentenario ★★★★ £E   Terrine ★★★ £D
Chianti Classico Riserva Torre a Destra ★★★ £E
Chianti Classico Riserva ★★ £D   Chianti Classico ★★ £C

Castello di Poppiano (Colli Fiorentini) *www.conteguicciardini.com*

This Colli Fiorentini estate has belonged to the Guicciardini from the mid-12th century and the current count Ferdinando can claim an ancestor who corresponded regularly with Machiavelli, who lived nearby. In wine terms this location is too often associated with something less impressive but the 120 ha of vines here produce some of the best wines of the Colli Fiorentini. The traditional wines include some Canaiolo and Colorino along with the Sangiovese. Il

Cortile is a fine example of Chianti from these hills. A denser Riserva must be given at least five years' age, yet misses a little of the style of the normale. Of the new-style reds, two in particular stand out. In Tricorno, Sangiovese combines with Cabernet Sauvignon and Merlot; well-oaked, concentrated and powerful, it is quite individual for this blend. Increasingly impressive Syrah, with a dash of blueberry and white pepper, includes 10% Sangiovese. In Tosco Forte the proportions are reversed. Vin Santo, produced from Malvasia, is of the old fashioned style; very biscuity and nutty yet with good concentration. Ancient as Poppiano is, it sustains new life in a 7-year-old property with 35 ha of vines in the Maremma. Adding to a regular Morellino di Scansano, the first Riserva was produced from the 2001 vintage. A small amount of Colpetroso, a blend of Cabernet (50%), Merlot (40%) and Petit Verdot (10%) is also made.

Castello di Poppiano
Recommended Reds:
Tricorno ★★★★ £E Syrah ★★★ £D Tosco Forte ★★ £C
Chianti Colli Fiorentini Riserva ★★ £C
Chianti Colli Fiorentini Il Cortile ★★ £B
Recommended Whites:
Vin Santo della Torre Grande ★★ £E Vernaccia ★ £B

Massi di Mandorlaia
Recommended Reds:
Morellino di Scansano Riserva ★★★ £C
Morellino di Scansano ★★ £B

Castello di Querceto (Chianti Classico) *www.castellodiquerceto.it*
This long-established family enterprise has 65 ha of vineyards centred on elevated plots around the castello but also includes parcels from further afield. In addition to usually good but not exceptional Chianti Classico, Riserva and single-vineyard Riserva Il Picchio (in each of which a little Canaiolo is used to complement the Sangiovese) there are four energetic and ageworthy premium bottlings produced from low yields. La Corte is 100% Sangiovese; Il Querciolaia, Sangiovese and Cabernet Sauvignon (65/35); Cignale, Cabernet with 10% Merlot; and Il Sole di Alessandro, a varietal Cabernet Sauvignon. All four show real intensity and flavour in the best vintages, if occasionally a little too much extract and oak. Vin Santo is old-fashioned, oxidative, almost dry, with a toffee and nut and dried fruits complexity. Also made are decent everyday examples of Vernaccia di San Gimignano and Querceto Chianti, the latter sourced from the Val d'Arno.

Recommended Reds:
Cignale ★★★★ £F Il Sole di Alessandro ★★★ £F
La Corte ★★★ £E Il Querciolaia ★★★ £E
Chianti Classico Riserva Il Picchio ★★★ £E
Chianti Classico Riserva ★★ £D Chianti Classico ★ £C

✿ Castello dei Rampolla *www.castellodeirampolla.it*
The Conca d'Oro south of the town of Panzano has long been considered one of Chianti Classico's finest sub-zones. Principe Alceo Di Napoli Rampolla favoured Cabernet Sauvignon over Sangiovese and more than half the current 42 ha of vineyard are planted to it. Sammarco was the wine that made the estate famous and only includes 20% Sangiovese with the Cabernet. It continues to be a firm, powerful and aristocratic red with great dimension and fine blackcurrant, herb and small-berried fruit. The estate is now run along biodynamic lines by son Luca and daughter Maurizia (with continued guidance from Giacomo Tachis), who have brought to fruition a project started by their father, La Vigna d'Alceo. Of particular interest is the high density (8–10,000 vines per hectare;

twice that of many Tuscan vineyards) and low spur-training. The wine is a blend of 85% Cabernet and 15% Petit Verdot. It has been sensational since its first vintage in 1996. Vigna d'Alceo spends less time in wood than Sammarco and has quite a contrasting texture and profile, but there is terrific purity, depth and intensity. Chianti Classico Riserva, which included a little Cabernet, has been phased out but it would be wrong to overlook the regular Chianti Classico, which usually shows how well Sangiovese does in these soils. With lots of class and intensity within a sturdy frame, it needs to be kept for at least 5 years from a good vintage.

Recommended Reds:
Vigna d'Alceo ✪✪✪✪✪ £H Sammarco ★★★★★ £G
Chianti Classico ★★★ £D

Castello Romitorio (Montalcino) *www.castelloromitorio.com*
Castello Romitorio is the property of Italian artist and sculptor Sandro Chia and his wines are labelled with representations of some of his work. Around half of the estate's 20 ha of vineyards are planted to Sangiovese from which increasingly good Brunello is produced under the guidance of consultant enologist Paolo Vagaggini. The wines are well balanced, expressive and intelligently made within the context of each vintage. A Reserva is altogether deeper and richer with some oak influence yet shows classic character and balance. Top vintages deserve 10 years' age. The regular Brunello isn't quite what it should be but Sant'Antimo Rosso (Sangiovese with 20% Cabernet Sauvignon) from the same vintage has good promise if a lightly coarse edge to the fruit. Give it at least another 5 years. Other wines include a Chianti Colli Senesi and a Morellino di Scansano coupled with a blockbuster Ghiaccio Forte, a Morellino with 15% Syrah added to the Sangiovese.

Recommended Reds:
Brunello di Montalcino Riserva ★★★★ £F
Brunello di Montalcino ★★★★ £E Rosso di Montalcino ★ £C
Ghiaccio Forte Morellino di Scansano ★★★★ £E
Sant'Antimo Rosso ★★★☆ £E

Castello del Terriccio (Terre di Pisa) *www.terriccio.it*
Castello del Terriccio lies not far to the north of Bolgheri and was one of the first of the many other fine estates that now dot the Tuscan coastline. Thanks to considerable investment and a determination to produce wines of the highest order, the estate, with 50 ha of vines, is now well known in fine wine circles. Winemaking expertise has come from Carlo Ferrini and Terriccio's fame has been spearheaded by two fine reds. Lupicaia is the high-priced flagship red (Cabernet Sauvignon (85%) with 10% Merlot and 5% Petit Verdot) and is intended to compete with Bordeaux's best. It is powerful, intense and oaky with deep lush blackcurrant and black cherry fruit but plenty of structure too, and though of high quality gives only a hint of its origins. The considerably cheaper Tassinaia, from roughly equal parts Cabernet Sauvignon, Merlot and Sangiovese, is similarly flattering, developing delicious chocolate and plum flavours with a little age. There is similar ambition to produce great whites. Early vintages showed some lovely ripe fruit but lacked structure or depth. Recently there's been a marked improvement in Con Vento which is 100% Sauvignon Blanc. Saluccio was a barrel-fermented and aged Chardonnay but it is a stainless steel-aged version, Rondinaia, that is being pursued. Since 2000 a tiny amount (just 6,000 bottles) of an exciting new blend was produced, but production of over 35,000 bottles has been achieved since 2006. Called simply Castello del Terriccio it blends Syrah (50%), Petit Verdot (25%) with Mourvèdre and Tannat. Also made is an

Tuscany

unwooded pure Sangiovese, Capannino.

Recommended Reds:
Lupicaia ★★★★☆ £G Castello del Terriccio ★★★★ £F
Tassinaia ★★★☆ £E

Recommended Whites:
Rondinaia ★★☆ £D Con Vento ★★☆ £C

Castello Vicchiomaggio (Chianti Classico) *www.vicchiomaggio.it*
John Matta's well-sited estate, topped by an impressive Renaissance
castle, has been transformed since it was bought by his family in
1966. It now runs to 33 ha and with help from Giorgio Marone,
produces three premium Sangiovese-based reds. The best of these
is the Chianti Classico Riserva La Prima which comes from the
estate's oldest vines (over 50 years) and has recently been aged in
100% new oak. The wine consistently shows good richness, depth,
a preserved black fruits character and a certain class. Older vintages
included small amounts of Canaiolo and Colorino but since the
03 vintage is straight Sangiovese. Made in greater quantities is
the Riserva Agostino Petri, which complements Sangiovese with
a small percentage of Cabernet Sauvignon and Canaiolo. It is
aged partly in *barrique* and partly in large wood and is long and
stylish but best with five years' age. The third fine Sangiovese is
Ripa delle More, previously almost pure Sangiovese but has lately
included increasing amounts of Cabernet Sauvignon and Merlot
and now shows a small berried and blackcurrant influence. Ripa
delle Mandorle is a less expensive but also less convincing red
from Sangiovese and Cabernet Sauvignon. A new attractive white
under the same label is based on unoaked Trebbiano with 20%
oak-fermented Chardonnay. The estate's more affordable Chianti
Classico, San Jacopo, shows better intensity and expression than
in the past. Also made is Semifonte di Semifonte, a premium red
from Cabernet Sauvignon, Sangiovese and Merlot grapes. A varietal
Merlot, from vines planted in 99, called FSM, after John Matta's
father, who founded the FS Matta wine importing company in
London in 1921, was first produced in 03, and now shows the
potential envisaged.

Recommended Reds:
Chianti Classico Riserva La Prima ★★★★ £E
Chianti Classico Riserva Agostino Petri ★★★ £E
Chianti Classico San Jacopo ★★ £C Ripa delle More ★★★☆ £F
Ripa delle Mandorle ★☆ £C

Recommended Whites:
Ripa delle Mandorle ★☆ £C

Castello di Volpaia (Chianti Classico) *www.volpaia.com*
While much is made of sub-zones like Panzano and Monti, there are
many other good small areas within the Chianti Classico zone, such
as the cluster of fine small estates in the hills north-east of Radda.
Giovanella Stianti and her husband Carlo Mascheroni, have long
made elegant, stylish wines. The wines are now made by Lorenzo
Regoli with consultancy from Riccardo Cotarella. This includes
Super-Tuscans Coltassala (redesignated a Chianti Classico Riserva
since the 1998 vintage), from Sangiovese and a little Mammolo, and
Balifico, which is Sangiovese complementd by Cabernet Sauvignon.
Coltassala in particular has shown the elegance, refinement and
grace that Sangiovese can attain. Occasionally the wines have
struggled for ripeness and adequate richness but recent form is very
good. Regular Chianti Classico is now labelled simply Volpaia. Some
Vin Santo and a little white are also made.

Recommended Reds:
Balifico ★★★★ £F

Chianti Classico Riserva Coltassala ★★★★ £E
Chianti Classico Riserva ★★★ £C Chianti Classico ★★ £B

Castiglion del Bosco (Montalcino) *www.castigliondelbosco.it*
This is a vast historic estate in the north-east corner of the Brunello
di Montalcino zone with 55 ha of vineyards. Under new ownership
since 2003, led by Massimo Ferragamo (of Ferragamo USA), brother
of IL BORRO's owner Ferruccio, it comes complete with its own
'village', castle ruins, hotel, restored luxury villas and Tom Weiskopf
designed championship golf course, and is being developed as
a private members club. There have been signs of improvement
before but it hasn't been consolidated on. However with a new
winery and direction there is at least the potential for a sustained
quality revival. Consultant Niccolò d'Afflitto has already stamped
his mark on the wines. That means ripe, concentrated, oak-lined
Brunello in a very modern style, particularly powerful and full in the
single vineyard Campo del Drago. Millecento, a Brunello Riserva,
is only produced in exceptional years and then only in magnums.
Rosso has lots of modern appeal too but with all wines there
doesn't seem to be sufficient quality from the fruit for the treatment
lavished on them. More time is needed to see what can be achieved
in the vineyard. Two supertuscans, Dainero, a Merlot based red
with 10% Sangiovese and Prima Pietra, (50% Merlot, 30% Cabernet
Sauvignon and 10% each of Cabernet Franc and Petit Verdot), show
promise as the vines age.

Recommended Reds:
Brunello di Montalcino Campo del Drago ★★★★ £G
Brunello di Montalcino ★★★☆ £F Rosso di Montalcino ★☆ £C

Cennatoio (Chianti Classico) *www.cennatoio.it*
Cennatoio produces fruity, round, attractive Tuscan reds of broad
appeal. They are generally sound, ripe and very drinkable but not
much more and lack real intensity, depth and definition. Chianti
Classico Oro now includes 5% Colorino while Riserva O'Leandro
includes 5% Cabernet Sauvignon yet there is little to distinguish
between them or where they come from. There are also several IGTs
with good fruit richness. Etrusco is pure Sangiovese, Mammolo is
pure Merlot and Arcibaldo (often the best of these) is Sangiovese/
Cabernet Sauvignon (50/50). Also made is Rosso Fiorentino
(Cabernet Sauvignon) and Vin Santo, including an Occhio di Pernice
version from Sangiovese and Canaiolo grapes.

Recommended Reds:
Arcibaldo ★★★ £E Etrusco ★★ £E Mammolo ★★ £E
Chianti Classico Riserva O'Leandro ★★ £D
Chianti Classico Riserva Oro ★★ £D

Cerbaiona (Montalcino)
Diego Molinara's 7 ha estate can be one of Brunello's greats. The
concentration, depth and power combined with a thrilling aromatic
and flavour complexity make it a superb cellaring investment even
at the price. However, of those vintages tasted there is marked
variation and the wines can lack for balance and cleanliness. The
rating therefore only applies to certifiable great vintages. Though
the estate now seems to be hitting its stride, other older vintages
should only be bought in any quantity (not that there's much to be
had) once tasted. A second wine labelled simply Cerbaiona adds
Cabernet Sauvignon, Merlot, Syrah and Malvasia Nera to Sangiovese,
and can also be variable.

Recommended Reds:
Brunello di Montalcino ★★★★★ £G Cerbaiona ★★★ £E

Giovanni Chiappini (Bolgheri) *www.giovannichiappini.it*
By piecing together some 20-odd hectares of land over more than
a decade, Giovanni Chiappini now has around 5 ha of vineyard from
which he produces wine with the help of the Alberto Antonini/
Attilio Pagli team. The leading wine is Guado de' Gemoli, made from
80% Cabernet Sauvignon and 20% Merlot. Successive vintages have
shown a steady rise in quality. Lienà (Leonardo in the local dialect,
named for his grandfather), which started out as a pure Merlot of
great promise, is now joined by a Liena Petit Verdot. The Merlot is a
full, powerful offering in the manner of ORNELLAIA's Masseto, a wine
of tremendous richness and sumptuous Merlot texture. A Liena
Cabernet Sauvignon and Cabernet Franc are promised to complete
this single varietal range. Felciaino is an unwooded second selection
(Sangiovese, Cabernet, Merlot) while Ferruggini (70% Sangiovese,
30% Cabernet Sauvignon) is more everyday fare, but both are
reasonably priced.
Recommended Reds:
Lienà Merlot ★★★★ £F   Guado de' Gemoli ★★★ £E
Felciaino ★★ £C

Ciacci Piccolomini d'Aragona *www.ciaccipiccolomini.com*
This substantial estate with a fine 17th-century palazzo and 35 ha
of vineyards is in the favoured south-east corner of the Brunello
zone. After making waves with the 1988 and 90 vintages it has
continued, first under Roberto Cipresso and now Paolo Vagaggini,
to make fine modern-styled Brunello and Rosso. Brunello is ripe and
full-textured, with good breadth and depth, relatively approachable
when released but generally better with 10 years' age. A ripe,
perfumed Rosso (previously labelled Vigna della Fonte) typically
has good richness and depth and with 3–5 years' age makes a
better bet than many a poor Brunello. The estate also has plantings
of French varieties. Ateo is from Sangiovese, Merlot and Cabernet
Sauvignon and is slightly anonymous and wants for a little more
depth while Fabius, which is based on Syrah is intense and very ripe,
not classic but with a wild Tuscan quality to it. In 2003, a new estate,
Santo Stefano, was acquired in the Montecucco DOC producing
a Montecucco Sangiovese (85% minimum Sangioivese in each
vintage) - a fruit-forward wine displaying spicy, cherry notes.
Recommended Reds:
Brunello di Montalcino Riserva Vigna di Pianrosso ★★★★☆ £F
Brunello di Montalcino Vigna di Pianrosso ★★★★ £E
Rosso di Montalcino ★★☆ £C   Sant'Antimo Fabius ★★★☆ £E
Sant'Antimo Ateo ★★☆ £D   Montecucco Sangiovese ★★☆ £D

Donatella Cinelli Colombini (Montalcino) *www.cinellicolombini.it*
In establishing her own winery, Donatella Cinelli Colombini has
come to symbolise the efforts the Donne del Vino movement for
the promotion of women in wine (as well as other spheres through
an annual local award), further enhancing what has already been
achieved by her mother, Francesca. Her brother Stefano now
runs the well-known family estate, Fattoria dei BARBI. Although
consultancy comes from Carlo Ferrini the style of Donatella's wines
is determined by an all-female jury and since the first vintages in the
mid-90s they have been attractive, modern and fruit-accented. The
regular Brunello is *barrique*-aged while Prime Donne is in a more
traditional style and shows greater elegance. While not of the first
order these wines show admirable consistency and drinkability with
impressive richness. A Riserva has more extract and structure and
deserves 10 years' age. A second estate under the same ownership
is Il Colle Trequanda. An expressive Orcia red from Sangiovese and
Foglia Tonda, Cenerentola is sourced from here as is now Il Drago e

le 8 Colombe which makes reference to Ferrini and the now 8 'doves'
(women) upped from seven by the arrival of the appropriately-
named Valerie Lavigne the new consultant winemaker. It is a
modern style blend of Sangiovese, Merlot and Alicante sealed with
an innovative closure. At Il Colle, a Chianti Superiore is produced as
well as the only white, San Chimento, made with Traminer grapes.
Unusually both estates offer hiking routes through the vineyards for
visitors.
Il Casato
Recommended Reds:
Brunello di Montalcino Riserva ★★★★ £F
Brunello di Montalcino Selezione Prime Donne ★★★ £F
Brunello di Montalcino ★★★ £E   Rosso di Montalcino ★★ £D
Il Colle
Recommended Reds:
Orcia Cenerentola ★★★ £D   Il Drago e le Sette Colombe ★★★ £D

Col d'Orcia (Montalcino) *www.coldorcia.it*
Col d'Orcia is one of the best known and most respected names
in Montalcino. Owner Francesco Marone Cinzano was elected
president of the Brunello consorzio in 2007. The large estate
includes 130 ha of vines but the wines are made to a high standard.
Ex-BANFI winemaker Pablo Harri now directs winemaking and
there is consultancy from Maurizio Castelli. Since 2010 the whole
estate has been certified organic, making it the largest organic
wine producer in Tuscany. The regular Brunello shows plenty of
fruit. A tendency to firm, slightly drying tannins can detract and
structure can be too dominant in the regular Riserva. The Riserva
Poggio al Vento comes from 5.5 ha of south-facing slopes and
can develop a marvellous complexity with a decade's ageing.
As well as Brunello there is a consistent and gutsy, characterful
Rosso di Montalcino, while Rosso degli Spezieri is a bright, fruity
blend of Sangiovese, Ciliegiolo and Merlot for early consumption.
Banditello is a kind of halfway house between Rosso and Brunello,
whilst Nearco Sant'Antimo is a rich blend of Merlot, Cabernet and
Syrah. New (from 2009) is a Chianti Gineprone from the Siena hills,
named after the juniper herb which abounds in the area. Olmaia
is the major concession to foreign varieties and is a very powerful,
rich, oaky Cabernet Sauvignon, although it still wants for a little
more refinement both in its structure and flavours. Moscadello di
Montalcino is very honeyed with intense, very ripe fruit yet is not in
the least heavy. Some Chardonnay (Ghiaie) and Pinot Grigio are also
made.
Recommended Reds:
Brunello di Montalcino Riserva Poggio al Vento ★★★★ £F
Brunello di Montalcino ★★★ £E   Rosso di Montalcino ★★ £C
Olmaia ★★★ £F   Rosso degli Spezieri ★ £B
Recommended Whites:
Moscadello di Montalcino Pascena ★★★ £D

Colle Santa Mustiola *wwwpoggioaichiari.it*
This small estate is in the extreme south-east of Tuscany, very
close to Umbria. The estate now produces three wines, the most
important being the 100% Sangiovese Poggio ai Chiari, which is
made from 4 of the 6 ha of densely planted vineyard (10,000 vines
per ha). Yields are low (1 kg per vine) and there is an extended
maceration, malolactic in 20 hl Slavonian oak for 3 years and no
fining or filtering. The wine is kept for a further 2 years in bottle
before release. A second wine, Vigna Flavia, Sangiovese with up to
5% Colorino, spends 2 years in Slavonian oak and one year in bottle.

Tuscany

Neither are blockbusters but are elegant, expressive, classy and pure. A little rosé, Kernos, is also made from 100% Sangiovese.

Recommended Reds:

Poggio Ai Chiari ★★★★ £E   Vigna Flavia ★★★ £D

Collelceto (Montalcino) *www.collelceto.it*

Rising Brunello star Elia Palazzesi has 7 ha of vines from which he produces classic, deep, savoury wines. Consultancy comes from the lately much respected Lorenzo Landi. Maceration times are relatively long and there is some use of *barriques* to enhance the structure, resulting in lush wines of good substance. There is decent Rosso from recent vintages too. The wines are approachable now but expect the Brunello to improve for a decade and the Riserva for longer still. A racy Sangiovese, Lo Spepo, vinified in stainless steel and marketed within the year is also produced for early drinking.

Recommended Reds:

Brunello di Montalcino Riserva Elia ★★★★ £F
Brunello di Montalcino ★★★ £E   Rosso di Montalcino ★★ £C

Collemattoni (Montalcino) *www.collemattoni.it*

These wines are showing much better form than previously. Marcello Bucci directs this small 7.5 ha estate that has been in the same family for generations. Production is characterised by relatively long maceration times and only large Slavonian oak is used for Rosso and Brunello. Brunello shows a dense, intense spicy complexity of ripe red and black fruits and herbs. Long and complete, it represents very good value for Brunello. Rosso is nicely concentrated and expressive. Again it is reasonably priced.

Recommended Reds:

Brunello di Montalcino ★★★★☆ £E   Rosso di Montalcino ★★☆ £C

Colombaio di Cencio *www.toscana4dreaming.com*

It is not every day that interesting new estates join the established order of Chianti Classico's hillsides. The focus here is on Chianti Classico (intially a Riserva, then as normale, now both are made) and a blended premium red, Il Futuro composed of Cabernet Sauvignon, Sangiovese and Merlot. Winemaking is directed by Jacopo Morganti with input from established enologist Paolo Vagaggini (FULIGNI and others). There's no mistaking the oak in Il Futuro but there's also powerful, ripe, deep, lush berry richness and a sleek texture. The length, intensity and promise is there but time is needed to see how much expression and finesse will be apparent with five years' age or more. Also made are a more everyday red, Monticello (from the same varieties as in Il Futuro) and blended white, Sassobianco.

Recommended Reds:

Il Futuro ★★★★ £E   Chianti Classico Riserva I Massi ★★★☆ £E
Chianti Classico I Massi ★★★ £D

Corzano & Paterno (Chianti) *www.corzanoepaterno.it*

For sleek, pure Tuscan reds, Corzano & Paterno is a label to seek out. From 15 ha of vineyard on the outer rim of the Classico zone, Alijoscha Goldschmidt produces a small but fine range of wines. Il Corzano, the premium red, is the finest expression and, though international in its composition and modern vinification, it is far removed from the many bland examples of this genre. A wine of splendid texture and complexity, it is a blend of mostly Sangiovese and Cabernet Sauvignon and a little Merlot. Oak is also present in stylish Chianti and Chianti Riserva but again it is set against pure fruit and good depth. The quality possible from Malvasia and Trebbiano grapes can be seen in a very fine and intense sweet white, Passito di Corzano (or in older vintages, Vin Santo). For dry white there an attractive unoaked blend of Trebbiano, Malvasia, Petit Manseng, Sémillon and sauvignon Blanc and Chardonnay, Il Corzanello. The Corzanello label has now been extended to include a red (Sangiovese, Cabernet Sauvignon and Merlot) and a rosé (100% Sangiovese) but these have not been tasted.

Recommended Reds:

Il Corzano ★★★☆ £E   Chianti Riserva Tre Borri ★★★ £D
Chianti Terre di Corzano ★★ £B

Recommended Whites:

Il Passito di Corzano ★★★☆ £E   Il Corzanello ★☆ £B

Costanti (Montalcino) *www.costanti.it*

Costanti was one of the first recorded producers of Brunello. Andrea Costanti, who has run this estate for two decades, now oversees both the high-altitude 7 ha vineyard area of Colle al Matrichese, east of Montalcino itself, and a further 4 ha in the Calbello vineyard at Montosoli, purchased in 1997. He works with Vittorio Fiore to produce elegant but long-lasting Brunello that starts out a little forbidding but shows considerable finesse and style with 10 years' age or more. There is richer fruit and less austerity than previously but similar ageing capacity in recent vintages. A Riserva is only produced in really exceptional years. Rosso di Montalcino shows both more breadth and refinement than is usual but needs at least five years' age. From the Calbello property are produced a second very good Rosso di Montalcino. Vermiglio is a partly *barrique*-aged 70% Sangiovese and 30% Cabernet and Merlot with the emphasis on the fruit character.

Recommended Reds:

Brunello di Montalcino Riserva ★★★★ £G
Brunello di Montalcino ★★★☆ £F
Rosso di Montalcino Calbello ★★☆ £E
Rosso di Montalcino ★★ £D

Tenimenti Luigi D'Alessandro *www.tenimentidalessandro.it*

The D'Alessandro family undertook the ambitious task of completely restructuring their estate situated in the relative viticultural wilderness of eastern Tuscany at Cortona. More than 50 ha were planted primarily to Syrah with some Chardonnay and Viognier - all at high densities for Tuscany (7,000 vines per hectare). Brothers Massimo and Francesco have been fastidious about producing the highest quality fruit from low yields. The estate focused on Fontarca, a rich, blended white from Chardonnay and Viognier, and Il Bosco, pure Syrah from the estates oldest vineyards, although a single vineyard Syrah, Migliara, produced from vines planted in 2000, has been added to the range and continues to improve with age. Both the Chardonnay and Viognier components of Fontarca were *barrique*-fermented and aged (the Chardonnay in new oak, the Viognier in used). The wine is ripe and aromatic, powerful and high in alcohol. It is not made for long cellaring but provides marvellous exotic, peachy fruit within a couple of years of the vintage. Since 2007, however, Fontarca is now only made with 100% Viognier and a new Viognier, Bianco del Borgo, is made purely for early drinking. Il Bosco offers similarly impressive fruit of the black plum, herb, spice and floral spectrum. It has a lovely intensity and richness but, importantly, framed within a more complete structure that suggests as much pleasure with five years' age or more. There is also made a Borgo Syrah from younger vines that is a second wine for Il Bosco. Increasingly good, it compares well with good Côtes du Rhône Syrah.

Recommended Reds:

Cortona Il Bosco ★★★★ £E   Borgo Syrah ★★☆ £C

Recommended Whites:
Fontarca ★★★ £C

Tenuta Degli Dei (Chianti Classico) *www.deglidei.it*
Originally worked as a horse breeding estate which has been owned by the fashion designer, Roberto Cavalli, since the early 1970s (it still is), it also had a small, neglected vineyard, but in the year 2000, with the active participation of his son, Tomasso and leading oenologist, Carlo Ferrini, turned to serious grape growing with a view to producing a truly "Super Tuscan" wine. Cavalli Collection and Cavalli Selection are blends of Merlot, Cabernet Franc, Cabernet Sauvignon, Petit Verdot and Alicante Bouchet which are labelled with different Roberto Cavalli designs for each vintage. The 25 hectares of vines are divided equally between their estate in Panzano and the vineyards next to Roberto Cavalli's villa just south of Florence. All the vines are south facing and provide a balance of fruit and structure from the combination of the loose, marl rich soil in Panzano and the clay based soil in the Florence vineyards. Production of the first vintage (2004) was only some 200 cases, increasing to 900 in 2005 and almost 2,000 in 2006 – the first commercially released vintage. The 2006 vintage Selection is a contrarian blend of grapes for the area (NO Sangiovese and deliberately so) and is deep and smooth with plenty of complex, concentrated fruit yet displaying a great deal of finesse. We haven't tasted the Collection blend (we are not sure whether this is a different blend or just a different labelling) but we are already impressed and feel that the wine can only improve in the future as the vines age. New from 2010 is Le Redini, a blend of 90% Merlot with 10% Alicante from young vines. By 2010, total production has risen to 22,000 bottles in all.
Recommended Reds:
Cavalli Selection ★★★★☆ £F

Dei (Montepulciano) *www.cantinedei.com*
Catherina Dei has 37 ha over which she lavishes much attention and the fruit intensity she procures is of a different order to run-of-the-mill Vino Nobile. Consultancy comes from one of Tuscany's best, Niccolò D'Afflitto, and the regular Vino Nobile has been supremely consistent since the mid-1990s. There is ripe, stylish, concentrated fruit but also an initial firmness that makes for better drinking with 3–5 years' age, when it has developed a spicy, savoury complexity. A Riserva, named for the single vineyard Bossona since 99, is aged partly in tonneaux and partly in *botti* adds more weight and structure. It should be given time, up to five years. More oak treatment (12 months in *barriques*) is given to an unusual premium blend, Sancta Catharina from a single vineyard of Sangiovese, Syrah, Cabernet Sauvignon and Petit Verdot. If more variable this has generally been a lush, ripe characterful wine since its inception in 1994. Rosso di Montepulciano is also made and is light (if with a little more richness in the best years), round and fresh if drunk with a couple of years' age. A dry white, Martiena, is made from Malvasia, Grechetto and Trebbiano for early drinking and a small amount of Vin Santo is made from the same blend of grapes (but in different proportions) but is capable of ageing up to 20 years. Prices are very reasonable by any reckoning.
Recommended Reds:
Vino Nobile di Montepulciano Riserva Bossona ★★★★ £E
Vino Nobile di Montepulciano ★★★ £C
Sancta Catharina ★★★☆ £D

Del Cerro (Montepulciano) *www.saiagricola.it*
Del Cerro is one of three leading wine estates of the Saiagricola

group but by no means least (also see CÒLPETRONE - Central Italy, and Montalcino estate, LA PODERINA). The large land holding includes 170 ha of vineyards. Despite its relatively large production, regular Vino Nobile (250,000 bottles) offers fine Vino Nobile fruit and character if sometimes slightly diminished by the defects of its vintage. Considerably superior is the Riserva with lovely depth, weight and texture. The vineyard selection, Antica Chiusina is more immediately arresting with a striking mineral, black fruits intensity and fruit-rich, concentrated palate but both wines are amongst the best in the appellation. Other wines are not of the same order. Manero, now 80% Sangiovese and 20% Merlot, although supple and expansive, can lack the balance, depth and distinction its price suggests. Btaviolo Bianco, 100% Trebbiano, is also made for early drinking as well as a Vin Santo, Sangallo, made from Trebbiano and Grechetto. Rosso di Montepulciano and Chianti Colli Senesi are usually adequate if from a decent vintage.
Recommended Reds:
Vino Nobile di Montepulciano Antica Chiusina ★★★★ £F
Vino Nobile di Montepulciano Riserva ★★★★ £E
Vino Nobile di Montepulciano ★★☆ £C   Manero ★★☆ £F

Fanti - San Filippo (Montalcino) *www.tenutafanti.it*
The Tenuta San Filippo includes 14 ha of vineyards in the south-east corner of the Montalcino zone. Owner Filippo Fanti completed three terms as president of the Brunello consorzio and, with the assistance of enologist Stefano Chioccioli, ensured that his own wines are up there amongst the best. The depth, drive and structure are most impressive. Deep colour and an oak influence are characteristic but there is also good balance and harmony between fruit and oak. There's also the promise of marvellous complexity and texture with 10 years' age or more. A Riserva from the Macchiarelle vineyard, shows even greater depth and complexity. Rosso di Montalcino is good too but in an internationally-styled Sant'Antimo Rosso (*barrique*-aged Sangiovese, Merlot, Syrah and Cabernet Sauvignon from young vines) the Sangiovese character has been somewhat snuffed out. A Sant' Antimo bianco (Vermentino, Trebbiano, Viognire and Malvasia) and Vin Santo is also made.
Recommended Reds:
Brunello di Montalcino Riserva ★★★★★ £F
Brunello di Montalcino ★★★★ £E   Rosso di Montalcino ★★ £C
Sant'Antimo Rosso ★ £B

❀ Fèlsina (Chianti Classico) *www.felsinawine.com*
Under Giuseppe Mazzocolin (whose wife's family also own Castello di Farnetella) and consultant Franco Bernabei this now substantial property (94 ha) has become one of Chianti Classico's quality heavyweights. Fèlsina always shows off the best of this southern commune, where the wines are more earthy, gutsy and fleshy (hinting at Brunello) than the more elevated, more northerly zones. The best wines, Riserva Rància, the premium oak-aged Sangiovese, Fontalloro, and increasingly the rich, dense Cabernet Sauvignon, Maestro Raro, all show greater complexity and add a touch of refinement but there are no wimps here. A Chardonnay, I Sistri, has never lacked for flavour either. Another white, Pepestrino is a basic quaffer based on Trebbiano. Regular Chianti Classico is best with at least three years' age, others with five or more. Vin Santo and a spumante made from Sangiovese, Pinot Noir and Chardonnay are also made. The best of the Castello di Farnetella wines (56ha) is the complex, stylish Poggio Granoni from Sangiovese, Cabernet Sauvignon, Merlot and Syrah. A Pinot Nero, Nero di Nubi is flavoursome but coarse while a Chianti Colli Senesi which includes

Tuscany

a little Merlot, shows good purity whilst the Riserva, in which Cabernet is added to the Merlot is a little more chunky. Sauvignon is fresh and herbal if drunk young. Also noted for its fine olive oil, Fèlsina now produces four single varietal examples in addition to a blended bottling.

Fèlsina Berardenga
Recommended Reds:
Fontalloro ★★★★☆ £F   Maestro Raro ★★★★ £F
Chianti Classico Riserva Rància ★★★☆ £E
Chianti Classico ★★☆ £C
Recommended Whites:
Chardonnay I Sistri ★★★ £C

Castello di Farnetella
Recommended Reds:
Poggio Granoni ★★★☆ £F   Chianti Colli Senesi Riserva ★★☆ £D
Chianti Colli Senesi ★★£C
Recommended Whites:
Sauvignon ★★ £C

Ambrogio e Giovanni Folonari   www.tenutefolonari.com
This is the project of the Folonari family members who were formerly part of RUFFINO. As well as taking possession of the Cabreo and Nozzole estates, the father-and-son team of Ambrogio and Giovanni Folonari have moved quickly to embellish their holdings. New Vino Nobile estate TorCalvano (Gracciano Svetoni) and Brunello producer La Fuga are complemented by an estate being developed in Bolgheri, Campo del Mare. The most outstanding of the ex-Ruffino wines is the Cabernet Sauvignon, Il Pareto, from the Nozzole estate but a Sangiovese/Cabernet Sauvignon blend (70/30), Cabreo Il Borgo, is just as well known and can show similar intensity and depth of fruit in top vintages. Both need 5 years' age but will keep for much longer. Cabreo La Pietra is a *barrique*-fermented and aged Chardonnay of long-standing and is typically rich and creamy with ripe fruit and plenty of depth and good length, but can be a little ungainly. The Spalletti estate in Chianti Rufina also forms part of the holdings.

Tenuta di Nozzole
Recommended Reds:
Il Pareto ★★★★ £F   Chianti Classico Riserva La Forra ★★ £C

Tenute del Cabreo
Recommended Reds:
Cabreo Il Borgo ★★★ £E
Recommended Whites:
Cabreo La Pietra ★★★ £D

Tenuta La Fuga
Recommended Reds:
Brunello di Montalcino ★★★ £E

Fontodi (Chianti Classico)   www.fontodi.com
Fontodi Chianti Classico is a benchmark example that most other producers, except a few makers of super-Chianti Classico, should be aiming to emulate. At its price position it is rarely (if ever) matched and shows marvellous vigour, intensity and style. Fontodi, with 70 ha of vineyards, is fortunate to have not only a great location (Panzano's Conca d'Oro) but also the dedication of Giovanni Manetti in the vineyards and long-term winemaking direction from Franco Bernabei. Chianti Classico Riserva Vigna del Sorbo includes 10% Cabernet Sauvignon and shows great refinement and style. Flaccianello della Pieve was one of the first great pure-Sangiovese Tuscan wines and still shows lovely dimension and evident class.

Syrah has also been made for several years and is beginning really to hit its stride with an intense fruit core, though it still lacks the refinement and style to compete with similarly priced examples from around the world. Pinot Nero has also improved but is less suited to the soils (and climate) than the Syrah. A white, Meriggio, is made from barrel-fermented Pinot Bianco and some Sauvignon Blanc. All the wines are certified organic. Extra virgin olive oil is first class.

Recommended Reds:
Flaccianello ★★★★☆ £F   Syrah Case Via ★★★ £E
Chianti Classico Riserva Vigna del Sorbo ★★★★ £E
Chianti Classico ★★★ £C

✿ Podere Forte (Orcia)   wwwpodereforte.it
Here on the hillsides in the Orcia Valley south-east of Montalcino, a new classic wine estate is emerging. 110 ha of farm land is being carefully restored and revitalised by its owner and includes a patchwork of both vines and olives. Initially there was only 5ha of densely planted vineyard - at 500-600m and with 7-10,000 vines per ha - in production but this has risen to 19 ha. A new vineyard on a very steep slope is at twice this density. To complement a dedicated team, expert outside help has been sought including that of one of Bordeaux's best, Stéphane Derenoncourt. The focus is on two wines, both aged in 100% new oak. Both Petrucci (100% Sangiovese) and Guardiavigna (Sangiovese, Cabernet Sauvignon, Merlot and Petit Verdot) are vibrant, ripe and well oaked but have excellent balance and dense, compact fruit that will continue to unfurl with age. Petrucci has the greater purity and originality and deserves 10 years' age while the black-fruited Guardiavigna more immediate and seductive and could be drunk sooner, or kept. Quantities of both are still small but already deservedly sought after. Petruccino is a second selection of Sangiovese, aged only in used *barriques* and equates to a fine Chianti Classico or Rosso di Montalcino. The farm also produces salami, flour, honey and olive oil - the latter in a refined grassy, peppery style.
Recommended Reds:
Orcia Petrucci ★★★★★ £F   Orcia Guardiavigna ★★★★☆ £F
Orcia Petruccino ★★★ £D

Fossacolle (Montalcino)   www.fossacolle.it
Sergio Marchetti is most definitely one of the leaders of the latest wave of new Brunello stars. He produces unashamedly modern, lush, approachable Brunello that is also solid and classy. Success is not confined to the stellar vintages either. Brunello is oaky with lots of extract but needs time. Rosso is perfumed and fruit-rich – modern, yes, but ripe and creamy. Brunello deserves 10 years and Rosso will keep too. A Rosso di Toscana, made from Cabernet Sauvignon, Petit Verdot and Merlot is also made but not tasted.
Recommended Reds:
Brunello di Montalcino ★★★★ £F   Rosso di Montalcino ★★★ £D

Frescobaldi   www.frescobaldi.it
The Frescobaldi empire is one of Tuscany's most historic and important. The 1,000 ha of vineyards spread over nine estates include some prime sites. Subject to the expertise of Lamberto Frescobaldi and Niccolò d'Afflitto many of the wines are richer and riper than they were in the 1980s and early 90s. The best wine is unquestionably the very fine Montesodi (from 20 ha of vineyards) from the Chianti Rufina estate, Nipozzano. Of long-standing reputation, it is a wine of real class with great length and structure; a wine to drink with a decade's age or more. The much bigger-volume

Nipozzano Riserva can also show a certain style and, with age, charm. Mormoreto, an intense Cabernet Sauvignon that includes some Cabernet Franc is also produced on this estate. From more elevated vineyards in the enclave of Pomino the whites in particular show recent improvement; Il Benefizio is a *barrique*-aged blend of predominantly Chardonnay. The other major outpost of quality is the Castelgiocondo estate in Montalcino. However, even if recently improved (the rating applies since 1997), earlier vintages of Brunello have been very disappointing and the Rosso di Montalcino, Campo ai Sassi, is rarely of a quality worthy of its appellation. Lamaione is a varietal Merlot of good fruit and consistency. The initially overhyped Luce that started out as a joint venture with Robert MONDAVI, also has its source in Montalcino. It is a blend of Sangiovese and Merlot in equal measure and recently impresses for extract and density but is now a little overdone and lacks the refinement that its price would suggest. Lucente, more Sangiovese than Merlot, is the second wine and has improved yet doesn't represent good value for money. Since 2003, 5 of the 77 ha on the Luce della Vite estate have been producing a DOCG Brunello. A range of modest varietals is also being produced under the Danzante label. A promising premium wine, Giramonte, 88% Merlot, 12% Sangiovese made since 1999, comes from the Castiglioni estate in the Colli Fiorentini, where another lesser blend, Tenuta Frescobaldi di Castiglioni, (50% Cabernet Sauvignon, 30% Merlot, 10% Cabernet Franc and 10% Sangiovese) is also produced. Seductive, stylish aromas precede a palate structure of slightly less sophistication but of wide appeal. Since 2006, wines have been produced from the Ammiraglia estate in the Maremma, Pietraregia Riserva (Morellino di Scansano DOCG) Ammiraglia IGT (100% Syrah), Terre More (Cabernet Maremma Toscana DOC) and Vermentino but have not been tasted. Basic Frescobaldi brands, including Rèmole Chianti, are just that: basic. New Morellino di Scansano Santa Maria is decent. Frescobaldi has also ventured into Friuli in North-East Italy, taking a controlling interest in Collio producer Attems.

Marchesi de' Frescobaldi
Recommended Reds:
Chianti Rufina Montesodi ★★★★★ £F
Chianti Rufina Riserva Nipozzano ★★☆ £C
Mormoreto ★★★ £E   Pomino ★ £C
Morellino di Scansano Santa Maria ★★☆ £C
Recommended Whites:
Pomino Il Benefizio ★★ £C

Tenuta di Castelgiocondo
Recommended Reds:
Brunello di Montalcino Riserva ★★★★ £F
Brunello di Montalcino ★★★ £E   Lamaione ★★★ £F

Tenuta di Castiglioni
Recommended Reds:
Giramonte ★★★ £F   Tenuta Frescobaldi di Castiglioni ★★ £C

Luce della Vite
Recommended Reds:
Luce ★★★ £G   Lucente ★★ £D

✿ Fuligni (Montalcino)   *www.fuligni.it*
At just 10 ha, this is one of the many small Brunello estates and one of the few that are really worth hunting down. The erudite Roberto Guerrini makes wine to contemplate and savour and while there is the classic Brunello muscle and size there is also more elegance than is typical. Quality has been consistently first-rate even in less good vintages, when many others are disappointing, the culmination of the collaboration between Guerrini and his

consultant Paolo Vagaggini. The SJ or San Jacopo, with a Merlot component, is lush with a seductive immediacy, while the Rosso shows terrific intensity and vibrancy of fruit. Brunello is reasonably priced vis-à-vis the competition.
Recommended Reds:
Brunello di Montalcino Riserva ★★★★★ £G
Brunello di Montalcino Vigneti dei Cottimelli ★★★★☆ £E
Rosso di Montalcino Ginestreto ★★★ £C   San Jacopo ★★ £C

Gagliole (Chianti Classico)   *www.gagliole.com*
Swiss banker Thomas Bär has a passionate commitment to making fine wine. Seven of 9 ha of vines on slopes in Castellina, not far from LA BRANCAIA, are currently in production. Consultancy, previously from Luca D'Attoma, has come from Stefano Ciocchioli since 03/04. Sangiovese-based Gagliole includes around 10% Cabernet Sauvignon and fermentation is in conical oak vats with a total maceration of 3–4 weeks. The result is a very complete modern, sophisticated red with a lush, creamy texture and rich blackberry fruit but it is also a wine of some style and individuality. More original and even better than Gagliole is Pecchia, from more than 30-year-old vines. Also made since 2004 is a decent Chianti Classico. New, from 2011 is a 50/50 blend of Sangiovese and Merlot, Valetta, with good balance and a degree of appealing upfront fruit, but will improve with cellaring for at least 5 years.
Recommended Reds:
Gagliole Pecchia ★★★★★ £F   Gagliole Rosso ★★★★ £E
Gagliole Valetta ★★★ £D   Chianti Classico Rubiolo ★★ £C

Tenuta di Ghizzano (Terre di Pisa)   *www.tenutadighizzano.com*
Ghizzano is the leading property in the Pisa hills, an increasingly good source of rich, ripe reds further up the coast from the famous Bolgheri zone. The large estate (350 ha) has belonged to this noble family since the 14th century and the relatively small vineyard of 16 ha is currently being expanded to 25 ha. The estate is managed by the owner's daughter, Ginevra, and two wines fashioned by enologist Carlo Ferrini have established the family's reputation as wine producers. Veneroso is primarily a blend of Sangiovese and Cabernet Sauvignon while Nambrot, originally a varietal Merlot, now includes 20% Cabernet Sauvignon and 10% Petit Verdot. Both are aged in new oak and made in a rich, lush modern style. Nambrot is a little fuller and more succulent but Veneroso has the greater class. An entry level blend of 85% Sangiovese, 15% Merlot, is produced, while a tiny quantity of Vin Santo, San Germano, is also made.
Recommended Reds:
Nambrot ★★★★ £E   Veneroso ★★★★ £E

Bibi Graetz   *www.bibigraetz.com*
Bibi Graetz has 10 ha at Fiesole just outside Florence. If this seems an unlikely place for making fine wines then try his Testamatta. Consultancy comes from the highly regarded Alberto Antonini team. The blend is very Tuscan with 70% Sangiovese balanced by mostly Colorino and Canaiolo but also a little Malvasia Nera and Moscato Nero. The fruit comes from vines that are 30–60 years old and vinification is in open fermenters. The result is an inky-black red of marvellous intensity and originality. Powerful and extracted, it should be cellared rather than used to impress your friends. It is concentrated, almost velvety yet structured and there are also miniscule amounts of new varietals from Colorino (Colore) and Canaiolo. Even more extraordinary is Bugìa, a white from Ansonica grapes grown on the Isola del Giglio (off the Maremma coast near Orbetello). All will be rated with further tastings.

Wine behind the label

Tuscany

Recommended Reds:

Testamatta ★★★★☆ £F

⊛ **Grattamacco/ Colle Massari (Bolgheri)** *www.collemassari.it*
Grattamacco was only the second estate to commercialise wine
production from the now-famous zone of Bolgheri. Piermario
Meletti Cavallari worked steadily to refine a great red wine of his
own but in 2002 leased his estate to Claudia Tipa of Colle Massari.
The red Grattamacco, a blend now dominated by Cabernet
Sauvignon with the balance from Sangiovese and Merlot comes
from 10 of the 14 ha of gently sloping vineyards on a 30 ha estate.
Over recent years the wine has become increasingly refined and
harmonious but without losing its individuality, its fine perfume of
spice, floral and herb scents and dark berried fruit. There is good
depth and a certain rigour to the structure but great length of
flavour. Older vintages (pre-1992) contain Malvasia Nera rather than
Merlot. Current vintages, following investment and input from Tipa,
are a step-up in quality. L'Albarello, produced from 2007, is a blend of
70% Cabernet Sauvignon, 25% Cabernet Franc and 5% Petit Verdot,
from a 2 ha vineyard with vines trained in such a way that each vine
is equisistant from the each other. A maximum of 1kg of grapes is
left on each vine prior to harvest and vinification takes place in open
conical vats during alcoholic fermentation before being transferred
to small *barriques* for malolactic fermentation and ageing. There is
good structure underneath plenty of racy fruit here and five years
or more ageing won't do it any harm. The perfumed white from 1
ha of Vermentino, half of it aged in oak, is now ripe, structured and
complex. Colle Massari is a 300 ha estate in the southern Maremma
with 66ha of vineyard. Both the Vermentino-based whites and
Sangiovese-based reds are sold under the Montecucco DOC. The
Irisse white adds in 15% Grechetto and half of it is aged in oak which
dominates slightly. The Rigoletto red adds 15% each of Ciliegiolo
and Montepulciano to Sangiovese and shows promise. Better is
the Montecucco Riserva coming from higher slopes and with 10%
Ciliegiolo and 10% Cabernet Sauvignon with good sweet fruit but
expect still more as the vines age. In 2011 Claudio and Maria Iris Tipa
purchased the POGGIO DI SOTTO estate in Montalcino. Wines from
all the estates are certified organic.

Grattamacco
Recommended Reds:

Bolgheri Superiore ★★★★ £F   Bolgheri Rosso ★★☆ £E
L'Albarello ★★★★ £F
Recommended Whites:

Bolgheri Bianco ★★★☆ £E

Colle Massari
Recommended Reds:

Montecucco Riserva ★★★ £D   Montecucco Rigoletto ★★☆ £C
Aleatico dell'Elba Alea Ludendo ★★☆ £C
Recommended Whites:

Montecucco Irisse ★★ £C   Montecucco Melacce ★☆ £C

Guado al Tasso (Bolgheri) *www.antinori.it*
Guado al Tasso is ANTINORI's vast estate in Bolgheri. From 300 ha
of vineyards is produced a consistently excellent estate red from
Cabernet Sauvignon and Merlot. Complex and refined, there is
the elegance and detail expected of a top class Bolgheri red. It is
typically composed of 60% Cabernet Sauvignon, 30% Merlot and
10% Syrah and aged for around 14 months in new French oak. First
made in 1990, recent vintages have been excellent. Rather than
compromise its reputation a new label, Il Bruciato was produced

- offering much of the Guado al Tasso quality but at a much more
affordable price. Of the other wines, Vermentino has good intensity
and length while the rosé is attractive and fresh if drunk within
a couple of years of the vintage. New (2011) are a 100% Merlot,
Cont'Ugo and Gherado, a rosato blend of Merlot and Cabernet
Franc with a little Syrah.
Recommended Reds:

Bolgheri Superiore Guado al Tasso ★★★★☆ £G
Bolgheri Superiore Il Bruciato ★★★☆ £E
Recommended Whites:

Bolgheri Vermentino Camillo ★★ £D
Recommended Rosés:

Bolgheri Rosato Scalabrone ★ £B

Gualdo del Re (Val di Cornia) *www.gualdodelre.it*
Under Barbara Tamburini's consultancy both the composition and
the quality of several wines here have had a serious makeover.
Generally there is successively better depth, concentration and
intensity in the three premium reds. I Rennero is now pure Merlot
but included Pinot Nero in the first vintages. It is more varietal,
with a mineral streak to its deep, ripe, black fruit character. Federico
Primo is 100% Cabernet Sauvignon, while Gualdo del Re is from
Sangiovese. Of the whites, Strale, 100% *barrique*-femented and
aged Pinot Bianco, used to be known as Lumen but is a good
spicy, creamy, Tuscan example of the variety. Vermentino is very
attractive if drunk very young, while basic Eliseo red and white have
good character if only moderate structure and substance. A sweet
Aleatico, Amansio, Cabraia, a blend of Cabernet Saubvignon and
Cabernet Franc and a Pinot Noir, Senzansia, are also made.
Recommended Reds:

Val di Cornia Suvereto Federico Primo ★★★★ £E
Val di Cornia Suvereto Gualdo del Re ★★★☆ £E
Val di Cornia Suvereto I Rennero ★★★☆ £E
Val di Cornia Rosso Eliseo ★☆ £B
Recommended Whites:

Strale ★★ £C   Val di Cornia Vermentino Valentina ★★ £B
Val di Cornia Bianco Eliseo ★☆ £B

Guicciardini Strozzi (San Gimignano) *www.guicciardinistrozzi.it*
This historic estate (recorded as early as AD994) is one of the
exceptions in a sometimes very disappointing appellation (for
red as well as white). While Vernaccia can be slightly coarse it has
good flavour (from skin contact) and more weight in the Riserva
version. The reds are soundly made with some style. Sòdole is from
Sangiovese and Millanni from Sangiovese, Cabernet Sauvignon
and Merlot. Both are typically ripe and oaky with intense fruit, and
usually best 5–6 years after the vintage. Further vineyards have been
acquired
Recommended Reds:

Millanni ★★★ £E   Sòdole ★★★ £D
Chianti Colli Senesi Titolato Strozzi ★ £B
Recommended Whites:

Vernaccia di San Gimignano Riserva ★★ £C
Vernaccia di San Gimignano Titolo Strozzi ★ £B
Vernaccia di San Gimignano Villa Cusona ★ £B

I Balzini *www.ibalzini.it*
Located in Barberino Val d'Elsa but outside the confines of Chianti
Classico, this small 5.4ha estate is planted on sloping terraces (i
balzini) to Sangiovese, Cabernet Sauvignon and Merlot. Since
1998 production has been divided between a White Label (50/50

Cabernet/Sangiovese) and Black Label which complements the Cabernet with 25% Sangiovese and 25% Merlot. White Label spends 12-14 months in oak and is characterful with ripe fruit, sometimes with a dash of pepper, leather or earth with a lightly tannic finish. Black label, with an extended maceration and up to 18 months in oak, is a bigger, more concentrated wine with preserved blackberry, heather, smoke and black plum as well as raisin and prune in hotter years. Recent vintages are particularly impressive, dense, lush example but exotic rather than refined. Older vintages tend to be slightly more rustic but show impressive complexity with 8-10 years' age. Both are sold as Colli della Toscana Centrale IGT. Green Label, (80% Sangiovese, 20% Mammolo), Red Label, (Merlot, Cabernet Sauvignon and Sangiovese) and Rosato Pink Label (Sangiovese and Merlot) are unoaked wines made for early drinking.

Recommended Reds:
I Balzini Black Label ★★★★ £E I Balzini White Label ★★★ £E

I Giusti & Zanza (Terre di Pisa) *www.igiustiezanza.it*
Nestled in Pisa's hills not far from the coast and Livorno, this estate comprises 15 ha of densely planted vineyards redeveloped since 1995. The owners have worked with consultant Stefano Chioccioli and have made steady progress. Dulcamara is Cabernet Sauvignon complemented by Merlot but in Belcore it is Sangiovese that forms the major part of the blend. Both can be a little aggressive in their youth (with sometimes a touch of greenness in Belcore) but these are powerful and concentrated wines with sweet, intense fruit, and added depth and extract in Dulcamara. Patience is the key: give Belcore 6 years, Dulcamara 8–10 years from the vintage. New from 2003 was a pure Syrah, Perbruno, from a vineyard planted in 1999. Its berry, plum, licorice and herb scents and intense ripe fruit are checked by relatively modest depth but the indications are that this will be very good with more vine age. Nemorino Rosso (Syrah, Sangiovese, Merlot) and a zesty Bianco (Trebbiano, Sémillon) are more for everyday drinking but offer good fruit, with plenty of substance in the red.

Recommended Reds:
Dulcamara ★★★★ £F Perbruno ★★★☆ £E
Belcore ★★★ £C Nemorino Rosso ★★ £B

Recommended Whites:
Nemorino Bianco ★★ £B

Tenuta Il Borro (Colli Aretini) *www.ilborro.it*
With money and expertise you can make a very good red almost anywhere in Tuscany it seems. East of the Chianti Classico zone in the Val d'Arno, the Ferragamo family (of fashion house fame) have transformed an entire borgo with their Euros. The 700 ha of surrounding land includes 40 ha of vines from which they have produced an estate red under the auspices of renowned consultant Niccolò d'Afflitto. The blend of mostly Merlot and Cabernet Sauvignon with a little Syrah and Petit Verdot is very much in the modern, very concentrated, black-fruited mould but it also shows impressive depth, length and considerable ageing potential. Il Borro is now complemented by Pian di Nova (mostly Syrah with some Sangiovese) and Polissena (100% Sangiovese) which offer impressive fruit and structure at more affordable prices.

Recommended Reds:
Il Borro ★★★★ £F Polissena ★★★ £E Pian di Nova ★★★ £C

Il Molino di Grace (Chianti Classico) *www.ilmolinodigrace.it*
American entrepreneur Frank Grace bought vineyards in Panzano in the late 90s and currently has 33 ha in production. He is committed to Chianti Classico based almost entirely on Sangiovese. Together with manager Gerhard Hirmer and enologist Franco Bernabei, he has already produced some excellent wines. Perfumed, stylish Chianti Classico and a denser, more structured Riserva are 90% Sangiovese with the balance from Cabernet Sauvignon, Merlot and Canaiolo. Both large and small oak are employed, both new and used. Better still are concentrated, powerful Riserva Il Margone, with lots of extract and requiring 8–10 year's ageing, and a small-volume, *barrique*-aged flagship wine, Gratius, which is 100% Sangiovese from near 60-year-old vines. The latter is concentrated, classy and seductive, and similarly deserves to be drunk with a decade's age. For everyday drinking there's Il Volano.

Recommended Reds:
Gratius ★★★★ £E Il Volano ★ £B
Chianti Classico Riserva Il Margone ★★★☆ £E
Chianti Classico Riserva ★★★ £D Chianti Classico ★★ £C

Il Palazzino (Chianti Classico) *www.podereilpalazzino.it*
Relatively few estates are as committed to the pursuit of a classic expression of Chianti Classico as Il Palazzino. Alessandro Sderci distinguishes between four different sites and achieves a quite different expression and level of quality from each. While technical assistance is sought, he is determined to avoid any style imposition from an outside consultant. The Sderci's finest plot of vines is Grosso Sanese, planted 35 years ago. 100% Sangiovese and sold as a vino da tavola from 1981 till 1993, it is now among the top flight of Chianti Classico. A small part of Grosso Sanese may be set aside as Riserva and given slightly longer ageing in *barriques*. These are 10-year wines. La Pieve comes from four parcels around a church, is *barrique*-aged (a third new) and has impressive depth, although also some of the austerity of the other wines if drunk too young. More fruit-driven but with less structure is Argenina, while La Cascina Girasole (sold as an IGT) is simpler and reflects its cooler origins. New is Bertinga, a single vineyard blend of Cabernet Sauvignon and Petit Verdot and and Stagi, 100% Colorino. We have not tasted these wines, but it looks as if both will require long cellaring before being ready to drink.

Recommended Reds:
Chianti Classico Riserva Grosso Sanese ★★★★ £E
Chianti Classico Grosso Sanese ★★★★ £D
Chianti Classico La Pieve ★★★ £D
Chianti Classico Argenina ★★ £C La Cascina Girasole ★ £B

Il Palazzone (Montalcino) *www.ilpalazzone.com*
American owner Dick Parsons has wasted no time producing a deep, powerful, modern-styled Brunello. Only half of the 8 ha of the high-altitude estate (480m) qualifies for Brunello production. In the hands of Paolo Vagagghini these grapes have been forged into a lush, intense, oak-influenced wine. But as with the best of modern examples, it also reveals plenty of rich, savoury, herb-andspice Brunello character. More oaky is the Riserva which has marvellously concentrated fruit to suggest a great wine with 15 years' age. Some wine, chosen not to be included in the Brunello is set aside for production of VDT Rosso di Palazzone from Sangiovese Grosso grown on the estate, which is bottled from time to time with wine from more than one vintage. Whilst bottlings do vary, they represent a good price/quality ratio. A supertuscan, Lorenzo and Isabelle made from Cabernet Franc (60%) Petit Verdot (2%) and the balance Sangiovese, was first produced in 2005 but this has not been tasted.

Tuscany

Recommended Reds:
Brunello di Montalcino Riserva ★★★★★ £G
Brunello di Montalcino ★★★★ £F Rosso di Palazzione ★★ £C

🌟 **Il Poggione (Montalcino)** *www.tenutailpoggione.it*
Il Poggione has made some excellent Brunello for 40-odd years,
in fact during all the time that Pierluigi Talenti (see TALENTI) was
winemaker here – from 1958 until his death in 1999. The large
estate with just over 100ha of vines is now under the direction of
Pierluigi's protégé – Fabrizio Bindocci. The wines have been slightly
old-fashioned: full and structured, always with a fair amount of
tannin but balanced and capable of long ageing, although already
exhibiting a deep, savoury complexity and richness soon after their
release; in fact everything that lighter, more superficial examples
lack. The balance can be more marginal in a lighter vintage but not
in recent years There is even more power, structure and breadth
in the long-lived Riserva. The Rosso, too, rarely lacks for depth or
intensity but shows more obvious plummy black fruits and plenty
of grip. Future vintages look likely to maintain the fine tradition if
perhaps tending to a more overt fruit richness that can also be seen
in San Leopoldo, a Sangiovese/Cabernet Sauvignon/Cabernet Franc
blend. The wines are very reasonably priced for the quality and
there's fine, spicy, grassy good olive oil too.

Recommended Reds:
Brunello di Montalcino Riserva ★★★★★ £F
Brunello di Montalcino ★★★★ £F Rosso di Montalcino ★★ £C
San Leopoldo ★★★ £E

Innocenti (Montepulciano) *www.cantineinnocenti.it*
These excellent authentic examples of Vino Nobile are not as
widely appreciated as they ought to be. Vittorio Innocenti, once
a philosophy teacher, together with his wife Maria Rosa and sons
Tommaso and Mario, makes wines from 12 ha in the less fashionable
north of the zone, between Montepulciano and Montefollonico.
The latter being the small medieval village where the cellars are. A
high percentage of Sangiovese is favoured (with a little Canaiolo)
and the wines are somewhat traditional in style but with impressive
expression and complexity. With intense flavour and slightly chewy
extract they are to an extent the antithesis of the lush, forward
modern style. Occasionally there is a hint of rusticity such as a touch
of reduction or brett but are otherwise sound and well-composed.
Riservas have more concentration, dimension and extract and if
approachable after 5 years deserve to be laid down for 10 years.
Rosso di Montepulciano, although perfumed is no simple quaffer
with depth and structure making it more comparable to a good
Rosso di Montalcino. As well as Chianti Colli Senesi, there are also
occasional quantities of a premium varietal Sangiovese, Acerone
sold as an IGT. Rarely produced is an example of Vin Santo, Occhio
di Pernice.

Recommended Reds:
Vino Nobile di Montepulciano Riserva ★★★☆ £E
Vino Nobile di Montepulciano ★★★ £D
Rosso di Montepulciano ★★☆ £B

🌟 **Isole e Olena (Chianti Classico)**
Paolo De Marchi is perhaps Tuscany's finest ambassador, effortlessly
combining dynamism and humility in a tireless pursuit of quality.
A vignaiolo first and winemaker second, over three decades he
has poured a massive amount of energy (and intelligence) into
reshaping an estate (now with 48 ha of vineyards) bought by his
family in the 1960s. The wines have been very good for a long time

but only now that he has developed his own clones of Sangiovese
and reclaimed the most taxing vineyards are the best fruits of
his labours being transformed into ever better wines. From the
great Cepparello (from Sangiovese) through powerful, long-lived
Cabernet Sauvignon and stylish Syrah to vibrant Chianti Classico
the wines are intense, complete and expressive with both depth
and elegance. A vertical tasting of any of the wines will show how
they also manage to reflect something of the vintage character yet
without the defects. Whites as well as reds are made and, though
the Chardonnay has had its ups and downs, it is usually one of
Tuscany's best examples, while the Vin Santo is consistently brilliant.
Paolo is now also making wines from his native region, Piedmont at
Proprietà SPERINO.

Recommended Reds:
Cepparello ★★★★★ £F
Cabernet Sauvignon Collezione De Marchi ★★★★ £F
Syrah Collezione De Marchi ★★★★ £F Chianti Classico ★★ £C
Recommended Whites:
Vin Santo ★★★★ £F Chardonnay Collezione De Marchi ★★★★ £E

La Braccesca (Montepulciano) *www.antinori.it*
ANTINORI's property in Montepulciano, has long been the source
of a good dependable Vino Nobile. Its wide distribution ensures
that drinkers get a decent bottle of wine from sometimes otherwise
dodgy restaurant wine lists. Since 2001 there has been more in the
shape of Santa Pia which adds flair and better depth. Wines from
Antinori's extensive Cortona vineyards (giving a total of 265 ha)
are also made here including a modern styled, if slightly inelegant,
Bramasole from Syrah (made since 2000) with good depth of
peppery black fruits.

Recommended Reds:
Cortona Syrah Bramasole ★★★★ £E
Vino Nobile di Montepulciano Santa Pia ★★★ £E
Vino Nobile di Montepulciano ★★ £D
Rosso di Montepulciano Sabazio ★ £B

La Brancaia (Chianti Classico) *www.brancaia.com*
Up until 1997 the La Brancaia wines were made at FONTERUTOLI.
Since 1999 the estate has been under the direction of Barbara
Widmer, daughter of the Swiss owners, who works with her
husband, Martin Kronenberg. The 65 ha comprise three estates, 9
ha Brancaia (in Castellina) and 10 ha Poppi (in Radda) and 'Brancaia
in Maremma' extending to 45 ha of vineyards. The first releases
of Ilatraia ffrom Maremma have been exceptionally good; 40%
Cabernet Sauvignon, 40% Petit Verdot and 20% Cabernet Franc is
the current blend, although Sangiovese has been used in the past.
The Chianti Classico Riserva is produced from the best Sangiovese
on the estate, with a touch of Merlot, while Brancaia II Blu (with a
blue label) is 50% Sangiovese with 45% Merlot and 5% Cabernet.
All wines see some new wood and this is evident in the finished
wines but they also show ripe stylish fruit and good depth. A third
wine, Tre, 80% Sangiovese with 20% of Cabernet and Merlot is made
from fruit taken from all three estates and usually shows good fruit
in a supple style. While quality has increased, so have the prices.
Since 2009, the estate has produced an unoaked fresh and fruity
white 'Il Bianco' made from mainly Sauvignon Blanc with some
Gewürztraminer, Sémillon and Viognier.

La Brancaia
Recommended Reds:
Brancaia II Blu ★★★★ £F Chianti Classico Riserva ★★★ £E
Tre ★★☆ £C

Recommended Whites:
Brancaia Il Bianco ★★ £C
Brancaia in Maremma
Recommended Reds:
Ilatraia ★★★★ £F

La Fiorita (Montalcino) *www.fattorialafiorita.it*

This is the estate of renowned enologist Roberto Cipresso. 7 ha are split between two sites: the first, with established vines, is at 200m altitude in the very south of the zone, while the second, a more recently planted vineyard at 350m. It is a very modern-style Brunello – open, deeply perfumed and appealing yet with good fruit depth and intensity too – for drinking quite young or with 10 years' age. The wine is now being released later than most other Brunello so that it is closer to its full potential when becoming available to drink. The treatment of the Riserva (not made in every vintage) doesn't differ from that of the regular wine but is released much later. The current release in 2014 is the 2006.

Recommended Reds:
Brunello di Montalcino Riserva ★★★★☆ £G
Brunello di Montalcino ★★★★ £F

La Gerla (Montalcino) *www.lagerlamontalcino.com*

What has happened here? Perfectly good, well-made but not exceptional Brunello has suddenly taken on an extra dimension. The same team of enologist Vittorio Fiore and agronomist Alberto Passeri has been in place for a number of years but from the 01 vintage are altogether better than earlier efforts. 11.5 ha of vineyard are split between those just north of Montalcino itself (6 ha, including the 1ha Gli Angeli vineyard) and the balance around Castelnuovo dell'Abate in the south. Certainly yields have been recently lowered but equally the promise of an excellent vintage has been fully realised. Brunello is in a lush, modern, forward style but now with extra intensity and style. Gli Angeli, sometimes made as a Riserva but not in 2001, is a fabulous effort in this vintage with marvellous depth, complexity and class. Seductive with super fine tannins it has wonderful appeal as a medium-term example but should age well too. A stylish and exuberant Rosso is also made, as is Birba, a *barrique*-aged Sangiovese and extra virgin olive oil.

Recommended Reds:
Brunello di Montalcino Vigna Gli Angeli ★★★★★ £F
Brunello di Montalcino ★★★★ £E   Rosso di Montalcino ★★★ £C

❀ La Massa (Chianti Classico) *www.lamassa.com*

Giampaolo Motta is now working with Stéphane Derenencourt to produce two very good modern wines in the Classico zone from 25 ha of vines., although due to blending of other varietals, can only be marketed as IGT Toscana. The experienced Motta now has over a decade of vintages behind him from these prime vineyards in the much vaunted Panzano sub-zone. Both wines are aged in *barriques* and are always full of ripe, intense fruit. La Massa is predominantly Sangiovese-based (usually around 60% with the addition of Cabernet Sauvignon and Merlot) and delivers consistently high quality and is best with 5 years' age or more, Giorgio Primo is now effectively a Bordeaux blend (around 60% Merlot, 35% Cabernet Sauvignon and 5% Petit Verdot aged for 18 months in French oak *barriques*, although proportions vary from year to year) and is built for long ageing with the potential of reaching as high a plane as any in the world for this blend.

Recommended Reds:
Giorgio Primo ★★★★★ £G   La Massa ★★★☆ £E

❀ La Pieve (Chianti) *www.lapieve.net*

Montaione is something of a backwater for quality Chianti production, lying to the west of Chianti Classico, but it has a remarkable young star in Simone Tognetti. A dedicated approach to both viticulture and vinification as well as the small size of the estate (15 ha of vines) ensures high quality is maintained even in difficult vintages. The regular Chianti includes up to 15% Canaiolo and has excellent fruit. Fortebraccio, made from 100% Sangiovese and effectively a Riserva, has lovely style and purity with balanced oak while Rosso del Pievano (equal parts Cabernet Sauvignon and Sangiovese) sees some new oak and is lush, deep and very long. Not only are the wines very good but they are very reasonably priced. A little white is also made, as well as a100% Syrah, Il Gobbo Nero.

Recommended Reds:
Rosso del Pievano ★★★★ £D   Chianti Fortebraccio ★★★☆ £C
Chianti La Pieve ★★★ £B

La Poderina (Montalcino) *www.saiagricola.it*

Saiagricola is the agricultural arm of investment banking group Fondiaria Sai and counts La Poderina, DEL CERRO (Vino Nobile) and CÒLPETRONE (Montefalco Sagrantino) as its blue-chip properties. The Brunello comes from around 20 ha in the south of the Montalcino zone and the production team is led by consultant Lorenzo Landi. It can be a striking wine with a singular spiced herb and black fruit complexity and a dense, well-defined texture. Both this and small-production Poggio Abate are *barrique*-aged. Rosso is more variable but a fine, unusually elegant Moscadello di Montalcino is also made, as is an entry level red, Virgulto, made from 100% Sangiovese grapes for early drinking.

Recommended Reds:
Brunello di Montalcino Poggio Abate ★★★★ £G
Brunello di Montalcino ★★★★ £F   Rosso di Montalcino ★ £C
Recommended Whites:
Moscadello di Montalcino Vendemmia Tardiva ★★★ £F

La Togata (Montalcino) *www.brunellolatogata.com*

This is 'heavy metal' Brunello: bold, and slightly rough-edged but with the real essence of Brunello character in the selection La Togata dei Togati and the robust, powerful Riserva. La Togata was established in 1996 and its various parcels of vineyard (including Montosoli) total 21 ha from which a rigorous grape selection is made. Winemaking is directed by Paolo Vagaggini and *barriques* are favoured, but so are long maceration times for the top wines. Togata dei Togati should be given at least 10 years, the Riserva 15 or more from a top vintage. As well as a good meaty Rosso, two other Sangiovese-based reds are made – the characterful Azzurreta offers considerably more than the light, quaffing Barengo.

Recommended Reds:
Brunello di Montalcino Riserva ★★★★★ £F
Brunello di Montalcino La Togata dei Togati ★★★★ £F
Brunello di Montalcino ★★★ £E   Rosso di Montalcino ★★ £D
Azzurreta ★★ £D   Barengo ★ £C

Mauricio Lambardi (Montalcino) *www.lambardimontalcino.it*

Committed grower Maurizio Lambardi's Canalicchio di Sotto, like a number of Brunello's small estates, doesn't produce that much wine but what there is can be very good. His wines have a depth and fullness that show off the quality of his fruit. Their lushness and richness mean that the wines are accessible early or for drinking with 10-15 years' ageing. Though not all are of the same standard, there is generally good quality across recent vintages. From the best

Tuscany

vintages, an intense vibrant Rosso needs 3–5 years to show at its best.
Recommended Reds:
Brunello di Montalcino ★★★☆ £D   Rosso di Montalcino ★★ £B

Lanciola (Chianti Classico) *www.lanciola.it*
The 80 ha estate of Lanciola, nearly half of it planted to vines, lies
at the top of the Classico zone. By rights the wines ought not be
anything special here but in recent vintages they have certainly
offered plenty of substance and vibrancy. At the level of Chianti
Classico Riserva and the premium red, Terricci (Sangiovese with
15% Cabernet Sauvignon and 5% Cabernet Franc), this translates
as broad, muscular wines that can be slightly overdone in terms
of oak and extract. Both shouldn't be drunk with less than five
years' age. Within their context, regular Chiantis, both Classico and
Fiorentini, are, however, more successful, with a vigour and intensity
well matched by a stylish fruit expression. In short, don't expect
great finesse here but you will get plenty of wine for your money.
Chardonnay (Ricciobianco), Pinot Nero (Riccineri) and Vin Santo are
also made.
Recommended Reds:
Terricci ★★★ £D   Chianti Classico Riserva ★★ £C
Chianti Classico Le Masse di Greve ★★ £B
Chianti Colli Fiorentini ★★ £B

Lavacchio (Chianti Rufina) *www.fattorialavacchio.com*
A proper working farm (with windmill) as well as a wine estate,
Lavacchio has been certfied organic since 2004. Consultancy now
comes from Alberto Antonini and good progress can be seen in
recent releases. Regular Chianti Rufina Cedro has the particular
enticing cherry fruit unique to Rufina, while the *barrique*-aged
Riserva with 10% Merlot has plenty of substance and grip and
deserves 6–7 years' age. Fontegalli is from 60% Merlot, with
the balance equally divided between Cabernet Sauvignon and
Sangiovese. Despite the blend it still has a distinctively Tuscan bitter
cherry edge to the fruit. Also made is a light dry white, Pachàr,
from Chardonnay, Sauvignon and Viognier. Charlotte is a one-off
moderately sweet wine made from late-harvested non-botrytised
Sauvignon and Gewürztraminer grapes with flavours running from
ripe apple to pear, quince and guava. More usual is Oro di Cedro
from botrytised Gewürztraminer.
Recommended Reds:
Fontegalli ★★★ £D   Chianti Rufina Riserva ★★★ £C
Chianti Rufina Cedro ★★ £B
Recommended Whites:
Charlotte ★★★ £D   Pachàr ★ £B

Le Bèrne (Montepulciano) *www.leberne.it*
A dedicated family concern, the Natalini family have 6 ha of prime
Cervognano vineyards close to those of Boscarelli in the heart of
the zone. Established back in the 1960s, they have been producing
their own Vino Nobile since 1995. Some serious quality input by
young Andrea Natalini and consultancy from Paolo Vagaggini is
giving excellent results. Vino Nobile has been 100% Sangiovese
but good quality Colorino (3% and 10% in the Riserva) has been
added in current releases. Ageing (for 2 years) is in a mix of large
oak and *barriques*. The quality of the fruit and concentration are
hallmarks together with plenty of extract. A supple Riserva gets an
extra years' ageing with slightly greater use of *barriques* and adds
more class, complexity and depth. Rosso is light but attractive. Very
small amounts of a fine Vin Santo, Ada are also made with moderate
sweetness, good intensity and a lively vein of acidity. Olive oil has

good purity and intensity.
Recommended Reds:
Vino Nobile di Montepulciano Riserva ★★★★ £E
Vino Nobile di Montepulciano ★★★☆ £C
Rosso di Montepulciano ★☆ £B
Recommended Whites:
Vin Santo di Montepulciano Ada ★★★ £E

Le Cinciole (Chianti Classico) *www.lecinciole.it*
Established in 1991, Luca Orsini and Valeria Viganò started to
produce Chianti on their small 30 ha family estate. Chianti Classico
is made complemented by a small quantity of Riserva (5000
bottles) in most years. 11 ha out of 13 ha of vineyard are currently
in production of which 4 ha known as Valle del Pozzo, are located
in Panzano's prized Conca d'Oro. Sangiovese is king with just a
small addition of Canaiolo (2-4%) to the normale. Do not drink
these wines too young as there is a tendency to flesh up and open
out giving greater harmony with more age. This means 3-5 years'
for Chianti Classico and a minimum of 6 years for the Riserva. The
latter comes from old vines in Valle del Pozzo with low yields (1kg
per plant) and is aged for a year in small French oak and another
in 20hl casks. At its best there is splendid depth, complexity and
concentration. From 2000, they ventured into international varietals,
commencing with Camalaione, 70% Cabernet Sauvignon, 15%
Syrah and 15% Merlot and then Cinciorosso, 60% Sangiovese, 20%
Cabernet Sauvignon, 15% Syrah and 5% Merlot, from young vines
for early drinking. Fine extra virgin olive oil is also made.
Recommended Reds:
Chianti Classico Riserva Petresco ★★★☆ £E
Chianti Classico ★★☆ £C

Le Corte/ Principe Corsini *www.principecorsini.com*
As recently as 1992 Duccio Corsini, the son of the Principe Corsini,
set out to produce high-quality wine with view to restoring the
historic Villa di Corsini. The Chianti Classico estate, in the family
since Renaissance times, covers 250 ha with 49 ha of vineyards.
Duccio Corsini is assisted by one of Tuscany's best consultant
winemakers, Carlo Ferrini. There are three fine Chianti Classicos, a
good normale (Le Corti), a more structured Riserva (Cortevecchia)
and the premium bottling, Don Tommaso. The wines are ripe,
intense and modern but typically Chianti Classico, with particularly
good structure and depth in Don Tommaso. A 100% Sangiovese,
Zac, an IGT Toscana has been produced since 2008 but not tasted.
The family also have a holding in the Maremma, Tenuta Marsiliana,
producing a deep, penetrating and characterful IGT primarily from
Cabernet Sauvignon and Merlot with a little Petit Verdot. A floral and
herb scented second wine is also produced from this estateas well
as a Vermentino. Also under the ownership of the Principe Corsini
is the Titignano estate in Umbria where the SALVIANO wines (see
Central Italy) are made.
Le Corti
Recommended Reds:
Chianti Classico Don Tommaso ★★★ £E
Chianti Classico Riserva Cortevecchia ★★ £D
Chianti Classico Le Corti ★★ £B
Tenuta Marsiliana
Recommended Reds:
Marsiliana ★★★ £E

Le Filigare (Chianti Classico) *www.lefiligare.it*
This attractive estate is at a relatively high altitude on lean, stony

soils and shows increasing promise with its wines. Carlo Burchi has doubled the original vineyard area to 12 ha and now works with his son Filippo and enologist Dr Luciano Bandini. Though the wines can be a little tight and compact if tasted very young, there is usually an underlying fruit richness which makes for sleek, elegant, stylish and fruity Chianti with a little age. In the regular version the Sangiovese is complemented by Canaiolo and Colorino, while the Riserva includes Colorino and Merlot and spends longer in oak. Podere Le Rocce is a blend of Cabernet Sauvignon and Sangiovese (65/35) that is quite sturdy but with the potential to add richness with age. Newish Pietro is a more ambitious premium blend of Merlot, Sangiovese and Syrah that is more powerful and extracted. In terms of keeping, Chianti Classico normale is best with two or three years, Riserva with 3–5, while even more time is needed for the Podere Le Rocce. A small amount of Vin Santo is also made.

Recommended Reds:
Podere Le Rocce ★★★ £E
Chianti Classico Riserva Maria Vittoria ★★★ £E
Chianti Classico ★★ £C

Fattoria Le Fonti (Chianti Classico) *www.fattoria-lefonti.it*
Tuscany needs more producers like this – small estates that are maximising the potential of a small but coherent range of wines. Le Fonti's success seems to owe much to Lorenzo Bernini, who is responsible for the 22 ha of vineyards, and consultant Paolo Caciorgna, who makes the wines. Vito Arturo is named for the Imberti brothers' father, who bought the estate in 1956. A single-vineyard varietal Sangiovese, it reveals both quality and intensity to the fruit in recent vintages. Only a notch or two lower is the Chianti Classico Riserva, also pure Sangiovese. The normale (with 5% Canaiolo) starts out a little lean but will fill out if given three years' age. Rather traditionally styled and of moderate sweetness, Vin Santo has a roasted nuts, date and walnut character but also dried citrus and a honeyed intensity. These wines shouldn't be confused with those of Azienda Agricola LE FONTI.

Recommended Reds:
Vito Arturo ★★★☆ £E   Chianti Classico Riserva ★★★ £D
Chianti Classico ★☆ £B
Recommended Whites:
Vin Santo del Chianti Classico ★★★ £E

❀ **Le Macchiole (Bolgheri)** *www.lemacchiole.it*
Le Macchiole is as outstanding a producer of Bolgheri as its neighbours ORNELLAIA or SASSICAIA. Eugenio Campolmi transformed both the 18 ha estate and the way the wines were made before his early death. His success owes much to enologist Luca D'Attoma, responsible for several of Tuscany's most exciting creations. Made in the greatest quantities, the estate red, Macchiole, is Sangiovese-based but with between 5% Cabernet Sauvignon and 10% each of Merlot and Cabernet Franc. The latter in particular seems to add character; sleek and compact, it opens out with age. Three other reds are made in small quantities. Paléo Rosso was originally a Cabernet Sauvignon based wine complemented by Sangiovese and Cabernet Franc. However the Cabernet Franc increased from15% in 1999 to 30% in 2000, while from then is entirely from Cabernet Franc. Despite this evolution, it has sustained a characteristic mineral-imbued, intense, small berry fruit character within a structured frame. At least five years' age is recommended, as it is for for reds that fully deserve their cult status. The quality of the tremendously rich, classically varietal Merlot, Messorio, and deep, structured, minerally Syrah, Scrio, is quite spellbinding. Paléo

Bianco, from Chardonnay and Sauvignon, is ripe and stylish. Bolgheri Rosso, produced since 2004, is 50% Merlot, 30% Cabernet Franc and 20% Syrah and was, we suppose, introduced as an entry level wine, but fights well above its weight with some juicy, deep and unctuous fruit.

Recommended Reds:
Messorio ★★★★★ £H   Scrio ★★★★★ £H
Paléo Rosso ★★★★ £F   Macchiole Rosso ★★★☆ £D
Bolgheri Rosso ★★☆ £D
Recommended Whites:
Paléo Bianco ★★ £D

Le Pupille (Morellino di Scansano) *www.fattorialepupille.it*
For long the one outstanding producer from the heart of the southern Maremma, Le Pupille was well established before a recent wave of newcomers from other parts of Tuscany rushed to join in. Quality (already good) soared in the 1990s under a string of top-flight consultants, the latest being ex-technical director of Bordeaux's Château LAFITE, Christian Le Sommer. Regular Morellino di Scansano has always shown off the character of Sangiovese in this zone with its wild herb and delightful berry fruit character supplemented by a little Alicante and Malvasia Nera. A fine Riserva with extra weight and structure is also produced and efforts are now going into further improving the quality of the excellent single-vineyard Poggio Valente, introduced in 1997. There is marvellous style and complexity in this wine that newer producers in Morellino will take some time to emulate. Even better and now a marvellously rich, concentrated wine is Saffredi, a blend of Cabernet Sauvignon, Merlot and Petit Verdot. All four reds need a little age: three years for the regular Morellino, five or more for Poggio Valente and Saffredi. Solalto, a delicious sweet wine with gently spicy dried peach and apricot fruit, is a late-harvested blend of Sauvignon, Traminer and Sémillon.

Recommended Reds:
Saffredi ★★★★☆ £F   Morellino di Scansano Poggio Valente ★★★ £E
Morellino di Scansano ★★ £C
Recommended Whites:
Solalto ★★★ £E

Le Sorgenti (Colli Fiorentini) *www.fattoria-lesorgenti.com*
Le Sorgenti can be found in the hills just beyond the south-eastern edge of Florence and is emerging as one of the stars of the Colli Fiorentini. There are two top reds. Gaiaccia is a classic blend of Sangiovese and Alicante from a single vineyard at 500m with berry/cherry fruit that sings out; Scirus, a Merlot,Cabernet Sauvignon Petit Verdot and Malbec blend with crushed berry fruit that is composed and seductive with a certain elegance. Although in a lighter style, the Chianti (100% Sangiovese) is juicy with good fruit intensity and plenty of charm, while Sghiràs is a ripe, melony dry white from Chardonnay and Trebbiano Toscana. Vin Santo is also made. New from 2011, is a 100% Malbec, Coda Rossa, but this has not been tasted.

Recommended Reds:
Scirus ★★★ £D   Gaiaccia ★★★ £C   Chianti Colli Fiorentini ★★ £B
Recommended Whites:
Sghiràs ★ £C

Cantine Leonardo da Vinci (Chianti) *www.cantineleonardo.it*
Formed in 1961, this modern and increasingly respected co-op made the switch from bulk production to quality wines only relatively recently. The grapes are drawn from around 500 ha, mostly

Tuscany

in the Montalbano hills west of Carmignano – the countryside around the birthplace of the great artist and inventor. Winemaking direction comes from Riccardo Pucci with consultancy from Alberto Antonini. All the wines are very soundly made with good fruit intensity and represent good value at their respective quality levels. Both straight Chianti and Brunello di Montalcino rarely leave you feeling short changed, only the Morellino is slightly weak. A vineyard site of particular merit is singled out for special bottlings. The dense, black-fruited Sant'Ippolito is a blend of Merlot (40%), Syrah, (40%) and Sangiovese (20%). It deserves to be drunk with 5–6 years' age or more. For white a ripe, attractive Chardonnay, Ser Piero, is produced. Among other wines made are a varietal Merlot, Merlot degli Artisti, and Vin Santo, Tegrino d'Anchiano. A range of wines are also sold under the da Vinci label. Also produced by the same group are the well made wines of Cantina di MONTALCINO.

Recommended Reds:
Sant'Ippolito ★★★★ £E   Chianti Riserva ★★☆ £C
Chianti ★★ £B   Brunello di Montalcino ★★ £C
Chianti Classico Leonardo ★★ £B   Morellino di Scansano ★☆ £B
Recommended Whites:
Ser Piero ★ £B

Lisini (Montalcino) *www.lisini.com*
Franco Bernabei is the consultant of choice for the Lisinis. From 12 ha of vineyards he ensures good consistency and attractive wines even in lesser vintages. Though there is real Brunello complexity and weight the wines are generally more for the medium than long term. The exception is the single-vineyard wine Ugolaia. Potentially very exciting, it can be just a little overdone in terms of structure, though the necessary balance for long keeping is usually there. The Rosso can also impress with its forward, lush and vibrant black fruit character. There is also an unoaked version of Sangiovese Grosso, San Biago, for early drinking.

Recommended Reds:
Brunello di Montalcino Ugolaia ★★★★☆ £G
Brunello di Montalcino ★★★★ £F   Rosso di Montalcino ★★ £C

Livernano (Radda in Chianti) *www.livernano.it*
Livernano is a restored medieval hamlet that, like a number of others, was abandoned in the post-war migration to the cities. It was revived by Swiss Marco Montanari but has recently come under new ownership. 15 ha of vines have been replanted at higher densities (and unusually trained alberello) under the guidance of eminent agronomist Remigio Bordini. Winemaking expertise comes from the highly respected Stefano Chioccioli. The Livernano blend (Cabernet/Merlot/Sangiovese) shows good intensity and structure as well as increasing depth and concentration, though for me more exciting (and aptly named) is Puro Sangue, a very pure, powerful expression of Sangiovese which promises much with 5–7 years' age. Similarly small quantities of L'Anima, an intense, exotic fruited but well-balanced *barrique*-aged white are also produced. Based on Chardonnay, it also includes Sauvignon, Gewürztraminer and Viognier. Chianti Classico and Chianti Classico Riserva (both 80% Sangiovese and 0% Merlot) are produced at Livernano, as well as at the Cuillo's other estate at Casalvento, which is the subject of work in progress.

Recommended Reds:
Purosangue ★★★★ £E   Livernano ★★★☆ £E
Recommended Whites:
L'Anima ★★☆ £E

Fattoria di Magliano *www.fattoriadimagliano.it*
A significant proportion of this 97 ha Morellino di Scansano estate is planted to young vineyards first established in 1998. A fine, fruit-intense Morellino di Scansano, Heba, i Sangiovese with 5% Syrah and has classic Maremma herbs and cherry, berry fruit. Better still is Poggio Bestiale from a large vineyard site planted to Merlot, Cabernet Sauvignon, Cabernet Franc and Petit Verdot. This wine shows just how well these varieties are suited to these soils. A varietal Syrah, Perenzo made an auspicious début from the 03 vintage and shows splendid aromatic complexity and style, suggesting great wine in the making. For white there's Pagliatura, an intense, fruit-driven Vermentino that is delicious if drunk from the most recent vintage. Organic farming has been practised since 2011 and the wines are expected to be certified organic from the 2014 vintage onwards.

Recommended Reds:
Perenzo ★★★★ £E   Poggio Bestiale ★★★☆ £D
Morellino di Scansano Heba ★★☆ £B
Recommended Whites:
Pagliatura ★★ £C

Malenchini (Colli Fiorentini) *www.malenchini.it*
There isn't an official campaign as such for 'real Chianti' but if there were, Malenchini would surely be a leading advocate. From 17.5 ha of vineyard close to Florence itself the Malenchinis produce a version from 90% Sangiovese and 10% Canaiolo that has classic vibrancy, purity and intensity and archetypal Tuscan flavours. It is neither big, overly complex nor a wine for keeping – but neither is it expensive. Cabernet Sauvignon is grown and is combined with 20% Sangiovese in Bruzzico, a ripe, characterful example that should be given at least 6–7 years from the vintage. Good Vin Santo is in the more traditional mould that goes so well with biscotti. New additions are Vino da Rosso, a basic everyday Sangiovese and Toscana Bianco, from equal parts of Chardonnay and Trebbiano Toscano.

Recommended Reds:
Bruzzico ★★★ £D   Chianti Colli Fiorentini ★★ £B
Recommended Whites:
Vin Santo ★★★ £D

Mannucci Droandi (Chianti Classico) *www.mannuccidroandi.com*
This 100 ha estate includes 32 ha of vineyards in two parts. Campolucci, where the winery is based, falls in the Colli Aretini while Ceppeto provides Chianti Classico from the Gaiole commune. Run along organic principles the family receives some input on the winemaking from Giorgio Marone. There is good depth and definition to all the wines with ripe fruit, ripe tannins and good textures, usually without any of the defects that too many producers still grapple with. Chianti Classico is particularly attractive with just a couple of years' age. Riserva adds more depth, concentration and style. More international in style is Campolucci, an IGT red which is 50% Sangiovese with 25% each of Cabernet Sauvignon and Merlot. The oak is more obvious but there's also good depth, texture and length. Rossinello is a rosato from Sangiovese. Experimental wines from Foglia Tondo, Pugnitello and Barsaglina have also been made in 2007 and 2008 while the extra virgin olive oil qualifies for the Chianti Classico DOP.

Recommended Reds:
Campolucci ★★★☆ £E
Chianti Classico Riserva Ceppeto ★★★ £D

Chianti Classico Ceppeto ★★☆ £C
Recommended Rosés:
Rossinello ★ £B

Marchesi Pancrazi *www.pancrazi.it*
Growing Pinot Nero in Tuscany might seem like a mistake and for
the most part it is. The Pancrazis unwittingly planted the variety,
which they believed to be Sangiovese, in the mid-70s. They had
received considerable recognition for their efforts by the early 90s
and 30 years on new vineyards are coming on stream and quality
continues to rise. There are two estates, 20km northwest of Florence:
14 ha San Donato at 400m and 5 ha Bagnolo at sea-level, which
is planted to Pinot only. Quantities are small, even of the main
bottling, Villa di Bagnolo, which is aged in 30% new French oak.
This is a fine, elegant style with real charm but intensity too. Tiny
amounts of Vigna Baragazza (from a single clone) are made and
show greater depth, intensity and concentration, deserving of 5–8
years' age. San Donato (an equal blend of Pinot and Gamay) is in an
attractive fruity style and it can sometimes leave most Bourgogne
Passetoutgrains and a good many Beaujolais crus in its wake. To a
family that has succeeded against the odds with Pinot Nero, making
a varietal Colorino may seem logical. Early versions of Casaglia (since
1998) have been much improved on. While still not an easy wine,
this wild-fruited Tuscan original (only a handful of others are made)
has lots of substance and a firm structure but is intense, ripe and
meaty – it needs food to be sure. There's good olive oil too.
Recommended Reds:
Pinot Nero Vigna Baragazza ★★★★ £F
Pinot Nero Villa di Bagnolo ★★★ £E   Casaglia ★★★ £D
San Donato ★★ £C

Mastrojanni (Montalcino) *www.mastrojanni.com*
One of the few really great Brunello producers, Mastrojanni
commands almost 19 ha of steep stony slopes in the south-eastern
confines of the DOCG. Both large and small wood are used for
ageing but it's not obvious in these deep, dark monsters. Structured,
with dense but ripe tannins, the wines always show an expansive
quality in the mouth that few of the more modern, oak-influenced
styles even approach. Sometimes the balance is not quite there
or the wine is a bit deficient, or relatively advanced though good,
but the depth, class and complexity from top vintages make this
an excellent investment for keeping for 10–15 years (i.e. 5–10 more
after release). A special selection, Schiena d'Asino (which may need
closer to two decades) is produced, as is (since 2006) a slightly
lighter and more approachable cru, Loreto. San Pio (80% Cabernet
Sauvignon, 20% Sangiovese) is more accessible in the short-term as
is a Rosso which can be excellent in good vintages, with Brunello-
like fullness but always needing another two or three years after its
release (at two years). Botrys is a late-harvested blend of Sauvignon,
Moscato and Malvasia.
Recommended Reds:
Brunello di Montalcino Schiena d'Asino ★★★★ £F
Brunello di Montalcino ★★★★ £F
Brunello di Montalcino Loreto ★★★ £E
Rosso di Montalcino ★★ £D   San Pio ★★★ £D

Mocali (Montalcino)
There are 9 ha of vineyard at this 32 ha estate in the western part of
the zone on the slopes of the Valle della Chiesa di Santa Restituta.
The wines, made by Tiziano Ciacci with advice from consultants
Barbara Tamburini and Vittorio Fiore, are just beginning to realise

their full potential. French tonneaux are used, at least in part, for all
Brunellos and Rosso too. Regular Brunello is dense, sweet-fruited
with a modern, oak-influenced texture. The same is largely true
of the single vineyard Vigne delle Raunate version. Powerful and
expansive, it delivers plenty of flavour and style, if best drunk with
10-15 years' age. Earlier vintages of Brunellos, including Riservas are
less convincing. Rosso is modern, round and attractive. Also made
are IGT red and white, a Morellino di Scansano and an example of
Moscadello di Montalcino.
Recommended Reds:
Brunello di Montalcino Vigneto delle Raunate ★★★★☆ £F
Brunello di Montalcino ★★★★ £E   Rosso di Montalcino ★★ £C

Monte Bernardi (Chianti Classico) *www.montebernardi.com*
Developed by Stak Aivaliotis since the late 1980s, this 53 ha estate
(with 6 ha of vines) is now run by the Schmelzer family. The first
wines made by Michael Schmelzer are from the 2004 vintage.
The intention has always been to produce pure wines with
minimal interference. A rigorous selection and – relatively unusual
for Tuscany – a prolonged pre-fermentation maceration were
employed as well as the use of a basket press. High-quality French
oak, some of it new, is used in the ageing of all the wines and this
has been evident in their structures and flavours. To date Sa'etta
(100% Sangiovese) has been intense, ripe and oaky. Chianti Classico
Bernardi is virtually 100% Sangiovese. Chianti Classico Riserva
includes a little Canaiolo. Tzingana is a spicy, berryish and plummy
blend of Merlot and Cabernet Sauvignon, Cabernet Franc and Petit
Verdot.
Recommended Reds:
Tzingana ★★★ £F   Sa'etta ★★★ £D
Chianti Classico Bernadi ★★ £C

Montecalvi (Chianti Classico) *www.montecalvi.com*
Jacqueline Bolli and her husband have just 3 ha of vines planted
mostly to Sangiovese (including some 1930s vines) but including
some Cabernet Sauvignon and Syrah too. The 10 ha estate was
established by her father Renzo Bolli in the late 80s. Until 2002 a
single estate red was made with guidance from consultant Stefano
Chioccioli. However in this difficult vintage Chianti Classico was
made instead of Montecalvi and both wines were produced for
another year. As from 2004, the Chianti Classico Montecalvi has
been made with 100% Sangiovese, whilst what was previously
called Montecalvi, has now been replaced by VV (vielles vignes)
from a vineyard planted in 1932 with Sangiovese (95%) and 5%
Cabernet Sauvignon planted 20 years ago to fill in the spaces where
the old plants had died. It's not produced in every vintage but has
great depth and concentration adding real distinction with a wild
berry fruits, herb and earth refinement. Planting more Cabernet and
a little Alicante Bouschet in 2001, has resulted in a new Cabernet-
based red, San Piero which was released from the 04 vintage. Also
made are tiny quantities of extra virgin olive oil.
Recommended Reds:
San Piero ★★★★ £G   VV ★★★★ £F
Chianti Classico Montecalvi ★★☆ £E

Montepeloso (Val di Cornia) *www.montepeloso.it*
This estate is one of Suvereto's stars, making wines of extraordinary
concentration from well-sited vineyards. The wines from 8 ha of
vines are made by consultant Fabrizio Moltard. Low yields and
barrique-ageing make for wines with deep, rich, powerful fruit and
fine, ripe tannins. Gabbro is from Cabernet Sauvignon, Cabernet

Franc and Petit Verdot, while Nardo is predominantly Sangiovese but with a little Marselan and Montepulciano. Both are made in very small quantities and highly sought after, so are not cheap. Eneo, predominantly Sangiovese and Montepulciano, but also including a little Marselan and Alicante, is made in greater quantities.

Recommended Reds:

Nardo ★★★★★ £H Gabbro ★★★★★ £G Eneo ★★★★ £E

Montevertine (Chianti Classico) *www.montevertine.it*

Sergio Manetti became one of the legends of the modern Tuscan wine renaissance after creating the pure-Sangiovese, single-vineyard Super-Tuscan Le Pergole Torte. The striking labels are the work of artist Alberto Manfredi. The small estate now has 10 ha of vineyards at high altitude, though not all are fully in production. Le Pergole Torte is subject to a lengthy maceration (25–30 days) before ageing, only initially in *barriques*. Besides Le Pergole Torte there is another top red, Montevertine (previously designated Riserva), which approximates to a regular traditional Chianti Classico, albeit a very good one, which includes a little Canaiolo and Colorino. Both can show marvellous quality, at once very stylish and harmonious, complex with excellent dimension on the palate, gaining in richness with age and with great length of flavour. It can be easy to underestimate quality when the wines are very young but usually with 5–8 years' age the full potential becomes apparent. Quality is not entirely consistent but tends to follow the best vintages. Pian del Ciampolo is a more recently introduced cheaper red with a bright, more forward, floral fruit character. Following his father's death in 2000, it seems that Martino Manetti has taken this fine estate along the same path continuing to be assisted by the venerable Giulio Gambelli. Since Gambelli's recent passing, consultancy is now continued by Paolo Salvi.

Recommended Reds:

Le Pergole Torte ★★★★☆ £F Montevertine ★★★ £E
Pian del Ciampolo ★ £B

Giovanna Morganti/ Le Boncie (Chianti Classico) *www.leboncie.it*

I've only ever tasted this wine twice but it is unquestionably a thoroughbred Chianti Classico. Very Tuscan, it is mostly Sangiovese but has always included a little of other indigenous varieties including Colorino and Ciliegiolo, coming from 4 ha of high density alberello trained vineyards in the south of the zone. It is pure, detailed and refined - very much the antithesis of the Merlot or Cabernet enriched, oak-lined, international style. Young vintages need time to settle down but the wine shows real promise.

Recommended Reds:

Chianti Classico Le Trame ★★★ £D

Moris Farms (Monteregio di Massa Marittima) *www.morisfarms.it*

The Moris family's substantial landholding in the Maremma includes 70 ha of vineyards. 37 ha of these fall under the Monteregio di Massa Marittima DOC and 33 ha qualify as Morellino di Scansano. Generally sound if robust examples of both are produced, particularly an intense, extracted Riserva of the latter. The Monteregio has a bit more substance than the standard Morellino due to lower yields. The real star however is Avvoltore, a powerhouse Sangiovese-based wine of great vigour and depth. Cabernet Sauvignon and Syrah (20 and 5% respectively) play an important part in its consistently rich, floral and crushed berry fruit complexity. It is balanced with great length and usually best with 6–8 years' age.

Recommended Reds:

Avvoltore ★★★★ £E

Morellino di Scansano Riserva ★★ £D
Morellino di Scansano ★ £C Monteregio di Massa Marittima ★★ £C

Silvio Nardi (Montalcino) *www.tenutenardi.com*

There can be little doubt about the Nardi family's desire to number among the élite of Brunello producers given the seriousness of their approach to both viticulture and vinification. The 80 ha of vineyards includes 72 ha planted to Sangiovese. Expert advice has included that from Bordeaux University's Dean of Enology, Professor Yves Glories. Clonal selection and low yields are central to the viticultural advances while the intelligent use of oak and balanced extract highlight the winemaking nous. The quality rise is best exemplified by the single-vineyard Brunello Manachiara, showing tremendous depth, complexity and class. Regular Brunello is very good too, pursued by a concentrated powerful Rosso. Sant'Antimo Merlot (from 04) has a spicy, plummy berry richness. Even newer (2005) is the Turan Sant Antimo Rosso, a blend of Petit Verdot, Sangiovese, Syrah and Colorino. If this isn't enough then buy the Nardi's stylish, complex olive oil with a long finish that keeps well for months after the harvest.

Recommended Reds:

Brunello di Montalcino Vigneto Manachiara ★★★★★ £G
Brunello di Montalcino ★★★★ £F
Rosso di Montalcino ★★★ £D Sant Antimo Merlot ★★★ £D

Nittardi (Chianti Classico) *www.nittardi.com*

This German-owned Chianti Classico estate with 13 ha of vineyard is best known for the often superb artist labels that have adorned a small batch of bottles in each vintage since the 1980s. In the past decade quality has risen perceptibly under consultant Carlo Ferrini and both normale (with 5% Canaiolo) and Riserva (with 5% Merlot) are now consistently fine examples. The Riserva shows impressive depth, complexity and length and should keep for a decade. New from 2003 is Nectar Dei, a blend based mostly on Cabernet Sauvignon and Merlot with a little Syrah and Petit Verdot from an estate being developed in the southern Maremma, which was quickly followed by Ad Astra, a blend of Sangiovese Cabernet Sauvignon, Merlot and Syrah with typical cherry and herbal fruit from the area and in 2012, the first Nittardi white wine, Ben, 100% Vermentino was released.

Recommended Reds:

Nectar Dei ★★★★ £F Ad Astra ★★ £D
Chianti Classico Riserva ★★★ £E Chianti Classico ★★ £C

Nottola (Montepulciano) *www.cantinanottola.it*

Around 300,000 bottles are produced here making this a medium-sized producer of Vino Nobile. With assistance from Riccardo Cotarella since 1995 there is a good standard to the winemaking. Vino Nobile comes only from Sangiovese and has two years of ageing in large casks. With good fruit, texture and balance and a certain orginality, it offers good value but deserves at least five years' ageing. Vigna del Fattore requires more patience; although more modern-styled due to spending six months of its ageing in *barrique*, it is dense and ripe-fruited with lots of extract and needs 8-10 years to open out fully. Ready sooner is Nottola's Rosso di Montepulciano which is amongst the best made; with raspberry leaf, spice and cherry, good substance and extract, it needs around three years to drink well. Made too are Chianti Colli Senesi, a basic IGT red and white Bianco Vergine Valdichiana. As well as wine the estate produces olive oil and offers accomodation for those visiting the area.

Recommended Reds:
Vino Nobile di Montepulciano Vigna del Fattore ★★★ £E
Vino Nobile di Montepulciano ★★☆ £C
Rosso di Montepulciano ★★ £B

Tenuta Oliveto (Montalcino) *www.tenutaoliveto.it*
Here is a young Montalcino enterprise making good progress. Starting from scratch in 1994, the first Brunello and Rosso were only made in 1997. With almost 12 ha of vineyards and winemaking expertise comes from Roberto Cipresso. Brunello is a modern, fruit-driven style and more accessible than bigger, more structured examples. Rosso di Montalcino Il Roccolo can also be fine, if sometimes a bit too ripe. A second Rosso, Castelnovo is a bit cheaper. Fruit from the youngest vines goes into Il Leccio; although lacking depth and finesse, it is well-priced at the level.

Recommended Reds:
Brunello di Montalcino ★★★☆ £F
Rosso di Montalcino Il Roccolo ★★★ £D
Il Leccio ★★☆ £C

☻ Tenuta dell' Ornellaia (Bolgheri) *www.ornellaia.it*
This celebrated estate has been under the control of Frescobaldi since 2006, which superceded a joint venture with the MONDAVI family. Originally it was the creation of Lodovico Antinori, Piero ANTINORI's younger brother, who was able to set up on his own in the 1980s due to his inheritance from his mother's family. He spared no expense in transforming 70 ha of mostly scrubby countryside into a model wine estate. The main focus of production continues to be the estate blend, Ornellaia, from Cabernet Sauvignon, Merlot, Petit Verdot and Cabernet Franc (now made in excess of 12,000 cases a year) which celebrated its 25th vintage in 2010. Le Serre Nuove, positioned as a second wine, has been made since 1997. Large volumes are made of Le Volte, the least expensive wine and a blend of Cabernet Sauvignon, Sangiovese, and Merlot; it has been somewhat irregular in terms of quality, rarely providing value for money. Made in more modest quantities, if not quite as scarce as it once was, is the pure Merlot, Masseto – the estate's most sought-after wine. The sheer opulence of the fruit in Masseto has no equal for some of its more impassioned fans. There's little doubt about the quality of this or of Ornellaia, though the ratings below only apply to the best vintages. The more classically structured Ornellaia requires the greater patience. Poggio alle Gazze, a ripe and zesty Sauvignon-based white, made until 2001, has been re-introduced with the 2008 vintage. Also produced (from 2011) is Ornus, a late harvest dessert wine made form 100% Petit Manseng.

Recommended Reds:
Bolgheri Rosso Superiore Ornellaia ★★★★★ £H
Masseto ★★★★★ £H   Bolgheri Rosso Le Serre Nuove ★★★ £E
Le Volte ★☆ £C

☻ Siro Pacenti (Montalcino) *www.siropacenti.it*
Giancarlo Pacenti has turned a good estate into an outstanding one in just a few short years. In recent vintages quality has been exemplary, in fact arguably it has become the best regular Brunello available since 1995, Some new oak is used but this does not overwhelm the marvellous quality of the fruit and extract. Not only is there superb richness, breadth and power but the wine possesses great length, really fine tannins and impeccable balance. Pacenti also makes a rich, concentrated Brunello-like Rosso di Montalcino, with the weight if not the dimension of a really decent example at that. Unfortunately some wine brokers are only too aware of the quality and its speculative potential but prices are not crazy when a merchant or retailer has bought first-hand. At least these wines can be bought in the confidence of finding out what great Brunello tastes like, whether drunk now or with another 10–15 years' age. A little Riserva is sometimes made but has not been tasted from recent vintages.

Recommended Reds:
Brunello di Montalcino ✪✪✪✪✪ £G   Rosso di Montalcino ★★★ £D

Panizzi (San Gimignano) *www.panizzi.it*
There was surely not a more dedicated grower in the San Gimignano zone than Giovanni Panizzi if the quality of his Vernaccia di San Gimignano is anything to go by. The regular version is well structured and has good weight and fruit. The Riserva is fermented and aged in oak and has a minerally, leesy, spiced preserved citrus character as well as breadth and intensity, almost like a slightly unusual white Burgundy. Evoe is a special *cuvée*, barrel fermented for 10 months in French conical casks and then bottled unfiltered. It's tight, tany and mineral, with quite a fair bit of structure. Made since 2003 is a very stylish single-vineyard version, Vigna Santa Margherita. There is also a premium red, Folgóre, from Sangiovese (around 75%) with Merlot and Cabernet Sauvignon. Fully ripe, plummy and stylish, like the whites it is among the very best in the zone. Expansion has come on a pace since the estate was purchased by the Nicolai family in 2005, with not only a Cabernet Sauvignon, Rubente, from San Gimignano to compliment the Folgore, but also a Chianti dei Colli Senese Riserva and a Rosso di Montalcino from an estate acquired in Montalcino with their first Brunello coming on stream with the 2013 vintage. Some entry level IGT Toscana reds are also being produced, so this new direction must be considered as work in progress. Ratings apply only to wines made by Giovanni Panizzi, who passed away in 2010.

Recommended Reds:
Folgóre ★★★☆ £E
Recommended Whites:
Vernaccia di San Gimignano Riserva ★★★ £D
Vernaccia di San Gimignano Vigna Santa Margherita ★★★ £C
Vernaccia di San Gimignano ★★ £C

☻ Pertimali/ Livio Sassetti *www.sassettiliviopertimali.com*
Pertimali is a 9 ha Montalcino estate producing slightly old-fashioned Brunello of great richness and depth within a sturdy frame. A meaty Rosso di Montalcino too can be full, ripe and savoury with a little age, showing the true character of Sangiovese in this zone. Vigna dei Fili di Seta, a blend of Sangiovese and Cabernet Sauvignon, is the only wine likely to have seen any small wood and is more modern, with rich, dense fruit to the fore. However, a note of caution, particularly for the Brunello – despite some really fine examples (for which the rating is given), quality can be uneven with sometimes questionable balance and stability. A very small amount of Riserva is also made and can be superb. In 1999, the Sassetti family purchased a property in the Maremma, La Querciolina, planted vineyards and are now producing wines from Sangiovese and Ciliego, but these have not yet been tasted.

Recommended Reds:
Brunello di Montalcino Riserva ★★★★★ £G
Brunello di Montalcino ★★★★ £F
Rosso di Montalcino ★★★ £D   Vigna dei Fili di Seta ★★★★ £D

Fattoria di Petroio (Chianti Classico) *www.fattoriapetroio.com*
An excellent family-run Classico estate with 13 ha in the very south

of the zone and a lineage running back 300 years. Its relatively low profile belies the quality of the wines. The focus is on a regular Chianti Classico, which is 80–85% Sangiovese topped up with Canaiolo, Malvasia Nera, Colorino and Merlot – an individual, complex example that is best with 3–5 years' age. A small amount of Riserva (of roughly the same blend) has greater breadth and extract and is best with 5 years or more. Both wines benefit from consultancy from Carlo Ferrini. Also made (and again of similar composition) is a more everyday IGT, Poggio al Mandorlo, a very fresh and juicy unwooded Sangiovese from young vines for early drinking.

Recommended Reds:
Chianti Classico Riserva ★★★ £D   Chianti Classico ★★ £B
Poggio al Mandorlo ★ £B

✿ Petrolo (Colli Aretini) *www.petrolo.it*
From the Colli Aretini (east, over the Monti del Chianti from Gaiole in Chianti Classico) this large historic estate is focussed on producing wines of the highest quality from 31 ha of vineyards. This includes one of Tuscany's finest pure Merlots. About 20,000 bottles are now made annually of Galatrona, which has not only remarkable richness and concentration but a depth, spice and individuality that compares with the very best Pomerol. But while the Merlot joins the spiral of cult wines, Luca Sanjust and his mother, with expert help, also produce a Sangiovese blend with 15% Merlot and 5% Cabernet Sauvignon that bears little relation to the humble status of the zone in which they are based. Torrione is for Sangiovese what Galatrona is for Merlot. Made in much greater quantities it has been very impressive since 1997, if not of the same concentration or proportions as Galatrona. Since 2004, a single vineyard Cabernet Sauvignon, Campolusso has been produced from vines planted in 2001, which as yet doesn't show the same depth as the Galatrona, but no doubt, time will tell. Boggina, since 2006, is another single vineyard variety, this time Sangiovese and as from the 2011 vintage, the estate is experimentally vinifying a small part of the grapes in that vineyard in terracotta amphorae where the wine is left for several months on its skins without adding sulphites. These are bottled separately under the label Bogginanfora and if successful, we can expect a greater portion of the harvest to be vinified in this way. Finally, InArno, 100% Sangiovese produced by Petrolo with grapes from neighbouring vineyards is in celebration of the new Val d'Arno di Sopra DOC. Olive oil production is also taken very seriously.

Recommended Reds:
Galatrona ★★★★☆ £G   Boggina ★★★★ £G
Bogginamfora ★★★★ £G   Torrione ★★★☆ £D
InArno ★★☆ £D

Piaggia (Carmignano) *www.piaggia.com*
Mauro Vannucci has many fans clamouring for his small production of Carmignano Riserva. It isn't quite like any other, the grapes being picked very ripe and at very low yields. It is very rich with concentrated black fruits; powerful with lots of extract but well balanced with good acidity and fine tannins too. After capitalising on the excellent vintages of 1997 and 99 and by working with Alberto Antonini he has done still more by producing outstanding efforts in every vintage since, including an uncommon 02 harvested in late October after the rains with many of the grapes being discarded. All vintages should be given at least 6–8 years' ageing. As good and complete a wine as it is, its modern, oak-lined sumptuousness does come slightly at the cost of originality and

class. Small quantities of Il Sasso are also produced with a very similar composition of Sangiovese, Cabernet Sauvignon and Merlot (70/20/10). Effectively a second wine, it is vineyard-specific and more international in style but lush, cedary and berryish with a little age. Two recent additions make up the range - Poggio de'Colli, unusually 100% Cabernet Franc which is meaty, fruity and smoky, perhaps lacking a little in finesse and a Sangiovese with a smidgen of Canaiolo, Pietranera, from young vines with a more racy mouth feel.

Recommended Reds:
Carmignano Riserva ★★★★☆ £E   Poggio de'Colli ★★★☆ £F
Il Sasso ★★★☆ £D   Pietranera ★★☆ £C

Pian dell' Orino (Montalcino) *www.piandellorino.com*
The heart of Caroline Pobitzer's recently revived small 6 ha estate lies next to Biondi-Santi at around 450m. The latest vintages confirm her and her husband as one of the young emerging producers in Montalcino. Organic status has lately been augmented by biodynamic treatments. The Brunello with a five week maceration and ageing only in large cask, is quite solid, compact with good depth and tipicité and should drink well with 10 years' age or more. Rosso, partly aged in tonneaux, is very good in a medium-weight, accessible style with pure floral (violet), spice and crushed blackberry aromas - drink with 3-4 years' age. As good as these both are, given the estate's relative infancy, caution should be taken with earlier vintages. Not tasted is an inexpensive IGT red, Piandorino in which Cabernet Sauvignon and Merlot were added to Sangiovese, but is now 100% Sangiovese.

Recommended Reds:
Brunello di Montalcino ★★★★ £F   Rosso di Montalcino ★★★ £D

Pian delle Vigne (Montalcino) *www.antinori.it*
There's arguably no Brunello more consistent than that of ANTINORI's. The 60 ha estate was only purchased in 1995 and more than half of it is planted to young vines of new clones. The wine is sophisticated, modern if not classically Brunello; improving from a good if not inspiring first (95) vintage, though with a suggestion of slightly too much oak from early tastings. Nonetheless it is clear from this wine that the intention of the Antinori winemaking team is to produce much more than a solid, dependable Brunello - rather one that competes with the zone's best. Indeed, a Riserva, Vigna Ferrovia was produced in 2004 with the intention of only producing the Riserva in great years. 2006 and 2007 are the only other vintages released so far.

Recommended Reds:
Brunello di Montalcino ★★★★ £F

Piancornello (Montalcino)
Claudio Monaci is now making some excellent wines from this small 10 ha estate at an altitude of 250m in the very south of the zone. Established in 1990, only now are the vines which are planted in stony, rocky soils starting to show more of their potential. Very fine Brunello has been produced, aged partly in *barrique* and partly in large oak, and carefully crafted combining concentration and depth with expression and vitality. There is lots of crushed berry and Montalcino herb character and a fine tannic structure that will slowly unfurl over the next 10 years. A Riserva is produced in exceptional years. Rosso is also a good example with plenty of breadth and intensity. Interesting too is the perfumed Poggio dei Lecci which adds 10% each of Syrah and Colorino to Sangiovese - and atypically good for a lighter style red from the area. Also made

are two excellent single variety olive oils, Olivastra and Correggiolo.

Recommended Reds:
Brunello di Montalcino ★★★★ £F
Rosso di Montalcino ★★★ £D   Poggio dei Lecci ★★ £B

⚘ Pieve Santa Restituta (Montalcino) *www.terlatomontalcino.com*
Angelo GAJA's first venture into Tuscany was this small, wonderfully sited Brunello estate. While all eyes are now on what comes out of his major undertaking in Bolgheri, CA' MARCANDA, the wines here are beginning to show the impact of his winemaker, Guido Rivella. Two Brunellos are made – Rennina, a superior selection from the best vines, and Sugarille, from a single-vineyard site. The original 11ha have been expanded and will eventually total 35 ha, still small by comparison with the zone's biggest producers. The wines already command high prices, whether by design or demand, but show an elegance and structure that since 1995 have set them apart from most other Brunello. The first vintages formulated with the Gaja magic are only beginning to be ready for drinking as both wines need at least 10–12 years' age (and should keep for considerably longer). From the 2005 vintage, the Gajas decided to produce a regular Brunello which was not vineyard designated. It's slightly more approachable than the single vineyard wines, but will still repay several years cellaring.

Recommended Reds:
Brunello di Montalcino Rennina ★★★★★ £G
Brunello di Montalcino Sugarille ★★★★★ £G
Brunello di Montalcino ★★★★ £F

Poggerino (Chianti Classico) *www.poggerino-chianti-italy.com*
This fine 43 ha estate is in some of Chianti Classico's highest hills (between 400 and 500m) north-east of Radda. After a remarkable Riserva made in 1990, the wines have maintained a high standard under the continued efforts and winemaking skill of Piero Lanza. A small amount of Merlot supplements the plantings of Sangiovese and is used in both a minor supporting role in the Chianti Classico and as an equal partner in the premium cuvée, Primamateria. While new oak and concentrated ripe fruit are much in evidence, there is also an elegance and stylishness to the wines derived at least in part from the elevation, aspect and soil of the vineyards. The Chianti Classico shows the fine spice, cherry and herb notes characteristic of Sangiovese and deserves 2 or 3 years' age. A small amount of a fine Riserva from a single vineyard, Bugialla, is made in good years and deserves 5 years' age. Primamateria (first made in 1997) shows intense sweet berry fruit depth, great length and superfine tannins and is very approachable but best with 5 years' ageing or more. For everyday drinking, Il Labirinto is made from young vines of Sangiovese and intended as a second selection for the Chianti Classico.

Recommended Reds:
Primamateria ★★★★ £E   Chianti Classico Riserva Bugialla ★★★ £E
Chianti Classico ★★ £B   Il Labirinto ★ £B

⚘ Poggio Antico (Montalcino) *www.poggioantico.com*
Under the direction of Paola Gloder Montefiori, Poggio Antico has been producing fine Brunello for an age from 30-odd hectares of elevated vineyards (450m) on a ridge running south of Montalcino itself. In current and recent releases the hand of enologist Carlo Ferrini can be seen in the extra drive and intensity added to the elegance that the site delivers. Improvement seem likely to continue with replanting at much higher densities than previously. Most impressive (from 1999) is the vineyard-specific Riserva (aged partly

in small oak) with great depth, class and a preserved-fruits intensity. Drink it with 10–15 years' age or more. The regular example (which sees 3 years in large Slavonian oak) is more classic, combining expression with concentration and depth. The tonneaux-aged Altero (previously IGT but now Brunello due to the reduced wood-ageing requirements) is slightly more international but has great style and complexity. Give both 10 years. The quality of the fruit destined for the Rosso di Montalcino is identical to that of the Brunello and of Altero. A small portion is made and bottled before the mandatory ageing time for Brunello thus allowing wine for earlier consumption. Rosso is not produced in every vintage as in the best years the whole crop goes into the Brunellos. It is certainly something worth having whilst waiting for the Brunellos to come round. New since 2001 is Madre, an equal blend of Cabernet Sauvignon and Sangiovese; oaky and robust but concentrated, it should show more refinement with 8–10 years' age. Newer still is Lemartine, mainly Sangiovese with Cabernet Sauvignon and Petit Verdot. 2010 was the first vintage released in 2012 and we look forward to an opportunity to taste it.

Recommended Reds:
Brunello di Montalcino Riserva ★★★★★ £G
Brunello di Montalcino Altero ★★★★☆ £G
Brunello di Montalcino ★★★★ £F   Madre ★★★ £D
Rosso di Montalcino ★★★ £D

Poggio Argentiera *www.poggioargentiera.com*
One of the most exciting of the many new names emerging from the Maremma. Production is focused on Morellino. An unwooded regular bottling, Bellamarsilia is ripe, spicy and characterful and includes 10% Ciliegiolo and 5% Alicante. Capatosta is from older vines of Sangiovese and also includes a little Alicante. It spends around 12 months in French oak (one-third new) following a relatively short fermentation. The style is relaxed and expressive yet with intense, concentrated fruit. There are also very small amounts of Finisterre (40% Cabernet Franc, 30% Syrah, and 30% Alicante), which spends longer in oak but only used oak. Stylish and complex, this has real character and lightly mineral intensity. All impress. Additionally, a few hundred bottles of Lalicante are made from late-harvested Alicante grapes which were subsequently dried, resulting in a red of moderate sweetness with intense, distinctive spicy fruit character. Also made are two unoaked dry whites, Ansonica & Vermentino (in equal proportions) and a 100% Vermentino, Guazz. New from young vines is a Syrah/Alicante 50/50 blend from the Maremma. The owners have also gone into partnership with Antonio Camillo, their estate manager, to produce a range of red and white wines under the Antonio Camillo label, which will be the subject of work in progress.

Recommended Reds:
Morellino di Scansano Capatosta ★★★★ £E
Morellino di Scansano Bellamarsilia ★★ £B   Finisterre ★★★★ £E

Poggio Gagliardo (Montescudaio) *www.poggiogagliardo.com*
Poggio Gagliardo has around 80 ha of vines planted mostly to Sangiovese in this still little-known zone north of Bolgheri. The slightly old-fashioned style favours flavour, complexity and originality over modernity and fruit. Of the whites, Linaglia is predominantly Vermentino fermented in stainless steel while Vignalontana is *barrique*-aged Chardonnay. Basic Rosso is good value with lots of Tuscan character from significant percentages of Ciliegiolo and Canaiolo. Malemacchie and Rovo are both predominantly Sangiovese but only the latter sees small barrels,

Tuscany

which impact on flavour, texture and structure. The powerful, complex Gobbo ai Pianacci adds 25% each of Merlot and Cabernet Sauvignon to Sangiovese and also has a distinctive oak influence, while Ultimosole is a blend of the two Cabernets. For something completely different there's Rovo Chinato (made in similar fashion to Barolo Chinato – cold macerated with an infusion of spices for 70 days). After a splendid aromatic panoply of spices comes a long finish of intense sweet fruit, spice, herbs and a cigar/chocolate complexity.

Recommended Reds:
Montescudaio Ultimosole ★★★ £E   Montescudaio Rovo ★★★ £D
Montescudaio Gobbo ai Pianacci ★★★ £D
Montescudaio Malemacchie ★★★ £C   Montescudaio Rosso ★★ £B
Recommended Whites:
Montescudaio Vignalontana ★★ £C   Montescudaio Linaglia ★★ £B
Montescudaio Bianco ★★ £B

Poggio alla Sala (Montepulciano) *www.poggioallasala.it*
There are few better introductions to the wines of Montepulciano than these. The balance, ripe round fruit character and pleasing textures don't ask too much of the taster. Yet there is good depth and style with a gentle minerality in a relatively soft, lightly structured Vino Nobile. The range produced from the 40 ha of vineyards which are gradually being redeveloped, is uncomplicated with just Rosso, Vino Nobile and Riserva rounded out by Chianti Colli Senesi, and of course olive oil. All the wines include 10% Canaiolo except the Riserva which is 100% Sangiovese. In contrast to the Vino Nobile, Rosso is lighter and more perfumed for early drinking while the Riserva is intense and concentrated.

Recommended Reds:
Vino Nobile di Montepulciano Riserva ★★★☆ £E
Vino Nobile di Montepulciano ★★☆ £C
Rosso di Montepulciano ★☆ £B

❀ Poggio San Polo (Montalcino) *www.poggiosanpolo.com*
Under the guidance of Silvia Fertonani this small but expanding Montalcino estate was one of the zone's rising stars. The original 5ha of San Polo are at 480m in the east of the zone and another 10 ha (Montheluc) have come on stream only since 2003. The good work started by the Fertonani family is now being continued by the ALLEGRINI family, one of the leading lights in the Veneto, who purchased the estate in 2007 and also own POGGIO AL TESORO in Bolgheri. Apart from the Brunello Riserva, of which only two vintages have been released (2004 and 2006), the only other new wine is Rubio, an entry level wine made mainly from Sangiovese, produced from 2006. Mezzo Pane, a powerful and complex blend of Sangiovese and Merlot, has shown a steady rise in quality, although it nonetheless misses the class of the Brunello. Good Rosso will be best with 5–6 years' age.

Recommended Reds:
Brunello di Montalcino ★★★★ £F
Mezzo Pane ★★★ £E   Rosso di Montalcino ★★ £D

❀ Poggio Scalette (Chianti Classico) *www.poggioscalette.com*
This small 12.5 ha estate was put together by top enologist Vittorio Fiore in the early 90s. Resurrecting an old vineyard with some very old vines he was able to expand the estate and keeps only the best grapes for Il Carbonaione. The wine has always been 100% Sangiovese and is a very fine example, with pure fruit, ample breadth and depth and lovely harmony. It has been consistently good since its first vintage in the difficult 1992 vintage. Though the

wine now qualifies as Chianti Classico, it retains IGT status as Alta Valle delle Greve, giving it some regional definition in the absence of Chianti Classico sub-zones. Piantonaia is a new varietal Merlot made since 03 and is now destined exclusively for the Enoteca Pinchiorri in Florence together with Richiari from Chardonnay . It is a bold Tuscan interpretation yet complex and without any hint of rusticity. Dark chocolate, carob and black plum lurk behind vanilla and blackberry essence that will show well with 10 years' or more. New, from 2007, is Capogatto, an equal blend of Cabernet Sauvignon Merlot, Cabernet Franc and Petit Verdot and a straight Chianti Classico (100% Sangiovese). Il Corto is the extra virgin olive oil.

Recommended Reds:
Il Carbonaione ★★★★★ £F   Piantonaia ★★★★ £F

Poggio al Solo (Chianti Classico) *www.poggioalsole.com*
Giovanni Davaz is one of a special group of Tuscan winemakers whose dedication in the vineyard and great care in maximising the potential of the grapes from a favoured site results in wines a breed apart from the increasing amounts of well-made wine in Tuscany. The 18 ha are in the vicinity of ANTINORI'S most famous vineyards. The majority of production is Chianti Classico, both a splendid, sleek, intense and stylish normale and a poised, elegant but graceful and beautifully defined Casasilia. There are also three concessions to international varieties: Trittico is a Merlot/Cabernet Sauvignon/Sangiovese blend made for early drinking while a Syrah, although lacking the concentration of a top Côte-Rôtie, has fine fruit and intensity and the length of flavour that characterises all the wines. A straight Cabernet Sauvignon is also made. Don't expect blockbusters or immediate gratification in these wines; instead, elegance triumphs over power. At least 3 years is needed for the regular Chianti Classico and 5 or more for the other wines.

Recommended Reds:
Chianti Classico Casasilia ★★★★ £E
Chianti Classico ★★★ £C
Syrah ★★★ £E   Trittico ★★ £B

Poggio di Sotto (Montalcino) *www.poggiodisotto.com*
This is a small carefully planned and researched organic estate located in the south-eastern corner of the Montalcino zone. Expertise was enlisted by the previous owner, Piero Palmucci, from the University of Milan and the highly respected Giulio Gambelli in an attempt to produce an authentic 'terroir-derived' expression of Brunello. To this end only large 25-35hl Slovenian oak is used for maturation. After a difficult start, these wines are now recognised as being amongst the appellation's finest. Whilst the Brunello and the Riserva have improved significantly over the years it is the Rosso that represents a great buy even with a significantly higher than average price tag for Rosso. Buy it instead of some of the more hyped commercial Brunellos available. There is a fine olive oil here too. In 2011, the estate was sold to Claudio and Maria Iris Tipa of COLLE MASARI and GRATTAMACCO who are committed to carrying on production here in the same vein.

Recommended Reds:
Brunello di Montalcino Riserva ★★★★★ £H
Brunello di Montalcino ★★★★☆ £G
Rosso di Montalcino ★★★☆ £E

>> Poggio al Tesoro (Bolgheri) *www.poggioaltesoro.it*
Poggio al Tesoro is a 70 ha property in Bolgheri acquired in 2002 by the ALLEGRINI family from the Veneto. Adjacent to the ORNELLAIA vineyard, the largest of the four vineyards owned by the estate, 'Le

Sondraie', situated just 35 metres above sea level, is where Merlot, Cabernet Franc, Cabernet Sauvignon, Syrah, Vermentino and a tiny amount of Petit Verdot are grown. The 'Solosole' Vermentino has become a bit of a cult Vermentino, zingy and vibrant, but can lack body in some years. The oldest vineyard, planted in 1994, 'Via Bolgherese' comprises 51% Cabernet Sauvignon and 49% Cabernet Franc, whilst 'Le Grottine' comprises 33% Cabernet Franc, 22% Cabernet Sauvignon and a whopping 45% Petit Verdot. The fourth vineyard, 'Valle di Cerbaia' was planted in 2008 with 34% Cabernet Franc, 33% cabernet Sauvignon and 33% Viognier. 'Mediterra' is their entry level red – 8 months in old oak - a blend of 40% Syrah, 30% Cabernet Sauvignon and 30% Merlot, displays easy drinking fresh fruit, whilst 'Sondraia' (65% Cabernet Sauvignon, 25% Merlot and 10% Cabernet Franc) spends 18 months in 50% new and 50% old oak has much more body with plenty of sweet fruit beneath the tannins. Some cellar ageing would be required here to get the best out of it. Top of the range is the 100% Cabernet Franc 'W Dedicato a Walter' (Walter Allegrini) – 18 month in new oak, again with nice sweet fruit and a long finish. 'Cassiopea' rosato is a one night stand between Merlot and Cabernet Franc, fruity but can finish a little short. The wines, by and large, have a good price/quality ratio. (NB)

Recommended Reds:
IGT Toscana 'W – Dedicato a Walter' ★★★★☆ £F
Bolgheri Superiore Sondraia ★★★★ £E
IGT Toscana 'Mediterra' ★★☆ £B
Recommended Whites:
Bolgheri Solosole ★★ £B
Recommended Rosés:
Bolgheri 'Cassiopea' ★★ £B

Poggio Uliveto (Chianti Classico) *www.fattoriapoggiopiano.it*
This estate forms part of the holdings of the amiable Conte GianLuigi Borghini Baldovinetti de' Bacci Venuti known collectively as Fattoria San Fabiano. Poggio Uliveto includes 20 ha of vineyards and from a new winery and cellar around 30,000 bottles of Vino Nobile are made. 10% of Canaiolo is included in the blend and a long maceration precedes ageing in both tonneaux and *barriques*. The resulting style is admirably balanced with lots of charm. Rosso di Montepulciano and Chianti Colli Senesi are also produced but haven't been tasted.
Recommended Reds:
Vino Nobile di Montepulciano ★★★ £D

Poggiopiano (Chianti Rufina) *www.fattoriapoggiopiano.it*
Not to be confused with Fattoria di Poggiopiano, this small property (Azienda Agricola Poggiopiano) is found in San Casciano Val di Pesa in the north-west of the Chianti Classico zone and is run by Stefano Bartoli and his brother Alessandro. Consultancy for the two wines comes from Luca D'Attoma. Most remarkable is the premium red, Rosso di Sera, which combines a high 15% of Colorino (an exciting grape but seldom used in a significant percentage) with Sangiovese. The wine has a delicious spicy, black-fruited depth and a lush texture but with a floral, cherry character that distinguishes it from less interesting efforts that include Merlot instead. A second vineyard now supplements the estate vineyards of only 9ha. The love of Colorino has led Stefano (from 2006) to produce a 100% version, Taffeta, whilst massively tannic and needing several years cellaring, nevertheless shows a lot of generosity of fruit and elegance underneath with great complexity. Mamma non M'ama is a Sangiovese IGT suplemented by a little Merlot wich completes the range. For more immediate drinking is a fine pure fruited Chianti Classico, with excellent breadth, intensity and depth.
Recommended Reds:
Taffeta ★★★★★ £G   Rosso di Sera ★★★★ £E
Chianti Classico ★★★ £C

Poliziano (Montepulciano) *www.carlettipoliziano.com*
In the past 2 decades Poliziano (named for the Renaissance poet, Politian) has been propelled to the top echelon of producers, not just in Montepulciano but in all of Tuscany, by its owner Federico Carletti. Assisted for a number of years by the brilliant Carlo Ferrini, he has given the wine range greater focus and taken the quality consistently higher. Most encouraging has been the quality of the regular Vino Nobile, with its atypical intensity and weight, which has continued to improve despite being made in increased quantities (in excess of 10,000 cases). However, it is the top two wines that are most exciting. Asinone, from a 9-ha vineyard, adds more breadth, complexity and sheer style over the regular version but with similar preserved cherry fruit intensity. Le Stanze is an outstanding Tuscan Cabernet Sauvignon with wonderful depth and intensity but also shows increasing elegance and style. Other wines include a Rosso di Montepulciano that is fuller and fleshier than any other versions and most resembles a good Chianti Classico normale. Elegia, was a fine oak-aged Sangiovese made until 1995. Poliziano's 120 ha of vineyard includes the Lohsa estate in the Maremma from which is produced very good Morellino di Scansano. It includes 15% Ciliegiolo and has a spicy, vibrant, pure fruit character and is adding more depth as new vines come on stream. Also from Lohsa is Mandrone di Lohsa (from 2001), a Cabernet Sauvignon-based wine that also includes Alicante and Petit Verdot.
Poliziano
Recommended Reds:
Le Stanze ★★★★☆ £F
Vino Nobile di Montepulciano Asinone ★★★★ £E
Vino Nobile di Montepulciano ★★★ £D
Rosso di Montepulciano ★☆ £B
Azienda Agricola Lohsa
Recommended Reds:
Morellino di Scansano ★★★ £D

Querceto di Castellina (Chianti Classico) *www.querceto.com*
The first wines were only produced here in 1999 having previously sold in bulk. Progress has been guided by consultant Gioia Cresti and 10ha of stony vineyards at 420-450m have been extensively replanted with new clones. From three varieties - Sangiovese, Merlot and Ciliegiolo - are produced just two modern style reds. In Chianti Classico L'Aura is now 95% Sangiovese and 5% Merlot. The wine spends 14 months in mostly used *barriques* and has an appealing, seductive quality. From 2006, a Riserva has been produced upping the quantity of Merlot to 10% giving it that much more roundness and depth. Podalirio started out as a predominantly Sangiovese blend topped up with Merlot (99, 2000 and 01) after a transitional 03 as an equal blend of the two varieties, it is now 100% Merlot with good purity, intensity and a touch of minerality. The Chiantis deserve 3-5 years while Podalirio should be given at least 6-8 years. Cinque (since 2008) is an unoaked entry level Sangiovese for early drinking whilst a small production of white, Livia (since 2010), 50% Viognier and 50% Roussanne looks interesting but has not yet been tasted.
Recommended Reds:
Podalirio ★★★☆ £E   Chianti Classico Riserva Belvedere ★★★ £E
Chianti Classico L'Aura ★★☆ £C

Tuscany

Italy

⚫ Querciabella (Chianti Classico) *www.querciabella.com*
One of Chianti Classico's grand estates, now fully organic and
biodynamic, Querciabella is run by Sebastiano (son of its founder
Giuseppe) Castiglioni, who is gently guided by winemaker Guido
De Santi. The range from 26ha of vineyards was until recently
restricted to just four wines. All the wines have a certain strength as
well as individuality – the structure amply supports a considerable
richness of fine intense fruit (from low yields). Chianti Classico
includes 5% Cabernet Sauvignon and retains a distinctive Tuscan
character. Palafreno (first made in 2000), is a rich, refined Merlot. In
fact this is made to a similar standard to the deservedly acclaimed
red Camartina, a wine of great class and intensity currently from
70% Sangiovese and 30% Cabernet Sauvignon. It is not made when
the quality is not up to scratch. Batàr, from Chardonnay and Pinot
Bianco is a rich, powerful, complex white with an almost exotic
fruit character. Earlier vintages were sometimes a little overblown
but there has been less oak and more elegance since 1998 yet it
is still not unlike a bold full-on Pouilly-Fuissé in character. Of the
reds, even the Chianti Classico needs 3 years' ageing or more,
Palafreno at least 5-6 years while Camartina deserves 8-10 years.
Look out for new wines from 36ha of vineyards at Alberese in the
Maremma. Mongrana IGT Maremma Toscana is a spicy, racy blend
of Sangiovese, Merlot and Cabernet Sauvignon, great to drink
whilst the more serious wines are waiting to come round. New
(since 2007) is Turpino, a blend of Cabernet Franc, Syrah and Merlot,
sourced equally from vineyards in both the Quercibella estates.
Recommended Reds:
Camartina ★★★★★ £F   Palafreno ★★★★☆ £F
Chianti Classico ★★☆ £C   Mongrana ★★☆ £C
Recommended Whites:
Batàr ★★★☆ £E

Rampa di Fugnano (San Gimignano) *www.rampadifugnano.it*
This Swiss owned estate is run along organic lines and rates
amongst San Gimignano's best. With only 10ha, volumes are quite
modest but working with consultant Paolo Caciorgna there is good
quality across the range - something few others in the zone achieve.
Regular Vernaccia di San Gimignano, Alata is a decent flavoursome
example while Privato can add a little more style and depth. Viognier
too is well-made with decent varietal character without becoming
heavy or oily. All should be drunk fairly young. The reds are more
interesting if relatively restrained. Beyond a supple, typical Chianti
(Sangiovese/Canaiolo) with good ripeness, there's varietal examples
of both Sangiovese and Merlot. Bombereto, the Sangiovese,
achieves good purity and intensity, particularly in the best years. The
star though is Gisèle which needs 6-10 years' age. With breadth and
elegance it is a stylish expression of Tuscan Merlot, only lacking a
little extra richness to be really fine. A Vin Santo, Topazio is also made
as is organic olive oil (labelled Poggialbosco).
Recommended Reds:
Gisèle ★★★☆ £E   Bombereto ★★☆ £D
Chianti Colli Senesi Via dei Franchi ★☆ £B
Recommended Whites:
Vernaccia di San Gimignano Privato ★★☆ £C
Vernaccia di San Gimignano Alata ★☆ £B   Vi Ogni è ★☆ £C

Ricasoli/ Castello di Brolio (Chianti Classico) *www.ricasoli.it*
This noble property had a rough ride under corporate ownership for
a couple of decades until it was re-acquired in 1993 by the Ricasoli
family, led by Francesco Ricasoli. Brolio's importance in the modern
era (Baron Bettino Ricasoli set out the parameters for Chianti

Classico in the 1870s) added more clout to a decision taken 4 years
later to establish a flagship Chianti Classico in a move to try to
restore the pre-eminence of its name in the zone. The wine is made
from 100% Sangiovese from a selection of the best vineyards and
aged in predominantly new French oak. Successive vintages, if quite
oaky, are increasingly expansive and stylish. As the vineyards (the
vast estate includes 227 ha of vines) continue to improve, so should
the wine. A Gran Selezione, Colledila, whilst not actually a Riserva, is
made from vines in selected plots on the estate and marketed as a
limited edition wine. That labelled simply Brolio and Brolio Riserva
are selected from the vast majority of Ricasoli's holding in Gaiole
and are 80% Sangiovese, 15% Merlot and 5% Cabernet Sauvignon.
Casalferro now 100% Merlot), produced from a single vineyard of
that name in Gaiole, is a consistently impressive red which shows
typical concentration, intensity and ageing potential. A classic nutty,
biscuity Vin Santo is also made under the Castello di Brolio label.
Some labels include wine from bought-in grapes, such as Rocca
Giucciardia (Chanti Classico), Campo Ceni (Sangiovese, Merlot and
Cabernet Sauvignon from young vines) and Torricella, *barrique-*
aged Chardonnay of increasing refinement while other wines of
improving quality include the inexpensive Formulae, based on
Sangiovese.
Recommended Reds:
Chianti Classico Castello di Brolio ★★★☆ £E
Chianti Classico Brolio ★★☆ £C
Chianti Classico Riserva Rocca Guicciarda ★ £C
Casalferro ★★★ £E
Recommended Whites:
Vin Santo Castello di Brolio ★★★ £D   Torricella ★★ £C

Riecine (Chianti Classico) *www.riecine.com*
Owned for more than two decades by Englishman John Dunkley,
this small jewel already had a considerable reputation before
coming under the control of American Gary Baumann in 1996/7.
Dunkley had the good fortune, in 1971, to buy a vineyard already
planted to a remarkably high-quality clone of Sangiovese and
further small increases in vineyard area from sites scattered around
the Gaiole commune have brought in more good fruit. The
wines, long made by Sean O'Callaghan have always shown great
concentration, intensity and a purity and elegance that have set
them apart from most examples. More recently they have shed
some of the austerity that some tasters found overwhelming,
though they were never intended to be drunk in their youth. The
wines will still age very well but now have a richer texture and
greater suppleness. Chianti Classico is still best with three to five
years' ageing, Riserva and La Gioia (also Sangiovese) with 6–10,
sometimes more. The stampede to the Maremma has even seduced
Riecine and La Gioia has been produced from Montecucco fruit.
Though not cheap, Riecine prices have always been a fair reflection
of quality.
Recommended Reds:
La Gioia ★★★★ £F   Chianti Classico Riserva ★★★★ £E
Chianti Classico ★★★ £D

Rocca di Castagnoli (Chianti Classico) *www.roccadicastagnoli.it*
This is an impressive estate and castello in the commune of Gaiole
with a well established track record for Chianti Classico Riserva and
other premium wines. Recently the wines have become even better.
Each one is named for the vineyard or vineyards it comes from.
Poggio a' Frati, the Riserva, (95% Sangiovese, 5% Canaiolo) is aged
in large barrels. Stielle, a Sangiovese/Cabernet Sauvignon blend

(80/20) is the best of the three non-Classico premium reds. Buriano is straight Cabernet Sauvignon and Le Pratola 100% Merlot; neither lack for ripe, intense fruit or character. Dry white Molino delle Balze is a Chardonnay at the riper end of the spectrum but is well balanced. Vin Santo is also good with a classic character and a restrained oxidative influence. Capraia used to be one of the Riservba wines of the Castagnoni estate, but latterly is labelled separately both as a regular Chianti Classico (90% Sangiovese and 10% Canaiolo) and as a Riserva (100% Sangiovese). A second estate, San Sano, is also in Gaiole but a little way south-west of the Castagnoli vineyards, near Lecchi. Here regular Chianti Classico includes a 10% Canaiolo and Vigneti della Rana 10% Ciliegio, while Borro al fumo is a similar blend to Stielle. All miss a little vigour and definition but show promise. Other wines produced are a Morellino di Scansano, Spiaggiole, from the Poggio Maestrino Estate in the Maremma and Nera d'Avola and Syrah from the recently acquired Poggio Graffetta Estate in Sicily

Rocca di Castagnoli
Recommended Reds:

Stielle ★★★★ £E Buriano ★★★ £E Le Pratola ★★★ £E
Chianti Classico Riserva Capraia ★★★ £D
Chianti Classico Riserva Poggio a' Frati ★★☆ £D
Chianti Classico Capraia ★★ £C Chianti Classico ★☆ £B

Recommended Whites:

Vin Santo del Chianti Classico ★★★ £E Molino delle Balze ★★ £C

Castello San Sano
Recommended Reds:

Borroalfumo ★★☆ £E Chianti Classico Vigneti della Rana ★★☆ £C
Chianti Classico ★☆ £B

✿ Rocca di Montegrossi *www.roccadimontegrossi.it*
Marco Ricasoli's 20 ha of vineyards were cleaved from those of CASTELLO DI CACCHIANO (under the control of his brother Giovanni) in the mid-nineties. They are related to the Ricasoli family of the area's most famous estate, Castello di Brolio (see RICASOLI). Ever finer Chianti Classico (Sangiovese with 5% Canaiolo and 5% Colorino) and Riserva (95% Sangiovese 5% Pugnitello) are becoming classic pure Tuscan wines. Geremia, 100% Sangiovese up to and including 98, but since the 01 vintage transformed to a Merlot and Cabernet Sauvignon blend (65/35). This emphasis on establishing the purity and typicity of Chianti Classico has set an example that more and more are following. There is real distinction to the bright, vibrant fruit character in these composed, refined wines, as well as a depth and structure that ensure they age well. Regular Chianti Classico needs 2–3 years' ageing, the Riserva five years and most vintages of Geremia need closer to 10 years. Marvellously rich Vin Santo is made in very small quantities. The vineyards have been farmed organically since 2006 and have been certified organic since 2010. Insomma, a first-division estate and one to follow.

Recommended Reds:

Geremia ★★★★☆ £F
Chianti Classico Riserva San Marcellino ★★★★ £E
Chianti Classico ★★★ £C

Recommended Whites:

Vin Santo ★★★★☆ £F

Romeo (Montepulciano) *www.massimoromeo.it*
Just 20,000 bottles of wine are made from this small estate. Its owner, Massimo Romeo is the current president of the Vino Nobile Consorzio. His wines are from the part of his property called Podere Corsica. Although there are 6 ha of vineyards, some are in the

process of being replanted. Regular Vino Nobile with 5% each of Canaiolo and Mammolo has good character usually with sufficient ripeness, plenty of extract and firm acidity. Particularly impressive is Lipitiresco which includes 10% Colorino and another 5% from Canaiolo and Mammolo. Slightly uncompromising when young with a mineral and red and black fruits intensity and some oak influence, it is worth keeping 8-10 years. Also made are a Riserva dei Mandorli, Rosso di Montepulciano and a Malvasia dominated Vin Santo only released with 10 years' age.

Recommended Reds:

Vino Nobile di Montepulciano Lipitiresco ★★★☆ £E
Vino Nobile di Montepulciano ★★★ £C

Ruffino *www.ruffino.com*
One of the most famous Tuscan houses, Ruffino was divided in 2000 (see Ambrogio e Giovanni FOLONARI) and some of its prized vineyards, including those of the Nozzole estate, have been lost. Yet there are still great swathes of vineyard scattered around the leading wine zones. Vino Nobile di Montepulciano Lodola Nuova is not overly concentrated but shows some of the character of the appellation and is better in a Riserva. Brunello from Il Greppone Mazzi can be an attractive, savoury example but not is not consistently so. Riserva is supple and savoury. The real excitement comes from the Chianti Classico zone, which produces a wine of great class and breadth in top vintages, Riserva Ducale Oro. Slightly old-fashioned in style, it needs at least 5–8 years' age but can last considerably longer. That without the gold (Oro) label is not of the same standard. Better still is Romitorio di Santedame (Colorino/Sangiovese), a highly original wine of great character and superb fruit but needing similar age to the Oro. Following the loss of the Cabreo wines, a new Chardonnay, Il Solatio, has been added. Modus is a relatively new red combining Sangiovese, Cabernet Sauvignon and Merlot with good balance and increasing style. Ruffino also makes an attractive white, Libaio (Chardonnay with a little Pinot Grigio) and the large-volume Chianti Classico Aziano. Constellation Wines took a 40% interest in Ruffino late in 2004 and acquired the rest of the company in 2011.

Tenimenti Ruffino
Recommended Reds:

Romitorio di Santedame ★★★★★ £G Modus ★★★ £F
Chianti Classico Riserva Ducale Oro ★★★★ £E
Chianti Classico Riserva Ducale ★★ £D
Chianti Classico Santedame ★★ £C

Il Greppone Mazzi
Recommended Reds:

Brunello di Montalcino Riserva ★★★ £F
Brunello di Montalcino ★ £E

Lodola Nuova
Recommended Reds:

Vino Nobile di Montepulciano Riserva ★★☆ £E
Vino Nobile di Montepulciano ★★ £E

Russo (Val di Cornia) *www.vinirusso.it*
If viticulture comes second to rearing cattle at this small estate, vinification is nonetheless given serious consideration, as the grapes are transformed into a pair of very appealing, seductive reds by consultant enologist Alberto Antonini. Sassobucato, from Merlot and Cabernet Sauvignon (70/30), has a distinctive black plum, cured meats and herb aroma, and is full and round with pristine sweet fruit. Barbicone Riserva (80% Sangiovese and the rest from Ciliego,

Tuscany

Cannaiolo, Giacomino and Colorino) reveals smoke, plum, cherry and herbs as well as a lush, supple texture. Ceppitaio is made in greater quantities and is more variable but at its best is ripe and characterful.

Recommended Reds:
Val di Cornia Riserva Barbicone ★★★★ £E
Val di Cornia Ceppitaio ★★ £B
Sassobucato ★★★★ £E

Salicutti (Montalcino) www.poderesalicutti.it
This small Montalcino estate has just 4 ha from four parcels of elevated vineyards (450–480m). A mixture of both tonneaux and larger oak are used and the wine is neither fined or filtered. Production is organic from low-yielding vines and the fruit quality can be very impressive. However, beyond this there is not the anticipated breadth nor always the purity or balance that its reputation suggests and most vintages also want for a little more refinement in the tannins. Yet clearly there is the potential here for a great Brunello. Dopoteatro, a Cabernet Sauvignon, includes 10% of Canaiolo.

Recommended Reds:
Brunello di Montalcino ★★★ £F
Rosso di Montalcino ★★ £D   Dopoteatro ★★ £E

❀ Salvioni/ La Cerbaiona (Montalcino) www.aziendasalvioni.com
This classic handmade Brunello of great elegance and complexity is made in small quantities but such is its quality and expression of Montalcino-grown Sangiovese that it deserves to be tasted at least once. Given the dedication of its makers, Giulio Salvioni and his son Davide, there is no need to track down the most raved-about vintage either, as the quality of the wines from the mid-1990s is being maintained. Traditionally produced without any new oak, the wine undergoes a long maceration followed by around two years in large Slavonian oak casks. The wine is rich, deep and powerful with superb texture and definition and great expression both in aroma and flavour. The elevated 2.26 ha site of Cerbaiola usually yields little more than 5,000 bottles a year but quantities are vintage-dependent as the production of a little Rosso is used to help maintain the very high standards.

Recommended Reds:
Brunello di Montalcino ✪✪✪✪✪ £G
Rosso di Montalcino ★★★ £E

San Fabiano (Chianti Classico) www.sanfabianocalcinaia.it
Cellole is one of two estates that make up 34 ha of vineyard; the second, San Fabiano, is at lower altitude and 10 km from Castellina. Top consultant Carlo Ferrini has helped raise the quality of the reds. His hand is most evident in Cerviolo Rosso, a very worthy flagship wine. It is now 90% Sangiovese mixed with 10% of other grapes and is nevertheless a very distinguished red of excellent concentration and density. Old vine fruit, earth and mineral notes add class and complexity. Regular Chianti Classico, aged only in one- and two-year oak is typically supple and stylish. The Riserva is potentially a lush, flattering red but is marked by too much oak in recent vintages. A Chardonnay is also made but the balance isn't quite right yet in this either. A Cabernet Sauvignon with 10% Petit Verdot is also produced but has not been tasted.

Recommended Reds:
Cerviolo Rosso ★★★★ £E   Chianti Classico Riserva ★★ £E
Chianti Classico ★★ £C

San Felice (Chianti Classico) www.agricolasanfelice.com
The property of insurance company Reunione Adriatica Sicurtà, this grand estate with 200 ha of vines is noted for its experiments with Sangiovese and other grapes (especially native varieties). During a long period of development under Enzo Morganti, both Vigorello, a blend of Cabernet Sauvignon,(50%) Merlot (45%) and Petit Verdot and a single-vineyard Chianti Classico Riserva Poggio Rosso (containing 10% of Colorino and 10% Pugnitello) were created. Both wines can be long-lived, intense and stylish. A second Chianti Classico Riserva, Il Grigio, made in much greater quantities, is not of comparable quality but can offer a dense, chewy mouthful. The regular Chianti Classico, though a big-volume wine (50,000 cases), can show good fruit and perfume, especially in good vintages. A Chardonnay, Ancherona, is also made, as well as a 100% Pugnitello. Also included in San Felice's production are 14ha of vineyards of the Campogiovanni estate in Montalcino from which some complex, expansive Brunello has also been produced. The rating applies to top examples only. A little Riserva Il Quercione is also made while the Rosso is intense and vibrant. In the Maremma, two reds and a Vermentino are produced but these have not yet been tasted.
San Felice
Recommended Reds:
Vigorello ★★ £E   Chianti Classico Riserva Poggio Rosso ★★ £C
Campogiovanni
Recommended Reds:
Brunello di Montalcino ★★★★☆ £F   Rosso di Montalcino ★★☆ £C

San Giusto a Rentennano www.fattoriasangiusto.it
This is a much venerated Chianti Classico estate run by brothers Francesco and Luca Martini di Cigala and all the wines are made to a very high standard. The focus is very much on Sangiovese and as natural as possible an expression of it. The wines are particularly notable for strength allied to an intense preserved fruits quality which makes for complex, classy wines with the necessary age. In top years even the Chianti Classico normale shows these attributes and easily surpasses some of the more expensive offerings. The Riserva (labelled as Le Baroncole since 2000) is more muscular but shows exquisite fruit and great length and is only bettered by the premium Sangiovese, Percarlo, made from 5.5 ha of the estate's 30 ha of vineyards. This big, structured wine is made from very ripe fruit and subject to long ageing in *barrique* (more than 50% new). It more closely resembles a top Brunello in style than most wines from the Classico zone and has a great track record. There's also an outstanding, wonderfully complex example of Vin Santo (based primarily on Malvasia) and from recent vintages a varietal blockbuster Merlot, La Ricolma, aged in 100% new oak, but quantities of both are minuscule. Regular Chianti Classico excepted, don't drink any of the wines with less than six years' age; 10 or more is often better. Prices are very fair.

Recommended Reds:
Percarlo ★★★★ £F   La Ricolma ★★★★ £F
Chianti Classico Riserva Le Baroncole ★★★★ £E
Chianti Classico ★★★☆ £C
Recommended Whites:
Vin Santo ★★★★ £F

San Vincenti (Chianti Classico) www.sanvincenti.it
Roberto Pucci works closely with enologist Carlo Ferrini to produce fine modern-style Chianti Classico and a single premium red, Stignano, from his 10 ha of south-facing vineyards. Chianti Classico is 100% Sangiovese and is ripe and concentrated with sufficient

extract to require another 2–4 years' ageing. A vibrant, powerful, minerally Riserva is very good indeed with more depth than most. Stignano is now 50% Sangiovese and 50% Merlot and is intense and concentrated, its black plum, spice and mineral fruit infused with oak. Relatively backward when young, it develops to become deeply seductive with age. Both top two reds need 6–8 years' age or more.

Recommended Reds:
Stignano ★★★★ £E
Chianti Classico Riserva ★★★☆ £D
Chianti Classico ★★★ £C

Sangervasio (Terre di Pisa) *www.sangervasio.com*
Sangervasio is just one of several estates in the Pisa hills earning credibility for this zone relatively close to the Tuscan coast. Part of a large estate, 22 ha of vineyards are cultivated biodynamically and planting densities are being radically increased. The great potential here seems certain to be realised by Luca Tomassini, who currently employs top consultant Luca D'Attoma (who works at LE MACCHIOLE among others) to produce two intense, tightly structured reds. A Sirio is Sangiovese-based but including 5% Cabernet Sauvignon while I Renai is oaky, powerful Merlot with a lot of extract but good ageing potential. Both wines need at least five years to show at their best. A second wine, Sangervasio (from Sangiovese, Merlot and Cabernet not used for the top reds) has been made since 2002. Also produced are Vin Santo, Recinaio, a dry white, a Cabernet Sauvignon, a Chardonnay and a Chianti.

Recommended Reds:
A Sirio ★★★ £E   I Renai ★★★ £E   Sangervasio ★ £B

Enrico Santini (Bolgheri) *www.enricosantini.it*
Enrico Santini has 10 ha in Bolgheri and is its most interesting new star. His first vintage was in 2000 and the vines are young but the leading wine, Montepergoli, is worth contrasting with the zone's heavyweights. Advice from near neighbour Michele SATTA and consultancy from Attilio Pagli have helped in producing a profound red of real vigour and intensity and lovely berry fruit aroma and flavour. The blend is mostly Cabernet Sauvignon, Merlot and Syrah with a little Sangiovese. The latter contributes more to an excellent spicy, perfumed second wine, Poggio al Moro, that represents much better value than equivalent wines from other Bolgheri producers. Both reds also show a refinement that Satta's can lack. A third red, I Montali, is a special selection made at the time of blending of 30% Merlot, 30% Cabernet Sauvignon, 20% Syrah and 20% Sangiovese, and is not made every year. Santini's white has good weight but could be more focused; from Sauvignon (30%) and Vermentino (70%), the latter seems to contribute more to its character.

Recommended Reds:
Bolgheri Rosso Montepergoli ★★★★ £E
Bolgheri Rosso Poggio al Moro ★★★ £D
Recommended Whites:
Bolgheri Bianco Campo alla Casa ★ £C

✿ Sassicaia/Tenuta San Guido (Bolgheri) *www.tenutasanguido.com*
Much has been written about what is arguably Italy's single most famous wine, including a book by Marco Fini. Currently directed by Sebastiano Rosa, its production has been much expanded from the original elevated Castiglioncello vineyard that provided the first commercial and much celebrated vintage, 1968. The vast San Guido estate now has about 60 ha of vineyards spread over four main plots, resulting in a production in excess of 12,000 cases

a year. The wine, for long sold as a vino da tavola, has since 1994 had its own special zone in the Bolgheri DOC, which the Marchese has done much to promote. It is now a blend of 85% Cabernet Sauvignon and 15% Cabernet Franc and is aged for up to two years in French *barriques* (a third new). The 5 star rating applies only to outstanding vintages and, while efforts in the 1990s generally don't match exceptional vintages like 1985, most years and particularly throughout the 2000s still reveal a beautifully composed wine with a delicious sweet black fruits intensity and elegant complexity that is sustained on a very long finish. Five years' ageing is a minimum, the best will improve for 20 or more. A second wine, Guidalberto, first made in the 2000 vintage, is more modestly priced and from different vineyards. This has been joined by a third and economically priced red, Le Difese. Composed of Merlot, Cabernet Sauvignon and Sangiovese, it is aged for 12 months in *barriques* and shows cool fruit and some sophistication.

Recommended Reds:
Bolgheri Sassicaia ★★★★★ £H   Guidalberto ★★★ £E

Michele Satta (Bolgheri) *www.michelesatta.com*
Michele Satta isn't one of Bolgheri's big names but makes some good wines from 30 ha of vineyards. Piastraia is the top wine, a blend of Sangiovese, Cabernet Sauvignon, Merlot and Syrah. It doesn't lack for extract or depth but sometimes wants for more refined tannins. Nonetheless it is usually full, complex and characterful. Cavaliere (previously Vigna al Cavaliere) is unusual in the zone in being pure Sangiovese and, if again characterful, it can be more angular than Piastraia. I Castagni is a single vineyard blend of 70% Cabernet Sauvignon, 20% Syrah and 10% Teroldego maturing for 24 months in *barriques* and then a further 18 months in bottle before release. It's a deep and unctuous wine, with the Teroldego giving the tannins some extra softness. Whites have always been important: Costa di Giulia, from Vermentino and Sauvignon, is aromatic and attractive if no more; Giovin Re, a varietal Viognier, is very ripe and oak-influenced but lacks the structure and definition of good Condrieu. Basic Bolgheri Rosato and Rosso are also produced.

Recommended Reds:
I Castagni ★★★ £F   Bolgheri Rosso Piastraia ★★★ £E
Cavaliere ★★ £E
Recommended Whites:
Giovin Re ★★ £E   Costa di Giulia ★ £B

Fattoria Selvapiana (Chianti Rufina) *www.selvapiana.it*
For years this noble estate, in the Giuntini family since 1827, was the only rival to FRESCOBALDI's Nipozzano estate in the small but exciting zone of Chianti Rufina. The combination of energy and austerity in the wines when young can seem daunting to wine drinkers used to soft, oak-rich reds but there is both a purity to the fruit and refinement in the wines that sets them apart from all but the best Chianti Classico. From 25 ha of vineyards, Federico Masseti and consultant Franco Bernabei have been producing very good wines for a number of years, especially a single-vineyard Riserva Bucerchiale. It shows great intensity and depth but always deserves to be kept for at least six or seven years and will keep for as long again. A second single-vineyard wine, Fornace (previously sold as Chianti Rufina Riserva), contains an increasing amount of Cabernet Sauvignon and is more obvious and fleshy but with good complexity. Vin Santo is very good too with rich ripe fruit and a refined nutty complexity while olive oil is another star product here.

Italy

Recommended Reds:
Chianti Rufina Riserva Bucerchiale ★★★★ £E
Fornace ★★★☆ £E Chianti Rufina ★★☆ £C
Recommended Whites:
Vin Santo ★★★★ £E

Sesta di Sopra (Montalcino) www.sestadisopra.it
If you're on the trail of leading small Brunello estates don't pass over this one, approximately halfway between Castelnuovo dell'Abate and Sant'Angelo in Colle. Assuming you find there's any wine left of course given production is restricted to just 2 ha of vineyard, resulting in only 4000 bottles of Brunello. 1999 was the first Brunello and has been followed by promising examples since. Although firmly structured and powerful there is impressive underlying purity and intensity that should reward those prepared to wait 10-15 years' (for a potentially 5-star wine). A riserva has been produced only in magnums for the 2004 vintage but in bottles for subsequent vintages. The small scale of the operation must facilitate a quality-led approach and the calibre of the fruit can also be seen in a seductive, concentrated modern-style Rosso.
Recommended Reds:
Brunello di Montalcino ★★★★☆ £F Rosso di Montalcino ★★★ £D

Sesti (Montalcino) www.sestiwine.com
From the Castello di Argiano, Sesti's wines have sometimes verged on the rustic but nonetheless show real intensity and depth. Ageing is traditional, involving 4 years (5 for Riserva) in cask with a stay in both large and smaller oak. The wines show lighter, more evolved colours (but there is at least no suspicion of manipulation) and are sometimes more developed and less concentrated than other examples yet there is always very impressive flavour and definite class especially in the expansive and complex Riserva. Terra di Siena is an intense, characterful blend of Cabernet Sauvignon and Merlot, while the less expensive Monteleccio is a light, supple, fragrant rendition of Sangiovese with spiced red fruits. The owner's passion for astronomy is reflected in the labels. Sesti olive oil (4-star) is vigorous and peppery, retaining its freshness well.
Recommended Reds:
Brunello di Montalcino Riserva Phenomena ★★★★ £F
Brunello di Montalcino ★★★☆ £F Rosso di Montalcino ★★ £C
Terra di Siena ★★★ £E Monteleccio ★★ £C

Sette Ponti (Colli Aretini) www.tenutasetteponti.it
This is a very slick and professional operation which has produced fabulous wines from the eastern side of the Valdarno in a very short space of time. Some 64 ha of vineyards are a mix of new and well-established plantings. The estimable Carlo Ferrini is the consultant winemaker. Oreno is now from Merlot, Cabernet Sauvignon and Petit Verdot. Crognolo, produced in slightly greater quantity, is 90% Sangiovese with the balance from Merlot and Cabernet Sauvignon. Both are rich yet gently textured wines with a beautifully detailed fruit intensity. Oreno, as might be expected, is the more international of the two but is concentrated and very harmonious; Crognolo expresses more of its origins in a sweet-fruited expression of Sangiovese. An unwooded Sangiovese, Vigna di Pallino is an attractive, cherryish base wine. New from the southern Maremma are the Poggio al Lupo wines. Morellino di Scansano has a full 15% Alicante. More promising is a dense, extracted estate blend that is three-quarters Cabernet Sauvignon with 20% Merlot and some Petit Verdot. Also worth looking out are the wines of FEUDO MACCARI from Noto in the south-east corner of Sicily.

Sette Ponti
Recommended Reds:
Oreno ★★★★ £F Crognolo ★★★☆ £D
Vigna di Pallino ★ £B
Poggio al Lupo
Recommended Reds:
Poggio al Lupo ★★★ £E Morellino di Scansano ★★ £C

Solaria (Montalcino) www.solariacencioni.com
Patrizia Cencioni is one of a growing band of women producing high-quality wines in Montalcino. Her lush, supple, very accessible Brunello and Rosso from 9 ha of vineyards are neither 'made' nor too modern. Brunello is not excessively powerful or weighty but has plenty of substance, good character and balance. Consistency is also impressive with no weakness in the Brunello and across recent vintages of the perfumed, stylish Rosso. New from 01 is a special selection of Brunello called simply '123'. This is going to require some patience but has great potential. Also made is Solarianne, from Cabernet Sauvignon and Sangiovese - gutsy and powerful. Prices are more reasonable than for other wines of similar quality.
Recommended Reds:
Brunello di Montalcino ★★★★ £E Rosso di Montalcino ★★☆ £C
Solarianne ★★★☆ £E

Soldera (Montalcino) www.soldera.it
Gianfranco Soldera's estate of just 8ha is Brunello's most controversial. Sourced from some of Montalcino's best slopes (next to Gaja's PIEVE SANTA RESTITUTA), the grapes are grown organically with great effort going into not only maximising the fruit quality but also enriching the ecosystem. The winemaking is natural, with no temperature control, and a long and rigorous maceration precedes a stay of (often) more than five years in large oak *botti*. The resulting wines of, at times, extraordinary breadth and complexity can make most modern-styled efforts seem rather simplistic and one-dimensional. In certain vintages Riservas are now produced from the two different vineyards of Intistieti and Case Basse but these are not released until 6–7 years after the vintage. In other years a single Brunello is produced (designated Riserva if considered worthy). Problems of stability due to high levels of volatility have occasionally been an issue in the past, but the greatest dilemma for most would-be drinkers is which car to sell in order to buy a case or two. (£H).

Sorbaiano (Montescudaio) www.fattoriasorbaiano.it
Montescudaio perhaps isn't that familiar to wine drinkers, even to fans of Tuscan wines. But think coastal Maremma for this zone lies between the Pisa stars and those of Bolgheri. Sorbaiano and Poggio Gagliardo are established leading estates (others of note include Aione, La Regola and Merlini). The emphasis here has been on Sangiovese with consistently excellent results in the distinctive Rosso delle Miniere which unusually adds in 30% Cabernet Franc and 10% Malvasia Nera. Pian di Conte is a varietal Sangiovese while from 2003 is Febo from Merlot. which has delicious blackberry and mineral purity, lots of extract but good balance and real promise. The estate's leading white is Lucestraia which adds 20% Vermentino and 30% Chardonnay to Trebbiano. A vibrant spice, peach, melon and grapefruit character just manages to restrain an oak influence from six months in *barrique*. The structure is good but drink with just two years' age. Basic Montescudaio red and white, Sangiovese and Trebbiano based respectively, offer good fruit and flavour at the price. Vin Santo and olive oil are also made. There is also ample accomodation here for those looking for a central base from which

to explore the coastal strip.
Recommended Reds:
Febo ★★★★ £E Montescudaio Rosso Rosso delle Miniere ★★★☆ £D
Pian di Conte ★★☆ £C Montescudaio Rosso ★☆ £B
Recommended Whites:
Montescudaio Bianco Lucestraia ★★☆ £C
Montescudaio Bianco ★☆ £B

Talenti (Montalcino) *www.talentimontalcino.it*

Riccardo Talenti's father was one of those instrumental in creating a worldwide reputation for Brunello. Pierluigi Talenti created his own estate in 1980 after receiving great acclaim for the Brunello of IL POGGIONE and has been a reliable source of fine Brunello ever since. Now with 20 ha of vines, Riccardo works with enologist Carlo Ferrini and early indications are of even better wines. Ageing is in a mix of tonneaux and larger barrels. The wines show classic character, breadth and style with nicely covered tannins and will maintain the reputation for ageing very well. Riserva, now designated Vigna del Paretaio (coming from a 2 ha vineyard) might be kept for 10 years or more. Rosso is intense and expressive and good with just 3-5 years' age. The reasonably priced Trefolo is a fruit-centred blend of Sangiovese, Syrah, Cabernet and Merlot, whilst Rispollo is a more serious blend of Cabernet Sauvignon Merlot and Petit Verdot. Fine olive oil is light and spicy.
Recommended Reds:
Brunello di Montalcino Riserva Vigna del Paretaio ★★★★☆ £G
Brunello di Montalcino ★★★★☆ £F
Rosso di Montalcino ★★☆ £C Trefolo ★★ £C

Terrabianca (Chianti Classico) *www.terrabianca.com*

Roberto Guldener's Terrabianca is a great source of consistent, supple and stylish reds from 52 ha of vineyards. To an extent style seems to triumph over substance with the emphasis on supple textures and drinkability but the best wines are also intense, complex and individual. There is no lack of expertise as consultancy comes from Vittorio Fiore and Remigio Bordini (viticulture). Ceppate, from Cabernet Sauvignon and Merlot, has a refined complexity with plummy fruits and cured meats. Campaccio instead combines Sangiovese with Cabernet (70/30) in a blend that is soft but distinctive with a little age; the Riserva version (50/50) is deeper and more oaky. Piano del Cipresso, with its crushed small red fruits and oak-enhanced complexity, is 100% Sangiovese and arguably the most authentic of these wines. 80% comes from from Chianti Classico vineyards and the rest from Maremma, so it is sold as an IGT. Chianti Classico Riserva Croce, though sometimes lacking intensity and depth, is also distinctly Tuscan. Other wines include Il Tesoro (Merlot from the southern Maremma), a sweet white from dried grapes, Il Fior di Fino, and a more everyday Chianti Classico, Scassino. There isn't an entirely logical relationship between quality and prices – which are perhaps as indicative of international demand as of intrinsic quality.
Recommended Reds:
Campaccio Riserva ★★★ £F Campaccio ★★ £E
Ceppate ★★★ £F Piano del Cipresso ★★★ £E
Chianti Classico Riserva Croce ★★ £C

Tornesi (Montalcino) *www.brunellotornesi.it*

This small unsung 7 ha Montalcino estate lies immediately north of the township. Consultant Paolo Vagaggini ensures a good balance between traditional and modern approaches to winemaking. The Rosso is partially *barrique*-aged while new medium to large (13-

25hl) Slavonian oak is used for the Brunello. Rosso can be drunk quite young while the round and fruit-centred Brunello is a good medium-term prospect. The Riserva is a much longer term prospect. Quantities are modest and prices are very reasonable both relative to the quality and vis-à-vis other producers.
Recommended Reds:
Brunello di Montalcino ★★★★ £F
Brunello di Montalcino Riserva ★★★★☆ £G
Rosso di Montalcino ★★☆ £D

❀ Tenuta di Trinoro *www.tenutaditrinoro.it*

From high up in the hills, a little way south of Montepulciano, is one of Tuscany's most isolated new estates - created by Andrea Franchetti from virgin wine territory in 1992. Passing over Sangiovese, Bordeaux varieties were chosen to be planted at high densities. At a range of altitudes (but around 600m) the 27 ha of vineyards would be too high further north in Tuscany. Here, near the Umbrian and Lazio borders, the summer heat is tempered by cool nights. Trinoro is the main wine and based on Cabernet Franc with small amounts of Cabernet Sauvignon and some Petit Verdot - the blend adjusted according to the success of each variety in a particular vintage. Clearly the *terroir* is something special, given not only the richness but also the originality of the wine. Yields are very low and there is marvellously pure, concentrated black fruit and a hint of wild herbs in a refined structure. An excellent second wine, Le Cupole di Trinoro, has been introduced with less domination by the Cabernet Franc (between 40% and 70% depending on the vintage) and offers something of the complexity of Trinoro at a more affordable price. Palazzi is 100% Merlot, with a lot of voluptuousness, sometimes a little overripe for some palates and doesn't mtch the price/quality ratio of either Trinoro or Le Cupole.. New from 2011 is Magnacosta, 100% Cabernet Franc from a parcel planted over 20 years ago on deep gravel near a stream. This the first separate bottling from this cru - only 1600 were produced and we have yet to taste it. Franchetti has also invested in establishing a new vineyard on the northern slopes of Mount Etna in Sicily called PASSOPISCIARO (see Southern Italy & Islands).
Recommended Reds:
Tenuta di Trinoro ✪✪✪✪✪ £H Palazzi ★★★★ £H
Le Cupole ★★★☆ £E

❀ Tua Rita (Val di Cornia) *www.tuarita.it*

Tua Rita and more recently Montepeloso have set the standards for Suvereto, one of Tuscany's brightest new zones since the mid-90s. The Merlot, Redigaffi, is among Tuscany's half-dozen top Merlots but continues to be made in tiny quantities in an opulent, flamboyant style. Rather more of Giusto di Notri, a Cabernet/Merlot blend is produced. This is roughly two parts Cabernet (including 10% Cabernet Franc) to one of Merlot; an equally powerful, dense, expansive style and with similarly excellent texture and balance. Both wines will keep for at least a decade. The wine currently made in the greatest quantity and often overlooked in all the hype is the red Perlato del Bosco. Produced from Sangiovese and Cabernet Sauvignon until the 2011 vintage, when it returned to it's original Sangiovese, it is also considerably more affordable and has seductive, forward fruit but good depth and style too. Whites, too, are worthy; the oak-fermented and aged Lodano (previously known as Sileno) is an aromatic, creamy blend of Chardonnay, Gewürztraminer and Riesling. Perlato di Bosco Bianco is also made from indigenous Trebbiano, Ansonica and Vermentino. Production has been increased over the years and there are now 30ha in

Italy

production. A small amount of Syrah is also made and Rosso di Notri (Sangiovese with some Merlot and Syrah) is a surprisingly good value red made from the farm of Stefano Frascolla that deserves at least three years' age.

Recommended Reds:

Redigaffi ★★★★★ £H   Giusto di Notri ★★★★★ £F
Perlato del Bosco ★★★☆ £E   Rosso di Notri ★★☆ £C

Recommended Whites:

Lodano ★★ £C

❀ **Valdicava (Montalcino)**   *www.valdicava.it*
One of Brunello's small growers, this estate has come to the fore under the direction of Vincenzo Abbruzzese (though it has belonged to his family for half a century) and the winemaking skills of Attilio Pagli. The style is for Brunello of real weight, power and richness and there is excellent complexity and dimension. The wines don't usually lack for depth and are now up amongst the best going. There is usually the structure to improve for at least a decade, and longer in the Riserva Madonna del Piano. Rosso di Montalcino is particularly good.

Recommended Reds:

Brunello di Montalcino Riserva Madonna del Piano ★★★★★ £G
Brunello di Montalcino ★★★★★ £F   Rosso di Montalcino ★★★ £D

Tenuta di Valgiano (Colline Lucchesi)   *www.valgiano.it*
The Lucchese hills are the northernmost of several pockets of viticulture gaining prominence on the western coast of Tuscany. Valgiano is arguably the leading estate but it is only one of several of emerging importance in the area. The 16 ha of vineyards are on poor gravelly soils at around 250m altitude, between the coast and the Apennines. Much importance is placed on ensuring that the wines express their origins and a sense of place; biodynamic practices are employed to this end. The estate red is 60% Sangiovese with the balance from Syrah and Merlot, and is rich and succulent with good depth and balance. Palistorti is a similar blend but from younger vines; effectively a second wine, it is lighter and more perfumed but has good depth and intensity too. Scasso dei Cesari, a pure Sangiovese from over 40-year-old vines from two contrasting soil types has now been discontinued and the vineyards have just been replanted. You will need to watch this space for further developments. A cooling Apennine influence favours the retention of acidity and the production of a characterful white, now re-named Giallo di Muri Bianco. A blend of mostly Vermentino, Trebbiano and Malvasia but also including a little Chardonnay. All the wines are now sold under the Colline Lucchesi DOC.

Recommended Reds:

Colline Lucchesi Tenuta di Valgiano ★★★★ £F
Colline Lucchesi Palistorti ★★☆ £C

Recommended Whites:

Colline Lucchesi Giallo dei Muri ★ £B

Fattoria Valtellina (Chianti Classico)   *www.fattoria-valtellina.com*
Valtellina is a small estate whose wines have commanded a premium ever since acquiring an enviable reputation under Giorgio Regni. In recent years the wines have been made by Andreas Stössel with some input from the much consulted Vittorio Fiore. They are not of the easy-going, quaffing type but rather firm, dense, powerful wines with lots of extract that can require some patience. There is a tendency to over-ripeness in the top wines in the best years but this doesn't compromise their ageing potential. If the wines could occasionally use a little more harmony and finesse they don't want

for flavour, complexity or power. Convivio is three parts Sangiovese to one part Cabernet Sauvignon while the newer Il Duca (di Montechioccioli) swells the ranks of varietal Tuscan Merlots.

Recommended Reds:

Il Duca ★★★ £G   Convivio ★★★ £E
Chianti Classico Riserva ★★★ £E   Chianti Classico ★★ £C

Vecchie Terre di Montefili   *www.vecchieterredimontefili.com*
The reputation of this Chianti Classico based estate, the property of the Acuti family since 1979, rests primarily with two very fine Super-Tuscans. The quality and symmetry of the wines was recognised in the 1980s and has been maintained due to the skill of Vittorio Fiore. Bruno di Rocca is a Cabernet Sauvignon/Sangiovese blend and usually a stylish but concentrated fusion of berryish fruit and elegant oak after some ageing. More distinctive, with a lovely complexity and acquiring an increasingly rich and smooth texture with age, is a pure Sangiovese, Anfiteatro. Regular Chianti Classico (also 100% Sangiovese) shows a stylish complexity and an authentic Tuscan stamp. A white, Villa Regis, is a *barrique*-aged blend of Chardonnay that includes some Sauvignon Blanc and Traminer; perfumed with an underlying intensity it should be drunk within 2-3 years of the vintage.

Recommended Reds:

Bruno di Rocca ★★★★ £F   Anfiteatro ★★★★ £F
Chianti Classico ★★☆ £C

Recommended Whites:

Vigna Regis ★★ £D

Villa Cafaggio (Chianti Classico)   *www.villacafaggio.it*
A very professionally directed estate, Villa Cafaggio is a dependable name for high-quality Chianti Classico and Tuscan blends. Stefano Farkas produces ripe, vibrant, almost chewy wines with lovely perfume and sweet fruit on the palate. There are 30ha of vineyards in Panzano's Conca d'Oro as well as a further 10 ha that are leased; they are planted mostly to Sangiovese but also to some Cabernet Sauvignon and Merlot. Efforts to maximise fruit quality include the selection of, and replanting with, superior clones as well as the adoption of green harvesting. In the winery, the use of concentrated must adds richness in lighter years, while micro-oxygenation has also been employed over the last decade. New oak is important to the style of the wines, enhancing both structure and flavour – 100% is used in the top two wines. San Martino, from a single vineyard, is now pure Sangiovese (older vintages include a little Cabernet), while Cortaccio is 100% Cabernet Sauvignon but used to include a little Sangiovese. Both add a little more concentration and style over a very good Chianti Classico Riserva. A single-vineyard Riserva Solatio Basilica (from 4 ha) is even better but has not been made in the most recent vintages due to replanting. All the wines benefit from a little extra age, Chianti Classico normale is best with three years, Riserva with four or five and Cortaccio and San Martino with at least five years. Prices are reasonable for the quality.

Recommended Reds:

Chianti Classico Riserva Solatio Basilica ★★★ £E
Chianti Classico Riserva ★★★ £D   Chianti Classico ★★ £C
Cortaccio ★★★ £E   San Martino ★★★ £E

Villa Mangiacane (Chianti Classico)   *www.mangiacane.it*
At the heart of this estate is an imposing 15th-century renaissance villa established by Niccolò Machiavelli's uncle, a cardinal, and recently given new life by its South African owner. Like the villa, the vineyards are being restored and with help from Alberto Antonini

very good Chianti Classico has already been produced. The regular version with 10% Canaiolo and 5% Colorino has a modern structure but classic flavours. A Riserva adds a little more but not as much as might be expected. There is also a 100% Merlot, Aleah, but this has not been tasted.

Recommended Reds:
Chianti Classico Riserva ★★★ £D   Chianti Classico ★★☆ £C

Villa Pillo *www.villapillo.com*
Villa Pillo is one of a number of estates to show that good wine is not restricted to the well-established areas or even the much vaunted newer regions of the coastal or southern Maremma. Being off the beaten track, north of San Gimignano, and with reds from non-native varieties may not endear the estate to everyone but the wines are both interesting and of good quality. Marco Chellini now makes the wines but 90s vintages were made by Paolo di Marchi of ISOLE E OLENA. Syrah has been the star wine, with some lovely pepper, berry and mineral character as well as a fleshy succulence. Merlot too shows good fruit intensity, while Vivaldaia from Cabernet Franc has an overly herbaceous, green component yet can also show good depth and texture. Vin Santo, only released with five years' age has good dried fruit, brazils and walnut complexity with good fruit richness. Borgoforte is a simple, fruity red of variable composition. Cingalino is an easy drinking blend of Merlot (65%) and Cabernet Franc, whilst Cypresses is a 100% Sangiovese with typical sour cherry undertones and which will repay some ageing. Both have an excellent price/quality ratio.

Recommended Reds:
Syrah ★★★☆ £E   Merlot Sant'Adele ★★★ £E
Cypresses ★★☆ £C   Vivaldaia ★☆ £E   Cingalino ★☆ £B
Recommended Whites:
Vin Santo del Chianti ★★★ £E

>> Villa Poggio Salvi (Montalcino) *www.villapoggiosalvi.it*
Villa Poggio Salvi has now broken away from its association with BIONDI SANTI and is ploughing its own furrow with considerable success. Pierluigi's grandson, Luca Belingardi, is now the winemaker and apart from the original 21ha of Sangiovese Grosso planted, the estate now also maintains other vineyards in the Chianti and Maremma regions, producing Chianti Colli Senese, Morellino di Scansano and other IGT Toscana wines. Their Vermentino has a touch of mineral austerity but finishes long and the entry level Merlot, Lavischio, can also lack generosity of fruit in some vintages. Tosto, 100% Sangiovese, by contrast is soft and supple after spending 8 months in oak. The two DOGCs, the unoaked Chianti Colli Senese 'Caspagnoso' (90% Sangiovese/10% Merlot) and the Morellino di Scansano 'Vaiao' (Sangiovese with just a splash of Merlot) display fresh vibrancy, the Morellino showing typical sour cherry flavours. But the reputation here is on the Montalcinos. The Rosso spends a year in big *botte*, toffee flavours come through here, but needs time to develop its full potential. The Brunello DOGC spends 18 months in *botte* and certainly needs the full 5 years before release before it becomes remotely approachable. The single vineyard Brunello 'Pomona' is more refined but could still be a little tannic in its youth. 30 months in oak does show. The Brunello Riserva, 36 months in oak, is only made in the good years, deep and unctuous, requiring a considerable amount of cellaring. The trait of all the wines seems to be austerity in their your but will well repay keeping. (NB)

Recommended Reds:
Brunello di Montalcino 'Pomona' ★★★☆ £G

Brunello di Montalcino Riserva ★★★★ £G
Brunello di Montalcino ★★★ £F
Rosso di Montalcino ★★☆ £C
Chianti Colli Senese 'Caspagnoso' ★★☆ £B
Morellino di Scansano 'Vaiao' ★★☆ £B
Toscana IGT Sangiovese 'Tosco' ★★☆ £B
Toscana IGT Merlot 'Lavischio' ★★ £B
Recommended Whites:
IGT Toscana Vermentino ★★ £B

Villa Sant' Anna (Montepulciano) *www.villasantanna.it*
Good progress has been made here in recent vintages in this self-styled 'women's winery'. Simona and her daughters Anna and Margherita run the estate with some winemaking input from top consultant Carlo Ferrini. Their profile has been boosted in part by the release of a special selection Vino Nobile, Poldo. Only 5000 bottles were made of the first vintage in 2001 but twice as much was made in certain years thereafter. Dense, lush and vigorous it is a shade too oaky yet otherwise impeccably balance with lots of potential. Like the regular Vino Nobile (around 30,000 bottles) it includes 10% of Cabernet Sauvignon and Merlot as well as 10% of Canaiolo and Mammolo with the Sangiovese but a higher proportion goes into tonneaux. Rosso di Montepulciano comes from younger vines but has plenty of substance while the Chianti Colli Senesi is a match for it, coming as it does from older vines lying outside the DOCG boundaries. Vin Santo is in a nutty, oxidised style but has lots of intensity.

Recommended Reds:
Vino Nobile di Montepulciano Poldo ★★★☆ £E
Vino Nobile di Montepulciano ★★★ £D
Rosso di Montepulciano ★★ £B   Chianti Colli Senesi ★★ £B

Other wines of note

Ambrosini
Recommended Reds: Val di Cornia Tabaro' ★★★ £C
Riflesso Antico (Montepulciano) ★★★★ £E
Ampeleia
Recommended Reds:
Ampelaia (Cab Franc/Sangiovese/Grenache/Others) ★★★☆ £E
Badia a Coltibuono
Recommended Reds: Chianti Classico Riserva ★★ £D
Sangioveto (Sangiovese) ★★★ £F
Badia di Morrona
Recommended Reds: Vigna Alta (Sangiovese) ★★★ £E
N'antia (Sangiovese/Cab Sauv/Merlot) ★★★ £E
Fattoria dei Barbi
Recommended Reds: Brunello di Montalcino Vigna Del Fiore ★★★ £E
Bindella
Recommended Reds: Vino Nobile di Montepulciano ★★ £C
Vino Nobile di Montepulciano I Quadri ★★★ £D
Borgo Salcetino
Recommended Reds: Chianti Classico Riserva Lucarello ★★ £D
Rossole (Sangiovese/Merlot) ★★ £D
Brunelli
Recommended Reds: Brunello di Montalcino ★★★ £E
Podere Capaccia
Recommended Reds: Chianti Classico ★ £C
Chianti Classico Riserva ★★ £D
Querciagrande (Sangiovese) ★★★ £E

Tuscany

Italy

Capoverso
Recommended Reds:
Vino Nobile di Montepulciano ★★★ £E
Cortona Syrah ★☆ £C

G Fuso Carmignani
Recommended Reds: For Duke (Syrah/Sangiovese) ★★★ £E

Casa Emma
Recommended Reds: Chianti Classico ★★ £C
Chianti Classico Riserva ★★★ £E   Soloio (Merlot) ★★★ £F

Casa Sola
Recommended Reds: Chianti Classico ★★ £C
Chianti Classico Riserva ★★★ £E
Montarsiccio (Cab Sav/Merlot/Sangiovese) ★★★☆ £F

Casafrassi
Recommended Reds: Chianti Classico ★★ £C

Casale-Falchini
Recommended Whites: Selva d'Oro (Vernaccia/Chardonnay) ★★ £B
Vernaccia di San Gimignano Vigna A Solatio ★★ £B
Vernaccia di San Gimignano Ab Vinea Doni ★★ £C

Podere Casina
Recommended Reds: Morellino di Scansano ★ £B
Morellino di Scansano Marchele ★★ £C   Aione (Sangiovese) ★★★ £B

Castello d'Albola (Zonin)
Recommended Reds: Acciaiolo (Sangiovese/Cab Sauv) ★★★ £E

Castello di Meleto
Recommended Reds: Chianti Classico ★★ £B
Chianti Classico Riserva Vigna Casi ★★☆ £D
Fiore (Merlot/Sangiovese) ★★★ £D
Rainero (Merlot/Cab Sauv/Sangiovese) ★★★☆ £D

Castello San Donato In Perano
Recommended Reds: Chianti Classico ★★ £C
Chianti Classico Riserva ★★★ £D

Cecchi
Recommended Reds: Spargolo (Sangiovese) ★★★ £E
Morellino di Scansano Riserva Val Delle Rose ★★ £C

Centolani
Recommended Reds: Brunello di Montalcino tenuta Friggiali ★★★ £E
Brunello di Montalcino Pietranera ★★★ £E

Cerro del Masso
Recommended Reds: Chianti ★★ £B

Cesani
Recommended Reds: Luenzo (Sangiovese/Colorino) ★★★ £E
Vernaccia di San Gimignano Sanice ★★★ £B

Cima
Recommended Whites: Vermentino ★ £C
Candia Dei Colli Apuani Vigneto Candia Alto ★★ £C
Recommended Reds: Anchigi (Sangiovese) ★★ £C
Romalbo (Sangiovese/Massaretta) ★★★ £D
Montervo (Merlot) ★★ £D   Gamo (Syrah) ★★★ £F

Coliberto
Recommended Reds:
Monteregio di Massa Marittima Riserva Thesan ★★ £C

Collelungo
Recommended Reds: Chianti Classico ★☆ £C
Chianti Classico Riserva ★★ £D
Chianti Classico Riserva Campocerchi ★★☆ £F

Collosorbo
Recommended Reds: Rosso di Montalcino ★★ £C
Brunello di Montalcino ★★★ £E
Brunello di Montalcino Riserva ★★★★ £F

Contucci
Recommended Reds: Vino Nobile di Montepulciano ★★ £C

Fassati
Recommended Reds: Vino Nobile di Montepulciano Pasiteo ★★ £C
Vino Nobile di Montepulciano Riserva Salarco ★★ £D

Fattoria di Fiano/Ugo Bing
Recommended Reds: Chianti Colli Fiorentini ★★ £B
Fianesco (Sangiovese & Others) ★★★ £D

Ferrero
Recommended Reds: Brunello di Montalcino ★★★ £E

Fornacina
Recommended Reds: Brunello di Montalcino ★★★ £E

Gualdo Al Melo
Recommended Reds: Bolgheri ★★★☆ £C

Il Bruscello
Recommended Reds: Val di Cornia Loco dei Frati ★★ £D

Il Carnasciale
Recommended Reds: Caberlot ★★★★ £F

Il Corno
Recommended Reds: Colorino Dell' Corno (Colorino) ★★★ £E

Incontri (Martelli & Busdraghi)
Recommended Reds: Val di Cornia Lago Bruno ★★★ £D

La Comandina
Recommended Reds: Vintore (Sangiovese/Colorino) ★★★☆ £D

La Novella
Recommended Reds: Chianti Classico ★★☆ £B
Chianti Classico Riserva ★★★☆ £D

Il Paradiso di Frassina
Recommended Reds: Brunello di Montalcino Montosoli ★★★ £E
Do - 12 Uve (Sangiovese/Cab Sauv/Petit Verdot/Syrah) ★★ £C

La Parrina
Recommended Reds: Parrina Rosso Muraccio ★★ £B
Parrina Rosso Riserva ★★ £C

La Querce
Recommended Reds: Chianti Colli Fiorentini La Torretta ★★ £C
La Querce (Sangiovese/Colorino) ★★★ £D

La Rasina
Recommended Reds: Brunello di Montalcino ★★★ £E

La Regola
Recommended Reds:
Montescudaio La Regola (Sangiovese/Merlot/Cab Sauv) ★★★ £D

La Rendola
Recommended Reds: L'Incanto (Sangiovese/Merlot) ★★ £C
La Pineta (Sangiovese) ★★ £C

La Selva
Recommended Reds: Prima Causa (Cab Sauv/Merlot) ★★ £D

Le Calcinaie
Recommended Whites:
Vernaccia di San Gimignano Vigna Ai Sassi ★★ £C
Recommended Reds: Teodoro (Sangiovese/Merlot/Cab Sauv) ★★ £C

Le Calvane
Recommended Reds: Chianti Colli Fiorentini Riserva Il Trecione ★★ £C
Borro Del Boscone (Cab Sauv) ★★ £D

Le Casalte
Recommended Reds: Vino Nobile di Montepulciano ★★ £C
Vino Nobile di Montepulciano Querce Tonda ★★★ £D

Le Fonti
Recommended Reds: Chianti Classico Riserva ★★ £C
Fontissimo (Sangiovese/Cabernet) ★★ £D

Le Macioche
Recommended Reds: Brunello di Montalcino ★★★☆ £E

Rosso di Montalcino ★★☆ £C

Costanza Malfatti
Recommended Reds: Morellino di Scansano ★★★ £D

Mantellassi
Recommended Reds: Querciolaia (Alicante) ★★★ £D
Morellino di Scansano Riserva Le Sentinelle ★★★ £D

Massa Vecchia
Recommended Whites:
Bianco (Vermentino/Sauvignon/Malvasia Candia) ★★★ £C
Recommended Rosés:
Rosato (Merlot/Malvasia Nera/Aleatico) ★★ £B
Recommended Reds: Rosso (Merlot/Cab Sauv) ★★☆ £C
La Querciola (Sangiovese/Alicante) ★★★ £D
Aleatico Passito ★★★☆ £D

Melini
Recommended Reds:
Chianti Classico Riserva Vigneti La Selvanella ★★★ £D

Merlini
Recommended Reds: Guadi Piani (Sangiovese/Cab Sauv) ★★ £C

Cantina di Montalcino
Recommended Reds: Brunello di Montalcino ★★★ £E
Rosso di Montalcino ★★ £C

Montellori
Recommended Reds: Salamartano (Cab Sauv/Merlot) ★ £D
Dicatum (Sangiovese) ★★★ £D

Monteti
Recommended Reds:
Caburnio (Cab Sauv/Merlot/Alicante) ★★★☆ £B
Monteti (Cab Sauv/Cab Franc/Petit Verdot) ★★★ £D

Panzanello
Recommended Reds: Chianti Classico ★★ £B
Chianti Classico Riserva ★★☆ £C

Paradiso
Recommended Reds: Saxa Calida (Cab Sauv/Merlot) ★★★ £E

Patrimonio Tringali-Casanuova
Recommended Rosés:
Bolgheri Rosato (Merlot/Sangiovese/Cab Sauv/Syrah) ★★ £B
Recommended Reds: Bolgheri Rosso (Cab Sauv/Merlot) ★★★ £D
Sangiovese di Toscana ★★☆ £C

Petra
Recommended Reds: Val di Cornia Rosso Ebo ★★ £C

Piazzano
Recommended Reds: Chianti Rio Camerata ★★ £B
Chianti Riserva Rio Camerata ★★★ £C

Enrico Pierazzuoli
Recommended Reds:
Carmignano Riserva Le Farnete ★★★☆ £D
Carmignano Le Farnete ★★☆ £B   Barco Reale Le Farnete ★ £B
Chianti Montalbano Riserva Tenuta Cantagallo ★★★☆ £C
Chianti Montalbano Tenuta Cantagallo ★ £B
Gioveto Tenuta Cantagallo (Sangiovese/Merlot/Syrah) ★★★ £D
Chianti Classico Matroneo ★★ £C

Poggio Tempesta
Recommended Reds: Brunello di Montalcino ★★★☆ £E

Poggio Verrano
Recommended Reds:
Dròmos (Sangiovese/Alicante/Cabernets/Merlot) ★★★★ £F

Quercia Al Poggio
Recommended Reds: Chianti Classico ★★ £C
Chianti Classico Riserva ★★☆ £D

Riseccoli
Recommended Reds: Chianti Classico Riserva ★★ £D
Saeculum (Sangiovese/Cab Sauv/Merlot) ★★★ £F
Recommended Whites: Vin Santo Del Chianti Classico ★★ £D

Rocca delle Macìe
Recommended Reds: Roccato (Sangiovese/Cab Sauv) ★★★ £E
Ser Gioveto (Sangiovese) ★★★ £E

Roccaccia
Recommended Reds: Fontenova (Sangiovese/Ciliegiolo) ★★ £C
Poggio Cavalluccio (Ciliegiolo) ★★★ £D

Salcheto
Recommended Reds: Vino Nobile di Montepulciano ★★★ £C
Rosso di Montepulciano ★★ £B   Chianti Colli Senesi ★ £B

San Filippo – Rosi
Recommended Reds: Brunello di Montalcino ★★★ £F

Sassotondo
Recommended Reds: Sovana Superiore Franze (Sangiovese) ★★ £C
San Lorenzo (Ciliegiolo) ★★★ £D

Serraiola
Recommended Whites:
Monteregio di Massa Marittima Violina (Vermentino) ★★ £C
Recommended Reds:
Monteregio di Massa Marittima Lentisco (Sangiovese) ★★ £C
Campo Montecristo (Sangiovese/Merlot/Syrah) ★★ £D

Suveraia
Recommended Reds:
Monteregio di Massa Marittima Bacucco di Suveraia ★★ £D

Terralsole
Recommended Reds: Brunello di Montalcino ★★★ £E

Terre del Sillabo
Recommended Reds: Niffo (Cabernets/Sangiovese/Merlot) ★★ £E

Teruzzi e Puthod
Recommended Whites:
Terre di Tufi (Vernaccia/Malvasia/Vermentino) ★★ £C
Carmen (Sangiovese – Vinified As A White) ★★ £C

Giuliano Tiberi
Recommended Reds: Le Vespe (Sangiovese Based) ★★ £C

Torraccia di Presura
Recommended Reds: Chianti Classico Il Tarocco ★★ £B
Chianti Classico Riserva Il Tarocco ★★ £C

Trerose (Tenementi Angelini)
Recommended Reds:
Vino Nobile di Montepulciano Simposio ★★☆ £E

Val di Suga (Tenementi Angelini)
Recommended Reds: Brunello di Montalcino ★★★ £E
Brunello di Montalcino Vigna Spuntali ★★★☆ £F

Valdipiatta
Recommended Reds: Vino Nobile di Montepulciano ★★ £C
Vino Nobile di Montepulciano Vigna D'alfiero ★★★ £E

Fattoria Varramista
Recommended Reds: Varramista (Syrah/Merlot/Sangiovese) ★★ £D

Verbena
Recommended Reds: Brunello di Montalcino ★★★ £E

Vignamaggio
Recommended Reds:
Chianti Classico Riserva Castello di Monna Lisa ★★ £D
Obsession (Cab Sauv/Merlot) ★★★ £E
Vignamaggio (Cab Franc) ★★★ £E
Recommended Whites: Vin Santo ★★ £E

Tuscany

Author's choice

Classic Tuscans reds

Ambra   Carmignano Riserva Le Vigne Alte Montalbiolo
Antinori   Solaia
Avignonesi   Vino Nobile di Montepulciano Riserva Grandi Annate
Boscarelli   Vino Nobile di Montepulciano Nocio Dei Boscarelli
Capannelle   50 & 50
Castello di Rampolla   Vigna D'alceo
Podere Forte   Orcia Petrucci
Gagliole   Gagliole Rosso
Il Molino di Grace   Gratius
Bibi Graetz   Testamatta
Isole e Olena   Cepparello
Le Pupille   Saffredi
Montevertine   Le Pergole Torte
Petrolo   Galatrona
Poggiopiano   Rosso di Sera
Poliziano   Vino Nobile di Montepulciano Asinone
Riecine   La Gioia
Ruffino   Romitorio di Santedame
Querciabella   Camartina
San Giusto a Rentennano   Percarlo
Sette Ponti   Crognolo
Tenuta di Trinoro   Tenuta di Trinoro
Vecchie Terre di Montefili   Anfiteatro

Outstanding Chianti

Castello di Ama   Chianti Classico Vigneto Bellavista
Castello di Fonterutoli   Chianti Classico Castello di Fonterutoli
Castello La Leccia   Chianti Classico Bruciagna
Castello di Volpaia   Chianti Classico Riserva Coltassala
Castello Vicchiomaggio   Chianti Classico Riserva La Prima
Fattoria di Felsina   Chianti Classico Riserva Vigneto Rancia
Fontodi   Chianti Classico
Frescobaldi   Chianti Rufina Montesodi
Il Palazzino   Chianti Classico Grosso Sanese
La Massa   Chianti Classico Giorgio Primo
La Pieve   Chianti Fortebraccia
Poggio al Sole   Chianti Classico Casasilia
San Giusto a Rentennano   Chianti Classico Riserva Le Baroncole
Fattoria Selvapiana   Chianti Rufina Riserva Bucerchiale
Rocca di Montegrossi   Chianti Classico Riserva San Marcellino

Diverse Top Quality Brunello

Banfi   Brunello di Montalcino Poggio Ale Mura
Tenuta Caparzo   Brunello di Montalcino Vigna La Casa
Casanova di Neri   Brunello di Montalcino Tenuta Nuova
Col d'Orcia   Brunello di Montalcino Riserva Poggio Al Vento
Fuligni   Brunello di Montalcino Vigneti Dei Cottimelli
Mastrojanni   Brunello di Montalcino Schiena D'asino
Silvio Nardi   Brunello di Montalcino Vigneto Manachiara
Siro Pacenti   Brunello di Montalcino
Pertimali/Livio Sassetti   Brunello di Montalcino Riserva
Pieve Santa Restituta   Brunello di Montalcino Sugarille
Poggio Antico   Brunello di Montalcino Altero
Poggio di Sotto   Brunello di Montalcino
Salvioni/La Cerbaiola   Brunello di Montalcino
San Filippo - Fanti   Brunello di Montalcino
Valdicava   Brunello di Montalcino

Coastal red marvels

Casanova della Spinetta   Sezzana
Castello del Terriccio   Lupicaia
Tenuta di Ghizzano   Veneroso
Grattamacco/Colle Massari   Bolgheri Rosso Superiore
Guado Al Tasso   Bolgheri Rosso
Gualdo del Re   Federico Primo
Le Macchiole   Scrio
Montepeloso   Nardo
Tenuta Dell'ornellaia   Bolgheri Rosso Superiore Ornellaia
Sangervasio   A Sirio
Enrico Santini   Bolgheri Rosso Montepergoli
Sassicaia/Tenuta San Guido   Bolgheri Sassicaia
Tua Rita   Redigaffi
Tenuta di Valgiano   Tenuta di Valgiano

Tuscan best buys (reds)

Fattoria di Basciano   Vigna Il Corto
Casa di Terra   Poggio Querciolo
Castello di Poppiano   Toscoforte
La Pieve   Chianti La Pieve
Lavacchio   Chianti Rufino Cedro
Le Miccine   Chianti Classico
Le Sorgenti   Gaiaccia
Cantine Leonardo Da Vinci   Chianti Riserva
Fattoria di Magliano   Morellino di Scansano Heba
Malenchini   Chianti Colli Fiorentini
Fattoria di Petroio   Chianti Classico Riserva
Poggio Argentiera   Morellino di Scansano Bellamarsilia
San Vincenti   Chianti Classico
Enrico Santini   Bolgheri Rosso Poggio Al Moro
Tua Rita   Rosso Dei Notri

"Caccia al tesoro"
Just as culturally there is so much to be discovered just beyond the
bounds of Tuscany so it is when it comes to viticulturally derived
masterpieces. This is not a section of also-rans but includes exciting
top-quality producers increasingly bringing the best out of a rich
heritage of native varieties. Of the growing number of fine reds,
the trio of Sangiovese, Sagrantino and Montepulciano offer the
greatest riches, but also to be unearthed are compelling Cabernet
Sauvignon/Merlot blends and stylish whites from Verdicchio and,
lately, Pecorino.

Emilia-Romagna
Emilia
Emilia is of course much celebrated for its gastronomic riches.
It doesn't share that world-wide reputation for its wines but in
(real) **Lambrusco** with four DOC zones of its own, it does have an
excellent food wine. Top examples from Cleto Chiarli (Chiarli 1860)
or Ermete Medici are a good bet. Emilia's two most significant other
DOCs are for wines from the low hills to the south of the cities of
Piacenza and Bologna. Both the **Colli Piacentini** (contiguous with
Lombardy's Oltrepò Pavese) and **Colli Bolognesi** (now DOCG)
can produce decent Cabernet Sauvignon and Barbera as well as
Chardonnay, Sauvignon and Malvasia. Gutturnio is a speciality of
the former, a blend of Barbera and Bonarda of good character and
quality from a handful of producers. If in Bologna, seek out Giuseppe
Beghelli, Floriano Cinti, Isola, Terre Rosse or Vallona. Alternatively if
stopping over in Piacenza consider La Stoppa, La Tosa or Luretta.
Romagna
More exciting in viticulture terms is Romagna, where the best
Sangioveses outside Tuscany are now produced. Though much
Sangiovese di Romagna is pretty basic, the best examples have
depth, intensity and excellent texture and concentration where
there is denser planting and lower yields. Several of the best
producers (including Calonga, Drei Donà, San Patrignano, San
Valentino, Tre Monti and Zerbina) combine their efforts through an
association, Convito di Romagna in an attempt to better promote
Romagna and Sangiovese. Most also make good wines from
Chardonnay, Cabernet Sauvignon and other imports. Both a slightly
nutty, dry and a sweet version of **Albana di Romagna** (DOCG) are
made; the latter, as passito, made from dried grapes, is usually far
superior (Zerbina's is exemplary).

Marche
Whites
This region is still best-known for **Verdicchio dei Castelli di Jesi**
but top examples are light years ahead of the cheap and cheerful
examples poured from amphora-shaped bottles 20-odd years
ago. Both the wines from the Castelli zone and the more inland
Verdicchio di Matelica will now display finesse and complexity
allied to good concentration and structure if bought from a top
producer. The best from Castelli di Jesi include those from Bucci,
Coroncino, Garofoli (Podium, Serra Fiorese), Marchetti (Cavaliere),
Montecappone (Utopia), Marotti Campi (Salmariano), Monte Schiavo
(Pallio di San Fiorese, Le Giuncare), San Lorenzo, Santa Barbara,
Sartarelli, Tavignano (Misco), Umani Ronchi, Velenosi, Vignamato,
and indeed, Fazi Battaglia's Massaccio. Most are dry and unwooded,
sometimes lees enriched, occasionally subtly oaked. Some
emphasise minerality, others refined fruit and floral characters. Those
from Matelica (always mineral-infused) to try are Bisci, Collestefano,
Del Carmine (Aja Lunga) and La Monacesca. Late-harvested, passito
(from Monte Schiavo, Pievalta, Santa Barbara or Vignamato) and

sparkling versions (Garofoli) highlight the grape's versatility. With
odd exceptions, Falerio (dei Colli Ascolani) tends to be much more
ordinary, its blend usually dominated by the boring Trebbiano.
Here as in Abruzzo, the Pecorino grape variety has recently shown
its potential, with many producers in the south of the region, now
having a white based partly or wholly on it. Good examples are
produced by Aurora, Ciù Ciù, De Angelis, Le Caniette, San Giovanni,
San Savino and Velenosi - some are sold as **Offida** Bianco.

Reds
With reds the picture is very exciting, if more complicated, with
an increasing number of DOCs as well as the regional IGT. The
great grape of both the Marche and Abruzzo (see below) is
Montepulciano with the most stunning reds based on it alone. Red
DOCs in the Marche include **Rosso Conero**, often coming from
vineyards lying within the beautiful Parco Cónero on the edge of the
Adriatic. This is a spicy, flavoursome red based on Montepulciano
with distinctive plummy cherry fruit. From the 2004 vintage Riservas
that are 100% Montepulciano qualify as **Conero Riserva** DOCG. Try
from Garofoli (Grosso Agontano), Le Terrazze (Sassi Neri), Marchetti
(Villa Bonomi), Strologo (Decebalo) or Umani Ronchi (Cùmaro). The
best **Rosso Piceno Superiore**, from a limited southern zone, are at
a similar level especially when the maximum 70% Montepulciano
to 30% Sangiovese is employed. Look for San Savino (Picus),
Saladini Pilastri (Monteprandone) or Velenosi (Roggio del Filare). Be
wary however of straight Rosso Piceno as it encompasses much
of the region (those from Le Caniette, San Lorenzo are stand-out
exceptions). Yet the many of top Montepulciano-based wines are
sold simply as IGT **Marche** (see Aurora, Maria Pia Castelli, Ciù Ciù,
De Angelis, Dezi, Fausti, Oasi degli Angeli, San Lorenzo, San Savino
and others). The IGT also covers exciting reds from foreign varieties
or unusual blends (those from Boccadigabbia, Dezi, Le Terrazze, or
Santa Barbara's Pathos). **Esino** (Rosso) covers some of the reds from
the Verdicchio zones. **Offida** Rosso is a blend of Montepulciano
and Cabernet Sauvignon - 70/30 is typical but they can include
20% of other varieties (check out Ciù Ciù or San Giovanni). The odd
sounding **Lacrima di Morro d'Alba** survived near extinction in
the 70s but in the past decade several Verdicchio producers have
planted Lacrima, a unique local variety produced in the Ancona
province around the village of Morro d'Alba. Many are light, highly
scented but with firm tannins yet otherwise offer better perfume
and texture than most rosés! For better structure and body and
an indication of the grape's true potential look out for those from
Conti di Buscareto, Luigi Giusti or San Lorenzo (tiny amounts
but stunning). **Colli Pesaresi** covers several of the diverse but
interesting wines of Luigi Mancini.

Umbria
Sangiovese is the leading red variety in Umbria and the regular red
from the region's most important zone, Montefalco is based on it.
Montefalco Rosso also includes a small percentage of Sagrantino
and in the very best examples offers a characterful alternative
to similarly priced Chianti or other Tuscan equivalents. Other
Sangiovese-based appellations include **Colli Amerini** and **Colli del
Trasimeno**, though both are becoming better known for rich, ripe,
modern reds based on Cabernet Sauvignon and/or Merlot. These
two grapes do exceedingly well in certain parts of Umbria (look for
examples from Caprai, Poggio Bertaio, Sportoletti and others). The
best wine from Montefalco is **Montefalco Sagrantino**, from a grape
that gives remarkable colour, extract, acid and alcohol. It needs
careful vinification but at best produces an intense, concentrated,

Central Italy

Italy

powerful yet original Italian red and the small plantings are on the increase. Those from Caprai, Còlpetrone, Paolo Bea, Goretti, Madonna Alta, Perticaia, Scacciadiavoli and Tabarrini should be tried. Sweet versions from dried grapes are labelled passito. **Colli Martani**, a much more extensive zone lying mostly to the west of Montefalco, can provide attractive whites from Grechetto. The other established white DOC is Orvieto (see Lazio). South of Perugia is the small zone of **Torgiano** (DOCG for Riserva) for Sangiovese based reds that also include Canaiolo and Ciliegiolo. The Lungarotti reds responsible for its status are at last making a sustained revival.

Lazio

The most important appellation in Lazio is now the regional IGT. Whether from the border with Umbria and Tuscany, the coast (Cerveteri) or the Colli Albani (Alban hills) many new wines are appearing. The majority are reds made from Cabernet Sauvignon and/or Merlot, though Sangiovese occasionally forms the main component. However the positive current trend to producing premium reds from 100% Cesanese (a local variety) might yet give Lazio a more distinctive red wine profile. There are three Cesanese DOCs now. The best examples (Cantine Ciolli for instance) combine texture and complexity within a refined structure. The established DOCs of **Est! Est!! Est!!!**, **Orvieto** (shared with Umbria) and **Frascati** are for the most part all based on the Trebbiano grape and offer little in terms of serious quality, but there are some reasonable examples of each and some good, late-harvested sweet styles. For Orvieto go for Castello della Sala, Decugnano dei Barbi, La Carraia or Palazzone. Frascati based on Malvasia tends to be much better - try those from Castel de Paolis, Fontana Candida and Villa Simone.

Abruzzo & Molise
Abruzzo reds

Abruzzo has two region-wide DOCs and the majority of wines are either **Montepulciano d'Abruzzo**, if red, or Trebbiano d'Abruzzo if white. There are an increasing number of good examples of the red from the characterful, peppery and good value everyday versions to so much more when the fruit is top-notch. There is an increasing number of ambitious examples and more are beginning to combine depth and substance with refinement and complexity achieved for so long by Valentini. If the combination of power, richness and class of Masciarelli's Villa Gemma is beyond your reach consider the best from Agriverde, Fratelli Barba, Caldora, Castorani, Cataldi Madonna, Farnese, La Valentina, Monti, Nicodemi, Emidio Pepe or Ciccio Zaccagnini or newer names such as Montipagano or Nicola Santoleri. Some of these producers now sell their top wines under the more restricted **Montepulciano d'Abruzzo Colline Termane** DOCG. The rosato version of Montepulciano, Cerasuolo is variable - both from producer to producer and vintage to vintage.

Abruzzo whites

Trebbiano d'Abruzzo can still be pretty dull but while Valentini's excellent example is usually cited as the one exception be sure to also taste those from Masciarelli (Marina Cvetic), Nicodemi (Notàri), Agriverde (Riseis di Recastro) or Fratelli Barba (Vigna Franca). As in the southern Marche an emerging white grape is Pecorino, occasionally transformed in to an intriguing white with good structure and flavour. (try from Agriverde, Contesa or Franco Pasetti). Decent examples of other varietals and blends, both red and white (including the interesting Passerina), can appear under the **Controguerra** DOC.

Molise

In Molise, **Biferno** was until recently its one important DOC. Like the reds of Abruzzo it is based on Montepulciano but additionally includes some Aglianico. The white is similar to Trebbiano d'Abruzzo. Newly created is a region-wide **Molise** DOC including essentially varietal examples of Aglianico, Montepulciano, Falanghina, Greco and Moscato. The leading producer is Di Majo Norante.

A-Z of producers by appellation/region

Regions
A Emilia-Romagna
B Marche
C Umbria
D Lazio
E Abruzzo
F Molise

Appellations
1 Colli Bolognesi
2 Albana di Romagna
3 Sangiovese di Romagna
4 Colli Pesaresi
5 Falerio dei Colli Ascolani
6 Verdicchio dei Castelli di Jesi
7 Verdicchio di Matelica
8 Rosso Conero
9 Rosso Piceno
10 Rosso Piceno Superiore
11 Colli del Trasimeno
12 Torgiano Rosso Riserva
13 Montefalco Sagrantino
14 Colli Martani
15 Orvieto
16 Est! Est!! Est!!!
17 Colli Amerini
18 Frascati
19 Montepulciano d'Abruzzo
20 Biferno

A-Z of producers - *Emilia-Romagna*

Giuseppe Beghelli (Colli Bolognesi) *www.collibolognesi.com*
Ever been in Bologna and wondered if decent wine was made in
the vicinity? Giuseppe Beghelli is a dedicated producer who makes
only a couple of thousand cases of red and white from 10 ha of
vines. The wines have the craft and concentration of a competent
and committed grower. The Barbera Riserva is a tour de force for the
Colli Bolognesi. Rich, ripe and oaky when young, it has formidable
concentration and depth and very fine tannins and deserves to be
drunk with at least 6–8 years' age. Cabernet is cool but full and for
once the hint of green pepper doesn't precede a harsh tannic finish,
but it deserves 5–6 years' age. If you're wondering what Pignoletto is,
try Giuseppe's scented, characterful and concentrated example (also
made frizzante). Tiny amounts of Sauvignon are also made to a high
standard.
Recommended Reds:
Colli Bolognesi Barbera Riserva ★★★ £C
Colli Bolognesi Cabernet Sauvignon ★★☆ £C
Recommended Whites:
Colli Bolognesi Pignoletto Classico ★★☆ £B

Stefano Berti (Sangiovese di Romagna) *www.stefanoberti.it*
Stefano Berti has only been making his own wine since 2000 but
with the 01 Calisto he has made a Sangiovese di Romagna of
such character and intensity as to add further proof of the quality
possible from this zone. Winemaking help is provided by the Attilio
Pagli/Alberto Antonini consultancy team. Fruit comes from both
older vines and newer plantings but easily absorbs 12 months in
new oak. The wine has drive, intensity and a stylish mineral, herb
and black fruits complexity. If there is not yet the extra breadth of
the very best examples, future vintages should add it. Quantities
are small if increasing. A second red, Ravaldo, which is only partially
barrique-aged benefitted from the grapes instead. This too, has
plenty of style and appeal. An entry level Sangiovese, Bartimeo,
made from young vines has been produced from the 2012 vintage
and a Sangiovese made without sulfites, Nona 2013, has just been
released this spring.
Recommended Reds:
Sangiovese di Romagna Superiore Calisto ★★★ £D
Sangiovese di Romagna Superiore Ravaldo ★★ £C

Castelluccio (Sangiovese di Romagna) *www.ronchidicastelluccio.it*
This was the first estate in Romagna to set out to prove that
Sangiovese from Romagna could compete with top examples
from Tuscany. Renowned Tuscan consultant Vittorio Fiore (POGGIO
SCALETTE), already involved with making the wines to a standard
not previously associated with Romagna, bought into the 16 ha
estate in 1999. The wines, made by Vittorio's son Claudio, used to
be sold as vino da tavola in order to distance them from the lowly
perception of the Sangiovese di Romagna DOC but most are now
sold under the Forlì IGT. As well as the revamping of winemaking
efforts, single crus – Ronco delle Ciliegi and Ronco delle Ginestre
– were planted as long ago as 1975 to high quality clones at a
higher density and continue to be improved by the viticulturalist,
Remigio Bordini. A third cru, Ronco della Simia, was also made until
very recently but there are now just the two original sites. Ciliegi
shows more class and elegance than an increasingly rich-fruited
and good-value Sangiovese di Romagna, Le More. Ginestre, the top
wine, comes from a 2 ha site and adds more weight, power and
complexity. Sauvignon Blanc is the other variety of choice. Lunaria

is a very distinctive mineral and very ripe citrus example that is
partially barrel-fermented, resulting in a gentle leesy influence.
Though not classically varietal, it can be more convincing than the
richer, more 'barriqued' Ronco del Re. All the reds need at least
two or three years to get going; the crus are best with five or more.
Whites can be drunk young or kept for a year or two. Massicone, a
blend of Cabernet Sauvignon and Sangiovese is promising, ripe and
intense.
Recommended Reds:
Ronco delle Ginestre ★★★★☆ £E
Ronco dei Ciliegi ★★★☆ £E   Massicone ★★★☆ £E
Sangiovese di Romagna Le More ★★ £B
Recommended Whites:
Ronco del Re ★★ £D   Lunaria ★★ £B

Floriano Cinti (Colli Bolognesi) *www.florianocinti.it*
Three distinctly different sites make up over 17 ha of vineyards from
which Giovanni Fraulini makes some of the best wines of the Colli
Bolognesi. Lightly sparkling Pignoletto frizzante compares well with
decent Prosecco and other whites are clean, varietal and soundly
made. Reds are rather more, especially the Sasso Bacco Merlot and
Cabernet Sauvignon. The Merlot is full and lush with plum, berry,
olive and cedar; Cabernet is more structured but a shade more
complex too. Both drink well with 4–5 years' age. Regular Merlot
and Barbera can show a hint of green but are plump, round and
fruit-centred. A passito-style sweet wine from Pignoletto grapes has
no botrytis but is intense and pure with a touch of honeysuckle.
Otherwise there's Rubrum Cor Laetificans. Made from Merlot, Pinot
Nero and Cabernet Sauvignon grapes left late on the vine, this is
more than a curiosity. In fact it is a super match for chocolate –
sweet and intense with a hint of bitter chocolate and licorice on the
nose, it is concentrated with chocolaty, cherry/berry fruit and lots of
acidity. Be sure to try it with some decent chocolate.
Recommended Reds:
Rubrum Cor Laetificans ★★★ £D
Colli Bolognesi Merlot SassoBacco ★★☆ £B
Colli Bolognesi Merlot ★★ £B
Colli Bolognesi Cabernet Sauvignon SassoBacco ★★☆ £B
Colli Bolognesi Barbera ★★☆ £B
Recommended Whites:
Colli Bolognesi Pignoletto Passito ★★★ £C
Colli Bolognesi Pignoletto Classico SassoBacco ★★ £B
Colli Bolognesi Chardonnay ★★ £B
Colli Bolognesi Sauvignon ★ £B
Colli Bolognesi Pignoletto Frizzante ★ £B

Drei Donà - La Palazza (Sangiovese di Romagna) *www.dreidona.it*
Claudio Drei Donà, together with his son Enrico and Tuscan
consultant Franco Bernabei, makes a small but very competent
range of wines from 27 ha of vineyards. Pruno, the best if not the
most expensive wine, is made from the oldest part of a single
vineyard. Notturno, Sangiovese from younger vines, is effectively
the second wine and reveals plenty of very attractive plum and
cherry fruit. Magnificat is varietal Cabernet Sauvignon with plenty
of substance and style and a chocolaty-coffee complexity from a
vineyard planted in the late 1980s. Graf Noir is a rich, characterful
blend of Sangiovese, Cabernet Franc and Negretto Longanesi. Il
Tornese is Chardonnay aged in double-sized *barriques* and large
wood with good intensity and evident lees-driven character, while
Varenne is an unoaked version. A Riserva, Cuvée Palazza, and a
wine from young vines, Le Vigne Nuove, both made from mostly

Sangiovese and some indigenous grapes, have recently been introduced to cover both ends of the spectrum.

Recommended Reds:

Graf Noir ★★★ £F   Magnificat ★★★ £E
Sangiovese di Romagna Superiore Riserva Pruno ★★★ £D
Notturno Sangiovese ★★☆ £C

Recommended Whites:

Il Tornese ★ £C

Isola (Emilia-Romagna/Colli Bolognesi)

Marco Franceschini works this small organic estate with his family, in particular with his second son, Gianluca. Two-thirds of some 12 ha of hillside vineyards are planted to the local Pignoletto grape with the balance to those French varieties well-established in the Colli Bolognesi. Newly planted vines are being treated biodynamically and the intention is to make a full conversion. The wines are very pure, intense as well as bright and cool in the way that makes examples from Bolognesi very attractive. The Superiore version of Pigoletto has spicy, lemony, chalky aromas, a suggestion of sweetness but is intense and fruit driven. Chardonnay is good in a fresh, direct unoaked version and retains good purity and precision in the oak-influenced Monte Gorgii version. The stylish Barbera Monte Gorgii spends 12 months in oak and is rich, ripe , firm but with lots of depth and balanced ripe tannins. Cabernet Sauvignon Monte Gorgii is also fine with oak spice, cedar, black plum, cassis, adding a carob complexity with a little age. There is also a frizzante style Pignoletto.

Recommended Reds:

Colli Bolognesi Barbera Monte Gorgii ★★★ £C
Colli Bolognesi Cabernet Sauvignon Monte Gorgii ★★★ £C

Recommended Whites:

Colli Bolognesi Chardonnay Monte Gorgii ★★☆ £C
Colli Bolognesi Chardonnay ★★ £B
Colli Bolognesi Pignoletto Superiore ★★ £B

La Stoppa (Emilia-Romagna/Colli Piacentini) www.lastoppa.it

Located a relatively short distance south of Piacenza this estate belongs as much in North-East Italy as Central Italy. One of the leading producers of the Colli Piacentini, with 30 ha of vineyard, a high standard has long been maintained here (Luretta, Il Poggiorello, La Tosa and Lusenti are others in the area worth investigation). La Stoppa's sweet Malvasia from dried grapes, Vigna del Volta (but including 5% Moscato) is consistently among the best wines here - deep, honeyed and concentrated, it also has excellent balance in top years. Ageno is a dry Malvasia-based style and shows the extraordinary colour that comes from a long maceration on the skins. Bottled unfiltered, the exotic aromas and rich flavour are only slightly let down by a light astringency on the finish. Of the reds, Macchiona (Barbera, Bonarda - 50/50) opens out with 5-8 years to reveal a splendid complexity with an intense, old viney component. Also excellent with similar intensiy and depth but not recently tasted are Cabernet Sauvignon Stoppa and Barbera della Stoppa. Other wines include a varietal Merlot, I Padri and when possible Buca delle Cane from botrytised Sémillon grapes.

Recommended Reds:

Macchiona ★★★☆ £D

Recommended Whites:

Colli Piacentini Malvasia Passito Vigna del Volta ★★★★ £E
Ageno ★★★ £E

✿ San Patrignano www.sanpatrignano.org

This remarkable community, founded by Vincenzo Muccioli and now run by his son, Andrea, is a centre of drug and social rehabilitation near Rimini. Part of the international Rainbow network, it is financed through private donations and activities such as wine production, in which it is fortunate to have the services of Riccardo Cotarella (see FALESCO). The wines are very good indeed, from mostly older vineyards, but new vineyards are coming on stream and a total of 100 ha is planned, half of which will be planted to Sangiovese. The top wine, Sangiovese di Romagna Riserva Avi, made in very small quantities, is bottled with a different label every year. Since 1999 it comes from new vineyards that are more densely planted to higher-quality clones. It is very concentrated, dense and structured but with a sleek and elegant texture. Also impressive is a second Riserva, Zarricante, which is aged in a mixture of old and new oak. A regular version, Aulente, spends 8 months in large wood and exhibits lovely pure cherry fruit and good depth. All three wines need time: three years for Aulente, at least five for the Riservas. Montepirolo is a classy Bordeaux blend that combines Cabernet Sauvignon with Merlot, Cabernet Franc and sometimes a little Petit Verdot. Structured, concentrated with great length, it requires 5–8 years' ageing. From 2001 is Noi, a blend of Sangiovese, Cabernet Sauvignon and Merlot (60/20/20). A varietal stainless steel-vinified Sauvignon Blanc, Vintàn is also made.

Recommended Reds:

Sangiovese di Romagna Riserva Avi ★★★★ £E
Sangiovese di Romagna Riserva Zarricante ★★★ £D
Sangiovese di Romagna Aulente ★★ £C   Montepirolo ★★★ £E

San Valentino (Sangiovese di Romagna) www.vinisanvalentino.com

A 14 ha estate on hills near Rimini on the Adriatic coast purchased by Giovanni Mascarin in 1990. Progressive changes and improvements over the last decade and a half are now resulting in some very impressive wines. His son Roberto took over in 1997, hired consultant Fabrizio Moltard in 2000 and oversees a new gravity-fed winery from 2005. Though most of the vines average around 10 years' age, high densities combined with leaf-plucking and green-harvesting result in low yields. The reds are now very good indeed. There are two fine Sangiovese di Romagna, pure ripe-fruited Scabi and classy intense Riserva Terra di Covignano, that also benefits from some old-vine fruit. A powerful Cabernet Sauvignon, with 20% Merlot, Luna Nuova has the blackberry, mineral and earth of good Romagna Cabernet. Also made but not tasted is Eclissi di Sole, 50% Sangiovese with 20% Cabernet Franc, 20% Merlot and 10% Syrah, a Montepulciano and a Syrah, and whites which include Fiore, a barrique-aged Chardonnay, and Alta Marea from Trebbiano and Chardonnay. Also a member of the Convito di Romagna.

Recommended Reds:

Sangiovese di Romagna Riserva Terra di Covignano ★★★★ £E
Sangiovese di Romagna Superiore Scabi ★★ £C
Luna Nuova ★★★ £E

Terre Rosse (Emilia-Romagna/Colli Bolognesi) www.terrerosse.it

This well-established producer has a deserved reputation for intense varietal wines made without any oak. Highlights include Adriana Vallania, a pure-fruited Malvasia with balanced residual sugar, and Riesling Malagò Vendemmia Tardiva (Riesling and Riesling Italico), which is usually rich and flavoursome. The pink-tinged Pinot Grigio is another star, characterful but structured too, while the Chardonnay Cuvée, now produced every year, is a real step up from the basic version and is deep, concentrated and creamy. Vallania is pure

Central Italy /Marche

Viognier and has good breadth if not the structure for more. Of the reds, Cabernet Sauvignon has also been successful, particularly the Cuvée version from an old clone. Also good is Grannero from Pinot Nero and a cherry-scented rosé, which has uncommon length and intensity.

Recommended Reds:

Il Rosso Cabernet Sauvignon Cuvée ★★★☆ £E
Il Rosso Cabernet Sauvignon ★★☆ £C
Petroso Merlot ★★☆ £C   Grannero Pinot Nero ★★ £C

Recommended Whites:

Colli Bolognesi Chardonnay Cuvée ★★★ £C
Colli Bolognesi Chardonnay ★★ £C
Colli Bolognesi Pinot Grigio ★★★ £C
Colli Bolognesi Pinot Bianco ★★ £C
Colli Bolognesi Sauvignon ★★ £C
Adriana Vallania ★★★ £C   Vallania Viognier ★★ £C
Riesling Malagò Vendemmia Tardiva di EV ★★ £D
Malagò di Elisabetta Vallania ★★ £C

Recommended Rosés:

Cabernet in Rosa ★★ £C

✿✿ Zerbina (Sangiovese di Romagna) *www.zerbina.com*
This 40 ha estate is brilliantly run by Cristina Geminiani whose wines have maintained or bettered consistent high standards over the past decade or more. Viticultural improvements, particularly planting at higher densities, continue to underpin quality. The top wine, Pietramora, from a single vineyard of old vines, shows an extra level of richness and dimension since 1997. Torre di Ceparano comes from more densely planted alberello (bush-trained) vines and has gained in texture and concentration as the vines have aged. The greatest part of the Sangiovese production comes in the shape of the unoaked Ceregio, a supple, fruity, earlier-drinking example. For Marzieno a little CabernetSauvignon, Syrah and Merlot are added to Sangiovese; lush, powerful and oaky, but doesn't quite reach the heights of Pietramora. Scaccomatto is probably the best rich, concentrated botrytised sweet wine in Italy, made from Albana grapes, while a lighter version, Arrocco, is made from second-choice fruit or in lesser vintages. A third, botrytised Albana "AR" is by contrast, only made in exceptional years and borders on ✿✿✿✿✿ in some vintages. An attractive, partly oak-fermented and aged dry white, Tergeno, is made from (mostly) Chardonnay with a little late-harvested Albana.

Recommended Reds:

Sangiovese di Romagna Superiore Riserva Pietramora ★★★★ £E
Sangiovese di Romagna SuperioreTorre di Ceparano ★★★ £C
Sangiovese di Romagna Superiore Ceregio ★★ £B
Marzieno ★★★☆ £E

Recommended Whites:

Albana di Romagna Passito Riserva AR ★★★★★ £H
Albana di Romagna Passito Scacco Matto ★★★★ £G
Albana di Romagna Passito Arrocco ★★ £D
Tergeno ★★ £C

A-Z of producers - *Marche*

Aurora (Marche/Rosso Piceno) *www.viniaurora.it*
Around 10 ha of this 30 ha organic estate in the hills of the southern Marche are planted to vines. A single wine, Barricadiero, has attracted the greatest attention but all the wines are made to a good standard. Barricadiero is Montepulciano complemented by Cabernet Sauvignon (70/30 in 2002). Aged in *barriques* for 12

months, it has good breadth and complexity but lots of extract too and requires a little patience. More forward but also with plenty of extract is Rosso Piceno Superiore, a 50/50 blend of Montepulciano and Sangiovese aged in medium-sized casks. The white Pecorino, Fiobbo, is partly fermented and aged in *barriques* and has impressive breadth and length with ripe stone fruits and quince flavours. A passito, made from 100% Passerina is also produced. More everyday are Falerio and regular Rosso Piceno. Incidentally, this appears to be an unpretentious holiday farm stay that should appeal to visitors – with the bonus that the wines are also good. Aurora is also one of the quality band known as Piceninvisibili (see SAN SAVINO).

Recommended Reds:

Barricadiero ★★★ £D   Rosso Piceno Superiore ★★ £B

Recommended Whites:

Offida Pecorino Fiobbo ★★★ £B

Bisci (Marche/Verdicchio)
This is a well-established producer with 25 ha in production, two-thirds to Verdicchio. With the exception of the Riserva, Bisci's Verdicchio see only stainless steel. Vigneto Fogliano offers considerably more than a very drinkable basic version while the grape's propensity for age can be seen in Senex (less fresh but with more depth, complexity) and Riserva (fuller with detectable oak) versions. The reds are all sold as IGT Marche. Rosso Fogliano is a basic quaffer - equal parts Montepulciano, Barbera, Merlot, Cabernet Franc - vinified and aged without wood. Much better are the two *barrique*-aged Sangiovese-based wines. In the Villa Castiglioni, containing Cabernet Sauvignon, both components are properly ripe and there is depth, intensity and already considerably complexity. Piangifame, dominated by Sangiovese has some very ripe cherry fruit in its savoury, slightly raisiny style.

Recommended Reds:

Villa Castiglioni ★★★ £C   Piangifame ★★★ £C
Rosso Fogliano ★ £B

Recommended Whites:

Verdicchio di Matelica Riserva ★★★ £C
Verdicchio di Matelica Vigneto Fogliano ★★☆ £C
Verdicchio di Matelica Senex ★★☆ £C
Verdicchio di Matelica ★☆ £B

Boccadigabbia (Marche/Rosso Piceno) *www.boccadigabbia.com*
Boccadigabbia, one of the leading red wine producers of the Marche comprises 28 ha from home vineyards and the more recently acquired 18 ha Villamagna estate. Under the extremely competent winemaking of Fabrizio Ciufoli, this includes some of the best Rosso Piceno going. The single-vineyard Saltapicchio (previously sold as Rosso Piceno) now, like most of the other wines, appears under the Marche IGT. It shows some herbs, smoke and cherry fruit together with good acidity and well-balanced tannin. An attractive, herb scented Mont'Anello white is based on Maceratino and Verdicchio, and there is also a Pecorino. French varieties have been planted at Boccadigabbia since the early 19th century (introduced when the region was under Napoleonic rule), so non-native varietals are no recent sell-out. Their quality is of a high standard, too – all the wines show ripe fruit and some oak influence but with good balance. Pinot Grigio, with ripe citrus, pear and spicy notes, is a rare good example outside North-East Italy but the best wine is a stylish, powerful but elegant, pure blackcurrant-fruited Cabernet Sauvignon, Akronte that has few rivals outside Tuscany. Newish Merlot, Pix is promising, at once powerfully structured and finely textured.

Recommended Reds:
Akronte ★★★★ £F Pix ★★★ £E Rosso Piceno ★★ £C
Sangiovese Saltapicchio ★★ £C Pinot Nero Il Girone ★ £D
Recommended Whites:
Chardonnay Montalperti ★★ £C Pinot Grigio La Castelletta ★★ £B
Colli Maceratesi Ribona Mont'Anello ★ £B

Bucci (Marche/Verdicchio) *www.villabucci.com*
Bucci is one of the best-known producers of Verdicchio, having long
been held in high regard for the Villa Bucci Riserva. It is produced
from 40-year-old vines and spends 18 months in large Slavonian
oak. Refined, complex and concentrated, it is almost always a very
complete and stylish example and most impressive in its ability to
age. The regular Verdicchio is soundly made if less exciting. Red from
5 ha of the 26 ha takes the shape of Rosso Piceno. A new Villa Bucci
version with more Montepulciano than Sangiovese (70/30) is richer
and rounder than the existing 50/50 Pongelli example.
Recommended Reds:
Rosso Piceno Villa Bucci ★★ £C Rosso Piceno Tenuta Pongelli ★ £B
Recommended Whites:
Verdicchio dei Castelli di Jesi Classico Riserva Villa Bucci ★★★ £D
Verdicchio dei Castelli di Jesi Classico Superiore ★★ £C

❂ Maria Pia Castelli (Marche) *www.mariapiacastelli.it*
This young estate, with the first wines in 2002 and 2003 seems to
be in very good hands. Maria Pia Castelli and her husband Enrico
Bartoletti are producing ambitious but exciting wines (all sold as
Marche IGT) including an unusual exotic white, an outstanding rosé
and two very promising reds. Stella Flora (50% Pecorino with 30%
Passerina and Trebbiano and Malvasia di Candia) is fermented on
the skins before spending 18 months in *barriques*. Deep in colour
and flavour, and full of exotic and old-fashioned fruits, the wine
is bold, lightly tannic yet surprisingly well-balanced. The reds are
varietal, Orano from Sangiovese - a dense, expansive and fleshy
example, while Erasmo Castelli (named for Maria Pia's father who
got the project started in 99) is a Montepulciano given two years
in *barriques*. Sant'Isidoro, the powerful rosé is an equal blend of
the two red varieties. Its deep cherry colour precedes a wonderful
complex floral nose and atypical depth and intensity on a lively,
fresh palate - in short, all the style and structure of a fine white but
with red fruits expression. A top notch rosé that shouldn't be missed.
Bravissimo!..
Recommended Reds:
Erasmo Castelli ★★★★ £D Orano ★★★☆ £C
Recommended Whites:
Stella Flora ★★★ £C
Recommended Rosés:
Sant'Isidoro ★★★ £C

Ciù Ciù (Marche) *www.ciuciu.it*
One of the grouping of eight in the southern Marche known as
Piceninvisibili, brothers Massimiliano and Walter Bartolomei, with
80 ha of vineyards, are also one of the zone's leaders. There are
good examples of all the typical wines including whites Falerio
Oris, (Pecorino, Passerina and Trebbiano) and Offida Pecorino (Le
Merlettaie). There is good minerality to the reds which show higher
acidity than those from other producers and occasionally a slightly
rawer edge to the tannins. Rosso Piceno Superiore (Gotico) is the
full 70/30 blend of Montepulciano and Sangiovese and there are
varietal examples of these two varieties sold as Marche Rosso IGT.
The Montepulciano, Oppîdium is usually the top wine; oak-lined,

fruit rich, lush, fat but structured. The Sangiovese, Saggio is very
intense and flavoursome but the acidity can be intrusive. Both
should be drunk with 7-8 years' age or more. Also look for Esperanto
(70% Montepulciano to 30% Cabernet Sauvignon), an example
of Offida Rosso that successfully combines mineral, blackberry
and vanilla flavours in a lush, chewy texture but again patience
is required. Also produced are blends - San Martino (Sangiovese/
Merlot), Bacchus (Montepulciano and Sangiovese) and San Carlo
(Sangiovese, Merlot and Barbera)
Recommended Reds:
Oppîdium ★★★☆ £D Saggio ★★★ £D
Offida Rosso Esperanto ★★★ £D
Rosso Piceno Superiore Gotico ★★☆ £C
Recommended Whites:
Offida Pecorino Le Merlettaie ★★☆ £B Falerio Oris ★☆ £B

❂ Coroncino (Marche/Verdicchio) *www.coroncino.it*
A better Verdicchio than Coroncino's Gaiospino is hard to find. The
husband and wife team started out in 1982 and have just 7ha of
vineyards. Gaiospino is sourced from the best vineyard, Spescia – a
steep 2.7 ha site – and part is fermented and aged in double-sized
barriques. The wine has continued to improve year on year and
is now an extremely stylish, refined Verdicchio with a pure citrus
and pear fruit intensity. A Fumé version has also been made, while
a well-structured, ageworthy Verdicchio, Stracacio was produced
in 2000. A second selection, Il Coroncino, comes from vineyards
around the winery and if less refined has good fruit richness. Il Bacco
is the most affordable but has good fruit and plenty of character if
best if drunk within 1-2 years. A new red, Ganzerello is made from
Sangiovese.
Recommended Whites:
Verdicchio dei Castelli di Jesi Classico Superiore Gaiospino ★★★★ £D
Verdicchio dei Castelli di Jesi Classico Superiore Stracacio ★★★ £E
Verdicchio dei Castelli di Jesi Classico Superiore Il Coroncino ★★★ £C
Verdicchio dei Castelli di Jesi Classico Superiore Il Bacco ★★☆ £C

De Angelis (Marche/Rosso Piceno) *www.tenutadeangelis.it*
Another of the southern Marche's well-established estates, De
Angelis comprises more than 50 ha of vines and another 10 ha of
olive trees. The star wine is Anghelos (70% Montepulciano, 30%
Cabernet Sauvignon) sold as Marche IGT. Dense, concentrated
and extracted it shouldn't be drunk too young. Other reds can
be less convincing with a tendency to slightly too much extract
in a characterful Rosso Piceno Superiore, and too much oak in an
otherwise ripe, concentrated and complex Oro version. Also made is
a decent Montepulciano d'Abruzzo with plenty of fruit and balanced
tannins. Of the whites the Falerio is a simple summertime quaffer,
while the unwooded Chardonnay made in a relatively lean style
offers just a little more. Much better is a varietal Pecorino with fine
fruit detail, good depth and structure.
Recommended Reds:
Anghelos ★★★ £D Rosso Piceno Superiore ★★ £C
Rosso Piceno Superiore Oro ★☆ £D
Montepulciano d'Abruzzo Villarey ★★ £B
Recommended Whites:
Pecorino ★★ £B Chardonnay Prato Grande ★ £B

Dezi (Marche)
The Dezi family have 20 ha of vineyard over which much care is
lavished. Production is organic and the quality of the fruit can be
seen in all the wines. The top wines are a much praised Sangiovese

called Solo and a less trumpeted pure Montepulciano, Regina del Bosco. Solo has finely detailed fruit and an elegance quite unexpected for the Marche. It is moderately concentrated and when young the effect of up to two years in new French oak is evident, but its class shows through. Regina del Bosco shows lots of style too. It is more structured, with the soft flesh and black-fruited complexity of Montepulciano. Dezio is a much more affordable Montepulciano that can include some Sangiovese and is aged in large oak botte. It is supple and expressive with good length. The perfumed white Le Solagne is a ripe, flavoursome blend of Malvasia and Verdicchio. All are sold as Marche IGT.

Recommended Reds:
Solo ★★★★ £E   Regina del Bosco ★★★ £E   Dezio ★★ £C
Recommended Whites:
Le Solagne ★ £B

❀ Fausti (Marche)
Initially known as Contrada Castelletta, this winery is still makes one of the Marche's best value reds. Domenico D'Angelo is the viticulturalist for SALADINI PILASTRI, where he has significantly improved the quality of fruit since the mid-90s. On a small 8 ha estate established with Cristina Fausti, he benefits from further collaboration with the Antonini team for his own wine, Vespro, a 70/30 Montepulciano/Syrah blend. Though the vines are young, yields are low with splendid black plum, spice, licorice and carob fruit in a modern style. Also made is Rosso Piceno, Fausto.

Recommended Reds:
Vespro ★★★★ £C

Garofoli (Marche/Verdicchio) *www.garofolivini.it*
Fourth-generation Carlo and Gianfranco Garofoli now head this large family firm which was founded in 1871 and has been making wines for over a century. They focus primarily on producing top-quality Verdicchio from low yields. While the simple Serra del Conte is a bit basic, Macrina is well worth extra money. Serra Fiorese is a Riserva aged in oak and can show considerable richness and depth with three or four years' age, but arguably the best Verdicchio is the unoaked Podium, with lovely breadth, weight and a refinement only seen in a handful of examples. Also made are a passito version from dried grapes, Brumato, and a sparkling wine from Verdicchio. Three Rosso Conero are all 100% Montepulciano. The premium version, Grosso Agontano (now Conero Riserva), aged in *barriques* for 12 months, has ample breadth and complexity and should be drunk with five years' age or more. Camerlano is a blend of Merlot, Cabernet Sauvignon and Montepulciano in varying proportions according to the vintage, whilst Monte Reale is a 100% Sangiovese. All the wines, but particularly the whites, are very well priced for the quality.

Recommended Reds:
Conero Riserva Grosso Agontano ★★★ £D
Rosso Conero Vigna Piancarda ★★ £C
Rosso Piceno Colle Ambro ★ £B
Recommended Whites:
Verdicchio dei Castelli di Jesi Classico Riserva Serra Fiorese ★★★ £D
Verdicchio dei Castelli di Jesi Classico Superiore Podium ★★★ £C
Verdicchio dei Castelli di Jesi Classico Superiore Macrina ★☆ £B
Metodo Classico Brut Riserva Vintage ★★☆ £C

Luigi Giusti (Lacrima di Morro d'Alba) *www.lacrimagiusti.it*
If you're new to Lacrima di Morro d'Alba these wines are a treat. At its best the grape gives wines with deep colour, seductive aromas,

as well as flavour, substance and breadth yet which are not in the least bit heavy. Piergiovanni Giusti works with Giancarlo Soverchia to make three excellent examples from 9 ha dedicated to the variety. The regular 'Lacrima' is a delight with lovely balance, the red rosé scented Rubbjano is a vineyard selection aged in small barrels and has more breadth and a refined finish. A third, Luigino is aged in new *barriques* and has greater weight and structure but promises much with 5 years' age or more - almost in the mould of an elegant Barolo. Despite there being only modest quantities of 'Lacrima' and very small amounts of the two selections, being little known in the English speaking world you shouldn't be beaten to their door by speculators. A rosé, Le Rose di Settembre is also made and a blend, Intruso, is made with Montepulciano, Lacrima di Morro, Sangiovese and Merlot. Visciola is a passito made from Lacrima di Morro d'Alba but has not been tasted.

Recommended Reds:
Lacrima di Morro d'Alba Rubbjano ★★★ £D
Lacrima di Morro d'Alba Luigino ★★★ £D
Lacrima di Morro d'Alba Lacrima ★★ £C

La Monacesca (Marche/Verdicchio) *www.monacesca.it*
La Monacesca, named for a settlement of Benedictine monks, is located in Matelica, the smaller, lesser known of Marche's two Verdicchio zones. Ripe and concentrated unoaked Verdicchio with good depth and character are produced from 27 ha of vineyards at 400m altitude. The superior bottling, gently nutty and buttery with spice, citrus and a minerally quality, shows greater refinement and definition than a well-made regular version. The top white, Mirum, is produced from late-harvested grapes, giving added richness and complexity. All three can be drunk young but keep well. Also made is a varietal Chardonnay, Ecclesia, and an increasingly good red, Camerte (70% Sangiovese/30% Merlot).

Recommended Reds:
Camerte ★★★ £D
Recommended Whites:
Verdicchio di Matelica Riserva Mirum ★★★ £D
Verdicchio di Matelica La Monacesca ★★ £C
Verdicchio di Matelica ★ £B

Lanari (Marche/Rosso Conero) *www.lanarivini.it*
10 years ago Rosso Conero was the leading red wine appellation in Marche. The picture has changed considerably with many of the best reds now sold as Marche Rosso, many of which come from the southern Marche. Nevertheless Rosso Conero has continued to improve, not least the examples made by Luca Lanari and his enologist Giancarlo Soverchia from 12 ha of vines. The regular version (with 10% Sangiovese) can be a touch rustic but is better than the more insipid offerings from some of the larger producers. Better are the single vineyard examples from 100% Montepulciano. D'Inclite spends 6-7 months in *barrique*, the oak being well married to its mineral, black fruited character. It is Fibbio however that has established Lanari's reputation. Coming from a higher vineyard, the wine has 12-15 months in oak and has considerably more style and complexity. The best vintages improve for at least a decade. A very small quantity of a new Riserva, Aretè is now made.

Recommended Reds:
Conero Riserva Fibbio ★★★☆ £E
Rosso Conero D'Inclite ★★☆ £C   Rosso Conero ★ £C

La Caniette (Marche/Rosso Piceno) *www.lecaniette.it*
This family claim to have been growing grapes in the region for four

centuries yet there is no lack of ambition in the wines, including the whites. The Lucrezia, 100% Passerina, is a powerful, full blown white. Although a bit overdone it is a refreshing change from run of the mill Pecorino Veronica. More 'off the wall' is a varietal Pecorino, "Io sono Gaia Non Sono Lucrezia" which is partially fermented on the skins. From its peach skin colour to unusual aromas and flavours this is very much a 'red wine' white with impressive intensity and balance. Due to location the reds are simply Rosso Piceno without the Superiore designation but for once it doesn't matter. The premium versions, Morellone (70% Montepulciano/30% Sangiovese) and Nero di Vite (50/50) are high in alcohol, dense and flavoursome. The latter is a significant step-up from the soft, fleshy Morellone; richer, more complex and better defined, it only lacks a touch more class and refinement to put it amongst the Marche's best. An unoaked version, Rosso Bello, made in equal parts with Montepulciano and Sangioivese with 10% Cabernet Sauvignon is also made. New is a heavyweight, Cinabro, made with 100% Bordo (a local clone of Grenache) aged in *barriques* for 30 months, but has not been tasted.

Recommended Reds:
Rosso Piceno Nero di Vite ★★★☆ £E
Rosso Piceno Morellone ★★ £C
Recommended Whites:
Offida Pecorino Io sono Gaia Non Sono Lucrezia ★★☆ £C
Offida Pecorino Veronica ★ £B   Marche Passerino Lucrezia ★☆ £B

❀ Le Terraze (Marche/Rosso Conero)   *www.fattorialeterrazze.it*
To rhythms of Bob Dylan, the laid-back Antonio Terni is steadily building production towards 10,000 cases of wine a year 20 ha of estate vineyards. Yet this is a very serious enterprise based on slopes at low elevation close to the sea within the Parco Conero. Birds are a big problem with all manner of devices to scare them off. Whatever they eat they haven't impacted on the high quality range of wines. A long period of consultancy from Attilio Pagli has ensured ever better reds. A regular Rosso Conero (100% Montepulciano) shows better ripeness and richness than most examples. Sassi Neri (now Conero Riserva), with an extended maceration (three weeks) and a year in *barriques* (a third new) shows real depth, succulence and elegance with three years' age or more. Just occasionally a very special selection, Visions of J, is produced. With age it can show added class and complexity but Sassi Neri represents better value. Chaos is another fine red, a lush, black-fruited blend of Montepulciano (50%), Syrah and Merlot aged in new oak. Made since the 02 vintage is Planet Waves. A blend of Montepulciano and Merlot it is very much in an international style but is full, concentrated and long. What's more it was produced at Bob Dylan's instigation. A little unoaked but well-made Chardonnay, Le Cave, is also made.

Recommended Reds:
Conero Riserva Visions of J ★★★★ £F
Conero Riserva Sassi Neri ★★★☆ £D
Rosso Conero ★★ £B   Chaos ★★★☆ £F
Planet Waves ★★★☆ £F
Recommended Whites:
Le Cave ★★ £B

Leopardi Dittajuti (Marche/Rosso Conero)   *www.leopardiwines.com*
Piervittorio Leopardi Dittajuti's collaboration with Riccardo Cotarella has been a most sucessful one. Some white as well as red is produced from 45 ha of well tended vineyards. From 2001 reds show richer, softer fruit and balanced tannins. The regular Rosso Conero is supple and fruit-driven – more should taste like this at this

level. Then there is Pigmento, deeper and more concentrated with well-integrated oak, resulting from a longer maceration on the skins and up to 24 months in new *barriques*. It has the potential to be very good indeed and needs five years' ageing. More international and less distinctive is Casirano, a blend of Cabernet Sauvignon, Syrah and Montepulciano (roughly a third of each), but this too is well made. Two Sauvignons are also surprisingly good. Fresh Bianco del Coppo is vinified in stainless steel, while stylish, oak-influenced Calcare has better structure. A Vermentino, Castelverde, is also produced, but this has not been tasted.

Recommended Reds:
Conero Riserva Pigmento ★★★☆ £D
Rosso Conero ★★☆ £C   Casirano ★★★ £D
Recommended Whites:
Calcare ★★ £D   Bianco del Coppo ★ £B

❀ Malacari (Marche/Rosso Conero)   *www.malacari.it*
Malacari continues a long heritage both of place (Offagna long pre-dates its formidable medieval fortress) and as a producer of wine and olive oil. Today, the wines made by Sergio Paolucci, are two excellent examples of what is possible from the Montepulciano grape in the Marche. The regular example boasts character and originality at a very affordable price while a much more limited production of Grigiano offers the concentration, muscularity and bold complexity of fully realised Montepulciano. The roasted nuts, black fruits, oak and extract combine for a rich, intense yet soft and expressive mouthful, especially if given 5-10 years' age. A Verdicchio, Vinea Misturi, is also produced.

Recommended Reds:
Conero Riserva Grigiano ★★★★ £D   Rosso Conero ★★☆ £B

Fattoria Mancini (Marche/Colli Pesaresi)   *www.fattoriamancini.com*
Luigi Mancini has got all sorts of weird ideas, but the intent and results deserve to be taken seriously. From slopes high above the rim of the Adriatic, Pinot Nero, which came with Napoleon's troops nearly 200 years ago, is the grape of choice. From it is made a white wine, Impero Bianco, of an exotic, almost decadent fruit character, vaguely similar to an over-the-top Alsace Pinot Gris. In a second white, the unoaked Roncaglia, Pinot Nero is again vinified as a white wine where it complements Albanella, a little-known variety said to have Albariño as a parent – though of modest structure, the wine is full of ripe nectarine and exotic fruits. The best Pinot however is kept for the reds. The regular Pinot Noir has rather old-fashioned Burgundian flavours albeit without the finesse of which Pinot is capable, but there's no disputing the character and complexity of these ripe, meaty but well-balanced examples. Rive shows more oak as well as a lot of extract and intensity and should be put aside for at least five more years. Blu, now 100% Ancellotto, is a powerful black-fruited wine also needing time but shows great promise. Sangiovese is also made.

Recommended Reds:
Blu ★★★ £E   Colli Pesaresi Focara Pinot Noir Rive ★★★ £D
Recommended Whites:
Colli Pesaresi Roncaglia ★★ £B   Impero Blanc de Pinot Noir ★★ £B

Marchetti (Marche/Rosso Conero)   *www.marchettiwines.it*
The distinctive crenulated Villa Bonomi, located in hills just west of Ancona, was being used for silk worm production at the time of its purchase by Maurizio Marchetti's grandfather. The family later became one of the first of four producers to make Rosso Conero when the DOC was first introduced. Maurizio's 18 ha of black grapes

Central Italy /Marche

are almost entirely given over to Montepulciano with just a little Syrah, Merlot and Cabernet Sauvignon. These are complemented by 9ha of vines near Jesi dedicated to Verdicchio production. The latter deserves mention as much as the reds, especially a good value premium bottling, Tenuta del Cavaliere. Coming from later harvested fruit, it is concentrated, gently minerally and well-balanced despite highish alcohol. Better known is Maurizio's very bold, ripe gutsy and long established Villa Bonomi red - sold as Conero Riserva since 2004. Aged for 14 months in both new and used oak, some of the richness and texture is derived from the use of governo alla toscana whereby must is added after the alcoholic fermentation helping induce the malolactic. While it misses a little of the finesse of other top Conero reds it is both complex and long-lived (and much improved on the efforts of a decade ago). Regular bottlings of both Rosso Conero and Verdicchio have plenty of fruit and good balance and offer more than the standard offerings from many of the larger producers of each.

Recommended Reds:
Conero Riserva Villa Bonomi ★★★ £D   Rosso Conero ★☆ £B
Recommended Whites:
Verdicchio Castelli di Jesi Classico Superiore Tenuta del Cavaliere ★★★ £C
Verdicchio dei Castelli di Jesi Classico ★☆ £B

Monte Schiavo (Marche/Verdicchio) *www.monteschiavo.com*
Big can be beautiful. Since 1995 this former co-op has formed part of the holdings of the Pieralisi family (manufacturers of industrial equipment). Monte Schiavo currently produce around two million bottles and own around 115 ha of vineyards, the majority of it planted to Verdicchio. Under guidance from enologist Pierluigi Lorenzetti the wines are expertly made and reasonably priced. All the Verdicchios, save a basic Ruviano offer both good body, fruit and expression. Pallio di San Floriano, from grapes harvested later than most, has good breadth and is lightly nuanced. Nativo (made in very small quanities) is slightly atypical as a result of spending a year on the lees; fuller in texture it also reveals a certain elegance. The Riserva Le Giuncare (released just over two years after the vintage) is now only lightly oaked and combines depth and weight with a spice, floral, herbal and almond complexity. Although this wine doesn't necessarily improve greatly with age (beyond an extra couple of years) all but the weakest vintages can be drunk with confidence with as much 8-10 years. The leading red is Adeodato, a concentrated and extracted version of 100% Montepulciano deserving of 5 years' ageing or more. Esio, sold as IGT Marche is mostly Cabernet Sauvignon and Montepulciano aged in new oak. 'Pieralisi for friends' is a new Sangiovese/Merlot blend sold under the Esino DOC. For a dessert white there's Archè, a passito (dried grapes) version of Verdicchio that is one of the better examples made. Monteschiavo also includes olive oil production from local varieties at their own Frantoio (oil making facility). The Pieralisi family also own three other wineries in Italy - in Abruzzo (VILLA BIZZARI), Puglia and Sicily.

Recommended Reds:
Rosso Conero Adeodato ★★☆ £C   Esio ★★ £C
Recommended Whites:
Verdicchio Castelli di Jesi Classico Superiore Riserva Le Giuncare ★★★ £C
Verdicchio Castelli di Jesi Classico Superiore Pallio di San Floriano ★★☆ £C
Verdicchio dei Castelli di Jesi Classico Superiore Nativo ★★☆ £B
Verdicchio dei Castelli di Jesi Classico Coste del Molino ★☆ £B

✿ Oasi Degli Angeli (Marche/Rosso Piceno) *www.kurni.it*
Marco Casolanetti and Eleonora Rossi produce just one very sought-

after wine, one of the region's benchmark reds. Kurni was first made in 1997 and is an outstanding, powerful, very ripe, complex expression of the Montepulciano grape. Although unlikely to be encountered now, a white from Trebbiano, Esedra, was also made in the first two vintages. Winemaker Giovanni Basso takes a rigorous approach to quality both in the vineyard and cellar which along with the tiny production has fuelled the wine's cult status. The wine is a majestic offering with splendid purity, complexity (preserved black fruits, smoke, grilled meats, mineral and graphite) within a very concentrated and massively structured frame - the the richness and extract being balanced by very fine tannins. Production, around 6,000 bottles, is slowly increasing, though seems unlikely to ever satisfy demand. The estate is another supporting the Piceninvisibili initiative (see SAN SAVINO) promoting the wines of Piceno.
Recommended Reds:
Kurni ★★★★★ £G

Saladini Pilastri (Marche/Rosso Piceno) *www.saladinipilastri.it*
The name Saladini Pilastri denotes an ancient lineage and an estate hundreds of years old but its wine production is only just getting into its stride. Since the arrival of Domenico D'Angelo in the mid-nineties viticulture has been switched to an organic basis. The fruits of these efforts are now being more fully realised thanks to consultancy from Alberto Antonini. The wines are better balanced and more expressive than previously, with plenty of extract but not the hardness of old. The top wine is Vigna Monteprandone (70% Montepulciano, 30% Sangiovese), a concentrated red with truffle, plum, blackberry and spice, but intense fruit is seen in all examples of Rosso Piceno including an increasingly good basic. In Pregio del Conte, Aglianico instead of Sangiovese complements the Montepulciano, adding style though still wanting for better harmony.

Recommended Reds:
Rosso Piceno Superiore Vigna Monteprandone ★★★ £C
Rosso Piceno Superiore Vigna Montetinello ★★☆ £C
Rosso Piceno Vigna Piediprato ★★☆ £B
Rosso Piceno ★☆ £B   Pregio del Conte ★★ £C

San Giovanni (Marche/Rosso Piceno) *www.vinisangiovanni.it*
Gianni Di Lorenzo now runs the 35 ha estate established by his father Silvano in 1990. His goal is for ever higher quality, seemingly at the risk of turning him into a Marche superstar! The straight Rosso Piceno, Ophites (50/50) is an excellent bright, fruit-driven example with good purity. Superiore Leo Guelfus shows some oak influence but a supple, relaxed style. Better still is the Axeé with the maximum 70/30 blend of Montepulciano and Sangiovese. With a cherry/berry, herbal and mineral profile, this has more precision and intensity whilst avoiding the high acidity and over-extraction seen in some examples. Zeii, which adds Cabernet Sauvignon (30%) and Merlot (20%) to Montepulciano has a very different flavour profile with a bramble, crushed berry and black plum character but similarly includes a mineral component. Both are accessible relatively young but have good ageing potential. Whites are also worthy with a flavoursome and well-structured Pecorino, and ripe grapefruit, herb and tropical-fruited Marta produced from late-harvested Sauvignon and Vermentino grapes. Also made but not tasted is a sweet wine from noblyrotted Passerina grapes.

Recommended Reds:
Offida Rosso Zeii ★★★☆ £D   Rosso Piceno Superiore Axeé ★★★ £D
Rosso Piceno Superiore Leo Guelfus ★★☆ £C
Rosso Piceno Ophites ★★ £B

Recommended Whites:
Offida Pecorino Kiara ★★ £B Marta ★★ £B

⚫ San Lorenzo (Marche) www.fattoriasanlorenzo.com
There can be no more talented nor passionate producer in the
Marche today than Natalino Crognaletti. His wines are superb and
with good reason. A commitment to producing the highest quality
fruit and extracting the best from it results in wines of both superb
fruit quality and structure. The 35 ha are farmed biodynamically but
this is no religion here but more a consequence of a commitment
to what Natalino views as a traditional style of viticulture. All the
wines are labelled with the vineyard origins. Reds are hand-plunged
prior to ageing in used oak of both larger and smaller capacity - the
oak serving only as a vessel to enhance structure with the barrels
being shaved and washed to diminish oak given flavours. Natalino
has even produced some of his own barrels at a cooper based in
Merano. While most are turning away from Sangiovese for quality
wines in the Marche, here it is used to complement Montepulciano
to marvellous effect in a Rosso Piceno of excellent purity and
expression (and value!). Only half the amount of Sangiovese (20%)
is used in a powerful concentrated Rosso Conero that needs
8-10 years' ageing. For a varietal version of Montepulciano there
is Vigneto del Solleone (sold as IGT Marche). which displays the
essence of the grape in this part of the Marche. Needless to say,
Natalino's Lacrima is superb with a depth and complexity that
goes way beyond what even good examples of this variety offer.
Verdicchios show a beautifully refined fruit with none of the slightly
coarser, Trebbianolike, more herbal aspects seen to some extent
in most examples. Even the inexpensive Vigna del Gino is vibrant
and full of life. Wine pilgrims seeking renewal can buy bottles at the
winery.
Recommended Reds:
Vigneto del Solleone ★★★★ £E
Rosso Conero La Gattara ★★★☆ £C
Rosso Piceno Vigna Burello ★★★ £C
Lacrima Vigna Paradiso ★★★☆ £C
Recommended Whites:
Verdicchio Castelli di Jesi Classico Riserva Vigna delle Oche ★★★☆ £C
Verdicchio Castelli di Jesi Classico Superiore Vigna delle Oche ★★★ £C
Verdicchio dei Castelli di Jesi Classico Vigna di Gino ★★☆ £B

⚫ San Savino - Podere Capecci (Marche) www.sansavino.com
Simone Capecci's 35 ha family estate is one of the most exciting
in Piceno, adding a new dynamism to the Marche as a whole. He
is also one of Piceninvisibili, a grouping of eight quality-minded
producers in the southern reaches of the Marche intent on working
together to gain a better understanding of their area as well as
raising its profile. The white from Pecorino is arguably the most
distinctive made. It is floral and mineral with lemon rind and spice
and is ripe, intense and flavoursome on the palate with a hint of
saltiness. Excellent reds include lush, complex, partly barrique-aged
Picus (60/40 Montepulciano/Sangiovese) and stylish if oaky Fedus
(100% Sangiovese). The pure, concentrated Ver Sacrum is 100%
Montepulciano and sees no oak. Rich, powerful and complete
Quinta Regio is also from Montepulciano but with 12 months in
barrique and two years in large oak. Inexpensive Collemura Rosso
Piceno and white Falerio are also made but have not been tasted.
Recommended Reds:
Quinta Regio ★★★★☆ £F   Ver Sacrum ★★★☆ £E
Fedus ★★★ £D   Rosso Piceno Superiore Picus ★★★ £C

Recommended Whites:
Offida Pecorino Ciprea ★★★ £C

Santa Barbara (Marche/Verdicchio) www.vinisantabarbara.it
The popular and dynamic Stefano Antonucci makes a fine and
consistent range of whites based primarily on Verdicchio. A very
creditable basic quaffing Verdicchio and more classic Pignotto
are surpassed by the unoaked Le Vaglie with a fine floral, herbal,
mineral character and good depth and structure. In contrast the
Riserva spends 12 months in barriques and compares well with an
elegant, mineral-intense, leaner style of white burgundy. Unusual is
the late harvested Tardivo ma non Tardivo, with added depth and
breadth. Botrytis is avoided and with its ripe stone fruit and spice
character is not unlike a Auslese Trocken style of German Riesling.
A Sauvignon Blanc and a Passerina are also made but have not
been tasted.There are also two excellent reds: Il Maschio da Monte
(100% Montepulciano) has a fine spicy depth but usually needs
time to fatten up. Better still is Pathos (Marche IGT), a very seductive
international blend of Merlot, Cabernet Sauvignon and Syrah. Other
reds are balanced and soundly made but lack for richness and
ripeness - that with the most potential is the Stefano Antonucci
Marche red, a blend of Montepulciano, Cabernet Sauvignon and
Merlot.
Recommended Reds:
Pathos ★★★☆ £F   Stefano Antonucci ★★ £C
Rosso Piceno Il Maschio da Monte ★★★ £D
Recommended Whites:
Verdicchio Castelli di Jesi Classico Tardivo ma non Tardivo ★★★☆ £D
Verdicchio Castelli di Jesi Classico Riserva Stefano Antonucci ★★★ £C
Verdicchio dei Castelli di Jesi Classico Le Vaglie ★★★ £C
Verdicchio dei Castelli di Jesi Pignotto ★★☆ £C
Verdicchio dei Castelli di Jesi ★☆ £B

Sartarelli (Marche/Verdicchio) www.sartarelli.it
This 51 ha estate is one of the best sources in the Marche for ripe,
flavoursome Verdicchio. The regular example is typically bright, fresh
and fruit-driven with ripe apple, floral and yellow plum flavours.
Tralivio is partially barrique-aged, resulting in a richer texture but
more of a leesy influence and less refinement and fruit purity. It is
better with at least three years' age. The Contrada Balciana, which
has a year in barrique, can start out a little awkwardly too but has
good intensity and lots of depth and character, though still seems to
miss a little refinement that would ensure a higher rating. A Passito
and a sparkling Brut using the Charmat method are also made from
Verdicchio grapes.
Recommended Whites:
Verdicchio dei Castelli di Jesi Classico Contrada Balciana ★★☆ £D
Verdicchio dei Castelli di Jesi ClassicoTralivio ★★ £C
Verdicchio dei Castelli di Jesi Classico ★★ £B

Silvano Strologo (Marche/Rosso Conero) www.vinorossoconero.com
Founded in 1998 this small estate has quickly made a name for
itself, especially since working with Giancarlo Soverchia. Only the
best fruit from 10 ha of vines at 250m is kept and used for three
Montepulciano-based reds and a little rosé, both still and sparkling
made from 90% Montepulciano and 10% Sangiovese. Regular
Rosso Conero Julius, with plump black cherry fruit generally keeps
well for 5-6 years. Traiano is more ample with greater depth and
more characteristic of the terroir here. Hot years show more of a
distinct amarena or bitter cherry quality from over-ripe fruit but
are otherwise rich and characterful. The top selection, Decebalo, is

Central Italy /Marche

subject to a long maceration (25-30 days) and given 18 months in new French oak on the fine lees with frequent rackings. Showing lots of promise this is more complete in every respect but only differs from Traiano in the winemaking and not the fruit selection. Whites include an entry level blend of Malvasia, Trebbiano and Moscato, a Moscato Giallo Passito and an unusual local grape, Incrocio Bruni 45, created in a laboratory by Professor Bruno Bruni from Sauvignon and Verdicchio.

Recommended Reds:

Conero Riserva Decebalo ★★★☆ £D
Rosso Conero Traiano ★★★ £C Rosso Conero Julius ★★ £C

Tenuta di Tavignano (Verdicchio) *www.tenutaditavignano.it*
Tavignano's elevated vineyards are topped by a villa of Roman origins. The 360 degree panoramic views from the 230 ha estate are splendid, taking in both the coast at Senigállia and Monte San Vicino to the west in the direction of the Appenines. Fine too are the mineral-imbued Verdicchios produced from around half of the 30ha of vineyard that were planted in the early to mid-90s. Misco, the top selection is a refined and classy example with fine ripe fruit, floral and mineral nuances. Its depth, intensity and a certain elegance put it amongst the very best made. A Riserva version adds a little more expression. The regular Tavignano bottling is also well-structured with a satisfying minerality. All are better with at least 2-3 years' age. The more basic Vigna Verde is a decent quaffer. Other whites include a Pecorino and a Passerina. A significant chunk of vineyard is also planted to Montepulciano and a lesser amount of Sangiovese. An easy-drinking regular Rosso Piceno, Castel Rosino adds 25% Sangiovese and 5% Cabernet Sauvignon to Montepulciano. In the more ambitious Libenter - of the same blend but given 14 months in *barriques* - there is plenty of rich, ripe extract but not as yet the refinement in the tannic structure needed in order to reveal its full potential. Cervidoni, 70% Montepuciano and 30% Sangiovese, is even fuller and rounder with a big mouthfeel but also lacks tannic structure. There is also a Lacrima di Morro d'Alba, Barbarossa, but this has not been tasted. A little of an attractive Sangiovese based rosé is also made. Not yet tasted is Sante Lancerio, Tavignano's passito Verdicchio.

Recommended Reds:

Rosso Piceno Libenter ★★ £C Rosso Piceno Cervidoni ★★ £C
Rosso Piceno Castel Rosino ★ £B

Recommended Whites:

Verdicchio Castelli di Jesi Classico Superiore Misco Riserva ★★★☆ £C
Verdicchio Castelli di Jesi Classico Superiore Misco Selezione ★★★ £C
Verdicchio dei Castelli di Jesi Classico Superiore Villa Torre ★☆ £B

Umani Ronchi (Marche & Abruzzo) *www.umanironchi.com*
Despite being a big volume producer in its more basic brands, in its best wines Umani Ronchi offers a good quality introduction to the wines from the central Adriatic coast. These include good Verdicchio in both stainless steel fermented examples (Villa Bianchi and single-vineyard Casal di Serra) and the partially oak-aged and fermented Riserva Plenio. Verdicchio is also combined with Chardonnay in the oak-aged Le Busche. Reds from the Montepulciano grape show good character too, especially in Rosso Conero San Lorenzo and Riserva Cúmaro. New from 2009, is another Conero Risrerva, Campo San Giorgio, with even greater intensity. In Pelago, the richer, oakier red flagship wine, Montepulciano has been successfully combined with Cabernet Sauvignon and Merlot (typically 50/40/10). Yet despite a pretty good record for consistency and flavour there's not quite the value for money of old. The wines can also sometimes lack

for balance and definition. As well made as they can be, it seems there should be more life and intensity to most of the range. A new Vecchie Vigne version of Casal di Serra shows more intensity and vigour. Among other wines made are a varietal Sangiovese, Medoro, good Lacrima di Morro d'Alba, and a sweet white from botrytised Sauvignon grapes, Maximo.

Recommended Reds:

Pelago ★★★ £E Conero Riserva Cúmaro ★★★ £D
Rosso Conero San Lorenzo ★☆ £B
Lacrima di Morro d'Alba Fonte del Re ★★ £B
Montepulciano d'Abruzzo Jorio ★☆ £B

Recommended Whites:

Verdicchio dei Castelli di Jesi Riserva Plenio ★★ £C
Verdicchio dei Castelli di Jesi Casal di Serra ★ £B
Le Busche ★ £C

✿ **Velenosi (Rosso Piceno & Verdicchio)** *www.velenosivini.com*
This is a very switched on producer with a consistently high quality range that makes it one of the Marche's best. Striking is their success with both more international varieties and those considered more classically Marche, as well as in white, red and sparkling styles but then expertise comes from both Attilio Pagli and, lately, Ronco Taraborelli (for fizz). The vintage-dated Brut Metodo (60% Chardonnay, 40% Pinot Nero) is stylish and flavoursome and compares well with premium Italian sparkling wines. 'The Rose' is a new Pinot Nero dominated sparkler but it is not of the same standard. Of the whites, the Falerio Vigna Solaria bears no relation to most labelled under this humble DOC while from 2005 there is also an attractive Verdicchio from Paolo Garbini's own vines. The unoaked Chardonnay, Villa Angela is remarkably good in this style and far better than most Australian examples, presumably due to working with better raw materials. A *barrique*-aged version, Rêve di Villa Angela is very 'peaches and cream' and might work better if barrel-fermented too. The mineral and lightly elderflower Sauvignon is also a surprise and compares well with good examples from the North-East. More recent expansions to the range include a Passerino and two Pecorinos (A Falerio from 2006 and an Offida since that appellation gained promotion to DOCG status in 2011). Reds include a quite sophisticated version of Rosso Piceno Superiore in Il Brecciarolo and an outstanding example in Roggio del Filare. Both are oak-aged and combine 60% Montepulciano with 40% Sangiovese, the latter spending 18 months in new French *barriques*. It is a beautifully composed whole with great 'Marche' style and expression. Ludi is another excellent red with Montepulciano complemented by Cabernet Sauvignon and Merlot (40/30/30). From a similar ageing regime and low yields it has a super fruit quality that masks a fine structure. Both top reds deserve to be drunk with at least 5-6 years' age. Other reds include a straight Montepulciano, a Lacrima di Morro d'Alba regular and superiore and a "Gold" version of Il Brecciarolo

Recommended Reds:

Rosso Piceno Superiore Roggio del Filare ★★★★ £D
Rosso Piceno Superiore Il Brecciarolo ★★ £B Ludi ★★★☆ £E

Recommended Whites:

Velenosi Brut Metodo Classico ★★★ £D
ChardonnayVilla Angela ★★★ £C
Verdicchio dei Castelli di Jesi Classico ★★☆ £C
Sauvignon Linagre ★★☆ £C
Pecorino Villa Angela ★★ £C
Falerio Vigna Solaria ★★ £B

Vignamato (Verdicchio & Rosso Piceno) *www.vignamato.com*
Maurizio Ceci has modernised and expanded the small operation established by his father, Amato in the 1950s. There are just 9ha of vineyards and the range of wines reflect a dedicated approach from the vineyard to what's in the bottle. The Valle delle Lame Verdicchio is very fresh, clean and spicy if drunk young. Versiano, the Superiore version, reveals more complexity, elegance and purity and needs 2-4 years' age. Another Verdicchio, Ambrosia (not tasted) is fermented in tonneaux and aged on the lees but is not made every year. For red there's a very perfumed (wild cherry) and flavoursome Esino Rosso with negligible tannin, produced half from Montepulciano and half from Sangiovese, Cabernet Sauvignon and Merlot. The Rosso Piceno, Campalliano (from Montepulciano) has 12 months in French oak and is deep, concentrated and flavousome, quite long and powerful but with a relatively soft, supple structure. However the best wine is Antares, the passito-style Verdicchio which is partly dried on the vine and partly on racks. It has a fine interplay between dried stone fruits and a gentle spicy botrytis character. Only moderately sweet, there is excellent intensity and balance to highlight the spice, honeycomb and preserved citrus flavours..

Recommended Reds:
Rosso Piceno Campalliano ★★★ £C
Esino Rosso Rosolaccio ★★ £B

Recommended Whites:
Verdicchio dei Castelli di Jesi Passito Antares ★★★☆ £E
Verdicchio dei Castelli di Jesi Classico Superiore Versiano ★★★ £C
Verdicchio dei Castelli di Jesi Classico Valle delle Lame ★☆ £B

A-Z of producers - *Umbria*

✿ **Paolo Bea (Umbria/Montefalco Sagrantino)** *www.paolobea.com*
Paolo Bea's family date back to the 1500s and he maintains a small family production that is organic, artisanal and traditional in the truest sense. Due to the care and diligence in the vineyard, intervention is minimal yet responsive to the growing conditions of the each particular year. The wines are aged in a mix of large oak and stainless steel. Every bottle is numbered and will throw a light sediment with age. The Montefalco Sagrantino (secco) is a wine of marvellous concentration, purity and complexity and is powerful, beautifully balanced but deserving of another 5-10 years' ageing. In more difficult vintages, Rosso de Vêo is made instead. With spiced preserved cherry and liquified raspberry, the wine shows marvellous fruit purity. An expressive, flavoursome Montefalco Rosso is also made. Sourced from Vigna San Valentino, it is Sangiovese-based with the balance of 30% from Montepulicano and Sagrantino. The Sagrantino Passito is made only after 5 months of natural drying on straw mats resulting in a very sweet and intense style with high acidity and showing a degree of evolution with 5 years' age or more. The wine is necessarily very expensive , the production is tiny. There is also some extra virgin olive oil, no doubt made with the same fastidious approach. Whether the wines are always of the standard for which they are rated remains to be confirmed but you're unlikely to be disappointed, assuming you can afford them in the first place.

Recommended Reds:
Rosso de Veo ★★★☆ £E   Montefalco Sagrantino ★★★★☆ £F
Montefalco Sagrantino Passito ★★★★ £G

✿ **Arnaldo Caprai (Montefalco Sagrantino)** *www.arnaldocaprai.it*
This modern powerhouse operation has brought the small Montefalco zone and its Sagrantino grape wide recognition both within Italy and on foreign markets. Since the late 1980s the

winery, vineyards (90 ha in production) and the wines have been transformed under Marco Caprai (Arnaldo's son) and his winemaking consultant Attilio Pagli. The leading Sagrantino wines are extremely concentrated, powerful and structured. These are not wines for early drinking but are complex and demanding, needing at least 10 years' age. The Sagrantino 25 Anni is an Italian classic, utterly compelling with terrific aromatic complexity and superb texture and dimension in the mouth. An unusual sweet (passito) version is very intense, with much of the wild berry character of Sagrantino but a certain finesse too. Montefalco Rosso Riserva, in contrast, is based on Sangiovese (70%) with the balance from Sagrantino and Merlot. A long maceration shows in the wine's breadth and rich texture. Lesser wines are also very good, including a stylish, intense regular Montefalco Rosso and an intense fresh and fruit-filled white from Grechetto. Montefalco Bianco combines Chardonnay, Trebbiano and Sauvignon with Grechetto. There are ongoing experiments with other varieties including international ones such as Syrah and Malbec. Umbria Outsider is a plush, deeply concentrated red from Merlot and Cabernet Sauvignon that rivals the region's best in this mould and there is a tiny production of Outsider Pinot Nero as well.

Recommended Reds:
Montefalco Sagrantino 25 Anni ✪✪✪✪✪ £G
Montefalco Sagrantino Collepiano ★★★★ £F
Montefalco Sagrantino Passito ★★★ £F
Montefalco Rosso Riserva ★★★ £E   Montefalco Rosso ★★ £C

Recommended Whites:
Grechetto dei Colli Martani Grecante ★★☆ £C

Castello della Sala (Umbria/Orvieto) *www.antinori.it*
The Castello della Sala is a major outpost of the ANTINORI family (see Tuscany), with 160 ha in the vicinity of the 14th-century castle after which the estate is named. It was acquired by Niccolò Antinori (father of Piero) in 1940. The principal wine, Cervaro della Sala, has an established track record as one of Italy's best Chardonnays, with a refinement and gentle minerality missing from most of the bigger, more concentrated examples. As much as 20% of the wine is Grechetto but its relative propensity to age also sets it apart from others. A second Chardonnay, now called Bramito del Cerro (previously simply Chardonnay) shows good richness and depth and is decent value for money. Conte della Vipera is Sauvignon with a small addition of Chardonnay while Muffato della Sala is an oak-aged botrytised sweet wine of moderate richness and sweetness made from varying percentages of Sauvignon, Grechetto, Gewürztraminer and Riesling. Orvieto is made in three versions: Superiore, Campogrande and an amabile (medium-dry) version, Casasole. From 2005 the improving Superiore has been repackaged as San Giovanni della Sala and in addition to the more usual Grechetto and Procanico, a quarter of the blend is comprised of Pinot Bianco, Riesling and Viognier.

Recommended Reds:
Pinot Nero ★★ £E

Recommended Whites:
Cervaro della Sala ★★★★ £E   Bramito del Cerro ★★★ £C
Muffato della Sala ★★ £E   Conte della Vipera ★★ £C
Orvieto Classico Superiore San Giovanni della Sala ★★ £B

Còlpetrone (Umbria/Montefalco Sagrantino) *www.saiagricola.it*
Còlpetrone has been part of the Saiagricola stable since 1995 (others are DEL CERRO in Montepulciano and LA PODERINA in Brunello di Montalcino – see Tuscany) and along with CAPRAI it is one of the established benchmarks for Sagrantino. The wines from

63 ha of vineyard are made by noted enologist Lorenzo Landi. The impressive black plum, smoke and herb-fuelled Sagrantino has formidable power, extract and intensity, often needing a decade or longer to show at its best. Montefalco Rosso too is typically concentrated with plenty of extract. One caveat: some recent bottles of both wines have revealed a slight musty wood character that suggests a possible cellar problem. Also made is an intense passito version, its complex flavours usually well checked by a good balance between sweetness and acidity. In some years, a "gold" Sagratino is produced in magnums.

Recommended Reds:
Montefalco Rosso ★★ £C   Montefalco Sagrantino ★★★★ £E
Montefalco Sagrantino Passito ★★★ £F

Goretti (Umbria/Montefalco Sagrantino) *www.vinigoretti.com*
The Goretti brothers have 15 ha in the Montefalco and are establishing a new winery there. Stefano and Gianluca work with Barbara Tamburini and Vittorio Fiore for three complex and appealing reds. The Goretti's Sagrantino shows classic character but also a distinctive blue/black berry fruit depth. There is both breadth and extract but 10 years is needed if it is to reach its full potential. Montefalco Rosso, in which 20% each of Sagrantino and Merlot complement Sangiovese, is very seductive with fine floral and berry fruit intensity, but finishing with slightly drying tannins. In L'Arringatore Merlot and Ciliegiolo add complexity and individuality to the Sangiovese core; again there are firm tannins but top vintages need another 2–3 years. Whites include a sound Grechetto vinified in stainless steel and barrel-fermented Il Moggio from grapes harvested 10–20 days later. Though slightly coarse, it is aromatic and flavoursome. Pinot Grigio and Chardonnay are also made.

Recommended Reds:
Montefalco Sagrantino ★★★☆ £E   Montefalco Rosso ★★ £C
L'Arringatore ★★★ £D
Recommended Whites:
Il Moggio ★ £C   Colli Perugini Grechetto ★ £B

La Fiorita Lamborghini (Umbria) *www.lamborghinionline.it*
Two very good reds are made at this beautiful estate at the southern end of Lago Trasimeno purchased by Ferruccio Lamborghini (Patrizia's father) in 1971. Riccardo Cotarella (see FALESCO) makes the wines and top vintages of Campoleone, an equal blend of Sangiovese and Merlot, are excellent. This is the more international of two wines, showing terrific intensity, powerful new oak and crushed small berry fruit - if not originality. The second wine, Trescone, is a sleek and intense blend of Sangiovese, Ciliegiolo and Merlot (50/30/20) with distinctive plum and cherry fruit. Both reds are subject to a long maceration. Trescone is aged in large wood as against the 12 month's ageing in new *barriques* that the Campoleone receives. Trescone needs at least three years' ageing in bottle, Campoleone twice that. Both are sold under the Umbria IGT. A third red, Torami, a pretty much equal blend of Cabernet Sauvignon, Sangiovese and Montepulciano, has been made since 2003, spends 10 months in French *barriques* and released after another 6 months of bottle ageing. It's smooth but concentrated with hints of liquorish, quinnine and sandalwood. A fourth, Era, is 100% Sangiovese produced since 2007 but has not been tasted.

Recommended Reds:
Campoleone ★★★★ £F   Torami ★★★ £D   Trescone ★★ £C

Lungarotti (Umbria/Torgiano) *www.lungarotti.it*
This almost legendary producer was once a beacon of brillance

for Umbrian and Italian winemaking. It remains a family concern with Giorgio's two daughters, Teresa and Chiara now at the helm. Sadly while the fame resulting from wines produced in the 60s and 70s has continued to maintain interest (and sales), quality has been through a long lean period. Much of the fame derives from two leading reds: the Torgiano Rubesco Riserva Vigna Monticchio (Sangiovese/Canaiolo, currently 70/30) and San Giorgio (a similar blend but with 50% Cabernet Sauvignon). Despite an emphasis on a respect for tradition there have been many disappointing examples of both wines over the past two decades. As both have only been released after long-ageing it means that changes, much vaunted by some commentators, take time to feed through. The wines are now released after 4-5 years, with much of the ageing in bottle. Current expertise includes that from Lorenzo Landi and Denis Dubourdieu. Vigna Monticchio could still use more richness while San Giorgio needs the greater time (another 10 years) for the tannins to mellow. Others wines are increasingly soundly made with quite large volumes of regular Rubesco and Torre di Giano white (Vermentino/Trebbiano/Grechetto). The supple, fruity Giubilante is from Sangiovese, Merlot and Syrah. For the wine tourist a visit to the Museo del Vino and the Museo dell'Olivo e dell'Olio is mandatory.

Recommended Reds:
San Giorgio ★★★★ £E
Torgiano Rosso Riserva Rubesco Vigna Monticchio ★★★☆ £E
Torgiano Rosso Rubesco ★ £C   Giubilante ★☆ £C
Recommended Whites:
Aurente Chardonnay ★★☆ £C
Torgiano Bianco Torre di Giano ★☆ £B

Madonna Alta (Montefalco Sagrantino) *www.madonnalta.it*
This small Montefalco estate is currently expanding from 14 ha to 20 ha. With consultancy from Emiliano Falsini (of the Alberto Antonini/Attilo Pagli team) it is now producing excellent examples of Montefalco Rosso and Montefalco Sagrantino. The Rosso has the classic core of Sangiovese complemented by Sagrantino and Merlot. Aged in used oak, it has a sprinkling of spice and good depth and breadth. The Sagrantino, aged in part in new *barriques*, has super fruit with clove, spice, floral characters, black cherry and black plum in a rich, full texture. There is abundant tannin but it is not drying or harsh, although the wine needs cellaring for 10 years. Falconéro is a fresh, fruity, more everyday red that includes a little Merlot and Cabernet Sauvignon with Sangiovese. Also made is an intense, extracted Passito version of Sagrantino and two whites vinified in stainless steel; the Falconéro Bianco includes some Chardonnay.

Recommended Reds:
Montefalco Sagrantino ★★★☆ £E
Montefalco Sagrantino Passito ★★★☆ £E
Montefalco Rosso ★★☆ £C   Falconéro Rosso ★☆ £B

Palazzone (Umbria/Orvieto) *www.palazzone.com*
While it's true that even good Orvieto is nothing to wax lyrical about, those from Palazzone can be among the very best. Terre Vineate (from Procanico and smaller amounts of Grecanico, Malvasia, Verdello and Drupeggio) has ripe, pure fruit and will still drink well with 2–3 years' age. Campo del Guardiano is richer with very ripe citrus fruit, even a touch of honey, but can sometimes develop quite quickly. Other whites include perfumed Grechetto, L'Ultima Spiaggia, an oaked Viognier, which still seems a work in progress but has sufficient fruit quality to suggest further potential. The estate's 25ha also produce reds. Rubbio, from mostly Sangiovese, can be a touch lean but has good intensity and purity. Less consistent are

Cabernet Sauvignon/Cabernet Franc blend Armaleo and Muffa Nobile, a sweet white from Sauvignon.

Recommended Reds:
Armaleo ★★ £D   Rubbio ★★ £C

Recommended Whites:
Orvieto Classico Campo del Guardiano ★★☆ £C
Orvieto Classico Terre Vineate ★★☆ £B
Muffa Nobile ★★ £E   Grechetto ★★ £B

Perticaia (Umbria/Montefalco Sagrantino) *www.perticaia.it*
Perticaia is one of a new wave of quality estates emerging from the Montefalco area. There are 14 ha in the sub-zone of Casale, half for Montefalco Sagrantino. The newer vineyards planted in the late 90s at higher densities are already giving good results thanks in part to winemaking from Emiliano Falsini. Montefalco Rosso (Sangiovese with Sagrantino and Colorino) is aged in French tonneaux and has wild raspberry and blackberry fruit and spice but also tannins that require 3–4 years to soften. Montefalco Sagrantino is oaky but with real breadth and promise, expect a complex, elegant four star example with 10 years' age or more. In 04 a new entry-level red was produced from Sangiovese with 10% Colorino and 10% Merlot. Soft and supple, it is unusually spicy for Sangiovese. Riserva versions for both the Sagrantino and Rosso are also made.

Recommended Reds:
Montefalco Sagrantino ★★★☆ £E
Montefalco Rosso ★★☆ £C   Umbria Rosso ★★ £B

Pieve del Vescovo (Umbria)
Named for the 14th century Castello di Pieve di Vescovo, much of the vineyard area (22 ha) of this 120ha estate has recently been replanted. Lucciaio is a blend of roughly equal parts Merlot and Cabernet Sauvignon with 15% Sangiovese, and is aged for 12 months in *barrique*, a third new. It shows both substance and style with good *terroir* expression but needs time to harmonise its structure. The relatively inexpensive Piovano by contrast is based on Sangiovese complemented by Canaiolo and Ciliegiolo and shows excellent, stylish fruit character. It promises to be very appealing with 3-4 years' age. Tezio (from 2002), an equal blend of Merlot and Cabernet Sauvignon is also impressive - if more pricey.

Recommended Reds:
Lucciaio ★★★☆ £E   Tezio ★★★☆ £E
Colli del Trasimeno Piovano ★★ £B

Poggio Bertaio (Umbria) *www.poggiobertaio.it*
There are parts of Umbria where Cabernet Sauvignon and Merlot really excel – SPORTOLETTI has really hit the jackpot, so too Poggio Bertaio with Crovèllo. Undoubtedly being the family estate of respected enologist Fabrizio Ciufoli lends a certain advantage too. The 20 ha of vineyards are in the hills close to Lago Trasimeno. The Merlot and Cabernet Sauvignon grapes are combined in generally equal proportions for Crovèllo, whereas Cimbolo is Sangiovese from 30-year-old vines, albeit at low densities. Both are *barrique*-aged but Crovèllo is richer with blackberry, mineral, oak spice and a touch of carob and licorice. More compact in profile and less of a blockbuster, Cimbolo is also consistently fine.

Recommended Reds:
Crovèllo ★★★★ £F   Cimbolo ★★★ £E

Scacciadiavoli (Umbria/Montefalco Sagrantino)
Whether you can really banish your demons, as the name suggests, by drinking Montefalco Rosso or Montefalco Sagrantino from

this producer is debatable. But it's at least worth a try, as thanks to Stefano Chioccioli they are both particularly good examples – modern, sweet-fruited wines with lush textures. The stylish Rosso is only 60% Sangiovese with the balance mostly Sagrantino (15%) and Merlot (25%). Sagrantino is bigger and oaky but with fine tannins on a long finish. It needs 6–10 years. Sagrantino Passito is also made.

Recommended Reds:
Montefalco Sagrantino ★★★☆ £E   Montefalco Rosso ★★ £C

Sportoletti (Umbria/Assisi) *www.sportoletti.com*
One of the best of a new wave of producers in Umbria and Lazio, many of whom have been helped by Riccardo Cotarella in producing high-quality reds. Brothers Ernesto and Remo have 20 ha of vines at around 400m on the hills of Spello and Assisi north of Montefalco and within a new Assisi DOC. The top red, Villa Fidelia, is an oak-aged blend of Merlot with Cabernet Sauvignon and Cabernet Franc (usually 70/20/10) from 4ha of vineyards. It has typical 'Cotarella' richness, depth and concentrated fruit but also a splendid smoke, sweet spice and mineral individuality and is potentially a classic. A second red, Assisi Rosso (Merlot/Sangiovese) is ripe and plummy with a lush, supple mouthfeel and is quite stylish for what can often be a rather boring blend. Villa Fidelia Bianco is an increasingly good white, an oak-aged blend of Chardonnay and Grechetto, while the texture of a varietal Grechetto has been subtly enhanced by oak. New since 2011, is a Grechetto Passito, but this has not been tasted.

Recommended Reds:
Villa Fidelia Rosso ★★★★★ £E   Assisi Rosso ★★ £B

Recommended Whites:
Villa Fidelia Bianco ★★ £C   Assisi Grechetto ★ £B

Tabarrini (Umbria/Montefalco Sagrantino) *www.tabarrini.com*
This is a young Montefalco enterprise, only bottling since 1999 and completing a new cellar in 2003. There are 11ha of vineyards but only 8 ha in production. Consultant enologist Emiliano Falsini has been employed since 2001 and his winemaking style shows in the wines. The Sagrantino is harvested very late to achieve fully ripe tannins and then spends up to a months on its skins before half is aged in new *barriques*, half in large casks. The oak is balanced and spice, floral and truffle aromas are followed by concentrated bitter chocolate, black cherry and black plum fruit on the palate. There is considerable depth, breadth and extract. Rosso is a typical blend of mostly Sangiovese with the addition of Cabernet Sauvignon, Sagrantino and Merlot. Sagrantino Passito is also made. From 04 is a white, Bianco Ad Armando, made from old-vine Trebbiano Spoletino picked in November which has good weight, texture and structure with a refined minerally/salty component.

Recommended Reds:
Montefalco Sagrantino Colle Grimaldesco ★★★★ £E
Montefalco Rosso Colle Grimaldesco ★★ £C

Recommended Whites:
Bianco Ad Armando ★★ £B

A-Z of producers - *Lazio*

Casale del Giglio (Lazio) *www.casaledelgiglio.it*
South of the Colli Albani and Castelli Romani (Frascati country), almost on the coast, this is virgin wine country, not unlike the coastal Maremma in Tuscany. So it is perhaps not surprising that Casale del Giglio have concentrated on French grape varieties, although some local grapes (Biancolella) and Spanish (Tempranillo)

Central Italy /Abruzzo & Molise

are also used in making wine. Production from 150 ha is quite significant but there is a good standard of modern winemaking from Paolo Tiefenthaler. There is also on-going experimentation with input from the renowned Attilio Scienza of the University of Milan. The best of the varietals is arguably the Petit Verdot but better are the blends - all are sold as Lazio IGT. Of the whites, the fruity Satrico is from Chardonnay, Sauvignon and Trebbiano while the fragant and richer textured Antinoo is one third Chardonnay two thirds Viognier. For red there's Madreselva (Merlot, Petit Verdot and Cabernet Sauvignon) which spends 16-18 months in new *barriques*, and the still more ambitious Mater Matuta (Shiraz, Petit Verdot - 85/15) with nearly two years in new oak. Both are quite intense and concentrated but don't have the depth, style or refinement seen further north. Aphrodisium (not tasted) is a late-harvested white, unusually combining Viognier, Fiano, Greco and Petit Manseng. Although overall quality is good the top wines don't reach the quality levels their prices suggest.

Recommended Reds:
Mater Matuta ★★★ £F Madreselva ★★★ £E
Petit Verdot ★★ £C Shiraz ★☆ £C
Recommended Whites:
Antinoo ★★ £C Satrico ★ £B

Castel de Paolis (Lazio) *www.casteldepaolis.it*
Set up in the early 90s, after a period of experimentation Giulio Santarelli's Castel de Paolis (with 12 ha of vines) has been a quality leader in the Frascati hills. Collaboration with Franco Bernabei, and most recently Carlo Corino has ensured no drop off in quality. Many of the wines are a successful combination of local, or at least Italian varieties with some foreign imports. The excellent Vigna Adriana with the addition of Viognier to Malvasia (and lately Sauvignon too) has attracted the most attention but the flavoursome if sometimes overly robust black-fruited red Quattro Mori (Syrah, Merlot, Cabernet Sauvignon, Petit Verdot) has also impressed for more than a decade. Other wines can be good too including the more regular Malvasia/ Trebbiano-based Frascati Superiore and herb and spice scented Campo Vecchio red (Syrah, Cesanese, Montepulciano, Sangiovese). As well as a botrytis affected, late picked, moderately sweet Cannellino style Frascati, also interesting is the sweet, perfumed late harvested Rosathea from Moscato Rosa.

Recommended Reds:
Quattro Mori ★★★ £E Campo Vecchio ★★ £C
Recommended Whites:
Vigna Adriana ★★★ £C Frascati Superiore ★★ £B
Recommended Rosés:
Rosathea ★★ £D

❀ Falesco (Lazio) *www.falesco.it*
This substantial 250 ha estate on the Lazio/Umbria border belongs to two of Italy's most famous winemaker brothers – Renzo Cotarella, ANTINORI's winemaker, and the widely consulted enologist Riccardo Cotarella. The local appellation is the normally nondescript Est! Est!! Est!!! but Poggio dei Gelsi is a bright, perfumed and fruity white of some style. A good, characterful if oaky, dry white, Ferentano, is made from one of the local grapes, Roscetto, and there is also an attractive Grechetto. But it is the reds have caused the most interest. Montiano is a high-quality, lush, showy Merlot, not classic but with lots of extract, complexity and excellent flavour length. Marciliano, an Umbria IGT, (produced since 1999) is at least as impressive with slightly roasted intense blackcurrant and blackberry fruit from Cabernet Sauvignon and Cabernet Franc, arguably with the

greater depth of the two. Both need 8–10 years' age. Other Umbrian wines are Trentanni (50/50 Mrerlot and Sangiovese) and RC2, a Sagrantino di Montefalco. At a more affordable level is a 'second' fruity Merlot (dell'Umbria), a Sangiovese and a Grechetto, and Vitiano, a supple, forward, aromatic blend of Cabernet Sauvignon, Merlot and Sangiovese made in large quantities. There is also Vitiano Bianco (Vermentino and Verdicchio) and Rosato (Merlot, Cabernet Sauvignon and Sangiovese with 10% Aleatico) to complete the range. Other single varietals are Soente (Viognier) and Tellus (Syrah). Pomele, first made in 2001, is a dessert wine made from Aleatico.

Recommended Reds:
Montiano ★★★★★ £E Marciliano ★★★★★ £E
Merlot ★★ £C Tellus ★★ £C Vitiano Rosso ★★ £B
Recommended Whites:
Soente ★★ £C Ferentano ★★ £C
Vitiano Bianco ★★ £B Est! Est!! Est!!! Poggio dei Gelsi ★★ £B

A-Z of producers - *Abruzzo & Molise*

Agriverdi (Abruzzo) *www.agriverde.it*
If you fancy bathing in grape skins this could be just the place for you. For as well as making wine Agriverde offer a range of health and beauty treatments including Vinoterapia - those involving grape skins or extracts. The very modern high-tech winery produces a plethora of labels from 75 ha of vineyards. The top wine is the Plateo Montepulciano d'Abruzzo, which has two years in *barriques* as well as two years in stainless steel. It is a powerful, ripe, complex and structured example with real finesse. Around 16,000 bottles are made and the Solàrea label includes an oaky Trebbiano d'Abruzzo, decent Cerasuolo, and a stylish, dark-fruited version of Montepulciano d'Abruzzo. There are also some good Riseis di Recastro wines including a well-structured Pecorino that would make a decent alternative for a good unoaked Chablis, as would the unoaked Chardonnay (both Terre di Chieti IGT). Both the Montepulciano d'Abruzzo and Trebbiano d'Abruzzo pair in this range are expressive and typical. An oaked Chardonnay, Capo di Vigne is concentrated and flavoursome but slightly clumsy while the inexpensive Natum wines are certified organic - the Montepulciano d'Abruzzo is soft and forward with lots of character. So if you do decide to stay, at least the wines will be good.

Recommended Reds:
Montepulciano d'Abruzzo Plateo ★★★★ £F
Montepulciano d'Abruzzo Solàrea ★★★ £D
Montepulciano d'Abruzzo Riseis di Recastro ★★ £C
Montepulciano d'Abruzzo Natum ★☆ £B
Recommended Whites:
Pecorino Riseis di Recastro ★★☆ £C £C
Trebbiano d'Abruzzo Riseis di Recastro ★★☆ £ £B
Chardonnay Riseis di Recastro ★★☆ £C £B
Recommended Rosés:
Montepulciano d'Abruzzo Cerasuolo Solàrea ★★☆ £ £C

Fratelli Barba (Abruzzo) *www.fratelli barba.it*
This modern operation is overseen by Giovanni Barba one of three professionally qualified brothers. Around 65 ha of a vast 680 ha estate is planted to vines which supplies all their needs. The most interest is at the Vigna Franca level in both Montepulciano d'Abruzzo and Trebbiano d'Abruzzo. The red subject to 14 months in French *barriques*, has good complexity and breadth but not the richness or depth of the best. Drink it with five years' age or more. The white Vigna Franca has good promise with well-integrated yellow fruits,

spice and oak. The Colline Morino versions are inexpensive. The red has good flavour but could use a little more charm while there is plenty of fruit and freshness in the white if it is drunk young.

Recommended Reds:

Montepulciano d'Abruzzo Vigna Franca ★★★ £C
Montepulciano d'Abruzzo Colle Morino ★★ £B

Recommended Whites:

Trebbiano d'Abruzzo Vigna Franca ★★☆ £B
Trebbiano d'Abruzzo Colle Morino ★☆ £B

Podere Castorani (Abruzzo) *www.poderecastorani.it*

First-rate Montepulciano d'Abruzzo is a relatively rare beast but this young enterprise, reviving part of a historic farm since 2000, promises something special. The name has a ring of motor racing about it and the partners include Formula One racing driver Jarno Trulli's father and his manager. Also on board is expert viticulturalist Bruno Cavuto who oversees the estate's 30ha of well established pergola-trained vines. The organically produced wines are made by the fourth partner, Luca Petricelli, whose experience includes winemaking in Bordeaux and Spain. The Castorani red is subject to a long maceration and 12 months in small oak; it is a stylish, beautifully balanced wine with concentrated black cherry and spice. Rich and deep with lots of Montepulciano flesh and individuality, it shows just what is possible with a good site and the right know-how in Abruzzo. New Jarno red (not tasted) is another varietal Montepulciano but from late-harvested grapes which are then partially dried. A more affordable Costa delle Plaie label offers well-made Montepulciano d'Abruzzo, Trebbiano d'Abruzzo, Pecorino and pink Cerasuolo. A basic red cuvée from Montepulciano is Majolica.

Recommended Reds:

Montepulciano d'Abruzzo Castorani ★★★☆ £E
Montepulciano d'Abruzzo Costa delle Plaie ★★ £C

Recommended Whites:

Trebbiano d'Abruzzo Costa delle Plaie ★☆ £B

Cataldi Madonna (Abruzzo) *www.cataldimadonna.com*

Montepulciano d'Abruzzo producer Luigi Cataldi Madonna is just beginning to realise the full potential of the fruit from his elevated vineyards beneath the Gran Sasso (the highest peak of the Appenines). The style is for bold, full flavoured reds with soft, ripe tannins. Not subtle, they still lack a little sophistication but have broad appeal. A regular example offers reasonable value but there is much more in the two top bottlings. Maladrino sees one-third new oak while in Tonì it is two-thirds. The power, flavour and concentration are all givens and there is added complexity and length in Tonì, though both wines can want for a little more definition. Cataldi Madonna's two Cerasuolos are among the better examples, made with good freshness and lively floral fruit if drunk young. A further red, Occhiorosso is Cabernet Sauvignon with a little Montepulciano.

Recommended Reds:

Montepulciano d'Abruzzo Tonì ★★★ £D
Montepulciano d'Abruzzo Maladrino ★★ £D
Montepulciano d'Abruzzo ★★ £C

Recommended Whites:

Trebbiano d'Abruzzo ★ £B

Di Majo Norante (Molise) *www.dimajonorante.com*

Alessio Di Majo's 60 ha estate is essentially organic and has been Molise's one really notable producer for more than a decade. Yet only more recently, with the input of consultant Riccardo Cotarella,

has there been real consistency and a further increase in quality across the range. Reds are now led by a premium example of greater breadth and intensity than previously seen. This Don Luigi comes from 90% Montepulciano with the balance from Aglianico and is a rich, oaky cuvée – just occasionally a little overdone. The long-established blend Ramitello Rosso is produced from Sangiovese and Aglianico and is ripe, balanced and characterful. Contado shows plenty of Aglianico fruit and style if not yet the depth and structure synonymous with the best examples of this grape, while a varietal Sangiovese needs a little more refinement. Whites are ripe and clean with plenty of fruit. A Greco has dried peach, apricot and spice if modest structure, whilst there are both regular and organic versions of Falanghina and Aglianico. Don Luigi excepted, the wines continue to be well-priced for the fruit and character they deliver.

Recommended Reds:

Molise Don Luigi ★★★ £E   Molise Aglianico Contado ★★ £B
Biferno Rosso Ramitello ★★ £B   Sangiovese ★ £B

Recommended Whites:

Molise Greco ★★ £B   Molise Falanghina ★★ £B

Farnese Vini (Abruzzo) *www.farnese-vini.com*

This is a big operation with around 10 million bottles produced annually. The volume though is in the basics especially Farnese Montepulciano d'Abruzzo and the Sangiovese sold as Terre di Chieti IGT. A notch up is the Casale Vecchio label with a juicy, forward Montepulciano d'Abruzzo, Sauvignon-based Luna Bianca and varietal Pecorino. Much more interesting however are the Montepulciano d'Abruzzo Colline Teramane DOCG wines including the Opis label Riserva, both being made in quite small volumes. To some extent they are 'big winery' wines in that they miss the purity, detail and definition of those from a top small producer but they are well-balanced with good fruit and depth, particularly the Riserva. There is also an Opis white from Chardonnay. The flagship is the red Edizione Cinque Autoctoni - the five native varieties being Montepulciano, Sangiovese, Primitivo, Negroamaro and Malvasia Nera. At once modern and original, with wild herbs, a melange of black fruits it is plump, flavoursome and long, even if there isn't the definition or class for fine. As it is sold as a Vino da Tavola look for the lot number in small print on the label in order to ascertain the vintage. Also made are the FEUDI DI SAN MARZIANO wines from Puglia, produced jointly with the local Cantina Sociale.

Recommended Reds:

Edizione Cinque Autoctoni ★★★☆ £E
Montepulciano d'Abruzzo Colline Teramane Riserva Opis ★★★ £D
Montepulciano d'Abruzzo Colline Teramane ★★ £C
Montepulciano d'Abruzzo Casale Vecchio ★☆ £B

La Valentina (Abruzzo) *www.lavalentina.it*

These wines have always shown potential but it has often been compromised by too much extract and tannin in the past. A total of 31 ha are either owned or leased while consultancy comes from Luca D'Attoma. Two special cuvées of Montepulciano d'Abruzzo, Spelt and Bellovedere, are subject to a long maceration and are impressively complex and structured. Spelt is only partly aged in *barriques* and misses the extra weight and dimension of Bellovedere. Binomio, produced in collaboration with Stefano INAMA (see North-East Italy) is now run as a separate operation. The grapes come from the 4-ha San Valentino vineyard at 500m altitude and are subject to shorter maceration times than the La Valentina reds but there is still lots of extract and power. The wine is aged in new French *barriques* and offers more cherry/berry and spice and less coffee and herb.

Central Italy /Abruzzo & Molise

Italy

Basic La Valentina Montepulciano and Trebbiano could be better but Cerasuolo is a decent example. Spelt Trebbiano and Cerasuolo are a cut above the basic versions. The ratings for Spelt and Bellovedere apply to the best vintages.

La Valentina
Recommended Reds:
Montepulciano d'Abruzzo Bellovedere ★★★★ £E
Montepulciano d'Abruzzo Spelt ★★★ £C
Recommended Rosés:
Montepulciano d'Abruzzo Cerasuolo ★ £B

Binomio
Recommended Reds:
Montepulciano d'Abruzzo Binomio ★★★ £E

Marramiero (Abruzzo) *www.marramiero.it*
Enrico Marramiero and winemaker Romeo Taborelli plough a good quality furrow in the heart of Abruzzo between the Grand Sasso and the sea, with three vineyards in Rosciano covering some 54 ha of vines and a further 6ha at Ofena, known as the "oven" of Abruzzo because of the high temperatures reached in the summer and a big difference of temperatures between night and day. An entry level range of Montepulciano, Trebbiano, Cerasuolo and Pecorino are suplememted by a "selection" range of superior wines. Inferi Montepulciano spends around 18 months in French and Slavonian oak and whilst smooth on the palate, the fruit can be sometimes masked by the wood, even after 4 or 5 years of bottle age. The stylish Abruzzo Pecorino shows good aromacy around the natural sharpness of this varietal to produce harmonious balance. Remarkable for the area, though, is a refreshing sparkling wine made from Chardonnay (65%) and Pinot Nero (35%) spending 3 years on its lees and displaying balanced flavours of fruitiness and biscuit. A rosé is also made. The flagship wine, however, is Dante Marramiero, made from 40-50 year old Montepulciano vines and aged for 4 years in wood and a further 6 years in bottle before commercial release, a 14.5% blockbuster with an underlying softness and lashings of spice and black fruits.
Recommended Reds:
Montepulciano d'Abruzzo Dante Marramiero ★★★★★ £H
Montepulciano d'Abruzzo Inferri ★★ £C
Recommended Whites:
Brut Sboccatura Autonno ★★★☆ £D   Abruzzo Pecorino ★★★ £C

Masciarelli (Abruzzo) *www.masciarelli.it*
In Gianni Masciarelli, the Abruzzo has another great star. Together with Marina Cvetic he has constantly improved quality to the point where this estate has become a flag-bearer for Montepulciano d'Abruzzo. Villa Gemma is the top wine and impresses for its fabulous texture, depth and richness of fruit that owes something to both tremendous fruit quality and a prolonged maceration in wood. Also increasingly good (and less expensive) is the Marina Cvetic version. Other reds include a less successful but improving Cabernet Sauvignon, now showing a more refined structure than previously. Masciarelli's top white is a wine of increasing stature too – the barrel-fermented Trebbiano d'Abruzzo has good depth and breadth with a pure herbal, mineral and oakinfluenced complexity. The non-barriqued Castello di Semivicoli version of Trebbiano is also stylish and expansive. Cerasuolo is also made while Villa Gemma Bianco is a stainless steel-fermented Trebbiano with 10% Cococciola (a variety not previously encountered). Regular Montepulciano and Trebbiano are good value.

Recommended Reds:
Montepulciano d'Abruzzo Villa Gemma ★★★★★ £F
Montepulciano d'Abruzzo Marina Cvetic San Martino Rosso ★★★★ £D
Cabernet Sauvignon Marina Cvetic ★★★ £E
Montepulciano d'Abruzzo ★★☆ £B
Recommended Whites:
Trebbiano d'Abruzzo Marina Cvetic ★★★☆ £E
Trebbiano d'Abruzzo Castello di Semivicoli ★★☆ £B
Chardonnay Marina Cvetic ★★ £D
Recommended Rosés:
Rosato ★★ £B

Antonio & Elio Monti (Abruzzo) *www.vinimonti.it*
This small operation draws from 15 ha of vineyards to make around 7,000 cases of wine each year. Its reputation is for powerful, structured if somewhat rustic reds, although recently there has been input from Riccardo Cotarella and the wines show more oak influence but also more vigour and fruit purity without sacrificing their marvellous complexity and flavour expression. The single vineyard Pignotto, of which only 11,000 bottles are made, is potentially an outstanding wine. Following a very long maceration, it is aged in French *barriques*. Wonderfully complex with earth, coffee, wild herbs, oak spice, plum and other black fruits, it also powerful and extracted. There is good integration between fruit and structure but it does demand 10 years' ageing from all but the most masochistic of drinkers of such big reds. There are two other bottlings: Senior has good structure and depth but needs at least 3-5 years' age; Voluptas is for everyday. Controguerra Riserva Rio Moro adds Cabernet Sauvignon, Merlot and Sangiovese to Montepulciano and is rich and concentrated if more international in style. A little white is also made. Beyond a decent Trebbiano d'Abruzzo, Dorato del Sole, there's Raggio di Luna, a characterful white in which Chardonnay is blended with Trebbiano, Passerina and Pecorino. Cerasuolo (Montepulciano vinified as a white) has more the colour of a light red rather than a rosé and has pretty fruit.
Recommended Reds:
Montepulciano d'Abruzzo Colline Teramane Pignotto ★★★★ £E
Montepulciano d'Abruzzo Colline Teramane Senior ★★★ £C
Montepulciano d'Abruzzo Voluptas ★ £B
Controguerra Riserva Rio Moro ★★★ £C
Recommended Whites:
Controguerra Raggio di Luna ★ £B

Nicodemi (Abruzzo) *www.nicodemi.com*
Nicodemi is a significant producer of certified organic wines making use of the new DOCG for a restricted part of Montepulciano d'Abruzzo, Colline Teramane. Neromoro is a powerful and extracted example from a single vineyard within the 38 ha of vines. Rich and meaty with plenty of oak from 16–18 months in new French *barriques*, give it 8–10 years. Not at the same level, Notàri has a good sweet fruit core but less well-integrated oak and firmer tannins. A white equivalent from Trebbiano – a small percentage *barrique*-fermented – stays on the lees with *bâtonnage*. This is stylish and harmonious with good complexity and a creamy texture. One to try.
Recommended Reds:
Montepulciano d'Abruzzo Colline Teramane Neromoro ★★★★ £F
Montepulciano d'Abruzzo Colline Teramane Notàri ★★ £D
Montepulciano d'Abruzzo ★ £B
Recommended Whites:
Trebbiano d'Abruzzo Notàri ★★☆ £C   Trebbiano d'Abruzzo ★ £B

Emidio Pepe (Abruzzo) *www.emidiopepe.com*

A small traditional producer of powerful long-lived Montepulciano d'Abruzzo, biodynamic since 2006 (previously organic). Wine has been made here since 1899 and bottled since 1964. Sisters Sofia and Daniela work with their father in what is an almost entirely manual operation including de-stalking, decanting and bottling by hand. The red is a bold, structured, deeply flavoursome example of impressive breadth and length. It is impressive with a dark plum, savoury, smoky, spicy grilled meats complexity, lots of extract but is well-balanced. It could be drunk now but will keep too. These are great wines for cellaring but don't come looking for sophistication or elegance. Also expect significant differences from vintage to vintage. Be sure and taste first any vintages you intend buying a significant quantity of. Trebbiano d'Abruzzo is also made in a simple way from foot-trodden grapes but no recent vintages have been tasted. A rosato and more recently a Pecorino are also made.

Recommended Reds:

Montepulciano d'Abruzzo ★★★★ £F

Torre Zambra (Abruzzo)

Laurentino di Cerchio, together with young winemaker Davide Dias, are creating some excellent *terroir*-driven wines. The unoaked entry level Montepulciano Villamagna Madia shows easy drinking smoothness with nice complexity on the finish A step up is the Collemaggio Montepulciano, refined in stainless steel for one year and then around 15-16 months in second year French oak. Even then, the oak dominates for some years and is best approached with at least 5-6 years maturity. There is a lot of fine, rich fruit beneath the tannins here. Further up the scale is Brune Rosse, a Montepulciano which has spent 24 months in French and Slavonian oak but this has not ben tasted. A Cerasuolo and four single varietal whites make up the rest of the Collemaggio range of which the best is the Pecorino Superiore which shows fresh, fruity flavours balanced with the natural steeliness of this particular varietal. All wines have an excellent price/quality ratio.

Recommended Reds:

Montepulciano d'Abruzzo Collemaggio ★★★ £C

Montepulciano d'Abruzzo Villamagna Madia ★★☆ £B

Recommended Whites:

Abruzzo Pecorino Superiore Collemaggio ★★★ £B

❀❀ Valentini (Abruzzo)

Francesco Valentini continues the work of his father, Edoardo who first provided one of the great alternatives to the modern school of winemaking. The greatest care goes into producing high-quality fruit from tendone-trained vines planted at low densities. From a total of 64 ha of vines, only a small quantity is released under Valentini's distinctive label. Much of the wine is sold off in bulk and if it is not up to standard then no wine is produced at all. There is no temperature control, only large old wood, and no fining or filtration. After the wine is bottled it is kept until it is considered ready to drink. At it's best, the red (100% Montepulciano) is a wine of great power and dimension that slowly releases it's complex aromas and flavours that include dried flowers, cedar, coffee, spice, pepper and berry fruit. It requires at least a decade's age. The splendidly textured complex white shows a range of floral, herbal and fruit-derived scents with striking depth, breadth and length; it only misses the class a nobler variety would bring. Some pink Cerasuolo is also made as is excellent spicy, intense extra virgin olive oil.

Recommended Reds:

Montepulciano d'Abruzzo ★★★★★ £G

Recommended Whites:

Trebbiano d'Abruzzo ★★★★ £F

Ciccio Zaccagnini (Abruzzo) *www.cantinazaccagnini.it*

Ciccio and son Marcello have buit this estate up from a production of 1,000 bottles in 1978 to over one million today from 150 ha of vines now planted. With the help of oenologist Concezio Marulli, Zaccagnini is now considered as one of the leading lights in the Abruzzo. Whilst there are some 20 different wines produced, size does not appear to have diminished quality. We haven't tasted all the range but consider what we have tasted as good value for money. Entry level Montelpuciano Tralcetto spends about 4 months in Slavonian oak, is full flavoured with soft tannins for easy drinking and fair complexity on the finish. San Clemente is a pretty big step up with oak ageing for 18 months with a further 12 in stainless steel and 6 months in bottle before release. The result is a robust, full-bodied and intense mouthfeel with plenty of fruit beneath a big tannic structure and great complexity on the finish. In between there are several cuvées of Montepulciano ranging from NOSO2 (no added sulfites - 12.5% abv) upwards to San Clemente. There is a fair range of whites, too and some sparkling and passiti - we like the Yamada Pecorino for its smooth and aromatic citrus flavours underneath a firm mineral structure.

Recommended Reds:

Montepulciano d'Abruzzo Terre di Casuria San Clemente ★★★★☆ £E

Montepulciano d'Abruzzo Tralcetto ★★★ £B

Recommended Whites:

Colline Pescaresi Pecorino Yamada ★★★ £B

Other wines of note

Emilia-Romagna

Calonga

Recommended Whites: Pagadebit di Romagna ★ £B

Zenaide (Chardonnay/Albana) ★☆ £C

Albana di Romagna Passito Kiria ★★★☆ £E

Albana di Romagna Dolce ★☆ £C

Recommended Reds: Balsamino (Balsamina) ★ £B

Ordelaffo (Sangiovese/Cabernet Sauvignon) ★☆ £B

Castellone (Cabernet Sauvignon) ★★★☆ £C

Sangiovese di Romagna Superiore Riserva Michelangiolo ★★★★ £D

Cleto Chiarli

Recommended Reds:

Lambrusco Grasparossa di Castelvetro Pruno Nero ★ £B

Lambrusco Grasparossa di Castelvetro Enrico Cialdini ★★ £B

Leone Conti

Recommended Whites:

Albana di Romagna Passito Non Ti Scordar di Me ★★ £D

Ferrari & Perini

Recommended Whites: Spumante Brut Non-Vintage ★★☆ £B

Malvasia Dolce (Spumante) Non-Vintage ★★☆ £B

Colli Piacentini Passito Malvagia ★★★ £D

Recommended Reds: Colli Piacentini Gutturnio Vivace ★★ £B

Graziano

Recommended Reds:

Fontana Boschi Autunno (Met. Classico Lambrusco di Modena) ★★☆ £C

Il Poggiorello

Recommended Whites:

Colli Piacentini Malvasia Perticato Beatrice Quadri ★★★ £C

Colli Piacentini Sauvignon Perticato Il Quadri ★★☆ £C

Colli Piacentini Chardonnay Perticato La Piana ★★ £C

Central Italy

Italy

L'alba E La Pietra (Malvasia/Sauvignon/Viognier) Annotre ★★★ £C
Recommended Reds:
Colli Piacentini Pinot Nero Perticato Le Giastre ★★ £D
Colli Piacentini Cabernet Sauvignon Perticato del Novarei ★★☆ £D
Colli Piacentini Barbera 'I Piston ★★★ £D
Colli Piacentini Gutturnio Perticato Valandrea ★★★ £C
Colli Piacentini Gutturnio Riserva La Barbona ★★★★ £E
Cantine Intesa
Recommended Reds: I Calanchi - Numi (Cab Sauv) ★★ £C
La Berta
Recommended Reds:
Sangiovese di Romagna Superiore Solano ★★ £B
Sangiovese di Romagna Riserva Olmatello ★★ £C
Almante (Alicante) ★★ £C
La Tosa
Recommended Reds:
Colli Piacentini Cabernet Sauvignon Luna Selvatica ★★ £D
Colli Piacentini Gutturnio Vignamorello ★★ £C
Tenuta La Viola
Recommended Reds:
Sangiovese di Romagna Superiore Il Colombarone ★★ £C
Luretta
Recommended Whites:
Colli Piacentini Malvasia Dolce Le Rane ★★★ £E
Colli Piacentini Sauvignon I Nani E Le Ballerine ★★ £C
Giovanna Madonia
Recommended Reds:
Sangiovese di Romagna Superiore Riserva Ombroso ★★★ £D
Ermete Medici & Figli
Recommended Reds:
Lambrusco Reggiano Secco Arte E Concerto ★★ £B
Paradiso
Recommended Reds: Barbarossa ★★ £D
Mito (Cab Sauv/Merlot/Syrah) ★★ £E
Terragens
Recommended Reds: Romio (Sangiovese) ★★ £C
Terre della Pieve
Recommended Reds: Sangiovese di Romagna A Virgilio ★ £B
Sangiovese di Romagna Superiore Nobis ★★★ £C
Recommended Whites: Albana di Romagna Passito Stilnoro ★★★ £D
Tre Monti
Recommended Whites: Trebbiano di Romagna Vigna Rio ★★ £B
Albana di Romagna Secco Vigna Rocca ★★☆ £B
Colli d'Imola Bianco Salcerella (Sauvignon/Chardonnay) ★★ £B
Colli d'Imola Chardonnay Ciardo ★★☆ £B
Colli d'Imola Bianco Thea (Albana/Chardonnay/Petit Manseng) ★★ £B
Albana di Romagna Passito Casa Lola ★★★☆ £D
Recommended Reds:
Colli d'Imola Boldo (Merlot/Sangiovese/Cabernets) ★★ £B
Sangiovese di Romagna Superiore Campo di Mezzo ★☆ £B
Sangiovese di Romagna Superiore Riserva Petrignone ★★☆ £B
Sangiovese di Romagna Superiore Riserva Thea ★★★☆ £C
Trere'
Recommended Reds:
Sangiovese di Romagna Riserva Amarcord D'un Ross ★★ £C
Vallona
Recommended Reds:
Colli Bolognesi Cabernet Sauvignon Selezione ★★★ £C
Colli Bolognesi Merlot Afederico ★★★ £C
Recommended Whites: Colli Bolognesi Pignoletto ★★ £B

Marche
Accadia
Recommended Whites:
Verdicchio dei Castelli di Jesi Classico Superiore Conscio ★★ £B
Verdicchio dei Castelli di Jesi Classico Superiore Cantori ★★☆ £B
Antica Cantina Sant'amico
Recommended Reds: Lacrima di Morro d'Alba Per Bacco ★ £B
Lacrima di Morro d'Albavenere Oro ★☆ £B
Belisario
Recommended Whites: Verdicchio di Matelica Vigneti Belisario ★★ £B
Verdicchio di Matelica Vigneti del Cerro ★★ £B
Verdicchio di Matelica Riserva Cambrugiano ★★ £C
Boccafosca
Recommended Whites: Verdicchio dei Castelli di Jesi Stellaria ★☆ £B
Recommended Reds: Lacrima Morro d'Alba Nerium ★ £B
Mario & Giorgio Brunori
Recommended Whites:
Verdicchio dei Castelli di Jesi Classico Superiore San Niccolò ★★ £B
Conte di Buscareto
Recommended Reds:
Lacrima Morro d'Alba Campagnia della Rosa ★★☆ £B
Recommended Whites: Verdicchio dei Castelli di Jesi Passito ★★ £C
Carminucci
Recommended Reds: Rosso Piceno Superiore Naumachos ★ £C
Casalfarneto
Recommended Whites:
Verdicchio dei Castelli di Jesi Classico Superiore Fontevecchia ★☆ £B
Collestefano
Recommended Whites: Verdicchio di Matelica ★★★ £B
Contrada Tenna
Recommended Reds: Marche Rosso (Montepulciano) ★★★☆ £D
Del Carmine
Recommended Whites: Verdicchio di Matelica Aja Lunga ★★ £B
Verdicchio di Matelica Petrara Bianco ★★ £B
Recommended Reds:
San Vicino (Sangiovese/Lacrima/Cabernet Sauvignon) ★★☆ £C
Fazi Battaglia
Recommended Reds: Rosso Conero Riserva Passo del Lupo ★★ £D
Recommended Whites:
Verdicchio dei Castelli di Jesi Classico Riserva San Sisto ★★ £D
Verdicchio dei Castelli di Jesi Classico Massaccio ★★★ £C
Verdicchio dei Castelli di Jesi Classico Superiore Le Moie ★ £B
Fattoria Laila
Recommended Whites:
Verdicchio dei Castelli di Jesi Classico Superiore Eklektikos ★★ £B
Recommended Reds: Rosso Piceno ★ £B
Rosso Piceno Lailum (Montepulciano) ★★☆ £D
Laurentina
Recommended Reds: Rosso Picenotalliano ★★ £C
Mauro Lucchetti
Recommended Reds:
Lacrima di Morro d'Alba Superiore Guardengo ★☆ £B
Stefano Mancinelli
Recommended Whites:
Verdicchio dei Castelli di Jesi Classico Superiore ★★ £B
Recommended Reds: Lacrima di Morro d'Alba Superiore ★ £B
Lacrima di Morro d'Alba Passito ★★★ £E
Cantine Marconi
Recommended Whites:
Verdicchio Castelli di Jesi Cl. Sup. Sapori di Gen. Etichetta Nera ★★☆ £B

Marotti Campi
Recommended Whites:
Verdicchio dei Castelli di Jesi Classico Superiore Luzano ★★ £B
Verdicchio dei Castelli di Jesi Classico Riserva Salmariano ★★★ £B
Verdicchio dei Castelli di Jesi Passito Onyr ★☆ £C

Terre Cortesi Moncaro
Recommended Whites:
Verdicchio dei Castelli di Jesi Classicoverde di Cà Ruptae ★★ £B
Verdicchio dei Castelli di Jesi Riserva Vigna Novali ★★ £C
Verdicchio dei Castelli di Jesi Passitotordiruta ★★★ £D
Recommended Reds:
Rosso Conero Riserva Vigneto del Parco ★★★ £C
Barocco (Montepulciano/Cab Sauv) ★★★ £C

Montecappone
Recommended Whites:
Verdicchio dei Castelli di Jesi Riserva Utopia ★★☆ £C
Recommended Reds: Rosso Piceno Montesecco ★★☆ £B

Claudio Morelli
Recommended Whites: Bianchello del Metauro Borgo Torre ★☆ £B

Moroder
Recommended Reds: Rosso Conero ★ £B
Rosso Conero Dorico ★★★ £D
Recommended Whites:
Oro (Moscato/Trebbiano Dorato/Malvasia) ★★ £E

Piantate Lunghe
Recommended Reds: Conero Riserva Rossini ★★ £C

Pievalta (Biodynamic)
Recommended Whites:
Verdicchio dei Castelli di Jesi Classico Superiore Dominè ★★ £B
Verdicchio dei Castelli di Jesi Passito Curina ★★★ £C

Alberto Quacquarini
Recommended Reds:
Vernaccia di Serrapetrona ★★ £C (Medium-Dry And Frizzante)

Poderi San Lazzaro
Recommended Reds: Grifola (Montepulciano) ★★★☆ £D

Terra Vignata
Recommended Whites: Verdicchio di Matelica ★☆ £B

Zaccagnini & C.
Recommended Whites:
Verdicchio dei Castelli di Jesi Classico Salmàgina ★★ £B
Verdicchio dei Castelli di Jesi Classico Pier delle Vigne ★★ £C

Umbria
Adanti
Recommended Reds: Montefalco Sagrantino ★★★ £C
Montefalco Sagrantino Passito ★★★ £D

Antonelli
Recommended Reds: Montefalco Rosso Riserva ★★ £D
Montefalco Sagrantino ★★ £E

Barberani
Recommended Reds:
Lago di Corbara Foresco (Sangiovese/Cabernets) ★★ £D
Lago di Corbara Villa Monticelli (Sangiovese/Merlot/Cabs) ★★★ £E

Cantina Colli Amerini
Recommended Reds: Colli Amerini Rosso Superiore Carbio ★★ £C

Decugnano dei Barbi
Recommended Whites: Orvieto Classico Superiore II ★★☆ £C
Recommended Reds:
II (Sangiovese/Montepulciano/Canaiolo) ★★★ £E

La Carraia
Recommended Whites: Orvieto Classico Poggio Calvelli ★★ £B

Recommended Reds: Fobiano (Merlot/Cab Sauv) ★★★ £D
Sangiovese ★★ £B Tizzonero (Montepulciano) ★★ £B

La Palazzola
Recommended Reds: Merlot ★★ £D
Rubino (Cab Sauv/Merlot) ★★★ £D

Le Velette
Recommended Reds: Gaudio (Merlot) ★★★ £C

Madre Vite
Recommended Reds:
Colli del Trasimeno Glanio (Sangiovese/Gamay/Merlot) ★★ £B

Rocca di Fabri
Recommended Reds: Montefalco Sagrantino ★★☆ £E
Faroaldo (Sagrantino/Cab Sauv) ★★☆ £E
Recommended Whites: Grechetto dei Colli Martani ★ £C

Salviano/Titignano
Recommended Reds:
Lago di Corbara Turlò (Sangiovese/Cab Sauv) ★★ £B

Spoletoducale Casale Triocco
Recommended Reds: Montefalco Rosso Casale Triocco ★★ £B
Montefalco Sagrantino Casale Triocco ★★★ £D

Tordi Maro
Recommended Reds: Sangiovese ★★ £B
Cabernet Sauvignon ★★ £B

Lazio
Cantine Ciolli
Recommended Reds: Olevano Romano Silene (Cesanese) ★★☆ £B
Olevano Romano Cirsium (Cesanese) ★★★☆ £C

Piero Costantini/Villa Simone
Recommended Whites: Frascati Superiore Villa dei Preti ★★ £B
Frascati Superiore Vigneto Filonardi ★★ £C

Colle Picchioni
Recommended Whites:
Le Vignole (Malvasia/Trebbiano/Sauvignon) ★★ £B
Marino Donna Paolo (Malvasia/Trebbiano/Sauvignon) ★★ £B
Recommended Reds:
Perlaia (Merlot/Sangiovese/Cabernet Sauvignon) ★★☆ £C
Vigna del Vassallo (Merlot/Cabernets) ★★★☆ £D

Fontana Candida
Recommended Whites: Frascati Superiore Terre dei Grifi ★ £B
Frascati Superiore Vigneto Santa Teresa ★★ £B
Recommended Reds: Kron (Merlot/Sangiovese) ★★ £C

Trappolini
Recommended Reds: Sangiovese Paterno ★★ £C

Abruzzo & Molise
Caldora
Recommended Whites: Chardonnay ★ £B
Colle dei Venti Pecorino ★★ £B
Recommended Reds: Montepulciano d'Abruzzo Yumé ★★★ £B

Tenuta Caracciolo
Recommended Reds:
Montepulciano d'Abruzzo Duchi di Castelluccio ★★ £B

Contesa (di Rocco Pasetti)
Recommended Whites: Pecorino ★★ £B
Trebbiano d'Abruzzovigna Corvino ★ £B
Recommended Reds: Montepulciano d'Abruzzo Vigna Corvino ★ £B
Montepulciano d'Abruzzo Contesa ★★ £C

Barone Cornacchia
RecommendedReds:Montepulcianod'AbruzzoPoggioVarano ★★ £B

Italy

Gran Sasso
Recommended Whites: Trebbiano d'Abruzzo ★☆ £B
Pecorino ★★☆ £B
Recommended Reds: Montepulciano d'Abruzzo ★☆ £B
Montepulciano d'Abruzzo Colline Teramane ★★★☆ £C

Illuminati
Recommended Reds:
Montepulciano d'Abruzzo Colline Teramane Riserva Zanna ★★ £C
Montepulciano d'Abruzzo Colline Teramane Riserva Pieluni ★★★ £E
Controguerra Rosso Riserva Lumen ★★★ £E

Marramiero
Recommended Reds: Montepulciano d'Abruzzo Incanto ★ £B
Montepulciano d'Abruzzo Inferi ★★ £C

Montipagano
Recommended Reds:
Montepulciano d'Abruzzo Colline Teramane ★★★ £D

Orsogno/Lunaria
Recommended Reds: Bucefalo ★★★ £B

Franco Pasetti
Recommended Whites: Pecorino ★★ £C

Casa Vinicola Roxan
Recommended Reds: Montepulciano d'Abruzzo Galelle ★★ £C
Montepulciano d'Abruzzo Taverna Nova ★ £A

Nicola Santoleri
Recommended Reds: Montepulciano d'Abruzzo Vignaladra ★★☆ £B
Montepulciano d'Abruzzo Crognaleto ★★★☆ £D

Talamonti
Recommended Reds: Montepulciano d'Abruzzo Tre Saggi ★★ £C

Terra d'Aligi/Spinelli
Recommended Reds: Montepulciano d'Abruzzo Tatone ★★☆ £B
Montepulciano d'Abruzzo Tolos ★★★ £C

Torre dei Beati
Recommended Rosés:
Montepulciano d'Abruzzo Cerasuolo Bella ★★ £B
Recommended Reds: Montepulciano d'Abruzzo ★★☆ £B
Montepulciano d'Abruzzo Cocciapazza ★★★ £C
Montepulciano d'Abruzzo Mazzomurello ★★★☆ £D

Valori
Recommended Reds: Montepulciano d'Abruzzo ★★ £B
Montepulciano d'Abruzzo Vigna Sant'angelo ★★ £C

Villa Bizzarri
Recommended Reds: Montepulciano d'Abruzzo Sasso Arso ★☆ £B
Montepulciano d'Abruzzo Girone dei Folli ★★ £B

Author's choice

Excellent Sangiovese di Romagna
Stefano Berti   Sangiovese di Romagna Superiore Calisto
Castelluccio   Ronco delle Ginestre
Calonga   Sangiovese di Romagna Superiore Riserva Michelangolo
Drei Donà - La Palazza   Sangiovese di Romagna Sup. Riserva Pruno
La Berta   Sangiovese di Romagna Superiore Riserva Olmatello
La Viola   Sangiovese di Romagna Superiore Il Colombarone
Giovanna Madonia   Sangiovese di Romagna Sup. Riserva Ombroso
San Patrignano   Sangiovese di Romagna Riserva Avi
San Valentino   Sangiovese di Romagna Riserva Terra di Covignano
Terre Della Pieve   Sangiovese di Romagna Superiore Nobis
Tre Monti   Sangiovese di Romagna Superiore Riserva Thea
Zerbina   Sangiovese di Romagna Riserva Pietramora

Top Montepulciano based Reds
Agriverde   Montepulciano d'Abruzzo Plateo
Maria Pia Castelli   Erasmo Castelli
Podere Castorani   Montepulciano d'Abruzzo
Cataldi Madonna   Montepulciano d'Abruzzo Tonì
Ciu Ciu   Opîdium
Di Majo Norante   Molise Don Luigi
Garofoli   Conero Riserva Grosso Agontano
Lanari   Rosso Conero Fibbio
Le Terrazze   Conero Riserva Sassi Neri
Leopardi Dittajuti   Rosso Conero Pigmento
Masciarelli   Montepulciano d'Abruzzo Villa Gemma
Antonio & Elio Monti   Montepulciano d'Abruzzo Pignotto
Nicodemi   Montepulciano d'Abruzzo Colline Teramane Neromoro
Oasi Degli Angeli   Kurni
San Lorenzo   Vigneto Del Solleone
San Savino - Podere Capecci   Quinta Regio
Silvano Strologo   Conero Riserva Decebalo
Valentini   Montepulciano d'Abruzzo
Velenosi   Rosso Piceno Superiore Roggio Del Filare

Individual Red Stars
Boccadigabbia   Akronte Cabernet Sauvignon
Caprai   Montefalco Sagrantino 25 Anni
Falesco   Montiano
Luigi Giusti   Lacrima di Morro d'Alba Rubbjano
La Fiorita Lamborghini   Campoleone
Le Terrazze   Chaos
Fattoria Mancini   Blu
Pieve del Vescovo   Lucciaio
Poggio Bertaio   Crovèllo
San Lorenzo   Lacrima Vigna Paradiso
Santa Barbara   Pathos
Sportoletti   Villa Fidelia Rosso
Tabarrini   Montefalco Sagrantino Colle Grimaldesco
Zerbina   Marzieno

Classy Verdicchio
Bisci   Verdicchio di Matelica Vigneto Fogliano
Bucci   Verdicchio dei Castelli di Jesi Classico Riserva Villa Bucci
Collestefano   Verdicchio di Matelica
Coroncino   Verdicchio dei Castelli di Jesi Classico Sup. Gaiospino
Garofoli   Verdicchio dei Castelli di Jesi Classico Superiore Podium
La Monacesca   Verdicchio di Matelica La Monacesca
Marchetti   Verdicchio dei Castelli di Jesi Class. Sup. Tenuta Cavaliere
Marotti Campi   Verdicchio dei Castelli di Jesi Class. Ris. Salmariano
Monte Schiavo   Verdicchio Castelli di Jesi Class. Sup. Ris. Le Giuncare
Sartarelli   Verdicchio dei Castelli di Jesi Class. Sup. Contrada Balciana
San Lorenzo   Verdicchio Castelli di Jesi Class. Sup. Ris. Vigna Delle Oche
Tenuta di Tavignano   Verdicchio dei Castelli di Jesi Class. Sup. Misco
Umani Ronchi   Verdicchio dei Castelli di Jesi Classico Riserva Plenio

Other Fine Dry Whites (without recourse to Chardonnay)
Castel De Paolis   Vigna Adriana
Maria Pia Castelli   Stella Flora
Ciu Ciu   Offida Pecorino Le Merlettaie
Falesco   Est! Est!! Est!!! Poggio dei Gelsi
Le Caniette   Offida Pecorino Io Sono Gaia
Fattoria Mancini   Pinot Nero Impero Bianco
Palazzone   Orvieto Classico Campo Del Guardiano
San Savino - Podere Capecci   Offida Pecorino Ciprea
Valentini   Trebbiano d'Abruzzo

'L'antico riscoperto'

The south of Italy has experienced a veritable explosion in quality and originality since mid- to late 90s. Once-isolated pockets of quality continue to mushroom and there is now quality as well as quantity from the ever swelling ranks of excellent producers in the Mezzogiorno. As in much of Italy the general standard of winemaking is at an unprecedented level. Add this to some high-quality vineyard sources, both new and old, and a rich hoard of ancient grape varieties (often Greek in origin) and you begin to see what is possible. The big three are Campania, Puglia and Sicily but don't ignore some brilliant wines from Basilicata, Calabria and Sardinia too. All six regions serve up both good-value bottles and world-class wines.

Campania

Taurasi is Campania's leading appellation, based on its most important grape, Aglianico. Its DOCG status may have once wanted for endorsement but now there are many good examples and a few outstanding wines which show the depth, structure and class that the grape can achieve when winemaking expertise is employed and the fruit quality has been maximised. Increasing amounts of good **Greco di Tufo** and **Fiano di Avellino** (both DOCG since 2003) are also produced in the Avellino hills but several of the best wines from this exciting area appear under the **Irpinia** IGT, the ancient name for the zone. Avellino's leaders are Mastroberardino and Feudi di San Gregorio but good examples come from several others.

To the north in the neighbouring province of Benevento another white, Falanghina, is starting to show real promise under the DOCs of **Sannio**, **Sant'Agata dei Goti**, **Solopaca** and **Taburno**. More good Aglianico also appears under each, especially the **Aglianico del Taburno**, which has now been granted DOCG status. Production is being led by the co-op, Cantina del Taburno. From vineyards in the Caserta province (nearer to Lazio), Aglianico is complemented by Piedirosso in increasingly good **Falerno del Massico** and reds from Aglianico vines on the slopes of the Roccamonfina volcano send the senses into overdrive (see Galardi). Red **Lacryma Christi del Vesuvio** from the slopes of Vesuvius is also based on Piedirosso.

If you're lucky enough to be visiting the island of **Ischia** or the **Costa d'Amalfi** there's potential from these vineyards too; even if you're not, at least try one of several fine whites based on Biancolella, from either Casa D'Ambra or Pietratorcia. Other new stars such as De Conciliis and Luigi Maffini are located in the south of Campania, revealing the potential of Fiano and Aglianico in the hills of Cilento.

Basilicata

In Basilicata, as in Campania, the great red grape is Aglianico. What's more it does exceedingly well here too with the right expertise. So if heading across to Puglia from Campania via the ancient city of Matera, first stop in the north where there now exists the opportunity to discover an ever increasing number of good sources of high quality examples of **Aglianico del Vulture**. The towns of Barile, Rionero in Vulture and Venosa are at the heart of an extensive DOC covering elevated slopes in the vicinity of the Monte Vulture volcano. **Aglianico di Vulture Superiore**, produced in the province of Potenza, has now been upgraded to DOCG status. Recent vintages of the top wines from Alovini, Le Querce, Cantine del Notaio or Elena Fucci, amongst others, may now be compared with those from Paternoster or D'Angelo, who are invariably the only sources of older wines of quality. Look out too for still newer names such as Giannattasio, Lelusi or the good value Grifalco. Good inexpensive examples also come from Cantine Sasso, and the Vulture and Venosa co-ops.

Puglia

More than anything else, Puglia provides value for money. **Salice Salentino** is the best-known of the many DOCs on the Salento peninsula that are based on the Negroamaro grape, but topped up with some Malvasia Nera. They range from simple gutsy, baked, raisiny examples to more complex, lush and sweet-fruited versions. Alezio, Copertino, Leverano and Squinzano offer similar reds if fewer good examples. The best Negroamaro comes from alberello (bush trained) vines and the reds of **Brindisi** are also based on it. Those who have long proven its potential, such as Cosimo Taurino and Vallone, are being joined by newer exponents including Conti Zecca, La Corte, Li Veli, Tenute Rubino, Tormaresca and Vetrere, accounting for a profusion of varietal examples (many excellent value) as well as blends based on Negroamaro but complemented by Montepulciano or Cabernet Sauvignon. **Primitivo di Manduria** (now DOCG) is the most important on the peninsula for Primitivo (a grape said to be identical to California's Zinfandel if of discernably different character according to some winemakers). Primitivo also appears under broader IGTs such as Tarantino and several of the Salento peninsula's best wines are sold as Salento IGT. There are now many good examples, several extremely good value for money. For something more unusual try an example of the Susumaniello grape, those from Tenute Rubino and Torre Guaceto (see Academia dei Racemi) highlight its potential.

On the high plateau of central Puglia, Primitivo is also DOC in **Gioia del Colle**. To the north lies **Castel del Monte** and here Uva di Troia (also known as Nero di Troia), Montepulciano and Aglianico feature. All three varieties have excellent potential as is becoming increasingly apparent from the likes of Torrevento, Rivera or Tormaresca. The latter, Antinori's southern outpost, is also using Cabernet Sauvignon. Uva di Troia is also an important planting on the rolling countryside in the very north of the region often as part of a **Cacc'e mmitte di Lucera** red (those from Alberto Longo and Petrilli are good). Rivera and Cantine Carpentiere are particularly instrumental in elevating the relatively unknown Castel del Monte wines to DOCG status as **Bombino Nera**, **Nero di Troioa Riserva** and **Rosso Riserva**. Falanghina and other varieties that are also common to neighbouring Molise are beginning to show promise here too.

Calabria

If Calabria is still seen as something of a backwater in more ways than one (both from the north and from outside Italy), its leading quality wine producers are more than making up for their relative lack of numbers. The best known DOC is **Cirò**, for a characterful red based almost exlusively on Gaglioppo, and a more ordinary white from Greco Bianco. Librandi are based here and have been a leader in the propagation of previously obscure, near extinct grape varieties. Two other DOCs, **Savuto** and **Scavigna**, used by Odoardi for wonderfully seductive reds, include a substantial proportion of Gaglioppo in the blend. Scavigna can also include significant percentages of Aglianico, Cabernet Sauvignon and Merlot.

Sicily (Sicilia)

The change in Sicily over the past decade has been extraordinary

Southern Italy & Islands

Italy

and the wave of often excellent new producers shows little sign of abating. Many of the top reds are sold as Sicilia IGT. There has been a strong focus on the international varieties, especially Cabernet Sauvignon, Merlot, Syrah and Chardonnay, but even more attention is now being paid to the high quality native varieties led by Nero d'Avola, Nerello Mascalese and white Inzolia. This mix of foreign and native seems to have helped in promoting Sicilian wines abroad – the success and acclaim with international varieties at worst serving as a kind of Trojan horse to facilitate a more sustained assault of native varieties.

The sea of vines in the west of Sicily is why the island vies with Puglia as Italy's most productive region. For long most of the wine has been pretty simple, dilute stuff but in the DOC zones of **Marsala** and **Alcamo**, as in pockets all over the island, there are also reds of unprecedented quality. From the central highlands, new names such as Feudo Montoni now add to the efforts of long standing producer Tasca d'Almerita in promoting quality. Other DOCs include **Contessa Entellina**, which covers a wide range of reds and whites of the producer Donnafugata and, in the south, **Cerasuolo di Vittoria** (DOCG from 2006) where Frappato is added to Nero d'Avola for a characterful, concentrated and perfumed red (try from COS, Planeta or Valle dell'Acate).

The vineyards on the lower slopes of Mount Etna are **Etna** DOC. Benanti is an established star and also the inspiration for something of a cult fringe that has developed on the northern slopes. As well as the Cambria brothers' revitalised estate (Cottanera), here can be found a cluster of high profile growers including Frank Cornelissen, Andrea Franchetti (Passopisciaro), Mick Hucknall of Simply Red fame (Il Cantante) and Marc De Grazia (Terre Nere). All share a passion for uncompromising quality based on the Nerello Mascalese grape and there are already some outstanding wines. Further evidence of this variety's nobility can be found north-east of Etna, in the small zone of Faro near Messina. Here its potential is harnessed in the brilliant reds of Palari.

Down in the south-eastern corner both **Moscato di Noto** (see Planeta) and **Moscato di Siracusa** (see Pupillo) are being revived but more importantly it is emerging as a leading area for Nero d'Avola (where in fact the town of Avola is located). Other impressive sweet whites come from offshore. Malvasia delle Lipari comes from this volcanic island group to the north and Moscato di Pantelleria from an especially windswept volcanic island that lies closer to Tunisia than Sicily. The richer, sweeter Passito di Pantelleria versions from dried grapes are the most exciting - be sure and try those from Benanti, De Bortoli, Donnafugata and Solidea.

Sardinia (Sardegna)

Several of Sardinia's DOCs are region-wide and typically account for everyday reds and whites of reasonable value if from a good source. These include **Cannonau di Sardegna**, **Monica di Sardegna** and **Vermentino di Sardegna**. There is an increasing amount of fine Cannonau di Sardegna including that from Alberto Loi and Antichi Poderi Jerzu. However, some of the best wines containing Cannonau (a clone of Grenache), from the likes of Argiolas, Dettori or Feudi della Medusa, do not come under the regional DOC but are wines of much greater depth and complexity.

Vermentino di Gallura, from a more restricted northern zone, is the island's only DOCG but examples of both Vermentinos can be

wonderfully fresh and aromatic (Capichera, Cantina Sociale Gallura, Giovanni Cherchi or Santadi for starters). Most of Sella & Mosca's red wines fall under **Alghero** DOC, named for the town on the north-west coast.

Carignano del Sulcis is also a more defined zone (in the south-west corner) where Santadi, the best of Sardinia's many co-ops, is based and makes some remarkably good Carignano-based reds. Try too Barrua from Agripunica. Another pocket of exceptional Carignano is at Arzachena in the far north (see Capichera). Cagnulari is another Sardinian red variety of some potential that is beginning to be realised (Giovanni Cherchi or Feudi della Medusa). **Vernaccia di Oristano** is a small zone producing oxidised, sherry-like wines – those from Attilio Contini are of high quality.

A-Z of producers by region

Appellations

1 Falerno del Massico
2 Greco di Tufo
3 Fiano di Avellino
4 Taurasi
5 Aglianico del Vulture
6 Castel del Monte
7 Gioia del Colle
8 Primitivo di Manduria
9 Brindisi
10 Salice Salentino
11 Cirò
12 Savuto
13 Faro
14 Etna
15 Cerasuolo di Vittoria
16 Contea di Sclafani
17 Marsala
18 Alcamo
19 Contessa Entellina
20 Vermentino di Gallura
21 Alghero
22 Vernaccia di Oristano
23 Carignano del Sulcis
24 Vermentino di Sardegna, Cannonau di Sardegna

Regions

A Campania
B Basilicata
C Puglia
D Calabria

A-Z of producers - *Campania*

Antonio Caggiano (Campania) *www.cantinecaggiano.it*
Antonio Caggiano is one of the stars of Taurasi yet only turned his attention to making fine wines in 1990. Now he makes a range of reds and whites, all to a consistently high standard. Foremost is the single-vineyard Taurasi Vigna Macchia dei Goti, from Aglianico which is then aged in one and two year- old wood. It shows some classic tar, earth, smoke and black plum fruit characters, with no lack of depth or character and fine tannins. Also from a single vineyard comes Salae Domini, which spends 10–12 months in *barrique* and is sold under the IGT Aglianico dell'Irpinia. Though oak is apparent it integrates well with a fine, ripe fruit character. Taurì, an inexpensive version of Aglianico displaying some of the grape's classic character, is also sold under the IGT. Béchar is a fruit-intense Fiano di Avellino that is not too structured – as wines from this appellation sometimes can be. FiaGre is a *barrique*-aged blend of 70% Fiano and 30% Greco. Fresh when young, it will also keep a couple of years. A potent Greco di Tufo, Devon, is now made. Also produced is a lovely, elegant sweet white, Mel, from dried Fiano and Greco grapes, with lightly spicy pear and quince among its delicious flavours.
Recommended Reds:
Taurasi Vigna Macchia dei Goti ★★★ £E   Salae Dominii ★★★ £D
Taurì ★★★ £C
Recommended Whites:
Mel ★★★ £E   Fiano di Avellino Béchar ★★ £C
FiaGre ★ £B

Caputo (Campania) *www.caputo1890.it*
A sizeable modern wine operation that continues to expand, Caputo produces examples of most of Campania's DOCs. Lesser wines are sound but for the most part unexciting; however, Greco di Tufo, Fiano di Avellino and Falanghina are good examples of these whites. Unusual are a dry white (Fescine) and sparkling wine (Caputo Brut), produced from Asprinio di Aversa grapes grown on an extraordinary canopy between poplar trees. On the red front, Caputo's varietal efforts with Casavecchia and Piedirosso grapes (the latter as Campanus) show great character and intensity, if austere and structured when young needing at least five years. Zicorrà and the Taurasi are the top reds, both produced from Aglianico and *barrique*-aged. The complex and sweet berry-fruited Ziccorà needs at least 6–8 years. The Taurasi is the class act; powerful and extracted, it needs 10 years' age but will keep for longer.
Recommended Reds:
Taurasi ★★★★ £E   Zicorrà ★★★ £D   Casavecchia ★★ £C
Lacryma Christi del Vesuvio Campanus ★★ £C
Recommended Whites:
Fiano di Avellino ★★ £C   Greco di Tufo ★★ £C
Campi Flegrei Falanghina Frattasi ★★ £C
Sannio Falanghina ★ £B

Casa D'Ambra (Campania/Ischia) *www.dambravini.com*
First established in 1888, D'Ambra is Ischia's leading producer but only after having been revitalised since the 1980s by Mario D'Ambra and more recently his youngest grandchild, Andrea. 80% of production are whites which are unoaked. The stunning clifftop terraces of Frassitelli (500m above the sea) are planted with 4 ha of Biancolella, and provides the finest varietal expression of this grape. Exuding a fusion of herbs, spice, broom, stone fruits and mineral the wine is at once dense and intense, yet lively with a fine lingering finish. Also based on Biancolella is the powerful, dry Kime

(Biancolella with 20% of other native varieties) with a ripe, almost late-harvested character and refined almondy finish. Euposia, a varietal from the Forastera grape, is less well-delineated but reveals a subtle salty, mineral quality. 15% of Forastera is also included in the ripe and vibrant regular Biancolella bottling. Reds are light but intense. The supple if cool regular Per'e Palummo (Piedirosso) contrasts with a more extracted and minerally Dedicato a Maria D'Ambra version that adds in Guarnaccia, and is partly oak-aged. While needing age, with a little more ripeness and richness it has the potential to be very interesting. If visiting there's also a small museum with winemaking artefacts..
Recommended Reds:
Ischia Rosso Dedicato à Mario D'Ambra ★★☆ £D
Ischia Per'e Palummo ★☆ £B
Recommended Whites:
Ischia Biancolella Frassitelli ★★★ £C   Ischia Biancolella ★★ £B
Ischia Bianco Kime ★★★ £C   Ischia Forastera Euposia ★★☆ £C

De Conciliis (Campania) *www.viticoltorideconciliis.it*
The De Conciliis family have been making wines from their 25 ha of vineyards close to the coast for less than 10 years and they grow almost exclusively only two varieties as the basis for all their wines: Fiano for the whites and Aglianico for the reds. Wines labelled Donnaluna are the standard versions, an intense solid red being more impressive than the white. Perella (not tasted) is a smaller volume Fiano while new is Antece, which is Fiano given an essentially red-wine vinification with a week on the skins. It is rich, structured and complex with flavours running from citrus to the exotic. The outstanding wine is Naima, a *barrique*-aged Aglianico subject to a long maceration. It is a lush, concentrated, splendidly complex and powerful example of this noble grape. Also made is Ra! from a small vineyard that is an inter-mixed planting of Aglianico and Barbera. Partially dried grapes are foot-trodden, resulting in a moderately sweet wine with an intense ripe fruit, spice and earth character. Ka! is a sweet white from Malvasia and Moscato grapes. There's also an attractive aperitif-style sparkler, Selim Brut, made by the Charmat method. All are sold as IGTs.
Recommended Reds:
Naima ★★★★ £E   Donnaluna Aglianico ★★ £C
Recommended Whites:
Ka! ★★★ £D   Antece ★★★ £C   Selim Brut ★ £C
Donnaluna Fiano ★ £B

✿ Masseria Felicia (Campania) *www.masseriafelicia.it*
What awesome vineyard sites there must exist in Campania! Here we have relatively young vines but already super wines. It helps to have Aglianico as the principal variety and being small (7.5 ha) sharpens the focus on quality but there is something magical here on the lower slopes of Monte Massico. Just two reds of tremendous extract and richness are produced, both based on an 80/20 blend of Aglianico and Piedirosso. Ariapetrina is partly aged in used French *barriques* and reveals a mineral, spice, berry, plum character with a hints of earth, chestnut and truffle. The Etichetta Bronzo version gets 12-14 months in new oak and adds a dense, smouldering earth and fruit derived richness. For white there's increasingly good Falanghina. Quantities of all wines are very small.
Recommended Reds:
Falerno del Massico Etichetta Bronzo ★★★★★ £F
Falerno del Massico Ariapetrina ★★★★ £D
Recommended Whites:
Anthologia Falanghina ★★★ £C

Benito Ferrara (Campania) *www.benitoferrara.it*

A long established estate recently expanded to 7 ha, the Ferrara family draws the best from the richly mineral soils. For a taste of really fine Greco di Tufo, Gabriella Ferrara's Vigna Cicogna more than suffices. A concentrated example with intense ripe fruit and a deep minerality it adds just a little more richness over a very good regular version. A single bottling of Fiano is scarcely less good than the Cicogna; fruit-rich but with depth and structure too. Due Chicchi is a simpler, less expressive but soundly made Greco sold under the Campania IGT. While the white grapes come from vineyards at around 500m, those for Aglianico are that bit higher. Those for Vigna Quattro Confini are at 600m from which a partially oaked fruit-intense example is made. The wine shows a distinctive cherry/ raspberry, red fruits pastille quality when young. This character becomes almost confected in a very juicy, fruity Passo del Lupo Aglianico sold under the Campania IGT. Give the Quattro Confini 3-5 years to round out fully.

Recommended Reds:

Irpinia Aglianico Vigna Quattro Confini ★★★ £C

Passo del Lupo ★★★ £B

Recommended Whites:

Greco di Tufo Vigna Cicogna ★★★☆ £E

Greco di Tufo ★★★ £D   Fiano di Avellino ★★★ £D

Due Chicchi ★☆ £B

✿✿ Feudi di San Gregorio (Campania) *www.feudi.it*

In a short space of time this winery based in the Avellino hills of Campania has risen to be the region's leading producer and one of the most exciting in Italy. Riccardo Cotarella now helps steer the ship but the reputation was established by Mario Ercolino (now working on projects elsewhere). Plenty of oak is used and the reds are modern but with fabulous fruit, concentration and depth. Piano di Montevergine, the single-vineyard version of Taurasi, has great class, style and excellent balance (a second Selve Luoti was previously made). Serpico is arguably southern Italy's finest red, a wine of majestic depth and length of flavour. Pàtrimo, made since 1999, is a prodigious varietal Merlot, with marvellous fruit and depth, if not quite the breadth of Serpico. The range of whites, often from steep sloping vineyards, is lead by excellent examples of Greco, Fiano and Falanghina including single vineyard versions of Fiano di Avellino (Pietracalda), Greco di Tufo (Cutizzi) and Sannio Falanghina (Serraciolo). Campanaro is late-harvested Fiano and Greco that have been fermented to dryness and partially *barrique*-aged, producing a rich, exotic but balanced wine. A passito-style sweet version from partly botrytised grapes, Privilegio, reveals intense ripe citrus fruit and moderate sweetness. Previously made, Idem is also sweet but includes Moscato, Greco, Falanghina and Coda di Volpe as well as Fiano. Merlot excepted, it is remarkable that the quality of all these wines is based on the native local varieties. While the top wines are no longer cheap there's both decent quality in the more moderately priced wines led by Rubrato, a varietal Aglianico now produced in relatively big volumes. Others include Lacryma Christi red and white, Trigaio (Aglianico-based) and Albente (Falanghina). A rosé is also made, Ros'aura, as well as Rosh, a kosher red wine, both from Aglianico. Besides burgeoning operations in Basilicata (VIGNE DIMEZZO) and Puglia (OGNISSOLE), ambitious sparkling wines (DUBL Greco and DUBL Aglianico) are made, thanks to collaboration with Anselme Selosse (Jacques SELOSSE) of Champagne..

Recommended Reds:

Taurasi Piano di Montevergine ★★★★★ £F

Taurasi ★★★★ £E   Serpico ★★★★★ £F

Pàtrimo ★★★★★ £F   Rubrato ★★ £C

Lacryma Christi Rosso ★★ £C   Trigaio ★★ £B

Recommended Whites:

Privilegio ★★★ £E   Fiano di Avellino Pietracalda ★★★ £D

Fiano di Avellino ★★★ £C   Greco di Tufo Cutizzi ★★★ £D

Greco di Tufo ★★ £C   Campanaro ★★★ £D

Sannio Falanghina Serrocielo ★★ £C   Albente ★ £B

Recommended Rosés:

Ros'aura ★ £B

✿ Galardi (Campania)

In the north of Campania, between the volcano of Roccamonfina and the sea, Galardi produces just one wine, Terra di Lavoro, from Aglianico (80%) and Piedirosso. There are now 10ha of vines wedged between groves of chestnut trees at 400 m. Production is gradually increasing towards a projected maximum 40,000 bottles of this new classic. With help from Riccardo Cotarella, Terra di Lavoro (Roccamonfina IGT) is now a superb, fabulously complex red of great depth and stunning length, with a wealth of black fruits, mineral and earth, spice and herbs. It has improved in nearly every vintage since it was first made in 1994 and shows, along with some of the other stunning wines of this region, what tremendous potential there is here. Cult status means high prices. Strict selection is required to maintain the high standards. Don't miss the chance to try any vintage, especially with some age.

Recommended Reds:

Terra di Lavoro ✪✪✪✪✪ £F

Il Cancelliere (Campania) *www.ilcancelliere.it*

The Romano family have been producing wine for 150 years and the current generation, led by Socorso Romano and agronomist Enrico Romano, is now producing some of the best Taurasi and Aglianico in the area. The vineyards consist of some 9 ha in the Taurasi district, between 450 and 550 metres above sea level Grapes are manually harvested between the first and second week in November and the wines are made without filtering and fining. The 'Gioviano' Aglianico is a big mouthful but there is plenty of ripe, dark fruit beneath the tannins. After 20 days of maceration at room temperature, the wine is aged in wood for 12 months with a further 4 months in bottle before it is commercially released. The 'Nero Né' is a full DOGC Taurasi – aged in wood for 24 months in 32 hectolitre Slovenian oak casks and another 12 months in bottle before release. Here we have an even bigger wine – coupled with a great deal more finesse than the IGT Aglianico. The Riserva is very impressive with enough in it to last 30 years or more with hints of liquorice and peppers adding to the underlying black cherry and plum fruit. (NB)

Recommended Reds:

Taurasi Nero Né Riserva ★★★★ £E

Taurasi Nero Né ★★★☆ £D   Campania Aglianico Giovano ★★★ £C

Le Vigne di Raito (Campania) *www.levignediraito.com*

In 2001, Patrizia Malanga found herself with 2 ha of half abandoned land and immediately began the process of planting a vineyard there. With the help of expert oenologists and agronomists, she planted her first vines in 2003 and produced her first wine in 2007 – a blend of 80% Aglianico and 20% Piedirosso. Like her nearby neighbour, Silvia Imparato of MONTEVETRANO, Patrizia is concentrating on a single wine which she endeavours to encapsulate all the fragrances and tastes of the local area. 2007 saw the first vintage of this wine – called 'Le Vigne di Raito' – just 4000 bottles produced - a smooth and elegant wine with hints of

Italy

garrigue, cherry, liquorice and myrtle. The grapes are hand picked and then vinified in temperature controlled stainless steel tanks for 15 days before being transferred into 500 litre French oak barrels and assembled before the malolactic fermentation begins. After a further 12 months the wine is bottled without filtration or fining. From 2008, the estate is now both organic and biodynamic and also produces a rosé (this time 80% Piedirosso and 20% Aglianico). (NB)

Recommended Reds:
IGT Colli di Salerno Ragis Rosso ★★★★ £D

Luigi Maffini (Campania) *www.maffini-vini.com*
Working primarily with Aglianico and Fiano, Luigi Maffini has expanded to 12 ha vineyard but continues to improve the balance and fruit purity that mark out his wines. The intense, fruit-driven white Kràtos (pure Fiano) has inviting scents of spice, herb, dried peach and apricot. While it doesn't have the structure for long keeping it is delightful when young. There is more depth and style in an oak-fermented and aged version, Pietraincatenata. The regular red cuvée, Klèos, from Aglianico, Piedirosso and Barbera (70/20/10), is relatively forward but again provides lots of attractive fruit. However it is Cenito, now 100% Aglianico (Cilento Aglianico DOC since 03) that shows the greatest promise. Despite an occasional excess of oak (given up to 14 months in new oak), there is also a depth and elegance only apparent with around 8–10 years' age. A sweet white from dried Fiano grapes, called simply Passito was first made in 2002. Given 40 days drying, any botrytis influence is minimal and a lush, dried stone fruits character is accentuated. A well-balanced Rosato, Denazzaro from Aglianico was first made in 06 and shows promise too. All wines, Cenito excepted, are sold under the Paestum IGT.

Recommended Reds:
Cilento Aglianico Cenito ★★★☆ £E   Klèos ★★☆ £C

Recommended Whites:
Passito ★★★☆ £E   Pietraincatenata ★★★☆ £D   Kràtos ★★☆ £C

Recommended Rosés:
Denazzaro ★★ £B

>> Guido Marsella (Campania) *www.guidomarsella.com*
Since planting the vineyard in 1995, Guido Marsella has striven to prove that Fiano di Avellino, which had hitherto been shipped to Piedmont as a base wine for vermouths, had some nobility. His 26 hectares of vineyard is also planted with Greco di Tufo and Falaghina. Harvesting as late as possible, the wines are fermented in 100% stainless steel tanks, and cellared on fine lees for a minimum of 15 months prior to release. The Fiano displays firm, voluptuous fruit in the mouth coupled with a good persistence on the palate whilst the Greco is tight and mineral, pure and clean. The Beneventano Falanghia is again very smooth with purity of fruit and a mineral finish. This is one of Campania's better growers. (NB)

Recommended Whites:
Fiano di Avellino ★★★ £D   Greco di Tufo ★★★ £C
Falanghina Beneventano ★★★ £C

✿ Mastroberardino (Campania) *www.mastroberardino.com*
For decades Mastroberardino was Campania's one producer of note and the first to promote the wines of Taurasi, Fiano di Avellino and Greco di Tufo. Having rebuilt following a devastating earthquake in 1980, the family now control 420 ha of vineyards and produce around 200,000 cases of wine a year. The estate is run by the 10th-generation Carlo and Piero Mastroberardino but winemaking is still overseen by their father, Antonio. A split between brothers

Antonio and Walter Mastroberardino in 1994 led to Walter and his family establishing TERREDORA. The leading wine here is the Taurasi Radici, which is aged in a mixture of large and small oak. Complex and refined with impressive dimension and power, it only shows at its best with around a decade's age. This is now complemented by a newer wine, Naturalis Historia (after Pliny the Elder's great work), which is also 100% Aglianico. It spends two years in small oak and is richer and more modern in style. A varietal Aglianico, Avellanio, also shows good fruit. The best versions of Greco di Tufo (Nova Serra) and Fiano di Avellino (Radici) are intense, ripe and varietal. The More Maiorum version of the latter is unusual in being oak-fermented and aged before a long bottle refinement (30 months) prior to release. From 1996 Mastroberardino was given responsibility for replanting historic vineyard sites (totally about 1ha) among the ruins of ancient Pompeii. The culmination of these efforts is Villa dei Misteri, a *barrique*-aged blend of Piedirosso and Sciascinoso (90/10), first produced in 2001. With intense red fruits, especially cherry and cranberry, it is an intriguing wine though its modest structure and depth maybe due to young vines. Also produced are three sweet wines - a botrytisised Fiano passito, Melizie, and an Aglianico passito, Antheres, and a lesser Aglianico passito, Hacolnero, more of a Recioto style. Relatively large volumes of Lacryma Christi del Vesuvio are also produced, the white from Coda di Volpe, the red from Piedirosso.

Recommended Reds:
Taurasi Riserva Radici ★★★★ £G   Taurasi Radici ★★★ £E
Naturalis Historia ★★★ £F   Avellanio Aglianico ★ £B

Recommended Whites:
Fiano di Avellino More Maiorum ★★ £D
Fiano di Avellino Radici ★★ £C   Greco di Tufo Nova Serra ★★ £C
Greco di Tufo Vignadangelo ★ £B

Moio (Campania) *www.cantinemoio.it*
Michele Moio fu Luigi is the full name for the wines made by one of southern Italy's leading lights, Luigi Moio. Professor of Enology at Naples University, he also consults for several other wineries. The Moio vineyards are situated in what was the territory of Roman Falernus. Unusually Primitivo, rather than Aglianico or Piedirosso, forms the basis of the reds. Very ripe fruit and long macerations make for powerful, vigorous, uncompromising wines of formidable intensity and complexity. The regular version from an arid, volcanic site spends 6–8 months in large Slavonian oak and can need 7–8 years to really shine. Moio 57, from a different vineyard, spends longer in oak and is more complex, while Guarano has rich fruit but tannins to match. Maiatico is the top selection of fruit and is aged in mostly new *barriques*; it tastes like a collision between fruit intensity and the earth from which it has burst forth, with a profusion of aromas and flavours including earth, plum, fig, clove, spice and tar. Drink early or keep another five years. Both whites are good examples of Falanghina, the Falerno a little riper, longer and more structured. Both will improve for a year or so.

Recommended Reds:
Falerno del Massico Maiatico ★★★★ £E
Falerno del Massico Primitivo ★★★ £C
Moio 57 ★★★ £C   Guarano ★★★ £C

Recommended Whites:
Falerno del Massico ★★ £C   Falanghina ★★ £B

✿ Salvatore Molettieri (Campania) *www.salvatoremolettieri.com*
Although only founded in 1995, this small cellar draws on the experience of a winegrowing family steeped in the land. The

intense, powerful Aglianico produced in the late 90s have been further improved with greater finesse, expression and balance in the most recent releases. 11 ha of vines cover gentle, well exposed slopes of the Valle del Calore at 550-600m. The four top reds are all produced from Aglianico grapes from the Cinque Querce vineyard. A mix of *barriques* and *botti* grandi are used - that with the shortest ageing is sold simply as Irpinia Aglianico. This is a pure, elegant example with smoke, plum, berry and coffee scents and a dense, chewy and expansive palate, needing 6-10 years' ageing. Campi Taurasini, from young vines, is a more approachable wine in its early years. On the other hand, Renonno is made from vines which had been replanted with the cuttings of pre-phylloxera vines which are over 100 years old combined with vines ranging from 5 years to 75 years old. Like the Cinque Querce wines, it needs a long cellaring time before the wine reaches its best. The Taurasi with 30 months in wood adds earth, spice and truffle notes, with an almost pre-phylloxera quality. More modern, it is also very classy with abundant fine tannin give it at least 10 years and amongst the best examples going. The longer aged, tarry Riserva is bigger, slightly more traditional but should prove to be a legendary example with 20 years' age. For a more forward and overt fruitiness go for the Aglianico-based Irpinia Rosso from the Ischia Piana vineyard that includes 15% of (mostly) Cabernet Sauvignon and a little Piedirosso. Whites include flavoursome Fiano di Avellino and bold but stylish Greco di Tufo. Insomma, this is not a cellar to miss, but especially if you have an addiction for Aglianico.

Recommended Reds:
Taurasi Vigna Cinque Querce ★★★★★ £F
Taurasi Riserva Vigna Cinque Querce ★★★★★ £F
Taurasi Renonno ★★★★ £E Irpinia Campi Taurasini ★★★★ £D
Irpinia Rosso Ischia Piana ★★☆ £C
Recommended Whites:
Greco di Tufo ★★★ £C Fiano di Avellino Apianum ★★☆ £C
Irpinia Bianco Alopecis ★★ £C

❀ Montevetrano (Campania) *www.montevetrano.it*
Production of Montevetrano is only slightly higher (at 28,000 bottles a year) than GALARDI's Terra di Lavoro, another of the super-Campanian wines made by Riccardo Cotarella. Silvia Imparato's few hectares are at San Cipriano Picentino in hills behind the bustling coastal city of Salerno. Here Cabernet Sauvignon (60% of the blend) and Merlot (30%) hold sway, while Aglianico makes up the balance. The wine sold under the Colli di Salerno IGT has great structure and depth with considerable complexity and elegance and is not simply another internationally styled red. Since 2011, a 100% Aglianico, Core, has been produced. It has spent 10 months in new French *barriques*. Perhaps a little too early to rate at the moment but a potential ★★★ wine (£D).
Recommended Reds:
Montevetrano ★★★★★ £F

❀ Pietracupa (Campania)
This small estate has risen quickly to produce some of the finest whites in not just Campania but southern Italy. The young Sabino Loffredo in collaboration with Carmine Valentino adds another dimension to Greco and Fiano in both regular and special selections. By eschewing wood the emphasis is on the fruit and the character of the vineyard. The wines are characterised by their perfumes, energy, intensity and minerality, with a density and purity in the mouth. There is floral, citrus and peach in Fiano which is more smoky, minerally and structured in the Il Cupo version which is only

made in years when Sabino feels that there is sufficient ripeness of fruit to warrant it, so is not produced in every vintage. Both Greco are ripe-fruited with a stone-fruits, herb and mineral intensity, and an almost atypical depth, weight and length. Reds include Quirico, a light, bright, expressive, supple unwooded Aglianico; like a fine Nebbiolo d'Alba complementing a more Barolo-like Taurasi. The latter is not big but pure and intense with a minerally finesse, only missing a little more richness to be really fine.
Recommended Reds:
Taurasi ★★★☆ £E Quirico ★★☆ £C
Recommended Whites:
Il Cupo ★★★☆ £E Fiano di Avellino ★★★ £C Greco di Tufo ★★★ £C

Tenuta Ponte (Campania) *www.tenutaponte.it*
Here is another source of good typical Campania whites. Not one but five small estates comprise the 35 ha of vineyard directed by one of the owners, Alessandro Di Stasio. The wines are made by Carmine Valentino (consultant for PIETRACUPA) and include a refined, elegant Falanghina (Beneventano IGT) that has good depth for the variety and is complemented by a full, concentrated Greco di Tufo and intense, perfumed Fiano di Avellino. Varietal Coda di Volpe is also made. For red there is a reasonably priced, dense, extracted, slightly old style Taurasi of good promise. Two other reds are made but haven't been tasted. Carazita is Aglianico-based but includes 10% each of Sangiovese and Merlot while Cossano is a *barrique*-aged Merlot. There is certainly plenty of promise here in anticipation of new releases.
Recommended Reds:
Taurasi ★★★ £E
Recommended Whites:
Greco di Tufo ★★★ £C Falanghina ★★★ £C Fiano di Avellino ★★ £C

San Paolo (Campania) *www.magistravini.it*
This fairly new operation has the winemaking expertise of Mario Ercolino (ex FEUDI SAN GREGORIO) behind it. There are fine examples of the three most established white varieties in Campania: Fiano di Avellino, Greco di Tufo, and Falanghina. All are true to type and properly ripe with good concentration; the Fiano and Greco also have the structure and intensity to improve with an extra year's age or more. Two Aglianico reds are even more impressive. An unwooded but potent IGT example has extraordinary colour and fruit for the price. The Taurasi ,with 14 months in French oak, has added style with classic plum, coffee, carob, berry and herb scents and flavours. More fruit-driven than some, it nonetheless shows lots of promise.
Recommended Reds:
Taurasi ★★★☆ £D Aglianico ★★ £B
Recommended Whites:
Fiano di Avellino ★★ £C Greco di Tufo ★★ £C Falanghina ★★ £B

❀ Cantina del Taburno (Campania) *www.cantinadeltaburno.it*
It is always a good sign when a region's co-ops start turning out high-quality wines. The decision to do so by the agrarian co-op of the Benevento province, with a winery close to the foot of Monte Taburno, is a recent one – helped by input from the University of Naples. Whites are a speciality with excellent examples of Falanghina, Fiano and hitherto obscure Coda di Volpe. The quality of regular Falanghina and Fiano has improved immeasurably in successive vintages. Small amounts of Falanghina are bottled as Cesco dell'Eremo and Folius, both with some *barrique* influence. A Fiano and a Coda di Volpe are also made. The spice, earth, smoke

Italy

and plum of fine Aglianico are well expressed in Delius, especially with four or five years' age, but a better-value Fidelis is a decent introduction too. The crowning achievement is the Bue Apis from vineyards on the slopes of Monte Taburno, an Aglianico of great breadth and structure that sees 18 months in new oak following a long maceration. Its price reflects both its quality and limited production of just a few thousand bottles. A passito Falanghina, Ruscolo, is also produced. Also produced but not tasted are a Taburno Piedirosso and an Aglianico and Piedirosso blend, Torlicoso.

Recommended Reds:
Bue Apis ★★★★ £F   Delius ★★★ £D
Aglianico del Taburno Fidelis ★★ £B
Recommended Whites:
Taburno Falanghina ★★ £C   Taburno Greco ★★ £C

Telaro/Lavoro & Salute (Campania)   *www.vinitelaro.it*
The three Telaro brothers produce a distinctive range of reasonably priced wines from Campania's leading grape varieties. The 40 ha of vines on their 85 ha estate on the lower slopes of the Roccamonfina volcano in northern Campania are farmed organically. Aglianico forms the basis of the reds and Falanghina, Fiano and Greco the whites. The top two reds are the Riservas, Ara Mundi from 100% Aglianico and Calivierno, which includes some 20% Piedirosso. Both show deep earth, mineral, herb and ripe fruit complexity, good density and ripe tannins as well as a proven ability to age well. Of similar style and character but more immediate and fruit-driven is Montecaruso, which also includes a little Piedirosso. Whites from Fiano and Greco are well made with good fruit. Falanghina shows extra style when made in a late-harvested Vendemmia Tardiva version. Unusual is a sweet Aglianico-based red made from dried grapes, Passito delle Cinque Pietre. Concentrated and intense, it shows reasonable balance if some astringency, avoids being too raisiny and releases a fusion of red fruit flavours and spice.

Recommended Reds:
Galluccio Riserva Ara Mundi ★★★ £D
Galluccio Riserva Calivierno ★★★ £D
Galluccio Montecaruso ★★ £B   Passito delle Cinque Pietre ★★ £D
Recommended Whites:
Falanghina Vendemmia Tardiva ★★ £B
Greco Le Cinque Pietre ★★ £B   Fiano Le Cinque Pietre ★★ £B
Galluccio Ripabianca Falanghina ★ £B

Terre del Principe (Campania)   *www.terredelprincipe.com*
Located in northern Campania, Terre del Principe is the new company formed in 2003 by Peppe Mancini after a split with his partner in his original creation, VESTINI CAMPAGNANO. The vineyards have been retained. so the wierd and wonderful grape varieties revived by Mancini (Casavecchia and Pallagrello Nero and Bianco) now attain similar high quality but under new labels. Of the two Pallagrello Bianco whites, Fontanavigna is the stainless-steel version with apple, melon, pear, spice and quince, and impressive breadth on the palate. Le Sèrole is *barrique*-fermented and tastes like an exotic Chardonnay but one with real structure and weight. For the reds, Castello delle Femmine combines the two black grape varieties and displays black plum, bilberry, spice, mineral and licorice in a soft yet discernably tannic structure. Centomoggia is the varietal Casavecchia made from mostly very old vines and aged in new *barriques*. With its concentrated spicy, blackberry, bilberry fruit and powerful tannins it needs 6–8 years' ageing. Ambruco is the equivalent wine from Pallagrello Nero and similarly needs time. It is produced from young vines and the concentrated and stylish fruit

seems a little overwhelmed by the oak and structure at present; the wine will be rated after further tastings.

Recommended Reds:
Centomoggia ★★★ £D   Castello delle Femmine ★★ £C
Recommended Whites:
Le Sèrole ★★★ £D   Fontanavigna ★★ £C

Terredora (Campania)   *www.terredora.com*
Fine examples of Greco and Fiano have always distinguished this producer since it was set-up following a break with Mastroberardino in 1994. The new operation was centred on estate vineyards that date from 78 and now total more than 150 ha. A composed and complete Fiano di Avellino Terre di Dora usually vies with Greco di Tufo Terre degli Angeli for top honours but the Loggia della Serra Greco is also ripe, structured and intense. All three are made in significant quantities (ranging from 150.000 to 200,000 bottles). A late-harvested Fiano, CampoRe is partly aged in *barrique* but hasn't worked. Decent Falanghina comes in two different bottlings, Irpinia and Campania bottlings. The Aglianico reds have been a little uneven in the struggle to find balance but come in three guises. A persuasive if relatively light Irpinia Aglianico can show good complexity. The regular Taurasi, Fatica Contadina reveals classic flavours and richness with 5-10 years' age but usually needs a little more restraint and better balance. CampoRe is made in small quantities (5000 bottles) but hasn't yet reached its true potential. Other wines include Lacryma Christi red and white, and a passito-style Fiano.

Recommended Reds:
Taurasi Fatica Contadina ★★★☆ £F   Irpinia Aglianico ★★☆ £B
Recommended Whites:
Fiano di AvellinoTerre di Dora ★★★ £C
Greco di TufoTerre degli Angeli ★★★ £C
Greco di Tufo Loggia della Serra ★★ £C   Irpinia Falanghina ★★ £C

Vesevo (Campania)   *www.vesevo.it*
Campania could do with more of this. That is, excellent examples of her best known grapes sold for reasonable prices. Valentino Sciotto and Marco Scarinci are behind several operations in central and southern Italy, including the GRAN SASSO label from Abruzzo. Fresh fruit-driven varietals result from careful attention to grape quality, low fermentation temperatures and avoidance of oxidation. Early releases were good but the wines have become more expressive in the last couple of vintages. The Falanghina is excellent value while fine Fiano and Greco are only missing that little extra structure, individuality or class of the region's finest. Even with more than five year's age the Taurasi is still backward but reveals something of Aglianico's fine fruit profile; there is enough extract and density to suggest a 10-15 year potential. Regular Aglianico (Beneventano IGT) delivers both great fruit and style at a very affordable price and in reasonable volumes.

Recommended Reds:
Taurasi ★★★☆ £E   Aglianico ★★ £B
Recommended Whites:
Fiano di Avellino ★★★ £C   Greco di Tufo ★★★ £C
Falanghina ★★☆ £B

❀ Villa Matilde (Campania)   *www.villamatilde.it*
The Avallone brothers were consistently successful with wines from their San Castrese property in the northern reaches of Campania, including Falerno del Massico, before adding more Falanghina and Aglianico from vineyards (Rocca dei Leoni) in the more inland

Beneventano province. New acquisitions in the Avellino hills add Greco and Fiano (Tenute di Altavilla) to the mix. Of the whites, the regular Falanghina (Roccamonfina IGT) and Beneventano examples are eclipsed by the Falerno del Massico Bianco (also Falanghina) which is more mineral and better structured. The later harvested Caracci is partly *barrique*-aged, usually resulting in a harmonious integration of concentrated ripe fruit and oak-derived flavours and texture but should be given 4-5 years' ageing. New Fiano and Greco are tight and concentrated and deserve 3-4 years. Reds are even better. A supple varietal Aglianico (Beneventano IGT) is surpassed by partly oaked Falerno del Massico Rosso (80% Aglianico, 20% Piedirosso) which can start out a little backward but will come into its own after five years or more. Camarato, the same blend but from a parcel of old vines and aged for 12 months in French oak, is sleek and stylish with excellent defintion and fruit intensity, only missing the extra depth of the region's finest reds. Cecubo is a real contrast - it retains the Piedirosso component but the Aglianico is replaced by Abbuoto (45%) and Primitivo (35%). Its multifaceted character ranges from bark, smoke and mineral through black plum and wild berries to cocoa and licorice. Dense and powerful, this is an intense, structured and stylish red - cellar for 10 years. Also made is a fresh and characterful (Aglianico) rosé, Terre Cerase. Eleusi is a passito-style sweet white from Falanghina grapes, partly dried on the vine and then in trays. Its spiced apricot, dried peach and floral aromas precede an exuberant fruit-intense palate, it is potentially a top example. Look out too for an exquisite new passito-style red from Aglianico grapes, Deira. Taurasi Tenuta di Altavilla, since 2004, is a powerful, complex, fruit-driven wine with many facets of expressive opulence. Will need 10 years of cellaring at least to be seen at its best..

Recommended Reds:
Taurasi Tenute di Altavilla ★★★★☆ £E Cecubo ★★★★ £E
Falerno del Massico Camarato ★★★★ £F
Falerno del Massico Rosso ★★★ £C
Aglianico Rocca dei Leoni ★★☆ £C

Recommended Whites:
Eleusi ★★★☆ £E Fiano di Avellino Tenute di Altavilla ★★★ £C
Greco di Tufo Tenute di Altavilla ★★★ £C
Falerno del Massico Caracci ★★★ £C
Falerno del Massico Bianco ★★★ £B
Falanghina Rocca dei Leoni ★★ £C Falanghina ★★ £B

Recommended Rosés:
Terre Cerase ★☆ £B

A-Z of producers - *Basilicata*

❋ **Alovini (Basilcata/Aglianico del Vulture)** *www.alovini.it*
Two complex, bold Aglianico are what make the vini of the Alò family special. The powerful, dense Alvolo shows the influence of 18 months in new *barriques* but also reveals a complex spicy, coffee infused black fruits richness. The second, Armànd hasn't quite the same definition or concentration yet still shows lots of style as well as breadth and depth with five years' age or more. If neither have quite the finesse of the very best Aglianico, Alvolo nevertheless has great potential and deserves at least a decade's ageing. For seekers after something more international there's Cabánico, an equal blend of Cabernet Sauvignon and Aglianico. Although reasonably well-combined the coarser, slightly rustic Cabernet component dominates. Under the Le Ralle label there's Aglianico del Vulture with decent fruit and structure, more modest fruit-driven Rosso (stainless steel vinified Aglianico), adequate Greco and basic off-dry Rosato.

Recommended Reds:
Aglianico del Vulture Alvolo ★★★★☆ £E
Aglianico del Vulture Armànd ★★★☆ £C
Aglianico del Vulture Le Ralle ★★ £C
Cabánico ★★☆ £C Rosso Le Ralle ★☆ £B
Recommended Whites:
Greco Le Ralle ★ £B

Basilisco (Basilicata/Aglianico del Vulture) *www.basiliscovini.it*
From the outset in the late 90s, Michele Cutolo focussed on producing premium Aglianico from around 10 ha of vineyard on a 20 ha estate. His Basilisco Aglianico del Vulture comes from volcanic soils on slopes at 400 m above sea level. Cool cellars carved out for oak ageing may contribute to quality which has risen steadily. The wine which spends 18 months in *barrique* (60% new) has a distinctive personality. Dense and concentrated, the amalgam of oak, black fruits, mineral and earth makes for an interesting comparison with other examples. Most vintages only show their full potential with 6–8 years' age. Teodosio is a recent addition with excellent purity and definition at a more affordable level. In 2011, the estate was purchased by FEUDI DI SAN GREGORIO, who under the direction of Valarie Malafarina and agronomist Pierpaolo Sirch are continuing the Basilisco philosophy in the same vein. A white wine, Sophia, 100% Fiano, has now been added to the range but has not been tasted.

Recommended Reds:
Aglianico del Vulture Basilisco ★★★★ £D
Aglianico del Vulture Teodosio ★★☆ £C

Bisceglia (Basilicata, Campania & Puglia)
This ambitious new project undertaken by Mario Bisceglia (who made money in mineral water) looks set to become a leading force in the promotion of the wines of Basilicata and southern Italy in general, perhaps complementing what Feudi di San Gregorio has achieved for Campania. Like FSG they have extended their reach to three regions; there are 30 ha in the Aglianico zone and a further 15 ha under lease which adds varietals from Campania and Puglia. A new winery has been constructed to receive people as well as grapes, and organic principles are adhered to. Further concessions to the international palate come in the shape of Tréje (Merlot and Syrah added to Aglianico) and Armille (30% Merlot to 70% Aglianico), both sold as Basilicata IGT. Both are good wines with character and intensity in Tréje and a rich, lush and seductive quailty in Armille if somewhat dumbed down by the Merlot. More exciting is the regular Aglianico del Vulture which spends 12 months in new *barriques*. The less expensive Terra di Vulcano series includes offers an attractive Falanghina, good everyday Aglianico and grippy, dense Primitivo. There is also a rosé from Negroamaro - this and the Primitivo are sold as Puglia IGT.

Bisceglia
Recommended Reds:
Aglianico del Vulture Riserva ★★★★ £E
Aglianico del Vulture ★★★☆ £D Armille ★★★ £D Tréje ★★☆ £C
Terra di Vulcano
Recommended Reds:
Primitivo ★★☆ £C Aglianico del Vulture ★★ £C
Recommended Whites:
Falanghina ★★ £B

Cantine del Notaio (Basilcata) *www.cantinedelnotaio.com*
This young operation is already making exciting Aglianico del

Vulture. The owner is one of several producers working with Aglianico to profit from the expertise of Luigi Moio, a professor of enology in Naples. The premium example Il Sigillo is produced from fully ripe, bordering toward late harvest grapes subject to a lengthy maceration of about a month and has 24 months in new French oak which adds complexity to a splendid expression of Aglianico fruit. Their other premium Aglianico, La Firma, has around a 25 day maceration period and spends 12 months in new French oak and has a more austere style than Il Sigillo. The wines haven't yet quite the same sophistication in structure as some of their rivals but are very promising, deserving of 6-8 years' age. A third example, Il Repetorio, has less depth but is more immediate and fruit-accented with attractive pepper, spice and berry notes, though still benefits from a little bottle age. Two dry whites are produced, La Raccolta, made with a white vinification of Aglianico di Vulture grapes with Fiano, Sauvignon and Chardonnay. Maceration is made in French oak for 15 days before being transferred to stainless steel for 12 months before release. Il Preliminare has Malvasia, Moscato and Chardonnay added to a white vinification of Aglianico with no oak maturity resulting in a wine which expresses a myriad of tropical fruit flavours for easy drinking. A sweet wine, L'Autentica, comes from Moscato and Malvasia grapes and is very apricotty and fruit-intense if relatively straightforward. A little sparkling white and rosé wine is made from Aglianico as well.

Recommended Reds:
Aglianico del Vulture Il Sigillo ★★★★ £F
Aglianico del Vulture La Firma ★★★★ £F
Aglianico del Vulture Il Repetorio ★★☆ £D
Recommended Whites:
La Raccolta ★★★ £D   L'Autentica ★★ £E
Il Preliminare ★★ £B

✪ D'Angelo (Aglianico del Vulture) *www.dangelowine.com*
The D'Angelo Aglianico del Vulture reds show impressive fruit and complexity when young but add greater richness, harmony and a deep, savoury complexity with age. An increasing percentage of production comes from estate fruit, including the single-vineyard Riserva, Caselle, from a 5 ha site. The Donato d'Angelo is version starts out more austere needing time to unfurl but is expansive and very long. Give it 8-10 years. Canneto is a selection of Aglianico from old vines and is aged in *barriques* but has a similarly profound structure and good ageing potential. Another estate vineyard, Serra delle Querce (6.2 ha), is the source of an increasingly persuasive *barrique*-aged blend of Aglianico and Merlot. Intense and minerally with smoke, pepper and berry fruit character despite the oak influence, this too deserves at least 5 years' age. A further Aglianico, Valle del Noce has recently been added. Vigna dei Pini is a fresh attractive white if drunk young.

Recommended Reds:
Aglianico del Vulture Donato D'Angelo ★★★★☆ £E
Aglianico del Vulture Riserva Vigna Caselle ★★★★ £D
Aglianico del Vulture ★★☆ £B   Canneto ★★★★ £E
Serra delle Querce ★★★★ £E

✪ Elena Fucci (Aglianico del Vulture) *www.elenafuccivini.com*
If you haven't yet been seduced by Aglianico del Vulture then the single wine made by this charming, petite goddess should do the trick. Elena, fresh from her studies at the University of Pisa has been working with her father, Salvatore, and enologist Sergio Paternoster, to produce Titolo from 3.5 ha (55-60 year old vines) of 6 ha of vineyard first worked by her grandfather. The volcanic 'pozzolana'

soils and altitude (650m) are typical of the zone, as are the late harvesting dates - around the end of October each year. First made in 2000 potent and expressive with mineral, black fruits, herbs and spices, it is a concentrated, modern interpretation deserving of 10-12 years' cellaring.

Recommended Reds:
Aglianico del Vulture Titolo ★★★★ £E

Giannattasio (Aglianico del Vulture) *www.giannattasio.net*
One of a further wave of small but promising operations making Aglianico del Vulture from the slopes below the Vulture volcano. Others include GRIFALCO, LAGALA, LELUSI and MACARICO which have followed the success of BASILISCO, Elena FUCCI and others. Arcangelo Giannattasio is assisted by his parents in bringing the best out of the La Gorizza estate that was known in the 19th century for Aglianico. Their 10ha includes both older vines and new established cordon-spur trained vines. The single Aglianico wine, Arcà is aged in new *barriques* for 12 months and already shows real class and complexity. Soft but expansive, a little more definition and depth should put it up with the best. Also in production are Moscato and extra virgin olive oil.

Recommended Reds:
Aglianico del Vulture Arcà ★★★★ £E

Grifalco (Basilicata/Aglianico del Vulture)
Grifalco della Lucania is the new enterprise of Fabrizio Piccin and his wife Cecilia Naldoni, Vino Nobile producers (Salcheto) for more than 20 years in Tuscany. Their 18 ha complete with brand new winery comprises four diverse parcels (Ginestra, Venosa, Maschito and Rapolla) with vines mostly ranging from 10 to 40 years in age. 30.000 bottles were produced from the first vintage to be commercialized (2004) rising to 60,000 bottles now. With only 20% of the wine given around 8 months in *barriques* the style is fresher, more fruit driven and berryish than others. It is also supple and almost immediately accessible and displays a certain elegance and, as importantly, is very reasonably priced. There are effectively, three cuvees now - the regular Grifalco, Gricos, from younger vines and for more immediate drinking and the single vineyard Damaschito, from 40 plus year old vines, a long maceration and 12 months in large Slavonian oak barrels which will only become approachable after a minimum of 10 years.

Recommended Reds:
Aglianico del Vulture Damaschito ★★★★ £D
Aglianico del Vulture Grifalco ★★★ £C
Aglianico del Vulture Gricos ★★ £B

✪ Tenuta Le Querce (Basilicata)
Le Querce has quickly became established as a major star and is recognised as one of the leading estates in the wider wine revolution in Basilicata. 70 ha of a 100 ha estate are planted to vines averaging 35 years of age at an elevation of 450 m. The regular example, Il Viola, is produced in ample quantities (150,000 bottles) yet has good fruit intensity and some style. Rosso di Costanza adds more density and shows impressive length as well as an oak influence from 12 months in *barrique* and needs five years' age. The crowning glory, however, is Vigna della Corona, of which less than 10,000 bottles are produced from a single plot of vines. This is a marvellously expansive wine but with a structure that demands at least 6–8 years' age following a very long maceration and 18 months in French oak. Much of the complexity, expression and nobility of Aglianico is ensnared here. Tiny amounts of Tamurro Nero have also

been produced from a distinctive variety identified in the estate vineyards. The Pietrafesa family also produce the wines of Cantina Sasso, a source of reasonably priced, soundly made Aglianico del Vulture.

Tenuta Le Querce
Recommended Reds:
Aglianico del Vulture Vigna Corona ★★★★★ £F
Aglianico del Vulture Rosso di Costanza ★★★☆ £E
Aglianico del Vulture Il Viola ★★☆ £C

Cantine Sasso
Recommended Reds:
Aglianico del Vulture ★★ £B

LeLuSi (Basilicata/Aglianico del Vulture) www.lelusivini.com
LeLuSi is another new entrant in the swelling ranks of quality Basilicata wine producers. The Labarbuta siblings (from whose names the acronym Lelusi is derived) have just 6ha (half of it newly planted) and thus far have produced a very ripe, powerful expression of Aglianico. A long maceration is favoured and the premium version, Lelusi, gets 18 months in new *barriques*. Although the fruit edges into the over-ripe, raisiny spectrum the wine is nonetheless rich and deep with a black fruit, earthy and truffly complexity and sweet tannins. Slightly more restraint, adding a little more finesse and structural definition would put it in the first division of Aglianico del Vulture. Shesh, a second Aglianico, only partly aged in *barriques* combines warmth and expression.

Recommended Reds:
Aglianico del Vulture Lelusi ★★★★ £D
Aglianico del Vulture Shesh ★★☆ £B

❀ Paternoster (Aglianico del Vulture) www.paternostervini.it
In the rush for the new wave of quality wines now coming out of Basilicata this venerable producer should not be overlooked. This is still very much a family winemaking enterprise, dating back to 1925. Vinification and ageing is relatively traditional and in the top example, Don Anselmo, produces a deep, powerful wine, classically tight and closed in youth but rich and mesmerising with age. Almost as good but in a different, more modern style is Rotondo, which is subject to a shorter maceration and spends 14 months in *barriques*. The wine is richer and more immediate but stylish and sophisticated too. The bigger-volume Synthesi (aged mostly in large Slavonian casks) is ripe and supple, not a big wine but with good structure and needing just a couple of years' age. Also made are a partially *barrique*-fermented white from Fiano, Biancorte, and a sweet white from Moscato grapes, Clino.

Recommended Reds:
Aglianico del Vulture Don Anselmo ★★★★☆ £F
Aglianico del Vulture Rotondo ★★★★ £E
Aglianico del Vulture Synthesi ★★☆ £C

A-Z of producers - *Puglia*

Accademia dei Racemi (Puglia) www.racemi.it
The idea of an umbrella organisation for a network of growers in Puglia's Salento peninsula was conceived and then realised by Gregory Perrucci of Pervini. Launched in 1999 it has done much to promote the good-value reds of this area, particularly from old Primitivo vines. Pervini itself is fired by the younger generation of the Perrucci family. The services of Roberto Cipresso put the winemaking on a solid footing with expertise lately coming from Cosimo Spina. Salvatore Mero is responsible for the vineyards,

including those of the family's own 45 ha estate, Felline. Typically all the wines have good fruit, balance and real character. Pervini's Bizantino Rosso is a blend of Negroamaro and Primitivo as is Felline's Alberello, while the new L'Evangelista is Primitivo with a little Montepulciano (90/10). Felline's Vigna del Feudo, previously a blend of Primitivo, Montepulciano and a little Cabernet and Merlot, is now Primitivo, Malvasia Nera and Ottavianello in equal proportions. Primo Amore is a sweet version of Primitivo. The wines from Masseria Pepe, Sinfarosa, and Casale Bevagna should not be overlooked, especially the Primitivos – Sinfarosa's excellent 'Zinfandel' or Pepe's complex Dunico. Newer wines from Tenuta Pozzopalo and Torre Guaceto (Sum, from the Susumaniello grape, and Dedalo from Ottavianello) are promising. Anarkos is the basic quaffing red.

Pervini
Recommended Reds:
Primitivo di Manduria Primo Amore ★★ £C
Primitivo di Manduria Archidamo ★★ £B Bizantino Rosso ★★ £B

Felline
Recommended Reds:
Primitivo di Manduria ★★★ £C Vigna del Feudo ★★ £B
Alberello ★★★ £B
Recommended Rosés:
Vigna Rosa ★ £C

Masseria Pepe
Recommended Reds:
Primitivo di Manduria Dunico ★★ £C
Primitivo del Tarantino Portile ★★ £B

Sinfarosa
Recommended Reds:
Primitivo di Manduria Zinfandel ★★★ £C Primitivo ★★ £B

Casale Bevagna
Recommended Reds:
Salice SalentinoTe Deum Laudamus ★★ £C

Tenuta Pozzopalo
Recommended Reds:
Primitivo di Manduria Giravolta ★★ £C

Torre Guaceto
Recommended Reds:
Sum ★★ £D Dedalo ★★ £B

Botromagno (Puglia) www.botromagno.it
Guided by consultant Severino Garofano, this co-op consistently turns out three excellent wines: a dry white, a red and a sweet white. The dry white is the perfumed and well-structured Gravina from Greco and Malvasia Bianca. The red, Pier delle Vigne, is a blend of Aglianico and Montepulciano and is very 'southern' in style with preserved black fruits and raisins but with excellent intensity and length too. Gravisano is now one of the top sweet wines of mainland southern Italy with a fine preserved fruits, honey and spice intensity that shows especially well with five years' age or more. Other wines, including a varietal Primitivo, are not as yet of the same level.

Recommended Reds:
Pier delle Vigne ★★★ £C Primitivo ★☆ £B
Recommended Whites:
Gravisano Passito di Malvasia ★★★ £E Gravina ★★☆ £B

Cantele (Puglia) www.cantele.it
The Battista family have held sway here since the 1950s, and over the last 60 years or so have continued to expand the production

Italy

of this estate in the heel of Italy to the extent that some 30 ha are under vine producing 11 different wines. Not all have been tasted but we have been impressed with the general overall standard. In what they describe as the 'Classic' range, the Negromano Rosato is fresh and intense with good persistence, whilst the regular Negromano red is chunky and solid, if perhaps lacking a bit of fruit. On the other hand, the Primitivo is akin to a juicy Zinfandel, very smooth and easy drinking. The Negromano 'Teresamanara' is a definite step up over the regular wine with deep black fruits beneath the tannins and will need some time to come round. However, the Amativo – 60% Primitivo and 40% Negromano has definiteNew World connotations with its capacity to be enjoyed young and to age for 5 years or more – a good combination of smoothness, complexity and balance. (NB)

Recommended Reds:
IGT Salento Amativo (Negroamaro/Primitivo) ★★★★ £D
IGT Salento Primitivo ★★★☆ £D
IGT Salento Teresa Manara (Negroamaro) ★★★☆ £D
Salice Salentino Riserva ★★☆ £B
IGT Salento Rosso (Negroamaro) ★★☆ £B
Recommended Whites:
IGT SalentoTeresa Manaro (Chardonnay) ★★☆ £B
Recommended Rosés:
IGT Salento Rosato (Negroamaro) ★☆ £B

Cantine Carpentiere (Castel del Monte) *www.cantinecarpentiere.it*
Enzo and Luigi Carpentiere run their family estate high up (450m) on the Le Murge plateau within the Parco della Murgia (a national park). All the grapes come from their 18 ha of vineyards which are cultivated along organic lines. A modern winery now processes the grapes harvested by hand. Aided by enolo-gist Franco Pastore, the first vintage was as recent as 2005 as earlier vintages were sold off. Most impressive of the wines (all are based on Uva di Troia, including a new white) is the varietal Pietra dei Lupi that sees 12 months in Slavonian oak. This is a classy, supple and expansive red which again flags up the considerable potential of Uva di Troia in the Castel del Monte DOC. Armentario (not yet tasted) follows a similar vinification but spends 24 months in oak. A third red, Colle dei Grillai adds in 15% each of Cabernet Sauvignon and Merlot and is given six months in French *barriques*. The result is a plump and flavoursome wine, at once ripe yet cool and expressive, and soundly structured. The Rosato is no run of the mill example with the style and finesse missing from too many of the vividly coloured concoctions the world over.

Recommended Reds:
Castel del Monte Pietra dei Lupi ★★★☆ £C
Castel del Monte Colle dei Grillai ★★☆ £C
Recommended Rosés:
Castel del Monte Rosato Esordio ★★ £B

❀ **Gianfranco Fino (Puglia)** *www.gianfrancofino.it*
Rescuing old bush-trained vines that were going to be uprooted, the Finos set out to uncompromisingly go for quality and as a result, since their first vintage of "Es" Primitivo di Manduria in 2004, their wines now have a cult following around the world. Aiming for low yields, minimal intervention and no irrigation to get a bit of extra stress out of the 60 year old vines, around 15,000 bottles of "Es" have been produced each year since 2004. The grapes are allowed to dry slightly on the vine and after selection and de-stemming, fermentation is in *inox* for two to three weeks before they are then racked into 50% new and 50% one year old French *barriques* for

9 months, bottled and kept for a further 9 months before being commercially released. The result is a very dense and complex wine, but with lots of upfront fruit, with bitter herbs contrasted with sweet chocolate on the palate. Around 4,500 bottles of a second wine, "Jo" Negroamaro Salento Rosso, from 40 year old alberello vines, have been produced each year since 2006 and have been vinified in a similar manner, save that the wine spends 12 months in oak and only 6 months in bottle before release. "Jo" is lighter than the Primitivo but with more finesse with cherry, myrtle and blueberry overtones. Both will easily cellar for several years. Also produced but not tasted are tiny quantities of Primitivo Dolce "Es Piu Sole" (£G) and a rosé "Simona Natale". (NB)

Recommended Reds:
"Es" Primitivo di Mandura ★★★★★ £F
"Jo" Negroamaro Salento Rosso ★★★★☆ £F

La Corte (Puglia)
Chris RINGLAND the cult Barossa winemaker has been recruited to work with La Corte's winemaker Giuseppe Caragnulo. Their aim is to produce great wines from Primitivo and Negroamaro. Primitivo is labelled as Zinfandel to the irritation of some Californian winemakers but the quality at least does their name no harm. Grapes are both bought-in and sourced from leased vineyards. The superior bottlings are labelled simply La Corte and come from old-vine fruit that has 12 months in oak. Both show very ripe fruit, considerable intensity and extract and while needing more age are a significant step up from the more affordable Zinfandel Anfora and Negroamaro Solyss. The top wine is Ré, a selection of the best Negroamaro and Primitivo, that shows greater complexity and style. The Renideo group also comprises La Rendola in Tuscany but these wines still want for both consistency and excitement.

Recommended Reds:
Ré ★★★ £E   Zinfandel La Corte ★★★ £C   Zinfandel Anfora ★★ £B
Negroamaro La Corte ★★★ £C   Negroamaro Solyss ★★ £B

Leone de Castris (Puglia) *www.leonedecastris.com*
Leone de Castris represent the more traditional face of Puglia, dating back to the 17th century. The large volume winery draws on around 400 ha of vineyards on the Salento peninsula. Among an extensive range of inexpensive wines basic Salice Salentino Maiana offers warm sun-ripened fruit but not much else. However a Riserva, subject to ageing in large oak casks, is a big step up and shows a classic dark raisiny character with black plum, black cherry and chocolate fruit. Better again is the Donna Lisa Riserva. In fact until recently this was a Salice like no other, with a significant oak contribution to its complex character. If sometimes a little overdone, it is very complete when successful and deserves 8–10 years' age. The white equivalent is, somewhat surprisingly, a *barrique*-fermented and aged Chardonnay. More interesting is the characterful unoaked Messapia from the native Verdeca. Other reds include an intense if slightly one-dimensional Primitivo, Santera, and Syrah Il Lemos. Five Roses is the widely seen rosé, also made in an Anniversario version. Both should be drunk very young. New from 2000 was Messere Andrea, a *barrique*-aged blend of Negroamaro and Cabernet Sauvignon (85/15). Other wines include Elo Veni, a varietal Negroamaro, and La Rena, a second varietal Primitivo.

Recommended Reds:
Salice Salentino Riserva Donna Lisa ★★★ £D   Il Lemos ★★ £D   Salice Salentino Riserva ★★ £B   Primitivo di Manduria Santera ★★ £B
Recommended Whites:
Salice Salentino Riserva Donna Lisa ★★ £C   Messapia ★★ £B

Masseria Li Veli (Puglia/Salice Salentino) *www.liveli.it*
This undertaking between Angelo Maci and Tuscan heavyweight
AVIGNONESI has already produced some excellent examples of
varietal Negroamaro. Passamante, sold as Salento IGT, is the least
expensive with just 6 months' ageing in wood and stainless steel
before bottling. It shows plenty of extract, fruit and soft, ripe tannins.
Deep, powerful and more structured is Salice Salentino Pezzo
Morgana, which promises to peak with 5–6 years' age, becoming
richer and more chocolaty. The longest ageing is given to a Salice
Salentino Riserva, MLV (18 months before a further 12 months in
bottle). The wine shows a marvellous complexity and a suggestion
of old-vine fruit with great depth and length of flavour. Prices are
not typical of Salice Salentino but then neither is the quality..
Recommended Reds:
Salice Salentino Riserva MLV ★★★☆ £D
Salice Salentino Pezzo Morgana ★★★ £C   Passamante ★★★ £C

Alberto Longo (Puglia) *www.albertolongo.it*
A new modern, quality driven operation, this 35 ha estate is located
in northern Puglia. Vineyards are split between two estates, Fattoria
Cavalli (where the winery is located) and Masseria Celentano (where
it is possible to stay). There are both established local varieties such
as Nero di Troia, Montepulciano and Bombino Bianco (in common
with Molise to the north), and others more associated with southern
Puglia (Negroamaro, Primitivo) and as well as some French varieties
(both Cabernets, Syrah and Merlot). Most vines are cordon spur
trained, yields are kept low and the grapes are hand-harvested. The
white, Le Fossette (Falanghina) and rosé, Donnadele (Negroamaro)
are soundly made for early drinking. Most of the reds are stainless
steel fermented and aged and currently miss a little depth yet show
very distinctive expressive fruit characters and good balance. The
DOC red, Cacc'e Mmitte, based on Nero di Troia and Montepulciano
with a little Bombino Bianco is reminiscent of a gentle southern
Rhône red. Capoposto (100% Negroamaro) is supple and red-fruited
while the almost Chinon-like Calcara Vecchia combines Cabernet
Franc and Merlot. The top red, Le Cruste (guyot and pagliarello-
trained) has the potential to be a really fine example of Nero di Troia
and already reveals added depth and complexity. Try it with five
years' age. The soils, location and winemaking expertise promise
much here - there is surely still more to come.
Recommended Reds:
Le Cruste ★★★ £D Capoposto ★★☆ £C Calcara Vecchia ★★☆ £C
Primitivo ★★☆ £C Cacc'e mmitte di Lucera ★★☆ £B
Recommended Whites:
Le Fossette ★★ £C
Recommended Rosés:
Donnadele Rosato ★★ £B

Rivera (Puglia/Castel del Monte) *www.rivera.it*
Rivera is the leading advocate of the Castel del Monte DOC, which
is relatively little known outside Italy, and has for years produced a
characterful wellpriced red in its Il Falcone. A considerably extended
range now includes a flagship red, Pier Apuliae, from Uva di Troia
(Nero di Troia). Made since the 2000 vintage, it shows much of
the personality and class of this grape as well as a fine structure.
In neither this nor in the more moderately priced Il Falcone (with
30% Montepulciano) is oak allowed to dominate. Both wines, but
particularly the deeper, more concentrated Pier Apuliae need time
to show their true complexity. Cappellaccio, a 100% Aglianico, is
increasingly fine, while Triusco is straight Primitivo, soundly made
and reasonably priced. Rupicolo is an inexpensive red from the

same grapes as Il Falcone but with the proportions reversed. Whites
are more than adequate too, with an existing Chardonnay Preludio
No.1 now complemented by a new, small-volume version, Lama di
Corvo. Sauvignon, Fiano and a rosé are also made.
Recommended Reds:
Castel del Monte Puer Apuliae ★★★★ £E
Castel del Monte Riserva Il Falcone ★★☆ £D
Castel del Monte Aglianico Riserva Cappellaccio ★★ £C
Castel del Monte Rupicolo ★ £B Triusco ★★ £B
Recommended Whites:
Castel del Monte Chardonnay Preludio No.1 ★★ £B

✿ **Tenute Rubino (Puglia/Brindisi)** *www.tenuterubino.it*
It has taken some time for the Rubino family's estate to really hit
its stride. The first wines were made in 1999 and most of the reds
from the early vintages struggled for ripeness and richness. Now
commanding an estate of 200 ha of vineyard Luigi Rubino, together
with winemaker Luca Petrelli and some consultancy from Riccardo
Cotarella, has an excellent range of modern vibrant wines that reveal
pristine ripe fruit and commensurate structures. Most outstanding
is Torre Testa which is set to become one of the classic wines of
southern Italy. 1.5 ha of old alberello trained vines produce the
rarely encountered Susumaniello grape. The wine oozes fine smoky,
minerally old vine fruit, impressive depth and complexity as well
as abundant fine tannins, making it comparable in structure and
quality to a top Aglianico or Barolo. Two selections of Primitivo are
also fine. Punta Aquila is from young vines, undergoes the shorter
maceration of the two, has less wood contact but reveals ample
very ripe fruit, good balance and length. Visellio from 15-year-old
vines has added richness with a preserved cherry, dark chocolate
and carob complexity deserving of five years' ageing or more.
Also remarkably improved is Jaddico, based on Negroamaro but
complemented by Montepulciano and Malvasia Nera (70/15/15).
Lighter and more fragrant, berryish Marmorelle Rosso adds 20%
Malvasia Nera to Negroamaro. Whites are good too, the well-
structured Giancòla (100% Malvasia Bianca) with a lightly mineral
streak should be drunk with 2-4 years' age. Both Marmorelle Bianco
(Chardonnay with 20% Malvasia Bianca) and Saturnino Rosato are
faultless examples of their type; perfumed, expressive and fresh if
drunk very young. Olive oil is also very good here. The extra virgin
half-litre bottling, a blend of three varieties, is particularly fine, surely
one of the best made in Puglia.
Recommended Reds:
Torre Testa ★★★★☆ £E Visellio ★★★☆ £C
Punta Aquila ★★★☆ £E Brindisi Rosso Jaddico ★★★☆ £C
Marmorelle Rosso ★★☆ £B
Recommended Whites:
Giancòla ★★★ £C Marmorelle Bianco ★★ £B
Recommended Rosés:
Saturnino Rosato ★★ £B

✿ **Cosimo Taurino (Puglia)** *www.taurinovini.it*
Francesco Taurino works with the estate's long-serving consultant,
Severino Garofano, who helped to produce most of Puglia's few
memorable wines before its recent awakening. Rich, robust yet
harmonious reds rely on the principles of picking very ripe fruit at
low yields and the intelligent use of new oak. It is now a 165 ha
estate but the top wine Patriglione comes from just 20 ha of vines,
with a high average vine age. It is a wonderfully rich, complex and
beautifully structured expression of southern Italy and its quality
is surely the best argument in favour of the Negroamaro grape

Italy

(though the wine also includes 10% Malvasia Nera). The modestly priced Notarpanaro, a similar blend, is also produced from old vines and is dense and flavoursome. Both wines qualify for the DOC Brindisi but are sold as Salento IGT. The popular Salice Salentino Riserva, produced in fair quantity (60,000 cases), typically shows good intensity of flavour. A white, I Sierri, is from Chardonnay and Malvasia while Scaloti is a decent rosé. Le Ricordanze is a dessert wine from Sémillon and Riesling.

Recommended Reds:
Patriglione ★★★★☆ £F   Notarpanaro ★★ £B
Salice Salentino Riserva ★☆ £B

Tormaresca (Puglia) *www.tormaresca.it*
You wouldn't expect anything less than an unqualified success from an ANTINORI venture into Puglia and so it's proving. A total of 350 ha of vineyards are split between two estates, which give their names to the top two reds. Both the Masseria Maime (100% Negroamaro), and Bocca di Lupo (90% Aglianico, 10% Cabernet Sauvignon) show great fruit definition, excellent texture and balance. Modern, yes, but characterful too. The deep spice and berry fruit of the Maime is one to contrast with other top examples of Negroamaro. At least as good is a deep, blackberry, earth and spice-rich Torcicorda, a varietal Primitivo from old vines. On a simpler level, there's good intensity in the regular and relatively inexpensive Tormaresca Rosso, a blend of Negroamaro with Cabernet Sauvignon, and new NèPriCa which is based on Negroamaro but as the name suggests, also includes Primitivo and Cabernet. Beyond a sound, attractive regular Chardonnay is the impressively rich if only moderately complex Pietrabianca.

Recommended Reds:
Masseria Maime ★★★ £D Castel del Monte Bocca di Lupo ★★★ £C
Torcicoda ★★★ £C NèPriCa ★★ £B Tormaresca Rosso ★☆ £B
Recommended Whites:
Castel del Monte Pietrabianca ★★★ £C Tormaresca Chardonnay ★ £B

Torrevento (Puglia) *www.torrevento.it*
Torrevento doesn't make the best wines in Puglia but quality has been steadily improved with Massimo di Bari now in charge of winemaking while prices remain low and although there's now lots of good value from any number of producers, few maintain it throughout the range so successfully. Located in the elevated Alta Murgia part of Puglia, Torrevento also provides an insight into the potential of the Nero di Troia grape as well as the more usual suspects, Negroamaro and Primitivo. Vigna Pedale is 100% Nero di Troia as is the DOCG Riserva Ottagono, a late harvest, almost Amarone-like fruit bomb, but at 13.5% abv doesn't hit you four square between the eyes. In Torre del Falco the wine is now only made with Nero di Troia instead of previously blended with Cabernet. The reds in particular show better balance and better expression than in the 90s. Newish Torrevento wine, Kebir, a dense, concentrated *barrique*-aged blend of Cabernet Sauvignon and Nero di Troia, is the only wine priced at significant premium. Ghenos Primitivo di Manduria, produced from 2007, 10 months in stainless steel and a further 6 months in *barrique*, is deeply flavoured with a slightly sweetish finish - it can be broached fairly young, but will also repay keeping. Dulcis in Fundo is an attractive and aromatic, light but intense sweet wine.

Torrevento
Recommended Reds:
Castel del Monte Riserva Vigna Pedale ★★★★ £D
Castel del Monte Ottagono Riserva DOCG ★★★☆ £D

Kebir ★★★ £D   Salice Salentino Riserva Sine Nomine ★★★☆ £C
Primitivo di Manduria Ghenos ★★★ £C
Salice Salentino ★★ £B Torre del Falco ★★ £B
Recommended Whites:
Moscato di Trani Dulcis in Fundo ★★ £B

Vallone (Puglia)
Vallone is comprised of three estates that include 170 ha of vines among other crops. As at some other top Puglian outfits, enologist Severino Garofano helps produce wines to a consistently high standard. The outstanding wine, Graticciaia, is a partially *barrique*-aged red made from (mostly) Negroamaro grapes that have been dried for around 3 weeks on mats (graticci) in the warm autumn sun. The resulting wine has powerful aromas of spice, very ripe berry, dried fruit and tobacco. There is rich, concentrated sweet fruit, depth and power but good balance and it may be drunk soon after release or kept. Other wines include Brindisi Rosso Vigna Flaminio (also made as a rosato), which shows very ripe fruit in a very supple structure while intensely flavoured Salice Salentino is one of the best made. Some Sauvignon Blanc is grown for both a dry white, Corte Valesio and a passito (dried grapes) version, Passo delle Viscarde, that also includes some Malvasia.

Recommended Reds:
Graticciaia ★★★☆ £F   Brindisi Vigna Flaminio ★★ £B
Salice SalentinoVereto ★☆ £B

Vetrere (Puglia) *www.vetrere.it*
The Bruni sisters, Annamaria and Francesca, have established a modern wine cellar in order to supplement their existing production of olive oil. The results have been very impressive, helped by consultancy from Mario Ercolino (ex-FEUDI DI SAN GREGORIO) and offer an accessible, affordable taste of Puglia. The whites are Chardonnay-based but the balance can include Malvasia, Verdeca or Fiano, which add personality. Laureato is the oaked version with better depth and mouthfeel but less harmony. The reds are pure Negroamaro or Primitivo. Tempio di Giano, the unoaked Negroamaro, has lovely fruit and can be as impressive as the oaked Lago della Pergola. Both versions of Primitivo are supple with ripe fruit and good varietal character; the oaked Barone Pazzo shows more depth and extract. Most of the wines are sold as Salento IGT.

Recommended Reds:
Barone Pazzo ★★★ £C   Lago della Pergola ★★☆ £C
Tempio di Giano ★★☆ £B Livruni ★★ £B
Recommended Whites:
Finis ★★ £B   Laureato ★★ £B

Conti Zecca (Puglia) *www.contizecca.it*
From across the Salento peninsula in Puglia, Conti Zecca pumps out some fairly serious volume across the basic range, Donna Marzia but this also affords enologit Dr Fernando Antonio Romano the opportunity to make more modest quantities of progressively better wines from the DOCs of Salice Salentino and Leverano at slightly higher prices. From a fine wine point of view it also makes possible a premium red of very impressive fruit richness and complexity that is simply called Nero. Only 25,000 bottles are made. Based on Negroamaro it also includes 30% Cabernet Sauvignon. Slightly less rich, more oaky yet very stylish Terra substitutes Aglianico for the Cabernet component. Both deserve five years' age. In whites, Luna a 50/50 blend of Chardonnay and Malvasia Bianca, sees 6 months in *barrique* before resting in botttle for a further 3 months before release, whilst Sole is a sweet offering of 85% malvasia Bianca and

15% Moscato Bianco is fermented in stainless steel at a controlled temperature and then stopped when all the natural sugar in the must has come out. It is then matured in cement tanks lined with epoxy resin.

Recommended Reds:
Nero ★★☆ £E   Leverano Riserva Terra ★★★ £C
Primitivo ★★☆ £B
Recommended Whites:
Salento Sole ★★ £B   Salento Luna ★☆ £B

A-Z of producers - *Calabria*

Roberto Ceraudo (Calabria) *www.dattilo.it*
Roberto Ceraudo has 20 ha of vineyards and more than twice that of olives within sight of the Ionian sea. Located just south of Cirò, these hills also formed part of the wine lands of ancient Greece. Ceraudo farms organically and produces aromatic, stylish wines. Petelia combines Chardonnay with Greco Bianco and exudes fruit with an exotic guava influence but has good structure and balance. Imyr is straight Chardonnay with a pronounced barrel spice and preserved peach character and is similarly well made. Of two light, off-dry, pale-coloured floral/fruity rosés (both labelled Grayasusi), the Etichetta Argento (or silver label) version spends some time in wood and shows a little more depth. Dattilo is 100% Gaglioppo but could use a little more substance. Better is Petraro (half Cabernet Sauvignon) which reveals a fine complex fusion between the two varieties. A little firmness to the extract detracts but should soften with seven or eight years' age.
Recommended Reds:
Petraro ★★★ £E   Dattilo ★ £D
Recommended Whites:
Imyr ★★☆ £C   Petelia ★★☆ £B
Recommended Rosés:
Grayasusi Etichetta Argento ★★ £B   Grayasusi ★☆ £B

Librandi (Calabria/Cirò) *www.librandi.it*
Librandi is the leading producer of Calabria from a base near Cirò Marina on the Ionian coast. A long-established enterprise, the family gradually moved from being growers into production of bulk wines before bottling their own wines. Vineyards have slowly been expanded to the present 230 ha and, building on the early involvement of enologist Severino Garofano, expertise since 1998 has come from top Piedmontese enologist, Donato Lanati. After initially planting international varieties which resulted in their top red, Gravello (Gaglioppo/Cabernet Sauvignon), much thought (with advice from Attilio Scienza) has gone into the planting of a 160 ha site at Rosaneti, where many Calabrian varieties are being revived. The first great success of this strategy is Magno Megonio, a *barrique*-aged varietal Magliocco. It is becoming increasingly persuasive with a more refined structure, showing a floral aspect to a preserved red and black fruit character that becomes carob-tinged with age. Best value is the Cirò Riserva Duca San Felice, a characterful red with gamey, earthy, black plum and herb characters and intense chocolaty flavours; slightly rustic but good. The non-DOC wines are sold under the Val di Neto IGT. Critone is a fresh, well-made blend of Chardonnay and Sauvignon Blanc, while Le Passule is a light yet intense honeyed and refined sweet wine from Mantonico. First produced in 2001 is Efeso, a rich dry and oaky version of Mantonico with lots of character and depth. Librandi also produced good rosé in the Terre Lontane rosato from Gaglioppo and Cabernet Franc. Simple Cirò Bianco, Rosso and Rosato are also made.

Recommended Reds:
Magno Megonio ★★★ £E   Gravello ★★★ £D
Cirò Rosso Riserva Duca San Felice ★★ £C
Recommended Whites:
Efeso ★★★ £E   Le Passule ★★★ £D
Recommended Rosés:
Terre Lontane ★ £B

❀ Odoardi (Calabria/Savuto & Scavigna) *www.cantineodoardi.it*
The Odoardi brothers are based on the opposite side of Calabria to LIBRANDI or CERAUDO and produce remarkable reds from the Savuto and Scavigna DOCs of seductive texture and considerable elegance. There is input from renowned enologist Stefano Chioccioli for these Gaglioppo-based wines. Most outstanding are the *barrique*-aged Vigna Mortillo and Vigna Garrone – the latter being a little richer and including a small percentage of Cabernet and Merlot. Both consistently show well with 6–8 years' age.
Recommended Reds:
Savuto Superiore Vigna Mortillo ★★★★ £E
Savuto ★★ £C   Scavigna Vigna Garrone ★★★★ £E

Senatore (Calabria/Cirò) *www.senatorevini.com*
The Senatores have been farming near the Ionian sea for over 100 years, producing not only typical DOC wines from the Gallioppo and Greco Bianco grapes, but also modern IGT wines from international varietals such as Cabernet Sauvignon, Merlot and Chardonnay. An entry level blend, "Alikia" of Greco Bianco (70%) and Traminer (30%) is clean and delicate, whilst a Cirò Bianco DOC, made with 100% Greco Bianco, shows a little more finesse than this fairly humdrum varietal usually produces. A fresh and fruity rosato is produced from the Gallioppo grape and there is a regular red and a riserva red (Arcano) with a little more substance – the regular spending about four months in oak and the riserva about two years which does emphasise the wood if broached too young. Another IGT is made from Nerello Calabrese which shows a bit more fruit that is not so masked by the wood since it only spends between 8-12 months in small *barriques*. "Ehos", a nice blend of Cabernet Sauvignon and Merlot (60/40) is produced in a modern way with minimum handling and again 8-12 months in oak whilst "Silo", a blend of Chardonnay, Sauvignon Blanc and Incrocio Manzoni is well balanced and fruity. (NB)
Recommended Reds:
Cirò Rosso Classico Riserva Arcano ★★★☆ £C
Cirò Rosso Classico Arcano ★★★ £B
IGT Calabria Rosso Nerello ★★★☆ £C
IGT Calabria Rosso Ehos ★★☆ £C
Recommended Whites:
Cirò Bianco Alei ★★ £B   IGT Calabria Bianco Silo ★★ £B
IGT Calabria Bianco Alikia ★★ £B
Recommended Rosés:
Cirò Rosato Puntalice ★★ £B

A-Z of producers - *Sicilia (Sicily)*

Abbazia Santa Anastasia (Sicilia) *www.abbaziasantanastasia.com*
This superbly sited estate high above the sea on the north coast of Sicily emerged as one of the island's brightest new stars in the 1990s. Its wines first grabbed attention after help from the Tuscan enologist Giacomo Tachis and are now made under guidance from Gianfranco Cordera. Most impressive is the top wine, Litra, made from 100% Cabernet Sauvignon since 1999 but previously including

Southern Italy & Islands /Sicily

Italy

Nero d'Avola. It is intense and ripe, with blackcurrant, black plum, mineral and a hint of herbs within a full, structured but balanced frame. Still-improving Passomaggio is Nero d'Avola with 30% Merlot. Other reds include Sens(i)nverso Syrah, 12 months in 20-30hl. *botti* and 6 months in bottle before release and Sens(i)nverso Nero d'Avola, spending double the time in wood. Given the vineyard altitude of 400–500 m above sea level, whites also have potential here. Sinestasia is a fragrant and fruity Sauvignon Blanc, while Zurrica is Chardonnnay with 20% Grillo. Sens(i)nverso Chardonnay sees the benefit of 5 months in 5hl. tonneaux. Least expensive are basic but well-made wines; Punto 5 Traminer and a Chardonnay/Viognier blend in white and Syrah and Merlot in red. Drink Litra with five years' age or more, other wines can be drunk young. The whole range is produced biodynamically.

Recommended Reds:

Litra ★★★★ £E Sens(i)nverso Nero d'Avola ★★☆ £D
Sens(i)nverso Syrah ★★ £D Montenero ★★ £D
Passomaggio ★★ £B

Recommended Whites:

Sens(i)nverso Chardonnay ★★☆ £D Sinestasia ★★ £C
Zurrica ★★ £C

Alessandro di Camporeale (Sicilia) *www.alessandrodicamporeale.it*
Brothers Rosolino, Antonino and Natale Alessandro currently produce two good-value reds. Donna Ta' is a good, supple everyday version of Nero d'Avola, while Kaid is an expressive, characterful Syrah with some propensity for ageing. The 30 ha of vineyards will also provide some native Cataratto as well as the usual foreign invaders.

Recommended Reds:

Kaid ★★★ £C Donna Ta' ★★ £B

Baglio di Pianetto (Sicilia) *www.bagliodipianetto.com*
High in the hills west of Palermo can be found yet another modern enterprise typical of the new face of Sicilian viticulture. While not yet achieving its full potential, good progress is being made. Tenuta di Pianetto is a new estate with 62 ha of vineyards and is complemented by another of 32 ha of vines (Tenuta di Baroni) in the far south-eastern corner of the island, at Noto. All the wines are either single varietals or dual varietal. In addition to the natives Nero d'Avola (Baroni sourced) and Inzolia have been planted imports Merlot, Petit Verdot, Syrah and Viognier. The two dry whites show good promise: Ginolfo (Viognier) and a perfumed, floral Ficiligno in which Viognier combines well with Inzolia. Reds are more uneven, sometimes let down by either lesser quality fruit or a slightly coarse oak influence. These include Shymer (Merlot/Syrah), Ramione (Merlot/Nero d'Avola) and Cembali (Nero d'Avola). Only those with reasonably consistent results, led by the varietal Merlot, Piana dei Salici, have been rated. Ra'ls is a fresh, perfumed, grapey, and fruit-centred Moscato di Noto. Light and moderately sweet, it has orange, peach and apricot flavours. Both estates also provide extra virgin olive oil.

Recommended Reds:

Salici Merlot ★★☆ £C Carduni Petit Verdot ★★ £C
Nero d'Avola ★☆ £B

Recommended Whites:

Moscato di Noto Ra'ls ★★ £C Ficiligno ★★ £B
Ginolfo Viognier ★☆ £C

Benanti (Sicilia/Etna) *www.vinicolabenanti.it*
The Benanti family have had vines on the lower slopes of Mount Etna since the late 19th century. Since 1988 Giuseppe Benanti has identified some of the best densely planted old-vine vineyards from the northern, southern and eastern slopes of Etna and experimented with, primarily, the local varieties in order to produce wines of great character and individuality. Single-varietal reds, were at times too firm in the first releases (1999) but are already showing finer structures and better harmony. Nero d'Avola, Nerello Mascalese and Nerello Cappuccio are made; all three are impressively complex and show the expression possible when grown in Etna's soils. An excellent Lamorèmio red has an established track record. Made from equal parts Nerello Mascalese, Nero d'Avola and Cabernet Sauvignon, it has a fascinating black fruits, mineral and herbs complexity. Rosso di Verzella, Rovittello and Serra della Contessa all combine Nerello Mascalese and Nerello Cappuccio but come from quite diverse locations and altitudes, the last having perhaps the most agreeable structure. Whites are increasingly good too with lots of style and individuality, led by Pietramarina, an intense scented varietal Carricante that is impressively structured and pure. It already has some age when released but will improve for 5-6 years. Less refined but flavoursome is Edèlmio, a blend of Carricante and Chardonnay. There's also the only known example of the obscure Minnella grape, made from vines growing amongst the Nerello Mascalese. Better, though, is the sweet Passito di Pantelleria that combines intensity and refinement in its spiced, honeyed apricot fruit and is one of the best going.

Recommended Reds:

Lamorèmio ★★★★ £E Nero d'Avola ★★★☆ £D
Nerello Mascalese ★★★☆ £D Nerello Cappuccio ★★★ £D
Etna Rosso Serra della Contessa ★★★ £E
Etna Rosso Rovittello ★★★ £E

Recommended Whites:

Passito di Pantelleria Coste di Mueggen ★★★ £E
Etna Bianco Superiore Pietramarina ★★★ £D
Minnella ★★☆ £D Edèlmio ★★ £C

>> Tenuta di Castellaro (Sicilia/Lipari) *www.tenutadicastellaro.it*
Massimo Lentsch, a marketing man from Bergamo, fell in love with the terrain in Lipari, one of the Aeolian Islands that form a volcanic outcrop off the coast of northern Sicily and in just the space of 6 short years, has established himself as one of the leading winemakers in Italy. Aided and inspired by Salvo Foti, the founder of the "Vigneri" consortium and with some state of the art equipment, he has managed to produce some of the few "natural" wines that haven't fallen short in structure, flavour and complexity. From various vineyard sites scattered around the island, four wines are being produced from bush vines in currently 9 ha, with a goal of planting 20 ha and a production of 120,000 bottles. Bianco Pomice (White Pumice) has 60% Malvasia delle Lipari, 30% Caricante and 10% "other native vines" some of which presumably have been around the island for a long time. The wine shows striking minerality with hints of both flora and fauna made from direct pressing of the fruit in a pneumatic press, with the Malvasia being fermented and aged in stainless steel for about 6 months and the Caricante seeing 3rd and 4th year oak for the same period. Nero Ossidiana, named after the volcanic glass soil that abounds on the island, is 60% Corinto, 20% Nero d'Avola and 20% "other native vines." Both whole and de-stemmed grapes are pressed and vinified without temperature control followed by a long maceration on the skins. The juice is then run off and placed in barrels for the malolactic fermentation. After around 8 months the wine is transferred into stainless steel tanks and decanted frequently to obtain natural

clarification. The wine shows remarkable balance and finesse with deep, brambly black fruit flavours and enough tannic structure to allow some cellaring. It's a bit early to tell at the moment because the wines are so new, but they bode enormous promise. Two other wines are made - a rosé Caolino (Kaolin) , treated in a similar way to the red but for a shorter period and Malvasia delle Lipari from dried grapes with a slow fermentation in oak barrels, but these have not been tasted. All wines are sold as IGT Sicilia. This is certainly a producer to watch. (NB)

Recommended Reds:
Nero Ossidiana ★★★★ £E
Recommended Whites:
Bianco Pomice ★★★ £E

Castello Solicchiata (Sicilia) *www.castellosolicchiata.it*
Castello Solicciata is said to be the first Bordeaux blend in Italy made from Cabernet Sauvignon, Cabernet Franc and Merlot from vines planted in 1855 by the then Barone Spitaleri on Etna's volcanic soils. The same blend is being produced today from 60 ha of vines by the current generation and shows good concentration of fruit coupled with a smooth finesse resulting in a wine of great complexity. It certainly bears cellaring for a minimum of 5 years to get the best out of it. A second wine from the same blend is also good but with less concentration of fruit. From a further 25ha Boschetto Rosso "Pinetna" Pinot Noir is produced with good varietal flavours and also a second wine Sant'Elia with a similar lack of intensity over the first but nevertheless is decent and flavoursome with good forward fruit. (NB)

Recommended Reds:
Castello Solicciata ★★★ £E   Secondo di Castello Solicciata ★★ £C
Boschetto Rosso ★★★ £E   Sant'Elia ★★ £C

Ceuso (Sicilia) *www.ceuso.it*
Though based in the Alcamo zone in western Sicily, best known for its dilute whites, the Melia family are establishing a fine track record for high-quality reds. With 25.5 ha of the estate planted to vines, they combine the best of the traditional and modern. The estate red, Ceuso is wonderfully characterful, concentrated and powerful with deep smoky, earthy aromas. It is composed of Nero d'Avola (around half) with the balance from Cabernet Sauvignon and Merlot. Though given 12 months in *barrique*, it is freshened up in vats before 12 months' bottle-age prior to release. As the vine age for Ceuso increases so does the wine's richness. Fastaia, added in 2000 has evolved into a blend of Cabernet Sauvignon, Merlot and Petit Verdot. It shows a deep smoky and powerful southern character as well as polished tannins. Both wines may be drunk young but will keep, Ceuso perhaps 10 years. Also made are Scurati red and white. The red is a very reasonably priced supple, expressive Nero d'Avola while the white is a fresh, perfumed example of Grecanico. New is Le Arbe, made from Zibbibo grapes, but has not yet been tasted.

Recommended Reds:
Ceuso ★★★★ £D   Fastaia ★★☆ £C   Scurati ★★☆ £B
Recommended Whites:
Scurati ★☆ £B

Frank Cornelissen (Sicilia/Etna) *www.frankcornelissen.it*
Frank Cornelissen and his Japanese wife Yoko Sano produce very small quantities of wine from the north slopes of Mount Etna. There are 12 ha in total, 8.5 ha planted to alberello grown vines, the rest to olive and fruit trees. The approach is both obsessive and uncompromising avoiding any treatments either in the vineyard

or during production. Other fruiting plants have also been added to the vineyard in order to avoid monoculture and enhance the ecosystem. New vines are planted on their own roots using existing pre-phylloxera cuttings. There is no separation of the wines from the pulp during maceration which lasts several months in 400 litre terracotta giarre (amphora-like) submerged in volcanic rock. A basket press is also employed while filtration, fining and the use of sulphur are avoided. Phew! The wines? What is considered the highest definition of *terroir* (from Nerello Macalese grapes) is designated Magma (£G)- made in three separate versions: Trefiletti, Marchesa and Calderrara. While difficult to assess employing the usual quality parameters, all are intensely mineral, smoky and complex but without the richness normally associated with wines produced from yields as low as 300g per vine. Mongibello (the arabic derived local name for Etna) is the considerably cheaper second wine, again from Nerello Mascalese while Rosso di Contadino combines an assortment of grapes for a more affordable everyday red. Whites are vinified in much the same fashion as the reds. Olive oil is also made with the same, almost fanatical devotion and bottled according to a similar three-tiered production (Magma-Mongibello-Contadino). The tiny amounts of Magma oil come only from the San Benedetto variety. Fruit and honey are also produced. As production varies significantly from year to year it precludes rating the wines in any sort of meaningful way. It is also too early to assess how well wines made in this way will develop and age so the best advice is to seek out a tasting and decide for yourself if they are essential for your cellar.

COS (Sicilia/Cerasuolo di Vittoria) *www.cosvittoria.it*
COS is the leading proponent of Cerasuolo di Vittoria and a long-standing advocate of quality wine from Sicily, having been founded by three students in 1980 (Giuseppina Strano provided the last letter of the acronym). Most of the wines are made without oak and are bottled unfiltered. Now DOCG, Cerasuolo di Vittoria usually combines Nero d'Avola and Frappato in a 60/40 blend. As well as a very good perfumed, expressive regular example, another, Pithos is made - unusual in being aged in terracotta *giarre* (amphora-like containers). In Vastunaca the percentages of Nero d'Avola and Frappato being practically the same. Nero d'Avola is also vinified on its own with excellent results in a relatively forward but intense and plummy Nero di Lupo. Also made is Contrada, a more pricy Nero d'Avola from 55 year old vines and aged for two years in French oak. In white, Ramí (50% Inzolia, 50% Grecanico) is a fine example of what can be produced from local varieties and without any recourse to oak. Its inviting ripe fruit and herb aromas are complemented by freshness, concentration and good balance in the mouth. Pithos Bianco is 100% Grecanico. All the wines are sold in distinct heavy squat bottles. Only those recently tasted have been rated. Locanda COS could serve as a useful base when exploring the region.

Recommended Reds:
Cerasuolo di Vittoria ★★★ £C   Nero di Lupo ★★★ £D
Recommended Whites:
Ramí ★★★ £C

Cottanera (Sicilia/Etna) *www.cottanera.it*
An important operation on the northern side of Mount Etna at 700 m altitude. Since 1995 the Cambria brothers have begun to transform the 43 ha of vines bought by their father over four decades ago. Consultancy comes from Leonardo Valenti and the first vintage was 1999. The wines at the top level – including Grammonte, a varietal Merlot; Nume, Cabernet Sauvignon; Sole

Southern Italy & Islands /Sicily

Italy

di Sesta, varietal Syrah; and L'Ardenza, varietal Mondeuse (surely Sicily's if not Italy's only example) – show remarkable fruit intensity, concentration and definition. All are aged in new French oak for 18 months. They are powerful and vibrant with great potential, but it is still early days and it remains to be seen how well the wines age and how much finesse time will add, but all should be given at least five years from the vintage. Considerably less expensive is Fatagione, a blend of Nerello Mascalese and Nero d'Avola (90/10), which shows very intense fruit and much of the potential complexity of Nerello Mascalese. The moderately priced Barbazzale red is a similar blend to Fatagione but more open and immediate, while the promising unoaked white version comes from old vineyards of Inzolia and Viognier.

Recommended Reds:
Grammonte ★★★☆ £E L'Ardenza ★★★☆ £E
Sole di Sesta ★★★ £E Nume ★★★ £E Fatagione ★★★ £D
Barbazzale Rosso ★★ £B
Recommended Whites:
Barbazzale Bianco ★★ £B

Cusumano (Sicilia) *www.cusumano.it*
Alberto and Diego Cusumano control 140 ha of vineyards and with the help of consultant Mario Ronco made a rapid start in Sicily's new age of wine. Two premium reds are based on Nero d'Avola, though the French varieties are also successful here. Sàgana is a varietal Nero d'Avola fermented and aged in 2,000-litre barrels and shows ripe, intense fruit. By contrast, Noà, which adds Cabernet Sauvignon and Merlot to Nero d'Avola, is aged in French *barriques*. It is even better, with more depth and complexity in a seamless harmonious blend. A *barrique*-fermented Chardonnay, Jalé, and varietal Inzolia, Cubìa, show fine fruit and each spends six months on its lees, though this works less well in the latter. Produced without any wood but good value are a brambly, spicy, blackberry Benuara, which adds Syrah to Nero d'Avola, and a fresh, stylish white from Inzolia and Chardonnay, called Angimbé. Inexpensive varietal examples of Nero d'Avola, Merlot and Syrah are more everyday but could use a little more ripeness and richness. Inzolia is more appealing.

Recommended Reds:
Sàgana ★★★ £D Noà ★★★ £D Benuara ★★ £B
Recommended Whites:
Cubìa ★★ £C Jalé ★★ £C Angimbé ★★ £C
Alcamo ★ £B Inzolia ★ £B

✿ Marco de Bartoli (Sicilia) *www.marcodebartoli.com*
A crusader for the original unfortified Marsala, for five years between 1995 and 2000 Marco de Bartoli was prevented by the authorities from making any wine. He now continues with his sons Renato (a trained winemaker) and Sebastiano and currently produces Vigna La Miccia, the youngest and freshest style fortified with a little mistella, and a Marsala Superiore (also fortified) from wines aged for around 10 years in a sort of *solera* system. Small amounts of extraordinary old wines are used for blending with younger wines, as in Vecchio Samperi Ventennale, an unsweetened and unfortified blend of older and younger vintages but with an average age of 20 years. This is a brilliant expression of what very ripe Grillo grapes can achieve with age with marvellous complexity and length - full of rich, toffeed dry fruits, candied peel, dates, walnuts and other nuances of flavour. In 2010 Marco produced a Trentennale, to commemorate the 30th anniversary of the winery by emptying 1,200 of the very first bottles of Vecchio Sampere produced in 1980 and re-bottling 999 from a special *solera*. Other wines include those from the

island of Pantelleria (the production of which was the source of the controversy); the very good Passito di Pantelleria Bukkuram, and a fine dry version of Zibibbo (Muscat of Alexandria) called Pietranera. Newish are a splendid dry white from Grillo, Grappoli del Grillo with soaring mineral/graphite aromas, and a Pignatello, Rosso di Marco. Entry level dry indigenous wines have more recently been produced as Vignaverde (Grillo). Sole e Vento (Grillo and Zibibbo) and Luce (Catarratto).

Recommended Whites:
Vecchio Samperi Ventennale ★★★★☆ £F
Passito di Pantelleria Bukkuram ★★★★ £F
Marsala Superiore 10 anni ★★★☆ £F
Grappoli del Grillo ★★★☆ £E Pietranera ★★☆ £E
Vigna La Miccia ★★☆ £D

Tenuta dell' Abate (Sicilia) *www.tenutadellabate.it*
More well-priced Sicilian reds and whites. The grapes come only from the estate's 60 ha of vineyards in central southern Sicily. The winemaking shows a certain sophistication. Terre del Palco red is a classy example of Nero d'Avola with good depth of bramble, plum fruit, best drunk with 3–4 years' age. Slightly more ambitious but with obvious potential is Giffarrò, a Cabernet Sauvignon/Syrah blend (60/40), with a stylish, gently cedary complexity, good concentration and fine tannins; drink this with five years' age. A Terre del Palco white is a fresh lemony Chardonnay that shows almost no *barrique* influence. two more Terre del Palco whites, Grillo/Viognier and Traminer/Sauvignon Blanc/Viognier are also produced but have not been tasted. Entry level wines under the Lissandrello label (Syrah/ Cabernet Sauvignon/Nero d'Avola, Cabernet Sauvignon and Inzolia) are also produced.

Recommended Reds:
Giffarrò ★★★ £C Terre del Palco Nero d'Avola ★★ £C
Recommended Whites:
Terre del Palco Chardonnay ★★ £C

✿ Donnafugata (Sicilia/Contessa Entellina) *www.donnafugata.it*
The Rallo family left only their name in Marsala production and have devoted themselves to making table wines in the last decade. In Contessa Entellina they even have what is effectively their own DOC for the top reds and whites grown at altitude in western Sicily. Reds from the late nineties had a tendency to over-extraction but input from Carlo Ferrini, one of Tuscany's very best consultants, has ensured richer, softer examples with finer tannins. The dense, intense complex and classy Mille e Una Notte, based on Nero d'Avola is an ageworthy flagship best with eight years age or more. Tancredi, based on Nero d'Avola but with around 30% Cabernet Sauvignon and Tannat shows the blackcurrant influence of the latter but also an increasingly fine structure over recent vintages. Angheli is Merlot and Cabernet Sauvignon and seems fullest and ripest when the Merlot is most successful. Whites include the scented Vigna di Gabri mainly Ansonica (Inzolia), depending on the vintage, which has real style and length, while the Chardonnay Chiarandà shows a southern richness but also has more structure and better balance than some. The usually fresh and aromatic Anthìlia is produced from Ansonica and Cataratto. From the family's vineyards in Pantelleria, Ben Ryé is very much in the dried fruit, apricot spectrum of these sweet wines but has excellent intensity and balance.

Recommended Reds:
Contessa Entellina Mille e Una Notte ★★★★☆ £F
Contessa EntellinaTancredi ★★★ £D Angheli ★★ £C

Recommended Whites:

Passito di Pantelleria Ben Ryé ★★★ £E
Contessa Entellina Chiarandà ★★ £E
Moscato di Pantelleria Kabir ★★ £D
Contessa Entellina Vigna di Gabri ★★ £C
Contessa Entellina Chardonnay La Fuga ★★ £B

Masseria del Feudo (Sicilia) *www.masseriadelfeudo.it*

The Cucurullo's farm includes 12 ha of organically cultivated vineyards (at 450m) in central southern Sicily. Recently restored farm buildings have been fitted out with stainless steel tanks and rows of *barriques*. With expert help three impressive wines are already being fashioned. The white Haermosa is 100% Chardonnay with the rich, ripe fruit and concentration typical of the best Sicilian examples, if not the dimension or nuance for more. A varietal Nero d'Avola, Rosso delle Rose, is an expressive, modern, very accessible example Grillo is spicy yet delicate with some complexity.

Recommended Reds:

Rosso delle Rose ★★★ £D

Recommended Whites:

Haermosa ★★ £D Grillo ★★ £C

Feudo Maccari (Sicilia) *www.feudomaccari.it*

This is the Sicilian outpost of Antonio Moretti (owner of SETTE PONTI in Tuscany). Parcels of low-altitude vineyards lying close to the sea are planted to bush vines, some new, some well-established. The estate wine is Saia, produced from Nero d'Avola vines with an average age of 20 years. After a moderate period of maceration it is aged in French *barriques*, resulting in a ripe, powerful and intense example. The wines deserve to be drunk with five years' age or more. A second wine, is also 100% Nero d'Avola but aged only in stainless steel. Maharis is a blend of Nero d'Avola, Cabernet Sauvignon and Syrah but has not been tasted.

Recommended Reds:

Saia ★★★ £D Nero d'Avola ★★ £B

◉ Feudo Montoni (Sicilia) *www.feudomontoni.it*

Having once sold grapes to TASCA D'ALMERITA, this is a rather special source of Nero d'Avola. In fact they claim to have a special clone and the evidence for this is pretty compelling. In all 30 ha are in production, in some instances grafted on to old pre-phylloxera rootstocks. Altitude also plays a part, with two sites in the central highlands – the first at 400m, the other at 680m (within the Contea di Sclafani DOC although the wines are sold as IGTs). A 25–30 day maceration is given to the top wine, Vrucara, a selection of the best grapes (from 70-year-old vines) aged in tonneaux of 500 litres for 12 months and bottled without fining or filtration. Eschewing a blockbuster style, it nonetheless possesses wonderful complexity including coffee, carob, mineral and plum aromas. Elegant, classy and expansive, it is likely to show at its best with 8–10 years' age. The regular version is also oak-aged and very stylish for this level. Feudo Montoni also produces two elegant whites from Catarratto and Grillo, with the latter producing more intense vibrancy, but it doesn't mean that the former does not represent good value for money.

Recommended Reds:

Vrucara Selezione Speciale ★★★★☆ £E Nero d'Avola ★★☆ £C

Recommended Whites:

Grillo ★★☆ £C Catarrato ★★☆ £B

Feudi Principi di Butera (Sicilia) *www.feudobutera.it*

The Zonin name is synonymous with large-volume modern Italian wines. The company's very extensive holdings include a large tract of vines (around 140 ha) at 300–400m near the coast in southern Sicily. The first reds were made in 2000, the first whites 2001. Two wines stand out but are not cheap. Best is the impressively complex Deliella from Nero d'Avola that just needs a little more depth and concentration to be really fine. Symposio (65% Cabernet Sauvignon, 30% Merlot and 5% Petit Verdot) shows definite class too, with a distinctive Silician take on these varieties. Most other varietals are soundly made for everyday drinking but don't have the fruit or interest of other examples at a comparable price level.

Recommended Reds:

Deliella ★★★ £F Symposio ★★☆ £E

Firriato (Sicilia) *www.firriato.it*

Firriato encapsulates what is possible in Sicily given the right direction and winemaking expertise. The time spent under the auspices of roving winemaker Kim Milne has resulted in a durable quality formula with international appeal. The consistency and quality from 200 ha would please many a New World producer. Top reds are made in moderate quantities: Harmonium (100% Nero d'Avola) is a consistently impressive example without a silly price tag. Ribeca 100% Perricone is classy and individual with a fine, almost silky texture. With a different flavour profile and structure, Camelot is a Cabernet Sauvignon/Merlot, it shows a cool, somewhat Bordeaux-like complexity. Dual variety Santagostino red (Nero d'Avola/Syrah) and white (Cattaratto/Chardonnay) from the Soria estate are produced in larger quantities but show good character and depth. Another star is the well-priced Chiaramonte white made from Ansonica (Inzolia) which edges a flavoursome Grillo for depth and structure. Inexpensive Etna Rosso (from both Nerello Mascalese and Nerello Capuccio, blended 80/20) has something of the smoke, floral, grilled meats, prunes and spice complexity that grander examples show.

Recommended Reds:

Camelot ★★★ £F Harmonium ★★★ £E Ribeca ★★★ £D
Santagostino Baglio Soria ★★ £D Altavilla della Corte ★☆ £B
Etna Rosso ★ £B

Recommended Whites:

Santagostino Baglio Soria ★★☆ £D Chiaramonte Ansonica ★★☆ £B
Altavilla della Corte Grillo ★★ £B

Gulfi (Sicilia) *www.gulfi.it*

Gulfi has two main growing areas: the 'home' vineyards at 400–500m in Val Canzeria north of Ragusa and some low-altitude plantings in Val di Noto between Noto and Pachino in the extreme south-east of Sicily. Two very good fruit-driven and mineral-imbued whites are produced at altitude. Valcanzjria is a blend of Carricante, Albanello and Chardonnay, while Carjcanti is a blend of Carricante and Albanello. All the reds are produced from Nero d'Avola with the Nerojbleo and Rossojbleo coming from the elevated Iblei slopes. Both show a cool, herbal aspect, with a little more substance and some oak influence in Nerojbleo. The four vineyard-designated Nero d'Avolas are all from free standing alberello (bush vines) averaging around 35 years' age, with densities of more than 7,000 vines per hectare. All four show real promise from the perfume and fruit of Nerosanlore and the elegance and persistence of Nerobufaleffj to the substance and density of Nerobaronj and the extract and power of Neromàccarj. All deserve at least five years' age..

Recommended Reds:

Nerosanlore ★★★ £E Nerobufaleffj ★★★ £E Nerobaronj ★★★ £D

Southern Italy & Islands /Sicily

Italy

Neromàccarj ★★★ £D Nerojbleo ★★ £C Rossojbleo ★☆ £B
Recommended Whites:
Valcanzjria ★★☆ £C Carjcanti ★★☆ £C

Hauner (Isola di Salina) www.hauner.it
Carlo Hauner, father of the incumbent Carlo, revived and refined the production of acclaimed Malvasia delle Lipari from this small volcanic island more than 30 years ago. The reputation remains intact with sweet whites of elegance, intensity and purity. The regular version shows lovely spice, floral, honeycomb and intense dried/preserved citrus and nectarine/peach fruit, while the Passito version from grapes dried on mats for 2–3 weeks is more classy, intense and apricotty, and very long. Just 3–5,000 bottles of a Riserva are made in exceptional vintages. The winery draws on 20 ha in total and is actually on Salina, where dry whites and reds are also produced. The Carlo Hauner white is from Inzolia and Cataratto; though lacking a little definition and intensity, it has an unusual salty aspect. Better are the reds: a light, slightly minerally, smoky Salina Rosso (Nero d'Avola, Nerello Mascalese) and Rosso Antonella (Nero d'Avola, Sangiovese and Corinto Nero) which develops considerable complexity with 4–5 years' or more. The Aeolian islands are also noted for capers and the Hauners have their own production from Salina.
Recommended Reds:
Rosso Antonella ★★ £C Salina Rosso ★ £B
Recommended Whites:
Malvasia delle Lipari Passito ★★★★ £F Malvasia delle Lipari ★★★ £C

Maurigi (Sicilia) www.maurigi.it
Francesco Maurigi only established his new estate (Tenuta di Budonetta) as recently as 1998 but has 40 ha planted at 550–700m in an area where previously there were no vines. It has also been planted entirely to French grape varieties. There are five estate wines in a ripe, stylish, polished mode, and they are already impressive despite coming from very young vines. Coste all'Ombra is 90% Sauvignon, 10% Chardonnay and shows good structure and intensity. A ripe, full and well structured Chardonnay, Terre di Sofia, just misses a little nuanced complexity to be really good. Red Saia Grande is an unusual but individual blend of Syrah, Merlot and Pinot Nero, while Terre di Maria adds in Cabernet Sauvignon that has been subject to 20 months in barrique. Terre di Ottavia, 100% Pinot Nero, was first produced in 2002 and impresses for its texture and cherry and wild raspberry fruit. Also good are Bacca Rosso and Bianco made from bought-in grapes and based on local varieties. In the supple, softly-textured red 20% of both Syrah and Cabernet Sauvignon complement Nero d'Avola, while in the intense, flavoursome white 20% Chardonnay marries well with Inzolia and Grecanico.
Recommended Reds:
Terre di Maria ★★★ £E Terre di Ottavia ★★☆ £E
Saia Grande ★★☆ £C Bacca Rossa ★★ £C
Recommended Whites:
Terre di Sofia ★★☆ £E Coste all'Ombra ★★☆ £C
Bacca Bianca ★★ £B

✿ Morgante (Sicilia) www.morgante-vini.it
Former growers and suppliers of wine for blending, the Morgante family have been producing their own wine since 1998 under the winemaking expertise of Riccardo Cotarella. From part of more than 200 ha of vines Nero d'Avola is made in two versions: a regular example (15,000 cases a year) has four months of oak-ageing, while

Don Antonio (3,000 cases) is a superior selection which spends 12 months in new French oak. The oak is quite prominent in the latter with depth, intensity too in an increasingly expansive frame. The regular example, with good character and intensity, can be drunk quite young; Don Antonio is better with 3–5 years' age and will keep for longer. Morgante also produces an entry level red from Nero d'Avola (Scinthili) and a white wine made from (unspecified) red grapes (Bianco di Morgante).
Recommended Reds:
Don Antonio ★★★★ £E Nero d'Avola ★★ £B

Salvatore Murana (Pantelleria)
Salvatore Murana is the top producer of Passito di Pantelleria, a delicious sweet wine made from Zibibbo grapes on the windswept volcanic island of Pantelleria between Sicily and Tunisia. The wines, especially at the top level, show greater refinement than others now being exported in increasing numbers. Murana's wines are named for the sub-zones from which they are produced. Martingana is the most concentrated and raisiny, a very powerful but stylish example. Khamma is also an excellent example with classic dried apricot and date aromas and flavours. Moscato di Pantelleria is a lighter style with lower alcohol and from grapes subjected to a shorter drying period. Mueggen has good intensity and a spicy, dried fruit character; Turbè is the least expensive version. New is a dry version of Zibibbo called Gadì.
Recommended Whites:
Passito di Pantelleria Martingana ★★★★ £G
Passito di Pantelleria Khamma ★★★ £G
Moscato di Pantelleria Mueggen ★★ £F

✿ Palari (Sicilia/Faro) www.palari.it
In the premium wine from the Palari estate we are witnessing the revival of a wine name famous in the 14th century: Faro. From steep slopes high above the Straits of Messina, Salvatore Geraci undertook to breath life back into a DOC that had almost ceased to exist. Working with his brother, Giampiero, he also enlisted the winemaking expertise of Donato Lanati. Only local grapes have been used – Nerello Mascalese and Nerello Cappuccio as well as smaller amounts of other obscure varieties – though vinification and maturation are modern with ageing in French barriques. The wine impresses most with its nuanced complexity, which includes red fruits, coffee, herb and dried flowers, and its dimension and length. But this is also a wine of refined, discreet structure: don't come seeking colour, extract or incredible fruit richness – this is from a different part of the quality spectrum. Rosso del Soprano is wonderfully complex for a second wine that shows very well with 3-4 years' age.
Recommended Reds:
Faro ★★★★★ £F Rosso del Soprano ★★★ £E

✿ Passopisciaro (Sicilia/Etna) www.passopisciaro.com
Named for its locality on the lower northern slopes of Mount Etna, this is Andrea Franchetti's (Tenuta di TRINORO, Tuscany) 8 ha estate in Sicily. It lies close to FRANK CORNELISSEN, TERRE NERE and others passionate about this emerging zone first singled out by BENANTI. Franchetti has in common too with these producers a belief in the potential of Nerello Mascalese to make great wines. The densely planted vineyards of 80 year old alberello trained vines are at 850m with some new plantings (propagated from the best old vines - sélection massale) at 1000m! The wine is aged in large 30hl oak for 18 months. Think in terms of a fine but approachable cru Barolo,

only at about half the price. Since 2008, several single vineyard crus have been created and these are the subject of work in progress together with the Petit Verdot/Cesanese Franchetti Flagship wine and a Chardonnay and we shall be reporting on these more fully in the next edition.

Recommended Reds:
Passopisciaro ★★★★☆ £E

Planeta (Sicilia) www.planeta.it
Planeta is a seemingly unstoppable engine that is producing marvellously consistent quality and doing wonders for Sicily's image in foreign markets. Building on an early reputation for international grapes some of the finest wines now also come from native varieties and more are being developed. The dynamic young Planetas have a wise and gifted winemaker in Carlo Corino. Total holdings now consist of six estates/wineries and 363 ha of vineyards: the Ulmo winery (near Sambuca) and the newer Dispensa winery (near Menfi) are in the west of Sicily but wines are also produced in Vittoria in the south, Feudo di Mezzo at Etna, La Baronia in Central Sicily and Noto in the south-east corner of the island (for new Moscato di Noto and Eloro DOC Nero d'Avola). The top wines are relatively expensive; the Santa Cecilia, from Nero d'Avola, and a pure Syrah are often the best with excellent fruit and length. Burdese, Cabernet Sauvignon (70%) and Cabernet Franc, is very good too and a rich, intense Merlot shows more class since 2001. Cerasuolo di Vittoria, made since 2001 is a classic blend of Nero d'Avola and Frappato (60/40) with distinctive perfume, spice and very ripe red fruits. Rich, ripe Chardonnay is complex and powerful and a very good example of this style, showing more refinement in cooler vintages. La Segreta Rosso and Bianco are much cheaper yet made to a high standard and represent the best value for money. The red is a blend of Nero d'Avola, Merlot and Syrah (60/20/20) and is consistanly good. The white is based on Grecanico but includes significant percentages of Chardonnay, Viognier and Sauvignon Blanc and the combination of citrus and more exotic fruit really sings out. Another white, Alastro, combines Grecanico and Chardonnay but a barrique-fermented component of the latter overwhelms the fruit somewhat. Cometa is an impressive powerful, concentrated, partly barrel fermented and oak-aged white from Fiano grapes – not subtle but rich in exotic and dried stone fruits aromas and flavours. In contrast there's an aromatic, grapey and well-balanced Moscato di Noto, fermented and aged only in stainless steel. Carricante and Nerello Mascalese wines from their Etna vineyards have not yet been tasted.

Recommended Reds:
Santa Cecilia ★★★ £D Burdese ★★★ £D Merlot ★★★ £D
Syrah ★★★ £D Cerasuolo di Vittoria ★★★ £C
La Segreta ★★ £B
Recommended Whites:
Cometa ★★★☆ £D Moscato di Noto ★★★ £D
Chardonnay ★★★ £D La Segreta ★★ £B Alastro ★ £B

Pupillo (Sicilia/Moscato di Siracusa) www.solacium.it
Here is something different. Of Greek origins, Moscato di Siracusa has had its own DOC since 1973 yet production was non-existent until Antonino Pupillo re-established it. These are naturally fermented Muscats from Moscato Bianco with around 14% alcohol. All show a fine, floral and particularly spicy pure expression. Pollio is little more than off-dry but the late-harvested Solacium is sweet, intense and apricotty whilst retaining adequate freshness with a little age. An IGT Moscato, Cyane, is a dry version scented with jasmine, rosé, blossom and ripe stone fruits that compares well with

other dry Muscats. A red, Re Federico, from Nero d'Avola is cool and herbal but shows promise too.

Recommended Reds:
Re Federico ★★ £B
Recommended Whites:
Moscato di Siracusa Solacium ★★★ £C
Moscato di Siracusa Pollio ★★ £C Cyane ★★ £B

Solidea (Pantelleria) www.solideavini.it
A worthwhile addition to the growing band of good sources for the sweet Muscats of Pantelleria. Production is artisanal with hand-picking of the Zibibbo grapes and careful attention during the drying phase prior to a lengthy fermentation. The D'Anconas' Passito is particularly lush, sweet and richly flavoured with powerful raisiney, grapey and dried apricot flavours as well as toffee, honey and other dried fruits. Both this and the lighter but spicy, intense Moscato di Pantelleria are particularly good. There is also a dry, aromatic Zibibbo called Ilios.

Recommended Whites:
Passito di Pantelleria ★★★ £E Moscato di Pantelleria ★★ £C

Spadafora (Sicilia) www.spadafora.com
An earthquake in 1968 was the trigger for the start of the modern era of production of this estate under Don Pietro Spadafora, father of the present owner and director Francesco. It has been Francesco however who provided the quality impetus in the 90s. The 100 ha of vineyards now contain a significant amount of introduced varieties including Syrah, Cabernet Sauvignon and Chardonnay. There is a barrique-aged varietal version of each sold under the Schietto label as well as a Nero d'Avola. The Syrah has concentrated crushed blacks fruits in a chewy, fleshy texture with plenty of extract and needs 5-8 years' ageing. The Cabernet is of comparable quality. Less expensive but well-made are a cedarey and Bordeaux-like Don Pietro red (Nero d'Avola, Cabernet Sauvignon and Merlot) and citrusey, lemon zest Don Pietro white (from Inzolia, Cattaratto and Grillo). The local DOC, Monreale is used for a lively vibrant unwooded Syrah that drinks well with a little age, and fresh unwooded white, Alhambra. Spadafora's flagship wine is Sole dei Padri, a premium Syrah from low-yielding vines aged in new barriques for 12 months. Although more expressive than the Schietto version, it is more oaky and international in style but needs 6-10 years for its full potential to be realized. Olive oil, like the wine is estate grown and produced. New from 2011 is Les Jeux sont faits, an unwooded Syrah that has spent 2 years in stainless steel and 6 months in bottle before release. All the wines are certified organic.

Recommended Reds:
Sole dei Padri ★★★☆ £F Schietto Syrah ★★★☆ £D
Schietto Cabernet Sauvignon ★★★ £D Don Pietro ★★ £C
Monreale Syrah ★★ £C
Recommended Whites:
Don Pietro Bianco ★★ £C

❂ Tasca d'Almerita (Contea di Sclafani) www.tascadalmerita.it
This large estate was acquired as long ago as 1830 and though much reduced by land reform in the 1950s currently has almost 600 ha of high-altitude vineyards. Direction comes from the current Count, Lucio Tasca d'Almerita, who is dedicated not just to continuing, but to improving on the standards that set the estate apart when wine from Sicily meant nothing more than plonk. Winemaker Luigi Guzzo has recently had consultant input from Carlo Ferrini and there is ongoing research into grape varieties.

Italy

Rosso del Conte (Mainly Nero d'Avola with other permitted red grapes for the appllelation) and Cabernet Sauvignon are the two leading reds, made to a consistently high standard. The Rosso del Conte, full of bramble, plum and spice fruit, is fleshy and ripe, adding chocolate and coffee flavours with age – composed yet characterful. The Cabernet is both powerful and remarkably refined. Nero d'Avola has been combined with Cabernet in Cygnus and with Merlot in Camastra, while Lamùri is a new varietal version. Whites are led by a rich, powerful Chardonnay which has good depth and well-integrated oak. Unwooded whites include the flavoursome Nozze d'Oro, from Inzolia and Sauvignon Tasca, and characterful Leone d'Almerita which combines Cataratto with Pinot Bianco, Traminer and Sauvignon. All wines used to appear under the Sicilia IGT, but the top wines now have their own DOC, Contea di Sclafani. Basic Regaleali red, white and rosé are made in big quantities and are excellent quaffing wines.

Recommended Reds:
Contea di Sclafani Rosso del Conte ★★★★ £E
Contea di Sclafani Cabernet Sauvignon ★★★★ £E
Camastra ★★ £C   Cygnus ★★ £C
Recommended Whites:
 Contea di Sclafani Chardonnay ★★★ £D
Contea di Sclafani Bianco Nozze d'Oro ★★ £C
Leone d'Almerita ★★ £B

Terre di Giurfo (Sicilia/Cerasuolo di Vittoria) *www.terredigiurfo.it*
A very promising young enterprise situated in the Cerasuolo di Vittoria DOCG zone. Wine was first only made here in 2002, although the property has been in the Giusino family for more than 200 years. The 90 ha at 550m elevation includes 34 ha of vineyard (a part new) and 24 ha of well-established olive groves. Both Cerasuolo and a varietal Syrah, Ronna are already very good, combining substance and structure with a certain poise and elegance. Nero d'Avola shows potential too whether unwooded as Kudyah or as the *barrique*-aged Kuntàri (the only wine that sees any oak). Although the latter is slightly over-oaked there is fine fruit too. Suliccènti is 100% Inzolia with quite concentrated rich fruit, infused with broom and herbs. Other than Syrah 'foreign' varieties run to Merlot and Chardonnay (not yet in production) but are also new plantings of Grillo and Frappato. The extra virgin olive oil is an excellent example of premium Sicilian quality; very fresh, pure and intensely green tomato and spicy, even six months or more after the harvest.

Recommended Reds:
Cerasuolo di Vittoria Maskarìa ★★★ £C   Ronna ★★★ £C
Kuntàri ★★ £C   Kudyah ★★ £B
Recommended Whites:
Suliccènti ★★☆ £B

✿ **Tenuta delle Terre Nere (Sicilia/Etna)** *www.tenutaterrenere.it*
Marco De Grazia is a name familar to Italian wine aficionados as a leading Italy-based distributor of fine Italian wines. He is also but one of several personalities to have a few hectares of old vines (almost all Nerello Mascalese) on the northern slopes of Mount Etna. Of 15 ha there is a mix of young trellised vines and older free-standing bush vines. From 2007 the estate had a new dedicated winemaking facility. Of three premium single vineyard wines Calderara Sottana is the only one made in anything approaching significant quantity (25,000 bottles). All three reds spend 18 months in 600l and 1200l oak (20% new) with the malolactic fermentation in wood too. Calderara Sottana is both supple and expansive with a stylish mineral, herb and black-fruited character. Feudo di Mezzo

(Il Quadro delle Rose) is the most forward, generous and smooth but with enough tannic substance to age gracefully. Since 2006 the fruit from pre-phylloxera Nerello Mascalese and Nerello Capuccio have been vinified separately and is the most individual with a mineral edge to an old-fashioned preserved red fruits character. Guardiola comes from the most elevated vineyards, and showcases the complexity, expansive qualities and class possible from old bush-vine Nerello Mascalese. With very pure mineral infused red fruit, impressive depth and breadth, and caressing Burgundian/Barolo-like texture it is, unquestionably, already one of the very best reds of Sicily and southern Italy. The Santa Spirito vineyard was acquired in 2007 and wine from the two main varietals has been made from its fruit but has not yet been tasted. A fresh and fruit-driven regular Rosso that includes 20% Nerello Cappuccio, has also been made since 2005 while a new Bianco combines Catarratto, Carricante, Grecanico and Inzolia. An intense stylish and expansive white, full of preserved citrus, spice and herb, it deserves at least 2-4 years' ageing. Again, since 2007, a superior Etna white, Cuvée delle Vigne Niche, has been produced, this time from 100% Carricante. A Rosato is also made.

Recommended Reds:
Etna Rosso Prephylloxera ★★★★★ £F
Etna Rosso Vigneto Guardiola ★★★★★ £E
Etna Rosso Feudo di Mezzo ★★★★ £E
Etna Rosso Calderara Sottana ★★★☆ £E   Etna Rosso ★★☆ £C
Recommended Whites:
Etna Bianco ★★★☆ £C

Valle dell' Acate (Sicilia) *www.valledellacate.com*
Directed by Gaetana Jacono, this is an interesting range of wines from 100 ha of vineyards, relying primarily on indigenous varieties for both reds and whites. It is slightly frustrating too in that while many of the wines really sing out, including a varietal, perfumed Frappato and stylish, expressive Cerasuolo di Vittoria, the top wine Tané is too ambitious. The latter is mostly Nero d'Avola but includes 15% Syrah and while much more concentrated than the other wines, is too oaky, with oak tannins on the finish and is a touch too alcoholic. Better balanced but with only moderate depth is a varietal Nero d'Avola, Il Moro. New unoaked Poggio Bidini is also from Nero d'Avola - a light but attractive quaffing example. Of the whites, the oak-aged Bidis (Chardonnay/Inzolia) is ripe and sweet-fruited but a bit heavy, lacking structure and vibrancy. Unwooded varietal Inzolia is also made (labelled Insolia) but hasn't been tasted. Of interest to the visitor are the restored old wine cellar and millstone.

Recommended Reds:
Cerasuolo di Vittoria ★★★ £C   Frappato ★★☆ £B   Tané ★★ £E
Il Moro ★★ £C   Poggio Bidini ★ £B
Recommended Whites:
Bidis ★ £B

Do Zenner (Sicilia) *www.zenner.it/terra-delle-sirene*
Do Zenner is the adopted Vietnamese son of Hans and Nina Zenner who moved from Switzerland to Sicily in 1975. In 79 they acquired a first small patch of vineyard in the historic vine growing zone of Bufaleffi near Noto. The vineyard has subsequently expanded and is now approaching 7 ha (4 ha in production) including better terraced parcels and, since 2002, an exceptional plot of old alberello trained vines. First commercialized in the late 90s thanks to help from enologist Salvatore Foti, the wine is just now starting to really come into its own. Yields are less than 1kg per vine and the wine undergoes a 20 day maceration with pumping over. Used barrels

are used for both the malolactic fermentation and ageing as Do is seeking structure as much as flavour and hopes to combine the character derived from soil/location with that from vinification. If early vintages had a tendency to a slight rusticity and very intense berryishness there is more expression and nuance in the latest releases. Dense and quite extracted, it promises to be a wine of real individuality as well as vigour with at least 5-6 years' age. New, is Goccia Rossa, 90% Nero d'Avola and 10% Syrah from younger vines. Without doubt this is an interesting estate to follow. Do's commitment and understanding bode well for a potentially great Italian wine.

Recommended Reds:
Terra delle Sirene ★★★☆ £C

⚫ Zisola (Sicilia) *www.mazzei.it*

The Mazzei family's (CASTELLO DI FONTERUTOLI, Tuscany) newest venture brings them to southeastern Sicily, just outside the town of Noto - further swelling the ranks of numerous outsiders who have taken a stake in the new Sicily for wine. 17 ha of the restored 50 ha estate is currently planted to alberello trained vines. At around 130m above sea level, some of the planting is new and some existing, mostly Nero d'Avola but also some Syrah, Cabernet Franc and Petit Verdot. Their first wine (Zisola) is a varietal Nero d'Avola aged for 10 months in French *barriques* (50% new). The wine is concentrated and sweet-fruited with dark raspberry, plum and spice and hints of clove and earth. It also has the balance, depth and class normally associated with a Mazzei creation. Keep it for at least 3-5 years. 2006 saw the first vintage of Doppiozetta, a stunning blend of Nero d'Avola, Syrah and Cabernet Franc, a hefty wine that will need some years ageing. In addition to wine production of a high quality extra virgin olive oil has been undertaken which will be rated in the future.

Recommended Reds:
Noto Rosso Doppiozeta ★★★★ £E   Zisola ★★★☆ £D

A-Z of producers - *Sardegna (Sardinia)*

Agripunica (Sardegna) *www.agripunica.it*

Is this Sardinia's Sassicaia? Certainly it has all the credentials to be. The principal owners are Sebastiano Rosa, who manages SASSICAIA/ TEN. SAN GUIDO, and SANTADI but also includes Ten. San Guido itself, Antonello Pilloni of Santadi and the celebrated Giacomo Tachis (architect of Sassicaia's quality and much more besides). The 150 ha estate was established in 2002. Production of the first wine, Barrua was small based on 10 ha of old Carignano vines. The same vineyard has another 20 ha of new plantings of Carignano, Cabernet Sauvignon and Merlot - the latter two grapes contributing 10% and 5% of the blend respectively. Another large site, Narcao (120 ha) has been planted and two further wines - a red and a white are now inproduction. The red, Montessu, is 60% Carignano, with equal parts of Syrah, Cabernet Sauvignon, Cabernet Franc and Merlot making up the rest. Aged for 15 months in used *barriques*, it doesn't have the depth or breadth yet of the Barrrua, but should improve as the vines age. Samas is a blend of 80% Vermentino and 20% Chaerdonnay, vinified separately in stainless steel and then blended and rested in concrete for a further 3 months. The Barrua (sold as Isola dei Nuraghi IGT) shows sophisticated winemaking with floral, crushed black fruits, carob and oak spice, an expansive stylish palate with balanced extract and a long finish.

Recommended Reds:
Barrua ★★★★ £F   Montessu ★★ £C

Recommended Whites:
Samas ★ £B

Argiolas (Sardegna) *www.argiolas.it*

Argiolas is one of Sardinia's two leading producers (the other is SANTADI). It is run by Franco and Giuseppe Argiolas, sons of Antonio Argiolas, but with assistance from leading enologist Giacomo Tachis. Since 1985 the 230 ha estate has been completely replanted with the emphasis on local Sardinian varieties. There are good examples of some of the island's more widely seen DOCs including Costamolino (Vermentino di Sardegna); Costera (Cannonau di Sardegna); Perdera (Monica di Sardegna); and S'elegas (Nuragus di Cagliari), a crisp dry white. The best wines, however, are sold under the IGT Isola dei Nuraghi. Is Argiolas is 100% Vermentino, while Angialis, a fine light sweet wine, is made from (mostly) Nasco and Malvasia. Newish Cerdeña is a (pricey) *barrique*-fermented and aged Vermentino. The top red is the deep but firmly structured Turriga, based on Cannonau but with 5% of each of Carignano, Malvasia Nera and the Sardinian variety Bovale. Similarly structured is Korem, from Bovale, Carignano and a little Cannonau. Most wines should be drunk young but Korem and Turriga (subject to a delayed release) usually need plenty more bottle-age after release; the Turriga is best with 10 years' age. New is Is Solinas which is almost entirely Carignano from 15 ha of new vineyard in the Golfo di Palmas. Seemingly more modern in style, it is more perfumed and refined than either Korem or Turriga. Its intense black fruit core will still need a minimum of 5-6 years to unfurl. SerraLori is a rosé made from a mix of grapes.

Recommended Reds:
Turriga ★★★☆ £F   Is Solinas ★★★☆ £E
Korem ★★★ £D Cannonau di Sardegna Costera ★★ £C
Monica di Sardegna Perdera ★ £B

Recommended Whites:
Angialis ★★★ £D   Is Argiolas ★★ £B
Vermentino di Sardegna Costamolino ★★ £B
Nuragas di Cagliari S'elegas ★ £B

Capichera (Sardegna) *www.capichera.it*

Brothers Fabrizio and Mario Ragnedda only began to produce their own wines from their family estate in the far north of Sardinia in the 1980s. There are now 60 ha of vines and quality from Vermentino (for whites) and Carignano (for reds) is very good indeed, although the wines do come with a price to match. 'Capichera' is the estate white, an intense, perfumed Vermentino. Vigna'ngena is a slightly more affordable version. Vendemmia Tardiva, late-harvested (but dry) and *barrique*-aged, is a splendid wine with refined, pure fruit and great length. Both Carignanos are ripe and classy; Assajé is stainless steel fermented and aged. The powerful *barrique*-aged Mantènghja has added depth and concentration but should be drunk only with 8 years' age or more. If only the wines were a bit cheaper!

Recommended Reds:
Mantènghja ★★★★ £F   Assajé ★★★ £E
Recommended Whites:
Capichera Vendemmia Tardiva ★★★ £F   Capichera ★★ £E
Vermentino di Gallura Vigna 'Ngena ★★ £C

⚫ Giovanni Cherchi (Sardegna) *www.vinicolacherchi.it*

This small Sardinian operation is worth tracking down for the quality of its Vermentinos alone but the soft, appealing, scented reds have a similar intensity and the same ability to evoke something of the

Wine behind the label

Southern Italy & Islands /Sardinia

Italy

essence of the island. The pear, citrus and spice character Cherchi achieves in his Vermentino makes for delightful whites for relatively early drinking. The *barrique*-aged Boghes, also from Vermentino shows a deft use of oak and lovely complexity with a couple of years' age. Most intriguing of the reds, a varietal Cagnulari is not a wine of great depth or structure but its delightful fruit character is now inspiring other growers to plant it. Luzzana is a blend of equal parts Cannonau and Cagnulari; scented and oak-influenced with preserved berry-fruit character, it is deserving of at least 3-4 years' age. Recent vintages have added more weight and depth. New is Soberanu, a Cagnulari wine selected from the oldest vineyards with the grapes given a long hang before harvesting, vinified in new and one vintage *barriques* for 14 months with a further 4 months in bottle (without filtration) before commercialisation. This is a big wine that will need 6-8 years before its luscious overlying fruit can poke its head above the tannins. The non-DOC wines are sold under the Isola dei Nuraghi IGT.

Recommended Reds:
Soberanu ★★★★☆ £E Luzzana ★★★☆ £D
Cannonau di Sardegna ★★ £C Cagnulari ★★ £C
Recommended Whites:
Boghes ★★★ £D Vermentino di Sardegna Tuvaoes ★★☆ £D
Vermentino di Sardegna Pigalva ★★ £C

Ferruccio Deiana (Sardegna) *www.ferrucciodeiana.it*
A relatively new family operation, trained winemaker Ferruccio Deiana now has 60 ha of vineyard (planted in part on limestone soils) with the typical Sardinian grapes. Of two Vermentino di Sardegna, Arvali is a selection from higher sites and is harvested later resulting in better definition and a little more elegance. Slightly over-ambitious is a pricy *barrique*-aged blend of Vermentino and Nasco (75/25) called Pluminus which delivers flavour but not sufficient finesse or balance. For red there's an adequate supple, juicy example of the usually uninspiring Monica. The Cannonau is a slightly better bet but the real interest comes in Ajana (local dialect for Deiana), which like Pluminus is sold under the Isola dei Nuraghi IGT. Based on Cannonau it adds in 30% Carignano and 20% Bovale Sardo and spends 18 months in *barrique*. A powerful, concentrated and complex red it has lots of substance and style; which deserves 8-10 years' age. The Deiana's sweet white Oirad (Dario, Ferruccio's son, in reverse) is based on Malvasia, Moscato and Nasco. It adds honeycomb, spice and dried citrus to a grapy core, and shows an added vibrancy and intensity. The estate also produces entry level Cannonau, Monica and Vermentino under the Sanremy label. A bonus for visitors, should you be in the vicinity of Cagliari, is a small museum that forms part of the recently expanded winery.

Recommended Reds:
Ajana ★★★★ £E Cannonau di Sardegna Sileno ★★☆ £C
Monica di Sardegna Karel ★★ £B
Recommended Whites:
Oirad ★★★ £D Vermentino di Sardegna Arvali ★★☆ £C
Pluminus ★★ £E Vermentino di Sardegna Donnikalia ★★ £B

✿ **Dettori (Sardegna)** *www.tenutedettori.it*
To appreciate these fabulous wines be prepared to take some time and leave your preconceptions behind. Alessandro Dettori is uncompromising in the making of his wine. His 13 ha of very low-yielding alberello (bush-trained) vines lie close to the sea (but at 250 m altitude) in Sénnori in north-west Sardinia. There is no oak whatsoever, no filtration, no fining, no additions or adjustments

and Alessandro accepts it might not always work but is undeterred. Vermentino shows uncommon weight, texture and pure, cool fruit but lacks the zest and freshness of more mainstream styles. Three single-vineyard Cannonau show diverse character. Tuderi, from 40-year-old vines is full and powerful yet mellow with deep fruit. An intense, licoricy Tenores (from 40- to 60-year-old vines) is the most extracted and discernably tannic, and highest in alcohol with highish acidity too, needing at least five years' age. Dettori (from 60- to 120-year-old vines) has fabulous red fruit and lightly mineral, floral complexity. There is lovely breadth and purity – a wine to savour and savour (in a decent glass) before trying to procure another bottle. Chimbanta is the result of Alessandro treatment of the much-derided Monica grape and shows good promise with cranberry and pomegranate fruit and atypical breadth for the variety. Ottomarzo is another red, this time from the Pascale grape. For sweet wine there's Moscadeddu, from a local variant of Moscato, which has a gorgeous nose of purest honeycomb, delicate apricot and allspice. Medium-dry, it is not as concentrated as might be expected. It remains to be seen how the wines will age, suffice to say they could be very special indeed.

Recommended Reds:
Dettori ★★★★☆ £F Tenores ★★★★ £F Tuderi ★★☆ £E
Chimbanta ★★☆ £D
Recommended Whites:
Vermentino ★★ £D Moscadeddu ★★ £D

Feudi Della Medusa (Sardegna)
Here comes another important contribution to the cannon of quality Sardinian wine. 40 ha of vineyard at Santa Margherita di Pula are but a short distance from the remains of the ancient Nora (south of Cagliari) while Cannonau and Cagnulari are drawn from a further 15 ha of well-established vineyards in the north. Donato Lanari has been employed to work his magic on both these and other local varieties (labelled Corona de Logu) together with imports including Chardonnay, Syrah and Cabernet Sauvignon. Two dry whites are fresh with restrained oak and plenty of ripe fruit character; both are based on Chardonnay but Sa Perda Bianca includes 20% Malvasia. Reds include two unoaked examples. Cannonau di Sardegna, with good purity and a herb and raspberry fruit intensity, has much more depth and flair than basic examples while Biddas Arrubias which adds 15% of Bovale Sardo and Cagnulari to Cannonau, it is ripe and characterful. An oak-aged Cagnulari is very distinctive with crabapple, cherry and pomegranate scents and good body. The top two reds are given 18 months in French oak and are more concentrated and structured. Gerione adds both Cabernets and Syrah to Bovale while Norace is mostly Bovale and Cannonau with 15% Syrah. Also made is Aristeo, a stylish passito style sweet wine from Nasco and Malvasia grapes. *Barrique*-aged, it is of medium weight, moderately sweet and well-balanced with honeycomb, spice and dried nectarine. All wines are sold as Isola dei Nuraghi IGT.
Recommended Reds:
Gerione ★★★☆ £E Norace ★★★☆ £E Cagnulari ★★☆ £D
Cannonau di Sardegna Corona de Logu ★★ £D
Biddas Arrubias Corona de Logu ★☆ £C
Recommended Whites:
Aristeo ★★★ £E Alba Nora ★★★ £C Sa Perda Bianca ★★☆ £D

Giuseppe Gabbas (Sardegna) *www.gabbas.it*
Like the other 'Giuseppe' located in the Barbagia region of Sardinia (see Giuseppe SEDILESU) Signor Gabbas knows how to make the most of Cannonau. Working with enologist Lorenzo Landi, his

494

fruit-driven Lillové has all the style of a fine cru Beaujolais with cool, supple inviting fruit. The Riserva Dule retains the exuberance of fruit but adds a little more breadth and depth. Both the top reds will keep but can be drunk with just 4-5 years' age.

Recommended Reds:
Cannonau Riserva Dule ★★★☆ £D Cannonau Lillové ★★☆ £B

Cantina Sociale Gallura (Sardegna) www.cantinagallura.net
This large co-op run by Dino Addis controls about 350 ha of vineyards and produces some of the best examples of Sardinian Vermentino. Those from Gallura zone are DOCG and here they give some credence to this status. As this style of wine needs to be drunk young for its floral, fruit and herb zestiness, it is important that it is not too heavy or over-ripe. Of four Vermentinos made in significant quantities only Gemellae and Canayli have been recently tasted but all are worth trying (Piras and Mavriana are the other two). Despite the volumes (one-third of a million bottles), Canayli has long been the quality reference point with added style and complexity to its herb, ripe stone fruit and tropical fruit character. It also has sufficient structure and the balance to keep for 3-4 years. Although Vermentino is the focus some red is also made including an adequate Cannonau di Sardegna and more characterful oak-aged Dolmen (Colli del Limbara IGT) - based on Nebbiolo with some Cabernet Sauvignon and Sangiovese. A sparkling wine, Moscato di Tempio Pausania is made too but hasn't been tasted. Very small quantities of a new premium Vermentino, Genesi were first produced from 04.

Recommended Reds:
Dolmen ★★ £C

Recommended Whites:
Vermentino di Gallura Superiore Canayli ★★★ £C
Vermentino di Gallura Gemellae ★★ £B

Alberto Loi (Sardegna) www.albertoloi.it
Sergio Loi and his siblings are taking forward the estate created by their father. Cannonau is the basis for nearly all the wines. Of the Cannonau di Sardegna, regular Sa Mola offers plenty of flavour if not much else, while the Riserva Cardedo has lots of soft red fruits and good concentration. The top Riserva, with a panoply of red fruits, has a lot more class, intensity and power though lacks a little definition. There are also three premium reds based on Cannonau (around 70%) but also including Carignano, Bovale and other local varieties. Stylish, concentrated Astrangia is surpassed by Tuvara which opens out beautifully with five years' age or more and adds more class, complexity and breadth. Loi Corona, aged only in barrique and including Cabernet Sauvignon, is intentionally more international in style but similarly impressive. Unusual is Leila, produced from Cannonau but avoiding skin contact and subject to a white wine vinification and a spell in barriques. It has the body and texture of a red with a preserved stone fruit/citrus character. A fresh, attractive Vermentino is also produced. The top reds are sold as IGT Isola dei Nuraghi.

Recommended Reds:
Tuvara ★★★ £E Loi Corona ★★★ £E Astrangia ★★ £D
Cannonau di Sardegna Jerzu Riserva Alberto Loi ★★★ £C
Cannonau di Sardegna Jerzu Riserva Cardedo ★★ £C

Recommended Whites:
Leila Vendemmia Tardiva ★★ £D

Masone Mannu (Sardegna) www.masonemannu.com
Olbia is on the north-eastern edge of Sardinia and Masone

Mannu's vineyards fall within the Vermentino di Gallura DOCG. Two decent examples are made: a scented and expressive, Petrizza for immediate consumption, and a more structured, Costarenas. The latter, partly aged in barriques, reveals intense peach and nectarine fruit following six months on the fine lees. Yet reds are at least as important in this very competently made range. Entu is half and half Cannonau and Carignano. Mannu is an elegant and individual red which adds 40% Bovale Sardo (here known as Muristellu) to 30% each of Cannonau and Carignano. It is given 18 months ageing, partly in new and second use barriques. It is cool, elegant and harmonious with ripe tannins and will build nicely in complexity with more age. Ammentu is made from botrytised and overripe Vermentino and Malvasia harvested at the end of October. A sweet wine of moderate weight and concentration it is very well-defined with the vibrancy and lift to carry its yellow plum, spice and marmalade flavours.

Recommended Reds:
Mannu ★★★☆ £E Entu ★★☆ £C

Recommended Whites:
Ammentu ★★★ £E
V ermentino di Gallura Petrizza ★★ £C
Vermentino di Gallura Superiore Costarenas ★★☆ £C

Pala (Sardegna) www.pala.it
A very creditable progressive Sardinian operation. Brothers Enrico and Mario Pala increasingly produce attractive, flavoursome whites and reds from 50 ha of vineyards first established by their father. Whites include a decent floral, herb and citrus Vermentino di Sardegna and a partly barrique-fermented blend of Vermentino, Chardonnay and some Malvasia called Entemari, which has a little more breadth and shows good balance and length. For red, the Cannonau I Fiori is perfumed and sweet-fruited with good character. Better is the Riserva, which spends 10 months in 3000 litre French oak barrels followed by 3 months in stainless steel and 3 months before bottling. The top red, S'Arai, 40% Cannonau, 40% Carignano, 30% Bovale, has added ripe red and black fruit intensity, breadth and depth. New is a late-harvested blend of Nasco and Vermentino, Assoluto. Other wines from Bovale, Syrah and Monica are produced but have not been tasted.

Recommended Reds:
S'Arai ★★★ £D Cannonau di Sardegnal Riserva ★★ £D
Cannonau di Sardegnal Fiori ★ £C

Recommended Whites:
Entemari ★★☆ £D Vermentino di Sardegna I Fiori ★★ £B

❀ Santadi (Sardegna) www.cantinadisantadi.it
The success and renown of the Santadi co-op is based around the Carignano grape (France's once humble Carignan). The key here, as with the top examples in the Languedoc, is that it ripens fully. Santadi has a deserved following for its combination of quantity and quality. The top wine is Terre Brune which also includes a tiny amount of Bovaleddu and is aged for 16–18 months in new French barriques. It is rich, powerful and structured, southern in its warmth and flavours and usually needs another 3–5 years' ageing after it is released (so is best with eight years' age or more). Rocca Rubia is made in much greater quantities (180,000 bottles) and has less weight and structure but plenty of style and can be drunk a little sooner. Araja is an unoaked Carignano that includes 15% Sangiovese. A basic yet stylish Carignano Grotta Rossa can be a good quaffing wine. Several good whites are also made. The Cala Silente has some lees contact for added complexity; citrusy, herbal

Southern Italy & Islands

Pedraia from Nuragus grapes is very fresh and appealing if drunk young; and Villa di Chiesa is a barrel-fermented blend of Vermentino and Chardonnay. The best white, however, is the sweet Latinia based on Nasco (as is the ARGIOLAS sweet wine), with lovely ripe fruit, real intensity, style and balance. Santadi are also partners in AGRIPUNICA, a project involving Tenuta San Guido, Giacomo Tachis and Sebastiano Rosa to produce a benchmark Carignano-based red.

Recommended Reds:
Carignano del Sulcis Superiore Terre Brune ★★★★ £E
Carignano del Sulcis Riserva Rocca Rubia ★★★ £C
Carignano del Sulcis Grotta Rossa ★☆ £B Araja ★★ £B
Recommended Whites:
Latinia ★★★ £E Vermentino di Sardegna Cala Silente ★★☆ £C
Vermentino di Sardegna Villa Solais ★☆ £B
Villa di Chiesa ★ £D Nuragus di Cagliari Pedraia ★ £B

Giuseppe Sedilesu (Sardegna) www.giuseppesedilesu.com
Located in the highland Barbagia region in central Sardinia (north of the Gennargentu mountains), the Sedilesu family cultivate 15 ha of alberello trained vines at 650m elevation. Almost all of it is Cannonau from which four different bottlings are produced. They are a revelation: stylish and expressive reds that are ripe, balanced (despite high natural alcohol levels) and well-structured. Mamuthone adds a little more precision and purity over a cool, intense 'Annada bottling. Better again is the Carnevale version, coming from lower yields, which given a 20-25 day maceration prior to ageing in *barriques* (one third new). More structured, it deserves 6-8 years' ageing. The top wine, Ballu Tundu comes from 100 year old vines aged in used 40 hectolitre *botti*. It is a classic example of its type, deeply flavoured with very ripe fruit. It is a slightly old-style red but in the best sense with fine tannins as well as a certain purity and elegance. The white grape, local to the area, is known as Granazza di Mamoiada and grows amongst the Cannonau. As with the reds, only natural yeasts are used with both fermentation and ageing in *barriques*. Grapefruit, quince and herb scented, the wine reveals significant (red wine-like) breadth and complexity with a slight bitter grapefruit, old-fashioned citrus quality as well as real style and length.

Recommended Reds:
Cannonau di Sardegna Riserva Ballu Tundu ★★★☆ £D
Cannonau di Sardegna Carnevale ★★★ £C
Cannonau di Sardegna Mamuthone ★★☆ £C
Cannonau di Sardegna 'Annada ★★ £B
Recommended Whites:
Perda Pintà ★★★ £C

Sella & Mosca (Sardegna) www.sellaemosca.com
Owned by the makers of Cinzano and Riccadonna, Sella & Mosca has been slimming down its range of wines from around 500 ha of vineyards in the north-west of Sardinia. Operations are directed by Mario Consorte, who combines the traditional and modern to produce an unusual range of wines. Reds include the firmly structured Tanca Farrà from Cannonau and Cabernet Sauvignon and Marchese di Villamarina, a varietal Cabernet. Terre Rare is a red from Carignano del Sulcis but in common with most of Sella & Mosca's reds, it could use a little more refinement. The Cannonau Riserva is aged two years in large Slavonian oak with a few more months in bottle before being commercially released. There is a good example of Vermentino, La Cala, grown near the sea which gives a slight saltiness to the wine, making it an excellent accompaniment to seafood. Terre Bianche is from the Torbato grape, only grown in the Alghero zone on Sardinia.

Recommended Reds:
Alghero Marchese di Villamarina ★★☆ £E
Alghero Tanca Farrà ★★ £C Cannonau di Sardegna Riserva ★★ £C
Carignano del Sulcis Riserva Terre Rare ★ £C
Recommended Whites:
Teere Bianchi Torbato Alghero ★★ £C
Vermentino di Sardegna La Cala ★ £B

Other wines of note

Campania
Alois
Recommended Reds: Campole (Aglianico) ★★☆ £C
Trebulanum (Casavecchia) ★★★ £D
Colli di Lapio/Clelia Romano
Recommended Whites: Fiano di Avellino ★★ £D
Grotta del Sole
Recommended Whites: Campo Flegrei Falanghina ★ £B
Greco di Tufo ★ £B
La Rivolta
Recommended Whites: Sannio Fiano ★★☆ £B
Recommended Reds: Aglianico del Taburno ★★ £B
Ocone
Recommended Reds: Taburno Piedirosso Calidonio ★★☆ £D
Pietratorcia (Ischia)
Recommended Whites: Scheria (Bianco) (Biancolella/Fiano) ★★☆ £B
Ischia Bianco Superiore Vigne di Chignole ★★☆ £B
Recommended Reds: Ischia Rosso Vigne di Janno Piro ★★ £C
Scheria (Rosso) (Aglianico/Syrah/Piedirosso/Guarnaccia) ★★☆ £D
Meditandum (Viognier/Malvasia) ★★★ £E
Alfonso Rotolo
Recommended Whites: Fiano Valentina ★★ £B
Greco di Tufo Loggia della Serra ★★ £C
Adolfo Spada
Recommended Whites: Gallicius (Bianco) (Falanghina) ★★ £B
Recommended Reds: Gallicius (Rosso) (Aglianico) ★★ £C
Sabus (Aglianico/Piedirosso/Montepulciano) ★★☆ £D
Gladius (Aglianico/Piedirosso) ★★★☆ £E
Cantina Terranera
Recommended Whites: Irpinia Coda di Volpe ★★ £B
Vestini Campagnano
Recommended Whites: Pallagrello Bianco ★★★ £D
Recommended Reds: Pallagrello Nero ★★★ £E
Vinosia
Recommended Whites: Soavemente (Greco/Fiano) ★★ £B
Recommended Reds: Vigna Marziacanale (Aglianico) ★★☆ £C

Basilicata
Terre degli Svevi
Recommended Reds: Aglianico del Vulture Re Manfredi ★★ £B
Consorzio Viticoltori Associati del Vulture
Recommended Reds: Aglianico del Vulture Carpe diem ★★ £B
Aglianico del Vulturevetusto ★★★ £D
Lagala
Recommended Reds: Aglianico del Vulture Nero Degli Orsini ★★☆ £C
Rosso del Balzo (Aglianico) ★☆ £B
Macarico
Recommended Reds: Aglianico del Vulture Macarì ★★★ £C
Aglianico del Vulture Macarico ★★★★ £E
Tenuta del Portale
Recommended Reds: Aglianico del Vulture ★★ £C
Starsa (Aglianico) ★★ £B

Puglia

A Mano
Recommended Reds: Prima Mano (Primitivo) ★★ £C

Adria Vini
Recommended Reds: Conviviale Primitivo ★★★ £B

Antica Masseria del Sigillo
Recommended Whites: Chardonnay ★☆ £B
Recommended Reds: Primitivo Sigillo Primo ★☆ £B
Terre del Guiscardo (Primitivo/Merlot/Cab Sauv) ★★★ £C

Apollonio
Recommended Reds: Copertino Rosso Riserva Divoto ★★☆ £B
Primitivo Terragnolo ★★ £B
Valle Cupa (Negroamaro /Primitivo) ★★☆ £B

Antiche Aziende Canosine
Recommended Whites: Tharen (Moscato Passito) ★★☆ £C

Castel di Salve
Recommended Reds: Il Volo di Alessandro (Sangiovese) ★☆ £C
Lama del Tenente (Primitivo/Malvasia Nera/Montepulciano) ★★☆ £D

Castello Monaci
Recommended Reds: Salice Salentino ★ £B Artas (Primitivo) ★★ £C

Cefalicchio (Biodynamic)
Recommended Reds: Rosso Canosa Vigne Alte ★☆ £B
Rosso Canosa Riserva Romanico (Uva di Troia) ★★☆ £C
Recommended Whites: Lefko (Chardonnay) ★☆ £B
Moscato Bianco Jalal ★☆ £B
Recommended Rosés: Ponte della Lama ★ £B

Tenuta Cocevola/Maria Marmo
Recommended Reds: Castel del Montevandalo (Uva di Troia) ★★ £B
Recommended Rosés: Castel del Monte Rosato (Uva di Troia) ★ £B

D'Alfonso del Sordo
Recommended Reds: Guado San Leo (Uva di Troia) ★★★ £D
Contrada del Santo (Uva di Troia/Merlot) ★★ £C

Diomede
Recommended Reds: Troia (Uva di Troia) ★★ £B
Nero di Troia (Uva di Troia) ★☆ £A

Cantine due Palme
Recommended Reds: Salice Salentino Riserva Selvarosa ★★☆ £B

Fatalone
Recommended Reds: Gioia del Colle Primitivo ★★☆ £B
Gioia del Colle Primitivo Riserva ★★★ £C

Feudi di San Marzano
Recommended Whites:
Bianco Salento (Verdeca/Malvasia Bianca) ★ £B
Recommended Reds: Negroamaro ★ £B Primitivo ★★ £B
Primitivo Sessantanni ★★★ £D

Cantine Cristiano Guttarolo (Organic)
Recommended Reds: Primitivo di Puglia ★★☆ £B
Antello delle Murge (Primitivo) ★★★☆ £C

Masseria Monaci
Recommended Reds: Copertino Eloquenzia ★★ £B
I Censi (Negroamaro/Primitivo) ★★ £C

Paolo Petrilli
Recommended Reds: Cacc'e Mmitte di Lucera Agramonte ★★ £C
Ferraù (Uva di Troia/Sangiovese) ★★★ £C

Cantine Paradiso
Recommended Reds:
Primitivo Puglia IGT Posta Piana ★★★☆ £B
Uva di Troia Puglia IGT Posta Piana ★★★ £B

Rosa del Golfo
Recommended Rosés: Rosato Rosa del Golfo ★ £B
Recommended Reds:
Quarantale Riserva Mino Calò (Negroamaro/Primitivo) ★★ £D

Cantine Sampietrana
Recommended Reds: Settebraccia ★★★ £C

Brindisi DOC Riserva ★★ £B

Cantine San Marzano
Recommended Reds: Vindoró Negroamaro IGP Salento ★★★☆ £D

Schenk Italia
Recommended Reds:
Brunilde di Menzione Primitivo di Manduria DOC ★★★☆ £C
Brunilde di Menzione Brindisi DOC Riserva ★★★ £C

Schola Sarmenti
Recommended Reds: Cubardi Primitivo IGT Salento ★★★★ £D
Nardo Riserva Nerìo (Negroamaro/Malvasia Nera) ★★★ £C
Nardo Roccamora (Negroamaro/Malvasia Nera) ★★☆ £B
Armentino (Primitivo/Negroamaro) ★★ £B
Recommended Whites: Fiano IGT Salento ★★☆ £C
Candòra (Chardonnay) ★★ £B

Conte Spagnoletti Zeuli
Recommended Reds:
Castel del Monte Vigna Grande (Uva di Troia) ★★★ £B

Torre Quarto
Recommended Reds: Tarabuso (Primitivo) ★ £B
Bottaccia (Uva di Troia) ★★ £B Sangue Blu (Negroamaro) ★★ £B
Quarto Ducale (Primitivo/Uva di Troia) ★★ £B

Valle dell' Asso
Recommended Reds: Salice Salentino ★☆ £B
Galatina Negroamaro ★★ £B Terra San Giovanni (Primitivo) ★☆ £B
Negroamaro Biologica ★★ £B Piromáfo (Negroamaro) ★★☆ £C

Varvaglione – Vigne & Vini
Recommended Reds: Papale di Manduria ★★★ £C

Calabria

Fattoria San Francesco
Recommended Reds: Cirò Rosso Rondo Dei Quattro Venti ★★★☆ £D
Donna Madda (Gaglioppo) ★☆ £C
Recommended Whites: Cirò Bianco ★ £B
Recommended Rosés: Cirò Rosé ★ £B

Sicily (Sicilia)

Calatrasi
Recommended Reds: D'Istinto Magnifico (Cab Sauv/Merlot) ★★★ £D

Cantine Colosi
Recommended Whites: Malvasia delle Lipari Naturale di Salina ★★ £C
Malvasia delle Lipari Passito di Salina ★★ £D
Moscato di Pantelleria ★★ £C Passito di Pantelleria ★★ £D

Duca di Salaparuta
Recommended Reds: Duca Enrico (Nero d'Avola) ★★★☆ £F
Triskelè (Nero d'Avola/Cab Sauv/Merlot) ★★★☆ £D
Recommended Whites: Bianco di Valguarnera (Inzolia) ★★ £D

Feotto dello Jato
Recommended Reds: Rosso di Turi (Merlot) ★ £C
Monreale Syrae (Syrah) ★ £C
Recommended Whites: Monreale Zabbya (Cataratto-Mod.Sweet) ★ £D

Feudo di Santa Tresa
Recommended Reds: Cerasuolo di Vittoria ★☆ £B
Avulisi (Nero d'Avola) ★★☆ £C

Cantine Florio
Recommended Whites: Marsalavergine Oro Terre Arse ★★★ £D
Marsalavergine Oro Baglio Florio ★★★ £D
Marsala Superiore Riserva Vecchioflorio ★★★ £C
Vino Liquoroso di Pantelleria Morsi di Luce ★★ £C

Tenute Galfano
Recommended Reds: Nero d'Avola ★★ £C
Recommended Whites: Moscato Passito ★★★☆ £D Zibbibo ★★ £C

Grottarossa
Recommended Reds: Rosso della Noce (Nero d'Avola) ★ £B

Pietradolce

Southern Italy & Islands

Recommended Reds: Rampante Etna Rosso ★★★ £E
Etna Rosso ★★☆ £C
Cantine Rallo
Recommended Reds: Syrah ★★★ £C Principe Nero d'Avola ★☆ £B
Recommended Whites: Gruali (Grillo) ★☆ £B
Cataratto Carta d'Oro ★☆ £B
Settesoli
Recommended Reds:
Mandrarossa Bonera (Nero d'Avola/Cab Sauv) ★£B
Mandrarossa Bendicò (Nero d'Avola/Merlot/Syrah) ★★ £C
Terreliade
Recommended Whites: Timpa Giadda (Grillo) ★☆ £B
Recommended Reds: Nirà (Nero d'Avola) ★ £B

Sardinia (Sardegna)
Antichi Poderi Jerzu
Recommended Reds: Cannonau di Sardegna Marghìa ★ £B
Radames (Cannonau/Cab Sauv/Carignano) ★★ £D
Attilio Contini
Recommended Whites: Vernaccia di Oristano Riserva ★ £C
Vernaccia di Oristano Antico Gregori ★★★ £E
Cantina Sociale Vermentino
Recommended Whites: Vermentino di Gallura Funtanaliras ★★ £B
Recommended Reds: Cannonau di Sardegnatàmara ★★ £C
Galana (Cab Sauv/Carignano/Cannonau/Cagnulari) ★★ £D
Mesa
Recommended Whites: Vermentino di Sardegna Opale ★★ £C
Recommended Reds: Carignano del Sulcis Buio ★★☆ £B
Buio Buio (Carignano) ★★★☆ £D
Malombra (Carignano/Syrah) ★★★☆ £E

Author's choice

Southern red stars
Abbazia Santa Anastasia   Litra
Agripunica   Barrua
Argiolas   Turriga
Benanti   Lamorèmio
Ceuso   Ceuso
COS   Scyri
Dettori   Cannonau Dettori
Donnafugata   Contessa Entellina Mille e Una Notte
Feudo Montoni   Vrucara Selezione Speciale
Librandi   Gravello
Montevetrano   Montevetrano
Morgante   Don Antonio
Odoardi   Scavigna Vigna Garrone
Palari   Faro
Passopisciaro   Passopisciaro
Odoardi   Scavigna Vigna Garrone
Rivera   Castel del Monte Puer Apuliae
Tenute Rubino   Torre Testa
Tasca d'Almerita   Contea di Sclafani Rosso del Conte
Cosimo Taurino   Patriglione
Vallone   Graticciaia
Villa Matilde   Cecubo
Conti Zecca   Nero
Do Zenner   Terra delle Sirene

Superior expressions of Aglianico
Alovini   Aglianico del Vulture Alvolo
Basilisco   Aglianico del Vulture
Antonio Caggiano   Taurasi Vigna Macchia Dei Goti
Cantine del Notaio   Aglianico del Vulture La Firma
D'Angelo   Canneto

Masseria Felicia   Falerno del Massico Etichetta Bronzo
Feudi di San Gregorio   Taurasi Piano di Montevergine
Elena Fucci   Aglianico del Vulture Titolo
Galardi   Terra di Lavoro
Tenuta Le Querce   Aglianico del Vulture Vigna Corona
Salvatore Molettieri   Taurasi Vigna Cinque Querce
Paternoster   Aglianico del Vulture Rotondo
Telaro/Lavoro & Salute   Galluccio Riserva Ara Mundi

Brilliant inexpensive reds
Accademia Dei Racemi/Felline   Vigna del Feudo
Accademia Dei Racemi/Sinfarosa   Primitivo di Mandura Zinfandel
Apollonio   Vale Cupa
Basilisco   Aglianico del Vulture Teodosio
Ceuso   Scurati
Grifalco   Aglianico del Vulture
Tenuta Le Querce   Aglianico del Vulture Il Viola
Leone De Castris   Salice Salentino Riserva
Masseria Li Veli   Passamante
Morgante   Nero d'Avola
Planeta   La Segreta Rosso
Tenute Rubino   Marmorelle Rosso
Conte Spagnoletti Zeuli   Castel del Monte Vigna Grande
Cosimo Taurino   Notarpanaro
Telaro/Lavoro & Salute   Galluccio Montecaruso
Cantina del Taburno   Aglianico del Taburno Fidelis
Torrevento   Castel del Monte Riserva Vigna Pedale
Valle dell'acate   Cerasuolo di Vittoria
Vallone   Salice Salentino Vereto
Vetrere   Tempio di Giano
Conti Zecca   Salice Salentino Riserva Cantalupi

Captivating whites
Benanti   Etna Bianco Superiore Pietramarina
Antonio Caggiano   Fiano di Avellino Béchar
Capichera   Capichera Vendemmia Tardiva
Giovanni Cherchi   Vermentino di Sardegna Tuvaoes
COS   Ramì
Cusumano   Cubìa
Casa d'Ambra   Ischia Biancolella Frassitelli
Marco de Bartoli   Grappoli del Grillo
Benito Ferrara   Greco di Tufo Vigna Cicogna
Feudi della Medusa   Alba Nora
Feudi di San Gregorio   Sannio Falanghina
Cantina Sociale Gallura   Vermentino di Gallura Superiore Canayli
Guido Marsella   Fiano di Avellino
Pietracupa   Greco di Tufo
Planeta   Cometa
Santadi   Vermentino di Sardegna Cala Silente
Tasca d'Almerita   Contea di Sclafani Nozze d'Oro
Tormaresca   Castel del Monte Pietrabianca

Delicious sweet whites
Argiolas   Angialis
Benanti   Passito di Pantelleria Coste di Mueggen
Botromagno   Gravisano Passito di Malvasia
Antonio Caggiano   Mel
De Bartoli   Passito di Pantelleria Bukkuram
Donnafugata   Passito di Pantelleria Ben Ryé
Feudi di San Gregorio   Privilegio
Librandi   Le Passule
Salvatore Murana   Passito di Pantelleria Martingana
Santadi   Latinia
Villa Matilde   Eleusi

While for years the quality of Spanish wine in the more established regions and DOs had been acceptable it could also have fairly been said that the real potential in the country remained untapped. However, the past half decade or so has seen dramatic change both in fine-wine production and in lesser regions. There are new-wave Riojas and an abundance of great reds from Castilla y León, but other, smaller regions like Priorat have also been providing some remarkable and striking wines in recent years. Further south, in the great centre of the country, relaxation of the regulations governing irrigation and a desire to harness the potential of the best hillside sites as well as some fine, old bush-vine plantings of regional varieties has brought increasing change. It remains depressing, however that despite all this there is still a sizeable amount of sometimes very mediocre wine being produced in almost all the established regions.

North-East Spain

País Vasco is the Spanish Basque country and home to three tiny DOs with barely 125 ha between them. All are close to the coast between Bilbao and San Sebastien. **Getariako Txakolina** is the furthest east, **Bizkaiko Txakolina** stretches around Bilbao, while directly to its south is **Arabako Txakolina**. The best are dry, quite steely whites based on Hondarribi Zuri.

The north-western sector of the **Rioja** DO stretches into País Vasco and includes some of the best of the region's sites in the Rioja Alavesa. The Rioja wine zone spreads out of the administrative region of Rioja, its borders stretching into Navarra to its north-east and Castilla y León to the west. The wine area is split into three sub-regions: Alavesa, Alta and Baja. Tempranillo performs well in the limestone soils of the Alavesa, which is moderated by cooling breezes, as is the Alta. The latter, though, has more clay in the soil, particularly suitable for Garnacha, which dominates the plantings in the hotter Baja sub-region. Graciano is also planted and makes an important impact on many blends as well as providing the odd striking varietal example. Most wines are a blend of the regions and, while generally the fruit of the Alavesa is the finest, there are outposts of quality in all three.

Whites are dominated by Viura with some Garnacha Blanca and Malvasia but few are of the quality of the reds. Of equal importance is the approach of the bodegas. The area has some very substantial producers but quality remains variable. The original ageing classifications of Crianza, Reserva and Gran Reserva are still in place but varietal labels are becoming far more commonplace and many fine new wave premium wines are being produced, which are generally vinified using French rather than American oak, many with the malolactic fermentation in barrel. Some, it has to be said, are very pricey as well.

Navarra shares the native Tempranillo, Garnacha and Viura with Rioja but also has considerable plantings of the international varieties; Cabernet Sauvignon, Merlot, Syrah and Chardonnay. Some impressive wines are produced but one often feels price is a key in the producer's approach and there should be more excitement than there is. To the east and stretching far towards the south of Navarra are the arid plains of Aragón. Bulk wine is generally the order of the day but there are four DOs worth considering: in **Campo de Borja** and **Somontano** some very good reds and the occasional Chardonnay and indeed Gewürztraminer stand out. Good, earthy and characterful reds are also produced in **Calatayud** and

Cariñena. Significant old bush-vine Garnacha is a very important resource in both DO's.

Running south from the Pyrenees and along the Mediterranean coast on the Costa Brava is **Cataluña**, home to a number of diverse wine regions and with its own vast DO which is a source of some top reds in particular. Right up close to the French border a few fine, traditional reds are made in the **Empordà** DO as well as some late-harvest wines similar to those found in France's Roussillon region. Some good red and white is produced from the **Costers del Segre** DO and a vast array of indigenous and international grapes are planted. To the immediate east are the vineyards of **Conca de Barberá**, cooled by altitude and a source of some good Chardonnay and Pinot Noir, but most of the fruit is sold on. Just inland from the coast and southwest of Barcelona are the vineyards of **Penedès**, established in a global sense by the considerable efforts of Miguel Torres. Some fine reds and whites are produced, again from a mix of local and international varieties but much of the output is relatively pedestrian. Interestingly the odd low-volume, garage-style red is appearing too. Similar styles are also being produced in the small DO of **Pla de Bages**, just to the north. Penedès is also the centre of the vast **Cava** DO. These sparkling wines are made by the traditional method from a combination of local Macabeo, Parellada and Xarel-lo as well as Chardonnay and Pinot Noir. Some very well-crafted vintage and non-vintage bottlings are produced but overall the quality tends to be sound at best. Many operations are very substantial and automation in the cellars is common. Cava at the lower levels can often display a marked rubbery character.

Immediately to the west of Penedès are the vineyards of **Tarragona**, which has two superior sub-regions, **Montsant** DO, which surrounds the small, very high-quality region of **Priorat** which, like Rioja is a DO Ca. Tarragona is planted to a range of varieties and fortified wines are still produced here. It is the reds, though, that excel and none more so than the superb old-vine plantings of Garnacha and Cariñena. The best can easily rival top-quality Châteauneuf-du-Pape. The reds in Priorat are the wines with the greatest potential. They include a fascinatingly variable blend comprising Garnacha, Cariñena, Cabernet Sauvignon, Syrah, Merlot and Pinot Noir. The vineyards are ideally planted in sparse, finely drained, stony soils and the climate is warm but not excessively so. The red wines of **Terra Alta**, to the south and inland of Montsant are also worth considering.

North-West Spain

The wines of north-western Spain are produced in Castilla y León and Galicia. Immediately to the west of Rioja is **Ribera del Duero** which, along with exceptional examples in Rioja and Priorat, produces most of the finest reds in the country. The historic Vega Sicilia bodega is based here and top reds are produced in and around the region as Vinos de Mesa and Vinos de la Tierra (VdT) as well as DO. While the greatest Ribera del Duero wines are both magnificent and pricey, too many remain depressingly mediocre with baked and often dried out fruit and hard tannins. The wines are based on Tinto Fino (Tempranillo) but may also include Cabernet Sauvignon, Merlot and Malbec in the blend.

To the north-west is the small DO of **Cigales**, where some good, structured reds are made, and to the west the white-wine DO of **Rueda**. Interesting barrel-fermented and single vineyard wines from both Sauvignon Blanc and the local Verdejo are produced.

Spain

Spain

The latter can be responsible for some very striking and potentially ageworthy whites. Immediately west of Rueda and also centred on the Duero river towards Zamora and Portugal is the warm red-wine area of **Toro**. The vineyard area here has always promised much but it is only relatively recently that wines of real depth have begun to emerge, some world-class. A local strain of Tempranillo, Tinto de Toro, is the mainstay of blends but Garnacha is also permitted and old vines contribute much to quality. A number of very impressive wines are also produced under the VdT (Vinos de La Tierra) Castilla y León classification. Look out also for the recently established DOs of **Arribes** and **Tierra del Vino de Zamora**. In the far west of the Castilla y León region is the small, visually striking DO of **Bierzo** which now produces both easy-drinking and truly exciting reds as well as a little white. On a note about classification VdT labelled wines are gradually being moved to the new IGP (Indicación de Origen Protegida) like France. Wines labelled VC (Vinos de Calidad) are from regions due to be upgraded to full DO status.

Virtually adjoining Bierzo but in fact in Galicia is **Valdeorras**. Reds are produced, like those in Bierzo, from Mencía but of particular note are the whites produced mainly from the unusual, indigenous Godello. The best are floral, ripe and respond well to handling in oak. Some attractive, fruity as well as more structured whites are also produced in **Ribeiro** but the greatest concentration of bodegas are found in the coastal vineyards of **Rías Baixas**. Their strikingly aromatic whites are generally best enjoyed young but the odd example is successfully barrel-fermented and will keep in the short to medium term, not dissimilar in this respect to more structured examples from Condrieu in the northern Rhône. Some exceptional mineral, elegant and nervy reds also emanate from the, at times near vertiginous, slopes of **Ribeira Sacra**. Fine reds and whites are also found at **Monterrei** on the Spanish/Portuguese border.

Central and South-East Spain

Over the past decade much has changed in the central and southern reaches of Spain. Identifying cooler mesoclimates and harnessing the sheer quality of some of the old bush vines and outcrops of well-drained soils are among the keys. The introduction of irrigation over the last decade has also given this arid area greater scope. Although this is more relevant in the production of bulk wines, of which a considerable volume are produced here. This is particularly the case with wines made from the lower and more fertile central plains.

The nation's capital city is home to the small DO of **Vinos de Madrid**. The vineyards stretch over a large area both to the immediate south-east of Madrid and some considerable distance to the west and include three sub-regions. Tempranillo is the most important red variety and Cabernet Sauvignon and Syrah are also permitted. Garnacha is also now assuming much greater importance. Whites include Chardonnay, Albillo and the local Malvar. The reds in particular can be very good and are more akin to a Ribera del Duero than a Rioja. A little further to the south-west of Madrid is the DO of **Mentrida**. This is mainly red wine country. Garnacha and Tempranillo are successful here as are the French interlopers, Cabernet Sauvignon, Merlot, Syrah and Petit Verdot. The vast central plains and particularly **La Mancha** are not generally associated with wines of any substance, this region after all is notable for its considerable number of co-ops. Things are beginning to change, though, and new and interesting wines are emerging, particularly from bodegas with higher altitude vineyards and

better sites. A strict control of yields is also a key factor. However, unfortunately for the DO, many impressive emerging wineries prefer to take the **VdT Castilla** because of the perception of quality from La Mancha. In the west of the region there are a number Vinos de Pago (single property) DOs, a classification taking increasing significance throughout the country. **Dominio de Valdepusa** has been well established for some time, **Dehesa de Carrizal** is more recently known on international markets. At Dehesa del Carrizal the focus is on French varieties, reds as well as Chardonnay, at Dominio de Valdepusa there is a little Graciano as well. A number of La Mancha bodegas also have holdings in the new small DO of **Uclés**, to the south-west of Madrid. Some rich and well made reds are now appearing. **Valdepeñas** used to be considered somewhat of a beacon amongst the other wine regions of the area but nothing of real consequence has emerged recently.

Some of the best potential for reds is to the east of the area, nearer the coast in the DO's of **Valencia**, **Manchuela** and **Utiel-Requena**. The indigenous Bobal and Monastrell are both proving very successful and fine Syrah, Malbec and Garnacha is also being made. Just to the south in the DOs of **Yecla**, **Jumilla** and **Bullas** some impressive and complex reds are being produced. A number of joint ventures with overseas expertise are being developed and some of the wines are not only impressive for their quality but notable for their high price as well. The newly created DOP **El Terrerazu** is a fine source of Tempranillo as well as Bobal. Some good fortified wine, Fondillon is produced from Monastrell at **Alicante**, as are some fine, sweet Moscatels. In the past decade some very well made reds and decent well-crafted whites have also been made here.

Southern Spain & Islands

The south is fortified-wine country, most specifically the sherries of **Jerez y Manzanilla**. Andalucía is also home to the fortified wines of **Montilla-Moriles** and **Málaga**. Most of the former are relatively ordinary but there are some exceptional wines from old soleras. The traditional wines of Málaga are very rare, a blend of sweet wine and grape juice, some of which is fortified. The sherry industry is centred around the towns of Jerez and Sanlúcar de Barrameda to the north of Cádiz. The wines are all raised in a *solera* system which is maintained by fresh young wines. Fino sherry in Jerez is very similar to Manzanilla at Sanlúcar. Both are best drunk on release for their fresh, salty character imbued by a period under *flor* yeast. Manzanilla Pasada is a nutty, aged wine, having been exposed to *flor* influence, as is Amontillado. Oloroso will have no *flor* character at all, having been immediately fortified above 18 degrees of alcohol. Palo Cortado is halfway in style between Fino and Amontillado. Rich and concentrated fortified Moscatel is also produced in the area as well as Pedro Ximènez. A recent development to ensure quality and character is a new set of classifications, VOS and VORS. VOS stands for Very Old Sherry and the wine must have an average age of at least 20 years. VORS stands for Very Old Rare Sherry and the average age of the wine must be a minimum of 30 years. Many of the best examples are older than this, although it is not a requirement for the classification to be used.

Over recent vintages the other major development in the south has been the emergence of some very impressive light wines both red and white. In the VdT **Cádiz** impressive and structured reds are being produced by one winery in particular, Huerta de Albala and from an area thought of simply as fortified wine country. A number of sherry bodegas are also taking advantage of the classification,

mainly for whites. To the east at Sierras de Málaga (sharing the DO with the fortified wines of Málaga) the high altitude vineyards inland are now a source of some very impressive Bordeaux style reds. A number of fine examples are also simply labelled as Vino de Mesa. Yet further still to the east is the large VC (Vinos de Calidad) **Granada** (VC being an interim classification before full upgrade to DO status). Among the eastern appellations of Andalucia are the vineyards of the VdT **Cumbres del Guadalfeo (formerly Contraviesa-Alpujarra)**, home to some of the very highest vineyards in Spain, a source of intense and mineral-scented whites and structured, characterful reds. Also of interest Inland of Almeria is the VdT **Ribera del Andrax**, where altitude also plays a part in producing balanced, rich and ripe reds.

As yet few wines have emerged on overseas markets from the either the Balearics or the Canaries. However a number of particularly impressive reds are produced in Mallorca from the DO's of **Binissalem Mallorca** and **Pla i Llevant**, as well as the VdT's of **Formentera**, **Mallorca** and **Iles Balears**. A number of varieties both red and white are proving successful, none more so than the indigenous red Callet. The Canaries would also seem to have genuine potential for whites with its sparse volcanic soils and fortifieds are also produced.

A-Z of producers by appellation/region

Spain

26 Yecla
27 Jumilla
28 Almansa
29 Valdepeñas
30 La Mancha
31 Vinos de Madrid
32 Montilla-Moriles
33 Málaga
34 Jerez-Xérès-Sherry, Manzanilla Sanlúcar de Barrameda

1 Rías Baixas
2 Ribeiro
3 Valdeorras
4 Bierzo
5 Toro
6 Cigales
7 Rueda
8 Ribera del Duero
9 Bizkaiko Txakolina
10 Getariako Txakolina
11 Rioja
12 Navarra
13 Campo de Borja
14 Somontano
15 Costers del Segre
16 Empordà
17 Conca de Barberá
18 Penedès
19 Tarragona
20 Priorat
21 Montsant
22 Terra Alta
23 Utiel-Requena
24 Valencia
25 Alicante

North-East Spain

Spain

Spanish vintages

Although there is a reasonably uniform climate in most of Spain's more southerly regions, the chart below should provide a good guide as to what to expect with the premium red-wine areas. The maturity guide applies to top wines. Spains fine reds are increasingly ageworthy and this as well as a move towards earlier releases requires the top crus to be cellared after release despite highly sophisticated modern winemaking in the best examples. Dry whites generally should be drunk on or shortly after release. The great fortified wines will be ready to drink on release.

Spanish vintage chart

	Rioja	Ribera del Duero	Priorat
	Top Wines	Top Wines	Top Wines
2015	★★★☆ A	★★★★ A	★★★★ A
2014	★★★★ A	★★★★ A	★★★★ A
2013	★★★☆ A	★★★★ A	★★★★ A
2012	★★★★ A	★★★★ A	★★★★ A
2011	★★★★☆ A	★★★★☆ A	★★★★ A
2010	★★★★☆ B	★★★★☆ A	★★★★ A
2009	★★★★ B	★★★★☆ A	★★★☆ B
2008	★★★☆ B	★★★☆ B	★★★☆ B
2007	★★★☆ B	★★★ B	★★★☆ B
2006	★★★★ C	★★★☆ B	★★★★ B
2005	★★★★ C	★★★★ B	★★★★ B
2004	★★★★ C	★★★★ B	★★★★ C
2003	★★★★ C	★★★★☆ B	★★★★ C
2002	★★★☆ D	★★★☆ C	★★★☆ C
2001	★★★★☆ C	★★★★☆ B	★★★★ C
2000	★★★ D	★★★ C	★★★☆ D
1999	★★★☆ C	★★★☆ C	★★★☆ D
1998	★★★ D	★★★☆ D	★★★★☆ C
1996	★★★ D	★★★★ C	★★★★ D
1995	★★★★ D	★★★★ D	★★★★ D
1994	★★★★☆ D	★★★★ D	★★★★☆ D

A-Z of producers - *North-East Spain*

Abadal (Pla de Bages) *www.abadal.net*
A key producer with 45 ha under vine from this small DO on the borders of Penedes. For the reds in particular a similar line up of French varieties is an important element of the mix as it is in the neighbouring DO. It is rare though in Penedes to find reds as richly textured as those here. As well as the Abadal blanco, Exòtic, a lees aged blend of Chardonnay, Sauvignon Blanc and Picapoll there is an interesting white Autòcton, made from Picapoll, which is a local variety, and full of ripe floral fruit and good acidity. A selection of the same variety from old vines, Nual, is also made. Simplest of the reds is the Cabernet Franc and Tempranillo blend which gets a short period of oak ageing. Merlot 5 comes from five different clones of the variety, all of which are vinified separately. The Reserva 3.9 is sourced from a single vineyard and blends mainly Cabernet Sauvignon with a little Syrah. Rich, dark fruited, almost jammy with supple tannins. The top wine the Selecció, like the 3.9 is unfiltered and blends both Cabernets with Syrah. 14 months oak ageing provides a complex minty, elegant red. Also look out for red Crianza and Reserva. (DM)

Recommended Reds:
Pla de Bages Selecció ★★★ £E   Pla de Bages 3.9 Reserva ★★★ £D
Pla de Bages Merlot 5 Reserva ★★☆ £C
Pla de Bages Cabernet Franc Tempranillo ★★☆ £C
Recommended Whites:
Pla de Bages Picapoll ★★☆ £C

Bodegas Acustic (Montsant) *www.acusticceller.com*
Small, excellent artisan winery producing barely more than a couple of thousand cases a year from old-vine Garnacha and Samsó. A combination of vines up to 75 years old and finely drained stony, sandy soils provides fruit of persuasive intensity. The Acústic is aged in one and two year old barrels, dark and spicy, with a marked mineral edge. Rounder, more opulent is the Braó, meaning brave, with a sweet edge from both the concentration of the fruit and around 30% new wood. You should expect both to develop well in bottle. Also now produced is a more expensive red, Auditori coming from very old Garnacha and a white Acústic Blanc from a blend of old vine Garnacha Blanca, Macabeo, Garnacha Gris and Pansal. The wines, not racked, are bottled unfined and unfiltered. (DM)
Recommended Reds:
Montsant Auditori ★★★★★ £F
Montsant Braó ★★★★ £E
Montsant Acustic Vinyes Velles Nobles ★★★☆ £C

Albet i Noya (Penedès/Cava) *www.albetinoya.cat*
Stylish Penedès as well as characterful Cava are both made here and the firm is committed to organic viticulture. A wide range of red and white grapes are cultivated on the 81 ha under vine at their Can Vendrell estate, including a number of experimental varieties. The estate vineyards are planted on the western slopes of the Ordal mountains in the Alt Penedès and the soils are low in fertility and consist of a mix of clay, sand and calcareous stone with just sufficient water retention. The Reserva Marti is the flagship red, Tempranillo dominates the blend which is also made up of Syrah, Cabernet Sauvignon and Merlot with spicy black fruits and a supple structure. Two other similarly priced examples are also made, La Milana from a blend including the local Caladoc as well as Tempranillo, Cabernet Sauvignon and Merlot and a very rare varietal Belat. The wines are aged for between 13 and 24 months, in the case of the Reserva Marti, in small French oak. The Lignum Negre is the volume premium red (Cabernet Sauvignon, Garnacha, Merlot) and a stylish peppery Col-Lecció Syrah is aged in used oak. Among the whites the Col-Lecció Chardonnay is barrel fermented and kept on stirred lees, while the El Fanio Xarel.lo is lees aged adding texture to its floral, elegant fruit. The Lignum Blanc is crisp and citrusy, three months for the Chardonnay component in oak adding texture and depth to Sauvignon Blanc. A crisp Macabeo, 3 Macabeus and a pricier small volume white El Blanc are also made. Good quality Cava ranges from the bright floral Petit Albet (Xarel.lo, Macabeo and Parellada) which spends around a year on lees to the more complex Brut Reserva, which also includes Chardonnay and Brut 21 (Chardonnay and Parellada) which is disgorge dated. The Cava range is completed by a Brut Nature Gran Reserva and a Rosat from Pinot Noir. A light red and white Petit Albet are also made in significant volume. (DM)
Recommended Reds:
Penedès Reserva Marti ★★★☆ £D
Penedès Syrah Col-Lecció ★★★ £C   Penedès Lignum ★★☆ £C
Recommended Whites:
Penedès Chardonnay Col-Lecció ★★★ £C

Penedès El Fanio ★★☆ £C Penedès Lignum ★★☆ £C
Cava Brut 21 Reserva NV ★★★☆ £D
Cava Brut Reserva Vintage ★★☆ £C
Cava Petit Albet Brut Reserva NV ★★ £C

❀ Alemany I Corrió (Penedès)

In comparison to many other premium Penedès operations this is
veritably tiny, a warehouse winery. A very passable second wine,
Pas Curtei, has been added to the Sot Lefriec to help ensure the
integrity and quality of the top wine. Both Laurent Corrio and
Irene Alemany studied enology in Burgundy and the partners now
have 8ha of their own vineyards planted to old-vine Cariñena (60
years) and 20-year-old Merlot and Cabernet Sauvignon. Both wines
are blends of the three varieties, with Merlot dominating and are
handled as naturally as possible by gravity and inert gas and bottled
unfined and unfiltered. Recently added are a couple of barrel-
fermented whites, Plou i Fa Sol from Xarel.lo as well as Principia
Matemathica from a blend of Xarel.lo and Malvasia. (DM)

Recommended Reds:
Penedès Sot Lefriec (Cabernet Sauvignon, Merlot, Cariñena) ★★★★ £E
Penedès Pas Curtei ★★★ £D

Bodegas Luis Alegre (Rioja) *www.luisalegre.com*

This impressive medium sized bodega, although originally founded
in 1968 was purchased in the late 1990s by a group of industrialists,
bringing the resources and considerable investment to produce
a range of wines of a uniformly impressive standard. There are
around 54 ha of fully owned vineyards and viticultural input is given
to their external sources as well. Winemaking expertise is provided
by Alexandra Schmedes and the team from Bodegas ERCAVIO and
a new winery has been completed with ultra modern vinification
equipment. Grape selection is done in the vineyard and micro-
vinifications can be done for individual parcels. The entry level wines
are immediately approachable, coming from younger vines. These
include a Tempranillo Rosado and a Blanco Joven from Tempranillo
and Viura respectively as well as a Tinto Joven red produced with
carbonic maceration from Tempranillo. A second Rosado, Provence
Flores is also made. The white citrus scented barrel fermented Finca
La Reñana has a little Malvasia as well as Viura and comes from 40
year old vines. Koden is a young red which sees six months in wood.
The Crianza benefits from 15% Graciano adding some structure
and complexity to the style. The Reserva similarly blends Graciano,
with a little Mazuelo and Garnacha, while the Parcela No 5 is solely
Tempranillo The Reserva Selección Especial is dominated by old
bush vine Tempranillo and offers real intensity and depth. The top
wine, Pontac is a fuller, rounder more modern style of Rioja. Blended
from Tempranillo (95%) and Graciano, it comes from the best parcels
and is both fermented and aged in wood with malolactic in barrel. A
couple of white Cavas, a Brut and a Brut Nature are also made. (DM)

Recommended Reds:
Rioja Pontac ★★★★☆ £F
Rioja Reserva Selección Especial ★★★★ £E
Rioja Parcela No 5 ★★★☆ £D Rioja Reserva ★★★☆ £D
Rioja Crianza ★★☆ £C Rioja Koden ★★☆ £C
Rioja Tempranillo ★★ £B

Recommended Whites:
Rioja Finca La Reñana ★★★ £D

❀❀ Finca Allende (Rioja) *www.finca-allende.com*

This is one of the very best producers in Rioja. Most of the fruit
comes from their own vineyards in the Rioja Alta although some
other growers are also used. Impressive Rioja Blanco, blended from
Viura and Malvasia is fermented and aged for a year in French oak.
Offering more depth and complexity is Mártires from a site of over
40 year old Viura. As well as the approachable Rioja Tinto there
are two other very concentrated and complex reds. Calvario is
Tempranillo with a bit of Garnacha and Graciano and comes from
a single vineyard planted in 1945. The richly dark-fruited varietal
Graciano was produced for the first time with the 2004 vintage.
The top wine, the pricey Aurus from 65-year-old vines, is unfiltered
with a rich, concentrated and supple texture. Both very complex
and harmonious, it will age gracefully. Paisajes y Viñedos is a joint
venture between Allende and Quim Villa, owner of Barcelona wine
merchant Vila Viniteca under the Uvas Felices banner. The wines
are all from single vineyards, La Pasada is a varietal Tempranillo
from old vines, Cecias is from 85 year old Garnacha in the south
eastern stretches of the DO and Valsalado comes from a blend of
varieties planted in a small vineyard near Logroño. A number of
other labels have also been produced in recent vintages. Finca
Coronado is the family's property in La Mancha, producing reds of
impressive density and character which take the regional Vinos de
La Tierra classification. Finca Coronado is a blend of Tempranillo,
Cabernet Sauvignon, Syrah, Petit Verdot and Merlot and of the two
more expensive varietals, the Graciano is a touch more sumptuous
and opulent. The firm is also producing a small range of modern,
approachable Riojas under the Finca Nueva label. The Reserva and
Crianza both stand out.(DM)

Finca Allende
Recommended Reds:
Rioja Aurus ⬤⬤⬤⬤⬤ £H   Rioja Calvario ★★★★★ £G
Rioja Graciano ★★★★☆ £G   Rioja ★★★ £C
Recommended Whites:
Rioja Mártires ★★★★☆ £G   Rioja Blanco ★★★☆ £E

Paisajes y Viñedos - Uvas Felices
Recommended Reds:
Rioja La Pasada ★★★☆ £E   Rioja Valsalado ★★★☆ £E
Rioja Cecias ★★★☆ £E

Finca Nueva
Recommended Reds:
Rioja Reserva ★★★ £C   Rioja Crianza ★★☆ £B
Rioja Cosecha ★★ £B
Recommended Whites:
Rioja Fermentado en Barrica ★★☆ £B Rioja Blanco ★☆ £B

Finca Coronado
Recommended Reds:
VdT Castilla Graciano ★★★★ £E VdT Castilla Petit Verdot ★★★★ £E
VdT Castilla Finca Coronado ★★★☆ £D

❀ Bodegas Altanza (Rioja) *www.bodegasaltanza.com*

A small and comprehensive range of Rioja is produced at Altanza
in the centre of the Rioja Alta. This is a sizeable 320 ha estate with
just under 200 ha planted to vines. Olive oil is also important here
and around 70 ha is also planted to olive trees. Unusually only
Tempranillo is planted and yields are kept low, green pruning is
practiced and the fruit is entirely hand harvested. A white is also
made which comes from a blend of Viura and Sauvignon Blanc. In
the winery vinification follows traditional lines with fermentation
of the reds in stainless steel and malolactic in large Allier oak
vats. The wines are then aged in a mix of new and older oak with
French accounting for 85% with some American and Russian
casks also used. There is a soft juicy rosado and the Capitoso is an

North-East Spain

approachable semi crianza style red. The Lealtanza reds are made in a traditional style but the wines fruit is always to the fore and not overwhelmed by oak. The Reserva Selección is also bottled under the Lealtanza label and is a fresher more approachable red being aged for just 12 months in bottle after cask ageing in comparison to the Gran Reserva which is held back three years. The Reserva Especial is richer and fuller and comes from a selection of very old Tempranillo. Pride of place though goes to the two Artistas Españoles wines. The Reserva Dali sees 12 months in new French oak, the Miro 18. Both are rich and sumptuous with a real old-vine complexity and dimension. A number of the wines are also released under the Edulis label. (DM)

Recommended Reds:
Rioja Artistas Españoles Reserva Miro ★★★★★ £G
Rioja Artistas Españoles Reserva Dalí ★★★★☆ £G
Rioja Reserva Selección ★★★★ £F
Rioja Reserva Especial ★★★☆ £E
Rioja Lealtanza Gran Reserva ★★★ £E
Rioja Lealtanza Reserva ★★★ £D
Rioja Lealtanza Crianza ★★☆ £C   Rioja Capitoso ★★ £B
Recommended Rosés:
Rioja Lealtanza ★☆ £B

❀ Bodegas Alto Moncayo *www.bodegasaltomoncayo.com*
A recently created bodega moving wine quality and indeed the price achievable in this lesser DO to new levels. Barossa Valley veteran Chris Ringland established the winemaking for the project. His hand has also be seen in the excellent wines to the south in Jumilla at Bodegas EL NIDO. The wines are based on old-vine Garnacha and 62 ha is planted in clay and red slate soils with some vines up to 100 years old. A continental climate and low summer rainfall, as well as organized canopy management and a green harvest ensures optimum ripeness. An artisan approach to winemaking means open top fermenters, use of basket presses and bottling without filtration. There is a well priced entry level wine, Veraton, the regular Alto Moncayo and a very limited production top label Aquilon which requires a pretty deep pocket. (DM)

Recommended Reds:
Campo de Borja Aquilon ★★★★★ £G
Campo de Borja Alto Moncayo ★★★★☆ £E
Campo de Borja Veraton ★★★★ £D

Alzania (Navarra) *www.alzania.es*
Undoubtedly, one of the best producers in Navarra and as such quite small in scale. Run by José Manuel Echeverria who is a native of Navarra and Maria Sáenx-Olazábal whose origins are in Rioja, between them they have produced one of the most exciting bodegas in the region. They produce wines of uncompromising interest and character. There is an entry level Syrah, labelled as such. Finca La Moneda is a touch richer and vinified without crianza ageing requirements. 21 del 10 is also a relative rarity, a 100% varietal Syrah, full of dark, spicy licorice scented fruit. It is aged for a year in French oak. The top wine Selección Privada is a big, rich modern red, a blend of Merlot and Tempranillo with ageing and malolactic in new oak. (DM)

Recommended Reds:
Navarra Selección Privada ★★★★ £F
Navarra 21 del 10 ★★★☆ £E   Navarra Finca La Moneda ★★★ £D

Ameztoi (Getariako Txakolina) *www.txakoliameztoi.com*
Small and impressive producer from this little appellation in the Pais Vasco. The wines are made from 18 ha of the Hondarrabi Zuri variety, native to the region. The naturally cultivated vineyards are carved into steep terraced slopes overlooking the Bay of Biscay, where apple and pear trees are as much of a feature of the landscape as vines. The wines taste fresh and green with stony, mineral characters. You are likely to encounter some CO_2 and they should always be drunk as young and fresh as possible. Both offer a zesty fruit intensity and depth rarely found in light whites.(DM)

Recommended Whites:
Getariako Txakolina Primus Circumdedisti Me ★★★ £D
Getariako Txakolina Ameztoi Txakoli ★★☆ £C

Joan d'Anguera (Montsant) *www.cellersjoandanguera.com*
The Anguera family have been based in the region for close to two centuries and the business is now run by brothers Joan and Josep. They have 31 ha spread across four separate sites. Based in the village of Darmós, the celler produces four dry reds and a sweet red D'Or from Garnacha. As well as the three dry wines rated below they also make a Joan d'Anguera label which blends Cabernet Sauvignon, Garnacha and Syrah. There is a fairly modern approach to vinification with a fermentation temperature restricted to just under 30 degrees celsius to promote fruit in the wines and an extended maceration of 25 to 35 days to polymerise and round the tannins. Planella (Cariñena, Syrah and Garnacha) and Finca L'Argatà (Garnacha and Syrah) are both single vineyard wines, El Bugador is the flagship and dominated by Garnacha with a little Syrah. (DM)

Recommended Reds:
Montsant El Bugador ★★★★ £E   Montsant Finca l'Argata ★★★☆ £C
Montsant La Planella ★★★ £C

Ardévol (Priorat)
The Ardévol family have origins at Porrera stretching back to the 13th Century and had vineyard holdings before phylloxera. More recently though the vineyards were abandoned and hazelnuts grown on the plots. They only decided to replant their vineyards in 1995 and Garnacha, Syrah, Cabernet Sauvignon and Merlot are all cultivated. Ageing is generally for 12 to 14 months in a mix of new and used French oak. The Terra d'Hom now consists of a blend of 90/10 Syrah to Cabernet and this very much shows through in its dark-fruited, spicy character. Again ageing in new and used French oak, generally for a little longer around 16 months. A more approachable red, Anjoli, comes from younger vines. (DM)

Recommended Reds:
Priorat Terra d'Hom ★★★★☆ £F

>> Aroa Bodegas (Navarra) *www.aroawines.com*
Small and impressive organically farmed bodega, cultivating 20 ha of vineyard. There are a range of red and white grapes planted and spread across seven separate vineyards in the Tierra Estella subzone of Navarra where the soils are dominated by clay and limestone. The white Laia is an attractive nutty cool fermented style with clean fresh citrus character. The Larrosa rosado gets 36 hours of maceration on skins and has just sufficient structure to work well with food or on its own, albeit the alcohol is fairly high around 14%. The Mutiko red offers lots of bright, vibrant berry fruit, with a cool fermentation and a relatively short period on skins. The second tier Jauna red is denser and fuller with bigger, firmer tannins. Ageing is in oak for 18 months after a separate vinification of each variety. The top label Gorena is impressive with a rich, concentrated berry fruit structure and supple finely polished tannins. The final composition will depend on the best results in the vineyard and may change year by year. (DM)

Recommended Reds:
Navarra Gorena (Final blend varies) ★★★☆ £D
Navarra Jauna (Cabernet Sauvignon, Merlot, Tempranillo) ★★★ £C
Navarra Mutiko (Tempranillo, Merlot) ★★☆ £B
Recommended Whites:
Navarra Laia (Garnacha Blanca) ★★ £B
Recommended Rosés:
Navarra Larrosa (Garnacha, Tempranillo) ★★☆ £B

✿✿ Artadi (Rioja) *www.artadi.com*
This is the brand name of the Cosecheros Alaveses bodega and an impressive range of new-wave Rioja is produced here from 75ha of vineyards. The range includes a well-crafted regular red which sees no oak. A level up are the Viñas de Gain Crianza and the more expensive Pagos Viejos Reserva. Both are rich, ripe and concentrated reds. There are also two other very impressive Reservas: Viña El Pisón comes from a single vineyard whereas the Grandes Añadas is a very limited special bottling. Both are very pricey. A fine modern source of Rioja, the company also now has an investment in the newly established Navarra property Artazu and in particular the old-vine Garnacha Santa Cruz de Artazu as well as some vibrant new Monastrell based reds from Alicante at El Seque. (DM)

Artadi
Recommended Reds:
Rioja Viña El Pisón ✪✪✪✪✪ £H   Rioja Grandes Añadas ★★★★☆ £G
Rioja Pagos Viejos ★★★★ £E   Rioja Viñas de Gain ★★★☆ £D
Rioja Joven ★★★ £C
Artazu
Recommended Reds:
Navarra Santa Cruz de Artazu ★★★★ £E
Navarra Pasos de San Martin ★★★ £C
El Sequé
Recommended Reds:
Alicante El Sequé ★★★★ £E

Artevino (Rioja) *www.grupoartevino.com*
This group of bodegas based in Rioja are producing some excellent results not only in Rioja but also in Ribera del Duero and Toro. Finca Villacreces is a source of some of the best wine in the Ribera DO. The vineyard is planted to Tinto Fino (Tempranillo), Merlot and Cabernet Sauvignon. As well as the regular red an additional and very pricey super-cuvée, Nebro, is also made in tiny quantities and now also an approachable young wine Pruno. At Vetus there are 20 ha under cultivation and the old vines here benefit from being grown at an altitude of up to 700 metres. The Vetus label is a big characterful example of the appellation being aged for 12 months in a mix of French and American oak. There is also a more forward Flor de Vetus and a premium Celsus is also produced. Of the two Rioja bodegas, Izadi's vineyards are planted in the Rioja Alavesa in the foothills of the Sierra Cantabria. The barrel-fermented white is mainly Viura with a touch of Malvasia, the supple approachable Crianza is blended from Tempranillo, Graciano and Mazuelo, the Reserva El Regalo is a touch more complex coming from Graciano and Garnacha in addition to Tempranillo. The top red Expresion comes from the oldest Tempranillo and is dense and elegant. Orben is the newest project of the group producing a modern styled Tempranillo from a selection of small parcels as well as an impressive richly textured premium red, Malpuesto. (DM)

Bodegas Izadi
Recommended Reds:

Rioja Expresión ★★★★ £F   Rioja Reserva El Regalo ★★★☆ £D
Rioja Crianza ★★★ £C
Recommended Whites:
Rioja Barrel Fermented ★★★ £C
Bodegas Orben
Recommended Reds:
Rioja Malpuesta ★★★★☆ £F   Rioja Orben ★★★☆ £E
Finca Villacreces
Recommended Reds:
Ribera del Duero Finca Villacreces Reserva ★★★★ £E
Ribera del Duero Finca Villacreces Pruno ★★☆ £C
Vetus
Recommended Reds:
Toro ★★★☆ £D   Toro Flor de Vetus ★★★ £C
Recommended Whites:
Rueda Flor de Vetus ★★★ £C

Bodegas Ateca (Calatayud) *www.bodegasateca.es*
Another small bodega in the Gil family's group. Other stars include EL NIDO in Jumilla and CAN BLAU in Montsant. Here at Ateca the potential shown in producing great value Garnacha from old bush-vines is very well expressed with slick Australian winemaking. The bodega was founded recently in 2005 and can draw on fruit from around 55 ha of vineyards. The slatey soils and over 50 year old vines add much to quality. The Honoro Vera Garnacha is a vibrant fruit driven style whereas the other two wines offer greater depth and some structure, particularly the Armas which is raised in barrels for 18 months. A white Rueda Honoro Vera is also made here from Verdejo. (DM)

Recommended Reds:
Calatayud Atteca Armas ★★★★ £E   Calatayud Atteca ★★★☆ £C
Calarayud Honoro Vera Garnacha ★★☆ £B

>> Bioenos (Cariñena) *www.bioenos.com*
This small operation produces just one wine from the rare Crespiello, or locally Vidadillo indigenous grape. Bioenos itself is principally a chemical wine analysis company, the wine bodega being established in 2001. The company have also been involved during the last couple of decades in the work to recover other grape varieties, including Tinta de Toro, Bobal and Albillo. The red is a rich round and characterful wine with dark fruits, herbs and spice notes all present. (DM)
Recommended Reds:
Cariñena Pulchrum (Crespiello) ★★★☆ £C

Bodegas Borsao (Campo de Borja) *www.bodegasborsao.com*
Long-established operation with over 400 members who between them control 1,450 ha of vineyards. It has justifiably been regarded as a source of well-made and well-priced regional Spanish reds. The fresh fruit driven Selección Tinto blends Garnacha with Syrah. More seriously structured are the Barrica and Reserva Selección labels. The Barrica, from Garnacha and Syrah is aged in French oak for three months, the Reserva, which includes Cabernet Sauvignon as well as Tempranillo, in a majority of French barrels for around 17 months. The most exciting wine, though, is the 100% Garnacha, Tres Picos, sourced from vineyards up to 60 years of age. A wine of structure and depth, offering complex dark berry fruit and aromas of herbal spices. (DM)
Recommended Reds:
Campo de Borja Tres Picos ★★★ £C

North-East Spain

Campo de Borja Reserva Selección ★★☆ £C
Campo de Borja Barrica Selección ★★ £B
Campo de Borja Selección ★☆ £B

Burgos Porta (Priorat) www.massinen.com

Husband and wife team Salvador Burgos and Conxita Porta have a total of 15 ha outside the village of Poboleda which are planted on steep terraces on the local Llicorella (schist) soils. The vineyards being up to 500 metres above sea level provide good natural acidity in the grapes and balance in the resulting wines. The vines, which are farmed organically, vary in age with the oldest up to 50 years. Just two wines are produced in the old stone winery, Negré a blend of Garnacha, Cabernet Sauvignon, Cariñena and a small amount of Syrah from a mix of young and old vines. It offers impressive smoky, spicy and dark berry and plummy fruit and good depth and persistence. The top wine, the dark-fruited and mineral Coster is a reserve bottling from roughly half Garnacha and half Cariñena from old vines and a smattering of Cabernet adding a subtle firm edge to the wines structure. Both are aged for 12 months in mainly French oak, with just a little American. Expect the Negré to show well within three or four years the Coster a little longer. (DM)

Recommended Reds:
Priorat Mas Sinén Coster ★★★★☆ £F
Priorat Mas Sinén Negré ★★★★ £F

>> Ca N'Estruc - Uvas Felices (Cataluña) www.canestruc.com

Made in partnership with Barcelona wine merchant Vila Viniteca, Francisco Marti Badia runs this 22 ha property with vineyards planted in a sheltered site protected from northerly winds by the Monserrat mountains. Modern wire trellising is used and a green harvest practiced before veraison to reduce yields and improve flavour intensity. Of the reds, Idoia Negre gets 12 months in French oak, while the Idoia Blanc is a mixed blend, which is barrel fermented. There are also two pricier wines under the L'Equilibrista label, a white and a red Garnatxa as well as entry level rosado and blancos. (DM)

Recommended Reds:
Cataluña L'Equilibrista (Syrah, Cariñena, Garnacha) ★★★☆ £C
Cataluña Idoia Negre (Syrah, Cab. Sauv, Garnacha) ★★★ £C
Cataluña Negre (Cabernet Sauvignon, Syrah) ★★ £B
Recommended Whites:
Cataluña Idoia Blanco (Xarello, Macabeo, others) ★★☆ £C

❁ Cellers Can Blau (Montsant) www.cellerscanblau.es

Based in the village of Mas Roig this newly established operation has 35 ha comprising Cariñena planted on sandy/clay soils, Garnacha on slate and Syrah on chalk. Nuria López Sarroca is in charge of crafting wines of splendid elegance as well as intensity. The Can Blau is dark, smokey and full of rich sweet fruit, the Mas de Can Blau more intense and complex, with a marked old-viney quality as well as a piercing minerality underpinning the wine. Both are bottled unfined and unfiltered. A more forward fruit driven example Blau is also made. (DM)

Recommended Reds:
Montsant Mas de Can Blau ★★★★ £F
Montsant Can Blau ★★★☆ £E
Montsant Blau ★★☆ £C

Can Grau Vell (Cataluña) www.grauvell.cat

Small but very impressive Cataluña property producing three wines, the top label Alcor is a red blend of persuasive depth and concentration. As is the case with so much of modern Spanish viticulture this a recently established project. The vineyards were planted in 2002 and there are around 3 ha cultivated. The soils are a mix of slate stones and clay but most important they are well drained and are planted at a density of 6,500 vines per hectare. Not the level of a close planted Bordeaux vineyard but very good for achieving fruit concentration from a steeply aspected site. The wine itself is a dense, spicy dark-fruited blend of Syrah, Garnacha, Cabernet Sauvignon, Monastrell and Marcelan. Vinification and fermentation is mainly in 500 litre oak barrels (open topped) with punch downs, the balance in fibre glass tanks with the must pumped over. Malolactic is then in oak with the wine aged for 18 months. The regime of minimal contact involves just one racking and a light fining. There is a softer second label red, Tramp and a rosado Quike which is briefly barrel aged for four months. (DM)

Recommended Reds:
Cataluña Can Grau Vell Alcor ★★★★ £E

❁ Can Rafols dels Caus (Penedes) www.canrafolsdelscaus.com

This is among the very best sources of Penedes and Cava, in particular a number of stunning white wines. Carlos Esteva began restoring the vineyards on the old family estate in 1979 after they had fallen into a state of some disrepair. His key to success is the approach in the vineyards which are farmed organically and pruning and harvesting is all done manually. The vineyards are located around 15 kms inland from the Mediterranean and enjoy a maritime climate and benefit from an altitude of 300 metres as well as cooling sea breezes. The terroir is ideal for high quality wine production with sparse and well-drained rocky soils with traces of limestone. The whites are particularly striking with a piercing minerality present in all the wines. Gran Caus is Xarello, Chardonnay and Chenin,Xarello Pairal 100 % varietal from a single vineyard, La Calma unusually Chenin Blanc and from a single vineyard with a very calcareous soil emphasised by the intense citrus and mineral qualities of the wine. The top wine here though is the brilliant EL Rocallís, rich nutty and concentrated as well as maintaining that mineral character. It comes from the rare Incroccio Manzoni. The Gran Caus rosado comes from Merlot and has sufficient structure to work well with food. The Gran Caus red is a Bordeaux style red blend of the two Cabernets and Merlot with some cedary complexity, Ad Fines a varietal Pinot Noir and the Caus Lubis a varietal Merlot of real dark, plummy depth and concentration. A number of other reds are also available, including a special limited release red 30 Aniversario. Entry level wines are also produced under the Petit Caus label along with three Cavas. (DM)

Recommended Reds:
Penedès Caus Lubis ★★★☆ £E   Penedès Ad Fines ★★★ £E
Penedès Gran Caus ★★☆ £D
Recommended Whites:
Penedès El Rocallís ★★★★☆ £E   Penedès La Calma ★★★★ £E
Penedès Xarel.lo Pairal ★★★★ £E   Penedès Gran Caus ★★★ £D
Cava Gran Caus ★★★ £C
Recommended Rosés:
Cava Gran Caus ★★☆ £C

Luis Cañas (Rioja) www.luiscanas.com

This substantial Rioja bodega produces a comprehensive and fine range both under the Luis Cañas label and under the premium Bodegas Amaren label where the wines are vinified in a separate facility. The vineyards are auspiciously sited in the heart of the Rioja Alavesa around the small town of Villabuena. There are around 120 ha under vine planted on a mix of clay and limestone. Tempranillo is

very much the dominant red variety although Graciano, Garnacha and Mazuelo are also grown. Viura is the only white variety the firm cultivates. The Luis Cañas wines are available at a range of price-points. There is one white under the Luis Canas label, which is barrel-fermented in new French oak. Among the reds the Crianza is the most approachable with a short three months in barrel, mainly French. The Reserva is denser and richer with concentrated blackberry fruit its texture and structure gained from 18 months in wood. The Reserva Selección de Familia is a prime selection which gets 24 months in new French oak and offers more complexity and concentration. The Gran Reserva is generally available on the market at close to 10 years of age. More evolved and elegant in style it still offers attractive dark cherry fruit and is approachable and will keep well for half a decade after release. Four wines are produced under the premium Amaren label. There is a barrel fermented white from older vines which is mainly Viura with a little Malvasia, a red blend Angeles de Amaren, a blend of Tempranillo and Graciano aged in a combination of French and American oak. Both the Amaren Tempranillo Reserva and Amaren Graciano are thoroughly modern in style with a rich texture following malolactic in barrel. The Graciano a touch denser and offering more dark-fruit. The pinnacle here though is the super-premium Hiro 3 Racimos, a blend of all four of the bodegas red varieties. Very deeply coloured in its youth with dark cherry and intense blackberry fruit it is a thoroughly modern style of Rioja requiring at least 5 years cellaring. (DM)

Amaren
Recommended Reds:
Rioja Tempranillo Reserva ★★★☆ £F   Rioja Graciano ★★★☆ £F
Rioja Angeles de Amaren ★★☆ £C
Recommended Whites:
Rioja Blanco ★★★ £E

Luis Cañas
Recommended Reds:
Rioja Hiro 3 Racimos ★★★★☆ £G   Rioja Gran Reserva ★★★☆ £E
Rioja Selección de Familia ★★★☆ £E   Rioja Reserva ★★★ £D
Rioja Crianza ★★☆ £C
Recommended Whites:
Rioja Fermentado En Barrica ★★ £C

Cellers Capafons-Ossó (Montsant) *www.capafons-osso.com*
This operation has two estates, one in Montsant and the second in Priorat, with a total of some 30ha under vine. Three wines are produced at the Masia Esplanes cellars in Montsant. A juicy, forward rosé, Roigenc, is 100% Syrah cool-fermented with 8 hours of skin contact. The Vessants red, a blend of Merlot, Garnacha, Cabernet Sauvignon and Cariñena, and the denser and more structured Masia Esplanes, blended from Cabernet Sauvignon, Merlot, Garnacha and Syrah, are aged for 10 to 12 months in French and American oak. Both wines are dominated by dark and spicy fruit rather than the more mineral, *sauvage* character often found in neighbouring Priorat. A white from the DO Ca, Enllac, is produced as well as three reds. Sirsell is a newly released fruit-driven blend which is softer and lighter than its stablemates. The Masos d'en Cubells is the more approachable of the two top wines. The Mas de Masos, is impressively rich, concentrated and darkly-spicy. Both have a subtle mineral undercurrent which is less ferocious than some. (DM)
Recommended Reds:
Priorat Masos de Masos ★★★★ £E
Priorat Masos d'En Cubells ★★★☆ £D
Priorat Sirsell ★★★ £C   Montsant Masia Esplanes ★★★☆ £D
Montsant Vessants ★★☆ £C

Recommended Rosés:
Montsant Roigenc ★★ £C

Celler de Capçanes (Montsant) *www.cellercapcanes.com*
One of Spain's finest co-operatives, established way back in 1933, it is also among the best in Europe. It was really only in 1995 that high quality was achieved as a result of the production of a remakable Kosher wine, Flor de Primavera. This initiative was promoted by the Jewish community of Barcelona who wished to produce a high-quality wine under strict Lo mebushal conditions, with everything carried out by a rabbi (with guidance) and no pasteurisation of the wine. It has evolved into a splendid pure Garnacha from old vines ranging from 85 to 105 years of age. Two further kosher reds are also made. With the resulting new investment that this development brought the range of reds here is now extensive and generally very impressive. The 120-strong membership provides some splendid old-vine Garnacha, Tempranillo and Cariñena as well as Merlot, Syrah and Cabernet Sauvignon, drawing on close to 250 ha of vineyards. The top-labelled reds are now classified under the recently established Monsant DO. Among the best wines are two ripe, berry-fruited styles, Mas Collet which sees some oak and Mas Donís Barrica, both have a big dollop of Garnacha. Mas Donís has some Syrah adding firm, tannic depth. Costers del Gravet is fuller and more structured – a blend of Cabernet Sauvignon, Garnacha, Cariñena and Tempranillo – but the tannin can be a touch raw in its youth. The Vall de Calàs, a blend of Merlot, Garnacha and Tempranillo is suppler and rounder with dark plum fruit. The top two wines, Mas Tortò and Cabrida, are both markedly extracted, dense and powerful reds. The former is dominated by old-vine Garnacha, with Cabernet Sauvignon and Syrah lending structure and perfume. Cabrida, 100% very old vine Garnacha (some close to 100 years), is macerated on skins for 4–5 weeks and has a modern touch with malolactic in barrel, most of the oak being French. It is immensely concentrated, just lacking that element of extra refinement for true greatness but very impressive and ageworthy nonetheless. All of the wines offer excellent value for money. (DM)
Recommended Reds:
Montsant Cabrida ★★★★ £E   Montsant Flor de Primavera ★★★☆ £D
Montsant Mas Tortò ★★★☆ £C   Montsant Costers del Gravet ★★★ £C
Montsant Vall de Calàs ★★☆ £B   Montsant Mas Collet ★★ £B
Montsant Mas Donís ★☆ £B

>> Cartoixa de Montsalvat (Priorat) *www.cellerscartoixa.com*
Francesc Sánchez-Bas established this small bodega with 8 ha in 1996 and produces three excellent wines. The Blanc de Montsalvat is barrel fermented and then kept in barrel with lees stirring for between three and five months. It has an attractive creamy, nutty texture with nicely balanced fresh citrus acidity. Montgarnatx with a touch more Garnacha is dark, savoury and complex with its Cariñena component being around 70 years old, ageing is for 8 to 10 months in 2 and 3 year old barrels to preserve its fruit character. The top red the Montsalvat is also marked by a rich, dark old-viney savoury, spicy quality. The blend here is dominated by very old Cariñena. The wine spends around 14 months in new French oak which is nicely judged. (DM)
Recommended Reds:
Priorat Montsalvat ★★★★☆ £F   Priorat Montgarnatx ★★★★ £E
Recommended Whites:
Priorat Blanc de Montsalvat ★★★★ £E

North-East Spain

Spain

⚙ Castell d'Encus (Costers del Segre) *www.encus.org*
Small property which is fast becoming a benchmark for the DO. It was established in 2001 by Raul Bobet, who had spent a decade and a half with TORRES. Just 23 of the 90 ha have been cleared of forest and planted at high density to a range of both red and white grape varieties. The vineyards are found at high altitude, up to 1,000 metres and the wines traditionally vinified in stone. The intention is not to produce above 6,000 cases a year and make wines solely from estate grown grapes. Four whites and three reds are currently made. SO2 like the Taleia is a blend of Sauvignon Blanc and Sémillon. Taika is a sparkling white with the bottle fermentation occuring naturally. Both the Ekam and Taleia are impressive. The Ekam Riesling and Albariño blend which has a touch of botrytis, is cool fermented to preserve and lift its aromatic qualitities, whereas the Graves style Taleia is part barrel fermented. The top three reds are all impressive, the Quest (Cabernet Sauvignon, Cabernet Franc, Petit Verdot and Merlot) and Thalarn, a varietal Syrah vinified in a mix of stone and wooden vats as well as stainless steel. Like the Acusp Pinot Noir they undergo the malolactic fermentation in barrel. (DM)

Recommended Reds:
Costers del Segre Acusp ★★★★ £E
Costers del Segre Quest ★★★★ £E
Costers del Segre Thalarn ★★★★ £E
Recommended Whites:
Costers del Segre Ekam ★★★☆ £D
Costers del Segre Taleia ★★★☆ £D

Castell del Remei (Costers del Segre) *www.castelldelremei.com*
Good to very good reds are made at Castell del Remei along with Blanc Panell, a tank-fermented blend of Macabeo, Sauvignon Blanc and Chardonnay, and Oda Blanc, which is vinified and aged on lees for six months in American oak. The reds really stand out. Gotim Bru is a ripe, forward blend of Tempranillo, Merlot and Cabernet Sauvignon with a spicy hint of cinnamon from 10 months' ageing in American wood, which is used for all the Castell del Remei reds. Oda is denser and more structured, a blend of Merlot, Cabernet Sauvignon and Tempranillo. The top label, 1780, is a firmly structured blend of Cabernet Sauvignon, Tempranillo and Merlot. Excellent results are also now being achieved at a separate property Cérvoles Celler. The fine and ripe darkfruited Cérvoles Negre blends Cabernet Sauvignon and Tempranillo with some Garnacha and Merlot, whereas the richer and more sumptuous Cérvoles Estrats has no Merlot in its blend and the Cabernet which dominates provides a firm and structured cedary undercurrent. A barrel fermented white is also made as well as two lower priced wines a white and a red both labelled Colors. (DM)

Castell del Remei
Recommended Reds:
Costers del Segre 1780 ★★★ £D   Costers del Segre Oda ★★☆ £C
Costers del Segre Gotim Bru ★★ £C

Cérvoles Celler
Recommended Reds:
Costers del Segre Cérvoles Estrats ★★★★ £E
Costers del Segre Cérvoles ★★★ £D

>> Castillo de Monjardín (Navarra) *www.monjardin.es*
This winery was founded in 1988 by winemaker Victor del Villar Tolosa with his wife Sonia Olano. They make well-made modern stylish wines of good value. The property is found in the northwest of the region, in the foothills of the Pyrenees with 220 ha planted at a significant altitude of around 600 metres helping promote a fresh edge and the warm summers are moderated by the "Cierzo" wind. Eleven wines are made in all and as well as those wines reviewed below there is a Pinot Noir from old vines, a rosado, Lagrima and a late harvest white Esencia Monjardín, from Chardonnay. Three other Chardonnays are made. There is a fruit driven unoaked style, El Cerezo. The Barrique example offers a richer texture, after a slow fermentation it is aged on lees for four months. Reserva Special Selección offers a touch more intensity with zesty subtle citrus fruit and the ability to develop nicely in bottle for up to half a decade. The Monjardín Clasico is a young wine style Tempranillo which gets a short four month period in barrel. Bright and forward with attractive red berry fruits. Crianza Coupage Selección combines Cabernet Sauvignon, Tempranillo and Merlot. There are well-developed berry fruits and a hint of mint and oak spice from 12 months in *barrique*. The old vine Garnacha is full of character with red and black fruits and a spicy herb scented quality. The vineyard is now 70 years old and planted, like most of the red varieties a little lower than the Chardonnay and Pinot Noir plots. The rich, dense and structured Reserva comes solely from the Los Carasoles site. Dominated by Cabernet Sauvignon with a little Tempranillo it is aged for two and a half years in barrel providing a supple and approachable as well as finely structured red. (DM)

Recommended Reds:
Navarra Reserva Los Carasoles ★★★☆ £D
Navarra Garnacha Old Vines ★★★☆ £C
Navarra Merlot Deyo ★★★ £C
Navarra Crianza Coupage Selección ★★★ £C
Navarra Monjardín Clasico ★☆ £B
Recommended Whites:
Navarra Chardonnay Reserva Special Selección ★★★☆ £D
Navarra Chardonnay Barrique ★★★ £C
Navarra El Cerezo Chardonnay ★★ £B

Castillo Perelada (Empordà) *www.perelada.com*
This is a substantial operation producing an extensive range of wines from the DO as well as a number of Cavas. Wine is not the only product with olive oils, vinegars and marc also made. Origins of winemaking here date back to the middle-ages although three generations of the Mateu family have run the estate since 1923. Over the past two decades the family have focussed above all on quality. Approachable fruit-driven wines are made as well as a number of varietal examples. Among the whites are a Garnacha, labelled Garnatxa Blanca, a Chardonnay and a Sauvignon Blanc. A Rosado comes from Cabernet Sauvignon. There is a vibrant Cabernet varietal red which is vinified at controlled temperatures and aged for up 16 months in a mix of American and French oak. The 3 (Garnatxa, Samsó, Cabernet Sauvignon and Merlot) and 5 Fincas (Cabernet Sauvignon, Garnatxa, Merlot, Syrah and Samsó) are respectively crianza and reserva styles. The 3 Fincas is more Mediterranean in style, the 5 Fincas more international. Both are aged in a mix of French and American wood. The bodega also produces four single vineyard wines from three sites. Finca Espolla is a blend of Monastrell and Syrah. From Finca La Garriga come both a red from Samsó and a white which is a blend of Cariñena, Chardonnay and Sauvignon Blanc. The spicy, dark-fruited red Garriga is from over 50 year old vines grown in silt, sand and gravel soils. It sees 16 months in American oak. The spicy, plummy Finca Malaveïna by contrast lends its style more to the Right Bank of Bordeaux and as such is aged in French rather than American wood. It combines Merlot, Cabernet Sauvignon, Syrah and Garnatxa. At the pinnacle

of the range both the Finca Garbet and Gran Claustro, which is a combination of Cabernet Sauvignon, Merlot, Garnatxa and Samsó, command high prices. The Garbet vineyard is solely planted to Syrah and the 7 ha directly overlook the Mediterranean. It is dense and concentrated although modern vinification with an extended 30 day maceration and hand plunging provides a rich dark-fruited and approachable red. The Gran Claustro is an impressive cedary red. An Ex Ex Colección red has been produced from an experimental vineyard and from a number of varieties. Examples have been made generally as a single varietal although the Ex Ex 1 and Ex Ex 5 have been blends. A number of very limited reds are also released under the Homage label and a late harvest wine, Garnatxa de l'Empordà is made from a mix of both red and white Garnacha. Perelada also own two Priorat bodegas, CIMS DE PORRERA and Casa Gran de Siurana.. (DM)

Recommended Reds:
Empordà Gran Claustro ★★★★ £F Empordà Finca Garbet ★★★★ £F
Empordà 5 Fincas Reserva ★★★ £D
Empordà Finca La Garriga ★★★☆ £D
Empordà Finca Malaveina ★★★ £D
Empordà Cabernet Sauvignon ★★☆ £C
Empordà 3 Fincas Crianza ★★ £C

Recommended Whites:
Cava Gran Claustro Vintage ★★★ £D Cava Brut Reserva NV ★★ £B

Recommended Rosés:
Cava Brut Rosado NV ★ £B

Castillo de Sajazarra (Rioja & Alella) *www.castillodesajazarra.com*
Fine Rioja red and an excellent white Alella, In Vita from Pansa Blanca and Sauvignon Blanc are produced here. A new rosado In Vita has also been added to the range. Among the Rioja reds there are Kosher wines produced with ELVI WINES from Ribera del Júcar, Herenza Kosher Crianza and Mati Kosher Semi Crianza. Sajazarra itself is just to the west of Haro in the northern stretches of the Rioja Alta. There are 49 ha under vine in Rioja, planted in calcareous and clay soils, 42 ha of which are Tempranillo and spread across 24 separate plots, which are all conveniently close to the bodega winery. The majority of the range is aged traditionally but the hallmark here is the attractive and approachable quality of the wine's fruit. The red cherry Vega Saja Crianza is aged in a mix of French and American oak, as is the Solar de Líbano. Both the Reservas are a step up. The cherry and vanilla scented Solar de Libano Reserva is, like the Crianza, a blend of Tempranillo, Graciano, Garnacha and a more traditional style spending 24 months in American barrels. The Castillo de Sajazarra Reserva is a touch rounder, more opulent. French and American wood is used and a small proportion of the wine is put through the malolactic fermentation in barrel. The top wine, Digma, like the Reserva solely from Tempranillo, is a modern style coming from a selection of the best fruit from two separate estates which are vinified separately. Elegant, stylish and supple the wine goes through the malolactic and is then aged in the French oak for just 14 months. A Digma Graciano is also now made. The Rioja reds are bottled unfiltered. (DM)

Recommended Reds:
Rioja Digma ★★★★☆ £F Rioja Reserva ★★★★ £E
Rioja Solar de Líbano Reserva ★★★☆ £D
Rioja Vega Saja Crianza ★★★ £C
Rioja Solar de Líbano Crianza ★★☆ £C

Recommended Whites:
Alella In Vita ★★★ £B

Recommended Rosés:
Alella In Vita ★★ £B

>> Chivite (Navarra) *www.chivite.com / www.granfeudo.es*
This substantial producer now produces wines under two separate banners, Chivite and the more economically priced Gran Feudo label. It is a substantial family owned bodega and one of the most important commercially in Navarra, based in the Ribera Baja subzone. As well as the wines here in Navarra, the bodega has interests in Rioja at Viña Salceda, produces a new Finca de Villatuerta premium range and owns the single Pago property Señorío de Arínzano in northern Navarra. At Chivite there is a substantial vineyard holding with plots owned in Rueda and Ribera del Duero now as well as in Navarra and the firm has a number of modern wine making facilities. The entry level wines take the Gran Feudo label and there is a Gran Feudo Edición label, where the wines are a touch more modern in style. The top Chivite wines go under the Colección 125 banner. The rosado is fresh and vibrant, a combination of Garnacha, Tempranillo and Merlot. Chardonnay ranges from forward and fruit driven, Gran Feudo, more complex and intense Gran Feudo Edición to rich and concentrated Colección 125. There are varietal as well as blended reds. Under the Edición banner there is a Crianza combining Tempranillo, Merlot and Cabernet Sauvignon with vibrant and soft red berry fruit. The Gran Feudo Reserva is a more evolved blend of Tempranillo, Cabernet Sauvignon and Merlot. The Gran Feudo Viñas Viejas is a Reserva style from Tempranillo and Garnacha offering real depth and a dark, spicy and berry fruit complexity. Aged solely in French oak it comes from vines planted between 1940 and 1960. The top red is the finely structured, rich and concentrated Colección 125. It comes solely from Tempranillo and barrel ageing is well judged, the wine spending around 14 months in French oak, just under half of it new. A Colección 125 Rosado is also now made from Tempranillo as well as a late harvest white from Moscatel. (DM)

Chivite
Recommended Reds:
Navarra Colección 125 Reserva ★★★☆ £D
Recommended Whites:
Navarra Colección 125 Blanco ★★★ £D

Gran Feudo
Recommended Reds:
Navarra Gran Feudo Vinas Viejas Reserva ★★★ £C
Navarra Gran Feudo Edición Crianza ★★☆ £C
Navarra Gran Feudo Reserva ★★ £B
Recommended Whites:
Navarra Gran Feudo Edición Chardonnay ★★☆ £B
Navarra Gran Feudo Chardonnay ★★ £B
Recommended Rosés:
Navarra Gran Feudo Edición Rosado ★★ £B

Cims de Porrera (Priorat)
One of an increasing number of top-quality performers from this small but great appellation. There are 55ha of vines here, producing a firmly structured, rich and concentrated Priorat, Clàssic dominated by Cariñena blended with Garnacha and just a touch of Cabernet Sauvignon. It is dark, spicy and beguiling in its fiery complexity. There are also two small-scale varietal labels Clàssic Garnatxa and Clàssic Caranyana. There is a good, much more forward second wine, Solanes. Produced from younger vines, it will provide an exciting example of what the DO has to offer at a relatively affordable price. (DM)

North-East Spain

Recommended Reds:
Priorat Clàssic ★★★★☆ £F Priorat Solanes ★★★☆ £E

❂ **Clos d'Agon (Cataluña)** www.closdagon.com
This small bodega is located in the far north-east of the country on the granite plateau of Girona and the vineyards are just a few kilometres from the Mediterranean coast and just south of the French border. The property is owned by a group of Swiss friends who retain Peter Sisseck (who vinifies PINGUS) as a consultant. The gravel, clay and granite soils and the maritime influence on the local mesoclimate provide an excellent environment for cultivating the Bordeaux red varieties. Clos d'Agon Tinto is a mix of Cabernet Sauvignon, Merlot and some Syrah amd a little Petit Verdot. The second wine Valmaña is good if quite a bit lighter and from a similar blend. A little stylish, barrel-fermented white is also made which is a nutty, peachy, citrus scented mix of Viognier, Roussanne and Marsanne. A tinta, a blanca and a rosado are also made under the Amic label from Garnacha Tinta and Blanca. (DM)
Recommended Reds:
Cataluña Clos d'Agon ★★★★ £E Cataluña Clos Valmaña ★★★ £D
Recommended Whites:
Cataluña Clos d'Agon ★★★ £D

Clos Figueras (Priorat) www.closfigueras.com
This is the home estate of Bordeaux-based wine broker Christopher Cannan, who also owns the excellent Montsant operation, Celler LAURONA. Clos Figueras is an excellent example of old-vine Garnacha and Cariñena, which account for around 80% of its blend. The Cannans acquired the estate in 1997 on advice from René Barbier and 10 ha out of a total of 17 ha are planted on the famous licorella schistous soils. A second label, Font de la Figuera, is from younger vines and is softer, rounder and much more approachable. It has less Garnacha and Cariñena in the blend and includes more Syrah, Mourvèdre and Cabernet Sauvignon. There are also some Viognier vines and these contribute to the CLOS MOGADOR white Nelin as well as the home Font de la Figuera white blend. An additional young red is also now being made and is dominated by Garnacha. (DM)

Recommended Reds:
Priorat Clos Figueras ★★★★ £F Priorat Font de la Figuera ★★★ £D

❂ **Clos i Terrasses (Priorat)**
Very small but very impressive 10 ha Priorat property established in 1989 and one of a number of emerging operations that have transformed this small DO from rustic backwater to an important wine region. Two wines are made here: the top wine, Clos Erasmus, is a super-rich blend of Garnacha, Cabernet Sauvignon and Cariñena; the well-priced second wine, Laurel, is produced from the younger vines. Clos Erasmus is given extended ageing in new oak and is a massively dense, powerful and exotic style of red. It is both very concentrated and complex, but very firm and structured when young. (DM)
Recommended Reds:
Priorat Clos Erasmus ✪✪✪✪✪ £G Priorat Laurel ★★★★ £F

❂ **Clos Mogador (Priorat)** www.closmogador.com
Talented owner and winemaker René Barbier advises at a number of other wineries, including Daphne Glorian's CLOS I TERASSES, as well as producing wine here at his own 20-ha property. Clos Mogador is yet another super-rich, extracted, deep and dense example of this

exciting appellation. The blend is Garnacha, Cabernet Sauvignon, Syrah and, unusually, Pinot Noir, which just adds a piercingly fragrant note. A big, structured wine, it will develop very well with age. As well as producing his brilliant red, René Barbier has long been interested in making a benchmark white Priorat. The final blend for the wine is a fascinating mix of Garnacha Blanca, Viognier, Pinot Noir (vinified as a white) and a little Roussanne, Marsanne and Maccabeo. The plots are located at high altitude on the hill of Ermita, one of the great sites of the appellation. Viognier is also supplied by Christopher Cannan of CLOS FIGUERAS, who mistakenly planted it instead of Syrah. The wine is part vinified in oak and part in stainless steel and has great style and intensity. Barbier is also involved at Vinyes de MANYETES. (DM)
Recommended Reds:
Priorat Clos Mogador ★★★★★ £G
Recommended Whites:
Priorat Clos Nelin ★★★★☆ £F

>> **Clos Pons (Costers del Segre)** www.clospons.com
Winemaking at the Pons family's small property in the Garrigues subzone of Costers del Segre is a recent phenomenon, although they are long established olive growers. Indeed it is olive and almond trees that dominate the dry, somewhat arid landscape. There are just over 30 ha currently under vine with vineyards planted at around 700 metres promoting structure and fresh acidity. Four wines are produced, three reds and a characterful floral and citrus scented white Sisquella. This is barrel fermented and aged for a short time, four months, on fine lees helping to define the wines rich texture. The red Alges is the most approachable of the reds with attractive spicy black fruit and supple well balanced tannins. Ageing is for nine months in mainly French and a little American oak in a combination of new, second and third fill barrels. Roc Nu is bigger and more structured the tannins firmer. Full of rich, concentrated blackberry scented fruit and nicely judged oak the wine is aged for longer, around 14 months in new and one year old barrels. A further red Serie 800 is a special selection, solely from Marselan. (DM)
Recommended Reds:
Costers del Segre Roc Nu (Tempranillo, Garnacha, Cab Sauv) ★★★☆ £D
Costers del Segre Alges (Tempranillo, Garnacha, Syrah) ★★★ £C
Costers del Segre Jan Petit (Garnacha, Syrah) ★★ £B
Recommended Whites:
Costers del Segre Sisquella (Garnacha Bl, Albariño, Moscatel) ★★★ £C

Coca í Fitó (Montsant) www.cocaifito.com
This is a fine small new Montsant bodega producing a small range of wines both from their own vineyards and from bought in fruit. The second label wines take the Jaspi brand, whereas the estate wines are simply labelled Coca i Fitó. Their vineyards are spread amongst a number of villages within the Falset Valley. The soils are quite varied and this helps in adding complexity and character in the wines. Traces of limestone, granite, slate and clay are all present. The vines range from 15 to 80 years of age. The vines are all farmed ecologically and as you would expect the harvest is done manually by hand. Of the two Jaspi wines, the Negre is the softest and most approachable and very much in a fruit-driven style. It blends Grenache, Carignan, Cabernet Sauvignon and Syrah. It gets a straightforward three months in French and American oak. The Jaspi is a touch more structured, coming from 12 months in wood and comes from a similar blend although it has a little more Syrah. It has more of a meaty, savoury and spicy quality. There is a very well made rosado from the brothers own vineyards which comes 100 %

from Syrah and gets three months in barrel. This is very much a food wine style. The top wine is the very good Coca i Fitó which is rich and concentrated with dark, licoricey and spicy fruit. It blends 50% Syrah with old-vine Grenache and Carignan. It is aged for 12 months in barrel. A further red label Tocat de L'Ala is a joint venture coming from Empordà, showing real potential. Priorat is now made and a stylish and intense red now comes from Ribeira Sacra. (DM)

Coca i Fitó
Recommended Reds:
Montsant Negre Coca i Fitó ★★★★ £E
Montsant Dolç Coca i Fitó ★★★☆ £E
Recommended Rosés:
Montsant Rosa Coca i Fitó ★★☆ £C

Jaspi
Montsant Jaspi Maragda ★★★☆ £D
Montsant Jaspi Negre ★★★ £C
Recommended Whites:
Terra Alta Jaspi d'Or ★★☆ £C
Terra Alta Jaspi Blanc ★★☆ £C

Samsara
Recommended Reds:
Priorat Samsara ★★★☆ £E

Tocat de L'Ala
Recommended Reds:
Empordà Tocat i Posat ★★★☆ £E
Empordà Tocat de l'Ala ★★★ £D
Recommended Whites:
Empordà Tocat de l'Ala ★★★ £D

Tolo do Xisto
Recommended Reds:
Ribeira Sacra Tolo do Xisto ★★★☆ £E

❂ Contino (Rioja) www.cvne.com
Contino is part-owned by CVNE and the wines are made by them. Indeed this was among the pioneering "Château style" wineries established in the Rioja region. There is a total of some 60 ha of vineyards, 4ha of which are Graciano. There is an attractive Reserva red which has good depth and is supple and velvety in texture. A traditionally styled Gran Reserva adds greater depth and is unusually available only in magnums. This along with a big dollop of Graciano will enable the wine to develop nicely in bottle. As well as these, there is a Blanco which is *sin crianza* in style and is a blend of Viura, Malvasia and Garnacha Blanca. The top two reds are among the best in the region and both are single vineyard wines. The Viña del Olivo comes from a blend of roughly 90% Tempranillo and the balance Graciano. It is a modern style with the malolactic taking place in French oak with further ageing for 15 months. The Graciano is similarly fermented in large French oak vats and then aged in new French and Hungarian oak. These are both impressive, structured ageworthy reds. (DM)

Recommended Reds:
Rioja Graciano ★★★★★ £G   Rioja Viña del Olivo ★★★★★ £G
Rioja Gran Reserva ★★★★☆ £F   Rioja Reserva ★★★☆ £E

Costers del Siurana (Priorat) www.costersdelsiurana.com
Sizeable operation by Priorat standards with 40 ha of estate vineyards. Carlos Pastrana was one of the earlier pioneers of the appellation, establishing his estate in the 1980s. Of the wines the dense and powerful Clos de l'Obac is a dark, fiery and impressively structured blend of Garnacha and Cabernet Sauvignon in equal parts, with a little Merlot, Syrah and Carineña. Dolç de l'Obac is an

unusual sweet red blended from Syrah, Garnacha and Cabernet Sauvignon. The Miserere bottling is a blend of Cabernet Sauvignon, Garnacha, Tempranillo and Merlot as well as Cariñena. It is lighter with reasonable depth and a soft rounded structure but, while good, has a leaner edge than others. A white Kyrie, from a blend of Garnacha Blanca, Macabeu, Xarel.lo and Muscat of Alexandria is also made. (DM)

Recommended Reds:
Priorat Dolç de l'Obac ★★★★ £F   Priorat Clos de l'Obac ★★★★ £F
Priorat Miserere ★★★☆ £E

Tomas Cusiné (Costers del Segre) www.tomascusine.com
Tomas Cusiné had spent twenty years working with his family property CASTELL DEL REMEI before deciding to branch out and produce two excellent reds from two small sites acquired in the north of the DO on land neighbouring Montsant and Conca de Barbera. He now has 29 ha under vine and plans to expand this to around 40 ha. The vineyard sites are at an altitude of around 700m and the strong diurnal swing in temperature ensures good acidity in his grapes whilst also being able to harvest at a good level of phenolic ripeness. As well as four Costers del Segre reds he also makes three fine whites, a fresh lightly mineral and fruity Auzells from a range of white varieties including Macabeu, Parellada and Sauvignon Blanc and a close to varietal Macabeu (it has a tiny amount of Albariño), Finca Racons. Auzells gets a touch of barrel-fermentation and is aged on lees. The third white Finca La Serra is a single vineyard Chardonnay. Of the reds, which are given a pre-fermentation cold-soak, Llebre is a fruit driven blend of Tempranillo, Merlot, Cabernet Sauvignon, Garnacha, Cariñena and Syrah. Villosell blends Tempranillo with Syrah. It is ripe brambly and forward. The Geol is firmer, a touch more structured but with a fine rounded quality to its tannins. The blend here comprises Samsó, Merlot and Cabernet Sauvignon. The malolactic takes place in barrel. The fourth red, Finca Comabarra combines Garnacha, Syrah and Cabernet Sauvignon. Under the Cataluña DO an attractive red blending Cariñena, Garnacha and Syrah, Dràc Magic is made along with a white. From high altitude vineyards in the Conca de Barberà DO come red and white labelled Cara Nord, the red a Rhône style blend offering impressive dark and spicy berry fruit and a characterful mineral edge. The top reds will drink very well with 3-4 years' age. (DM)

Recommended Reds:
Costers del Segre Geol ★★★☆ £E   Costers del Segre Villosell ★★★ £D
Costers del Segre Llebre ★★☆ £C
Conca de Barberà Cara Nord ★★★ £C
Cataluña Dràc Magic ★★☆ £C
Recommended Whites:
Costers del Segre Finca Racons ★★★ £C
Costers del Segre Auzells ★★★ £C

❂ CVNE (Rioja) www.CVNE.com
This firm make some of the most traditional styles of Rioja under a number of brand umbrellas. Cune, Monopole, Real de Asúa and Imperial labels are produced at the Cune bodega, Viña Real and the single estate CONTINO reds in separate wineries. There is also a separate cellar within a cellar where the Real de Asúa and Imperial wines are vinified and aged. The firm is one of the oldest in the region and was established in 1879. The fifth generation of the founding family are still involved in the management of the operation. The majority of the Cune *terroir* is found in the Rioja Alta, the westernmost of the three sub-zones. From here they

North-East Spain

obtain close to half of their red grape requirements from a mix of calcareous and alluvial soils. The Vina Real vineyards are found on the Cerro de la Mesa hill in the heart of the Rioja Alavesa. Monopole is Spain's oldest white wine brand. It is now a modern, fresh style produced solely from Viura and cool fermented in stainless steel. An attractive, fruity strawberry scented Cune rosado spends a short time on skins gaining a little structure and fruit. This like the Cune Crianza is bottled under screw cap. The Cune Reserva is a traditionally vinified and aged example spending 24 months in a mix of French and American oak. The Imperial reds are classic old style Riojas and in the best sense. They are characterised by elegant red berry and cherry fruit, offer a supple rounded texture and are immediately enjoyable on release. Both are aged in a mix of French and American oak. The Vina Real winery is a modern state of the art facility where technology aids the vinification of a range of traditionally styled wines. A white is barrel-fermented while the reds are vinified with strict temperature control and ageing is in a mix of French and American oak, just American for the Crianza. Two icon wines, Real de Asua and Pagos de Vina Real are also produced. Real de Asua is given a lengthy vatting with fermentation in large oak vats. Pagos de Viña Real is modern in style, ageing is in French oak and the malolactic takes place in barrel. (DM)

Recommended Reds:
Rioja Viña Real Pagos de Viña Real ★★★★★ £G
Rioja Real de Asua ★★★★★ £G
Rioja Imperial Gran Reserva ★★★★ £F
Rioja Imperial Reserva ★★★☆ £E
Rioja Viña Real Gran Reserva ★★★☆ £E
Rioja Viña Real Reserva ★★☆ £D   Rioja Viña Real Crianza ★★ £C
Rioja Cune Reserva ★★☆ £C   Rioja Cune Crianza ★★ £B
Rioja Monopole ★☆ £B
Recommended Whites:
Rioja Monopole ★☆ £B
Recommended Rosés:
Rioja Cune ★☆ £B

Vinyes Domènech (Montsant) *www.vinyesdomenech.com*
Based around the village of Capçanes, this is one of the best bodegas in the DO. Proprietor Joan Ignasi Domènech's roots are in the Priorat region but his involvement in wine is recent, establishing his family property in 2002. There are 10 ha under vine, the whole property measuring a little more, 15 or so ha. The vines are protected both by the Montsant mountains and more immediately by surrounding forest. The clay/calcareous soils also have a high stone content aiding permeability and flavour intensity. The vineyards are currently planted to a mix of varieties which range from 15 to over 70 years, the quality backbone being provided by the holding of old Garnacha. As well as the top two reds a white Rita comes from Garnacha Blanca and Macabeo and a well priced young red, Bancal del Bosc, is comprised of Garnacha, Cabernet Sauvignon and Syrah. Of the top two reds, Furvus is the more approachable with a small proportion of younger Merlot included with Garnacha. Ageing is now in almost all French oak. The top wine Teixar is one of the benchmarks for Montsant. It comes from the oldest Garnacha vines and is full of beguiling, complex, smoky, spicy dark fruit. It is aged in French oak but second and third fill barrels are used as well as new to achieve the wines impeccable balance. (DM)

Recommended Reds:
Montsant Teixar ★★★★☆ £E   Montsant Furvus ★★★☆ £D

❂ Domini de La Cartoixa (Priorat) *www.closgalena.com*
There are 11 ha of vineyards here which are farmed organically. The wines tend to be more fruit driven and a touch less mineral and *sauvage* in style than some others. The Formiga de Vellut is the most approachable of the three estate wines, coming from Garnacha, Cariñena and Syrah and aged in barrel for eight months. The dense and dark-fruited Galena is the second label, a blend of Garnacha, Cabernet Sauvignon, Merlot and Cariñena. Vatting is for 15 days and the wine aged in mainly French oak for a year. The Clos Galena is altogether denser, more concentrated. A blend of Garnacha, Cariñena, Merlot, Syrah and Cabernet, the wine has a higher proportion of old-vine fruit and is more mineral and nervy in character. Expect the top two wines to develop well for five years and more. Another red is made from other sources under the Crossos label. (DM)

Recommended Reds:
Priorat Clos Galena ★★★★★ £F   Priorat Galena ★★★★ £E
Priorat Formiga de Vellut ★★★ £D

>> Doniene Gorrondona *www.donienegorrondona.com*
This bodega is found in the Bakio Valley in Bizkaiko Txakolina and sited in a perfect amphitheatre, with steeply sloping vineyards south facing from the Bay of Biscay. The soils are well drained and the 12 ha here, with some vines dating back to pre-phylloxera times, farmed organically. The Doniene white is fresh crisp and with subtle apple scents and a hint of citrus. The Gorrondona white, also from Hondarrabi Zuri is a touch more intense with more apparent minerality. A barrel fermented white, Doniene and a red Gorrondona are also made. (DM)

Recommended Whites:
Bizkaiko Txakolina Gorrondona ★★★ £C
Bizkaiko Txakolina Doniene ★★☆ £B

Celler Dosterras (Montsant) *www.dosterras.com*
Two very good reds are made at this small environmentally friendly bodega. Garnacha is the dominant variety but Samsó is also important. Vine age is also important and the plants range from 40 to up to 100 years old. The soils are also closer to typical Priorat being a mix of clay, chalk and slate. The fruit is hand harvested into small boxes and the wines then vinified naturally with a lengthy maceration of up to 30 days in small French oak vats. The wines are then aged in a mix of 225, 300 and 500 litre barrels to emphasise the fruit and the malolactic is carried out in wood. The Vespres which combines Garnacha and Samsó is opulent and full of dark fruit, the tannins polished and the oak well judged. Coming from the oldest Garnacha, the Dosterras offers a touch more depth with a real old vine complexity. A further premium red (DM)

Recommended Reds:
Montsant Dosterras ★★★★ £E   Montsant Vespres ★★★☆ £D

Edetària (Terra Alta) *www.edetaria.com*
A recently established bodega, founded in 2003 by Joan Àngel Lliberia. He only produces wines from his own 24 ha of vineyards and from a substantial holding of old vines with many over 50 years of age. The climate here is Mediterranean and the low summer rainfall stresses the vines just sufficiently to encourage good ripening in the fruit after *veraison*. The harvest is manual and there is a careful selection before individual parcel by parcel vinification in small tanks. Some well priced wines are produced under an entry level label, Via Terra, the red from Garnacha, the white from Garnacha Blanca. They come from younger vines and are made

to emphasise their fruit. The Edetana white (Garnacha Blanca and Viognier) and red (Garnacha) are both a touch more serious. The white gets a short period in oak, 300 litre barrels are used like all the wines here, for around four months. The top white Edetaria Selecció is a nutty, tangy and mineral scented wine coming from Garnacha Blanca and barrel fermented. The Edetana red is vibrant, spicy and full of dark berry fruit. Vines up to 40 years old and ageing for 10 months in barrel add to the wines character. The top red, the Edetaria Selecció offers real character and value at this level. It is dominated by Garnacha with Syrah and Cariñena and aged for 12 months in French oak. A Dolç style is also made. (DM)

Recommended Reds:

Terra Alta Edetària Selecció ★★★☆ £D

Terra Alta Vía Edetana ★★★ £C

Terra Alta Vía Terra ★★ £B

Recommended Whites:

Terra Alta Edetària Selecció ★★★ £C

Terra Alta Vía Edetana ★★☆ £C

Terra Alta Vía Terra ★★ £B

Finca Egomei (Rioja) *www.egomei.es*

Egomei is a part of the A & B Bodegas group which also owns Bodegas CAMILO CASTILLA in Navarra, which produces some very good late harvested Moscatel. The vineyards around Alfaro in south-east Rioja have been planted since 1975. Of 100 ha including olive groves, 35 ha are planted to vines. There is a stylish, modern winery and after the harvest a careful grape selection is followed by fermentation in temperature controlled stainless tanks. Two reds are made, both blends of Tempranillo and Graciano. The Egomei is marginally the more approachable of the two, and very much the more affordable. Spicy black fruit is nicely underpinned by subtle oak. It's a modern style spending 14 months in French barrels on its fine lees. The pricier Alma is lent extra structure from a higher proportion (25%) of Graciano. There is a similar vinification regime, although the malolactic fermentation is in barrel with further ageing on fine lees for three months. The wine spends a total of 18 months in oak providing a stylish, concentrated dark berry fruited red with polished tannins and impressive depth. (DM)

Recommended Reds:

Rioja Alma ★★★★ £E   Rioja Egomei ★★★☆ £D

❀❀ Eguren (Rioja & Toro) *www.sierracantabria.com*

The Eguren family are one of the most important producers in Rioja and have been largely instrumental in ensuring the visibility the muscular reds now have in Toro. Indeed their timely sale of the NUMANTHIA bodega to LMVH for a very tidy sum seems to have been a very astute move prior to the credit crunch. This they have replaced with a potentially very fine new property, Teso La Monja, from where they produce a vibrant Almirez from younger vines, the sturdy and structured Victorino from 45 to 70 year old vines and a small amount of a limited release cuvée, Alabaster from pre-phylloxera vines. A joven style and aged just six months in barrel, Romanico is also made. Rioja though is the heart of the operation. Both traditional and modern styles are produced. Based in the region since 1870, Sierra Cantabria was the first of the current brands to be established and four well made, traditionally crafted reds are vinified, Cosecha, Crianza, Reserva and Gran Reserva. There are 100 ha of vineyards planted to a south to south-east exposition in the Sierra Cantabria Mountains. As well as the traditional styles other wines are made. Cuvée Especial is from older vines and aged in a mix of French and American oak. Organza is the single white

that the Egurens make, a concentrated, nutty, citrus infused and barrel fermented blend of Viura, Malvasia and white Garnacha. Three premium reds are also made at Sierra Cantabria. Colección Privada comes from over 50 year old vines and is aged in a mix of French and American oak. Amancio comes from a single high-altitude, organically fertilized vineyard and is aged in "200% new French oak". Finca El Bosque, which also comes from calcareous based soils sees a little less time in wood and while equally opulent is a touch more elegant than Amancio. There are two other Rioja properties. At Señorio de San Vicente, just one wine is made. It comes from a rare and low-yielding strain of Tempranillo, Peludo. Viñedos de Paganos is some way to the east of the other two estates although it is also in the shadows of the Cantabria range. The vineyards have a high calcareous clay and sandstone content and offer a marked mineral quality in the two super-premium wines produced. The more economically priced El Puntido is aged for 18 months in new French oak, while La Nieta is from a 1.75 ha small vineyard and from restricted yields of barely more than 20 hl/ha. Both wines are from high density planted vineyards. You can expect the top wines to develop well for a decade and more. The Eguren range is completed by some attractive fruit driven wines which are sourced from a range of areas and released under the Dominio de Eguren label. (DM)

Sierra Cantabria

Recommended Reds:

Rioja Finca El Bosque ★★★★★ £G   Rioja Amancio ★★★★☆ £G

Rioja Colección Privada ★★★☆ £E   Rioja Gran Reserva ★★★ £D

Rioja Cuvée Especial ★★☆ £C   Rioja Reserva ★★☆ £C

Rioja Crianza ★★ £B   Rioja ★☆ £B

Recommended Whites:

Rioja Organza ★★★ £D

Señorio de San Vicente

Recommended Reds:

Rioja San Vicente ★★★★ £F

Viñedos de Páganos

Recommended Reds:

Rioja La Nieta ★★★★★ £G   Rioja El Puntido ★★★★☆ £F

Teso La Monja

Recommended Reds:

Toro Alabaster ★★★★★ £F   Toro Victorino ★★★★ £E

Toro Almirez ★★★ £D

Enate (Somontano) *www.enate.es*

One of the three big wineries here. Reds are the dominant wines although as well as Chardonnay, Gewürztraminer is particularly striking among the whites and also offering good value. The bodega has around 400 ha under vine and 85% of this is accounted for by red varieties. As well as a crisp fresh and nutty cool fermented Chardonnay, Barrica, a barrel fermented example is also made. The Gewürztraminer is striking, it shows much of the pungency of Alsace which is rare. There is a fairly wide range of reds including varietals and blends. The Reserva is solely Cabernet Sauvignon and aged in French oak for a year. A level up is the Reserva Especial, this is a Cabernet dominated Bordeaux red with a little Merlot, full of black fruit, cassis and a rich toasty character. The wine is matured in French oak for 18 months. Two limited release premium labels are also produced, a red Uno which blends Cabernet with Merlot and Syrah and a white Uno which is a barrel fermented Chardonnay. (DM)

Recommended Reds:

Somontano Reserva Especial ★★★ £D

North-East Spain

Spain

Somontano Cabernet Sauvignon Reserva ★★☆ £C
Somontano Cabernet Merlot ★☆ £B
Recommended Whites:
Somontano Chardonnay Barrica ★★★ £C
Somontano Gewürztraminer ★★☆ £B

Cellers de L'Encastell (Priorat) www.roquers.com

One of an increasing number of fine small bodegas emerging from this part of Priorat. The family had originally sold their fruit on but decided to vinify wines from their own two estates, Mas d'en Capçador and Mas d'en Ferran in 1999. They have a total of 7.5 ha. Their vines are grown on the classic licorella and schist soils of the area and produce full bodied robust wines with a characteristic mineral undercurrent, although the Marge is much more obviously a fruit-driven style. Roquers de Porrera is altogether tighter, more structured and backward in its youth with a fiery, mineral undercurrent with notes of dark cherry. The old vine quality of the Cariñena component in the blend clearly showing through. It also does in the Roquers de Samsó, which is 100 % Cariñena. The wines certainly offer good value for the region.(DM)

Recommended Reds:
Priorat Roquers de Porrera ★★★★ £F
Priorat Roquers de Samsó ★★★☆ £E   Priorat Marge ★★★ £D

❀ Escoda Sanahuja www.celler-escodasanahuja.com

A serious stand out producer in the small Conca de Barberá DO with vines planted at altitudes of 450 to 600 metres. Joan Escoda farms his small holding of 10 ha, which includes olive groves and almond trees as well as vines, biodynamically. A permanent vegetative cover on the soil ensures sufficient moisture and optimum conditions for ripening. The artisan approach continues in the cellar where sulphur additions are avoided, minimal processing of any kind is the norm and the wines bottled without fining or filtration. Oak ageing is also kept to a minimum with no more than 6 to 8 months for the reds and a maximum of 4 months for the whites. The results are impressive. Each of the top wines is named after the single small vineyard it comes from. The exception is the elegant raspberry fruited red blend Nas del Gegant which comes from Merlot, Garnacha, Cariñena and Cabernet Franc and the same site as a second fruit driven white Els Bassotets. This like the similarly named Els Bassots is from Chenin Blanc. Els Bassots is rich and nutty with the slightly evolved character of minimally handled whites. Coll de Sabater is a Bordeaux Right Bank blend of Cabernet Franc and Merlot, rich, plummy and with an underlying fresh mineral quality. La Lloptera is very good for Spanish Pinot Noir with a hint of dark fruit and subtle gamey notes with a tight structure and good nervy acidity. Perhaps the most characterful of the wines is Les Paradetes. It blends Carignan and Garnacha with the very rare local Sumoll grape and offers intense wild berry fruits and a classic Mediterranean herb spiced undercurrent. (DM)

Recommended Reds:
Conca de Barberá La Lloptera ★★★★ £D
Conca de Barberá Les Paradetes ★★★★ £D
Conca de Barberá Coll del Sabater ★★★★ £D
Conca de Barberá Nas del Gegant ★★★ £C
Recommended Whites:
Conca de Barberá Els Bassots ★★★☆ £D

Bodegas Escudero (Rioja) www.familiaescudero.com

The Escudero family produce wines under two labels Escudero and Vinsacro and vinify their wines in two facilities. The Escudero wines,

which include some Cavas are well crafted and the Solar de Becquer wines traditionally made. They also produce a red and white labelled simply Becquer and more recently two super premium reds Arvum and Vidau as well as Crianza, Reserva and Gran Reserva Serna Imperial reds. The Valsacro red comes from vines planted in poor, rocky calcareous soils in the Rioja Baja. 40% of the wines fruit is sourced from their Vidau vineyard, which is 80–100 years old and is planted to Garnacha in the main, with some Tempranillo, and a sprinkling of Mazuelo. It is rich and concentrated with dark fruits and cinnamon. The splendidly complex and intense Dioro comes solely from Vidau fruit and is modern and fleshy in style with malolactic in French oak barrels. The wine combines Tempranillo, Graciano and Mazuelo with a dominant proportion of over 70 year old Garnacha. Both the reds will benefit from some ageing and the Dioro will continue to evolve for a decade and or more. (DM)

Bodegas Vinsacro
Recommended Reds:
Rioja Dioro ★★★★ £F   Rioja ★★★☆ £E
Bodegas Escudero
Recommended Reds:
Rioja Solar de Becquer Reserva ★★ £C
Rioja Solar de Becquer Crianza ★★ £B

Espelt Viticultors (Empordà) www.espeltviticultors.com

An extensive range of wine is made at this well equipped medium sized bodega. The Espelt family have had vinegrowing origins in the Empordá region for a century although the modern winemaking approach is more recent with the curent winery facility being built in 2000. Reds, whites, rosés, sweet and sparkling wine is all made. There are some 200 ha of vineyards dotted about the DO and planted in the sparse gravel, granite and slate soils of the area. Vaillet is a fresh, fruit-driven blend of white Garnacha and Macabeo while the Quize Roures is richer and fuller with a little structure provided by a touch of barrel-fermentation. It combines both Garnacha Gris and Blanca. Mareny, a blend of Sauvignon Blanc and Muscat as well as Chardonnay are also made. The soft and approachable Sauló is a blend of Garnacha and Cariñena and full of spicy, herb-scented Mediterranean character. The other reds are a mix of both native and international grape varieties. Vidiví blends Garnacha with Merlot, the more structured black pepper spiced Terres Negres impressively combines Cariñena with Cabernet Sauvignon. The top red, Comabruna comprises Syrah, Cariñena and the rare Marselan (a crossing of Grenache and Cabernet Sauvignon). It is rich, dense and offers big chewy tannins, a fine mineral undercurrent as well as subtle black pepper and spices. Airam comes from white and black Garnacha. It is a naturally sweet style and vinified and aged in a lightly oxidative style in a form of *solera* which now dates back 14 years. Three other sweet wines are offered from Garnacha and Muscat and the range is completed by a couple of rosés and a Traditional Method sparkling white, Escuturit Brut.(DM)

Recommended Reds:
Empordà Comabruna ★★★☆ £E   Empordà Terres Negres ★★★ £C
Empordà Vidiví ★★★ £C   Empordà Sauló ★★☆ £B
Empordà Airam ★★★☆ £E
Recommended Whites:
Empordà Quinze Roures ★★☆ £C   Empordà Vailet ★★ £B

❀ Bodegas Exopto (Rioja) www.exopto.net

An impressive recently established winery based in Rioja's Alavesa. Owner Tom Puyaubert draws on 10 ha planted to Tempranillo which

comes from the Rioja Alta, as well as Graciano and Garnacha from the Rioja Baja. The late-ripening local climate and finely drained clay/limestone in the Rioja Alta and the rocky soils of the Baja provides for excellent intensity in the grapes. Most approachable and excellent value is the young wine Bozeto which is a blend of Garnacha, Tempranillo and Graciano, aged in a mix of concrete and wooden vats to emphasise the wines fruit. The citrus scented, creamy textured Horizonte de Exopto Blanco has most recently been added. It is barrel-fermented in French oak and aged on fine lees for 12 months. It is a blend of 30 to 60 year old Viura, Malvasía and Garnacha Blanca. The Horizonte Tinto comprises a blend of 80% Tempranillo with the balance Graciano and Garnacha. Supple and immediately appealing it gains from 12 months in both new and used French oak. Exopto is denser, more firmly structured with 60% Graciano and 30/10 Tempranillo and Garnacha. 18 months in a high proportion of new French oak demands time for the fruit to integrate with a rich texture added by the malolactic fermentation in barrel. Five or six years patience will undoubtedly be rewarded. (DM)

Recommended Reds:
Rioja Exopto ★★★★☆ £F   Rioja Horizonte de Exopto ★★★☆ £D
Rioja Bozeto ★★☆ £B
Recommended Whites:
Rioja Horizonte de Exopto ★★★☆ £D

Celler Fuentes (Priorat)   www.granclos.com
Small Priorat producer making an impressively structured and concentrated Gran Clos *cuvée* as well as a decent second wine, El Puig, and a straightforward nutty white Vinya Llisarda. To this have been added a red blend of Garnacha and Cariñena, Cartus and a fruit driven blend of Garnacha, Cariñena and Merlot, Solluna. There are 32ha under vine planted in schistous soils and much of the production is sold internationally. Gran Clos is blended from mainly Garnacha with Cariñena and a touch of Cabernet Sauvignon. A wine of formidable extract but with beguiling dark, spicy berry fruit, it will develop well with 5–7 years' ageing. (DM)

Recommended Reds:
Priorat Gran Clos Joset Maria Fuentes ★★★★☆ £F

Fernández de Piérola (Rioja)   www.pierola.com
Three fine reds and a relatively light barrel-fermented wild yeast white are made at this estate located in the north of the region in the Rioja Alavesa. While the majority of the region's output is still blended from different sites, these wines are all *terroir*-driven. The Moreda, a tributary of the Ebro, helps moderate the climate and provides nourishment for the deep-rooted, low-yielding vines. High altitude, protection provided by the Sierra Cantabria mountains and finely drained soils high in minerals also contribute to style and quality. The reds are marked by their purity of fruit and elegant intensity. The red 393 North East Spain Litium Reserva is richer and fuller with more obvious creamy oak character than the more piercingly fruit-driven Crianza and Reserva. (DM)

Recommended Reds:
Rioja Litium Reserva ★★★☆ £E   Rioja Reserva ★★★ £D
Rioja Crianza ★★☆ £C
Recommended Whites:
Rioja Fermentado en Barrica ★★ £C

Ferrer Bobet (Priorat)   www.ferrerbobet.com
Some elegant and stylish Priorat is made at this small bodega between Falset and Porrera. Two wines are made and are dominated by very old Cariñena and Garnacha from high elevation steeply sloped vineyards. 22 ha has now been planted to a number of varieties at one of the highest points in the appellation and on soils with some of the highest Llicorella content. Sophisticated vinification includes fermentation in small oak vats and ageing in tightly grained French oak with the malolactic fermentation in barrel. Selecció Especial is made in very small quantities. The Ferrer Bobet red is a stylish, elegant and very intensely flavoured Priorat with a piercing mineral complexity, rich texture and very polished tannin structure. (DM)

Recommended Reds:
Priorat Ferrer Bobet ★★★★☆ £F

>> Vinyes d'en Gabriel (Montsant)   www.vinyesdengabriel.com
The family origins of this small biodynamically farmed bodega stretch back over 150 years and it is now one of the quality benchmarks in Montsant. Based around the village of Darmós, the vineyards are in reasonably close proximity to the Mediterranean at an altitude of up to 200 metres above sea level. There is though enough of a diurnal swing in temperature to ensure good fresh acidity in the wines. The soils are comprised of a mix of chalk, clay and granite and the vineyards planted to Cariñena and Garnacha, some very old, as well as younger Syrah. The three L'Heravi red blends all offer real character and great value. L'Heravi is a Joven style, the Seleccio and Criança more structured aged wines. An old vine Cariñena, Mans de Samsó, was released for the first time with the 2009 vintage. It is considerably more expensive. (DM)

Recommended Reds:
Montsant L'Heravi Criança ★★★☆ £D
Montsant L'Heravi Selecció ★★★☆ £D
Montsant L'Heravi ★★★ £C

>> Genium Celler (Priorat)   www.geniumceller.com
Genium Celler was formed in 2002 when six winegrowing families amalgamated their holdings and now produce a small range totalling eight wines. Among these are a Rosado produced from Garnacha, Rosers's and a young red Fresc which is a blend of Garnacha and Cariñena. More serious are Poboleda Vi di Vila from Garnacha, Cariñena and a little Merlot aged for 12 months in barrel and the flagship, pricey red Excel-lent from mainly old Cariñena as well as Garnacha and a smattering of Merlot. All the wines are produced exclusively from the estate owned vineyards of the partners eight separate properties. The majority of the vines are old Garnacha and Cariñena and are planted on costers, non terraced slopes, which are naturally low yielding. The white Ximenis is dominated by Pedro Ximénez. It is given a long cool fermentation in barrel to preserve its subtle citrus, nutty fruit. The restrained dark cherry and very lightly mineral Ecològic is given close to four weeks maceration and aged in barrel for around six months. The Celler red has a similar winemaking regime, it sees a small proportion of new oak and is a touch more exotic and spicy in character. The Costers red is dark, herb-spiced and concentrated with a rich opulent gamey character and a marked old vine complexity. Aged in new French oak for 14 months a sizeable proportion of the fruit comes from 100 year old vines. (DM)

Recommended Reds:
Priorat Excel-lent ★★★★☆ £G
Priorat Costers ★★★★ £E   Priorat Celler ★★★☆ £E
Priorat Ecològic ★★★ £D
Recommended Whites:
Priorat Ximenis ★★☆ £D

North-East Spain

Spain

✿ Gramona (Penedès) *www.gramona.com*
Well-established Penedès producer founded in 1921, with an extensive range of both still wines and fine Cavas. The Gramona family have or control 150ha of vineyard. The range of Cavas includes dry and medium styles and focuses heavily on the indigenous varieties of the area with generally very good results. The Imperial Gran Reserva has some 10% of Chardonnay in support of Xarel-lo and Maccabeo. The III Lustros is solely indigenous varieties, Xarel-lo (70%) and Maccabeo. It gets an extended period of 5–6 years on its lees. The wines offer reasonable value and are interesting alternatives to lesser Champagnes. A premium Celler Battle Grand Brut gets up to 8 years on its yeast lees, while Argent has a much higher proportion of Chardonnay. Of the still wines the Gessami is a fresh, vibrant, fruit-driven blend of Muscat, Sauvignon Blanc and Gewürztraminer with impressive depth and intensity. The Sauvignon Blanc is barrel-fermented on its lees for 3–6 months and offers a subtle melange of citrus, green apple and nutmeg flavours. A Chardonnay is also produced and there is an Ice Wine, Vi de Glass, from Gewürztraminer and another from Riesling. A Pinot Noir Brut de Pinot Noir is matured in wood, some new. (DM)

Recommended Whites:
Penedès Vi de Glass Gewürztraminer ★★★☆ £E
Penedès Font Jui Xarel-lo ★★★ £C
Penedès Sauvignon Blanc ★★★ £C
Cava Celler Battle GR Brut ★★★★☆ £F
Cava III lustros GR Brut Nature ★★★★ £E
Cava Imperial Gran Reserva ★★★☆ £D
Cava La Cuvee Gran Reserva Brut ★★★ £C

>> Hacienda Grimón (Rioja) *www.haciendagrimon.es*
This small bodega, owned by the Oliváns family produces a range of six wines solely from their own 22 ha of organically farmed parcels in the Rioja Alta. The hand harvested vineyards are planted to a mix of Tempranillo, Garnacha and Graciano and the vines range from 10 to 45 years old. As well as the reds, a rosado is also made which comes solely from Garnacha. The Tempranillo is an unoaked style although unlike other jovens it is not vinified with carbonic maceration. The wine offers really attractive bright berry fruit and an impressively rich texture and structure. The Crianza is vinified from similar fruit sources as the Tempranillo, three different, separate vineyard parcels. Ageing is in a mix of French and American oak. The Reserva offers more depth and structure with a slightly firmer edge to its tannins. Ageing is for 16 months in barrel and 15% Graciano adds to the wine. Labarona is also a Reserva style, spending 18 months in barrel and from the oldest 45 year old Tempranillo and Graciano. A varietal Tempranillo, Finca La Oración is also made as well as a Graciano Desvelo. (DM)

Recommended Reds:
Rioja Labarona ★★★☆ £D
Rioja Reserva ★★★ £C
Rioja Crianza ★★☆ £C
Rioja Joven ★★☆ £B

>> Guelbenzu (VdT Ribera de Queiles) *www.guelbenzu.com*
This is the stand out producer in this small VdT region and is a member of the Taninia group of wineries which also includes SEÑORIO DE SARRIA in Navarra, PALACIO DE BORNOS in Rueda, TORESANAS in Toro and Vallebueno in Ribera del Duero. The bodega has 46 ha under vine in Vierlas, right in the heart of the Queiles valley, straddling the Navarra and Aragon communities. Strong north winds dry the local climate and the presence of the Moncayo mountain is an additional influence. The wines have been produced in a new state of the art winery since 2001. A total of six wines are made, all red. The entry level examples include the Guelbenzu Red, a soft fruit driven style coming from Merlot and Vierlas a Syrah aged in a mix of American and French oak for 6 months. The spicy, berry fruited Azul Tempranillo undergoes a similar cellar regime. Among the top wines, Lombana comes from Graciano and like the ripe blackcurrant scented Evo sees 12 months in barrel, although the Evo from Cabernet Sauvignon is solely raised in French oak. The top wine Lautus is a varied blend sourced from the best vineyards in the vintage. It gains depth and a rich texture and structure from 18 months in new French oak. (DM)

Recommended Reds:
VdT Ribera del Queiles Lautus ★★★☆ £D
VdT Ribera del Queiles Evo ★★☆ £C
VdT Ribera del Queiles Azul ★★ £B

Ijalba (Rioja) *www.ijalba.com*
A number of reds, two whites and a rosé are produced at this 80-ha property.The Múrice Tinto Crianza is a good modern, fruit-driven style. The Graciano Tinto is precisely that, an unusual, varietal Graciano which is full of dark brambly fruit. It is structured and will age well and is quite unlike most Rioja in style. Continuing the unusual approach is a new varietal Maturana Tinto, Dionisio Ruiz Ijalba. A level up, the Reserva is 90% Tempranillo, while the small-production Selección Especial is an equal blend of Tempranillo and Graciano. Both are full, deep and extracted styles with surprising weight and depth. Better with 4 or 5 years' ageing. (DM)

Recommended Reds:
Rioja Reserva ★★★ £D   Rioja Murice ★★☆ £C
Rioja Graciano ★★☆ £C

Inurrieta (Navarra) *www.bodegainurrieta.com*
One of the larger operations in Navarra, producing a sound range of well priced wine in the Ribera Alta subzone. The bodega has a modern well equipped winery and 230 ha of vineyards to draw on. The soil is diverse and the altitude ranges from 300 to 480 metres which enables successful cultivation of a range of grapes. 26 ha is put aside for Sauvignon Blanc with the rest of the holding accounted for by red varieties. A fruit driven white Orchidea is cool fermented in tank and there is a soft berry fruited rosado, Mediodia which gains some weight with four months on fine lees. A more structured, mineral grassy fruited white Orchidea Cuvée is barrel fermented and aged in French oak for 8 months. The Norte (Merlot/Cabernet Sauvignon) and Sur (Garnacha/Syrah) reds both offer good value, being what the bodega feels are good Atlantic and Mediterranean expressions of their fruit. The Norte is aged 6 months in French oak, the Sur a similar time in American barrels. The Cuatrocientos Crianza combining Cabernet Sauvignon, Merlot and Graciano, and Altos de Inurrieta Reserva from Cabernet Sauvignon as well as Garnacha are bigger more structured wines. The Crianza gains some attractive spicy character from the small proportion of Graciano included in the blend, the Reserva is more of a pure Bordeaux style and aged only in French oak for 15 months as opposed to 14 months in a mix of barrels with the Crianza. The top wine is the characterful Laderas de Inurrieta, a rich dark and spicy example of Graciano aged in new American oak for a little over a year. A further red Puro Vicio from Syrah is of a comparable price to the Laderas. (DM)

Recommended Reds:
Navarra Laderas de Inurrieta ★★★☆ £E

Navarra Altos de Inurrieta ★★★ £C
Navarra Norte ★★☆ £C Navarra Cuatrocentos Crianza ★★☆ £C
Navarra Sur ★★ £B
Recommended Whites:
Navarra Orchídea ★★☆ £B
Recommended Rosés:
Navarra Mendiodia ★★ £B

>> Itsasmendi (Bizkaiko Txakolina) *www.bodegasitsasmendi.com*
Itsasmendi was established in 1994 and is now one of the best
equipped in the area with a modern winery with stainless steel and
temperature control to optimise the subtle and delicate flavours
of the indigenous varieties. There are 30 ha now under vine and
these are farmed organically. As well as Hondarrabi Zuri, there are
very small holdings of Riesling and Izkiriot Handi, a variety also
found in Jurançon in France. The Itsasmendi white is a fresh, green
apple scented Hondarrabi Zuri, while the Uretzi is a subtle and
intense style with restrained apple and honeysuckle aromas aged in
small French oak. A further dry white Itsasmendi 7 includes a small
proportion of Riesling and the red Eklipse blends Pinot Noir with
Hondarrabi Beltza. (DM)
Recommended Whites:
Bizkaiko Txakolina Uretzi ★★★☆ £D
Bizkaiko Txakolina Itsasmendi ★★★ £C

⚫ Vinya Ivo (Empordà)
A recently established and impressive small new celler producing
two characterful examples of this small DO. It is run by Ivo Pagès
who has 40 years experience working in wine with spells in various
regions in France including Bordeaux and Burgundy as well as in
Spain and Italy. He has now set up his own project in his native
Empordà. The vineyards are on steep schistous slopes and the *terroir*
bears more than a passing similarity with sites in Priorat, Montsant
and the heart of the Roussillon just to the north of the French and
Spanish border. The top wine S'Alqueria is by no means cheap
but is one of the finest examples produced from the region. It is a
blend of very old Samsó (Cariñena), somewhat youger Garnacha
as well as a little Macabeo and Petit Verdot. Both the Carignan and
Petit Verdot are aged in small oak. The wine is full of black fruits,
spices and with a very pure mineral intensity. The second label
Pirata is more approachable with lifted fruit aromas and a supple
texture. It emanates from a varied blend of Samsó, Garnacha, Syrah,
Petit Verdot, Monastrell and Marselan which is a cross of Cabernet
Sauvignon and Grenache. S'Alqueria will benefit from four or five
years patience. (DM)
Recommended Reds:
Empordà S'Alqueria ★★★★ £F Empordà Pirata ★★☆ £B

Bodegas y Viñedos del Jalon *www.castillodemaluenda.com*
Del Jalon grew out of the foundations of the Calatayud San Isidro
co-operative in the 1960s. The company was established in 1999
and is now controlled by the Aragon government, financial
institutions and three bodegas. The combined project is able to
draw on up to 1,000 ha of vineyards. A wide range of wines is made
and old bush vine Garnacha is one of the cornerstones of quality.
There are two main brands which share many of the same wines,
Viña Alarba which is more commonly seen on export markets and
Castillo de Maluenda. A third brand Navitum is kept exclusively for
young and fresher wine styles and further brands are Claraval, La
Dolores and Teorema with an old vine Garnacha. Five further reds
are also made under the Las Pizarras Collection label. Under the

Viña Alarba brand the Tempranillo Roble and characterful dark,
spicy Garnacha/Syrah are young wines which see no wood. The
Garnacha Viñas Viejas sees just two months which lends just a little
extra structure to the wines rich old vine character. The Crianza and
Reserva are both more traditional in style being aged in American
oak and then in bottle before release, the Reserva combining
Tempranillo, Syrah and Garnacha. A pricier Pago San Miguel
dominated by Garnacha is also made. The pinnacle though are the
Las Pizarras Collection wines. As well as three old vine Garnachas
which also includes Fabla with limited oak ageing, Siosy is a Syrah
and Volcan is an unwooded Tempranillo. For the top two wines,
vinification is at a controlled temperature for up to three weeks and
the dense and complex old vine Alto Pizarro is aged for 11 months
in French oak between 225 and 500 litres to retain the character of
the fruit. (DM)
Recommended Reds:
Calatayud Alto Las Pizarras Viñas Viejas ★★★★ £D
Calatayud Las Pizarras Viñas Viejas ★★★☆ £C
Calarayud Viña Alarba Reserva ★★☆ £C
Calatayud Viña Alarba Garnacha Viñas Viejas ★★☆ £B
Calatayud Viña Alarba Garnacha/Syrah ★★ £A
Calatayud Viña Alarba Tempranillo ★☆ £A

Bodega Niño Jesús (Calatayud) *www.satninojesus.com*
The output of this co-op used to be sold off in bulk but recently
the members have decided to make a range of their own wines
from some excellent old Garnacha and Tempranillo bush vines
ranging from 60 to over 80 years of age. The local Xirac has also
recently been introduced and there is a little white Maccabeo. A
new state-of-the-art winery has been completed and the range of
wines is now marketed under the Estecillo label. Quality is aided by
high-altitude vineyards planted at 650–880m. The reds are produced
using gentle basket presses and the quality of the reds is very
striking. Drink the wines relatively young to enjoy their vibrant fruit,
although they will stand a little age. (DM)
Recommended Reds:
Calatayud Estecillo Legado Garnacha ★★★ £C
Calatayud Estecillo Garnacha Syrah ★★☆ £C
Calatayud Estecillo Garnacha Tempranillo ★★ £B

⚫ La Calandria (Navarra) *www.puragarnacha.com*
Javier Continente makes a small range of exceptional Garnacha reds
which are among the very finest examples in Navarra and compare
favourably with the best from other regions. The vineyards are on
the borders of Navarra and Aragon and are farmed organically as
well as being naturally low yielding from very old bush vines, some
well over 100 years. As well as the reds a vibrant and refreshing
rosado Sonrojo, is made with sufficient depth and structure from
old vine fruit to work well as both an aperitif and a match for light
summer lunches. The most approachable of the three reds, the
Volandera is unusually bottled with a Grolsch style bottle stopper.
It is a wine to be enjoyed for its exhuberant deep, smoky and
essentially juicy fruit qualities. A refreshing edge provides balance
and there is that underlying old vine depth. Cientruenos is just a
touch more complex. There is a firmer edge, although the wine
is vibrant and approachable with a combination of red and dark
berry fruits as well as restrained use of oak. The top wine, Tierga is
an impressively serious and finely crafted, cellarworthy Garnacha
that stands comparison with some of the best examples from the
likes of Chateauneuf-du-Pape. It is denser, more concentrated than
the other two wines. From the best parcels and very oldest vines

Spain

it offers complex dark fruit aromas, hints of cassis and spice and underpinned by polished tannins, not inconsiderable alcohol and a fresh, mineral edge. It will evolve well for a decade. (DM)

Recommended Reds:

Navarra Tierga Pura Garnacha ★★★★☆ £E
Navarra Cientruenos ★★★☆ £C   Navarra Volandera ★★★ £C

Recommended Rosés:

Navarra Sonrojo ★★☆ £B

La Cova dels Vin (Montsant) www.lacovadelsvins.cat
Small project created by Francesc Perello, who is the winemaker at the Celler de CAPÇANES, with his father from an old plot of ancient vines that had fallen into disuse. Like so many vineyards it is only recently that the potential of these old vineyards can be fully appreciated. Potentially great quality grapes ended up being sold in bulk. There are now a number of sites ranging in altitude from 200 to 700 metres and planted in a mix of chalk, clay and slate which aids complexity in the wines. Red, white and rosado are all now made. Young wines are released under both the Deler and Ombreta brands, the Ombreta labels offering a little more depth. The red is from Garnacha. Both the Ombra (Garnacha, Samsó, Cabernet Sauvignon) and Terròs (Garnacha, Samsó, Syrah) reds are a good deal more serious and structured. They are aged in French oak barrels for 14 months and 300 litre barrels are preferred to emphasise the dark spicy fruit character of the wines rather than the oak. The Terròs is a touch more sumptuous coming from older vines and the malolactic fermentation taking place in barrel rather than tank. (DM)

Recommended Reds:

Montsant Terròs ★★★★ £E   Montsant Ombra ★★★☆ £D
Montsant Ombretta ★★☆ £C

❀ La Vinya del Vuit (Priorat)
The name of this winery refers to the eight partners involved in the project. Just one red is produced each year, a Priorat of persuasive depth and character combining dark-berried fruit with an elegant perfumed mineral complexity. The project is led by husband and wife winemaking team Sara Perez (MAS MARTINET) and René Barbier Jnr (CLOS MOGADOR). The wine is produced from extremely old, near centenarian, Carineña and Garnacha vines on the schistous soils outside the village of Gratallops. The richly textured fruit is underpinned by sturdy youthful tannins and creamy oak. It is aged for just under two years in a large proportion of new oak which is well judged and integrated. (DM)

Recommended Reds:

Priorat La Vinya del Vuit El 8 ★★★★★ £G

❀ Bodegas Lan (Rioja) www.bodegaslan.com
Lan is a significant bodega producing an excellent range of wines in both traditional and modern styles. The firm has a 70 ha estate, Viña Lanciano, and although bought in fruit contributes towards the lower level wines the top reds are only made from estate owned and produced grapes. The growers the bodega does work with ensure low yields and ripe fruit. The Crianza is a classic, supple red cherry fruited style, with ageing for 12 months in a mix of French and American wood and comes solely from Tempranillo. The Reserva offers more depth and hints of spice and ripe black fruits. A similar period in oak is followed by a couple of years in bottle before release. A proportion of Mazuelo adds a further dimension. The Gran Reserva, solely from estate Tempranillo, Mazuelo, Garnacha fruit, is a traditionally slightly evolved style with elegant red cherry

fruit and soft tannins. Both Mazuelo and Garnacha add character. The D12 is a modern, fleshy well priced red, a varietal Tempranillo, with dark blackberry and cocoa spiced fruit spending 10 months in both French and American barrels. The Viña Lanciano is from the firm's own vineyards and from over 30 year old vines. It is curiously aged for six months in Russian and then 12 months in French oak. The blend is Tempranillo and Mazuelo. The Lan Edición Limitada is a thoroughly modern style and comes from a single vineyard Pago El Rincón and a blend of Tempranillo, Mazuelo, Graciano, on the Lanciano estate. It goes through the malolactic in barrel and is aged in both French and Russian wood but only for nine months which lifts the quality of its rich, rounded black fruit texture. The top wine is the Culmen, a blend of Tempranillo and Graciano, also from Pago El Rincón and from the oldest vines. This is a structured, richly textured wine with intense spicy, berry fruit character and real depth. The malolactic fermentation in French oak is followed by ageing for a total of 18 months and then 18 in bottle before release. (DM)

Recommended Reds:

Rioja Culmen Reserva ★★★★★ £G
Rioja Lan Edicion Limitada ★★★★☆ £G
Rioja Viña Lanciano ★★★★☆ £F   Rioja Gran Reserva ★★★★ £F
Rioja Lan D12 ★★★★ £E   Rioja Reserva ★★★☆ £D
Rioja Crianza ★★★ £C

Celler Laurona (Montsant) www.cellerlaurona.com
Owned by Christopher Cannan, who also owns the Priorat property CLOS FIGUERAS, and Rene Barbier of CLOS MOGADOR, this joint venture was established in 1999. There are two wines, both rich and concentrated. Laurona is blended from a mix of Garnacha, Cariñena, Syrah, Cabernet Sauvignon and Merlot, while the Seleccio de 6 Vinyes comes from a more conventional 60% Garnacha and 40% Cariñena. A fair proportion of new oak is used for ageing but it is the larger 500-litre casks; the Seleccio is also fermented in new oak after a long maceration. Malolactic is in barrel and the wines are kept on their lees during maturation. (DM)

Recommended Reds:

Montsant Selecció de 6 Vinyes ★★★★ £F
Montsant Laurona ★★★☆ £D

Vinya L'Hereu (Costers del Segre) www.vinyalhereu.com
The full name of this small high quality bodega is Vinya l'Hereu de Sero. It is one of the benchmarks for Costers del Segre DO, along with Tomas CUSINE and CASTELL DEL REMEI with their their fine Cérvoles labels. Just two organically produced reds are crafted here from 14 ha of vines planted in dense clay and limestone soils at an altitude of 450 metres above sea level. The area is arid and with a semi-continental climate although it also benefits from the further influences of both the Pyrenees and Mediterranean. The Petit Grealó is supple, fleshy and approachable with an impressive, firm structure and a rich savoury quality to its fruit. It blends Syrah with Merlot and Cabernet Sauvignon and is vinified and aged in stainless steel to emphasise its fruit. The Flor de Grealó is fuller, richer and more structured. Merlot is the dominant variety at around 40% of the blend with equal amounts of Cab Sauv and Syrah. The wine is aged for 12 months in French oak although this is reined in, just 20% is new and 300 litre barrels are used. As a result the wine has a subtle slightly mineral quality and the character of the dark, licoricey fruit is apparent. Both wines are released with a little age and are immediately approachable.((DM)

Recommended Reds:

Costers del Segre Flor de Grealó ★★★☆ £E

Costers del Segre Petit Grealó ★★★ £C

Lobban Wines (Calatayud & Cataluña) *www.lapamelita.com*
This is the small project of Pamela Geddes who was a winemaker for Seppelts in Australia and also runs one of the best small Tapas bars in Barcelona. She also works as a consultant at one of the bigger Catalan co-ops. It is her experience in Australia making classic sparkling Shiraz that has enabled her to produce two of the regions more exciting and unusual sparkling wines. La Pamelita is a red sparkler produced from Syrah, the fruit coming from Calatayud. A seven day skin contact brings out the colour and the wine gains complexity from 36 months on lees in bottle. Like its best Australian counterparts it's a wonderfully fruit driven wine with ripe berry fruit and spices in abundance, albeit with a touch less residual sugar than tends to be found in Aussie examples. Her rosado sparkler, La Rosita is really no less impressive. This is Garnacha and a touch of Syrah and is quite dry with a low *dosage* and is rich and biscuity with hints of ripe berry fruit in the background. Pamela's third wine is a very characterful Calatayud red, a blend of very old Garnacha, young trellised Syrah and a little Tempranillo. Very characterful and with an underlying old-viney component, only the Syrah is raised in small oak. All three wines are excellent value. (DM)
Recommended Reds:
Caltayud El Gorditos ★★★ £C Espumoso La Palmelita ★★★ £C
Recommended Rosés:
Espumoso La Rosita ★★☆ £C

López de Heredia (Rioja) *www.lopezdeheredia.com*
López de Heredia is famous for some of the finest traditionally styled wines in Rioja. It is often referred to by its well established Tondonia brand with classic Reserva and Gran Reserva reds and a Reserva white. The bodega was founded in 1877 and they own 170 ha in Rioja Alta with vineyards planted along the River Ebro. Viña Tondonia is much the largest of their holdings with over 100 ha under cultivation. The processes in the winery follow the traditional approach with red wine musts fermented in oak vats and ferments rising fairly high towards the middle 30 degrees Celsius. Barrel ageing can be followed by quite extensive bottle ageing and the firm have their own cooperage. The wines are labelled by vineyard. Among the whites, the lightly toasty citrus scented Viña Gravonia Crianza from Viura is aged for 4 years in oak. A touch more evolved on release is the honeyed Viña Tondonia Reserva (Viura and Malvasía) which is raised for six years in barrel. Of the reds, which all include Tempranillo, Garnacha and Mazuelo the Viña Cubillo Crianza is more immediately marked by red cherry fruit, it sees just three years in cask. The Viña Bosconia is complex and evolved, further complexity is added with 15% Garnacha and the wine is raised in barrel for up to five years. The Viña Tondonia Reserva is just a touch more complex with a little more depth. It sees a further year in wood and has just 75% Tempranillo. Garnacha, Graciano and Mazuelo are all included adding a further dimension. The Viña Tondonia Gran Reserva, which also includes a little Graciano, is the greatest of the reds. It is a subtle, beguiling and complex wine aged in barrel for no less than 9 years. Among other wines released there is a white Tondonia Gran Reserva and a Bosconia Gran Reserva which sees a little less time in barrel than the Tondonia. While the wines are given limited rackings and are lightly fined for stability they are all bottled without filtration. (DM)
Recommended Reds:
Rioja Gran Reserva Viña Tondonia ★★★★☆ £F
Rioja Reserva Viña Tondonia ★★★★ £E

Rioja Reserva Viña Bosconia ★★★☆ £E
Rioja Crianza Viña Cubillo ★★★ £C
Recommended Whites:
Rioja Reserva Viña Tondonia ★★★☆ £E
Rioja Crianza Viña Gravonia ★★★ £D

Domaines Lupier (Navarra) *www.domaineslupier.com*
Among the better Garnacha reds are made at this small bodega, not just in Navarra but in Spain as well. Over recent years owners Enrique Basarte and Elisa Úcar have been recovering old parcels of Garnacha from high altitude Navarra vineyards. They now have 27 separate parcels planted at altitudes ranging from 400 to 750 metres. The oldest vines date back to 1903. The couple have acquired an old manor house in the heart of the vineyards and have created a small purpose built winery. With a capacity to produce 50,000 bottles, quality and not volume will always be the priority. Two wines are currently made. El Terroir has a touch less depth, it comes from marginally lower sited parcels. La Dama Viñas Viejas is sourced from slightly higher sites and older vines. Both wines are aged in a mix of 225, 300 and 500 litre barrels to ensure the character of the fruit. These are dark berry fruited, dense and complex examples of the grape. (DM)
Recommended Reds:
Navarra La Dama ★★★★ £E Navarra El Terroir ★★★☆ £D

Marco Abella (Priorat) *www.marcoabella.com*
The Marco family have roots in the village of Porrera dating back to the 15th century although they only founded their property in 2001. Some excellent reds though are now emerging from this small bodega. A barrel-fermented and aged white, Olbia is also made in small quantities, less than a thousand cases a year. It blends Pedro Ximenez with Macabeo, and Garnacha Blanco. A fresh, fruit driven styled red blending Garnacha and Cariñena complements the two big reds. The vineyard which extends to 30 ha comprises slate soils and there is an altitude at the upper terraced slopes of 1,500 metres all helping to provide an intense, complex, mineral quality in the wines. Green harvesting is practiced and there is a careful crop selection at harvest. The modern winery facility has been built into the hillside and cellar processes are carried out by gravity. Individual plots are vinified separately in order to retain the character of the *terroir*. Fermentation takes place in a mix of cement and wooden vats. The dark, elegant Mas Mallola comes from 15 year old vines and a mix of mainly Garnacha and Cariñena and a little each of Syrah and Cabernet Sauvignon. It is aged in oak for up to 18 months. The top wine the structured, richly textured and subtly mineral Clos Abella is crafted from the oldest vines. It is again dominated by Garnacha and Cariñena. (DM)
Recommended Reds:
Priorat Clos Abella ★★★★☆ £F Priorat Mas Mallola ★★★☆ £E
Priorat Loidana ★★★☆ £E

Magaña (Navarra) *www.vinamagana.com*
This is one of the top bodegas in Navarra. Juan Magaña established the property in 1968 and now has around 100 ha (247 acres) planted in one of the warmer sub-regions of the DO. The resulting wines tend to be richer than many from the region and avoid the leafy tones that can often be found in other red Navarra examples. The soils provide an ideal growing environment consisting of a mix of gravel and limestone and a gravel subsoil providing good drainage. A number of wines are crafted under the Viña Magaña home bodega label as well as Torcas, Merlot and Calchetas which

North-East Spain

are all rarer and a good deal pricier. Dignus is a crianza style red which is a typical blend of Tempranillo, Merlot and Cabernet Sauvignon. The wine is aged for around a year and French oak is preferred. Barón de Magaña is a more international style, still crianza, with a blend dominated by Tempranillo with the balance Cabernet and Merlot. The wine is fleshier and a touch more opulent with 70% rather than 50% new wood used. Calchetas is Merlot, Cabernet and Malbec, the richly textured and firmly structured Torcas, which is only bottled in the best years and is a truly international mix of Merlot, Cabernet Sauvignon, Syrah and Malbec. The wine is given a lengthy maceration during fermentation and aged for 20 months or so in oak. Expect the top wines to develop well for 5 to 10 years. (DM)

Recommended Reds:
Navarra Calchetas ★★★★ £F   Navarra Torcas ★★★☆ £E
Navarra Merlot ★★★☆ £E   Navarra Barón de Magaña ★★★ £C
Navarra Dignus ★★☆ £B

Magrez Espagne (Priorat) *www.bernard-magrez.com*
Bordeaux merchant Bernard Magrez, the owner of PAPE-CLEMENT and much else besides, produces these wines in Spain and is based in the village of Porrera. In Toro there are close to 9 ha under vine with a proportion of the holding up to 100 years of age. As a result of this the vines are bush-pruned although leaf and bunch thinning are practiced to optimise quality. The top wine Paciencia has more concentration and power than the second label Temperencia. Paciencia is an excellent example of the muscular and structured style of the DO and no doubt benefits from a low yield of only 20 to 30 hectolitres per hectare. Vinification utilises small vat fermentation and maceration and the juice and wine is moved by gravity without recourse to pumps. Confianza is a third wine from the Paciencia plots and is a softer, more forward fruit-driven style. In Priorat, the Herència de Padri comes from a blend of Carignan, Grenache, Merlot and Cabernet Sauvignon and a second Priorat label, Alegria is also made which combines Grenache, Carignan, Merlot and Cabernet. Most recently a VdT Vastilla red, Prudencia is made from Tempranillo and from Jumilla comes a blend of Monastrell and Syrah, Luz del Palacio. (DM)

Recommended Reds:
Toro Paciencia ★★★☆ £E   Toro Temperencia ★★★ £C
Priorat Herència de Padri ★★★☆ £F

✿ Vinyes de Manyetes (Priorat)
This is another property with valuable input from winemaker René Barbier Ferrer, the owner of CLOS MOGADOR and consultant to Daphne Glorian at CLOS I TERASSES. Output is relatively small, so the wines are inevitably scarce. Manyetes is dark and almost impenetrable in its youth, with a very marked, deep, spicy character from Cariñena, which dominates a blend also comprising Garnacha. The vines are grown in slate soils and, while Cariñena may not be being heavily replanted in the region, examples like this demonstrate the real personality that it can give. The second label Solertia, is much more than just a second wine. It is dominated by Garnacha, with a little less Cabernet Sauvignon and Syrah. Manyetes deserves cellaring for at least 5 years. (DM)

Recommended Reds:
Priorat Manyetes ★★★★★ £G   Priorat Solertia ★★★★ £F

Marques de La Concordia (Rioja) *www.unitedwineries.com*
New-wave collection of estates owned by the giant United Wineries Group who also own Berberana, Marques de Monistrol,

Lagunilla and the Rioja labelled Marques de Griñon (as opposed to the wines of DOMINIO DE VALDEPUSA). Although some less than overwhelming wine is made at lower price levels five projects come under the Marques de la Concordia umbrella. As well as Marques de la Concordia in Rioja other operations are in the Duero Valley (Hacienda Zorita), in Rueda (Vega de La Reina) and also in the south at Principe de Hohenlohe in Andalucía. For convenience we have reviewed them together in this entry. Marqués de la Concordia consists of two estates totalling just 32ha, the Hacienda La Concordia in the Rioja Alavesa and the Hacienda de Susar in the Rioja Baja. There is a straightforward, fruit-driven Tempranillo and a better, more structured Crianza which gets 18 months in French and American oak. Pride of place goes to the splendid Hacienda de Susar, sourced entirely from that vineyard. A blend of Tempranillo, Syrah, Cabernet Sauvignon and Merlot, this supple and concentrated red is among the region's more exciting new wines. Reds are also now made at Hacienda Abascal in Ribera del Duero. Hacienda Zorita, formerly Durius is a name that has been associated with the Duero for some years and the wines are now genuinely interesting. The good, well-priced estate-sourced Tinto is a varietal Tempranillo, while Durius Magister MM series is a rich and fleshy blend of Tempranillo, Malbec, Merlot and Syrah sourced from the firm's best vineyards in Arribes. Of real interest is the Andalus red from Principe Alfonso de Hohenlohe, a vino de mesa produced solely from Petit Verdot. Dark, blackberry fruit and subtle oak are seamlessly integrated. A number of well crafted whites are also produced in Rueda at Vega La Reina. Top reds will benefit from a little age, particularly the Hacienda de Susar. (DM)

Marques de La Concordia (Hacienda Susar)
Recommended Reds:
Rioja Hacienda de Susar ★★★★ £F
Rioja Crianza ★★☆ £C
Rioja Tempranillo ★☆ £B
Marques de La Concordia (Hacienda Zorita)
Recommended Reds:
Arribes Durius Magister MM ★★★☆ £E
VdT Castilla y León Tempranillo Natural Reserve ★☆ £B
Bodegas Principe Alfonso de Hohenlohe
Recommended Reds:
Vino de Mesa Andalus ★★★☆ £E
Vega de La Reina
Recommended Whites:
Rueda Verdejo ★★☆ £C
Rueda Sauvignon Blanc ★★ £C

✿ Marques de Murrieta *www.marquesdemurrieta.com*
This most conservative of the Rioja bodegas produces traditional reds and whites which are exposed to considerable periods of oak-ageing. There are some 300 ha of vineyards and production is sizeable at 250,000 cases or so a year. Gran Reservas are now all released under the Castillo d'Ygay label and Reservas are now simply Murrieta. The white Capellania is citrusy with very marked vanilla essence – oaky but good. The red Reserva and Gran Reserva can be more variable with occasionally very high volatile acidity. At their best they are splendidly rich, particularly the Castillo d'Ygay Especial which can be of a different order. In a concession to new-wave Rioja styles a premium red, Dalmau, is now produced. It is firm, structured and above all elegant and it should develop well with 5 or 6 years' cellaring. In Rías Baixas a peachy, lightly exotic white Pazo de Barrantes is made, which should be drunk young. This has been joined by a single vineyard example La Comtesse de Pazo Barrantes.

(DM)

Marques de Murrieta

Recommended Reds:

Rioja Dalmau Reserva ★★★★☆ £F

Rioja Gran Reserva Especial Castillo d'Ygay ★★★★ £F

Rioja ★★★ £D

Recommended Whites:

Rioja Capellania ★★★ £D

Pazo de Barrantes

Recommended Whites:

Rías Baixas Albarino ★★★☆ £D

Marques de Riscal (Rioja) *www.marquesderiscal.com*

Much development and expense has been put into this noble old bodega in recent years. Paul Pontallier of Château MARGAUX in Bordeaux has provided additional guidance in the winery. Good traditional reds are produced along with some more modern styled wines. The Barón de Chirel Reserva is very impressive: rich but structured and firm in its youth. It will make excellent drinking with 5 or 6 years' bottle-development. As well as the Baron de Chirel there is a Tempranillo, Graciano blend Finca Torrea from old vines and the Gehry Selection from old Tempranillo. The firm is also a source of consistently good fresh Rueda whites. The fresh Verdejo and Sauvignon should both be enjoyed young; the Limousin is lightly oaky and leesy and will benefit from keeping for 2 or 3 years. (DM)

Recommended Reds:

Rioja Reserva Baron de Chirel ★★★★☆ £G

Rioja Gran Reserva ★★★☆ £E   Rioja Reserva ★★★☆ £D

Recommended Whites:

Rueda Limousin ★★★ £C   Rueda Finca Montico Verdejo ★★☆ £B

Rueda Sauvignon Blanc ★★☆ £B

Marques de Vargas (Rioja) *www.marquesdevargas.com*

This 65-ha family-owned property, which is a part of the same group that owns Pazo SAN MAURO in Rías Baixas and CONDE DE SAN CRISTOBAL in Ribera del Duero, is unusual for the region in producing wines solely from its own vineyards. Recently quality has been increasingly high, with major investment in a new winery facility and consultancy from Michel Rolland. The style is traditional but the winemaking and the purity and depth in the wines are second to none. The vineyards are tended naturally, avoiding herbicides and pesticides, yields are kept tightly under control and green-harvesting is carried out prior to *veraison*. The Reserva is 75/10/5/10 Tempranillo, Mazuelo, Garnacha and other varieties. Ageing is in a combination of American, Russian and French oak, just under a third new. The Reserva Privada is 60% Tempranillo, 10% each of Mazuelo and Garnacha and the balance other varieties. There is also a top label Reserva Especial, Hacienda Pradolagar, which requires a very deep pocket. The wines will benefit from 3 or 4 years' cellaring. (DM)

Recommended Reds:

Rioja Reserva Privada ★★★★ £F   Rioja Reserva ★★★☆ £E

Celler Marti Fabra (Emporda)

This property has been in family hands since the 12th century and the style of the wines is very traditional. The DO is right in the north-eastern corner of Spain, in very close proximity to the vineyards of the Roussillon in France. Understandably the wines share quite a similarity with the better examples from that region. The vineyards themselves benefit from drying maritime breezes and as such

require minimal treatment and intervention. The meagre slatey soils ensure a low-yielding crop of intensely flavouful grapes. There are two very characterful wines under the Masia Carreras label. The spicy, herb scented berry-laden red blends Garnacha, Cariñena and a touch each of Cabernet Sauvignon, Tempranillo and Syrah. The white, a blend of mainly Carignan Blanc and Gris with a little Grenache Blanc and Gris and a touch of Piquepoul, is a richly nutty, herby style with a lovely toasty undercurrent. Both wines possess a real mineral backbone. The musky, citrussy Verd Albera is much more fruit driven in style. In part this is down to its vinification and part to its 50% Muscat component. The range is completed by two late harvest sweet wines. There is a Muscat and particularly characterful a rich, intensely nutty and complex Garnatxa, coming from old-vine Garnacha Blanca and Rosada and aged in barrel for five to 10 years. (DM)

Recommended Reds:

Empordà Masia Carreras ★★★☆ £D

Empordà Garnatxa Masia Pairal Can Carreras ★★★☆ £D

Recommended Whites:

Empordà Masia Carreras ★★★ £C   Empordà Verd Albera ★★☆ £C

❀ **Mas Alta (Priorat)** *www.bodegasmasalta.com*

This new Belgian owned property seems certain to emerge as one of the greats of Priorat. Already the wines have achieved a rare level and refined quality. 60 ha have been purchased near to Daphne Glorian's CLOS I TERASSES and the vines range from 60 to over 100 years of age. Wine consultancy comes from the Rhône specialist Michel-Tardieu of TARDIEU-LAURENT with oak being supplied by his Burgundian partner Dominique LAURENT. The bright, forward Artigas comes from younger vines, and blends Garnacha, Cariñena and a touch of Cabernet and offers just a hint of minerality on the finish. A further red Cirerets, blending Garnacha and Cariñena slots into the red range just above Artigas. The other two wines are firmer, more structured and backward. Old-vine Cariñena is the most important component of both wines and they both have more new wood in evidence. The powerful rich and concentrated La Creu Alta demands five to seven years cellaring, a year or two longer than La Bassetta. The range is completed by a nutty, characterful white, Artigas which includes Garnacha Blanca and Macabeu and a forward red under the same brand. (DM)

Recommended Reds:

Priorat La Creu Alta ★★★★★ £G   Priorat La Basseta ★★★★☆ £F

Priorat Cirerets ★★★★ £F   Priorat Artigas ★★★☆ £E

Recommended Whites:

Priorat Artigas ★★★☆ £E

Mas Blanch I Jove (Costers del Segre) *www.masblanchijove.com*

Newly established Costers del Segre property founded in 2006. Their vineyards are located close to the western borders of the Priorat region and at significant altitude, around 700 metres above sea level with a high diurnal swing in summer and early autumn day and night temperatures promoting a fresh acidity and structure in the wines. Only fruit from the bodegas own five vineyards is used for the wines and the soils, comprising a mix of clay and chalk have low organic matter and are excellent for producing intensely flavoured grapes and low yields. There are currently five wines including a characterful white produced solely from Macabeu. Fermentation and ageing is for 6 months in medium toast French oak and the wine offers a rich and nutty complexity with an underlying subtle citrus intensity. The most approachable of the reds is the black cherry laden Abrivat which is a blend of Tempranillo, Garnacha,

North-East Spain

Cabernet Sauvignon and Merlot. Ageing is in a combination of French and American oak but very well judged, a clear mineral component in the background underpins the wine. The top wine the red Expressiu is like all the wines here very favourably priced. It is a blend dominated by Garnacha with additional Cabernet Sauvignon providing structure and also Tempranillo. The wine is macerated at controlled temperatures to emphasise its fruit and is aged in moderate toast mainly French oak. It is dark, spicy and full of mineral intensity. A second red, Petit Saó and a rosé, Saó Rosat are also made. (DM)

Recommended Reds:
Costers del Segre Saó Expressiu ★★★☆ £D
Costers del Segre Saó Abrivat ★★★ £C
Recommended Whites:
Costers del Segre Saó Blanc ★★★ £C

❀ Mas Doix (Priorat) *www.masdoix.com*
Although the Doix family have been involved in viticulture here since the 19ᵗʰ century, it wasn't until Ramon Llangostera took over the running of the property with major investment creating a new winery in 1998 that Celler Mas Doix was born. It has emerged as one of the finest bodegas of the region. The vineyards around the village of Poboleda are planted on naturally very low yielding slopes and with Garnacha and Cariñena of between 75 and 100 years of age the potential is tremendous. The Doix Costers de Vinyes Velles is almost totally vinified from Garnacha and Cariñena and from yields often as low as 15 hl/ha. This brilliantly dense and intensely mineral infused red gets a vatting of 30 to 40 days and is in new French oak for 16 months. The second label Salanques is more obviously fruit driven, coming from marginally younger vines and with a touch of Merlot, Cabernet and Syrah blended in. It is more accessible and will drink well with three or four years ageing. A third label, Les Crestes sourced from the youngest Garnacha and Cariñena as well as young Syrah is the softest most approachable of the wines. Expect the Doix Costers de Vinyes Velles to develop well for up to a decade or more. (DM)

Recommended Reds:
Priorat Doix Costers de Vinyes Velles ★★★★★ £G
Priorat Salanques ★★★★ £E   Priorat Les Crestes ★★★ £D

Mas d'En Gil (Priorat) *www.masdengil.com*
This small Mas was founded in 1998 by the Rovira Carbonell family with much investment going into both their 45 ha of vineyards planted in the characteristic slate licorella soils of the area and in the cellars. The result is not only excellent reds but a very characterful white, Coma Blanca, which blends Garnacha Blanca with Macabeo. Rich and nutty with underlying citrus and mineral notes it gains weight and texture from six months in French oak. Coma Vella, the most accessible of the reds is a fruit driven blend of Garnacha, Cariñena, Cabernet, Syrah and Merlot. The Clos Fontá, mainly Garnacha and Cariñena with a quarter Cabernet adding some minty dark fruit, is denser, firmer and more structured with a powerful mineral undercurrent. It demands four or five years cellaring to show at its best. A very small amount of a reserva label Gran Buig is also made in exceptional years from the oldest plots of Garnacha and Cariñena. It is by no means cheap.(DM)

Recommended Reds:
Priorat Clos Fontà ★★★★☆ £F   Priorat Coma Vella ★★★☆ £E
Recommended Whites:
Priorat Coma Blanca ★★★☆ £E

>> Mas Igneus (Priorat) *www.masigneus.com*
A sound range of four red and two white Priorat is produced at this organic and biodynamically pioneering bodega founded in 1996. Based at their Coster de l'Ermita property just outside Gratallops, they have two other estates and source grapes from a number of growers around Poboleda all of whom farm their vines organically. There are old vine holdings of Garnacha and Cariñena as well as newer plantings of Syrah, Cabernet Sauvignon and Merlot and for the whites, Garnacha Blanca, Moscatel, Pedro Ximenez and Macabeo. The cellar is well equipped and each parcel can be vinified separately. There is an approachable red and a white, which are both labelled Barranc dels Clossos. The top white FA104 is solely from Garnacha Blanca and is barrel fermented and aged for a short time in oak, around four months with bâtonnage. There are two FA labelled reds. FA206 is the lighter of the two, it is dominated by Garnacha and is aged for around six months in used oak to emphasise its forward berry fruit. FA112 is more structured with a rich dark fruited character and toasty oak. A blend of Garnacha, Cariñena and Cabernet Sauvignon, like the Coster the malolactic fermentation is carried out in barrel. The low volume, top label red, Coster de L'Ermita is an unfiltered blend of Garnacha and Cariñena of around 70 years of age, it commands a pretty substantial price. (DM)

Recommended Reds:
Priorat Fa 112 ★★★★ £E   Priorat Fa 206 ★★★ £C

>> Mas de L'Abundancia (Montsant) *www.masdelabundancia.com*
A small bodega which was founded in 2002 and is based in the village of El Masroig. Owner, winemaker Jesus del Rio though has origins in the DO that go back to the 1300's. 4.5 ha are farmed and Cariñena and Garnacha are the significant varieties. This has been supplemented by recent plantings of Cabernet Sauvignon. Three reds are made, the flagship Mas de l'Abundància and second label Fluminis as well as a fruit driven style He-Ma. Fluminis unusually has a small proportion of the previous vintage included in its blend and a further portion goes through malolactic fermentation in barrel. The Mas de l'Abundancia is more structured and firm. It is vatted for up to four weeks and is aged for around 12 months in French oak. It is full of dark fruit with a minty quality from its Cabernet component, blended with Mazuelo and Garnacha. A white, Decalpino is also made from old Garnacha Blanca. (DM)

Recommended Reds:
Montsant ★★★☆ £D   Montsant Fluminis ★★★ £C

>> Mas La Mola (Priorat) *www.maslamola.com*
This property has been in the hands of the Ferrando family for over 150 years, although, the winemaking and viticulture are now looked after by Jordi Masdeu Català and Alessandro Marchesan. 7 ha are cultivated and include a mix of old Cariñena, Garnacha, Garnacha Blanca which is planted on steep slate terraces as well as Macabeo planted in gravel. Four wines are made in a small celler in the village of Poboleda. Mas La Mola Blanc comes from a blend of mainly Macabeo as well as Garnacha Blanca. There is a young red label, L'Atzar, produced from younger parcels and blended from Syrah, Garnacha, Cariñena, Cabernet Sauvignon and Merlot. A very limited release top red, La Vinyeta Vella is blended from 65 to 90 year old Garnacha and Cariñena. The dark fruited, lightly herb spiced and mineral La Mola Negre comes from mainly old Garnacha and Cariñena. The winemaking regime involves a long maceration, a separate vinification for each variety and ageing in a mix of new and one year old French oak for around 15 months. (DM)

Recommended Reds:
Priorat Mas La Mola ★★★★ £E

❀ **Mas Martinet (Priorat)** *www.masmartinet.com*
Small family-run operation producing some excellent results in this high-quality DO. The Pérez Ovejero family possess some 7ha of vineyards which yield a marvellously complex, structured wine. In Clos Martinet they handcraft a wine with more elegance and less raw power than some of the wines of their neighbours but rarely with less intensity or finesse. It is a blend of Garnacha, Syrah, Cabernet Sauvignon and Cariñena. Recently added to this are two very rich, structured and intense single vineyard bottlings. Els Escurçons is from a mass selection of Grenache and Syrah, planted at 600 metres, Cami Pesseroles is a blend of old-vine Garnacha and Cariñena. Both possess real depth and weight. One of the winemakers here, José Luis Perez, was also involved with CIMS DE PORRERA. The entry level wine, Martinet Bru, is very well priced and relatively soft and accessible. (DM)

Recommended Reds:
Priorat Cami Pesseroles ★★★★☆ £F
Priorat Els Escurçons ★★★★☆ £F
Priorat Clos Martinet ★★★★☆ £F   Priorat Martinet Bru ★★★☆ £D

Mas Perinet (Priorat) *www.masperinet.com*
This now well established Priorat project was started in 1998 with vineyard holdings in both the Priorat and Montsant appellations. There are a total of some 32 ha now under cultivation but the property covers an area of 269 ha, so there is plenty of scope to develop. The first releases were only at the end of 2004. An increasing number of wines are being added to the range. The white Montsant is a blend of Garnacha Blanco, Chenin Blanc and a little Muscat à Petits Grains. Barrel-fermented in French oak, it offers impressive purity and subtle, nutty, citrus and herb-spiced fruit. The Priorat is in a lighter style than many of the more ferocious examples found elsewhere and is dominated more by elegant dark berry fruit than their raw, mineral *sauvage* quality. A property to watch. Two other reds Perinet Plus and Gotia have also been released. (DM)

Recommended Reds:
Priorat ★★★☆ £E
Recommended Whites:
Montsant Clos Maria ★★★ £C

❀ **Masia Serra (Emporda)** *www.masiaserra.com*
Top class wines are produced at this bodega on the far north-east Mediterranean coast of the country. Established in 1995 there are now 10 ha under vine. The Gneis, named after the soil of the *terroir*, is a finely structured, elegant and concentrated blend of Cabernet Sauvignon, Garnacha and Merlot. Herbal spices are underpinned by a cedary depth adding complexity. Ageing is in French oak for a year and a half and the wine is bottled unfiltered. A second wine lo comes from a very similar blend, it is softer and a touch lighter. A further red Aroa, from a blend of Garnacha and Marselan has also been added. Ctònia is a barrel-fermented white which is 100% Garnacha Blanca offering a creamy nutty complexity. The small range is completed by sweet white Ino which is fortified early leaving considerable sweetness and is a blend of different vintages, a form of *solera* is created before bottling. Deep golden in colour with a nutty, honeyed richness and just a touch of lemon acidity to add balance. The range is now completed by a sparkling Cremant white.(DM)

Recommended Reds:
Empordà Gneis ★★★★ £E   Empordà lo ★★★ £D
Recommended Whites:
Empordà Empordà Ino Garnatxa de L'Empordà ★★★ £E
Empordà Ctònia ★★★ £D

Agustí Torelló Mata (Penedès/Cava) *www.agustitorellomata.com*
One of the stand out Cava producers and making almost exclusively sparkling wines, which are of a consistently impressive quality. A cool fermented white XII and Esperit, a marc distilled from Cava skins are also made. Of the range of Cavas the Rosat Trepat is a fresh fruit-driven rosé with some complexity, the Brut Reserva dry and elegant and with good depth from 24 months on lees. There are three characterful Gran Reservas, one released in a Magnum size only from old vines and a Barrica in which the primary fermentation is partly in barrel. This is made solely from Macabeo, the other white Cavas from a Macabeo, Xarel.lo, Parellada blend. The top wine, Kripta is among the very best Cavas and is also produced from old vines. The Gran Reservas and Kripta are all released without *dosage*. The Bayanus wines are solely available in halves, the rosado is also vinified from Trepat. (DM)

Recommended Whites:
Penedès XII Subirat Parent ★★☆ £C
Cava Brut Nature Kripta Gran Reserva Vintage ★★★★ £F
Cava Brut Nature Gran Reserva Vintage ★★★☆ £E
Cava Brut Nature Gran Reserva Barrica Vintage ★★★☆£E
Cava Brut Nature Bayanus Reserva Vintage ★★★☆ £D
Cava Brut Reserva Vintage ★★★ £D
Recommended Rosés:
Cava Brut Nature Bayanus Rosat Reserva Vintage ★★★ £D
Cava Rosat Reserva Vintage ★★☆ £D

❀ **Melis (Priorat)** *www.melispriorat.com*
This impressive, small Priorat operation is part owned by Santa Barbara based Victor Gallegos who also spearheads the viticulture at SEA SMOKE CELLARS in California's coastal Sta. Rita Hills AVA. The vineyards are planted at between 250 and 350 metres above sea level in the classic volcanic schist and licorella slate soils of the region. Work on the vineyards began in 2000 and new plantings of close-spaced and spur pruned Garnacha, Cariñena, Syrah and Cabernet Sauvignon have been added to some ancient Cariñena already planted. Low yielding fruit and meticulous care in the vineyard provide two wines of excellent dark fruit intensity, purity and balance as well as an underlying mineral quality from the soils. Elix, which like its sister wine, comes from a blend of the vineyards grape varieties along with some Merlot and is softer and more approachable. Melis is tighter, more structured and offers greater depth and dimension. Both wines are very polished examples of the appellation and are bottled unfined and unfiltered. (DM)

Recommended Reds:
Priorat Melis ★★★★★ £F   Priorat Elix ★★★★ £E

❀ **Bodega Abel Mendoza Monge (Rioja)**
One of an emerging number of high-quality small bodegas. A number of red and white Rioja's are made here. The two whites are barrel-fermented and aged and impressive and well-priced varietal examples. The Joven and Crianza reds are solely from Tempranillo and aged in French rather than American oak. The 18ha of vineyards in the shadow of the Sierra Cantabria mountains are planted in clay/limestone and stony, sandy soils, which provide an excellent *terroir*. The entry-level red is a vibrant, fruit-filled, exuberant wine

Spain

produced by carbonic maceration for drinking young. The Jarrarte is a stylish, well-structured barrel aged (older barrels are used) Rioja, with rich fruit and supple, well-rounded tannins. It will develop well over 4–5 years. The Selección Personal, is aged in new oak. Powerful, dense and impeccably balanced it has the depth and structure to develop very well over 8–10 years. Equally ageworthy are two very impressive varietal examples of Tempranillo and Graciano. These are rich, sumptuous modern style Riojas with the malolactic in barrel. (DM)

Recommended Reds:
Rioja Graciano ★★★★☆ £G   Rioja Tempranillo ★★★★ £E
Rioja Selección Personal Crianza ★★★★ £E
Rioja Jarrarte Crianza ★★★☆ £C
Rioja Jarrarte Joven ★★ £B
Recommended Whites:
Rueda Malvasia ★★★ £C   Rueda Viura ★★☆ £C

Merum Priorati (Priorat) *www.merumpriorati.com*
This is a new venture benefiting from the winemaking expertise of Don Lewis, the former head winemaker at MITCHELTON in Australia. The property is based in the eastern sector of the Priorat DO, in Porrera. Two red wines are produced, both of which are vinified in small open fermenters with hand plunging. The wine is then matured by individual parcel and blended at bottling after 12 months. The lighter, more approachable Ardiles is a mix of mainly Garnacha and Cariñena from both newer and older vines, with a small amount of Syrah and Cabernet to add both structure as well as an additional flavour dimension. Ageing is in a combination of new and older *barriques*. The denser and powerfully structured Osmin is more obviously mineral with a spicy dark undercurrent and old-viney character to its fruit. It is a blend of 80 to 100 year old Garnacha and Cariñena as well as younger Syrah, Cabernet and Merlot. A toasty note is added to the meaty, flinty character of the fruit from 100% new oak and the wine will undoubtedly benefit from at least five years ageing. A white is also now made which comes from Viognier. (DM)

Recommended Reds:
Priorat Osmin ★★★★☆ £F   Priorat Ardiles ★★★☆ £E

>> Bodegas Montecillo (Rioja) *www.bodegasmontecillo.com*
This is the Rioja branch of the giant Osborne sherry based wine group. Just four traditionally styled wines are made of uniformly sound quality. The bodega, the third oldest in the region, is now run by family member Rocío Osborne. She is one of the sixth generation of the Osborne family. This is a substantial operation with a large modern winemaking facility and a stock of 20,000 barrels for ageing. There is though a move for the fruit to be more expressive than in the past, particularly in the Crianza. The fruit for all the wines comes from La Rioja Alta and gives them a fine and fresh edge. Crianza now gets around 10% Graciano blended with Tempranillo. Vinification remains traditional but fermentation temperature is controlled before ageing for 18 months in American oak. The other three wines are all so far solely from Tempranillo. Resreva fermentation is again controlled with a slightly longer three week vatting before ageing in a mix of Frenach and American barrels for 24 months. The Gran Reserva now enjoys a similarly modern approach. A marginally longer 26 months in is spent in oak. The Gran Reserva Selección Especial is different, the current release being the 2001. The primary fermentation, vatting and ageing period were not that different to the Gran Reserva. The wine has just been aged for much longer, well over 10 years. (DM)

Recommended Reds:
Rioja Gran Reserva Selección Especial ★★★★ £F
Rioja Gran Reserva ★★★☆ £D   Rioja Reserva ★★★ £D
Rioja Crianza ★★☆ £C

❀ Bodegas Muga (Rioja) *www.bodegasmuga.com*
This family-owned bodega is relatively small by Rioja standards. The approach is fiercely traditional for most of the range and at best the wines can be very good. Fermentation is in wooden vats and ageing in oak and the Reserva, Selección Especial and Gran Reserva can display classically mellow, rounded Tempranillo character with vanilla and coconut notes infused from extended time in cask. Tempranillo is blended with Garnacha, Mazuelo and Graciano in the Reserva, Selección Especial and Prado Enea; with Mazuelo and Graciano in the impressive and expensive new, modern-style Torre Muga, which is loaded with vibrant blackberry fruit and velvety tannin. The top wine is the splendidly complex Aro, a blend of 60 year old Tempranillo and Graciano aged for 18 months in new Franch oak. Good white Fermentado en Barrica shows some depth and some decent, fruity rosé completes the range. (DM)

Recommended Reds:
Rioja Aro ★★★★★ £H   Rioja Torre Muga ★★★★☆ £F
Rioja Gran Reserva Prado Enea ★★★☆ £E
Rioja Selección Especial Reserva ★★★☆ £E
Rioja Muga ★★★ £D
Recommended Whites:
Rioja Blanco ★★ £C
Recommended Rosés:
Rioja Rosado ★☆ £B

❀ Bodegas Ostatu (Rioja) *www.ostatu.com*
A family-run bodega – still quite rare in this region of large commercial interests – producing Rioja of exemplary quality, white as well as red. They have just 26ha in the higher-altitude vineyards of the Rioja Alavesa planted on chalkyclay soils. There are a total of six reds now made including a young red wine vinified in part by carbonic maceration one white, tank fermented and aged on fine lees as well as a rosé. The top reds are all very modern in style. The Crianza is Tempranillo, Garnacha and Graciano aged in a combination of French and American oak; it offers real depth at this level. The Reserva is aged for 16 months in largely French oak. Rich, dense, darker and smokier than you would normally find from the region, it blends 90% Tempranillo with some Graciano. The Laderas del Portillo is almost all Tempranillo with a tiny amount of Viura. Ageing is in French oak and the modern approach continued with the malolactic fermentation in barrel. The top wine, Gloria de Ostatu, is amongst the best modern reds in Rioja. It is 100% Tempranillo, sourced from the family's oldest vines on steep south-west facing slopes and aged in all-new French oak. This wine needs and demands time to come into balance and a splendid depth and complexity here should emerge with 5 or 6 years' ageing. (DM)

Recommended Reds:
Rioja Gloria de Ostatu ★★★★☆ £F
Rioja Laderas del Portillo ★★★★ £E
Rioja Reserva ★★★☆ £D   Rioja Crianza ★★★ £C
Recommended Whites:
Rioja ★★☆ £C

Oxinbaltza (Bizkaiko Txakolina) *www.oxinbaltza.com*
Three excellent whites and a red example of Bizkaiko are made at this small bodega from Hondarrabi Zuri. There are 23 ha of vines

under cultivation and these are planted, in the main, on terraces, or steeply aspected slopes and despite the close proximity of the Bay of Biscay, at an altitude of 200 to 400 metres. The harvest is all manual and in the cellar there is temperature control and the wines bottled without filtration. The Katan is crisp, fresh and full of zesty apple scented fruit with a restrained mineral undercurrent. The Oxinbaltza is barrel fermented, adding weight and a rounder texture but with equally impressive intensity. Maiora is a stylish late harvest wine. The red Mauma comes from Hondarrabi Beltza. (DM)

Recommended Whites:

Bizkaiko Txakolina Oxinbaltza ★★★★ £D
Bizkaiko Txakolina Maiora ★★★☆ £C
Bizkaiko Txakolina Katan ★★★ £C

>> Pago de Cirsus (Navarra) *www.pagodecirsus.com*

Owner Inaki Nunez comes from a significant background in film distribution and production. He established his bodega in 2002 and built a striking tower which is in homage to medieval Navarra. The project is based in the Ribera Baja in the south of the Navarra DO where there are 135 ha under vine. A range of modern well-made wines is produced, white, rosado and red with technical guidance from Bordeaux consultant Jean Marc Sauboua. Chardonnay comes in two guises. There is a clean and fresh, cool fermented example, which is then aged for 12 months in French oak. More serious, richer and with a creamy texture and intense citrus fruit is the Fermentado en Barrica, which is barrel fermented and aged with lees stirring. The characterful dark cherry and plum scented Vendimia Seleccionada has a hint of underlying toasty oak and is aged for 14 months in French wood and combines Tempranillo, Merlot and Syrah. The Cuvée Especial (Tempranillo, Merlot and Syrah) is a touch richer enjoying a similar period in small barrels. The varietal Tempranillo Seleccion de Familia is a little pricier and a special selection. A small amount of a further red Opus II, which blends Tempranillo and Syrah is also made along with late harvest Moscatel. (DM)

Recommended Reds:

Navarra Selección de Familia ★★★☆ £D
Navarra Cuvée Especial ★★★ £C
Navarra Vendimia Selecciónada ★★☆ £B

Recommended Whites:

Navarra Chardonnay BFB ★★★ £C
Navarra Pago de Cirsus Chardonnay ★★ £B

Pago de Larrainzar (Navarra) *www.pagodelarrainzar.com*

This is a very newly established bodega, fouded in 2001 and located in the far northern reaches of the Navarra DO. Two wines are made and quality is the the keyword here. Owner Miguel Canalejo was a successful Navarran businessman and a similar commitment and dedication is clearly showing through in his family's wines. The vineyard area covers 13 ha and is planted to a mix of Tempranillo, Cabernet Sauvignon, Merlot and Garnacha from different clones planted in sparse stony, clay and sandy soils. Harvesting is by hand and there is a rigorous selection both in the vineyard and at the winery. Vinification is in stainless steel and all four varieties are fermented separately. Ageing is in a mix of new and one and two year old barrels in a temperature and humidity controlled cellar. Pago de Larrainzar Reservea Especial, the top wine wine is one of the finest in the appellation, rich and concentrated with supple tannins and with a sumptuous, velvety quality. The second wine Raso de Larrainzar is barely less impressive. While immediately approachable on release, expect the Pago de Larrainzar to evolve well for a decade. A Cabernet Sauvignon and a third wine, Angel de

Larrainzar, are also now made. (DM)

Recommended Reds:

Navarra Pago de Larrainzar Reserva Especial ★★★☆ £E
Navarra Raso de Larrainzar ★★★ £C

>> Pagos del Moncayo *www.pagosdelmoncayo.com*

As well as ALTO MONCAYO this is the other top quality small winery in Campo de Borja. The bodega is only just over a decade old but crucially some of the fruit in the wines comes from vines over 80 years old. Situated in the shadow of the Sierra del Moncayo, the sparse calcareous soils and continental climate provide for fruit with real flavour intensity and excellent potential structure in the wines. Four reds are made. The Pagos del Moncayo is a Joven style, vibrant and full of juicy dark berry fruit. The top varietal wines are both impressive. The Garnacha has just a touch more structure, spending around 10 months in barrel but maintaining a core of ripe, sweet dark fruit and spice. The Syrah has a similar cellar regime as the Garnacha and is in a ripe dark fruited style, with more opulent candied fruit than black pepper. A marginally pricier (£E) blend of the two, Privé, is also made. (DM)

Recommended Reds:

Campo de Borja Garnacha ★★★★ £D
Campo de Borja Syrah ★★★☆ £D
Campo de Borja Pagos del Moncayo ★★★ £C

Palacios Remondo (Rioja)

As well as producing his own extraordinary range in Priorat, Alvaro PALACIOS has also had a significant recent contribution to the family property in the Rioja Baja. The 150 ha of vineyards are covered with large pebbles and provide a formidable resource for intensely flavoured fruit. There is a lightly oaked white Plácet, as well as a range of reds here which impress. La Vendimia is partly vinified by carbonic maceration, which provides a wine of immediate appeal. Dark and spicy La Montesa Crianza spends up to a year in French oak. Propriedad is the new flagship red and is fermented in large wooden casks and then transferred to *barrique* for malolactic. It is supple, harmonious and richly extracted. (DM)

Recommended Reds:

Rioja Propriedad H Remondo ★★★☆ £E
Rioja La Montesa Crianza ★★★ £D   Rioja La Vendimia ★★☆ £C

Recommended Whites:

Rioja Plácet ★★★☆ £D

✸✸ Alvaro Palacios (Priorat)

Alvaro Palacios established this excellent small property in the late 1980s and he produces some very good to quite exceptional examples of the Priorat DO from his 10ha of vineyards. Experience gained in the Napa Valley has enabled him to produce modern, very finely crafted examples from this small but great region. The entry level Camins del Priorat is a forward, perfumed blend of Garnacha, Cariñena, and a little Cabernet Sauvignon and Syrah. Les Terasses has a higher proportion of Cariñena, some of it very old and the result is always harmonious and impressive, the wine displaying supple tannin and an exotic, dark fruit quality. Gratallops is a bit pricier and is dominated by Garnacha and Cariñena with again a smattering of Cab Sauv and Syrah as well as Picapoll and comes from vineyards in Gratallops. The magnificently concentrated L'Ermita is produced from very old Garnacha vines. Finca Dofi has around 4/5ths Garnacha, with a firm structure provided by the inclusion of a little Cabernet Sauvignon, Syrah, Merlot and Cariñena. It is very complex, with an almost floral, cedary character as well as

Spain

the rich, dark fruit of the Garnacha. Finca Dofi and L'Ermita are both extremely refined and very ageworthy, improving effortlessly for a decade or more. Palacios also looks after the wines at his family bodega in Rioja, at Palacios Remondo and is also involved with his nephew Ricardo Perez at Descendientes de J Palacios in Bierzo.(DM)

Recommended Reds:
Priorat L'Ermita ✪✪✪✪ £H   Priorat Finca Dofi ★★★★★ £F
Priorat Gratallops ★★★★☆ £F   Priorat Les Terrasses ★★★★ £E
Priorat Camins del Priorat ★★★☆ £D

Pardas (Penedès) www.cellerpardas.com
Small bodega established in 1997 in the Alt Penedès. There are 30 ha under vine and a small range of both local and international grapes are grown. The vines are planted on terraces in a mixed clay and calcareous soil and yields are actively controlled. The small winery is well equipped and laid out to operate the winemaking and cellar handling processes by gravity. The Rupestris Blanc (Xarel·lo, Xarel·lo Vermell, Malvasía and Macabeo) is a fresh and crisp style, fermented in tank and bottled early. A touch more serious is the Xarel.lo, barrel fermented and aged. Of the reds, the supple, approachable Negre Franc (Cabernet Sauvignon, Cabernet Franc, Merlot and Sumoll) is full of ripe dark cherry fruit. It is aged for 11 months in French oak with the smaller Cabernet Sauvignon component going through malolactic fermentation in barrel. More structured and offering greater depth is the rich dark berry fruited Aspriu which is vinified from both Cabernet Sauvignon and Franc. A long maceration on skins for up to a month is followed by 13 months in new French oak. A similar approach to the malolactic provides a wine with a rich texture and creamy, toasty oak. A rosado Sumoll comes from the local variety of the same name and the variety is blended with Marselan in another red, Collita Roja. The range is completed with a second, premium priced Aspriu Xarel.lo.. (DM)

Recommended Reds:
Penedès Aspriu ★★★★ £E   Penedès Negre Franc ★★★ £C
Recommended Whites:
Penedès Xarel.lo ★★★ £C   Penedès Rupestris ★★☆ £C

✿ Parés Baltá (Penedes & Priorat) www.paresbalta.com
This sizeable and ancient Penedes producer, established in 1790, has an extensive range which includes both still wines and Cava. There are 174ha under vine and the total output is now approaching 70,000 cases a year. The regular Cavas and still wines offer decent value for money and the Mas Elena red stands out, a soft, lightly herbal, forward blend of Cabernet Sauvignon, Merlot and Cabernet Franc, Mas Petit is Cabernet Sauvignon and Garnaxta (grenache). Of the two rosado styles Ros de Pacs blends Cabernet Sauvignon and Merlot, Radix is a juicy Shiraz with just four hours skin contact. The soft fruity Blanc de Pacs blends Macabeo, Xarello and Parellada, Calcari is a more complex Xarello aged on stirred lees. Ginesta is a fine and spicy, varietally pure Gewürztraminer sourced from high altitude vines. The Special Selection wines, produced in small volume and from the lowest yielding sites, are where some of the most impressive results are being achieved. Long maceration and new oak are the order of the day for the reds, with barrel-fermentation on lees for the premium white, Electio, vinified from Xarello. There are four sturdy and characterful premium reds. Mas Irene blends Cabernet Franc and Merlot, whereas Absis is a mix of Tempranillo, Merlot Cabernet Sauvignon and Syrah. Hisenda Miret is a spicy, herb scented Garnaxta, Marta de Baltá a densely packed, licoricey Syrah. The Absis in particular requires a minimum of 6–7 years to shed its burly tannins. There are also two very good sweet

wines Music white and red. The white is fully Chardonnay, the red Tempranillo and Cabernet. The winery also produces the very limited-production Dominio Cusiné 1790. Cava is also important here and Blanca Cusiné and the 100% Chardonnay Cuvée de Carol are both notable. Both have primary fermentation in barrel. The family also own the Gratavinum winery in Priorat where they are producing fine, more fruit driven reds than some of the more ferocious examples elsewhere in the region. Their 17 ha in Gratallops are farmed organically and planted on terraces. Two well made wines are made. 2PR is in a marginally more fruit driven style, whereas the GV5 is firmer and more structured. Both wines are aged for up to a year in a mix of French and, unusually, Hungarian oak. (DM)

Parés Baltá
Recommended Reds:
Penedès Absis ★★★★ £G Penedès Marta de Baltá ★★★★ £F
Vino de Mesa Music ★★★☆ £E   Penedès Hisenda Miret ★★★☆ £D
Penedès Mas Irene ★★★ £C   Penedès Mas Elena ★★ £B
Penedès Mas Petit ★★ £B   Penedès Indigena ★★ £B
Recommended Whites:
Vino de Mesa Music ★★★☆ £E   Penedès Electio ★★★ £E
Penedès Ginesta ★★★ £D   Penedès Calcari ★★☆ £C
Penedès Blanc de Pacs ★☆ £B   Cava Blanca Cusiné ★★☆ £C
Cava Cuvée de Carol ★★ £C
Recommended Rosés:
Penedès Radixs ★★ £B   Penedès Ros de Pacs ★☆ £B
Gratavinum
Recommended Reds:
Priorat GV5 ★★★★ £F   Priorat 2PR ★★★☆ £E

✿ Parmi Priorat (Priorat) www.parmipriorat.com
This is a recently established, Italian owned operation confirming the considerable interest in this special appellation which now has owners and winemakers from across the wine world. A small range is produced and quality is good to very good, in particular the splendid La Coma. Here, as is the case with other small producers, the potential greatness of Cariñena is being confirmed. A second old vine red is produced from the variety, Il Mas de Salut, which we plan to bring further news of later in the year. Younger vines are also important and the decision at Parmi is to focus on Garnacha to complement their old Cariñena vines. The most approachable of the wines is the young vine L'Infant de Porrera, sourced from a number of sites around the village of Porrera and from mainly Garnacha vines up to 15 years old. A good deal more serious and structured is the Cariñena and Garnacha blend, L'Esperit de Porrera, sourced from 40 to 60 year old bush vines. La Coma is of a different order. It comes from tiny yields and 80 to 100 year old vines and the wine possesses a subtle and very elegant mineral quality as well as intense dark, spicy black fruits. While much of the vineyard here is very venerable, vinification is thoroughly modern. There is a carefully organised triage, fermentation is in *inox* and the wines are aged in French oak with the malolactic in barrel. (DM)

Recommended Reds:
Priorat La Coma ★★★★★ £G   Priorat L'Esperit de Porrera ★★★★ £F
Priorat L'Infant de Porrera ★★★☆ £E

Partida Bellvisos (Priorat)
This is a very small bodega jointly owned by René Barbier Jnr from CLOS MOGADOR and his winemaker wife Sara Perez whose family own MAS MARTINET. Through their company they also produce the excellent Montsant wines at VENUS LA UNIVERSAL. The annual

production is just 1,000 bottles a year at present and the wine is produced from steeply sloping vineyards planted on finely drained licorella soils, a form of schist. Around four hectares are cultivated and the vines are of a significant age, over 60 years which contributes to the rich, spicy old-vine tarry, blackberry complexity of the wine. Partida Bellvisos is a blend of Garnacha Peluda (a variant of Grenache with the underside of the leaves having a hairy appearance) and Carineña. The wine is aged for 20 months in 300 litre barrels to emphasise the quality of its fruit. (DM)

Recommended Reds:
Priorat Gratallops Partida Bellvisos ★★★★☆ £F

Pasanau Germans (Priorat) *www.cellerpasanau.com*
Small Priorat property producing wines of impressive style and excellent value in a region not especially noted for it. Pasanau has some of the highest vineyards in the appellation on the viticultural boundary between Priorat and Montsant. The Finca La Planeta comes from a 3ha plot planted on meagre rocky soils with a gravelly top soil. The growing conditions are excellent for cultivating Cabernet Sauvignon and this dominates the blend but Garnacha contributes 20% and gives the wine a rich opulent character as well as a firm mineral structure. The Ceps Nous is softer, more forward with more obvious berry fruit. It combines Garnacha, Cariñena, Merlot and Syrah. Newly added is a single vineyard old-vine Cariñena, El Vell Coster. (DM)

Recommended Reds:
Priorat Finca La Planeta ★★★★ £E   Priorat Ceps Nous ★★★☆ £D

✿ Celler Vinos Piñol (Terra Alta) *www.vinospinol.com*
One of the very best producers in this small DO in the far north-east of the country. Part of the key to quality here is the altitude of the 37 ha of vineyards at some 450m. The whites are good enough at the top level although they lack the quality and depth of the reds. The soft and lightly fruity Señora del Portal is dominated by Garnacha Blanco with a little Sauvignon and Maccabeo. The barrel-fermented and aged L'Avi Arrufí is again dominated by Garnacha but is very heavily oaked. The reds have a splendid dark berry and herb-spice character with some real old-vine complexity showing through in the top wines. Raig de Raim is soft and supple, made from Garnacha with a hint of Merlot. Señora del Portal is 20% each of Garnacha, Tempranillo, Cabernet Sauvignon, Merlot and Shiraz, given 6 months in oak for extra weight and flesh. The Sacra Natural is a characterful blend of very old Cariñena with a little Merlot, Syrah and Tempranillo. The red L'Avi Arrufí, sourced from the highest vineyards on the estate and from 50-year-old vines, is really dark, spicy and minerally. The top wine is the Mather Teresina, a selection of the oldest vines and a non-vintage blend.(DM)

Recommended Reds:
Terra Alta Mather Teresina ★★★★ £E
Terra Alta L'Avi Arrufí ★★★☆ £E   Terra Alta Señora del Portal ★★★ £E
Terra Alta Sacra Natural ★★★ £C   Terra Alta Raig de Raïm ★★☆ £C

Recommended Whites:
Terra Alta L'Avi Arrufí ★★★ £E   Terra Alta Señora del Portal ★★☆ £B

Celler del Pont (Priorat) *www.cellerdelpont.com*
Recently established small Priorat property producing a sturdy, powerful and richly mineral-laden red, Lo Givot. The wine is a blend of Garnacha, Cariñena, Cabernet Sauvignon and Syrah. At present the vineyard area stretches over around 5 ha, and half of the vines are over 50 years old, planted on free-draining shale hillside slopes. All of the varieties are vinified separately in stainless steel and

maturation takes place in mainly French and some American oak for 12–14 months. The wine is full of dark, spicy Grenache varietal character and is less austerely mineral and *sauvage* in style and character than some others from the appellation. It deserves 5 or 6 years' ageing to show at its best. (DM)

Recommended Reds:
Priorat Lo Givot ★★★★☆ £F

Portal del Montsant (Montsant) *www.glevaestates.com*
This is now a part of the Gleva Estates group of bodegas who have interests not just in Montsant but also further afield in Rioja, Ribera del Duero, Rueda, Alella and Cava. Although these Montsant wines are generally in a forward berry fruited, rather than intensely mineral style, nonetheless they do offer impressive depth and complexity throughout the small range. The vineyards are planted in a range of soils including clay, chalk and sand with the highest elevation at up to 800 metres. Add to this some very old vine Cariñena and there is real potential here. The entry level red and white are both labelled Bruberry, the red is bright and vibrant. A touch more depth can be found in the Brunus red and a Rosado is also made under the same label. The top two wines are the red and white Santbru. The dark, spicy and complex red is full of old vine character. (DM)

Recommended Reds:
Montsant Santbru ★★★☆ £D
Montsant Brunus ★★★ £C

Recommended Whites:
Montsant Santbru ★★★☆ £D

Portal del Priorat (Priorat) *www.portaldelpriorat.com*
Alfredo Arribas sold his sister Montsant operation, PORTAL DEL MONTSANT in late 2010. He now focuses not only on Priorat both under the renamed Clos de Portal label as well as a fruit driven well priced red Gotes but also Montsant red and whites under a new brand Trossos. The top red and white are labelled Tros Negre and Tros Blanc and second wines Trossos Sants white and Trossos Vells red have been made from the 2011 harvest. There are three very good to fine reds made under the Clos de Portal banner. 14 ha are cultivated organically on a mix of roughly half costers (slopes) and half terraces. As well as Cariñena and Garnacha; Cabernet Franc, Syrah and experimental Monastrell are also grown. The concentrated dark fruited, spicy Negre de Negres (Garnacha, Cariñena, Cabernet Sauvignon, Syrah) is the most approachable of the wines with real depth and intensity nonetheless. The Somni from a mix of Cariñena, Syrah and Garnacha is dark, richly berry fruited and with a fine mineral undercurrent, it is a touch more concentrated. The top red the Tros de Clos comes from very old one hundred year old vines. (DM)

Recommended Reds:
Priorat Clos del Portal Tros de Clos ★★★★☆ £F
Priorat Clos del Portal Somni ★★★★☆ £F
Priorat Clos del Portal Negre de Negres ★★★☆ £E
Priorat Gotes ★★★ £D
Montsant Trossos Tros Negre ★★★★ £F

Recommended Whites:
Montsant Trossos Tros Blanc ★★★★ £F

✿ Pujanza (Rioja) *www.bodegaspujanza.com*
A very impressive winery based in the Rioja Alavesa producing dense modern style Rioja's. The bodega was established in 1998 and there is a vineyard holding of some 40 ha around the village of Laguardia planted in clay and limestone soils. The Pujanza Hado

North-East Spain

Spain

bottling is a 100% Tempranillo coming from 20 year old vines and aged solely in French oak. Rich, ripe and supple the wine is full of dark-berry fruit and well judged oak. The Norte which comes from older vines and mainly Tempranillo sees longer in new French oak is denser and firmer with really impressive depth and concentration. The top wine the Cisma is a seriously rich and structured red of considerable depth and dimension. It comes with a seriously high price tag as well. A further Tempranillo based red Finca Valdepoleo is made as well as a white Viura based white Rioja Añadas Frías (DM)

Recommended Reds:
Rioja Pujanza Cisma ★★★★★ £G Rioja Pujanza Norte ★★★★☆ £F
Rioja Pujanza Hado ★★★☆ £D

Recaredo (Penedes & Cava) *www.recaredo.es*
Some very good Penedès and excellent Cava is made at this bodega founded in 1924 by Josep Mata Capellades. The cellars are still in the family house in Sant Sadurní d'Anoia. There are 50 ha under vine, planted at an altitude of up to 300 metres and spread across six vineyards, all of which are farmed organically. The most approachable of the white Penedès is the Aloers, a crisp fresh style coming from vines grown in calcareous soils and a blend of Xarel.lo, Macabeo and Parellada. The wine comes solely from biodynamically farmed estate vineyard fruit and gets a very short barrel fermentation and ageing period of just over a month to add to the wine's structure. Can Credo by contrast is a varietal Xarel.lo. The Cavas are all quality benchmarks. They are all Brut Nature, completely dry in style and are manually disgorged with the remuage all done by hand. Local varieties are also key in the style of the wines. The Brut Nature (Xarel.lo, Macabeo, Parellada) is fresh, structured and its citrus fruit underpinned by subtle yeast notes. The Brut de Brut (Xarel.lo, Parellada) is a more complex and beguiling wine. It comes from older vines and gets well over five years on its lees in bottle. The Reserva Particular (Macabeo, Xarel.lo) is a step up in both quality and price. It's intense, structured and very complex with subtle fruit and yeast notes underpinned by a real mineral quality. The wine spends over six years on lees in bottle. The bodega also make a rosado, Intens, a further vintage Brut Nature, Subtil Gran Reserva and a second very pricey special cuvée Turo d'en Mota from very old vines and solely coming from Xarel.lo. (DM)

Recommended Whites:
Cava Reserva Particular ★★★★★ £G
Cava Brut de Brut ★★★★☆ £F Cava Brut Nature ★★★★ £E
Penedès Can Credo ★★★☆ £E Penedès Aloers ★★★ £D

❀ Remelluri (Rioja) *www.remelluri.es*
Remelluri is now established as one of the best of the new-wave Rioja producers although the vineyard origins date back to the 19th century. The bodega was also the first single estate property in the region. Telmo RODRÍGUEZ, responsible for building the reputation of the bodega and once again the winemaker, has a number of other projects as well, growing vines and producing wines in many of Spain's major appellations under his own banner, Compania de Vinos Telmo Rodríguez. There are 105 ha planted here in the Rioja Alavesa and the vineyards are tended organically. French rather than American oak is used during the wine's *élevage* and the style provides greater fruit than ha been the case in the region. A white is now made from a mix of varieties and is fermented and aged in French oak for 12 months. A newly added red, Lindes de Remelluri is bright and forward and vinified from bought in fruit. The Reserva and Gran Reserva, particularly, are structured and will stand some ageing. (DM)

Recommended Reds:
Rioja Gran Reserva ★★★★☆ £F Rioja Reserva ★★★★ £E

❀ Remírez de Ganuza (Rioja) *www.remirezdeganuza.com*
Top-quality Rioja bodega based in the Rioja Alavesa with 57 ha under vine. Four good to exceptional reds of real distinction are produced and the Trasnocho is one of the region's great wines. In addition an easy-drinking, forward wine, Erre Punto R, is mainly produced by carbonic maceration and there is a white counterpart vinified from Viura and Malvasía. The richly textured Fincas de Ganuza Reserva is an immediately appealing blend. The tannin is supple and rounded and it will drink well young. The Reserva is more classically structured. Tight and restrained in its youth, this is a wine marked more by elegance than sheer weight or concentration. By contrast, the opulent and exotic Trasnocho is a massive, extracted but very well balanced Tempranillo: pricey but one of the very best of the new wave of Rioja reds. It can be surprisingly open; however, this is a wine that will add complexity with age. (DM)

Recommended Reds:
Rioja Trasnocho ★★★★☆ £G
Rioja Remirez de Ganuza Reserva ★★★★ £F
Rioja Fincas de Ganuza Reserva ★★★☆ £E
Rioja Erre Punto ★★☆ £C
Recommended Whites:
Rioja Erre Punto ★★★ £D

❀ La Rioja Alta (Rioja) *www.riojalta.com*
This is one of the most fiercely traditional of the old Rioja bodegas. It is a moderately sizeable operation with a production of around 40,000 cases a year. It was originally founded in 1890 and some founding families still have a share in the company. It is renowned for some of the very best traditional Reservas and Gran Reservas. Interests include the Bodega Torre de Oña, also in Rioja, where a modern, fruit-driven Baron de Oña is made and the Rías Baixas property Lagar de Cervera, where an attractive, peachy, fruit-driven white Rías Baixas is produced. At the La Rioja Alta winery the wines are given considerable cask-ageing. The Viña Alberdi Reserva is the most modern with a mere 2 years in oak, a high proportion of it new. The Gran Reservas 904 and 890 spend respectively 5 and 8 years in cask. There is no doubt that the sheer quality of the fruit and the wines' intensity is exemplary but releases tasted throughout the last 10 years have been somewhat variable. A new state-of-the-art winery has also been completed in the Ribera del Duero and the first wines are now being marketed under the Aster brand. Ripe and spicy examples of the DO they are not yet at quite the level of leaders of the appellation. Prior to this the fruit from the first seven harvests was sold to other producers. (DM)

La Rioja Alta
Recommended Reds:
Rioja 890 Gran Reserva ★★★★☆ £G
Rioja 904 Gran Reserva ★★★★☆ £F
Rioja Viña Ardanza Reserva ★★★☆ £E
Rioja Viña Arana Reserva ★★★ £D
Rioja Viña Alberdi Reserva ★★★ £D
Bodega Torre de Oña
Recommended Reds:
Rioja Barón de Oña Reserva ★★★ £D
Bodega Aster
Recommended Reds:
Ribera del Duero Reserva ★★★ £E

Lagar de Cervera
Recommended Whites:
Rías Baixas Lagar de Cervera ★★★ £D

Cellers Ripoll Sans (Priorat) *www.closabatllet.com*
This is a very good small Priorat estate. Both red and white examples are made in artisan style and quantity. Marc Ripoll has some excellent terraced vineyards and vines up to 100 years of age which contribute significantly to the dense, black-fruited, mineral-laden Closa Batllet red. Firmly structured and ageworthy, it is a blend of Cariñena, Garnacha with small amounts of Cabernet Sauvignon and the balance Syrah. The wine is aged in a mix of French and American oak for just over a year. A number of other reds are also now made. Torroja Ronçavall is a single vineyard old vine Cariñena, while 2 Vinyes is from the same grape and 90 to 100 year old vines and two vineyard sources. A third Cariñena, 5 Partides, comes from five separate parcels of again very old vines up to 100 years of age. Artai is a younger vine red from a blend of varieties. There are also a couple of whites. One is produced solely from the local Escanyavella and is barrel fermented for around four months, while the Closa Batllet Blanco is also aged for a short time in oak and the Escanyavella blended with Garnacha Blanca. ((DM)
Recommended Reds:
Priorat Closa Batllet ★★★★ £F

✪ **Roda (Rioja & Ribera del Duero)** *www.roda.es*
Roda is an impressive 76 ha Rioja property producing two Reservas and a new-wave Rioja super *cuvée*, the very pricey Cirsion as well as an approachable forward younger wine style Sela which comes from youthful vines. The property was established in 1987 although much of the vineyard is well over 30 years old. Current plantings comprise mainly Tempranillo with a smattering of Graciano and Garnacha. Roda I is the flagship of the two Reservas, powerful and concentrated but with an underlying spicy, berry fruit character. Roda is a touch lighter but still much more than a second wine. Cirsion, aged in all new French oak, is rich, structured and cedary – a wine of great finesse and breeding. The firm have also established a new project, La Horra, in Ribera del Duero, after spending 4 years researching the best potential sites for Tinto Fino in the region. La Horra is a joint venture partnership with local growers who farm 40 ha of old vine parcels in the province of Burgos. Currently two wines, both branded Corimbo are crafted. The Corimbo is a more forward approachable style, particularly in the context of this appellation. Corimbo I is bigger, fuller and with a richer texture and more structured. Average vine age is now over 20 years and vinification is traditional in a mix of stainless steel and wooden vats and ageing in mainly French and a little American oak, the Corimbo I seeing a little longer in barrel, 16 months as opposed to 12 for the Corimbo.
Bodegas Roda
Recommended Reds:
Rioja Cirsion ✪✪✪✪✪ £H   Rioja Roda I Reserva ★★★★☆ £F
Rioja Roda I ★★★★ £E   Rioja Sela ★★☆ £C
Bodega La Horra
Recommended Reds:
Ribera del Duero Corimbo I ★★★★ £E
Ribera del Duero Corimbo ★★★ £D

✪✪ **Telmo Rodríguez** *www.telmorodriguez.com*
Telmo Rodríguez is one of Spain's great winemaking stars. From his base in Logroño he produces an extensive range of wines from throughout the country in highly diverse styles and now with significant vineyard holdings across a number of appellations which are farmed organically. He is also once more in charge of winemaking at his family bodega, REMELLURI. A good, fresh, fruit-driven Rueda, Basa Blanco, is vinified mainly from Verdejo. This is joined by a more structured and much lower volume 100% Verdejo, El Transistor vinified and raised in a mix of small oak, cement and stainless steel. Three good to very good examples of Ribera del Duero are produced including the exceptional Matellana which is rich, dense and full of dark fruit and smoky spices. It will improve for a decade or more. The Rioja Lanzaga is intense and elegant with a supple structure and vibrant dark berry fruit, whereas the Altos de Lanzaga is rich, stylish and impressively structured with well-integrated oak and very good depth. Toro offers the well-priced Dehesa Gago and opulent, spicy, ageworthy Pago La Jara. Some fine reds are also produced from less established areas. From Cigales comes the leafy, light berry-fruited Viña 105. The Pegaso Pizarra comes from old bush vines planted in slatey soils in the far south of Castilla y León, around the village of Cebreros. It is tight and well crafted, with a mix of dark herb scented fruit and a piercing, very classy mineral quality from the slate soils it comes from. A further Cebreros red Pegaso Granito comes from granite based soils. Of equal interest is the splendid Moscatel-based Málaga, Molino Real, which has remarkable richness and intensity. A second Málaga MR is more fruit driven, raised in stainless steel rather than oak and there is a Sierra de Málaga Moscatel as well from old bush vines, Mountain Blanco. Other wines to consider are well priced red and white from Valdeorras, Gaba do Xil, respectively from Mencia and Godello as well as tiny amounts of two premium examples from the same DO, the red As Caborcas and white Branco de Santa Cruz. A young red style Al Muvedre from Alicante, comes from bush vine Monastrell. All the top reds will develop very well with age.
Recommended Reds:
Rioja Altos de Lanzaga ★★★★☆ £F   Rioja Lanzaga ★★★☆ £D
Ribera del Duero Matellana ★★★★★ £G
Ribera del Duero M2 ★★★★☆ £F   Ribera del Duero Gazur ★★★☆ £E
Cigales Viña 105 ★★★☆ £D   Toro Pago La Jara ★★★★☆ £F
Toro Dehesa Gago ★★★☆ £D   Valdeorras Gaba do Xil ★★★☆ £D
VdT Castilla y León Pegaso Pizarra ★★★★ £E
Recommended Whites:
Málaga Molino Real ★★★★★ £F   Málaga MR Moscatel ★★★☆ £D
Valdeorras Gaba do Xil ★★★☆ £D

✪ **Benjamin Romeo (Rioja)** *www.bodegacontador.com*
One of the leading names in Rioja, Benjamin Romeo's top wines have achieved close to cult status. Romeo was originally the winemaker at another great Rioja bodega, ARTADI. He is dedicated to making wines of the highest quality and his vineyards are farmed organically and biodynamically. In the winery red fermentation as well as ageing is carried out in wood. Sulphur levels are kept to an absolute minimum and the wines are bottled without filtration. His modern styled reds are uncompromisingly rich and concentrated examples of the region, nevertheless possessing a subtle underlying finesse and balance that underpins the deep and dark-fruited Tempranillo from which they are mainly vinified. The Predicador, by contrast with the other reds is approachable both in terms of its supple fruit-driven structure and its price tag. La Cueva del Contador, like the other wines gets a pre-fermentation cold-soak and then malolactic in barrel and is aged for 18 months in oak. La Viña de Andrés comes from a single small plot and is named after Benjamin's father. It is a touch more extracted than La Cueva and gets longer on its skins, over three weeks. The formidably dense and

North-East Spain

structured Contador is among the greatest reds in Rioja and comes from very ancient vines, over 80 years old. Ageing for a minimum of 10 years is recommended. A traditional Gran Reserva, Carmen is also now made as well as a *joven* red, A Mi Manera. In addition to the reds two Rioja whites, Qué Bonita Cacareaba, which is barrel fermented and a Predicador Blanco are also produced.

Recommended Reds:

Rioja Contador ✪✪✪✪✪ £H
Rioja La Viña de Andrés Romeo ★★★★☆ £G
Rioja La Cueva del Contador ★★★★☆ £G
Rioja Predicador ★★★☆ £E

Rotllan Torra (Priorat) *www.rotllantorra.com*

This bodega is located in Torroja del Priorat, in the heart of the region. The operation is now well established and the first bottles were released back in 1984. There are 24 ha of vines with plantings in some instances upwards of 70 years of age. They also work with other grape growers who own a further 60 ha. A total of seven reds are now produced and there are a couple of sweet wines including a Moscatel. The Balandra blend is aged for 10 months in American oak. The more sophisticated Amadis is aged in finer French oak. The Tirant includes very old (up to 100 years) Garnacha and Cariñena. Aged in new French oak with malolactic fermentation in barrel, this is the richest and finest of the trio and will improve in bottle for up to 15 years. The firm also have a new project Autor producing a further Priorat red. ((DM)

Recommended Reds:

Priorat Tirant ★★★★☆ £F   Priorat Amadís ★★★☆ £E
Priorat Balandra ★★★ £D

Bodegas San Alejandro (Calatayud) *www.san-alejandro.com*

This sizeable Aragon co-op was established in 1962 and now numbers around 300 growers who between them control around 1,100 ha of vineyards. As a result of this a wide range of wines is offered and the Baltasar labelled reds stand out. A number of similar Garnacha wines are released under the Las Rocas banner and a premium Garnacha, Evodia is made for the American market. The Gracian Reserva is produced from some of the best and oldest vineyard blocks owned by the members. The wine is blended from a combination of around 70% 50 to 70 year old Garnacha and younger Tempranillo and Cabernet Sauvignon. Aged in a combination of French and American oak with malolactic fermentation in barrel, the wine is full of spicy, dark berry fruit and just the merest hint of vanilla. Other wines to consider are the limited production Garnacha Nativa, the splendid Garnacha Viñas Viejas, full of herb spice old-viney character and there is a Crianza blended from Garnacha, Tempranillo and Syrah. A roble style red is also made from Tempranillo along with a rosado from Garnacha and a white from Macabeo. ((DM)

Recommended Reds:

Calatayud Baltasar Gracián Garnacha Viñas Viejas ★★★☆ £D
Calatayud Baltasar Gracián Nativa ★★★☆ £D
Calatayud Baltasar Gracián Reserva ★★★ £C

Celler Joan Sangenis (Priorat)

Like many of the producers here, Joan Sangenis established their winery very recently, in 1995. However the Sangenis family are one of the oldest in the region, originally selling their grapes to the local co-op. There are 80ha under vine planted on south-facing slopes and the winery is modern and well equipped with stainless steel and temperature control. The Cal Pla labels are lighter and more

fruit-driven, the white coming from a blend of Garnacha Blanca, Macabeo and Moscatel, the red from Garnacha and Cariñena. This, like the Crianza Mas d'En Compte, is bottled without fining or filtration. The Mas d'En Compte comes from all old vines, Cariñena (45%), Garnacha (50%) and just 5% of Cabernet Sauvignon. It is aged for 14 months in French oak. Rich and full, it is more fruit-driven in style than some of the more fiery examples of Sangenis' neighbours. The Barrel-Fermented white comes from 60% Garnacha Blanca, the balance being Picapoll and Pansal, and each variety is fermented and aged separately in French oak for 6 months. It is ripe and tropical with a hint of minerality but the oak is quite apparent in the wine's youth and needs a year or so for balance. Less than 60 cases are produced a year of Planots, a blend of Garnacha and 100-year-old Cariñena from the oldest vineyard. ((DM)

Recommended Reds:

Priorat Mas d'en Compte Crianza ★★★★ £E   Priorat Cal Pla ★★☆ £D

Recommended Whites:

Priorat Mas d'en Compte Barrel-Fermented ★★★☆ £E
Priorat Cal Pla ★★☆ £D

Saó del Coster (Priorat) *www.saodelcoster.com*

Small artisan bodega owned by Swiss Spaniard Fredi Torres. His approach is to make a more elegant style of Priorat, more about finesse than raw power. He produces a number of wines in small lots from his 6 ha which is farmed biodynamically on a mix of terraces and slopes. Half the holding is comprised of old vines the other half are recently planted and include some international varieties. S de Saó de Coster is the softest of the wines while Planassos, the top *cuvée*, comes from very old Cariñena. Terram is produced in reasonable volume relative to the scale of the operation, around 500 cases or so annually. A pre-fermentation cold soak is followed by vinification at controlled temperature for around three weeks preserving the wines elegant dark berry fruit and maintaining its fresh edge. Ageing is for 15 months in a mix of new and used French oak. (DM)

Recommended Reds:

Priorat Terram ★★★★ £E

Señorio de Otazu (Pago de Otazu) *www.otazu.com*

This is now one of Spain's single Pago DOs properties. The estate is sizeable with 115 ha of the 350 ha given over to vineyards. As well as Tempranillo, Merlot and Cabernet Sauvignon, Chardonnay is grown. The higher volume wines are labelled Otazu, the top cuvees take the Señorio de Otazu brand. There are two whites, both Chardonnays, the more expensive cru being barrel-fermented. The regular bottling is in a light, melon-fruited style with decent depth and reasonable intensity; the barrel fermented example has a richer texture with hints of toast and a lightly buttery character. The Premium Cuvée red is from Tempranillo, Merlot and Cabernet Sauvignon. It is dark, plummy, ripe and spicy with a relatively soft structure for early drinking. The cedary, slightly minty Pago de Otazu comes from a similar blend and is aged in French oak for 18 months. Altar, is a blend of Cabernet Sauvignon and Tempranillo. It is a clear step up with altogether greater flesh and depth. Ageing is in new oak with malolactic in barrel. An additional, very pricey Cabernet Sauvignon-based red, Vitral is also made. ((DM)

Recommended Reds:

Navarra Señorio de Otazu Altar ★★★★ £F
Pago de Otazu Señorio de Otazu ★★★☆ £D
Navarra Otazu Premium Cuvée ★★☆ £C

Recommended Whites:
Pago de Otazu Señorio de Otazu Chardonnay BFB ★★★ £D
Navarra Otazu Chardonnay ★★ £B

Celler Joan Simo (Priorat) *www.cellerjoansimo.com*
Small bodega based in Porrera producing small volumes of good
red. The operation only began in 1999 and the family work 15 ha
of mainly Garnacha, of which around a half are around 100 years
old. Coming from old-vine Garnacha and aged in barrel, Les Sentius
is full of of ripe, dark-berry fruit, a hint of minerality and supple
and approachable tannin. Les Eres has an altogether denser, more
complex old vine quality to its fruit and a clear Priorat *sauvage*
quality. Winemaking is modern with a long period of 3 to 5 weeks
on skins at a controlled temperature and the malolactic for both
wines is in barrel. (DM)
Recommended Reds:
Priorat Les Eres ★★★★☆ £F   Priorat Les Sentiuss ★★★☆ £E

>> Talai Berri (Getariako Txakolina) *www.talaiberri.com*
Both red and white Chacoli are made here. The bodega, founded in
1992 is found on some of the sunniest slopes of Mount Tali Mendi
and the winery located in the heart of the firms 12 ha of vines.
Manual harvesting, in small crates, followed by temperature control
during vinification helps to ensure quality. The white Txakoli is crisp
and fresh with subtle green fruit and mineral aromas. The red, very
characterful with crisp and very fresh red berry fruit and a slightly
bitter dark cherry edge. A second white Jakue is vinified on lees with
bâtonnage. (DM)
Recommended Reds:
Getariako Txakolina Talai Berri (Hondarribí Beltza) ★★★ £C
Recommended Whites:
Getariako Txakolina Talai Berri (Hondarrabi Zuri) ★★☆ £B

>> Terra Personas (Montsant) *www.terrapersonas.com*
A small range of bright, forward and immediately approachable
wines is produced here. There is a rosado as well as the nutty, lightly
aromatic white and two reds. The bodega is owned by the Dutch
Persoon family. The vineyard consists of 10 ha which are protected
by the Montsant mountains and planted at around 200 metres
altitude. The Blanco from Garnacha Blanca and Macabeo is part
tank fermented in stainless steel at cool temperatures, its Garnacha
Blanca component in small oak. Of the two reds the Terra Vermella
(Carinena, Garnacha and Syrah) is more approachable and fruit
forward. The Terra Negra is more complex, the influence of around
80% of old Cariñena in the blend with Garnacha and Syrah is
immediately apparent on tasting. (DM)
Recommended Reds:
Montsant Terra Negra ★★★ £C   Montsant Terra Vermella ★★☆ £B
Recommended Whites:
Montsant Terra Blanca ★★ £B

Terra Remota (Empordà) *www.terraremota.com*
Terra Remota is one of the newer Empordà names, established
in 2006 and located on the higher slopes of the Alt Empordà.
Marc Bournazeau has extensive winery experience having
previously been a co-owner of operations in both France and
Chile. He has used this in the design of the winery, which involves
as many processes as possible being carried out under gravity
and operations in both the vineyards and cellar are as natural as
possible. Five wines are now being produced, the Caminito Rosado
(Syrah, Garnacha and Tempranillo), Caminante Blanco (Garnacha

Blanca, Chenin Blanc and Chardonnay) as well as Camino red
(Syrah, Garnacha, Cabernet Sauvignon and Tempranillo), are all
approachable fruit driven styles. The rosé has sufficient structure
to work well as a food wine as well as being enjoyed on its own. A
proportion of the wine is barrel fermented and it is aged on lees
for six months. The white is also aged on lees for 6 to 8 months and
unusually includes around a third of Chenin Blanc which provides
a hint of Stellenbosch rather than Touraine in the wine. The mixed
blend Camino red comes from some of the younger vines and
the vinification is traditional with the malolactic fermentation
carried out in larger vats before transfer to smaller barrels for
ageing. A combination of 225 and 500 litre vessels contribute to
the forward berry fruit qualities of the wine. The top two reds are
more structured, dense and powerful. Clos Adrien is significantly
dominated by Syrah with some Garnacha and this shows in the
dark, spicy and black pepper notes encountered. A long maceration
is followed by malolactic fermentation and then ageing in 225 litre
French oak. The top red, Usted has a touch more Garnacha than
Syrah and is rounder and a touch richer, more velvety. While the
Syrah is similarly vinified, the Garnacha is aged first in *inox* before
transfer to barrel. (DM)
Recommended Reds:
Empordà Usted ★★★★ £F Empordà Clos Adrien ★★★★ £E
Empordà Camino ★★★ £D
Recommended Whites:
Empordà Caminante ★★☆ £C
Recommended Rosés:
Empordà Caminito ★★☆ £C

⊛ Terra de Verema (Priorat) *www.terradeverema.com*
Like so much that is emerging in this now classic region, this is a
new small high quality operation. Two very impressive reds are
covred here and additional releases are planned in future vintages
including a limited production wine Licorelium. Both current
releases are marked by a piercing, intense mineral and spicy dark
fruit quality with real depth and concentration. The Corelium is a
stunning example of modern Priorat but the Triumvirat in particular
is a great value buy as well at the moment. Founded in 2005, the
property is spread across five separate parcels and totals currently
8.3 ha, of which close to 4 ha are now farmed biodynamically. In
the cellar the wines are sensitively vinified and handled, and ageing
varies from 12 to 16 months in a mix of new and used French oak.
The maximum long term production will not exceed 50,000 bottles.
Top quality olive oil will also be produced. (DM)
Recommended Reds:
Priorat Corelium ★★★★★ £G   Priorat Triumvirat ★★★★ £E

Vinyes del Terrer (Tarragona) *www.terrer.net*
Excellent small producer and a rarity in the DO now that Montsant
has its own appellation status. Two reds and a white are made from
7 ha of vines planted within a close proximity of the Mediterranean
at an altitude of just 20 metres. The resulting effect of the sea
breezes helps moderate the local climate and the nights are cooled
during the summer. Four varieties, Garnacha, Cabernet Sauvignon,
Sauvignon Blanc and Moscatel are planted across the bodegas 9
small vineyard parcels. The white is dominated by Sauvignon Blanc
which makes up around 80% of the blend. The wine is a fresh,
cool fermented style with crisp green fruit, a hint of minerality
and a subtle aromatic quality imparted by the Moscatel. The Terrer
d'Aubert Cabernet Sauvignon offers vibrant dark berry fruit and
good depth. The Garnacha component combined with Cabernet

North-East Spain

in the Nus de Terrer provides a slightly sweeter, meaty quality with a herbal spiced edge. Both wines are given a cold soak prior to fermentation. (DM)

Recommended Reds:

Tarragona Nus de Terrer ★★★☆ £D

Tarragona Terrer d'Aubert ★★★ £D

Recommended Whites:

Tarragona Blanc del Terrer ★★★ £C

Terres de Vidalba (Priorat) *www.terresdevidalba.com*

Just one very good Priorat, Tocs, is made at this bodega. The vineyards are found in the Poboleda area in the north-eastern stretches of the appellation bordering Montsant. The vines are planted on steep terraced slopes and are planted to a mix of Garnacha, Syrah, Cabernet Sauvignon and Merlot. The family currently have 8 ha under vine, although Tocs is produced from just one single vineyard, Barranc de la Bruixa. Unsurprisingly yields are restricted and the grapes handpicked at harvest. The blend comprises from roughly or just under a third each of Garnacha, Syrah and Cabernet while the Merlot is included in much smaller proportions. Vinification is handled by MAS MARTINET as a part of their Mas Martinet Assessoraments operation which provides winemaking and viticultural consultancy. The wine is richly textured and full of sweet dark fruits and well judged oak which is almost all new. A second label Vidalba is also made. (DM)

Recommended Reds:

Priorat Tocs ★★★★☆ £F

✿ Terroir Al Limit (Priorat) *www.terroir-al-limit.com*

This small partnership headed up by Dominik Huber with input from South Africa's Eben SADIE from Swartland is producing a small range of brilliant reds with a real stamp of their individual terroirs and with a balance and elegance often missing here. The partners started individually with Dominik producing Arbossar and Eben, Dits del Terra. However they decided to merge their operations in 2005 and now have their own winery facility. The wines are crafted from a number of tiny sites planted on steep slopes around the village of Torroja with vines ranging from 50 to 100 years old grown in the typically sparse llicorella soils of the area. The most approachable of the wines, Torroja a blend of Carignan and Grenache is a village wine sourced from a number of sites in the direct area. In the longer term it is planned to incorporate as much declassified fruit from the other crus as possible to provide a clear indication of the partners approach to the husbandry of their land. It has the dark-fruited but elegant character of the other wines if not the depth and intensity. Arbossar and Dits del Terra are both 100% very old Carignan. They are also exceptional examples of the variety, the Dits from south facing slopes perhaps a touch fuller and more exhuberant, the Arbossar from three north facing sites a touch more structured and restrained. A third red from their own plots, Pedra de Guix has also been been added. At the pinnacle here are two single vineyard wines which are surely likely to emerge as consistent ✿✿✿✿✿ examples of the appellation in the future. Les Tosses is again a varietal Carignan and from a very high altitude vineyard. Intense, powerful and with a tight, structured and very mineral quality it demands at least five years of cellaring. Les Manyes is a 100% Grenache, very spicy, dark and concentrated with a sumptuous texture and a subtle mineral undercurrent. Expect the wines, in particular the crus, to age very well for a decade. (DM)

Recommended Reds:

Priorat Corelium Les Manyes ★★★★★ £H

Priorat Les Tosses ★★★★★ £H Priorat Dits del Terra ★★★★★ £F

Priorat Arbossar ★★★★★ £F Priorat Torroja ★★★★ £E

✿ Torres (Penedes & other regions) *www.torres.es*

Very important producer, now making wines from grapes sourced throughout Cataluña. The Penedès firm of Jean León has been added to the operation and its wines are now of a uniformly much higher quality than they were before the acquisition by Torres. In 2014 some of the facilities of Bodegas El Albar LURTON in Rueda were purchased to develop Torres' recently established Rueda Verdeo brand. Overseas interests have been established in Chile with the MIGUEL TORRES brand for many years however they have not quite matched the quality of the Penedès wines. By contrast Miguel Torres' sister MARIMAR TORRES produces well-made and well-priced, cool-climate Chardonnay and Pinot Noir in California's Sonoma Green Valley. The Torres range is extensive and the regular wines are often less exhilarating than they might be. You have to look for the mid-range and top-flight labels to find real excitement. Among the reds, Atrium is a plummy, ripe Merlot, and Gran Coronas a blend of mainly Cabernet Sauvignon and Tempranillo. New to the range is Nerola, mainly Syrah with some Monastrell. The top reds include the Mas Borrás Pinot Noir which has still to show the quality achieved elsewhere with this tricky variety. The Mas la Plana Cabernet Sauvignon is structured and cedary, and the Grans Muralles is of real interest – a very local blend of Monastrell, Garnacha Tinta, Cariñena, Garró and Samsó, full of exotic dark fruit. Reserva Real is a very impressive blend of Cabernet Sauvignon, Merlot and Cabernet Franc. A new and potentially fine Priorat, Salmos has recently been added to the range. Of the whites, the commercial Viña Esmeralda is a blend of Moscatel and Gewürztraminer and has a dollop of residual sugar. More serious is Fransola, a lightly-oaked blend of mainly Sauvignon Blanc with some local Parellada. Milmanda is the pricey top Chardonnay from Conca de Barberá and Waltraud is a fine lime and mineral-scented Riesling. Top reds are undoubtedly ageworthy; Reserva Real requires considerable patience. Crisp, fresh and elegant green fruited Rías Baixas now comes from Pazo das Bruxas. (DM)

Torres

Recommended Reds:

Penedès Reserva Real ★★★★☆ £H

Penedès Mas La Plana ★★★★ £F Penedès Gran Coronas ★★ £B

Cataluña Gran Sangre de Toro ★★☆ £C

Penedès Atrium Merlot ★☆ £B

Conca de Barberá Grans Muralles ★★★★★ £G

Priorat Perpetual ★★★☆ £F Priorat Salmos ★★☆ £D

Ribera del Duero Celeste Crianza ★★☆ £D

Recommended Whites:

Conca de Barberá Milmanda ★★★☆ £E

Penedès Fransola ★★★ £D Penedès Waltraud ★★☆ £C

Penedès Gran Viña Sol ★★ £B Cataluña Viña Esmerelda ★★ £B

Jean León

Recommended Reds:

Penedès Zemis ★★★★ £E

Penedès Cabernet Sauvignon Gran Reserva La Scala ★★★☆ £D

Penedès Cabernet Sauvignon Reserva ★★☆ £C

Penedès Pago Merlot ★★☆ £C

Recommended Whites:

Penedès Pago Chardonnay ★★☆ £C

Pazo das Bruxas
Recommended Whites:
Rías Baixas ★★☆ £C

Trio Infernal (Priorat) *www.linfernal.es*
Increasingly persuasive Priorat is being produced by the partnership of French based *vignerons* Laurent COMBIER and Jean-Michel GERIN, both from the Northern Rhône Valley, and Peter Fischer from CHÂTEAU REVELETTE in the Côteaux d'Aix en Provence. The vintages of the reds have been improving year on year here as the partnership begin to extract the best from their site. As well as the red bottlings an impressive barrel-fermented white Riu, is also being produced from 40 to 50 year old Garnacha Blanca and Macabeu. Particularly impressive is the Aguilera Viñas Viejas which has a real mineral as well as dark fruit component. It comes from over 100 year old Cariñena grown on steep hillside slopes and gets 18 months in French oak. As the partnership has refined their approach they are also now making a further Carinena, Fons Clar, a 100% Syrah Cara Nord and an old vine Garnacha, El Casot. The supple and approachable fruit driven red, Riu includes Syrah as well as Garnacha and Cariñena. (DM)
Recommended Reds:
Priorat Aguilera Viñas Viejas ★★★★☆ £F
Priorat Riu ★★★☆ £E
Recommended Whites:
Priorat Riu ★★★☆ £E

>> Trossos del Priorat (Priorat) *www.trossosdelpriorat.com*
Trossos is a new bodega, established in 2004 producing just one red and one white. It is owned and run by husband and wife team Juli and Mercè Mestre. They have also benefitted from technical guidance from Toni Coca who has his own bodega in Montsant, COCA I FITÓ. Their vines are planted on *Llicorella* costers and naturally low yielding. The small winery has been partially buried in the vineyard slopes and as a result operates by gravity. The white Abracadabra (Garnacha Blanca, Macabeo) is part aged in new French oak and offers relatively attractive lightly citrus and herb scented fruit and good depth. The red Lo Mon is impressive, dark, spicy and smoky with a characteristic mineral edge, the wine is aged in used barrels and the complex old vine qualities of Garnacha and Cariñena are balanced by a firm tannin edge provided by younger Syrah and Cabernet Sauvignon. An additional white Llum d'Alba combines Garnacha Blanca, Viognier and Macabeo and three further reds are made including a further premium example Pam de Nas from old Garnacha and Cariñena.
Recommended Reds:
Priorat Lo Món ★★★★ £E
Recommended Whites:
Priorat Abracadabra ★★★ £D

Valencisco (Rioja) *www.valencisco.com*
The full name of this bodega is Compañía Bodeguera de Valenciso and just one red and a single white are currently made, both of impressive quality. It was founded in 1998 and is very much boutique in size and approach, just 100,000 bottles or so are made a year. There are plots in 12 separate vineyards in the Rioja Alta, which are all farmed sustainably. Yields are kept in check and no more than 5 tons per hectare are harvested. A small modern winery facility was completed in 2006 and is well equipped with solely French barrels used for ageing. The elegant Rioja Reserva Tinto has a nicely rounded, supple texture and impressively intense notes of dark cherry and ripe berry fruits with finely judged restrained hints of creamy oak in the background. The Tempranillo fruit is all hand harvested and the individual plots picked at optimum maturity. Vinification is in concrete vats and then ageing is for 16 months in French oak, a third new. The wine is then further settled for a year in concrete tanks before bottling. An excellent citrus infused white is also made. Viura is blended with old Garnacha Blanco adding a rich texture and a restrained nutty character. Only made in tiny quantities it is sourced from very old vines planted in clay-limestone soils. Barrel-fermentation is followed by 9 months ageing in French barrels. Both are well worth searching out. (DM)
Recommended Reds:
Rioja Valencisco Reserva Tinto ★★★★ £E
Recommended Whites:
Rioja Valencisco Blanco ★★★☆ £D

Celler Vall Llach (Priorat) *www.vallllach.com*
Singer Luis Llach founded this first-class Priorat property in the early 1990s. He also has an interest in CIMS DE PORRERA. The first vintage bottled at Vall Llach was 1998. An important key to quality here has been the acquisition of some very old vineyards, varying from 70–100 years of age and sited on slatey slopes. Viticulture is generally organic and chemicals are avoided. New plantings of Garnacha, Cabernet Sauvignon, Merlot and Syrah have been undertaken and these generally make up the bulk of the third wine, Embruix and are siginificant in the second label Idus which still has a significant proportion of old vine fruit. The younger vines also contribute texture and complexity. Vall Llach itself is dominated by old-vine Cariñena, with Garnacha and Cabernet Sauvignon blended in. It is a dark, spicy, brooding beast, full of fiery *sauvage* character. It will require 4 or 5 years' cellaring to soften its raw youthful edge. An old vine Cariñena, Porrera de Vall LLach is also made and a very limited flagship red, Finca Mas de la Rosa was added with the 2010 vintage and comes from a single vineyard of the same name. 10% Cabernet compliments old Cariñena. A white, Aigua de Llum de Vall Llach is also made. (DM)
Recommended Reds:
Priorat ★★★★☆ £F   Priorat Idus ★★★★ £E
Priorat Embruix ★★★☆ £D

Valserrano (Rioja) *www.valserrano.com*
The origins of this fine small bodega stretch back to the middle of the nineteenth century. A small range of wines are produced. As well as the five covered here there are two further varietal bottles, a Garnacha and a Mazuelo a pricier Premium Blanco (£F) and a newly released top red Nico by Valserrano (£F). There is also a traditionally styled Gran Reserva. Today this is a family firm owned by Juan Pablo de Simón and his brothers. There are 65 ha of vineyards which are planted on the sunny lower slopes of the Cantabrian mountains and the vines vary in age with some old holdings and an average of around 25 years. There is an underground cellar in the winery where temperature and humidity are naturally controlled and also a modern vinification area with temperature controlled stainless steel for vinification and a substantial holding of oak barrels roughly 50/50 French and American. The white from Viura is barrel-fermented and comes from the highest vineyards aiding acidity in the wine. It is typically citrussy and lightly toasty. The Crianza is the most approachable of the reds, it is a blend of Tempranillo (90%) and Mazuelo and gets a cold pre-fermentation maceration before ageing in barrel for 17 months. The Reserva is richer and more structured and includes Graciano rather than Mazuelo. It

North-East Spain

is traditionally aged for 24 months in barrel, the majority French oak. The Graciano is a well made example of a difficult variety to vinify, it is a fine, firm and perfumed example aged for 14 months in tight grained Allier oak. The Finca Monteviejo is a single vineyard blend of over 60 year old Tempranillo, Graciano and Garnacha. Yields are naturally low and there is an additional sorting at harvest. Vinification is modern with a pre-fermentation cold-soak and ageing in new French oak. (DM)

Recommended Reds:

Rioja Valserrano Finca Monteviejo ★★★★ £F

Rioja Graciano ★★★☆ £E   Rioja Valserrano Reserva ★★★ £D

Rioja Valserrano Crianza ★★☆ £C

Recommended Whites:

Valserrano Fermentado en Barrica ★★☆ £C

Venus La Universal (Montsant)

This is another winemaking partnership between husband and wife winemakers Sara Pérez and René Barbier Jnr. Sara's family own Mas Martinet, René's Clos Mogador. There is a small holding of Garnacha, Cariñena, Cabernet Sauvignon and Merlot planted on steep, rocky schist and granite terraces. Fruit is harvested as late as possible to ensure phenolic ripeness and the wines get a lengthy 3-4 week maceration. Dido is the softest and most approachable of the wines. It is a blend of Garnacha, Cabernet Sauvignon and Merlot. Ageing is for 10 months in mainly 2- and 3-year-old oak and a small proportion in tank. Venus is altogether fuller, richer and more concentrated. A blend of 50% Syrah grown in granite soils and 50% Cariñena grown in schist this is full of dark berry fruit and supported by firm but supple tannins. A characterful, nutty barrel fermented Dido white is also made which blends Macabeu, Garnacha Blanca and Xarel.lo coming from chalk and clay based soils and 70 year old vines. Undoubtedly these are benchmark wines for the appellation. (DM)

Recommended Reds:

Montsant Venus ★★★★ £E   Montsant Dido ★★★☆ £D

Recommended Whites:

Montsant Dido ★★★ £D

Viñas del Vero (Somontano) www.vinasdelvero.com

One of the major producers in Somontano. The premium Blecua red is a separate project It is a separate flagship winery and provides a wine that is a selection of the firm's best fruit sources and made from the best seven Viñas del Vero vineyards and combining Garnacha, Tempranillo, Merlot and Cabernet Sauvignon. There is an artisan approach to the harvest which is done by hand and the wine is fermented and then macerated in French wooden fermentation vats. The malolactic fermentation then follows with the wine transferred to new Allier French oak barrels. The final wine comes from the best selection of the individual four varieties, which are assembled after 12 months and then aged for a further 8 months before being bottled unfiltered and unfined. The Secastilla reds are also marketed as a separate label. As well as the splendid old vine Secastilla from Garnacha, a second wine La Miranda de Secastilla is made from a blend of old Garnacha as well as Syrah and Parraleta grapes. Both wines are sourced from "Pagos" (estates) in the north-eastern stretches of Somontano. Under the Viñas del Vero brand both Cabernet Sauvignon and Chardonnay are well established, however the Rhône varieties and Gewürztraminer are increasingly important. The wines are split into three distinct ranges. The Tradición wines are soft and approachable, whereas the Colección examples more structured and from superior lower yielding fruit

sources. The two Reservas are among the benchmarks for the DO. The Gran Vos red is an unspecified blend, the white Clarion a combination of Chardonnay and Garnacha Blanca. (DM)

Blecua

Recommended Reds:

Somontano Blecua Reserva ★★★★ £E

Secastilla

Recommended Reds:

Somontano Secastilla ★★★★ £E

Viñas del Vero

Recommended Reds:

Somontano Gran Vos Reserva ★★★☆ £D

Somontano Syrah Colección ★★★ £C

Somontano Cabernet Sauvignon Colección ★★★ £C

Recommended Whites:

Somontano Clarión Reserva ★★★☆ £D

Somontano Gewürztraminer Colección ★★★ C

Somontano Chardonnay Colección ★★★ C

>> Vinyes dels Aspres (Empordà) www.vinyesdelsaspres.cat

This small property is found in the northerly stretches of the appellation in the foothills of the Pyrenees. The vineyards have been in the family hands for generations and there are some 30 ha cultivated, planted in gravel and shale soils, ideal for producing good, intensely flavoured grapes. The winery is well equipped with stainless steel vats and temperature control. The nutty, citrus and herb spiced Blanc dels Aspres from Garnacha is barrel fermented and aged on fine lees with *bâtonnage*. Among the reds the Xot is the most approachable; it is a vibrant juicy fruited style that is early bottled. The Negre dels Aspres is a more structured red, the 35 year old Cariñena and Garnacha playing a prominent role with dark berry fruit and spicy hints apparent. S'Alou, the top red is dominated by the bodegas oldest Garnacha and both this and the Negre are aged for around a year and a half in small French oak. (DM)

Recommended Reds:

Empordà S'Alou ★★★★ £E   Empordà Negre dels Aspres ★★★ £D

Empordà Oriol ★★☆ £C

Recommended Whites:

Empordà Blanc dels Aspres ★★★ £D

>> Viña Zorzal (Navarra) www.vinazorzal.com

Zorzal started life in 1989 created by Antonio Sanz, a winemaking project now run by his three sons. They make a range of red, white and rosado styles from a range of varieties. As well as the Graciano and Garnacha based Viña Zorzal reds There is a Chardonnay, a Rosado Garnacha, a Garnacha Blanca as well as two Tempranillo reds, one from Rioja Alavesa. There are also now two premium single vineyard wines. Señora de las Alturas is a blend of mainly Garnacha with around one-fifth Graciano, Corral de los Altos is a varietal Garnacha. The Navarra vineyards are in the south of the appellation and are generally dry during the growing season but the altitude provides for acidity and structure. The Zorzal Graciano is a striking vibrant blackcurrant and raspberry scented red full of juicy fruit. The Garnacha also impresses, albeit with a touch less exhuberance. Vinification emphasises the wines fruit character with a relatively cool fermentation and short maceration. A touch more concentrated, the Malyeto, also Garnacha is given 9 months cask ageing. (DM)

Recommended Reds:

Navarra Viña Zorzal Graciano (Graciano) ★★★ £C

Navarra Viña Zorzal Garnacha (Garnacha) ★★★ £C

Other wines of note - *North-East Spain*

Cataluña & Aragon

Cellers Alta Alella
Recommended Reds: Alella Dolç Mataró ★★★ £D
Alella Orbus ★★★ £D
Alella Parvus Syrah ★★☆ £C
Recommended Whites: Alella Lanius (★★★ £C
Alella Pansa Blanca ★★☆£B

Agnès de Cervera
Recommended Reds: Priorat Kaios ★★★★ £E
Priorat Lytos ★★★ £C   Priorat Argeles ★★☆ £C
Priorat La Petite Agnès ★★ £B

Altavins Viticultors
Recommended Reds: Terra Alta Domus Pensi ★★★☆ £D
Terra Alta Tempus ★★★ £CTerra Alta Almodí ★★★ £C   Terra Alta
Almodí Petit Negre ★★ £B
Recommended Whites: Terra Alta Ilercavònia ★★★ £C
Terra Alta Almodí Petit Blanc ★★ £B

Bodegas Aragonesas
Recommended Reds:
Campo de Borja Coto de Hayas Garnacha Centenarias ★★★ £C
Campo de Borja Coto de Hayas Reserva ★★☆ £B
Campo de Borja Coto de Hayas Crianza ★★ £B

Bodegas Aylés
Recommended Reds: Pago de Aylés A de Aylés ★★☆ £B
Cariñena Aylés Garnacha ★★☆ £B
Cariñena Aylés Merlot/Tempranillo ★★☆ £B
Recommended Whites: Cariñena Dorondon ★★ £B

Celler Avgvstvs Forum (Avgvstvs)
Recommended Reds: Penedès Trajanvs ★★★ £D
Penedès Cabernet Franc ★★☆ £C
Penedès Cabernet Sauvignon/Merlot ★★☆ £C
Penedès Merlot/Syrah (Merlot, Syrah) ★★ £C
Recommended Whites:
Penedès Chardonnay Barrel Fermented ★★★ £C

Otto Bestué
Recommended Reds:
Somontano Finca Santa Sabina ★★★ £C
Somontano Finca Rableros ★★☆ B

Buil Giné
Recommended Reds: Priorat Pleret Negre ★★★☆ £E
Priorat Joan Giné Giné ★★★ £D   Priorat Giné Giné ★★☆ £C
Montsant Baboix ★★★ £D   Montsant 17 XI ★★☆ £C

Can Feixes
Recommended Whites: Penedès Chardonnay ★★★☆ £D

Canals Canals
Recommended Whites:
Cava Brut Nature Gran Reserva Vintage ★★★☆ £D
Cava Brut Nature Reserva NV ★★☆ £C

Canals Nadal
Recommended Whites:
Cava Antoni Canals Nadal Cupada Selecció Reserva Vintage ★★★☆ £E
Cava Brut Nature Gran Reserva Vintage ★★★ £C
Cava Brut Nature Reserva Vintage ★★★ £C
Cava Brut Reserva Vintage ★★☆ £C   Cava Brut NV ★★ £B
Recommended Rosés: Cava Brut NV ★★ £B

Care
Recommended Reds: Cariñena XCLNT ★★★☆ £D
Cariñena Bancales ★★★ £CCariñena Crianza ★★☆ £B
Cariñena Joven ★☆ £B

Recommended Whites: Cariñena Chardonnay ★★ £B
Recommended Rosés: Cariñena Rosado ★☆ £B

Carmenet
Recommended Whites:
Cava Opus Evolutium Gran Reserva Brut Nature ★★★☆ £D
Cava Laietá Brut Nature (★★★ £C

Castellroig
Recommended Whites: Cava Brut Reserva Vintage ★★★ £C

Castillo di Monesma (Dalcamp)
Recommended Reds:
Somontano Castillo de Monesma Reserva ★★★ £C
Somontano Castillo de Monesma Crianza ★★ £B
Somontano Castillo de Monesma ★☆ £A

Celler Cercavins
Recommended Reds: Costers del Segre Bru De Verdú ★★★ £C

Codorníu
Recommended Whites: Cava Jaume Brut Especial Reserva ★★★ £D
Cava Reina Maria Cristina Blanc de Noirs Reserva ★★☆ £C
Cava Extra Brut NV ★★☆ £C
Cava Anna de Codorniu Blanc de Noirs NV ★★ £B
Cava Anna de Codorniu Brut NV ★★ £B
Cava Clasico Brut 1872 NV ★☆ £B   Rías Baixas Leiras ★★☆ £C
Recommended Rosés: Cava Anna de Codorniu Rosado NV ★☆ £B

Colet
Recommended Whites:
Penedès Extra Brut Assemblage Vintage ★★★★ £E
Penedès Extra Brut Grand Cuvée Vintage ★★★☆ £D
Penedès Brut A Priori NV ★★★☆ £D
Penedès Extra Brut Vatua! NV ★★★☆ £C
Penedès Extra Brut Tradicional NV ★★★ £C
Recommended Rosés: Penedès Brut A Posteriori NV ★★ £C

Colet Navazos
Recommended Whites: Penedès Extra Brut Reserva NV ★★★★☆ £E
Penedès Extra Brut NV ★★★★ £E

De Muller
Recommended Reds: Priorat Lo Cabaló ★★★ £E
Tarragona Porpores de Muller ★★ £D   Priorat Legitum ★★ £C
Recommended Whites: Tarragona Chardonnay ★★☆ £C

Doniene Gorronda Txakolina
Recommended Whites: Bizkaiko Txakolina Gorrondona ★★★ £C
Bizkaiko Txakolina Doniene ★★☆ £B

Celler El Masroig
Recommended Reds: Montsant Mas Roig ★★★★ £E
Montsant Les Sorts Vinyes Velles ★★★☆ £D
Montsant Sycar ★★★ £C   Montsant Castell Les Pinyeres ★★★ £C
Montsant Les Sorts ★★☆ £B   Montsant Sola Fred ★★ £B
Recommended Whites: Montsant Les Sorts ★★ £B
Montsant Sola Fred ★☆ £B
Recommended Rosés: Montsant Les Sorts ★★☆ £B

Falset-Marçà
Recommended Reds: Montsant Verema Sobremadurada ★★★★ £E
Montsant Verema Tardana ★★★☆ £D
Montsant L'Esparver ★★★★ £E
Montsant Ètim Selection Syrah ★★★ £D
Montsant Ètim Selection Garnacha ★★★ £C
Recommended Whites: Montsant Verema Tardana ★★★☆ £D

Celler Bárbara Forés
Recommended Reds: Terra Alta Coma d'En Pou ★★★☆ £E
Terra Alta El Templari ★★★ £C
Recommended Whites: Terra Alta El Quinta ★★★ £D
Terra Alta Barbará Forés ★★☆ £C

North-East Spain

Spain

Freixenet
Recommended Whites: Cava Brut Reserva Vintage ★★☆ £C
Cava Elyssia Gran Cuvée NV ★★☆ £C
Cava Elyssia Pinot Noir NV ★★☆ £C
Cava Cordon Negro Brut NV ★★ £B
Recommended Rosés: Cava Cordon Rosado NV ★☆ £B
Grand Recosind (Cellers Santamaria)
Recommended Reds: Empordà Reserva ★★★ £D
Empordà Crianza ★★☆ £C
Grandes Vinos y Viñedos
Recommended Reds:
Cariñena Corona de Aragón Special Selection ★★★ £C
Cariñena Beso de Vino Selección ★★★ £C
Cariñena Beso de Vino Garnacha ★★☆ £B
Cariñena Corona de Aragón Crianza ★★☆ £B
Heretat Navàs
Recommended Reds: Montsant Heretat Navas ★★☆ £C
Bodegas Irius
Recommended Reds:
Somontano Absum Colección Tempranillo ★★★ £C
Somontano Absum Colección Merlot ★★☆ £C
Somontano Absum Varietales ★★☆ £B
Recommended Whites:
Somontano Absum Colección Chardonnay ★★☆ £C
Somontano Absum Colección Gewürztraminer ★★☆ £C
Jaume Giró i Giró
Recommended Whites:
Cava Bombonetta Brut Gran Reserva Vintage ★★★ £D
Cava Elaboración Artesana BN Vintage ★★☆ £C
Cava Elaboración De Cal Rei Brut Reserva NV ★★☆ £C
Juve y Camps
Recommended Whites: Cava Gran Reserva Brut Vintage ★★★☆ £D
Cava Reserva de La Familia BN Gran Reserva Vintage ★★★ £C
Cava Cinta Púrpura Brut NV ★☆ £B
La Conrería d'Scala Dei
Recommended Reds: Priorat Iugiter Selección ★★★★ £F
Priorat Iugiter ★★★☆ £E
Priorat La Conreria Black Slate Escaladei ★★★☆ £D
Priorat La Conreria ★★★ £C
Recommended Whites: Priorat Les Brugueres ★★★☆ £D
La Perla del Priorat
Recommended Reds: Priorat Comte Pirenne Reserva ★★★☆ £E
Priorat Clos les Fites ★★★ £D
La Vinyeta
Recommended Reds: Empordà Puntiapart ★★★ £C
Empordà Llavors ★★☆ £C   Empordà Heus Negre ★★ £B
Recommended Whites: Empordà Heus Blanco ★★ £B
Recommended Rosés: Empordà Heus Rosado ★★ £B
Bodegas Latidos de Vino
Recommended Reds: VdT Valdejalón I Love Barrica ★★★ £C
VdT Valdejalón I Love Tinto ★★☆ £B
Recommended Whites: VdT Valdejalón I Love Moscatel ★★★ £D
VdT Valdejalón I Love Blanco ★ £B
Recommended Rosés: VdT Valdejalón I Love Rosado ★★ £B
Bodegas Laus
Recommended Reds: Somontano Reserva ★★★ £C
Somontano Crianza ★★☆ £C   Somontano Roble ★★ £B
Recommended Whites: Somontano Flor de Chardonnay ★★☆ £C
Somontano Flor de Gewurztraminer ★★ £B
Bodegas Leceranas
Recommended Reds: VdT Bajo Aragon Evohé Garnacha ★★★ £B

VdT Bajo Aragon Evohé Tempranillo ★★☆ £B
Les Cousins
Recommended Reds: Priorat La Sagesse ★★★★ £E
Priorat L'Inconscient ★★★ £D
Recommended Whites: Priorat L'Antagonique ★★★ £D
Licorella Vins
Recommended Reds: Priorat Aónia ★★★ £D
Priorat Gran Nasard ★★★★ £E   Priorat Mas Saura ★★★★ £F
Llopart
Recommended Reds: Penedès Castell de Subirats ★★★ £D
Recommended Whites:
Cava Leopardi Gran Res. Brut Nature Vintage ★★★★ £E
Cava Brut Nature Reserva Vintage ★★★☆ £C
Cava Brut Reserva Vintage ★★★ £C Penedès Clos des Fossils ★★★ £C
Recommended Rosés: Cava Brut Reserva Vintage ★★☆ £B
L'Olivera
Recommended Whites: Costers del Segre Eixadurs ★★★ £C
L'Origan - Uvas Felices
Recommended Whites: Cava L'O de Brut Nature NV ★★★ £C
Recommended Rosés: Cava L'O de Brut Rosat NV ★★★ £C
Celler Los Trovadores
Recommended Reds: Montsant Gallicant ★★★☆ £D
Montsant Citareus ★★★ £C   Montsant Karma de Drac ★★☆ £C
Celler Malondro
Recommended Reds: Montsant Latria ★★★☆ £D
Mas Candí
Recommended Whites: Cataluna Desig ★★★ £C
Mas Estela
Recommended Reds: Empordà Estela Solera ★★★☆ £D
Empordà Vinya Selva de Mar ★★★☆ £D Empordà Quindals ★★★ £C
Recommended Whites: Empordà Moscatell Dulce ★★★ £D
Empordà Vinya Selva de Mar ★★☆ £C
Mas Foraster
Recommended Reds:
Conca de Barberá Josep Foraster Selecció ★★★ £D
Conca de Barberá Josep Foraster Crianza ★★☆ £C
Mas Rodó
Recommended Whites: Cava Penedès Macabeo ★★★☆ £D
Penedès Riesling ★★★ £C   Penedès Montonega ★★☆ £C
Mestres
Recommended Whites:
Cava Brut Reserva Mas Vía Vintage ★★★★☆ £G
Cava Brut Nature Gran Reserva Clos Nostres Senyor Vintage ★★★★ £E
Cava Brut Nature Gran Reserva Visol Premium Vintage ★★★☆ £D
Cava Brut Reserva Cupage 50 Años NV ★★★☆ £D
Cava 1312 Brut Reserva Especial NV ★★★ £C
Cava Mont Ferrant
Recommended Whites:
Cava Berta Bouzy Brut Reserva Vintage ★★★☆ £D
Cava Brut Gran Reserva Vintage ★★★ £D
Vinyes d'Olivardots
Recommended Reds: Empordà Gresa ★★★ £D
Empordà Finca Olivardots ★★☆ £C
Recommended Whites: Empordà Blanc de Gresa ★★☆ £C
Família Nin-Ortiz
Recommended Reds:
Priorat Nit de Nin ★★★★★ £G   Priorat Planetes de Nin ★★★★☆ £E
Priorat Planetes de Nin Garnatxes en Amfora ★★★★ £E
Recommended Whites: Priorat Selma de Nin ★★★★ £F
Priorat Planetes de Nin ★★★ £D

Olivera
Recommended Whites: Costers del Segre Eixadurs ★★★ £C
Bodegas Pablo
Recommended Reds:
Cariñena Gran Viu Garnacha del Terreno ★★★☆ £D
Cariñena Gran Viu Selección ★★★☆ £D
Cariñena Menguante Selección Garnacha ★★★ £C
Cariñena Menguante Tempranillo Roble ★★☆ £B
Cariñena Menguante Garnacha ★★☆ £B
Parxet/Raventós de Alella
Recommended Whites: Cava Brut Titiana Vintage ★★★☆ £D
Cava Brut Nature ★★☆ £C   Cava Brut Reserva ★★☆ £C
Cava Cuvée 21 ★☆ £B
Alella Raventós de Alella Pansa Blanca ★★☆ £B
Recommended Rosés: Cava Brut Titiana ★★★ £D
Pascona
Recommended Reds: Montsant Evolució ★★★ £C
Montsant Tradició ★★☆ £B
Bodega Pirineos
Recommended Reds: Somontano Marboré ★★★☆ £D
Somontano Señorío de Lazan Reserva ★★★ £C
Somontano Montesierra Crianza ★★ £B
Somontano Merlot-Cabernet ★☆ £A
Recommended Whites: Somontano Mesache ★★☆ £C
Somontano Gewürztraminer ★★ £B
Prior Pons
Recommended Reds: Priorat Prior Pons ★★★☆ £E
Priorat Planets de Prior Pons ★★☆ £C
Vinicola del Priorat
Recommended Reds: Priorat Onix Clàssic ★★★ £C
Raïmat
Recommended Reds: Costers del Segre Vallcorba ★★ £C
Recommended Whites: Cava Gran Brut NV ★★ £C
Costers del Segre Castell del Raimat Viña 27 ★★ £B
Costers del Segre Castell del Raimat Viña 24 ★☆ £A
Raventós i Blanc
Recommended Whites: Cava La Finca Vintage ★★★★ £E
Cava de Nit ★★★☆ £D   Cava L'Hereau Reserva Brut ★★★ £C
Penedès Silencis ★★★ £C   Penedès Perfum de Vi Blanc ★★☆ £C
Rimarts
Recommended Whites: Cava Uvae ★★★★ £F
Cava Reserva Especial Chardonnay Vintage ★★★☆ £E
Cava Gran Reserva 40 Vintage ★★★☆ £D
Recommended Rosés: Cava Brut Rosae ★★☆ £C
Bodegas Santo Cristo
Recommended Reds:
Campo de Borja Cayas Selección Garnacha ★★★ £C
Campo de Borja Viña Ainzón Reserva ★★ £B
Campo de Borja Viña Ainzón Crianza ★★ £B
Scala Dei
Recommended Reds: Priorat Cartoixa ★★★ £E
Priorat Prior ★★ £D   Priorat Negre ★☆ £C
Costers del Sió
Recommended Reds: Costers del Segre Siós Selección ★★★☆ £E
Costers del Segre Alto Siós ★★★ £C
Terrasses del Montsant
Recommended Reds: Montsant Heretat Navas ★★☆ £C
Jané Ventura
Recommended Reds: Penedès Mas Vilella ★★★ £D
Penedès Finca Els Camps Ull de Llebre ★★★ £D
Penedès Negre Selecció ★★☆ £B

Recommended Whites: Penedès Finca Els Camps Macabeu ★★☆ £C
Cava Brut Reserva de la Música ★★☆ £C
Bodegas Victoria
Recommended Reds: Cariñena Longus ★★★☆ £E
Cariñena Dominio de Longaz ★★☆ £C   Cariñena Pardina ★★ £B
Vinya El Vilars
Recommended Reds: Costers del Segre Leix ★★★☆ £D
Costers del Segre Villars ★★★ £C

Rioja, Navarra & Pais Vasco
Ad Libitum
Recommended Reds: Rioja Maturana Tinta ★★★ £D
Recommended Whites: Rioja Tempranillo Blanco ★★★ £C
Finca Albret
Recommended Reds: Navarra La Viña de Mi Madre ★★★☆ £D
Navarra Albret Reserva ★★★☆ £D   Navarra Albret Crianza ★★★ £C
Amézola de La Mora
Recommended Reds: Rioja Iñigo Amézola ★★★☆ £D
Antiguas Viñas de Rioja
Recommended Reds: Rioja El Tractor ★★★★☆ £E
Rioja Audius ★★★☆ £D   Rioja Marqués de Arviza Reserva ★★★ £D
Rioja Hacienda Calavia Reserva ★★★ £D
Rioja Marqués de Arviza Crianza ★★☆ £C
Rioja Viña Maria Luisa Crianza ★★☆ £C
Bodegas Ameztoi
Recommended Whites:
Getariako Txakolina Primus Circumdedisti Me ★★★ £C
Getariako Txakolina Ameztoi Txakoli ★★☆ £B
Señorio de Andión
Recommended Reds: Navarra Señorio de Andión ★★★☆ £D
Artuke
Recommended Reds:
Rioja La Condenada ★★★★★ £G   Rioja K4 ★★★★☆ £F
Rioja Finca de Los Locos ★★★★ £E   Rioja Pies Negros ★★★☆ £D
Rioja Artuke ★★☆ £B
Asensio
Recommended Reds: Navarra Reserva ★★★ £C
Navarra Crianza ★★☆ £C   Navarra Roble ★★ £B
Azul y Garanza
Recommended Reds: Navarra Seis de Azul ★★★ £C
Navarra Abril de Azul ★★☆ £B
Baigorri
Recommended Reds: Rioja Garage ★★★★☆ £E
Rioja Reserva ★★★★ £D   Rioja Belus ★★★☆ £D
Rioja Crianza ★★★ £C
Beldui
Recommended Whites:
Arabako Txakolina Santi Victoris et Santi Jacobi Brut Nature ★★☆ £C
Arabako Txakolina Beldui Txakolina ★★ £B
Beronia
Recommended Reds: Rioja III a C ★★★★☆ £F
Rioja Gran Reserva ★★★ £D   Rioja Mazuelo ★★★ £D
Rioja Graciano ★★★ £D   Rioja Reserva ★★☆ £C
Rioja Tempranillo Elaboración Especial ★★☆ £C
Recommended Whites: Rioja Blanco Barrel Fermented ★★★ £C
Rioja Beronia Blanco ★★★ £C
Recommended Rosés: Rioja Beronia ★☆ £B
Dominio de Berzal
Recommended Reds: Rioja Maceración Carbónica ★☆ £B
Rioja Crianza ★★☆ £C   Rioja Seleccion Privada ★★★ £E

North-East Spain

Bodegas Bilbainas
Recommended Reds: Rioja La Vicalanda Reserva ★★★ £D
Rioja Viña Pomal Reserva ★★☆ £C   Rioja Viña Pomal Crianza ★☆ £B

Ramón Bilbao
Recommended Reds: Rioja Mirto de Ramón Bilbao ★★★★ £E
Rioja Gran Reserva ★★★☆ £D   Rioja Reserva ★★★ £C
Rioja Crianza Edición Limitada ★★★ £C   Rioja Crianza ★★☆ £B

Biurko Gorri
Recommended Reds: Rioja BK ★★★☆ £D   Rioja Graciano ★★★ £C
Rioja Arbanta ★★☆ £B

Campillo
Recommended Reds: Rioja Reserva Especial ★★★☆ £E
Rioja Gran Reserva ★★★ £D   Rioja Reserva ★★★ £C

Campo Viejo
Recommended Reds: Rioja Dominio de Conte ★★★ £D
Rioja Gran Reserva ★★ £C   Rioja Reserva ★★ £B
Rioja Crianza ★☆ £B

Bodegas Camillo Castillo
Recommended Whites:
Navarra Capricho de Goya Vino Licor ★★★★ £E
Navarra Montecristo Dry Muscat ★★☆ £B

Cassado Morales
Recommended Reds:
Rioja Laderas Sur ★★★★☆ £F   Rioja Gran Reserva ★★★★ £E
Rioja Reserva ★★★ £D   Rioja Crianza ★★ £C
Rioja Graciano ★☆ £B   Rioja Dimidium ★☆ £B

Bodegas Corral
Recommended Reds: Rioja Altos de Corral ★★★☆ £E
Rioja Don Jacobo Gran Reserva ★★☆ £C
Rioja Don Jacobo Reserva ★★☆ £B

Dinastia Vivanco
Recommended Reds: Rioja Parcelos de Garnacha ★★★★☆ £E
Rioja Parcelos de Graciano ★★★★☆ £E
Rioja Parcelos de Mazuelo ★★★★☆ £E
Rioja 4 Varietales ★★★★ £E   Rioja Reserva ★★★☆ £D
Rioja Crianza ★★★ £C
Recommended Whites:
Rioja Blanco ★★☆ £B
Recommended Rosés:
Rioja Rosado ★★☆ £B

Bodegas Faustino
Recommended Reds:
Rioja Autor Reserva Especial ★★★☆ £E
Rioja Faustino I Gran Reserva ★★★ £C
Rioja Faustino V Reserva ★★☆ £B   Rioja Faustino Crianza ★★ £B
Recommended Whites: Rioja Faustino V Blanco Sin Crianza ★☆ £B
Recommended Rosés: Rioja Faustino V Rosado ★☆ £A

Heras Cordon
Recommended Reds: Rioja Reserva ★★★ £D
Rioja Vendimia Selecciónada ★★☆ £C

Heredad Ugarte
Recommended Reds: Rioja Anastasio ★★★★☆ £F
Rioja Martin Cendoya Reserva ★★★★ £E
Rioja Dominio de Ugarte Reserva ★★★ £C
Rioja Crianza ★★ £B
VdT Castilla Mercedes Eguren Shiraz Tempranillo ★★☆ £B
Recommended Whites: Rioja Martin Cendoya Malvasía ★★★ £C

Bodega Domeco de Jarauta
Recommended Reds: Rioja Viña Marro Reserva ★★☆ £C
Rioja Viña Marro Crianza ★★ £B
Rioja Viña Marro Vendimia Seleccionada ★★ B

Rioja Viña Marro ★☆ £A

Bodegas del Jardin
Recommended Reds: VdT Ribera del Queiles 2 Pulso ★★★ £C

Bodegas Lacus
Recommended Reds: Rioja H12 ★★★☆ £D
Rioja Inédito S ★★★ £C   Rioja Inédito 3/3 ★★☆ £B
Recommended Whites: Rioja Inédito Blanco ★★★ £C

Lar de Paula
Recommended Reds: Rioja Reserva ★★★ £C
Rioja Crianza ★★☆ £C

Lezaun
Recommended Reds: Navarra Reserva ★★☆ £B
Navarra Crianza ★★☆ £B   Navarra Egiarte Crianza ★★ £A
Navarra Tempranillo ★★ £A

Maetierra Dominum
Recommended Reds: Rioja Quatro Pagos ★★★★ £E
Rioja Gavanza ★★★ £C   Rioja Montesc ★★ £C
Recommended Whites: VdT Valle de Sadacia Melante ★★★☆ £C
VdT Valle de Sadacia Libalis ★★☆ £B

Marco Real
Recommended Reds: Navarra Reserva de Familia ★★★ £C
Navarra Colección Privada ★★☆ £C
Recommended Rosés: Navarra Homenaje ★★ £B

Marqués de Cáceres
Recommended Reds: Rioja Gaudium Gran Vino ★★★☆ £E
Rioja Reserva ★★☆ £C Rioja Crianza Vendimia Selecionnada ★★ £B
Recommended Rosés: Rioja Rosado ★☆ £A

Martinez Laorden
Recommended Reds: Rioja Por Ti Graciano ★★★ £D

Miguel Merino
Recommended Reds: Rioja Gran Reserva ★★★☆ ££D
Rioja Reserva ★★★ £C

Nekeas
Recommended Reds:
Navarra El Chaparral de Vega Sindoa Old-Vine Garnacha ★★☆ £C
Navarra Reserva ★★☆ £C   Navarra Crianza ★★ £B
Recommended Whites:
Navarra Chardonnay Cuvée Allier ★★☆ £C

Bodegas Obalo
Recommended Reds: Rioja Altino ★★★☆ £D
Rioja Obalo Crianza ★★★ £C   Rioja Obalo Tinto ★★☆ £B

Ochoa
Recommended Reds: Navarra Reserva ★★☆ £C
Navarra Serie 8a Mil Gracias ★★ £B   Navarra Tempranillo ★★ £B
Recommended Whites: Navarra Moscatel Dulce ★★☆ £C
Recommended Rosés: Navarra Rosado de Lágrima ★★ £B

Bodegas Olabarri
Recommended Reds: Rioja Bikandi Reserva ★★★☆ £E
Rioja Bikandi Crianza ★★☆ £C   Rioja Gran Reserva ★★☆ £D
Rioja Reserva ★★ £C   Rioja Crianza ★☆ £B

Bodegas Ondalán
Recommended Reds: Rioja 100 Abades ★★★☆ £D
Rioja Tempranillo ★★☆ £B

Hermanos Pecina
Recommended Reds: Rioja Chobeo de Pecina ★★★★☆ £F
Rioja Pecina Reserva Vendimmia Seleccionada ★★★★ £E
Rioja Señorío de Pecina Gran Reserva ★★★☆ £E
Rioja Señorío de Pecina Reserva ★★★ £D
Rioja Señorío de Pecina Crianza ★★☆ £C
Recommended Whites: Rioja Chobeo de Pecina ★★ £C

Principe de Viana
Recommended Reds: Navarra 1423 ★★★☆ £D
Navarra Garnacha Old Vines ★★☆ £B   Navarra Crianza ★★ £B
Recommended Whites: Navarra Chardonnay ★★ £B

Bodegas Ramirez de La Piscina
Recommended Reds: Rioja Crianza ★★☆ £C
Rioja Crianza Selección ★★★ £D

Bodegas Riojanas
Recommended Reds:
Rioja Gran Albina ★★★ £D   Rioja Viña Albina Reserva ★★★ £C
Rioja Monte Real Reserva ★★☆ £C
Rioja Monte Real Crianza ★★ £B

Olivier Rivière
Recommended Reds: Rioja Ganko El Cabezota ★★★★ £D
Rioja Rayos Uva ★★★☆ £C
Recommended Whites: Rioja Jequitibá ★★★☆ £C

Viña Salceda
Recommended Reds: Rioja Conde de Salceda Reserva ★★★☆ £D
Rioja Reserva ★★★ £C   Rioja Crianza ★★☆ £B

Señorio de Sarria
Recommended Reds: Navarra Sotés ★★☆ £C
Navarra Tinto No 7 ★★ £B   Navarra Crianza ★☆ £B
Recommended Whites: Navarra Chardonnay ★☆ £A
Recommended Rosés: Navarra Rosado No 5 ★★ £B
Navarra Rosado ★☆ £A

Bodega Solabal
Recommended Reds: Rioja Esculle de Solabal ★★★★ £E
Rioja Reserva ★★★ £D   Rioja Crianza ★★☆ £C

Bodega Tandem
Recommended Reds:
Navarra Ars Mácula ★★★ £D   Navarra Ars Nova ★★ £C

Viñedos del Ternero
Recommended Reds: Rioja Sel de Su Merced Reserva ★★★★☆ £F
Rioja Picea 650 ★★★★☆ £F

Bodegas Tobia
Recommended Reds: Rioja Alma Tobia ★★★★☆ £F
Rioja Tobia Graciano ★★★☆ £D
Rioja Oscar Tobia Reserva ★★★ £D
Rioja Selección Crianza ★★★ £C   Rioja Viña Tobia ★★☆ £B
Recommended Whites: Rioja Oscar Tobia Reserva ★★☆ £C
Rioja Viña Tobia ★★ £B
Recommended Rosés: Rioja Alma Tobia ★★★ £D
Rioja Viña Tobia ★☆ £B

Txomin Extaniz
Recommended Whites: Getariako Txakolina Txomin Etxaniz ★★☆ £C

Bodegas Pedro Benito Urbina
Recommended Reds: Rioja Gran Reserva Especial ★★★☆ £D
Rioja Selección ★★★ £D   Rioja Reserva Especial ★★☆ £C
Rioja Crianza ★☆ £B   Rioja Garnacha ★☆ £A

Bodegas Valdelana
Recommended Reds: Rioja Centum Vitis ★★★★☆ £F
Rioja Ladrón de Guevara Autor Crianza ★★★☆ £D
Rioja Ladrón de Guevara Reserva ★★★☆ £D
Rioja Ladrón de Guevara Autor Roble ★★★ £C
Rioja Ladrón de Guevara Crianza ★★★ £C
Rioja Ladrón de Guevara ★★ £B
Recommended Whites: Rioja Ladrón de Guevara ★★ £B

Bodegas Valdemar
Recommended Reds:
Rioja Inspiracion Edición Limitada ★★★★ £F
Rioja Inspiracion Graciano ★★★★ £F

Rioja Conde de Valdemar Gran Reserva ★★★ £E
Rioja Inspiracion Tempranillo ★★★ £E
Rioja Inspiracion ★★★ £D
Rioja Conde de Valdemar Reserva ★★☆ £C
Rioja Conde de Valdemar Crianza ★★ £C
Rioja Conde de Valdemar Tempranillo ★☆ £B
Recommended Whites: Rioja Conde de Valdemar Viura ★☆ £B

Emilio Valerio
Recommended Reds: Navarra Laderas de Montejurra ★★★ £C

Finca Valpiedra
Recommended Reds: Rioja Reserva ★★★ £E

Work in progress!!

Producers under consideration for the next edition
Bodegas Albamar (Rías Baixas)
Bodegas Alodia (Somontano)
Viña Blanca del Salnés (Rías Baixas)
Espectacle Vins (Montsant)
Clos Berenguer (Priorat)
Clos Dominic (Priorat)
El Escocés Volante (Calatayud)
Casa Gran del Siurana (Priorat)
Maius Viticultors (Priorat)
Celler Malondro (Montsant)
Mas Basté (Priorat)
Massard Brunet (Priorat)
Noguerals (Montsant)
Orto Vins (Montsant)
Ritme Celler (Priorat)

Author's choice - *North-East Spain*

A selection of the best of Cataluña
Reds:
Clos d'Agon   Cataluña Tinto
Alemany I Corrio   Penedès Sot Lefriec
Cartoixa de Montsalvat   Priorat Montsalvat
Castell d'Encus   Costers del Segre Thalarn
Clos I Terasses   Priorat Clos Erasmus
Vinyes Domènech   Montsant Teixar
Vinya Ivo   Empordà S'Alqueria
La Vinya del Vuit   Priorat El 8
Mas Doix   Priorat Doix Costers de Vinyes Velles
Alvaro Palacios   Priorat L'Ermita
Portal del Priorat   Priorat Clos del Portal Somni
Terroir al Limit   Priorat Les Tosses
Torres   Grans Muralles Conca De Barberá
Whites:
Cans Rafols dels Caus   Penedès El Rocallís
Clos Nelin   Priorat
Escoda Sanahuja   Conca de Barberá Els Bassots
Gramona   Cava Iii Lustros
Mas Alta   Priorat Artigas
Mas Perinet   Montsant Clos Maria
Recaredo   Cava Reserva Particular

Established and emerging Rioja red classics
Finca Allende   Aurus
Bodegas Altanza   Artistas Españoles Reserva Miro
Artadi   Viña El Pisón Reserva

North-West Spain

Spain

Castillo de Sajazarra   Digma
Contino   Graciano
Bodegas Exopto   Exopto Cuvée Luca
Bodegas Lan   Culmen Reserva
López de Heredia   Gran Reserva Viña Tondonia
Bodegas Muga   Rioja Aro
Marqués de Murrieta   Dalmau
La Rioja Alta   890 Gran Reserva
Bodegas Orben   Malpuesto
Bodegas Ostatu   Gloria de Ostatu
Viñedos de Páganos   La Nieta
Bodegas Pujanza   Cisma
Remelluri   Gran Reserva
Remirez de Ganuza   Trasnocho
Bodegas Roda   Cirsion
Benjamin Romeo   Contador
Sierra Cantabria   Finca El Bosque

A-Z of producers - *North-West Spain*

✿ Aalto (Ribera del Duero) *www.aalto.es*
Very impressive estate producing a richly concentrated, dense, modern style of Ribera del Duero. The operation is relatively small, Aalto owns 42 ha which are effectively farmed organically across a number of plots in the provinces of Valladolid and Burgos. All the vines are well over 45 years old and yields can easily be kept to a minimum. Among the small group of partners Mariano Garcia looks after winemaking; formerly he spent 30 years as the enologist at VEGA SICILIA and now is also involved with the exceptional V d T Bodega MAURO as well MAURODOS in Toro. Javier Zaccagnini runs the new wave Rueda bodega OSSIAN. The winemaking regime ensures careful sorting and ageing in 70% new French oak. The wine is powerful, supple and very complex, full of dark fruits and oriental spices. The PS bottling adds an extra dimension and is only released in the best vintages. (DM)
Recommended Reds:
Riberra del Duero Aalto PS ★★★★★ £G
Riberra del Duero Aalto ★★★★☆ £F

✿ Abadia Retuerta (VdT Castilla y Leon) *www.abadia-retuerta.com*
An impressive and sizeable project based just outside the boundaries of the Ribera del Duero DO in the village of Sardón del Duero, a short distance to the east of the city of Valladolid. There are now over 200 ha of vineyards and quality is uniformly impressive. Considerable investment has been put into the operation, which includes a state of the art, gravity-fed winery. Wines range from the softer Selección Especial to the powerful and structured super premium Petit Verdot, PV. They do offer good quality for the prices.The Bordeaux red varieties are planted as well as Tempranillo and Syrah. The Abadía Retuerta Selección Especial red is full and structured and with notable oak. Limited amounts of four special top *cuvées* represent the pinnacle here: Pago Valdebellón from Cabernet Sauvignon, Pago Negrallada from Tempranillo, Pago La Garduña from Syrah and PV produced from Petit Verdot. A white Le Domaine is also made from a combination of Sauvignon Blanc and Verdejo. These top reds are very ageworthy and the PV very pricey. (DM)
Recommended Reds:
VdT Castilla y León Pago Valdebellón ★★★★★ £G
VdT Castilla y León Pago Negrallada ★★★★★ £G
VdT Castilla y León Selección Especial ★★★★☆ £E

✿ Agro de Bazán *www.agrodebazan.com*
Small, first class producer in this potentially high quality DO. Many Albariño based whites are produced for early consumption and can lack grip and structure, as is the case with the approachable, but attractively aromatic Granbazán Verde. However, the Granbazán Ambar is richer and more concentrated, resembling a good Condrieu. It has a pure mineral structure and the depth to develop well over several years, becoming richly harmonious with a little bottle development. The top wine is the Granbazán Limousin which is barrel fermented in Allier oak. The A Lambonada is a late harvested Albariño with a hint of residual sugar, an ideal aperitif. Most approachable is the well priced Albariño Contrapunto. The firm also make some attractive fruit driven reds in the Utiel Requena DO under the Mas de Bazán label, with a characterful Bobal crianza style standing out. A white Cava is also made in a fruit driven style from Macabeo, Chadornnay and a little Xarel-lo as well as a fresh zesty Bobal dominated rosado. (DM)
Agro de Bazán
Recommended Whites:
Rías Baixas Granbazán Limousin ★★★★ £E
Rías Baixas Granbazán Ambar ★★★☆ £D
Rías Baixas A Lambonada ★★★ £C
Rías Baixas Granbazán Verde ★★★ £C
Rías Baixas Contrapunto ★★ £B
Mas de Bazán
Recommended Reds:
Utiel-Requena Mas de Bazán Reserva ★★★ £C
Utiel-Requena Mas de Bazán Bobal ★★★ £C
Utiel-Requena Mas de Bazán Cabernet Sauvignon ★★☆ £C
Utiel-Requena Mas de Bazán Crianza ★★ £B
Recommended Whites:
Cava Mas de Bazán ★☆ £B
Recommended Rosés:
Utiel-Requena Mas de Bazán Rosado ★☆ £B

≫ Almaroja (Arribes) *www.almaroja.com*
This excellent small bodega is owned by winemaker Charlotte Allen. Before establishing her artisan project in this remote appellation bordering northeast Portugal, Charlotte worked in the British wine and wine broking trades dealing with top quality boutique wineries. Before embarking on establishing her own bodega she worked vintages in France and South Africa, enabling her to balance a technical winemaking understanding with an artisan terroir based approach. Almaroja was established in 2007 and she now has around 12 ha under vine spread across a number of small plots and a number of varieties, some indigenous to the region. Farming is organic and increasingly biodynamic and she has a small cellar in the town of Fermoselle. Cielos & Biesos is is a vibrant approachable blend of Juan García and other unspecified grapes. The Pirita Blanca shows attractive green, floral spicy fruit with hints of citrus and nutmeg from a blend of Malvasía, Albillo, Godello, Puesta en Cruz. The red Pirita is mainly Juan García with a plethora of other varieties. Deep black fruits and an edgy minerality give real character. Ageing is in used barrels. The top red is Charlotte Allen, a blend of Juan García, Bruñal, Rufete, Tempranillo aged in a mix of new and used wood. Structured and with real depth and concentration it will be the better for three or four years in bottle. (DM)
Recommended Reds:
Arribes Charlotte Allen ★★★★ £E
Arribes Pirita ★★★☆ £D
Arribes Cielos & Besos (Juan García & others) ★★★ £C

Recommended Whites:
Arribes Pirita Blanca ★★★ £C

❀ Alonso del Yerro (Ribera del Duero) www.alonsodelyerro.com
The del Yerro family produce two modern, fleshy examples of Ribera del Duero. The bodega is based in the town of Roa, in Burgos in the heart of the DO. Winemaking consultancy comes from Bordelais Stéphane Derenencourt and the wines certainly have the elegance and purity he nearly always weaves into the reds he produces. Vineyards were purchased very recently in 2002 and the family have 30 ha spread across four separate plots. Only Tempranillo is planted and the altitude of the various sites varies between 800 and 840m. This coupled with meagre soils, yielding barely 30 hl/ha, contributes to the quality. The vineyard is as yet still young at 15 years so the potential is all there. Hand harvesting is followed by a rigorous sorting and the fruit is fed under gravity to the fermentation tanks. An extensive vatting of a month or more is followed by malolactic in barrel. The wines are kept on their lees with some stirring and micro-oxygenation. The resulting wines are dark, spicy and finely structured with added dimension in the Maria cuvée. An impressive Toro, Paydos is also now being made from just under 9 ha with vines dating back to the 1930s. (DM)

Recommended Reds:
Riberra del Duero Maria ★★★★☆ £F
Riberra del Duero ★★★★ £E   Toro Paydos ★★★★ £E

Bodegas Arrocal (Ribera del Duero) www.arrocal.com
The Arrocal family founded their bodega in 2002 and they have built a highly efficient gravity-fed winery to handle their carefully sorted handpicked fruit. They currently farm 23 ha and 20 ha of this is Tempranillo. Vinification is modern, with a careful control of the fermentation temperature and avoiding over-extraction in the wine. For the time being a fairly conservative period of around two weeks is utilised to macerate the fruit and the regular Arrocal is given just 8 months in oak, the Selección around 14 months. As well as the reds there is also a well-priced modern, fruit driven rosado. Two premium reds are also now released and both are sourced from single vineyards. Ángel comes from 70 year old vines. The top red Máximo is thoroughly modern in style and gets 200% new oak, the wine is aged in new oak and then racked to completely fresh new barrels. (DM)

Recommended Reds:
Ribera del Duero Máximo ★★★★☆ £G
Ribera del Duero Ángel ★★★★ £F
Ribera del Duero Arrocal Selecció ★★★☆ £E
Ribera del Duero Arrocal ★★☆ £C

Recommended Rosés:
Ribera del Duero Arrocal ★★ £C

❀ Ismael Arroyo (Ribera del Duero) www.valsotillo.com
Fine, quality producer of dense, powerful and tannic Ribera del Duero. The wines can be among the best in the DO. Top wines from the small 16 ha estate vineyard go under the Val Sotillo label and include Crianza, Reserva and Gran Reserva. Even the Crianza is very structured while the Gran Reserva has formidable extract with concentrated, dark fruit, subtle, spicy oak and real refinement. The splendid Reserva VS is a special selection from 100% Tempranillo. It is aged for 24 months in American oak. A further approachable red, Finca Buenavista is aged for six months in barrel. The VS demands to be cellared. (DM)

Recommended Reds:
Ribera del Duero Val Sotillo Reserva VS ★★★★☆ £F
Ribera del Duero Val Sotillo Gran Reserva ★★★★ £E
Ribera del Duero Val Sotillo Reserva ★★★☆ £D
Ribera del Duero Val Sotillo Crianza ★★★ £C
Ribera del Duero Val Sotillo ★★☆ £C
Ribera del Duero Mesoneros de Castilla y León Roble ★★ £B

Arzuaga Navarro www.arzuaganavarro.com
This is a reasonably substantial Ribera property making traditional sturdy examples of the appellation. However, some recent releases are showing a defter touch in handling the sometimes aggressive tannins of the Tempranillo here. There are currently 140 ha under vine with the majority, some 125 ha, accounted for by Tempranillo (known here as Tinto Fino). There are a further 10 ha of Cabernet Sauvignon and 5 ha of Merlot. La Planta, made in a semi-joven style, offers straightforward cherry fruit. The Arzuaga Crianza is a clear step up. A blend of Tempranillo (90%) and Cabernet Sauvignon, the wine is aged in a mix of French and mainly American oak. It is robust and structured but with some good sweet fruit as well. The Reserva is sturdier in style; French oak is dominant for ageing and both Cabernet Sauvignon and Merlot are blended in. The Gran Reserva is aged for an extended 40 months in French oak. There is a steady move towards fleshier, suppler styles now including the Gran Reserva which has the malolactic fermentation in barrel. The Special Reserve is produced from over 90-year-old vines and is 100% Tinto Fino aged in French oak, again with the malolactic in barrel. The top wine is the Gran Arzuaga. Not only is the wine supple, rich and very concentrated but it simply has a marvellous vibrancy not present in some of the older vintages made here. A more modern style, Amaya is also now made which is aged in French barrels for 20 months. The Arzuaga-Navarro family also own a promising property in La Mancha, Pago Florentino, producing ripe, fleshy, full-flavoured Tempranillo. The property is now one of the 14 single Pago properties in the country. They also own the La Colegiada property in the recently established DO of Arlanza. The Gran Arzuaga and Special Reserve need time but the Reserva and Gran Reserva are ready to drink on release. (DM)

Bodegas Arzuaga
Recommended Reds:
Ribera de Duero Gran Arzuaga ★★★★☆ £H
Ribera de Duero Special Reserve ★★★★ £F
Ribera de Duero Gran Reserva ★★★ £G
Ribera de Duero Reserva★★★ £E   Ribera de Duero Crianza ★★ £D

Bodega La Colegiada
Recommended Reds:
Arlanza Tinto Lerma Crianza ★★☆ £D

Bodegas y Viñedos La Solana
Recommended Reds:
Pago Florentino Pago Florentino Tinto ★★☆ £D

Bodegas As Laxas (Rías Baixas) www.bodegasaslaxas.com
This is a very old estate originally established way back in 1860, although it has only been under its current ownership since 1982. The 19 ha of vineyards have an ideal south-facing aspect. A number of wines are produced, most based on the Albariño. The Laxas is relatively cool-fermented in stainless steel and has marked grassy, floral aromas with just a hint of citrus and a subtle minerality. The Bágoa de Miño comes from the single-vineyard O Pucha estate and is more intense and piercing in character than its stablemate. Both wines should be enjoyed young. Two further dry wine labels are also

North-West Spain

now made, Val do Sosego is 100% Albariño, Condado Laxas also has 10% each of Loureiro and Treixadura. Sensum is a traditional method sparkler from Albariño. (DM)

Recommended Whites:
Rías Baixas Rías Baixas Bágoa de Miño ★★★☆ £D
Rías Baixas Laxas ★★★ £C

❀ **Bodegas Avanthia (Valdeorras)** *www.jorgeordonez.es*
This small Valdeorras property was established in 2006 and is owned by a partnership of US importer Jorge ORDOÑEZ and Bodegas GODEVAL. A very fine and quite pricey red Avanthia as well as a classic Valdeorras white are made. In addition the winery is also now making a more approachable second red Avanthia Mosteiro as well as a Rosado. There are 10 ha planted and most of this is Godello with just a small holding of very old Mencia. The vineyards are found at altitude, around 550 metres above sea level and planted on steep slopes. The *terroir* consists of Ordovician slate soils which offer excellent drainage and being dark retain heat and reflect back at night, which aids ripening. Harvesting is all done by hand and there is a careful selection prior to vinification. The white is barrel-fermented and aged for 7 months but in larger 500 to 600 litre barrels to retain balance. It is full of elegant green fruits with a nutty, lightly toasted mineral undercurrent. The Avanthia Mencia is vinified traditionally and aged in French oak for 14 months. This is a serious and complex example of the variety full of dark fruits spices and minerals with silky tannins and well judged oak. It is an undoubted rival to some of the best from Bierzo. (DM)

Recommended Reds:
Valdeorras Mencia ★★★★☆ £F
Recommended Whites:
Valdeorras Godello ★★★★ £E

Baden Numen (Ribera del Duero) *www.badennumen.es*
Small and newly established bodega, founded in 2003, with some well-sited vineyards on the finely drained limestone soils on south-facing slopes just to the east of Valbuena del Duero. Carlos Niño is finding his way but is already making wines of impressive quality as well as good value in a region not famed for bargains. He only uses French oak and the wines show more refinement and elegance than many of his neighbours. The approachable and fruity Baden Numen B bottling sees just six months in wood, the more serious Crianza N generally around 14 months. He has most recently added a premium Crianza bottling AU which is quite a bit pricier. (DM)

Recommended Reds:
Riberra del Duero Crianza N ★★★☆ £D
Riberra del Duero B ★★☆ £C

Balvinar (Cigales)
The partners here have rapidly established this boutique bodega as one of the very best names to look for in the small Cigales DO, just to the west of Ribera del Duero. This is the only wine made here and in small quantities, barely more than 4,000 bottles a year and only in better vintages. It is a thoroughly modern red, full of rich, sumptuous dark berry fruit and made from 100% Tempranillo (known locally as Tinta Fina). The fruit is all hand harvested from old vines planted in four separate vineyards outside the small town of Cubillas de Santa Marta. After fermentation, the wine goes through 100 % malolactic fermentation in barrel and ageing is for 16 months in a mix of French, American and Hungarian oak. It would be best to allow a further 12 months of cellaring. (DM)

Recommended Reds:
Cigales Balvinar ★★★★ £E

❀ **Belondrade (Rueda)** *www.belondrade.com*
Strikingly impressive and rich Rueda is produced at this small bodega established in 1994. Verdejo is the sole varietal used to produce both the whites here. The Rueda is barrel fermented with a rich texture, mineral and citrus complexity and a depth and persistence often lacking in the region. The Quinta Apolonia bottling is lighter and more obviously fruit driven in style but with an attractive vibrant citrus quality. The Quinta Clarisa is a ripe fruit driven rosado produced from Tempranillo. The Rueda will stand a little ageing although all three wines are immediately approachable.

Recommended Whites:
Rueda Belondrade y Lurton BFB ★★★★ £E
VdT Castilla y León Quinta Apolonia ★★☆ £C
Recommended Rosés:
VdT Castilla y León Quinta Clarisa ★★ £B

❀ **Juan-Manuel Burgos** *www.byvjuanmanuelburgos.com*
One of the best sources of Ribera del Duero. There are 30 ha of vineyards and these include some very old vineyard holdings, some dating to pre-phylloxera, and yields are kept strictly under control. The vineyards themselves are planted at an altitude of around 800 metres and on clay and sandy soils mixed with limestone and rock. As well as the more serious Avan labelled wines Burgos produces an excellent, modern fruit-driven red Fescenino which he vinifies from bought in fruit. The Avan reds are a good deal more serious. The Nascimento is the simplest and comes from Burgos' youngest vines, just around 15 years of age. The Concentratión gains additional richness and depth from older 50 to 70 years old vines. It gets around 14 months in French oak. The Viñedo del Terrubio is sourced from 65 to 70 year old vines and is aged a little longer for 18 months in new French oak. Terrunyo de Valdehernando is sourced from just one single plot established in 1934 providing a wine of beguiling depth and complexity. The Cepas Centenarias is less approachable, big and very structured young but with formidable depth and concentration.

Recommended Reds:
Ribera del Duero Avan Cepas Centenarias ★★★★☆ £G
Ribera del Duero Avan Terruño de Valdehernando ★★★★☆ £F
Ribera del Duero Avan Viñedo del Terrubio ★★★★ £F
Ribera del Duero Avan Concentratión ★★★☆ £E
Ribera del Duero Avan Nacimento ★★★ £C
Ribera del Duero Fescenino ★★ £C

❀ **Bodegas Felix Callejo** *www.bodegasfelixcallejo.com*
An impressive Ribera property established in 1989 by Félix Callejo and his three children have joined him in the family enterprise. There is now in excess of 100 ha planted at over 850 metres on south facing limestone rich soils. Under a secondary label, Viña Pilar, roble and crianza styles are both produced. Under the full Callejo banner the Flores de Callejo is ripe and approachable with just a touch of firm tannin. Both the crianza styled Callejo and Majuelos de Callejo are fuller, rounder with suppler tannins after a vatting of 25 to 28 days. Ageing is a mix of modern and traditional with 12 months in French oak for the Callejo and 18 months for the reserva styled Majuelos de Callejo. Both wines now complete the malolactic fermentation in barrel. Originally the Gran Reserva was aged solely in new American oak for 24 months although a mix

of French and American is now used and the malolactic again is completed in barrel. The result is a more elegant balanced style and the wine is fresher and livelier than many other Gran Reservas. It is now labelled Gran Callejo. The top wine, the Selección Vinedos de la Familia, is more modern. Aged for around 18 months in French oak after a lengthy vatting followed by malolactic in barrel it is an excellent example of why modern style vinification and handling is becoming increasingly popular here. In its most recent project, Finca Valderoble, the family produce red wines under the VdT Castilla y León classification from vines grown at an altitude of close to 1,000 metres. Tempranillo, Merlot and Syrah are all planted in sparse limestone soils. (DM)

Recommended Reds:
Ribera del Duero Seleccion Vinedos de la Familia ★★★★☆ £G
Ribera del Duero Gran Callejo ★★★★ £F
Ribera del Duero Majuelos de Callejo ★★★☆ £E
Ribera del Duero Callejo ★★★ £D
Ribera del Duero Flores de Callejo ★★☆ £C

⚙ Cámbrico (Sierra de Salamanca) www.cambrico.com
Based in the heart of the Sierra de Francia Natural Park high above the city of Salamanca in the newly established VC Sierra de Salamanca, the vineyards here are at an altitude of 800 to 900 metres in a climate and environment that's brilliant for producing intensely flavoured grapes and fine wines. The vine has been cultivated in these hills since Roman times. The vineyards are planted in a mix of granite and slate soils on steeply escarped terraces with vines ranging from 40 to 100 years of age. Tempranillo and the indigenous Rufete are the main grapes cultivated and the farming is organic. The fruit is manually harvested and the berries hand de-stemmed before fermentation in stainless steel and the winery processes carried out by gravity. The wines are aged in French oak with the malolactic taking place in barrel. Five wines are made. The 575 Uvas de Cámbrico is rich and black fruited with a round, approachable texture. Both the Rufete and Tempranillo are more structured, the Rufete very elegant and mineral. Barrel ageing varies between 15 and 18 months. A Calabrés is also made as well as a forward fruit driven Viñas del Cámbrico

Recommended Reds:
VC Sierra de Salamanca Cámbrico Tempranillo ★★★★☆ £F
VC Sierra de Salamanca Cámbrico Rufete ★★★★☆ £F
VC Sierra de Salamanca 575 Uvas de Cámbrico ★★★☆ £D

Caro Dorum (Toro)
The full name of the winery here is Bodegas Carmen Rodríguez Mendez. Guillermo Díez Rodríguez' family has been growing grapes in Toro for generations but Guillermo is the first formal winemaker in his family. Aware of the tremendous potential of his fruit, the first vintage sold here was 2003. There are 16 ha in a number of small plots and everything is done by hand and the vineyards farmed organically. Production remains small at less than 2,000 cases a year, so inevitably they won't be that easy to find. There is a light, fresh and nutty Malvasia white although it is the reds that stand out. Unlike others in the appellation only French oak is used and the top Selección Especial gets 18 months in new wood. Issos comes from the youngest vines, although these are over 25 years and provides an impressively dark, smoky fruited firmly structured red. The Caro Dorum is in the same mould but coming from vines over 40 years old it has a greater old-vine, meaty complexity. The Selección is dense and powerful and very firmly structured. Time is needed for it to unfurl. All the wines will benefit from five years ageing. The

Selección positively demands it. (DM)
Recommended Reds:
Toro Seleccion Especial ★★★★ £F
Toro Caro Dorum ★★★☆ £E   Toro Issos ★★★ £C
Recommended Whites:
Toro Malvasia ★★☆ £C

>> Casal de Armán (Ribeiro) www.bodegascasaldearman.com
Casal de Armán is a small to medium sized bodega, owned by the González Vázquez family producing around 7 to 8,000 cases a year of both red and white Ribeiro. Founded in the late 1990s the bodega has close to 20 ha of vineyards planted on terraces at an altitude of 200 to 350 metres. The fruit is all hand harvested and kept in refrigerated storage prior to vinification. The small winery is modern and well equipped with stainless steel tanks, pneumatic presses, stem removing machines and temperature control for fermentation. Four whites and a couple of reds are made. The whites are all dominated by Treixadura and the Casal de Armán label is immediately approachable with fresh, crisp green apple scented fruit. The Armán Barrica and Armá Sobre Lias are both more structured whites. The characterful Lias spends 8 months on its fine lees giving added depth while the stylish creamy Barrica is barrel fermented then aged in French oak, also for 8 months. The Armán tinto (Brancellao, Souson, Caiño) is bright and full of red berry fruit and a second red Barrica is aged in oak. (DM)
Recommended Reds:
Ribeiro Casal de Armán ★★★ £C
Recommended Whites:
Ribeiro Casal de Armán Finca Misenhora ★★★★ £D
Ribeiro Casal de Armán Finca Os Loureiros ★★★★ £D
Ribeiro Casal de Armán ★★★☆ £C

⚙ Casar de Burbia (Bierzo) www.casardeburbia.com
This small family owned bodega may be relatively new in an equally newly emerging fine wine appellation but it is now firmly established among the leaders in terms of the quality of, particularly, its striking reds. The family only began purchasing vineyards in 1989 but had recognized the potential of the neglected hillside vineyards on the mountain of Valtuille de Arriba. Most Bierzo was then coming from the fertile lower lying plains of the appellation. The average altitude of the Casar de Burbia plots is around 700 metres above sea level and the slopes are very steep with inevitably good drainage and a wide variation in day and night summer temperatures. A considerable effort has gone into establishing the vineyards in there current state. Many of the original plots were planted to Palomino and these have since been grafted over to Mencia in production of the reds here. Two whites, Casar Godello are also now made, one is barrel fermented and the wine aged in oak for 12 months. Of the reds the entry level Casar de Burbia is aged for 8 months in American oak. It is supple and approachable with a slightly smoky undercurrent. The splendid Hombros by contrast only sees French oak and comes from 100 year-old vines, a more elegant and intense wine, and great value. The Tebaida comes from higher altitude plots with a high stone content in the soils. It's an elegant, structured and very mineral red which will age well. The equally mineral Tebaida 5 has that extra dimension. it is sourced from a number of 100 year old plots and demands at least four or five years cellaring. (DM)
Recommended Reds:
Bierzo Tebaida 5 ★★★★ £F   Bierzo Tebaida ★★★☆ £D
Bierzo Hombros ★★★☆ £C
Bierzo Casar de Burbia ★★★ £C

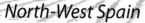

North-West Spain

Spain

>> Castro Ventosa (Bierzo) *www.castroventosa.com*

This is the family bodega of the Pérez family. Raúl PÉREZ has established himself as one of the winemaking stars of central western and north western Spain. He produces a fine range of very low volume wines under his own label and consults to Bodegas MARGON in Tierra de León and QUINTA DA MURADELLA in Monterrei. He has also made a very stylish red Garnacha, El Reventon with Méntrida based Daniel LANDI. The bodega is named after its vineyards, which are planted on the slopes of the hill that is the base of an ancient Roman fort, meaning "Windy Castle". The family origins in viticulture here date back to the 1750's and today they have 75 ha under cultivation, all of it Mencia and one of the most significant holdings of the variety in the appellation. The Vino Joven comes from younger vines, between 20 and 40 years old so by no means young and is vinified and aged for four months solely in stainless steel to emphasise the wines fruit. El Castro de Valtuille comes from older vines, up to 85 years old and the wine is a more complex and structured example which is part fermented in oak and aged in French barrels for a year or so. The very stylish and intense Cepas Centenarias is made from, as the name suggests over 100 year old vines.

Recommended Reds:

Bierzo Cepas Centenarias ★★★★☆ £F
Bierzo El Castro de Valtuille ★★★★ £E
Bierzo El Castro de Valtuille Joven ★★★☆ £C

❀ Viñas del Cenit (Bierzo) *www.bodegascenit.com*

A new and rapidly established benchmark winery for Zamora. The wines being produced here are clearly far superior to many lesser producers from much more established appellations. The *terroir* is excellent with similar soils to Toro, gravel over sand, with a bed rock of red clay. The vines are all old-vine ungrafted Tempranillo. The intense and spicy Venta Mazarrón offers not only impressive depth and intensity with lovely rich, dark sweet black fruit but excellent value. The top two wines are a bit pricier. Both get extensive ageing in oak and offer great depth and refinement. Recently added is Vía Cénit, a crianza style aged for 12 months in barrel.

Recommended Reds:

Tierra del Vino de Zamora Cénit VDC ★★★★☆ £F
Tierra del Vino de Zamora Cénit ★★★★ £F
Tierra del Vino de Zamora Venta Mazarrón ★★★☆ £D

>> Conde de San Cristobal *www.marquesdevargas.com*

This Ribera del Duero bodega is under the same ownership as MARQUÉS DE VARGAS in Rioja, and PAZO SAN MAURO in Rías Baixas. The bodega and vineyards are found close to Peñafiel, in the western stretches of the DO. There are 80 ha under vine, which are farmed organically and the bodega is fully self sufficient for its grape growing requirements. The first vintage produced at the well-equipped modern winery was from 2003. A well priced ripe, spicy and dark fruited example of Ribera, Conde de San Cristobal, is made from a blend of Tinto Fino, Cabernet Sauvignon, Merlot. The fruit is manually harvested and the vines are still relatively young, 15 to 30 years old. Vinification and handling is modern in the gravity fed winery. The fruit gets a cold soak for 3 to 5 days and then a fermentation at a cool 20 to 24 C followed by a further two weeks on skins to round and soften the wines tannins. This is followed by partial malolactic fermentation in small oak. The total barrel ageing is for 12 to 14 months in a mix of wood and the wine bottled without filtration. A second premium label Raíces Reserva Especial is also now made. (DM)

Recommended Reds:

Ribera del Duero ★★★☆ £D

Coto de Gomariz (Ribeiro) *www.cotodegomariz.com*

One of the best producers from this somewhat remote and very rural DO. The output is also relatively sizeable at over 10,000 cases a year from a vineyard holding of some 20 ha. The Ribeiro and the Gomariz are both well priced with the Gomariz X unusually vinified solely from Albariño. It offers more of a mineral character than the very floral and aromatic Ribeiro. The top white is a blend of Treixadura, Godello and Loureiro with a richer texture from four months in oak. Of the reds Abadia de Gomariz is the most obviously forward with spicy red berry fruit and is a blend Sousón, Ferrón and Mencia. Both the VX bottlings are produced solely from the local Sousón and get quite extensive ageing in oak, which is certainly very apparent when the wines are young. Both will certainly benefit from four or five years ageing. (DM)

Recommended Reds:

Ribeiro VX Cuveé Primo ★★★☆ £E
Ribeiro VX Cuveé Caco ★★★ £D
Ribeiro Abadia de Gomariz ★★☆ £C

Recommended Whites:

Ribeiro Colleita Seleccionada ★★★☆ £D
Ribeiro Gomariz X ★★★ £C   Ribeiro ★★☆ £B

Dehesa de Cadozos (VdT Castilla y León) *www.cadozos.com*

Located near to Portugal by the Duero, the Dehesa de Cadozos estate is planted at 830 metres above sea level. The combination of both the altitude and sandy, gravelly, meagre soils provides an excellent environment for the production of fine wine. Organically cultivated Tinto Fino and Pinot Noir are the sole varieties grown and currently the Cadozos red is an elegant, dark cherry scented example. Crop-thinning, drip irrigation and hand harvesting at optimum maturity all help to ensure a good balance of ripe tannin, sufficient acidity and good fruit intensity in the wine. Vinification is in small fermenters and ageing is for 15 months in French oak. A slightly pricier varietal Pinot Noir and an approachable blend, Sayago 830 are also made.

Recommended Reds:

VdT Castilla y León Cadozos PN ★★★☆ £F
VdT Castilla y León Cadozos ★★★☆ £E

❀ Descendientes de J. Palaciosos (Bierzo)

This is one of the Bierzo benchmarks and shows the tremendous character and individuality that can be wrought from the Mencia grape. Established in 1999 by Priorat maestro Álvaro PALACIOS and his nephew Ricardo Perez there are 15ha cultivated biodynamically with a substantial holding of old vines. These are spread across 60 small and diverse parcels around the village of Corullón. The softest and most accessible of the wines the Petalos del Bierzo comes from vines ranging from 40 to 90 years and the wine, which is aged in barrel for four months is ripe dark, smoky and impressively concentrated at this level. The Corullón is a selection from distinct old vine parcels planted on very steep slopes and very low-yielding. The wine is dense and minerally with a piercing intensity to its dark berry fruit. Moncerbal is produced from a single vineyard planted at an elevation of 600 to 750m and is poised, structured and offers greater depth and elegance than the Corullón. Three additional single vineyard wines are also produced, the pricey La Faraona, Las Lamas and San Martin. All the wines are bottled unfined and unfiltered. (DM)

Recommended Reds:
Bierzo La Faraona ★★★★★ £G   Bierzo Las Lamas ★★★★★ £G
Bierzo Moncerbal ★★★★☆ £F   Bierzo Corullón ★★★★ £E
Bierzo Petalos del Bierzo ★★★☆ £D

❀ Dominio de Atauta (Ribera del Duero) *www.dominiodeatauta.com*

Before selling his operation to the Avanteselecta group of small
wineries Michael Sanchez had been acquiring plots of very old
Tempranillo in Ribera del Duero for two decades and the bodega
is now a source of some benchmark wines for the appellation.
These are thoroughly modern reds and very different in style from
some of the Reservas and Gran Reservas made elsewhere. From
vineyards located in the cooler eastern stretches of the DO these
are wines which positively demand cellaring. There are a number
of very impressive and pricey limited bottlings including La Mala
and Valdegatiles. These are rich, supple and characterful with really
impressive depth and loads of dark, smoky, black fruit as well as
intense minerality. Three more forward styles are also made, a
modern style Atalayas de Golbán, as well as a Crianza and Reserva
Torre de Golbán, all from Tinto Fino. (DM)

Recommended Reds:
Ribera del Duero Valdegatiles ★★★★★ £G
Ribera del Duero La Mala ★★★★★ £G
Ribera del Duero Atauta ★★★★ £E
Ribera del Duero Torre de Golbán Reserva ★★★ £D

❀ Dominio do Bibei (Ribeira Sacra) *www.dominiodobibei.com*

Dominio do Bibei is a major new bodega with a focus on reds but
producing two very fine whites also. Javier Dominguez who runs
the project has benefitted from advice from Priorat stars Sara Pérez
and René Barbier Jnr in the creation of his excellent small range. In
this rugged semi mountainous terrain, the bodega is in the process
of restructuring its vineyard terraces. They now have 45 ha under
vine. The gravity fed winery contains only cement and wooden
vessels and the artisan approach shows through in the quality of the
wines. The entry level white Lapola is a multi variety blend, it is cool
fermented in larger barrels and then aged on lees in a combination
of larger vats and concrete tanks on lees for over a year. The subtle,
structured, mineral and citrus scented Lapena is fermented in barrel
and aged in a mix of vessels on lees for up to 20 months. The entry
level red, is the splendid vibrant and black-fruited Lalama. It is mainly
Mencia and finely structured and lower in alcohol than most other
Spanish reds. A level up in both quality and price is the Lacima. It
sees 20 months in oak, but older barrels. The splendid top red is the
Dominio do Bibei, a wonderfully complex and beguiling red, full of
dark fruits, minerals and spice.

Recommended Reds:
Ribeira Sacra Dominio do Bibei ★★★★★ £F
Ribeira Sacra Lacima ★★★★☆ £F   Ribeira Sacra Lalama ★★★★ £E
Recommended Whites:
Ribeira Sacra Lapena ★★★★ £E   Ribeira Sacra Lapola ★★★☆ £D

❀❀ Dominio de Pingus (Ribera del Duero)

Now a cult wine among the top Ribera del Duero reds and rivalled
for price only by VEGA SICILIA and the top limited cuvées from
Priorat. Pingus was in fact only established as recently as 1995. Very
modern in style and approach, the wine is massively extracted
but has remarkably intense, pure, dark and spicy fruit. Malolactic
fermentation in barrel provides a supple, velvety texture resulting
in a wine which is not only approachable but very ageworthy.
The second label, Flor de Pingus, is also impressive and pricey and

there is a micro-cuvée Amelia which is a single barrel selection.
A completely separate project is PSI which can be purchased for
considerably less. (DM)

Recommended Reds:
Ribera del Duero Valdegatiles ✪✪✪✪✪ £G
Ribera del Duero Flor de Pingus ★★★★ £G
Ribera del Duero PSI ★★★☆ £E

Dominio de Tares (Bierzo) *www.dominiodetares.com*

This is a recently established Bodega which is proving the
tremendous potential of this DO. As well as the four Mencía-based
reds there is a fine, mineral and citrusy, nutty Godello-based white,
FB which is barrel-fermented. The Baltos is soft, forward and nicely
rounded, but with a nice structured mid palate. Aged in American
oak, this will drink well relatively young. The Cepas Viejas, from
60-year-old vines, is dense and concentrated with an earthy dark
berry character. It is aged in both French and American oak of up
of to 5 years of age whereas the more opulent Bembibre is aged
only in French oak and the dark and spicy fruit gets a rich and toasty
edge with an impressive depth and complexity from 80 year old
vines. The top red, the Tares P3, is altogether subtler and finer. From
a single plot of 100 year old vines it is very structured in its youth,
demanding at least 5–6 years to open out. Malolactic is carried
out in barrel for a proportion of the wine and it is bottled without
filtration. (DM)

Recommended Reds:
Bierzo Tares P3 ★★★★ £F   Bierzo Bembibre ★★★★ £E
Bierzo Cepas Viejas ★★★ £D   Bierzo Baltos ★★☆ £C
Recommended Whites:
Bierzo Godello Fermentado en Barrica ★★★ £D

Dominio del Bendito (Toro) *www.bodegadominiodelbendito.com*

French born Antony Terryn produces three Toro reds and a Vin de
Paille. He started his own small bodega in 2004 having previously
worked at Quinta de La QUIETUD. He now has 10 ha of Tinta de
Toro to draw on, ranging in age from 15 to 80 years old, all of which
is farmed organically. As well as the Gold Label red there is a Silver
label which is a younger wine style aged in oak for 6 months. The
three Toro bottlings are completed by El Titan, a big, full modern red.
Indeed this style is also reflected in the sturdy muscular Gold Label,
which comes from 45 year old vines and is aged like all the reds only
in French oak. The muscular El Titan sees new oak and needs time
to shed its immediate impact. There is a *Vin de Paille* made in tiny
quantities, less than 100 cases a year.

Recommended Reds:
Toro El Titan ★★★★ £E   Toro Gold Label Las Sabias ★★★☆ £D
Toro Silver Label El Primer Paso ★★★ £C

Dominio Dostares *www.dominiodostares.com*

DOMINIO DE TARES in Bierzo and LUSCO in Rías Baixas. Located in
the west of Castilla y León, the red and rosado wines are produced
from the characterful and piercing Prieto Picudo variety. The
operation is not inconsiderable with 115 ha under vine and an
output of around 15,000 cases a year. Much of the key to quality
are vines that range from upwards of 80 to over 100 years of age.
There are two very well priced entry level wines, Tombú is a ripe
and juicy rosé which should be drunk young and the characterful
Estay is a supple and softly structured Crianza style which gets six
months oak ageing. The Leione is a step up, richly textured with the
malolactic fermentation in a mix of oak types. The top wine Cumal
is dense, structured and impressively concentrated with rich, spicy

Spain

darkberried old-vine fruit and real complexity. Plan on giving these four to six years from the vintage. A white, Brysal is also made from a blend of Albarín, Verdejo and Doña Blanca. (DM)

Recommended Reds:
VdT Castilla y León Cumal ★★★★ £F
VdT Castilla y León Leione ★★★☆ £E
VdT Castilla y León Estay ★★☆ £C

Recommended Rosés:
VdT Castilla y León Tombú ★★☆ £C

>> Adega Eidos (Rías Baixas) *www.adegaeidos.com*
Fine small bodega, located in the Salnés Valley. It is a source of three whites as well as the local Oruje brandy and two liqueurs. The vineyards are planted on slopes, which overlook the Pontevedra estuary. Founded in 2000, the property has just over 8 ha spread across around 100 different small parcels. The winery not only has temperature control but the facilities to micro-vinify some of the plots of ungrafted vines that are grown. Both the Eidos and Veigas de Padriñán are impressively complex and mineral. The Veigas includes fruit from ungrafted parcels and is kept on fine lees for up to 11 months. The third white Contraaparede is kept for an extended period in stainlees steel before bottling.

Recommended Whites:
Rías Baixas Veigas de Padriñán (Albariño) ★★★☆ £C
Rías Baixas Eidos de Padriñán (Albariño) ★★★☆ £C

Bodegas Estancia Piedra (Toro) *www.estanciapiedra.com*
Fine newly established Toro property. Scottish lawyer Grant Stein founded the operation in 1998 although the age of some of the vineyard is considerably older. There is a block of over 40 year old Tinto de Toro and Garnacha and the single vineyard 'Paredinas', the source for the wines of the same name, which is over 100 years old. A new premium red Pride of Paredinas is the flagship red. Considerable investment has gone into the cellars and the wines are modern in style and very well made. Intervention in both vineyard and cellar though is kept to a minimum. Fruit is rigorously sorted prior to fermentation and predominantly French rather than American oak is used to age the wines. The Roja Crianza is soft and approachable, offering good berry fruit and some depth. La Garona unusually has quite a high proportion of Garnacha (25%) and is dark, smoky and more firmly structured. The Piedra Platino Selección is a more traditional style, 100% Tinto de Toro and aged for 18 months in French (90%) and American oak. The top wine the Paredinas is impressively rich and shows lovely complex, dark old-vine fruit character. It is aged for 22 months in 100% new French oak which is very well harnessed. Expect the wines to drink well on release, as they are held back for a year or two after bottling. There is also a regular every day well-priced Toro Azul, a fresh white Rueda and a rosé. (DM)

Recommended Reds:
Toro Paredinas ★★★★ £F   Toro Piedra Platino Selección ★★★☆ £D
Toro Lagarona ★★★ £D   Toro Etiqueta Roja Crianza ★★☆ £D
Toro Piedra Azul ★★ £C

Recommended Whites:
Rueda Verdejo ★★ £C

Bodegas Estefania (Bierzo) *www.tilenus.com*
Bierzo is now firmly established as a serious source of good to very good reds. This is undoutedly the case here with reds of striking depth, character and quality made with the guidance of Raúl PÉREZ under the Tilenus label as well as a good value budget young wine called simply Tilenus Vendimia and a further approachable red, Roble which spends a little less than a year in a mix of French and American oak. The property was established in 1999 and the first vintage was in 2000. There are approaching 40 ha under vine. Old bush vines make a significant contribution to the quality of the wines and here they are mostly up to 100 years old and more. The wines are produced solely from the local Mencia grape which offers an original array of flavours not found elsewhere. In the past the variety was often cropped to high levels in the region and consequently light, simple wines used to be the norm. However the dark, spicy depths achieved in the Pagos de Posada give an indication of just what is possible. While the Pieros is denser, more concentrated it is more obviously fleshy and oaky, the Pagos de Posada offering more mineral character. Both the top reds will develop very well in the medium term with 5 or 6 years' age. A single white is also made from Godello while an organically farmed red Castillo de Ulver comes from a plot of younger vines. (DM)

Recommended Reds:
Bierzo Tilenus Pieros ★★★★ £F
Bierzo Tilenus Pagos de Posada ★★★★ £E
Bierzo Tilenus La Florida Crianza ★★★☆ £D
Bierzo Tilenus Roble ★★★ £C   Bierzo Tilenus Vendimia ★★☆ £C

>> José Estévez Fernández (Ribeiro) *www.mauroestevez.com*
This is a small bodega where the family involvement in viticulture stretches back to the 1940s although it is recently that they have been making a small amount of wine commercially. Output is tiny, barely 700 cases a year and most of this is white. A tiny amount of red is produced from a blend of Caiño, Sousón and Brancellao. The white, Mauro E Álvarez is, like most whites in the DO, dominated by Treixadura with a touch of Albariño and Loureiro. It is intense and rich and less grassy and more honeyed than many from the region.

Recommended Whites:
Ribeiro Mauro Estevez ★★★☆ £D

❀❀ Alejandro Fernández *www.grupopesquera.com*
VEGA SICILIA may be the most famous property in this potentially great DO but Alejandro Fernández isn't far behind. His two wineries, Pesquera and Condado de Haza, produce some of the best examples here at all quality levels. The Pesquera Crianza is stylish and concentrated whereas the Reserva and Gran Reserva are real benchmarks – very dark, powerful and marked by subtle, cedary oak and, in the case of the Gran Reserva, a formidable structure. The Cuvée Janus is made only in great years and is not only massive in extract but remarkably fine. Sadly it is made in tiny quantities. The Condado de Haza wines don't quite match their stablemates but are impressive nonetheless. The Crianza is surprisingly forward in style, the Alenza more extracted and inevitably rich and heady. Both the Alenza and the Reserva, which spends longer in bottle, demand to be cellared. Two interesting projects are DEJHESA LA GRANJA and EL VINCULO. The former is in Zamora, where Fernández is producing a 100% Tempranillo that is aged for 24 months in American oak. At El Viniculo in La Mancha he produces two further Tempranillo varietals, one a Crianza aged for 6 months, the other a Reserva which sees 12 months in cask. In both cases American oak is used to complement the rich, and ripe warm-grown fruit. (DM)

Pesquera

Recommended Reds:
Ribera de Duero Gran Reserva ✪✪✪✪✪ £H
Ribera de Duero Reserva ★★★★☆ £F
Ribera de Duero Crianza ★★★ £D

Condado de Haza
Recommended Reds:
Ribera de Duero Alenza★★★★☆ £F
Ribera de Duero Reserva★★★☆ £E
Ribera de Duero Crianza ★★☆ £D
Dehesa La Granja
Recommended Reds:
VdT Castilla y Leon Dehesa La Granja ★★★ £D
El Vinculo
Recommended Reds:
La Mancha Reserva★★★ £D   La Mancha Crianza ★★★ £C

Bodegas Emeterio Fernández (Cigales) *www.lalegua.com*
Winemaking was established here in 1997. There are 80 ha of potentially great vineyards planted in alluvial soils with finely drained topsoils which are a mix of stones and pebbles. The vineyard currently comprises mainly Tempranillo with a small holding each of Garnacha and Cabernet Sauvignon. Two entry-level fruit-driven reds are produced, a Joven from Tempranillo and Garnacha and a juicy fruited Roble. Quality is impressive and the wines show a great depth and intensity of fruit. As winemaker Carlos Ayala Sanz continues to refine the winemaking a special cuvée Capricho has also now joined the Crianza and Reserva bottlings. This is hand destemmed grape by grape and is richer and fuller, more modern and fleshy in style. (DM)
Recommended Reds:
Cigales La Legua Capricho ★★★★ £F
Cigales La Legua Reserva ★★★☆ £D
Cigales La Legua Crianza ★★★ £C
Cigales La Legua Roble ★★☆ £B
Cigales La Legua Tempranillo ★★ £B

>> Bodegas Fillaboa (Rías Baixas) *www.bodegasfillaboa.com*
This is now one of the most established names in the DO. There are 70 ha under cultivation and the bodega produces four whites which are all produced from estate grown fruit. The Masaveu family purchased the property in 2000. A new entry level Albariño, Atlantik has recently been added to the small range. The Fillaboa is full of ripe peach and aromatic fruit, with a subtle mineral quality. The Finca Monte Alto single vineyard wine comprises 12 separate plots on some of the highest slopes on the property. Richly textured and complex it gains depth from 9 months on its fine lees. The small range is completed by the Fermentado en Tino, which is fermented in a larger 2,000 litre vat and then kept on fine lees for 18 months, first in vat and then in stainless steel. (DM)
Recommended Whites:
Rías Baixas Selección Finca Monte Alto ★★★☆ £D
Rías Baixas Fillaboa ★★★ £C

>> Adega Manuel Formigo (Ribeiro) *www.fincateira.com*
The Formigo family has been involved with viticulture in this region for generations although the bodega was founded very recently in 2006. Their small output is dominated by whites although a red, Finca Teiro Tinta is also made from a blend of Sousón, Caiño, Brancellao and Garnacha. There are 4.5 ha under vine and spread across five vineyards and planted on stony, granite soils. The whites are all cool fermented for around two weeks, the crisp and fresh Finca Teira (Treixadura, Godello, Torrontés) and Formigo (Treixadura, Palomino Fino, Godello; Torrontés, Albariño, Loureiro) in reasonable quantities. The top white, the Teira X which blends Treixadura, Alvilla, Albariño and Loureiro comes from older vines. While it retains a fresh and crisp, mineral and green-fruited character it also offers more depth and a richer texture. A small amount of a varietal Loureira, Cholo has just been released and a pricy Dulce Treixadura solera aged Tostado de Teira has also been made. (DM)
Recommended Whites:
Ribeiro Teira X ★★★★ £E   Ribeiro Finca Teira ★★★☆ £C
Ribeiro Formigo ★★★ £C

O. Fournier (Ribera del Duero) *www.ofournier.com*
A producer with not only a range of powerful and characterful Ribera del Duero reds but also some impressive wines at their property in Mendoza in Argentina and now Chile also. See O. FOURNIER in the South American section for additional details. There are now 60 ha under vine with some vineyard plots over 50 years and much of the bodegas holding is planted in soils with a high proportion of pebblestones. There is a modern forward red which gets just four months oak ageing and is excellent value, Urban Ribera. The top three wines are the benchmarks. The Spiga and Alfa Spiga are both bottled unfiltered and aged in mainly French and a little American oak, the former for 12 to 13 months, the Alfa Spiga for 18 to 20. These are big, dense and concentrated reds and typically go through malolactic in barrel. The flagship red from the 2004 vintage is O Fournier. The big blockbuster style is achieved with a vatting of up to 40 days, ageing in 100% new French oak and again malolactic in barrel. Filtration is once again eschewed. All three will add weight and complexity with five or more years cellaring. (DM)
Recommended Reds:
Ribera del Duero O. Fournier ★★★★ £F
Ribera del Duero Alfa Spiga ★★★☆ £E
Ribera del Duero Spiga ★★★ £D
Ribera del Duero Urban Ribera ★★☆ £C

Gallego Zapatero *www.bodegasgallegozapatero.com*
A small range of reds are produced at this family run Ribera del Duero bodega with all the wines released under their Yotuel brand. The parents of the current generation established the vineyards although it is more recently that a range of modern, well crafted wines are made. There are 9 ha under cultivation in the heart of the DO around Anguix with an altitude of around 800 metres above sea level. This provides for good balance and structure although there is often the risk of frosts in the spring. Farming is organic and the yields kept purposefully low. The small winery is well equipped and the harvested fruit is vinified strictly by plot. The soils are propitious, low in organic matter with traces of sand and limestone. The Roble is vibrant, dark and spicy with some underlying tannins, it is aged for 7 months in French barrels. The Seleccion is bigger, fuller and more structured it spends longer in barrel, 13 months and comes from vines over 75 years old. The Vinas Viejos will no longer be made because the direction here is towards some very impressive dark-fruited, elegant and mineral scented single vineyard wines from now on. Of the three currently released the Finca Valdepalacios is produced in the biggest volume but not large generally less than 2,000 bottles. The vinification and ageing are modern the malolactic occurring in barrel and ageing is for no less than 15 months. La Nava which is aged in larger 500 litre barrels has a particularly piercing, edgy dark and spicy character. All three of the single vineyard sites are well over 75 years old. (DM)
Recommended Reds:
Ribera del Duero Yotuel Finca San Miguel ★★★★ £E
Ribera del Duero Yotuel Viñas Finca Valdepalacios ★★★★ £E

North-West Spain

Spain

Ribera del Duero Yotuel Finca La Nava ★★★★ £E
Ribera del Duero Yotuel Viñas Viejas ★★★☆ £E
Ribera del Duero Yotuel Selección ★★★ £C
Ribera del Duero Yotuel Roble ★★☆ £B

⊛ **Gancedo (Bierzo)** *www.bodegasgancedo.com*
One of the more exciting properties from an exciting region. Established as recently as 1998, there are a mere 11.5 ha under vine producing both reds and whites of impressive quality. Of the whites, which are dominated by Godello with a little Doña Blanca, the nutty, characterful Capricho is vinified in older wood and held on lees for 12 months. By contrast the Herencia de Capricho is barrel-fermented in a proportion of new French oak with a similar lees influence. This has a rounder, more citrus infused quality but both wines have a fine underlying mineral character. The reds are produced from the Mencia variety, The Gancedo and Xestal are both dark and smoky with a piercing nervy mineral edge. The Ucedo is fuller, rounder with more obvious new wood. All three reds will continue to develop for at least five years, the Ucedo a touch longer. (DM)
Recommended Reds:
Bierzo Seleccion Ucedo ★★★★☆ £E
Bierzo Xestal ★★★★ £D Bierzo Gancedo ★★★☆ £D
Recommended Whites:
Bierzo Herencia del Capricho ★★★☆ £D
Bierzo Capricho ★★★☆ £C

>> **Garmón Continental (Ribera del Duero)**
This is the third project of the Garcia family along with their MAURO and MAURODOS winery's. Currently just one wine is being made, a classy Ribera del Duero vinified from Tinto Fino. The intention is very much to keep this limited with an output of no more than 80,000 bottles a year. A new winery facility is being developed. The wine comes from fruit grown in a selection of vineyards in the eastern stretches of the Ribera del Duero DO. The vineyards are characterised by their altitude, 850 to around 1,000 metres which provides the wine with its fresh edge and structure as well as vines ranging from 30 to 100 years old grown in clay, sandy-clay and limestone soils. The wine is marked by dark fruits, a hint of spice and with structured but polished tannins and a fresh balanced edge. Vinification is thoughtful, avoiding overextraction. Vatting lasts for 14 days and the spontaneous natural fermentation temperature kept at around 28 degrees celsius. Cellar ageing is for 16 months in French. This is a stylish modern Ribera red with great potential. (DM)
Recommended Reds:
Ribera del Duero Garmón ★★★★ £E

Godelia (Bierzo) *www.godelia.es*
Godelia is now one of the leading producers in Bierzo after a major restoration of the property. They have 35 ha spread across three different properties and planted at varied elevations and in a mix of clay, quartz and slate. The fruit is always hand harvested into small crates and carefully sorted prior to vinification. Four reds and two whites are made. The floral, citrus fruited Godelia Blanco is dominated by Godello and aged for five months on lees (sobre lías), while its Doña Blanco component comes from very old vines adding complexity. The Godelia Selección is solely 80 year old Godello and barrel fermented and aged on lees for 8 months. The Viernes is a juicy, blackberry fruited Joven style coming from young vines up to 20 years old. It stays in tank on lees before bottling. The Godelia red is a more firmly structured style, aged in oak for

12 months and offering a complex array of dark berry fruit and an impressive mineral quality. The Selección has a touch more depth and a richer texture with 16 months in French oak (400 litre barrels for balance) and the malolactic in cask. Particularly unusual and full of interest is a red dulce style, Libamus, full of dark, unctuous berry fruit and a pure underlying minerality. A white and red Selección are both also made. (DM)
Recommended Reds:
Bierzo Libamus Dulce de Mencía ★★★★☆ £E
Bierzo Godelia Selección ★★★★ £D
Bierzo Godelia 12 Meses ★★★☆ £D Bierzo Viernes ★★★ £C
Recommended Whites:
Bierzo Godelia Selección ★★★☆ £D Bierzo Godelia ★★★ £C

Bodegas Godeval (Valdeorras) *www.godeval.com*
Originally founded in 1987 this is one of the best producers in an increasingly exciting region for top class whites. With 17 ha planted exclusively to Godello, on sharply sloping hillside vineyards with finely drained slate soils, the conditions are all in place for the production of intensely flavoured grapes. The regular white is fermented relatively cool and offers a fine mineral and citrus, green fruited intensity. The Cepas Vellas comes from the oldest vines on the property and is aged on lees for six months which adds a rich and rounder texture to the wines intense, mineral qualities. (DM)
Recommended Whites:
Valdeorras Viña Godeval Cepas Vellas ★★★☆ £D
Valdeorras Viña Godeval ★★★ £C

>> **Adegas Guimaro (Ribeira Sacra)** *www.guimaro.es*
Much of the quality of the reds now emerging from this region is due to the successful recovery of old terraced vineyards on the regions precipitous slopes. This is certainly the case here, Mencia based wines of subtlety and sheer elegance are produced rather than overmade blockbusters. The intense blackberry fruited Guimaro is a young Joven style, full of depth and character and impressive class for its price. It's also worth looking out for some special vineyard wines, Fincas Meixemán, Capeliños and Pombeiras. Two whites from Godello are also made.
Recommended Reds:
Ribeira Sacra Guimaro Joven (Mencia) ★★★☆ £C

⊛ **Hacienda Monasterio** *www.haciendamonasterio.com*
Like the now cult wine Pingus this Ribera del Duero based project has its winemaking led by Dane, Peter Sisseck. It was founded in 1991 by a group of private investors and much investment in both vineyards and wineery facilities has followed, the estate was in serious decline when the group took it over. The estate consisted of 115 ha of which 70 ha were planted to vines. The property is located in the excellent stretch of the DO just to the west of Peñafiel and between Pesquera and Valbuena. There are three wines and all share a quality and elegance that is very often missing in this region. While the the wines are crafted in a traditional Crianza and Reserva style, the approach in the winery is thoroughly modern and sophisticated, malolactic is carried out in barrel and only French oak is used for ageing. Tinot Fino is the main variety but there are supplementary holdings of Cabernet Sauvignon, Merlot and Malbec. These are only blended into the wines if the Tinto Fino endures unusually difficult ripening conditions. The Cosecha bottle is a crianza in style and gets 15 months in new French oak. There are two Reserva bottlings which are more intense and complex, in particular the stunning Reserva Especial. (DM)

Recommended Reds:
Ribera del Duero Reserva Especial ★★★★★ £G
Ribera del Duero Reserva ★★★★☆ £F
Ribera del Duero Cosecha ★★★★ £E

Hornillos Ballesteros (Ribera del Duero)

This family owned and run bodega with small cellars in Roa in the centre of the DO was only recently founded in 2002. The wines are striking and generally offer some very good values. Javier and Miguel Ballesteros run the operation with input from Juan-Manuel BURGOS, an established star of the region. Their Burgos vineyards tend to be cool for the appellation, producing elegant wines with intense aromatic character and well balanced acidity. They have a number of vineyard sources planted on varying soils and with some vines of up to 75 years of age. The fresh, fruit driven Mibal Joven sees no wood, while the Mibal tinto and Mibal Selección get respectively 12 and 16 months in French oak with the malolactic in barrel. Their approach is to have a fairly high level of toasting of the barrels, so the wood can be quite pronounced when the wines are young. (DM)

Recommended Reds:
Ribera del Duero Perfil ★★★★ £F
Ribera del Duero Mibal Seleccion ★★★ £E
Ribera del Duero Mibal ★★☆ £C
Ribera del Duero Mibal Joven ★★ £C

Bodegas La Cana (Rías Baixas) *www.jorge-ordonez.es*

This is another new and very promising project developed by Jorge Ordóñez. Founded in 2008, there are 20 ha planted in Sisán Ribadurnia in the Salnés Valley sub-region in the far north of the Rías Baixas DO and with a pronounced maritime climate. At present two wines are being made, La Caña and the marginally pricier (£E) La Caña Navia, both of which are 100% Albariño . It is an intensely aromatic and fresh style with vibrant acidity and is partially barrel fermented in oak and gains richness and depth from a period of several months on its lees. It is characterised by hints of green fruits, peach and has a subtle herbaceous, mineral undercurrent. (DM)

Recommended Whites:
Rías Baixas La Caña ★★★☆ £D

>> Lagar de Besada (Rías Baixas) *www.lagardebesada.com*

A small range of very decent whites is produced at this small bodega with just 3 ha under vine in the Salnés subzone. In addition to the Rías Baixas whites there is an unusual, albeit quite pricey Espumoso sparkler produced from Albariño. The bodega is longer established than many here, being founded in 1988. This is also now the brand name for the entry level white, a well priced cool fermented Albariño. Also offering great value is the Lagar de Besada which is fresh, zesty and lightly aromatic. It gains additional richness from 6 months on lees. The Baladiña cuvée is also cool fermented but spends longer "sobre lias", around a year. The leading white is the very impressive Añada de Baladiña. A vineyard selection aged on lees for 24 months and with minimum sulphur additions.

Recommended Whites:
Rías Baixas Añada de Baladiña (Albariño) ★★★☆ £D
Rías Baixas Baladiña (Albariño) ★★★ £C
Rías Baixas Lagar de Besada (Albariño) ★★ £B

>> Lagar da Condesa (Rías Baixas) *www.lagardacondesa.com*

This is a fine, newly established bodega by the Gil family with vineyards planted in the Val do Salnés sub region. Albariño is the sole variety and the first crop vinified with the 2013 vintage. The winery is traditionally styled although the best modern winemaking processes are utilised and everything from harvest onwards done by hand. The vines are planted in sand and granite with a south-west exposition and excellent drainage. During the vinification, the fruit is de-stemmed and then fermentation is partly in 500-600 litre barrels and partly in stainless steel. The wine remains in contact with the lees for four months. Green fruits are interwoven with restrained citrus and a hint of background peach. A second fresh styled Rías Baixas, Kentia is also released under the Orowines label, which the Gil family use for fruit driven, fresh, approachable styles. Again it is made solely from the Albariño variety. At Juan GIL in Jumilla a bright vibrant red, Comoloco is also made from Monastrell. (DM)

Lagar da Condesa
Recommended Whites:
Rías Baixas Lagar da Condesa ★★★ £C
Orowines
Recommended Whites:
Rías Baixas Kentia ★★ £B

Lagar de Costa (Rías Baixas) *www.lagardecosta.com*

An excellent small bodega which is very well established, being founded back in 1950. Based in the Salnés Valley, the 6 ha of vines are planted in sandy loam soils which are naturally poor for water retention and therefore aid fruit ripening and flavour intensity in the grapes. The output of the bodega is distinctly artisanal, around 5,000 cases a year and the vast majority of this is accounted for by the regular Lagar de Costa, which like all three whites is solely from Albariño. Coming from 30 year old vines there is an added dimension and the wine is cool fermented and aged on lees. The top two wines are very impressive. The Barrica is a selection from similarly aged vineyards with fermentation in larger 500 litre French and Hungarian oak before ageing on fine lees. The top wine the Maio comes from the oldest vines which are over 50 years of age and from three distinct plots. It is aged for two years on lees but in stainless steel not oak. A red Viva la Vid—a, comes from Espadeiro. Fewer than 600 bottles are made. (DM)

Recommended Whites:
Rías Baixas Maio de Lagar de Costa ★★★★ £E
Rías Baixas Barrica ★★★ £C   Rías Baixas Lagar de Costa ★★☆ £C

>> Lagar do Mérens (Ribeiro) *www.lagardomerens.com*

A very good small bodega established just over a decade ago. The winery is located in an old converted stone warehouse and is well organized with modern fermentation and storage equipment. There are 3.5 ha under vine, which is planted in loamy soils covering a granite base. The wines are strikingly structured and mineral. Three wines are made. As well as the two excellent whites there is a red 30 Copelos, which is a blend of Sousón, Caíño, Ferrón and Garnacha, aged in a mix of French, Hungarian and American oak. Both whites have a sizeable proportion of Treixadura (around 70%), the regular white is attractive, green fruited and with a citrus undercurrent. Fermented at a medium temperature, just over 17 C it is kept on fine lees for 8 months which adds depth and a richer texture. Quite a bit pricier is the concentrated Barrica. The wine displays a combination of fresh green fruit and a toasty component from the new wood. Ageing is in 300 litre barrels on fine, stirred lees.

Recommended Whites:
Ribeiro Lagar do Meréns Barrel Fermented ★★★ £D
Ribeiro Lagar do Meréns ★★☆ £C

North-West Spain

Recommended Reds:
Ribeiro Lagar do Meréns 30 Copelos ★★★ £E

>> Lagar de Sabariz (VdM Galicia) *www.lagardesabariz.com*
Two exceptional wines are made at this small artisan bodega from vineyards bordering the Ribeiro DO, hence its theoretically humble status. The brilliant A Pita Cega white is made from Treixadura, Albariño and a number of unspecified grapes. It is a match for any of the top whites coming from its neighbouring appellation. The property is biodynamically farmed and planted to local varieties with vineyards ranging from 300 to 500 metres in altitude. The wines are fermented in stainless steel and aged on fine lees. A Pita Cega is full of intense green fruits, youthfully reserved with edgy acidity and a piercing mineral quality expect it to evolve further for a couple of years. A second marginally cheaper white, A Pita Miuda comes solely from Treixadura. If you can track the wines down they are well worth trying. (DM)
Recommended Whites:
VdM Galicia A Pita Cega ★★★★☆ £F
VdM Galicia A Pita Miuda ★★★★ £E

La Mejorada (VdT Castilla y Leon) *www.lamejorada.es*
This new bodega is found to the south of the city of Valladolid and the wines take the Vinos de la Tierra Castilla y León classification. The climate is continental with cold winters and warm dry summers. The bodega is actually situated in a fifteenth century monastery, so while the project is very new the surroundings are not. A range of vines have been planted since the acquisition of the land in 1999 and there are a total of 42.5 ha now under vine. The soils are quite diverse and include traces of sand and granite over a clay subsoil. The new well-equipped winery has been established in what was the monastery cloister. The releases are all red, Villalar the most obviously approachable, although it is dominated by Cabernet Sauvignon (90%) with the balance Tempranillo. Vinification is modern with a cold soak, an extended vatting and malolactic in barrel with ageing a total of 12 months. A further Villalar, Oro has also been made which is 100% Tempranillo. Las Norias is vinified in a very similar manner and is again 100% Tempranillo, it offers a more pronounced cherry fruit intensity. The top red, Las Cercas is a clear step up on the other wines. It blends Tempranillo with Syrah and offers dark fruited flavours with a spicy, mineral background and a supple structure. All three wines below are bottled unfiltered. ((DM)
Recommended Reds:
VdT Castilla y León Las Cercas ★★★☆ £E
VdT Castilla y León Las Norias ★★★ £C
VdT Castilla y León Villalar ★★★ £C

Bodegas La Val (Rías Baixas) *www.bodegaslaval.com*
Good quality, medium sized Rías Baixas bodega producing textbook examples of the DO. A small range of wines are produced and include a number of other wines than those profiled here but these should be worth seeking out. The bodega was founded in 1985, a relative veteran by current Spanish standards, and is planted to a combination of Albariño, Loureiro and Treixadura. There is now an extremely modern wine making facility and there are 35 ha under vine. The regular Rías Baixas is attractive and forward with classy grass scented fruit and good intensity. Finca de Arantei is one of the firm's single vineyard bottlings and is a clear level up in quality. Both wines are traditionally vinified without recourse to oak although the bodega does make a barrel-fermented example also. (DM)

Recommended Whites:
Rías Baixas Finca de Arantei ★★★ £C
Rías Baixas Albariño ★★☆ £C

⚙ Leda Viñas Viejas *www.bodegasleda.com*
This is an exciting project along the lines of MAURO and ABADIA RETUERTA, producing first-class red wine not just from within the boundaries of the Ribera del Duero DO. Winemaker César Munoz, who is also responsible for the up-and-coming Ribera wines at Bodegas MONTEBACO is one of the partners here. Currently some of the 100% Tinto Fino fruit is sourced from Ribera and some from the Cigales DO; the average age of the vines is 50 years. There is a good lighter red Mas de Leda, a spicy and characterful example which joins the deep, dark and formidably extracted Leda. The top wine nevertheless possesses a fine balance and supple structure. It will age very well for a decade or so. Under the same ownership is the impressive Toro bodega Bienvenida de Vinos, source of a typically dense, powerful and structured 100% Tinto de Toro which offers a fine balance of dark fruit and well judged and integrated new oak. (DM)
Leda Viñas Viejas
Recommended Reds:
VdT Castilla y Leon Leda Viñas Viejas ★★★★☆ £F
VdT Castilla y Leon Mas de Leda ★★☆ £C
Bienvenida de Vinos
Recommended Reds:
Toro Sitio de 'El Palo' Bienvenida ★★★★☆ £F

Lezcano Lacalle (Cigales) *www.lezcano-lacalle.com*
A small family owned property making wines of real quality from 16 ha of south facing dry-farmed vineyards planted in sand and clay soils topped by well drained gravel. An altitude of 800 metres and high summer diurnal (day to night) temperature fluctuations provides grapes with a high concentration of flavour as well as excellent acidity. There is a rosado, Docetiñidos and a crianza style, Maudes which is aged for 12 months in oak. Of the reservas, both wines are vinified traditionally with a lengthy 20 plus day vatting and the Du bottling given malolactic in barrel which adds a rounded, richer texture and a more complex character. Expect both wines to develop well in bottle for five years at least. (DM)
Recommended Reds:
Cigales Reserva Du ★★★☆ £E   Cigales Reserva ★★★ £D

>> Leyenda del Paramo *www.leyendadelparamo.com*
This project is led by Pedro Gonzalez Mittelbrunn and was established with the 2009 harvest. Three ranges of wine are made. Red, white and rosado examples are made under the Flor del Páramo, Rescatado and the premium Leyendas de Vida labels. The main variety cultivated is the local Prieto Picudo, which has great potential and the project is working hard at acquiring increased old vine holdings of the grape. The white Albarín is also important. The climate is cool maritime and the sunny summers are balanced by the altitude of around 900 metres and the influence of the Cantabrian Mountains. The Flor del Páramo wines offer great value, essentially bright and fruit driven. The white is made from Verdejo, the rosado and tinto from young Prieto Picudo. El Restacado is a range of organic wines, rosado and red again coming from Prieto Picudo, the white from Albarín Blanco. The grapes are all from the bodegas own organic plots. The blanco and rosado are fresh, cool fermented and the malolactic fermentation avoided. The tinto, while

a young wine style, gets three months in used barrels adding a little structure. The five wines under the Leyendas de Vida banner also offer good value. Blanco, rosado and tinto are all released under the El Aprendiz label. Although all three take the Tierra de León DO they are from a combination of own vineyards and bought in grapes. The approach to vinification is very similar to the Restacado wines. The top two reds are a step up both in quality and price, albeit still offering good value. Both offer a dark, edgy black-fruited character. El Músico spends three months longer in wood and new French oak is used. In El Médico a combination of French and American barrels are used with 25% new oak resulting in a touch more elegance and minerality. A rounded texture comes from carrying out the malolactic in barrel in both. (DM)

Recommended Reds:
Tierra de León El Músico ★★★☆ £D
Tierra de León El Médico ★★★☆ £C
Tierra de León El Aprendiz ★★☆ £B
Tierra de León El Restacado ★★☆ £B
VdT Castilla y León Flor del Páramo ★☆ £A

Recommended Whites:
Tierra de León El Aprendiz ★★☆ £B
Tierra de León El Restacado ★★☆ £B
VdT Castilla y León Flor del Páramo ★☆ £A

Recommended Rosés:
Tierra de León El Aprendiz ★★☆ £B
Tierra de León El Restacado ★★☆ £B
VdT Castilla y León Flor del Páramo ★☆ £A

Liberalia Enologica (Toro) *www.liberalia.es*
Good quality emerges throughout this small range from a producer with some very old vineyards ranging from upwards of 30 to over 100 years of age. The creation of the bodega though is a far more recent event in 2000. Of the reds Cero is from some of the younger vines and is fermented unusually in new American oak with the malolactic following. The wine is marked by its upfront sweet fruit and the oak is very apparent in the wine's youth. The Tres Roble is very much in the fruit driven mould with just four months cask ageing. The wine is unusually rich and firm for the style, not least coming from over 40 year old vines. The Cuatro is a Crianza style with 12 months in both French and American oak. The tannin is not inconsiderable and the wine offers impressive depth and persistence. Give it at least four or five years from the vintage. The Cabeza de Cuba is a similar style but subtler, less overtly tannic and with an impressive lift to its fruit coming from 70 year old vines. Similar patience, as with the Cuatro, will be rewarded. The marginally more expensive Cinco from 100 year old vines has real depth and a chewy concentration. Its big muscular tannin demands seven or eight years patience. The flagship Liber is only made in the greatest vintages. A pleasant sweet white Toro, Uno is also produced from Moscatel and Albillo. (DM)

Recommended Reds:
Toro Liber ★★★★☆ £F   Toro Cinco ★★★★ £F
Toro Cabeza de Cuba ★★★☆ £E   Toro Cuatro Crianza ★★★ £D
Toro Tres Roble ★★★ £C   Toro Cero ★★☆ £C

Recommended Whites:
Toro Uno ★★ £C

Loess (Ribera del Duero & Rueda) *www.loess.es*
This is a recently established small high quality bodega producing wines from both the Rueda and Ribera del Duero appellations. The wines all show great promise. There is an excellent Rueda

which is crisp, mineral and with a really striking, piercing citrus and green fruit intensity. The juice is given a short cold soak for a few hours with pressing and fermentation following at a cool rather than cold temperature and then given a brief period on its fine lees. Three other wines are also made. There is a marginally pricier Rueda Collection, which comes from older vines, the vineyard first planted in 1936. The wine is barrel-fermented and aged with regular lees stirring and bottling is in July after the harvest. In Ribera del Duero again an appellation label as well as a Collection wine are produced. The regular bottling is in a more obviously fruit driven style, the Collection seeing over two years in barrel. Traditional ageing classifications are avoided and French rather than American oak used for ageing. A mix of 225 litre and 500 litres vessels are used which helps reduce the influence of some of the leaner wood tannins found in other examples in the DO. (DM)

Recommended Reds:
Ribera del Duero Collection ★★★★ £E
Ribera del Duero ★★★☆ £D

Recommended Whites:
Rueda Collection ★★★☆ £D   Rueda Verdejo ★★★ £C

Los Astrales (Ribera del Duero) *www.astrales.es*
Very impressive Ribera bodega producing benchmark modern examples of the DO. As well as the Ribera bottling covered here, there is also a second label Christina which is just a touch pricier however, you should expect similarly impressive results. The Romera de la Cruz family have 15 ha of vineyards with a proportion of the holding up to 70 years of age and yields are very low around 1.5 tons to the acre. A further 14 ha have also now been established. Planted in a mix of clay and sandy soils, promoting finely textured tannins, the vines are traditional head trained and the climate is cooler than is normally encountered here. No chemicals are used and the vines farmed as naturally as possible. The result is elegant wines that have excellent fruit as well as structure and a fresh balancing acidity. The technical director is Eduardo Garcia who also makes the wines at nearby MAURO, the Bierzo PAIXAR project and is a partner at Bodegas LEDA. Everything in the winery is gravity fed and the wine is pumped over during vatting and then aged in mainly French and a little American oak for up to 18 months. New oak is restricted to just a third. Los Astrales is elegant dark-fruited with hints of blackberry and spice with big, firm but very supple tannins and a classic mineral backbone. Expect it to develop well for a decade and more. (DM)

Recommended Reds:
Ribera del Duero Astrales ★★★★ £E

Losada (Bierzo) *www.losadavinosdefinca.com*
Three very good Bierzo reds are made at Losada or Losada Vinos de Finca to give the bodega its full name. Much of the DO is planted on slate soils. The focus here though has been to concentrate on recovering very old vines planted in clay. The firms' holding is spread across a wide array of small parcels. The property includes a modern well equipped winery overlooked by the Castro Ventosa hill. The fruit is all hand harvested and sorted prior to vinification. Of the wines the Losada red is full of dark berry fruit, spice and violet aromas and approachable tannins; it is sourced from local growers and from old vines. Ageing is for 12 months in second and third fill barrels. The Altos de Losada is a touch richer, more complex with more mineral character. It comes from 20 individual old vine parcels which are vinified separately with the wine then aged in French oak for 15 months. The third red, La Bienquerida, is equally impressive. It

North-West Spain

comes from a single old vineyard which is planted in clay, shale and slate soils to mainly Mencia as well as a small number of unidentified varieties. Vinification and ageing is similar to the Altos de Losada. A forward fruit driven red Pájaro Rojo and a rosado 5 Rosas are also made. (DM)

Recommended Reds:

Bierzo La Bienquerida ★★★★ £E

Bierzo Altos de Losada ★★★☆ £D   Bierzo Losada ★★★ £C

Bodega El Albar Lurton (Toro)   *www.francoislurton.com*

François Lurton has been producing wine in Rueda for a number of years which is released under the Hermanos Lurton label. There is a good regular Rueda white and a richer barrel-fermented Cuesta de Oro. More recently he has expanded to include some very well made reds from the Toro area. The vineyards are planted at high altitude on well-drained sand and gravel soils and yields are naturally very low. He releases five wines under his own El Albar label, three reds, a white Verdejo and a rosado, as well as producing an extraordinarily dense and concentrated Toro in partnership with roving global consultant Michel Rolland, Campo Eliseo and a second label Campo Alegre. This is made in a seriously full blown, high alcohol style. Rich and concentrated though certainly impressive. The Excelencia, now VdT labelled, is quite different, lighter, less intense but the wine possesses an excellent balance and elegance so often lacking in Toro. There is also a lighter easier drinking red, Barricas which is more Crianza than Reserva in style as it receives just one year in oak. Both Excelencia and Campo Eliseo will benefit from a further 2 or 3 years ageing after release. Toro. VdT and Rueda wines are now being vinified at a recently created winery facility at Villafranca del Duero in the eastern extremities of the Toro DO. As a result of this in 2014 some of the firms facilities and vineyards in Rueda were sold to Penedès based Bodega TORRES. (DM)

Recommended Reds:

Toro Campo Eliseo ★★★★ £F

VdT Castilla y León El Albar Excelencia ★★★☆ £E

Recommended Whites:

Rueda Hermanos Lurton Cuesta de Oro ★★★ £C

Rueda Hermanos Lurton ★★☆ £C

Maldivinas (VdT Castilla y León)   *www.maldivinas.es*

A small top quality operation based at Cebreros and producing first class Garnacha reds. It is recently established and the vineyards are farmed along organic principles. The vines are in an area called La Movida which is just outside Cebreros in the direction of Ávila. The combination of vines over 60 years old, steeply aspected plots and slate soils provides for grapes with very impressive flavour intensity. Winemaking is typically modern with minimal intervention. There is a pre-fermentation cold soak followed by vatting for up to a month and then ageing in largely used French oak for a year or just over. A number of reds have been released in very small quantities; La Movida, La Movida Laderas, La Movida and Doble Punta as well as a white Albillo Combate. (DM)

Recommended Reds:

VdT Castilla y León Doble Punta Garnacha ★★★★☆ £F

VdT Castilla y León La Movida Laderas ★★★★ £E

VdT Castilla y León La Movida Granito ★★★☆ £D

VdT Castilla y León La Movida ★★★☆ £D

Recommended Whites:

VdT Castilla y León Albillo Combate ★★★☆ £D

Mar de Envero (Rías Baixas)   *www.mardeenvero.es*

The Mar de Envero bodega was founded in 2007 by two partners, winemaker Miguel Angel Moreira who is a native of the area and Breixo Reymóndez. They produce two impressive and approachable whites, both from the Albariño variety. After harvesting and pre-vinification the pressed fruit gets a cold soak to enhance primary fruit aroma and then this is followed by a cool fermentation and ageing on fine lees in stainless steel. The Troupe is the more approachable of the two. It is ripe and aromatic with opulent passion fruit and fresh, balancing acidity. The top wine, the Mar de Envero is more structured. It offers an impressive depth of zesty, peachy fruit but an intense mineral quality also. (DM)

Recommended Whites:

Rías Baixas Mar de Envero ★★★ £C   Rías Baixas Troupe ★★☆ £C

Margon (Tierra de León)   *www.bodegasmargon.com*

An excellent small bodega emphasising the potential of the local Prieto Picudo variety. The owners have invested heavily in the project and have a state of the art modern winery and winemaking input from Bierzo based winemaking star Raúl PÉREZ. A small range of red, white and rosado wines is made and the two dry whites, Pricum Albarín Barrica and Pricum Albarín Valdemuz both come from the same grape. A sweet white Pricum Aldabaran Vendimia Tardia, is made from Verdejo. Two rosados are also made, again from Prieto Picudo, the regular is fermented in stainless steel and there is also a Rosado Barrica. Of the reds the Pricum Primeur is the most approachable, the Pricum Preto Picudo is a touch more serious. It comes almost exclusively from estate grown grapes and from old vines. The reds are vinified in large French oak vats and ageing is in small wood. A single vineyard red Paraje de El Santo and a further red Valdemuz from over 100 year old vines are also made. (DM)

Recommended Reds:

Tierra de León Prieto Picudo ★★★★ £D

Tierra de León Primeur ★★★☆ £D

❀ Viña de Martin (Ribeiro)

This small bodega produces both whites and the rarer, certainly on the export market, Ribeiro reds. It also stands out as one of the DOs beacons of quality. Unlike a number of other high quality small scale producers around the country Viña de Martin is not a recent flash in the pan. While by no means venerable the bodega has been established for over 20 years and has been consistently providing evidence of the potential from the region. Both the whites are dominated by Treixadura, with the balance Torrontés, Lado and Albariño. The subtle citrus and green fruited Escolma Blanco also gets 8 months in oak. The reds, with a fresh green, but not under-ripe edge to their fruit offer an interesting alternative to many of, not only Spain's, but also other wine regions overblown and over-ripe reds. These are certainly worth trying. (DM)

Recommended Reds:

Ribeiro Escolma ★★★☆ £E   Ribeiro A Torna dos Pasás ★★☆ £C

Recommended Whites:

Ribeiro Escolma ★★★★ £D   Ribeiro Os Pasás ★★★ £C

>> Bodegas Martin Codax (Rías Baixas)   *www.martincodax.com*

Martin Codax is one of the best known Rías Baixas names on international markets and can be found in over 40 different countries. The bodega was founded in 1986 and is named after one of the most famous of Galicia's troubadours. The vineyards consist of 420 hectares of Albariño between the member growers. Most vineyards are located in the Salnés Valley are spread across

a number of small parcels and the fruit is all hand harvested. The wines are cool fermented in stainless steel and go through malolactic fermentation. The Martin Codax label is a cool fermented fresh style, while the Organistrum is barrel fermented and then transferred to stainless steel and aged on lees. Two additional whites are made. Burgans is a cool fermented fresh style, Lías fermented and aged on fine lees with *bâtonnage*. Vindel is part barrel and part stainless steel vinified providing intense stone fruit aromas. The flagship of the Códax Rías Baixas range Gallaecia is a real rarity. Although coming from 100% Albarino, the wine is vinified from botrytised grapes but is fermented dry. The wine is marked by aromas of peach and apricot and has a rich and rounded texture almost hinting of sweetness but finishing with a dry intensity. Two further whites are also released under the Alma Atlántica banner. These include a Godello, Mara from Monterrei and a Rías Baixas, Alba which is a varietal Albariño. Also owned is a small bodega in Bierzo, Cuatro Pasos. Three reds and a rosado are made and sourced from vineyards of over 80 years of age around Otero, Hornija, Corullón and Valtuille. Coming from 100% Mencia, the vines are planted in well drained slate soils in some of the higher elevations in the DO. The Cuatro Pasos red is bright, juicy and full of attractive forward dark berry fruit with supple approachable tannins. It is aged for just two months in small oak. There are two more structured reds; the Black label sees six to seven months in French and American oak while Pizarras de Otero is another characterful blackberry and floral scented young wine style which sees no wood. (DM)

Bodegas Martín Códax
Recommended Whites:
Rías Baixas Gallaecia ★★★★☆ £G
Rías Baixas Vindel ★★★★ £E Rías Baixas Lías ★★★☆ £D
Rías Baixas Organistrum ★★★☆ £D
Rías Baixas Burgáns ★★★ £C Rías Baixas Martin Codax ★★☆ £B

Alma Atlántica
Recommended Whites:
Rías Baixas Alba Martín Albariño ★★☆ £B
Monterrei Mara Martin Godello ★★☆ £B

Bodegas Cuatro Pasos
Recommended Reds:
Bierzo Black Label ★★★ £C Bierzo Pizzaros de Otero ★★☆ £B
Bierzo Cuatro Pasos ★★ £B

Matarredonda (Toro) www.matarredonda.com
Matarredonda was recently founded in 2000, with a first vintage in 2001. There are 25 ha planted in one of the warmer sectors of the DO and the vines consistently ripen before the late September rains. Both reds are dense and powerful, very muscular examples coming from vines that range from 80 to an extraordinary 140 years old. Some of these planted in sandy soils are pre-phylloxera and have real potential. Both wines are aged in a mix of French and American oak, the marginally lighter Juan Rojo for 8 months the dense and firmly structured, dark and spicy Libranza for 14 months. Both demand at least five years patience.

Recommended Reds:
Toro Libranza ★★★☆ £EToro Juan Rojo ★★★ £C

⚙ Mauro (VdT Castilla y Leon) www.bodegasmauro.com
Mauro is an impressive small to medium sized bodega where slightly more than 25,000 cases are made from 70 ha. There is a sister winery in Toro, MAURODOS. The vineyards are planted mainly to Tempranillo but also to Syrah and soils are well drained and stony. Three reds are produced: a supple, opulent, forward style simply

labelled Mauro; a Vendimia Seleccionada, which is richer and firmer; and a single-vineyard *cuvée*, Terreus, which is produced in limited volumes and only when the vintage conditions are particularly fine. It comes from very old vines and requires five years cellaring. (DM)

Recommended Reds:
VdT Castilla y León Terreus ★★★★★ £F
VdT Castilla y León Mauro Vendimia Seleccionada ★★★★☆ £F
VdT Castilla y León Mauro ★★★☆ £E

⚙ Maurodos (Toro) www.bodegasanroman.com
As well as the excellent wines he has been involved in developing at MAURO under the VdT Castilla y León classification, enologist Mariano Garcia established this benchmark Toro property in the mid 1990s. Two wines are now made, San Román is a dense, opulent and richly textured red, full of dark berry fruit and supple, polished tannins. The considerable structure and initially firm grip from both the tannins and oak will necessitate a little patience. Given 5 or 6 years' ageing the wine should provide ample reward. A second label Prima, is great value and offers a typically full-bodied, dark-fruited style and is a touch more accessible. (DM)

Recommended Reds:
Toro San Román ★★★★☆ £F Toro Prima ★★★☆ £D

Viña Mein (Ribeiro) www.vinamein.com
Small Ribeiro bodega which is the source of a couple of very well crafted whites. A tiny quantity of a fine minerally red with elegant cherry fruit is also produced. Javier Alén established his vineyard and winery in 1988 and he cultivates some 16 ha on free-draining south and west facing slopes and has a modern and well equipped winery. The mineral and citrus scented Viña Mein white is the mainstay of the winery with around 100,000 bottles produced each year. It is a blend of mainly Treixadura, about 80%. The barrel-fermented bottling comes from a similar blend and is aged for 18 months in oak after fermentation. This is well judged and nicely integrated with a subtle toasty element underpinning the green, mineral and lightly herbaceous fruit. Both whites should be enjoyed relatively young; the red will stand three or four years ageing. (DM)

Recommended Reds:
Ribeiro Viña Mein Clásico ★★★ £D
Recommended Whites:
Ribeiro Fermentado en Barrica ★★★☆ £D
Ribeiro Viña Mein ★★★ £C

⚙ Bodegas Menade www.menade.es
The Sanz family siblings, Ricardo, Marco and Alejandra make a range of wines from Rueda, Toro and in partnership in Bierzo under three distinctive labels and projects. The bodega was originally known as Sitios de Bodega. A range of well-made, as well as extremely well-priced whites from Rueda are available under the Bodegas Menade brand. These are very good clean and fresh examples of the region all aged on their fine lees for a time to add weight and depth, the Verdejo in particular really standing out. The Menade Terruño wines are a clear step up in both quality and price. The V3 (Verdejo) is barrel-fermented at a low but not cool temperature and aged on lees for up to 8 months in barrel, adding both depth and a rich creamy complexity. Morfeo is a very fine Toro coming from vineyards which range from 80 to 120 years of age with many vines dating back to pre-phylloxera times. The wine is both barrel-fermented as well as aged in new French oak. Equally striking are the two reds from Bierzo. This is in fact a partnership between Ada Prada Amigo and the Sanz's. The de 2 is the most approachable of

the two reds, Ambos a selection of the oldest vines and plots being aged in barrel for up to eight months. In addition to the wines covered here, a white Nosso is also released which is from their Finca Menade vineyard and fully organic. (DM)

Mencia de-Dos
Recommended Reds:

Bierzo Ambos ★★★★ £E   Bierzo de-Dos★★★☆ £D

Menade Terruño
Recommended Reds:

Toro Morfeo Cepas Viejas ★★★★ £E

Recommended Whites:

Rueda V3 Viñas Viejas ★★★★ £E

Menade
Recommended Whites:

Rueda Verdejo ★★★ £B   Rueda Sauvignon Blanc ★★☆ £B
Rueda Menade Dulce ★★ £B

✿ Gerardo Méndez *www.bodegasgerardomendez.com*

A small and very good Rías Baixas winery which is planted to just 5 ha of organically farmed vineyards. Of this though 3 ha are over 50 years old and one vineyard, planted on granite and stone soils, of just a hectare is up to 200 years old and predates any other sites in the DO. The Albariño bottling comes from all eight of the plots that are farmed and is a crisp, fresh and lightly mineral style gaining weight and depth from six months lees ageing. The Cepas Vellas gets longer on lees, up to 11 months and offers a level of richness, complexity and concentration that is rarely encountered elsewhere in the DO. An Albariño Barrica is also made. (DM)

Recommended Whites:

Rías Baixas Do Ferreiro Cepas Vellas ★★★★ £E
Rías Baixas Do Ferreiro Albariño ★★★ £D

Montebaco (Ribera del Duero) *www.bodegasmontebaco.com*

This quality conscious Ribera property was established relatively recently and produced wines for the first time from the 1994 vintage. There are 45 ha of vines, most around Valbuena de Duero in the western sector of this substantial DO close to the city of Valladolid. The mesoclimate is distinctly continental with harsh winters and warm summers. The vineyard altitude at 800 to 850 metres also helps in providing acidity and balance in the wines. Cultivation is as natural as possible and chemicals are avoided. Where vines are replanted they are established from clones sourced from some of the oldest vineyards in the appellation. Considerable investment has also gone into the bodega and the latest winery equipment is used for fermentation and handling. There are additionally 5 ha in Rueda where a single white is produced from Verdejo with fermentation in stainless steel and a short period on lees. The three Ribera reds are all crianza styles and are more fruit driven in style than many other examples from the area. The lighter Semele gets 12 months ageing the Montebaco and the Vendimmia Seleccionada, a little longer between 13 and 18 months. The top two reds are impressively ageworthy, particularly the dark, densely structured and elegant VS. (DM)

Recommended Reds:

Ribera del Duero Montebaco Vendimia Seleccionada ★★★★ £E
Ribera del Duero Montebaco ★★★☆ £D
Ribera del Duero Semele ★★☆ £C

Recommended Whites:

Rueda Verdejo ★★ £C

Montecastro (Ribera del Duero) *www.bodegasmontecastro.es*

Two very fine and relatively well priced red Ribera del Duero reds are made here. These are very intense, subtle and structured wines, in marked contrast to many other examples you're likely to encounter from the DO. The property was established quite recently, in 2000. They own six separate vineyard parcels and vines range from young to over 100 years of age. Winemaking is under the guidance of French oenologist Jean-François Hébrard, who also makes the Toro reds at Quinta de La QUIETUD. The Alconde, solely Tinto Fino, is the more obviously forward of the two wines although there is a classy elegance and intensity along with crafted tannins. The more structured and firm Montecastro y Llanahermosa Comes from Tinto Fino, Cabernet Sauvignon as well as Merlot and requires at least five years cellaring from the vintage.

Recommended Reds:

Ribera del Duero Montecastro y Llanahermosa ★★★★☆ £E
Ribera del Duero Alconte ★★★☆ £D

Elias Mora (Toro) *www.bodegaseliasmora.com*

Victoria Benavides has now split up with Victoria PARIENTE and is running her own Toro bodega at Elias Mora while her former partner in "Dos Victorias" Victoria Pariente is running her family bodega in Rueda. Of the Toro bottlings the Roble is by far the softest and most fruit-driven in style. Both the Crianza and the splendid Gran Elias Mora are much more serious. The Crianza is aged in a mix of French and American oak for 12 months, the Gran Elias Mora in French oak for 18 months. The latter is very tight and restrained when young and needs at least 5 years to unfurl. Two further and pricier premium reds are also made. Elias Mora Reserva (£F) spends 24 months in barrel, the top label 2V (£F)spends a little less time in wood but its all new. (DM)

Recommended Reds:

Toro Gran Elias Mora ★★★★ £E   Toro Crianza ★★★☆ £D
Toro Viñas Elias Mora Roble ★★☆ £C

✿ Emilio Moro (Ribera del Duero) *www.emiliomoro.com*

Emilio Moro is one of the benchmark bodegas in Ribera, now run by Jose Moro, the third generation of his family here. The vineyards are planted on sites that range from 750 to 1,000 metres above sea level and in varied chalk, clay and loam soils. There are four distinct vineyards which are all planted to Tinto Fino, the oldest of them Valderramiro was established in 1924 in clay and chalk. It is responsible for the special cuvée top wine Malleolus de Valdeorrama, a very concentrated, rich and spicy mineral scented and structured red. A small range is produced. The entry level wine is the forward, straightforward cherry scented Finca Resalso which comes from young vines less than 15 years old. The other wines are more structured, with greater depth. The Emilio Moro label is now a crianza style rather than labelled as such to emphasise its fruit. The Malleolus red too eschews traditional ageing characteristics and sees 18 months in new French oak. It is dark, spicy and concentrated and needs cellaring. As well as the splendid Valdeorrama two other small volume and very high price reds are also made, Malleolus Sanchomartin from the Pago de Sanchomartin vineyard in Pesquera de Duero and the Clon de La Familia of which barely 1,000 bottles a year are made. At the firm's second winery, Cepa 21, the approach is a little different where two modern, well priced examples of the appellation are made. The bodega has just over 50 ha under vine, all from a clone derived from 100 year old vines close to Pesquera de Duero, most of which is planted close to the winery in silt and clay-sandy soils at an altitude ranging from 780 to 850 metres. Seasonal

attention is given to both canopy management and crop thinning to provide good flavour intensity during ripening. A modern winery and barrel cellar have been created along with a temperature and humidity controlled bottle cellar for ageing the wine before release. The Hito is an approachable younger wine style with ageing in French oak for around 8 months. The Cepa 21 offers more depth, density and structure with longer ageing, 14 months in French and American oak which gives a touch of spicy vanilla to the wine's ripe black fruit character. A Hito Rosado is also made along with a small amount, just 500 cases or so, of an additional premium red, Malabrigo. (DM)

Emilio Moro
Recommended Reds:
Ribera del Duero Malleolus Valderramiro ★★★★★ £G
Ribera del Duero Malleolus ★★★★ £E
Ribera del Duero Emilio Moro ★★★ £D
Ribera del Duero Finca Resalso ★★☆ £C

Bodegas Cepa 21
Recommended Reds:
Ribera del Duero Cepa 21 ★★★ £C Ribera del Duero Hito ★★☆ £D

❀ Bodegas Naia (Rueda) www.bodegasnaia.com
A bodega crafting seriously impressive examples of this DO. The 40 ha of vineyards are planted in finely drained gravel soils, around the village of La Seca, the source of some of the region's very best sites. Founded in 2002, four wines are now being produced. There is an entry level white Las Brisas, originally a blend now just Verdejo. K Naia is most recently added which is a fresh crisp 85/15 blend of Verdejo and Sauvignon Blanc. The top two wines are both varietal Verdejo's. Naia is tank fermented with just a hint of wood from the use of some oak staves in a proportion of the tanks. It offers an immediately appealing style with a fine green fruit, citrus and mineral intensity. Tighter and more firmly structured is the barrel-fermented Naiades. The wine will benefit from a year or two in bottle to integrate the impressively concentrated fruit with the oak. (DM)

Recommended Whites:
Rueda Naiades ★★★★ £E Rueda Naia ★★★ £C

❀ Bodegas Neo (Ribera del Duero) www.bodegasneo.com
A small to medium sized bodega making some good to very good reds from its own as well as other local vineyard holdings. There are also a couple of very well-priced fruit driven Ribera wines from bought-in fruit. The Vivir, Vivir is moved straight from tank to bottle, the El Arte de Vivir gets around four months in American oak. The excellent value Sentido bridges the gap between the Vivir wines and the Neo bottling and a Rioja example is also now produced. It is aged for 9 months in a mix of French and American oak with the malolactic in barrel. The top two Neo wines are Ribera del Duero benchmarks in the modern style. This means emphasising the character of the wines fruit with a firm ageworthy structure underpinning it. The wines are sourced from vineyards varying from 50 to 80 years old both from other growers and from vineyards the partnership are acquiring themselves. The wines get a vatting of around three weeks, with Neo aged for 18 months mainly in French and a little American oak the Punta Essencia 24 months in new French barrels. Both wines are bottled without recourse to filtration. Other wine projects include a Priorat, Prior de Neo, Disco, a red Ribera del Duero aged in oak for six months and Crazy Tempranillo, a rosado also from Ribera del Duero and somewhat younger vines. Two forward styles of Ribera del Duero take the Obra label and a

varietal Verdejo produced under the Motivo brand. Contemporary music is also a passion of the team here and this is almost certainly the only winery in the world with an on site recording studio to complement the nearby fermentation vessels. They provide support and assistance to local rock musicians. (DM)

Recommended Reds:
Ribera del Duero Neo Punta Essencia ★★★★☆ £F
Ribera del Duero Neo ★★★★ £E
Ribera del Duero Sentido ★★★ £C
Ribera del Duero El Arte de Vivir ★★☆ £B
Ribera del Duero Vivir, Vivir ★★ £B

❀ Viña Nora (Rías Baixas) www.vinanora.com
A very recently established and excellent source of top quality Albariño based whites, now a part of the Avanteselecta group of wineries. The vineyards have an excellent exposition overlooking the Miño river and the vines are planted in finely drained gravel soils both of which contribute in no small degree to the quality of the wines. As well as the top wine the Nora de Neve, there are two entry level wines, Val de Nora and Nora which are also 100% Albariño. The Nora de Neve is both barrel-fermented and then aged in Allier oak. Unlike most examples of the appellation this will develop well in bottle for up to five years or so. (DM)

Recommended Whites:
Rías Baixas Nora de Neve ★★★★ £E

❀ Bodega Numanthia Termes (Toro) www.bodegaseliasmora.com
Numanthia is one of the highest profile wineries in Toro. The Rioja based EGUREN family founded the bodega in 1998. They have since sold Numanthia to LMVH for a tidy sum. The winery is named after the town that was famed for its local resistance to the legions of Rome. There are 40 ha under vine and some of the holding planted in sandy soils dates back to pre-phylloxera times. The warm and sunny mesoclimate of the vineyards as well as the high temperature variation between night and day in summer ensure old-vine fruit of considerable depth and intensity. Vinification is thoroughly modern with malolactic in barrel and the wines are bottled without fining or filtration. The small quantities of the top wine Termanthia achieve very high prices indeed. (DM)

Recommended Reds:
Toro Termanthia ★★★★★ £H
Toro Numanthia ★★★★ £F Toro Termes ★★★ £D

❀ Ossian (Rueda) www.ossian.es
The Ossian project is devoted solely to producing premium quality white wines from the Verdejo grape and is based around the small town of Nieva. It is now under the same ownership as Pago de Carra. Viticulture is all organic and the additional key to quality is some very old vines planted in sandy soils. They are therefore resistant to phylloxera and as a result many are ungrafted and up to 160 years old. The winemaking approach for the Ossian white is distinctly Burgundian with both barrel fermentation and ageing on stirred lees. The junior wine Quintaluna is not barrel fermented but gets additional weight and a richer texture from ageing on its lees for two months. The wines are marked by impressive concentration with subtle restrained citrus and white fruit aromas and an underlying mineral intensity. A low volume top label Capitel, is also made, like Ossian it is released under VdT Castilla y León classification. (DM)

Recommended Whites:
VdT Castilla y León Ossian Capitel ★★★★☆ £F

North-West Spain

VdT Castilla y León Ossian ★★★★ £E
Rueda Quintaluna ★★★ £C

✿ Pago de Carraovejas www.pagodecarraovejas.com

This top Ribera del Duero operation was founded in 1988. There are 60 ha of vineyards planted to a mix of 75% Tempranillo and 25% Cabernet Sauvignon. The winery is modern and very well equipped with stainless steel and temperature control equipment. No vino joven is made. Ageing is in a mix of new and one-and two-year-old French and American oak. The Crianza is rich and concentrated with impressive dark berry fruit and full, supple tannins. The Reserva, which gets longer ageing, is fuller and offers greater depth and dimension. These are sturdy, initially backward and powerful wines which demand to be cellared. The richly textured El Anejón comes from a single plot planted in mineral, limestone dominated soils. Ageing is just for 12 months in barrel. It edges the very pricey and concentrated limited cuvée "Cuesta de Las Llebres" for elegance and definition, perhaps because Las Llebres spends 24 months in new French oak. (DM)

Recommended Reds:

Ribera del Duero Cuesta Las Llebres ★★★★★ £H
Ribera del Duero El Anejón ★★★★★ £G
Ribera del Duero Reserva ★★★★ £F
Ribera del Duero Crianza ★★★☆ £E

Pago de Los Capellanes www.pagodeloscapellanes.com

This medium sized bodega was founded quite recently in 1996 and the family holding now stretches to 110 ha and modern viticulture and training methods employed. As elsewhere an altitude of 800 metres with warm summers and cold nights ensures good acidity in the grapes and a potentially excellent structure in the resulting wines. The forward, fruit-driven Joven Roble nevertheless possesses a sufficiently firm edge to its tannin. Bigger, fuller are both the Crianza and Reserva bottling which gain additional refinement from ageing in French oak for respectively 12 and 18 months. The top two wines are thoroughly modern examples of the DO. Both are produced from 100% Tempranillo and output is very low, just over 1,200 cases of El Nogal and a mere 250 cases of El Picón. El Nogal is marked by ripe and sumptuous dark-berry fruit, El Picón is subtler, more restrained and demands cellaring. (DM)

Recommended Reds:

Ribera del Duero El Picón ★★★★☆ £G
Ribera del Duero El Nogal ★★★★ £F
Ribera del Duero Reserva ★★★☆ £E
Ribera del Duero Crianza ★★★ £C
Ribera del Duero Joven Roble ★★☆ £C

✿ Paixar (Bierzo)

This small joint venture project is establishing itself as one of the benchmarks of Bierzo. Alberto and Eduardo Garcia, sons of the legendary Mariano Garcia have teamed up with Gregory Perez and Alejandro Luna of LUNA BEBERIDE. The tremendous quality being achieved here is due to a combination of 50 to 80 year old Mencia vines, sparse slatey soils to optimise the flavour intensity in the grapes and an altitude of 700 to 900 metres enabling the grapes to be harvested later than most other Bierzo sites. The wine offers wonderfully intense black. spicy fruit and there is a classic minerality which adds to the wines complexity. (DM)

Recommended Reds:

Bierzo Mencia ★★★★☆ £F

Palacio de Bornos www.palaciodebornos.com

One of the better modern producers of Rueda. As well as white wine interests in Rueda the owners, the Taninia Group, also produce impressive Toro at the Bodegas TORESANAS, Navarra at SENORIO DE SARRIA, fine V T Ribera del Queiles at GUELBENZU in the Autonomous Community of Navarra and Ribera del Duero at their Vallebueno winery. Among a fine line-up of Rueda whites under the Palacio de Bornos label there is a grassy, fresh Sauvignon Blanc that should be drunk young and four wines based on Verdejo. The Verdejo, is similarly fresh, grassy and herbaceous in style, La Caprichosa richer and more complex coming from old vines. Other wines are handled in oak. The Fermentado en Barrica is rich, toasty and buttery, while the Vendimia Seleccionada is more structured, with the pure green Verdejo fruit always making itself felt. A semidulce is also made from Sauvignon Blanc and there are also a number of sparkling wines.

Recommended Whites:

Rueda Palacio de Bornos Vendimia Seleccionnada ★★★ £D
Rueda Palacio de Bornos La Caprichosa ★★★ £D
Rueda Palacio de Bornos Fermentado en Barrica ★★☆ £C
Rueda Palacio de Bornos Verdejo ★★ £B
Rueda Palacio de Bornos Sauvignon Blanc ★★ £B

✿ Palacio de Fefiñanes (Rías Baixas) www.fefinanes.com

This first class winery is based in a magnificent baronial palace which dates back to 1647. Indeed the Bodega itself has been running since 1904. Output though has always remained relatively modest, today just over 10,000 cases a year and quality is high. The vineyard holding is tiny and the winery has a series of long-term grape supply contracts with technical input from the Fefiñanes wine-making team. Three wines are produced. The Albariño de Fefiñanes is fermented cool in stainless steel and is marked by its youthful green fruit and underlying minerality. Drink it young and fresh. There is a barrel-aged bottling 1583, which sees both French and American oak. The top wine, the Albariño de Fefinanes III, is also cool-fermented and delivers an impressive array of herbaceous scents, a piercing minerality and also a fuller, more complex character. This is achieved by six months ageing on lees in tank with *bâtonnage*, followed by a further 24 months prior to bottling. Drink shortly after release. (DM)

Recommended Whites:

Rías Baixas Albariño de Fefiñanes III ★★★★ £E
Rías Baixas Albariño de Fefiñanes 1583 ★★★☆ £D
Rías Baixas Albariño de Fefiñanes ★★★ £C

✿ Rafael Palacios (Valdeorras) www.rafaelpalacios.com

Rafael Palacios is arguably producing the best wine in a region that is fast establishing itself as one of the most exciting in Spain for crisp and fresh, striking white wines. One of the key elements in the quality of the wine here is the vineyard plots which are almost all to be found at an altitude of around 600 metres. Much of the DO is planted at lower levels and on valley floor vineyards. Vinification is very traditional and artisan with fermentation in large old wood and then ageing for several months on lees. The more forward, citrus infused Louro do Bolo has a hint of Treixadura, the top label AS Sortes is varietal Godello. It is richly concentrated and with a piercing mineral undercurrent, surely one of Spain's great whites. (DM)

Recommended Whites:

Valdeorras AS Sortes ★★★★☆ £E
Valdeorras Louro ★★★★ £D

>> **Pardevalles (Tierra de León)** *www.pardevalles.com*
Pardevalles was established by the Alonso family over six decades ago although until recently, along with so many others, the fruit was sold off in bulk. It is the current generation who have been realising the potential of the property. There are currently 31 ha under vine, the majority of which is Prieto Picudo along with a smattering of Albarín. The altitude of the vineyards ranges from 760 to 820 metres and the poor, rocky, alluvial soils are propitious for growing intensely flavoured grapes. The white Pardevalles is cool fermented after a short period on skins and is full of zesty bright citrus fruit and a subtle mineral quality. The most approachable of the reds, the Pardevalles is like all three 100% varietal and is a bright Joven style with ripe berry fruit. The other two reds are more structured with ageing in barrel, although all the wines are given a cold soak which lifts the bright berry fruit character of the Prieto Picudo. The Gamonal is aged for around 8 months or so, the top red the Carroleón longer, around 15 months. A Rosado is also made, again coming from Prieto Picudo.

Recommended Reds:
Tierra de León Pardevalles Carroleón ★★★☆ £D
Tierra de León Pardevalles Gamonal ★★★☆ £C
Tierra de León Pardevalles Tinto ★★☆ £B

Recommended Whites:
Tierra de León Pardevalles Albarín ★★☆ £B

Recommended Rosés:
Tierra de León Pardevalles Rosado ★★☆ £B

Jose Pariente (Rueda) *www.josepariente.com*
The two "Dos Victorias" who marketed their Toro and Rueda wines together have decided to split up and go their separate ways. Victoria Pariente is now running her family bodega in Rueda. The holding across the DO is dominated by plantings of Verdejo but also now includes some Sauvignon Blanc and a characterful varietal example of this is made. The Jose Pariente Verdejo Rueda is beautifully crafted with pure green and citrus fruit and great purity despite coming from the properties younger vines. The barrel-fermented example is equally impressive offering a fuller and rounder texture and adding a touch more structure from the influence of the wood. A Special Cuvée is also now released as well as a *dulce* style, Apasionado. (DM)

Recommended Whites:
Rueda Verdejo Fermentado en Barrica ★★★☆ £D
Rueda Verdejo ★★★ £C   Rueda Sauvignon Blanc ★★☆ £C

Pazo Baión (Rías Baixas) *www.pazobaion.com*
This small, high quality project is seeking to establish itself as the first true "Pago" property in the region. One wine is made solely from fruit cultivated on the estate property. It also has an important social function in providing an environment for individuals rehabilitating from drug problems. The estate has 22 ha under vine, solely Albariño, split into eight separate parcels with many vines up to 40 years of age so there is a real potential for the fruit. The Art Deco styled winery is well organised with all the latest fermentation and wine storage equipment. The wine is fresh, floral and complex with marked mineral and citrus notes under its bright, peachy fruit. (DM)

Recommended Whites:
Rías Baixas Pazo Baión ★★★☆ £D

❀ **Pazo de Señorans (Rías Baixas)** *www.pazodesenorans.com*
One of the most consistent properties in the Rías Baixas appellation, the property purchased in 1979. Output remains small at barely 4,000 cases a year. The regular bottling is supported by a limited-release Selección de Añadas which unlike the regular wine is held in tank and matured for over two years before bottling. A barrel aged example Sol de Señorans is also made which is tank fermented and then aged on lees in barrel for six months. The Rías Baixas label is bottled early and displays some of the best peachy, tropical, mineral and grassy characters to be found in the aromatic Albariño grape. The wines should be drunk soon after release, although the Selección de Añadas has the structure to continue to develop further. (DM)

Recommended Whites:
Rías Baixas Selección de Añadas ★★★★ £E
Rías Baixas Sol de Señorans ★★★☆ £D
Rías Baixas Pazo de Señorans ★★★ £C

Pazo San Mauro (Rías Baixas) *www.marquesdevargas.com*
This single estate was purchased by the MARQUÉS DE VARGAS in 2003. The vineyards overlook the Miño River right on the border between Spain and Portugal and are in the most southerly and mountainous of the Rías Baixas sub-zones, Condado de Tea. The varietal Albariño is ripe and opulent with rich, almost tropical, nutty notes. It is typically cool-fermented at 17–18C to emphasise the fruit. The Sanamaro, which is 95% Albariño and 5% Loureiro, comes from the highest slopes. Aged on its fine lees for 3 months, it has a little more structure than is normally encountered in the region. The wines should be drunk young and fresh. (DM)

Recommended Whites:
Rías Baixas Sanamaro ★★★☆ £D   Rías Baixas Albariño ★★★ £C

Pazos del Rey (Monterrei) *www.pazosdelrey.com*
This is one of the best small producers in this remote north-western DO. Three wines are now made, an impressive, crisp, minerally white dominated by Godello with a little Treixadura, a varietal Godello Sila and a red Sila from Mencia. The Pazo de Monterrey brand takes its name from the palace of the same name, a significant fortress that dominates the landscape of the area. There are mainly hillside vineyard plots planted on granite and slatey soils. The river Támera, a tributary of the Duero, influences the local climate and a wide variation in day and night temperatures approaching the ripening period ensures good fresh acidity in the grapes. The winemaking team has enjoyed new world expertise and as one might expect the wines are typically clean, fresh and zesty. (DM)

Recommended Reds:
Monterrei Sila Mencia ★★★ £C

Recommended Whites:
Monterrei Pazo de Monterrey ★★★ £C

Bodegas Peique (Bierzo) *www.bodegaspeique.com*
The Peique family are now among the benchmarks in Bierzo. They established their bodega in 1999 and produce three characterful and diverse reds from 10 ha of vineyards on some of the steepest unirrigated slopes of the DO. The Peique Tinto Mencia comes from their youngest vines, albeit these are 50 years or so, and is very much in a joven style but with vibrancy and real fruit depth. A further more approachable red Ramón Valle is also made. The Viñedos Viejos comes from even older vines, over 70 years of age and is bigger, fuller and demanding of four or five years patience. The old-vine, complex, dark, spicy and minerally fruit is well supported by 12 months in a mix of French, American and Russian oak. The splendid top label Selección Familiar gets 18 months in oak which is very well integrated with rich, intense dark old vine fruit

North-West Spain

from a vineyard section and vines averaging over 90 years of age. One of the best wines of the region expect it to continue to develop in bottle for a decade or so. The small range is now completed by a rosado and a white from Godello as well as a premium red Luis Peique. (DM)

Recommended Reds:

Bierzo Peique Seleccion Familiar ★★★★ £E

Bierzo Peique Seleccion Viñedos Viejos ★★★☆ £D

Bierzo Peique Ramón Valle ★★★☆ £D

Bierzo Peique Tinto Mencia ★★★ £C

>> Adega Pena das Donas (Ribeira Sacra) www.penadasdonas.com

Very good piercingly mineral white and red is made at this small bodega with sustainably farmed south facing vineyards planted on precipitously steep old terraced, low yielding vineyards. These overlook the River Sil and are planted in slate and stone soils. There are 5 ha found at an altitude ranging from 450 to 600 metres, of which the Godello is between 80 and 100 years old, although the bodega itself was only recently established in 2005. The vibrant red fruited Verdes Matas is solely Mencia of 30 to 40 years of age. The wine is aged in oak but only for a short time, around four months in both French and American barrels. The Almalarga from Goedello is intense and pure, subtle green fruit notes underpinned by zesty citrus acidity. Additional weight comes from four months ageing on fine lees. The second white Almalarga Barrica (Godello and Treixadura) is just a touch rounder, richer and is very subtly oaked.

Recommended Reds:

Ribeira Sacra Verdes Matas Tinto ★★★☆ £D

Recommended Whites:

Ribeira Sacra Almalarga Barrica ★★★★ £D

Ribeira Sacra Almalarga ★★★☆ £C

✿ Raúl Pérez (Bierzo)

This is the small personal bodega and label of winemaking consultant Raúl Pérez. His family own the small Bierzo property CASTRO VENTOSA. As well as making his own exceptional small range of wines, Pérez is a consultant to QUINTA DE MURADELLA in Monterrei and makes El Reventon from old Garnacha under the VdT Castilla y León classification with Méntrida based Dani LANDI. He is also now in charge of winemaking direction at TILENUS. As well as red and white Bierzo, Pérez has made his own wines in Rías Baixas, Ribeira Sacra, Tierra de León, Monterrei and VdT Castilla y León. Additional wines to consider are the pricey Monterrei red blend A Trabe, the Prieto Picudo from 100 year old vines in Tierra de León as well as a white Albarín from the same DO and a reasonably priced Rías Baixas, Muti which is a varietal Albariño. A red Rías Baixas Muti comes from Caiño and there are two further Ribeira Sacra wines, both labeled Sacrata from Mencia and Godello. His top red Bierzo, Ultreia de Valtuille comes from very old Mencia vines. It offers intense sweet dark, spicy berry fruits and is finely structured spending 12 months in Austrian Fudres (1,500 litre casks) on lees. The much more economically priced Ultreia Saint Jacques is full of vibrant, approachable fruit although with impressive depth and concentration. A further well priced Bierzo red Vico is also made. The red El Pecado is also from a blend of very old Mencia, Caiño Tinto and Merenzao vines grown in slaty soils, it is dark, subtle and with restrained spices and a piercing minerality. It is vinified with a substantial proportion of whole clusters and gets a maceration of up to two months. Cellaring is for 12 months in small oak. The white Bierzo Ultreia La Claudina comes from Godello and a single vineyard of the same name. It is richly textured with opulent fruit and an

impressive mineral intensity. The wine is vinified in oak barrels of varied sizes. The Rías Baixas Sketch from Albariño, one of the stand out wines of the DO, is made in tiny quantities and has a price tag to match. It comes from granite soils in the Val do Salnés just a stone's throw from the sea. Ageing is on fine lees for 12 months in older oak. Very unusually the wine is experimentally aged in bottle under water at very low natural temperatures. All the wines are made in very small lots. (DM)

Recommended Reds:

Bierzo Ultreia de Valtuile ★★★★★ £G

Ribeira Sacra El Pecado ★★★★☆ £F

Bierzo Ultreia Saint Jacques ★★★☆ £C

Recommended Whites:

Bierzo Ultreia La Claudina ★★★★☆ £F

Rías Baixas Sketch ★★★★☆ £F

Pérez Pascuas (Ribera del Duero) www.perezpascuas.com

This is one of an increasing number of top-quality producers in this great north-western appellation. The operation was established in 1980 and has some 120ha of vineyards planted mainly to Tempranillo but also some Cabernet Sauvignon and Merlot. The wines are powerful and quite extracted and are now aged in a mix of French and American oak. Under the Viña Pedrosa label there are fine, structured Crianza and Reserva, as well as a denser, richer Gran Reserva with considerable tannin – a wine that demands patience. Pérez Pascuas Gran Seleccion, from a single vineyard, is very refined and complex as well as powerful and firmly tannic when young. A silky, velvety texture will emerge with age, though. The Cepa Gavilan and La Navilla are modern early bottled styles. (DM)

Recommended Reds:

Ribera del Duero Pérez Pascuas Gran Seleccion ★★★★☆ £G

Ribera del Duero Viña Pedrosa Gran Reserva ★★★★ £F

Ribera del Duero Viña Pedrosa Reserva ★★★★ £F

Ribera del Viña Pedrosa La Navilla ★★★★ £F

Ribera del Duero Viña Pedrosa Crianza ★★★☆ £E

Ribera del Duero Cepa Gavilan ★★★ £D

Pittacum (Bierzo) www.terrasgauda.com

Under the same ownership as TERRAS GAUDA in Rías Baixas and now QUINTA SARDONIA in Castille, this is one of a wave of impressive over-achieving bodegas in this splendid small region. Like many it has not been established very long, in this case only since 2001. However the ability to draw on some very well-sited old vineyards with modern well organized winemaking sees reds of real character and quality. The Pittacum red is a Joven style with just six months ageing in oak. The quality of the fruit from vines between 50 and 80 years old provides the raw material for a beguilingly charracterful, exciting and well priced red. The Aurea understandably is more serious in both density and structure. Fruit comes from vines over 100 years old and the wine is aged new French oak for 14 months. While the new wood is very apparent in the wines youth expect the sheer character and quality here to begin to emerge with four or five years ageing. It will surely keep a good deal longer. Also worth noting now is a further red La Prohibición which unusually comes solely from Garnacha Tintorera and an approachable Petit Pittacum. A simple rosado, Tres Obispos is also made. (DM)

Recommended Reds:

Bierzo Aurea ★★★★ £E   Bierzo Pittacum ★★★☆ £D

✿ César Principe (Cigales) www.cesarprincipe.es

A stand out producer in the Cigales DO. The Bodega was founded in

Wine behind the label

1980 and there are 40 ha under vine. The quality is exemplary in the top wine and a Crianza red with shorter wood ageing and a rosado are also made. The César Principe is no doubt helped by Tempranillo vines that are over 60 years of age as well as a control of yields. Ageing in new French and a little American oak is for 14 months. Deeply coloured, dark and spicy fruit is very well integrated with the oak and further development and complexity are sure to be gained with five or more years ageing.

Recommended Reds:
Cigales César Principe ★★★★ £E

✿ Quinta da Muradella (Monterrei)

A region benchmark. Jose Luis Mateo has 14 ha of a bewildering array of red and white grapes all biodynamically farmed and producing wines that range from really pretty good value to somewhat expensive. In this endeavour he is very ably assisted by Bierzo based winemaking guru Raúl Pérez. Much of the character of the wines comes from the diversity of soils in which the vineyards are planted, ranging from slate and granite to schist and quartz and a fine edged minerality is always present. The entry level wines are labelled Alanda and the white comes from Godello, Treixadura and Doña Blanca. The elegant piercingly intense berry fruited red from Mencia, Bastardo, Garnacha Tintorera and gets a cold soak and is aged for just over a year in older barrels. The Gorvia red and white are both a step up. The wonderfully pure and structured peachy, green fruited, zesty Blanco from Doña Blanca is given a short period on its skins and then racked off to commence fermentation in stainless steel before passage to older 500 litre French oak barrels. Contact with the fine lees is maintained for two months and ageing is continued for just under a year in barrel and then tank. The Gorvia Tinto from Mencia is full of ripe, perfumed dark berry fruit with a subtle spiciness running through the wine. The vinification regime is similar to the Alanda, although with a proportion in new oak. Small volumes of a number of other reds, some from single vineyards and single varieties, are also produced. These are understandably quite a bit pricier. These include Albarello (the variety is also referred to as Brancellao), Berrande which is a varietal Mencia, a 100% single vineyard Bastardo, Finca Notario which is a single vineyard field blend and a 100% Sousón. (DM)

Recommended Reds:
Monterrei Quinta da Muradella ★★★★ £D
Monterrei Quinta da Muradella Alanda ★★★ £C
Recommended Whites:
Monterrei Quinta da Muradella Gorvia ★★★★ £D

✿ Quinta de La Quietud (Toro) *www.quintaquietud.com*

This 22 ha Toro estate was established in 1999. Winemaker Jean-François Hébrard is from Bordeaux and among others he has worked for include Jean-Luc Colombo. The French influence comes shining through in the wines, which are subtle and elegant. The vineyard contains some very old vines, the age range is 10 to 90 years and this shows through in the quality of the wine. The Corral de Companas comes from the youngest vines and is intended to ensure the integrity of the regular Toro. This is aged in one-third new oak with the mix being 70% French and the balance American. A new wine La Mula has been added as well and this gets around 18 months in French oak and is a more international style. The small range also includes a sweet white dulce style. Now made are three additional wines under the Ababol label which come from co-owner Eusebio Sacristán's family estate outside Vallalodid. A

fresh fruit driven white Verdejo is joined by a more complex barrel-fermented and aged example from the same variety and a punchy red aged in stainless steel for six months.

Recommended Reds:
Toro La Mula ★★★★☆ £F   Toro Quinta de la Quietud ★★★★ £E
Toro Corral de Campanas ★★★ £D
VdT Castilla y León Ababol ★★ £B
Recommended Whites:
Vino de Mesa La Dulce Quietud ★★★ £D
VdT Castilla y León Gran Ababol Verdejo ★★★ £C
VdT Castilla y León Ababol Verdejo ★★☆ £C

>> Quinta do Buble (Monterrei) *www.quintadobuble.com*

A handful of well-priced whites and a red are made at this small bodega, founded in 2001. The property has 25 ha currently being cultivated largely organically and a further 15 ha is also owned for future use. The vineyards with a hillside aspect and planted at over 700 metres provides balance and a crisp, fresh character. The modern well-equipped winery and cellar are partially built into the landscape providing natural thermal control. The Quinta do Buble Godello Blanco is nicely textured with zesty citrus fruit and has an underlying mineral quality. The Quinta do Buble Tinto from Mencia is aged in a mix of French and American oak and is marked by spicy red fruits and a leafy, peppery note with a toasty oak component in the background. There are two secondary labels, Terra do Lobo and Roncal. (DM)

Recommended Reds:
Monterrei Quinta do Buble Barrica ★★☆ £C
Recommended Whites:
Monterrei Quinta do Buble ★★★☆ £C

✿ Quinta Sardonia (VdT Castilla y León) *www.terrasgauda.com*

Based in the village of Sardón del Duero the vineyards at this small property are located just to the west of the Ribera del Duero DO boundaries and it is now a part of the same group that owns TERRAS GAUDA in Rías Baixas and PITTACUM in Bierzo. Jerome Bougnaud runs the property and valueable input comes from Peter Sisseck, notable for vinifying PINGUS. The 22 ha of vineyards, planted at an altitude of 700 to 800 metres are farmed biodynamically and just two wines are made in a Bordeaux/international style. The *grand vin* is very modern in approach with well defined dark black fruits, well judged oak and real depth and concentration. The supple and very well rounded tannins should enable the wine to be enjoyed with just a few years of ageing. A second wine is also now made, QS2.

Recommended Reds:
VdT Castilla y León Quinta Sardonia ★★★★☆ £F

Rejadorada (Toro) *www.rejadorada.com*

Rejadorada is new and was founded only in 1999, although their vineyards are some of the oldest in the region and include a number of plots that date back to pre-phylloxera times. There are four wines, Rejadorada is light and vibrant the Semi Crianza and is typically forward in style. The Novellum is a crianza and by contrast is more seriously structured as a result of 12 months ageing in oak. The Sango Reserva is rich, dense and powerful, full of dark spicy fruit and underpinned by quite marked toasty vanilla oak. A fourth premium red Bravo is also now produced which spends a shorter time in wood, just over a year.

Wine behind the label

North-West Spain

Spain

Recommended Reds:
Toro Sango Reserva ★★★ £E   Toro Bravo ★★★ £E
Toro Novellum Crianza ★★★ £C
Toro Rejadorada Semi Crianza ★★☆ £B

Ribera de Pelazas (Arribes) *www.bodegasriberadepelazas.com*
This small bodega established in 1997 on the borders of Spain and Portugal is among the best sources of fascinating and characterful reds from the newly emerging region of Arribes del Duero which has recently acquired DO status. Much of the key to quality is a combination of 60 to over 100 year old vines and an excellent granite, calcareous *terroir*. There are just 15 ha under vine and five wines are produced. In addition to a white produced from Malvasia, both the Abadengo and the really characterful Gran Abadengo come from the very rare local Juan Garcia variety. Full of dark, spicy almost floral scented fruit, in the case of the Gran Abadengo a 35 day vatting and 18 months in oak do not overwhelm the wine. Both may be broached with just a little age. A third Abadengo has also now been added, Special Selection which combines a little Bruñal with Juan Garcia. The Bruñal which comes from the indigenous grape of the same name is an altogether bigger, firmer and much more backward style and much pricier. Aged for just 12 months in wood for perfect balance the wine is sourced from a handful of small growers who cultivate the variety. A minimum of five years is required for the wine to begin to show its true quality. (DM)
Recommended Reds:
Arribes Bruñal ★★★★★ £G   Arribes Gran Abadengo ★★★☆ £E
Arribes Abadengo ★★☆ £C

Bodegas Rodero (Ribera del Duero) *www.bodegasrodero.com*
This bodaga belongs to a long-established family of growers in the Duero Valley who until 1990 sold their fruit to VEGA SICILIA. They now focus on producing a fine traditional range of appellation wines. There are a total of just over 80ha of vineyards, mostly planted at altitude on well-drained sites that are naturally low in rainfall. This well-stressed environment provides grapes of great flavour intensity. The average age of the vineyard is now over 35 years and as well as the local Tinta del Pais (Tempranillo), a small amount of Cabernet Sauvignon and Merlot are also planted. Barrel maturation is in a mix of French and American oak. The top wines are impressively ageworthy. The Reserva is structured and concentrated while two special bottlings are a level up. Pago de Valtarreña comes from a single vineyard of over 40 year old vines, Traditional in approach with ageing in a combination of French and American oak. Very characterful is a new blend of Tempranillo, Cabernet as well as Merlot, TSM which is the fleshiest and most beguiling of the wines. It has real depth and power. (DM)
Recommended Reds:
Ribera del Duero TSM ★★★★☆ £F
Ribera del Duero Pago de Valtarreña ★★★★☆ £F
Ribera del Duero Reserva ★★★☆ £E
Ribera del Duero Crianza ★★★ £D
Ribera del Duero 9 Meses ★★☆ £C   Ribera del Duero Joven ★★ £C

Rodriguez Sanzo (VdT Castilla y Leon) *www.rodriguezsanzo.com*
A recently established operation based in the city of Valladolid, just to the immediate north of the Rueda DO is producing a small range of wines with a number of small bodegas in different appellations under the guidance of winemaker Javier Rodríguez. It initially took the label of Valsanzo for its wines. An increasingly wide range is now being made. As well as those covered here there are examples from

Rioja, Priorat, Rías Baixas and VdT Castilla y León as well as a red from across the border in the Douro. They are well made modern styles as much marked by their vibrant fruit as anything else. In addition to the ripe, dark berry scented Toro Damalisco Crianza there is also now a Reserva Terras JR. Bierzo JR is ripe, spicy and forward with that nice underlying minerality so prevalent in the Mencia grape. The Vall Sanzo Crianza Ribera del Duero is very much in a modern style and a premium Parajes is also made. There is additionally a range of striking whites from Rueda sourced from some of the higher altitude sites of the DO. The Viña Sanzo Verdejo is intense, mineral and citrus scented. (DM)
Recommended Reds:
Ribera del Duero Vall Sanzo Crianza ★★★ £D
Bierzo Terras JR ★★☆ £C   Toro Damalisco Crianza ★★ £B
Recommended Whites:
Rueda Vina Sanzo Verdejo Sobre Lías ★★★ £C

✿ Emilio Rojo (Ribeiro)
Emilio Rojo makes one of the most striking examples in Ribeiro. He has no trouble in selling his minimal output of barely 700 cases a year and achieving an impressively high price for the DO. He established his small property in 1987 and has just two ha of terraced hillside vineyards planted on sparse granite soils. As one would expect with a small, quality driven operation the vines are farmed along organic principles. The wine is marked by intense green fruits with honeyed notes and a classic minerality. It is best enjoyed within five years of the vintage. (DM)
Recommended Whites:
Ribeiro Emilio Rojo ★★★★ £E

>> Adega Manuel Rojo (Ribeiro) *www.adegamanuelrojo.es*
A small bodega making both red and white Ribeiro, the red in very small volumes, barely 300 cases a year. Founded in 2003, the property is in the heart of the appellation and to ensure the quality of the wines there is a small well equipped winery with stainless steel vinification tanks and temperature control. The impressive white (Treixadura, Godello, Albariño and Lado) is made in larger volume but is still very artisan, production is approaching a 1,000 cases a year. It is rich, concentrated and subtly aromatic. (DM)
Recommended Whites:
Ribeiro Manuel Rojo ★★★☆ £D

Rompesedas (Toro) *www.rompesedas.com*
Impressive new bodega producing just three reds. As well as the fine regular Rompesedas there is a small output of a limited release Finca Las Parvas, which comes from a small 2.5 ha plot and is vinified in 500 litre oak barrels and a young wine RD 6 Months in Barrel. All the bodega fruit is sourced from very old vines which are naturally low yielding and planted in a combination of sandy, clay soils with calcareous traces. Harvesting is by hand and all the fruit is kept fresh in a cool room before vinification. The regular Coral Duero Rompsedas is rich, opulent and spicy, full of concentrated dark cherry fruit. After a four day cold soak fermentation and maceration is at controlled temperature for just over four weeks before ageing for 18 months in a mix of mainly French and a little American oak. (DM)
Recommended Reds:
Toro Coral Duero ★★★★ £E

>> Santiago Ruiz (Rías Baixas) *www.bodegasantiagoruiz.com*
Owned for many years by Bodegas LAN in Rioja the Santiago

Ruiz bodega is run by Rosa Ruiz whose family has origins in local viticulture dating back to the 1860s. The property is in the O Rosal sub region and there are 38 ha under vine. Both the Atlantic Ocean and the Miño River have an influence on the local climate. While others are devoting themselves solely to Albariño, this is a more traditional operation and a number of grapes are planted and incorporated in the final assemblage of the Santiago Ruiz. Until very recently just one wine was made here, no special cuvées, or selections. A varietal Albariño, Rosa Ruiz (£D) is also now made. The Santiago Ruiz (Albariño, Loureiro, Godello,Treixadura and Caíño Blanco) is a rich, grassy, subtle and quite restrained example of the DO. (DM)

Recommended Whites:

Rías Baixas Santiago Ruiz ★★★☆ £D

Sameiras (Ribeiro)

Good and very well-priced wines are produced at this small bodega with an output of just a few thousand cases a year. Antonio Cajilde produced his first wines with the 2002 vintage. The wines tend to be fruit-driven in style but offer lots of depth and complexity, particularly the striking white. This is achieved by harvesting at optimum ripeness, restricting yields and with the white Ribeiro ageing on lees to add richness and intensity. It is a blend of Treixadura, Godello, Albariño and small amounts of Lado and Loureiro. The grapes that make up the red are hardly household names either. A barrica white is also now produced. A couple of additional approachable wines, one red and one white are also now made and branded Viña do Avó. (DM)

Recommended Reds:

Ribeiro ★★★ £C

Recommended Whites:

Ribeiro ★★★ £C

>> Santa Marta Bodegas (Valdeorras) *www.vinaredo.com*

Some good to very good reds and whites are made at this family owned bodega with vineyards planted at around 600 metres. Although the project was only founded in 1998 some of the Mencia and Godello vineyard plots are much older, approaching 50 years, planted in reflective slate soils. The bodega has 12 ha of owned vineyards and also works with other growers in cultivating a further 18 ha. There are two entry-level wines, both labelled, Valsadal, a white from Palomino and Godello and a red from Mencia and Garnacha Tintorera. Barrel aged wines, labelled Barrica are also made from both Mencia and Godello. There is also a Garnacha Centenaria (Garnacha Tintorera) and a Viñaredo Tostado, a late harvest Godello made from dried grapes. The fresh, mineral and subtly peachy Viñaredo Godello is given a short period of cold maceration before a cool fermentation. The Viñaredo Mencia shows lovely dark cherry fruit and a slight hint of minerality. Both the Mencia and rare Sousón reds get a cold soak before vinification and the dark cherry fruited Sousón is aged in small oak for eight months. (DM)

Recommended Reds:

Valdeorras Viñaredo Barrica ★★★ £D
Valdeorras Sousón ★★★ £D
Valdeorras Viñaredo Mencia ★★★ £C

Recommended Whites:

Valdeorras Viñaredo Godello ★★☆ £B

Sanclodio (Ribeiro)

A very good example from this remote north-western region is produced at this small bodega owned by reporter and filmmaker

José Luis Cuerda. The origins of the estate that the wine is produced from date back to the 1500s although successful winemaking is a much more recent occurrence with the vineyards being planted in 2002. There are now 6 ha under vine planted on three individual sites in the Gomariz Valley planted on terraced granite slopes. The vineyards are farmed sustainably and a careful control of yields helps to ensure the quality of the wine. Five traditional grapes of the north-west are planted; Treixadura (which accounts for over 70% of the plantings), Loureiro, Godello, Torrontés and Albariño. Immediately after harvest the wine is pressed and then cold-settled for 48 hours before fermentation which takes place at a medium temperature of 20 degrees Celsius providing a range of flavours. Two months on the fine lees are then followed by bottling. The wine has a beguiling green fruits and mineral quality with really impressive intensity. It is best enjoyed with a year or two. (DM)

Recommended Whites:

Ribeiro ★★★☆ £D

Bodegas Shaya (Rueda) *www.shaya.es*

This is a new Rueda bodega founded in 2008, run and distributed by the Gil family and Enrique Busto. There are 30.5 ha under vine and the vast majority goes into the Shaya, a zesty and herb scented white with a classic mineral edge. A small amount of a barrel-fermented Rueda, Shaya Habis sees around 7 months in oak while both wines gain lees enrichment prior to bottling. Old Verdejo vines add a rich depth and breadth and yields are low at just 2.5 tons to the acre. The vines are planted on sandy soils mixed with gravel on a clay base. Many are actually ungrafted. A fresh fruit driven example Aristo is also now made. Winemaking expertise is Australian under the direction of Belinda Thomson.

Recommended Whites:

Rueda Shaya Habis ★★★★ £D
Rueda Shaya ★★★ £C   Rueda Arindo ★★ £B

Viña Somoza (Valdeorras) *www.vinosomoza.com*

One of the better producers from this small but very good low-fertility, generally white wine producing DO. The bodega was founded two generations back by Victor Fernández. Today the winery is modern and very well equipped with the latest pneumatic press, stainless steel tanks, sorting tables and temperature control. The vineyards are planted solely to Godello and the hillside vineyards have a well-drained slate sub soil which also helps to impart a pronounced mineral quality in the wines. In the winery after the grape selection the must is pressed and cold settled. The Neno de Viña Sobre Lias is fermented in stainless steel and aged on fine lees before bottling. It has a fresh zesty quality with hints of green fruits and citrus and a touch of minerality. The lees add substance but the wine should be enjoyed young. The Selección is fuller and a touch more structured with a rounder creamier character, developing a lightly honeyed, peachy character over two or three years. Barrel fermentation and ageing for six months on lees provides a richer texture and depth in the wine. (DM)

Recommended Whites:

Valdeorras Selección Sobre Lías ★★★☆ £D
Valdeorras Neno de Viña Sobre Lías ★★★ £C

❂ Terras Gauda (Rías Baixas) *www.terrasgauda.com*

Founded in 1990, this is one the best properties in Rías Baixas. They have also recently established a second winery, exploiting the potential for great reds at Bierzo at Bodegas PITTACUM and have acquired QUINTA SARDONIA in the Duero Valley. The vineyards

North-West Spain

here in the Rosal Valley are close to the River Miño, which provides a benevolent mesoclimate. All of the wines are based on the aromatic Albariño, with a small amount of Loureiro and Caiño Blanco, the characterful less aromatic Lar Mar being dominated by Caiño. The Abadía de San Campio is marked by its piercing, almost peachy, aromatic fruit, while the Terras Gauda label offers more depth and concentration. Both are cool-fermented to emphasise their fruit. The Terras Gauda Black Label is vinified in oak, a portion new, with *bâtonnage*. The wine has a weighty oak character but loses some of its exuberant fruit in the process. (DM)

Recommended Whites:
Rías Baixas Terras Gauda Black Label ★★★★ £E
Rías Baixas La Mar ★★★★ £D   Rías Baixas Terras Gauda ★★★☆ £D
Rías Baixas Abadía de San Campio ★★☆ £B

Toresanas www.toresanas.com
Attractive, forward and approachable Toro reds are produced here. As well as their interests in Toro the owners, the Taninia Group, also produce impressive Rueda at the PALACIO DE BORNOS, Navarra at Señorio de Sarria, fine VdT at GUELBENZU and Ribera del Duero at their Vallebueno winery. They have 20 ha under vine planted in clay and sandstone soils with a limestone sediment. Three wines are produced and are in very much a forward fruit driven style without some of the firm, sometimes hard tannin found in other examples in the DO. The Novillo sees no wood, the dark cherry fruited Roble is aged for 6 months in a mix of French and American barrels, the Orot is a touch more structured and sees a year in wood.

Recommended Reds:
Toro Orot Crianza ★★★ £D Toro Amant Roble ★★ £C
Toro Amant Novillo ★★ £B

Torremilanos (Ribera del Duero) www.torremilanos.com
Established by the Penalba Lopez family in 1975, winemaking at this estate dates back to 1903. There is also a very impressive hotel where you could certainly consider staying if you are visiting the region. There are now over 200 ha under vine with some plots approaching 100 years old. A small range of both traditional and modern Ribera del Duero is produced including a white Peñalba López. In addition this is one of those instances where there is a Cava produced outside Cataluña. The simplest Ribera bottlings are the rosado Tempranillo with bright strawberry fruit and the supple approachable Roble which gets just four months in oak. Both take the Monte Castrillo label. There are two further fruit driven styles, Los Cantos de Torremilanos and Torremilanos. Also under the Torremilanos label there is a Crianza which shows a good balance of fruit, and French oak is used for ageing for around 13 months. There are two Reservas, Torremilanos is solely Tempranillo, the Torre Albériz includes a little Cabernet Sauvignon and Merlot adding just an additional dimension. The quality of the Gran Reserva is now being lifted with ageing in French oak. Cyclo is very different in style and approach. Vinification is more modern, with richly textured dark-berry fruit and well judged sweet oak. A very pricey top label red, Torremilanos El Roble Viejo comes from 90 year old vines planted in the family Roble Viejo vineyard. (DM)

Recommended Reds:
Ribera del Duero Cyclo ★★★★☆ £F
Ribera del Duero Torremilanos Gran Reserva ★★★★ £F
Ribera del Duero Torre-Albeniz Reserva ★★★☆ £E
Ribera del Duero Torremilanos Reserva ★★★☆ £D
Ribera del Duero Torremilanos Crianza ★★★ £C
Ribera del Duero Monte Castrillo Roble ★★☆ £C

Recommended Whites:
Cava Peñalba López ★★☆ £C
Recommended Rosés:
Ribera del Duero Monte Castrillo Tempranillo ★★☆ £B

Traslanzas (Cigales) www.traslanzas.com
Just a single red is made here at Translanzas and its one of the better examples of the appellation. Production is small, barely more than 1,200 cases a year so the wine won't be easy to find but given it's quality and price its well worth considering if you come across it. The continental climate provides Tempranillo of piercing elegant intensity, marked as much by its acidity as its tannin. A rounded, supple and velvety component is provided by malolactic in a mix of French and American oak. Being released at three to four years from the vintage, gives the wines an additional couple of years in bottle to add greater weight and flesh. (DM)

Recommended Reds:
Cigales ★★★ £D

Vinos Trico (Rías Baixas)
This is one of the more exciting recent developments in Rías Baixas. José Antonio López has been involved previously with both Adegas MORGADIO and LUSCO. This is his own project from which he is producing just one very fine example of the DO. He currently has just 5 ha of Albariño but it provides him with fruit of tremendous depth and intensity. The early releases have all shown a rich green fruit and citrus intensity with a classic underlying mineral purity. The wine is made using traditional methods being aged in tank for around 11 months and kept on fine lees prior to bottling. At present it represents a major bargain. A second label Tabla de Sumar is a little cheaper. (DM)

Recommended Whites:
Rías Baixas Tricó ★★★★ £D

Bodegas Tridente (VdT Castilla y Leon) www.bodegastriton.es
This project from the partnership of the Gil family and Enrique Busto is based near Zamora producing a range of very good and well priced reds all labelled Tridente under the VdT Castilla y León umbrella. The bodega was founded in 2008 and is able to draw on 63 ha of vineyards. Tempranillo, Mencia and Prieto Picudo are all planted in both León as well as in Bierzo. The main source is from within the Toro boundaries and the vines are very old, dating back to 1910 in a number of the 30 or so parcels. The richly textured, dark-fruited Tridente Mencia is sourced from Bierzo, Toro and around Zamora. It gets a short ageing in French oak and is very international in style but has that mineral edge often encountered in the variety. Tridente Tempranillo is a touch less opulent but offers good concentration and depth. Two further Tempranillo's are made. Entresuelos is a forward fresh style with limited barrel ageing (6 months), while the premium Tempranillo Rejón comes from within the Toro boundaries and 130 year old vines. A red Tridente Prieto Picudo is made in very small volumes. (DM)

Recommended Reds:
VdT Castilla y León Rejón ★★★★ £E
VdT Castilla y León Tridente Mencia ★★★☆ £D
VdT Castilla y León Tridente Tempranillo ★★★ £D
VdT Castilla y León Tridente Entresuelos ★★ £C

Bodegas Trus (Ribera del Duero) www.bodegastrus.com
Trus is an organically run bodega producing four wines, very much in a single estate style and solely from Tinto Fino. They are

thoroughly modern and wines are produced under the two labels. The estate vineyards are located in the propitious western half of the DO just to the north of Pesquera de Duero and enjoy a south to south-west aspect. The almost extreme continental climate with very warm summers provides wines with real depth of flavour and extract. The elevation aids acidity though and sophisticated modern vinification provides for reds with rich, plummy, berry-laden fruit and firm but approachable tannins. The Tramuz label is more forward and approachable and a Joven is made. The Trus wines are more structured and a Roble, Crianza as well as a Reserva are produced. (DM)

Recommended Reds:
Ribera del Duero Trus Reserva ★★★★ £F
Ribera del Duero Trus Crianza ★★★ £D

>> Bodegas Valdesil (Valdeorras) *www.valdesil.com*
The family origins of vine growing at this bodega stretch back to the 1880s. In its modern form though, the bodega has been running for a decade and a half. Old vineyard plots are being recovered from original family holdings and included in this are 11 small parcels of very old vines planted in slatey soils. Among them is the Pedrouzos vineyard, which was established at the end of the 19th century. As well as the impressive Godello whites, two reds are also made from Mencia, Valderoa and in the best years a special selection Valderoa Carballo. Montenovo is the entry level white from younger 20-year old vines, fresh and forward and marked by attractive zesty fruit. It is cool fermented and early bottled. The Valdesil white is richer, more complex coming from older over 30-year old vines and aged for four months on fine lees. The Pezas de Portela is a rich, round and complex white with subtle creamy oak notes as well as fresh green and peachy fruit and a classic minerality. It is barrel fermented in barrels of varying size and comes from older 50 plus-year old plots. A very small amount of the single vineyard Pedrouzos is made and is released solely in magnums as well as now a second premium white Parcela O Chao. (DM)

Recommended Whites:
Valdeorras Pezas de Portela Cepas Viejas ★★★★ £E
Valdeorras Valdesil Godello Sobre Lías ★★★☆ £D
Valdeorras Montenovo ★★★ £C

Adegas Valmiñor (Rías Baixas) *www.valminor.com*
A further example of the potential from Spain's most established fine white wine region. It was established in 1997, with fruit purchasing arrangements having been established with an extensive network of fine quality local growers. Strict criteria are applied here including the age of the vineyard, its aspect and the mineral composition as well as quality and drainage of its soil. There are two forward entry level whites, Serra da Estrela and Torroxal, both from Albariño. The regular Valmiñor, which is also varietal Albariño, is forward, fresh and full of appealing citrus and mineral notes. The Dávila is altogether more serious, a blend of Albariño, Loureiro and Treixadura gaining from a period on lees which clearly adds to its depth and complexity. The range is completed by two premium, low volume releases, Davila M 100 which is a blend and Davila L 100 which is an unusual Loureiro varietal. (DM)

Recommended Whites:
Rías Baixas Dávila ★★★☆ £D   Rías Baixas Valmiñor ★★★ £C

●● Vega Sicilia (Ribera del Duero & Toro) *www.vega-sicilia.com*
This is Spain's most famous red wine producer. The quality of its wines in Ribera del Duero in recent years has been challenged by

the likes of ALEJANDRO FERNANDEZ and DOMINIO DE PINGUS but Vega Sicilia remains quite distinct in style and approach. The top wine, Unico, which is a blend of Tinto Fino and Cabernet Sauvignon, is still given extended cask-maturation, although this has been reduced to help preserve the wine's freshness. A non-vintaged Reserva Especial is also produced – very expensive and evolved in style and very intense and complex. The second wine, Valbuena, produced from Tinto Fino, Malbec and Merlot, has more obvious fruit character. In a move to provide a more contemporary approach but to retain the quality of Vega Sicilia, a new winery, Alión, was established in 1991. These are impressive, structured and dense modern examples of the DO produced solely from Tinto Fino and full of dark, spicy fruit, supple tannins and cedary oak. The wine has shown an added dimension consistently over the past decade. The rich, powerful and smoky Pintia in Toro is also establishing itself as benchmark in that DO produced from old Tinto de Toro vines. Alión will benefit from at least 5 years' cellaring. Both Unico and Valbuena are accessible on release but will develop very well in bottle. The Alvarez family have also invested in Hungary in the Tokaji operation OREMUS. (DM)

Bodegas Vega Sicilia
Recommended Reds:
Ribera del Duero Reserva Especial ✪✪✪✪✪ £H
Ribera del Duero Unico ✪✪✪✪✪ £H
Ribera del Duero Valbuena ★★★★ £F
Bodegas y Viñedos Alión
Recommended Reds:
Ribera del Duero Alión ★★★★★ £G
Bodegas y Viñedos Pintia
Recommended Reds:
Toro Pintia ★★★★ £F

● Vidal Soblechero (Rueda) *www.clavidor.com*
A fine small family bodega making an almost bewildering array of wines from their 42 ha of vineyards. There are a number of well sited parcels "pagos" and a considerable holding of old vines. Some plots of Verdejo are now over 70 years old. The family is able to exploit a range of soils and the vineyards themselves benefit from a higher altitude than most in the region. Good to very good red and white is produced under both the Rueda DO and VdT Castilla y León classifications. Reds are ripe and juicy, fully Tinta Fina (Tempranillo). The Tinta Fina S gains an additional dimension from partial malolactic in small barrel and 12 months in new and used, mainly French oak. The white Rueda wines offer great varietal purity along with an underlying minerality. There is a real depth to the Cepas Viejas, which blends very old 60 to 70 year old Verdejo and Viura. A short pre-fermentation period of skin contact ensures good fruit to complement the wine's structure, particularly the Cepas Viejas and Verdejo. The top reds and whites are the single vineyard, Pagos de Villavendimia bottlings. The red Finca Perdiz is a rich, well-structured Tinta Fina gaining a rounded texture from malolactic in new wood. The piercing, mineral Finca El Jardin is a Sauvignon bottled after six months on stirred lees. The elegant and characterful lightly citrus scented Finca Varrastrojuelos is a 100% Viura produced from very old vines, some over 90 years. A number of very impressive single vineyard Verdejos, Fincas Buenavista, Matea and El Alto are also produced and are barrel-fermented. The range is completed by three well priced modern wines, a Sauvignon and two rosados, including the Capricho 1031. (DM)

Recommended Reds:
VdT Castilla y León Finca Perdiz ★★★☆ £E

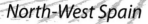

North-West Spain

VdT Castilla y León Finca Las Sernas ★★★ £D
VdT Castilla y León Tinta Fina S ★★☆ £C
VdT Castilla y León Tinta Fina C ★★☆ £C
VdT Castilla y León Tinto Joven ★★ £B
VdT Castilla y León Tinta Fina ★☆ £B
Recommended Whites:
VdT Castilla y León Finca El Alto ★★★★ £D
VdT Castilla y León Finca Buenavista ★★★★ £D
VdT Castilla y León Finca Matea ★★★☆ £D
VdT Castilla y León Finca Varrastrojuelos ★★★ £D
VdT Castilla y León Finca El Jardin ★★★ £D
Rueda Cepas Viejas ★★☆ £C   Rueda Verdejo ★★☆ £C
Rueda Sauvignon Blanc ★★ £B
Recommended Rosés:
Rueda Capricho 1031 ★★ £B

Hermanos del Villar (Rueda) *www.orodecastilla.com*
A striking producer of Verdejo-based whites. Owner and winemaker Pablo de Villar has around 70 ha of Verdejo planted in a number of sites in stony alluvial soils. There is also 15 ha planted to Sauvignon Blanc and a further 20 ha to Tempranillo. The Verdejo whites offer the most interest. The regular bottling is cool-fermented in tank and Villar has isolated his own wild yeast strain. While the regular bottling has some straightforward grassy flavours and just a hint of tropical fruit, the Oro de Castilla is of a different order. Finely structured with subtle creamy tones and rich almost honeyed peachy fruit, this is one of the better examples of the appellation. It should develop well in bottle for 2 or 3 years. (DM)
Recommended Whites:
Rueda Oro de Castilla Verdejo ★★★ £C
Rueda Valdelapinta Verdejo ★★☆ £C

Vinum Terrae (Rías Baixas)
This small operation was established just a few years ago with vineyards in the heart of the Rías Baixas region in the Valle do Salnés. Investment continues in new winery equipment and some fruit is still bought in while the estate vineyards gradually come on stream. The original wine at the Agnusdei bodega is 100% Albariño, tank-fermented and full of enticing minerally, steely floral fruit. Both fresh and intense, it is best drunk young for its perfume – say within its first 12–18 months. A second Rías Baixas is also now been added which is in a rounder fleshier style, You & Me. This is undoubtedly a winery to watch in the region as its vineyards age. The most recent development is a new bodega in Ribera del Duero, Tierra Adentro. (DM)
Recommended Whites:
Rías Baixas Agnusdei Albariño ★★★ £C
Rías Baixas You & Me ★★☆ £C

❀ Vizcarra-Ramos (Ribera del Duero) *www.vizcarra.es*
Founded in 1991, this is one of the more exciting among the new wave of bodegas in this top quality DO. There are 26 ha planted at an altitude of around 850 metres. Yields are kept to a minimum in the well drained clay/limestone and stony soils and a small cover crop is planted to optimise ripening. The Senda del Oro is full of dark-berry fruit and a spicy, peppery character. It offers surprising depth for the style. The 15 Meses, full of coffee and tobacco scents and with a rich, spicy intensity is aged in a mix of French and American oak. The Torralvo is fuller, darker with a richer texture from malolactic and ageing in French oak, it is sourced from a vineyard with an average age of around 60 years. The impressively

concentrated and densely textured top two cuvées are special selections and both are produced in very small volumes. Inés has a small proportion of Merlot included in the blend and a more pronounced berry fruit character, Celia a touch of Garnacha. They are named after Juan-Carlos Vizcarra-Ramos' two daughters. (DM)
Recommended Reds:
Ribera del Duero Inés ★★★★★ £G
Ribera del Duero Celia ★★★★★ £G
Ribera del Duero Torralvo ★★★★ £F
Ribera del Duero 15 Meses ★★★☆ £D
Ribera del Duero Senda del Oro ★★★ £C

Yllera (Rueda) *www.grupoyllera.com*
Substantial north-western operation producing an extensive range of wines from the DOs of Rioja (the Coelus brand), Rueda, Ribera del Duero and Toro as well as a number of examples of V T Castilla y León. Among the latter wines, as well as the Reserva and Crianza bottlings a top end wine is also produced, Dominus, a selection from 50 year old vines and aged in French rather than the combination of American and French oak used for the other VdT reds. As well as these the range also now includes an old vine Toro, Garcilaso. Fine, green fruited, minerally Rueda is released under the Viña Cantosan brand, as is a crisp Brut sparkling white. As well as this Yllera Verdejo and Sauvignon are made. Of the Ribera del Duero reds the unoaked Viña del Val is the softest and most accessible, marked by its bright red berry fruit more than its structure. The Bracamonte Roble has more depth and a little grip from soft supple tannins, while still marked by attractive darker berry fruit there is a touch of oak spice in the background. The rich, ripe blackberry scented Crianza offers a fine mix of dark fruits and sweet oak. Aged for just 6 months in *barriques* it offers a more attractive style and better value than the Reserva which spends 24 months in oak and is a touch drier and less exuberant. Top reds are approachable within 3 or 4 years and will develop well in bottle. (DM)
Recommended Reds:
Ribera del Duero Bracamonte Reserva ★★★ £E
Ribera del Duero Bracamonte Crianza ★★★ £C
Ribera del Duero Bracamonte Roble ★★☆ £C
Ribera del Duero Viña del Val ★★ £B
VdT Castilla y León Vendimia Seleccionada ★★★ £D
VdT Castilla y León 12 Meses en Barrica ★★☆ £C
Recommended Whites:
Rueda Yllera Verdejo Vendimia Nocturna ★★ £B
Rueda Viña Cantosan Viñas Viejas ★★ £B
Rueda Viña Cantosan Brut ★★ £B

❀ Zárate (Rías Baixas) *www.bodegas-zarate.com*
This bodega is based in the favourable Salnés Valley subregion and as such enjoys a beneficial maritime climate. The Zárate family have been based here since 1920, so unlike many other emerging quality bodegas they are no flash in the pan. The winemaker Eulogio Pomares has studied in both Bordeaux and Germany. Since his first vintage in 2000 the investment in winemaking technology has been considerable but equally important is the work in developing the quality of the fruit, in both the bodegas own vineyards and growers they buy from. New viticultural developments include biodynamics and planting without rootstocks. Among the wines the Zárate Albariño is the most approachable; it offers notes of green fruit and peach as well as a pure underlying minerality. Tras da Viñas is richer, fuller and creamier but with marked nervy acidity. It spends 30 months on its fine lees, enriching its texture. It should

develop well over five years or more. There are also two other single vineyard vines which are a touch pricier; El Palomar and El Balado. The richly textured peachy El Palomar comes from centenarian vines. As well as the whites, three reds are made, a Loureiro tinto, a Caiño tinto and an Espadeiro. The bodega also has a joint venture with Barcelona merchant Vila Viniteca making a varietal Albariño, El Jardín de Lucia, which is marketed as a part of the Uvas Felices selection. Pomares also makes a small number of excellent wines under his own label. (DM)

Zárate
Recommended Whites:
Rías Baixas El Palomar ★★★★ £E
Rías Baixas Tras da Viñas ★★★☆ £D
Rías Baixas Albariño ★★★ £C

Uvas Felices - El Jardín de Lucia
Recommended Whites:
Rías Baixas El Jardín de Lucia ★★★ £C

Eulogio Pomares
Recommended Whites:
Rías Baixas Albariño Crianza Oxidativa ★★★★☆ £E

❀ **Zerberos** *www.winesdanielramosvinos.blogspot.com*
Daniel Ramos refers to himself as a Span-Aussie. He brings a modern new world approach to his wines while seeking to harness the tremendous potential available from some of this regions old vine Garnacha. The town of Cebreros is the heart of this small traditional sub-region of Castilla y León located to the south-west of Madrid. His south facing vineyards are planted at an altitude of between 800 and 1,000 metres in a mix of granitic sand and slatey schist, providing a piercing mineral quality in the wines with the more approachable wines coming from the granite sand. There are four reds, three of which are now partly labelled after the soil type they are grown in. The Sand and Schist/Arena Pizarra bottling is sourced from vines grown in both soil types. It's ripe, creamy and full of dark-berry fruit and possesses a real old-vine character. His second red, Slate Schist/Pizarra comes solely from schist and is more structured and mineral in style. The third wine, Arena/Granitic Sand is the most opulent of the wines. Daniel is also involved with a number of partners in a new small scale project, Bodega Garnacha Alta Alberche, again focussing on old 40 to over 85 year old Garnacha grown in the Alto Alberche Valley. The Roble is bright and fruit driven, the Selección a touch more structured. A Joven and a Rosado are also made as well as two premium label wines, Finca Catalino and Finca Faustina. (DM)

Zerberos
Recommended Reds:
VdT Castilla y León Granitic Sand Arena ★★★★☆ £F
VdT Castilla y León Schist Pizarra ★★★★ £E
VdT Castilla y León El Berraco ★★★☆ £D
VdT Castilla y León Sand and Schist Arena Pizarra ★★★ £C
Recommended Whites:
VdT Castilla y León Vino Precioso ★★★☆ £D
VdT Castilla y León Viento Zephyros ★★★ £C

Bodega Garnacha Alta Alberche
Recommended Reds:
VdT Castilla y León 7 Navas Finca Faustino ★★★★ £F
VdT Castilla y León 7 Navas Finca Catalino ★★★☆ £D
VdT Castilla y León 7 Navas Selección ★★★ £C
VdT Castilla y León 7 Navas Joven Roble ★★☆ £B

Other wines of note - *North-West Spain*

Castilla y León
Bodega del Abad
Recommended Reds:
Bierzo Dom Bueno Barrica ★★★ £C
Recommended Whites:
Bierzo Dom Bueno Barrica ★★★ £C
Akilia
Recommended Reds: Bierzo Lombano ★★★★ £E
Bierzo Villarín ★★★★ £D   Bierzo Chano Villar ★★★☆ £D
Bierzo Villa de San Lorenzo ★★★ £C
Recommended Whites: Bierzo K ★★★★ £D
Bierzo Valdesacia ★★★☆ £D
Alta Pavina
Recommended Reds: VdT Castilla y León Citios Pinot Noir ★★★☆ £E
VdT Castilla y León Selecto ★★★ £E
Alto Sotillo
Recommended Reds: Ribera del Duero Rubiejo Evolución ★★★☆ £E
Ribera del Duero Roble ★★☆ £C   Ribera del Duero Joven ★★ £B
Àlvarez y Diaz
Recommended Whites: Rueda Mantel Blanco FB ★★★ £C
Rueda Mantel Blanco Verdejo ★★☆ £B
Rueda Mantel Blanco Sauvignon Blanc ★★ £B
Rueda Monte Alina ★☆ £A
Àngel Lorenzo Cachazo
Recommended Whites: Rueda Martivili Verdejo FB ★★★ £C
Rueda Martivili Verdejo ★★ £B
Àngel Lorenzo Cachazo - Uvas Felices
Recommended Whites: Rueda Fenomenal ★★★ £C
Rueda El Perro Verde ★★★ £C
Hernando y Sourdais Bodegas Antidoto
Recommended Reds:
Ribera del Duero 'La Hormiga de Antidoto' ★★★★☆ £F
Ribera del Duero Antidoto ★★★☆ £D
Bodegas JA Calvo (Casajús)
Recommended Reds:
Ribera del Duero Casajús Antiguos Viñedos ★★★★ £E
Ribera del Duero Casajús Vendimia Seleccionada ★★★☆ £D
Camino del Norte
Recommended Reds: Bierzo El Tesón ★★★★ £E
Bierzo El Soradal ★★★ £D
Cillar de Silos
Recommended Reds: Ribera del Duero Viña de Amalio ★★★★☆ £F
Ribera del Duero Torresilo ★★★☆ £E
Ribera del Duero Cillar de Silos ★★★ £D
Ribera del Duero Joven ★★☆ £C
Bodega Cuatro Rayas (Agricola Castellana)
Recommended Whites: Rueda Cuatro Rayas ★★★ £C
Rueda Azumbre Vendimia Selecciónada ★★ £B
Bodega Cyan
Recommended Reds:
Toro Selección Personal Carlos Moro ★★★★ £E
Toro Pago de La Calera ★★★★ £E
Toro Prestigio ★★★☆ £D   Toro 12 Meses ★★★ £C
Dominio del Águila
Recommended Reds: Ribera del Duero Reserva ★★★★★ £F
Ribera del Duero Pícaro del Aguila Viñas Viejas ★★★☆ £D
Recommended Rosés: Ribera del Duero Pícaro Clarete ★★★☆ £E
Dominio de Es
Recommended Reds: Ribera del Duero La Diva ★★★★★ £H

North-West Spain

Spain

Ribera del Duero Viñas Viejas de Soria ★★★★★ £G

Don Juan del Águila
Recommended Reds:
VdT Castilla y León Gaznata Finca Mariano ★★★ £C
VdT Castilla y León Gaznata Concrete ★★☆ £B
VdT Castilla y León Gaznata Joven ★☆ £A

Pedro Escudero
Recommended Whites: Rueda Fuente Elvira ★★☆ £C
Rueda Valdelainos ★★ £B

Bodegas Farina
Recommended Reds: Toro Gran Colegiata Campus ★★★ £D
Toro Gran Colegiata Reserva ★★☆ £C
Toro Gran Colegiata Crianza ★★☆ £C
Toro Gran Colegiata Roble Francés ★★☆ £C
Toro Gran Colegiata Barrica ★★ £B   Toro Colegiata ★☆ £B
Recommended Whites: Toro Colegiata (Malvasia) ★☆ £B

Garcia Figuero
Recommended Reds: Ribera del Duero Tinus ★★★★☆ £H
Ribera del Duero Noble ★★★★☆ £G
Ribera del Duero Seleccionada ★★★★ £F
Ribera del Duero 15 Meses en Barrica ★★★☆ £E
Ribera del Duero 12 Crianza ★★★ £D
Ribera del Duero 4 Roble ★★ £C

Bodegas Hiriart
Recommended Reds: Cigales Crianza ★★★ £C
Recommended Rosés: Cigales Lágrima ★★☆ £B

Bodegas Gil Luna
Recommended Reds: Toro Gil Luna ★★★☆ £D
Toro Tres Luna ★★★ £C

Hijos Antonio Polo (Pagos Peñafiel)
Recommended Reds:
Ribera del Duero Pagos Peñafiel Vendimia Selecciónada ★★★★ £E
Ribera del Duero Pagos Peñafiel Reserva ★★★☆ £E
Ribera del Duero Pagos Peñafiel Crianza ★★★ £C

Finca La Rinconada
Recommended Reds:
VdT Castilla y León Barcolobo Selección ★★★☆ £E
VdT Castilla y León Barcolobo ★★★ £D
Recommended Whites:
VdT Castilla y León Barcolobo Fermentado en Barrica ★★★ £C

Viña Mambrilla
Recommended Reds:
Ribera del Duero Alidis Expresión ★★★☆ £E
Ribera del Duero Aldis VS ★★★ £F
Ribera del Duero Reserva ★★★ £D
Ribera del Duero Crianza ★★☆ £C

Marqués de Irun
Recommended Whites: Rueda ★★ £B

Matarromera
Recommended Reds:
Ribera del Duero Solanas Reserva Especial ★★★★★ £G
Ribera del Duero Prestigio ★★★★☆ £F
Ribera del Duero Reserva ★★★☆ £E
Ribera del Duero Crianza ★★★ £C   Ribera del Duero Melior ★★ £B

Bodegas Mocén
Recommended Whites: Rueda Mocén Verdejo ★★☆ £B
Rueda Mocén Sauvignon Blanc ★★ £B
Rueda Mocén ★★ £B

Bodegas Monte la Reina
Recommended Reds:
Toro Castillo Monte La Reina Vendimia Seleccionada ★★★☆ £D

Toro Castillo Monte La Reina Crianza ★★☆ £C
Recommended Whites:
Toro Castillo Monte La Reina Verdejo ★★ £B

Viñedos de Nieva
Recommended Whites: Rueda B Nieva Pie Franco ★★★ £C
Rueda B Nieva ★★☆ £B

Ovidio Garcia
Recommended Reds: Cigales Esencia ★★★ £C
Cigales Selección Barrica ★★☆ £C

Prieto Pariente
Recommended Reds:
VdT Castilla y León El Origen de Prieto Pariente ★★★★ £E
VdT Castilla y León Prieto Pariente ★★★☆ £D
Recommended Whites: VdT Castilla y León Viognier ★★★☆ £D

Bodegas Protos
Recommended Reds: Ribera del Duero Selección ★★★★ £E
Ribera del Duero Reserva ★★★☆ £E
Ribera del Duero Crianza ★★★ £D
Ribera del Duero Roble ★★☆ £C
Recommended Whites: Rueda Protos Verdejo ★★☆ £B

Real Sitio de Ventosilla (Prado Rey)
Recommended Reds:
Ribera del Duero Prado Rey Reserva ★★★☆ £E
Ribera del Duero Prado Rey Finca Valdelayegua Crianza ★★★ £C
Ribera del Duero Prado Rey Roble ★★☆ £B
Recommended Whites: Rueda Prado Rey Verdejo ★★☆ £B

Teófilo Reyes
Recommended Reds: Ribera del Duero Crianza ★★★ £C

Viña Sanz (Finca La Colina)
Recommended Whites:
Rueda Finca La Colina Verdejo Cien x Cien ★★★ £C
Rueda Verdejo ★★☆ £B   Rueda Sauvignon Blanc ★★ £B

Viña Sastre
Recommended Reds: Ribera del Duero Regina Vides ★★★★☆ £G
Ribera del Duero Pago de Santa Cruz ★★★★ £E
Ribera del Duero Viña Sastre Crianza ★★★ £C
Ribera del Duero Viña Sastre Roble ★★☆ £B

Sei Solo
Recommended Reds: Ribera del Duero Sei Solo ★★★★☆ £F
Ribera del Duero Preludio ★★★☆ £D

Finca Sobreno
Recommended Reds: Toro Special Selection ★★★ £E
Toro Crianza ★★☆ £C   Toro Roble ★★ £B

Tabula
Recommended Reds: Ribera del Duero Gran Tabula ★★★★☆ £F
Ribera del Duero Tabula ★★★★ £E
Ribera del Duero Damana Crianza ★★★☆ £D
Ribera del Duero Damana 5 ★★☆ £B

Bodegas Tardencuba
Recommended Reds: Toro Valnuevo Selección ★★★ £E
Toro Autor ★★★ £D   Toro Crianza ★★☆ £C   Toro Roble ★★ £B

Bodegas Tera y Castro
Recommended Whites: Rueda Dilectum ★★★ £C
Rueda Pentio ★★☆ £B

Bodegas Uvaguilera
Recommended Reds: Ribera del Duero Palomero ★★★☆ £F

Valpiculata
Recommended Reds: Toro Valpiculata ★★★☆ £E
Toro Puertas Novas ★★★ £C

Valsardo
Recommended Reds:
Ribera Del Duero Reserva Superior ★★★☆ £F
Ribera Del Duero Valsardo ★★★☆ £E
Ribera Del Duero Valdeyuso ★★★ £C
Vega Sauco
Recommended Reds: Toro Adoremus ★★★ £C
Toro Tó ★★☆ £B
Bodegas Veracruz
Recommended Whites: Rueda Ermita Veracruz ★★★ £C
Ángel Rodriguez Vidal
Recommended Whites: Rueda Martinsancho Verdejo ★★★ £C
Bodegas Villacezán
Recommended Reds: Tierra de León Seis Meises ★★★ C
Tierra de León Doce Meses ★★☆ £C
Tierra de León Dehesa de Villacezán ★★ £B
VdT Castilla y León Mar de Castilla y León ★★ £B
Recommended Whites: Tierra de León Albarín ★★☆ £B
Bodega Viñagueriña
Recommended Reds: Toro Munia Especial ★★★ £E
Toro Munia Crianza ★★☆ £C Toro Munia ★★ £B
Bodegas Vizar
Recommended Reds: VdT Castilla y León Syrah ★★★☆ £D
VdT Castilla y León Selección Especial ★★★☆ £D
VdT Castilla y León 12 Meses ★★★ £D
VdT Castilla y León 5 Meses ★★☆ £C
VdT Castilla y León Joven ★★ £B
Enologica Wamba
Recommended Reds: VdT Castilla y León Ambisna ★★☆ £C
VdT Castilla y León Zarzanas ★★ £C
VdT Castilla y León Lyna ★☆ £B
Recommended Whites: Rueda Ambisna ★★☆ £B
Zumaya
Recommended Reds: Ribera del Duero Reserva ★★★ £E
Ribera del Duero Crianza ★★☆ £C
Galicia
Viña Almirante
Recommended Whites: Rías Baixas Vanidade ★★★☆ £D
Rías Baixas Vicius Barrica ★★★ £C
Rías Baixas Pionero Mundi ★★★ £C
Adegas d'Altamira
Recommended Whites: Rías Baixas Selección ★★★ £C
Rías Baixas Brandal ★★☆ £C
Altos de Torona
Recommended Whites: Rías Baixas Altos de Torona ★★★ £C
Bodegas Aquitania
Recommended Whites: Rías Baixas Aquitania ★★☆ £C
Rías Baixas Bernon ★★☆ £B
Bodegas Attis
Recommended Whites: Rías Baixas Sitta Ancestros ★★★★ £F
Rías Baixas Nana ★★★★ £E Rías Baixas Embaixador ★★★☆ £D
Rías Baixas Mar ★★★☆ £D Rías Baixas Attis ★★★ £C
Rías Baixas Xión ★★☆ £B
Bodegas d'Berna
Recommended Reds: Valdeorras Tinto ★★☆ £C
Bouza do Rei
Recommended Whites: Rías Baixas Castel de Bouza ★★★ £C
Rías Baixas Bouza do Rei ★★☆ £B
Adega O Casal
Recommended Reds: Valdeorras Casal Novo ★★☆ £C
Recommended Whites: Valdeorras Casal Novo ★★☆ £C

Adegas Castrobrey
Recommended Whites:
Rías Baixas Sin Palabras Edicion Especial ★★★☆ £D
Rías Baixas Nice to Meet You ★★★ £D
Rías Baixas Sin Palabras Castrovaldés ★★★ £C
Rías Baixas Castro Valdés ★★☆ £C
Adega Castrocelta
Recommended Whites: Rías Baixas Castrocelta ★★☆ £C
Adegas A Coroa
Recommended Whites: Valdeorras A Coroa ★★☆ £B
Bodegas Coto Redondo
Recommended Reds:
Rías Baixas Señorio de Rubiós Vino Novo ★★ £C
Recommended Whites:
Rías Baixas Señorio de Rubiós Condado Blanco Tea ★★★ £C
Rías Baixas Señorio de Rubiós ★★☆ £B
Crego e Monaguillo
Recommended Whites: Monterrei Crego e Monaguillo ★★☆ £C
Adega Cruceiro
Recommended Reds: Ribeira Sacra Cruceiro Rexio ★★★ £D
Ribeira Sacra Cruceiro ★★☆ £C
Bodegas Docampo
Recommended Whites: Ribeiro Señorío da Vila ★★★ £C
Ribeiro Viña do Campo ★★ £B
Bodega Eidosela
Recommended Whites: Rías Baixas Etra Condado ★★★ £C
Rías Baixas Arbustrum ★★☆ £C Rías Baixas Etra ★★☆ £B
Envinate
Recommended Reds:
Ribeira Sacra Lousas Vino de Aldea ★★★☆ £C
Adegas Gallegas
Recommended Whites: Rías Baixas D. Pedro Neve ★★★ £D
Rías Baixas Veigadares ★★★ £D
Rías Baixas D. Pedro de Sotomayor ★★☆ £C
Rías Baixas Dionisios ★★ £C
Bodega Cooperativa Jesús Nazareno
Recommended Reds: Valdeorras Valdouro Barrica ★★ £B
Recommended Whites: Valdeorras Viña Abad ★★ £B
La Maleta Hand Made Wines (Ribeiro)
Recommended Reds: Ribera del Duero Finca La Viajera ★★★☆ £C
Rioja Marquesado del Alto Crianza ★★★☆ £C
Recommended Whites:
Rías Baixas El Príncipe y el Birrete ★★★☆ £C
Rías Baixas El Rubio Infante ★★☆ £B
Valdeorras El Precipio ★★★☆ £C
Rías Baixas El Rubio Infante ★★☆ £B Rueda Pizpireta ★★☆ £B
Bodegas y Viñedos La Senda
Recommended Reds: Bierzo La Senda 1984 ★★★☆ £C
Bierzo La Senda ★★★ £B
Bodegas La Tapada
Recommended Whites:
Valdeorras Guitián Barrica de Acacia ★★★☆ £D
Valdeorras Guitián ★★★ £C
Lar de Ricobao
Recommended Reds:
Ribeira Sacra Selección do Val 10 Lunas ★★★ £D
Ribeira Sacra Selección do Val ★★☆ £C
Recommended Whites: Ribeira Sacra Ouro do Val ★★☆ £C
Ribeira Sacra Godello ★★ £C
Luna Beberide
Recommended Reds: Bierzo Luna Beberide ★★★☆ £D

North-West Spain

Recommended Whites: Bierzo LB ★★★ £C

Maior de Mendoza
Recommended Whites: Rías Baixas 3 Crianzas ★★★ £C
Rías Baixas Sobre Lías ★★★ £C   Rías Baixas Fulget ★★☆ £C

Adegas Morgadío
Recommended Whites: Rías Baixas Morgadío ★★☆ £C

Adegas Moure - Abadía da Cova
Recommended Reds:
Ribeira Sacra Abadía da Cova de Autor ★★★★ £E
Ribeira Sacra Abadía da Cova ★★★ £C
Ribeira Sacra A Fuga ★★☆ £B
Recommended Whites: Ribeira Sacra Abadía da Cova ★★★☆ £D

Rubén Moure Fernández
Recommended Reds: Ribeira Sacra Finca Cuarta ★★★☆ £C

Nairoa
Recommended Whites: Ribeiro Alberte ★★☆ £C

Notas Frutales de Albariño
Recommended Whites: Rías Baixas Finca Garabelos ★★★ £D
Rías Baixas La Trucha ★★☆ £C

Adega Pazo do Mar
Recommended Whites: Ribeiro Expresión Barrica ★★☆ £C
Ribeiro Expresión ★★ £B

Pazos del Rey
Recommended Reds: Monterrei Sila Mencia ★★★ £C
Recommended Whites: Monterrei Pazo de Monterrey ★★★ £C

Eduardo Peña
Recommended Whites: Ribeiro Eduardo Peña ★★☆ £B
Ribeiro María Andrea ★★ £B

Pombal a Lanzada
Recommended Whites: Rías Baixas As Batea ★★★★ £D
Rías Baixas Arcan ★★★☆ £C   Rías Baixas Mytilus ★★★ £C

José Carlos Quintas Pérez (O Rei de Campoverde)
Recommended Whites: Rías Baixas O Rei de Campoverde ★★☆ £B

Quinta de Couselo
Recommended Whites:
Rías Baixas Quinta de Couselo Selección ★★★☆ £E
Rías Baixas Quinta de Couselo ★★★ £C

Joaquin Rebolledo
Recommended Reds: Valdeorras Tinto Barrica ★★★ £D
Recommended Whites: Valdeorras Godello ★★★ £C

Ronsel do Sil
Recommended Reds: Ribeira Sacra Pórtico da Gloria ★★★★ £E
Ribeira Sacra Alpendre ★★★★ £E
Ribeira Sacra Arpegio (Mencía) ★★★☆ £D
Ribeira Sacra Vel'uveyra (Mencia) ★★★ £C
Recommended Whites: Ribeira Sacra Ourive Doña Branca ★★★☆ £D
Ribeira Sacra Ourive ★★★☆ £D   Ribeira Sacra Vel'uveyra ★★★ £C

Bodegas Santiago Roma
Recommended Whites:
Rías Baixas Santiago Roma Selección ★★★ £C
Rías Baixas Santiago Roma ★★☆ £B

Adegas Rosalia de Castro
Recommended Whites: Rías Baixas Paco & Lola ★★★ £C
Rías Baixas Rosalia de Castro ★★☆ £C   Rías Baixas Lolo ★★ £B

Bodegas Tapias Mariñan
Recommended Whites: Monterrei Pazo de Mariñan ★★☆ £B

Bodega Tabú
Recommended Whites: Monterrei Stibadía ★★☆ £B

Terra de Asorei
Recommended Whites: Rías Baixas Nai e Señora ★★★ £D
Rías Baixas Terra de Asorei ★★☆ £B

Terra do Castello
Recommended Whites:
Ribeiro Selección (Treixadura) ★★☆ £C
Ribeiro Treixadura (Treixadura) ★★ £B

Tomada de Castro
Recommended Whites:
Rías Baixas (Albariño) ★★★ £C

Alan de Val
Recommended Reds:
Valdeorras Pedrazas Mencia (Mencia) ★★☆ £C
Valdeorras Alan de Val Mencia (Mencia) ★★ £C
Recommended Whites:
Valdeorras Alan de Val Godello ★★ £C

Valdamor
Recommended Whites:
Rías Baixas Valdamor Barrica (Albariño) ★★★☆ £D
Rías Baixas Valdamor (Albariño) ★★★ £C

Adegas Valdavia
Recommended Reds:
Ribeiro Cuñas Davia (Brancellao, Caíño Tinto, Mencía, Sousón)
★★☆ £C
Recommended Whites:
Ribeiro Cuñas Davia Barrica (Treixadura, Albariño) ★★★ £C
Ribeiro Cuñas Davia (Treixadura, Godello, Lado, Albariño) ★★☆ £C

Adega Valdés
Recommended Whites:
Rías Baixas Gundian (Albariño) ★★★ £C
Rías Baixas Pazo Viladomar (Treixadura, Albariño) ★★☆ £C

Adegas Valtea
Recommended Whites:
Rías Baixas Valtea (Albariño) ★★★ £C

Via Romana
Recommended Reds:
Ribeira Sacra Barrica (Mencia) ★★★ £C
Ribeira Sacra (Mencia) ★★ £B

Work in progress!!

Producers under consideration for the next edition
Bodegas Adria (Bierzo)
Bodegas Albamar (Rías Baixas)
Adega Algueira (Ribeira Sacra)
Allegro Con Spirito (Toro)
Viña Blanca del Salnés (Rías Baixas)
Bodegas de Blas Serrano (Ribera del Duero)
Bodegas Convento de Las Claras (Ribera del Duero)
Bodegas Lopez Cristobal (Ribera del Duero)
Bodegas Divina (Toro)
Bodegas El Paraguas (Ribeiro)
Forjas del Salnés (Rías Baixas)
Bodegas Garcia de Aranda (Ribera del Duero)
Goyo Garcia Viadero (Ribera del Duero)
Bodegas Gormaz (Ribera del Duero)
Antonino Izquierdo (Ribera del Duero)
Bodegas La Milagrosa (Ribera del Duero)
Bodegas La Setera (Arribes del Duero)
Bodega Matsu (Toro)
Mengoba (Bierzo)
Bodegas Nanclares (Rías Baixas)
Veronica Ortega (Bierzo)

Pagos de Matanegra (Ribera del Duero)
Adega da Pinguela (Valdeorras)
Adega Ponte da Boga (Ribeira Sacra)
Hacienda Solano (Ribera del Duero)
Hacienda Terra d'Uro (Toro)

Author's choice - North-West Spain

20 Exemplary Castilla y León reds

Aalto   Ribera del Duero Aalto PS
Abadía Retuerta   Pago Valdellón Vino de Mesa
Bodegas Alion   Ribera del Duero
Cámbrico   VC Sierra de Salamanca Cámbrico Rufete
Viñas del Cénit   Tierra del Vino de Zamora Cénit VDC
Descendientes de J Palacios   Bierzo La Faraona
Gallego Zapatero   Ribera del Duero Yotuel Finca San Miguel
Hacienda Monasterio   Ribera del Duero Reserva Especial
Leda Vinas Viejas   Viña Leda
Mauro   Mauro Vendimia Seleccionada
Pesquera   Ribera del Duero Gran Reserva Cuvée Janus
Gancedo   Bierzo Seleccion Ucedo
Emilio Moro   Ribera del Duero Malleolus Valderramiro
Pago de Carraovejas   Ribera del Duero Cuesta Las Llebres
Paixar   Bierzo Paixar
Dominio de Pingus   Ribera del Duero Pingus
Quinta Sardonia   VdT Castilla y León Quinta Sardonia
Teso La Monja   Toro Alabaster
Vega Sicilia   Ribera del Duero Unico
Bodegas Vizcarra   Ribera del Duero Inés

A selection of the finest whites from North-West Spain

Agro de Bazán   Rías Baixas Granbazán Ambar
Bodegas Avanthia   Valdeorras Godello
Belondrade   Rueda Belondrade y Lurton BFB
Dominio do Bibei   Ribeira Sacra Lapena
Lagar de Costa   Rías Baixas Maio de Lagar de Costa
Pazos de Lusco   Rías Baixas Pazo Piñeiro
Menade Terruño   Rueda V3 Viñas Viejas
Gerardo Méndez   Rías Baixas Do Ferreiro Cepas Vellas
Bodegas Naia   Rueda Naiades
Viña Nora   Rías Baixas Nora de Neve
Ossian   VdT Castilla y León Ossian Capitel
Palacio de Fefiñanes   Rías Baixas Albarino de Fefiñanes III
Rafael Palacios   Valdeorras AS Sortes
Raúl Pérez   Bierzo Ultreia La Claudina
Quinta da Muradella   Monterrei Gorvia
Emilio Rojo   Ribeiro
Pazo de Señorans   Rías Baixas Selección de Añadas
Terras Gauda   Rías Baixas Le Mar
Bodegas Vidal Soblechero   VdT Castilla y León Finca El Alto
Zárate   Rías Baixas El Palomar

A-Z of producers - Central, Southern Spain & the Islands

Bodegas Almansenas (Almansa)   www.ventalavega.com

This is arguably the benchmark bodega in this small DO in south-eastern Spain with wines produced from mainly Garnacha Tintorera and Monastrell on their home Venta La Vega estate. Whites are also produced here as well. La Huella is a fresh and approacchanle blend of Verdejo, Sauvignon and unusually Monastrell vinified as a white. More serious is the Adaras Blanco a special barrel-fermented selection of Verdejo and Sauvignon Blanc. The altitude of the vineyards at around 850 metres is what gives the wine is vital acidity and structure. The Tintorera strain of the Garnacha, with dark flesh, was for long considered to be only of real benefit in adding colour to blends. When blended with Monastrell though the wines appear to have real potential. Four reds are produced. Calizo is a young wine which has a relatively short vatting and should be enjoyed for its young, vibrant fruit. La Huella de Adaras is a blend of the estates two main varieties as well as a little Syrah. It is a soft and juicy fruited wine which gets a touch of depth and structure from ageing in stainless steel vats on lees for 12 months. Venta La Vega Old Vines is solely Garnacha Tintorella and Monastrell. It is a sturdier and firmer red, gaining character from a mix of ageing in both oak and cement vats. The top wine Adaras is solely Garnacha Tintorera and sourced from the best old vine plots. It offers impressive grip and a supple ripe structured with dark and spicy berry fruit as well as impressive fruit intensity. It is aged for around 14 months in French oak and will drink well at three or four years of age.(DM)

Recommended Reds:
Almansa Adaras ★★★☆ £D
Almansa Venta La Vega Old Vines★★★ £C
Almansa La Huella de Adaras ★★☆ £B
Almansa Calizo de Adaras★★ £B

Recommended Whites:
Almansa Adaras ★★★ £C   Almansa La Huella de Adaras ★★ £B

Alto Landon (Manchuela)   www.altolandon.com

Along with Finca SANDOVAL and PONCE this is one of the benchmarks for this small DO to the west of La Mancha. There are a total of 60 ha under vine and the vineyards benefit considerably from their altitude of over 1,000 metres. A considerable array of red varieties is planted, among whites as well as Chardonnay, there is also a little Petit Manseng and Moscatel Petit-Grain. Particularly characterful among the reds is an impressive varietal Malbec. Rich, ripe and full of dark berry fruit and underlying tobacco, the wine is aged for 14 months in French barrels. The Alto Landon red is in a very ripe style, ageing is in a mix of French and American oak and the wine blends 50% of Syrah with the balance comprising Cabernet Franc and Garnacha. Rayuelo is dark and spicy coming from Bobal, Malbec and Monastrell. A fourth red CF de Alto Landon (Cabernet Franc) is also made. The Alto Landon White is a blend of Chardonnay and Petit Manseng one of the better examples from southern Spain. It is barrel-fermented and then aged for just six months in the same barriques to take up sufficient oak to add a dimension to the ripe citrus and tropical character of the wine's fruit. (DM)

Recommended Reds:
Manchuela L'Ame Malbec ★★★☆ £E
Manchuela Alto Landon Red ★★★ £D
Manchuela Rayuelo ★★★☆ £D

Recommended Whites:
Manchuela Alto Landon White ★★★ £D

Alvarez Nölting (Valencia)   www.alvareznolting.com

This bodega, founded in 2002, had to take the Viño de Mesa Valencia classification for its first few releases. Sourced from a vineyard that now covers 22 ha, the Alvarez Nölting red is a rich, full, spicy and dark fruited blend. The wine is aged for around 12 months in both French and American oak and gets another 12 months ageing in bottle before release. Expect it to gain further depth with an additional three to four years in the cellar. A number of other wines have now been added to a small expanding range.

Central, Southern Spain & the Islands

Spain

There are a couple of Chardonnay's, one with short three month oak ageing, while the other reds also number a Syrah, El Gran Loco and Finca Alvarez both from Bobal as well as a natural *dulce* style, which is vinified from Monastrell. (DM)

Recommended Reds:
Valencia Alvarez Nölting ★★★☆ £E

Alvear (Montilla-Moriles) www.alvear.es
This is one of the great names of Montilla-Moriles, founded in 1729 and still run by the Alvear family. A small but outstanding range is produced. As well as their wines here, the firm also owns PALACIO QUEMADO in Ribera del Guadiana, producing an interesting and characterful range. In Montilla-Moriles the Pedro Ximénez (PX) variety dominates the wines. Among the keys to quality is the *terroir* of the vineyards which have a marked *albariza* component, namely soils high in limestone. The fruit is late ripening and natural *flor* yeasts are successfully produced to aid the wines classic style. The Fino en Rama comes from a single vintage, the citrusy, nutty character evolving from 30 months in oak under *flor*. The Fino CB differs, coming from *solera* and is similarly kept in American oak. Best of the Finos is the Capataz, with a subtle and intense nutty complexity. It spends on average over five years in *solera*. Impressive and characterful Amontillado is produced. The rich, nutty and concentrated Amontillado Carlos VII has a slight tang of saltiness due to its Fino origins. Ageing is for around six years and again 500 litre American oak is used. The wine has a touch of residual sugar. An Oloroso Fundación is also made. Rich, sweet Pedro Ximénez labels are also important. There is an excellent Cosecha vintage wine which comes from sun dried fruit, full of baked figs and underlying nutty, toasty tones with a proportion of the ageing in new small oak. The Pedro Ximénez Solera comes from an original date of 1927. It is full of complex dried fruit character. Both wines have over 400 g/ltr residual sugar. They can either be sipped or poured over top quality ice cream. An exceptional old Reserva is also made from an 1830 Solera as well as a very old Amontillado Solera Fundación. (DM)

Recommended Whites:
Montilla-Moriles Alvear PX Solera 1927 ★★★★☆ £E
Montilla-Moriles Amontillado Carlos VII ★★★☆ £C
Montilla-Moriles Pedro Ximénez de Añada ★★★ £C
Montilla-Moriles Fino en Rama de Añada ★★☆ £B
Montilla-Moriles Fino Capataz ★★☆ £B
Montilla-Moriles Fino CB ★★ £B

✿ Anima Negra (VdT Mallorca) www.annegra.com
One of Mallorca's outstanding wineries and the first to put the wines from this island on the international map. The local Callet for the reds and the Prensal among the whites are the two key varieties here. The first harvest was in 1994 and Cabernet Sauvignon was the dominant variety. The winery has consistently moved towards championing native varieties. There are currently 14 ha of owned vineyards and some fruit is also bought in. The An 2 is the softest and most accessible of the reds with spicy, minty fruit, the blend dominated by Callet with a little local Manto Negro and Fogoneu along with some Syrah. The temperature during fermentation is kept under control at around 28 C and the wine is then aged for a year in a mix of mainly French and some American oak after the malolactic in tank. The An bottling is firmer, more structured, with spicy dark fruit and subtle hints of licorice and minerals. It blends mainly old Callet, from vines up to 60 years old and is traditionally vinified and aged in French oak for up to 18

months. One white is made from mainly Prensal and a little Muscat, Quibia. There is also a small amount of a limited production red, Son Negre, which is a good deal pricier than the An. (DM)

Recommended Reds:
VdT Mallorca An ★★★★ £E   VdT Mallorca An 2 ★★★ £D

Bodegas Anfora Enix (VdT Ribera del Andarax) www.vegaenix.com
This bodega is to be found in the far east of Andalucia and is a source of some very ripe, opulent sun kissed reds. The vineyard site, at an altitude of 750 metres was decided on in 1995 and 13 ha were planted. Yields are kept deliberately restricted because of the vine's youth and the resulting wines are certainly impressively concentrated. A small range of wines are made, now numbering 10 different labels. The dark plum and cherry, almost raisin scented Xolair is solely Merlot. It is traditionally vinified and aged in French oak for 12 months. The Aristeo is perhaps better balanced, a combination of Cabernet Sauvignon, Syrah and Merlot, it offers a complex array of ripe dark black fruits with an underlying spicy, tobacco character. With malolactic in barrel and ageing for 14 months in French oak this is both sumptuous and richly textured. The red the Laurenti, which is solely Cabernet Sauvignon, is vinified in a similar fashion and while the wine offers real weight and concentration it lacks some of the balance and poise of the Aristeo. These are approachable styles and will drink well at three or four years. (DM)

Recommended Reds:
VdT Ribera del Andarax Laurenti ★★★☆ £E
VdT Ribera del Andarax Aristeo ★★★ £D
VdT Ribera del Andarax Xolair ★★★ £D

Arrayan (Mentrida) www.arrayan.es
Emerging as one of the best new producers in this DO to the south-west of Madrid and bordering Toledo, Arrayán was established in 1999 with 26 ha planted at their Finca La Verdosa property. The continental climate and an altitude of 470 to 510 metres above sea-level provides a benevolent environment for cultivating the French varietals Cabernet Sauvignon, Syrah, Petit Verdot and Merlot. Two of the varietals are produced independently and there is a blended red, labelled Premium, which is one of the bodega's top two wines. All see around 12 to 15 months in solely French Allier barrels. The sunny summers are evident in the wines which regularly attain alcohol levels of around 14% but remain elegant and finely balanced. Syrah and Petit Verdot seem to have proved more successful than the other two Bordeaux varietals as single varietal wines in recent vintages. Petit Verdot is impressively deep, spicy and concentrated while the Syrah is full, rich and chocolatey with just a hint of black pepper. The Premium offers not only depth and concentration but has a balance and elegance that the varietals just struggle to equal. All will benefit from four or five years cellaring. A fresh rosado and an approachable red blend Selección are also made as well as a second quite pricey premium red blend Estela de Arrayán. To this has been added a further range of three approachable reds under the La Verdosa label. (DM)

Recommended Reds:
Mentrida Premium ★★★★ £E   Mentrida Syrah ★★★☆ £E
Mentrida Petit Verdot ★★★☆ £E

Bodegas Atalaya (Almansa) www.bodegasatalaya.es
This small bodega was recently established in 2007. The Gil Family group has interests in a wide range of DOs and among other key

names are Bodegas EL NIDO in Jumilla and Cellers CAN BLAU in Montsant. Three wines are currently produced and the vineyards are planted in limestone soils and at an altitude of 700 to 1,000 metres above sea level. There are both continental and Mediterranean influences on the local climate. The Atalaya del Camino red is blended from Monastrell as well as the local Garnacha Tintorera. This variety has long been regarded as little more than blending material to add colour to wines because of its red flesh. Here, as at ALMANSENAS, the potential that can be obtained from the grape is clearly being realised. Vinification is modern and under Australian direction and the wine is aged for around 12 months in French oak before bottling. Full of vibrant raspberry fruit, enjoy it within two or three years of the vintage. A fruit driven entry level wine, Laya is aged for a short time in word, around 4 months and a small volume of a more expensive premium red Alaya Tierra is also made and which is solely old vine Garnacha Tintorera aged for 15 months in mainly French barrels as well as a small proportion of American oak to compliment the variety. (DM)

Recommended Reds:
Almansa Alaya Tierra ★★★☆ £D
Almansa La Atalaya del Camino ★★★ £C
Almansa Laya ★★☆ £B

Bodega Balcona (Bullas) *www.partal-vinos.com*
The Fernández family made their first vintage as recently as 1998, having been inspired by José Luis Pérez Verdú of MAS MARTINET in Priorat. They have been grape growers for generations and as such have a tremendous resource in extensive plantings of old-vine Monastrell, many plots now over 50 years of age. The climate here is benign with warm summer days contrasting with cool nights as a result of the altitude of the vineyards (around 825m). The soils are a combination of clay and limestone, which provides an excellent base for high quality vine growth. Investment has been extensive in the winery with stainless steel tanks, temperature control and French and American oak for maturation. Three wines are currently being produced. The 37 Barricas is mainly Monastrell and is the simplest of the wines. The Partal, also dominated by Monastrell, is vibrant and intense with piercing dark, spicy berry fruit and supple, well-rounded tannins. There is also an additional third blend Casa de la Cruz comprising Syrah, Cabernet Sauvignon, Merlot and a little Monastrell. (DM)

Recommended Reds:
Bullas Partal ★★★ £C   Bullas 37 Barricas ★★☆ £C

Barbadillo (Jerez y Manzanilla) *www.barbadillo.com*
Barbadillo is based in Sanlúcar de Barrameda and the key focus is the production of good and often exceptional Manzanilla. The key volume brand is Solear and there is an unfiltered En Rama, which is very intense with a real salty, yeasty depth and a piercing background citrus character. There are also a number of other excellent, classic examples including the rich, powerful and heady Cuco Oloroso, nutty Principe Amontillado, citrussy and spicy Obispo Gascón Palo Cortado and unctuous La Cilla Pedro Ximénez. A number of remarkable old wines from venerable soleras are available and labelled VORS, including Amontillado, Oloroso Seco and Palo Cortado. Rich and concentrated Pedro Ximénez, Palo Cortado, Amontillado and Oloroso Reliquia are also made. These wines are understandably very pricey but are surely at the pinnacle of great sherries. Barbadillo also own Vega Real in Ribera del Duero and PIRINEOS in Somontano. (DM)

Recommended Whites:
Jerez y Manzanilla Obispo Gascón Palo Cortado ★★★☆ £E
Jerez y Manzanilla Cuco Oloroso Seco ★★★☆ £E
Jerez y Manzanilla Principe Amontillado ★★★☆ £E
Jerez y Manzanilla En Rama Solear Manzanilla ★★★☆ £D
Jerez y Manzanilla La Cilla Pedro Ximénez ★★☆ £C
Jerez y Manzanilla Solear Manzanilla ★★ £B
Jerez y Manzanilla Eva Cream ★★ £B

Barranco Oscuro (VdM Andalucia) *www.barrancooscuro.com*
The origins of this bodega in the high mountains of Granada are not new, they date back to 1872. The quality of the wines being produced now is strikingly impressive. The 1368 red is so called because it comes from Spain's highest cultivated vineyards. All of the bodegas 15 ha is farmed as naturally as possible and no chemicals or fertilizers are employed. The stony soils and high summer temperature variations provide wines of striking, nervy acidity and real intensity. The very well priced Blancas Nobles is a multi-varietal blend. Fine lifted grassy, citrus fruit is supported by nervy minerality. The Tempranillo y Mas red offers great value with spicy, smoky fruit, a blend aged in French and American oak. The Borgoñón Granate is earthy, ripe and dark fruited with a marked underlying acid grip. The top two wines though are the 1368 and the newly added Rubaiyat. Both are likely to age very well for up to a decade.

Recommended Reds:
VdM Andalucía 1368 Pago Cerro Las Monjas ★★★☆ £E
VdM Andalucía Rubaiyat ★★★☆ £E
VdM Andalucía Borgoñón Granate ★★☆ £C
VdM Andalucía Tempranillo y Mas ★★☆ £C
Recommended Whites:
VdM Andalucía Blancas Nobles Clasico ★★ £B

Ricardo Benito (Vinos de Madrid) *www.ricardobenito.com*
One of the most important bodegas in the Vinos de Madrid region, Ricardo Benito, founded in 1940, is located in the heart of Madrid's Nalcarnero sub region, just to the south-west of the capital. The sand and clay soils here provide some exceptional old-vine Tempranillo from microscopic yields which is used in the production of one of Spains greatest reds, Divo. Vinification is modern with ageing in new French oak and malolactic in barrel. This sumptuously rich and complex red with its velvety tannins is bottled unfined and unfiltered and has a price tag to match its reputation. A second label, Dividivo is also now made which blends Tempranillo with Merlot, Syrah, Garnacha and Cabernet Sauvignon. The rest of the range is, by contrast, extremely well-priced and offers great value. The Castizo labelled wines are soft, fruity and immediately approachable, while the Tapon de Oro label offers just a touch more depth and concentration. The Señorio de Medina Sidonia is a traditional reserva style from 100% Tempranillo with secondary flavours developing from ageing for 12 months in a mix of both American and French oak and then a further three years in bottle. The Duán is altogether more modern in style, a blend of Tempranillo, with lesser proportions of Merlot, Cabernet Sauvignon and Garnacha, it is aged for around 8 months with malolactic in barrel and then bottled unfined for an early release. The second wine in the range after Divo, Asido is a blend of Tempranillo, Merlot and just around 10% of Cabernet Sauvignon. Ageing is in French oak for 14 months and 80% is new. Again unfined the wine offers very good quality and value. (DM)

Recommended Reds:
Vinos de Madrid Divo ★★★★★ £H

Wine behind the label

Central, Southern Spain & the Islands

Vinos de Madrid Asido ★★★ £C   Vinos de Madrid Duan ★★★ £C
Vinos de Madrid Señorío de Medina Sidonia Reserva ★★☆ £C
Vinos de Madrid Tapon de Oro Crianza ★☆ £C
Vinos de Madrid Castizo ★ £B
Recommended Whites:
Vinos de Madrid Tapon de Oro ★ £B

⚫ **Bernabeleva (Vinos de Madrid)** *www.bernabeleva.com*
New as well as very promising small bodega producing great, well-priced reds and impressive whites in the western San Martin sub-zone of the Vinos de Madrid DO to the south-west of the Capital. Garnacha is the dominant variety and it is now well accepted that some of the region's finest reds are likely to emerge from old-vine plantings of the variety here in the future. Bernabeleva itself has a long history. The property was purchased in 1923 when the original vineyards were established. Modern winemaking and viticulture is far more recent. The vineyards are now farmed biodynamically and have been certified as such since 2009. Five wines are currently made. The red Navaherreros and Cantocuerdas white are, if you like, the generics although this by no means does them justice. All the reds come from varietal Garnacha, Of the whites, Cantocuerdas comes from the potentially characterful Albillo. It is fermented in large oak *foudres* and has a southern style weight and oily richness but a nutty, fresh, apple-scented character as well. Navaherreros is a blend of Albillo and Macabeo. It is a touch more fruit driven and is barrel fermented in 500 litre oak. The top three reds are very good indeed and a clear level up from the Navaherreros. All four get a short cool soak and are then vinified with a proportion of whole bunches to add both structure and complexity. The reds will all benefit from 4 or 5 years cellaring. A Cantocuerdas Moscatel is also produced. (DM)
Recommended Reds:
Vinos de Madrid Viña Bonita ★★★★ £E
Vinos de Madrid Carril del Rey ★★★★ £E
Vinos de Madrid Arroyo de Tórtolas ★★★★ £E
Vinos de Madrid Navaherreros ★★★☆ £D
Recommended Whites:
Vinos de Madrid Cantocuerdas ★★★☆ £D
Vinos de Madrid Navaherreros ★★★☆ £D

⚫ **Bernabe Navarro (Alicante)** *www.bodegasbernabenavarro.com*
This is now one of Central and South Eastern Spain's finest sources of Monastrell based reds with vines of 40 to 50 years of age, although the bodega itself was only founded in 2000. Coming from 40 ha of family owned vineyards planted at 600 metres above sea level, the wines are all stylish, refined and very well crafted. French, rather than American oak is used in the cellar and each variety is vinified separately. The Beryna blends Monastrell with a mix of Tempranillo, Cabernet Sauvignon, Syrah and Merlot offering complex dark berry fruit and herbal spices. The Casa Balaguer is a more international rounded style with a similar blend but just 50% of Monastrell. The top red, the denser and fuller Beryna Selección is again 50% Monastrell with 40% Tempranillo and just 10% Cabernet Sauvignon adding some firm tannin. The wine sees 50% new oak for 18 to 20 months and demands at least five or six years ageing. The other two reds can be approached a year or two earlier. An additional premium label Curro which blends Monastrell and Tempranillo has also been added. (DM)
Recommended Reds:
Alicante Beryna Selección ★★★★☆ £E
Alicante Casa Balaguer ★★★★ £E

Alicante Beryna ★★★★ £D

⚫ **Dominio Buenavista** *www.dominiobuenavista.com*
This is one of the key producers from the VdT region of Cumbres de Guadalfeo, formerly Contraviesa-Alpujarra. The bodega is recently established and helps makes the case for the potential quality of high altitude Granada vineyards. As well as the wines rated here you would be well advised to look for the winery's other wines including Chardonnay and red late harvested Don Miguel and the Tempranillo dominated well priced Sierra Sol (£B). The indigenous Vijiriega Veleta white is a wine of real character, arguably the most interesting in the range. The subtle citrus and honeyed fruit underpinned by a wonderful nervy acidity. Cabernet Sauvignon too works well in the high altitude vineyards. Rich, dark berry fruit is supported by classic cassis and an unusual black pepper element. The Tempranillo, aged like the Cabernet for one year in American oak offers just a touch less depth and concentration but impresses nonetheless. These nervy wines are well worth trying.
Recommended Reds:
VdT Cumbres de Guadalfeo Nolados ★★★ £D
VdT Cumbres de Guadalfeo Cabernet Sauvignon ★★☆ £C
VdT Cumbres de Guadalfeo Tempranillo ★★☆ £C
Recommended Whites:
VdT Cumbres de Guadalfeo Vijiarega ★★☆ £C
Recommended Rosés:
VdT Cumbres de Guadalfeo Tempranillo Rosado ★★ £B
Cava Rosado ★★ £B

⚫ **Rafael Cambra (Valencia)** *www.rafaelcambra.es*
Wine quality generally in the DOs of the south-east of Spain is moving from strength to strength and none more so than at this excellent bodega only founded in 2001. Rafa Cambra is able to draw on 25 ha for his own four reds but is also responsible for the viticulture and vinification of his family's own very well made fruit driven wines at Bodega EL ANGOSTO. He has just added a soft easy drinking style, Bon Homme which is is marketed with three different label designs. It is a 50/50 Cabernet Sauvignon and Monastrell. His Dos bottling is a striking Saint-Emilion lookalike blend of Cabernet Sauvignon and Cabernet Franc in almost equal proportions and just a small amount of Monastrell. The wine unquestionably has a touch of the aroma of CHEVAL BLANC about it. There is though a vibrant ripe black fruit character that you wouldn't find in Bordeaux. Ageing is for 10 months in oak so as not to overwhelm the fruit. Uno is a 100 % Monastrell of great depth, complexity and intensity. 14 months in small oak is easily absorbed, with a marked meaty, savoury quality underpinning the dark, spicy fruit in much the same way as the very best Bandols. The top wine is the newly added, rich and sumptuous Minimum, a blend of Monastrell from the highest and lowest yielding part of the vineyard and around a third of Cabernet Franc. Expect all the wines to offer more with five to six years ageing. (DM)
Recommended Reds:
Valencia Minimum ★★★★☆ £E   Valencia Uno ★★★★☆ £E
Valencia Dos ★★★★ £D   Valencia Bon Homme ★★☆ £C

⚫ **Canopy (Méntrida)** *www.bodegascanopy.com*
Four low volume and very good quality wines emerge from this small operation. Just over 3,000 cases are produced a year from what are distinctly Rhône style reds and very good ones they are too. Both Garnacha and Syrah are cultivated, the former cordon trained and grown on sandy soils, the latter traditionally head-trained and from siliceous granite soil. The vineyards are planted

574

Wine behind the label

Central, Southern Spain & the Islands

Spain

at an altitude of around 750 metres and this helps to promote natural acidity and preserve primary flavours and aromas in the wines with cool summer nights. Sustainable viticulture is practiced and intervention is kept to an absolute minimum. The rich, dark berry fruited Tres Patas has a real old-vine complexity. It is a blend of mostly Garnacha and the balance Syrah. The varieties are vinified separately and after a couple of weeks vatting the malolactic then takes place in barrel. Neither the oak nor the rich character of the malolactic are allowed to take over the wine. Although 50% new oak is used, this is only for eight months and in larger 500 litre barrels. A very similar regime is maintained with the peppery, licorice and spice scented Malpaso, a 100% Syrah and not dissimilar to a top level Cornas. La Viña Escondida comes from older Garnacha vines, around 65 years old. It is aged and the malolactic fermentation carried out in 2,000 litre *foudres*. The fourth red, Congo is only available in tiny quantities, less than 100 cases a year. It is again from old Garnacha planted in the southern hills of the Sierra de Gredos. (DM)

Recommended Reds:
Méntrida La Viña Escondida ★★★★☆ £F
Méntrida Malpaso ★★★★ £E   Méntrida Tres Patas ★★★☆ £D

🔹 **Cap de Barbaria (VdT Formentera)** *www.capdebarbaria.com*
This is another first class producer from the Balearics and two reds are produced here in a quiet spot on the island of Formentera. As well as the winery and vineyard the property also boasts a small luxury hotel. The Cap de Barbaria red is produced from a mixed blend of Cabernet Sauvignon, Merlot, Monastrell and the local Fogoneu. There are two small plots totalling just one and a half hectares and includes 40 to 50 year old Monastrell and Fogoneu with the larger plot planted at a high density to the Cabernet and Merlot. All four varieties are both harvested and vinified separately and the fermentation is relatively cool at 26 to 28 degrees celsius to enhance the wines fruit intensity. Added richness is achieved with malolactic in barrel but the resulting wine offers a fine balance of rich fruit and subtle integrated oak. Expect the wine to drink well at a young age but also develop well for a decade and more. A second label Ophiusa is also now made from the same varieties. (DM)

Recommended Reds:
VdT Formentera Cap de Barbaria ★★★★ £E

>> **Bodega Carabal (Ribera del Guadiana)** *www.carabal.es*
This is one of the small stand out producers from the DO. The vineyards are located in the foothills just to the west of the Toledo Mountains. Owner Antonio Ferré Banús purchased the property in 1989 and the bodega has been developed on a small scale since then. 52 ha of vines are planted in clay and quartz soils, including Syrah, Cabernet Sauvignon, Tempranillo and Graciano and these are divided up into 35 different plots. The most recent vines are trellis trained and harvested mechanically. Primary fermentation is straightforward in stainless steel with the malolactic following. The Rasgo roble style is dominated by Syrah and is full of ripe and dark, spicy vibrant cherry fruit. It gets a short five months in mainly French and some American oak. The top label Carabal Gulae is more complex, balancing dark cherry and other black fruits with toasty, vanilla oak. Barrel ageing is for 10 months and again mainly Frenck oak is employed. A third red Carabal Gulae sits in the middle and combines all four varieties.

Recommended Reds:
Ribera del Guadiana Carabal Gulae ★★★☆ £D
Ribera del Guadiana Rasgo ★★☆ £B

🔹 **Casa Castillo (Jumilla)** *www.casacastillo.es*
Casa Castillo is among the rising stars from Spain's southern regions. Despite the hot, arid climate of the area the vineyards here are planted at an altitude of over 700m and this elevation and the limestone soils provide old bush-vine Monastrell (Mourvèdre) of exceptional quality. The Monastrell is full of vibrant juicy fruit and approachable young. The dark, spicy Valtosca is the odd man out in the range with no Monastrell just Syrah. Las Gravas has a small proportion of Garnacha and Syrah in a blend providing dark, brambly old-vine fruit. It is aged in French oak and like all three top wines malolactic is in barrel. Pie Franco is 100% Monastrell from ungrafted vines that are over 65 years old. Rich, dense and spicy, the wine is aged for 22 months in French oak. So far these all offer very good value. (DM)

Recommended Reds:
Jumilla Pie Franco ★★★★ £E   Jumilla Las Gravas ★★★☆ £D
Jumilla Valtosca ★★★☆ £C   Jumilla Monastrell ★★☆ £B

🔹 **Bodegas Castaño (Yecla & others)** *www.bodegascastano.com*
The dynamic Castaño family make an extensive range based mainly on old vine Monastrell from this south-western region. The basic reds, white and rosé are labelled Dominio Espinal. The two reds are the best bets among these clean, well-made, fruit-driven wines; the Dominio Espinal Seleccion has a little extra depth and a soft, round structure. Monastrell clearly stands out among the varietal wines and is given 25% carbonic maceration and is a vibrant, spicy red which sees no oak. The Hecula bottling by contrast gets 12 months in a mix of French and American oak, some new. It comes from unirrigated old vines and has impressive dark berry varietal character. A partially barrel-fermented Macabeo/Chardonnay offers some light tropical fruit, while the Rosado Monastrell is bright, spicy and strawberry fruited. The Pozuelo-labelled reds are more traditional in style with less upfront fruit. The Crianza is aged for 10 months in American oak, the Reserva for 20 months. The impressive Colección is an 80/20 blend of Monastrell and Cabernet Sauvignon aged for up to14 months in a mix of French and American oak. Dark berry fruit is nicely underpinned by characterful notes of black pepper. The Monastrell Dulce is a late-harvest fortified red with considerable residual sugar and a rich, slight raisiny character. A further red GSM (Garnacha, Syrah, Monastrell) is also now made as well as the premium Casa de la Cera, a blend of 50% Monastrell and 50% of Garnacha Tintorera, Cabernet Sauvignon, Syrah and Merlot. The second premium red, the dense, concentrated and characterful Casa Cisca, is 100% old Monastrell from high-altitude vineyards planted on limestone soils. A recent project is Altos del Cuadrado in Jumilla, a source of an attractive approachable red, and the more serious Triple V from dry-farmed Monastrell and a little Petit Verdot. There are two further small joint ventures. Viña al Lado de la Casa, in association with Barcelona wine mechant Vila Viniteca, produces a fine modern, spicy dark-fruited Yecla of the same name which is mainly Monastrell and Detrás de la Casa from which there is a Syrah and a blend of Cabernet and Garnacha Tinto. There is also a partnership with American importer Eric Solomon providing a spicy and approachable red, Solanera. (DM)

Bodegas Castaño
Recommended Reds:
Yecla Casa Cisca ★★★★ £E   Yecla Dulce Monastrell ★★★☆ £D
Yecla Colección ★★★☆ £C   Yecla Solanera ★★★ £C
Yecla Hecula Monastrell ★★☆ £C
Yecla Castaño Red Monastrell ★★ £B
Yecla Dominio Espinal Selección ★★ £B

Central, Southern Spain & the Islands

Yecla Pozuelo Reserva ★★ £C Yecla Pozuelo Crianza ★☆ £B
Recommended Whites:
Yecla Castaño Macabeo Chardonnay ★★ £B
Recommended Rosés:
Yecla Castaño Rosé Monastrell ★☆ £B
Altos del Cuadrado
Recommended Reds:
Jumilla Triple V ★★★ £D Jumilla Altos del Cuadrado ★★☆ £C
Viña al Lado de la Casa - Uvas Felices
Recommended Reds:
Yecla Viña al Lado de la Casa Monastrell ★★★☆ £E
Yecla Detrás de la Casa Cab Sauv /Garnacha Tintorera ★★★☆ £E
Yecla Detrás de la Casa Syrah ★★★☆ £E

>> Cerro del Águila (VdT Castilla)

This new project is partnership of five friends led by sommelier
Alvaro Parilla and is a further example of the potential of great old
vine Garnacha based wines in west central Spain. Based in the
Toledos Mountains, Cerro del Aguila have 10 old plots of Garnacha
totaling 5.2 ha which they are in the course of properly recovering.
The vines were planted between 1964 and 1989 and the extreme
continental climate allied to altitudes of 770 to 1,000 metres gives
tremendous potential in the wines. In the winery individual lots
are vinified separately and as yet total output is less than 5,000
bottles annually. Vinification begins with a cold soak, followed by
spontaneous fermentation and the malolactic occurs naturally in
barrel and new wood is avoided to preserve the character of the
fruit. In this they are very successful. The dense and concentrated
Puerto Carbonero combines a little Syrah with old Garnacha. The
equally impressive Vereda del Lobo is solely Garnacha, full of intense
herb scented dark berry fruits. The Malabra is just a touch more
approachable. (DM)
Recommended Reds:
Vino de Mesa Puerto Carbonero (Garnacha, Syrah) ★★★★ £E
Vino de Mesa Vereda del Lobo (Garnacha) ★★★★ £E
Vino de Mesa Malabra (Garnacha) ★★★☆ £C

>> Cien y Pico (Manchuela) *www.cienypico.com*

This is a small recently developed partnership, which focuses on
some good reds made largely from the once unheralded Garnacha
Tintorera grape. The name of the bodega means "one hundred and
something" and is a specific reference to the very old Garnacha
Tintorera and Bobal vines planted here. Although the climate is
very hot during the summer growing season, the vines are deep
rooted, naturally very low yielding because of their age, and the
altitude of close to 1,000 metres provides moderation and balanced
acidity in the fruit. The Doble Pasta is a touch more approachable.
Full of dark and spicy ripe berry fruits and a hint of cocoa the wine is
fermented and macerated in small vats for a moderate time, around
10 days and a fifth aged in French oak for 19 months. The Knights
Errant, referring both to the fictional Don Quixote as well as to the
winemakers themselves, who come from different corners of the
globe, is a fruit selection from the best parcels. A similar vinification
regime ensures the vibrancy and character of the Garnacha
Tintorera but more structure is lent to the wine with 85% being
aged in new French oak. Two additional wines have been added to
the range; En Vaso from Bobal (£D) and `Winemaker`s-Gallant` also
from Bobal (£E).
Recommended Reds:
Manchuela Knights Errant ★★★☆ £D
Manchuela Doble Pasta ★★★ £C

✹ Comando G (Vinos de Madrid)

This is a fabulous and unusual project, named after the young
winemaker partners comic strip heroes of their childhood and a
welcome diversion from the many over pious fine wine projects
around the globe. The aim is very serious though, to make some
of Spain's greatest Garnacha reds from a small and auspicious
holding planted at 1,000 metres in the far west of the appellation.
It is a partnership between Daniel Jiménez-Landi of Dani LANDI in
Méntrida and Fernando Garcia Alonso at Bodegas MARAÑONES.
Based in Vinos de Madrid, Comando G also has a joint venture
making reds in partnership with Barcelona wine merchant Vila
Viniteca under the Uvas Felices banner. The Vinos de Madrid red
Las Umbrías has all the hallmarks of true greatness, possessing
extraordinary depth and exceptional intensity of flavour along with
mineral purity. The team also now make a further red, Rumbo Al
Norte which it seems has similar potential as does Tumba del Rey
Moro. There is also a further red, La Bruja Averia which is very well
priced. A white, El Tamboril is made from Garnacha Blanca and
Garnacha Gris. Organic viticulture, minimal handling and an absence
of filtration are inevitable. The wines as yet are only available in very
small quantities but do seek them out. (DM)
Commando G
Recommended Reds:
Vinos de Madrid Comando G Las Umbrías ★★★★★ £F
Vinos de Madrid Comando G La Bruja Averia ★★★☆ £C
Commando G - Uvas Felices
Recommended Reds:
Vinos de Madrid Comando G La Mujer Cañón ★★★★☆ £E
Vinos de Madrid Comando G El Hombre Bala ★★★★ £D

>> Cortijo Los Aguilares *www.cortijolosaguilares.com*

This 200 ha Sierras de Málaga estate was purchased in 1990 by José
Antonio Itarte and his wife Victoria. As well as vines, olive trees are
grown and free range pigs farmed. The first vines were established
in 2000 with Pinot Noir, Cabernet Sauvignon, Merlot and Petit Verdot
all being planted and farmed organically. Part of the original farm
property has been converted into a winery and storage facility
with thermo-regulated stainless steel tanks and temperature and
humidity control in the barrel cellar. Young and aged styles are
both made. The best wines are the top label reds. Very impressive
is the Tadeo, like other examples from the appellation proving that
Petit Verdot works very well here. The Tempranillo and Bordeaux
style blend Pago El Espino doesn't quite have the same depth and
concentration but is full of rich, spicy black fruit and a hint of toasty
oak. Both wines spend 16 to 17 months in tight grained French oak.
A Pinot Noir and a Tinto are also made.
Recommended Reds:
Sierras de Málaga Tadeo de Los Aguilares (Petit Verdot) ★★★★ £E
Sierras de Málaga Pago El Espino (Tempranillo, Merlot, Cabernet
Sauvignon, Petit Verdot) ★★★★ £E
Sierras de Málaga Tinto ★★★ £D

>> Crápula Wines (Jumilla) *www.crapulawines.com*

This is a new name in the Jumilla DO in the south east of Spain
established in 2008. Generally very modern style wines are made
under both the Crápula and NdQ banners. An excellent fruit driven
example, the NdQ 3 Meses is a young Joven style with minimal
oak ageing. It shows the vibrant dark fruit youthful potential of
the Monastrell (blended with a little Syrah) and I preferred it to
the marginally more expensive NdQ Selección which is a more
traditional style spending longer in wood, more classically Spanish

in style. Under the Crápula banner Crápula Gold 5 Meses combines Monastrell with a little Syrah, dark and spicy with a supple texture gaining from five months in both French and American oak. Cármine is a vibrant and approachable style dominated again by Monastrell with vibrant black fruits it gets a little structure from 12 months in a mix of French and more unusually Central European oak. The Crápula red is a mix of Cabernet Sauvignon, Monastrell and Syrah. Ageing is for 12 months in French barrels with rounded berry fruit, it lacks the vibrancy of the Carmine. The top wine is the modern, supple and well-rounded Soul. Richly textured with dark, spicy fruits it combines Cabernet Sauvignon, Monastrell, Petit Verdot and Syrah which are aged in French oak for 15 months. (DM)

Recommended Reds:
Jumilla Crápula Soul (Garnacha, Syrah) ★★★☆ £D
Jumilla Crápula Carmine Crianza ★★★ £C
Jumilla Crápula ★★☆ £C
Jumilla Crápula Gold 5 Meses ★★ £B
Jumilla NdQ Seleccion ★★ £B
Jumilla NdQ Roble ★★☆ £B

Dehesa del Carrizal *www.dehesadelcarrizal.com*
The rules governing the establishment of single appellation properties do not necessarily guarantee quality, however this is certainly not the case here, and a small range of fine wines are produced. The property is in the province of Ciudad Real to the south of Toledo, the hilly northerly aspect of the vineyards and high altitude (800 to 900 metres) all contribute to the elegant style achieved throughout the range. The soils of clay, quartz and gravel provide an excellent growing environment and a range of French grapes is planted as well as Tempranillo. There are now 22 ha under vine. There is a restrained and subtle style of Chardonnay. The oak treatment is minimised with just four months barrel-ageing and one-third new wood. Of the reds, Cabernet Sauvignon is 100% varietal with finely structured tannins and a marked minty component. Syrah sees mainly older wood in the style of the Northern Rhône and is full of spicy, black-peppered fruit and a nicely ripe underlying licoricey character. Similarly impressive and concentrated is the MV, comprising approximately one-third each of Cabernet Sauvignon, Merlot and Syrah. It is the most obviously oaky of the wines, being aged in a mix of 60% French as well as American and East European wood. The top wine, the Colección Privada is from the same blend as the MV and generally with a little less Cabernet. It is more strikingly opulent and offers greater depth and a richer texture. The quality is determined not only by a selection from the best parcels on the property but also by a barrel selection of those parcels. Expect all the reds to continue to improve for a minimum of five years, the Colección Privada for up to a decade. A varietal Petit Vedot is also released. (DM)

Recommended Reds:
Dehesa del Carrizal Colección Privada ★★★★ £E
Dehesa del Carrizal Syrah ★★★☆ £D
Dehesa del Carrizal MV ★★★☆ £D
Dehesa del Carrizal Cabernet Sauvignon ★★★ £D

Recommended Whites:
Dehesa del Carrizal Chardonnay ★★★☆ £D

Alvaro Domecq (Jerez y Manzanilla) *www.alvarodomecq.com*
Good quality small sherry producer, now a part of the Avanteselecta Groups distribution operation. The wines, particularly at the lower levels offer excellent value for money. In addition to the wines rated below the bodega also produce a sound Oloroso, Alburejo, also

very competitively priced as well as a 1730 labelled Palo Cortado and Amontillado Viejo. La Jaca is the lightest of the wines with an attractive citrus intensity and a classic salty undercurrent. La Janda is fuller and a touch more concentrated with nutty, almondy tones, good fresh acidity and an earthy, salty *flor* yeast quality. The Aranda Cream is in marked contrast to many of the commercially available examples of the style. It is sweet and quite unctuous but with a fresh, zesty acidity holding it all together. In addition to the Palo Cortado and Amontillado there are two other top class wines under the premium 1730 label. The Pedro Ximénez is rich, very dark and concentrated with considerable sweetness but a fine citrussy tang giving balance. The average age of the Oloroso 1730 solera is over 30 years and the depth and dry, nutty intensity of the wine is both rich and complex.

Recommended Whites:
Jerez y Manzanilla 1730 Oloros VORS ★★★★☆ £F
Jerez y Manzanilla 1730 Pedro Ximénez ★★★★ £E
Jerez y Manzanilla La Janda Fino ★★☆ £C
Jerez y Manzanilla Aranda Cream ★★☆ £C
Jerez y Manzanilla La Jaca Manzanilla ★★ £B

Dominio de Aranleón (Utiel-Requena) *www.aranleon.com*
Although this bodega has been in existence since 1927 it is in recent vintages that real strides have been made in both wine quality and the inventiveness in which they produce their wines. As well as Utiel-Requena, wines come from Valencia and a Cava, Deshora is also made as well as a number of wines under the Ahora, Aranleón and Encuentro brands. The Blés reds all take the Valencia DO, coming from 120 ha of organically farmed vineyards and a Joven and a Roble are also made. Both the Crianza and characterful, dense Reserva combine Monastrell with Tempranillo. Both wines have the malolactic fermentation carried out in barrel, unusually Hungarian oak being the vessel of choice and the Reserva aged for 12 rather than the six months for the Crianza. The Soló red offers a really characterful dark and spicy fruit intensity. It comes from mainly Bobal as well as a smattering of Tempranillo and Syrah and spends a couple of months on lees in barrel during 12 months ageing. The best wine, the El Arbol de Aranleón is cellared in French oak after the malolactic and the wine is kept on its fine lees for the duration. It is one of the benchmarks of the DO.

Recommended Reds:
Utiel-Requena El Arbol de Aranleón ★★★★ £E
Utiel-Requena Soló ★★★☆ £D   Valencia Blés Reserva ★★★ £C
Valencia Blés Crianza ★★★ £C

El Angosto (Valencia) *www.bodegaelangosto.com*
This is the family bodega of Valencia star winemaker Rafael CAMBRA and he is involved in an advisory capacity. A small range of good to very good reds and whites is made. The Cambra family have had a long established vine nursery business supplying the market for 150 years but the family bodega is much more recent being established in 2004. There are 90 ha of vineyards which are planted on hillside calcareous soils. Of the wines the aromatic and fruit driven El Angosto Blanco is fresh and fragrant and this has been joined by a premium white Viña Los Almendros which combines Sauvignon Blanc with Verdejo. The El Angosto Blanco also includes Muscat and Chardonnay. The reds are classic Mediterranean styles. The El Angosto tinto is dark, spicy and approachable. La Tribu is richer, fuller and a touch more structured. The top wine is the very impressive and well-priced Viña Los Almendros. This dense, dark-fruited red is thoroughly modern in style, it is fermented in barrel

Central, Southern Spain & the Islands

and the malolactic then also takes place in oak with ageing for 14 months in new oak. A further premium red, El Jefe de La Tribu is also now made. (DM)

Recommended Reds:
Valencia Viña Los Almendros ★★★★ £E
Valencia La Tribu ★★★ £C   Valencia El Angosto ★★☆ £B
Recommended Whites:
Valencia El Angosto ★★ £B

❂ **El Maestro Sierra (Jerez y Manzanilla)** *www.maestrosierra.com*
A small bodega which was originally founded in 1832 by Jose Antonio Sierra who was a master carpenter and barrel maker for many leading sherry houses. However his background ensured a rocky road in his ambitions of making top quality sherry. The result today is a holding of some of the finest old soleras in the region which are being brought to market in small quantities by the current owner, Pilar Pla Pechovierto and her winery manager Ana Cabestrero. The Capataz (cellar master), Juan Clavijo has been at the bodega for over 50 years and has lovingly maintained its treasures. As well as an excellent range of traditionally styled releases there are a number of exceptional old wines. These include the Amontillado 1830, Oloroso 1/14, Pedro Ximénez Viejisimo whose soleras are certainly well over 50 years old. The very old Extra Viejo Oloroso 1/7 (of which there are just 7 butts) through natural evaporation has reached an alcohol level of close to 25 degrees. Both the intensely citrus, and salty, yeasty Fino and richly nutty, complex Oloroso are brilliant value buys. (DM)

Recommended Whites:
Jerez y Manzanilla Oloroso ★★★★ £C
Jerez y Manzanilla Fino ★★★☆ £C

❂ **Bodegas El Nido (Jumilla)** *www.bodegaselnido.es*
A new Jumilla benchmark, El Nido is a partnership between Australian Chris RINGLAND, a significant wine maker in the Barossa Valley and Bodegas JUAN GIL. At El Nido, Ringland can draw on 60 plus year old Monastrell as well as Cabernet Sauvignon grown in chalky stone and sandy soils. As elsewhere in central and southern Spain, the key to quality is warm summers with cool nights providing the necessary acidity in the fruit. The wines are rich, fleshy and concentrated modern styles with dense, powerful tannins and not inconsiderable new oak. The Clio is lighter, more typically Jumilla in style with a higher proportion of Monastrell. They will develop well, the El Nido for up to a decade. The 2009 vintage saw the first release of Corteo which is a varietal Syrah. (DM)

Recommended Reds:
Jumilla El Nido ★★★★★ £G   Jumilla Clio ★★★★ £E

El Regajal (Vinos de Madrid) *www.elregajal.es*
Three reds are now produced at this small Madrid winery in the Arganda sub-region of the DO. The area is marked by the influence of limestone in the soils and this helps provide balance and freshness to the big, rich and full-bodied wines produced here. The vineyards are farmed along organic lines and everything is done by hand with the harvest brought in, in small lots. As is the case with a number of the top wines from Madrid, in the Selección Especial Tempranillo is blended with Cabernet Sauvignon, Syrah and Merlot. Fermentation is in stainless steel and then the wine is aged for 15 months with the malolactic in barrel providing a typically fleshy and concentrated style. The wine is currently marked by its excellent value. A second wine, Las Retamas de El Regajal is also now made and this has been joined by a premium label Galia which is solely

Tempranillo. (DM)
Recommended Reds:
Vinos de Madrid Selección Especial ★★★☆ £E

Elvi Wines (Ribera del Júcar) *www.elviwines.com*
As well as being the benchmark for the small DO of Ribera del Júcar this is also one of the key producers of Kosher wines in Spain. As well as from the bodegas home appellation, wines also emerge from Montsant as well as Priorat, Rioja, Utiel Requena and Cava. The Ribera wines offer good value as well as quality. The white Ness is crisp and fresh with a subtle aromatic quality from Moscatel. The Cava Adar is very much in a crisp green fruit style with ageing on lees for 12 months. The Ness red (Tempranillo, Syrah, Merlot, Cabernet Sauvignon) is nicely structured with ripe berry fruit as a result of a pre-fermentation cold soak, a vatting at controlled temperatures and for close to three weeks then ageing in barrel for 12 months. The top Ribera del Júcar, Adar (Bobal, Tempranillo, Merlot, Petit Verdot, Cabernet Sauvignon) is richer, more concentrated, it is unfined and only very lightly filtered after 12 months in wood. The dark plum fruited Makor from Utiel Requena is full of Bobal character, the variety dominates the wine with a touch of Cabernet Sauvignon adding grip. The Rioja Herenza Crianza and Mati Semi Crianza, both varietal Tempranillo are made in association with CASTILLO DE SAJAZARRA from their fruit and both wineries collaborate in the Alta Alella white Invita. Ageing is in a mix of French and American oak for 14 months. The top wine and the priciest comes from Priorat. The El26 from a blend of Cabernet Sauvignon, Garnacha, Cariñena and Syrah has a marked blackberry, blackcurrant quality as well as a subtle minerality as a result of the Cabernet included. (DM)

Recommended Reds:
Priorat El 26 ★★★☆ £E   Rioja Herenza Crianza ★★★ £D
Rioja Mati Semi Crianza ★★☆ £C   Ribera del Júcar Adar ★★★ £C
Ribera del Júcar Ness ★★☆ £B   Utiel-Requena Makor ★★☆ £B
Recommended Whites:
Cava Brut Adar ★★ £C   Ribera del Júcar Ness ★★ £B

Bodegas Ercavio (VdT Castilla) *www.bodegasercavio.com*
This is a partnership of three winemaking friends, Margarita Madrigal, Gonzalo Rodriguez and Alexandra Schmedes who have been working together since 1998. The winery is also known as Mas Que Vinos. Wishing to make their own wines as well as working with other producers they settled on an area a short distance to the east of Toledo, the Mesa de Ocaña. A combination of altitude (750 metres), a continental climate with dry summers and cool nights as well as calcareous-clay soils provides an ideal viticultural environment for perfectly matured grapes. Four fruit-driven wines are produced under their Ercavio label as well as two denser, more seriously structured and ageworthy reds. The Blanco is mainly low-yielding Airen with a little Sauvignon Blanc. It is cool-fermented and aged on lees for around 10 weeks. A second white, La Malvar de Ercavio is barrel fermented and comes from the Malvar variety. A fruit driven style is achieved with the Tempranillo Joven which is bottled unwooded. The Tempranillo Roble is more traditionally vinified and gets five months ageing in a mix of French and American oak, while the Selección Limitada is mainly Tempranillo and a little Merlot and is a selection aged for longer, up to a year in barrel and offers more depth and a tighter, more elegant style. Of the top reds, La Meseta is 50/50 Syrah and Tempranillo, whereas the La Plazuela is mainly very old Tempranillo with some bush vine Garnacha adding a beguiling, complex old-vine herb spice

character. All the barrel aged reds are bottled unfiltered. Both La Meseta and La Plazuela will continue to add greater complexity for at least six or seven years. A further premium red, El Señorito de Ercavio sourced from a single vineyard, a sparkling white Espumoso, and a dulce red from Tempranillo are also made. Most recently added is a Rioja red produced from 50 year old bush vines, La Buena Vid de Mas Que Vinos.

Recommended Reds:
VdT Castilla La Plazuela ★★★★ £E
VdT Castilla La Meseta ★★★☆ £D
VdT Castilla Ercavio Selección Limitada ★★☆ £C
VdT Castilla Ercavio Tempranillo Roble ★★☆ £B
VdT Castilla Ercavio Tempranillo Joven ★★ £B

Recommended Whites:
VdT Castilla Ercavio ★☆ £C

Fernando de Castilla *www.fernandodecastilla.com*
This venerable old bodega founded in 1837 is now run with considerable enthusiasm and skill by Norwegian Jan Pettersen. These are very classic and traditional sherries and are absolutely bone dry, with the exception of the gloriously rich and nutty, aromatic Antique PX. The Classic labelled wines are simpler than the complex Antique wines but both the Fino and Manzanilla offer excellent value and exactly what one would expect from the styles at a higher quality level than many better known big brands. The Antique wines though are a clear step up here. The Fino is aged for up to seven years under its *flor* yeast cover, much longer than most examples, because of its structure and stability in barrel. The Amontillado has a rich nutty, almost austere quality with a subtle citrus and salty undercurrent. The Oloroso is a touch less austere with great concentration and a rich and unctuous texture. Perhaps the stand out wine is the Palo Cortado, which offers wonderful intensity and a very pronounced citrus quality.

Recommended Whites:
Jerez y Manzanilla Antique Pedro Ximénez ★★★★☆ £F
Jerez y Manzanilla Antique Palo Cortado ★★★★☆ £F
Jerez y Manzanilla Antique Oloroso ★★★★ £E
Jerez y Manzanilla Antique Amontillado ★★★★ £E
Jerez y Manzanilla Antique Fino ★★★☆ £D
Jerez y Manzanilla Classic Dry Fino ★★★ £C
Jerez y Manzanilla Classic Manzanilla ★★★ £C

>> Bodegas Juan Gil (Jumilla) *www.bodegasjuangil.com*
This is one of the oldest bodegas in south-east Spain, established in 1916 and now run by the fourth generation of the family. The family also have investments in a number of small boutique operations throughout the country. The key to the quality of the wines here in this very dry arid region is the altitude of the vineyards, 700 to 850 metres, the well-drained sand and limestone soils and a wide variation in day and night temperature during the growing season promoting a balanced fresh edge in the wines. Vinification and ageing is now in a modern winery facility with stainless steel and temperature control for both fermentation and ageing. There are two fine entry level Monastrell reds Honoro Vera, both very well priced, one coming solely from Organic certified vineyards. The Juan Gill Yellow label red is a young wine style full of bright red and black fruits, a hint of oak spice and solely from Monastrell. Ageing is for just four months in a combination of French and American oak. The Silver Label red is vinified from some of the family's older Monastrell, adding to the wines complexity with copious spicy black fruits and supple nicely rounded tannins. It gets 12 months ageing in small

French oak. The top red the Juan Gil Blue Label gains depth and structure from blending both Cabernet Sauvignon and Syrah with old Monastrell. The wine is aged for 18 months in both French and American barrels. The small range is completed by a Dry Muscat white. (DM)

Recommended Reds:
Jumilla Blue Label ★★★★ £E
Jumilla Silver Label ★★★☆ £C
Jumilla Yellow Label ★★☆ £B
Honoro Vera Monastrell ★★ £A
Honoro Vera Organico ★★ £A

⚙ González Byass (Jerez y Manzanilla) *www.gonzalezbyass.com*
One of the most famous names in sherry production with a large volume of sound, regular Fino and Amontillado. The Tio Pepe brand in particular, while produced in very large quantity, is nonetheless an impressive Fino – salty and intense with piercing citrus notes. A more impressive *En Rama* version is also now being sold. Of a different order are a number of super-rich Amontillados and Olorosos. These include the full, rich Alfonso, Apóstoles, and most notably Matusalem. Two other very impressive, full-bodied styles are made. The Amontillado Del Duque is dry, very intense and almost overwhelms one with its full, rich and toffeed *rancio* character. The Noé Pedro Ximénez is unctuously sweet, very rich and heady but refined too. An extremely complex vintage Palo Cortado is also made, most recently from 1982.

Recommended Whites:
Jerez y Manzanilla Añada Palo Cortado ✪✪✪✪✪ £H
Jerez y Manzanilla Del Duque Amontillado VORS ★★★★★ £F
Jerez y Manzanilla Matusalem Oloroso VORS ★★★★☆ £F
Jerez y Manzanilla Apóstoles Oloroso VORS ★★★★ £F
Jerez y Manzanilla Noé Pedro Pedro Ximénez ★★★★ £F
Jerez y Manzanilla Leonor Palo Cortado ★★☆ £C
Jerez y Manzanilla Viña AB Dry Amontillado ★★☆ £C
Jerez y Manzanilla Tio Pepe Fino En Rama ★★★ £D
Jerez y Manzanilla Tio Pepe Fino ★★☆ £C
Jerez y Manzanilla Alfonso Oloroso ★★ £C

Gosalbez Orti/Qubél (Vinos de Madrid) *www.qubel.com*
Another example of a newly established winery showing the exciting potential of Spain's so called lesser regions. Although only founded in 2000 the latest releases continue to move from strength to strength. All three wines take the Qubél brand and you may be as likely to find them listed as this rather than under the bodega name. The vineyards are all farmed organically and are located to the south east of Madrid at an altitude that ranges from 750 to 900 metres. This coupled with mountains to the north provides an excellent growing environment with warm sunny summers and cool nights. Very limited drip irrigation is also employed simply to avoid excessive vine stress. The vibrant, spicy, herb scented Excepción comes from 35 to 40 year old Garnacha vines and is aged in a mix of American and French oak. It makes an interesting alternative to a southern Rhône red. Both the Naturé and the Paciencia are based largely on Tempranillo, blended with a little Cabernet Sauvignon and Syrah. Both are firmer, more structured wines than the Excepción, although they are nevertheless supple, ripe and will drink well at three or four years. The Paciencia will benefit from a year or two longer. Two additional wines are now released under the Mayrit label, a white from Albillo and a red blend. A further Qubél red blend, Revelación is also made. (DM)

Central, Southern Spain & the Islands

Recommended Reds:
Vinos de Madrid Qubel Paciencia ★★★★ £E
Vinos de Madrid Qubel Naturé ★★★☆ £D
Vinos de Madrid Qubel Excepción ★★★☆ £C

● **Gutierrez Colosia (Jerez y Manzanilla)** *www.gutierrez-colosia.com*
This is a splendid old bodega with origins going way back to 1838. The operation is now run by Juan Carlos Gutiérrez, who only began estate bottling in the late 1990s. Prior to this much of the wine was sold in bulk to some of the larger Sherry houses. The cellars are located very close to the riverside in El Puerto de Santa Maria and it is this proximity which helps provide the humidity to produce intense *flor* yeast character in the wines. They are some of the best examples of the region at all quality and price levels. The regular styles all offer excellent concentration and depth although the top Solera Familiar wines are of a clearly different order. The Fino En Rama is among a new breed of Finos being offered by a number of bodegas. The wine is unfiltered and comes straight of its fine lees in cask. (DM)

Recommended Whites:
Jerez y Manzanilla Solera Familiar Palo Cortado ★★★★★ £F
Jerez y Manzanilla Solera Familiar Amontillado ★★★★☆ £F
Jerez y Manzanilla Solera Familiar Oloroso ★★★★☆ £F
Jerez y Manzanilla Solera Familiar Pedro Ximénez ★★★★ £E
Jerez y Manzanilla En Rama Fino ★★★★ £D
Jerez y Manzanilla Soleado Pedro Ximénez ★★★ £D
Jerez y Manzanilla Soleado Moscatel ★★★ £D
Jerez y Manzanilla Manzanilla ★★★ £C
Jerez y Manzanilla Fino ★★★ £C
Jerez y Manzanilla Oloroso ★★★ £C
Jerez y Manzanilla Amontillado ★★★ £C
Jerez y Manzanilla Cream ★★☆ £C

>> **Bodegas Habla (VdT Extremadura)** *www.bodegashabla.com*
A new small bodega which has invested considerably in both its vineyards and modern winemaking and cellar facilities. The labelling over recent vintages has been more than a little difficult to follow. The wines have been released under a series of brand names depending on the conditions and the vintage and as No 1, 2, 3 and so on. The blend composition has varied a little but as Habla No 14 has now been released a pattern is emerging. Habla 13 is a dense and structured Cabernet Sauvigon, Habla 14 a stylish Syrah. A more obviously forward fruit driven secondary wine, Habla del Silencio is also now being made, which is a blend of Syrah, Cabernet Sauvignon and Tempranillo. The bodega is located in the north eastern stretches of Extremadura, the vineyards planted to a mix of varieties. Of the top two wines the Cabernet is the firmer of the two. Big and firm youthful tannins will take two or three years to soften and the wine offers a mix of dark fruits and cedar. The Syrah is a touch softer, marked by dark pepper and a hint of oriental spices. Two whites and a rosado are also now made. (DM)

Recommended Reds:
VdT Extremadura Habla No 14 ★★★★ £E
VdT Extremadura Habla No 13 ★★★★ £E
VdT Extremadura Habla del Silencio ★★★ £D

Heretat de Taverners (Valencia) *www.heretatdetaverners.com*
Good and well-priced wines are crafted at this small bodega, originally a farmhouse dating back to the 1660s. The vineyard now totals 25 ha and a range of varieties planted including Chardonnay and Sauvignon Blanc for whites as well as reds. As well as the reds

rated here one white Reixiut is produced from the holding of white grapes. The El Vern Crianza is a blend of Tempranillo, Monastrell, Cabernet with Merlot and is the most traditional of the reds. Well defined fruit though is apparent with a wine fermented at relatively cool temperatures. Ageing is for 10 months in American and French oak and a further 12 months in bottle prior to release. Mallaura is a vibrant, opulent style seeing 14 months in oak. Dominated by Monastrell, the blend also has small proportions of Garnacha Tintorera, Cabernet Sauvignon and Tempranillo. Pride of place though goes to the excellent Graciano. It is a more densely structured and concentrated red than the other bottlings. Full of dark cherry and notes of plum the wine is nicely underpinned with subtle creamy French oak and will benefit further from two or three years in bottle. A further red Ben Viu as well as a late harvest red Punt Dolc are also made. (DM)

Recommended Reds:
Valencia Graciano Reserva ★★★☆ £D
Valencia Mallaura Reserva ★★★ £C
Valencia El Vern Crianza ★★☆ £C

● **Bodegas Hidalgo-La Gitana** *www.lagitana.es*
This is a large Sanlúcar-based operation with some impressive sherry brands. Bestknown is La Gitana Manzanilla, which provides consistently good value with fresh, tangy, lightly salty fruit. It particularly needs to be drunk young. A more intense En Rama example is also now made. There is a volume range, Hidalgo Clasica producing all the classic sherry styles. Superior to these are the Premium range. These include the Napoleon Amontillado which is slightly toffeed and nutty but dry, and there is a Cream Alameda and an evolved and nutty Oloroso Seco Faraón and a concentrated Pedro Ximénez Triana and a nutty, citrus scented Palo Cortado, Wellington which is classified as VOS (Very Old Sherry). The Manzanilla Pastrana comes from the firm's single vineyard of the same name. It is an aged Pasada, with an evolved, nutty character as well as an underlying hint of citrus. The range is completed by the impressive collection of rare Viejo wines. These are now classified as VORS (Very Old Rare Sherries). They are all stunningly complex. (DM)

Recommended Whites:
Jerez y Manzanilla Oloroso Faraón Viejo VORS ★★★★★ £G
Jerez y Manzanilla Palo Cortado Wellington Viejo VORS ★★★★★ £G
Jerez y Manzanilla Pedro Ximénez Triana Viejo VORS ★★★★☆ £G
Jerez y Manzanilla Amontillado Napoleón Seco Viejo VORS ★★★★☆ £F
Jerez y Manzanilla Palo Cortado Wellington VOS ★★★★ £E
Jerez y Manzanilla Manzanilla Pasada Pastrana ★★★ £D
Jerez y Manzanilla Oloroso Faraón Seco ★★★ £D
Jerez y Manzanilla Pedro Ximénez Triana ★★☆ £C
Jerez y Manzanilla Amontillado Napoleón Seco ★★☆ £C
Jerez y Manzanilla Manzanilla La Gitana En Rama ★★☆ £C
Jerez y Manzanilla Manzanilla La Gitana ★★ £B

Huerta Albalá (VdT Cádiz) *www.huertadealbala.com*
Considerable investment has gone into this property producing benchmark reds in an area known principally for its fortified sherries. The vineyards now planted to a mix of Syrah, Merlot, Cabernet Sauvignon and the local Tintilla de Rota on a mix of silt, sand and chalk and most recently Chardonnay from which a White Barbazul has been added to the small range. The quality of the *terroir* provides for wines of very impressive quality. Pink Barbazul from Syrah is a bright juicy rosado which gets a short maceration and then a period on lees to give it a little structure. There is a soft and approachable red Barbazul which is a blend of all the varieties

and gains a little extra depth from 5 months in barrel. The regular Taberner is ripe and cedary with dark and spicy berry fruit and rich creamy oak and youthfully assertive tannins. The Taberner No 1 is denser, fuller with a really roasted opulent character. Both of these are modern supple wines which will be accessible at a relatively young age. (DM)

Recommended Reds:
VdT Cádiz Taberner No 1 ★★★★ £E
VdT Cádiz Taberner ★★★☆ £E VdT Cádiz Barbazul ★★☆ £C
Recommended Rosés:
VdT Cádiz Barbarosa ★★ £B

Vinos Jeromin (Vinos de Madrid) *www.vinosjeromin.com*
A medium sized bodega and source of some of the best wines from the eastern sector of the Madrid DO. An extensive range is made with approachable well made reds and whites under the Puerta de Alcalá and Puerta de Sol labels. The varietal de Sol Tempranillo, a crianza style and Reserva Alcalá, from the same variety and aged for 15 months in oak both stand out. The Grego labelled reds are modern and impressive fruit driven styles. They all offer great quality for the price. The Roble is mainly Syrah with Tempranillo while the Crianza also has a little old vine Garnacha as well. The Félix Martínez Cepas Viejas red is a traditional reserva style dominated by Tempranillo, aged for 18 months in a mix of French and American oak and there is also a crianza Cinco Añadas. The Manu is a more modern red with ripe, dark fruit nicely underpinned by supple well-structured tannins. It includes Syrah, Tempranillo and Garnacha in a blend which varies a little year by year. Two further premium reds are also made. Pasarela Cibeles combines Tempranillo and Syrah while Dos de Mayo Crianza is a varietal Tempranillo. Manuel Martínez is also involved in a separate project, Vinos Sin-Ley producing a number of well priced fruit-driven wines for the United States market.

Recommended Reds:
Vinos de Madrid Manu Vino de Autor ★★★★ £E
Vinos de Madrid Félix Martínez Cepas Viejas ★★★☆ £D
Vinos de Madrid Grego Crianza ★★★ £C
Vinos de Madrid Grego Garnacha Centenarias ★★★ £C
Vinos de Madrid Grego Roble ★★☆ £B
Vinos de Madrid Puerta de Sol Tempranillo Crianza ★★☆ £B
Vinos de Madrid Puerta de Alcalá Reserva ★★ £B
Vinos de Madrid Puerta de Alcalá Crianza ★☆ £B
Recommended Whites:
Vinos de Madrid Puerta de de Sol Blanco ★☆ £B

✿ Jiménez-Landi (Méntrida) *www.jimenezlandi.com*
This is one of the leading producers in this small region to the south-west of Madrid where the Jiménez-Landi family have been producing very impressive wines from old-vine Garnacha. Syrah is also planted but it is the character of the reds produced from Garnacha that offer something special here. The most approachable of the wines, the dark-berried, spicy and mineral Sotorrondero is a blend of mainly Syrah with a little Garnacha from old vines. The other wines are all Garnacha and an old-vine complexity shines through in all with the Pielago coming from a number of sites. More complex and intensely mineral in style are the three top reds from specific vineyards and *terroirs*. Dark and spicy as well as very mineral, the Ataulfos comes from a biodynamically farmed east facing 60 year old plot planted in siliceous soils. El Fino del Mondo is from a 1,000 metre vineyard of 70 year old vines. It is very nervy and tightly structured and will be splendid given five years or so. Dani LANDI

who made the wines has now branched out on his own.
Recommended Reds:
Méntrida El Fino del Mundo ★★★★☆ £F
Méntrida Ataulfos ★★★★☆ £F
Méntrida Piélago ★★★★ £E Méntrida Sotorrondero ★★★☆ £D

✿ La Bota De - Equipo Navazos *www.equiponavazos.com*
A new operation which was founded in late 2005. The Bota De team work hand in hand with a number of other bodegas producing very good to exceptional very limited production bottlings from both Jerez and Montilla. A range of outstanding sherries, all produced in small quantity and from selected butts (casks) and from some of the best old soleras in the region are made. Most styles of sherry are made with individually numbered releases. Wines come from Jerez and Montilla-Moriles and most recently a couple of vintaged sparkling wines, Collet-Navajos Extra Brut and Extra Brut Reserva, made using the traditional method but the *dosage* coming from wines made in southern vineyards with some *flor* character. The range of wines is as far removed from some of the large scale commercial producers volume output as it is possible to imagine. Almost all are given a numbered bottle brand and also a dated release from the *solera* on each individual bottle. The range of releases is now quite extensive with wines having been released under Numbers 1 to well over 40 now. There is also an old Brandy and the unctuously rich and nutty Pedro Ximénez Casa del Inca from Montilla is released without a number. There is also a new unfortified white from Palomino, Navajos Niepoort, which is made in collaboration with Port producer Dirk Niepoort. All the sherry styles can be found in the range and all will be worth seeking out. Among the outstanding highlights are the intense and salty Manzanilla Pasada Bota Punta and a couple of stunning Pedro Ximénez wines.
Recommended Whites:
Montilla-Moriles Pedro Ximénez de Montilla-Moriles ★★★★★ £G
Jerez y Manzanilla Pedro Ximénez de Jerez ★★★★★ £G
Jerez y Manzanilla Manzanilla Pasada Bota Punto ★★★★★ £F
Jerez y Manzanilla Viejo Cream Bota NO ★★★★★ £F
Jerez y Manzanilla Manzanilla Navazos ★★★★☆ £E
Jerez y Manzanilla Amontillado Navazos ★★★★☆ £E
Jerez y Manzanilla Fino Macharnudo Alto ★★★★ £D
VdM Andalucia Navazos-Niepoort ★★★★ £D

Finca La Estacada (VdT Castilla) *www.fincalaestacada.com*
Although La Estacada is based in the south-eastern sector of the La Mancha DO, their wines take the VdT Castilla classification. Wine quality here though is very good. Reds undoubtedly star. The Blanco offers simple straightforward grassy fruit and a superior Secua Blanco is also now offered. The 6 Meses means simply aged for six months in *barrique*. If one were to quibble it would be that the 6 and 12 Meses would show their vibrant fruit better with just a touch less time in new oak. The top three wines achieve a better balance and harmony. The Selección Varietales is aged for 18 months in American and French oak with good depth and balance. The top two reds are a clear step up over the rest of the range. La Estacada, a blend of Syrah and Merlot offers particularly good value. Secua blends Cabernet with Syrah and while denser and more powerful misses a touch of the elegance and subtlety of La Estacada.
Recommended Reds:
VdT Castilla Secua ★★★☆ £E
VdT Castilla La Estacada ★★★☆ £E
VdT Castilla Selección Varietales ★★★ £D
VdT Castilla 12 Meses ★★★ £C

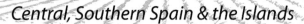

Central, Southern Spain & the Islands

Spain

VdT Castilla 6 Meses ★★☆ £B
Recommended Whites:
VdT Castilla Blanco ★☆ £B
Recommended Rosés:
VdT Castilla Rosado ★☆ £B

Celler La Muntanya (VdM Valencia) *www.cellerlamuntanya.com*
This is an interesting project based in the Alicante mountains and established in 2004, producing a small range of excellent wines and olive oil, the wines taking simply Table Wine status on the label. The bodega has no vineyards and the fruit is supplied under an an agreement known as Microviña, a joint venture between both the grower and the bodega. La Muntanya provide guidance and support in maintaining sustainably farmed vineyards as well as advice with new vine plantings. The celler has all the winemaking and ageing facilities. The vineyards for all the wines are farmed completely sustainably. Currently there are two dry whites, four reds, and a Dolç style sweet white from Malvasia. The nutty, characterful Albir white aged for 6 months in oak. A level up and arguably the best of the range is the richly textured, mineral and citrus scented Lliure Albir which is a typical Mediterranean blend. Of the reds the Celler La Muntanya is a supple dark-berry fruited multi variety blend. The top red, the Almoroig is chunkier and sturdier. The whites are quickly cooled and then pressed after the harvest, followed by fermentation in a mix of vats and smaller oak. The red varieties are vinified separately and then aged in a combination of larger vats and small oak for 8 to 9 months on lees. The third red, Paquito El Chocolatero is a blend of Monastrell, Garnacha and Garnacha Tintorera. (DM)
Recommended Reds:
VdM Valencia Almoroig ★★★☆ £D
VdM Valencia La Muntanya ★★★ £C
Recommended Whites:
VdM Valencia Iliure Albire ★★★☆ £D
VdM Valencia Albir ★★★ £C

⚫ Dani Landi (Méntrida) *www.danilandi.com*
Dani Landi has left his family bodega, JIMÉNEZ-LANDI where he had contributed substantially in establishing it as perhaps the stand out producer in this small region to the south-west of Madrid He continues on his own in making stunning wines from old-vine, organically and biodynamically farmed Garnacha. There are three stunning single vineyard examples of the grape. The supple and intensely complex and concentrated Cantos del Diablo (Stones of the Devil), although the site is planted at 900 metres, it is reasonably warm and east facing and the fruit is not de-stemmed prior to fermentation as a result. Daniel also makes a brilliant Garnacha red, El Reventon, from over 70 year old vines grown in slatey, limestone soils around the key village of Cebreros. The wine offers a beguiling mineral, dark-fruited rich and sumptuous complexity. It is unquestionably one of Central Spain's stand out reds. A further single vineyard wine comes from a 60 year Garnacha site, Las Iruelas grown on slate soils at an altitude of 1,000 metres. Very edgy and mineral. A more approachable Garnacha red Uvas de La Ira is also made as well as a similarly labelled white from Albillo. Daniel is also involved with Fernando Garcia Alonso of Bodegas MARAÑONES in creating further pure Garnacha reds at COMANDO G.
Recommended Reds:
VdT Castilla y León El Reventon ★★★★★ £F
VdT Castilla y León Las Iruelas ★★★★★ £F

Méntrida Cantos del Diable ★★★★★ £F
VdT Castilla y León Uvas de La Ira ★★★★ £E
Recommended Whites:
VdT Castilla y León Uvas de La Ira ★★★★ £E

⚫ Bodegas Lavia (Bullas) *www.bodegaslavia.com*
This bodega was only very recently established in 2004 but the early results would suggest excellent potential and one of the appellation benchmarks for Bullas. Monastrell is the most important variety and this is supplemented by Syrah on the 8 ha of vineyards planted at an altitude of 800 metres. As elsewhere in southern Spain this along with sparse soils low in organic matter provides grapes of impressive flavour intensity. Winemaking is thoroughly modern with small stainless steel fermenters and French oak used for ageing. The must and wine is handled by gravity and the wines vinified with natural yeasts. Good, dark-fruited and vibrant wines are produced, the Lavia + offering a touch more depth and concentration. A pricier single vineyard Lavia + Finca Paso Malo is also made although not yet tasted. (DM)
Recommended Reds:
Bullas Lavia + ★★★★ £D   Bullas Lavia ★★★☆ £D

Bodegas Licinia (Vinos de Madrid) *www.bodegaslicinia.es*
New small and high quality production from another fine boutique operation. Licinia is run by winemaker Olga Fernandez and the bodega is notable for the quality of its signature red Licinia. The wine is hand harvested and the fruit temperature controlled before sorting. Vinification is modern in stainless steel and the wine aged for 12 months in small French oak. A second, attractive fruit driven red Altos del Tajuña also helps to ensure the consistent depth and quality of Licinia. The property is located to the south-east of Madrid and Licinia was the Roman name for the small town of Morata where the operation is based. (DM)
Recommended Reds:
Vinos de Madrid Licinia ★★★★ £E
Vinos de Madrid Altos del Tajuña ★★★ £D

Bodegas Los Frailes (Valencia) *www.bodegaslosfrailes.com*
One of Valencia's better sources of modern, characterful reds. Monastrell, some of it of considerable age, is the key variety along with a little Cabernet Sauvignon and Tempranillo. Although the Velázquez family has owned the property since 1771, it was only very recently in 1999 that the modern project was developed. There are 130 ha of organically cultivated vineyards that can be drawn on. The vines are planted in sandy, calcareous soils and the high stone content provides excellent drainage. The Efe labels are approachable young wine styles, in particular the Efe Monastrell which comes from some of the younger vines of the variety, around 15 to 20 years and ageing is for a short time in tank. The Efe Barrica is a touch more concentrated with older 45 year Monastrell blended with 20% of young Cabernet Sauvignon. The top two wines are firmer and marked more by their texture and depth than by their fruit. Bilogía is a 50/50 Monastrell and Tempranillo blend, full of dark spice, and a subtle minerality it is aged in American oak. Trilogía has a greater proportion of Monastrell and the 20% of Cabernet Sauvignon adds to the wine's firm, tannic structure, with a small proportion of Tempranillo. A late harvest red After 3 from Monastrell is also made. Trilogía in particular demands at least five years patience. (DM)
Recommended Reds:
Valencia Trilogía ★★★☆ £E

Valencia Bilogía ★★★ £C Valencia Efe Barrica ★★☆ £C
Valencia Efe Monastrell ★★ £B

Emilio Lustau (Jerez y Manzanilla) *www.lustau.es*
This is a sizeable sherry operation supplying a considerable
international own-label market. It also has a splendid range of
high-quality sherries sold under its own label. In 2008 the Domecq
sherry brands including La Ina were acquired. A good and extensive
Solera range includes salty, good-value Puerto Fino, Península
Palo Cortado, Don Nuño Oloroso as well as Amontillado Los Arcos
and Escuadrilla. Very unusual and very rich, almost overly so, is
the Moscatel Superior Emilin. The Almacenista label offers very
impressive, nutty Manzanilla Amontillado, a beautifully evolved, very
lightly salty Manzanilla Pasada, stylish Palo Cortado Vides and the
richly concentrated Amontillado del Puerto. The Emperatriz Eugenia
Oloroso is more developed and shows greater *rancio* character. The
East India Solera is full of nutty, burnt toffee aromas. As well as an
En Rama range recently released, a number of very fine old wines
are also offered from the company's oldest soleras including various
VORS labels and the Rich Oloroso vintage wine. (DM)
Recommended Whites:
Jerez y Manzanilla East India Solera Oloroso ★★★★ £F
Jerez y Manzanilla Empertriz Eugenia Gran Reserva Oloroso ★★★☆ £E
Jerez Manzanilla Almacenista Manzanilla Amontillada ★★★ £D
Jerez y Manzanilla Manzanilla Almacenista Pasada ★★★ £D
Jerez y Manzanilla Palo Cortado Almacenista Vides ★★★ £D
Jerez y Manzanilla Amontillado Almacenista del Puerto ★★★ £D
Jerez y Manzanilla Península Palo Cortado Solera ★★★☆ £D
Jerez y Manzanilla Moscatel Emilin Solera ★★★☆ £D
Jerez y Manzanilla Puerto Fino Solera ★★☆ £C
Jerez y Manzanilla Fino La Ina ★★ £C

>> Mahara (VdT Cádiz) *www.mahara.es*
This is an excellent small artisan operation, producing just one
stylish red from the rare Tintilla de Rota variety. Based in the Jerez
region the Albariza soils have a high proportion of limestone, which
proves very beneficial as it does in the production of Sherry. There
are 7 ha under vine and the combination of limestone and low
organic matter along with good water retention provides for good
growing conditions with the warm summers. Cooling sea breezes
also provide a balanced local climate. There is an artisan approach
to winemaking, harvest is judged by tasting the grapes, everything
is done by hand and in the winery there is minimal intervention,
spontaneous fermentation, no sulphur additions and bottling
without filtration. The wine offers concentrated black fruit aromas
with dark spices and a fresh balanced edge. It will develop nicely for
four or five years in bottle. (DM)
Recommended Reds:
VdT de Cádiz Mahara ★★★★ £E

Malaga Virgen (Malaga) *www.bodegasmalagavirgen.com*
This large, family-owned operation has been making the wines
of Málaga since before the arrival of the phylloxera vine louse.
Throughout the last century production of these wines based
on Pedro Ximénez and Moscatel has declined dramatically. The
bulk of the 400,000-case output here is sourced from the family's
180 ha of vineyards and the wines are produced using sun-dried
grapes aged on mats. An extensive range is made from both PX
and Moscatel, the majority being sweet in style. A straightforward
dry white and rosado are also made under the Barón de Rivero

label as well as a red Pernales which is 100% Syrah. Best of the
PX range is the Reserva de Familia which has a lightly nutty and
raisiny character and reasonable depth. A fine grapy, concentrated
Moscatel is also released under the same label. Most exciting are
three splendid Transañejo bottlings which are aged in *solera* and
average around 50 years of age. The Seco is nutty, concentrated and
almost shockingly dry on the palate with a lingering citrus intensity
underpinnong its rich, nutty fruit. Dark and extraordinarily rich, the
Moscatel has remarkable depth and a piercing intensity. All are truly
among Spain's vinous gems. (DM)
Recommended Whites:
Málaga Transañejo Moscatel Don Salvador ★★★★☆ £G
Málaga Transañejo PX Don Juan ★★★★☆ £G
Málaga Transañejo Seco Don Juan ★★★★ £F
Málaga Moscatel Reserva de Familia ★★☆ £C
Málaga PX Reserva de Familia ★★☆ £C

❀ Mano a Mano (VdT Castilla) *www.bodegamanoamano.com*
This new small bodega is now a part of the Avanteselecta group
of small high quality boutique properties. Although based in La
Mancha the bodega chooses to take the Vinos de La Tierra Castilla
classification for their reds rather than the DO. The well priced
Mano a Mano red is an excellent,fleshy and vibrant, forward red
offering great value. The wine is produced from low yields of
Cencibel and the vineyards planted in sandy soils over a bedrock
of clay, limestone and pebbles. This local strain of Tempranillo is
well suited to the semi-drought conditions found in La Mancha
and the resulting wines are rich and robust but very much in a
joven style. The wine is aged for up to six months in small oak and
needs a few months after release to achieve a rounded harmony
of fruit and wood. The Venta La Ossa red comes from just 15 ha
and is dominated by old-vine Tempranillo which is dry-farmed,
with around 95% in the blend along with 5% of Syrah to round
things off. The wine is aged for around 12 months in small oak. Full
of dark,spicy berry fruit and hints off chocolate there is quite a bit
of youthful new oak which will take a year or two to integrate. An
additional red, Venta La Ossa Syrah is also made which sees a similar
period in small oak, both French and American as well as a young
wine style, Manon Roble, 100% Tempranillo. (DM)
Recommended Reds:
VdT Castilla Venta La Ossa ★★★★☆ £F
VdT Castilla Mano a Mano ★★★☆ £C

❀ Bodega Marañones *www.bodegamaranones.com*
Youthful owner Fernando Garcia Alonso is based in the western
Vinos de Madrid San Martín subregion. He is a source of tremendous
Garnacha reds and Albillo based whites from old bush trained
vines. Fernando practices organic farming and produces five wines
from vineyards ranging from 30 to over 80 years of age. There are
various parcels, totalling around 15 ha, with the vines planted in a
mix of sandy loams, sand and granite at an altitude of between 650
to 850 metres. A high diurnal swing in summer temperature and
vines protected from northern winds provides fruit with excellent
potential balance and fresh acidity as well as rich concentration.
The result is red wines of intense fruit and classic minerality along
with two whites. Picarana, which gains weight and a richer texture
from barrel-fermentation with lees stirring and has a rich, citrus
infused character. It is now joined by a second white, Piesdescalzos,
also coming from Albillo and from a single plot of 50 year old vines.
The reds get a brief cold soak before fermentation in small open

Central, Southern Spain & the Islands

barrels with *pigéage*. Cellaring is then in larger wooden barrels to emphasise the quality of the fruit. The wines all offer excellent quality for the price and are bottled unfined and unfiltered. Fernando is also involved in the exciting COMANDO G project. (DM)

Recommended Reds:

Vinos de Madrid Marañones ★★★★☆ £E
Vinos de Madrid Peña Caballera ★★★★☆ £E
Vinos de Madrid Labros ★★★★☆ £E
Vinos de Madrid Treinta Mil Maravedíes ★★★☆ £D

Recommended Whites:

Vinos de Madrid Piesdescalzos ★★★★☆ £E
Vinos de Madrid Picarana ★★★★ £D

E Mendoza (Alicante) *www.bodegasmendoza.com*
This is one of the benchmark producers in Alicante and a source of consistent well made and modern styled wines with impressively vibrant and accessible fruit. The family run bodega was established quite recently in 1989 and there are some 70 ha now being cultivated. The Chardonnay is a crisp unoaked style of good ripe intensity. A barrel fermented example is also made. Both the Petit Verdot and Merlot are ripe, forward and accessible, the Merlot showing a hint of oak and the Petit Verdot very good depth and character at the price. The Shiraz has excellent varietal purity with a restrained dark pepper and licorice character you would'nt necessarily expect in this southerly region. The bodega now make a varietal Pinot Noir as well. The Santa Rosa bottling is mainly a Bordeaux style blend with the majority Cabernet Sauvignon joined by Merlot and a little Syrah. It is aged for 19 months in 225 litre French oak and offers a ripe blacurrant and mineral fruit character and good carry and intensity. Perhaps the standout red here is the Estrecho, a varietal Monastrell which is ripe and concentrated with dark blackberry and damson fruit, a spicy mineral undercurrent and persuasive intensity. There are two further reserva reds; Peñón de Ifach combines Cabernet Sauvignon, Merlot and Petit Verdot and a Cabernet Shiraz blend is also made. The Moscatel de Marina offers lots of pure muscat fruit and nicely balanced acidity. (DM)

Recommended Reds:

Alicante Monastrell Estrecho ★★★★ £E
Alicante Reserva Santa Rosa ★★★★ £E
Alicante Shiraz ★★★ £C   Alicante Petit Verdot ★★★ £C
Alicante Merlot ★★☆ £B

Recommended Whites:

Alicante Moscatel de la Marina ★★★ £C
Alicante Chardonnay ★★☆ £B
Alicante Young White Chardonnay ★☆ £B

Bodega Monastrell (Bullas) *www.bodegamonastrell.com*
Along with LAVIA and BALCONA, this bodega is a further indicator of the potential quality possible in this small DO. The vineyards are a small distance inland from the Mediterranean and benefit from an altitude of 850 to 900 metres above sea level. As elsewhere in the south, this contributes to the balance and structure of the wines. Monastrell is the main variety planted and provides the fruit for the dark, spicy, ripe and fruit driven Chaveo as well as the more firmly structured and ageworthy Valché. Almudi Uno is produced from Petit Verdot. The fruit for this is sourced from vines planted as high as 1,200 metres and farmed organically. An Almudi Tres blend and a Dulce style from Monastrell are also made. (DM)

Recommended Reds:

Bullas Valché ★★★☆ £D   Bullas Almudi Uno ★★★ £D
Bullas Chaveo ★★★ £C

✿ Mustiguillo (DOP Pago El Terrerazo) *www.bodegamustiguillo.com*
A very impressive producer with some 89 ha of vineyards close to Valencia in the small El Terrerazo appellation which has now been classified as a single Pago property as of 2011. Much of the vineyard is planted to very old, unirrigated Bobal, which provides potentially exceptional raw material. Tempranillo, which is by no means young at 35 plus years, and Cabernet Sauvignon is also planted. Five wines are now produced. Mestijaze from Bobal, Tempranillo, Cabernet Sauvignon, Merlot and Syrah is forward and full of dark, brambly fruit. Finca Terrerazo comes from Bobal and is supple and reasonably approachable, the more forward of the two Pago labels; it is aged for 18 months in French oak. The pricier Quincha Corral, also Bobal, is more structured and firm. Winemaking is distinctly modern, with primary fermentation completed in barrel followed by the malolactic. These are rich, concentrated wines full of dark fruit and cedar. They are likely to improve in bottle for 5 years or more. Two whites are additionally made mainly from the rare Merseguera grape. The Vino de España classified Mestizaje Blanco also includes a little Malvasia and Viognier and is tank fermented and aged on lees, while the Finca Calvestra which is barrel fermented as well as being aged on lees is solely from Merseguera. (DM)

Recommended Reds:

Pago El Terrerazu Quincha Corral ★★★★☆ £F
Pago El Terrerazu Finca Terrerazo ★★★★ £E
Pago El Terrerazu Mestizaje ★★★ £C

Bodegas Olivares (Jumilla) *www.bodegasolivares.net*
The operation here is not small, with 275 ha under vine, and it has been established since the 1930s. One of the keys in Jumilla is the presence of sandy soils which made it one of the few areas to escape phylloxera. The result is a high proportion of not only old but also ungrafted Monastrell vines. The Joven (Monastrell, Garnacha and Syrah) is a vibrant, fruit-driven blend. Denser and fuller with altogether more structure is the impressive Altos de la Hoya (Monastrell and Garnacha). Particularly rare is the rich, concentrated, purely varietal, late-harvested and occasionally botrytis-affected Dulce Monastrell. A Crianza red solely from Monastrell and Rosado combining Monastrell and Syrah are also made. (DM)

Recommended Reds:

Jumilla Dulce Monastrell ★★★☆ £D
Jumilla Altos de la Hoya ★★★ £C   Jumilla Joven ★★☆ £B

✿ Jorge Ordoñez (Malaga) *www.jorge-ordonez.es*
This project was established by US wine importer Jorge Ordoñez in 2004 and a small range of mainly sweet white Moscatels are produced. As well as the No 1 Seleccion Especial, there are two other smaller volume wines, No 2 Victoria and No 3 Viejas Viñas. Both are quite a bit more expensive than the well priced No 1. The final wine in the quartet is the No 4 Esencia, made in tiny quantities. The wines are all produced from old vines on slate soils inland of Málaga and are marked by their pure upfront sweetly intense, grapey fruit. They are in marked contrast to some of the aged *solera* styles produced by other top producers in the DO. A dry Moscatel, Botani is also now made as well as a sparkling Botani muscat, an additional sweet Moscatel, Victoria Conarte, and a red Botani from Garnacha.

Recommended Whites:

Málaga Seleccion Especial No 3 Viejas Viñas ★★★★★ £G
Málaga Seleccion Especial No 2 Victoria ★★★★☆ £F
Málaga Seleccion Especial No 1 Selección Especial ★★★★ £E
Málaga Botani ★★★ £C

Pago Casa Gran (Valencia) *www.pagocasagran.com*
While grapes have been cultivated in the Casa Gran vineyards since the 1960s it is only since 2006 that the family have been releasing wines under their own label. Like so many small, quality conscious producers wine production is a very recent undertaking. The vineyards are being farmed organically and full certification has been achieved in 2008. Monastrell is an important component in all the wines here and gives an almost salty character to the more familiar dark, brambly fruit of the variety. The approachable, fruit driven Reposo is also blended with Merlot, Cabernet and Syrah. Both the top two wines are more serious and structured. They differ from the Reposo, being hand-harvested. The Casa Gran, blended from Monastrell, Garnacha, Syrah and Cabernet is part aged in French oak before bottling. The top wine the Arenal is solely Garnacha and Monastrell. Vinification is similar to the Casa Gran with fermentation and the malolactic carried out conventionally in stainless steel. Ageing though is solely in French oak for around 14 months with a proportion of new wood. A Reposo white is also produced from Moscatel and Gewürztraminer. An additional four wines are also now made since 2008 from a neighbouring estate and labelled Casa Benasal. These are in a more forward fruit driven style. (DM)

Recommended Reds:
Valencia Falcata Arenal ★★★☆ £D
Valencia Falcata Casa Gran ★★★ £C
Valencia Falcata Reposo ★★☆ £B
Recommended Whites:
Valencia Falcata Reposo ★★☆ £B

Pago de Vallegarcia (VdT Castilla) *www.vallegarcia.com*
This is one of Central Spain's most exciting new producers, located just to the east of DEHESA DEL CARRIZAL, also a fellow member of the small group Grandes Pagos d'Espana which represents and promotes the interests of a number of high quality small wine producers. The quality and purity of the wines here is exemplary. Not least the Viognier which is so often fat and overblown in other hands. Barrel-feremented and aged on lees for six months, the wine shows a lovely balance of peachy, mineral fruit and very subtle background oak. It should be drunk young, Both the top two reds are finely crafted in an elegant and piercing style but with really fine fruit, particularly the gloriously smoky and intense black pepper-scented Syrah. The Hipperia is a Bordeaux styled blend of Cabernet Sauvignon, Merlot and Cabernet Franc. A second label Petit Hipperia is also made as well as Miriade a second Viognier. (DM)

Recommended Reds:
VdT Castilla Syrah ★★★★ £E   VdT Castilla Hipperia ★★★☆ £E
Recommended Whites:
VdT Castilla Viognier ★★★☆ £D

Pago del Ama (VdT Castilla) *www.cigarralsantamaria.com*
Although this family group is better known for some of the finest restaurants in not only Toledo but Spain, some fine wines, particularly reds are also produced here at their small bodega "Cigarall Santa Maria". The holding is tiny just 5 ha and certainly much of the production is consumed locally. However these are really splendid reds and worth hunting down, not least enjoying if you happen to be visiting Toledo. The Merlot is one of the best examples in Spain, so often the variety tends towards a vegetal undercurrent. Not here, the wine is dense, rich and full of dark, spicy berry and plum fruit. Syrah is arguably a touch better but only just. It is dark, smoky and complex with just a hint of black spicy pepper. Look out also for a Cabernet Sauvignon and the Colección

Especial which blends Tempranillo with small proportions of Merlot, Cabernet Sauvignon and Syrah. (DM)
Recommended Reds:
VdT Castilla Syrah ★★★★ £E   VdT Castilla Merlot ★★★★ £E

Pagos de Familia *www.pagosdefamilia.com*
Pagos de Familia consists of two estates. Dominio de Valdepusa was among the pioneer properties in La Mancha producing fine, modern reds. The Marques de Griñon also has a second property, El Rincón where a red is made under the Vinos de Madrid appellation. Dominio de Valdepusa is planted in the Montes de Toledo on limestone subsoils and at a high vine density. El Rincón, to the south-west of the capital was established only a decade ago and planted on granite and sand over clay to both Syrah and Garnacha. Very well crafted and stylish wines are made. The key is a commitment to viticulture with sophisticated modern trellising as well as irrigation only when needed. Good to very good reds are produced: Cabernet Sauvignon, Petit Verdot, Syrah as well as blends of all three, Eméritus and Summa Varietalis. The Syrah is rich and smoky and the Petit Verdot scented yet firm – it needs more time than the others, 5 or 6 years. The Cabernet, surprisingly, can show a leafy note. The Éméritus and Summa Varietalis are both rich, dark and concentrated, with a big dollop of Syrah adding a black pepper spiced complexity. A further premium red AAA is made in small volume and named for Marques de Griñon's three daughters. (DM)
Recommended Reds:
Dominio de Valdepusa Émeritus ★★★★ £G
Dominio de Valdepusa Summa Varietalis ★★★☆ £E
Vinos de Madrid El Rincón ★★★☆ £D
Dominio de Valdepusa Syrah ★★★☆ £D
Dominio de Valdepusa Petit Verdot ★★★☆ £D
Dominio de Valdepusa Cabernet Sauvignon ★★★ £D

Perez Barquero (Montilla-Moriles) *www.perezbarquero.com*
A range of first class Montilla *flor* influenced, fortified and sweet wines are made here. Established in 1905 the bodega has some excellent vineyard plots in the lime rich Sierra de Montilla and Moriles Alto areas. As well as the traditional Montilla styles the bodega makes a fresh, fruit driven white Viña Amalia from a blend of Pedro Ximénez, Moscatel, Verdejo and Torrontés . It is low in alcohol, around 10.5 % and has a touch of residual sugar. Of the Finos, the Los Amigos is aged under *flor* in American oak for 3 to 4 years. A touch more complex and rich is the Gran Barquero, aged for longer in *solera* with an average of 8 to 10 years. A third fino is also made, spending a shorter time in cask, Solera 13. The Gran Barquero Amontillado is very concentrated, nutty and charcterful. The Gran Barquero Oloroso is rich, unctuous and concentrated without quite the elegance and finesse of the Amontillado. Some excellent Pedro Ximénez is also made. There is an approachable, rich and sweet Cosecha and Los Amigos bottling. A good deal more complexity and intense dried fruit notes, fig and prune can be found in the Gran Barquero. The top PX is the splendid La Cañada. It is very rich, intense and with extraordinary complexity and great balance and subtlety. The bodega also have a number of very rare bottles, an Amontillado, Oloroso and PX from a 1905 dated *solera*. (DM)
Recommended Whites:
Montilla-Moriles Pedro Ximénez La Cañada ★★★★☆ £E
Montilla-Moriles Oloroso Gran Barquero ★★★ £C
Montilla-Moriles Amontillado Gran Barquero ★★★ £C
Montilla-Moriles Fino Gran Barquero ★★★ £C
Montilla-Moriles Pedro Ximénez Gran Barquero ★★☆ £C

Wine behind the label

Central, Southern Spain & the Islands

Spain

Montilla-Moriles Pedro Ximénez Cosecha ★★ £B
Montilla-Moriles Fino Los Amigos ★★ £B
Montilla-Moriles Viña Amalia ★ £A

❂ Bodegas Ponce (Manchuela)
Ponce is a relative newcomer in Manchuela but really showing the potential to be achieved from old vine Bobal planted in clay and calcareous limestone soils. Indeed most of the wines are vinified solely from the variety and the total output is barely more than 3,000 cases a year. Quality though is very good throughout the small range and the wines are good value and very characterful. There are a total of around 22 ha under cultivation and many of the vines are now well over 60 years of age, adding to the complexity of the wines, particularly the three single vineyard "Finca" bottlings. The vineyards, which are farmed as naturally as possible with no chemicals, are at an altitude of close to 900 metres and this helps promote acidity and balance in the resulting wines. Because of the arid summer climate and low rainfall the vineyard is planted at a low density of just over 1,000 vines to the hectare. All the wines are aged in French oak, the Clos Lojén for 8 months the other wines for just under a year. Buena Pinta differs from the other reds being a blend of Garnacha and Moravia Agria, which lends acidity. A white, El Reto from Albillo is rich, concentrated and minerally. (DM)
Recommended Reds:
Manchuela La Casilla Finca Moján Blanco ★★★★☆ £E
Manchuela La Casilla Finca La Estrecha ★★★★ £D
Manchuela La Casilla Finca Luján ★★★★ £D
Manchuela PF ★★★☆ £D   Manchuela Pino ★★★ £C
Manchuela Buena Pinta ★★★ £C
Manchuela La Casilla ★★★ £C
Manchuela Clos Lojen ★★★ £C
Recommended Whites:
Manchuela El Reto ★★★☆ £D

Ramos-Paul (Malaga) www.ramos-paul.com
José Manuel Ramos-Paul Ruano and his wife Pilar Martínez-Mejías Laffitte established their wine business, Bodegas y Viñedos El Chantre in 1999, believing firmly in the potential of the Serrania de Ronda sub-region for the production of top quality reds. The vineyards are found at an altitude of 1,000 metres providing for grapes of not only rich extract but also high acidity. They are planted to a mix of Tempranillo, Cabernet Sauvignon, Syrah (referred to here as Shiraz) and Merlot. The first release, the 2004, showed much potential, and subsequent vintages taking quality a stage further. The final *assemblage* is a blend of mainly Cabernet, with Tempranillo and Syrah. (DM)
Recommended Reds:
Sierras de Málaga Ramos-Paul ★★★★ £F

>> Bodegas Recuero (VdT Castilla) www.bodegasrecuero.com
This is another example of the potential of quality wine making in Toledo. The Recuero family have been vinegrowers for a number of generations since 1873 and their cellars are in the northeast of the Province. The vineyards are found in the valley of the Gigüela River, which is a tributary of the Guadiana. The vines are planted in limestone soils, which are poor in organic matter and with a low density of bush vines. The summers are very warm and cold growing season nights are important. As well as the four reds covered below a white sparkler Methode Traditionelle, Often Sigilo is also made, mainly from Airen and aged for 36 months in bottle. A dry light white Gordal Sigilo comes from the grape of the

same name. The red Sigilo Viña Maldita is unusual for the area, a light cherry fruited Pinot Noir. Offering more depth and intensity is the Sigilo Moravia from the local Moravia Agria variety, full of earthy, characterful blackberry fruits and with a dark spicy edge. Both Sigilo reds are aged in French oak for 12 months. There are two Tempranillo reds. The first bright and forward with red berry fruits, the Guarda Familiar more structured. Bearing similarity with a modern styled Rioja it is aged in small French oak for 14 months. Jesús is also involved with another small winery project, Antier, in the Sierra de Gata in the northwest of the Extremadura. (DM)
Recommended Reds:
VdT Castilla Guarda Familiar ★★★☆ £E
VdT Castilla Sigilo Moravia ★★★☆ £D
VdT Castilla Tempranillo ★★☆ £C
VdT Castilla Sigilo Viña Maldita ★★ £D

Bodegues Ribas (VdT Mallorca) www.bodeguesribas.com
The Ribas family have been cultivating vines on the island of Mallorca since 1711 and it is still very much a small dedicated family operation. The new generation of Araceli and Xavier Ribas have gained valuable experience working in other major regions and have brought this knowledge to supplement the quality of grapes being produced in the family's 40 ha of rocky sparse and well-drained soils. The growing conditions naturally produce very low yields and fruit with great fruit intensity from vines with an average age of over 50 years. Of the wines the Ribas label provides the softest and most accessible wines. There is a rosado blending Mantonegro, Callet and Merlot as well as the fresh citrus fruited blanco produced from Pensal Blanc and Chardonnay and the juicy fruited tinto coming from Mantonegro, Syrah, Cabernet Sauvignon and Merlot with extra depth and structure provided by 10 months in oak. The ripe and spicy red Sió is the most important wine in the small portfolio. Produced from a similar blend to the Ribas red it is aged in oak, a proportion of which is new and around 25% American, the balance French. Rich and very characterful with deep, dark and spicy berry fruit as well as a marked mineral quality is the Ribas de Cabrera tinto. The wine, which is dominated by the indigenous Mantonegro, is aged for 15 months in French oak. As well as these the family also make a Sió blanco which gets six months in oak with a little Viognier as well as Prensal and Chardonnay, a further red Sió Contrast made from another indigenous grape the Gargollasa and a couple of Dulce bottlings. Soma is a white from Viognier which is a newly established joint venture project. These are excellent examples if you are visiting the island and worth hunting for elsewhere.(DM)
Recommended Reds:
VdT Mallorca Ribas de Cabrera ★★★☆ £E
VdT Mallorca Sió ★★★ £C   VdT Mallorca Ribas ★★☆ £B
Recommended Whites:
VdT Mallorca Ribas ★★ £B

❂ Celler del Roure (Valencia) www.cellerdelroure.es
Recently founded bodega, in 1995, since when Celler del Roure has established itself as one of the benchmarks in the Valencia DO. Three good to very good reds and a white are produced. The fruit comes from the family vineyard planted some way inland at an altitude of 500 to 600 metres above sea level and giving a fresh acidity and balance to the wines. Monastrell is the main component of ripe dark-berried, brambly Les Alcusses and a number of other varieties have been included in the blend. The top wine Maduresa, more structured, rich and sumptuously ripe has less Monastrell and also

includes a little rare indigenous Mandó. Vinification is modern and the wines are aged for a few months on lees in cask. The Maduresa in particular has the fine mineral structure to enable further development over half a decade and more. The white Cullerot was recently added to the small range. Two juicy, forward red blends (£B) are also made. Parotet is dominared by Mandó, while Vermell combines Garnacha Tintorera, Monastrell and a little Mandó (DM)

Recommended Reds:
Valencia Maduresa ★★★★ £E   Valencia Les Alcusses ★★★ £C
Valencia Setze Gallets ★★☆ £B
Recommended Whites:
Valencia Cuillerot ★★★ £C

❁ Finca Sandoval (Manchuela)
This bodega is perhaps unfairly known as much for being owned by top Spanish wine journalist Victor de la Serna as for the quality of its very fine red wines. There is an excellent regular red Manchuela bottling, a fine secondary label Salia and a new cuvée Cecilia has also been added. There is also a more expensive special cuvée "TNS" blending Touriga Nacional and Syrah which is bottled in magnums. The regular Sandoval bottlings blend both Syrah and Monastrell and provide wines of dark, spicy and mineral scented fruit. Expect them to age well for five years or more. Two further reds have been released, a Signo Garnacha and Signo Bobal. (DM)

Recommended Reds:
Manchuela TNS ★★★★☆ £F
Manchuela Finca Sandoval ★★★★ £E
Manchuela Salia ★★★☆ £C   Manchuela Cecilia ★★★ £C

❁ Sedella Vinos (VdM Andalucia) *www.sedellavinos.com*
Lauren Rosillo makes one excellent red, which he refers as a Mediterranean Mountain Wine. He crafts it from ancient vines, many up to 100 years old, planted at high altitude, approaching 1,000 metres, on the slopes of the Sierras de Málaga appellation. While the farming is distinctly artisanal and organic, the winemaking is carried out in an architecturally striking new winery that overlooks the vineyards and integrates well with the landscape of the area. The Sedella Tinto is made from the indigenous Romé, Garnacha Tinto as well as a smattering of other local varieties. It is in contrast to a number of other wines from the area, which are dominated by Bordeaux red grapes. The fruit was all hand-harvested and after sorting fermentation followed with natural yeasts and then the malolactic fermentation in cement amphora. Ageing was for 16 months in French oak. The wine is full of striking black berry fruits and the subtle herb-scented aromas of the region. On the palate it is richly textured and finely balanced by polished tannins with a crisp acidity lending intensity to the wines dark berry fruit. (DM)

Recommended Reds:
Vino de Mesa Andalucia Sedella Tinto ★★★★☆ £E

❁ Señorio de Barahonda (Yecla) *www.barahonda.com*
A wide range of wines is produced here at Barahonda. Local Monastrell constitutes much of the quality and a resource that includes 110 ha of owned vines of 40 to 65 years is certainly significant. The winery is also able to call on further resources so it is not limited. Carro is a soft fruit driven blend of 50% Monastrell with the balance Syrah, Tempranillo and Merlot. Monastrell Sin-Madera is varietal and in a similar style, vinification is solely stainless steel. Both the Crianza and Barrica are a blend of Monastrell with Cabernet Sauvignon lending structure. The Barrica is fresher and with greater vibrancy. Newly offered Organac combines 40 year old Monastrell

with 20 year old Syrah. Summum is a characterful small volume Monastrell from ungrafted vines and aged in American and a small amount of French oak in a rich and toasty black-fruited style. The Heredad Candela Monastrell comes from 80 year old vines and the quality of the fruit really shines through, the wine being aged in solely 500 litre French oak for 9 months with the malolactic in barrel. There is also an impressive Petit Verdot. Structured and full of varietal dark spicy fruit the wine is aged in smaller 225 litre oak. Look out also for a number of other wines. Tranco is a red blend of Cabernet Sauvignon and Monastrell, both Campo Arriba and Cueva Negra combine variable proportions of Monastrell, Syrah and Garnacha Tintorera and Zona Zepa is produced in tiny quantities from pre-phylloxera Monastrell. (DM)

Recommended Reds:
Yecla Monastrell Heredad Candela ★★★★ £D
Yecla Summum ★★★★ £D
Yecla Petit Verdot Heredad Candela ★★★☆ £D
Yecla Summum ★★★★ £D   Yecla Organac ★★★ £C
Yecla Barrica ★★☆ £B   Yecla Crianza ★★ £B
Yecla Monastrell ★★ £B   Yecla Carro ★☆ £B

►► Sierra Salinas (Alicante) *www.mgwinesgroup.com*
This property was purchased in from the CASTAÑO family in 2013 by the MG Wines group who also own ESTEFANIA in Bierzo and LAVIA in Bullas. Some splendid reds are made from Monastrell, Cabernet Sauvignon, Garnacha Tintorera, Petit Verdot and Syrah. There are just over 50 ha of vines and the bulk of these are old bush vine Monastrell. A state of the art gravity flow winery has been built and the wines are aged in an underground cellar. The rich, complex and concentrated black fruited top label 1237 is named after the altitude of the highest peak in the Sierra Salinas Mountains. It is aged on lees for 21 months in barrel. Mira Salinas comes from a mixed blend and sees 14 months in wood. The Puerto Salinas is a touch more approachable with juicy, spicy blackberry fruit and a supple structure gained from ageing in a mix of new and used barrels for around a year. The most approachable of the reds is the vibrant Mo, which gains just a little structure from 4 months in used oak. This has been joined by a fruit driven white Puerto Salinas, which is a Chardonnay partly barrel fermented in 500 litre vessels. (DM)

Recommended Reds:
Alicante 1237 ★★★★☆ £F   Alicante Mira Salinas ★★★★ £D
Alicante Puerto Salinas ★★★ £C   Alicante Mo ★★☆ £B
Recommended Whites:
Alicante Puerto Salinas ★★☆ £B

❁ Son Vell/4 Kilos (VdT Mallorca) *www.4kilos.com*
This small and extremely impressive Mallorcan bodega, is also known just as 4 Kilos. It was established very recently and produced its first wine with the 2006 vintage. Output is fairly small, currently at around 5,000 cases a year. The wines are very fairly priced for their quality. The vineyards are planted with natural cover crops and the wines made with minimal intervention. The blend of the 4 Kilos red is dominated by the indigenous Callet with a healthy dollop of Cabernet Sauvignon and the balance from Syrah. The fruit is sourced from two small vineyards. The wine offers a richly textured and darkly spicy character to its fruit and is vinified in a distinctly modern fashion. Fermentation and ageing is in small French oak with malolactic in barrel. Supple and approachable, the wine should nevertheless devlop well for a decade or so. A more approachable, fruit-driven second label 12 Volts is nevertheless full of depth and

Central, Southern Spain & the Islands

character and comes from Callet, Syrah, Cabernet Sauvignon and Merlot. The bodega is also involved in another project producing a red, Gallinas y Focas, from a blend of Manto Negro and Syrah. It is a collaboration involving those with mental disabilities and their families. (DM)

Recommended Reds:

VdT Mallorca 4 Kilos ★★★★ £E   VdT Mallorca 12 Volts ★★★☆ £D

Bodegas Tagonius (Vinos de Madrid) *www.tagonius.com*
Founded in 2000 with considerable investment, this is one of the quality leaders in the DO of Madrid. The vineyards are found in a sheltered local climate to the south-east of the city. There is a Tagonius Blanco and an approachable Cosecha but it is the leading Tagonius reds that are the stand out wines. The dark berry Roble comes from Tempranillo, Cabernet Sauvignon, Merlot and Syrah and is aged in mainly used wood for around 6 months. Crianza is more structured with dusty, earthy tannins and good depth. The wine is aged for a year in a mix of French and American wood and half surprisingly, is new. The Reserva gets a touch longer 14 months and gains from the inclusion of a substantial proportion of Cabernet Sauvignon as well as a little Syrah. There are two interesting and characterful mono-varietals which are more modern and international in style. Merlot is dark, spicy and plummy while the Syrah is ripe, licoricey and with classic dark pepper spice character. Both are aged in solely new oak but only for 6 months to protect the character of the fruit. Mariage is a blend of Cabernet Sauvignon and Merlot, richly sweet fruited with black and spicy notes and creamy new oak. It is aged in a high proportion of new wood for up to two years. A further premium red Gran Via Reserva combines Merlot and Tempranillo. The top wine the Gran Vino is one of Central Spain's best reds. It is a blend of Cabernet Sauvignon, Syrah and just a touch of Tempranillo. The approach is thoroughly modern with new oak used and malolactic in barrel. The wine is first aged in smaller 225 litre oak and then transferred to larger 500 litre barrels. Dark, sumptuous and opulent it is immediately approachable but will add greater complexity with half a decade's cellaring and more. (DM)

Recommended Reds:

Vinos de Madrid Tagonius Gran Vino ★★★★ £F
Vinos de Madrid Mariage ★★★☆ £E
Vinos de Madrid Syrah ★★★☆ £E
Vinos de Madrid Reserva ★★★☆ £E
Vinos de Madrid Merlot ★★★ £D
Vinos de Madrid Crianza ★★★ £D
Vinos de Madrid Roble ★★☆ £C

Bodega Tikalo (VdT Castilla) *www.bodegatikalo.com*
Based in the heart of central Spain in the province of Ciudad Real, Tikalo produces good quality well-priced reds. The bodega was founded in 2002 and has a holding of around 400 ha of Tempranillo, Garnacha and Cabernet Sauvignon. The high altitude of the vineyard, around 850 metres above sea-level, ensures cool nights and the vineyard is dry-farmed with a considerable holding of older bush vines. The average age of the vineyard is now over 30 years providing fruit of real character, particularly from the lower yielding parcels. The range includes two simple fruit driven wines under the Albaliza label, the red offering somewhat more than the soft, fruity rosé. Rubens has a really vibrant quality to its fruit. Seeing no wood it is for early consumption and offers great value. The top three wines all take the Kios label and vinification is modern with malolactic in barrel. The Kios Tempranillo has a ripe dark fruit character and a touch of woody tannin, the Cabernet Sauvignon a very pronounced

minty overtone and a surprisingly firm structure. The Elite comes from a single low-yielding plot. It is impressively concentrated with a real old-viney quality beginning to emerge as well as a very smoky, coffee scented character from the new wood. It will be better with three or four years. (DM)

Recommended Reds:

VdT Castilla Kios Elite ★★★ £D
VdT Castilla Kios Cabernet Sauvignon ★★☆ £C
VdT Castilla Kios Tempranillo ★★☆ £C
VdT Castilla Rubens ★★☆ £B   VdT Castilla Albaliza ★★ £B

✿ Bodegas Tradición *www.bodegastradicion.com*
Although only established in 1998 by three members of old Jerez families, Bodegas Tradicion has an enviable holding of superb old sherry soleras. All the wines take the VOS classification (Very Old Sherry) for wines over 20 years. As such all the wines are entitled to take the appellation Jerez - Xèrés - Sherry which covers only the oldest and finest wines in the region. The old south-east facing cellars offer an ideal mix of wind and humidity for the soleras. All four wines have a depth and intensity of fruit rare indeed here. The nutty, tobacco scented Amontillado has an average age of 40 years and its origins go back to the 19th century. The rich and concentrated nutmeg scented Oloroso is a touch older. Palo Cortado is exquisitely intense, with a piercing citrus undercurrent lifting the wine. The rich and unctuous Pedro Ximenez offers a glorious mix of cocoa, roasted coffee and marvellous balance and structure, so rare to find in these wines. All four are well worth searching out and are well priced for their quality. (DM)

Recommended Whites:

Jerez y Manzanilla Oloroso VORS ★★★★★ £F
Jerez y Manzanilla Amontillado VORS ★★★★★ £F
Jerez y Manzanilla Palo Cortado VORS ★★★★★ £F
Jerez y Manzanilla Pedro Ximénez VOS ★★★★☆ £F

✿✿ Valdespino (Jerez y Manzanilla) *www.grupoestevez.com*
Valdespino is a marvellous, old-fashioned sherry producer, now under new ownership, with an impressive holding of old soleras providing some of the best examples to be found in Jerez. The salty and intense Fino Inocente has a marked *flor* yeast character but should be drunk as soon after purchase as possible to enjoy its fresh, pungent, citrus character. The Señorita Manzanilla is fresh and delicate. There is a rich and toffee-like Pedro Ximénez El Cantado which can only really be sipped. The Palo Cortado is one of the very best examples of this unusual style. There are a number of dry Amontillados. Tio Diego has an almost austere, tangy finish. The Contrabandista has just a touch of sweetness from the addition of a little PX. Far more interesting is the remarkable, intense, nutty and fragrant Coliseo, one of the greatest of all sherries. There an excellent old Oloroso full of depth and complexity. Proprietors, Grupo Estevez also own two other bodegas with wines showing real potential, La Guita and Real Tesoro. (DM)

Recommended Whites:

Jerez y Manzanilla Manzanilla Amontillado Coliseo VORS ✪✪✪✪✪ £H
Jerez y Manzanilla Palo Cortado Cardenale VORS ✪✪✪✪✪ £G
Jerez y Manzanilla Oloroso Don Gonzalo VOS ★★★★ £E
Jerez y Manzanilla Amontillado Contrabandista ★★★☆ £D
Jerez y Manzanilla Pedro Ximénez El Candado ★★★ £D
Jerez y Manzanilla Amontillado Tio Diego ★★★ £C
Jerez y Manzanilla Fino Inocente ★★★ £C
Jerez y Manzanilla Manzanilla Señorita ★★ £B

>> Bodegas Vegalfaro www.vegalfaro.com

This bodega has joined the small list of properties, which are entitled to their own single estate DO. As well as wines from this property they also make Cava and release wines from the Utiel-Requena appellation. There are a total of 60 ha under vine, all certified organic. The most approachable of the wines, the Rebel. lia labels, also includes a soft fruity rosado. The white is a crisp, cool fermented green-fruited blend of Chardonnay and Sauvignon Blanc. The red offers vibrant dark berry and cherry fruits and gains a little extra depth and structure from four months in Hungarian oak. Under the Caprasia label a white and a rosado are also made from respectively Chardonnay and a Bobal/Merlot blend. The Caprasia Roble, which blends Bobal and Merlot is a fresh black fruited, spicy red with a supple rounded texture after three months in small oak. The Bobal Crianza is a fuller, more structured wine. A modern approach to vinification sees a 14 month period in barrel including the malolactic fermentation and then five further months in amphorae. At Pago Los Balaguesses as well as the two reds a Chardonnay is also made from a small holding of 3 ha grown in chalk soils. The Garnacha Tintorera Merlot is deeply coloured and gets an extended period on skins during vinification. Marked by spicy black fruits, there is a rich toasted character. The Syrah enjoys a similar vinification regime and is a touch more elegant with black fruits and black pepper notes and a fine rounded texture with supple, polished tannins. (DM)

Recommended Reds:

Pago Los Balaguesses Syrah ★★★☆ £D
Pago Los Balaguesses Garnacha Tintorera Merlot ★★★☆ £D
Utiel-Requena Caprasia Bobal Crianza ★★★ £C
Utiel-Requena Caprasia Roble ★★☆ £B
Utiel-Requena Rebel.lia ★★☆ £B

Recommended Whites:

Utiel-Requena Rebel.lia ★★ £B

Bodega Vetas (Malaga) www.bodegavetas.com

Juan Manuel Vetas established his small winery in 2000 and he produces two wines of really impressive depth and dimension. Output is tiny though, barely 500 cases and he possesses just 1 ha. However these are the epitome of what great artisan wines and wines of *terroir* are all about, so they are worth looking for, particularly if you are in the area. The Petit Verdot is dark and smoky with ripe and firmly structured tannins and a mineral quality adding complexity. Similarly impressive is the Vetas Selección, a Bordeaux style blend. Both wines will benefit from at least five year's patience, they are however very well made, modern examples so you may broach them early without too much trepidation. (DM)

Recommended Reds:

Sierras de Málaga Vetas Selección ★★★★ £E
Sierras de Málaga Vetas Petit Verdot ★★★★ £E

Bodega Volver (La Mancha) www.bodegasvolver.com

The wines here were originally labelled Mano a Mano before a change in ownership took that label to the Avanteselecta group. Unlike a number of neighbouring wineries who prefer to take the VdT Castilla classification rather than DO La Mancha, this is not the case at Volver. Winemaker Rafael Canizares can draw on around 100 ha of Tempranillo and a little Merlot, with the majority of the vines well over 40 years old. The vineyards are planted at altitude, around 600 metres in the more favourable eastern sector of the appellation in sandy soils and on a stony, rocky bedrock. The ripe and spicy Paso a Paso offers impressive depth and intensity at a very fair price, while the top label Volver is dense, rich and impressively concentrated. The Paso a Paso white offers excellent varietal fruit and fresh balanced acidity. A second label Tarima Hill is a source of Alicante Monastrell reds and a white from a blend of Merseguera, Macabeo and Moscatel. A vibrant bright fruited red, Wrongo Dongo is also made from Jumilla fruit. Two Tempranillo reds are made at a second bodega Venta Morales. (DM)

Recommended Reds:

La Mancha Volver ★★★★ £E
La Mancha Paso a Paso Tempranillo ★★★ £C
Jumilla Wrongo Dongo ★★ £B

Recommended Whites:

La Mancha Paso a Paso Verdejo ★★☆ £C

Other wines of note - *Central & Southern Spain & The Islands*

Madrid & Castilla La Mancha

Casa Alarcón

Recommended Reds: VdT Castilla Don Jaime ★★☆ £C
VdT Castilla Nea ★★☆ £C

Alonso Cuesta

Recommended Reds: Méntrida Alonso Cuesta ★★★☆ £D
Recommended Whites: Méntrida Alonso Cuesta ★★ £B

Finca Antigua

Recommended Reds: La Mancha Crianza ★★☆ £C
La Mancha Garnacha ★★☆ £B La Mancha Tempranillo ★★ £B

Arva Vitis

Recommended Reds:

VdT Castilla Grial de Avalon ★★★☆ £D
VdT Castilla Avalon ★★★ £C
VdT Castilla Selección Privada ★★☆ £B
VdT Castilla Tempranillo Merlot ★☆ £A

Bodegas Campos Reales

Recommended Reds: La Mancha Gladium Viñas Viejas ★★★ £C
La Mancha Canforrales Selección ★☆ £A

Casal del Blanco (DOP Pago Casal del Blanco)

Recommended Reds:

Casa del Blanco Quixote Merlot/Tempranillo/Petit Verdot ★★☆ £D
Casa del Blanco Quixote Cabernet Sauvignon/Syrah ★★☆ £D

Casalobos

Recommended Reds:

VdT Castilla Casalobos ★★★☆ £D

Finca Constancia

Recommended Reds:

VdT Castilla Altos de la Finca ★★★☆ £D
VdT Castilla Parcela 23 ★★★ £C
VdT Castilla Finca Constancia ★★☆ £B

Bodegas Fontana

Recommended Reds:

VdT Castilla Quercus ★★★☆ £D
VdT Castilla Dueto de Fontana ★★★☆ £D
Uclés Esencia de Fontana ★★★ £C
VdT Castilla Gran Fontal Vendimia Seleccionada ★★★ £C
La Mancha Fontal Crianza ★★ £B La Mancha Fontal Roble ★☆ £A

Bodega Iniesta

Recommended Reds:

Manchuela Finca El Carril ★★☆ £C

Recommended Whites:

Manchuela Finca El Carril Valeria ★★★ £C
Manchuela Corazón Loco ★★ £B

Central, Southern Spain & the Islands

Spain

Bodega Los Aljibes
Recommended Reds: VdT Castilla Selectus ★★★☆ £E
VdT Castilla Aljibes ★★★ £C
VdT Castilla Aljibes Cabernet Franc ★★☆ £C
Dehesa Los Llanos
Recommended Reds: VdT Castilla Mazacruz Cima ★★★ £C
Recommended Whites: VdT Castilla Mazacruz Cima ★★☆ £C
Manuel Manzaneque (DOP Pago Finca Élez)
Recommended Reds: Finca Élez Nuestra Selección ★★★☆ £E
Finca Élez Nuestra Syrah ★★★ £D   Finca Élez Crianza ★★☆ £C
Bodegas Martúe La Garda (DOP Pago Campo La Guardia)
Recommended Reds: Campo La Guardia Martúe Especial ★★★ £D
Campo La Guardia Martúe ★★☆ £C
Bodegas Nueva Valverde
Recommended Reds: Vinos de Madrid 750 ★★★ £E
Vinos de Madrid Tejoneras Alta Selección ★★☆ £C
Pago del Vicario
Recommended Reds: VdT Castilla Agios ★★★ £E
VdT Castilla Monagós ★★★ £D
VdT Castilla 50-50 ★★☆ £C   VdT Castilla Penta ★★ £B
VdT Castilla Merlot Dulce ★☆ £B
Recommended Whites: VdT Castilla Talva ★★ £C
VdT Castilla Blanco de Tempranillo ★☆ £B
VdT Castilla Corte Dulce ★☆ £B
Recommended Rosés: VdT Castilla Petit Verdot Rosado ★☆ £B
Pinuaga
Recommended Reds: VdT Castilla 200 Cepas ★★★ £D
VdT Castilla Pinuaga ★★★ £D   VdT Castilla La Senda ★★☆ £B
Bodegas Piqueras
Recommended Reds: Almansa Gran Marius ★★☆ £B
Almansa Valcanto Monastrell ★★ £A
Almansa Castillo de Almansa Colección ★☆ £A
Almansa Marius ★☆ £A
Dominio de Punctum
Recommended Reds: VdT Castilla Lobetia Tempranillo ★★☆ £C
VdT Castilla Punctum Roble ★★ £B
VdT Castilla Punctum Graciano Syrah ★★ £B
Recommended Whites: VdT Castilla Lobetia Chardonnay ★★★ £C
VdT Castilla Punctum Viognier ★★ £B
Luis Saavedra
Recommended Reds:
Vinos de Madrid Corucho Garnacha Cepas Viejas ★★★☆ £D
Recommended Whites: Vinos de Madrid Corucho ★★☆ £C
Señorio de Val Azul
Recommended Reds: Vinos de Madrid Fabio ★★★☆ £D
Bodega Tintoralba
Recommended Reds: Almansa Crianza Selección ★★★ £B
Almansa Higueruela Selección ★★☆ £B
Almansa Altitud 1100 ★★ £A
Recommended Rosés: Almansa Higueruela ★☆ £A
Uribes Madero (DOP Pago de Calzadilla)
Recommended Reds: Pago Calzadilla Syrah Especial ★★★☆ £D
Pago Calzadilla Opta ★★☆ £C

Communidad Valenciana & Murcia
Bodega J Belda
Recommended Reds: Valencia Ca'Belda ★★★ £C
Valencia Pinot Noir ★★☆ £D   Valencia Migjorn ★★☆ £C
Bleda
Recommended Reds: Jumilla Divus ★★★ £C
Jumilla Amatus ★★☆ £C   Jumilla Castillo de Jumilla Crianza ★☆ £B

Bodegas Bocopa
Recommended Reds:
Alicante Laudum Monastrell Especial ★★★ £C
Recommended Whites: Alicante Marina Espumante ★★☆ £B
Recommended Rosés: Alicante Terreta Rosado ★★☆ £B
Hacienda del Carche
Recommended Reds: Jumilla Tavs ★★☆ £C
Jumilla 4 Cepas Viejas ★★☆ £C
Bodegas Carchelo
Recommended Reds: Jumilla Canalizo ★★★☆ £D
Jumilla Altico A ★★☆ £C   Jumilla Carchelo C ★★☆ £B
Casa de La Ermita
Recommended Reds: Jumilla Petit Verdot ★★★ £D
Jumilla Idílico ★★☆ £C   Jumilla Crianza ★★☆ £C
Jumilla Roble ★★ £B   Jumilla Joven ★☆ £B
Recommended Whites: Jumilla Joven ★☆ £B
Chozas Carrascal (DOP Pago Chozas Carrascal)
Recommended Reds: Utiel-Requena Las Ocho ★★★ £D
Utiel-Requena Los Dos Ces ★★☆ £B
Recommended Whites: Utiel-Requena Las Tres ★★☆ £C
Bodegas Viña Elena
Recommended Reds: Jumilla Pacheco Cuvée Elena ★★★ £C
Jumilla Familia Pacheco Selección ★★★ £C
Jumilla Familia Pacheco Roble ★★ £B
Bodegas Enguera
Recommended Reds: Valencia Megala ★★★☆ £D
Valencia Dis Tinto ★★☆ £C
Bodegas Silvano Garcia
Recommended Reds: Jumilla Viñahonda Allier-Finesse ★★★ £C
Jumilla Dulce Monastrell ★★☆ £C
Jumilla Viñahonda Crianza ★★☆ £C
Jumilla Viñahonda Monastrell ★★☆ £B
Jumilla Viñahonda Joven ★★ £B
Bodega Francisco Gomez
Recommended Reds: Alicante Serrata Reserva ★★★ £D
Alicante Boca Negra ★★★ £D   Alicante Moratillas Crianza ★★ £B
Recommended Whites: Alicante Fruto Noble Sauvignon Blanc ★★ £B
Gutiérrez de La Vega
Recommended Reds: Alicante Viña Ulises ★★★ £C
Alicante Príncipe de Salinas ★★☆ £B
Recommended Whites:
Alicante Moscatel Casta Diva Reserva Real Solera ★★★★★ £G
Alicante Moscatel Casta Diva La Diva ★★★★☆ £E
Alicante Moscatel Casta Diva Miel ★★★ £C
Alicante Moscatel Casta Diva Dorada ★★☆ £B
Bodegas Hispano Suizas
Recommended Reds: Utiel-Requena Bassus Pinot Noir ★★★★ £E
Recommended Whites: Utiel-Requena Impromptu ★★★☆ £D
La Bascula
Recommended Reds: Yecla The Gauntlet ★★★ £C
Rioja The Charge ★★☆ £B   Jumilla Turret Fields Monastrell ★★☆ £B
Recommended Whites: Alicante Casta Diva ★★★★☆ £E
Terra Alta The Catalan Eagle ★★☆ £B   Rioja The Charge ★★☆ £B
Bodegas La Purisima
Recommended Reds: Yecla Trapio ★★★☆ £E
Yecla Valcorso Monastrell ★★ £B   Yecla Valcorso Syrah ★★ £B
Bodegas Los Pinos
Recommended Reds: Valencia Brote Reserva ★★☆ £C
Valencia Los Pinos ★★ £B
Valencia Dominio Los Pinos Crianza ★★ £B
Valencia Dominio Los Pinos Barrica ★☆ £B

Bodegas Luzon
Recommended Reds: Jumilla Altos de Luzón ★★★ £D
Jumilla Finca de Luzón ★★☆ £C
Jumilla Luzón Monastrell ★★☆ £C
>> Mas L'Altet
Recommended Reds: Alicante Luka ★★★★ £E
Alicante Nineta ★★★☆ £D
Alicante Avi Monastrell Especial ★★★☆ £D
Bodegas Murviedro
Recommended Reds:
Valencia Expresión Solidarity Cuvée ★★★★☆ £F
Valencia Colección Petit Verdot ★★☆ £C
Valencia Reserva ★★ £C Valencia Crianza ★☆ £B
Utiel-Requena Cueva de la Culpa ★★★☆ £E
Utiel-Requena Corolilla Crianza ★★ £B
Bodegas Olivares
Recommended Reds: Jumilla Dulce Monastrell ★★★☆ £D
Jumilla Altos de la Hoya ★★★ £C Jumilla Joven ★★☆ £B
Pago de Tharsys
Recommended Reds: Utiel-Requena Dominio de Requena ★★ £A
Recommended Whites: Cava Brut Nature ★★ £B
Recommended Rosés: Cava Brut Reserva Rosado ★★★ £B
Pago del Molino
Recommended Reds: Utiel-Requena Arras de Bobal ★★★★ £E
Utiel-Requena Fusión de Bobal ★★★ £C
Salvador Poveda
Recommended Reds:
Alicante Fondillón Vintage Gran Reserva ★★★★ £E
Alicante Toscar Monastrell ★★ £B
Primitivo Quiles
Recommended Reds:
Alicante Fondillon Gran Reserva Generoso ★★★☆ £D
Alicante Raspay Reserva Especial ★☆ £C
Recommended Whites:
Alicante Moscatel Gran Reserva ★★★☆ £D
Bodegas del Rosario
Recommended Reds: Bullas 3000 Años ★★★★ £E
Bullas Las Reñas Selección ★★★ £C
Bullas Las Reñas Crianza ★★☆ £B
Bullas Las Reñas Monastrell ★★☆ £B
Recommended Whites: Bullas Las Reñas ★☆ £A
Recommended Rosés: Bullas Las Reñas ★★ £A
Finca San Blas
Recommended Reds:
Utiel-Requena Labor del Almadeque Merlot ★★★ £C
Utiel-Requena Labor del Almadeque Reserva ★★★ £C
Utiel-Requena Lomalta ★★☆ £B
>> Sexto Elemento
Recommended Reds: Alicante Respeto ★★★★ £E
Valencia David & Goliath ★★★☆ £D
Valencia Sexto Elemento ★★★☆ £D
Tres P
Recommended Reds: Bullas Tres P ★★★ £B
Dominio de la Vega
Recommended Reds: Utiel-Requena Bobal ★★☆ £B
Recommended Whites: Cava Brut Reserva NV ★★★ £D
Cava Brut Natur NV ★★☆ £B
Vera de Estenas
Recommended Reds:
Utiel-Requena Casa don Ángel Bobal ★★★☆ £D
Utiel-Requena Casa don Ángel Malbec ★★★ £C

Utiel-Requena Vera de Estenas Reserva ★★★ £C
Utiel-Requena Vera de Estenas Crianza ★★☆ £B

Extremadura & Andalucia
Aecovi-Jerez
Recommended Whites:
Jerez y Manzanilla Manzanilla Mira La Mar ★★☆ £B
Viñas de Alange-Palacio Quemada (Alvear)
Recommended Reds: Ribera del Guadiana PQ ★★☆ £C
Ribera del Guadiana Palacio Quemado Reserva ★★☆ £C
Ribera del Guadiana Palacio Quemado Crianza ★☆ £B
Ribera del Guadiana PQ Primicia ★★ £B
Ribera del Guadiana Señorio de Alange Ensamblaje ★★ £B
Ribera del Guadiana Señorio de Alange Tempranillo ★☆ £A
Alto Almanzora
Recommended Reds:
VdT Sierras de las Estancias y Los Filabres Valmediano ★★★ £C
VdM Andalucia Este ★★☆ £B
Recommended Whites: VdM Andalucía Este ★★ £B
Recommended Rosés: VdM Andalucia Este ★★ £B
Bodega Anchurón
Recommended Reds: VdT Altiplano de Sierra Nevada ★★★☆ £D
VC de Granada ★★☆ £C
Recommended Rosés: VC de Granada ★★ £B
Herederos de Argüeso
Recommended Whites:
Jerez y Manzanilla Manzanilla San León Reserva de La Familia ★★★★ £D
Jerez y Manzanilla Manzanilla San León ★★★ £C
Jerez y Manzanilla Manzanilla Las Medallas ★★☆ £B
Bodegas Bentomiz
Recommended Whites:
Málaga Ariyanas Naturalmente Dulce ★★★★ £E
Málaga Ariyanas Seco Sobre Lías ★★★ £C
Bodegas y Viñedos de La Capuchina
Recommended Reds:
Sierras de Málaga Capuchina Vieja ★★★☆ £E
Cruz Conde
Recommended Whites:
Montilla-Moriles Solera Fundación ★★★★ £E
Montilla-Moriles PX Cruz Conde ★★☆ £C
Montilla-Moriles Fino Cruz Conde ★☆ £B
Delgado Zuleta
Recommended Whites:
Jerez y Manzanilla Palo Cortado Monteagudo ★★★ £D
Jerez y Manzanilla Amontillado Monteagudo ★★★ £D
Jerez y Manzanilla Oloroso Monteagudo ★★☆ £C
Jerez y Manzanilla Manzanilla La Goya ★★☆ £B
Díez Mérito
Recommended Whites:
Jerez y Manzanilla Amontillado Fino Imperial VORS ★★★★☆ £F
Jerez y Manzanilla Pedro Ximénez Vieja Solera VORS ★★★★☆ £F
Jerez y Manzanilla Oloroso Don Bertola ★★★ £C
Jerez y Manzanilla Pedro Ximénez Bertola ★★★ £C
Jerez y Manzanilla Fino Bertola ★★☆ £B
Bodega Doña Felisa
Recommended Reds: Sierras de Málaga Chinchilla ★★★ £E
Bodegas Excelencia
Recommended Reds: Sierras de Málaga Los Frontones ★★★ £E
Marques de Valdueza
Recommended Reds:
VdT Extremadura Marques de Valdueza Etiqueta Roja ★★★★ £E

Central, Southern Spain & the Islands

Spain

Finca Moncloa
Recommended Reds: VdT Cádiz Finca Moncloa Barricas ★★★☆ £E
VdT Cádiz Finca Moncloa ★★★ £C
Finca Onegar
Recommended Reds:
VdT Sierras de las Estancias y Los Filabres Expresión ★★★ £E
VdT Sierras de las Estancias y Los Filabres Tempranillo ★★☆ £D
Pago Los Balancines
Recommended Reds:
Ribera del Guadiana Huno Mantanegra ★★★☆ £D
Ribera del Guadiana Huno ★★★ £C
Ribera del Guadiana Crash ★★☆ £B
Recommended Whites: Ribera del Guadiana Alunado ★★★☆ £D
Pago del Mare Nostrum
Recommended Reds: VdM Andalucia 1500 Pinot Noir ★★★☆ £D
Sanchez Romate Hermanos
Recommended Whites:
Jerez y Manzanilla Old & Plus Oloroso ★★★★☆ £E
Jerez y Manzanilla Old & Plus Amontillado ★★★★☆ £E
Jerez y Manzanilla Pedro Ximénez Cardenal Cisneros ★★★ £D
Jerez y Manzanilla Oloroso Don José ★★★ £D
Jerez y Manzanilla Palo Cortado Regente ★★★ £C
Jerez y Manzanilla Amontillado NPU ★★★ £C
Jerez y Manzanilla Fino Marismeño ★★ £B

F. Schatz
Recommended Reds:
Sierras de Málaga Finca Sanguijuela ★★★☆ £E
Sierras de Málaga Petit Verdot ★★★ £E
VdM Andalucia Acinipo ★★☆ £D
Sierras de Málaga Pinot Noir ★★☆ £E
Recommended Whites:
Sierras de Málaga Chardonnay ★★☆ £C
Recommended Rosés:
VdM Andalucia Rosado ★★ £C
Toro Albalá
Recommended Whites:
Montilla-Moriles Amontillado Viejísimo Solera 1922 ★★★☆ £E
Montilla-Moriles Don PX Gran Reserva ★★★☆ £D
Montilla-Moriles Don PX ★★☆ £C
Bodegas Valdivia
Recommended Whites:
Jerez y Manzanilla Sacromonte Oloroso ★★★★ £D
Jerez y Manzanilla Sacromonte Amontillado ★★★★ £D
Jerez y Manzanilla Sacromonte Pedro Ximénez ★★★★ £D
Jerez y Manzanilla Pedro Ximénez Dulce ★★★ £C
Jerez y Manzanilla Amontillado Dorius ★★★ £C
Jerez y Manzanilla Fino Seco ★★☆ £B
Williams & Humbert
Recommended Whites: Dos Cortados Palo Cortado ★★★★ £E
Dry Sack Solera Especial ★★★ £D

The Balearics & The Canaries
José Luis Ferrer
Recommended Reds: Binissalem-Mallorca Crianza ★★★ £C
Binissalem-Mallorca Crianza ★★☆ £C
Vins Miquel Gelabert
Recommended Reds:
Pla i Llevant Torrent Negre Selecció Privada Syrah ★★★☆ £D
Pla i Llevant Torrent Negre Selecció Privada Cabernet ★★☆ £D
Pla i Llevant Torrent Negre ★★☆ £C

Recommended Whites:
Pla i Llevant Chardonnay Roure Selecció Especial ★★☆ £C
El Grifo
Recommended Reds: Lanzarote El Grifo Tinto Barrica ★★★ £C
Lanzarote El Grifo Tinto ★★★ £C
Recommended Whites: Lanzarote El Grifo Canari Licor ★★★★ £E
Lanzarote El Grifo Seco Barrica ★★★ £C
Lanzarote El Grifo Semidulce Colección ★★★ £C
Lanzarote El Grifo Seco Colección ★★★ £C
Bodegas Los Bermejos
Recommended Reds: Lanzarote Maceración Carbónica ★★☆ £B
Recommended Whites:
Lanzarote Malvasía Naturalmente Dulce ★★★☆ £D
Lanzarote Brut Nature Vintage ★★☆ £D
Lanzarote Malvasía Fermentado en Barrica ★★☆ £C
Lanzarote Malvasía Semidulce ★★☆ £B
Lanzarote Malvasía Seco ★★☆ £B
Macià Batle
Recommended Reds:
Binissalem-Mallorca Reserva Privada ★★★☆ £D
VdT Mallorca Pagos de María ★★★ £C
Binissalem-Mallorca Crianza ★★☆ £C
Binissalem-Mallorca Crianza ★★ £B
Recommended Whites:
Binissalem-Mallorca Blanc de Blancs ★★ £C
Jaume Mesquida
Recommended Reds: Pla i Llevant Cabernet Sauvignon ★★☆ £D
Pla i Llevant Negre ★★☆ £C
Recommended Whites: Pla i Llevant Chardonnay ★★ £C
Miquel Oliver
Recommended Reds: Pla i Llevant Ses Ferritges ★★★☆ £D
Pla i Llevant Aia ★★★ £D   Pla i Llevant Syrah Negre ★★☆ £C
Recommended Whites: Pla i Llevant Son Caló ★☆ £C
Finca Son Bordils
Recommended Reds: VdT Mallorca Syrah ★★☆ £C
VdT Mallorca Cabernet Sauvignon ★★☆ £C
VdT Mallorca Negre ★★☆ £C
Recommended Whites: VdT Mallorca Chardonnay Bóta ★★☆ £C
Bodega Stratvs
Recommended Whites:
Lanzarote Naturalement Dulce ★★★★☆ £E
>> Suertes del Marqués
Recommended Reds:
Valle de La Orotava Candio ★★★★ £D
Valle de La Orotava El Esquilón ★★★☆ £C
Valle de La Orotava La Solana ★★★☆ £D
Valle de La Orotava El Lance ★★★☆ £C
Valle de La Orotava 7 Fuentes Tinto ★★★ £C
Recommended Whites:
Valle de La Orotava Vidonia ★★★★ £D
Valle de La Orotava Trenzado ★★★ £C

Work in progress!!

Producers under consideration for the next edition
4 Monos (Vinos de Madrid)
Emilio Hidalgo (Jerez y Manzanilla)
La Moradas de San Martín (Vinos de Madrid)
Vinessens (Alicante)

Author's choice - *Central, Southern Spain & the Islands*

A selection of the best of Central, Southern Spain & the Islands

Reds:

Ricardo Benito   Vinos de Madrid Divo

Bernabe Navarro   Alicante Beryna Selección

Rafael Cambra   Valencia Minimum

Canopy   Mentrida La Viña Escondida

Cap de Barbaria   VdT Formentera Cap de Barbaria

Casa Castillo   Jumilla Pie Franco

Comando G   Vinos de Madrid Las Umbrías

Bodegas El Nido   Jumilla El Nido

Huerta Albalá   VdT Cádiz Taberner No 1

Dani Landi   Mentrida Cantos del Diable

Bodegas Lavia   Bullas Lavia +

Mano a Mano   VdT Castilla Venta La Ossa

Mustiguillo   Pago El Terrerazu Quincha Corral

Ponce   Manchuela La Casilla Finca Moján Blanco

Sedella Vinos   VdM Andalucia Sedella Tinto

Son Vell   VdT Mallorca 4 Kilos

Whites:

Bernabeleva   Vinos de Madrid Cantocuerdas

Celler La Muntanya   VdM Valencia Iliure Albire

Bodega Marañones   Vinos de Madrid Piesdescalzos

Pago de Vallegarcia   VdT Castilla Viognier

Some top values

Reds:

Bodegas Almanseñas   Almansa Venta La Vega Old Vines

Atalaya   Almansa La Atalaya

Celler del Roure   Valencia Setze Gallets

Elvi Wines   Ribera del Júcar Ness

Bodegas Ercavio   VdT Castilla Ercavio Selección Limitada

Finca La Estacada   VdT Castilla 6 Meses

Bodegas Los Frailes   Valencia Efe Monastrell

Bodegas Monastrell   Bullas Chaveo

Whites:

Bodegas Castaño   Yecla Castaño Macabeo Chardonnay

El Angosto   Valencia El Angosto Blanco

E Mendoza   Alicante Chardonnay

Pago Casa Gran   Valencia Falcata Reposo

Bodegas Volver   La Mancha Paso a Paso Verdejo

Rosés:

Huerta Albalá   VdT Cádiz Barbarosa

Bodegas Sierra Salinas   Alicante Mo

Dominio de Buenavista   VdT Cumbres de Guadalfeo Tempranillo

Portugal

The Portuguese winemaking revolution started in the 2000's continues apace. At the cutting edge are some brilliant winemakers making both everyday wines of great value and character and also exciting new wines of unprecedented quality for this ancient wine- producing country. The Douro, followed by Alentejo, provides the greatest riches and the Dão renaissance continues but there are exciting wines from nearly all the major regions. A country that long made its fame for fortified wines, is now gathering accolades for its table wines – red particularly but increasingly white wines too. For white wines, which have improved in leaps and bounds, Vinho Verde leads the way with some exceptional varietal Alvarinho and Loureiro wines and, at the highest level, the Douro impresses. There is still much poor wine at lower end but the best wines from leading producers can be tried with confidence. If we are honest, overproduction is still a problem. Portugal's burgeoning middle classes consume the lion's share of the best wines and have pushed up prices somewhat but increasing quantities are exported and many new, exciting wines are being introduced every year. Value for money- wise, Portugal still remains the best there is in Western Europe.

Port & the Douro
Port tradition
The five leading varietals in this spectacular region were identified in the 1970s as Touriga Nacional, Tinta Roriz, Touriga Franca (previously called Touriga Francesa), Tinta Barroca and Tinto Cão. Some consider a sixth, Tinta Amarela, to be equally important. Though all were often planted as field blends that might include any number of other varieties, there has been an increasing trend towards planting by single variety. Where it is feasible on the steep schistose slopes, quality-conscious producers now favour vertical plantings (as used in the Mosel) with a resultant increase in density. But these vineyards co-exist with old-fashioned (occasionally single-row) terracing (socalcos) and the bulldozed terracing (patamares) that were introduced in the 1970s and allowed for greater mechanization.

In the west of the region the Serra do Marão range of mountains has a significant effect on the climate. There is a successive drop-off in average rainfall in stages from relatively rain-soaked Porto to Régua (Baixo Corgo – the westernmost of three sections), to Pinhão (Cima Corgo), to the dry, flatter lands of the Douro Superior (close to the eastern border with Spain) where there is some use of irrigation. Producers have shown it is possible to get grapes fully ripe in the Baixo Corgo around Régua, though they are likely to be hardest hit in rain-affected vintages. Cima Corgo is the classic port country with the greatest concentration of 'A' classified vineyards (vines are classified A to F) and most of the famous quintas.

A quinta defines a farm or estate which may be composed of vineyards of more than one grade. The quintas overlooking the Douro are important but so are those found on several small tributaries, especially those from the valleys of the Rio Pinhão and the Rio Torto. Here the greatest differences in character, structure and styles are discernible from individual terroirs. Although many of the classic Vintage Ports are sourced from here fine port is also made in the Douro Superior which has seen a frenzy of planting for table wine as well as port by some of the region's leading players.

Port has traditionally been stored at the port lodges in Vila Nova da Gaia (opposite the city of Porto, on the north bank of the Douro), but since 1986 it has been permitted to make, store and ship port at its source in the Douro. Quinta do Noval and Quinta de la Rosa were two of the first to take advantage of this but it is necessary to have cool cellars if the wines are not to take on a distinctive baked character known as Douro bake. New lodges are air conditioned with humidity carefully controlled.

Although autovinification is common for most ports, the best Vintage Ports are made by fermenting in lagares. Traditionally this involves treading by foot (though this is now being closely imitated by robotic devices) which allows the rapid but gentle extraction of colour, tannin and extract in the 48 hours or so before the fermentation is arrested by the addition of port brandy. Temperature control of lagares and the chilling of brandy are also used to harmonise this addition and avoid a spirity component in the resulting port.

Red revolution
Most table reds were previously made from inferior grapes or sites, but in the past two decades leading producers have established potentially high-quality sites (or harnessed the potential of existing sites) specifically for Douro reds, resulting in a remarkable revolution in both the quality and quantity of premium examples. Port grapes have been deployed to produce fine table vines, both younger plantings and established vines too. Elevation and cooler north-facing sites come into their own for table wine, especially the whites. The best wines impress not only with splendid fruit, depth and structure but also the stylish minerality that vine age and the Douro's soils can bring. The best estates are now producing terroir-driven wines targeting the fine wine sector that compare favourably to fine Bordeaux.

As with port, some of it is coarse, baked or unattractively earthy but the best are rich, elegant, complex, perfumed and characterful. Douro has been long-regarded by the Portuguese as the country's finest wine region for red table wine (and whites too). Some Douro reds can honestly be described as some of the world's finest wines and whilst prices are creeping up, they are still very affordable by Bordeaux / Burgundy / Tuscan / Napa (etc.) standards. The list of top wines is now too extensive to summarize here but Alves de Sousa, Lemos & van Zeller, Niepoort, Poeira, Pintas, Quinta do Crasto, Duas Quintas, Vale Dona Maria, Vallado, Wine and Soul, Quinta do Passadouro and Quinta do Vale Meão all include at least one of the region's benchmark examples.

Other regions
Minho/Vinho Verde
Minho is very unlike most of the wine growing regions of Portugal. It is warm but damp – sometimes very damp due to its coastal Atlantic influence - think of a muggy summer's day in the UK. Whereas Vinho Verde used to be a bit of a joke, it should now be taken seriously from the best producers. Really decent **Vinho Verde** (or Vinho Regional Minho) made in the Rios do Minho region, has been, at least until recently, very rare. Despite changes to viticulture, a tradition of high yields and the damp climate can make it difficult to get Alvarinho (the best grape), Loureiro, Trajadura or other grapes fully ripe for the white version that is widely exported. However several good producers, including Quinta do Ameal, Anselmo Mendes and the particularly refined Alvarinho from Antonio Esteves Ferreira (Quinta do Soalheiro) lead the quality charge and are attracting a flurry of new names like Galician Marcial Dorado.

Beiras/Bairrada & Dão

Beiras, a large, predominantly agricultural region to the south of the Douro, includes both the Bairrada and Dão DOCs. Labels showing simply Beiras Vinho Regional can be wines that fall outside the regulations for these DOCs as well as wines from the wider region. The Portuguese do not consider Beiras a good region for wine and excellent vintages can be few and far between in **Bairrada**. The biggest problem is rain and the diseases which can result from it. The heavy clay soils are largely planted to the Baga grape which is high in both tannin and acidity and it can be difficult to achieve full ripeness in its tannins. Nonetheless wines of great depth and character, if idiosyncratic style and flavour, are possible and much progress has been made in recent years. The out and out star is Luis Pato (and increasingly his daughter Filipa – see below) but there are several other good producers including Dão Sul (Quinta do Encontro), Campolargo (who work with French varieties as well as Portuguese), the much under-rated excellent traditional style of Sidonio de Sousa as well as offerings from the estimable Caves Aliança, Sogrape and others. Also try the modern-styled, Beiras labelled Calcário from Filipa Pato (Luis's talented daughter) and Quinta das Bageiras. The best wines come from silty soils of the valley bottoms rather than the underlying clay.

The **Dão** has granitic sandy soils and is less exposed to the coast than Bairrada. Though once associated with tough, tannic reds that only occasionally showed well with considerable age (and having a reputation with the Portuguese as only fit for marinating meat!), the last decade has seen a dramatic improvement in quality and there has been increased planting of Touriga Nacional and Tinta Roriz on well-sited hillsides. Both grapes have been produced varietally as have Jaen, Alfrocheiro Preto and even some Tinta Cão, though these grapes generally perform better as part of a blend. The best estates now offer rich, ripe but characterful reds, among the country's most food-friendly. Fine quality whites have also been made from Malvasia Fina and Encruzado, the latter particularly promising in gently oaked varietal examples. There is an increasing diversity of styles - every wine student needs to jot down Quinta dos Roques/Maias and Alvaro Castro (Quintas Pellada and Saes) at the top of their shopping list but there is plenty more besides including the top reds from Sogrape's Quinta dos Carvalhais and Dão Sul. Top Beiras reds are also made by João Portugal Ramos (especially Quinta de Foz de Arouce). Rarely encountered outside Portugal are wines from the **Beira Interior** region, sandwiched between Dão and the Spanish border to the east, most famous for its city of Castelo Branco. It is a low-lying, mainly dairy farming region with largely deeply weathered clay soils, which would not be an obvious choice for wine production but watch this space - there are exciting pockets of ambition. Look out for Quinta da Baixo and .

Lisboa & Tejo

Lisboa, previously known as **Estremadura**, covers undulating hillsides north of Lisbon but despite its proximity to the coast it avoids much of the cloud cover and rain of more northerly maritime-influenced areas such as Bairrada and Vinho Verde. It has long produced more wine than any other region, much of it from large co-ops. But here, too, things have improved and a handful of individual estates are emerging with some creditable wines. **Alenquer** is the most important sub-regional DOC. The region still needs more excellent estates like the Tavares da Silva family's Quinta de Chocapalha and José Bento dos Santos' Quinta do Monte d'Oiro in order to gain a wider international recognition.

DFJ Vinhos are based here too but also make good wines from other regions. In **Tejo**, previously known as Ribatejo, despite many high-yielding vineyards, there is some good value to be had where a top winemaker has been contracted to make the wines. Newcomer Vale da Algares has raised the stakes with its no expense spared state of the art winery and upmarket white Viognier and Viognier blends. It will be interesting to see how their reds perform with a bit more vine age. Both regions have a smattering of foreign varieties, including Cabernet Sauvignon and Syrah, but premium, sometimes varietal, examples of Portugal's best grapes are far more important.

Península de Setúbal /Setúbal

One grape, Castelão (Periquita), brought to the region by José Maria da Fonseca in 1830, dominates production in **Península de Setúbal** (previously known as Terras do Sado) and nowhere else does it work varietally quite so well. The best smoky, minerally, earthy, spicy examples are sold as **Palmela** (a more defined area of mostly sandy soils on the Setúbal peninsula) or Península de Setúbal. A new wave of producers are fashioning some promising if sometimes, over-ambitious premium and super-premium wines with the help of leading consultants like Mouchão's Paulo Laureano at Soberanas and Pegoes' Jaime Quendera (Casa Ermelinda Freitas). These are typically sourced from relatively young vineyards planted to Portugal's flagship varieties (especially Touriga Nacional and Aragones) and French varieties (notably Cabernet Sauvignon, Syrah and Alicante Bouschet). Based on Muscat of Alexandria variants, **Setúbal** and **Moscatel de Setúbal** (predominantly Moscatel) are famous fortified wines of good quality, particularly from José Maria da Fonseca and Bacalhôa.

Alentejo

The still relatively small, scattered vineyards of **Alentejo** lie close to the Spanish border on the eastern side and are drier and less maritime-influenced. Viticulture in the modern era is a relatively recent phenomena but quality estates now abound. Most of the top Alentejo reds are blends based on Trincadeira and Aragonês (Tinta Roriz), with Castelão, Alicante Bouschet or even Cabernet Sauvignon as minor components. Syrah has been made varietally and shows promise in a rich, powerful if slightly earthy, robust way. Ripe, sound, attractive whites are on the increase (grapes include Roupeiro, Antão Vaz and, for acidity, Arinto) but only a handful show sufficient depth or structure to improve with age, though this is slowly changing. Unsurprisingly top estates look to their premium reds to underpin their emerging reputations but the future looks exciting. Those that must be tasted include the best wines from Herdade do Mouchão, Fundação, Eugénio de Almeida, Cortes de Cima, Esporão, Quinta do Mouro, Quinta do Zambujeiro and João Portugal Ramos. Relative newcomers have also shown their worth, notably Malhadinha Nova, but also, Herdade do Rocim, Herdade dos Grous and Quinta de Dona María established by Julio Tassara de Bastos after he sold the Quinta do Carmo brand.

Algarve

In the very south of Portugal there has not been the same level of quality hitherto but progress is being made. Not considered to be a sensible wine growing region by many Portuguese, it has relied in part on outside investment and ideas. Monte da Casteleja and Quinta do Frances also show promise, with *terroir*-driven wines. Cliff Richard (Adega do Cantor) is using a similar mix of grapes to the Alentejo to good effect in his Vida and Onda Nova reds and whites. In recent years there has been increasing experimentation with non-

Portugal

indigenous varietals such as Syrah and Sangiovese, with varying success.

Madeira

Madeira is made by a small number of shippers who for the most part buy grapes from the island's many small growers. Tinta Negra Mole dominates their vineyards but the best Madeira comes from the slowly increasing amounts of the traditional varieties. The wine needs to be made from at least 85 per cent of either Malvasia (Malmsey), Bual (Boal), Verdelho or Sercial to be labelled as such. As well as being fortified, fundamental to Madeira's style is a high level of acidity and a degree of caramelisation due to heating. Most Madeira, especially the stuff used for cooking, undergoes the estufagem process which involves a period in a hot store (estufa). The best wines, however, are made by the canteiro system, whereby the wine is only subjected to natural heating in cask over a period of three years or more. As a result the wines are less coarse and have less of a burnt-sugar flavour.

Each of the traditional varieties is associated with a certain degree of sweetness. The greater the sweetness, the higher the percentage of spirit in the wine as the fermentation is arrested at an earlier stage to retain a higher sugar level. The richest and sweetest, Malmsey – often pungent, full and toffeed – is usually the most easily appreciated but most examples miss the elegance and definition associated with the smoky, spicy, dried-fruits Bual (Boal), which is less sweet but still a dessert-style wine. The best Verdelho (of moderate sweetness) is often tangy yet lightly honeyed with dried citrus fruits and a certain delicacy of flavour and aroma. The dry Sercial, often with daunting acidity, can show a fine citrusy (orangey), nutty and dried-fruit complexity with age.

The best commercial styles are the 10-year-old and 15-year-old wines. The age indicated will be an average as the wines are blended to maintain a consistent style. Even from the best shippers, 3-year-old Madeira will almost invariably be made from Tinta Negra Mole and is likely to involve the addition of caramel and the use of concentrated must. Traditional vintage Madeira will have spent at least 20 years in cask but many of the very best have spent 50 years or even 100 years in wood. Once bottled it continues to age but at a very slow rate. As they are only made in tiny quantities and sell for high prices it is imperative to consult a specialist. An exciting recent development is Colheita Madeira – wines made from Mole from a single year crafted with traditional varieties or Tinta Negra Mole and which have spent at least 5 years in cask. Brighter in style than Frasqueiras, they combine charming upfront appeal without sacrificing complexity or structure and are kinder on the pocket! Rare examples of two other traditional grapes, Moscatel and Terrantez, are also occasionally encountered.

Port styles

The English Gentlemen's drink of old is undergoing a renaissance and even at the finest level, represents very good value for money (compared to say top Bordeaux or Tuscany) for the opportunity to try some of the world's finest wines. There are two basic styles of port: those matured in bottle and those aged in wood. Of the former, **Vintage Port** applies to any port that meets the requirements of the IVP (Instituto do Vinho do Porto or Port Wine Institute) and is usually bottled before the summer of the second year after the harvest. While the title implies the 'declared' vintages bearing a house name, it applies equally to single-quinta ports and

'off-vintage' ports (or 'second label' – a shipper's port from a non-declared year, increasingly made as a true single-quinta example). These wines, which may be bought through a wine merchant or agent prior to being shipped, will always require decanting. Late Bottled Vintage Port (or **LBV**) – a style purportedly invented by Taylors - spends four to six years in large vats and the majority are fined and filtered to avoid any sediment forming in the bottle and are ready to be consumed when released. 'Unfiltered examples (labelled Traditional' until 2002) however, more closely resemble Vintage Ports in character and depth and, though they must be aged for a further three years in bottle before release, are not necessarily ready to drink when released. Some, having only the minimum bottle-age, will improve for a further five or six years. LBVs are often remarkably good value but only the very best can approach a Single Quinta vintage port in the quality – the latter often not being much more expensive (usually double the price but LBVs are not that expensive). Though the name is very important in the port houses' pecking order, it is more than just a name – there are clear differences in style. For example, the two 'big boys' – Grahams and Taylors make noticeably different styles – the former being sweeter and fruiter, the latter being richer and drier with the distinctive violets aroma.

Crusted Port, like Traditional LBVs and Vintage Port, will throw a sediment but is a blend of two or three vintages rather than one and the year given is that of its bottling. Of the wood-matured styles the most credible are those tawnies with an indication of age. Though extensively blended to maintain a house style, these gently oxidised styles can show considerable complexity and refinement. The quality of **10-year-old Tawny Port** is, however, extremely variable and in many instances the quality doesn't match the price. At worst they are simple, coarse and tired but better, fresher, balanced examples can show a date, nut, fig and toasty complexity that is seen more often in examples of the more pricey **20-year-old Tawny Port**. **30-and 40-year-old** examples are variable (sometimes excessively volatile) and expensive but at their best have an intense, nutty *rancio* character and complexity not dissimilar to an aged sherry. **Colheita Port** is effectively a tawny port of a single vintage and is labelled with both the year of the colheita (harvest) and bottling year. They have a minimum of seven years in cask and can have all the qualities of the best tawnies with an indication of age but don't always have the fruit to further improve with extended bottle age. Colheita tawnies from the best houses, such as Calem and Ramos Pinto are truly superb examples of the port maker's craft and represent some of the best wines that Portugal can offer. The most commercially important port is the relatively inexpensive **Vintage Character** or **Premium Ruby**. The best offer good fruit intensity in an easy drinking style. Brand names supplant style in the minds of consumers. Regular **Ruby Port** is very young, fruity port (at best) while some basic **Tawny Port** is simply a poor Ruby cut with some **White Port**. The latter, from white grapes but turning amber with age, is usually best avoided as many taste sweet and doctored. A few are dry and nutty with some refinement. As of 2005, it has also been possible to market aged dated white ports - Andresen, Quinta de Santa Eufemia specialise in this category and make excellent wines, nutty, but lighter and more elegant in style than their tawny counterparts. Finally, as of 2009, Rosé Port has received official recognition on the back of "Croft Pink", the pioneering rosé launched in 2008. Best served chilled or on ice, it's finding its niche as a cocktail

Douro/Port

Domingos Alves de Sousa	600
C.A.R.M	601
Calabriga	619
Casa de Casal de Loivos	616
Champalimaud	612
Churchill	603
Cockburn	603
Croft	603
Delaforce	604
Dow	605
Duas Quintas	618
Duorum	604
Ferreira	606
Casa Ferreirinha	606
Fonseca	606
Gould Campbell	619
Graham	607
Lavradores de Feitoria	608
Niepoort	610
Pintas	620
Poeira	611
Prats & Symington	619
Quarles Harris	619
Quinta da Estação	601
Quinta da Gaivosa	601
Quinta da Portela Vilariça	615
Quinta da Urze	602
Quinta das Castas	615
Quinta das Heredias	612
Quinta das Tecedeiras	604
Quinta de la Rosa	615
Quinta de Macedos	613
Quinta de Roriz	615
Quinta do Coa	602
Quinta do Côtto	612
Quinta do Crasto	612
Quinta do Infantado	613
Quinta do Noval	614
Quinta do Passadouro	614
Quinta do Portal	614
Quinta do Urze	602
Quinta do Vale da Raposa	601
Quinta do Vale Doña Maria	616
Quinta do Vale Meão	616
Quinta do Vallado	616
Quinta do Vesuvio	617
Quinta dos Quatro Ventos	600
Ramos Pinto	618
Real Companhia Velha	618
Roquette & Cazes	612
Sandeman	618
Silva & Cosens	619
Smith Woodhouse	618
Taylor's	619
Warre	620
Wine & Soul	620

Vinho Verde/Minho

Anselmo Mendes	609
Paço de Teixeiro	612
Quinta do Ameal	611
Quinta do Soalheiro	616

Beiras

Caves Alianca	600
Filipa Pato	610
Quinta de Foz de Arouce	618

Beira Interior

Quinta dos Currais	612
Quinta dos Termos	616

Bairrada

Campolargo	602
Luis Pato	610
Quinta da Dona	600
Quinta das Baceladas	600
Quinta do Encontro	604
Sidónio de Sousa	618

Dão

Alvaro Castro	602
Dão Sul	604
Quinta da Garrida	600
Quinta da Pellada	602
Quinta das Maias	615
Quinta de Saes	602
Quinta dos Carvalhais	619
Quinta dos Roques	615

Lisboa

Quinta da Cortezia	611
Quinta de Chocapalha	611
Quinta do Monte d'Oiro	613
Quinta da Murta	611

Tejo

Casal Branco	602
Vale d'Algares	620

Península de Sétubal/Palmela

Bacalhôa	601
Herdade da Comporta	603
Jose Maria da Fonseca	607

Alentejo

Cortes de Cima	603
Ervideira	604
Esporão	606
Fund. Eugénio de Almeida	607
Herdade Grande	608
Malhadinha Nova	609
Monte da Ravasqueira	609
Herdade do Mouchao	609
Quinta da Terrugem	600
Quinta da Viçosa	618
Quinta do Mouro	613
Quinta do Zambujeiro	617
Quinta Dona Maria	613
Joao Portugal Ramos	617

Madeira

Barbeito	601
Blandy's	608
Cossart Gordon	609
D'Oliveira	605
Henriques & Henriques	608
Leacocks	609
Madeira Wine Company	608

Other

DFJ Vinhos	604
Sogrape	619
Symington	619

1. Vinho Verde
2. Douro, Port
3. Bairrada
4. Dão
5. Alenquer
6. Palmela, Setúbal

Wine behind the label

Portugal

Port vintages

It used to be so simple. Vintage Port was made when the port shippers 'declared' a particular vintage was of sufficient quality to justify the bottling of a house port from that year. In other years, the same wine would be bottled under the name of a leading estate or quinta. But in a swing towards estate-based ports, some true single quintas make a port more in the mould of a Bordeaux château, that is to say in almost every year. Nonetheless general declarations are still important and still tend to highlight the very best years, though examples from a top source – whether a true single quinta or that of an 'off-vintage' quinta name – can surpass weaker efforts from a declared year. As the declarations are made 15 months to two years after the harvest there is always a second vintage coming under consideration, leading sometimes to a so-called 'split declaration' as some shippers decide to wait and declare the younger wine instead. For a true guide to longevity both the vintage assessment and that of the individual producer's style and reputation must be taken together. **Those years underlined denote a wide declaration.**

2015: A very hot summer across most of Portugal meant that port houses began the harvest before the end of August. These wines have not been tasted yet but disease levels were low and ripeness not a problem – most port houses are confident of making very fine wines and this could be a declared vintage of excellent quality.

2014: a problematic vintage and no Port houses are making suggestions that this should be declared. Only just being tasted at time of writing. Many areas of the Douro were affected by torrential rain during the harvest. The best houses will make good Single Quinta ports though it not likely to be a classic for vintage port overall.

2013: The general consensus here is that some Quinta wines will be declared as in 2012.

2012: Few of the major houses have declared this as a vintage year although some just declared from a single Quinta. 2011 has been a hard act to follow although the quality of the 2012 harvest was good. A lukewarm take up of wines from the superb 2011 vintage has led to many of the houses doubting the wisdom of making a declaration this year, although what has been declared should work out as good value for money.

2011: With ripeness and tannic structure - and ideal weather - 'legendary vintage' and 'vintage of the century' are terms that have been applied to 2011, which has now been announced as a Declared Vintage by most port houses– the first since 2007. The trade tastings in May 2013 generally put vintage ports from Fonseca, Graham's, Taylor's and Warre's at the top of the tree, with typical scores of 19/20 (or 96 Parker Points). But these are early days and a lot can happen in cask and bottle before the drinking window (2030 to 2050?) is approached. Many fine Single Quinta vintage ports were made too (the top vintage ports of each house are blended from the best quintas, rather than grapes from a single estate) and will command high prices to accompany their justifiably high tasting scores. Quinta do Noval and Quinta do Vesuvio have stormed the single quinta tastings.

2010: A very wet winter of 2009/10 was followed by a record-breaking wet spring. But a long summer drought followed and the winter rains had recharged water tables, ensuring the vines were not subjected to undue water stress in many locations. Picking started rather later than usual – from mid to late-September. Some port houses made Single Quinta ports to very good effect but there was no general declaration, despite much speculation that there would be. It was clear by October 2011 that fine wine had been made in some estates but it was too patchy to make a declaration.

2009: A cool start to the growing season until mid-August after which the first of two heat spikes hit the region, the second, in mid-September. Dry, hot weather, including unusually warm nights, prevailed until a huge storm in early October by which time most grapes had been harvested, 10-12 days earlier. Though yields were low and grapes healthy, the prolonged hot spell proved challenging in terms of achieving phenolic ripeness and retaining balance. Elegance and structure will be at a premium, but expect powerful wines from those who got it right.

2008: A cool and mainly unsettled growing season after a wet April and May retarded maturity. The vintage was only saved by a spell of gentle, sunny autumn days which commenced in mid-September and prevailed throughout the harvest to the end of October (with some notable exceptions). This was just as well considering that the growers needed to wait longer than usual for the grapes to ripen. Fortunately many did wait and although the quantity was well down, some excellent wines were produced, notably at Quinta do Noval who declared back-to-back vintages in 2007 and 2008.

2007: A cool and damp early summer threatened the vintage, but perfect weather conditions during the harvest starting in late September, produced evenly ripe grapes which augured well for the quality of the vintage. The wines show intensely dark colour with wonderful perfume, rich fruit and silky tannins which will allow the wines to be drunk comparatively early, but which will also have great ageing capacity. The overall quality has led this to become a generally declared vintage.

2006: A succession of heat waves from May through to September did the greatest harm to the prospects of a good vintage in 06 (stressing the vines) even though existing ground water levels were good from winter rain. Hail also reduced significantly the crop for some while spells of summer rain also caused problems for others. Don't expect consistency or greatness but there were some individual successes.

2005: This proved to be an exceptionally dry vintage in the Douro (and the year of serious forest fires in much of the country). It was dry not just during the growing season but also during the winter that preceded it. Early September rains were beneficial and very healthy fruit with good acidities should translate to refined, elegant ports. Quantities are down 20% on 04.

2004: Like 2005 a very dry year in the Douro but a very wet August and wet and overcast early September intervened before a sunny end. Potential alcohol levels were high and there isn't the backbone of a great year. Results amongst young single quinta ports are variable. Some display a slightly cooked aspect, others lack depth yet there are also wines with good fruit richness and fine structures as well as the purity evident in the best table wines.

2003: In the year of Europe's extreme heat Portugal's Douro fared better than most. The preceding wet winter and continued spells of heavy rain meant that in most cases the vines were able to draw on sufficient ground water to avoid stress or raining during a spell of extreme heat in early August. Top names already show deeply perfumed, richly berried wines of great potential.

2002: This is a year the rains fell to spoil a potentially fine vintage. September's 'Friday the 13th' was lucky for only a few (mostly in the Douro Superior) in the sense that they had picked most of the grapes already before the start of more than a month of miserable weather. Nonetheless, some good, forward, fruit-emphasised single-quinta ports were made by those who care about quality.

2001: The winter preceding this growing season was incredibly wet resulting in the widely televised tragic bridge collapse over the river

on March 4. Despite the reasonably dry growing season and good harvest conditions, the moisture absorbed in the early part of the year has dampened quality to some extent, though volumes are up.

2000: Rain in the early part of the growing season and a poor flowering were compensated for by a hot, dry ripening period. Yields were very low but the best wines have an incredible intensity of fruit and fine ripe tannins. There is not perhaps quite the size or power of certain other excellent vintages but the wines promise to be long-lived with great expression and classic character in the top names.

1999: Though characterised by irregular, low rainfall much of it fell at harvest as the rain set in from mid-September. Top quality was hard to achieve and while most small estates made Vintage Port, the shippers opted for their single quinta

ports. Good quality but it will be overshadowed by 2000.

1998: Due to an irregular growing season with intermittent heavy rain at harvest, and despite very low yields, this year is one of good rather than great quality. The best single-quinta ports are reasonably concentrated and intense but more modestly structured and lack real stuffing. Some attractive medium-term drinking.

1997: The season had something of a hole in the middle, with a cool, wet midsummer. The return of the sun and real heat more than saved the vintage. The wines have quite firm but ripe structures and the best are well-concentrated too. Less successful than 1994 or 2000 yet still a very promising vintage with many excellent wines. The very best may come from Fonseca, Niepoort and Noval (Nacional) as well as Dow, Graham, Taylor and Vesúvio.

1995: A very hot August ensured a vintage of good concentration to follow 1994. The wines are often very ripe and there are more raisiny characters and a lack of flavour finesse in some. At least half a dozen shippers declared, though most of the top names opted for single-quinta port instead.

1994: The most outstanding port vintage in recent times. Universally declared, the wines initially showed a remarkably seductive fruit but a deep, tannic back bone that suggests classic wines with 20, 30 or more years' age. Now is not the time to drink them, especially when many older vintages, that are drinking so well, often cost less.

1992: A very high-quality vintage but only declared by a handful of shippers who preferred this to 1991. The cynical dismissed Taylor-Fonseca motives in the tricentenary year of Taylor's founding yet, as at Vesúvio and Niepoort, port of real class and concentration was made.

1991: Given the mixed form of the 80s, 1991 is emerging as something of a turning point in vintage fortunes. It was also the start of a much brighter era for port's commercial prospects. The wines are full and firm, not a seductive or elegant vintage but with plenty of power in the best examples. Despite more than a decade's age the best examples such as Dow, Graham and Warre deserve considerably longer.

1987: Few declarations but whether Vintage or single-quinta, such as Warre's Cavadinha or Graham's Malvedos, one for drinking up. Also includes a colheita from Niepoort.

1985: A much-touted vintage on the basis of extremely favourable vintage conditions but while exceptional for a few, generally it is very patchy. The heat at vintage time precipitated winemaking problems which, though remedied in subsequent vintages, led to washed-out, sometimes volatile wines. Generally a success for the well-equipped Symington group (Graham is superb); only a few others, including Fonseca capitalised on nature's benevolence.

1983: Muscle and structure typified many of the wines from this vintage but the best have added flesh and richness with age.

Another Symington year and while Taylor and Niepoort are also very good, bottles from Cockburn and Ramos Pinto can be more variable.

1982: The hasty chose to declare this instead of the superior 1983 and got it badly wrong. A few, including Sandeman and Niepoort, did rather better but these and the best single-quinta should now be drunk up.

1980: A year unjustly overlooked and for a time considered second-rate but those from the Symington stable in particular have done much to restore its reputation. To those in the know, Dow, Graham and Warre have long provided a remarkably good and well-priced source of port.

1977: A classic year but with many examples now near their best, it doesn't seem to have quite the staying power of 1966 or 63. Variation has been noted in Taylor and more recently in Dow. Fonseca has been consistently brilliant and Graham, Niepoort and Smith Woodhouse seem to have got better and better while Warre too has proven its worth down the years.

1975: There were few exceptions to what turned out to be a relatively light and fast-maturing vintage.

1970: Up until and including 1970 much Vintage Port was bottled in the UK rather than at source and this fine vintage does sometimes show the variations in quality this can bring. Nonetheless a very good vintage with most wines showing excellent balance and fine tannins, often displaying the particular style of a shipper's port to good effect. The likes of Dow, Graham, Fonseca, Noval's Nacional, Niepoort and Taylor will continue to improve.

1966: An excellent vintage of very powerful ports, the best of which are likely to last even longer than the classic 1963. However there are slightly fewer really great wines and of those most do not possess the extra finesse or harmony of its predecessor. Nonetheless very fine examples from Cálem, Delaforce, Dow, Fonseca, Graham, Noval's Nacional and Taylor. Drink now or keep.

1963: The finest proven vintage of the second half of the 20th century, and remarkably consistent too. Cockburn, Croft, Delaforce, Dow, Fonseca, Graham, Noval's Nacional, Taylor and Warre provide the evidence. Of recent declarations only 1994 poses any sort of threat to its supremacy. As well as continued age worthiness, it is the balance and marvellous refinement in the wines that set them apart from other top years. Drink now or keep.

Earlier Years: Great port years extend back the length of the entire 20th century but those still truly alive and great become increasingly scarce with the years (as well as hard to find and prohibitively expensive). 1960 is a fully mature vintage but good bottles exist from a number of shippers; Cockburn's seems the most likely to keep a lot longer. 1955 has always had more vigour and richness and while many are tiring, well-sourced bottles of Dow, Graham, Fonseca and

the regular Noval will live on. Older vintages (48, 45, 35, 34, 31, 27 and others) should only be bought where the wines have been impeccably stored and from a reliable bottler (see 1970).

Portuguese red wine vintages

While not covered in the vintage commentary above, the best Portuguese table wines have considerable ageing potential. In general, the best reds, whatever their origins, will keep for 5-10 years but the majority of such wines have been made in the last few years and do not come from earlier vintages. Therefore while the vintage chart needs to be considered in conjunction with comments in the specific producer entry, in most instances buy from a recent good vintage whether for drinking young or to cellar for a substantial period.

Wine behind the label

Portugal

2015: A very hot summer especially in the inland of Dao and Alentejo away from the ameliorating coastal breezes. An early vintage in most regions and the few wines that have been tasted from the serious estates at this point suggest this will be a fine vintage.

2014: the coolest summer for 80 years was followed by a wet harvest in northern Portugal affecting table wine as well as port. Coastal areas of Minho and Bairrada had a problematic vintage. Not likely to be a classic but the best producers will make fine wine in small quantities.

For earlier years use the chart ratings.

Port & Portugal vintage chart

Vintage Port			Douro	Dão	Alentejo
2015	NYR	2015	★★★★ A	★★★★ A	★★★★ A
2014	★★☆ A	2014	★★★★ A	★★★ A	★★★ A
2013	★★★☆ A	2013	★★★☆ A	★★☆ A	★★★☆ A
2012	★★★☆ A	2012	★★★ A	★★☆ A	★★★☆ A
2011	★★★★☆ A	2011	★★★★ A	★★★☆ A	★★☆ B
2010	★★★ A	2010	★★★ B	★★☆ B	★★☆ B
2009	★★★ A	2009	★★★☆ A	★★★☆ A	★★★★ B
2008	★★★★ A	2008	★★★☆ B	★★★ B	★★★★ B
2007	★★★★★ A	2007	★★★★★ A	★★★★ B	★★★★ B
2006	★★★ A	2006	★★★ B	★★★ C	★★★★ B
2005	★★★☆ A	2005	★★★★☆ B	★★★★ C	★★★☆ B
2004	★★★ A	2004	★★★★☆ B	★★★☆ C	★★★☆ B
2003	★★★★☆ A	2003	★★★★☆ B	★★★★ C	★★★☆ B
2000	★★★★☆ A	2002	★★★ C	★★☆ C	★★★☆ B
1997	★★★☆ A	2001	★★★★☆ C	★★★★ C	★★★★ C
1995	★★★ B	2000	★★★★☆ C	★★★★ C	★★★★ C
1994	★★★★★ A	1999	★★★☆ C	★★★ D	★★★☆ D
1992	★★★★ B	1998	★★☆ D	★★ D	★★☆ D
1991	★★★☆ B	1997	★★★★ C	★★★★☆ C	★★★★ D
1987	★★☆ C	1996	★★☆ D	★★★★ D	★★☆ D
1985	to ★★★★ B	1995	★★★☆ D	★★★☆ D	★★★★ D
1983	★★★★ C	1994	★★★★☆ C	★★★☆ D	★★★ D
1980	★★★ C	1992	★★★★ D	★★★☆ D	★★☆ D
1977	★★★★☆ C	1991	★★★★ D	★★★☆ D	★★★☆ D
1970	★★★★ C				
1966	★★★★☆ C				
1963	★★★★★ C				

A-Z of producers

Caves Aliança (Beiras) *www.alianca.pt*
Once associated with the mediocrity of much Portuguese table wine, Caves Aliança has undergone a major transformation in the past decade and now provides much-improved quality at all levels. The company, which is majority owned by Group Bacalhôa, owns large estates in the Douro Superior, Beiras Interior, Dão and Alentejo. The basics are simple but increasingly well made, but much more interesting are the reasonably priced Bairrada Garrafeira, Douro Foral Grande Escolha, Palmela Particular and Dão Particular. From a good vintage these all show regional character and gain a savoury intensity with 3–5 years' age. New premium wines see winemaker Francisco Antunes working with Pascal Chatonnet to produce high quality reds from individual estates: Quinta das Baceladas (Bairrada),

Quinta da Garrida (Dão), Quinta dos Quatro Ventos (Douro) and Quinta da Terrugem in Alentejo. The latter, a blend of Aragonês (Tinta Roriz) and Trincadeira (70:30), is well made with a spicy, earth, berry and black plum character. First made in 99, T da Terrugem (90% Aragonês) is complex and classy, combining power and finesse, and promises to be a new classic Portuguese red - the 01 is also very fine. Quatro Ventos, primarily Touriga Franca and Tinta Barocca and a Reserva (mostly Tinta Roriz and Touriga Franca) are also well executed. The Baceladas Merlot/Cabernet Sauvignon/Baga blend is individual but with true Bairrada character while two Bagas from Quinta da Rigodeira, especially Quinta da Dona (which is only made in top years from a single parcel within Rigodeira), are classy reds with well-managed firm but ripe tannins. Dão red Quinta da Garrida shows a classic Dão personality imbued with floral and mineral notes. A Touriga Nacional from Garrida is more concentrated and structured.

Aliança
Recommended Reds:
Douro Foral Grande Escolha ★★ £B Bairrada Garrafeira ★★ £B Dão Particular ★★ £B Palmela Particular ★★ £B

Quinta das Baceladas
Recommended Reds:
Bairrada Quinta das Baceladas ★★★ £B

Quinta da Dona
Recommended Reds:
Bairrada Quinta das Dona ★★★★ £E

Quinta da Terrugem
Recommended Reds:
Alentejo T da Terrugem ★★★★★ £F
Alentejo Quinta da Terrugem ★★★ £C

Quinta dos Quatro Ventos
Recommended Reds:
Douro Reserva ★★★☆ £D Douro ★★★ £C

Quinta da Garrida
Recommended Reds:
Dão Reserva ★★★☆ £D DãoTouriga Nacional ★★★ £C
Dão ★★☆ £B

⚙ Domingos Alves De Sousa (Douro) *www.alvesdesousa.com*
Quinta da Gaivosa is one of the five estates of Domingos Alves de Sousa located in the Lower Douro north of Régua. Domingos is now working with his son Tiago and his regular Gaivosa wine is one of the most stylish and refined reds of the Douro; there is not the weight or richness of other examples but it is long and distinguished and drinks well with 3 years' age or more. The smaller Quinta do Vale da Raposa ('Valley of the Fox') is the source of several reds, including a round, fruity, regular Douro, three good varietal expressions and a deep, powerful Grande Escolha, which has excellent ageing potential. Like Gaivosa it is based on Touriga Nacional, Tinta Cão and Tinta Roriz. Three other estates, Estação, Caldas and Aveleira provide mostly inexpensive but generally well-made reds - Estação Colheita Seleccionada shows extra vigour and intensity. White wine is also made if of more variable quality. Also produced from old vines in the Gaivosa vineyards is Alves de Sousa Reserva Pessoal red. It is more powerful, and earthy than Gaivosa if less refined and composed. The white equivalent is a complex and flavoursome *barrique*-fermented and aged blend of local varieties. Also produced is the new Vinha de Lordelo from Gaivosa's oldest vines. In the Gaivosa mould, it also includes Sousão and Tinta Amarela and has super fruit and added depth. Even better is

Abandonado, another premium bottling from neglected 80-year-old vines planted in schistose soils that captures the essence of old vine Douro expression and intensity. Cume is a new inexpensive red with a smart modern label; simple but supple and berryish. Vintage Port is a very good prospect with 8-10 years' age.

Recommended Reds:

Reserva Pessoal Alves de Sousa ★★★☆ £E

Recommended Whites:

Reserva Pessoal Alves de Sousa ★★☆ £D

Quinta da Gaivosa

Recommended Reds:

Douro Vinha de Lordelo ★★★★ £F   Douro ★★★☆ £E
Vintage Port ★★★★ £E

Quinta da Estaçao

Recommended Reds:

Douro Colheita Seleccionada ★★☆ £C

Quinta do Vale da Raposa

Recommended Reds:

Douro Abandonado ★★★★★ £F   Douro Grande Escolha ★★★ £E
Douro Touriga Nacional ★★★ £C   Douro Tinta Roriz ★★ £D
Douro Tinto Cão ★★ £D   Douro ★☆ £B

Bacalhôa (Peninsula de Setúbal)   *www.bacalhoa.com*

Bacalhôa Vinhos de Portugal is the new name for J P Vinhos, a significant producer in the Peninsula de Setúbal with some 500-600 ha of vineyards, some in the neighbouring regions of Alentejo and Lisboa. The best have good flavour and intensity. Tinto da Ânfora is a good, occasionally variable, gutsy example of Alentejo fruit and personality – mostly Aragonês (Tinta Roriz) with a little Trincadeira, Castelão and Alfrocheiro Preto, oak-aged in wood of mixed origins. Much better but at a price is a Grande Escolha version made in the best years. Full and concentrated with deep spice, cedar and savoury notes, it is aged in 100% new Allier oak for 8 months. The age worthy Quinta do Bacalhôa is a single-estate wine, mostly Cabernet Sauvignon but with 10% Merlot, that tastes not unlike a slightly rustic, earthy Graves – a ripe, meaty, characterful example with ample earthy blackcurrant fruit and depth. With a *terroir* not dissimilar to the Left Bank in Bordeaux, this wine is clearly aimed at the claret lover. The wine is very age worthy. The fleshier Palacio de Bacalhôa features more Merlot. Whites, too, are not without character, especially recent addition Quinta do Bacalhôa, a rich, ripe twist on a Bordeaux blend with Alvarinho fleshing out the Sauvignon Blanc and Sémillon. Cova da Ursa is a barrel-fermented Chardonnay that is flavoursome but better balanced and more restrained than in early efforts. Other well-known brands include a light, dry Catarina based on Fernão Pires with a barrel-fermented Chardonnay component, and adequate fruity Monte das Ânforas red and white. J P Tinto and Branco are the basic red and white. Sparkling wine, both Loridos Bruto, (from Castelão and Fernão Pires), and Loridos Chardonnay are produced from grapes grown in Lisboa. Newish varietals under the Só label ('Só' meaning 'only') are Syrah (from 99) and Touriga Nacional (2001). Both are now powerful and concentrated with impressive depth and flavour length. Fortified vintage and rare Rosso Moscatel de Setubal are very good, with lovely depth of flavour and balance.

Recommended Reds:

Moscatel de Setúbal Rosso ★★★★ £E
Tinto da Ânfora Grande Escolha ★★★ £D
Só Syrah ★★★ £C   Só Touriga Nacional ★★★ £C
Quinta do Bacalhôa ★★☆ £B   Tinto da Ânfora ★☆ £B

Recommended Whites:

Moscatel de Setúbal Vintage ★★★☆ £D
Quinta do Bacalhôa ★★☆ £B   Moscatel de Setúbal NV ★★ £C
Cova da Ursa ★ £B

✿ Barbeito (Madeira)   *www.vinhosbarbeito.com*

Barbeito has an interesting range of commercial Madeiras as well as small stock of very old vintage examples. Operations are directed by the dynamic Riccardo de Freitas, who has been involved in the winemaking since 1991. All the grapes are bought in and all the wines, save for the 3 year olds, are canteiro wines, subject only to natural heating. The wines are generally drier and racy, with higher acidities than some due to a policy of not de-acidifying. Nor are the wines caramelised as is more usually the case. Single Harvest, made only from Tinta Negra Mole, and with dried fruits, nut, fig and date flavours, shows what is possible from this variety. VB is an innovative fruity medium dry blend of Verdelho and Bual. The Boal (Bual) Reserva (previously labelled Veramar) averages 5 years' age and has excellent fruit and intensity for this level. For more classic fire power, the range of 10-year-old wines should be tried. Again the Boal is fine, while Special Reserve 20 and 30 year old Malvasias show still more power, intensity and length. The breadth and potency of both of these contrast with the elegance and purity in a very small-production single cask and two cask Boal and Colheitas. Verdelho Frasqueira (Vintage, the 1981 follows on from 1980) is a very fine example of the elegance and style of good Verdelho. These and other treasures besides deserve a wider audience; the use of contemporary packaging and 50cl bottles should help.

Recommended Whites:

Madeira 30-year-old Special Reserve Malvasia ★★★★★ £H
Madeira 20-year-old Special Reserve Malvasia ★★★★ £F
Madeira Verdelho Frasqueira ★★★★☆ £G
Madeira Single Cask Malvasia Colheita ★★★★☆ £F
Madeira Single Cask Boal Colheita ★★★★☆ £F
Madeira Boal Reserva ★★★☆ £E   Madeira VB ★★★☆ £E
Madeira 10-year-old Boal Reserve ★★★ £E
Madeira 10-year-old Sercial Reserve ★★★ £E
Single Harvest ★★★ £D

C.A.R.M (Douro)   *www.carm.pt*

C.A.R.M stands for Casa Agrícola Roboredo Madeira. The Madeira family have 62 ha of vineyards and 220 ha of olive groves in the Douro Superior, spread across seven quintas. Trained winemaker Rui Madeira makes three excellent wines under the C.A.R.M label and several others named for individual quintas. A characterful Classico (half Touriga Nacional) sees a little oak. More concentrated and better defined is a Reserva which is 50% *barrique*-aged Touriga Nacional and Touriga Franca. Premium spends 12 months in new Allier *barriques* and is deep and seductive with lots of tannin but excellent balance in 2000. It is likely to improve for up to 10 years. Conversely, a bottle of C.A.R.M. DOP Douro, an unsulphured Touriga Nacional first produced in 2009, tasted tired. Quinta da Urze varietals are aromatic with expressive varietal character and balanced tannins and can be drunk fairly young. Quinta do Côa is in the Côa Valley where the Palaeolithic rock carvings have been designated a World Heritage Site. Its two well balanced, spicy reds are both made from certified organic grapes.

C.A.R.M

Recommended Reds:

Douro Premium ★★★★ £E   Douro Reserva ★★★ £C

Portugal

Douro Classico ★★ £B
Quinta da Urze
Recommended Reds:
Douro Touriga Nacional ★★ £B   Douro Tinta Roriz ★★ £B
Douro Touriga Franca ★★ £B
Quinta do Côa
Recommended Reds:
Douro Reserva ★★★ £C   Douro ★★ £B

Campolargo (Bairrada)   *www.campolargovinhos.com*
Manuel dos Santos Campolargo to give it its full name, is the
enterprise of the larger-than-life Carlos Campolargo who has
invested heavily in both replanting most of his vineyards and
building a brand new winery to process what are now a wide
range of grape varieties and wines. The invasion of mostly
Bordeaux varieties won't please the purists but several of the
wines are still based on quality natives such as Baga, Tinta Roriz
and Touriga Nacional. As the team works out what grows best
where and which varieties best complement one another, the
varietal composition of the wines in his burgeoning portfolio is
liable to change year on year. At the lower priced end of the scale
there is a characterful supple Entre II Santos in which Merlot is
used to soften the Baga component. For Vinho de Putto, another
entry level red, a dash of Cabernet Sauvignon brings a touch of
darker fruit and freshness to this blend of Touriga Nacional, Tinta
Roriz and Syrah and, for upmarket Contra a Corrente, backbone
and finesse. A Pinot Noir shows good varietal character and is
sometimes blended with old vine Baga - curiously it has something
of the scented mineral character of a good Dão and a little more
backbone than vintages of straight Pinot Noir. Vinha da Costa is a
single vineyard blend of Tinta Roriz with some Merlot and Syrah
which reveals lots of intensity and berry fruit character. Two other
premium reds are more international. Calda Bordelezza is indeed
a Bordeaux blend but unusual in combining equal parts of Merlot
and Cabernet Sauvignon with 20% of Petit Verdot. It is very dense
and concentrated with the Petit Verdot evident in its distinctive
character; being both balanced and promising but likely to need
8-10 years. 'Diga' red is a backward, intense varietal Petit Verdot with
the acidity, extract and power not uncommon to such ambitious
examples that are, however, only rarely convincing. 'Diga?' white, a
somewhat herbal, green-tinged Viognier has yet to hit its straps, but
it is early days. Otherwise whites come in the shape of two barrel-
fermented varietals, Arinto and Bical and Entre Deux Santos, a part
barrel-fermented Sauvignon Blanc blend all of which are well made
if not as characterful or refined as the reds. Recent developments
include solid if a tad uninspiring sparkling wines and, most
promising of all, A Dão red currently made at Alvaro Castro's cellar.
Also made but not tasted is Termeao from Touriga Nacional (with
Cabernet Sauvignon and Castelão).
Recommended Reds:
Vinha da Costa ★★★☆ £F   Calda Bordelezza ★★★☆ £E
Bairrada Contra a Corrente ★★★☆ £E
Bairrada Diga? ★★☆ £E
Bairrada Campolargo ★★☆ £C   Bairrada Entre II Santos ★★☆ £B
Recommended Whites:
Arinto ★★ £C

Casal Branco (Tejo)   *www.casalbranco.com*
The Casal Branco estate is more famous for breeding pure Lusitano
horses than for wine but much progress has been made here over

the past decade. Direction comes from José Vasconcellos and his
family's large estate includes 140 ha of vineyards on predominantly
sandy soils. Merlot, Cabernet Sauvignon and Petit Verdot under the
Capucho label all show good varietal character and ripe tannins
although the Merlot and Cabernet can be cool and leafy and there's
a tendency to use too much oak. Made in very small quantities,
Petit Verdot (from 2003) is produced from low yields and has much
more concentrated and intense fruit. More original is Falcoaria,
produced from Castelão and Trincadeira. The regular example is ripe
and savoury but a Reserva has more depth and cedary, herbal black
fruits and shows very well with 5–6 years' age. The barrel-fermented
white version is made from Fernão Pires and has good structure
but again, can be too oaky. Inexpensive dual-variety Terra de Lobos
white (Fernão Pires and Sauvignon Blanc £B) and red (Castello/
Cabernet Sauvignon) have succeeded the Cork Grove brand and are
well made. (sold in the UK).
Recommended Reds:
Ribatejo Falcoaria Reserva ★★★ £C
Ribatejo Falcoaria ★★ £B   Petit Verdot Capucho ★★★ £E
Merlot Capucho ★★ £C   Cabernet Sauvignon Capucho ★★ £C
Recommended Whites:
Ribatejo Falcoaria★ £B

✿ **Alvaro Castro (Dão)**   *www.quintadapellada.com*
In Alvaro Castro we have one of Portugal's finest and most
individualistic winemakers, now joined by his daughter, Maria. An
opportunity to do a comprehensive tasting of the wines from two
estates can prove elusive but more than worth the effort. Castro
owns two mountain slope Quintas in the west of the Dão region,
high up in the rugged foothills of the Serra da Estrela. Quinta
de Saes is SE-facing with less sun at the end of the day than the
higher (520m) but warmer south west facing Quinta de Pellada.
As well as mixed old vines of local varieties, Castro has 5 trial plots
of Touriga Nacional, Tinta Roriz, Cabernet Sauvignon, Merlot and
Syrah at Saes. A splash of Cabernet is finding its way into an elegant
but flavoursome new rosé. A fine white Reserva is produced in
an old vines version and displays intense ripe fruit and impressive
breadth. The red Reserva (Estágio Prolongado) which comes from
an old vineyard that includes Touriga Nacional and Alfrocheiro, is
concentrated with an elegant fruit expression within a compact
structure. The more ordered Quinta da Pellada is the source of the
quince and minerals-driven Primus, also several good reds including
a varietal Touriga Nacional of excellent purity and fruit intensity.
In a similar vein is Carrocel but, as Castro puts it "200% new oak is
used" both for the fermentation and again for the ageing. Although
intense and backward when young the oak is well integrated; time
will show whether an underlying depth will emerge with age. In
'Pape' Touriga is combined with Baga and gives very complete and
classy wines. Looking beyond the Dão, it seems great minds do
think alike and sometimes even collaborate. The meeting of minds
between one Dão great and the Douro visionary Dirk Niepoort has
resulted in Doda (originally called Dado). A roughly equal blend
from both regions, this is another fine red.
Recommended Reds:
Dão Pape ★★★★☆ £E   Dão Pape ★★★★ £E
Dão Carrocel ★★★☆ £F
Doda ★★★★ £F
Quinta da Pellada
Recommended Reds:
DãoTouriga Nacional ★★★☆ £E   Dão ★★★☆ £C

Quinta de Saes
Recommended Reds:
Dão Reserva Estagio Prolongado ★★★☆ £C   Dão ★★☆ £C
Recommended Whites:
Dão Primus ★★★☆ £E   Dão Reserva (old vines) ★★★ £C
Dão Reserva ★★☆ £B

Churchill (Port & Douro) *www.churchills-port.com*
The port house established in 1981 by Johnny Graham and his brothers has come a long way in just over 30 years. In the early days port was made in rented, cramped quarters and solely from bought-in grapes but now the company has expanded and it acquired two important quintas of its own in 1999: Quinta da Gricha and Quinta do Rio. The ports have always been made to a high standard, for a time drawing on grapes from the Fojo and Manuela quintas, and generally show rich, ripe fruit and good balance, avoiding over ripeness or an excessive spirity character. The Vintage Port, in particular, has got better with successive declarations. Best recent years are 2003, 2000, 97, 94 and 91. Other ports are competitively priced and often better value than the equivalents from the biggest names. Served slightly chilled, the amber-coloured dry white port is a rare good example. The single-quinta Quinta da Gricha port (from 04, 01 2000 and 99) and Quinta do Rio (01) now complement the fine Agua Alta made in 1998, 96, 95 and 92. Several Douro reds are now also being made by the talented João Brito e Cunha, who also makes finely honed wines under his own Azeo and Quinta de S. José labels.
Recommended Reds:
Vintage Port ★★★★ £F   Vintage Port Quinta da Gricha ★★★☆ £F
20-year-old Tawny Port ★★★ £E   10-year-old Tawny Port ★★ £C
Crusted Port ★★★ £C   Late Bottled Vintage Port Unfiltered ★★ £C
Finest Reserve Port ★★ £B
Recommended Whites:
White Port Dry Aperitif ★ £B
Churchill Estates
Recommended Reds:
Douro Grande Reserva ★★★ £E   Douro Reserva ★★ £C
Douro Quinta da Gricha ★★ £C
Douro Touriga Nacional ★★ £C
Douro ★☆ £C
Recommended Rosés:
Douro Touriga Nacional ★ £B

Cockburns (Port) *www.cockburns.com*
Established in 1815, Cockburn is one of the best-known port names. Much of its recent popularity is down to the success of the simple, sweet Special Reserve, a Vintage Character port. Quinta do Tua and, since 1989, Quinta dos Canais are two excellent quintas that form part of a substantial vineyard resource. The Vintage Port, for many years of only moderate quality or worse, has returned to form and, since Symington Family Estates acquired first the assets in 2006, then the brand (in 2010) they have made the ports and invested heavily in new production facilities. Mature vintages such as 1963, 60 and 55 or even older bottles can be superb (the rating only applies to the best vintages). The single quinta Touriga Nacional dominated Quinta dos Canais shows a lovely fruit purity and intensity and if it is less long-lived than the Vintage it still shows the quality of fruit that it brings to the blend. LBV is modest but tawnies (now packaged in 50cl bottles) show good intensity and length of flavour.

Recommended Reds:
Vintage Port ★★★★ £F   Vintage Port Quinta dos Canais ★★★ £E
20-year-old Tawny Port ★★ £F   10-year-old Tawny Port ★ £E

Herdade da Comporta *www.herdadedacomporta.pt*
A fine up-and-coming winery owned originally by the now defunct Espirito Santo banking group, producing hearty and terroir-driven wines from the Setúbal area of Lisboa. Vineyards are ca. 35 ha, the location being an interesting warm, estuarine low-lying zone at the mouth of the Sado river, with sandy soils. Unsurprisingly, the area was important for rice production in the last century. Plantings started in 2001- red grapes are Aragonez, Trincadeira, Alicante Bouschet and Touriga Franca, and the white grapes are Arinto and Antão Vaz. Wine production is overseen by Francisco Pimenta, and Parus, a wine first released in 2010 has received wide acclaim. The red wine is complex, elegant with hints of allspice and crystallized fruits on the nose. (GW)
Recommended Reds:
Parus Red ★★★☆ £D   Comporta Red ★★★ £C
Herdade da Comporta red ★★ £B
Recommended Whites:
Parus White ★★★ £C   Herdade da Comporta White ★★ £B
Recommended Rosés:
Herdade da Comporta Rosé ★★ £B

Cortes de Cima (Alentejo) *www.cortesdecima.pt*
Cortes de Cima, for ripe, modern-styled reds, is located in Vidigueira, the southern most of the Alentejo's subzones, and the wines are made by the owner, Dane Hans Kristian Jørgensen. There are now 130 ha of vineyards many which have been converted to the Smart Dyson training system, thanks to input from viticultural expert Richard Smart. Since 1997 the wines have been consistently good; fruit-driven with excellent varietal expression, particularly from the Portuguese grapes. The ripe, fleshy Cortes de Cima varies in composition but always includes Syrah, Aragonês and Trincadeira. A dark, dense Reserva (Syrah and Aragonês in 01 but additionally with Trincadeira in 03) marries new oak to a splendidly complex fruit character and is usually the top wine. A powerful varietal Syrah, Incógnito, is deep and concentrated and adequately balanced despite being high in alcohol. It has lots of character but is at the very ripe end of the spectrum and misses the finesse of a top Rhône example. A signature grape, Cortes de Cima now make an estate single varietal Syrah and Hans Christina Andersen Syrah, which is midway between the two. An enticingly aromatic Touriga Nacional shows super fruit. Varietal Aragonês (labelled Aragonez) is usually impressive too but then there are no poor wines here. The more forward, soft, fruity Chaminé is good value, while Courela is the basic red. From 2003 the first white, Clara (100% Antão Vaz) shows good fruit and has now been joined by Chamine white, which is sound if unexciting. A barrel sample of Petit Verdot looked promising - the variety seems well suited to the region. Extra Virgin olive oil is now being made here too.
Recommended Reds:
Cortes de Cima Reserva ★★★★ £E
Cortes de Cima Hans Christina Andesen Syrah ★★☆ £D
Cortes de Cima ★★☆ £C   Touriga Nacional ★★★☆ £D
Incógnito ★★★ £E   Aragonez ★★★ £D
Trincadeira ★★☆ £C   Chaminé ★☆ £B
Recommended Whites:
Clara ★ £B

Portugal

Croft (Port) *www.croftport.com*

What later became known as Croft had its beginnings in 1678 and its leading quinta, Quinta da Roêda, has provided the backbone of all its best Vintage Ports in the 20th century. Prior to the 1990s it is necessary to go back to 1977, 70, 66, 63, 60 or 55 for a really great Croft Port but Croft's real salvation has come from its recent purchase by the estimable Taylor-Fonseca group. Croft's Vintage 2003, the first foot trodden vintage since 1963 (for which the rating is given), showed a quantum leap in quality and has an exotic quality, good depth and a certain elegance. Of the other ports, a decent 10-year-old Tawny is made while the LBV with some upfront fruit is of the filtered type. 'Distinction' is the Vintage Character port and this along with Fine White, Fine Ruby and Fine Tawny are the big-volume basic ports, now joined by the pioneering Croft Pink, a rosé Port.

Recommended Reds:
Vintage Port ★★★★ £F   Vintage Port Quinta da Roêda ★★ £E
10-year-old Tawny Port ★★ £E

DFJ Vinhos *www.dfjvinhos.com*

DFJ was originally formed out of a partnership between Portuguese winemaker José Neiva and the two partners of UK wine shippers, D&F. Only Neiva remains. A huge range of fruit driven wines aimed squarely at the export market is produced from growers primarily in Lisboa, but also from other regions stretching from the Douro to the Algarve. Nearly all the wines are based on native varieties and offer reasonable flavour and supple textures even at very modest price points. Pink Elephant, an off dry but well balanced rosé which was conceived as an ideal match with curry has rightly received both critical and popular acclaim. But as you ascend in price, there's usually much more interest to be had from boutique producers. Premium reds include the extensive Grande Arte range. The "Icon" range includes Esacada, Francos, Consensus and, a recent addition, Quinta do Rocio, an award winning Lisboa red blend of Touriga Nacional, Shiraz, Merlot and, unusually, Grenache only available on allocation in Portugal.

Recommended Reds:
Tejo Consensus ★★★★ £D   Alentejo Francos Reserva ★★★★ £D
Grand' Arte Touriga Nacional Special Selection ★★★☆ £C
Grand' Arte Touriga Franca ★★☆ £B
Grand' Arte Alicante Bouschet ★★ £B   Grand' Arte Tinta Roriz ★★ £B
Grand' Arte Shiraz ★★ £B   Grand' Arte Touriga Nacional ★★ £B
Douro Escada ★★★ £C   Douro Patamar Reserva ★★ £B
Alenquer Francos ★★★ £C   Manta Preta ★★ £B
Senda do Vale Reserva ★★ £B   Lisboa Quinta do Rocio ★☆ £E
Recommended Whites:
Grand' Arte Alvarinhlo ★★ £B   Segada Fernão Pires ★ £B
Grand' Arte Chardonnay ★ £B

Dão Sul (Global Wines) (Dão) *www.daosul.com*

Established in the Dão region in 1989, Dão Sul has rapidly become one of Portugal's leading players. It is one of the few Portuguese producers able successfully to juggle a portfolio that encompasses super-premium single quinta wines with volume commercial brands, not to mention experimenting with quirky inter-regional and international "hybrid" wines (see below). Quality is strong across the board. The Dão, where it all started, remains a key strength and is home to two historic estates (both with good restaurants), Quinta de Cabriz, and Casa de Santar/Paço dos Cunhas do Santar, also Quinta dos Grilos. Red blends under the Cabriz and Santar labels are contemporary but characterful and very good value for money;

flagship Cabriz CCCC is a modern yet formidably structured wine, with terrific concentration of ripe fruit. Lees-ageing and batonnage make for among the region's most complex Encruzado under the Santar labels. The characterful, rounded red Quinta do Ribeiro Santo comes from winemaker Carlos Lucas' home estate. In 2000, Dão Sul expanded into the Douro (Quinta das Tecedeiras & Quinta Sá de Baixo), Bairrada (Quinta do Encontro), Estremadura/Lisboa (Martim Joanes Gradil), Alentejo (Herdade Monte da Cal), also Brazil. Without exception, the wines are well made, the most exciting deriving from Quinta do Encontro, which also has a restaurant housed in an arrestingly designed circular building. One off hybrids include Pião (a blend of Nebbiolo from Piedmont's Marchesi di Gresy with Dão Touriga Nacional), Duorat (a blend of Touriga Nacional from the Douro with Garnatxa Roja from Priorat) and Homenagem (a Portuguese collaboration made with fruit from Cabriz and Luis Pato in Bairrada). (SA)

Dão
Recommended Reds:
Casa de Santar Reserva ★★★☆ £C
Quinta de Cabriz Reserva ★★★ £C
Quinta de Cabriz Touriga Nacional ★★★ £C
Quinta de Cabriz Colheita Seleccionada ★★☆ £B
Quinta do Ribeiro Santo ★★☆ £B
Recommended Whites:
Paço dos Cunhos do Santar Vinho do Contador ★★★☆ £C
Casa de Santar Encruzado ★★★ £B
Quinta de Cabriz Encruzado ★★ £B
Quinta de Cabriz Colheita Seleccionada ★★ £B

Estrenadura/Lisboa
Recommended Reds:
Berco do Infante ★ £B

Douro
Recommended Reds:
Quinta das Tecedeiras Vintage Port ★★★ £F
Quinta das Tecedeiras Reserva ★★★ £D
Quinta Sá de Baixo Sá de Baixo ★★ £B

Bairrada
Recommended Reds:
Quinta do Encontro Grande Encontro ★★★★ £F
Quinta do Encontro Encontro 1 ★★★★ £E
Quinta do Encontro Bairrada Superior ★★★ £C

Alentejo
Recommended Reds:
Herdade Monte da Cal Vinha de Saturno ★★★ £F
Herdade Monte da Cal Reserva ★★ £B

Delaforce (Port)

Delaforce, like Croft became part of the Taylor-Fonseca group in 2001 but, though they still make the ports, the brand was acquired by Real Companhia Velha in 2009. The wines are noted for being fruit-rich, stylish and refined at their best. That 'best' vanished after 1977 but the 92, 94 and 2000 made by Nick Delaforce show some lovely fruit, although they are not in the blockbuster mould. 2003 (for which the rating is given) is very ripe, intense and fruit-filled. Older vintages still very much alive are 1966, 63, 60 and 55. The sculptured terraces of Quinta da Corte (adjoining Ramos Pinto's Bom-Retiro) are a key component of fruit quality and have been the source of a delicious if relatively forward, medium-weight single-quinta port when a vintage isn't declared. Recent vintages are 2004, 01, 97, 95 and 91. Late Bottled Vintage, if more superficial, can

also reveal good fruit, while the tawnies and Colheitas show more finesse than most yet have good intensity too. There seems little doubt that the wines will get even better under the new regime.

Recommended Reds:
Vintage Port ★★★★ £F   Vintage Port Quinta da Corte ★★ £E
20-year-old Tawny Port Curious and Ancient ★★★ £E
10-year-old Tawny Port His Eminence's Choice ★★ £D
Late Bottled Vintage Port ★ £C

D'Oliveira (Madeira) *www.vinhosmadeira.pt*
Pereira D'Oliveira with substantial stocks of old wine are one of the best sources for top quality Madeira. Wines date back to 1850 when the company was founded by João Perreira D'Oliveira. The company, currently run by Aníbal and Luís D'Oliveira, supplements its own grape supply with that from small growers. The style is for real concentration allied to intense flavour with increasingly complexity and finesse in older bottles. Those with an indication of age (10-year, 15-year-old styles) include Tinta Negra Mole and are labelled according to sweetness. If not that refined, they are characterful and intense; the 15-year-old Medium-Dry perhaps currently the most stylish of these. It is difficult to do justice to the many fine Colheita and especially Vintage (confusingly labelled Reserva) bottlings here. Verdelho from 1981, Boal from 1983 or Malvasia from 1987 are good Colheita examples of these varieties but there is more refinement in older Reservas such 1977 Boal (£G) or 1966 Verdelho (£G). D'Oliveira have long made the rarer Terrantez too and a reasonably priced example can be had from 1977 (£G). Extraordinary old wines still available include a 1937 Reserva Sercial - illustrating the splendid complexity Sercial can achieve with age - a 1908 Reserva Boal (a classic example of long-aged Boal) and 1905 Reserva Verdelho but these are justifiably more expensive (all £H) There are many more jewels to track down, several much older but you'll need deep pockets.

Recommended Whites:
Madeira 15-year-old Sweet ★★★☆ £F
Madeira 15-year-old Medium-Dry ★★★☆ £F
Madeira 10-year-old Sweet ★★★ £E
Madeira 10-year-old Dry ★★★ £E

❀ Dow (Port) *www.dows-port.com*
Though a part of the Symington empire, as Silva & Cosens, the Dow port brand has a very distinct profile. There is a weight and dimension to the top years that, combined with an elegance and poise, puts them among the best, as recently seen in 1994, 97, 2000, 03 and 07. The latter is structured, expansive and classically Dow's. Vintages that can be drunk now include 1985, 83, 80, 77, 70, 66, 63, 55 and 45. Even older vintages can still have some life, as does a fully-mature 1960 – although the 77 is now showing some variability. It is quite a structured port but its fine tannins are covered in layers of ripe fruit. In lesser years the wine can appear more muscular and occasionally a hint of spirit can also show through. However, Quinta do Bomfim, from slopes close to Pinhão in the heart of the Douro, was until recently the most important quinta in the region and some fine ports have been made under this name in non-declared years including 2001, 1999, 98, 95, 92, 90, 87, 86 and 84. Dow also includes the exciting Quinta Senhora da Ribeira, which lies across the Douro from Quinta da Vesúvio in the Douro Superior. Once owned by Silva & Cosens and still part of its grape resources during recent years, its acquisition by the Symingtons in 1998 resulted in excellent single-quinta ports in 98, 99 and 2001, 2004, 2005, 2006 and 2008 made at the quinta now with state-of-the-art

automated systems. Winemaking facilities have also been boosted by the high-tech Quinta do Sol, where many of the ports are made. Crusted Port shows something of the Dow (elegant, drier) style at a moderate price and Late Bottled Vintage, though of the filtered type, can have good fruit richness and some depth. Tawnies tend to be quite vigorous but with good complexity at the 20-and 30-year level, while Trademark is an acceptable Vintage Character port.

Recommended Reds:
Vintage Port ✪✪✪✪✪ £G
Vintage Port Quinta do Bomfim ★★★★ £F
Vintage Port Quinta Senhora da Ribeira ★★★★ £F
30-year-old Tawny Port ★★★ £F
20-year-old Tawny Port ★★★ £F
10-year-old Tawny Port ★★ £E   Crusted Port ★★★ £D
Late Bottled Vintage Port ★★ £D

Duorum (Port & Douro) *www.duorum.pt*
Although the relaxation of regulations governing Port production in 1986 has led to a growth of independent Port producers typically these comprise existing estates who previously sold their grapes or wines to shippers. It takes nerve to start up from scratch as with Duorum, but then the two men behind this new joint project are two of Portugal's best known oenologists, João Portugal RAMOS and Jose Maria Soares Franco, the latter of whom oversaw production of FERREIRA's Barca Velha for 27 years. The pair purchased Castelo Melhor, 150 ha of elevated (350-550m) vineyard in the Douro Superior, which they planted in 2008. Meantime, fruit is sourced from a combination of rented old vineyards and growers in the Cima Corgo and the Douro Superior. Since the aim is to produce a modern, fruit-led style with good ageing capacity, the duo prefer fruit from elevated vineyards (350-500m). Freshness is prized and the wines are concentrated but fleshy, the Vintage Port, vivid in its fruity purity, with powerful but ripe supporting tannins. A Late Bottled Vintage Port (not tasted) is also made. A very promising venture. (SA)

Recommended Reds:
Vintage Port ★★★☆ £F   Douro Reserva ★★★ £D
Douro Colheita ★★ £C

Ervideira (Alentejo) *www.ervideira.pt*
This ambitious, modern enterprise is headed by Duarte Leal da Costa. Wines have been made here since 1998 from re-established family vineyards on two estates, Monte da Ribeira and Herdadinha. Fruit sourced only from these 160 ha, is transformed by oenologist Paulo Laureano into around 75,000 cases of consistent and characterful wine. Least expensive are the Terras d'Ervideira red and white, which are well made with ripe fruit and good structures. Both are typical Alentejo blends, the herbal, citrusy white from Antão Vaz, Roupeiro and Arinto, and the bright red fruited red from Trincadeira, Aragonês and Castelão. In the Vinha d'Ervideira red the Castelão component is replaced by Alicante Bouschet and Cabernet Sauvignon (together making 30%) and has more depth and extract. The most ambitious of the reds is the Conde d'Ervideira Reserva from a similar blend but subject to 8 months in new oak. This needs a minimum of 5–6 years' age in order to show its full potential. A white equivalent is 100% Antão Vaz fermented and aged in oak, its mealy, spicy character is slightly overdone but it has good fruit and structure and won't fall apart. Also made are a series of varietal reds, including Trincadeira, Aragonez and Touriga Nacional under the Castas d'Ervideira label.

Recommended Reds:
Conde d'Ervideira Reserva ★★★ £D

Portugal

Terras d'Ervideira ★★ £B   Vinha d'Ervideira ★★ £B
Recommended Whites:
Terras d'Ervideira ★★ £B   Conde d'Ervideira Reserva ★★ £B

✿ Esporão (Alentejo) www.esporao.com

Herdade do Esporão represents a massive investment and real faith in the potential of the Alentejo region. Dr Jose Roquette, brother of Quinta do Crasto's Jorge Roquette (behind QUINTA DO CRASTO) has been very successful in developing what is now 600ha of vineyards spread across five different sites. Despite the size, winemaker David Baverstock (a leading influence in the development of modern, quality Portuguese wines) has set a high standard in both red and white wines. The Esporão-labelled and varietal wines are bold, powerful, ripe, intense, fruit-driven and oak-influenced. The Esporão Reserva is currently a blend of Trincadeira, Aragonês and Cabernet Sauvignon aged in American oak for 12 months and shows good richness and depth with 3–4 years' age. Newish Private Selection/ Garrafeira is powerful with lots of oak, extract and breadth and needs a decade to show at its best. Flagship Torre de Esporão first released in 2004 is muscular and impressive but requires time in bottle to really prove its worth. The pick of a series of varietal examples are the Alicante Bouschet, Aragonês, and Touriga Nacional which, with production slashed from 20,000 to 6,000 bottles, have moved up a gear in quality. Vinha da Defesa includes red, white and rosé. The red is based on Aragonês while the white, with good tangy, citrusy fruit, is produced from Antão Vaz, Arinto and Roupeiro. The same white varieties are oak-aged to give a ripe, spicy, creamy and peachy if unsubtle Esporão Reserva with moderate ageing potential. Private Selection white is Sémillon with Marsanne (90/10) and could easily be mistaken for a concentrated Barossa example. At an everyday level the best vintages of Monte Velho red can provide decent value and the Monte Velho and Duas Castas whites are very well made, fruity but refreshing wines that betray the Aussie touch. Least expensive are the Alandra red and white. Sparkling wine, a sweet wine and a range of olive oils and cheeses are also produced. The acquisition of Quinta dos Murças in the Douro, where Baverstock started his Portuguese career, promises to deliver if initial trial wines are anything to go on. Watch this producer closely – a great future.

Recommended Reds:
Alentejo Esporão Private Selection/Garrafeira ★★★★☆ £F
Alentejo Esporão Torre do Esporão ★★★★ £F
Alentejo Esporão Reserva ★★☆ £D
Alicante Bouschet ★★★ £D
Aragonês ★★★ £D   Touriga Nacional ★★★ £D
Trincadeira ★★ £C   Vinha da Defesa ★ £B
Monte Velho ★ £A
Recommended Whites:
Alentejo Esporão Private Selection ★★★ £D
Alentejo Esporão Reserva ★★☆ £C   Roupeiro ★ £B
Vinha da Defesa ★ £B

Ferreira (Port)

Ferreira was built up by one of the legends of the Douro, Dona Antónia Adelaide Ferreira (whose diminutive name 'Ferreirinha' is used for the company's table-wine production). Ferreira makes the most gutsy, earthy example among the leading Vintage Ports; it is often very ripe and raisiny but with plenty of raw intensity and can age impressively. It is declared more frequently than most, including good years that were not generally declared (recently 2011 and 2010) as well as 2009, 08, 07, 03, 99, 97, 95, 94 and 91. Late Bottled Vintage with character and depth is not shy, while the tawnies maintain fruit intensity; spice and dried fruits in the Quinta do Porto, with additional refined, nutty complexity in the Duque de Bragança. Four important quintas are included in the Ferreira holdings: Quinta do Porto, Quinta do Seixo, Quinta do Caedo and Quinta da Leda. The last is the centre of production for table wines including Barca Velha, first produced in 1952 and for long Portugal's most famous red. Now aged in new French oak (previously Portuguese), it is based on Tinta Roriz but also includes Touriga Nacional, Touriga Franca, Tinta Barroca and Tinta Amarela and is only blended and subsequently released when deemed ready (with 5–10 years' age). The fruit sources have changed but the current signs suggest that future vintages of the Leda reds will be at least as good as the best to date. The current vintage for Barca Velha is 2009, which follows 04, but in addition good (rather than great) years are released as Casa Ferreirinha Reserva (previously Reserva Especial), although some vintages of this have had finesse at the expense of richness. Of the new reds, Quinta da Leda is based on Touriga Nacional but complemented by varying percentages of Tinta Roriz and Touriga Franca. With more depth, extract and structure than some of the other new wave Douro reds it should be given 7–10 years to develop fully. A varietal Touriga Nacional has previously been made but greater potential can be seen in a classy, muscular 04 Vinha do Pombal that needs even more time. Also made but not tasted is Vinha da Ribeira. For Callabriga, see SOGRAPE.

Ferreira
Recommended Reds:
Vintage Port ★★★ £F
20-year-old Tawny Port Duque de Bragança ★★★ £F
Tawny Port 10-year-old Quinta do Porto ★★ £E
Late Bottled Vintage Port ★★ £D

Casa Ferreirinha
Recommended Reds:
Douro Barca Velha ★★★★☆ £H
Douro Quinta da Leda Vinha do Pombal ★★★★☆ £E
Douro Quinta da Leda ★★★☆ £E
Douro Quinta da Leda Touriga Nacional ★★★ £C
Douro Casa Ferreirinha Reserva ★★ £E
Douro Vinha Grande ★★ £B

✿ Fonseca (Port) www.fonseca.pt

Fonseca is one of the truly great Vintage Ports and a name most serious port drinkers know well. Though under the same ownership as Taylor it has a very distinct identity of its own. Fruit comes from the Cruzeiro, Santo António (both in the Pinhão Valley) and Panascal quintas and the wines are fashioned by David Guimaraens, following the successful tenure by his father (Bruce Guimaraens) before him. Fonseca has a rich and expansive style with often explosive fruit intensity and marvellous depth of flavour, yet doesn't lack for structure. Great vintages include 2003, 2000, 97, 94, 92, 85, 77, 70, 66, 63 and 55. Fonseca Guimaraens is the name of the consistently very fine 'off-vintage' port, made in good years when there isn't a declaration; it can generally be bought with confidence at a somewhat more affordable price. A single-quinta, Quinta do Panascal (which may be visited), is also sometimes made in these years. The standard is generally high in the other ports, too, with good vigour and intensity in the tawnies and usually good fruit in a filtered-type LBV. Terra Prima is an attractive, fruit-driven certified organic reserve ruby Port. Bin 27 is one of the best of the big-brand Vintage Character ports. A dry White Port, Siroco, is also made.

Recommended Reds:
Vintage Port ✪✪✪✪✪ £G
Vintage Port Fonseca Guimaraens ★★★★ £E
Vintage Port Quinta do Panascal ★★★ £E
20-year-old Tawny Port ★★★ £F   10-year-old Tawny Port ★★ £E
Late Bottled Vintage Port ★ £C
Terra Prima Reserve Ruby Port ★ £C
Bin No. 27 ★ £C

José Maria Da Fonseca (Peninsula de Setúbal)   *www.jmf.pt*

This long-established family producer has 850 ha of vines at its disposal between the two regions of Peninsula de Setúbal and Alentejo. These include the large Algeruz vineyard purchased in 1989 and subsequently used to develop better clones of local Portuguese varieties but also trialling Syrah, Tannat, Viognier and Sauvignon Blanc. The wines are made by seventh-generation Domingos Soares Franco. Some of the big-volume brands can show attractive fruit if lacking structure and concentration. Whites including Quinta de Camarate and Primum are generally sound but like the reds want for more intensity and excitement. Red Primum (from Touriga Nacional and Touriga Franca) could use a little more richness. The Periquita brand has been extended and, save for the Clássico, is no longer made exclusively from the Castelão grape. The Clássico, released with some age, shows more of the classic spicy, berry, savoury and chocolaty Castelão character. White, rosé and reserve Periquitas are well made and good value. Better still are the Garrafeira wines, RA, CO (both from Castelão), TE (Castelão/ Cabernet) and more recently FSF (Shiraz, Trincadeira and Tannat in 2001), which show excellent complexity, depth and intensity; all are best with 6–10 years' age. New in 2000 is a powerful, oaky Hexagon, produced from the grape varieties of FSF plus Touriga Nacional, Tinta Cão and Touriga Franca. Like FSF it is foot-trodden in lagares and aged in new French and American oak. Colecção Privada Domingos Soares Franco are experimental wines, notably a Moscatel Roxo rosé, though arguably this rare grape is best put to its traditional, fortified use. From the Douro come the Domini wines, a joint venture with Cristiano van Zeller (QUINTA DO VALE DOÑA MARIA). Domini Plus shows classic Douro character and intensity in a modern style. The other great strength is Setúbal (fortified sweet Moscatel and other varieties), ranging from a youngish vintage-dated Alambre that is grapey and fresh with citrus peel, ripest peach and apricot character, to a deep-coloured, honeyed Moscatel Roxo with an orange peel aroma, through to a rich, gently oxidised Superior (recent vintages are 1962, 64, 65, 66 and 71) with a sweet intensity of dates and nuts. Most extraordinary, however, is a limited-release bottling called Trilogia (a blend of 1900, 34 and 65). Very intense yet not excessively sweet, it has marvellous finesse to its honeyed, citrus peel and nutty aromas and flavours.

José Maria da Fonseca
Recommended Reds:
Garrafeira FSF ★★★☆ £C   Garrafeira CO ★★☆ £C
Garrafeira RA ★★☆ £C   Hexagon ★★★ £F
Periquita Clássico ★★ £C
Recommended Whites:
Setúbal Superior ★★ £E
Setúbal Moscatel Roxo 20-year-old ★★ £E
Domingos Soares Franco & Cristiano Van Zeller
Recommended Reds:
Douro Domini Plus ★★★ £E   Douro Domini ★★ £B

Fundação Eugénio De Almeida (Alentejo)

Fundação Eugénio de Almeida is a charitable foundation that was founded in 1963 by Vasco Maria Eugénio de Almeida whose family had owned the land since the late eighteenth century, including the original 17th century winery in Évora where Carthusian monks made wine (and wines are stilled cellared). In 2007, production shifted to an enormous new state-of-the-art winery. Production has doubled from 1.5 million to 3 million kilos of grapes since the move. Grapes, 75% of which are hand-picked are sourced from 550 ha, of which the Fundação owns 310 ha. With its extensive cool rooms, selection tables and gravity transfers, quality (in terms of fruit purity and tannins) as well as quantity has increased. While the wines are showing brighter fruit and more refined tannins, save for the Scala Coeli label, they are drier in style and more structured than those made by more export-focused producers. Flagship Péra-Manca red, one of Portugal's best-known wines, has sinew and heft. Rich and spicy, with dried as well as fresh fruits, it develops savoury, gamey notes with age. It is very much a food wine, as is as Péra-Manca white, a blend of Antão Vaz and Arinto. Also traditional in style, it is not dissimilar from Hermitage, in fact Pedro Batista, the winemaker, is now experimenting with Roussanne. The winery also produces well-made reds under the Cartuxa, Foral de Évora and EA (everyday drinking), also some reasonable whites. Scala Coeli is a relatively new label which takes a less traditional path (though the tannin structure remains firm). Pricey Scala Coeli wines utilise varieties that are foreign to Alentejo – the 2007, a Touriga Nacional is perfumed, with a freshness that Touriga can deliver in this region, in 2006 a Syrah is spicy and fleshy; on the other hand, Scala Coeli Branco 2008 made from Alvarinho falls flat, lacking the zip associated with this Vinho Verde variety. (SA)
Recommended Reds:
Alentejo Péra-Manca ★★★★☆ £H   Alentejo Scala Coeli ★★☆ £F
Alentejo Cartuxa Reserva ★★★ £E   Alentejo Cartuxa ★★ £E
Recommended Whites:
Alentejo Péra-Manca ★★★☆ £E

✿ Graham (Port)   *www.grahams-port.com*

In terms of quality if not quantity, Graham's reputation is anchored by its brilliant Vintage Port, which tends to be a sweeter style than Taylor's. If not quite as sought after as Taylor or Fonseca in the last decade, it nonetheless has proven itself to be one of the top ports in almost every widely declared vintage (and possibly the highest scoring port in tastings for the recently declared 2011 vintage), perhaps the most consistently fine of all. The wines are big, rich and sweet-fruited with a lush opulence that conceals ripe, compact tannins. The same intensity of fruit holds up magnificently over 20, 30, 40 years or more. Excellent vintages include 2011, 2007, 2003, 2000, 97, 94, 91, 85, 83, 80, 77, 70, 66, 63, 55 and 45. In non-declared years the wine has long been produced as the often excellent Malvedos Vintage Port, named for Quinta dos Malvedos (at Tua, upriver from Pinhão) where 70ha of vineyards were replanted in the 1980s. Other important components of the Vintage Ports are Quinta das Lages and Quinta da Vila Velha in the Rio Torto, south of Pinhão. Graham's The Tawny is a youthful sumptuous wood aged tawny. The age dated Tawnies are, as you would expect from Graham, rich with a hint of Douro bake in the 20-year-old version yet the balance is good. Small amounts of 30- and 40-year-old versions are also made. The LBV (of the filtered type) is fruity, round and agreeable if lacking real depth. An intense, grapey Six Grapes is one of the better examples of the Premium Ruby or Vintage Character style. A Crusted Port is now also made.

Portugal

Recommended Reds:
Vintage Port ✪✪✪✪ £G   Vintage Port Malvedos ★★★★ £E
20-year-old Tawny Port ★★ £F
10-year-old Tawny Port ★ £E
Six Grapes ★ £D   The Tawny Port ★ £D
Late Bottled Vintage Port ★ £C

Henriques & Henriques (Madeira)
A leading Madeira producer equipped with a modern winery and making excellent, consistent commercial Madeiras, especially the 10-year-old and 15 year-old versions of the noble varieties, Sercial, Verdelho, Malmsey and Bual. Extra dry aperitif Monte Seco is mouth-wateringly good and "Single Harvest" Bual and Tinta Negra Mole Colheitas refined. The historic family firm was started in 1850 but the family have been landowners on Madeira for centuries. Most impressive is their ability to produce high quality in all styles (some shippers manage only one or two) across vibrant citrusy Sercial, elegant honeyed Verdelho, rich nutty Bual and still richer, sweeter but less refined Malmsey. The 15-year-old versions generally add that bit more intensity and richness which better balances the assertive acidities. Very small amounts of outstanding Vintage Madeira (at very high prices) are available from specialist stockists – a 1900 Century Malmsey has a marvellous aged complexity yet sparkles with life - some vintage-dated from the late 19th century and other even more venerable examples without a specific vintage date.

Recommended Whites:
Madeira 15-year-old Bua ★★★★ £E
Madeira 15-year-old Verdelho ★★★★ £E
Madeira 15-year-old Malmsey ★★★☆ £E
Madeira 15-year-old Sercial ★★★ £E
Madeira 10-year-old Bual ★★★☆ £D
Madeira 10-year-old Verdelho ★★★ £D
Madeira 10-year-old Malmsey ★★☆ £D
Madeira 10-year-old Sercial ★★☆ £D
Madeira 5-year-old Bual ★★ £C
Madeira 5-year-old Verdelho ★★ £C
Madeira Single Harvest Colheita Bual ★★★☆ £E
Madeira Single Harvest Colheita Tinta Negra Mole ★★★ £E
Madeira Monte Seco ★ £B

Herdade Grande (Alentejo) www.herdadegrande.pt
António Lança is a qualified viticulturalist who has been producing his own wines since 1996 from 60 ha of vines in a 350 ha estate that also includes olives and other crops. The winemaking facilities have been considerably expanded in the last 3 or 4 years and more of the grapes are now turned into Herdade Grande wines (rather than being sold to Esporão). Production is planned to peak at around 40,000 cases. There has been a corresponding rise in quality. A soundly structured estate white made from Antão Vaz sees negligible oak and shows a subtle mineral quality. The red estate wine comes from Aragonês and Trincadeira (plus 10% Cabernet and Syrah) and is a good, intense, berryish wine of adequate breadth and structure. Altogether more exciting is a premium red from 50-year-old vines (90% Aragonês) that spends 12 months in (mostly) American oak. It is rich, concentrated and powerful with lots of oak and extract but with the fruit to match, displaying a liquorice, chocolate, carob and berry succulence. It is likely to be best with 8–10 years' age. Herdade Grande Reserve (not tasted) is only made in top years. Second label Condado das Vinhas red and white are soundly made but don't show the same fruit quality as the Herdade Grande wines.

Recommended Reds:
Alentejo Herdade Grande Colheita Seleccionada ★★★★ £E
Alentejo Herdade Grande ★★ £B

Recommended Whites:
Alentejo Herdade Grande Colheita Seleccionada ★★ £B

❁ Lavradores de Feitoria (Douro) www.lavradoresdefeitoria.pt
This new project gathers in grapes from 15 estates that were previously sold to port companies. The winemaking team of Paulo Ruão, José Carlos Fernandes and Raul Perreira shows a lot of skill in selecting and blending the grapes for an expanding range of wines. Três Bagos is an already successfully established brand, the grapes being drawn from all 3 of the Douro sub-regions. The red from Tinta Roriz, Touriga Nacional and Touriga Franca offers plenty of character and fruit, while a white from local varieties is fresh and perfumed with good intensity. An unexpectedly good Sauvignon is also made. Basic Douro bottlings, both the red and a white from 100% Malvasia, are forward, fruity quaffers. The wines to seek out, however, are the Grande Escolha red which has a classy black-fruited depth and lots of breadth and the spicy, red-fruited Meruge, the so-called Feitoria blood brother of Niepoort Charme (Dirk Niepoort has been involved in the project from the outset). A special single-quinta bottling, Quinta da Costa das Aguaneiras No. 6 (mostly Touriga Nacional), has lush, plummy old-vine fruit that suggests there are more good things in store here.

Recommended Reds:
Douro Três Bagos Grande Escolha ★★★★ £E
Douro Meruge ★★★☆ £D   Douro Três Bagos ★★ £B
Douro Quinta da Costa das Aguaneiras No. 6 ★★★ £D

Recommended Whites:
Douro Três Bagos ★★ £B   Douro ★ £B

Madeira Wine Company www.madeirawinecompany.com
This is the leading producer of Madeira and includes the well-known brand names of Blandy's, Cossart Gordon and Leacocks. Some marvellous Vintage Madeiras are made but only in small quantities, usually only a few thousand bottles at best. The bigger-volume, so-called commercial Madeiras with an indication of age can show plenty of style too, if not the same concentration or complexity. Wines labelled with one of the noble varieties (most are almost 100% rather than the required minimum of 85%) are now only made using the canteiro system and used American oak casks are employed for ageing. Blandy's wines are generally richer and sweeter than those of Cossart Gordon but the wines are similarly made. Cossart Gordon's 10-year-old Verdelho and Bual are particularly fine for this level, the delicacy and harmony of the Verdelho contrasting with the tangy, orangey, peel-and-spice fruit intensity of the richer Bual. Blandy's 5-year-old Alvada is an innovative rich and soft, vanilla-edged blend of Bual and Malmsey aimed at winning a new audience for Madeira. Blandy's 15-year-old Malmsey is both concentrated and elegant and is a significant step up from the 10-year-old version. A series of 'Colheita' Madeira from relatively recent vintages are also made under the Cossart Gordon and Blandy's label - both excellent. For the many fine old Vintage Madeiras see a specialist; both Cossart Gordon and Blandy's include rare vintages of Terrantez. A 1968 Verdelho Blandy's is very tangy and intense while a 1958 Bual (either Cossart Gordon or Blandy's) is very fruit-rich and is fine now but should be stashed away for another 50 years. Alternatively, don't wait, go directly for a 1908 Bual Cossart Gordon (bottled 1985) for wonderful richness, complexity,

texture and length.

Blandy's
Recommended Whites:
Madeira 15-year-old Malmsey ★★★☆ £E
Madeira 10-year-old Verdelho ★★★ £D
Madeira 10-year-old Bual ★★★ £D
Madeira 10-year-old Malmsey ★★☆ £D
Madeira 5-year-old Malmsey ★★ £C
Madeira 5-year-old Alvada ★ £C   Madeira Colheita ★ £C

Cossart Gordon
Recommended Whites:
Madeira 15-year-old Bual ★★★ £E
Madeira 10-year-old Bual ★★★ £D
Madeira 10-year-old Verdelho ★★★ £D
Madeira 5-year-old Bual ★★ £C

Leacocks
Recommended Whites:
Madeira 10-year-old Bual ★★ £D

Malhadinha Nova (Alentejo) *www.malhadinhanova.pt*
Here is yet more evidence of the continued quality advance in the Alentejo. As the Soares brothers set about restoring a 200 ha estate located in the sparsely populated south of the region in the late 90s, they sought consultancy from the respected oenologist Luis Duarte (also QUINTA DO MOURO) for 20 ha of vineyard. Only in production since 2003, the Soares brothers have achieved meteoric success with their ambition and attention to detail. Though the vines are youthful, free-draining schist soils account for a well-structured estate red (made from Alicante, Aragones and Tinta Miuda with a dash of Touriga Nacional and Cabernet Sauvignon), which shows terrific concentration, combined with balancing freshness. In 2006, the Soares produced a new top tier wine, the muscular Marias de Malhadinha, as with the estate red, it is deeply concentrated with a mineral undertow. Time will tell if it warrants the price tag. The composition of the flagship white is still evolving. It is a blend of Arinto, Viognier and Chardonnay. Early versions have been impressive if perhaps a little too oaky and generous. Aside from these top wines, the small but perfectly formed gravity fed winery produces a surprisingly wide range. The Peceguina wines are the most affordable with a sound rosé and white and well-made ripe but juicy red from Aragonês, Touriga Nacional, Alfrocheiro and Alicante. The estate white is barrel-fermented and aged Antão Vaz that is flavoursome and oak-infused but not heavy. Pequeno João is another premium red but with Cabernet Sauvignon and Syrah complementing Aragonês. It manages to retain something of a Portuguese twist despite an assertive black fruit component from the imported varieties.
Recommended Reds:
Malhadinha Marias ★★★★ £G   Malhadinha ★★★☆ £F
Pequeno João ★★★☆ £E   Monte da Peceguina ★★☆ £D
Recommended Whites:
Monte da Peceguina ★ £C
Recommended Rosés:
Rosé da Peceguina ★ £B

Anselmo Mendes (Vinho Verde) *www.anselmomendes.com*
Anselmo Mendes makes Vinho Verde under his eponymous label and consults widely to, among others, Quinta do Ameal, Casa de Cello (both Vinho Verde) and Douro producer Alves de Sousa. Mendes was born in Moncao, together with Melgaco, Vinho Verde's hotspot for Alvarinho, a grape which he's "studied" for 20 years

and to good effect – he is a master of the variety. His Alvarinhos come in many guises (unwooded, wooded, sweet and sparkling). Whatever the style and, irrespective of price point, the common thread is that they deliver on quality and finesse. Meticulous canopy management ensures that fruit is ripe. A slow fermentation with natural and selected yeasts followed by lees-ageing/stirring accounts for a silky texture. Muros Antigos, the entry-level range, comprises an Alvarinho/Loureiro blend and single varietal wines; the single varietal Alvarinho develops limes on toast and lemon butter with a few years ageing while maintaining its freshness and persistence. Contacto, first introduced in 2008, is a ripe, peachy wine which owes its exuberant mid-palate to skin contact. A more serious and structured Muros de Melgaco Alvarinho 2009 is fermented and aged in untoasted French oak for 6 months, of which 10% is new. It benefits from a couple of years in bottle. Barrel samples of two 2009 vintage single vineyard Alvarinhos (both four star wines), one new and as yet unnamed, the second called Curtimenta (first trialled in 2005) show fabulous precision and minerality. A passito method dessert wine at the drier end of the spectrum is textured and complex. (SA)
Recommended Whites:
Curtimenta Alvarinho ★★★★ £E
Muros de Melgaco Alvarinho ★★★☆ £E
Contacto Alvarinho ★★★☆ £D
Muros Antigos Alvarinho ★★☆ £C
Muros Antigos Alvarinho/Loureiro ★ £B
Muros Antigos Loureiro ★ £B

Monte da Ravasqueira (Alentejo) *www.ravasqueira.com*
A new but promising operation in Alentejo. It is a family venture with a projected 30,000 cases from 34 ha of vineyards, made by the widely experienced Rui Reguinga. The very reasonably priced Fonte da Serrana (a second label) is based on Aragonês, Trincadeira and Cabernet Sauvignon and shows good richness and lots of character. Monte da Ravasqueira adds in some Alicante and Touriga Nacional and is slightly more concentrated but seems set to develop a stylish, savoury complexity with a hint of carob and will be best with 5–6 years' age.
Recommended Reds:
Monte da Ravasqueira ★★★ £C   Fonte da Serrana ★★ £B

Herdade do Mouchão (Alentejo) *www.mouchaowine.pt*
Mouchão enjoys a good reputation amongst drinkers of bold, characterful reds. The estate is a massive 900 ha cork grove that includes 32 ha of vineyards. The vineyards have been re-established since 1986 when the land was returned to the family having lost control of their property during the revolution of 1974. Viticulture is modern with a double trellising system used to train the mostly Alicante Bouschet vines - there is also Trincadeira and small amounts of Aragonês and other varieties. The wines, made by Paolo Laureano, follow a traditional vinification with the grapes foot-trodden in lagares prior to ageing in (mostly) large oak and (20-25%) new French *barriques*. Mouchão, the main wine (70-80% Alicante, the balance mostly Trincadeira), is typically bold, savoury and expressive with a dense, chewy palate and plenty of extract. It also offers good value. Tonel 3-4, essentially a selection of the best cuvées, is more singular, intense and very sweet-fruited with a dense black plum and prune richness. It needs a decade before it opens out fully. Due in part to being based on Alicante, these wines are markedly different from the new wave of quality and they add something special to vista of the Alentejo wines. A second label, Dom Rafael

Wine behind the label

includes a good value, flavoursome, quite traditionally styled red and a correct white. Ponte das Canas, first made in 2005, is a fruit-driven but polished blend of Portuguese and French grapes which gives Mouchão a foot in the modernist camp too.

Recommended Reds:
Mouchão Tonel 3-4 ★★★★ £F   Mouchão ★★★☆ £D

❀❀ Niepoort (Douro & Port)   *www.niepoort-vinhos.com*
Dirk Niepoort, fifth generation of this Dutch-owned shipper, is obsessed with wine to the benefit of wine lovers everywhere. Working with José Nogueira, and also since 2004 with Nick Delaforce (for port), he has long produced both outstanding Douro table wines and an extraordinary array of fine ports in almost every style imaginable. Niepoort has two quintas of its own: Quinta do Carril and Quinta de Nápoles, where the table wines are made at an impressive new (2007) state-of-the-art, schist clad winery. The outstanding Vintage Port is marked by its raw power and vigour in youth but with almost unequalled intensity and length of flavour and will be stunning. Secundum is effectively a second selection to the Vintage Port but increasingly impressive (particularly 03). Much of Niepoort's early reputation was for tawnies and colheitas of great refinement. 10-year-old Tawny Port combines vigour and complexity in a class of port that is too often overpriced for the quality. The very fine colheitas are from a string of vintages that run from 1995 back to the early part of the 20th century. Senior (aged Tawny) and Junior (Ruby) are superb, accessible styles - easily better than most other examples in their respective categories. Dirk also makes the best White Port going, with atypical elegance and freshness. Then there are the red wines produced with right hand man Luis Seabra from old, low-yielding vines which have excellent structure and weight. Redoma has been produced for a decade and while its price has crept up with the quality there is marvellous fruit and a rugged Douro complexity but a certain elegance too, especially now he is using bigger format barrels. The age worthy Redoma white is quite remarkable for Portugal: from grapes grown at altitude, it is a barrel-fermented and aged white of real depth and structure. The Reserva is more elegant and minerally. A relatively new white, Tiara, from cool, high vineyards is also promising. Redoma Rosé, given a little wood ageing, remains fresh and characterful for several years from a vintage. Flagship red, Batuta (like Redoma sourced from north-facing slopes), was first produced in 1999; deep, intense and powerful but already splendidly complex, it is already one of the Douro's (and Portugal's) greatest reds. More affordable is Vertente, which combines accessibility and fine fruit with good richness and texture; as the name suggests, Drink Me (UK name) is an even more accessible entry level red. Entry level ports Tawny Dee and Ruby Dum are similarly upfront and packaged in a fun bottle. Other top tier reds include, Charme, first made in 2000, puts the emphasis on elegance from old vine Tinta Franca and Tinta Roriz that is not de-stemmed. It can be quite Burgundian in style with seductive red fruits, spice and some, but not excessive, oak influence. Robustus, the name of Dirk's very first red from 1990 (Hermitage-like and still vigorous 20 years on) was revived in 2004 and has been refined with lengthy ageing in large, old wooden vats. "Projectos" experimental wines include a Pinot Noir, also a Riesling, both of which show promise. Niepoort also produces Gira Sol, a delicate, floral Vinho Verde made from Loureiro at QUINTA DE SOALHEIRO where Dirk consults.

Recommended Reds:
Vintage Port ❂❂❂❂❂ £G   Vintage Port Pisca ★★★★ £G
Vintage Port Secundum ★★★★ £F   Colheita Port ★★★★ £F

30-year-old Tawny Port ★★★★ £H
10-year-old Tawny Port ★★★★ £E   Senior Tawny Port ★★★ £C
Late Bottled Vintage Port ★★★ £D   Junior Tinto Port ★★ £C
Douro Batuta ★★★★★ £G   Douro Robustus ★★★★★ £G
Douro Charme ★★★★☆ £G   Douro Redoma ★★★★ £E
Douro Vertente ★★★ £C   Douro Drink Me ★ £B
Recommended Whites:
Douro Redoma Reserva ★★★★ £F   Douro Redoma ★★★☆ £E
Douro Tiara ★★ £E   White Port ★★ £C   Vinho Verde Gira Sol ★☆ £C
Recommended Rosés:
Douro Redoma ★★ £B

❀ Filipa Pato (Beiras)   *www.filipapato.net*
Filipa Pato is the daughter of Luis PATO (below) and is at the vanguard of a talented new generation of winemakers. Her wines are made in Bairrada and sourced from diverse vineyard sources in Beiras including Bairrada and Dão. For this reason, all the wines are sold as Beiras Vinho Regional. Her winemaking experience includes stints in Australia and Argentina. The elegant, stylish *terroir*-driven premium Lokal wines are from leased vineyards. Calcário is from old vine Baga (80 years old) from Bairrada and is both fermented and aged in oak (50% new). Silex comes from a single Dão vineyard and is a blend of Touriga Nacional (75%) and Alfrocheiro Preto. Like Calcário, it is modern and well-made with excellent structure and ripe tannins. Ensaios wines are less expensive but are bright-fruited and soundly structured. The white from Arinto and Bical, half aged in used wood, is floral, citrusy and fruit-driven while the red which is lightly mineral and spicy is a blend of Jaen, Baga and Tinta Roriz. Wines under the Vinhos Doidos label are made in conjunction with her husband and include Bossa, a relatively fruit-driven but leesy, tangy blend of Bical and Maria Gomes (excellent value for money), whereas Nossa Branco is powerful, textured traditionally vinified Bical - an excellent food wine - which needs time to unfurl.

Recommended Reds:
Lokal Silex ★★★★☆ £E   Lokal Calcário ★★★★ £E
Ensaios Tinto ★★ £C
Recommended Whites:
Vinhos Doidos Nossa Branco ★★☆ £E   Ensaios Branco ★★ £C
Vinhos Doidos Bossa Branco ★ £B

❀ Luis Pato (Bairrada)   *www.luispato.com*
Luis Pato has been Bairrada' great moderniser, introducing green harvesting, complete de-stemming, temperature control and *barrique*-ageing to fashion the region's and some of Portugal's top wines. He remains an innovator, lately fashioning FLP and the Abafado range of sweet "molecular" (cryoextracted) wines and even a Touriga Nacional red (João Pato - not tasted), but it is his way with the local Baga grape that sets the pulse racing. The flavours of Baga are not to everyone's taste but these are excellent, age worthy examples of what is possible. A combination of new and one year old Allier *barriques* are used for the top single-vineyard wines. The best of these, from 70-year-old vines in a 0.7 ha vineyard, is Vinha Barrosa, with terrific intensity and dimension and a remarkable earthy, truffly, old-vine richness. Vinha Pan and Vinha Barrio are almost as good, the Pan perhaps more tannic and intense than the more mineral Barrio. Quinta do Moinho from younger vines is arguably the least of these wines yet doesn't lack for intensity, breadth or style. A very small amount of wine is produced from ungrafted vines and fermented in new oak and bottled as Baga Pé Franco. Though very structured it has extraordinary aromas and flavour including earth, truffles, smoke, coffee, black plum;

it probably needs to be kept for a minimum of a decade before drinking. As might be expected the wine is bottled without fining or filtration. A regular Baga has more forward, spicy, black plum fruit and is lightly structured. It is worth trading up to Vinhas Velhas red for that bit more intensity and structure. Vinhas Velhas white, a blend of Bical. Cerceal and Sercialinho, is also very good. Flagship white Vinha Formal, made from 100-per-cent Bical that is fermented and aged in oak hails from a single vineyard. The oak is not allowed to dominate and the wine reveals subtle yet intense, ripe fruit with excellent breadth and structure to improve for several years.

Recommended Reds:
Quinta do Ribeirinho Baga Pé Franco ★★★★☆ £H
Vinha Barrosa ★★★★ £E   Vinha Pan ★★★☆ £E
Vinha Barrio ★★★☆ £E
Quinta do Moinho ★★★ £D
Maria Gomes ★★ £C   Vinhas Velhas ★★ £C
Baga ★ £B
Recommended Whites:
Vinha Formal ★★★☆ £D

⊕ Poeira (Douro) *www.poeira.pt*
Jorge Moreira consults for QUINTA DE LA ROSA and has recently returned to Real Companha Velha, where he started out, to make wine there. However he also makes a few thousand bottles of his own from Quinta de Terra Feita de Cima in the Pinhão Valley. The exact composition of the Poeira red is unclear as it is produced from a field blend of old vines. Jorge's philosophy is to put the emphasis on acidity for elegance and to avoid making a heavy tannic wine. The result is indeed elegant, a classy Douro red characterised by both red and black fruits. While not in a blockbuster mould, it shows intensity and depth and evident ageing potential. The range has now been extended. Innovative well-structured blend Poeira CS 2007 includes 23% Cabernet Sauvignon for backbone, 21% Sousao for freshness and 56% Touriga Nacional for perfume. New second tier wines Po de Peira Branco (a unique blend of Alvarinho and Gouveio) and Po de Peira Tinto reflect Moireira's elegant, intense style.

Recommended Reds:
Douro Poeira ★★★★☆ £F   Douro Poeira CS ★★★☆ £E
Douro Po de Poeira ★★★ £D
Recommended Whites:
Douro Po de Poeira ★★★ £D

Quinta do Ameal (Minho) *www.quintadoameal.com*
Pedro Araújo is a great grandson of Adriano Ramos Pinto. Vineyards have been long established in this northern part of the Vinho Verde DOC but yields from 12 ha have been reduced to well below the norm. Under the winemaking expertise of Anselmo Mendes, Loureiro forms the basis of both a fresh and focused unoaked version that is sold as a Vinho Verde most recently showing increased minerality and depth. A more concentrated and detailed, oak fermented and aged (6 months new French) Escholha sold as Vinho Regional Minho. The latter needs at least 2-3 years age to show at its best. Also made is an unoaked Arinto with plenty of ripe fruit depth if not quite the finesse that Loureiro brings, a complex, structured traditional method Espumante (Arinto) and Special Harvest, a delicious passito method sweet Loureiro.

Recommended Whites:
Escholha Loureiro ★★★☆ £D   Arinto ★★★ £C
Vinho Verde Loureiro Ponte da Lima ★★☆ £C

Quinta de Chocapalha (Lisboa) *www.chocapalha.com*
Quinta de Chocapalha is the family estate of talented winemaker Sandra Tavares da Silva (Pintas). It comprises 40 ha of vineyards in a particularly blessed part of Lisboa. Quinta de Chocapalha adjoins QUINTA DA CORTEZIA but the wines are made in a contrasting way. For the red wines the grapes are foot-trodden in stone lagares (in robotic lagares from 2003) and fermented in French oak vats. All are then aged in French *barriques*, and show excellent fruit and extract but also a depth and texture not encountered in other good Lisboa reds. An intense, pure and classy Chocapalha Reserve is the best wine yet. The regular Quinta de Chocapalha includes Castelão and Alicante in the blend with Touriga Nacional and Tinta Roriz. Also made is a distinctive *barrique*-aged (50% new) Cabernet Sauvignon with a mineral quality to its berry and blackcurrant fruit. Also showing great promise is the Quinta de Chocapalha reserva Branco white from Chardonnay and Arinto (60/40) with the Chardonnay component fermented and aged in *barriques*. There is also a dry, racy, Riesling like Arinto (Quinta de Chocopalha Arinto) and a fresh, unoaked blend of Arinto, Viosinho and Vital (Quinta de Chocopalha Branco).

Recommended Reds:
Chocapalha Reserve ★★★★ £E
Cabernet Sauvignon Quinta de Chocapalha ★★★ £D
Quinta de Chocapalha ★★☆ £D
Recommended Whites:
Quinta de Chocapalha Reserva Branco ★★ £D
Quinta de Chocapalha Arinto ★★ £B
Quinta de Chocapalha ★★ £B

Quinta da Cortezia (Lisboa) *www.quintadacortezia.com*
Miguel Reis Catarino is a trained viticulturalist and winemaker who has worked as a consultant in the Alentejo but also has his own estate in Lisboa. Here his obsession with light and soils has resulted in remarkable fruit quality from 66 ha of family vineyards that have been replanted in stages since 1991. Only a percentage is currently produced under the Cortezia label, led initially by three varietals (made since 1997). The wines are dense and compact when young but with a pure varietal intensity and fine, ripe tannins. The wines perhaps lack flair but deserve to be drunk with at least 5 years' age. More impressive than the varietal examples is the Reserva from Touriga Nacional, Tinta Roriz and Merlot. There is more complexity, extract and structure as well as depth and richness. Making use of a new gravity-fed winery from 2004, white wines are now being produced for the first time from Chardonnay, Fernão Pires and Arinto grapes that were previously sold to other producers. To date an attractive, fruity white has been made under the Vinha Conchas label, already source of a good value, light, supple and berryish red for early drinking. There is also now a Quinta da Cortezia white and the Vinha Concha label is augmented by a Special Selection red, (neither tasted).

Recommended Reds:
Quinta da Cortezia Reserva ★★★ £C   Merlot ★★ £C
Touriga Nacional ★★ £C   Tinta Roriz ★★ £C
Vinha Conchas ★ £B
Recommended Whites:
Vinha Conchas ★ £B

>> Quinta da Murta (Lisboa-Bucelas) *www.quintadamurta.pt*
French producer and owner Franck Bodin has transformed this property in the Lisboa region. First planted some 20 years ago, Quinta da Murta is making a real impact, especially with the white

wines, termed the 'Wine of Shakespeare' (see Henry VI part 2). The parent material of the soil is Jurassic calcareous marl and limestone and the vineyards are planted on south and south-east facing slopes at ca. 250m elevation. Arinto is the main white varietal grown and the wines are typically fresh, zesty and acidic. Aromas of lemon and vanilla dominate and though they may be enjoyed young, these wines will benefit from some cellar age. The classico is a superb food wine. The Touriga Nacional and Syrah red is an interesting development and worth watching.

Recommended Reds:

Murta red ★★ £B

Recommended Whites:

Quinta da Murta Classico ★★★ £C   Quinta da Murta ★★ £B
Quinta da Murta Espumante Reserve Brut Nature ★★ £C

Recommended Rosés:

Murta Espumante Rosé Extra Brut ★ £B

Quinta do Côtto (Douro & Port) *www.quinta-do-cotto.pt*
Owner and winemaker Miguel Champalimaud has made Douro reds from the early 1980s, long before the recent explosion in their production. The Côtto wines from 50 ha of vineyards are concentrated and muscular but with much greater refinement in recent years than the slightly tough, brawny, if characterful efforts from the 1980s and early 1990s, though they lack the finesse of the best producers. The Grande Escolha does in fact mean what are considered by their maker to be the great years, when a selection of Touriga Nacional, Tinta Roriz and Touriga Franca grapes undergo an extended maceration prior to ageing in new Portuguese oak. Still rather forbidding in its youth, there is good dimension as well as increasing complexity with age; it shouldn't be drunk with less than 6–8 years' cellaring. The regular Côtto needs time too, often 5 years. As well as a flavoursome white Douro, decent Vinho Verde (from a mix of varietals subject to some oak influence) has good fruit and ripeness but more elegant are varietal Loureiro and Avesso sold as Vinho Regional Minho. Good Vintage Port is also made occasionally.

Quinta do Côtto

Recommended Reds:

Douro Grande Escolha ★★★ £E   Douro ★★ £C

Recommended Whites:

Douro ★ £B

Champalimaud

Recommended Reds:

Vintage Port ★★★☆ £E

Paço de Teixeiró

Recommended Whites:

Loureiro ★★ £B   Avesso ★★ £B
Vinho Verde ★ £B

❀ **Quinta do Crasto (Douro & Port)** *www.quintadocrasto.com*
With a superbly sited winery and 70 ha of vineyards, Crasto has built an enviable reputation for both splendid table wines and fruit-rich ports. The Roquettes have recently acquired Quinta da Cabreira, a 120 ha estate in the Douro Superior, 100ha of which have been newly (block) planted. Winemaking is currently overseen by Dominic Morris, Manuel Lobo and Tomás Roquette. New entry-level Flor do Crasto, a bright, floral red contrasts nicely with the (also unoaked) but more structured regular Crasto Douro red which offers good Douro character within a grippy but modern structure. From young vines in the Douro Superior, Crasto Superior is an oaked, generously fruity, spicy red, which brings a point of difference to

the range. Crasto's first white wine, an unpretentious fresh, unoaked quaffer, also hails from the Douro Superior. An intense black-fruited Reserva from Quinta do Crasto old vines can age impressively and represents excellent value for money. Varietal reds are occasionally made, a powerful but balanced Tinta Roriz and Touriga Nacional. Two small-volume premium reds, only made in outstanding years, Vinha da Ponte and Vinha Maria Teresa, were first produced from the 1998 vintage. Both show a structure, depth and dimension that put them among the Douro's very best. Maria Teresa, aged in French oak comes from a single vineyard of 22 inter-planted varieties and 100 year old vines. Vintage Port (made in 1994, 95, 97, 99, 00, 01, 03, 04, 07, 08, 09, 10, 11 and 12) is consistently good with added depth and concentration in the most recent vintages - a very good 10-15 year port that should keep for longer. A traditional Late Bottled Vintage Port is more forward but with an attractive, moderately sweet fruit character. Xisto, a joint venture between Jorge Roquette and Bordeaux's Jean-Michel Cazes, comes from the Douro Superior. Named for the schist soils, it is a blend of Touriga Nacional, Tinta Roriz and Touriga Franca. While flavoursome it lacks the finesse and pedigree of the Crasto top wines.

Quinta do Crasto

Recommended Reds:

Douro Vinha da Ponte ★★★★★ £G
Douro Vinha Maria Teresa ★★★★★ £G
Douro Reserva ★★★☆ £E   Douro Crasto Superior ★★★ £E
Douro ★☆ £C   Douro Flor de Crasto ★ £B
Vintage Port ★★★★ £F   Late Bottled Vintage Port ★★★ £E

Roquette & Cazes

Recommended Reds:

Douro Xisto ★★★☆ £F

Quinta dos Currais (Beira Interior) *www.quintadoscurrais.com*
Production in Beira Interior (a large region inland to the east of the Dão and bookmarked by the Douro Superior to the north and Alentejo to the south) has traditionally been driven by co-operatives and focused on white table wine. This is changing fast with some exciting pockets of ambition. With consultancy from Vines and Wines (who have done much to raise standards in the Dão), Quinta dos Currais are at the vanguard of the region's quality revolution. Founded in 1989 by José Diogo Tomás, he started the project from scratch with quality not quantity in mind and it shows. The vines are planted on schist soils on a north-south facing 30 ha site at around 500m. Varieties include Arinto, Síria, and Fonte-cal (whites) and for reds, Castelão, Touriga Nacional, Tinta Roriz, Jaen and Rufete. The basic red, a blend of Touriga Nacional, Aragonez, Castelao and Rufete is fresh and unworked with summer compote fruit, floral notes and spice. A heady Reserva, which benefits from time in bottle, shows ample concentration and impressive fruit purity wed to ripe but structured tannins. Unoaked whites include a benchmark single varietal Síria (the region's classic white), with ripe, tropical fruit cut with mouthwatering citrus acidity. The Colheita Seleccionada is a complex, flinty blend of 50% Fonte Cal (for minerality and mouthfeel), 25% Síria and 25% Arinto. All the wines, but especially the reds, represent very good value for money. (SA)

Recommended Reds:

Beira Interior Reserva ★★★ £C   Beira Interior ★★ £B

Recommended Whites:

Beira Interior Colheita Seleccionado ★★ £B
Beira Interior Síria ★ £B

Quinta das Heredias (Port) *www.quintadasheredias.com*
This emerging port house has already produced some very fine ports despite being only recently established. Mauricette Mordant, who helped found Champagne house Vranken, bought the historic monastery of Quinta do Convento (San Pedro das Aguias) on the Rio Távora outright from Vranken in 1996. It also includes the quintas of Espinhos and Calcado as well as Heredias – comprising 82 ha in the Cima Corgo. All the ports will eventually be entirely estate produced, most of the grapes having been sold off until 1999. Winemaker Jean Hugues Gros makes well defined, balanced ports with expressive fruit across a range of styles. Though some wines necessarily include older bought-in wines, all are impressive including a marvellously complex 40-year old Tawny. Ruby has excellent fruit for this level while Vintage Port from 2001 shows both elegance and depth. A traditional Late Bottled Vintage also shows good style while a dry White Port from 100% Malvasia Fina has good balance between spiced fruit characters and more nutty tertiary flavours. Some Douro red is also made but the emphasis is on port.

Recommended Reds:
40-year-old Tawny Port ★★★★★ £H
20-year-old Tawny Port ★★★★ £E   10-year-old Tawny Port ★★★ £D
Vintage Port ★★★★ £F   Late Bottled Vintage Port ★★ £D
Ruby Port ★★ £B

Recommended Whites:
White Port Meio Seco ★★ £C

Quinta do Infantado (Port) *www.quintadoinfantado.com*
The Roseira family have been making their own wines since 1978 from 45 ha of vineyards on a small northern tributary of the Douro downstream from Pinhão. João Roseira works with the talented Luís Soares Duarte and all the wines, even a Ruby, are made in lagares and are richly extracted. The incremental addition of spirit results in less being added and an avoidance of the spirit character seen in some Vintage Ports. Infantado's Vintage Port is powerful, intense and extracted, with more finesse in vintages since 1997. Also made is a traditional (i.e. throwing a sediment) Late Bottled Vintage of great extract and intensity. Needless to say a 10-year-old Tawny is vigorous and refined, unlike some of the rather tired, relatively simple examples that exist. The Quinta also produces table wines and João Roseira and Luis Duarte independently make the table wines of Bago de Touriga.

Recommended Reds:
Vintage Port ★★★★ £E   Late Bottled Vintage Port ★★★ £D
10-year-old Tawny Port ★★★ £E   Douro Reserva ★★ £E
Douro ★☆ £C

❀ **Quinta de Macedos (Douro)** *www.quintamacedos.com*
This is a very promising small property on the Rio Torto, which has been sympathetically revived by Paul Reynolds and his brother Raymond, a UK wine shipper. It runs to just 6.8 ha but much of it is planted to old vines. Viticulture is organic and old terraces of varying aspect have a mixed planting of Douro varieties (but led by Touriga Franca). Replanting has been undertaken where necessary and buildings have been restored including the stone lagares. A vertical basket press has also been installed for further extraction. The leading wine, Quinta de Macedos (first made in 2000) is produced from the oldest vines (60–80 years old) and spends 20 months in new French oak. The result is a deep, very rich, very ripe concentrated red with classic Douro complexity. It avoids over-ripeness, over-extraction or excess oak but has a structure and density that deserves at least 10 years' ageing. Lagar de Macedos

with more Tinta Roriz comes from slightly younger vines and spends less time in oak. Although it is soft and approachable the abundant fine tannins suggest more time is needed. A third, more accessible but still well-structured wine, Pinga do Torto is from younger vines of Tinta Roriz, Touriga Nacional and Touriga Franca.

Recommended Reds:
Douro Quinta de Macedos ★★★★☆ £E
Douro Lagar de Macedos ★★★☆ £E
Douro Pinga do Torto ★★ £C

Quinta do Monte d'Oiro *www.quintadomontedoiro.com*
The decision to modernise this winery, now one of the stars of both Lisboa and Portugal, was taken back in 1990. Engineer, businessman and talented amateur chef José Bento dos Santos was inspired by the great reds of Côte Rôtie and set out to emulate them on his 'hill of gold' near Alenquer. The results of an initial replanting of less than 3 ha to Syrah were such that since 1998 the balance of 15 ha of vineyard now also includes new Touriga Nacional, Tinta Roriz and Touriga Franca along with a little Viognier and Petit Verdot. The food-friendly wines are made by Graça Gonçalves with consultancy from Maison CHAPOUTIER who also consult on biodynamic treatments in the vineyard. The winery rapidly forged its reputation for world class wines with the release of the 1999 bottling of Homenagem a António Carqueijeiro. This is Syrah-based with 6% Viognier and essentially the same blend is used in the estate Reserva (with around 4% Viognier). The latter is no longer aged in 100% new French *barriques*, which delightfully showcases its refined deep raspberry/blackberry fruit, making for a more finely poised wine that rewards time in glass. It has a white Rhône companion in Madrigal, a part barrel-fermented aromatic but subtle Viognier with good finesse. There is lots of potential too in Aurius which has a fine interplay of preserved red and black fruits if not yet the concentration or depth for really fine wine. This blend includes the new fruit from Touriga Nacional, Tinta Roriz and Petit Verdot as well as Syrah. Also made are Têmpera, based on Tinta Roriz and the entry level Lybra, a bright, fresh and stylish red fruited Syrah. Since 2006 Santos and Michel Chapoutier have worked together under their eponymous label Bentos e Chapoutier, making Ex Aequo, a sumptuous blend of 75% Syrah and 25% Touriga Nacional (★★★).

Recommended Reds:
Quinta do Monte d'Oiro Reserva ★★★★ £E
Aurius ★★★☆ £E   Lybra ★★ £E

Recommended Whites:
Madrigal ★★☆ £D

❀ **Quinta do Mouro (Alentejo)** *www.quintadomouro.com*
Miguel Viegas Louro's small estate is one of the quality leaders in the Alentejo. There are 14 ha of vineyards, planted in the main to Aragonês, Cabernet Sauvignon and Alicante. Yields are kept low and the wines have maintained a consistent standard thanks to winemaker Luis Duarte. The estate red (around 3,000 cases), aged in both Portuguese and French oak, is an excellent firmly structured, spicy, black-fruited expression that develops classic Alentejo savoury complexity with more age. Made for the long haul, it is neither fined nor filtered. Slightly more is made of a second wine, Casa dos Zagalos (5,000 cases), which also has good fruit intensity and balance, true to the house style. A very small quantity of a 'gold label' version, aged for longer only in (new) French oak, first trialled in 1999 and has subsequently been made in exceptional vintages. Tasted in 2009, these are superb, immensely concentrated wines buttressed by ripe but firm tannins - made for the even longer haul!

Portugal

Recommended Reds:
Quinta do Mouro Gold Label ★★★★★ £F
Quinta do Mouro ★★★★☆ £E   Casa dos Zagalos ★★ £C

Quinta Dona Maria (Alentejo)   www.donamaria.pt

The Quinta, also known as Quinta do Carmo, is an arrestingly beautiful 18th century estate in Estremoz at around 400m. Owner Julio Tassara de Bastos, who still resides there, clearly has a knack with wines because his very first, Quinta do Carmo Garrafeira 1986 (made by João Portugal RAMOS), created waves following its release. Tasted in 2009, it was still impressively spicy, structured and vigorous. Not long afterwards, he was approached by Domaines Barons de Rothschild (Lafite), to whom he sold 50% of the company, including the Quinta do Carmo brand, in 1992. Under Lafite, winery operations were moved to Herdade das Carvalhas and Bastos sold his interest in the company around 2000, retaining only the Alicante Bouschet vineyard. Bastos has restored the old winery at Quinta Dona Maria, with its huge marble lagares and cement tanks. Reds feature old vine Alicante Bouschet and grapes from younger plantings of Alicante Bouschet, Petit Verdot, Syrah, Cabernet Sauvignon (to which he reckons Lafite cuttings lend a capsicum note), Aragones and Touriga Nacional, Viognier and Sémillon for whites. Julio Bastos is a powerful, sinewy and mineral old vine Alicante Bouschet, regarded as among Portugal's best and priced accordingly. The red Reserva is an elegant, beautifully structured blend of Alicante Bouschet, Petit Verdot and Syrah with a dusty minerality. Amantis red (Syrah, Petit Verdot and Alicante Bouschet, Cabernet Sauvignon and dash of Touriga Nacional) and white (Viognier with a dash of Sémillon) are more accessible but are nonetheless polished wines. Dona Maria Branco has a more traditional core of Antão Vaz, with Arinto and Douro variety Viosinho for balance, the latter varieties bringing freshness and minerality. The estate makes a good textured just dry rosé too. All in all, this is a class act with much potential. (SA)

Recommended Reds:
Dona Maria Reserva ★★★★☆ £F   Julio Bastos ★★★☆ £F
Amantis ★★ £D
Recommended Whites:
Anantis Branco ★★ £D   Dona Maria Branco ★☆ £C

✿ Quinta do Noval (Douro/Port)   www.quintadonoval.com

Today direction at Noval comes from Christian Seely of AXA-Millésimes (the corporate owner of CH. PICHON-LONGUEVILLE and other prestigious properties) while the wines are made by António Agrellos. But it got its start in modern times from António José da Silva, who first isolated the famous 2.5 ha of ungrafted vines that produce Nacional, the most sought-after of all ports. A port of great breadth, power and dimension, with a distinctive earthy, spicy dark plum character, it adds flesh and richness with age to become an often riveting port after 20, 30 or more years. Production from the low-yielding vines that average 35–40 years' age is tiny (200–300 cases) and bottles are hard to secure. The regular Quinta do Noval Vintage (which benefits from Nacional fruit when that wine is not made) has been a very exciting port in recent vintages after a lean spell prior to the 90s. It, too, is structured but profound and very age worthy. Silval, though named after one of Noval's own vineyards, is essentially a second selection but still a high-quality, medium-full style. Noval for a time made the ports from the excellent QUINTA DE RORIZ but the property is now owned by the Symingtons. Noval's Late Bottled Vintage is in the traditional sediment-throwing style and is a fine, concentrated example, particularly in top

vintages. There is also a fine range of aged tawnies and vintage-dated colheitas with dates ranging from 1987 back half a century. Other commercial styles are adequate if not more. Raven is a new, distinctly packaged Premium Ruby. A new vat room dedicated to making red table wine was completed in 2004 and Noval successfully released their first super premium red, Quinta do Noval in 2006. Cedro do Noval an elegant, very good value for money "second wine" is an unusual blend of traditional Douro varieties with Syrah. In 2010, Noval launched Labrador, an exciting 100% Syrah Vinho Regional Duriense with Douro gout de terroir.

Recommended Reds:
Vintage Port Nacional ✪✪✪✪✪ £H
Vintage Port ★★★★★ £G
Vintage Port Silval ★★★★ £E
40-year-old Tawny Port ★★★ £G
20-year-old Tawny Port ★★★ £F
10-year-old Tawny Port ★★ £D
Colheita Port ★★★ £E   Late-Bottled Vintage Port ★★ £C
LB ★ £B   Quinta do Noval ★★★☆ £F
Labrador ★★☆ £D   Cedro do Noval ★★☆ £C

Quinta do Passadouro   www.quintadopassadouro.com

Owned by the Bohrmann family since 1991 and now in partnership with winemaker Jorge Serôdio Borges of Pintas who had already established a track record under Niepoort management. This superb quinta in the Pinhão Valley includes 18 ha of vineyards, in part planted to old vines including some Sousão. The estate's old vine fruit is now augmented with fruit from a new 20 ha vineyard of south-facing 25-30 year old block planted vines at Quinta do Sibio in the Roncao Valley. Yields are low and the grapes are foot-trodden in stone lagares before 18 months in French barriques. The wine has become increasingly stylish, expressive and complex with successive vintages, with black fruits, spice, clove and floral characters that become more savoury with 5 years' age or more. A superb old-vines Reserva is also made, it is very concentrated with intense, sweet fruit and has excellent balance; its youthful black olive, truffle, earth and preserved black fruits character should give still more with 10 years' age. New from 04 is 'Passa' a more moderately priced version from young vines that offers good value if needing some 5-6 years' to show at its best. Port has been a fine single-quinta example and there is now an LBV also. In 2008, Passadouro released its first white, made from bought-in grapes.

Recommended Reds:
Douro Reserva ★★★★☆ £F
Douro Passadouro ★★★☆ £C
Douro Passa ★★★ £C   Port Quinta do Passadouro ★★★★ £F
Late-Bottled Vintage Port ★★☆ £C
Recommended Whites:
Douro Passadouro ★★★ £C

Quinta do Portal (Douro & Port)   www.quintadoportal.com

Quinta do Portal is not one quinta but four. Portal itself was once known as Quinta do Casal de Celeirós while the estates also include the Quinta do Confradeiro at Celeirós in the Pinhão Valley. Money and expertise have not been spared and the most recent vintages show that it is now all starting to come together. The style is for oaky wines but recently this has been matched by a ripe, intense fruit expression. Previous wood-taint problems have been addressed with help from one of the leading experts in this field, Pascal Chatonnet. Varietal Tinta Roriz, Touriga Franca and Touriga Nacional are expressive with good intensity. Grande Reserva is oaky

but also stylish and minerally with a convincing fruit depth and richness that should harmonise with 8–10 years' age. Vintage Port, made since 1995, comes from Quinta dos Muros grapes and shows good promise. In addition a small portion is bottled separately as Portal+. Fortified Moscatel Galego (Muscat á Petit Grains) has become something of a niche speciality and in 2009, Portal released its maiden 2007 late harvest blend of Moscatel, Rabigato and Viosinho. Growing demand for dry whites has encourage significant new plantings, 84ha of which major on white varieties (especially Viosinho and Gouveio).

Recommended Reds:

Vintage Port ★★★★ £F   10-year-old Tawny Port ★★☆ £E

Douro Grande Reserva ★★★★ £E

Douro Touriga Nacional ★★★☆ £D

Douro Tinta Roriz ★★☆ £D

Douro Touriga Franca ★★☆ £D

Douro Reserva ★★ £C   Douro Frontaria ★☆ £B

Douro ★ £B

Recommended Whites:

Moscatel Galego Reserve★★★ £D

Moscatel Galego★★☆ £C

Quinta da Portela da Vilariça (Douro)

Only 15 ha of this 400 ha estate sited among ancient village ruins in the harsh, dry reaches of the Douro Superior are planted to vines. Direction comes from 5th-generation Joaquim Morais Vaz. The estate red from Touriga Nacional, Touriga Franca, Tinta Roriz and a little Tinta Cão, is complemented by a varietal Touriga Nacional. Both are perfumed, with depth and intensity, although they are at the very ripe end of the spectrum and occasionally raisiny and slightly rustic. In complete contrast is a new red, Quinta das Castas, from 80-year-old Touriga Nacional vines near Vila Real. This shows cool, expressive fruit in the difficult 2002 vintage and is a wine to seek out.

Quinta da Portela da Vilariça
Recommended Reds:

Douro Touriga Nacional ★★★ £E   Douro ★★ £C

Quinta das Castas
Recommended Reds:

Douro ★★★ £C

Quinta dos Roques (Dão)

In the space of just a few years, Quinta dos Roques has emerged as arguably one of the Dão's leading estates, producing modern, accessible wines from continual experimentation with different varieties, blends and refinements to vinification. Vineyards now total 40 ha and the winemaking benefits from the expertise of well-known consultant Rui Reguinga who succeeds Professor Virgílio Loureiro. The characterful, medium weight regular dos Roques red is based on Touriga Nacional but also includes Alfrocheiro Preto and Tinta Roriz. All three grapes have also been vinified varietally (since 1996) giving excellent fruit expression and good concentration and structure. The Touriga Nacional has additional breadth and a deep plum and violet character with a hint of pine and white pepper, and is the best of these. Better still is a Reserva made from an old vineyard of mixed plantings that includes Tinta Roriz and Touriga Nacional. The Quinta do Correio wines are an inexpensive second label red and white from estate grapes. Wine from the nearby estate of Quinta das Maias is also made here, the reds reflecting the importance of the local Jaen in the 12ha of vineyards at 700m. Both

the regular Maias red and varietal Jaen can show a slightly smoky, spicy, wild berry fruit; the varietal example adds more flesh, intensity and structure. A Colecção version of Jaen is from very old vines and is very exciting A herb-scented Malvasia is a rare good Dão white but a subtly oaked Encruzado with refined peach and exotic notes is even better. Some sparkling rosé is also made. In 2005 and 2007 (exceptional vintages) a powerfully oaked new flagship wine, Maias Flor das Maias, has been made at Quinta das Maias.

Quinta dos Roques
Recommended Reds:

Dão Reserva ★★★★ £D

Dão Touriga Nacional ★★★ £D

Dão Tinto Cão ★★ £C   Dão Alfrocheiro Preto ★★ £C

Dão Tinto ★★ £B   Quinta do Correio ★☆ £B

Recommended Whites:

Dão Encruzado★★★ £C   Quinta do Correio ★☆ £B

Quinta das Maias
Recommended Reds:

Dão Jaen Colecção ★★★☆ £C   Dão Tinto ★☆ £B

Recommended Whites:

Dão Malvasia Fina ★☆ £B

✪ Quinta de Roriz (Port & Douro)   *www.quintaderoriz.com*

Quinta de Roriz was famous as an individual-quinta port in the 19th century but was re-established as an independent operation by the van Zeller family and has now been acquired by Symington. The Vintage Port was made by others for most of the 20th century. There are currently 42 ha within a sheltered amphitheatre some distance up-river from Pinhão but still within the Cima Corgo. Its revival is being achieved with help from the SYMINGTON Family who, before the acquisition in 2009, made the wines for some time. Under the new ownership, Roriz will become the home of Prats & Symington, the joint table wine venture between the Symingtons and Bruno Prats (ex-Cos d'Estournel), as well as the Roriz wines and ports. Grapes for Prats & Symington Chryseia have been sourced from Roriz for some time but the wines will now also be made at Roriz. The Vintage Port (100% foot-trodden and interestingly containing a small percentage of Sousão) is already a classic. What marks it out is its sheer class, with a dimension, definition and complexity seen only among the top names - cellar for at least 20 years. Two Douro table wines have made rapid strides and are distinguished from the Prats & Symington wines by their firmer, less refined tannins. The stylish Reserva (Touriga Nacional/Touriga Franca/Tinta Roriz) is aged in new French *barriques* and has good depth and extract and benefits from time in bottle. Prazo de Roriz, the entry level wine is relatively forward but retains good character for its price point.

Recommended Reds:

Vintage Port ✪✪✪✪✪ £G

Douro Quinta de Roriz Reserva ★★★ £C

Douro Prazo de Roriz ★★ £B

Quinta de la Rosa (Port & Douro)   *www.quintadelarosa.com*

The Bergqvist family took back control of its vineyards in the 1980s, producing their own port for the first time in 1988. Quinta de la Rosa has in fact demonstrated how successful a more estate-centred approach can be (given sufficiently cool storage) and makes a Vintage Port in every vintage (1993 excepted) in the manner of a Bordeaux château. Tim Bergqvist, first with help from David Baverstock but especially more recently working with Jorge Moreira (POEIRA) has steadily improved quality as the extensive

Portugal

winery buildings have been renovated and vineyards upgraded and in some instances replanted. Vintage Port shows the balance and excellent fruit intensity that characterises these ports. In 1999 an excellent single-vineyard example was made from old vines in Vale do Inferno (now replanted). Finest Reserve is essentially a Vintage Character port but far better than the norm, with real elegance and intensity, while a traditional Late Bottled Vintage shows more depth than filtered examples. Quinta de la Rosa table wines are just as important as the ports and both a partially oaked regular example (from Tinta Roriz, Touriga Franca and Tinta Barocca) and more oaky but increasingly refined Reserva impress. Jorge Moreira has produced more seamless wines with better purity and vibrancy. In 2005 Moreira and the Bergqvist family released Quinta das Bandeiras Passegem made in joint venture, a rich fuller-bodied red from a 100 ha estate they have planted in the Douro Superior. Also made are a perfumed white and cheaper white, a rosé and (unwooded) red under the Da Rosa label.

Recommended Reds:
Vintage Port ★★★★☆ £F
10-year-old Tawny Port Tonel No. 12 ★★★ £D
Late Bottled Vintage Port ★★★ £C
Finest Reserve ★★★ £C
Ruby Port Lote 601 ★★ £B
Douro La Rosa Reserve ★★★★ £E
Douro ★★★ £C Douro Vale da Clara ★★ £B
Recommended Whites:
Douro ★☆ £B

❀ **Quinta de Soalheiro (Vinho Verde)** *www.soalheiro.com*
Located in Melgaço, Vinho Verde's warmest, driest sub-region, production at Soalheiro is focused on Alvarinho, known as Albarino in neighbouring Galicia, Spain. It is Vinho Verde's star variety and Soalheiro are one of its finest exponents. Antonio Cerdeira illegally planted 4 ha of Alvarinho in 1974 and, following changes in the law, released his first Alvarinho in 1982. Today his daughter, Maria tends the estate's 10 ha of organically certified vines, while her brother Luis makes the wines. The classic is aromatic with lingering fruit salad flavours in its youth. A vertical tasting back to 1995 provided ample demonstration of its potential to age – like a Riesling, it retained its acidity while developing complex, weightier toast, lime, lemon cordial and butter flavours. The flagship Soalheiro Reserva is fermented in oak, but the wine to seek out is Soalheiro Primeiras Vinhas, an old vine selection with a small percentage of barrel-fermented fruit. It shows remarkable concentration, complexity and length without losing the region's trademark levity. Primeiras Vinhas is made with input from Dirk NIEPOORT. Luis in turn has a hand in Niepoort Gira Sol Vinho Verde, which is made from the Loureiro grape. (SA)
Recommended Whites:
Soalheiro Primeiras Vinhas ★★★★★ £E
Quinta de Soalheiro Alvarinho ★★★★ £D
Quinta de Soalheiro Reserva ★★★ £E
Espumante Soalheiro ★★★ £E

>> **Quinta dos Termos (Beira Interior)** *www.quintadostermos.pt*
Located near Belmonte, between the cities of Covilha and Guarda on the slopes of the Sierra Estrela, this Beiran winery is making waves and producing distinctive terroir-driven wines in a location seemingly fairly unpropitious for wine making. Main varietals are Touriga Nacional, Tinta Roriz, Trincadeira, Refete, Castelao, Baga and Jaen. The wines generally undergo long maceration in French oak.

Tannic and earthy when young, these wines have a good drinking window of 5 – 15 years and at the top end, produce elegant wines with some finesse. (GW)
Recommended Reds:
Quinta Dos Termos Vinhas Seleccao DOC ★★★ £C
Quinta Dos Termos Vinhas Velhas Reserva DOC ★★★ £C
Quinta Dos Termos Reserva DOC ★★★ £C
Beira Interior DOC ★★ £A

❀ **Quinta do Vale Doña Maria** *www.quintavaledonamaria.com*
Cristiano van Zeller's family once owned QUINTA DO NOVAL but now he is involved in some capacity in the production, direction or distribution of several Douro estates as well as one or two from further afield. The 10 ha vineyard of Vale Doña Maria (in his wife's family for generations) on the Rio Torto is an old-fashioned, mixed planting, with many of the vines 50–60 years old. Grapes are foot-trodden in lagares, for a rich, fleshy, characterful and seductive red. Also produced in most vintages is an increasingly fine Vintage Port. Both are made by Sandra Tavares da Silva (Pintas) with some input from Francisco Olazabal of QUINTA DO VALE MEÃO. The VZ negociant label includes an excellent if ambitiously priced Graves-like white. Cristiano van Zeller also has a joint venture with Domingos Soares Franco (see José Maria da FONSECA), producing both a Vintage Port and Domini table wines from properties in the Douro Superior (Alto Douro). CV a richly concentrated yet elegantly drawn red from older vineyards on north, northwest and west-facing vineyards opposite do Vale Do. Maria is produced in conjunction with Pintas. The characterful, supple Casa de Casal de Loivos red is also produced by Lemos & Van Zeller.
Quinta do Vale Doña Maria
Recommended Reds:
Douro CV ★★★★☆ £F Douro ★★★★ £D
Vintage Port ★★★★ £E
Casa de Casal de Loivos
Recommended Reds:
Douro ★★★ £C

❀ **Quinta do Vale Meão (Douro & Port)**
Francisco Javier de Olazabal was president of FERREIRA until 1998 and his 62 ha of vineyards (part of a 270 ha estate established by Olazabal's ancestor, Doña António Adelaide Ferreira) used to provide the basis of Barca Velha. The best grapes from this estate are in a bend in the Douro only 30 km or so from the Spanish border are now made into an outstanding estate red by his son Francisco, a trained winemaker. Comprising Touriga Nacional (60%), Touriga Franca (20), Tinta Roriz (10) and 5% each of Tinto Cão and Tinta Barroca, the wine is initially foot-trodden and spends 2 years in new Allier oak. Distinctively spicy, there is a depth and breadth, as well as elegance and class, to this wine that put it with Douro's elite – the same qualities (not surprisingly) that distinguish the best vintages of Barca Velha. Since 2005, Francisco has favoured oak coopered by Taransaud for its relative neutrality and match with Touriga Nacional and the wines show an extra level of class. A stylish second wine, Meandro, represents very good value for money. Aged in used oak, it is medium-bodied and reveals intense, juicy, plummy fruit. A complex, aromatic Vintage Port is rich, quite forward and spicy - an attractive medium term proposition. Thirteen hectares of new vineyard were planted in 2008 on granite slopes with outcrops of schist at 350m, high above the original estate – insurance against global warming.

Recommended Reds:
Douro Quinta do Vale Meão ★★★★★ £F
Douro Meandro ★★★ £C   Vintage Port ★★★★ £F

Quinta do Vallado (Douro) *www.quintadovallado.com*
Vallado is a revitalised estate in the Lower Douro (Baixo Corgo) on the Rio Corgo run by Francisco Ferreira and João Ferreira Alvares Ribeiro. A new winery was completed in the late 1990s to handle the fruit from new and restructured vineyards totalling 64 ha and, so revitalised is this estate that, in 2008, they built a second, state-of-the-art winery and barrel room in anticipation of doubling production. Like others, Valldo has acquired 50 ha in the Douro Superior which they started planting in 2011. An unwooded, regular estate red (from a field blend of varieties) shows the earthy, smoky, dark, plum fruit of the Douro in a well-balanced, concentrated (and affordable) form. The wines are made by QUINTA DO VALE MEÃO'S Francisco Olazabal. A Reserva, aged in new French oak, has been made since 1999 (but not in 02 or 01) and has shown more sophistication as well as extra depth and concentration, especially from 2004 onwards. Vallado also make one of the Douro's best single varietal ranges, the best of which is a rich, exuberant Touriga Nacional, followed by a Tinta Rorz and a Sousão grape which is very intense, concentrated and intriguing with the variety's trademark freshness and deep colour (it is a teinturer variety). Flagship red, Adelaide, first made in the 2005 vintage (and only to be made in top years), comes from a single vineyard at 400m, home to the estate's oldest fruit. Tiny yields account for its dense concentration and impressive structure – a wine whose potential has yet to be revealed. As well as three white wines, an aromatic, dry Moscatel and an unoaked and oaked blend, Port is also produced in the shape of 10-year and 20-year-old tawnies and, from 04, Vintage and LBV too.

Recommended Reds:
Douro Adelaide ★★★★ £G   Douro Reserva ★★★☆ £E
Douro Touriga Nacional ★★★☆ £E
Douro Tinta Roriz ★★★ £E
Douro Sousão ★★★ £E
Douro ★★ £C
Recommended Whites:
Moscatel Gallega ★ £C

✿ Quinta do Vesuvio (Port) *www.quinta-do-vesuvio.com*
This estate of 400-odd ha spread over seven hills was one of the grand properties of the 19th century. In 1989 it was bought by the Symington family and turned into one of the new breed of true (château-like) quintas. The wine from the expanding vineyard (currently 100 ha of vines) is made and matured on the estate. Though its massive lagares and winery buildings have been renovated, it remains the last bastion of foot-treading in the Symington portfolio (other port houses use robotic lagares). Vesuvio has produced wine of high quality made in almost every vintage since 1989 and the wines are frequently among the very best of the declaration. Other years can be very good too, there being much less vintage variation in the dry Douro Superior than further downstream. At its best the extraordinary ripeness in the tannins, as well as the fruit from low-yielding vines, can make the wine tempting when quite young but it will also be very interesting to see how well it might show with 20 or 30 years' age. Touriga Franca, Touriga Nacional, Tinta Roriz and Tinta Barroca all contribute to its unique character. Since 2007, the full potential of the vineyards, carefully parcellated by the Symingtons, has been realised in the production of both a second vintage Port and two red table wines, Quinta do Vesuvio and Pombal. The limited production (250 cases) Vesuvio Capela Port is a formidably structured, deeply concentrated blend of Touriga Nacional, Touriga Franca and Sousão designed to contrast with the sweeter, softer Vesuvio Vintage. It promises to be long lived. The first vintages of the table wine show promise if not yet the refinement or concentration of the Douro's top wines.
Recommended Reds:
Vintage Port ✪✪✪✪✪ £F
Capela Vintage Port ★★★★★ £H

✿ Quinta do Zambujeiro (Alentejo) *www.zambujeiro.com*
This Swiss-owned estate with 30 ha of vineyards only made its first wines in 1999 but they were impressive from the outset. The releases are of a different order to all but the very best wines from the Alentejo. Only around 5,000 bottles of the outstanding estate wine is made in each year. Yields are very low, and maceration can last up to 6 weeks before 2 years in new French oak. The wine is neither fined nor filtered and is very expansive, lush and complex with excellent depth and expression. At around half the price, a second wine, Terra do Zambujeiro, may seem expensive but it also has impressive depth and complexity despite drawing on some younger-vine fruit. There is only 50% new oak but the wine shows similar composure and style. A third wine, Monte da Castanheiro, is more affordable.
Recommended Reds:
Zambujeiro ★★★★★ £G
Terra do Zambujeiro ★★★☆ £E

João Portugal Ramos (Alentejo) *www.jportugalramos.com*
For more than 20 years, João Ramos has been the leading consultant oenologist in the south of Portugal, working for some of Alentejo's best cooperatives. His own project has gained increasing momentum in the past decade, producing wines under his own label on his estate near Estremoz but also working for others as a consultancy. The top wine is the Marqués de Borba Reserva, a powerful but composed blend of Aragonês, Trincadeira and some Alicante Bouschet and Cabernet Sauvignon, with excellent dimension and weight, needing 5–10 years to show at its best. Vila Santa, with the same varieties (if more based on Trincadeira), shows style and harmony, even elegance and continues to be excellent value for money, as is the vibrantly fruity Vila Santa white, a blend of Antão Vaz, Arinto and Verdelho, new in 2008. Varietal examples of Trincadeira and Aragonês show good fruit definition and supple structures. A varietal Syrah of considerable black fruit intensity, if more marginal balance has been made since 2000. More unusual, if not unique, is a supple, perfumed varietal Tinta Caiada. A simple Marqués de Borba white and varietal Antão Vaz are good, clean whites for early consumption. Of the other wines, Quinta de Viçosa provides a very ripe and powerful Syrah/Trincadeira and lush black-fruited Single Vineyard (Touriga Nacional and Merlot) from the Alentejo. Also worth tracking down are the wines of Quinta de Foz de Arouce in the Beiras, owned by João's father-in-law. A new single-vineyard wine, Vinha de Santa Marta, has been produced since 2001. It shows a classic rugged, black fruited character and including Touriga Nacional is very classy. Production of a white was resumed in 2004. Ramos also owns Falua in Tejo, source of good value export-focused brands Tagus Creek and the more upmarket Conde de Vimioso white and red. DUORUM is his exciting Douro joint venture with former Barca Velha winemaker José Maria Soares Franco.

Portugal

João Portugal Ramos
Recommended Reds:
Alentejo Marqués de Borba Reserva ★★★★ £E
Alentejo Marqués de Borba ★ £B
Vila Santa ★★★ £B
Trincadeira ★★ £B Aragonês ★★ £B
Syrah ★★ £B Tinta Caiada ★★ £B
Recommended Whites:
Alentejo Marqués de Borba ★★ £B Antão Vaz ★ £B

Quinta da Viçosa
Recommended Reds:
Syrah/Trincadeira ★★★ £C Single Vineyard ★★★ £C

Quinta de Foz de Arouce
Recommended Reds:
Quinta de Foz de Arouce Vinha Velhas de Santa Maria ★★★★ £E
Quinta de Foz de Arouce ★★★ £C

Ramos Pinto (Port & Douro) *www.ramospinto.pt*
It was the father of Ramos Pinto's director and winemaker, João Nicolau de Almeida, who created Barca Velha (see FERREIRA), the Douro's first great red wine, and Ramos Pinto has been one of the leading proponents in the recent revival of table wines (last made in any quantity before port evolved into a fortified style). Duas Quintas wines are named for the high vineyards (600m) of Bon Ares and the lower Ervamoira (both deep in the Douro Superior). The reds are now consistently good, stylish with excellent fruit intensity and refined, if firm, in structure. A deep, vigorous and classy Reserva Especial from a field blend of 50 year-old vines (actually from Bom-Retiro, the company's leading estate on the Rio Torto) shows a wonderful seam of minerality and promises to age well for a decade plus. The Reserva and Collection are also very good, the latter, fleshier and more approachable but nonetheless well structured. An attractive white for early drinking is also made. Most consistent and refined of the ports is a 20-year-old Tawny from Bom-Retiro. It has depth and intensity (sometimes missing in this category) as well as complexity and refinement. Vintage Port has been better in recent vintages (2011 and 1997 at least) but although it has a certain individuality, it wants for more depth and richness. Late Bottled Vintage can be remarkably full and powerful while a modest Vintage Character port is named for a fourth quinta, Urtiga. Tawny ports are luscious and good value for money.

Duas Quintas
Recommended Reds:
Douro Reserva Especial ★★★★☆ £F Douro Reserva ★★★★ £E
Douro Collection ★★★☆ £D Douro ★ £C
Recommended Whites:
Douro ★★ £C

Ramos Pinto
Recommended Reds:
Vintage Port ★★★ £G Late Bottled Vintage Port ★★ £D
20-year-old Tawny Port Quinta do Bom-Retiro ★★★ £F
10-year-old Tawny Port Quinta da Ervamoira ★ £E

Real Companhia Velha (Douro/Port) *www.realcompanhiavelha.pt*
The Douro's largest landowner and biggest maker of port enjoys wide distribution around the globe. Its Royal Oporto brand is familiar to most consumers even if they haven't drunk it. Its inclusion here, however, is for its revitalised production of Douro table wines, one or two of which are worthy of more than passing mention. The Evel red offers plenty of fruit while the Porca de Murça Riserva adds more structure and complexity. But for those interested in premium Douro reds it is a Grande Escholha version of Evel (from Touriga Nacional, Touriga Franca and Tinta Cão) and the revived Grantom label (which adds Cabernet Sauvignon to the two Tourigas) that should be tasted. Both these reds have quite a forbidding structure but the Evel Grande Escholha in particular shows a capitivating complexity and intensity. Unusual for the Douro is a Chardonnay from low-yielding vines on the Quinta do Cidrô that delivers good flavour and texture. In 2010, Jorge Moreira (Poeira) who started out here, succeeded Jerry Luper as Technical Director. Expect the wines to attain new levels of refinement.
Recommended Reds:
Douro Grantom ★★★ £E Douro Evel Grande Escholha ★★★ £D
Douro Porca de Murça Reserva ★★ £B Douro Evel ★ £B
Douro Quinta dos Aciprestes ★ £B
Recommended Whites:
Quinta do Cidrô Chardonnay ★ £B

Sandeman (Port) *www.sandeman.com*
Like Graham's, Sandeman is of Scottish origins and its familiarity to occasional port drinkers has been reinforced by the famous brand logo of the Sandeman 'Don'. In the 50 years since the company went public it has had a torrid time quality-wise under changing ownership. A revival has been started in the past decade following the purchase, and subsequent replanting, of Quinta do Vau since 1988. Its newest owners perhaps offer the best chance of a sustained revival given the example of Ferreira's form under the same ownership. Sogrape have invested in a new winery and impressive visitor facility at Quinta do Seixo and the impressive 2007 Vintage Port sees increased complexity and depth (reflected in the rating below). The newly-tasted 2011 suggests great things. Of older vintages, some very good ports were made in the 50s and 60s, although most of these are tiring now and are not as good as the top examples. Tawnies are a strength, however, with particular elegance and finesse in the 20-year-old Tawny. Recently on very good form is the Vintage Character port, Signature (known as Founders Reserve outside the UK).
Recommended Reds:
Vintage Port Vau ★★★★ £F 20-year-old Tawny Port ★★★ £F
Imperial Aged Tawny Port ★★ £C
Signature ★★ £B

Sidónio de Sousa (Bairrada)
The wines are made very traditionally at this small estate of 12 ha. The oldest, vines (around 100 years) were grubbed up having become uneconomical (2005 being the last year of production), leaving an average vine age of 15 years. Touriga Nacional and Merlot have been planted. Vintages subsequent to 2005 have yet to be tasted. Winemaker Rui Moura Alves, who also makes the wines at Casa de Saima, Quinta de Baixo and Quinta das Bágeiras, uses natural yeasts, favours the retention of stems, uses concrete lagares and wooden plungers, and ages the wine where appropriate in large, old Portuguese wood. This approach, even more than at the other properties, really works here – perhaps because of the quality of the fruit. Both wines are 100% Baga. In the past, a Reserva has shown good intensity, a silky mouthfeel and a stylish, savoury complexity. The remarkable, powerful Garrafeira, with deep savoury fruit, great depth and intensity and enveloping but refined tannins, is only made in exceptional vintages (just a few thousand bottles of 1995, 97 and 2000 were made). There's also a sparkling red made from 100% Baga.

Wine behind the label

Recommended Reds:
Bairrada Garrafeira ★★★★ £E   Bairrada Reserva ★★★ £C

Smith Woodhouse (Port)   *www.smithwoodhouse.com*
Another Symington group, noted for its consistent high quality but reasonably priced Vintage Port. It is based on the Madalena quinta in the Rio Torto Valley but also including grapes from Penedo do Salto quinta, has a certain spicy individuality and is typically succulent, intense and well-balanced. A good Madalena port has been made in certain non-declared years. A traditional (i.e. it leaves a sediment) Late Bottled Vintage maintains the house style and integrity. Other wines include Lodge Reserve, which is a decent Vintage Character port, and a 10-year-old Tawny.

Recommended Reds:
Vintage Port ★★★★★ £F   Vintage Port Madalena ★★★ £D
Late Bottled Vintage Port ★★★ £C
Lodge Reserve ★ £B

Sogrape   *www.sograpevinhos.com*
Portugal's largest producer includes the port companies of Ferreira, Offley and Sandeman but the focus of table-wine production is in Dão, where the flagship estate of Quinta dos Carvalhais has been developed. Varietal wines from here have been quite impressive but the vines are still relatively young and, though both Touriga Nacional and Tinta Roriz have been reasonably full with good breadth, they have lacked a little richness. Powerful Carvalhais Reserva (Touriga Nacional/Tinta Roriz/Alfrocheiro Preto) is profound and complex with excellent dimension and length but needs 8–10 years' age. A varietal Encruzado, fermented and aged in French oak for 6 months, adds a little richness with a couple of years' age. Herdade de Peso in Alentejo produces a solidly made range of estate wines. Well made, very good value single estate Vinho Verde is made at Quinta de Azevedo while Morgdio da Torre Alvarinho shows good fruit concentration and layer. Sogrape also produces regional wines under its Grao Vasco, Callabriga brands and Pena de Pato brands. While relatively consistent and successful, aimed at the export market, they rarely show the character or depth of others' estate produced wines and can taste comparatively "sweet".

Sogrape
Recommended Reds:
Herdade do Peso Aragonês ★★★☆ £C
Douro Reserva ★★☆ £B   Dão Reserva ★★☆ £B
Alentejo Reserva ★★☆ £B
Recommended Whites:
Vinho Verde Quinta de Azevedo ★ £B

Callabriga
Recommended Reds:
Douro Reserva ★★☆ £E   Douro ★★ £D
Alentejo Reserva ★★☆ £E   Alentejo ★★☆ £D

Quinta dos Carvalhais
Recommended Reds:
Dão Reserva ★★★ £E   Dão Tinta Roriz ★★ £E
Dão Touriga Nacional ★★ £E
Recommended Whites:
Dão Encruzado ★★★ £C

Symington   *www.symington.com*
The Symington family runs the Douro's leading port shippers, owning COCKBURN, DOW, GRAHAM, QUINTA DO VESÚVIO, RORIZ, SMITH WOODHOUSE and WARRE, and, through the MADEIRA

WINE COMPANY, is also the leading producer of Madeira. Gould Campbell is one of two lesser labels made in widely declared Years and is increasingly well regarded. Rich and broad, it can represent excellent value for money in stellar vintages. The other minor port brand, Quarles Harris, is based on the Quinta de Cabanas and is consistently good. Attractive and well-balanced with intense sweet fruit, it will drink well with 10 years' age. Though late in joining the revival in table-wine production, the Symingtons are rapidly making up lost ground. The Altano brand, first introduced in 1999 has been augmented by a basic white to join the red, the latter offering decent quality and Douro typicity at its price point. Meanwhile, the well-made if oaky Altano Reserva (introduced in 2000 and aged in American and French oak) has been joined by a stylish, characterful red from the organically certified Quinta de Assares (from 2007), while Quinta Ataide is an elegant, floral 100% Touriga Nacional (from 2008). As of 2010, the Symington's holdings in the Vilariça valley, Douro Superior, which is the principal source of Altano will be farmed organically. In collaboration with Bruno Prats (the former owner of CH. COS D'ESTOURNEL), the Symingtons make Chryseia and PS under their Prats & Symington label which, as of 2009, is based at RORIZ. The aim from the outset was to create an elegant and very seductively textured red. Though powerful, the wine is less extracted and spends less time in oak than many Douro reds at this price point. Nonetheless, it is ageworthy. Post Scriptum is the quite striking, well-balanced second wine, introduced in 2002 when no Chryseia was made; it is a stylish wine for the money.

Gould Campbell
Recommended Reds:
Vintage Port ★★ £F   Late Bottled Vintage Port ★ £C
Quarles Harris
Recommended Reds:
Vintage Port ★★★ £F
Silva & Cosens
Recommended Reds:
Douro Altano Reserva ★★ £C   Douro Altano ★ £B
Prats & Symington
Recommended Reds:
Douro Chryseia ★★★★ £E   Douro Post Scriptum ★★★ £C

❀ Taylor's (Port)   *www.taylor.pt*
Taylor's tend to produce a drier style of port compared to its great rival Graham's and is characterised by the classic 'violets on the nose'. An exemplary port producer – some say the finest - under the same ownership as FONSECA, and CROFT. Vintage Port is based on the famous Quinta de Vargellas in the Douro Superior and the larger Terra Feita quinta in the Rio Pinhão valley, but new vineyards have recently been purchased in both of these sectors of the Douro. Fruit from the Pinhão provides the greater structure while the Douro Superior gives a more floral perfume and great intensity of fruit. Taylor's structure, marvellous depth and class set it apart from most other ports and occasionally it is unrivalled for its completeness. In good non-declared years, Quinta de Vargellas is made and can be a stunning port in its own right, while Terra Feita has also been produced as a single-quinta port which is possibly one of the best value ports available. Quinta de Vargellas Vinha Velha is a thrillingly powerful yet flamboyant very limited production old vine selection made in 1995, 1997, 2000, 2003, 2005, 2007, 2008, 2009 and 2011. Iron fist in velvet glove, it is worth seeking out if understandably pricey given its rarity. Other ports are generally less exciting, 10-year-old Tawny is disappointing against the best

examples, though the 20-year-old is significantly better and very good 30 and 40-year-old versions are also made in small quantities. Late Bottled Vintage (a style allegedly created by Taylor's) is a spicy, fruity and characterful filtered example while First Estate (Vintage Character) is similarly good of its type. A well-made White Port called Chip Dry is also made.

Recommended Reds:
Vintage Port Quinta de Vargellas Vinha Velha ✪✪✪✪✪ £H
Vintage Port ✪✪✪✪✪ £G
Vintage Port Quinta de Vargellas ★★★★ £E
Vintage Port Quinta de Terra Feita ★★★ £E
20-year-old Tawny Port ★★ £F   10-year-old Tawny Port ★ £D
Late Bottled Vintage Port ★★ £C   First Estate ★ £B

Vale d'Algares (Tejo)
From 2009, the Vinho Regional Ribatejano has a snappy new moniker, Tejo, the name of the river which cuts a swathe through the region before emptying into the Atlantic swell at Lisbon. It reflects the reinvention of a region whose fertile river plains used to produce a sea of indifferent wine, but whose more conscientious producers have grubbed up vineyards along the river and concentrated production on poorer soils. Their efforts have attracted a wave of ambitious newcomers, of whom Vale d'Algares is the most high profile. Starting from scratch, in 2003 and 2004 it planted around 30ha of calcareous clay soils to Portuguese and international varieties. A no-expense-spared state of the art winery was built in 2004 and young gun Pedro Pereira Gonçalves recruited in 2006 to make a range of premium plus wines. Given the youth of the vines, whites are very much the forte. Though prices are high, flagship Vale d'Algares (a fruity but restrained part barrel-fermented and aged Viognier) and second tier "Selection" (an unusual, aromatic blend of Viognier and Alvarinho) set a new standard for the region. Guarda Rios white, rosé and red are well-made, modern fruit-driven wines. (SA)

Recommended Whites:
Vale d'Algares Branco ★★☆ £E
Vale d'Algares Selection Branco ★★ £D   Guarda Rios Branco ★ £C
Recommended Rosés:
Guarda Rios Rosé ★ £C

Warre (Port)   *www.warre.com*
Last but not least in the Symington portfolio of great port houses, Warre makes a consistently fine Vintage Port. It is perfumed, with a rich, spice, fig and black fruit intensity and a lushness that together form part of a distinctive character that alone makes it worth cellaring. In certain top vintages it will age for 40 years or more. Quinta da Cavadinha in the Rio Pinhão valley, not far from either QUINTA DO NOVAL or TAYLOR's Terra Feita, forms the main component of the Vintage Port and can be excellent when released in non-declared years. The other significant long-standing component of the Vintage Port comes from Quinta do Bom Retiro Pequeno (adjacent to that of Ramos Pinto) in the Rio Torto valley. This estate with 34 ha of mostly old vines was added to the Symington family's holdings in 2006. The traditional (unfiltered) Late Bottled Vintage is rightly considered one of the best made and the current release usually has around 10 years' age yet can still be kept. Tawnies include a fine, complex, 20-year-old, and the mould-breaking lifter and elegant Otima (with a clear-glass bottle), now made in both 10-year-old and 20-year-old versions. Warrior, a Vintage Character port, though of modest structure, actually tastes something like the Vintage Port and is one of the best in its

category.
Recommended Reds:
Vintage Port ★★★★★ £F
Vintage Port Quinta da Cavadinha ★★★ £E
Late Bottled Vintage Port ★★★ £D
20-year-old Tawny Port ★★★ £F
20-year-old Tawny Port Otima ★★ £F
10-year-old Tawny Port Otima ★☆ £D
10-year-old Sir William ★ £D   Warrior Special Reserve ★ £B

❀ Wine & Soul (Douro & Port)   *www.wineandsoul.com*
From a 1.8 ha south-facing vineyard previously used for port production comes another profound Douro red. The small property belongs to Jorge Serôdio Borges (ex NIEPOORT and still responsible for QUINTA DO PASSADOURO wines) and his wife, Sandra Tavares (her family's estate is QUINTA DECHOCAPALHA in Estremadura). Grapes from a field blend of mixed planting (more than 30 different grape varieties of 80-year-old vines) are fermented and foot-trodden in lagares. The malolactic fermentation is completed in barriques in which the wine is aged for 15 months. A full-bodied but mineral "second" red wine, Character now comes from old vine fruit. In 2009, a new flagship red joins the ranks, Manoella, which is sourced from the prized 12ha vineyard of that name; it once belonged to Borges' grandfather, but has now come into the Wine & Soul fold. There are two Manoella wines, the regular, displaying a great deal of elegance and finesse and a second, from a parcel of very old vines and aged for 20 months in oak has real grip and demands long cellaring, but promises to be a classic. The vintage port is dense, powerful and very promising and shares something of the elegance and purity of Pintas. A new white, Guru is a barrique-fermented and aged blend of local varieties. Although oak-influenced in flavour and texture, it is not overdone but intense, vibrant and expressive with a lightly mineral aspect. Sandra Tavares also works with Cristiano van Zeller at QUINTA DO VALE DOÑAMARIA. (NB)

Recommended Reds:
Douro Quinta da Manoella VV ★★★★★ £F
Douro Pintas ★★★★☆ £F   Douro Manoella ★★★☆ £C
Vintage Port ★★★★☆ £F
Recommended Whites:
Douro Guru ★★★★ £E

Other wines of note

Afros (Vinho Verde)
Recommended Whites: Vinhao ★★ £B
Loureiro ★★★ £B
Azamor (From 2004)
Recommended Reds: Alentejo Azamor ★★☆ £B
Boas Quintas
Recommended Reds:
Dão Quinta da Fonte Do Ouro Touriga Nacional ★★★☆ £D
Recommended Whites:
M Borges H Madeira 10-Year-Old Sercial Old Reserve ★★☆ £D
Madeira 10-Year-Old Boal Old Reserve ★★☆ £D
Madeira 15-Year-Old Malmsey ★★★ £E
Cálem
Recommended Reds: Vintage Port ★★★ £E
Colheita Port ★★★ £D   20-Year-Old Tawny Port ★★★ £E
40-Year-Old Tawny Port ★★★ £G
Adega Do Cantor (Algarve)
Recommended Whites: Vida Nova Branco ★ £B

Recommended Rosés: Vida Nova Brut Rosé Espumante ★★ £D
C.A.R.M.I.M. (Reguengos de Monsaraz Co-Op)
Recommended Reds:
Alentejo Reguengos Garrafeiras Dos Sócios ★★ £D
Casa Cadaval (Tejo)
Recommended Reds: Padre Pedro ★ £A
Herdade de Muge ★★ £B
Trincadeira ★★ £C
C. da Silva
Recommended Whites: Dalva Port Golden White ★★★☆ £G
Casa Ermelinda Freitas (Peninsula de Setúbal)
Recommended Reds: Dona Ermilinda ★★ £B
Recommended Whites: Terras do Pó ★ £B
Moscatel de Setúbal ★★ £B
Casa de Mouraz (Organic)
Recommended Reds: Dão ★★ £C
Recommended Whites: Dão ★☆ £C
Casa de Paços (Vinho Verde)
Recommended Whites: Loureiro/Arinto ★ £B
Fernão Pires ★★ £B
Casa de Saima
Recommended Whites: Bairrada ★☆ £C
Recommended Reds: Bairrada Reserva ★★ £C
Bairrada Garrafeira ★★★★ £E
Conceito
Recommended Reds: Port Vintage ★★★ £F   Douro ★★★ £E
Douro Bastardo ★★★ £E   Douro Contraste ★★ £D
Recommended Whites: Douro ★★ £D
Cunha Martins
Recommended Reds: Dão ★★ £C
Domingos Damsaceno (Península de Setúbal)
Recommended Reds: Domingos Damsaceno ★☆ £C
Vinhos D. Joanna/Encostas de Estremoz (Alentejo)
Recommended Reds: Touriga Nacional ★ £B
Alicante Bouschet Selecção ★★ £C
Trincadeira Selecção ★★ £C   Touriga Nacional Selecção ★★ £C
Touriga Franca Selecção ★★ £C
Paulo Laureano Vinus (Alentejo)
Recommended Reds: Dolium Reserva ★★☆ £C
Dolium Selectio Touriga Nacional ★★☆ £C
Reserva ★★☆ £D   Reserva Vinea Julieta Talhao ★★★ £E
Recommended Whites: Dolium Branco Escolha (Antão Vaz) ★☆ £C
Falua Sociedade de Vinhos (Tejo)
Recommended Reds:
Conde de Vimioso Reserva (Touriga N/Tinta Roriz/Cab S) ★★★ £E
Tagus Creek Touriga Nacional Reserva ★★ £B
Fita Preta (Alentejo)
Recommended Reds:
Sexy (Touriga Nacional/Cab S/Alicante Bouschet/Aragonês) ★★ £B
Fita Preta (Touriga Nacional/Cab S) ★★★☆ £E
Recommended Whites: Sexy (Antão Vaz, Verdelho And Arinto) ★ £B
Palpite (Antão Vaz, Verdelho And Arinto) ★★★ £D
Fojo
Recommended Reds: Douro Vinha Do Fojo ★★ £C
Douro Fojo ★★★★ £F
Herdade dos Coelheiros (Alentejo)
Recommended Reds:
Tapada de Coelheiros (Cab S./Trincadeira/Aragonês) ★★ £C
Tapada de Coelheiros Garrafeira (Cab S/Aragonês) ★★★ £D
João Brito e Cunha/ Quinta de S. Jose (Douro)
Recommended Whites: Azeo Branco ★★ £C

Azeo Branco Reserve ★★★ £D
Recommended Reds: Quinta de S. José Colheita ★★☆ £D
Quinta de S. José Reserva ★★★☆ £E   Azeo Reserva ★★★☆ £E
Justino Henriques
Recommended Whites:
Madeira Broadbent 3-Year-Old Rainwater ★☆ £C
Madeira Broadbent 5-Year-Old Fine Rich Reserve ★★☆ £C
Madeira Broadbent 10-Year-Old Malmsey ★★★☆ £D
Martinez
Recommended Reds: Vintage Port ★★★ £E
Vintage Port Quinta da Eira Velha ★★★ £E
10-Year-Old Tawny Port ★★ £C
Vinha Paz
Recommended Reds: Dão ★★ £B   Dão Reserva ★★★ £D
Pegos Claros (Campanhia das Quintas)
Recommended Reds: Palmela Reserva ★★ £B
Herdade do Arrepiado (Alentejo)
Recommended Reds: Velho Colheita ★★★☆ £E
Herdade dos Grous (Alentejo)
Recommended Reds: Alentejo 23 Barricas ★★★ £E
Alentejo Moon Harvest ★★★ £E
Alentejo Reserva ★★★☆ £E
Herdade do Perdigâo (Alentejo)
Recommended Reds: Herdade do Perdigão Reserva ★★★ £C
Herdade da Pestana (Alentejo)
Recommended Reds: Tapada Grande ★★ £C
Pinhal da Torre/Quinta do Alqueve (Tejo)
Recommended Reds:
Quinta do Alqueve Touriga Nacional/Syrah ★★★ £D
2 Worlds ★★ £B   Quinta do Alqueve Tradicional ★☆ £B
Nova Safra ★ £A
Poças
Recommended Reds: Vintage Port ★★★ £F
Late Bottled Vintage Port ★★ £D
Douro Reserva ★★ £D
PV
Recommended Reds: Douro VT' ★★★☆ £F
Quevedo
Recommended Reds: Oscar's Tinto ★ £B   Ruby Port ★☆ £C
Vintage Port ★★★ £E
Recommended Whites: White Port ★ £C
Recommended Rosés: Rosé Port ★ £C
Quinta de Abrigada
Recommended Reds: Alenquer ★ £B
Alenquer Vinha Nobre ★★ £B
Quinta da Alorna (Tejo)
Recommended Reds: Casa da Alorna ★★ £B
Quinta da Alorna Reserva ★★ £C
Quinta da Bica
Recommended Reds: Dão ★★☆ £B   Dão Reserva ★★★☆ £C
Quinta das Bágeiras
Recommended Reds: Bairrada Reserva ★★ £C
Recommended Whites: Bairrada ★★★☆ £C
Quinta de Baixo
Recommended Reds: Bairrada Reserva ★★★ £C
Bairrada Garrafeira ★★ £C
Recommended Whites: Bairrada Reserva ★★★ £C
Quinta do Corujão
Recommended Reds: Dão ★★☆ £B   Dão Reserva ★★★☆ £D
Quinta de Linhares (Vinho Verde)
Recommended Whites: Colheita Seleccionada ★★ £C

Portugal

Avesso ★★ £B
Quintas de Melgaço (Vinho Verde)
Recommended Whites: QM ★★★ £D
Castrus De Melgaço ★★★ £E
Quinta do Cardo (Beira Interior)
Recommended Reds: Quinta do Cardo ★★ £B
Recommended Whites: Siria ★★ £C
Quinta do Carmo (Alentejo)
Recommended Reds: Dom Martinho ★☆ £B
Quinta do Carmo ★☆ £D
Quinta do Carmo Reserva ★★★☆ £E
Quinta da Carvalhosa (Douro)
Recommended Reds: Campo Ardosa ★★★ £E
Quinta do Centro (Alentejo)
Recommended Reds: Pedra Basta ★★ £C
Quinta do Condoso
Recommended Reds: Douro ★★★ £D
Quinta da Falorca (Dão)
Recommended Reds: T-Nac ★★ £C   Reserva ★★★ £E
Touriga Nacional ★★★☆ £E
Garrafeira ★★★ £E   Garrafeira Old Vines ★★★☆ £E
Quinta do Feital (Vinho Verde)
Recommended Whites: Dorado Alvarinho Superior ★★★★ £E
Dorado Auratus ★★★ £D
Quinta de Fundo de Vila (Douro)
Recommended Reds: Douro Terrus ★★★ £D
Quinta da Lagoalva (Tejo)
Recommended Reds: Reserva ★★ £C
Alfrocheiro ★★ £B   Syrah ★★ £B
Tinta Roriz/Touriga Nacional ★★ £B
Recommended Whites: Arinto/Chardonnay ★★☆ £E
Quinta do Louridal (Vinho Verde)
Recommended Whites: Poema ★★★ £D
Quinta de Nossa Senhora do Carmo (Douro)
Recommended Reds: Douro Grainha ★★☆ £C
Douro Colheita ★★ £B
Douro Grande Reserva ★★★☆ £D
Douro Grande Reserva Referencia ★★★★ £E
Port Reserve ★★ £C   Port LBV ★★ £C
Recommended Whites: Douro Grainha ★★ £C
Quinta de Paços (Minho)
Recommended Whites: Vinho Verde Casa do Capitão ★★ £B
Casa De Paços Arinto ★★ £B
Casa De Paços Morgado do Perdigão Arinto/Loureiro ★★ £C

Quinta de Pancas (Lisboa)
Recommended Reds:
Cabernet Sauvignon Special Selection ★★ £D
Touriga Nacional Special Selection ★★ £D   Grande Escolha ★★ £D
Quinta do Romaneira (Bucelas)
Recommended Whites: Prova Regia ★☆ £B
Morgado Santa Catherina ★★ £D
Quinta do Romaneira (Douro, Port)
Recommended Reds: Port Vintage ★★ £F   Douro ★★☆ £E
Douro R de Romaneira ★★☆ £C
Recommended Whites: Douro ★★ £C
Quinta da Sequeira
Recommended Reds: Douro ★★ £B
Douro Grande Escolha ★★★ £C
Recommended Rosés: Douro Rosé ★ £B
Quinta do Sobredos (Douro)

Recommended Reds: Douro Aneto ★★ £C
Recommended Whites: Douro Aneto ★★ £C
Douro Aneto Reserva ★★★ £E
Quinta do Tourais (Douro)
Recommended Reds: Douro Miura ★★★☆ £C
Douro Tourinio ★★★☆ £C
Douro Darani ★★★☆ £E
Quinta Edmun do Val (Vinho Verde)
Recommended Whites: Alvarinho ★★★☆ £C
Quinta do Zimbro/Manuel Pinto Hespanhol
Recommended Reds: Douro Zimbro ★★☆ £B
Douro Zimbro Grande Reserva ★★☆ £D
Douro Calços Do Tanha ★★☆ £B
Douro Calços do Tanha Reserva ★★★ £C
Recommended Rosés: Douro Calços do Tanha ★★ £B
Reguengo de Melgaço (Vinho Verde)
Recommended Whites: Quinta De Reguinga ★★★ £C
Rui Reguinga (Alentejo)
Recommended Reds: Terrenus Reserva ★★★☆ £D
Terrenus ★★☆ £C
Recommended Whites: Terrenus ★★☆ £C
Herdade do Rocim (Alentejo)
Recommended Reds: Rocim Tinto ★★☆ £C
Grande Rocim ★★★☆ £F
Santo Isidro de Pegoes (Peninsula de Setúbal)
Recommended Whites: Stella Blanco ★☆ £B
Caves São João
Recommended Reds:
Dão Reserva Seleccionada Porta dos Cavalheiros ★★ £C
Herdade de Sao Miguel (Alentejo)
Recommended Reds: Desobridores Reserva ★★★☆ £E
Herdade Sao Miguel ★★★ £C
Herdade Sao Miguel Montinho ★★ £B
Skeffington (Fladgate Partnership)
Recommended Reds: Vintage Port ★★★ £E

Work in progress!!

Producers under consideration for the next edition
Van Zeller & Co
Casal de Ventozela (Minho)

Author's choice

Classic Vintage Ports
Dow's Vintage Port
Duorum Vintage Port
Fonseca Vintage Port
Gould Campbell Vintage Port
Graham's Vintage Port
Niepoort Vintage Port
Niepoort Pisca Vintage Port
Quinta do Noval Vintage Port
Quinta do Noval Vintage Port Nacional
Quinta do Vesuvio Vintage Port
Quinta do Vesuvio Capela Vintage Port
Sandeman Vintage Port
Smith Woodhouse Vintage Port
Taylor's Vintage Port
Warre's Vintage Port

Alternative Single Quinta Type Vintage Ports
Cockburn   Vintage Port Quinta dos Canais
Dow   Vintage Port Senhora da Ribeira
Fonseca   Vintage Port Guimaraens
Graham   Vintage Port Malvedos
Pintas   Vintage Port
Quinta do Noval   Vintage Port Silval
Quinta do Passadouro   Vintage Port
Quinta das Tecedeiras   Vintage Port
Quinta do Vale Meao   Vintage Port
Taylor's   Vintage Port Quinta de Vargellas Vinhas Velhas
Taylor's   Vintage Port Quinta de Vargellas
Taylor's   Vintage Port Quinta de Terra Feita
Warre   Vintage Port Quinta da Cavadinha

Leading New Order Portuguese Reds
Alves de Sousa   Douro Lordelho
Alvaro Castro   Dão Quinta de Pellada Reserva
Conceito   Douro Bastardo
João Brito e Cunha   Douro Quinta de S. José Reserva
Dão Sul   Bairrada Encontro 1
Esporão   Alentejo Garrafeira
Herdade da Malahdinha Nova   Alentejo
Herdade da Malahdinha Nova   Alentejo Marias
Herdade do Mouchão   Alentejo Mouchão
Herdade do Mouchão   Alentejo Mouchão Tonel 3-4
Niepoort   Douro Redoma
Niepoort   Douro Robustus
Niepoort   Douro Batuta
Filipa Pato   Beiras Lokal Silex
Filipa Pato   Bairrada Vinhos Doidos Nossa Branco
Fundação Eugénio de Almeida H Alentejo Pera-Manca
Luis Pato   Vinha Barrosa
Luis Pato   Quinta do Ribeirinho Baga Pé Franco
Poeira   Douro
Quinta do Crasto   Douro Vinha Maria Teresa
Quinta do Crasto   Douro Vinha da Ponte
Quinta da Falorca   Dão Garrafeira Old Vines
Quinta dos Maias   Dão Flor de Maias
Quinta do Monte d'Oiro   Reserva
Quinta do Mouro   Alentejo
Quinta do Passadouro   Douro Reserva
Quinta dos Roques   Dão Reserva
Quinta do Vale Meão   Douro
Ramos Pinto   Douro Reserva Especial
Ramos Pinto   Douro Duas Quintas
João Portugal Ramos   Alentejo Marqués de Borba Reserva
Rui Reguinga   Alentejo Terrenus
Quinta do Zambujeiro   Zambujeiro
Van Zellars   Douro CV
Wine & Soul   Douro Pintas

Leading New Order Portuguese Whites
Alvaro Castro   Dão Quinta de Saes Reserva
Anselmo Mendes   Vinho Verde Curtimenta
Niepoort   Douro Redoma Reserva Branco
Fundação Eugénio de Almeida   Alentejo Pera-Manca
Filipa Pato   Bairrada Vinhos Doidos Nossa Branco
Quinta do Ameal   Vinho Verde
Quinta das Bágeiras   Bairrada Garrafeira
Quinta da Murta   Lisboa

Quinta do Feital   Vinho Verde Dorado
Quinta do Soalheiros   Vinho Verde Primeiras Vinhas
Wine & Soul   Douro Guru

Good Value Portuguese Reds and Whites
Reds:
Alves de Sousa   Douro Quinta Do Vale da Raposa Touriga Nacional
Caves Aliança/Quinta da Garrida   Dão
Campolargo Vinha do Putto   Bairrada
Conceito   Douro Contraste
Dão Sul   Dão Quinta de Cabriz Colheita Seleccionada
Esporão   Alentejo Reserva
Luis Pato   Vinha Velhas Beiras
Quinta da Bacalhôa   Setubal
Quinta do Coa   Douro
Quinta dos Currais   Beira Interior Reserva
Quinta da Falorca   Dão T-Nac
Quinta do Noval   Douro Cedro do Noval
Quinta do Passadouro   Douro Passa
Quinta de La Rosa   Douro
Quinta do Vallado   Douro
Symington Altano Reserva Red   Douro
Whites:
Anselmo Mendes   Vinho Verde Contacto
João Portugal Ramos   Vila Santa
Quinta do Cardo   Beira Interior
Santo Isidro de Pegoes   Península de Setúbal Colheita Seleccionada
Quinta dos Termos   Beira Interior

Germany

Germany's often exquisite white wines deserve wider recognition and support. Wines are now riper and cleaner and are increasingly marketed in a direct modern way with a growing number of consistently well made dry or off-dry Rieslings. More clarity is still needed in terms of what degree of sweetness to expect but there are ever more outstanding producers. Those with an established reputation have recently been joined by increasing numbers of fine, often small, newer operations. Apart from the sweet wines, which are expensive to produce and made in tiny quantities, many of the wines are very reasonably priced for the quality. There are also excellent examples of Weissburgunder (Pinot Blanc), Silvaner and other white grapes, as well as some wonderful reds from Spätburgunder (Pinot Noir).

Making sense of German wine styles

There are two basic quality levels, QbA (*Qualitätswein bestimmter Anbaugebiete*) and QmP (*Qualitätswein mit Prädikat*). Fine quality begins with the latter which includes six Prädikat (or classifications) of ripeness - for each a minimum must weight (sugar level in the grape) must be obtained. **Kabinett** is the lowest level and should mean a light, dry white but quality is producer dependent. **Spätlese** (meaning late-harvest) wines are riper - dry examples are labelled Trocken (off-dry is Halb-Trocken), otherwise expect some sweetness. **Auslese** wines are made from riper grapes again (sometimes botrytis affected) and are usually sweeter, but Trocken versions are also made. Still riper and sweeter categories of **Beerenauslese** and the rare **Trockenbeerenauslese** (TBA) are made only from handpicked, shrivelled grapes, almost invariably enriched by noble rot (botrytis). **Eiswein**, high in both sugar and acidity, is made from frozen grapes which, when they are crushed, leave the water behind. Critical to quality in all levels is the balance between residual sugar and acidity.

Most Prädikat wines also come from a single site - an *Einzellagen* name, usually suffixed with a village name (often dropped in the Pfalz). These names are emphasised in bold throughout the German section. Certain sites lend themselves to favour the production of one style but not necessarily another. Within the same Prädikat level (usually Auslese) the best parcels from a single top site (or the resulting cuvées) may be differentiated as *Goldkapsel* (Gold Capsule) or even *Lange Goldkapsel* (Long Gold Capsule), usually correlating with a greater degree of botrytis character. Alternatively small stars may appear on the label to distinguish between bottlings of increasing quality ('1 Stern', '2 Sterne' or '3 Sterne') Only where these are being made on a fairly regular basis have they been included within producer entries.

Many of Germany's top estates belong to the VDP (*Verband Deutscher Prädikats-und Qualitätsweingüter*) consortium (labels bear its emblem of an eagle) and their best and rarest sweet wines are sold at the VDP auction (as Versteigerungswein). Specialist wine merchants may stock such wines following a successful bid. The VDP has also been important in promoting the establishment of a vineyard classification system. Since 1999 an increasing number of producers have labelled some or all of their wines from the best vineyards under the top level of the classification. In 2007 this category was officially declared (if not yet legally recognised) as *Erste Lage* and needed to be a minimum of Spätlese must weight. Dry wines (Trocken) are known as *Grosses Gewächs* (already in use in the Pfalz, Franken and other regions and identified as GG on labels), or *Erstes Gewächs* (in the Rheingau). From the 06 vintage all *Erste*

Lage can be recognised by a special bottle (used by some in Pfalz since 02) with an embossed symbol: a figure '1' next to a bunch of grapes. In 2000, two new categories were introduced for dry wines. Both basic Classic level and premium Selection wines are varietal but the latter also come from a single vineyard.

From the 2012 vintage, however, a new classification system was put in place. The top level remains *Erste Lage*, with the 1 next to the bunch of grapes: these are wines from the best vineyards in Germany. The vineyards are narrowly demarcated, the grape varieties are designated, the maximum yield is 50 hectalitres per hectar (50hl/ha), there is a minimum must weight (the level of sugar in the grape-juice), and the grape must be selectively harvested by hand. Fruity wines with natural sweetness are denoted by the traditional Prädikats, as set out above, whilst dry wines are labeled Erstes Gewächs, if the wine is from the Rheingau region, or Grosses Gewächs if from the other regions of Germany. The second level of classification is Klassifizierte Lage/Ortswein/Terroirwein, which are wines from classified wines of 'Superior' quality, from a small group of traditional vineyards, with a maximum yield of 65hl/ha. The lowest level is Gutswein, with a maximum yield of 75hl/ha. When looking for good-quality wines from Germany, avoid wines bearing a village name in conjunction with a Grosslage name (looking much like the name of a specific site but actually referring to a broader sweep of inferior vineyards). Piesporter Michelsberg and Niersteiner Gutes Domtal are infamous examples that have been allowed to demean the reputation of a fine village and mislead the consumer.

Germany's wine regions
Mosel

The Mosel, as it is now officially known, also incorporates wines from two tributaries, the Ruwer and the Saar (the latter can still be used on labels). Riesling is king here and the top wines are almost exclusively from this grape. The vines are planted individually on often perilously steep slopes above the exaggerated twists and turns of the river below. The river Mosel flows along the Luxembourg border (here Moselle - see Other Europe) before turning towards Trier and it is almost immediately joined by the most important tributary, the **Saar**. Viticulture is marginal but the wines can be extraordinary. In the best years (plenty of those recently), and only then in the best sites, are sublime steely, minerally wines made, sometimes with piercing acidity but developing a marvellous, vibrant, honeyed intensity with age. Farthest from the Mosel are the vineyards of **Serrig**, most notably **Schloss Saarstein**; downstream **Saarburg** is distinguished by the **Rausch** vineyard. These, like most of the top vineyards, lie obliquely to the river. Further downstream are **Ockfener Bockstein**, the **Kupp** vineyard from behind **Ayl**, and **Scharzhofberg** from one of Germany's great names, Egon Müller. The village of **Oberemmel** and its fine vineyards, including **Hütte**, lie in a recess away from the Saar and are often overlooked. **Braune Kupp** by contrast is on the river itself, north of **Wiltingen**, as is **Altenberg**, another great site, opposite the village of **Kanzem**. The Ruwer is a trickle by contrast with the Mosel but boasts some exceptional sites that produce exquisite, elegant wines in exceptional vintages. In the village of **Kasel** are the fine **Kehrnagel** and **Nies'chen** sites but the greatest vineyards are those of **Eitelsbach**, with **Karthäuserhofberg** and the **Abtsberg** vineyard of Maximim Grünhaus/von Schubert.

Obtaining full ripeness (and thus potential greatness) on the Mosel proper is a problem, and only in its middle section, the Mittel Mosel, are the great gems of Mosel viticulture consistently superb. Travelling downstream from Trier, opposite the village of **Leiwen**, the very steep **Laurentiuslay** is the first fine site, from which several good interpretations are made. **Trittenheim's** best vineyards are **Leiterchen** and **Apotheke**, which can show a cool, delicate minerality, but the really outstanding sites in this section of the river are the south-facing vineyards either side of **Piesport**, **Goldtröpfchen** and **Domherr**, which can show a marvellous intensity of blackcurrant, peach and citrus fruit. **Kesten** marks another fine stretch of vineyard beginning with **Paulinshofberg** and culminating in the **Juffer** and, especially, the **Juffer-Sonnenuhr** sites opposite the village of **Brauneberg**. These wines show a marvellous mineral intensity from a number of top growers. Between here and Bernkastel are some good vineyards around **Lieser (Niederberg Helden)** and **Mülheim (Helenenkloster)** but the most impressive are on the dramatic steep slopes that run northwards along the Mosel from behind **Bernkastel**. These begin with the small celebrated **Doctor** vineyard, **Graben** and **Lay**, but stretch on to **Domprobst**, the great site of **Graach**, flanked on either side by the fine **Himmelreich** and **Josephshof** vineyards. The same great slope then continues with the **Sonnenuhr** vineyard opposite **Wehlen**, which extends as far as **Zeltingen**. Many of the Mosel's finest producers are located in this section and wines from the likes of Willi Schaefer, Dr Loosen, Markus Molitor, Joh Jos Prum, Max Ferd Richter and Selbach-Oster offer high quality but differing interpretations. The Bernkastel wines can tend either to be very expensive without always showing their full potential or, as this is a much misused name, have little to do with the great vineyards behind the village. Two *Grosslage* names to be aware of are Badstube (often fine as it is restricted to the best sites) and the much wider Kurfürstlay. Just downstream of Zeltingen is arguably the last brilliantly exposed segment of the Mittel Mosel. The last two great village names are **Ürzig**, with its famous **Würzgarten** ('spice garden') vineyard, and **Erden**, which lies opposite the almost sheer **Prälat** and similarly south-facing **Treppchen** vineyard.

The last stretch of the Mosel before it reaches the Rhine at Koblenz is known as the Terrassenmosel for its narrow terraces. Though not held in the same esteem as those vineyards in the Mittel Mosel, there is undoubted potential here beginning to be realised by a number of small growers. In particular, quite powerful, minerally examples have been realised from the **Röttgen** and **Uhlen** vineyards of **Winningen**.

Mittelrhein

The scattered vineyards on the picturesque north-running stretch of the Rhine constitute the small region of Mittelrhein. They can be seen both north and south of Koblenz but the best wines come from a handful of producers around **Bacharach** which has several good sites with slatey soils. As in the Mosel, Riesling is king and good examples have a distinctive floral, mineral intensity.

Nahe

The Nahe has more land planted to vineyards than the Rheingau but much less Riesling, yet its best examples can combine the best qualities of both the Mosel and Rheingau. The greatest stretch of vineyards lies south of the spa town of **Bad Kreuznach**. The town itself has potentially outstanding sites in **Kahlenberg**, **Krötenpfuhl** and **Brückes** but, though improving, quality has not

been maximised. Most famous are the vineyards of **Niederhausen**, especially **Hermannshöhle**. Dönnhoff is a brilliant producer which has also underscored the quality of Brücke (associated with **Oberhausen**, across the river) and **Kupfergrube**, which along with **Felsenberg** is one of the great vineyards of **Schlossböckelheim**. The village of **Norheim** has good south-facing sites in **Dellchen**, **Kafels** and **Kirschneck** while **Traisen** has **Bastei** and **Rotenfels** but this section of the Nahe needs others besides Dönnhoff to make more of its inherent potential. **Bockenauer Felseneck** on the Ellerbach tributary is another great site which sparkles in the hands of Schäfer-Fröhlich who, along with Emrich-Schönleber, also produces refined Rieslings much further upstream on the Nahe, at **Monzingen** - from the **Halenberg** and **Frühlingsplätzchen** vineyards. Downstream from Bad Kreuznach, and nearer to the Rhine, is **Dorsheim**, where the top sites of **Burgberg**, **Goldloch** and **Pittermännchen** show good richness from Schlossgut Diel. The **Pittersberg**, **Dautenpflänzer** and **Rheinberg** sites of **Munster-Sarmsheim** can also be a source of good quality Riesling.

Rheingau

One glance at a map of German wine regions makes it obvious why this particular region has been held in high regard for so long. Tight contours above the Rhine, as it swings west south-west for 30 km, indicate an ideal swathe of vineyards, some of which have long belonged to some of Germany's most aristocratic estates. Despite the potential, quality remains mixed and is as likely to come from an emerging smaller grower with less well-known sites as from a more famous name. As the river starts to swing north again, Spätburgunder is planted in the **Höllenberg** vineyard above **Assmannshausen** but Riesling otherwise dominates these vineyards as in no other German region. In the main section, where some of the leading villages are to be found, the vines stretch well back from the river. The best wines show a riper, richer fruit intensity that contrasts with the generally lighter, more elegant examples from the Mosel. The citrus, apple and white peach flavours more prevalent in the Mosel are replaced more often by peach, nectarine and apricot, even at Kabinett and Spätlese levels of ripeness.

Rudesheim's best vineyards lie opposite Bingen almost directly above the river, **Berg Schlossberg** and **Berg Rottland** on the steepest slopes are the finest but several others can also produce high quality. Moving east, Geisenheim, famous for its wine school, includes the vineyards of Kläuserweg and Rothenberg, while perched high above it is the historic estate of **Schloss Johannisberg** with its own separate *Einzellage* identity. Behind the neighbouring village of Winkel, **Schloss Vollrads** too is an *Einzellage* in its own right and efforts are being made to restore its flagging reputation. **Winkel** also has two fine vineyards in **Jesuitengarten** and **Hasensprung**. Further east, **Oestrich** deserves to be better known as both the **Doosberg** and **Lenchen** sites can provide top-quality Riesling in the right hands (Kühn or Spreitzer). The village of Hallgarten lies high above Oestrich but it is only with Hattenheim and Erbach, from vineyards close to the river, that better sites are found. **Hattenheim** includes **Wisselbrunnen**, **Nussbrunnen** and, in **Mannberg**, has the extension of **Erbacher Marcobrunn**, from which some of the Rheingau's most powerful, flavoursome Rieslings can be made. Erbach also includes fine sites in Siegelsberg, Schlossberg and Hohenrain.

Kiedrich lies a long way back from the river but has steep slopes in **Grafenberg** and a high-profile producer in Robert Weil. The

Germany

vineyard of **Wasseros** also has the potential for top quality. To the east of Kiedrich is **Rauenthal**, a village from which stylish, spicy, minerally Riesling can be made from several outstanding sites. Until very recently at least the potential of **Baiken** and **Gehrn** has not been realised while fine examples of **Nonnenberg** and **Rothenberg** from both recent and older vintages can be found. Neighbouring Martinsthal (Langenberg) and other villages closer to Wiesbaden also contain fine if lesser-known vineyards such as **Wallufer Walkenberg**. At its eastern end, the Rheingau vineyards are not on the Rhine at all but on the river Main as it flows west into the Rhine. **Hochheim** includes several top sites from a relatively narrow wedge of vineyard, including **Domdechaney**, **Kirchenstück** and **Hölle**.

Rheinhessen

Germany's most extensively planted and productive region is also the source of a significant amount of its poorest wine. The leading grapes are Müller-Thurgau and Silvaner, much of it destined for oceans of bland semi-sweet blends. It is yet again Riesling grown at the Rhine's edge that produces the best wines. **Bingen**, in the region's north-west corner, at the juncture of the Nahe and the Rhine rivers, has one important vineyard, the **Scharlachberg**, but it is a famous stretch of vineyards from around Oppenheim and up to Nackenheim that produces the great Rieslings. The steep east- and southeast-facing escarpment of the Roter Hang hill that runs from behind Nierstein towards Nackenheim includes most of the top sites, particularly those on the sweep of the Rhine itself. Fine **Niersteiner** vineyards include the **Orbel**, **Heiligenbaum**, **Ölberg**, **Hipping**, **Brudersberg** and **Pettenthal**, while **Rothenberg** (whose top producer is Gunderloch) comes under **Nackenheim**. Behind **Oppenheim** (like Nierstein, sullied by a *Grosslage* name), lie **Herrenberg** and **Sackträger**, two more potentially outstanding sites. At Flörsheim-Dalsheim, in the southern hinterland, Weingut Keller has highlighted the potential of this area and established the reputation of the **Dalsheimer Hubacker** vineyard, while to the north the Wittmann family are forging a reputation for the best vineyards of Westhofen.

Pfalz

Riesling is the most planted variety in the Pfalz but occupies only 21 % of the vineyard, so there are many other grapes that assume an important role here as well. There is very fine Rieslaner and excellent Scheurebe and the wines are noted for a lush richness checked by a vibrant acidity. Good examples of the 'Pinots' – Grauburgunder, Weissburgunder and Spätburgunder – are made too. The Pfalz is effectively a continuation of Alsace, and the Haardt mountains offer similar protection to the Vosges, often ensuring a sunny, dry autumn. The region's best producers are no longer confined to the Mittelhaardt, a rich vein of sites made famous by Bassermann-Jordan, Bürklin-Wolf and von Buhl.

On hillside slopes on the western edge of the villages (running northwards) of Ruppertsberg, Deidesheim and Forst are some of the finest sites. The best from **Ruppertsberg** include **Gaisböhl**, **Hoheburg** and **Reiterpfad**, while those from **Deidesheim** include **Hohenmorgen**, **Leinhöhle**, **Kieselberg**, **Kalkofen** and **Grainhübel**. **Forst** has two outstanding sites in **Jesuitengarten** and **Kirchenstück** but also **Freundstück**, **Pechstein** and **Ungeheuer**. The last fine sites in this stretch are clustered together just south of **Wachenheim** and includes **Gerümpel**, **Goldbächel** and **Rechbächel**. From here the vineyards continue virtually unbroken and north of the spa town Bad Dürkheim, from close to

Ungstein (Herrenberg) and **Kallstadt (Saumagen)**, there is still more potential for outstanding wines. Many producers now make a Riesling Spätlese Trocken from a top site and label it as *Erste Lage* (previously *Grosses Gewächs*) in the manner of an Alsace Grand Cru. A growing number of good producers make fine Rieslings from outside this particularly well-protected belt. The most high-profile of these, Müller-Catoir, is as successful with Rieslaner, Scheurebe and Muskateller as with Riesling.

Baden

This fast-growing, resurgent region (now Germany's third most important in terms of quantity), lies directly across the Rhine, here forming the border with Germany, from Alsace. Production is dominated by large co-operatives but exciting small, private producers are more responsible for its growing reputation for quality. Though a quarter of the planting is Müller-Thurgau, the leading variety is red. Spätburgunder (Pinot Noir) accounts for almost a third of the vineyard area. Grauburgunder (or Ruländer as it is also called here) and Weissburgunder in both oaked and unoaked styles are also important, as is Traminer. From this elongated stretch of vineyards, those from the areas of Kaiserstuhl and Ortenau produce some of the finest wines. In Kaiserstuhl's volcanic soils all three 'Pinots' do particularly well from around the towns of **Achkarren**, **Burkheim**, **Ihringen** and **Oberrotweil**. Further north, Riesling (as Klingelberger) assumes some significance in **Durbach** (especially from the **Plauelrain** vineyard) and in the Ortenau, where the quality obtained by Laible suggests its true potential is only just beginning to be realised.

Franken

In Franken, as in the Rheinhessen, the variety that dominates production is Müller-Thurgau, though not from a quality perspective. Silvaner is the most important quality grape and Franken is where this grape shows the greatest interest and complexity. Riesling hardly figures at all, in part because the more continental growing season isn't always long enough to achieve full ripeness. Yet from certain locations, usually close to the broad, snaking Main river, it shows a style and complexity that owes something to the soils (often limestone-rich) as well as the grape. **Escherndorf** has one outstanding site, **Lump**, where brilliant wines from Horst Sauer, including Riesling and Silvaner, deserve the widest recognition. **Iphofen** to the south is blessed with excellent vineyards in **Julius-Echter-Berg** and **Kronsberg**. Other locations with good sites include Würzburg (the famous **Würzburger Stein**) and those of **Randersacker (Sonnenstuhl)**. Top grower Paul Fürst (Rudolf Fürst) showcases the quality of **Bürgstadter Centgrafenberg** Riesling and Spätburgunder while Fürst Lowenstein is a leading advocate of **Homburger Kallmuth**. If the squat Bocksbeutel bottle comes as a surprise, and is more difficult to pour from, don't be dissuaded from trying the quality inside.

Other regions

Good Spätburgunder is made in the very small region of Ahr, named for a northerly tributary of the Rhine, while the modest amounts of wine produced in Hessische Bergstrasse is mostly Riesling. There are substantial vineyards areas in Württemberg where reds are as important as whites, and increasingly good quality, if from a select number of producers. Wine quality from the small Saale-Unstrut and Sachsen regions, at the extreme northern latitudes of continental European viticulture, has improved since Germany's reunification, but there are no stars yet.

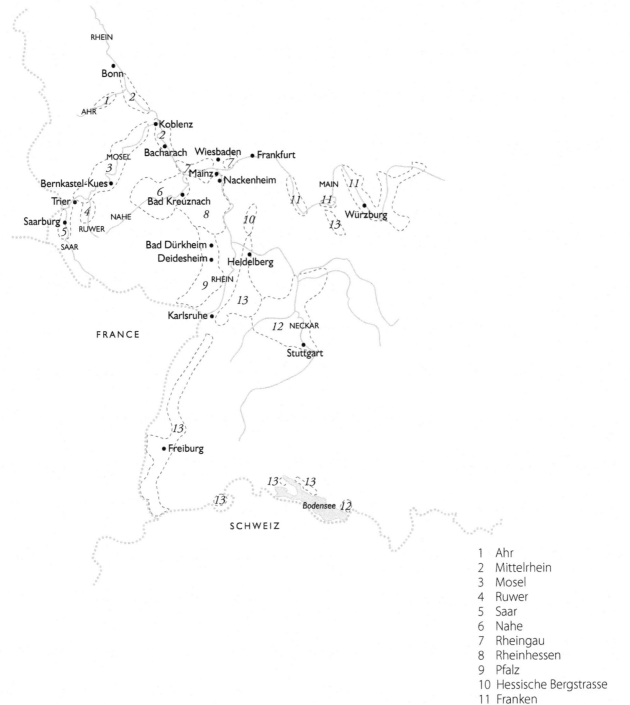

RHEIN

Bonn

1

2

AHR

Koblenz

2

MOSEL

Bacharach   Wiesbaden   Frankfurt

3

7   7

Mainz

Bernkastel-Kues

6   Nackenheim

Trier

Bad Kreuznach   MAIN   11

4   8   11

Saarburg   NAHE

5   RUWER   10   11

SAAR   Würzburg

13

Bad Dürkheim   Heidelberg

Deidesheim

9   RHEIN

13

Karlsruhe

FRANCE   12   NECKAR

Stuttgart

13

Freiburg

13   13

13   Bodensee   12

SCHWEIZ

1   Ahr
2   Mittelrhein
3   Mosel
4   Ruwer
5   Saar
6   Nahe
7   Rheingau
8   Rheinhessen
9   Pfalz
10   Hessische Bergstrasse
11   Franken
12   Württemberg
13   Baden

Germany

A-Z of producers by region

Germany vintages

What is produced each year from German vineyards is dependent on the climatic conditions – especially during the months of October and November. Top years provide greater ripeness and plentiful Spätlese and Auslese and, if the conditions are right, botrytis enrichment for Beerenauslese and Trockenbeerenauslese styles. In a poor year only Kabinett and a little Spätlese might be made. When to drink wines and potential longevity are very producer-dependent but the table below is based on Spätlese and Auslese levels of ripeness. An example from the Mosel is likely to need a little more time than one from the warmer Rhine but the producer will be of much greater significance. While well-made Kabinett can be drunk within a year or two of the vintage, most Spätlese or Auslese needs 3 or 4 years' age to start to show well. Whether they will keep for another couple of years or a further 5, 10 or 15 (or more) depends on the specific wine and vintage quality. Eiswein from a fine vintage like 98 or 04 can age very impressively, but even when well-balanced from the outset it usually retains its penetrating acidity.

Recent vintages

Recent vintages are very exciting. Since 2001 producers in Germany have been unmatched by any other fine wine region for such a run of vintages. Global warming may threaten the livelyhoods of growers in some parts of the world but here, recently at least, its influence is more benign.

2015: Unlike the 2014 vintage, there are very few caveats for this one – indeed, it creeps towards the exceptional. There was a long, hot and dry summer, which gave rise to some worries about too much stress on the vines, but enough rain fell in early September, and then in mid-October, to prevent the feared consequences. Fortunately, it remained cool during most of the rain, and this prevented rot and mildew. There are no real variations in quality amongst the regions: overall, the results are terrific.

2014: the winter was mild and dry, the spring was warm and sunny, and buds were bursting during the first fortnight in April. Early May saw a bit of frost damage in the Mosel and Franken. Flowering began in the first week of a very hot June and was pretty well complete by July. So far, so good. July finally saw ample rain, as a result of which there was vigorous growth, and growers had repeatedly to remove excess foliage. By the end of July, grapes were three weeks ahead of the average, which meant that skins were softened. Not only did this make them prone to rot, but a new threat flew in: the Asian fruit fly invaded and attacked, spreading rapidly and widely. This was disastrous for red-wine grapes such as Dornfelder and Regent, but not so for Spätburgunder, which is a late ripener. August saw cold temperatures combined with huge downpours. Some producers picked in early September, when the rain threatened all-conquering rot, settling for average to good wines, rather than no wines at all; others picked very quickly and sorted very selectively. As a result, there are some very good wines and a lot of very drinkable wines.

2013: A cold winter followed by cool weather retarded flowering and whilst the weather was kind during the summer months, the harvest was spoilt by wet weather in late September and early October and producers struggled to pick before the onset of rot. Noble rot, however, fared a lot better and some excellent noble sweet wines will be made. Quantities are considerably down owing to the short picking time but most dry white wines produced will be of reasonable quality, although displaying a high amount of acidity. The best producers would have picked at higher residual sugar levels to offset this acidity. Reds are light in colour, quantity

and quality, particularly Pinot Noirs.

2012: A warm spring was followed by cool and damp weather right up to the end of July. August was very hot and dry with good weather carrying on throughout September. However, a combination of uneven flowering and the heat spikes in August left some producers harvesting both underripe and overripe grapes. Those who managed to effect a selective early harvest followed by a later than usual main harvest succeeded in producing high quality wines, satisfying the aficionados of minerality on the one hand and ripeness on the other. A lack of botrytis and low yields, however, means that Auslese and up will be in very short supply. This was a good vintage for reds with Spätburgunders showing very well in particular.

2011: The vagaries of the weather were maddening. First there was the hottest and driest April in decades; there was lots of rain in June, which continued into July, but there was not the feared appearance of much rot. At the end of August there were two huge hailstorms, which hit the Mittel Mosel particularly, but also cut a swathe through a part of the Pfalz and Rheinhessen. The question facing producers then was, do you pick your early-ripening varieties now, for fear of losing the bulk of your crop, or wait, hoping for an Indian summer? The better producers held on, and were rewarded with sunny days, cool nights, and no more rain. Their results were outstanding, with many commentators already referring to it as the vintage of the century. This verdict should wait a bit longer, but there will be some superlative wines.

2010: After a decade of vintages ranging from very good to superlative, 2010 came as a shock. First of all, many crops were reduced by early frosts. Then September, which is, ideally, warm and sunny, was cold and rainy, whilst October was cool. As a result, there were very high levels of acidity and galloping rot in many vineyards. A lot of deacidification went on, especially in the Mosel. Indeed, the Mosel suffered the worst: production was down drastically, with some of the best producers losing 50% of their crop. There are some terrific German wines, with both high acidity and high sugar, but a lot more mediocre ones. Wines from the Nahe, Franken and parts of Baden generally performed the best.

2009: This has the potential of being a great vintage, particularly for the dryer wines. Superb conditions in August, September and October has resulted intop quality fruit across the board, so there will be many wines below spätlese quality from the best producers. On the other hand irregular flowering has led to an overall reduction in yields - about 15% down on last year. Only small quantities of beerenauslese and trockenbeerenauslese have been made due to the late arrival of botrytis, but the quality is superb. Red wine growers are also delighted, with the Spätburgunder producing as good results as can be remembered.

2008: This is a more classical, leaner vintage than 2007, similar perhaps to that of 2004, with crisp and fresh wines with fruity acidity being the norm. Good with some fulsome wines of Kabinett and Spätlese quality. Because of cool weather in September there was a lack of botrytis and few dessert wines were made, although those that did are extremely satisfied with the quality. A few producers even managed to make some Eiswein at the end of December. Reds are also reported as more than satisfactory.

2007: German vintages continue to scale the heights. Reports from all 13 German wine growing regions record a superb year both in quality and quantity. As a result there are increased quantities of Auslese, Beerenauslese and Trockenbeerenauslese wines for all to enjoy. Qualitätswein, Kabinett and Spätlese were considerably above average in flavour, freshness and acidity. The long growing season also allowed high quality reds to be produced with ripe tannins and plenty of body.

2006: Could Germany do it again in 2006? In short, yes but with some variability from region to region. The Mittel Mosel and Nahe were the most outstanding, surpassing 05 with some astonishing wines that beg to be cellared. In the Saar some were hit by hail and cooler weather in late September drastically compromising yields although quality is still very good. Franken also improved over 05.

2005: Another splendid vintage to follow 04. The combination of some rain followed by excellent October weather has resulted in some fantastic sweet styles from Auslese to TBA, especially in more northern regions. Prospects are good for reds too.

2004: A fine vintage, characterised in particular by excellent late-harvested Spätlese with fine acidities and cool but fully ripe fruit. There is a refinement and intensity if not the exotic panache of the best 03s or the electric structures of 02s. Some superb Eiswein compensates for a paucity of rich botrytised styles.

2003: Germany felt the heat too. This extraordinarily hot European summer seared nearly every part of the continent but for the most part the vineyards here provided better balanced wines than in her more southerly neighbours. The super-rich, ripe 03s can be exceptional, if atypical, when the balance is right.

2002: 02 is characterised by some exceptional ageworthy wines (if very little of the very sweet styles). Some wines closed up some after bottling and some growers believe their wines too austere but there is also ample evidence of wines with intense, fully ripe fruit lying beneath a steely backbone. One to continue to keep.

2001: Hailed as an outstanding vintage following a relatively uneven finish to the late 90s. The best wines show classic styles and flavours with excellent balance. Both drier and sweeter styles can be drunk now.

Older vintages: include some exceptional years where the wines can provide an unbelievable drinking experience that illustrates the nobility of the Riesling grape from sites of unequalled *terroir*. 1998 is arguably the best vintage of the rather uneven late 90s from a German wide perspective with fine quality in both dry and sweet styles. There is also a string of older, almost legendary vintages going back to the early 20th century but these are diverse in terms of region specificity and also highly producer dependent, and then often to the point of manifest differences between separate bottlings (sometimes only distinguished by a different AP nummer). Auction prices (in Germany) are probably the surest indicator of quality.

Wine behind the label

Germany

Germany vintage chart

	Mosel Riesling	Rhine Riesling	Pfalz Riesling
2015	★★★★★ A	★★★★★ A	★★★★★ A
2014	★★★★ A	★★★★ A	★★★★ A
2013	★★★ A	★★★ A	★★★ A
2012	★★★★★ A	★★★★★ A	★★★★★ A
2011	★★★★★ A	★★★★★ A	★★★★★ A
2010	★★★ B	★★★ B	★★★ B
2009	★★★★★ A	★★★★★ A	★★★★★ A
2008	★★★★ B	★★★★ B	★★★★ B
2007	★★★★★ B	★★★★★ B	★★★★★ B
2006	★★★★★ B	★★★★ B	★★★★ B
2005	★★★★★ B	★★★★★ B	★★★★☆ B
2004	★★★★ C	★★★★ C	★★★★ C
2003	★★★★☆ C	★★★★☆ C	★★★★☆ C
2002	★★★★☆ C	★★★★☆ C	★★★★☆ C
2001	★★★★☆ C	★★★★☆ C	★★★★☆ C
2000	★★★☆ C	★★★ C	★★☆ C
1999	★★★☆ C	★★★☆ C	★★★★ C
1998	★★★★ C	★★★★ C	★★★★☆ C
1997	★★★★ C	★★★☆ C	★★★☆ C
1996	★★★☆ C	★★★★ C	★★★★☆ C
1995	★★★★☆ C	★★★☆ C	★★★☆ C
1994	★★★★ C	★★★★ C	★★★☆ C
1993	★★★★ C	★★★★ C	★★★★ C
1992	★★★☆ D	★★★☆ D	★★★☆ D
1990	★★★★★ C	★★★★★ C	★★★★★ C

A-Z of producers

Gerhard Aldinger (Württemberg) *www.weingut-aldinger.de*
Aldinger is one of the two top producers from Württemberg. Typically he has quite a variety of reds and whites in his large range of wines. Fortunately almost anything is worth a try. The highlights from 28 ha of vineyards are Riesling and Lemberger (Blaufränkisch) from Fellbacher Lämmler, and Spätburgunder from Untertürckheimer Gips. The Riesling is cool, concentrated and minerally, especially in Erste Lage (Grosses Gewächs, GG) and Auslese versions. The rich, lush reds can be a touch over-oaked but are more harmonious with a little age. There's also an unexpectedly good licorice-and-berry Merlot which includes 5% Petit Verdot and needs at least 6 years' ageing. Other good whites include Sauvignon and Gewürztraminer that are elegant and expressive. Don't overlook the supple, flavoursome basic red and white Bentz blends for everyday drinking either.

Recommended Reds:
Spätburgunder 3 Sterne ★★★ £E   Cuvée M Merlot ★★★ £E
Bentz Rotwein Cuvée ★ £B

Recommended Whites:
Fellbacher Lämmler Riesling GG ★★★ £E
Fellbacher Lämmler Riesling Auslese ★★★ £C
Cuvée S Sauvignon Blanc ★★ £C
Untertürckheimer Gips Gewürztraminer 2 Sterne ★★ £C
Bentz Weisswein Cuvée ★★ £B

Bassermann-Jordan (Pfalz) *www.bassermann-jordan.com*
This famous Pfalz estate (Weingut Geheimer Rat Dr von

Bassermann-Jordan is its full name) has been revitalised since the mid-1990s. With 50 ha, the estate is large but includes vineyards in some of the best sites of Forst and Deidesheim. Under the direction of Ulrich Mell and Gunter Hauck are produced intense, ripe Rieslings (at the Spätlese level and higher) with good balanced acidities. Erste Lage (Grosses Gewächs, GG) versions and Sweet wines can be very good too. The wines below are only a selection of what is made, but almost anything of Spätlese level or above made since 1997 is worth trying.

Recommended Whites:
Deidesheimer Mäushöhle Riesling Beerenauslese ★★★★ £H
Deidesheimer Hohenmorgen Riesling Eiswein ★★★ £H
Deidesheimer Hohenmorgen Riesling Auslese ★★★ £F
Deidesheimer Hohenmorgen Riesling GG ★★★ £D
Deidesheimer Kalkofen Riesling GG ★★★ £D
Forster Pechstein Riesling GG ★★★★ £D
Forster Kirchenstück Riesling Auslese ★★★ £D
Forster Jesuitengarten Riesling Spätlese Trocken ★★ £C
Riesling QbA Trocken ★★ £B   Weissburgunder Trocken ★★ £B

Friedrich Becker (Pfalz) *www.weingut-friedrich-becker.de*
Friedrich Becker junior is now building on his father's achievements, the family having left the local co-op in the early 70s. At the southern most extent of the Pfalz - the vineyards (18 ha) actually straddle the French border they make very good whites but have achieved greater recognition for reds, particularly those from Spätburgunder. The good value 'B' Trocken is an attractive, concentrated and well-balanced example. Much more ambitious is the 'Res' version which spends 18 months in new French and German oak. With input from Stefan Dorst the 96 version raised expectation of what was possible. Now the top version is labelled simply Pinot Noir (£F/G) and while rich with impression, depth and dimension, the oak can be too much both in terms of flavour and structure. 'Res' is marginally cheaper but in the same mould. Erste Lage versions have also been made. Other reds include a dense and characterful Guillaume (from Cabernet Sauvignon, Merlot, Pinot Meunier and Dornfelder) and a richly black-fruited oaky extracted Die Verbotene Frucht (forbidden fruit) from Cabernet Sauvignon from the vineyards lying in Germany. Whites in a full, flavoursome, well-structured style are increasingly successful. Weisser Burgunder Spätlese Trocken (10% barrel fermented) is concentrated and expressive but a Kalkgestein example is also characterful and intense. Riesling has strength and depth in either Spätlese Trocken or Spätlese Difussion versions. A Schweigener Sonnenberg Erste Lage (Grosses Gewächs, GG) version is also made. Grauburgunder, as Kabinett or Spätlese Trocken, has lots of vitality and shouldn't be ignored either. Gewürztraminer is also made. Ratings for Spätburgunder 'Res' and Die Verbotene Frucht are based on their potential with age and shouldn't be drunk young.

Recommended Reds:
Spätburgunder 'Res' ★★★ £F   Spätburgunder 'B' Trocken ★★ £C
Die Verboten Frucht ★★★ £E   Rotweincuvée Guillaume ★★☆ £C

Recommended Whites:
Riesling Diffusion Spätlese ★★★ £D
Riesling Spätlese Trocken ★★☆ £C
Weisser Burgunder Spätlese Trocken ★★ £C
Weisser Burgunder Kalkgestein ★★☆ £C
Grauer Burgunder Spätlese Trocken ★★ £B

❀ **Wgt. Bercher (Baden)** *www.weingutbercher.de*
Bercher has 25 ha of vines in the Kaiserstuhl in southern Baden

Wine behind the label

and plantings are dominated by the three Pinots. More than 70% of production comes from Spätburgunder, Weissburgunder or Grauburgunder. Burkheimer Feuerberg wines qualify as Erste Lage (Grosses Gewächs, GG) and are particularly good, with real richness and depth. Weissburgunder is stylish, intense and long, while the Spätburgunder shows splendid flavour complexity. Limberg II, a *barrique*-aged blend of Cabernet Sauvignon, Merlot, Limberger and Spätburgunder, was first produced in 2001. Also very good is an intense and refined Gewürztraminer Auslese (not unlike a very good Alsace Vendange Tardive). Some very good, well-balanced Eiswein is also made when conditions allow; it is intense and tangy, full of ripe nectarine and dried peach fruit. The dry whites should be drunk within 3 to 4 years of the vintage. They recently replaced their Gewürztraminer, from which they had made a terrific auslese, with Scheurebe. This is one of the top producers in the Kaiserstuhl.

Recommended Reds:
Burkheimer Feuerberg Spätburgunder GG ★★★ £E
Jechtinger Eichert Spätburgunder Spätlese Trocken ★ £C
Recommended Whites:
Königschaffhauser Hasenberg Gewürztraminer Auslese ★★★★ £D
Burkheimer Feuerberg Weissburgunder GG ★★★ £C
Weissburgunder Kabinett Trocken ★★ £B
Burkheimer Feuerberg Grauburgunder GG ★★★ £C
Chardonnay Spätlese Trocken ★★ £C

Bergdolt (Pfalz) *www.weingut-bergdolt.de*
This 23 ha estate has been in the same family since the mid-18th century. The recent run of favourable vintages has produced dependably fine quality from the two main grapes, Riesling and Weissburgunder. Differences due to soil type (including loess and sandstone) are brought out too. Weissburgunders are atypically good – intense, concentrated and pure, especially in the Kirrweiler Mandelberg Erste Lage (Grosses Gewächs, GG) version. Riesling is excellent whether from Ruppertsberger Nussbien, Ruppertsberger Reiterpfad or Duttweiler Kreuzberg. Reds include an increasingly good Spätburgunder that sees 30% new oak, with breadth, purity and a cool, forest-floor expression. The slightly firm tannins will soften with 3–5 years' ageing. A little sweet wine is also made from Riesling and Weissburgunder.

Recommended Reds:
Duttweiler Kalkberg Spätburgunder Trocken ★★ £C
Recommended Whites:
Ruppertsberger Reiterpfad Riesling GG ★★★ £C
Ruppertsberger Nussbien Riesling Kabinett ★★ £B
Duttweiler Kreuzberg Riesling Spätlese Trocken ★★★ £B
Kirrweiler Mandelberg Weissburgunder GG ★★★ £C
St Lamprecht Weissburgunder Spätlese Trocken ★★★ £B
St Lamprecht Weissburgunder Kabinett Trocken ★★ £B

Josef Biffar (Pfalz) *www.weingut-biffar.com*
Following the death of Josef Biffar, the estate has been bought by the Japanese family Tokuoka in 2013. Tokuoka Fumiko, a trained oenologist, has recently taken up the reins at this 12 ha estate in the heart of the Pfalz, 80% of which is planted to Riesling. Some excellent wines were produced from the late 1980s onwards as the cellars were gradually modernised until a hiccup in the late 90s in part due to successive changes in winemaking personnel. Wines made since 2001 by Heiner Maleton and later, Tina Herrbruck, show a crystalline purity, poise and intensity; the winemaker is now Michael Lieblaw who has worked with Tokuoka Fumiko for a number of years. Both Wachenheimer Gerümpel and Deidesheimer

Grainhübel Rieslings give full justification to the sites' Erste Lage status. There is excellent definition too in the racy sweeter styles. The wines rated below relate only to wines made prior to the recent change of ownership.
Recommended Whites:
Deidesheimer Kalkofen Riesling Eiswein ★★★★ £G
Deidesheimer Kieselberg Riesling Auslese ★★★ £E
Deidesheimer Grainhübel Riesling GG ★★★ £C
Wachenheimer Gerümpel Riesling GG ★★★ £C
Wachenheimer Altenberg Riesling Spätlese Trocken ★★ £C

Georg Breuer (Rheingau) *www.georg-breuer.com*
Bernhard Breuer was passionate about Rheingau Riesling and was one of its leading advocates until his death in 2004. His legacy is not only an estate of some 33 ha but also joint ventures in South Africa (MONT DU TOIT) and Portugal's Douro (QUINTA DA CARVALHOSA). The Rheingau vineyards include 2.6ha in the highly rated Rüdesheimer Berg Schlossberg, 1ha in Berg Rottland and the entire 5 ha of Rauenthaler Nonnenberg. All three sites are classified as Erste Lage, giving ample scope for making fine (Erstes Gewächs) Rheingau Rieslings. The wines improved considerably in the 1990s and in recent vintages have been particularly good. Sweeter styles generally show good botrytis richness, with good intensity and length of flavour in the Goldkapsel Auslese wines; the Rauenthal Nonnenberg is most stylish and distinctive. Just a little more focus and refinement would put the wines among the very best from the Rheingau. Some Grauburgunder and Spätburgunder are also made. Prices are high for the quality. Old varieties Orleans and Heunisch are also being replanted here.
Recommended Whites:
Rüdesheimer Berg Rottland Riesling Auslese Goldkapsel ★★★★ £G
Rüdesheimer Bischofsberg Riesling Auslese Goldkapsel ★★★ £G
Rüdesheimer Berg Riesling Auslese Goldkapsel ★★★ £G
Rüdesheimer Berg Rottland Riesling Trocken ★★ £D
Rüdesheimer Berg Schlossberg Riesling Trocken ★★ £D
Rauenthaler Nonnenberg Riesling Auslese Goldkapsel ★★★★ £G
Rauenthaler Nonnenberg Riesling Trocken ★★ £D
Riesling Trocken Montosa ★★ £B

Reichsrat von Buhl (Pfalz) *www.reichsrat-von-buhl.de*
It has taken some time but Japanese investment has put this once famous estate established in 1849 back on the map of the Pfalz's best (it is leased to a consortium of Japanese wine merchants). With 62 ha of vineyards spread across some enviable sites it would be a shame if the wines were not special and, the Yen having been spent, the wines have been back on form since 1994. It is difficult to separate the top Rieslings for quality, coming as they do from some out-and-out top Pfalz vineyards, yet no two are alike. The very classy, mineral-imbued Forster Pechstein is hard to better in a top vintage but the initially more austere Ruppertsberger Reiterpfad has underlying concentration, a white peach fruit intensity and a touch of spice. Others are scarcely less good. As is the trend in the Pfalz there is now much emphasis on the production of Erste Lage (Grosses Gewächs, GG) but some fine sweet wines are made too, including Riesling from Forster Ungeheuer and Scheurebe from Ruppertsberger Reiterpfad.
Recommended Whites:
Forster Pechstein Riesling GG ★★★★ £E
Forster Kirchenstück Riesling GG ★★★ £E
Forster Jesuitengarten Riesling Spätlese ★★★ £D
Deidesheimer Paradiesgarten Riesling GG ★★★ £E

Germany

Ruppertsberger Reiterpfad Riesling GG ★★★ £E

❀ **Bürklin-Wolf (Pfalz)** www.buerklin-wolf.de
Since the mid-1990s Christian von Guradze has restored the
reputation of this large and historic estate. Its 86 ha of vineyards
include several of the Pfalz's top sites which under the new
classification system have been designated Erste Lage (for Grosses
Gewächs, GG). The focus has been to produce a top full-bodied dry
Riesling in each and these wines, all Spätlese Trocken, much more
closely resemble top Alsace wines than anything from other areas
in Germany. Forster Jesuitengarten is rich and minerally with real
weight and an Alsace-like oiliness; the Kirschenstück is a brilliant
wine with terrific minerality, great intensity, concentration and
excellent ageing potential; Deidesheimer Hohenmorgen shows an
unusual, spicy character and deep, pure fruit; while Ruppertsberger
Gaisböhl is broader but long and classy. Less expensive, the 'B'-rated
Wachenheimer Rechbächel and Ruppertsberger Hoheburg are a
little lighter but have good length and intensity. Cheaper again is
a Bürklin Estate Riesling, which offers good fruit character. Other
good wines include a very sweet Scheurebe Beerenauslese that is
just rescued by its acidity and a very intense sweet Muskateller TBA
with rich, vibrant, apricotty fruit that also teeters on the brink. Some
Chardonnay and Spätburgunder are also made.
Recommended Whites:
Forster Kirschenstück Riesling GG ★★★★★ £E
Forster Ungeheuer Riesling GG ★★★★ £E
Forster Jesuitengarten Riesling GG ★★★ £D
Forster Pechstein Riesling GG ★★★ £D
Wachenheimer Rechbächel Riesling TBA ★★★★ £H
Wachenheimer Rechbächel Riesling GG ★★★ £C
Deidesheimer Hohenmorgen Riesling GG ★★★ £D
Ruppertsberger Gaisböhl Riesling GG ★★★ £D
Ruppertsberger Hoheburg Riesling GG ★★★ £C
Bürklin Estate Riesling ★★ £B   Scheurebe Beerenauslese ★★ £F
Muskateller TBA ★★★★ £H

❀ **Weingut Clemens Busch (Mittel Mosel)** www.clemens-busch.de
The new kid (a member since 2007) on the VDP block-the
association of top growers-is Clemens Busch of Pünderich, a little
known Mittel-Mosel village going downstream from the big names
of Bernkastel, Wehlen, Zelingen and Erden. Opposite the village
is the spectacular Marienberg vineyard with real potential for the
finest quality. The estate has 11 ha. All wines recommended are
Riesling. Father Clemens and his wife have followed the organic
route since 1986 and son Florian has now taken production to the
biodynamic level. An exciting modern approach operating from
a house dated 1663 right on the river (the cellars are on a higher
altitude above the village to avoid cellar flooding problems). Natural
wild yeasts are used for most wines, cultured yeasts only for the
sweet botrytised wines. This is one of the most *terroir* focussed
estates in Germany. vom Roten Schiefer is from red slate soil which
gives a spiciness and roundness in the nose. Falkenlay is from grey
slate, less floral but more mineral. Fahrlay is from blue slate, very
concentrated and even more mineral; this is most expressive in
Fahrlay Terrassen from 65 year old vines on terraced vineyards. Red
soils dominate perhaps their finest vineyard Marienberg Rothenpfad
from which they make their top dry Grosses Gewächs wine as
well as, in 2007, wonderfully concentrated sweet wines. Their
Punderiches Marienburg Riesling TBA is outstanding. Nonnengarten
too has rich red soil. Extraordinary wines, worth seeking out; prices
are very reasonable explained by the comparative obscurity of the
village. Note that as the estate is now a member of the VDP, it will
have to conform to the association's requirements for labelling
from 2009 onwards: the VDP wishes to phase out the dry Prädikat
appellation and allow a single vineyard designation only for the
Grosses Gewächs top dry wines.
Recommended Whites:
Punderliches Marienburg Riesling TBA ★★★★★ £H
Marienberg Rothenpfad Riesling GG ★★★★ £D
Marienberg Spätlese Riesling ★★★★ £C
Fahrlay Terrassen Riesling ★★★★ £C
Vom Roten Schiefer Riesling ★★★ £C
Nonnengarten Riesling ★★★ £C
Falkenlay ★★★ £C   Riesling Spätlese Trocken ★★★ £C
Riesling Kabinett Trocken ★★★ £B

Castell (Franken) www.castell.de
This historic and aristocratic estate (Fürstlich Castell'sches
Domänenamt in full), which has been in the family since the 11th
century, encompasses a whole village, its vineyards (65 ha) and
bank. Under the current Graf (prince) the past decade has seen a
renewed emphasis on quality. There is quite a daunting range of
wines and quality levels with different bottle shapes to boot. A
Bordeaux bottle is used for a more international style (indicated
by variety first) while the Bocksbeutel is retained for the classic
traditional styles. Several good examples of each are made but the
latter wines are the ones to look out for, including powerful, well
structured Silvaner from Casteller Schlossberg and Casteller Hohnart
and concentrated Rieslaner Spätlese from Casteller Kugelspiel.
They can also be impressively ageworthy as a splendid, complex
example of the Rieslaner from 1993 amply demonstrates. Unusual
but well-made is Silvaner 10 Apriles Anno 1659, an oaked version.
Beerenauslese and TBA of high quality are also produced from
Silvaner and Rieslaner but only in very small quantities. The best red
is a very good if pricey and slightly overoaked Spätburgunder from
Reitsteig, part of Schlossberg with a good southern exposure. Wines
labelled Castell-Castell are the basics.
Recommended Whites:
Casteller Schlossberg Rieslaner Auslese ★★★ £F
Casteller Schlossberg Silvaner GG ★★★ £E
Casteller Schlossberg Riesling GG ★★★ £E
Casteller Kugelspiel Rieslaner Spätlese ★★★ £D
Casteller Hohnart Silvaner Kabinett Trocken ★★ £B
Riesling Hohnart ★★ £B   Silvaner 10 Apriles Anno 1659 ★★ £C
Silvaner Kugelspiel ★★ £B   Silvaner+Traminer Trautberg ★ £B
Müller-Thurgau Bausch ★ £B

A Christmann (Pfalz) www.weingut-christmann.de
Steffen Christmann was elected the new president of the VDP in
2007. His 19.5 ha of vineyards include four leading Pfalz vineyard
sites (Deidesheimer Hohenmorgen, Gimmeldinger Mandelgarten,
Königsbacher Idig and Ruppertsberger Reiterpfad), each designated
Erste Lage (for Grosses Gewächs, GG). The Idig site is on limestone
soils and produces more piquant wine styles. Mandelgarten is
more powerful with a zesty finish. All the wines show intense,
ripe fruit and a full, lush, almost creamy character yet with good
intensity and acidity. Though they are made in a Trocken style
there is also a little sweetness, similar to many of the Alsace grands
crus in recent vintages. Christmann's own sweet wines are very
sweet, intense and succulent but generally well-balanced, with
the richness underpinned by a vibrant structure. Small amounts
of Trockenbeerenauslese and Eiswein are also made as is a

Spätburgunder (Pinot Noir) from Königsbacher Idig.

Recommended Whites:
Königsbacher Idig Riesling Trocken GG ★★★★ £E
Königsbacher Idig Riesling GG ★★★ £E
Königsbacher Idig Riesling Auslese ★★★ £E
Gimmeldinger Mandelgarten Riesling GG ★★★ £E
Ruppertsberger Reiterpfad Riesling GG ★★★ £E
Deidesheimer Hohenmorgen Riesling GG ★★★ £E

✿ JJ Christoffel (Mittel Mosel) *www.moenchhof.de*
The recently retired Hans Leo Christoffel has leased his minute holding (4 ha) of Riesling vines to neighbour Robert Eymael (MÖNCHHOF/ROBERT EYMAEL), who has taken full responsibility for the wines' production and sale. However a separate identity has been maintained for the wines, over which Christoffel still has some influence. The Ürziger Würzgarten wines are excellent with lovely spice, citrus (and riper peach and nectarine in the riper styles), and penetrating intensity and depth, particularly in reasonably priced special selections. Fine Rieslings are also produced from Erdener Treppchen.

Recommended Whites:
Ürziger Würzgarten Riesling Eiswein ★★★★★ £H
Ürziger Würzgarten Riesling Auslese 3 Sterne ★★★★ £E
Ürziger Würzgarten Riesling Auslese 1 Stern ★★★ £D
Ürziger Würzgarten Riesling Spätlese ★★ £D
Ürziger Würzgarten Riesling Kabinett ★★ £C

Dautel (Württemberg) *www.weingut-dautel.de*
Dautel is proof that there is good wine to be had from Württemberg, even if many fans of German Riesling would have trouble locating the region. Ernst Dautel stopped selling his grapes to the local co-op in the late 70s and now makes a large range from 13 ha. Riesling from the best site, Bönnigheimer Sonnenberg, includes a promising, powerful Erste Lage (Grosses Gewächs, GG) version. For other wines Ernst uses his own star system to differentiate between different quality levels. In fact these stars (Sterne) are a pretty good indication of what to expect with sound quaffers at 2 Sterne, more interest at 3 Sterne (including a stylish, elegant Wurmberg Riesling Trocken) and some very good wines at 4 Sterne. Of the latter, a rich, stylish barrel-fermented Weissburgunder and toasty, spicy, plummy 'S' Lemberger (Blaufränkisch) particularly stand out. Besides Spätburgunder (Pinot Noir), that is slightly overoaked at 4 Sterne, other reds include a fruity if simple Samtrot (a mutation of Pinot Meunier) and Vision, an equal blend of Lemberger and Pinot Noir. Blended premium red and white Kreation are consistently impressive too (3 or 4 Sterne depending on the vintage) – the oak-fermented white from Riesling, Kerner and Pinot Blanc, the red from Merlot, Cabernet Sauvignon and Lemberger. Also made but not tasted are TBA and Eiswein from Bönnigheimer Sonnenburg.

Recommended Reds:
Kreation 3/4 Sterne ★★★ £D   Lemberger 'S' 4 Sterne ★★★ £D
Spätburgunder 'S' 4 Sterne ★★ £D
Bönnigheimer Sonnenberg Spätburgunder 3 Sterne ★★ £B
Lemberger 4 Sterne ★★ £C

Recommended Whites:
Bönnigheimer Sonnenberg Riesling GG ★★★ £D
Bönnigheimer Wurmberg Riesling Trocken 3 Sterne ★★★ £C
Bönnigheimer Sonnenberg Riesling Trocken ★★ £B
Weissburgunder Trocken 4 Sterne ★★★ £D
Kreation 3/4 Sterne ★★★ £D

Domdechant Werner'sches *www.domdechantwerner.com*
This Rheingau estate of 18 ha dates back to 1780 when it was acquired by the dean (Domdechant) of the cathedral at Mainz. The current Dr Franz Werner Michel provides a solid range of wines particularly from the Domdechaney and Kirchenstück sites. There is plenty of intensity together with spice, citrus and riper fruit flavours and good balance, though in most there is not yet the style, richness or persistence for really fine quality. In 2001 a superior Riesling Spätlese Trocken Lange Goldkapsel was made from Domdechaney. Eiswein is made from both Kirchenstück and Domdechaney when conditions permit. Beginning in 2009, some very nice Spätburgunder is now being made.

Recommended Whites:
Hochheimer Kirchenstück Riesling Erstes Gewächs ★★★ £E
Hochheimer Kirchenstück Riesling Spätlese ★★★ £C
Hochheimer Domdechaney Riesling Erstes Gewächs ★★★ £E
Hochheimer Domdechaney Riesling Auslese ★★★ £E
Hochheimer Domdechaney Riesling Spätlese ★★★ £C
Hochheimer Domdechaney Riesling Spätlese Trocken ★★ £C

✿ Dönnhoff (Nahe) *www.doennhoff.com*
Helmut Dönnhoff is quite rightly regarded as one of Germany's most celebrated winemakers. A traditionalist, he favours large oak casks. He makes prodigious Rieslings from 25 ha of vineyards, mostly from sites in Schlossböckelheim, Niederhausen and Oberhäusen, where the Brücke vineyard is Alleinbesitz (solely owned). Even QbA can be distinctive if more modest in cooler years, while excellent examples of Riesling Kabinett include an Oberhäuser Leistenberg that shows both *terroir* and ripe fruit. Spätlese and Auslese wines show splendid concentration, a fine minerally intensity and considerable elegance. The range of vividly expressed flavours, from cool blackcurrant, apple and citrus to ripe peach, is matched by a lingering intensity of fruit. Schlossböckelheimer Kupfergrube Spätlese is intense and long and adds a dash of spice to a delicious ripe peach and blackcurrant character. Particularly concentrated and very classy, if initially less expressive, are Spätlese and Auslese from Oberhäuser Brücke that can appear with a Goldkapsel designation. The Eiswein from the same vineyard is quite exquisite, very sweet and intense and pure but beautifully balanced with honeyed, spicy, dried stone-fruit flavours that go on and on. Those named for a day of the week add a slight premium. The Dellchen wines are intensely mineral while more powerful are those from the Hermmshöhle vineyard. Some Weissburgunder and Grauburgunder are also made.

Recommended Whites:
Oberhäuser Brücke Eiswein ✪✪✪✪✪ £H
Oberhäuser Brücke Riesling Auslese ★★★★★ £F
Oberhäuser Brücke Riesling Spätlese ★★★★ £E
Niederhäuser Hermannshöhle Riesling Auslese ★★★★★ £F
Niederhäuser Hermannshöhle Riesling Grosses Gewächs ★★★★ £E
Niederhäuser Hermannshöhle Riesling Spätlese ★★★ £D
Norheimer Dellchen Riesling Grosses Gewächs ★★★★ £E
Norheimer Dellchen Riesling Kabinett ★★ £C
Schlossböckelheimer Felsenberg Riesling Spätlese ★★★ £D
Schlossböckelheimer Kupfergrube Riesling Spätlese ★★★ £D
Oberhäuser Leistenberg Riesling Kabinett ★★★ £C
Riesling QbA ★★ £C

Duijn (Baden) *www.weingut-duijn.com*
Ex-sommelier Jacob Duijn is a Pinot Noir specialist based in Baden with 6.6 ha of vines. The grapes are hand-picked at low yields and this translates to fully ripe, intense fruit. Laufer Gut Alsenhof, the

basic version from youngish vines in a vineyard of the same name, sees only used French *barriques* while Jannin, from 25-year-old vines, is aged partly in new oak. Most impressive is the SD, with greater depth, complexity and finesse. The wines have only been tasted very young but expect them to fill out with age. The basic needs a couple of years to soften, Jannin 3–5 years from the vintage, SD slightly longer. All are now labelled Pinot Noir rather than Spätburgunder.

Recommended Reds:

Pinot Noir SD ★★★ £F   Pinot Noir Jannin ★★★ £E
Pinot Noir Laufer Gut Alsenhof ★★ £D

⚫ Emrich-Schönleber (Nahe) *www.emrich-schoenleber.de*
This is now arguably the second great estate of the Nahe (after Dönnhoff). Though still small (at 17 ha), it has been improved and much enlarged by Werner Schönleber. Through careful selection and attentive winemaking he produces tight, sleek, intense Rieslings with lovely balance and great length of flavour from the previously unsung village of Monzingen. Riesling Kabinett from Frühlingsplätzchen shows a lovely elegant, gently spicy, minerally intensity and makes great everyday drinking. The estate also includes 4ha of the steep Halenberg vineyard, a source of wines with minerally, refined flavours. A regular Spätlese from this site is medium-dry but both Halbtrocken and Trocken versions are also produced, while energised Auslese also come in a super 3 Sterne *Goldkapsel* version. Halenberg Eiswein is beautifully delineated and is one of those where citrus flavours, especially grapefruit and lime, often prevail over riper peach or apricot. A little Eiswein is also produced from the Frühlingsplätzchen vineyard. A ripe Grauburgunder emphasises fruit.

Recommended Whites:

Monzinger Halenberg Riesling Eiswein ★★★★★ £H
Monzinger Halenberg Riesling Auslese 3 Sterne ★★★★★ £G
Monzinger Halenberg Riesling Auslese ★★★★ £E
Monzinger Halenberg Riesling Spätlese ★★★ £D
Monzinger Frühlingsplätzchen Riesling Beerenauslese ★★★★☆ £F
Monzinger Frühlingsplätzchen Riesling Spätlese ★★★ £D
Monzinger Frühlingsplätzchen Riesling Kabinett ★★ £C
Monzinger Grauburgunder Spätlese Trocken ★ £C
Riesling QbA Lenz ★☆ £B

Weingut Joachim Flick (Rheingau) *www.flick-wein.de*
This Rheingau estate of 19.5ha lies at the eastern extremity of the region, beyond Hochheim and close to Frankfurt. Some excellent Riesling is produced from the alleinbesitz (wholly owned) Wickerer Nonnberg, as well as Wickerer Mönchsgewann and Hochheimer Hölle. There is highish acidity in more basic examples but usually ripe fruit too. Apart from more occasional sweeter styles it is the Erstes Gewächs from Mönchsgewann and Nonnberg that really stand out. Both are refined and classy, with a touch more density in the Nonnberg but they do need to be drunk with a minimum of 5 years' age or more. There's fine Gewürztraminer from Nonnberg too that is pure and ageworthy while for everyday drinking good examples of the inexpensive 'Classic' level have been made since 2005. For red the Spätburgunder from Nonnberg is balanced and supple.

Recommended Reds:

Wickerer Nonnberg Spätburgunder Spätlese Trocken ★★☆ £C
Recommended Whites:
Wickerer Mönchsgewann Riesling Erstes Gewächs ★★★★ £E
Wickerer Nonnberg Riesling Erstes Gewächs ★★★★ £E

Wickerer Nonnberg Riesling Auslese ★★★☆ £E
Wickerer Nonnberg Gewürztraminer Spätlese Trocken ★★★ £C
Hochheimer Hölle Riesling Spätlese Trocken ★★☆ £C
Hochheimer Hölle Riesling Kabinett ★★ £B
Wickerer Nonnberg QbA Riesling Trocken ★★ £B
Wickerer Stein Riesling Kabinett Trocken ★☆ £B
Riesling Classic QbA ★★ £B

Rudolf Fürst (Franken) *www.weingut-rudolf-fuerst.de*
Paul Fürst (one of the Trias five – see Fürst Löwenstein) has 18.7 ha of vineyards, at least half of which are planted to black varieties, mostly Spätburgunder. There is a sophistication that too many German Pinots still lack, with better balance, finer tannins and more measured use of oak. The wines are elegant and long if occasionally needing to be a touch riper and richer. Particularly good is the Spätburgunder Hunsruck R. Also impressive are the Volnay-like Frühburgunders, particular the deep, pure 'R' version. Parzival combines Pinot Noir and Domina, again with a significant step-up in quality in the 'R' bottling. Whites are led by a Riesling 'R' Spätlese with real weight and intensity but a regular version of Weissburgunder and atypically stylish Müller-Thurgau will not disappoint. Sweet wines are made in exceptional years.

Recommended Reds:

Bürgstadter Centgrafenberg Spätburgunder 'R' ★★★ £F
Bürgstadter Centgrafenberg Spätburgunder ★★ £D
Spätburgunder Tradition ★★ £C   Parzival 'R' ★★★ £F
Bürgstadter Centgrafenberg Frühburgunder 'R' ★★★ £F
Bürgstadter Centgrafenberg Frühburgunder ★★ £D
Recommended Whites:
Bürgstadter Centgrafenberg Riesling Eiswein ★★★★ £H
Bürgstadter Centgrafenberg Riesling 'R' ★★★ £D
Bürgstadter Centgrafenberg Riesling Spätlese ★★ £D
Bürgstadter Centgrafenberg Weissburgunder Trocken ★★ £C
Müller-Thurgau ★ £B

Weingut Göttelmann (Nahe)
Götz Blessing and his wife Ruth Göttelmann-Blessing are both trained enologists and have worked very hard to improve both the quality of their grapes and the resulting wines. There are now 13.5 ha of vineyards of classic steep slate-covered slopes, 66% of which are planted to Riesling. A long, cool, natural fermentation is favoured resulting in wines of often piercing minerally citrus and blackcurrant fruit. The acidity can be a little too sharp in some of the drier styles but a reduction in yields seems to contribute to good flavour length. The Dautenpflänzer Riesling Spätlese shows a Mosel-like elegance while a Selection bottling is intense and nuanced. All the Rieslings need age and promise to be very lively even with 5–10 years' age at Spätlese level or higher. A pure lemony, minerally Weissburgunder and intense Chardonnay open out with a little age.

Recommended Whites:

Münsterer Rheinberg Riesling Auslese 3 Sterne ★★★★ £F
Münsterer Rheinberg Riesling Beerenauslese ★★★ £G
Münsterer Dautenpflänzer Riesling Selection ★★★ £D
Münsterer Dautenpflänzer Riesling Spätlese ★★ £C
Münsterer Kapellenberg Riesling Spätlese Trocken ★★ £C
Münsterer Rheinberg Riesling Spätlese ★★ £C
Münsterer Riesling Kabinett Trocken ★ £B
Münsterer Weissburgunder Spätlese Trocken ★★ £C
Münsterer Chardonnay Spätlese Trocken ★★ £C

Grans-Fassian (Mittel Mosel) *www.grans-fassian.de*
Gerhard Grans is credited with generating increased acclaim for Leiwen and its leading site, Laurentiuslay, following a series of impressive wines in the late 1980s. The estate dates back to 1624 and is located in the tight horseshoe bend of the Mosel between Leiwen and Trittenheim. 11 ha of vineyards include the top sites of Trittenheimer Apotheke and Piesporter Goldtröpfchen. The wines have ample ripe fruit and excellent structure too, the exotic richness in the sweeter styles well checked by balancing acidity. Grans' efforts received further endorsement in 2001 with membership of the VDP.

Recommended Whites:
Leiwener Laurentiuslay Riesling Eiswein ★★★★ £H
Leiwener Laurentiuslay Riesling Spätlese ★★ 'S' £C
Trittenheimer Apotheke Riesling Beerenauslese ★★★★ £H
Trittenheimer Apotheke Riesling Auslese ★★★ £E
Trittenheimer Apotheke Riesling Spätlese ★★ £D
Piesporter Goldtröpfchen Riesling Auslese ★★★ £E
Piesporter Goldtröpfchen Riesling Spätlese ★★ £D

❀ Gunderloch (Rheinhessen) *www.gunderloch.de*
Fritz and Agnes Hasselbach's 14 ha of vineyards are steeply sloping and well protected. The famed Rothenberg site with its distinctive red slaty soils is as steep as some of those on the Mosel and produces some of the richest, most intense Rieslings in Germany. There is an explosive richness of fruit at Spätlese level with ever-increasing intensity, power and structure at higher levels of ripeness. The wines are also generally very well balanced, enabling them to be drunk fairly young, though most should be kept for 5 years or considerably longer. A little wine is also made from the Niersteiner Oelberg and Niersteiner Pettenthal sites. Drei Sterne Auslese is a good example of characterful Trocken style Auslese, while Jean-Baptiste is an off-dry Kabinett estate wine. Newish Red Stone Riesling is a light, racy, commercial example.

Recommended Whites:
Nackenheimer Rothenberg Riesling Beerenauslese ✪✪✪✪✪ £H
Nackenheimer Rothenberg Riesling Auslese Goldkapsel ★★★★★ £F
Nackenheimer Rothenberg Riesling Auslese ★★★★ £E
Nackenheimer Rothenberg Riesling Auslese 3 Sterne ★★★ £E
Nackenheimer Rothenberg Riesling Spätlese ★★★ £D
Nackenheimer Rothenberg Riesling Kabinett ★★ £C
Jean Baptiste Riesling Kabinett ★★ £C   Red Stone Riesling QbA ★ £B

❀ Weingut Fritz Haag (Mittel Mosel) *www.weingut-fritz-haag.de*
This historic estate known as Dusemonder Hof of 14 ha produces some of the finest, most elegant Rieslings in the Mosel from the heart of its one of its greatest sites, Brauneberger Juffer-Sonnenuhr. The village of Dusemond was only renamed Brauneberg in 1925 due to the fame of its vineyards. Wilhelm Haag is not only one of the region's leading winemakers but also a leader in promoting quality throughout the region. A seamless succession seems assured as his highly competent winemaker son Oliver Haag, who revitalised production at WEGELER, assumed control in 2005. The wines start out very taut and concentrated with a remarkably fine, minerally intensity and gradually open out with age. There is increasing weight and richness in Spätlese level and higher, culminating sometimes in a small amount of Beerenauslese or TBA. Bottlings of Spätlese wines and higher from individual numbered casks are also made and prices vary according to the considered quality of each. A cool, floral, appley QbA is a decent basic. Oliver's brother Thomas makes excellent wines at SCHLOSS LIESER.

Recommended Whites:
Brauneberger Juffer-Sonnenuhr Riesling Aus. Goldkapsel ✪✪✪✪✪ £G
Brauneberger Juffer-Sonnenuhr Riesling Auslese ★★★★★ £F
Brauneberger Juffer-Sonnenuhr Riesling Spätlese ★★★★ £E
Brauneberger Juffer Riesling Spätlese ★★★☆ £D
Brauneberger Juffer Riesling Kabinett ★★☆ £C
Riesling QbA ★☆ £B

Weingut Willi Haag (Mittel Mosel) *www.willi-haag.de*
This, at 6 ha the smaller of the two Haag estates, doesn't enjoy the same reputation as that of Wilhelm Haag (Fritz HAAG). It has been under the direction of Marcus Haag for the past decade, whose father Dieter received part of the family estate when it was split back in the early 60s, and some good wines have emerged from the run of recent good vintages. More of the wines come from the heavier, less slaty soils of Juffer as opposed to Juffer-Sonnenuhr. There isn't the purity of those from Wilhelm Haag nor the individuality of those from Theo Haart (Rheinhold HAART) yet there has lately been good ripeness, intensity and balance in most of the wines. The quality of Brauneberger Juffer and more especially Juffer-Sonnenuhr site does come through if sometimes wanting more better definition and detail. Drier styles are decent while at riper levels (Spätlese and higher) there is plenty of substance and style.

Recommended Whites:
Brauneberger Juffer Riesling Beerenauslese ★★★★ £F
Brauneberger Juffer Riesling Auslese ★★★ £D
Brauneberger Juffer Riesling Spätlese ★★☆ £C
Brauneberger Juffer Riesling Spätlese Halbtrocken ★★ £C
Brauneberger Juffer Riesling Kabinett ★☆ £C
Brauneberger Juffer-Sonnenuhr Riesling Auslese ★★★★ £E
Brauneberger Juffer-Sonnenuhr Riesling Spätlese ★★★☆ £C

Weingut Reinhold Haart (Mittel Mosel) *www.haart.de*
This small 7.5 ha estate is centred on Piesporter Goldtröpfchen, one of the great sites of the Mittel Mosel. Piesport, a name shamelessly debased by commercial exploitation in the latter half of the 20th century, actually played an important part in the propagation of Riesling in preference to lesser varieties in the 18th century. Theo Haart's wines are made naturally without any overarching style imposition, maximising quality in the context of the vintage and by reducing yields. The intensely blackcurrant fruit is characteristic, so too is a profusion of peach, apricot and citrus in many Spätlese and Auslese wines as well as exotic fruits in the sweetest styles. It is this flavour and intensity that marks out the wines' quality, supported by a subtle minerality and perfectly balanced acidity. Other sites such as Dronhofberger give cooler green apple and citrus flavours but share this intensity. Wintrich Ohligsberg (which like Goldtröpfchen qualifies as Erste Lage) offers spice and ripe peach at the Auslese level. The true potential of these wines is only revealed with age. Some Goldkapsel bottlings are made as are a little Beerenauslese or TBA, though the last can be difficult to obtain as they are usually set aside as Versteigerungswein (wines for auction). There are also two Grosses Gewächs dry wines; the Ohligsberg is sharper than the fuller Goldtröpchen. Haart to Heart is a light attractive quaffing Riesling.

Recommended Whites:
Piesporter Goldtröpfchen Riesling Auslese Erste Lage ★★★★ £E
Piesporter Goldtröpfchen Riesling Spätlese Erste Lage ★★★☆ £C
Piesporter Goldtröpfchen Riesling Kabinett Erste Lage ★★ £B
Piesporter Domherr Riesling Auslese ★★★★ £D
Piesporter Domherr Riesling Spätlese ★★★☆ £C
Piesporter Grafenberg Riesling Spätlese ★★★ £C

Wintricher Ohligsberg Riesling Auslese Erste Lage ★★★ £C
Dhron Hofberger Riesling Spätlese ★★ £C

Dr Heger (Baden) *www.heger-weine.de*
As with many Baden estates, much of what is produced here (20 ha) is based on the three Pinots, but a quarter of the plantings are Riesling. All the Dr Heger wines come from two very good sites, the loess soils of Ihringer Winkelberg and the volcanic soils of Achkarrer Schlossberg, both in the Kaiserstuhl. Fine, ripe, oak-infused Spätburgunders come from both sites as does another example, Mimus (named for Joachim's father). The top examples of Weissburgunder and Grauburgunder are rich, full and generally well balanced. Riesling from old vines on Achkarrer Schlossberg is ripe and intense but can lack subtlety and nuance. Muskateller and Gewürztraminer at Auslese level are in a similar vein with impressive flavour and balance, just wanting a little more elegance to be really fine. A second range of wines is made under the Weinhaus Joachim Heger label.

Recommended Reds:
Ihringer Winklerberg Spätburgunder 3 Sterne ★★★ £F
Mimus Spätburgunder ★★★ £E   Spätburgunder QbA ★ £C

Recommended Whites:
Ihringer Winklerberg Gewürztraminer Auslese ★★★ £E
Ihringer Winklerberg Muskateller Auslese ★★★ £E
Ihringer Winklerberg Weissburgunder GG 3 sterne ★★ £E
Achkarrer Schlossberg Riesling GG 3 sterne ★★ £E

Prinz von Hessen (Rheingau) *www.prinz-von-hessen.com*
One of several improving domaines in the Rheingau. Following much investment in renewing the cellars, including direction for a time from Markus Sieben, much more has been made of the potential of 33 ha of vineyards. Sweet styles are now very good indeed and progress can also be seen in several of the drier styles, with better richness and texture in the Erste Lage (Erstes Gewächs) The wines are increasingly showing both the texture and structure and the ripe fruit that are sadly rarer than they should be in the Rheingau. The gentle spice and concentrated very ripe fruit in the sweeter styles of Johannisberger Klaus is particularly captivating. A little red Frühburgunder (a strain of Pinot Noir) is also made.

Recommended Whites:
Johannisberger Klaus Riesling Beerenauslese ★★★★ £G
Johannisberger Klaus Riesling Auslese ★★★ £E
Johannisberger Klaus Riesling Erstes Gewächs ★★★ £C
Johannisberger Klaus Riesling Kabinett ★ £B
Winkeler Hasensprung Riesling Erstes Gewächs ★★ £C
Winkeler Jesuitengarten Riesling Erstes Gewächs ★★ £C

Heyl zu Herrnsheim (Rheinhessen) *www.heyl-zu-herrnsheim.de*
Nierstein has few estates of real quality but the Rieslings produced here in recent vintages under the direction of winemaker FelixPeters gives a real lead to others in the area. The 12 ha of vineyards encompass all the top sites between Nierstein and Nackenheim, including sole ownership of the small Brudersberg site. All the wines are much improved but riper styles of the vineyard-designated examples (Brudersberg, Oelberg and Pettenthal) show the most emphatic progress, with greater depth and intensity. These are sweet, intense and concentrated wines with ripe fruit in the finish. Niersteiner Pettenthal Erste Lage (Grosses Gewächs, GG) can be minerally, dry and rather austere but is intense, concentrated with an exotic exuberance. Above the basic estate bottlings of Riesling, Weisser Burgunder and Silvaner are superior Rotschiefer versions that come only from the red slate soils. A little Beerenauslese and TBA from the Pettenthal and Brudersberg sites are also made.

Recommended Whites:
Niersteiner Oelberg Riesling Auslese Goldkapsel ★★★★ £F
Niesteiner Brudersberg Riesling Auslese ★★★ £F
Niersteiner Pettenthal Riesling Auslese ★★★ £E
Niersteiner Pettenthal Riesling Trocken GG ★★★ £D
Niersteiner Pettenthal Riesling Spätlese ★★ £C
Riesling Trocken Rotschiefer ★★ £C   Riesling Kabinett Feinherb ★ £B
Weisser Burgunder Trocken Rotschiefer ★★ £C

✿ Heymann-Löwenstein (Terrassenmosel) *www.hlweb.de*
Reinhard Löwenstein's 15 ha of vineyard cling to extremely steep terraces in the Terrassenmosel, only a short distance from Koblenz and the juncture of the Mosel with the Rhine. He makes some magnificent dry wines from stone walled slopes perfectly angled to the low sun. The atypically warm mesoclimate combines with a long ripening season and low yields to produce excellent fruit. The slate soils are distinct from those in the Mittel Mosel and the resulting wines are a very different expression of the Mosel too. They tend to be either fermented to dryness or made in more fully sweet styles (Auslese and above), though the winemaking approach is very 'hands-off'. Sweet wines show exquisite fruit and definition. The Erste Lage wines from parcels of vines within Winninger Uhlen deliver intense, mineral elegance in the Laubach, more depth and weight in Roth Lay and cooler promise in Blaufüsser Lay. The length of flavour and complexity in all three is most impressive. Of other names used that don't refer to a vineyard site, Schieferterrassen indicates a vineyard blend while a vom Blauem Schiefer Riesling comes from a different 'blue' type of slate within Uhlen.

Recommended Whites:
Schieferterrassen Riesling Eiswein ★★★★★ £H
Winninger Uhlen Riesling 'Roth Lay' Auslese ★★★★ £F
Winninger Uhlen Riesling 'Blaufüsser Lay' Erste Lage ★★★ £D
Winninger Uhlen Riesling 'Laubach' Erste Lage ★★★ £D
Winninger Uhlen Riesling 'Roth Lay' Erste Lage ★★★ £D
Winninger Rottgen Riesling Auslese ★★★ £F
Winninger Rottgen Riesling ★★★ £D
Hatzenporter Kirchberg Riesling ★★ £C
Vom Blauem Schiefer Riesling ★★ £C
Schieferterrassen Riesling ★ £C

✿ Weingut von Hövel (Saar) *www.weingut-vonhoevel.de*
One of the Saar's long-established estates (11 ha), von Hövel is of monastic origins. Most wines come from the excellent Scharzhofberg or Oberemmeler Hütte sites – the latter is an Alleinbesitz (sole ownership). The wines (100% Riesling) have long been good but have sometimes been too marked by sulphur or other 'off ' odours. However this seems much less of a problem than previously and there is real intensity to the fruit from a lemony Kabinett to nectarine in the riper styles. There is a pure, racy quality to the Scharzhofberger Auslese and terrific intensity allied to excellent definition in the supremely pure, intense, long and honeyed Lange Goldkapsel Oberemeler Hütte. Even the light, basic, off-dry QbA is well balanced with surprising length of flavour.

Recommended Whites:
Oberemmeler Hütte Riesling Auslese Lange Goldkapsel ★★★★★ £F
Oberemmeler Hütte Riesling Auslese ★★★☆ £E
Oberemmeler Hütte Riesling Spätlese ★★☆ £C
Oberemmeler Hütte Riesling Kabinett ★★ £C
Scharzhofberger Riesling Auslese ★★★ £D

Scharzhofberger Riesling Spätlese ★★☆ £C
Riesling Balduin von Hövel QbA ★ £B

Bernhard Huber (Baden) *www.weingut-huber.com*
This is a 28 ha estate in the Kaiserstuhl with well-established vineyards (65% Pinot Noir) that has been producing its own wines since the late 80s. Previous tastings of the top wines have found them to be too overblown and oaky, especially in Chardonnay and Pinot Noir;they are still ripe, full, concentrated and toasty but also better balanced.Indeed, a number are now excellent to outstanding. Four different Pinot Noirs go from Junge Reben (young vines) through Malterdinger Bienenberg to Alte Reben (old vines) and then the top bottling, 'R'. This is from low-yielding 40-year-old vines and spends 18 months in new oak. Weissburgunder and Muskateller are also good, intense and expressive if not showing the refinement found in the best from Alsace. Most wines drink well with 2–3 years' age but the best Pinot Noirs will improve for twice as long.
Recommended Reds:
Spätburgunder 'R' ★★★ £E
Malterdinger Bienenberg Spätburgunder GG ★★ £C
Recommended Whites:
Chardonnay 'R' ★★★ £E Chardonnay Qualitätswein ★★ £D
Malterdinger Bienenberg Weissburgunder GG ★★ £B
Malterdinger Bienenberg Muskateller ★★ £B

Weingut Karl H Johner (Baden) *www.johner.de*
Situated in the Kaiserstuhl, with volcanic soil mixed with clay, Johner is notable amongst German winemakers because all of the wines produced on their 17 ha estate, including the most expensive, are bottled under screwcap. They began bottling with screwcap in 2003, moving fully to it with the 2004 vintage; as a result, some custom was lost, but they are convinced that opinion is swinging around. Meanwhile, they experiment to develop ways of modifying wine-making techniques to exploit the possibilities of screwcap. The family also have a wine estate in New Zealand (the NZ wines are available at the winery), encouraging the transmission of approach and technique, and some, although not all, of their wines have a New World style. Many are high in alcohol – the majority of the twenty-two tasted came in at 14% or higher – but Patrick Johner maintains that wine with that level of alcohol will thrive under screwcap. He argues that high alcohol in a wine can be coped with if the structure is good, but with ageing under cork, the fruit normally declines; however, under screwcap, the fruit and structure are preserved and thus keep the alcohol in line. The tannin matures more slowly, so the red wines can be too tough during the first couple of years. The Merlot has barrel ageing for well over two years before bottling, to try to soften the tannins; some fruit is sacrificed, but there is still a good deal, with a lot of spice. One way they develop their richer wines is to harvest when the bunches are mixed in size, so that the fruitier grapes and the more acidic ones together provide balance. The wines have lovely noses, and can be very fresh; indeed, the Sauvignon Blanc has an incredibly intense nose. The Weissburgunder SJ has a creamy nose and lovely length, whilst the Grauburgunder SJ is big and rich, but with very good acid. The remarkably inexpensive Spätburgunder von Kaiserstuhl has lots of fruit and balancing acid. (KB)
Recommended Reds:
Bischoffinger Steinbuck Pinot Noir ★★★ £E
Blauer Spätburgunder ★★ £D Spätburgunder vom Kaiserstuhl ★ £B
Recommended Whites:
Grauer Burgunder SJ ★★★ £E Sauvignon Blanc ★★ £C

Weingut Toni Jost (Mittelrhein) *www.tonijost.de*
Peter Jost has almost 15 ha of vineyards, with the majority of the wines coming from Bacharacher Hahn, the region's leading site. The wines are typically perfumed, citrus and zingy, adding riper peach and apricot flavours in the sweet styles. A basic Riesling Trocken can be a little lean; the Kabinett is usually riper and with better intensity and a little sweetness. Spätlese and Auslese show intense, mineral and floral characters, with increased sweetness though not the extra depth and concentration expected at these levels of ripeness. A Beerenauslese, however, is typically very ripe, with an accentuated botrytis character and good balance between intense, sweet fruit and a vibrant acidity that ensures long ageing. A little wine is also made from the Rheingau as is some Spätburgunder. Recent vintages lack the poise and definition that were once the hallmarks of these wines.
Recommended Whites:
Bacharacher Hahn Riesling Beerenauslese ★★★★ £H
Bacharacher Hahn Riesling Auslese ★★★ £E
Bacharacher Hahn Riesling Spätlese ★★ £C
Bacharacher Hahn Riesling Kabinett ★ £B

Juliusspital (Franken) *www.juliusspital.de*
Founded in 1576, the hospice of Juliusspital has a long history of wine production as well as care for the needy. With 172 ha of vines, production is not insubstantial. Of the most interest are the top Spätlese wines from some of Franken's best sites. These are elegant and refined, with good definition that lets the fruit sing out with a little bottle-age. The Silvaner and Riesling are bottled in the distinctive dark green Bocksbeutel bottles. Volkacher Karthäuser Weisser Burgunder is bottled in a Burgundy-type bottle and the light touch employed in the winemaking shows just how well this grape (Pinot Blanc) can perform here. The Wurzburger Stein Riesling Grosses Gewächs has also emerged as one of the very best examples of the style in the region. As well as those rated below, good wines are made from other top sites such as Randersackerer Pfülben and Escherndorfer Lump.
Recommended Whites:
Würzburger Stein Riesling Grosses Gewächs ★★★★ £E
Würzburger Stein Riesling Spätlese Trocken ★★★ £D
Iphöfer Julius-Echter-Berg Riesling Spätlese Trocken ★★ £D
Würzburger Stein Rieslaner Auslese ★★★ £E
Volkacher Karthäuser Weisser Burgunder Spätlese Trocken ★★ £D
Würzburger Stein Silvaner Spätlese Trocken ★★ £C
Würzburger Innere Leiste Silvaner Spätlese Trocken ★★ £C
Iphöfer Julius-Echter-Berg Silvaner Spätlese Trocken ★★ £C

❀ Karlsmühle (Ruwer) *www.karlsmuehle.com*
Peter Geiben's 14.5 ha of vineyards are spread over some excellent Ruwer sites, namely those in Lorenzhöf (Felsay and Mäuerchen) and Kasel (Nies'chen and Kehrnagel). The wine quality since the late 1990s puts him among the best growers in the Mosel-Saar-Ruwer. The wines have excellent ripeness (in a cool, mineral, citrus/apple vein) and intensity, ranging from the light, stylish and fruit-intense Mäuerchen Kabinett to sweet, concentrated and elegant Nies'chen Auslese. An incredibly sweet and tangy Eiswein, the Kehrnagel, has smoky, spicy, mineral and honeyed aromas and dried fruit flavours, deserving plenty of age. All the wines are extremely well priced for the quality.
Recommended Whites:
Kaseler Kehrnagel Eiswein★★★★★ £H
Lorenzhöfer Riesling Eiswein★★★★ £G

Germany

Lorenzhöfer Riesling Auslese Goldkapsel ★★★ £E
Lorenzhöfer Riesling Spätlese ★★ £B
Lorenzhöfer Mäuerchen Riesling Kabinett ★★ £B
Kaseler Nies'chen Riesling Auslese Lange Goldkapsel ★★★★ £F
Kaseler Nies'chen Riesling Spätlese ★★★ £B

❀ Weingut Karthäuserhof (Ruwer) *www.karthaeuserhof.com*
Christoph Tyrell's historic Ruwer estate is one of the great names
of the Mosel-Saar-Ruwer. The 19 ha of vineyards are based on the
famous Eitelsbacher Karthäuserhofberg site, which produces vivid,
intense, elegant expressions of Riesling. Ludwig Breiling has made
the wines in recent vintages and a very high quality standard has
been set. Flavours range from apple, white peach, blackcurrant,
citrus and mineral in Kabinett and Spätlese (usually produced in a
Trocken or Feinherb version as well) to nectarine, peach and exotic
fruits in Auslese and Eiswein. The latter show marvellous richness as
well as the same vibrant acidity and long finish seen in all the wines.
In any given vintage 4- to 5-star bottlings of Auslese from individual
numbered casks can be superb, their purity and class are apparent
even when starting out intense and closed. QbA Riesling has decent
weight and flavour and a dry Weissburgunder is also made.

Recommended Whites:
Eitelsbacher Karthäuserhofberg Eiswein ✪✪✪✪ £H
Eitelsbacher Karthäuserhofberg Riesling Auslese ★★★☆ £E
Eitelsbacher Karthäuserhofberg Riesling Spätlese ★★★ £D
Eitelsbacher Karthäuserhofberg Riesling Spätlese Trocken ★★☆ £D
Eitelsbacher Karthäuserhofberg Riesling Kabinett ★★ £C
Eitelsbacher Karthäuserhofberg Riesling QbA ★ £B

Wgt. Franz Keller Schwarzer Adler (Baden) *www.franz-keller.de*
This neighbourhood of the Kaiserstuhl is home to several excellent
producers, of which Weingut Franz Keller is one. It forms part of an
organisation which includes a wine import company, a Michelin-
starred restaurant and a lovely small hotel. Indeed, the initial
purchase of 5 ha of vineyard (there are now 48 ha) was made purely
in order to produce wine for the restaurant, which itself is over a
century old. Possibly as a consequence, the winery concentrates on
making wines which pair well with food. Franz Keller, who died in
2007 at the age of 80, was an important pioneer in Germany of fully-
fermented dry wines and the use of *barriques*. The wine used to
be made on the site behind the hotel, with the barrels being rolled
across the road to the tunnels used for ageing and storage, and
which extend 150 meters into the hill. From the summer of 2012,
however, wine production has moved a kilometre away to a large,
customer-friendly, purpose-built winery and wine centre. They grow
a wide range of grape varieties: more than half of the vineyards are
planted with Grauburgunder (Pinot Gris) and Spätburgunder (Pinot
Noir), with the remainder made up of Weissburgunder (Pinot Blanc),
Müller-Thurgau, Silvaner, Gewürztraminer, Chardonnay, Riesling,
Sauvignon Blanc, Merlot, Cabernet Sauvignon and Lemburger. There
are six vineyards, which can be, very roughly, divided between those
which are dominated by volcanic soils, which produce wines of
great minerality, and those which are primarily loess, which produce
fruitier wines: Achkarrer Schlossberg and Oberbergener Pulverbuck
are primarily volcanic, whilst Oberbergener Basgeige, which can be
seen from the back of the hotel, is primarily loess – although they all
have patches of the other type. Organic fertilisers are used, green
harvest and the halving of bunches are utilised, and the grapes are
picked manually. Depending on the vineyard and the grapes, both
stainless steel and oak are used for vinification and ageing. The
Spätburgunders are especially good, being concentrated, juicy, and

elegant, with the premium Grauburgunder, Weissburgunder and
Chardonnay not far behind. Their entry-level wines can be intensely
flavourful and very good value. It is notable that the labels of their
top wines often do not include the vineyards. (KB)

Recommended Reds:
Spätburgunder 'A' trocken ★★★☆ £E
Spätburgunder 'S' trocken ★★★ £E

Recommended Whites:
Chardonnay 'S' trocken ★★★ £D   Weissburgunder 'A' trocken ★★ £E
Weissburgunder trocken ★ £B
Oberbergener Bassgeige Grauburgunder Trocken ★ £B

❀ Weingut Keller (Rheinhessen) *www.keller-wein.de*
Away from the Rheinterrassen (the steep slopes between
Oppenheim and Nackenheim), the Rheinhessen doesn't have that
much to offer, yet Klaus Keller and his son Klaus-Peter are showing
that outstanding wines are possible in the hilly countryside around
Flörsheim-Dalsheim, where they have 15.8 ha, almost half planted to
Riesling but a quarter to Weissburgunder and Grauburgunder. They
produce some fine dry wines but better still are the marvellously
exuberant sweeter styles with scintillating fruit richness and
excellent balance and length of flavour. There is not perhaps the
sheer class or elegance that more northern sites can bring but
the rich, exotic fruit intensity is hard to resist. As well as very small
amounts of outstanding TBA, some Spätburgunder is made. All the
better wines deserve some age and will keep for a decade.

Recommended Whites:
Dalsheimer Hubacker Riesling Auslese 3 Sterne ★★★★ £G
Dalsheimer Hubacker Riesling Auslese ★★★ £F
Dalsheimer Hubacker Riesling Spätlese ★★ £C
Dalsheimer Hubacker Riesling Spätlese Trocken ★★ £C
Dalsheimer Hubacker Riesling Kabinett Trocken ★ £B

August Kesseler (Rheingau) *www.august-kesseler.de*
At the end of the Rheingau around Assmannshausen Pinot Noir is
as important as Riesling, especially in August Kesseler's vineyards
where about 45% of his 23 ha are planted to it. Drawing on top
sites including Assmannhäuser Höllenberg and Rüdesheimer Berg
Schlossberg, intense concentrated Spätburgunder is produced with
a much better fruit spectrum than in many German examples. These
wines are comparable to good if not great Burgundy and something
of the *terroir* also comes through, if less so initially in the new-oaked
vineyard-designated versions. Riesling has depth and intensity and
the class of Berg Schlossberg and Berg Roseneck come through
particularly at Spätlese level. Berg Schlossberg is also his best site
for dry, mineral and intense Rieslings. This is unquestionably a
high-quality estate; the only problem is the prices. Astronomical
tags on the tiny amounts of Beerenauslese and TBA are somewhat
understandable but for the Spätburgunders? It's not even that far to
drive to Burgundy.

Recommended Reds:
Assmannshäuser Höllenberg Spätlese 1 Stern ★★★ £F
Cuvée Max Spätlese ★★ £E

Recommended Whites:
Rüdesheimer Bischofberg Auslese Goldkapsel ★★★ £F
Rüdesheimer Bischofberg Riesling Kabinett ★ £B
Rüdesheimer Berg Schlossberg Riesling Spätlese Trocken ★★★ £D
Rüdesheimer Berg Schlossberg Spätlese Goldkapsel ★★★ £D
Rüdesheimer Berg Roseneck Spätlese Goldkapsel ★★★ £D
Rüdesheimer Berg Roseneck Riesling Spätlese Trocken ★★ £D
Lorcher Schlossberg Riesling Kabinett ★★ £C

Reichsraf von Kesselstatt (Mosel) *www.kesselstatt.com*
The Günter Reh family possess 35 ha of vineyard land in the Mosel, all of it planted to Riesling and much of it in leading sites. Yields are moderate and the aim is for natural, unmanipulated wines. Fermentation is in stainless steel with extended ageing on the fine lees. Typically the wines are properly ripe and clean with fruit emphasised and good acid balance, though sulphur levels can detract from the wines. At their best they also reflect something of their origins if not necessarily competing with the top examples from a given site. Those rated below include wines from most but not all the famous sites that are regularly made. The top Grosses Gewächs sites are among the most convincing dry wines of the region and preserve a fruit richness to balance the acidity. There are several more good wines besides, though 'RK' Riesling and new dry Palais Kesselstatt Riesling are not amongst them.

Recommended Whites:
Scharzhofberger Riesling Eiswein ★★★★ £G
Scharzhofberger Riesling Spätlese Lange Goldkapsel ★★★ £E
Kaseler Nies'chen Riesling Eiswein ★★★★ £G
Kaseler Nies'chen Riesling Riesling Spätlese ★★ £C
Kaseler Nies'chen Riesling Kabinett ★ £B
Piesporter Goldtröpfchen Riesling Auslese ★★★ £E
Piesporter Goldtröpfchen Riesling Spätlese ★★★ £D
Josephöfer Riesling Spätlese ★★ £C Josephöfer Riesling Kabinett ★ £B
Graacher Domprobst Riesling Spätlese ★★ £C

Knipser (Pfalz) *www.weingut-knipser.de*
This estate is not quite what you might expect. There is top-quality Riesling but also a lot of red wine from 40 ha of vineyards – and not just Spätburgunder, the most planted variety, but also St-Laurent, Dornfelder, Cabernet Sauvignon, Merlot and Cabernet Franc. The latter three make up 'X' which spends 2 years in new oak, resulting in a cool, elegant and cedary but Bordeaux-like effort at its best. Spätburgunder and St-Laurent can also be good but the latter in particular doesn't have the depth or richness to match the oak treatment. In Cuvée Gaudenz, the Bordeaux varieties are complemented by Dornfelder, making a reasonable quaffer but overly light. However, the Riesling Spätlese from the best sites are really fine – intense, vibrant and concentrated. The yields are distinctly lower for the Steinbuckel example from Laumersheimer Mandelberg. A good unoaked blend of Chardonnay and Weissburgunder with pure peachy fruit is also produced, as is a little TBA.

Recommended Reds:
Cuvée X ★★★ £E
Grosskarlbacher Burgweg St-Laurent Trocken ★★ £D
Grosskarlbacher Burgweg Spätburgunder Spätlese ★★ £D

Recommended Whites:
Laumersheimer 'Steinbuckel' Mandelberg Riesling GG ★★★★ £D
Dirmsteiner 'Himmelsrech' Mandelpfad Riesling GG ★★★ £D
Sommersheimer Kappellenberg Riesling Spätlese ★★★ £C

✿ Koehler-Ruprecht (Pfalz) *www.koehler-ruprecht.com*
The predisposition here is for dry wines with good structure. With only a little more than half the 10 ha estate planted to Riesling there are also examples of Pinot Blanc, Pinot Gris, Chardonnay and Pinot Noir. Barrel fermented versions of the whites are labelled 'Philippi'. All show good ripeness, usually with integrated lees and oak character. Pinot Noir can be particularly good in the warmest vintages. Some Gewürztraminer and Scheurebe are also made but Riesling is once again the main attraction. It comes from the very good Kallstadter

Saumagen site where limestone soils give vigorous, ripe fruited and minerally examples. 'R' bottlings are particularly good with added concentration and character, usually with a spicy botrytis influence. After a delayed release 'R' wines will continue to age superbly. Generally speaking, all the Rieslings age very well (losing any youthful reductive aromas) though there have been occasional exceptions. Bernd Philippi is also a partner in the Douro estate QUINTA DA CARVALHOSA.

Recommended Reds:
Pinot Noir Philippi 'R' ★★★ £E   Pinot Noir Philippi ★★ £D
Recommended Whites:
Kallstadter Saumagen Riesling Eiswein ★★★★★ £G
Kallstadter Saumagen Riesling Auslese 'R' ★★★★ £E
Kallstadter Saumagen Auslese Trocken ★★★ £D
Kallstadter Saumagen Riesling Spätlese Trocken ★★ £C
Pinot Blanc Philippi ★★ £C   Chardonnay Philippi ★★ £C

Kruger-Rumpf (Nahe) *www.kruger-rumpf.com*
This estate of 21.5 ha offers good-value, attractive, well-made Riesling. The Dautenpflänzer is the best site and the dry, powerful and structured Erste Lage (Grosses Gewächs, GG) shows good ageing potential. Spätlese from the same site has refined, spicy, minerally fruit. Rieslings from Pittersberg, Kapellenberg and Rheinberg are also good if less stylish. Only the lesser of two Spätburgunders, 'M', has been tasted (the other is 'R'); though soundly made it needs a bit more stuffing. Basic examples of Riesling, Weissburgunder and Grauburgunder aren't bad.

Recommended Whites:
Münsterer Dautenpflänzer Riesling Auslese ★★★ £E
Münsterer Dautenpflänzer Riesling GG ★★★ £D
Münsterer Dautenpflänzer Riesling Spätlese ★★★ £C
Münsterer Dautenpflänzer Riesling Kabinett ★★ £B
Binger Scharlachberg Riesling Spätlese ★★★ £C
Münsterer Pittersberg Riesling Spätlese ★★ £B
Münsterer Rheinberg Riesling Kabinett ★★ £B
Münsterer Kapellenberg Riesling Kabinett ★★ £B
Grauburgunder Trocken ★ £B

Peter Jakob Kühn (Rheingau) *www.weingutpjkuehn.de*
Quality has been on the up and up here for the past decade and more and Peter Jakob Kühn now makes exemplary Rheingau Rieslings from his long-established family estate with 19ha of organically tended vineyards. Kühn's Oestrich Lenchen wines combine the richness of the Rheingau with the elegance of the Mosel. Off-dry Riesling Kabinett is one of the very best in Germany at this level, with beautifully defined fruit and bright but not harsh acidity. The Spätlese has exquisite sweet fruit and lovely balance, while the Auslese is very pure, concentrated, wonderfully poised and complex. Outstanding Beerenauslese with a waxy, honeyed quality and superb preserved-fruit and botrytis richness contrasts with a vibrant, very sweet, but less rich or complex Eiswein. Doosberg provides complex, expressive, minerally dry wines. All the wines deserve some age and the sweeter styles should have at least 5 years. Some Spätburgunder is also made. The debate surrounding closures is also having an impact in Germany. While the Stelvin cap is now increasingly widely used Peter Jakob Kühn has bottled some of his wines under a 'crown seal' in order to eliminate taint of any kind.

Recommended Whites:
Oestricher Lenchen Riesling Beerenauslese ★★★★★ £H
Oestricher Lenchen Riesling Eiswein ★★★★ £H

Germany

Oestricher Lenchen Riesling Auslese ★★★★ £F
Oestricher Lenchen Riesling Spätlese★★★ £D
Oestricher Lenchen Riesling Kabinett★★★ £C
Oestricher Doosberg Riesling Erste Lage★★★ £D
Oestricher Doosberg Riesling Zwei Trauben QbA★★ £C

Franz Künstler (Rheingau) *www.weingut-kuenstler.de*
Since the mid-1990s Gunter Künstler has been able to draw upon extensive vineyards spread over the Hochheim slopes, having added those of the Aschrott estate to an existing estate first established by his father in 1965. The 36 ha include the top sites of Hochheimer Hölle, Kirchenstück and Domdechaney. The more traditionally made wines, such as a fine Kirchenstück Spätlese, show wonderful peach and nectarine richness, well checked by good acidity. Gunter Künstler has also made a feature of producing completely dry wines from an Auslese level of ripeness, with a powerful honeyed Kirchenstück and a splendidly complex, ripe and distinctive Hölle version. A characterful, weighty example from the Stielweg vineyard shows a coarser, botrytised influence and is not as convincing. Non-dry examples of Auslese, such as that from Domdechaney show lovely fruit richness and depth. There's also very sweet, deep, rich Beerenauslese and TBA. Other wines include a stylish, elegant if oaky cherry-fruited Pinot Noir (Spätburgunder) Auslese, its price presumably pushed up by local demand, and an attractive sparkling wine, Non Plus Cuvée M (Pinot Noir/Chardonnay), in which the strawberry, cherry notes of Pinot dominate.
Recommended Reds:
Pinot Noir Auslese ★★ £F
Recommended Whites:
Hochheimer Hölle Riesling TBA ★★★★★ £H
Hochheimer Hölle Riesling Beerenauslese ★★★★ £H
Hochheimer Hölle Riesling Auslese Trocken ★★★ £E
Hochheimer Hölle Riesling Spätlese Trocken ★★ £D
Hochheimer Kirchenstück Riesling TBA ★★★★★ £H
Hochheimer Kirchenstück Riesling Auslese Trocken ★★★ £E
Hochheimer Kirchenstück Riesling Spätlese ★★★ £D
Hochheimer Domdechaney Riesling Auslese ★★★ £E
Hochheimer Stielweg Riesling Auslese Trocken ★★ £E
Hochheimer Reichstal Riesling Kabinett ★★ £C

✿ Sybille Kuntz (Mittel Mosel) *www.sybillekuntz.de*
This small estate of 10 ha run by Sybille Kuntz and her husband is a rising star in the Mosel. The vineyards are well established, primarily in Lieser Niederberg-Helden, and the focus is on dry wines. A regular bottling is surpassed by Gold-Quadrat and Dreistern. The latter has unusual breadth and depth for dry Mosel Riesling as well as a stylish mineral, herb and citrus character. While these wines are not in the classic Mosel mould, optimal ripeness is sought from the old vines and they do seem to work; the claim to be good food wines seems justified too. Even an Auslese Goldkapsel is produced in a Halb-Trocken style. At the other end of the sweetness spectrum there are small quantities of fine Beerenauslese and very sweet, very intensely flavoured TBA. Occasionally sulphur levels detract in some of the wines but this should be less of a problem with age.
Recommended Whites:
Lieser Niederberg Helden Riesling TBA ★★★★ £H
Lieser Niederberg Helden Riesling Beerenauslese ★★★ £H
Lieser Niederberg Helden Riesling Auslese Halbtrocken ★★★ £E
Lieser Niederberg Helden Riesling Spätlese Trocken Dreistern ★★★ £E
Riesling Gold-Quadrat ★★ £D   Riesling Trocken ★★ £C

✿ Andreas Laible (Baden) *www.weingut-laible.de*
This relatively little-known (outside of Germany at any rate) producer makes wines of a quality unprecedented in the Ortenau area of Baden. From just 7.5 ha of vineyards there is consistently high quality, not just in Riesling (Klingelberger as it is called here) but also in Gewürztraminer and Scheurebe. All the wines come from the Durbacher Plauelrain site and the top examples have lovely concentrated, fruit, with depth, body and good acidity. The top wine is the Riesling Auslese Trocken, a rich, honeyed yet dry, concentrated and complex example with great length of flavour. A richer Achat bottling of Riesling Spätlese Trocken contrasts with a racier regular version that offers a cooler spectrum of fruit flavours. Gewürztraminer is lush, ripe and intense and there is a cocktail of fruit in a rich but well-balanced Scheurebe. Chardonnay, Grauburgunder and Spätburgunder are also made to a high standard.
Recommended Whites:
Durbacher Plauelrain Riesling Auslese Trocken ★★★★ £E
Durbacher Plauelrain Riesling Spätlese Trocken Achat★★★ £C
Durbacher Plauelrain Riesling Spätlese Trocken★★ £C
Durbacher Plauelrain Gewürztraminer Auslese★★★ £D
Durbacher Plauelrain Scheurebe Auslese★★★ £D

✿ Hans Lang (Rheingau) *www.weingut-hans-lang.de*
Johann Maximilian, who is also called Hans like his father who established the estate, has 20 ha of vineyards. He makes mostly Riesling from Hattenheim's top sites but also Weissburgunder and Spätburgunder. Quality at the basic level is sound but various special bottlings and Spätlese level and higher bring more concentration and style. A Charta bottling is good value. Vom Bunten Schiefer Riesling comes from a slaty site, reflected in a pure, minerally and concentrated wine. Erste Lage (Erstes Gewächs) is produced from both Hassel and Wisselbrunnen. The latter is powerful yet elegant, deserving of 5 years' age. Wisselbrunnen quality also shines through in Auslese and Eiswein examples. The regular version of Spätburgunder shows a bit too much extract and oak for the fruit quality.
Recommended Whites:
Hattenheimer Wisselbrunnen Riesling Eiswein ★★★★★ £G
Hattenheimer Wisselbrunnen Riesling Auslese ★★★★ £E
Hattenheimer Wisselbrunnen Riesling Erstes Gewächs ★★★★ £D
Hattenheimer Schutzenhaus Riesling Auslese ★★★ £D
Hattenheimer Hassel Riesling Spätlese ★★★ £C
Riesling vom Bunten Schiefer ★★★ £C
Riesling Johann Maximilian ★★ £B   Riesling Charta ★★ £B
Riesling Kabinett Trocken ★ £B   Weissburgunder Trocken ★ £B

✿ Langwerth von Simmern *www.langwerth-von-simmern.de*
The number of good estates in the Rheingau is on the increase and often, as here, it is due to the revival of a famous estate. Dating back to 1464, Langwerth von Simmern has enjoyed periods of much acclaim and quality has come roaring back in the last 10 years. The 31.5 ha of vineyards include many of the Rheingau's most outstanding sites. Even Kabinett-level wines show off the class of vineyards such as Rauenthaler Baiken, Hattenheimer Nussbrunnen and Erbacher Marcobrunn. The intensity, definition, vibrancy and splendid expression make for excellent drinking whether the wines are young or aged. A Blaukapsel (blue capsule) Riesling Spätlese is a special selection from Hattenheimer Mannberg (90% ownership) which is also the source of an Erste Lage (Erstes Gewächs) bottling.

Recommended Whites:
Hattenheimer Wisselbrunnen Riesling Beerenauslese ★★★★ £F
Hattenheimer Wisselbrunnen Riesling Spätlese ★★★ £C
Hattenheimer Nussbrunnen Riesling Auslese ★★★★ £E
Hattenheimer Nussbrunnen Riesling Kabinett ★★★ £B
Hattenheimer Mannberg Riesling Spätlese Blaukapsel ★★★★ £D
Rauenthaler Baiken Riesling Spätlese ★★★ £C
Rauenthaler Baiken Riesling Kabinett ★★ £B
Erbacher Marcobrunn Riesling Kabinett ★★★ £B
Riesling QbA ★★ £B

Weingut Josef Leitz (Rheingau) *www.leitz-wein.de*
With 41 ha of vines in some of Rudesheim's best vineyards,
Johannes Leitz is is developing into one of the Rheingau's more
important producers. The results of improved vineyard health
and more natural winemaking shine through in the wine quality.
Vineyards such as Berg Schlossberg particularly lend themselves
to the elegant, intense style of Rheingau Riesling he is making.
Quality runs throughout the many different bottlings produced
from ripe, attractive QbA or Kabinett examples to richer yet
elegant, ripe mineral, peach and apricot fruited Spätlese, Auslese
and Beerenauslese. Eiswein, such as that from Klosterberg, is tight,
intense and long. Prädikat styles produced from each site vary from
year to year.

Recommended Whites:
Rudesheimer Klosterberg Riesling Eiswein ★★★★ £H
Rudesheimer Drachenstein Riesling Beerenauslese ★★★★ £H
Rudesheimer Kirchenpfad Riesling Auslese ★★★★ £F
Rudesheimer Berg Roseneck Riesling Spätlese ★★★ £D
Rudesheimer Berg Roseneck Riesling Kabinett ★★ £B
Rudesheimer Berg Schlossberg Riesling Spätlese ★★★ £D
Rudesheimer Magdalenenkreuz Riesling Spätlese ★★ £C

❀ Carl Loewen (Mittel Mosel) *www.weingut-loewen.de*
Karl-Josef Loewen has been a champion of the very good
Laurentiuslay vineyard which lies at the heart of his 12 ha estate.
Here he produces Rieslings with lovely finesse and expression:
minerally and spicy with a suggestion of elderflower. They are also
characterised by excellent balance and length of flavour. Bottlings
from individually numbered casks can be exceptionally good.
Varidor is a dry generic Riesling while an Alte Reben (old vine)
version is also dry, if full and more New World-like. There is also a
bright intense fruit in the wines from the under-rated Thörnicher
Ritsch. When conditions permit he produces a splendid classy
Leiwener Klostergarten Eiswein, with an interplay of preserved citrus
and tropical fruit flavours. This, like all the wines, is very fairly priced.

Recommended Whites:
Leiwener Klostergarten Riesling Eiswein ★★★★★ £F
Leiwener Klostergarten Riesling Kabinett ★★ £C
Thörnicher Ritsch Riesling Auslese ★★★★ £C
Thörnicher Ritsch Riesling Spätlese ★★★ £C
Leiwener Laurentiuslay Riesling Spätlese ★★★ £C
Leiwener Laurentiuslay Riesling Auslese ★★★ £C

❀ Dr Loosen (Mittel Mosel) *www.drloosen.com*
Probably the best-known quality producer from the Mosel today,
Ernst Loosen has achieved a remarkable transformation in both
the quality and image of a 22 ha estate with some choice Mittel
Mosel plots. The approach is organic and non-interventionist and
the wines have lovely depth and intensity but also real elegance
and a distinctive expression of their origins. Whether the splendid

succulent fruit richness of Wehlener Sonnenuhr, the spice-lined
finesse of Ürziger Würzgarten or the more exotic class of Erdener
Prälat, there is excellent ripeness, definition and concentration
that owes much to old vines and low yields. Wines are also made
from the Erdener Treppchen and Graacher Himmelreich sites. All
the wines should be kept for at least 3–4 years, except perhaps
the widely seen Dr L, which can have good intensity and attractive
fruit. A little Beerenauslese and TBA is also made. Ernst Loosen also
produces excellent dry Rieslings at the J L WOLF estate, and another
(Eroica) in Washington State in conjunction with CH. STE MICHELLE.

Recommended Whites:
Bernkasteler Lay Riesling Eiswein ★★★★★ £H
Bernkasteler Lay Riesling Kabinett ★★☆ £C
Wehlener Sonnenuhr Riesling Auslese Goldkapsel ★★★★★ £F
Wehlener Sonnenuhr Riesling Auslese ★★★★ £E
Wehlener Sonnenuhr Riesling Spätlese ★★★ £D
Wehlener Sonnenuhr Riesling Kabinett ★★☆ £C
Erdener Prälat Riesling Auslese Goldkapsel ★★★★★ £F
Erdener Prälat Riesling Auslese ★★★★ £F
Erdener Treppchen Riesling Auslese ★★★★ £E
Erdener Treppchen Riesling Spätlese ★★★ £D
Erdener Treppchen Riesling Kabinett ★★☆ £C
Ürziger Würzgarten Riesling Auslese ★★★★ £E
Ürziger Würzgarten Riesling Spätlese ★★★ £D   Riesling Dr 'L' ★★☆ £B

Fürst Löwenstein (Franken & Rheingau) *www.loewenstein.de*
Fürst Löwenstein comprises two estates: 30 ha in Franken including
part of the imposing and historic terraced Kallmuth escarpment,
and also 22 ha in Rheingau that were leased for several years (until
1997) to Schloss Vollrads. Direction for both has come from Robert
Haller for the past decade and quality is now very good. In Franken,
the estate is one of a group of five called Trias (Triassic) committed
to making more of three distinct terroirs. Silvaner in the top version,
Asphodill (a Mediterranean plant rare in these parts), is ripe and
exotic with spicy, floral, earthy and minerally flavours. Coronilla, the
Riesling equivalent, is stylish, concentrated and more seductive.
Equally good is the classy Tradition which combines the two. The
Rheingau vineyards are centred on Hallgartner Schönhell and
Jungfer. Recent vintages show Riesling of good intensity and flavour
even at Kabinett level. The top Rheingau Spätburgunder, labelled
Pinot Noir, comes from French clones and is classy and Burgundian.
Sweet wines are also made – Beerenauslesen from Kallmuth and
TBA and Eiswein from the Rheingau – but have not been tasted.
Fürst Löwenstein also owns a Tokaji estate in Hungary..

Franken
Recommended Reds:
Bürgstadter Centgrafenberg Spätburgunder Auslese Trocken ★★ £E
Recommended Whites:
Homburger Kallmuth Riesling Spätlese Trocken GG Coronilla ★★★ £D
Homburger Kallmuth Silvaner Spätlese Trocken GG Asphodill ★★★ £D
Homburger Kallmuth Silvaner Kabinett Trocken ★★ £C
Silvaner Trocken ★ £B   Homburger Kallmuth Tradition ★★★ £C
CF Weissburgunder ★ £B

Rheingau
Recommended Reds:
Hallgarten Schönhell Pinot Noir Spätlese Trocken ★★★ £E
Hallgarten Schönhell Spätburgunder Spätlese Trocken ★★ £C
Hallgarten Schönhell Spätburgunder+Frühburgunder Trocken ★ £B
Recommended Whites:
Hallgarten Schönhell Riesling GG ★★★ £D

Germany

Hallgarten Jungfer Riesling Spätlese Trocken ★★ £C
Hallgarten Jungfer Riesling Kabinett Trocken ★★ £B

❀ Meyer-Näkel (Ahr) *www.meyer-naekel.de*

Arguably no producer in Germany has a higher reputation for red wine than Meyer-Näkel. With 15.2 ha, the wines include the very light, very cherryish QbA Trocken, the light, pure Blauschiefer (grown on blue slate) and classy, 'S' selection aged in used *barriques*. The top wines however are the single vineyard examples. Those tasted come from Dernauer Pfarrwingert (labelled Auslese Trocken) and Neuenahrer Sonnenberg (Erste Lage). Others come from Walporzheimer Kräuterberg. Top wines are aged in between 70% and 100% new oak. The more raspberryish and Volnay-like Pfarrwingert Frühburgunder ripens earlier and can show the better balance while the Pfarrwingert Spätburgunder has perhaps the greater potential complexity, but both are intense, deep and long. Best of all is the Sonnenberg Erste Lage which is very classy, complex and complete if not with the same mineral nuances of the very best Burgundies. The standard here is very high indeed but the wines shouldn't be rushed as there is greater fruit richness and better balance with oak and alcohol with increasing bottle age.

Recommended Reds:

Dernauer Pfarrwingert Spätburgunder GG ★★★★ £F
Dernauer Pfarrwingert Spätburgunder Auslese Trocken ★★★☆ £F
Neuernahrer Sonnenberg Spätburgunder Erste Lage ★★★★ £F
Spätburgunder Trocken Selection 'S' ★★★ £E
Spätburgunder Trocken Blauschiefer ★★ £D
Dernauer Pfarrwingert Frühburgunder Auslese Trocken ★★★★ £F

Markus Molitor (Mittel Mosel) *www.markusmolitor.com*

Markus Molitor has 38 ha of vineyards from which he produces ripe and sweet styles of Riesling. The best of these are from the excellent Zeltinger Sonnenuhr in the heart of the Mittel Mosel. The wines are extraordinarily rich, concentrated, intense and ripe for the Mosel but they succeed in retaining sufficient acidity and balance to allow them to be either drunk young or kept (at least in the medium term). While a Riesling Kabinett can be disappointing, there is a honeyed, ripe, peach richness in versions of Riesling Spätlese and the best Auslese and a Beerenauslese show a deep marmalady botrytis character and a luscious richness. Eiswein has vibrant preserved citrus and grapefruit flavours but lacks the complexity of the very best. Sadly prices are very high and the TBA are reserved to be sold as *Versteigerungswein* (at auction).

Recommended Whites:

Bernkasteler Badstube Riesling Eiswein ★★★★ £H
Zeltinger Sonnenuhr Riesling Beerenauslese ★★★★ £H
Zeltinger Sonnenuhr Riesling Auslese 3 Sterne ★★★★ £H
Zeltinger Sonnenuhr Riesling Auslese ★★★ £E
Zeltinger Sonnenuhr Riesling Spätlese ★★★ £C

Mönchhof/Robert Eymael (Mittel Mosel) *www.moenchhof.de*

Robert Eymael has been running the ancient Mönchhof estate since 1994. His 10 ha of vineyards are planted only to Riesling and concentrated on three of the finest sites of the Mittel Mosel: Ürziger Würzgarten, Erdener Treppchen and the great Erdener Prälat. The wines show classic delicacy, intensity and refined fruit flavours, especially at Spätlese and Auslese levels of ripeness. Wines from the Würzgarten (spice garden) of Urzig are famed for their spicy character. The Mönchhof examples show this characteristic spiciness, as well as hints of mineral, ripe peach and nectarine fruit. While there's currently not the concentration or length of flavour

seen in the very best examples from these sites, prices aren't excessive for the quality. Also under Robert Eymael's direction (and an interesting contrast) are the wines of the small estate of J J CHRISTOFFEL.

Recommended Whites:

Ürziger Würzgarten Riesling Auslese ★★★★ £D
Ürziger Würzgarten Riesling Spätlese ★★★ £C
Erdener Treppchen Riesling Auslese ★★★ £D
Erdener Treppchen Riesling Spätlese Trocken ★★ £C
Erdener Treppchen Riesling Kabinett ★★ £B
Erdener Prälat Riesling Auslese ★★★ £D

Georg Mosbacher (Pfalz) *www.georg-mosbacher.de*

80% of the Mosbacher family's 20 ha is planted to Riesling. Richard Mosbacher works with his daughter Sabine and her husband Jürgen Düringer to give excellent expression to plots of vines in some of the leading Pfalz vineyards. The Erste Lage wines possess fresh, ripe intense fruit and good flavour depth yet there is real differentiation between each site. The striking mineral intensity and depth in the powerful Forster Ungeheuer (grown on mid-slope sandstone soils) contrasts with the open, expressive Deidesheimer Kieselberg (from stoney sandy soils), which includes some exotic fruit flavours. Vines from the small Forster Freundstück site also provide Erste Lage Riesling as well as favouring Eiswein production. Good Rieslings are also made from lesser-known sites around Deidesheim and Forst. There is also some Weissburgunder and Gewürtraminer.

Recommended Whites:

Forster Ungeheuer Riesling GG ★★★ £E
Forster Freundstück Riesling GG ★★★ £E
Deidesheimer Kieselberg Riesling GG ★★★ £E

❀❀ Egon Müller/Scharzhof (Saar) *www.scharzhof.de*

Egon Müller IV now runs an estate with a reputation like no other in Germany. The fame of the Scharzhofberg site and the prices that the top sweet wines command align it with the most prestigious domaines in the world. The closest village to the south-east-facing slopes is Wiltingen but this is not included in the wines' names. As well as the wines from 8 ha of estate vineyards the wines from the 4 ha Le Gallais estate are produced here. The latter come from Braune Kupp north of Wiltingen, which, unlike those of Scharzhofberg (in a side valley), lies above the river Saar itself. The top sweet wines start out firm, intense and taut but have tremendous underlying concentration with the potential to last for decades. Small amounts of brilliant Trockenbeerenauslese and Eiswein (both of super 5-star quality) are made when conditions permit. As well as pure and expressive regular versions of Spätlese and Auslese, several superior, numbered versions are also released. All need at least 10 years' age. Almost all the wines are sold at auction (so prices can vary considerably). Only a basic Schwarhof Riesling, a Kabinett and a Spätlese are reasonably affordable, if not great value.

Recommended Whites:

Scharzhofberger Riesling TBA ✪✪✪✪✪ £H
Scharzhofberger Riesling Beerenauslese ✪✪✪✪✪ £H
Scharzhofberger Riesling Auslese Goldkapsel ★★★★★ £H
Scharzhofberger Riesling Auslese ★★★★ £G
Scharzhofberger Riesling Spätlese ★★★☆ £E
Scharzhofberger Riesling Kabinett ★★☆ £C
Riesling QbA Schwarzhof ★☆ £B

Le Gallais
Recommended Whites:

Wiltinger Braune Kupp Riesling Auslese Goldkapsel ★★★★ £H

Wiltinger Braune Kupp Riesling Spätlese ★★ £D

⚫ Muller-Catoir (Pfalz) *www.mueller-catoir.de*
The 20 ha of vineyards are not on the Pfalz's most famous sites, but very intense, fine wines are produced across a range of lesser-known vineyards. The wines provide a real contrast to the exquisite balance and finesse seen in the top Mosel wines as, although well-balanced and fine, they are characterised more by their power and thrilling intensity, which have earned them an almost fanatical following. Those from Rieslaner (a crossing between Riesling and Sylvaner) are the most individual and characterful of all, with remarkable sweetness and power at Auslese level and higher. Riesling, though intense, doesn't always have quite the depth or concentration seen in other top Pfalz examples. Sweet, exotic Scheurebe and good dry examples of Grauburgunder, Weissburgunder and Muskateller are also made.

Recommended Whites:
Mussbacher Eselshaut Rieslaner TBA ✪✪✪✪✪ £H
Mussbacher Eselshaut Rieslaner Auslese ★★★ £E
Mussbacher Eselshaut Rieslaner Spätlese ★★ £D
Haardter Bürgergarten Rieslaner Beerenauslese ★★★★ £H
Gimmeldinger Schlössel Rieslaner Spätlese Trocken ★★ £C
Gimmeldinger Mandelgarten Riesling Auslese ★★★ £F
Haardter Bürgergarten Riesling Spätlese Trocken ★★ £D
Haardter Herrenletten Riesling Spätlese Trocken ★★ £D
Haardter Mandelring Scheurebe Auslese ★★★ £F
Haardter Mandelring Scheurebe Spätlese ★★ £C
Haardter Bürgergarten Muskateller Trocken ★★ £C

Von Othegraven (Saar) *www.von-othegraven.de*
The von Othegraven estate is centred on the Kanzem Altenberg site in the Saar, with 7.5 ha of a total 16 ha of vineyards sited in this south-south-east facing amphitheatre with reddish slatey soils. During 2010 owner Heidi Kegel sold the property to Gunther Jauch, a distant relative and German TV entertainer. The character is of ripe, minerally, slightly spicy citrus/preserved citrus fruit with increasing concentration at higher Prädikat levels. The wines are very well made with a pulsating exoticism. As well as some Goldkapsel Auslese, a little Riesling is also made from the good Wiltinger Kupp and Ockfener Bockstein sites. This is a name that deserves to be better known. The dry wines are amongst the most successful in the Saar with mineral intensity giving weight to the austere purity of the style.

Recommended Whites:
Kanzemer Altenberg Auslese Erste Lage ★★★★ £E
Kanzemer Altenberg Riesling Erste Lage ★★★ £C
Kanzemer Altenberg Riesling Kabinett Erste Lage ★★ £B
Riesling Qualitätswein ★ £B

Paulinshof (Mittel Mosel) *www.paulinshof.de*
The Jünglings, father and son, make excellent reasonably priced Trocken and Halbtrocken styles from 9 ha spread over several different sites (including the solely owned Brauneberger Kammer) in the Mittel Mosel. There are two outstanding dry wines, both Auslese Trocken, from Kerstener Paulingshofberg, very mineral from deep blue slate but with a rich viscous texture and Brauneberger Kammer, planted on light brown shale. This is softer with racier acidity. The wines are impressive, whether from the recent run of top vintages or slightly more difficult vintages. They are taut but poised and properly ripe with a fruit intensity that ensures they are long-lived. Sweet Auslese wines are good too with added concentration and

depth.

Recommended Whites:
Kestener Paulinshofberger Riesling Auslese Trocken ★★★☆ £D
Kestener Paulinshofberger Riesling Auslese ★★★ £E
Brauneberger Kammer Riesling Auslese Trocken ★★★☆ £D
Brauneberger Juffer-Sonnenuhr Riesling Spätlese Trocken ★★★ £C
Brauneberger Kammer Riesling Spätlese Halbtrocken ★★ £C
Brauneberger Juffer Riesling Spätlese ★★ £C

Pauly-Bergweiler (Mosel) *www.pauly-bergweiler.com*
This producer comprises two estates totaling 16.2 ha. In addition to the Pauly-Bergweiler estate are the vineyards of Peter Nicolay that have come from Dr Pauly's wife's family. Lighter, simpler styles of Riesling are better made than most, while there is lovely definition and refinement in the Prädikat wines. The family is fortunate to have nearly 2ha of vineyards in the Bernkasteler Badstube am Doctorberg; wines from here retain a minerally elegance whilst building in richness with age. Riesling Spätlese (and sometimes higher ripeness levels) is also made from Graacher Himmelreich and Wehlener Sonnenuhr. Wines from the Peter Nicolay estate include Riesling Spätlese and Auslese from Ürziger Goldwingert and Erdener Prälat.

Recommended Whites:
Bernkasteler Badstube am Doctorberg Riesling Auslese ★★★ £D
Bernkasteler Badstube am Doctorberg Riesling Spätlese ★★★ £C
Erdener Treppchen Riesling Selection ★★ £B
Riesling Dr Pauly Noble House ★£B Riesling Dr Pauly Classic ★ £B

⚫⚫ Joh Jos Prüm (Mittel Mosel) *www.jjpruem.com*
The famed 20 ha estate of Dr Manfred Prüm is centred on the great Wehlener Sonnenuhr site but also includes Zeltinger Sonnenuhr, Graacher Himmelreich and Bernkasteler Lay. The wines are justly renowned for their longevity and the refinement that ageing brings. In fact, a wonderful, racy intensity and minerally elegance used only to become apparent with several years' age but the most recent vintages can be drunk quite young. After a decade or more a Spätlese can show a delicate toastiness and subtle, honeyed perfume preceding a beautifully delineated, fruit-filled palate. The Auslese-level wines retain a finesse and delicacy seen in Kabinett and Spätlese wines but add more depth and intensity to riper fruit flavours, including peach and apricot, rather than white peach and apple. 5-star Beerenauslese and TBA wines are sold at auction and can be difficult to obtain. Late bottling means the wines are usually a year behind most other producers, becoming available only in the second year after the vintage.

Recommended Whites:
Wehlener Sonnenuhr Riesling Auslese Goldkapsel ✪✪✪✪✪ £H
Wehlener Sonnenuhr Riesling Auslese ★★★★ £E
Wehlener Sonnenuhr Riesling Spätlese ★★★☆ £D
Wehlener Sonnenuhr Riesling Kabinett ★★☆ £C
Bernkasteler Badstube Riesling Auslese ★★★★ £E
Graacher Himmelreich Riesling Spätlese ★★☆ £D
Graacher Himmelreich Riesling Kabinett ★★ £C

⚫ Ratzenberger *Mittelrhein www.weingut-ratzenberger.de*
On the basis of recent vintages this is now one of the best two or three estates in the Mittelrhein. The 13.8 ha of vineyards include Steeger St Jost, Bacharacher Posten and Bacharacher Wolfshöhle, all a continuation of the same slopes. There is lovely purity in the Steeger St Jost wines while the best Wolfshöhle wines are stylish and classy with the distinctive mineral, floral and preserved nectarine quality of the Mittelrhein. An Erste Lage (Grosses Gewächs,

GG) version shows real promise, with the concentration to match its strength and structure. Even basic QbAs are decent, a tangy Trocken version better than Caspar R which has marked sweetness to balance the acidity. The very sweet, powerful, intense (and enamel shattering) Eiswein has also been made in an incredibly concentrated 1 Sterne version.

Recommended Whites:
Bacharacher Kloster Fürstental Riesling Eiswein ★★★★★ £F
Bacharacher Wolfshöhle Riesling GG ★★★★ £E
Bacharacher Wolfshöhle Riesling Spätlese 1 Sterne ★★★ £D
Bacharacher Posten Riesling Spätlese Halbtrocken ★★ £C
Steeger St Jost Riesling Spätlese Trocken ★★ £C
Steeger St Jost Riesling Kabinett Halbtrocken ★★ £B
Riesling Trocken ★★ £B   Riesling Caspar R ★ £B

✿ Ökonomierat Rebholz (Pfalz) *www.oekonomierat-rebholz.de*
Although he is based in the less-celebrated southern part of Pfalz, Hansjörg Rebholz manages to make some of the region's best wines - very fine and intelligently crafted gems. Don't expect the power or weight of the likes of other top Pfalz producers, rather a pure, intense, *terroir*-derived expression of Riesling. The cool, pure mineral intensity of the Kastanienbusch from red slate soils contrasts with the minerally warmth derived from the gravel and sandstone of the Im Sonnenschein site. Good as these are, only 40% of the estate's 20 ha of vineyard are planted to Riesling. Another 48% is comprised of the Pinots (Blanc, Gris and Noir) and Chardonnay. The Siebeldingen Im Sonnenschein Weisser Burgunder is a superb example of this grape. It comes from a more fossil-rich part of the vineyard than the Riesling and is very composed, pure and complex, on an altogether different quality level from most German examples (or indeed, anywhere else). Chardonnay has 9 months in 60-70% new oak and is very fine, elegant with both poise and intensity. Spätburgunder, aged in particularly fine grained oak, is cool, stylish and expressive with impressive length. Other wines include Silvaner, Grauburgunder and some sweet Auslese versions as well as some sparkling wine.

Recommended Reds:
Siebeldingen im Sonnenschein Spätburgunder GG ★★★☆ £F

Recommended Whites:
Birkweiler Kastanienbusch Riesling GG ★★★★ £E
Siebeldingen im Sonnenschein Riesling GG ★★★★ £E
Siebeldingen im Sonnenschein Weisser Burgunder GG ★★★★ £E
Weissburgunder Spätlese Trocken ★★★☆ £D
Chardonnay Spätlese Trocken ★★★★ £E

Balthasar Ress (Rheingau) *www.balthasar-ress.de*
The Ress wines have a slightly chequered past in terms of quality, at times lacking a little definition or depth depending on the wine and vintage, and occasionally ageing a little quickly. Father (Stefan) and son manage a substantial 42 ha of vineyards that includes parcels in some of the best sites around Hattenheim. The recent run of excellent vintages has made for a more consistent showing with many of the Rieslings typified by an attractive and elegant expression of citrus and nectarine fruit (and a mineral influence in some) backed by fine acidity. There's still not the extra intensity, depth or concentration of the Rheingau's best but their accessiblity and refined, pleasing style will deservedly attract more wine drinkers to German Riesling. Flavoursome, gently creamy Weissburgunder is also made. The wines listed below are but a few from an extensive range.

Recommended Whites:
Hattenheimer Nussbrunnen Riesling Erste Lage ★★★ £E
Hattenheimer Nussbrunnen Riesling Auslese ★★★ £E
Rüdesheimer Berg Schlossberg Riesling Erste Lage ★★★ £E
Rüdesheimer Berg Rottland Riesling Erste Lage ★★★ £E
Hochheimer Steilweg Riesling Spätlese Trocken ★★ £C
Hattenheimer Schutzenhaus Riesling Kabinett Trocken ★★ £B
Weissburgunder Trocken ★ £B

✿ Max-Ferd Richter (Mittel Mosel) *www.maxferdrichter.com*
Dr Dirk Richter is the current director of this family estate, established over 300 years ago. The 17 ha of vineyards are in some of the Mittel Mosel's best sites. There is a characteristic ripeness and intensity, and the fine acidity and the class of the top vineyards comes through. No two wines are quite the same: a complex, intense, apricotty Juffer-Sonnenuhr Spätlese, for instance, contrasts with the more citrus elegance of Graacher Himmelreich Spätlese. The small Alleinbesitz (solely owned vineyard) of Mülheimer Helenenkloster consistently produces an outstanding Eiswein – a sweet and tangy potion of citrus peel, dried peach, spice and more exotic flavours that lingers long in the mouth. The Veldenzer Elisenberg vineyard is also under the sole ownership of the family and the source of fine Rieslings, including an excellent Cask 60 Auslese. Prices are fair, a good Richter Estate QbA included.

Recommended Whites:
Mülheimer Helenenkloster Riesling Eiswein ★★★★★ £H
Brauneberger Juffer-Sonnenuhr Riesling Auslese ★★★★ £E
Brauneberger Juffer-Sonnenuhr Riesling Spätlese ★★★ £D
Graacher Domprobst Riesling Auslese ★★★ £D
Graacher Domprobst Riesling Spätlese Halbtrocken ★★ £C
Graacher Himmelreich Riesling Spätlese ★★★ £C
Graacher Himmelreich Riesling Kabinett ★★ £B
Oehlener Sonnenuhr Riesling Spätlese ★★★ £C
Oehlener Sonnenuhr Riesling Kabinett ★★ £B
Brauneberger Juffer Riesling Spätlese ★★★ £C
Brauneberger Juffer Riesling Kabinett ★★ £C

Weingut Josef Rosch (Mittel Mosel)
Werner Rosch and his wife have only 7.5 ha, but are producing some marvellously pure, well-defined Riesling, especially at Spätlese level and higher. The elegant wines from Trittenheimer Apotheke are probably the best going while the Selection JR 3 Sterne is a beautifully composed example with cool citrus and white peach fruit. Auslese combines elegance and richness. Leiwener Klostergarten is the source of an excellent refined, intense Eiswein (made in most years) and, surprisingly, a lean but attractive sparkling wine.

Recommended Whites:
Leiwener Klostergarten Riesling Eiswein ★★★★★ £F
Leiwener Klostergarten Riesling Brut ★★ £C
Leiwener Klostergarten Riesling QbA Trocken ★ £B
Trittenheimer Apotheke Riesling Auslese ★★★★ £E
Trittenheimer Apotheke Riesling Spätlese ★★★ £D
JR Selection Riesling Spätlese Trocken 3 Sterne ★★★ £D
JR Junior Riesling Trocken ★★ £B

Salm-Dalberg Schloss Wallhausen (Nahe) *www.salm-salm.de*
Michael Prinz zu Salm-Salm spent 17 years as president of the VDP until 2007. His son Felix (32nd generation!) is becoming involved in the winemaking and there are definite signs of improvement in the Schloss Wallhausen estate wines. The 12.5 ha of vineyards

include several good sites and the intention is eventually to produce only one wine from each. *Barrique*-aged Spätburgunder has good flavour but is slightly over-extracted and oaky. Also under the same ownership are the wines of VILLA SACHSEN where quality is also being revitalised. (KB)

Recommended Whites:
Wallhäuser Felseneck Riesling Spätlese ★★★ £C
Wallhäuser Johannisberg Riesling GG ★★ £D
Roxheimer Berg Riesling Spätlese ★★ £C
Schloss Wallhausen Riesling Kabinett ★★ £B
Schloss Wallhausen Riesling Halbtrocken ★ £B

Sankt. Urbans-Hof (Saar & Mittel Mosel) *www.urbans-hof.de*
For fine Mosel wines that are fully ripe with extra intensity yet without sacrificing their elegance or individuality, this estate is hard to beat. Young Nik Weis is making the most of his family's considerable viticultural resource of 32 ha planted mostly to Riesling and his winemaker Rudolf Hoffmann is clearly able to harness the potential of fruit that is riper and more concentrated than most. Piesporter Goldtröpfchen wines, from a particularly steep part of the vineyard just above the river's edge, show rich, intense blackcurrant, citrus and peach fruit, yet elegance too. From the Saar, the Ockfener Bockstein wines are splendidly individual with a smokey and mineral, very ripe citrus character at Auslese level. The wines from Leiwener Laurentiuslay, a particular warm site for the Mosel, are of similar quality and include a vibrant intense (and reasonably priced) Erste Lage from 04. Highish sulphur levels can detract at Kabinett level, but these wines too will age and will then taste immeasurably cleaner. A small amount of wine is usually designated Goldkapsel and Eiswein is also produced from Leiwener Klostergarten.

Recommended Whites:
Wiltinger Schlangengraben Riesling Auslese Goldkapsel ★★★★ £F
Piesporter Goldtröpfchen Riesling Auslese ★★★★ £E
Piesporter Goldtröpfchen Riesling Spätlese ★★★ £C
Piesporter Goldtröpfchen Riesling Kabinett ★★ £B
Ockfener Bockstein Riesling Auslese ★★★★ £E
Ockfener Bockstein Riesling Spätlese ★★★ £C
Ockfener Bockstein Riesling Kabinett ★ £B
Leiwener Laurentiuslay Riesling GG ★★★☆ £D

Salwey (Baden) *www.salwey.de*
Salwey makes really good examples of the three Pinots, especially at the top level. The wines are ripe and complex with lots of intensity and breadth whether from Weissburgunder, Grauburgunder or Spätburgunder. Their 41 ha of warm, protected vineyards of Oberrotweil in the Kaiserstuhl are fundamental to quality: Eichberg and Henkenberg (both especially good for Grauburgunder) are mostly decomposed volcanic soils, Käsleberg is loess (for faster-developing but stylish, lightly minerally wines) and Kirchberg (where Spätburgunder excels) has rocky volcanic soils. The various white wine cuvées are many and varied but the best are rich and characterful if lacking the finesse that would really set them apart. There is more class but also evident oak in the top Spätburgunders (the Henkenberg version is easily the best value). Regular (QbA Trocken) examples are light, sound and modestly structured. As well as sweet, opulent Auslese, rich, intensely sweet TBA and Eiswein from Grauburgunder have also been made when possible.

Recommended Reds:
Oberrotweiler Kirchberg Spätburgunder GG 3 Sterne ★★★ £F
Oberrotweiler Kirchberg Spätburgunder Spätlese RS Tr. ★★★ £E
Oberrotweiler Henkenberg Spätburgunder Trocken ★★★ £C

Recommended Whites:
Oberrotweiler Eichberg Grauburgunder Spätlese Trocken ★★★ £E
Grauburgunder Auslese 3 Sterne ★★★ £E
Oberrotweiler Henkenberg Grauburgunder Spätlese Tr. ★★★ £D
Oberrotweiler Henkenberg Grauburgunder Kabinett Tr. ★★ £B
Oberrotweiler Käsleberg Grauburgunder Kabinett Trocken ★★ £B
Oberrotweiler Kirchberg Weissburgunder GG 3 Sterne ★★★ £D
Oberrotweiler Käsleberg Weissburgunder Kabinett Trocken ★★ £B

✿✿ Horst Sauer (Franken) *www.weingut-horst-sauer.de*
In the space of a few vintages, Horst Sauer has emerged as the best producer in Franken and one of the new stars of Germany; the winemaker now is his daughter Sandra Sauer. There is both complexity and individuality in all the better wines, while elegance and well-detailed fruit are evident even in Riesling Kabinett. From a total of 16.5 ha of vineyards in one of Franken's most prized vineyard sites, Escherndorfer Lump, there is Silvaner of similar quality to Riesling and both have excellent balance and composure in dry and sweeter styles. Quite superb Riesling Beerenauslese and Riesling and Silvaner TBA all combine richness and expression; intense spice, mineral and dried fruit flavours linger long on the finish. A Scheurebe Spätlese is an excellent example of this variety too and even Müller-Thurgau has good intensity and shows a light minerally elegance. Partially barriqued Sennsucht Silvaner is a successful diversion in a more international style. Some Pinot Noir rosé is also made.

Recommended Whites:
Escherndorfer Lump Riesling TBA ✪✪✪✪✪ £H
Escherndorfer Lump Riesling Eiswein ★★★★★ £H
Escherndorfer Lump Riesling Beerenauslese ★★★★★ £G
Escherndorfer Lump Riesling Auslese ★★★★ £E
Escherndorfer Lump Riesling Spätlese Trocken ★★★ £C
Escherndorfer Lump Riesling Kabinett Trocken ★★ £B
Escherndorfer Lump Silvaner TBA ✪✪✪✪✪ £H
Escherndorfer Lump Silvaner Auslese ★★★★ £E
Escherndorfer Lump Silvaner Spätlese Trocken ★★★ £C
Sehnsucht Silvaner Spätlese Trocken ★★☆ £C
Eschendorfer Lump Scheurebe Spätlese ★★★ £C

Willi Schaefer (Mittel Mosel)
There are arguably no finer examples of Rieslings from the village of Graach than those from Willi Schaefer's extremely modest 4 ha. These pure, intense wines are not in the least overpowering but are wonderfully expressive and long with more richness at Auslese level. Those from Domprobst are superior to those from Himmelreich, being consistently finer, riper and fuller. That said, even the Himmelreich Kabinett can show fine apple, grapefruit and lemon that contrast with the peachier, mineral intensity in Domprobst Kabinett and Spätlese. A perfect balance of acidity and concentrated, riper fruit is typical in the Domprobst Auslese. Some individually numbered casks of Auslese from both Domprobst and Himmelreich are also made, as is a little Beerenauslese.

Recommended Whites:
Graacher Domprobst Riesling Auslese ★★★★ £E
Graacher Domprobst Riesling Spätlese ★★★ £D
Graacher Domprobst Riesling Kabinett ★★ £B
Graacher Himmelreich Riesling Spätlese ★★ £C
Graacher Himmelreich Riesling Kabinett ★ £B

✿ Schäfer-Fröhlich (Nahe) *www.weingut-schaefer-froehlich.de*
With his 17.5 ha, Tim Fröhlich, a new star in the Nahe, has produced

since 2002 some quite superb wines. The quality of his wines has further enhanced the reputation of the very steep slate and quartz Monziger Halenberg vineyard and even steeper blue slate, basalt and quartz Bockenauer Felseneck site. Kabinett and Spätlese from both are very refined with excellent balance and definition. There is Weissburgunder too, a lovely pure example fermented in stainless steel and a richer, more textured, lightly oaked 'S' version. As well as super regular Auslese, sweeter styles of Riesling from Felseneck include exquisite TBA and Eiswein as well as *Goldkapsel* versions.

Recommended Whites:
Bockenauer Felseneck Riesling TBA ★★★★★ £H
Bockenauer Felseneck Riesling Eiswein ★★★★★ £G
Bockenauer Felseneck Riesling Auslese ★★★★ £E
Bockenauer Felseneck Riesling Spätlese Trocken ★★★ £C
Bockenauer Felseneck Riesling Spätlese ★★★ £C
Bockenauer Felseneck Riesling Kabinett Trocken ★★ £B
Monzinger Frühlingsplätzchen Riesling GG ★★★ £E
Monzinger Halenberg Riesling Spätlese ★★★ £C
Monzinger Halenberg Riesling Kabinett Trocken ★★ £B
Bockenauer Weisser Burgunder 'S' ★★★ £C
Bockenauer Weisser Burgunder Trocken ★★ £B

❀ Schloss Lieser (Mittel Mosel) *www.weingut-schloss-lieser.de*
Thomas Haag, who is the son of Wilhelm Haag (and brother of Oliver) of the Fritz HAAG estate, has been responsible for the much-improved quality that has revitalised this once-famous 11.5 ha estate centred on the Lieser Niederberg Helden site. His taut, intense and ripe Rieslings add richness and complexity in the higher Prädikat styles and with age. Auslese wines (there is typically more than one bottling) in particular attain the exquisite combination of finesse and richness that exemplifies the best sites of the Mittel Mosel. A mineral, grapefruit and subtly orange blossom Brauneberger Juffer-Sonnenuhr Riesling Spätlese can be excellent too, while a stunning Auslese *Lange Goldkapsel* has also been made from this vineyard. An occasional tendency to an excessive sulphur or sulphides taint can detract although most will lose this with additional bottle age. A little 3 Sterne Auslese and some Beerenauslese or TBA are made when conditions permit. The wines are reasonably priced.

Recommended Whites:
Brauneberger Juff-Sonnenuhr Ries Aus Lange Goldkapsel ★★★★★ £F
Brauneberger Juffer-Sonnenuhr Riesling Spätlese ★★★☆ £D
Lieser Niederberg Helden Ries Auslese Goldkapsel 2 Sterne ★★★★ £E
Lieser Niederberg Helden Riesling Auslese ★★★ £D
Lieser Niederberg Helden Riesling Spätlese ★★☆ £C
Riesling Kabinett ★★☆ £B   Riesling QbA ★☆ £B

Schloss Saarstein (Saar) *www.saarstein.de*
Christian Ebert runs this 10 ha estate bought by his father in 1956. It is based, for the most part, on the wholly-owned Serriger Schloss Saarsteiner vineyard, where steep slopes on forest-topped hillside afford the best protection in what is otherwise at the margins for successful viticulture. The grapes struggle to get fully ripe, resulting in a very cool green fruits character, especially in cooler vintages. The best acid/sugar balance is usually seen in Auslese level wines; below this the sweetness can initially mask the fruit purity underneath (*Süssreserve* sometimes being added to check the high acidity levels). Patience is needed but the crushed blackcurrant leaf, green apple, citrus and mineral complexity becomes increasingly enticing with age. Alcohol levels are always low, even by Mosel standards. Occasionally sulphur levels can be intrusive, at least when

the wines are young. As well as a little Beerenauslese and Eiswein, some Weissburgunder is also produced.

Recommended Whites:
Serriger Schloss Saarsteiner Riesling Auslese Goldkapsel ★★★★ £F
Serriger Schloss Saarsteiner Riesling Auslese ★★★☆ £E
Serriger Schloss Saarsteiner Riesling Spätlese ★★☆ £C
Serriger Schloss Saarsteiner Riesling Kabinett ★★ £B

Schloss Schönborn (Rheingau) *www.schoenborn.de*
Schloss Schönborn has a collection of 50 ha of the very best vineyard land in the Rheingau, including Erbacher Marcobrunn, that must be the envy of many a small grower. Despite some quality ups and downs there are indications of a more sustained revival over recent vintages. As well as improvement in the sweeter styles there is increasing depth and texture in Erste Lage (Erstes Gewächs) bottlings. Most wines show a little sulphur when young but this is less marked with age and the best vintages will age very well indeed.

Recommended Whites:
Rüdesheimer Berg Schlossberg Riesling Auslese ★★★ £E
Rüdesheimer Berg Rottland Riesling Auslese ★★★ £E
Hattenheimer Pfaffenberg Riesling Erstes Gewächs ★★ £D
Hattenheimer Pfaffenberg Riesling Spätlese ★★ £C
Erbacher Marcobrunn Riesling Erstes Gewächs ★★ £D
Erbacher Marcobrunn Riesling Spätlese ★★ £C
Erbacher Marcobrunn Riesling Kabinett ★ £C

Schloss Vollrads (Rheingau) *www.schlossvollrads.com*
This celebrated Rheingau estate with a history stretching back to the 14th century has been put on a new footing since come under the ownership of a bank. Since 1999 the estate and winemaking direction has come from Dr Rowald Hepp and quality from a massive 63 ha of vineyards, planted entirely to Riesling, is seeing a slow but steady return. There has been a significant leap forward with good minerality and depth even at Kabinett level, but there is still the potential for even better wines. Intense ripe peach and citrus fruit at Spätlese level (and apricot at higher ripeness levels) combined with good balanced acidity promises wines of good concentration, definition and ripeness. Some Beerenauslese and TBA are also made.

Recommended Whites:
Schloss Vollrads Riesling Auslese ★★★ £E
Schloss Vollrads Riesling Spätlese ★★★ £D
Schloss Vollrads Riesling Kabinett ★★ £C
Schloss Vollrads Riesling QbA ★ £B

❀ Schlossgut Diel (Nahe) *www.diel.eu*
Armin Diel, a leading expert on German wines and a German television celebrity, finds time to make some very good wines from 24 ha centred on Dorsheim's top sites. His Rieslings are rich and intense but usually well balanced. Even Kabinett from the Dorsheimer Pittermännchen is ripe, full and delicious while Spätlese makes for a fascinating contrast. All share a floral, herbal, mineral, blackcurrant and nectarine profile. Diel also makes *barrique*-fermented Pinot Gris, Pinot Blanc (Cuvée Victor is a blend of the two) and Pinot Noir. Cuvée Caroline is plump, with good depth of ripe red fruits and oak if missing the dimension and class of fine Burgundy. Diel de Diel is a characterful basic blend of the three white varieties. The estate also makes four top dry Grosses Gewächs wines; Burgberg is a minerally example with citrus notes; Goldloch has a honeyed riper style; Pittermannchen is all fruity charm but

Schlossberg is bigger, more backward.

Recommended Whites:

Riesling Eiswein ★★★★★ £H
Dorsheimer Pittermännchen Riesling GG ★★★★ £E
Dorsheimer Pittermännchen Riesling Auslese ★★★★ £F
Dorsheimer Pittermännchen Riesling Spätlese ★★★ £D
Dorsheimer Pittermännchen Riesling Kabinett ★★ £C
Dorsheimer Burgberg Riesling Auslese ★★★★ £E
Dorsheimer Burgberg Riesling Spätlese ★★★ £D
Dorsheimer Burgberg Riesling Kabinett ★★ £C
Dorsheimer Goldloch Riesling Auslese ★★★ £E
Dorsheimer Goldloch Riesling Spätlese ★★ £D
Dorsheimer Schlossberg Riesling GG ★★★★ £E
Dorsheimer Goldloch Riesling Kabinett ★★ £C
Cuvée Victor ★★ £E   Grauburgunder ★★£C
Weissburgunder ★★ £C

Schmitt's Kinder (Franken) *www.schmitts-kinder.de*

Schmitt's Kinder, another of the Trias five (see Fürst LÖWENSTEIN), has 14 ha of fine vineyards in the Randersacker sites Sonnenstuhl and Pfülben. The latter is a steep, south-west-facing slope with Muschelkalk (fossilised limestone) soils. The quality is best illustrated in the Erste Lage versions of Silvaner and Riesling. The stylish, ripe yellow plum, subtle spice and mineral of the Silvaner is slightly outdone by the complex, powerful and concentrated Riesling. There is also Rieslaner (a crossing of Riesling and Sylvaner) Auslese from Sonnenstuhl with the typical structure and texture of the grape. Decent Bacchus, adequate Müller-Thurgau and grapefruity Scheurebe are also worth a try.

Recommended Whites:

Randersackerer Pfülben Riesling GG ★★★ £E
Randersackerer Pfülben Riesling Kabinett Trocken ★★ £B
Randersackerer Sonnenstuhl Rieslaner Auslese Goldkap 'S' ★★★ £E
Randersackerer Pfülben Silvaner GG ★★★ £E
Randersackerer Sonnenstuhl Silvaner Spätlese Trocken ★★ £C
Randersackerer Sonnenstuhl Scheurebe Spätlese Trocken ★★ £C
Randersackerer Ewig Leben Bacchus Kabinett Trocken ★ £B

Von Schubert/Maximin Grünhaus (Mosel) *www.vonschubert.com*

The most famous estate of the Ruwer Valley is based on the Maximin Grünhaus vineyards which, like those of Karthäuserhof on the other side of the river, face south-east on slopes running obliquely to the small Ruwer river. Dr Carl-Ferdinand von Schubert worked with winemaker Alfons Heinrich for nearly 2 decades. In 2004 winemaking responsibilities passed to Stefan Kraml. The heart of the solely owned site of 31 ha is the Abtsberg vineyard, which produces sublime Rieslings of outstanding expression and definition. Class and finesse are paramount to the style of the wines; overwhelming power and concentration are not sought. Apart from the ripest styles, delicious lime, mineral, floral, apple and white peach flavours prevail, but there is also the structure and intensity to age for years. Most splendid are the numbered Ausleses of varying richness (and price, £E to £F) but almost always at least 4-star quality. Some Beerenauslese is also sometimes made. Eiswein shows great finesse and lots of concentration and rich, ripe fruit in the best years but with cooler flavours and less concentration in less successful years. All the wines need at least 3–4 years' ageing.

Recommended Whites:

Maximin Grünhauser Abtsberg Riesling Beerenauslese ★★★☆ £H
Maximin Grünhauser Abtsberg Riesling Eiswein ★★★★☆ £H
Maximin Grünhauser Abtsberg Riesling Auslese ★★★★ £F
Maximin Grünhauser Abtsberg Riesling Spätlese ★★★ £D
Maximin Grünhauser Abtsberg Riesling Kabinett ★★ £C
Maximin Grünhauser Herrenberg Riesling Spätlese ★★ £D

Selbach-Oster (Mittel Mosel) *www.selbach-oster.de*

This 20 ha estate has been in the family since 1661 and is now run by Johannes Selbach and his wife. Some fine Mosel wines are made, with depth, elegance and fine, cool, apple, citrus and white peach flavours. Particularly stylish is a classy Zeltinger Sonnenuhr Riesling Auslese, though this and other wines have sometimes suffered from a excessive level of sulphur. Recently the wines are better, cleaner, aided no doubt by healthy fruit from the run of top vintages since the turn of the century. A little Beerenauslese and TBA are also made from Zeltinger Sonnenuhr. Wines labelled J&H Selbach are produced from bought-in grapes as part of a *négociant* business.

Recommended Whites:

Zeltinger Sonnenuhr Riesling Auslese 1 Stern ★★★★ £E
Zeltinger Sonnenuhr Riesling Auslese ★★★ £E
Zeltinger Sonnenuhr Riesling Spätlese ★★★ £C
Graacher Domprobst Riesling Auslese ★★ £E
Graacher Domprobst Riesling Spätlese ★★ £C
Zeltinger Schlossberg Riesling Spätlese ★★ £C
Wehlener Sonnenuhr Riesling Kabinett ★★ £B

Spreitzer (Rheingau) *www.weingut-spreitzer.de*

The Spreitzer brothers have 17 ha of vineyards and like KÜHN are realising the potential of Oestrich's best sites. There is an emphasis on low yields and the wines are kept on the lees for as long as possible. Great care is taken not to damage the skins prior to whole-bunch pressing. The flatter Lenchen site gives intense, ripe, fruity but well-defined Riesling, while the steep, stony Doosberg gives a very mineral, cold steel character with very intense, deep, minerally peachy fruit, requiring a little more patience. Fine Erste Lage (Erste Gewächs) bottlings from Oestrich Lenchen and Hattenheimer Wisselbrunnen are also produced. There is yeastiness to some of the wines if drunk very young but this is not a problem with some bottle-age. There's particularly fine Kabinett quality, often declassified Spätlese, but sweeter styles can also be superb, including Beerenauslese and TBA, made when conditions are right.

Recommended Whites:

Oestricher Lenchen Riesling Auslese Goldkapsel ★★★★ £E
Oestricher Lenchen Riesling Kabinett ★★★ £C
Oestricher Lenchen Riesling Kabinett Halbtrocken ★★★ £C
Oestricher Doosberg Riesling Spätlese Trocken ★★★ £D

Weingut Jean Stodden (Ahr) *www.stodden.de*

Alexander Stodden works with his father Gerhard to make some of Germany's best Spätburgunder, here labelled as Pinot Noir on export labels. Production from 6.5 ha is 95% red and almost all of that is Pinot. The grapes have 14 days of skin contact including a 4-day cold pre-fermentation maceration. Ageing is in Allier *barriques*, with new ones used for the top JS Auslese wines. The leading site is Recher Herrenberg, the light slatey soils giving elegant expressive Pinot but with added concentration in an Auslese 3 Sterne version from a selection of 20-year-old vines. The heavier soils of Dernauer Hardtberg make for a fuller, chewier style. Sometimes there is a tendency to use too much oak and the wines do show some astringency when young but this is less likely to be a problem with the 3–5 years' age they deserve. Amongst a wide range of *cuvées*, Jeanne is a well-composed blend of Pinot Noir, Dornfelder and Dunkelfelder aged in used *barriques*.

Germany

Germany (side tab)

Recommended Reds:
Recher Herrenberg Pinot Noir JS Auslese 3 Sterne ★★★ £F
Recher Herrenberg Pinot Noir JS ★★ £E
Dernauer Hardtberg Pinot Noir JS Auslese ★★★ £E
Pinot Noir JS ★★ £C Jeanne ★★ £C

Studert-Prüm (Mittel Mosel) *www.studert-pruem.com*
This is a small 5 ha estate run by brothers Stephan and Gerhard
Studert (12th generation) but resulting from the amalgamation of
the Studert family's vines (here since 1581) with those of Peter Prüm.
The steep slopes of Wehlener Sonnenuhr forms the core of a range
of increasingly well-made whites – interestingly, 80% of the vines
are ungrafted. There is not quite the precision or purity of others,
and drier styles can sometimes be harsh and under-ripe, but there
is generally good intensity and balance in the wines with added
concentration in the ripest styles. Auslese 2 Sterne is deep and
concentrated while the TBA has richly botrytised flavours and exotic
honeyed fruit. Most of the wines can be drunk fairly young but will
also be good in the medium term - with 6-7 years' ageing.

Recommended Whites:
Wehlener Sonnenuhr Riesling TBA ★★★★ £F
Wehlener Sonnenuhr Riesling Auslese 2 Sterne ★★★☆ £E
Wehlener Sonnenuhr Riesling Spätlese 3 Sterne ★★★ £D
Wehlener Sonnenuhr Riesling Spätlese ★★☆ £C
Wehlener Sonnenuhr Riesling Kabinett ★★ £B
Bernkasteler Graben Riesling Spätlese ★★ £C
Graacher Himmelreich Riesling Kabinett ★★ £B

Tesch (Nahe) *www.weingut-tesch.de*
Dr Martin Tesch, a biochemist, has been uncompromising in taking
his family estate forward since 1996. He has focused mostly on
dry wines, and from 2003 exclusively so. Almost 19ha are planted
predominantly to Riesling and a contrasting range of full, expressive
examples are produced. Clean uncomplicated labels indicate only
the vineyard (as many Pfalz producers now do). Karthäuser, Krone
and St Remigiusberg are from Laubenheim; Königsschild and Löhrer
Berg from Langenlonsheim. Karthäuser is at once fruit-driven and
vigorous but has a certain subtlety as well, Königschild impresses
with size and ripeness of spiced citrus fruit and Krone (from mixed
soils) is more mineral and herbal, but all are fine. The least expensive
Riesling Unplugged is a good example of the new image, a quality
dry Riesling certain to attract more consumers to German wines.
Tastings of St Remigiusberg, potentially the top example, are
insufficient for a rating. Good examples of riper, sweeter styles have
also been made.

Recommended Whites:
Karthäuser Riesling Spätlese Trocken ★★★ £C
Königsschild Riesling Spätlese Trocken ★★★ £C
Krone Riesling Spätlese Trocken ★★★ £C
Löhrer Berg Riesling Spätlese Trocken ★★ £C

✿ Van Volxem (Saar) *www.vanvolxem.com*
High quality combined with Roman's outsized physique and
flamboyant personality seems to have provoked a little envy as
well as an almost cult following since he purchased the estate in
2000. Much of the controversy seems to boil down to his pursuit
of drier styles in a region that has traditionally promoted great
sweet wines. After all, some of Germany's top estates can be found
in the Saar and their greatest wines are sweet. The estate lies in
the wine-producing village of Wiltingen, best known for its top
vineyard, Scharzhofberger. It also possesses parcels in the heart of
the most famous vineyards in Wiltingen - Braunfels, Klosterberg,
Gottesfuss, as well as Scharzhofberger. This excellent portfolio was
further enhanced in 2002 with the purchase of 2.5 ha of the best
part of the famous Kanzemer Altenberg and again with purchases
of 8ha in the Wawerner Goldberg. The 42 ha of steep-slate vineyards
here are planted with roughly 40 year old vines, 96% Riesling and
4% Pinot Blanc. In the first growth Wiltinger Gottesfuss, one of the
steepest and most renowned Saar vineyards, Van Volxem possesses
an extreme rarity, 125 year old pre-phylloxera vines. With low
yields barely over 30 hl/ha, Roman produces finely textured, fruity,
and elegant *terroir* wines with enormous depth and complexity,
persistence on the palate as well as ageing potential. From the
early days of his replanting programme, the use of pristine genetic
material of mostly ungrafted vines (no modern clones), labour
intensive growing work including organic and biodynamic methods,
low yields of small berries in small clusters, and highly-selective
hand harvesting have been important factors in the success of
the estate. The goal for these handcrafted wines is to retain the
characteristics from each specific vineyard within the bottle. In
order to keep the unique style of each vineyard, indigenous yeasts
are favoured over selected, cultured yeasts and the wines are never
chaptalised. With the exception of the botrytis specialities, Von
Volxem wines are an ideal partner with many aromatic dishes with
all reaching an acceptable level of alcohol by volume of between
10 and 12%. This is a remarkable diversion from the generally held
notion that German wines are either too sweet or excruciatingly
acid.

Recommended Whites:
Scharzhofberger Riesling Auslese Goldkapsel ★★★★☆ £G
Scharzhofberger Pergentsknopp Riesling ★★★★☆ £E
Kanzemer Altenberg Riesling Alte Reben ★★★★ £E
Wiltinger Gottesfuss Riesling Alte Reben ★★★★ £E
Scharzhofberger Riesling ★★★★ £D
Wiltinger Volz Riesling ★★★☆ £D
Wiltinger Kupp Riesling ★★★☆ £D Riesling Alte Reben ★★★☆ £D
Rotschiefer Riesling Kabinett ★★★ £C Saar Riesling ★★★ £C
Schiefer Riesling ★★☆ £B Weissburgunder ★★☆ £B

Geheimrat J Wegeler (Rheingau, Mosel & Pfalz) *www.wegeler.com*
The Wegeler family have some outstanding vineyard sites totalling
some 80 ha, the majority in the Rheingau (48 ha) but with significant
holdings in the Mosel (14 ha) and Pfalz too. Andreas Holderrieth has
taken over from Oliver Haag (of Weingut Fritz HAAG) as winemaker
for the Rheingau wines. There is refinement and lovely definition
in Winkeler Jesuitengarten, more weight and power in Berg
Schlossberg. Other examples come from Berg Rottland, Oestricher
Lenchen and Geisenheimer Rothenberg. From the Mosel there's
a range of fine Spätlese and higher ripeness level wines from the
Wehlener Sonnenuhr and Bernkasteler Doctor sites that show
depth, richness and ripeness. More wines will be rated with further
tastings. The wines from the Pfalz are wholly unimpressive.

Gutshaus Oestrich
Recommended Whites:
Winkeler Jesuitengarten Riesling Erstes Gewächs ★★★ £D
Rüdesheimer Berg Schlossberg Riesling Erstes Gewächs ★★★ £D
Gutshaus Bernkastel
Recommended Whites:
Bernkasteler Doctor Riesling Auslese ★★★★ £E
Bernkasteler Doctor Riesling Spätlese ★★★ £D
Wehlener Sonnenuhr Auslese ★★★ £E

Wehlener Sonnenuhr Riesling Spätlese ★★★ £D
Wehlener Sonnenuhr Riesling Kabinett ★★ £C

Dr Wehrheim (Pfalz) *www.weingut-wehrheim.de*

The Dr Wehrheim estate is in the southern Pfalz, some 20 km south of Neustadt. Only 40% of 15 ha are planted to Riesling; the balance comes mostly from Weissburgunder, Spätburgunder, Silvaner and St-Laurent (possibly related to Pinot Noir). Vineyard names are only used for two Erste Lage, Kastanienbusch and Mandelberg, other wines being named for their soil types. Despite a reputation for top-quality Weissburgunder and Spätburgunder, the best wines are from Riesling. The finest examples have cool, intense, minerally nectarine fruit. They are tight, even austere when young but have great depth and power with added class in the Kastanienbusch version. The best Weissburgunders are the fruit-intense, lightly minerally Buntsandstein and slightly fuller Muschelkalk – these outshine the leesy, oaked (and more pricey) Erste Lage (Grosses Gewächs, GG). Spätburgunder is softly textured, complex and flavoursome but too much oak compromises the structure and finish. Cuvée Carolus is a Bordeaux blend.

Recommended Reds:

Birkweiler Mandelberg Spätburgunder GG ★★ £E

Recommended Whites:

Birkweiler Kastanienbusch Riesling GG ★★★★ £E
Riesling Rotliegendes ★★★ £C
Riesling Kabinett Trocken ★ £B
Birkweiler Mandelberg Weisser Burgunder GG ★★ £D
Weisser Burgunder Buntsandstein ★★ £B
Weisser Burgunder Muschelkalk ★★ £B
Silvaner Kabinett Trocken ★ £B

✿ Robert Weil (Rheingau) *www.weingut-robert-weil.com*

Wilhelm Weil continues the revitalisation of this large Rheingau estate with 80 ha of vineyards planted almost exclusively to Riesling (with 1% Spätburgunder). Since the 1990s the wines have shown remarkable intensity and richness, especially in the sweeter styles. At the top level the wines really excel but also sell for very high prices, at least partly fuelled by an almost cult following. At the heart of the domaine is one of the finest vineyards in the Rheingau, Kiedricher Gräfenberg, a site of historical significance and reputation. Everything possible is done to ensure that grapes are as rich, ripe and concentrated as possible and this is particularly apparent at the Auslese level and higher. The rich, sweet, apricot and dried-peach fruit, braced by tangy acidity, becomes more honeyed and magnificent with age. It is a shame to drink these wines too young. Wines from other vineyards, sold as Weil Estate Riesling, though reasonably lush and concentrated, don't show the elegance or lingering fruit intensity of the Kiedricher Gräfenberg wines. An *Erste Lage (Erstes Gewächs)* bottling from the Grafenberg site is now a cut above other Rheingau examples. Spätburgunder and tiny amounts of outstanding TBA are also made.

Recommended Whites:

Kiedricher Turmberg Riesling TBA ✪✪✪✪✪ £H
Kiedricher Gräfenberg Riesling Eiswein ✪✪✪✪✪ £H
Kiedricher Gräfenberg Riesling Beerenauslese Goldkap ✪✪✪✪✪ £H
Kiedricher Gräfenberg Riesling Auslese Goldkapsel ★★★★★ £H
Kiedricher Gräfenberg Riesling Auslese ★★★★ £F
Kiedricher Gräfenberg Riesling Erstes Gewächs ★★★★ £F
Kiedricher Gräfenberg Riesling Spätlese ★★★ £E

Hans Wirsching (Franken) *www.wirsching.de*

This 75 ha Franken estate has been in the same family for 14 generations and includes a large chunk of the famed Julius-Echter-Berg site. Winemaking direction for the last 12 years has come from Dr Uwe Matheus, although the winemaker is Werner Probst, and viticulture is essentially organic. Silvaner, at 35% the most planted variety, shows good character and depth from both Julius-Echter-Berg and Kronsberg. Riesling too is fine, including a powerful *Erste Lage (Grosses Gewächs, GG)* version from Kronsberg, which should keep for 5-10 years. Good Weissburgunder and Scheurebe are also produced from Kronsberg. Both are intense but balanced and the Scheurebe is particularly exuberant and exotic. 'S' versions add more intensity and complexity. Sweeter styles include a rich, stylish and well-balanced Rieslaner (a Riesling and Sylvaner crossing) from Julius-Echter-Berg. St. Veit is a soundly made (dry) blend of Silvaner, Scheurebe and Riesling.

Recommended Whites:

Iphöfer Julius-Echter-Berg Rieslaner Beerenauslese ★★★★ £G
Iphöfer Kronsberg Silvaner Spätlese Trocken 'S' ★★★☆ £D
Iphöfer Julius-Echter-Berg Silvaner Auslese ★★★ £E
Iphöfer Julius-Echter-Berg Silvaner GG ★★ £D
Silvaner QbA Trocken ★☆ £B
Iphöfer Kronsberg Riesling GG ★★★☆ £D
Iphöfer Julius-Echter-Berg Riesling GG ★★ £D
Iphöfer Kronsberg Scheurebe Spätlese Trocken ★★★☆ £C
Iphöfer Kronsberg Weisser Burgunder GG ★★ £D
St. Veit QbA Trocken ★☆ £B

✿ Weingut Wittmann (Rheinhessen) *www.wittmannweingut.com*

Quality from the excellent 25 ha Wittmann estate, now committed to biodynamic production, continues to rise and, like Weingut KELLER, breathing new life into Rheinhessen. It is very much a family enterprise with tireless effort going into improving the health of the vineyard, which is certified as organic. 65% of the plantings are Riesling, the best examples of which, both dry and sweet, are now really first class and stand comparison with top examples from other regions. 'S' selection wines have an extra intensity and rich fruit on the finish as well as the vibrant acidity that is common to all the range. The Auslese 'S' from Westhofer Morstein pulsates with honey, botrytis and ripe fruit. Patience is required for powerful but austere *Erste Lage (Grosses Gewächs, GG)* bottling from the top vineyards, Aulerde, Kirschspiel and Morstein. The Aulerde starts out the tightest but has excellent potential, Kirschspiel shows excellent fruit and length, and the stylish Morstein has a subtle spice, mineral/fruit complexity. Some Chardonnay is also produced, while more esoteric wines include sweet versions of Huxelrebe and Albalonga (a Rieslaner-Silvaner crossing).

Recommended Whites:

Westhofener Aulerde Riesling TBA ★★★★ £H
Westhofener Aulerde Riesling GG ★★★ £E
Westhofener Morstein Riesling GG ★★★★ £E
Westhofener Morstein Riesling Auslese 'S' ★★★★ £E
Westhofener Morstein Riesling Spätlese ★★★☆ £D
Westhofener Kirschspiel Riesling GG ★★★☆ £E
Riesling QbA Westhofener Trocken 'S' ★★★ £C
Riesling QbA Trocken ★★ £B
Scheurebe QbA Trocken 'S' ★★☆ £C
Silvaner Trocken 'S' ★★ £C
Weisser Burgunder Trocken 'S' ★★ £C

Germany

J L Wolf (Pfalz) *www.jlwolf.com*

Expertise and investment from Ernst Loosen quickly realised the potential from 8.4 ha of vineyards belonging to the country estate of Villa Wolf. The majority of the vines are Riesling planted in some of the Pfalz's most vaunted sites. Applying the same organic approach used for the DR LOOSEN wines in the Mosel, as well as reducing yields and improving vinification, has resulted in a high quality but contrasting range of wines. They are naturally broader and more powerful than Mosel styles but also very complex and classy at what is called 'grand cru' level, which includes Pechstein, Ungeheuer and Jesuitengarten from Forst, and Leinhöhle from Deidesheim. So called 'premier crus' from Wachenheim are also fine: Wachenheimer Belz is dry, intense and gently refined. There's good character too in 'village' wines, especially Wachenheimer Riesling. Least expensive are the 'estate' varietal wines under the Villa Wolf label; most widely seen is the Grauburgunder, exported as Pinot Gris. More pricey 'J L' labelled Spätburgunder and Grauburgunder are also made.

Recommended Whites:

Forster Pechstein Riesling Spätlese Trocken ★★★★ £D
Deidesheimer Leinhöhle Riesling Spätlese Trocken ★★★ £D
Wachenheimer Belz Riesling Spätlese Trocken ★★★ £C
Wachenheimer Riesling ★★ £B Forster Riesling ★★ £B

Weingut Ziereisen (Baden) *www.zieriesen.de*

Here is another new high quality essentially red wine estate to emerge from Baden. The Ziereisens have 11 ha and are focussed on producing high quality Spätburgunder/Pinot Noir. Hans Peter Ziereisen believes that something of the individual character or *terroir* of the different parcels can be brought out. The most basic of the crus is Tshuppen which is aged only in used wood but is a soft, plummy style capable of a little age. A second, Schulen comes from a recently purchased but well-established vineyard with 30-year-old vines; *barrique*-aged (50% new), the oak is evident but there is better breadth. Rhini by contrast is aged in 100% new oak but has greater richness and intensity to the fruit and promises much with at least 5-6 years' age. 2003 saw the first vintage of an Alte Reben version from a single plot of vines. Concentrated and powerful there is ample evidence of old-vine fruit; like the Rhini there is lots of potential here. Also first made in 03 was a Syrah from young vines All the top reds are bottled unfiltered. Whites include a little Weissburgunder, Grauburgunder - Harett Pinot Gris comes from old vines and has a ripe late-harvested fruit character - and an oak-aged Chardonnay.

Recommended Reds:

Pinot Noir Alte Reben ★★★☆ £F Pinot Noir Rhini ★★★☆ £E
Pinot Noir Schulen ★★ £D Pinot Noir Tshuppen ★☆ £C
Syrah ★★★ £F

Recommended Whites:

Pinot Gris Harett ★★ £B

✿ Zilliken (Saar) *www.zilliken-vdp.de*

Forstmeister Geltz-Zilliken is the full name for the estate of Hans-Joachim Zilliken, which is based in large part on the fine Saarburger Rausch vineyard. The Rieslings from 11 ha are ripe and intense with no harshness and flavours range from cool lemon and lime fruit in Kabinett to nectarine and peach at higher levels. There is also a fine mineral undercurrent which varies with vintage and age. Sweeter styles, Auslese and above, are the real stars with much greater concentration, superb definition and a stylish elegance that showcases the vineyard. There may be several versions of Auslese and Eiswein and all the most select bottlings including the more

occasional Beerenauslesen and TBA, are sold at the VDP auction (so prices are averaged). A little Riesling also comes from Ockfener Bockstein.

Recommended Whites:

Saarburger Rausch Riesling TBA ✪✪✪✪✪ £H
Saarburger Rausch Riesling Eiswein ✪✪✪✪✪ £H
Saarburger Rausch Riesling Beerenauslese ★★★★★ £G
Saarburger Rausch Riesling Auslese Lange Goldkapsel ★★★★★ £G
Saarburger Rausch Riesling Auslese Goldkapsel ★★★★ £F
Saarburger Rausch Riesling Spätlese ★★☆ £C
Saarburger Rausch Riesling Kabinett ★☆ £B

Other wines of note

Acham-Magin (Pfalz)
Recommended Whites:
Forster Kirchenstück Riesling Trocken GG ★★ £D
Ruppertsberger Reiterpfad Riesling Trocken GG ★★ £D
Bastian (Mittelrhein)
Recommended Whites:
Bacharacher Posten Riesling GG ★★★ £D
Bacharacher Posten Riesling Auslese ★★★ £D
J B Becker (Rheingau)
Recommended Whites:
Wallufer Walkenberg Riesling Spätlese Trocken ★★ £C
Wallufer Walkenberg Auslese Trocken ★★★ £D
Dr Crusius (Nahe)
Recommended Whites:
Traiser Rotenfels Riesling Spatlese ★★☆ £C
Traiser Rotenfels Riesling Auslese ★★★☆ £D
Traiser Bastei Riesling Spätlese Trocken ★★ £C
Schlossböckelheimer Felsenberg Riesling Spätlese ★★ £C
Schlossböckelheimer Kupfergrube Ries Spätlese Halbtrocken ★★☆ £C
Diefenhard (Rheingau)
Recommended Whites:
Martinsthaler Langenberg Riesling Erste Lage ★★ £C
Groebe (Rheinhessen)
Recommended Whites:
Westhofener Riesling Kabinett ★★ £B
Westhofener Kirschspiel Riesling Spätlese ★★ £B
Westhofener Aulerde Riesling GG ★★★ £C
Kurt Hain (Mosel)
Recommended Whites:
Piesporter Goldtröpfchen Riesling Spätlese ★★ £B
Piesporter Goldtröpfchen Riesling Auslese ★★★ £C
Freiherr Von Heddesdorff (Mosel)
Recommended Whites:
Winninger Röttgen Riesling Spätlese ★★ £B
Winninger Röttgen Riesling Auslese ★★★ £D
Weingut Johannishof (Rheingau)
Recommended Whites:
Johannisberger Klaus Riesling Spätlese ★★★ £C
Rüdesheimer Berg Rottland Riesling Auslese ★★★ £E
Heribert Kerpen (Mosel)
Recommended Whites:
Wehlener Sonnenuhr Riesling Spätlese ★★ £B
Lingenfelder (Pfalz)
Recommended Whites:
Freinsheimer Goldberg Riesling Spätlese Trocken ★★ £B
Grosskarlbacher Osterberg Riesling Spätlese Halbtrocken ★★ £B

Meulenhof (Mosel)
Recommended Whites:
Erdener Treppchen Riesling Spätlese ★★ £B
Erdener Treppchen Riesling Auslese ★★ £C

Gutsverwaltung Niederhausen Schlossbockelheim (Nahe)
Recommended Whites:
Niederhauser Hermannshöhe Riesling Spätlese Halbtrocken ★★ £C
Schlossböckelheimer Kupfergrube Riesling Spätlese ★★★ £C
Niederhauser Hermannsberg Riesling Auslese ★★★☆ £D

Weingut Pfeffingen (Pfalz)
Recommended Whites:
Ungsteiner Herrenberg Riesling Spätlese Trocken ★★ £B

S A Prüm (Mosel)
Recommended Whites:
Wehlener Sonnenuhr Riesling Spätlese ★★ £C
Wehlener Sonnenuhr Riesling Auslese Goldkapsel ★★★★ £H
Graacher Himmelreich Riesling Eiswein ★★★★ £H

Querbach (Rheingau)
Recommended Whites:
Oestrich Doosberg Riesling Erste Lage ★★ £C

Johann Peter Reinert (Saar)
Recommended Whites:
Kanzemer Altenberg Riesling Spätlese ★★ £B
Kanzemer Altenberg Auslese ★★★ £C

Johann Ruck (Franken)
Recommended Whites:
Iphöfer Julius-Echter-Berg Silvaner Spätlese ★★★ £C
Iphöfer Julius-Echter-Berg Riesling Spätlese Trocken ★★★ £D

Schloss Johannisberg
Recommended Whites:
Schloss Johannisberger Riesling Spätlese ★★ £C
Schloss Johannisberger Riesling Auslese ★★★ £F
Schloss Johannisberger Beerenauslese ★★★ £H

Schloss Reinhartshausen (Rheingau)
Recommended Whites:
Erbacher Marcobrunn Riesling Erste Lage ★★ £D

Sekthaus Solter (Rheingau)
Recommended Whites:
Rheingau Riesling Brut Reserve ★★ £C

Weingut Am Stein (Franken)
Recommended Whites:
Würzburger Innere Leiste Riesling GG ★★★ £D
Stettener Stein Riesling Eiswein ★★★★ £H

Weingut J Storrlein (Franken)
Recommended Whites:
Randersackerer Sonnenstuhl Riesling Spätlese Trocken ★★★ £D
Randersackerer Sonnenstuhl Weissburgunder GG ★★ £C

Dr H Thanisch (Erben Thanisch) (Mosel)
Recommended Whites: Bernkasteler Lay Riesling Spätlese ★★ £C
Bernkasteler Badstube Riesling Kabinett ★ £B
Bernkasteler Badstube Riesling Spätlese ★★ £C
Bernkasteler Badstube Riesling Auslese ★★★ £F
Bernkasteler Doctor Riesling Kabinett ★★ £B
Bernkasteler Doctor Riesling Spätlese ★★★ £C
Bernkasteler Doctor Riesling Auslese ★★★★ £F

Villa Sachsen (Rheinhessen)
Recommended Whites: Riesling Classic ★ £B
Riesling Spätlese Trocken ★★ £C
Binger Scharlachberg Riesling Spätlese ★★★ £C

Dr Wagner (Saar)
Recommended Whites:
Saarburger Rausch Riesling Kabinett ★☆ £B
Saarburger Rausch Riesling Spätlese ★★☆ £C
Ockfener Bockstein Riesling Spätlese ★★☆ £C
Ockfener Bockstein Riesling Auslese ★★★ £E

Dr F Weins-Prüm (Mosel)
Recommended Whites:
Graacher Himmelreich Riesling Kabinett ★ £B
Graacher Domprobst Riesling Spätlese ★★★ £C
Wehlener Sonnenuhr Riesling Spätlese ★★ £C
Wehlener Sonnenuhr Riesling Auslese Goldkapsel ★★★★ £E

Wöhrwag (Württemberg)
Recommended Whites:
Untertürkheim Herzogenberg Rivaner Trocken ★☆ £B
Untertürkheim Herzogenberg Ries Kabinett Trocken Goldkapsel ★☆ £B
Untertürkheim Herzogenberg Ries Spätlese Trocken GG ★★☆ £D
Untertürkheim Herzogenberg Riesling Beerenauslese ★★★☆ £F
Recommended Reds:
Moritz (Dornfelder/Cabernet Sauvignon) ★☆ £C

Author's choice

Classic dry or off-dry Mosel Riesling
Grans-Fassian   Leiwener Laurentiuslay Riesling Spätlese 'S'
Wgt. Fritz Haag   Brauneberger Juffer-Sonnenuhr Riesling Spätlese
Wgt. Reinhold Haart   Piesporter Goldtröpfchen Riesling Spätlese
Heymann-Löwenstein   Winninger Uhlen Riesling 'Roth Lay' Erste Lage
Karlsmühle   Kaseler Nies'chen Riesling Spätlese
Wgt. Karthäuserhof   Eitelsbacher Karthäuserhofberg Ries Spät Trock
Dr Loosen   Wehlener Sonnenuhr Riesling Spätlese
St. Urbans-Hof   Ockfener Bockstein Riesling Spätlese
Willi Schaefer   Graacher Domprobst Riesling Spätlese
Schloss Lieser   Lieser Niederberg Helden Riesling Spätlese

More superior dry or off-dry Riesling
Bassermann-Jordan   Forster Pechstein Riesling Spätlese Trocken GG
Bürklin-Wolf   Forster Kirchenstück Riesling GG
Christmann   Gimmeldingen Mandelgarten Riesling Trocken GG
Dönnhoff   Niederhäusen Hersmannshöhle Riesling Spätlese
Emrich-Schönleber   Monzinger Frühlingsplätzchen Ries Spätlese
Wgt. Göttelmann   Münsterer Dautenpflänzer Riesling Selection
Wgt. Keller   Dalsheimer Hubacker Riesling Spätlese Trocken
Peter Jakob Kühn   Oestricher Lenchen Riesling Kabinett
Franz Künstler   Hochheimer Hölle Riesling Auslese Trocken
Andreas Laible   Durbacher Plauelrain Riesling Auslese Trocken
Weingut Joseph Leitz   Rudesheimer Berg Schlossberg Ries Spätlese
Ökonomierat Rebholz   Birkweiler Kastanienbusch Ries Spät Trocken GG
Schäfer-Fröhlich   Bockenauer Felseneck Riesling Spätlese Trocken
Schlossgut Diel   Dorsheimer Pittermännchen Riesling Spätlese
Van Volxom   Scharzhofberger Pergentsknopp Riesling
Wgt. Wittmann   Westhofener Kirschspiel Riesling GG

Stupendous German sweet wines
Georg Breuer   Rauenthal Nonnenberg Riesling Auslese Goldkapsel
Dönnhoff   Oberhäuser Brücke Riesling Eiswein
Gunderloch   Nackenheimer Rothenberg Riesling Beerenauslese
Dr Loosen   Bernkasteler Lay Riesling Eiswein
Markus Molitor   Zeltinger Sonnenuhr Riesling Beerenauslese
Müller-Catoir   Mussbacher Eselshaut Rieslaner Tba
Joh Jos Prüm   Wehlener Sonnenuhr Riesling Auslese Goldkapsel

Germany

Max Ferd. Richter   Mülheimer Helenenkloster Riesling Eiswein
Horst Sauer   Escherndorfer Lump Riesling TBA
Egon Müller/Scharzhof   Scharzhofberger Riesling TBA
Robert Weil H Kiedricher Gräfenberg Riesling Auslese Goldkapsel

Fine German whites not from Riesling
Wgt. Bercher   Königschaffhauser Hasenberg Gewürz Auslese
Emrich-Schönleber   Monzinger Grauburgunder Spätlese Trocken
Dr Heger   Ihringer Winklerberg Muskateller Spätlese 3 Sterne
Andreas Laible   Durbacher Plauelrain Gewürztraminer Auslese
Müller-Catoir   Haardter Mandelring Scheurebe Auslese
Horst Sauer   Escherndorfer Lump Silvaner Auslese
Juluisspital   Würzburger Stein Silvaner Spätlese Trocken
Wgt. Salwey   Oberrotweiler Kirchberg Weissburgunder GG 3 Sterne
Hans Wirsching   Iphofer Julius-Echter-Berg Rieslaner Beerenauslese

Wonderful Spätburgunder
Meyer-Näkel   Dernauer Pfarrwingert Spätburgunder GG
Franz Keller   Spätburgunder 'A' trocken
Ökonomierat Rebholz   Siebeldingen im Sonnenschein
Spätburgunder GG

From a growing band of small producers, Austria provides the world with outstanding dry whites, superb sweet wines and ever more interesting, good quality reds. Yet international recognition and appreciation of the great strides made has been slow in coming. From the steep hillside vineyards above the Danube (Donau) come the great Rieslings and Grüner Veltliners of the Wachau, as well as from the neighbouring regions of Kremstal and Kamptal. Around the Neusiedlersee, a broad shallow lake in the east that extends into Hungary, are spread the vineyards providing the grapes for the outstanding sweet wines as well as many of the raw materials for the current revolution in red wine production.

The regions

Niederösterreich's best: Wachau, Kremstal & Kamptal

The WACHAU is the leading wine region of Niederösterreich (Lower Austria) and together with Kremstal and Kamptal produces the majority of Austria's top dry Rieslings and Grüner Veltliner. Wachau's Rieslings are generally much closer in style to Alsace than Germany: full and powerful, with a marvellous concentration and purity of fruit within a vibrant structure. The very best have great class and age impressively. The more traditional grape of Grüner Veltliner also excels, with great depth and power to its peppery fruit character. There are three levels within the Wachau's system of ripeness: Steinfeder, Federspiel and Smaragd. The relatively low-alcohol style of Steinfeder is for early drinking but the best Federspiel are more structured and concentrated and will keep for at least three or four years. The best quality however always comes from the Smaragd examples, named after a little green lizard. German classifications of ripeness are used for sweeter styles (Auslese, Beerenauslese, etc.), made in small quantities by some growers when conditions permit. Wines from leading vineyards can sometimes be labelled with the vineyard only (*Ried* Klaus for example) and not the associated village. Behind Spitz are the top sites of **Hochrain** and **Singerriedel**, given brilliant expression by Hirtzberger, while Weissenkirchen includes the **Steinriegl**, **Achleiten** and **Klaus** sites close to the village. Further downstream are the particularly favoured steep terraces running from Dürnstein around past Oberloiben and Unterloiben; top vineyards include **Kellerberg**, **Loibner Berg**, **Schütt** and **Steinertal** but fine examples are also made from several other sites.

Wachau merges seamlessly into KREMSTAL, though there is not the same number of outstanding vineyards or producers here. In order to avoid much of what is in fact decidedly ordinary, look for wines from Nigl or Salomon, the latter highlighting the splendour of the **Kögl** vineyard. Kremstal is included among a number of regions under Austria's recently established DAC (Districtus Austriae Controllatus) a new regulatory category of controlled origins for the country's wines and grape varieties which has now being extended to a number of regions, in this case for Grüner Veltliner and Riesling. KAMPTAL (now included as a DAC region also for Grüner Veltliner and Riesling) in the valley of the Kamp is away from the Danube but the potential of vineyards around the wine town of Langenlois is increasingly being realised. Until recently only one producer, Bründlmayer, stood out but there are now several good sources. The top vineyards are Zöbinger **Heiligenstein** and Strasser **Gaisberg** from which several producers make good wines. As other excellent producers such as Fred Loimer or Schloss Gobelsburg come to the fore so does recognition of other great vineyard sites including Langenloiser **Steinmassl** or Kammerner **Lamm**.

Other regions of Niederösterreich

TRAISENTAL (now a DAC region for Grüner Veltliner and Riesling), is east of the Wachau and centred on another Danube tributary, the Traisen, was only officially recognised as a distinct wine region in 1995. Though it lacks the imposing terraces of the Wachau and it can be more of a struggle to get fully ripe fruit, it does boast at least one good producer in Neumayer. The large region of DONAULAND has two poles of potential quality and sensibly both have recently been given independent regional status. Foremost in quality terms is WAGRAM which adjoins Kamptal. It can be the source of excellent value Grüner Veltliner. Some also do surprisingly well with Pinot Noir. Leading producers include Fritsch, Leth and Ott. At the eastern end of Donauland is KLOSTERNEUBURG which lies just north of Vienna. The historic Stift Klosterneuburg is being stirred back into life with promsing St-Laurent reds and sweet whites. WIEN (Vienna) itself has a lot of land planted to vines for everyday dry whites. However, Wieninger and Zahel produce fine whites from the celebrated **Nussberg** site. South of the capital is the THERMENREGION, once famous for the sweet whites of Gumpoldskirchen from Zierfandler and Rotgipfler grapes but now making mostly dry whites and reds. North of Vienna is WEINVIERTEL, where again there's not a lot of real excitement, though producers such as Pfaffl and Graf Hardegg show there is potential for good dry whites. Weinvertel received Austria's first DAC.

Burgenland

Formerly part of Hungary, the edge of Burgenland forms all of Austria's entire border with its eastern neighbour. The best wines are the sweet whites made around the shores of the Neusiedlersee. On its western shore in NEUSIEDLERSEE-HÜGELLAND, around the town of **Rust**, the traditional Ausbruch style is made, now generally a full, sweet white with higher alcohol than wines made in the Germanic style (but with a must weight between those of Beerenauslese and TBA). The leading wine town for sweet whites on the eastern shore of the NEUSIEDLERSEE is Illmitz and the low-lying vineyards produce Austria's most stunning examples, led by those of Kracher. In both regions Welschriesling, Muskat Ottonel, Pinot Blanc, Pinot Gris and Chardonnay are the most important white grapes, with Chardonnay in both sweet and dry styles.

Reds are also increasingly important in Burgenland, from Neusiedlersee (especially around Gols and Mönchhof) now a DAC for Zweigelt and Neusiedlersee-Hügelland but also MITTELBURGENLAND and SÜDBURGENLAND. Grapes include Zweigelt, St-Laurent, Pinot Noir, Blaufränkisch (DAC in Mttelburgenland) and also Cabernet Sauvignon and Merlot. All appear either varietally or as a blend of some combination of these, often aged in new oak. Previously rather robust, earthy and brambly, Blaufränkisch-based reds are showing increasing refinement. For the sceptical or those already hooked on great Grüner or Riesling do try the diverse but top quality reds from the likes of Kollwentz, Feiler-Artinger, Triebaumer or Juris. Pannobile (made in white as well as red) is produced by nine growers around Gols - quality and composition varies from producer to producer.

Steiermark (Styria)

In Steiermark, especially SÜDSTEIERMARK close to the Slovenian border, some aromatic, lively whites including Sauvignon Blanc, Chardonnay (here called Morillon) and Gewürztraminer are made. Lighter, unoaked examples are sold as *Steirische Klassik*. More serious single vineyard efforts from the likes of Gross, Tement or Wohlmuth can be a revelation with a sosphisticated use of oak, and unexpected weight, poise and complexity. These now contrast with the region's previous reputation for wines with unbalanced alcohol levels and excessive oak.

Wine behind the label

Austria

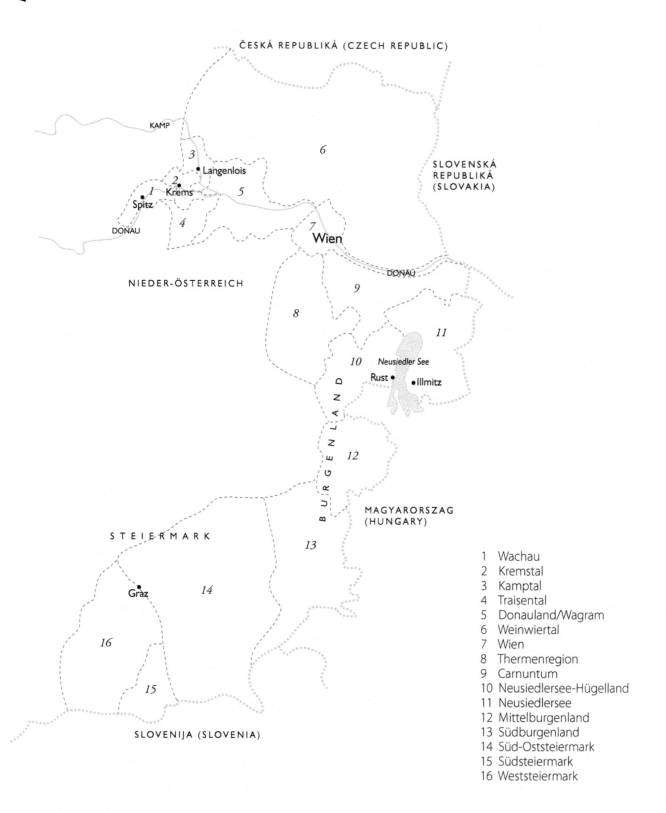

ČESKÁ REPUBLIKÁ (CZECH REPUBLIC)

KAMP

SLOVENSKÁ REPUBLIKÁ (SLOVAKIA)

3

Langenlois
2 Krems
1
Spitz
DONAU
4
5
6

Wien *7*

DONAU

NIEDER-ÖSTERREICH

9

8

11

10
Neusiedler See
Rust Illmitz

B U R G E N L A N D

12

MAGYARORSZAG (HUNGARY)

STEIERMARK

13

Graz
14

16

15

SLOVENIJA (SLOVENIA)

1 Wachau
2 Kremstal
3 Kamptal
4 Traisental
5 Donauland/Wagram
6 Weinwiertal
7 Wien
8 Thermenregion
9 Carnuntum
10 Neusiedlersee-Hügelland
11 Neusiedlersee
12 Mittelburgenland
13 Südburgenland
14 Süd-Oststeiermark
15 Südsteiermark
16 Weststeiermark

A-Z of producers by region

Wachau		Donauland/Wagram	
Leo Alzinger	657	Bernhard Ott	664
Franz Hirtzberger	660	**Weinwiertel**	
Holzapfel	660	Graf Hardegg	659
Josef Jamek	660	Pfaffl	664
Emmerich Knoll	661	**Neusiedlersee-Hügelland**	
Lagler	662	Feiler-Artinger	658
Nikolaihof	663	Kollwentz-Römerhof	661
F-X Pichler	665	Prieler	666
Rudi Pichler	665	Heidi Schröck	667
Weingut Prager	665	Ernst Triebaumer	667
Schmelz	667	**Neusiedlersee**	
Domäne Wachau	668	Paul Ach	657
Kremstal		Juris	660
Felsner	659	Kracher	661
Mantelhof	663	Helmut Lang	662
Nigl	663	Anita & Hans Nittnaus	664
Salomon-Undhof	666	Gut Oggau	664
Petra Unger	668	Velich	668
Kamptal		**Mittelburgenland**	
Kurt Angerer	657	Arachon T FX T	657
Bründlmayer	658	**Südburgenland**	
Ehn	658	Schiefer	666
Birgit Eichinger	658	Krutzler	662
Hiedler	659	**Thermenregion**	
Hirsch	660	Heinrich Hartl	659
Jurtschitsch Sonnhof	661	**Südsteiermark**	
Loimer	662	Lackner-Tinnacher	662
Rudolf Rabl	666	Erich & Walter Polz	665
Schloss Gobelsburg	666	Gross	659
Traisental		Tement	667
Neumayer	663	Wohlmuth	668

Austria vintages

With variable growing conditions from year to year, vintages are important in Austria. More difficult vintages can not only result in a lack of richness and ripeness but can fail to provide the balance essential for ageing. The ratings below for Riesling and Grüner apply to the best Wachau Smaragd examples or similar styles from Kremstal or Kamptal. Top wines need 3-5 years' age but will keep for a decade or longer from a top vintage. The sweet wines of Neusiedlersee and Neusiedlersee-Hügelland, while producer-dependent, will nearly always benefit from at least 5 years' age and will keep for a decade or more. Austria's increasingly good reds are also vintage dependent but vary more significantly in style and ageing potential from producer to producer.

2016: As of October 2016, it has been a difficult year. The frost from the 26th to the 29th of April was devastating for many: one grower in Kremstal lost 20% of his crop, whilst another in the Wachau lost 60%. After the frost came sultry heat and frequent masses of rain, followed by powdery mildew. In Lower Austria this put the Grüner Weltliner grape at risk, although Riesling looks good. Growers in the Steiermark and eastern Austria, especially in Burgenland, fared badly from the frost as well as from the heat, frequently above 30° centigrade over all of Austria, and the rain. Overall, the size of the crop will be considerably less than in 2015.

2015: Weather conditions were much better than in 2014, and winemakers were on the whole happy with the results. There were exceptions. Hailstorms in the first week of May wiped out 3,000 ha in Lower Austria, although the Wachau escaped, and in the Steiermark, a single hailstorm cost many growers 25-30% of their crop. Overall, the summer saw hot days and nights, but fortunately, there was enough rain in mid-August followed by heat; good weather then prevailed through the harvest. There were relatively robust alcohol levels, unlike in 2014, and fruit-driven aromatics. On the whole there were a lot of excellent wines made across Austria; it will take time to see if 2015 develops into a great vintage.

2014: For grape growers and winemakers, this was a year to be forgotten. Virtually everywhere in Austria it was very warm and very rainy, and the inevitable result was rapidly-spreading and destructive rot. In the Wachau, one grower said that he had had so many grapes that he took off 50% of his Grüner Weltliner in June; then one month before harvest, from mid-August to mid-September, there were 40 mm of rain and rot exploded. Another lost 30% of his grapes from the rain. Overall, although many of the wines were aromatic, losses came to 40%. Similarly, they suffered weather damage in the Neusidlersee, but in their case, the year was rainy and cold, and as a result, there were fewer good wines than usual. In Styria, they not only had rain and the resultant rot, but they also had hail; some growers lost 50% of their crop. There are young whites that are a pleasure to drink, but this is not a year to lay down many wines in the cellar. Having said that, some of the best wines in Lower Austria are more complex and impressive than their 2015 versions.

2013: A little bit of coulure in the Grüner Veltliner during the flowering season has led to reduced yields and the formation of extra sweet berries on the vines which has led to fruity wines with perhaps a little less structure than desired. Because of late flowering, Rieslings did not always reach sufficient ripeness to ensure balance, but the excessive acidity, when corrected, will allow good keeping qualities for the wines. Not a lot of sweet wines were made owing to a lack of botrytis, but what has been made is of excellent quality. Reds this year are a little on the light side, showing soft tannins and elegant fruitiness.

2012: The frosts of May 17 and 18 put paid to a great deal of quantity and yields were well down on the figures for 2011. However, what was produced was of excellent quality due to ideal growing conditions for the rest of the summer. The wines are tighter and leaner than those of 2011 but nevertheless the ripeness of the grapes ensured good aromacy and fruitiness in the dry whites whilst the Prädikat wines, produced in reasonable quantities this year, are showing good balance between sweetness and acidity. It was also another fine year for the reds, whilst showing a little less exuberance than the 2011s, are extremely well balanced with the best of them quite suitable for extended cellaring.

2011: After a very cold winter, benign spring weather resulted in even early flowering and despite a rather humid June, fine weather in August and September produced just the right growing conditions for an excellent vintage - in quantity as well as quality after two rather lean years. White wines are therefore ripe with low acidity, full and aromatic, which will not only drink early but will also have sufficient backbone for some ageing. It has also been an excellent year for the reds which are showing generosity of fruit as well as fine tannic structure. The best will be superb and even wines from the lesser appellations will show a degree of class not see since 2006. The only downside to this vintage is that frosts early and late in the year did much to restrict noble rot and so with few exceptions, this is not a year for the sweetest of wines although

Austria

some who risked leaving their grapes on the vine were rewarded with some fine Eiswein harvested in February 2012.

2010: Colder and wetter weather than average has once again played havoc with this vintage. Yields are well down again and with the shortage of wine from the 2009 vintage there will be an inevitable increase in prices. After a rainy September, those who decided to pick early in October fared better than those who waited because the rain returned again at the end of the month. The saving grace is that what has been produced is of good quality - fruity and aromatic. Reds are expected to be on the light side but not lacking in finesse and balance.

2009: The weather in spring and summer 2008 was all over the place - storms, floods and mud slides, record lightning and hot tropical conditions, according to the Austrian Marketing Board. From 1959 onwards, Austrian vintages ending in 9 have often been exceptional but there were few triumphs over 2009's apocalyptic weather cycle. Flowering was early and fruit set poor (especially for the Riesling) so the potential size of the harvest was reduced. There was a lot of rain towards the end of the summer that led to botrytis, with smaller volumes of wine at Federspiel level. However, there is evidence of good concentration of acidity, though the wines are not especially exuberant.

2008: Weather conditions in 2008 were almost the reverse of 2007. After a normal spring, there was a great deal of rain up to the end of July that produced challenging conditions of disease and rot, not to mention a general under ripeness of the fruit. Many growers, worried by the health of the grapes, picked early, but warm October winds rewarded those who took the risk of delaying the harvest. As a result, this is a vintage of uneven quality and careful selection needs to be made. In attune to the reverse conditions of the previous vintage, Riesling fared better than Grüner Veltliner and in the reds, Zweigelt did better than Blaufränkisch in the reds. Warm, damp weather in the Burgenland ensured average quantity and quality of sweet wines.

2007: Fine summer weather gave way to long periods of rain at the beginning of September which left the growers with a dilemma as to when to pick. Those who waited, however, (some didn't pick until the beginning of November) were rewarded with drying winds that helped to limit the amount of rot. Whilst overall quantities produced were a little above average, quality was mixed, with Grüner Veltliner generally faring better than Riesling in the whites and Blaufränkisch faring better than the thinnerskinned Zweigelt in the reds. In the south, the Styrian whites were crisp and aromatic, whilst good conditions prevailed in the Burgenland to enhance the development of noble rot.

2006: After the ordeals of 2005, 06 looks a more consistent bet for quality throughout Austria. The long preceding winter built up moisture levels that were needed to support the vine in the heat of July and generally there was good health and high sugar levels. Yields were down slightly in Wachau/Kremstal/Kamptal but quality is high. In Burgenland reds look promising but there was little incidence of botrytis for the sweet wines.

2005: With quantities down quality in 05 was somewhat salvaged by a decent late burst of weather in October but rot and underipeness will mar lesser examples. Stick with a good name for refined whites and spare, refined reds. Sweet wine prospects are better.

Older vintages: include 2002 and 2003 for very good reds from Burgenland and Styria. The dramatic flooding of the Danube in 2002 resulted in ruined grapes from vines on the flat ground in and around the Wachau region but quality is surprisingly good from

terraced vineyards. In 2001, October made the vintage and late picking ensured rich, structured wines now really coming into their own. Also consider, very ageworthy 99s from the Wachau, Kremstal and Kamptal while the 97s from the same regions were, and can still be, super. Keeping with the odd years, good wines can also be had from 95 and 93.

Austria vintage chart

	Wachau/Kremstal Kamptal Riesling	Wachau/Kremstal Kamptal Grüner Veltliner	Neusiedlersee N-Hügelland Sweet whites
2015	★★★☆ A	★★★☆ A	NYR
2014	★★☆ B	★★☆ B	★★☆ A
2013	★★★☆ B	★★★☆ B	★★★★ A
2012	★★★★ B	★★★★ B	★★★★ B
2011	★★★★☆ B	★★★★☆ B	★★★ B
2010	★★★ C	★★☆ C	★★★ C
2009	★★★☆ B	★★★☆ C	★★★☆ B
2008	★★★ C	★★☆ C	★★★ C
2007	★★★ C	★★★☆ C	★★★★ B
2006	★★★★☆ B	★★★★☆ B	★★ C
2005	★★★ C	★★★ C	★★★☆ C
2004	★★★★ C	★★★★ C	★★★★☆ B
2003	★☆/ ★★★★ C	★☆/ ★★★★ C	★★★★☆ B
2002	★★★☆ C	★★★☆ C	★★★★ C
2001	★★★★☆ C	★★★★☆ C	★★★☆ C
2000	★★★★ C	★★★★ C	★★★★☆ C
1999	★★★★★ C	★★★★★ C	★★★★ C
1998	★★★☆ C	★★★☆ C	★★★★ C
1997	★★★★★ C	★★★★★ C	★★★★ C
1995	★★★★ C	★★★★ C	★★★★★ C
1993	★★★☆ D	★★★☆ D	★★★★ D
1991	★★☆ D	★★★☆ D	★★★★ D
1990	★★★★☆ D	★★★★☆ D	-

Changes in the labels

Long-mooted changes in the Austrian wine law have resulted in changes on wine labels. The DAC classification (Districtus Austria Controllatus) has been extended and developed, the process of identifying mapping top vineyard sites is continuing, with the resulting single-vineyard names on labels, and sparkling wines are being more rigorously regulated. First of all, regional names are being simplified: the four regions whose names included Burgenland or Neusidlersee are now all just Burgenland. Secondly, single-vineyard wines must now be labelled Ried plus the name of the vineyard. Thirdly, in Burgenland, all of those sweet wines which were called Ruster Ausbruch are now labelled trockenbeerenauslese wines; only those from the town of Rust itself may be labelled Ruster Ausbruch. And fourthly, sparkling wines (sekt) will have a series of slightly confusing labels, but the thing to remember is that Austrian Sekt with Protected Designation of Origin can be sold only when labelled with one of the defined terms Klassic, Reserve, or Grosse Reserve.

In **Kamptal**, **Kremstal**, **Traisental** and **Wagram**, all part of **Niederösterreich** (Lower Austria), the Österreichische Traditionsweingüter (Austrian Traditional Wine Estates) or ÖTW, have, from the 2016 vintage, introduced a three-tier classification system; this, however, for the time being leaves out Wagram, which does not yet have an established DAC system. The tiers are Gebietswein, which is a regional wine, such as Kamptal or Kremstal; Ortswein, which is a village wine, such as Langenlois or Spitz; and

Riedenwein, which is a single-vineyard wine, such as Gaisberg or Heiligenstein. Within the Ried or single-vineyard classification, work has been going on for some time to identify the best vineyards as Erste Lagen or first growths or premier crus; as of September 2016 there were 62 of them. The intention is also to identify the Grosse Lagen or grand crus. The Erste Lagen wines have 1ÖTW on their labels.

The **Wachau** have their own organisation, the Vinea Wachau Nobilis Districtus, and their own system of quality control. There are three levels: Steinfeder, which is the lightest, may be gently sparkling, and is to be drunk young, has an alcohol level of 11-11.5%; Federspiel, which is made from riper grapes, has an alcohol level of 11.5-12.5%; and Smaragd, made from the ripest grapes, has a minimum alcohol level of 12.5%, and the potential to age. They are normally the highest quality wines. The Vinea Wachau permits only wines made from white grapes in the classification.

In the **Steiermark** in the south, the Styrians have their own association, the Steirische Terroir & Klassic Weingüter, or STK; they have their own vineyard classification system, with Premier Cru STK Vineyards and Grand Cru STK Vineyards.

A-Z of producers

Paul Achs (Neusiedlersee) *www.paul-achs.at*
With 95% of his production from 23 ha red wine it would be reasonable to describe Paul Achs, a third generation wine grower, as a red wine specialist! He works with Ronny Rebscher to make arguably the most consistent range of quality reds within the vicinity of Neusiedler See. Blaufränkisch, in several versions, and Pinot Noir are particularly good. The top wines are oak-aged, partly in new wood but its use is vintage dependent. Probably the best wine, the Ungerberg Blaufränkisch from a vineyard close to Gols comes from old vines. Aged in in *barriques* and 300-litre Fässern, it is dense with a creamy, smoky, blackberry intensity and is expressive and well-balanced but needs time, typically 6-10 years. Altenberg and others have also been produced. A fine Edelgrund version is aged only in used oak but also needs time. New oak (usually about 60%) is used for the complex and intense Pinot Noir and 5 years should ensure a good balance between oak and fruit. The Pannobile red is a good example too, concentrated and flavoursome with refined tannins - Paul's blend is from Zweigelt, Blaufränkisch and St. Laurent. A little Merlot and Syrah are also planted which can find their way into this wine. As well as a decent St. Laurent, the regular Blaufränkisch, and Zweigelt make excellent everyday drinking. A little Sauvignon is made, as is Chardonnay.

Recommended Reds:
Blaufränkisch Ungerberg ★★★☆ £E
Blaufränkisch Edelgrund ★★★ £D
Blaufränkisch ★★ £B Pinot Noir ★★★☆ £E
Pannobile ★★★☆ £E St. Laurent ★★☆ £C
Zweigelt ★★ £B

Leo Alzinger (Wachau) *www.alzinger.at*
The wines of this small 8 ha estate are difficult to obtain but are some of the best of the Wachau. Leo Alzinger now works with his son (also called Leo) to produce slightly more Grüner Veltliner than Riesling from top sites including Loibenberg and Steinertal. These wines are typically intense, taut and steely when young but with an underlying richness and concentration. As they evolve, their true class, minerality and considerable complexity become apparent. At least 5 years' age is required. More accessible if slightly less classy are

Riesling and Grüner Veltliner from Liebenberg while there's a fine concentrated example of Grüner (especially the Smaragd version) from the Mühlpoint site below Steinertal. As well as Riesling and Grüner Veltliner from other sites, a little of a Reserve Grüner Veltliner and a Chardonnay are also made but have not yet been tasted.

Recommended Whites:
Deidesheimer Mäushöhle Riesling Beerenauslese ★★★★ £H
Loibner Loibenberg Riesling Smaragd ★★★★ £E
Loibner Steinertal Riesling Smaragd ★★★★ £E
Loibner Steinertal Grüner Veltliner Smaragd ★★★ £E
Dürnsteiner Liebenberg Riesling Smaragd ★★★ £D
Dürnsteiner Liebenberg Grüner Veltliner Smaragd ★★★ £D
Loibner Mühlpoint Grüner Veltliner Smaragd ★★★ £D
Loibner Mühlpoint Grüner Veltliner Federspiel ★★ £C

⊙ **Kurt Angerer (Kamptal)** *www.kurt-angerer.at*
Three unoaked Grüner Veltliners from differing soils are arguably the most consistent and balanced of this increasingly fine and diverse range of whites and reds from 27 ha. Kies from red gravel is harvested first and made in the biggest volume and has plenty of intensity and good structure. Significantly better is Loam from loess soils, which is riper and more distinctive, while Spies from granite soils is tight when young but promising. Eichenstraude is another bottling of Grüner from a small parcel of late-harvested fruit from old vines. It has added breadth but also an intrusive leesy oak influence. Better is Unfiltriet, which, though barrel-fermented and aged, is well balanced and has impressive breadth and expression that would not shame many a Meursault producer. A flavoursome, spicy, creamy Pinot Blanc that sees similar treatment is less good. Donatus Riesling is very ripe, concentrated and powerful. Reds are also successful with good fruit intensity and varietal character but in general could use a little more depth and less oak. Merlot includes a little Cabernet Sauvignon.

Recommended Reds:
Merlot ★★★ £C Zweigelt Granit ★★ £D
Zweigelt Barrique ★ £C St Laurent ★★ £C
Cabernet Sauvignon/Zweigelt ★★ £C
Recommended Whites:
Grüner Veltliner Unfiltriert ★★★ £D
Grüner Veltliner Loam ★★★ £C Grüner Veltliner Spies ★★★ £B
Grüner Veltliner Eichenstraude ★★ £C
Grüner Veltliner Kies ★★ £B Riesling Donatus ★★★ £C
Pinot Blanc ★★ £C

⊙ **Arachon T FX T (Mittelburgenland)**
This high-profile project, which commenced with the 1996 vintage involves the collaboration of three leading winemakers of diverse backgrounds: F-X PICHLER, Manfred TEMENT and Tibor SZEMES. Grapes are sourced from 25 ha of vineyard in Horitschon belonging to 37 growers who have been encouraged to reduce yields and achieve full ripeness. The main focus is Arachon evolution – originally intended as an internationally styled red, it has a distinct Austrian personality with half the blend from Blaufränkisch and the balance from Zweigelt, Merlot and Cabernet Sauvignon (varying in proportion according to the vintage). It is also much more refined in structure in the most recent vintages with increasing class to its smoky, cedary, spicy, plummy complexity. Since the 2000 vintage only French oak has been used. Made since 2001 is a decent second wine, a'Kira – a 100% Blaufränkisch that needs a couple of years to fill out. Arachon should be given 5–10 years' age.

Austria

Recommended Reds:
Arachon evolution ★★★★ £D a'Kira ★★ £B

❁ Bründlmayer (Kamptal) *www.bruendlmayer.com*
Willi Bründlmayer's organically run estate is the best dry white wine producer in Austria outside the Wachau and it rivals the best of those. About 60ha of lyre-trained vineyards occupy sites around the town of Langenlois. The most outstanding of these is Zöbinger Heiligenstein, producing superb Rieslings with depth, power and vibrant ripe fruit; still fuller and more complex is an Alte Reben (old vines) example. A fine mineral-edged Steinmassel Riesling is also produced but Grüner Veltliner is at least as important, with full, flavoursome examples with green peppercorn and yellow plum fruit, particularly lush and ripe in the Ried Lamm bottling. Top examples of each deserve to be drunk with 4–5 years' age, while regular Kamptaler Terrassen examples (from a blend of sites), which show good fruit if not the same style or concentration, can be drunk young. Though Grüner Veltliner (Ried Loiser Berg and Ried Kaferberg are two more fine examples) and Riesling account for more than half of what is produced, a well-balanced, ripe, medium-weight Chardonnay that avoids being too oaky or leesy is also good. Traditional-method sparkling wine and some Pinot Noir (Cécile) are also made, as are occasional sweet but superb Beerenauslese and TBA from both Grüner Veltliner and Riesling.

Recommended Whites:
Riesling Alte Reben ★★★★★ £E
Zöbinger Heiligenstein Riesling ★★★★ £D
Langenloiser Steinmassel Riesling ★★★ £C
Riesling Kamptaler Terrassen ★★ £C
Grüner Veltliner Alte Reben ★★★★ £D
Kammerner Lamm Grüner Veltliner ★★★ £D
Langenloiser Berg Vogelsang Grüner Veltliner ★★ £C
Grüner Veltliner Kamptaler Terrassen ★★ £C Chardonnay ★★ £C

Ehn (Kamptal) *www.ehnwein.at*
Michaela Ehn is one of the quality stars among a group of 11 'Women and their Wines' promoting female winemaking/wine production in Austria (others include Birgit EICHINGER, Silvia PRIELER, Heidi SCHRÖCK and Petra UNGER). Michaela runs 14ha planted mostly to Grüner Veltliner and Riesling and individual bottlings of both can be very good. The Titan version of Grüner from the Spiegel vineyard is one of the full-blown, partly oaked examples that are on the increase. It is, however, intense, concentrated and minerally as well as better balanced than some. Rieslings from Zöbinger Heiligenstein are especially fine, concentrated and structured. Other whites include a complex, exotic blend from a mixed planting of old vines (8 varieties) called Jubiläumswein, which is deep, concentrated and well structured. Sauvignon has good purity and intensity. Also produced is a Titan version of Chardonnay fermented and aged in *barrique* while a richly honeyed and botrytised Chardonnay Beerenauslese (made only from 2001) has excellent balance and purity. Red Tizian is a soft, juicy-fruited crowd-pleasing blend.

Recommended Whites:
Zöbinger Heiligenstein Riesling Reserve ★★★★ £E
Zöbinger Heiligenstein Riesling ★★★★ £D
Loiserberg Riesling ★★★ £D Grüner Veltliner Titan ★★★★ £D
Oberer Panzaun Grüner Veltliner ★★★ £C
Harein Grüner Veltliner ★★★ £C Panzaun Grüner Veltliner ★★ £C
Alter Panzaun Jubiläumswein ★★★ £C
Sauvignon Blanc ★★ £C Gelber Muskateller ★★ £C

❁ Birgit Eichinger (Kamptal) *www.weingut-eichinger.at*
In Austria, as elsewhere, female winemakers tend to be a small minority but as is often the case the amount of quality wine they produce is not commensurate with their numbers. Birgit Eichinger is one of the emerging stars of Kamptal where her 8 ha of vines include the two top sites, Heiligenstein and Gaisberg. Both Grüner Veltliner and Riesling from Gaisberg are fine, with a touch of minerality in the first and a pure classy, citrus depth to the latter. Riesling from Heiligenstein is bigger yet structured with great style and depth with the 2016 showing quite a lot of fruit. Grüner Veltliner from Wechselberg also highlights the potential of this site. The ripest Grüner grapes from Gaisberg and Heiligenstein go into a partially oaked wine called Goliath that has good richness, length and complexity, if struggling a little for balance. Also made is a very good example of unoaked Chardonnay (from Strasser Gaisberg), while a second Chardonnay, Strasser Stangl, is oaked and more international, yet still with good fruit purity.

Recommended Whites:
Zöbinger Heiligenstein Riesling ★★★★ £D
Strasser Gaisberg Riesling ★★★ £C
Strasser Gaisberg Grüner Veltliner ★★★ £C Grüner Veltliner Goliath ★★★ £D
Strasser Wechselberg Grüner Veltliner ★★ £C
Strasser Gaisberg Chardonnay ★★ £C
Strasser Strangl Chardonnay ★★ £C

❁ Feiler-Artinger *www.feiler-artinger.at*
Kurt Feiler works with his father to make fine, elegant sweet whites plus some dry whites and reds on his family's 30 ha estate. Sweet whites start with Ruster Ausbruch, the traditional sweet wine of Rust which varies in composition but can include Pinot Blanc, Chardonnay and Welschriesling whilst a Pinot Cuvée version with the Pinot Blanc component fermented in new oak, adds in Pinot Gris. True to the style, the wines are more fully fermented than sweet German wines and have an alcohol level (13.5%) similar to Sauternes. The wines are honeyed and refined with lots of ripe botrytised fruit intensity but vary in richness and style according to the vintage. The creamy, refined and pure-fruited Pinot Cuvée shows a lovely balance between sweetness and acidity. An Essenz bottling is an intensely sweet unctuous style with great purity, depth and length and should be tried at least once. Other sweet wines include a good Beerenauslese (Weissburgunder, Chardonnay and Welschriesling) along with Traminer Beerenauslese, Muskat Ottonel Beerenauslese and occasionally an unusual dried cherry-fruited Zweigelt Beerenauslese. Dry varietal whites are made too as is the barrel fermented Gustav from Chardonnay, if previously also including Pinot Gris and Neuburger, which has creamy pear, quince and melon fruit. Reds have become increasingly important, lately accounting for more than half the winery's output. The complex, smoky black-fruited Solitaire is based on Blaufränkisch (usually with Merlot and Cabernet Franc). It now receives up to 100% new oak and has become increasingly ripe and concentrated, deserving of 7-8 years' ageing. A very convincing, gutsy yet elegant Cabernet Sauvignon/Merlot blend needs a similar amount of time. It is numbered with successive vintages: the 2007 vintage, for example, is 1013. Other reds include a brambly, characterful 'Zweigelt & More' (with a little Cabernet Franc) and a dense Pinot Noir aged in 75% new oak. A Cabernet Franc and a rosé from Blaufränkisch are also made.

Recommended Reds:
Solitaire ★★★★ £E Cabernet/Merlot ★★★☆ £E

Zweigelt Beerenauslese ★★★ £E Pinot Noir ★★★ £E
Blaufränkisch Umriss ★★☆ £C Zweigelt & More ★★☆ £C
Recommended Whites:
Ruster Ausbruch Essenz ★★★★★ £G
Ruster Ausbruch Pinot Cuvée ★★★★☆ £F
Ruster Ausbruch ★★★☆ £E Beerenauslese ★★★☆ £E
Traminer Beerenauslese ★★★☆ £E
Welschriesling Auslese ★★☆ £C Gustav ★★ £C

Felsner (Kremstal) *www.weingut-felsner.at*
Manfred Felsner produces good, reasonably priced Grüner Veltliner and Riesling from his family's 16.5 ha estate in Kremstal. There is not the style, complexity or concentration seen from top Wachau producers but the wines are generally soundly made with good varietal expression. Grüner Veltliner is grown on loess soils and shows yellow plum, lentil, spice and pepper in several different bottlings. The 2015 Grüner Veltliner from the Moosburgerin vineyard is fruity and very pleasant, an expressive, stylish Riesling from the Gebling vineyard is the best of those tasted. Reds include soft, supple St-Laurent and a spicy, flavoursome Zweigelt.
Recommended Reds:
Zweigelt Weitgasse ★★ £B St. Laurent ★ £B
Recommended Whites:
Gebling Riesling ★★★ £C Grüner Veltliner Alte Reben ★★ £C
Grüner Veltliner Lössterrassen ★★ £C
Vordenberg Grüner Veltliner ★★ £C
Moosburgerin Grüner Veltliner Kabinett ★★ £C
Gebling Grüner Veltliner ★★ £C

Gross (Südsteiermark) *www.gross.at*
Alois Gross has nearly 50 ha in southern Styria, well over 90% of it planted to a wide but typical range of varieties for the region. A range of Steirische Klassik varietals are expressive if relatively straightforward. All benefit from 3–4 months on their lees, the Chardonnay (Morillon) additionally from ageing in 25hl casks. Only a limited number of the single-vineyard wines have been tasted but it is surely these that have established the Gross name as they are focused, properly structured wines with poise and intensity. An elderflower-and-mineral Sauvignon from Sulz contrasts with a fuller, richer, spicy, complex and composed Ratscher Nussberg example. The latter receives 10 months in large oak and shows just how seamless this integration should be. Also super is Gewürztraminer from Ratscher Nussberg; distinguished by its subtlety, length and intensity it could pass for an Alsace grand cru. Others include Weissburgunder from both Nussberg and Kittenberg as well as Gelber Muskateller from the Perz vineyard. Gewürztraminer is also produced occasionally in a very sweet style such as TBA or Eiswein.
Recommended Whites:
Gewürztraminer Eiswein ★★★★ £E Sulz Sauvignon Blanc ★★★ £D
Ratscher Nussberg Gewürztraminer ★★★ £D
Sulz Sauvignon Blanc ★★★ £D
Ratscher Nussberg Sauvignon Blanc ★★★ £D
Sauvignon Blanc Steirische Klassik ★★ £B
Gelber Muskateller Steirische Klassik ★★ £B
Morillon Steirische Klassik ★★ £B
Weissburgunder Steirische Klassik ★ £B
Welschriesling Steirische Klassik ★ £B

Graf Hardegg (Weinviertel) *www.grafhardegg.at*
Well-travelled Peter Veyder-Malberg makes an increasingly high standard of wines here from 43 ha of vineyard in what is a comparative wilderness for quality wines in Austria. Some 40% of the plantings are Grüner Veltliner, responsible for a number of good examples including: a lively Veltlinsky; a more mineral, intense and pure example, Graf Hardegg, that qualifies under new appellation rules as Weinviertel DAC; and a richer example from the Steinbügel site. A further Grüner is released under the Schloss banner from vineyards surrounding the property. But the estate has received more attention for wines such as Viognier (Austria's first), Cabernet Sauvignon, Merlot and Pinot Noir. The Rote Reserve (not tasted) is a blend of Cabernet Sauvignon, Merlot and a little Zweigelt. The Viognier is fermented on the skins and has good concentration and flavour but the alcohol can be obtrusive (if now better balanced than previously). Pinot Noir from Steinbügel shows promise but a dense Riesling from the same site is more impressive. A peculiarity is Forticus, a fortified red from Blauburger and Merlot grapes. Also released under the Graf Hardegg label is a Zweigelt and a rosé from Zweigelt and Pinot Noir. Schloss Riesling and Pinot Noir examples are made and Brut Sekt white and rosé are also released.
Recommended Reds:
Pinot Noir Steinbügel ★★ £C
Recommended Whites:
Grüner Veltliner Steinbügel ★★★ £C
Grüner Veltliner Veltlinsky ★★ £B
Weinviertel Graf Hardegg Grüner Veltliner ★★ £B
Riesling Steinbügel ★★★ £C Viognier V ★★ £E

Heinrich Hartl (Thermenregion) *www.weingut-hartl.at*
Seventh generation winemaker Heinrich Hartl is in charge of the 15 ha family property, plus 3 rented ha – producing 100,000 bottles, 70/30 red/white. The family still get involved in tastings, but ultimately, Hartl makes the decisions. The estate's reds comprise Pinot Noir; St Laurent; Zweigelt (including over 50-year old vines); as well as Cabernet, Merlot and Blauburger; and the rest, local varietals. Whites include Rotgipfler (including 35-40 year old vines); Weissburgunder; Sauvignon Blanc; Muskateler; and the rest, Chardonnay, Gewurztraminer and locals. Hartl offers updated versions of tried and true styles, sticking to what he feels works best for the region's cold winters and warm summers. Whites are soft and aromatic, with ripe – but not overripe – fruit, good acidity and depth of flavour. Natural yeasts coax the best from the heavier whites. For all wines, Hartl loves experimenting with different variables - hang time, fermentation temperature, keeping parcels separate – and vinifies in tanks from 800-3500l and then blends the lots. Reds ferment in stainless steel, temperature-controlled open vats. Best bets include the powerful and interesting Rotgipfler, a wine with a point of view – and the two red reserves, which are fruit-forward but bright rather than explosive, 100% faithful versions of their varietal. Pinot Noir has unassuming, silky tannins and a touch of sweetness but no flavour from a bit of new oak. (MR)
Recommended Reds:
Pinot Noir Reserve ★★★☆ £E Pinot Noir Classic ★★☆ £C
St Laurent Reserve ★★★☆ £E St Laurent Classic ★★☆ £C
Zweigelt ★★☆ £C
Recommended Whites:
Rotgipfler ★★★☆ £C Gruner Veltliner ★★☆ £C

Hiedler (Kamptal) *www.hiedler.at*
The Hiedlers are an Austrian-Spanish husband-and-wife team. They make a wide range of styles including sweet wines, reds, and Chardonnay, Muskat Ottonel and Weissburgunder/ Pinot Blanc from 20 ha of vineyards around Langenlois. But the real focus is of

Austria

course Grüner Veltliner, accounting for over half the vineyard area, and Riesling. With the emphasis on fruit intensity the wines are in marked contrast to many other producers. There is also impressive depth and minerality to the top wines if not the extra class or expression of some. Grüner Veltliner Thal adds more depth over a soundly made Spiegel version. Rieslings Steinhaus and Heiligenstein show atypically rich fruit whilst Riesling Maximum is a big, rich, powerful, somewhat Alsace in style offering but develops well. Riesling is also made from Gaisberg and Urgestein and there are further examples of Grüner Veltliner. A cool, minerally Sauvignon Blanc shows some potential too.

Recommended Whites:
Riesling Maximum ★★★★ £E
Steinhaus Riesling ★★★ £C   Heiligenstein Riesling ★★★ £D
Thal Grüner Veltliner Novemberlese ★★★ £C
Spiegel Grüner Veltliner ★★ £C   Steinhaus Sauvignon Blanc ★★ £C

✪ Hirsch (Kamptal) www.weingut-hirsch.at
Hirsch, with 20 ha of vineyards in production, is owned by Johannes Hirsch, one of Austria's most interesting winemakers, with a rapidly rising reputation, and one from whom much is expected. They have been biodynamic since 2006. Great care is taken to achieve full physiological ripeness while natural yeasts and whole-bunch pressing are employed in order to enhance a natural expression of *terroir*. This is best seen in two contrasting premium Rieslings. The Gaisberg from mica-schist soils shows a mineral, citrus and subtle spice character and impressive flavour intensity whilst the sandstone of Heiligenstein imparts ripe fruit, mineral and spice but with great purity and expression. Both are long and best with at least 3-4 years' age. Both Grüner Veltliner are stylish and expressive; Heiligenstein more classic, Lamm more mineral. The Grub Grüner Veltliner Is rich and fruity on the palate, with nice acid and a long length. The single vineyard wines are not bottled until the July following the harvest so only available in bottle with a minimum of a years' age. All wines are bottled with screwcaps, the first in Austria to use them.

Recommended Whites:
Zöbinger Heiligenstein Riesling ★★★★ £D
Zöbinger Gaisberg Riesling ★★★☆ £D   Zöbinger Riesling ★★★ £C
Kammerner Lamm Grüner Veltliner ★★★ £D
Kammener Grub Grüner Veltliner ★★★ £D
Zöbinger Heiligenstein Grüner Veltliner ★★★ £D

✪ Franz Hirtzberger (Wachau) www.hirtzberger.com
The differences between the Wachau's élite are more stylistic than qualitative and it is common to find that one producer pleases more one year or on one particular occasion and another at a different time. From 12 ha of rocky soils there is a pure pristine fruit intensity to Hirtzberger's examples of Grüner Veltliner and Riesling. Most of the vineyards are directly behind the winery in the centre of Spitz. The Grüner Veltliner, which needs deeper soils than does the Riesling, Is planted on the flat and lower terraces, whilst the Riesling is higher up; the Weissburgunder is at midpoint. The wines are structured examples, taut and concentrated, but beautifully balanced. Of the top Rieslings in the (ripest) Smaragd style, Hochrain is a classic Wachau example with great length of flavour, whilst the splendid minerally Singerriedel has superb structure underpinning the fruit richness. There is an underlying strength and intensity to Honivogl Grüner Veltliner, which, like the Rieslings, deserves 5 years' ageing before drinking. Smaragd Grüner from Axpoint and Rotes Tor are also classic, Federspiel from the latter an excellent, more

affordable example of balanced Grüner Veltliner. In addition some Grauburgunder is also produced.

Recommended Whites:
Singerriedel Riesling Smaragd ★★★★★ £F
Hochrain Riesling Smaragd ★★★★ £F
Setzberg Riesling Smaragd ★★★★ £E
Steinterrassen Riesling Federspiel ★★★ £D
Axpoint Grüner Veltliner Smaragd ★★★★ £E
Honivogl Grüner Veltliner Smaragd ★★★★ £E
Rotes Tor Grüner Veltliner Smaragd ★★★★ £E
Rotes Tor Grüner Veltliner Federspiel ★★★ £D
Spitzer Steinporz Weissburgunder Smaragd ★★★★ £E

Holzapfel (Wachau) www.holzapfel.at
The 9.5 ha estate of Karl Holzapfel maintains a relatively low profile outside Austria but produces clean, pure if relatively austere examples of fine Wachau Grüner Veltliner and Riesling. At the Federspiel level this equates to cool, green-fruited and herb-tinged wines that avoid being harsh and which open out with a minimum of 2–3 years' age. Smaragd wines impress with their length, depth and structure. Achleiten Grüner Veltliner has classic character and intensity, showing the real essence of the grape and vineyard, whilst Vorderseiber Riesling has a pure citrusy fruit and delicate spice-filled depth.

Recommended Whites:
Ried Achleiten Grüner Veltliner Smaragd ★★★★ £D
Ried Achleiten Grüner Veltliner Federspiel ★★ £C
Zehenthof Grüner Veltliner Federspiel ★★ £C
Vorderseiber Riesling Smaragd ★★★★ £D
Zehenthof Riesling Federspiel ★★★ £C

Josef Jamek (Wachau) www.jamekweingut.at
Josef Jamek was one of the pioneers of the dry styles of Riesling and Grüner Veltliner that have re-established Austria's winemaking reputation. The 25 ha estate is now run by one of his daughters, Jutta, and her husband, Hans Altmann. Low yields contribute to an intense varietal expression as well as something of the individual *terroir*. The wines are pure, intense and very classy in the case of the Ried Klaus Riesling, with a floral, mineral aspect and citrus and nectarine fruit. Similar class can be seen in Ried Freiheit. Concentrated but firm when young they generally need time to soften and become easier to drink. Chardonnay and Weissburgunder is also made while reds include Zweigelt and Spätburgunder. The stylish Sekt is an unusually good example of sparkling wine from this part of Europe.

Recommended Whites:
Ried Klaus Riesling Smaragd ★★★★ £E
Ried Freiheit Riesling Smaragd ★★★★ £E
Ried Achleiten Grüner Veltliner Smaragd ★★★ £D
Ried Achleiten Grüner Veltliner Federspiel ★★ £C
Grüner Veltliner Sekt Brut ★★ £C

Juris (Neusiedlersee) www.juris.at
With viticultural roots that extend back at least 400 years, Axel and Herta Stiegelmar are the current generation producing an almost endless range of good whites, reds and sweet whites on 23 ha at Gols on the eastern shore of the Neusiedlersee. A total of 80% of production is red but the dry whites include a distinctive elderberry-scented Sauvignon and a clean, pure Chardonnay (Altenberg) that sees only large oak. Reserve Chardonnay and Villa Juris Pinot Gris (the latter from Hungarian vineyards) are a little too steeped in

oak but have good texture and depth. Selection reds are round, supple and flavoursome, mostly notably the Blaufränkisch and St-Laurent. Wolfsjäger is a supple, brambly blend of Blaufränkisch and Zweigelt. Reserves show generally well worked oak and an elegant, stylish complexity – Pinot Noir and St-Laurent are really good Austrian examples (St Georg combines the two grapes) and the same can be said of Blaufränkisch and Cabernet Sauvignon. The inviting Ina'mera Reserve is a very successful blend of Blaufränkisch, Cabernet Sauvignon and Merlot. Most diverting, however, are the sweet wines. There's an intensely perfumed and stylish Strohwein from Scheurebe grapes dried on reeds for 3 months, while a richer Chardonnay TBA (made in minute quantities) has great sweetness and spiced honeyed fruit intensity. A real oddity is a Pinot Noir TBA, with very intense preserved stone fruits character.

Recommended Reds:
Cabernet Sauvignon Reserve ★★★ £E
Ina'mera Reserve ★★★ £E Pinot Noir Reserve ★★★ £D
Pinot Noir Selection ★ £C St. Laurent Reserve ★★★ £D
St. Laurent Selection ★★ £C Blaufränkisch Reserve ★★★ £D
Blaufränkisch Selection ★★ £C Wolfsjäger ★★ £C

Recommended Whites:
Chardonnay TBA ★★★★ £F Chardonnay Reserve ★★ £C
Chardonnay Selection Altenberg ★★ £B
Strohwein ★★★ £F Sauvignon Blanc Selection ★★ £B

Jurtschitsch Sonnhof (Kamptal) www.jurtschitsch.com
This traditional family estate of 60 ha, now under the stewardship of Alwin and Stefanie Jurtschitsch, is run along ecological principles and with parcels in some of Kamptal's top sites, is making excellent progress, now producing wines of a quality close to the top tier of Wachau/Kamptal dry whites. In the vineyards particular attention is paid to reducing yields, a dedication reflected in the both the intensity and length of flavour achieved with Grüner Veltliner and the particularly fine fruit and gentle minerality in the best Rieslings. Most wines drink well with just 2 or 3 years' age. Whilst the selection of wines varies somewhat from year to year it usually includes those listed below. Small quantities of sweet wines (Trockenbeerenauslese and even Eiswein) from Riesling, Grüner Veltliner and Chardonnay are made when conditions favour it.

Recommended Whites:
Zöbinger Heiligenstein Riesling Reserve ★★★★ £E
Zöbinger Heiligenstein Riesling Auslese ★★★ £D
Zöbinger Heiligenstein Riesling ★★★ £C Riesling Alte Reben ★★★ £D
Grüner Veltliner Trockenbeerenauslese ★★★★ £F
Grüner Veltliner Reserve ★★★ £D Grüner Veltliner Alte Reben ★★★ £C
Ried Schkenbickl Grüner Veltliner ★★★ £C
Ried Steinhaus Grüner Veltliner ★★ £C

❀ Emmerich Knoll (Wachau) www.loibnerhof.at
This historic family vineyard of some 15 ha, planted mostly to Grüner Veltliner and Riesling, is another that shows just how good the top Wachau whites are. Emmerich Knoll's wines can be difficult to taste when young but can become almost overwhelming in their intensity and concentration with a little age or time in the glass. Any youthful aggression also tends to dissipate as both a strong varietal character and terroir influence emerge. The Smaragd version of Loibenberg Loibner Riesling has great vigour and superb length of flavour - indeed, it is quite delicious. Both this and the elegant, refined Dürnsteiner Schütt can age for a decade or more in top vintages. Pure, ripe Riesling is also made from Ried Pfaffenberg from outside the Wachau area. Examples of Grüner

Veltliner show classic peppery varietal fruit but with balanced levels of alcohol. Loibner Kreutles Grüner Veltliner hasn't usually the extra concentration or style of the Loibenberg Loibner or Loibner Schütt examples but nonetheless shows a lovely fruit character. A little of a special selection of the ripest (but non-botrytised fruit) is reserved for 'Vinothekfüllung' Grüner Veltliner and Riesling, whilst some Beerenauslese is also made when conditions permit.

Recommended Whites:
Loibenberg Loibner Riesling Smaragd ★★★★★ £E
Loibenberg Loibner Riesling Federspiel ★★ £C
Dürnsteiner Ried Schütt Riesling Smaragd ★★★★★ £E
Pfaffenberg Steiner Riesling Kabinett ★★★ £C
Loibenberg Loibner Grüner Veltliner Vinothekfüllung ★★★★ £E
Loibenberg Loibner Grüner Veltliner Smaragd ★★★ £D
Loibner Schütt Grüner Veltliner Smaragd ★★★ £D
Loibner Ried Kreutles Grüner Veltliner Federspiel ★★ £C
Loibner Ried Kreutles Grüner Veltliner Smaragd ★★ £C

Kollwentz-Römerhof (Neusiedlersee-Hügelland)
One of Burgenland's leading estates, well-known in Austria and its German-speaking neighbours, it is deserving of wider recognition, particularly for its deep, complex and original reds. Grapes have been adapted to a range of different soil types in 20 ha of vineyard. Selective picking and much work in the vineyard results in moderate yields of high quality grapes. The Steinzeiler from Blaufränkisch, Cabernet Sauvignon and Zweigelt has marvellous complexity, with earth, truffle, plum, tobacco and coffee hints, if not the dimension of a world-class red. Cabernet Sauvignon is very good in a cooler style with round, plump berry fruit and well-integrated oak after a little bottle age, though it can sometimes struggle for fully ripe tannins. Relatively high levels of volatility can sometimes impede their otherwise undoubted ageing potential. Varietal Blaufränkisch and Zweigelt are also produced in a number of guises, as is Eichkogel, an equal blend of the two varieties. Single vineyard Chardonnays including Tatschler and Gloria are made from different parts of the Leithagebirge, which has calcareous soils, but while the potential is there they don't currently have the depth or fruit intensity to match their powerful, oaky frames. Better balanced is a vibrant minerally unoaked Sauvignon Blanc, Steinmühle. Very ripe, intense, honeyed sweet wines are also made, not of the explosive concentration of Kracher yet very sweet, richly botrytised and well-balanced. Prices are high due to local demand.

Recommended Reds:
Steinzeiler ★★★☆ £E Cabernet Sauvignon ★★★ £E

Recommended Whites:
Trockenbeerenauslese ★★★ £G Sauvignon Steinmühle ★★★ £C

❀❀ Kracher (Neusiedlersee) www.kracher.at
The sweet wines of the late Alois Kracher are, quite frankly, some of the best In the world, and constitute 75% of their production, with the remainder dry. Based in Ilmitz, the family continues to work together on their 40 ha to produce consistently outstanding wines, making the most of the favourable conditions for botrytis enrichment afforded by Lake Neusiedl and surrounding small lakes (known as Seewinkel). Those labeled Zwischen den Seen ('between the lakes') are unoaked examples, usually from naturally spicy, aromatic indigenous varieties, whilst the Nouvelle Vague wines are oaked. The pick of several very sweet, very intense Trockenbeerenauslese are Grande Cuvée (No.6, usually Chardonnay dominated but with a significant percentage of Welschriesling), Nouvelle Vague Chardonnay (No.7, of sublime sweetness and

Austria

impeccable balance), and Zwischen den Seen Welschriesling (of varying sweetness depending on the bottling and vintage but always refined). Perfumed, honeyed, grapy Muskat Ottonel is also delicious. A reasonably affordable introduction is the Cuvée Beerenauslese (typically Chardonnay and Welschriesling), a good, rich, not excessively sweet example with concentrated botrytised fruit and the finely balanced acidity so characteristic of these wines. Reds include an attractive supple spicy Zweigelt aged only in used oak and Blend I and Blend II, both made from Zweigelt, Cabernet Sauvignon and Merlot. These are aged in new *barriques*, the persuasive, elegant medium-bodied Blend I is predominately Zweigelt whilst Blend II is roughly one-third of each grape. Though all sweet wines are numbered, they are listed below without any as the numbers sometimes change with a new vintage. Also there can be a second (or even third) version, of greater sweetness, of certain varietals.

Recommended Reds:
Blend I ★★★☆ £D Zweigelt Ilmitz ★★ £C
Recommended Whites:
Grande Cuvée TBA ✪✪✪✪✪ £H
Chardonnay Nouvelle Vague TBA ✪✪✪✪✪ £H
Welschriesling Zwischen den Seen TBA ★★★★☆ £F
Scheurebe Zwischen den Seen TBA ★★★★☆ £F
Muskat Ottonel Zwischen den Seen TBA ★★★★☆ £F
Traminer Nouvelle Vague TBA ★★★★ £F
Cuvée Beerenauslese ★★★☆ £D

Krutzler (Südburgenland) www.krutzler.at
Brothers Erich and Rheinhold Krutzler have less than 10 ha of vineyards that are almost entirely given over to Blaufränkisch. Great care goes into maximizing fruit quality. The basic version from younger vines has 6 months in tank and large oak resulting in a supple, open, round style full of plum, berry and cherry fruit. The Reserve is from older vines and partly *barrique*-aged and adds class as well as much more depth and dimension. It needs 3–4 years to show at its best. The top wine, Perwolff, is made in small quantities. This includes up to 10% Cabernet Sauvignon and spends 18 months in *barrique*. Although the oak is apparent when the wine is young so is its class and it must be given 8–10 years' age to realise its full potential. It has depth and extract to complement its refined cedar, plum, bramble and black cherry character. Also made but not tasted is a Weissburgunder Auslese from well-established vines.
Recommended Reds:
Perwolff ★★★★ £E
Blaufränkisch Reserve ★★★ £D
Blaufränkisch ★★ £C

Lackner-Tinnacher (Südsteiermark) www.tinnacher.at
Fritz Tinnacher's 17 ha of vines run up and down slopes in the very south of Southern Styria, just north of the border with Slovenia. There is good quality throughout the range, especially in the best wines from the Eckberg and Steinbach vineyards. Sauvignon is good even in a basic Steireiche Klassik bottling but significantly better in a mineral-edged Steinbach and richer, more complex Welles examples. Both Chardonnays (Morillon) are stainless steel vinified then aged in large oak. There is a purity and minerality akin to a Saint-Véran in the Eckberg, and both density and minerality in the ageworthy Steinbach version. Grauburgunder is rich and detailed, a dry flavoursome Roter Traminer releases rose and blossom scents while an intense, sweet Eiswein has better definition, complexity and sheer style than Beerenauslese. There is also a red called simply Steinbach from Zweigelt and St. Laurent but this hasn't yet been tasted.

Recommended Whites:
Ried Türken Riesling Eiswein ★★★★ £E Beerenauslese ★★★ £C
Welles Sauvignon Blanc ★★★ £C Steinbach Sauvignon Blanc ★★☆ £C
Sauvignon Steirische Klassik ★☆ £B
Steinbach Morillon ★★★ £E Eckberg Morillon ★★☆ £C
Steinbach Grauburgunder ★★★ £C
Steinbach Weissburgunder ★★☆ £B
Eckberg Weissburgunder ★★ £B Ried Türken Roter Traminer ★★ £C
Steinbach Welschriesling ★☆ £B Ried Gamitz Gelber Muskateller ★☆ £B

Lagler (Wachau) www.laglers.at
Almost half this 12.5 ha Wachau estate is planted to Grüner Veltliner and a quarter to Riesling. There are fine examples of each, both Federspiel and Smaragd, from leading sites. Particularly good is Riesling from Ried Steinborz (from 40–50-year-old vines) with a spicy component to its deep, stylish fruit character. Beyond the good vineyard-specific Grüners there is a late-picked Elisabeth Selection, made from a selection of the best grapes. Rich and powerful it is usually well balanced. A rarity is a Müller-Thurgau TBA. 'Perish the thought!' you might think, but if any comes your way don't hesitate to try it. This is an extraordinary wine for the Müller-Thurgau – very concentrated and very sweet with exotic aromas and a rich toffee, honey and butterscotch palate, all remarkably well balanced.
Recommended Whites:
Müller-Thurgau TBA ★★★★★ £F
1000 Eimerberg Riesling Smaragd ★★★ £D
Ried Steinborz Riesling Smaragd ★★★ £D
Riesling von den Terassen Federspiel ★★ £C
Ried Steinborz Grüner Veltliner Smaragd ★★★ £D
Grüner Veltliner Elisabeth Selection ★★★ £D
1000 Eimerberg Grüner Veltliner Smaragd ★★★ £C
Ried Vorderseiber Grüner Veltliner ★★★ £C
Ried Burgberg Grüner Veltliner Federspiel ★★ £B
1000 Eimerberg Neuburger Smaragd ★★ £C

Helmut Lang (Neusiedlersee) www.helmutlang.at
Based in Illmitz, Helmut Lang makes both reds and whites from 13.5 ha of vineyards that include the typical varieties of the area. But it is the sweet wines, from Samling 88 (Scheurebe), Chardonnay and Welschriesling in the main, that have made his reputation. From limited tastings it seems almost anything is worth a try. Beerenauslese, Ausbruch and TBA styles are richly botrytised, often very sweet and concentrated but well balanced and capable of long ageing. Pinot Blanc has also been produced in a TBA style; it is very sweet with rich cream, spice and toffee as well as baked apple and clove. Eiswein (usually primarily Samling 88 and with some boytrytis influence) is slightly less convincing. Sweet wines of forceful personality, if lacking a little refinement, have also been made from Sauvignon Blanc. .
Recommended Whites:
Samling 88 TBA ★★★★ £F Samling 88 Eiswein ★★★ £E
Pinot Blanc TBA ★★★★ £E Sauvignon TBA ★★★ £E

❁ Loimer (Kamptal) www.loimer.at
Lorimer has been biodynamic since 2006, and was an early member of Respekt-BIODYN, an association of wineries in Austria, Germany, Italy and Hungary, all of whom use the absolute minimum of sulphur. Like most in Kamptal, Fred Loimer has more than half of his estate planted to Grüner Veltliner but a quarter of his 25 ha is

also planted to Riesling. He excels at producing both. The wines are precise but pure and expressive with real depth and length. He has now arguably become one of the established Wachau/Kamptal superstars, which include BRÜNDLMAYER, HIRTZBERGER, KNOLL, F-X PICHLER and PRAGER. There is excellent Grüner Veltliner, a classic full and sophisticated Käferberg and more elegant and expressive Spiegel. Three cru Rieslings are beautifully made, a spicy, citrus and mineral Seeberg with a very intense nose, a Steinmassl with breadth, concentration and a white peach fruit purity, and a Kaferberg that demonstrates a rich palate balanced with acid, a lovely wine. LOIS is a light but expressive introductory Grüner Veltliner. For more depth and intensity try the regular Langenlois varietals, which are excellent value for money. Also made are Chardonnay, a Chardonnay/Grauburguner blend called simply 'Fred Loimer', and Pinot Noir. For a new joint venture, 'Loimer and friends', grapes are sourced from Gumpoldskirchen in the Thermenregion region. Since 2013, he has made two sparkling wines, an Extra Brut made from Grüner Veltliner, Zweigelt and Pinot Noir, and an Extra Brut Rosé made from Zweigelt, Pinot Noir and Chardonnay; both have tiny, sustained bubbles in the mousse and a long length..

Recommended Whites:
Steinmassl Riesling ★★★★ £E
Seeberg Riesling ★★★★ £D Riesling Langenlois ★★★ £C
Spiegel Grüner Veltliner ★★★ £E Käferberg Riesling ★★★★ £D
Käferberg Grüner Veltliner ★★★ £E
Grüner Veltliner Langenlois ★★ £C LOIS ★ £B

>> Mantlerhof (Kremstal) *www.mantlerhof.at*
This is an organic estate of 14 ha, whichh has been owned by the family since the 14th century. The vineyards are primarily loess, which provides plenty of the nutrients needed by Grüner Veltliner, and normally produces relatively soft and full-bodied wines. They make both Rieslings and Grüner Veltliners, but, unusual and notable, they also make wines from the Roter Veltliner. This is a very old grape, and Mantlerhof were amongst the very few who had single vineyard grapes. The Roter Veltliner Gedersdorfer Reisenthal is a Klassic wine to be drunk young and is very agreeable. The Gedersdorfer Mosburgerin Grüner Veltliner has a very aromatic, floral nose and bone-dry palate with fruit and mineral notes. The Riesling Beerenauslese has a fragrant nose and Is not too heavily sweet and is well-balanced with moderate acid; it is quite delicious. They are one of the few wine producers to make a Neuberger: it's a very vigorous vine which grows sideways and down with lots of leave, and this supports a microclimate in the vine whichh encourages fungi. Their Neuberger Hommage wine has an aromatic nose and palate. (KB)

Recommended Whites:
Riesling Beerenauslese ★★★ £C Neuberger Hommage ★★ £B
Gedersdorfer Ried Mosburgerin Grüner Veltliner ★★ £B

Neumayer (Traisental) *www.weinvomstein.at*
Due east of the Wachau region, on the Traisen, a tributary of the Danube, Ludwig Neumayer has 8 ha of scattered parcels of vineyard. Despite the relative obscurity he makes better wines than some of those with parcels in the Wachau's highly rated sites. His best wines are derived from Grüner Veltliner and Riesling although Weissburgunder, Chardonnay and Sauvignon are also important. In difficult vintages the wines could potentially struggle for full ripeness but there is an artisanal approach that ensures good intensity to cool citrusy fruit. The Wein vom Stein wines in particular, from a selection of the best parcels, show fine fruit expression, purity

and length of flavour, even if they are slightly austere in their youth. Both Grüner Veltliner and Riesling are classy and mineral and best with at least 2 or 3 years' age. Weissburgunder from the same site (unoaked but long on the lees) has good concentration and purity. Also interesting is IKON Sauvignon Blanc; from late-harvested fruit and partly barrel-fermented it retains a certain purity and balance that many others in this style lack.

Recommended Whites:
Der Wein vom Stein Riesling ★★★☆ £D
Rothenbart Riesling ★★★ £D Berg Riesling ★★ £C
Der Wein vom Stein Grüner Veltliner ★★★ £D
Engelberg Grüner Veltliner ★★ £B Rafasetzen Grüner Veltliner ★★ £B
Der Wein vom Stein Weissburgunder ★★ £C
IKON Sauvignon Blanc ★★ £C Chardonnay ★ £B

✿ Nigl (Kremstal) *www.weingutnigl.at*
The wines have steadily increased in quality over the past 15 years and now range from very good to excellent. A wide range of Grüner Veltliner and Riesling from 30 ha of the top sites in Kremstal are made and the best are now very good indeed. As well as these among whites are a Sauvignon Blanc and a Gelber Mukateller, and reds include a fragrant and balanced Pinot Noir. Contrasting Rieslings range from the racy, minerally, elegant Piri to the taut, intense and concentrated Hochäcker or the deep, pure and stylish Privat (a selection from Piri and old vines). The Privat version of Grüner Veltliner is full-bodied and powerful with very ripe fruit, yet remains balanced and is profound for this variety. All have good ageing potential; Rieslings in particular show at their best with at least 3–5 years' age or more. As well as those below, other wines include Grüner Veltliner from Ried Zwelt, and Riesling from Kremser Kremsleiten. Late harvest examples are also made TBA from both Grüner and Riesling as well as a Grüner Eiswein. Of particular note in 2016 were the Senftenberger Riesling Privat Pellingen Reserve 2015, which grew in the mouth, and a spectacularly good Senftenberger Hochächer Riesling 2011.

Recommended Whites:
Grüner Veltliner Privat ★★★★ £E
Senftenberger Piri Grüner Veltliner ★★★ £E
Kremser Freiheit Grüner Veltliner ★★ £C Riesling Privat ★★★★ £E
Senftenberger Hochäcker Riesling ★★★★ £E
Senftenberger Piri Riesling ★★★ £E
Recommended Reds:
Pinot Noir ★★ £C

✿ Nikolaihof (Wachau) *www.nikolaihof.at*
Nikolaus and Christine Saahs make fine biodynamically (Demeter certified) produced Riesling, Grüner Veltliner and Gelber Muskateller from 22 ha of vineyards that have been a source of wine for more than a thousand years. The vines have a high average age and recent vintages have added a little extra intensity to wines that have good definition and style. Riesling is particularly long-lived, whether the restrained, minerally vom Stein or intense, refined Im Weingebirge (both from the Wachau) or steely, elegant Steiner Hund from just outside the area, in Kremstal. Even the fine Federspiel version of vom Stein will improve for 5 years or more. The Saahs' characterful Im Weingebirge Grüner Veltliner shows a smoky, earthy influence in a quite full, fat Smaragd version and good ripeness in a Federspiel version. Both can be drunk young and the Smaragd version with up to 5 years' age. Of other varieties grown, Weissburgunder shows good depth and structure. The Rosé Sekt, made from Zweigelt, has a nice, although not long-lasting, mousse

Austria

of tiny bubbles, and a strong taste of the grape.

Recommended Whites:
Steiner Hund Riesling Reserve ★★★★☆ £E
Vom Stein Riesling Smaragd ★★★★ £E
Vom Stein Riesling Federspiel ★★★ £D
Im Weingebirge Riesling Smaragd ★★★☆ £E
Im Weingebirge Grüner Veltliner Smaragd ★★★☆ £E
Im Weingebirge Grüner Veltliner Federspiel ★★☆ £C
Hefeabzug Grüner Veltliner ★★☆ £C

Anita & Hans Nittnaus (Neusiedlersee) *www.nittnaus.at*
Reds take centre-stage at this 25 ha family-run estate that produces the wines as naturally as possible. Zweigelt and Blaufränkisch are the most widely planted varieties and form the basis of the regular blends. The elegant Heideboden is the principal estate wine and can also include St-Laurent, Pinot Noir or Cabernet Sauvignon, Merlot and Syrah and shows good complexity if only moderate concentration. Varietal Pinot Noir has lots of class in a medium-bodied style. The two top reds are Comondor and Pannobile, both deep and stylish. Comondor is mostly from Merlot, Blaufränkisch and Zweigelt, whilst Pannobile is Zweigelt with Blaufränkisch. Both have lots of extract and intensity and need time to soften and fill out; Comondor can be a fraction too tannic. The white blends, Heideboden and Pannobile, are from Chardonnay and Pinot Blanc; the minimally oaked Heideboden is unexpectedly classy and composed. For sweet wine there's a dense, concentrated TBA based on Chardonnay, Sauvignon and Weissburgunder and/or Neuburger.

Recommended Reds:
Comondor ★★★ £E Pannobile ★★★ £D
Pinot Noir Kurzberg ★★ £D Heideboden ★★ £B
Zweigelt ★ £B

Recommended Whites:
TBA ★★★★ £F Heideboden ★★ £B

Gut Oggau (Neusiedlersee) *www.gutoggau.com*
You can't tell a wine by its label, but Gut Oggau aims to try. Distinctive marketing gives each of the estate's nine wines a human face, name and personality. Perfect for the Facebook generation, sure – but these wines aren't just pretty faces. Since 2007, its first vintage, Oggau has produced on 11.5 ha of rented vineyards (adding another 1.5 in 2010) planted with Grüner Veltliner (4); Zweigelt (2), Weissburgunder (1.5) and 1 with Gewürztraminer and Welschriesling. The vineyards are Demeter-certified, cultivated biodynamically, by hand (crush is by foot) - with no *verboten* treatments or fining and when possible, no filtering. All wines ferment spontaneously without cooling, and are sulphured only shortly before bottling. Whites go into stainless steel and large barrels (over 500l), and sit on the lees for 8 months, and may age up to 2 years. Reds ferment in stainless steel, open boxes and concrete tanks – and age in barrels and concrete tanks. Mechthild (an elegant, austere Grüner with a luscious streak) and Bertholdi (Blaufrankish, not tasted) are vinified in an old wooden press. At the "entry level", Theodora (Grüner Veltliner/Welschriesling) is bright, fresh and zingy while her red "brother" Atanasius (Zweigelt/Blaufränkisch) is highly quaffable but carefully composed, with deep fruit that lingers – excellent value. Timotheus (Grüner Veltliner/Weissburgunder) with his super-aromatic nose, does not deliver quite as much on the palate. The white blend Emmeram (Gewürztraminer) was the business, spicy and electric. Another red; a rosé; and a Beerenauslese have not yet been tasted. (MR)

Recommended Reds:
Atanasius ★★★ £C
Recommended Whites:
Mechtild ★★★★ £F
Emmeram ★★★☆ £E
Theodora ★★★☆ £C
Timotheus ★★☆ £E

Bernhard Ott (Wagram) *www.ott.at*
Bernhard Ott's 16 ha are in Wagram, since 2007 an independent region rather than just a quality zone within Donauland. The loess soils are highly suited to Grüner Veltliner. All the whites are fermented and aged in stainless steel, with no oak, and 90% are from Grüner. The estate is biodynamic. The wines develop from a cool, spicy Am Berg to Fass 4, a selection of the best vineyards, through late-harvested old-vine Der Ott, to the powerful Rosenberg 1. Lage from over 50-year-old vines are expressive, pure and characterful – more fruity, less concentrated or structured than top Wachau examples but good drinking and well-priced. Further top level examples come from Feuersbrunner Spiegel, particularly a complex Grüner Veltliner, and Engabrunner Stein, with an aromatic Grüner Veltliner, whilst other wines include von Rottem Schotter Riesling..

Recommended Whites:
Rosenberg Reserve Grüner Veltliner ★★★ £D
Der Ott Grüner Veltliner ★★★ £C
Feuersbrunner Spiegel Grüner Veltliner ★★★ £C
Engabrunner Stein Grüner Veltliner ★★ £C
Fass 4 Grüner Veltliner ★★ £C Am Berg Grüner Veltliner ★☆ £B
Von Rotem Schotter Riesling ★★ £C

R & A Pfaffl (Weinviertel) *www.pfaffl.at*
Weinviertel is the little known region in the north-eastern corner of Austria, north of Vienna. Roman Pffafl's 53 ha, spread over 10 villages, actually lie (mostly) just outside of Vienna (and the Wien wine zone). Now working with his son, who is also called Roman, he has proved what is possible here with particularly good Riesling and Grüner but also good Sauvignon and soundly made reds. A good Grüner, Zeiseneck is like all the single vineyard examples produced under the new DAC, but better are a cool, minerally Hundsleiten Reserve (from sandstone soils) and deeper, more detailed Goldjoch Reserve (loamy soils), which is fermented in and then aged for 12 months in large oak. Also to be considered is a DAC Hiedviertel example and Hommage, a DAC Reserve from a vineyard selection. Arguably there is a bigger quality differential between two Rieslings, a fine Mosel-like Terrassen Sonnleiten (from stony terraces) and the excellent pure, ripe (but botrytis free) Am Berg which has lovely balance. Sauvignon is distinctive and elderflower scented with crunchy pure fruit and good structure while a barrique-aged and fermented Chardonnay Rossern can be rich but balanced. Of the reds both St. Laurent (also coming from Waldgärten) and Pinot Noir are intense and fruit expressive, and best drunk with 3-5 years' age. Zweigelt also comes from two further vineyards Sandstein and a reserve from Burggarten. Both 'Excellent' (not tasted) and Heidrom are blends of Cabernet Sauvignon and Merlot with some Zweigelt in "Excellent". Also made are Chardonnay Exklusiv and Weissburgunder Nussern. Wien 1 and Wien 2 are inexpensive white and red blends respectively from vineyards in the Wien zone.

Recommended Reds:
Pinot Noir ★★★ £C Heidrom ★★☆ £D
St. Laurent Altenberg ★★☆ £C Blauer Zweigelt ★ £C

Recommended Whites:
Riesling Am Berg ★★★☆ £E Riesling Terrassen Sonnleiten ★★☆ £C
Grüner Veltliner Goldjoch ★★★ £C
Grüner Veltliner Hundsleiten ★★★ £C
Sauvignon Seiser Am Eck ★★☆ £C Weinviertel DAC Zeiseneck ★☆ £B

✿✿ F-X Pichler (Wachau) *www.fx-pichler.at*
Franz Xaver Pichler is acclaimed by many to be the Wachau's finest producer, and it's hard to dispute, given the extremely high quality in his top Smaragd Riesling and Grüner Veltliner of great extraction and concentration. Certainly no effort is spared in maximising the quality potential from 7.5 ha of vineyards. The Loibner Berg is consistently the classiest and most concentrated of the Rieslings but that from the steep Dürnsteiner Kellerberg vineyard has great refinement, purity and length of flavour, whilst the Urgestein Terrassen shows terrific richness and intensity in outstanding vintages. If more youthfully austere, Steinertal has a beauty and definition that becomes increasingly apparent after 5 years or more. The off-dry Riesling Reserve 'M', from Loibenberg and Kellerberg, is only made when there is a stuck fermentation, and they make a virtue out of necessity; it's rich with some honey character and a very long length. The Grüner Veltliners are marvellous too; a deep, dense and structured Loibner Berg is perhaps the finest of several made but a full, vibrant Kellerberg and intense, long Urgestein Terrassen are also top wines. More forward Federspiel examples are produced from the Loibner Klostersatz and Frauenweingarten sites. Of great potential if somewhat less typical are the special supercharged selections of Riesling (Unendlich – endless or never-ending) and Grüner Veltliner ('M'), both highly concentrated old-vine versions that are high in alcohol.

Recommended Whites:
Loibner Berg Riesling Smaragd ✪✪✪✪✪ £F
Dürnsteiner Kellerberg Riesling Smaragd ★★★★★ £F
Urgestein Terrassen Riesling Smaragd ★★★★ £F
Steinertal Riesling Smaragd ★★★★ £F
Riesling Reserve 'M' ★★★★ £F
Loibner Berg Grüner Veltliner Smaragd ★★★★ £E
Dürnsteiner Kellerberg Grüner Veltliner Smaragd ★★★★ £E
Urgestein Terrassen Grüner Veltliner Smaragd ★★★ £E

✿ Rudi Pichler (Wachau) *www.rudipichler.at*
The grapes come from his 15 ha of vineyards, from which Rudi Pichler makes wines that are meant to be different, aiming for greater concentration and structure as well as ripe, intense fruit flavours. The use of indigenous yeast and higher fermentation temperatures can add an almost exotic quality to the riper styles. He does not like malo-lactic fermentation becausee It would interfere with the purity of the wine from a specific vineyard. Yet the balance is excellent with good definition and minerality. There is real strength and depth in the top crus at Smaragd level, not the austerity of some but still requiring at least 5 years' ageing to show at their best. Of the single vineyard (Ried) wines, both Kollmütz and Hochrain Grüner Veltliner illustrate his style very well. An intensely mineral Steinriegl, and an Achleiten with great length and class, do the same for Riesling. Blended Terrassen Smaragd Riesling and Grüner Veltliner are very good too and even Wachauer Federspiel wines, with cooler citrus flavours but no underripeness, show plenty of vigour and intensity. If less well-known than other Wachau producers, this is now a name to track down. Some but not all of the wines are rated below. Roter Veltliner Smaragd and Weissburgunder Kollmütz Smaragd are also notably made.

Recommended Whites:
Weissenkirchner Achleiten Riesling Smaragd ★★★★★ £E
Weissenkirchner Steinriegl Riesling Smaragd ★★★★ £E
Terrassen Riesling Smaragd ★★★★ £D
Wachauer Riesling Federspiel ★★★ £C
Wösendorfer Hochrain Grüner Veltliner Smaragd ★★★★ £D
Wösendorfer Kollmütz Grüner Veltliner Smaragd ★★★★ £D
Terrassen Grüner Veltliner Smaragd ★★★★ £D
Wachauer Grüner Veltliner Federspiel ★★ £C

Polz (Südsteiermark) *www.polz.co.at*
This is a long-established family estate bolstered by the purchases of prime vineyards by Erich and Walter Polz in the eighties. There is now more than 50 ha and typically for southern Styria there is a quite a large range of wines, mostly dry whites but also reds and a sweet white. Steirische Klassik varietals are nothing special but excellent Grauburgunder and Traminer are produced from the Grassnitzberg's sandstone soils. Aged only in large oak, both are concentrated, pure and expressive. A third in a trio comes from Weissburgunder. Excellent Sauvignon comes from the steep Hochgrassnitzberg slopes right on the border with Slovenia. Barrel-fermented and aged there is lots of structure and finesse in a regular version Another Sauvignon 'Therese' from the 450m Thereseinhöhe vineyard has good fruit and structure and is also a good bet. Chardonnay (Morillon), with the exception of the excellent 'Moth' example is generally a touch less assured, the fruit in Obegg and Hochgrassnitzberg somewhat overwhelmed by the winemaking. Urbani is a convincing deep, oak-lined but well-balanced blend of Zweigelt, Cabernet Sauvignon and Blaufränkisch. There is potential too in Pinot Noir – produced from vines only planted in 2000. A fine Hochgrassnitzberg TBA from Morillon (Chardonnay) and Sauvignon Blanc has very sweet, concentrated botrytised fruit and good balance.

Recommended Reds:
Urbani ★★★ £C
Recommended Whites:
Hochgrassnitzberg TBA ★★★★ £F
Hochgrassnitzberg Sauvignon Blanc Reserve ★★★☆ £E
Hochgrassnitzberg Sauvignon Blanc ★★★ £E
Sauvignon Blanc Therese ★★☆ £C
Sauvignon Blanc Steirische Klassik ★☆ £C Moth ★★★ £C
Grassnitzberg Traminer ★★★ £C
Grassnitzberg Grauburgunder ★★☆ £C
Morillon Steirische Klassik ★ £B

✿ Prager (Wachau) *www.weingutprager.at*
Franz Prager did much to establish the pre-eminence of top dry whites from the Wachau. His daughter Ilse and her winemaker husband Toni Bodenstein have sought to produce dry wines of ever-greater harmony and longevity as well as making some fine sweet wines when conditions permit. They farm 16.5 ha. From the village of Weissenkirchen come several fine Smaragd Rieslings, including a superb minerally, peachy Steinriegl that is firm when young but with great depth and length, adding richness and complexity with age. Both Riesling and Grüner Veltliner from the Achleiten site are also very fine and can show a little spice as well as an intense fruit depth. Fine Auslese and occasional TBA examples are also made from this site. Of the other fine Rieslings, a very refined Wachstum Bodenstein Riesling (from the highest vineyard at 460m) contrasts with a bolder, more forward Kaiserberg example and a distinctive, minerally, cool-fruited Klaus. All wines benefit from even more age

Austria

than is typical for the best Wachau whites; Rieslings need 5 years but will keep for a decade. An intense, fruit-rich Chardonnay Smaragd is also made and has good structure and depth.

Recommended Whites:

Weissenkirchen Achleiten Riesling Smaragd ★★★★☆ £E
Weissenkirchen Klaus Riesling Smaragd ★★★★☆ £E
Weissenkirchen Wachstum Bodenstein Riesling Smaragd ★★★★ £E
Weissenkirchen Steinriegl Riesling Smaragd ★★★★ £E
Weissenkirchen Steinriegl Riesling Federspiel ★★ £C
Dürnsteiner Kaiserberg Riesling Smaragd ★★★ £D
Dürnsteiner Hollerin Riesling Smaragd ★★★ £D
Weissenkirchen Achleiten Grüner Veltliner Smaragd ★★★☆ £E
Weissenkirchen Weitenberg Grüner Veltliner Smaragd ★★★ £D
Hinter der Burg Grüner Veltliner Federspiel ★★☆ £C

Prieler (Neusiedlersee-Hügelland) *www.prieler.at*

The Prieler family has 20 ha of vineyards on hillside slopes to the west of Neusiedlersee. Silvia Prieler and her younger brother Georg transform the high quality fruit produced by their father into an intelligent range of dry whites and reds. The whites show good purity and are unoaked except for a stylish Chardonnay from Seeberg that is nicely restrained with a good minerally aspect to it. There is also an unoaked version from the Sinner vineyard. Silvia Prieler is passionate about Pinot Noir (which comes from the same calcareous soils), which she makes under her own label, and there is real complexity and character following 18 months in partly new barriques. Arguably the best red is the Goldberg Blaufränkisch grown on slaty soils. Full of brambly black fruits, herbs and mineral intensity, it has lots of extract and power and promises much with 6–8 years' age. Cabernet Sauvignon appears to struggle more for ripeness, with firm tannins but also deep cedary, chocolaty fruit. Also worth trying is a ripe, lush, berryish Schützner Stein, which is Blaufränkisch topped up with Merlot. There also now two releases under the Leithaberg DAC, a Blaufränkisch and a Pinot Blanc which have not been tasted.

Recommended Reds:

Goldberg Blaufränkisch ★★★ £E
Johanneshöhe Blaufränkisch ★★ £C
Pinot Noir Hochsatz ★★★ £D   Schützner Stein ★★★ £C
Ungerbergen Cabernet Sauvignon ★★ £D

Recommended Whites:

Seeberg Pinot Blanc ★★ £C   Seeberg Chardonnay ★★ £C

>> Rudolf Rabl (Kamptal) *www.weingut-rabl.at*

At 80 ha, this is a relatively large estate, to whichh they add grapes purchased from anotherr 20 ha. They are certified sustainable, whichh means no pesticides if at all possibler, and no fertilizers, so they use manure. They grow Frühroter Veltliner (no relation to Grüner Veltliner), a grape not widely seen. They have part of the Rote Erde (red earth) part of Ried Steinhaus, red because of the iron in the soil; the Riesling Steinhaus Rote Erde Kamptal Reserve has lots of fruit and crisp acid with some Intensity. The Riesling Schenkenbichl Alte Reben Reserve Is a lovely wine, with a good balance and a big palate. There are some nice Grüner Veltliners, especially Dechant Alte Reben Reserve and the Käferberg Alte Reben. A good red wine is Der Rote 'C-B-Z', made from Cabernet Sauvignon, Blauberger and Zweigelt, with dark fruit and some rubber on the nose and lots of good fruit and a balanced structure on the palate. There are also some very nice sweet wines, in particular the Traminer Beerenauslese, which has quite an intense nose and enough acid to balance the sweetness, so that it isn't syrupy, and the Blauer

Zweigelt Eiswein, which is really nice, with lots of acid and nice fruit on the palate. A drawback of Rabl, however, is the vast number of different wines they make - in 2016 I tasted 47 different wines - which must prevent enough attention being paid to some of the wines. Discussion about cutting back on the numbers, however, is currently taking place.

Recommended Whites:

Riesling Steinhaus Rote Erde Kam;tal Reserve ★★ £C
Riesling Schenkenbichl Alte Reber Reserve ★★ £C
Dechant Grüner Veltliner Alte Reben Reserve ★★ £C
Käferberg Grüner Veltliner Alte Reben ★★ £C

Recommended Reds:

Der Rote 'C-B-Z' ★★ £C   Blauer Zweigelt Eiswein - ★★ £C

Salomon-Undhof (Kremstal) *www.undhof.at*

This estate has remained in the same family since 1792. Bertold Salomon returned to take up the mantle from his older brother Erich in 2002. Von Stein Grüner Veltliner comes from two small plots of eroded rocky soils producing a wine of lovely minerality and intensity that starts out quite austere. Another fine Grüner comes from old vines in Lindberg, the lower part of Wachtberg. The terraces of Kögl provide fine Riesling with extra depth and concentration in a Reserve that is in essence a very pure, elegant style. While Salomon's 20 ha of vineyards are almost exclusively Grüner Veltliner or Riesling, a little Gelber Traminer is also made. A very attractive wine, it combines good fruit intensity with a mix of spice, floral and lychee characters.

Recommended Whites:

Kremser Kögl Riesling Reserve ★★★★ £D
Kremser Kögl Riesling ★★★ £C   Pfaffenberg Riesling ★★ £C
Von Stein Grüner Veltliner Reserve ★★★ £D
Undhof Wieden Grüner Veltliner ★★ £B
Grüner Veltliner Hochterrassen ★ £B
Gelber Traminer Noble Reserve ★★ £D

Schiefer (Schiefer) *www.weinbau-schiefer.at*

Uwe is another Blaufränkisch man, with the potential to become the Blaufränkisch man. He is also Schist man, from both his name and the soils in which his 5.2 ha of vines grow. The regular Eisenberg Blaufränkisch is made from bought-in grapes and aged only in large oak, but is an excellent bright, pure, well-defined and unmanipulated example of the grape. From estate grapes Szapary is vinified in open-fermenters and aged in 1- and 2-year French oak and is denser and more extracted but with riper tannic quality that too many examples from other producers miss. The Reihburg, which is comprised of four parcels of old vines, sees new oak (500 litre), the percentage depending on the vintage. This really oozes class and has lovely depth and complexity but needs 5 years to really open out. Small amounts of other wines are also made including Pinot Noir, Merlot, dry whites and a new rosé. The vineyards also extend into Hungary. Another Blaufränkisch (here K Kékfrankos) and a dry white are made.

Recommended Reds:

Blaufränkisch Eisenberg R Reihburg ★★★★ £E
Blaufränkisch Eisenbeg S Szapary ★★★☆ £D
Blaufränkisch Eisenberg E Eisenberg ★★★ £C

❀ Schloss Gobelsburg (Kamptal) *www.gobelsburg.at*

This ancient estate of 70 ha still belongs to a Cistercian monastery and the castle itself was built in the early 18th century. Under the winemaking direction of Michael Moosbrugger, with consultancy

from Willi BRÜNDLMAYER since 1996, the wines have made amazing progress over recent vintages. 35 ha of vineyards give both Grüner Veltliner and Riesling that are fully ripe and intense but of superb definition and concentration too. There is great style and refinement in a rich yet poised and elegant Riesling (from Gaisberg) with a sublime pure fruit character, while a composed, concentrated and classy Ried Zöbinger Heiligenstein is also marvellous. Regular Gobelsburger Riesling and Renner Grüner Veltliner are good value. Sparkling wine, reds (a Cuvée Bertrand blend, Pinot Noir, St Laurent and Zweigelt, the latter under the Domäne Gobelsburg label), and Messwein (altar wine, meaning that it must be natural, with no added sugar or acid, under the Gobelsburger name) are also made. Moosbrugger is a keen historian of the estate and its wines, and points out that the Cistercians had links with their brothers in Burgundy and brought Pinot Noir to the region; the Pinor Noir Reserve has a very prominent nose and minerals over the fruit on the palate, and is delicious.

Recommended Reds:
Pinot Noir ★★ £D

Recommended Whites:
Zöbinger Heiligenstein Riesling ★★★★★ £F
Riesling Gaisberg ★★★★☆ £E
Riesling Gobelsburger ★★ £B
Kammerner Lamm Grüner Veltliner ★★★★ £E
Kammerner Grub Grüner Veltliner ★★★ £E
Kammerner Renner Grüner Veltliner ★★★ £D

❀ Schmelz (Wachau) *www.schmelzweine.at*
This is very much a family business and one with a relatively low profile, at least outside the German-speaking countries, but which deserves to be better known. Production from 10 ha is roughly two-thirds Grüner Veltliner and one-third Riesling. The wines are all vinified and aged in stainless steel. 60% of the production is Federspiel because it Is easier to sell In Austria - Austrians are showing a decided preference for lower-alcohol wines (the permitted alcohol level is 11.5% to 12.5%).Vineyard sites include Pichl Point with loess soils, which give a ripe, very fruit-rich Smaragd Grüner (Smaragd wines have a minimum alcohol level of 12.5% to beyond 14%). It is also sometimes made in an 'XL' version (beyond Smaragd ripeness) of tremendous richness and texture; even if the balance seems precarious, it can age for up to 10 years. In contrast Grüner from Höhereck (40-year-old vines on stony soils) is more floral and mineral in style. For Riesling, both the pure, citrusy Steinriegl and concentrated, more structured Dürnsteiner Freiheit are excellent examples.

Recommended Whites:
Grüner Veltliner XL ★★★★ £E
Höhereck Grüner Veltliner Smaragd ★★★★ £E
Pichl Point Grüner Veltliner Smaragd ★★★ £D
Steinwand Grüner Veltliner Federspiel ★★ £C
Steinriegl Riesling Smaragd ★★★★ £E
Dürnsteiner Freiheit Riesling Smaragd ★★★★ £E
Weingebirge Riesling Federspiel ★★★ £C

Heidi Schröck (Neusiedlersee-Hügelland) *www.heidi-schroeck.com*
On her 10 ha, Heidi Schröck achieves the same heights with sweet wines that other female Austrian winemakers do with dry whites or reds (see EHN, EICHINGER, PRIELER and UNGER). Her Ruster Ausbruchs are very good indeed – pure, spicy and concentrated but elegant too. The composition varies but can include Furmint, Welschriesling, Weissburgunder, Grauburgunder and Sauvignon.

A wonderfully honeyed single-vineyard example, Turner, is 100% Furmint and even better. But there's more from 8ha of vineyards than small quantities of sweet wines. Dry whites include Furmint – actually off-dry but with a marvelous intensity of spicy citrusy fruit and a long finish – and a late-picked Weissburgunder which is very ripe, intense and lees-enriched. The Gelber Muskateller and reds are promising too. There's good fruit-driven Blaufränkisch and a more oaky Junge Löwen, 50/50 Blaufränkisch/Zweigelt.

Recommended Reds:
Blaufränkisch Kulm ★★ £D
Junge Löwen ★★ £D

Recommended Whites:
Ruster Ausbruch Turner ★★★★ £F
Ruster Ausbruch ★★★ £F
Furmint ★★ £C
Weissburgunder ★ £C
Gelber Muskateller ★ £C

❀ Tement (Südsteiermark) *www.tement.at*
One of the standard-bearers for southern Styria, Manfred Tement makes some superbly balanced and expressive whites, the majority from 45 ha of estate vineyards. Beyond a range of sound, varietally pure Steirische Klassik basics, he makes some very good Chardonnay (Morillon) and at times brilliant Sauvignon. The latter from Grassnitzberg vineyards (limestone) has strength and purity requiring a little ageing while another from Sernau (gravel and sand) has even better structure and can keep for up to a decade. Zieregg is Sauvignon more in a Bordeaux mould and is richly textured, powerful but balanced. It can result from as many as eight pickings from very steep slopes. Of the Chardonnay, Sulz Morillon sees used *barriques* and large oak that enhances an attractive minerality. The example from Zieregg is more powerful and oakier but has greater depth and potential. Tement's sweet wines are floral, elegant examples in contrast to deeper, richer wines from other Austrian producers. There is also a little red but more important are those produced in collaboration with F-X Pichler (see ARACHON T FX T).). In 2016, the frost In April caused the loss of more than 90% of his crop.

Recommended Whites:
Zieregg Sauvignon Blanc ★★★★ £E
Zieregg Sauvignon Blanc Beerenauslese ★★★ £F
Sernau Sauvignon Blanc ★★★ £E
Grassnitzberg Sauvignon Blanc ★★ £D
Sauvignon Blanc Steirische Klassik ★★ £B
Zieregg Morillon ★★★ £E
Sulz Morillon ★★★ £D
Welschriesling Steirische Klassik ★ £B
Weissburgunder Steirische Klassik ★ £B

Ernst Triebaumer (Neusiedlersee-Hügelland) *www.triebaumer.com*
Ernst Triebaumer (or ET) is one of the best-known names of Burgenland. From a total of 16 ha of vineyard, his sons Herbert and Gerhard are responsible for a wide range of styles. There are sheep living in the vineyards, who help with the crops: they eat all of the grass, thus removing the need for much use of tractors, and they strip the low leaves from the vines and eat them. There is no Intervention in the cellar. What is made in a given vintage depends to some extent on the climatic conditions. Whites include Chardonnay and Sauvignon Blanc as well as a light, elegant aromatic Gelber Muskateller and Grüner Veltliner. The latter has a significant amount of fruit on the back palate and a very nice acid structure;

Austria

the taste is rather different from those produced in Lower Austria. However, the best grape is Blaufränkisch and up to 3 versions are made: Gmärk, Oberer Wald and the quite excellent Ried Marienthal. The last-named comes from a vineyard of fossilised limestone soils and sees 70% new oak but is only made in exceptional years. All Blaufränkisch develop well over 5 years or more; tasted too young they can seem a little harsh or lean but with age the wines soften and become increasingly complex. Maulwurf, which is quite a fruity wine with a good balanced structure, is a pricey blend of Blaufränkisch with Cabernet Sauvignon and Merlot. The Blaufränkisch Cabernet Sauvignon can benefit on occasion from a little more ripeness. Two other interesting blends, Hauptsache, a blend of St-Laurent, Merlot and Shiraz, and Tridendron, comprising Merlot, Cabernet Sauvignon and Blaufränkisch, are also made; the latter is a very assertive wine which, after three years in bottle, still had tannins which gripped the gums. For sweet wines there's fine Ruster Ausbruch made from Chardonnay, Weissburgunder and Welschriesling, which has a gorgeous nose but not always enough acid; an example is the 2013 when it fell a victim to the weather and was a touch syrupy In most vintages, however, it Is an impressive wine. An Essenz is made in very small quantities.

Recommended Reds:
Blaufränkisch Ried Marienthal ★★★★ £E
Blaufränkisch/Cabernet Sauvignon ★ £C

Recommended Whites:
Ruster Ausbruch ★★★★ £F   Chardonnay Ried Pandkräftn ★★ £C
Grüner Veltliner ★★ £B   Gelber Muskateller ★ £B

Petra Unger (Kremstal)   www.ungerwein.at
Lately helped by her brother Axel, Petra Unger has been running this moderately large (40 ha) Kremstal estate since 1999. The vineyards incorporate those leased by her father from the Benedictine Abbey of Gottweig in 1987. Approachable and easy drinking wines are made under the Q label. Whilst other varieties make a significant contribution, including Zweigelt, Pinot Noir, Chardonnay and Pinot Gris, the focus is on Grüner Veltliner (almost half of the plantings) and Riesling, which are responsible for the quality of the wines. A Reserve bottling has stylish citrus and nectarine fruit richness and is long and generally well balanced. It ages impressively, becoming toasty and honeyed. The Alte Reben Reserve Grüner from Oberfeld is slightly exotic but full and concentrated with sufficient balance and structure to improve for at least 3 years. Sweet wines include a vibrant Eiswein from Sprinzenberg that is mostly Neuberger but sometimes includes Grüner. A late harvested Wachau Riesling also comes from the Silberbügel site and there is a TBA Chardonnay.

Recommended Whites:
Ried Sprinzenberg Eiswein ★★★★ £E
Ried Gaisberg Riesling Reserve ★★★ £C
Ried Steinterrassen Riesling Classic ★★ £B
Ried Oberfeld Grüner Veltliner Alte Reben Reserve ★★★ £C
Ried Gottschelle Grüner Veltliner Reserve ★★ £C
Ried Oberfeld Grüner Veltliner ★ £B

Velich (Neusiedlersee)   www.velich.at
On their 12 ha, Velich make a number of interesting wines. From Apetlon in the Neusiedlersee, a short distance from the Hungarian border, the Velich brothers make Austria's finest Chardonnay. Tiglat is a single vineyard example, 100% *barrique*-fermented and aged (50% new oak), that combines depth and richness with real poise and elegance. It is neither too ripe nor too oaky or leesy as some Austrian examples are. A second Chardonnay, Darscho is a

blend from different vineyards hasn't the quite the same depth yet but good dimension and intensity. Cuvée TO (previously OT) is a relatively inexpensive blend of Chardonnay with some Welschriesling and Sauvignon Blanc – a perfumed, peachy white for early drinking. Neusiedlersee is of course more famous for its sweet wine production and Velich make some fine examples. Seewinkel Beerenauslese is based on Welschriesling and other varieties and can show good botrytis richness and sweet dried apricot fruit. Welschriesling TBA is sweet, intense and very refined.

Recommended Whites:
Welschriesling TBA ★★★★ £F
Seewinkel Beerenauslese ★★★ £E
Apetlon Chardonnay Tiglat ★★★☆ £E
Apetlon Chardonnay Darscho ★★★ £D
Cuvée TO ★★ £B

Domäne Wachau (Wachau)   www.domaene-wachau.at
This Wachau co-op with around 600 growers produces some of the most readily available and affordable examples of Grüner Veltliner and Riesling from the Wachau. Whilst the wines are not at the same level as the very best private estates, standards are nonetheless quite impressive. Volume examples are released under the Wachau Klassik label and they generally show good definition and intensity. The Domäne Wachau label was originally introduced for wines from individual vineyard sites, although all wines are now released under this banner. As well as the leading wines listed below, individual bottlings from other sites such as Singerriedel and 1000-Eimer-Berg are also produced. Dry wines are generally best with between 2 and 5 years' age, though they will keep longer in top vintages.

Recommended Whites:
Dürnsteiner Kellerberg Riesling Smaragd ★★★ £C
Loibener Loibenberg Riesling Smaragd ★★★ £C
Riesling Exceptional ★★★ £C
Weissenkirchener Achleiten Riesling Smaragd ★★★ £C
Terrassen Riesling Smaragd ★★ £C
Weissenkirchener Achleiten Grüner Veltliner Smaragd ★★★ £C
Dürnsteiner Kellerberg Grüner Veltliner Smaragd ★★ £C
Terrassen Grüner Veltliner Federspiel ★★ £B

Wohlmuth (Südsteiermark)   www.wohlmuth.at
Gerhard Wohlmuth oversees what is one of southern Styria's larger quality estates. The 60 ha of vineyards include some leading sites planted to more than a dozen varieties, 70% white. These are the real stars, including two starkly contrasting Sauvignons. Steinriegel comes from very steep schist slopes, is mostly fermented in stainless steel and has ripe, mineral-infused fruit and good breadth and intensity. Three other premium Sauvignons are also released. Edelschuh and Hochsteinriegl are also single vineyards whilst the Kitzecker example comes from a number of sites. Premium Terroir and Single Vineyard Riesling, Chardonnay, Gelber Muskateller, Pinot Gris and Sémillon are also made as well as an old vine Gewürztraminer and a green fruited stainless steel fermented Pinot Blanc Gola. Reds include an attractive plummy Aristos (Blaufränkisch and Cabernet Sauvignon) and a much more ambitious Rabenkropf from Blaufränkisch but from a lower-yielding single vineyard with over 45-year-old vines. Both are from Burgenland. The latter sees 100% new oak, a little too evident in both structure and flavour, but there is potential here. A Rabenkropf Privat is also released in the very best vintages, the latest being a 2007. Also made but not yet tasted are varietal Blaufränkisch and Pinot Noir as well as kosher red and white.

Recommended Reds:
Rabenkropf ★★ £D Aristos ★★ £C
Zweigelt ★ £B
Recommended Whites:
Steinriegel Sauvignon Blanc ★★★ £C Sauvignon Blanc ★★ £C
Gewürztraminer Alte Reben ★★ £C
Gola Pinot Blanc ★★ £C

Other wines of note

Johann Donabaum (Wachau)
Recommended Whites:
Loibner Garten Grüner Veltliner Smaragd ★★ £C
Fritsch (Wagram)
Recommended Whites: Steinberg Grüner Veltliner ★★☆ £B
Schlossberg Grüner Veltliner ★★★ £C
Riesling Wagram ★★☆ £C Riesling Reserve ★★★☆ £C
Recommended Reds: Pinot Noir Grand Select ★★ £C
Pinot Noir 'P' ★★★ £D Zweigelt Red Soil ★☆ £B
Foggathal No.12 (Zweigelt/Cabernet Sauvignon/Merlot) ★★★☆ £D
Gesellmann (Mittelburgenland)
Recommended Reds: Blaufränkisch Creitzer ★★ £B
Zweigelt ★★ £B Syrah ★★★☆ £D
OP Eximium Cuvée (Blaufränkisch/Zweigelt) ★★☆ £D
Bela Rex (Cabernet S/Merlot) ★★★☆ £E
Gesellmann 'G' (Blaufränkisch/St. Laurent) ★★★☆ £F
WGT. Giefing (Neusiedlersee-Hügelland)
Recommended Whites: Grüner Veltliner ★☆ £B
Ruster Ausbruch (Neuburger/Chardonnay) ★★★☆ £E
Recommended Reds:
Cardinal (Blaufränkisch/Zweigelt/Cabernet Sauvignon) ★★★ £E
Glatzer (Carnumtum)
Recommended Whites: Grüner Veltliner Dornenvogel ★☆ £C
Recommended Reds: St. Laurent ★ £B
St. Laurent Altenberg ★★ £C
Zweigelt Dornenvogel ★★☆ £C
Gotinsprun (Blaufränkisch/Merlot/Zweigelt/St. Laurent) ★★★ £D
Gernot Heinrich (Neusiedlersee)
Recommended Reds: Red (Zweigelt/Blaufränkisch) ★ £B
Zweigelt ★ £B Blaufränkisch ★ £B St Laurent ★ £B
Pannobile (Zweigelt/Blaufränkisch) ★★ £D
Gabarinza (Zweigelt/Blaufränkisch/Merlot/St. Laurent) ★★★ £E
WGT. Leth (Wagram)
Recommended Whites: Sauvignon Blanc Classic ★☆ £C
Riesling Classic ★☆ £C
Brunnthal Sauvignon Blanc Lagenreserve ★★★ £C
Brunnthal Grüner Veltliner Lagenreserve ★★☆ £C
Scheiben Grüner Veltliner Lagenreserve ★★★ £C
Scheiben Roter Veltliner Lagenreserve ★★ £C
Riesling Wagramterrassen Lagenreserve ★★★ £C
Recommended Reds: Pinot Noir Reserve ★★ £C
St. Laurent Reserve ★★ £C Gigama (Zweigelt) ★★★ £E
Malat (Kremstal)
Recommended Whites: Höhlgraben Grüner Veltliner ★★ £B
Dreigarten Grüner Veltliner Reserve ★★★ £C
Steinbühel Riesling ★★ £C Silberbühel Riesling Reserve ★★★ £D
Brunnkreuz Sauvignon Blanc Reserve ★★ £C
Gelber Muskateller Reserve ★★ £B Am Zaum Pinot Blanc ★★ £B
Gerhard Markowitsch (Carnuntum)
Recommended Whites: Sauvignon Blanc ★★☆ £C
Grüner Veltliner Ried Schonzäcker ★★ £B

Grüner Veltliner Alte Reben ★★★ £C Blaufränkisch ★★ £B
Recommended Reds:
Carnuntum Cuvée (Zweigelt/Pinot Noir) ★★ £B
Rubin Carnuntum (Zweigelt) ★★☆ £C
Pinot Noir Reserve ★★★ £E St. Laurent Rothenberg ★★★ £D
Redmont (Zweigelt/Cabernet S/Syrah) ★★☆ £D
Rosenberg (Zweigelt/Merlot/Cabernet S) ★★★ £E
Moric (Neusiedlersee-Hügelland)
Recommended Reds: Blaufränkisch ★★ £B
Neckenmarkt Blaufränkisch Alte Reben ★★ £D
Lutzmannburg Blaufränkisch Alte Reben ★★★ £D
Netzl (Carnuntum)
Recommended Whites: Chardonnay ★ £B
Grüner Veltliner Selection Bärnreiser ★★ £B
Recommended Reds: Rubin Carnuntum (Zweigelt) ★★ £C
Cabernet Sauvignon ★★★ £D Edles Tal (Zweigelt/Merlot) ★★☆ £D
Anna-Christina (Zweigelt/Cabernet S/Merlot) ★★★☆ £E
Willi Opitz (Neusiedlersee)
Recommended Whites: Eiswein (Welschriesling) ★★★ £G
Weisser Schilfmandl Muskat Ottonel TBA ★★★ £G
Goldackerl Beerenauslese (Welschriesling/Scheurebe) ★★ £F
Goldackerl TBA (Welschriesling/Scheurebe) ★★★★ £G
Recommended Reds: Opitz One Stohwein (Zweigelt) ★★★ £G
Gerhard Pittnauer (Neusiedlersee)
Recommended Reds: Pinot Noir Reserve ★★ £C
St. Laurent Alte Reben ★★ £C
Pannobile (Zweigelt/Blaufränkisch/St. Laurent) ★★ £D
Red Pitt (Zweigelt/St. Laurent/Cabernet S/Merlot) ★☆ £C
Wgt. Pöckl (Neusiedlersee)
Recommended Reds:
Rosso e Nero (Zweigelt/Blaufränkisch/Cabernet S/Merlot) ★★ £D
Admiral (Zweigelt/Blaufränkisch/Cabernet S/Merlot) ★★☆ £E
Pretterebner (Neusiedlersee)
Recommended Reds: Blaufränkisch ★★★ £C St. Laurent ★★ £C
Stift Klosterneuberg (Klosterneuberg)
Recommended Whites: Hengsberg Grüner Veltliner ★ £B
AltweingartenChardonnay ★☆£B Eiswein(Welschriesling) ★★★☆£E
Recommended Reds: Raflerjoch Pinot Noir ★☆ £B
Stiftsbreite St. Laurent Ausstich ★★ £B
Stiftsbreite St. Laurent Barrique ★★★ £C
Stölzerhof (Neusiedlersee)
Recommended Reds: Trockenbeerenauslese Zweigelt ★★★ £F
Recommended Whites:
Trockenbeerenauslese Samling 88 (Scheurebe) ★★★ £F
Tibor Szemes (Mittelburgenland)
Recommended Reds: Horitschoner Blaufränkisch Tradition ★★ £C
Horitschoner Imperial CJ (Blaufränkisch/Cab. Sauvignon) ★★★ £D
Tegernseerhof (Wachau)
Recommended Whites: Loibenberg Grüner Veltliner ★★ £C
Durnsteiner Bergdistel Grüner Veltliner ★★ £C
Durnsteiner Höhereck Grüner Veltliner ★★ £C
Loibenberg Riesling ★★★ £C Steinertal Riesling ★★★☆ £D
Durnsteiner Kellerberg Riesling ★★★☆ £D
Grüner Veltliner Creation ★★★ £E Riesling Creation ★★★ £E
Tinhof (Neusiedlersee-Hügelland)
Recommended Reds: Gloriette (Blaufränkisch) ★★ £D
Feuersteig (Blaufränkisch/Zweigelt/St Laurent) ★ £C
Recommended Whites:
Fuchsenriegl (Neuburger/Weissburgunder) ★ £C
Trockenbeerenauslese (Weissburgunder) ★★★ £F

Austria

Umathum (Neusiedlersee)
Recommended Reds:
Haideboden (Zweigelt/Blaufränkisch/Cabernet) ★☆ £C
Ried Hallebühl (Zweigelt/Blaufränkisch) ★★★☆ £E
Pinot Noir Unter den Terassen zu Jois ★★☆ £E
St. Laurent Bom Stein ★★☆ £D
Recommended Whites: Beerenauslese Chardonnay ★★★☆ £F
Trockenbeerenauslese Scheurebe ★★★★☆ £G

Weinrieder (Weinviertel)
Recommended Whites: Grüner Veltliner Alte Reben ★★☆ £B
Riesling Bockgärten I (Trocken) ★☆ £B
Riesling Bockgärten II (Halbtrocken) ★☆ £B
Schneiderberg Riesling Eiswein ★★★☆ £F
Poysdorfer Kugler Weissburgunder ★★★☆ £F
Poysdorfer Hohenleiten Chardonnay TBA ★★★☆ £F

Rainer Wess (Wachau & Kremstal)
Recommended Whites: Grüner Veltliner Wachauer ★☆ £B
Grüner Veltliner Terrassen ★★☆ £C
Loibenberg Grüner Veltliner ★★★ £D
Pfaffenberg Grüner Veltliner ★★★☆ £D
Riesling Wachauer ★★☆ £B Riesling Terrassen ★★★ £C
Loibenberg Riesling ★★★☆ £D Pfaffenberg Riesling ★★★☆ £D

Wieninger (Wien)
Recommended Whites: Nussberg Riesling ★★ £B
Nussberg Riesling Alte Reben ★★☆ £C
Nussberg Riesling Alte Reben Reserve ★★★☆ £D
Herrenholz Grüner Veltliner ★★ £B Chardonnay Select ★★ £B
Recommended Reds: Pinot Noir Grand Select ★★ £C
Wiener Trilogie (Zweigelt/Merlot/Cabernet Sauvignon) ★☆ £B

Zahel (Wien)
Recommended Whites: Grüner Veltliner Grinzing ★ £B
Wiener Gernischter Satz (Grüner Veltliner/Riesling/Chardonnay) ★ £B
Nussberg Riesling ★★ £B Sauvignon Blanc ★☆ £B
Nussberg Grande Reserve (field blend of varieties) ★★★☆ £D
Recommended Reds: Zweigelt Wiener ★☆ £B
Wiener Komposition (Zweigelt/St. Laurent/Blaufränkisch) ★★ £B
St. Laurent Reserve ★★☆ £C
Antares Grande Res. (St. Laurent/Zweigelt/Cab S/Merlot) ★★★☆ £E

Author's choice

Superior Austrian Riesling
Leo Alzinger Loibner Loibenberg Riesling Smaragd
Bründlmayer Zöbinger Heiligenstein Riesling Alte Reben
Hirsch Zöbinger Gaisberg Riesling
Franz Hirtzberger Spitzer Singerriedel Riesling Smaragd
Jurtschitsch Sonnhof Zöbinger Heiligenstein Riesling Alte Reben
Emmerich Knoll Dürnsteiner Ried Schütt Riesling Smaragd
Loimer Langenloiser Käferberg Riesling
Nigl Senftenberger Riesling Privat Pellingen Reserve
Nikolaihof Baumpresse Riesling Im Weingebirge
F-X Pichler Dürnsteiner Kellerberg Riesling Smaragd
Rudi Pichler Weissenkirchener Achleiten Riesling Smaragd
Prager Weissenkirchen Achleiten Riesling Smaragd
Wieninger Nussberg Riesling Alte Reben Reserve

Superb Grüner Veltliner
Bründlmayer Kammerner Lamm Grüner Veltliner
Birgit Eichinger Strasser Gaisberg Grüner Veltliner
Hiedler Thal Grüner Veltliner Novemberlese
Franz Hirtzberger Honivogl Grüner Veltliner Smaragd

Josef Jamek Ried Achleiten Grüner Veltliner Smaragd
Emmerich Knoll Loibenberg Loibner Grüner Veltliner Smaragd
Loimer Langenloiser Käferberg Grüner Veltliner
Nigl Grüner Veltliner Alte Reben
Nikolaihof Im Weingebirge Grüner Veltliner Smaragd
F-X Pichler Loibner Berg Grüner Veltliner Smaragd
Prager Weissenkirchen Achleiten Grüner Veltliner Smaragd
Schloss Gobelsburg Kammerner Lamm Grüner Veltliner

Sweet Whites
Reds:
Hans & Anita Nittnaus Trockenbeerenauslese
Ernst Triebaumer Ruster Ausbruch
Whites:
Bründlmayer Zöbinger Heiligenstein Riesling Trockenbeerenauslese
Feiler-Artinger Ruster Ausbruch Pinot Cuvée
Kracher Grande Cuvée Trockenbeerenauslese Nouvelle Vague
Helmut Lang Samling 88 Trockenbeerenauslese
Heidi Schröck Ruster Ausbruch
Umathum Scheurebe Trockenbeerenauslese
Velich Welschriesling Trockenbeerenauslese

Leading Reds
Paul Achs Blaufränkisch Ungerberg
Arachon T FX T Arachon Evolution
Feiler-Artinger Solitaire
Gesellmann Gesellmann 'G'
Juris St. Laurent Reserve
Kollwentz-Römerhof Steinzeiler
Kracher Blend 1
Krutzler Perwolff
Netzl Anna-Christina
Anita & Hans Nittnaus Pannobile
Pretterebner Blaufränkisch
Schiefer Blaufränkisch Eisenberg Reihburg
Ernst Triebaumer Ried Marienthal Blaufränkisch

Best Value Austrians
Reds:
Anita & Hans Nittnaus Heideboden
Whites:
Kurt Angerer Grüner Veltliner Spies
Ehn Oberer Panzaum Grüner Veltliner
Birgit Eichinger Strasser Gaisberg Riesling
Felsner Grüner Veltliner Moosburgerin Kabinett
Graf Hardegg Weinviertel Dac Grüner Veltliner
Loimer Riesling Langenlois
Neumayer Rafasetzen Grüner Veltliner
Bernhard Ott Der Ott Grüner Veltliner
Heidi Schröck Furmint
Salomon Undhof Wieden Grüner Veltliner
Rainer Wess Riesling Wachauer

Wine behind the label

This is a diverse geographical section, even a motley collection but one that sparkles here and there with real vibrancy. Our focus here naturally is to support the exciting, emerging regions and nations rather than waste space on those perenially under-achieving countries (those that continue to service the bulk and own-label market places rather than seek to establish any quality reputation of their own). Happily England finds a place as one the promsing band, where the greatest potential for fine wine continues to be of the sparkling variety. Luxembourg too does fizz and some good aromatic whites while Switzerland has established quality credentials, if not value. Elsewhere in Central and Eastern Europe isolated viticultural outposts suggest scope for the future. However it is the sweet wine renaissance at Tokaji in Hungary that best illustrates just what investment, technology and a commitment to excellence can achieve. In a drier vein, the majority of the premium reds and whites come from Greece, Slovenia, Israel or Lebanon where top quality producers have made the most of the potential afforded by site and climate. Take a look too at what is emerging from Algeria and Morocco.

Western Europe
England

In England growers' annual challenge of bringing in an adequate quality grape harvest has been eased by the hot summers of 2003, 2005 and 2006 as well as a precocious 2007, although later years have proved less propitious until a promising 2013 was followed similarly in 2014 and 2015 with excellent September weather. For several decades the industry has struggled with modest varieties and crossings of mostly German origin. The problem, at least until the recent escalation of the impact of global warming, was finding adequate 'quality' grape varieties that will ripen sufficiently in a generally cool and damp northerly climate. Bacchus, a crossing of German origins (whose parents include Riesling, Silvaner and Müller-Thurgau) with somewhat Sauvignon-like qualities, has arguably emerged as the leading white variety. Others include Reicheinsteiner, Ortega and Seyval Blanc. The latter has proved to work particularly well here but has faced opposition from EU regulators due to being a hybrid.

Others have gone further, planting the high quality Champagne grapes of Chardonnay, Pinot Noir and Pinot Meunier, with Chardonnay and Pinot Noir now being the most widely planted grape varieties in England. The key to their success has been planting and sourcing fruit from vineyards on the southern English downland chalk soils (the same strata as in Champagne). The results are some first-class sparkling wines. Building on the success of the best vintages of the 90s, it is quite probable that the hot summers of 03, 05, 06 and 13 will produce wines of a quality unprecedented in England. The quality leader for the past decade has been Nyetimber Vineyard but Ridgeview, another sparkling specialist, and others such as Hush Heath Estate (for the new Balfour Brut Rosé made by Owen Elias) offer serious quality too. For production of dry whites (but also including sparkling wines) Denbies, Chapel Down, Three Choirs and Stanlake Park head the established quality leader board.

Luxembourg

This small, pretty and well ordered country is increasingly a western European transport hub with travellers making haste to Germany, France, Belgium or perhaps catching a plane to London. Yet it is also a relaxed, civilised holiday destination. If your itinerary does include a night (or even a few hours) in the Grand Duchy then insist on drinking the local wines as the quality will surprise you.

Luxembourg shares with England a northerly latitude, missing the latter's maritime amelioration but compensating with continental summers. If seemingly too far north in French terms, viticulture here is in fact on the upper reaches of the Moselle (Mosel) river where it forms the border with Germany before turning east and wrapping itself around those extraordinary sites in the Mosel-Saar-Ruwer. The river and its proximity to often steep and well-drained slopes is crucially important as have been the recent string of hot summers. From 1300 ha of vines along a 42 km stretch that extends north from Schengen (the reknown tri-cornered border with France and Germany), the best vineyards have been classified as *Grands Premiers Crus* (GPC). Parcels within some of these *lieux-dits* are the source of the most exciting wines but they must come from a top producer (see below).

Central & Eastern Europe
Hungary

In Hungary, apart from Tokaji, few wines of real quality have been produced. Again, investment has been centred on the bottom of the market. There is potential, particularly with the reds from the southern **Villány-Siklós** region. **Tokaji**, though, is a different matter. Investment aplenty has flooded into the region and some of the results are stunning.

All Tokaji is based on the Furmint grape, but usually including a smaller amount of Hárslevelú (the two varieties account for 90% of the vineyard area) and . The great sweet wines are *Aszú* wines, derived from dried (usually botrytised) grapes but only make up a very small percentage of the region's production. Individual berries are made into a paste-like consistency which is soaked in the must before completing fermentation in casks. The level of *puttonyos* now reflects a minimum level of sugar and extract in the wine, ranging from 3 *puttonyos* to 6 *puttonyos*. The degree of oxidation that occurs with ageing has been much reduced by many of the new school of producers with the result that the wines are now altogether fresher, more intense and with some truly splendid botrytis character in the best examples. The top names are Disznókö, Oremus, Istvan Szepsy, Royal Tokaji and Tokaji Classic but Château Megyer, Château Pajzos and Crown Estates are also decent sources. Szepsy even makes a sweet example following more classic reductive winemaking practices (labelled Noble Late Harvest). Essencia (*Eszencia*) refers to wines of higher than 6 *puttonyos* and is made from the most concentrated juice that is characterized by its low alcohol and exceedingly high residual sugar levels. It also characterised by high acidity and potential longevity.

Good dry whites which are made and labelled varietally are also on the increase. Those from Furmint show the greatest promise. Also occasionally encountered is *Szamorodni*, a dry or off-dry style of higher alcohol and extract due to the inclusion of some botrytised fruit. Among the great recent years for the sweet wines to look out for are 2000, 99, 96, 95, 93 and 88. It's a shame that the same technology has failed to reach that part of the appellation that lies across the border in Slovakia.

Switzerland

In Switzerland there is both quality and diversity, if at a price - this being the price the local market supports. Now producing slightly more red wine than white, well-established viticultural areas include the Vaud, Valais and Ticino but wine is also made around Geneva, in Neuchâtel and in the north-east. In fact it is the latter that has produced some of Switzerland finest wines. The Pinots from Daniel & Martha Gantenbein stand comparison with top German examples.

Other Europe, North Africa, Middle East & Asia

Other Europe & Med

Jean-René Germanier sets the standard for the mostly French-speaking **Valais** where the mountain valley viticulture is made possible by the presence of the Rhône. Here, hundreds of miles from its more famous associations in France, vines flank a roughly south-western stretch of the river before it turns and runs north-west towards Lac Léman (Lake Geneva). Successful local varieties include Fendant for firm dry whites, Humagne and the increasingly fashionable Cornalin for characterful reds. Dôle is from Gamay and Pinot Noir; the latter can be impressive varietally too.

In the **Vaud**, spectacular vineyards arc on steep terraces above Lac Léman in the region of Lavaux where Chasselas is king. The best from well-established ACs such as Dézaley, Saint-Saphorin and Epesses display minerality and tension. Most, however, are more humdrum. Other regions within the Vaud include Chablais, east of Lac Léman in the Rhône valley (Aigle and Yvorne are leading communes) and La Côte, running west of Lausanne towards Geneva. In French speaking **Neuchâtel** the vineyards, planted almost entirely to Chasselas and Pinot Noir, extend along the northern shore of Lac Neuchâtel as far as Lac Bienne. **Ticino**, the Italian bit of Switzerland, has focused almost exclusively on Merlot. They have a good local reputation but are plagued by variability both from grower to grower and year to year. Christian Zündel is the quality leader but several others (Daniele Huber, Luigi Zanini) have made ripe, lushly-textured examples that are true to the variety. The two Cabernets often contribute to blends and there are also very small amounts of Pinot Noir and Chardonnay (Zanini's is the stand-out white).

Bulgaria

Bulgaria ought to produce much more in the way of quality than it does. That said, things might finally have taken a turn for the better with the arrival of Stéphan von Niepperg (owner of the brilliant Ch. La Mondotte in Saint-Emilion) whose investment is already bearing fruit in early releases of the Enira wines from the Bessa Valley winery. Other increasingly good wines are also coming from the Thracian Valley, Melnik and Ustina.

Other Central & Eastern Europe

While Hungary's Tokaji region doesn't lack for history, investment and direction and Switzerland isn't short of money or connoisseurship, other parts of Central Europe (other than a revitalised Austria - see separate section) continue to do less well. The Czech Republic and Slovakia both produce some decent dry whites. In the **Czech Republic** whites from the likes of Grüner Veltliner and Gewürztraminer are produced in **Bohemia** and **Moravia** and in **Slovakia** some well-made reds originate from the **Nitra** region, as well as good stylish whites from **Pezinok** just north of Bratislava. Perhaps most significant is the emergence of Château Bela, producing fine Rieslings in **Stúrovo**, just north of Hungary. Further east, nothing of real note has yet emerged from the **Ukraine** or **Moldova** despite there being some modern winemaking input in the latter. In **Romania** the best potential would appear to rest with the sweet botrytised wines of **Cotnari** and **Murfatlar** but some outside investment would be an immense advantage.

South-Eastern Europe
Greece

This is a country with real potential and an increasing number of stylish modern whites and rich plummy reds are now being made as well as a few established classics like the sweet Muscats from the island of **Samos**. Arguably nowhere has advanced the winemaking revolution here more than in the Peloponnese (Peloponessos), a cradle of ancient viticulture but until recently best known for a tradition of sweet wines (from Muscat and Mavrodaphne) under the **Patras** appellation. Independent producers are now exploiting more high-potential viticultural sites planted chiefly to Agiorgitiko for red. 100% of the variety is required to qualify for the leading red wine appellation **Nemea** while a minimum of 85% of the white Moschofilero is mandatory in the **Mantinia** appellation. The peninsula's leader is Gaia Estate. Other good producers, including Skouras and Antonopoulos, addtionally promote international varieties. The same is true of the dynamic Evharis estate located east of isthmus of Corinth just outside Athens in the foothills of the Gerania mountains.

Several new pockets of quality have also emerged in northern Greece. In the elevated lake district around Amydeon the Greek varieties of Xinomavro and Mavrodaphne are shown as much respect by Alpha Estate as imported Sauvignon, Syrah or Merlot. Further east, Gerovassiliou have put Thessaloniki firmly on the wine map with impressive varietals from French grapes but have also successfully revived the ancient Malagousia variety (as a varietal white) as well as indigenous black grapes (including Limnio) for a premium red blend. Further east is Biblia Chora on the slopes of Mount Pangeon (of Dionysus legend), succeeding as much with Agiorgitiko and Assyrtiko (the latter being combined with Sauvignon) as Cabernet or Chardonnay. A similar duality is echoed in the wines of Ktima Pavlidis, located north of here near **Drama**. Another part of Greece that has made huge strides is the beautiful volcanic island of **Santorini**. The potential for outstanding mineral-imbued dry whites from Assyrtiko has already been realized by Hatzidakis, Gaia estate and Sigalas. The quality of Vinsanto from dried grapes shouldn't be ignored either. Also in a sweet wine vein are the famous Muscats of **Samos**. Here the island co-op continues its long and consistent production that combines quality and value.

Slovenia

Quietly but assuredly wines of world class quality are emerging from this small, outwardly looking and progressive European star. Of three main wine regions, west is best. Known as Primorska it encompasses the wine producing areas of (Goriska) Brda, Kras, Istria and Vipava. Most impressive are the wines made in Brda, in the western hills that form the border with Italy. In fact the Collio hills of Friuli-Venezia Giulia, source of the Slow Food coined 'super whites' extends into Slovenia. And there's no less potential here. There are growers with vineyards in Italy just as there are Italian producers with vineyards in Slovenia. The likes of Edi Simcic, Marjan Simcic, Batic and others deserve to be as familiar to wine drinkers as Italy's Jermanns, Gravners, Vie di Romans and the like. In fact, Gravner and his radical non-interventionist winemaking philosophy is an inspiration for many. For some at least this equates to no temperature control or yeast addition, and often prolonged skin maceration or even vinification on the skins, for the white wines. Others follow a more conservative approach but the best all favour hard work in the vineyard for the best results. Winemaking is also undergoing significant changes in Slovenia's more northerly and eastern regions. Podravje which is centred on the valley of the Drava river, in part close to the Austrian border makes significant quantities of mostly sweet and sparkling styles. To the south, Posavje extends along the Sava river, near Croatia.

Croatia

Croatia is a land of more than a thousand islands, and also a land of vineyards, with more than 300 geographically defined wine districts. The two primary wine regions, Primorska Hrvatska ("coastal Croatia") and Kontinentalna Hrvatska ("continental Croatia"), are divided into a total of 12 sub regions, themselves further divided into smaller vinogorje or wine hills, which spread northeast from the Dalmatian coast to the plains of the Danube River. It was here that the Zinfandel was supposed to have originated although this may be disputed by the people of Puglia in Italy!

In a way, Croatia is still work in progress for us, but we do now have sufficient information to list a few producers here.

Middle East & Asia

Israel

The industry in Israel is still largely focused on the production of kosher wines, many from the **Golan Heights**, but an increasing number of very stylish reds and whites are being produced there as well. In fact, a technical revolution has occurred over the past few years in as much as new investment in planting noble varieties, state-of-the-art technology and better understanding of the *terroir* has put Israeli wines firmly on the international map. There are now over 200 wineries, some of which have grown into internationally established operations such as Barkan Wine Cellars with their Segal label and the Golan Heights Winery with their well-established Yarden label, whilst others have distinctly remained in the area of boutique wineries, producing premium wines, sometimes with prices to match.

Lebanon

In Lebanon, after decades of war and strife, new producers, fortified by outside investment and expertise have surpassed the emblematic and long established Chateau Musar in producing dense, powerful wines of heady character. The new kids on the block are Massaya, Chateau Kefraya and Chateau Ksara.

Turkey

Turkey is another country showing impressive potential. In Turkish Thrace the Bordeaux red and white varieties and Syrah are all being successfully cultivated. In the west of the country in the Aegean region, Cabernet Sauvignon, Merlot, Syrah, Cabernet Franc, Petit Verdot, Grenache, Mourvedre, Cinsault, Chardonnay, Viognier and the indigenous Narince have all been planted by the Selendi winery.

Georgia

For such a relatively small country – it is abut the same size as Switzerland – Georgia has an extraordinarily diverse climate. Traditional wines, both red and white are made in *Qvevri* (or *Kwevri*) and they can be dauntingly tannic. The Qvevri is a clay vessel buried underground up to the neck in the *marani* (wine cellar) to create a simple form of temperature control. After fermentation (including skins, stalks and pulp) the wines can stay in the vessel for up to two years. Whites can have the glowing amber colour of maple syrup. Some fine Saperavi and wines from other native varieties are now being released.

India

It only seems a few years ago that India was best known for the Omar Khayyam sparkling wine brand. However the countries potential is now beginning to be realised. The Nashik Valley is just inland from the west coast of central India with the vines planted at altitude. The Soul Tree winery have planted Shiraz, Cabernet Sauvignon, Sauvignon Blanc and Chenin Blanc. The key to quality as well as the altitude of the vineyards is a double pruning during the growing season ensuring just one annual harvest.

North Africa

Fine reds are also emerging from **Algeria** and **Morocco** from old bush vines. If historically wines from North Africa were used to bolster many a well-known Rhône or Burgundy, there's evident potential too, given enough expertise and care.

A-Z of producers - *England*

Astley Vineyards (Worcestershire)

Astley is one of the oldest commercial vineyards in the UK that is still in production. It was, for a short while, also the most northerly vineyard in the world. The first real commercial vintage did not take place until 1983 with the current owners increasing the number of varietals planted, and continuing with an eye for quality rather than quantity by deliberately Other Europe /England restricting yields. Wines are produced from a single 5 acre (2 ha) vineyard site with no bought-in grapes. Jonty's objective is to achieve a consistency of production which endeavours to emulate the traditional goal of the winemaker that a wine should reflect a specific geographical location or *terroir*. Husbandry is based on an overall pest management approach that limits chemical intervention and, wherever possible, adheres to natural controls rather than industrial ones. Main grape varieties are Kerner, Madeleine Angevine, Siegerrebe (especially for late harvest), Phoenix and Bacchus. "George Eckert" vintage brut is 100 per cent Kerner – gentle bubbles, although a little bit austere and very dry on the attack, it smooths out to give a more rounded fruit-driven perception at the finish. "Phoenix" is a single low-yielding varietal wine with good aromatic fruit and nicely balanced acid. "Veritas" is the first wine they have ever made without having to chaptalise – 100 per cent Kerner, very full in the mouth, hints of grapefruit and gooseberry and a complex finish. Reserve Fumé is a blend of Madeleine Angevine and Kerner fermented separately, this has light green apple fruit, with a restrained grassy undercurrent although somewhat dominated by oak. (NB)

Recommended Whites:

Veritas ★★★ £C   Reserve Fumé ★★☆ £C

George Eckert Brut Vintage ★★ £D

Late Harvest ★★ £D

Phoenix ★★ £B

Bolney Wine Estate (West Sussex)   *www.bolneywineestate.com*

The Bolney Wine Estate (formerly known as Bookers Vineyard) owes its success to the winemaking skills of Sam Linter, the daughter of Rodney and Janet Pratt, who originally bought the estate in 1972. From the modest start of 3 acres (1.2 ha), the estate has now expanded to 33 acres (13.4 ha), not yet all of it in production. Chardonnay, Pinot Noir, Dornfelder, Rondo, Pinot Grigio, Würzer, Müller-Thurgau and Merlot are the varietals grown and from these, 12 different wines are produced. Latterly, there has been a change of emphasis from red to sparkling wines which now number six. The sparkling Rosé, with lovely red fruit undertones, made from 100% Pinot Noir and the yeasty Blanc de Blanc, from 100% Chardonnay grapes are now joined by a full Pinot Noir red. A still Pinot Noir 2009 is already showing promise with nice juicy fruit and Lychgate Red,

a blend of Dornfelder and Rondo is soft, juicy and round. The estate was one of the first in the UK to plant Merlot which is not under cover – the wine is light but can only improve in weight as the vines mature. What does have weight, though, is the Bacchus, with hints of green pepper and gooseberry with excellent balance between fruit and acidity. (NB)

Recommended Reds:
Pinot Noir ★★ £C Lychgate Red ★☆ £B
Recommended Whites:
Bacchus ★★★ £B Blanc de Blancs ★★ £D
Recommended Rosés:
Cuvée Rosé ★★☆ £C

Camel Valley (Cornwall) *www.camelvalley.com*
One of the best producers in the south-west of England and indeed in the country. The Lindo family produced their first vintage in 1992 and have since turned their vineyard and visitor centre into one of Cornwall's most popular tourist attractions. While the sales achieved through their cellar door are fundamental to the Lindo's, quality is a key consideration. The vines are planted on a steep southerly slope looking down towards the river Camel near Bodmin. Of course yield is all important in England but it is also as much a question of achieving a crop in the first place. The vines are all trained to single guyot to optimise light exposure and aid ripening. As almost everywhere in England now sparkling wine is of considerable import. The Cornwall Brut is produced from a blend of Seyval Blanc, which works particularly well here, Reichensteiner and Huxelrebe. It is subtly aromatic with a hint of bready, yeasty complexity and gets 15 months ageing on lees. The rosé sparkler is solely from Pinot Noir, with a restrained raspberry note to its fruit it offers better depth and verve than many equivalents from Champagne. The grassy, citrus and mineral scented Bacchus is produced in a completely dry style while the Camel Valley Rosé is a vibrant fruit-driven style from Pinot Noir pressings and Dornfelder. A further white sparkler is produced from Pinot Noir and there is a juicy fruited red from a blend of Dornfelder, Triomphe, Pinot Noir and Rondo as well as a rounder style white, Atlantic. There are a couple of self-catering cottages for those visitors who wish to stay. (DM)

Recommended Reds:
Camel Valley Red ★☆ £B
Recommended Whites:
Cornwall Brut Vintage ★★★ £D
Camel Valley Bacchus ★★ £B
Recommended Rosés:
Sparkling Pinot Noir Vintage ★★★ £D
Camel Valley ★☆ £B

Chapel Down (Kent) *www.chapeldown.com*
This is the main brand of the English Wines Group and has now grown since its inception in 1992 to become the biggest wine producer in England. The original wines were made from the Chapel Down Farm on the Isle of Wight. In 1995 the operation was expanded by the purchase of the Tenterden Vineyard and then in 2000 the acquisition of Lamberhurst Vineyard. Wines are produced not only from estate owned vineyards but also from a wide network of small growers who supply a considerable amount of companies needs. As elsewhere considerable effort is being put into the cultivation of both Chardonnay and Pinot Noir. Not surprisingly sparkling wine is an important element in the range. The Three Graces is the stand out wine, a blend of Pinot Noir, Pinot Meunier and Chardonnay with a subtle yeasty as well as a citrus and light

red fruits quality and impressive intensity. Good, without the same complexity and depth is the Pinot Reserve, a blend of Pinot Noir and Pinot Blanc, a more obviously fruit-driven style. There is also a very good sparkling rosé made from 100% Pinot Noir. Of the still wines the Bacchus whites in particular stand out. In addition to the Sauvignon like Tenterden Estate there is also a bottling from variuos vineyards in the South-East. The English Rose comes from a range of typically English style varieties and some Pinot Noir. It is fresh, and full of attractive red fruit aromas. The Flint Dry from a range of aromatic varieties is light, clean and fresh with a hint of grapefruit. (DM)

Recommended Whites:
Pinot Prestige Vintage ★★★☆ £E
Pinot Reserve Brut Vintage ★★☆ £D
Bacchus Reserve Tenterden Estate ★★☆ £C
Bacchus Reserve ★★ £B Flint Dry ★ £B
Recommended Rosés:
Brut Rosé ★★★ £D English Rose ★☆ £B

Davenport (East Sussex) *www.davenportvineyards.co.uk*
Will Davenport owns 8 ha (20 acres) of vineyards in both Kent and East Sussex. He organically produces just three wines a red Pinot Noir, a dry white Horsmoden produced from a number of aromatic varieties and most notable a finely crafted and almost austerely structured sparkling white Limney Estate from the vineyard of the same name. A blend of Pinot Noir (55%) and the balance Auxerrois, the wine is aged on lees for two years prior to disgorging. Expect all the wines to drink well on release. (DM)

Recommended Whites:
Limney Estate Vintage ★★ £D

Denbies (Surrey) *www.denbiesvineyard.co.uk*
Very substantial operation with 107 ha planted on limestone soils near Dorking, of which 94 ha is currently in production. It was founded in 1986 by Adrian and Gillian White and when selecting the site the potential ripening of the grapes was very carefully evaluated. Denbies is also far and away England's most visited vineyard with around 300,000 visitors a year and a wide number of varieties have been planted over the years and this has now been honed with Pinots Noir and Meunier along with Chardonnay planted on the best hillside plots. More Bacchus has also been established and this is a plus for still wine production with a fine intense nettley character. Vineyard Select bottlings of this variety, Pinot Gris, which is a touch off-dry and barrel-fermented and oak aged Ortega are all successful. The popular and very commercially successful Surrey Gold is a finely tuned off-dry blend of Ortega, Reichensteiner, Müller-Thurgau and Bacchus. As elsewhere, sparkling wines have good potential, the Greenfields Cuvée is a blend dominated by Pinot Noir, with additional Chardonnay and Pinot Meunier, it gains complexity from three years on lees while retaining a classic floral English quality. The Rosé Cuvée is fully Pinot Noir and slightly off-dry like all the Denbies sparklers. The Redlands is a supple, lightly perfumed berry-fruited red blended from roughly equal proportions of Pinot Noir and Dornfelder. A fresh young rosé Rose Hill and two whites, Juniper Hill from Bacchus and Schönburger and Flint Valley from Seyval Blanc and Reichensteiner are also noteworthy. Among recent developments, a new sparkling Blancs de Noirs, Cubitt Reserve, has been produced from the 2006 vintage from 100% Pinot Noir.

Recommended Whites:
Greenfields Cuvée Vintage ★★★ £E

Bacchus Vineyard Select ★★ £C
Pinot Gris ★★ £C   Ortega Vineyard Select ★★ £C
Surrey Gold ★☆ £B
Recommended Rosés:
Rosé Cuvée Vintage ★★☆ £D

Gusbourne (Kent) *www.gusbourne.com*
In 2004 Andrew Weeber fulfilled a dream by planting classic
Champagne vines (Chardonnay, Pinot Noir and Pinot Meunier) on
70ha of vineyards in Kent and West Sussex. Many of the Chardonnay
and Pinot Noir were Burgundy clones, whose lower yielding vines
produced extra richness of fruit. This has enabled the estate to
produce still wines in those years where it has been allowed to by
the vagaries of the English climate. There have, so far, been two
Chardonnay vintages and three Pinot Noir. They do both display a
degree of astringency as one would expect from a cool climate -
the Chardonnay is certainly more Chablis than California - but the
Pinot Noir does display a little more richness. But it is the sparkling
wines which shine here. The first vintage was in 2006 (there are
no NV wines yet) and with a policy of keeping the wine at least 36
months on their lees, this was not released until 2010. The current
release is the 2010 vintage. The Brut Reserve (as it is called) displays
fine biscuity flavours and has gained in weight with each successive
vintage. The Blanc de Blancs shows the creaminess that one would
expect from Chardonnay. The first Rosè, which is about to be
released (2010), has fine cherry fruit flavours but is completely dry
on the finish. Some of the 2007 bottles have been held back and
will soon be released as a late disgorged version, the 60 months on
its lees allowing it to display extra richness and finesse and could be
on the cusp of ★★★★★ when released . This is a very successful
operation and the wines have shot to the forefront in the hierarchy
of English wine producers in a very short space of time, mainly due
to the skills of head winemaker Charlie Holland, who has learned
his craft all over the world. The operation has attracted investors
and now Gusbourne is a public company listed on the UK AIM stock
market, the first English wine producer to achieve this. (NB)
Recommended Whites:
Blanc de Blancs ★★★★ £F   Brut Reserve ★★★☆ £E
Chardonnay "Guinevere" ★★ £D
Recommended Reds:
Pinot Noir ★★☆ £D

✿ Nyetimber (West Sussex) *www.nyetimber.com*
The ancient Nyetimber Manor, which dates back to before the
Domesday Book was compiled, is now the base for one of the
very best wine producers in England. Eric Heerema purchased the
property in early 2006 from Andy Hill and Cherie Spriggs has joined
as winemaker after Dermot Sugrue moved on to develop a new
venture at Wiston Park Estate nearby. The close-spaced vineyards
were established in the mid-1980s and are planted on ideally
exposed south-facing slopes of greensand over limestone soils. The
first vintage was in 1992. Pinot Noir, Pinot Meunier and Chardonnay
are all now planted. With Eric Heerema's purchase of the property
there has been a dramatic growth in vineyard planting and there
are now no less than 152 ha under cultivation. Potential output
could rise from the 100,000 bottles produced in the 2004 vintage to
upwards of 700,000 bottles in the future. It remains to be seen how
this will impact on the wines quality in the future. Two excellent
sparkling wines are produced solely from first press juice and are
aged on their lees for 5 years or so before disgorging. The Classic
Cuvée blends mainly Chardonnay with lesser amounts of the Pinots.

The Blanc de Blancs is leaner, more intense and piercing and will
add more with a little age after release. Given the regular problems
of the English climate, it is interesting to consider the potential of
warmer years, but vintages like 2012, which Claire Spriggs decided
not to bottle because of the inferior quality of the fruit, will still
crop up to test the resolve of the winemaker. Five cuvées are
now produced, a rosé and a *demi-sec* as well as a single vineyard,
Tillington, from 2009.
Recommended Whites:
Classic Cuvée Vintage ★★★☆ £E
Première Cuvée Blanc de Blancs Vintage ★★★☆ £E

✿ Ridgeview (East Sussex) *www.ridgeview.co.uk*
The first vintage here was in 1996 and the late Mike Roberts
established Ridgeview as one of England's finest sources of
top sparkling wines. The vineyard is planted on limestone over
sandstone and clay soils and to a combination of the Champagne
varieties. A number of other vineyards also supply grapes and these
are either utilised for the Ridgeview labels or produced for the
owners as finished wines. The wines are made using Champagne
techniques and a Coquard press is utilised for whole bunch
pressing and the wines all go through malolactic fermentation.
The Bloomsbury Brut coming from all three of the grapes is the
mainstay of production, accounting for around 60 to 70% of the
winery output. It nevertheless has impressive complexity and an
attractive creaminess. The Cavendish has more red fruit in the blend
and should be broached first of the trio. The rosé is the most striking
of these wines and gains depth and structure from a blend that is
dominated by Chardonnay. Subtle red berry fruits are underpinned
by a lightly herbal character. There are a number of other labels to
look out for as well. Victoria is a Rosé saignee made from Pinopt Noir
and Pinot Meunier for early drinking, Grosvenor is a Blanc de Blancs
style and Knightsbridge is a Blanc de Noirs. (DM)
Recommended Whites:
Bloomsbury Brut Vintage ★★★☆ £E
 Cavendish Brut Vintage ★★☆ £D
Recommended Rosés:
Fitzrovia Brut Rosé ★★★☆ £E

Sharpham (Devon) *www.sharpham.com*
The origins of this scenic estate are recorded in the Domesday Book
with construction of the splendid Sharpham House beginning in
1770. There are 3.2 ha (8 acres) planted and unusually 90% of this is
Madeleine Angevine which works particularly well here. Much care
is taken in the south-facing vineyards which benefit from gentle sea
breezes drifting up the River Dart and many of the vines have been
converted to Scott-Henry trellising to improve fruit ripening. Today
the estate is run by winemaker Mark Sharman who makes perhaps
England's best and most striking red wine the Beenleigh Red from a
blend of Cabernet Sauvignon and Merlot which has a pronounced
Loire leafiness but good depth and structure. The vines for this are
cultivated on Mark's own property and in poly tunnels. This seems
to work here because of the steep aspect and airflow through
the tunnels. Humidity and excessive canopy growth can be real
problems for growers taking this route with international varieties.
The Sharpham Red is markedly different, a fresh and berry-scented
100% Rondo, giving it good colour. The Sharpham Estate Selection
is 100% Madeleine Angeveine as is the Barrel Fermented white.
The former full of fragrant green fruit, the latter gaining weight and
dimension from the malolactic as well as oak fermentation and
ageing. The Sharpham Rosé offers a little structure with good fresh

Other Europe etc /England

acidity and will develop for two or three years. A sparkling white and rosé are also now being made and is disgorged at THREE CHOIRS and a Dart Valley Reserve white and a Pinot Noir Précose are also made. (DM)

Recommended Reds:
Beenleigh Red ★★★ £E   Sharpham Red ★★ £C
Recommended Whites:
Sharpham Estate Selection ★★ £C
Sharpham Barrel-Fermented ★★ £C
Recommended Rosés:
Sharpham Rosé ★★ £B

Stanlake Park (Berkshire) *www.stanlakepark.com*
The 11 ha of vineyard here are a modern addition to an ancient estate documented since the 12th century. Vineyards were first planted in 1979, and Thames Valley Vineyards (as it was first called), was a pioneer in the renaissance of English wine. Early success was derived from consistent acclaim for a classic and ageworthy oak-aged, English dry white (now Kings Fumé) based on some of the most successful white varieties grown in England (Bacchus, Ortega, Regner and Scheurebe). With uncharacteristic breadth and structure, the wine shows good complexity and length and will usually keep for up to 5 years. To this has been added both reds and fine sparkling wines. The latter include Brut Superior Rosé from Pinot Noir and Chardonnay grapes and their flagship Stanlake Brut, made mainly from Pinot Noir with Chardonnay and sometimes some Gamay grapes.. A varietal Pinot Noir is also made when conditions are most favourable. Stanlake is an important source of contract winemaking as well and wines are made not only for local growers but many from much further afield as well. The Darts on acquiring the property in 2005 invested heavily in their winemaking facility and this would appear to be paying off. (DM)

Recommended Reds:
Ruscombe Red ★★ £C
Recommended Whites:
Stanlake Brut ★★☆ £E   King's Fumé ★★ £C
Hinton Grove ★☆ £B
Recommended Rosés:
Pinot Blush ★☆ £B

Three Choirs (Gloucestershire) *www.three-choirs-vineyards.co.uk*
Top-quality and long established English property founded in 1973 and now with 30 ha (75 acres) of vineyards, the majority planted to a generally southerly aspect on well-drained sandstone soils. There is a warm meso-climate in this corner of Gloucestershire and crucially lower than average rainfall. Good dry and sweet whites are made as well as sparkling non-vintage and vintage bottlings. Reds also include some good Pinot Noir. Considerable effort has gone into grape crossing and hybrid research because of the vagaries of the English climate and the results have been generally very successful. The Bacchus dry white has long been a key wine here and winemaker and vineyard director Martin Fowke would like to plant more but it offers a very poor crop in difficult years. The Siegerrebe is also impressive, fresh and zesty. Willow Brook is an aromatic off-dry white blend of Siegerrebe, Seyval Blanc, Reichensteiner and Orion. The rosé is a combination of Triomphe for colour and Seyval Blanc providing a good backbone and fresh lively acidity. Sparkling wine is also made, although the feeling here is that the English explosion in new vineyard planting for sparkling wine production may be

over ambitious. The Classic Cuvée Brut is made in a deliberately fruit driven style rather than looking for more complex secondary yeast derived flavours. Three Choirs is also a significant resource for contract winemaking for small vineyard clients across the country providing state of the art winemaking facilities as well as providing sparkling wine ageing and disgorging. For visitors there is a gourmet restaurant and hotel overlooking the vineyards and also now a number of exclusive chalets among the vines. (DM)

Recommended Reds:
Ravens Hill Red ★★ £C
Recommended Whites:
Bacchus ★★☆ £C
Classic Cuvée Brut Non-Vintage ★★ £C
Siegerrebe ★★ £B   Willow Brook ★★ £B
Recommended Rosés:
Rosé ★★ £B

Wickham Vineyard *www.three-choirs-vineyards.co.uk/wickham*
Wickham is arguably Hampshire's best vineyard and winery, although a number of other small operations are gaining in importance and quality. The vineyards here are long established in English terms being planted in 1984. The property has 7.3 ha (18 acres) on fairly heavy clay and gravel based soils so for this reason the vineyards are trained to a Geneva Double Curtain to reduce vine vigour and manage canopy growth. Just recently, the vineyard has been acquired by THREE CHOIRS who will be refurbishing the existing buildings and re-planting the vineyard commencing from the winter of 2014/2015 to help establish a productive vineyard in the years to come. In the meantime, the shop will continue to sell wines made by the previous owners whilst stocks last. The ratings below refer solely to the previous owners' wines. Two decent reds have been produced, the softer and more accessible Row Ash red is dominated by Triomphe and chock full of juicy fresh fruit. A good deal more serious and structured is the Special Reserve which is a blend of Rondo offering concentration, colour and structure and Pinot Noir adding elegance and finesse. Among the whites, the oak aged Fumé is a blend of Seyval, Bacchus and Reichensteiner while the Limited Release White is made from the aromatic Wurzer. A number of other wines are also produced and available from the vineyard shop.

Recommended Reds:
Special Reserve Red ★★ £C   Row Ash Red ★☆ £B
Recommended Whites:
Special Release Fumé ★★ £B
Limited Release White ★☆ £B

>> Wiston Estate (West Sussex) *www.wistonestate.com*
The 6000 acre Wiston Estate has been farmed by the Goring family since 1743 but it's only since 16 acres of Pinot Noir, Pinot Meunier and Chardonnay had been planted in 2006, that it has shot to prominence. Enticing Dermot Sugrue away from NYETIMBER as head winemaker, has put this estate to the forefront of English fizz. Produced by sustainable farming methods, these young wines are beginning to show power, finesse and elegance. What stands out in all the wines is the balance of fruit and acidity together with precision on the palate. As the vines age, more structure will develop in the wines. (NB)

Recommended Whites:
Wiston Blanc de Blancs Vintage ★★★☆ £F
Wiston Cuvée Brut Vintage ★★★☆ £E

Wiston Cuvée Brut NV ★★★ £D
Recommended Rosés:
Wiston Rosé Vintage ★★★☆ £F

Yearlstone (Devon) *www.yearlstone.co.uk*

Yearlstone has become an increasingly important location for winemaking in Devon and the south-west of England. The first reason is the excellent value wines produced and the second because many other local vineyards have their wines produced here including those of PEBBLEBED VINEYARD. The vineyard is run by husband and wife team Juliet and Roger White. Juliet looks after the winemaking, while Roger takes responsibility for managing their 3 ha (7.5 acres) of vineyards spread across two sites. The vines have a southerly exposition and are planted in well-drained Devon sandstone soils. Among the whites the stand out wine is the No 6, a blend of Pinot Blanc and Madeleine Angevine. Unfortunately, none was made in 2013. It is less floral and aromatic than the other whites but has additional structure from a limited period in small oak and has a nice mineral undercurrent. The No 5 is intensely floral and aromatic, coming from Siegerrebe which is not dissimilar in style to a Gewürztraminer. Of the other two whites, No 2 is a floral blend of Madeleine Angevine and Riechensteiner, again not made in 2013, whilst the No 1 entry level wine is a zingy 100% Reichensteiner. Sparkling wine is relatively new but shows quite some potential. The solid Sparkling Brut Vintage, currently the 2010, comes from a blend of Pinot Blanc and Seyval Blanc which provides all the necessary acidity. If you are visiting there are great panoramic views over the vineyards from the Terrace Café. (DM)

Recommended Whites:
Yearlstone Sparkling Brut Vintage ★★☆ £C
Yearlstone No 6 ★★ £B
Yearlstone No 5 ★☆ £B
Yearlstone No 4 ★☆ £B
Yearlstone No 1 ★ £B
Yearlstone No 2 ★ £B
Recommended Rosés:
Yearlstone No 3 ★☆ £B

A-Z of producers - *Luxembourg*

✿ Aly Duhr (Wormeldange) *www.alyduhr.lu*

With just 8.5ha of carefully tended vines on rolling slopes above the Moselle, producing some 80,000 bottles annually, this family domaine is one of Luxembourg's finest. Son Abi is no longer hands on at the estate but still acts as a consultant whilst he concentrates on his own CH. PAUQUE. From each of the usual range of Luxembourg varieties are made several high quality cuvées. Most are subject to a short period of skin contact prior to fermentation. What sets them apart is the added definition and detail with gentle herb, floral, fruit, mineral and spice complexities realised from high quality fruit. They are also characterised by their balance and finesse with none of the clumsiness, coarseness or heavyness that sometimes mars Gewürztraminer, Pinot Gris and the like. All the wines are designated with vineyard lieux-dits (a little Rivaner and Elbling excepted), the best of which are labelled Domaine et Tradition with the next range down as Grand Premier Cru. As well as the pure and expressive Pinot Gris from Hohfels are Auxerrois from (Wormeldange) Koeppchen and Riesling from (Ahn) Palmberg. Those rated below are but a few of the extensive range but it worth giving anything a try from Aly Duhr - even an oak-aged Elbling, labelled Bromelt, is decent for this difficult variety. A *barrique*-

aged red from Pinot Noir shows great elegance and is improving with every vintage and the *barrique*-aged whites (Auxerrois and Chardonnay), labelled Monsalvat, are impressive. The wines also represent an excellent price/quality ratio.
Recommended Reds:
Pinot Noir Barrique ★★★ £C
Recommended Whites:
Riesling Grand Premier Cru Nussbaum Vendange Tardive ★★★★ £E
Riesling Palmberg Domaine et Tradition ★★★ £D
Riesling Gollebour Grand Premier Cru ★★ £B
Riesling Nussbaum Grand Premier Cru ★★ £C
Chardonnay Monsalvat ★★★★ £E
Pinot Gris Hohfels Domaine et Tradition ★★★☆ £D
Pinot Gris Hohfels Grand Premier Cru ★★☆ £C
Pinot Gris Nussbaum Grand Premier Cru ★★☆ £C
T'OK Pinot Gris Barrique ★★☆ £C
Pinot Gris Ongkaft Grand Premier Cru ★★ £C
Auxerrois Monsalvat ★★★ £E
Auxerrois Koeppchen Grand Premier Cru ★★★ £D
Crémant 64 Pinot Blanc/Pinot Noir ★★☆ £D
Crémant 62 Riesling ★★ £D
Pinot Blanc Pietert ★★☆ £C
Pinot Blanc Barrique ★★ £C
Rivaner Convicts ★★☆ £B
Rivaner ★★ £B   Bromelt ★★ £B

Dom. Mathis Bastian (Remich) *www.mathisbastian.lu*

Luxembourg, as with any other wine region, could do with more like this - small, focussed and committed estates. Mathis and his wife Anouk seem right on the money with fruit-emphasised, well-structured varietals from Auxerrois, Pinot Gris, Pinot Blanc, Riesling and Gewürztraminer produced from their 13 odd ha of vineyard. The added concentration and definition over most other Luxembourg wines help them to stand out. It may have been warmer along these slopes these past few summers yet the Bastian's also have wines of proven ageing potential that were made in the late 80s and early 90s. The warmest vintages can be slightly full-blown, cooler ones retain their austerity yet most are vibrant, intense with good varietal character and something of their origins too. Riesling and Pinot Gris are particularly good but all others scarcely less so. A little Pinot Noir and Pinot Noir Rosé is also made.
Recommended Whites:
Riesling Wellenstein Kurschels ★★★ £C
Pinot Gris Wellenstein Foulschette ★★★ £C
Pinot Blanc Remich Goldberg ★★☆ £C
Auxerrois Remich Goldberg ★★☆ £C

Gales (Remich) *www.gales.lu*

The well-established Gales winery is directed by third generation Marc Gales. Crémant provides the volume, the vast majority of it in Brut or Extra Brut styles. The bulk of it is also non-vintaged, the exception is an excellent Crémant Jubilee from 100% Riesling. Elegant and stylish it might not have the complexity or breadth of top Champagne but is without doubt a fine example of its type. All production is based in a modern winery where the seried ranks of gyropalettes look and sound like a set from a 60s futuristic movie. These can be contrasted with the extensive underground cellars of Caves St Martin (under the same ownership since 1985) which were carved out under the cliffs at Remich shortly after World War I. This range includes some attractive inexpensive drinking including a bright Pinot Blanc and an off-dry fruit-driven Crémant Rosé. The

Other Europe & Med

superior Gales label includes several good still wines, labelled either GPC or Domaine et Tradition. Pinot Gris, Auxerrois and Riesling are all strengths with commendable balance, structure and concentration, if a little weaker in 04 than 05.

Gales
Recommended Whites:

Crémant Jubilee Riesling Brut Vintage ★★★ £C
Crémant Heritage Brut Non-Vintage ★★ £B
Pinot Gris Wellenstein Foulschette ★★☆ £C
Pinot Gris Domaine et Tradition ★★☆ £C
Riesling Domaine et Tradition ★★☆ £C
Riesling Wellenstein Kurschels ★★ £C
Pinot Blanc Domaine et Tradition ★★ £B
Auxerrois Remich Hôpertsbour ★★ £B
Auxerrois Domaine et Tradition ★★ £B

Caves St. Martin
Recommended Whites:

Pinot Blanc GPC De Nos Rochers ★★ £B
Pinot Gris GPC De Nos Rochers ★★ £B
Auxerrois GPC De Nos Rochers ★☆ £B

Recommended Rosés:

Crémant Rosé Brut Non-Vintage ★☆ £B

✪✪ Ch. Pauqué (Grevenmacher)

Abi has now made a clean break with the family vineyards at Ahn and is now ploughing his own furrow making wines from his vineyards spread over 6 villages from Schengen to Wasserbillig – about 5 ha. in all. Two lines of wines are produced - the classic ones (Riesling & Pinot Gris) and ones with Burgundian characteristics, focused on wines fermented and aged in oak barrels. The grapes are normally harvested from the beginning of October to mid November in order to get the best possible maturity. The botrytised grapes do not see skin contact. Long fermentations, with natural yeasts give Château Pauqué wines a characteristic creamy harmony. With over 50% of Riesling (some of the vineyards have been planted more than 60 years ago) the Château Pauqué Estate has one of the highest Riesling percentages in Luxembourg. Additionally, Abi grows Elbling, Auxerrois, Pinot Blanc, Pinot Gris and Chardonnay. He makes a large range of wines – but just a few hundred bottles of each – starting with his entry level Bromelt, made from the normally boring Elbling grape, but even here, he manages to give it a 'lift'. A quintet of Rieslings starting with wines from two different locations – "Grevenmacher Fels" and "Paradäis", show delicate finesse and good length, with the former showing more mineral characteristics than the latter, which has a bit more citrussy fruit. The "Grevenmacher Fels" is available in *moelleux* in the 2006 vintage, whilst there is a Veilles Vignes version of the "Paradäis" with more intensity of fruit. A straight Veilles Vignes is also made from vines planted in 1942 and here the wine reaches an apogée of class with great spätlese characteristics. There is again a "Paradäis" Vendange Tardive, which does truly bring the wine into an auslese quality. Whilst Riesling can be said to be the mainstay, it's what Abi achieves with other, native and non-native grapes which is truly remarkable. Pinot Gris "Paradäis" shows good varietal spiciness and "Fossiles" is another great blend of Pinot Blanc and Auxerrois, nutty and with good length. It is in the treatment of the Auxerrois, however, not normally noted for its noble character, which takes on a new dimension under the "Clos du Paradis" label - 100% Auxerrois with full, rich, nutty, intense and creamy complexity. His Chardonnay, at so north a latitude, confusingly labelled just "Château Pauqué", is smooth and rich, but with a great tannic structure displaying perfect

balance between the fruit and the acidity. A new Chardonnay *cuvée* (first vintage 2008) "Clos de la Falaise", deliberately has more minerality. Finally "Montée des Seigneurs" is a late harvest Auxerrois, smooth and unctuous, without being sickly sweet. (NB)

Recommended Whites:

Montée des Seigneurs ★★★★★ £F
Auxerrois Clos du Paradis ★★★★☆ £E
Chardonnay Clos de la Falais ★★★★ £E
Chardonnay Château Pauqué ★★★★ £E
Riesling Paradaïs Vendanges Tardives ★★★★☆ £E
Riesling Paradaïs Vieilles Vignes ★★★★ £D
Riesling Vieilles Vignes ★★★★ £D
Riesling Sur la Roche ★★★☆ £D
Riesling Grevenmacher Fels ★★★☆ £C
Riesling Paradaïs ★★★☆ £C
Pinot Gris Paradaïs ★★★ £C
Fossils ★★★ £C   Bromelt ★★ £B

Dom. Alice Hartmann (Wormeldange) www.alice-hartmann.lu

There is, seemingly, almost an identity crisis at this professionally run and presented estate that sits just above a pleasant, deceptively placid stretch of the Moselle. With an emphasis on Chardonnay, Pinot Noir (as well as Riesling) and a premium sparkling wine from the same grapes, this small 4 ha vineyard is anything but the norm for Luxembourg. If this were not enough there are wines too from small parcels owned in Germany's Mittel Mosel (Trittenheimer Apotheke) and Burgundy's Côte de Beaune (Saint-Aubin); each made in their respective regions. But if there is not the 'Luxembourg' stamp of other good producers, quality is high throughout the range. Riesling comes from the very best part of Luxembourg's most famous vineyard, the Koeppchen vineyard at Wormeldange (it is worth noting that the Koeppchenn name is now applied to a large area and is little guarantee of quality in itself). A 'Les Terrasses' bottling comes from precipitous calcareous slopes which almost topple over a small bluff high above the river, giving an attractive Riesling of good intensity and distinguished by an underlying minerality and great persistence. Slightly cheaper is a more than adequate, cool-fruited second bottling designated 'La Chapelle'. Very small amounts of a third, 'Selection' Riesling are made from the best later picked fruit, but only in the best years. This is richer and more complete but it seems probable that all 3 bottlings could still offer more. Soundly made oak-infused Chardonnay and Pinot Noir from Grevenmacher vineyards (further north on the Moselle), show good potential and are reasonably priced. However they do miss the underlying fruit depth and purity more easily obtained in Burgundy, for instance. The estate's Crémant de Luxembourg is one of the best made with a distinctive fusion of floral, fruit, grilled nuts and oak-given characters. Although non-vintaged, recently disgorged stock will benefit from keeping for an extra year or two. Spätlese and Auslese versions of Trittenheimer Apotheke are especially good if much more pricey (see Germany). Also made are a little of a special bottling of Crémant, an Eiswein and a series of marcs.

Recommended Reds:

Pinot Noir Grevenmacher Clos du Kreizerberg ★★☆ £C

Recommended Whites:

Riesling GPC Wormeldange Koeppchen Selection ★★★ £C
Riesling GPC Wormeldange Koeppchen Les Terraces ★★☆ £C
Riesling La Chapelle ★★ £B
Crémant de Luxembourg Brut ★★☆ £C
Chardonnay Grevenmacher Clos du Kreizerberg ★☆ £C

Wine behind the label

Other Europe etc /Hungary/Switzerland

Other Europe & Med

A-Z of producers - *Hungary*

Disznókö (Tokaji) www.disznoko.hu
Disznókö was created in 1992 and, as with a number of Tokaji producers, considerable investment has been put into this operation, including major new cellars. The estate spreads over 150 ha of which 100 ha on volcanic clay soils are farmed. Of these 60 ha contain very old vines. Although newly established in its latest manifestation, the estate has a history stretching back over 300 years and was classified as a First Growth by royal decree in 1772. A full range of Tokaji styles is produced and the top sweet wines have marvellous botrytis complexity. With as much care being lavished on the base wine as the Aszú, the wines are very opulent and exotic but have comfortably enough acidity for balance. (DM)
Recommended Whites:
Tokaji Aszú 6 Puttonyos ★★★★☆ £G
Tokaji Aszú 5 Puttonyos ★★★★ £F

❂ Oremus (Tokaji) www.tokajoremus.com
Oremus was created in 1993 as a joint venture between Tokaji Kereskedöhóz (the former state-run commercial house) and Bodegas VEGA SICILIA (see Spain). It is named after the vineyard where the original Tokaji was produced in 1650. A full range of styles is produced, from an excellent dry Furmint - Mandolás combines elegance with depth and intensity - to an exceptional and heady Essencia. Modern technology is taken advantage of: rotofermenters, for example, are used to macerate the Aszú berries. The Essencia wine (and it is on the borderline of not being classified as such – some vintages have been as low as 3% of alcohol) is astonishing: residual sugar is in excess of 400 g/l but fierce acidity provides an extraordinary balance. All the sweet wines are impressive. (DM)
Recommended Whites:
Tokaji Essencia ✪✪✪✪✪ £H
Tokaji Aszú 5 Puttonyos ★★★★ £F
Tokaji Furmint Mandolás ★★★ £C

❂ Istvan Szepsy (Tokaji) www.szepsy.hu
Istvan Szepsy was originally a director of the co-operative in Mád. In recent years he has been establishing his own small vineyard holding with some of the best sites in the region. He has reverted his vineyards to traditional bush-vine pruning and keeps yields under tight control. He now has around 7.5 ha in rocky, volcanic soils. The quality is reflected in wines which are unusually fresh for the region. Indeed there has been a general move to produce wines with less oxidative character and these perhaps more than any others really reflect this new approach. Dry styles are very impressive with a real depth and mineral purity, particularly the outstanding Szent Tamás Grand Cru. The Aszú 6 Puttonyos is remarkably intense. Szepsy was also originally involved with American financier Anthony Hwang in a new venture, Királyudvar, where similarly impressive fresh Tokaji styles are being produced. (DM)
Recommended Whites:
Tokaji Aszú 6 Puttonyos ✪✪✪✪✪ £H
Tokaji Cuvée ★★★★★ £F
Tokaji Furmint Szent Tamás Grand Cru ★★★★ £F
Tokaji Hárslevelú ★★★★ £E

❂ Royal Tokaji Wine Company (Tokaji) www.royal-tokaji.com
This was the first of the foreign investments in the Tokay region in 1989. A consortium including Danish winemaker Peter Vinding-Diers and wine writer Hugh Johnson formed the company in partnership with 63 growers, providing a formidable resource of top vineyard sites. The attention in the vineyard is undoubtedly paying off and yields have been almost halved to an average of around 40 hl/ha. The wines are rich and intense, without a hint of oxidation, and have a more overtly orange peel and nutty character than other examples. (DM)
Recommended Whites:
Tokaji Essencia ✪✪✪✪✪ £H
Tokaji Aszú Nyulaszo 6 Puttonyos ★★★★ £G
Tokaji Blue Label 5 Puttonyos ★★★ £E

Tokaj Classic (Tokaji) www.tokaj-classic.com
Musician Andras Bruhács' family were involved in winemaking before World War II, with a small winery and vineyard in the south of Hungary near Pécs. Together with fellow musicians Martin Schneider and Carl Gustav Settelmeier he has revived this under the Villa Makar label, where they produce Chardonnay grown on limestone soils. They have also established the Tokaj Classic cellar in Tokaji, where they are producing some excellent examples of the appellation. The Noble Late Harvest is both rich and elegant with a subtle, sweet peachy character. The 5 Puttonyos is richer, fuller and impressively intense with piercing botrytis character. The magnificent, rich and opulent 6 Puttonyos is one of the best examples from the region. All can be enjoyed on purchase but will continue to evolve over a decade and more. (DM).
Recommended Whites:
Tokaji Aszú 6 Puttonyos ★★★★★ £G
Tokaji Aszú 5 Puttonyos ★★★★ £F
Tokaji Noble Late Harvest ★★★ £D

A-Z of producers - *Switzerland*

Dom. Louis Bovard (Vaud) www.domainebovard.com
The wines of Louis Bovard serve as an inspiration to other Swiss growers. Based in Cully on pretty terraced slopes above Lac Léman (Lake Geneva), brothers Antoine and Louis-Philippe Bovard produce Lavaux Chasselas-based wines without equal. The wines are remarkably stylish and finely balanced with mineral, citrus, apple and a delicately nutty character. In the Dézaley Grand Cru Médinette there is added depth, structure and intensity and the wines can easily age for five years or more. From Saint-Saphorin, a varietal Chasselas, L'Archevesque, is another elegant white with an intense long finish. This too is better with a little age and should keep for five years or more. As well as some Sauvignon, some red is made from Merlot, Pinot Noir and Syrah, and sold as Dézaley Grand Cru.
Recommended Whites:
Dézaley Grand Cru Médinette ★★★ £E
Calamin Cuvée Speciale ★★ £D
Saint-Saphorin L'Archevesque ★★ £D
Aigle Cuvée Noe ★★ £D
Epesses Terre à Boire ★★ £C

>> Thierry Constantin (Sion) www.thierryconstantin.ch
Thierry Constantin farms 5.5 hectares on the right bank of the Rhône in the communes of Vétroz and Sion. He grows a number of international and indigenous grapes to produce a range of well-crafted wines. There is a crisp, entry level Fendant, but his Petite Arvine has more depth and class. Pinot Noir 'Vieilles Vignes', unoaked, is on the light side but finishes with good length. "Aguares" Cornalin is rich and deep with hints of black cherry beneath the soft tannins. The wine is matured in large *foudres* for

679

Other Europe & Med

24 months and then kept in stainless steel for a further 6 months before bottling. (NB)

Recommended Reds:
Aguares Cornalin ★★★☆ £E
Pinot Noir Vieilles Vignes ★★☆ £D
Recommended Whites:
Petite Arvine ★★★ £E
Le Fendant ★★☆ £D

Donatsch (Graubünden) www.donatsch.info

The estate had been in the hands of the Donatsch family for over 100 years, when in 1973, Thomas Donatsch visited the Domaine de la Romanee Conti and befriended the then winemaker, Andre Noblet, who not only gave him instruction on how to make good Pinot Noir, but sent him away with three used *barriques* from the DRC to get on with it on his own. With application and experimentation, and aided and abetted by his son, Martin, who is now in charge of winemaking, Donatsch has emerged as one of the leading exponents of Pinot Noir in the world outside Burgundy. Three levels of Pinot Noir are now produced - the entry level "Tradition", 1er Cru equivalent "Passion" and Grand Cru equivalent "Unique", if such a analogy can be made. Each level is a step up, "Tradition" is clean with real purity of fruit, "Passion" displays an unctuousness with cherry-like fruit embraced by some real Burgundian farmyardy flavours, whilst "Unique", displaying a darker hue, is full and complex in the mouth with a long finish. But the most intriguing of the wines they produce is from the autochthonal Completer grape of which there are only 5 ha of it in the world, so you may have to visit the vineyard, or their inn, "Zum Ochsen" to taste it. A whiff of pineapple on the nose suggests a fruit bomb but this is far from the case. The taste is a kind of cross between Chardonnay, Riesling, Chenin Blanc and Pinot Blanc - very marginally off-dry and as it is vinified in oak, like the Chardonnay, it gives a touch of vanilla. They produce a host of other wines in pretty small quantities - Chardonnay, (at three levels as in the Pinot Noir), Pinot Gris, Pinot Blanc, a blend of Cabernet, Merlot and Pinot Noir and a sparkling Pinot Blanc by the methode traditionelle. The family own and the business is operated from their wine bar "Zum Ochsen" where no doubt all their wines can be consumed with impunity. (NB)

Recommended Reds:
Pinot Noir "Unique" ★★★★☆ £F
Pinot Noir "Passion" ★★★☆ £D
Pinot Noir "Tradition" ★★★ £C
Recommended Whites:
Completer "Malansrebe" ★★★☆ £E

✿ Jean-René Germanier (Valais) www.jrgermanier.ch

Germanier is one of the very finest producers in Switzerland, making top-class red and white from native as well as international varieties. The estate has been in the same family since it was founded in 1896. The vineyards in the small Vétroz appellation of the spectacularly sited Valais region are cultivated organically and the average vine age of 40 years along with restricted yields helps ensure fruit of impressive flavour intensity. The wines are all impressively ripe and full but their firm structure and particularly their acidity reminds the drinker of their cool-climate origins. The range includes a number of wines under the Classique label. A level up are the three Vétroz Grand Cru bottlings. The Fendant is firm and minerally with subtle green apple, citrus and melon notes. It will develop well in bottle for

5 years or more. The dry Amigne is ripe and sappy with a long finish. The Pinot Noir is bigger and firmer with real grip and persistence. Among the Reserve bottlings the Humagne du Valais rouge is from the local variety of the same name. It is ripe and berry-laden with a hint of oak from ageing in one-third new barrels and is bottled unfiltered. Cornalin, too, another local varietal, from a single parcel, Champmarais, is intense and spicy and their top priced red. Cayas, made from 100% Syrah, captivates the palate with cool climate freshness and true varietal flavours. The rich and very concentrated and intense Amigne de Vétroz is from an extremely rare variety exclusive to the Valais of which just 18 ha are planted. This characterful late-harvest white is aged in new oak for 11 months and offers complex flavours of honey, peach and a hint of citrus. The top reds will develop well in the medium term. (NB)

Recommended Reds:
Cornalin Champmarais ★★★★ £F
Cayas Syrah du Valais ★★★★ £E
Vétroz Pinot Noir Grand Cru ★★★ £D
Valais Humagne du Valais ★★★ £D
Recommended Whites:
Valais Mitis Amigne de Vétroz ★★★★ £G
Valais Amigne Vétroz Grand Cru ★★★ £D
Vétroz Fendant Grand Cru ★★★ £D

A-Z of producers - *Slovakia*

Ch. Belá (Stúrovo)

This grand property is in the Stúrovo region, just inside Slovakia, close by the Danube and only about 60km north of Budapest in Hungary. Originally the property of Egon MÜLLER'S wife's family, the property was lost to the family in World War II and has only recently been bought back. Resuming production in 2001 and given the winemaking direction from one of the Saar's great names, the estate white (from Riesling) already shows good depth and an attractive minerality, herbal aspect within a reasonably powerful frame. Generally the wines are more in an Austrian than Germanic style with body and power allied to definition and purity. In 04 a Reserve as well as two dry versions were made. Off-dry in style, the stylish Reserve shows fine balance and definition. They don't need to be rushed - drink with 5 years' age or more.

Recommended Whites:
Château Belá Reserve ★★★ £D
Château Belá ★★☆ £C

A-Z of producers - *Bulgaria*

Bessa Valley Winery (Bulgaria) www.bessavalley.com

The Bessa Valley project started in 2001 by a consortium led by Count Stephan von Neipperg of Ch. CANON-LA-GAFFALIÈRE in Saint-Emilion, whose experience has helped to establish the quality of the wines produced. Four cuvées are now made - the largest volume (240,000 bottles) is marketed under the Enira label. In 2008 this was a blend of 55% Merlot, 27% Syrah, 13% Petit Verdot and 5% Cabernet Sauvignon with an average yield of 45 hl/ha. The wine displays nice upfront fruit without being jammy, although it does lack a bit of complexity. The Enira Reserva (125,000 bottles) is a blend of 42% Merlot, 25% Petit Verdot, 20% Syrah and 13% Cabernet Sauvignon with the same average yield as the regular wine. Here there is much more elegance and complexity with less obvious fruit although it is certainly there beneath the tannins. Two

small productions of superior selections complete the quartet. The "BV" blend is composed of equal parts of Merlot, Syrah, Cabernet Sauvignon and Petit Verdot yielding only 30 hl/ha and is aged for over 18 months in 100% new oak *barriques* producing some 7,500 bottles. The wood is much more obvious here but again it doesn't quite mask all of the splendid fruit which lurks underneath - a long, complex finish shows its class. Finally, there is a very small production of a 100% Syrah wine (1,300 bottles). The varietal flavour of the Syrah was not quite as pronounced as expected, but it was unmistakable and probably this will be redressed as the vines age over the years. (NB)

Recommended Reds:

BV ★★★★ £D   Enira Reserva ★★★☆ £C

Syrah by Enira ★★★ £D

Enira ★★★ £B

>> Minkov Brothers (Thracian Valley)   www.minkovbrothers.bg

With local wineries giving up the ghost and finding it more profitable to grub up their vines and grow fruit, it was commendable that a conglomerate of local industrialists clubbed together to resuscitate one of Bulgaria's most famous wineries, formed in 1875. Today, over a million bottles are produced from four large vineyards in the area. These are all planted with international grape varieties, eschewing the indigenous ones so much favoured by the boutique producers. They produce a wide variety of quality wines, from simple, entry-level wines to some premium wines which would not look out of place on the international stage. The grapes are harvested by hand are put in trays and transported to the winery for sorting and with state-of-the-art equipment the musts are macerated and fermented in non-corrosive *cuves* at controlled temperatures. Depending on their style, some wines mature in *barriques* made of French and American oak placed in special tunnels dug underneath the ground. A lot of the vines are still young and the wines will certainly gain more structure as the vines age. We haven't tasted their whole range but below we have rated some of the better ones. (NB)

Recommended Reds:

Syrah and Viognier "Jamais Vue" ★★★☆ £C

Cabernet Sauvignon, Cabernet Franc and Merlot "Tri-Cycle" ★★★ £C

Syrah "Le Photographe" ★★☆ £C

Recommended Whites:

Rheinriesling "Le Photographe" ★★★ £B

Viognier "Cycle" ★☆ £A

Chardonnay Minkoff Brothers ★☆ £A

>> Villa Melnik (Melnik)   www.villamelnik.com

The Zikatanovs are a family with a longstanding tradition of growing grapes and of winemaking. A few years back, Nikola decided to modernise the estate and together with his wife, Lyubka, replanted the vineyards and built the winery. They planted their vineyards with both indigenous and international grape varieties to lead the renaissance of the region. Their new, modern winery opened its doors in 2013, with state-of-the art wine-making equipment and a dedicated highly-qualified staff, with local Head Winemaker, Rumyana Stoilova, who graduated with a degree in oenology in Bordeaux. In 2015, Militza, Luybka and Nikola's daughter joined the family business to help create the modern image of Melnik. The winery is built on three levels, and the cellars are dug into the sandy hill. The wine-making process is organized so that the flow of the wine moves by the force of gravity through the three levels of the building, thus allowing the wines to be treated gently. From 30 ha

under cultivation, a number of different wine are made, from the entry level Family Tradition range, through the lightly oaked Bergolé range, to their top Aplauz range which includes some limited edition wines. The Bergolé Viognier/Chardonnay (60/40) spends 6 months in old oak, has good aromacy, but tends to retain oakyness in its youth. Syrah, with 10% Viognier, has good varietal flavours but lacks body. Bergolé straight Syrah has even more tarryness but still on the light side. The indigenous Melnik in this range is quite rustic but finishes long. In the Aplauz range, the Viognier has lovely apricot and peach flavours but again is somewhat dominated by the oak. Premium Reserve Syrah spends 18 months in oak and displays good fruit beneath the tannins although a little rustic, whilst Aplauz Premium Reserve Cabernet is much smoother with riper fruit. Finally, Melnik 55, is a new crossing of the Melnik grape with unctuous smooth fruit and a good degree of finesse. (NB)

Recommended Reds:

Aplauz Premium Reserve Syrah ★★★☆ £C

Aplauz Premium Reserve Cabernet Sauvignon ★★★☆ £C

Aplauz Melnik 55 ★★★☆ £C

Bergolé Syrah ★★★ £C

Bergolé Melnik ★★★ £C

Bergolé Syrah and Viognier ★★☆ £B

Recommended Whites:

Applauz Viognier ★★★ £C

Bergolé Viognier/Syrah ★★ £B

>> Villa Yustina (Ustina)   www.villayustina.com

Milko Tzvetkov became the owner of a steel-making factory after the break up of the communist regime and supplied many wineries with their stainless steel cuves. Seeing how well they were doing he decided to start his own winery in 2008 with vines planted in 2007. The first vintage of their own wines was in 2010 but had ben making wine since 2008. Her has three ranges – entry level Villa Yustina, 4 Seasons, representing wines for Winter, Spring, Summer and Autumn and his premium Monogram wines. Villa Yustina Blanc is 40% Chardonnay, 35% Sauvignon Blanc and 25% Sémillon. It's quite aromatic but perhaps a little short on the finish. 4 seasons Pinot Noir, representing Autumn, has good varietal flavours with some length on the palate although lacing a bit of body. This will certainly improve as the vines age. Monogram Mavrud and Rubin is deep and unctuous with a chunky mouthfeel and a rounded finish. This is a promising estate whose wines will certainly improve as the vines age. (NB)

Recommended Reds:

Monogram Mavrud and Rubin ★★★ £B

4 Seasons Autumn Pinot Noir ★★☆ £B

Recommended Whites:

Villa Yustina Blanc ★☆ £A

A-Z of producers - *Greece*

Alpha Estate (Amyndeon)   www.alpha-estate.com

The partnership of Mavridis the grape grower and Latridis the winemaker established this 33 ha property in the Amyndeon region in northern Greece at the end of the 1990s. They currently have a mix of grapes planted, most of them international varieties, as well as 2 ha of Mavrodaphne and 4.5 ha of ungrafted Xinomavro. The vineyards are at a very high altitude of 620–710m and the sandy clay soils are sparse and well drained. The Alpha White is currently 100% Sauvignon, with a piercing varietal character and intensity to match some of the best examples elsewhere. The characterful Xinomavro

Other Europe & Med

red is produced in two cuvees, a single vineyard Hedgehog, spending 12 months in French oak and a Reserve Vielles Vignes, spending double the time in oak. Both need to be kept for at least five years before becoming approachable. The top wine, the Alpha red, is a 60/20/20 blend of Syrah, Merlot and Xinomavro aged for 12 months in French oak. It is rich and impressively concentrated and driven by a dark, peppery Syrah character. Firmly structured, it will benefit from 4–5 years' patience. A simple, fresh and nicely balanced dessert wine blends Gewürztraminer and a little Malvasia. (DM)

Recommended Reds:
Alpha Estate Red Macedonia ★★★ £D
Alpha Hedgehog Single Vineyard Xinomavro ★★ £C
Recommended Whites:
Alpha Estate Sauvignon Blanc Florina ★★ £C
Alpha Estate Dessert White Florina ★★ £C

Biblia Chora Estate (Pangeon) *www.bibliachora.gr*
The two owners of this recently established operation are both enologists and their wines are marked by impressive pure fruit character. The 150 ha of vineyards are planted in the sparse flinty soils of Mount Pangeon in the north of the country. This location combines with cooling breezes from the nearby Strymonic Gulf to provide ideal growing conditions. Greek varieties Assyrtiko and Agiorgitiko have both been planted as well as Sauvignon Blanc, Chardonnay, Sémillon, Syrah, Merlot and Cabernet Sauvignon. The number of different wines produced there has now grown to 10. The Estate White blend of Sauvignon Blanc with Assyrtiko has well-judged oak and good peachy, citrus fruit. The Estate Red is currently a classic Bordeaux blend of Merlot and Cabernet Sauvignon. Twelve months in new oak provide a rich, characterful wine with marked dark berry fruit. The red will develop well over 4 or 5 years; the other wines should be broached young, particularly the rosé. Red and white are also released under the Plagios, Areti and Ovilos labels. (DM)

Recommended Reds:
Estate Biblia Chora Red Pangeon ★★★ £D
Recommended Whites:
Estate Biblia Chora White Pangeon ★★☆ £D
Recommended Rosés:
Estate Biblia Chora Rosé Pangeon ★ £B

Evharis Estate (Gerania) *www.evharis.gr*
Small 30 ha Greek estate located between Athens and Corinth with vineyards planted in the foothills of the Gerania Mountains. Indigenous white Assyrtiko, Roditis and Athiri along with red Agiorgitiko are joined by international varieties Chardonnay, Sauvignon Blanc, Syrah, Merlot and Grenache. A good floral and intense tank-fermented Estate White blends Assyrtiko with Chardonnay and Mavrodaphne and is marked by the herbal character of the Assyrtiko. The Estate Red blends 60% Syrah with 40% Merlot and displays fine, rich berry fruit, with an undercurrent of herbs and thyme and impressive intensity. It is aged in French oak for 12 months, lending it depth and structure. Estate bottlings of Syrah, Merlot and Chardonnay are also produced. The Syrah is particularly striking with impressive depth and a firm structure provided by grapes grown at altitude. The wines are now bottled without filtration. An impressive varietal Assyrtiko white is also produced, fermented and aged in French oak for 6 months with very subtle oak tones and aromas of citrus and summer fruits. The budget Ilaros red and white are decent fruit-driven and immediately appealing wines. The top reds should be aged for at least a couple

of years in bottle. (DM)
Recommended Reds:
Estate Red Gerania ★★★ £D
Syrah Estate Gerania ★★★ £D
Merlot Estate Gerania ★★ £C
Ilaros Red Gerania ★ £B
Recommended Whites:
Estate White Gerania ★★ £B
Asyrtiko Estate Gerania ★★ £B
Ilaros White Gerania ★ £B

Gaia Estate (Nemea & Santorini) *www.gaia-wines.gr*
Founded in 1994, this is one of the finest producers in Greece. The company run two separate wine estates. It established the Thalassitis property on the volcanic island of Santorini in 1994 and followed this up in 1996 with a property at Koutsi in Nemea. Production in Nemea is focused around three reds all made from the indigenous Agiorgitiko. The Notios red is soft, brambly and forward; a varietal Agiorgitiko is fuller and better structured. Very impressive is the dense and concentrated top red, Gaia Estate, with a firm structure and real depth. A juicy rosé is also produced from a variety known as 14-18h. The Koutsi range is completed by Notios white, a blend Moschofilero and Roditis, and a benchmark for retsinas, Ritinitis Nobilis, vinified from Roditis grown in a cool climate at high altitude. Two intense, piercing, mineral-scented whites are produced from Santorini: Thalassitis and Thalassitis Oak. The key to quality here lies in the 70- to 80-year-old very low-yielding ungrafted Assyrtiko vines. The regular Thalassitis is cool-fermented but not to the detriment of the naturally intense mineral and honeysuckle aromas. The Thalassitis Oak is fermented in new oak and aged on lees for 5–6 months. The oak is very well integrated, lending increased structure rather than flavour, and the wine will develop well in the short term. Gaia Estate is capable of further development for up to 10 years. Enjoy the other wines young. Also capable of long ageing is Gaia S, a blend of 70% Agiorgitko and 30% Syrah, aged for 12 months in small French *barriques* and bottled without fining or filtration. (DM)

Recommended Reds:
Gaia Estate Nemea ★★★★ £E
Gaia S ★★★ £D
Agiorgitiko Nemea ★★ £B   Notios Nemea ★ £B
Recommended Whites:
Thalassitis Santorini ★★★ £D
Thalassitis Oak Santorini ★★★ £D
Notios Nemea ★ £B   Ritinitis Nobilis Retsina ★ £B
Recommended Rosés:
14-18h Nemea ★ £B

Gerovassiliou (Epanomi) *www.gerovassiliou.gr*
This thoroughly modern wine estate of 45 ha is to be found just 25km south of Thessaloniki in northern Greece. Well-drained sandy soils and, for Greece, cool summers provide an excellent environment for good-quality wine production. An interesting mix of international and local varieties are cultivated to produce both red and white wines. Owner and winemaker Evangelos Gerovassiliou was trained in Oenology and Viticulture at the University of Bordeaux and to some extent this comes across in the wines, which are subtle and restrained. The Viognier has a marked floral and lightly peachy character and should be drunk young. The Chardonnay is in a subtle, light, melony style with just a hint of toasty new oak. Particularly characterful is the Malagousia, a rare local variety marked by hints of citrus and and underlying

spicy herbs. The Syrah/Merlot/Limnio red is tight and restrained in a very peppery style. It would benefit from just a touch more flesh. Evangelo is an interesting blend of Petit Syrah and Viognier. The Viognier stabliises and softens the harshness of the Petit Syrah and adds aromacy to the wine. The best red is the Avaton, which is produced from Limnio, Mavroudi and Mavrotragano. It is rich and spicy with abundant dark berry fruit. Give it 2 or 3 years. (DM)

Recommended Reds:
Evangelo ★★★ £E   Epanomi Avaton ★★★ £E
Epanomi Syrah/Merlot ★★ £C

Recommended Whites:
Epanomi Chardonnay ★★★ £D
Epanomi Malagousia ★★★ £C
EpanomiViognier ★★ £C

◉ Hatzidakis (Santorini)   *www.hatzidakiswines.gr*

The barren landscape of the island of Santorini in the heart of the Cyclades is home to another first-class producer of top whites. This small family venture was established in 1997 and Haridimos Hatzidaki makes some of the most piercing and mineral organic examples from the island in his underground cellars. Indeed, these are such some of the most exciting dry whites to have emerged from Greece in recent years. There are two very good citrus and mineral unoaked dry whites: Santorini blends Assyrtiko, Aidani and Athiri, while Aidani is the more citrusy of the two. Nikteri Santorini is produced from some of the oldest vines on the property. Aged in wood, it is richer and more opulent than the other whites, more honeyed than mineral. Mavrotragano, produced predominantly from a local grape of the same name, is now an excellent mineral-infused red of real class and individuality Haridimos also makes a very good, piercingly intense Vinsanto from dried grapes. Aged in cask for 3 years, it is marked by complex dried fruits and honey and has excellent balance and a firm acidic backbone. (DM)

Recommended Reds:
Mavrotragano Santorini ★★★ £D

Recommended Whites:
Vinzanto Santorini ★★★★ £F
Aidani Santorini ★★★ £C
Nikteri Santorini ★★★ £C   Santorini ★★★ £C

Ktima Pavlidis (Drama)   *www.theta.apogee.gr*

Small and impressive estate in northern Greece with just 30 ha planted to a mix of international and indigenous varieties. The vineyards are planted in calcareous soils and at an altitude of around 300m This along with a careful control of yields ensures top-quality fruit. The Thema white is a blend of Sauvignon Blanc and Assyrtiko which is cool-fermented with a touch of skin contact. The Assyrtiko gives the wine really fine fresh acidity and there is a marvellous piercing citrus and mango quality to the fruit. A barrel-fermented Chardonnay is also produced. The Thema red is an impressively structured blend of Syrah and Agiorgitiko aged in French (80%) and American oak with malolactic in barrel. Good and firm tannin needs 3 or 4 years but there isn't a hint of leafiness here. Rich and berry-laden varietal bottlings of Syrah and Tempranillo are also released. Essentially fruit-driven, they are aged in oak for around 14 months. (DM)

Recommended Reds:
Thema Red ★★ £C
EmphasisTempranillo ★★ £C
Emphasis Syrah ★★ £C

Recommended Whites:
Thema White ★★ £B

Samos Co-Operative (Samos)   *www.samoswine.gr*

Fine, long-established producer of sweet Muscat. The total scope of the operation is vast with 4,000 members and production approaching 800,000 cases a year. Vines are planted right across the island with some at altitudes of up to 800m. This contributes to the quality of the top wines – indeed, all of the Muscats are sourced from mountain-grown grapes. The Vin Doux, Grand Cru and Anthemis are fortified in a similar manner to other Muscats in France and elsewhere. Vin Doux offers simple, straightforward grapey fruit, while the Grand Cru is sourced from higher-altitude vineyards and has more developed and complex flavours. Anthemis is aged in cask for 5 years and has impressive depth and structure. The Nectar differs in that it is vinified from dried grapes and is not fortified. The wine has significantly less oxidative character than the Anthemis along with a quite marked high-toast oak character and a real piercing intensity. (DM)

Recommended Whites:
Samos Nectar ★★★ £D   Samos Anthemis ★★ £C
Samos Grand Cru ★★ £C   SamosVin Doux ★ £B

Sigalas (Santorini)   *www.sigalas-wine.gr*

This is another example of the tremendous potential of the wines from this small volcanic island in the Aegean Cyclades. Established in 1991 the founding partners Pari Sigala, Christo Markozane and Gianni Tounda have 5.25 ha (13 acres) of vineyards which they have organically certified. Their other contract growers also provide them with fruit grown under similar conditions. The Assyrtiko white is the mainstay of the domaine with around 3,500 cases produced a year. It is a modern stainless steel, cool-fermentation style with a nice citrus fruit and a mineral undercurrent. The Kavalieros remains on the lees for 18 months and offers more depth and intensity, while the Assyrtiko barrel-fermented white is understandably fuller and fatter, although it has a restraint, structure and balance that similar wines from other regions would do well to emulate. Vinification is modern and the wine is kept on its lees and it will benefit from a year or two to harness the oak. The stylish, intense and sweet Vinzanto has a lovely balance of sweet fruit and a steely mineral acidity cutting through it. A nutmeg, orange and spice character emanates from sun dried grapes providing a wine of real length and intensity.

Recommended Whites:
Santorini Sigalas Vinzanto ★★★☆ £E
Santorini Sigalas Assyrtiko Barrique ★★★ £C
Santorini Sigalas Assyrtiko ★★☆ £B
Santorini Sigalas Kavalieros ★★★ £C

A-Z of producers - *Slovenia*

Batic (Vipava)   *www.batic.si*

Miha Batic has 15 ha of densely planted vineyards in Vipava and is one of a group of Slovenian winemakers who has been influenced by the winemaking philosophy and success of Josko Gravner (see North-East Italy). The approach is organic with a huge commitment in the vineyard to obtaining optimum ripeness and health. Winemaking incorporates much of the Gravner treatment, especially with the top wines. That means no added yeasts, no fining, no filtration, no temperature control and long skin maceration times for, yes, white wines. If there is a tendency to more variability here

than with those sticking to more conventional practices there are also some thrilling, vibrant wines that are complex and pure. Most show a surprising lightness of touch. A varietal Pinela is elegant and racy with lemon zest, spice and lots of finesse. In Bonisimus, the same grape is combined with Chardonnay, Rebula (Ribolla Gialla) and Pinot Grigio for a fine fusion of floral, herbal ahead of real breadth and persistence on the palate. Miha's Chardonnay develops a deep citrus rind and grapefruit complexity allied to a slightly oxidative nuttiness and a fine creamy texture yet often with a freshness and vibrancy unexpected with 5 years' age or more. The top white (Batic) is a Gravner-esque blend of great structure, complexity and vibrancy from Chardonnay, Malvasia and Rebula grapes given 10 days skin contact. Drink with 5 years' age or more. Reds include a varietal Cabernet Franc, arguably more vintage dependent than the whites; a cool but intense and persistent style. New is Cuvée Zaria which combines Rebula, Chardonnnay, Moscato Rosa, Pinela and other oddities. Very perfumed, intense and stylish with spiced strawberry and citrus and a powerful yellow and red fruits palate, it too has real potential. At a simpler and softer level, the rosé is in an off-dry style made from 100% Cabernet Sauvignon not unlike a rosé d'Anjou. Other wines include a refined yet powerful sweet wine (Valentino) from dried Rebula and Pinela grapes.

Recommended Reds:
Cabernet Franc ★★☆ £D
Recommended Whites:
Bonisimus ★★★☆ £F   Cuvée Zaria ★★★ £D
Chardonnay ★★★ £D
Pinela ★★★ £D
Rebula ★★ £C
Recommended Rosés:
Rosé ★☆ £B

>> **Gomila (Northeast Slovenia)** *www.pfwineries.com*
The Puklavec Family took over the local cooperative at Ljutomer-Ormož in 2009. Not that they weren't familiar with it since Martin Puklavec and his heirs have been involved with the co-operative since the 1930s. Aided and abetted by talented winemaker, Mitja Herga, an impressive range of white wines are produced, together with a little red (Cabernet/Merlot) and some sparkling (Furmint and Pinot Noir). The Exclusive Furmint is bone dry, with a little bit of saltiness on the tongue, with balanced minerality which is not too austere. The Exclusive Sauvignon Blanc is smooth and light but perhaps is lacking a little in definition. Better is the Furmint/Sauvignon Blanc blend which displays more zing and liveliness. Furmint/Pinot Blanc is smooth and tasty, with the biscuity flavour of the Pinot Blanc restraining the acidity of the Furmint. The Cabernet Sauvignon/Merlot has balanced fruit and acidity with a complex finish. (NB)
Recommended Reds:
Gomila Cabernet Merlot ★★★☆ £B
Recommended Whites:
Gomila Exclusive Furmint ★★★ £B
Gomila Furmint Sauvignon Blanc ★★☆ £B
Gomila Exclusive Sauvignon Blanc ★★ £B

⊕ **Edi Simcic (Brda)** *www.edisimcic.si*
Here is both the present and future of Slovenian winemaking. Edi and his son Aleks make first class wines from 7.4 ha close to the Italian border. Quality is built upon a base of low yields and a stringent fruit selection that results in concentrated, powerful wines

with rich, ripe fruit. The range includes outstanding Chardonnay and fine, almost Graves-like Sauvignon and lush, structured Rebula (Ribolla Gialla). Slightly less successful are Sivi Pinot (Pinot Gris) and Beli Pinot (Pinot Blanc); neither lack for flavour, character or texture but both miss the purity of the other whites. Sauvignon and Chardonnay make up 70% of the blend in Triton, a concentrated, harmonious fruit-filled blend. The balance is made up of either Pinot Blanc or Pinot Gris, depending on the vintage. Red comes in the form of the Merlot dominated Duet (complemented by Cabernet Franc), a cool red-fruited medium-bodied red that is more plummy and black fruited in the warmest vintages. Smaller quantities of premium versions are also made. Kozana Chardonnay, coming from a single site, has all the richness and balance possible associated with a top flight Pouilly-Fuissé vineyard. Triton Lex, again from Chardonnay and Sauvignon but complemented by 40% Rebula in 04, adds more depth and structure over the regular Triton. The top red Duet Lex sees 100% new oak and has rich yet pure, elegant fruit nestled in vanillan oak (slightly better integrated in 02 than 03). Tiny amounts of two sweet wines are also made but haven't been tasted. Edijev Izbor (Rebula but also some Chardonnay, Sauvignon and Verduzzo) is produced from grapes dried for 6 months. Bosa Rosa is a red equivalent, similarly made from dried grapes (mostly Merlot but also both Cabernets). Both spend 3 years in cask. Whites can be aged for up to 5 years, the Chardonnays probably much longer; Duet Lex needs 6-10 years' ageing.
Recommended Reds:
Duet Lex Goriska Brda ★★★☆ £D   Duet Goriska Brda ★★ £B
Recommended Whites:
Chardonnay Kozana Goriska Brda ★★★★ £D
Chardonnay Goriska Brda ★★★☆ £D
Triton Lex Goriska Brda ★★★★ £D
Triton Goriska Brda ★★☆ £D
Sauvignon Goriska Brda ★★★☆ £D
Rebula Goriska Brda ★★★ £C
Sivi Pinot Goriska Brda ★★☆ £D
Beli Pinot Goriska Brda ★★☆ £D

Valter Sirk (Dobrovo) *www.valtersirk.com*
The Sirk family have been vine growers for many generations but in 1991, Valter Sirk decided to make his own wine and the firm has gone from strength to strength ever since. The marl and sandstone vineyards produce crisp whites from a number of different autochthonal and international grapes. Ribulla is firm and crisp whilst their Pinot Grigio shows good spiciness and crispness. Chardonnay is crisp and clean but possibly lacks a little fruit drive, but both the Malvasia and Sauvignonasse (Tocai Fruilano) which benefit from 10% of the production in wood are both aromatic and complex. Of all the whites, the Sauvignon Blanc is the most successful with the gooseberry, grassy taste of a fine Sancerre. The Merlot is matured in both old and new oak and is a splendid example displaying nuances of cederwood and cigar box with a lot of underlying black summer fruit. (NB)
Recommended Reds:
Merlot Goriska Brda ★★★★ £E
Recommended Whites:
Sauvignon Blanc Goriska Brda ★★★ £B
Sauvignonnasse Goriska Brda ★★☆ £B
Rebula Goriska Brda ★★☆ £B
Malvazija Goriska Brda ★★☆ £B
Pinot Grigio Goriska Brda ★★☆ £B
Chardonnay Goriska Brda ★★ £B

Zanut (Brda) *www.zanut.si*

This property is situated in western Brda where Slovenia borders on to Italy, just a few kilometres from Gorizia. It's in a hot micro-climate with the hot breezes from the sea and the strong north wind (burja), coupled with the marl soil, helps to give the wines extreme minerality, coupled with excellent character of fruit, all from their own vineyard. It's not a large organisation - around 50,000 bottles of wine are produced annually consisting of two red and six white varieties. Their wines basically reach the market in two groups - young, fresh, and easy drinking wines - Merlot, Pinot Grigio, Pinot Bianco and Sauvignonasse (aka Tocai Fruilano) and more complex wines, produced with a great deal more care and attention. The regular Merlot is matured in large old oak barrels for three years – showing aromas of sour cherries and leather and is full of ripe black fruit on the palate, whilst the Pinot Grigio displays crisp, spicy acidity, tempered by the small amount of wood it touches in the maturation process. Amongst the more complex wines are a fresh and crisp Rebula and a Sauvignon Blanc which owes more to New Zealand than to Italy or even the Loire Valley with it's intense grassiness. Jama is a late harvest selection of Sauvignonasse grapes producing a warm, full-bodied, rich and complex finish and the Merlot Brja, only produced in exceptional years from the best grapes, spends up to four years in new 500 litre barrels. There's real complexity in the finish of this wine, displaying nuances of black fruits, vanilla, chocolate and tobacco. A regular and reserve Cabernet Sauvignon are also produced but these have not been tasted. (NB)

Recommended Reds:

Merlot Brajac̆ Goriska Brda ★★★★☆ £E

Merlot Goriska Brda ★★★ £B

Recommended Whites:

Jama Goriska Brda ★★★☆ £D

Sauvignon Blanc Goriska Brda ★★★☆ £C

Rebula Goriska Brda ★★☆ £C

Pinot Grigio Goriska Brda ★★ £B

A-Z of producers - *Croatia*

>> Ilock Wine Cellars (Croatian Danube) *www.ilocki-podrumi.hr*

The first written evidence of the cultivation of grapes on the right bank of the Danube, in Croatia, dates back to Illyrian times, before the Roman conquest, and the Romans confirmed the right of Ilok as an ideal location for growing grapes and wine production. Here Ilok Wine Cellars continues the millennia-old tradition of wine growing producing wines from 990 ha of vineyards, with a total annual production about 4 million litres of wine. Ilok is also a destination tourist location with many attractions built around the wine cellars and the reputation of its wines. Since 1970 significant investment has been made in the reconstruction of neglected and war-devastated vineyards, cellar and other outbuildings with the result of the wines now being readily available on the international stage. The indigenous Graševina is the main grape varietal grown, but Chardonnay and Traminer are also produced as well as Frankovna (Blaufränkisch) and Cabernet Sauvignon. As you can imagine, large quantities are produced, but nevertheless have a good price/quality ratio. The entry level Graševina is, perhaps, a little basic, but the Premium oaked cuvee has a good balance of fruit and acidity coupled with a judicious use of the oak. Chardonnay displays good citrusy flavours with reasonable persistence on the finish, whilst the Traminer (Traminac) is quite fruity and spicy. The reds, which are blended into a single wine, has not been tasted. (NB)

Recommended Whites:

Malvasia Festigia Riserva Vinzinada ★★★☆ £C

Iločki Podrumi Graševina Premium (Vrhunsko) ★★★ £C

Iločki Podrumi Chardonnay ★★☆ £B

Iločki Podrumi Traminer ★★☆ £C

Iločki Podrumi Graševina ★ £A

>> Kabola Winery (Istria) *www.kabola.hr*

The Markežić family have been winemakers since 1891 when the first cornerstone was laid with the Momjan Muscat. Since then gradual improvements and innovations have led to the creation of their modern winery, Kabola. The estate is situated in the north-west part of the Istrian peninsula, 275 m above sea level, but nevertheless, close enough to the sea to be influenced by it. The soil consists mainly of clay and is rich in marl, which also characterises the wines. A unique feature here is that some of the wines are still traditionally being produced in amphoras. Buried in the earth and through prolonged fermentation, the family believe that the ageing of the wine without removal of the grape skins has enhanced the noble features of the Malvasia. This also keeps the wine fresh before transfer to the cellars for the final crafting of the wines. The amphora Malvasia, which is only produced in the better vintages, certainly shows more intensity of fruit than the regular wine, nuances of dried stone fruits and good minerality. The Muscat is much more grapey and verges on being medium-sweet. The red Teran is soft and fruity but with a fair degree of complexity whilst the rosé is quite full-bodied with a dry, fresh finish. Cabernet Sauvignon, erlot and a sparkling wine from Pinot, Chardonnay and Malvasia are also produced but these have not been tasted. (NB)

Recommended Reds:

Kabola Teran ★★★ £D

Recommended Whites:

Kabola Malvasia Istriana Amphora ★★★☆ £E

Kabola Malvasia Istriana ★★ £B

Kabola Muscat ★★ £B

Recommended Rosés:

Kabola Teran Rosé ★★ £C

>> Vina Laguna (Istria) *www.vinalaguna.hr*

Vina Laguna produces wines from 600 ha of vineyards in the Istrian peninsular. Their wines fall into three categories, crisp, lively and fruity entry level wines, more serious Festigia range and the premium Festigia Reserva range. Malvsia is the main grape varietal and here they run 4 cuvées of it. The entry level Malvasia is minerally and light – can be a bit astringent in some vintages but generally finishes with some persistence. A step up is the premium "Festigia" Malvasia which shows just that bit more fruit and complexity. Not made every year is Vinzinda Reserva Malvasia which shows more finesse. There is also an oaked version, Malvasia Akacija, again not made in every vintage, which is full in the mouth but can be dominated by the wood. The unoaked versions are for early drinking, but the Akacija should improve with a little ageing. Amongst other entry level wines are a zingy Pinot Gris and a blend of Teran, Borgonja Crna and Merlot called "Terra Rossa" which is easy drinking, smooth and fruity. A straight Merlot in the Festigia range is smooth with seamless oak integration and will repay cellaring for 3 or 4 years. Castello, a blend of 50% Merlot, 30% Syrah and 20% Cabernet Sauvignon, from the Terra Rossa soils in the west of the Istrian peninsular, is a great food wine with good concentrated fruit and complexity. Top of the range, Cabernet Sauvignon Reserva also displays good complexity and will repay cellaring. The wines are

Other Europe & Med

excellent value for money. (NB)

Recommended Reds:

Cabernet Sauvignon Festigia Riserva ★★★★ £D

Merlot Festigia ★★★☆ £C

Castello Festigia ★★★☆ £C

Terra Rossa ★★ £B

Recommended Whites:

Malvasia Festigia Riserva Vinzinada ★★★☆ £C

Malvasia Festigia Riserva Akacija ★★★☆ £C

Malvasia Festigia ★★★ £B

Pinot Gris ★★ £B

Malvasia Select ★★ £A

A-Z of producers - *Lebanon*

Ch. Kefraya (Bekaa Valley) *www.chateaukefraya.com*

Kefraya is situated in the heart of the Bekaa Valley with vineyards planted on steep terraces at an altitude of between 950 and 1,100 metres above sea level. This, combined with the meagre clay, lime and stony soils provides the environment for potentially intense fruit. The property consists of 300 ha and the range of wines includes red, white and rosé. The lightly aromatic and honeyed Blanc de Blancs blends Chardonnay with Sauvignon Blanc and Viognier. A short period of ageing on lees adds to the wines depth and texture. Unusual and characterful is the fortified Lacrima d'Oro, produced from 100% Clairette. rich and sweet with just sufficient acidity for balance. Of the reds there is a more fruit driven style, Les Bretèches as well as the impressive Château red and imposingly structured Comte de M. Château Kefraya blends Cabernet Sauvignon with Mourvèdre and a big dollop of Syrah. A long four to five week vatting gives a wine of considerable dimension with dark, spicy blackberry fruit and firm tannins, five years of age will certainly add more. The Comte de M is a rich, meaty, cedary blend of Cabernet Sauvignon and Syrah in roughly equal proportions. Cellaring for at least five years and more from the vintage is recommended. (DM)

Recommended Reds:

Comte de M ★★★☆ £E

Château Kefraya ★★★ £D

Recommended Whites:

Lacrima D'Oro ★★ £E

Château Kefraya Blanc de Blancs ★★ £C

Ch. Musar (Bekaa Valley) *www.chateaumusar.com*

Not only the most famous name in Lebanese wine making but also one of the most recognizeable in the whole world of wine, the Hochar family overcame great obstacles in continuing to vinify their wines during the difficult civil strife in Lebanon in the early 1980s. Although there are certainly other important producers here now, Musar remains consistent to the style and character of its wines of those years. As well as the top red and white there is a decent enough Château Musar rosé as well as second and third label wines released as Hochar Père et Fils and Musar Cuvée. A red, white and rosé are released under all three labels. Each of the reds is produced from a blend of Cabernet Sauvignon, Cinsault and Carignan, the whites from the local indigenous Merwah and Obaideh varieties. The style of the Château Musar red remains striking, a touch of volatility and intense sweet berry fruit with an underlying structure that supports a real propensity for age. Some of the early bottles from the 1970s and 1980s held up well for a decade and a half. It will be interesting to see if the most recent vintages emulate this. (DM)

Recommended Reds:

Château Musar Bekaa Valley ★★★ £D

Hochar Pere et Fils Bekaa Valley ★★ £C

Recommended Whites:

Château Musar Bekaa Valley ★★ £C

Hochar Pere et Fils Bekaa Valley ★ £C

✹ Massaya (Bekaa Valley) *www.massaya.com*

Arguably now the finest producer in the Lebanese Bekaa Valley. The Massaya range of wines is produced at the Ghosn family's restored Tanaïl property which includes an Arak distillery, boutique and barbecue facilities as well as the Massaya winery. In 1998 the family formed a partnership with the Bruniers of VIEUX-TÉLÉGRAPHE in Châteauneuf-du-Pape, Hubert de Boüard de Laforest of Château ANGELUS and Dominique Hebrard of Château TRIANON in Saint-Emilion to provide the expertise to make top-quality wine from the Bekaa. Three reds are now made as well as a couple of whites and a soft fruity rosé, a blend of Cinsault, Syrah and Cabernet Sauvignon. The classic white is soft, nutty and approachable, a blend of Sauvignon Blanc and Clairette. The Silver Selection is a step up; it is 70% Sauvignon Blanc and 30% Chardonnay. Both are cool-fermented to emphasise their fruit. The three reds are the key wines here. The Classic is a forward and fruit driven blend of Cinsault, Cabernet Sauvignon and Syrah. The Silver Selection is bigger and sturdier with firm tannins and some depth. It blends Cinsault and Grenache with a little Mourvèdre and Cabernet Sauvignon. The top Gold Reserve red is dense, powerful and concentrated, 50% Cabernet Sauvignon 40% Mourvèdre and 10% Syrah. It will benefit from at least 5 years' ageing. The quality of the wines is improving vintage by vintage so expect more to come. (DM)

Recommended Reds:

Gold Reserve Bekaa Valley ★★★★ £E

Selection Bekaa Valley ★★★ £C

Classic Bekaa Valley ★★☆ £C

Recommended Whites:

Classic Bekaa Valley ★☆ £C

A-Z of producers - *Israel*

➤➤ Alexander Winery (Upper Galilee) *www.alexander-winery.com*

Ex cameraman for Israeli television Yoram Shalom founded the winery in 1996 and production has increased from 12,000 bottles in 1999 to over 60,000 bottles today. Since the 2006 vintage all the wines are kosher. Fruit is grown in three vineyards in the Upper Galilee area at heights between 700 and 850 metres and consists of Cabernet Sauvignon, Cabernet Franc, Merlot, Syrah, Petit Verdot, Mourvèdre, Grenache, Sauvignon Blanc and Chardonnay. After the alcoholic fermentation the wine is transferred to new French and American *barriques* for around two years and another 12 months is spent in bottle before commercial release. Reds are produced in a definite New World style and could certainly compete with the best in California and Australia. Cabernet Franc has great depth and concentration of black forest fruit although there is a slight tendency to be on the jammy side. Alexander the Great Amarolo is a blend of all the six red grapes used dominated by Cabernet Sauvignon and Merlot (80%0 between them which produces a really smooth finish despite its 15.5% abv. It is in an inordinately heavy bottle and one can't help having the feeling that the marketing exceeds the quality in the bottle. Alexander the Great Cabernet Sauvignon has good upfront fruit dominated by blackberry flavours, well balanced with the tannins. Gaston is again 80% Cabernet Sauvignon and Merlot

but this time the balance is made up with Syrah, which whilst being well balanced is a little less exuberant then the others. A little white (Chardonnay and Sauvignon Blanc) is also made but has not been tasted.

Recommended Reds:

Alexander The Great Amarolo ★★★★ £G
Alexander The Great Cabernet Sauvignon ★★★★ £F
Alexander Cabernet Franc ★★★★ £D
Alexander Gaston ★★★ £D

Barkan Wine Cellars (Hulda) *www.barkan-winery.co.il*
Barkan Wine Cellars is Israel's second largest winery with a diversified vineyard portfolio covering all of Israel's top terroirs. They make a range of wines from quality driven to affordable. The winery was founded by a group of grape growers and their internationally trained team of winemakers is headed by Edward Salzberg, Yolam Sharon and Irit Boxer Shank. State-of-the-art equipment is used to produce quality and consistency. Their flagship Superieur Cabernet Sauvignon is a blend from their best vineyards in the Upper Galilee, including around 10% Merlot from the cool climate Dovev vineyard and aged for 18 months in new French *barriques*, which with age produces a smooth, velvety and complex wine with hints of black summer fruits and a long finish. Reserve Altitude Cabernet Sauvignon +624 is a single vineyard wine, 100% Cabernet Sauvignon whilst a little less open than the Superieur, displays good expression of the terroir. There is also Cabrnet Sauvignon from vineyards at Altitude +412 and +720. Their Reserve Cabernet Sauvignon is produced from 5 different vineyards, 2 in the Golan Heights and 3 in the Upper Galilee. The grapes are picked at optimum ripeness and produce a wine with a very smooth finish after being aged for 20 months in French and American oak but lacks a little of the complexity of the other two wines. Reserve Shiraz is harvested mainly from a vineyard on terra rossa terraces above Jerusalem with the addition of some fruit from the Golan Heights. Aged for 14 months in French and American oak, of which only 25% is new, a small amount (5%) of Cabernet Sauvignon and 2% Petit Verdot is added at the final blending to give it more complexity and length. A Reserve Merlot is produced from several vineyards in the Golan Heights and Upper Galilee, aged for 14 months in *barriques*, one-third new, resulting in a smooth and balanced wine but perhaps lacking a little of the clout of the Cabernets. Finally, a Reserve Pinotage from the Judean foothills in one of the rare vineyards outside South Africa producing this varietal, shows good varietal f lavours and a fair finish. Barkan produces a large selection of other red and white wines ranging from entry level to their Superieur series, of which the above are just a small selection. (NB)

Recommended Reds:

Superieur Cabernet Sauvignon Upper Galilee ★★★★ £F
Reserve Altitude Cabernet Sauvignon +720 Upper Galilee ★★★★ £E
Reserve Altitude Cabernet Sauvignon +624 Upper Galilee ★★★☆ £E
Reserve Cabernet Sauvignon Golan Heights ★★★☆ £D
Reserve Shiraz Jerusalem Hills ★★★☆ £D
Reserve Merlot Golan Heghts/Upper Galilee ★★★ £D
Reserve Pinotage Judean Hills ★★☆ £C

Dalton Winery (Upper Galilee) *www.dalton-winery.com*
Dalton was one of the first wineries to be located in the picturesque Upper Galilee region of Israel, being established in 1995. All their vineyards lie at an elevation of between 700 and 900 metres above sea level. Since their first vintage, producing 20,000 bottles, the scope and size of the winery has now grown to a production of around 850,000 bottles of Cabernet Sauvignon, Merlot, Cabernet Franc, Shiraz, Zinfandel, Barbera, White Riesling, Sauvignon Blanc, Chardonnay, Viognier and Moscato. Not all their wines have been tasted, but we have been impressed by the efforts of local winemaker Na'ama Mualem, trained at Roseworthy College in South Australia. She is ably abetted by experienced consultant winemaker, John Worontschak. Shiraz and Cabernet are the mainstays of production and the Shiraz Reserve (95% Shiraz, 5% Viognier) has big tarry and spicy flavours with a long finish. Cabernet Sauvignon Reserve is sophisticated and complex, smooth with soft tannins and good balance between fruit and acidity. Alma, a meritage blend of Cabernet Sauvignon, Merlot and Cabernet Franc, doesn't quite match up to the complexity of the other two reds, but is nevertheless smooth and rich. Two more Alma blends have been added to the range - a Syrah-Mourvèdre-Viognier and a Chardonnay-Viognier but these have not yet been tasted. All reserve reds are aged between 12 and 18 months in *barriques*. There is an unusually large range of whites here for Israel since Israel is not really noted for its white wine production and even here it is evident that the whites do not match the reds for quality. Sauvignon Blanc Reserve has good cut grass flavours but lacks a bit of the nervous zingyness that one would expect from a prime example. An unoaked Chardonnay (not a reserve wine) was very clean and was a bit more uplifting on the palate. The Viognier vines were probably not sufficiently aged to produce distinctive aromacy, but this again was clean and will show more promise in subsequent vintages. For the religious and curious, all the wines produced by Dalton are strictly Kosher which is not always the case with top Israeli wineries. (NB)

Recommended Reds:

Shiraz Reserve Upper Galilee ★★★★ £F
Cabernet Sauvignon Reserve Upper Galilee ★★★☆ £E
Alma Cab-Merlot Upper Galilee ★★★☆ £D

Recommended Whites:

Sauvignon Blanc Reserve Upper Galilee ★★★☆ £D
Chardonnay Unoaked Upper Galilee ★★★ £D
Wild Yeast Viognier ★★☆ £C

Golan Heights Winery (Golan Heights) *www.golanwines.co.il*
One of Israel's best known and oldest wineries, the eponymous Golan Heights Winery put the area on the map as Israel's premier wine producing area. Marketing under the Yarden, Gamla and Golan labels, they have been one of the flag carriers internationally for Israel since their formation in 1983. We haven't tasted all the range but have been happy to receive recent confirmation at a tasting in London of their continuing quality. Sparkling Gamla Brut is an equal blend of Chardonnay and Pinot Noir without being too effervescent whilst their Yarden Viognier, fermented partly in French oak barrels and partly in stainless steel, is one of the few Israeli ones that produces true varietal flavours. Yarden Katzrin Chardonnay disappointed in much the same way as some white Burgundies have in the recent past. The reds are an altogether different kettle of fish. A Yarden Syrah, aged for 18 months in French oak, displayed good tarryness and spice that one would expect from this Rhône varietal whilst the Yarden Cabernet Sauvignon, aged for the same time in small oak *barriques*, showed intensity of black summer fruits with good complexity. Finally, the Yarden Heights Gewürztraminer, an "ice wine" made from whole cluster frozen grapes fermenting slowly over a period of months, is a delightful dessert wine displaying all the tropical fruit nuances of the varietal accompanied by a sweet, rich and long finish. (NB)

Other Europe & Med

Recommended Reds:
Yarden Syrah Galilee/Golan Heights ★★★★ £D
Yarden Cabernet Sauvignon Galilee/Golan Heights ★★★★ £D
Recommended Whites:
Yarden Gewürztraminer Galilee/Golan Heights ★★★★ £F
Yarden Viognier Galilee/Golan Heights ★★★ £D
Gamla Brut Galilee/Golan Heights ★★☆ £E
Yarden Katzrin Chardonnay Galilee/Golan Heights ★ £D

✿ **Margalit Winery (Hadera)** *www.margalit-winery.com*
Founded in 1989 by Dr Yair Margalit, a scientist and physical chemist, Margalit Vineyard is considered to be the leading boutique winery in Israel. Ably abetted by his winemaking son, Asif, the winery concentrates on Bordeaux varieties and produces 4 different labels from their holdings of Cabernet Sauvignon, Merlot and Cabernet Franc. Annual production is around 20,000 bottles. Only free-run wine is used in their production and after two rackings the wine is aged in small oak *barriques* (95% French, 5% American) of which one third are new, for around 12 months. The wines are not fined but coarse-filtered and blended together before the final *assemblage*. The winery owns two vineyards, one in the upper Galilee mountains where Cabernet Sauvignon and Merlot are planted and another near Binyamina on the Mediterranean coast which consists of Cabernet Franc vines. They maintain organic fertilisation just before the winter rains. Israel is dry in the summer with no rainfall at all and they rely solely on the winter rains and do not irrigate the vineyards otherwise. This forces the vines to dig its roots deeply which allows the vines to produce excellent grapes. Cabernet Sauvignon Kadita Vineyard always has a small proportion of Merlot, varying between 6% and 10% according to the vintage, and has nice complexity with good summer berry flavours, although it can be a little too herbaceous in some years. The Cabernet Franc from the coastal vineyard at Binyamina, with around 5% Cabernet Sauvignon blended in is smooth but probably with a little less complexity than the Cabernet Sauvignon from the higher vineyard. The flagship "Enigma", predominately Cabernet Sauvignon but with substantial chunks of Merlot and Cabernet Franc from both vineyards, varying from year to year, is the most complete wine that the estate produces with smooth complexity, black berry fruits and cigar box nose being the most akin to a good classed growth Bordeaux. In some years, when they think it is merited, Special Reserve wines are produced. (NB)
Recommended Reds:
Enigma Galilee Mountains/Coast ★★★★ £G
Cabernet Sauvignon Kadita Vineyard Galilee Mountains ★★★☆ £F
Cabernet Franc Binyamina Vineyard Coast ★★★ £F

Segal Wines (Hulda)
The Segal family has been producing wine in Israel for nearly 100 years and were pioneers in planting vineyards in the Upper Galilee. Segal merged with BARKAN WINE CELLARS in 2001 but retain complete autonomy in making wines from their own vineyards, with winemaker Avi Feldstein at the helm. They own three vineyards, the most challenging of which is the Dovev Vineyard near the Lebanese border at an altitude of 740 metres. Among the varietals grown here is the unique to Israel Argaman, meaning deep crimson, developed from crossing the French Carignan with the Portuguese Souazo in order to add colour to everyday wines in warm regions in the plains of Israel. However, the extreme climatic conditions and poor soil found at the altitude of the Dovev Vineyard presents different challenges from the high-yielding vineyards of the plains.

Here, the vines have responded with producing an intense, fruity and aromatic wine, dark and brooding, but without the clumsiness normally associated with this varietal. Their flagship wine is their Unfiltered Cabernet Sauvignon, made with 65% of the fruit from the Dishon Vineyard and 25% Cabernet Sauvingon and 10% Merlot from the Dovev Vineyard. The wines are aged for approximately 2 years in mainly new French oak *barriques* and then bottled without fining or filtration. The result is a harmonious balance between the raciness of the fruit from the high altitude Dovev Vineyard and the more lush Cabernet from the lower Dishon Vineyard producing a wine of great elegance, complexity and length. (NB)
Recommended Reds:
Segal's Unfiltered Cabernet Sauvignon Upper Galilee ★★★★☆ £F
Segal's Single Vineyard Dovev Argaman Upper Galilee ★★★ £E

Tulip Winery (Galilee) *www.tulip-winery.co.il*
The winery is situated at Kfar Tikva (Village of Hope) a residential community for people with special needs, some of whom are employed at the winery. It was established only in 2003 and sources fruit mainly from vineyards in Upper Galilee and the Judean Hills with the objective of producing high quality wines at affordable prices. Itzhak Itzaki, the founder is the force behind the winery whilst son Roy has now taken up the reins as CEO in order to drive the winery towards international success. Tamir Arzy is the winemaker, responsible for the production of 95,000 bottles under 8 labels. White Tulip (60% Gewürztraminer, 40% Sauvignon Blanc) is the only white produced and is nice and fruity but with perhaps not enough overt spiciness to make the Gewürztraminer count. Nevertheless, a very drinkable wine. Just Merlot is a 100% single vineyard Merlot, aged in French oak for 8 months and displaying tones of ripe red fruits and simple drinkability. Mostly Cabernet Franc (85% Cabernet Franc and 15% Cabernet Sauvignon) was aged for 14 months in French and American oak barrels, producing a wine with excellent varietal flavours, the savouriness of the Franc coming through well against the fruitiness of the Sauvignon. Cabernet Sauvignon Reserve (90% Cabernet Sauvignon, 10 % Cabernet Franc) by contrast is round and smooth with fullness in the mouth and nice complexity on the finish of fine red fruit. The Syrah Reserve (90% Syrah, 10% Cabernet Sauvignon) 15% abv and aged in French oak for 18 months, is big and chunky with fair tarry fruit, but with enormous length on the finish. One for keeping. The flagship wine, Black Tulip, consists of 60% Cabernet Sauvignon, 20% Merlot, 13% Cabernet Franc and 7% Petit Verdot and is very smooth and complex with nuances of ripe black forest fruits. The wine is aged for about 30 months in new French oak, but there is certainly no oak domination because of the ripeness of the fruit. (NB)
Recommended Reds:
Black Tulip Judean Hills ★★★★☆ £F
Syrah Reserve Upper Galilee ★★★☆ £E
Cabernet Sauvignon Reserve Judean Hills/Upper Galilee ★★★☆ £E
Mostly Cabernet Franc Judean Hills ★★★☆ £D
Just Merlot Judean Hills ★★☆ £C
Recommended Whites:
White Tulip Upper Galilee ★★ £C

A-Z of producers - *Turkey*

>> Gulor (Thrace)
Gulor's winery and estate vineyards are located in Tekirdag on the north shore of the Marmara Sea in the region of Thrace, just outside the town of Sarkoy, which for centuries was the historical

centre of Turkish wine production. The estate is planted to Cabernet Sauvignon, Merlot, Petit Verdot, Malbec, Syrah and Sauvignon Blanc in addition to Italian varieties including Sangiovese and Montepulciano. Gulor also owns vineyards in Anatolia and contracts with producers there for indigenous varieties like Okuzgozu and Bogazkere. The winery produces approximately 150,000 bottles of wine annually across five tiers of wine. Professor Nicolas Vivas from the University of Bordeaux, has directed all phases of production and winemaking there for the last two decades. Since 2012, winemaking at Gulor has been in the hands of Antoine Bastide d'Izard, a seventh-generation winemaker from the family estate of Domaine de Beaumont in Languedoc. We have had a limited experience of tasting these wines but what we have seen promises well. A Sauvignon Blanc is grassy, nettley and peppery, whilst a Cabernet Sauvignon/ Merlot blend has good underlying fruit beneath firm tannins. This is a work in progress which will be further explored in future editions. (NB)

Recommended Reds:
Cabernet Sauvignon/Merlot ★★☆ £B
Recommended Whites:
Sauvignon Blanc ★★★ £B

>> Selendi (Aegean) *www.selendi.com.tr*
Selendi Wines was established in 2000 from a former tobacco field and turned into a vineyard and a boutique winery. The 1.5 hectares vineyard was planted with Cabernet Sauvignon, Merlot and Syrah. As the hobby turned into a business, the Ongor family purchased more land in 2005. The second vineyard was established in Sarnic village, 800m high from the sea level. The 19 hectares there comprise of separate plots planted to Cabernet Sauvignon, Merlot, Syrah, Cabernet Franc, Petit Verdot, Grenache, Mourvedre, Cinsault, Chardonnay, Viognier and Narince. The Sarnic vineyard is organically certified. The grapes are hand-picked before sunrise, and transported in 13kg small baskets to the air-conditioned winery. The grapes are hand selected to ensure optimum ripeness before being put through the de-stemmer. Each varietal is fermented separately in stainless-steel tanks. Maturation is then continued in medium-toasted French oak barrels for 20 months. The Red Blend is mainly Merlot, with Cabernet Sauvignon, Cabernet Franc and Syrah with the proportions varying with each vintage. It does repay long cellaring but has deep and complex red fruit beneath the tannins. Each vintage has a different contemporary painting by a Turkish artist on its label. The Merlot is a bit softer and more approachable with good persistence on the finish. (NB)

Recommended Reds:
Merlot ★★★ £D
Red Blend ★★★ £D

A-Z of producers - *Georgia*

>> Ch. Mukhrani (Mukhrani) *www.mukhrani.com*
Not far from Mukhrani is the village of Dzalisa, where a second century Greek mosaic of Dionysus mosaic was discovered in 1974. Wine has been made here for a long time. Prince Ivane Bagrationi (1812-1893), scion of the Bagrationi dynasty that once ruled Georgia, established the palace and winery at Château Mukhrani. The estate's sparkling wines in particular were widely praised and won Bagrationi the honour of "Officier du Mérite Agricole" in Paris in 1889. He supplied wines to the Russian Imperial Court. The "new" Château Mukhrani was established in 2001 with help from Tatiana Fabergé, whose great-grandfather was a brother of Prince Ivane. The

92 ha of vineyards are cheek by jowl with the palace, which will be refurbished after the winery and cellars have been finished in 2011. There are also ambitious plans for wine-related "cultural events" such as a museum, a restaurant, classical music concerts, weddings, horse riding and so on. The first bottled vintage was 2007. About 300,000 bottles were made in 2010. According to Mukhrani's winemaker Lado Uzunashvili this will rise over the next few years to about 850,000. (SG)

Recommended Reds:
Saperavi ★ £B

>> Pheasant's Tears (Sighnaghi) *www.pheasantstears.com*
Growing up in the USA, John H. Wurdeman V became passionate about Georgian music and culture. Smitten by the ancient walls and the mists of Sighnaghi, where he now lives with his wife and children, he started to make wine because "in Georgia you need wine for guests – so I made my own!" In 2005 he met Gela Patalishvili, who warned him that the old traditions were in danger and they could be the generation that oversaw the death of Qvevri winemaking. This meeting led to the creation of Pheasant's Tears, which now produces 40,000 bottles per year of seven varietal wines. "The idea was to make a traditional wine and to make it right," says John about his Qvevri winemaking methods, which sometimes produce dauntingly tannic white and red wines. The Rkatsiteli is from the dry Kartli region but Pheasant's Tears' other wines are from Kakheti. (SG)

Recommended Reds:
Saperavi ★★★★ £F   Tavkveri ★★★ £F
Shavkapito ★★★ £F
Recommended Whites:
Mtsvane ★★★ £F   Rkatsiteli ★★ £F
Chinuri ★★ £F   Kisi ★★ £F

>> Schuchmann Wines (Kisiskhevi) *www.schuchmann-wines.com*
German businessman Burkhard Schuchmann came to Georgia because "here you can develop things." He recruited third-generation winemaker Georgi Dakishvili to oversee his estate at Kisiskhevi in the Kakheti wine region. Schuchmann produces a less tannic and oxidative style of kwevri wine than some other producers. (SG)

Recommended Reds:
Vinoterra Saperavi ★★★ £D   Saperavi ★★ £C
Recommended Whites:
Vinoterra Rkatsiteli ★★★ £D

A-Z of producers - *India*

>> Soul Tree Winery (Nashik Valley) *www.soultreewine.co.uk*
The brainchild of two British businessmen of Indian descent, Soul Tree has become one of the best respected boutique wineries in India. With vineyards located in the traditional wine producing area of the Nashik Valley in Maharastra, winemaker Rajash Racal is crafting a range of classy wines from young vines, whilst giving new skills to small independent local farmers. Wines are honed with spicy Indian food in mind, but they shouldn't necessarily be confined to that cuisine. Whilst weather conditions in India would actually allow two harvests in a single year, Soul Tree's policy is to use a double pruning, single cropping strategy to ensure fruit concentration, with the vines being harvested in February/March each year. Pruning before and after the monsoon ensures minimum intervention during the growing season. The Ayika sparkling wine is made by the

Other Europe, North Africa, Middle East & Asia

Charnat method from Chenin Blanc, Sauvignon Blanc, Shiraz and Symphonie and is decidedly off-dry, but cuts well with the spiciness of Asian cuisine. Both the straight Sauvignon Blanc and Chenin Blanc wines are crisp and dry with some degree of minerality. Unoaked Shiraz and Cabernet Sauvignon are quite light, easy-drinking wines with good red fruit flavours beneath soft tannins. The premium Shiraz (60%)/Cabernet Sauvignon (40%) Reserve is barrel aged for 12 months in French oak and displays depth of brambly fruit with a good degree of complexity. All the red wines have a not-for-children minimum 14% abv kick to them. (NB)

Recommended Reds:
Shiraz/Cabernet Sauvignon Reserve ★★★ £C
Cabernet Sauvignon ★★☆ £C
Shiraz ★★☆ £B

Recommended Whites:
Sauvignon Blanc ★★☆ £B
Chenin Blanc ★★☆ £B
Ayika Sparkling NV ★★ £C

Other wines of note - *Western Europe*

England
A' Beckett's
Recommended Whites: Estate Sparkling Wiltshire ★★ £C
Estate Blend Worcestershire ★☆ £B
Recommended Rosés: Estate Rosé Wiltshire ★☆ £B
Biddenden
Recommended Whites: Gribble Bridge Sparkling Kent ★★ £D
Gribble Bridge Ortega Kent ★★ £B
Recommended Rosés: Rosé ★☆ £B
Recommended Reds: Gamay ★☆ £B
Breaky Bottom
Recommended Whites: Cuvée Brian Jordan East Sussex ★★☆ £D
Kir Royal ★★ £E
Brightwell
Recommended Reds: Oxford Regatta Oxford ★☆ £C
Recommended Whites: Sparkling Chardonnay Oxfordshire ★★★ £D
Bacchus Oxfordshire ★☆ £B   Oxford Flint Oxfordshire ★☆ £B
Recommended Rosés: Oxford Rosé Wiltshire ★★ £B
Eglantine
Recommended Whites: Northstar Nottinghamshire ★★★☆ £F
Hush Heath Estate
Recommended Whites:
Leslie's Reserve NV ★★★ £D
Sky Chardonnay ★★★ £ C
Recommended Rosés:
Balfour Brut Rosé Vintage Kent ★★★ £E
Kenton Vineyard Recommended Whites: Ortega Devon ★★ £B
Recommended Rosés: Estate Rosé Devon ★☆ £B
Leventhorpe
Recommended Whites: Seyval Yorkshire ★ £B
Madeleine Angevine Yorkshire ★☆ £B
Marlings
Recommended Reds: Three Cows Hampshire ★☆ £B
Recommended Whites: Three Cows Hampshire ★☆ £B
Recommended Rosés: Three Cows Hampshire ★☆ £B
Parva Farm
Recommended Whites: Bacchus Monmouthshire ★★ £B
Pebblebed
Recommended Rosés: Sparkling Rosé Vintage Devon ★★★ £E
Rosé Devon ★☆ £B

Setley Ridge
Recommended Reds: Setley Ridge Red Hampshire ★☆ £B
Welcombe Hills
Recommended Reds: Pinot Noir Warwickshire ★☆ £B
Pinot Noir Précoce Warwickshire ★☆ £B

Luxembourg
Cep d'Or
Recommended Whites:
Crémant Signature Vintage (Pinot Noir/Chardonnay) ★★ £B
Pinot Blanc Gpc Stadtbredimus Goldberg ★ £B
Auxerrois Gpc Stadtbredimus Primerberg ★★ £B
Pinot Gris Stadtbredimus Primerberg Signature ★★ £B
Riesling GPC Stadtbredimus Fels Signature ★☆ £B
Gewürztraminer Stadtbredimus Côteaux Signature ★★ £B
A Gloden & Fils
Recommended Whites:
Crémant de Luxembourg Brut Non-Vintage (Riesling) ★★ £B
Pinot Gris Wellenstein Foulschette Tradition Du Domaine ★★ £B
Riesling Wellenstein Kurschels Tradition Du Domaine ★★ £B
Recommended Rosés: Rosé de Noirs Brut Non-Vintage ★ £B
Dom. Mathes
Recommended Whites: Riesling GPC Wormeldange Koeppchen ★ £B
Crémant Steel Non-Vintage (Riesling/Chardonnay/Pinot Blanc) ★☆ £B
Caves Henri Ruppert
Recommended Whites: Riesling Côteaux de Schengen ★ £B
Pinot Gris Côteaux de Schengen ★☆ £B
Caves St. Remy - Desom
Recommended Whites:
Crémant de Luxembourg Millesimé (Riesling/Pinot Blanc) ★★ £B
Riesling GPC Wormeldange Koeppchen ★★☆ £B
Les Domaines de Vinsmoselle
Recommended Whites: Rivaner Côtes de Remich ★ £B
Auxerrois Côtes de Grevenmacher ★☆ £B
Riesling GPC Wormeldange Wousselt ★★ £B

Other wines of note - *Central & Eastern Europe*

Hungary
Château Megyer
Recommended Whites: Tokaji Aszú 5 Puttonyos ★★★ £E
Château Pajzos
Recommended Whites: Tokaji Aszú 5 Puttonyos ★★★ £E
Crown Estates
Recommended Whites: Tokaji Aszú 5 Puttonyos ★★☆ £D

Switzerland
Daniel & Martha Gantenbein
Recommended Reds: Pinot Noir ★★★☆ £D
Daniele Huber
Recommended Reds:
Montagna Magica (Merlot/Cabernets) ★★★ £E
Luigi Zanini
Recommended Reds: Merlot Del Ticino Castello Luigi ★★★ £F
Recommended Whites:
Bianco Di Besazio Castello Luigi (Chardonnay) ★★★ £F
Christian Zundel
Recommended Reds: Orrizonte (Merlot/Cabernet) ★★★ £E

Other wines of note - *South-Eastern Europe*

Greece
Antonopoulos
Recommended Reds: Cabernet Nea Dris Patras ★★ £C
Areti
Recommended Whites: Macedonia Assyrtiko ★★ £B
Macedonia Assyrtiko Oak-Aged ★★ £C
Gentilini
Recommended Whites: Robola Cephalonia ★★ £B
Harlaftis
Recommended Reds: Argilos Attika ★ £B
Chateau Harlaftis Attika ★★ £B
Recommended Whites: Chardonnay ★★ £B
Kir-Yianni
Recommended Reds: Yianakohori Imathia ★★ £D
Recommended Whites: Sauvignon Blanc Florina ★★ £C
Manousakis-Nostros
Recommended Reds:
Vatolakos Mourvèdre - Crete ★★★☆ £D
Vatolakos "The Blend" - Crete ★★★★ £D
Vatolakos Grenache - Crete ★★★☆ £C
Recommended Whites:
Vatolakos White - Crete ★★★ £C
Vatolakos Rousanne - Crete ★★ £C
Megapanos
Recommended Reds: Nemea Agiorgitiko ★★ £B
Dom. Mercouri
Recommended Reds: Domaine Mercouri Red ★★ £C
Recommended Whites: Foloi ★ £B
Moraitis (Paros)
Recommended Whites: Monemvasia ★★ £B
Recommended Rosés:
Rosé (Manteleria/Assyrtiko) ★☆ £B
Recommended Reds: Aidani/Cabernet Sauvignon ★★ £B
Nemeion (Peloponnese)
Recommended Reds: Reserve ★★★ £C
Serpieri Estate
Recommended Reds: Mavrodaphne ★★★★☆ £G (1946)
Dom. Skouras
Recommended Reds: Nemea Saint George ★★ £B
Nemea Grand Cuvée ★★★ £C
Vin de Pays de Peloponesse Cuvée Prestige ★★ £B
Vin de Pays de Peloponesse Megas Oenos ★★ £C
Recommended Whites:
Viognier Vin de Pays de Peloponesse Larsinos Estate ★★ £B
Viognier Vin de Pays de Peloponesse Eclectique ★★ £B
Chardonnay Vin de Pays de Peloponesse Oak Fermented ★★ £B
Dom. Vassiliou
Recommended Whites: Ambelones Koropi ★ £B
Recommended Reds: Erythros Attika ★★ £C
Nemea Agiorgitiko ★★★ £C
Wine Art Estate
Recommended Reds: Drama Syrah ★ £B
Drama Merlot ★ £B   Drama Nebbiolo ★★ £B
Recommended Whites: Drama Techni Alipias ★ £B
Drama Assyrtiko ★★ £B   Drama Chardonnay ★★ £B

Slovenia
Cotar
Recommended Reds: Terra Rossa ★★★ £D

Movia
Recommended Whites: Veliko Belo Brda ★★ £C

Other wines of note - *Middle East & North Africa*

Israel
Bazalet Ha Golan
Recommended Reds: Cabernet Sauvignon Reserve ★★★ £D
Dom. du Castel
Recommended Reds: Petit Castel ★★ £C
Grand Vin ★★★ £C
Chillag Winery
Recommended Reds: Cabernet Sauvignon Orna ★★ £C
Saslove Winery
Recommended Reds: Cabernet Sauvignon Adom ★★★ £D
Carmel Blend ★★★ £D
Tzora Vineyards
Recommended Reds: Stone Hill Vineyard Estate Reserve ★★★ £D
Ilan Misty Hills ★★★ £D

Lebanon
Château Ksara
Recommended Reds: Château Ksara Rouge ★★★ £C
Château Marsyas
Recommended Reds:
Château Marsyas (Cab Sauv/Syrah/Merlot) ★★★☆ £D

Syria
Bargylus
Recommended Reds:
Bargylus (Cab Sauv/Syrah/Merlot) ★★★☆ £D

Turkey
Pendore Okuzgozu Bogazkere
Recommended Reds: Okuzgoru Bogazkere ★★☆ £C
Syrah ★★★☆ £D
Chamlija Winery (Thrace)
Recommended Reds:
Cabernet Sauvignon ★★ £C
Recommended Whites:
Sauvignon Blanc ★★☆ £B
Kastrotireli (Izmir)
Recommended Reds:
Syrah/Mourvédre ★★★ £C

Georgia
Orovela
Recommended Reds: Saperavi ★★★★ £E

India
York Winery (Maharastra)
Recommended Whites: Chenin Blanc ★☆ £B
Grover Zampa (Nandi Hills)
Recommended Whites: Viognier Art Series ★★☆ £B
Sula Vineyards (Nashik Valley)
Recommended Reds: Shiraz ★★★ £C

Morocco
Cahina
Recommended Reds: Cahina ★★★ £E

Other Europe, North Africa, Middle East & Asia

France

Lumière
Recommended Reds: Guerrouane Cuvée Lumière ★★★☆ £F

Algeria
Dom. de Saint Augustin
Recommended Reds: Côteaux de Tlemcen Cuvée Monica ★★★ £E

Dynamic pace among small, high-quality wine producers is evident throughout California, and this is as much the case here as elsewhere in the state. As well as the more established cooler areas like the Russian River, new vineyards are now being developed on the Sonoma Coast with great success. Wine prices remain buoyant – a wealthy local market combined with scarcity among the top wines ensures this. There are great Cabernets here but this is generally Chardonnay and Pinot Noir territory, with some exceptional Zinfandel in warmer sites. Some magnificent wines, yes, but without the stratospheric prices of the Napa Valley collectors' Cabernets.

Geography

The North Coast of California is a vast area. It takes in Mendocino and Lake Counties, over 100 miles to the north of San Francisco, as well as Sonoma County, which runs southwards west of the Mayacamas Mountains and then takes in the western end of Carneros. The whole viticultural area is encompassed under the **North Coast** AVA. What enables such diverse vinegrowing is cool breezes and sea fogs that drift in through coastal gaps. The most significant of these – the Petaluma gap – provides an effective cooling fan for the vast Sonoma vineyard, north and south of the town of Santa Rosa. It is only thanks to these cooling breezes and sea fogs, which dominate the summer months along the state's coastline all the way south towards Santa Barbara, that fine wine production is possible in California at all.

Mendocino and Lake Counties

Mendocino is a large, sprawling vinegrowing area, mostly cool and suitable for Pinot Noir and Chardonnay. The **Anderson Valley**, which opens up to the ocean, produces a number of restrained, stylish examples and is also an excellent source of sparkling wine. To the north-east are the warmer AVAs of **Redwood Valley** and **Potter Valley**. Some increasingly impressive Syrah, Zinfandel and Cabernet are grown here. Lake County and the **Clear Lake** AVA, **Guenoc** and **Benmore Valley** sub-AVAs are located to the east, across the Mayacamas Mountains. Clear Lake and Guenoc are best-suited to growing reds – Cabernet Sauvignon and Zinfandel – as well as a ripe style of Chardonnay and Sauvignon Blanc. Benmore Valley by contrast is significantly cooled by elevation and provides tighter, more restrained Chardonnay.

Northern Sonoma

This is really the heartland of North Coast vinegrowing and it includes the warm red-grape areas of **Dry Creek Valley** and **Alexander Valley** to the northeast. These are located to the west and east respectively of the meandering northern sections of the Russian River which runs through the towns of Asti, Geyserville and Healdsburg. Tremendous Zinfandel and Syrah can be found in both AVAs. Excellent restrained Chardonnay, structured Cabernet and meritage styles are all sourced from the higher mountain slopes of the Alexander Valley. To the immediate east of here is the **Knights Valley**, source of some first-class Chardonnay and Cabernet Sauvignon. **Chalk Hill** AVA is just to the south and is dominated by the winery of the same name. South of Healdsburg the considerable expanse of the **Russian River Valley** AVA opens out. To the far west on the Sonoma coast some very impressive Chardonnay and Pinot Noir is now being produced and takes the **Sonoma Coast** AVA. The Russian River area is now very well established as a source of exemplary Pinot Noir and Chardonnay and, in the warmer eastern sites, very good Syrah and Zinfandel. To the south-west is the distinctly cool. **Green Valley of Russian River Valley** AVA, a source

of top-quality sparkling wines and restrained styles of Chardonnay and Pinot Noir. Just to the south of Santa Rosa and nestled into the Sonoma Mountains is the **Bennett Valley** appellation which is an exciting source of both Pinot Noir and Chardonnay and some fine Syrah and Merlot.

Sonoma Valley

The **Sonoma Valley** AVA itself is located to the south of Santa Rosa and is home to some of the largest producers on the North Coast. The valley is bordered by the Mayacamas range to the east and the Sonoma Mountains to the west. The appellation runs from north to south-east through the towns of Oakmount, Kenwood, Glen Ellen and Sonoma itself. The western range has its own AVA, **Sonoma Mountain**, and provides impressive examples of restrained Chardonnay, Pinot Noir and Cabernet Sauvignon. In general the better reds are planted in the warmer northern sections of the AVA while the southern sector that borders Carneros produces stylish whites but also good Pinot Noir. Some of the best and sturdiest Cabernet blends and Zinfandels are sourced from the higher slopes leading into the Mayacamas Mountains.

A-Z of producers by region

California North Coast

California

Green Valley of Russian River		**Sonoma Valley**		Landmark	703	St Francis Vineyards	710
Hartford	701	Arrowood	695	Lioco Wines	704	Verité	711
Hartford Court	701	Chateau St Jean	697	David Noyes	706	**Other**	
Iron Horse	702	Hanzell	701	Ravenswood	707	Thackrey & Co	711
Marimar Torres	711	Kamen Estate	702	Spann Vineyards	709		

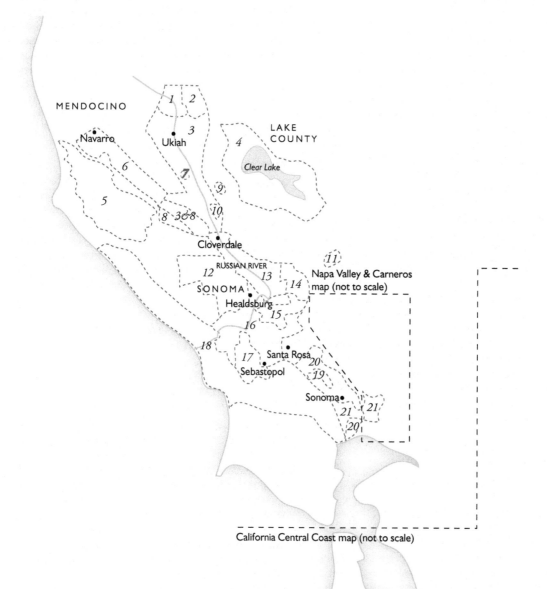

California North Coast vintage chart

	Pinot Noir	Chardonnay	Zinfandel	Cabernet Sauvignon
2015	★★★★☆ A	★★★★☆ A	★★★★☆ A	★★★★☆ A
2014	★★☆ A	★★★★ A	★★★★☆ A	★★★★ A
2013	★★★★☆ A	★★★★☆ A	★★★★☆ A	★★★★ A
2012	★★☆ B	★★★★ B	★★★★☆ A	★★★★ A
2011	★★☆ B	★★☆ B	★★☆ B	★★★ A
2010	★★★ B	★★★ B	★★☆ B	★★☆ B
2009	★★★★☆ B	★★★★☆ B	★★★★☆ B	★★★★ B
2008	★★★☆ B	★★★☆ C	★★★★ B	★★★★ B
2007	★★★★ B	★★★★ B	★★★☆ B	★★★★☆ B
2006	★★★☆ C	★★★☆ C	★★★ C	★★★★ B
2005	★★★★ C	★★★★ C	★★★ C	★★★★ C
2004	★★★★ C	★★★★ C	★★★ C	★★★★ C
2003	★★★★ C	★★★★ C	★★★★ C	★★★★ C
2002	★★★★ C	★★★★ C	★★★ C	★★★★☆ C
2001	★★★★ C	★★★★ C	★★★★ C	★★★★☆ C
2000	★★★☆ D	★★★☆ D	★★★ D	★★☆ D
1999	★★★★ D	★★★★ D	★★★★ D	★★★☆ C
1998	★★★★ D	★★★★ D	★★☆ D	★★★ C
1997	★★★★ D	★★★★ D	★★★☆ D	★★★★ D
1996			★★★☆ D	★★★☆ D
1995				★★★★☆ D
1994				★★★★☆ D

A-Z of producers

🌢 **Adrian Fog (Russian River Valley)** *www.adrianfog.com*
This is a small Pinot Noir only operation producing wines of very high quality. As well as the Oppenlander Pinot wine has also been released from the Two Sisters vineyard in the Russian River Valley, the Sonoma Coast Hunnicutt Vineyard which comes from a site just a few miles inland of the coast and the Savoy Vineyard in the Anderson Valley. The Oppenlander Vineyard provides a wine of remarkable depth and persistence. The site is planted to a range of clones adding to the wines potential complexity. The climate is cool with the vineyard planted at significant altitude. This shows in a wine which is tight and structured. Subtle blueberry fruit needs time to express itself. A very low volume barrel selection (less than 100 cases) is also made and labelled "Monster". All the wines are aged in a mix of new and used oak and are bottled unfined and unfiltered. (DM)

Recommended Reds:
Pinot Noir Oppenlander Vineyard Mendocino County ★★★★★ £F

Arrowood (Sonoma Valley) *www.arrowoodvineyards.com*
Dick Arrowood has sold his interest in this medium-sized operation which is now a part of the Jackson Family wine estates portfolio. The wines themselves are all sourced from Sonoma Valley fruit. The wines are all now released under the Arrowood label. There is a fairly extensive range of bottlings: classy citrusy Chardonnay from Sonoma County as well as Chardonnay and Cabernet Sauvignon under the Réserve Spéciale label. Single vineyard Chardonnay also comes from the Russian River Alary Ranch. Malbec, Merlot and Rhône styles are of equal importance, the best of which are from Saralee's Vineyard. The Arrowood range is completed by a number of additional single vineyard Cabernets, which like the Réserve

Spéciale are fairly pricey (£F-G). (DM)

Recommended Reds:
Cabernet Sauvignon Réserve Spéciale Sonoma County ★★★★ £G
Syrah Saralee's Vineyard Russian River Valley ★★★★ £F
Syrah Sonoma Valley ★★★☆ £E
Cabernet Sauvignon Sonoma County ★★★ £F

Recommended Whites:
Chardonnay Sonoma County ★★★☆ £D
Viognier Saralee's Vineyard Russian River Valley ★★★ £E

Bella Vineyards (Dry Creek Valley) *www.bellawinery.com*
This small Dry Creek operation has the benefit of some very old Zinfandel and the wines offer excellent value. The Adams, who began making wine in 1999, farm a number of vineyards in the Dry Creek and Alexander Valleys. Winemaking input comes from former RIDGE winemaker Michael Dashe who also makes wine under his own Dashe Cellars label. At the winery site caves for cellaring the wine provide an ideal temperature and humidity controlled environment for the cellars. There is a spicy and exuberant rosé which is blended from Syrah and Cabernet Sauvignon. More serious though are the reds. Small quantities are also produced of Petite Sirah and some additional single vineyard Syrah and Zin. The Big River Ranch Syrah is a blend of all three vineyards and is a vibrant, forward example with ripe spicy licorice fruit and hints of black pepper. The Alexander Valley Zinfandel includes some very old vine fruit and is supple, ripe and forward with a rich, silky texture. The Big River Ranch single vineyard bottling is firmer and more structured but still possesses copious quantities of dark, spicy fruit. This and the Syrah will develop well with five years ageing. A range of limited release wines are also available direct from the tasting room. (DM)

Recommended Reds:
Syrah Big River Ranch Alexander Valley ★★★★ £E
Syrah Sonoma Valley ★★★☆ £E
Zinfandel Big River Ranch Alexander Valley ★★★★ £E
Zinfandel Alexander Valley ★★★ £D

Recommended Rosés:
Rosé Sonoma County ★★ £D

>> Benovia (Russian River Valley) *www.benoviawinery.com*
Benovia is a relative newcomer, founded in 2003 when Joe Anderson and Mary Dewane bought the Cohn Vineyard, followed by the Martaellen Vineyard in 2005 complete with winery, (both in the Russian River AVA) and more recently the cool climate Tilton Hill vineyard (Sonoma Coast) which has just had its first release (2012 Pinot Noir) in late 2014. Mike Sullivan co-owns the winery and is responsible for the winemaking and the day to day management of the estate. Between their own vineyards and other bought in fruit from high quality neighbouring vineyards they produce just a few hundred cases of each of their 8 wines currently available. What perhaps sets them apart from other producers is the judicious use of oak, less than 24 months in oak and perhaps more importantly, between 21% and 46% of new oak used in the maturation process which provides a clear stamp of balance and finesse without being weedy and "too French"! Chardonnay and Pinot Noir are the mainstay of their operation with a little Zinfandel from the Cohn vineyard's 40 plus year old vines. There is high octane Russian River Valley Chardonnay from the Martaellen vineyard, which has now gone over to organic farming, a beautifully balanced combination of citrus and stone fruits – refined and restrained but unmistakably Californian. La Pommeraie Chardonnay from George Martinelli's vineyard is on a par with great balance between fruit and acidity

and a long finish. Seaview Chardonnay from Lee Martinelli's Charles vineyard is the tightest of the three, needing perhaps at least 5 years cellaring before its complex aromas come to the fore and is a little less intense than the other two. The Cohn Vineyard Pinot Noir is the pick of the bunch from vines planted in the 1970s and now producing intense, ripe and complex nuances of judiciously oaked red fruit. There is a Russian River blend from the Martaellen, Cohn, Martinelli and Tilton vineyards which is their biggest production (1780 cases) with perhaps not the same amount of finesse and complexity as the Cohn, but nevertheless amongst the best of Californian Pinot Noirs. The single vineyard Martaellen Russian River Pinot Noir sits between the two in weight and complexity. La Pommeraie Pinot Noir is a little more lightweight and less intense. The Zinfandel is a model of restraint with harmonious brambly fruit and a long finish. Not tasted are the Tilton Hill single vineyard Pinot Noir (first release) and a Grenache from Mike Sullivan's family vineyard but as only 74 cases of the Grenache 2012 were made, you will need to fall over yourselves to get some when it is released in the spring of 2015. (NB)

Recommended Reds:
Pinot Noir Cohn Vineyard ★★★★★ £F
Pinot Noir Russian River Valley ★★★★ £E
Pinot Noir Martaellen ★★★★ £F
Pinot Noir La Pommeraie ★★★☆ £F
Zinfandel Sonoma County ★★★★ £E
Recommended Whites:
Chardonnay Russian River Valley ★★★★☆ £E
Chardonnay La Pommeraie ★★★★☆ £E
Chardonnay Seaview ★★★★ £E

Benziger (Sonoma Mountain) *www.benziger.com*
Large, family-run operation producing an extensive range of wines from vineyards that are farmed using sustainable practices. The best are very good and by comparison with many other California examples offer good value. The family also owns the Imagery Estate winery, which sells a good-quality range Syrah, Sangiovese, Mourvèdre and a white blend at the tasting room only. Sonoma County wines are approachable and good value and there are numerous limited-production, vineyard-designated wines made, with some of the vineyards farmed biodynamically. (DM)
Recommended Reds:
Cabernet Sauvignon Sonoma County ★★☆ £C
Recommended Whites:
Chardonnay Pratt Vineyard Russian River Valley ★★★ £E
Sauvignon Blanc North Coast ★★☆ £C

>> Bevan Cellars (Sonoma County) *www.bevancellars.com*
Russell Bevan is a perfect example of passion and dogged pursuit of perfection paying off. While living in the Midwest, he and his business and life partner, Victoria, took trips to California in pursuit of their love of wine. Soon they were meeting the most fascinating winemakers, vintners and growers. Bevan credits the venerable Philip Togni and Greg LaFollette as his early inspirations. Soon they were searching for their own property, eventually acquiring eight acres in Bennett Valley. The sought advice from the well-known and vintner Kal Showket. Kal offered Russell a ton of his Cabernet Sauvignon to test his winemaking prowess… the rest, as they say, is history. Bevan has several high-profile consulting projects; his mainstay, however, is his own brand, Bevan Cellars, that has been winning critics and consumers since the beginning. His winemaking at its core is all about texture and tannin management,

achieved mainly by watchful eye during the growing season, as well as extended maceration/cold soak techniques in the cellar. The portfolio is extensive, ranging from a Sauvignon Blanc with "cult-like" following, to RRV Chardonnays, Sonoma Coast Pinot Noirs and several reds, dominated by a 5-strong portfolio of vineyard-designated Cabernet Sauvignons. All the wines are made from carefully hand-picked, top-notch vineyards in Napa and Sonoma. The Tin Box Vineyard, located in Oakville is a stunning wine. Deep, dark and immensely enticing, it is crafted from old vines and will cellar for several decades. Bench Vineyard, located in Stag's leap, boasts classic SLD flavor profiles and rich mouthfeel. Boxer's fist in a velvet glove, it's a yet another perfect example of age-worthy Napa Cab. (IT)
Recommended Reds:
Cabernet Sauvignon Tin Box Vineyard Oakville ✪✪✪✪✪ £H
Cabernet Sauvignon Bench Vineyard Stags Leap District ★★★★★ £G
Cabernet Sauvignon McGah Vineyard Rutherford ★★★★☆ £G
Cabernet Sauvignon Wildfoote Stags Leap District ★★★★☆ £G
Recommended Whites:
Sauvignon Blanc Dry Stack Vineyard Bennett Valley ★★★★ £F

✿ Carlisle (Russian River Valley) *www.carlislewinery.com*
Mike Officer is making some of the most exuberant and characterful Zinfandel in California, mainly from single vineyard sources and very old vine plantings. He is also fast becoming a regional benchmark for Syrah. As with many of the best small producers in Sonoma he is warehouse based. As well as the wines rated below Mike also makes a Sonoma County Syrah and a Sonoma County Zinfandel as well as a plethora of other single vineyard examples and Rhône styled red blends which occasionally vary vintage to vintage. Recent vintages have seen the addition of whites; a Grüner Veltliner from the Sonoma Mountain Steiner Vineyard and a couple of blends. Derivative combines Sémillon, Muscadelle and Palomino. Compagni Portis is a mixed field blend including Gewürztraminer, Trousseau Gris, Riesling and a number of other varieties. Expect these to be of a uniformly high standard and the appellation wines a touch easier on your wallet although the value to quality ratio here is extremely good. A number of very good Zinfandels are produced from single vineyard sources. Most of these sites were planted up to and over a century ago by Italian immigrants. Often the Zinfandel is interplanted with other varieties which undoubtedly adds complexity and character to Russian River examples. The dry-farmed Bacchi Ranch comes from the northern "Crucible" of the Russian River, Dry Creek and Alexander Valleys. The wine is ripe, spicy and with all the super concentration and jammy characteristics of low-yielding, warm grown Zin. Perhaps the finest example, with the greatest purity of fruit, is that from the home Carlisle Vineyard. Almost 100% Zinfandel the wine offers an elegance and freshness less evident in the other wines. The Two Acres Red comes from a vineyard planted in 1910 and planted to an unusual mix of Mourvèdre, Mondeuse, Petite Sirah, Syrah, Carignane, Peloursin and Alicante Bouschet. There are also a few Zinfandel vines and a cross of Zinfandel and Mondeuse, Helena. The wine is loaded with dark berry fruit and oriental spices and would make for an interesting comparison with the very greatest of Bandol. Syrah emerges in a number of guises. The Dry Creek Valley wine is perhaps the fattest and most opulent. Rich, spicy fruit and black pepper are all in evidence. The Papa's Block bottling, is picked late, at the beginning of November and is more structured and refined with a lovely pure minerality to its fruit. Last to come in is the Bennett Valley Syrah, it offers more elegance and a marvellous depth and persistence of

fruit. All of these wines are ageworthy, in particular the Syrahs and all are well worth seeking out.. (DM)

Recommended Reds:
Syrah Papa's Block Russian River Valley ★★★★★ £F
Syrah Bennett Valley ★★★★★ £F
Syrah Dry Creek Valley ★★★★☆ £E
Two Acres Red Two Acres Vineyard Russian River Valley ★★★★★ £F
Zinfandel Carlisle Vineyard Russian River Valley ★★★★★ £E
Zinfandel Bacchi Ranch Russian River Valley ★★★★☆ £E
Zinfandel Dry Creek Valley ★★★★☆ £E

Chalk Hill Winery (Chalk Hill) *www.chalkhill.com*
This producer, now owned by Bill Foley who owns FOLEY and LINCOURT in Santa Barbara County, unusually possesses its own AVA and has been for many years committed to maximising the quality of the fruit from estate vineyards. The whites are made in a full, ripe style with judicious use of new oak for both Sauvignon and the richly textured Estate Chardonnay. Chardonnay from the Russian River, Syrah and a Pinot Noir Estate have also added to the range. The reds express attractive, berry fruit character. A small production of a rich and luscious botrytised Sémillon Chairman's Selection is produced when vintage conditions permit. (DM)

Recommended Reds:
Estate Red Chalk Hill ★★★★ £F

Recommended Whites:
Chardonnay Estate Chalk Hill ★★★☆ £E
Sauvignon Blanc Chalk Hill ★★★ £D

Chateau St Jean (Sonoma Valley) *www.chateaustjean.com*
The original and striking 'Chateau' here was built in 1920, pre-Prohibition. The current winery was founded in 1973 and the estate comprises some 100 ha (250 acres), of which 32 ha (80 acres) are planted to vines. These, along with three additional vineyards, Robert Young, Belle Terre and La Petite Etoile, provide the foundation for the fine Reserve and vineyard-designated wines. Sonoma County wines are all well-priced and regularly offer good to very good-value drinking. A number of speciality and limited-release wines are sold exclusively at the tasting room.(DM)

Recommended Reds:
Pinot Noir Sonoma County ★★ £C
Merlot Sonoma County ★★ £C

Recommended Whites:
Chardonnay Belle Terre Vineyard Alexander Valley ★★★ £D
Chardonnay Sonoma County ★★ £C
Fumé Blanc La Petite Etoile Russian River Valley ★★★ £C
Fumé Blanc Sonoma County ★★☆ £C
Gewürztraminer Sonoma County ★★☆ £C

Clos du Bois (Alexander Valley) *www.closdubois.com*
Large-volume winery producing close to half a million cases annually. The straightforward Sonoma Classic range, mainly under the North Coast AVA, is the mainstay of the winery but they can be impressive. Appellation Reserve wines are a step up, but it is the vineyard-designated and Winemakers Reserve cuvées which are the benchmarks here. Winemakers Reserve Cabernet and Marlstone in particular are dense, concentrated and well structured, the latter a blend of Cabernet Sauvignon, Merlot, Cabernet Franc, Malbec and Petit Verdot from the vineyard of the same name. For value and style the two top Chardonnays are subtly oaked, with good citrusy, leesy depth and a certain finesse.(DM)

Recommended Reds:
Cabernet Sauvignon Winemakers Reserve Alexander Valley ★★★☆ £F
Cabernet Sauvignon Briarcrest Vineyard Alexander Valley ★★★ £F
Marlstone Alexander Valley ★★★☆ £F
Tempranillo Reserve Alexander Valley ★★☆ £E

Recommended Whites:
Chardonnay Calcaire Russian River Valley ★★★ £D
Chardonnay Reserve Russian River Valley ★★★ £D

Collier Falls (Dry Creek Valley) *www.collierfalls.com*
Collier Falls Vineyard was originally planted with 8 acres (3.2 ha) of Zinfandel in 1982. When Barry and Susan Collier bought the Vineyard in 1991, they added a further 11 acres (4.5 ha) of Zinfandel, Petite Sirah and Primitivo and 7 acres (2.8 ha) of Cabernet Sauvignon, Cabernet Franc and Petit Verdot. The wines are lush and alcoholic and winemaker Mike Lancaster ages in both French and American oak to give the wines a distinctive Californian style. There are vintage variations and Zinfandel can easily be 15.5% of abv and their Primitivo is even higher with 16.5% which perhaps masks the fruit a little more than the Zinfandels. Nevertheless, there is a distinct rasiny fruit result with tastes of dried currants and nutmeg coming through. A late harvest Primitivo disappoints by being neither sweet enough or fruity enough and with its nuances of Earl Gray tea would be difficult to match with any food. (NB)

Recommended Reds:
Zinfandel Dry Creek Valley ★★★☆ £F
Primitivo Dry Creek Valley ★★★☆ £E
Late-Harvest Primitivo Dry Creek Valley ★★ £E
Cabernet Sauvignon Dry Creek Valley ★★★☆ £F

✿ Dehlinger (Russian River Valley) *www.dehlingerwinery.com*
Dehlinger remains among the very top echelon in the Russian River, continually crafting outstanding unfiltered Pinot Noir, Syrah and Chardonnay. Cabernet Sauvignon does not quite hit the same heady heights, although it is rich, structured and impressive in top years. There are quantities of single-vineyard Pinot Noir from the Goldridge site but availability is very limited but well worth seeking out, as is the East Face Syrah. The reds are not only powerful and structured but very refined as well, and will drink well in the medium term. (DM)

Recommended Reds:
Pinot Noir Estate Russian River Valley ★★★★☆ £F
Syrah Estate Russian River Valley ★★★★☆ £F
Cabernet Sauvignon Estate Russian River Valley ★★★★ £F

Recommended Whites:
Chardonnay Estate Russian River Valley ★★★★ £E

>> Donelan Family Vineyards *www.donelanwines.com*
The Donelan Family produce an extensive range of small batch wines throughout Sonoma County from their Santa Rosa base including wines from Chardonnay, Pinot Noir, Syrah, Grenache, and Roussanne. They work with four key sites; Obsidian (Knights Valley), Richard's Family Vineyard (Sonoma Valley), Kobler Vineyard (Green Valley of the Russian River Valley) and Walker Vine Hill Vineyard (Russian River Valley). Some quite exceptional Syrah comes from a range of sources. All are dark fruited, spicy and offer tremendous depth, rich fruit and concentration. A further Rhône style Moriah combines almost all Grenache with a little Syrah, much in the manner of a plush, fleshy modern Châteauunf- du-Pape. Pinot Noir is very good if not quite at the level of the Syrah's. As well as a fine, restrained Chardonnay, the Venus white comes from Roussanne and

California North Coast

Viognier. (DM)

Recommended Reds:

Syrah Obsidian Vineyard Russian River Valley ★★★★★ £G

Syrah Cuvée Keltie Sonoma County ★★★★★ £G

Syrah Walker Vine Hill Vineyard Russian River Valley ★★★★★ £F

Syrah Kobler Family Vineyard Russian River Valley ★★★★☆ £F

Syrah Cuvée Christine Sonoma County ★★★★☆ £F

Cuvée Moriah Sonoma County ★★★★☆ £F

Pinot Noir Two Brothers Russian River Valley ★★★★☆ £F

Recommended Whites:

Chardonnay Nancie Sonoma County ★★★★☆ £F

Venus Sonoma County ★★★★☆ £F

Dry Creek Vineyard (Dry Creek Valley) www.drycreekvineyard.com
Medium-sized winery notable for good, well-priced Fumé Blanc
in a very much more herbaceous style than many and a number
of rich and impressive Zinfandels. The latter have been produced
consistently over a number of vintages and while full and vibrant
they are rarely overblown. With old-vine Zinfandel fruit increasingly
in demand throughout the state, Dry Creek has established its own
'Heritage' clone, propagated from old-vine cuttings on phylloxera-
resistant rootstock. A small quantity of premium Cabernet both a
Sailor's Hill and Endeavour have also been released along with single
vineyard Zinfandel from the Dry Creek Valley Spencer's Hill Vineyard
as well as from the Beeson and Somers Ranches.(DM)

Recommended Reds:

Zinfandel Old Vine Sonoma County ★★★☆ £D

Zinfandel Heritage Clone Sonoma County ★★★ £C

Merlot Dry Creek Valley ★★ £D

Cabernet Sauvignon Dry Creek Valley ★★ £D

Recommended Whites:

Chardonnay Estate Block 10 Russian River Valley ★★☆ £D

Fumé Blanc Sonoma County ★★☆ £C

✿ DuMOL (Russian River Valley) www.dumol.com
Some very good Burgundian style wines are produced here along
with a couple of excellent Syrahs. Much of the fruit comes from
Russian River Valley vineyards. The wines are themselves labelled
by individual brands rather than by vineyards with the exception
of Pinot and Chardonnay releases from the DuMOL estate
vineyard. Stylistically the wines are very structured and require
a little patience. The area's climate provides grapes with ample
richness and concentration. Chardonnay is barrel-fermented and
aged on lees for 18 months and natural yeasts are relied on for
both fermentation and the malolactic. The Isobel is impressively
structured coming from the Charles Heintz Vineyard in the Russian
River. The style of the wine is achieved by combining both an
early and a later harvest ensuring excellent acidity as well as
underlying richness. The Chloe *cuvée* comes from the Ritchie,
which is some distance inland. The wine has a marvellous balance
of intense fruit, real weight and concentration all underpinned by
a mineral purity. Of the Pinot bottlings, the Aidan is opulent and
impressively rich coming solely from Dijon clones. The Ryan is a
touch more structured. Both offer concentrated dark plum and
berry fruit and the mineral purity that characterises all the wines
here. Aidan is touch more gamey, Ryan more floral and aromatic.
The best of the Pinots is Finn which comes from two Russian River
vineyards: Occidental Road and the DuMOL estate site. The wine has
excellent acidity and fruit of great intensity with a rich dark-cherry
fruit character. All the wines get a cold soak for five days and are
fermented with native yeasts with malolactic in barrel. Eddie's Patch

Syrah is sourced from steep east facing hillside slopes providing
fruit of very impressive intensity. It is the most complete but both
examples are very full and concentrated with dark, spicy blackberry
fruit and a mineral edge. In addition to the above, Russian River
Pinot Noir, Syrah and Chardonnay are produced as well as a Viognier,
Lia which is vinified without malolactic, a Chardonnay Clare from
the Hyde Vineyard in Carneros and a further Pinot Noir Eoin which
comes from the Sonoma Stage Vineyard on the Sonoma Coast. The
wines will develop very well, the Syrahs for a decade and more.(DM)

Recommended Reds:

Pinot Noir Finn Russian River Valley ★★★★★ £G

Pinot Noir Aidan Russian River Valley ★★★★☆ £G

Pinot Noir Ryan Russian River Valley ★★★★☆ £G

Syrah Eddie's Patch Russian River Valley ★★★★★ £F

Syrah Jack Robert's Run Russian River Valley ★★★★☆ £F

Recommended Whites:

Chardonnay Chloe Russian River Valley ★★★★★ £G

Chardonnay Isobel Russian River Valley ★★★★☆ £F

Dutton-Goldfield (Russian River Valley) www.duttongoldfield.com
Very impressive Chardonnay and Pinot Noir from a range of sites,
mostly in the cool Green Valley. Chardonnay and Pinot Noir are both
sourced from the cooler Dutton Ranch, which is family owned. The
east-facing Rued Vineyard is planted to Chardonnay now over 40
years old. The resulting wine has both a firm structure and subtle
minerality underpinning its lightly piercing tropical, citrus fruit. The
Dutton Ranch bottling is more obviously fruit-driven without quite
the depth or persistence. Both wines are barrel-fermented on lees
from a mix of natural and added yeasts. Of the Pinots, McDougall
Vineyard from the northwestern Sonoma Coast and the Dutton
Ranch are the most obviously cool climate, with the McDougall
bottling offering impressive depth and intensity. Fuller and more
marked by dark plum fruit is the Devil's Gulch Ranch from some of
the steepest, lowest-yielding protected vineyards in Marin County.
Pinot Noir also now comes from three other sources; Angel Camp
Vineyard in the Anderson Valley, the Azaya Ranch in Marin County
and the Dutton Ranch Emerald Ridge Vineyard in the Green Valley.
Additional releases include Zinfandel from the Russian River Morelli
Lane Vineyard, a red blend of Syrah, Zinfandel and Pinot Noir,
Spectrum Red, a Pinot Blanc labelled Shop Block, A Riesling from the
Chileno Valley Vineyard in Marin County and a very late harvested
Riesling, Sticky Finish from the same site. The Pinots get 5–7 days'
cold soaking to lift their fruit and all the wines are bottled with
minimal processing and will benefit from 3–5 years' ageing. (DM)

Recommended Reds:

Pinot Noir Devil's Gulch Ranch Marin County ★★★★ £F

Pinot Noir McDougall Vineyard Sonoma Coast ★★★★ £F

Pinot Noir Dutton Ranch Russian River Valley ★★★★ £F

Recommended Whites:

Chardonnay Dutton Ranch Rued Vineyard Green Valley ★★★★ £E

Chardonnay Dutton Ranch Russian River Valley ★★★☆ £E

Edmeades (Anderson Valley) www.edmeades.com
Mendocino-based winery, producing an extensive range of full,
brambly Zinfandels as well as a Gewürztraminer. The Mendocino
vineyards for the Zinfandel are above the coastal fog line and the
warm sunny days are complemented by cool nights, providing
good acidity for structured wines. They are typically big and brawny,
offering weight and power rather than finesse. They are vinified
using wild yeast fermentation and, as in all the best Jackson family
wines, handling is kept to a minimum and fining and filtration

eschewed. The focus is now on single-vineyard Zins. Top cuvées can be very impressive. (DM)

Recommended Reds:

Zinfandel Mendocino ★★★ £C

Merry Edwards (Russian River Valley) *www.merryedwards.com*
Merry Edwards has been working with wine since 1974 and produces a small and impeccable range of Pinot Noir, Chardonnay and Sauvignon Blanc. She is now very aware that this is the era of the winegower and not the winemaker and her wines reflect this. A dry Sauvignon Blanc is produced from Russian River fruit. The wine is almost piercingly gooseberry scented but has magnificent structure being fermented and aged in small French oak, a small proportion of which is new and lees stirring is employed. A late harvested version is also made and there is a Chardonnay from Olivet Lane. There are now eight different Pinot Noir bottlings with a number of single vineyard examples, and in addition to those listed below are wines from her own Meredith Estate and Coopersmith vineyards, as well as from the Flax and Georganne Russian River sites. The simplest and most accessible is the Sonoma Coast wine which is marked by its cool climate coastal *terroir* with intense red cherry fruit. A high proportion of new oak is used but is brilliantly integrated. The Russian River Valley wine is more opulent in style with a cold soak pre-fermentation and a richly supple texture. It will drink very well young. Some superb single vineyard wines are also produced. The Olivet Lane example is very finely structured with a piercing red cherry character. By contrast, the Klopp Ranch bottling is much fuller and loaded with rich plummy fruit and a real savoury character. Like all the wines here a cold soak is employed adding depth and substance. (DM)

Recommended Reds:

Pinot Noir Klopp Ranch Russian River Valley ★★★★ £F
Pinot Noir Olivet Lane Russian River Valley ★★★★ £F
Pinot Noir Russian River Valley ★★★☆ £E
Pinot Noir Sonoma Coast ★★★ £E

Recommended Whites:

Sauvignon Blanc Russian River Valley ★★★ £D

>> Emeritus Vineyards *www.emeritusvineyards.com*
Former SONOMA-CUTRER owner Brice Jones continued with his love of Pinot Noir by purchasing a 115 acre Russian River Valley apple orchard from Don and Marcia Hallberg two miles north of Sebastopol and immediately began to plant Pinot Noir vines. He had also purchased a plot of land on the Sonoma Coast near Annapolis which he was convinced would be ideal for Pinot Noir and named it the William Wesley vineyard. In 2004 he persuaded Pinot Noir specialist Don Blackburn to come on board as the winemaker. Unfortunately, Don passed away just after the 2008 harvest and his assistant, French born Nicolas Cantacuzane stepped into the breach and has remained the head winemaker up to today. A combination of an American born, French trained winemaker and a French born American trained winemaker has led to the production of balanced wines displaying a great deal of finesse. The Hallberg Ranch Pinot Noir is comfortably delicate whilst displaying vibrant fruit and a good streak of balancing acidity as well as being well priced for the quality. There are some other special releases (not tasted) getting up to the £G price category, but one should be more than content with the vineyard designated Pinot Noir *per se*. (NB)

Recommended Reds:

Pinot Noir Hallberg Ranch ★★★★☆ £E

Gary Farrell (Russian River Valley) *www.garyfarrellwinery.com*
This winery has become notable for stylish, elegant Chardonnay and Pinot Noir with the wines being made now by Theresa Heredia who moved from the Joseph PHELPS owned Sonoma County Freestone Winery. The Rochioli vineyard remains an important source of fruit here for both varieties. An increasing number of vineyard designates have also added and in addition to the wines covered below both varieties are sourced from the Russian River Bacigalupi Vineyard. Pinot Noir also comes from the Bien Nacido Vineyard, as well as from the Hallberg, Stiling and Toboni Vineyards in the Russian River. Further Chardonnay is made from Westside Farms again in the Russian River, the Durell Vineyard in the Sonoma Valley and Russian River Selection Syrah and Sauvignon Blanc are also produced as well as a second Zinfandel from the Russian River Maffei Vineyard. Chardonnay is made in a rich, tropical style but with well-judged oak, while Pinot is ripe, full and packed with dark plum and berry fruit. Zinfandel is good but not quite at the level of the Chardonnays and Pinots. (DM)

Recommended Reds:

Pinot Noir Rochioli-Allen Vineyard Russian River Valley ★★★★ £F
Pinot Noir Rochioli Vineyard Russian River Valley ★★★★ £F
Pinot Noir Selection Russian River Valley ★★★ £E
Zinfandel Bradford Mountain Dry Creek Valley ★★★ £E

Recommended Whites:

Chardonnay Rochioli-Allen Vineyard Russian River Valley ★★★★ £F
Chardonnay Rochioli Vineyard Russian River Valley ★★★★ £F
Chardonnay Selection Russian River Valley ★★★ £D

⚫ Fisher Vineyards (Russian River Valley) *www.fishervineyards.com*
The Fishers run one of the longest-established properties in the region, founded in 1973, producing top class reds and whites from some superbly sited high density vineyards in both Sonoma and Napa. Of the two great single-vineyard Cabernets, the Napa Valley-sourced Lamb Vineyard bottling is marginally richer, more chocolaty. The Sonoma County Wedding Vineyard offers a touch more elegance with a fine minty undercurrent. Most accessible of the reds is the RCF Vineyard Merlot from the Napa – rich, forward and fruit driven with dark, spicy plum fruit and supple tannins. The Cameron Red is a varying blend dominated by Cabernet Sauvignon (sometimes produced as a varietal) and complemented by Merlot and Malbec. Sourced from the Fishers' youngest Napa Valley vines, it offers a fine balance of opulent berry fruit, nicely judged new wood and impressive persistence. The blackcurrant- and tobacco-scented Coach Insignia Cabernet Sauvignon is blended with a little Merlot with fruit coming from the north-east of the valley along the Pallisade Mountains and the eastern hills above Oakville as well as some Merlot from Sonoma Mountain. Chardonnay is both very impressive and well priced. The firm structure of both bottlings is achieved by using fruit grown at altitude and partial malolactic fermentation. The Whitneys Vineyard has just a touch more citrus intensity and depth but both will develop well with 4 or 5 years' age. A further Cabernet is produced from the Mountain Estate vineyard, the 1 5 7 Merlot comes from Sonoma County and is blended with a little Merlot and a Syrah Hidden Terrace Vineyard is also made from the south facing slopes of the wineries Mountain Estate site. A second label UNITY is also a source of well priced Cabernet, Pinot Noir, Chardonnay and a rosé (Pinot Noir, Syrah and Malbec) from a range of vineyard sources throughout the Napa, Sonoma and Mendocino counties. Top reds are notably ageworthy. (DM)

Recommended Reds:

Cabernet Sauvignon Lamb Vineyard Napa Valley ★★★★★ £H

California

Cabernet Sauvignon Wedding Vineyard Sonoma County ★★★★☆ £H
Cabernet Sauvignon Coach Insignia Napa Valley ★★★★☆ £F
Cameron Red ★★★★ £F Merlot RCF Vineyard Napa Valley ★★★★ £F
Recommended Whites:
Chardonnay Mountain Estate Sonoma County ★★★★ £F
Chardonnay Whitneys Vineyard Sonoma County ★★★★ £F

✿ Flowers (Sonoma Coast) *www.flowerswinery.com*
This is now part owned by the firm that includes Napa Valley
QUINTESSA in its portfolio. It is a very good Sonoma coastal
property with vineyards planted in volcanic soils and moderated
by cooling maritime breezes making for an ideal environment for
cultivating Chardonnay and Pinot Noir. Vinification follows age-
old Burgundian techniques for both varieties. As well as the wines
rated here, Pinot Noir is also made from the home Sea View Ridge
vineyard and a further red Perenial is a varying blend dominated
by Pinot Noir, Syrah and Pinot Meunier, with very small proportions
of Dolcetto and Chardonnay. The Moon Select bottlings are a
special vineyard selection from within the family's estate property.
Chardonnay is restrained and minerally with a fine balance of citrus
fruit and subtle, lightly toasty oak. Pinot is full of bright berry fruit
and hints of smoky cherries. The depth and intensity of the Camp
Meeting Ridge *cuvée* suggests 3 or 4 years' ageing will be rewarded.
(DM)
Recommended Reds:
Pinot Noir Moon Select Sonoma Coast ★★★★★ £G
Pinot Noir Estate Camp Meeting Ridge Sonoma Coast ★★★★☆ £F
Pinot Noir Sonoma Coast ★★★★ £E
Recommended Whites:
Chardonnay Moon Select Sonoma Coast ★★★★☆ £F
Chardonnay Estate Camp Meeting Ridge Sonoma Coast ★★★★☆ £F
Chardonnay Sonoma Coast ★★★★ £E

Foppiano (Russian River Valley) *www.foppiano.com*
The Foppiano family own some 64 ha (160 acres) of prime Russian
River vineyards. There are a number of good solid wines here with
the two Petite Sirah cuvées showing real quality. The Russian River
Estate bottling offers concentrated dark berry fruit and spicy black
pepper undercurrents, while the Lot 96 is juicy, rich and forward
but with fine concentration. It represents particularly good value.
Also made are a characterful, cherry fruited Zinfandel, a medium
bodied Pinot Noir, a restrained barrel-fermented Chardonnay, a zesty
Sauvignon Blanc and a Rosé, all now from Estate vineyards. (DM)
Recommended Reds:
Petite Sirah Estate Russian River Valley ★★★☆ £D
Petite Sirah Lot 96 Sonoma County ★★☆ £C

Frick (Dry Creek Valley) *www.frickwinery.com*
Small Rhône specialist with further interesting releases from
Carignane, Mourvèdre, Grenache Blanc, Grenache Noir and
Counoise are made as well as the wines below. Bill Frick produces
bespoke wines from 2 ha (5 acres) of vines on a small property
established in 1976 in a cooler sector of the Dry Creek Valley. Key to
the style here is a naturally stressed vineyard planted on steep, well-
drained slopes. The result is vines which struggle just sufficiently
in order to achieve fruit with real intensity. The wines are not huge
blockbusters but nevertheless show rich and concentrated fruit
with balance and finesse. A Cinsault rosé is also produced and
new is C Squared, a Rhône-style blend of Cinsault and old vine
Carignane and C Cubed a combination of Cinsaut, Carignane and
Counoise. Dry Creek is also the source of two further blends Côtes

du Dry Creek White and Red as well as Garibaldi a very unusual field
blend that includes Carignane, Grenache, Muscat Blanc, Zinfandel,
Petite Sirah, Valdeque, Mission, Palomino and Burger. The range is
completed by Lucia which combines Cinsaut, Syrah and Counoise.
All offer good value. (DM)
Recommended Reds:
Syrah Owl Hill Dry Creek Valley ★★★☆ £D
Cinsault Dry Creek Valley ★★★ £D
Recommended Whites:
Viognier Gannon Vineyard Dry Creek Valley ★★★ £D

Fritz Winery (Dry Creek Winery) *www.fritzwinery.com*
Fritz was established as long ago as 1979 and production is still
small and bespoke. Grapes come from both the Dry Creek Valley
and the cooler Russian River, which provides an excellent source
for Chardonnay, particularly the famed Dutton Ranch. Helen Turley
of MARCASSIN spent a couple of years consulting here and the
quality shines through. Minimalist practices such as native yeast
fermentation are employed. The Zins are vibrant and full of rich fruit,
the Chardonnay broad, nutty and toasty. The range is completed by
a Russian River Pinot Noir including a Reserve example, a Sauvignon
Blanc, a pricier Reserve Chardonnay (£F) and a restrained cedary
Cabernet Sauvignon. (DM)
Recommended Reds:
Zinfandel Estate Reserve Dry Creek Valley ★★★☆ £E
Zinfandel Estate Dry Creek Valley ★★★ £D
Recommended Whites:
Chardonnay Russian River Valley ★★★ £D

Gallo of Sonoma (Dry Creek Valley) *www.gallosignatureseries.com*
One of the world's largest wine companies, E & J Gallo, is known the
world over for its Gallo and Turning Leaf volume labels – the former
hugely successful and very commercial. There is also a Coastal range
from the giant facility at Modesto in California's Central Valley, but it
is the top two wines now produced from the substantial Sonoma
County vineyard holdings which provide the real interest. Seven
vineyards are owned, spread throughout Sonoma County covering
the Russian River Valley, Dry Creek Valley, Alexander Valley and
Sonoma Valley AVAs. Further vineyards have also been added in the
Napa Valley and in Monterey. Both the Cabernet and Chardonnay
are made from the best fruit of the Sonoma estate vineyards for the
vintage. As well as Sonoma Coast the Chardonnay has also been
released under the Russian River banner. The wine is richly textured
and barrel-fermented followed by the malolactic and then aged for
a total of around a year and a half in barrel. The dark fruited Cabernet
is given a pre-fermentation cold soak and aged for just under two
years in mainly new French oak. Four additional premium wines are
also released under the Signature Series label and sourced from a
range of estate owned vineyards. There are both a Sonoma Coast
and Russian River Valley Chardonnay, a Pinot Noir from the Santa
Lucia Highlands as well as a Napa Valley Cabernet Sauvignon. (DM)
Recommended Reds:
Cabernet Sauvignon Estate Northern Sonoma ★★★★ £G
Recommended Whites:
Chardonnay Estate Sonoma Coast ★★★☆ £F

Geyser Peak (Alexander Valley) *www.geyserpeakwinery.com*
This is a substantial operation with an extensive range. The California
Series varietal wines are generally sound and tend to emphasize
straightforward fruit characters. With the exception of the Sonoma
County Chardonnay the other wines take the California appellation.

Wine behind the label

A level up are the wines produced under the Appellation Series banner and as well as the Sauvignon Blanc River Ranches, Water Bend Chardonnay comes from the Alexander Valley, Pluto's Fury Pinot Noir from the Russian River, Walking Tree Cabernet Sauvignon also from the Alexander Valley and a Tectonic Red Blend which combines Cabernet Sauvignon and Petit Verdot. The Reserve wines including a cedary Cabernet and a meritage Bordeaux blend, which are both aged in French oak for 18 months and are crafted from the winery's best vineyards and lots. An Inkstand Cabernet is also now released which includes a little Petit Verdot, Petite Sirah and Malbec. If you are visiting there are also a number of wines made in small runs of barely more than 150 cases and available solely from the winery. These include the top Bin series Cabernet Sauvignon from the Alexander Valley. (DM)

Recommended Reds:
Alexandre Meritage Reserve Alexander Valley ★★★ £E
Cabernet Sauvignon Reserve Alexander Valley ★★★ £E
Recommended Whites:
Sauvignon Blanc River Ranches Russian River Valley ★★ £C
Chardonnay Sonoma County ★☆ £B Sauvignon Blanc California ★☆ £B

Goldeneye (Anderson Valley) *www.goldeneyewinery.com*
Dan and Margaret DUCKHORN are responsible for distinctive, once almost ferocious Napa Merlots as well as the Paraduxx Zinfandels. Goldeneye is their Anderson Valley property, specialising in Pinot Noir and also now making Pinot Gris from the Split Rail Vineyard and estate grown Confluence Vineyard Gewürztraminer. The vineyards stand out for their cool climate and the proximity of the Pacific coastline. The Anderson Valley example is now sourced from four different estate vineyards. It is dominated by bright strawberry fruit, supple tannin and a marked vanilla character after spending 18 months in new French oak. It will drink very well with 2–3 years' age. Estate single vineyard wines are also released and the top wine Ten Degrees Estate Grown is a special selection and is fairly pricey (£G). (DM)

Recommended Reds:
Pinot Noir Anderson Valley ★★★☆ £F

Halleck (Russian River Valley) *www.halleckvineyard.com*
Ross Halleck produces a number of brilliant Pinot Noirs as well as very good Sauvignon Blanc and a particularly unusual and very striking, minerally Gewürztraminer. The first vintage was in 1999. His home vineyard is tiny just 0.4ha (1 acre) planted solely to Pinot Noir and although not tasted the wine produced is likely to be of at least a similarly high standard. The second Pinot Noir Three Sons Cuvée is sourced from a number of carefully selected sites and with both components tasted out of barrel and tasted from bottle the wine offers an impressive mix of dark, spicy fruit, a lovely savoury character and an impressive underlying minerality. A further example, Hillside includes a small proportion of estate fruit. The piercingly pure Sauvignon Blanc is fermented in a combination of stainless steel to preserve its fresh character and neutral oak to add depth and structure. It offers a fine mix of green, gooseberry fruit with a nice mineral core. The Gewürztraminer is subtle and restrained when compared with many Alsatian examples but there is a really impressive underlying richness and viscosity. The whites will develop well with a little age, the Pinots deserve a little more patience. (DM)

Recommended Reds:
Pinot Noir Three Sons Cuvée Russian River Valley ★★★★☆ £F

Recommended Whites:
Sauvignon Blanc Little Sister Russian River Valley ★★★☆ £D
Gewürztraminer Piner Creek Ranch Russian River Valley ★★★☆ £D

❀ **Walter Hansel (Russian River Valley)** *www.walterhanselwinery.com*
Stephen Hansel's small Russian River winery is very low key in terms of publicity but he produces some of the most strikingly impressive and well priced Pinot Noir and Chardonnay in the Sonoma Valley, and California for that matter. The property was established by the late Walter Hansel, Stephen's father and it remains small and commited to quality. All the fruit for the Chardonnay and Pinot Noir comes from estate owned vineyards. A very decent Sauvignon Blanc is produced from bought-in Russian River fruit, particularly in vintages when the Chardonnay volumes are a little short. For the first time in 2013 a little rosé was made from Pinot Noir. All the Chardonnays are marked by a rich texture and a pure mineral character. The Cahill Lane bottling a touch more structured and poised than the full-throttle Russian River Valley wine. The splendidly dense and very concentrated Cuvée Alyce is a barrel-selection from the best barrels earmarked from the best blocks and gets a touch longer on lees. Of a splendid range of Pinot Noirs, the Cahill Lane is perhaps the tightest, most elegant while the South Slope is more opulent and exotic in style than a more structured North Slope example. A Three Rows bottling accounts for barely 50 cases a year and is loaded with dark and restrained berry fruit and beautifully judged oak. The top Pinot Noir is Cuvée Alyce which like the Chardonnay, is a selection both by the barrel and from blocks that yield barely more than three-quarters of a ton to the acre (the average across the vineyard is closer to two tons). It is an extraordinarily dense, rich and truly opulent example of the variety. Given the very fair prices these wines are a must for any discerning drinker. (DM)

Recommended Reds:
Pinot Noir Cuvée Alyce Russian River Valley ★★★★★ £F
Pinot Noir Three Rows Russian River Valley ★★★★★ £E
Pinot Noir North Slope Russian River Valley ★★★★☆ £E
Pinot Noir South Slope Russian River Valley ★★★★☆ £E
Pinot Noir Cahill Lane Russian River Valley ★★★★☆ £E
Recommended Whites:
Chardonnay Cuvée Alyce Russian River Valley ★★★★★ £F
Chardonnay Cahill Lane Russian River Valley ★★★★☆ £E
Chardonnay Estate Russian River Valley ★★★★ £D
Sauvignon Blanc Russian River Valley ★★★ £C

Hanzell (Sonoma Valley) *www.hanzell.com*
Small producer located high up in the Mayacamas Mountains. Hanzell was established way back in 1953 and has long been a pioneer of first-class Chardonnay and Pinot Noir from its hillside estate vineyard. The operation is built on the quality of this mountain *terroir*. The Chardonnay is a tight, structured example in its youth with well-judged oak and subtle citrus notes, altogether different from many fuller, fatter examples produced by its neighbours. The Pinot is rich and vibrant, with concentrated dark berry flavours and just a hint of game. Both wines will age well and will benefit from 4 or 5 years' ageing. A number of single vineyard wines are also additionally released now which are selections from the best plots on the property. These include Chardonnay and Pinot examples from the Ambassador 1953 and De Brye vineyards as well as Ramos Vineyard Chardonnay and Sessions Vineyard Pinot Noir. The small range is completed by a Sebella Chardonnay which is from young vines. (DM)

California North Coast

Recommended Reds:
Pinot Noir Estate Sonoma Valley ★★★★ £G
Recommended Whites:
Chardonnay Estate Sonoma Valley ★★★★ £F

Hartford Family Winery *www.hartfordwines.com*
Founded in 1993 by Don Hartford and his wife Jennifer Jackson-Hartford, of the KENDALL-JACKSON clan, this Green Valley of Russian River Valley based operation is dedicated to producing Pinot Noir, Zinfandel and Chardonnay. Winemaker Mike Sullivan purposely crafts very Burgundian styles of Chardonnay and Pinot – tighter, more structured wines than many of their neighbours'. Both are good medium-term cellar propositions. Zinfandel is produced in a ripe, full style but retains real finesse. The Hartford label now encompasses just Zinfandel from the Russian River with a number of single vineyard wines from Dina's, Fanucchi-Wood Road, Hartford, Jolene's and Highwire vineyards. In addition to this an extensive range of single-vineyard Chardonnay and Pinot Noir cuvées are made under the Hartford Court label. Pinot Noir comes from a number of sources: there are wines from Velvet Sisters Vineyard in Anderson Valley, the Sevens Bench Vineyard in Carneros and Far Coast and Seascape sites on the Sonoma Coast. A Land's Edge example comes from a number of Sonoma Coast sources with a marked maritime influence. Russian River Pinot is produced from the Arrendell and Jennifer's vineyards. A single site Marin County example is also made. Impressive Chardonnay comes from the Far Coast, Stone Côte and Seascape vineyards on the Sonoma Coast, the Fog Dance Vineyard in the Green Valley as well as the Four Hearts bottling from the Russian River. All stand out. (DM)
Hartford
Recommended Reds:
Zinfandel Russian River Valley ★★★☆ £E
Hartford Court
Recommended Reds:
Pinot Noir Arrendell Vineyard Russian River Valley ★★★★☆ £G
Pinot Noir Velvet Sisters Vineyard Anderson Valley ★★★★ £F
Recommended Whites:
Chardonnay Four Hearts Vineyard Russian River Valley ★★★★ £E

Paul Hobbs (Sonoma County) *www.paulhobbs.com*
Winemaker Paul Hobbs spends the northern-hemisphere spring months vinifying wines in South America, where he has helped in shaping the style at VALDIVIESO in Chile and CATENA in Argentina. Indeed he also produces his own premium Argentine Malbec, COBOS, from high altitude vineyards in the Upper Mendoza. Equally important, he also produces benchmark wines in California from Cabernet Sauvignon, Merlot, Pinot Noir, Syrah and Chardonnay. His main focus is on single-vineyard wines, particularly an extensive number from Chardonnays, produced in very small quantities. Handling is minimal and the wines are vinified with wild yeasts. Oak is carefully integrated and the primary objective is to provide wines of balance and finesse. Top selections for Chardonnay and Pinot Noir, labelled Cuvée Agustina, are unquestionably very impressive and both very pricey and in short supply. (DM)
Recommended Reds:
Pinot Noir Hyde Vineyard Carneros ★★★★☆ £G
Pinot Noir Russian River Valley ★★★★ £F
Cabernet Sauvignon Napa Valley ★★★★ £G
Recommended Whites:
Chardonnay Russian River Valley ★★★★ £F

Iron Horse Vineyards (Green Valley) *www.ironhorsevineyards.com*
Like MARIMAR TORRES, Iron Horse is located in the cool Green Valley of Russian River Valley AVA (which may very shortly become officially known as Green Valley), where it produces some of the best sparkling wines in California. These are sourced from the lower-lying sites most affected by early-morning fog, which provide fruit with ideal acidity. There is a stylish Pinot Noir-dominated Wedding Cuvée, the Russian Cuvée with a slightly higher *dosage* and the Classic Vintage Brut, which is a blend of roughly 60/40 Pinot Noir and Chardonnay. Impressively structured and elegant, the Blanc de Blancs is only a touch below the quality of the much pricier Brut LD. An extensive range of Pinot Noir and Chardonnay still wines is also produced. From the cool climate Green Valley come both Estate Chardonnay and Pinot Noir. An unoaked Chardonnay is also made as well as a more expensive (£E) Heritage Clone example. As well as the Estate wine there are a number of more expensive Pinot Noir (£F) releases from specially selected estate vineyard blocks. (DM)
Recommended Reds:
Pinot Noir Estate Green Valley ★★★☆ £E
Recommended Whites:
Brut LD Green Valley ★★★★ £F
Blanc de Blancs Sonoma-Green Valley ★★★☆ £E
Classic Vintage Brut Sonoma-Green Valley ★★★ £E
Russian Cuvée Sonoma-Green Valley ★★★ £E
Wedding Cuvée Sonoma-Green Valley ★★★ £E
Chardonnay Estate Sonoma-Green Valley ★★★ £D

Kamen Estate (Sonoma Valley) *www.kamenwines.com*
Estate in the south-western Mayacamas range with vineyards at an altitude of 335-440 m (1,100-1,450 ft), growing the Bordeaux varieties Cabernet Sauvignon and Cabernet Franc as well as Petite Sirah, Grenache, Sauvignon Blanc, Viognier and Syrah. The meagre, volcanic, rocky soils rarely produce yields beyond 1.5 tons/acre, resulting in wines with great intensity and depth. Three reds are now produced, a pure varietal Estate Cabernet Sauvignon, a Syrah, a Grenache and Writers Block, an interesting blend of Syrah, Cabernet Sauvignon and Petite Sirah. A white is also now made from estate grown Sauvignon Blanc and Sauvignon Musqué and a Viognier is also produced. Winemaking consultancy is provided by Mark Herold who also produces his own Mark Herold Wines and was the former owner/winemaker at the Merus winery. (DM)
Recommended Reds:
Cabernet Sauvignon Sonoma Valley ★★★★ £G

Kendall-Jackson (Sonoma County) *www.kj.com*
Vast, private family owned wine company, founded by the late Jess Jackson, producing an extensive range under its own label and also owning or part-owning a considerable number of wine operations in the premium-wine sector throughout California. Leading brands include ARROWOOD, EDMEADES, and LA CREMA and the company also has interests in Italy (Tenuta di Arceno), Chile (Calina), Argentina (Tapiz) and Australia. The family also have connections with the HARTFORD FAMILY WINERY and MATANZAS CREEK, as well as owning LA JOTA, CAMBRIA, BYRON, FREEMARK ABBEY, STONESTREET and VÉRITÉ, and a number of independently run estates have been set up to produce top-quality reds. The LOKOYA wines emanate from singlevineyard, mountain-vineyard sites, while the ATALON labels are drawn from varied sources. The super-premium CARDINALE is blended from Napa and Sonoma fruit sources. Under the Kendall-Jackson logo, an extensive array of affordable wines are offered as K-J Avant and Vintners Reserve red and whites. The Grand

Reserve label is a step up, producing winemaker barrel selections from a range of vineyards. The top wines under the K-J label are the newly established Highland Estates, a range of single estate wines under the Jackson Estate banner and the very pricey Stature series of a Chardonnay and a red Bordeaux blend of Cabernet Sauvignon, Merlot, Petit Verdot and Malbec. (DM)

Recommended Reds:
Cabernet Sauvignon Stature Napa Valley ★★★★ £G
Cabernet Sauvignon Grand Reserve California ★★★ £D
Recommended Whites:
Chardonnay Stature Napa Valley ★★★★ £G
Chardonnay Grand Reserve California ★★ £C

❀❀ Kistler (Russian River Valley) *www.kistlervineyards.com*
This has long been a name associated with some of the greatest California Chardonnay. More recently Steve Kistler has been producing some marvellous, rich and vibrant Pinot Noirs as well. Both varieties are made in very small lots from a number of different sites throughout Sonoma County as well as Carneros. The Kistler Vineyard, Durell Vineyard, Dutton Ranch, Hudson Vineyard and McCrea Vineyard, have all been sources of wines that are invariably of at least ★★★★ quality. Cuvée Cathleen is the top Chardonnay. The Chardonnays are characterised by full, rich, honeyed notes along with an elegant, mineral core; the Pinots can be explosive with youthful, weighty tannins, suggesting real cellaring potential. Kistler is also now making a series of Pinot Noirs under a new brand, Occidental. Expect these to be top notch. (DM)

Recommended Reds:
Pinot Noir Kistler Vineyard Sonoma Valley ✪✪✪✪✪ £H
Pinot Noir Sonoma County ★★★★ £F
Recommended Whites:
Chardonnay Kistler Vineyard Sonoma Valley ✪✪✪✪✪ £H
Chardonnay Hudson Vineyard Carneros ✪✪✪✪✪ £H
Chardonnay Dutton Ranch Russian River Valley ★★★★★ £H
Chardonnay Sonoma County ★★★★ £F

La Crema (Russian River Valley) *www.lacrema.com*
A significant winery in the Kendall-Jackson empire, La Crema was originally established in 1979. It produces a now extensive range of good, well-crafted and reasonably priced Pinot Noir and Chardonnay, along with Pinot Gris, and Viognier. There are particularly good value wines taking the Sonoma Coast and Monterey appellations. An extensive and impressive array of wines are also made from a number of smaller AVAs, including marginally pricier Fog Veil and Shell Ridge Vineyard Pinots from the Russian River. The winery have also ventured outside California for the first time and have established Pinot Noir vineyards in the Willamette Valley in Oregon. The Chardonnay is typically ripe and exotic with tropical notes and evident oak, the reds are marked by forward, ripe berry fruit. Russian River and Carneros bottlings are a step up in depth and intensity. A special selection of pricier Chardonnay (£F) and Pinot Noir (£G) is released under the Nine Barrels label which is a selection of the best barrels from the wineries Russian River fruit. (DM)

Recommended Reds:
Pinot Noir Carneros ★★★ £E
Pinot Noir Russian River Valley ★★★ £E
Pinot Noir Sonoma Coast ★★☆ £C
Recommended Whites:
Chardonnay Russian River Valley ★★★ £D
Chardonnay Sonoma Coast ★★☆ £C

❀ La Follette (Russian River Valley) *www.lafollettewines.com*
Founded by Greg Bjornstadt and Greg la Follette and originally named Tandem, La Follette is now a partnership of Greg La Follette and Pete Kight who also owns QUIVIRA Vineyards. Bjornstadt has established his own new label, Bjornstadt Cellars, while La Follette remains to direct operations here. He was responsible for establishing FLOWERS and more recently has provided consultancy to other small scale operations including HALLECK. Fruit comes from some of the best growers in the area. Pinot Noir is the key variety but Chardonnay and a Pinot Meunier from the van der Kamp Vineyard are also made. Vineyard sources are Sangiacomo, Van der Kamp, Manchester Ridge in Mendocino and DuNah in the Russian River Valley for Pinot Noir as well as Sangiacomo, Manchester Ridge and Lorenzo in the Russian River for Chardonnay. Pinot Noir is supple and forward drinking well young and improving for five years. Rich, Burgundian styled Van der Kamp Pinot offers real depth and persistence, the Sangiacomo is a touch more firmly structured with a smoky concentration and a gamey, truffley undercurrent. (DM)

Recommended Reds:
Pinot Noir Van der Kamp Vineyard Sonoma Mountain ★★★★☆ £F
Pinot Noir Sangiacomo Vineyard Sonoma Coast ★★★★☆ £F

Landmark (Sonoma Valley) *www.landmarkwine.com*
Very fine and stylish Chardonnays and Pinot Noirs are made on this property by winemaker Eric Stern. During the mid-1990s roving wine consultant Helen Turley of MARCASSIN provided additional input and direction. There is a commitment here to producing wines from the ripest fruit from low-yielding, meticulously-tended vineyards and with minimal intervention. Chardonnay is the main focus, the Overlook label providing good value. A marginally pricier Rodgers Creek Chardonnay also comes from the Sonoma Coast and a Pinot Gris is also made. The Chardonnays are in the rich, lightly tropical vein with nutty oak but decent grip and structure as well. The Grand Detour Pinot Noir is sourced from the high-altitude Van der Kamp vineyards of Sonoma Mountain and the wine is structured and concentrated with a gamey undercurrent. In addition a small amount of Pinot Noir is also produced from the Rodgers Vineyard as well as from the Santa Lucia Highlands and the Mirabelle Vineyard in the Russian River Valley. The small range of reds is completed by a Steel Plow Grenache from the Sonoma Valley. (DM)

Recommended Reds:
Pinot Noir Grand Detour Sonoma Coast ★★★☆ £E
Pinot Noir Overlook Sonoma County ★★☆ £D
Recommended Whites:
Chardonnay Damaris Reserve Sonoma Coast ★★★☆ £E
Chardonnay Overlook California ★★☆ £C

Laurel Glen (Sonoma Mountain) *www.laurelglen.com*
Small operation with some 16 ha (40 acres) of prime vineyards planted to Cabernet Sauvignon, Merlot and Cabernet Franc. Cabernet Sauvignon is very much the dominant variety. The property has thin, rocky and superbly drained soils which provide an excellent base for producing explosive Cabernet Sauvignon and a second wine Counterpoint. The Cabernet is 100% varietal and comes from slopes planted at close to 1,000 feet. Counterpoint is softer and more approachable with vibrant blackberry fruit qualities. Dominated by Cabernet Sauvignon there is a small amount of Merlot to soften the palate. A rosé is also made, Crazy Old Vine Rosé, which comes from estate grown fruit and a mix of Cabernet Sauvignon and a number of unspecific other varieties. A further

Cabernet, The Laureate, will be released under the guidance of consulting winemaker David RAMEY. The first release from 2010 is less than 100 cases. (DM)

Recommended Reds:
Cabernet Sauvignon Sonoma Mountain ★★★★ £F
Counterpoint Sonoma Mountain ★★★ £E

>> Lioco Wines (Sonoma Valley) *www.liocowine.com*
Lioco Wines source fruit from Sonoma, Mendocino and Santa Cruz counties. While their artisan range is dominated by Pinot Noir and Chardonnay they also source Carignan from old vines for their Santa Rosa winemaking base. They refer to themselves as a European style *négociant* and produce wines with a restrained elegance often missing in the State. The Sativa Carignan is an impressive red which bears comparison with the best examples of the variety from France's Midi regions. The vines are 70 years old, are head-pruned, dry-farmed and have an ideal southerly exposition. Vinification is from whole bunches and aging is in neutral oak. There is a really characterful old-vine complexity and a beguiling array of dark berry fruits and herb spices. Pinot Noir Laguna comes from Sonoma Coast sites and is marked by edgy red fruit qualities. Aged for 11 months and new oak kept to a minimum, around 15%. The Sonoma Chardonnay is both elegant and approachable. Vinification is in a mix of stainless tanks and older wood with ageing on lees to preserve the fruit character. The top Estero Vineyard Chardonnay is in a rich, lightly honeyed style with fresh citrus and mineral qualities. The vines are all dry-framed and of signicant age, the oldest blocks close to 50 years old. (DM)

Recommended Reds:
Pinot Noir Laguna Vineyard Sonoma Coast ★★★★ £E
Carignan Sativa Mendocino County ★★★★ £E
Recommended Whites:
Chardonnay Estero Vineyard Russian River Valley ★★★★ £E
Chardonnay Sonoma Valley ★★★ £D

● Lynmar Estate (Russian River Valley) *www.lynmarestate.com*
Very good now well established Russian River winery with vineyards at their own Quail Hill Ranch. The first vintage released was 1996. Production is mainly concentrated on hand-crafted Chardonnay and Pinot Noir. The regular estate bottlings now take the Russian River Valley label. Reserves and a host of single vineyard examples of both varieties are produced from the home Quail vineyards and a number of other sites which are more restrained in style with greater depth and intensity. The Quail Hill Chardonnay, particularly, is marked by super-ripe opulent fruit and layer upon layer of flavour. Five Sisters Pinot Noir is a selection of the very best home estate fruit and only made in exceptional vintages. The Pinot Noirs are full of of rich dark berry fruit and spicy new and used oak, in varying proportions. Russian River Valley Syrah and a Russian River Rosé of Pinot Noir are also now being made. (DM)

Recommended Reds:
Pinot Noir Five Sisters Russian River Valley ★★★★★ £G
Pinot Noir Quail Hill Vineyard Russian River Valley ★★★★ £F
Pinot Noir Russian River Valley ★★★☆ £E
Recommended Whites:
Chardonnay Quail Hill Vineyard Russian River Valley ★★★★ £F
Chardonnay Russian River Valley ★★★☆ £E

Macrae Family (Sonoma County) *www.macraewinery.com*
David Macrae sources Chardonnay and Pinot Noir grapes from the Bacigalupi Vineyard and Cabernet Sauvignon and Merlot from the

Stagecoach Vineyard owned by the Krupp Bothers at VERAISON in the Napa Valley. Winemaker Kerry Damskey is charged with making wines that are true to their *terroir*, all being from single vineyards. The Chardonnay displays typical sweet Californian fruit, with hints of grapefruit and pomelo, with good complexity and length. However, it seems to lack just a bit of extra 'grip' to make it a truly top class wine. The Pinot Noir displays similar characteristics, certainly not a blockbuster, but with complexity on the finish and plenty of finesse although it could do with a bit more structure. By contrast, the Cabernet Sauvignon has a great balance between fruit and acidity with layers of blackcurrant, blueberry and other summer fruits beneath gentle, supple tannins. A very fine wine, indeed. A Merlot from the Stagecoach vineyard is also made. (NB)

Recommended Reds:
Cabernet Sauvignon Stagecoach Vineyard Napa Valley ★★★★☆ £F
Pinot Noir Bacigalupi Vineyard Russian River Valley ★★★☆ £E
Recommended Whites:
Chardonnay Bacigalupi Vineyard Russian River Valley ★★★☆ £E

✿✿ Marcassin (Sonoma Coast)
Helen Turley has achieved a cult reputation among California winemakers, consulting to some of the top producers throughout the North Coast. In 1990 she and her husband John Wetlaufer established the Marcassin winery and have developed their own vineyard, planted to Pinot Noir and Chardonnay which is now their main focus. Other Chardonnay cuvées have also been produced from the Lorenzo Vineyard, Three Sisters and Upper Barn, with Pinot Noir coming from Blue Slide Ridge and the Three Sisters Vineyard. The wines are produced in tiny amounts, only a couple of hundred cases per bottling, and will be nigh on impossible to find. Their reputation is formidable and they are very expensive. (DM)

Recommended Reds:
Pinot Noir Marcassin Vineyard Sonoma Coast ✪✪✪✪✪ £H
Pinot Noir Marcassin Three Sisters Sonoma Coast ★★★★★ £H
Pinot Noir Blue Slide Ridge Sonoma Coast ★★★★★ £G
Recommended Whites:
Chardonnay Marcassin Vineyard Sonoma Coast ✪✪✪✪✪ £H
Chardonnay Three Sisters Sonoma Coast ★★★★★ £G

✿✿ Martinelli (Russian River Valley) *www.martinelliwinery.com*
As well as her own MARCASSIN wines, here at Martinelli winemaker Helen Turley produces brilliant Zinfandel, some of the very best in the state; the Jackass Hill is a benchmark for all. Look out too for releases from the Russian River Vellutini Ranch and the barrel selected Vigneto di Evo. You can also find very classy Chardonnay and Pinot Noir here sourced from a number of sites. These are wines of real complexity and style, with a sense of *terroir* and place. Pinot is produced in very small quantities but you can invariably expect wines of at least ★★★, often ★★★★ or more. There is a Sonoma Coast example and additional releases come from the Zio Tony Ranch and the Three Sisters Vineyard on the Sonoma Coast. The Chardonnay is honeyed and toasty but always with an intense, mineral complexity. There are a number of single site releases of this too, with additional wines from Bella Vigna, the Lolita Ranch and the Three Sisters Vineyard. The Muscat of Alexandria, produced in tiny quantities, is made from 100 year-old vines, it is grapey and sugary but not syrupy. Syrah is also now released from a number of sites including the Russian River Valley Chico's Hill Vineyard, Terra Felice (blended from a number of sites) as well as from the Vellutini and Zio Tony Ranches. The reds will undoubtedly benefit from a little ageing. (DM)

Recommended Reds:
Zinfandel Jackass Hill Russian River Valley ✪✪✪✪✪ £F
Zinfandel Jackass Vineyard Russian River Valley ★★★★★ £F
Zinfandel Giuseppe & Luisa Russian River Valley ★★★★★ £F
Pinot Noir "Water Trough Vineyard" Green Valley ★★★★★ £F
Pinot Noir Lolita Ranch Russian River Valley ★★★★☆ £F
Pinot Noir Blue Slide Ridge Sonoma Coast ★★★★ £F
Pinot Noir Bella Vigna Russian River Valley ★★★☆ £E
Recommended Whites:
Chardonnay Zio Tony Ranch Russian River Valley ★★★★★ £F
Chardonnay Woolsey Road Russian River Valley ★★★★ £E
Chardonnay Charles Ranch Sonoma Coast ★★★★ £E
Chardonnay Martinelli Road Russian River Valley ★★★★ £E
Muscat of Alexandria Jackass Hill Russian River Valley ★★★★ £F

Matanzas Creek (Russian River Valley) *www.matanzascreek.com*
Medium-sized operation producing mainly Chardonnay, Sauvignon Blanc, Merlot and an increasing amount of impressive Pinot Noir. Matanzas Creek produced some stunning wines during the late 1980s and early 90s, and the winery looks to be right back in the top division. Small amounts of a powerful Reserve Merlot, a very pricey Journey meritage blend, a Bennett Valley Pinot Noir and Chardonnay and Sauvignon Blanc from the same AVA are also now being made. Sauvignon Blanc is vinified in part tank and part barrel to balance fresh flavours with a rich texture, while the cool qualities of the Bennett Valley provide a subtle Chardonnay of impressive intensity. As well as these premium Chardonnay and Sauvignon Blanc are also released under the Journey label. (DM)
Recommended Reds:
Merlot Sonoma County ★★★ £D
Recommended Whites:
Chardonnay Bennett Valley ★★★★ £E
Sauvignon Blanc Bennett Valley ★★★☆ £D

Mayo Family (Sonoma County) *www.mayofamilywinery.com*
Sizeable family run winery producing an extensive and generally impressive range of wines sourcing fruit from both the Sonoma and Napa Valleys and producing wines in relatively small lots. In addition to the wines profiled here Pinot Gris from the Balleto Vineyard on the Sonoma Coast and an easy drinking red blend Libertine offer good value drinking. Pinot Noir comes from the Laurel Hill Vineyard in the Sonoma Valley with a pricier Reserve (£F) also made. Well priced Barbera is made and there is a Primitivo from the Rossi Ranch in the Sonoma Valley. Also coming from the Sonoma Valley is a Merlot Los Chamizal Vineyard, "Meredith's Cuvée". There also two Rhône style reds; The Gypsy "Jessica's Cuvée" is a Sonoma Valley Grenache, Syrah, Mourvèdre blend, while the Page/Nord Vineyard "Lilyann's Block" is a Napa Valley Syrah. Laurel Hill Chardonnay is straightforward and fermented in stainless steel and there is an oaked example as well. Viognier is rich and peachy, going through 100% malolactic it should be drunk young and fresh. Zinfandel from the Ricci Vineyard shows lots of old vine character and rich and complex raspberry scented fruit. Perhaps the top red though is the splendid Sodoni Vineyard Petite Sirah. Coming from a vineyard planted in the 1940s this is deep, dark and full of dark berry fruit and spices and with powerful but surprisingly supple tannins. If you are visiting the winery tasting room in Healdsburg its worth trying the Zinfandel Port which is also sourced from the Ricci Vineyard. (DM)
Recommended Reds:
Petite Sirah Sodoni Vineyard Russian River Valley ★★★★ £F
Zinfandel Port Ricci Vineyard Russian River Valley ★★★☆ £F

Zinfandel Old Vine Ricci Vineyard Russian River Valley ★★★☆ £E
Recommended Whites:
Viognier Saralee's Vineyard Russian River Valley ★★★ £E
Chardonnay Laurel Hill Vineyard Sonoma Valley ★★☆ £D

❀ Peter Michael (Knights Valley) *www.petermichaelwinery.com*
Sir Peter Michael's Knights Valley winery has, for nearly three decades, been producing very fine cool climate wines, with mountain vineyard sources a key element. The Chardonnay cuvées are all very impressive with a combination of rich, ripe, honeyed fruit and deftly handled oak. The combination of different clones, native yeast fermentation and careful selection in the vineyard and cellar all contribute and the wines have been increasing in both subtlety and complexity. As well as the vineyard releases, there are two Barrel Selection Cuvées: Cuvée Indigene and Point Rouge which is a winemaker selection from the very best barrels of the vintage. Sauvignon Blanc Les Après-Midi is stylish and not dissimilar to top white Graves – it is barrel-fermented with lees-ageing and *bâtonnage* but is tight and structured with a mineral restraint. Coeur à Coeur, is by contrast a blend of Sémillon and Sauvignon. The Moulin Rouge Pinot is a more recent addition from the famed Pisoni Vineyard in the Santa Lucia Highlands and there are three other Pinot releases from the Seaview Estate vineyard on the Sonoma Coast. The top red, Les Pavots, is from the vineyard of the same name and is a dark, brooding blend of Cabernet Sauvignon, Merlot and Cabernet Franc. It is among the finest Bordeaux blends in California and requires a minimum of 6–7 years' age to show at its best. Two other Bordeaux styles are also made. Au Paradis is a blend of the two Cabernets from Oakville, L'Esprit des Pavots comes from younger vines on the Les Pavots site. (DM)
Recommended Reds:
Les Pavots Knights Valley ✪✪✪✪✪ £H
Pinot Noir Le Moulin Rouge Pisoni Vineyard ★★★★ £H
Recommended Whites:
Chardonnay Cuvée Indigene Sonoma County ✪✪✪✪✪ £H
Chardonnay Mon Plaisir Sonoma County ★★★★★ £H
Chardonnay Belle Côte Knights Valley ★★★★★ £G
Chardonnay La Carrière Knights Valley ★★★★☆ £G
Sauvignon Blanc Les Après-Midi Sonoma County ★★★★☆ £G

Robert Mueller (Russian River Valley) *www.muellerwine.com*
The Muellers established their small family winery in the centre of Healdsburg in 1991. Since then production has gradually risen to a few thosand cases a year of good, rich and stylish Syrah Block Eleven, Zinfandel Old Vines, Sauvignon and Chardonnay as well as Pinot Noir from a number of sites, all in the Russian River. Other Pinot Noirs to consider are August Reecher, Tempi, Cuvée X and Hogans Run. Chardonnay LB is in a ripe, classically forward California style and should be approached in its youth. The Pinots show impressive deep berry fruit, with some gamey elements and supple, well-balanced fine tannins. (DM)
Recommended Reds:
Pinot Noir Emily's Cuvée Russian River Valley ★★★★ £F
Recommended Whites:
Chardonnay LB Russian River Valley ★★★☆ £E

Novy (Russian River Valley) *www.novyfamilywines.com*
Novy was recently purchased by KJ, having been run by Adam and Dianna Lee of SIDURI and Dianna's family, the Novys. The wines which are dominated by Rhône styles, including a Russian River Viognier, are made at the Siduri facility in Santa Rosa. The intention is

for Siduri to remain focussed on Pinot Noir while Novy also produce Zinfandel, Sauvignon Blanc, Gewürztraminer, Chardonnay, unusual varietal Pinot Meunier and a Pinot Noir vinified as a white, both from the Van der Kamp Vineyard as well as a Four Mile Creek Red Table Wine which is a blend of Grenache, Syrah and Zinfandel. Grenache comes from the Judge Family Vineyard and is rich and full with dark and spicy fruit and a touch of firm tannin gives the wine backbone. Ageing is in neutral French oak. As well as a lighter Russian River Syrah, there is also a bottling from the Judge Family site which is richer and fuller with spicy dark pepper underpinning its fruit. Gary's Vineyard in the Santa Lucia Highlands has been a source of very opulent, dark, almost jammy, chocolatey Syrah, while the Rosella's Vineyard example now stands out for its depth, structure and a fine intensity and minerality which underpins its licorice and black pepper character. It is clearly the benchmark wine of the range. While both the fruit sources and the wines change to some degree from year to year, high quality is maintained. Vineyard sources are expected to remain the same. (DM)

Recommended Reds:
Syrah Rosella's Vineyard Santa Lucia Highlands ★★★★☆ £F
Syrah Gary's Vineyard Santa Lucia Highlands ★★★★ £F
Syrah Judge Family Vineyard Bennett Valley ★★★★ £F
Syrah Russian River Valley ★★★☆ £E
Grenache Judge Family Vineyard Bennett Valley ★★★☆ £E

David Noyes Wines (Sonoma Valley) *www.davidnoyeswines.com*
David Noyes started his winemaking career at RIDGE in 1970 and worked with several wineries in the area until he created the Kunde Estate Winery in 1989. He stayed with the Kunde family until 2006, when he left to concentrate full-time on his own label wines, which he started in 2001. He owns no vineyards, but fruit is sourced from various premium vineyards in the Sonoma County and he makes his wine at the Wellington Vineyards facility at Glen Ellen. Since 2005, Noyes has been using a hybrid natural/synthetic cork called Diam for closing all his wines and he has found this instrumental in substantially reducing the amount of TCA affected corks. Whilst concentrating on Chardonnay and Pinot Noir, the Rued Vineyard Chardonnay being very restrained and refined with judicious oaking, the fairly straightforward Sonoma Coast Pinot Noir gets outdone in weight and complexity by the single vineyard Dutton Ranch version. A Sonoma Valley Zinfandel and a well priced Rosé of Pinot Noir are also made. This is a small producer but there is a strong local following and a thriving wine club. (NB)

Recommended Reds:
Pinot Noir Dutton Ranch Russian River Valley ★★★★ £E
Pinot Noir Sonoma County ★★★☆ £D
Recommended Whites:
Chardonnay Rued Vineyard Russian River Valley ★★★☆ £E

Papapietro Perry (Russian River Valley) *www.papapietro-perry.com*
The first commercial vintage was as recent as 1998 at this very new, small but high-quality warehouse winery with a range of single vineyard Pinot Noirs and two special clonal selections, Pommard Clones and 777 Clones, which are touch pricier. There is also a small amount of Zinfandel from the Dry Creek Valley including two single vineyard examples, Pauline's and Elsbree as well as Chardonnay which also comes from the Peters Vineyard. A number of classic Pinot techniques are used. The wines get a three day cold soak and are fermented by vineyard lot in small containers. The wines are regularly hand plunged to aid extraction and to keep the temperature of the fermenting must under control. The dark

and richly concentrated wines are aged in 60% new oak which is seamlessly integrated. They are bottled unfined and unfiltered. (DM)
Recommended Reds:
Pinot Noir Peters Vineyard Russian River Valley ★★★★ £F
Pinot Noir Russian River Valley ★★★☆ £F

⊛ **Vineyard of Pasterwick** *www.pasterickwine.com*
Gerry Pasterick makes only Syrah and Viognier including now a Rosé of Syrah from his Russian River Valley base. He produces around 600 cases, mainly the Estate Syrah from his steep hillside vineyard in the Dry Creek Valley. He augmented his holding with several plantings in 1990, 1998, 1999 and 2001. In 2001 he planted a small block of Viognier, with a second block in 2006. Gerry is meticulous about his Syrah and tries as far as possible to follow the traditional Northern Rhône method of blending around 3% Viognier with the Syrah and maturing the wine in barrel for 3 years. It is then bottle aged for a further year before it is released. The wine is gamey with big fruit and strong flavours, almost black in colour, with nuances of violet, black fruit, spice, and tar. A long, complex finish completes the journey but the wine should really be cellared for several years before it reaches its full potential. The excellent price/quality ratio is an added bonus. A tiny amount of a single block on the steepest slope on the site, Angle of Repose (£F) is also made. (NB)
Recommended Reds:
Syrah Dry Creek Valley ★★★★☆ £E

⊛ **Pax Wine Cellars (Russian River Valley)** *www.paxwine.com*
After a period of ownership disputes it is good that this very impressive warehouse winery is continuing to produce some of the best small-lot Syrah, Grenache and Rhône blends in California. The wines are characterised by ripe, opulent, full-blown dark fruit, loads of depth and concentration, and marvellous varietal purity throughout. There is also a further Syrah which is a blend of Alder Springs, Castelli-Knight and Griffins Lair. The Castelli-Knight is markedly opulent and laden with dark spicy fruit while the Griffins Lair shows a dark, brambly, tarry character. The Alder Springs stands out for its depth, grip and power as well as an impressive array of dark fruits. The small range is completed by a Grenache from the James Berry Vineyard in Paso Robles and there is a blend, The Vicar which is comprised of Grenache, Mourvèdre and Syrah and is the winery ode to Châteauneuf-du-Pape. While these exciting wines are certainly high in alcohol they are also finely balanced. (DM)
Recommended Reds:
Syrah Alder Springs Vineyard Mendocino County ★★★★★ £F
Syrah Castelli-Knight Ranch Russian River Valley ★★★★★ £F
Syrah Griffins Lair Vineyard Sonoma Coast ★★★★★ £F

⊛ **Peay Vineyards (Sonoma Coast)** *www.peayvineyards.com*
This is a partnership between winemaker Vanessa Wong, vinegrower Nick Peay and marketeer Andy Peay who established their small, remote Sonoma Coast vineyard in the mid 1990s. They produce a small range of elegant and intensely flavoured wines from the Rhône varieties as well as Chardonnay and Pinot Noir. The whites tend to be more a touch more exuberant than the reds but still retain a fine cool grown mineral core. The Viognier is aged for 11 months on lees and, despite full malolactic, retains fresh acidity, giving the wine elegance and a little structure. Roussanne/Marsanne is subtle, restrained, nutty and balanced with a lovely minerality which gives the wine real character. It is aged, like the Viognier, in older wood and kept on lees after the malo. Estate Chardonnay is piercingly intense with citrus and stony, mineral notes underpinned

by a toasty richness from barrel-fermentation (40% new oak is used). A second Sonoma Coast example is also made. Pinot Noir comes in five guises. There is an impressive Sonoma Coast example and one from the Anderson Valley Savoy Vineyard. The three estate Pinot releases are Ama and Scallop Shelf as well as a third label Pomarium. These are tight, structured and very well crafted and need a little time. Ama is a touch more opulent and brooding than Scallop Shelf but both are very clearly elegant, cool grown styles. The Syrah's are more Côte-Rotie than Cornas like and the cool climate character of the estate vineyards again shows through in the wines. La Bruma has a real mineral quality, while Les Titans is more dark-fruited and a touch weightier with more of a rich licorice character. The wines are given a cold-soak and aged in around 10% new wood. All are bottled unfined and unfiltered. (DM)

Recommended Reds:
Pinot Noir Ama Sonoma Coast ★★★★☆ £F
Pinot Noir Scallop Shelf Sonoma Coast ★★★★☆ £F
Pinot Noir Sonoma Coast ★★★★ £E
Syrah Les Titans Sonoma Coast ★★★★ £F
Syrah Estate La Bruma Sonoma Coast ★★★★ £F
Recommended Whites:
Chardonnay Estate Sonoma Coast ★★★★ £E
Roussanne/Marsanne Estate Sonoma Coast ★★★★ £E
Viognier Estate Sonoma Coast ★★★☆ £E

Porter Creek Vineyards *www.portercreekvineyards.com*
Small family-owned Russian River Valley winery producing four separate Pinot Noirs, two Chardonnays, a Syrah, an old-vine Zinfandel and a striking example of old-vine Carignane. The George's Hill Chardonnay is in a tighter, leaner style than others from the region, with notes of apple and pear, rather than more exotic tropical notes, and an impressive mineral core. The Fiona Hill Pinot Noir is relatively light but elegant, with fine and persistent red berry fruit dominating the palate. Expect these wines to develop well for 5 years or more. (DM)

Recommended Reds:
Pinot Noir Fiona Hill Russian River Valley ★★★☆ £E
Carignane Old Vines Alexander Valley ★★★ £C
Recommended Whites:
Chardonnay George's Hill Estate Russian River Valley ★★★ £D

❋ **A Rafanelli (Dry Creek Valley)** *www.arafanelliwinery.com*
Dave Rafanelli has some excellent hillside vineyard sites in the Dry Creek Valley from which he ensures top quality fruit for his own estate wines. He not only produces superlative old-vine, highly complex and characterful Zinfandel, but some impressive Cabernet Sauvignon as well. The estate vineyards are dry farmed (i.e. without recourse to irrigation) and yields are always kept to a minimum. A tiny quantity, just 250 cases or so are made of a special selection, Terrace Select, which is raised in new French barrels for 36 months. (DM)

Recommended Reds:
Cabernet Sauvignon Dry Creek Valley ★★★★☆ £F
Zinfandel Dry Creek Valley ★★★★ £E

❋ **Radio Coteau (Russian River Valley)** *www.radiocoteau.com*
Eric Sussman established this operation in partnership with Bill and Joan Smith, former owners of LA JOTA and WH SMITH, producing fine Sonoma Coast Pinot Noir. Before venturing out on his own project Eric gained invaluable experience both in the States and elsewhere. Those he has worked for include Comte ARMANDE in

Pommard, BONNY DOON and most recently, DEHLINGER where he shaped his knowledge and understanding of North Coast estate grown Pinot Noir. The wines are hand-made and advocating sustainable farming has been one of the key factors in establishing grower links. Pinot Noir is the main variety here. The Anderson Valley provides a fine Savoy Vineyard example. A hillside aspect and cool summer nights ensure a wine with piercing red berry fruit, great minerality and a firm structure. Cool Sonoma Coast is the source of the rich dark-berry fruited Terra Neuma which comes from biodynamically farmed vines. The wine possesses excellent acidity. La Neblina (Spanish for fog) differs in that it is from a blend of two vineyards. Full of dark-cherry fruit it is softer and more approachable. The Alberigi is full, dark and smoky and possesses a firm structure demanding of 3 or 4 years' patience. Two additional Pinots are also released from the Laguna Vineyard in the Russian River and the Dierke Vineyard and Clos Platt Vineyards, both on the Sonoma Coast. Syrah from the Cherry Camp Vineyard is rich and full of dark berry fruit with sumptuous chocolatey undertones despite its cool climate origins. It is picked very late often in the beginning of November. A second Sonoma Coast Syrah is also released from the Dusty Lane Vineyard. Timbervine is sourced from elevated hillside plantings. Cooling breezes provide a fine structured mineral edge to the wine's dark berry and roasted coffee fruit with subtle notes of black pepper. Las Colinas, like La Neblina, is a blend of cool climate sites and is characterised more by its elegance than its weight. Just one Zinfandel is produced which comes from the Radio Coteau Estate Vineyard Robert's Block. Zin was originally sourced from Von Viedlich Vineyard and will be worth a try if you come across any. The range is completed by an elegant and very Burgundian styled Chardonnay from the Savoy Vineyard. Subtle citrus and mineral notes are underpinned by a rich leesy complexity on the palate. A Riesling also comes from the recently planted Platt Vineyard on the Sonoma Coast. The wines deserve cellaring, particularly the top Syrahs. (DM)

Recommended Reds:
Pinot Noir Savoy Vineyard Anderson Valley ★★★★★ £F
Pinot Noir Terra Neuma Sonoma Coast ★★★★★ £F
Pinot Noir Alberigi Vineyard Russian River Valley ★★★★☆ £F
Pinot Noir La Neblina Sonoma Coast ★★★★ £F
Syrah Cherry Camp Sonoma Coast ★★★★★ £F
Syrah Timbervine Russian River Valley ★★★★★ £F
Syrah Las Colinas Russian River Valley ★★★★ £E
Zinfandel Von Viedlich Vineyard Russian River Valley ★★★★☆ £E
Recommended Whites:
Chardonnay Savoy Vineyard Anderson Valley ★★★★☆ £F

Ravenswood (Sonoma Valley) *www.ravenswood-wine.com*
No longer small, this Sonoma winery has a major focus on good to very good Zinfandel. The winery was founded in 1976 by winemaker Joel Peterson and partner Reed Foster, who have now sold a controlling interest to Constellation Brands. Vintners Blend is a good budget label, including Zinfandel, Merlot and Chardonnay. In the second tier are the County Series wines, sourced from vineyards throughout the state, including several Zinfandels. The top wines are in the Single Vineyard-Designated series. Along with the Zinfandels offered there is an interesting meritage red, Pickberry. A further premium red Icon Mixed Blacks has also been released which is a blend of Zinfandel, Carignane, Petite Sirah and varying small amounts of other varieties. Top reds are fine cellar prospects. (DM)

Recommended Reds:
Zinfandel Teldeschi Vineyard ★★★★ £E
Zinfandel Old Vine Napa Valley ★★★ £C

California North Coast

Zinfandel Amador County ★★☆ £C
Cabernet Sauvignon Sonoma County ★★ £C
Merlot Sonoma County ★★ £C

J Rochioli (Russian River Valley) www.rochioliwinery.com

The Rochioli family have been grape growers for far longer than they have been wine producers. They do however produce some of the best Pinot Noir and Chardonnay from the Russian River, along with impressive Sauvignon Blanc. A Pinot Noir rosé is also made and Estate Syrah and Valdigué are also now available. A sparkling Blanc de Noir is also made. As well as the estate Pinot Noir and Chardonnay, there are a number of single-vineyard bottlings of each produced in very small quantities, almost invariably rating ★★★★ or more. (DM)

Recommended Reds:
Pinot Noir Estate Russian River Valley ★★★★ £F
Recommended Whites:
Chardonnay Estate Russian River Valley ★★★★ £E
Sauvignon Blanc Estate Russian River Valley ★★★ £D

Roederer Estate (Anderson Valley) www.roedererestate.com

Champagne house Louis Roederer has set up its California outpost in the cool Anderson Valley. Unlike a number of their competitors they concentrate on producing just four wines. The regular Brut NV, made from all three Champagne grapes, and Rosé, from Pinot Noir, provide good value and a riper, fuller style than their French counterparts. The Brut L'Ermitage is altogether more serious, a very well structured blend of Pinot Noir and Chardonnay that is both long and complex. A small volume of Brut L'Ermitage Rosé is also made. (DM)

Recommended Whites:
Brut L'Ermitage Anderson Valley ★★★★ £F
Brut NV Anderson Valley ★★★ £E
Recommended Rosés:
Brut Rosé NV Anderson Valley ★★☆ £E

⚫ Seghesio (Dry Creek Valley) www.seghesio.com

The Seghesio family have been based in the Sonoma Valley since 1895, although they only decided to bottle their own fruit as recently as 1983. Today there are 162 ha (400 acres) of prime vineyard sites which are producing some of the best Zinfandel and Italian-style wines in California. The Zins, of which there are eight wines now released, all have marvellous depth and purity – full of ripe fruit but complex and very intense. There's good to very good Sangiovese and Barbera. Varietal Aglianico is also now released as well as a Petite Sirah, Il Cinghiale. A number of blends are also included in the range. Defiant combines Aglianico, Syrah and Cabernet Sauvignon, Marian's Reserve is from Zinfandel, Petite Sirah and Carignane, while Nonno's Rosso blends Zinfandel, Alicante Bouschet and Syrah with Mourvèdre. There are also two single vineyard Russian River Pinot Noirs, sourced from the Dutton-Manzana and Peters sites. While reds dominated the output here there are a couple of well priced whites. A Vermentino is made as well as the mineral and green-fruited Arneis which is a touch riper and fuller than many Italian examples. (DM)

Recommended Reds:
Zinfandel Old Vine Sonoma County ★★★★ £E
Zinfandel Cortina Vineyard Dry Creek Valley ★★★★ £E
Zinfandel Home Ranch Alexander Valley ★★★★ £E
Zinfandel Sonoma Valley ★★★ £C
Barbera Alexander Valley ★★★ £D

Sangiovese Alexander Valley ★★★ £D
Recommended Whites:
Arneis Russian River Valley ★★★★ £F

Selby (Russian River Valley) www.selbywinery.com

A relatively small operation producing small lots across a fairly extensive range with several wines only available at the tasting room in Healdsburg. However if you are travelling in the area it is well worth a visit. Throughout the range the wines offer generally excellent value for money. The winery was established in the early 1990s by Susie Selby's late father, David. She has since taken on the winemaking mantle and takes a very hands on approach. There is a good and fresh rosé made from Syrah with limited skin contact. Of the whites, the Sonoma County Sauvignon is light, fresh and grassy while the Russian River Chardonnay offers subtle tropical fruit, spicy oak and a rich texture from ageing on lees. A Dave Selby Reserve is also made. An extensive range of reds are also produced. Merlot is soft and plummy but more serious is a Malbec, blended with a little Cabernet Sauvignon, which has a ripe tobacco and dark-fruited character. Cherry-scented Pinot Noir from the Russian River is bottled unfined and unfiltered and sees some new French oak. Again a Reserve is also made, Calegari. Cabernet Sauvignon also receives new oak and offers an impressive intensity of fine red berry and plum fruit in a ripe and full style. Decent Syrah from Sonoma County is joined by a very impressive limited bottling from the Vesenaz Vineyard. It is very characterful and loaded with dark blackberry fruit and spicy pepper notes. There is also a very impressive and well-priced old vine Zin from the Dry Creek and Alexander Valleys. A Bobcat version is a limited bottling from 65 to 85 year old vines and is arguably the most exciting wine produced here. It is rich and concentrated with just a slight hint of raisin showing through. The range is completed by a port-style wine, made from Zinfandel and a sweet white called Fancy Nancy, a blend of Gewürztraminer, Sauvignon Blanc and Muscat. Additional reds include a Russian River Valley Sangiovese, a Dry Creek Valley Carignane and an Alexander Valley Petit Verdot. (DM)

Recommended Reds:
Zinfandel Bobcat Sonoma County ★★★☆ £E
Zinfandel Port Sonoma County ★★★ £D
Zinfandel Old Vines Sonoma County ★★★ £D
Syrah Vesenaz Vineyard Dry Creek Valley ★★★☆ £E
Syrah Sonoma County ★★★ £D
Malbec Alexander Valley ★★★☆ £D
Cabernet Sauvignon Asevedo Reserve Sonoma County ★★★ £E
Pinot Noir Russian River Valley ★★★ £D
Merlot Sonoma County ★★☆ £C
Recommended Whites:
Fancy Nancy Sonoma County ★★★ £D
Chardonnay Russian River Valley ★★★ £D
Sauvignon Blanc Sonoma County ★☆ £B

⚫ Siduri (Russian River Valley) www.siduri.com

An extensive range of fine and stylish Pinot Noirs, as well as impressive Syrah under the NOVY label have been made by this small warehouse operation on the outskirts of Santa Rosa since its first vintage in 1994. Diana and Adam Lee recently sold their operation to Kendall-Jackson and have practiced an absolutely minimalist approach to winemaking and to date no wine they have bottled has been either fined or filtered. The objective is to produce wines that are expressive of the region or individual *terroir* from which they have been sourced. A range of single-vineyard bottlings

have included the high-profile Pisoni Vineyard among them. Pinot is now sourced all the way from the Willamette Valley in Oregon down to the Sta. Rita Hills AVA in Santa Barbara County – the only problem being that there's not very much about. Vineyard sources are expected to remain the same under the new ownership for the time being. (DM)

Recommended Reds:

Pinot Noir Pisoni Vineyard Santa Lucia Highlands ★★★★★ £G
Pinot Noir Van der Kamp Vineyard Sonoma Mountain ★★★★ £F
Pinot Noir Santa Lucia Highlands ★★★★ £F
Pinot Noir Sonoma County ★★★☆ £E

Simi (Alexander Valley) *www.simiwinery.com*
This winery was originally established in 1876 by the immigrant Italian Simi family and is now a part of the Constellation Brands Icon Estate range. The wines here have been improving across recent vintages, they are altogether more accessible than previously, particularly in the case of the lower priced Sonoma County wines. Sauvignon Blanc is cool-fermented and gains additional depth from a small addition of Sémillon. The wineries big volume brand is Chardonnay with an output of well over 100,000 cases a year and it shows; the wine has straightforward melon scented fruit and gets a touch of new French oak but lacks the vibrancy of the Sauvignon. Bigger, fuller and richer is the Reserve Chardonnay from Russian River vineyards. The wine was originally based on the Goldfields Vineyard but a number of other sites are now included. Around two-thirds is aged in new oak and this a typically full, rich style and moderately priced. A marginally pricier Alexander Valley (£E) example is also made. However it is the reds which are more impressive. Merlot comes from a range of sites. Cabernet Sauvignon by contrast is from solely Alexander Valley fruit and includes unusually a little Syrah and Petite Sirah as well as Merlot and Cabernet Franc. This is the winery's other big volume brand and it is intense and structured with vibrant blackberry fruit. It is the top two Cabernets though that are the stand out wines. The Landslide Vineyard bottling has only been released since the 1999 vintage but has emerged as a well priced premium quality example of the variety. The vineyard is planted to a range of clones and the wine offers rich blackberry and plum fruit as well as a lush texture and will drink well young. The Reserve Alexander Valley example, sourced from a range of Alexander Valley sites, is denser and fuller. It is given 24 months in 100% new oak, then aged for a further year before release. Pinot Noir, including a Russian River Reserve and Pinot Gris are also made. (DM)

Recommended Reds:

Cabernet Sauvignon Reserve Alexander Valley ★★★★ £G
Cabernet Sauvignon Landslide Vineyard Alexander Valley ★★★☆ £F
Cabernet Sauvignon Alexander Valley ★★☆ £D
Merlot Sonoma County ★★ £D

Recommended Whites:

Chardonnay Reserve Russian River Valley★★☆ £D
Sauvignon Blanc Sonoma County★★ £C
Chardonnay Sonoma County★☆ £C

Skewis Wines (Russian River Valley) *www.skewiswines.com*
Specialist producer of small-lot Pinot Noir. Output is rarely above 200 cases per wine, so bottles will be difficult to find – but very much worth the search. Yields are around 2 tons to the acre and the Skewises work closely with their vineyard suppliers on crop thinning prior to *veraison* when necessary. Fermentation is in small bins and completed in barrel. The wines are marked more by elegance and

persistence on the palate than by sheer weight. The Salzgeber-Chan from the Russian River is the lightest and most approachable. Also from the Russian River, Montgomery (last released from the 2009 vintage) is more gamey with strawberry character. Also released from the Russian River is a Lingenfelder Vineyard wine and a further release from the Peters Vineyard on the Sonoma Coast. The finely structured Anderson Valley Reserve offers impressive intensity and depth with stunning character and purity. This has not been released for a few years but other single site examples from Anderson Valley include the Wiley, Greenwood Ridge and Ridley Vineyards and should certainly be worth looking for. Expect all the wines to develop very well for 4 or 5 years. (DM)

Recommended Reds:

Pinot Noir Anderson Valley Reserve ★★★★☆ £F
Pinot Noir Montgomery Vineyard Russian River Valley ★★★★ £F
Pinot Noir Salzgeber-Chan Vineyard Russian River Valley ★★★★ £E

WH Smith (Sonoma County) *www.whsmithwines.com*
Bill Smith established his reputation for making great California reds when he ran the LA JOTA winery on Howell Mountain, creating massive and powerful Cabernet Sauvignon and Petite Sirah – some of legendary proportions. The Smiths have now sold some of their interest here on the Sonoma Coast to David DEL DOTTO. As well as the intense and complex Hellenthal Vineyard, a Sonoma Coast and a number of other bottlings are also offered as well as two Howell Mountain Cabernet Sauvignons, Brown and Purple labels from land he recently planted. The Pinot style is one of elegance rather than power, with an attractive undercurrent of piercing, red berry fruit and well-judged oak. (DM)

Recommended Reds:

Pinot Noir Hellenthal Vineyard Sonoma Coast ★★★★ £F

Sonoma-Cutrer (Russian River Valley) *www.sonomacutrer.com*
Originally established as a top-notch producer of Chardonnay in 1973 by Brice Cutrer Jones. The wines are consistent well priced, particularly the two leading cuvées below. With the exception of Les Pierres, which is just to the north of Carneros, the vineyard plots are all Russian River. The Russian River Ranches bottling is a blend of all the winery's vineyards throughout the region, while the two single-vineyard wines are classified as its Grand Cru program. The tiny-production top wine is the Founders Reserve, selected from the five best barrels of the vintage and bottled without filtration. This is not a vineyard selection but purely the very best barrels from the three vineyards. Pinot Noir is also now made, with examples from the Russian River, the Vine Hill and Owsley vineyards and a Founders Reserve label is also made. (DM)

Recommended Whites:

Chardonnay Les Pierres Sonoma Valley ★★★ £E
Chardonnay The Cutrer Russian River Valley ★★★ £E
Chardonnay Russian River Ranches Russian River Valley ★★☆ £D

Spann Vineyards (Sonoma Valley) *www.spannvineyards.com*
Another small artisan winemaking husband and wife team who first got the bug through drinking wine (Betsy lived in Bordeaux for a while and Peter was a wine buyer for restaurants, and seemed to be doing an admirable job at it, too). Whilst Betsy is the hands-on winemaker, Peter sources fruit from other vineyards as well as their own, allowing them to create some interesting blends. Betsy's Backacher Bottle Blonde is a blend of roughly two-thirds Sémillon and one-third Chardonnay – an easy drinking medium-bodied quaffing wine with immediate appeal as the entry level white. On a

California North Coast

more serious note, Yin Yang is a Chardonnay and Viognier blend that has the stone fruit flavours of the Viognier jostling with the full and rich character of Chardonnay. A barrel-fermented Chardonnay from the Gustaffson Estate in Carneros is also available but in very small quantities. Mo Zin is a delightful blend of Zinfandel, Mourvèdre, Syrah and Primitivo, offering brambly fruit with hints of lavender, herb and *garrigue*, full, rich, herby and spicy. A number of other reds are made – Cabernet Sauvignons from the Cross Creek Vineyard in the Sonoma Valley and the Mayacamus Range. A Mourvèdre is sourced from Lake County. From Amador County there is a Zinfandel, a Primitivo, a Cabernet Franc as well as a Tempranillo Two Barrels. A Petit Verdot and a Malbec are made from Sonoma County fruit while a Cinsault is made under the Sonoma Valley AVA. There are also a number of red blends. Classic Four is a Bordeaux styled combination of Cabernet Sauvignon, Cabernet Franc, Merlot and a decent proportion of Petit Verdot, while OMG blends just Cabernet Sauvignon and Merlot. Mojo 15 barrels is a super-Tuscan lookalike combining Cabernet Sauvignon, Sangiovese, Syrah, Merlot and Cabernet Franc. S&M from Sonoma Valley is from Syrah and Merlot while Powerlifter is made from a combination of Petite Sirah, Cinsault, Grenache and Syrah. A red Betsy's Backacher is also made and is a mixed blend similarly priced to the white. (NB)

Recommended Reds:
Mo Zin California ★★★☆ £D
Recommended Whites:
Chardonnay/Viognier Sonoma County ★★★☆ £D
Betsy's Backacher Bottle Blonde California ★★☆ £C

St Francis Vineyards (Sonoma Valley) *www.stfranciswine.com*
Impressive, medium-sized Sonoma winery founded in 1971. An extensive range is produced, mainly from Sonoma County fruit and at the top end the quality is striking. Zinfandels, both Old Vines and Three Valleys, are big, brooding, ripe examples of the variety. Two other examples from the Anacieto and Bacchi vineyards are Russian River Valley sourced. The Sonoma County Terra Rossa is named after the red clay soils found throughout its Dry Creek, Russian River and Sonoma Valley vineyard sources. The Cabernet Kings Ridge Reserve, the top label, from Sonoma Valley is powerful, refined and very well crafted. It will age gracefully and needs a minimum of 6 years. Merlot, Pinot Noir, Chardonnay and a Gewürtraminer are also made. A fairly extensive range of reserve labels are also available solely from the winery. (DM)

Recommended Reds:
Cabernet Sauvignon Kings Ridge Vineyard Reserve ★★★★☆ £G
Cabernet Sauvignon Sonoma County ★★☆ £C
Zinfandel Three Valleys Sonoma County ★★★ £E
Zinfandel Old Vines Sonoma County ★★☆ £C
Merlot Sonoma County ★☆ £C
Recommended Whites:
Chardonnay Reserve Behler Vineyard Sonoma Valley ★★☆ £E
Chardonnay Sonoma County ★☆ £C

Steele (Lake County) *www.steelewines.com*
Jed Steele has enormous experience of the wine business in California, having previously been the founding winemaker at KENDALL-JACKSON. He established his own label in 1991 and he now produces an extensive range of reds and whites, with the top-of-the-line examples coming from an almost bewildering array of single-vineyard sources. These are not only impressive and stylish but represent very good value for money. Chardonnay is on the one hand rich and opulent, on the other balanced by a fine

mineral undercurrent, and there is an unusual late-harvest example produced from very low yields. The reds are supple, well-structured and accessible at a young age. They will however develop well in bottle. Writers Block and Shooting Star are the winery's secondary labels, providing good fruit-driven wines at very fair prices. Often these will be ★, sometimes ★★ plus wines. The top label is Steele Stymie from which a Merlot and Syrah are produced which are not expensive (£E). (DM)

Recommended Reds:
Pinot Noir Bien Nacido Vineyard Santa Maria Valley ★★★☆ £E
Pinot Noir Sangiacomo Vineyard Carneros ★★★ £D
Pinot Noir Carneros ★★☆ £C
Syrah Parmalee-Hill Vineyard Russian River Valley ★★★☆ £E
Syrah Lake County ★★☆ £C
Cabernet Franc Lake County ★★★ £C
Merlot Lake County ★★☆ £C
Zinfandel Catfish Vineyard Lake County ★★★ £D
Recommended Whites:
Chardonnay Cuvée California ★★★ £C
Pinot Blanc Santa Barbara County ★★ £C

✿ **Stonestreet (Alexander Valley)** *www.stonestreetwines.com*
One of a number of high-quality, medium-sized wineries in the Jackson family empire. Chardonnay, Cabernet Sauvignon both in various guises, and the Bordeaux style red Legacy, a blend dominated by Cabernet Sauvignon, are all impressive with fruit coming from the estate's high altitude Alexander Mountain property in the Alexander Valley AVA and a number of individual vineyard sites. Chardonnay is in a rich, tropical style, with the top bottlings showing both refinement and the structure for mid-term cellaring. The reds are big, powerful and brooding, marked by high alcohol. They are rich almost chocolaty, with just the occasional leafy note in cooler vintages. Three additional whites are also released. Aurora Point is a Sauvignon Blanc, Terrace Point a Sémillon/Sauvignon blend and a varietal Riesling is also made. (DM)

Recommended Reds:
Cabernet Sauvignon Christopher's Vineyard ★★★★★ £G
Legacy Alexander Valley ★★★★★ £G
Recommended Whites:
Chardonnay Upper Barn Vineyard Alexander Valley ★★★★☆ £F

Joseph Swan (Russian River Valley) *www.swanwinery.com*
This is the oldest established winery in the Russian River. It was founded by the original owner, Joe Swan, Lynn Berglund's father in 1967. Four decades later the wines reflect the history of the property and are both traditional and characterful. Pinot Gris is rich and honeyed with a firm mineral structure, the fruit will take 2 or 3 years to open out. Zinfandel comes from both the Russian River and Sonoma Valley and is characterful, well priced if generally very ripe in style. The example from the Stellwagen Vineyard is round and full with sweet fruit dominating the mid palate. The Mancini Ranch is a touch lighter with a leafy, peppery component. Saralee's Vineyard Pinot Noir is gamey and quite Burgundian in style. No doubt some of its complexity coming from the six different clones planted in the vineyard. The Trenton Estate home vineyard is a fine source for both Syrah and Pinot Noir. The Syrah is dark and peppery with a firm structure, while the Pinot is rich and shows lovely ripe strawberry fruit and an underlying truffly character. Although the reds are generally accessible on release, the Pinots and particularly Syrah will benefit from 3 or 4 years of further ageing. (DM)

Recommended Reds:
Pinot Noir Trenton Estate Russian River Valley ★★★☆ £F
Pinot Noir Saralee's Vineyard Russian River Valley ★★★ £E
Syrah Trenton Estate Russian River Valley ★★★ £E
Zinfandel Stellwagon Vineyard Sonoma Valley ★★★ £D
Zinfandel Mancini Ranch Russian River Valley ★★☆ £D
Recommended Whites:
Pinot Gris Trenton Station Russian River Valley ★★☆ £C

Thackrey & Co (Marin County) *www.thackreyandcompany.com*
Sean Thackrey produces a small range of top-flight reds from Pinot Noir, Sangiovese, Petite Sirah and his long established Syrah, Orion. This is sourced from the Rossi Vineyard in St Helena and is a massive, burly wine with tremendous potential, requiring at least 5 years' cellaring to shed its tannin. The Pleiades by contrast is a ripe, altogether more forward non vintage blend from a varying mix of Syrah, Grenache, Mourvèdre and Petite Sirah and may be enjoyed on release. Also now produced are Pinot Noir Andromeda from Devil's Gulch Ranch in Merin County, Sangiovese Aquila from the Eaglepoint Ranch in Mendocino and Petite Sirah Sirius from the same source. A Viognier, Lyra comes from the Noble Vineyard in the Knights Valley. It is also well worth visiting the "Library" on Sean's website which is the world's finest resource for texts on the history of wine-making. (DM)
Recommended Reds:
Orion Rossi Vineyard Napa Valley ★★★★☆ £G
Pleiades California ★★★★ £F

Tin Barn (Sonoma County) *www.tinbarnvineyards.com*
This small winery is a collaboration of five friends, including winemaker Michael Lancaster who manages its daily operation. The business name emanates from the old barn found on the Sonoma Coast where Lancaster sources his earthy, cool climate Syrah. Other wines include grassy and lightly citrusy Sauvignon Blanc from Carneros, where the winery tasting room is based. The wine is 80% tank fermented with the balance in oak to add a little weight and structure. A Cabernet Sauvignon from Sonoma Valley has a marked dark berry and plummy fruit character. A splendidly dark, savoury Zinfandel from the Russian River has a lovely blackberry and mineral character. Arguably the best wine here, however, is the Coryelle Fields Vineyard Syrah from the Sonoma Coast. It has dark spicy fruit that is well balanced by smoky new oak as well as impressive depth and substance. The reds, particularly Cabernet and Syrah, will develop nicely over four or five years. Pinot Noir also comes from the Ricci Vineyard in Carneros, Merlot from the Desnudos Vineyard in the Sonoma Valley and a rosé, Joon Rose of Syrah is also sourced from the Coryelle Fields Vineyard. (DM)
Recommended Reds:
Zinfandel Chamizal Vineyard Russian River Valley ★★★☆ £D
Syrah Coryelle Fields Vineyard Sonoma Coast ★★★☆ £D
Cabernet Sauvignon Sonoma Valley ★★★ £E
Recommended Whites:
Sauvignon Blanc Hi Vista Vineyard Carneros ★★☆ £C

Marimar Torres (Green Valley) *www.marimarestate.com*
Based in the cool Green Valley appellation, Miguel Torres" sister Marimar established this operation in 1986, planting the small 33 ha (81 acre) Don Miguel vineyard equally between Chardonnay and Pinot Noir. Small plantings of Albariño, Syrah and Tempranillo have followed. A varietal Albariño as well as blends of Chardonnay/Albariño and Syrah/Tempranillo are now released. A new property

in the Freestone Valley on the Sonoma Coast, Doña Margarita Vineyard has been planted to Pinot Noir. There is a European approach to viticulture with high vine density helping to ensure low-yielding, piercing fruit. The vineyards have been tended entirely organically since 2003 and cover crops are planted to control vigour and provide a better balance. Vinification is typically Burgundian. The Chardonnay is barrel-fermented and aged on lees with 100% malolactic and a second label Acero is also released. Pinot Noir is vinified by separate parcel and clone with a small proportion of whole bunches adding complexity. As well as the La Masía release, Mas Cavalls comes from the Doña Margarita Vineyard and there are three very limited releases from the Don Miguel Vineyard which are wine club exclusives, Pinot Noir Cristina as well as Pinots from the Stony and Earthquake Blocks. The wines are always restrained and well balanced with good medium-term cellaring potential. (DM)
Recommended Reds:
Pinot Noir La Masía Don Miguel Vineyard Green Valley ★★★★ £F
Recommended Whites:
Chardonnay La Masía Don Miguel Vineyard Green Valley ★★★★ £E

◉ Vérité (Sonoma Valley) *www.veritewines.com*
Recently established Jackson family premium operation specialising in Bordeaux red styles. The wines are all hand-crafted from various sites throughout Sonoma County. The vineyard sources are classic mountain terroirs and winemaker Pierre Seillan is able to source what the winery refers to as micro crus, producing wines from the very best blocks of a number of estates. Fruit comes from the Alexander, Bennett and Knights Valleys as well as Carneros and Atlas Peak. La Joie emulates the Left Bank of Bordeaux and is a blend of roughly two-thirds Cabernet Sauvignon with the balance Merlot. Youthfully backward and firmly structured, it is nevertheless very concentrated with fine, intense, very ripe dark berry fruit. La Muse, mainly Merlot and a small amount of Cabernet Sauvignon, is more forward and opulent. Full of dark plum and spicy oak, the wine is richly textured, supple but finely structured. Without doubt the option of being able to source superb fruit from a number of sites adds complexity. The third wine in the portfolio is Le Désir, a Saint-Emilion style blend of Cabernet Franc and Merlot with a touch of Cabernet Sauvignon. (DM)
Recommended Reds:
La Joie Sonoma County ★★★★★ £H
La Muse Sonoma County ★★★★★ £H
Le Désir Sonoma County ★★★★★ £H

❀ Williams Selyem (Russian River Valley) *www.williamsselyem.com*
The Dysons purchased this classic Sonoma property from founders Burt Williams and Ed Selyem in 1998. Winemaker Bob Cabral has stayed on and continues to make the same artisan styles of Chardonnay, Pinot Noir and Zinfandel as Williams and Selyem. The Pinots are rich and concentrated, marked by their powerful, earthy tannins, while the Chardonnay can be lusciously rich but with none of the overt tropical notes found in neighbouring wines and an unoaked example is also made. The Zinfandels are striking, concentrated and very pure. A plethora of single-vineyard labels are produced every vintage and rarely are these less than ★★★★. These are Sonoma wines for the longer haul. There have also been releases of two very interesting, rich and intense sweet wines from Gewürztraminer (San Benito County) and Muscat. Both are opulent in style but well-structured with a fine mineral-fresh acid balance. A late harvested Port style red also comes from the Vista Verde Vineyard combining the traditional Portuguese varieties of Touriga

California North Coast

National, Tinta Cão, Tinta Francesca and Tinta Madeira. (DM)

Recommended Reds:

Pinot Noir Hirsch Vineyard Sonoma Coast ★★★★★ £F

Pinot Noir Estate Russian River Valley ★★★★★ £F

Zinfandel Bacigalupi Vineyard Russian River Valley ★★★★ £F

Recommended Whites:

Chardonnay Allen Vineyard Russian River Valley ★★★★ £F

Chardonnay Heintz Vineyard Sonoma Coast ★★★★ £F

Gewürztraminer Late Harvest Vista Verde ★★★★★ £G

Muscat Canelli Late Harvest Russian River Valley ★★★★ £G

>> **Wind Gap Wines (Russian River Valley)** *www.windgapwines.com*
Wind Gap are based in Sebastopol in the Russian River Valley but make a range of characterful wines from a number of areas under the guiding eye of winemaker Pax Mahle who has also made some exceptional Rhône styles at the PAX WINES company. The Trousseau Gris, a rare example of the variety in California is sourced from the Russian River Valley. Like all the wines here cool climate sources are sort to provide a fresh edge and drinkability. There is a traditional vinification with a brief skin contact, fermentation in a mix of stainless tanks and concrete, and then aging in neutral oak and stainless steel to lend the wine a little structure and emphasise the quality of its fruit. The result is impressive weight on the palate with an interesting array of floral and exotic fruit aromas. Woodruff Chardonnay is an elegant, almost Burgundian style. Fermentation is in stainless steel and the wine is aged in small oak, around 20% for less than a year. Grenache from over 85 year old vines is full of old vine complexity and vinified and aged traditionally in concrete. (DM)

Recommended Reds:

Grenache Old Vine Sceales Sonoma County ★★★☆ £E

Recommended Whites:

Chardonnay Woodruff Santa Cruz Mountains ★★★★ £F

Trousseau Gris Russian River Valley ★★★ £C

Other wines of note

Alexander Valley Vineyards

Recommended Reds: Cyrus Alexander Valley ★★★☆ £F

Cabernet Sauvignon Estate Alexander Valley ★★★ £D

Zinfandel Old Vine Alexander Valley ★★★ £E

Redemption Zin Alexander Valley ★★★ £D

Sin Zin Alexander Valley ★★☆ £D

Temptation Zin Alexander Valley ★★☆ £C

Alluvia Rhône Blend Alexander Valley ★★★ £E

Recommended Whites: Chardonnay Estate Alexander Valley ★★☆ £C

"Gewurz" Mendocino County ★★ £B

Recommended Rosés: Sangiovese Alexander Valley ★★ £B

Anakota

Recommended Reds:

Cabernet Sauvignon Helena Montana Knights Valley ★★★★★ £F

Anthill Farms Winery

Recommended Reds: Pinot Noir Anderson Valley ★★★★ £E

Arnot-Roberts

Recommended Reds: Syrah Sonoma Coast ★★★★ £F

Bogle Vineyards

Recommended Reds: Zinfandel Old Vine California ★☆ £C

Bonterra

Recommended Reds: Syrah Mendocino County ★★ £B

Recommended Whites: Chardonnay Mendocino County ★★ £B

Viognier North Coast ★★ £B

August Briggs

Recommended Reds: Pinot Noir Russian River Valley ★★★ £E

Recommended Whites:

Chardonnay Leveroni Vineyard Carneros ★★★ £D

Capiaux

Recommended Reds:

Pinot Noir Widdoes Vineyard Russian River Valley ★★★★ £F

Pinot Noir Pisoni Vineyard Santa Lucia Highlands ★★★★☆ £F

Chateau Souverain

Recommended Reds:

Cabernet Sauvignon Winemakers Reserve Alexander Valley ★★★☆ £E

Recommended Whites:

Chardonnay Winemakers Reserve Carneros ★★★☆ £E

Cobb Wines

Recommended Reds:

Pinot Noir Coastlands 1906 Sonoma Coast ★★★★☆ £F

Pinot Noir Jack Hill Sonoma Coast ★★★★ £F

BR Cohn

Recommended Reds:

Cabernet Sauvignon Olive Hill Estate Sonoma Valley ★★★☆ £F

Recommended Whites:

Chardonnay Sangiacomo Vineyard Carneros ★★★☆ £D

Copain Wines

Recommended Reds:

Pinot Noir Kiser en Haut Anderson Valley ★★★★☆ £F

Syrah Les Voisins Yorkville Highlands ★★★☆ £E

Pinot Noir Tous Ensemble Mendocino County ★★★☆ £E

Syrah Tous Ensemble Mendocino County ★★★☆ £E

Recommended Whites:

Chardonnay Dupratt Vineyard Mendocino County ★★★★ £F

Davis Bynum

Recommended Reds: Pinot Noir Russian River Valley ★★★☆ £E

De Loach

Recommended Reds: Zinfandel OFS Russian River Valley ★★★☆ £E

Recommended Whites:

Chardonnay OFS Russian River Valley ★★★☆ £E

Drew Family

Recommended Reds:

Pinot Noir Gatekeepers Mendocino Ridge ★★★★ £E

Failla Wines

Recommended Reds: Pinot Noir Sonoma Coast ★★★☆ £E

Recommended Whites: Chardonnay Sonoma Coast ★★★☆ £E

Ferrari Carano

Recommended Reds: Merlot Sonoma County ★★★ £D

Recommended Whites: Fumé Blanc Sonoma County ★★★ £C

Chardonnay Sonoma County ★★☆ £D

Fetzer

Recommended Reds: Zinfandel Valley Oaks California ★☆ £A

Cabernet Sauvignon Valley Oaks California ★ £A

Recommended Whites: Chardonnay Sundial California ★ £A

Freeman

Recommended Reds: Pinot Noir Sonoma Coast ★★★☆ £E

Hanna

Recommended Reds:

Cabernet Sauvignon Reserve Red Ranch Alexander Valley ★★★★ £F

Cabernet Sauvignon Red Ranch Alexander Valley ★★★ £E

Zinfandel Bismark Mtn. Vineyard Moon Mtn. Sonoma Valley ★★★☆ £F

Recommended Whites:

Chardonnay Elias Estate Russian River Valley ★★★☆ £F

Haywood

Recommended Reds:

Zinfandel Los Chamizal Vineyard Sonoma Valley ★★☆ £C

Hirsch Vineyards
Recommended Reds:
Pinot Noir San Andreas Fault Sonoma Coast ★★★★☆ £F

J Wine Company
Recommended Whites:
Chardonnay Strata Russian River Valley ★★★ £E
Pinot Gris Russian River Valley ★☆ £C
Vintage Brut Russian River Valley ★★★ £E

Jolie-Laide Wines
Recommended Reds:
Grenache Syrah Rossi Ranch Sonoma County ★★★★ £E

Jordan
Recommended Reds:
Cabernet Sauvignon Estate Alexander Valley ★★★☆ £F
Recommended Whites:
Chardonnay Estate Russian River ★★★☆ £E

Kenwood Vineyards
Recommended Reds:
Cabernet Sauvignon Artists Series Sonoma Valley ★★★☆ £F
Cabernet Sauvignon Jack London Sonoma Valley ★★★ £E
Zinfandel Jack London Sonoma Valley ★★★ £D

Knez Winery
Recommended Reds:
Pinot Noir Cerise Vineyard Anderson Valley ★★★★☆ £F
Recommended Whites:
Chardonnay Demuth Vineyard Anderson Valley ★★★★ £E

Kunde Estate
Recommended Reds:
Zinfandel Reserve Century VinesSonoma Valley ★★☆ £E

Kutch Wines
Recommended Reds:
Pinot Noir McDougall Ranch Sonoma Coast Highlands ★★★★☆ £F
Pinot Noir Sonoma Coast ★★★☆ £E

Lancaster Estate
Recommended Reds:
Lancaster Estate Cabernet Sauvignon Alexander Valley ★★★★ £F

Lazy Creek
Recommended Whites: Gewürztraminer Anderson Valley ★★☆ £C

Limerick Lane
Recommended Reds:
Zinfandel Russian River Valley ★★★★ £D

Marietta Cellars
Recommended Reds:
Christo Rhone Blend NV Sonoma/Mendocino Counties ★★★☆ £D
Old Vine Red California ★★★ £C

Murphy-Goode
Recommended Reds:
Cabernet Sauvignon Terra a Lago Alexander Valley ★★★ £E
Zinfandel Liars Dice Sonoma Coast ★★ £C
Recommended Whites:
Reserve Fumé Sauvignon Blanc Alexander County ★★ £C
The Fumé Sauvignon Blanc North Coast ★ £C
Chardonnay California ★☆ £C

Nalle Winery
Recommended Reds: Zinfandel Dry Creek Valley ★★☆ £E

Navarro Vineyards
Recommended Reds: Pinot Noir Anderson Valley ★★ £C
Recommended Whites: Gewürztraminer Anderson Valley ★★ £C

Optima
Recommended Reds:
Cabernet Sauvignon Alexander Valley ★★★☆ £F

Petrichor
Recommended Reds: Les Trois Sonoma County ★★★★ £E

Pezzi King
Recommended Reds:
Zinfandel Old Vine Dry Creek Valley ★★★☆ £E

Raen
Recommended Reds:
Pinot Noir Royal St. Robert Cuvee Sonoma Coast ★★★★ £F

Random Ridge
Recommended Reds: Cabernets Reserve Mount Veeder ★★★☆ £E
Zinfandel Old Wave Sonoma Valley ★★★ £D

Martin Ray Vineyards
Recommended Reds: Synthesis Napa Valley ★★★★☆ £F
Cabernet Sauvignon Sonoma County ★★☆ £D
Recommended Whites: Chardonnay Russian River Valley ★★☆ £C

Red Car Wine Co
Recommended Reds: Pinot Noir Estate Sonoma Coast ★★★★ £F
Recommended Whites:
Chardonnay Estate Sonoma Coast ★★★★ £F

Quivira
Recommended Reds: Zinfandel Dry Creek ★★★ £D
Recommended Whites:
Sauvignon Blanc Fig Tree Vineyard Dry Creek Valley ★★☆ £C

Sadler Wells
Recommended Reds: Pinot Noir Sonoma Coast ★★★ £E
Recommended Whites: Chardonnay Carneros ★★★ £D

Sbragia Family
Recommended Reds:
Merlot Home Ranch Dry Creek Valley ★★★☆ £D
Recommended Whites:
Chardonnay Gamble Ranch Napa Valley ★★★★ £E
Chardonnay Home Ranch Dry Creek Valley ★★★☆ £D

Scharffenberger Cellars
Recommended Whites:
Brut Non Vintage Excellence Anderson Valley ★★☆ £C
Recommended Rosés:
Brut Vintage Rosé Excellence Anderson Valley ★★☆ £D

Scherrer Vineyard
Recommended Reds: Pinot Noir Russian River ★★★☆ £E
Zinfandel Old and Mature Vines Alexander Valley ★★★ £D

Sebastiani
Recommended Reds:
Cabernet Sauvignon Cherry Block Sonoma Valley ★★★★ £F

Philip Staley
Recommended Reds:
Grenache Staley Vineyard Russian River Valley ★★★ £D
Recommended Whites:
Viognier Staley Vineyard Russian River Valley ★★★ £C
Sémillon Dry Creek Valley ★★★ £C
Duet Sonoma County ★★☆ £C

Leo Steen
Recommended Whites:
Chenin Blanc Saini Vineyard Dry Creek Valley ★★★ £E

Stuhlmuller
Recommended Reds:
Cabernet Sauvignon Estate Alexander Valley ★★★☆ £E
Recommended Whites:
Chardonnay Estate Alexander Valley ★★★ £C

Trentadue
Recommended Reds: Old Patch Red Alexander Valley ★★ £C
Petite Sirah La Storia Alexander Valley ★★★☆ £D

California North Coast

California

Zinfandel La Storia Alexander Valley ★★★☆ £D
Wei Chi Vineyards
Recommended Whites:
Semillon Lucksinger Vineyard Lake County ★★★☆ £D
Wellington Vineyards
Recommended Reds:
Zinfandel Meeks Hilltop Ranch Sonoma County ★★★ £D
Wilde Farm
Recommended Reds:
Pinot Noir Donnelly Creek Anderson Valley ★★★★ £E

Work in progress!!

Producers under consideration for the next edition

Amapola Creek
Anaba Wines
Anakota
Bedrock Wine Co
Boar's View
Gamba Vineyards
Gundlach-Bundschu
Hidden Ridge
Kosta Browne
Mantra
Morgado Cellars
Peirson Meyer
Ram's Gate Winery
Relic
Sojourn Cellars
Wayfarer

Author's choice

A selection of Sonoma blockbuster reds

Dehlinger Syrah Estate
Carlisle Two Acres Red Two Acres Vineyard Russian River Valley
Gallo of Sonoma Cabernet Sauvignon Estate Northern Sonoma
Hartford Zinfandel Russian River Valley
Kendall Jackson Cabernet Sauvignon Stature Napa Valley
Martinelli Zinfandel Jackass Hill Russian River Valley
Peter Michael Les Pavots Knights Valley
Seghesio Zinfandel Cortina Vineyard Dry Creek Valley
DuMOL Syrah Eddie's Patch Russian River Valley
Laurel Glen Cabernet Sauvignon Sonoma Mountain
Pax Wine Cellars Alder Springs Vineyard Mendocino County
Fisher Vineyards Wedding Vineyard Sonoma County
Stonestreet Legacy Alexander Valley
Vérité La Muse Sonoma County
Vineyard of Pasterwick Syrah Dry Creek Valley

Benchmark Pinot Noirs

Adrian Fog Pinot Noir Oppenlander Vineyard Mendocino County
Dutton-Goldfield Pinot Noir Devil's Gulch Ranch Marin County
Gary Farrell Rochioli Vineyard Russian River Valley
Hanzell Pinot Noir Estate Sonoma Valley
Hartford Court Arrendell Vineyard Russian River Valley
Paul Hobbs Pinot Noir Hyde Vineyard Carneros
Kistler Pinot Noir Kistler Vineyard Vineyard Sonoma Valley
Lynmar Winery Five Sisters Russian River Valley
Papapietro Perry Pinot Noir Peters Vineyard Russian River Valley
J Rochioli Pinot Noir Estate Russian River Valley

Walter Hansel Pinot Noir Cuvée Alyce Russian River Valley
Williams Selyem Pinot Noir Hirsch Vineyard Sonoma Coast
Marimar Torres Pinot Noir La Masía Don Miguel Vineyard
Peay Vineyards Pinot Noir Scallop Shelf Sonoma Coast
Radio Coteau Pinot Noir Savoy Vineyard Anderson Valley
Skewis Pinot Noir Anderson Valley Reserve
La Follette Pinot Noir Van der Kamp Vineyard Sonoma Mountain

A selection of cool climate Sonoma whites

Arrowood Viognier Saralee's Vineyard Russian River Valley
Halleck Gewürztraminer Piner Creek Ranch Russian River Valley
Kistler Chardonnay Dutton Ranch Russian River Valley
La Crema Chardonnay Russian River Valley
Landmark Chardonnay Damaris Reserve Sonoma Coast
Lynmar Winery Chardonnay Quail Hill Vineyard Russian River Valley
Martinelli Chardonnay Charles Ranch Sonoma Coast
Peter Michael Cuvée Indigene Sonoma County
David Noyes Wines Chardonnay Rued Vineyard Russian River Valley
Peay Vineyards Roussanne/Marsanne Estate Sonoma Coast
Radio Coteau Chardonnay Savoy Vineyard Anderson Valley
Steele Chardonnay Durrell Vineyard
Williams Selyem Chardonnay Heintz Vineyard Sonoma Coast
Dutton-Goldfield Dutton Ranch Rued Vineyard Green Valley

A selection of affordable Sonoma values
Recommended Reds:
Dry Creek Zinfandel Old Vine Sonoma County
Edmeades Zinfandel Mendocino
Flowers Pinot Noir Sonoma Coast
Foppiano Petite Sirah Lot 96 Sonoma County
Zinfandel Heritage Clone Sonoma County
Steele Cabernet Franc Lake County
Seghesio Zinfandel Sonoma Valley
Papapietro Perry Pinot Noir Russian River
Porter Creek Carignane Old Vines Alexander Valley
Recommended Whites:
Ferrari Carano Fumé Blanc Sonoma County
Frick Viognier Gannon Vineyard Dry Creek Valley
Iron Horse Vineyards Chardonnay Estate Sonoma-Green Valley
Lazy Creek Gewürztraminer Anderson Valley
Martinelli Chardonnay Martinelli Road Russian River Valley
J Rochioli Sauvignon Blanc Estate Russian River Valley
Sbragia Family Chardonnay Home Ranch Dry Creek Valley
Selby Sauvignon Blanc Sonoma County
Joseph Swan Pinot Gris Trenton Station Russian River Valley

The Napa Valley has now been producing high-quality wine for over three decades and indeed many properties go back to pre-Prohibition times. As in the other major viticultural regions of California, dynamic change is continuous and new operations, particularly boutique and very small scale premium red producers, are emerging all the time. Of one thing there is no doubt: winemakers here and particularly those working with classic Bordeaux varieties, are able to charge super-premium prices. These days the top Bordeaux reds can seem relative bargains in comparison to some of their Napa counterparts. There is no question that an increasing number of truly world-class wines continue to emerge from Napa but also that there are as many that are priced too highly and quite simply struggle to justify their lofty tags. If you are looking for some very serious bottles they're certainly here, but some care and research is needed before purchasing.

Geography

The **Napa Valley AVA** runs along an extensive river valley stretching from north of Calistoga along the Napa River to south of the town of Napa itself and just edging towards San Pablo Bay at the northern end of San Francisco Bay. South-west of Napa, the Carneros AVA is located south of the Mayacamas Mountains and effectively divides the Sonoma and Napa Counties viticultural regions. In Napa, like Sonoma and Mendocino, the climate is moderated by cool marine breezes and coastal fog..

Northern Napa

Calistoga's benchland vineyards are the warmest in the Napa Valley, because little of the moderating sea breeze drifts this far. The topography becomes semimountainous to the west with the **Spring Mountain District** AVA and to the east the **Howell Mountain** AVA, which is an extension of the Coastal Ranges. There are a number of exceptional Cabernet Sauvignons, Merlots and meritage blends, produced from vineyards within these mountain AVAs. Equally impressive wines are also emerging from sites similarly cooled by altitude but on the lower slopes, both to the west, and east of the valley. These sites are characterised by excellent aspects and soil drainage, both of which are hallmarks in the production of great wine. The key to these wines is their structure; their mountain origin gives them a unique stamp. They can be the least approachable when young but among the longest-lived and most refined of Napa's great reds. This is essentially Cabernet country but there are some good Chardonnays, one or two stylish Syrahs and Viogniers and some very good Zinfandel.

Central Napa

The central section of the Napa Valley is the heart of its best benchland vineyards for Cabernet Sauvignon and Bordeaux-style red blends. This takes in an area that runs from **St Helena** in the north to cooler Yountville in the south and encompasses the AVAs of **Rutherford** and **Oakville**. It is difficult to generalise as wine quality is by no means determined by the traditional Rutherford Bench yardstick: the bench is a narrow strip of vineyard stretching north of the town of Rutherford with gravel and sandy-clay soils producing potentially great wines, but in recent years a whole host of other small vineyard sites have proven to have excellent growing conditions, many of them taking the Napa Valley AVA. However, in general the wines to the north at St Helena are the ripest and most opulent, while those from Yountville have the tightest structure. These generalisations are offset by exceptional producers outperforming their neighbours and by many sites which

are influenced by the sloping hills of Howell Mountain to the east and Spring Mountain and the Mayacamas to the west. As well as the Bordeaux styles, good Zinfandel and Syrah are grown throughout this stretch of vineyards.

Southern Napa

To the east of Yountville are the AVAs of **Stags Leap District** and **Atlas Peak**. To the west **Mount Veeder** provides sturdy reds with Zinfandel and Syrah increasingly successful; some fine, tightly structured Chardonnay and peachy Viognier are also produced. Stags Leap is somewhat of a conundrum. There are some very fine wines produced in these gravel soils but also a number of underperformers. Atlas Peak has so far disappointed. The winery of the same name has experimented with only moderate success with Sangiovese, Cabernet Sauvignon and Chardonnay. To the west of Napa, towards the **Wild Horse Valley**, the Bordeaux varieties and Chardonnay have all been successful. The newly created AVA of **Coombsville** would appear to offer much potential.

Carneros

Part-Sonoma County and part-Napa County, **Carneros** AVA is just inland to the north of San Pablo Bay and directly affected by those cool, marine breezes. This is key for the production of sparkling base wine and it is no surprise that a number of sparkling-wine operations are based here, including California offshoots of some of the big European names. Pinot Noir and Chardonnay are successful and, more surprisingly, in warmer mesoclimates so is spicy, black pepper-styled Syrah, notably from the Hudson Vineyard.

A-Z of producers by region

Wine behind the label

Napa & Carneros

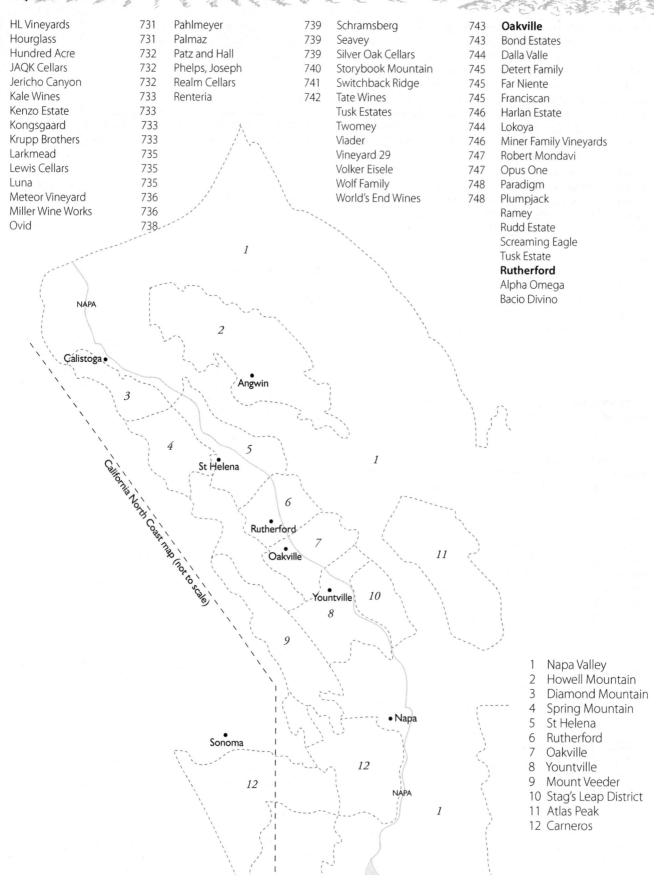

1 Napa Valley
2 Howell Mountain
3 Diamond Mountain
4 Spring Mountain
5 St Helena
6 Rutherford
7 Oakville
8 Yountville
9 Mount Veeder
10 Stag's Leap District
11 Atlas Peak
12 Carneros

California North Coast map (not to scale)

Beaulieu Vineyard
Cakebread Cellars
Caymus
Peter Franus
Frog's Leap
Grgich Hills
Lail Vineyards
Mumm Napa
Prisoner Wine Co
Quintessa
Rubicon Estate
Scarecrow
Staglin Family
Swanson
Spring Mountain
Barnett Vineyards
Behrens Family Winery
Cain Cellars
Fantesca
Juslyn
Newton
Pride Mountain Vineyards
Sherwin Family
Stony Hill
Spring Mountain Vineyard5
Philip Togni
Stag's Leap District
Pine Ridge
Quixote
Shafer
Stag's Leap Wine Cellars
St Helena
Aubert
Benessere Vineyards
Beringer
Bure
Dana Estates
Duckhorn
Fairchild
Flora Springs
Forman
Grace Family
Heitz Cellars
Kuleto
Littorai
Melka
Morlet Family
Nine Sun's
Rombauer
Spottswoode
Tor Kenward
Turley Cellars
Tusk Estates
Vineyard 29
Volker Eisele
Wolf Family Vineyards
Yountville
Domaine Chandon
Dominus
Larkin Wines

California Napa & Carneros vintage chart

	Cabernet & Meritage Blends	Zinfandel	Pinot Noir	Chardonnay
2015	★★★★☆ A	★★★★☆ A	★★★★☆ A	★★★★☆ A
2014	★★★★☆ A	★★★★☆ A	★★★★☆ A	★★★★☆ A
2013	★★★★☆ A	★★★★☆ A	★★★★☆ A	★★★★☆ A
2012	★★★★☆ A	★★★★☆ A	★★★★☆ A	★★★★☆ A
2011	★★★ A	★★★ B	★★★ A	★★★☆ B
2010	★★★☆ A	★★★ B	★★★ B	★★★ B
2009	★★★★☆ A	★★★★☆ A	★★★★☆ A	★★★★☆ B
2008	★★★★ A	★★★★ B	★★★★ B	★★★★ B
2007	★★★★☆ B	★★★☆ B	★★★★ B	★★★★ C
2006	★★★★ B	★★★ B	★★★☆ B	★★★★ C
2005	★★★★ B	★★★ C	★★★★ B	★★★★ C
2004	★★★★ A	★★★ C	★★★★ B	★★★★ C
2003	★★★★ B	★★★★ C	★★★★ C	★★★★ C
2002	★★★★☆ B	★★★ C	★★★★ C	★★★★ C
2001	★★★★☆ C	★★★★ C	★★★★ C	★★★★ D
2000	★★☆ C	★★★ D	★★★☆ D	★★★☆ D
1999	★★★☆ C	★★★★ C	★★★★ C	★★★★ D
1998	★★★ C	★★☆ D	★★★★ D	★★★★ D
1997	★★★★ C	★★★☆ D	★★★★ D	★★★★ D
1996	★★★☆ D	★★★ D	★★★☆ D	-
1995	★★★★ D	★★★☆ D	★★★☆ D	-

A-Z of producers

✪✪ **Abreu (Napa Valley)** *www.abreuvineyard.com*
David Abreu is best-known among his fellow winegrowers as a superlative viticulturalist. Numbered among his distinguished clientele are GRACE FAMILY, VIADER and PAHLMEYER. As well as his many vineyard-management commitments, he fashions a number of massive, super-ripe Cabernets. The Madrona Ranch with a hint of Merlot and Cabernet Franc. The wine is one of the most 'collectable' in California and as such is very pricey and almost impossible to find. Three further vineyard bottlings are also made, Thorevilos, Las Posadas Howell Mountain and Cappella. Check the winery website if you are interested in joining the waiting list. (DM)
Recommended Reds:
Cabernet Sauvignon Madrona Ranch Napa Valley ✪✪✪✪ £H
Cabernet Sauvignon Thorevilos Napa Valley ★★★★★ £H
Capella Proprietary Red St Helena ★★★★★ £H
Las Posadas Howell Mountain ★★★★★ £H

Acacia (Carneros) *www.acaciavineyard.com*
Acacia has always produced wines that are soundly made and represent reasonable value for money if sometimes lacking a touch of character or sense of place in the volume labels. The wines are particularly marked by their ripe fruit and for opulent reds and tropically styled whites at competitive prices they are all decent bets. Chardonnay is forward, oaky and richly textured. The Carneros is the volume wine; it has a sizeable output and gets 9 months ageing in one third new French oak. The Sangiacomo Vineyard output is a good deal less. Aged in a sizeable proportion of new French oak it is a step up in quality. There is also a small amount of a barrel-selection from the Russian River. Pinot Noir in its various

Napa & Carneros

guises offers bright berry fruit with greater depth and power in the single vineyard examples which include Winery Lake and St Clair Vineyard examples from Carneros, as well as a Thornton Vineyard example from the Sonoma Coast. Orogeny is a pricey Russian River Valley Pinot. A Pinot Noir rosé is also produced as well as a Syrah. (DM)

Recommended Reds:
Pinot Noir Carneros ★★☆ £E
Recommended Whites:
Chardonnay Sangiacomo Vineyard Napa Valley ★★★☆ £E
Chardonnay Winery Lake Vineyard Carneros ★★★ £E

>> Alpha Omega (Rutherford) *www.aowinery.com*
A partnership of a business power couple Michelle and Robin Baggett and notable winemaker Jean Hoefliger, also counts world-famous Michel Rolland as a consultant. A harmonious union of New World terroir and Old World techniques create a perfect blend of classic meets modern. The portfolio is extensive, featuring Cabernet Sauvignons, Red blends, Chardonnays, Merlot, a Petit Verdot and a couple of Sauvignon Blancs. Of note are their Cabernets, sometimes available in library releases to the wine club members. Using stellar fruit sources, such as Beckstoffer To-Kalon vineyard, Mission Hopper and Las Piedras, Hoefliger crafts wines of enormous concentration, solid structural core and great finish. The whites are quite fetching as well, particularly the hybrid of Bordeaux-style and New Zealand Sauvignon Blanc, which presents as a lively cross of dynamic acidity and classic fruit flair. (IT)
Recommended Reds:
Proprietary Red Napa Valley ★★★★ £E
Cabernet Sauvignon Napa Valley ★★★★ £E
Recommended Whites:
Sauvignon Blanc Napa Valley ★★★★☆ £E
Chardonnay Napa Valley ★★★★ £F

Amici Cellars (Napa Valley) *www.amicicellars.com*
The first commercial vintage at Amici was in 1992 and the winery remains small with an output of just a few thousand cases a year. Winemaker Jeff Hansen sources fruit from throughout the Napa for the Cabernet, while the Pinot Noir comes from the Costa Vineyard in Mendocino. Both wines are aged in French oak, 40–50% new, and the Pinot Noir is regularly hand-punched during fermentation to add complexity. The Pinot Noir is in a relatively tight style with bright strawberry fruit. The Cabernet is ripe and full with a dark, almost tarry character. The Cabernet in particular will benefit from 5 or 6 years' cellaring. A more expensive Reserve Cabernet is also released along with pricier still (£G) examples from Spring Mountain and the Morisoli Vineyard in Rutherford. A Sauvignon Blanc is also made. (DM)
Recommended Reds:
Cabernet Sauvignon Napa Valley ★★★☆ £F
Pinot Noir Mendocino County ★★★ £E

✿ Andersons Conn Valley *www.connvalleyvineyards.com*
Todd Anderson creates his family's small range of wines both from home Conn Valley as well as other vineyards with winemaker Mac Sawyer. The reds here in particular during the last decade have emerged as some of the finest and best priced examples from an area notable for its inflated prices. Todd also has his own micro garage style operation GHOST HORSE VINEYARDS from which he produces three wines that compete with the world's very best for both high quality and for high prices. There are now 11ha (26.5

acres) under vine - the property was originally planted back in 1983 and the first vintage 1987. Sauvignon Blanc is relatively new and comes from Lake County where the warm climate produces a ripe and opulent barrel-fermented example which gains additional depth from just over 20% Sémillon in the blend. Chardonnay from the cool Green Island Vineyard in southern Napa is in a ripe, peachy, tropical style, full and impressively concentrated with a rich underlying leesy character and sufficient acidity (the malolactic is avoided). However, it is the Bordeaux styled reds which truly stand out. The softest and most accessible of these is the Right Bank red, a blend of Cabernet Franc and Merlot. The wine is dark, cedary and with an underlying mocha character from its oak and has very impressive depth. Cabernet Sauvignon is 100% varietal and comes solely from estate grown grapes. As one would expect the wine is tighter and more firmly structured with subtle cassis notes and finely chiselled tannins. The top wine, Éloge is a blend of mainly Cabernet Sauvignon, with Cabernet Franc and a little Merlot and Petit Verdot. It is richly textured and opulent but with an elegance rarely found in the Napa. Bottled without filtration expect the top reds here to age extremely well. (DM)
Recommended Reds:
Éloge Red Napa Valley ✪✪✪✪✪ £G
Cabernet Sauvignon Reserve Estate Napa Valley ★★★★★ £F
Right Bank Red Napa Valley ★★★★ £F
Recommended Whites:
Chardonnay Green Island Vineyard Napa Valley ★★★★ £E
Sauvignon Blanc Lake County ★★★☆ £E

✪✪ Araujo (Napa Valley) *www.araujoestatewines.com*
These formidable wines are all produced from the Eisele Vineyard, originally owned by JOSEPH PHELPS, in the north-eastern part of the Napa Valley. As well as the Cabernet Sauvignon there is a first class Syrah and most recently Altagracia, a Bordeaux red blend of Cabernet Sauvignon, Petit Verdot and Merlot. Both are sadly produced in tiny quantities. Even scarcer is the occasional bottling of Viognier. The variety is mainly planted to blend with the Sauvignon Blanc and to provide fragrance for the Syrah. Since its purchase by former owner Bart Araujo in 1990, a considerable effort has been put into the vineyard with its superbly drained stony soils and mountain-moderated climate. The approach is as one would expect, delivering wines with rich, immensely concentrated fruit and supple and rounded tannins. The Cabernet is blended with a little Cabernet Franc, Petit Verdot and Merlot. The Sauvignon Blanc has a hint of Viognier and is part barrel- and part tank-fermented and then aged on lees for 6 months. With a total of just 16.6 ha (41 acres) under vine there is an inevitable scarcity here. Release prices are very fair but the auction market quickly gets a hold. All the reds are immensely ageworthy, however you might consider broaching them with 5 or 6 years' age, particularly if you're lucky enough to have a case or two. The property was sold in the summer of 2013 to the Pinault family whose other wine interests include Château LATOUR. (DM)
Recommended Reds:
Cabernet Sauvignon Eisele Vineyard Napa Valley ✪✪✪✪✪ £H
Recommended Whites:
Sauvignon Blanc Eisele Vineyard Napa Valley ★★★☆ £E

✿ Arietta (Napa Valley) *www.ariettawine.com*
John KONGSGAARD consults widely for other wineries as well as producing some superb Rhône styles under his own label. Here he has established a partnership with Fritz Hatton to produce very

small-scale, high-quality reds modelled mainly on the wines of Bordeaux. The Merlot is 100% varietal, dark, cedary, exceptionally balanced and very long and complex. The Hudson H Block is more Saint-Emilion than Pomerol in style; it blends Cabernet Franc with the balance Merlot. It is the firmest of the trio. The Variation One is dominated by Syrah and blended unusually with Merlot. Opulent, exotic and loaded with smoky, dark fruit it is the most approachable of the wines. Given some of the stratospheric prices elsewhere, the wines look like pretty good value. All will benefit from at least 4–5 years' cellaring and will keep very well. A varietal Cabernet Sauvignon is also produced and there is a pricey 88 Keys made from just two select barrels. Quartet combines the two Cabernets with Merlot and a touch of Petit Verdot while a white, On The White Keys, is a white Bordeaux lookalike coming from Sauvignon Blanc and Sémillon. (DM)

Recommended Reds:
Variation One Red Napa Valley ★★★★★ £H
H Block One Red Napa Valley ★★★★★ £H
Merlot Napa Valley ★★★★★ £G

>> Arkenstone (Howell Mountain) *www.arkenstone.com*

Nestled high atop the west side of Howell Mountain, the vineyard cultivated by Susan and Ron Krausz, oozes sophistication. Their vines hit the ground in 1998, and despite its youth, the infant vineyard soon delivered. The reds are broad, tense, anchored, high-acid and embrace powerful minerality; while whites tend to be more elegant and intellectual. The formidable Bordeaux blend of Cabernet Franc, Cabernet Sauvignon, Malbec, Merlot and Petit Verdot titled "Obsidian" is a blend made from grapes grown at high elevations and sourced from the estate vineyard's top blocks. It is aged for 22 months in new oak. The other significant wine is their Sauvignon Blanc, (with a dash of Semillon) which ferments in both barrel and concrete egg, and enjoys an 18-month bottle rest. Planted in rocky volcanic soils, the stress-burdened vines produce an intense result. The brand's wines are predominantly sold via mailing list and due to low production, sell out quickly. (IT)

Recommended Reds:
Obsidian Estate Howell Mountain ★★★★★ £H
Recommended Whites:
Sauvignon Blanc Estate Howell Mountain ★★★★★ £F

Atalon (Napa Valley) *www.atalon.com*

Recently established premium winery owned by the Jackson family, producing wines which are intended to complement their LOKOYA and CARDINALE brands. A wide range of Napa vineyard sources are being called on. The Cabernet Sauvignon is impressive, dense and powerful, offering dark fruits, berry and cherry aromas and a subtle cedary note. An additional dimension is added by the inclusion of a little Merlot, Malbec, Petit Verdot and Cabernet Franc. In addition to the Cabernet, a blend dominated by Merlot Pauline's Cuvée offers decent value and a fresh cool fermented Sauvignon Blanc is also made. (DM)

Recommended Reds:
Cabernet Sauvignon Napa Valley ★★★☆ £E
Pauline's Cuvée Napa Valley ★★★ £D

>> Aubert (Napa Valley) *www.aubertwines.com*

Owner/proprietor Mark Aubert is a resident of Napa Valley, where his parents owned a vineyard. With a degree from UC Fresno, he worked under the tutelage of the legendary winemaker Helen Turley at Peter Michael Vineyards and subsequently at Colgin Cellars. He had

also consulted for Bryant Family, Futo and Sloan "cult" wineries. His namesake brand launched in 1999 with his vineyard-designated Pinot Noirs and Chardonnays. There are four Pinot Noirs: CIX, Reuling, Ritchie, Sonoma Coast and UV-SL Vineyard and eight single vineyard Chardonnays: CIX, Eastside, Larry Hyde & Sons, Lauren, Ritchie, Sugar Shack, UV and UV-SL. All are worth seeking. Standouts are the stunning Eastside Chardonnay, from a vineyard planted to a Montrachet clone. Intense, delineated and precise, it delivers plenty of tropical and stone fruit, and is inherently age-worthy. Pinot Noir from UV vineyard, owned and farmed by Ulysses Valdez, planted to Calera and Vosne-Romanee clones, is an embarrassment of riches. Wealth of black and blue fruit, earth and exotic spice gives way to a long-lasting finish. (IT)

Recommended Reds:
Pinot Noir UV Vineyard ★★★★☆ £G
Pinot Noir Ritchie Vineyard Sonoma Coast ★★★★ £G
Recommended Whites:
Chardonnay Hudson Vineyard Carneros ★★★★★ £G
Chardonnay Larry Hyde and Sons Vineyard Carneros ★★★★★ £G
Chardonnay Sugar Shack Estate Vineyard Napa Valley ★★★★★ £G

Bacio Divino (Rutherford) *www.baciodivino.com*

Claus Janzen's small operation is now the source of a number of labels. The Bacio Divino red is a very stylish, impressive and unusual blend of Cabernet Sauvignon, Sangiovese and Petite Sirah. Part of Claus Janzen's inspiration was tasting the red at Domaine de TREVALLON in Provence, itself a blend of unconventional varieties. The Bacio Divino is a rich, smoky and succulent wine, accessible and ripe with velvety tannins and great depth. Pazzo is a blend of Sangiovese, Cabernet Sauvignon and Petite Sirah and is produced in a lush, forward style to be enjoyed sooner rather than later. Among other labels recently added to the range Vagabond includes a Syrah (£F) and Petite Sirah (£E) and Lucie a Chardonnay (£E) and a couple of Pinot Noirs (£F). Under the Janzen label there is a reasonably priced Napa Valley Cabernet Sauvignon (£E) as well as a number of much more expensive Janzen Vineyard Designate Cabernets (£H) from the Beckstoffer To Kalon and Missouri Hopper as well as the small estate Cloudy's Vineyard on the high eastern slopes of the Napa Valley. These are available in magnums or jeroboams. (DM)

Recommended Reds:
Bacio Divino Napa Valley ★★★★★ £G
Pazzo Napa Valley ★★★ £D

>> Barbour Vineyards (Napa Valley) *www.barbourvineyards.com*

Jim Barbour is one of, if not the most admired viticulturalists in the US. While planting, and tending to some of the most coveted vineyards in Napa Valley for several decades he also hired famed Celia Welch (Corra, Keever, Lindstrom, Scarecrow) to make miniscule, 300+cs lots of his own namesake wine. Made from Jim Barbour's dry-farmed, hand-harvested estate vineyard, it rests for 22 months in 60% new French Oak and is sold exclusively via mailing list. The wine is nothing short of perfection personified. Dark and heady, the intense, concentrated aromas of black and blue waft from the glass, giving way to dry herbs and notes of tobacco leaf and a beautifully composed mid-palate. Its clarity, purity and breadth is virtually unmatched, as wine wows you with layers upon layers of flavor. The superbly structured tannins are elegant and refined, defying logic for the wine of this size and complexity. It will long outlast us, yet entirely irresistible now. If there is ever a wine that unambiguously deserved a perfect score, this is it. (IT)

Napa & Carneros

California

Recommended Reds:
Barbour Cabernet Sauvignon Napa Valley ✪✪✪✪✪ £G

Barlow Vineyards (Napa Valley) *www.barlowvineyards.com*
Small 20 ha (50-acre) property south of Calistoga, founded in 1994. As well as Merlot and the Barrouge blend (Cabernet Sauvignon and Merlot), the Smiths produce varietal Cabernet Sauvignon and Zinfandel, a Sauvignon Blanc and a little rosé However with a planned production ceiling of just 2,000 cases the wines will always be fairly scarce. Quality is impressively high and the wines at present offer very good value for Napa. The style is fat and showy but with sufficient grip and acidity provided by cool nights during the summer. The wines are bottled unfiltered and should benefit from 5 years' ageing. (DM)

Recommended Reds:
Barrouge Napa Valley ★★★★ £E
Merlot Napa Valley ★★★☆ £E

Barnett Vineyards (Spring Mountain) *www.barnettvineyards.com*
The Barnetts have one of the most spectacularly sited properties on Spring Mountain, with steeply terraced vineyards at an elevation of 600m (2,000ft). Because they sit above the fog line they gain up to three extra hours of sunlight a day compared with the valley floor, providing for a long, even ripening period. The first Cabernet release from the 16 ha (40 acre) property was in 1989 and quality has been consistently fine. The highest point on the property, Rattlesnake Hill, provides a superbly intense and balanced super-premium Cabernet. The vineyard here will produce barely more than a ton to the acre and this is reflected in a wine that offers brilliant depth and intensity. A rich and plummy Merlot comes from both the home vineyards and neighbouring York Creek. Pinot Noir originally sourced from the Santa Lucia Highlands now comes from the Savoy and Donnelly Creek vineyards in the Anderson Valley and also from the Tina Marie Vineyard in the cool Green Valley AVA. Chardonnay in a fat, citrusy style, with just 70% malolactic to preserve acidity, is sourced from Sangiacomo Vineyard in Carneros. A second release also comes from the Savoy Vineyard. The range is completed with a fresh and vibrant gooseberry-laden Sauvignon Blanc which should be enjoyed young. The Spring Mountain reds in particular will develop very well in bottle; the Rattlesnake Hill deserves up to a decade. (DM)

Recommended Reds:
Cabernet Sauvignon Rattlesnake Hill Spring Mountain ★★★★★ £H
Cabernet Sauvignon Spring Mountain ★★★★ £F
Merlot Spring Mountain ★★★★ £E

Recommended Whites:
Chardonnay Sangiacomo Vineyard Carneros ★★★ £E
Sauvignon Blanc Napa Valley ★★ £C

Beaulieu Vineyard (Rutherford) *www.beaulieuvineyards.com*
Historic Napa winery founded in 1900. The Beaulieu reputation was established by the legendary André Tchelistcheff. While quality was distinctly variable during the 1980s, the late 90s though saw a marked improvement. An enormous range of wine is offered under Coastal, Maestro Collection, Napa Valley and Reserve labels and some good wines can be found at the lower price levels. The Reserve and Maestro Collection wines are a clear step up in quality. The latter particularly can offer excellent value as well. Beauzeaux is a juicy blend of Zinfandel, Valdiguié, Charbono, Petite Sirah and Grenache. The top-end Cabernets are particularly impressive. The premium Tapestry is a typical Bordeaux-style blend. (DM)

Recommended Reds:
Cabernet Sauvignon Clone 6 Napa Valley ★★★★ £H
Cabernet Sauvignon Clone 4 Napa Valley ★★★★ £H
Cabernet Sauvignon Georges de Latour Napa Valley ★★★★ £G
Cabernet Sauvignon Coastal Estates ★★ £C
Tapestry Reserve Napa Valley ★★☆ £F
Zinfandel Maestro California ★★★ £D
Zinfandel Coastal Estates ★ £C
Pinot Noir Reserve Carneros ★★ £E
Pinot Noir Coastal Estates ★☆ £C
Beauzeaux Maestro Napa Valley ★★ £C

Recommended Whites:
Chardonnay Reserve Carneros ★★☆ £D

Behrens Family Winery *www.behrensfamilywinery.com*
Formerly known as Behrens & Hitchcock this is a very impressive small Spring Mountain producer specialising in tiny lots (often barely more than 100 cases of a *cuvée*) of startling, massive, super-rich reds from a number of varieties sourced throughout the North Coast. The range includes the Cemetery a 100% Cabernet Sauvignon, top Syrah dominated red Sainte Fumee and Petite Sirah from Kick Ranch, along with some concentrated, powerful blends. Ode to Picasso, the last vintage was 2008, combines Syrah, Cabernet Sauvignon, Merlot and Cabernet Franc. The Front Man is dominated by Merlot, whereas Head in the Clouds is mainly Cabernet Sauvignon. The Road Less Travelled is mainly a meritage blend but with a small proportion of Tempranillo included. Labor of Love is a Saint-Emilion mix of Cabernet Franc, Cabernet Sauvignon and Petit Verdot, while by contrast The Heavyweight is dominated by Cabernet Sauvignon. The whole range is marked by a style that emphasises full, sumptuous fruit with formidable depth and extract. Although there is a greater structure and grip in the Cabernet-based cuvées, these are wines that offer supple tannins, rich fruit and not inconsiderable alcohol. (DM)

Recommended Reds:
The Cemetery Napa Valley ★★★★★ £G
Ode to Picasso Napa Valley ★★★★☆ £G

Benessere Vineyards (St Helena) *www.benesserevineyards.com*
Good, well-priced wines with a focus on Italian varieties. While these have often struggled to achieve the quality in California that they do at home, those of Benessere are among the better examples. The top label Phenomenon is a Sangiovese-dominated blend with some Cabernet Sauvignon, Syrah and Merlot. It is a softer, more opulent and vibrant example of the style than its Tuscan counterparts, although firmer and more structured than the lighter, more fruit-driven Sangiovese. There are also a couple of vibrant, characterful Zinfandels. Pinot Grigio has a light, nutty intensity. Along with the Phenomenon, two further premium reds are released. Sorridonte is only available from the winery and blends Aglianico with Merlot and Syrah, and there is a rare varietal Sagrantino. Expect the Zinfandel Collins Holystone and particularly the Phenomenon to evolve well with half a decade's ageing. (DM)

Recommended Reds:
Phenomenon Napa Valley ★★★★ £F
Zinfandel Collins Holystone Old Vines Napa Valley ★★★ £E
Zinfandel Black Glass Napa Valley ★★★ £E
Sangiovese Napa Valley ★★ £D

Recommended Whites:
Pinot Grigio Napa Valley ★★ £D

Beringer (St Helena) *www.beringer.com*

Now a part of the global Beringer Blass group, this winery was established 125 years ago and has always produced wines of good to very good quality at all price levels. Much of this success must be attributed to the skills of winemaking chief Ed Sbragia whose top cuvées remain some of the very best in California. He has handed over the operational winemaking reins to his deputy Laurie Hook, while spending more time on his own SBRAGIA FAMILY wines. Estate vineyards continue to be developed and for a number of the premium labels the home St Helena vineyard, planted on well-drained soils in the Spring Mountain foothills, remains a key to quality. The two entry-level ranges provide sound, everyday wines. The Classics range emphasises the classic varieties whereas the Los Hermanos wines are made in a fruit forward and off-dry style for the whites. The Founders Estate range is a level up and generally some oak, new and old, is used to lend structure and an added dimension to the wines. Regional wines, mostly from Napa and Knights Valley are produced with more of an emphasis on *terroir*. Some new French oak is used for ageing and some good bottles can be found. There are also a small number of Distinction Series wines released which include the Knights Valley Reserve Cabernet along with a Luminus Chardonnay and Quantum a red blend. At the pinnacle are the Private Reserve and Single Vineyard labels. A number of top Cabernets come from a range of single vineyards. A small range of wines (£C-£D) are also available under the Modern Heritage brand and includes examples from Pinot Noir and Riesling. (DM)

Recommended Reds:

Cabernet Sauvignon Private Reserve Napa Valley ✪✪✪✪✪ £H
Cabernet Sauvignon Bancroft Ranch Howell Mountain ★★★★ £F
Cabernet Sauvignon Knights Valley ★★★ £E
Merlot Bancroft Ranch Howell Mountain ★★★★ £F
Merlot Napa Valley ★★☆ £D

Recommended Whites:

Chardonnay Private Reserve Napa Valley ★★★★ £F
Chardonnay Napa Valley ★★☆ £D
Sauvignon Blanc Napa Valley ★★ £C

✿ **Robert Biale (Napa Valley)** *www.robertbialevineyards.com*

This operation has owned vineyards in the Napa Valley for decades but more recently they have established themselves as a very impressive small producer of mainly old-vine Zinfandel from a range of sources including their home vineyard, along with Petite Sirah and a Barbera and Sangiovese. The Hill Climber label has also offered some brilliantly concentrated Syrahs. The key to quality here is tight control of yields both in their own vineyards and through working closely with the small growers who also supply grapes. With so much California Zin now massively extracted and overblown, these examples show remarkable refinement and balance. This is artisan California winegrowing at its best. The Zins will drink very well young as well as aging gracefully, while the Petite Sirah and Hill Climber wines need five or six years and will keep very well. (DM)

Robert Biale

Recommended Reds:

Zinfandel Monte Rosso Vineyard ★★★★ £F
Zinfandel Aldo's Vineyard Napa Valley ★★★★ £F
Petite Sirah Royal Punishers Napa Valley ★★★ £F

Hill Climber

Recommended Reds:

Syrah Rolly Akers Vineyard Napa Valley ★★★★ £F
Syrah Pilgrimage Vineyard Napa Valley ★★★★ £F
Syrah Jack and Jill Vineyard Napa Valley ★★★ £E

Blackbird Vineyards (Napa Valley) *www.blackbirdvineyards.com*

In 2003 Michael Polenske bought the 10 acre (4 ha) Blackbird Vineyard from Mia Klein of SELENE Winery and immediately set about installing Aaron Pott (ex QUINTESSA, but cut his teeth at Châteaux TROPLONG-MONDOT and Latour Figeac in St. Émilion for five years) as winemaker. Whilst the majority of the vineyard's fruit was already contracted to other top wineries in the Napa Valley (SHAFER and VIADER among them), a small amount was held back for Pott to produce a 100% Merlot that continued the fine reputation that the Blackbird label had already achieved under Mia Klein. Five wines are currently produced in minute quantities. The entry level rosé, aptly named 'Arriviste', is Cabernet Sauvignon, Merlot and Cabernet Franc and is akin to an Anjou rosé but with less obvious sugar. 'Arise' is mainly Merlot, with both Cabernets and has a neatness about it with a good deal of charm. 'Illustration' is their main wine, a blend of more than 75% Merlot with the balance Cabernet Franc and Cabernet Sauvignon producing a rich wine with soft tannins and the feel of polished leather. 'Paramour' is spicy and concentrated, big structured although the alcohol is less than in 'Illustration'. Made with just under 10% Cabernet Sauvignon and the rest divided between Merlot and Cabernet Franc, it reminds one of Saint Émilion as opposed to the Pomerol style of the former. Finally 'Contrarian' which is a blend of the three main grape varietals has big fruit on the nose – close knit, with stylish nuances of dark bitter chocolate on the palate. All the reds spend just over 20 months in French oak with 'Arise' having the least amount of new oak (about half) as opposed to the others with around 75% new. This is possibly why it impressed the most. The wines don't quite have the persistence of the very best. (NB)

Recommended Reds:

'Contrarian' Proprietary Red Napa Valley ★★★★ £G
'Paramour' Proprietary Red Napa Valley ★★★★ £G
'Illustration' Proprietary Red Napa Valley ★★★★ £G
'Arise' Proprietary Red Napa Valley ★★★★ £F

Recommended Rosés:

'Arriviste' Napa Valley ★★☆ £C

Blockheadia Ringnosii (Napa Valley)

Michael Ouellette founded Blockheadia in 1992. Well priced, characterful Zinfandel, Petite Sirah, Pinot Noir and Sauvignon Blanc are now produced. Fruit comes from a number of sources and is always hand-picked. The wines are very much in the fruit-driven mould with minimal oak influence. The Zins are marked by spicy, dark fruits and they are medium weight rather than blockbusters. The Sauvignon Blancs are vinified without oak and offer a mix of lightly tropical fruit with a soft mineral undercurrent. They are also well-balanced and tend to avoid some of the excessively alcohol levels found elsewhere. The wines are all approachable on release. (DM)

Recommended Reds:

Zinfandel Lorenza Lake Napa Valley ★★★ £E
Zinfandel Sonoma County ★★☆ £E

Recommended Whites:

Sauvignon Blanc Napa Valley ★★ £C

✿ **Bond Estates (Oakville)** *www.bondestates.com*

The Bond label was established in 1996 by Bill Harlan to produce a small range of bespoke reds from exceptional vineyard sites to compliment his great HARLAN ESTATE Oakville red. The first releases followed in 1999. The wines are all individually branded rather than labelled by vineyard source in order to ensure long

Napa & Carneros

term continuity and all are predominantly Cabernet Sauvignon. At a time when an increasing number of small volume Napa reds are being released and sold solely through mailing lists it is refreshing that a sizeable proportion here is purposely distributed through the wine trade. The same commitment to quality is maintained as with the two Harlan Estate reds. Vinification is in small lots with some whole berry fermentation in oak. Each of the wines is then aged in its own cellar. Matriarch is a second label used to ensure the integrity of the five premium labels. It is in a softer, more accessible style but nonetheless offers impressive depth and concentration. The Melbury comes from a south-eastern exposed site off Howell Mountain Road overlooking Lake Hennessey. It is the lightest of the quartet but displays intense red cherry fruit and great elegance. St Eden comes from red volcanic soils on the eastern side of Oakville, north of the Oakville Crossroad. Loaded with rich, dark fruit it is a very opulent and seductive style with a rounded texture and very supple tannins. Vecina comes from an eastern exposure in the foothills above Oakville. It is a dense and very structured wine with a subtle and restrained core of very rich, blackberry essence and almost chocolatey Cabernet fruit. It demands cellaring for at least 6 or 7 years. Pluribus was introduced with the 2003 vintage. Coming from a vineyard with a south-eastern exposure on Spring Mountain, while rich and opulent in style there are some very sturdy mountain tannins which need some patience. A large portion of the Vecina and Pluribus is barrel-fermented to round and soften the palate when young. The newest addition to the portfolio is Quella, added with the 2006 vintage after 8 years of experimenting with the site. It originates from an uplifted riverbed east of Rutherford. The intention has been to produce a subtle, graceful wine with sumptuous blueberry fruit and retain fine grained tannins and an alluring minerality. Although this wine has not yet been tasted you can expect undoubted class and at least ★★★★★ quality (DM)

Recommended Reds:

Vecina Red Napa Valley ✪✪✪✪✪ £H
Pluribus Red Napa Valley ✪✪✪✪✪ £H
Melbury Red Napa Valley ★★★★★ £H
St Eden Red Napa Valley ★★★★★ £H
Matriarch Red Napa Valley ★★★★ £F

>> Brand Napa Valley (Napa Valley) *www.brandnapavalley.com*
Ed and Deb Fitts fell in love with the gorgeous Pritchard Hill, and set out on a mission to craft the best wine possible from this challenging rocky site. They discovered untapped potential that led them to hire rock-star winemaker Phillip Melka and create a "Brand" that reflects their passion and values. Eight acres of vineyards planted on twelve blocks at 1300-1600ft elevations, overlook Lake Hennessey. Meticulously selected clones are grafted on a variety of rootstocks to achieve diversity and optimize the site. Cabernet Franc, Cabernet Sauvignon and Petit Verdot thrive there, producing wines of integrity and distinct character. There are three wines: Brand Cabernet, Proprietary Blend and Brio. 400-cs Cabernet is a powerhouse that demonstrates the breadth and depth of flavor that mountain fruit can deliver. 200-cs Proprietary is a blend dominated by Cabernet Franc that showcases variety's finesse and dimension. Brio, another 400-cs Cabernet-based blend is a pure delight, with seductive chocolate and tobacco notes, along with smooth tannins. (IT)

Recommended Reds:

Brand Cabernet Sauvignon Napa Valley ★★★★★ £H
Brand Proprietary Red ★★★★☆ £G

Brown Estate (Napa Valley) *www.brownestate.com*
Fine Zinfandel and Cabernet Sauvignon are produced from the Brown family property in the Chiles Valley District in the eastern Napa. Of the 16 ha (40 acres) under vine, two-thirds are planted to Zinfandel. The first vintage of Zinfandel was only in 1996, but it is one of the very best examples from the region, with vibrant, spicy, dark bramble fruit underpinned by tangy acidity and marvellous intensity and depth. A second Zin Westside is also made from estate grapes, but labelled Napa Valley rather than Chiles Valley. The subtly oaked Cabernet Sauvignon is 100% varietal and is loaded with vibrant blackberry and spicy fruit. It will evolve well with 5 years' ageing. The small range is completed by an estate-grown Chardonnay and Chaos Theory a blend of Zinfandel, Cabernet Sauvignon and Petite Sirah. (DM)

Recommended Reds:

Cabernet Sauvignon Estate Napa Valley ★★★★ £F
Zinfandel Estate Chiles Valley ★★★★ £E

❂ Bryant (Napa Valley) *www.bryantwines.com*
With production of just over a 1,000 cases the Bryant Cabernet has become one of a handful of blue-chip California examples of the variety alongside such illustrious names as ARAUJO, COLGIN, GRACE FAMILY, HARLAN and SCREAMING EAGLE. The property is located in the Pritchard Hill sector of the Napa, close to CHAPPELLET and the Bryants evidently achieve much more from the area than their neighbours. The vineyards benefit from cooling breezes channelled directly from Lake Hennessey on the eastern slopes of the valley. While the wine has immense depth and power, it is also supple and rounded, approachable at 5 or 6 years. In part this is achieved with a five-day cold soak prior to fermentation. Two further low volume wines are also now released, DB4 and Bettina. The wine is bottled without filtration. Expect the Estate wine to age gracefully and be prepared to pay a very high price for it. (DM)

Recommended Reds:

Cabernet Sauvignon Estate Napa Valley ✪✪✪✪✪ £H

>> Bure Family Wines (Napa Valley) *www.burefamilywines.com*
What happens when a professional hockey player and a famous Hollywood actress get married and start a family? They buy a vineyard in Napa, of course! Valeri Bure, who counts two Olympic games, and a decade of professional hockey, developed an interest in wine while playing in Canada. When he and Candace Cameron Bure (Full House) got married, they began travelling to Napa Valley for leisure; soon after searching for a perfect property. After a long hunt, it revealed itself in a form of a St Helena estate, that was not even for sale. The Bures convinced the owners to part with it and soon Bure Family Wines was born. Prominent winemaker, Luc Morlet, a long-time friend and confidant took on the task of winemaking. Tiny lots of meticulously composed wines comprise Bure's prized portfolio, which sells out quickly to his group of dedicated fans. Duration, a Cabernet crafted from fruit collected from the vineyard planted to Clone 4 selection from Beckstoffer Missouri Hopper vineyard is pure indulgence in a glass. Silky texture, gobs of blue and black fruit and nuanced finish. Thirteen, a Cabernet made from a hillside vineyard boasts richness of flavor, sexy red/black fruit, forest floor and subtle hints of wood. Both will age nicely for at least a decade or two. (IT)

Recommended Reds:

Thirteen St Helena ★★★★★ £H
Duration Oakville ★★★★ £G

Cafaro (Napa Valley) *www.cafaro.com*
Joe Cafaro is a successful consultant winemaker who has made wine for the likes of ACACIA and DALLA VALLE. He also owns a small winery where he produces stylish, supple and complex Cabernet, Merlot and most recently a small amount of Syrah, which like all the wines from the Cafaro Family Vineyard. His property is on slopes just to the south of Stags Leap. The wines are all marked by their purity of fruit and fine, elegant structure, without some of the aggressive tannin found elsewhere from mountain-grown reds. Ripe, intense berry fruit is well balanced with lightly spicy oak. Compared with much of the competition these wines are great value. (DM)
Recommended Reds:
Cabernet Sauvignon Family Vineyard Napa Valley ★★★★ £F
Syrah Cafaro Family Vineyard Napa Valley ★★★★ £F
Merlot Family Vineyard Napa Valley ★★★★ £F

Cain Cellars (Spring Mountain) *www.cainfive.com*
This is a spectacularly sited Spring Mountain estate planted to Cabernet Sauvignon, Merlot, Malbec, Cabernet Franc and Petit Verdot, which make up the flagship Cain Five – a medium-full, ripe, chocolaty and lightly cedary blend. The Concept, another meritage blend dominated by Cabernet Sauvignon, along with smaller proportions of Merlot, Cabernet Franc and Petit Verdot is sourced from benchland as well as hillside vineyards. This is softer and more approachable than its mountain-grown big brother. Cain Cuvée is a non-vintage Bordeaux blend in a soft, forward style. (DM)
Recommended Reds:
Cain Five Napa Valley ★★★★ £G Cain Cuvée Napa Valley ★★ £D
Cain Concept Napa Valley ★★★☆ £F

Cakebread Cellars (Rutherford) *www.cakebread.com*
Now a fairly substantial operation which the Cakebread family have been running for well over two decades. Production now runs to 18 wines, including an extensive premium range. Chardonnay and Sauvignon are both rich and oaky in style, with the Reserve Chardonnay adding an extra element of depth and texture. Regular Merlot and Cabernet are well crafted and both are big, powerful and quite alcoholic reds. Pinot Noir now comes in a number of guises both appellation examples from Carneros and the Anderson Valley as well as three single vineyard wines. Pinot is the dominant variety in the Rubaiyat red, a tank-fermented forward, fruit-driven, easy-drinking blend. Napa Valley Syrah includes a little Petite Sirah and Grenache and there is a Zinfandel from the Red Hills AVA in Lake County. The top cuvées are the three super-premium Cabernets. As well as the excellent Benchland Select, very small quantities of Vine Hill Ranch and Dancing Bear Ranch are also made. (DM)
Recommended Reds:
Cabernet Sauvignon Benchland Select Napa Valley ★★★★☆ £H
Cabernet Sauvignon Napa Valley ★★★★ £G
Merlot Napa Valley ★★★ £E
Recommended Whites:
Chardonnay Reserve Napa Valley ★★★☆ £F
Chardonnay Napa Valley ★★☆ £E Sauvignon Blanc Napa Valley ★★ £C

Oliver Caldwell (Napa Valley) *www.caldwellcellars.com*
The Caldwells now produce just one Cabernet Sauvignon having sold their Aida Vineyard to VINEYARD 29. The pure varietal Esedra Cabernet Sauvignon comes from the Bella Vista (Calistoga), Beckstoffer (Silverado Trail) and Vybony (Oakville) vineyards. It is impressively rich and concentrated with a chocolaty, lightly spicy cedar character and a supple, finely honed structure. A series of

contemporary artworks are used for the labels. A densely structured, powerful Petite Sirah from Aida was one of the better examples from the region, if you can still find any. Cabernet Sauvignon and Zinfandel continue to be made by Vineyard 29 from the site. 2001 is the most recent available vintage of the Esedra through the winery website. It should make excellent drinking now. (DM)
Recommended Reds:
Cabernet Sauvignon Esedra Napa Valley ★★★★ £G

Cardinale (Oakville) *www.cardinale.com*
This very pricey red is the jewel in the crown of the KENDALL-JACKSON empire. It is a blend of Cabernet Sauvignon and Merlot sourced from prime vineyards both benchland as well as mountain plots on Mount Veeder, Diamond Mountain, Spring Mountain and Howell Mountain. A massively powerful and concentrated red with copious quantities of super-ripe cassis and hints of cedar underpinned by high-toast oak, in the best vintages the wine convincingly earns ★★★★★. Yet you do feel that just a hint more refinement would add that final dimension. (DM)
Recommended Reds:
Cardinale Proprietary Red Napa Valley ★★★★☆ £H

Caymus (Rutherford) *www.caymus.com*
Two good to very good Cabernet Sauvignons are vinified here. The Wagner family also produce very stylish Chardonnay at their Central Coast winery MER SOLEIL as well as Pinot Noir under the BELLE GLOS label. Conundrum is a classy white, blended from an unusual mix of Sauvignon Blanc, Sémillon, Chardonnay, Viognier and Muscat Canelli. It is ripe and aromatic with a hint of new oak and comes from a diverse source of vineyards in Napa, Monterey, Santa Barbara and Tulare counties. The wines now stand alone as separate brands rather than being a subsidiaries of the Caymus label. The Special Selection, one of California's top reds, needs cellaring and will improve in bottle for 5–10 years. The grapes are harvested lot by lot and vinified with extended maceration on skins and ageing in new French oak. A Napa Valley Caymus Zin is also made. (DM)
Recommended Reds:
Cabernet Sauvignon Special Selection Napa Valley ★★★★ £H
Cabernet Sauvignon Napa Valley ★★★ £F
Recommended Whites:
Conundrum California ★★☆ £C

Chappellet (Napa Valley) *www.chappellet.com*
This winery, located on Pritchard Hill close to BRYANT, has had a variable record in recent years. Most interesting is the impressive Chenin Blanc. Vinified from old vines with just a hint of oak this is a striking and unusual example of the variety for California. Las Piedras Cabernet Sauvignon and Signature Chardonnay have both shown recent form as should be expected from first class vineyards with meagre, well-drained stony soils. Napa Valley Merlot is blended with Cabernet Sauvignon, Malbec and Petit Verdot. The Cultivation, a forward meritage blend, is an additional Cabernet-based wine here. Pinot Noir, Malbec and Zinfandel are also produced as well as an expensive Pritchard Hill Estate Vineyards Cabernet Franc. The range is completed with a small volume of a single clone Cabernet Sauvignon, Clone 337. (DM)
Recommended Reds:
Cabernet Sauvignon Las Piedras Napa Valley ★★★☆ £F
Merlot Napa Valley ★★☆ £D
Recommended Whites:
Chardonnay Signature Napa Valley ★★★ £E

Napa & Carneros

Chardonnay Napa Valley ★★☆ £D
Chenin Blanc Old Vine Cuvée Napa Valley ★★★ £D

Chateau Montelena (Napa Valley) www.montelena.com

One of a few genuinely historic Napa wineries dating back to the 1880s. Nowadays the winery is best- known for one of the greatest Cabernet-based reds from the US. Even in lesser years the Montelena Estate red has a reputation for real quality. It is a backward and powerfully structured wine that stands in marked contrast to the many ripe and supple, opulent styles that have emerged more recently. A minimum of 10 years is required to enjoy it at its best; often opening a bottle early will cause great disappointment as with some of the great wines of France. A varietal Zinfandel has now replaced the St Vincent which blended Zinfandel and Sangiovese. It is a typically fine, elegant and structured example of the grape in keeping with the winemaking approach here. The Chardonnay is a particularly restrained, tight and mineral-laden example, stylish and impeccably balanced. Unlike many examples from California it will develop well with age. A fresh style of Napa Valley Sauvignon Blanc is also made as well as a small amount of Riesling from the Potter Valley which has a small amount of botrytis and a touch of residual sugar. (DM)

Recommended Reds:
Cabernet Sauvignon Montelena Estate Napa Valley ★★★★★ £H
Cabernet Sauvignon Napa Valley ★★★☆ £F
Zinfandel Montelena Estate Napa Valley ★★★☆ £E

Recommended Whites:
Chardonnay Napa Valley ★★★☆ £E

Chateau Potelle (Mount Veeder) www.chateaupotelle.com

The Fourmeaux family origins are in the French wine trade but Marketta and Jean-Noël have made a very good job of producing classically original, stylish California wines. The VGS labels are particularly impressive, none more so than the Zinfandel and Cabernet Sauvignon vinified from estate-grown mountain fruit. These are big, structured wines which need time, 5 years or so, to soften their youthfully aggressive, at times angular tannins. Chardonnay is barrel-fermented with nicely judged oak, Sauvignon Blanc is fresh and floral but further complexity is added with a small amount of Sémillon and a portion of the fruit barrel-fermented on lees. Other VGS labels also include Merlot, Syrah, Petite Sirah and Cabernet Franc. while a red blend Illegitimate comes from Cabernet Sauvignon, Merlot, Zinfandel and Syrah. A Grenache Blanc, Inevitabel White from Chardonnay, Gewürztraminer and Viognier, and a Riviera Rosé from Cinsault and Syrah complete the range. (DM)

Recommended Reds:
Zinfandel VGS Mount Veeder ★★★☆ £F
Cabernet Sauvignon VGS Mount Veeder ★★★☆ £F

Recommended Whites:
Chardonnay VGS Mount Veeder ★★★ £E
Sauvignon Blanc Napa Valley ★★ £D

>> Checkerboard Vineyards www.checkerboardvineyards.com

Perched high atop the southeastern slope of Diamond Mountain, the property cascades down for two and a half miles to the valley floor. It is a confluence of four vineyard sites, Aurora, at 1200ft, Coyote Ridge at 900ft, Meadows at 600ft, Nash Creek at 2000ft, a cave and a winery. All farming practices are sustainable. Custom French oak casks house separate lots of wine in the cave compound, consisting of six separate chambers for winemaking and wine

aging. State-of-the-art technology monitors each individual barrel humidity levels. Superstar winemaker Martha McClellan lends her talents to the brand from the very beginning, assuring a meticulous quality control. The wines are fruit-driven yet intensely precise. Aurora Vineyard is an aromatic symphony of interwoven blue and red fruit, intermitted with led pencil and hints of cedarwood. Coyote Ridge entices with distinct minerality and baking spice. Nash is the belle of the ball with its haunting, striking cherry cordial and dark chocolate notes. Hints of star anise add to the intrigue, followed by a thunderous, satisfying finish. (IT)

Recommended Reds:
Cabernet Sauvignon Aurora Vineyard ★★★★★ £G
Cabernet Sauvignon Nash Vineyard ★★★★☆ £G
Cabernet Sauvignon Coyote Ridge Vineyard ★★★★ £G

✿ Cline Cellars (Carneros) www.clinecellars.com

Along with Randall Grahm of BONNY DOON, Fred Cline was one of the original Rhône Rangers. From his 142 ha (350 acre) property he produces a plethora of Zins and some first-class Rhône styles. The family have some of the most extensive plantings of Rhône varieties in the state and account for no less than 85% of all Mourvèdre plantings, although fruit is also sourced widely elsewhere and both the Single Vineyard and Ancient Vines wines stand out. Some solid whites are also produced but they lack the same excitement as the reds, with their vibrant, spicy, berry fruit character. At the top end they posses not only rich, concentrated fruit but marvellously honed, supple tannins – wines of weight and finesse. The fact that they represent great value is another major plus. An extensive range of reds and whites are now also made from Sonoma County. (DM)

Recommended Reds:
Mourvèdre Small Berry Vineyard Contra Costa County ★★★★ £E
Mourvèdre Ancient Vines Contra Costa County ★★★ £D
Syrah Estate Carneros ★★★☆ £E   Syrah Sonoma County ★★☆ £C
Zinfandel Big Break Vineyard Contra Costa County ★★★☆ £E
Zinfandel Bridgehead Vineyard Contra Costa County ★★★☆ £E
Zinfandel Live Oak Vineyard Contra Costa County ★★★☆ £E
Zinfandel Ancient Vines Contra Costa County ★★★ £D
Zinfandel Lodi ★★☆ £C
Carignane Ancient Vines Contra Costa County ★★☆ £D

Recommended Whites:
Viognier North Coast ★★ £C

Clos Pegase (Napa Valley) www.clospegase.com

A fairly extensive range is produced at this Calistoga winery, although our most recent tastings only cover the Napa Cabernet. The other key wines are the Mitsuko Vineyard Merlot, Pinot Noir and Chardonnay. A special label Hommage Cabernet Sauvignon and Chardonnay are also released each year with the labels taken from works among the Shrem's own extensive art collection. The Cabernet is full, dark and spicy with a lightly cedary undercurrent and reasonable depth. Give it 4 or 5 years. (DM)

Recommended Reds:
Cabernet Sauvignon Napa Valley ★★★ £F

✿ Colgin Cellars (Napa Valley) www.colgincellars.com

Colgin now offers a number of super-premium bottlings. All are extremely expensive (the winery release prices can also be rapidly dwarfed by trading prices at auction) and two are based on Cabernet Sauvignon, although the Cariad red is Cabernet Sauvignon, Merlot and Cabernet Franc (all sourced from the Madrona Vineyard) blended with some fruit from Thorevilos and

Howell Mountain. Unblended Cabernet Sauvignon in two guises is produced from the Herb Lamb (most recent vintage 2007) and Tychson Hill vineyards. The main focus is gradually moving to two estate wines, the Estate Napa Valley Red (same blend as the Cariad with a little Petit Verdot) and Estate Syrah. The wines are neither fined nor filtered and spend around two years in new French oak. All undoubtedly offer considerable weight, depth and rich textures. The winemaking reins are now in the hands of Allison Tauziet, vineyard expertise is provided by David ABREU and further consultation comes from Bordelais Alain Raynaud producer of Château QUINAULT in Saint-Émilion. (DM)

Recommended Reds:
Cabernet Sauvignon Herb Lamb Vineyard ✪✪✪✪✪ £H
Cabernet Sauvignon Tychson Hill ✪✪✪✪✪ £H
IX Estate Red Blend ★★★★★ £H
Cariad Red Blend ★★★★★ £H   IX Estate Syrah ★★★★★ £H

>> Continuum (Napa Valley) www.continuumestate.com
Continuum was born as a passionate tribute by Tim Mondavi and Marcia Mondavi Borger to the late Robert Mondavi, who was a partner in the project. It symbolizes Mondavi's legacy, the continuation of excellence, inspired stewardship of the land and constant innovation. Located high on Pritchard Hill, 60-acre hillside, organically farmed vineyards are planted to Bordeaux varietals: Cabernet Sauvignon, Cabernet Franc, Merlot and Petite Verdot. They boast terrific volcanic and rocky soils, exposures and elevations of up to 1600ft and diurnal temperature shifts – all factors facilitating bold, highly structured, age-worthy wines. The carefully chosen rootstock is ideally suited for specific blocks. The yields are low, hovering at less than 2 tons per acre. Two wines are made: Continuum, a blend of Cabernet Sauvignon, Cab Franc, Merlot and Petit Verdot and Novicium, Latin for "young" – a blend of Merlot, Cab Franc and Cabernet Sauvignon, that is made utilizing the fruit collected from younger vines. (IT)

Recommended Reds:
Continuum Napa Valley ★★★★☆ £H
Novicium Napa Valley ★★★★ £G

Corison Winery (Napa Valley) www.corison.com
Cathy Corison produces a small amount of Napa Cabernet Sauvignon sourced from a variety of top quality benchland vineyard sites. Unlike many wines produced by her Napa neighbours, the Corison Cabernet is not overblown and has considerable depth and finesse. Aged in around 50% new French oak the wine shows remarkably well young but will evolve impressively with cellaring. A very limited amount of a special *cuvée* from the Kronos Vineyard is also produced, which requires more patience and a deeper pocket. A Gewürztraminer is also made from the Anderson Valley and a Helios labelled Cabernet Franc from the Napa Valley. (DM)

Recommended Reds:
Cabernet Sauvignon Kronos Vineyard Napa Valley ★★★★☆ £G
Cabernet Sauvignon Napa Valley ★★★★ £F

❀ Robert Craig (Napa Valley) www.robertcraigwine.com
Small, very high-quality Napa operation established in 1992 and sourcing fruit from a number of locations. Affinity is a Bordeaux-style blend of Cabernet Sauvignon, Petit Verdot, Merlot, Cabernet Franc and Malbec. Ripe, supple and surprisingly elegant it can be approached relatively young. For Napa it is a brilliant value. The three Cabernets are equally stylish, but have a denser, firmer edge. They require a little more time to tame their mountain tannins but

they are more approachable than many. The Howell Mountain is particularly fine with elegant, dark cedary fruit and a pure mineral edge. The spicy Zinfandel is a rich, vibrant, dark-fruit style but has a nice fresh underlying acidity. The Chardonnay doesn't quite have the intensity of the reds but nevertheless has a good, rich texture with ripe citrus fruit and a subtle tropical character. The wine gets additional depth from 60% barrel-fermentation, although the fruit is to the fore with a minimum of new oak. Drink the reds over three to ten years. A well priced fruit forward blend Mt George Cuvée (£D) blends Cabernet and Merlot and a rosé La Fleur is also made. (DM)

Recommended Reds:
Cabernet Sauvignon Howell Mountain ★★★★★ £F
Cabernet Sauvignon Mount Veeder ★★★★☆ £F
Cabernet Sauvignon Spring Mountain Mountain ★★★★☆ £F
Affinity Napa Valley ★★★★☆ £E
Zinfandel Howell Mountain ★★★★ £E
Recommended Whites:
Chardonnay Durrell Vineyard Sonoma Valley ★★★☆ £E

Culler (Napa Valley) www.cullerwines.com
Karen Culler makes a small range of excellent value Napa Valley reds. She established her small property in the late 1990s after a decade or so at ROBERT MONDAVI and now makes wine at a number of other properties. In addition to her Syrah's she also makes Cabernet Sauvignon with wines released under both the Culler and Caesedra labels. In the winery intervention is kept to a minimum, racking is done by gravity and both wild and cultured yeasts are used to instigate fermentation. Of the Syrah reds there is a big full blown Napa Valley bottling marked by dark, spicy fruit and smoky oak. The two vineyard bottlings are subtler, more poised and structured. The Griffins Lair Vineyard, from a site just to the south of the Petaluma gap is rich and licoricy with a fine underlying minerality. The Sawi Vineyard is the tightest and most structured of the trio, coming from a site planted at 1,400 feet. A wine of very impressive grip and substance produced from a John ALBAN sourced Syrah clone. (DM)

Recommended Reds:
Syrah Sawi Vineyard Sonoma Coast ★★★★ £F
Syrah Griffins Lair Vineyard Sonoma Coast ★★★★ £F
Syrah Napa Valley ★★★☆ £E

Cuvaison (Napa Valley) www.cuvaison.com
Medium-sized operation producing sizeable volumes of Chardonnay. Fruit is sourced from its own vineyards, including a property in Carneros, as well as from elsewhere; the recently acquired Brandlin Ranch on Mount Veeder also now provides further resources of estate fruit for vintages to come and a top end Cabernet Sauvignon/Merlot blend Two Estates has now been released. The wines are well-crafted, well-priced and always reliable. They are also very well priced in a California context. Most impressive is the Single Block Kite Tail Chardonnay from south facing slopes which gets 15 months in mainly new high-quality French oak. Syrah from Carneros estate fruit and other Single Block wines have been added to the the range. Expect these to have good potential. (DM)

Recommended Reds:
Pinot Noir Estate Carneros ★★★ £E
Recommended Whites:
Chardonnay Single Block Kite Tail Carneros ★★★☆ £E
Chardonnay Estate Carneros ★★☆ £D
Sauvignon Blanc Solitaire Carneros ★★☆ £C

Wine behind the label

Napa & Carneros

California

❀ **Dalla Valle (Oakville)** www.dallavallevineyards.com
One of Napa's small-volume, super-premium wineries with a first-class hillside site to the east of Oakville. The vines are planted in sparse red clay and volcanic soils which forces them to struggle for excellence. Also crucial to quality here is the extra sunshine the vineyard receives compared with those of the valley floor 120m (400ft) below, which results in grapes of exquisite flavour and concentration. Three wines are produced under the guidance of winemaker Andy Erickson and roving consultant Michel Rolland. The main focus of production is Cabernet Sauvignon plus a small amount of the even more impressive Maya, from the vineyard of the same name. Both are dominated by Caberenet Sauvignon with a small proportion of Cabernet Franc blended in. A third red Collina comes from the estates younger vines. The Cabernet Sauvignon and Maya are dense, massive and hugely extracted wines requiring a minimum of 6–7 years' ageing; the Collina can be approached much sooner. (DM)
Recommended Reds:
Cabernet Sauvignon Estate Oakville ★★★★★ £H

>> **Dana Estates (St Helena)** www.danaestates.com
Nestled at the foothills of Mayacamas Mountains, Dana Estates, which translates from Sanskrit as "generous spirit," was formerly the property of John and Diane Livingston. It was purchased by Korean businessman Hi Sang Lee in 2005. Five years in the making, the winery received a much-needed spectacular facelift, courtesy of celebrity architect Howard Backen. Philippe Melka came on board soon after to create world-class wines. The130x26ft cave was designed with perfection in mind, with barrels resting under 16ft steel arches outfitted with lights. There are four estate vineyards – Crystal Springs, Helms, which is in Rutherford Bench, Hershey – on Howell Mountain and Lotus which sits at 1200ft elevation on Vaca Mountain. Only the best grapes are used. Melka is a consultant, and along with winemaker Cameron Vawter, creates prodigious wines of undeniably purity and decadence. Three distinct Cabernets and a blend called Onda, composed from several sites, showcase smart viticulture and impeccable winemaking. Lotus is ridiculously pleasurable, with gobs of black fruit and dense tannin structure. Hershey is about bright fruit and distinct minerality. Onda is a layered and voluptuous blend, that is a pleasure to consume, but will age happily as well. (IT)
Recommended Reds:
Cabernet Sauvignon Helms Vineyard Rutherford ✪✪✪✪✪ £H
Cabernet Sauvignon Lotus Vineyard Napa Valley ★★★★★ £H
Cabernet Sauvignon Hershey Vineyard Howell Mountain ★★★★☆ £H
Recommended Whites:
Sauvignon Blanc Howell Mountain ★★★★ £G

Darioush (Napa Valley) www.darioush.com
Darioush Khaledi established this winery in 1997 but the results are already impressive. He owns 13 ha (33 acres) of vineyards around the site of the spectacular new winery building, along with 10 ha (25 acres) in the Mount Veeder and Atlas Peak AVAs. Most of the wines are released under the Signature label. The Signature reds are rich, vibrant and impressively dense and powerful. Cabernet Sauvignon is blended with Merlot, Cabernet Franc and Petit Verdot. A Russian River Valley Pinot Noir Signature is also made. In addition a premium release red, Darius II comes from mainly Cabernet Sauvignon and is sourced from the Sage Vineyard on Mount Veeder and the Apadana Block on the Darioush Estate. The wines have minimal handling in the cellar and the reds are bottled without filtration. Expect them to age well over the medium term. (DM)
Recommended Reds:
Cabernet Sauvignon Signature Napa Valley ★★★☆ £G
Shiraz Signature Napa Valley ★★★☆ £F
Merlot Signature Napa Valley ★★★ £F
Recommended Whites:
Chardonnay Signature Napa Valley ★★★ £F
Viognier Signature Napa Valley ★★☆ £E

Del Dotto (Napa Valley) www.deldottovineyards.com
David Del Dotto is a relatively new name in the Napa Valley wine community but he has one of the most unconventional approaches to selling and marketing his wines. Only a proportion of his resources go into producing the wines rated below which he sells in general distribution as well as at the winery tasting room. What is most unusual is that wines are also sold in barrel as futures and his customers can, with a little guidance, effectively select their own blend. Currently based in both the south eastern Napa Valley, as well as at a new cellar just to the south of St Helena which will no doubt become an important visit for quality minded consumers. A further development is some very promising Pinot Noir being produced from vineyards purchased from Bill Smith of WH SMITH on the Sonoma Coast as well as Chardonnay from a site neighbouring MARCASSIN. A number of vineyards are now estate owned and this will be increased over time with all being farmed organically. Sangiovese is vibrant, well structured and full of dark-cherry fruit. Syrah offers very good varietal purity in a full-bodied dark and sweet fruited style with a hint of black pepper and spice. The ripe, chocolatey Napa Valley Cabernet Sauvignon is 100% varietal and sourced from vines grown on the Rutherford Bench. A very good elegant and ripe black fruited Cabernet Franc is produced from both estate and other vineyards. Howell Mountain is the source of a firmly structured Cabernet Sauvignon that is marked by not only rich dark fruit but also an elegant mineral character. Among a wide range of small lot super premium reds is the David Red, which is a blend of Cabernet Sauvignon, Merlot and Cabernet Franc. It is very much in the lush, open and richly textured house style and offers impressive depth and concentration. Finally if you pay a visit there are a number of characterful port style fortifieds to try. (DM)
Recommended Reds:
The David Red Napa Valley ★★★★★ £H
Cabernet Sauvignon Howell Mountain ★★★★☆ £G
Cabernet Sauvignon Napa Valley ★★★★ £G
Syrah Sonoma Coast ★★★★ £G   Sangiovese Napa Valley ★★★☆ £F

>> **Detert Family (Oakville)** www.detert.com
Detert's family roots run deep. Great grandma fell in love with a picturesque Oakville property that partly comprised the now world-famous To-Kalon vineyard. She passed the reigns to her son Gunther, who worked tirelessly to establish their vineyard as one of the most sought-after in Napa Valley. They grew Cabernet Sauvignon and Cabernet Franc that went into Mondavi Reserve and Opus One programs, as well as several other famous brands. In 2000, three of her grandsons made a momentous decision to continue the legacy by creating a Detert brand bottling, honoring the fruit of the family's vineyard. Low-intervention techniques are the hallmark of the winemaking; the philosophy revolves around showcasing the purity of what the land had delivered. The fruit is hand-sorted, and pressed directly in to a mix of new and used oak barrels. Their 165cs Cabernet Franc is a benchmark of what can be achieved with an extraordinary site and minimalistic approach in the cellar. Gorgeous

floral and red fruit aromas, baking spices, forest floor, dry herbs, framed by rich, dark chocolate comes together in this phenomenal example of a young wine that is begging for the cellar yet hard to resist now. The 200cs Cabernet is no sloucher, either. Great mouthfeel and minerality, savory notes intermixing with sweet fruit – it all makes sense and lingers nicely. (IT)

Recommended Reds:
Cabernet Franc Sauvignon Oakville ★★★☆ £G
Cabernet Sauvignon Oakville ★★★★ £F

◆◆ Diamond Creek *www.diamondcreekvineyards.com*
The late Al Brounstein died in June 2006 but his great achievement was to produce supreme Cabernet Sauvignon for a great deal longer than most of the new generation of super-cuvées. These are not just wines of massive extract and weight, sourced from prime mountain sites and each individually stating its own *terroir*, they are wines of grace, power and above all immense refinement. Volcanic Hill is the fullest and longest lived. Red Rock Terrace, like Volcanic Hill, comes from a warm site and is the most accessible of the trio whereas Gravelly Meadow – from the coolest of the three sites – is tight and restrained. You would be well-advised to cellar for at least 10 years to enjoy one of these bottles at its best. A fourth vineyard, Lake, is the coolest and smallest of the five plots on the property. Occasionally it produces extraordinary wines; there have only been eight vintages of it since 1972 and it almost always fetches a small fortune at auction. The fifth plot, called Petit Verdot and planted entirely to the variety, has now come on stream and provides additional blending resources for all the wines. (DM)

Recommended Reds:
Cabernet Sauvignon Gravelly Meadow ✪✪✪✪✪ £H
Cabernet Sauvignon Volcanic Hill ✪✪✪✪✪ £H
Cabernet Sauvignon Red Rock Terrace ✪✪✪✪✪ £H

Diamond Terrace (Diamond Mountain) *www.diamondterrace.com*
The Taylors purchased their 6.5 ha (16 acre) vineyard in 1998. Cabernet Sauvignon was originally planted in 1984 and the vineyard brought up to its present size in 1992. They have now decided to retire and 2008 was the last vintage. Production was tiny and for Napa the wine reasonably priced. It is an elegant and structured mountain red but with a sufficiently supple feel to its tannin. Aged in a mix of French and American oak, it shows both dark, spicy fruits and a toasty hint on the finish. A Howell Mountain Cabernet was also released from 2008. (DM)

Recommended Reds:
Cabernet Sauvignon Diamond Mountain ★★★★ £F

Domaine Carneros (Carneros) *www.domaine.com*
California outpost of the Champagne house TAITTINGER. As well as the sparklers it has recently been producing some stylish and reasonably impressive Pinot Noirs. These are in a ripe and full berry fruit style. Famous Gate is aged for 10 months in one half new oak and has a little structure; the Domaine bottle is softer and more immediately accessible. Avante-Garde, an entry-level example, has now been added. The Le Rêve Blanc de Blancs is the pinnacle of the sparkling range which now totals eight wines. It is a wine of some considerable style, almost exclusively Chardonnay with a tiny proportion of Pinot Blanc. Real complexity is gained from the 5 years spent on lees. (DM)

Recommended Whites:
Brut Blanc de Blancs Le Rêve Carneros ★★★☆ £F
Brut Vintage Cuvée Carneros ★★☆ £D

Domaine Chandon (Yountville) *www.chandon.com*
Probably the best-known among the California sparkling wine producers and established way back in 1973, Chandon is also producing a limited amount of Carneros-sourced still wine from the traditional Champagne varieties bottled as varietals, with the Carneros Reserve Pinot Noir the highlight, as well as Cabernet Sauvignon from the Napa Valley and Mount Veeder. Of the sparkling wines, Reserve Brut and Blanc de Blancs are refined and reasonably intense; the Yountville Vintage Brut is bigger and fuller with marked toasty, bready notes; while the small amount of the rare Mount Veeder *cuvée*, a Blanc de Blancs which spends four years on lees, is tight, well-structured and stylish. (DM)

Recommended Whites:
Vintage Brut Yountville ★★★☆ £F
Reserve Brut Sonoma/Napa Counties ★★★ £E
Reserve Blanc de Blancs Mount Veeder ★★★ £E
Brut Classic California ★★ £C

Recommended Rosés:
Reseve Pinot Noir North Coast ★★☆ £E

✪ Dominus Estate (Yountville) *www.dominusestate.com*
Christian Moueix is a member of the Bordeaux dynasty responsible for Château Petrus. Some of the exotic but firm youthful elements of that great wine are reflected in Dominus despite it being a blend dominated by Cabernet Sauvignon. The key is in the winemaking and while the ripe fruit character of the Napanook Vineyard shows through it still possesses a classically powerful tannic structure. It requires up to a decade or more of ageing to show at its best, providing a wine of balance, subtlety and refinement. The Napanook is an impressive second label first produced in 1996. It is considerably more forward than the *grand vin* and can be approached easily with 3 or 4 years' development. (DM)

Recommended Reds:
Dominus Napa Valley ✪✪✪✪✪ £H
Napanook Napa Valley ★★★☆ £F

Duckhorn (St Helena) *www.duckhorn.com*
This has evolved into a mid-sized operation since it was founded in 1978. The main focus of the operation is Merlot. A good regular Napa Valley bottling is joined by top-end examples from estate fruit as well as two other premium labels from the Rector Creek Vineyard and the Three Palms Vineyard. Examples are also released from Atlas Peak and Carneros. Cabernet Sauvignon is also good. As well as the Napa bottling, two single-vineyard wines, Monitor Ledge and Rector Creek, are also produced. The style was of an iron fist but is tamer these days, with suppler tannin. The wines will still benefit from 4 or 5 years' cellaring and the top wines will keep very well. Decent whites are also made and as well as a Bordeaux style Sauvignon Blanc (with a little Sémillon) a similarly priced barrel fermented Chardonnay is also made. The Duckhorn label also includes a Cabernet Franc and a Petit Verdot. The Paraduxx Z Blend is an unusual blend of Zinfandel with a touch of Cabernet, while the Decoy label from Napa and Sonoma Coast maintains the integrity of the top wines offering good and forward approachable wines. A new winery facility for the Paraduxx has now been completed and a range of reds and whites are produced along with a rosé. The Duckhorns have also purchased vineyards and a winery in the cool Anderson Valley to produce stylish Pinot Noir under the GOLDENEYE label and under the Migration brand premium Chardonnay and Pinot Noir is produced from both AVA and single vineyard sources. Details of all the wines can be found on the Duckhorn website. (DM)

Wine behind the label

Napa & Carneros

California

Recommended Reds:

Cabernet Sauvignon Napa Valley ★★★★ £G
Merlot Three Palms Napa Valley ★★★★ £G
Merlot Napa Valley ★★★☆ £F   Paraduxx Napa Valley ★★★☆ £E
Decoy Napa Valley ★★ £D   Decoy Merlot Napa Valley ★★ £D

Recommended Whites:

Sauvignon Blanc Napa Valley ★★☆ £D

❀ Dunn Vineyards (Howell Mountain) *www.dunnvineyards.com*
Randy Dunn was one of the pioneers of great mountain-grown
Cabernet. He established his own operation in 1979 during the time
he was winemaker at CAYMUS. Output is now capped at around
4,000 cases a year. The estate bottling, Howell Mountain, is a massive
wine almost always offering formidable concentration and depth
with real finesse as well. Ageing is for 2 years in half new and half
used oak. The Napa Valley Cabernet is in a marginally softer style
but is nevertheless a considerable and seriously structured wine.
Both wines get a light filtration which Dunn believes adds stability
but are not fined; retaining tannin is key to their longevity. Both
understandably require cellaring, the Estate Howell Mountain for a
minimum of a decade. Also noteworthy is the value offered by both
wines in these days of extraordinarily high prices for Napa reds. (DM)

Recommended Reds:

Cabernet Sauvignon Estate Howell Mountain ✪✪✪✪✪ £H
Cabernet Sauvignon Napa Valley ★★★★☆ £ G

Dyer (Diamond Mountain) *www.dyerwine.com*
The Dyers have both been active in the Califirnia wine industry for
the past quarter of a century and more. Bill was the winemaker at
STERLING VINEYARDS before moving on to consult in the Napa,
Sonoma and in Canada. Dawnine was the winemaker at DOMAINE
CHANDON. They purchased their 5ha (12 acres) on Diamond
Mountain in 1992 and their vineyards are just to the south of
REVERIE and VON STRASSER. Indeed they make the wine in space
rented at the Von Strasser winery. Just one very elegant and cedary
mountain Cabernet Sauvignon is produced from their mostly dry-
farmed vineyard grown in finely drained volcanic soils which yields
barely 2 tons to the acre. The aspect is north-east facing and the fruit
ripens very late, so there is no need for excessive extended hang-
time here. The typical annual output is a mere 400 cases and most
is sold through their small mailing list. If you prefer a more subtle
and elegantly structured style rather than the increasingly popular
big fleshy extracted styles emerging right across the Valley then it is
well worth considering. The Dyers are also now involved in the new
super premium METEOR operation. (DM)

Recommended Reds:

Cabernet Sauvignon Diamond Mountain Napa Valley ★★★★ £F

Elizabeth Spencer (Napa Valley) *www.elizabethspencerwines.com*
Elizabeth Pressler and Spencer Graham founded the Elizabeth
Spencer winery in 1998, a year after they got married. Elizabeth
was a well-known figure in Californian wine circles, having been
involved in marketing, hospitality and brand development with
several leading luminaries such as ARAUJO, DALLA VALLE, ETUDE,
FRANCISCAN, HARLAN, KAMEN, SEAVEY, Soter, SPOTTSWOODE,
VIADER and others. Spencer Graham was originally a restaurateur
and chef and with his innate tasting ability, became the winery's
first winemaker. Sourcing grapes from a number of high quality
vineyards, they set about providing value for money wines which
would be both accessible and show the character of their *terroir*.
The whites generally are more restrained than the reds, which

display more vibrant fruit – particularly the Bordeaux varietals which
also show more persistence on the palate. The range of wines
produced is quite broad but in very limited quantities – starting
from their entry level certified organic Mendocino Sauvignon Blanc
(not tasted) through Chenin Blanc, Grenache, Zinfandel and Petite
Sirah, also from Mendocino, Chardonnay, Syrah and Pinot Noir from
Sonoma and the big guns – Merlot and Cabernet Sauvignon from
Knight's Valley, Mount Veeder and the Napa Valley. A number of
select wines are also available through the winery members club
and released under the ExS banner. (NB)

Recommended Reds:

Cabernet Sauvignon Mount Veeder ★★★☆ £F
Cabernet Sauvignon Napa Valley ★★★ £F
Pinot Noir Block Seven Sonoma Coast ★★★ £E
Syrah Sonoma Coast ★★☆ £E

Recommended Whites:

Chardonnay Wente Clone Sonoma Coast ★★★ £D
Chenin Blanc Mendocino ★☆ £D

>> Fairchild (St Helena) *www.fairchildwines.com*
Larry Fairchild grew up on a farm and studied crop genetics at
University of Nebraska. His career pursuits took him to the House of
Representatives Int'l Affairs department work, but his agricultural
roots stayed intact. An eventual move to the Bay Area and a
budding love of wine led him to Napa Valley, where he eventually
acquired a carefully selected site. In 1999 he planted a 2-acre
vineyard on the south-facing slopes of Lake Hennessey. He named
it "Sigaro" to commemorate his love of fine cigars. His vision for his
wines centered around a classic combination of Bordeaux-style
with their integrity and age-worthiness and classic, unapologetic
California fruit. He retained Jim BARBOUR to tend to his vines and
Philippe MELKA to make the wine. All his choices, from land to
people selections would ultimately pay off handsomely, as his brand
experienced a meteoric rise. His first commercial release was in 2005
to an instant buzz from the trade community. Fairchild produces
the estate Sigaro, GIII and Stones, from fruit sourced from Oakville's
Beckstoffer Georges III, To-Kalon and Stagecoach vineyard on
Pritchard Hill. (IT)

Recommended Reds:

Cabernet Sauvignon Sigaro Vineyard Napa Valley ✪✪✪✪✪ £H
Cabernet Sauvignon Georges III Vineyard Napa Valley ✪✪✪✪✪ £H
Cabernet Sauvignon Stones No 2 Napa Valley ✪✪✪✪✪ £H
Cabernet Sauvignon Stones No 1 Napa Valley ★★★★★ £H

Fantesca (Spring Mountain) *www.fantesca.com*
Tiny property producing initially just 400 cases a year of Cabernet
Sauvignon from around 4 ha (10 acre) vineyard in the south-eastern
reaches of the small Spring Mountain AVA. To this have been added
a Chardonnay, a Pinot Noir King Richards Reserve both from the
Russian River, as well as a red blend All Great Things. The vines on
the property are above the fog line and complexity is aided by a
wide variation in aspect and slope as well as a long ripening period.
The Cabernet, made by Heidi Barrett, is a big, sturdy mountain
wine with firm tannins and dark, spicy black fruits, and will require a
minimum of 5–7 years' ageing to soften. (DM)

Recommended Reds:

Cabernet Sauvignon Spring Mountain ★★★★☆ £G

Far Niente (Oakville) *www.farniente.com*
There are just two main wines at this well-established (first vintage
1979) estate in the heart of Napa. The original winery here dates

back to 1885 and was created from gold-rush money. Fruit quality is maintained through ownership of vineyards in five sites and covering no less than 95 ha (235 acres). The Cabernet is a typically powerful Napa expression requiring several years' cellaring to be enjoyed at its best. The Chardonnay has been fine-tuned over recent vintages and is an unusually elegant and refined style with a well-honed, tight oak influence, a blocked malolactic fermentation and the balance to offer real promise with age. Its taut mineral style is in marked contrast to other Napa examples of the variety. The winery is also involved in a new Russian River Valley Pinot Noir and Chardonnay venture, EnRoute. (DM)

Recommended Reds:
Cabernet Sauvignon Oakville ★★★★☆ £G
Recommended Whites:
Chardonnay Napa Valley ★★★★ £F

Flora Springs (St Helena) *www.florasprings.com*
Sizeable family-owned and run operation with a broad selection of wines. The Komes' now own nearly 200 ha (500 acres) of Napa vineyards, providing a considerable resource for their range. Among the flagships are the Cabernet Sauvignon Rutherford Hillside Reserve and the proprietary red Trilogy, a blend of Cabernet Sauvignon, Merlot, Cabernet Franc and Malbec. Both are ageworthy and display a fine balance of ripe fruit and harmonious tannin. Both these and the Wild Boar Vineyard Cabernet require 5 years' ageing. Three further single vineyard varietal Cabernets have now been added to the range from the Holy Smoke Vineyard at Oakville, the Out of Sight Vineyard in the southern Napa and the Rennie Reserve from St Helena. The Napa Merlot is more accessible than the Cabernet as you would expect. Along with the Trilogy Red, white Signature wines include the part barrel fermented Sauvignon Blanc Soliloquy Vineyard and the Barrel Fermented Chardonnay. A well priced (£C) Napa Valley Chardonnay is also made which is partly vinified in barrel. (DM)

Recommended Reds:
Cabernet Sauvignon Rutherford Hillside Reserve ★★★★☆ £G
Cabernet Sauvignon Wild Boar Vineyard Napa Valley ★★★★ £F
Cabernet Sauvignon Napa Valley ★★★☆ £F
Trilogy Napa Valley ★★★★ £F   Merlot Napa Valley ★★★ £E
Recommended Whites:
Barrel Fermented Chardonnay Napa Valley ★★★ £D
Sauvignon Blanc Soliloquy Vineyard Oakville ★★★ £C

Forman (St Helena) *www.formanvineyard.com*
Ric Forman makes impressive examples of both Chardonnay and Cabernet Sauvignon which also includes Merlot, Cabernet Franc and Petit Verdot. Vineyards established in the early 1980s are the source of his excellent raw material. Planted mainly in volcanic gravel and sand, they are sparse and provide naturally low-yielding fruit. The Chardonnay is rich and lightly tropical with a pure mineral edge and well-integrated oak. It has unusually good grip and structure for a Napa example, being fermented and aged in oak but without the malolactic fermentation. The Cabernet Sauvignon is rich, concentrated and cedary, with subtle cassis notes in the background. The wine is firmly structured and possesses the depth and fruit quality to develop well in bottle for 5 or more years and keep considerably longer. The wines are notable for their excellent value. (DM)

Recommended Reds:
Cabernet Sauvignon Napa Valley ★★★★ £F

Recommended Whites:
Chardonnay Napa Valley ★★★★ £F

Franciscan (Oakville) *www.franciscan.com*
Agustin Huneeus sold Franciscan to Canandaigua in 1999 along with the two sister wineries ESTANCIA and Mount Veeder Winery, although he retained his prestige QUINTESSA operation. The wines here are good and in most cases offer reasonable value for money. They are very much in a rich California vein, being very ripe, upfront and fruit-driven. They will show well young. Cuvée Sauvage is in a very rich, high-toast oak style and is vinified entirely with natural yeasts. The ripe, supple, cedary and forward Magnificat red will develop well with 5 years' ageing or so. Other premium reds are Cabernet Sauvignons from Oakville, a Napa Valley Winemakers Reserve, a Napa Valley Clos Reserve and a Napa Valley Stylus label. Most exciting though of the wines marketed through Franciscan are the characterful reds produced from Mount Veeder. Elegant, pure and minerally with finely chiselled tannins the wines needs five or six years at a minimum, the Reserve longer. (DM)

Franciscan
Recommended Reds:
Magnificat Napa Valley ★★★☆ £F   Merlot Napa Valley ★★ £C
Cabernet Sauvignon Napa Valley ★★☆ £E
Recommended Whites:
Chardonnay Cuvée Sauvage Napa Valley ★★★☆ £E
Chardonnay Napa Valley ★★ £E
Mount Veeder Winery
Recommended Reds:
Cabernet Sauvignon Napa Valley Reserve ★★★★ £G
Cabernet Sauvignon Elevation 1550 Napa Valley ★★★☆ £F

Peter Franus (Rutherford) *www.franuswine.com*
Impressive small producer with a range sourced from a number of committed grape growers. The style is very much one of minimal intervention and the wines are impressive without being overdone. Cabernet comes from a number of Napa sources. Zinfandel is always stylish and vibrant: the Napa-sourced example is impressive but better is the stylish and complex Mount Veeder wine from the Brandlin Vineyard. A Napa Valley Bordeaux blend is also made as well as a Cabernet Franc, a Merlot and a Rhône style Red Hills Red from Lake County. Sauvignon from the Stewart Vineyard in Carneros sees no new wood and is fresh zesty and striking. Whites also come from Chenin Blanc and Albariño. (DM)

Recommended Reds:
Cabernet Sauvignon Napa Valley ★★★☆ £F
Zinfandel Brandlin Vineyard Mount Veeder ★★★☆ £E
Zinfandel Napa Valley ★★★ £D
Recommended Whites:
Sauvignon Blanc Stewart Vineyard Carneros ★★☆ £C

Frog's Leap (Rutherford) *www.frogsleap.com*
John Williams established Frogs Leap with Larry Turley, who went on to make superstar Zins at TURLEY CELLARS. The emphasis of the marketing here is on fun, reflected in the labelling. Pull a cork and you'll see what I mean. However, the wine is serious and can be very impressive. The style is for forward, ripe, fleshy reds with sufficient structure to age nicely in the medium term and for rich, fruity whites. A small amount of Petite Sirah is now produced from Rutherford as well as an unusual red the Heritage Blend which combines Charbono with Petite Sirah, Carignane, Valdiguié and Riesling. There are also a few hundred cases of juicy rosé labelled La

Napa & Carneros

Grenouille Rougante "Pink" made from old-vine Valdiguié. (DM)
Recommended Reds:
Cabernet Sauvignon Napa Valley ★★★☆ £E
Merlot Rutherford ★★★☆ £E Zinfandel Napa Valley ★★★☆ £D
Recommended Whites:
Chardonnay Napa Valley ★★★ £D
Sauvignon Blanc Rutherford ★★★ £C

Gargiulo Vineyards (Oakville) www.gargiulovineyards.com
Small boutique winery producing Cabernet Sauvignon and
Merlot from the Money Ranch Vineyard, as well as a red blend
Aprile Super Oakville. This is dominated by Sangiovese with a little
Cabernet Sauvignon to add grip. The wine is in a light, elegant style
but offers impressive intensity at this price level. It is supple and
approachable and will drink well with a couple of years' ageing.
Cabernet Sauvignon is fuller, more concentrated, with dark, spicy,
berry fruit and supple approachable tannins. Aged in close to 80%
new French oak, it lacks the elegance and intensity of the Aprile. A
smaller volume 575 OVX Cabernet Sauvignon is also made as well as
a Cabernet Sauvignon based blend G major 7. (DM)
Recommended Reds:
Cabernet Sauvignon Money Ranch Vineyard Oakville ★★★☆ £E
Aprile Super Oakville Blend Oakville ★★★☆ £E

Gemstone (Napa Valley) www.gemstonewine.com
Small property producing an impressive meritage red from a
blend of Cabernet Sauvignon with a little Merlot and Cabernet
Franc as well as a Cabernet Sauvignon blended with a little Petit
Verdot. Second label Facets has much more Merlot, the last
vintage currently available is 2008. A tiny amount of Chardonnay is
available only on the mailing list. Philip Melka is now overseeing the
winemaking and the wines should become increasingly impressive.
The Gemstone Red is dense and full with dark, spicy fruit and a
cooler minty undercurrent. It will benefit from at least 5 years'
cellaring. (DM)
Recommended Reds:
Proprietary Red Napa Valley ★★★★☆ £G

❀ **Ghost Horse Vineyards (Napa Valley)** www.ghosthorseworld.com
This is the tiny scale home project of Todd Anderson who runs his
family's estate and winery ANDERSONS CONN VALLEY. The family
labels offer some of the better values in the Napa whereas his
approach here is somewhat different. Output is absolutely tiny,
just 200 cases or so a year and the wines, all Cabernet Sauvignons,
are produced by tiny lot fermentation and using every small scale
hand crafted method available. Whole berry fermentation, vatting in
small oak and multiple, daily hand punching down are all employed
and vinification is determined by individual blocks within Todd's
small 1ha (3 acre) property in the hills of south eastern Napa where
prestigious neighbours include PAHLMEYER. All the wines have
an extraordinary depth and intensity of sweet fruit with a truly
beguiling and astonishing level of complexity. The very best fruit is
reserved for the top two bottlings although given the prices of $500
a bottle and upwards it's all relative. There is a splendid Napa Valley
bottling, while more expensive are the Fantome and Apparition,
the sturdiest of this trio. A fourth label with very limited production
is the Spectre. The wines can only be acquired by visiting the
family winery in Conn Valley by appointment but you will be given
the opportunity to taste all of them. They will also be delivered
anywhere in the world. (DM)
Recommended Reds:

Cabernet Sauvignon Apparition Napa Valley ✪✪✪✪✪ £H
Cabernet Sauvignon Fantome Napa Valley ✪✪✪✪✪ £H
Cabernet Sauvignon Napa Valley ✪✪✪✪✪ £H
Gloria Ferrer (Carneros) www.gloriaferrer.com
The style here is for rich, ripe sparkling wines sourced mainly
from estate vineyards in Carneros. While the wines are typically
Californian, the impressive winery and cellar, referred to by the Ferrer
family as 'Champagne Caves', is designed in an unusual hacienda
style. The Chardonnay is a style that should be enjoyed young.
The Pinot Noir and Merlot, which also come from Carneros, will
stand just a little age. The sparkling wines, which all benefit from
sufficiently lengthy lees-ageing, are ready on release. The Royal
Cuvée spends an extended 6 years on its yeast, while the flagship
Carneros Cuvée has a high proportion of reserve wine and 7 years
on its lees. A small volume of two premium Pinot Noir labels, José S.
Ferrer and WillMar are available exclusively from the winery. (DM)
Recommended Whites:
Carneros Cuvée Carneros ★★★ £FRoyal Cuvée Carneros ★★☆ £D
Blanc de Noirs Carneros ★★ £D
Sonoma Brut Sonoma County ★☆ £D Chardonnay Carneros ★★☆ £D
Recommended Rosés:
Brut Rosé Carneros ★★ £D

Grace Family Vineyards (St Helena) www.gracefamilyvineyards.com
This tiny operation was the first of the now numerous California cult
wineries and the Grace Family is one of the most exalted premium
Cabernets in California. It commenced production in 1978 and
barely 400 cases are made annually from the family vineyard. This
was one of the first vineyards to be planted with close-spaced vines,
avoiding the need for herbicides or pesticides, and biodynamic
farming is being evaluated at present. Part of the production is
auctioned for charity so the remainder is extremely rare. Big, richly
textured and immensely powerful, it is a wine respected for its
balance and finesse as much as its sheer concentration. If you can
find any, expect to pay a very high price. Some very decent olive oil
is also made. (DM)
Recommended Reds:
Cabernet Sauvignon Napa Valley ★★★★☆ £H

Green & Red Vineyard (Napa Valley) www.greenandred.com
Small estate in the Chiles Valley on the eastern side of the Napa
Valley whose main focus is Zinfandel. Consultancy input from Helen
Turley of MARCASSIN has provided the stimulus for well-crafted ripe
and supple examples of the variety. All of the wines are now made
from estate grown fruit. The Chiles Mill is an estate single-vineyard
bottling, as the Tip Top Zin. These are a level up on the Chiles
Canyon Zin sourced from all three of the estate sites. The range also
now includes a Petite Sirah, as well as a Sauvignon Blanc. The Petite
Sirah comes from the Tip Top Vineyard, white the Sauvignon Blanc
from the Catacula site sees a touch of oak during fermentation
and malolactic is blocked to preserve freshness. The wines are all
reasonably priced. (DM)
Recommended Reds:
Zinfandel Chiles Mill Vineyard Chiles Valley ★★★☆ £E
Zinfandel Chiles Canyon Vineyards Chiles Valley ★★★ £D

Grgich Hills Estate (Rutherford) www.grgich.com
Mike Grgich made his reputation at CHATEAU MONTELENA before
going on to establish a formidable track record under his own
label. All the wines are now coming solely from estate fruit and the
vineyards are farmed biodynamically. Chardonnay is big, full and

typically opulent in a classic ripe and forward tropical Napa style. It is aged in French oak and should be enjoyed in its first 2 or 3 years. The ripe and lightly grassy Fumé Blanc has its malolactic blocked for freshness, as does the Chardonnay and should be drunk young. Two powerful and firmly tannic Cabernets, including a pricey limited release Yountville Selection, are joined by a Zinfandel that is rich and heavily extracted with vibrant dark berry fruit, full of depth but a touch short on refinement. This is joined by a limited production Zin Miljenko's Old Vine which is available at the winery as well as a round and plummy Merlot. Petite Sirah also comes from the Miljenko's Vineyard. A fine late-harvest botrytised white, Violetta is also produced from a field blend of Sauvignon Blanc, Riesling, and Gewürztraminer. (DM)

Recommended Reds:
Cabernet Sauvignon Yountville Selection Napa Valley ★★★★ £H
Cabernet Sauvignon Napa Valley ★★★☆ £F
Merlot Napa Valley ★★★ £E   Zinfandel Napa Valley ★★★ £E
Recommended Whites:
Violetta Napa Valley ★★★★ £G
Chardonnay Napa Valley ★★★ £E
Fumé Blanc Napa Valley ★★☆ £D

✿✿ Harlan Estate (Oakville) *www.harlanestate.com*
Odds are, if you have heard of any famous California wines, you have heard of Harlan Estate. Founded in Oakville in 1984 by Bill Harlan, it is a 240-acre estate ranging in elevations from 225 to 1225ft, with forty acres under vine. The terraced vineyards are predominantly planted to Cabernet Sauvignon, supplemented by Bordeaux varietals such as Merlot, Cabernet Franc and Petite Verdot. Bill Harlan, a real estate developer and visionary, desired to not just build a winery, but to create a perfect fusion of form and function. This one of the most architecturally admired wineries in California is home to the winemaker of record, Bob Levy, whose deep faith in capturing the magic of what the land and the vineyard delivers, and uncompromising pursuit of excellence has earned him total peer and consumer admiration and plenty of perfect scores from a variety of critics. Two wines are made – Harlan Estate and Maiden. Harlan Estate debut vintage was 1990, released in 1996, production hovers in a 2000 case range. Maiden inaugural vintage was 1995, rereleased in 1999, with an annual production of 900 cases. Both are exceptionally age worthy. Harlan Estate has cult-like following, with a long waiting list. It is widely regarded as one of the best Bordeaux blends in the New World. Remarkable power, wealth and depth of flavor and complexity are the hallmarks of the brand. (IT)
Recommended Reds:
Estate Red Napa Valley ✪✪✪✪✪ £H
The Maiden Red Napa Valley ★★★★ £G

Havens (Napa Valley) *www.havenswinery.com*
A good, small range of wines with the Bordeaux varieties a key element in the portfolio. Certainly rich and impressive when at their dark fruited best, the wines can be marked by oak. Bourriquot is a Bordeaux style blend, but Right Bank rather than Left, being a stylish blend of Cabernet Franc and Merlot. A second Meritage blend is also produced as well as a Napa Valley Cabernet Sauvignon. Chardonnay is the one white currently made in a rich, opulent style with lots of oak. The wines will develop well in the medium term and the Bourriquot is a real cellaring proposition. (DM)
Recommended Reds:
Bourriquot Napa Valley ★★★☆ £F   Meritage Napa Valley ★★★ £E

Heitz Cellars (St Helena) *www.heitzcellar.com*
One of the original benchmark producers of premium Napa reds, particularly the great Martha's Vineyard Cabernets. Quality has been up and down during the 1980s and 1990s but the wines are now sounder and they seem generally to be improving. The Bella Oaks and Trailside bottlings are a touch lighter than Martha's Vineyard but impressive nevertheless. Chardonnay is in a tighter style than some of its neighbours and is only lightly oaked. There are a total of 142 ha (350 acres) of estate vineyards spread throughout Napa and as well as Cabernet and Chardonnay some Grignolino and Zinfandel are produced. (DM)
Recommended Reds:
Cabernet Sauvignon Martha's Vineyard Napa Valley ★★★★☆ £H
Cabernet Sauvignon Trailside Vineyard Napa Valley ★★★★ £F
Cabernet Sauvignon Napa Valley ★★★☆ £F
Recommended Whites:
Chardonnay Napa Valley ★★☆ £D Sauvignon Blanc Napa Valley ★★☆ £C

Hess Collection (Mount Veeder) *www.hesscollection.com*
An unusual operation in that Donald Hess also provides visitors with access to his extensive art collection. The wines here are impressive, particularly the Cabernet Sauvignon and Chardonnay, produced under the Hess Collection label and vinified from estate Mount Veeder fruit. A new pricey top wine The Small Block Reserve from the Napa Valley is a varietal Cabernet Sauvignon. A number of other Hess Collection wines are also released under the Small Block banner. Cabernet Sauvignon and Chardonnay under the Hess Select label are released respectively under the North Coast and Monterey appellations. They are soft, forward and economically priced. A Malbec also comes from Salta in Argentina and there is a Winemakers Blend "Treo". The third label Artezin offers reasonably priced Zinfandel, Carignan, Charbono, Petite Sirah, Mourvèdre and a white Verdelho from Amador County. Donald Hess also has an interest in GLEN CARLOU in South Africa and Bodega COLOME in Argentina. (DM)
Recommended Reds:
Cabernet Sauvignon Collection Mount Veeder ★★★☆ £F
Cabernet Sauvignon Collection Allomi Napa Valley ★★★ £E
Cabernet Sauvignon North Coast Hess Select ★☆ £C
Recommended Whites:
Chardonnay Collection Mount Veeder ★★★ £E
Chardonnay Monterey Hess Select ★☆ £B

HL Vineyards (Napa Valley) *www.herblambvineyard.com*
The Lamb famed vineyard is a mere 3 ha (7.4 acres) and was the source for some benchmark wines from COLGIN Cellars. Located just below Howell Mountain on the elevated slopes to the east of St Helena, the vineyard yields less than 2 tons to the acre of piercingly intense Cabernet Sauvignon grapes. The first vintage for the HL estate wine here was as recent as 1997 and production remains tiny, so there is an inevitable scarcity. A second label Two Old Dogs helps ensure quality and a Sauvignon Blanc is also made in tiny quantities from Yountville fruit. The HL Cabernet is a rich, powerful and brooding red that needs at least 5–7 years' cellaring. (DM)
Recommended Reds:
Cabernet Sauvignon HL Napa Valley ★★★★★ £H

Hourglass (Napa Valley) *www.hourglasswine.com*
A handful of reds and an Hourglass Vineyard Sauvignon Blanc (£E) are made here. The Hourglass site is a tiny 1.6ha (4 acre) vineyard planted in 1992 in close proximity to the COLGIN Tychson Hill,

Napa & Carneros

California

VINEYARD 29 and GRACE FAMILY vineyards. Spread across the hillside as well as the valley floor, the soil is made up of a rocky/gravelly loam mix ideal for low yielding vines and producing top quality, intensely flavoured grapes. A second larger vineyard Blueprint was acquired in 2006 and more economically priced reds from Cabernet Franc (£G), Cabernet Sauvignon (£G), Merlot (£F) and Malbec (£F) are also now made from these plots. The Hourglass Cabernet Sauvignon is produced from 100% varietal fruit and is in a very rich, ripe style. Ageing is for 18 to 20 months in a mix of new and used French oak. (DM)

Recommended Reds:

Hourglass Cabernet Sauvignon Napa Valley ★★★★★ £H

⚫ Hundred Acre (Napa Valley) *www.hundredacre.com*

Jayson Woodbridge is now making some of the most exciting full blown Cabernet Sauvignon in the Napa. The first vintage was only in 2000. His Kayli Morgan site is in the eastern hills of the Napa. The well drained, meagre soils provide an excellent *terroir*; the eroded clay holds moisture and to aid the ripening process a fine mist method of irrigation is employed. As well as providing sufficient moisture for the vines during heat spikes the process lowers the ambient temperature of the plants micro-climate and ensures an optimum even phenolic ripening. The wine is 100% Cabernet Sauvignon and is vinified block by block using only small lot vatting. There is no crushing and fermentation is by whole berry. Depending on the vintage yields have varied between 1.4 and 2.5 tons to the acre. The wines are sumptuous and concentrated style and will drink well young but deserve at least five or six years' patience. Further Cabernets, Ark Vineyard on Howell Mountain, Precious and Few and Far Between have also been recently released. (DM)

Recommended Reds:

Cabernet Sauvignon Kayli Morgan Napa Valley ⚫⚫⚫⚫⚫ £H
Cabernet Sauvignon Few and Far Between Napa Valley ★★★★★ £H
Cabernet Sauvignon Ark Vineyard Howell Mountain ★★★★★ £H

⚫ Inglenook Estate (Rutherford) *www.inglenook.com*

This historic estate and trademark has been re-established with wines made under the former Rubicon Estate banner now being made under the Inglenook banner by Francis Ford Coppola. This began as a small operation when film director Coppola first became involved in winegrowing, but there is now a sizeable output through the Francis Coppola Winery in the Sonoma Valley at Healdsburg. An extensive range is released there. Under the Sofia label you'll find approachable sparklers, the Rosso & Bianco label is for everyday reds and whites, while the Diamond Series is a range of red and white varietals sourced throughout the state and generally taking the California appellation. These are straightforward, reliable, fruit-driven wines and well priced. The Directors Cut series is a step up with a small range of wines from Sonoma County and there is an additional range under the Francis Coppola Reserve label. Two further reds are also made, a Bordeaux blend Archimedes and Eleanor which combines an interesting mix of Zinfandel, Petit Verdot, Cabernet Franc, Cabernet Sauvignon and Petite Sirah from Rutherford and Alexander Valley sources. It is though the top Inglenook labels that really impress. As well as the wines listed below there is a small production of RC Reserve Syrah and Sauvignon Blanc. Zinfandel Edizione Pennino is rich and powerful with dense, brambly fruit. At the pinnacle there are two flagship wines. Blancaneaux is a blend of Roussanne, Marsanne and Viognier. Rubicon is a very structured, firm and powerful meritage red aged for 26 months in French oak and requires at least 6–7 years' patience.

It is firmly established as one of Napa's great reds. (DM)

Recommended Reds:

Rubicon Rutherford ⚫⚫⚫⚫⚫ £H
Cask Cabernet Estate Rutherford ★★★★☆ £G
Cabernet Franc Estate Rutherford ★★★★ £F
Zinfandel Edizione Pennino Rutherford ★★★★ £F

Recommended Whites:

Blancaneaux Rutherford ★★★★☆ £F

JAQK Cellars (Napa Valley) *www.jaqkcellars.com*

Is this serious or is it humorous? Wine drinking poker players should be thrilled with this new conception of marketing wine. The brainchild of Joel Templin and Katie Jain, already at the forefront of graphic design, have teamed up with Craig MacLean, one time winemaker for CAIN CELLARS and SPRING MOUNTAIN VINEYARDS, to produce wines that are themed on card play. JAQK itself, of course, stands for Jack, Ace, Queen and King and the clever labelling and packaging makes an exciting visual impact on the consumer. But you have to be reminded that it is not the label that one drinks. Behind the label (and this is one of the *raisons d'être* for this guide) is the knowledge that some serious winemaking hides beneath a somewhat gimmicky exterior. All the wines are named after gaming terms, which may or may not make them easier to remember. Black Clover Napa Valley Merlot is smooth with soft tannins and good finesse, very approachable now but will keep for some years. High Roller Napa Valley Cabernet Sauvignon has layers of upfront black fruit and an unctuous and long finish. Soldier of Fortune Napa Valley Syrah is a big wine with good varietal flavours without being too aggressive. There are wines from other parts of California going under exotic names such as Pearl Handle Chardonnay from Sonoma Coast, Charmed Sauvignon Blanc, Her Majesty Chardonnay, Bone Dance Merlot and 22 Black Cabernet Sauvignon from vineyards around California. Since they major on packaging, there are a number of gift box choices that are attractive to the eye. Prices seem a little elevated. (NB)

Recommended Reds:

Cabernet Sauvignon 'High Roller' Napa Valley ★★★★ £G
Merlot 'Black Clover' Napa Valley ★★★☆ £F
Syrah 'Soldier of Fortune' Napa Valley ★★★☆ £F

>> Jericho Canyon (Napa Valley) *www.jerichocanyonvineyard.com*

For Marla and Dale Bleecher, proprietors it was love at first sight. Three years into their exhaustive search, they found a stunning ranch just outside Calistoga. They divided their forty-acre vineyard into 24 blocks and planted Cabernet Sauvignon, Merlot and Cabernet Franc. Careful viticultural practices throughout the growing season ensures that their small-lot Bordeaux-style blends are complex, balanced wines. In 2006 the winery and a 6000-sq. ft cave were complete. David Ramey was the original winemaker, followed by Aaron Pott and their own son, Nicholas, stepping in to contribute. Michel Rolland has been part of the blending team since 2010. The Reserve Cabernet Sauvignon was chosen from 38 top lots on the estate. Larger than life, brimming with dark fruit and spices, it is deftly balanced and oozes grace and sensuality. The Estate Cab is, in contrast, quite elegant and somewhat restrained, showing the purity of terroir and gorgeous multi-layered textures. Chimera Proprietary blend is a showgirl of rich, opulent fruit, creamy mouthfeel and sleek tannins. There is also a Jericho Creek Cab, a new and fantastic Rosé, made from the estate Bordeaux varietals, and an outstanding, wildly aromatic Sauvignon Blanc, that features a seductive array of tropical/citrus fruit aromas, as well as stone fruit

undertones. Its bright acidity and terrific finish makes for a dreamy experience. (IT)

Recommended Reds:
Estate Cabernet Sauvignon Napa Valley ★★★★☆ £G
Chimera Proprietary Blend Napa Valley ★★★★ £G
Recommended Whites:
Sauvignon Blanc Napa Valley ★★★★☆ £F

Juslyn (Spring Mountain) *www.juslynvineyards.com*
Founded in 1997 by British expatriates, this is an impressive source of Cabernet that should be worth following. The Butlers' 17 ha (42 acre) Spring Mountain property is the source of the Estate Cabernet Sauvignon. The wine is rich and full, with impressive concentration and a fine cedary undercurrent adding further complexity. An additional Meritage style red Perry's Blend comes from a combination of Cabernet Sauvignon, Merlot, Cabernet Franc and Petit Verdot. A Sauvignon Blanc comes from Napa County fruit. (DM)
Recommended Reds:
Cabernet Sauvignon Estate Spring Mountain ★★★★☆ £G

>> Kale Wines (Napa Valley) *www.kalewines.com*
Kale specializes in boutique wines from top sustainably farmed vineyards planted to Rhône varietals. Kale Anderson grew up in Sonoma, surrounded by the wine industry and the great outdoors that nurtured his love of land. He graduated from UC Davis and did his first harvest at J Winery in RRV, subsequently working at Cliff Lede, COLGIN CELLARS, PAHLMEYER, STAGS LEAP and Terra Valentine. With fifteen vintages under his belt, Anderson moved on to consulting projects and launched his own brand in 2008. His Alder Springs Vineyard-Spirit Rock Syrah comes from a site with "heroic" viticulture, as the hilly, steep coastal range vineyards are challenging to access and farm. Spirit Rock sits at 2700ft elevation, and produces miniscule yields and tiny berries. The ensuing wine is tense, with a tightly wound core of uber-concentrated fruit. 'Home Run Cuvee" made from Kick Ranch Syrah, sourced from a site in Sonoma County's newest AVA, Fountaingrove, is an entirely different offering. Deep, dark, pure fruit is lush and generous, balanced by bright acidity, minerality and round mouthfeel. "Heritage" from McGah Vineyard in Rutherford gets plenty of sunlight and is known for its ripe fruit due to its eastern exposure. Dark and concentrated, the Grenache and Mourvèdre are outstanding. Stagecoach is one of the largest Napa vineyards, with a great diversity of soils and exposures. Kale Syrah and Grenache, planted to ALBAN clone, comes from the Pritchard Hill area at 1500ft elevation, so the fruit is uber-intense and glorious. There is also a very pretty rosé, fashioned in a concrete egg. (IT)
Recommended Reds:
Home Run Cuvee" Kick Ranch Vineyard Sonoma County ★★★★ £F
Heritage McGah Vineyard Rutherford ★★★★ £F

>> Kenzo Estate (Napa Valley) *www.kenzoestate.com*
Kenzo Tsujimoto, a Japanese businessman, founder of Capcom, has been intrigued with Napa Valley since the days of the historic 1976 Paris tasting. A couple of decades of extensive search later he acquired a 4000-acre property on the slopes of Mt. George. Plantable parcels were carefully selected, and in 1998 the ground prep had begun. By 2001, first grapes were harvested and David ABREU was hired to manage the vineyard, who convinced him to replant it to his specifications. In 2002, replanting of several Bordeaux varietals had begun, and a year later another superstar

had joined the team – eminent winemaker Heidi Barrett, who made some of Napa's most famous cult wines. In 2005, the second go-around of the brand-new harvest under the careful tutelage of Abreu has proven to be a success, with the fruit coming in complex and concentrated. The wine rested for 20 months in new French wood and one year in bottle, and was released in 2008. There were three offerings: Rindo, Murasaki and Ai. All three wines showed impressive prowess for such a young vineyard. With the release of 2007 vintage Asatsuyu, Heidi's only Sauvignon Blanc, the brand was quickly establishing itself as a source of unique and high impact luxury wines. Soon after the winery and caves were built, insuring that all the processes are done in house, with every available tool to achieve perfection. Rindo remains a flagship wine, a composition of Bordeaux varietals from multitude of blocks. Asuka, a Cabernet Franc blend is an intense, red-fruit driven effort with laser-like precision and subtle hints of wild flowers and baking spices. Ai or "indigo" is predominantly a Cabernet, true to its name it is dark, inky, bold and beautiful, a powerhouse full of unlimited potential. Murasaki or "purple" is a Cab and Merlot blend, an homage to the "Right Bank" of Bordeaux. It is quite pleasant now, but will clearly benefit from aging. Asatsuyu Sauvignon Blanc continues to impress with its amplified varietal character, gorgeous tropical fruit and melon medley. There is rosé called "Yui" made from Merlot and Cab Franc, and even a sweet wine, Muku, a blend of Sauvignon Blanc and Semillon, to round out the portfolio. It is gloriously feminine and fragrant (think rose petals and apple blossom), yet shows amazing acidity. (IT)
Recommended Reds:
Rindo Napa Valley ★★★★★ £G
Asuka Cabernet Franc Napa Valley ★★★★☆ £G
Murasaki Napa Valley ★★★★☆ £G
Recommended Whites:
Asatsuyu Sauvignon Blanc Napa Valley ★★★★ £F

❀ Kongsgaard (Napa Valley) *www.kongsgaardwine.com*
John Kongsgaard produces wines of formidable weight and concentration. The approach is one of minimal intervention in the cellar allied to wild yeast fermentation and the wines are neither fined nor filtered. The Chardonnay is a very impressive example of the variety, combining the best subtle elements of great Burgundy with a richly textured, almost explosive dose of honeyed Napa fruit. The finish is very long and complex. A small volume super premium example, The Judge, is also now released. While the Chardonnay is not exactly made in abundance (around 1,500 cases), there is only a tiny amount of two Rhône styles – a ViognierRoussanne blend, Viorous, rich in texture with a fine, intense nutty complexity, and a very powerful and impressive Syrah produced from Carneros fruit. This will comfortably stand alongside the finest examples of the variety from the northern Rhône and is of undoubted ✪✪✪✪✪ quality. Napa Valley Cabernet Sauvignon, Merlot and a blend of the two, Fimasaurus are also released under the Kongsgaard label. A second label, Kings Farm, is available through the mailing list and these are more approachable styles, albeit made in small quantities. (DM)
Recommended Reds:
Syrah Napa Valley ✪✪✪✪✪ £H
Recommended Whites:
Chardonnay Napa Valley ★★★★★ £G
Roussanne/Viognier Napa Valley ★★★★★ £G

Napa & Carneros

✤ Krupp Brothers (Napa Valley) *www.kruppbrothers.com*
The Krupp family began by planting a vineyard with their own name in 1991 and completed their estate holdings by planting the Stagecoach Vineyard on Pritchard Hill in 1996. While the majority of the wines come from the Stagecoach vineyard, a varietal Merlot is released from the Krupp vineyard. All the wines rated below are produced from the Stagecoach site. The more approachable Bordeaux styled wines take the Veraison label while the Black Bart label is used for Rhône styles, and the Krupp Brothers label for the top reds. The dark, spicy and well structured Veraison Cabernet Sauvignon is blended with a smattering of Cabernet Franc, Merlot and Malbec. The Krupp M5 Cabernet is a dense and brooding red, dominated by Cabernet Sauvignon and sourced only from the best blocks on Stagecoach. The Synchrony blend is a varying combination of all the Bordeaux grapes and when dominated by Cabernet Franc offering a subtle, characteristic leafy undercurrent to the fruit. The Doctor has a Spanish influence being a blend of Tempranillo, Merlot, Malbec, Cabernet Sauvignon and Cabernet Franc. Of the two Rhône style wines the Black Bart's Bride is a very characterful peachy and honeyed Viognier, on occasion blended with Marsanne. The Black Bart Syrah is a robust and spicy example with a minerally structure emerging from grapes grown at an altitude of around 1,700 feet. In addition to the wines covered here under the Krupp Brothers label they also produce a Veraison Red blend, a Black Bart Port style Syrah and a Chardonnay. A characterful range of wines produced from yields varying from just over 1 ton to around 3 tons to the acre. (DM)
Krupp Brothers
Recommended Reds:
Cabernet Sauvignon M5 Stagecoach Vineyard ★★★★☆ £G
The Doctor Stagecoach Vineyard Napa Valley ★★★★ £F
Synchrony Stagecoach Vineyard Napa Valley ★★★★ £F
Black Bart
Recommended Reds:
Syrah Stagecoach Vineyard Napa Valley ★★★★☆ £F
Recommended Whites:
Black Bart's Bride Stagecoach Vineyard Napa Valley ★★★☆ £F
Veraison
Recommended Reds:
Cabernet Sauvignon Stagecoach Vineyard Napa Valley ★★★★ £F

Kuleto (St Helena) *www.kuletoestate.com*
Pat Kuleto began establishing vineyards on this eastern Napa ranch in 1993 and there are now plantings of Cabernet Sauvignon, Syrah, Sangiovese, Malbec, Cabernet Franc and Chardonnay, all now released varietally, as well as some Muscat. A Rosato is also produced from Sangiovese. Production is approaching 10,000 cases a year, small in winery terms yet dwarfing that of some of the winery's neighbours. The vineyards range in altitude from 250–450m (800–1,450ft) and both the Syrah and the Cabernet Sauvignon are marked by their elegance, purity of fruit and finely honed structure. Low yields of barely 1.5 tons/acre contribute to their quality. The dark, smoky and peppery Syrah is aged in 500 litre puncheons, which helps preserve the varietal character, while the rich and cedary Cabernet sees a high proportion of new French oak. Both will benefit from half a decade's cellaring. A series of Cabernets are now released and are also labelled Villa Vista, Lone Acre and Native Son. The Danielli Cabernet is now the estate's top red and marginally pricier than the other Cabs. Bill Foley of FOLEY Vineyards purchased Kuleto in 2009 and is providing additional winemaking and farming resources to ensure continuity of quality. (DM)

Recommended Reds:
Cabernet Sauvignon The Point Estate Napa Valley ★★★★ £G
Syrah Estate Napa Valley ★★★★ £F

Lagier Meredith (Mount Veeder) *www.lagiermeredith.com*
This property high up on Mount Veeder was purchased by Lagier and Meredith in 1986. Remote and seemingly far away from the humdrum of Napa Valley grape growing, the redwood forests nearby are home to mountain lions and coyotes. Originally one wine was made here, a richly textured, very pure and intense Syrah. The first vines were planted in 1986 and the first wine released from the 1996 vintage. The total area under vine is very small at less than 2 ha (4.5 acres) and as well as Syrah, Mondeuse, Malbec and most recently Zinfandel are planted. The site is above the night time valley fog resulting in more even daily temperatures. This allied to finely drained, volcanic soils means the fruit gets a naturally lengthy hang time producing grapes of impressive flavour intensity and fine tannins. Bottled without filtration, expect this Syrah to develop very well over 5–7 years. The only problem is there's very little available. Small amounts of the other varietals are made as well as a rosé and a port style Syrah. The couple have also teamed up with their neighbours Aaron and Claire Pott of Pott Wine in producing wines under a second label Chester's Anvil, with wines made from a number of sources and at very fair prices. (DM)
Recommended Reds:
Syrah Mount Veeder ★★★★ £F

Lail Vineyards (Rutherford) *www.lailvineyards.com*
Although this is a newly established small-scale winery, owner Robin Daniel Lail's family history goes back to the beginnings of viticulture in Napa itself. One of her ancestors, Gustav Niebaum, established the original Inglenook winery in 1879. Five wines are now made here. The J Daniel Cuvée is a Bordeaux blend of two-thirds Cabernet Sauvignon and one-third Merlot. It is sourced from a mere 2.3 ha (5.6 acres). The second red the Blueprint is a blend of Cabernet Sauvignon and Merlot. A gooseberry scented Sauvignon Blanc was added with the 2007 vintage. Winemaker Philippe Melka continues to produce increasingly stylish, elegant and very finely structured meritage reds. A further Cabernet from Howell Mountain, Mole Hill as well as a second serious Sauvignon Blanc, Georgia are also made. (DM)
Recommended Reds:
J Daniel Cuvée Napa Valley ★★★★ £F
Blueprint Red Napa Valley ★★★☆ £E
Recommended Whites:
Blueprint Sauvignon Blanc Napa Valley ★★★ £D

La Jota (Howell Mountain) *www.lajotavineyardco.com*
Throughout the 1980s and 90s La Jota has been a source of some of the most powerful and impressive examples produced in the Howell Mountain AVA. The winery has become famed for massive dense and tannic reds that need considerable cellaring but develop very well in bottle. Ownership has passed from Bill Smith (now vinifying Sonoma Valley Pinot Noir under his own W H SMITH label) to MARKHAM vineyards. Winemaker Christopher Carpenter continues to maximise the potential of the 11 ha (28 acres) of prime mountain vineyards. The Heritage Release is 100% Cabernet Sauvignon; the Howell Mountain has some Merlot, Cabernet Franc and Petit Verdot blended in and is supple and rounded for a mountain red and is softer in its youth. As well as the Cabernet Sauvignons, a few hundred cases of Cabernet Franc and Merlot are

also produced. (DM)

Recommended Reds:

Cabernet Sauvignon Heritage Release Howell Mountain ★★★★ £G
Cabernet Sauvignon Howell Mountain ★★★☆ £F

Larkin Wines (Yountville) *www.larkinwines.com*

Wine broker Sean Larkin's small Yountville operation produces a very fine Cabernet Franc-based red, one of the best of this style in the region as well as now a Cabernet Sauvignon also and the first vintage was only 1999. Very small amounts are exported and it would be well worth joining the mailing list. Cabernet Franc is blended with Merlot as well as small amounts of Cabernet Sauvignon and Petit Verdot which add weight and depth. Marked by its elegance and well-honed, supple tannins, the wine is lighter than many other meritage blends but offers very impressive fruit persistence on the palate. The plush, well-honed, cedary Cabernet Sauvignon has small amounts of Merlot and Petit Verdot. Give both at least 5 years. Another Cabernet Sauvignon and Merlot are also released under the Jack Larkin label and similarly priced. (DM)

Recommended Reds:

Cabernet Franc Napa Valley ★★★★☆ £F
Cabernet Sauvignon Napa Valley ★★★★☆ £F

Larkmead (Napa Valley) *www.larkmead.com*

This winery dates back to the end of the 19th century and has always focused on estate wines. The Bordeaux red varieties are the main focus of the operation but new blocks of Sauvignon Blanc and Tocai Friulano have been established and released, the Sauvignon Blanc under the Lillie brand and vinified in oak in the style of a top white Graves. Regular Cabernet Sauvignon is produced as well as a premium meritage LMV (£G) and a more economically priced Bordeaux blend Firebelle (£F), which offers rich, concentrated, dark plummy fruit and a hint of vanilla spice from 55% new French oak. Finely structured and balanced, the wines generally avoid some of the quite heavily extracted characteristics found in many of their peers. The top label Cabernet Sauvignon Solari Reserve is a pure varietal sadly only available in tiny quantities direct from the winery. The wine is loaded with mouth-coating dark, spicy fruits and just a hint of subtly integrated spice from 100% new wood. It comes from the oldest Cabernet vines and needs at least 6 or 7 years' cellaring to do it justice. (DM)

Recommended Reds:

Cabernet Sauvignon Solari Napa Valley ★★★★★ £G

Lewis Cellars (Napa Valley) *www.lewiscellars.com*

If like me you're a motor racing fan you'll be delighted by the quality of the powerful, dense Cabernet-based reds hand-crafted by former Indy 500 star Randy Lewis and his wife Debbie. This small, bespoke range is marked by rich fruit and in the top reds power and structure. They are quintessential California wines but serious and very impressive. For the Cabernet Reserve you need to wait for the tannins to subside but it will be worth it. Cuvée L was added with the 2004 vintage, which is a good deal more expensive than the Reserve and a premium Hillside Vineyard example is also released. Good Chardonnay, including excellent Reserve and Bacaglia Lane bottlings, is also produced and Syrah and Sauvignon Blanc have been added to the portfolio. The range is completed by Alec's Blend, an unusual fruit-driven combination of Syrah, Merlot, Cabernet Sauvignon and Petit Verdot. (DM)

Recommended Reds:

Cabernet Sauvignon Reserve Napa Valley ★★★★☆ £H
Cabernet Sauvignon Napa Valley ★★★★ £G

Merlot Napa Valley ★★★★ £F

❀ Littorai (St Helena) *www.littorai.com*

Before establishing his own St Helena-based winery, Ted Lemon gained considerable winemaking experience in Burgundy as well as California. This is reflected in a range of Chardonnays and Pinot Noirs which are distinctly Burgundian in style. The winery name derives from the Latin litor and means 'the coasts'; Lemon's objective is to make the best examples he can of the Burgundy varieties from North Coast vineyard sources. Chardonnay is subtle, structured and only lightly tropical. Pinot Noir shows intense, subtle berry fruits and is always well meshed by firm but supple tannin. As well as the Charles Heintz and BA Thieriot bottlings, Chardonnay comes from Mays Canyon in the Russian River and The Tributary on the Sonoma Coast. A further Sonoma Coast white, Lemons Folly is a field blend of Sauvignon Blanc and Gewürztraminer. Pinot also emerges from Mays Canyon as well as the One Acre, Cerise and Roman vineyards in the cool Anderson Valley. Wines from The Haven, The Pivot and Mays Canyon vineyards on the Sonoma Coast are also made. That classic cool-climate red berry character is particularly apparent in the Savoy Vineyard Pinot; the BA Thieriot has more dark fruit and plum, being fuller and richer in texture. Expect the Chardonnays to develop well over 5–7 years. The Pinots and particularly the Savoy Vineyard will keep a little longer. (DM)

Recommended Reds:

Pinot Noir Savoy Vineyard Anderson Valley ★★★★★ £G
Pinot Noir Hirsch Vineyard Sonoma Coast ★★★★☆ £F
Pinot Noir BA Thieriot Vineyard Sonoma Coast ★★★★☆ £F

Recommended Whites:

Chardonnay Charles Heintz Vineyard Sonoma Coast ★★★★☆ £F
Chardonnay BA Thieriot Vineyard Sonoma Coast ★★★★☆ £F

Lokoya (Oakville) *www.lokoya.com*

This is Kendall-Jackson's super-premium label, producing distinctive Cabernet Sauvignons that showcase the best single-vineyard characteristics of prime mountain-grown fruit. The wines are vinified in the same facility as the flagship CARDINALE, which by contrast is a blend of sources. While vineyard source and low yields of 2–3 tons/acre are key to the great fruit in the wines, vinification is aimed at maximising their potential. Long vatting times, basket-pressed grapes, 20–21 months in top-quality French oak all contribute and the wines are neither fined nor filtered. These are all very big, dense and powerfully structured wines, needing time to shed their early youthful austerity. The Diamond Mountain is the most opulent and has had varying small portions of Merlot and Cabernet Franc blended in depending on the year. The other cuvées thus far have been 100% Cabernet Sauvignon. The Spring Mountain is more perfumed, while the Howell Mountain and Mount Veeder are the firmest of the quartet. (DM)

Recommended Reds:

Cabernet Sauvignon Diamond Mountain ★★★★☆ £H
Cabernet Sauvignon Howell Mountain ★★★★☆ £H
Cabernet Sauvignon Mount Veeder ★★★★☆ £H
Cabernet Sauvignon Spring Mountain District ★★★★☆ £H

Luna (Napa Valley) *www.lunavineyards.com*

Luna focuses on Italian varietals and a number of reds. John KONGSGAARD provided the early winemaking direction. Both the regular Pinot Grigio and Sangiovese are good value for money, while the pricier Canto is a proprietary Super-Tuscan-style blend of Sangiovese, Cabernet Sauvignon and Merlot with a little Petite

Napa & Carneros

Sirah adding additional grip. Indigenous yeasts are used, the Pinot Grigio unusually gets just a hint of new barrel-fermentation with lees-enrichment and the reds are all aged in fine-grained French oak and bottled without fining or filtration. A Sangiovese Reserve is also now produced along with Pinot Grigio and Chardonnay Reserves. Top flight Napa Valley Cabernet Sauvignon is also included in the portfolio along with a Petite Sirah and a white late harvested Pinot grigio, Mille Baci. In general the wines will drink well young and the Canto, Cabernet Sauvignon and Sangiovese Reserve will all benefit from short ageing. (DM)

Recommended Reds:
Canto Napa Valley ★★★★ £F
Sangiovese Reserve Napa Valley ★★★★ £F
Sangiovese Napa Valley ★★★ £D
Cabernet Sauvignon Napa Valley ★★★☆ £F
Recommended Whites:
Pinot Grigio Napa Valley ★★★ £C

>> **Melka Wines (St Helena)** *www.melkawines.com*
Phillipe Melka rising star ascended quickly in the wine circle, as word spread around the valley about a talented and thoughtful winemaker who trained at HAUT-BRION and took guidance from PÉTRUS proprietors. His resume includes consulting at BRAND, DANA ESTATES, LAIL, VINEYARD 29 and other clients, for many of which he attained a plethora of perfect and near-perfect scores from critics such as Robert Parker. His reputation as a supreme *terroir* guy and an uber-intuitive blender helped propel him into the ranks of the most highly regarded winemakers of our time. Originally from Bordeaux, Melka worshipped the notion of the land as the primary reason for greatness in wines. His stint at Haut-Brion was followed by studying soils at DOMINUS in Napa. He counts some of the top industry luminaries as his mentors. In 1994 he came to reside in Napa full-time, and in 1996 Melka brand was launched, with the idea of making wines that sing the soil. Four labels were created, Metisse and CJ from Napa, Mekerra from Sonoma, Majestique worldwide. Metisse is a blend of Bordeaux varietals, Mekerra, which pays homage to Melka's father, is a Knight's valley blend. Majestique, true to the original intent, represents fruit sources from around the world, from Saint Emilion's Cabernet Franc to California's Central Coast Syrah. CJ acknowledges Phillip and his wife Cherie's two children: Chloe and Jeremy. It's a superb blend of very enjoyable young wine. (IT)

Recommended Whites:
Mekerra Proprietary White Sonoma Valley ★★★★☆ £G
Recommended Reds:
Montbleau Vineyard Napa Valley ★★★★★ £H
Metisse Jumping Goat Vineyard Napa Valley ★★★★☆ £H
Mekerra Proprietary Red Sonoma Valley ★★★★ £G

Miller Wine Works (Napa Valley) *www.millerwineworks.com*
Impressive new small operation producing Rhône style reds from the Napa Valley and now Pinot Noir from the Kendric Vineyard in Marin County. Chef turned winemaker Gary Miller gained experience with LA JOTA, MARTINELLI and Robert BIALE before establishing his own Napa based operation. Grenache from the High Valley AVA in Lake County is produced in tiny quantities and is super-ripe in style with loads of dark-berry and herb scented fruit. It gains additional weight and colour from Syrah and Mataro with ageing in neutral oak. Syrah from Sage Canyon is opulent and showy but still possesses a firm structure from vineyards grown at 900 to 1,400 feet. It gets around one-third new French oak ageing

for 16 months but it is never intrusive. Other Rhône reds include a number of blends. Sierra Works from El Dorado County combines Mourvèdre, Petite Sirah, Grenache and Syrah. The Works from Napa Valley fruit is a mix of Syrah, Grenache, Mataro and unusually Tinta Cão. The Jordan's Journeys Red is a blend of mainly Mataro, with Syrah and a smattering of Grenache. The Lake County sourced GM blend comprises Petite Sirah, Tinta Cão, Mataro and Grenache. A Sierra Hills Mourvèdre is blended with a little Grenache. A white, Harvest Blanc, which combines mainly Roussanne with Viognier, Marsanne and Grenache Blanc as well as an El Dorado rosé, Ruddy Bloom, and a port style, Teodoro, complete the small and well-priced range. (DM)

Recommended Reds:
Syrah Sage Canyon Vineyard Napa Valley ★★★★ £E
Grenache Shannon Ridge Vineyard High Valley ★★★☆ £E

❀ **Meteor Vineyard (Napa Valley)** *www.meteorvineyard.com*
One of the latest in a long line of cult wines, no expense has been spared by Barry Schuler, the ex-CEO of AOL, to realise his dream of making world class Cabernet Sauvignon. Teaming up in partnership with Bill and Dawnine DYER, one of Napa Valley's leading husband and wife winemaking teams, they have produced a wine of outstanding quality with their first release from the 2005 vintage. With the vineyard being located in an ideal growing climate, 500 feet above sea level and planted with three selected Cabernet Sauvignon clones not long after the Schulers bought it in 1999, the quality of the fruit produced on its white volcanic soil was soon recognised by some of Napa's top wine producers who purchased fruit from the Schulers. Recognising that the fruit was of outstanding quality, they decided to make a small amount of wine solely from this vineyard under their own label. Like many great wines of the world, there is a cool climate elegance combined with lush, ripe fruit, giving it a seamless balance and a long, lingering finish. Quite remarkable for vines which are barely over a decade old. Only around 700 cases are made with a further 90 cases of Special Family Reserve Cabernet Sauvignon. Of course, these wines are not cheap, the Special Family Reserve being well off the radar of our most expensive price category; and whilst the wine is approachable now it may be better to buy it sooner rather than later – it's certainly going to be drinking well into the next decade or more and it won't get any cheaper. (NB)

Recommended Reds:
Special Family Reserve Cabernet Sauvignon Coombsville ✿✿✿✿✿ £H
Perseid Cabernet Sauvignon Coombsville ✿✿✿✿✿ £H

❀ **Miner Family Vineyards (Oakville)** *www.minerwines.com*
Established relatively recently, Miner Family Vineyard was founded in 1998. The principle source of fruit for the range is the Oakville Ranch, where Dave Miner was president. Other Napa vineyards are also used as well as Gary's, Sierra Mar and Rossella's vineyards in the Santa Lucia Highlands for striking Pinot Noir, and the Simpson Vineyard in Madera County for a floral, medium-bodied Viognier. A Wild Yeast example is now made from the site as well. Merlot comes from the Stagecoach Vineyard. Fine, impressively structured Cabernet Sauvignon comes from Oakville, along with the Stagecoach Vineyard and there is now a red meritage, The Oracle, which blends Cabernet Sauvignon, Merlot, Cabernet Franc as well as a little Malbec and Petit Verdot. A Cab Franc and Malbec are also made. Grenache, Sangiovese, Tempranillo and Petite Sirah are also now offered as is a small amount of Sauvignon Blanc which comes from vineyards near Yountville and is part barrel and part stainless

steel-fermented. The Chardonnays, particularly the Wild Yeast, are very impressive. The wines are barrel-fermented with full malolactic and handled in mainly new oak. The Wild Yeast bottling is exotically tropical, rich and very concentrated. A number of similarly priced examples are released from single vineyard sources. La Diligence is a fine smoky, black and spicy Syrah produced in association with François VILLARD of Condrieu and a key auction favourite at the annual Hospices du Rhône weekend in May. A white example is also made from Marsanne. Look out also for a Roussanne and The Iliad, a blend of Marsanne, Roussanne and Viognier. In general the wines are very approachable young, although the Cabernet based reds need a little time. (DM)

Recommended Reds:
The Oracle Napa Valley ★★★★☆ £G
Pinot Noir Gary's Vineyard Santa Lucia Highlands ★★★★ £F
La Diligence Napa Valley ★★★★ £F
Cabernet Sauvignon Oakville ★★★★ £F
Merlot Stagecoach Vineyard ★★★☆ £F
Syrah Napa Valley ★★★☆ £D

Recommended Whites:
Chardonnay Wild Yeast ★★★★ £F
Chardonnay Napa Valley ★★☆ £D
Viognier Simpson Vineyard ★★★ £E

Robert Mondavi (Oakville) *www.robertmondavi.com*
Arguably the most famous wine name in California now purchased by Constellation Brands. The late Robert Mondavi must take much of the credit for the positive public face of California wine when it re-emerged as a quality region in the 1970s. The company has very widespread wine interests in California although most overseas investments and partnerships have now been sold. In addition to the large-scale premium operation at Oakville Mondavi also owns the Woodbridge winery facility in the Central Valley which produces straightforward everyday reds and whites. The BYRON winery on the Central Coast has been a Mondavi label for some years and the prestigious ARROWOOD operation in Sonoma is also owned. OPUS ONE was the first of the Mondavi winery partnerships, established in 1979 with MOUTON ROTHSCHILD. The core of the Oakville operation, though, is the firm's premium wines and Cabernet has always been exceptional. The Reserve comes mainly from the great To Kalon vineyard and a second release solely from To Kalon is also now offerred. The wines are either classified as Napa or other district bottlings as well as Reserves. Fumé Blanc as a style has always been successful here and an additional special bottling is now offerred from the very low-yielding I Block on the To Kalon vineyard, planted in 1945 and believed to be the oldest in North America. (DM)

Recommended Reds:
Cabernet Sauvignon Reserve Napa Valley ⭕⭕⭕⭕⭕ £H
Cabernet Sauvignon Oakville ★★★★ £F
Cabernet Sauvignon Napa Valley ★★★ £E
Pinot Noir Reserve Napa Valley ★★★ £F
Pinot Noir Napa Valley ★★ £D   Merlot Napa Valley ★★☆ £D

Recommended Whites:
Chardonnay Reserve Carneros ★★★☆ £F
Chardonnay Napa Valley ★★ £C   Fumé Blanc Napa Valley ★★ £D

>> Moone-Tsai (St Helena) *www.moonetsai.com*
A synergistic partnership between Larry and MaryAnn Tsai and Mike Moone with combined several decades of experience in leadership roles at the highest levels of a variety of businesses yielded a venture that added yet another superstar brand to a

Napa galaxy of exceptional wines. They wisely retained Phillipe MELKA, whose winemaking talents are some of the most coveted in California. Their quest to craft wines of exceptional balance and finesse was rooted in embracing and harnessing the power of great fruit, attracting top winemaking talent and utilizing every available resource. As a symbol of Lion, gracing the label is an homage to a wise and powerful creature, protector of Bacchus. The fruit for Cor Leonis Cabernet Sauvignon, was sourced from Beckstoffer To-Kalon, St Helena and Caldwell vineyards in Coombsville. Bold, with tons of blue/black fruit, hints of coffee and Valrhona chocolate and light spice the tannins dance gracefully on the palate despite the wine's youth. There is plenty to admire in the Napa Valley Cabernet as well – black fruit, pencil shavings, a touch of licorice, and assertive spice. The Howell Mountain Merlot blend is all about big, vibrant flavors and sensations. Wet earth, white truffle and hints of cedar accompany black and blue forest floor fruit. The structure is dazzling and well suited for this gentle giant. Black List is a gorgeous wine, with exotic spice, tealeaf, espresso and a wealth of black fruit. Great balance and agility. There are two Chardonnays, one from Mt Veeder; the other sourced from Sonoma Coast famed Charles Heintz vineyard. It is a great effort, profound and palate pleasing. Lots of floral tones, tropical and citrus fruit framed by lively acidity, and subtle creamy oak. (IT)

Recommended Reds:
Cabernet Sauvignon Cor Leonis Napa Valley ★★★★★ £H
Hillside Blend Howell Mountain ★★★★☆ £G
Black List Proprietary Blend Napa Valley ★★★★ £G

Recommended Whites:
Chardonnay Charles Heintz Vineyard Sonoma Coast ★★★★☆ £G

>> Morlet Family Vineyards (St Helena) *www.morletwine.com*
Luc and Jodie Morlet launched their brand in 2006 with a goal of crafting vineyard designates of Cabernet Sauvignon and Cabernet Franc from Napa and Chardonnay, Pinot Noir, a Syrah, a Proprietary white and a Late Harvest wine from Sonoma fruit. They found a home for their production in a historic St Helena estate that was a pre-Prohibition winery. Their St. Helena estate is planted to Cabernet Sauvignon and is precisely farmed. Morlet's "Mon Chevalier" vineyard is located in Knights Valley and is planted to Bordeaux varietals: Cabernet Sauvignon, Cabernet Franc, Merlot, Malbec and Petit Verdot. "Cœur de Vallée" vineyard is located on the Oakville Bench has Cabernet Sauvignon and Cabernet Franc. In addition to the estate vineyards, they farm the vineyards in Bennett Valley, Dry Creek, Fort Ross-Seaview, Napa, and Russian River Valley. Luc, who comes from a family of sparkling wine producers in France, studied business in Dijon. He has been making wines and consulting at such illustrious wineries as Peter MICHAEL, STAGLIN, VINEYARD 7 & 8, amongst others. At the heart of his winemaking lie Old World techniques from Burgundy and Bordeaux that are modified to reflect his New World presence and stylistic preferences. He practices low-intervention techniques to craft wines that are deftly balanced, rich and complex. The wines are aged in 100% new French oak barrels.(IT)

Recommended Reds:
"Passionnement" Cabernet Sauvignon Oakville Bench ⭕⭕⭕⭕⭕ £H
"Mon Chevalier" Cabernet Sauvignon Knights Valley ★★★★★ £G
"Morlet Estate" Cabernet Sauvignon St Helena ★★★★☆ £G
"Cœur de Vallée" Cabernet Sauvignon Oakville ★★★★☆ £G
"En Famille" Pinot Noir Fort Ross-Seaview Sonoma Coast ★★★★★ £G
"Coteaux Noires" Pinot Noir Fort Ross-Seaview ★★★★☆ £F

Napa & Carneros

Recommended Whites:
"Billet Doux" Late Harvest White Alexander Valley ★★★★★ £H
"Ma Princesse" Chardonnay Russian River Valley ★★★★☆ £G
"Ma Douce" Chardonnay Fort Ross-Seaview ★★★★☆ £F
"La Proportion d'Oree" Proprietary White Sonoma County ★★★★☆ £F

Mumm Napa (Rutherford) *www.mummnapa.com*
One of several California sparkling-wine operation with a leading Champagne house as owner. The regular Champagne from the parent can occasionally disappoint but the California Brut Cuvée Prestige offers a very attractive, well-priced alternative. It is fresh and forward with just a touch of bready yeast character. A Reserve Brut is also offered. The DVX Vintage *cuvée* is of a different order, combining forward fruit with a rich, leesy character and a firm, balanced structure for short ageing on release. The range has now been extended with another premium wine, Cuvée M, which blends the Pinot Noir with Muscat. A red version is also now made and combines mainly Pinot with a little Syrah. A small number of wines are available solely at the winery and include a DVX Vintage rosé, premium Brut Santana wines and a number of still wines. (DM)

Recommended Whites:
Cuvée DVX Vintage Napa Valley ★★★☆ £F
Blanc de Blancs Napa Valley ★★☆ £D
Brut Cuvée Prestige Napa Valley ★★☆ £D

Recommended Rosés:
Brut Reserve Napa Valley ★★☆ £D

Newton (Spring Mountain) *www.newtonvineyard.com*
This well-established Napa operation is part of the expanding portfolio of Moët Hennessy premium wineries around the world which include the likes of CLOUDY BAY. The wines here have always been impressive and reasonably priced. At the lower level the decent Red Label Chardonnay is joined now by a red blend labelled Claret and red Label Cabernet Sauvignon. The best wines are the impressive Unfiltered bottlings produced with natural fermentation and handled by gravity in the winery. Recently added is a top-quality premium Cabernet Sauvignon, Le Puzzle, which is sourced from soils with a higher chalk, gravel and loam content. Chardonnay may be approached young; the Merlot and Cabernet bottlings require longer. Le Puzzle will both benefit from 4–5 years' cellaring; expect Le Puzzle to be very ageworthy. (DM)

Recommended Reds:
Cabernet Sauvignon Le Puzzle Napa Valley ★★★★☆ £G
Cabernet Sauvignon Unfiltered Napa Valley ★★★★ £F
Merlot Unfiltered Napa Valley ★★★★ £F

Recommended Whites:
Chardonnay Unfiltered ★★★★ £F
Chardonnay Red Label ★★★ £E

>> Nine Suns (St Helena) *www.ninesuns.com*
An extraordinary venture took place with an inception of the Chang family purchasing a 40-acre property on Pritchard Hill. It is now known as Houyi Vineyard, a covered fruit source for some of the most desired Napa Valley brands. At nearly 1,400 feet above sea level on south-sloping acreage, Houyi sits above the fog line. Twenty-two acres are planted primarily to Bordeaux varietals, with several Rhone blocks. Situated in the Vaca Mountains – the eastern-most range of the Napa Valley – the Hambright soils of Houyi Vineyard originate from volcanic basalt flows. To develop and farm Houyi Vineyard, vast quantities of boulders were excavated from the top five feet of soil. Stones remaining below the five-foot datum provide deep fissures

for grapevine roots to forage down, seek out moisture and draw nutrients. The vineyard was originally planted in 2004 and had nine different grape contracts. That has since changed to reflect ongoing sales to fewer clients, such as Juan Mercado of Realm, a rock star producer and a close friend. The rest of the fruit will be bottled under the Nine Suns brand. The winery will be run by a team of two brothers and a sister, all with diverse and impressive backgrounds in architecture, business and engineering. The trio other friends and advisors include Michael Rolland and Benoit Touquette. (IT)

Recommended Reds:
Cabernet Sauvignon Houyi Vineyard Napa Valley ★★★★★ £H

Opus One (Oakville) *www.opusonewinery.com*
This MONDAVI/Rothschild (Mouton-Rothschild) joint venture was conceived in 1978, the first vintage being in 1979 and remains independent from Constellation in its vineyard management and administration. At the time, super-premium Napa styles of Cabernet had not really materialised and Opus One was uniquely highly priced among its peers. During the 1990s the Mondavi Reserve Cabernet Sauvignon from the great To-Kalon vineyard was of a consistently higher standard, although the Q Block part of that same vineyard contributes to Opus One. The wine, a blend of all five Bordeaux varieties, has never quite fulfilled its potential but the scale of the production means there aren't the scarcity problems found with some other top Californian reds. The wine is always given a very lengthy *cuvaison* of up to 40 days and is aged in 100% new French oak. (DM)

Recommended Reds:
Opus One Napa Valley ★★★★☆ £H

Recommended Whites:
Chardonnay Unfiltered ★★★★ £F

>> Outpost Wines (Howell Mountain) *www.outpostwines.com*
Born in 1998, Outpost was established on the rugged Howell Mountain to create authentic 100% varietal bottlings, such as Cabernet, Grenache, Petite Sirah and Zinfandel, planted on the organically farmed 28-acre vineyard. Red rocky soil, high altitudes, unique weather patterns – all factors contributing to the greatness of the brand's offerings. Thomas Rivers Brown, whose own philosophies of land stewardship aligned perfectly with the proprietors, has been the winemaker from the very beginning. Hand-harvested small lots of intense mountain fruit are processed with minimal intervention. All blocks are fermented separately, and the wines are un-fined and unfiltered. The fruit is superb, and wildly expressive, resulting in artisanal wines with a distinct sense of place. The brand is best known for their Zinfandel and Grenache, however their Petite Sirah and Cabernets are also exceptional. The "Immigrant" red blend comprised of Cabernet Franc, Cabernet Sauvignon and Merlot is a terrific effort – jammy and sexy to the last drop. (IT)

Recommended Reds:
"Immigrant" Red Blend True Vineyard Howell Mountain ★★★★★ £G
Cabernet Sauvignon True Vineyard Howell Mountain ★★★★☆ £G
Grenache Howell Mountain ★★★★ £F
Zinfandel Howell Mountain ★★★★ £F
Petite Sirah Howell Mountain ★★★★ £F

>> Ovid (Napa Valley) *www.ovidvineyards.com*
Named after a Roman poet who lived in 43 BC and wrote Metamorphoses, a retelling of the Greek myths, that celebrate change, it symbolizes transforming grapes into something far

more meaningful and inspirational. The winery's motto is carried throughout, from sustainable farming methods, to creating a visionary wine estate that would infinitely thrive, to crafting wines that are change agents in human experience. The founding partners, Dana Johnson, Mark Nelson and Janet Pagano had a clear vision in mind. To implement it, they have enlisted the talents of viticulturalist David ABREU, consulting winemaker Andy Erickson and a young winemaking super-talent Austin Peterson who took the brand on a whole other level. Planted in 2000, the 15-acre parcel is organically farmed. It is divided into acre blocks, each planted on a diverse rootstock and clonal selections of Cabernet Sauvignon, Cabernet Franc, Merlot and Petit Verdot. The winemaking facility is state-of-the-art, gravity flow, outfitted with every possible gadget and piece of equipment useful in high-quality, modern production. The winery is drop dead gorgeous, constructed from top-notch craftsman materials and powered by solar panels. Some of the best views in the Valley are here. The fruit from their Pritchard Hill vineyards is carefully sorted; post aging only select barrels are used for blending. Ovid Estate is a blend of the four Bordeaux varietals: Cabernet Sauvignon, Cabernet Franc, Merlot and Petit Verdot, varying in proportion from year to year but always eloquently conveying this special place. Hexameter is the meter that Ovid used in his poem: Metamorphoses. The verses speak of inspirational, timeless tales, and their Cabernet Franc reflects that spirit. Hexameter is not available every vintage. A term used in footnotes, Loc. Cit. is an abbreviation of the of the Latin phrase Loco Citato, which means "in the place cited" or "from the same place." Loc. Cit. wine comes from a continually distinctive parcel of the vineyard. Only in select years there is enough fruit to make Loc. Cit. Cabernet Sauvignon. The idea of experimentation in all facets of grape growing and winemaking is a hallmark of the estate. Experiment wines are a derivative of this process. Each vintage small amounts of different wines are made that are of special value, allowing the consumer to experience new aspects of Ovid's vineyard and winemaking. (IT)

Recommended Reds:
Ovid Napa Valley ✪✪✪✪ £H
Hexameter Napa Valley ★★★★★ £H
Loc.Cit Napa Valley ★★★★☆ £H

⚙ Pahlmeyer (Napa Valley) *www.pahlmeyer.com*
This is a top-quality, low-volume winery producing three super-premium wines, although occasional declassified lots under the Jayson label can also be very good. A committed approach to viticulture throughout Pahlmeyer's vineyard sources, with reduced yields and careful canopy management, combines with inventive winemaking to produce wines of depth, concentration and great finesse. In the winery the reds are partly whole-bunch fermented, helping to provide both a supple texture and a firm structure. While they should undoubtedly be cellared for at least half a decade the tannin is just a touch more balanced and harmonious than in some others. A Sonoma Coast Chardonnay and a Pinot Noir are also both made as well as a Petit Verdot from the home Waters Ranch. Both Chardonnays are fermented with wild yeasts in 100% new oak and bottled with neither fining nor filtration. A small volume of Pinot Noir is also now being made under the Wayfarer label. (DM)

Recommended Reds:
Proprietary Red Napa Valley ★★★★★ £G
Merlot Napa Valley ★★★★★ £G
Recommended Whites:
Chardonnay Napa Valley ★★★★☆ £F

>> Palmaz (Napa Valley) *www.palmazvineyards.com*
One of the most impressive state of the art wineries is, undoubtedly, Palmaz. The Palmaz family had purchased the property, previously tended to by Henry Hagen during the nineteenth century in 1990s and set out to bring back its former splendor. Julio and Amalia Palmaz, along with their children, Florencia and Christian Gastón decided to create a winery that seamlessly fuses tradition and technology. With tremendous effort and investment their 600-acre estate with 64 acres of vineyards has become a hallmark of the sacrifices and triumphs achievable in pursuit of the art of consummate winemaking. Two generations of the Palmaz family have sought to bring innovation and invention to the ancient art of making wine. Their background in the sciences, passion for living life to the fullest and years of backbreaking work have resulted in a unique winery situated inside an 18-story cave that combines cutting-edge technology with a respect for winemaking tradition. Producing great wine begins with the vineyard, and tending to the vines at Palmaz is done with a full-time vineyard team. Lead by viticulturist Mike Wolf, the vineyard team is a tight-knit group of passionate farmers dedicated to the craft of growing exceptional wines. Tina Mitchell, a UC Davis graduate, moved to Napa in 1981. Her previous stints include Louis Martini and Niebaum Coppola, where she worked under famed Andre Tchelistcheff. She joined Palmaz in 2003 as a full-time winemaker. Mia Klein, one of the most sought-after Napa Valley winemakers, serves as a winemaking consultant. (IT)

Recommended Reds:
Cabernet Sauvignon Gaston Napa Valley ★★★★☆ £G
Brasas Napa Valley ★★★☆ £F
Recommended Whites:
Chardonnay Amalia Napa Valley ★★★☆ £F

Paradigm (Oakville) *www.paradigmwinery.com*
The Harris's sizeable vineyard property in the heart of Oakville underpins the admirable quality achieved at this excellent small estate. Production is very small at around 5,000 cases. Winemaking expertise is provided by Heidi Peterson Barrett and in the principal wine, the Cabernet Sauvignon (blended with Cabernet Franc and Merlot for harmony), she achieves a round supple style with richly textured blackberry fruit and a hint of vanilla and spice from ageing in high quality toasty new oak. She also handcrafts very good Merlot, a tiny amount of Zinfandel and, most recently, Cabernet Franc. (DM)

Recommended Reds:
Cabernet Sauvignon Estate Oakville ★★★★ £F

Patz and Hall (Napa Valley) *www.patzhall.com*
The two partners here first worked for FLORA SPRINGS and during this association they determined to establish a small winemaking operation in order to produce top-quality Pinot Noir and Chardonnay. The regular bottlings of Pinot Noir from the Sonoma Coast and Napa Valley Chardonnay are impressive but even more so are the small-volume runs produced from a number of single vineyards. Top Pinot Noir is now sourced from the Alder Springs, Gap's Crown, Jenkins, Hyde, Burnside and Pisoni vineyards. Chardonnay emerges from Alder Springs, Durrell Ranch, Dutton Ranch, Hyde and recently the Zio Tony Ranch in the Russian River. The wines see a high proportion of new oak and, as with so many top-quality producers now, indigenous yeasts are favoured and they are always bottled unfiltered. These are big, forward, explosive examples of both varieties. (DM)

Wine behind the label

Napa & Carneros

California

Recommended Reds:

Pinot Noir Hyde Vineyard Carneros ★★★★☆ £F
Pinot Noir Chenoweth Ranch Russian River Valley ★★★★☆ £F
Pinot Noir Sonoma Coast ★★★☆ £F

Recommended Whites:

Chardonnay Hyde Vineyard Carneros ★★★★☆ £F
Chardonnay Dutton Ranch Russian River Valley ★★★★ £E
Chardonnay Sonoma Coast ★★★☆ £E
Chardonnay Napa Valley ★★★☆ £E

❀ **Joseph Phelps (Napa Valley)** *www.jpvwines.com*
Now a fairly large operation, originally founded in 1972, Phelps has
built a reputation based on top-quality Bordeaux-style red varietals
and blends. The full range encompasses those other usual suspects
Chardonnay and Sauvignon Blanc, a small volume of an excellent
late-harvest Eisrébe Scheurebe white, Pinot Noir in various guises as
well as Syrah and Viognier. The regular Napa Valley Cabernet, Syrah
and Sauvignon Blanc are good and immediately approachable.
Various single vineyard Pinot Noirs and Chardonnays are more
serious. The top label Cabernet Sauvignon from the Backus Vineyard
and the magnificent Insignia are of a different order. The former is
produced from 100% Oakville Cabernet Sauvignon and is a massive,
structured wine with very ripe, black fruit and supple tannin. The
Insignia is a meritage blend of all five Bordeaux red varieties. Equally
powerful and dense, this is more sumptuous and exotic than the
Backus Cabernet but equally ageworthy. A new winery has also
been established producing the Pinot Noir and Chardonnay from
the Sonoma Coast the Fog Dog label offering good value. (DM)

Recommended Reds:

Insignia Napa Valley ✪✪✪✪✪ £H
Cabernet Sauvignon Backus Vineyard Oakville ★★★★★ £H
Cabernet Sauvignon Napa Valley ★★★☆ £F
Syrah Napa Valley ★★★☆ £F
Merlot Napa Valley ★★★☆ £E
Le Mistral California ★★★ £E

Recommended Whites:

Chardonnay Ovation North Coast ★★★ £E
Viognier Napa Valley ★★☆ £D   Sauvignon Blanc Napa Valley ★★ £C

Pine Ridge (Stags Leap) *www.pineridgewinery.com*
Founded in 1978, this is now a relatively large property producing
just mid- to premium-range wines. There are some 80 ha (200
acres) planted in 16 different vineyard locations throughout the
Napa Valley. Indeed, estate-grown grapes account for some 95%
of the winery's production. The focus is mainly on the Bordeaux
varieties. Cabernet Sauvignon now comes from Oakville and Howell
Mountain as well as Rutherford and Stags Leap and there is a Cave 7
label with a touch of Malbec. A rare and well-priced blend of Chenin
Blanc and Viognier is cool-fermented to emphasise its fruit. Carneros
is increasingly important for Chardonnay and a premium example
Le Petit Clos (£F) is also made. Onyx, is also unusual for California,
a blend of Merlot, Malbec and Tannat (most commonly associated
with the dark wines of Madiran). Three other cuvées, blends of the
Bordeaux varieties, are the well-priced Charmstone and Tessitura
as well as the pricier Fortis (£G) . The fine meritage Andrus Reserve
(the latest release was 2006, is sourced from close-planted estate
vineyards in the Mayacamas). Aged in 100% high-toast new oak with
malolactic fermentation in barrel, this is a spicy, big, and youthfully
backward wine. A Petit Verdot is also released and there is a super
premium Cabernet Sauvignon (£H), Epitome which is released only
in exceptional years. (DM)

Recommended Reds:

Andrus Reserve Napa Valley ★★★★☆ £H
Cabernet Sauvignon Stags Leap District ★★★★ £F
Cabernet Sauvignon Rutherford ★★★★ £F
Cabernet Sauvignon Napa Valley ★★★ £E
Merlot Carneros ★★☆ £D

Recommended Whites:

Chardonnay Dijon Clones Carneros ★★★☆ £E
Chenin Blanc-Viognier Clarksburg ★☆ £C

Plumpjack (Oakville) *www.plumpjackwinery.com*
The Plumpjack winery is just a part of a leisure-based operation that
specialises in food and wine and includes the luxury Squaw Valley
Inn at Olympic Valley. Good to very good Cabernet Sauvignon,
Merlot and Chardonnay are produced and Syrah has also now been
added to the small range. The winery is nestled into the hills in the
eastern side of the valley and surrounded by some 19.5 ha (48 acres)
of estate vineyards planted in 1992. As the vines age their best is
still to come if the same winemaking philosophy is maintained. The
Chardonnay is ripe, forward and toasty, the Cabernet powerful and
structured. The very expensive Reserve offers an extra dimension at
a not inconsiderable premium. A new winery CADE has also been
established on Howell Mountain producing Sauvignon Blanc and
Cabernet Sauvignon. The group also includes the Odette Estate
Winery in Stags Leap producing from the 2012 vintage Cabernet
Sauvignon in both Estate and Estate Reserve versions. (DM)

Recommended Reds:

Cabernet Sauvignon Reserve Oakville ★★★★★ £H
Cabernet Sauvignon Estate Oakville ★★★★☆ £G
Merlot Napa Valley ★★★☆ £F

Recommended Whites:

Chardonnay Reserve Napa Valley ★★★☆ £F

Pride Mountain (Spring Mountain) *www.pridewines.com*
The late Jim Pride established Pride Mountain as one of the finest
sources of great Napa red and his family will continue this tradition.
The vineyards here are characterised by a southerly exposure as well
as mountain, volcanic and sandstone soils with a very high stone
and gravel content, providing exceptional drainage. Quality is then
emphasised with careful canopy management. There are 32 ha (80
acres) under vine planted to the key Bordeaux red varieties as well as
Syrah, Sangiovese, Chardonnay and Viognier. The beautifully poised
and balanced Cabernet Sauvignon is 100% varietal and offers a level
of depth and finesse rarely achieved for the variety in the Napa. It
would be a waste to broach before 7 or 8 years of age. Vintner Select
versions of Cabernet Sauvignon, Merlot and Chardonnay have been
added to the small range. The top wines here – both very pricey and
very scarce – are the Reserve Cabernet Sauvignon and the Reserve
Claret, a blend of Cabernet Sauvignon and Merlot with a little
Cabernet Franc and Petit Verdot. These are made in tiny quantities
and kept only for the winery's very best customers. Best to visit or
join the mailing list. (DM)

Recommended Reds:

Cabernet Sauvignon Napa Valley ★★★★☆ £F

>> Prisoner Wine Co *www.theprisonerwinecompany.com*
The Prisoner Wine Co made in partnership with QUINTESSA, while
based at Rurtherford produce some rarer wine styles. The Prisoner
Red also includes a small proportion of Cabernet Sauvignon,
however the rest of the blend is distinctly less Napa like. The wine
is dominated by Zinfandel and also includes Syrah, Petite Sirah and

Charbono as well as Cabernet resulting in a unique blend with winemaker Jen Beloz sourcing fruit from a number of small farmers. Marked by intense dark berry fruits, hints of raspberry, pepper spices and coffee, the wine offers impressive depth, intensity and concentration. Aging in oak is not overdone, 30% of the barrels are new with a combination of both French and American wood used. We can certainly certainly also recommend the white blend Blindfold which combines a base of Chardonnay with an interesting mix of Roussanne, Viognier, Grenache Blanc, Marsanne and Chenin Blanc. It comes from diverse fruit sources in Sonoma, Santa Barbara and Yountvlle. Three additional wines are made. Cuttings is their Cabernet Sauvignon, Saldo a Zinfandel while Thorn is a Merlot including a little Syrah and Malbec. (DM)

Recommended Reds:
The Prisoner Estate Napa Valley ★★★★ £F
Recommended Whites:
Blindfold California ★★★☆ £E

>> Quixote Winery (Stag's Leap District) www.quixotewinery.com

In the heart of Stags Leap District resides a whimsical winery that produces some of the most exciting wines in the Valley. Aaron Pott, one of Napa Valley's most coveted winemakers, lends his talent to this unique operation, specializing in Petite Sirah. Five diverse soil types and careful viticultural practices by reknown vineyardist Michael Wolf facilitates wines of exceptional concentration and complexity. The wines rest for 20 months in custom crafted French Oak, a unique practice that allows for wines to develop in distinct and nuanced ways. In addition to Petite Sirah there is Cabernet Sauvignon, Malbec and Rosé. The individually designated Block 12 Petite Sirah is pure ink, packed with dark fruit, exotic spice, chocolate and coffee notes. The energy, given the size and girth of the wine is phenomenal, and nearly defies logic. Tannins are huge yet graceful. Age-worthy and exciting, it is easily the best Petite Sirah made in Napa, and possibly in the US. Their Cabernet Sauvignon is equally gorgeous, juicy and well structured. Malbec, due to its long fermentation process, doesn't lack for bright, lush fruit aromatics, vibrant mid-palate and opulent, unctuous tannins. The finish lasts for a full minute. (IT)

Recommended Reds:
Petite Sirah Helmet of Mambrino Stag's Leap District ✪✪✪✪✪ £G
Cabernet Sauvignon Quixote Stag's Leap District ★★★★☆ £G
Malbec Lotus Vineyard Stag's Leap District ★★★★ £F

Quintessa (Rutherford) www.quintessa.com

This winery was originally part of FRANCISCAN. Quintessa is now solely owned by Agustin Huneeus whose other properties/partnerships include the Chilean winery VERAMONTE and the Sonoma Coast FLOWERS winery as well as a number of other projects. Illumination is a Sauvignon Blanc made from a small plot established at the Quintessa property. Faust is a Cabernet Sauvignon sourced from a range of Napa Valley appellations. Finally The PRISONER includes a number of wines made in partnership with a number of top growers. The rigorously selected Quintessa single estate red, vinified in the gravity fed winery, is a rich and powerful, very ripe Napa meritage blended from Cabernet Sauvignon, Merlot, Cabernet Franc, Petit Verdot and Carmenère that is loaded with richly textured dark fruit and raised for 20 months in oak. (DM)

Quintessa
Recommended Reds:
Quintessa Red Napa Valley ★★★★☆ £G

Recommended Whites:
Illumination California North Coast ★★★★ £E
Faust
Recommended Reds:
Cabernet Sauvignon Napa Valley ★★★★ £F

Ramey (Oakville) www.rameywine.com

David Ramey has had a vast winemaking influence on the style of a number of leading producers, among them CHALK HILL and RUDD ESTATE, where he is still the general manager. Under his own Ramey label he produces remarkably fine Chardonnay, impressive for its finesse, intensity and sheer quality as much as for its weight and texture. While the same gamut of winery techniques may be employed here as elsewhere – natural yeast fermentation, lees-enrichment, new oak for barrel-fermentation and ageing et al. – the key to these wines is their sheer balance and refinement. Of the single-vineyard bottlings the Hudson has greater weight, the Hyde a tighter, more mineral structure. Two other similarly priced single vineyard examples also emerge from Platt Vineyard on the Sonoma Coast and from the Ritchie Vineyard in the Russian River AVA. Recently added to the Chardonnays are some first-class reds. The Napa Valley Claret red comes from a number of sites. There are four Cabernet Sauvignons, ranging in price from the Napa Valley example (£F) to the top label coming from the Pedregal Vineyard in Oakville (£H). Premium priced Cabernet Franc emerges from a mix of Oakville and other Napa fruit sources and there are two Syrahs; an economically priced example from the Sonoma Coast (£E) and pricier one (£F) from the Russian River Valley Cole Creek Vineyard. (DM)

Recommended Reds:
Cabernet Sauvignon Pedregal Vineyard Oakville ★★★★★ £H
Recommended Whites:
Chardonnay Hyde Vineyard Carneros ★★★★★ £F
Chardonnay Hudson Vineyard Carneros ★★★★★ £F
Chardonnay Russian River Valley ★★★★☆ £E
Chardonnay Carneros ★★★★☆ £E

>> Realm Cellars (Napa Valley) www.realmcellars.com

Juan Mercado, an Army medic, followed his heart and leveraged every penny he had saved to launch his brand. He eventually left a lucrative hospital job and poured himself into wine. Some of his early mentors and peers were John KONGSGAARD, Wells Guthrie (COPAIN WINES), PAX MAHLE, Jeff Smith and Thomas Rivers Brown. After tasting several "cult" wines, Juan set out to create his own version of an irresistible Napa Valley wine. He, and his then-wife Paige, bought a home in Napa and Juan went to work harvests at notable Napa wineries. In early the 2000s, he managed to secure some fruit and his first winemaker, Mike Hirby ("Relic"). He managed to get some grapes from Andy Beckstoffer who took a chance on a young passionate entrepreneur. Fruit purchases from DOMINUS, Farella, SHERWIN and ABREU followed, and the first wines under the Realm brand were released in 2004. After a rocky start that included a Vallejo warehouse arson that destroyed the entire 2003 vintage and plunged the emerging brand into a seven-figure hole, Juan and his partners emerged victorious. The wines were fabulous and exceptionally well received by consumers and press. Production went up every year, and the brand found a perfect home in St Helena. The wines are now made by Benoit Touquette, an extremely talented winemaker, originally from Bordeaux. The Realm story is a powerful testimony of passion and determination. (IT)

Napa & Carneros

California

Recommended Reds:
Cabernet Sauvignon "Beckstoffer Dr. Crane" Napa Valley ✪✪✪✪✪ £H
Cabernet Sauvignon blend "Houyi Vineyard" Napa Valley ✪✪✪✪✪ £H
Cabernet Sauvignon blend "The Tempest" Napa Valley ★★★★★ £G
Cabernet Sauvignon blend "The Bard" Napa Valley ★★★★★ £G
Cabernet Sauvignon "Beckstoffer To-Kalon" Napa Valley ✪✪✪✪✪ £H

Renteria Wines (Napa Valley) *www.renteriawines.com*
Salvador Renteria arrived in the Napa Valley from Mexico in 1962 and soon became one of the most sought after vineyard managers in the area. In 1987, he started his own vineyard management company which now looks after more than 1,500 prime acres. In 1993, he handed over control to his son, Oscar, who is now the driving force behind the business. In 1997 they decided to make wines under their own label with their expert knowledge in sourcing fruit. They now have 53 acres (21 ha) of their own vineyards and are in the course of constructing a new winery on Mount Veeder. Although they are based in the Napa Valley, they do also produce Pinot Noirs from Sonoma as well as from Carneros. The Sonoma Coast Pinot Noir has good varietal flavour but lacks a bit of weight and complexity. The Russian River Pinot Noir is a little sweeter, plummy and viscous with good length and will probably be good for five years or more. Their Stag's Leap District Cabernet Sauvignon has great complexity with nice, inky fruit and is quite Bordeaux-like as one would expect from this appellation. Not tasted were a Carneros Chardonnay, a Pinot Noir single vineyard (Knittel), (also from Carneros) and a Cabernet Sauvignon from Mount Veeder. All wines are produced in tiny quantities at the moment but they hope to be able to produce up to 5,000 cases once their winery is finished. (NB)

Recommended Reds:
Cabernet Sauvignon Stag's Leap District ★★★★ £F
Pinot Noir Russian River Valley ★★★☆ £E
Pinot Noir Sonoma Coast ★★★ £E

Reverie (Diamond Mountain) *www.reveriewine.com*
Consultancy for winemaking at this 16 ha (40-acre) property with steep southfacing slopes in close proximity to DIAMOND CREEK has been provided from the outset by Ted Lemon of LITTORAI. Of the wines the AS Kiken is produced from all five red Bordeaux varieties. Coming from the lower-lying blocks of the estate, the wine is softer, more forward than the Special Reserve. The Barbera is bright, foward and essentially fruit-driven, although it still offers good grip from the variety's trademark high acidity and has really piercing fruit intensity. Cabernet Franc is one of the best in the region. Loaded with rich, dark and spicy fruit and well-judged oak it has only the barest leafy, minty note to suggest the variety. The Special Reserve is emerging as one of Napa's better premium reds and is not excessively priced. A blend of Cabernet Sauvignon, Petit Verdot and Merlot, it is a big, rich and structured wine with an almost chocolaty edge to its fruit. Other reds include El Sueno a blend of Grenache, Tempranillo and Cabernet Sauvignon and the only white is a Rousanne. (DM)

Recommended Reds:
Cabernet Sauvignon Special Reseve Napa Valley ★★★★☆ £G
Cabernet Sauvignon Unfiltered Napa Valley ★★★★ £F
Cabernet Franc Napa Valley ★★★★ £F
Barbera Napa Valley ★★★ £E   AS Kiken Napa Valley ★★★ £E

>> Rombauer Vineyards (St Helena) *www.rombauer.com*
Koerner Rombauer moved to Napa Valley in 1972 with a single goal in mind: crafting food-friendly wines. His great aunt, Irma Rombauer, authored a book called Joy of Cooking, now in its 8th edition. The winery launched in 1980, and has been growing exponentially ever since. Their wines became legendary, and whites-practically synonymous with California-style Chardonnay. There is so much more to the brand, though. Their single vineyard-designates, such as Buchli and Home Ranch are terrific and very limited efforts, showcasing the best of Carneros grape growing and masterful winemaking. They are the only winery in the US that boasts two optical sorters, which are used during the crush to sort all the fruit that comes in during harvest, from their wildly popular Sauvignon Blanc, to single vineyard Cabernets, all whites and reds get the same meticulous treatment. One of those, Stice Lane, sourced from a vineyard in St Helena is brimming with red and black fruit, refined tannins and lengthy finish. In addition, there is a hedonistic, richly textured Diamond Selection and bright, backward Atlas Peak that is followed by lush, unctuous, inky and agile Le Meilleur du Chai – a blend that represents top barrel selections. There is a crisp, balanced Sauvignon Blanc and several Zinfandels made that represent top fruit sources from Amador, El Dorado, Lake and Napa. (IT)

Recommended Reds:
Le Meilleur du Chai Napa Valley ★★★★☆ £G
Cabernet Sauvignon Diamond Selection Napa Valley ★★★★ £G
Cabernet Sauvignon L Stice Lane Vineyard St Helena ★★★★ £G

Recommended Whites:
Sauvignon Blanc Napa Valley ★★★★☆ £E
Chardonnay Buchli Station Vineyard Carneros ★★★★ £F
Chardonnay Home Ranch Vineyard Carneros ★★★★ £F

✿ Rudd Estate (Oakville) *www.ruddwines.com*
Leslie Rudd purchased the 22 ha (55 acres) that comprise his estate property in the heart of Oakville in 1996. His prestigious near-neighbours include SCREAMING EAGLE, HARLAN, and SILVER OAK. The high-density vineyards are planted in rocky soils on the eastern side of the Oakville benchland, almost into the foothills of the Vaca Mountains. In order to assist wine quality both during vinification and ageing, cellars with both temperature and humidity controls have been dug underneath the winery. The Sauvignon Blanc, barrel-fermented with natural yeasts, sees a proportion of new wood. It is marked by a fresh, citrus, grassy mineral character. It will develop well in the short term. The Cabernet has a small proportion of Merlot and Malbec blended in and is tight, lean and structured in its youth but with real depth and intensity. The Estate Red is fuller and richer by contrast with dollops of oak and ripe, spicy dark fruit, yet it also has a really fine, firmly structured core that suggests great complexity with 6 or 7 years' age. (DM)

Recommended Reds:
Estate Red Oakville ★★★★★ £H
Samantha's Cabernet Sauvignon Oakville ★★★★★ £G

Recommended Whites:
Sauvignon Blanc Mount Veeder ★★★★ £E

Saintsbury (Carneros) *www.saintsbury.com*
Long established as one of the top producers of the Burgundian varietals in Carneros. Volume has risen considerably since the winery was founded in 1981 with Pinot Noir accounting for the bulk of the output. The Carneros and Brown Ranch Chardonnays are serious and refined examples of the Carneros style. The By George Pinot Noir is a straightforward, fruit-laden example of the grape coming from a number of single vineyards. A small amount of Pinot Noir

from the estate-owned, single vineyard Stanly and Brown Ranch are bottled individually. There is also a release of Pinot Noir from the Cerise Vineyard in Anderson Valley and recently a further Carneros single vineyard Toyon Farm. Despite the fact that yields reach a surprisingly high 3.5–4 tons/acre, the wines retain a really piercing fruit quality. The only other variety produced is a tiny amount of Pinot Gris and a rosé Vin Gris is also made. (DM)

Recommended Reds:
Pinot Noir Brown Ranch Carneros ★★★★☆ £G
Pinot Noir Stanly Ranch Carneros ★★★★ £F
Pinot Noir By George Carneros ★★★ £E
Recommended Whites:
Chardonnay Brown Ranch Carneros ★★★★ £F
Chardonnay Carneros ★★★ £D

>> **Scarecrow (Rutherford)**   *www.scarecrowwine.com*
Decidedly a "cult" winery since inception, the brand story starts with J.J. Cohn planting eighty acres of Cabernet in 1945. His fruit eventually made its way into the likes of OPUS ONE, Niebaum-Coppola, DUCKHORN and PHELPS Insignia. While most other vineyards were planted on rootstock that was highly vulnerable to phylloxera, Cohn's was content to stay with the original St. George clone. Because of this genius move, his wines survived and thrived during the phylloxera invasion. J.J. found an immense success in Hollywood, becoming a chief of production at MGM. Cohn counts such classics as Ben Hur, Mutiny on the Bounty, and of course, the legendary Wizard of Oz, among his films. Named after a cultural icon, the Scarecrow brand embodies the great legacy of American originality and optimism. Under the careful stewardship of Michael Wolf, the fruit is superb. Two wines are made: Scarecrow and M. Etain. Winemaker Celia Welch crafts wines that fuse power and elegance, abundance of sophisticated fruit and spice and bright acidity. The finish on the Scarecrow is astonishing, lingering for days. Both wines will age nicely. (IT)

Recommended Reds:
Cabernet Sauvignon Scarecrow Rutherford ✪✪✪✪✪ £H
M. Etain Napa Valley ★★★★ £G

❀ **Schramsberg (Calistoga)**   *www.schramsberg.com*
A labor of love by Schramsberg founders, Jack and Jamie Davies, who came to Napa in search of fulfillment, and a simpler life. The winery was founded in 1965, after the Davies's discovered an enchanting, but badly neglected Schramsberg winery, perched on a mountain in St Helena. They set out to not just restore a legacy but to make world-class sparkling wines. Davies are credited with being first in using commercial Chardonnay in American sparkling wine. Their son Hugh took over the reins in Together with Sean Thompson, senior winemaker, they craft an extensive portfolio of sparkling and still wines made from cool climate sites in Napa, Marin, Mendocino and Sonoma counties. Over 110 different vineyards are utilized annually, to make 250 base wines for future blending. (IT)

Recommended Reds:
Cabernet Sauvignon J. Davies "Jamie" Napa Valley ★★★★★ £H
Cabernet Sauvignon J. Davies ★★★★ £F
Recommended Whites:
J Schram North Coast ★★★★★ £G
Reserve North Coast ★★★★☆ £F
Extra Brut North Coast ★★★★☆ £F
Blanc de Blancs North Coast ★★★ £E
Blanc de Noirs North Coast ★★☆ £E

Crémant Demi-Sec North Coast ★★ £E
Recommended Roses:
J Schram Rosé North Coast ★★★★★ £G

❀ **Screaming Eagle (Oakville)**   *www.screamingeagle.com*
Perhaps first among all the recent Cabernet and meritage superstars of the Napa, certainly if rated by price achieved at auction. Jean Phillips sold her interest here in 2006 and the direction has followed on similar lines. Approximately 20 ha (50 acres) of Cabernet Sauvignon, Merlot and Cabernet Franc around Oakville are cultivated with enough of the crop retained to produce around 500 cases of a super-concentrated, immense and profound Cabernet Sauvignon. The wine is currently sold exclusively via a mailing list and to prestigious restaurants. As such it is nigh-on impossible to find except at the major auction houses, where the prices obtained will defy belief. (DM)

Recommended Reds:
Cabernet Sauvignon Oakville ✪✪✪✪✪ £H
Cabernet Sauvignon Second Flight Napa Valley ★★★★☆ £H

❀ **Seavey (Napa Valley)**   *www.seaveyvineyard.com*
As with ANDERSONS CONN VALLEY, this small property shows the excellent potential for this vineyard area in the foothills to the east of St Helena. The Seaveys purchased the property in 1979 but its origins go back a 100 years before that. The original stone barn on the property has been renovated and is now used as both the winery and tasting room. Up until 1990 all the fruit was sold on but after completing a major replanting program the Seaveys decided to produce their own wines. There are 16 ha (40 acres) overlooking Lake Hennessey and the south-east facing slopes provide naturally low-yielding fruit of excellent quality. As well as their top flight Cabernet Sauvignon, they also produce a Chardonnay, Merlot as well as a second estate Cabernet Sauvignon, Caravina. The Cabernet Sauvignon has been a model of consistency throughout the last 20 plus years and is one of the best examples in the appellation. When compared with many of their neighbours it is very fairly priced. It includes a small amount of Petit Verdot and sometimes Merlot is blended in depending on the conditions of the year. The wine is traditionally vinified in stainless steel and aged in oak for 18 to 19 months. True to the poised, structured style of the wine the oak is never overdone and varies between one-third and a half new wood. It is ripe and full with lovely cassis notes and a subtle cedary quality and deserves cellaring for at least 6 or 7 years. (DM)

Recommended Reds:
Cabernet Sauvignon Napa Valley ★★★★★ £G

❀ **Shafer (Napa Valley)**   *www.shafervineyards.com*
John Shafer is a Napa Valley legend. He arrived in 1972, leaving a successful career in the publishing world, to pursue his passions for winegrowing. He bought a 210-acre parcel in SLD and proceeded to replant the existing vineyards dating back to the 1920s. The first fruit came in 1978, John's son Doug came on board in 1983, after graduating from UC Davis, and in 1984 Elias Fernandez joined the winemaking team. He has been with the brand ever since, becoming the winemaker of record in 1994. More land acquisition followed, and today Shafer Vineyards is considered one of the most successful brands in Napa Valley, with an extensive portfolio of high-quality wines. Their flagship, Hillside Select is sourced from a vineyard many consider to be in the top two dozen worldwide. Rocky soil, exposure diversity, cool San Pablo Bay breezes contribute to intense fruit. Shafer Hillside select bottling is highly allocated and

Napa & Carneros

sells out in weeks. It had justly achieved several perfect scores over the years, as it is, in fact as close to Cabernet perfection as it gets. Despite its $265 price tag is a relative bargain, given its superiority and aging potential. There is also a lush, supple Cabernet Sauvignon, the inky, ripe and satisfying Relentless - a blend of Syrah, Petite Sirah, a Cab/Merlot blend and a luscious Chardonnay. (IT)

Recommended Reds:
Cabernet Sauvignon Hillside Select Stags Leap District ✪✪✪✪✪ £H
Cabernet Sauvignon One Point Five Stags Leap District ★★★★☆ £F
Relentless Napa Valley ★★★★★ £F   Merlot Napa Valley ★★★★ £E
Recommended Whites:
Chardonnay Red Shoulder Ranch Carneros ★★★★☆ £F

Sherwin (Spring Mountain) *www.sherwinfamilyvineyards.com*
Small Spring Mountain property 600m (2,000ft) above sea level producing a top-class Cabernet Sauvignon. The 6 ha (15 acres) of vineyards are also planted to a little Merlot and Cabernet Franc to add complexity. Yields are kept tightly in check and cover crops not only protect the mountain soils but also aid ripening. Production is currently less than 2,000 cases a year with a ceiling of around 2,500 cases with a new gravity- flow winery that they hope to lift the wine to a new level. Ageing is in 100% new oak, seamlessly integrated with the rich and concentrated dark berry-laden fruit. Give it at least 5 years. As well as the *grand vin* a Syrah is released from the Dry Creek Valley, Cellar Scraps is a mixed blend red and a Sonoma Coast Chardonnay is also made. A small volume of a further red Patriotic Pour is made in aid of the families of the victims of the September 11 attack on New York with bottles donated to charity and available at the winery. Finally a further Cabernet Sauvignon, Cobalt is made from mountain fruit in association the Cobalt boat building company. (DM)
Recommended Reds:
Cabernet Sauvignon Spring Mountain ★★★★☆ £G

Silver Oak Cellars (Napa Valley) *www.silveroak.com*
Two powerful and supple Cabernets are produced at Silver Oak Cellars. The estate was established as a partnership between Ray Duncan and the late Justin Meyer, the original winemaker. Daniel Baron took over those reins and continues to produce wines of substance and quality, particularly in the case of the Napa Valley bottling, despite production now running at around 70,000 cases a year. The style is classic northern California: the wines are rich, ripe and full but offer an accessible, rounded texture and surprisingly soft tannins; the Napa Valley label has additional finesse and depth. A newer venture is a premium Merlot planted in finely drained volcanic soils at the Soda Canyon Ranch in south-eastern Napa. This is marketed under the Twomey label and a winery has been established in Calistoga where Sauvignon Blanc is also being produced from estate vineyards. In 2007 a further development was a winery set up for the production of Pinot Noir in Healdsburg with a dedicated tasting room. (DM)
Silver Oak Cellars
Recommended Reds:
Cabernet Sauvignon Napa Valley ★★★★ £G
Cabernet Sauvignon Alexander Valley ★★★☆ £F
Twomey
Merlot Napa Valley ★★★☆ £F

⊛ **Spottswoode (St Helena)** *www.spottswoode.com*
This historic estate was originally established in 1882 and comprises a lavish Victorian farmhouse and a modern winery constructed

in 1999. The estate has 15 ha (37 acres) planted to Cabernet Sauvignon, Cabernet Franc and Sauvignon Blanc, the latter just a single hectare (2.5 acres). The Cabernet is sourced fully from estate fruit, with a small component of Cabernet Franc in the blend. It is a deep, finely structured wine, with refined tannins and great ageing potential. The Sauvignon, sourced from estate fruit as well as vineyards in Napa and Sonoma Counties, is in a quintessentially California style: part barrel-fermented with lees-enrichment which is ripe, stylish and long. Small amounts of a second Cabernet Lindenhurst and a Syrah, Field Book are also made. (DM)
Recommended Reds:
Cabernet Sauvignon Napa Valley ★★★★★ £G
Recommended Whites:
Sauvignon Blanc Napa Valley ★★★☆ £E

Spring Mountain Vineyard *www.springmountainvineyard.com*
Grand Spring Mountain District property that has been up and down over the years but is now producing wines of real style that are representative of the area. The estate vineyards total some 92 ha (225 acres) and owner Jacqui Safra has also acquired three adjoining properties, bringing the total size of the estate to a substantial 342 ha (845 acres). All wines come solely from estate fruit and Syrah and Pinot Noir are produced in addition to the wines rated below. The Sauvignon Blanc is partly aged in new French oak, around 20%, which does not obscure the ripe gooseberry-scented varietal fruit. The Cabernet Sauvignon is blended with Merlot and Petit Verdot and is crafted in an elegant mediumweight style with dark berry fruit underpinned by a hint of cedar. The top red Elivette is aged for 21 months in new French oak. A blend of Cabernet Sauvignon with just a little Merlot and Petit Verdot, it is richer and more opulent with dark and spicy berry fruit and a subtle hint of oak spice in the background. Both reds will benefit from 4 or 5 years' ageing. (DM)
Recommended Reds:
Elivette Estate Napa Valley ★★★★☆ £G
Cabernet Sauvignon Estate Napa Valley ★★★☆ £F
Recommended Whites:
Sauvignon Blanc Estate Napa Valley ★★☆ £D

Stag's Leap Wine Cellars (Stags Leap) *www.cask23.com*
Stag's Leap Wine Cellars will forever be famous in wine circles as a result of the 1976 Paris tasting, when the Cask 23 outgunned the best from Bordeaux to the astonishment of the French judges on that day. The wine world has come a long way in the last 40-odd years and while Cask 23 remains an impressive example of hillside Napa Cabernet there is equal quality, if not the restrained character of this great red, from neighbouring properties. The lower-level Fay and SLV bottlings are also very good although inevitably recently, prices have been creeping up. Softer and more immediately accessible examples include the recently released Artemis, which uses a fair proportion of Fay vineyard fruit in its blend. The whites include some good Sauvignon Blanc, while Chardonnay from the Arcadia vineyard is mainly barrel-fermented with rich fruit and good concentration. The top Cabernets will age very well. Reasonably priced red and white varietals are also released under the Hawk Crest brand, the best being the Vineyard Selections Cabernet Sauvignon and Merlot. (DM)
Recommended Reds:
Cabernet Sauvignon Cask 23 Stags Leap District ★★★★☆ £H
Cabernet Sauvignon SLV Stags leap District ★★★★ £G
Cabernet Sauvignon Fay Estate Stags Leap District ★★★★ £F
Cabernet Sauvignon Artemis Napa Valley ★★★ £E

Merlot Napa Valley ★★★ £F
Recommended Whites:
Chardonnay Arcadia Napa Valley ★★★ £E
Chardonnay Karia Napa Valley ★★☆ £D
Sauvignon Blanc Aveta Napa Valley ★★ £C

⚜ **Staglin Family (Rutherford)** *www.staglinfamily.com*
The Staglins founded their small winery in 1985 with 20 ha (50 acres) of vineyard which had originally been a source for André Tschelistcheff when blending his legendary vintages of the BEAULIEU VINEYARDS Private Reserve Georges de la Tour Cabernet. Production now runs at just under 10,000 cases a year, the majority Cabernet Sauvignon, with just a few hundred cases of a Sangiovese Stagliano as well as Chardonnay. The estate Chardonnay and Cabernet are both very impressive. A second label Salus is now released to ensure the integrity of the estate wines. Although the Salus wines are lighter and more obviously fruit-driven, all the wines are marked by their weight, rich texture and extract. The Rutherford bottlings achieve this with ease and the Cabernet Sauvignon in particular is very refined. Both reds and whites will age well, the Rutherford Cabernet requiring 5 years or so. (DM)
Recommended Reds:
Cabernet Sauvignon Rutherford ★★★★★ £H
Cabernet Sauvignon Salus Rutherford ★★★★ £G
Recommended Whites:
Chardonnay Rutherford ★★★★☆ £F
Chardonnay Salus Rutherford ★★★☆ £E

⚜ **DR Stephens (Howell Mountain)** *www.drstephenswines.com*
An attorney by trade, Don Stephens fell in love with wine during his days of running a restaurant that helped fund his education. As his legal career blossomed, and evolved, his interest in wine steadily stayed. In 1996 he and his wife Trish purchased their 35-acre dream property on Howell Mountain, planting a 9-acre Moose Vineyard shortly after. In 1999, their first Cab was released, with much acclaim from trade and consumer community. With the support of their fans, the brand, featuring ultra-premium, highly allocated wines, took off and has been going strong ever since. One of the most sought after viticulturalists, Michael Wolf, manages the vineyards. Michael Hirby, winemaker, along with Don's son Justin, share winemaking duties. There are three Cabs, Moose Valley, Walther River Block and Napa Valley, a Star Chardonnay, Silver Eagle Pinot Noir and Noble Block Moose Valley Sauvignon Blanc. Their gorgeous Chardonnay is a best-kept secret. Made from fruit grown in Rutherford. , Moose Valley Cabernet never disappoints with its wealth and depth of flavor. (IT)
Recommended Reds:
Cabernet Sauvignon Moose Valley Howell Mountain ★★★★★ £G
Cabernet Sauvignon Walter River Block Howell Mountain ★★★★ £F
Recommended Whites:
Chardonnay Star Vineyard Napa Valley ★★★★☆ £F

Storybook Mountain (Napa Valley) *www.storybookwines.com*
This is a Zinfandel-only winery and a very good one, located on the red clay and loam slopes of the Mayacamas. The estate vineyards surrounding the property were originally planted in the 1880s and these hillside plots continue to show the potential of the variety. Insecticides and herbicides are avoided and the wine is vinified and aged in century-old caves which provide an ideal environment with even year-round temperatures and just the right level of humidity. A combination of French, American and Hungarian oak is used to age the wines. They are full-bodied and structured, tight and firm in their youth but with the kind of cellaring potential the variety very often lacks. A top estate reserve is regularly produced with an occasional limited-production, special vintage selection Eastern Exposures which has a small amount (less than 5%) of Viognier to add fragrance. Understandably pricier Seps Estate Cabernet Sauvignon, including a Reserve and Antaeus a blend of Zin and the Bordeaux varieties as well as a Viognier and two rosés complete the small range. (DM)
Recommended Reds:
Zinfandel Eastern Exposures Napa Valley ★★★☆ £F
Zinfandel Mayacamas Range Napa Valley ★★★ £E

Swanson (Rutherford) *www.swansonvineyards.com*
Impressive and stylish wines are produced at this family-run Napa winery established in 1985. Although production is not small quality has remained good to very good. As well as the three principal releases, Sangiovese, Petite Sirah, Zinfandel, super premium Face Cabernet Sauvignon, Chardonnay, Sauvignon Blanc and two late harvest whites have been produced in recent vintages. Crespicule is from Sémillon while Tardif comes from Chardonnay. Neither is cheap (£H). Merlot has been made since the winery was founded; it is crafted in a medium-full, supple style with an emphasis on ripe, forward, plummy fruit and well-judged oak. The premium Alexis blends mainly Cabernet Sauvignon with Merlot now from the estate Oakville Gold Coast Vineyard. The style is modern with an extending vatting of around four weeks and malolactic in barrel. The wine is ripe and supple with quite marked background oak spice. Give it 4–5 years. (DM)
Recommended Reds:
Alexis Napa Valley ★★★★ £F Merlot Napa Valley ★★★☆ £E
Recommended Whites:
Pinot Grigio Napa Valley ★★ £D

Switchback Ridge (Napa Valley) *www.switchbackridge.com*
The small Peterson Ranch in the north-eastern part of the Napa Valley now has 8 ha (20 acres) under vine planted to Cabernet Sauvignon, Merlot and Petite Sirah. Finely-drained rocky soils produce naturally low-yielding grapes of impressive flavour intensity. Only estate-grown fruit is used and winemaking is in the hands of Robert Foley, who also produces wines under his own label. As well as the excellent Cabernet Sauvignon, varietal Merlot and Petite Sirah are also produced. The richly textured Cabernet is opulent and loaded with exotic dark fruits and smoky, spiciness and subtle oak. Expect it to drink well at a surprisingly young age. (DM)
Recommended Reds:
Cabernet Sauvignon Napa Valley ★★★★★ £G

▶▶ **Tate Wines (Napa Valley)** *www.tatewine.com*
Tate was founded in 2011 by winemaker David Tate, who has dedicated the last two decades working at some of the top Napa Valley wineries. A Canadian native, he has spent the last decade as the winemaker and GM at BARNETT Vineyards, a premium winery on Spring Mountain. Prior to that, he worked at RIDGE Vineyards, and at wineries around the world, from Provence, France, to Australia and New Zealand. His own brand was born out of passion for making micro-lots of wines from boutique vineyards that embrace the very essence of Napa Valley terroir. His exceptional rosé (of which a just single barrel was made) called Miss Gay is one of the best saignée-style rosés I have ever tasted. Top wines are Spring Street Chardonnay, Merlot, Cabernet. For Mt Veeder Cab

Napa & Carneros

Jack's Vineyard Howell Mountain – think ink, black fruit, licorice, cocoa, truffle. (IT)

Recommended Reds:
Cabernet Sauvignon Jack's Vineyard Howell Mountain ★★★★☆ £G
Cabernet Sauvignon Mt. Veeder ★★★★ £F

Recommended Whites:
Chardonnay Spring Street Napa Valley ★★★☆ £D

❀ Philip Togni (Spring Mountain) www.philiptognivineyard.com
Philip Togni is a vastly experienced winemaker, having worked at a number of major wineries during a career spanning well over 4 decades. From his own estate vineyards on Spring Mountain he produces one of the more impressive Cabernets to be found in the Napa. It is a dense, powerful wine, with considerable tannin reinforcing its mountain origins, its texture rounded by malolactic fermentation in barrel. Powerful and long-lived it requires 8–10 years in the cellar. A second bottling from younger vines Tanbark Hill has joined the *grand vin*. Togni also produces a tiny amount of a fine sweet dessert wine from Black Muscat under the Ca Togni label. (DM)

Recommended Reds:
Cabernet Sauvignon Spring Mountain ★★★★★ £G
Cabernet Sauvignon Tanbark Hill Napa Valley ★★★★ £F
Ca Togni Napa Valley ★★★★★ £G

Tor Wines (St Helena) www.torwines.com
Tor Kenward makes small amounts of top-class Cabernet Sauvignon, a little Syrah labelled Hommage Allan, Grenache Cuvée Cooper from Paso Robles and Chardonnay both from the Hudson and Durrell Vineyards in Carneros. Cabernet Sauvignon comes from a vineyard south of Yountville established with the help of David Abreu using a field selection of clones from five different Napa sources, from the To Kalon Beckstoffer Vineyard as well as from Howell Mountain, Oakville and a Napa Valley example is also made. The Cimarossa Howell Mountain Cabernet is sturdy, full and with firm, rounded youthful tannins. Syrah has also emerged from the Hudson Vineyard which was ripe, smoky and opulent. Chardonnay is made in a rich, ripe, peach- and citrus-laden style. The oak is finely judged and the wines are dominated by a rich, rounded texture on the palate. The Cabernets require 3 or 4 years, longer for the Howell Mountain. (DM)

Recommended Reds:
Cabernet Sauvignon Cimarossa Howell Mountain ★★★★★ £G
Cabernet Sauvignon Tierra Roja Vineyard Oakville ★★★★★ £G

❀❀ Turley Cellars (St Helena) www.turleywinecellars.com
Larry Turley produces perhaps the modern benchmark for Zinfandel – massive, dark, brooding examples of the variety. The wines are increasingly made from a wide range of sources and generally bottled as single-vineyard cuvées. What is remarkable about these wines is that despite having alcohol levels more akin to fortified wines – 16% and upwards is not uncommon – there is still a remarkable balance and purity as well as extraordinarily concentrated, ripe, berry fruit. Styles vary from younger full-throttle Napa Valley bottlings, old vineyard examples from Contra Costa County to minerally Paso Robles with its limestone soils. Very good Petite Sirah is also produced from estate as well as other vineyards. These are very powerful and long-lived wines whereas the Zins can be approachable with just 2 or 3 years and at their optimum are the finest wines here. Both the firmly structured mountain grown, fiercely tannic and blackberry laden Rattlesnake Ridge and the

suppler, lusher and more opulent Hayne Vineyard are benchmark examples of the variety. All of the wines are produced in small lots, often fewer than 200 cases, with the majority sold by mailing list, some exclusively or at the winery's Paso Robles tasting room. Bottling is without fining or filtration and some of the wines can offer remarkable value. (DM)

Recommended Reds:
Petite Sirah Rattlesnake Ridge Howell Mountain ✪✪✪✪✪ £F
Petite Sirah Hayne Vineyard Napa Valley ✪✪✪✪✪ £F
Petite Sirah Estate Vineyard Napa Valley ★★★★☆ £F
Zinfandel The Grist Vineyard Dry Creek Valley ★★★★☆ £F
Zinfandel Mead Ranch Atlas Peak ★★★★☆ £F
Zinfandel Dusi Vineyard Paso Robles ★★★★☆ £F
Zinfandel Old Vines California ★★★★ £E
Zinfandel Estate Napa Valley ★★★★ £F
Zinfandel Duarte Vineyard Contra Costa County ★★★★ £F
Zinfandel Dragon Vineyard Howell Mountain ★★★★ £F
Zinfandel Juvenile California ★★★☆ £D

>> Tusk Estates (Napa Valley) www.tuskestates.com
A venture of three long-time friends, Michael Uytengsu, Tim Martin and Phillippe Melka who have dedicated their lives to perfection in the food and beverage industry was destined for greatness. Michael traded his background in investment banking for the family food business, which has since seen exponential growth. Tim's storied restaurant business-related past led him to a momentous meeting with Robin LAIL, resulting in the creation of his branding firm, Gauge. This focuses on marketing and business development for such rock star brands as Flanagan, Lail, MELKA and many more. Phillipe, originally from Bordeaux, started his career at HAUT BRION and earned a Master's in agronomy and enology. His terroir-study driven journey to Napa Valley led him to learn from such luminaries as Christian Moueix, Paul Draper (RIDGE) and Daniel Baron (SILVER OAK) and later around the world, eventually leading him back to Napa. The last couple of decades were spent consulting for high-profile brands and building his own, Melka wines. The brand launched in 2007, with a unifying motto of producing unique wines from the top appellation/vineyard sources that raise the bar in a high sweepstakes luxury Napa market. The partners agonized over every detail, from meticulous fruit selection to the best designed packaging money can buy. 2013 Tusk Estate (250 cases) is a Cabernet blend of 7 vineyards, aged 30mo in French oak 2011 Tusk Estate (150 cases) is made from fruit crafted from Oakville and Pritchard Hill appellations, aged in new French oak for 27 months. (IT)

Recommended Reds:
Cabernet Sauvignon Estate Oakville ✪✪✪✪✪ £H

❀❀ Viader (Napa Valley) www.viader.com
Very stylish and refined red wines are crafted at this small estate nestled in the foothills of Howell Mountain. Production is less than 5,000 cases a year. The vineyard is planted on well-drained volcanic soils and yields fruit of real depth and intensity. The Viader red is a blend of Cabernet Sauvignon and Cabernet Franc and is the mainstay of the winery. It is powerful, intense and supple with malolactic taking place in barrel and although there is close to 100% new wood, it is seamlessly integrated, refined and harmonious. Unusually the Cabernet Franc component is aged in Russian oak. The Petit Verdot V is a rare and impressively structured example of the variety, blended with Cabernet Sauvignon and Cabernet Franc. Rich, spicy dark berry fruit is interwoven with

subtle hints of cedar and finely judged wood. The wine is dense, powerful and very ageworthy. The estate Syrah comes from both Barossa Valley and Hermitage clones, which provides both weight and structure. It is aged in 600-litre new puncheons so the oak is nicely restrained and the rich, exotic dark licorice and black pepper fruit is finely balanced by plush, supple tannins. The wine is beguiling young but expect it to add further complexity with 5 or 6 years' cellaring. A Viader Black label red has also been added to the range. This is well priced (£F) and is a blend of Cabernet Sauvignon, Syrah, Malbec and Petite Sirah. The estate wines are very well complemented by an excellent dark-berry fruited Cabernet Franc and elegant red berry laden Tempranillo produced from other fruit sources as well, both wines taking the Dare label and a Dare Cabernet Sauvignon is also made as well as a rosé, Viader Dry which is mainly Cabernet Sauvignon. (DM)

Recommended Reds:
Viader Estate Napa Valley ✪✪✪✪✪ £G
Viader V Estate Napa Valley ★★★★★ £G
Syrah Estate Napa Valley ★★★★★ £F
Dare Tempranillo Napa Valley ★★★★ £E
Dare Cabernet Franc Napa Valley ★★★★ £E

✿ Vineyard 29 (St Helena) *www.vineyard29.com*

The McMinns state of the art winery at their Vineyard 29 site just to the north of St Helena is where they vinify their top wine, a Cabernet Sauvignon, as well as a Bordeaux red blend and a Zinfandel from the potentially great Aida Vineyard which they purchased from Oliver and Karen Caldwell of OLIVER CALDWELL in 2001. Found two miles to the north of Vineyard 29, Aida is warmer but is moderated by afternoon breezes. Both properties are looked after by vineyard specialist David ABREU. The Aida Zinfandel is in the very ripe and berry laden style spectrum but with a subtle minerality. The Aida Red is big, rich and opulent; dominated by Cabernet Sauvignon with just over a third Merlot, malolactic is in barrel and the wine aged in 100% new French oak for 18 months. The Vineyard 29 Cabernet comes from estate vineyards planted in the lower eastern facing Mayacamas slopes just above Highway 29, hence the name of the property. The site benefits from good early morning sunlight and avoids the excessive heat of the afternoons here. Dark fruit, cedar and oak spice are all apparent although the wine possesses an impressive mineral elegance as well. The top two reds will develop very well in bottle. A Cabernet Franc and a Sauvignon Blanc are also now made from the Vineyard 29 estate blocks and a second Cru label includes a Cabernet Sauvignon, a Pinot Noir and a Sauvignon Blanc. (DM)

Recommended Reds:
Vineyard 29 Cabernet Sauvignon Napa Valley ★★★★★ £H
Aida Red Napa Valley ★★★★ £G
Aida Zinfandel Napa Valley ★★★☆ £F

>> Vineyard 7 & 8 (Spring Mountain) *www.vineyard7and8.com*

7&8 is one of the best examples of deliberate, thoughtful winemaking. The Steffens family patiently searched for their perfect property, one with an established vineyard suitable for premium grapes. In 1999 they had purchased the forty-acre parcel on Spring Mountain, originally planted in the early 1980s. Launny Steffens had a great interest in numerology, and 7 and 8 represents an homage to both Western and Eastern lucky digits. The focus is on maximizing the fruit that the vineyards deliver via a low-intervention process in the cellar. Winemaker Martha McClellan along with an associate winemaker Lesley Steffens,

Launny's son, are determined to make wines with a sense of place and distinct varietal character. High-elevation vineyards that lie above fog line feature a long growing season and produce perfectly physiologically ripe fruit. This results in wines of superior cellar-worthiness. The cellar practices are all about hand-sorting, small ferments and emphasis on a watchful eye over every detail. Three wines are made: Estate Chardonnay, Cabernet and Correlation (IT)

Recommended Reds:
Cabernet Sauvignon Estate Spring Mountain ★★★★★ £G
Correlation Spring Mountain ★★★★ £F

Volker Eisele (St Helena) *www.volkereiselefamilyestate.com*

Volker Eisele 3080 Lower Chiles Valley Road, St Helena, CA 94574
Tel: 707 965-2260 Fax: 707 965-9609

The Eisele family established this small Chiles Valley property in the early 1970s and the original Cabernet vines were planted in 1975. The vineyards are planted at an altitude between 900 to 1100 feet above sea level and this helps in promoting acidity and gives a slightly mineral edge to the wines. There are now 24 ha (60 acres) under vine, all farmed (and certified) organic. The Gemini White is a Graves style blend of Sémillon and Sauvignon Blanc. Fresh and quite forward in style with zesty citrus fruit and a honeyed undercurrent, the wine is fermented in stainless steel and then aged in oak, a proportion new, for four months. Enjoy this relatively young. The mainstay of the winery, Cabernet Sauvignon is blended with occasionally Cabernet Franc and Merlot. Aged in French oak (50% new) for 24 months, this is ripe, chocolatey with a structure and elegance imparted from Eisele's cool altitude assisted site. The top wine Terzeto is a blend of one-third each of Cabernet Sauvignon, Merlot and Cabernet Franc. Aged in mainly new French oak for 24 months, the wine is rich, elegant and structured with a real mineral purity. Expect the reds, particulalrly the Terzeto to develop very well over the medium term. (DM)

Recommended Reds:
Terzeto Red Napa Valley ★★★★☆ £G
Cabernet Sauvignon Napa Valley ★★★☆ £E

Recommended Whites:
Gemini White Napa Valley ★★★ £D

Waterstone (Spring Mountain) *www.waterstonewines.com*

Founded in 2000 with an objective to "create luxury wines at affordable prices", Philip Zorn and Brent Shortridge have come a long way towards achieving that goal. They own no vineyards nor any winemaking facility, but in view of their strong relationship with top growers and wineries, they have been able to bring about a remarkable rapport qualité/prix for their wines. A Syrah made from cool climate fruit in the Carneros district displays typical spiciness with good upfront tarry tones and soft tannins. There is a really judicious use of oak – only 12 months in French oak, of which around a third is new, providing an attractive soft texture. The fruit for their Merlot is sourced half from cool Carneros and half from the hotter Chiles Valley. This combination has allowed the wine to develop a little jammy smoothness coupled with very good finesse. Ripe fruit and good intensity again characterizes their Napa Valley Cabernet Sauvignon, with the majority of grapes being sourced from hillside vineyards in Oakville and Rutherford, but with the addition of some Diamond Mountain fruit adding structure. Although the wine is vinified in mainly new French *barriques* for 18 months, there is remarkable balance between of fruit, tannin and acidity. Chardonnay and Pinot Noir from Carneros are less impressive, well made but lacking the same finesse and varietal

Napa & Carneros

flavour. The winery also produces a rosé Napa Valley Cabernet Sauvignon, a Reserve Napa Valley Cabernet Sauvignon which have not been tasted as well as a Napa valley Zinfandel and Sauvignon Blanc. Philip Zorn is an intelligent winemaker who obviously handles his fruit very carefully and the gentle pricing of the finished product (with perhaps, the exception of the Reserve Cabernet Sauvignon) is an added bonus. (NB)

Recommended Reds:
Cabernet Sauvignon Napa Valley ★★★★ £D
Merlot Napa Valley ★★★★ £D
Syrah Napa Valley ★★★★ £D
Pinot Noir Carneros ★★☆ £D
Recommended Whites:
Chardonnay Carneros ★★☆ £D

Wolf Family St Helena) *www.wolffamilyvineyards.com*
The Wolfs acquired the historic old Inglewood estate and winery in 1997. The vineyard comprises Cabernet Sauvignon planted in 1996 and just 0.4 ha (1 acre) of Cabernet Franc, established in the mid-80s. Total output is tiny at just over 600 cases. The vineyards are naturally low-yielding and the crop rarely comes in much above 3 tons to the acre, without recourse to crop thinning. Both wines are in the exuberant high-alcohol style of modern Napa. The Cabernet Franc, which includes a little Cabernet Sauvignon is aged in a sizeable proportion of new wood and is vatted for just over two weeks. The dark and spicy black fruit has a subtle leafy undercurrent from the Cabernet Franc. Cabernet Sauvignon sees a little more new oak and is macerated for around a week longer. The dark black fruit also has a pronounced minty undercurrent. Both wines are in a lighter, more elegant and less extracted style than many of their peers and will benefit from 4 or 5 years' ageing. A second label Phaedrus is produced from the youngest vines and a tiny amount of Sauvignon Blanc is also made. (DM)

Recommended Reds:
Cabernet Sauvignon Estate Napa Valley ★★★★ £F
Cabernet Franc Estate Napa Valley ★★★☆ £E

❀ World's End Wines (Napa Valley) *www.maltus.com*
Jonathan Maltus, of CH. TEYSSIER and LE DOME fame in Saint-Émilion, has switched allegiance from South Australia, where he produced the Colonial Estate range of wines, to the Napa Valley from the 2008 vintage onwards, to produce a range of big, fruit-driven wines which would make a Bordeaux purist wince. Mind you – he has been doing that for the last 17 years or so in Bordeaux, so why should he care? He owns just one vineyard in Napa, but has also contracted to buy fruit from some of the most prestigious vineyards in the area to produce luscious blockbusters in his own inimitable style. Aided by his head winemaker in Bordeaux, Neil Whyte and consultant oenologist Gilles Pauquet, who works also with Chx. CHEVAL BLANC, FIGEAC and CANON (to name but three), six wines under the World's End label vie with some of the best in California. There are three single vineyard wines – Good Times, Bad Times, a 100% Cabernet Sauvignon from Beckstoffer's To Kalon Vineyard, Crossfire, another Cabernet Sauvignon from Missouri Hopper vineyard and Wavelength, a Syrah/Cabernet Franc blend from the Sugarloaf Mountain Vineyard. From 2009, three Napa Valley Reserve wines, If Six was Nine (mainly Cabernet Sauvignon), Little Sister (Merlot) and Against the Wind (Cabernet Franc) have been sourced from quality vineyards from Coombsville to Sugerloaf Mountain and added to the range. All display a rich, opulent, velvety mouthfeel, with the single vineyard wines expressing that

much more complexity and structure. The reserve wines may be approached immediately, but have enough to last a good 15 years – the single vineyard wines could well do with a little cellaring time – 5 years would not be unreasonable, but have the capacity to last for two decades or more. Prices are reasonable for the quality – especially the Reserve wines. (NB)

Recommended Reds:
Good Times Bad Times ★★★★★ £H
Crossfire ★★★★★ £G   Wavelength ★★★★★ £F
Against The Wind ★★★★☆ £E
If Six Was Nine ★★★★ £E   Little Sister ★★★★ £D

Other wines of note

29 Songs
Recommended Reds: Syrah Napa Valley ★★★ £E
Altamura
Recommended Reds: Cabernet Sauvignon Napa Valley ★★★☆ £F
Antica
Recommended Reds: Cabernet Sauvignon Napa Valley ★★★★☆ £F
Recommended Whites: Chardonnay Carneros Reserve ★★★☆ £E
Artesa
Recommended Reds: Pinot Noir Reserve Carneros ★★ £E
Recommended Whites: Chardonnay Carneros Reserve ★★☆ £D
Bell Wine Cellars
Recommended Reds: Cabernet Sauvignon Napa Valley ★★★ £E
Cabernet Sauvignon Claret Napa Nalley ★★★ £E
Bennett Lane
Recommended Reds: Cabernet Sauvignon Napa Nalley ★★★☆ £F
Cabernet Sauvignon Reserve Napa Valley ★★★★ £G

Buccella
Recommended Reds: Merlot Napa Nalley ★★★★☆ £G
Cabernet Sauvignon Napa Valley ★★★★★ £G
Buena Vista
Recommended Reds: Pinot Noir Carneros ★★☆ £D
Pinot Noir Private Reserve Carneros ★★★☆ £E
Recommended Whites:
Chardonnay Private Reserve Carneros ★★★☆ £E
Chardonnay Carneros ★★☆ £D
Cartlidge and Browne
Recommended Reds: Zinfandel North Coast ★★☆ £C
Recommended Whites: Chardonnay California ★★★ £C
Chiarello Family
Recommended Reds: Petite Sirah Roux Old Vine Napa Valley ★★★ £D
Chimney Rock
Recommended Reds: Elevage Stags Leap District ★★★★ £G
Cabernet Sauvignon Stags Leap District ★★★☆ £F
Clos du Val
Recommended Reds: Primitivo Napa Valley ★★★☆ £E
Cabernet Sauvignon SLD Stags Leap District ★★★★ £F
Recommended Whites: Chardonnay Carneros ★★★ £D
Conn Creek
Recommended Reds: Cabernet Sauvignon Napa Valley ★★☆ £C
Anthology Napa Valley ★★★☆ £E
Cornerstone
Recommended Reds: Cabernet Sauvignon Napa Valley ★★★ £F
Edge Hill
Recommended Reds: Zinfandel Napa Valley ★★★☆ £E
El Molino
Recommended Reds: Pinot Noir Napa Valley ★★★☆ £F

Recommended Whites: Chardonnay Rutherford ★★★☆ £F

Elyse

Recommended Reds: Nero Misto California ★★★ £ £C

Cabernet Sauvignon Morisoli Vineyard Napa Valley ★★★☆ £F

Zinfandel Morisoli Vineyard Napa Valley ★★★☆ £E

Etude

Recommended Reds: Pinot Noir Carneros ★★★☆ £E

>> Freemark Abbey

Recommended Reds: Cabernet Sauvignon Napa Valley ★★★☆ £E

Cabernet Sauvignon Bosché Estate Napa Valley ★★★★ £F

Girard

Recommended Reds: Petite Sirah Napa Valley ★★★☆ £D

Recommended Whites: Sauvignon Blanc Napa Valley ★★☆ £C

Groth

Recommended Reds: Cabernet Sauvignon Napa Valley ★★★ £E

Cabernet Sauvignon Reserve Napa Valley ★★★☆ £H

Recommended Whites: Chardonnay Napa Valley ★★☆ £D

Hartwell Vineyards

Recommended Reds:

Cabernet Sauvignon Stags Leap District ★★★★ £G

Hendry Ranch

Recommended Reds: Cabernet Sauvignon Napa Valley ★★★★ £F

Red Wine Napa Valley ★★★☆ £E

Zinfandel Block 28 Napa Valley ★★★☆ £E

Zinfandel Block 7 Napa Valley ★★★ £E

Recommended Whites: Chardonnay Napa Valley ★★★ £D

Pinot Gris Napa Valley ★★ £C

Honig

Recommended Whites: Sauvignon Blanc Napa Valley ★★ £C

Howell Mountain

Recommended Reds: Zinfandel Howell Mountain ★★★☆ £E

Judd's Hill

Recommended Reds: Cabernet Sauvignon Napa Valley ★★★ £E

Keenan

Recommended Reds: Merlot Napa Valley ★★★☆ £F

Cabernet Sauvignon Reserve Spring Mountain ★★★★☆ £F

Larson Family

Recommended Whites: Gewürztraminer Estate Carneros ★★☆ £C

Lewelling

Recommended Reds: Cabernet Sauvignon Napa Valley ★★★★ £F

Livingston Moffett

Recommended Reds: Gemstone Yountville ★★★★☆ £G

Cabernet Sauvignon Moffett Vineyard Rutherford ★★★★ £F

Cabernet Sauvignon Stanley's Selection Napa Valley ★★★★ £F

Syrah Mitchell Vineyard Napa Valley ★★★★ £F

Macrostie

Recommended Whites: Chardonnay Russian River Valley ★★★☆ £E

Marilyn Wines

Recommended Reds: Merlot Marilyn Napa Valley ★★★ £D

Marston Family

Recommended Reds: Cabernet Sauvignon Napa Valley ★★★☆ £F

Louis M Martini

Recommended Reds:

Cabernet Sauvignon Monte Rosso Sonoma Valley ★★★★ £F

Mason Cellars

Recommended Whites: Sauvignon Blanc Napa Valley ★★☆ £C

>> Matthiasson

Recommended Reds: Cabernet Sauvignon Napa Valley ★★★★ £F

Recommended Whites: Chardonnay Linda Vista Napa Valley ★★★ £E

>> Mayacamas

Recommended Reds:

Cabernet Sauvignon Mount Veeder ★★★★★ £G

Merryvale

Recommended Reds: Profile Napa Valley ★★★★ £G

Recommended Whites: Chardonnay Silouette Napa Valley ★★★★ £F

Monticello

Recommended Reds:

Cabernet Sauvignon Corley Reserve Napa Valley ★★★ £F

Recommended Whites: Chardonnay Napa Valley ★★☆ £C

>> Mount Brave

Recommended Reds: Merlot Mount Veeder ★★★★ £F

Cabernet Sauvignon Mount Veeder ★★★★☆ £F

Neyers

Recommended Reds:

Syrah Old Lakeville Road Sonoma Coast ★★★☆ £E

Recommended Whites: Chardonnay Carneros ★★★ £D

Oakville Ranch

Recommended Reds: Cabernet Sauvignon Napa Valley ★★★★☆ £F

Cabernet Franc Napa Valley ★★★★☆ £G

Recommended Whites: Chardonnay Napa Valley ★★★★ £E

Paloma

Recommended Reds:

Merlot Spring Mountain Estate Spring Mountain ★★★★ £E

Provenance

Recommended Reds: Cabernet Sauvignon Rutherford ★★★ £E

Kent Rasmussen

Recommended Reds: Pinot Noir Carneros ★★★ £E

Raymond Vineyards

Recommended Reds:

Cabernet Sauvignon Reserve Napa Valley ★★★★ £F

Cabernet Sauvignon Family Classic Sonoma & Napa County ★★★ £D

Renard

Recommended Reds: Tres Niños Napa Valley ★★★☆ £E

Recommended Whites:

Roussanne Westerly Vineyard Santa Santa Barbara County ★★★☆ £D

Saddleback Cellars

Recommended Reds: Zinfandel Old Vines Napa Valley ★★★ £D

Cabernet Sauvignon Estate Napa Valley ★★★☆ £E

St Clement

Recommended Reds: Cabernet Sauvignon Napa Valley ★★★☆ £E

Merlot Napa Valley ★★☆ £D

Recommended Whites:

Chardonnay Abbot's Vineyard Carneros ★★☆ £D

St Supéry

Recommended Reds: Meritage Red Napa Valley ★★★★ £F

Cabernet Sauvignon Napa Valley ★★★☆ £E

Recommended Whites: Chardonnay Napa Valley ★★☆ £D

Sauvignon Blanc Napa Valley ★☆ £C

Selene

Recommended Reds:

Merlot Frediani Vineyard Napa Valley ★★★★ £E

Recommended Whites:

Sauvignon Blanc Hyde Vineyard Carneros ★★★ £C

Sequoia Grove

Recommended Reds: Cabernet Sauvignon Napa Valley ★★★ £E

Cabernet Sauvignon Reserve Rutherford ★★★★ £F

Recommended Whites: Chardonnay Carneros ★★☆ £D

Showket

Recommended Reds: Cabernet Sauvignon Oakville ★★★ £F

Napa & Carneros

Signorello
Recommended Reds: Syrah Estate Napa Valley ★★★★ £F
Cabernet Sauvignon Estate Napa Valley ★★★★ £F
Recommended Whites:
Chardonnay Hope's Cuvée Napa Valley ★★★★ £E
Silverado Vineyards
Recommended Reds:
Cabernet Sauvignon Estate Napa Valley ★★★☆ £E
Merlot Mt George Vineyard Napa Valley ★★☆ £D
Robert Sinskey
Recommended Reds: Pinot Noir Carneros ★★★ £E
Cabernet Sauvignon SLD Estate Stags Leap District ★★★☆ £G
Merlot Carneros/Napa Valley ★★★ £E
Recommended Whites: Chardonnay Carneros ★★★ £D
>> Smith-Madrone
Recommended Reds:
Cabernet Sauvignon Spring Mountain ★★★☆ £F
Recommended Whites: Riesling Spring Mountain ★★★ £E
>> Snowden
Recommended Reds:
Cabernet Sauvignon The Ranch Napa Valley ★★★☆ £E

Work in progress!!

Producers under consideration for the next edition
Adamvs Estate
Amuse Bouche
B Cellars
Beau Vigne
Blankiet
Bressler
Caldwell
Carter Cellars
Carver-Sutro
Chayeau Boswell
Cliff Lede
Crocker And Starr Wines
Favia
Gandona Estate
Hall Winery
Harbison Estate
Harris Estate
Hestan
Jones Family
Kapcsandy Family
Kobalt
Lewelling
Levy & McClellan
Louis Martini
Maybach
Merus
Myriad Cellars
Odette Estate
Paras Vineyard
Pott Wine
Revana
Robert Foley Vineyards
Schrader Cellars
Sloan Estate
Orin Swift
The Debate

Venge Vineyards

Author's choice

Some premium Napa reds
Andersons Conn Valley   Éloge Red Napa Valley
Araujo   Cabernet Sauvignon Eisele Vineyard
Arietta   H Block One Red Napa Valley
Bacio Divino   Bacio Divino Red Napa Valley
Colgin Cellars   Cabernet Sauvignon Herb Lamb Vineyard
Dalla Valle   Cabernet Sauvignon Estate Oakville
Diamond Creek   Cabernet Sauvignon Volcanic Hill
Lokoya   Cabernet Sauvignon Diamond Mountain
Dunn Vineyards   Cabernet Sauvignon Estate Howell Mountain
Harlan Estate   Estate Red Napa Valley
Meteor   Special Family Reserve Cabernet Sauvignon Coombsville
Robert Mondavi   Cabernet Sauvignon Reserve Napa Valley
Shafer   Cabernet Sauvignon Hillside Select
Pahlmeyer   Proprietary Red Napa Valley
Viader   Cabernet Sauvignon Napa Valley

A selection of diverse Napa whites
Far Niente   Chardonnay Napa Valley
Frog's Leap   Sauvignon Blanc Rutherford
Kongsgaard   Roussanne/Viognier Napa Valley
Luna   Pinot Grigio Napa Valley
Miner Family   Chardonnay Wild Yeast
Inglenook Estate   Blancaneaux Rutherford
Pahlmeyer   Chardonnay Napa Valley
Staglin Family   Chardonnay Rutherford

The best of Carneros
Reds:
Cline Cellars   Syrah Estate Carneros
Kongsgaard   Syrah Napa Valley
Saintsbury   Brown Ranch Carneros
Whites:
Cuvaison   Chardonnay Single Block Kite Tail Carneros
Domaine Carneros   Brut Blanc de Blancs Le Rêve Carneros
Peter Franus   Sauvignon Blanc Stewart Vineyard Carneros
Gloria Ferrer   Carneros Cuvée Carneros
Pine Ridge   Chardonnay Dijon Clones Carneros
Ramey   Chardonnay Hudson Vineyard
Shafer   Chardonnay Red Shoulder Ranch Carneros

The best Napa red values
Storybook Mountain   Mayacamas Range Napa Valley
Green & Red   Chiles Canyon Vineyards Chiles Valley
Brown Family   Zinfandel Estate Chiles Valley
Peter Franus   Zinfandel Napa Valley
Grgich Hills   Merlot Napa Valley
Benessere   Zinfandel Collins Holystone Old Vines Napa Valley
Gargiulo Vineyards   Aprile Super Oakville Blend Oakville
Luna   Sangiovese Napa Valley
Turley Cellars   Zinfandel Juvenile California

The coastline from around Santa Barbara to just south of San Francisco has over the last decade and a half emerged as an excellent alternative to the larger regions on the North Coast and along the Napa Valley for a number of quality wine styles. Production is more scattered but includes some very good cool-climate whites and reds and impressive Rhône styles and Zinfandels. Here, as elsewhere, new and innovative producers are emerging. Prices are rising although only Pinot Noir and Syrah are getting anywhere near the stratospheric levels of the super-premium Cabernet blends on the North Coast. In order to cover the remainder of California's wine growing areas Central Valley and the Temecula region to the south of Los Angeles are also included in this section, as well as the far superior wines of Amador County, Livermore Valley and the Sierra Foothills.

Santa Barbara County

Santa Barbara County is to the north of Los Angeles and follows the coastline embracing the regional AVAs of **Santa Maria** to the north of the county, **Santa Ynez** and the recently established **Sta. Rita Hills**. Santa Rita, located between the towns of Lompoc and Buellton, includes the great Sanford and Benedict Vineyard within its boundaries. This is an excellent source of top Pinot Noir and Chardonnay and is notably affected by cooling sea breezes – more so than the neighbouring Santa Ynez Valley, which is further inland. The coolest western sectors provide ripe, tropical Chardonnay, while further east some increasingly impressive Syrah, Grenache and white Rhône varieties are grown, as well as Cabernet Sauvignon and Merlot. To the north of the county the Santa Maria Valley provides some of the best Pinot Noir in the state and some excellent Chardonnay. Pinot Blanc and Syrah are also successful here.

San Luis Obispo County

The northern tip of the Santa Maria AVA lies within San Luis Obispo County, which stretches northwards along the coast and a considerable way inland to north of Paso Robles. Four AVAs are contained within its boundaries. **Arroyo Grande** and **Edna Valley** are both relatively cool. The former is a fine source of Chardonnay and Pinot Noir, whereas the Edna Valley has also provided some excellent Rhône styles and Sauvignon Blanc and Sémillon. Further to the north **Paso Robles** is warmer and the wines are fuller and riper in style. This is generally red wine territory with very good Cabernet Sauvignon, Merlot, Zinfandel and Syrah. There are also white Rhône varieties planted closer to the ocean along with good Chardonnay. **York Mountain** to the west of Paso Robles is also cooled by altitude.

Monterey County

This extensive area gives its name to an AVA that stretches down from the coast at the town of Monterey along the Salinas River valley almost to Paso Robles. On the coast just to the south of Monterey are the **Carmel Valley** and, further inland, the **Santa Lucia Highlands** AVAs. The former has a surprisingly protected balmy climate and Cabernet Sauvignon and Merlot are successful; the latter is a source of some of the most impressive recent bottlings of Pinot Noir, some of it very pricey indeed. A number of top producers have sourced from the highly regarded Pisoni Vineyard. To the east of Soledad and the Salinas River is the tiny *monopole* appellation of **Chalone**. First-class Chardonnay, Pinot Blanc and Pinot Noir are grown here. Going south down the Salinas Valley from Soledad are the AVAs of **Arroyo Seco** and **San Lucas**.

Santa Cruz and Santa Clara Counties

Santa Cruz is the principal AVA taken for the best wines, stretching across these two counties. The area includes a whole range of mesoclimates and runs from the southern San Francisco Bay south to Santa Cruz and inland southeast almost to San Benito County, which has just one winery of note (Calera) and the tiny **Mt. Harlan** AVA. Chardonnay and Pinot Noir are successful in Santa Cruz as well as warmer-grown Cabernet Sauvignon. Two of California's great reds originate here: the Ridge Monte Bello and Katherine Kennedy Cabernet Sauvignon.

Sierra Foothills, Central Valley and the South

The huge geographical area of the Sierra Foothills encompasses Amador County and stretches into the Sierra Mountains. The AVAs here are **El Dorado**, **Fiddletown** and the **California Shenandoah Valley**. The area is mainly a source of top old bush vine Zinfandel but a number of Italian varieties, particularly Barbera, also enjoy some success. It is also a very important source of top quality Rhône styles and varieties. To the south is the giant irrigated Central Valley, heart of California's vast bulk wine industry. To the far south towards San Diego is the region of Temecula but no real wines of note have emerged.

A-Z of producers by region

Amador County		Justin	764
Renwood	769	L'Aventure	765
Arroyo Grande		Linne Calodo	765
Laetitia	765	Nadeau	767
Talley Vineyards	773	Peachy Canyon	768
Carmel Valley		Pipestone	768
Bernardus	756	RN Estate Vineyard	770
Chalone		Saxum Vineyards	771
Chalone	758	Summerwood	772
Contra Costa County		Tablas Creek	772
Precedent Wine	768	Tobin James Cellars	774
Edna Valley		Treana	774
Alban	753	Villa Creek Cellars	775
Edna Valley	760	**Santa Barbara County**	
Madera County		Andrew Murray Vineyards	754
Quady	769	Black Sheep Finds	756
Monterey County		Bonarccorsi	757
Belle Glos	766	Carina Cellars	758
Mer Soleil Winery	766	Fox, Blair	761
Morgan Winery	767	Hitching Post	763
Robert Talbott	772	Jaffurs Cellars	764
Paso Robles		Kunin Wines	765
Adelaida Cellars	753	Lincourt	765
Anglim	755	Loring Wine Co	766
Austin Hope	755	Margerum	766
Calcareous	757	Municipal Winemakers	767
Castoro Cellars	758	Piedrasassi	768
Chateau Margene	758	Tensley Wines	773
Denner	759	Tercero Wines	773
Dover Canyon	760	Three Saints	760
Eberle Winery	760	Zaca Mesa	776
Four Vines	761	**San Benito County**	
Robert Hall	762	Calera	757
Halter Ranch	762	**Santa Cruz Mountains**	
Terry Hoage	763	Big Basin	756
Jada Vineyard	764	Bonny Doon	757

Central Coast & Sierra Foothills

California

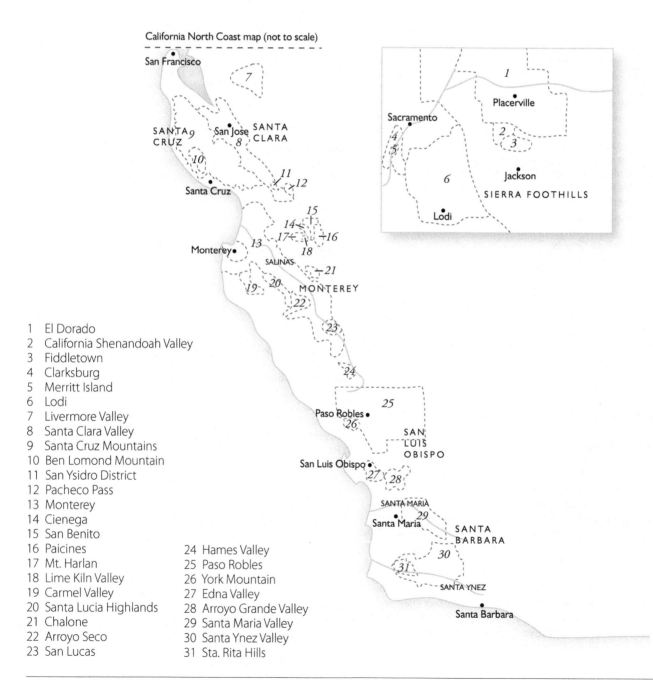

California North Coast map (not to scale)

SIERRA FOOTHILLS

1 El Dorado
2 California Shenandoah Valley
3 Fiddletown
4 Clarksburg
5 Merritt Island
6 Lodi
7 Livermore Valley
8 Santa Clara Valley
9 Santa Cruz Mountains
10 Ben Lomond Mountain
11 San Ysidro District
12 Pacheco Pass
13 Monterey
14 Cienega
15 San Benito
16 Paicines
17 Mt. Harlan
18 Lime Kiln Valley
19 Carmel Valley
20 Santa Lucia Highlands
21 Chalone
22 Arroyo Seco
23 San Lucas
24 Hames Valley
25 Paso Robles
26 York Mountain
27 Edna Valley
28 Arroyo Grande Valley
29 Santa Maria Valley
30 Santa Ynez Valley
31 Sta. Rita Hills

Wine behind the label

California Central Coast vintage chart

	Pinot Noir South Central Coast	Syrah South Central Coast	Cabernet Sauvignon Santa Cruz Area	Zinfandel Amador County
2015	★★★★☆ A	★★★★☆ A	★★★★☆ A	★★★★☆ A
2014	★★★★ A	★★★★ A	★★★★☆ A	★★★★ A
2013	★★★★ A	★★★☆ A	★★★★☆ A	★★★★ A
2012	★★★★ A	★★★★ A	★★★☆ A	★★★★ A
2011	★★★☆ A	★★★☆ A	★★★ A	★★★☆ A
2010	★★★★ A	★★★★ A	★★★☆ A	★★★★ A
2009	★★★★☆ B	★★★★ A	★★★★☆ A	★★★★ B
2008	★★★★ B	★★★★ B	★★★★ A	★★★★ B
2007	★★★★ B	★★★★ B	★★★★ A	★★★★ B
2006	★★★★ B	★★★★ B	★★★★ B	★★★★ B
2005	★★★★ C	★★★★ B	★★★★ B	★★★★ B
2004	★★★★ C	★★★☆ B	★★★☆ B	★★★☆ C
2003	★★★★ C	★★★★ C	★★★★ B	★★★★ C
2002	★★★★ C	★★★★ C	★★★★ B	★★★★ C
2001	★★★★ D	★★★★ C	★★★★ B	★★★★ C
2000	★★★★ D	★★★☆ C	★★★★ C	★★★★ C
1999	★★★☆ D	★★★☆ D	★★★☆ C	★★★☆ D
1998	★★★☆ D	★★★☆ D	★★★★ C	★★★☆ D
1997	★★★★ D	★★★★ D	★★★★ C	★★★★ D
1996	★★★★ D	★★★☆ D	★★★★ C	★★★☆ D
1995	-	★★★☆ D	★★★☆ D	-

A-Z of producers

A Donkey and Goat (Berkeley) *www.donkeyandgoat.com*
An exciting and recently established producer providing juicy, exuberant Rhône style reds and Pinot Noir as well as rosé and both a Roussanne and a couple of Chardonnays. The Brandts worked in the Rhône and Burgundy before deciding to establish their own operation in 2003, which is warehouse based. The Grenache rosé is ripe and characterful, gaining an added dimension from fruit sourced from pre-prohibition vines. The real excitement here though are the reds. The Fenaughty bottling comes from El Dorado and offers impressive structure and grip as well as dark, spicy fruit from vines planted in decomposed granite. A touch of Viognier is included in the blend which adds to its spicy character. A number of additional Syrahs are also made from El Dorado, Mendocino Ridge and Anderson valley sources. Yields are small and the wines are bottled unfiltered. New sources and wines are being added all the time. Following the wineries website is a must. (DM)
Recommended Reds:
Syrah Fenaughty Vineyard El Dorado ★★★★ £E
Recommended Rosés:
Grenache Rosé Isabel's Cuvée California ★★☆ £C

Adelaida Cellars (Paso Robles) *www.adelaida.com*
This family-owned winery was established in 1981 and can be found just inland of the Pacific with estate vineyards planted at altitude and enjoying the benefit of considerable day to night temperature variations providing ripe, well balanced grapes with great acidity. The mountain limestone based soils also help in providing fruit of naturally very low yields. The HMR Vineyard Pinot Noir from the winery's own Hoffman Mountain Ranch may be pricey but loaded with rich, exotically spicy dark fruit it is impressively structured and refined. The vineyard was planted in 1964. The finely structured, tight and elegant Cabernet also comes from the HMR Vineyard and a pricier example is also made from the firm's Viking Vineyard. Dark, peppery Syrah comes from Adelaida's high elevation Anna's Vineyard. Unfined and unfiltered bottling ensures good depth and intensity. Other reds include Nebbiolo, Mourvèdre and two blends; Version which is pure Rhône varieties and Tribe which also includes a little Petite Sirah and Cabernet Franc. Of the whites the rich, citrus and nutmeg scented Burgundian style Chardonnay also comes from the HMR Vineyard, similarly planted around 45 years ago. The Viognier provides a piercing minerality as well as a restrained citrus and lightly aromatic character. (DM)
Recommended Reds:
Pinot Noir HMR Estate Vineyard Paso Robles ★★★★ £F
Cabernet Sauvignon HMR Estate Vineyard Paso Robles ★★★☆ £F
Syrah Anna's Vineyard Paso Robles ★★★☆ £E
Recommended Whites:
Viognier Anna's Vineyard Paso Robles ★★★☆ £E
Chardonnay HMR Estate Vineyard Paso Robles ★★★☆ £E

✪✪ Alban (Edna Valley) *www.albanvineyards.com*
Over a period of 10 years or so John Alban has established himself as one of the finest Rhône specialists on the Central Coast. He has around 20 ha (50 acres) planted to vines in the Edna Valley from which he has been turning out increasingly fine examples. His estate vineyards are located in a cool sector of the Edna Valley, and this is reflected in the style, intensity and refinement of his wines. As well as the estate Viognier he makes a good basic example from various Central Coast sources. The estate Roussanne is one of the state's better examples, while Grenache is sourced from warmer Paso Robles. It is the remarkable Syrah bottlings, though – all of them intense and very well crafted – which stand out. Reva is the most approachable, Lorraine and the pricey Seymour sturdier and more structured. Limited-release Pandora is a cellar blend of Alban's best lots of Syrah and Grenache. Pinot Noir is also now being made under the North banner. (DM)
Recommended Reds:
Syrah Seymour Vineyard Edna Valley ✪✪✪✪ £H
Syrah Lorraine Edna Valley ★★★★★ £G
Syrah Reva Edna Valley ★★★★★ £G
Grenache Paso Robles ★★★★ £F
Recommended Whites:
Roussanne Estate Edna Valley ★★★★ £F
Viognier Estate Edna Valley ★★★★ £E
Viognier Central Coast ★★★ £D

✪ D'Alfonso Curran *www.dalfonso-curranwines.com*
Santa Ynez Valley based Bruno d'Alfonso and Kris Curran are both experienced winemakers – he as head winemaker at SANFORD Winery for over 20 years and she as assistant winemaker at CAMBRIA and then head winemaker at Koehler, SEASMOKE and FOLEY. Both had been producing small amounts of wine under their own labels using the facilities of their then employers (with their blessing) until 2007 when they established their new operation. Although they own no vineyards, they can source fruit from impeccable sources and opened their showcase tasting room in Solvang in 2008. Bruno markets under two labels – Di Bruno for Italian varieties and The Badge for Chardonnay and Pinot Noir whilst Kris just has the Curran label to cover a multitude of wine varietals. D'Alfonso's long established unoaked, Pinot Grigio, is fresh, spicy and lively, whilst

California

his other white wine, a Chardonnay from the Sierra Madre Vineyard, is quite steely, vinified in stainless steel. The wine is full of flavour albeit a touch one-dimensional. Pinot Noir from vineyards in the Sta. Rita Hills spends 48 months in oak offering nuances of toffee and quite juicy fruit. Premium Pinot Noir and Chardonnay are also now marketed under the new d'Alfonso-Curran label. Di Bruno Sangiovese is sourced from the STOLPMAN vineyard and matured in oak. Kris Curran's contribution to this ménage à deux kicks off with a Grenache Blanc, which also sees no wood, is very fresh and aromatic. Grenache Rosé is nicely complex and spicy, fully dry with good intensity. Sangiovese is sourced from various vineyards in the Santa Ynez Valley. Kris reaches the heights with her Syrahs, though. The Reeves' Ranch Reserve has spent 34 to 36 months in new French oak and is pretty tarry and voluptuous with good length and complexity, but this is out-gunned by the Black Oak Vineyard Reserve, which has an explosion of mace, spice, animal and *garrigue* in a smooth, complex, deep overlay of tar. 3 years in new oak again. New World Tempranillo can be juicier than the Spanish counterpart and hers is no exception. It's not as noble as the Syrah, of course, but it is quite complex. This is an exiting new partnership. (DM)

Di Bruno
Recommended Reds:
Sangiovese Stolpman Vineyard Santa Ynez Valley ★★★★ £E
Recommended Whites:
Pinot Grigio Santa Barbara County ★★★ £C

The Badge
Recommended Reds:
Pinot Noir Double Barrel Sta. Rita Hills ★★★★ £F
Recommended Whites:
Chardonnay Blue Steel Santa Barbara County ★★★☆ £E

Curran
Recommended Reds:
Syrah Black Oak Vineyard Reserve Santa Ynez Valley ★★★★☆ £F
Syrah Reeves Ranch Reserve Santa Ynez Valley ★★★★☆ £F
Sangiovese Santa Ynez Valley ★★★★ £E
Tempranillo Santa Ynez Valley ★★★★ £D
Recommended Whites:
Grenache Santa Ynez Valley ★★★ £D
Recommended Rosés:
Grenache Gris Santa Ynez Valley ★★★ £C

Alma Rosa (Sta. Rita Hills) *www.almarosawinery.com*
Richard Sanford is one of the most famous names of not only the Sta. Rita Hills but of Santa Barbara County. He was one of the founders of the great Sanford and Benedict Vineyard, a source of some legendary Pinot Noir and he also established the SANFORD Winery. He and his wife Thekla have now created a new winery based on organic farming practices and producing a range of well made and priced varietal reds and whites as well a number of vineyard designated wines from their own La Encantada and El Jabali vineyards in the Sta. Rita Hills. The regular whites covered here are essentially clean, pure fruit driven styles, the Pinot Gris very spicy and Alsatian in style, the Pinot Blanc aged in used oak adding structure and the Chardonnay getting just a touch of new oak for fermentation. The malolactic though is blocked to preserve the fresh character of the wine. Of the two Pinot Noir bottlings, the Sta. Rita Hills is bright and forward, marked by vibrant strawberry and cherry scented fruit. La Encantada by contrast offers a more spicy, complex, earthy character with less obvious primary fruit and impressive structure and grip. Give it two or three years cellaring to add a

further dimension. (DM)
Recommended Reds:
Pinot Noir La Encantada Vineyard Sta. Rita Hills ★★★★ £F
Pinot Noir Sta. Rita Hills ★★★☆ £E
Recommended Whites:
Chardonnay Santa Barbara County ★★★ £C
Pinot Gris Santa Barbara County ★★★ £C
Pinot Blanc Santa Barbara County ★★☆ £C

⚘ Ampelos Cellars (Sta. Rita Hills) *www.ampeloscellars.com*
After high pressure careers in the corporate world, Rebecca and Peter Work opted for a financially less rewarding but far more satisfying lifestyle in the stunning Sta. Rita Hills. They purchased their small ranch in 1999 and the events of September 11, 2001 when they were in New York convinced them of the value of making a living from their land. Ampelos is the Greek term for vine and with ties in Greece (where they have a small holiday villa) it seemed a logical name for their new venture. A number of their wines are also branded with Greek symbols. From their small home vineyard, now farmed biodynamically, and sourcing from other carefully selected sites the Works are producing an excellent small range of Rhône and Burgundian style wines. Elegant and finely crafted they are marked more by *terroir* and place than by some of the more extractive techniques of a number of their neighbours. As well as their own wines they also supply a small amount of fruit to other wineries, among them JAFFURS, BREWER-CLIFTON and Samsara. There is a characterful fruit driven rosé produced solely from Syrah with a hint of pepper as well as fresh berry fruit. Viognier is cool fermented and offers an attractive mineral purity. Both should be drunk young. The Syrache is a blend of mainly Syrah and Grenache, rich and vibrant with a fine mix of dark blackberry fruit and a spicy herbal tone from the Grenache. Syrah is solely from estate fruit. An impressively rich and black pepper scented wine with a lovely piercing minerality. There are now two Pinot Noirs from estate fruit and oak-aged with 35% new wood in the 'lambda' and 50% in the 'rho'. The 'lambda' is ripe and full of dark berry fruit with a touch of sous bois. The richer and more gamey 'rho' comes from a top barrel selection. An additional Pinot Noir is made from a number of sources including the Ampelos home vineyard. The estate vines are still very young and the potential is particularly good. This along with some very reasonable prices means this is a producer to keep track of. (DM)
Recommended Reds:
Pinot Noir Ampelos Vineyard rho Sta. Rita Hills ★★★★☆ £F
Pinot Noir Ampelos Vineyard lambda Sta. Rita Hills ★★★★ £E
Syrah gamma Ampelos Vineyard Sta. Rita Hills ★★★★ £E
Syrache Santa Barbara County ★★★☆ £D
Recommended Whites:
Viognier Santa Ynez Valley ★★★ £C
Recommended Rosés:
Rosé of Syrah Santa Ynez Valley ★★☆ £C

Andrew Murray *www.andrewmurrayvineyards.com*
Andrew Murray Vineyards is a relatively new and good Rhône specialist based in the Santa Ynez Valley AVA. The range is dominated by Syrah. There is an approachable fruit driven example Tous Les Jours as well as a number of single vineyard wines. Vineyard sources have included Stolpman, Thompson, Watch Hill and Terra Bella. Esperance is a stylish blend of Grenache, Syrah and Mourvèdre, full of ripe berry fruit, spices and herbs. All the components are vinified separately before final blending and ageing. Cinsault and Mourvèdre are also now produced from the

Curtis Vineyard in the Santa Maria Valley. Reds also include fruit driven Pinot Noir and Cabernet Sauvignon under the This is E11even label. The Viognier is cool-fermented to emphasise its peachy, exotic character and should be drunk young. In addition an RGB white is a blend of Roussanne and Grenache Blanc, a varietal Roussanne was originally made as well. An entry level white This is E11even Unplugged combines Chenin and Sauvignon Blanc. These are stylish and complex wines which show a deft handling of fruit and oak in the top reds. (DM)

Recommended Reds:
Esperance Santa Ynez Valley ★★★☆ £E
Syrah Tous Les Jours Sanya Ynez Valley ★★☆ £C
Recommended Whites:
Viognier Santa Maria Valley ★★★☆ £E

Anglim Winery (Paso Robles) *www.anglimwinery.com*
The Anglim's small range of wines is mainly focussed on Rhône styles with Cabernet Sauvignon, Cabernet Franc and Zinfandel as well as Pinot Noir from the Fiddlestix Vineyard in the Sta. Rita Hills (see FIDDLEHEAD CELLARS). Output remains strictly boutique at around 3,000 to 4,000 cases per year with all the wines produced in pretty small lots, although they are all very fairly priced. Generally French oak only is used for ageing and this with restraint to allow the fruit to shine through. The Central Coast Syrah is elegant, stylish and black-fruited with a hint of spiciness. Cabernet Sauvignon is very much in an approachable fruit driven style, aged in used oak and given extra fragrance with the addition of a little Syrah. Zinfandel from the St. Peter of Alcantara Vineyard is a classically Paso, berry-laden example. It is an exception with a small amount of American oak used for ageing which compliments the sweet-fruited style of the wine. Ripe honeyed, spicy Viognier comes from the Bien Nacido Vineyard and is given a three day maceration, then fermented and aged in used oak with regular lees stirring. Look out also for a blend, Cameo, which comprises Viognier, Grenache Blanc and Roussanne and a Rosé which complete the range. (DM)

Recommended Reds:
Syrah Central Coast ★★★ £D
Cabernet Sauvignon Starr Ranch Paso Robles ★★★ £D
Zinfandel St. Peter of Alcantara Vineyard Paso Robles ★★★ £C
Recommended Whites:
Viognier Fralich Vineyard Paso Robles ★★★ £D

✿ Arcadian (Sta. Rita Hills) *www.arcadianwinery.com*
The key here is the quality of the fruit. Joe Davis wherever possible leases vineyard blocks rather than purchasing grapes, providing him with a better vineyard control. He always minimises his yields, focusing on the yield per vine rather than per hectare to optimise the balance of the vineyard. An artisan approach to winegrowing results in stylish, opulent Chardonnay and intense, finely structured Pinot Noir along with a small amount of Syrah from a number of sources. The Chardonnays possess more structure and grip than commonly found on the Central Coast while retaining an exciting level of lightly citrusy, smoky fruit. Pinot comes from a number of cool-climate sites including a pricey but magnificently rich, concentrated and piercingly intense Pisoni Vineyard bottling. Monterey is also the source of a Gary's Vineyard Pinot, a rich and gamey wine with some smoky oak. It doesn't attain quite the depth of the Pisoni but a firmly structured backbone will ensure further complexity with 4 or 5 years' age. This has now been superseded by a Santa Lucia Highlands example. The Fiddlestix Vineyard was added with the 2001 vintage from Kathy Joseph's (FIDDLEHEAD

CELLARS) Sta. Rita Hills site. It is the epitome of cool-climate Pinot in which subtle strawberry fruit is beautifully meshed with subtle oak and the wine posseses the acidity and finely honed mineral structure to promise much with age. Vinification for all the Pinots includes whole-cluster fermentation, cold soaking and completing fermentation in barrel. The wines are bottled without fining or filtration. (DM)

Recommended Reds:
Pinot Noir Pisoni Vineyard Santa Lucia Highlands ★★★★★ £G
Pinot Noir Fiddlestix Vineyard Sta. Rita Hills ★★★★☆ £F
Pinot Noir Gary's Vineyard Santa Lucia Highlands ★★★★☆ £F
Recommended Whites:
Chardonnay Sleepy Hollow Vineyard Monterey County ★★★★ £F

✿✿ Au Bon Climat (Santa Maria Valley) *www.aubonclimat.com*
One of the very finest exponents of Pinot Noir and Chardonnay in California. Very different to many of their peers, these are wines marked by their restrained elegance, almost Burgundian in style. This applies particularly to the Chardonnays, which are tight and surprisingly backward in their youth but with a potential and depth rarely found outside the finest examples on the Côte de Beaune. The top cuvées need 3 or 4 years to unfold. Jim Clendenen will often pick a small portion of the fruit early to increase the natural acidity in the wine. Pinot Noir ranges from the approachable Santa Barbara example to the supreme Cuvée Isabelle, a barrel-selection of the best barrels in a single vintage from a range of sites and Knox Alexander, the vines for the latter still being relatively young. A whole range of single-vineyard cuvées of both Chardonnay and Pinot are produced. The red La Bauge is generally sourced from the vast and sprawling Bien Nacido Vineyard which has been a vital source for Au Bon Climat over the last decade and a half. Both varieties have also been regularly sourced from the great Sanford and Benedict Vineyard. The Hildegard white blends Pinot Gris, Pinot Blanc and a small amount of Aligoté in a tight and restrained alternative to Chardonnay. The Clendenen Family Chardonnay is released under a separate label to the Au Bon Climat wines. Jim also vinifies both Chardonnay and Pinot Noir in partnership at ICI/LA BAS in Oregon as well as under the Barham Mendlesohn label in the Russian River and makes a range of Italian-style reds and whites under the Clendennen Family banner. (DM)

Recommended Reds:
Pinot Noir Cuvée Isabelle California ✪✪✪✪✪ £F
Pinot Noir Knox Alexander Santa Maria Valley ★★★★★ £F
Pinot Noir Sanford and Benedict Sta. Rita Hills ★★★★★ £F
Pinot Noir Talley Vineyard Arroyo Grande Valley ★★★★☆ £F
Pinot Noir La Bauge au-dessus Santa Maria Valley ★★★★☆ £E
Pinot Noir Santa Barbara County ★★★ £D
Recommended Whites:
Chardonnay Sanford and Benedict Sta. Rita Hills ★★★★★ £F
Chardonnay Nuits Blanches au Bouge Santa Maria Valley ★★★★★ £F
Chardonnay Clendenen Family Santa Maria Valley ★★★★★ £F
Chardonnay Talley Vineyard Arroyo Grande Valley ★★★★ £E
Chardonnay Santa Barbara County ★★★ £D
Chardonnay Wild Boy California ★★ £C
Hildegard Santa Maria Valley ★★★★ £F

Austin Hope (Paso Robles) *www.austinhope.com*
As well as making the wine at his own small property here, Austin Hope is the winemaker for his family's winery TREANA. The focus here is purely on the Rhône Valley. The Syrah is sourced from the the Los Alamos Valley in northern Santa Barbara County. These are

Wine behind the label

Central Coast & Sierra Foothills

California

Hope Family Vineyard to the west of Paso Robles, which has a high limestone content. The vines are planted at a high density and yields are rarely more than 1.5 tons to the acre. Fermentation is in small open-top tanks and ageing is in 100% new French oak. . This big, full-blown, vibrant wine offers loads of rich, dark and spicy fruit and not inconsiderable oak character. A Grenache is also now made alongside the Syrah and is similarly priced. A Roussanne, originally from the Mer Soleil Vineyard in the Santa Lucia Highlands, now coming from the home Hope Family Vineyard is also released. (DM)

Recommended Reds:

Syrah Hope Family Vineyard Paso Robles ★★★☆ £E

Babcock Vineyards (Sta. Rita Hills) www.babcockwinery.com
Small to medium-sized operation producing an extensive range. Located in the centre of the newly established Sta. Rita Hills AVA, the 32 ha (80 acres) of vineyards close to the ocean are cooled by regular morning mists and afternoon sea breezes. The results are generally impressive, particularly with Pinot Noir; with very exciting limited bottlings "Terroir Exclusives". Stylish and structured Syrah now goes under the Upper Crust Label. Merlot comes from the Santa Ynez Valley there are a number of stylish Cabernets from the eastern stretches of the Santa Ynez Valley, including the Classic Rock Cuvée and the pricier Block 15 both from the Estelle Vineyard. Among the whites Pinot Grigio is clean and nutty; Sauvignon Blanc is part barrel-fermented, the majority vinified in tank. Chardonnay is also barrel-fermented and put through malolactic to add weight and texture. Prices have always been consistently good here. (DM)

Recommended Reds:

Syrah Upper Crust Santa Ynez Valley ★★★☆ £E
Classic Rock Santa Ynez Valley ★★★ £C
Pinot Noir Santa Barbara County ★★☆ £D

Recommended Whites:

Chardonnay Santa Barbara County ★★☆ £D
Sauvignon Blanc Estate Sta. Rita Hills ★★☆ £C
Pinot Gris Naughty Little Hillsides Sta. Rita Hills ★★ £C

Beckmen Vineyards (Santa Ynez) www.beckmenvineyards.com
Tom Beckmen established this operation in 1994 when he bought a Santa Barbara ranch which he replanted with different rootstocks. In 1996 he added the Purisma Mountain Vineyard property which is planted at altitude and unusually on limestone-based soils. Warm summer days are complemented by cool nights which provide additional structure in the wines. Tom Beckmen and his son Steve, the winemaker, have been experimenting with biodynamic farming. The Cuvée Le Bec is a soft, forward blend of Grenache, Syrah, Mourvèdre and Counoise. More akin to a top Côtes du Rhône than a Châteauneuf-du-Pape this is ripe, fleshy and spicy for drinking over its first 3 or 4 years. The Purisma Grenache is altogether more serious. Dark berry and herb-spiced fruit is not impeded by new oak and the wine offers a firm enough structure to develop well for 6 or 7 years. The original estate vineyards now also provide Sauvignon, Marsanne and some top Syrah. The Purisma Mountain Vineyard is a source not only for Grenache but also Roussanne, Syrah, Mourvèdre and a little Cabernet Sauvignon. An attractive source for Rhône styles, the range is also excellent value. (DM)

Recommended Reds:

Syrah Purisma Mountain Vineyard Santa Ynez Valley ★★★★ £F
Grenache Purisma Mountain Vineyard Santa Ynez Valley ★★★★ £F
Grenache Estate Santa Ynez Valley ★★★ £D
Cuvée Le Bec Santa Barbara County ★★☆ £C

Recommended Whites:

Marsanne Purisma Mountain Vineyard Santa Ynez Valley ★★★ £D
Le Bec Blanc Santa Ynez Valley ★★☆ £C

Recommended Rosés:

Grenache Purisma Mountain Vineyard Santa Ynez Valley ★★☆ £C

Bernardus (Carmel Valley) www.bernardus.com
The 20 ha (50 acres) of estate vineyards here are all planted to the Bordeaux varieties. Winemaker Mark Chesebro is committed to making traditional ageworthy reds. The Marinus, crafted from high-density plantings of Cabernet Sauvignon, Merlot, Cabernet Franc and Petit Verdot, is traditionally vinified with regular pumpovers for extraction. It spends 12 months in new oak after malolactic is completed in tank. The wine is structured and ageworthy – give it 5 or 6 years. There are also now two further estate properties. From Ingrid's Vineyard comes Pinot Noir and Chardonnay, while Cabernet Sauvignon is produced from Parrot Ranch. A number of vineyard designated wines are also made from Pinot Noir, Chardonnay and Sauvignon Blanc. Monterey County Sauvignon Blanc and Chardonnay are subtly oaked with barrel-fermentation and lees-stirring. The Sauvignon has a small proportion of Sémillon and is richly textured, more Graves in style than other New World herbaceous examples. Both offer good value. (DM)

Recommended Reds:

Marinus Carmel Valley ★★★★ £F   Merlot Carmel Valley ★★★☆ £E

Recommended Whites:

Chardonnay Monterey County ★★★ £E
Sauvignon Blanc Monterey County ★★★ £D

Big Basin (Santa Cruz Mountains) www.bigbasinvineyards.com
A new name in the Santa Cruz Mountains, established in 1998, producing rich, characterful chocolatey Syrah from high altitude mainly estate-owned vineyards. These were originally planted nearly 100 years ago by French immigrants but the site had fallen into serious decay by the 1960s. Bradley Brown undertook a major project in restoring the site. The Rattlesnake Rock site, planted in 2000, is the source of the top wine and further home vineyard blocks are being developed, planting includes Syrah, Grenache and Roussanne with selections from John ALBAN. In the winery minimal intervention is key to ensuring quality and both must and wine are handled as gently as possible. The Rattlesnake Rock Syrah is oak-aged (90% new French) and is rich, structured and opulent with hints of cocoa and licorice as well as dark black fruit. The wine is bottled unfined and unfiltered and should develop very well in bottle. Two additional Syrah's are now released, Old Corral from home estate blocks and from the Coastview Vineyard, the highest site in Monterey County. Blended reds are also important. Odeon is Syrah blended with Cabernet, while Paderewski Vineyard as a GSM. Homestead is a mix of varieties. As well as the Rhône styles a range of no fewer than six Pinot Noirs are now also made. The range of small lot wines is completed with a GSM rosé, a Roussane from home vineyard blocks and a Riesling. (DM)

Recommended Reds:

Syrah Rattlesnake Rock Santa Cruz Mountains ★★★★ £E

Black Sheep Finds (Santa Barbara) www.blacksheepfinds.com
Peter Hunken was originally part of the Holus Bolus partnership with Sashi Moorman of PIEDRASASSI. A range of wines is now made under the Black Sheep Finds banner and they are very fairly priced. As well as the Holus Bolus Syrah, there are three single vineyard examples from the Watch Hill Vineyard in Santa Ynez, the Rim Rock

Vineyard in the Santa Maria Valley and the White Hawk Vineyard in now joined by a Holus Bolus Blanc made from Roussanne. A second label Syrah, Hocus Pocus is a well priced blend of cool and warm fruit, and a Hocus Pocus Pinot Noir is also made from the Sta. Rita Hills. The small range is completed by a Santa Ynez Valley Bordeaux red blend, Genuine Risk, which blends Cabernet Sauvignon with lesser amounts of Petit Verdot, Cabernet Franc and Merlot. The Hocus Pocus Syrah is a rich and extracted example full of dark, brambly fruit, more defined by its weight and power than by its origin, it is impressively concentrated. (DM)

Recommended Reds:
Syrah Holus Bolus Santa Barbara County ★★★★ £E

Bonaccorsi (Santa Barbara County) *www.bonawine.net*
The late Michael Bonaccorsi was of one of America's top sommeliers. With his wife Jenne Lee he founded Bonaccorsi to produce top-quality wines from Pinot Noir, Chardonnay and the Rhône varieties. She continues their work. Grapes are sourced from some of the cooler sites in the Santa Maria Valley and Sta. Rita Hills. The Pinot Noirs are all very impressive. There is now an entry level JL Bonarccorsi as well as a number of vineyard designated wines. The tight and youthfully restrained Fiddlestix bottling needs two or three years to soften its mineral structure but offers great persistence and depth. All the wines will develop very well in the short to medium term. (DM)

Recommended Reds:
Pinot Noir Fiddlestix Vineyard Sta. Rita Hills ★★★★ £F

Bonny Doon (Santa Cruz Mountains) *www.bonnydoonvineyard.com*
Randall Grahm's Bonny Doon operation may have an eccentric and off-the-wall approach to marketing and labelling but the wines are impressive and generally very fairly priced. Grahm has sold his interest in the Big House labels and his output is much closer to his original boutique size of operation. The Rhône varieties are the backbone of the range, indeed Grahm is often thought of as the original 'Rhône Ranger'. Le Cigare Volant (Grenache and Syrah) and Old Telegram (Mourvèdre) are both modelled on the great wines of Châteauneuf-du-Pape. Syrah is sourced from a number of vineyards, the key to making consistently elegant examples which emphasise the beguiling feminine character of the grape. The approachable and vibrant Clos de Gilroy has been made on and off over the past couple of decades and is mainly Grenache from a number of sites and regions. The Rhône whites have included various bottles vinified from Roussanne and Viognier over the years. Among a major re-branding exercise there is a new label 'Dewn' under which an extensive range of wines are now being released and available for purchase through the winery website. (DM)

Recommended Reds:
Le Cigare Volant California ★★★★ £E
Old Telegram California ★★★★ £E
Syrah Le Pousseur Central Coast ★★★ £D
Clos de Gilroy California ★★ £C

Brander (Santa Ynez Valley) *www.brander.com*
Bordeaux varieties, both red and white, are the focal point at this property. Decent reds are made in a markedly structured style but the Sauvignon Blancs are perhaps the most striking wines. Like the reds they are more Bordeaux-like than many other New World examples. The Santa Ynez bottling is softly structured with a hint of subtle gooseberry fruit and a touch of minerality discernible on the palate. Au Naturel and Cuvée Nicolas are limited-production

bottlings, the latter with 25% Sémillon and part barrel-fermentation. Merlot is soft and forward, as is the regular Cabernet Sauvignon. The Reserve Cabernet is blended with a little Merlot and comes from vines now over 25 years old that yield barely more than a ton to the acre. Youthfully hard and quite austere this needs 4 or 5 years to begin to soften. Syrah and Cabernet Franc are also made. (DM)

Recommended Reds:
Cabernet Sauvignon Reserve Santa Ynez Valley ★★★☆ £F
Merlot Santa Ynez Valley ★★☆ £D

Recommended Whites:
Sauvignon Blanc Cuvée Nicolas Santa Ynez Valley ★★★☆ £D
Sauvignon Blanc Au Naturel Santa Ynez Valley ★★★ £D
Sauvignon Blanc Santa Ynez Valley ★★☆ £C

❀ Brewer Clifton (Sta. Rita Hills) *www.brewerclifton.com*
Small, operation producing tiny amounts of very rich and extracted, full-blown Chardonnay and Pinot Noir from a number of vineyards in the Sta. Rita Hills. The Pinots are fermented with whole clusters, see some new oak and are neither fined nor filtered. The oak is also reined in on the Chardonnays but they do undergo full malolactic, producing wines which are both richly textured and very full-bodied. As well as the wines rated here Pinot is produced from the AMPELOS, Cargasacchi, Machado and Hapgood vineyards and Chardonnay is sourced from Hapgood and Gnesa. Expect similarly rich and concentrated wines. All will stand a little age but can be enjoyed young. Steve Clifton also makes a range of very low-volume excellent Italian varietals under the PALMINA label. It will be interesting to see how these evolve compared with other California attempts. Greg Brewer is also the winemaker at the MELVILLE Winery just outside Lompoc in the Sta. Rita Hills. (DM)

Recommended Reds:
Pinot Noir Melville Vineyard Sta. Rita Hills ★★★★☆ £F

Recommended Whites:
Chardonnay Mount Carmel Sta. Rita Hills ★★★★★ £F
Chardonnay Sweeney Canyon Sta. Rita Hills ★★★★☆ £F

Calcareous Vineyard (Paso Robles) *www.calcareous.com*
Another recently created boutique Paso Robles operation producing low volume wines. Sisters Dana Brown and Erika Messer established Calcareous in 2000 with their father Lloyd Messer. Sourcing fruit from a range of sites but focusing on mainly their own classic limestone planted Westside vineyards, they produce Rhône, Bordeaux and Burgundian wine styles and their property consists of no less than 179 ha (442 acres) providing them with great future scope. Blackberry and black pepper notes mark the Syrah. Cabernet Sauvignon offers typically ripe aromas of black fruits, cassis and just a hint of tobacco and cedar, gaining from ageing in a proportion of new French oak. The wines, particularly the red Rhône and Bordeaux styles are showing increasing quality in the latest releases. A well priced second range is labelled Twisted Paso. (DM)

Recommended Reds:
Syrah Devils Canyon Paso Robles ★★★☆ £E
Cabernet Sauvignon York Mountain ★★★☆ £E
Pinot Noir York Mountain ★★★ £E

❀ Calera (San Benito County) *www.calerawine.com*
Best-known for its quartet of single-vineyard Pinot Noirs that have at times approached cult status. Josh Jensen's objective is to handcraft wines that have more to do with classic Burgundy than with some of the more typically fruit driven, squeaky-clean examples from his California contemporaries. On occasion the results are less than

California

perfect but generally these are benchmarks for the state. There are now two further vineyard sources for Pinot Noir, Ryan and de Villiers which were both planted in the late 1990s. The regular Central Coast wines are good if unspectacular and the Viognier is very good when not overly alcoholic. Aligoté is also now made in very small quantities. The winery was the first to be completely gravity-fed. (DM)

Recommended Reds:
Pinot Noir Reed Vineyard Mount Harlan ★★★★☆ £F
Pinot Noir Selleck Vineyard Mount Harlan ★★★★☆ £F
Pinot Noir Jensen Vineyard Mount Harlan ★★★★☆ £F
Pinot Noir Mills Vineyard Mount Harlan ★★★★☆ £F
Pinot Noir Central Coast ★★★☆ £E
Recommended Whites:
Chardonnay Mount Harlan Vineyard Mount Harlan ★★★★☆ £E
Chardonnay Central Coast ★★★☆ £D
Viognier Mount Harlan Vineyard Mount Harlan ★★★★ £E

Cambria (Santa Maria Valley) *www.cambriawine.com*
Part of the giant KENDALL JACKSON Group, Cambria is its Central Coast flagship. It is by no means small with the total area under vine now some 565 ha (1,400 acres). Top-flight Pinot Noir is ripe and full of red-berry fruit, and particular noteworthy are a number of Pinot Clone listed bottlings as well as Chardonnays which are barrel-fermented with lees-ageing to add weight and complexity. Nicely structured Syrah has good brambly fruit intensity, more Saint-Joseph than Hermitage. (DM)

Recommended Reds:
Pinot Noir Bench Break Vineyard Santa Maria Valley ★★★☆ £E
Pinot Noir Julia's Vineyard Santa Maria Valley ★★★ £D
Syrah Tepusquet Vineyard Santa Maria Valley ★★★ £D
Recommended Whites:
Chardonnay Bench Break Vineyard Santa Maria Valley ★★★☆ £E
Chardonnay Katherine's Vineyard ★★★☆ £D

Carina Cellars (Paso Robles) *www.carinacellars.com*
David Hardee works with winemaker Joey TENSLEY making a small and impressive range of Rhône style reds and whites. After the purchase in 2006, of a ranch, on the Westside of Paso Robles, all wines made since 2009 come from estate grapes, grown on steep vineyard sites. The Iconoclast, originally a Napa Valley-sourced red, is a richly textured blend of Syrah and Cabernet Sauvignon. The Estate Viognier includes about 10% Grenache Blanc, with lots of minerality and finely balanced acidity. The intriguingly named Syrah 7 Percent (a reference to the Viognier component) is rich, supple and almost chocolatey with a piercing quality to its fruit. Two other estate Rhône blends; Clairvoyant and Sibylline are also made, with varying percentages of Syrah, Mourvèdre and Grenache. A well priced Zinfandel is also made. Top reds and particularly the Iconoclast need a few years. (DM)

Recommended Reds:
Iconoclast Estate ★★★★ £F   Syrah 7 Percent Estate ★★★☆ £E
Recommended Whites:
Viognier Estate ★★★ £D

Castoro Cellars (Paso Robles) *www.castorocellars.com*
Niels Udsen has a sizeable custom crush business in the eastern stretches of Paso Robles as well as making a small range of well-priced, mainly Paso Robles sourced reds and whites. The Udsens are also adding their own vineyards, three of which are now run organically. Cool, tank-fermented Fumé Blanc is full of clean, fresh,

lightly varietal Sauvignon Blanc fruit with a hint of residual sugar and offers great value for the region. Cabernet Sauvignon is in a medium weight style, a touch angular with bright cherry fruit and a hint of oak spice. Richer and offering greater concentration is the Reserve Zin. It is low-yielding, densely textured Paso Robles Zinfandel with a lovely dark, smoky quality. Other top end labels include a mixed blend red Pasofusion, a Brut Champenoise sparkler from Chardonnay and Pinot Noir, two Syrah's and a Charbono. (DM)

Recommended Reds:
Zinfandel Reserve Paso Robles ★★★ £D
Cabernet Sauvignon Paso Robles ★★ £C
Recommended Whites:
Fumé Blanc Paso Robles ★★ £B

❀ **Chalone (Chalone)** *www.chalonevineyard.com*
This is the original estate founded by the late Richard Graff who went on to establish the Chalone Wine Group. The Group has now been sold to Diageo and interests include ACACIA, Provenance, ROSENBLUM CELLARS, and BEAULIEU VINEYARDS among others in California, Monte Xanic in the California Baja in Mexico and a partnership with Domaines Baron Philippe de Rothschild SA in Château Duhart-Milon in Bordeaux. The Chalone white wines are intense, subtle and slow-developing; the Chardonnay Heritage is particularly fine, the Chenin Blanc a benchmark for the variety in California. In part this is helped by the vineyard's location 520m (1,700ft) above the Salinas Valley close to the Pinnacles National Monument. Indeed the estate possesses its own AVA. The Pinot Noir by contrast with the whites has often disappointed in recent vintages. Estate Syrah and Grenache have now been added to the Pinot and Merlot, Cabernet Sauvignon and Sauvignon Blanc are also made. Time will tell how the wines develop under their current ownership. (DM)

Recommended Reds:
Pinot Noir Estate Chalone ★★★ £E
Recommended Whites:
Chardonnay Heritage Chalone ★★★★☆ £F
Chardonnay Estate Chalone ★★★★ £E
Pinot Blanc Estate Chalone ★★★☆ £E
Chenin Blanc Estate Chalone ★★★☆ £E

Chateau Margene (Paso Robles) *www.chateaumargene.com*
This small winery was established in 1998 and focuses on reds from the Bordeaux varieties. They draw on not only their own 2.5 ha (6 acre) estate vineyard but also from other sites as well, both Westside and Eastside. Yields are kept low, around 2 tons to the acre and the estate property is run using sustainable farming practices. The Cabernet Sauvignon and Cabernet Sauvignon Reserve wines come from not only the Margene property but also a number of other vineyards. Like the top wine, Beau Mélange, a cold soak is employed for both prior to fermentation and ageing is in a mix of French and American oak. The output of Beau Mélange is tiny, around 100 cases a year. It is produced only from estate fruit and blends 50% Cabernet Sauvignon with a quarter each of Merlot and Cabernet Franc. Ageing is for over 30 months in a large proportion of new French oak, around a half the period the wine stays on lees. All three wines are in a very rich and very ripe fruited style and are bottled unfined and unfiltered. (DM)

Recommended Reds:
Beau Mélange Paso Robles ★★★★ £G
Cabernet Sauvignon Reserve Paso Robles ★★★ £F
Cabernet Sauvignon Paso Robles ★★★ £E

Clos LaChance (Santa Cruz Mountains) *www.closlachance.com*
This operation founded in 1987 is producing an ever increasing number of wines. Most expensive are the Designate Series, details of which can be found on the winery website. Among the Reserve and Estate Series wines, Pinot Noir comes from the Santa Cruz Mountains, the estate Cabernet and Merlot are both good and well-priced. Recent releases to look out for include Estate Petite Sirah and Estate Grenache. The Murphy's now own a vineyard development company, which they believe will ensure a good continuity of grape supply in the fairly unstable California vineyard fruit supply chain. (DM)
Recommended Reds:
Cabernet Sauvignon Reserve Santa Cruz Mountains ★★☆ £E
Pinot Noir Reserve Santa Cruz Mountains ★★☆ £E
Merlot Estate Central Coast ★★ £D
Recommended Whites:
Chardonnay Reserve Santa Cruz Mountains ★★★ £C

Cold Heaven (Santa Maria Valley) *www.coldheavencellars.com*
Morgan Clendenen's objective with her wines is to find the best possible cool-grown Viognier, believing that the best examples with the finest structure from Condrieu emerge from those producers who harvest with plenty of acidity. Excessive alcohol is avoided and the wines are fermented in used oak and aged until malolactic has been completed. They are cold-stabilised and lightly fined but bottled unfiltered. The Sanford and Benedict has been the best example thus far and the wine is classic cool-climate, fruit-driven Viognier with marked floral perfume and a fine, mineral undercurrent lending depth and finesse. Morgan also releases a Viognier made in association with Yves CUILLERON, Domaine des Deux Mondes Saints & Sinners, including Sanford and Benedict fruit. She also releases a little Pinot Noir and Syrah as well as a Viognier from the Le Bon Climat Vineyard. The Viogniers may be enjoyed young but will evolve nicely for 3 or 4 years. (DM)
Recommended Whites:
Viognier Sanford and Benedict Vineyard Sta. Rita Hills ★★★☆ £E
Viognier Le Bon Climat Vineyard Sta. Rita Hills ★★★☆ £E
Viognier Santa Ynez Valley ★★★ £D

Core (Santa Barbara County) *www.corewine.com*
Small, recently established Rhône-style specialist based in Santa Maria but sourcing fruit under a long term leasing arrangement from the high altitude Alta Mesa vineyard in Santa Barbara County. Planted at an altitude of 3,200 feet (just under 1,000 metres) to Mourvèdre and Grenache the site provides fruit for wines that have both of impressive intensity as well as good stucture and racy acidity. The Core white is dominated by Grenache Blanc with Marsanne and Roussanne. It is nutty and lightly floral and fermented in stainless steel. A Core labelled Grenache and a Viognier are also made along with a Kuyam labelled Sauvignon Blanc. From a third label Turchi, Malbec, Syrah and Cabernet are produced. The Hard Core red comes from Grenache, Mourvèdre and Cabernet Sauvignon. Structured and surprisingly elegant there is a marvellous persistence of dark berry fruit. Candy Core is an unusual late-harvested Grenache which is rich, unctuous and concentrated. A number of other reds should also be considered, Elevation Sensation (Grenache, Mourvèdre and Syrah), Mister Moreved (Mourvèdre with a little Grenache), a Bordeaux styled blend Kuyam Cuvée Nolan and the premium Cuvée Fletcher from a variable blend of Grenache and Mourvèdre. (DM)

Recommended Reds:
Candy Core Santa Barbara County ★★★★ £E
Hard Core Santa Barbara County ★★★★ £E
Recommended Whites:
Core White ★★★☆ £D

>> Domaine de La Côte (Sta. Rita Hills) *www.domainedelacote.com*
Domaine de la Côte is a collection of forty acres of vineyards, many of which are located at high elevations at the western part of the Sta. Rita Hills AVA. The brand is owned by Raj Parr and well-regarded winemaker, Sashi Moorman (PIEDRASSASI). They also make Chardonnay and Pinot at SANDHI Wines. The vineyards were custom-planted to heritage selections per Moorman's specifications. The vineyards are farmed organically. The cellar practices focus on low intervention methodologies. The winery produces several versions of intense, energetic, low-alcohol Pinot Noirs. (IT)
Recommended Reds:
Pinot Noir "La Côte" Sta. Rita Hills ★★★★ £F
Pinot Noir "Memorious" Sta. Rita Hills ★★★★ £F
Pinot Noir Mt. Carmel "Old Vines" Sta. Rita Hills ★★★★ £F
Pinot Noir "Blooms Field" Sta. Rita Hills ★★★★ £F
Pinot Noir Estate Sta. Rita Hills ★★★★ £F
Pinot Noir "Rinconada" Sta. Rita Hills ★★★☆ £F

Denner Vineyards (Paso Robles) *www.dennervineyards.com*
The Denners established their vineyard here in 1999. Farmed entirely by sustainable practices the calcareous soils are also a source of top quality fruit for other producers including Justin Smith at SAXUM. The Viognier is a rich, full style with unctuous fruit and should be enjoyed young. The Syrah is ripe, full and marked by a spicy black pepper character and the rich almost jammy character of the variety here. The Ditch Digger blends Grenache, Syrah and Mourvèdre and possesses a touch more minerality and is firmer and more classically structured. Cabernet, Grenache and Zinfandel are also made along with a Bordeaux blend Mother of Exiles. Expect the reds to develop well over the medium term. (DM)
Recommended Reds:
Ditch Digger Paso Robles ★★★★ £E   Syrah Paso Robles ★★★★ £E
Recommended Whites:
Viognier Paso Robles ★★★ £E

✿ Dierberg (Santa Ynez Valley) *www.dierbergvineyard.com*
The Dierbergs own three vineyards in the Santa Ynez area. Their first, purchased in 1996 is called Star Lane Vineyard, in one of the warmest spots in the area and considered suitable for growing Cabernet Sauvignon and other Bordeaux varietals and two in the cooler areas of Santa Maria and the Sta. Rita Hills, near the Pacific Ocean which are used to grow Chardonnay and Pinot Noir grapes, both aptly named Dierberg Vineyards. Premium varietal wines are made by winemaker Nick de Luca individually from the three vineyards under the Dierberg and Star Lane labels, whilst less expensive bottles are blended from all three vineyards and sold under the Three Saints label. The Dierberg Vineyard Chardonnay is whole-cluster pressed for minimum skin contact then afterwards goes through malolactic fermentation on its own. After 16 months in barrel, the finished wine is bottled unfiltered. Youthful oak tends to mask the underlying fruit, but this is something that should integrate in time. The Pinot Noir shows class and finesse with good varietal flavours. The Star Lane Vineyard Sauvignon Blanc has good fruit, but the part maturation in oak seems to have inhibited the vibrancy of the wine a little. Star Lane Cabernet Sauvignon has good

California

soft tannins with elegance and finesse and here the 18 months spent in 100% French oak does not seem to overpower the fruit. A premium Cabernet Sauvignon "Astra" is also produced from selected plots in the vineyard but this not yet been tasted. The Three Saints Chardonnay showed good lemony notes, finely balanced between fruit and acidity and not over oaked. Syrah, Cabernet Sauvignon and Pinot Noir are also produced under the Three Saints Label as well as a Merlot from Star Lane and a Syrah from the Dierberg vineyards. (NB)

Dierberg
Recommended Reds:
Pinot Noir Estate Vineyard Santa Maria Valley ★★★★☆ £F
Recommended Whites:
Chardonnay Estate Vineyard Santa Maria Valley ★★★ £E

Star Lane
Recommended Reds:
Cabernet Sauvignon Santa Ynez Valley ★★★★ £F
Recommended Whites:
Sauvignon Blanc Santa Ynez Valley ★★★ £E

Three Saints
Recommended Reds:
Cabernet Sauvignon Santa Barbara County ★★ £D
Recommended Whites:
Chardonnay Santa Barbara County ★★★ £D

Dover Canyon (Paso Robles) www.dovercanyon.com
This small artisan winery was established in 1994 while Dan Panico was still the winemaker at EBERLE. The main emphasis is on bespoke small lot Zinfandel and Syrah from Paso Robles Westside fruit. Small volumes of Rhône whites as well as red blends and some Bordeaux style reds are also produced. Zinfandel comes from a number of sources and the wines are small lot bottlings from either single vineyards or special selections. Both the Old Vine Benito Dusi and Bella Vineyard wines are marked by a real intensity of spicy brambly fruit. The Benito Dusi a touch rounder and fuller, the Bella Vineyard tighter, more minerally. Production is tiny just eight barrels of Benito Dusi and four barrels of the Bella Vineyard emerged from the 2003 vintage and both were on the cusp of four stars. Winemaking for all the reds is the same with vinification in small open top fermenters. Viognier is in a richly textured style with very subtle peachy fruit and and a hint of citrus and has emerged from the Hansen and Chequera vineyards. The wines are bottled without recourse to filtration. (DM)
Recommended Reds:
Zinfandel Old Vine Benito Dusi Vineyard Paso Robles ★★★☆ £E
Zinfandel Bella Vineyard Paso Robles ★★★☆ £E

Eberle (Paso Robles) www.eberlewinery.com
With an increasing number of newly emerging names in Paso Robles Eberle stands out as one of the earliest established operations here and has been running for over 30 years. Gary Eberle produces a well made range of reds and whites which are all marked by their ripe, forward character and richly-textured style. While they may not be the opulent blockbusters of some of their neighbours they nevertheless offer excellent value for money. Among the reds the single vineyard Syrah stands out. The Estate Cabernet Sauvignon is also impressively dense and concentrated and a Reserve version is also available but it isn't cheap (£G). Cabernet, Chardonnay and Muscat Canelli come from the Estate vineyard which is planted on well drained gravel and granite soils.

Both the nearby Steinbeck and Mill Road vineyards are planted on rocky loam soils which suit the Rhône varieties. The reds will all stand a little age. (DM)
Recommended Reds:
Syrah Steinbeck Vineyard Paso Robles ★★★ £D
Cabernet Sauvignon Estate Paso Robles ★★★ £E
Cabernet Sauvignon Vineyard Selection Paso Robles ★★☆ £C
Recommended Whites:
Viognier Mill Road Vineyard Paso Robles ★★ £C
Chardonnay Estate Paso Robles ★★ £C
Muscat Canelli Estate Paso Robles ★☆ £C

⦿ **Edmunds St John (Berkeley)** www.edmundsstjohn.com
Small warehouse winery, a benchmark among California Rhône Rangers. Very impressive Syrah, which can stand comparison with some of the best of the northern Rhône, is made from a number of sources. Fenaughty Vineyard is planted at 900 metres and the volcanic clay-loam soils provide an excellent growing environment. Aging is in old wood to preserve the character of the wine. The Bassetti Vineyard Syrah is the stand out wine. Planted in sparse rocky soils there is a significant maritime influence with the vines planted just a couple of miles from the coast. A structured Rhône red, Shell and Bone, has been made from the Rozet Vineyard with its excellent calcareous soils is a blend of Mourvèdre, Grenache, Syrah and Counoise. There is also a fine, fresh and aromatic white, Heart of Gold, which blends Vermentino and Grenache Blanc and a rosé, Bone-Jolly is also made from Gamay (DM)
Recommended Reds:
Syrah Bassetti Vineyard San Luis Obispo ★★★★☆ £F
Syrah Fenaughty Vineyard El Dorado ★★★★ £E

Edna Valley (Edna Valley) www.ednavalleyvineyard.com
The Niven Family who own the Paragon Vineyard established this partnership with the CHALONE Wine Group in 1980 to produce a range of well-priced varietal wines that emphasise the cool-climate characteristics of the Edna Valley. Key here are the coastal fogs which drift inland to cool the vineyards at night during the summer growing season and the clay and volcanic rock soils. Chardonnay dominates the production of well over 100,000 cases a year and it stands out. Quality remains impressive despite the volume and the wines are good value. Chardonnay from the Paragon Vineyard is barrel-fermented and shows nicely judged lees and oak with subtle tropical and melon fruit notes. Both Syrah and Pinot are now also sourced from the Paragon Vineyard. Sauvignon Blanc comes from the Central Coast and Merlot and Cabernet Sauvignon are both sourced from Paso Robles. The Syrah is bright and spicy with vibrant raspberry fruit. The Pinot is more marked by forward berry fruit than complex secondary flavours. There are a number of limited release wines available including pricier Reserves. (DM)
Recommended Reds:
Pinot Noir Paragon Vineyard Edna Valley ★★☆ £C
Syrah Paragon Vineyard Edna Valley ★★☆ £C
Recommended Whites:
Chardonnay Paragon Vineyard Edna Valley ★★★ £C
Viognier Paso Robles/San Luis Obispo ★★ £C

⦿ **Fiddlehead (Sta. Rita Hills)** www.fiddleheadcellars.com
A native of Chicago and a bio-chemist, Kathy Joseph established her small operation in 1989 and makes just Sauvignon Blanc and Pinot Noir. A Pinot rosé was added for the first time with the 2005 vintage. The three dry Sauvignons are sourced from a mix of cooler

and warmer Santa Ynez sites. The Happy Canyon bottling comes from vineyards within the recently established AVA of the same name, which is a sub region of Santa Ynez. It is ripe and lightly tropical in style and gets a rich creamy texture from a combination of fermentation and short ageing in 50/50 new and neutral oak; one-third is vinified in stainless steel. Goosebury is a blend of the Vogelzang and McGinley vineyards and is cool-fermented with malolactic blocked to provide a piercingly pure and minerally green fruited style in the manner of the best of Sancerre. Best of the trio is the Honeysuckle, a more structured example which is vinified and aged in 100% new wood. It comes solely from the Vogelzang vineyard and is entitled to the Happy Canyon appellation. The cool nights here together with a blocked malolactic ensures good acidity and structure in the wine. It always gets three years ageing in bottle before being released. Of the Pinots, both the 728 and Lollapalooza come from the estate Fiddlestix Vineyard which has been a source of other fine examples from the likes of AMPELOS and ARCADIAN. The wines are firm and structured with opulent sweet berry character in warm years. 728 refers to the mile marker on the Santa Rosa road where the Fiddlestix vineyard is sited. Lollapalooza is a barrel selection of wine sourced from the best blocks. In very exceptional years (2010 is currently available) a single exceptional barrel, Doyle, is selected and bottled with a small series of artists labels. It is by no means cheap (£H). An Oldsville Reserve Pinot comes from the Willamette Valley and is in marked contrast to the Fiddlestix wines; tighter and more elegant with lighter red berry and herb scented fruit. Like the Lollapalooza, it is oak-aged (40% new) but the oak is similarly seamlessly integrated. A single barrel selection is again made in the very best years and labelled Alloro. There is also a characterful late-harvest white made from dried Sauvignon grapes with just a touch of botrytis. It is also sourced from the Happy Canyon of Santa Barbara AVA. (DM)

Recommended Reds:
Pinot Noir Lollapalooza Sta. Rita Hills ★★★☆ £F
Pinot Noir Oldsville Reserve Willamette Valley ★★★★ £F
Pinot Noir 728 Sta. Rita Hills ★★★★ £E
Recommended Whites:
Sauvignon Blanc Honeysuckle Santa Ynez Valley ★★★☆ £E
Sauvignon Blanc Goosebury Santa Ynez Valley ★★★☆ £E
Sauvignon Blanc Happy Canyon Santa Ynez Valley ★★★ £D
Sauvignon Blanc Sweetie Santa Ynez Valley ★★★☆ £E
Recommended Rosés:
Pink Fiddle Sta. Rita Hills ★★☆ £C

Flying Goat Cellars (Santa Ynez Valley) www.flyinggoatcellars.com
Small operation specialising in Pinot Noir but lately making a little Pinot Gris too as well as sparkling white, red and rosé. The wines now come from a range of selected vineyards. Owner and winemaker Norman Yost has over 25 years winemaking experience in both the Russian River Valley and Oregon, ideal qualifications for making serious Pinot Noir and Pinot Gris. The Sierra Madre Vineyard white is from Santa Maria with a marked maritime influence. The wine is cool-fermented and bottled fresh after a few months. It is an exuberant peachy, forward style to be enjoyed young. As well as the Rio Vista bottlings tasted here, examples are also produced from the Dierberg, Bien Nacido, Solomon Hills and FOLEY Rancho Santa Rosa Vineyards. The regular Rio Vista bottling comes from a range of Dijon Clones clones and is aged for 12 months in a mix of new and old French oak. Clone 2A shares a similar élevage, but comes instead from a single clone (designated 2A) which was one of the first planted in California. The Rio Vista is more classically Santa

Maria in style with dark fruits and a rich opulent texture. 2A is more characterful and marked by red cherry fruit and a gamey, earthy quality. Both will develop well after two or three years aging. (DM)
Recommended Reds:
Pinot Noir Rio Vista Vineyard Sta. Rita Hills ★★★★ £E
Pinot Noir Rio Vista Vineyard Clone 2A Sta. Rita Hills ★★★★ £E
Recommended Whites:
Pinot Gris Sierra Madre Vineyard Santa Maria Hills ★★★ £C

Foley (Sta. Rita Hills) www.foleywines.com
Bill Foley has one of the largest vineyard holdings in the Sta. Rita Hills AVA. In addition to this he also owns the LINCOURT winery further inland at Solvang where he produces a range from Santa Barbara County fruit. His Rancho Santa Rosa property is planted to 93 ha (230 acres) and has been isolated into 59 micro blocks which are farmed and vinified separately. The site is mainly Pinot Noir (planted on the higher slopes), Chardonnay and a little Syrah and Pinot Gris. A second site Rancho Las Hermanas is also now owned comprising 86 ha (213 acres). There are two separate vineyards, Lindsay's planted to red varieties and Courtney's planted to whites. The mainstays of the winery are Pinot Noir and Chardonnay. The Rancho Santa Rosa vineyards are marked by traces of limestone in the soils and an array of clones are planted. Pinot Noir is aged for around 14 months in oak (around one-third new) and is medium weight with a combination of dark and red fruits as well as a note of cocoa and vanilla from the oak. Chardonnay comes from low yields, barely 2 tons to the acre, and is barrel-fermented and aged 10 months in oak (40% new). Citrus and cooler notes of pears and green fruits and underpinned by a rich, creamy, leesy texture and a subtle minerality. Small-lot bottlings of both Pinot Noir and Chardonnay are also made which are both site and barrel selections from both estates. (DM)
Recommended Reds:
Pinot Noir Rancho Santa Rosa Sta. Rita Hills ★★★☆ £E
Recommended Whites:
Chardonnay Rancho Santa Rosa Sta. Rita Hills ★★★ £D

Four Vines (Paso Robles) www.fourvines.com
The output at this winery, famed for "off the wall" labelling and an essentially fun approach to wine is now not inconsiderable. However the wines remain true to their origins, well made full of fruit and with the kind of balance and structure that supports drinking with food, something so many fruit-bomb high point scorers so singularly fail to achieve. Spicy, vibrant Zinfandel sourced from a range of sites but always with the complexity of older vines as well as the Naked Chardonnay make up the core of a very well-priced range of wines along with the red Truant which is mostly Zinfandel. There is a range of old vine Zin offerings along with Petite Sirah. A level up in both quality and price is a small range of red blends, known to the winery as the "Freakshow", as well as a Petite Sirah, the "The Heretic", we can vouch for the Anarchy, a rich, dense and brambly, peppery blend of Syrah, Mourvèdre and Zinfandel. (DM)
Recommended Reds:
Anarchy Paso Robles ★★★☆ £E
Zinfandel Old Vine OVC California ★★☆ £B
Recommended Whites:
Chardonnay Naked Santa Barbara County ★★☆ £B

⊛ **Blair Fox Cellars (Santa Barbara County)** www.blairfoxcellars.com
Blair Fox is the head winemaker for Fess Parker but has his own

Central Coast & Sierra Foothills

California

boutique operation where he has been producing notable wines for some years now. A specialist in Rhône varietals, he won the Andre Tchelistcheff Winemaker of the Year Award at the 2008 San Francisco International Wine Competition. Great attention to detail hallmarks the quality of his wines which are produced in very small quantities. The red, iron rich, nutrient deprived soils of the high altitude Paradise Road vineyard has produced a Viognier with tiny berries, small clusters and very concentrated and rich flavours of apricot and peach. From the same vineyard, a massively structured Syrah is produced with layers and layers of thick, tarry fruit. 26 months in French and American oak, it is also kept for one more year in bottle before being released. Another Syrah, this time from the Tierra Alta Vineyard in the Santa Ynez Valley was punched down by hand until fermentation was complete, then basket pressed and aged for twenty months in 100% French oak. The result is a wine of great complexity with intense, full fruit and good persistence.. As well as these a Grenache and Petite Sirah are made from the Fox Family Vineyard as well as a red blend the Ambush. Under the Blair Fox Cellars label a rosé, Haylee's and a white Vermentino Fox Family Vineyard are also made. An additional range of reds and whites are also released under the Fox Wine Co. brand and mostly from Santa Barbara fruit sources. They are a touch cheaper (£D-£E). (NB)

Recommended Reds:
Syrah Tierra Alta Vineyard Santa Ynez Valley ★★★★☆ £F
Syrah Paradise Road Vineyard Santa Barbara County ★★★★☆ £F
Recommended Whites:
Viognier Paradise Road Vineyard Santa Barbara County ★★★★ £E

Foxen (Santa Maria Valley) *www.foxenvineyard.com*
While there have been a plethora of new names emerging in these increasingly fashionable small wine regions, the Foxen boys, as they are affectionately known, have been around it seems for an eternity. They have consistently and continue to produce some of the best and most characterful wines from the area. Fruit comes from a number of sources including their own estate Tinaquaic Vineyard and the high altitude steeply sloping Block 8 of the giant Bien Nacido Vineyard. The regular Pinot Noir is elegant, cherry-fruited and softly structured but offers impressive depth and persistence, a large part of the fruit coming from Block 8. The Bien Nacido bottling itself is altogether firmer and fuller with a ripe gamey character and an impressive depth of complex dark fruit and smoky oak. A Block 43 is released from the same vineyard and there are releases from a number of other vineyards in the Sta. Rita Hills AVA. A range of Bordeaux styles are now being released under the Foxen 7200 label along with a Sangiovese and Sangiovese Merlot blend, Volpino. Chardonnay from the home Tinaquaic vineyard has long been one of the better examples from the region combining a rich, toasty and creamy character with subtle citrus and lightly tropical fruit. Chardonnay also comes from Bien Nacido. Of equal interest is one of the best Chenin Blanc in California. The Ernesto Wickenden Vineyard provides fruit of the highest quality with real varietal purity. Both Chardonnay and Chenin Blanc are barrel fermented and will develop further with a little ageing as will the reds, particularly the Block 8 and the Foothills Reserve. (DM)

Recommended Reds:
Pinot Noir Bien Nacido Vineyard Block 8 Santa Maria Valley ★★★★ £F
Pinot Noir Santa Maria Valley ★★★☆ £E
Recommended Whites:
Chardonnay Tinaquaic Vineyard Santa Maria Valley ★★★★ £E
Chenin Blanc Ernesto Wickenden Vineyard Santa Maria Valley ★★★ £C

Gainey (Santa Ynez Valley) *www.gaineyvineyard.com*
Small to medium-sized and long established operation. The Gainey Home Ranch of some 36 ha (91 acres) is planted to the red Bordeaux varieties in addition to Sauvignon Blanc. The property itself is much larger at 730 ha (1,800 acres) and the family also farm cattle. Chardonnay, Pinot Noir and Syrah have been planted across 38 ha (98 acres) at two vineyards in the cooler Sta. Rita Hills, Evan's Ranch and Rancho Esperanza. The winery facility is now gravity-fed to provide the gentlest environment possible in which to vinify the grapes. The Limited Selection Merlot, Pinot Noir, Chardonnay and Sauvignon Blanc have been impressive in recent vintages. The Merlot is bottled without filtration. Sauvignon Blanc gets some oak-ageing and the Limited Selection Chardonnay is fermented and aged in barrel on lees. The Estate labels are a touch cheaper., however the wines generally represent good value. The 2001 vintage saw the release of a Limited Release Cabernet Franc, Cabernet Sauvignon and a premium Bordeaux blend Patricks Vineyard are also released. (DM)

Recommended Reds:
Limited Selection Merlot Santa Ynez Valley ★★★ £E
Recommended Whites:
Chardonnay Estate Sta. Rita Hills ★★★ £D
Limited Selection Sauvignon Blanc Santa Ynez Valley ★★☆ £C
Riesling Santa Ynez Valley ★★☆ £C

Robert Hall (Paso Robles) *www.roberthallwinery.com*
A good small range of well-priced wines is made at this mid-sized property with 121 ha (300 acres) under vine across four vineyards. The wines are all marked by clean and pure varietal fruit and the reds are quite firm and structured. The fresh and crisp Sauvignon Blanc is part barrel-fermented and aged in tank for 4 months on lees, which adds both weight and depth. Cabernet Sauvignon comes from both benchland as well as hillside sites on the Hall home ranch. It is a touch firm and tannic but offers attractive cedary fruit; give it at least 4 years. The two Syrah's are notably striking, providing dark and spicy wines with a forward brambly character. Like the Cabernet, these are aged in European oak with malolactic being completed in barrel. A pricier Meritage red are also produced the latter from Cabernet Sauvignon, Merlot, Cabernet Franc and Petit Verdot. (DM)

Recommended Reds:
Syrah Reserve Paso Robles ★★★ £D
Syrah Paso Robles ★★☆ £D   Merlot Paso Robles ★★☆ £D
Cabernet Sauvignon Paso Robles ★★ £D
Zinfandel Paso Robles ★★ £C
Recommended Whites:
Sauvignon Blanc Paso Robles ★★ £B
Orange Muscat Paso Robles ★☆ £C

Halter Ranch (Paso Robles) *www.halterranch.com*
Swiss-born financier Hansjoerg Wyss purchased 364 ha (900 acres) of the 3,000 acre Halter Ranch in 2000. Some of the property had already been planted to vines but Hansjoerg has now taken that holding to 101 ha (250 acres). Much of his wish to do so is the aspect and site of the vineyards, which are 550 metres above sea level and planted on limestone-rich soils. Amongst an increasingly extensive range two well-made reds are crafted and reviewed here. In addition a Rhône style red blend Côtes de Paso, a Zinfandel and two premium labels Syrah Block 22 and Ancestor, a Bordeaux style are also made. At the foot of the red range is a well priced Cabernet/Syrah, Synthesis. The whites comprise a Sauvignon Blanc and a

white Côtes de Paso. Both the Syrah and Cabernet undoubtedly benefit from their limestone low yield *terroir*. The Cabernet is full of tobacco and rich, ripe blackcurrant fruit, the Syrah dark pepper and spice. Both wines are aged for 16 months in 40% new wood. They should drink very well with two or three year's age, the Cabernet is a touch more structured. (DM)

Recommended Reds:

Syrah Paso Robles ★★★☆ £E

Cabernet Sauvignon Paso Robles ★★★☆ £E

Harrison Clarke (Santa Ynez Valley) *www.harrisonclarkewine.com*
Harrison Clarke are based in the picturesque Santa Ynez Valley region of Santa Barbara County in the Purisima Hills. The soils of the vineyards which combine clay, clay-loam and limestone provide excellent conditions for the production of rich, ripe black-fruited Grenache and Syrah. Both wines should be considered if you can get hold of them, they are real bargains. Grenache is super-ripe and full of black fruit with a pure varietal character showing through, albeit not the kind of restrained strawberry fruit you might expect from the Southern Rhône. Both also come from very low yields, particularly the dark, smoky Syrah, barely more than one and a half tons to the acre, and also key to their quality is the use of small open top fermenters and basket presses. The Grenache in particular is immediately approachable and the Syrah will add a further dimension with three or four years patience. A second special selection Syrah, Cuvée Charlotte, is made in even smaller quantities and well priced Grenache red and a Grenache rosé are released under the Harrison-Clarke Sorrellina label. (DM)

Recommended Reds:

Syrah Harrison-Clarke Vineyard Santa Ynez Valley ★★★★ £E

Grenache Harrison-Clarke Vineyard Santa Ynez Valley ★★★☆ £D

Herman Story (Santa Maria Valley) *www.hermanstorywines.com*
A small range of explosively rich reds have been produced by Russell From since 2001 at his small Santa Maria winery which he now shares with MCPRICE MYERS. An extensive range of vineyards and regions now form the core of his fruit sources. As well as the reds he also makes a little Santa Barbara Viognier labelled Tomboy, a single vineyard Syrah from the John Sebastiano Vineyard and a rosé, After Hours. Production is at present very small but its well worth subscribing to his mailing list. The Grenache is a deep, dark and blackberry laden red, full and explosively rich. Syrah is a touch more structured and needs a little more time. Prices are very good and the wines made in very small lots so its worth checking the website. (DM)

Recommended Reds:

Syrah Nuts and Bolts California ★★★★ £E

Grenache On the Road California ★★★★ £E

Hitching Post (Santa Barbara) *www.hitchingpostwines.com*
Restaurateur Frank Ostini's Hitching Post II in Buellton was featured in the film Sideways. He and friend Gray Hartley also produce a number of fine small-lot reds from Pinot Noir, Syrah and the red Bordeaux varieties, drawing on a range of Santa Barbara County vineyard sources. The wines were originally vinified at the AU BON CLIMAT/QUPÉ facility and production remains small. Fermentation takes place in small vats and the wines are only racked just before bottling without filtration. The Generation Red is based on Cabernet Franc with some Merlot and, unusually, Syrah blended in. It offers some characterful berry fruit in a medium-weight style. Syrah comes from a number of sources, with the best bottling from the

excellent Purisima Mountain Vineyard. Pinot Noir is the main focus and a number of vineyard-designated bottlings are made including Fiddlestix, Bien Nacido, Cargasacchi and Julia's Vineyard. The top Pinot, Highliner, is a barrel selection from the best lots of the best vineyards. All the wines will stand a little age. (DM)

Recommended Reds:

Pinot Noir Highliner Santa Barbara County ★★★★☆ £F

Syrah Purisima Mountain Vineyard Santa Ynez Valley ★★★★ £E

Generation Red Santa Barbara County ★★★☆ £D

❀ **Terry Hoage (Paso Robles)** *www.terryhoagevineyards.com*
This small bespoke winery is fast becoming one of the best sources of characterful, opulent Rhône styled reds from the Paso Robles AVA. The winery and vineyards are located in the western hills of the appellation, with vines planted on steep slopes and in some of the regions most propitious limestone soils. Dark, smoky and characterful Syrah is aged in 90% new French oak offering a pronounced toasty undercurrent but it in no way overwhelms the rich concentration of the wine's fruit. The Grenache and Syrah "The 46" blend has less new oak, and the wine is more obviously fruit driven with rich and ripe blackberry fruit in abundance. The Pick is a classic southern Rhône blend comprising Grenache, Syrah, Mourvèdre and Counoise. As such there is less oak influence and the wine is characterised not just by dark, spicy fruit but also a subtle herb-scented character. Other reds to consider are a pure Grenache Skins, 5 Blocks a blend of Mourvèdre, Grenache and Cinsault as well as a second Syrah Three-Four. The range is completed by a white The Gap comprising Grenache Blanc, Picpoul and Roussanne. The reds will drink well with a year or two of ageing, although Syrah may benefit from a little more patience than will the blends. (DM)

Recommended Reds:

Syrah The Hedge Paso Robles ★★★★☆ £F

Grenache Syrah The "46" Paso Robles ★★★★ £E

Cuvée The Pick Paso Robles ★★★★ £E

❀ **JC Cellars (Oakland)** *www.jccellars.com*
Jeff Cohn was the Vice-President of production at the increasingly sizeable ROSENBLUM CELLARS. He now continues only in a consultancy role as his time is increasingly taken up producing some exceptional Syrah reds under his own JC Cellars label. The wines were originally made at the Rosenblum facility but he has recently moved to a separate nearby location in Oakland. The Syrahs are among California's most striking examples. They range in style from elegant and subtle to rich and very concentrated. Some cuvées result in just 200 cases or so. Vinification is carried out in very small lots and the vats are individually hand punched between four and five times daily during fermentation. Ageing is in French oak for around a year and a half (varying up to 100% new). The Rockpile Vineyard Haley's Reserve is from a newly established AVA of the same name and is rich, structured and very mineral in character. Zinfandel is also important and there are releases from a number of vineyards. The Imposter and Smoke and Mirrors wines are Zinfandel and mostly Rhône variety blends. Broken Compass is solely a Rhône blend but dominated by Carignane whereas Misc Stuff is dominated by Grenache. A varietal Grenache, The Fallen Angel comes from the El Diablo Vineyard in the Russian River, a Mourvèdre, Twist of Fate is mainly from Paso Robles fruit. The red range is completed by a Cabernet from the Stagecoach Vineyard in Atlas Peak and a Pinot Noir from the Lancel Creek Vineyard in the Russian River. First Date is a lightly nutty, floral Rhône style blend of Roussanne and Marsanne from a mix of Paso Robles and Atlas Peak sources. It is part barrel

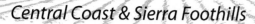

Central Coast & Sierra Foothills

fermented in French oak. There are also a couple of Viogniers, one a late harvested example and a rosé from Grenache, Syrah and Mourvèdre. The top reds are very ageworthy. (DM)

Recommended Reds:
Syrah Rockpile Vineyard Haley's Reserve Rockpile ★★★★★ £F
Recommended Whites:
First Date California ★★★ £D

Jada Vineyard (Paso Robles) *www.jadavineyard.com*
Jack Massina, a New York heart surgeon, purchased the land in 1998 and in the following year 68 (27.5 ha) of the 100 acres (40.5 ha) purchased were planted to Syrah and a mix of Bordeaux varietals by John Crossland, the vineyard manager of the Beckstoffer Vineyard in the Napa Valley. Until 2005, grapes were sold but in that year they engaged Scott Hawley, who previously worked for FETZER and SUMMER WOOD as their winemaker. Currently, the winemaker is David Galzignato, who was previously the winemaker at Charles Krug. In 2007, some of the vines were replanted by adding clonal variations of Syrah as well as the introduction of Grenache, Mourvèdre and white Rhône Varietals including Viognier, Roussanne, and Grenache Blanc. At the same time, vine density was increased to over 1800 per acre to encourage extra low yields. The site, located in the Templeton Gap, is cooled by ocean breezes and this coupled with rocky and calcareous soil makes it an ideal location for both Rhône and Bordeaux varietals. The wines, mainly blends, are all given a significant personalised name. "Hell's Kitchen" (Syrah, Grenache, Mourvèdre, Viognier and Roussanne) combines leather, bitter chocolate and spice with big tannins. It needs 5 years to show its full potential but can be approached young. "Jersey Girl" (100% Syrah) has excellent varietal flavours, smooth tarry-ness without overpowering the wine. "Jack of Hearts" (45% Cabernet Sauvignon, 40% Petit Verdot and 5 % Merlot) is smooth, dark and inky, the Petit Verdot giving it extra depth and colour. "Passing By" is 95% Cabernet Sauvignon and 5% Merlot – smooth and silky, the dark berry fruit is tempered by slight herbaceous flavours and a little sweetness on the finish. A tiny quantity of a Viognier/Roussanne/Grenache Blanc blend is made but this was only tasted in barrel. It is now labelled XCV on release. The hand-picked grapes are sorted and gravity fed into small open-top fermenters with most of the fruit being destemmed although some lots receive some whole clusters. A 4 to 6 week fermentation skins follows before basket pressing. The malo-lactic is in French Oak barrels (between 40% and 80 % new, depending on the blend) and then ageing is for around 8 to 12 months for the white and 18 to 36 months for the reds, receiving only one further racking for blending before being transferred to tank for final blending and bottling unfined and unfiltered. At present output is restricted to the ultimate goal of reaching not more than 3,000 cases which has just recently been attained. (NB)

Recommended Reds:
Jack of Hearts Paso Robles ★★★★ £F
Jersey Girl Paso Robles ★★★★ £F
Hell's Kitchen Paso Robles ★★★★ £F
Passing By Paso Robles ★★★★ £F

Jaffurs Wine Cellars (Santa Barbara County) *www.jaffurswine.com*
An impressive small range of Rhône styles is made at Craig Jaffurs climate-controlled winery in Santa Barbara. The first vintage here was 1994 and production is still small and quality high. Syrah is the main focus and is sourced from the Ampelos, Thompson, Larner, Kimsey, Verna's and Bien Nacido vineyards. Roussanne comes from the Stolpman Vineyard while a Grenache Blanc is sourced

from the Thompson Vineyard. Viognier is richly textured, full and fat with subtle varietal character and hints of peach and citrus fruit. The Santa Barbara Syrah is typically dark and spicy with ripe black pepper notes and impressive weight for a regional bottling. At just over 1,400 cases a year, it is the largest-volume wine. The much smaller-volume single vineyard bottlings are fuller, richer and altogether more complex. Bottled unfined and unfiltered expect them to benefit from at least 3 or 4 years' cellaring. (DM)

Recommended Reds:
Syrah Ampelos Vineyard Sta. Rita Hills ★★★★ £F
Syrah Thompson Vineyard Santa Barbara County ★★★★ £E
Syrah Santa Barbara County ★★★☆ £E
Grenache Santa Barbara County ★★★☆ £E
Recommended Whites:
Roussanne Stolpman Vineyard Santa Ynez Valley ★★★☆ £D
Viognier Bien Nacido Vineyard Santa Santa Maria Valley ★★★☆ £D

❀ Justin (Paso Robles) *www.justinwine.com*
Very good operation producing some of the best Bordeaux-style reds on the Central Coast. These wines may share similar grapes to their French counterparts but are altogether fuller and riper without any hint of the rusticity or jamminess often found in warm-climate Cabernet. Isosceles is a blend of Cabernet Sauvignon, Cabernet Franc and Merlot, marginally more refined than Justification, which is just over half Cabernet Sauvignon, the balance Merlot. To these has been added a very dense, impressive Isosceles Reserve which blends all five red Bordeaux varieties. Dominated by Cabernet Sauvignon it is bottled unfiltered. A Paso Robles Syrah is now made as well as Merlot, Petit Verdot, Malbec and Zinfandel. Three further premium reds are made. Focus is a varietal Syrah, Right Angle is a blend of Cabernet Sauvignon, Petit Verdot, Petite Sirah and Malbec while Savant combines Syrah and Cabernet Sauvignon. Chardonnay and Sauvignon Blanc are aged in top-quality French oak and there is a limited-release reserve Chardonnay bottling which is worth considering. A number of interesting special labels can be sourced directly from the winery. Prices are pretty good. (DM)

Recommended Reds:
Isosceles Reserve Paso Robles ★★★★☆ £F
Isosceles Paso Robles ★★★★☆ £F
Justification Paso Robles ★★★☆ £E   Syrah Paso Robles ★★★ £D
Cabernet Sauvignon Paso Robles ★★★ £D
Recommended Whites:
Chardonnay Paso Robles ★★★ £D
Sauvignon Blanc Paso Robles ★★ £C

❀ Kathryn Kennedy *www.kathrynkennedywinery.com*
The late Kathryn Kennedy took up winemaking at her small 3 ha (8 acre) Santa Cruz Mountain property in her 40s. The Estate Cabernet is highly sought after by local collectors and the most likely way of obtaining any at all is to join the mailing list. A secondary label, Small Lot, is also produced, again in very small quantities, from selected Cabernet plots throughout the Santa Cruz AVA. A sparkling wine Cuvée Twenty Seven is also now made from the Burgundy varieties. A part barrel, part tank-fermented cool-climate Sauvignon Blanc was added with the 2003 vintage. Vinification for the reds is in small lots and the approach throughout is one of care and minimal handling. The Cabernets, particularly the Estate, will comfortably add great complexity with 10 years' age. (DM)

Recommended Reds:
Cabernet Sauvignon Estate Santa Cruz Mountains ★★★★★ £G

Kunin Wines (Santa Barbara County) *www.kuninwines.com*
Well-priced Syrah, Viognier and red and white blends are all made at this small Santa Maria winery as well as Sauvignon Blanc from the Happy Canyon area. The regular Santa Barbara Syrah accounts for just over 1,000 cases a year and is marked by its rich, fleshy, forward fruit. Aged in a mix of French and American oak, a third of it new, this is an accessible, supple Syrah that can be broached with a couple of years' age. More serious and complex, although only marginally more expensive, the Alisos Vineyards bottling is again aged in one-third new French and American oak. It offers greater depth and dimension, albeit in a similarly opulent, rich, brambly vein. Give it 3 or 4 years. An additional Syrah is also now released from the Santa Ynez Larner Vineyard. (DM)

Recommended Reds:
Syrah Alisos Vineyards Santa Ynez Valley ★★★★ £D
Syrah Santa Barbara County ★★★ £E

Labyrinth (Santa Maria Valley) *www.labyrinthwine.com*
Ariki "Rick" Hill produces top grade Pinot Noir in Santa Barbara County. The first wines emerged in 2000 when Rick joined forces with another Santa Barbara Pinot Noir star, Lane TANNER, now his wife. The name of the winery represents the problems of successfully growing and even more importantly gaining optimum flavour ripening from this most difficult of varieties. The ripe and intense Santa Barbara County Pinot comes from a mix of the Bien Nacido and Cambria Vineyards. It is subtle and elegant with excellent underlying acidity. The wine gets a cold soak prior to fermentation and some whole bunches adds to complexity. New oak is kept to a minimum, emphasising the wine's elegant fruit and racking is avoided during 20 months barrel-ageing. It will gain from three or four year's patience. Ther range has now been expanded with a number of very small lot released wines, mainly from Paso Robles fruit and released under the Haka by Labyrinth label. (DM)

Recommended Reds:
Pinot Noir Santa Barbara County ★★★☆ £D

Laetitia (Arroyo Grande) *www.laetitiawine.com*
Selim Zilkha was among a number of partners who purchased Laetitia from Champagne DEUTZ in the late 1990s. He has acquired sole ownernership. Sound, well-priced sparklers were the foundation of production here and are still being made but the real focus of the winery now is on good-quality estate and single-vineyard Chardonnay, Syrah and Pinot Noir. Other wines are released under the Nadia label. The vast majority of the output is still wines. The wines are good and well made with reasonable depth, intensity and concentration of flavour. Estate wines are produced from Chardonnay, Pinot Gris, Syrah and Pinot Noir; and there are pricier single-vineyard Pinot Noirs from the La Colline, Les Galets and La Coupelle vineyards. The estate wines are generally very fairly priced; the single-vineyard Pinots will stretch the pocket a little more. (DM)

Recommended Reds:
Pinot Noir Reserve du Domaine Arroyo Grande★★★ £E
Pinot Noir Estate Arroyo Grande★★ £D
Syrah Estate Arroyo Grande★★★ £D

Recommended Whites:
Chardonnay Estate Reserve Arroyo Grande★★☆ £D
Chardonnay Estate Arroyo Grande★★ £C
Brut Cuvée Arroyo Grande★★☆ £D Laetitia XD Arroyo Grande★★ £C

Recommended Rosés:
Brut Rosé Arroyo Grande ★★★ £D

⚙ **L'Aventure (Paso Robles)** *www.aventurewine.com*
Top-quality operation set up by Frenchman Stephan Asseo. His 51 ha (127 acre) property is located in the favourable climes of Paso Robles Westside and the vineyard is planted on meagre, finely drained soils with a high limestone content. This, allied to the long sunny days of the Westside, provides fruit of excellent quality. The vineyard is close-planted and yields less than two tons to the acre. As well as the Bordeaux varieties and Syrah; Roussanne and Viognier are also cultivated. Among the wines Optimus is an impressive combination of Syrah, Cabernet Sauvignon, and Petit Verdot aged in 100% new wood and bottled unfiltered. The top two red blends are wines of really impressive depth and dimension. The fabulously rich, dark, spicy Cuvée Côte à Côte Estate red is a Rhône blend of Grenache, Syrah and Mourvèdre. The Grenache yields barely a ton to the acre. The top Estate Cuvée is produced from Syrah (50%), Cabernet Sauvignon (45%) and a little Petit Verdot, which adds additional grip and dimension. Very backward and restrained when young, it is a wine that demands cellaring for 7–10 years. Newly added but not yet tasted is Le Grand Verdot a red dominated by Petit Verdot with Cabernet Sauvignon and Syrah for balance. (DM)

Recommended Reds:
Estate Cuvée Paso Robles ★★★★★ £G
Cuvée Côte à Côte Estate Paso Robles ★★★★★ £G
Cabernet Sauvignon Estate Paso Robles ★★★★☆ £G
Optimus Estate Paso Robles ★★★★ £F

Lincourt (Santa Barbara County) *www.lincourtwines.com*
Bill Foley established this operation in 1996 where he produces wines from mainly Santa Maria and Santa Ynez fruit sources. More recently he has also established his own vineyard property Rancho Santa Rosa from where he produces estate grown Sta. Rita Hills Pinot Noir and Chardonnay under his FOLEY winery label. Both Santa Maria and the Sta. Rita Hills are important components for Pinot Noir and Chardonnay. The Pinot Noir is classically vinified with punching down of the cap during fermentation and vatting and the wine aged for 15 months in oak. A series of additional and pricier (£E) single vineyard Pinots are also released. The lightly tropical Chardonnay is tank aged and is whole cluster pressed. There are also a number of more expensive examples of the variety which are ably handled from single vineyards. While these wines are relatively simple straightforward, fruit driven examples they all offer good value. Cabernet Sauvignon and Sauvignon Blanc are also made. (DM)

Recommended Reds:
Pinot Noir Lindsay's Vineyard Sta. Rita Hills ★★★ £D
Recommended Whites:
Chardonnay Steel Sta. Rita Hills ★★☆ £C

⚙ **Linne Calodo (Paso Robles)** *www.linnecalodo.com*
Some of the finest and most vibrantly exciting Rhône-style reds and Zinfandel, not only along the Central Coast but in California, are being produced at this small Paso Robles Westside property. Matt Trevisan sources fruit from a number of vineyards and from different clones within varieties. The key is low yielding fruit of the highest quality from some of the finest vineyards in the area. The name of the winery refers to the particular calcareous soils of the Westside. Winemaking is minimalist in terms of intervention but the art of blending is at a very high level here. There is also a very good white which gets around 6 months in used oak prior to bottling. The richly textured Contrarian is mainly Grenache Blanc and blended with small and varying amounts of Picpoul Blanc, Viognier and

California

Roussanne. The sturdy Rising Tides is a blend of Syrah, Mourvèdre and Grenache in fairly similar proportions. The Cherry Red is dominated by Zinfandel with a little Syrah and Mourvèdre blended in. The extraordinary Zinfandel fruit here yields barely more than half a ton to the acre. Problem Child, again mainly Zinfandel, was named after an earlier vintage when the fermentation stuck. The Trevisans opted to let nature take its course and the wine eventually completed its natural vinification many months later – a reminder to Matt that, for him, the minimalist approach is always best. Of two great Rhône blends, Nemesis is dominated by Syrah with smaller parts of Mourvèdre and Grenache. Sticks and Stones blends mainly Grenache with Syrah and the balance Mourvèdre. All the wines deserve a minimum of 5 or 6 years in your cellar. Three additional reds are also made. Outsider is dominated by Zinfandel while Perfectionist is a Rhône style focussed on Syrah and Overthinker is Grenache with smaller amounts of Syrah and Mourvèdre. (DM)

Recommended Reds:
Nemesis Paso Robles ★★★★★ £G
Sticks and Stones Paso Robles ★★★★★ £G
Problem Child Paso Robles ★★★★☆ £F
Cherry Red Paso Robles ★★★★☆ £F
Rising Tides Paso Robles ★★★★☆ £F
Recommended Whites:
Contrarian Paso Robles ★★★★☆ £F

Longoria Wines (Santa Ynez Valley) *www.longoriawine.com*
Although he started his own label over 30 years ago, Rick Longoria, an experienced winemaker in the area, has only been running his own family winery since 1997. Production, as with many of his contemporaries, remains small and he is one of a number of producers with a warehouse facility in Lompoc. Albariño, Pinot Grigio, Chardonnay, Tempranillo, Pinot Noir, Bordeaux blends, Syrah and Cabernet Franc – in the guise of the Longoria Blues label of which it dominates the blend– are all produced. With poor consumer acceptance of the variety, Rick named his Cab Franc after his love of blues music. Elegant and cedary, it gains a hint of dark, spicy plum from the addition of a little Merlot. Syrah, originally from a number of sites now comes from the Clover Creek Vineyard in Santa Ynez. The wine is in a lighter, spicier style than some of his neighbours' offerings. Firm and lightly stalky Pinot Noir Lovely Rita from the Sta. Rita Hills has some attractive gamy notes as well as impressively piercing dark cherry fruit. Single vineyard examples are also made from the Bien Nacido Vineyard and the Sta. Rita Hills Fe Ciega site. The Chardonnay Cuvée Diana is made in very small quantities and offers lightly tropical fruit with a full, richly textured mid-palate and just a hint of oak spice. A Sta. Rita Hills example is also made. The Longoria Blues in particular will benefit from 3 or 4 years' patience. (DM)

Recommended Reds:
Syrah Clover Creek Vineyard Santa Ynez Valley ★★★ £E
Pinot Noir Lovely Rita Sta. Rita Hills ★★★ £E
Longoria Blues Santa Barbara County ★★★ £E
Recommended Whites:
Chardonnay Cuvée Diana Sta. Rita Hills ★★★ £E

Loring Wine Co (Santa Barbara) *www.loringwinecompany.com*
Pinot Noir, in various vineyard guises, is the main wine made by Brian Loring at his Lompoc warehouse winery, and very impressive it is too. Grenache, Cabernet Sauvignon and Mourvèdre, branded Not Pinot, are also made as well as a series of Chardonnays, most of which are single vineyard wines. Fruit for the Pinots comes from

some of the best vineyard sites for the variety and the wines are marked by their rich texture and piercing varietal purity. The grapes are given a cold soak prior to fermentation and then gently basket-pressed before ageing in 50% new French oak. Both the Cargasacchi and Clos Pepe bottlings come from the cool Sta. Rita Hills. The Cargasacchi is a surprisingly rich and opulent wine with weight and a rich sweet texture to its fruit. The Clos Pepe is less gamey, more dark minerally with a tight, firm structure. It should age very well. As well as single vineyard wines a number of AVA releases are also available from the Russian River, Santa Lucia Highlands, San Luis Obispo and Santa Barbara County as well as a Sta. Rita Hills wine. (DM)

Recommended Reds:
Pinot Noir Cargasacchi Vineyard Sta. Rita Hills ★★★★ £F
Pinot Noir Clos Pepe Vineyard Sta. Rita Hills ★★★★ £F

Margerum (Santa Barbara) *www.margerumwinecompany.com*
Doug Margerum had been in the wine business for 20 years before establishing his own small volume boutique winery operation. He operates out of a small space just behind the BRANDER winery, outside Los Olivos. His is a garage sized operation and like many newly established producers he is creating handcrafted wines from a range of sites and terroirs. With the exception of his Columbia Valley Pinot Gris from Washington State including a second label Klickitat, the wines are from warmer climate Santa Barbara yet all the wines have a vibrancy and fresh poised character. Sauvignon Blanc Sybarite is from a number of sites in the Happy Canyon area of Santa Ynez. Among the range of reds there are Rhône red blends, two Grenaches and a Pinot Noir. The two Syrahs included below are particularly striking. The Colson Canyon bottling is the most subtle and least obvious but opens up with lovely fleshy fruit on the palate and impressive length. The Black Oak Vineyard is savoury and spicy with marked licorice and black pepper in abundance. They are structured and ageworthy. A top blend of Santa Barbara County Syrah's, ÜBER, comes from a number of sites. (DM)

Recommended Reds:
Syrah Black Oak Vineyard Santa Ynez Valley ★★★★ £F
Syrah Colson Canyon Vineyard Santa Ynez Valley ★★★★ £F
Recommended Whites:
Sauvignon Blanc Sybarite Happy Valley Santa Ynez Valley ★★★☆ £D
Pinot Gris Margerum Ranch Columbia Valley ★★☆ £C

Mer Soleil Winery (Monterey) *www.mersoleilvineyard.com*
Several different varieties are cultivated at this small vineyard and winery near Santa Lucia. The focus is mainly on the full-on Chardonnay which is stylish and powerful and possesses an excellent balance of ripe fruit and well-judged oak. The Wagner family also runs CAYMUS in the Napa Valley and supplies the fruit for an attractive, nutty Marsanne/Viognier blend under the TREANA label in partnership with Paso Robles grape growers the Hope family. The small range is completed by a number of single vineyard Pinot Noirs under the Belle Glos label and an unoaked Chardonnay, Silver. (DM)

Mer Soleil
Recommended Whites:
Chardonnay Reserve Santa Lucia Highlands ★★★☆ £E
Belle Glos
Recommended Reds:
Pinot Noir Taylor Lane Vineyard Sonoma Coast ★★★☆ £F

Pinot Noir Las Alturas Vineyard Santa Lucia Highlands ★★★ £F
Pinot Noir Clarke and Telephone Vineyard Santa Maria Valley ★★★ £F

Morgan Winery (Monterey County) *www.morganwinery.com*
Small to medium-sized warehouse winery. Chardonnay, Pinot Noir and Syrah are mainly sourced from the Santa Lucia Highlands and Monterey with a small amount of Chardonnay also coming from Arroyo Seco. These are first-class sources for the Burgundy varieties. Pinot Noirs come from Rosella's, Double L, Tondre Grapefield and Gary's vineyards in the Santa Lucia Highlands and are a step up from the regular bottling. Chardonnays from two different vineyards – Double L and McIntyre – have replaced the Reserve bottling. The Syrah G17 is classy in a cooler, spicier style with a touch of Grenache and Tempranillo included and there are additional examples from the Double L Vineyard and a Santa Lucia Highlands vineyards blend Tierra Mar. Look out also for a southern Rhône-style Côtes du Crow's, a blend of Syrah and Grenache. The cool-grown Monterey Sauvignon Blanc is good value, full and ripe with a hint of Alexander Valley fruit adding complexity. It is part barrel-fermented. An additional and well priced range of approachable wines has also been added under the Lee Familly Farm umbrella. These include Grenache, Tempranillo and a Portuguese style red blend Rio Tinto as well as a rosé and whites from Albarino and Torrontes. Most of the wines will drink well young; the single-vineyard bottlings will stand a little age. (DM)
Recommended Reds:
Syrah Tierra Mar Monterey County ★★★☆ £F
Syrah G17 Monterey County ★★★ £D
Pinot Noir Twelve Clones Santa Lucia Highlands ★★★ £E
Recommended Whites:
Chardonnay Monterey County ★★★ £D
Sauvignon Blanc Monterey County ★★☆ £C

Mount Eden Vineyards (Santa Cruz) *www.mounteden.com*
The whole Mount Eden range is characteristic of the best of the Santa Cruz Mountains. The wines are deep, powerful and reserved. All will benefit from cellaring. The Pinot is a big, rich style, whereas the Cabernet Sauvignons are tight and backward in their youth with considerable structure and grip. An Old Vine Reserve Cabernet is also released. They need time to soften the initially austere mountain tannins. Chardonnay is particularly good: restrained in style with subtle citrus fruit and fine-grained nutty, spicy oak held in the background. A Reserve is also made. The wines have real depth and complexity. More approachable wines are released under the Domaine Eden umbrella and there is also now a Chardonnay Edna Valley Wolff bottling. (DM)
Recommended Reds:
Pinot Noir Estate Santa Cruz Mountains ★★★☆ £F
Cabernet Sauvignon Estate Santa Cruz Mountains ★★★ £F
Recommended Whites:
Chardonnay Estate Santa Cruz Mountains ★★★★☆ £F

Municipal Winemakers *www.municipalwinemakers.com*
Although a native Californian, Dave Potter spent his formative winemaking years in Australia, graduating at Curtin University in Margaret River and working for Fosters on a number of their leading brands, as well as stints at HENSCHKE in the Barossa Valley, Ch. de Montfaucon in the Rhône Valley and Fess PARKER in his native Santa Barbara County. His Australian experience has led him to a down to earth philosophy about what his wines should be and where they stand in the market place which gives them an outstanding

quality/price ratio. He makes a Kabinett style Riesling, labelled Bright White, reminiscent of a Riesling from the Clare Valley in South Australia – citrussy and aromatic with a little steeliness underneath. The redcurrant scented Bright Red (Grenache/Cinsault/Counoise and Syrah) is more a food wine that a show wine. An increasing and diverse range of wines are now being made and its worth checking out the winery website for full details. At the pricier end these include a Kick On Riesling, a Grenache from the Fox Family Vineyard and a Pinot Noir, Rita's Crown from the highest slopes in the Sta. Rita Hills. (NB)
Recommended Reds:
Bright Red Santa Barbara County ★★☆ £C
Recommended Whites:
Bright White Santa Barbara County ★★☆ £C

Nadeau (Paso Robles) *www.nadeaufamilyvintners.com*
Small Zinfandel specialist based to the West of Paso Robles also producing small quantities of Grenache, Mataro and Petite Sirah. A rosé and two red blends are also made. RVR is a Rhône style, Mixed Black comprising Zinfandel, Petite Sirah and Grenache. The vineyards are planted on well-drained slopes and are dry-farmed. An ideal exposure ensures long sunny days, the vineyards being just above the fog line that drifts in through the Templeton Gap. The Bouncer, produced from a number of vineyard sites, is the most obviously upfront, vibrant and juicy of the wines, showing just a touch of new American oak. The massive, brambly and spicy, Critical Mass is the most exciting of the wines and is softer and suppler. (DM)
Recommended Reds:
Zinfandel Critical Mass Paso Robles ★★★ £D
Zinfandel The Bouncer Paso Robles ★★☆ £C

✿ Ojai (Ventura County) *www.ojaivineyard.com*
Originally involved with Jim Clendenen at AU BON CLIMAT, Adam Tolmach founded his own operation in the mid-1980s. Top Syrah has always been a focal point here and these are always classy, superbly crafted wines – subtle and restrained with real depth, and very different from the many overblown, overripe examples produced elsewhere. Chardonnay, Pinot Noir and Sauvignon are also very impressive in a bewildering number of vineyard guises, often varying from year to year. The very good value Ojai White combines Sauvignon Blanc and Chardonnay while the whites also include a late harvested Riesling as well as an exotic dry version from the Kick On Ranch and a Roll Ranch Viognier. . (DM)
Recommended Reds:
Syrah Bien Nacido Vineyard Santa Maria Valley ★★★★☆ £F
Syrah Santa Barbara County ★★★☆ £E
Pinot Noir Bien Nacido Vineyard Santa Maria Valley ★★★★ £F
Recommended Whites:
Chardonnay Bien Nacido Vineyard Santa Maria Valley ★★★★ £E
Sauvignon Blanc McGinley Vineyard Santa Ynez Valley ★★★☆ £D

✿ Palmina (Santa Ynez Valley) *www.palminawines.com*
Steve Clifton produces Burgundian varietals in partnersip with Greg Brewer at BREWER-CLIFTON as well as this his own label, which are among the most exciting Italian style wines from the Central Coast and indeed in California. Steve and wife Chrystal are regular travellers to Italy, visiting producers there to gain as much insight as possible into the characteristics of the wines they produce, while retaining their own Santa Barbara identity from the myriad of mesoclimates that the County posesses. Whites are all fermented in stainless steel to emphasise their subtle varietal perfume while

reds are aged in mainly used oak supporting the strong fruit and fresh acidity of Sangiovese and Nebbiolo. The Traminer is lightly aromatic, more Italian than Alsatian. There is a good, clean fresh and lightly nutty Santa Barbara Pinot Grigio. This is also the source for a lighter, elegant Arneis and a convincing intense, grassy, nutty Tocai Friulano. The range of whites are completed by a fine ripe intensely aromatic Malvasia Bianca along with Subida, a Tocai Friulano vinified with extended skin contact which has not yet been tasted. Nebbiolo comes from a number of sites, the Sisquoc Vineyard bottling below offering greater depth and a firmer structure than the Stolpman. The wines both offer impressive varietal purity without some of the sturdier tannin and acidity you are likely to encounter in top examples from Piedmont. In addition a Santa Barbara example is also well priced (£D) and there are more expensive wines from the Honea Vineyard (£F) and a special cuvée Rocca (£F) made in tiny quantities. The Alisos cuvée is a blend of 75% Sangiovese and the balance Merlot which rounds the palate out and softens the wines structure. The Undici is more seriously structured, the Cliftons touching their caps to Tuscany's best examples of Sangiovese. Barbera is also made from Santa Barbara County sources as well as examples from the Alisos Vineyard and Walker Vineyard in Santa Ynez. A Santa Barbara County is well priced (£C) while the much pricier Savoia (£F) is a blend of Nebbiolo, Barbera and Syrah. The top reds have real density and substance and will develop well in bottle for up to a decade. (DM)

Recommended Reds:
Nebbiolo Sisquoc Vineyard Santa Maria ★★★★ £E
Undici 11 Santa Ynez Valley ★★★★ £E
Nebbiolo Stolpman Vineyard Santa Ynez ★★★★ £E
Alisos Alisos Vineyard Santa Ynez ★★★☆ £E

Recommended Whites:
Tocai Friulano Honea Vineyard Santa Ynez ★★★☆ £D
Malvasia Bianca Santa Barbara County ★★★☆ £D
Arneis Honea Vineyard Santa Ynez Valley ★★★ £D
Pinot Grigio Santa Barbara County ★★★ £C
Traminer Alisos Vineyard Santa Barbara County ★★★ £C

Recommended Rosés:
Botasea Rosato di Palmina Santa Barbara County ★★☆ £C

Peachy Canyon Winery (Paso Robles) *www.peachycanyon.com*
Long established Zinfandel specialist on the Central Coast with a range dominated by reds. A Chardonnay and a Viognier are also made as well as a Port style late harvest red. The red Zins are ripe and spicy with decent berry fruit, particularly the concentrated Especial from the Mustang Springs. Doug Beckett also produces a number of other solid reds. Incredible Red and Westside are now solely Zin, the Westside used to have a touch of Carignane. As well as the Old School House Cabernet Sauvignon there is a premium bottling, Devine Cab, which is a blend of the better estate vineyards. Para Siempre combines Merlot with the Cabernets Sauvignon and Franc. The range now also includes Paso Robles Syrah and further Zins, Vortex, Snow Vineyard, Mustard Creek and Mustard Springs. Petite Sirah is also made along with Cirque de Vin a well priced (£C) mainly Bordeaux blend and Sin Nombre, an unusual blend of Caladoc, Marselan and a little Cabernet Sauvignon. (DM)

Recommended Reds:
Zinfandel Especial Paso Robles ★★★ £E
Zinfandel Westside Paso Robles ★★ £C
Para Siempre Paso Robles ★★★ £E
Cabernet Sauvignon Old School House Paso Robles ★★ £D
Incredible Red Paso Robles ★☆ £B

⊛ Piedrasassi (Santa Barbara County) *www.piedrasassi.com*
This very small volume label is led by Sashi Moorman the winemaker at STOLPMAN VINEYARDS. The Piedrasassi Syrah is sourced from a number of vineyard sites including Sebastiano, HARRISON-CLARKE, Rim Rock and Spanish Springs Vineyards. The varied components provide a wine of intense weight and concentration as well as surpising complexity, with a markedly *sauvage* quality and real mineral purity. Vinification is strictly artisanal and a sizeable proportion of whole bunches are used and the fruit is given around a months cold soak. Aging is in neutral larger oak up to 500 litres. The wine should develop well for at least a decade. The small range has now been expanded to include a slightly pricier cool climate Rim Rock Syrah from San Luis Obispo, a second approachable, fruit driven Syrah PS, a Lompoc Wine Co. Pinot from the Sta. Rita Hills and a Central Coast White from Albariño and Sauvignon Blanc. A Santa Barbara Syrah and a Chardonnay are available exclusively from the small tasting room under the Vineland label. (DM)

Recommended Reds:
Piedrasassi Syrah Central Coast ★★★★☆ £F

Pipestone (Paso Robles) *www.pipestonevineyards.com*
This small property is located on the Westside of Paso Robles and its vineyards overlook the Templeton Gap. The rocky, calcareous soils and a *terroir* cooled by evening breezes off the Pacific provide an excellent environment for growing top quality Rhône varieties. The wines have a piercing and impressive fruit character with a striking minerality and lashings of oak in the reds. The Viognier is very aromatic in style with a marked peachy, spicy character in contrast to many more restrained and textured examples found elsewhere. The Viognier is aged on fine lees in oak for just over 6 months. The Rhône Style Red is a blend of Grenache, Syrah and Mourvèdre and is more obviously fruit driven than the Estate Syrah, which is firmer and more structured and gets a little new French and American oak for ageing. A Grenache, Mourvèdre, Zinfandel and Syrah/Cabernet Sauvignon are also produced along with two Reserves a Syrah and a blend Chateauneuf du Pipe. (DM)

Recommended Reds:
Syrah Estate Paso Robles ★★★☆ £D
Rhône Style Red Paso Robles ★★★ £D

Recommended Whites:
Viognier Paso Robles ★★★ £D

>> Precedent Wine (Contra Costa County) *www.precedentwine.com*
Precedent is a small artisan operation based in Contra Costa County to the east of San Francisco. Owner/winemaker Nathan Kandler is a firm believer in terroir and bringing a real sense of place to his wines. His vineyard sources are sustainably farmed, wine making is with natural yeasts and bottling with minimal sulphur, unfined and unfiltered. His Old Vine White is a Riesling sourced from the Wirz Vineyard and a patch of dry-farmed, head trained old vines now over 60 years old. Vinification is distinctly different from many established "classic" examples you may be familiar with from Germany, Alsace or Austria. Whole bunch pressing then slow barrel fermentation in used French oak followed by the malolactic fermentation. The result is a wine with a rich opulent texture, zesty fresh acidity and hints of floral, citrus and peach fruits. Nathan Kandler also makes a dry Chenin Blanc from Clement Hills in Lodi. Among his reds he also currently produces a Zinfandel, which is also Contra Costa County sourced from the Evangelho Vineyard. Earlier releases included a Syrah from the Bennett Valley in Sonoma County and a Pinot Noir from Marin County. (DM)

Recommended Reds:
Zinfandel Evangelho Vineyard Contra Costa County ★★★★ £E
Recommended Whites:
Old Vine White Wirz Vineyard Cienega Valley ★★★☆ £D
Chenin Blanc Sec Clement Hills Lodi ★★★☆ £D

Quady (Madera County) *www.quadywinery.com*
Fortified- and sweet-wine specialist based in the arid Central
Valley. Red Starboard is a port style produced from Amador County
Zinfandel while the whites are produced from Muscat: Essencia from
Orange Muscat and Elysium from Black Muscat. These are good,
well-crafted examples if lacking the richness and finesse of the very
best European and Australian equivalents. A vintage port style is
also made along with a Palomino Fino sherry style aged under a *flor*
yeast cover in the traditional style. (DM)
Recommended Reds:
Starboard Amador County ★★☆ £D
Recommended Whites:
Essencia Madera ★★★ £D   Elysium Madera ★★☆ £D

❀ Qupé (Santa Maria Valley) *www.qupe.com*
One of the first and still one of the finest of the California Rhône
Rangers, Bob Lindquist's winery has recently been purchased by
Charles Banks and his Terroirs Selections operation which owns
MAYACAMAS in the Napa and MULDERBOSCH and other operations
in South Africa. Lindquist shares winemaking facilities and a similar
vision with Jim Clendenen at AU BON CLIMAT. The wines here are
of a uniformly high standard; both reds and whites are subtle and
elegant and very well crafted. The Bien Nacido Vineyard is the main
source of fruit but Lindquist also farms the Ibarra-Young Vineyard
on biodynamic principles and has established his own Sawyer
Lindquist Vineyard in the Edna Valley from which Viognier and
Marsanne as well as Syrah and Grenache are now being released.
The white Bien Nacido Cuvée blends Chardonnay and Viognier. The
fresh and forward, black fruited Maxtap Cuvée is a combination
of Syrah, Grenache, Tempranillo and Mourvèdre. Richer and more
serious is the Los Olivos Cuvée a Rhône blend of Syrah, Mourvèdre
and Grenache. There are a couple of Bien Nacido Syrahs, the Hillside
Estate often of 5-star quality, as well as a regular Central Coast
bottling which is lighter and quite peppery. Recent Syrah additions
to the range now include bottlings from Stolpman, Alisos and
Purisima Mountain vineyards. A barrel selection Syrah "Sonnies" (£F)
is also now made from the Sawyer Lindquist property and only in
exceptional vintages comes a Syrah Bien Nacido X Block which is
pretty pricey compared with the rest of the range (£G). The whites
should be broached relatively young; the top reds will evolve very
well over 5 or 6 years. (DM)
Recommended Reds:
Syrah Bien Nacido Hillside Estate Santa Maria Valley ★★★★☆ £F
Syrah Sawyer Lindquist Vineyard Edna Valley★★★★ £E
Syrah Bien Nacido Vineyard Santa Maria Valley★★★★ £E
Syrah Alisos Vineyard Santa Barbara County ★★★★ £E
Syrah Purisima Mountain Vineyard Santa Ynez Valley ★★★★ £E
Syrah Stolpman Vineyard Santa Ynez Valley ★★★★ £E
Syrah Central Coast ★★★ £C
Los Olivos Cuvée Santa Ynez Valley ★★★★ £E
Maxtap Cuvée Central Coast ★★★ £C
Recommended Whites:
Roussanne Bien Nacido Hillside Estate Santa Maria Valley ★★★★☆ £F
Chardonnay Bien Nacido Reserve Santa Maria Valley ★★★★ £E
Chardonnay Y Block Santa Barbara County ★★★ £D

Viognier Ibarra Young Vineyard Santa Ynez Valley ★★★★ £E
Marsanne Bien Nacido Vineyard Santa Maria Valley ★★★☆ £D
Bien Nacido Cuvée Santa Maria Valley ★★★ £D

Rancho Sisquoc (Santa Maria Valley) *www.ranchosisquoc.com*
This is a relatively long-established name in Santa Barbara County
among a plethora of new and emerging producers. Some 130
ha (320 acres) of vineyard are now planted on the vast 15,000
ha (37,000 acre) Flood ranch. From a fairly extensive range, the
Bordeaux varieties particularly stand out. The vineyards are among
the warmer sites in the Santa Maria Valley but get some respite from
the summer heat as a result of cooling winds and morning fog that
drifts in through the coastal ranges. Sylvaner is a rare impressive
example from California with lightly tropical fruit and a hint of
residual sugar. Chardonnay offers good weight, subtle tropical notes
and and rich texture at this level. Both the Merlot and Sisquoc River
are fruit-driven styles, the latter a cherry-scented blend of Cabernet
Sauvignon, Merlot, Syrah, Sangiovese and Malbec. The Cabernet
Sauvignon is a more seriously structured red, although it is in a
lighter style than others and offers a subtle minty intensity to its
fruit. The top red, Cellar Select, blends Merlot, Cabernet Sauvignon,
Malbec, Cabernet Franc and Petit Verdot, again in a light, subtle
style but with great depth and intensity and just that subtle minty
undercurrent. The top two reds will develop well in bottle. (DM)
Recommended Reds:
Cellar Select Meritage Santa Barbara County ★★★★ £E
Cabernet Sauvignon Santa Barbara County ★★★ £D
Merlot Santa Barbara County ★★☆ £C
Sisquoc River Red Santa Barbara County ★★☆ £C
Recommended Whites:
Chardonnay Santa Barbara County ★★★ £D
Sylvaner Santa Barbara County ★★☆ £B

Renwood (Amador County) *www.renwood.com*
The Italian and Rhône-style wines here are all impressive but it
is the great Zinfandels from old bush vines that really stand out.
Renwood's vineyards are planted at altitude, generally well over
300m (1,000ft) above sea level, and the warm days and cool
summer evenings enable good structure and acidity to be built
up in the fruit. The top Zinfandels, including the Grandpere, are
what super-ripe, concentrated old-vine Zinfandel is all about.
Other premium releases include Merida, Flutist and Musicians Zins.
Good-value can be found in the Premier Old Vine example and fresh
fruit-driven styles with the California and BBQ labels. As well as the
Zinfandels, good quality Barbera and Syrah are made and other reds
also include Tempranillo, Primitivo and a Zinfandel and Syrah blend,
Clarion. In general the wines should be drunk fairly young but the
top Zinfandels will add further complexity with a little age. Among
the small range of whites are Viognier, a Sauvignon Blanc and the
White Wine which blends Vermentino with Sauvignon. (DM)
Recommended Reds:
Zinfandel Amador Ice Wine Amador County ★★★☆ £E
Zinfandel Grandpere Amador County ★★★☆ £E
Zinfandel Premier Old Vine Amador County ★★★ £C
Zinfandel California ★★ £B   Barbera Amador County ★★★ £C
Syrah Amador County ★★★ £C
Recommended Whites:
Viognier Amador County ★★☆ £C

❀❀ Ridge Vineyards (Santa Cruz Mountains) *www.ridgewine.com*
This is one of California's great wineries producing some

Central Coast & Sierra Foothills

outstanding, particularly single vineyard wines. It is worth looking at the website to see the full range. Chardonnay, both Santa Cruz Mountains and the premium Monte Bello, is in a classically Burgundian style, intense but restrained. Some utterly superb and very complex Zinfandels are handcrafted from a range of sources. These include the Pagani Ranch, which contains some Alicante Bouschet and Petite Sirah, and York Creek, with increasing amounts of Petite Sirah. There is also one of the best examples of varietal Petite Sirah (so often hard and unyielding). The great Geyserville red is usually around two-thirds Zin with both Carignane and Petite Sirah in the blend. A Syrah/Grenache blend and varietal Syrah and Grenache are also now produced from the Lytton Estate and, sticking with the southern California theme, Paul Draper also now produces a Carignane from Buchignani Ranch. The greatest Ridge wine is the meritage Monte Bello, unquestionably one of the state's finest and longest-living Cabernet-based reds. Whether some of the newer Napa Valley super-premium examples will stand the test of time like these remains to be seen. (DM)

Recommended Reds:
Monte Bello Santa Cruz Mountains ✪✪✪✪✪ £H
Cabernet Sauvignon Estate Santa Cruz Mountains ★★★★ £E
Geyserville Alexander Valley ★★★★★ £E
Zinfandel Lytton Springs Vineyard Dry Creek Valley ★★★★☆ £E
Zinfandel Pagani Ranch Sonoma Valley ★★★★☆ £E
Zinfandel York Creek ★★★★ £E Petite Sirah Lytton Estate ★★★★ £E
Recommended Whites:
Chardonnay Estate Santa Cruz Mountains ★★★★ £E

⊛ RN Estate Vineyard (Paso Robles) *www.rnestate.com*
French émigré and hotelier Roger Nicolas released his first vintage here in 2005. Specialising in Rhône and Bordeaux varietals from his own vineyard, he also produces a little Pinot Noir which he buys in. One could say that a Gallic influence prevails, for the wines are uniformly balanced with a great deal of finesse. Pinot Noir from the Fiddlestix Vineyard in the Sta. Rita Hills has deep colour, supple tannin with good fruit and body. A second and marginally more expensive example comes from the Solomon Hills Vineyard in the Santa Maria Valley. East Knoll Cuvée is a blend of Syrah and Zinfandel which are fermented together for 20 months in French and American barrels. Although approaching 14% abv, the wine is surprisingly light, but elegant – probably one to drink young. Cuvée des Artistes is Syrah, Cabernet Sauvignon, Zinfandel and now a touch of Petit Verdot– it's elegant, too. His top blend is a classic Bordeaux style, Harmonie des Cépages combining Cabernet Sauvignon, Cabernet Franc, Merlot, Malbec and Petit Verdot aged for 20 months in French oak, this wine is supple, fruity and elegant with lovely complexity, good length and an explosion of black fruit. It is to be noted that Roger is really a small producer with around 120 to 250 cases of the reds made each year. (NB)

Recommended Reds:
Harmonie des Cépages Paso Robles ★★★★☆ £F
Pinot Noir Fiddlestix Vineyard Sta. Rita Hills ★★★★ £F
Cuvée de Artistes Paso Robles ★★★☆ £F
East Knoll Cuvée Paso Robles ★★★ £E

Rosenblum Cellars (Alameda) *www.rosenblumcellars.com*
The Rosenblum warehouse winery is located in the San Francisco Bay area in central Alameda. The main focus here is on Zinfandel and very good it is too. Even in a difficult years the wines stand out for their intensity, purity and depth and the top examples show really splendid complexity. Numerous bottlings are sourced from

a diversity of regions – Contra Costa to Paso Robles to Sonoma's Alexander Valley. Among other wines the main focus is on the Rhône Valley. There are good budget level wines (£B) released under the Vintners Cuvée label. There are also some impressive late-harvest bottlings including an excellent Black Muscat from the Gallagher Ranch in Madera County. Former winemaker Jeff Cohn also produces a small amount of very good Syrah under his own JC CELLARS label and has done much to create the splendid substance of this range. (DM)

Recommended Reds:
Zinfandel Maggie's Reserve Sonoma Valley ★★★★ £F
Zinfandel Winemaker Selection Sonoma County ★★★★ £F
Zinfandel Richard Sauret Reserve Paso Robles ★★★☆ £E
Zinfandel Carla's Reserve Contra Costa County ★★★☆ £E
Zinfandel Eagle Point Ranch Mendocino County ★★★ £D
Syrah England Shaw Vineyard Solano County ★★★☆ £E
Black Muscat Gallagher Ranch Madera County ★★★ £E

Rusack (Santa Ynez Valley) *www.rusackvineyards.com*
The Rusacks produce a good small range of reds and whites from across Santa Barbara County. As well as the three main varietals of Chardonnay, Pinot Noir and Syrah they also produce Sauvignon Blanc, a Bordeaux blend of Merlot and Cabernet Franc called Anacapa, Zinfandel and Sangiovese, all from Santa Ynez fruit. Then there's a rosé from Syrah and Pinot Noir. The three Santa Barbara County labelled wines rated below offer good varietal character and are softer and more accessible than the Reserve bottlings. Pinot Noir also comes in a Santa Maria Valley bottling. The Santa Maria Reserve Chardonnay is aged in nearly all new wood and gets 9 months ageing as does the generic bottling. It is tighter, more structured with less obvious fruit than the regular Santa Barbara wine. Both wines go through around 50% malolactic to both preserve acidity and add weight and texture. The Reserve Pinot Noir is sourced from cooler Sta. Rita Hills fruit, including the Huber, Fiddlestix and Rancho Santa Rosa vineyards. Both Pinot Noirs are given a cold soak and aged in French oak (around one-third new). The Reserve is much the more backward of the two with dark and intense mineral fruit slowly opening out on the palate. Syrah from Santa Barbara County is supple and forward, the Ballard Canyon Reserve darker, loaded with spicy black pepper fruit and rounded out by well chiselled tannins. Both are given a cold soak and the Ballard Canyon sees a touch more new wood although this is very well integrated. Pinot Noir, Chardonnay and Zinfandel are also now being released from the Santa Catalina Island Vineyards the Rusacks have established on the small island just to the south west of Los Angeles. The top two reds covered will benefit from four or five years, particularly the Syrah. (DM)

Recommended Reds:
Syrah Ballard Canyon Reserve Santa Ynez Valley ★★★★ £E
Pinot Noir Reserve Sta. Rita Hills ★★★☆ £E
Pinot Noir Santa Barbara County ★★★ £D
Recommended Whites:
Chardonnay Reserve Santa Maria Valley ★★★☆ £E
Chardonnay Santa Barbara County ★★★ £D

>> Sandhi Wines (Sta. Rita Hills) *www.sandhiwines.com*
Yet another venture of Raj Parr and Sashi Moorman (Domaine de la CÔTE), Sandhi is a boutique brand that focuses on Pinot Noirs and Chardonnays from top vineyards from the Sta. Rita Hills. *Terroir*, viticulture and cellar practices make a trifecta of the elements necessary to produce stellar wines. Their vineyards utilize

fruit sources that are carefully selected, taking into consideration the quality and balanced character. The farming is done in a collaborative fashion, in accordance with Moorman's specifications. The wines boast high acidity, salinity and minerality and are undeniably elegant. Moorman's background includes stints as a chef, working alongside Adam Tolmach at the OJAI Vineyard, and multi-year employment at STOLPMAN Vineyard. All wines are fermented using wild yeasts. Pinot Noirs see 100% stem inclusion to add energy, complexity, and structure. (IT)

Recommended Reds:

Pinot Noir "La Côte" Sta. Rita Hills ★★★★ £F
Pinot Noir "Sanford and Benedict" Sta. Rita Hills ★★★☆ £F

Recommended Whites:

Chardonnay Rita's Crown Sta. Rita Hills ★★★★☆ £F
Chardonnay Mt. Carmel Sta. Rita Hills ★★★★ £F
Chardonnay "Bentrock" ★★★★ £F
Chardonnay "Sanford and Benedict" Sta. Rita Hills ★★★☆ £F

Sanford Winery (Sta. Rita Hills) *www.sanfordwinery.com*
Located in the cool Sta. Rita Hills, Sanford produces good to very good Chardonnay and Pinot Noir. Richard Sanford has now sold his interest so it remains to be seen how quality will emerge in the longer term. One of the key assets here is the great Sanford and Benedict Vineyard, from which a number of winemakers have crafted some of the finest examples of Pinot Noir and Chardonnay to have emerged from California. Pinot Noir bottlings, particularly La Rinconada and a couple of premium labels from the same vineyard, Vista Al Rio and Dominio Del Falcon, are laden with intense berry fruit and well-judged oak. Chardonnay is in a ripe tropical style, with plenty of wood. (DM)

Recommended Reds:

Pinot Noir La Riconada Vineyard Sta. Rita Hills ★★★★ £F
Pinot Noir Sta. Rita Hills ★★☆ £E

Recommended Whites:

Chardonnay Sanford and Benedict Vineyard Sta. Rita Hills ★★★★ £F
Chardonnay La Rinconada Sta. Rita Hills ★★★☆ £E
Chardonnay Sta. Rita Hills ★★☆ £D

✪✪ Saxum (Paso Robles) *www.saxumvineyards.com*
This recently established Rhône style specialist has rapidly emerged as an icon producer among the new wave of Paso Robles. Syrah is the leading variety with the varietal Bone Rock. There are also four Rhône style blends: Broken Stones, James Berry, Heartstone and Terry Hoage vineyards from a varying mix of Grenache, Mourvèdre, Syrah and Counoise. The recently added Paderewrski Vineyard red combines Zinfandel with Mourvèdre, Tempranillo and Petite Sirah. The Syrah Bone Rock comes from his family's James Berry vineyard. Broken Stones is in fact mainly Syrah with the balance Grenache, Mourvèdre and a small proportion of Petite Sirah. The fruit is sourced not only from the home James Berry vineyard but also from the Denner and Heartstone vineyards. A small winery has now been established, the wines were originally produced at the now closed Garretson facility. All the vineyard sources for the wines are located on the Westside of Paso Robles and offer fruit of brilliant intensity and depth. The approach in the winery is as one would expect, very minimalist, with low sulphur levels and the wines are kept on their fine lees. Despite alcohol levels often over 15% all the wines retain an excellent balance and purity in much the same way as the great traditional reds from Châteauneuf-du-Pape. Rich, spicy black pepper fruits, with a hint of minerality and real depth mark the wines. Expect all to develop very well over five to seven years and keep

considerably longer. Auction prices are now stupendous. (DM)

Recommended Reds:

Syrah Bone Rock Paso Robles ✪✪✪✪✪ £G
Broken Stones Red Paso Robles ✪✪✪✪✪ £G
James Berry Vineyard Red Paso Robles ★★★★★ £G
Heartstone Vineyard Red Paso Robles ★★★★★ £F

✪ Sea Smoke Cellars (Sta. Rita Hills) *www.seasmoke.com*
Newly established operation with some spectacularly sited vineyards in the western Sta. Rita Hills to the north of the Santa Ynez river overlooking the Sanford and Benedict and Fiddlestix sites and planted on south facing bluffs. Pinot Noir comes in three guises and these are some of the best examples from the area. They are produced solely from the Sea Smoke property, which is rare for the region. In the winery a cold soak is employed for all the fruit and all three wines are bottled unfiltered. The Botella version is ripe and forward, a selection across the various blocks of the property. The Southing is richer and fuller with firmer tannins and an impressively intense mineral undercurrent. More new wood is used (around 65%) although in many respects this is more successful than Ten, the fullest and densest example with formidable concentration, which is aged in 100% new wood after a longer vatting of up to a month. Expect the top two wines to develop well for up to a decade. Most recently added are Sea Spray a Blancs de Noirs sparkler and Streamside a premium Sta. Rita Hills Chardonnay. (DM)

Recommended Reds:

Pinot Noir Ten Sta. Rita Hills ★★★★☆ £G
Pinot Noir Southing Sta. Rita Hills ★★★★ £F
Pinot Noir Botella Sta. Rita Hills ★★★☆ £E

✪✪ Sine Qua Non (Ventura County) *www.sinequanon.com*
This really is the quintessential California garage winery. Warehouse style wineries have been an established feature of the industry in California for many years. Until recently the Krankl's owned no vineyards themselves and the wines can be very difficult to follow due to alarmingly regular name changes. They are though the epitome of the finest quality artisan winemaking: rich, opulent and always produced from the finest fruit. Pinot Noir is no longer made however an example of impressive purity and rich berry fruit (★★★★★) was sourced from the Shea Vineyard in Oregon. Most recently labelled Omega, previously it has been named A Capella, Veiled and Left Field. A second Pinot Noir has also been released which is sourced from a number of California sites and 2005 saw the last Pinot Noir, Over and Out from Santa Barbara. If you encounter these wines they are likely to be at their peak bur ir is a case of *caveat emptor* with their age. There is a blend of Roussanne, Viognier and Chardonnay mainly from Central Coast sources. Petit Manseng in small proportions is also now included. Krankl has also made a 100% Roussanne and Vin de Paille straw wine styles have also come from Marsanne and Rousanne. A varietal Chardonnay from the Bien Nacido has also now been made from the 2012 vintage, Pearl Clutcher. Recent releases of Syrah have included a little Grenache and Petite Sirah, in 2012 the wine labelled Syrah Stock. A number of Grenache dominated reds are also now made with an increasing use of recently developed estate vineyards. They are impressive rivals to some of the great single vineyard and special *cuvée* bottles from Châteauneuf-du-Pape. Indeed Krankl is also involved in a partnership with CLOS SAINT JEAN producing a single top wine from that appellation. The home Cumulus Vineyard is also a source of two reds under the Next of Kyn banner, a Syrah and a Rhône styled blend of Grenache, Syrah, Mourvèdre, Petite Sirah and Touriga

California

Nacional. Krankl has also made Eiswein from either Gewürztraminer or Viognier, a Vin de Paille from Sémillon and occasional botrytis Viogniers. The wines are not only of the highest quality but inevitably extremely pricey and very scarce. (DM)

Recommended Reds:

Grenache/Syrah/Mourvèdre California ✪✪✪✪✪ £H

Recommended Whites:

Roussanne/Viognier/Chardonnay California ✪✪✪✪✪ £H

⚜ **Stolpman (Santa Ynez Valley)** *www.stolpmanvineyards.com*
The wines here have developed considerably in recent vintages with a new focus on white and red Rhône varietals. In addition Sangiovese is also now planted in the home vineyards. Jeff Newton provides vital input in the vineyards and the vines are now much closer planted. The winemaker Sashi Moorman creates wines of really impressive depth and rich concentration. He is also involved in his own micro garage style label PIEDRASASSI. and is a partner in Domaine de la Côte with Rajat Parr and Sandhi Wines with Parr and Charles Banks, former owner of SCREAMING EAGLE. The home vineyard property is sizeable around 90 ha (220 acres) and is located in Ballard Canyon which benefits from cool nights as well as warm sunny days. The top white L'Avion is from Roussanne and is rich, nutty and forward, marked more by its texture than upfront fruit, being fermented at high temperature and aged on fine lees with *bâtonnage*. Ageing in 500 litre 2nd fill barrels also helps to avoid any oakiness. Viognier, including a late harvest version, Sauvignon Blanc and a second Roussanne are also made. La Croce is a vibrant blend of co-fermented Sangiovese and Syrah, both varieties ripening at very similar times, the combined vinification adding further complexity. The dark fruit character of the Syrah adds weight and dimension to the bright dark cherry notes evident in the Sangiovese. Small lot fermentation is the order of the day in small new oak. There is a very good Estate Syrah from a mix of clones. The very fine top Syrah, Angeli which comes from a selection of the best blocks on the property. While the Estate Syrah is vinified in stainless steel, the Angeli is vatted in small oak and is dark and impressively concentrated, spicy and complex. An extended range of reds also includes a Petite Sirah, a Grenache, an Estate Sangiovese, a number of additional Syrah based reds and La Cuadrilla an approachable Syrah/Sangiovese/Grenache/Petite Sirah blend. (DM)

Recommended Reds:

Angeli Estate Santa Ynez Valley ★★★★☆ £F
La Croce Estate Santa Ynez Valley ★★★★ £F
Syrah Estate Santa Ynez Valley ★★★☆ £E

Recommended Whites:

L'Avion Estate Santa Ynez Valley ★★★☆ £E

Summer Wood (Paso Robles) *www.summerwoodwine.com*
This relatively small winery includes a luxurious four star small guest house on its Paso Robles Westside estate which would make a good base for exploring the area. The vast majority of the winery's output is sold through the tasting room and via their mailing list. Rhône styles are particularly exciting here and include both Syrah and Viognier. Zinfandel is also produced as is Chardonnay and Cabernet Sauvignon. The estate has 19 ha (46 acres) under vine and fruit is sourced from home as well as other Paso Robles vineyards. The Syrah is sourced from three separate vineyards and is aged in 40% new wood. The impressively concentrated Diosa red is dominated by Syrah and comes from among others the highly rated DENNER Vineyard. Ageing is in a mix of French, Hungarian and a little American oak. The Diosa Blanc is a blend of Marsanne, Roussanne and Viognier, the Roussanne giving a really spicy, citrus and lightly nutty edge to the fruit. It enjoys a long cool fermentation and as such should be enjoyed in its relative youth. Both reds will stand a little age. Recent developments have seen single vineyard Syrah and Marsanne from the Alta Colina site added as well as two super-premium reds, the Reserve Cabernet and Sentio labels. Grenache, Grenache Blanc, Viognier and a GSM red blend are also produced. (DM)

Recommended Reds:

Diosa Red Paso Robles ★★★☆ £F   Syrah Paso Robles ★★☆ £E

Recommended Whites:

Diosa Blanc Paso Robles ★★★☆ £F

⚜ **Tablas Creek (Paso Robles)** *www.tablascreek.com*
This is the first major overseas investment for the Perrin brothers of CHÂTEAU DE BEAUCASTEL in Châteauneuf-du-Pape. Along with Robert Haas they have established an important nursery for Rhône Valley planting material and are now producing increasingly impressive red and white blends as the vineyards mature. The range of wines has been consistently increasing over recent vintages and now includes some of the best Rhône style wines on the Central Coast. The red and white Côtes de Tablas are in the mould of top-quality Côtes du Rhône. The red a blend of Grenache, Syrah, Mourvèdre and Counoise, the white Viognier, Grenache Blanc, Marsanne and Roussanne. There is a vibrant and spicy Dianthus rosé which contains a large proportion of Mourvèdre and shares some of the structure of a good Bandol albeit it with with a riper more opulent fruit character. Approachable red, white rosé Patelin de Tablas examples are also made at a marginally lower price.. The top red and white Esprit de Tablas (formerly Esprit de Beaucastel) cuvées are consistently excellent with real depth and persistence. The white a blend of Roussanne, Grenache Blanc and just a touch of Viognier, the red is dominated by Mouvèdre with a small amount of Syrah and less Grenache and Counoise. Offering a firmer structure and grip than many of its neighbours it also offers a softer more accessible approach than can be found in the Beaucastel wines. A 100% Roussanne is one of an increasing number of varietal wines made. It is part barrel-fermented and there are tiny amounts of Antithesis, a full-blown style of Chardonnay, as well as Panoplie, a wine based on Mourvèdre and made when vintage conditions favour and recently Full Circle Pinot Noir. Additional white varietal labelled wines now made are Petit Manseng, Marsanne, Picpoul Blanc, Vermentino and Viognier. Reds are from Syrah, Tannat and Mourvèdre. The range is completed by a small amount of three Vin de Paille wines and a new En Gobelet label has been added coming from dry farmed and head pruned vines, it combines Grenache, Mourvèdre, Syrah and Tannat. (DM)

Recommended Reds:

Esprit de Tablas Paso Robles ★★★★☆ £F
Côtes de Tablas Paso Robles ★★★☆ £D

Recommended Whites:

Esprit de Tablas Paso Robles ★★★★☆ £E
Roussanne Paso Robles ★★★★ £E
Côtes de Tablas Paso Robles ★★★☆ £D

Recommended Rosés:

Dianthus Rosé Paso Robles ★★★ £C

Robert Talbott (Monterey County) *www.talbottvineyards.com*
Small operation with vineyard resources in the Salinas Foothills and Santa Lucia Mountains. There are four regular Chardonnays, Kali-Hart, Logan, Sleepy Hollow and the pricier Diamond T Estate,

which is a marvellously stylish cool-climate example, delivering very fine fruit from low yields with very well judged, fine-grained oak and a rich leesy complexity. It is bottled unfined and unfiltered. The Diamond T is among the best on the Central Coast and has been joined by another limited release, Cuvée Sarah. Look out also for recently added Pinot Noir, which include the same brands as the Chardonnays as well as two super premium wines Sarah and RFT. Expect quality to match the whites. (DM)

Recommended Whites:
Chardonnay Diamond T Estate★★★★☆ £F
Chardonnay Sleepy Hollow★★★★ £E
Chardonnay Kali-Hart Vineyard★★★☆ £E
Chardonnay Logan★★★ £D

Talley Vineyards (Arroyo Grande) *www.talleyvineyards.com*
First-class estate Chardonnay and Pinot Noir are made here using sustainable farming practices at this family owned winery. The Rosemary and Rincon vineyards have tremendous potential and as yet are still relatively young. Both are capable at times of providing wines of 5-star quality. Pinot Noir is produced from very low yields and wild yeasts and new French oak are used in the winery. Chardonnay is reared in the finest French oak and aged on lees to provide additional weight and a rich texture. The Talleys also produce the variety from their Edna Valley Olivers Vineyard site, which is planted exclusively to the variety. Edna Valley is also the source of both an AVA Chardonnay and Pinot Noir. Bishops Peak is their label for a range of nicely crafted, straightforward budget wines. The Talleys are also important suppliers to other producers such as AU BON CLIMAT. (DM)

Recommended Reds:
Pinot Noir Rosemary's Vineyard Arroyo Grande ★★★★ £F
Pinot Noir Rincon Vineyard Arroyo Grande ★★★★ £F
Pinot Noir Estate Arroyo Grande ★★★☆ £E

Recommended Whites:
Chardonnay Rosemary's Vineyard Arroyo Grande ★★★★ £F
Chardonnay Rincon Vineyard Arroyo Grande ★★★★ £F
Chardonnay Estate Arroyo Grande ★★★☆ £E

❀ Tantara Winery (Santa Maria Valley) *www.tantarawinery.com*
The Fink and Cates partnership is responsible for a classy Chardonnay and some of the best Pinot to emerge from the Central Coast. Cadence Chardonnay is produced in an opulently tropical style, with a marked citrus undercurrent. A number of single-vineyard bottlings have also been made which offered real depth and style, with a mineral undercurrent and impressive structure. Of the Pinots, the regular Santa Maria bottling is soft, ripe and forward. Of the single-vineyard wines the Santa Maria-sourced Solomon Hills Ranch is rich and showy with loads of dark and spicy fruit; the Dierberg, similarly rich, offers greater depth and dimension from very low yields. The Bien Nacido Adobe is sourced from four separate plots and is surprisingly tight and structured. Typically elegant, piercing and very intense dark fruit is apparent in the Sta. Rita Hills-sourced Rio Vista Vineyard. Two top wines stand out. Evelyn, a homage to Bill Cates' mother produced in minute quantities, is sourced from a number of Santa Maria sites and is loaded with sweet and opulent fruit. In complete contrast, the Pisoni bottling is less exotic, more restrained, but offers remarkable depth and purity. Additional Pinot vineyard sources now include the Bien Nacido Corral blocks, Tondre Grapefield in the Santa Lucia Highlands, La Colline in the Arroyo Grande Valley and from 2012 from the Zotovich Vineyard in the Sta. Rita Hills. Carousal Blanc de

Blancs and Blanc de Noirs sparklers were also made in the 2009 vintage. Give all of the wines 2 or 3 years; the Pisoni Vineyard in particular need 4–5 years to evolve. (DM)

Recommended Reds:
Pinot Noir Evelyn Santa Maria Valley ★★★★★ £G
Pinot Noir Pisoni Vineyard Santa Lucia Highlands ★★★★★ £F
Pinot Noir Adobe Bien Nacido Vineyard ★★★★ £E
Pinot Noir Dierberg Vineyard Santa Maria Valley ★★★★ £E
Pinot Noir Rio Vista Vineyard Rio Vista Vineyard ★★★★ £E
Pinot Noir Solomon Hills Ranch Santa Maria Valley ★★★★ £E
Pinot Noir Santa Maria Valley ★★★☆ £E

Recommended Whites:
Cadence Chardonnay Santa Maria Valley ★★★ £E

❀ Tensley Wines (Santa Barbara County) *www.tensleywines.com*
Joey Tensley has built up an incredible reputation for his Syrah wines since he started up in 1998. Owning no vineyards, but obtaining his fruit from impeccable sources, he has built up production of his vineyard designated wines from 100 cases in his first year to over 3,000 cases now. Wife Jennifer has created her own brand – "Lea", producing Syrah Rosé, Chardonnay and Pinot Noir. The grapes for the Rosé come from a single vineyard, Tierra Alta, and a single Syrah clone, Tablas 99. Yields are low, three tons per acre and the grapes are crushed by foot. Half the fruit had skin contact for only three hours whilst the other half stayed on the skins overnight. There is rich fruit in the wine, and reasonable depth. Under the Tensley label, the Camp 4 Vineyard Blanc is a field blend of Grenache Blanc and Rousanne. It is bottled after a month and a half to preserve freshness. Aromatic with ripe fruit and overtones of pomelo distinguish this wine which can be drunk early or be drunk over the next 2 to 3 years. Joey makes a range of different vineyard designated Syrahs – two were tasted at our last visit. Turner Vineyard Syrah, is vinified in one year old barrels on the gross lees with some 25% to 30% of the grapes being included in whole clusters. The wine is elegant with the impressive finesse of this cool climate vineyard. The Colson Canyon Vineyard Syrah has much more depth and good tarry fruit, a touch of herbaceousness with supple tannins. A new and unusual experiment has resulted from a meeting in California with Cécile Dusserre, the owner and winemaker of the Domaine du MONTVAC in Vacqueras in the southern Rhône Valley. She shipped in bulk some of her Gigondas wine (Grenache, Syrah and Mourvèdre) to Joey who blended it with Syrah from the Colson Canyon Vineyard. The result is a complex blend of fleshy California with the subtle and savoury Gigondas. Two significantly pricier Syrah's are made from a blend of sites. OGT blends Colson Canyon, Thompson Vineyard and Tierra Alta fruit, while BMT comes from Colson Canyon and Rodney's Vineyard and includes around a quarter Grenache with the Syrah components. (NB)

Recommended Reds:
Tensley Syrah Colson Canyon Vineyard Santa Ynez Valley ★★★★☆ £E
Tensley Syrah Turner Vineyard Sta. Rita Hills ★★★★ £E
Détente Colson Canyon Vineyard/Gigondas ★★★★ £F

Recommended Whites:
Tensley Blanc Camp Four Vineyard Santa Barbara County ★★★ £E

Recommended Rosés:
Lea Syrah Rosé Tierra Alta Vineyard Santa Ynez Valley ★★☆ £D

Tercero Wines (Santa Barbara County) *www.tercerowines.com*
Larry Schaffer is the oenologist at Fess PARKER Vineyards but finds a little time to do his own thing as well. Specialising in Rhône red and white varietals, he also produces a notable Gewürztraminer,

Central Coast & Sierra Foothills

The Outlier. With typical lychee aromas, one would expect a much sweeter wine than the full, unctuous dry style produced here. Balanced alcohol making it quite food-friendly too. Camp 4 and Larner Vineyards Mourvèdre is meaty, spicy and deep with hints of leather and violets, whilst his "Cuvée Christie" (Grenache, Syrah, Mourvèdre and Petite Sirah) has all the complex spice, leather and *garrigue* that one would expect from such a blend. A barrel sample of Grenache from the cool-climate Watch Hill Vineyard also showed a great deal of promise on tasting. (NB)

Recommended Reds:
Cuvée Christie Santa Barbara County ★★★★ £E
Mourvèdre Camp 4/Larner Vineyards Santa Ynez Valley ★★★☆ £E
Recommended Whites:
The Outlier Dry Gewürztraminer Santa Barbara County ★★★ £C

Terre Rouge & Easton Wines *www.terrerougewines.com*
Amador County based Bill Easton was one of the very first Rhône Rangers, along with the likes of Randall Grahm at BONNY DOON. Today he produces Rhône styles under the Terre Rouge label, while his Easton label supplies good fruit-driven, spicy Barbera and more serious Zinfandel as well as H House, (a soft easy blend of Cabernet and Syrah), Cabernet Sauvignon and a Sauvignon Blanc. He is based in Amador County and his Shenandoah Valley vineyards are cooled due to their elevation. Syrah is the dominant red variety but in addition there is a Mourvèdre from the Sierra Foothills, minerally Viognier as well as Rousanne including an oxidized style Rox, a Muscat from the Shenandoah Valley and a white blend Enigma (Marsanne, Viognier and Roussanne). The Syrahs as yet offer a little more and are the main focus. The Tête a Tête (Syrah, Mourvèdre & Grenache) is soft and forward, as is the Syrah Côte de l'Ouest. More serious are both the Sierra Foothills and Sentinel Oak Vineyard Pyramid Block Syrahs. At its best the Sentinel bottling is structured and firm with good intensity, more in the style of Côte-Rôtie than Hermitage. Ascent Syrah is a fine barrel selection which sees more new oak: rich, almost opulent with impressive depth and concentration. Top reds will benefit from 4 or 5 years' ageing. (DM)

Domaine de la Terre Rouge
Recommended Reds:
Syrah Ascent Sierra Foothills ★★★★ £G
Syrah Sentinel Oak Vyrd Pyramid Block Shenandoah Valley ★★★☆ £E
Syrah Sierra Foothills ★★★ £D
Syrah Côte l'Ouest California ★★☆ £C
Tête a Tête Sierra Foothills ★★ £C
Recommended Whites:
Viognier Shenandoah Valley ★★★ £E

Easton
Recommended Reds:
Zinfandel Shenandoah Valley ★★★ £D
Barbera Shenandoah Valley ★★☆ £D

✿ **Testarossa (Santa Cruz Mountains)** *www.testarossa.com*
The focus here is top-quality Pinot Noir and Chardonnay along with two red blends the Cabernet based Los Gatos Rob's Red and a Santa Cruz Mountains Meritage. Originally the wines were sourced from Monterey vineyards but the Jensens now scour the whole Central Coast to produce the best possible examples. The range covers no fewer than 25 single-vineyard cuvées as well as appellation wines, which are invariably good to very good indeed, with consistently impressive results. The Pinots are rich and gamey with no shortage of oak; the Chardonnays are riper and fuller than some of the more

minerally, restrained styles elsewhere. They possess a marvellously rich weight and texture and can be enjoyed with just a year or two in bottle. (DM)

Recommended Reds:
Pinot Noir Rosella's Vineyard Santa Lucia Highlands ★★★★☆ £F
Pinot Noir Santa Lucia Highlands ★★★★ £F
Pinot Noir Monterey County ★★★☆ £E
Recommended Whites:
Chardonnay Bien Nacido Vineyard Santa Maria Valley ★★★★ £F
Chardonnay Rosella's Vineyard Santa Lucia Highlands ★★★★ £F
Chardonnay Santa Lucia Highlands ★★★★ £F
Chardonnay Monterey County ★★★☆ £E

✿ **Tobin James Cellars (Paso Robles)** *www.tobinjames.com*
This sizeable Paso Robles operation produces an extensive but exemplary range of wines at all price levels. There is also a sense of fun, with the wines which all have tongue in cheek brand names, many relating to less than lawful characters from the old American West. The winery is built on the site of an old stagecoach stop and the tasting room features an original 1860s Brunswick mahogany bar. The regular range of wines indeed offer a sense of fun and accessible drinking. The Sauvignon Blanc Sundance is bright and grassy but the reds are the mainstay. All impress for their vibrant, spicy fruit character and the rich and brambly Zinfandel Ballistic really stands out. The Chardonnay James Gang Reserve is, like the Sauvignon, sourced from cooler Monterey. Subtle melon and citrus mark the wine more than showy tropical fruit. Reserve reds are the basis of the reputation for quality here and all are very well worth seeking out. You may have to join the mailing list or visit the winery to get hold of them. The Meritage Private Stash is a restrained and elegant Bordeaux blend. Blue Moon Zinfandel is an extraordinarily dense, fiery and muscular example, the epitome of full-blown, dark, spicy Paso Robles Zin. The James Gang Reserve Syrah is opulent, dark and typically spicy, while the benchmark Syrah is the remarkable Blue Moon, sourced like all the best reds here from Westside fruit. The limestone-based, steeply sloped vineyards are barely more than a decade and a half old and stubbornly refuse to produce much more than half a ton per acre. The result is a wine of really impressive density, dimension and fiery intensity. Top reds deserve cellaring. (DM)

Recommended Reds:
Syrah Blue Moon Paso Robles ★★★★☆ £G
Zinfandel Blue Moon Paso Robles ★★★★ £F
Syrah James Gang Reserve Paso Robles ★★★★ £F
Meritage Private Stash Paso Robles ★★★ £F
Cabernet/Syrah James Gang Reserve Paso Robles ★★★ £F
Zinfandel Ballistic Paso Robles ★★★ £C
Syrah Rock-n-Roll Paso Robles ★★ £C
Cabernet Sauvignon Notorious Paso Robles ★★ £C
Sangiovese Primo Paso Robles ★★ £C
Recommended Whites:
Chardonnay James Gang Reserve Monterey County ★★★ £E
Sauvignon Blanc Sundance Monterey County ★☆ £C

Treana (Paso Robles) *www.hopefamilywines.com*
Winemaker AUSTIN HOPE also produces Rhône-style reds under his own label. Here he has long been established as the family winemaker, producing premium Treana wines as well as budget-level wines under the Liberty School label, including Cabernet Sauvignon, Pinot Noir, Merlot, Chardonnay and a blend Cuvée which combines Syrah, Cab Sauv, Grenache, Petite Sirah and a touch

of Viognier. A level up The Treana white is a spicy, peachy blend of Marsanne and Viognier. It is vinified in a mix of stainless steel, neutral oak and just 15% new French oak to emphasise its nutty fruit character. The Treana red is a blend of Syrah and Cabernet Sauvignon. Good structure and a ripe, spicy, almost chocolaty character dominate the wine which offers good depth at a fairly high price. It will be better with 4–5 years' ageing. Merlot and Zinfandel from various sites are released under the Candor label, while the Troublemaker is a non-vintaged Rhône style red blend. These offer decent value (£C). (DM)

Recommended Reds:
Treana Red Paso Robles ★★★☆ £F
Liberty School Cabernet Sauvignon Paso Robles ★☆ £B
Recommended Whites:
Treana White Central Coast ★★★ £E
Liberty School Chardonnay Central Coast ★☆ £B

Villa Creek Cellars (Paso Robles) www.villacreekwine.com
Warehouse operation run by restaurateur Cris Cherry. The wines are the epitome of modern, fleshy, vibrant Paso Robles reds and are undoubtedly among the best and most exciting reds in an already exciting region. The fact that they are extremely affordable is another great bonus. The Avenger and Willow Creek red are both Rhône blends, the Willow Creek bottling with a higher proportion of Syrah, the Avenger dominated more by Grenache. Garnacha is 100% Grenache, with lovely ripe herb spice berry fruit character. Like all the wines here the pH is high but the wines are never manipulated or acidified. The Mas de Maha is a new development, a blend of Tempranillo, Grenache, Mourvèdre and Carignan very much in the style of new wave Rioja but with more exuberant fruit. The most recent vintage being 2009. The top label High Road is Syrah, Mourvèdre and Grenache. Very dense and powerfully structured, it is one of the region's top reds. The fruit comes from the James Berry Vineyard, itself one of the best sources in the region and from which a varietal example is also now released. Continuing the Rhône theme Syrah has also been released from the Bassetti Vineyard and other red releases have included a Mourvèdre labelled Damas Noir, La Boda a Syrah and Mourvèdre blend and Trovador which combines Syrah and Carignan. A premium Cabernet Sauvignon (£F) is also now made from the coastal Carver Vineyard at York Mountain. A well priced white (£D) and labelled as such is a blend of Grenache and Roussanne which comes from the James Berry Vineyard as does a varietal Roussanne. Unlike the other, more accessible reds the High Road deserves 4 or 5 years' patience. (DM)

Recommended Reds:
High Road Paso Robles ★★★★ £F
Avenger Paso Robles ★★★☆ £E
Garnacha Paso Robles ★★★☆ £E
Willow Creek Paso Robles ★★★☆ £E
Mas de Maha Paso Robles ★★★☆ £E

❀ Kenneth Volk (Santa Maria Valley) www.volkwines.com
Ken Volk's winemaking career took off with the creation of the WILD HORSE Winery and Vineyards in 1981 and he remained at the helm for 22 years before selling out to Peak Wines International, a division of Jim Beam Brands Worldwide. Not one for sitting around doing nothing, he purchased the "original" Byron Winery facility from the Robert MONDAVI Corporation in 2004 and renamed the property Kenneth Volk Vineyards. The first wines released under this label were in 2006. Although he primarily focuses on Chardonnay and

Pinot Noir, he produces a long list of other varietals and blends and his total output comes to some 20,000 to 22,000 cases in propitious years. Fruit from estate-owned vineyards accounts for just over a third of the total and the rest is sourced from superior vineyard growers with whom he works, even to the extent of participating directly in the management of the fruit. Ken spent a lot of time and money upgrading the winery in 2005 endowing it with some state of the art equipment and improved infrastructure. The entry level Chardonnay is the unoaked "Jaybird", with aromatic upfront citrussy flavours, good texture and reasonable length, whilst the Santa Maria Cuvée, with fruit coming from the Kenneth Volk Estate, Bien Nacido and Sierra Madre vineyards is smooth and buttery, with some apparent new oak. The vineyard-designated Chardonnays are a cut above, with the Sierra Madre showing a little more restraint and less exuberance than the blend. There is one blended Pinot Noir and three single vineyard ones and again, there is an obvious step up in quality in the latter ones. The Santa Maria Cuvée has good varietal flavour, nicely restrained with typical Californian sweet fruit – not a lot of weight but complex in the mouth. The Sierra Madre Cuvée, however, has more depth and concentrated fruit with soft tannins and good persistence. Garey Vineyard Pinot Noir is dark and strong, tightly knit, which suggests that it could well do with long cellaring, although the soft tannins should make it approachable in 2 or 3 years. The Bien Nacido shows a great deal of elegance – a step up in finesse with very luscious and seductive fruit. This can be broached now but will repay keeping as well. Apart from his Bordeaux varietals (not yet tasted) Ken is very keen on what he calls "Heirloom Wines" – wines that are not mainstream varietals (at least in the United States) and need a harder sell to get them readily appreciated. He has taken up the challenge which he says he finds "fun and educational". A Malvasia Blanca from Monterey which is 25% barrel fermented (the rest in stainless steel) has pear and lychee overtones, nice aromacy and reasonable length. On the red side, the Enz Vineyard Lime Kiln Valley Zinfandel, including fruit from vines planted in 1895, displays sweet, brambly fruit, pretty and spicy and not clumsy by any means with a great deal of elegance considering its 15% plus abv. The Mourvèdre, from the same vineyard, planted in 1922, is deep and unctuous, very full with fine complexity. (NB)

Recommended Reds:
Pinot Noir Bien Nacido Vineyard Santa Maria Valley ★★★★☆ £F
Pinot Noir Sierra Madre Vineyard Santa Maria Valley ★★★★☆ £F
Pinot Noir Garey Ranch Vineyard Santa Maria Valley ★★★★☆ £F
Pinot Noir Santa Maria Cuvée Santa Maria Valley ★★★★ £E
Zinfandel Enz Vineyard Lime Kiln Valley ★★★★ £E
Mourvèdre Enz Vineyard Lime Kiln Valley ★★★★ £E
Recommended Whites:
Chardonnay Sierra Madre Vineyard Santa Maria Valley ★★★★ £E
Chardonnay Santa Maria Cuvée Santa Maria Valley ★★★☆ £D
Chardonnay "Jaybird" Santa Maria Valley ★★★ £D
Malvasia Blanca Monterey ★★★ £D

Westerly Vineyards (Santa Maria Valley) www.westerlywines.com
Some impressive wines are produced here, particularly from the Bordeaux red varieties. The vineyards are located in the newly established Happy Canyon AVA, notable for success with the Bordeaux grapes. Pinot Noir and Chardonnay are sourced from the cooler Sta. Rita Hills. The Sauvignon Blanc, which includes a little Sémillon, is vinified in stainless steel and neutral oak and the malolactic is blocked to retain freshness. It is subtly tropical, with a gooseberry and mineral undercurrent. A similarly priced Fletcher White is also made which includes a touch of Viognier

Central Coast & Sierra Foothills

with Sauvignon Blanc. The Fletcher Red is a blend of Cabernet Sauvignon, Merlot, Cabernet Franc and Petit Verdot. The wine is aged for 24 months in wood with the malolactic fermentation in barrel. It is impressively structured with marked but supple tannins and a hint of smoky oak and there is a subtle minty edge to the dark berry fruit. The Merlot is vibrant, forward and plummy. The Fletcher Red in particular will benefit from a few years' ageing. A Cabernet Sauvignon is also made as well as Côte Blonde, a Syrah with a touch of Viognier. (DM)

Recommended Reds:
Fletcher Red Happy Canyon of Santa Barbara ★★★★ £F
Merlot Happy Canyon of Santa Barbara ★★★ £D
Recommended Whites:
Sauvignon Blanc Happy Canyon of Santa Barbara ★★★☆ £D

Zaca Mesa (Santa Barbara County) *www.zacamesa.com*
A fairly long-established property for Santa Barbara with a focus on the Rhône varieties. The exception to the Rhône theme is a Chardonnay very much in the tropical-fruit style. It has the malolactic blocked for freshness and gains some complexity from the addition of a touch of Viognier and Roussanne. The varietal Viognier offers simple, straightforward fruit and an impressively piercing peachy varietal purity often edging ★★★. A white blend Z Blanc is also now made which combines the wineries three white grape varieties. Syrah is ripe, dark and smoky in a more medium-weight style than some: more Saint-Joseph in style than Cornas. The dark, juicy Z Cuvée, a blend of Grenache, Mourvèdre, Syrah and Cinsault, is laden with herb, spice and berry flavours and offers great value for money. Like the other wines it will drink well young. The dark, dense and impressively structured Z Three is Syrah, Mourvèdre and Grenache. Also made are two additional Syrah's the Mesa Reserve and Black Bear Block. This is produced from the oldest vineyard block of the variety and is a touch pricier than the Z Three. (DM)

Recommended Reds:
Z Three Santa Ynez Valley ★★★★ £F
Z Cuvée Santa Ynez Valley ★★★ £D
Syrah Santa Ynez Valley ★★☆ £D
Recommended Whites:
Roussanne Santa Ynez Valley ★★★ £D
Viognier Santa Ynez Valley ★★☆ £C
Chardonnay Santa Ynez Valley ★★ £C

Other wines of note

Aaron
Recommended Reds: Petite Sirah Paso Robles ★★★★ £E
Ahlgren
Recommended Reds:
Cabernet Sauvignon Bates Ranch Santa Cruz Mountains ★★★ £E
Baileyana
Recommended Reds:
Syrah Grand Firepeak Cuvée Edna Valley ★★★☆ £D
Recommended Whites:
Chardonnay Grand Firepeak Cuvée Edna Valley ★★★ £D
Bassetti Vineyards
Recommended Reds: Syrah Madolyn San Luis Obispo ★★★ £D
Bien Nacido Vineyards
Recommended Reds: Syrah Santa Maria Valley ★★★☆ £E
Pinot Noir Santa Maria Valley ★★★☆ £E

Recommended Whites: Chardonnay Santa Maria Valley ★★★☆ £E
Broc Cellars
Recommended Reds: Zinfandel Vine Starr Sonoma County ★★★☆ £E
Nero d'Avola Mendocino County ★★★☆ £E
Syrah Cuvee 11.9 Santa Lucia Highlands ★★★☆ £E
Valdigue Solano Green Valley ★★★ £D
Ken Brown Cellars
Recommended Reds: Pinot Noir Cargasacchi Sta. Rita Hills ★★★★ £E
Pinot Noir Sta. Rita Hills ★★★☆ £E
David Bruce
Recommended Reds: Pinot Noir Estate Santa Cruz ★★★ £E
Byron
Recommended Reds: Pinot Noir Santa Maria Valley ★★★ £D
Recommended Whites: Chardonnay Santa Maria Valley ★★★ £D
C.G. Di Arie
Recommended Reds:
Zinfandel Southern Exposure Shenandoah Valley ★★★ £C
Cedarville
Recommended Reds: Grenache Estate Fair Play ★★★ £D
Syrah Estate Fair Play ★★★ £D
Recommended Whites: Viognier Estate Fair Play ★★★ £D
Chamisal
Recommended Reds:
Pinot Noir Chamisal Vineyard Edna Valley ★★★☆ £E
Chanin Wine Co
Recommended Reds: Pinot Noir Bien Nacido Vineyard ★★★★ £E
Recommended Whites: Chardonnay Bien Nacido Vineyard ★★★★ £E
Clautiere Vineyard
Recommended Reds: Mon Beau Rouge Estate Paso Robles ★★☆ £D
Syrah Estate Paso Robles ★★☆ £D
Recommended Whites: Viognier Estate Paso Robles ★★ £C
Curtis
Recommended Reds: Syrah Santa Barbara County ★★★ £D
Mourvèdre Santa Barbara County ★★★ £D
Heritage Red Santa Barbara County ★★★ £C
Recommended Whites: Roussanne Santa Barbara County ★★★ £C
Viognier Santa Ynez Valley ★★☆ £C
Heritage White Santa Barbara County ★★☆ £C
Epiphany
Recommended Reds: Revelation Santa Barbara County ★★★☆ £E
Recommended Whites:
Grenache Blanc Camp 4 Vineyard Santa Barbara County ★★☆ £C
Recommended Rosés: Grenache Rosé Santa Barbara County ★☆ £C
Estancia
Recommended Reds: Meritage Reserve Paso Robles ★★★ £E
Pinot Noir Stonewall Vineyard Santa Lucia Highlands ★★☆ £D
Recommended Whites: Chardonnay Monterey ★★ £C
Fess Parker
Recommended Reds:
Syrah Rodneys Vineyard Santa Barbara County ★★★★ £E 3.5
Syrah Santa Barbara ★★★ £C
Recommended Whites: Chardonnay Santa Barbara ★★★ £C
Viognier Santa Barbara ★★☆ £C
Firestone
Recommended Whites: Chardonnay Santa Ynez Valley ★★ £B
Thomas Fogarty
Recommended Reds: Pinot Noir Santa Cruz Mountains ★★★☆ £D
Recommended Whites: Chardonnay Santa Cruz Mountains ★★★ £D
Hahn Family
Recommended Reds: Syrah Santa Lucia Highlands ★★★☆ £E
Pinot Noir Santa Lucia Highlands ★★★ £E

Recommended Whites:
Chardonnay Santa Lucia Highlands ★★☆ £D
Pinot Gris Santa Lucia Highlands ★★ £D
Heller Estate
Recommended Reds:
Cabernet Sauvignon Estate Carmel Valley ★★★ £E
Recommended Whites: Chardonnay Carmel Valley ★★☆ £C
J Dusi
Recommended Reds:
Zinfandel Dante Dusi Vineyard Paso Robles ★★★☆ £D
Jackhammer
Recommended Reds: Pinot Noir Central Coast ★★★ £D
Recommended Whites:
Chardonnay Central Coast ★★★ £D
Paul Lato
Recommended Reds:
Syrah Il Padrino Bien Nacido Vineyard Santa Maria Valley ★★★★☆ £F
Syrah Cinematique Larner Vineyard Santa Ynez Valley ★★★★☆ £F
Liquid Farm Winery
Recommended Whites:
Chardonnay White Hills Vineyard Sta. Rita Hills ★★★★ £E
Lompoc Wine Co
Recommended Whites: Chardonnay Sta. Rita Hills ★★★★ £E
Recommended Reds: Pinot Noir Sta. Rita Hills ★★★★ £E
Lucas & Lewellen
Recommended Reds: Merlot Santa Barbara County ★★ £C
Cabernet Sauvignon Santa Barbara County ★★ £C
Lucia
Recommended Reds:
Pinot Noir Gary's Vineyard Santa Lucia Highlands ★★★★ £E
Recommended Whites:
Chardonnay Santa Lucia Highlands ★★★★ £E
Lutum
Recommended Whites:
Chardonnay Durrell Vineyard Carneros ★★★★ £E
Marilyn Remark
Recommended Reds:
Syrah Tondre Grapefield Vineyard Monterey County ★★★ £D
Recommended Whites: Marsanne Monterey County ★★★ £D
McPrice Myers
Recommended Reds:
Syrah Larner Vineyard Santa Ynez Valley ★★★★ £E
Syrah Les Galets Vineyard Arroyo Grande ★★★★ £E
Grenache L'Ange Rouge Santa Barbara County ★★★★ £E
Melville
Recommended Reds:
Syrah Estate Donna's Sta. Rita Hills ★★★★☆ £F
Syrah Estate Sta. Rita Hills ★★★★ £E
Recommended Whites:
Viognier Estate 'Vernas' Sta. Rita Hills ★★★★ £E
Murrieta's Well
Recommended Reds:
Los Terseros Meritage Livermore Valley ★★★ £E
Los Terseros Zinfandel Livermore Valley ★★☆ £E
Recommended Whites:
Los Terseros Meritage Livermore Valley ★★ £D
Moraga
Recommended Reds: Moraga Red Bel Air ★★★★ £H
Nichols Winery
Recommended Reds:
Pinot Noir Edna Ranch Vineyard Edna Valley ★★★ £E

Recommended Whites:
Chardonnay Edna Ranch Vineyard Edna Valley ★★★ £E
Norman
Recommended Reds: Zinfandel The Monster Paso Robles ★★★ £D
Paraiso
Recommended Reds: Pinot Noir Santa Lucia Highlands ★★☆ £E
Rosenthal - Malibu Estate
Recommended Reds: Merlot Malibu Newton Canyon ★★☆ £E
Cabernet Sauvignon Malibu Newton Canyon ★★★ £E
Recommended Whites:
Chardonnay Malibu Newton Canyon ★★☆ £E
Stephen Ross
Recommended Reds: Pinot Noir Edna Valley ★★★ £E
Pinot Noir Bien Nacido Vineyard Santa Maria Valley ★★★ £E
Recommended Whites:
Chardonnay Bien Nacido Vineyard Santa Maria Valley ★★★ £D
Stephen's Cellars
Recommended Reds:
Pinot Noir Estate Vineyard San Luis Obispo ★★★ £E
Recommended Whites:
Chardonnay MacBride Vineyard York Mountain ★★☆ £E
Shadow Canyon
Recommended Reds:
Amila Shadow Canyon Vineyard York Mountain ★★★★ £E
Syrah Shadow Canyon Vineyard York Mountain ★★★★ £E
Solomon Hills Vineyards
Recommended Whites: Chardonnay Santa Maria Valley ★★★☆ £E
Tatomer Wines
Recommended Whites:
Gruner Veltliner Meeresboden Santa Barbara County ★★★☆ £F
Tolosa
Recommended Reds: Syrah Edna Valley ★★★ £D
Pinot Noir Edna Valley ★★☆ £D
Recommended Whites: Chardonnay Edna Valley ★★★ £D
A Tribute to Grace Winery
Recommended Reds:
Grenache Highlands Vineyard Santa Barbara County ★★★★ £F
Varner Wines
Recommended Whites:
Chardonnay El Camino Vineyard Santa Cruz ★★★ £D
Viano Vineyards
Recommended Reds:
Sangiovese Reserve Shenandoah Valley ★★☆ £D
Valdigué Reserve Shenandoah Valley ★★ £C
Cabernet Sauvignon Shenandoah Valley ★★ £C
Recommended Whites: Hillside White California ★☆ £B
Vino Noceto
Recommended Reds: Sangiovese Shenandoah Valley ★★★ £C
Whitcraft
Recommended Reds: Pinot Noir Santa Barbara County ★★★ £D
Recommended Whites:
Chardonnay Bien Nacido Santa Maria Valley ★★★ £D
Wild Horse Winery
Recommended Reds: Merlot Paso Robles ★★ £C
Syrah Paso Robles ★★ £C
Syrah Unbridled Label Paso Robles ★★☆ £E
Recommended Whites: Chardonnay Central Coast ★★ £B
Windward Vineyard
Recommended Reds: Pinot Noir Monopole Paso Robles ★★★ £E

Wine behind the label

Central Coast & Sierra Foothills

California

Work in progress!!

Producers under consideration for the next edition
Alta Colina
Ambullneo Vineyards
Blackjack Ranch
Booker Vineyard
Caliza Winery
Carmel Road Winery
Cattleya Wines
Clos Solene
Copia Vineyards
Consilience
DAOU Vineyards
Deovlet Wines
Epoch Este Wines
Hammell Wine Alliance
Hilliard Bruce
The Hilt
Jelly Roll
Jonata
Domaine de La Côte
La Sirena
Law Estate Wines
Ledge Vineyards
Greg Linn Wines
Mail Road Wines
Next of Kyn
Pali Wine Co
Pharaoh Moans
Pisoni Vineyards and Winery
ROAR Wines
Samsara
Sanguis
Sinor-LaVallee
Jacob Toft
Torrin Wine
Tyler Winery
Wenzlau Vineyard

Author's choice

A diverse selection of Central Coast reds
Ampelos Cellars   Pinot Noir Ampelos Vineyard Rho Sta. Rita Hills
Alban   Syrah Seymour Vineyard Edna Valley
Au Bon Climat   Pinot Noir Cuvée Isabelle
Bonny Doon   Le Cigare Volant California
Calera   Pinot Noir Jensen Vineyard Mount Harlan
Edmunds St John   Syrah Bassetti Vineyard San Luis Obispo
Terry Hoage   Syrah The Hedge Paso Robles
JC Cellars   Syrah Rockpile Vineyard Haley's Reserve Rockpile
Justin   Isosceles Reserve Paso Robles
L'Aventure   Estate Cuvée Paso Robles
Paul Lato   Syrah Il Padrino Bien Nacido Vineyard Santa Maria Valley
Linne Calodo   Sticks And Stones Paso Robles
Loring Wine Co   Pinot Noir Cargasacchi Vineyard Sta. Rita Hills
Melville   Syrah Estate Donna's Sta. Rita Hills
Ojai   Syrah Bien Nacido Vineyard Santa Maria Valley
Ridge Vineyards   Monte Bello Santa Cruz Mountains
RN Estate   Harmonie des Cépages Paso Robles
Saxum   Broken Stones Red Paso Robles

Shadow Canyon   Amila Shadow Canyon Vineyard York Mountain
Stolpman   Angeli Estate Santa Ynez Valley
Tablas Creek   Esprit de Tablas Paso Robles

A selection of exciting whites
Andrew Murray   Viognier Santa Maria Valley
Blair Fox   Viognier Paradise Road Vineyard Santa Barbara County
Brewer Clifton   Mount Carmel Sta. Rita Hills
Linne Calodo   Contrarian Paso Robles
Chalone   Pinot Blanc Estate Chalone
Cold Heaven   Viognier Sanford and Benedict Vineyard Sta. Rita Hills
Fiddlehead Cellars   Sauvignon Blanc Happy Canyon Santa Ynez
Mount Eden Vineyards   Chardonnay Estate Santa Cruz Mountains
Qupé   Viognier Ibarra Young Vineyard Santa Ynez Valley
Talbott   Chardonnay Diamond T Estate Monterey County
Testarossa   Chardonnay Rosella's Vineyard Santa Lucia Highlands
Talley   Chardonnay Estate Arroyo Grande

A selection of sound values from the Central Coast
Reds:
Beckmen Vineyards   Cuvée Le Bec Santa Barbara
Eberle   Syrah Steinbeck Vineyard Paso Robles
Harrison-Clarke   Grenache Harrison-Clarke Vineyard Santa Ynez
Herman Story   Grenache On the Road California
Hitching Post   Generation Red Santa Barbara County
Jaffurs Wine Cellars   Syrah Santa Barbara County
Labyrinth   Pinot Noir Santa Barbara County
Renwood   Barbera Amador County
Domaine de la Terre Rouge   Syrah Côte l'Ouest California
Tobin James Cellars   Zinfandel Ballistic Paso Robles
Whites:
Brander Vineyards   Sauvignon Blanc Santa Ynez Valley
Bonny Doon   Critique Of Pure Riesling
Flying Goat Cellars   Pinot Gris Sierra Madre Vineyard Santa Maria
Foxen   Chenin Blanc Ernesto Wickenden Vineyard Santa Maria Valley
Margerum   Sauvignon Blanc Sybarite Happy Valley Santa Ynez Valley
Palmina   Malvasia Bianca Santa Barbara County
Rancho Sisquoc   Sylvaner Santa Barbara County
Tercero Wines   The Outlier Dry Gewürztraminer Santa Barbara
Three Saints   Chardonnay Santa Barbara County

Wine behind the label

The total area of vineyards in the north-west of the United States is small, certainly when compared to the sprawling expanses of California, but is nevertheless spread across a vast geographical area. Pinot Noir, Pinot Gris, Pinot Blanc and Chardonnay have now been well-established in Oregon for close to three decades. A whole host of small to medium-sized wineries have emerged and new ones continue to do so. Most of these are to be found in the Willamette Valley. Washington State is the second largest state in terms of quality wine production behind California, but has only recently become really well-known. New and exciting sources of top reds, from both the Bordeaux and more recently the Rhône varieties, are increasing and it seems certain that this trend will continue.

Oregon

As well as the **Willamette Valley** there are several other AVAs to the south, including the **Umpqua Valley**, **Red Hills Douglas County** and in the far south of the state **Rogue Valley** and **Applegate Valley**. The southern appellations are also now included in a generic **Southern Oregon** AVA. The Umpqua Valley region sits in the river valley of the same name, with coastal ranges to the west and the Cascades range of volcanic peaks to the east. Some exciting reds and whites are emerging. The Rogue Valley is marked by relatively high-altitude vineyards and cool-climate whites, including Gewürztraminer and Pinot Gris, are planted with some success in the westerly sectors of the AVA, as are increasingly impressive reds. In the north-east both the Columbia and Walla Walla valley AVAs extend over the state line, with a few wineries based on the Oregon side. The **Columbia Gorge** further west also straddles the two States..

The main viticultural activity, though, is in the Willamette Valley, a vast stretch of vineyards with varied soils and an extensive array of mesoclimates running from Eugene in the south to Portland in the north. At its widest the AVA is in excess of 80 km (50 miles) and it runs north-south for 320 km (200 miles). The majority of vineyards are found in the northern half of the region between Monmouth and Portland; the greatest concentration in Yamhill County, in the centre of that area. Here six new smaller AVAs have been established. These are the north-western **Yamhill-Carlton District**, to its east the **Chehalem Mountains** which includes the **Ribbon Ridge** appellation and stretches the furthest north. Immediately south the **Dundee Hills** and to the south-west **McMinnville**. The most southerly of the sub AVAs are the **Eola-Amity Hills**. This is mainly Pinot Noir country and the hunt for unique sites continues apace as wineries seek to establish different *terroirs*. Because of the small agricultural nature of the industry there is a real air of co-operation. Many producers are now farming biodynamically or sustainably.

A number of white varieties are also successful, among which Pinot Gris and Pinot Blanc have the best potential. Inevitably Chardonnay is extensively planted but really striking examples are still limited.

Washington State

The vineyard area here is vast and is dominated by the giant **Columbia Valley** AVA, within which there are three sub-AVAs, the **Yakima Valley** in the west, the **Horse Heaven Hills** that borders it and the **Walla Walla Valley** in the east. A sizeable part of both Columbia Valley and Walla Walla in fact stretches into northern Oregon. The Yakima Valley also includes three further sub-regions: **Red Mountain**, **Rattlesnake Hills** and most recently **Snipes Mountain**.

A newly established AVA close to the coast is **Puget Sound**, yet it appears to be too cool and damp to provide wines of any substance. The Columbia Valley by contrast is dry and necessarily irrigated. Located to the east of the Cascade Mountains, it is suitable for quality wine because of its northerly latitude and consequently longer, sunnier days. Excellent Bordeaux-style reds are produced along with good Chardonnay. The Yakima Valley is also successful with these grapes and with Syrah. Perhaps the greatest potential is actually for the Rhône varieties rather than those of Bordeaux. Excellent wines of both styles have now been made in Walla Walla as well.

Oregon & Washington State vintages

With such a sprawling viticultural expanse, providing any meaningful detail on vintages is difficult. The following provides an idea of what to look for.

Oregon: 2015 saw a cool autumn after late summer rains achieved balance in the vineyards. Pinot Noir should be good and restrained elegant wines are likely. 2014 has proved to be good in Oregon with some potentially great Pinot Noir and a bumper crop. The summer was warm without excessive heat spikes and dry through the harvest. In 2013 what looked like a fine vintage in the Willamette was adversely effected by late harvest rains. Earlier picked Pinot Noir and Pinot Gris look good, some decent Chardonnay has been made and sound reds will emerge from the southern regions. A warm summer in 2012 saw good nicely ripened wines made. In 2011 there were very difficult summer growing conditions and the vintage was saved by an Indian summer. Expect elegant and reasonably intense wines from the best producers. 2010 proved to be an above average year for the State. In 2009 fruit quality was decent in all areas of Oregon. 2008 provided some good to very good Pinot. 2007 was difficult for Pinot Noir but some good whites have been made. In 2006 the wines are were forward and approachable young with rich fruit and moderate acidity and should now be being drunk. 2005 produced elegant and structured Pinot Noir and crisp whites. 2004 was a tricky vintage and those who harvested late did reasonably well. 2003 was good but some wines struggled for balance with high alcohol. 2001 was reasonable. Prior to this 2002, 2000, 1999 and 1998 were good to very good but only the best will be holding up.

Washington State: 2015 has seen an excellent growing season with warm weather throughout the summer. Grapes showed good colour and flavour with good acidity as well. 2014 will be a very good year with excellent reds made. Summer was warm and dry and the harvest was early and conducted in fine conditions. In 2013 the best reds should be very good, particularly Syrah. Some producers did though pick quite early and some underripe flavours may be found in some wines. 2012 provided some excellent dense and concentrated reds. 2011 was a lighter vintage with generally good and elegant wines. 2010 provided good, concentrated reds on a par with the previous vintage. 2009 in Washington State saw some impressive reds. 2008 provided some lighter but elegant wines from the best producers. 2007 by contrast produced some fine structured reds. 2006 was very promising, 2005 was good for whites although there was some uneven ripening in the reds. 2004 was exciting for reds with good physiological ripeness and not excessive alcohol. 2003 and 2002 wee also very good. Top reds will hold well for a decade, often longer.

Pacific North-West

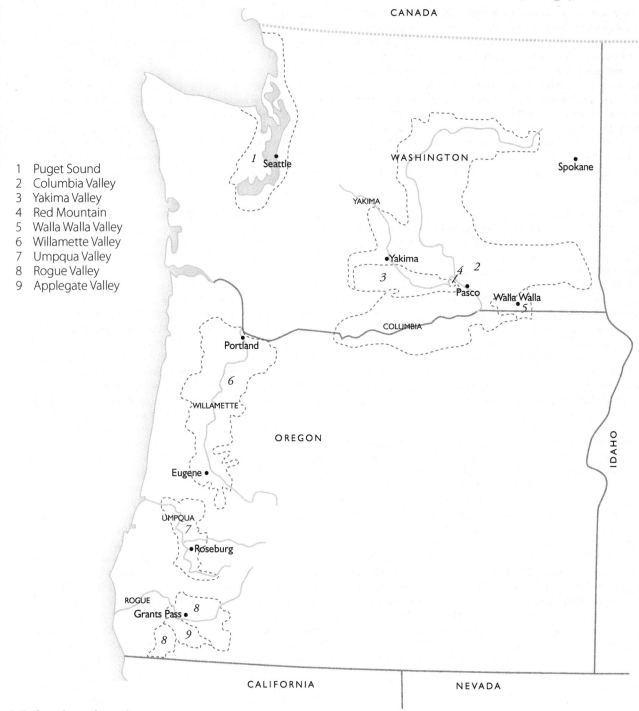

1. Puget Sound
2. Columbia Valley
3. Yakima Valley
4. Red Mountain
5. Walla Walla Valley
6. Willamette Valley
7. Umpqua Valley
8. Rogue Valley
9. Applegate Valley

A-Z of producers by region

A-Z of producers *Oregon*

A To Z Wineworks (Chehalem Mountains) *www.atozwineworks.com*
This partnership of four friends, Deb and Bill Hatcher and Cheryl Francis and Sam Tannahill was established in 2000 and have grown to become Oregon's largest winery group. As well as A to Z they produce wines under their own premium labels: Deb and Bill make HATCHER Pinot Noir while Cheryl and Sam have a small range under their FRANCIS-TANNAHILL label. They have also now acquired the REX HILL winery. The A to Z wines provide them with real volume and enable them to source fruit from throughout Oregon producing a well priced range of accessible easy drinking fruit accented reds and whites. While not complex, the wines have a vibrancy and fresh fruit quality at this level that has long been missing in the State. The usual Oregon suspects, Pinot Noir, Pinot Gris and Riesling, are all important components of the range as is increasingly, Chardonnay. Sangiovese is the primary variety providing an interesting light red cherry character in the rosé. The whites and the rosé should be drunk young and fresh, the Pinot Noir is great young but will cellar for a short time. (DM)
Recommended Reds:
Pinot Noir Oregon ★★★ £C
Recommended Whites:
Riesling Oregon ★★★ £C
Chardonnay Oregon ★★☆ £C
Pinot Gris Oregon ★★☆ £C
Recommended Rosés:
Rosé Oregon ★☆ £B

Abacela (Umpqua Valley) *www.abacela.com*
The Jones produce an excellent small range of Spanish and Rhône style wines and are showing the real potential of these styles in

the Umpqua Valley. The fruit is sourced mainly from the estate Fault Line vineyards. Both whites are also fermented in stainless steel to emphasise their pure fruit character. The clean and lightly mineral Viognier comes from estate vineyards and Steelhead Run in the Applegate Valley. A touch more aromatically intense is a very characterful floral, citrusy Albariño. Characterful Garnacha (Grenache), aged in neutral oak, is firmly structured with ripe chalky tannins and dark berry and herb-scented fruit. Syrah is co-fermented with a little Viognier adding a touch of spiciness to its dark blackberry fruit, black pepper and subtly vanilla scented oak. Ageing is in small French oak with 20% new. Equally impressive is a full, big and powerfully structured Tempranillo, more in the style of a Toro than a Rioja. A little new oak, around 10%, is used. Both this and the Syrah will develop well for 5 or 6 years. A rosé is also made from Grenache and reds Tannat, Malbec and a further premium Tempranillo, Paramour. (DM)
Recommended Reds:
Tempranillo Estate Umpqua Valley ★★★☆ £E
Syrah Estate Umpqua Valley ★★★☆ £D
Garnacha Umpqua Valley ★★★ £C
Recommended Whites:
Albariño Estate Umpqua Valley ★★★☆ £C
Viognier Umpqua Valley ★★★ £C

Adea (Willamette Valley) *www.adeawine.com*
This family operation began life under the Fisher label but this had to change because of a winery name conflict. Adea is now named after the members of the family. The family estate vineyard was planted in 1990 with aid from Michael Etzel of BEAUX FRÈRES and the first wine produced in 1995. The Adea name has been utilised since 1998. The range of Pinot Noirs includes two very ripe opulent single vineyard bottlings from the Hawks View and Durrant Vineyards as well as forward supple Willamette bottling labelled Dean-Os which is the most accessible of the wines. The wines are dark, dense and full of black cherries and mineral notes. All are marked by their full-blown style and the wines can be in excess of 15% alcohol. It is also worth looking out for the Willamette Valley Chardonnay which we have not tasted. (DM)
Recommended Reds:
Pinot Noir Hawks View Vineyard Willamette Valley ★★★☆ £E
Pinot Noir Durant Vineyards Willamette Valley ★★★☆ £E
Pinot Noir Dean-Os Willamette Valley ★★★ £E

✿ **Adelsheim (Chehalem Mountains)** *www.adelsheim.com*
This is now a long established Willamette producer, founded in 1971, with vineyards at 11 different sites in the Chehalem Mountains, Eola-Amity Hills and Ribbon Ridge. A state of the art gravity flow winery was completed in 1997. In addition to the wines covered here an unoaked Chardonnay, a Pinot Noir rosé called Deglacé, as well as a number of other single vineyard Pinots are produced. Auxerrois is a rare Oregon example of the variety. Cool fermented and vinified and aged without the malolactic, it is fresh, grassy and aromatic. For a well-crafted Pinot Blanc a small proportion is fermented in small neutral oak, adding some weight to the wine which has fresh green fruit with a hint of minerality. Pinot Gris is also cool fermented, although partial malolactic adds textural richness and impressive substance. The Caitlin's Reserve Chardonnay comes from two sites in the Dundee Hills and Chehalem Mountains. The wine is whole cluster pressed and barrel-fermented in partial new wood and aged *sur lie* for around 15 months. Richly leesy, with some oak apparent when young, it is an impressively structured example of the variety.

Oregon

The Pinot Noirs are de-stemmed and get a cold soak. The Willamette Valley bottling is sourced from a range of sites and offers richly dark cherry scented fruit and good structure and intensity. The Elizabeth's Reserve is a barrel selection from the winery's best lots; dark plum fruit and a complex truffle character are underpinned by a firm minerality. A very small quantity of single vineyard wine is produced from various sites. Calkin's Lane is superbly poised and structured but needs to be kept for 3 or 4 years. (DM)

Recommended Reds:
Pinot Noir Calkins Lane Vineyard Willamette Valley ★★★★☆ £F
Pinot Noir Elizabeth's Reserve Willamette Valley ★★★★ £F
Pinot Noir Willamette Valley ★★★☆ £E

Recommended Whites:
Chardonnay Caitlin's Reserve Willamette Valley ★★★★ £E
Pinot Gris Willamette Valley ★★★ £C
Pinot Blanc Chehalem Mountains ★★★ £C
Auxerrois Willamette Valley ★★☆ £C

>> Amalie Robert (Willamette Valley) *www.amalierobert.com*
This winery is based in the south of the region a small distance from the small town of Salem. Dena and Ernie like others left the frantic corporate world behind to become winegrowers. They completed the planting of their 34 acres of vines in 2000 and they now have Pinot Noir, Chardonnay, Pinot Meunier, Syrah and Viognier planted. Her Silhouette is a great value un-oaked estate grown Chardonnay full of zesty, citrus and melon fruits with the malolactic fermentation blocked for freshness. Pricier although still good value is the Chardonnay Heirloom Cameo. Again estate grown, this is barrel-fermented and aged on lees adding a rich, creamy texture with intense and zesty lemon and lime flavours. Larger 500 litre puncheons are used to keep the fruit and oak nicely balanced. Among their small range they also produce Viognier, Syrah and of course Pinot Noir. Among a range of fine Pinit Noirs, The Reserve is the top label and mighty impressive it is. Fermented in small lots, block by block it offers a rich and rounded texture, firm and balance tannin structure with intense and concentrated dark cherry fruit. (DM)

Recommended Reds:
Pinot Noir The Reserve Willamette Valley ★★★★☆ £G
Pinot Noir Estate Selection Willamette Valley ★★★★ £F
Pinot Noir Amalie's Cuvee Willamette Valley ★★★★ £F
Pinot Noir Dijon Clones Willamette Valley ★★★☆ £E
Pinot Noir Pinot i Pinot Willamette Valley ★★★☆ £D
Pinot Noir The Uncarved Block Willamette Valley ★★★ £D
Syrah Satisfaction Willamette Valley ★★★☆ £D

Recommended Whites:
Chardonnay Heirloom Cameo Willamette Valley ★★★★ £E
Chardonnay Her Silouette Willamette Valley ★★☆ £C

Amity Vineyards (Willamette Valley)
Medium-sized Willamette Valley operation founded in the mid-1970s. Pinot Noir is reasonably fragrant with soft, red berry fruit but can be lacking in depth and substance. Single-vineyard bottlings have been added from the Schouten and Sunnyside vineyards as well as an Estate Vineyard bottling. These offer similar quality and value to the Winemakers Reserve. As well as the Pinots there is a light, berry-scented Gamay, which is upfront and fotward. The whites though are very good with clean, characterful fruit and impressive depth. They possess a mineral purity that is often missing here. The class act and undoubted value for money here is the stylish, lightly pungent Gewürztraminer, one of the better examples

in the state and really quite Alsatian in style. (DM)

Recommended Reds:
Pinot Noir Winemakers Reserve ★★★ £E
Pinot Noir Willamette Valley ★★ £C
Gamay Noir Willamette Valley ★☆ £D

Recommended Whites:
Gewürztraminer Oregon ★★★ £C
Riesling Oregon ★★☆ £C
Pinot Blanc Willamette Valley ★★☆ £C

Anne Amie Vineyards (Yamhill-Carlton) *www.anneamie.com*
A sizeable range of wines is available at this property with vineyards in the Yamhill-Carlton and Chehalem Mountain regions. The estate was purchased by Robert Pamplin in 1999 and much investment has gone into the project with now close to 45 ha under vine. There are three essential ranges of wines. The Cuvée A labels are young and fresh intended for early drinking. The Cuvée A Amrita is a well-priced multi varietal blend with a grassy, easy green fruited character. The Cuvée A Pinot Noir is full of juicy, vibrant strawberry fruit. The wine is lent a little extra structure with a cold soak, an extended period on skins and around 10 months barrel ageing. The Willamette Valley bottling is given a similar vinification but just has a touch more depth. Pinot Gris and Pinot Blanc both offer good crisp fruit, particularly the Pinot Blanc. Both are cold fermented and aged on lees, the Pinot Blanc for 18 months and with some barrel ageing adding weight. The Riesling is more serious and has some mineral as well as green fruit intensity. The estate plantings date back to 1979 and this provides additional complexity. Of particular interest here is the Pinot Noir Prismé which is vinified as a white. It gets a gentle pressing and then is barrel fermented and aged on fine lees in barrel for 18 months. It has good acidity and structure and a rich texture. An Estate Pinot Noir red is also made and there is also a pricier L'iris Pinot. (DM)

Recommended Reds:
Pinot Noir Prismé Willamette Valley ★★★☆ £E
Pinot Noir Willamette Valley ★★★ £D
Pinot Noir Cuvée A Willamette Valley ★★☆ £D

Recommended Whites:
Riesling Estate Yamhill-Carlton District ★★★ £C
Pinot Blanc Willamette Valley ★★☆ £C
Pinot Gris Willamette Valley ★★☆ £C
Cuvée A Amrita Willamette Valley ★★☆ £C

Archery Summit (Dundee Hills) *www.archerysummit.com*
Small, bespoke operation owned by the Andrus family, who founded the large premium PINE RIDGE operation in Napa's Stags Leap District. Very classy Pinot Noir is produced here along with Pinot Gris. The focus is on specially selected lots of Pinot Noir, providing not only style and class but individuality too. To that end over 40 ha (100 acres) of high-density vineyards have now been established. In addition to Arcus and Premier Cuvée, three other examples are produced from Renegade Ridge, Looney Vineyard, Red Hills and the home Archery Summit estates. The latter is the top premium bottling and very expensive. (DM)

Recommended Reds:
Pinot Noir Arcus Estate Willamette Valley ★★★★☆ £G
Pinot Noir Premier Cuvée Willamette Valley ★★★☆ £E

Argyle (Dundee Hills) *www.argylewinery.com*
Now a part of the Australian Lion Company group, which owns PETALUMA, this sizeable operation produces good Pinot Noir as well

as top-quality sparkling wine. For both Chardonnay and Pinot Noir, the bigger-volume Willamette Valley and Reserve bottlings offer good value; limited releases under the Nuthouse label offers a notch up in quality. The Nuthouse Pinot Noir is in a big, full style with dark fruit and evident oak. Fine Nuthouse Chardonnay is toasty, leesy and quite Burgundian in style. None are excessively priced. Also produced is stylish Riesling, including a Nuthouse example and a late harvest Minus Five. (DM)

Recommended Reds:
Pinot Noir Nuthouse Eola-Amity Hills ★★★★ £F
Pinot Noir Reserve Willamette Valley ★★★☆ £E
Pinot Noir Willamette Valley ★★☆ £D

Recommended Whites:
Chardonnay Nuthouse Willamette Valley ★★★☆ £E
Chardonnay Willamette Valley ★★☆ £D
Riesling Nuthouse Eola-Amity Hills ★★★ £D
Brut Knudsen Vineyard Willamette Valley ★★★☆ £F
Brut Willamette Valley ★★★ £E

Belle Vallée (Willamette Valley) *www.bellevallee.com*
The three partners here, winemaker Joe Wright along with Steve Allen and Mike Magee produced their first harvest with the 2002 vintage. Joe Wright worked originally for Willamette Valley Vineyards before moving on to this new operation. The winery is based in downtown Corvallis in the heart of the Willamette. There are arrangements with some of the best vineyards in the State in both the Willamette and Rogue Valleys. Willamette Pinot is the backbone of the operation and wide range of styles are created. The regular Pinot offers attractive ripe black cherry fruit and supple tannins. The Reserve is firmer with a little structure and grip supporting ripe cherry fruit. Darker, smokier with quite a bit more substance is the impressive Grand Cuvée. It comes from a number of sites and is aged in 100% new oak for around 15 months or so. The Rogue Valley is also important as a source for well-priced plummy Merlot, ripe and minty Cabernet Sauvignon as well as a ripe, chocolatey Syrah that finishes with a hint of black pepper. The range is completed by a lightly nutty, and honeyed Pinot Gris. (DM)

Recommended Reds:
Pinot Noir Grand Cuvée Willamette Valley ★★★☆ £E
Pinot Noir Reserve Willamette Valley ★★★ £E
Pinot Noir Willamette Valley ★★☆ £D
Syrah Rogue Valley ★★★ £D
Merlot Rogue Valley ★★☆ £D
Cabernet Sauvignon Rogue Valley ★★☆ £D

Recommended Whites:
Pinot Gris Oregon ★★ £C

❂ Beaux Frères (Ribbon Ridge) *www.beauxfreres.com*
Undoubtedly a producer of some of the best Pinot Noir in the Willamette Valley, this operation is as well known for the involvement of wine critic Robert M Parker as for anything else. The Beaux Frères vineyard in the Ribbon Ridge was planted in 1988. As with most of the current run of vineyards, vine density is high at over 2,200 vines per acre and the latest Dijon clones are planted. Vinification occurs naturally with indigenous yeasts from the vineyard and malolactic is also allowed to occur naturally. The results are impressive. The wines are powerful and structured with greater grip and concentration than most of their contemporaries. The Willamette Valley, formerly Belles Soeurs, is not a secondary label but sourced from other excellent Willamette vineyards and a third wine The Upper Terrace, from a new vineyard in the Ribbon Ridge AVA

has now been added. (DM)

Recommended Reds:
Pinot Noir Beaux Frères Vineyard Ribbon Ridge ★★★★★ £G
Pinot Noir The Upper Terrace Ribbon Ridge ★★★★★ £G
Pinot Noir Willamette Valley ★★★★ £F

❂ Bergström (Chehalem Mountains) *www.bergstromwines.com*
This small and impressive winery produces a fairly extensive range of wines including fine Burgundian style Chardonnay, Pinot Gris, Sauvignon Blanc and Riesling as well as Pinot Noir. It is for the latter wines that the winery stands out and in particular a range of excellent single vineyard bottlings. These include a generic well-priced Willamette Valley "Old Stones" bottling, a Cumberland Reserve and single vineyard wines from the Shea, Broadley, De Lancellotti and Nysa Vineyards. These consistently offer a rich, ripe and concentrated Pinot character, full of dark, plummy fruit and firm striking tannins. The home vineyard is perhaps more important than the other single vineyard bottlings, in that it accounts for over 500 cases a year, more than any of the other vineyard designate wines. It is planted on south, south-easterly slopes and offers a very meagre annual yield of less than one and a half tons to the acre. The resulting wines are deep and structured, requiring patience, at least four or five years, for the tight and reserved mineral and cherry-spiced fruit to fully evolve. (DM)

Recommended Reds:
Pinot Noir Bergström Vineyard Dundee Hills ★★★★★ £F
Pinot Noir Shea Vineyard Vineyard Yamhill Carlton ★★★★☆ £F
Pinot Noir De Lancelloti Vineyard Chehalem Mountains ★★★★☆ £F
Pinot Noir Cumberland Reserve Willamette Valley ★★★★ £E
Pinot Noir Old Stones Willamette Valley ★★★☆ £E

Recommended Whites:
Chardonnay Sigrid Willamette Valley ★★★★☆ £G
Chardonnay Old Stones Willamette Valley ★★★☆ £E

❂ Brooks Wine (Eola-Amity Hills) *www.brookswine.com*
A small range of very fine white and red is produced at this Eola-Amity Hills based winery. The late Jimi Brooks had been been winemaker and vineyard manager at MAYSARA while building his own small label focussing only on organic and biodynamic vineyard practices for his wines. This legacy is carried through in the wines today. Jimi Brooks passed away in 2004 before the harvest. His winemaking friends though rallied round to ensure the vintage was produced. Different lots were produced at different wineries. In 2006 Chris Williams became the full-time winemaker for Brooks, himself coming from Maysara. Jimi's sister Janie Brooks Heuck has taken on the responsibility of running the business in order to provide a future for Jimi's son Pascal, who is the sole owner, and sustain her brother's label and work. The wines are exemplary, the Rastaban comes from the Momtazi and Hyland Vineyards with dark, intense black cherry fruit with a structured, mineral undercurrent. It is one of those rare Oregon Pinots that will develop well for a decade. The softer, more immediately approachable Janus comes from a range of sites with something of that dark, dense character as well. There is a very good regular Pinot Noir, which offers great value. Ara is one of the State's best examples of citrus laden, zesty, mineral Riesling. The regular Willamette bottling is a touch less intense and structured but very good. Amycas is a fresh green-fruited aromatic blend of Pinot Gris, Pinot Blanc, Riesling, Gewürztraminer and Muscat. Enjoy it young and fresh. (DM)

Recommended Reds:
Pinot Noir Rastaban Willamette Valley ★★★★☆ £F

Oregon

Pinot Noir Janus Willamette Valley ★★★★ £E
Pinot Noir Willamette Valley ★★★ £C
Recommended Whites:
Riesling Ara Willamette Valley ★★★☆ £D
Riesling Willamette Valley ★★★ £C
Amycas Oregon ★★ £B

Carabella (Chehalem Mountains) *www.carabellawine.com*
Mike and Cara Hallocks wines are all sourced from the family's
own vineyards. Their site is found in the south-eastern tip of the
Chehalem Mountains on Parrett Mountain. The approach as with
other contemporary Oregon Pinot Noir growers is to plant blocks
of different clones separately. The 58 acre site now consists of seven
different Pinot Noir clones which are planted on a southeast facing
slope at an altitude of 500 to 600 feet on gravelly volcanic soils.
This provides a *terroir* perfect for dry farming low yielding vines and
producing fruit of impressive depth and intensity. The blending
options, from a range of microclimates and clones, is considerable.
The regular Pinot is elegant and full of both red cherry and darker
black fruits with well judged oak. Both the Inchinnan and Mistake
Block (which unexpectedly turned out to be planted to top quality
Pommard clones) Pinots are fuller, more opulent with darker richer
fruit notes apparent. As well as the Pinot Noir, there are two blocks
of Pinot Gris planted on the western side of the vineyard, producing
an elegant green fruited, lightly peachy white with a rich buttery
undercurrent from one third barrel-fermentation in neutral oak.
There are also two separate blocks of Chardonnay, resulting in a
finely structured almost Burgundian barrel fermented style with
elegant melon and citrus fruit underpinned by a creamy texture
from lees and nicely judged restrained oak. (DM)
Recommended Reds:
Pinot Noir Mistake Block Chehalem Mountains ★★★★ £E
Pinot Noir Inchinnan Chehalem Mountains ★★★☆ £E
Pinot Noir Chehalem Mountains ★★★ £D
Recommended Whites:
Chardonnay Chehalem Mountains ★★★ £D
Pinot Gris Chehalem Mountains ★★☆ £C

Chehalem (Willamette Valley) *www.chehalemwines.com*
Winemaking at Chehalem commenced in 1990. The winery is also
now co-owned by Bill and Cathy Stoller of STOLLER VINEYARDS
and Harry Peterson-Nedry is a part owner in their winery. There are
now three estate vineyard sources, Ridgecrest, Stoller and Corral
Creek, the total area under vine being some 106 ha (262 acres). Pinot
Noir makes up the bulk of the grapes, the rest being Chardonnay,
Riesling, Pinot Gris and a little Gamay Noir. 3 Vineyards is a blend
of the sites. As well as this and the three vineyard bottlings of
Pinot Noir a special *cuvée* is produced, the Reserve (formerly Rion
Reserve), which is firmer and more impressively structured. It should
evolve well over 4 or 5 years. The wines are generally very ripe and
full of exotic dark fruits and new oak is kept to a minimum. The Ian's
Reserve Chardonnay is barrel-fermented and gets full malolactic
and lees-ageing and stirring. The Inox is fresh and richly peachy with
impressive intensity. As the name suggests it is tank fermented and
sees no oak. The current range is completed by a Riesling and Pinot
Gris made in both dry and late-harvest styles. (DM)
Recommended Reds:
Pinot Noir Reserve Willamette Valley ★★★★ £F
Pinot Noir Ridgecrest Vineyards Willamette Valley ★★★☆ £F
Pinot Noir Stoller Vineyards Willamette Valley ★★★☆ £F
Pinot Noir 3 Vineyards Willamette Valley ★★★ £D

Recommended Whites:
Chardonnay Ian's Reserve Willamette Valley ★★★☆ £E
Chardonnay Inox Willamette Valley ★★☆ £C

>> Cowhorn (Applegate Valley) *www.cowhornwine.com*
The Applegate Valley AVA is in southern Oregon and proving a good
spot for Rhône style wines and Cowhorn is an excellent exponent.
Amongst their small range Spiral 36 is a blend of Viognier, Marsanne
and Roussanne with the varieties all co-fermented. The wine gets
three months in oak, which is kept in the background with just 20%
of new barrels with the wine showing attractive citrus fruit. The
wine offers excellent value. A touch pricier but still good value is
the Syrah 20, which is a 100% varietal example getting 10 months
in wood, again well reined in. The dark berry fruit is balanced by an
attractive black pepper spice quality. Look out also for fresh Viognier,
a Marsanne/Roussanne, which both get a short period in a small
proportion of new oak, with the malolactic fermentation blocked as
well as a Grenache. A Reserve Viognier and Reserve Syrah are also
made. (DM)
Recommended Reds:
Syrah 20 Applegate Valley ★★★★ £E
Recommended Whites:
Marsanne Roussanne Applegate Valley ★★★★ £E
Viognier Applegate Valley ★★★☆ £E
Spiral 36 Applegate Valley ★★★ £D

Coeur de Terre (Willamette Valley) *www.cdtvineyard.com*
The Neals established their property in 1998. Their vineyard is
planted to Pinot Noir as well as Syrah, a small amount of Viognier to
co-ferment with the Syrah in future releases, Rieslng and unusually
for Oregon, Gruner Veltliner. Pinot Noir is the main focus though
understandably and there are a number of different blocks with a
range of clones as well as both single and double guyot trellising.
Of the wines, the estate Pinot is selected from across the vineyard
holdings and offers a classic strawberry scented, elegant Pinot style.
The Renelle's Block Reserve is the first of the reserve wines here to
be released. It is darker and more structured with black cherry fruit
and supple tannins. It is complex and will develop well with three
or four years of ageing. The Riesling is marked by a combination of
green apple and underlying citrus with nicely balanced acidity and
impressive carry and intensity. It will be interesting to see the other
varieties in future because quality and value are good here. (DM)
Recommended Reds:
Pinot Noir Renelle's Block Reserve Willamette Valley ★★★★ £F
Pinot Noir Estate Willamette Valley ★★★☆ £E
Recommended Whites:
Riesling McMinnville ★★☆ £C

⦿ Cristom (Willamette Valley) *www.cristomwines.com*
Established in 1992, this small operation is now producing a range
of excellent Pinot Noirs and some good whites. As well as the lightly
oaked, quite restrained Chardonnay and floral Viognier there is a
stylish, mineral-scented Pinot Gris and most recently a Syrah. The
main focus is Pinot Noir, produced in a number of cuvées and from
a number of estate-owned single vineyards. The Mount Jefferson
Cuvée comes from a number of sites around the Valley. Impressive
single-vineyard bottlings come from Louise, Eileen, Jessie and
Marjorie, Louise the biggest and fullest of the wines. The Reserve is
mainly sourced from the four estate vineyards. A barrel selection, it is
a full, opulent style, which gets extended cask-ageing. The top Pinot
is the Signature Cuvée, a special selection. Expect to age the Pinots

successfully in the short to medium term over four to six years. (DM)

Recommended Reds:

Pinot Noir Marjorie Vineyard Willamette Valley ★★★★☆ £F

Pinot Noir Jessie Vineyard Willamette Valley ★★★★☆ £F

Pinot Noir Louise Vineyard Willamette Valley ★★★★☆ £F

Pinot Noir Eileen Vineyard Willamette Valley ★★★★ £F

Pinot Noir Reserve Willamette Valley ★★★☆ £E

Pinot Noir Mt Jefferson Cuvée Willamette Valley ★★★ £D

Recommended Whites:

Viognier Willamette Valley ★★★☆ £D

>> **De Lancellotti** *www.delancellottifamilyvineyards.com*

McMinnville based De Lancellotti, who are related to the BERGSTRÖM family, are located just to the northwest of Newberg produce a number of very worthy Pinot Noirs, including the Willamette Valley AVA Onelia and very well priced La Sorella. The Famiglia comes from their own biodynamically grown vines and new oak is minimal, just 15% for balance. The Lachini Vineyard is located in the Chehalem Mountains, and the vines also farmed biodynamically from a couple of clones. New oak is again minimally used, just 10% and the wine has an elegant red fruits character with restrained intensity and fine structure. Expect at least half a decade's development with ageing. It's also worth taking note of their excellent Anderson Vineyard Chardonnay from the Anderson Vineyard in the Dundee Hills. (DM)

Recommended Reds:

Pinot Noir Lachini Chehalem Mountains ★★★★☆ £F

Pinot Noir Onelia Willamette Valley ★★★★ £F

Pinot Noir Famiglia Willamette Valley ★★★☆ £E

Pinot Noir La Sorella Willamette Valley ★★☆ £C

Recommended Whites:

Chardonnay Anderson Dundee Hills ★★★★ £F

❀ **Domaine Drouhin (Dundee Hills)** *www.domainedrouhin.com*

Established in the late 1980s by Joseph DROUHIN and run by Véronique Drouhin, who controls the winemaking. The approach to viticulture from the outset was distinctly Burgundian: at the time she was one of the few focusing on high-density vineyard planting. The estate has some 35 ha (85 acres) under vine in the Red Hills area, which has a climate remarkably similar to that found on the Côte d'Or. The resulting wines are in a tight, restrained style but very pure with real depth and concentration. There is a powerful, dark berry character to the Pinot and the Cuvée Laurène has the refined, tannic structure to promise much with age. A very low-volume special release has also been added, the Cuvée Louise, which is a special barrel selection of the best of the material used in the Cuvée Laurène. There are two Chardonnays; Cuvée Arthur, is elegant and understated but with a piercing, mineral and citrus undercurrent. It is stylish with well-judged oak. A further label Edition Limitée is also made. The small Domaine Drouhin range is completed with an Edition Rosé of Pinot Noir. From the Eola-Amity Hills two further wines are made under the Roserock label and the Drouhin owned vineyard of the same name. These are well-priced and elegant wines full of character. The Pinot is vinified individually by vineyard block, of which there are 35. The wine is restrained, offering dark cherry fruit and a fresh, balanced structure. There are three further blocks of Chardonnay, which are like the Pinot sustainably farmed. Fermentation is part barrel and part tank, followed by the malolactic. Restrained melon and green fruit aromas are underpinned by fresh and zesty acidity and just a subtle hint of oak. (DM)

Domaine Drouhin

Recommended Reds:

Pinot Noir Cuvée Laurene Dundee Hills ★★★★☆ £F

Pinot Noir Dundee Hills ★★★★ £E

Recommended Whites:

Chardonnay Cuvée Arthur Dundee Hills ★★★★ £E

Roserock

Recommended Reds:

Pinot Noir Roserock Eola-Amity Hills ★★★☆ £D

Recommended Whites:

Chardonnay Roserock Eola-Amity Hills ★★★ £D

Elk Cove (Chehalem Mountains) *www.elkcove.com*

A long established winery founded in 1974. They have 120 acres of vineyards planted on three northern Willamette sites. South facing slopes and a combination of finely drained Willakenzie and Laurelwood soils provides an excellent growing environment. The winery is now gravity flow and the wines are achieving new levels of quality. Pinot Blanc is crisp and nutty with a lightly aromatic Alsatian character showing through. Pinot Gris comes from estate vineyards which are close planted and are crop thinned for low yields. Cool fermented, the wine offers great varietal purity and a marked floral, aromatic character. The Willamette Pinot Noir, like the single-vineyard wines, is produced from low-yielding fruit – often less than 2 tons to the acre. It is the softest of the wines with ripe and dark fruit and reasonable depth with quite apparent oak. The single vineyards are a clear level up in quality. The Roosevelt Vineyard is finely structured with firm tannins and a mineral undercurrent. The earlier ripening Mount Richmond is riper, fatter with a hint of truffle as well as rich dark cherry fruit. La Bohéme is perhaps the best of these with rich, dark fruit and a firm structure and spicy toasty oak which needs a little time to integrate. A Reserve is also made as well as three others, Windmill, Five Mountain and Clay Court. (DM)

Recommended Reds:

Pinot Noir La Bohéme Willamette Valley ★★★★☆ £F

Pinot Noir Mount Richmond Vineyard Willamette Valley ★★★★ £E

Pinot Noir Roosevelt Vineyard Willamette Valley ★★★★ £F

Pinot Noir Willamette Valley ★★★ £D

Recommended Whites:

Pinot Gris Willamette Valley ★★★ £C

Pinot Blanc Willamette Valley ★★★ £C

Erath Vineyards (Dundee Hills) *www.smwe.com/estates/details/erath*

Dick Erath moved to Oregon in 1968 and produced his first vintage in 1972. Over forty years later this is now a substantial operation. The backbone of the winery is the Oregon Pinot Noir, which comes from a number of sites in both the Willamette and Umpqua Valleys. The wine is soft and forward with just a slight vegetative hint and offers very good quality for the price. Pinot Blanc is 100% tank fermented and vinified without malolactic. It is bright and forward with good varietal purity and refreshing acidity. The Pinot Gris is Willamette sourced (80%) with the balance from warmer Umpqua. It is both ripe and lightly tropical with a good minerally undercurrent and excellent acidity. The Estate Selection Pinot Noir is a clear level up in quality. It comes from 100% Estate grown Dundee Hills fruit. Aged for 13 months in French oak (around one-third new), it has a lightly vegetal edge along with good weight and flesh and a truffly richness. The Prince Hill bottling gets a similar oak regime although it is darker richer and offers a suppler rounder palate. It is one of a bewildering array now of single vineyard wines being offered. The top two Pinots here will both develop nicely with a little age. (DM)

Pacific North-West

Recommended Reds:
Pinot Noir Prince Hill Vineyard Willamette Valley ★★★☆ £E
Pinot Noir Estate Selection Dundee Hills ★★★☆ £E
Pinot Noir Oregon ★★☆ £C
Recommended Whites:
Pinot Gris Oregon ★★☆ £C
Pinot Blanc Willamette Valley ★★ £C

Four Graces (Dundee Hills) *www.thefourgraces.com*
Steve and Paula Black purchased their 110 acre (44.5 ha) vineyard in 2003 and named it in honour of their four daughters. They have not ignored their son Nicholas though, he is recognized as the "keeper of the Four Graces" on their reserve label Pinot. Indeed it is no surprise that Pinot Noir is the main focus here. As well as their original Black Family vineyard, a second site the Doe Ridge Vineyard in Yamhill-Carlton was purchased in 2005 and a second single vineyard Pinot is released from here. The Black Family site is planted to a combination of Pinot Noir, Pinot Blanc and Pinot Gris. The original Pinot Noir holding was established in 1990 to a range of clones and the Alsace varieties in 1993. The developing age of the vineyard can be seen in the quality of the fruit in the wines. Both whites are restrained and elegant, the Pinot Blanc lightly honeyed with a classic hint of hazelnut, the Pinot Gris subtly floral and spicy with hints of grapefruit and cool fermented to emphasise the fruit. The Willamette Valley Pinot Noir comes from both the family's vineyards and is a lighter, immediately accessible red fruited style and very well priced. Oak influence is carefully handled and 10 months in French barrels gives just sufficient structure and grip in the wine. The Black Family Vineyard Pinot is much fuller and more structured. 13 months in new oak is well integrated and the wine is full of complex plum and dark cherry fruit. It will develop well with three or four years cellaring. (DM)
Recommended Reds:
Pinot Noir Black Family Estate Dundee Hills ★★★★ £F
Pinot Noir Willamette Valley ★★★ £D
Recommended Whites:
Pinot Blanc Dundee Hills ★★☆ £C
Pinot Gris Dundee Hills ★★☆ £C

✿ Francis-Tannahill (Dundee Hills) *www.francistannahill.com*
Cheryl Francis and Sam Tannahill are both involved with A TO Z WINEWORKS producing large volumes of well-made easy drinking fruit accented wines from around Oregon. Under their own label they make much smaller quantities of very rich, concentrated reds and whites from a number of sources. Gewürztraminer comes from the Dragonfly Vineyard near the Hood River. The vines here were planted in 1962 and are biodynamically farmed and produce barely one ton to the acre. With great varietal purity and a subtle minerality, the wine has been fermented in stainless steel and aged for a year on lees. A further white, Blind Love comes from a blend of Roussanne and Marsanne, very rare for Oregon. The Hermit Pinot Noir, regrettably, is produced in tiny quantities and comes from the Pearl vineyard in the Red Hills stretches of the Dundee Hills. A third is vinified as whole clusters and the wine is bottled unfined and unfiltered, shows fine edgy acidity and is loaded with rich, dark plummy fruit and black cherry. A further red, Sundown Red Wine is mainly Syrah but also includes a small amount of Viognier. It comes from the Rogue Valley AVA. It is also bottled without fining or filtration. Both reds will develop well with bottle age. (DM)
Recommended Reds:
Pinot Noir The Hermit Dundee Hills ★★★★☆ £F

Sundown Red Wine Oregon ★★★★ £E
Recommended Whites:
Gewürztraminer Dragonfly Washington ★★★☆ £D

Patricia Green Cellars (Ribbon Ridge) *www.patriciagreencellars.com*
Impressive property established by former Torii Mor winemakers Patty Green and Jim Anderson. The focal point of the operation is the 21 ha (52 acre) Estate Vineyard in Ribbon Ridge, which the pair purchased in 2000. As well as the Estate bottling wines have been made from a range of other vineyards too. These include Balcombe, Ana, Anden, Bonshaw and Whistling Ridge. Shea Vineyard has also been produced along with a number of other labels for tiny lot productions, including grapes sourced from the Hirsch Vineyard in the Russian River. Vinification is carried out with native yeasts and lees are often added back during barrel ageing. They are rich and concentrated, almost animal, gamey styles of Pinot Noir. The Estate Vineyard shows impressive concentration. Well-priced Sauvignon Blanc is becoming increasingly important as well. (DM)
Recommended Reds:
Pinot Noir Estate Vineyard Old Vine Ribbon Ridge ★★★★ £E

Hamacher (Yamhill-Carlton District) *www.hamacherwines.com*
Eric Hamacher makes a small amount of both Chardonnay and Pinot Noir and founded his winery operation in 1995. The wines are all sold to consumers through the Carlton Winemakers Studio of which he was one of the founders. As well as providing a tasting room it is a winery facility for a small number of producers, a form of small scale co-operative which has enabled the partners to benefit from modern sophisticated winemaking facilities. Fruit comes from four separate vineyards planted in a range of soils and at varied altitudes. All are farmed sustainably or organically. As well as his signature wine, his Pinot Noir there are H series releases of both Pinot and Chardonnay which are more approachable and spend a shorter time in barrel. The top Chardonnay is the Cuvée Forets Diverses which is whole cluster pressed and vinified from Dijon clones. The Pinot Noir though is the top wine here. It is very ageworthy for Willamette Pinot, in part because it comes from very old vines, most well over 30 years of age. You can expect it to cellar well for up to a decade. (DM)
Recommended Reds:
Pinot Noir Willamette Valley ★★★★ £E

✿ William Hatcher (Dundee Hills) *www.williamhatcherwines.com*
Just the one wine is produced here. Owner Bill Hatcher who is a partner in A TO Z WINEWORKS also spent years as the winemaker at DOMAINE DROUHIN so has a very fine Willamette pedigree. As with a number of other top level Oregon Pinots the wine offers excellent value. While many other producers are focussing on single vineyard wines Bill Hatcher believes the best of Willamette is shown through blending of different sites and sources fruit from four different vineyards. There is a very stringent selection to get the very best results and the Hatchers are in the enviable position of moving surplus wine to the A to Z label. The wine is very pure and elegant offering very intense subtle red cherry fruit and very well judged oak. (DM)
Recommended Reds:
Pinot Noir Willamette Valley ★★★★☆ £F

✿ JK Carriere (Chehalem Mountains) *www.jkcarriere.com*
Jim Prosser is the source of some of the finest Pinot Noir in Oregon. Indeed with the exception of a single Chardonnay, Lucidité, this is a

Pinot Noir only winery. The top reds are impressive, very structured in style and always have high acidities and demand some patience. The winery was established in 1999 in Yamhill County and is very small in volume. Some of the areas best vineyards are sources of fruit including Shea, the Gemini Vineyard in the Chehalem Mountains, the Anderson Family Vineyard in the Dundee Hills and Temperance Hill in the Eola Hills. There are now some 9 acres of young estate vineyards which for the time being are included in the approachable Provocateur. The Glass Pinot Noir is a particularly unusual and very characterful wine. Jim Prosser refers to it as a white Pinot Noir, although in bottle it has a light salmon pink colour. It is whole cluster pressed, barrel-fermented at a cool temperature and aged on Chardonnay lees. This is very much in line with age-old techniques used by the French for Champagne and helps reduce the colour. The Provocateur is sourced from a number of favoured sites and is vinified as the other wines with wild yeasts and aged in used oak. The wine is softer and more accessible than the Vespidae Willamette Valley example. For this again a selection of sites are used and this is the main focus of the winery accounting for around two-thirds of the annual output. It gets a little new oak, some 20% and is dark, cherry-scented and very mineral with a great backbone and impressive intensity. Each year a number of single-vineyards are determined to represent the ultimate in what is vinified here. Arguably the finest wine the Antoinette, has a depth and firm, mineral character rarely found in the State. It will continue to develop well for a decade but needs at least 3 or 4 years' ageing and decanting. A Blanc de Noir sparkler has also recently been added to the small range. (DM)

Recommended Reds:
Pinot Noir Antoinette Willamette Valley ★★★★★ £G
Pinot Noir Anderson Family Vineyard Willamette Valley ★★★★☆ £F
Pinot Noir Shea Vineyard Yamhill-Carlton ★★★★☆ £F
Pinot Noir Vespidae Willamette Valley ★★★★ £E
Pinot Noir Provocateur Willamette Valley ★★★☆ £D
Recommended Rosés:
Pinot Noir Glass Willamette Valley ★★★ £C

King Estate (Willamette Valley) *www.kingestate.com*
This is now a sizeable operation and the largest producer of Pinot Noir in Oregon. Quality ranges from good to very good and the wines are widely sourced throughout the state. The wines produced include the flagship Domaine and also well-priced Signature labels including a fine luscious ice-wine style Vin Glacé from estate grown Pinot Gris. Approachable easy drinking styles are labelled Acrobat. A number of low-volume limited release wines are also marketed and include reserves of Chardonnay, Pinot Gris and Pinot Noir. As well as these, Cabernet Sauvignon comes from a number of Oregon's warmer sites, there is a Late Harvest Riesling and Syrah sourced from the north of the state in the Columbia Valley. The range is completed by a number of vineyard designate Pinot Noirs from a number of vineyards. (DM)

Recommended Reds:
Pinot Noir Domaine Oregon ★★★★ £F
Pinot Noir Signature Oregon ★★☆ £C
Recommended Whites:
Pinot Gris Domaine Oregon ★★★ £D
Pinot Gris Signature Oregon ★★ £C
Chardonnay Signature Oregon ★★☆ £C
Vin Glace Signature Oregon ★★★ £D

Lemelson Vineyards *www.lemelsonvineyards.com*
This Willamette operation was established in 1999 with the completion of its winery facility. A small and impressive range of well priced Pinot Noirs are produced along with a good Chardonnay, dominated by melon and lightly mineral, spicy flavours rather than others which can be excessively tropical and oaky. Riesling and Pinot Gris are also made. The key wines though, as elsewhere throughout the Willamette are the Pinot Noirs. The firm has a considerable resource in the ownership of vineyards, which they farm organically, across a range of sites and soil types and yields are always kept in check and careful attention paid to canopy management to optimise fruit ripening. The Six Vineyards bottling is soft, fruit driven and forward, a blend of all the different sources. Thea's Selection, is a rich, fruit driven style, with soft supple tannin. The Stermer Vineyard bottling and the top wine Jerome Reserve are firmer and sturdier. The Jerome Reserve is additionally aged for up to 18 months in a mix of new and used oak. Concentrated and powerful it should develop well in bottle for 5 years or more. (DM)

Recommended Reds:
Pinot Noir Jerome Reserve Willamette Valley ★★★★ £F
Pinot Noir Stermer Vineyard Willamette Valley ★★★☆ £E
Pinot Noir Thea's Selection Willamette Valley ★★★ £D
Pinot Noir Six Vineyards Willamette Valley ★★☆ £C
Recommended Whites:
Chardonnay Reserve Willamette Valley ★★★ £D

Maysara (McMinnville) *www.maysara.com*
The Momtazis are as well known for the quality of fruit emerging from their biodynamically farmed home estate vineyard as they are for their fine wines. They purchased their vineyard in 1997 and initially began farming organically before deciding biodynamic preparations were the best way forward - in order to produce fruit of the highest quality and ensure a sense of place in wines with a real stamp of *terroir*. The Pinot Gris comes from both the Momtazi vineyard and several other local vineyards. Very finely structured with excellent fruit purity and very good acidity, it is whole cluster pressed and goes through partial malolactic, which adds weight and texture. The Pinot Noirs though provide the real excitement here and all come from the home vineyard. The Jamsheed version is produced from a mix of clones across all the blocks on the property. Big, full and loaded with ripe dark chery and plum fruit the wine is the most accessible and forward of the trio. The Cyrus comes solely from Pommard clones planted in the lower lying Block 13. More restrained in style with a very fine structure, it has a real dimension and quality to its dark cherry fruit. The Delara comes from best block on the property with the oldest vines. Ageing is in French oak (50% new) and offers up very rich dark fruit, a silky supple texture and impressive intensity. (DM)

Recommended Reds:
Pinot Noir Delara McMinnville ★★★★ £F
Pinot Noir Cyrus McMinnville ★★★★ £E
Pinot Noir Jamsheed McMinnville ★★★☆ £D
Recommended Whites:
Pinot Gris Arsheen Willamette Valley ★★★ £C

Montinore Estate (Willamette Valley) *www.montinore.com*
Rudy Marchesi is putting considerable investment into this sizeable operation since purchasing the winery in January 2006. The latest white vintages are already very promising and the Pinot Noirs consistently improving. The property consists of more than 84 ha (210 acres) of vineyards and is now farmed biodynamically. Of

Pacific North-West

the two premium labeled Pinot Noirs the Graham's Block is solely Pommard clones and aged in 70% new oak whereas the Parsons' Ridge gets a little less new wood. Both are vinified in small lots. Pinot Gris is a fresh crisp and forward style, with good acidity and just a touch of residual sugar. The Gewürztraminer is the best of the wines covered here, offering fruit with a very pure lychee varietal character and just a touch of sweetness on the wines finish. Riesling and Müller-Thurgau are also planted. (DM)

Recommended Reds:
Pinot Noir Cataclysm Estate Willamette Valley ★★★☆ £E
Pinot Noir Graham's Block 7 Estate Willamette Valley ★★★☆ £E
Pinot Noir Parsons' Ridge Estate Willamette Valley ★★★☆ £E
Pinot Noir Reserve Willamette Valley ★★★ £D
Recommended Whites:
Gewürztraminer Willamette Valley ★★★☆ £C
Pinot Gris Willamette Valley ★★☆ £C

✿ Owen Roe (Willamette Valley) *www.owenroe.com*
This small Newberg-based winery produces wines under two labels. The Owen Roe label is for top-quality, small-lot wines, while the Sharecroppers generics includes a Cabernet as well as the berry-laden, lightly gamey Pinot Noir. Quality is extremely high and the Owen Roe wines consistently offer a level of subtlety, elegance and purity of fruit rarely encountered in either state. Very small volumes of the various Owen Roe labels are available. Inevitably the wines are fairly scarce. Cabernet Franc from the Rosa Mystica Block of the Yakima Valley Roza Hills Vineyard is elegant and pure with subtle, leafy varietal character and fine intensity. The Red from the Dubrol Vineyard from the Yakima Valley is a Bordeaux styled blend produced from microscopic yields of late-picked fruit and offers formidable depth as well as impeccable balance. Pinot Noir The Kilmore from Pommard clones grown in Willakenzie soils produces a rich, dark-berry example of impressive persistence. The Owen Roe wines will benefit from a little age, particularly the Dubrol Red. (DM)
Owen Roe
Recommended Reds:
Red Wine Dubrol Vineyard Yakima Valley ★★★★★ £F
Pinot Noir The Kilmore Yamhill-Carlton ★★★★ £E
Cabernet Franc Yakima Valley ★★★☆ £D
Sharecroppers
Recommended Reds:
Pinot Noir Willamette Valley ★★☆ £C

Panther Creek (Willamette Valley) *www.panthercreekcellars.com*
This is an excellent producer of first-class Pinot Noir as well as Pinot Gris. The winery purchases fruit from a range of different vineyard sources throughout the Willamette Valley and, with long-term arrangements with growers, maintains a tight grip on viticulture. Careful sorting (triage) takes place prior to vinification and the practice of minimal intervention is carried through to bottling, with virtually no fining or filtration. There is a plethora of single-vineyard bottlings of Pinot Noir covering many of the major AVAs with a diversity of style. The Winemakers Cuvée comes from a blend of vineyards in both the Willamette and Umpqua Valleys. (DM)
Recommended Reds:
Pinot Noir Reserve Willamette Valley ★★★★ £F
Pinot Noir Schindler Eola-Amity Hills ★★★★ £F
Pinot Noir Kalita Vineyard Yamhill-Carlton ★★★★ £F
Pinot Noir De Ponte Dundee Hills ★★★☆ £E
Pinot Noir Winemakers Cuvée Willamette Valley ★★★ £D

Penner-Ash (Willamette Valley) *www.pennerash.com*
Ron and Lynn Penner-Ash produce some rich and concentrated Willamette Valley Pinot Noir as well as small quantities of hand-crafted Syrah and Viognier. The Syrah comes from several different Oregon growers, while the Viognier is sourced from vineyards in the Rogue and Columbia Valleys. The Pinot Noir, a blend from a number of sites gets 9 months in French oak, 40% of the barrels being new. The wine is rich and concentrated, firmly structured with dark berry fruit and a savoury edge to the palate. The Shea bottling is again rich, dark, plummy and smoky with additional weight and concentration. Both will keep well for 6 or 7 years and also drink well within a year or so of release. A wide range of single vineyard wines are now made. (DM)
Recommended Reds:
Pinot Noir Shea Vineyard Yamhill-Carlton ★★★★ £F
Pinot Noir Willamette Valley ★★★★ £E
Recommended Whites:
Viognier Oregon ★★★☆ £D
Recommended Rosés:
Roseo Oregon ★★ £D

Ponzi (Chehalem Mountains) *www.ponziwines.com*
Ponzi is a long-established Willamette Valley producer with a deservedly high reputation for its Pinot Noir. Luisa Ponzi has now taken on the winemaking mantle. Regular Willamette Classico Pinot Noir is certainly good in a ripe, gamey and earthy style. There is a superior Reserve bottling, which offers more depth and greater structure as well as the tiny-production Abetina, Vigneto Reserves (£G). Of particular interest here is one of the better Pinot Gris and a good fruit-driven Arneis. These offer particularly good value. Chardonnay comes in regular and Reserve examples along with two special cru wines, Avellana and Aurora (both £F). Pinot Blanc, Riesling and Dolcetto are also made. (DM)
Recommended Reds:
Pinot Noir Reserve Willamette Valley ★★★★ £F
Pinot Noir Classico Willamette Valley ★★★☆ £E
Recommended Whites:
Chardonnay Reserve Willamette Valley ★★★☆ £E
Pinot Gris Willamette Valley ★★★ £C
Arneis Willamette Valley ★★☆ £D

Raptor Ridge (Willamette Valley) *www.raptoridge.com*
The Schulls produce a small and impressive range of single-vineyard Pinot Noirs from a range of sources as well as one of the best value Willamette bottlings to be found in the State. They founded their winery in 1995 and have since planted a 7.5 ha (18 acre) site, which is farmed organically in the Chehalem Mountains. Output is now around 7,500 cases a year. As well as the Pinot Noir bottlings there is an attractive fresh minerally pure Pinot Gris, which is fermented in a mix of stainless steel and some used oak. Micro-oxygenation is used to develop the wine in the cellar. The Willamette comes from a range of sites that the Schulls feel will provide them with an attractive fruit driven style of Pinot. The rich and darkly fruited Reserve Pinot is vinified with a small proportion of whole clusters and aged in one-third new wood. From the McMinnville area is the Meredith Mitchell bottling. The very rocky soils provide for a more dark and spicy wine with added dimension from the well-integrated oak. The Shea vineyard is earthy and gamey with a dark-fruit core and a rich, truffle undercurrent together with a firm mineral structure that underpins the wine. The home estate vineyard, Tuscowallame is also now released and Pinot Noir also comes from

the Olenik and Black Hole Vineyards in the Chehalem Mountains, the Goodrich and Gran Moraine Vineyards in Yamhill-Carlton as well as the Crawford Beck Vineyard in the Eola-Amity Hills. An excellent, well-priced small range, the single vineyard wines all deserve cellaring for 4 or 5 years. A Pinot rosé is also made along with a Tempranillo and unusually now a Grüner Veltliner from the estate vineyard. (DM)

Recommended Reds:
Pinot Noir Meredith Mitchell Vineyard McMinnville ★★★★ £F
Pinot Noir Shea Vineyard Yamhill-Carlton ★★★★ £F
Pinot Noir Reserve Willamette Valley ★★★☆ £E
Pinot Noir Willamette Valley ★★★ £D
Recommended Whites:
Pinot Gris Willamette Valley ★★☆ £C

Rex Hill (Chehalem Mountains) *www.rexhill.com*
The four partners at A TO Z WINEWORKS purchased this operation in 2007. With 23 ha (56 acres) of owned vineyards (Estate and Jacob-Hart) planted almost exclusively to Pinot Noir and Chardonnay and sourcing fruit from elsewhere this winery has consistently produced first-class wines and in particular, Pinot Noir from a number of sites. There is a good regular Willamette Valley bottling and a very consistent Reserve. The partners believe that as yet only a limited number of vineyard sites have yet proved themselves in the longer term and quality can be achieved as much with a varied range of fruit sources as much as single sites. The Reserve and Jacob-Hart vineyard examples possess that extra dimension. While reasonably pricey, they are not excessively so. Of equal interest is a very good Pinot Gris from the Jacob-Hart Vineyard as well as a richly textured, creamy Chardonnay from the Willamette Valley. (DM)

Recommended Reds:
Pinot Noir Reserve Willamette Valley ★★★★ £F
Pinot Noir Willamette Valley ★★★ £E
Recommended Whites:
Chardonnay Seven Soils Willamette Valley ★★★ £D
Pinot Gris Jacob-Hart Vineyard Willamette Valley ★★★ £D

Andrew Rich (Willamette Valley) *www.andrewrichwines.com*
Andrew Rich established his operation a little over a decade ago and produces wines from both Oregon and Washington sources. As well as Pinot Noir, Sauvignon Blanc and Gewürztraminer a range of Rhône varieties including Grenache, Mourvèdre and Roussanne as well as Syrah contribute to his small range. Sauvignon Blanc has been produced from the Croft Vineyard for a number of vintages and is finely structured with impressively ripe tropical as well as green fruit notes. Pinot Noir Prelude comes from a blend of vineyard sources. Rich and characterful, there is a fine mix of red berry and darker plum fruit and very well judged oak. Unfortunately the dark, smoky and richly textured Syrah Prometheus is made only in tiny quantities. It is more reminiscent of the best from Cornas than further north in the Rhône. Sourced from a blend of three of Washington's best sites, the Ciel du Cheval, Klipsun and Red Willow vineyards, the wine will add further complexity with 4 or 5 years' of ageing. (DM)

Recommended Reds:
Pinot Noir Prelude Willamette Valley ★★★★ £F
Syrah Prometheus Columbia Valley ★★★★ £E
Recommended Whites:
Gewürztraminer Dessert Wine Willamette Valley ★★★★ £F
Sauvignon Blanc Croft Vineyard Willamette Valley ★★★☆ £D

St Innocent (Willamette Valley) *www.stinnocentwine.com*
Mark Vlossak established his small operation in 1988 with a number of other investors producing just a few hundred cases in his first vintage. Today the output remains relatively small and he makes some of the most striking wines in the AVA, with two-thirds accounted for by Pinot Noir. A big and structured Pinot Gris is more marked by minerality than by primary fruit. It offers tremendous intensity and carry on the palate. Pinot Blanc is no less impressive with rich nutty fruit and a silky texture. Chardonnay also comes from the Freedom Hill Vineyard and is quite Burgundian in style with some subtle citrus notes and a rich, creamy lees infused character. Pinot Noir is produced in a number of single-vineyard guises. As well as the bottlings covered here wines are released from the Vitae Springs, Zenith, Justice and Momtazi vineyards. A rich and concentrated dark fruited example is produced from the Shea Vineyard with hints of plum and black cherry and a touch of oak and truffle on the finish. The single vineyard Pinot Noirs will develop well in the medium term in bottle. (DM)

Recommended Reds:
Pinot Noir Shea Vineyard Yamhill-Carlton ★★★★ £E
Pinot Noir Freedom Hill Vineyard Willamette Valley ★★★★ £E
Recommended Whites:
Chardonnay Freedom Hill Vineyard Willamette Valley ★★★★ £E
Pinot Blanc Freedom Hill Vineyard Willamette Valley ★★★☆ £C
Pinot Gris Vitae Springs Vineyard Willamette Valley ★★★☆ £C

⊛ Domaine Serene (Dundee Hills) *www.domaineserene.com*
This is a top-class producer of both Pinot Noir and Chardonnay. Considerable investment has gone into the estate and the results are impressive. Yields are kept to a minimum – around 2 tons to the acre – and the harvest is always carried out by hand. Minimal intervention in the cellars means the Pinot Noir is only racked at bottling and is neither fined nor filtered. Chardonnay, made using only the Dijon clone, is barrel-fermented and aged on its lees for up to 15 months. Tiny lots of various single-vineyard bottlings are available through the winery and there is also a flagship Pinot Noir, Grace Vineyard. The Pinot Noirs are marked by their firm structure and dark, rich and concentrated berry fruit. Time is needed to integrate the new oak in both the Evenstad Reserve and Mark Bradford. The two Chardonnays are lightly tropical, with a fine, spicy, toasty oak character but with the firm structure that earmarks their cool-grown origins. The Clos du Soleil is the tighter, more mineral of the two. A vibrant Syrah, Rockblock SoNo, is a non-vintage example from Oregon Walla Walla fruit while the R Rosé is a barrel aged style. (DM)

Recommended Reds:
Pinot Noir Grace Vineyard ★★★★★ £G
Pinot Noir Mark Bradford Vineyard ★★★★☆ £G
Pinot Noir Evenstad Reserve ★★★★ £F
Pinot Noir Yamhill Cuvée ★★★☆ £E
Recommended Whites:
Chardonnay Clos du Soleil ★★★★ £E
Chardonnay Côte Sud ★★★★ £E

⊛ Sokol Blosser (Dundee Hills) *www.sokolblosser.com*
The Sokol Blossers purchased their first vineyard land in 1970. Their winery is now fully organically farmed. Wines from the home vineyards now take the Dundee Hills AVA. There are a couple of easy drinking wines: the white and red Evolution as well as a white sparkling Evolution. The white is lightly floral a real concoction of grapes. Cool fermentation aromas and a apple green character mark

the wine which has just a touch of residual sugar. The non-vintage Evolution red is a blend of Syrah, Montepulciano and Sangiovese and marked by ripe vibrant and forward red berry fruit. Pinot Noir is used to produce a fresh and characterful strawberry scented rosé. Finely structured, minerally Pinot Gris comes from a significant holding of estate vineyards as well as neighbouring sites within the Dundee Hills appellation. The Dundee Hills Pinot Noir is solely from estate grown fruit. Given a pre-fermentation maceration and vatted for around a month, ageing is in a sizeable proportion of new oak and the wine has a ripe, savoury character. The Estate Cuvée comes from the best blocks on the property with some of the fruit from vines around 35 years old. Darker and smokier in style with characterful dark cherry fruit and supple, rounded tannins, the wine is likely to improve with 3 or 4 years' bottle age. A number of premium Block series Pinot Noirs are also now made in small quantities. (DM)

Recommended Reds:
Pinot Noir Estate Vineyard Dundee Hills ★★★★ £F
Pinot Noir Dundee Hills ★★★☆ £E
Evolution NV America ★★☆ £C
Recommended Whites:
Pinot Gris Willamette Valley ★★★ £C
Evolution NV America ★★☆ £C
Recommended Rosés:
Rosé of Pinot Noir Dundee Hills ★★ £B

Soter Vineyards (Yamhill-Carlton) *www.sotervineyards.com*
This estate, Mineral Springs Ranch, was established by Tony Soter who founded his own ETUDE wines in California and consulted to a number of luminary wineries including ARAUJO, SHAFER, VIADER and DALLE VALLE. Planting began in 2002 and there are now 12 ha of Pinot Noir vines and slightly less than a hectare of Chardonnay which is reserved exclusively for their sparkling wines, a Brut white and rosé. The vineyard aspect here is ideal with consistent south-east to south-west slopes and the vines planted in loamy soils which provide excellent drainage. Sustainable farming is practiced to optimise the quality of the wines. For the North Valley Pinot Noir, Soter works with a number of growers, all with vineyards within a 10 mile radius of Carlton, to provide a well-priced example of the area. It is a wine marked by bright strawberry fruit and sees minimal new oak. The estate bottling is altogether more structured and richly textured. The fruit gets a cold soak before fermentation and an extended vatting on the skins. Ageing is then in a mix of 60% to 40% new to used French barrels and for around 12 to 15 months to balance the fruit and oak. The eventual planned output from the home vineyard is 3,000 cases a year. (DM)

Recommended Reds:
Pinot Noir Mineral Springs Ranch Yamhill-Carlton ★★★★ £F
Pinot Noir North Valley Willamette Valley ★★★☆ £E

Stangeland (Eola-Amity Hills) *www.stangelandwinery.com*
The vineyards at this estate are to be found just to the north of Salem and gain the maximum light exposure from the sun, picking up its benefit from early morning. The property, located on a hilltop with a south facing aspect, was originally planted in 1978 to a combination of Pinot Noir, Chardonnay and Pinot Gris. The developing age of the vineyards is beginning to show through in the quality of the wines and a number of other growers also supply fruit. Pinot Noir is the main focus and a broad range of wines is produced. The Estate example is in an attractive dark fruit style. The top two Pinots are impressively dense, structured and intense,

with the Winemakers Estate Reserve offering additional mineral depth and persistence. Both will benefit from three or four year's patience. The unusual and fascinating Chardonnay Decadence is an ice-wine style with the late-harvest fruit frozen and concentrated leaving a sweet and unctuous richness. The dry whites are all very well priced. The Pinot Gris and Gewürztraminer are in a very crisp and elegant Alsatian style, the Chardonnay restrained and citrusy gaining additional structure from 11 months barrel-fermentation and ageing. (DM)

Recommended Reds:
Pinot Noir Winemakers Estate Reserve Willamette Valley ★★★★ £F
Pinot Noir Estate Reserve Willamette Valley ★★★☆ £E
Pinot Noir Estate Willamette Valley ★★★ £D
Recommended Whites:
Chardonnay Decadence Estate Willamette Valley ★★★☆ £E
Pinot Gris Eola-Amity Hills ★★☆ £C
Chardonnay Estate Willamette Valley ★★☆ £C
Gewürztraminer Willamette Valley ★★ £C

Stoller Vineyards (Dundee Hills) *www.stollervineyards.com*
This is the sister property of Harry Peterson-Nedry's CHEHALEM. The Stollers are co-owners there and the same applies here. One of the key differences between the two operations being that the wines here are produced from estate fruit whereas at Chehalem a range of examples from a number of sources are created. Vineyard plantation work started in 1995, and the vines are close spaced, mostly to Pinot Noir. The south facing exposition, free-draining rocky soils and a range of different clones adds to both complexity and quality. The well-priced rosé is solely Pinot Noir and is vinified from a combination of direct pressing and a short skin maceration. The Dundee Hills Pinot Noir is, as you would expect, the softer of the Pinot bottlings with both getting a cold-soak prior to fermentation. Ageing is similar, around 10 to 11 months in wood with the more structured and complex mineral qualities of the Reseve Pinot determined by a selection both from the best vineyard plots and the best barrels. The Reserve Chardonnay is rich and honeyed with a concentrated buttery texture as well as sufficient mineral acidity for balance. The wine is in a typical barrel-fermented Chardonnay style, vinified on lees although only partial malolactic ensures that freshness of fruit. (DM)

Recommended Reds:
Pinot Noir Reserve Dundee Hills ★★★★ £E
Pinot Noir Dundee Hills ★★★ £C
Recommended Whites:
Chardonnay Reserve Dundee Hills ★★★☆ £E
Recommended Rosés:
Pinot Noir Dundee Hills ★★☆ £C

>> Torii Mor (Willamette Valley) *www.vidonvineyard.com*
Torii Mor was established with planting on the site of what is now the Olson Estate Vineyard in the Dundee Hills in 1972, so the vines now have some significant age and an Old Vine Reserve selection is also made. The Estate Pinot Noir made by French winemaker Jacques Tardy, is fermented conventionally without whole bunches and also has restrained use of new oak. Full of complex, dark berry fruits the wine offers a fine underpinning structure with supple tannins and nicely edgy acidity. We can also recommend readers to look for premium Pinots from the Nysa, Alloro and La Colina vineyards. The Dundee Vineyard and Yamhill-Carlton Select examples both offer good value, as does the very well priced Willamette Valley bottling. (DM)

Recommended Reds:
Pinot Noir Olson Chehalem Mountains ★★★☆ £F
Pinot Noir La Colina Vineyard Chehalem Mountains ★★★★ £F
Pinot Noir Alloro Vineyard Chehalem Mountains ★★★★ £F
Pinot Noir Nysa Vineyard Chehalem Mountains ★★★★ £F
Pinot Noir Yamhill Carlton Select ★★★☆ £E
Pinot Noir Dundee Hills Select ★★★☆ £E
Pinot Noir Willamette Valley ★★★ £D
Recommended Whites:
Pinot Gris Dundee Hills Reserve ★★★ £D

Vidon Vineyard (Willamette Valley) *www.vidonvineyard.com*
This is a recently established small operation, producing Pinot Noir
red and rosé as well as Tempranillo and Pinot Gris. The first vintage
was in 2003 and the Pinot Noir is now labelled 3 Clones. As ever with
small volume winemaking keeping a track of your favourite wines
is not easy. Production of all the wines is small. The estate vineyard
is planted on a south-west facing slope at an elevation of 400 to
500 feet in the Chehalem Mountains just to the north of Newberg.
The warm and sunny days here are moderated by cooling ocean
breezes. This provides fruit enriched with a long, easy ripening
period. Finely structured and elegant in style with just 10% new
wood the 3 Clones bottling comes from a yield of barely 2 tons to
the acre. Expect it to develop nicely for four or five years at least.
(DM)
Recommended Reds:
Pinot Noir 3 Clones Chehalem Mountains ★★★☆ £D

Willakenzie (Willamette Valley) *www.willakenzie.com*
This is a substantial operation with estate vineyards under
cultivation just to the north-east of Yamhill. As well as Pinot Noir,
which is the main focus, Pinot Blanc, Pinot Gris, Pinot Meunier and
Gamay are also planted. As with many other estates in the region
sustainable farming is practiced. For Pinot Noir ten different clones
are planted, providing additional complexity and the property is
named after the sedimentary soil that the vineyards are planted in.
The Pierre Leon bottling comes from a selection of all the vineyard
blocks and gets a typical cold soak and is aged for 12 months in oak
(60% new). It is full, fat and well rounded. The Kiana bottling gets
less new wood (40%) and is bottled unfiltered and unfined. The
Emery shows dark-cherry fruit with a rich plummy character and big
and supple tannins.(DM)
Recommended Reds:
Pinot Noir Emery Willamette Valley ★★★☆ £E
Pinot Noir Kiana Vineyard Willamette Valley ★★★☆ £E
Pinot Noir Pierre Leon Willamette Valley ★★★ £E

Willamette Valley Vineyards (Willamette Valley) *www.wvv.com*
Jim Bernau established his winery and estate vineyards in 1983.
The site is planted on south and south-west facing slopes. The
vineyards are now farmed sustainably and in 1997 the Tualatin
Estate vineyard and winery was added to the portfolio. Estate Pinot
Noir, Chardonnay, Pinot Blanc and Pinot Gris are all available. Pinot
Gris is a clean, fresh example, which is fermented cool in stainless
steel. The Whole Cluster Pinot Noir is a vibrant forward style. Like
the Pinot Gris it is an important volume brand for the winery. The
other Pinots are quite a step up and understandably produced in
much lower quantities. The Estate Vineyard wine is given a 5-day
cold soak and offers bright strawberry fruit with a slight green
pepper undercurrent. The Signature Cuvée is subtler with red cherry
fruit and good intensity. A number of AVA series wines are also

now made from the Dundee Hills, McMinnville, Ribbon Ridge and
Yamhill-Carlton regions. The top two wines will develop well over 4
or 5 years. (DM)
Recommended Reds:
Pinot Noir Signature Cuvée Willamette Valley ★★★★ £E
Pinot Noir Tualatin Estate Willamette Valley ★★★☆ £E
Pinot Noir Estate Willamette Valley ★★★ £E
Pinot Noir Whole Cluster Willamette Valley ★★☆ £D
Recommended Whites:
Pinot Gris Willamette Valley ★★ £B

◉ Ken Wright (Willamette Valley) *www.kenwrightcellars.com*
Ken Wright has established himself as the Willamette champion
of single-vineyard Pinot Noir, seeking to show in his wines the
best individual site characteristics in a single bottling, what the
French refer to as *terroir*. Now working with a considerable number
of vineyard owners, he produces wines from a wide range of
Willamette Valley sites. The Guadalupe Vineyard is among the
most successful bottlings here over a number of vintages. Sourced
like the McCrone Vineyard Pinot from the Yamhill foothills this is
opulent, lush and forward and will drink well at a young age. A
Chardonnay, comes from the Columbia River, Celilo Vineyard site.
A small amount of floral, subtly oaked Pinot Blanc is also produced.
Because production is limited, the various cuvées are hard to find.
However you can expect the wines to be almost invariably of 3 plus
star quality, often 4 star, and although not cheap, they are priced
very fairly. A new label, Tyrus Evan, has been established for non-
Burgundian styles and so far Syrah, Cabernet Franc, Malbec and a
Bordeaux red blend "Claret" are produced. A number of sites have
been sourced from including the Ciel du Cheval, Pepper Bridge and
Seven Hills Vineyards in Washington State and the Del Rio Vineyard
in the Rogue Valley in Oregon. Smoky, opulent black fruited Walla
Walla Syrah comes from the Seven Hills Vineyard, the Del Rio is a
touch more structured and firm. The Del Rio Claret is a blend of
Cabernets Franc and Sauvignon, Malbec and Merlot. It will need four
or five years, a little longer than the Ciel du Cheval, an opulent richly
textured blend of Merlot with Cabernet Franc and Petit Verdot. (DM)
Ken Wright
Recommended Reds:
Pinot Noir Guadalupe Vineyard Yamhill-Carlton ★★★★ £F
Pinot Noir Canary Hill Vineyard Willamette Valley ★★★★ £F
Pinot Noir McCrone Vineyard Yamhill-Carlton ★★★★ £F
Tyrus Evan
Recommended Reds:
Syrah Del Rio Vineyard Rogue Valley ★★★★ £F
Syrah Walla Walla Valley ★★★★ £F
"Claret" Ciel du Cheval Vineyard Rogue Valley ★★★★ £F
"Claret" Del Rio Vineyard Rogue Valley ★★★☆ £F

Z'IVO Wines (Eola Amity Hills) *www.zivowines.com*
Low volume and very good quality wines are being released under
this winery label. The main focus is on Pinot Noir but a couple of
whites are also released. As well as the Mika, there is a further white
Three which comes from a mix of Oregon and Washington State
fruit and is a blend of Melon de Bourgogne, Sauvignon Blanc and
Chardonnay. The Z'Ivo home vineyard was established in 1995 and
is close planted to a mix of clones on well-drained volcanic soils on
the eastern slopes of the Amity Hills. It is these soils which provide
the wines with the classic black fruited qualities which the Eola
Amity Hills are noted for. Much attention is spent on the vineyards
during the growing season with shoot positioning to ensure light

exposure as well as ventilation and crop thinning is also practiced. The Mika white is a blend of roughly two-thirds Chardonnay and one-third Pinot Gris which is aged in neutral oak for 11 months to give it additional weight and substance. The Eola-Amity Hills Pinot comes solely from estate grown fruit and is full of dark red berry fruit and the oak is well judged, ageing is for just 11 months and a third new wood is used. The Whole Cluster bottling is offered for a similarly very reasonable price and has just a touch more depth and intensity. As you would expect from the name of the *cuvée* the wine is vinified from only whole bunches. It is otherwise the mirror image of its sibling. (DM)

Recommended Reds:
Pinot Noir Eola Amity Hills Whole Cluster ★★★★ £E
Pinot Noir Eola Amity Hills ★★★☆ £D
Recommended Whites:
Mika Willamette Valley ★★☆ £C

A-Z of producers *Washington State*

Andrew Will (Washington State) *www.andrewwill.com*
Very good quality wines here for nearly two decades. Winemaker Chris Camarda produces elegant, very finely made reds. The wines come from a range of sources and there is a general move away from the varietal dominated bottlings of a few vintages ago. Camarda obviously feels blended wines is the way to go now. The Sorella is a fine, spicy mix of Cabernet Sauvignon, Cabernet Franc, Merlot and Petit Verdot. Ciel du Cheval, Champoux and Two Blondes are all Bordeaux blends from individual vineyards. If you are buying also look out for Cabernet Franc and Cabernet Sauvignon from the Columbia Valley and there is a single vineyard Cabernet Sauvignon from the Discovery Vineyard in the Horse Heaven Hills. (DM)

Recommended Reds:
Sorella Washington State ★★★★★ £F
Champoux Horse Heaven Hills ★★★★☆ £F
Ciel du Cheval Red Mountain ★★★★☆ £F
Two Blondes Yakima Valley ★★★★ £F

>> Betz Family Winery *www.betzfamilywinery.com*
This is one of Washington States finest red wine producers with exemplary Bordeaux and Rhône styles both made. Wines are sourced from a number of vineyards throughout the Colmbia Valley including Horse Heaven Hills, Red Mountain, Snipes Mountain as well as the Yakima Valley. Among the Rhône styles the Besoleil Red is Grenache based and offers great value and also includes Counoise, Cinsault, Syrah and Mourvèdre. There are also a number of Syrah's made. La Serenne comes from higher altitudes and with sufficient ripeness is ofter vinified with whole bunches. La Cote Rousse is a dark, spicy and brooding red of impressive depth. A Réserve du Soleil based in the main on Mourvèdre as well as a further premium Syrah, La Côte Rousse are also made. Some equally fine Bordeaux reds are also made. Cuvée Frangin is a supple and approachable combination of Cabernet Sauvignon, Merlot, Petit Verdot and Syrah, the Syrah of course being the odd man out but who cares. Clos de Betz is a rich, dense and opulent Right Bank blend of Merlot and Cabernet Sauvigon but gets around a fifth of Petit Verdot which lends further definition and structure. The Père de Famille is dominated by Cabernet Sauvignon, providing a wine of dark black fruits, backgound hints of cassis and impressive density and concentartion. Ageing is in all new French barrels. All the wines will continue to develop for a minimum of five years in bottle. (DM)

Recommended Reds:
Père de Famille Columbia Valley ★★★★★ £F
Clos de Betz Columbia Valley ★★★★★ £F
Cuvée Frangin Columbia Valley ★★★★ £E
Syrah La Côte Rousse Red Mountain ★★★★★ £F
Syrah La Serenne Boushey Vineyard Yakima Valley ★★★★☆ £F
Besoleil Red Columbia Valley ★★★★ £E

Bookwalter Winery (Columbia Valley) *www.bookwalterwines.com*
The Bookwalters have been producing premium Washington State wines since 1983 and fruit comes from a number of sources including top Columbia Valley vineyards. The Bookwalters also have their own vineyard, the Bookwalter Estate. The rich, supple, dark and plummy Merlot has a little Cabernet Sauvignon, Malbec and Petit Verdot blended in for structure. The Cabernet Sauvignon is firmer and offers berry fruit and an opulent cassis character. The Suspense is a sumptuous and rich red, very supple and forward, and like the other wines it will drink well relatively young. The blend comprises Merlot and Cabernets Sauvignon and Franc as well as Malbec. The wines are aged in new and used oak with the malolactic fermentation in barrel. As well as the wines rated here there is a soft multi-vintage red blend Notebook, an approachable Cabernet Subplot, decent Doubleplot Chardonnay, Notebook Riesling, a Chardonnay/Viognier blend Couplet and a late harvested Viognier Novella. Most recently added is a rosé, Scarlet Hexflame Rosé. Two further premium reds Conflict and Protagonist (£F) as well as a super premium varietal Cabernet Sauvignon the Volume Series (£G). (DM)

Recommended Reds:
Suspense Columbia Valley ★★★★ £F
Cabernet Sauvignon Foreshadow Columbia Valley ★★★ £E
Merlot Foreshadow Columbia Valley ★★★ £E

Canoe Ridge Vineyard *www.canoeridgevineyard.com*
Formerly owned by the California-based CHALONE Winery, Canoe Ridge, based in the Columbia Valley, has been owned by its current proprietors since 2011. It is a reliable producer of good, well-made, ripe and toasty Chardonnay along with Merlot and Cabernet Sauvignon that are soft, forward reds enjoyable in their relative youth. Merlot sees American oak; Cabernet is aged in French barrels. Stylish and more expensive Reserves are also available in more limited quantity as well as a Cherry Red Reserve from a blend of Syrah, Malbec and Grenache. A small quantity of Pinot Gris is also produced. (DM)

Recommended Reds:
Expedition Cabernet Sauvignon Columbia Valley ★★★ £E
Expedition Merlot Horse Heaven Hills ★★☆ £D
Recommended Whites:
Expedition Chardonnay Columbia Valley ★★☆ £D

✿✿ Cayuse Vineyards (Walla Walla Valley) *www.cayusevineyards.com*
Christophe Baron's family roots are in Champagne and there is a marked French influence in his wines. They tend to be tighter and more structured than a number of his neighbours' offerings, with a subtler, defter hand and very well integrated fruit and oak. They are far from showy blockbusters, though. Cayuse has also established itself as the first winery in Washington to work its vineyards biodynamically. A total of 24 ha (60 acres) are currently farmed and no fewer than 13 wines are produced in small quantity. The Rhône and Bordeaux varieties are the dominant plantings and there is also some Tempranillo, Grenache and Viognier. Both of these Syrahs are tight and well structured with dark, spicy fruit and a real minerality

showing through. The En Cerise is the more open and opulent of the two. Not yet tasted but worth trying is the En Chamberlin Vineyard bottling. Camaspelo is a Bordeaux blend of Cabernet Sauvignon and Merlot. This is the subtlest and lightest of the wines with a touch of leafiness, almost reminiscent of Loire reds. Given time and patience it will open up very well. (DM)

Recommended Reds:
Syrah Cailloux Vineyard Walla Walla Valley ⚬⚬⚬⚬⚬ £H
Syrah En Cerise Vineyard Walla Walla Valley ⚬⚬⚬⚬⚬ £H
Camaspelo Walla Walla Valley ★★★★★ £G

❋ Chateau Ste Michelle (Columbia Valley) *www.ste-michelle.com*
This is the largest producer in Washington State and the jewel in the Ste Michelle Wine Estates crown. The wines from Chateau Ste Michelle seem somehow more complete and exciting than those from sister winery COLUMBIA CREST, even at the lower levels. A considerable array of wines is produced here, including a number in overseas partnerships. The Columbia Valley is the focal point of the winery's operations and there is a new vinification facility at the Canoe Ridge Estate Vineyard, the River Ridge Winery. Other key vineyard sources are Cold Creek, Horse Heaven and Indian Wells. The Indian Wells wines now come from a combination of the Indian Wells vineyard and other sites. The regular Columbia Valley bottlings can offer very good value, particularly among the whites, with the single-vineyard series offering style, quality and diversity. There are some very good Artists Series and Ethos Reserve labels, now including Syrah sourced from a number of vineyards. The Meritage red has been consistently good over the last few vintages. Of particular interest are two joint partnerships. Eroica, results in a marvellously intense, opulent but crisp, mineral-scented Riesling made in partnership with Ernst LOOSEN from the Mosel-Saar-Ruwer. A superior Gold Riesling and both an Ice Wine and a Single Berry Select sweet wine are also made under the partnership. In tandem with Tuscany's ANTINORI is the premium red Col Solare, an opulent blend of Cabernet Sauvignon, Merlot, Cabernet Franc and Malbec. (DM)

Col Solare
Recommended Reds:
Col Solare Columbia Valley ★★★★☆ £G

Eroica
Recommended Whites:
Riesling Eroica Columbia Valley ★★★☆ £D

Chateau Ste Michelle
Recommended Reds:
Meritage Artists Series Columbia Valley ★★★★ £F
Cabernet Sauvignon Ethos Reserve Columbia Valley ★★★☆ £E
Cabernet Sauvignon Cold Creek Columbia Valley ★★★ £E
Cabernet Sauvignon Indian Wells Columbia Valley ★★☆ £C
Cabernet Sauvignon Columbia Valley ★★ £C
Syrah Ethos Reserve ★★★☆ £E
Syrah Columbia Valley ★☆ £C
Merlot Ethos Reserve Columbia Valley ★★★☆ £E
Merlot Canoe Ridge Columbia Valley ★★☆ £D
Merlot Indian Wells Columbia Valley ★★ £C
Merlot Columbia Valley ★☆ £C

Recommended Whites:
Chardonnay Ethos Reserve Columbia Valley ★★★☆ £D
Chardonnay Cold Creek Columbia Valley ★★★☆ £D
Chardonnay Canoe Ridge Columbia Valley ★★★ £D
Chardonnay Indian Wells Columbia Valley ★★☆ £C
Chardonnay Columbia Valley ★★ £C

Riesling Columbia Valley ★★ £B
Sauvignon Blanc Horse Heaven Columbia Valley ★★☆ £C
Sauvignon Blanc Columbia Valley ★☆ £B
Pinot Gris Columbia Valley ★ £B
Gewürztraminer Columbia Valley ★ £B

Columbia Crest (Columbia Valley) *www.columbia-crest.com*
Originally conceived as a junior label for CHATEAU STE MICHELLE this is now a stand-alone operation. The wines are all reasonably crafted, particularly at the top end, although there is a certain uniformity of style and you yearn for a little more character and individuality. The operation draws on extensive estate vineyards for much of its needs. A line-up of varietals appear under the Columbia Valley label. The Grand Estates wines are a step up and the range is completed by some impressive Reserve reds, as well as Chardonnay, some of which are available exclusively through the winery and online. The Walter Clore Private Reserve is a powerful meritage blend of Cabernet Sauvignon and Merlot in almost equal parts, it too is now a winery online exclusive. A small amount of late-harvest Viognier is produced. (DM)

Recommended Reds:
Walter Clore Private Reserve Columbia Valley ★★★ £E
Cabernet Sauvignon Reserve Columbia Valley ★★★ £E
Cabernet Sauvignon Grand Estates Columbia Valley ★★ £C
Merlot Grand Estates Columbia Valley ★★ £C

Recommended Whites:
Chardonnay Grand Estates Columbia Valley ★☆ £B

❋ Delille Cellars (Washington State) *www.delillecellars.com*
The focus of Dellille Cellars is principally on producing top-quality Bordeaux blends from a range of Yakima Valley fruit sources, the majority from the Red Mountain AVA and now including their own Grand Ciel site. To this end they succeed very well, with the wines close to the state pinnacle. Both the Chaleur Estate and the D2 are made in an open-knit, ripe, supple style, particularly the soft, more obviously forward D2 which is dominated by Merlot. The Estate – Cabernet Sauvignon, Merlot, Cabernet Franc and Petit Verdot – certainly has depth and a fine tannic structure, but very much in an opulent, bold fashion with vibrant, dark chocolaty fruit. Harrison Hill differs from Chaleur in that it is a single-vineyard meritage in a tighter, more backward style. The impressive white Chaleur Estate is a blend of ripe Sauvignon Blanc and Sémillon. An additional range of wines is now produced under the Doyenne label. These include a Roussanne, a Syrah, a red Rhône blend labelled Métier, Aix which includes a little Cabernet Sauvignon (Provençale in approach), and a rosé. As well as the Grand Ciel Vineyard Syrah, there is also a super premium Grand Ciel Cabernet Sauvignon (£H). (DM)

Recommended Reds:
Delille Chaleur Estate Red Mountain ★★★★☆ £F
Delille Harrison Hill Snipes Mountain ★★★★☆ £F
Grand Ciel Syrah Vineyard Red Mountain ★★★★☆ £F
Delille D2 Columbia Valley ★★★☆ £E

Recommended Whites:
Delille Chaleur Estate Columbia Valley ★★★☆ £E

Domaine Ste Michelle *www.michellesparkling.com*
Ste Michelle Wine Estates Washington label for sparkling wine focuses on straightforward, attractive fizz from the Columbia Valley produced at keen prices. The range comprises a Cuvée Brut, from red and white grapes, an Extra Dry and a rosé. A touch pricier is the vintages Luxe. The style is for marked fruit character rather than

Washington State

yeasty, bready complexity and a drink-now style. The Luxe is a little more elegant. (DM)

Recommended Whites:
Luxe Vintage Columbia Valley ★★☆ £D
Cuvée Brut Non-Vintage Columbia Valley ★★ £C

❀ Gramercy Cellars (Walla Walla Valley) www.gramercycellars.com
Greg Harrington was a very youthful Master Sommelier before becoming a winemaker and establishing this project. His objective is to produce a small range of wines that offer a sense of place, emphasising their *terroir* and create them with minimal intervention. A number of wines have now been made with the focus on The Rhône Valley and Bordeaux. In addition a Tempranillo Inigo Montoya from the Walla Walla Valley has also been released. It includes a touch of both Mourvèdre and Syrah. A Columbia Valley GSM red (Grenache,Syrah and Mourvèdre) is labelled Third Man. L'Idiot du Village comes from Mourvèdre and Syrah. A Walla Walla Pepper Bridge blend combines Merlot, Cabernet Sauvignon and Petit Verdot, while the Cabernet Sauvignon from the Columbia Valley has a hint of the Left Bank about it, with a small amount of Merlot, Cabernet Franc and Petit Verdot included. A third, more economically priced, Bordeaux style red Lower East Cabernet Sauvignon is also made. Harrington believes Grenache will emerge as one of the top three red grapes in Washington State in the years ahead. The dark-fruited, spicy and lightly mineral Columbia Valley Grenache comes from the Horse Heaven Hills area. It is blended with around 20% Syrah which provides balance and structure. The elegant intense, black-fruited lightly gamey and peppery Syrah Lagniappe comes from some of the cooler sites in the Columbia Valley. Like Côte-Rôtie a hint of Viognier is included. A Columbia Valley Syrah is also made and there is a pricier Reserve example John Lewis. (DM)

Recommended Reds:
Syrah Lagniappe Columbia Valley ★★★★☆ £F
Syrah Columbia Valley ★★★★ £E
Grenache Columbia Valley ★★★★☆ £F
L'Idiot du Village Columbia Valley ★★★★☆ £E
Cabernet Sauvignon Lower East Columbia Valley ★★★★☆ £F

Januik Winery (Washington State) www.noveltyhilljanuik.com
Established on his own now for some years, former CHATEAU STE MICHELLE head winemaker Mike Januik makes wines in small lots. He works with a whole host of vineyards and draws on Cold Creek for his Chardonnay and Champoux for an elegant and poised single-vineyard Cabernet Sauvignon. The regular Cabernet is good but doesn't quite have the depth or intensity. Merlot is rich and plummy and like all the reds has a marked spicy oak character in its youth. The Syrah is rich and supple with marked blackberry and black pepper aromas. The reds will all benefit from a little patience – 3 or 4 years at least. The Cold Creek Chardonnay is very richly textured with plenty of extract, oak and a full creamy weight on the palate. It will drink well young and keep a little while. A second range of well priced wines, Novelty Hill, is made by Mike Januik from the wineries own Stillwater Creek vineyard in the Columbia Valley. (DM)

Recommended Reds:
Cabernet Sauvignon Champoux Vineyard Columbia Valley ★★★★ £F
Cabernet Sauvignon Columbia Valley ★★★☆ £E
Merlot Columbia Valley ★★★☆ £E
Syrah Columbia Valley ★★★☆ £E

Recommended Whites:
Chardonnay Cold Creek Vineyard Columbia Valley ★★★☆ £E

Kiona (Yakima Valley) www.kionawine.com
This is one of the longest-established Washington wineries, started in 1975, and is located in the Yakima Valley's Red Mountain sub-appellation. A fairly extensive range is produced, both red and white. The top wines are the Estate bottling's from the firm's own Red Mountain vineyards, of which there are now over 80 ha (200 acres). As well as the wines rated below there are also Chardonnay, Zinfandel, Sangiovese, Riesling, Chenin Blanc and Lemberger examples. Most are very economically priced. Cabernet Sauvignon, no doubt helped by vines that are now over 30 years of age, and Merlot are the best bets here. Both have good, ripe and characterful fruit, suppler and more accessible in the Merlot. The Syrah has lots of dark, peppery fruit and good intensity if not quite the depth of the other two wines. All can be approached with 2 or 3 years' age but the Cabernet will benefit from a little longer. The Red Mountain Cyclops red (£F) is a Rhône blend, there is a premium Zinfandel the Red Mountain Big Kiona, while most expensive of all is the Single Berry Select Chenin Blanc from botrytised fruit. (DM)

Recommended Reds:
Cabernet Sauvignon Red Mountain Estate Yakima Valley ★★★☆ £F
Merlot Red Mountain Estate Yakima Valley ★★★☆ £F
Syrah Red Mountain Estate Yakima Valley ★★★☆ £E

❀ L'École No 41 (Walla Walla Valley) www.lecole.com
Established over 30 years ago, L'École No 41 has consistently produced good quality wine, both red and white. The reds are well crafted and stylish with refined supple tannins; not blockbusters, rather good, medium-term cellar prospects. The Apogee red is sourced from the Pepper Bridge vineyard and is a concentrated, cedary meritage blend of Cabernet Sauvignon and Merlot. Equally impressive is the earthy, structured Perigee, a blend of Cabernet Sauvignon, Merlot and Cabernet Franc. Syrah, also from the Estate Seven Hills Vineyard in Walla Walla is dark and brooding with a spicy black pepper character underpinning the fruit. The principal varieties here are Merlot and Sémillon and the winery is one of the very best sources of the latter. Subtle use of oak, and a marvellously waxy, honeyed character shows through. A straightforward red blend Recess Red is also produced from Merlot, the two Cabernets, Carmenère and Syrah. (DM)

Recommended Reds:
Apogee Pepper Bridge Walla Walla Valley ★★★★☆ £F
Perigee Estate Seven Hills Vineyard Walla Walla Valley ★★★★☆ £F
Merlot Estate Seven Hills Vineyard Walla Walla Valley ★★★★ £E
Merlot Columbia Valley ★★★☆ £E
Syrah Estate Seven Hills Walla Walla Valley ★★★★ £E
Cabernet Sauvignon Columbia Valley ★★★ £E
Cabernet Sauvignon Walla Walla Valley ★★★ £E

Recommended Whites:
Sémillon Columbia Valley ★★★ £C
Chardonnay Columbia Valley ★★☆ £C

❀❀ Leonetti Cellar (Walla Walla Valley) www.leonetticellar.com
Leonetti is one of the very best producers of Bordeaux-style reds in Washington State. The Reserve is of formidable proportions – a powerful wine that is sturdy but refined and very long-lived – an approach that has been perpetuated here for over three decades. High quality is maintained in the home vineyards, which are on fine, well-drained hillside slopes. Sustainable viticulture is practised and yields are kept down, rarely exceeding three tons to the acre. Green harvesting is also practiced. As well as the impressive Cabernet and Merlot, stylish Sangiovese is also produced in a softer, lighter style,

displaying very good intense, dark cherry fruit. The magnificent Reserve meritage red is made in very small quantities. (DM)

Recommended Reds:
Reserve Walla Walla Valley ✪✪✪✪✪ £H
Cabernet Sauvignon Walla Walla Valley ★★★★★ £G
Merlot Columbia Valley ★★★★★ £F
Sangiovese Walla Walla Valley ★★★★ £F

❀ **Long Shadows (Walla Walla Valley)** *www.longshadows.com*
This is a very interesting project run by Allen Shoup who for 20 years headed up the Stimson Lane Wine group whose wineries include CH. STE MICHELLE and COLUMBIA CREST. He is producing a small range of wines, each a joint venture with some of the worlds most notable winemakers. In support of this seven vineyards from a range of AVAs have been identified to provide the ideal character and *terroir* for each of the cuvées. Poets Leap is a crisp, fresh and lightly mineral Riesling with a touch of residual sugar produced with Armin Diel from Schlossgut DIEL in Germany. In addition to this Poets Leap Botrytis and Ice Wine Rieslings are also made which are understandably a good deal pricier. Saggi, made with Ambrogio and Giovanni FOLONARI from Tuscany, is a classic Super-Tuscan style red blending Sangiovese, Cabernet Sauvignon and Syrah with hints of dark cherries, strawberries and a silky texture. Chester Kidder is a Left Bank style blend made with Gilles Nicault, winemaker for nearby WOODWARD CANYON. Pirouette made with Philippe Melka and Agustin Huneeus, Sr is also from a Medoc blend and has a tiny proportion of Malbec as well as the varieties blended in the Chester Kidder; Cabernet Sauvignon, Merlot, Cabernet Franc and Petit Verdot. The Pedestal is dominated by Merlot, with a small proportion of Cabernet Sauvignon, Cabernet Franc and Petit Verdot. Made with Michel Rolland who as well as an expansive knowledge of winemaking around the globe advises to many Right Bank properties as well as making wine at his own Fronsac estate Ch. FONTENIL. Randy DUNN has made classic Cabernet Sauvignon at his Howell Mountain winery on the slopes of the Napa Valley for over three decades and here is also crafting in the Feather a 100% Cabenet Sauvignon, with notes of cherry, mint and a hint of chocolate. Sequel, made with former PENFOLDS winemaker John Duval is, as you would expect a Syrah, with a tiny hint of Cabernet in the blend. Full of ripe, dark-berry fruit with a hint of spice and black pepper. A dry Riesling, Carmina Burana is also made by Gilles Nicault. (DM)

Recommended Reds:
Pedestal Columbia Valley ★★★★☆ £F
Feather Columbia Valley ★★★★☆ £F
Sequel Columbia Valley ★★★★☆ £F
Pirouette Columbia Valley ★★★★☆ £F
Chester Kidder Columbia Valley ★★★★☆ £F
Saggi Columbia Valley ★★★★ £E

Recommended Whites:
Poets Leap Columbia Valley ★★★☆ £D

❀ **McCrea Cellars (Washington State)** *www.mccreacellars.com*
The McCrea Cellars winery is located around an hour's drive from downtown Seattle on the western, seaboard side of the Cascade Mountains. As at a number of other warehouse operations, production remains small and bespoke. All the wines, both white and red, are Rhône styles. There are a number of vineyard sources including Boushey Vineyards, Elephant Mountain and the Sugarloaf Vineyard in the Yakima Valley, as well as Ciel du Cheval in the Red Mountain AVA. Syrah is the key red here although Mourvèdre and

Counoise are produced as well as a lighter Rhône blend, Sirocco. The ripe, stylish, peachy Viognier has a little Roussanne blended in, no doubt giving a floral, slightly structured edge. The Viognier component is fermented in stainless steel, the Roussanne in older oak. Of the Syrahs the Cuvée Orleans echoes Côte-Rôtie with a small proportion of Viognier blended in. The Boushey Vineyard is ripe and a touch fuller with dark, spicy fruit and a hint of oak, while the Ciel du Cheval is perhaps the most opulent and rounded of the trio. Look out for also for bottlings including the red blend Sirocco, Counoise from Red Mountain, Mourvèdre from Ciel du Cheval as well as a late harvest Roussanne. All the reds get a cold soak prior to fermentation and are bottled without fining or filtration. (DM)

Recommended Reds:
Syrah Cuvée Orleans Yakima Valley ★★★★☆ £F
Syrah Boushey Vineyard Yakima Valley ★★★★ £E
Syrah Ciel du Cheval Red Mountain ★★★☆ £E

Recommended Whites:
Viognier Red Mountain ★★★ £D

Northstar (Walla Walla) *www.northstarmerlot.com*
Merlot is very much the focus at this operation, which saw its first vintage in 1994. The emphasis is on small lots. Early winemaking input came from consultant Jed STEELE from Sonoma although it is now under the direction of head winemaker David "Merf" Merfeld. A dark and plummy regular Columbia Valley Merlot has been joined by a more concentrated and marginally more opulent Walla Walla Valley bottling sourced in part from SPRING VALLEY. Oak is apparent in the wines when young and they are certainly on the ripe side. They offer real depth and character for the variety, though. Expect them to drink very well with 3–4 years' age. A third premium Merlot Premier (£G) is also made as well as a Cabernet Sauvignon (£E), a Cabernet Franc (£E), a Petit Verdot (£E), a Malbec (£E), a Syrah (£E) and a white Sémillon Stella Blanca (£C). (DM)

Recommended Reds:
Merlot Walla Walla Valley ★★★★ £F
Merlot Columbia Valley ★★★☆ £E
Stella Maris Columbia Valley ★★★ £D

Pepper Bridge Winery *www.pepperbridge.com*
This estate produces Bordeaux style reds solely from the Walla Walla Valley AVA and their own Pepper Bridge Vineyard and the Seven Hills Vineyard (in which they are partners). The vineyards are also an important source for a number of other leading Washington producers. The winery is gravity fed from crushing to barrel ageing. Vinification is straightforward with *pigéage* and 7–8 days on skins. Malolactic is carried out in barrel and ageing is for up to 18 months in French oak. Both Merlot and Cabernet Sauvignon offer reasonable depth and concentration. A touch of additional complexity is added in the Merlot, which has a smattering of Cabernet Franc and Malbec, the Cabernet Sauvignon a small proportion of each of the other four Bordeaux grapes. A further Bordeaux blend Trine is also made and there are two winery/wine club exclusives from the Pepper Tree and Seven Hills vineyards respectively. (DM)

Recommended Reds:
Merlot Walla Walla Valley ★★★★ £F
Cabernet Sauvignon Walla Walla Valley ★★★★ £F

❀❀ **Quilceda Creek Vintners** *www.quilcedacreek.com*
For many, this is Washington State's greatest source of Cabernet Sauvignon and Merlot. Certainly along with LEONETTI they vie for that accolade. Originally founded in 1978 by Alex Golitzen,

Washington State

the nephew of the legendary André Tchelistcheff, the main focus and volume here is the Cabernet Sauvignon, now made by Alex Golitzin's son Paul. The wine is sourced from several different prime vineyards. If not fully Cabernet Sauvignon, it is almost so, occasionally with a tiny proportion of Merlot blended in to add some flesh. In addition to the Cabernet a very small amount of a Columbia Red, another blend from the Palengat Vineyard and a further Cabernet from the Galitzine Vineyard are also produced. The family have now purchased the Champoux Vineyard as well as planting their own Estate Galitzine and Palengat vineyards in a drive to reinforce the quality of their wines. (DM)
Recommended Reds:
Cabernet Sauvignon Columbia Valley ○○○○○ £H

Reininger Winery (Walla Walla Valley) *www.reiningerwinery.com*
The Reiningers started their winery located in a small facility at Walla Walla airport in 1997 and they intend to restrict production under their Reininger label. 113 ha (280 acres) are now owned with a number of other partners in western Walla Walla at the Ash Hollow Vineyard and fruit from here was used for the first time with the 2001 vintage with both Cabernet and Syrah being produced. They also source fruit from the PEPPER BRIDGE, Seven Hills and SPRING VALLEY vineyards. Fruit from a number of vineyards is sourced for the winery's good value Helix label. The Helix Pomatia is a supple, soft, berry-laden blend of Syrah, Merlot, Cabernet Sauvignon, Petit Verdot and Cabernet Franc. It is aged mainly in used American and French oak, emphasizing the wine's fruit but lending it additional structure. Helix Cabernet Sauvignon, Merlot, Syrah, Sangiovese and a red Rhône style SoRho are also joined by whites Chardonnay, Viognier and a rosé. The denser and more seriously structured varietal labels see more French oak and the Cabernet around half new wood whereas the Syrah is aged entirely in used barrels to emphasise its dark peppery fruit. These are all wines of some depth and will develop further for a number of years. (DM)
Recommended Reds:
Syrah Walla Walla Valley ★★★★ £E
Cabernet Sauvignon Walla Walla Valley ★★★☆ £E
Merlot Walla Walla Valley ★★★☆ £E
Helix Pomatia Columbia Valley ★★☆ £D

Seven Hills (Walla Walla Valley) *www.sevenhillswinery.com*
A good and well-priced range of wines is produced at this Walla Walla based operation. The wines profiled here are the best the winery produces although a number of additional varietal wines both red and white are also produced, taking either the Walla Walla Valley or Columbia Valley AVA. The project was established in 1988 by Casey Mclellan and the focus of the winery is around the Bordeaux varieties and styles. The Pentad red is the top label, an interesting blend of Cabernet Sauvignon, Petit Verdot, Carmenère, Cabernet Franc and Malbec. Rich, ripe and with a smoky character and well judged oak. The elegant red cherry infused Ciel du Cheval comes from the vineyard of the same name in the Red Mountain AVA and combines Cabernet Sauvignon, Merlot, Petit Verdot and Cabernet Franc. The Klipsun Cabernet is a varietal example with well defined berry and red cherry fruit and polished tannins. The Seven Hills Merlot is less obviously upfront than other examples of the variety in the area and again shows a restrained, elegant quality with subtle, dark plummy fruit and nice well judged cedary, tobacco scented oak in the background. (DM)
Recommended Reds:
Pentad Red Walla Walla Valley ★★★★ £F

Ciel du Cheval Red Mountain ★★★☆ £E
Cabernet Sauvignon Klipsun Vineyard Walla Walla Valley ★★★☆ £E
Merlot Seven Hills Vineyard Walla Walla Valley ★★★☆ £E

✿ Spring Valley *www.springvalleyvineyard.com*
This property Walla Walla Valley produces wines mainly from its own estate vineyards. There is a small range of reds that not only offer the opulence of the region but a fine and supple structure and purity that is rarely achieved by their neighbours. There is a lot of oak here as elsewhere, but it is very well judged. The Uriah is a richly opulent Merlot blend with dark, spicy plum and berry fruit and very impressive depth. The Frederick is based on Cabernet Sauvignon and is the firmest of the wines, deserving 5 years' patience. The Nina Lee is a 100% Syrah with lots of dark pepper, oriental spices and exotic dark fruits. A number of other reds are also made. These include a varietal Merlot Mule Skinner a Cabernet Sauvignon Derby, a Cabernet Franc Katherine Corkrum and a Petit Verdot Sharilee. All should be well worth looking at. (DM)
Recommended Reds:
Uriah Spring Valley Vineyard Walla Walla Valley ★★★★☆ £F
Frederick Spring Valley Vineyard Walla Walla Valley ★★★★ £F
Nina Lee Spring Valley Vineyard Walla Walla Valley ★★★★ £F

Three Rivers (Walla Walla Valley) *www.threeriverswinery.com*
The partners here established this medium sized winery amidst picturesque surroundings in the Walla Walla in late 1999. A fairly extensive range of wines is produced from across Washington's AVAs by long term winemaker Holly Turner. The wines generally offer good value in a ripe but elegant style. The entry level Red Table Wine comes from a blend of Syrah, Cabernet Sauvignon, and Cabernet Franc and is sourced like most of the wines throughout the Columbia Valley. As well as the two reds covered here Columbia Valley labelled Sauvignon Blanc, Riesling, Chardonnay, Merlot and a Merlot Malbec blend are also released. Best of the Columbia Valley labelled wines is the cedary, blackberry and dark cherry fruited Svelte, a blend of four Bordeaux red varieties and dominated by Cabernet Sauvignon. There are also a number of single vineyard wines. Look out for Cabernet Sauvignon from the Champoux Vineyard in the Columbia Valley and Cabernet Franc from the Weinbau Vineyard in Wahluke Slope. For visitors there is a large attractive tasting room and if you feel inclined you can also practice your swing on three short holes of golf. (DM)
Recommended Reds:
Svelte Red Columbia Valley ★★★☆ £E
Cabernet Sauvignon Walla Walla Valley ★★☆ £D

Woodward Canyon (Walla Walla Valley) *www.woodwardcanyon.com*
In Washington State terms this fine small producer is a relative veteran. An extensive range of wines is produced. In addition to the medium-weight, finely structured Artists Series Cabernet Sauvignon there are additional bottlings including the soft, approachable Nelms Road and the premium Old Vines. The Estate Red is a blend of the best lots of Cabernet Sauvignon, Merlot and Cabernet Franc. There is a good Washington State Chardonnay and a more complex Estate Reserve. It is almost Burgundian in style but with a rich, toasty character. Small amounts of Dolcetto, Sauvignon Blanc and Riesling are also made. (DM)
Recommended Reds:
Estate Red Walla Walla Valley ★★★★ £F
Cabernet Sauvignon Artist Series ★★★★ £F
Cabernet Sauvignon Old Vines ★★★★ £F

Merlot Columbia Valley ★★★☆ £E
Recommended Whites:
Chardonnay Estate Reserve Walla Walla Valley ★★★★ £E
Chardonnay Washington State ★★★☆ £E

Other wines of note

Oregon

Alloro Vineyard
Recommended Reds:
Pinot Noir Estate Riservata Willamette Valley ★★★★☆ £G
Pinot Noir Estate Riservata Willamette Valley ★★★★ £F
Pinot Noir Estate Willamette Valley ★★★ £E
Recommended Whites:
Chardonnay Estate Willamette Valley ★★☆ £D

Anam Cara
Recommended Reds:
Pinot Noir Reserve Estate Chehalem Mountains ★★★★ £E
Pinot Noir Nicholas Estate Chehalem Mountains ★★★☆ £E

Antica Terra
Recommended Reds:
Pinot Noir Willamette Valley ★★★★ £E

Art & Science
Recommended Reds:
Syrah Stella Maris Vineyard Applegate Valley ★★★☆ £E
Pinot Noir Armstrong Vineyard Ribbon Ridge ★★★☆ £E

Ayres Vineyard
Recommended Reds:
Pinot Noir One Ribbon Ridge ★★★★☆ £G
Pinot Noir Pioneer Ribbon Ridge ★★★★☆ £G
Pinot Noir Lewis Rogers Lane Ribbon Ridge ★★★★☆ £G
Pinot Noir Perspective Ribbon Ridge ★★★★ £F
Pinot Noir Willamette Valley ★★★ £E

Benton Lane
Recommended Reds:
Pinot Noir Estate First Class Willamette Valley ★★★★ £F

Bethel Heights
Recommended Reds:
Pinot Noir Estate Willamette Valley ★★★☆ £E
Recommended Whites:
Chardonnay Estate Willamette Valley ★★★ £D

Brick House
Recommended Reds:
Pinot Noir Tonnellier Willamette Valley ★★★ £E

Broadley
Recommended Reds:
Pinot Noir Claudia's Choice Willamette Valley ★★★ £E

Cameron
Recommended Reds:
Pinot Noir Clos Electrique Willamette Valley ★★★ £E

Coelho Winery
Recommended Reds:
Pinot Noir Zeitoun Vineyard Eola–Amity Hills ★★★★ £F
Pinot Noir Paciência Willamette Valley ★★★★ £F
Pinot Noir Atração Willamette Valley ★★★☆ £D
Recommended Whites:
Pinot Gris Renovação Willamette Valley ★★☆ £C

Colene Clemens Vineyards
Recommended Reds:
Pinot Noir Margo Willamette Valley ★★★☆ £E

Cooper Mountain Vineyard
Recommended Reds:
Pinot Noir Terroir Meadowlark Willamette Valley ★★★☆ £F
Pinot Noir Life Willamette Valley ★★★ £E
Pinot Noir Willamette Valley ★★☆ £D
Recommended Whites:
Pinot Gris Willamette Valley ★★☆ £C

Dobbes Family Estate
Recommended Reds:
Pinot Noir Symonette Willamette Valley ★★★★ £F
Pinot Noir Patricia's Cuvee Willamette Valley ★★★☆ £F
Pinot Noir Griffin's Cuvee Willamette Valley ★★★☆ £F

Eyrie Vineyard
Recommended Reds:
Pinot Noir Original Vines Willamette Valley ★★★★ £F
Pinot Noir Willamette Valley ★★★☆ £E
Recommended Whites:
Pinot Gris Willamette Valley ★★★☆ £E

Kelley Fox
Recommended Reds:
Pinot Noir Momtazi Vineyard McMinnville ★★★★☆ £F
Pinot Noir Mirabai Willamette Valley ★★★★ £E

iOTA Cellars
Recommended Reds:
Pinot Noir Pelos Sandberg Vineyard Eota-Amity Hills ★★★☆ £E
Pinot Noir Not One iOTA Eota-Amity Hills ★★★ £D

Johan Vineyards
Recommended Reds:
Pinot Noir Three Barrel Willamette Valley ★★★★ £F
Pinot Noir Estate Willamette Valley ★★★☆ £E
Recommended Whites:
Chardonnay Estate Visdom Willamette Valley ★★★☆ £E
Grüner Veltliner Estate Willamette Valley ★★★☆ £E

Lachini Vineyards
Recommended Reds:
Pinot Noir Cuvée Giselle Willamette Valley ★★★★ £F
Pinot Noir Estate Willamette Valley ★★★☆ £E

Longplay Vineyards
Recommended Reds:
Pinot Noir Lucky 13 Chehalem Mountains ★★★☆ £E
Pinot Noir Jory Bench Reserve Chehalem Mountains ★★★☆ £E

Mckinlay
Recommended Reds:
Pinot Noir Special Selection Willamette Valley ★★ £E

Patton Valley
Recommended Reds:
Pinot Noir Estate Willamette Valley ★★★☆ £E

Phelps Creek
Recommended Reds:
Pinot Noir Cuvée Alexandrine Columbia Gorge ★★★★ £F
Pinot Noir Columbia Gorge ★★★ £E
Recommended Whites:
Chardonnay Lynette Columbia Gorge ★★★☆ £E

Silvan Ridge
Recommended Reds:
Pinot Noir Willamette Valley ★★☆ £C

Trathen Hall
Recommended Reds:
Pinot Noir Antiquum Willamette Valley ★★★ £E

Oregon & Washington State

Van Duzer
Recommended Reds:
Pinot Noir Saffron Fields Willamette Valley ★★★★ £F
Pinot Noir Dijon Blocks Willamette Valley ★★★★ £F
Pinot Noir Westside Blocks Willamette Valley ★★★★ £F
Pinot Noir Eola-Amity Hills ★★★☆ £E
Yamhill Valley Vineyards
Recommended Reds:
Pinot Noir Willamette Valley ★★☆ £E

Washington State
Amavi
Recommended Reds:
Cabernet Sauvignon Columbia Valley ★★★☆ £E
Syrah Columbia Valley ★★★☆ £E
Recommended Whites:
Semillon Columbia Valley ★★★ £C
Apex
Recommended Reds:
Cabernet Sauvignon Columbia Valley ★★☆ £E
Recommended Whites:
Chardonnay Columbia Valley ★★★ £C
Barnard Griffin
Recommended Reds:
Cabernet Sauvignon Columbia Valley ★★ £C
Merlot Columbia Valley ★★ £C
Recommended Whites:
Chardonnay Columbia Valley ★★ £B
Basel Cellars
Recommended Reds:
Syrah Columbia Valley ★★★☆ £E
Cadence
Recommended Reds:
Tapteil Red Washington ★★★☆ £E
Ciel du Cheval Red Washington ★★★☆ £E
Dunham Cellars
Recommended Reds:
Cabernet Sauvignon Columbia Valley ★★★☆ £E
Hedges Family Estate
Recommended Reds:
Red Mountain Red Columbia Valley ★★★ £E
Lauren Ashton Cellars
Recommended Reds:
Proprietor's Cuvée Red Mountain ★★★★ £F
Cuvee Arlette Columbia Valley ★★★★ £F
Maryhill Winery
Recommended Reds:
Winemakers Red Columbia Valley ★★ £B
Recommended Whites:
Pinot Gris Columbia Valley ★★ £B
Matthews Cellars
Recommended Reds:
Columbia Valley Claret Yakima Valley ★★★ £E
Mark Ryan Winery
Recommended Reds:
Cabernet Sauvignon Dead Horse Red Mountain ★★★★☆ £F
Long Haul Bordeaux Blend Columbia Valley ★★★★ £F
BTR The The Chief Columbia Valley ★★★ £D
BTR The Shift Columbia Valley ★★★ £D
BTR Vincent Red Columbia Valley ★★☆ £C
Recommended Whites:

Viognier Columbia Valley ★★★☆ £D
BTR Vincent Chardonnay Columbia Valley ★★ £B
Savage Grace
Recommended Reds:
Cabernet Franc Yakima Valley ★★ £D
Recommended Whites:
Chardonnay Columbia Gorge ★★★ £D
Charles Smith/ K Vintners
Recommended Reds:
The Klein Bordeaux Blend Walla Walla Valley ★★★★★ £F
Cabernet Sauvignon Chateau Smith Washington State ★★★ £D
Cabernet Sauvignon Substance Washington State ★★★ £C
The Hidden Syrah Wahluke Slope ★★★★★ £F
The Beautiful Syrah Walla Walla Valley ★★★★☆ £F
Syrah Boom Boom Washington State ★★★ £D
Merlot The Velvet Devil Washington State ★★☆ £C
Recommended Whites:
Chardonnay Sixto Frenchman Hills Washington State ★★★★ £E
Chardonnay Eve Washington State ★★☆ £C
Riesling Kung Fu Girl Columbia Valley ★★★ £C
Vino Pinot Grigio Washington State ★★ £C
Tamarack Cellars
Recommended Reds:
Cabernet Sauvignon Columbia Valley ★★★☆ £E
Merlot Columbia Valley ★★★☆ £E
Tenet
Recommended Reds:
GSM Columbia Valley ★★★★☆ £F
The Pundit Syrah Columbia Valley ★★★☆ £E
Walla Walla Vintners
Recommended Reds:
Cabernet Sauvignon Columbia Valley ★★★ £E

Work in progress!!

Producers under consideration for the next edition

Oregon
Arterberry Maresh
Ayoub Wines
Big Table Farm
Le Cadeau Vineyards
Evening Land
Lenne Estate
Scott Paul Wines
Shea Wine Cellars
Sineann
Solena

Washington State
Abeja
Adams Bench
Alleromb
Amaurice
Ross Andrew Winery
Ashan Cellars
Avenia
Boudreaux Cellars
Buty Winery
Corliss
Cote Bonneville
Fidelitas

Figgins Estate
Force Majeure
Horsepower Vineyards
Latta
Maison Bleue
Rasa Vineyards
Reynvaan
Rotie Cellars
Sheridan
Sixto
Sleight of Hand
Tranche Cellars
Two Vintners
Via Piano
Waters Winery

Reininger Syrah Walla Walla Valley
Seven Hills Pentad Red Walla Walla Valley
Spring Valley Nina Lee Boushey Vineyards
Tyrus Evan Syrah Del Rio Vineyard Rogue Valley
Whites:
Januik Chardonnay Cold Creek Vineyard Columbia Valley
L'Ecole No 41 Semillon Columbia Valley
Woodward Canyon Chardonnay Estate Reserve Walla Walla Valley

Author's choice

The best of the Willamette Valley
Reds:
Adelsheim Pinot Noir Calkins Lane Vineyard Willamette Valley
Archery Summit Pinot Noir Arcus Estate Willamette Valley
Beaux Frères Pinot Noir Beaux Frères Vineyard Ribbon Ridge
Bergström Pinot Noir Bergström Vineyard Dundee Hills
Brooks Pinot Noir Rastaban Willamette Valley
Cristom Pinot Noir Marjorie Vineyard Willamette Valley
Francis-Tannahill Sundown Red Wine Oregon
Patricia Green Cellars Estate Vineyard Old Vine Ribbon Ridge
JK Carriere Pinot Noir Antoinette Willamette Valley
Penner Ash Pinot Noir Shea Vineyard Yamhill-Carlton
Ken Wright Cellars Pinot Noir Guadalupe Vineyard Yamhill-Carlton
Z'IVO Wines Pinot Noir Eola Amity Hills Whole Cluster
Whites:
Chehalem Chardonnay Ian's Reserve Willamette Valley
Domaine Drouhin Chardonnay Cuvée Arthur Willamette Valley
Ponzi Chardonnay Reserve Willamette Valley
Raptor Ridge Pinot Gris Willamette Valley
Andrew Rich Gewürztraminer Dessert Wine Willamette Valley
St Innocent Pinot Blanc Freedom Hill Vineyard Willamette Valley
Domaine Serene Chardonnay Clos du Soleil Dundee Hills
Rosés:
Sokol Blosser Rose of Pinot Noir Dundee Hills
Stoller Vineyards Pinot Noir JV Estate Dundee Hills

A selection of new classics from Washington State
Reds:
Andrew Will Sorella Washington State
Bookwalter Suspense Columbia Valley
Cayuse Vineyards Syrah Cailloux Vineyard Walla Walla Valley
Chateau Ste Michelle Col Solare Columbia Valley
Delille Cellars Chaleur Estate Red Mountain
Dunham Cellars Cabernet Sauvignon Columbia Valley
Gramercy Cellars Syrah Lagniappe Columbia Valley
Leonetti Cellar Reserve Walla Walla Valley
Long Shadows Pedestal Columbia Valley
McCrea Cellars Syrah Cuvée Orleans Yakima Valley
Northstar Merlot Walla Walla Valley
Owen Roe Red Wine Dubrol Vineyard Yakima Valley
Pepper Bridge Winery Merlot Walla Walla Valley
Quilceda Creek Vineyards Cabernet Sauvignon Columbia Valley

Rest of North America

North America

Besides California, Oregon and Washington State, quality wine production is limited to just a handful of states. However grapes other than vinifera varieties are grown throughout the country. In New York State, for example, hybrid varieties are popular in the production of kosher wines and grape juice. Wines from these tend to have what is quaintly referred to as a 'foxy' character. A very damp pet dog smells not dissimilar. The best developments have been in Virginia, New York, in particular Long Island, in Maryland and to the far south in Arizona. The odd reasonable bottle has also emerged from Texas and the state may have real potential. Canadian quality wine has traditionally been Niagara icewine, but the developing region of the Okanagan Valley in British Columbia is also providing an increasing number of stylish dry whites and reds.

Virginia

Over the past decade, Virginia has emerged as a wine-producing region deserving serious attention. Quality has improved dramatically. Furthermore, their so-called signature grapes, Viognier and Cabernet Franc (with the upcoming Petit Manseng and Petit Verdot), are a welcome change from the hybrid varieties which used to dominate, the use of which had two unfortunate results: first, the wines could be distinctly unattractive both in aroma and taste, and secondly, wine made from hybrid grapes could not be exported to Europe, which only allows wines made from grapes which are Vitis vinifera. Having said that, some of the state's best wines are blends led by the Cabernet Sauvignon grape. As of late 2013, there were 230 wineries, up from five in 1980. Many of these, however, are small and depend on sales from their tasting rooms; a number also market themselves as venues for weddings and anniversary celebrations. The Virginian wine industry overall remains inward looking. Nevertheless, there are some very serious wine-makers. All of Virginia suffers from an unforgiving climate. First of all, the winters are long and can be very cold, with varying amounts of snow, so that the vines only begin to put out buds in late April. These are followed by suffocatingly hot and humid summers, which include frequent, sometime torrential, downpours, and not infrequent tropical storms and even hurricanes. This is a major reason for the popularity of the Viognier grape. Because its berries are small and thick-skinned, and the loose clusters of grapes allow the air to circulate, it withstands the humid summers and the accompanying fungal diseases better than, for example, the Chardonnay grape. Cool nights begin to appear only in September. All this means that Virginia has a relatively short growing season and one that begins relatively late. In the circumstances, it is impressive that Virginian winemakers make so many good, and a number of outstanding, wines.

The major wine-producing areas are in Northern and Central Virginia to the east of the Blue Ridge Mountains. These areas can, at this point, be largely narrowed down to two American Viticultural Areas, or AVAs, in which most of the best producers work: **Middleburg** AVA in Northern Virginia and **Monticello** AVA in Central Virginia. The soils vary across the state from granite in the west to sandy loam near Chesapeake Bay. Most of the soils, however, have a greater or lesser clay content, and thus growers look for slopes which will drain rapidly after the all-too-frequent downpours.

Prices can be high for Virginia wines. Some deserve it, a number of which are featured below, but, all too often, the quality of the wine does not deserve the high price asked for it. Ideally, this situation will improve.

Virginia Vintages

There are, of course, vintage variations, but there is a certain climatic sameness: winters are always cold, frost can be a problem in the spring, and summers normally see lots of rain, which can continue into the autumn harvest period. Therefore, variations between vintages can be less acute than in many other regions.

Recent vintages

The 2002 vintage suffered from drought, and the wines were of uneven quality. 2003 and 2004 were both wet vintages, and the wines were light. The 2005 vintage was very good: the warm growing season produced reds which were ripe and balanced, and whites which were more forward than usual. 2006 was a moderately cool vintage, producing crisp whites and light reds. 2007 was an excellent vintage: it was a particularly hot and dry year, which produced very ripe fruit and strong tannins – some producers called it a 'perfect' season. 2008 was a moderately cool vintage, which was good for chardonnay and for lighter reds, but left some sauvignon blancs with higher than usual acidity; 2009 was also cool, and it seemed to rain incessantly, but in this case there were some excellent vibrant whites; reds were a bit uneven, although some of the lighter styles were fresh. This will probably be one of the best vintages. With 2010, we are back to a very hot vintage, which was good for big reds but less good for some viogniers. This was followed by a very wet 2011, especially in September, and yields were down across the state. Whites and reds were both lighter in style. Finally, the weather in 2012 was more 'normal', although budburst was very early and so was the beginning of ripening. Rot was a problem as well as uneven ripening for reds. The whites were nicely aromatic. **2013:** there was a very wet spring and early summer – producers referred to almost endless rain - but fortunately the sun came out in early August and remained shining until mid-October. As a result, the white wine grapes ripened very well; indeed, it was a very good vintage for whites. The red wine grapes had more difficulties: because there was so little sun in July, they had problems ripening enough before more rain arrived in mid-October. On the whole, some Cabernet Franc and Nebbiolo grapes fared rather better than Cabernet Sauvignon and Petit Verdot. **2014:** the brutal winter cold badly damaged viognier and tannat grapes, whilst merlot refused to ripen in a number of areas. However, a cool and mostly dry summer allowed most growers to bring most of the other varieties to ripeness whilst maintaining acidity. Unfortunately, those in the Montecello AVA in central Virginia suffered a week of rain in the middle of October, and growers had to choose whether to pick early before optimal ripeness or wait for the sun. Success was variable, although the vintage is praised for its freshness. **2015:** early summer rains were extremely worrying, but July dried the vineyards and the weather through the harvest was very good. The rainfall, fortunately, came with cool weather, and this allowed fruit development and the retention of acid, as well as fewer problems with rot. It was an excellent year for white wines, especially for viognier. Reds, however, suffered when Hurricane Joaquin dumped heavy rains in the midst of the harvest, so whilst a number are good, this was not a red wine year.

A-Z of producers - *Virginia*

>> Barboursville (Monticello) *www.barboursvillewine.com*
Barboursville Vineyards was founded in 1976 by Gianni Zonin, whose family had been winemakers in Italy for 150 years, this is undeniably one of the top vineyards in Virginia, a leader in replacing hybrid

grapes with vinifera varieties and the producer of wines of high quality. With 172 acres of vines, it produces a wide range of varietals, including Italian varieties such as Nebbiolo and Vermentino, as well as Virginia's two 'signature' grapes, Viognier and Cabernet Franc. It also produces a notably delicious dessert wine called Malvaxia, with 50% each of the American hybrid Vidal for its acidity and 50% Muscato Ottonelle for its fragrance. It is also worth knowing that the estate complex includes a notably excellent restaurant, Palladio. Under the leadership of Luca Paschina, winemaker for over 20 years, Barboursville has concentrated massive effort on their vineyards, from the soil to trellis to canopy to grape clones. This has ensured very high quality grapes for Paschina to use in producing the wine. In making the Viognier Reserve, he uses no oak but ferments on the lees for up to a year, stirring every fortnight; with the aid of the great acidity, the wine is crisp and aromatic with very good ageing potential. They produced their first Vermentino in 2010. The Vineyard Nebbiolo Reserve is tannic in the front but on the journey to the back palate it develops a silkiness, with good fruit and lots of minerality. The Cabernet Franc Reserve has a wonderfully balanced structure, integrated fruit and minerals, and an endless finish; it is gaining an increasingly high reputation in Great Britain, as well as in the US. Octagon, made only in exceptional years and akin to a Right Bank claret, in 2009 was led by the Merlot grape, but included low percentages of Cabernet Franc, Cabernet Sauvignon and Petit Verdot; the 2012 contains no Cabernet Sauvignon. (KB)

Recommended Reds:
Cabernet Franc Reserve ★★★★ £D
Octagon ★★★ £E   Nebbiolo Reserve ★★ £D
Recommended Whites:
Viognier Reserve ★★★ £D   Malvaxia Reserve Passito ★★ £D

Boxwood Winery (Middleburg)   *www.boxwoodwinery.com*
Boxwood Winery breathes money. Situated in Virginia's hunt country, the 16-acre vineyard was laid out by viticulturalist Lucie Morton (sometimes referred to as 'legendary') after a great deal of examination of soils and aspects; as a result, Cabernet Sauvignon, Merlot, Petit Verdot and Malbec vines were planted. The wine consultant is the Bordeaux expert Stéphane Derenoncourt, appropriate given that Boxwood's aspiration is to produce first-rank Bordeaux-style wines. They currently produce Boxwood in a Left Bank style (led by Cabernet Sauvignon), and Topiary in a Right Bank style (led by Cabernet Franc), the latter a rich and fruity wine. In addition, they produce two rosés, based on Cabernet Franc and on Merlot, and Trellis, a blend of all of the grapes. The grapes are picked by hand, the bunches are de-stemmed, the grapes are hand-sorted, and they are then fermented in stainless steel without crushing. The free-run and the pressed juices are kept separate; the wine is then put in French oak barrels and aged for up to twelve months. Boxwood is not only a winery, it is an impressive marketing operation, having established two tasting rooms in Virginia and two in Maryland. The executive vice-president and daughter of the owners, Rachel Martin, was trained in Bordeaux. She oversees the winemaking, but can also be found in Great Britain, showing the wines and encouraging their adoption by wine merchants and restaurants. As a result, Boxwood wines are increasingly available in Britain as well as in the US. The wine called Boxwood is a blend of Cabernet Sauvignon, Merlot and Petit Verdot, and more New than Old World in its boldness. Topiary combines Cabernet Franc and Merlot; it is quite fruity, with some spice. The rosé, made by combining Cabernet Franc and Merlot, is fresh, fruity and subtle. It is considered by some to be the best rosé in Virginia. (KB)

Recommended Reds:
Boxwood ★★ £E   Topiary ★★ £E
Recommended Rosés:
Rosé ★★ £B

Linden Vineyards (Middleburg)   *www.lindenvineyards.com*
The genuinely interested visitor to Linden will be introduced first to the soil, then to the vines, and only then to the wines. The origins of Linden Vineyards was the purchase in 1983 of an abandoned hardscrabble farm (in the Blue Ridge, 'hardscrabble' refers to steep, poor rocky slopes) with primarily granitic soil. From the current 20 acres of the estate's Hardscrabble Vineyard and the two related vineyards of 5 acres each, Avenius and Boisseau, which are farmed by close colleagues, 4,000 cases of wine are made each year at Linden. The owner, than whom it is impossible to be more hands on, is Jim Law. He situates himself firmly in the French tradition, insisting that soil, site and micro-climate are much more important than grape varieties. His method of planting is high-density, to make the vines work for a living. To restrain the vigorous growth of the vines in a climate with so much rain, he plants crab grass between the vines: it grows low under the vines and emerges just at the time of véraison, when the grapes begin to ripen, so that it competes with the vines to produce the stress necessary for good grapes. The focus is overwhelmingly on the viticulture; the idea is that if the grapes themselves are outstanding, intervention in the winery can be minimal. He looks to make wines which are meant to be drunk with food, with good acidity, tamed tannins and moderate alcohol. Although a range of grapes is grown, the best wines are the Bordeaux-style red blends and the single-site sauvignon blanc and chardonnay, the letter vinified in a Burgundian style. The white wine grapes are hand-picked and -sorted and then de-stemmed; the chardonnay and late harvest wines are fermented in barrel, whilst the other white wines are fermented in stainless steel. The red wine grapes particularly show vintage variations, in that Cabernet Sauvignon prefers dry, hot weather whilst Merlot prefers more water - of which there is not a shortage in Virginia. The grapes are hand-picked and then double-sorted: before de-stemming, and then afterwards, the latter to remove stem fragments and pink unripe berries. The single-vineyard reds are aged in French oak for 9-22 months in 30-50% new oak; for the claret/Bordeaux blends, no new oak is used. (It is perhaps indicative that Jim Law uses the term claret, the English term for a Bordeaux-blend.) The wine is lightly filtered but not refined. There are a range of wines. The Avenius single-vineyard Sauvignon Blanc is of very high quality; it has a classic nose, and, tasted blind, it would be difficult to tell that it was not from the Loire. The Hardscrabble Chardonnay is clearly Burgundy-influenced; barrel-fermented and -aged, it has well-balanced fruit and acid on the palate with undertones of oak. The Hardscrabble Red can vary from year to year in composition, but all of them have very well-balanced acid and tannin, in some years more assertive than others, lots of Old World-type fruit (not so assertive), and good length. Petit Manseng, is the basis for an utterly delicious sweet wine, the sweetness balanced with good acidity and with a mouthfilling flavour. (KB)

Recommended Reds:
Hardscrabble Red ★★★ £E
Recommended Whites:
Hardscrabble Chardonnay ★★★ £D
Sauvignon Blanc ★★★ £C   Petit Manseng ★★ £C

Virginia

Rappahannock Cellars *www.rappahannockcellars.com*

Rappahannock, based in Middleburg, was founded in 1998 by John Delmare. He emphasises that it is a family concern, and, given that he and his wife have twelve children, all of whom have, at some time in their lives, worked on the farm, the term is more apposite than usual. Situated in the Virginia Piedmont at the base of the Blue Ridge Mountains, there are approximately 25 acres under vines comprising a range of varietals. They themselves supply two-thirds of the grapes necessary for their production, with one-third produced by other growers with whom they have worked for some years. The soil is sandy loam, which allows good drainage, and the vineyards are above 900 feet, which helps to minimise frost damage. In the vineyards, a great deal of effort has been made towards a sustainable method of agriculture. They compost the vineyard waste and use it as fertiliser for about one-third of the acreage and they use cover crops under the vines, thereby nearly eliminating the use of herbicides. The humid climate means that fungicides are required to combat mildew and rot, but natural compounds, probably akin to the traditional Bordeaux mixture of lime, copper sulphate and water, are used as much as possible. The red wine grapes are sorted in the vineyard before being picked by hand and then de-stemmed. For the fruity wine meant to be drunk young, they use whole berry (non-crushed) fermentation; for the Meritage and other more substantial wines, the grapes are crushed and fermented in stainless steel; the Meritage is aged in French oak for 16-18 months, whilst the Cabernet Franc and Petit Verdot are aged in a combination of French, American and Hungarian oak. For the whites, the grapes are also sorted in the vineyard, hand-picked, and then subject to whole-cluster pressing. The Chardonnay receives a combination of stainless steel- and barrel-fermentation; only French oak is used. The lees from the Chardonnay are used in the red wine ageing. the 'No-Oak' Chardonnay, which is aged on the lees, follows a Chablis model; it has a creamy nose and lovely fruit and minerality on the palate, with a clean finish. Depending on the year, the Cabernet Franc can resemble a Loire red more than one from the New World; the Petit Verdot has more acid than the Cabernet Franc but the acid and tannins are well-balanced. The 2006 and 2007 Meritage vintages were led by Cabernet Sauvignon, with Petit Verdot close behind and Malbec and Merlot way in the rear; in the 2010 vintage, however, Merlot is in the lead. Either way, it is rather more tannic than the other reds, thanks to the Cabernet Sauvignon, but well-integrated. (KB)

Recommended Reds:

Meritage ★★ £D   Petit Verdot ★ £D
Cabernet Franc ★★ £C

Recommended Whites:

'No-Oak' Chardonnay ★★ £C

R d V Vineyards (Middleburg)   *www.rdvvineyards.com*

The founder of RdV, Rutger de Vink, is a former US marine and holder of an MBA who decided that he wanted to make wines which could hold their own against Bordeaux First Growths and big California cult wines – indeed, he has said that he wants to make a cult wine himself. The outcome thus far has been wines which share characteristics of both. In 2001 he spent the year with Jim Law at Linden Vineyards, immersing himself in the viticultural methods of a man wholly dedicated to quality in the vineyard. De Vink then went out on a quest for land for his own vineyard and winery. And never mind the wine – the winery itself is a stunning marvel in concept combined with practicality. What De Vink was looking for was land which sloped and had shallow soil to limit its

water-holding propensity. After a three years' search and 100 test holes, he found hills with granitic soil 50 centimeters/21 inches deep; he now farms 6.5 hectares/16 acres. These are shared out with 40% Cabernet Sauvignon, 40% Merlot, 12% Petit Verdot and 8% Cabernet Franc, providing the raw materials for his Bordeaux blends: Lost Mountain, his flagship wine (previously called RdV), is a Left Bank type led by Cabernet Sauvignon; Rendezvous is led by Merlot, although it diverts from the Right Bank model by being nearly a quarter Cabernet Sauvignon. His wine consultant is Eric Boissenot, known for his work in the Médoc in the Left Bank. He made his first vintage for sale in 2009 (two years before, he had helped to make the vintage at Linden Vineyards). After picking the fruit, they chill it down to 7 degrees, give it a cold soak for two days, and macerate it for three weeks. Ageing the wine is seen as the most important step, and it is barrel-aged for 18-24 months. The alcohol level of the wines is at least 14%, with the 2010 Lost Mountain coming in at 14.5%. The wine itself, in spite of this level, is fresh and vibrant, showing lots of fruit balanced by its elegant structure. The Rendezvous is rich but not sweet. (KB)

Recommended Reds:

Lost Mountain ★★★★ £G   Rendezvous ★★★ £F

Veritas Vineyard & Winery *www.veritaswines.com*

Monticello based Veritas was founded in 1999 by Andrew Hodson, who was also the winemaker; his daughter Emily Pelton has now succeeded him in the latter position. Indeed, it is a family winery, with his wife Patricia in charge of the viticulture and his son George acting as the general manager. It is noticeable that the estate also includes a bed & breakfast and restaurant called The Farmhouse, a Retreat, and a wedding business; the inclusion of the last-named is often a warning of mediocre wines, but here it is not the case. The members of the family devote themselves to the wines. There are currently 52 acres, the predominate soil of which is a type of degenerate granite called 'Edneytown'. A wide range of grape varieties is planted, the most important vinifera varieties being Sauvignon Blanc, Chardonnay, Viognier, and Petit Manseng for white wines and Cabernet Franc and Petit Verdot for the reds. The grapes are picked by hand, cooled down (to 40° F/10° C for about 24 hours in the case of Viognier), de-stemmed, and then left to 'sit on the skins' for a period before being pressed. A varied mixture of new and old French and American oak is used for some of the wines, although not for the Viognier. Curiously, some of the whites tend to have higher rates of alcohol that the reds. Veritas produces a number of excellent wines. The Sauvignon Blanc has very nice acid, fruit and nettles on the palate, and has more finesse than many of this genre from New Zealand; a key to the quality is that the vineyard is at 1,300 feet, where the cool air protects this thin-skinned grape from the heat and the humidity (the latter is the parent of rot). The Viognier sits on its lees for six months, with the result that the wine is both round and aromatic. The two chardonnays are made in two different styles. The 'Saddleback' is fermented in stainless steel and is modelled on the style of a Chablis; the wine is high in acidity, clean, and rich with great flavour intensity. The 'Harlequin' is more in the style of a burgundy to the south of Chablis: it is barrel-fermented and aged in oak for six months, resulting in a butterscotch nose and a roundness balanced by good acid on the palate. The Petit Manseng, aged in neutral French oak, has a tropical nose and is springwater rather than syrupy sweet. The Cabernet Franc is quite elegant, with vibrant fruit and lovely flavour intensity. Finally, the Petit Verdot 'Paul Shaffer Edition' [it has various Editions – the current one is the 4th] shows rich fruit, a good amount of spice, and some

earthy notes, with a lovely integrated structure and very good length. (KB)

Recommended Reds:
Cabernet Franc ★★★ £D
Petit Verdot 'Paul Shaffer 4th Edition' ★★★ £E
Recommended Whites:
Reserve Sauvignon Blanc ★★★ £C
Saddleback Chardonnay ★★★ £C
Harlequin Reserve Chardonnay ★★★ £C
Viognier ★★ £D   Petit Manseng ★★ £C

Other wines of note

Barrel Oak Winery
Recommended Reds:
Petit Verdot ★ £E
Chateau O'Brien
Recommended Reds:
Tannat Limited Reserve ★ £F
Gardino Cellars
Recommended Whites:
Chardonnay ★ £C
Glen Manor Vineyard
Recommended Reds:
Hodder Hill [Bordeaux blend] ★★ £D
Recommended Whites:
Sauvignon Blanc ★ £C
Veramar Vineyards
Recommended Reds:
Cabernet Franc ★ £C
Recommended Whites:
Seyval Blanc ★ £C
White Hall Vineyards
Recommended Whites:
Petit Manseng ★★ £B

Work in progress!!

Producers under consideration for the next edition
Chrysalis
Glen Manor Vineyard
Horton Vineyards
Keswick Vineyards
Veramar Vineyards
White Hall Vineyards

Author's choice

A selection of interesting reds and whites
Reds:
Barboursville Vineyards   Cabernet Franc
Linden Vineyards   Hardscrabble Red
RdV   Lost Mountain [Bordeaux blend]
Veritas Vineyard & Winery   Petit Verdot 'Paul Shafer 4th Edition'
Whites:
Barboursville Vineyards   Viognier Reserve
Linden Vineyards   Hardscrabble Chardonnay
Veritas Vineyard & Winery   Reserve Sauvignon Blanc

New York State

New York State remains one of the better bets for quality wines outside the big sources on the western coast. In the north-west of the state the **Finger Lakes** region, just to the south of Lake Ontario, has a protected, very localised climate moderated by the lakes themselves. Both Chardonnay and Riesling are successful here along with a few sparkling wines. Among the best wineries, Fox Run, Dr Konstantin Frank, Lamoreaux Landing and Hermann J Wiemer stand out.

Directly north of New Jersey is the small **Hudson River** AVA where some decent Chardonnay is produced. Perhaps of most significance from a quality point of view are the wineries of **Long Island** and particularly **The North Fork of Long Island**. The climate is strongly maritime and both regions have proved to be impressive sources in recent years of Cabernet Sauvignon, Merlot and Cabernet Franc, along with the occasional striking Chardonnay. Bedell, Corey Creek, Gallucio, Jamesport, Palmer, Paumanok and Pellegrini are all worth a look.

Wines of note

Fox Run
Recommended Reds:
Cabernet Franc/Lemburger ★★☆ £C
Lakewood Vineyards
Recommended Reds:
Lemburger ★☆ £C
Recommended Whites:
Medium Riesling ★★ £C
Leonard Oaks Winery
Recommended Whites:
Late Harvest Vidal ★☆ £D
Red Newt Cellars
Recommended Whites: Hornet Vineyard Riesling ★★ £C
Tango Oaks Vineyard Riesling ★★ £C
Thirsty Owl Wine Company
Recommended Whites: Dry Riesling ★★☆ £D
Gewürztraminer ★★ £C
Villa Bellangelo
Recommended Whites:
Seyval Blanc ★☆ £B
Wölffer Estate Vineyard
Recommended Whites:
Late Harvest Chardonnayl ★★☆ £D

Arizona

There are two wineries that stand out in Arizona: Callaghan Vineyards, based in the Sonoita AVA and Dos Cabezas with some decent reds and whites from Cochise County near Tucson. The Sonoita region is cooled by its elevation and the Callaghan winery has some impressive, well-drained, gravel-dominated vineyards. An extensive range of varieties is planted and the Caitlin's Cuvée is a notable Bordeaux-style red dominated by Petit Verdot.

Wines of note

Callaghan Vineyards
Recommended Reds:
Caitlin's Selection Sonoita ★★★ £E

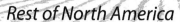

Rest of North America

North America

Claire's Selection Sonoita ★★★ £D
Dos Cabezas
Recommended Reds:
La Montaña Cochise County ★★★ £E
El Norte Cochise County ★★☆ £C

Rest of the USA

To the south of New York, a few good wines are being produced in **Maryland** which, with its warm maritime climate, has real potential despite the odd wet harvest. Better mesoclimates are being established and one winery in particular, Basignano, stands out for the impressive quality of its Cabernet Sauvignon and Meritage wines.
From a volume rather than a qualitypoint of view, **Idaho** is significant and home to the giant Ste Chapelle Winery. Quality so far has been sound but uninspirational with simple, straightforward red and white varietals.

Canada

The country has one sizeable wine region at Niagara in Ontario and more recently one in the far west in British Columbia. Wine production is now controlled by the VQA (Vintners Quality Alliance) and under these regulations the Ontario and generic British Columbia appellations were established. As well as in Niagara Peninsula good whites and icewine are also produced in Ontario from Pelee Island and Lake Eyrie North Shore. The vast majority of the country's vineyard area and wine production is still focused on Ontario. It is the icewines that make give Canada its unique stamp. **Key names** to look out for in Ontario include Cave Spring Cellars, Chateau des Charmes, Henry of Pelham, Konzelmann, Peller, Pillitteri and Reif Etate.

However in British Columbia and in particular in the **Okanagan Valley**, although those same magnificent icewines are crafted, there are an increasing number of dry table wines of note as well. Pinot Gris, Chardonnay, Merlot and Syrah have all shown potential in this dry, sparse inland region to the immediate north of the international border with Washington State. **Key names** in Okanagan are Blue Mountain, Gehringer Brothers, Inniskillin Okanagan, Jackson Triggs, Mission Hill, Quails Gate and Sumac Ridge.

Mexico

To date no wine in significant quantities of any substantial quality has been forthcoming here. This is largely down to a scarcity of local consumers to support a small wine industry. However, the potential of the area is there and in particular in the Baja Peninsula. The only wines to have had any worthwhile distribution so far are those of the LA Cetto company, although there is now Mexican investment in the Roussillon region in southern France.

Wine behind the label

Though it may still be a struggle to find fine South American wine on the wine list of a top restaurant in London, informed wine enthusiasts and professionals know how the growing reputation of this continents's wines, especially Argentina and Chile, is fully deserved. From the finer estates, age-worthy wines can hold their head up high amid Old World competition. Whilst Cabernet Sauvignon from Chile can still disappoint, except from the best estate, its Malbecs, Merlots and Carmeneres are breaking out of their cheap-and-cheerful, fruit-forward, early drinking reputation. Syrah is the new high altitude wonder varietal in Chile whilst Malbec from Argentina and increasingly Chardonnay continue to impress. Some impressive premium wines have emerged, suggesting real potential. There is some way to go before either country can compete in absolute quality terms with either Australia or California but new wines and producers are continuing to surface. The only other countries with potential for fine wine are Brazil and Uruguay. Some decent wines are emerging from the far south of Brazil, while Tannat is widely planted in Uruguay but as yet there are only a handful of reasonable examples.

Argentina

Argentina is as yet less established internationally than Chile and many wineries seem to have some way to go to match the fruit quality achieved at lower levels by her neighbour across the Andes. The country is, however, the fifth largest wine producer in the world, with a vast bulk-wine industry centred around the main region of Mendoza, which accounts for around nine out of every ten bottles produced. Argentina does appear to have real promise for good and indeed premium wine production and a number of impressive reds and whites are now being made. Outside expertise from the likes of Michel Rolland is increasing as is investment in new vineyards and wineries.

In the north of the country are the hot and dry vineyards of **Salta**, **Tucumán** and **Catamarca**. The lower lying vineyards are too warm for quality wine production and irrigation is vital. Within these regions, though, there are a number of better sites with vineyards planted at high altitude, in particular those in the Calchaquies Valley at **Cafayate**. Some good results are being achieved with both Malbec and Cabernet Sauvignon as well as the aromatic Torrontés. The bulk of Argentina's vineyards are in the Cuyo region to the south of Salta. Most northerly of the areas is high altitude **La Rioja**, a source of good reds and Torrontés. The centre of the country's wine production though is to the south at **Mendoza**. Areass that are of particular note are **Luján de Cuyo, Maipú** and the **Uco Valley**. The best of the vineyard area is planted at considerable altitude and some of the wines are world class. Malbec is very successful here but there are also widespread plantings of Cabernet Sauvignon, Syrah and Sangiovese. Bonarda is important both varietally and as a component in many wine blends and is the most widely planted red variety. Chardonnay inevitably is important and produces really striking wines in cooler sites.

To the south in Patagonia are the regions of **Neuquén** and particularly **Río Negro**. The climate is cool and early ripening Sauvignon Blanc, Sémillon and Chardonnay have all been grown with some success here. However, stylish, elegant examples of the red Bordeaux varieties and Syrah are also appearing and there are ongoing efforts to realise the potential complexity of Pinot Noir.

Chile

The country is split into five viticultural zones. Running from north to south, they are: **Atacama, Coquimbo, Aconcagua, Valle Central** and the **Región del Sur**. These zones contain a number of sub-regions and these may also be further subdivided. Atacama and Coquimbo are well to the north of the country. These are hot and dry, requiring mass flood irrigation, and generally produce basic table grapes as well as Pisco, the local brandy. There are new vineyard plantings at Coquimbo nearer the coast, where the climate is moderated by sea breezes. Some good rich and full-bodied reds are also now being produced both from the Bordeaux varieties and from Syrah further inland at altitude in **Limari**. You have to travel further south, though, to find vineyards capable of providing good quality wines in any volume. The region of Aconcagua includes the important sub-regions of **Casablanca** and **San Antonio**, where the vineyards are cool and nearer the coast. These is now a well-established source for some of the better white wines in the country with fine Syrah and Pinot Noir also emerging from San Antonio. Chardonnay, Gewürztraminer and Sauvignon Blanc are all successful. The **Valle del Aconcagua** itself is warmer and and becomes increasingly hot further inland. Eastern Aconcagua is largely red-wine territory. Some of the best sites are on well-drained slopes and the super-premium Seña blend is sourced from the area. The Valle Central is a substantial zone, which includes Chile's capital city Santiago to the north. The suburbs encroach into the vineyards of **Maipo**, the northernmost of the zone's sub-regions. The valley runs 400 km north to south, taking in Rapel, Maule and Curicó. The two key elements which influence grape growing here are the coastal fogs, which drift a long way inland and moderate the climate, and the Andes Mountains. The latter provide an important water source for irrigation. One of the problems encountered over the past decade has been over vigorous and over productive vineyards. Increased use of sophisticated drip irrigation systems is helping to overcome such vineyard problems. More wines are offering ripe and vibrant fruit now as opposed to some of the overtly green flavours that were so widespread just a few years ago. The best reds from Maipo have traditionally been Cabernet-based but increased plantings of Rhône varieties is a continuing trend. **Rapel** is very promising for fine wine production with Cabernet Sauvignon, Merlot and particularly Carmenère successful in the warmer south of the region at **Colchagua**, while earlier-ripening varieties including Chardonnay, Sauvignon Blanc and Pinot Noir are more successful in cooler **Cachapoal**. There are both promising reds and whites to be found at **Curicó**. Growing conditions are aided by large mid-season temperature fluctuations which help in preserving the acidity in the grapes. **Maule** to the south is largely dominated by white varieties but there is some good Merlot too. The coastal vineyards of **Leyda** offers fine whites as well as good Pinot Noir. To the south is the Región del Sur including the two sub-regions of **Itata** and, immediately to the south, **Bío Bío**. Unsurprisingly, this being the most southerly of the grape-growing regions, the climate is cool and rainfall is also high. Sophisticated trellising and the planting of early-ripening Pinot Noir and Chardonnay as well as Alsace varieties has shown some potential. The best results so far have come from Bío Bío.

Brazil

Bento Gonçalves, a city of 105,000 people, is the Bordeaux of Brazil. It lies at the centre of the **Vale dos Vinhedos** (Wine Valley), a sub-zone of the **Serra Gaúcha** wine region in Brazil's southern-most state Rio Grande do Sul. Money, mostly private, is being pumped into the Brazilian wine industry like newly fermented wine into an empty steel tank. Export markets are being targeted enthusiastically. Located at parallel 29°, Serra Gaúcha has an average winter temperature of 12°C. In the summer, temperatures average 22°C,

much cooler than in the north. The humidity caused by high rainfall means that spraying is essential. The lush landscape implies very fertile soils, which, because they encourage excessive vegetation, are not always the best for growing grapes for quality wine. The prevailing soil type is argillaceous, with plenty of clay. This suits Merlot well and also tempers the acidity promoted by the region's high altitude. Bento Gonçalves is at 690 metres above sea level, though vineyards in the Vale dos Vinhedos tend to be a bit less than that. Vinifera rather than hybrid vines are now universal for "fine wines."

The rest of South America

The only other country to have any real potential for quality wine production is Uruguay. Hybrid varieties are still important in the area planted but high quality vinifera varieties are becoming more significant. Cabernet Sauvignon, Merlot, Chardonnay and Sauvignon Blanc are all cultivated. Most important from a quality wine perspective is the Tannat. Elsewhere the climate is too hot and humid.

South America vintages

Any vintage assessment within the wine zones and regions here has to be very general because of both size and the effect of local mesoclimates. Increasingly reds are ageworthy, however whites, even those that are barrel-fermented should be approached young.

2016 was a wet year in Chile, though there should be some good results from earlier ripening whites. The weather was also an issue in Argentina although further away from the Andes less so. In **2015**, rain affected harvests both sides of the Andes, though in some parts of Chile, a hot and dry spell (relatively speaking for Chile) forced an early harvest. **2014** in Chile saw excellent growing and ripening conditions and full and concentrated reds are likely to develop well. In Argentina rain at harvest meant more variable results. In **2013** in Chile and Argentina the growing season was cool and the harvest late. Some good elegant and fresh wines have been made but growers required patience for the best results. Late ripening varieties did best, early ripeners like Sauvignon struggled. In **2012** in Chile it was a very ripe and early vintage whereas in Argentina the harvest was in marked contrast to Chile with cool harvesting conditions and wines that are likely to be more elegant than in recent years. In **2011** in Chile was a good year for quality with cool growing conditions however yields were lower than normal. In Argentina a cool growing period was followed by balmy ripening conditions and wines that are ripe and full but with fresh crisp acidity as well. **2010** in Chile although the vintage was overshadowed by the devastating earthquake in February, some good elegant wines will emerge, albeit with a lower than normal yield. and growers are very bullish and a number regard this as the best years since 2002. In **2009** in Argentina quality was good but yields were down, in Chile some fine reds were made albeit with some variability in the quality of the Cabernet and Carmenère. Good to very good wines, particularly red emerged in **2008** in both countries. **2007** was promising in both, **2006** was a step up on **2005**, particularly in Argentina with some elegant reds emerging from a long growing season. **2005** was sound in Chile, while Argentina enjoyed cooler late summer temperatures than normal and good wines were produced. **2004** was good for reds and whites in Chile, whereas in Argentina reds have benefitted from the hot year. **2003** and in particular **2002** were good for Malbec in Argentina. **2003** was good both red and white in Chile.

A-Z of producers by region

Argentina

Mendoza

Achaval-Ferrer	807
Viña Alicia	808
Alta Vista	808
Anubís	808
Susana Balbo	811
Ben Marco	811
Luigi Bosca	808
Walter Bressia	808
Buen Orden	808
Carinae	809
Bodegas Caro	809
Catena	809
Cheval des Andes	814
Clos de Los Siete	810
Viña Cobos	810
Crios	811
Cuvelier Los Andes	810
Bodega DiaMandes	810
Dominio del Plata	811
El Porvenir	811
Eral Bravo	811
O Fournier (Argentina)	811
Kaiken	812
Luca	809
Mendel	812
Bodega Monteviejo	812
Nieto Senetiner	812
Bodega Norton	813
Piedra Negra	813
Poesia	813
Pulenta Estate	814
Carlos Pulenta	813
Finca Sophenia	814
Terrazas de los Andes	814
Tikal	809
Val de Flores	815

Rio Negro

Bodega Chacra	809
Noemia Patagonía	812

Salta

Bodega Colomé	810
Michel Torino	814
Yacochuya	815

Chile

Aconcagua

Errázuriz	818
Seña	821
Viña Von Siebenthal	822

Cachapoal

Viña Altair	815

Viña Aquitania	815

Casablanca

Viña Casablanca	817
Casas del Bosque	816
Loma Larga	819

Colchagua

Hacienda Araucano	815
Neyen	821
Viu Manent	822

Curicó

Montes	820
Valdivieso	822

Leyda

Viña Leyda	820

Maipo

Almaviva	815
Carmen	816
Viñedo Chadwick	817
Concha y Toro	817
Cousiño Macul	818
De Martino	818
El Principal	818
Alvaro Espinoza	819
Haras de Pirque	819
Odfjell Vineyards	821
Viña Pérez Cruz	821
Santa Rita	821
Undurraga	822

Rapel

Casa Silva	816
Cono Sur	817
Lapostolle	819

San Antonio

Casa Marin	816
Viña Garces Silva	819
Matetic	820

Brazil

Serra Gaúcha

Lidio Carraro	823
Vinicola Miolo	823
Casa Valduga	823

BOLIVIA

JUJUY

SALTA
Salta

16

CHILE

CATAMARCA

PARAGUAY

Asunción

PARANÁ

ATACAMA

LA RIOJA

SALADO

BRASIL

La Serena 1

2

COQUIMBO 3

SAN JUAN
San Juan

URUGUAY

ARGENTINA

San Felipe

ACONCAGUA

ACONCAGUA 4
Valparaíso 5

15 Mendoza

URUGUAY

MAIPO 6 Santiago

14

Rancagua 13 MENDOZA

VALLE 7 San Fernando

Buenos Aires
Montevideo

CENTRAL Curicó
Talca 8

MAULE
9

COLORADO

10

REGIÓN Concepción
DEL SUR 11

Temuco Neuquén 12 12

NEGRO

12

PATAGONIA

1	Elqui
2	Limari
3	Choapa
4	Aconcagua
5	Casablanca
6	Maipo
7	Rapel
8	Curicó
9	Maule
10	Itata Balley
11	Bío Bío
12	Rio Negro
13	Valle de Uco/Tupungato
14	Luján de Cuyo
15	Maipú
16	Cafayate

A-Z of producers - *Argentina*

❀ **Achaval-Ferrer (Mendoza)** *www.achaval-ferrer.com*
Small top-quality Mendoza winery. It is an Argentine/Italian
partnership of four friends: Santiago Achaval Becu, Manuel Ferrer
Minetti, Italian winemaker and roving consultant Roberto Cipresso
and former world rally champion Tiziano Siviero. There are three
estate-owned vineyards which are planted at altitude (730–
1,100m) and there are some leasing arrangements with a number
of other vineyard owners. Vinification includes both pumping over
and punching the cap during maceration and malolactic takes
place in barrel. The Finca Altamira and Finca Mirador are both
100% Malbecs from single vineyards and produced from very

low-yielding old vines. A third vineyard source, Finca Bella Vista is
also now made, again from Malbec The mainstays of the winery
are the Quimera red, a blend of Malbec, Cabernet Sauvignon and
Merlot and a Malbec from a number of sites around Vistalba. These
are dense and powerful wines which will keep well for a decade or
more but can be broached with 3 or 4 years' age. (DM)

Recommended Reds:

Malbec Finca Mirador Mendoza ★★★★★ £F
Malbec Finca Altamira Mendoza ★★★★★ £F
Malbec Finca Bella Vista Mendoza ★★★★★ £F
Quimera Mendoza ★★★★ £E
Malbec Mendoza ★★★☆ £D

Wine behind the label

Argentina

South America

❀ Alta Vista (Mendoza) www.altavistawines.com

This new venture in Argentina's high-quality Luján de Cuyo region was established by the late Jean-Michel Arcaute and Patrick d'Aulan with the objective of producing cool-grown Malbec and Cabernet Sauvignon of real style and quality. Additional input is now provided by Michel Rolland of BON PASTEUR. There are around 61ha of vineyards and a wide range of wines is produced. There are varietal Classic labelled Malbec, Cabernet and Torrontés while the Premium labelled wines are a step up and include fresh aromatic Torrontés and an oaky Chardonnay. Premium Malbec is chunky and full of forward, easy-going, brambly fruit; more serious are the Malbec Terroir Selection and three excellent single vineyard wines, Alizarine, Serenade and Temis. Atemporal is a blend of Malbec, Cabernet Sauvignon, Syrah and Petit Verdot. The Alto is a very powerfully structured blend of Malbec and Cabernet Sauvignon and has an excellent balance of dark, spicy fruit, supple firm tannins and well-judged oak. The wine is neither fined nor filtered. (DM)

Recommended Reds:
Alto Vistalba ★★★★☆ £F
Malbec Alizarine Luján de Cuyo ★★★★ £E
Malbec Serenade Luján de Cuyo ★★★★ £E
Malbec Temis Luján de Cuyo ★★★★ £E
Malbec Terroir Selection Luján de Cuyo ★★★ £D
Atemporal Blend Luján de Cuyo ★★★ £D
Premium Malbec Luján de Cuyo ★★☆ £B
Recommended Whites:
Premium Torrontés Luján de Cuyo ★★ £B
Premium Chardonnay Luján de Cuyo ★☆ £B

Anubís (Mendoza)

The first vintage for this relatively new operation was only 1999 but the results so far have been promising and the wines offer excellent value for money. It is a partnership between Susana Balbo, who also produces wine under her own label at DOMINIO DEL PLATA, and Alberto Antonini, formerly of ANTINORI. Fruit is sourced from Luján de Cuyo and Tupungato and a range of vibrant varietals is now being produced. Cabernet Sauvignon and Malbec stand out. These are modern, stylish, richly extracted reds that are approachable and supple and may be enjoyed young. Antonini is also involved with estate owner Rodolfo Massera producing a further Malbec, LA REMONTA, from cool La Consulta to the south of Mendoza. (DM)

Recommended Reds:
Cabernet Sauvignon Mendoza ★★ £C   Malbec Mendoza ★★ £C

❀ Bodega Luigi Bosca (Mendoza) www.luigibosca.com.ar

The Arizu family have a sizeable family wine business producing close to 800,000 cases a year. The family now possess 668 ha of owned vineyards across seven sites. Quality across the board is generally very good with some excellent value to be found in the Finca La Linda label as well as fine Reserva Malbec and Cabernet Sauvignon. Los Nobles Chardonnay is in a rich, full tropical style with fermentation and ageing in new French oak. A very characterful Los Nobles Malbec gains additional complexity from some interplanted Petit Verdot. Of the top Gala labels the white Gala 3 is a vibrant fruit driven blend of Viognier, Chardonnay and a touch of Riesling. The Gala 4 is largely Cabernet Franc with a little Malbec, Gala 2 is dominated by Cabernet Sauvignon, while perhaps the most impressive is the Gala 1, 80% Malbec with Petit Verdot and just 5% of Tannat. The splendid and pricey top red Icono blends Malbec with Cabernet Sauvignon. The Viña Alicia wines are lower volume, almost boutique style wines. The project owned by Alberto Arizu's wife

Alicia emerged from experimental clones brought to Argentina from all over the world. The wines are some of the best in the country coming from high density plantings and low yields. Fermentation is by individual vineyard lot and the wines are unfiltered. Cuarzo is mainly Petit Verdot with a little Grenache and Carignan and Syrah and Nebbiolo are also now released as is a mutation of Malbec, "Brote Negro" from over 90 year old vines. An additional label Paso de Piedra provides more fruit driven styles aged in used barrels. The top reds under both labels will develop well in bottle for up to a decade. (DM)

Luigi Bosca
Recommended Reds:
Icono Lujan de Cuyo ★★★★☆ £G
Malbec Verdot Finca Los Nobles ★★★☆ £E
Gala 1 Mendoza ★★★☆ £E   Gala 2 Mendoza ★★★ £E
Gala 4 Mendoza ★★★ £E   Malbec Mendoza ★★★ £C
Cabernet Sauvignon Mendoza ★★☆ £C
Malbec Finca La Linda Mendoza ★★ £B
Recommended Whites:
Gala 3 Mendoza ★★★☆ £E
Chardonnay Finca Los Nobles Mendoza ★★☆ £C
Sauvignon Blanc Mendoza ★★ £C

Viña Alicia
Recommended Reds:
Cuarzo Viña Alicia Lujan de Cuyo ★★★★ £F
Brote Negro Viña Alicia Lujan de Cuyo ★★★★ £F
Malbec Viña Alicia Lujan de Cuyo ★★★☆ £E
Morena Cabernet Sauvignon Viña Alicia Lujan de Cuyo ★★★☆ £E

Buen Orden (Mendoza)

The Posada de Buen Orden Estate comprises 40 ha of vineyards planted at around 700 metres above sea-level on the higher slopes of Mendoza. Most of the vines are over 30 years old providing the raw material for wines of depth and character. This is aided no doubt by a high diurnal swing in summer temperatures ensuring excellent acidity in the grapes. Although the vineyards have been established here for some decades, it wasn't until 2004 that the family decided to start producing wines themselves. Fernando Oltra and his son Gonzalo have installed modern winery equipment and are crafting the wines with additional input from Luis Barraud who is also a co-owner at Viña COBOS. There is an unfiltered Tempranillo which sees 6 months ageing in a mix of French and American oak and a piercingly aromatic and characterful Torrontés which offers a depth and rich texture very rarely encountered with the variety. A relatively cool fermentation ensures the wine's bright aromatic character. (DM)

Recommended Reds:
Posada de Buen Orden Tempranillo Mendoza ★★★ £D
Recommended Whites:
Posadas de Buen Orden Selección Mendoza ★★☆ £C

❀ Walter Bressia (Mendoza) www.bressiabodega.com

Walter Bressia is a small scale wine producer as well as being one of Argentina's better known consultant winemakers. Production is strictly artisanal so these excellent wines will not be that easy to find. The grapes come from both his own small holdings as well as other parcels. The Monteagrelo bottling is a varietal Malbec of fine purity and depth, loaded with dark, spicy tobacco-scented ripe fruit. The Profundo is a touch more structured with Malbec blended with Cabernet Sauvignon, Syrah and Merlot. As elsewhere no small

808

element of the quality of the wines is achieved by incorporating Malbec of approaching 80 years of age. Both wines are aged in a mix of both French and American oak and will evolve well for at least five years. The range now extends to nine wines and includes a sparkler from Chardonnay and Pinot Noir and the premium Ultima Hoja. (DM)

Recommended Reds:
Profundo Mendoza ★★★☆ £E   Monteagrelo Mendoza ★★★ £C

Carinae (Mendoza)   *www.carinaevinos.com*
This small boutique winery was established in 2003 by Philippe Subra, an engineer who originates from south-west France. The key to the quality of his wines, partucularly his Malbec, has been in buying up small plots of sometimes very old, low-yielding vines. These are modern, vibrant, very fruit-rich wines and it comes as no surprise that winemaking consultancy comes from Michel Rolland. The old-vine quality of the fruit though undoubtedly shines through. Part of the Rolland style includes a saignée, a draining off of some of the juice to aid extraction during vinification. As well as the reds a fine aromatic and very fresh Torrontés comes from cooler climate vineyards in Salta. Of the reds the Cabernet Sauvignon Reserva has lots of rich, ripe fruit, more blackberry and dark cherry than cassis scented. It is excellent value as is the Malbec Reserva which has just a touch more depth and complexity. Syrah is also impressive. The Cabernet gets just five months in small oak in contrast to the Malbec which spends a year in wood. Newly added are Finca Deneza, a single vineyard Malbec and Brigitte a blend dominated by Malbec with a little Cabernet lending structure. The Syrah and Malbec Gran Reservas and Prestige, a blend of Malbec, Cabernet and Shiraz, are both produced in very small quantities with only a few hundred cases of each a year. The wines tend to be aged for 13 to 15 months in new French oak which is well judged and nicely integrated. Much of the complex character of the Malbec Gran Reserva in particular comes from old vines of up to 90 years of age. The top wines in particular will age very nicely for up to a decade. (DM)

Recommended Reds:
Prestige Perdriel ★★★★ £E
Malbec Gran Reserva Perdriel ★★★☆ £E
Syrah Gran Reserva Mendoza ★★★☆ £E
Malbec Reserva Mendoza ★★★ £C
Syrah Reserva Maipú ★★★ £C
Finca Deneza Perdriel ★★★ £C
Cuvée Brigitte Maipú ★★★ £C
Cabernet Sauvignon Reserva Mendoza ★★★ £C
Recommended Whites:
Torrontés Salta ★★☆ £B

Catena Zapata (Mendoza)   *www.catenawines.com*
The Catena operation is considerable with a number of ranges produced at all price levels. Good straightforward varietal styles are produced under the Argento label, while the Alamos range is a step up. Both the Chardonnay and the Malbec are worth considering. Good to very good whites and reds with real depth and style are produced under the Catena label and are very modern approachable wines. The premium bottlings appear under the Catena Alta label and include Chardonnay, Cabernet Sauvignon and Malbec. Alta Chardonnay from the Historic Rows in 2011 and 2012 approached a Grand Cru Burgundy in quality and indicates what Catena is capable of in the right locations. The top wine is the super-premium Cabernet Sauvignon Zapata, which has been joined by a

number of single vineyard labels; Argentino, Adrianna and Nicasia. All are sourced from vineyards at Luján de Cuyo. Daughter Laura produces an impressive range independently under the Luca brand which includes powerfully structured Malbec, Syrah and Cabernet Sauvignon and toasty Chardonnay from Mendoza, while son Ernesto produces stylish, modern reds: Patriota, a blend of Bonarda and Malbec; Jubilo which is based on Cabernet Sauvignon; and Amoria, based on Malbec. These are all comfortably worth three stars in the latest releases. The style throughout the premium ranges is modern and approachable and only limited cellaring will be required. Caro, a blend of Malbec and Cabernet Sauvignon, is a new joint venture with Baron de Rothschild of LAFITE-ROTHSCHILD. The partnership also produces two further wines; Amancaya has more Malbec while Aruma is pure Malbec. (DM/GW)

Catena
Recommended Reds:
Nicolás Catena Zapata Luján de Cuyo ★★★★ £G
Catena Zapata Malbec Argentino Luján de Cuyo ★★★★ £G
Cabernet Sauvignon Alta Luján de Cuyo ★★★ £E
Cabernet Sauvignon Catena Luján de Cuyo ★★ £C
Malbec Alta Luján de Cuyo ★★★★ £E
Malbec Catena Luján de Cuyo ★★☆ £C
Malbec Alamos Mendoza ★☆ £B
Recommended Whites:
Chardonnay Alta Luján de Cuyo ★★★☆ £E
Chardonnay Catena Luján de Cuyo ★★☆ £C
Chardonnay Alamos Mendoza ★ £B
Bodegas Caro
Recommended Reds:
Caro Mendoza ★★★ £E
Luca
Recommended Reds:
Syrah Mendoza ★★★ £E
Malbec Mendoza ★★★ £E
Recommended Whites:
Chardonnay Mendoza ★★★ £E
Tikal
Recommended Reds:
Jubilo Mendoza ★★★ £E   Patriota Mendoza ★★★ £D

✿ **Bodega Chacra (Rio Negro)**   *www.bodegachacra.com*
Piero Incisa della Rocchetta purchased the vineyards here in 2004. He is now producing the finest Pinot Noir, not only in Argentina but in South America. Rio Negro is in the arid central desert of Argentina but the vineyards have a temperate local climate moderated by the Neuquen and Limay rivers flowing eastwards out of the Andes and converging with the Rio Negro. Although summers are warm and sunny, the diurnal temperature change between day and night is high and ensures good acidity in the fruit. Biodynamic farming is practiced and the sparse gravel and alluvial soils with significant limestone traces provide grapes of impressive flavour intensity. There were three existing vineyards planted respectively in 1932, 1995 and 1967. A fourth site has since been planted on rootstocks from the 1932 and 1955 sites. The Barda Pinot is sourced from all the sites. The Treinta y Dos and Cincuenta wines see a higher proportion of new French oak, around 50% as opposed to 25% for the Barda. All three are aged for around 11 months in wood and the malolactic occurs naturally on lees. Bottling is without recourse to fining or filtration. The Barda is more obviously fruit-driven and comes from a higher (albeit not high) yield of 40 hl/ha. The single vineyard wines

offer greater depth and intensity. The Treinta y Dos possesses a really rich, dark-fruited old-vine complexity. An approachable plummy and pepper-spiced Merlot, Mainqué has also been added to the Pinots with a first vintage in 2007. The vines for this are planted next to the 1955 Pinot site. (DM)

Recommended Reds:
Pinot Noir Treinta y Dos Rio Negro ★★★★★ £G
Pinot Noir Cincuenta y Cinco Rio Negro ★★★★☆ £F
Pinot Noir Barda Rio Negro ★★★★ £E
Merlot Mainqué Rio Negro ★★★☆ £D

Clos de Los Siete (Mendoza) *www.closdelossiete.com*
A winery with a stellar reputation. This is a major new French investment in Argentina which includes international wine consultant Michel Rolland, who has already established his own successful YACOCHUYA label. In total 250 ha have been planted, 80 km south of Mendoza, covering 7 vineyards. The wines are produced at the Bodega MONTEVIEJO, owned by Catherine Péré-Vergé, the owner of Château MONTVIEL in Pomerol. The Clos de Los Siete red, is a blend of Malbec, Merlot, Cabernet Sauvignon and Syrah. It is full of upfront dark, brambly fruit and is aged one-third in vats and two-thirds in new oak. There is real potential here and it will be interesting to see how things develop as the vineyards age. (DM)
Recommended Reds:
Clos de los Siete Mendoza ★★★ £C

☙ Viña Cobos (Mendoza) *www.vinacobos.com*
This is a parnership between California winery owner and roving consultant Paul HOBBS and the Argentine husband and wife viticulture/winemaking team of Luis Barraud and Andrea Marchiori. The Marchiori family vineyard, located in the high altitude Perdriel area of Upper Mendoza is the source for the wines. There is an impressive holding of old Malbec between 50 and over 80 years of age. Three labels are released, including the good value Nativo Collection wines, the pricier Bramare label as well as the super-premium Cobos. While not exactly boutique in size production is small by South American standards. Three red Felino examples are produced. Merlot is ripe and plummy, Cabernet Sauvignon is supple, and marked by dark cherry fruit, while the vibrant dark berry-fruited Malbec is the best of the three. All get a 3-4 day cold-soak and are aged in French and American oak for 9 months and bottled with neither fining nor filtration. While reds dominate here there are a few hundred cases of a very respectable Chardonnay under the superior and much pricier Bramare Marchiori Vineyard label and this has been joined by a Felino example as well. Rich, nutty and leesy with real breadth the Bramare is barrel-fermented with natural yeasts in 50% new wood, very much in the Hobbs Sonoma mould. There is only a tiny amount of Bramare Cabernet Sauvignon produced but a bit more of a dark, spicy Malbec. Both are aged in a mix of mainly French and some American oak. The Marchiori Vineyard is also now an additional source of Malbec and Cabernet. The top wine, Cobos is one of, if not the most expensive in Argentina but is a magnificent full, rich and immensely concentrated old-vine Malbec of real depth and impressive structure. This and the other two Bramare reds will develop well in bottle but show very well young if you enjoy big, fleshy and opulent reds. (DM)
Recommended Reds:
Cobos Luján de Cuyo ★★★★★ £H
Bramare Malbec Luján de Cuyo ★★★★☆ £F
Bramare Cabernet Sauvignon Luján de Cuyo ★★★★ £F
Felino Malbec Perdriel ★★★ £C

Felino Cabernet Sauvignon Perdriel ★★★ £C
Felino Merlot Perdriel ★★★ £C
Recommended Whites:
Bramare Chardonnay Marchiori Luján de Cuyo ★★★★ £F

Bodega Colomé (Salta) *www.bodegacolome.com*
Colomé was purchased by Hess Family Estates during 2001 and currently has 135 ha under vine and a number of vines range from 60 to 150 years old with some vineyards of pre-phylloxera age. There are plans to plant a further 150 ha. The property is in the Calchaquí Valley in Salta in the north of the country. The climate is very dry which is auspicious for biodynamic farming and the cool nights ensure good fresh acidity in the fruit. A small range of reds are now produced along with a white Torrontés. This is one of the best regions for the variety and the property's example is one of the countries best, perfumed, aromatic and dry with impressive intensity. The Estate Malbec has a small proportion of Cabernet Sauvignon, Tannat, Petit Verdot and Syrah included in its blend. The vineyard sources range from very old (90-150 years old) to young vines. The top red is one of Argentina's top wines, the Reserva Malbec. It is rich, concentrated and profound with real intensity and underpinned by supple, velvety tannins. Malbec comes from the oldest plots and around 20% Cabernet Sauvignon adds backbone and structure. It will be best with five or six years in bottle. (DM)
Recommended Reds:
Reserva Malbec Salta ★★★★★ £G
Estate Malbec Salta ★★★ £D
Recommended Whites:
Torrontés Salta ★★ £B

Cuvelier Los Andes (Mendoza) *www.cuvelierlosandes.com*
This Mendoza winery and vineyard, established in 1999, is owned by the Cuvelier family who also own Château LÉOVILLE-POYFERRÉ in Bordeaux's Saint-Julien appellation. They are also partners in and contribute to the CLOS DE LOS SIETE project so with this and the Bordeaux connection it is no surprise that consultancy advise comes from Michel Rolland. There are now 55 ha under vine and plans to plant a further 10 ha. Quality is helped by the well drained stony, alluvial, gravel soils. Acidity and balance are achieved in the grapes with cool summer nights, the vineyards being between 1,015 and 1,045 metres above sea level. There is a modern state of the art winery and the harvest, all hand picked is carefully sorted prior to vinification. The fruit is given a pre-fermentation cold soak and fermentation and vatting lasts for 30 to 40 days. The well priced spicy, brambly Colección is a blend of nearly two-thirds Malbec with about 20% Cabernet Sauvignon along with a little Syrah, Merlot as well as a touch of Petit Verdot. It gets 12 months in French oak. The *grand vin* has a little more Malbec and a firmer, bigger structure although showing more obvious brambly Malbec character. 15 months is spent in around 50% new oak and the balance in first fill barrels. The top wine, the Grand Malbec is a sole varietal and gets a similar period in oak, all of it new though, which will require a minimum of four to five years to integrate. (DM)
Recommended Reds:
Grand Malbec Mendoza ★★★★ £F
Grand Vin Mendoza ★★★★ £E   Colección Mendoza ★★★☆ £D

Bodega DiaMandes (Mendoza) *www.diamandes.com*
The new DiaMandes bodega was founded by the Bonnie family of Château MALARTIC-LAGRAVIÈRE in 2005 when they established a 130 ha single estate in the heart of the CLOS DE LOS SIETE holding

Wine behind the label

Argentina

South America

in the Uco Valley. The success of Clos de Los Siete has shown the tremendous potential of this area of Mendoza. The vineyards are planted at an altitude of around 1,100 metres, so there's plenty of acidity in the grapes. The soil is a mix of clay and sand and also crucially has a substantial pebble component in the topsoil. A range of wines are now made, including three Malbec dominated reds, the top wine being the Uco Gran Reserva. This is a rich, concentrated and structured blend of Malbec and Cabernet Sauvignon. The second red Uco de Malbec has tiny proportions of Merlot, Syrah and Petit Verdot included. A third red, Perlita, comes from Malbec and a little Syrah. There is also a soft and approachable easy drinking rosé, a saignée selection labelled L'Argentin de Malartic. The range also includes two whites, a varietal Chardonnay and a varietal Viognier. Vineyard management follows modern techniques and a green harvest and leaf thinning are practised with harvesting by hand. Michel Rolland is the consultant winemaker and as you would expect vinification is modern. Whole bunches are gravity fed to stainless steel tanks which are completely insulated. Ageing is more typical –in French oak, the top wine spending two years in cask. (DM)

Recommended Reds:
DiaMandes de Uco Gran Reserva Valle de Uco ★★★★ £F

Dominio del Plata (Mendoza) www.dominiodelplata.com
This is the home winery of Pedro Marchevsky and Susana Balbo who are the manager and winemaker at ANUBÍS. The Crios label offers some attractive, fruit-driven wines including a fine floral Torrontés and two reds, a Cabernet Sauvignon and a Syrah/Bonarda blend. The top Dominio del Plata wines are a serious step up in both quality and price. Of the three labels the Susana Balbo and Nosostros wines offer greater depth and power. They are also produced in much smaller volumes. Expresivo is a blend of Malbec from cool La Consulta as well as Cabernet Sauvignon, Bonarda, Tannat and a little Merlot. Each variety is vinified separately and the wine aged in at least 50% new wood. The top label Nosostros is a richly textured old Malbec. Brioso, which like Nosostros is aged in new French oak, means strength and the wine is both deep and concentrated with great poise and refinement. It blends Cabernet Sauvignon, Cabernet Franc, Malbec and Petit Verdot and will develop well for up to a decade. A new reasonably priced Malbec, Zohar has also recently been added (DM)

Susana Balbo
Recommended Reds:
Nosostros Mendoza ★★★★☆ £G
Brioso Mendoza ★★★★ £F   Malbec Mendoza ★★★☆ £E
Cabernet Sauvignon Mendoza ★★★ £E

Ben Marco
Recommended Reds:
Expresivo Mendoza ★★★☆ £E   Malbec Mendoza ★★☆ £D
Crios
Recommended Reds:
Crios Malbec Mendoza ★★☆ £B
Crios Syrah Bonarda Mendoza ★★☆ £B
Recommended Whites:
Crios Torrontés Cafayate ★★ £B

El Porvenir (Cafayate) www.bodegaselporvenir.com
By Argentine standards this is, as yet, a relatively small producer crafting an impressive range of reds and sound Torrontés whites. There is a top single "super-premium" red Porvenir which it has to be

said is a good deal better priced than a number of other examples from competitor wineries. The other two ranges both red and white are Laborum and Amauta. The bodega has 77 ha (192 acres) spread across two estates, both in Cafayate and both farmed by sustainable methods. A combination of sparse sandy soils, and an altitude of 1,750 metres, long sunny days and a high temperature variation during the summer between the days and nights helps to ensure good flavour and balance in the grapes. Winemaking is handled by Luis Ismet and back-up is provided by Sonoma based Paul HOBBS who also consults at Viña COBOS. Top label Porvenir is an impressively dense and concentrated blend of the four red varieties here; Malbec, Cabernet Sauvignon, Tannat and Syrah. The Laborum wines are also impressive and include two Torrontés, a dry white and a late-harvested example which gets a little time in French oak. The Amauta reds like their Laborum counterparts are aged in a combination of both French and American wood. The Laborum Malbec and Tannat are both particularly striking. (DM)

Recommended Reds:
Porvenir Cafayate ★★★★ £F
Laborum Malbec Cafayate ★★★☆ £E
Laborum Syrah Cafayate ★★★☆ £E
Laborum Tannat Cafayate ★★★☆ £E
Laborum Cabernet Sauvignon Cafayate ★★★ £E
Amauta I Cafayate ★★★ £D
Amauta II Cafayate ★★☆ £D
Recommended Whites:
Laborum Late-Harvest Torrontés Cafayate ★★★ £D
Laborum Torrontés Cafayate ★★☆ £C

Eral Bravo (Mendoza) www.eralbravo.com
This is a newly established project of the Nieto family who have now sold their interest in the NIETO SENETINER winery. Output here is considerably less, just 7,500 cases as compared to over 130,000 cases a year at the old family operation. As well as vineyards around their winery base in the Luján de Cuyo, they can also draw on fruit from Uco Valley to the south and they have a total resource of around 250 ha, so lots of scope for expansion. The wines are all marked by an excellent vibrant dark berry fruit character, with an extra dimension in the Eral Bravo bottlings., which are aged solely in French oak for at least 12 months, 16 in the case of the Malbec, Cabernet and Syrah blended YBS. All are immediately approachable although the YBS will benefit from a little age. (DM)

Recommended Reds:
Eral Bravo YBS Mendoza ★★★☆ £E
Eral Bravo Malbec Mendoza ★★★ £C
Eral Bravo Cabernet Sauvignon Mendoza ★★★ £C
Urano Malbec Mendoza ★★☆ £B
Urano Cabernet Sauvignon Mendoza ★★☆ £B
Urano Syrah Mendoza ★★☆ £B

O Fournier (Mendoza) www.ofournier.com
This Spanish family owned operation not only produces fine red and white wines here in the Uco Valley sub region of Mendoza but also some very well crafted reds in Spain's Ribera del Duero, at Bodegas y Viñedos O FOURNIER. As yet the reds here don't quite have the depth and dimension of their Spanish counterparts but there is great potential. Wines are now also being produced in Chile, with plans for Rioja and Portugal's Douro Valley. As well as the Alpha and B Crux labels, named after the brightest stars in the Southern Cross constellation, accessible fruit driven wines are also released under the Urban Uco label. The family possess around 100 ha with some

811

vines over 30 years old and the vineyards are farmed biodynamically. A certain amount of fruit is also bought-in to supplement their requirements. The B Crux Sauvignon Blanc gets a short skin contact and is then fermented in stainless steel. The reds also benefit from a period of pre-fermentation maceration giving wines of bright, vibrant dark fruit with good intensity. They are bottled unfiltered. The blends are dominated by Tempranillo and both the Alfa Crux red and Alpha Malbec will gain further complexity with half a decades age. (DM)

Recommended Reds:

Alpha Crux Malbec Mendoza ★★★☆ £E

Alpha Crux Mendoza ★★★☆ £E

B Crux Mendoza ★★☆ £C

Recommended Whites:

B Crux Sauvignon Blanc Mendoza ★★ £B

Kaiken (Mendoza) www.kaikenwines.com

This newly established winery is named after the wild geese which criss-cross the Andes between Argentina and Chile. It is also under the same ownership as MONTES in Chile and under the winemaking guidance of Aurelio Montes, From a first vintage in 2002, Kaiken has produced a good range of well priced and approachable reds. A Premium Malbec, Mai has been added to the range along with a sparkling white, Kaiken Brut from Pinot Noir and Chardonnay and three Terroir Series wines a white and two reds. Output is substantial, and there are 70 ha of owned vineyards at Agrelo. The winery focuses mainly on Malbec and Cabernet Sauvignon for reds, along with a little Bonarda and Petit Verdot and Torrontés is used in the Terroir Series white. The wines are impressively ripe and characterful, in particular the spicy, brambly Ultra Malbec. All are immediately approacheable with the top two wines coming from considerably lower yields and aged in French as opposed to American oak used for the Reservas. (DM)

Recommended Reds:

Ultra Malbec Mendoza ★★★ £D

Ultra Cabernet Sauvignon Mendoza ★★☆ £D

Malbec Reserva Mendoza ★★☆ £C

Cabernet Sauvignon Reserva Mendoza ★★☆ £C

❀ Mendel (Mendoza) www.mendel.com.ar

This small, bespoke bodega is a source of some excellent old vine Malbec. Cabernet Sauvignon is also significant in the Unus blended red. Winemaking expertise is provided by Roberto de la Mota who previously made another benchmark red, Cheval des Andes at TERRAZOS DE LOS ANDES. Output here is small although the approach is highly sophisticated. The vineyards are located at altitudes ranging from 900 to 1,100 metres above sea level in the Luján de Cuyo sub-region of Mendoza. Much of the key to the quality of the wines are the old vineyards, up to 80 years in some plots, and the sparse mineral rich soils. The vines are flood irrigated block by block to manage the vines growth stress and this also helps in guarding against phylloxera with many vines being ungrafted. The summers at this altitude are never excessively hot and the summer nights cool, aiding the development of acidity in the grapes. Vinification, while sophisticated and well organized is nevertheless artisan in approach and philosophy. The fruit is carefully sorted and a long vatting of up to five weeks carried out. The spicy, complex old-viney Malbec is aged for 12 months in roughly one-third new wood. The Unus gets a little longer 16 months and in all new oak. The Malbec which accounts for roughly 70% of the blend is combined with Cabernet Sauvignon aiding the

grip and structure of the wine taking up the new wood. There is also a considerably pricier Malbec Finca Remola from an ungrafted 60 year old vineyard which is given the modern treatment of 200% new wood, being given a period in new barrels and passed again into a completely new set of barrels. A softer fruit driven Malbec, Lunta and a characterful low volume Sémillon add further interest to the range. Both the Malbec and the Unus are notable for their value as well as quality. (DM)

Recommended Reds:

Finca Remota Mendoza ★★★★★ £G

Unus Mendoza ★★★★ £E   Malbec Mendoza ★★★☆ £D

Lunta Mendoza ★★☆ £C

Recommended Whites:

Sémillon Mendoza ★★★ £D

Bodega Monteviejo (Mendoza) www.monteviejo.com

Catherine Péré-Vergé, the owner of Château MONTVIEL in Pomerol also vinifies the CLOS DE LOS SIETE red here at her Vista Flores winery. She is able to draw on 125 ha of vineyards planted between 900 and 1,200 metres and output currently is still modest at a mere 6,000 cases a year. The potential of the ultra modern winery is much greater, around 120,000 cases although 50,000 cases are accounted for by the Clos de Los Siete brand. Festivo is a soft, supple and immediately approachable fruit driven Malbec. Both the impressively dense, structured and characterful varietal Malbec Lindaflor red and the second label Petite Fleur, blending Malbec with Cabernet Sauvignon, Merlot and Syrah, are of a much greater dimension. The Petite Fleur is understandably lighter, with a subtle almost European style restraint. The Lindaflor Chardonnay also shares some of that restraint, although it offers lots of weight and a rich underlying leesy depth. Expect the top two reds to develop well the Lindaflor Malbec for up to a decade. (DM)

Recommended Reds:

Lindaflor Malbec Mendoza ★★★★ £F

Petite Fleur de Lindaflor Mendoza ★★★ £D

Festivo Mendoza ★★ £B

Recommended Whites:

Lindaflor Chardonnay Mendoza ★★★☆ £E

Nieto Senetiner (Mendoza) www.nietosenetiner.com

This is a large operation producing a range of both varietal and blended reds and a white Torrontes Nieto Reserva. Among the red Nieto Reservas are an oaky, dark Bonarda, as well as a lightly oaked Malbec. A step up is the Don Nicanor produced from a selection of old Malbec vines grown at significant altitude in Agrelo as well as an excellent Bonarda Limited Edition. A further Malbec red, Terroir Blend is an icon example of the grape and sourced from three separate estate vineyards. Best of all is the splendid premium Malbec, Cadus, made from over 80-year-old vines – a rich, long and very characterful wine offering much better value than many of its peers. (DM)

Recommended Reds:

Malbec Cadus Tupungato ★★★★ £E

Bonarda Limited Edition Mendoza ★★★ £D

Don Nicanor Malbec Mendoza ★★☆ £C

Malbec Nieto Reserva Mendoza ★★ £B

Bonarda Nieto Reserva Mendoza ★★ £B

❀ Bodega Noemia Patagonía (Rio Negro) www.bodeganoemia.com

This partnership between Contessa Noemi Marone Cinzano (of Tenuta ARGIANO in Tuscany) and Hans Vinding-Diers is responsible

for one of Argentina's most expensive and impressive reds. They acquired a vineyard planted to Malbec in the 1930s in the remote Rio Negro region in Patagonia in the south-east of the country. The area benefits from the climatic influence and natural irrigation from the rivers Neuquen and Limay. Growing conditions are ideal for the tiny 1.5 ha vineyard with warm summers, cool nights and temperate autumns during ripening. As well as the Noemia Malbec two other reds are also produced. Both have a little Merlot as well as Malbec and the J. Alberto a touch more depth and structure with a greater proportion of new wood. The Noemia is destemmed by the individual berry and carefully vinified with indigenous yeasts at a surprisingly low temperature of 26C with gentle *pigéage* and given a maceration of three weeks. It is aged in all new wood, with a third of the wine run back into new oak a second time, and the malolactic fermentation follows naturally in barrel. The wine is neither fined nor filtered and is aged on its gross lees for up to 24 months in oak. It is impressively rich and opulent, loaded with dark spicy berry fruit but firmly structured too, with a great potential to develop with age in bottle. (DM)

Recommended Reds:
Noemia Rio Negro ★★★★★ £G
J. Alberto Rio Negro ★★★★ £E   A. Lisa Rio Negro ★★★ £D

Bodega Norton (Mendoza)   *www.norton.com.ar*
This substantial property has origins here going back to the end of the 19th Century. Under the current ownership there are now close to 700 ha under vine with just over 500 ha that are available for planting. The key to the quality of the top Malbec blends are vines in certain plots up to 80 years old. The winery's output is considerable, over 1.3 million cases are produced a year, most of which is dominated by a range of straightforward whites and reds released as Finca La Colonia. These are joined by a number of superior Barrel Select reds, as well as wines released as Colección Varietales. Three sparkling wines are also made, the stand out being the Cosecha Especial Extra Brut NV. A number of wines are also released as Reservas, with a spicy, black-fruited Malbec standing out. As well as the wines listed below a Merlot and a Chardonnay are also made and the reds are aged in 1st and 2nd fill barrels to emphasise their fruit, the Chardonnay is barrel fermented in French oak. Privada is a blend of Malbec, Cabernet Sauvignon and Merlot which is aged for 16 months in French oak. A new icon label, Gernot Langes which blends Malbec with a little Cabernet Sauvignon and Franc has recently been introduced. (DM)

Recommended Reds:
Privada Mendoza ★★☆ £C
Cabernet Sauvignon Reserva Mendoza ★★ £C
Syrah Reserva Mendoza ★★ £C
Malbec Reserva Mendoza ★★ £C

Bodega Piedra Negra (Mendoza)   *www.francoislurton.com*
Francois Lurton has been involved with Argentine wine since 1992 and among his clients was CATENA ZAPATA. He established his own operation in 1996, originally with his brother Jacques purchasing vineyard land in Vista Flores at an altitude of 1100 to 1200m. He now has 136 ha under vine at his Chacayes estate from where his wines emanate. An extensive generic range of wines are produced under the Alta Colección label including Cabernet Sauvignon, Malbec, Chardonnay, Pinot Gris and Torrontés. A step up are the Reserve wines which include Malbec and Chardonnay as well as a white Pasitea, a *passerillé* style blend of Torrontés and Pinot Grigio. However, it is the premium reds which really stand out. The Gran

Lurton is the lightest of the trio, a ripe and cedary varietal Cabernet Sauvignon this has been produced since 1992. Piedra Negra is 100% Malbec, a rich and chewy, tobacco scented example with real character. The pricey Chacayes is dominated by Malbec and marked by very concentrated dark, smoky fruit. It comes from the best plots on the Chacayes property and is aged in oak for 24 months. Expect it to develop well in bottle for up to 10 years. (DM)

Recommended Reds:
Chacayes Uco Valley ★★★★ £F
Piedra Negra Uco Valley ★★★☆ £E
Gran Lurton Uco Valley ★★★ £D
Recommended Whites:
Pasiteaa Uco Valley ★★★ £C   Torrontésa Uco Valley ★★☆ £B

Bodega Poesia (Mendoza)   *www.bodegapoesia.com*
Hélène Garcin owns some key properties in Bordeaux, among them CLOS L'EGLISE in Pomerol and the sumptuous wines of BRANON in the Graves. In 2002 she discovered this vineyard planted to some remarkably old Malbec dating back to 1935 as well as a little Cabernet Sauvignon. The vineyard is now being run completely naturally without herbicides or pesticides. Fermentation for the top reds is in 60hl Bordelaise wooden vats and some new French oak is used in the cellar. Both the Clos des Andes reds are purely Malbec – rich, spicy and brambly with lots of depth and character. The very elegant and intense Poesia is an altogether more serious blend of 60% Malbec with 40% Cabernet Sauvignon to add grip and a tight structure, aged for 18–20 months in all-new oak. A number of well priced varietals are also produced as well as a supple and approachable blend, Pasodoble coming from Malbec, Cabernet Sauvignon, Syrah and Bonarda. (DM)

Recommended Reds:
Poesia Mendoza ★★★★ £F
Clos des Andes Reserva Mendoza ★★★☆ £D
Clos des Andes Mendoza ★★★ £C
Pasodoble Mendoza ★★☆ £C   Malbec Mendoza ★★ £B
Bonarda Mendoza ★★ £B
Recommended Whites:
Torrontés Mendoza ★☆ £B

Carlos Pulenta (Mendoza)   *www.bodegavistalba.com*
Some good and excellent value wines are made at this bodega under both the Vistalba and Tomero labels. These are separate vineyard holdings as well as wine brands. The Tomero vineyard is found in the Uco Valley, 130 kms southeast of Mendoza. It is considerable with over 400 ha under vine although it now has some age being planted over 30 years ago. Drip irrigation is used in the sparse sandy alluvial soils and acidity is aided by the altitude, around 1,200 metres above sea level. The Vistalba property is in the heart of the Lujan de Cuyo sub region and a modern highly equipped winery was constructed here in 2002. As ever in Mendoza, the cool summer nights help in providing freshness and structure in the wines. Some 50 ha is cultivated, the majority old Malbec with many of the vines now 60 years old. They also gain lots of mineral nutrition with soils that are rocky and alluvial, enabling the roots to burrow deep. Channel irrigation is practiced here and this provides protection against phylloxera with many vines on their own roots. The Tomero wines are fresh and approachable. The Torrontés coming from fruit bought from Cafayate in Salta is an excellent fresh aromatic example with good weight and texture. The Malbec is attractively vibrant and spicy and gets a little structure from 20% ageing in oak for around 8 months. The Reserva is altogether more

Argentina

serious with real depth and a supple tannic structure underpinning the rich berry fruit. It is fully aged in oak for up to 17 months. A Sauvignon Blanc and a Cabernet Sauvignon are also made at a similar price to the Malbec and Torrontés. The Vistalba reds are all blends. The fruit-driven Corte C and fully oak-aged Corte B are blends of Malbec, Cabernet Sauvignon and Bonarda. The top red, the super-rich and ripe black, spicy-fruited Corte A is 90% old Malbec with a little Cabernet Sauvignon adding more grip and a supple tannic structure. It gets 18 months in French oak. (DM)

Recommended Reds:
Tomero Malbec Reserva Uco Valley ★★★☆ £D
Vistalba Corte A Mendoza ★★★☆ £D
Vistalba Corte B Mendoza ★★★ £C
Vistalba Corte C Mendoza ★★☆ £B Tomero Malbec Uco Valley ★★ £B
Recommended Whites:
Tomero Torrontés Salta ★★ £B

Pulenta Estate (Mendoza) *www.pulentaestate.com*
By the standards of some of the giants of Argentine wine production this is a relatively small operation, producing around 40,000 cases, mainly reds of impressive depth and character. Although the winery was only founded in 2002, the family have been involved in Argentine viticulture for three generations. Brothers Hugo and Eduardo Pulenta look after 15 ha of vines planted at an altitude of 1,000 metres above sea level. As elsewhere, the high diurnal variation (between day and night temperatures) ensures grapes of excellent acidity as well as good phenolic ripeness. There are some good entry level wines under the La Flor label but it is the Pulenta Estate labels that stand out. Nutty, citrus scented Chardonnay is part vinified in oak and part in tank. The characterful varietal reds are all aged for twelve months in new French oak which is well judged and integrated. The top wine the Gran Corte is a blend of Malbec, Merlot, Cabernet, Tannat and Petit Verdot and with a touch longer in barrel offers greater depth and an impressive underlying elegant quality to its fruit and tannin. It will develop well for half a decade and more. Look out also for Pinot Noir, a Malbec/Cabernet blend as well as a superior Gran Malbec and a Gran Cabernet Franc. (DM)

Recommended Reds:
Gran Corte Mendoza ★★★☆ £E Malbec Mendoza ★★★ £D
Merlot Mendoza ★★★ £D Cabernet Sauvignon Mendoza ★★★ £D
Recommended Whites:
Chardonnay Mendoza ★★☆ £C

Finca Sophenia (Mendoza) *www.sophenia.com.ar*
Based in Tupungato at an altitude of around 1200m, this operation was established in 1997 and consultancy for vinification comes from Michel Rolland. There are 120 ha of vineyards now planted to a mix of Cabernet Sauvignon, Chardonnay, Merlot, Sauvignon Blanc and of course Malbec. Under the Altosur label a range of attractive easy fruit driven wines are produced. Malbec Rosé gets a short cold-soak, Sauvignon is cool-fermented and reds are aged in a mix of French and American oak for 3-4 months. The Finca Sophenia wines are more serious and structured. Reds are given a cold-soak and aged in oak for 10-12 months. The Cabernet is firm and structured while the Malbec is very characterful with a fine tobacco-scented fruit intensity. The Sophenia Synthesis is a blend of Merlot, Cabernet Sauvignon and Malbec. The wine is a selection of the best barrels of each variety and is aged in oak for 18 months. To this have now been added Roberto L with a blend dominated by Malbec and aged in French oak for 18 months and sophisticated Sauvignon Blanc.

Varietal wines are also made under a well priced ES Vino label. (DM)
Recommended Reds:
Sophenia Synthesis Mendoza ★★★☆ £E
Synthesis Malbec Mendoza ★★★☆ £D
Finca Sophenia Reserve Malbec Mendoza ★★★ £C
Altosur Malbec Mendoza ★★☆ £C
Finca Sophenia Reserve Cabernet Sauvignon Mendoza ★★☆ £C
Altosur Cabernet Sauvignon Mendoza ★★ £C
Recommended Whites:
Synthesis Sauvignon Blanc Mendoza ★★★ £D
Altosur Sauvignon Blanc Mendoza ★☆ £C
Recommended Rosés:
Altosur Malbec Rosé Mendoza ★☆ £C

Terrazas de Los Andes (Mendoza) *www.terrazasdelosandes.com*
This operation, which is a subsidiary of Moet Hennessy, was established in the late 1990s renovating a winery site dating back to 1898. Three ranges of wines are produced under the Terrazas de Los Andes brand and a joint venture has also been established with CHEVAL BLANC from Saint Émilion. Cabernet Sauvignon, Malbec, Torrontés and Chardonnay are all cultivated from high altitude vineyards at 600 to 1600m in the hills above Mendoza. The bottlings under the Altos del Plata label are soft, forward and fruit driven in style. A step up are the Reservas, one from each of the four varieties planted. Rich, oaky Chardonnay is barrel-fermented and aged for 7-8 months in 100% new wood but retains good balancing acidity. Both the Malbec and Cabernet Sauvignon are given a 3-5 week maceration and ageing is in one-third new wood; 20% American oak being used in the Malbec. The top two wines under the Terrazas de Los Andes banner are from single vineyards. The Malbec comes from a 75 year old vineyard at Vistalba Las Compuertas and both wines are aged in 100% new wood for 18 months. The Malbec is rich, smoky and complex, the Cabernet perhaps more elegant than might be expected with a minty undercurrent. The joint venture Cheval des Andes is a blend of 60% Cabernet Sauvignon and the balance Malbec. Vinification is completed with input from both parties and the result is an impressively rich, opulent and concentrated red with real depth and a firm ageworthy structure. (DM)

Cheval des Andes:
Recommended Reds:
Cheval des Andes Mendoza ★★★★ £F
Terrazas de Los Andes:
Recommended Reds:
Single Vineyard Malbec Mendoza ★★★☆ £E
Reserva Malbec Mendoza ★★★ £C
Single Vineyard Cabernet Sauvignon Mendoza ★★★ £E
Reserva Cabernet Sauvignon Mendoza ★★☆ £C
Recommended Whites:
Reserva Chardonnay Mendoza ★★☆ £C

Michel Torino (Salta) *www.micheltorino.com.ar*
The vineyards here in the hot Cafayate region in the north of Argentina succeed because of their high altitude. There are 360 ha under vine and the quality end of the spectrum is covered by the Colección, Cuma, Don David and Ciclos labels. The new flagship red is the rich, brambly Altimus which combines Malbec, Cabernet Sauvignon and Syrah. Under the Ciclos label there is a well made 50/50 blend of Malbec and Merlot. There is also a good, spicy, brambly Colección Malbec and a better, more concentrated Don

David. Cabernet Sauvignon under the Don David label has some piercing blackcurrant character with a lightly herbal note creeping in. Don David Torrontés is sound but not at the same level as the reds. (DM)

Recommended Reds:
Altimus Cafayate ★★★ £E
Malbec/Merlot Ciclos Cafayate ★★☆ £D
Cabernet Sauvignon Don David Cafayate ★★ £C
Malbec Don David Cafayate ★★ £C
Malbec Colección Cafayate ★★ £B

ValdeFlores(Mendoza) *www.michelrolland-argentinaexperience.com*
This operation has been created and managed by Michel and Dany Rolland. The wine is vinified at Bodega MONTEVIEJO along with Rollands other big Mendoza project CLOS DE LOS SIETE. Very much in the Rolland Bordeaux mould the wine is rich, ripe and opulent, significantly more so than Monteviejo's top Lindaflor red. Produced from 100% Malbec, it is vatted for around 14 months and then aged in new French oak and comes from vines planted in the 1950s. Bottled unfined and unfiltered it is both forward and accessible but has the depth and structure to suggest cellaring for five or more years will be handsomely repaid. (DM)

Recommended Reds:
Val de Flores Mendoza ★★★★ £E

❀ **Yacochuya (Salta)** *www.michelrolland-argentinaexperience.com*
This small winery owned by Michel Rolland and a number of friends is based in warm Salta, but crucially the Calchaquies Valley vineyards here are planted at high altitude, some 2,000m above sea level. Of equal importance is the age of the vines, which are now over 80 years old. The Yacochuya, a blend of Malbec and Cabernet Sauvignon, is very dense with marvellous depth and a rich sumptuous texture on the palate. Malolactic takes place in barrel and the wine is aged on lees with micro-oxygenation. It is bottled with minimal fining and without filtration and will develop very well over a decade or so. It is undoubtedly one of the very finest reds to have emerged from South America in recent years. A second red, San Pedro de Yacochuya, is also being made to ensure the integrity of the *grand vin*. Rolland is the owner of Le BON PASTEUR in Pomerol, he is also now involved in the recently established CLOS DE LOS SIETE operation, and his own VAL DE FLORES winery. (DM)

Recommended Reds:
Yacochuya Cafayate ★★★★☆ £F

A-Z of producers - *Chile*

❀ **Almaviva (Maipo)** *www.almavivawinery.com*
This is a joint venture between CONCHA Y TORO and Baroness Philippine de Rothschild (MOUTON-ROTHSCHILD). The ambitious project is aimed at producing one of, possibly the finest red wine yet from Chile. Considerable investment has already gone into both vineyards and winery. Almaviva is undoubtedly impressive but as yet falls a little way short of its lofty price tag and on a global scale faces formidable opposition. It is to be hoped that the style will surpass that other Mouton-Rothschild investment OPUS ONE. (DM)

Recommended Reds:
Almaviva Red Maipo Valley ★★★★☆ £G

Viña Altair (Cachapoal) *www.altairwines.com*
This is a new joint venture between the Dassault family of Château DASSAULT in Saint-Emilion and Guillermo Luksic who owns VIÑA

SAN PEDRO. Just two premium reds are made with the first vintage of both in 2002. The vineyards are in the Upper Cachapoal, one of the cooler areas of the country, nestled into the foothills of the Andes. There is a marked variation in day and night temperatures here along with natural cooling breezes, all of which contributes to the acidity in the fruit and improving the natural structure of the wines. Sideral is effectively the second wine but is sourced from other vineyards as well as estate fruit. It is a blend of Cabernet Sauvignon, Merlot and Syrah. As with the top wine, fermentation is in wooden vats and ageing is in some new oak. It is supple and approachable, if a touch leafy and peppery, and is made for immediate drinking altough it will develop well in the medium term. Altaïr is more serious and is impressively structured and concentrated. Blended from Cabernet Sauvignon, Carmenère, Cabernet Franc and Syrah, this comes solely from estate fruit. Expect it to develop well over a decade. (DM)

Recommended Reds:
Altaïr Cachapoal ★★★★ £F   Sideral Cachapoal ★★★ £D

Viña Aquitania (Maipo Valley) *www.aquitania.cl*
This property was originally established as Domaine Paul Bruno in 1984 by the Bordelais' Bruno Prats of COS D'ESTOURNEL and Paul Pontallier the winemaker at MARGAUX. They purchased around 18 ha (44 acres) in 1990 at Quebrada de Macul, in the heart of the Maipo at the foot of the Andes. They have since been joined by Chilean oenologist Felipe de Solminihac and Champagne oenologist Ghislain de Montgolfier. The wines are distinctly French in style with just a touch of the vibrant fruit that the best from Chile has become famed for. The mineral and subtly citrus scented Chardonnay Sol de Sol is sourced from the south of the country in cool Malleco, which is barrel fermented in 40% new wood and aged for 10 months with full malolactic and lees stirring. A Pinot Noir is also now produced from the area. The second red Aquitania Reserve is from Cabernet Sauvignon. A relatively cool post-fermentation maceration for a couple of weeks helps soften the wine and lift its vibrant berry fruit. Ageing is in a mix of older oak and stainless steel. The Lazuli is a rich, concentrated smoky and cedary 100% Cabernet Sauvignon which is traditionally vinified, vatting is for over three weeks with fermentation at medium to high temperatures and ageing in 60% new wood for 16 months. Expect the wine to develop well over five to seven years. (DM)

Recommended Reds:
Cabernet Sauvignon Lazuli Maipo ★★★☆ £E
Aquitania Reseve Cabernet Maipo ★★ £B
Recommended Whites:
Chardonnay Sol de Sol Malleco Valley ★★☆ £C

Hacienda Araucano (Colchagua) *www.francoislurton.com*
François Lurton has been making wine in Chile since 1992. It was only in 2000 though that he established his own operation in the Colchagua Valley, purchasing a 200 ha property and commencing planting completely afresh, at that time with his brother Jacques. The vineyards are planted on chalky/clay soils, farmed organically with a coastal moderating influence on the climate, so should have much potential. There is a range of good value varietals produced under the Araucano label including Carmenère, Cabernet Sauvignon, Chardonnay and Sauvignon Blanc. Clos de Lolol is an elegant, red berry-fruited 50/50 blend of Carmenère and Cabernet. A Cabernet Sauvignon is also produced under the Gran Araucano label and a premium Pinot Noir, Humo Blanco also comes from a cool microclimate around Lolol. Gran Araucano Chardonnay is a

Chile

rich and toasty, lightly tropical fruited barrel-fermented example being aged for 12 months in 50% new wood and bottled unfiltered. Particularly striking is the fresh, zesty and piercingly intense Humo Sauvignon Blanc, one of the best examples from the country and comfortably edging three and a half stars. The top red, the spicy, dark-cherry infused Alka, is one of Chile's best wines and surely the stand out example produced from Carmenère. Yields are very low and the vineyards are completely dry farmed. Expect it to develop well over the medium term. (DM)

Recommended Reds:

Alka Carmenère Colchagua ★★★★ £F
Clos de Lolol Colchagua ★★★ £E
Pinot Noir Humo Blanco Colchagua ★★★ £E
Cabernet Sauvignon Gran Araucano Colchagua ★★★ £D

Recommended Whites:

Chardonnay Gran Araucano Colchagua ★★★ £D
Sauvignon Blanc Humo Blanco Colchagua ★★★ £C

Carmen (Maipo) *www.carmen.com*

Carmen is owned by the large SANTA RITA operation. Production here itself is not inconsiderable with vineyard holdings now spread across many of the major regions. As a result an extensive range is produced, both red and white. The regular whites and particularly the reds are well-crafted and full of vibrant, ripe and crunchy fruit. The best wines, though, are produced under the Reserva, Gran Reserva and Winemakers Reserve labels. Gran Reservas now include Cabernet Sauvignon and Merlot from the higher Maipo; Carmenère and Syrah from Apalta as well as Chardonnay from Casablanca and Sauvignon Blanc from Leyda. The Reserva label now includes Sauvignon Blanc, Chardonnay, Carmenère, Cabernet Sauvignon and Merlot. The flagship red is the impressive Gold Reserve, which is produced from a small 45-year-old parcel of vines in Maipo. Top reds, particularly the Gold Reserve, will improve with cellaring. (DM)

Recommended Reds:

Cabernet Sauvignon Gold Reserve Maipo ★★★☆ £F
Cabernet Sauvignon Gran Reserva Maipo ★★☆ £C
Cabernet Sauvignon Reserva Colchagua ★★ £C
Winemakers Carmenère Blend Reserve Apalta ★★★ £E
Carmenère Gran Reserva Maipo ★★☆ £C
Carmenère Reserva Apalta ★★ £B
Syrah Gran Reserva Maipo ★★☆ £C
Merlot Reserva Colchagua ★★ £B

Recommended Whites:

Sauvignon Blanc Gran Reserva Leyda ★★ £C
Chardonnay Reserva Casablanca ★☆ £B

Casa Marin (San Antonio) *www.casamarin.cl*

This pioneering family owned winery , just 4 km from the ocean, is in the vanguard of the new and potentially very fine coastal wine region. Founded in 2000 Casa Marin is is now planted to 50 ha of the original varietals of Pinot Noir, Syrah, Sauvignon Blanc, Sauvignon Gris, Gewürztraminer and Riesling and is now joined by 2 ha of new plantings of Grenache which is due to be made into wine in 2014. The property is divided into a number of vineyard sites planted on a mix of clay, limestone, marine sediment and sand and drip irrigation is used. The proximity to the sea produces wines of low PH and high acidity. The elegant red berry scented Pinot Noir Lo Abarca Hills is impressively intense with just a hint of truffle, mocha and game. An additional Pinot, Tres Viñedos also impresses. The Miramar vineyard is a source of fine, minerally Riesling, showing the petrolly characteristics with age of the finest from Alsace. Syrah is also grown

in the Miranar vineyard and whilst it can be dark and peppery in some years, the proximity to the ocean can give it ripening problems in cooler years, with a resultant lack of alcoholic strength. Good Gewürztraminer is classic and full of varietally pure lychee fruit character. The cool-fermented single vineyard Sauvignon Blancs have an intense zesty citrus character, a hint of minerality and fine underlying acidity giving both the wines good structure, with that from the Cypresses vineyard edging it with grassy and asparagus tones - a good cross between the tropical fruitiness of New Zealand Sauvignon Blancs and the lawn mower scent of those from the Loire Valley. Sauvignon Gris is impressively intense with an underlying structure aided through partial barrel-fermentation. Maria Luz now shares winemaking duties with her son, Felipe, who is gradually taking over the reigns. (NB)

Recommended Reds:

Pinot Noir Lo Abarca Hills San Antonio ★★★★ £E
Pinot Noir Tres Viñedos San Antonio ★★☆ £C
Syrah Miramar Vineyard San Antonio ★★★ £E

Recommended Whites:

Sauvignon Blanc Cipreses Vineyard San Antonio ★★★★ £C
Sauvignon Blanc Laurel Vineyard San Antonio ★★★ £C
Riesling Miramar Vineyard San Antonio ★★★★ £C
Sauvignon Gris Estero Vineyard San Antonio ★★★ £C
Gewürztraminer Casona Vineyard San Antonio ★★★ £C

Casa Silva (Rapel) *www.casasilva.cl*

Among the best of Chile's newly established winery operations, Casa Silva was set up in 1997 and winemaking is supervised by the experienced Mario Geisse Garcia. The winery owns three different estates and has a total of some 830 ha of vineyards, so is not a small operation by any means. All of the vineyards are located in the potentially excellent Colchagua Valley. Among the best bets are the Reserva labels under both the Casa Silva and Doña Dominga brands. In particular, the dark, brambly and intensely spicy Carmenère Reserva and Quinta Generación Tinto, a blend of both Cabernet and Carmenère, are both ageworthy and will improve for 3 or 4 years. A number of impressive vineyard reserve wines have now been released including Gran Reserva Syrah, Cabernet Sauvignon and Merlot. Particularly striking is the Carmenère Micro Terroir label from Los Linques. An impressively dense and concentrated pricey top luxury *cuvée*, Altura is also offerred, a blend of Carmenère, Cabernet Sauvignon and Petit Verdot. (DM)

Recommended Reds:

Altura Colchagua ★★★★ £F
Carmenère MicroTerroir de Los Linques ★★★☆ £E
Carmenère Reserva Colchagua ★★★ £C
Quinta Generación Colchagua ★★★☆ £C
Merlot Gran Reserva Angostura ★★☆ £C
Merlot Reserva Colchagua ★★ £C
Syrah Gran Reserva Lolol Colchagua ★★☆ £C
Syrah Reserva Colchagua ★★ £C
Cabernet Sauvignon Gran Reserva Los Linques Colchagua ★★ £C
Cabernet Sauvignon Reserva Colchagua ★★ £C

Recommended Whites:

Quinta Generación Colchagua ★★ £C
Sauvignon Blanc Reserva Colchagua ★★ £B

Casas del Bosque (Casablanca) *www.casasdelbosque.cl*

Founded in 1993 by Juan Cuneo Solari, Casas del Bosque has grown from a boutique winery to one producing around 1 million bottles a year. All wines are tank fermented with commercial yeasts

but nevertheless, some wines of high quality are produced. Gran Reserva and Pesqueñas Producciones (small production) wines are particularly fine. There are 226ha of vines in production in the Casablanca Valley planted to Chardonnay, Sauvignon Blanc, Pinot Noir, Syrah and Riesling with another 18 or so producing premium Cabernet Sauvignon and Carmenère in the Rapel and Maipo Valleys. The Gran Reserva Sauvignon Blanc spends around two months in old oak after fermentation and has typical grassy and tropical fruit notes with good clean fruit. But the Pesquiñas Producciones Sauvignon Blanc has more weight and spends more time in wood, giving it just that bit more roundness and complexity. Similarly, Reserva Chardonnay, which spends 6 months in old oak, whilst having some tropical fruit flavours, does not compare with the Grand Reserve Chardonnay, spending almost a year in old oak and made from run-off juice as opposed to press wine for the Reserva. Small production Pinot Noir - 14 months in half new and half 3 year old barrels is round and complete with soft tannins, spice and damson overtones, whilst Small Production Syrah, grown at high altitude and matured for 14 months in around 85% new and 15% one year old barrels, shows great complexity, weight, length and true varietal tar and pepper on the palate. Carmenère from the Rapel Valley is racy and slick but without the concentration of the other reds. Gran Bosque is 100% Cabernet Sauvignon from Maipo and is their premium wine limited to around 5000 bottles each year. It's a whopping 15% abv and spends 22 months in new oak before release. The result is a smooth and concentrated wine showing mocha, smoke, dark chocolate and black fruits which will need at least 5 years of cellaring. The Late Harvest Riesling is not botrytis affected and is a little one dimensional and sugary. (NB)

Recommended Reds:

Gran Bosque Cabernet Sauvignon Maipo ★★★★☆ £F
Pinot Noir Pesqueñas Producciones Casablanca ★★★☆ £D
Syrah Pesqueñas Producciones Casablanca ★★★★☆ £E
Carmenère Reserva Rapel ★★★ £C

Recommended Whites:

Chardonny Gran Reserva Casablanca ★★★☆ £D
Chardonny Reserva Casablanca ★★☆ £B
Sauvignon Blanc Pesqueñas Producciones Casablanca ★★★ £D
Sauvignon Blanc Gran Reserva Casablanca ★★☆ £C
Late Harvest Riesling Casablanca ★☆ £C

Viña Casablanca (Casablanca) *www.casablancawinery.com*
Established by SANTA CAROLINA well over 10 years ago this has been a consistently impressive producer of good, sometimes very good cool-grown whites. Reds are produced as well and these wines are mostly now vinified from warmer growing areas. There is a fairly wide range of wines produced under the Céfiro label and a number of superior El Bosque and Nimbus wines which have a touch more depth. The top red is the Neblus, a pricey blend of Cabernet Sauvignon, Merlot and Carmenère which comes from Casablanca Valley fruit. Gewürztraminer is good, with some varietally pungent character; Sauvignon Blanc is equally stylish, with grassy, tropical notes showing through its piercing fruit. Chardonnay is among the better examples in the country, particularly the barrel fermented EL Bosque, which is very intense with marked citrus and subtle lees and oak character. It will develop well with limited ageing. (DM)

Recommended Reds:

Neblus Casablanca ★★☆ £E
Syrah Nimbus Maipo Casablanca ★★ £C
Syrah El Bosque Rapel Casablanca ★★ £C

Merlot Céfiro Maipo ★☆ £B

Recommended Whites:

Chardonnay Nimbus Casablanca ★★☆ £C
Chardonnay El Bosque Barrel Fermented Casablanca ★★☆ £C
Sauvignon Blanc Nimbus Casablanca ★★☆ £C
Gewürztraminer Nimbus Casablanca ★★ £C

Viñedo Chadwick (Maipo) *www.vinedochadwick.cl*
A recently established premium label owned by ERRAZURIZ, with a vineyard located on the northern bank of the Maipo river into the foothills of the Andes. The 300 ha property has been in the Chadwick family since 1945. The vineyard covers a mere 15 ha of the best stony/clay soils. It is now planted to the best field selections from both Maipo and the Don Maximiano vineyard of Cabernet Sauvignon, Cabernet Franc and Carmenère. The wine is aged in 100% new French oak. It complements the other top Errazuriz red, SEÑA, and shows some of the character that can be achieved in the Maipo as well as the Panquehue sub-region of Aconcagua where Errazuriz is based. At present it has impressive depth but is leaner and less opulent than Seña. Firmly structured with a cedary edge to its fruit, it needs at least 5 years to soften. (DM)

Recommended Reds:

Viñedo Chadwick Maipo ★★★★☆ £F

Concha y Toro (Maipo) *www.conchaytoro.com*
This is a massive operation with a huge range of commercial wines throughout the vinous spectrum at all price points. However, the wines are quality driven at all price points It is also involved with MOUTON ROTHSCHILD of Bordeaux in the super-premium ALMAVIVA project. Production is now well over 10 million cases a year and the company possess more than 4,500 ha of vineyards. Ignacio Recabarren left VIÑA CASABLANCA to provide consultancy input here and the results have filtered through. Both Trio and Casillero del Diablo offer good value in both red and white while the Terrunyo label has been created to emphasise real regional character. Marqués de Casa Concha is a recently added mid-range label producing some good reds and whites, of which the Chardonnay is notably good. Of the top labels Amelia Chardonnay is ripely tropical and toasty but with good depth. The Don Melchor Cabernet Sauvignon is sourced from the Puente Alto vineyard in the Maipo. It is a powerful, dusty red with dark berry fruit and a lightly leafy, minty component. Two additional premium reds are also made. Carmín de Peumo is dominated by Carmenère while Gravas del Maipo is mainly Syrah with just a small proportion of Cabernet Sauvignon sourced from poor gravel and stony soils. (DM/GW)

Recommended Reds:

Cabernet Sauvignon Don Melchor Maipo ★★★★ £F
Cabernet Sauvignon Terrunyo Maipo ★★☆ £D
Carmenère Terrunyo Rapel ★★★ £D

Recommended Whites:

Chardonnay Amelia Casablanca ★★★ £D
Chardonnay Trio Casablanca ★☆ £B
Sauvignon Blanc Terrunyo Casablanca ★★☆ £C
Sauvignon Blanc Trio Casablanca ★★ £B

Cono Sur (Rapel) *www.conosur.com*
This operation was established in 1993. There are extensive estate-owned vineyards and the company sources fruit from Casablanca, Maipo, Rapel and the Bío Bío Valley. Under the Bicicleta label some attractively fruity reds and whites are produced. Reserva Especial labelled Cabernet Sauvignon, Merlot and Pinot Noir are all decent

and well priced, while the Visión range is a step up and coming from specific terroirs. A small range of organic wines are also now being made and are released as Organic. Top wines are the 20 Barrels Pinot Noir, Merlot, Cabernet Sauvignon and Sauvignon Blanc. Pinot Noir is also produced in a limited edition bottling under the Ocio brand and is Chile's first super-premium bottling of the variety, although it appears to have some way to go to match other new world examples. The Cabernet and Merlot are extracted and forward as is the case with so many premium Chilean reds and characterised by dark berry, fruit. Pinot Noir shows a decent balance of strawberry, lightly savoury fruit with marked high-toast oak. (DM)

Recommended Reds:
Pinot Noir Ocio Colchagua ★★★☆ £F
Pinot Noir 20 Barrels Colchagua ★★☆ £D
Cabernet Sauvignon 20 Barrels Colchagua ★★☆ £C
Cabernet Sauvignon Reserva Especial Colchagua ★☆ £B
Merlot 20 Barrels Colchagua ★★ £C

Viña Cousiño-Macul (Maipo)   *www.cousinomacul.cl*
This is one of the oldest wineries in Chile and has remained under the ownership of the same family since its foundation in 1856. Particularly striking in comparison with many other more recently established and larger operations is that the family only produce wines from their own two Maipo properties. No fruit has been purchased in the past and the family remain committed to this approach. A comprehensive range of well made regular varietal wines are produced including Sauvignon Blanc and Gris, Riesling, an unoaked Chardonnay as well as reds from Cabernet Sauvignon and Merlot. The Reservas though are the particularly striking wines here, especially the reds. Antiguas Reserva Chardonnay is full, fat and round with rich tropical fruit and marked oak. Coming from the higher slopes of the Maipo there is sufficiently fresh acidity from the cool summer nights. The Don Matias Cabernet Sauvignon is full of attractive dark berry fruit and firm slightly dry tannins that need a little time to integrate. A Don Matias Merlot and Syrah are also made along with an Antiguas Reservas Syrah. The top two reds are Finis Terrae, a blend of roughly two-thirds/one-third Cabernet Sauvignon and Merlot and the premium Lota which has a touch more Cabernet. Finis Terrae has a supple texture and fine concentration. In part this is due to two-thirds new oak and a proportion of the wine going through malolactic in barrel. Not surprisingly the icon Lota sees nearly all new wood and is full of rich, dark spicy fruit and real depth. Expect both wines to develop well for five to eight years and keep longer. A Finis Terrae white is also made from a blend of Chardonnay, Riesling and Viognier. (DM)

Recommended Reds:
Lota Maipo ★★★★ £F   Finis Terrae Maipo ★★★☆ £E
Don Matias Cabernet Sauvignon Maipo ★★★ £C

Recommended Whites:
Antiguas Reservas Chardonnay Maipo ★★☆ £C

De Martino (Maipo)   *www.demartino.cl*
This Maipo based winery produces a fine range of reds and whites not just from the home vineyards but from a number of other areas as well. The winery and its new winemaker Eduardo Jordan place considerable emphasis in finding the best potential areas for each varietal. The Estate wines as is the case with all those produced here come from organically managed vineyards and are upfront and approachable. The Estate is a blend of Cabernet Sauvignon, Syrah, Petit Verdot and Malbec. There are two specifically organic labelled wines, the Cabernet coming from the home Isla de Maipo

vineyard. A Sauvignon Blanc is also produced and the wines vinified with a minimum of sulphur. The Legado labels are a step up and include Chardonnay from Limarí and Sauvignon Blanc from Maipo as well as a smoky, spicy Syrah from the newly established Choapa region. A number of impressive single vineyard wines are also released. Gooseberry and citrus scented Sauvignon comes from the coolest sector of Casablanca. Syrah is ripe and perfumed with a rich blackberry character. Perhaps best of all is the Carmenère, dark, spicy and very characterful. The top wine is the fine, intense cedary Familia, a blend of Cabernet Sauvignon, Carmenère and Malbec. (DM)

Recommended Reds:
Familia Maipo ★★★☆ £E   Syrah Legado Choapa ★★ £B
Syrah "Alto Los Toros" Maipo, Cachapoal & Maule ★★★ £D
Carmenère "Alto de Piedras" Maipo, Cachapoal & Maule ★★★ £D
Cabernet Sauvignon Organics Maipo ★★ £B
Estate E Maipo ★★ £B

Recommended Whites:
Sauvignon Blanc Single Vineyard Parcela 5 Casablanca ★★☆ £C

El Principal (Maipo Valley)   *www.elprincipal.cl*
This 54 ha Maipo estate has been developed by Bordelais Patrick Valette, with the vineyard planted to Cabernet Sauvignon, Carmenère and Merlot. El Principal is a modern Bordeaux style and as at many Bordeaux properties a second wine, Memorias, is produced to ensure the integrity of the *grand vin* and to this is now added a third label, Calicanto. Yields are kept low at 30 hl/ha and El Principal is aged in 100% new oak with malolactic in barrel. Memorias is a good, medium-weight style. El Principal is normally a blend of Cabernet Sauvignon with around a third of Carmenère and the wine offers greater richness and a rounder, suppler texture. (DM)

Recommended Reds:
El Principal Maipo ★★★☆ £E
Memorias Maipo ★★★ £D

✿ Errázuriz (Aconcagua)   *www.errazuriz.com*
Errázuriz is based in the Panquehue sub-region of Aconcagua and has several hundred ha of vineyards. Fruit is generally sourced from the home vineyards but also from cool Casablanca for whites. The range is comprehensive and there are some well-made, stylish wines at all levels. The regular varietals show well-defined fruit character. Superior selections come under the Max Reserva label and there are two striking Wild Ferment wines: a Chardonnay full of citrus and lightly smoked oak, and a forward, vibrant Pinot Noir marked by sappy cherry and wild strawberry aromas. Sangiovese and Carmenère Single Vineyard labels are both impressively concentrated as is the newly added La Cumbre Shiraz. A further icon label, Kai is dominated by Carmenère. The top reds include the Don Maximiano Founders Reserve and the super-premium SEÑA, which has real potential. An additional range of premium varietals is made at the LA ARBOLEDA ESTATE. 1999 was also the first vintage of VINEDO CHADWICK, a super-premium blend of Cabernet Sauvignon and Carmenère from a 15 ha vineyard in the Maipo Valley. The wine promises much. Also jointly owns CALITERRA. (DM)

Recommended Reds:
Kai Aconcagua ★★★★☆ £F
Don Maximiano Founders Reserve Aconcagua ★★★☆ £E
Shiraz La Cumbre Aconcagua ★★★☆ £E
Shiraz Aconcagua ★★☆ £C
Sangiovese Single Vineyard Aconcagua ★★☆ £C
Cabernet Sauvignon Max Reserva Aconcagua ★★☆ £C

Pinot Noir Wild Ferment Casablanca ★★☆ £C
Carmenère Single Vineyard Aconcagua ★★ £D
Merlot Max Reserva Aconcagua ★★ £C
Merlot Curico ★☆ £B
Recommended Whites:
Chardonnay Wild Ferment Casablanca ★★☆ £C
Chardonnay Max Reserva Casablanca ★★ £C

❀ Viña Alvaro Espinoza (Maipo Valley)

Alvaro Espinoza was originally the winemaker at CARMEN, where he looked after the winemaking from 1992 until 1999. He is a champion of both organic and biodynamic wine farming and is involved in Geo Wines producing wines with third party growers. There are three principal labels: Rayún, the budget label, Cucao, and the more expensive Chono wines. It is also worth looking out for Quinta de Viluco and Pargua for Maipo Valley Cabernet Sauvignon. He is also a consultant with clients including APALTAGUA and VINA LEYDA. His most exciting two wines though are the splendid reds he produces from his small home vineyards in the Maipo. By Chilean standards output is miniscule with around 500 to 800 cases being made of each wine. The exceptionally priced Kuyen is a blend of Syrah (70%) with the balance Cabernet Sauvignon. Rich and full of dark berry and black pepper fruit the wine is aged in a mix new and used French oak. The splendid Antiyal is one of Chile's greatest reds and very fairly priced in comparison to some of the other super-cuvées produced elsewhere in the country. It comes from a blend of 45% Carmenère, 30% Cabernet Sauvignon and 25% Syrah. It is dark, smoky and with a very pure minerality running through it. Expect it to age very well. (DM)
Recommended Reds:
Antiyal Maipo Valley ★★★★☆ £F   Kuyen Maipo Valley ★★★☆ £D

Viña Garces Silva (San Antonio)   *www.vgs.cl*

The first vintage here was as recent as 2003 and the quality being obtained from cool, coastal Leyda zone vineyards to the seaward side of the coastal mountains is impressively fine. Sauvignon Blanc, Chardonnay and Pinot Noir are produced from vineyards planted in well-drained clay/loam soils. Gewürztraminer has also now been planted and should have much potential. Output is very small by Chilean standards and there are a total of just over 70 ha under vine and only a third of the harvest goes into the Amayna wines. They are rich and viscous with sufficiently fresh acidity to provide balance despite alcohol levels upwards of 14%. Chardonnay is barrel-fermented and offers a weight and texture on the palate more reminiscent of a top example from California's Sta. Rita Hills than Chile. Regular Sauvignon Blanc is vinified in *inox*, the Barrel Fermented bottling carries good varietal green fruit but with concentration and a rich texture along with exotic tropical notes as well. The wines should be enjoyed fairly young. A Syrah has also now been added to the line-up. (DM)
Recommended Reds:
Pinot Noir Amayna San Antonio ★★★☆ £E
Recommended Whites:
Chardonnay Amayna San Antonio ★★★☆ £D
Sauvignon Blanc Barrel Fermented Amayna San Antonio ★★★☆ £D
Sauvignon Blanc Amayna San Antonio Leyda ★★★ £C

Haras de Pirque (Maipo)   *www.harasdepirque.com*

Eduardo Matte acquired this 600 ha estate in the higher reaches of the Maipo Valley in 1991 and over the next couple of years planted 120 ha of Cabernet Sauvignon, Merlot and Carmenère as well as Chardonnay and Sauvignon Blanc. The property is perhaps better known as one of Chile's best thoroughbred horse breeding studs. With vineyards planted at an altitude of between 550 and 660metres above sea level the local climate provides fruit of excellent ripeness and well balanced acidity. There are two well-priced ranges Equus and Haras offering good well-made essentially fruit driven styles. There are also three superior wines which take the Character label, including finely structured spicy and restrained Syrah, leafy Cabernet Sauvignon-Carmenère as well as Chardonnay. Just below the summit of the winery's production are the Elegance Chardonnay and Cabernet Sauvignon, which also includes a little Syrah and Cabernet Franc. Chardonnay is big and opulent with marked tropical fruit. The Cabernet shows its high altitude origins with a firm structure and minty undercurrent to its fruit. The top red, Albis is well-structured firm and in an elegant and quite restrained style with reined in new wood and a supple rounded texture from malolactic in barrel. A blend of Cabernet Sauvignon and Carmenère it offers good depth and intensity, as it should as one of Chile's more expensive reds. Cellaring for five years is advisable. (DM)
Recommended Reds:
Albis Maipo ★★★☆ £F
Cabernet Sauvignon Elegance Maipo ★★★ £D
Cabernet Sauvignon Character Maipo ★★☆ £C
Syrah Character Maipo ★★★ £D
Recommended Whites:
Chardonnay Elegance ★★☆ £D

❀ Lapostolle (Rapel)   *www.lapostolle.com*

This is now established as one of the best red wine producers in Chile. Winemaking direction has been provided for a number of years by Michel Rolland of BON PASTEUR. The Chardonnay in both regular Casa and Cuvée Alexandre versions is moderately rich and oaky, the Sauvignon Blanc quite piercingly tropical and grassy. It is the reds, though, that lift the winery onto a separate quality plateau. Cabernet Sauvignon Cuvée Alexandre is well structured but lacks the sheer opulence of the rich, supple, almost exotic Merlot Cuvée Alexandre. Dark smoky Syrah has also now been added as has a second red blend Borobo which comes from Syrah, Pinot Noir, Carmenere, Cabernet Sauvignon and Merlot. Currently a serious contender for the best red from Chile is the dense, powerful, opulent and richly textured Clos Apalta. The wine is structured and ageworthy but has all the hallmarks of Rolland's great wines from St-Émilion. A second more obviously fruit driven second Clos Apalta red is also made, Canto de Apalta. (DM)
Recommended Reds:
Clos Apalta Apalta-Colchagua ★★★★☆ £G
Borobo Regional Blend ★★★★ £F
Syrah Cuvée Alexandre Apalta-Colchagua ★★★ £D
Merlot Cuvée Alexandre Apalta-Colchagua ★★★ £D
Merlot Casa Rapel ★★ £C
Cabernet Sauvignon Cuvée Alexandre Apalta-Colchagua ★★☆ £D
Cabernet Sauvignon Casa Rapel ★★ £C
Recommended Whites:
Chardonnay Cuvée Alexandre Casablanca ★★★ £D
Chardonnay Casa Casablanca ★☆ £B
Sauvignon Blanc Casa Rapel ★☆ £B

Loma Larga (Casablanca)   *www.lomalarga.com*

This family owned winery has now been established for over a decade. Their vineyards are located in a protected valley providing a warmer climate than some parts of the region and protecting

South America

their sites from the cold southerly breezes prevalent in the region. As a result some of the greener notes that can be apparent in other reds from the region are thankfully absent here. No doubt a careful control of yields and well drained stony soils also contribute to quality. Both the fruit-driven Sauvignon Blanc and lightly tropical Chardonnay are ripe and reasonably concentrated. Pinot Noir is full of attractive red cherry fruit, supple and very approachable. Cabernet Franc is not often encountered in Chile and this is a well-crafted and elegant example with toasty, cassis tones. Best of the reds though is the spicy, black pepper noted Syrah. Supple, and with nicely integrated tannin, continued improvement is likely with four five years in bottle. Merlot, Malbec, Rapsodia, a blend of Syrah, Malbec and Cabernet Franc and Quinteto five variety blend would also appear to have much promise. A small range of economically priced varietal labels are also made under the Lomas del Valle brand. (DM)

Recommended Reds:
Syrah Casablanca ★★★ £D
Cabernet Franc Casablanca ★★★ £D
Pinot Noir Casablanca ★★★ £D
Recommended Whites:
Chardonnay Casablanca ★★☆ £C
Sauvignon Blanc Casablanca ★★☆ £C

Viña Leyda (Leyda) *www.leyda.cl*
Based in the sub-region of the same name this winery has vineyards a few kilometres further inland than those of the nearby San Antonio region just to the north-west. The cooling effect of the ocean provides a benevolent environment for impressive Pinot Noir and Chardonnay. Planting of the 249 ha of vineyards was first commenced in 1997 and the first vintage in 2001 showed the area's potential. Sauvignon Blanc from Leyda, as well as Cabernet Sauvignon, Carmenère and Syrah from warmer sites are also being produced. The simplest fruit driven releases take the Reserva /Classic label. There are also a number of well-made and very reasonably priced single-vineyard wines. Falaris Hill Chardonnay is barrel-fermented with a small proportion of new oak used. It offers lightly citrus toasty notes and good intensity. Las Brisas Pinot Noir is aged in older barrels and is marked by attractive, ripe red cherry fruit. A clear step-up are the impressive estate Lot wines. The rich, opulent Lot 5 Chardonnay is vinified with wild yeasts and barrel-fermented and aged in French oak. Pinot Noir Lot 21 is a ripe, dark fruited style of Pinot with real depth and marked toasty new oak. Immediately approachable it will continue to evolve nicely with three or four years ageing. (DM)

Recommended Reds:
Pinot Noir Lot 21 Leyda ★★★☆ £D
Pinot Noir Las Brisas Leyda ★★★ £C
Recommended Whites:
Sémillon Estate Franschhoek ★★★☆ £E
Chardonnay Lot 5 Leyda ★★★ £D
Chardonnay Falaris Hill Vineyard Leyda ★★☆ £C

Matetic (San Antonio) *www.mateticvineyards.com*
This impressive operation was only founded in 1999 but is proving the real potential of San Antonio in the production of both top quality reds and whites. A sommelier at a top London Michelin-starred restaurant conceded to the author that Matetic was one of the true hidden gems of the wine world. The vineyards enjoy a moderating maritime influence and have just sufficiently cold nights in the summer to ensure good acidity in the fruit. They are

farmed organically and there are now 90 ha under vine. Three good well-priced wines are released under Corralillo label. The subtle, leesy Chardonnay is barrel-fermented and gets an additionally rich texture from part malolactic. The reds are both fairly oaky but some pre-fermentation maceration lifts the fruit. The EQ wines are a clear level up. The Sauvignon Blanc has an impressively rich depth and concentration for the variety, rarely found in Chile. Certainly this will be helped by part barrel-fermentation in French oak and part in small volume stainless steel tanks, giving the wine a better contact with its lees. Chardonnay is typically barrel-fermented on lees and aged for a further 11 months, and offers a rich texture and subtle underlying citrus character. The cherry and plum fruited Pinot Noir gets a five day cold-soak with fermentation following with a mix of Burgundian style extraction techniques. The dark, smoky, spicy EQ Syrah, which gains from a similar 5 day pre-fermentation maceration and is then aged in roughly one-half new oak for 12 months. Impeccably balanced, expect this to gain additional gamey complexity with five years ageing. This is one of the finest new wines to come out of Chile in the last 10 years and one of the few Chilean Syrahs that could hold its head up to Southern Rhone. Be aware too of a new top label Syrah, released from the 2005 vintage and simply labelled Matetic. It comes from the best block of the firm's vineyards. (DM/GW)

Recommended Reds:
Syrah Matetic San Antonio ★★★★ £E
Syrah EQ San Antonio ★★★☆ £D
Syrah Corralillo ★★☆ £C
Pinot Noir EQ San Antonio ★★★☆ £D
Merlot/Malbec Corralillo ★★☆ £C
Recommended Whites:
Chardonnay EQ San Antonio ★★★☆ £D
Chardonnay Corralillo ★★☆ £C
Sauvignon Blanc EQ San Antonio ★★★ £C

Montes (Curicó) *www.monteswines.com*
This is a large producer with an extensive range of estate-grown and externally sourced wines. A decent and approachable range of fruit driven wines is produced under the Classic Series and Twins labels but the best are available under the Montes Alpha label and there are a number of other special bottlings. Chardonnay is in a rich tropical style but has a little finesse, while Cabernet Sauvignon is sound if a little light on occasion. However, it is the Montes Alpha reds, premium Montes Folly and premium Montes Alpha M that really stand out. The dark, smoky Syrah is one of Chile's best examples. Now added to this is the special Montes Folly bottling from the firm's Apalta Mountain Estate in Colchagua, a hand-picked 100% Syrah aged in new French oak, of which less than 1,000 cases are produced. The flagship Montes Alpha M, a Bordeaux blend from the single La Finca estate in Colchagua, is rich, earthy, extracted and concentrated. These two premium reds have now been joined by a Carmenère, Purple Angel which is blended with a little Petit Verdot. A late harvest white is also now offered, a blend of 50/50 Gewürztraminer and Riesling. (DM)

Recommended Reds:
Montes Alpha M Colchagua ★★★★ £F
Montes Folly Santa Cruz ★★★★ £F
Montes Purple Angel Colchagua ★★★★ £F
Montes Alpha Syrah Colchagua ★★★ £D
Montes Alpha Carmenère Colchagua ★★★ £D
Montes Alpha Cabernet Sauvignon Colchagua ★★★ £D
Malbec Classic Series ★★ £B

Recommended Whites:

Montes Alpha Chardonnay Curicó ★★☆ £C

Neyen (Colchagua Valley) *www.neyen.cl*

This newly established winery is producing just one super-premium red. It was purchased in late 2010 by Huneeus Vintners, which also owns Veramonte. While the winery and property were founded only in 2002, the origins of the estate and the oldest vine plantings go back to the 1890s. The original adobe stone winery has been completely renovated and now has a state of the art vinification, cellar and barrel ageing facility. The vineyards in the horseshoe shaped Apalta Valley are protected from maritime winds by the Coastal Range and also have sufficient diurnal temperature variation to aid acidity in the grapes. The oldest vines are found on the plots of around 30 ha that were purchased with the property and have been added to with new hillside plantings of Carmenère, Cabernet Sauvignon, Syrah and Merlot. There is a total now of 135 ha planted although only the oldest 30 ha are used for the Espiritu du Apalta and the wine is dominated currently by very old Carmenère and a little Cabernet Sauvignon. The wine is made under the consultancy guidance of Patrick Valette of EL PRINCIPAL, who includes Château PAVIE on his resumé. The yield is very low just 5 to 6 tons to the hectare and the fruit is dominated by blackberry, spice and cassis tones all underpinned by a rich texture and powerful, supple tannins. Aged for 12 to 14 months in new french oak the wine is likely to develop well for a decade and more. (DM)

Recommended Reds:

Esporitu du Apalta Maipo ★★★★ £F

Odfjell Vineyards (Maipo) *www.odfjellvineyards.com*

Daniel and Laurence Odfjell have established vineyards in Maipo very recently. By Chilean standards this is a small, almost boutique style of operation with a production of fewer than 40,000 cases a year across their range. Winemaking consultancy input is provided by Californian winery operator Paul HOBBS, as well as French enologist Arnaud Hereu. There is a budget Armador label with a ripe, plummy Carmenère standing out. The Orzada wines are a level up and some very characterful Cabernet Franc, Carmenère and unusually a Carignan stand out. The Cabernet Sauvignon is a touch less impressive. Top of the range are a 100% Cabernet Sauvignon Aliara which is full and rich with dark berry fruit and a ripe, chocolaty character and a 100% Carignan, Oddfjell. (DM)

Recommended Reds:

Odfjell Maipo ★★★★ £F   Aliara Maipo ★★★☆ £E
Carmenère Orzada Maule ★★★ £D
Carmenère Armador Maule ★★ £B
Cabernet Franc Orzada Maule ★★☆ £D
Cabernet Sauvignon Orzada Maule ★★☆ £C
Carignan Orzada Maule ★★☆ £C
Merlot Armador Maule ★☆ £B

Viña Pérez Cruz (Maipo) *www.perezcruz.com*

The first vintage at this winery based on the higher slopes of the Maipo was only 2002. They have established themselves though among the best from this, the oldest of Chile's red wine regions. Syrah and Carmenere stand out. Their Liguai farm is blessed with finely drained alluvial soils with a high rock content and the resulting grapes offer real fruit intensity. Resident winemaker Germán Lyon works with consultant Álvaro ESPINOZA and between them a fine range of wines emerges. The simplest, the Cabernet Reserva is ripe and approachable. The Limited Edition labels offer an additional dimension and come from lower yields. The Cot (Malbec) is ripe and spicy with a nice tobacco scented undercurrent. It is lighter, with less obvious black fruit than you might find in equivalents from Mendoza across the Andes. Syrah offers an approachable dark-fruited style with a hint of black pepper. Best of the three though is the Carmenère, rich and full of dark and spicy brambly berry fruit and real intensity. The Liguai blends Syrah, Cabernet and Carmènere. There is real depth and quality with a rich, round texture aided by malolactic in barrel underpinned by firm but restrained tannins. The top red Quelen is a similarly structured, dense and even more powerful blend unusually dominated by Petit Verdot with Carmènere and Cot. Five years ageing will undoutedly ensure further development for both these reds. A further red Chaski, which is dominated by Petit Verdot is also made. (DM/GW)

Recommended Reds:

Quelen Maipo ★★★☆ £E   Liguai Maipo ★★★☆ £E
Carmenère Limited Edition Maipo ★★★ £D
Cot Limited Edition Maipo ★★☆ £D
Syrah Limited Edition Maipo ★★☆ £D
Cabernet Sauvignon Reserva Maipo ★★ £C

Santa Rita (Maipo) *www.santarita.com*

Long-established, traditional old Chilean winery which had a wake-up call in the late 1990s and is beginning to produce an increasingly fine range of midmarket and premium wines. The 120 range offers some reasonable straightforward easy drinking; the reds are a better bet generally than the whites. Reserva whites are sound but no more; the reds again are better as is the case with the Medalla Real wines. Chardonnay, though, is well crafted in a tropical, toasty style. Both the Cabernet Sauvignon and Merlot Reservas display attractive, moderately concentrated, dark, spicy fruit. The wines that really stand out are the red Triple C, the Pethuén Carmenère and Casa Real Cabernet Sauvignon. Triple C is a blend of Cabernet Franc, Cabernet Sauvignon and Carmenère. Casa Real Cabernet is quite traditional in style with well-judged oak, both concentrated and reasonably refined. Australian winemaking guru Brian Croser has provided guidance here. (DM)

Recommended Reds:

Cabernet Sauvignon Casa Real Maipo ★★★☆ £F
Cabernet Sauvignon Floresta Colchagua ★★★ £D
Cabernet Sauvignon Medalla Real Maipo Valley ★★ £B
Carmenère Pethuén Maipo ★★★☆ £E
Triple C Maipo ★★★☆ £E

Recommended Whites:

Chardonnay Medalla Real Maipo ★★ £B

❀ Seña (Aconcagua) *www.sena.cl*

This wine was established as a partnership between Eduardo Chadwick at ERRÁZURIZ and California's ROBERT MONDAVI and vies with Clos Apalta from LAPOSTOLLE, ALMAVIVA and others for the accolade of best super-premium red from Chile. Since the takeover of Mondavi by Constellation Eduardo Chadwick has taken sole ownership of the project. It is now marketed alongside Chadwick's Errazuriz, ARBOLEDA and CALITERRA ranges. Seña is currently a blend of Cabernet Sauvignon, Merlot, Carmenère, Cabernet Franc and Petit Verdot. The wine is sourced from the Seña vineyard a 350 ha property in the western Aconcagua with 42 ha of ideal north facing slopes and high-density vineyard planting. The wine is also now produced biodynamically. It is impressively dense, structured and concentrated. (DM)

Chile

Recommended Reds:
Seña Aconcagua Valley ★★★★★ £G

Undurraga (Maipo)   www.gvp.cl
This estate was founded by Don Francisco Undurraga Vicuña in 1885 but is now co-owned by the Picciotti family from Colombia and José Yuraszeck, a Chilean entrepreneur, and between them they have now formed a holding company, Grupo Vinos del Pacifico, that owns Undurraga, Volcanes de Chile, a small production winery and TIB, which specialises in producing own label wines for clients. Winemaking philosophy has changed dramatically since 2006 and whilst they still produce some 1.5 million bottles annually from their 900 hectares of land, a lot of effort has gone into their TH (Terroir Hunter) range, highlighting production of only some 1,000 to 5,000 cases of each line. They have also been busy expanding their range of sparkling wines, mostly by the Charmat method, although they do have a small range of ultra premium wines produced by the *méthode champenoise*. The regular sparkling wines are divided into two ranges, one for export and one for local consumption. Curiously enough, that produced for local consumption is the better quality, having spent more time on the lees, so you will have to travel to Chile to taste the best! The reason for this seems to be that selling Chilean sparkling wines on the international market is a bit of a tough job, so they are cutting corners a bit in order to keep the price down. Nevertheless, they are all clean and racy for easy drinking with the traditionally produced Titillum range spending 3 years on the lees and showing good body and style. The TH range is a collection of *terroir* driven wines, either from their own vineyards, or bought in grapes from selected growers. Some wines of real quality are being made under this label. Sauvignon Blanc from the Leyda Valley has a nice grassy nose and Loire-like sweet-sour fruit, with lots of minerality, whilst one from Lo Abarca, even nearer to the ocean, is just as minerally but has more restrained fruit, more akin to a Bordeaux Sauvignon Blanc. Riesling from the San Antonio Valley has good varietal flavours but may lack a bit of acidity. Pinot Noir from Leyda displays good, fresh berry fruit, soft tannins and balancing acidity, whilst Carmenère from the much warmer Colchuaga Valley is unusually dark with deep-flavoured black fruit. Cool climate Syrah, on the other hand, shows minerality and spiciness, but can lack a little depth. Alto Maipo Cabernet Sauvignon from 30 year old vines, is smooth, rounded and well balanced and shows the maturity of the plant, but Carignan from 50 year old bush vines in the Maule Valley is really intense with high natural acidity and high alcohol which is definitely not for elegant sipping. Super premium wines include Founders Collection Cabernet Sauvignon from different plots in Maipo Valley, with vines over 30 years old displaying deep and unctuous black fruit and dark chocolate and their iconic blend from Alto Maipo of Cabernet Sauvignon (around 80%) Carmenère (8%), Syrah (8%) and Carignan (4%) named Altazor, showing classic structure and a good balance of fruit and acidity in a more European style and needing a minimum of 5 years cellaring. Percentages do vary slightly from year to year. The winemaking team of Rafael Urrejola, Carlos Concha and Patricio Lucera have certainly made great strides in bringing up the quality of Undurraga wines. (NB)

Recommended Reds:
Altazar Alto Maipo ★★★★★ £G
Founders Collection Cabernet Sauvignon Maipo ★★★★☆ £E
TH Pinot Noir Leyda ★★★★ £C
TH Cabernet Sauvignon Alto Maipo ★★★★ £C
TH Syrah Limari ★★★☆ £C
TH Carignan Maule ★★★☆ £C

Sybaris Carmenère Colchagua ★★★ £C
Recommended Whites:
Titillum Banc de Noirs NV ★★★★ £E
Undurraga Brut NV ★★★ £C   Undurraga Rosé NV ★★★ £C
Export Brut NV ★★☆ £C TH Riesling San Antonio ★★★ £C
TH Sauvignon Blanc Leyda ★★★ £C
TH Sauvignon Blanc Lo Abarca San Antonio ★★★ £C

Valdivieso (Curicó)   www.vinavaldivieso.cl
Kiwi winemaker Brett Jackson and a successful marketing-driven operation produce an extensiverange of wines at all levels. Regular red and white varietals are produced under the Valdivieso Classic label. At best these offer straightforward easy glugging. Some impressive red is produced under the Reserva label, though whites disappoint in comparison. Good Single Vineyard Cabernet Franc and Malbec particularly stand out amongst this range. Among the top wines the non-vintaged Caballo Loco is a winemaker's blend that changes by the year and comes from varied vineyard sources. A new Rhône style blend, Éclat from a mix of Carignan, Mourvèdre and Syrah has also been added. Top reds particularly Caballo Loco will stand a little age. (DM/GW)

Recommended Reds:
Caballo Loco Valle Central ★★★ £E   Éclat Maule ★★★ £D
Malbec Single Vineyard Maule ★★★ £C
Cabernet Franc Single Vineyard Colchagua ★★☆ £C
Merlot Single Vineyard Apalta ★★☆ £C

❀ Viña Von Siebenthal (Aconcagua)   www.vinavonsiebenthal.com
This recently established, Swiss-owned estate has three vineyards in the warm Panquehue. Hillside sites with sandy, stony soils are planted to Cabernet Sauvignon, Carmenère, Syrah and Petit Verdot, while the lower lying plots, which have clay-limestone soils, are planted to Merlot and Cabernet Franc, to a certain extent mirroring the approach in Bordeaux. A number of wines are produced. The soft, juicy, fruit-driven Parcela 7 is blended from Cabernet Sauvignon, Merlot and Cabernet Franc. Drink this young or with a little age. There is a very characterful Carmenère which like the Parcela is vinified in stainless steel and aged for just 4 months in oak. The Carabantes is dominated by Syrah, with Cabernet Sauvignon and Petit Verdot included in the blend. Aged for 6 months in oak, this is vibrant and spicy with impressive ripe blackberry fruit. The cedary Montelìg which is blended from Cabernet Sauvignon, Petit Verdot and just a little Carmenère, will develop very well with 4 or 5 years' cellaring. Recently added and at a similar level to Montelig is an intriguing and very characterful 100% Petit Verdot, Toknar. The top red, Tatay de Christobal is a 90/10 blend of Carmenère and Petit Verdot. It is a red of serious dimension and structure, its also very pricey. (DM)

Recommended Reds:
Tatay de Christobal Valle de Colchagua ★★★★★ £H
Toknar Panquehue Valle de Aconcagua ★★★★ £F
Montelig Valle de Colchagua ★★★★ £F
Carabantes Panquehue Valle de Aconcagua ★★★ £D
Carmenère Panquehue Valle de Aconcagua ★★☆ £D
Parcela 7 Panquehue Valle de Aconcagua ★★ £C

Viu Manent (Colchagua)   www.viumanent.cl
This family owned operation produce a sizeable range of well made wines from a current holding of 260 ha of vineyards, all in the Colchagua Valley. Fruit also comes from the Casablanca and Leyda regions for some of the firm's Sauvignon Blanc output. The climate

at Colchagua is warm albeit with the combined benefit of cooling breezes filtering inland from the ocean and sufficient altitude at 500 metres to promote excellent acidity in the grapes. The wines fit into three distinct ranges. The varietal wines are simple straightforward accessible and fruit driven and generally offer very good value. A level up are the Secreto wines which along with very modern labelling keep a component of their blend and detail secret. The top wines are the single vineyard bottlings along with the prestige red the very impressive red Viu 1. The Secreto Sauvignon comes itself from the lower Casablanca Valley, it is cool fermented with some skin contact. Among the Secreto reds Carmenère is spicy and and dense, Syrah full of black pepper fruit. Both benefit from a cold soak pre-fermentation. Single Vineyard Malbec is dense and concentrated with an earthy tobacco scented complexity. The Viu 1 is similarly dominated by Malbec and it is perhaps this variety that shines most here. Indeed this is one of those rare examples that stands fair comparison with the better examples from Mendoza. Aged for 20 months in mostly new French oak this is dense, powerful and complex. There is also a decent fresh, citrus scented late-harvest Sémillon which is worth consideration. (DM)

Recommended Reds:

Viu 1 Colchagua ★★★☆ £E

Malbec Single Vineyard Colchagua ★★★ £C

Carmenère Secreto Colchagua ★★☆ £B

Syrah Secreto Colchagua ★★☆ £B

Recommended Whites:

Sémillon Late Harvest Colchagua ★★☆ £C

Sauvignon Blanc Secreto Casablanca ★★ £B

A-Z of producers - *Brazil*

Lidio Carraro (Serra Gaúcha) *www.lidiocarraro.com*

Established in 1998 and debuting on the market in 2004, this self-proclaimed "boutique winery" has a philosophy of "pure wine". No oak is used, nor is there any filtering, micro-oxygenation or any other form of alchemy. The estate has two labels – SulBrasil and the "premium" Lidio Carraro range. The labels are essentially defined by their yields and the effects thereof: SulBrasil wines are cropped at 3kg per plant, Lidio Carraro at 1.4kg. So twice as much of the former is made than the latter. SulBrasil vineyards are planted on the usual argillaceous soils but the Carraro vineyards are mainly on granite. The prices are and alcohol levels are sometimes dizzyingly high, culminating in the 16% / (£G+) Tannat Grande Vindima. (SG)

Recommended Reds:

Lidio Carraro Merlot Grande Vindima ★★★ £F

Lidio Carraro Elos Touriga Nacional Tannat ★★★ £E

Lidio Carraro Tannat Grande Vindima ★★ £G

SulBrasil Agnus Merlot ★★ £C

SulBrasil Dadivas Pinot Noir ★★ £C

SulBrasil Dadivas Merlot Cabernet Sauvignon ★★ £C

Recommended Whites:

SulBrasil Dádivas Chardonnay ★★ £C

Recommended Rosés:

SulBrasil Dadivas Rosé ★ £C

Vinícola Miolo (Serra Gaúcha) *www.miolo.com.br*

Miolo is the slickest operation in the region and claims to be the largest producer of "fine wine" and Champagne-method fizz in Brazil. Michel Rolland advises on winemaking. In 2008 Miolo received 120,000 cellar door visitors. It also hosts one day wine courses. Brut Millésime is an equal blend of Chardonnay and Pinot Noir, nicely

balanced and very well made. The whites are clean and simple. The red wines are very much in the Rolland style, all ripe fruit and new oak. Quinta do Seival Casta Portuguesas is from Campanha Gaúcha vineyards near the border with Uruguay, 500km from Bento Goncalves, where altitude and rainfall are both lower and the average temperatures are higher. A light Pinot Noir is also made. (SG)

Recommended Reds:

Lote 43 ★★★ £D   Merlot Terroir ★★★ £D

Quinta do Seival Casta Portuguesas ★★★ £D

Recommended Whites:

Chardonnay ★★ £C   Brut Millésime ★ £D

Pinot Grigio ★ £C

Casa Valduga (Serra Gaúcha) *www.casavalduga.com.br*

This smart estate, with accommodation and excellent restaurants, is owned by the third-generation Valduga brothers Erielso, Juarez and João. It produces 1 million litres of quality wine per year, half of which is sparkling. It began to export in 2002. The 200-metre long "Champagne cellar" has a 6-million bottle capacity though it will not be full for at least 20 years. (SG)

Recommended Reds:

Gran Reserva Cabernet Sauvignon ★★ £E

Premium Cabernet Franc ★★ £C

Recommended Whites:

Gran Reserva 130 Brut ★★ £D   Premium Chardonnay ★ £C

Other wines of note

Argentina
Alpamanta
Recommended Reds:

Natal Malbec Mendoza ★★★★ £D

Estate Malbec Mendoza ★★★★ £D

Estate Cabernet Franc Mendoza ★★★☆ £D

Terroir Malbec Mendoza ★★ £C

Recommended Whites:

Breva Sauvignon Blanc Mendoza ★★★ £C

Terroir Sauvignon Blanc Mendoza ★★★ £C

Altos Las Hormigas
Recommended Reds:

Malbec Mendoza Reserva Valle de Uco ★★★☆ £E

Malbec Mendoza Clasico Mendoza ★★★☆ £D

Angulo Innocenti
Recommended Reds:

Unisono Uco Valley (Malbec/Cab Sauv/Cab Franc/Syrah) ★★★☆ £C

Cabernet Sauvignon Uco Valley ★★★ £B

Malbec Uco Valley ★★★ £B

Nonni Uco Valley (Malbec/Cabernet Sauvignon) ★★☆ £A

Antucura
Recommended Reds: Antucura Red Mendoza ★★★☆ £E

Cavulcura Red Mendoza ★★★ £C

Atamisque
Recommended Reds: Atamisque Blend Mendoza ★★★☆ £E

Atamisque Malbec Mendoza ★★★ £E

Atamisque Cabernet Sauvignon Mendoza ★★★ £E

Catalpa Malbec Mendoza ★★☆ £D

Catalpa Merlot Mendoza ★★☆ £D

Catalpa Pinot Noir Mendoza ★★☆ £D

Recommended Whites:

Catalpa Chardonnay Mendoza ★★☆ £D

Wine behind the label

South America

Belasco de Baquedano
Recommended Reds: Swinto Malbec Mendoza ★★★☆ £E
AR Guentota Malbec Mendoza ★★★ £C
Llama Malbec Mendoza ★★☆ £B
Bodegas Benegas
Recommended Reds:
Benegas Lynch Meritage Mendoza ★★★★ £F
Benegas Lynch Cabernet Franc Mendoza ★★★☆ £F
Benegas Malbec Mendoza ★★★☆ £C
Benegas Syrah Mendoza ★★★ £C
Recommended Whites:
Clara Benegas Mendoza ★☆ £B
Recommended Rosés: Carmela Benegas Mendoza ★☆ £B
Bienvenuto de La Serna
Recommended Reds:
Red Blend Valle de Uco ★★☆ £B
Mil Piedras Viogniervalle de Uco ★★ £B
Cabernet de Los Andes
Recommended Reds: Plenilunio Malbec Catamarca ★★★☆ £D
Plenilunio Cabernet Sauvignon Catamarca ★★★☆ £D
Vicien Malbec Reserve Catamarca ★★☆ £B
Vicien Bonarda Reserve Catamarca ★★☆ £B
Domingo Hermanos
Recommended Reds: Palo Domingo Yacochuya ★★★☆ £F
Rupestre Quebrada de Las Flechas ★★★☆ £E
Domingo Molina Malbecyacochuya ★★★ £C
Domingo Molina Quebrada de Las Flechas ★★★ £C
Finca Domingo Malbec Yacochuya ★★☆ £C
Recommended Whites:
Domingo Molina Torrontés Cafayate ★★☆ £C
Finca Domingo Torrontés Cafayate ★★ £C
Viña Doña Paula
Recommended Reds:
Malbec Selección de Bodega Mendoza ★★★☆ £F
Alluvia (Cabernet Franc) Mendoza ★★★ £C
Shiraz-Malbec Mendoza ★★☆ £B   Malbec Mendoza ★★☆ £B
Cabernet Sauvignon Mendoza ★★☆ £B
Recommended Whites: Chardonnay Estate Mendoza ★★ £C
Naked Pulp (Viognier) Mendoza ★★★ £C
Etchart
Recommended Reds: Arnaldo B Reserva Cafayate ★★ £C
Fabre Montmayou
Recommended Reds: Grand Vin Vistalba ★★★ £D
Gran Reserva Malbec Vistalba ★★☆ £C
Fin del Mundo
Recommended Reds: Special Blend Patagonia ★★★☆ £E
Cabernet Franc Single Vineyard Patagonia ★★★ £D
Malbec Reserva Patagonia ★★★ £D
Finca El Retiro
Recommended Reds: Syrah Mendoza ★★ £B
Malbec Mendoza ★★ £B
Finca Flichman
Recommended Reds: Dedicado Maipú ★★☆ £C
Enrique Foster
Recommended Reds:
Edición Limitada Malbec Mendoza ★★★☆ £F
Malbe Terruño Vistalba Mendoza ★★★ £D
Malbe Terruño Lunlunta Mendoza ★★★ £D
Malbec Reserva Mendoza ★★★ £D
Gauchezco Vineyard & Winery
Recommended Reds: Oro Malbec Maipú ★★★★ £D

Plata Malbec/Cabernet Franc Uco Valley ★★★☆ £C
Reserva Malbec Maipú ★★★☆ £B   Classic Malbec Maipú ★★☆ £B
Reserva Petit Verdot Maipú ★★ £B
Recommended Whites:
Sparkling Extra Brut Pinot Noir Maipú ★★☆ £C
Classic Torrontes Cafayate Valley ★★ £B
Finca Koch
Recommended Reds: Malbec Tupungato ★★ £B
Bodegas Krontiras
Recommended Reds:
Doña Silvina Reserva Malbec Luján de Cuyo ★★★★ £D
Doña Silvina Malbec Maipú ★★★ £C
Doña Silvina Fresh Malbec Maipú ★★☆ £C
Solar del Alma Malbec Luján de Cuyo ★★ £C
Doña Silvina Petit Verdot Single Vineyard Reserva Maipú ★★ £C
Recommended Rosés: Doña Silvina Rosado Malbec ★★☆ £C
La Bienvenida
Recommended Reds: Malbec Mendoza ★★ £C
Bodega Lagarde
Recommended Reds:
Henry Gran Guardo No 1 Mendoza ★★★ £D
Lagarde Guarda Mendoza ★★☆ £C
Recommended Whites: Henry Late Harvest ★★☆ £C
Felix Lavaque
Recommended Reds: Felix Lavaque Salta ★★★ £D
Mauricio Lorca
Recommended Reds:
Gran Lorca Poetico Blend Mendoza ★★★☆ £E
Lorca Poetico Syrah Mendoza ★★★ £D
Lorca Opalo Malbec Mendoza ★★★ £D
Lorca Fantasia Malbec Mendoza ★★ £C
Mapema
Recommended Reds: Primera Zona Mendoza ★★★ £E
Marta's Vinyard
Recommended Reds: Signature Malbec Mendoza ★★☆ £D
Tempranillo Reserve Mendoza ★★ £C
Masi Tupungato
Recommended Reds: Corbec Mendoza ★★★ £D
Paso Doble Mendoza ★★☆ £C
Navarra Correas
Recommended Reds: Malbec Limited Release Mendoza ★★☆ £C
Renacer
Recommended Reds:
Enamore(Malbec/CabSau/Bonarda/CabFranc)LujándeCuyo★★★£C
Punto Final Malbec Reserve Uco Valley ★★☆ £C
Punto Final Cabernet Sauvignon Luján de Cuyo ★★ £B
Punto Final Malbec Classico Luján de Cuyo ★☆ £B
RJ Viñedos
Recommended Reds: Malbec Premium Mendoza ★★★ £E
Merlot Premium Mendoza ★★★ £E
Blend de Selección Mendoza ★★☆ £C
Bodega Ruca Malén
Recommended Reds: Kinien Malbec Mendoza ★★★ £D
Malbec Mendoza ★★☆ £C
Cabernet Sauvignon Mendoza ★★☆ £C
Recommended Whites:
Chardonnay Uco Valley, Mendoza ★★☆ £C
Felipe Rutini
Recommended Reds: Apartado Tupungato ★★★ £D
Malbec Tupungato ★★☆ £C

Wine behind the label

Bodegas Salentein
Recommended Reds: Primus Malbec Mendoza ★★★☆ £E
Numina Reserve Mendoza ★★★ £D
Malbec Reserve Mendoza ★★☆ £C

Bodegas Santa Ana
Recommended Reds: La Mascotta Mendoza ★★★ £C
Malbec La Mascotta Mendoza ★★★ £C
Malbec Cepas Privada Mendoza ★★☆ £B
Shiraz Mendoza ★★ £B
Recommended Whites: Viognier Cepas Privada Mendoza ★☆ £B

Famiglia Schroeder
Recommended Reds:
Saurus Barrel Fermented Malbec Patagonia ★★★ £C
Alpataco Malbec Patagonia ★★☆ £C

Bodega Tacuil
Recommended Reds: Tacuil RD Salta ★★★☆ £E
33 de Davalos Salta ★★★★ £F

Tapiz
Recommended Reds: Malbec Reserve Mendoza ★★☆ £C
Malbec Mendoza ★★ £C

Pascual Toso
Recommended Reds: Magdalena Toso Mendoza ★★★★☆ £G
Finca Pedregal Mendoza ★★★★ £F
Alta Reserva Syrah Mendoza ★★★ £E
Malbec Reserve Mendoza ★★☆ £C
Recommended Whites: Chardonnay Barrancas Mendoza ★☆ £B
Sparkling Extra Toso Chardonnay Nv Mendoza ★★ £C
Sauvignon Blanc Barrancas Mendoza ★☆ £B

Trapiche
Recommended Reds: Iscay Maipú ★★★ £E
Malbec Broquel Mendoza ★★☆ £C
Cabernet Sauvignon Broquel Mendoza ★★ £C
Malbec Oak Cask Mendoza ★★ £B
Recommended Whites: Chardonnay Broquel Mendoza ★★ £B
Chardonnay Oak Cask Mendoza ★★ £B

Universo Austral
Recommended Reds: Kooch Malbec Rio Negro ★★★☆ £E
Kooch Pinot Noir Rio Negro ★★★ £E
Calafate Gran Reserva Neuquen ★★★ £D
Calafate Reserva Neuquen ★★☆ £C

Valentin Bianchi
Recommended Reds: Enzo Bianchi Mendoza ★★★★ £E
Particular Malbec Mendoza ★★★☆ £D
Particular Bianchi Malbec Mendoza ★★★ £D
Famiglia Bianchi Malbec Mendoza ★★☆ £D

Viniterra
Recommended Reds: Cabernet Sauvignon Luján de Cuyo ★☆ £B
Malbec Luján de Cuyo ★★ £B

Domaine Vistalba
Recommended Reds: Infinitus Malbec/Syrah Río Negro ★★★ £D

Weinert
Recommended Reds: Malbec Luján de Cuyo ★★★ £C
Cavas de Weinert Luján de Cuyo ★★ £C

Zorzal Wines
Recommended Reds: Climax Malbec Mendoza ★★★☆ £E
Climax Blend Mendoza ★★★ £E
Malbec Reserve Mendoza ★★☆ £C
Cabernet Malbec Reserve Mendoza ★★ £C
Cabernet Sauvignon Reserve Mendoza ★★ £C

Familia Zuccardi
Recommended Reds: Zuccardi Zeta Q Mendoza ★★★ £E

Malbec Q Mendoza ★★☆ £C   Tempranillo Q Mendoza ★★ £C

Chile
Viña Amaral
Recommended Whites: Chardonnay Leyda ★★☆ £B
Sauvignon Blanc Leyda ★★☆ £B

Anakena
Recommended Reds: Pinot Noir Ona Casablanca ★★☆ £B
Carmenère Rapel ★★ £B
Recommended Whites: Sauvignon Blanc Valle Central ★★ £B

Apaltagua
Recommended Reds: Carmenère Colchagua ★★ £B
Envero Colchagua ★★☆ £B   Grial Colchagua ★★★ £D

Bisquertt
Recommended Reds:
Carmenère Gran Reserva Casa La Joya Colchagua ★☆ £C

Viñedos Julio Bouchon
Recommended Reds: Carmenère Reserva Especial Maule ★☆ £B
Assemblage Maule ★★ £C

Caliterra
Recommended Reds: Cenit Colchagua ★★★★ £F
Edicion Limitada Shiraz Cabernet Viognier Colchagua ★★★ £C
Tributo Malbec Colchagua ★★☆ £C
Carmenère Reserva Colchagua ★★ £B
Merlot Reserva Colchagua ★☆ £B

Canepa
Recommended Reds:
Cabernet Sauvignon Magnificum Curicó ★★ £C
Carmenère Private Reserve Valle Centrale ★ £B

Casa Rivas
Recommended Reds: Carmenère Gran Reserva Maipo ★★ £C

Casas del Toqui
Recommended Reds:
Cabernet Sauvignon Reserve Prestige Cachapoal ★★☆ £B

Viña Chocalan
Recommended Reds: Gran Reserva Chocolan Maipo ★★★☆ £D
Syrah Reserva Maipo ★★★ £C
Cabernet Franc Reserva Maipo ★★★ £C
Carmenère Selección Maipo ★★☆ £B
Syrah Selección Maipo ★★☆ £B
Recommended Whites:
Sauvignon Blanc Malvilla San Antonio ★★☆ £C

Dos Andes
Recommended Reds: Gracia Carmenère Maipo ★☆ £B

Echeverria
Recommended Reds:
Cabernet Sauvignon Family Reserva Valle Central ★★ £C
Carmenère Reserva Valle Central ★☆ £B

Luis Felipe Edwards
Recommended Reds: Cabernet Reserva Colchagua ★☆ £B
Merlot Reserva Colchagua ★☆ £B

Espiritu de Chile
Recommended Reds: Cabernet Sauvignon Gran Reserva ★★ £C

Viña Estampa
Recommended Reds: Syrah Gold Assemblage Colchagua ★★★ £D
Carmenère Gold Assemblage Colchagua ★★★ £D
Cab Sauv/Carmenère/Petit Verdot Reserve Colchagua ★★☆ £B

Viña Intriga
Recommended Reds: Cabernet Sauvignon Maipo ★★★☆ £C

South America

O. Fournier (Chile)
Recommended Reds: Centauri Maule ★★★☆ £D
Urban Cabernet Sauvignon Maule ★★☆ £B
Recommended Whites:
Sauvignon Blanc Alpha Centauri San Antonio ★★★☆ £D
La Arboleda
Recommended Whites: Chardonnay Casablanca ★☆ £B
Recommended Reds:
Carmenère Colchagua ★★ £C Syrah Colchagua ★★ £C
Michel Laroche/Jorge Coderche
Recommended Reds: Piedra Feliz Casablanca ★★ £B
Colina Negra Casablanca ★★ £B
Recommended Whites: Rio Azul Casablanca ★★ £B
Los Vascos
Recommended Reds: Le Dix de Los Vascos Colchagua ★★★ £D
La Rosa
Recommended Reds:
Merlot Gran Reserve La Palmeria Rapel ★★ £B
Montgras
Recommended Reds: Ninquén Colchagua ★★★☆ £E
Antu Ninquén Syrah Colchagua ★★★ £C
Cabernet Sauvignon de Gras Reserva Colchagua ★★☆ £C
Carmenère de Gras Reserva Colchagua ★★☆ £C
Recommended Whites:
Chardonnay de Gras Reserva Colchagua ★★☆ £B
Viña Quebrada de Macul
Recommended Reds: Domus Aurea Maipo ★★★ £D
Viña San Pedro
Recommended Reds: Cabo de Hornos ★★★☆ £D
Tierras Moradas Carmenère Maule ★★★☆ £F
Cabernet Sauvignon Reserva Castillo Di Molina ★★ £B
Santa Carolina
Recommended Whites: Chardonnay Reservado Maipo ★☆ £B
Tabali
Recommended Reds: Payen Syrah Limari ★★★★ £F
Pinot Noir Talinay Limari ★★★☆ £E
Syrah Reserva Especial Limari ★★☆ £D
Syrah Reserva Limari ★★ £B Carmenère Reserva Limari ★★ £B
Recommended Whites: Chardonnay Talinay Limari ★★★ £C
Tarapacá
Recommended Reds: Syrah Privada Reserva Maipo ★★ £C
Milenium Maipo ★★★ £C
Terranoble
Recommended Reds: Carmenère Gran Reserva Maule ★★ £C
Torreón de Paredes
Recommended Reds: Don Amado Cachapoal ★★ £D
Miguel Torres
Recommended Reds: Manso de Velasco Curicó ★★☆ £D
Viña Ventisquero
Recommended Reds: Pangea Colchagua ★★★★ £F
Vertice Colchagua ★★★★ £E
Cabernet Sauvignon Reserva Castillo Di Molina ★★ £B
Veramonte
Recommended Reds: Primus Casablanca ★★ £C
Villard Estate
Recommended Reds: Equis Maipo ★★☆ £C

Uruguay
Bodega Bouza
Recommended Reds: Tannat Las Violetas Canelones ★★ £C
Merlot Las Violetas Canelones ★★ £B

Recommended Whites:
Albarino Las Violetas Canelones ★★ £B

Work in progress!!

Producers under consideration for the next edition
Finca Agostino (Mendoza, Argentina)
Antinori-Matte (Maipo, Chile)
Aristos (Cachapoal, Chile)
Bravado (Casablanca. Chile)
Clos des Fous (Chile)
Bodega Fernando Dupont (Maimará, Argentina)
Flaherty Wines (Chile)
Garage Wine Co (Chile)
Graffito (Mendoza, Argentina)
Finca Don Martino (Lujan de Cuyo, Argentina)
Viña Santa Ema (Maipo, Chile)
Tres 14 (Mendoza, Argentina)

Author's choice

A top Argentine selection
Reds:
Achaval-Ferrer Quimira
Viña Cobos Cobos Luján de Cuyo
Susana Balbo Brioso Mendoza
Ben Marco VMS Mendoza
Catena Zapata Nicolás Catena Zapata Luján de Cuyo
Bodega Chacra Pinot Noir Treinta y Dos Rio Negro
Tikal Corazon Mendoza
Bodega Monteviejo Lindaflor Mendoza
Nieto Senetiner Malbec Cadus Tupungato
Yacochuya Yacochuya Red Cafayate
Poesia Poesia Mendoza
Bodega Noemia Partagonia Malbec Mendoza
Whites:
Luca Chardonnay Mendoza

A top Chilean red selection of reds
Almaviva Almaviva Red Maipo Valley
Viña Altaïr Altaïr Cachapoal
Casa Lapostolle Clos Apalta Rapel
Viñedo Chadwick Red Maipo Valley
El Principal El Principal Maipo
Errázuriz Don Maximiano Aconcagua Valley
Montes Montes Folly Santa Cruz
Odfjell Vineyards Aliara Maipo
Seña Seña Aconcagua Valley
Viña Von Siebenthal Tatay de Christobal Valle de Colchagua

Wine behind the label

The extent to which Australia's global success derives from its easy to- understand appeal - from mostly varietal labelling of wine names to the direct and overt fruitiness that still characterises many of the wines - can not be underestimated. Yet there are also fine wines with great depth and structure and others of real style, elegance and nuance. The first years of the new century have witnessed a sea change in placing much greater emphasis on diversity and regionality. The correlation between price and quality is also improving but care is needed when purchasing more expensive bottles. In order to give some coherence to Australia's ever burgeoning vineyard area we have made four broad geopolitical divisions: **South Australia, Victoria & Tasmania, New South Wales & Queensland,** and **Western Australia.**

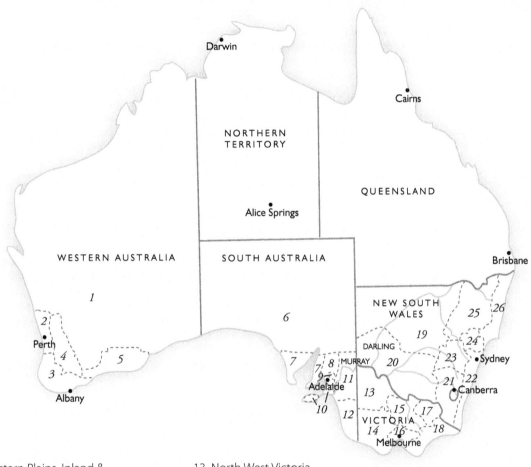

1 Eastern Plains, Inland & North of Western Australia	13 North West Victoria
2 Greater Perth	14 Western Victoria
3 South West Australia	15 Central Victoria
4 Central Western Australia	16 Port Phillip
5 Western Australian South East Coastal	17 North East Victoria
6 Far North	18 Gippsland
7 The Peninsulas	19 Western Plains
8 Mount Lofty Ranges	20 Big Rivers
9 Barossa	21 Southern New South Wales
10 Fleurieu	22 South Coast
11 Lower Murray	23 Central Ranges
12 Limestone Coast	24 Hunter Valley
	25 Northern Slopes
	26 Northern Rivers

South Australia

Almost half of all Australian wine comes from South Australia. The bulk of the cheaper wine comes from the Riverland area, on the Murray River close to Victoria, while many premium wines (red, white and fortified) are made from regions that range from baking hot to distinctly cool. Quality in all the established regions is producer-dependent, as many have chosen to maximise profits by concentrating their efforts on marketing and distribution rather than producing ever better wines. From both the latest wave of high-quality small producers and some of the more established names, the wines are increasingly vineyard-specific and less about winemaking technique but great wines also continue to be blended from a range of mesoclimates. There is also a trend in favour of experimenting with alternative varieties, notably Italian and Spanish, but also Austrian and Portuguese. It can result in some exciting, textured wines at the drier end of the spectrum, though prices tend to be high, especially if these wines are compared with their European counterparts.

Barossa

This GI zone, incorporating the Barossa Valley and the Eden Valley, witnessed the greatest revival amongst Australia's many historic winemaking areas during the 1990s.

Barossa Valley

Since the 1840s both English and Silesian immigrants have played an important part in establishing what has become the heart of the Australian wine industry. But in the modern revival of Australian table wines Barossa lost ground to newer areas and its rich viticultural resource of often unirrigated, old-vine Shiraz, Grenache and Mourvèdre began to rapidly disappear under Vine Pull schemes of the 1980s. Fortunately Peter Lehmann, Grant Burge, Charlie Melton and others rode to the rescue by producing wines of a quality that the world couldn't ignore and has since not been able to get enough of. Besides rich, lushly textured old-vine Shiraz and Rhône-style blends, Cabernet Sauvignon has an important place for its distinctive dense, black-fruited blockbusters; such Barossa classics often owe their sweet casing to ageing in American oak but the trend, even for classics like Peter Lehmmann Stonewall, is in favour of French oak. Barossa also has a great history of fortified wines and very high-quality examples, often blended from old wines, continue to be made. Though full-flavoured, whites are less suited to the conditions. Chardonnay, whose appeal in the 80s soon waned, does less well than Sémillon in the heat. Moscato d'Asti style fizz, on the other hand, works very well.

EdenValley

The most successful of the whites in the Barossa zone is Riesling, but from over the eastern ranges of the Barossa Valley in the significantly cooler, more elevated vineyards of the Eden Valley. Riesling particularly excels in the higher, more southern reaches where the Mount Lofty Ranges run through from the Adelaide Hills to the south. These areas are known as **High Eden** (a recently approved sub-region), home to Mountadam, Eden Springs, Heggies and Pewsey Vale (see Yalumba), and **Springton** and are the source of high-quality Chardonnay, Pinot Noir and Merlot. Viognier shows real potential too, though current quality has been a little overhyped. Great reds, particularly Shiraz but also Cabernet, are also produced from lower altitudes, most notably those from Henschke, near Keyneton.

Mount Lofty Ranges

Though geographically disparate, the Clare Valley and Adelaide Hills both form part of the Mount Lofty Ranges, where altitude plays a significant role in the style of the wines.

Clare Valley

Lying to the north-west of Barossa, the Clare Valley might be expected to be even hotter, but altitude changes the equation and is critical to the success of individual varieties. However, it is warm and even with irrigation vines can suffer water stress in particularly hot years. Several sub-regions have already emerged, including **Auburn**, **Polish Hill River**, **Sevenhill**, **Watervale** and around the township of **Clare** itself – though none have yet received official GI sanction. Most Rieslings from the Clare Valley offer less immediate fruit sweetness than those from the Eden Valley but have better structure and greater style. The best examples can be relatively austere in youth but develop an intense limey, mineral toastiness with 10 years' age or more. Shiraz is the most widely planted variety and the higher west-facing vineyards in particular provide some excellent examples with a captivating smoke, earth and mineral character (superbly illustrated by the likes of Kilikanoon). Cabernet Sauvignon is also a leading variety and if generally less compelling than the best Shiraz it also shows a distinctive regional stamp. Chardonnay, Sémillon and Merlot are the most important of the other varieties.

Adelaide Hills

The Adelaide Hills, in the ranges along and beyond the eastern edge of the state capital, form part of the southern extension of the Mount Lofty Ranges. Elevation is again critical and the reputation of this relatively small vineyard area grows apace, now way beyond its size, since being pioneered by Brian Croser (founder of Petaluma) in the 1970s. Chardonnay, especially from the sub-regions of **Lenswood** and **Piccadilly Valley**, rivals, even surpasses the best in the country but there has also been compelling quality from Pinot Noir and Sauvignon Blanc. The patchwork of vineyards, resulting in part from the perils of spring frost, contrasts with the swathe of low-altitude vineyards that carpet the floor of the McLaren Vale a short distance to the south.

Fleurieu

The Fleurieu Peninsula is dominated by production from the historic and important McLaren Vale but in the past decade wines of quality have begun to emerge from lesser-known neighbouring regions.

McLaren Vale

In the McLaren Vale, tucked between the hills and the coast, the heat is relieved by sea breezes and Shiraz, Grenache, Mourvèdre and Cabernet Sauvignon assume ascendancy. However, care must be taken if the wines are to show balance and depth as well as a lush texture. A re-energising of established producers (such as D'Arenberg) together with the emergence of the likes of Clarendon Hills, Fox Creek, or more recently, Gemtree and Mitolo, have, in conjunction with the general revival in the fortunes of Rhône varieties in South Australia, brought about both greater diversity in red wine styles and ever higher quality. So-called "Cadenzia" blends put the empasis on Grenache. Given the region's mix of soil types it is also encouraging to see increasing identification of the various sub-zones and individual vineyards. Soon the likes of Blewitt Springs, Clarendon and Kangarilla should be as well known for their location as for the wineries named after them. Whites are less exciting. Some

producers persist with Sauvignon Blanc and Chardonnay, the best of which come from the cooler northern end (Clarendon, Kangarilla) of the region where the Adelaide Hills begin, but the long-term success of whites in the heartland seems more suited to Rhône and other warmer-climate varieties.

Other Fleurieu regions

Flood-irrigated **Langhorne Creek** on the other side of the Fleurieu Peninsula has long provided soft, ripe Shiraz and Cabernet fruit that contributes to many a well-established blended South Australian red. An absence of high-profile producers has contributed to a lack of identity but Bleasdale, Bremerton, Lake Breeze, Heartland and others will bring greater recognition. Other pockets of vineyard that have recently been given their own official sanction are **Currency Creek** and **Southern Fleurieu** which lie either side of Langhorne Creek. **Kangaroo Island**, a large (4,350 km2), sparsely populated island 110 km southwest of Adelaide, has but a few vines yet shows good potential for Bordeaux style reds. Jacques Lurton established the Islander on Kangaroo Island in 2000.

Limestone Coast

The south-eastern corner of the state is geographically an extension of Victoria. The Limestone Coast zone is essentially flat yet its magic emerges from low limestone ridges topped with the famous *terra rossa* (or terra rosa) soil. The most established of these is, of course, Coonawarra.

Coonawarra

Coonawarra only emerged as a high-quality region in the latter half of the 20th century. Despite its renown, quality from this elongated, relatively exposed and coolish region with its terra rossa soils and high water table was highly variable. The combination of intermittent summer heat and cold, wet winters is as significant to quality as the fabled free-draining soils. Cooler vintages in particular demand high standards of viticulture yet mechanically harvested fruit that comes from high-yielding Cabernet Sauvignon vines fails to get fully ripe as does that from less suitable more water-retentive soils at the limits of the region. Many of the high-volume blends that result denigrate the Coonawarra name. Fortunately viticultural standards are on the up. Wynns, the region's biggest producer and a growing number of small or medium-sized estates (such as Bowen Estate or Hollick) are showing the sort of quality that is possible, and from Shiraz as well as Cabernet. There has been much fuss over Coonawarra boundaries but wiser producers are investing their energies on developing other similar, and very promising regions.

Padthaway

Northernmost of the Limestone Coast regions, Padthaway has a far less established reputation than Coonawarra. Despite being the warmer of the two, Padthaway already has a considerable reputation for Chardonnay. There are also substantial plantings of Cabernet Sauvignon and Shiraz and significant amounts of Riesling, Merlot and Pinot Noir. The Limestone Coast is destined to be better known as a grape growing rather than winemaking region.

Mount Benson and Robe

Mount Benson and adjoining Robe lie to the west of Coonawarra and Wrattonbully, right on the coast. Vineyards were non-existent here until 1989. Temperatures during the growing season are lower than in Coonawarra and both wind and frost can be a problem. Cabernet Sauvignon and Shiraz lead the plantings; Shiraz in particular, shows real promise. Interest has been heightened by the development of Kreglinger Estate (Norfolk Rise).

Wrattonbully

To the north of Coonawarra, Wrattonbully is now rapidly emerging as an important region for quality wines. Slightly warmer than Coonawarra, it has similar if older, terra rosa soils underneath the gently undulating surface and also slightly less risk of frost. The lion's share of planting has been to Cabernet Sauvignon but there are also significant amounts of Merlot and Shiraz. It is to some degree the Right Bank to Coonawarra's Left Bank. Wines from the region often form part of a Limestone Coast blend.

The rest of the Limestone Coast

Smaller newer areas that have yet to take on any real significance include Mount Gambier (in the extreme south of the state), Lucindale (on another Limestone ridge between Mount Benson and Wrattonbully), and Bordertown. The last already has significant plantings used in Limestone Coast blends.

A-Z of producers by region

Barossa Valley		Leabrook Estate	843
Barossa Valley Estate	832	Nepenthe	847
Rolf Binder	833	Petaluma	849
Wolf Blass	833	Pike & Joyce	849
Burge Family	834	Riposte Wines	851
Grant Burge	834	Shaw & Smith	852
Dutschke	837	The Lane Wine Co.	853
John Duval	837	Geoff Weaver	855
Elderton	837	**Adelaide Plains**	
Glaetzer	838	Primo Estate	850
Greenock Creek	838	**Clare Valley**	
Hemera	839	Tim Adams	831
Jacob's Creek	841	Annie's Lane	832
Kalleske	841	Jim Barry	833
Langmeil	843	Crabtree	836
Peter Lehmann	844	Grosset	838
Charles Melton	845	Kilikanoon	842
Mt Billy	846	Knappstein	842
Penfolds	848	Leasingham	843
Chris Ringland	851	Mitchell	845
Rockford	851	Mount Horrocks	846
Saltram	852	Neagles Rock	847
Sami-Odi	852	O'Leary Walker	847
Seppeltsfield	852	Pikes	849
St Hallett	851	Reilly's Wines	850
Thorn-Clarke	853	Wakefield	854
Torbreck	853	Wendouree	855
Turkey Flat	854	**McLaren Vale**	
Yalumba	856	Cascabel	834
Eden Valley		Chapel Hill	835
Heathvale	839	Clarendon Hills	835
Henschke	840	Coriole	836
Mountadam	846	D'Arenberg	836
Pewsey Vale	849	Fox Creek	837
Tin Shed	853	Gemtree	838
Adelaide Hills		Hamilton	838
Ashton Hills	832	Hardys	839
Barratt Wines	832	Kay Brothers	842
Chain of Ponds	835	Maglieri	844

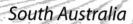

South Australia

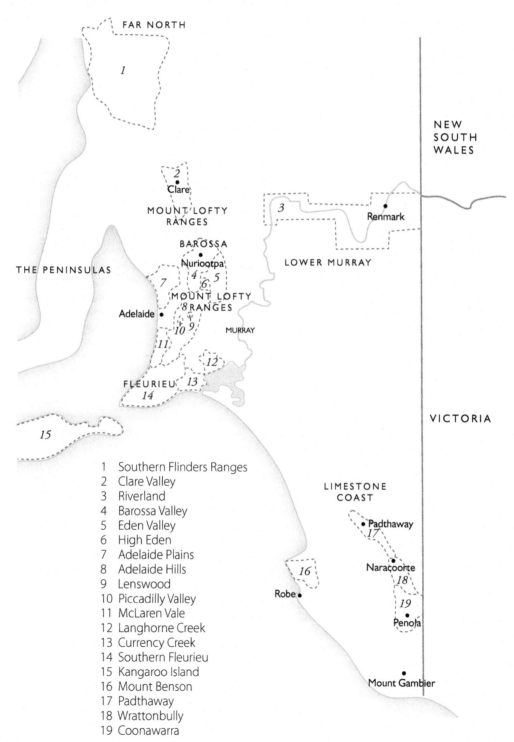

1 Southern Flinders Ranges
2 Clare Valley
3 Riverland
4 Barossa Valley
5 Eden Valley
6 High Eden
7 Adelaide Plains
8 Adelaide Hills
9 Lenswood
10 Piccadilly Valley
11 McLaren Vale
12 Langhorne Creek
13 Currency Creek
14 Southern Fleurieu
15 Kangaroo Island
16 Mount Benson
17 Padthaway
18 Wrattonbully
19 Coonawarra

South Australia vintages

The generalised Vintage charts cover some of the most ageworthy styles but needs to taken together with comments on style and ageing given in individual A-Z producer entries.Many wines can be drunk young but an increasing number will not be at their best for at least 5 years, both powerful, full-bodied reds or a more structured example of Clare Valley Riesling. Top-quality Chardonnay and Pinot Noir need 3-6 years' ageing. In terms of longer-term cellaring potential, great Australian Rieslings have been shown to age for a decade or more, while some famous Australian reds have been proven to age for 30 or even 40 years. Both the vintage ratings and when to drink assessments generally only apply to the top rated examples (3-star or higher).

Recent vintages

2016 This turned out to be a fairly early vintage and good balanced wines look likely although it was challenging for growers. The summer was hot and some cooler areas had to irrigate. Rain in January was well received. Barossa Shiraz should be very good and the Clare Valley not far behind. Riesling looks very promising in both the Clare and Eden Valleys. It was another good year for Coonawarra reds and for Adelaide Hills whites and Pinot Noir.

2015 This was a challenging vintage for growers in the Barossa and Clare Valleys with hot weather in February requiring a careful control of harvesting and sugar levels in the reds. Good wines have resulted though and some good to excellent Riesling in the Clare and Eden Valleys. Coonawarra once again produced fine Cabernet and Shiraz, a trend since 2012. Despite a threat from January bushfires warm late season weather and low rainfall resulted in a great vintage in the Adelaide Hills.

2014 Winter frosts, strong spring winds, summer heat spikes and some untimely rain at harvest once again reduced yields. Those who picked after the rain brought in fruit produced wines with richness and character with good varietal flavours at lower levels of alcohol. Low yields once again produced top cuvées in this vintage, the third quality vintage in a row.

2013 A dry winter and a few heat spikes dramatically reduced crop yields and those who had irrigated early had the best chance of protecting the grapes from shrivelling on the vines. Overall quality is only a little down on the outstanding vintage of 2012. Shiraz, Grenache and other Rhône varietals fared particularly well whilst Bordeaux varietals show good colour, fruit and tannins. Of the whites, the Rieslings once again displayed outstanding minerality although the Chardonnays were a little affected by the heat.

2012 In contrast to 2011, growing conditions were extremely favourable in 2012 and some outstanding wines were made. The only downside was that yields were in some places severely below average. Intense Shiraz, gracious Cabernets, lush Chardonnays and steely Rieslings have been the order of the day.

2011 One of the wettest growing seasons on record produced havoc, particularly amongst the reds, with Shiraz coming off worst. Whilst some producers made no Shiraz at all, there were some good quality wines made, but there is little of it that is worthy. Cabernet Sauvignon in Coonawarra fared slightly better, but even then the wines have tended to be a little hollow with low alcohol and sharp tannins. Adelaide Hills Chardonnays were plagued with botrytis and only the Rieslings generally over the whole State seemed to have done well with those from the Clare and Eden Valleys producing some outstanding wines.

2010 An early, low yielding year with poor fruit set followed by dry conditions and warm temperatures throughout the growing season, marked by an unseasonably warm spring and higher night-time temperatures than usual. Overall fruit quality is high, with some excellent reds made, though whites lack the structure and finesse of top years.

2009 A longer growing season than previous years despite a heatwave in late January/early February. This resulted in lower yields and heat stress in hotter regions. Where heat stress was managed, and in temperate and cooler regions where *veraison* had not yet occurred, flavour intensity, balance and tannin quality was very good to excellent.

2008 Fine growing conditions with the exception of some regions in South Australia which were hit by a heat wave in early March. Quantities were down by up to 20% in those areas.

2007 Yields were drastically down due to frost and severe drought conditions. Yet quality is promsing particularly in the cooler regions or where growers aren't dependent on irrigation.

2006 A third successive large harvest. After a cool February, a hot earlyMarch accelerated ripening in most parts. Cooler and wetter conditions affected those harvesting late.

South Australia vintage chart

	Barossa/ Eden Valley Shiraz	Coonawarra Cabernet	Clare/ Eden Valley Riesling	Adelaide Hills Chardonnay
2016	★★★★☆ A	★★★★☆ A	★★★★☆ A	★★★★ A
2015	★★★★ A	★★★★☆ A	★★★★ A	★★★★★ A
2014	★★★★ A	★★★★☆ A	★★★★ A	★★★★ B
2013	★★★★☆ A	★★★★☆ A	★★★★☆ B	★★★☆ B
2012	★★★★☆ B	★★★★☆ B	★★★★☆ B	★★★★☆ B
2011	★★ B	★★☆ B	★★★★☆ B	★★★ C
2010	★★★★☆ B	★★★★ B	★★★ B	★★★ C
2009	★★★★ B	★★★★ B	★★★★ B	★★★☆ C
2008	★★★★ C	★★★★ B	★★★★ C	★★★☆ C
2007	★★★★ C	★★★★ C	★★★★ C	★★★☆ C
2006	★★★★ C	★★★★ C	★★★★ C	★★★☆ C
2005	★★★★☆ C	★★★★☆ C	★★★★ C	★★★★☆ C
2004	★★★☆ D	★★★★☆ C	★★★ D	★★★★☆ C
2003	★★☆ D	★★★★ D	★★★☆ C	★★★★ D
2002	★★★★☆ C	★★★★☆ C	★★★★★ C	★★★★★ C
2001	★★★★ D	★★★☆ D	★★★☆ D	★★★ D
2000	★★★ D	★★★★☆ D	★★★☆ D	★★★ D

A-Z of producers

🌑 **Tim Adams (Clare Valley)** *www.timadamswines.com.au*
This is a brilliant Clare Valley producer with marvellously consistent reds and whites of great depth and character. Aberfeldy, the top red, has a certain elegance as well as masses of fruit and American oak, in which it spends the best part of two years. The Fergus takes its name from a grower who first supplied the Grenache around which a little Shiraz, Cabernet Sauvignon and Cabernet Franc are now woven; at once complex and appealing, it has a deserved following. Adams was inspired by MUGA (Isaac Muga worked the vintage here) to experiment with Tempranillo and Muga would be proud of the plush but spicy outcome. Riesling and Sémillon both have excellent varietal definition and good structure; the just off dry but well balanced Pinot Gris shows bright pear and a hint of spice (it is part barrel fermented). Prices continue to be exemplary for the quality. Adams acquired substantial vineyard holdings from LEASINGHAM,

so there is more to come from this established but progressive producer.

Recommended Reds:

Shiraz Aberfeldy ★★★★★ £E

Shiraz ★★★ £D

Cabernet Malbec ★★★☆ £C

Reserve Tempranillo ★★★ £D

The Fergus ★★☆ £C

Recommended Whites:

Reserve Riesling ★★★☆ £D

Riesling Botrytis ★★★ £C

Riesling ★★★ £C

Sémillon ★★★ £C

Pinot Gris ★★☆ £C

Annie's Lane (Clare Valley) *www.annieslane.com.au*

This Clare Valley range of wines is one of the best of the many in the former BERINGER BLASS Australian stable now owned by Treasury Wine Estates (formerly known as Fosters). Named after Annie Wayman, a local personality in the late 19th/early 20th century, the wines were previously made at the historic Quelltaler winery but are now made at the impressive Wolf BLASS facilities in the Barossa. The wines glow with fruit and are full and ripe with good balance and varietal expression. As might be expected for Clare Valley, Riesling and Shiraz particularly shine, as does Shiraz/Grenache/Mourvèdre blend that contains around 50% Shiraz. The premium Copper Trail Shiraz is made in open fermenters from unirrigated vines with part of the wine receiving an extended maceration prior to two years' ageing in mostly French oak barrels. The Riesling, the best value of the lot, harnesses lovely Clare Valley fruit which is checked by good acidity but like all the whites should be drunk young. Reds are better with 3 years' ageing or more but will keep considerably longer.

Recommended Reds:

Shiraz CopperTrail ★★★ £E

Shiraz ★★☆ £C

Shiraz/Grenache/Mourvèdre ★★★ £C

Cabernet/Merlot ★★ £C

Recommended Whites:

Riesling ★★ £B   Chardonnay ★ £B

Sémillon Sauvignon ★ £B

Ashton Hills (Adelaide Hills) *www.adhills.com.au*

Stephen George is a winemaker of considerable talent, especially given the diverse range of wines he produces to a such high standard. To be equally at home producing fine sparkling wines as cool Adelaide Hills Riesling, Pinot Noir and Chardonnay or rich powerfuls reds from the Clare Valley, as he is in forging the GALAH wines and making wines at WENDOUREE, is remarkable. The small estate-based 3.5 ha Ashton Hills is known first and foremost for two refined yet ripely fruity sparkling wines. The pale pink Salmon Brut is threequarters Chardonnay yet its strawberry and delicate biscuity flavours owe as much to the balance of Pinot Noir. An intense Riesling has a structure that puts it with the best from Eden Valley, Clare or Adelaide Hills. Pinot Noir (occasionally made as a Reserve) shows great fruit intensity, and increasingly a texture and breadth uncommon to most Australian examples. Chardonnay, too, shows off the potential of the Adelaide Hills.

Recommended Reds:

Pinot Noir ★★★ £D

Recommended Whites:

Riesling ★★★☆ £C

Chardonnay ★★★ £D

Blanc de Blancs ★★ £C

Recommended Rosés:

Salmon Brut ★★★ £D

✿ Balnaves (Coonawarra) *www.balnaves.com.au*

The winning combination of Doug Balnaves fruit and Peter Bissell's winemaking has propelled this 52-ha estate near the southern end of Coonawarra into the top echelon of Coonawarra producers. The flagship is The Tally, a big, powerful, oaky Cabernet Sauvignon that needs at least 5–8 years' ageing. Cabernet Sauvignon is also in a powerful mould with good breadth and style as well as intensity – a really good expression of Coonawarra fruit. Ripe, concentrated Shiraz can be at least as good. At a more affordable level, The Blend (typicallyMerlot/Cabernet Franc/Cabernet Sauvignon) and Cabernet Sauvignon/Merlot, are both ripe, round and pleasurable drinking if nothing more. This being Coonawarra there isn't much white but a Chardonnay with delicious fruit and well-worked oak is amongst the better examples from the Limestone Coast. A sweetish Sparkling Cabernet is a decent example of its type. Doug Balnaves and son Peter also manage vineyards and make wines for others in the district.

Recommended Reds:

The Tally ★★★★☆ £G

Cabernet Sauvignon ★★★★ £D

Shiraz ★★★☆ £D

Sparkling Cabernet ★★ £D

The Blend ★★ £C

Cabernet Sauvignon/Merlot ★★ £C

Recommended Whites:

Chardonnay ★★☆ £C

Barossa Valley Estate (Barossa Valley) *www.bve.com.au*

Established as a co-op (rare in Australia) by around 80 local growers in 1985, BVE is now 50% owned by HardyWine Company (ConstellationWines owned) and 50% by Barosssa Growers Holdings Ltd. The estate includes some of the best parcels of very old Shiraz vines in the Barossa. The pricey flagship E & E Black Pepper Shiraz is an explosively rich, powerful but balanced expression of old-vine Barossa fruit, full of preserved black fruits, prunes, licorice and tar and with great length too. Ebenezer Shiraz is full of berry fruit and American oak and is a good classic expression of the style. Entourage Cabernet is made in a similarly full-flavoured style. Under winemaker Stuart Bourne, Ebenezer Chardonnay has been dropped, though BVE still makes a Chardonnay under the new EMinor entry level range (£C) which includes a Shiraz and CabernetMerlot. The slightly more concentrated Barossa Valley Estate range also (£C) includes a Shiraz, Shiraz Tempranillo and Eden Valley Riesling.

Recommended Reds:

Shiraz E & E Black Pepper ★★★★ £G

Shiraz Ebenezer ★★★ £E

Cabernet Sauvignon/Merlot Entourage ★★ £C

Barratt Wines (Adelaide Hills) *www.barrattwines.com.au*

One of the Adelaide Hills' small gems directed by Lindsay Barratt. The Barratts now have their own winemaking facility at Lobethal and from just 8.9 ha in two different vineyards (Uley and Bonython) they highlight the region's affinity for Pinot Noir and Chardonnay. Since 2001 Pinot Noir production has been divided between a single-vineyard Bonython version and a superior Reserve. All the grapes are hand-picked and a portion of the fruit is fermented as

whole bunches, around 40% in the case of the Reserve. While the wines are quite powerful, they avoid being heavy – the alcohol being kept in check by the richly textured fruit. Chardonnay will keep for at least 5 years, Reserve Pinot even longer. Merlot is, like the Pinots, fermented in open fermenters and aged in French oak (part of it new). 2002 was the first vintage of an unwooded Sauvignon and the first from which the Pinots have been bottled unfiltered. The range now includes a Picadilly Sunrise, a Pinot Noir rosé (not tasted).

Recommended Reds:
Pinot Noir Reserve ★★★ £E
Pinot Noir Bonython ★★ £C
Recommended Whites:
Chardonnay Piccadilly Valley ★★★ £E
Sauvignon Blanc Piccadilly Valley ★★ £C

✿ Jim Barry (ClareValley) *www.jimbarry.com*
From a large number of some of Clare's best sites Peter and Mark Barry continue to build on what their father made famous over four decades, but whether the wines will now show more individuality or refinement remains to be seen. Reds are the mainstay: deep, impressively rich and concentrated if relatively unsubtle are Shiraz McRae Wood and Cabernet Sauvignon First Eleven. A premium Cabernet Benbournie is also made. However, it is for The Armagh that Jim Barry is best known. Considered one of the region's super-reds, it is an uncompromisingly big, thick, extracted and oaky Shiraz with a long track record dating back to 1985. It is made from very old, unirrigated vines and nearly always achieves the balance that some mega-Shirazes lack but must be kept for a minimum of a decade. Riesling is sourced from the Florita vineyard (in Watervale), first made famous by Leo Buring. Lodge Hill is toasty, limy and flavoursome with moderate structure but 'The Florita' has much greater expression, density and structure and is now recognized as one of the region's leading examples. Watervale Riesling (only available in Australia) shows good typicity and represents good value for money. Production is a substantial 60,000 cases, though much of that is accounted for by more ordinary reds and whites.
Recommended Reds:
Shiraz The Armagh ★★★★★ £H
Shiraz McCrae Wood ★★★★ £E
Shiraz Lodge Hill ★★☆£C
Cabernet Sauvignon McCrae Wood ★★★☆ £D
Cabernet/Malbec McCrae Wood ★★★☆ £D
Recommended Whites:
Riesling The Florita ★★★★ £D
Riesling Lodge Hill ★★ £B

Rolf Binder (Barossa Valley) *www.rolfbinder.com*
Rolf Binder and his sister Christa Deans draw upon mostly estate vineyards for an annual production of around 35,000 cases. The reds have returned to form with greater oomph and richness on the back of a succession of great vintages. They are deep, powerful, extracted wines, primarily from Rhône varieties, but there's animation too. The most acclaimed wines to date are the Heysen Vineyard and Hanisch Shirazes, the former combining an intense, preserved black fruits, earth and licorice character with a powerful structure and requiring at least 8–10 years' age to show its full potential. A Shiraz/Mataro Pressings (subtitled Binder's Bull's Blood) has rich black plum and berry fruit, while Heinrich is a more backward, extracted Shiraz/Mataro/ Grenache blend. Halcyon Cabernet Sauvignon/Merlot (usually 70% Cabernet) has intense brambly, cassis fruit and

ripe tannins to match. One that doesn't need cellaring is a more forward, supple, raspberryish Shiraz/Grenache under the Halliwell label. Two whites, Helios Sémillon and Highness Eden Valley Riesling are also made. The wines remain well priced despite the early hype. Inexpensive Retro 55 red and white are well-made. (SA)
Recommended Reds:
Shiraz Hanisch Vineyard ★★★★ £E
Shiraz Heysen Vineyard ★★★★ £E
Shiraz/Mataro/Grenache Heinrich ★★★★ £D
Shiraz/Mataro Pressings Hubris ★★★ £D
Cabernet Sauvignon/Merlot ★★★ £C
Shiraz/Grenache Halliwell ★★ £C
Shiraz Hales ★★ £B
Recommended Whites:
Riesling Highness★★★ £B
Sémillon Helios★★ £B

Wolf Blass (Barossa Valley) *www.wolfblass.com.au*
The Wolf Blass label is now one of the biggest brands in the Treasury Wine Estates portfolio of heavyweight Australian labels. As with any top brand the marketing success has been underscored by supreme consistency even if the wines no longer measure up to the personality and energy of the man who started it all. Of the more affordable ranges, Shiraz, Cabernet or blends of the two under the various red, yellow and Eaglehawk façades have been pretty uninspiring and, if showing some very recent improvement, they haven't been of the standard they were a decade or more ago. Whites are much improved though there is still better value to be had from elsewhere in Australia or further afield. At a higher price point, Grey Label reds offer a lot of upfront fruit and oak and adequate depth and structure. None of these labels however, should be confused with the wines near the top of the hierarchy where quality is much higher and the wines' origins are more discernible. Platinum Label Shiraz and Cabernet are based on single vineyards and aged in French oak, and finally deliver on depth, structure and balance, but platinum is also required to buy them. The wines with perhaps the most convincing price/quality ratio are the Gold Label range (an extension from an existing good-quality Gold Label Riesling). All (a vintage-dated sparkling Pinot Noir/Chardonnay excepted) are region-specific and do portray something of their origins. Lastly, the richly textured Black Label Cabernet Sauvignon/Shiraz (subjected to a delayed release) is consistently fine.
Recommended Reds:
Cabernet Sauvignon/Shiraz Black Label ★★★★ £F
Recommended Whites:
Riesling Gold Label Eden/Clare Valleys ★★ £C
Chardonnay Gold Label Adelaide Hills ★★ £C

Bleasdale (Langhorne Creek) *www.bleasdale.com.au*
Winemaker Michael Potts is fifth generation, making wines in a National Trust-classified winery and still utilising a lever press constructed in the 19th century. His family's vineyards are flooded annually by the Bremer River. All the wines show an accentuated varietal character and lots of flavour intensity. While most still want for a little more definition and structure this is not the case with Frank Potts, a savoury, cedary Cabernet Sauvignon-based blend that includes Malbec and Petit Verdot, nor with a profound, complex Generations Shiraz (from a parcel of old vines) that is perhaps the essence of Langhorne Creek with its earth, eucalypt, plum and berry character. Petrel Reserve is another premium Shiraz, first produced in 1999. Sweet, berryish Sparkling Shiraz lacks poise but has smooth

Australia

tannins. For white wines, cutting the concentrated, spicy fruit of the low yielding old vine Verdelho with a dash of Sauvignon Blanc brings crispness, if at the expense of a bit of character. It is now labelled Potts' Catch.

Recommended Reds:
Shiraz Generations ★★★★ £E
Shiraz Bremerview ★★★ £C
Frank Potts ★★ £C
Cabernet Sauvignon Mulberry Tree ★★ £B
Shiraz/Cabernet The Broad-Side ★★ £B
Sparkling Shiraz ★★ £B
Recommended Whites:
Verdelho Potts Catch ★★ £B

⚙ **Bowen Estate (Coonawarra)** www.bowenestate.com.au
Doug Bowen's smallish 33 ha estate continues to maintain a relatively low profile among the Coonawarra giants, though the wines are widely exported. The reds are of consistently high quality: deep, fleshy and textured with very ripe flavours and a certain idiosyncratic style. The grapes are picked very late and a good dose of oak ensures the wines have a sweet succulence particularly in the warmer years. Perhaps surprisingly for Coonawarra, Shiraz is even better than the Cabernet Sauvignon. The Blend is composed of Cabernet Sauvignon, Merlot and Cabernet Franc. A ripe and creamy Chardonnay is also made while Ampelon is a new single-vineyard Shiraz.

Recommended Reds:
Shiraz ★★★★ £D
Cabernet Sauvignon ★★★★ £D
The Blend ★★★☆ £D
Recommended Whites:
Chardonnay ★★☆ £D

Bremerton (Langhorne Creek) www.bremerton.com.au
Sisters Rebecca and Lucy Willson now run this large Langhorne Creek winery. The first vines were only planted in 1991 after the property was purchased by their parents in 1985 and most of the grapes come from their own 120 ha of vineyards. The best wines are the top reds, especially the Old Adam Limited Release Shiraz, which is aged in 100% new American oak and shows an oaky, vanilla and ripe black fruits style that is very concentrated, deep and intense – an old-style blockbuster but with fine structure and lots of character. Walter's Cabernet Sauvignon (100% new French oak) is in a similar very ripe-fruited mould but doesn't have quite the same depth or definition. Selkirk Shiraz is more earthy and jammy than Old Adam but has good concentration and depth, while Tamblyn is a blend of Cabernet Sauvignon, Shiraz, Malbec and Merlot that has plenty of fruit, if also a cooler leafy component, and light tannins. Of the whites, Verdelho with spiced citrus fruit and really good weight and structure stands out. Sauvignon Blanc is attractive if drunk young.

Recommended Reds:
Shiraz Old Adam ★★★★ £D   Shiraz Selkirk ★★★ £C
Cabernet Sauvignon Walter's Reserve ★★★ £D
Tamblyn ★★ £C
Recommended Whites:
Verdelho ★★ £C

⚙ **Grant Burge (Barossa Valley)** www.grantburgewines.com.au
Grant Burge has an impressive resource of 200 ha from which to make top Barossa wines. Nearly all are now prefixed with a vineyard name and are made in the recently reacquired old Krondorf winery.

Shiraz is naturally the strongest hand, starting with a sweet-fruited Miamba, progressing to a fuller, richer, oaky but characterful Filsell, and, from the same vineyard, Meschach, a pricey but powerful, super-stylish classic American-oaked Barossa Shiraz from 80-year-old vines that is more than a cut above the rest. Balthasar, a Shiraz Viognier, is made from mostly Eden Valley fruit in a more seductive, velvety style. The Cabernet equivalent to Meschach is Shadrach. a deep, rich and intense red, immersed in heather and blackcurrant and aged in French oak. Some early efforts of both wines lacked balance but this is not true of recent releases. Holy Trinity, composed of Grenache, Shiraz and Mourvèdre (40/40/20), mercifully is more modestly priced and is developing into an increasingly complex red; new French oak and an extended maceration on the skins are now employed to good effect. Two whites are oaky and flavoursome, a Summers Chardonnay surpassed by Zerk Sémillon Viognier. Other good whites include Thorn Riesling, Kraft Sauvignon and late-picked Lily Farm Muscat. Barossa Vines is a decent second label for varietal Shiraz, Sémillon and Chardonnay. Good sparkling and fortified wines are also made; the 20-year-old Tawny is particularly powerful, plump and appealing.

Recommended Reds:
Shiraz Meschach ★★★★★ £G
Shiraz Filsell Barossa ★★★★ £E
Shiraz Miamba Barossa ★★ £B
Cabernet Sauvignon Shadrach ★★★★ £E
Cabernet Sauvignon Cameron Vale ★★ £D
Merlot Hillcot Barossa ★ £C   Holy Trinity ★★★☆ £E
Tawny 20 Year-old ★★★☆ £E
Recommended Whites:
Sémillon Viognier Zerk★★ £C
Chardonnay Summers Eden Valley★ £B
Riesling Thorn★ £B

Burge Family (Barossa Valley) www.burgefamily.com.au
Rick Burge makes classic oak-lined, rich, lush, sweet-fruited Barossa reds. The wines have lots of depth, extract and intensity as well as the varietal expression typical of each grape variety as they perform in the Barossa. The wines have highish alcohol (around 14.5 for most of the reds) but are well balanced, only occasionally showing an excess of oak. Two reds in particular stand out. The decent Olive Hill, which was roughly equal proportions of Shiraz, Grenache and Mourvèdre, is now Mourvèdre and Grenache. Better still is Draycott Shiraz, which has lovely depth and style with a lingering, sweet, fruit-intense finish. Rick Burge's Garnacha, mostly old-vine Grenache but also including a little Shiraz and Mourvèdre, has a sweet crushed berry fruit depth but can struggle to balance the high alcohol. Sémillon has plenty of rich Barossa citrus and herb character though is not for long keeping. Also made is G3, a premium blend of Grenache, Shiraz and Mourvèdre. The range is completed by an Olive Hill Riesling and two inexpensive blended reds, Clochemerle and 'A Nice Red'.

Recommended Reds:
Shiraz Draycott ★★★★ £E
Mourvèdre Grenache Olive Hill ★★★ £D
Grenache Garnacha ★★ £D
Recommended Whites:
Sémillon Olive Hill ★★ £D

Cascabel (McLaren Vale) www.cascabelwinery.com.au
This is still a very young operation, having only made wines since

the late 1990s, yet this experienced couple seem to have both the know-how and a clear idea of the sort of wines they wish to fashion. All the wines are characterised by bright, pure fruit and definite restraint in terms of alcohol and oak. Round, soft and agreeable, they are not without substance and are always fruit rich on the finish. Only relatively small quantities are made of each wine, with the range varying and new wines added. 'Grenache et al' (85% Grenache) includes Shiraz and Mourvèdre. Shiraz has the usual fruit accent but is also individual with a distinctive smoke and heather character as well as real weight and depth. The style of most of the wines means that they can be drunk quite young. However also interesting are Tempranillo/Graciano (70/30) with very ripe berry fruit character and real intensity. A varietal Mourvèdre (here given its Spanish name, Monastrell) has strongly varietal black fruits appeal. Among current releases are reds Tempranillo El Sendero (£D) and a Rhône blend Tipico (£D) as well as the white Couloir Roussanne (£C)..

Recommended Reds:
Shiraz Fleurieu ★★★£D
Tempranillo/Graciano ★★ £D
Monastrell ★★ £D
Grenache et al ★★ £C
Recommended Whites:
Riesling Eden Valley ★★ £C

Chain of Ponds (Adelaide Hills) *www.chainofponds.com.au*
Established only in 1993 by the Amadio family, this is a relatively small producer and with originally among Adelaide Hills most sizeable vineyards (200 ha). However, there are now a series of grower contracts and the winery is looking into establishing a new cellar door facility in the the Adelaide Hills. The wines are currently vinified at Langhorne Creek. Quality has always been high, particularly for Corkscrew Road Chardonnay and the Amadeus Cabernet; the latter is remarkably profound and tightly furled when young, revealing a deep fruit core with at least 5 years' ageing. Top of the range The Cachet (not tasted), is a highly acclaimed Adelaide Hills blend of Cabernet, Shiraz and Merlot renowned for its generous style. Also from Adelaide Hills are Shirazes, Ledge and Graves Gate. Diva is a crisp, fresh green fruited sparkler. Zesty Sauvignon Blanc Black Thursday has a fine balance of gooseberry and citrus. Amelia's Letter Pinot Grigio has a well rounded creamy texture and a white fruits character. Innocence Rosé is a dry style with restrained berry fruits, 100% Pinot Noir. The extensive range also includes the excellent value-focused Novello label, Rosé is mainly Sangiovese with a little Pinot Noir, Sauvignon Blanc and Barbera. Dolcetto Shiraz and Pinot Gris are forward fruit driven styles. (DM)

Recommended Reds:
Cabernet Sauvignon Amadeus ★★★ £D
Pinot Noir Morning Star ★★★ £D
Shiraz Grave's Gate ★★★ £D
Shiraz Ledge ★★★ £D Novello Dolcetto Shiraz ★☆ £B
Recommended Whites:
Chardonnay Corkscrew Road ★★★ £D
Sauvignon Blanc Black Thursday ★★☆ £C
Diva NV (Chardonnay/Pinot Noir) ★★ £C
Amelia's Letter Pinot Grigio ★★ £C
Novello Pinot Gris ★☆ £B
Recommended Rosés:
Innocence Rosé ★★ £C
Novello Rosé ★☆ £B

Chapel Hill (McLaren Vale) *www.chapelhillwine.com.au*
Under winemaker Pam Dunsford, Chapel Hill, now Swiss-owned, built a solid reputation for consistent Cabernet and Shiraz. Her successor, Michael Fragos, has continued the good work. Quantity may be rising, but prices are not excessive for wines based on high-quality fruit from 44 ha of McLaren Vale vineyards. Medium-bodied Il Vescovo is a supple and attractive blend of Sangiovese and Cabernet Sauvignon. In line with current trends, it has been joined by Il Vescovo Pinot Grigio, Savagnin (originally labelled Albarino), Sangiovese and Tempranillo (not tasted). Shiraz is full and berryish. The Vicar, a blend of Cabernet and Shiraz in roughly equal proportions, is more ambitious and, shows greater refinement and balance as well as tremendous extract. Some of the Cabernet for both this and a varietal Cabernet Sauvignon comes from Coonawarra. Gorge Block Chardonnay from the estate (not tasted) has received critical acclaim for its structure and represents a quantum leap from the previous reserve Chardonnay. An unwooded Chardonnay is less appealing than a tasty, lipsmacking Verdelho. (SA)

Recommended Reds:
The Vicar ★★★★ £E
Shiraz ★★★☆ £C
Il Vescovo ★★ £C
Cabernet Sauvignon ★★★☆£C
Recommended Whites:
Verdelho ★★ £B

⊛⊛ **Clarendon Hills (McLaren Vale)** *www.clarendonhills.com.au*
If you've drunk Astralis then either you or your friends are not short of money. Bratasiuk's unfiltered and unfined, ripe, extracted reds, aged in French oak, are subjected to a long *cuvaison* and exhibit a depth and dimension that most Australian reds don't even approach. Some early vintages had questionable balance and marginal levels of volatility but all is being mastered and refined as the range expands and gains better definition through the use of vineyard or sub-regional names. With no less than 19 single vineyard single varietal wines, Bratasiuk, though not the first to do so, is providing an alternative to the brand-name-only marketeers who reveal precious little about their sources (likewise yields), even at a premium level. Reds, particularly Shiraz (labelled Syrah) and Grenache are powerful, broadly structured as well as very concentrated, marvellously complex and long in the best bottlings. All the names refer to a specific vineyard or vineyards located in three sub-zones of McLaren Vale, Clarendon, Blewitt Springs and Kangarilla. Other wines (not tasted) include Brookman Merlot, Onkaparinga Syrah and Grenache, Hickenbottom Grenache and Liandra Mourvèdre. A new vineyard planted high in the Clarendon Hills promises further exciting developments producing a new premium Syrah, Domaine Clarendon while Mourvèdre now comes from Liandra and Merlot from the Brookman Vineyard.

Recommended Reds:
Syrah Astralis ⊛⊛⊛⊛⊛ £H
Syrah Piggot Range ★★★★★ £H
Syrah Brookman ★★★★☆ £G
Syrah Hickinbotham ★★★★☆ £G
Syrah Liandra ★★★★☆ £G
Syrah Moritz ★★★★ £F
Grenache Romas ★★★★☆ £F
Grenache Blewitt Springs ★★★★ £F
Grenache Clarendon ★★★★ £F
Grenache Kangarilla ★★★★ £F
Cabernet Sauvignon Hickinbotham ★★★★☆ £F

South Australia

Cabernet Sauvignon Brookman ★★★★ £F
Cabernet Sauvignon Sandown ★★★☆ £F

Coriole (McLaren Vale) www.coriole.com

Coriole, now with 33 ha of vineyards in the Seaview region, has been known for its intense Shiraz almost since its inception in 1967, having inherited some already old vines and planted new ones which now have a few years behind them too. The wine is consistently richly textured with deep, ripe fruit and has been particularly good in recent vintages. The Soloist is an earthy, characterful single vineyard Shiraz with intense, spicy liquorice. The very complete, stylish Lloyd Reserve Shiraz, made only in very small quantities, is the premium version, with a long-established track record and more structure and oak (French instead of American from 2002) than the regular version. The powerful, minty, spicy, eucalypt Mary Kathleen is from Cabernet Sauvignon and Merlot but hasn't the same depth or class. Both require patience. Coriole is also known for its Sangiovese, which it pioneered in Australia with its first plantings in 1985. Coriole now makes three straight Sangiovese wines, Vita Reserve (in outstanding years only - 1998 and 2007 thus far), a new single clone Sangiovese, Brunello and the estate Sangiovese. The latter shows good varietal character flavourwise – cherryish with a savoury, earthy undertow (Vita Reserve and Brunello not tasted). There is also a fleshier, more sweet-fruited Sangiovese Shiraz in the entry level classic range. Other Italian varieties such as Fiano, Barbera and Nebbiolo have followed. The Fiano is increasingly textured with persistent underlying lemony acidity. Sagrantino is the most recent addition with Coriole's first vintage from 2007 (not tasted) just released to critical acclaim. Nero d'Avola and Prosecco will come into production shortly. The Dancing Fig Shiraz Mourvèdre is dark, intense and meaty. Among the whites, as well as the Fiano, a decent fruity Australian Chenin Blanc a Sémillon/Sauvignon Blanc and a single vineyard Chenin, the Optimist are also made.

Recommended Reds:
Shiraz Lloyd Reserve ★★★★☆ £F
Shiraz The Soloist ★★★ £E   Shiraz ★★★ £D
Shiraz Mourvèdre The Dancing Fig ★★☆ £C
Cabernet/Merlot Mary Kathleen Reserve ★★★☆ £E
Sangiovese ★★☆ £C
Recommended Whites:
Fiano ★☆ £C

Crabtree (Clare Valley) www.crabtreewines.com.au

Crabtree of Watervale is a small Clare operation with its own vineyards. Since 2007, it has been owned by Richard Woods & Rasa Fabian who brought in talented ex-Leasingham winemaker Kerri Thompson (who now has her own label KT & The Falcon). Some of the vines for the Riesling date from the 60s and yields are low resulting in a tight, minerally but scented Riesling that has both concentration and good balance. Shiraz from the Picnic Hill vineyard has a deep black plum, blackberry intensity with a spice and mineral complexity. Cabernet Sauvignon can show a cooler, more herbal aspect but is similarly well made. Newish Tempranillo has a slightly firm edge to the extract but shows good potential. Zibibbo is a light dry Muscat (named for the version grown on the island of Pantelleria, south of Sicily). Whites will keep and improve and although most reds need 3–5 years' but Shiraz should be given 6-8 years'.

Recommended Reds:
Shiraz Picnic Hill Vineyard ★★★☆ £C

Cabernet Sauvignon Windmill Vineyard ★★★ £C
Tempranillo Watervale ★★☆ £C
Recommended Whites:
Riesling Watervale ★★★ £C

D'Arenberg (McLaren Vale) www.darenberg.com.au

Jazzed up in the late nineties, this is a much trumpeted and sizeable producer with a seemingly ever-expanding range totalling 180,000 cases per year. Nearly all the wines are good but only a handful are really exciting; some are a little overhyped. The myriad exotic names don't make this an easy range to negotiate but they surely help with sales. The best reds have exuberant fruit and highish alcohol levels (and plenty of oak to help them on their way), making for enjoyable youthful drinking, but with enough structure to stand a bit of age. Recent vintages are more refined and lifted thanks to earlier picked fruit, more ruthless selection, less oak and less racking (to keep the fruit). Additionally, Chief Winemaker Chester Osborn attributes a greater minerality to not fertilising in the last 15 years. The best of the premium wines is the Dead Arm Shiraz, with super fruit, excellent concentration, lots of extract and intensity but balanced if needing time; best with 8-10 years' age. Footbolt is very easy to appreciate but faces stiff competition as South Australia has an abundance of fine Shiraz at this level, some with better texture and more depth. The powerful Ironstone Pressings (Grenache, Shiraz, Mourvèdre - 70/25/5) is recently very good, concentrated yet expressive - oozing depth and character. Bonzai Vine offers the same blend at a more affordable price but deserves a little patience. At a similar level to the Ironstone Pressings is the distinctive and characterful Coppermine Road Cabernet Sauvignon with an olive, black plum, spice and fig intensity. Sweet-fruited Custodian Grenache often shows some extraordinary flavours if at the cost of elegance and harmony. Another from the Derelict Vineyard is from late-harvested fruit. Varietal Mourvèdre seems more effortless with better depth and structure. Gutsy Galvo Garage is a blend of both Cabernets, Merlot and Petit Verdot from Southern Fleurieu. More unusual is an intense, spicy and concentrated Sticks & Stones which combines Tempranillo, Grenache and Souzao. Whites, from grapes only planted in 1995, are fruit-driven if sometimes a little coarse and lack the structure for long keeping. Riesling, Sémillon and Gewürztraminer have been made in a rich late-harvested style with some success. The Stump Jump red and white are forward, fruity gluggers. Lucky Lizard Chardonnay and Feral Fox Pinot Noir incorporate fruit from the Adelaide Hills. New kids on the block include The Cenosilicaphobic Cat (Sagrantino/Cinsault), and The Wild Pixie (Shiraz/Roussanne). A sparkling Chambourcin called Peppermint Paddock and a fortified Shiraz are also made.

Recommended Reds:
Shiraz Dead Arm ★★★★★ £E
Shiraz Footbolt ★★★ £C
Shiraz/Viognier Laughing Magpie ★★ £D
Shiraz/Grenache D'Arry's Original ★★ £C
Grenache/Shiraz/Mourvèdre Ironstone Pressings ★★★★ £E
Cabernet Sauvignon Coppermine Road ★★★★ £E
Cabernet Sauvignon High Trellis ★ £C
Mourvèdre Twenty-Eight Road ★★★ £D
Grenache Custodian ★★ £C
Grenache Derelict Vineyard ★★£D
Sticks & Stones ★★★ £C
Galvo Garage ★★ £C
Recommended Whites:
Roussanne Money Spider ★★ £C

Viognier Last Ditch ★★ £C
Sauvignon Broken Fishplate ★ £C
Riesling Dry Dam ★£B
Chardonnay Olive Grove ★ £B
Marsanne/Viognier Hermit Crab ★ £B

◉ Dutschke (Barossa Valley) *www.dutschkewines.com*
Shiraz is the thrust of this operation for wines made by Wayne
Dutschke from vines belonging to his uncle, Ken Semmler. St Jakobi,
with an almost coconutty American-oak influence (60%), displays
a deep fruit succulence and plenty of extract. Although oaky it
has depth and character and deserves to be judged with 5 years'
bottle age or more. By contrast, Oscar Semmler, the top *cuvée*, is
aged in 100% French oak. It is marvellously profound with terrific
potential if cellared for at least 5–8 years. While not cheap, quality is
commensurate with price. Willowbend (a second label), Chardonnay
both still and sparkling, Merlot, Cabernet and Shiraz/Merlot/
Cabernet are enthusiastically consumed locally. Some fortified wines
are also made to a high standard.
Recommended Reds:
Shiraz Oscar Semmler ★★★★★ £E
Shiraz St Jakobi ★★★★★ £E

◉ John Duval (Barossa Valley) *www.johnduvalwines.com*
After 29 years at PENFOLDS, during which time he was Chief Wine
Maker for 16 years, John Duval struck out on his own in 2003.
Unsurprisingly for the man who made Grange for many years,
old vine Barossa Valley Shiraz is at the heart of what he does.
However, Duval is not seeking to recreate the powerful, muscular
style of Grange. Rather, his source of inspiration is Penfolds RWT
Barossa Valley Shiraz, a wine which he was instrumental in creating
because he wanted to realise the Barossa's potential to produce
elegant Shiraz using French oak. Grapes are sourced from pockets
of excellence across the Barossa. The wines are long and layered,
characterised by fleshy berry fruit of terrific purity supported by ripe,
polished tannins. Plexus shows the characteristic red cherry notes
of Grenache, but the style is more restrained and pleasingly drier in
perception than is typical for the Barossa. Though rich and involving,
Entity Shiraz shows a light hand in terms of oak and extraction.
Flagship Eligo is more iron fist in velvet glove, showing denser layers
of fruit well met by powerful but ripe tannins. A white Plexus is also
made from a blend of Marsanne, Roussanne and Viognier. (SA)
Recommended Reds:
Eligo Shiraz Barossa Valley ★★★★☆ £F
Entity Shiraz Barossa Valley ★★★★ £E
Plexus (Shiraz/Grenache/Mourvèdre) Barossa Valley ★★★☆ £D

Elderton (Barossa Valley) *www.eldertonwines.com.au*
An unashamedly oaky, full-throttle style has earned this winery a
devoted following. The wines are not to everyone's taste but the
best examples have a rich fruit core as they are based on old-vine
Barossa Valley fruit. The estate is small in Australian terms with less
than 30ha of vineyards, together with a more recently acquired 16
ha in Eden Valley. Another recent development is biodynamic trials
and the environmental credentials are underlined by the winery's
carbon neutral status . American oak has been traditionally favoured,
the oak once found in nearly all South Australian wineries, which
adds intense vanilla, spice, even coconut flavours to the wines. The
most successful and sought after wine is the Command Shiraz. It is
very singular and concentrated, the essence of fruit and oak, usually
still a baby even with 5-10 years' age. The equivalent Cabernet

Sauvignon, the single vineyard Ashmead with rich fruit is aged only
in French oak - as is Merlot. Estate Shiraz and Cabernet Sauvignon
are opulent with good fruit intensity. Ode to Lorraine (CSM has been
renamed after co-founder Lorraine Ashmead) is not a Rhône blend
but what is now an unusual blend of Cabernet Sauvignon, Shiraz
and Merlot. Similarly, with effect from the 2008 Vintage, co-founder
Neil Ashmead is honoured with Neil Ashmead GTS (Grand Tourer
Shiraz), a limited production wine from a biodynamic trial block
which is aged in 100% new French oak barrels on gross lees (not
tasted). Riesling and Chardonnay are also made and offer plenty
of upfront flavour if not much else and are best drunk with just a
couple of years' age (Eden Valley Chardonnay has not been tasted).
An intensely flavoured dessert wine, Botrytis Sémillon (or Golden
Sémillon), is made from Riverina fruit, while the E Series Shiraz/
Cabernet is a flavoursome budget red from wider origins. (SA)
Recommended Reds:
Shiraz Command ★★★★ £F
Shiraz ★★☆ £D
Cabernet Sauvignon Ashmead Single Vineyard ★★★☆ £F
Cabernet Shiraz Merlot Ode to Lorraine ★★ £E
Cabernet Sauvignon ★★☆ £D
Merlot ★★☆ £D

Ralph Fowler (Mount Benson) *www.ralphfowlerwines.com.au*
Established in the up-and-coming coastal area of Mount Benson
in 1999. The 40 ha of estate vineyards include Merlot, Shiraz
and Viognier. Ralph Fowler (of diverse Australian winemaking
experience) currently makes Shiraz from a blend of Mount Benson
and Coonawarra fruit. The wine shows good fleshy texture, depth
and definition. The winemaking has been entrusted to Sarah Squires
since 2005. Merlot, and Viognier are also made as well as a Shiraz
Viognier blend and the Sticky from Viognier and Sauvignon Blanc.
Recommended Reds:
Shiraz Limestone Coast ★★★☆ £D

Fox Creek (McLaren Vale) *www.foxcreekwines.com*
This young but already much acclaimed McLaren Vale operation
is based on vineyards established by the Watt family in 1985.
Since 1995 Fox Creek has made rich, ripe and succulent reds with
a measure of (mostly) American oak, sometimes lacking finesse
and real style. The first wines were made by Sparky Marquis of
Mollydooker but are now made by Scott Zrna. Reserve Shiraz is
the leading red and more than any other displays the potency and
character of McLaren Vale. Though the varieties are different, there
is also classic expression in a more forward but ripe and stylish JSM
Shiraz/Cabernet Franc (and a little Cabernet Sauvignon). Reserve
Cabernet is rich and earthy with a firm finish. Other reds are less
exciting. Merlot and a new Cabernet/Merlot, Duet, show adequate
balance and ripeness but lack style and definition. Vixen is a well-
balanced if not first-division example of a sparkling Shiraz-based red
(but includes both Cabernets). The pick of the whites is a Verdelho
with an intense, flavoursome varietal character. Sauvignon Blanc
and Sémillon/Sauvignon Blanc have delicious ripe tropical fruit and
citrus flavours but need to be drunk very young.
Recommended Reds:
Shiraz Reserve ★★★★ £F
Shiraz Short Row ★★ £C
Shiraz/Cabernet Franc JSM ★★★ £C
Sparkling Shiraz/Cabernet Franc Vixen ★★ £C
Cabernet Sauvignon Reserve ★★ £D
Merlot Reserve ★ £D

Australia

Recommended Whites:

Chardonnay ★ £B
Verdelho ★★ £B
Sémillon/Sauvignon Blanc ★ £B
Sauvignon Blanc ★ £B

🌿 **Gemtree (McLaren Vale)** *www.gemtreewines.com*

The Buttery family have more than 130 ha of vines and have been grape growers since 1980 if only producing their own range of wines since 1998. A 10 ha wetlands project was also initiated in the same year. Since 2008, the entire estate has been farmed biodynamically by viticulturalist Melissa Buttery whose winemaker husband Mike Brown uses open-fermenters and a hands-off approach to vinification. Brown is not afraid to experiment and the style (and portfolio) is evolving beyond richly-textured, expressive fruit-accented reds also to encompass wines of exciting vibrancy. A case in point is White Lees Shiraz, aged on Chardonnay lees which Brown has discovered increases the total acidity. Tatty Road is a Cabernet-based Bordeaux blend with a substantial proportion of Petit Verdot. Bloodstone Shiraz oozes flavour and complexity while Bloodstone Tempranillo (now called Luna Roja) shows more sinewy, savoury tannins. Perhaps the most striking wine is the Uncut Shiraz with pristine McLaren fruit richness and depth. Obsidian Shiraz is still deeper and darker but more pricey too. For white, the Tatty Road Chardonnay is a flavoursome peach and melon fruited example for drinking fairly young. New from the 2005 vintage is The Phantom, a varietal Petit Verdot.

Recommended Reds:

Shiraz Obsidian ★★★★☆ £E
Shiraz White Lees Shiraz ★★★★ £D
Shiraz Uncut ★★★★ £D   Shiraz Bloodstone ★★★☆ £C
Tempranillo Luna Roja ★★★ £D
Tatty Road ★★★ £B

Recommended Whites:

Chardonnay Tatty Road ★★ £B

🌿 **Glaetzer (Barossa Valley)** *www.glaetzer.com*

Colin Glaetzer and his son (and winemaking whizz) Ben (also see MITOLO) have really lifted the quality of their own wines in recent vintages. Grapes come from unirrigated vineyards in the Ebenezer district of the Barossa Valley. The top wines are now very good indeed, not the blockbusters of old but more sophisticated, expressive wines with at least a suggestion of *terroir*. Tiny amounts are made of Amon-Ra, an unfiltered Shiraz produced from 100 year old vines and aged in French and American oak. Very concentrated and very intense, it has a fabulous fruit expression with plum, carob, blackberry and preserved black fruits but above all is very complete and very classy – best with at least 5-10 years age. More affordable are Bishop Shiraz and Wallace Shiraz/Grenache. These are supple and characterful with plenty of fruit, the latter almost like a Côtes du Rhône. Anaperenna, made since 04 and initially labelled Godolphin, is a Shiraz Cabernet Sauvignon blend (70/30) that is very ripe, concentrated and powerful, needing at least 6 years age.

Recommended Reds:

Amon-Ra Shiraz ★★★★★ £F
Anaperenna Shiraz Cabernet ★★★★★ £F
Bishop Shiraz ★★★ £D
Wallace Shiraz/Grenache ★★☆ £C

Greenock Creek (Barossa Valley) *www.greenockcreekwines.com.au*
The aim here is for very low yields from unirrigated plots. The

grapes are harvested very late, and the wines reveal unusual, almost exotic, ripe flavours and a preserved fruits character. The alcohol levels are high but the wines are balanced. For Shiraz, the Apricot Block is perhaps the most promising vineyard but is quite young; shortcomings in initial releases will be overcome with a little more age. The best wine (at least of those without a completely silly price) is the Seven Acre Shiraz. It has a particularly pronounced preserved fruits profile and reveals real power and intensity on the palate. Cornerstone Grenache (from old vines) and Cabernet Sauvignon usually also show what is possible from the best unirrigated vines. All the wines are expensive due to very low yields, the resultant meagre quantities and their cult status. Made in tiny quantities but sold for astronomical prices are Roennfeldt Road Cabernet Sauvignon and Shiraz.

Recommended Reds:

Shiraz Seven Acre ★★★★☆ £F
Shiraz Apricot Block ★★★★ £G
Grenache Cornerstone ★★★★ £F
Cabernet Sauvignon ★★★☆ £F

🌿 **Grosset (Clare Valley)** *www.grosset.com.au*
Jeffrey Grosset is an Australian superstar and deserves to be as well-known as the country's many sporting greats (in some circles he is). Outstanding Riesling, Chardonnay and Gaia Bordeaux blend all show pristine fruit, wonderful symmetry and excellent concentration and have proven ageability. There are now three Rieslings. First, the fine, intense floral and lime Springvale Watervale (now made from 100% own fruit) is made in greater quantity though there is still not much of it; Polish Hill is tighter and characterised by minerals; starting out austere, it particularly benefits from ageing. Both deserve 5 years or more. New from the 2010 vintage is the Off-Dry Riesling. Like the Rieslings and Chardonnay, a pure understated Sémillon/ Sauvignon blend is one of the best Australian examples of its type. Drink young or with 5 years or more. The compelling Gaia, 75% Cabernet Sauvignon with the balance from Cabernet Franc and Merlot, impresses for its style, complexity and depth. It makes a stark contrast to some of the overoaked, alcoholic monsters made by others. Grosset produces a little Pinot Noir from two vineyards in the Adelaide Hills. It is increasingly refined with a velvety texture and good detail and dimension. All the wines are made in relatively small quantities and are reasonably priced for the quality.

Recommended Reds:

Gaia ★★★★ £F
Pinot Noir ★★★☆ £E

Recommended Whites:

Riesling Polish Hill ★★★★★ £E
Riesling Springvale ★★★★★ £D
Riesling Off-Dry ★★★☆ £D
Chardonnay Piccadilly ★★★★☆ £E
Sémillon/Sauvignon Blanc ★★★☆ £D

Richard Hamilton (McLaren Vale) *www.hamiltonwines.com*
Richard Hamilton's McLaren Vale operation shouldn't be confused with Hugh Hamilton, though the extensive family connections run back to one of South Australia's first winemakers. His winemaking team produces some intense, characterful McLaren Vale wines, even if in some years they have lacked balance. Centurion 100-Year-Old Vines Shiraz, Shiraz and Burton's Vineyard Old Bush Vine Grenache show good depth and weight, very ripe fruit and often a measure of mint, eucalyptus and gamey notes. A GSM blend Colton's has now been added with the 2012 vintage. Other wines include Hut

Wine behind the label

Block Cabernets, which has a percentage of Merlot and Cabernet Franc but a tendency to slightly underripe tannins, and Merlot Lot 148. Of the whites, the Almond Grove Chardonnay accentuates ripe melony flavours and oak but not at the expense of balance, while Slate Quarry Riesling is also made, somewhat surprisingly, from local McLaren Vale fruit. The Hamilton Wine Group also own LECONFIELD.
Recommended Reds:
Shiraz Centurion 100 Year Old Vines ★★★☆ £F
Shiraz ★★ £C
Grenache Burton's Vineyard ★★★ £D
Recommended Whites:
Chardonnay Almond Grove ★★ £B

Hardys (McLaren Vale) *www.hardys.com.au*
Hardys is one of the great names of Australian wine even if the premium Hardys wines are marginally less well-known than those of some of their rivals. The Eileen Hardy label is reserved for an outstanding Shiraz, a rich, powerful if occasionally slightly over-oaked Chardonnay and new in 2010, a deep fruited, velvety Pinot Noir. These are sourced from the company's best vineyards, which can extend as far as Tasmania for the Chardonnay and Western Australia for the Shiraz. Brawny, extracted Thomas Hardy Cabernet, made since 1989, is now sourced entirely from Coonawarra. It has terrific depth and can evolve into an equally impressive, if less consistent red. Without the cult status of these flagship wines, under the Tintara label a Shiraz and Cabernet Sauvignon are now released. Hardys sparkling wines show an extra degree of finesse and intensity over most Australian sparklers, as seen in the top two examples, the vintage-dated Sir James Vintage and premium Arras, both Tasmania and Yarra Valley-sourced Pinot Noir/Chardonnay blends. Of the cheaper, everyday brands Nottage Hill varietals are slightly more expensive than the Stamps of Australia dual-variety blends, but offer more than the price differential suggests. The Oomoo range, relaunched to celebrate Hardys' 150th anniversary in 2003, revives a 19th-century label, meaning good.
Recommended Reds:
Shiraz Eileen Hardy ★★★★★ £F
Pinot Noir Eileen Hardy ★★★☆ £F
Cabernet Sauvignon Thomas Hardy ★★★★ £F
Shiraz Oomoo ★★ £C
Recommended Whites:
Chardonnay Eileen Hardy ★★★ £E
Chardonnay Oomoo Hardy ★★ £C

Heartland (Langhorne Creek) *www. heartlandwines.com.au*
This joint venture draws in grapes from the Limestone Coast, McLaren Vale, Langhorne Creek and Barossa Valley, mostly from vineyards owned by the four partners who include winemaker Ben Glaetzer (GLAETZER) and viticulturalist Geoff Hardy (PERTARINGA). They manage to combine both quality and volume with the bonus of reasonable prices. Particularly impressive is the Limestone Coast-sourced Directors Cut Shiraz (with a Langhorne Creek component since 2003). Profound, intense and concentrated, this is a stylish and individual wine with a subtle cool streak running through it. Also good are Limestone Coast Shiraz and Cabernet Sauvignon. There's lots of fruit and character too in the unusual blends, white Pinot Gris with a dash of Viognier (originaly a Viognier/Pinot Gris, now labelled Pinot Gris) and red Dolcetto/Lagrein. Inexpensive Stickleback red and white are well made with good fruit.
Recommended Reds:
Shiraz Directors' Cut ★★★☆ £D

Shiraz Langhorne Creek/Limestone Coast ★★★ £C
Cabernet Sauvignon Langhorne Creek/Limestone Coast ★★☆ £C
Dolcetto/Lagrein Langhorne Creek ★★☆ £C
Stickleback Red ★☆ £B
Recommended Whites:
Pinot Gris Langhorne Creek ★★ £C
Stickleback White ★ £B

Heathvale (Eden Valley) *www. heathvale.com*
The Heathvale Vineyard has vinous roots going back to 1865 but its modern incarnation begins with the new planting begun by Trevor and Faye March in 1987. The first wines came 10 years later and there are now 10 ha split between Cabernet Sauvignon, Shiraz, Chardonnay and Riesling. A trained viticulturalist, Trevor March enlists the help of Ben Radford and Jim Irvine for intense, ripe, richly textured wines. From 2008, wines are made on site in the new winery. Shiraz is given a cold soak (pre-fermentation maceration) and aged in mostly French, mostly used oak. It is very distinctive with concentrated very ripe fruit and a hint of eucalyptus and smoke. Chardonnay is whole-bunch pressed but doesn't go through a malolactic fermentation although it does have extended ageing on lees (with *bâtonnage*). It has excellent fruit – ripe stone fruits and a tropical component – and good breadth and balance. Cabernet Sauvignon and Riesling will be added with further tastings.
Recommended Reds:
Shiraz Eden Valley ★★★ £E
Recommended Whites:
Chardonnay Eden Valley/Barossa ★★★ £D

>> Hemera (Barossa Valley) *www.teusner.com.au*
This property was originally known as Ross Estate Wines before it was purchased by Winston Wine in 2013. Significant further investment has gone into the project. The vast majority of the wines produced come solely from estate grown fruit across 45 ha and the vines are up to 100 years old in some plots. The property is in the southern stretches of the Barossa where there are cooler growing conditions and the rolling hills range from 200 to 250 metres altitude. Quite varied vine microclimate conditions are created. There are four distinct ranges and these include a number of wines under the Evolution label, which are for easy drinking and priced accordingly (£B). The Estate range is extensive, as well as the wines included below Merlot, Chardonnay, Semillon and a Sparkling Semillon Chardonnay are also available. The Estate Shiraz and Bordeaux styled reds are in a big and dark fruited style and just around a third new wood is used to provide balance. The stand out Estate reds are the Old Vine Grenache with very impressive and intense red and dark berry fruits and the darker, more structured GSM. The Limited Release Cabernet Franc is more restrained than the other Bordeaux reds here, with subtle black fruits although not the leafy element you might find in a top Loire example. The Lynedoch blend is a fuller style with blackberry and blackcurrant fruits and a rich texture it is aged in 50% new oak for 18 months but in hogsheads. Aurora Shiraz is the top of the tree among the Limited Release wines, in both price and quality. The fruit comes mainly from the Ebenezer sub region in the north of the Valley and is in a full throttle style with dense concentrated dark fruits and spice. Also released (not tasted) under the Limited Release banner are Block 3 A Shiraz (£F), 100 Year Grenache (£F), Marsanne (£C) and Semillon (£C). Tier 1 is the first of two Icon reds, a classic blend of Shiraz and Cabernet Sauvignon. It is first a selection of the best blocks and then a selection of the best barrels of the two varieties.

Dark berry fruits and plum are underpinned by creamy oak. There is the structure and tannin for a decades cellaring and development. The JDR Shiraz comes from the very best Shiraz blocks. Hemera Estate vineyards at Lyndoch are on a clay over limestone based soil and this is complimented by fruit from a neighbouring block grown on rocky, shallow loams. Dark and spicy, this is a really concentrated Shiraz, a wine of rich texture rather than fruit, somewhat in the style of Grange. (DM)

Recommended Reds:

JDR Shiraz ★★★★★ £G
Tier 1 Shiraz Cabernet Sauvignon ★★★★☆ £G
Limited Release Aurora Shiraz ★★★★ £F
Limited Release Cabernet Franc ★★★☆ £E
Limited Release Lynedoch ★★★☆ £E
Hemera Estate GSM ★★★☆ £D
Hemera Estate Old Vine Grenache ★★★☆ £D
Hemera Estate Cabernet Sauvigon ★★★ £D
Hemera Estate Shiraz ★★★ £D
Hemera Estate Right Bank ★★★ £D

Recommended Whites:

Hemera Estate Riesling ★★★ £C
Hemera Estate Basket Press Marsanne ★★☆ £C

Henry's Drive (Padthaway) *www.henrysdrive.com*
Mollydooker winemakers Sparky and Sarah Marquis have been succeeded by Renae Hirsch at this large Padthaway estate established in 1998. It is planted in the main to Cabernet Sauvignon and Shiraz but also to Chardonnay and Merlot. The Shiraz has a gravelly, toasty, spicy, berry fruit and is aged in new American oak. Reserve Shiraz was added in 1999 and is more full-on with more extract and structure. Definitely a producer to watch as this range continues to develop. A Sparkling Shiraz is also made and Pillar Box range, first produced in consultation with Chris RINGLAND in 2004, represents good bang for buck.

Recommended Reds:

Shiraz Reserve ★★★★ £F
Shiraz ★★★☆ £D

❀❀ Henschke (Eden Valley) *www.henschke.com.au*
In the mid-to-late 1980s many of these fabulous reds could be bought for a song but eventually the rest of the world got to taste them and this, added to the explosion in wine prices in the 90s, now usually means making do with something cheaper. Since 1979, Stephen Henschke has been fine-tuning these already well-established single-vineyard-based reds while his wife Prue has maintained and gradually renewed the existing vineyard resources. There are now 115 ha of estate vineyards recently converted to biodynamic regime; the largest segment (50 ha) in the Eden Valley. Carefully seasoned American oak is favoured and red wine fermentations are now finished in new oak. Fabulous fruit in a full, supple, lushly textured wine is the classic Henschke style, with additional depth and dimension in the top wines. The most celebrated, and necessarily expensive vineyard, the 8 ha Hill of Grace, includes a parcel of vines (Grandfathers Block) that date in part from the 1860s. A second label Hill of Roses also comes from the Hill of Grace vineyard. From close by, Mount Edelstone (the first to be bottled separately in 1952) is arguably more consistent, with more pepper and spice character, if missing the extra majesty of Hill of Grace. Cyril Henschke Cabernet, previously entirely Cabernet Sauvignon, now includes a little Merlot and Cabernet Franc and shows superb pure blackberry, cassis fruit and fine grained tannins.

The ageing potential of all three top reds is well proven. Abbott's Prayer is based on Merlot but supplemented by both Cabernets and sees only French oak. Like the recently introduced Grenache-dominated blend, Johann's Garden, it is almost immediately drinkable but has real depth and concentration too. Newish Henry's Seven is is a stylish blend of Shiraz, Grenache and Viognier. From a start in the early 1990s whites have steadily improved, particularly the intense, taut and concentrated (and ageworthy) Lenswood Croft Chardonnay and Eden Valley Louis Sémillon. There's good varietal intensity in Crane's Chardonnay, Julius Riesling and Joseph's Hill Gewürztraminer, all from Eden Valley fruit. A second Riesling, Green's Hill is sourced from the Adelaide Hills as is Littlehampton Pinot Gris (£D). Also made but not tasted are Sauvignon (Coralinga - £D) and Pinot Noir (Giles - £E). Tilly's Vineyard is a very gluggable blend of Sémillon, Chardonnay and Sauvignon.

Recommended Reds:

Shiraz Hill of Grace ⭕⭕⭕⭕⭕ £H
Shiraz Mount Edelstone ★★★★★ £F
Cabernet Cyril Henschke ★★★★☆ £F
Abbott's Prayer ★★★★ £F
Shiraz/Cabernet/Merlot Keyneton Euphonium ★★★☆ £E
Grenache/Mourvèdre/Shiraz Johann's Garden ★★★ £D
Henry's Seven★★★ £D

Recommended Whites:

Chardonnay Croft ★★★☆ £E
Chardonnay Crane's ★★★☆ £C
Sémillon Louis ★★★☆ £D Riesling Julius ★★★ £D
Riesling Green's Hill ★★☆ £C
Gewürztraminer Joseph's Hill ★★☆ £D

Hewitson *www.hewitson.com.au*
Dean Hewitson secured long-term contracts for fruit from some remarkable old vineyards in the Barossa, Eden Valley and McLaren Vale. As both a Roseworthy and UC Davis graduate, and with extensive winemaking experience both at PETALUMA and abroad, he also has the know-how to make an accomplished range of wines, especially now he has built a made-to-measure winery. Beyond an intense, powerfully flavoured if broad Riesling are five fine reds plus Private Cellar, a blend of "the best and most idiosyncratic from each vintage" (not tasted). Miss Harry Dry Grown & Ancient is from old-vine Barossa Grenache, Shiraz and Mourvèdre and is flavoursome, balanced and a very drinkable style. Two Shirazes provide a fascinating contrast: the fig, prune and black plum Barossa character of Ned & Henry's is a foil for the more ambitous and extracted McLaren Vale example with its mint, eucalypt and intense berry fruit depth. Good as these are, they are surpassed by a superb Mourvèdre from the Old Garden vineyard probably the oldest vineyard (planted 1853) of this variety in the world. There is a marvellous old-viney, pre-phylloxera earth, spice and black fruits complexity to this most individual wine. Fruit for spicy Baby Bush Mourvèdre, first made in 2006, is sourced from Old garden cuttings and readily reveals its heritage. Also made but not tasted is Mermaids Muscadelle, a rare dry varietal version of this grape.

Recommended Reds:

Shiraz Mad Hatter McLaren Vale ★★★☆ £F
Shiraz Ned & Henry's Barossa Valley ★★★ £D
Mourvèdre Old Garden Barossa Valley ★★★★ £E
Mourvèdre Baby Bush ★★★ £D
Miss Harry Dry Grown & Ancient ★★ £C

Recommended Whites:

Riesling Eden Valley Gun Metal ★★ £C

Hollick (Coonawarra) *www.hollick.com*

Now a first-rate producer that shows what Coonawarra is all about across a range of varieties. The Hollicks have 52ha of vineyards in Coonawarra and another 20 ha in the emerging Wrattonbully region – small amounts by Coonawarra standards. Ian Hollick oversees a diverse range of very well-made wines with good intensity and extra depth in a range of top (Icon) reds that add refinement and complexity with age. All three have a black label; Ravenswood comes from the best parcels of Cabernet Sauvignon, while Wilgha Shiraz and newish Neilson's Block Merlot are site-specific. Ravenswood shows good varietal definition and intelligent use of oak and becomes sleek and stylish with 5 years' age or more. The range also includes whites: Chardonnay, the barrel fermented Bond Road, and a Sauvignon Blanc/Savagnin/Sémillon the Savagnin included for the first time in 2010. Other reds include distinctive stylish (and good value) Pinot Noir, Shiraz/Cabernet Sauvignon (predominantly Shiraz), a Wrattonbully Shiraz (not tasted) and regular Coonawarra Cabernet Sauvignon. This last (around 20% Merlot) shows increased richness in the most recent vintages. From Wrattonbully, alternative varieties Tempranillo and Sangiovese, the latter blended with Cabernet and labelled "Hollaia", show promise. As well as an intensely berryish Sparkling Merlot, a Pinot Noir/Chardonnay sparkler is produced. An attractive, light sweet wine, The Nectar, is also produced and is composed of around 80% Riesling with the balance from Sauvignon Blanc and/or Sémillon.

Recommended Reds:
Cabernet Sauvignon Ravenswood ★★★★ £D
Cabernet Sauvignon Coonawarra ★★★☆ £C
Merlot Neilson's Block ★★★ £D   Shiraz Wilgha ★★★★ £E
Tempranillo Wrattonbully ★★★ £C
Sangiovese/Cabernet Sauvignon Hollaia Wrattonbully ★★☆ £C
Pinot Noir ★★★ £C   Sparkling Merlot ★★ £D
Recommended Whites:
Chardonnay Bond Road ★★★ £C
Sauvignon Blanc/Savagnin/Sémillon Coonawarra ★★ £C

Jacobs Creek/Orlando (Barossa Valley) *www.jacobscreek.com.au*

The success of a single brand, namely Jacob's Creek, seems to have swallowed the image of the parent company here. Internationally at least, once-premium Orlando labels are giving way to the expanding Jacob's Creek range. Riesling has long been a strength here and is well suited the house style, which aims for approachable but balanced varietal expressions. Other varieties that stand out in the classic entry level include the Cabernet Sauvignon, Shiraz Cabernet, Merlot and Tempranillo, the latter probably the best Australian version at this price point. Jacob's Creek Reserves are generally a significant improvement on the basics and 2010 sees the release of single region reserve wines which should deliver added personality. At the top of the tree is the Super Premium range. It comprises Johann Shiraz Cabernet, a well-structured, deeply concentrated multi regional blend, and two single region wines:St Hugo Cabernet Sauvignon from Coonawarra, a medium weight, savoury style and Steingarten Riesling from the Barossa – a complex and ageworthy Riesling with impressive minerality. Relatively inexpensive Jacob's Creek sparkling Chardonnay/Pinot Noir is also made and has recently been joined by a well made Blanc de Blancs. Also new is the Winemakers Collection range including a Shiraz red and rosé and a Chardonnay.

Recommended Reds:
Shiraz Jacob's Creek Reserve ★★ £B
Shiraz/Cabernet Jacob's Creek Johann ★★★☆ £F
Cabernet Sauvignon Jacob's Creek St Hugo ★★★ £E
Cabernet Sauvignon Jacob's Creek Reserve ★★ £B
Recommended Whites:
Riesling Steingarten ★★★☆ £C
Riesling Jacob's Creek Reserve ★★ £B
Chardonnay Jacob's Creek Reserve ★★ £B
Chardonnay Jacob's Creek Blanc de Blancs ★ £C

❀ Kalleske (Barossa Valley) *www.kalleske.com*

This is a relatively new Barossa enterprise but with a deep heritage of grape growing near Greenock. Troy Kalleske working with his brother Tony only made the first wines in 2004 (previously the grapes were sold to the likes of Penfolds) but has already made a huge impact with the quality of the wines. Certified organic, the nearly 50 ha of vineyard which is still worked by their father, John, has a high average vine age (nearly 60 years old). While Shiraz and Grenache dominate there is also a sprinkling of other varieties including Mourvèdre and even Tempranillo and Zinfandel. Already remarkably impressive is the Greenock Shiraz which is fermented in open-top fermenters and basket pressed prior to ageing in a combination of new French and American oak. Concentrated, elegant and old viney it exhibits fabulous style without being the least bit heavy. It is very reasonably priced for the quality. Also made is a tiny amount of Johann Georg Shiraz from vines the first of which were planted in 1875, an Old Vine Grenache which have not yet been tasted, Eduard Shiraz, Moppa Shiraz, all single vineyard wines. Clarry's is a moderately priced Grenache-based blend topped up with Shiraz (20%) which has splendid purity and expression. Other wines include Florentine Chenin Blanc and Rosina Rosé which will be added with further tastings. Finally, Pirathon is a Shiraz made from prime growers' fruit, all sourced from the North West of the Barossa, which the Kalleskes rate most highly.

Recommended Reds:
Shiraz Greenock Barossa Valley ★★★★★ £E
Shiraz Eduard Barossa Valley ★★★★ £F
Shiraz Pirathon Barossa Valley ★★★☆ £D
Clarry's Barossa Red GSM ★★★☆ £D

Katnook Estate (Coonawarra) *www.katnookestate.com.au*

As part of the Wingara Wine group (which also includes RIDDOCH and Deakin Estate), this Coonawarra stalwart was acquired the Cava giant FREIXENET in 2001. It continues to be directed, however, by Wayne Stehbens, who has made the wine in a 19th-century stone woolshed (used in the region's early vintages) for the past 20-odd years. Much of the grape production has been sold to others but Katnook's reds have been characterised by their intense, concentrated, ripe (often very ripe), sweet fruit and tight structures when young. Whites can show good intensity too but typically lack subtlety and refinement. While the estate Cabernet impresses, limited release Cabernet Sauvignon Odyssey and Shiraz Prodigy are of a different order to the regular Katnook Estate versions. With impressive complexity, depth and sheer class they age beautifully and, in top vintages, will keep 20 years plus. All the Katnook reds need at least 5 years' age; Riesling and Chardonnay are usually better with three years. Cabernet is the best of a second label range called Founder's Block. The Caledonian range, Cellar Door only, breaks out of the single varietal straight jacket and comprises small parcels of blended wines.

Katnook Estate
Recommended Reds:
Cabernet Sauvignon Odyssey ★★★★☆ £F

South Australia

Cabernet Sauvignon ★★★ £D
Merlot ★★ £D Shiraz Prodigy ★★★★☆ £F
Shiraz ★★ £D
Recommended Whites:
Chardonnay ★★ £D
Sauvignon Blanc ★★ £C
Founders Block
Recommended Reds:
Shiraz ★★ £C Cabernet Sauvignon ★☆ £C
Recommended Whites:
Chardonnay ★☆ £B Sauvignon Blanc ★☆ £B

⦿ Kay Brothers (McLaren Vale) *www.kaybrothersamerywines.com*
Kay Brothers Amery Vineyard is a true Australian original. Founded by Herbert and Frederick Kay in the late 19th century the winery has assumed a legendary status on account of an adherence to tradition and wines of remarkable complexity, structure and impressive longevity. The winery has the feel of a working museum as an original basket press and open-top fermenters continue to be used. Much of the fuss surrounds the scrum for a few bottles of Block 6 Shiraz. Many of the vines from this vineyard date from 1892 and are very lowyielding. After a moderately long-fermentation under a submerged cap the wine is aged for more than two years in a mix of new American and Eastern European oak. The wine shows a fabulous old vines complexity, quite unexpected elegance and purity and super intensity and length. Remarkably it can be drunk with just 5 or 6 years age but will keep for 20 or more. If you have to settle for the Hillside Shiraz you won't be missing that much. Concentrated and powerful with very fine crushed blackberry fruit and mineral, licorice nuances, this wine actually needs 10 years or more before it is ready. Readily affordable are the excellent regular Basket Pressed Shiraz and Cabernet Merlot. These are a comparative disappointment after the top Shirazes but still pack a lot of intensity, density for relatively young vines and start to open up after 4 or 5 years' ageing. A little fortified Muscat is also made.
Recommended Reds:
Shiraz Block 6 ✪✪✪✪✪ £G
Shiraz Hillside ★★★★☆ £E
Shiraz Basket Pressed McLaren Vale ★★★☆ £C
Cabernet Merlot Basket Pressed McLaren Vale ★★★☆ £C

⦿ Kilikanoon (Clare Valley) *www.kilikanoon.com.au*
Kilikanoon owns or controls over 500 ha of prime vineyards throughout South Australia but if you want to know what wines from the Clare can taste like try Kevin Mitchell's now outstanding range. Although he lacked his own winemaking facility until 2004, the grapes had always come from 20 ha of estate vineyards. Shiraz in particular is a star - very old vine flagship Attunga 1865 (£F) is made only in exceptional years but, at less than half the price, Oracle and Covenant Shiraz command just as much respect, showing off the regional characteristics superbly and tremendously concentrated as well. The Oracle has a more floral, berryish accent in contrast to a more classic, smoke, mineral- and earth-imbued intensity in the Covenant. An expressive Blocks Road Cabernet Sauvignon shows both its orgins and the style and balance typical of the wines here with added concentrated and depth in recent vintages. Mort's Block Riesling has deep fruit intensity and is very well-structured in the most recent vintages needing at least 3-4 years to show at its best. Even better is the Reserve with exceptional concentration and length, not unlike a top Pfalz Grosses Gewächs in style. Another Riesling, Blacket's Vineyard is sourced from Eden Valley. Second

Fiddle is a well-balanced, fruity Grenache-based rosé. The latest releases are particularly impressive and still very good value. Medley is a very stylish blend of Grenache, Shiraz and Mourvèdre and Parable Shiraz - an intense eucalypt, herb and berryish McLaren Vale expression. Also new are the Killerman's Run wines which include Cabernet Sauvignon, Shiraz and Grenache/Shiraz - the last (the only one tasted) shows superb fruit and good depth. Several other limited production Shiraz are produced by Kevin Mitchell beyond the Clare from very low yielding vines. These include Testament Shiraz, Barossa 'R', a Greens Reserve (from the Greens Vineyard) in the Barossa and 'M' Reserve from McLaren Vale. (SA)
Kilikanoon
Recommended Reds:
Shiraz Oracle Clare Valley ★★★★★ £F
Shiraz Covenant Clare Valley ★★★★☆ £D
Shiraz Parable McLaren Vale ★★★★ £D
Grenache Prodigal ★★★☆ £D
Medley ★★★ £D
Cabernet Sauvignon Blocks Road Clare Valley ★★★★☆ £D
Recommended Whites:
Riesling Mort's Block Reserve Watervale ★★★★ £D
Riesling Mort's Block Watervale ★★★☆ £C
Killerman's Run
Recommended Reds:
Shiraz/Grenache ★★★ £B
Shiraz ★★☆ £B
Cabernet Sauvignon ★★ £B

Knappstein (Clare Valley) *www.knappstein.com.au*
An increasingly dependable producer with 100 ha of well-established vineyards. Recently the wines have been made by Glenn Barry and the reliable varietals remain moderately priced and widely available. The premium reds now include a number of single vineyard wines including Shiraz from Yertabulti in both regular and fortified styles. The Single Vineyard Enterprise Cabernet Sauvignon offers real depth and concentration. Of the improving whites, Sémillon/Sauvignon is at the rich, ripe end of the spectrum. Riesling adds more intensity and is very good indeed including the Hand-Picked Clare Valley version and a Watervale Ackland Vineyard version, coming from low-yielding unirrigated vines. An exotic new white called simply Three is based on Gewürztraminer, Riesling with a little Pinot Gris. A sparkling Shiraz as well as a Sparkling Riesling have also been introduced along with a dry light rosé. The range is completed with a late harvest Riesling.
Recommended Reds:
Cabernet Sauvignon Single Vineyard ★★★☆ £E
Shiraz ★★ £C
Cabernet/Merlot ★★ £C
Recommended Whites:
Riesling Watervale Ackland Vineyard ★★★ £C
Riesling Hand Picked ★★★ £B
Sémillon/Sauvignon Blanc ★★ £B
Three ★★ £B
Chardonnay ★ £B

Lake Breeze (Langhorne Creek) *www.lakebreeze.com.au*
One of the emerging quality producers from Langhorne Creek (on the opposite, eastern side of the Fleurieu Peninsula to McLaren Vale). Greg Follett makes the wines from a portion of his family's large holdings, the Folletts having been grape growers since the 1930s. The reds are very competently made; Bernoota is from

Shiraz and Cabernet Sauvignon (generally equal parts of each) with good complexity and a well-defined palate, Cabernet Sauvignon is of similar quality. Arthur's Reserve, a well composed blend of Cabernet Sauvignon and Petit Verdot has been made since 2001. Under a Selection 54 label a Shiraz is also made along with an Old Vine Grenache. Three whites are made, a Reserve Chardonnay a Vermentino and a refreshing frizzante style Moscato. In 1999, the Follet family established the False Cape vineyard in the cool, maritime climate of Kangaroo Island (wines not yet tasted). Three easy drinking examples labelled Bullant are also made from Lake Breeze grown fruit including a Shiraz, a Cabernet Merlot and a Chardonnay.

Recommended Reds:
Shiraz Winemaker's Selection ★★★☆ £E
Arthur's Reserve ★★★☆ £D
Cabernet Sauvignon ★★★ £E
Shiraz/Cabernet Bernoota ★★★ £D

Langmeil (Barossa Valley) www.langmeilwinery.com.au
Langmeil is a young enterprising family-owned Barossa operation offering classic succulent, expressive Barossa reds at very reasonable prices. From 14.5 ha of vineyards and contract grown fruit Paul Lindner brings out the real character of the Barossa through the use of a basket press and open-fermenters. There is arguably not the sophistication of the likes of Glaetzer yet there is much of the Barossa *terroir* and old vine style. Both Blacksmith's Cabernet Sauvignon and Valley Floor Shiraz offer good richness as well as depth. Both deserve 5-8 years' ageing although the Shiraz can be drunk sooner. Three Gardens is a soft, supple Shiraz/Grenache/Mourvèdre blend that can be drunk young or with 5 years' age. Small quantities of two premium reds are also made - Jackaman's Cabernet Sauvignon and The Freedom Shiraz. The latter comes from a single dry-farmed plot first planted in 1843 and has the same super concentration, formidable depth and terrific length of first division Barossa reds. It is also reasonably priced in this context. Other wines include Resurrection Mataro, Orphan Bank Shiraz, The Fifth Wave Grenache, sparklers Shiraz and Ondenc, new varietals Durif and Malbec as well as whites Viognier, Chardonnay and Eden Valley Riesling.

Recommended Reds:
Shiraz The Freedom ★★★★★ £G
Cabernet Sauvignon Blacksmith's★★★☆ £D
Shiraz Valley Floor★★★☆ £D
Three Gardens★★★ £C

Leabrook Estate (Adelaide Hills)
From close-planted high density vineyards and the use of minimal irrigation to the use of high quality French cooperage and a prolonged cold soak for some of the reds, former owner Colin Best succeeded in producing wines of considerable intensity and depth. The first commercial quantities were only produced in 2000. The Reserve Pinot Noir is deep and complex, almost overwhelming in flavour but balanced and long, needing 6-8 years' age from a top vintage. Chardonnay has impressive richness and weight in a slightly exaggerated Burgundy style, just missing the refinement and purity that would put it amongst top Meursault. His methods work just as well with other varieties including a dense Cabernet Franc with raspberry and blackcurrant leaf intensity, full-flavoured Pinot Gris, fruit-rich Sauvignon and powerful spicy blackfruited Cabernet/Merlot. Three Region Shiraz and Cabernet Sauvignon are also Adelaide Hills sourced but include a small component of

fruit from the Adelaide Plains and Langhorne Creek. While rich, ripe and intense there is a coarseness of flavour which may owe something to their origins - the Shiraz is much the better of the two with greater purity. Generally a little more purity and expression throughout the range would make it really first-rate. Arguably some the wines would benefit from a slightly more relaxed, hands-off approach but at least you won't feel short-changed for flavour and substance.

Recommended Reds:
Pinot Noir Reserve ★★★☆ £E
Cabernet Franc ★★★☆ £D
Merlot ★★☆ £E
Cabernet/Merlot ★★★ £D
Cabernet Sauvignon Three Region ★★☆ £E
Shiraz Three Region ★★★☆ £E

Recommended Whites:
Chardonnay ★★★★ £E
Sauvignon Blanc ★★★ £D
Pinot Gris ★★☆ £D

Leasingham (Clare Valley) www.leasingham-wines.com.au
The long-established winery which became Constellation Wines centre for Clare Valley excellence under Kerri Thompson (now making wine under her own label, KT & The Falcon and at Crabtree) has been mothballed and three of its four vineyards sold. Supplemented with bought in fruit the range remains simple and consistent. The Classic Clare wines are the most exciting, high in alcohol but packed full of rich, ripe fruit and abundant new oak; the Shiraz comes from the Schobers Vineyard and the Cabernet from Provis Vineyard. The oak theme continues in very good and reasonably priced Bin 61 Shiraz and Bin 56 Cabernet/Malbec. I suspect few of these reds are drunk with much age but all deserve 4 or 5 years. Mind you, a rich, untamed infusion of fruit and oak might appeal on some occasions. Prices of these dense, bold Classic Clare reds have risen considerably. Riesling is good with excellent limey, mineral intensity to the Bin 7. Classic Clare Riesling is made in a tighter, more ageworthy style.

Recommended Reds:
Shiraz Classic Clare ★★★ £F
Shiraz Bin 61 ★★ £D
Cabernet Sauvignon Classic Clare ★★★ £F
Cabernet/Malbec Bin 56 ★★ £D
Sparkling Shiraz Classic Clare ★★ £C

Recommended Whites:
Riesling Bin 7 ★★ £C
Riesling Magnus ★☆ £C

Leconfield (Coonawarra) www.leconfield.com.au
Leconfield was established by Sydney Hamilton in the early 1970s but sold to his nephew Richard HAMILTON in 1981. The leading wine over more than two decades has been the Cabernet, which made a lasting impact with the 1980 vintage. Yet while some vintages have been very impressive with a deep, rich, assertive berry fruit character, other years have been somewhat leafy and unexpectedly light. Still, it delivers plenty of character and Coonawarra typicity for the money. Cabernet includes a little Merlot, Cabernet Franc and Petit Verdot but most other wines are 100% varietal. Of these, a more plummy, berryish, at times slightly herbal Merlot has been more consistent than a Shiraz which has occasionally been slightly lean after a much celebrated 1995. However all have refined structures and show archetypal Coonawarra character and fruit

South Australia

Australia

intensity when on form. Recent vintages of Chardonnay have shown more elegance, if not the intensity of the more one-dimensional early vintages. Flavoursome yet refined Riesling is also made from surviving 1970s vines.

Recommended Reds:
Cabernet ★★★★ £D
Shiraz ★★★★ £C
Merlot ★★★ £C
Recommended Whites:
Chardonnay ★★★ £C
Riesling Old Vines ★★ £C

Peter Lehmann (Barossa Valley) *www.peterlehmannwines.com*
The late Peter Lehmann was a Barossa institution and a consistently sound bet for accessible but fruit-rich and well-structured Barossa reds. Production is large with much of the fruit grown under contract under the watchful eye of the Lehmann viticultural team. The top wine, Stonewell Shiraz is released with 5 years' age and is based on low-yielding old vines in the Stonewell vineyards but also includes premium fruit from other Barossa districts. Previously aged only in American oak, the French component has steadily risen and currently stands at 90%. It shows terrific concentration, depth and intensity and has majestic proportions, just missing the extra refinement for classic status. Eight Songs, aged only in French oak, has more recently shown greater character and complexity if not yet the refinement suggested by the artistic efforts to which its presentation is linked. Mentor, the premium Cabernet-based blend usually includes a significant percentage of Merlot, Malbec and Shiraz. Dense and structured, it is best with at least 6–10 years' age. New (since 2001) licorice, berry and plum The Futures Shiraz is a significant step up from the H & V (Hills and Valleys) Barossa Valley Shiraz, which nonetheless remains reasonably priced for an impressive mouthful of fruit as does its Cabernet counterpart. A powerful, ageworthy reserve Riesling from Eden Valley now named Wigan after Chief Wine Maker Andrew Wigan is outstanding and easily the best of the whites closely followed by the Masters Sémillon (recently named Margaret in honour of Peter Lehmann's wife): both are only released with 4–5 years' bottle-age and show complex tertiary characteristics. Clancy's red is an everday Barossa blend of Shiraz, Cabernet Sauvignon, Merlot and Cabernet Franc. Three premium wines are now made under the VSV (Very Special Vineyard) label and include Shiraz Orrock and 1885 as well as Cabernet Sauvignon Ruediger. As well as the H & V wines which also include Sauvignon Blanc from the Adelaide Hills and Pinot Gris from the Eden Valley, a number of similarly priced Barossa Valley wines are made under the Portrait label. Weighbridge is a budget label for Shiraz and Chardonnay. Layer's Red (not tasted), first made in 2008 is a blend of traditional and alternative varieties (Shiraz, Mourvèdre, Grenache, Tempranillo and Carignan).

Recommended Reds:
Shiraz Stonewell ★★★★★ £F
Masters Shiraz Eight Songs ★★★★ £E
Shiraz The Futures ★★★ £C
H & V Shiraz Barossa ★★ £C
Masters Mentor ★★★★ £D
H & V Cabernet Sauvignon Barossa ★★ £C
Clancy's ★ £B
Recommended Whites:
Riesling Masters Wigan Eden Valley ★★★★☆ £C
H & V Riesling Eden Valley ★★☆ £B
Sémillon Masters Margaret Barossa ★★★☆ £C

Lindemans (Coonawarra) *www.lindemans.com.au*
In Coonawarra, Lindemans (also see Victoria) makes a trio of top reds which can be traced back to the mid-1980s, in the case of Pyrus (a Bordeaux blend), and even longer for St George Cabernet and Limestone Ridge Shiraz/Cabernet. But despite some impressive past vintages these wines don't now stack up against the best from Coonawarra (which includes the premium WYNNS wines from the same stable). An initial fullness and fleshy texture and a pleasing complexity are let down by a lack of fruit intensity on the finish and a stalky, sappy quality that is often apparent. This seems to suggest a mix of good quality fruit and that of more mediocre origins. All 3 wines are significantly cheaper than the Wynns flagship wines but there are many better Coonawarra wines in their price range. By contrast generally good value is to be had in the Padthaway wines, particularly the Reserve Chardonnay with its pronounced barrel-fermentation character and rich fruit.

Recommended Reds:
Pyrus Coonawarra ★★★ £E
Cabernet Sauvignon St George ★★ £E
Shiraz/Cabernet Limestone Ridge ★★ £E
Shiraz Padthaway Reserve ★★ £C
Shiraz Padthaway ★ £B
Recommended Whites:
Chardonnay Padthaway Reserve ★★ £C
Chardonnay Limestone Coast ★ £B

Maglieri (McLaren Vale)
Captured in 1999 by Mildara Blass, this relatively small McLaren Vale winery had already made a name for itself with premium reds under the direction of Steve Maglieri as for its locally popular 'Lambrusco'. The reds, currently made by Trevor Tucker, generally show intense ripe fruit and well-integrated oak. Shiraz displays classic McLaren Vale character with slightly smoky, eucalyptus, very ripe dark berry/cherry/plum fruit and a hint of earth, building up dark-chocolate flavours with age. The Steve Maglieri version is more structured, extracted and oaky and needs the best part of a decade's ageing. Merlot is soundly made but, like many South Australian examples, is hardly a classic expression of the grape. The Cabernet is more convincing. Sémillon and Chardonnay are both well crafted and better than is typical for McLaren Vale. Quality across the range dipped a little in the 1999 vintage (which was poor in McLaren Vale) but premium reds should continue to be a good bet if the fruit sources are retained.

Recommended Reds:
Shiraz Steve Maglieri ★★★☆ £E
Shiraz ★★★ £C
Cabernet Sauvignon ★★ £B
Merlot ★ £B
Recommended Whites:
Chardonnay ★ £B
Semillon ★ £B

Majella (Coonawarra) *www.majellawines.com.au*
A label gaining in recognition and importance as more and more of the Cabernet and Shiraz grapes from prime Coonawarra land that were previously sold under contract (the Lynns have been an important supplier to WYNNS since 1980) are now being used for Majella wines. From the late 1960s vines began to compete with sheep for space and the first wines were produced in the early 90s and are today made on site by full-time winemaker, Bruce Gregory. The Cabernet/ Shiraz blend once common to many premium

South Australian wines but now mostly seen in budget wines has, since 1996, been the basis of a very impressive flagship, Malleea. Very dense, rich and concentrated fruit takes up the French oak treatment and fine tannins promise a long life. Varietal Shiraz and Cabernet are in a similar mould with potent berry fruit and evident oak but are a little more accessible when young. Significantly cheaper than Malleea and a run below the varietal reds in price, the Musician Cabernet/Shiraz is relatively forward and shows good Coonawarra typicity with a herbal edge to its black berry and currant fruit. Riesling shows a better, tighter structure than is usual in Coonawarra Riesling. Sparkling Shiraz is also a good example with subtle tannins and a berryish finish. Recent additions include a Merlot (since 2007) and Melody, a Shiraz rosé.

Recommended Reds:

Malleea ★★★★ £F   Cabernet ★★★ £D
Shiraz ★★★ £D   Sparkling Shiraz ★★★ £E
Cabernet/Shiraz The Musician ★★ £C

Recommended Whites:

Riesling ★ £C

❀ **Charles Melton (Barossa Valley)** *www.charlesmeltonwines.com.au*
Charlie Melton is one of the saviours of Australian Shiraz along with Rocky O'Callaghan (ROCKFORD), Bob McLean (ST HALLETT) and others. In the late 1980s and early 90s he produced wines of such character and richness from dry-farmed (unirrigated) Barossa old-vine fruit that it rescued the grape from the also-ran category assigned to it in the Cabernet-fixated wine scene that prevailed in Australia at the time. Though Melton is based in the heart of the Barossa, grapes (whether owned, leased or bought-in) are sourced from throughout the area. Both French and American oak are used but the past decade has seen a trend towards the former. Shiraz is arguably the best Melton wine made and he now focuses his energies on Kirsche Vineyard Shiraz from Flinders fruit and two limited releases, Voices of Angels (from the eden Valley) and Grains of Paradise (Barossa Valley). A straight Shiraz and Laura Shiraz are no longer made. One of Australia's best rosés is based on Grenache, while Nine Popes is a blend of Shiraz, Grenache and Mourvèdre. Cabernet shows the rich, ripe fruit and oak character typical to all the reds. Made by the traditional method and from Cabernet as well as Shiraz, the Sparkling Red is a very good example of its type; it shows a rich plum, berry and chocolate character with a little age. More exotic again is Sotto di Ferro, made from Pedro Ximenez and Muscadelle grapes (90/10) dried 'under the iron' – beneath a corrugated iron roof. It is well-balanced and complex, including roasted nuts, honey, nougat and dried apricot flavours, with real depth and intensity. All the reds benefit from having at least 5 years' age. Also made is Richlieu Grenache. Most recently, not one to rest on his laurels, Melton acquired 73 acres in High Eden in 2008 which has been planted primarily to Shiraz, Grenache together with a small field planting of those Châteauneuf-du-Pape varieties which he has managed to get through quarantine.

Recommended Reds:

Nine Popes ★★★★ £E
Shiraz Grains of Paradise ★★★★ £E
Shiraz Voices of Angels ★★★★ £E
Cabernet Sauvignon ★★★ £E
Sparkling Red ★★★£E
Sotto di Ferro ★★★£F

Recommended Rosés:

Rose of Virginia ★★☆ £D

Geoff Merrill (McLaren Vale) *www.geoffmerrillwines.com*
Geoff Merrill hardly needs any introduction to many wine consumers as he is one of the most instantly recognisable great characters of the Australian wine scene. The wines, made at the renovated Mount Hurtle winery since 1988, can seem a bit anonymous and simple, apparently at odds with the larger than life personality of their maker. At their best they do achieve a certain elegance and subtlety but more often there isn't the necessary fruit quality there to deliver the regional and varietal expression that is sought. The red Reserves, though showing greater intensity and complexity can want for better balance with an exaggerated cedary oakiness. The super premium Henley Shiraz is sold at a stratospheric price but does have remarkable depth and complexity within a relatively unobtrusive frame. This, like the Reserves (including Chardonnay), is only released with extended bottle-age. Regular varietals under the Wickham Park and Pimpala Road labels, which are now included under the Premium banner, at their best (when fully ripe), are generally soft, supple and attractive, even if they don't have the greatest weight or intensity. Wines under the Mount Hurtle label can have upfront if simple fruit character. Merrill also makes a small wine range in partnership with cricketers Ian Botham and Geoff Willis, Botham Merrill Willis.

Recommended Reds:

Shiraz Henley ★★★★☆ £G   Shiraz Reserve ★★★ £E
Cabernet Sauvignon Reserve ★★★ £D

Recommended Whites:

Chardonnay Reserve★★ £C
Chardonnay Wickham Park★☆ £C

>> **Ministry of Clouds (McLaren Vale)** *www.ministryofclouds.com.au*
Julian Forewood and Bernice Ong's Ministry of Clouds wines are marked by their excellent price/quality ratio. Like a few excellent winemakers in other parts of the world, their usp is the fact that as yet, they don't own any vineyards, and having worked in the wine trade for other producers for many years in the past, they have connections with some of the best growers in different regions in Australia. Mainly using the facilities of Tim Geddes at his winery in McLaren Vale, they are turning out wines with enormous purity of expression, balance and complexity with true varietal flavours, ably abetted by some uncanny (or is it canny) fruit selection from top growers. The icing on the cake, though, is the gentle pricing of the wines. (NB)

Recommended Reds:

Mataro McLaren Vale ★★★★☆ £D
Shiraz ★★★★ £D
Grenache McLaren Vale ★★★★ £D

Recommended Whites:

Chardonnay Tasmania ★★★★ £E

Mitchell (Clare Valley) *www.mitchellwines.com*
The Mitchell winery was established in 1975 and is now a medium-sized Clare producer (30,000 cases) with a strong track record for consistent, well-structured reds and whites. Save for a part barrel-fermented well structured Sémillon, the whites are made without any oak as is Grenache GSM from old unirrigated bush vines which includes a little Sangiovese and Mourvèdre. Both Peppertree Vineyard Shiraz and Sevenhill Vineyard Cabernet Sauvignon show a relatively subdued oak influence. Though the wines sometimes lack a little extra flair they nonetheless show typical Clare characteristics and Cabernet, Shiraz and Riesling are capable of long ageing. After some weaker efforts in the late 90s the Riesling is once again intense

Australia

and concentrated – an all-too-rare inexpensive wine worth cellaring. McNicol Riesling (not tasted £E) is a single vineyard wine from a later ripening stony quartzite site at 500m. Sparkling Shiraz, from the Peppertree vineyard, is also produced.

Recommended Reds:

Cabernet Sauvignon Sevenhill Vineyard ★★★ £D

Shiraz Peppertree Vineyard ★★★ £D Grenache GSM ★★ £C

Recommended Whites:

Riesling Watervale ★★★☆ £C

Sémillon ★★★ £C

⚜ Mitolo (McLaren Vale) *www.mitolowines.com.au*

Mitolo Wines was formed in 2000 after Frank Mitolo decided to expand on early efforts and commercialise his production. Through the winemaking services of Ben Glaetzer a (also a partner in the business) remarkably high standard has been achieved from the outset. Fermentation is completed in primarily French oak (new) in which the wines are subsequently aged for up to 16 months. Three differing Shirazes are notable for their depth, extract and detailed, complex fruit expressions. The fullest demonstration of fruit and *terroir* is revealed in the potentially outstanding McLaren Vale Savitar Shiraz. All must be given at least 5 years' age. Jester is a second-label Shiraz with good berryish McLaren Vale character. It is attractive but of some substance too. First produced in 2002 is Serpico, a Cabernet Sauvignon made from grapes dried on racks. It is very concentrated and powerful but balanced with black plum and black cherry fruit and avoids any overt raisiny character. Jester rosé from Sangiovese is a gutsy but well-balanced example and is now complemented by Jester Vermentino white. All the wines come complete with a Latin inscription which sheds some light on their names.

Recommended Reds:

Shiraz Savitar McLaren Vale ★★★★☆ £F

Shiraz G.A.M McLaren Vale ★★★★ £E

Shiraz Reiver Barossa Valley ★★★★ £E

Cabernet Sauvignon Serpico McLaren Vale ★★★★☆ £E

Cabernet Sauvignon Jester McLaren Vale ★★★ £C

Shiraz Jester McLaren Vale ★★☆ £C

Recommended Rosés:

Jester Sangiovese Rosé ★★ £B

Mt Billy (Barossa Valley) *www.mtbillywines.com.au*

Mt Billy, named for a local hill, is a small property at Victor Harbor in Southern Fleurieu. However, most of the wines are produced from grape purchases in the Barossa. Until recently they have been contract-made by Torbreck but have the services of Peter Schnell and Dan Standish from 2006. The focus is on two Barossa reds, both aged in French oak. Harmony is a blend of Shiraz, Mourvèdre and Grenache and can be slightly baked but has lovely depth with herbs and grilled meats and good balance – south Rhône-like in an overheated sort of way. Antiquity is from very old-vine Barossa Shiraz and is a classic complex expression, a touch overripe but with heather, smoke and dense black plum and prune fruit. It hasn't quite the extra depth or quality of the very best but is a fine example. A little Riesling from Eden and, from the Southern Fleurieu, Chardonnay (dry and sweet), a Shiraz and rosé have also been made.

Recommended Reds:

Antiquity Shiraz Barossa Valley ★★★★ £E

Harmony Barossa Valley ★★★ £D

Mount Horrocks (Clare Valley) *www.mounthorrocks.com*

This is a classy range of wines which all have good structure and

ripeness, especially now all fruit is 100% estate grown. Winemaker/proprietor Stephanie Toole now owns vineyards which total 10 ha across three sites, two in Watervale and one in the warmer Auburn sub-region which is dedicated to Cordon Cut Riesling. Great care is taken in producing the best possible fruit from unirrigated vines and also in their vinification (carried out at Jeffrey GROSSET's winery). Riesling is getting better and better, taut with vibrant fruit (lime and grapefruit with floral notes) and great length. Toole no longer makes a Chardonnay but the waxy, barrel fermented Sémillon is much more interesting than most Clare Chardonnays and shows good breadth and weight as well as the firm acidity that gives all the whites a certain austerity when young. Its citrus and mineral notes are not in the least overwhelmed by the oak. Cabernet/Merlot is what others would call simply Cabernet Sauvignon, as it only contains 5-10% Merlot, and shows a fine cool 'Clare' minerality and a certain supple seductive elegance. Toole is a Rhône fan and the distinctive peppery Shiraz deviates from the fuller bodied norm, showing excellent definition and a similar cool elegance. It deserves to be kept for 6-8 years. A sweet version of Riesling, Cordon Cut, is made by allowing the grapes to dehydrate on the vine by severing the cane from the trunk (the French term is *passerillage*; there is no botrytis but a *passerillé* or dried-grape character is achieved). It is one of Australia's finest desert wines - intense, pure, limey and honeyed with sublime balancing acidity.

Recommended Reds:

Shiraz ★★★☆ £D Cabernet/Merlot ★★★ £D

Recommended Whites:

Riesling Cordon Cut ★★★★☆ £F

Riesling Watervale ★★★★ £D

Semillon Watervale ★★★★ £D

Mountadam (Eden Valley) *www.mountadam.com.au*

A high-profile and often overhyped winery, Mountadam has had some successes but has never been totally convincing as one of South Australia's leading small producers. Established by the late David Wynn on the elevated High Eden Ridge, it was purchased by local businessman David Brown in 2006 who has installed winemaker Con Moshos, formerly Brian Croser's right hand man at PETALUMA. At times many of the wines have lacked real depth and complexity, if managing to wow some wine drinkers with their oak and at times beguiling fruit veneer. The High Eden Chardonnay has some style and structure and has been the most consistent wine but doesn't match the very top Adelaide Hills examples. Eden Valley Riesling can show exquisite fruit flavours and has had better structure of late than previously combined with a stony minerality. The Red is a blend of primarily Cabernet Sauvignon and Merlot and if it sometimes exhibits rather leafy, underripe characters, it can also develop a cedary, plummy complexity with age. Patriarch Shiraz is rich, composed and seductive. New are a Barossa range of unwooded Chardonnay, Cabernet/Merlot and Shiraz. Though of only modest depth and concentration, Shiraz in particular shows good expression while the unoaked Barossa Chardonnay's ripe fruit but well balanced acidity reveals its dual sourcing from the Eden Valley and Barossa floor.

Recommended Reds:

Shiraz DW High Eden ★★★★ £D

The Red High Eden ★★★ £D Cabernet/Merlot Barossa ★ £B

Recommended Whites:

Chardonnay High Eden ★★★ £D

Chardonnay Barossa ★ £B

Riesling Eden Valley ★★☆ £C

Neagles Rock (Clare Valley) *www.neaglesrock.com*
A small, young yet already well-established Clare producer. Both Jane Willson and Steve Wiblin had long experience in the corporate world of Australian wine before starting out in 1997 with just 8 ha of vineyards. They now have 26 ha and a successful vineyard restaurant. The wines are of a consistently high standard and, as with any good Clare producer, bring out much of the minerality and distinctive fruit expression the region offers. The Riesling is an excellent style for drinking young. Shiraz is expressive and complex with a cool-fruited elegance. It deserves 5-10 years ageing but could be drunk sooner. It is also very reasonably priced. Still cheaper is Hope Grenache/Shiraz (previously known as Misery because of the neglected, now nurtured vines from which it is sourced) for more everyday drinking but there is no lack of style to the supple juicy fruit. Other wines include a Sparrkling Pinot/Chardonnay, Sangiovese, Sémillon/Sauvignon Blanc and Mr Duncan Cabernet/Shiraz.

Recommended Reds:
Shiraz A Lovers Retreat Clare Valley ★★★★ £D
Grenache/Shiraz Hope Clare Valley ★★☆ £C
Recommended Whites:
Riesling Clare Valley ★★☆ £C

Nepenthe (Adelaide Hills) *www.nepenthe.com.au*
Much has changed at this Adelaide Hills pioneering winery since founder Ed Tweddell died in 2006. It was acquired by McGuigan Simeon, now known as Australian Vintage Limited in 2007. The winery was closed in 2009 and the wines are now made in the Barossa by Andre Bondar at Yaldara in the Barossa, which brand is also owned by Australian Vintage. Nonetheless, the vineyards located in prime sites in Lenswood, Charleston, Balhannah and Hahndorf remain intact so the new regime seems certain to continue to realise the cool climate potential of a multitude of varieties. Predominantly French oak is used, usually a mix of new and used. All the wines have excellent fruit but good texture and balance too. Pinot Noir is particularly impressive with great breadth and intensity on the palate. The Good Doctor Pinot Noir is in the top tier Pinnacle range, whose reds include Gate Block Shiraz from Balhannah. Whites in the Pinnacle range include Ithaca Chardonnay and, from 2009, Petraea Sauvignon Blanc, which is fermented and aged in large oak casks. Pinot Noir also appears in Charleston designation when sourced exclusively from a second, larger vineyard site. The Tempranillo shows good varietal character with a spicy blueberry component and, with vine age, shows a little more depth and structure. Intense, expressive whites include a lightly oaked and unwooded Chardonnay, the former under the Altitude label, both nicely composed with good fruit richness. Altitude Pinot Gris is fruity and floral while Altitude lightly oaked Sauvignon is a classic example of the herbal and ripe gooseberry, tropical Adelaide Hills character. Most affordable are unusual blends Tryst red with berry fruit and a leafy component, and white , whose varietal mix changes from year to year.

Recommended Reds:
Pinot Noir The Good Doctor ★★★£E
Shiraz Gate Block ★★★ £E
Tempranillo Altitude ★★ £C
Tryst Shiraz Cabernet Sauvignon ★ £B
Recommended Whites:
Chardonnay Ithaca ★★★★ £D
Chardonnay Altitude ★★ £C
Pinot Gris Altitude ★★ £C

Sauvignon Blanc Petraea ★★★ £D
Sauvignon Blanc Altitude ★★ £B
Tryst Sauvignon Blanc Semillon ★ £B

O'Leary Walker (Clare Valley) *www.olearywalkerwines.com*
Fantastic progress has been made here in next to no time. David O'Leary and Nick Walker started out in 2001 (02 was the first vintage) but this already has the look and feel of a long-established top Clare producer. Both partners are winemakers and Roseworthy graduates with a long and successful immersion in the Australian industry. Although based in the Clare Valley, they have estate vineyards in the Adelaide Hills and source fruit from other regions with an established reputation for a particular variety. To date the stars are the excellent value Clare Rieslings and some super Clare Shiraz, including a stunning Reserve. The latter has power, depth and classic Clare expression within a sophisticated structure. The regular Shiraz is fruit rich and beautifully delineated with touch of Clare minerality but actually includes 20% McLaren Vale fruit which adds a little lift and spiceness. Adelaide Hills Sauvignon and Pinot Noir are bright and fruit-filled and true to their origins. Hurtle sparkling wine is also sourced from the Adelaide Hills and reveals good breadth and ripe fruit. Most of the wines are remarkably well-priced.

Recommended Reds:
Shiraz Reserve Clare Valley ★★★★★ £F
Shiraz ★★★☆ £C   Pinot Noir Adelaide Hills ★★★ £C
Cabernet Sauvignon Clare Valley ★★☆ £C
Recommended Whites:
Riesling Polish Hill ★★★☆ £C
Riesling Watervale ★★★ £B
Hurtle Pinot Noir/Chardonnay Vintage Adelaide Hills ★★★ £C
Sauvignon Blanc Adelaide Hills ★★★ £B

❂ S.C. Pannell (Mclaren Vale/Adelaide Hills) *www.pannell.com.au*
Steve Pannell's background is as eclectic as his flagship range, which encompasses McLaren Vale stalwarts Grenache, Shiraz and Shiraz/Grenache but also an Adelaide Hills Nebbiolo. Pannell, a Western Australian, is the son of Dr Bill Pannell, founder of Margaret River's MOSS WOOD and PICARDY WINES in Pemberton. However, he has avidly pursued winemaking opportunities elsewhere, notably spending 10 years at HARDYS, where he was chief red winemaker, but also working vintage at Domaine des COMTES LAFON in Burgundy, Château MOUTON ROTHSCHILD in Bordeaux and G.D. VAJRA in Barolo. In 2004, he struck out on his own and has fast established a reputation for wines that skilfully combine ripe fruit and tannins with a sense of place. Careful vineyard selection (Pannell owns neither vineyards nor winery) and hands off winemaking in open top fermenters with natural yeast, hand plunging, no acidification and minimal use of new oak results in food friendly wines of impeccable balance. The Shiraz Grenache, his strongest suit, is an elegant rendition of the blend with ample spice, ripe but present tannins and impressive freshness, even in difficult years like 2007 and 2008. A floral Grenache without an ounce of fat exemplifies Pannell's take on this variety as "warm climate Pinot Noir." The Shiraz shows similar restraint and line when compared with McLaren Vale's traditional style, which is typified by a generous mid-palate. Though the Nebbiolo is widely regarded as Australia's best, youthful plantings can only take you so far. At this price point while it shows good varietal character, not least quite stern tannins, it lacks the finesse of similarly priced Italian counterparts. Only time will tell if Pannell's carefully selected new clones will reduce the gap. Aptly named entry level Pronto red and white are soft, exuberant but

South Australia

interesting blends, easier on both palate and pocket. In the works, a blend of Touriga Nacional and Tempranillo. (SA)

Recommended Reds:

Shiraz/Grenache ★★★★☆ £E   Shiraz ★★★★ £E

Grenache ★★★★☆ £E

Nebbiolo ★★☆ £E   Pronto ★☆ £B

Recommended Whites:

Pronto ★☆ £B

❀ Parker Coonawarra Estate   www.parkercoonawarraestate.com.au

This singular Coonawarra estate established by John Parker in 1985 produced some great wines during the 1990s, but only very recently added its own winemaking facility. The wines are made by Peter LEHMANN. The focus of production is a single premium wine only made in top vintages - a Bordeaux-like approach that is also reflected in the provocative name, Terra Rossa First Growth. In other years (unlike Médoc classed growths) only the second wine, Terra Rossa Cabernet Sauvignon, is released. First Growth is based on Cabernet Sauvignon but also includes Merlot and Cabernet Franc and is aged in 100% new French oak. It is fully ripe and concentrated, if at times a little oaky, with an intense pure fruit core wed to ripe but powerful, textured tannins - it takes the best part of a decade to unfurl. The second wine, which is now aged exclusively in French oak, has recently been only a shade behind, nudging 4 stars. A Merlot is also made but is only available in very small quantities direct from the winery. Entry level wines under the Coonawarra Series label include a Cabernet Sauvignon and a Shiraz.

Recommended Reds:

Terra Rossa First Growth ★★★★★ £F

Cabernet Sauvignon Terra Rossa ★★★☆ £D

Paxton (Mclaren Vale)   www.paxtonvineyards.com

Though established in 1979, the first Paxton wine was not released until 2000. The secret to this family-owned producer's rapid success lies in the quality of the biodynamically farmed fruit. David Paxton is one of Australia's leading viticulturists and the family own six vineyards, which puts over 100ha of prime McLaren Vale dirt at their disposal. David's son Michael is in charge of winemaking and produces several estate grown wines, the best of which derive from aged vines. Jones Block Shiraz, Quandong Farm Shiraz and the flagship wine, EJ Shiraz, are concentrated yet exceptionally well balanced single vineyard wines with terrific fruit purity and a sense of place. The latter derives from vines over 100 years old. AAA is a delightfully unshowy, juicy-fruited blend of two vineyards and two varieties (Shiraz and Grenache). Paxton also make a Tempranillo (not tasted). A Syrah Rosé courts popularity with more than a touch of residual sugar but, part barrel-fermented, it has the depth of flavour and freshness to partner food. As for whites, Thomas Block Chardonnay demonstrates that, in the right place (and with sensitive viticulture and winemaking), McLaren Vale can produce classy, poised whites. A Pinot Gris which lacks freshness is the only duff note. (SA)

Recommended Reds:

Shiraz EJ ★★★★ £F

Shiraz Quandong ★★★☆ £D

Shiraz Jones Block ★★★☆ £E

Shiraz/Grenache AAA ★★ £C

Recommended Whites:

Chardonnay Thomas Block ★★☆ £D

Recommended Rosés:

Shiraz Rosé ★ £C

❀ Penfolds (Barossa Valley)   www.penfolds.com.au

The leading Australian brand since the renaissance of Australian wine in the early 1950s, Penfolds remains high in consumers' estimation despite recent upheavals. Grange, Australia's most consistently great wine over 5 decades, is the pinnacle of production. Like all established investment wines, Grange has a crazy price tag but prices of all the top wines here reflect demand as much as production costs or intrinsic quality. Some top Penfolds reds are produced from a wide range of vineyard sources, which can certainly optimise complexity and aid consistency, although on the downside it might be argued there is less individuality. Grange is primarily Barossa and McLaren Vale Shiraz aged in American oak but typically contains around 5% Cabernet; while not the most refined expression of Shiraz, it is very powerful and complete, and fabulously complex with age. The RWT is 100% Barossa Shiraz aged in French oak; it has good drive and intensity but is oaky too. Intense Magill Estate is vineyard-specific but can be almost overripe and slightly coarse. St Henri, which includes around 5% Cabernet, is aged in large used oak barrels. The top Cabernet is Bin 707, which includes Coonawarra, Padthaway and Barossa fruit and, like Grange, is aged in American oak; there's terrific flesh and blackberry fruit depth in an uncompromising structure. Bin 407 is based primarily on Coonawarra and Padthaway fruit and aged in both French and American oak. Of the other Bin-labelled reds, the Barossa-sourced Bin 138 Old Vine Shiraz/Grenache/Mourvèdre and long-established Bin 389 stand out, 2009 saw the release of the inaugural Bin 23 Pinot Noir, a solid effort (although there are better buys out there). White wines have only taken on real significance here in the last decade. Flagship Chardonnay Yattarna has started to fly following a dramatic reduction in the percentage of new oak, reflecting its 100% cool climate origin (predominantly Tasmanian fruit, the balance from Adelaide Hills and Henty). The distinctly Australian style hinges around vivid fruit of lovely purity. A series of Bin-numbered Chardonnays has also been very impressive, especially the showy, oakier and funkier Reserve Bin A. For more affordable reds and whites, the refined Thomas Hyland range delivers good bang for buck. The Koonunga Hill brand covers some of the same varietals and dual-variety blends. It must take considerable skill to maintain these ranges but consistency can make for somewhat uninteresting wines; new release Seventy Six Shiraz Cabernet and Autumn Riesling successfully inject some lifeblood into the Koonunga Hill range.

Recommended Reds:

Grange ✪✪✪✪✪ £H   Shiraz RWT ★★★★☆ £G

Shiraz Magill Estate ★★★★ £G

Shiraz St Henri ★★★☆ £F

Shiraz Bin 150 Marananga ★★★☆ **£F**

Shiraz Bin 28 ★★★ £D   Shiraz Bin 128 ★★★ £D

Cabernet Sauvignon Bin 707 ★★★★☆ £G

Cabernet Sauvignon Bin 407 ★★★☆ £E

Shiraz/Grenache/Mourvèdre Bin 138 Old Vine ★★☆ £D

Cabernet Shiraz Bin 389 ★★★☆ £E

Shiraz/Mourvèdre Bin 2 ★★ £B

Recommended Whites:

Chardonnay Yattarna ★★★★ £G

Chardonnay Reserve Bin A ★★★☆ £F

Chardonnay Adelaide Hills ★★ £C

Penley (Coonawarra)   www.penley.com.au

Kym Tolley's ancestry and past link him to PENFOLDS but since 1991 he has produced a small but consistently high-quality range of wines under his own label. There are more than 90 ha of estate

plantings including nearly 40 ha of Coonawarra Cabernet. The style is for rich, ripe, smooth wines with lush fruit and unobtrusive tannins but with good ageing potential. French oak is favoured for Merlot, with a mix of the two for Cabernet and Shiraz. Cabernet Sauvignon Reserve (the same wine was known simply as Cabernet Sauvignon before 1998) has been consistently impressive while Special Select is a pricey flagship Shiraz, mostly from McLaren Vale fruit, but including 10% Cabernet Sauvignon. Phoenix and Hyland are lighter, more forward versions of Cabernet and Shiraz respectively. Chardonnay lacks a little elegance but is not short of richness or flavour. Tolley also makes a sparkling Pinot Noir and a (table wine) Pinot Noir, the latter cellar door only.

Recommended Reds:
Cabernet Sauvignon Reserve ★★★ £F
Cabernet Sauvignon Phoenix ★★ £C
Merlot Gryphon ★★ £C
Shiraz Special Select ★★★ £F
Shiraz Hyland ★★ £C
Shiraz/Cabernet Condor ★★ £C
Recommended Whites:
Chardonnay ★★ £C

Petaluma (Adelaide Hills)   *www.petaluma.com.au*
Brian Croser is no longer consulting here but the winery remains resolutely focused on the production of estate-grown site-specific wines. Petaluma was purchased by Lion Nathan in 2001, who were themselves bought by Japan based brewer Kirin Holdings in 2009. The formation of the Petaluma group (also KNAPPSTEIN, MITCHELTON, SMITHBROOK and STONIER) seemed to benefit all participants, at least quality- wise. The Petaluma range has always been small and total production is relatively modest. All the wines are site-specific. Riesling is long-established – an excellent, tightly structured, minerally example (now labelled Hanlin Hill for its Clare Valley origins) which needs a minimum of 2–3 years' age but is capable of much more. The most exceptional white is the brilliant, individual Tiers Chardonnay from the first vineyard planted in the Piccadilly Valley. With great depth, power and a mineral, citrus intensity, its structure and relative austerity when young demand patience. Founder Brian Croser, whose wife owns the Tiers vineyard, retains half of the fruit for his own label, TAPANAPPA Tiers. It is fascinating to compare and contrast the two; Petaluma's version carries more flesh and overt oak. Regular Piccadilly Valley Chardonnay, from other vineyards as well as Tiers also shows a minerally aspect as well as finesse and class that others lack. Again it ages well. Complex berry-fruited Coonawarra could use a little more weight in cooler years but always reveals greater concentration with age. Croser is an elegant traditional method sparkling wine, generally around half Chardonnay and half Pinot Noir, that has been consistently fine for more than a decade. A Late Disgorged version has also been produced. All wines have a structure not seen in many of the more immediate premium Australian sparkling wines and must be drunk with some bottle-age. Relatively recent additions include a promising Shiraz, including 5% Viognier, in an elegant, expressive style. Viognier has developed greater intensity with vine age and is an accomplished wine. Both come from the B&V Vineyard on the (warmer) eastern edge of the Adelaide Hills. Sharefarmers wines including a red (Cabernet/Malbec-based) are sourced from one of two Coonawarra vineyards. Also made from time to time are concentrated, honeyed sweet wines such as a fine Botrytis Sémillon Essence from Sharefarmers Vineyard. Bridgewater Mill Three Districts wines are blended from sites in Clare, Adelaide Hills and Coonawarra

and include Sauvignon Blanc, Chardonnay, Pinot Grigio, a Pinot Noir Rosé and Shiraz.

Recommended Reds:
Coonawarra ★★★★ £E
Shiraz Adelaide Hills ★★★ £E
Merlot Coonawarra ★★★ £D
Recommended Whites:
Chardonnay Tiers ★★★★☆ £F
Chardonnay Piccadilly Valley ★★★★ £D
Riesling Hanlin Hill ★★★★ £C
Viognier Adelaide Hills ★★★ £E
Croser ★★★☆ £D

Pewsey Vale (Eden Valley)   *www.pewseyvale.com*
Pewsey Vale is a historic vineyard established in the mid 19th century by Englishman Joseph Gilbert and revived by YALUMBA in 1961. The distinctive contoured vineyard was planted primarily to an old clone of Riesling that continues to be repropagated. During the 1980s the Riesling gained a considerable following as a leading example of Australian Riesling. However for a time during the 90s the wine retained its flavour but little else. Since the late 90s it has been re-invigorated and shows greater intensity and definition in more recent vintages. Yalumba's star winemaker Louisa Rose, who has been particularly successful with whites, has overseen the transformation. A distinctive strongly lime scented wine with ripe citrus and tropical notes, it doesn't have the nuance or structure of good European Rieslings but it is individual as well as ageworthy. For added weight and intensity there is a bold Contours version released only with several years bottle age which hails from the oldest vines and coolest, south-facing slopes. It is well worth the modest uplift in price and will keep 10 years plus. New in 2007 is Prima Riesling, a classy kabinett style with around 20g/l residual sugar, but more than enough balancing acidity to keep it in line.

Recommended Whites:
Riesling The Contours ★★★★ £C
Riesling Eden Valley ★★☆ £C
Riesling Prima Eden Valley ★★☆ £B

Pike & Joyce (Adelaide Hills)   *www.pikeandjoyce.com.au*
Pike and Joyce is a partnership in which the winemaking expertise of Neil Pike (see PIKES below) is applied to the Joyce family's 13 ha of vineyards in the Lenswood zone of the Adelaide Hills. Only 4000 cases are produced but the standard is impressively high. The wines are striking in the way the quality of the fruit has combined good structure and defintion. Pinot Gris is amongst the best produced in Australia while Sauvignon Blanc is an excellent example of Adelaide Hills fruit and intensity. Pinot Noir has a lovely purity and depth with refinement and balance missing in more ambitious examples. Only Chardonnay tends to excess in terms of the winemaking influence yet it is deep and concentrated with good ageing potential. The quality to value ratio here is hard to beat.

Recommended Reds:
Pinot Noir ★★★☆ £D
Recommended Whites:
Chardonnay ★★★☆ £D
Pinot Gris ★★★ £C
Sauvignon Blanc ★★★ £C

Pikes (Clare Valley)   *www.pikeswines.com.au*
Pikes is a medium-sized producer with 38 ha of estate vineyards at Polish Hill River and without doubt one of the most reliable names

South Australia

Australia

from Clare Valley. The wines are full and flavoursome with weight and intensity across the range. Both Shiraz and Cabernet Sauvignon (which includes 5% Cabernet Franc) show good Clare character with a mineral, earth influence in the rich berry fruit aromas and are ripe, plush and well balanced with restrained oak character. Shiraz/ Grenache/Mourvèdre (of varying composition) is a fragrant, nicely textured example of this now common Australian threesome. Riesling typically shows a floral, toasty and minerally intensity and increasingly good structure especially in a good year. The wines are decent value although occasional very good Reserves including Riesling (Merle) and Shiraz (EWP) are significantly more expensive. Sauvignon Blanc/Sémillon is also made, along with Sangiovese (Premio) and, since 2001, a pure, stylish Viognier. Luccio (Italian for pike) red and the Mullet white and red are relatively inexpensive blends. The supple, savoury Luccio red adds Sangiovese to Cabernet Sauvignon and Merlot. The Red Mullet is a ripe but savoury blend of Grenache, Shiraz, Mourvèdre and Tempranillo, while the vibrant, well defined The White Mullet is from Riesling, Viognier, Chenin and Sauvignon Blanc. Luccio white, once a blend, is now 100% Pinot Grigio. Also well composed is The Dogwalk Cabernet/Merlot. See PIKE & JOYCE (above) for Adelaide Hills wines.

Recommended Reds:
Shiraz Eastside ★★★☆ £C
Cabernet Merlot The Dog Walk ★★★ £C
Shiraz/Grenache/Mourvèdre The Assemblage ★★★ £C
Luccio ★★☆ £C The Red Mullet ★☆ £B
Recommended Whites:
Riesling Merle ★★★★ £E Riesling ★★★ £C
Viognier Gill's Farm ★★★ £C Pinot Grigio Luccio ★☆ £B
The White Mullet ★☆ £B

⚙ **Primo Estate (McLaren Estate)** *www.primoestate.com.au*
From an unpromising location, the hot Adelaide Plains, comes a quite exceptional range of wines, the result of innovation and talent that any wineproducing country would be proud of and which cautious winemakers can only dream of. Joe Grilli was clearly no ordinary Roseworthy graduate and he had both the confidence and ability to go where others are still frightened to follow, building on his Italian heritage and inspired by travels in Italy. He took on the running of his father's vineyard in 1979 and hasn't stopped experimenting since. Estate plantings are now supplemented from vineyards just south of Adelaide and in McLaren Vale proper as well as by bought-in grapes. All premium wines are labelled Joseph. His Cabernet/Merlot (90% Cabernet) uses partially dried grapes mostly from McLaren Vale. Dubbed Moda (Amarone) by Grilli, this is a richly textured, exuberant wine full of ripest cassis, blackberry and black plum fruit with plenty of oak, at its best with 5-10 years' age. La Magia is a late-harvested Riesling with a long history of experimentation; currently it is composed primarily of botrytised Eden Valley fruit and has also included Traminer on occasion. A fleshy, mellow, complex Sparkling Red is produced a unique blend of museum vintages from the last forty years combined with *"solera"* hogsheads of Moda Cabernet Merlot and Primo Estate Shiraz. Made since the 2001 vintage is ripe, perfumed Pinot Grigio d'Elena, a flavoursome but zippy expression of the variety. Under the Primo Estate label are Il Briccone, Shiraz/Sangiovese (with a little Cabernet, Nebbiolo and Barbera), and a zesty tropical and citrus-fruited La Biondina (mostly Colombard with Riesling and Sauvignon). Also made are a tiny amount of fortified Frontignan (Muscat), Fronti, Shale Stome Shiraz, Zamberlan Cabernet Sangiovese made using the ripasso method, Merlesco Merlot (unoaked) and vintage-dated

olive oils and vinegars.
Joseph
Recommended Reds:
Sparkling Red ★★★★☆ £F
Cabernet Sauvignon/Merlot Moda ★★★★ £F
Shiraz Angel Gully ★★★★ £E
Nebbiolo ★★☆ £E
Recommended Whites:
La Magia ★★★★ £D Pinot Grigio d'Elena ★★ £C
Primo Estate
Recommended Whites:
Il Briccone ★★☆ £C La Biondina ★☆ £C

>> **Reillys Wines (Clare Valley)** *www.reillyswines.com.au*
A comprehensive range of small lot wines is made at this small to medium sized winery (output is around 25,000 cases a year). There are essentially four ranges with good values throughout. Originally established in 1993 the Ardill's now have 115 ha of owned vineyards across the region. Visitors can also stay at the property, there are two luxury B & B accommodations and there is a restaurant at the cellar door. There are some excellent buys under the Barking Mad label. Riesling is crisp and fresh with an underlying zesty citrus quality. Grenache Shiraz and Shiraz are among a number of impressive Rhône styles made here at all levels. Both are aged in used hogsheads adding a little structure to the vibrant fruit. Reillys Riesling comes from elevated vineyards grown on limestone, based soils at Watervale. It is a refined, elegant example with intense green and citrus aromas and a subtle minerality. The Saignée is a surprisingly full-bodied rosé, almost a light red in style. A blend of Grenache, Sangiovese, Tempranillo along with a touch of Pinot Noir, it is kept on skins for three days. Reillys Shiraz is loaded with lifted black fruits and a hint of pepper and vanilla. Vinification is in open fermenters and aging in oak for 18 months. The Dry Land reds offer a touch more depth and come from un-irrigated plots offering naturally low yielding fruit. Cabernet Sauvignon is hand picked, fermented in open vat and aged in hogsheads for 24 months. Full of mint and blackcurrant the wine is firm but supple. Shiraz is similarly harvested and vinified although ageing is in a mix of French and American oak. The Old Bush Vine Grenache is an excellent value, full of dark berry and oriental fruits and a real old vine complexity from vineyards originally planted in 1919. RCV is the top label, coming from the best years with the caps being basket pressed before ageing in small French oak. The Dancer Cabernet Sauvignon is marked by elegant, cassis and mint flavours, firmly structured with impressive depth and dimension. The Epitaph Shiraz comes from the 1919 dry farmed block and offers rich, elegant black-fruited varietal character, a rich texture and impressive intensity, length and concentration. It spends over two years in barrel. Expect both RCV reds to evolve and improve for a decade and more. (DM)

Recommended Reds:
RCV Epitaph Shiraz ★★★★☆ £F
RCV 'The Dancer' Cabernet Sauvignon ★★★★ £E
Dry Land Cabernet Sauvignon ★★★☆ £D
Dry Land Shiraz ★★★☆ £D
Old Bush Vine Grenache ★★★☆ £C
Reillys Shiraz ★★★ £C
Reillys Cabernet Sauvignon ★★★ £C
Barking Mad Grenache Shiraz ★★☆ £C
Barking Mad Shiraz ★★☆ £C
Recommended Whites:
Reillys Watervale Riesling ★★★☆ £C

Barking Mad Riesling ★★☆ £B
Recommended Rosés:
Reillys Saignée ★★☆ £C

Reynell/Reynella (McLaren Vale) *www.hardywines.com.au*
Reynella or Chateau Reynella is a historic property with its origins dating from 1838 when the nation was still in its infancy (and its story is told in any decent book on Australian wine). Bought by the Thomas Hardy company in 1982, it now serves as the corporate headquarters for the much expanded Constellation Wines empire to which it belongs. Seemingly forever there has been a wealth of old-vine McLaren Vale material and in the 1990s deep, intense, muscular wines were fashioned. Open fermenters and old basket presses are utilised – Basket Pressed is the name that now adorns the reds. These are now wines of great depth, complexity and structure yet with ripe, smooth tannins. The wines are sold in Australia as Reynell.
Recommended Reds:
Cabernet Sauvignon Basket Pressed ★★★☆ £F
Shiraz Basket Pressed ★★★☆ £F

Chris Ringland (Barossa Valley) *www.chrisringland.com*
Chris Ringland's eponymous label (previously known as Three Rivers) is profiled here out of purely academic interest. Chris Ringland, who also makes the wines at LA CORTE in Italy's Puglia region and in Spain at ALTO MONCAYO and EL NIDO, makes minute amounts of Shiraz from unirrigated 100-year-old vines from a single vineyard on the eastern fringe of the Barossa Valley. Grapes cropped at the equivalent of 1 ton/acre are vinified in open fermenters before pressing in a basket press and completion of fermentation in 100% new French oak, where it can remain for more than 3 years. Its reputation is for tremendous richness and concentration. The four labels are Dimchurch, Reservation, Barossa Ranges and CR Barossa.

Riposte Wines by Tim Kappstein *www.timknappstein.com.au*
Tim Knappstein started out in the Clare Valley before founding Lenswood(now T K Wines) in the Adelaide Hills, where he makes wine for a number of labels. In 2002 Tim sold the Lenswood vineyard, but he continues to access its fruit which goes into his latest venture, Riposte, which he launched in November 2006. Knappstein's aim with this label is to make affordable cool climate premium wines. Focusing on strong suits Sauvignon Blanc, a just off-dry Traminer and a Pinot Noir, his brief is well met. They may not be as complex or concentrated as the wines he made at Lenswood, but they punch above their weight for the price point. A secondary Pinot Noir, The Dagger and a Shiraz, The Cutlass are additional reds while white Pinot Gris, The Stiletto and Scimitar Riesling are also made.
Recommended Reds:
Pinot Noir The Sabre ★★★ £E
Recommended Whites:
Sauvignon Blanc The Foil ★★★ £C
Traminer The Rapier ★★ £B

❀ **Rockford (Barossa Valley)** *www.rockfordwines.com.au*
Rockford wines still taste like true classics. Having been in the vanguard of the Barossa revival, Rocky O'Callaghan seems to have stayed true to the cause better than most. Commercial expansion to fund a fleet of Ferraris has never been the end goal. As a result the wines can be hard to find but they've not been compromised either. Basket Press Shiraz is very concentrated with the essence of old-vine Barossa fruit and should be given time to unfurl (10 years

or more). Cabernet Sauvignon is very intense and concentrated too if not overly elegant and needs similar ageing. Ready sooner are Moppa Springs, a very ripe, very flavoursome Grenache-based blend with Shiraz and Mourvèdre, and Rod & Spur (made only since 2000), a savoury, black fruited Shiraz/Cabernet Sauvignon blend. Whites deliver on flavour and character too; Eden Valley Riesling is picked late with plenty of skin contact giving a very full-flavoured example but at the expense of the finesse and other qualities this grape can deliver. The Sparkling Shiraz is one of the most famous examples going but the difficulty in getting hold of it and its cult status-fuelled price mean there's pain before pleasure.
Recommended Reds:
Shiraz Basket Press ★★★★★ £F
Sparkling Shiraz Black Shiraz ★★★★☆ £F
Cabernet Sauvignon Rifle Range ★★★★ £E
Rod & Spur ★★★ £D
Moppa Springs ★★★ £C
Recommended Whites:
Sémillon Local Growers ★★★ £C
Riesling Hand-Picked Eden Valley ★★☆ £C

Rosemount (Mclaren Vale) *www.rosemountestates.com*
Rosemount makes several of its best red wines at the McLaren Vale winery. Most famous of these is the McLaren Vale Shiraz sold as Balmoral Syrah, a wine with a real harmony of oak, fruit richness and weight as well as an extra dimension most other Australian examples miss. The Show Reserve Cabernet is sourced from Coonawarra and both French and American oak are utilised in its ageing. Show Reserve Shiraz, by contrast, comes from McLaren Vale (predominantly) and Langhorne Creek and like the Balmoral is aged only in American oak. Traditional is a Bordeaux blend of Cabernet Sauvignon, with 20% Merlot and a smaller amount of Petit Verdot, but the oak used is American not French. GSM stands for Grenache/Shiraz/Mourvèdre (typical percentages 50/40/10), and is one of the most high-profile of these now popular blends. Again, in the classic Australian mould, the oak is American. All the wines show lush fruit and oak, good depth and fine tannins, and if there is less refinement in the GSM there is also more character. Any of these reds will keep for up to 10 years but are most rewarding with just 5 or 6 years' age. Also see ROSEMOUNT (under New South Wales & Queensland).
Recommended Reds:
Syrah Balmoral ★★★★☆ £E
Shiraz Show Reserve ★★★ £C
Cabernet Sauvignon Show Reserve ★★★ £C
Traditional ★★★ £C   GSM ★★★ £C

St Hallett (Barossa Valley) *www.sthallett.com.au*
A decade ago, powered by Bob McLean, St Hallett was one of the bright new stars of Barossa. Now a successful medium-sized operation, it is perhaps the best-known but compared to Charles MELTON, ROCKFORD and others it has now lost some of its lustre. Sound, with good fruit and supple structures, the wines have lost some of their excitement and individuality. Young blood in the form of Matt Gant, now Toby Barlow has provided an injection of energy and flagship Old Block Shiraz, which was disappointing from late 90s vintages, has made something of a return to form, while, at the other end of the price spectrum, Poacher's Blend delivers good bang for buck. Blackwell Shiraz offers lots of Barossa character at a more affordable price. An intense, lemony Eden Valley Riesling is rich and weighty in its dotage and can be impressive. Biggest volumes come from the blended reds and a white, labelled Gamekeeper's

and Poacher's Blend. There are three Gamekeepers, a Shiraz, a Shiraz Cabernet and a Shiraz, Grenache Touriga blend which has an attractive floral lift. New are also a number of single vineyard Shiraz.

Recommended Reds:
Shiraz Old Block★★★★ £E
Shiraz Blackwell★★★ £D
Shiraz Faith★☆ £C
Recommended Whites:
Riesling Eden Valley★★ £C

Saltram (Barossa Valley) www.saltramwines.com.au
Saltram was once one of the most respected names in Australian wine but commercial growth and a lack of focus on the leading reds meant it wasn't the first name on the lips of the many new foreign converts to high-quality Australian wine in the last decade or so. Between 1992 and 2007 when he retired Nigel Dolan successfully restored some pride to these historic wines. Occasional great bottles from the late 50s, 60s and 70s can still be unearthed from Australian cellars (many made by Nigel's father Brian). BERINGER BLASS took control in 1996, the same year Barossa once again became the sole grape source. The wines, particularly the top reds, now show great richness and depth. Mamre Brook now offers decent value.

Recommended Reds:
Shiraz No. 1 Reserve ★★★ £E
Shiraz Mamre Brook ★★ £C
Cabernet Sauvignon Mamre Brook ★★ £C
Recommended Whites:
Chardonnay Mamre Brook★ £B

>> Sami-Odi (Barossa Valley) www.sami-odi.com
Perhaps the most boutique of the wineries is the one-third of a hectare owned by Fraser McKinley in the Barossa Valley and dedicated to organically produced Syrah. He does, however, farm some other small vineyards, but nevertheless his total production is very small. He makes a number of different bottlings almost, as it seems, on a whim. They go under the label of Sami-Odi, which is apparently named after a Turkish boat and an Italian book. Quantities of each wine are tiny, just a few hundred bottles of each, but there is no doubt about the high quality of the wines made by this dedicated winemaker. "Little Wine" is a series of bottlings of mixed vintages and the recent offering, #5, is full and fruity, with a wonderful soft mouthfeel and good balance between the fruit and acidity. Syrah "XIV" is the latest (2014) vintage of his top cuvee, displaying real finesse, balance, complexity and true varietal flavours. (NB)

Recommended Reds:
Syrah XIV ★★★★☆ £G
"Little Wine #5" Syrah ★★★★ £F

Seppeltsfield (Barossa Valley) www.seppeltsfield.com.au
Seppelt's historic Seppeltsfield winery is the centre of production for some splendid Australian fortified wines labelled Seppeltsfield but they can be difficult to obtain outside Australia, though this is starting to change, at least for the higher volume wines. KILIKANOON bought the estate from TreasuryWine Estates (who retain the Seppelt brand for table and sparkling wines) in August 2007 and have a long term lease for these 'icon' wines. All are very individual but common to each is a marvellous complexity derived from *rancio* flavours and tertiary bottle-aged characters. The intensity and power of the wines (almost all non-vintage) is not for the faint of heart but the spirit integration is finely handled.

While some approximate to a Spanish or Portuguese equivalent, flavours and structures are quite different. Outstanding examples include 'sherries' Amontillado DP 116, Show Fino DP 117 (now Flora Palomino) and Show Oloroso DP 38; and Show 'port' Tawny DP 90 (Now called Rare Tawny DP90 NV).Para Liqueur Port is produced in 2 versions, non-vintage and a 100-year-old version (1910 is the most recent release). The 100-year-old version (rating below based on the 1910 release) shows explosive spice box aromas and flavours of almost painful intensity, such is the concentration. From Rutherglen come outstanding Muscat (Show Reserve DP 63) and Tokay (Show Reserve DP 57). Also see SEPPELT GREAT WESTERN (Victoria & Tasmania).

Recommended Reds:
Para 100 Year Old Vintage Tawny ★★★★★ £H
Para 21 Year Old Vintage Tawny ★★★★ £G
NV DP 90 Rare Tawny ★★★★ £G
Para Grand Tawny ★★★☆ £D
Recommended Whites:
Rutherglen Muscat Grand ★★★☆ £D
Flora Palomino Extra Dry Fino DP117 ★★☆ £D

⚫ Shaw & Smith (Adelaide Hills) www.shawandsmith.com
The warehouse winemaking operation begun by Martin Shaw and Michael Hill Smith in 1989 has evolved into an estate-based (Balhannah and Woodside), small to medium-sized operation with a stunning new winery. Early success was fuelled by a Sauvignon that proved it was possible to make a distinctive and attractive early-drinking example in the Adelaide Hills. The most impressive wine was a deep, complex and ageworthy Reserve Chardonnay, replaced since 2000 by a single-vineyard example. The M3 vineyard at Woodside is named for Martin, Matthew and Michael. The wine is crafted around a core of pristine Adelaide Hills fruit and has excellent texture but is likely to show the greatest expression with around 5 years' age. Unoaked Chardonnay typically shows nicely concentrated fruit but there are better examples. Added with the 2005 vintage was a Pinot Noir. Also available is a superb Shiraz: which shows mineral, white pepper, concentrated plum and blackberry fruit, excellent structure, flesh and real class. Incognito is a secondary label and includes a Shiraz, a Pinot Noir and a Barbera which are all well priced (£B).

Recommended Reds:
Shiraz Adelaide Hills ★★★★ £D
Pinot Noir Adelaide Hills ★★★☆ £E
Recommended Whites:
Chardonnay M3 Vineyard ★★★★ £D
Sauvignon Blanc Adelaide Hills ★★★ £C

⚫ Tapanappa (Wrattonbully) www.tapanappawines.com.au
Brian Croser's new project is a partnership with Bordeaux's Jean-Michel Cazes (Ch. LYNCH-BAGES) and BOLLINGER - who were a former partner with Croser at PETALUMA. Tapanappa acquired the Koppamurra Vineyard prior to 2003 and have restructured the vines and renamed the site the Whalebone Vineyard. The Wrattonbully region has similar but older weathered limestone (Terra Rossa/Terra Rosa) soils to those found in Coonawarra. It is also slightly warmer. The grapes are hand-picked, a cold soak is employed and following malolactic fermentation in *barriques* the wine is aged in new French oak for 20 months. The first Cabernet Shiraz (mostly Cabernet Sauvignon) was made in 03. In addition Croser's now celebrated Tiers Chardonnay is being produced under the Tapanappa label - and is once again a wine of remarkable structure, intensity and

mineral purity. Look for older vintages of Tiers under the Petaluma label. The opulent Whalebone Vineyard, Wrattonbully Merlot is probably Australia's best expression of this variety. From 2007 this is now blended with Cabernet Franc. Tapanappa's portfolio also now encompasses Foggy Hill Pinot Noir made from vines planted in 2003 on the Fleurieu Peninsula. A further small range "Wines of Terroir" ais also made and includes a Pinot Noir Fleurieu Peninsula as well as a Shiraz and a Cabernet Shiraz from Wrattonbully.

Recommended Reds:
Cabernet Shiraz Whalebone Vineyard ★★★★☆ £F
Merlot Whalebone Vineyard ★★★★☆ £F
Pinot Noir Foggy Hill ★★★ £E
Recommended Whites:
Chardonnay Tiers ★★★★★ £F

The Lane Vineyard (Adelaide Hills) *www.thelane.com.au*
John Edwards' estate wines (previously known as Ravenswood Lane) come from 28 ha near Hahndorf in the central part of the Adelaide Hills. Much effort has gone into the packaging and image, and fortunately into the wines too, all vivid in expression and intensity. An exciting lush, peppery, fleshy Shiraz has real potential and does reflect something of the South Australia/Rhône hybrid style claimed for these wines. There is potential too in an intense, lemony Chardonnay Beginning that reveals the depth and dimension of a serious Côte de Beaune example. Two new Heritage wines (RG Chardonnay and JC Shiraz) have now been released and the other top tier wines comprise the Black Label range, while the entry level tier (once called Starvedog Lane) bears a white label and, going forward, most wines will also feature a Block Series number. The Gathering Sauvignon Sémillon is barrel-fermented and adds breadth without losing its razor sharp focus. The Shiraz Reunion shows earth and pepper to its sweet core of fruit. An unwooded 'No Oak' Chardonnay, Black Label Viognier, dessert wine and a traditional-method sparkling Chardonnay/Pinot Noir/Pinot Meunier are also made. There are no bargains here but nicely textured interesting wines at prices commensurate to quality. Though originally made in collaboration with Hardys, since 2005, all wines are estate grown and made on site at the Edwards' new small batch facility.

Recommended Reds:
Shiraz Reunion ★★★☆ £E
Cabernet Sauvignon 19th Meeting ★★★☆ £E
Recommended Whites:
Chardonnay RG Vineyard ★★★★ £F
Chardonnay Beginning ★★★ £D
Sauvignon Blanc Sémillon Gathering ★★☆ £C
Block 3 Chardonnay ★★ £C
Block 2 Pinot Gris ★★ £C

>> Thorn-Clarke (Barossa Valley) *www.thornclarkewines.com.au*
This is a substantial family owned business established in 1987 with a holding of close to 270 ha in the Barossa and an output now of 80,000 cases a year. A wide range of wines is made under a number of labels and includes Cabernet Sauvignon, Merlot, Nebbiolo, Pinot Gris and Chardonnay as well as a sparkler and a fortified tawny. The winery style is generally one of approachable wines offering good value with vibrant fruit albeit with some depth and structure in the Shotfire wines. Mount Crawford Riesling is a crisp green fruit rather than citrus infused example and comes from the Eden Valley. The Terra Barossa range offer good value including the dark berry fruited Shiraz. It is cool fermented and then barrel aged for 12 months. The Shotfire Shiraz is very Barossa in style rich, ripe and

opulent black fruits with a rich oak background after spending 14 months in 40 % new American oak hogsheads. The Quartage is a full-bodied Bordeaux style blend of Cabernet Sauvignon, Cabernet Franc, Petit Verdot and Merlot. More restrained in style and aged in French barrels it doesn't quite have the depth of the Shiraz with a slightly tarry edge. The William Randell Shiraz is stylish and very intense, offering not only class but value too. A selection of the best Shiraz lots, after controlled fermentation and vatting the wine went through the malolactic in barrel before ageing for 14 months in total. A William Randell Cabernet Sauvignon is also made as well as a very limited Ron Thorn Shiraz, produced only in what the winery considers their best years. (DM)

Recommended Reds:
William Randell Shiraz ★★★★ £E
Shotfire Shiraz ★★★ £C
Shotfire Quartage ★★☆ £C
Terra Barossa Shiraz ★★ £B
Recommended Whites:
Mount Crawford Riesling ★★ £B

Tin Shed (Eden Valley) *www.tinshedwines.com*
This new small Eden/Barossa operation, originally a joint venture between viticulturalist Andrew Wardlaw and the owner/chef of the renowned Vintners Bar & Grill in the Barossa, Peter Clarke is now wholly owned by Clarke and his wife. Their wines are made without added yeasts, enzymes or acidity. Indeed the wines are vibrant, fruit-intense and expressive in stark contrast with some of the more 'made', manipulated styles emanating from the Barossa. Wild Bunch Riesling, while only modestly structured, has exaggerated limey, toasty aromas and bursts with flavour and real fruit intensity. The stylish Melting Pot Shiraz, which includes some Mourvèdre and Grenache, has exuberant very berryish fruit intensity and good depth and length. Single Wire Shiraz, from Barossa and Eden Valley fruit, is foot-trodden before ageing in French oak. There is fabulous fruit expression, well-integrated oak and impressive depth and length if not the dimension on the palate to put it amongst the very best. Also made but not tasted is OMG Mataro and All Day Barossa Rosé.

Recommended Reds:
Shiraz Single Wire ★★★★ £E
Shiraz Melting Pot ★★★ £C
Recommended Whites:
Riesling Wild Bunch Eden Valley ★★ £C

◉ Torbreck (Barossa Valley) *www.torbreck.com*
Established in the mid-1990s, Torbreck became one of the most raved-about Barossa wineries by the turn of the century and is one of the few which produces genuinely outstanding wines that matched some of the hype. David Powell managed to buy small parcels of fruit from very old unirrigated, low yielding vineyards and turned them into wine with great aroma, deep fruit, structure and balance. All the reds have highish but balanced alcohol levels and a breadth and extract many other Barossa/Clare/McLaren Vale blockbusters lack. Runrig, the top wine first made in 1995, is Shiraz with a little Viognier; the fruit here is sensational. As well as great depth and class, this wine has the sort of dimension and structure only encountered in the very best Côte-Rôties and needs 8–10 years' ageing. In 2005, Powell got hold of Shiraz from Malcolm and Joylene Seppelt's old Gnadenfrei vineyard which he had coveted, regarding it as even "head and shoulders" above the Runrig components (Torbreck had made wine for the Seppelts). The

South Australia

Australia

result is The Laird, which is aged in extra thick staved French oak for 3 years and sadly not tasted! Descendant (a vineyard established from Runrig cuttings) includes a little Viognier, which contributes to its more open, perfumed character, but it has good extract and intensity too. The Factor, made since 1998 from 100% Shiraz from old unirrigated vines, is tighter, more compact and less expressive yet promises to have the greater ageing potential. The Struie, new since 2001, is a super, stylish blend of equal parts Barossa and Eden Valley fruit, while Juveniles and The Steading are southern Rhône-style blends of Grenache, Shiraz and Mourvèdre. Both of the latter pair are perfumed with lovely fruit and are supple and long; The Steading, aged in used and large oak, shows the better structure, but not the vibrancy or purity of Juveniles. Woodcutters red (Shiraz) and white (Sémillon) are the more affordable basics and offer good fruit, as does a white Woodcuttters RVM (Roussanne, Viognier and Marsanne). Torbreck also make The Pict, (Greenock Mataro), Les Amis (Seppeltsfield Grenache), The Gask (EdenValley Shiraz), Saignée, a bone dry Mataro rosé and The Bothie, a sweet Muscat. Craig Isbel now heads the winemaking team but the direction is clearly laid down by the path first trodden by David Powell.

Recommended Reds:
Runrig ✪✪✪✪✪ £H
The Factor ★★★★★ £G
Descendant ★★★★☆ £G
The Struie ★★★☆ £E
The Steading ★★★☆ £E
Juveniles ★★★ £D
Woodcutter's Shiraz ★★ £C
Recommended Whites:
Woodcutter's Sémillon ★☆ £C

❀ **Turkey Flat (Barossa Valley)** *www.turkeyflat.com.au*
Turkey Flat has a priceless resource of old-vine Barossa fruit. Some of the vines were planted in the 1840s. The winery has established its credentials particularly with Shiraz but also Grenache and Mataro. Shiraz is easily the best wine – succulent and full of old-viney fruit without being overwhelmed by oak. Grenache is even more approachable but lacks a little richness and depth by comparison. A Mataro shows good meaty depth, saddle soap and sinewy tannins. Butcher's Block is named for a vineyard planted to Mataro, Shiraz and Grenache and although an attractive, perfumed wine it misses the interest and intensity of better examples. Few rosés are worth seeking out but Turkey Flat's fragrant cherry and berry-fruited off-dry example (from Grenache, Cabernet, Shiraz and Mataro) is delicious, fresh and balanced if drunk very young. The Barossa Valley white is a blend of Marsanne, Viognier and Roussanne, still finding its feet, but promising. Marsanne also finds its way into The Last Straw, a vin de paille and the estate also produces two fortified sweet wines, Shiraz VP and a Pedro Ximenez which, while powerful, is more citrus and caramel inflected than its Spanish counterparts – no bad thing. The line up is completed by a sparkling Shiraz (not tasted).

Recommended Reds:
Shiraz ★★★★ £E
Grenache ★★☆ £C
Mataro ★★★ £C
Butchers Block ★★☆ £C
Recommended Whites:
Pedro Ximenez ★★☆ £F
Butchers Block ★ £C
Recommended Rosés:
Rosé ★★ £C

Two Hands *www.twohandswines.com*
There have been a lot of changes here since the initial (and justified) hype quickly turned this into a sought-after label. Grape sources, winemaker and production levels have all changed – the latter significantly with a profusion of limited-production labels – since the first vintage in 2000. The winemaker is Matt Wenk with consultancy from Rolf BINDER, where the wines used to be made until 2004. The standard of the reds is generally very high, most with both style and a sense of place allied to an intense, super-concentrated fruit expression. These are not wines for the feint hearted though, at best, balance and use of oak are good. Lily's Garden McLaren Vale Shiraz is arguably the most consistently fine of the reds and is made in a blockbuster style; Gnarly Dudes shows fine balance and structure and represents good value. A very intensely flavoured Riesling, The Wolf, wants for better definition and structure. Better is Brilliant Disguise Moscato (in the style of Moscato d'Asti) which, light and fluffy, could not be more different from the blockbuster reds. Small amounts of flagship Ares (Shiraz), Aphrodite (Cabernet Sauvignon) and Aerope (Grenache) are also made as well as a number of single vineyard Shiraz from the Barossa.

Recommended Reds:
Shiraz Lily's Garden McLaren Vale ★★★★ £E
Shiraz Angel's Share McLaren Vale ★★★ £C
Shiraz Gnarly Dudes Barossa Valley ★★★ £C
Shiraz/Cabernet Sauvignon The Bull and the Bear ★★★ £E
Shiraz/Grenache Brave Faces Barossa Valley ★★★ £D
Recommended Whites:
Riesling The Wolf Clare Valley ★★ £D
Moscato Brilliant Disguise Barossa Valley ★★ £D

Ulithorne (McLaren Vale) *www.ulithorne.com.au*
In 1997, a 12 ha McLaren Vale vineyard (planted in 1971 to Shiraz and Cabernet Sauvignon) was revived by artist Sam Harrison and Rose Kentish. A further 15 ha were subsequently added (including some Merlot) and Rose made a single wine, Frux Frugis Shiraz. in late 2006, the couple sold the vineyard but not the brand; Rose continues to make wine under the label from the Ulithorne vineyard and lately has made a Cabernet Shiraz blend called Paternus and a GSM blend.

Recommended Reds:
Shiraz Frux Frugis ★★★★ £F
Cabernet Shiraz Paternus ★★★★ £F
Dona Grenache Shiraz Mourvèdre ★★★ £D

Wakefield (Clare Valley) *www.wakefieldwines.com.au*
Established in 1969, Taylor's, as it is known in Australia (if not on export markets due to a certain port that's been around for a little longer), is still family owned. It is also the Clare Valley's biggest producer with 500 ha of vineyards but don't let that put you off as there are some good wines here. Best are the premium St Andrew's varietals and the super premium Visionary Cabernet. Intense toasty, limey Riesling has splendid depth and complexity with 5 years' age or more while Chardonnay is full, complex and oaky but with a good backbone of citric acidity to balance. Shiraz (American oaked) has a classic Clare berry/mineral stamp but Cabernet Sauvignon (aged in French oak) is at least as good with terrific complexity and dimension, and no lack of class. Estate reds are simpler and lighter but ripe with plenty of fruit intensity, best with at least 3–4 years' age. All estate and St Andrew's wines come from Clare Valley fruit. Also made under the Taylor's label are Jaraman varietals which combine fruit from different regions. A Clare Valley/Eden

Valley Riesling has plenty of push and pull - very flavoursome and complete. A budget range of varietals are produced under the Eighty Acres (£B) and Promised Land labels (£C).

Recommended Reds:
Cabernet Sauvignon The Visionary ★★★★☆ £G
Cabernet Sauvignon St Andrews ★★★★ £F
Cabernet Sauvignon Estate ★★ £C
Shiraz St Andrews ★★★ £F   Shiraz Estate ★★ £C
Merlot Estate ★★ £C

Recommended Whites:
Riesling St Andrews ★★★★ £E
Riesling Jaraman ★★★ £B   Riesling Estate ★★ £B
Chardonnay St Andrews ★★★☆ £E
Chardonnay Estate ★ £C

Geoff Weaver (Adelaide Hills) *www.geoffweaver.com.au*
From 11 ha of Lenswood vineyards established in the mid-1980s and at over 500 m elevation, Geoff Weaver (ex HARDYS) makes a modest amount of intensely flavoured, finely honed wine. Whites are best and benefit from time in bottle. An intensely flavoured and ageworthy Chardonnay vies with an intense toasty, limey and even more cellarworthy Riesling as the best of these. A stylish Sauvignon with ripe gooseberry fruit and a hint of smoke and blackcurrant leaf is also ageworthy. Ferus Sauvignon (not tasted), made only in top years, is naturally fermented and aged on the lees for around a year in second use oak. Cabernet/Merlot (typically more than 80% Cabernet) needs a warm year really to succeed; otherwise cooler leafy, sappy characters become too dominant and the texture too lean; it seems to have fallen by the wayside. Pinot Noir, on the other hand shows good texture, depth and better structure than previously.

Recommended Reds:
Pinot Noir ★★ £E

Recommended Whites:
Chardonnay ★★★ £E
Riesling ★★★ £C
Sauvignon Blanc ★★ £C

❀ Wendouree (Clare Valley)
This Clare Valley producer maintains a cult following by sticking rigidly to a formula of maximising the extraordinary fruit produced from 12 ha of vines. The winery dates from 1895 and little seems to have changed in the 100 years or so since. The reds are massive and uncompromising, extracted and tannic yet with dense, earthy impenetrable fruit when young. Balance and ripeness are nearly always there, ensuring these wines will, after 20 years or more, be complex and compelling. Shiraz/ Mataro (Mourvèdre) and Shiraz/ Malbec are predominantly Shiraz-based and, together with the varietal Shiraz, are perhaps more consistent than the Cabernet-based reds. None of the wines are made in much more than 500-case lots, so total production remains tiny. The prices are reasonable for the quality, given the considerable demand. Above all they are a cellaring investment for wine drinkers with patience.

Recommended Reds:
Shiraz★★★★☆ £F   Shiraz/Mataro★★★★☆ £F
Shiraz/Malbec★★★★☆ £F
Cabernet/Malbec★★★★ £F
Cabernet Sauvignon★★★★☆£F

Wirra Wirra (McLaren Vale) *www.wirra.com.au*
Wirra Wirra is a substantial operation (especially with the

acquisition of the Rayners vineyard in 2007, formerly the source of Brokenwood's Rayner Shiraz) with a long-established reputation. In recent years it has recruited expert help from the likes of Dr Tony Jordan and Tim James (from HARDYS) but the most recent accolades have deservedly gone to senior winemaker Samantha Connew who is now suceeded by her right hand man Paul Smith, who is himself suceeded as Assistant Winemaker by recently crowned McLaren Vale Bush King Paul Carpenter. Quality is uniformly very high and the top reds will repay keeping for 10 years' or more. Powerful, complex flagship reds are Cabernet Sauvignon, The Angelus / Dead Ringer (now labelled as the latter outside of Australia due to possible confusion with the famous Bordeaux château with the same name) and Shiraz, RSW. Absconder is a Grenache coming from some of the oldest blocks of the variety in McLaren Vale. In addition occasional Vineyard Series reds have been released from exceptional vintages including a Penley Coonawarra Cabernet Sauvignon and Chook Block McLaren Vale Shiraz as well as a straight Grenache (Allawah). Also very impressive is the regular McLaren Vale Shiraz now called Woodhenge. At a more everyday level, Church Block is a long-standing blend of Cabernet, Shiraz and Merlot. Wirra Wirra whites are flavoursome but do not match the reds for quality. Adelaide Hills wines are on the up, the Sauvignon Blanc (Hiding Champion) now picked early showing good line and intensity; 12th Man Chardonnay is also much improved. The Scrubby Rise brand includes both a red and a white blend as well as Shiraz and Chardonnay. Sparkling wines are also made, both The Cousins from Pinot Noir and Chardonnay and The Anthem, a Sparkling Shiraz. For fortifieds there's VP Vintage Fortified Shiraz.

Recommended Reds:
Cabernet Sauvignon The Angelus/Dead Ringer ★★★★ £F
Shiraz RSW ★★★★ £E
Shiraz Woodhenge McLaren Vale ★★★☆ £E
Cabernet/Shiraz/Merlot Church Block ★★☆ £C

Recommended Whites:
Chardonnay 12th Man Adelaide Hills ★★★ £C
Riesling Lost Watch Adelaide Hills ★★ £B

Woodstock (Mclaren Vale) *www.woodstockwine.com.au*
Woodstock is one of McLaren Vale's well-established wineries able to draw on its own vineyards for a solid, reasonably priced range of wines. As well as 22 ha in McLaren Flat, 33 ha of vineyards are located in Langhorne Creek (Angas Vineyard) and a further 27 ha in Limestone Coast (Wirrega Vineyard). The leading variety unsurprisingly is Shiraz, particularly The Stocks, the flagship wine made since 1991. The fruit from very old vines stands up very well to the new American oak in which it is aged. Regular Shiraz and a Cabernet Sauvignon are both rich, ripe and concentrated if lacking a little flair. More straightforward is a Shiraz Cabernet blend. Whites include Sémillon/Sauvignon Blanc, Riesling and Chardonnay. All show attractive, ripe, generous flavours but only the Chardonnay can stand a bit of age. Botrytis Sweet White is a blend of Chenin Blanc, Riesling and Sémillon and is ripe and intense if not that refined. A small amout of fortified wine is also made.

Recommended Reds:
Shiraz The Stocks ★★★☆ £E
Shiraz ★★★ £C
Cabernet Sauvignon ★★★ £C
Shiraz Cabernet Sauvignon ★☆ £B

Recommended Whites:
Chardonnay ★☆ £C   Sémillon Sauvignon ★☆ £C
Botrytis Sweet White ★☆ £C

South Australia

Wynns (Coonawarra) www.wynns.com.au

The most famous producer name in Coonawarra is a veritable colossus with 900 ha, around a third of the terra rossa soils. The oldest vines dating back to the 60s underwent a nerve-wracking renovation in the late 90s, during which time Wynns did not make flagship reds John Riddoch Cabernet Sauvignon for four years or Michael Shiraz between 1998 and 2003. After cutting back the build up of dead wood , not all the vines bounced back but those that did are now producing wines with "added freshness and ripeness". It shows in a brighter fruit quality and more supple tannins with better integrated wood. John Riddoch Cabernet is a magnificent rich, powerful rendition of Cabernet that makes no apology to any other great Cabernet region and needs to be drunk with 10 years' age or more. Michael Shiraz is the Shiraz equivalent of John Riddoch it is equally rich and powerful. Both Michael and John Riddoch wines now use only a fraction of the very best fruit available. The famous estate-based Black Label Cabernet is now a big-volume wine but is still relatively inexpensive with the same intense blackcurrant/blackberry fruit, oak and tannin balance it has always had. Shiraz is often at least as good and from a top vintage can add the little extra richness that makes it an excellent buy. Cabernet/Shiraz/Merlot includes only a little Merlot and the Cabernet and Shiraz components invariably merge for a ripe, supple, fruity red. Chardonnay delivers fine fruit and real complexity, a far cry from some of the overoaked earlier efforts. Riesling can be one of Australia's best bargain whites, consistently delivering a floral, limey, fruit-driven intensity. Despite its size, Wynns stands out thanks to its remarkable viticultural resources.

Recommended Reds:

Cabernet Sauvignon John Riddoch ★★★★★ £F
Cabernet Sauvignon Black Label ★★★ £D
Shiraz Michael ★★★★ £F
Shiraz ★★ £C Cabernet/Shiraz/Merlot ★ £C

Recommended Whites:

Chardonnay ★★ £B Riesling ★☆ £B

❀ **Yalumba (Barossa Valley)** www.yalumba.com

Yalumba is the only big Australian wine company still to be family-owned and, founded in 1849, is Australia's oldest family-owned company at that. Winemaking, led by Brian Walsh since the late 1980s, is now headed by the talented Louisa Rose. With more than 650 ha of vines from diverse sources, the range is necessarily large and continually evolving and, though some wines have a long history, there is no shortage of innovation here. Indeed, for such a large operation, the company is remarkably fleet of foot. It is at the vanguard of environmentally sustainable practices, pioneered Viognier Down Under and has been bang on trend with its recent introduction of several single vineyard reds, designed to showcase old vine fruit from different Barossa sub-zones. Ageworthy premium Barossa reds are traditional in the sense that they are full bodied with ripe, powerful tannins and no shortage of oak. But there is also a terrific concentration, purity and animation to the fruit, especially in recent years. Premium wines begin with The Reserve, a very limited-production Cabernet Sauvignon/ Shiraz blend made in 1990, 92, 96, 98, 2001, 2002 and 2004. Others produced on a more regular basis include Octavius, an expensive, richly oaky old-vine Barossa Shiraz (recently joined by plummy junior Barossa Shiraz, Patchwork), and The Signature (two-thirds Barossa Cabernet, one-third Barossa Shiraz), a suave, flattering blend streaked with vanilla in which the Cabernet lends gravitas to the more exuberant Shiraz. Yalumba's faith in this blend is underlined by the re-introduction of

the super-intense FDR1A Cabernet Shiraz (reviving a label first used in 1974) and The Scribbler, a new junior tier, this one more forward, with Shiraz the dominant partner. Coonawarra is the source of The Menzies range, a Cabernet, Merlot and Cabernet/Shiraz. New to the Coonawarra range is The Cigar, a glossy, more approachable young vine Cabernet with impressive concentration. MGS (Mourvèdre/Grenache/Shiraz) from the Hand-Picked range is a ripe, spicy berry-fruited example of this style of Barossa red. Other reds in this range include an expressive, floral Bush Vine Grenache, velvety Shiraz Viognier and an innovative Tempranillo Grenache Viognier blend (not tasted). There is also an Adelaide Hills Chardonnay, FDW (Fine Dry White) sourced from select growers. It shows some of the stylish complexity and subtlety typical of the best examples. Much has been made of Yalumba's efforts with Viognier (it pioneered plantings of the variety in South Australia) and vine age, the introduction of new clones together with a more oxidative approach to winemaking is paying dividends. With ripe, but not overripe, apricot and increasingly savoury lees nuances, top tier Virgilius can give Condrieu a run for its money, while the mid-priced Eden Valley wine shows good fruit purity and balance, representing good value for money. Late-harvested/botrytis styles now include Riesling, Sémillon and Viognier under a Noble Pick label. Dolcetto, Nebbiolo and other varieties have also been released locally under the Vinnovation Collection label. Y is a series of relatively inexpensive varietals including an unwooded Chardonnay, Riesling, Viognier, Pinot Grigio, Merlot and Shiraz; for a small premium, certified organic versions of Shiraz and Viognier are now available. Even cheaper are the simple, innocuous wines of budget brand, Oxford Landing, produced from Riverlands fruit. Other wineries owned by the family include the Eden Valley estates of PEWSEY VALE and Heggies as well as JANSZ from the Pipers River area of northern Tasmania. A very impressive Mesh Riesling, made in collaboration with Jeffrey GROSSET, shows a touch more fruit weight and punchier acidity than other Eden Valley examples, gravitating towards the Clare Valley in this respect. The Heggies wines are made by Peter Gambetta and include Riesling (occasionally also made in a botrytised version) with a pure citrus and mineral character and elegant, complex Chardonnay. Reserves of both are also made. The only red is a variable yet sometimes stylish Merlot. Smith & Hooper wines come from Wrattonbully fruit and include an ambitious Reserve Merlot. (SA)

Yalumba

Recommended Reds:

The Reserve Barossa ★★★★☆ £F
Shiraz The Octavius ★★★★ £F
Shiraz Swingbridge Vineyard Vineyard Craneford Eden Valley ★★★★ £F
Shiraz/Viognier Handpicked ★★★ £D
Shiraz Patchwork Barossa ★★ £C
Cabernet Sauvignon Coonawarra The Menzies ★★★ £E
Cabernet Sauvignon Coonawarra The Cigar ★★☆ £C
Cabernet/Shiraz The Signature ★★★★☆ £E
Cabernet/Shiraz FDR1A Barossa ★★★☆ £D
Cabernet/Shiraz The Scribbler Barossa ★★★ £C
Grenache Handpicked Tri-Centenary Vines ★★★★ £D
Grenache Barossa Bush Vine ★★☆ £C

Recommended Whites:

Muscat Museum Release ★★★★ £E
Chardonnay FDW Adelaide Hills ★★★ £C
Chardonnay Eden Valley ★★ £C
Viognier Virgilius ★★★ £E

Viognier Eden Valley ★★ £C
Viognier Organic ★☆ £B
Viognier Y ★ £B
Heggies
Recommended Reds:
Merlot Eden Valley ★★ £C
Recommended Whites:
Chardonnay Eden Valley ★★ £C
Riesling Eden Valley ★★ £B
Grosset - Hill-Smith
Recommended Whites:
Riesling Mesh ★★★☆ £D
Smith & Hooper
Recommended Reds:
Merlot Reserve ★★★ £D
Cabernet Sauvignon/Merlot ★★ £B

Zema Estate (Coonawarra) *www.zema.com.au*
Nearly 50 ha of estate vineyards were built up in Coonawarra by this family during the 1980s and early 90s, the core being in the very heart of the region. The wines express much of the best of Coonawarra with dense, powerful fruit lent a little more structure from oak-ageing. However, the oak is restrained, making for less obvious, slightly firmer wines that really benefit from at least 3–5 years' bottle-age. The oak is more in evidence, but not overdone, in the lusher Family Selection Cabernet Sauvignon. Harvesting is mechanical as in most vineyards in Coonawarra but the vines are still hand-pruned, which arguably makes a positive impact on quality. If slightly less good in cooler years, the wines really shine from good to great years. Cluny, a somewhat lighter, softer Bordeaux blend (adding Merlot, Cabernet Franc and Malbec to Cabernet Sauvignon) is the most accessible. A Family Selection Shiraz is also made. New is Saluti, a Cabernet Sauvignon/Shiraz blend with considerable concentration, but not at the expense of finesse. Greg Clayfield (ex-Lindemans) has now replaced long-term winemaker Tom Simons.
Recommended Reds:
Cabernet Sauvignon ★★★ £E
Cabernet Sauvignon Family Selection ★★★☆ £E
Cabernet Sauvignon/Shiraz Saluti ★★★★ £F
Shiraz ★★★ £E
Cluny ★★★ £D

Other wines of note

Angas The Bull
Recommended Reds: Cabernet Sauvignon ★★☆ £C
Arrivo (Adelaide Hills)
Recommended Rosés:
Nebbiolo Rosato Di Nebbiolo ★☆ £C
Australian Domaine Wines
Recommended Reds:
The Hattrick (Shiraz/Grenache/Cabernet) ★★★ £E
Battle Of Bosworth
Recommended Reds: Cabernet Sauvignon ★★★ £C
Shiraz ★★★ £C
Bellwether (Coonawarra)
Recommended Reds: Cabernet Sauvignon ★★★ £E
Art Series (Shiraz/Malbec Wrattonbully) ★★★ £D

Recommended Whites:
Chardonnay Tamar Valley Tasmania ★★★ £E
Art Series Heathcote Victoria (Vermentino) ★★ £D
Bethany (Barossa Valley)
Recommended Reds: Shiraz ★★ £C
Cabernet/Merlot ★ £C
Recommended Whites: Sémillon ★★ £B
Bird in Hand (Adelaide Hills)
Recommended Reds: Shiraz Two in The Bush ★★☆ £B
Shiraz Bird in Hand ★★★☆ £C
Merlot Adelaide Hills ★★★☆ £C
Cabernet Sauvignon Nest Egg ★★★ £C
BK Wines (Adelaide Hills)
Recommended Reds: Gower (Pinot Noir) ★★★☆ £E
Skin 'n Bones (Pinot Noir) ★★☆ £D
Red Blend (Grenache, Mataro, Syrah) ★★★☆ £E
Cult (Syrah) ★★★ £D
Nouveau (Syrah) ★★★ £D
Recommended Whites: Swaby (Chardonnay) ★★★ £E
One Ball (Chardonnay) ★★★ £D
Skin 'n Bones (Savagnin) ★★☆ £D
Blewitt Springs/Hillsview
Recommended Whites: Chardonnay Coonawarra ★★ £C
Recommended Reds: Shiraz Adelaide ★★★ £C
Malbec Langhorne Creek ★★ £C
Cabernet Sauvignon Langhorne Creek ★★ £C
Brand's Laira of Coonawarra
Recommended Reds:
Shiraz Stentiford's Reserve Old Vine ★★★ £F
Brothers in Arms (Langhorne Creek)
Recommended Reds: Shiraz ★★★ £C
Leo Buring
Recommended Whites:
Riesling Leonay Eden Valley ★★★ £E
Riesling Watervale ★★★ £D
Cape Jaffa (Mount Benson)
Recommended Reds:
Shiraz Mount Benson ★★☆ £C
Ceravolo (Adelaide Plains)
Recommended Reds: Shiraz ★★★ £C
Petit Verdot ★★★ £C
Sangiovese ★☆ £C
Claymore (Clare Valley)
Recommended Reds:
Shiraz Reserve Nirvána ★★★★ £E
Shiraz Dark Side Of The Moon ★★★ £C
Shiraz Walk On The Wild Side ★★☆ £C
Recommended Whites:
Riesling Joshua Tree ★★★ £C
clos Clare (Clare Valley)
Recommended Whites:
Riesling Watervale ★★★☆ £D
Creed (Barossa Valley)
Recommended Whites:
Riesling Wild Child ★★★☆ £C

South Australia

Recommended Reds:

The Pretty Miss (Shiraz/Cabernet Franc/Viognier) ★★☆ £D

Dog Ridge (Mclaren Vale)

Recommended Whites:

Sauvignon Blanc Mclaren Vale ★☆ £B

Recommended Reds:

Cabernet/Merlot The Pup ★☆ £B

Cabernet Sauvignon DV3 Mclaren Vale ★★★ £D

Shiraz DV7 Mclaren Vale ★★★☆ £D

Linda Domas

Recommended Whites:

Viognier/Chardonnay Vis à Vis ★★☆ £B

Sauvignon Blanc Salience ★★☆ £C

Recommended Reds:

Shiraz Egidio Mclaren Vale ★★ £D

Eden Springs (Eden Valley)

Recommended Whites: Riesling High Eden ★★★★ £C

Eperosa (Barossa Valley)

Recommended Reds:

Stonegarden (Grenache) ★★★★ £F

Synthesis (Mataro/Grenache/Syrah) ★★★★ £E

Elevation (Syrah) ★★★☆ £E

First Drop

Recommended Reds:

Shiraz Mothers Milk Barossa ★★★ £C

Shiraz Minchia Montepuciano Adelaide Hills ★★★ £C

Five Geese (Mclaren Vale)

Recommended Reds:

Shiraz Reserve Jon's Block ★★★☆ £D

Grenache Reserve ★★★☆ £D

Grenache/Shiraz Ganders Blend ★★★ £C

Fox Gordon

Recommended Reds:

By George Cabernet Tempranillo Adelaide Hills/Barossa Valley ★★★ £D

The Dark Prince Nero d'Avola Adelaide Hills ★★★ £C

Shiraz Eight Uncles Barossa Valley ★★☆ £C

Recommended Whites:

Princess Fiano Adelaide Hills ★★★ £C

Abby Viognier Adelaide Hills ★★★ £C

David Franz (Barossa Valley)

Recommended Whites:

Semillon Ancient Vine Long Gully ★★★☆ £C

Galah

Recommended Reds:

Cabernet/Malbec/Shiraz Clare Valley ★★ £C

Shiraz Clare Valley ★★ £C

Cabernet Sauvignon Clare Valley ★★ £C

Gibson Wines (Barossa Valley)

Recommended Reds:

Wilfreda (Shiraz/Mourvèdre/Grenache) ★★★ £D

God's Hill/ Scalzi Estate (Barossa Valley)

Recommended Reds: Shiraz Menzel ★★★★ £F

Tim Gramp (Clare Valley)

Recommended Whites:

Riesling Watervale ★★ £B

Recommended Reds:

Cabernet Sauvignon Watervale ★★ £B

Shiraz Mclaren Vale ★★★ £D

Shiraz Mount Lofty Ranges ★★★ £C

Haan Wines (Barossa Valley)

Recommended Whites: Viognier ★★ £C

Recommended Reds: Merlot Prestige ★★★ £D

Wilhelmus ★★★★ £E

Hahndorf Hill Winery (Adelaide Hills)

Recommended Whites: Sauvignon Blanc ★★★ £C

Hugh Hamilton (McLaren Vale)

Recommended Reds:

Shiraz Saperavi Black Ops ★★★☆ £D

Hentley Farm (Barossa Valley)

Recommended Reds:

Shiraz Mount Lofty Ranges ★★★☆ £C

Heritage Wines/Stephen Hoff

Recommended Reds: Shiraz Barossa ★★ £B

Cabernet/Malbec ★★ £C

Hillstowe (Adelaide Hills)

Recommended Reds: Shiraz Buxton ★★ £B

Shiraz Mary's Hundred ★★★★ £C

Pinot Noir Udy's Mill ★★★ £C

Recommended Whites:

Chardonnay Udy's Mill ★★ £C

Hobbs (Barossa Ranges)

Recommended Whites:

Viognier Single Vineyard ★★★ £E

Recommended Reds:

Shiraz Gregor (Late Harvest) ★★★★ £F

Grenache (Dessert Wine) ★★★★ £F

Hugo (Mclaren Vale)

Recommended Reds:

Shiraz ★★★☆ £C

Recommended Whites:

Chardonnay ★★ £B

Irvine (Eden Valley)

Recommended Reds:

Merlot Grand Eden Valley ★★★★ £F

Merlot Spring Hill Eden Valley ★★☆ £C

Zinfandel Reserve Eden Valley ★★★ £E

The Baroness (Merlot/Cab Franc/Cab Sauv) ★★★☆ £E

Merlot Cabernet Barossa ★★ £C

Islander Estate (Kangaroo Island)

Recommended Reds:

The Red ★★★ £D

Jeanneret (Clare Valley)

Recommended Reds:

Shiraz Rank And File ★★★★ £D

Cabernet Sauvignon Curly Red ★★★ £C

Recommended Whites:

Riesling Doozie ★★★ £E

Stephen John (Clare Valley)

Recommended Whites:

Riesling Watervale ★★ £C

Trevor Jones (Barossa Valley)
Recommended Reds:
Shiraz Dry Grown ★★★ £F
Recommended Whites:
Chardonnay Virgin ★★★ £C
KT & The Falcon (Clare Valley)
Recommended Whites:
Riesling Peglidis Watervale ★★★★ £D
Riesling Melva Watervale ★★★★ £D
Kaesler (Barossa Valley)
Recommended Reds:
Shiraz Stonehorse ★★★ £E
Kanta Wines (Adelaide Hills)
Recommended Whites:
Riesling Kanta ★★★★ £E
Kopparossa
Recommended Reds:
Cabernet Merlot Coonawarra ★★★ £C
Kurtz Family/Siebenschlafer
Recommended Reds:
Seven Sleepers Barossa (Malbec/Cab Sauv/Merlot/Other) ★★★☆ £C
Larrikin's Ghost
Recommended Reds:
Shiraz Mclaren Vale ★★★ £C
Lengs & Cooter
Recommended Reds:
Shiraz Old Vines Clare Valley ★★★ £C
Longview (Adelaide Hills)
Recommended Whites: Viognier Beau Sea ★★ £C
Chardonnay Blue Cow Unwooded ★ £C
Riesling Iron Knob ★★ £C
Sauvignon Blanc Whippet ★ £C
Recommended Reds: Shiraz Yakka ★★★ £D
Nebbiolo Black Crow ★ £C
Mclean's Farm (Barossa Valley)
Recommended Reds:
Barossa Reserve (Shiraz/Cabernet Sauvignon) ★★ £C
Shiraz Trinity Corner Barossa Valley ★★★ £C
Recommended Whites:
Riesling (Edenvalley) ★★★ £C
Massena (Barossa Valley)
Recommended Reds:
The Eleventh Hour (Shiraz) ★★★★ £E
Maxwell (Mclaren Vale)
Recommended Reds:
Shiraz Minotaur Reserve ★★★★ £F
Shiraz Eight Bells ★★☆ £C
Cabernet Sauvignon Reserve Lime Cave ★★★ £C
Cabernet Merlot Little Demon ★★ £C
Recommended Whites:
Chardonnay Adelaide Hills ★★☆ £C
Verdelho Little Demon Adelaide Hills ★★ £B
Recommended Rosés:
Grenache Little Demon ★★ £B

Mollydooker
Recommended Reds:
Shiraz The Boxer ★★★ £D
Two Left Feet (Shiraz/Cabernet Sauvignon/Merlot) ★★★ £D
Cabernet Sauvignon Maitre D' ★★★ £D
Morambro Creek (Padthaway)
Recommended Reds:
Shiraz Padthaway ★★★ £C
Cabernet Sauvignon Padthaway ★★★ £C
Shiraz Jip Jip Rocks Limestone Coast ★★☆ £B
Murray Street Vineyards (Barossa Valley)
Recommended Reds:
Shiraz Black Label ★★★ £C
Recommended Whites:
Semillon Black Label ★★★ £C
Noon (Mclaren Vale)
Recommended Reds:
Shiraz/Grenache Eclipse ★★★★ £E
Norfolk Rise Vineyard (Mount Benson)
Recommended Reds:
Shiraz Noolook ★★★☆ £D
Cabernet Sauvignon Noolook ★★★☆ £C
Merlot Mount Benson ★★★ £C
Ochota Barrels (Adelaide Hills)
Recommended Reds: 186 (Grenache) ★★★★ £F
Texture Like Sun (Pinot Noir/Grenache) ★★★★ £E
A Sense of Compression (Grenache) ★★★☆ £F
Fugazi (Grenache) ★★★ £E
Impeccable Disorder (Pinot Noir) ★★★ £F
A Forest (Pinot Noir) ★★☆ £E
Shellac (Syrah) ★★★ £E
I am the Owl (Syrah) ★★☆ £E
Recommended Whites: 5V 0V (Chardonnay) ★★★ £F
The Slint (Chardonnay) ★★☆ £E
Weird Berries in the Wood (Gewürztraminer) ★★ £D
The Other Wine Company (Adelaide Hills)
Recommended Reds:
Grenache McLaren Vale ★★★☆ £C
Recommended Whites:
Pinot Gris ★★☆ £C
Paulett (Clare Valley)
Recommended Whites:
Riesling Polish Hill River ★★ £B
Riesling Antonina ★★★★ £F
Riesling Trillains Sparkling ★★ £B
Chardonnay Polish Hill River ★★ £B
Recommended Reds:
Cabernet/Merlot Polish Hill River ★★ £D
Shiraz Polish Hill River ★★★ £D
Pertaringa (Mclaren Vale)
Recommended Reds:
Shiraz Over The Top ★★★★ £E
Shiraz Undercover ★★★☆ £C
GSM Two Gentlemens ★★★ £D
Cabernet Sauvignon Rifle And Hunt ★★★★ £E

South Australia

Cabernet Sauvignon Understudy ★★★ £C
Recommended Whites:
The Full Fronti Blanc Frontignac Fortified ★★★ £E
Sauvignon Blanc Scarecrow ★★☆ £C
Teusner (Barossa Valley)
Recommended Reds:
Avatar (Grenache/Mataro/Shiraz) ★★★☆ £E
The Riebke Ebenezer Road (Shiraz) ★★★☆ £E
Joshua (Grenache/Shiraz/Mourvèdre) ★★★ £D
Pirramimma (Mclaren Vale)
Recommended Reds:
Petit Verdot Reserve ★★★ £C
Shiraz Reserve ★★★ £C
Possums Vineyard (Mclaren Vale)
Recommended Reds:
Shiraz Mclaren Vale ★★★☆ £C
Punters Corner (Coonawarra)
Recommended Reds:
Shiraz ★★★ £C
Cabernet Sauvignon ★★★ £D
Pycnantha Hill (Clare Valley)
Recommended Reds:
Shiraz ★★★ £C
Quattro Mano (Barossa Valley)
Recommended Reds:
Duende ★★★☆ £C
Le Reto Tempranillo ★★★★ £D
RBJ Vintners
Recommended Reds:
Theologicum (Mourvèdre/Grenache) ★★ £C
Redheads Studio (Mclaren Vale)
Recommended Reds:
Red Heads Tomahawk Shiraz ★★ £B
The Good Doctor Tannat, Cabernet & Shiraz ★★★☆ £E
Reschke (Coonawarra)
Recommended Reds:
Cabernet Sauvignon Vitalus ★★★ £C
Cabernet Sauvignon Bos ★★★★ £D
Cabernet Sauvignon Empyrean ★★★★☆ £F
Recommended Whites:
Sauvignon Blanc Fume ★★☆ £C
Rookery (Kangaroo Island)
Recommended Reds:
Sangiovese ★★☆ £C
Ruggabellus (Barossa Valley)
Recommended Reds:
Archaeus (Syrah, Mataro, Grenache, Cinsault) ★★★☆ £E
Timaeus (Grenache, Mataro, Cinsault) ★★★ £E
Efferus (Mataro, Syrah, Grenache, Cinsault) ★★★ £E
Fluus (Grenache, Mataro, Cinsault) ★★☆ £D
Rusden (Barossa Valley)
Recommended Reds:
Cabernet Sauvignon/Shiraz Ripper Creek Barossa Valley ★★★☆ £E
Cabernet Sauvignon Boundaries Barossa Valley ★★★☆ £F
Recommended Whites:
Chenin Blanc Christina ★★☆ £D
Rusty Mutt (McLaren Vale)
Recommended Reds: Shiraz Original ★★★ £D
Recommended Whites:
Viognier Catnip ★★☆ £C

Rymill (Coonawarra)
Recommended Reds:
Cabernet Sauvignon ★★★ £C
Shiraz ★★ £C
MC2 (Merlot/Cab Sauv/Cab Franc) ★★ £B
Schild Estate (Barossa Valley)
Recommended Whites:
Sémillon/Sauvignon Blanc ★★☆ £C
Recommended Reds:
GMS (Grenache/Mourvèdre/Shiraz) ★★★ £C
Shiraz Barossa Valley ★★★★ £D
Shiraz Reserve Barossa Valley ★★★★ £F
Shiraz Moorooroo Barossa Valley ★★★★ £F
Setanta (Adelaide Hills)
Recommended Whites:
Chardonnay Emer ★★☆ £C
Recommended Reds:
Cabernet Sauvignon Black Sanglain ★★★★☆ £C
Sevenhill Cellars (Clare Valley)
Recommended Whites:
Riesling Clare Valley ★★ £B
Riesling St Aloysius Clare Valley ★★★ £D
Recommended Reds:
Shiraz Clare Valley ★★★☆ £C
Grenache ★★ £C
Cabernet Sauvignon ★★☆ £C
Shingleback (Mclaren Vale)
Recommended Reds:
Shiraz Mclaren Vale Block Reserve ★★★★ £D
Shirvington (Mclaren Vale)
Recommended Reds:
Shiraz ★★★ £F
Shobbrook (Barossa Valley)
Recommended Reds:
Shiraz ★★★★ £E
Recommended Whites:
Didier Semillon ★★★ £D
Skillogalee (Clare Valley)
Recommended Whites:
Riesling Clare Valley ★★☆ £C
Riesling Trevarrick Single Contour Clare Valley ★★★★☆ £D
Gewürztraminer Clare Valley ★★☆ £C
Recommended Reds:
Shiraz Basket Press Clare Valley ★★★ £C
Spinifex (Barossa Valley)
Recommended Reds:
Esprit (Grenache/Shiraz/Mourvèdre/Cinsault) ★★★☆ £D
Recommended Rosés:
Rosé Barossa Valley (Grenache/Cinsault) ★★☆ £B
Standish Wine Co
Recommended Reds:
Shiraz The Standish ★★★★ £F
Stringy Brae (Clare Valley)
Recommended Whites:
Riesling Clare Valley ★★★ £C
Teusner (Barossa Valley)
Recommended Reds:
Avatar (Grenache/Mataro/Shiraz) ★★★☆ £E
The Riebke Ebenezer Road (Shiraz) ★★★☆ £E
Joshua (Grenache/Shiraz/Mourvèdre) ★★★ £D

Wayne Thomas (Mclaren Vale)
Recommended Reds:
Petit Verdot Mclaren Vale ★★★★ £D
Torzi Matthews (Eden Valley)
Recommended Reds:
Shiraz Frost Dodger ★★★☆ £E
Viking (Barossa Valley)
Recommended Reds:
Grand Shiraz ★★★ £F
Vinteloper (Adelaide Hills)
Recommended Reds:
Shiraz Adelaide Hills ★★★★ £D
Touriga Nacional Langhorne Creek ★★★☆ £D
Recommended Whites:
Riesling Watervale Clare Valley ★★★★ £D
Uleybury Wines (Mount Lofty)
Recommended Reds:
Primitivo Bap Pipicella Reserve ★★☆ £E
Recommended Whites:
Sémillon Show Reserve ★★★★ £E
The Willows Vineyard (Barossa Valley)
Recommended Reds:
Cabernet Sauvignon Barossa ★★ £C
Shiraz Barossa ★★★ £D
Recommended Whites:
Sémillon Barossa ★★ £C
Willunga 100 (Mclaren Vale)
Recommended Reds: Grenache ★★ £B
Shiraz Barossa ★★ £B
Cabernet Sauvignon/Shiraz ★★ £B
Viognier ★☆ £B
Wilson Vineyard (Clare Valley)
Recommended Whites:
Riesling Gallery Series ★★ £B
Yangarra Estate (Mclaren Vale)
Recommended Reds:
Grenache Old Vine Mclaren Vale ★★★☆ £D
Grenache High Sands Mclaren Vale ★★★★ £F
Shiraz Mclaren Vale ★★★☆ £D
Cadenzia (Grenache/Shiraz/Mourvèdre) ★★★☆ £D

Work in progress!!

Producers under consideration for the next edition
Anvers Wines (Adelaide Hills)
Brini Estate Wines (Mclaren Vale)
Eden Hall (Eden Valley)
Foggo Wines (Mclaren Vale)
Radford Wines (Eden Valley)
Salomon Estate (Currency Creek)
Schubert Estate (Barossa Valley)
Shobbrook (Eden Valley)
Some Young Punks (South Australia)
Tait Wines (Barossa Valley)

Author's choice

Powerful Barossa/Eden Valley Shiraz-based reds
Barossa Valley Estate   Shiraz E&E Black Pepper
Grant Burge   Shiraz Meschach
Burge Family   Shiraz Draycott
Dutschke   Shiraz Oscar Semmler
John Duval   Shiraz Entity
Glaetzer   Shiraz Amon-Ra
Greenock Creek   Shiraz Seven Acre
Henschke   Shiraz Mount Edelstone
Kalleske   Shiraz Greenock
Peter Lehmann   Shiraz Stonewell
Charles Melton   Shiraz Voices Of Angels
Mt Billy   Shiraz Antiquity
Rockford   Shiraz Basket Press
Rolf Binder   Shiraz Hanisch
St Hallett   Shiraz Old Block
Torbreck   Shiraz The Factor
Yalumba   Shiraz Swingbridge Vineyard Craneford

Other top Shiraz
Tim Adams   Shiraz Clare Valley Aberfeldy
Jim Barry   Shiraz Clare Valley The Armagh
Bowen Estate   Shiraz Coonawarra
Coriole   Shiraz Mclaren Vale Lloyd Rserve
D'Arenberg   Shiraz Mclaren Vale Dead Arm
Gemtree   Shiraz Obsidian
Katnook   Shiraz The Prodigy
Kay Brothers   Shiraz Block 6
Kilikanoon   Shiraz Clare Valley Covenant
Mitolo   Shiraz Mclaren Vale Savitar
SC Pannell   Shiraz
Reynella   Shiraz Mclaren Vale Basket Pressed
Wendouree   Shiraz Clare Valley

Leading Cabernet-based reds
D'Arenberg   Cabernet Sauvignon Coppermine Road
Grosset   Gaia
Henschke   Cabernet Sauvignon Cyril Henschke
Hollick   Cabernet Sauvignon Ravenswood
Katnook   Cabernet Sauvignon The Odyssey
Leconfield   Cabernet Coonawarra
Mitolo   Cabernet Sauvignon Serpico
Parker Coonawarra   Terra Rossa First Growth
Penfolds   Cabernet Sauvignon Bin 707
Penfolds   Cabernet Sauvignon Bin 389
Penley Estate   Cabernet Sauvignon Reserve
Primo Estate   Cabernet Sauvignon/Merlot Joseph
Wendouree   Cabernet Sauvignon/Malbec Clare Valley
Wynns   Cabernet Sauvignon John Riddoch
Wynns   Cabernet Sauvignon/Shiraz Signature
Zema Estate   Cabernet Sauvignon/ Shiraz Saluti Coonawarra

Ageworthy whites
Tim Adams   Sémillon Clare Valley
Barratt   Chardonnay Piccadilly Valley
Jim Barry   Riesling The Florita
Grosset   Chardonnay Piccadilly
Grosset   Riesling Polish Hill
Peter Lehmann   Riesling Wigan

South Australia

Mount Horrocks   Riesling Watervale
Petaluma   Chardonnay Tiers
Pewsey Vale   Riesling The Contours
Shaw & Smith   Chardonnay M3 Vineyard
Tapanappa   Chardonnay Tiers
Uleybury   Show Reserve Semillo

Best buys
Reds:
Tim Adams The Fergus
Five Geese   Old Vine Grenache/Shiraz
Mitolo   Shiraz Jester
Penfolds   Cabernet Sauvignon Thomas Hyland
Quatro Mano   Duende
Taylors/Wakefield Cellars   Shiraz Clare Valley
Torbreck   Woodcutters Red
Wynns   Cabernet Sauvignon Coonawarra
Whites:
Annie's Lane   Shiraz Clare Valley
D'Arenberg   Roussanne Money Spider
Tim Gramp   Riesling Watervale
Kilikanoon   Riesling Clare Valley Morts Block
Penfolds   Chardonnay Thomas Hyland
Yalumba   The Cigar Y

Viticulture was more important in Victoria than in either South Australia or New SouthWales in the 19th century but the arrival of phylloxera triggered a decline for much of the state. In the late 1960s the first steps were taken towards a revival that has rapidly gained pace since the early 1980s. Victoria offers a diversity of site and climate permutations arguably unequalled in Australia, while much more is being made of Tasmania's cool climatic conditions. As an example of an increasing regionality, Heathcote Shiraz and Tasmanian Pinot Noir – which previously only boasted isolated successes – are now emerging as two potentially outstanding regional styles following a mini-explosion in quality. For Pinot Noir, Mornington Peninsula is also emerging as one of the country's finest regions for the variety while in the more established Yarra Valley, producers are exploring sub-regionality with interesting results. Other regions such as Henty, Gippsland or Macedon Ranges also seem set to gain wider recognition amongst consumers of quality wines.

North-West Victoria

The most productive area of Victoria, its regions of **Murray Darling** and **Swan Hill** are shared with the Big Rivers zone of New South Wales. It makes a significant contribution to Australia's big volume brand production from highly mechanized viticulture and winemaking.While the grapes from these high yielding irrigated vineyards are never going to produce wines of real quality, they can be sound as well as inexpensive and are usually much better than the equivalent from most other bulk wine producing areas around the world. at all.

North-East Victoria

Around the towns of **Rutherglen** and **Glenrowan** is the most significant area of Victoria viticulture to have survived its fall. Unique, intensely sweet fortified wines made from raisined Muscat and Muscadelle (once labelled Tokay but now being sold as Topaque) grapes are often subject to long ageing in hot conditions. A classification of the Rutherglen wines has recently been introduced. Beyond a basic Rutherglen category, in ascending order, are the Classic, Grand and Rare quality levels. Robust, earthy reds are also made from Shiraz, Durif and Cabernet Sauvignon. The heat of Rutherglen is in contrast to the cooler areas to the south-east. **Beechworth** has forged a reputation for fine Chardonnay and Pinot Noir thanks to Giaconda, but Rhône varieties are exciting too, especially at Castagna. Meanwhile, in the **Alpine Valleys** (including Ovens Valley) and **King Valley**, vineyards extend from the heat of Milawa into the lower reaches of the Australian Alps, part of the Great Dividing Range, where altitude is critical to cooler-climate viticulture in New South Wales. A wide range of grapes is grown but an unusual development is the propagation of Italian varieties.

Western Victoria

One of the strengths of Victoria is the great diversity of Shiraz styles, with top class examples from Henty, Grampians, Pyrenees and Bendigo, the latter in Central Victoria. **Grampians** (or Great Western as it used to be known), another survivor of Victoria's 19th-century viticulture, has long been famous for its Shiraz including one of Australia's very best fromMount Langhi Ghiran. Elevation makes it cooler than might otherwise be expected, as is the case with the rolling hills of **Pyrenees** where both Shiraz and Cabernet Sauvignon are made, to very high standards in the case of Dalwhinnie and now Michel Chapoutier and Anthony J. Terlato. . Chardonnay can also be impressive. The **Henty** region is still little known but encompasses a large area in the south-west corner of Victoria. There are climatic and soil similarities with the Limestone Coast (in South Australia) which lies but a short distance to the west. As Drumborg, it is more familiar as the source of the fine sparkling wines produced by the region's pioneer, Seppelt. Riesling and Pinot Noir also show much promise.

Central Victoria

Bendigo is now synonymous with great Shiraz, particularly the examples from the now separate region of **Heathcote**. In fact, Bendigo achieved fame for its Shiraz in the 19th century and this is once again a very exciting area with a recent surge of new wines set to challenge the leading estate of Jasper Hill. In **Goulburn Valley** another pocket of Victoria's wine production has been maintained. The region is vast, but the best producers are concentrated in the south, in the subregion of **Nagambie Lakes**, an area not a great distance east of Heathcote. Shiraz is brilliant from its leading producers, Tahbilk and Mitchelton, but Cabernet Sauvignon and Riesling as well as Marsanne and other white and red Rhône varieties are beginning to excel. Vineyards in the **Upper Goulburn** and **Strathbogie Ranges** are most suited to aromatic white varieties.

Port Phillip

The leading region among those lying close to the state capital of Melbourne is the **Yarra Valley**. First developed in the 19th century, its modern revival dates from the 1960s.Within its substantial confines there exist any number of mesoclimates but it is generally cool and damp by Australian standards. The Yarra Valley provides great examples of Pinot Noir and Chardonnay but also fine Bordeaux blends, though there can be a struggle for ripeness in cooler vintages. Shiraz is less important but of high quality from the likes of Yarra Yering. The best wines are fruit-rich but softly textured and stylishly complex, though there is a trend in favour of more restrained, medium bodied wines designed better to showcase vineyard character. There is also fine fizz although most examples include grapes sourced from outside the region. The Port Phillip zone also includes **Geelong**, **Sunbury** and the **Mornington Peninsula**. Geelong, thanks mostly to Gary Farr, formerly of Bannockburn, now of By Farr, has a reputation for intense, powerful Shiraz, Pinot Noir and Chardonnay. The same theme is echoed in the cool Mornington Peninsula whose many small producers, though focusing on Pinot Noir and Chardonnay, now among the country's best, can produce elegant, stylish Shiraz too. Similarly in Sunbury but more especially the higher-altitude **Macedon Ranges**, quality from Chardonnay and Pinot Noir can be outstanding. Bindi is the star but others are challenging. Other reds are at the margins for achieving full ripeness yet wines such as Craiglee's Shiraz or the Virgin Hills Cabernet Sauvignon-based blend can be super in the warmest vintages.

Gippsland

Gippsland is a vast, cool zone in the south-east of Victoria with some exceptional isolated pockets of vineyards, but its marginal climate is always likely to deter all but a mad few. Yet quality can be very high even if quantities are scarce. Try to find the Pinot Noirs of Bass Phillip and young Turk William Downie who also makes Pinot Noirs from the Yarra and Mornington Peninsula.

Tasmania

Across Bass Strait in Tasmania, the cooler, wetter climate has deterred the industry giants from invasion and its modern

Wine behind the label

Victoria & Tasmania

development has only really taken off in the past decade. The once dominant Pipers Brook group is no longer the only sizeable player. Constellation's investment in Bay of Fires and the recent acquisition of Tamar Ridge by Brown Brothers signals that major mainland producers are no longer content solely to source grapes from the island. Nonetheless, there are now dozens of tiny holdings from which tiny quantities of increasingly fine Pinot Noir are produced by a just a few talented winemakers. Riesling and Chardonnay are also successful, the latter important (with Pinot Noir) in the island's flourishing premium sparkling wine production. There is also a greater focus on aromatic white varieties other than Riesling, especially Sauvignon Blanc and Pinot Gris/Grigio.

1 Murray Darling
2 Swan Hill
3 Rutherglen
4 Glenrowan
5 Beechworth
6 Alpine Valleys
7 King Valley
8 Henty
9 Grampians
10 Pyrenees
11 Bendigo
12 Heathcote
13 Goulburn Valley
14 Nagambie Lakes
15 Strathbogie Ranges
16 Upper Goulburn
17 Yarra Valley
18 Mornington Peninsula
19 Geelong
20 Sunbury
21 Macedon Ranges

A-Z of producers by region

Rutherglen & Glenrowan

All Saints	866
Baileys of Glenrowan	866
Buller & Son, RL	868
Campbells	868
Chambers Rosewood	868
Morris	876
Stanton & Killeen	878

Beechworth

Castagne	868
Giaconda	872

Grampians

Armstrong Vineyards	866
Best's	867
Mount Langi Ghiran	876
Seppelt Great Western	878

Pyrenees

Dalwhinnie	870
Summerfield	879
Taltarni	879
Terlato & Chapoutier	880
Domaine Tournon	880

Henty

Crawford River	867

Bendigo

Balgownie	866
Pondalowie	877

Heathcote

Heathcote Winery	873
Jasper Hill	873
Wild Duck Creek	880

Nagambie Lakes

Mitchelton	875
Tahbilk	879

Upper Goulburn

Delatite	870

Yarra Valley

Domaine Chandon	868
Coldstream Hills	869
De Bortoli (Victoria)	870
Diamond Valley	870
William Downie	871
Giant Steps	872
Luke Lambert	874
Mac Forbes	874

Timo Mayer	875
Metier Wines	875
Mount Mary	876
PHI Wines	877
Seville Estate	878
Tarrawarra	879
Yarra Yering	880
Yarrabank	881
Yering Station	881
Yeringberg	881

Mornington Peninsula

Dromana Estate	871
Kooyong	873
Main Ridge	875
Moorooduc Estate	876
Paringa Estate	876
Port Phillip Estate	877
Stonier	879
Ten Minutes by Tractor	880

Geelong

Bannockburn	867
Eldridge Estate	871
By Farr	872
Lethbridge Wines	874
Scotchmans Hill	877
Shadowfax	878

Sunbury

Craiglee	869

Macedon Ranges

Bindi	867
Cobaw Ridge	869
Curly Flat	869
Hanging Rock	872
Virgin Hills	880

Gippsland

Bass Phillip	867

Tasmania

Bay of Fires	867
Clover Hill	879
Domaine A	871
House of Arras	873
Kreglinger	873
Stefano Lubiana	874
Moorilla Estate	875
Pipers Brook	874

Victoria & Tasmania vintages

The generalised Vintage charts below cover some of the most ageworthy styles and will prove most useful when taken together with comments on style and ageing within individual producer entries.Many powerful, full-bodied red can be drunk young but an increasing number will not be at their best for at least five years. Top-quality Chardonnay and Pinot Noir are likely to show at their best only with three to six years' ageing. In terms of longer-term cellaring potential, great premium Victorian Shiraz or Cabernet-based reds can improve for at least a decade. Both the vintage ratings and when to drink assessments generally only apply to the top rated examples (3-star or higher).

Recent vintages

2016 This was an early harvest in many regions with a warm summer and low rainfall. Despite this the Yarra Valley looks set to produce some fine Pinot Noir and Chardonnay. Reds from Bendigo and the Grampians are likely to offer good depth and concentration. Tasmania too had a very warm summer and the harvest was early, yields were up and prospects look good rather than great.

2015 This is emerging as a potentially great year throughout Victoria. The summer was warm rather than hot and the harvest was relatively early with cool late season night temperatures promoting good acidity in the fruit. There is classy Pinot Noir and Chardonnay from the Yarra, Mornington Peninsula and Geelong. Some excellent Shiraz has been produced in the central Victoria regions. In Tasmania it was a similar story. A balanced growing season and cool nights during the late season has resulted in wines of impressive depth and excellent acidity.

2014 It was a tough vintage in the cooler areas such as Yarra, a cold wet spring followed by some unwelcome heat spikes in January has led to some uneven results, but what was produced was of very good quality. October frosts played havoc in Beechworth resulting in greatly reduced yields and it was all in all, a challenging vintage.

2013 The weather during the 2013 growing season was warm and dry with just a few heat spikes thus allowing growers to produce more balanced wines than in the two previous vintages. Ripening came all at once and the growers had to be fast in harvesting if they were to avoid rot. Reds are high in alcohol and should repay long keeping, whilst whites are rich and aromatic.

2012 Ideal growing conditions lasted until March when heavy rainfall put a damper on things, so to say. Those who managed to pick before the rains have produced some excellent wines and early maturing varietals such as Pinot Noir have benefitted from this. Shiraz and Cabernet Sauvignons are more variable, but some top quality wines have been produced. The secret once more was careful selection, but there is a lot more good stuff than in the previous vintage.

2011 Wet weather throughout the spring and early summer led to downey mildew and rot, resulting in greatly reduced yields. Results were therefore variable and so careful selection is needed for this vintage. Whites generally fared better than reds although early maturing Pinot Noirs have produced some elegant wines. Much Shiraz and Cabernet Sauvignons failed to achieve a sufficient degree of ripeness and whilst they are generally showing good colour, they lack structure and generosity of fruit.

2010 Rainfall in winter and spring returned to more typical levels after a series of drought years which, the previous year, culminated in the tinder box conditions that led to Black Saturday. For some, rainfall at harvest required producers to hold their nerve but fortune smiled on the Yarra Valley, which experienced an excellent vintage, especially for the reds, as did other leading regions like Heathcote and Mornington Peninsula.

2009 A cool, late vintage in Tasmania resulted in excellent quality. Conversely, on the mainland, a record heat wave on 27-31 January resulted in scorching, sunburn and major crop loss. Worse followed. On Black Saturday, 7 February, bush fires ravaged Victoria, the North West of the Yarra Valley taking the brunt. About 25% of the region was directly impacted by fire. Elsewhere in the Yarra and in several other regions, smoke taint affected later ripening varieties. Regions that fared well include the Mornington Peninsula, Alpine Valley and Pyrenees, the Pyranees, Heathcote and Macedon Ranges.

2008 Drought was a major problem and the heat spike in early March resulted in many varieties maturing at the same time which

Australia

gave the wineries fermentation problems. Those who made an early start and harvested during February's cooler conditions fared better and quality is good. In Tasmania, warmer than normal temperatures throughout the growing season and an early harvest was good for quality.

2007 Victoria looks the worst affected of Australia's major wine producing states. Drought conditions resulting in a much smaller harvest and cronic water shortages were compounded by bushfires in the King and Alpine Valleys. The extent and duration of these fires will spoil fruit further afield too. However prospects for quality are good in some of the cool climate areas. Tasmania produced an early, relatively healthy crop.

2006 looks to be another good quality vintage in both Victoria and Tasmania with an early harvest in most regions and success with both Pinot Noir and Shiraz. Tasmania was particularly early with substantially lowered yields and increased concentration in both reds and whites.

2005 in Victoria was a plentiful harvest (a record crop in Australia) with a mild summer followed by hot conditions in early March. Many producers are confident of a high quality vintage including those in Tasmania.

2004 in Victoria, as with the other eastern states, saw quantity bounce back after the small, drought-affected early harvest of 03. Quality-wise, 04 was very good in the Yarra Valley which although generally cool (suiting Chardonnay) early warmth facilitated full ripening in Bordeaux varieties. Pinot Noir was less good here but very promising from Mornington Peninsula. Shiraz from Central and Western Victoria has concentrated ripe fruit from those vineyards that avoided excessive heat stress. In Tasmania cool weather meant a much prolonged season (into June for some) with a struggle for ripeness and healthy fruit. Yet wines from producers who achieved full ripening are very good – with good acidities and flavour complexity.

Victoria & Tasmania vintage chart

	Bendigo/ Heathcote Shiraz	Grampians/ Pyrenees Shiraz	Yarra Valley/ Pinot	Tasmania Pinot Noir
2016	★★★☆ A	★★★☆ A	★★★☆ A	★★★☆ A
2015	★★★★☆ A	★★★★ A	★★★★ A	★★★★☆ A
2014	★★☆ A	★★☆ A	★★★★☆ A	★★★ A
2013	★★★★ A	★★★★☆ A	★★★★ B	★★★★☆ A
2012	★★★★ A	★★★★ A	★★★★☆ A	★★★★ A
2011	★★☆ B	★★☆ B	★★★☆ B	★★★★☆ B
2010	★★★★☆ B	★★★★☆ B	★★★★☆ B	★★★★ B
2009	★★★☆ B	★★★☆ B	★★/★★★ B	★★★★☆ B
2008	★★★☆ C	★★★☆ B	★★★☆ C	★★★★☆ B
2007	★★★★ B	★★★★ B	★★☆ C	★★★★ C
2006	★★★★ C	★★★★ C	★★★★ C	★★★★ C
2005	★★★★☆ C	★★★★☆ C	★★★★☆ C	★★★★☆ C
2004	★★★★ C	★★★★ C	★★★ D	★★★ C
2003	★★★★☆ C	★★★★ C	★★★★☆ C	★★★★ D
2002	★★★★★ C	★★★★☆ C	★★★★★ D	★★★★☆ D
2001	★★★★★ D	★★★★☆ D	★★★★ D	★★★☆ D
2000	★★★★ D	★★★☆ D	★★★★☆ D	★★★★ D

A-Z of producers

All Saints (Rutherglen & Glenrowan) *www.allsaintswine.com.au*
The late Peter Brown bought this high-quality producer of Rutherglen Muscat and Topaque from his family (BROWN BROTHERS) in 1999. The estate is run by his children. The fortifieds already have quite a reputation while the table wines are rapidly improving. The Classic-level versions are relatively youthful and raisiny, the Grand add more richness and complexity, but Rare examples are that much more refined with terrific length of flavour. As overwhelming as these wines can be, Rare is a good place to start. Otherwise there's rich, characterful Shiraz and Durif if you're looking for something muscular and meaty. The Shiraz needs at least 5 years' ageing, the Durif needs 10 or more.
Recommended Reds:
Durif Family Cellar ★★ £E   Shiraz Family Cellar ★★ £E
Recommended Whites:
Rutherglen Topaque Rare ★★★★★ £G
Rutherglen Topaque Grand ★★★ £F
Rutherglen Topaque Classic ★★ £C
Rutherglen Muscat Rare ★★★★ £G
Rutherglen Muscat Grand ★★★ £F
Rutherglen Muscat Classic ★★ £C

Armstrong Vineyards (Grampians)
This is the project of Tony Royal who runs the Portavin bottling and packaging plant in Adelaide. Grapes from 5 ha of well-established, low-yielding vines are given a prolonged cold soak (pre-fermentation maceration) before being vinified in small open fermenters. Aged in 70% new oak, Armstrong is very much in the powerful blockbuster mould with the real essence of very ripe, concentrated Great Western Shiraz. In 2003 a second, more forward, expressive example was made with 5–6% Viognier and herbal, mineral, berryish fruit. With good texture, plenty of extract and fine tannins it should be at its best with 5–8 years' age.
Recommended Reds:
Armstrong Shiraz Great Western ★★★★☆ £E
Shiraz Viognier Great Western ★★★☆ £D

Baileys of Glenrowan *www.baileysofglenrowan.com.au*
In acquiring Baileys in 1996, Mildara Blass (now BERINGER BLASS) added some rich, original fortified Australian Muscat and Topaque to its portfolio. Apart from these sometimes outstanding fortified wines, Baileys was known for one of Victoria's most robust and gutsy Shirazes. However, in the most recent vintages the Shiraz has taken on more refinement with finer structure, yet retaining good fruit intensity. 1904 Block and 1920 Block Shiraz are named for when the vineyards on which they are based were planted. The fortifieds are particularly rich, sweet examples, lacking the elegance or refinement of others but with plenty of power and flavour. The finest versions are Winemaker's Selection but these are made only in tiny quantities and are difficult to obtain.
Recommended Reds:
Shiraz 1904 Block ★★★☆ £E   Shiraz 1920 Block ★★☆ £E
Cabernet Sauvignon ★ £C
Recommended Whites:
Liqueur Topaque Founder ★★★ £D
Liqueur Muscat Founder ★★ £D

Balgownie (Bendigo) *www.balgownie.com*
After a long period of ownership by Mildara Blass Balgownie is

finally returning to the form it originally showed under its founder Stuart Anderson. Major vineyard expansion has extended plantings to 35 ha and the quality of recent releases of Shiraz and Cabernet Sauvignon in particular has been generally very good. A small amount of single vineyard Chardonay and Pinot Noir for cellar door release only are also made. In 2003, Balgownie planted 7 ha of Chardonnay and Pinot Noir in the Yarra Valley to (not tasted), where the family have also established a cellar door and spa hotel.

Recommended Reds:

Shiraz ★★★☆ £D   Cabernet Sauvignon ★★★☆ £D

Recommended Whites:

Chardonnay ★★☆ £D

Bannockburn (Geelong)   *www.bannockburnvineyards.com*
Original winemaker Gary Farr's achievement is all the more remarkable given the relatively low profile of Geelong as a wine-producing region. Having established a considerable reputation by the mid-1980s he managed to keep the quality and the profile of Bannockburn among the country's leaders. New winemaker Michael Glover seeks to do the same. Cabernet was the fashionable variety and Pinot Noir almost unheard of in Australia when a deep, rich extracted example was first produced by Farr. Many of Farr's practices for handling Pinot Noir, both in terms of viticulture (including high-density planting) and winemaking (part whole-bunch pressing), were modelled on Domaine DUJAC in Burgundy. The wine's deep spice, plum and savoury, undergrowth (at times, stemmy) character has always been individual; never noted for finesse, it is complex, ageworthy and impressively structured. Serré, S.R.H, Range and and Stuart are all recently added and special vineyard and barrel selections of the grape. Shiraz also has superb texture and complexity and the concentrated Chardonnay can be very impressive, the SRH savoury. Sauvignon Blanc and Riesling are also made. The new wines from Gary Farr's own vineyards (BY FARR) or indeed those of his son Nicholas (FARR RISING) make for an interesting comparison.

Recommended Reds:

Pinot Noir ★★★★ £E   Shiraz ★★★★ £E

Recommended Whites:

Chardonnay SRH ★★★☆ £E

Chardonnay ★★★☆ £E

Bass Phillip (Gippsland)   *www.bassphillip.com*
Phillip Jones has gone out on a limb, opting for the vast, cool expanse of Gippsland for his winemaking venture. There are other notable wine producers here but they are as remote from each other as from other regions. Leongatha is further south and east than Mornington Peninsula and not far from Wilson's promontory, the mainland's most southerly point. The downside is variable vintage conditions, producing very ripe fruit on occasions, but just as often the vines can struggle for ripeness. From very closely spaced vineyards (at least in Australian terms) he has produced Pinot Noir of a quality that puts it among the very best in Australia. Early vintages, in the mid- to late 1980s, were made in minuscule quantities but the vineyard area has been gradually increased. The quality of the wines shows in the structure and length on the palate and the purity of the fruit. Only grapes of the requisite standard make the successive levels, from the most forward yet still serious regular Pinot through more intense, complex Premium to a deep, structured Reserve that needs at least 5 years' age. A tiny amount of Chardonnay and Gamay are also made. The wines are very expensive, in part due to their cult status. Two slightly less expensive

versions of Pinot Noir, the Crown Prince and the Village, have also recently been produced.

Recommended Reds:

Pinot Noir Reserve ★★★★ £H

Pinot Noir Premium ★★★★ £G

Pinot Noir ★★★ £F

Bay of Fires (Tasmania)   *www.bayoffireswines.com.au*
The draw of Australia's coolest climate proved too hard to resist for Constellation who established the winery at Bay of Fires in the north eastern corner of Tasmania in 2002. Fruit is sourced from the property's 23 ha of Chardonnay, Pinot Noir, Sauvignon Blanc, Pinot Gris and Riesling, which is supplemented with additional fruit from across Tasmania. Under winemaker Fran Austin, it has fast established a reputation for its wines which combine good fruit weight with cool climate brightness and definition. The top Pinot Noir shows extra depth and finesse. (SA)

Recommended Reds:

Pinot Noir ★★★☆ £E

Recommended Whites:

Sauvignon Blanc ★★☆ £E   Riesling ★★☆ £E

Pinot Gris ★★ £E   Sparkling Cuvée Brut ★★ £E

Recommended Rosés:

Sparkling Cuvée Rosé ★★ £E

Best's (Grampians)   *www.bestswines.com*
Best's had its beginnings in 1866 under Henry Best and a family tradition of grape growing and winemaking has been continued by the Thomson family since 1920. Ben Thomson is the current incumbent, ably assisted by Justin Purser, Ben taking over the reigns from his father Viv. The Concongella vineyards particularly favour medium bodied yet intense styles of Shiraz, which can be very good indeed, whether the approachable Bin 1, consistently deep, super-spicy and peppery Bin O or a very limited-release and pricey Thomson Family version, which needs time to unfurl. An idiosyncratic old vine Pinot Meunier is intense and spicy. Riesling is very good too, floral yet focused and long; Wadewitz is experimenting with an off dry style, The House Block Riesling, which looks promising. Recent Chardonnays show nicely defined varietal character. Merlot, Cabernet Franc and Pinot Noir are also made. Museum Releases can be pretty special too if rarely encountered.

Recommended Reds:

Shiraz Bin O Great Western ★★★★☆ £E

Shiraz Bin Thomson Family Great Western ★★★★ £E

Shiraz Bin 1 Great Western ★★★☆ £E

Cabernet Sauvignon Great Western ★★ £D

Old Vine Pinot Meunier Great Western ★★★ £E

Recommended Whites:

Chardonnay Great Western ★★★ £D

Riesling Great Western ★★★☆ £C

Bindi (Macedon Ranges)   *www.bindiwines.com.au*
Bindi is the leading producer in the Macedon Ranges and one of Australia's best boutique growers. Michael Dhillon makes very small quantities of outstanding cuvées of both Chardonnay and Pinot Noir. The vineyards are at 500m with differences in soil type and exposure between the 3 different Pinot Noir vineyards, Original Vineyard, the most recent elevated Block K, quartzladen Composition 8 and the more sheltered Block 5. Very low yields and a relatively low percentage of new French oak contribute to supremely rich and concentrated wines with excellent balance

Victoria & Tasmania

(without the high alcohol often associated with top-end Australian or North American examples) and an intense fruit-filled finish, particularly in the Chardonnays. Both Chardonnays and Original and Composition Vineyard Pinot Noir deserve to be drunk with at least 5–10 years' age but can easily be approached much sooner. Block 5 Pinot, made in minute quantities, has not been tasted. Also made is Pyrette Shiraz from Heathcote fruit and a little sparkling wine, which shows tremendous drive combined with bright creamy fruit.

Recommended Reds:
Pinot Noir Original Vineyard ★★★★ £F

Recommended Whites:
Chardonnay Quartz ★★★★☆ £F
Chardonnay Composition ★★★★ £E
Sparkling Chardonnay/Pinot Noir ★★★★☆ £E

❀ R L Buller and Son (Rutherglen) *www.buller.com.au*
The Buller family operations include both fortifieds and table wines from wineries in Rutherglen (Calliope) and Beverford in the Swan Hill region. Most exceptional are the outstanding (Rare) Topaque and Muscat from unirrigated Rutherglen vineyards. Made only in very small quantities, there is splendid complexity and superb flavour length as well as sheer age in both. The Premium Fine Old (or Premium Fine) examples are also made in a *solera* system and have great intensity, complexity and length as well as surprising elegance for the style. Another premium fortified, Premium Fine Old Tawny, more in the style of an aged Tawny Port, has not been tasted. Powerful, robust Calliope Shiraz is also made and other Limited Release reds include Durif and blends styled on the Rhône and Bordeaux. Prices for the fortifieds are keener than for most Rutherglen examples and represent exceptional value.

Recommended Whites:
Rutherglen Topaque Calliope Rare ★★★★★ £H
Rutherglen Topaque Premium Fine Old ★★★★ £D
Rutherglen Muscat Calliope Rare ★★★★★ £H
Rutherglen Muscat Premium Fine Old ★★★★ £D

❀ Campbells (Rutherglen) *www.campbellswines.com.au*
As always in Rutherglen the reputation of this producer depends on the quality of the fortified wines, and here they are consistently good. Impressively flavoursome in the cheaper examples, there is marvellous complexity, intensity and refinement in the Rare-level Isabella Topaque and Merchant Prince Muscat. Campbells reds, in particular The Barkly Durif, can show real intensity in a robust, gutsy style. Alcohol levels have been pared back especially for the Bobbie Burns Shiraz which represents good value.

Recommended Reds:
Durif The Barkly ★★ £E   Shiraz Bobbie Burns ★☆ £C

Recommended Whites:
Rutherglen Topaque Rare Isabella ✪✪✪✪✪ £H
Rutherglen Topaque Grand ★★★★★ £G
Rutherglen Topaque Classic ★★★★ £E
Rutherglen Topaque ★★★ £D
Rutherglen Muscat Rare Merchant Prince ★★★★★ £H
Rutherglen Muscat Grand ★★★★ £G
Rutherglen Muscat Classic ★★★ £E
Rutherglen Muscat ★★★ £D

❀ Castagna (Beechworth) *www.castagna.com.au*
There are few biodynamic estates in Australia but this is already the most important. The small estate is based just outside Beechworth at 500m elevation and benefits from hot days and cool nights.

The Beechworth region has been slow to take off despite the reputation of GIACONDA but as Castagna and others become better known this seems certain to change. Julian Castagna has decided to concentrate on Syrah and Viognier with some Sangiovese in contrast to the mostly Burgundian orientated Giaconda. Given the biodynamic stance, he also relies only on indigenous yeasts, again unusual in Australia, running counter to mainstream thinking in the industry. The top two wines are the Genesis Syrah which is intense, dense example with lots of extract and Un Segreto, a beautifully weighted, intense blend of Sangiovese and Shiraz with lifted incense spice and liquorice. Both are relatively cool, individual and highly expressive examples of Shiraz/Syrah and Sangiovese. In order to show its full potential Genesis Shiraz needs to be given 10 years, while Un Segreto just starts to hits straps at five years and will keep going 10 years plus. A second Shiraz, Sauvage offers some of the same wild black and red fruits intensity along with a mineral, licorice aspect, if not the same concentration or extra depth and complexity but this too needs some time - at least 5 years. A bold and powerful rosé Allegro also comes from Shiraz but is less interesting than La Chiave from Sangiovese which is sleek, stylish and almost certainly the best yet made in Australia. Viognier, bottled as Ingénue, rounds out the range and has decent structure and an elegance rarely seen in this variety 'down under'. The wines are bottled unfiltered. Adam's Rib White and Red (not tasted) are the entry level wines.

Recommended Reds:
Syrah Genesis ★★★★☆ £F
Sauvage ★★★☆ £E
Un Segreto ★★★★☆ £F
La Chiave ★★★☆ £F

Recommended Whites:
Ingénue ★★★☆ £F

Recommended Rosés:
Allegro ★★☆ £D

❀ Chambers Rosewood *www.chambersrosewood.com.au*
Many of the great fortified-wine producers of North-West Victoria have their beginnings in late-Victorian times; Chambers, based in Rutherglen, goes as far back as 1858. It is the stocks of extremely old wines that contribute not only to the incredible concentration and intensity of the Rare versions of Rutherglen Muscat and Topaque, the latter now labelled Topaque Muscadelle (previously sold simply as Old Liqueur Topaque and Old Liqueur Muscat) but also their remarkable texture and extraordinary flavour complexity. The tea-leaf elegance of the Topaque contrasts with the more dried-fruits, raisiny character of the Muscat. The Special bottlings, now classified Grand, are also very fine, although at the regular, if relatively inexpensive level, there is good richness but the balance and flavours are much less inspiring. Table wines are also made. Prices below are based on a 75cl bottle, though they are sold in halves.

Recommended Whites:
Rutherglen Topaque Muscadelle Rare ✪✪✪✪✪ £H
Rutherglen Topaque Muscadelle Grand ★★★★★ £H
Rutherglen Topaque Muscadelle ★★★ £E
Rutherglen Muscat Rare ✪✪✪✪✪ £H
Rutherglen Muscat Grand ★★★★☆ £H
Rutherglen Muscat ★★☆ £E

Dom. Chandon *www.chandon.com.au*
Now labelled Domaine Chandon (formerly Green Point), this prestigious Yarra Valley operation is one of the most important of the Moët-Hennessey foreign investments. It could probably

survive on the tourists alone but, under the stewardship of senior winemaker Dan Buckle (ex-MOUNT LANGI GHIRAN), an increasing number of still and sparkling wines are made to a high standard. Still and sparkling Pinot Noir and Chardonnay are characterised by clarity, intensity and good breadth. Shiraz is good too, widely-sourced it includes a little Viognier. Of the sparkling wines the Vintage Brut (roughly half Pinot Noir, half Chardonnay) is the quality standard bearer but a little Blanc de Blancs and Brut Rosé are also made. All show fine texture, ripe fruit and good richness and improve with a little age. A Non-Vintage blend is not of the same order yet a decent sparkler, far better than much basic Champagne.

Recommended Reds:
Shiraz Heathcote ★★ £D   Pinot Noir ★☆ £E

Recommended Whites:
Vintage Brut ★★★ £E   Vintage Blanc de Blancs ★★★ £D
Non-Vintage Brut ★★ £C   Chardonnay ★★ £D

Cobaw Ridge (Macedon Ranges) *www.cobawridge.com.au*
Established in 1985, the Cooper's Macedon Ranges six hectare vineyard is planted at 610 metres where, it transpires, Northern Italian Sudtirol variety Lagrein flourishes. However, the less than successful Vermentino was removed after five years having yielded a grand total of about 15 kg! A vertical of the inky Lagrein, Australia's first commercial quantities of the variety, showed great consistency and typicity with sappy, sour plum and cherry fruit underscored by ripe but present tannins. An aromatic, spicy, finely honed Shiraz (labelled Syrah) co-fermented with a dash of Viognier showcases the region's cool climate credentials too. The Coopers are also renowned for Chardonnay, while Pinot Noir (the smallest production wine) is now building a following (neither tasted). Certified organic in 2009, all wines are 100% estate grown and neither filtered nor fined. Additions are kept to the bare minimum so as not to interfere with vineyard expression and the wines have distinctly unforced feel about them. (SA)

Recommended Reds:
Pinot Noir ★★★ £F   Lagrein ★★ £E
Syrah ★★☆ £F

Recommended Whites:
Chardonnay ★★★ £D

Coldstream Hills (Yarra Valley) *www.coldstreamhills.com.au*
This high-profile Yarra Valley winery, founded in 1985 by wine critic James Halliday, is now part of the Treasury Wine Estates portfolio of small to medium-sized wineries. Production has risen from a little under 500 cases in the first vintage to over 30,000 cases while now the company owns or manages vineyard holdings totalling some 100 ha across five sites in the Upper and Lower Yarra. The wines are made by Andrew Fleming with consultancy from Halliday. Reserves are made from the best fruit and see a greater percentage of new French oak. Burgundy is the inspiration for both Pinot Noir and Chardonnay that are ageworthy but nevertheless emphasise attractive youthful fruit. Whole bunches are used in vinifying the Pinot Noir while Chardonnay undergoes a cool fermentation (and only a small amount of malolactic fermentation) as well as extensive lees contact. Reserve Cabernet Sauvignon shows good texture and intensity. Shiraz (including a Reserve), Sauvignon Blanc and Sparkling wines are also made along with two single vineyard Chardonnays and three Pinots.

Recommended Reds:
Pinot Noir Reserve ★★★☆ £F   Pinot Noir ★★ £D
Cabernet Sauvignon Reserve ★★★ £F

Merlot ★★ £D

Recommended Whites:
Chardonnay Reserve ★★★☆ £F
Chardonnay ★★☆ £D

Craiglee (Sunbury) *www.craiglee.com.au*
Craiglee is a tiny cool-climate winery and vineyard an hour or so north of Melbourne. In 1976 Pat Carmody replanted vines on the site of 19th-century vineyards. He and his family continue to make small quantities of wines in the original winery building. The emphasis here is on structured, elegant, wellcrafted wines with a real capacity to age. Chardonnay is marked by a restrained melon character, with well-judged, subtle use of oak. Like nearby VIRGIN HILLS with its Cabernet Sauvignon, the Shiraz here is at the extreme margin for achieving full ripeness. Certainly in the warmer years, it is one of the best in the state. In cooler or more variable vintages the classic pepper and spice character can be slightly overwhelmed by a minty influence. Very small amounts of Cabernet Sauvignon, Pinot Noir and Sauvignon Blanc are also made.

Recommended Reds:
Shiraz ★★★☆ £E

Recommended Whites:
Chardonnay ★★★ £D

Crawford River (Henty) *www.crawfordriverwines.com*
A long-established boutique operation, John Thomson's winery in the still little-known Henty region remains small but is making better wines than ever. Riesling is consistently the best variety with impressive depth, intensity and concentration. Long and stylish, it sometimes lacks the extra structure and tautness to rival top European examples. However, a beautifully balanced Reserve is even better with the weight, expression and minerality to rival at top example from Germany's Pfalz. Sémillon has real style and length too, with vivid herb and ripe citrus fruit. Cabernet Sauvignon comes from old vines and is much less consistent but can be superb in a warm year (for which the rating is given). With floral, berry and herbal complexity, it is taut, intense and complex with ripe tannins. Also made is a Cabernet/Merlot and elegant, moderately sweet white, Nektar.

Recommended Reds:
Cabernet Sauvignon ★★★ £E

Recommended Whites:
Riesling Reserve ★★★★☆ £F   Shiraz ★★★★ £D
Sémillon ★★ £C

Curly Flat (Macedon Ranges) *www.curlyflat.com*
Curly Flat is one of a small but growing band of high-quality producers located in the Macedon Ranges. Phillip and Jeni Moraghan's 14 ha of vineyards are at 575m and planted predominantly to Pinot Noir. Experience gained in North America has been supplemented by help from Gary Farr and the wines have been made in their own winery since 2002. Both Pinot Noir and Chardonnay are both complex and well balanced, with well-defined cool climate fruit and, picked on acid not sugar, have good underlying freshness. Declassified fruit goes into a second label, Williams Crossing. As well as a sparkling wine, Pinot Grigio a rosé and a premium Pinot have also been added to the range. In recent years there has been a shift towards farming biodynamically.

Recommended Reds:
Pinot Noir ★★★★☆ £F

Victoria & Tasmania

Recommended Whites:
Chardonnay ★★★★☆ £E

❀ Dalwhinnie (Pyrenees) www.dalwhinnie.com.au

This is the best winery in the Pyrenees region and one of the best both in the state and Australia. The 18 ha of organically tended vineyards are planted in granite soils at a higher altitude than many of the neighbouring estates and produce wines of real structure and finesse. With an established reputation for outstanding Shiraz and Chardonnay, the Jones have enlisted outside consultancy and the quality of the wines continues to improve. As well as Shiraz and Chardonnay, Pinot also comes from the Hut Vineyard on the Moonambel Valley floor. A small amount of Eagle Series Shiraz is made from a tiny 1.2 ha vineyard which is very intense, classy and complete but needs 10 years' ageing. Chardonnay is deep yet restrained with real intensity and structured for medium-term cellaring. Both the Moonambel Cabernet and Moonambel Shiraz will improve in bottle for 5, often 10 years.

Recommended Reds:
Shiraz Pyrenees Eagle Series ★★★★★ £G
Shiraz Moonambel ★★★★ £E
Cabernet Sauvignon Moonambel ★★★☆ £F
Pinot Noir The Hut ★★★ £F
Recommended Whites:
Chardonnay Moonambel ★★★★ £E

De Bortoli - Victoria (Yarra Valley) www.debortoli.com.au

De Bortoli is well-known for its big-volume inexpensive blends and varietals from Riverina but the better wines (the sweet Noble One excepted – see De Bortoli, New South Wales) are made in and, for the most part, sourced from the Yarra Valley. The winemaking is headed by Stephen Webber whose wife Leanne De Bortoli directs operations. Stylish Chardonnay, intense, dark cherry and plum Pinot Noir, and increasingly stylish, intense spicy Shiraz (including very limited quantities of a denser, more complex Reserve) appear under the Yarra Valley label, but the regular Pinot Noir and Chardonnay can lack the depth and expression of better examples. Reserves are however much more impressive - concentrated, complex and ripe if still not especially expressive of the Yarra. There has been a sea change with leading varieties Pinot Noir and Chardonnay, which are now picked at lower ripeness in pursuit of more elegant, *terroir* driven styles with fresh natural acidity. In the winery, natural yeasts and malolactic fermentations prevail. There is also a shift away from new oak, especially with the Chardonnays. This, together with techniques aimed at introducing a subtle phenolic character has resulted in greater complexity and layers of texture. In consequence, the wines benefit from a little more time in bottle. The flagship Melba Reserve, primarily from Cabernet Sauvignon is made in small quantities and released with several years' bottle age. Melba Lucia is an intense, well structured blend of Cabernet and Sangiovese. Gulf Station wines are less expensive but also sourced from the Yarra Valley. The Shiraz and Chardonnay stand out and provide good value, though other Gulf Station varietals can sometimes be surpassed by the cheaper Windy Peak wines, which include fruit from wider sources. The silky Windy Peak Pinot Noir (£B) is a case in point. New King Valley sourced innovative red and white blends under the Bella Riva label show promise. And innovation is also the watchword with a textured, off-dry Yarra Valley Reserve Release Riesling.

De Bortoli Yarra Valley
Recommended Reds:
Pinot Noir Reserve Release ★★★☆ £E
Pinot Noir ★★☆ £D
Syrah Reserve Release ★★★☆ £E
Shiraz/Viognier ★★★ £C
Melba Reserve ★★★ £E
Recommended Whites:
Chardonnay Reserve Release ★★★☆ £D
Chardonnay ★★☆ £C
Riesling Reserve Release ★★☆ £C
Bella Riva
Recommended Reds:
Sangiovese/Merlot King Valley ★★☆ £B
Gulf Station
Recommended Reds:
Shiraz ★ £C
Recommended Whites:
Chardonnay ★ £C

Delatite (Upper Goulburn) www.delatitewinery.com.au

Mansfield in the Central High Country of Victoria is one of the state's many cool outposts to be exploited. Wines have been made from these steep slopes with views across to the alpine retreat of Mount Buller since 1982. The wines are lighter and exhibit cooler flavours than the majority of Australian wines but have impressive fruit intensity. Aromatic white varieties are a forte. There's an aromatic, very floral Riesling that is intense and characterful. Even better is a wonderfully expressive Gewürztraminer which has good richness and depth and great length. Both only miss a little extra structure. The range now features some impressive late harvest styles. A waxy Pinot Gris is also made in a euro-centric style, with nutty, spicy notes to its pear fruit, as is the delightful, sweet late harvest Catherine Gewürztraminer. Chardonnay shows some style too, though it lacks a little depth. Reds are markedly cool and minty in style but do increasigly achieve ripe tannins in the Cabernet or Cabernet-based Devil's River, a blend of Cabernet Sauvignon, Malbec and Shiraz. Dungeon Gully (Merlot, Malbec, Cabernet Sauvignon and Shiraz) too, though very minty can be supple with soft tannins A number of other varietals are made including Sauvignon Blanc, Pinot Noir, Merlot, Nebbiolo, Tempranillo and Shiraz. Some sparkling wine, Delmelza Pinot/Chardonnay and Polly Gewürztraminer, is also made.

Recommended Reds:
Devil's River ★★ £D   Dungeon Gully ★★ £C
Recommended Whites:
Gewürztraminer Dead Mans Hill ★★★ £C
Gewürztraminer Catherine ★★☆ £C
Riesling ★★ £C   Chardonnay ★★ £C
Pinot Gris ★★ £C

Diamond Valley (Yarra Valley) www.diamondvalley.com.au

Small winery established in 1982 producing around 7,000 cases a year. While the Yarra Valley Blue Label range is well crafted with good varietal fruit, it is the White Label Estate wines, in particular the superb Pinot Noir, which stand out. The Chardonnay is rich and lightly tropical with well-judged oak, while the Estate Pinot is marked by concentrated – almost gamey – forward plum and black fruit, all underpinned by a not inconsiderable oak influence. Showy in its youth but with real structure too, it will be all the better for 5 years' ageing.

Recommended Reds:
Pinot Noir White Label ★★★★ £F
Pinot Noir Blue Label ★★ £C
Cabernet Merlot White Label ★★★ £F
Cabernet Merlot Blue Label ★★ £C
Recommended Whites:
Chardonnay White Label ★★★ £E
Chardonnay Blue Label ★★ £C

Domaine A (Tasmania) *www.domaine-a.com.au*

Peter and Ruth Althaus' Stoney Vineyard is but a short distance from Tasmania's capital Hobart in the Coal River Valley. Something of the viticultural and winemaking philosophy echoes that of many small producers in similarly marginal vine-growing regions in Europe. 11 ha of a 20 ha estate are planted at relatively high densities and both pruning and harvesting are carried out by hand. Domaine A is the top selection, Stoney Vineyard effectively a second label. Cabernet Sauvignon is a particularly good example of cool-grown elegance and much better than many underperforming classed growth Médocs. Domaine A Pinot Noir shows rich plum and cherry fruit and has length and style if missing a little extra depth or dimension to fully justify the price tag. The structure of Lady A, a barrel-fermented and aged Sauvignon is impressive too if the oak influence can teeter on being overdone. The Stoney Vineyard varietals are cool and elegant, generally with sufficient ripeness in fruit and tannins in the Cabernet. All in all an estate deserving of attention.

Domaine A
Recommended Reds:
Pinot Noir★★★ £F   Cabernet Sauvignon★★★ £F
Recommended Whites:
Sauvignon Blanc Lady A ★★★☆ £E

Stoney Vineyard
Recommended Reds:
Cabernet Sauvignon ★★ £D
Recommended Whites:
Sauvignon Blanc ★★ £C

✿ William Downie (Yarra Valley) *www.williamdownie.com.au*

William (Bill) Downie established his eponymous label in 2003. His passion is Pinot Noir and he makes no less than three from the Yarra Valley, Mornington Peninsula and Gippsland in Victoria, where he is planting his own high density (11,000 vines/ha) biodynamic vineyard. Meantime, fruit is rigorously sourced, where possible from vineyards farmed organically or biodynamically. Downie's love of Pinot stems from working for BASS PHILLIP, then DE BORTOLI in the Yarra Valley. Whilst at De Bortoli he oversaw their investment in Burgundy from 2001 until 2005. He brings a hands off approach to winemaking which is readily apparent in the delicate hue and subtle flavour profile of his intense Pinots. Fruit is de-stemmed and, after a natural cold soak for a few days, fermentation is in open-topped wooden fermenters. The wines are not plunged until dryness and are then aged in barrel for about 15 months. The Gippsland Pinot Noir is the funkier of the three, while the Mornington Peninsula wines show the brightest fruit. The Yarra Valley Pinot lies somewhere in between. But all three share great length and persistence thanks to fruit that is intense, but not in the least overbearing. Animated acidity and fine but present tannins complete the package and provide the structure for ageing. These are wines that benefit from four to five years in bottle to really start hitting their straps. (SA)
Recommended Reds:
Pinot Noir Yarra Valley ★★★★☆ £F

Pinot Noir Morning Peninsula ★★★★ £F
Pinot Noir Gippsland ★★★★ £F

Dromana Estate *www.dromanaestate.com.au*

Established by Garry Crittenden in 1982, whose son Rollo for some time made the wines, the Mornington Peninsula estate is now majority-owned by investors. The premium label is Dromana Estate for wines from estate-grown fruit. The focus is on Pinot Noir and Chardonnay but also includes a somewhat leafy but increasingly ripe, spicy berry-fruited Cabernet/Merlot and a stylish, cool but ripe Shiraz. Both Chardonnay and Pinot Noir are good examples but the relatively restrained, complex Reserves offer much more. Mornington Estate wines come from a separate 20 ha vineyard on the peninsula but much of the interest in Dromana comes from the production of Italian varietals, all sold under the "i" label. Current winemaker Duncan Duchanan has worked several vintages in Northern Italy and the range is generally attractive and well made. The Arneis, and a Pinot Grigio from Mornington Peninsula really come close to the intensity and character of good Italian examples while a Nebbiolo and Sangiovese from Heathcote shows increasingly fine fruit and tannins. The group has also expanded into the Yarra Valley with wines from Yarra fruit labelled as Yarra Valley Hills. Also under the same ownership is David Traeger of Nagambie Lakes.

Dromana Estate
Recommended Reds:
Pinot Noir★★ £D
Recommended Whites:
Chardonnay ★★ £D
i label
Recommended Reds:
Sangiovese ★★ £B
Nebbiolo ★★ £B
Recommended Whites:
Arneis ★★ £B   Pinot Grigio ★★ £B

✿ Eldridge Estate *www.eldridge-estate.com.au*

In 1995, David & Wendy Lloyd acquired Eldridge Estate. The vineyard, originally planted in 1984, is located on a north facing slope at 225 metres above sea level on rich terra rossa volcanic loam. Protected from harsh winds by natural land forms, the ripening period is long and cool. With a latitude of 38 22' 16" and longitude 145 1' 11, in altitude and climate, it is similar to Burgundy. Unsurprisingly, the focal point of the range is three Chardonnays and three Pinot Noirs (during their tenure, the Lloyds have grafted the vineyard over to the latest clones: six of Pinot Noir, five of Chardonnay). The Lloyds also make a sparkling wine (using all three Champagne varieties), an oaked Sauvignon Blanc and a Gamay. One hundred percent focused on the business, they work the seven acre vineyard and make the wines themselves. Production is small (between 800 and 1000 cases a year), but then the wines, all estate grown and bottled, are perfectly formed. Long and intense, the Estate and Clonal Blend Pinot Noirs are particularly refined, lifted and silky. The Estate Chardonnay shows the region's classic fleshy white peach, deftly balanced by a long thread of citrus acidity. (SA)
Recommended Reds:
Pinot Noir Clonal Blend ★★★★☆ £F
Pinot Noir ★★★★ £F
Recommended Whites:
Chardonnay ★★★★ £E

Victoria & Tasmania

⊕ By Farr (Geelong) www.byfarr.com.au

In 1999 Gary Farr released four new varietals from 4.8 ha of his own vineyards adjacent to BANNOCKBURN. Initially the wines were known as Bannockburn by Farr but are now simply By Farr. The wines are made in a purpose built winery but, coming from new clones on differing soil types and aspects, the wines are distinctly different. Shiraz, Chardonnay and no less than three cuvees of Pinot Noir (Farrside, Sangreal and Tout Pres, the latter almost twice the price and not tasted) all show a little more elegance and refined varietal character. Viognier is the major point of difference and seems set to show the hallmark Bannockburn weight and structure and therefore eclipse the high-alcohol but structure-deficient character of many Australian examples of this variety.

Recommended Reds:

Pinot Noir Farrside ★★★★ £F

Pinot Noir Sangrel ★★★★ £F

Shiraz ★★★ £F

Recommended Whites:

Viognier ★★★★☆ £F   Chardonnay ★★★★ £F

⊕⊕ Giaconda (Beechworth) www.giaconda.com.au

Production here remains small at around 2,500 cases per year, although the 3 ha vineyards planted in the 1980s have now doubled in size thanks to more recent plantings. A small amount of wine is exported but most of it is accounted for by a dedicated mailing list. Rick Kinzbrunner's Pinot Noir and Chardonnay are Australian cool-climate classics, almost Burgundian in style with an approach to vinification that mirrors the best of the Côte d'Or. Kinzbrunner has now even created a vast underground cellar in which to age the wines. The Pinot Noir is expansive and classy, the Chardonnay structured and immensely refined; it requires a minimum of 5 years' ageing to fully unfurl but is nearly always amongst Australia's finest examples. Cabernet is a classic Bordeaux blend of Cabernet Sauvignon, Merlot and Cabernet Franc. However 2012 was the last vintage with vines being grafted over to Shiraz. There is a Nantua Cabernet from 2014. More recently the range has been extended to include: Nantua Les Deux, a full-on Chardonnay with a small amount of Roussanne and a richly textured, stylish Shiraz from the neighbouring Warner vineyard. A Nebbiolo is now made as is an Estate Shiraz. Another new project is a joint venture with Michel CHAPOUTIER, Ergo Sum Shiraz which comes from the Nantua Vineyard. All the wines age very well. Prices reflect both quality and demand.

Recommended Reds:

Shiraz Warner Vineyard ★★★★★ £F

Pinot Noir ★★★★☆ £F

Cabernet ★★★☆ £F

Recommended Whites:

Chardonnay ★★★★★ £F

Nantua Les Deux ★★★★☆ £F

⊕ Giant Steps (Yarra Valley) www.innocentbystander.com.au

Phil Sexton it seems has a thing about Chardonnay. More than 20 years ago he established Devil's Lair in the Margaret River and soon produced a leading example. In 1997 he and his family took an almighty leap eastwards and took root again in the Yarra Valley. Of a range of impressive single vineyard wines now made those from one variety are the most thrilling: Chardonnay. Seven different Chardonny clones are planted and the wines are made as naturally as possible with hand harvesting, whole bunch pressing, no added yeasts, and minimal use of sulphur. Sexton Vineyard Chardonnay

has real dimension, weight and a slightly Chassagne-like fruit and style. Tarraford vineyard is slightly more Puligny-like with its intensity and drive. Both wines can lose a little definition in a very warm vintage but otherwise do consistently well. well. Arthur's Creek Chardonnay lies somewhere between the too, tight yet with a rich, intense core of fruit. Pinots, derived from five clones, are are also among the better examples made in the Yarra Valley with good expression and a certain elegance but need at least 5-6 years' age to open out fully. Still more can be expected as the vines age. Shiraz is also made - in the slightly exotic, succulent Miller vineyard example, a small amount of Viognier was fermented together with the Shiraz. Tiny amounts of Jones Block Shiraz are produced from very old McLaren Vale vines for a very dense and concentrated style that needs plenty of time. Harry's Monster, made from equal parts Cabernet Sauvignon, Cabernet Franc, Merlot and Petit Verdot is a fleshy, affable character only missing a little depth and refinement. Innocent Bystander wines are soundly made range from mostly bought-in fruit. A third label, Mea Culpa, now accounts for premium Chardonnay and Shiraz (£E).

Giant Steps

Recommended Reds:

Pinot Noir Gladysdale Vineyard ★★★★ £E

Pinot Noir Tarraford Vineyard ★★★☆ £E

Pinot Noir Sexton Vineyard ★★★ £D

Shiraz Jones Block ★★★☆ £E   Shiraz Miller Vineyard ★★★ £E

Harry's Monster Sexton Vineyard ★★★☆ £E

Merlot Giant Steps Vineyard ★★☆ £C

Recommended Whites:

Chardonnay Tarraford Vineyard ★★★★ £E

Chardonnay Arthur's Creek Vineyard★★★★ £E

Chardonnay Sexton Vineyard★★★☆ £D

Innocent Bystander

Recommended Reds:

Pinot Noir ★★ £B

Recommended Whites:

Chardonnay ★★ £B   Pinot Gris ★★ £B

Recommended Rosés:

Pink Moscato ★★ £C

Hanging Rock (Macedon Ranges) www.hangingrock.com.au

Both John and Ann (née Tyrrell, daughter of the late Murray TYRRELL) are steeped in winemaking experience, having been involved with some of the country's leading producers before securing their own property in 1985. Their vineyards on the Jim Jim, an extinct volcano, are as cool as any in Australia and are planted predominantly to Pinot Noir and Chardonnay for one of Australia's top sparkling wines, Macedon Cuvée, a blend of vintages. Consistency for a very rich, intense style is maintained by drawing from a substantial resource of reserve wines for each successive release. A more expensive Macedon Brut LD is a late-disgorged example spending 15 years on lees. The flagship rich, intense Shiraz is from the warmer Heathcote region. Production resumed in 1997, after a break of 5 years, from new vineyards (chiefly Athol's Paddock and Colbinabbin Estate) and has been a powerful expression of fruit and oak in every vintage since. A second premium Shiraz, Cambrian Rise is also from Heathcote and is cooler but stylish. Other premium wines include a cool, crisp well-structured Sauvignon Blanc from the Jim Jim vineyards and a fresh and grapey late harvest Riesling. Yellow label wines come from diverse sources including cool, supple Cabernet Sauvignon Prospect. Rock is the budget label.

Recommended Reds:
Shiraz Heathcote ★★★★ £F
Shiraz Cambrian Rise ★★★ £C
Cabernet Sauvignon Prospect ★★ £C
Recommended Whites:
Macedon Cuvée Non-Vintage ★★★☆ £E
Sauvignon Blanc Jim Jim ★★ £C

Heathcote Winery (Heathcote) *www.heathcotewinery.com.au*
Established in 1978, Heathcote Winery was among the first wave of commercial wineries in Heathcote, its first vintage in 1983. In 1997 the winery was purchased by an independent group of wine enthusiasts led by lawyer Stephen Wilkins. Significant investment has reaped dividends. Impressively layered and structured, the estate grown Curagee Shiraz (sourced from the 14 ha Newlans Lane Vineyard) has built a loyal following. The plusher, more overtly fruity Mail Coach Shiraz is predominantly estate grown and, like the Curagee, features a subtle splash of Viognier. In 2000, Heathcote Winery acquired the four hectare The Slaughterhouse Paddock vineyard (the region's second oldest), from which comes a third premium Shiraz (not tasted). Other reds made are the premium Wilkins Shiraz and a Cravens Place Shiraz. Heathcote Winery also produces Cravens Place MCV White, a blend of Viognier, Marsanne and Chardonnay as well as a Cravens Place Sauvignon Blanc and a Mail Coach Viognier. (SA)
Recommended Reds:
Shiraz Curagee ★★★★☆ £F
Shiraz Mail Coach ★★★☆ £D

⊕ House of Arras (Tasmania) *www.houseofarras.com.au*
Though House of Arras wines are made at HARDYS' McLaren Vale winery, where Constellation's sparkling wine supremo Edd Carr is based, the fruit for Constellation's flagship sparkling brand is rigorously sourced from Tasmania, latterly exclusively from Eastern Tasmania. Carr draws on a range of techniques to forge a supple yet sophisticated range a world away from the fruit-focused sparkling wines of old. All wines feature 100% malolactic fermentation (well balanced by Tasmania's ample acidity) and an element of oak ageing (whether for the base wine itself or *dosage* liqueur). Time on lees extends up to 10 years for the remarkably fresh and focused EJ Carr Late Disgorged Chardonnay /Pinot Noir. (SA)
Recommended Whites:
EJ Carr Late Disgorged Chardonnay/Pinot Noir Vintage ★★★★★ £H
Grand Vintage Chardonnay/Pinot Noir ★★★★ £F
Blanc de Blancs Vintage Chardonnay ★★★★ £F
Brut Elite Cuvée NV Pinot Noir/Chardonnay ★★★☆ £F

⊕ Jasper Hill (Heathcote) *www.jasperhill.com*
The production here is small and the wines can be very difficult to track down but it is worth the effort. As with the finest producers in the northern Rhône, the approach is one of minimal intervention: no irrigation, minimal vineyard treatments and virtually sulphur-free reds. Yields are tiny from the sparse, granite-based soils, between 1 and 2 tons to the acre. The two Shirazes are remarkable: both rich, concentrated and full of exotic dark berry fruit and spice, with a marvellous supple texture underpinning them. The Georgia's Paddock is slightly more opulent while a dash of Cabernet Franc in Emily's Paddock brings aromatic lift. They are amongst Australia's very finest. While they will easily age for 20 years or more they can be broached with just a few years in the cellar. while a dash of Cabernet Franc in Emily's Paddock brings aromatic lift. For long just

one white was also produced, a powerful stuctured Riesling, full of subtle citrus but minerally and toasty with 3 or 4 years' ageing. Very small quantities of Nebbiolo have been made since 2001. In 2009, Laughton made a Viognier, Emily's Paddock (not tasted). Also new is La Pleiade Shiraz (known as Cluster M45 in the USA), as well as an Agly Valley red from the Côtes du Roussillon in a joint venture with Michel CHAPOUTIER.
Recommended Reds:
Shiraz/Cabernet Franc Emily's Paddock ★★★★★ £G
Shiraz Georgia's Paddock ★★★★★ £F
Grenache Cornella Vineyard ★★★★★ £F
Recommended Whites:
Riesling Georgia's Paddock ★★★☆ £E

⊕ Kooyong (Mornington Peninsula) *www.portphillipestate.com.au*
This newish Mornington Peninsula winery, located in the warmer north of the peninsula on low vigour sandy clay soils, is one of its largest with 34 ha of vineyard to draw on. The wines are the work of Australian-trained winemaker Sandro Mosele who also makes wine at sister estate, PORT PHILLIP ESTATE which is home to the cellar door and a new bottling line and barrel hall, though the wines are made at Kooyong. Though Kooyong grows a small amount of Pinot Gris and Viognier, the focus here is on and he is making an expanding range of single-vineyard Chardonnay and Pinot Noir. For Massale Pinot Noir and Clonale Chardonnay, estate grown fruit is supplemented by bought in fruit; brighter and breezier than the estate wines nonetheless, these are elegant wines with no little finesse. A regular The Estate Pinot Noir is structured, powerful and dense with immaculate concentrated ripe cherry/berry fruit and five spice. The Estate Chardonnay is similarly powerful but with good depth and structure as well as a touch ofminerality, and will improve for at least 4–5 years'. Single-vineyard examples are even more impressively structured, the Pinot Noirs showing more backbone and savoury layers, especially Ferrous and Meres; they benefit from a few years bottle age before broaching. Chardonnay from the Faultline and Farrago Vineyard vineyards is tight knit and mineral, the former racier; again both promise to develop for several years, especially now the white wines are bottled under screwcap.
Recommended Reds:
Pinot Noir Meres★★★★☆ £F
Pinot Noir Ferrous ★★★★☆ £F
Pinot Noir Estate ★★★☆ £E
Pinot Noir Massale ★★★ £D
Recommended Whites:
Chardonnay Farrago ★★★★☆ £E
Chardonnay Faultline ★★★★☆ £E
Chardonnay Estate ★★★☆ £E
Chardonnay Clonale ★★★ £D
Pinot Gris Kooyong Buerrot ★★ £D

Kreglinger (Tasmania) *www.kreglingerwineestates.com*
Dr Andrew Pirie founded Pipers Brook back in 1974 and it has since risen to become the dominant force in the tiny Tasmanian wine industry with more than 200 ha of vineyards. The majority of shares are held by Kreglinger Australia, part of the Belgian de Moor family's Kreglinger group, which has also established a new venture in South Australia's Mount Benson region. The focus here has always rightly been on cool-climate varieties, in particular Pinot Noir, Chardonnay and Riesling. The wines generally show lovely varietal fruit character with extra nuance and richness. Sparkling wine has also been a strength since the much-heralded launch of Pirie, now presented

Victoria & Tasmania

Australia

as Kreglinger Vintage Brut. The wines don't offer exceptional value but are fairly priced for the quality compared to other Australian examples or equivalent Burgundian quality in Pinot or Chardonnay. With the 1999 vintage a small amount of single-site Pinot Noir (The Blackwood and The Lyre from sections of the Heemskerk Vineyard) joined a Chardonnay (The Summit) made since 1997 from 2 ha. Ninth Island is a separate entity drawing largely from the former Rochecombe vineyards; as well as very creditable Chardonnay and Pinot Noir the range includes several other varietals and a non-vintage Brut..

Pipers Brook
Recommended Reds:
Pinot Noir Estate ★★★ £D
Recommended Whites:
Chardonnay Estate★★ £D
Riesling ★★ £C
Gewürztraminer ★★ £C
Kreglinger
Recommended Whites:
Kreglinger Vintage Brut ★★★★ £E
Recommended Rosés:
Kreglinger Vintage Brut Rosé ★★★★ £E
Ninth Island
Recommended Reds:
Pinot Noir ★ £C
Recommended Whites:
Chardonnay ★ £C

>> Luke Lambert Wines *www.lukelambertwines.com.au*
Luke Lambert is a small and impressive boutique producer based in the Yarra Valley, whose single vineyard wines are made from handpicked fruit, wild fermented and with no temperature control, fining or filtration. Luke sources his fruit from vineyards that give a true expression of *terroir* and the result is that the wines reflect that expression together with vibrant juicy fruit and true varietal flavours. LL Chardonnay is juicy with good balance between the fruit and the acidity if perhaps lacking just a little bit of complexity. Crudo Shiraz, on the other hand, combines this juicy fruit, coupled with the tarryness of the grape and a judicious use of oak. LL Syrah (why one is called Shiraz and the other Syrah is something I haven't been able to fathom out) has that extra bit of complexity and a great deal of persistence on the finish. Whilst they are all approachable now, long cellaring will be additionally rewarding. Prices are very reasonable for the quality. (NB)
Recommended Reds:
LL Syrah ★★★★☆ £E
Crudo Shiraz ★★★★ £D
Recommended Whites:
LL Chardonnay ★★★☆ £D

>> Lethbridge Wines (Geelong) *www.lethbridgewines.com*
Lethbridge Wine is a partnership of Ray Nadeson, Maree Collis and Adrian Thomas. All coming from a medical background, these somewhat cult wines are much sought after by Melbourne doctors. Now venturing internationally, there is a chance for the rest of the world to appreciate theses well-made wines. Dr Nadeson Riesling (Ernie Loosen, eat your heart out!) already displays from its youth that peculiar petrolly sensation on the palate and has a fine complex finish, but the entry level Lethbridge Chardonnay disappointed a bit with some excess of residual sugar. Lethbridge's strength,

however are in their reds, starting with the well-balanced Ménage á Noir Pinot Noir – easy drinking and smooth. The Negroamaro is also easy drinking, but like its counterpart in Southern Italy, is not very complex. Where Lethbridge really steps up is with the Pinot Meunier, good colour, balance and length and one of the best examples of this component of Champagne wines I have tasted. Both the Lethbridge Shiraz and the Lethbridge Pinot Noir display true varietal flavours coupled with good complexity and a long finish. (NB)
Recommended Reds:
Lethbridge Shiraz ★★★★ £E
Lethbridge Pinot Noir ★★★★ £E
Ménage á Noir Pinot Noir ★★★☆ £D
Lethbridge Pinot Meunier ★★★☆ £D
Lethbridge Negroamaro ★★☆ £D
Recommended Whites:
Dr Nadeson Riesling ★★★ £D
Lethbridge Chardonnay ★★ £E

Stefano Lubiana (Tasmania) *www.slw.com.au*
This small Tasmanian operation is a veritable giant compared to some of the micro-boutique operations that make just a few hundred cases. The small vineyard at Granton, lying above the Derwent River, forms part of a much larger property but produces Pinot Noir and Chardonnay of a persuasive style and refinement, the former rich and velvety with attractive spaice. The fruit in each is very pure and intense, the wines elegant and vibrant and capable of at least 3 or 4 years' age. Sasso (not tasted) is the ultra-premium Pinot Noir. As well as a premium Chardonnay Collina and lower priced versions of both Chardonnay and Pinot Noir (Primavera), Sauvignon Blanc and Pinot Grigio are made. The fresh, appley non-vintage Brut sparkling wine is based on Pinot Noir with a little Chardonnay, while the vintage is taut, textured and characterful.
Recommended Reds:
Pinot Noir ★★★★ £F   Merlot ★★ £C
Recommended Whites:
Brut Vintage ★★★☆ £F
Brut Non-Vintage ★★☆ £E
Chardonnay★★★ £F   Riesling★★★ £C

☻ Mac Forbes *www.macforbes.com*
Before setting up his eponymous Yarra Valley/Strathbogie Ranges label, Mac Forbes' CV included stints in the Yarra Valley at Mount Mary and in Europe, including Austria, where he still makes wine. Unsurprising then that his approach is *terroir* driven. Sourcing fruit under long term contract from several vineyards in the Yarra Valley and Strathbogie Ranges, Forbes has a foot in two cutting edge camps. He is at the vanguard of producers seeking to express the Yarra's sub-regionality, also those crafting off-dry Riesling. At the time of writing, in addition to a generic Yarra Pinot Noir (not tasted) he makes five single vineyard Pinot Noirs of differing structure and intensity, depending on site - Coldstream, Woori Yallock, Gruyere, Dixon's Creek (not tasted) and Yarra Glen. From a cool, elevated site at 600m, Forbes' off-dry Strathbogie Ranges Riesling is perhaps Australia's most deftly balanced example of this niche but growing style, with ample line and tension despite over 30 grams of residual sugar (Rieslings are labelled by reference to the amount of residual sugar). In the winery, hands off rather than ultra-protective winemaking favours site over fruit, making for particularly subtle, complex Pinot Noir and Riesling, the latter finding particularly funky, mineral expression in Tradition Riesling, which sees three months

skin contact. These aromatic, relatively delicate varieties from cool climate sites seem to suit Forbes' ripe but crunchy low alcohol style better than his slightly lean Chardonnay and Cabernet Sauvignon (Syrah not tasted) or "Project Wines," a King Valley Barbera and Yarra Valley Arneis. They also bode well for his next project in Strathbogie Ranges: planting the currently quarantined Grüner Veltliner for which he has sourced cuttings from his Austrian (Carnuntum) project. As of the 2007 vintage, Hugh Cabernet has metamorphosed into a Bordeaux blend which should soften its edges. (SA)

Recommended Reds:
Coldstream Pinot Noir ★★★☆ £E
Woori Yallock Pinot Noir ★★★☆ £E
Gruyere Pinot Noir ★★★☆ £E
Yarra Glen Pinot Noir ★★★ £E
Hugh Cabernet Sauvignon ★★ £D

Recommended Whites:
Off-dry Riesling ★★★☆ £D
Tradition Riesling ★★★ £E
Woori Yallock Chardonnay ★★☆ £D

Main Ridge (Mornington Peninsula) www.mre.com.au
Tiny Mornington Peninsula estate dedicated to Chardonnay and Pinot Noir established back in 1975. In contrast to other pioneering operations such as STONIER and DROMANA ESTATE, Main Ridge has chosen to remain small and artisanal in its production. Nat White, who owns the property with his wife Rosalie, continues to make the wines in a traditional, hands off manner.. Although they can show some vintage variation, at best they are elegant and classy yet with plenty of drive and personality. Prices are high but not dissimilar to those of their neighbours. Pinot Noir comes in two versions, a regular example, labelled The Acre and a Reserve, Half Acre, made from a vineyard with shallow topsoil which is more structured. A Pinot Meunier (£E) is also made.

Recommended Reds:
Pinot Noir Half Acre ★★★☆ £F
Pinot Noir The Acre ★★★ £E
Recommended Whites:
Chardonnay ★★★ £E

>> Timo Mayer (Yarra Valley) www.timomayer.com.au
Timo Mayer has just 2.5 ha of vines in a single vineyard, Bloody Hill (so called because of its bloody steepness) in the Yarra Valley. The sheer purity of the fruit comes over strongly in the unfined and unfiltered wines and whilst not cheap exude quality in every direction. Bloody Hill Pinot Noir is very fine with excellent varietal flavours with soft tannins and a long finish. The vines are planted 3000 to the hectare for this wine but there is a part of the vineyard where the planting is at 6000. From these vines he produces his Close Planted Pinot Noir, which has that extra bit of concentration in the wine. The Doktor Pinot Noir is made from the close planted vines but here the selection for fermentation is 100% whole bunch, which while certainly austere in its youth, will repay long cellaring. His Syrah, also with 100% whole bunch fermentation, displays the essential tarryness and black fruit qualities of the grape, corpulent without being over-blowsy with firm, but gentle tannins. (NB)

Recommended Reds:
Close Planted Pinot Noir ★★★★☆ £F
Doktor Pinot Noir ★★★★☆ £F
Bloody Hill Pinot Noir ★★★★ £F
Syrah ★★★★ £F

Métier Wines (Yarra Valley)
Métier is a small wine operation and owner and winemaker Martin Williams is also a partner in Master Winemakers, which provides contract winemaking facilities. Métier's Tarraford Vineyard Chardonnay (from a 2 ha Yarra Valley site) is extremely well crafted with subtle use of oak and lees. Pinot Noir from the same vineyard has a fine texture but is more variable in its fruit quality and ageing potential. Yarra Valley Pinot Noir and Chardonnay have also been made from the 1.4 ha Schoolhouse Vineyard. A tiny amount of Viognier is produced from the high-altitude Kanumbra Vineyard in the Upper Goulburn. Also sourced from this region is Manytrees Shiraz/ Viognier. A second range, Milkwood, includes Sauvignon Blanc, Chardonnay, Pinot Noir and Shiraz.

Recommended Reds:
Pinot Noir Schoolhouse Vineyard ★★☆ £E
Pinot Noir Tarraford Vineyard ★★ £D

Recommended Whites:
Chardonnay Schoolhouse Vineyard ★★★★ £E
ChardonnayTarraford Vineyard ★★★★ £D

Mitchelton (Nagambie Lakes) www.mitchelton.com.au
Located on the banks of the Goulburn River in the Nagambie Lakes region, Mitchelton is part of a prestigious grouping that includes PETALUMA, KNAPPSTEIN and STONIER. A well-established portfolio of wines of which the top red, Print Shiraz, can exude a class and finesse not seen in the Barossa blockbuster styles. French oak is favoured for reds and a concerted move to lower yields since the mid-90s has brought increased concentration to many of the wines. Many of the whites combine citrusy flavours with more exotic, tropical notes, together with both vigour and good acidity; the wines are increasingly textural too. The intense floral and lime-scented Blackwood Park Riesling is also made in a Botrytis version. Mitchelton was also one of the first to develop red and white Rhône blends, the Airstrip white, comprising Marsanne, Roussanne and Viognier, and Crescent red is from Shiraz, Mourvèdre and Grenache. Varietal Marsanne is a speciality with intense honeysuckle aromas and flavours and has even been made in a vin de paille version. Just below the Print Shiraz in price is a new example from Heathcote and a fruit driven sparkler NV Cuvée and a Cabernet Sauvignon are also made.

Recommended Reds:
Shiraz Print ★★★★ £F   Shiraz ★★ £C
Shiraz/Mourvèdre/Grenache Crescent ★★★ £C
Recommended Whites:
Marsanne ★★☆ £C
Marsanne/Roussanne/Viognier Airstrip ★★ £C
Riesling Blackwood Park ★★★ £C
Chardonnay ★ £C

Moorilla Estate (Tasmania) www.moorilla.com.au
The impressive new Moorilla museum of antiquities appears likely to become more of a magnet for visitors than the wines. Yet this long-surviving Tasmania winery, though no longer family-owned, was resurgent under Alain Rousseau who has been succeeded by Michael Glover. Since 2007, the wines have been made by Conor van der Reest. The top wines are labelled Muse, while the Praxis wines offer a more approachable fruit driven style. Good cool, citrusy whites include a tight, minerally, appley Muse Riesling. A Muse Pinot Noir of increasing ripeness and richness, but with impressive texture and complexity too, is one of a growing number

of fine Tasmanian Pinots – difficult as they are to acquire. Sourced from the warmer Tamar Valley, the Muse Series Cabernet/Merlot might once have tasted rather tough and unripe but in recent good vintages the wines have been ripe and concentrated. Dense, powerful Syrah also shows much promise. (SA)

Recommended Reds:
Pinot Noir Muse Series ★★★ £E
Pinot Noir Praxis Seriesl ★★☆ £D
Cabernet/Merlot Muse Series ★★ £E
Recommended Whites:
Chardonnay Praxis Series ★★☆ £D
Riesling Praxis Series ★★☆ £C
Vintage Brut Muse Series ★★ £E

◉ Moorooduc Estate *www.moorooducestate.com.au*
Moorooduc Estate in northerly Mornington Peninsula was established in 1981 by Richard and Jill McIntyre, who planted the McIntyre vineyard in 1983, mainly to Pinot Noir and Chardonnay (with a small amount of Shiraz). In recent years, Bernard clones of Pinot Noir have been planted (sometimes grafted onto original plantings). Chardonnay, Pinot Noir and Pinot Gris are also sourced from three nearby vineyards, the Robinson vineyard (which is owned by Moorooduc's viticulturist, Hugh Robinson), the Garden Vineyard (which is leased) and the Osborn Vineyard (which is managed with input from Robinson and forms the basis of the entry level Devil Bend Creek wines). Richard McInytre, a practising surgeon, makes the wines at Moorooduc's winery. Though McIntyre is a cerebral winemaker, winemaking has become increasingly hands off in order to showcase the broad palette with which McIntyre works. Three subtly different cuvées of each of Chardonnay and Pinot Noir express the different aspects, soils types and clones to which he has access. Less new oak is used than in the early days and, after successful experimentation with the Chardonnay, McIntyre practices spontaneous wild yeast ferments across the range. The Pinot Noirs and Chardonnays (which undergo malolactic fermentation) are relatively weighty but with great texture and complexity, they are sensual wines with no shortage of finesse. (SA)

Recommended Reds:
Pinot Noir Robinson Vineyard ★★★★☆ £E
Pinot Noir McIntyre Vineyard ★★★★ £F
Pinot Noir Estate ★★★☆ £D
Shiraz McIntyre Vineyard ★★★★☆ £E
Recommended Whites:
Chardonnay Robinson Vineyard ★★★★ £E
Chardonnay McIntyre Vineyard ★★★★ £E
Chardonnay Estate ★★★☆ £D

Morris (Rutherglen & Glenrowan) *www.morriswines.com*
Although owned by Orlando since 1970, the tradition of family winemaking, producing some of Australia's excellent fortified wines, continues here – David Morris having taken over from his famous father Mick Morris in 1993. There is great age in these intelligently blended wines, particularly in the Old Premium versions of fortified Muscat and Topaque (Muscadelle). The regular Liqueur Muscat, tasting of intense, rich, slightly toffeed sweet raisins, is very typical of the style, but with a measure of delicacy, even fragrance. The Old Premium version of Muscat offers similar intensity and fragrance but more complexity and length, while in the spice-fuelled Old Premium Topaque there is excellent richness, depth and layer but arguably less of the classic Topaque flavours of other examples. Nonetheless the quality, richness and complexity in all the Liqueur Muscat and Liqueur Topaque wines can't be disputed. Old Premium 'Amontillado' and 'Tawny Port' are also made, the latter showing the complex *rancio* quality of aged components which creates an impression of dryness to the finish. Red wines including Shiraz and Durif can be sound but lack refinement.

Recommended Whites:
Old Premium Rare Liqueur Topaque ★★★★★ £G
Classic Liqueur Topaque ★★★☆ £C
Old Premium Rare Liqueur Muscat ★★★★★ £G
Classic Liqueur Muscat ★★★ £C

◉ Mount Langi Ghiran (Grampians) *www.langi.com.au*
This dynamic, go-ahead organic vineyard (now totalling 90 ha) and winery operation owes its reputation to winemaker, the late Trevor Mast. It has recently come under the same ownership as top Yarra Valley producer YERING STATION and the wines are now made by Ben Haines, who is sensitively stamping his own mark. Most celebrated is a remarkable and stylish famously peppery Shiraz, among Australia's top half-dozen examples of the variety. It is made from over 50-year-old vines and the fruit is flying, thanks to French oak and a significant element of whole bunch fermentation. Two further Shiraz, Cliff Edge and Hollows are chasing on the Langi's heels, while the reasonably priced Billi Billi (now straight Shiraz from contract grown fruit but initially including some Grenache and Cabernet) has plenty of style if not the greatest depth. Whites are well fashioned including a popular, fruit-driven Cliff Edge Pinot Gris, while Rieslings have become a speciality, with classic dry styles Langi and Cliff Edge (though even here, natural yeasts are used and lees stirred to build weight and texture).

Recommended Reds:
Shiraz Langi ★★★★★ £F
Shiraz Cliff Edge ★★★ £D
Shiraz Billi Billi ★★ £B
Recommended Whites:
Riesling Langi ★★★☆ £D
Riesling Cliff Edge ★★ £C
Pinot Gris Cliff Edge ★★ £C

Mount Mary (Yarra Valley) *www.mountmary.com.au*
The Middleton's Mount Mary is one of Victoria's holiest of holies, where the quality is whispered about by devotees, in complete contrast to the ballyhoo that emanates from South Australia's big guns. Quantities are small and grapes come from the estate's unirrigated vineyards. Quintet (Cabernet Sauvignon, Merlot, Cabernet Franc, Malbec and Petit Verdot) is graceful and refined with intense berry and cassis flavours, a wine that will easily keep for 20 years from a good vintage. The Pinot Noir can age for about half as long, starting out deceptively light but building on its pure fruit core with age. Two whites, a Chardonnay and Triolet (a blend of Sauvignon, Sémillon and Muscadelle) show restrained fruit and oak but can age well too.

Recommended Reds:
Quintet ★★★★☆ £G   Pinot Noir ★★★★ £G
Recommended Whites:
Triolet ★★★★ £F   Chardonnay ★★★★ £F

◉ Paringa (Mornington Peninsula) *www.paringaestate.com.au*
Top-notch small estate now producing upwards of 15,000 cases annually. McCall is a Burgundy fan and aims to make well structured, ageworthy wines. What is most remarkable about Paringa is not only the quality of the Chardonnay and Pinot Noir but also its Shiraz.

Certainly this tends to work best in warmer years but when vintage conditions are benign the wine benefits from an unusually long ripening period. Powerful yet refined, especially the Paringa label which easily soaks up its new oak, it is savoury with dried herbs and pepper. The Peninsula label is from a combination of bought-in fruit and younger Paringa vines. The flagship Paringa Chardonnay and Paringa Pinot Noir and Shiraz are from the best performing vines and offer greater concentration of fruit, complexity and later, well supported by supple acidity and well structured tannins respectively. These are keepers..

Recommended Reds:

Pinot Noir Paringa ★★★★★ £F
Pinot Noir Estate ★★★☆ £E
Pinot Noir Peninsula ★★☆ £C
Shiraz Paringa ★★★★★ £F
Shiraz Estate ★★★★ £E

Recommended Whites:

Chardonnay Paringa★★★★ £E
Chardonnay ★★★ £E
Chardonnay Peninsula ★★☆ £C
Pinot Gris ★★ £D
Riesling ★★☆ £C

PHI Wines (Yarra Valley) *www.phiwines.com*

Derived from the 21st letter of the ancient Greek alphabet, PHI symbolises perfect balance and harmony. This unusual joint venture between the De Bortoli and Shelmerdine has not only been harmonious, but has also been at the vanguard of cutting edge developments in the Yarra Valley. Production is focused on specific vine rows from a single vineyard, the densely planted Lusatia Park Vineyard, which is owned by Shelmerdine and was established in 1985. The wines, made by Steve Webber at De Bortoli, are fermented naturally with as little intervention as possible. Restraint is the watchword. In consequence, they are true ambassadors of their elevated, relatively cool, maritime influenced site, textured with elegant layers of fruit, aromatic lift and a savoury undertow. This makes the Sauvignon Blanc among Australia's most interesting expressions of the variety and a welcome antidote to the New Zealand wannabes. A Heathcote Syrah Grenache blend is also now being made. (SA)

Recommended Reds:

Pinot Noir ★★★★ £E

Recommended Whites:

Chardonnay ★★★☆ £D   Sauvignon Blanc ★★★ £D

Pondalowie (Bendigo) *www.pondalowie.com.au*

Dominic Morris (some time winemaker at QUINTA DO CRASTO in Portugal's Douro) has brought his considerable experience to bear at his own small winery in Bendigo. Plantings include Tempranillo, a little Malbec and Touriga Nacional as well as Cabernet Sauvignon and Shiraz. If Shiraz is the star, the unwooded MT Tempranillo with vibrant blueberry fruit and excellent substance should be tried too (labelled heathcote in 2007 because frost wiped out own plantings). Wines under the Special release Label, made only in peak years, offer more complexity and better dimension. particularly impressive are the Special Release Tempranillo (2003, 2006 and 2008) and Shiraz (2003, 2006 and 2008) both wines for the long haul. Vineyard Blend is composed of Shiraz, Cabernet Sauvignon and Tempranillo and shows the influence of the latter grape with a suggestion of a smoky, meaty character in an otherwise supple, ripe, fruit-driven wine. There's plenty of fruit too in a floral, black fruited Shiraz/

Viognier that is supple, flavoursome and long but in need of at least 5-6 years from the vintage. Cabernet/Shiraz, Cabernet Malbec and a vintage fortified have also been made.

Recommended Reds:

Shiraz ★★★★ £C
Shiraz Special Release ★★★★ £E
Shiraz/Viognier ★★★☆ £D
Vineyard Blend ★★★ £C
Tempranillo MT ★★★ £C
Tempranillo Special Release ★★★ £D

Port Phillip Estate *www.portphillipestate.com.au*

Mornington Peninsula winery Port Phillip is under the same ownership as KOOYONG and its impressive new cellar door and restaurant with bottling facility serves both estates. Both wines are made by highly rated winemaker, Sandro Mosele. The Port Phillip Estate wines from deeper, red soils are characterised by fine pure fruit, good texture and soft ripe tannins in the reds, more generous than those from Kooyong. Pinot Noir reveals fruit in the ripe plum, cherry and strawberry spectrum and is long and fruit-rich adding a more complex, gamey aspect with 4–5 years' age. As with many examples, the highish alcohol is scarcely contained and it lacks the extra dimension to put it amongst the very best Australian Pinots, though the darker, more powerful flagship Morillon Pinot Noir sets out to achieve that distinction and, with ferments in open *foudre* for better texture and tannin integration. Shiraz is if anything more interesting for while sometimes displaying a cool, minty green edge it also has impressive mineral and berry fruit and good depth and flesh. Cool vintages should be avoided but keep the wine for at least 5 years. Salasso is a textured, food-friendly Shiraz rosé. A rich, mealy, oaky Chardonnay has a ripe stone-fruit core and should also age well. A part barrel-fermented Sauvignon Blanc and, under the Quartier label, Italian varieties Arneis and Barbera are also made. A flagsip Shiraz, Serenne is also now made.

Recommended Reds:

Pinot Noir Morillon ★★★★ £F
Pinot Noir Estate ★★★★ £E
Shiraz Estate ★★★ £E

Recommended Whites:

Chardonnay Estate ★★★☆ £D

Recommended Rosés:

Rosé Salasso ★★ £C

Scotchmans Hill (Geelong) *www.scotchmanshill.com.au*

Situated on the Bellarine Peninsula just south-east of Geelong the vineyards enjoy a cool maritime climate. Production is sizeable for the region, accounting for 40% of the total production from Geelong but quality remains admirable, particularly considering the prices. The Pinot Noir is a strength, with ripe plum fruits, nicely handled oak and a seductive texture, while Shiraz and Cabernet Sauvignon can be individual and appealing, if sometimes struggling for ripeness. The Chardonnay is restrained with just a hint of oak showing through in the background. The Sauvignon is grassy and nettly, and marked by lightly tropical cool-fermentation aromas. Small quantities are also made of a very pricey premium pair; an oaky but expansive Pinot Noir Norfolk Vineyard and intense, impressively structured Chardonnay Sutton Vineyard. Swan Bay is the second label mainly produced from a second property, Spray Farm, while a separate range of wines made from fruit sourced throughout South Eastern Australia is labelled The Hill. The experimental Cornelius range is made in miniscule quantities while

Wine behind the label

Victoria & Tasmania

Australia

Ferryman is made in Geelong with fruit from Mornington Peninsula.
Recommended Reds:
Pinot Noir Norfolk Vineyard ★★★☆ £F
Pinot Noir ★★★ £D
Pinot Noir Swan Bay ★ £B   Shiraz ★★★ £C
Recommended Whites:
Chardonnay Sutton Vineyard ★★★☆ £F
Chardonnay Cornelius ★★★☆ £F   Chardonnay ★★ £C
Sauvignon Blanc ★★ £C

Seppelt Great Western (Grampians) www.seppelt.com.au
This is Seppelt's renowned sparkling-wine operation, which also
includes a very good range of table wines, recently rationalised
but still focussed on cool-climate areas where the company has
significant plantings. Aside from the Regional Range which is
comprised from 100% Victorian fruit, the portfolio includes four GI-
specific labels. The Drumborg varietals, which come from the cool
south-west corner of Victoria now called Henty, are some of the best
wines in the range. Riesling and Pinot Noir highlight the potential.
Pinot Grigio and two Chardonnays (one named Jalaka) are sourced
from the same area. The Vineyard Shiraz range comprises flagship St
Peters (the Grampians), Benno (Bendigo) and Mount Ida (heathcote).
Silverband features grampians Shiraz (still and sparkling) while
Aerins Vineyard introduces a new lower tier range including a Shiraz
and Grenache Shiraz Mourvèdre from Heathcote and a Pinot Grigio
from Mornington Peninsula. The traditional method sparkling wine
range is led by a distinctive creamy, citrusy Salinger (Chardonnay,
Pinot Noir and Pinot Meunier). Vintage Brut Fleur de Lys and NV
are less expensive and more overtly fruity but with some leesy
influence. However, most exceptional of the traditional-method
sparkling wines made here is the red Great Western Show Sparkling
Shiraz (which spends 6 years on its lees and is only available around
10 years after the vintage), arguably the most intriguing and
complex example of its type. The cheaper Original version comes
from South Australian fruit and the range is now augmented by
Silverband Grampians Sparkling Shiraz (not tasted). Inexpensive
varietals and blends are sold under the Moyston label. The best
wines unfortunately are not always easy to find outside of Australia.
Recommended Reds:
Shiraz Great Western St Peters ★★★ £F
Sparkling Shiraz Vintage Show ★★★ £F
Shiraz Chalambar ★ £D
Pinot Noir Drumborg ★★ £F
Recommended Whites:
Riesling Drumborg ★★☆ £D
Salinger Vintage ★★ £E

Seville Estate (Yarra Valley) www.sevilleestate.com.au
Seville Estate, founded by Dr Peter McMahon, was one of the Yarra
Valley's pioneers (of the modern era) and has produced small
volumes of fine varietals, particularly Shiraz, during the past 30
years. After a period of majority ownership under BROKENWOOD
when the wines were made by winemaker, Iain Riggs, the property
is once again family owned and the original founders' grandson,
Dylan McMahon makes the wines. The vineyards are on the cooler
side of the valley and accordingly suffer a little in cooler vintages.
At their best however they are powerful and fruitaccented with
well-integrated oak and good definition both in terms of structure
and flavour. Chardonnay can improve for up to 5 years; reds need
as long or more. Small amounts of Reserve Cabernet and Shiraz
have recently been produced from vines more than 30 years old;

the former plush yet refined, the latter in a savoury, earthy style. The
Barber range includes fruit driven approachable wines.
Recommended Reds:
Cabernet Sauvignon Old Vine Reserve ★★★★ £F
Shiraz Old Vine Reserve ★★★☆ £F
Pinot Noir ★★★ £D   Shiraz ★★★ £D
Recommended Whites:
Chardonnay ★★ £D

✿ Shadowfax (Geelong) www.shadowfax.com.au
Shadowfax (a name taken from Tolkien's Lord of the Rings)
established in 2000, is an exciting operation based in Werribee
Park between Melbourne and Geelong. Sourcing small parcels of
the best grapes from a number of districts, young Matt Harrop has
the responsibility of producing wines to match the high standards
set by the acclaimed Mansion Hotel, but has a stunning winery in
which to do so. There is a full but tightly structured Chardonnay,
characterful, textured Pinot Noir (both made from Geelong and
Yarra Ranges fruit), and vibrant, spicy, fruit-driven Shiraz from a
number of sites. Premium single vineyard wines in heavy black-
labelled bottles promise still more. A Macedon Ranges Chardonnay
is tautly structured but with ample flesh to its bones. Geelong Pinot
Noir is bold and full-flavoured with lots of breadth and extract (if
deficient in charm for the present). Two single-vineyard Shirazes
from lowyielding Heathcote fruit were also first made in 2001: both
Pink Cliffs and One Eye are concentrated, meaty, intense examples
with obvious potential but requiring 10 years' cellaring. Viognier,
Pinot Gris and unusual K Road Sangiovese/Merlot/Shiraz have also
been produced.
Recommended Reds:
Pink Cliffs Heathcote ★★★★ £F
One Eye Heathcote ★★★★ £E
Shiraz Victoria ★★★ £C   Pinot Noir ★★ £D
Recommended Whites:
Chardonnay Macedon Ranges ★★★★ £E
Chardonnay ★★★★ £D

Stanton&Killeen (Rutherglen) www.stantonandkilleenwines.com.au
The key to top drawer Rutherglen Muscat is old vines and aged
blending stock. It shows in this seventh generation Rutherglen
producer's portfolio. Stanton & Killeen's rich yet floral style is partly
due to the original vineyards which, still in production, were planted
by Jack Stanton in 1921. The Grand Rutherglen Muscat is particularly
impressive and the Rutherglen Topaques (not tasted) are also
reputed. At least as impressive are the vintage fortifieds, made in
the elegant, drier style pioneered by the late Chris Killeen, so-called
"Prince of Port". Classic duo Shiraz and Durif are blended with
Touriga Nacional, Tinta Câo, Tinta Roriz and Tinta Barroca, picking
these Portuguese varieties at lower ripeness. In 2008, Killeen's son
Simon made The Prince Reserva Red, a Portuguese varietal blend,
in tribute to his father. Medium bodied and less overtly fruity than
Stanton & Killeen's robust, full bodied Durif and Shiraz/Durif table
wines, it is available only by mail order or at the cellar door. (SA)
Recommended Reds:
Durif ★★☆ £E   Shiraz/Durif ★☆ £C
Recommended Whites:
Rutherglen Muscat Grand Rutherglen ★★★★ £G
Rutherglen Muscat Rare Rutherglen ★★★☆ £G
Rutherglen Muscat Classic ★★☆ £E
Rutherglen Muscat ★★ £D

Stonier (Mornington Peninsula) *www.stoniers.com.au*
Established in 1978 by Brian Stonier, this operation was one of the first premium wineries to emerge from the Mornington Peninsula. The potential first highlighted by Stephen Hickinbotham was cemented under his successor Tod Dexter and since the mid-1990s the winemaking mantle has gradually been assumed by Geraldine McFaul, now Michael Symons. Stonier came under the same ownership as PETALUMA (South Australia) in 1998 and, though initially this served to highlight the quality here, there has been a loss of form of late. As well as more than 20ha of estate vineyards, grapes are sourced from elsewhere on the peninsula. Recent releases of regular Chardonnay and Pinot Noir show good fruit but lack balance; while the Reserves perhaps try too hard, especially the Chardonnay which tends towards a sweetness. The use of oak could be more refined for both. Stonier have also produced small quantities of single-vineyard Pinot Noir and Chardonnay from the KBS Vineyard and, most recently, Windmill Pinot Noir.

Recommended Reds:
Pinot Noir Windmill ★★★ £F
Pinot Noir KBS ★★☆ £F
Pinot Noir Reserve ★★ £E   Pinot Noir ★★ £C
Recommended Whites:
Chardonnay Reserve ★★☆ £E
Chardonnay ★★ £C

Summerfield/ Syan (Pyrenees) *www.summerfieldwines.com*
This predominantly red-wine producer has been making wines since 1979, having first established vineyards in 1970. The first real leap in quality came with consultancy from Drew NOON (South Australia), the then state oenologist, in the late 1980s. Mark Summerfield is now responsible for the winemaking. He has set about reducing yields and the powerful reds are richer, riper, deeper and more consistent than previously but always with a noticeable dash of oak. Shiraz is the real star, particularly the Reserve (Estate in older vintages). Saieh is a barrel selection Shiraz available at the cellar door only. The muscular, minty Reserve Cabernet is now beginning to benefit from the use of some French oak. Both Reserves will keep for a decade or more. A varietal Merlot is also made, while Tradition is a blend of Shiraz with Bordeaux varieties. Syan is the international label.

Recommended Reds:
Shiraz Reserve ★★★★ £E   Shiraz ★★★ £D
Cabernet Sauvignon Reserve ★★★☆ £E
Cabernet Sauvignon ★★ £D
Merlot ★★ £D

Tahbilk (Nagambie Lakes) *www.tahbilk.com.au*
Historic winery which along with HENSCHKE has some of the oldest plantings of Shiraz anywhere in the world. One plot dates back to 1860. Production is not inconsiderable at close to 100,000 cases a year and an extensive range of wines is available at the cellar door. Vinification of the reds is very traditional and open-top wooden fermenters are used. In no small part the considerable age of the vines contributes to the structured, tannic style of the wines when young. They are very ageworthy but demand patience, up to 10 years for the Eric Stevens Purbricks and 1860 Vines. Of good fruit-driven whites, the Marsanne is a regional benchmark and the largest single planting, it is claimed, anywhere in the world. Though tight and lean young, it fleshes out with a few years in bottle showing attractive honeysuckle with stone fruits and will hold for a decade or more. Some of the vines were planted in 1927 and an early picked

cuvée, 1927 Vines Marsanne, tight knit and concentrated should last for even longer. New and promising too are varietal Roussanne and Viognier.

Recommended Reds:
Shiraz 1860 Vines ★★★★★ £G
Shiraz Eric Stevens Purbrick ★★★★ £F
Shiraz ★★☆ £C
Cabernet Sauvignon Eric Stevens Purbrick ★★★☆ £F
Cabernet Sauvignon ★★☆ £B
Recommended Whites:
Marsanne 1927 Vines ★★★☆ £E
Marsanne ★★☆ £B
Chardonnay ★★ £B   Riesling ★★ £B

Taltarni (Pyrenees) *www.taltarni.com.au*
With 132 ha, this is the Pyrenees' biggest producer. Taltarni, like CLOS DU VAL in the Napa Valley, was established in 1972 by John Goelet. For a long time Dominique Portet crafted the wines here – and his brother Bernard continues to oversee the Clos du Val wines. By the mid-1980s Taltarni was widely admired for its gutsy, structured varietals that highlighted the potential of the Pyrenees. Some wines have been too tough and extracted, others have lacked balance but the best bottles have aged superbly. Dominique Portet departed to make his own wines and under Peter Steer the wines became richer, oakier and more modern. The current winemaker is Loïc Le Calvez. The change is perhaps encapsulated in the Reserve Shiraz/Cabernet, a new flagship red that seamlessly combines Shiraz and Cabernet Sauvignon. The other great facet to Taltarni is the sparkling-wine production which reaches its zenith in the classy Clover Hill. This taut, ripe and structured sparkler comes from a dedicated Tasmanian estate with 21ha planted to Chardonnay, Pinot Noir and Pinot Meunier. The rosé is also very good. Three Monks Sauvignon, now part barrel fermented and labelled Fumé Blanc includes a Tasmanian component (from 2003) while the independent Lalla Gully range from a second, smaller Pipers River vineyard owned by Taltani is the source of Lalla Gully Sauvignon Blanc. Both red and white T-label are newish, fruit-accented second-label blends made from both estate and bought-in grapes.

Taltarni
Recommended Reds:
Reserve Shiraz/Cabernet ★★★★ £F
Shiraz Pyrenees ★★★ £E
Cabernet Sauvignon Pyrenees ★★★ £E
Recommended Whites:
Brut Vintage ★★☆ £D
Brut Taché Vintage ★★☆ £D
Fumé Blanc ★★ £D
Clover Hill
Recommended Whites:
Clover Hill Classic Vintage ★★★☆ £E
Recommended Rosés:
Clover Hill Exceptionelle Vintage Rosé ★★★☆ £E

Tarrawarra (Yarra Valley) *www.tarrawarra.com.au*
Tarrawarra has been single-minded in its aim of producing top-quality Chardonnay and Pinot Noir modelled on white and red Burgundy. Its success in turning out rich, structured, concentrated and complex examples of both owes much to the dedication and skill of winemaker Clare Halloran. Increasing vine age and growing skill in producing high-quality fruit are also driving quality. Chardonnay is 100% barrel-fermented with some use of bâttonage.

Victoria & Tasmania

The Pinot Noir receives a cold pre-fermentation maceration, open fermenters are used and around 25% of the oak is new. Both wines benefit from age and are best at least 3 to 5 years after the vintage. As you would expect, reserve wines show even greater depth and layer. These are powerful wines which require time for the oak to integrate and show at their best. Kosher Chardonnay and Shiraz are made under the Kidron label. Owner Marc Besen is also the wealthy benefactor behind the Tarrawarra Art Museum. In 2009, a new, very limited edition flagship range was introduced with the MDB label for Chardonnay and Pinot Noir (not tasted).

Recommended Reds:
Pinot Noir Reserve ★★★☆ £F Pinot Noir ★★★ £D
Recommended Whites:
Chardonnay Reserve ★★★☆ £E
Chardonnay ★★★ £D

❁ **Ten Minutes by Tractor** www.tenminutesbytractor.com.au
Ten Minutes by Tractor derives its name from three vineyards, each owned by (and named after) the founding families and located 10 minutes apart from each other in Mornington Peninsula. In 2004, businessman Martin Spedding bought Ten Minutes by Tractor, entering into long-term leases with the families to secure the fruit. Since 2008, fruit is also sourced from the younger Spedding Vineyard which, farmed organically from the outset, was certified organic in 2009. Though the wines are made by Richard McIntyre at MOOROODUC ESTATE, they are quite different from McIntyre's own label, with more acid drive and finer tannins, reflecting the vineyards' location within the Main Ridge sub-region, one of the coolest and highest parts of the Mornington Peninsula. In addition to the estate's vibrant 10X Pinot Noir and 10X Chardonnay, both vineyard blends, Ten Minutes by Tractor produces single vineyard Pinot Noirs and Chardonnays which reflect the different altitude, aspect and clone of each site. At 206m (at its highest point) the Judd vineyard is the more elevated, cooler site and produces a particularly lifted, floral Pinot Noir. The McCutcheon vineyard (highest point 200m) is closer in style to Judd, while the Wallis vineyard (highest point 142m) tends to produce Pinot Noir and Chardonnay of great depth of flavour. Though the single vineyard range is very good, it is a little pricier than other leading wines from the region. The range also includes a 10X Pinot Gris and 10X Barrel Fermented Sauvignon Blanc (the latter not tasted). (SA)

Recommended Reds:
Pinot Noir Wallis Vineyard ★★★★☆ £F
Pinot Noir Judd Vineyard ★★★★ £F
Pinot Noir McCutcheon Vineyard ★★★★ £F
Pinot Noir 10X ★★★ £D
Recommended Whites:
Chardonnay Wallis Vineyard ★★★★ £F
Chardonnay McCutcheon Vineyard ★★★☆ £F
Chardonnay 10X ★★☆ £D
Pinot Gris 10X ★☆£D

Dom.Tournon/Terlato&Chapoutier www.mchapoutieraustralia.com
The prestigious Rhône Valley producer CHAPOUTIER has made a sizeable commitment in Australia, originally establishing their operation in Mount Benson but having now moved to the Pyrenees in Victoria. The rating for the Mount Benson Shiraz is included because readers may still encounter the wine. Viticultural practices model those in the Rhône and progress has been made towards a fully biodynamic regime. Already the reds show a fine fruit intensity and structure and are improving with each successive

vintage, adding more refinement and depth. As a part of the project Chapoutier is involved with Anthony J Terlato, who owns the SANFORD winery on California's Central Coast, at Domaine Terlato & Chapoutier. The duo make a Shiraz-Viognier *négoce* wine and Lieu dit Malakoff Shiraz from their jointly owned 22 ha single vineyard of that name in the Victorian Pyrenees. More recently, the Domaine Tournon range has been extended to include a Victorian Mathilda Shiraz and Chapoutier has acquired 34 ha in Victoria (Landsborough Estate, Lady's Lane and Shays Flat) for the Domaine Tournon label from which the maiden vintage was 2009. A number of pricier single vineyard wines are made from these sites. The Tournon range also includes a Mathilda white from Viognier and Marsanne as well as a rosé from Grenache. At the pricier end of the spectrum there is a Terlato & Chapoutier L Block Shiraz (£F) and a further Syrah, Domaine Beechworth Ergo Sum (£G).

Recommended Reds:
Dom Terlato & Chapoutier Lieu dit Malakoff Pyrenees ★★★★ £E
Dom Terlato & Chapoutier Shiraz-Viognier Victoria ★★★☆ £D
Dom. Tournon Shiraz Mathilda Victoria ★★★★ £D
Dom. Tournon Shiraz Mount Benson ★★★☆ £D

Virgin Hills (Macedon Ranges) www.virginhills.com.au
Just one wine is made here, a blend of Cabernet Sauvignon, Shiraz and Merlot. The winery and vineyard are now owned by Michael Hope of HOPE ESTATE in the Hunter Valley after several recent changes in ownership. While there is some vintage variation, the wine is usually amongst the best Cabernet-based reds in Victoria. Vineyard practice is organic, minimal intervention is employed during vinification and the wine is virtually sulphur-free. As the location is at the limit of ripening for these varieties the wine is not produced every year. At its best it is a magnificent, elegant, cedary red; in cooler years there can be a marked green undercurrent.
Recommended Reds:
Virgin Hills ★★★★ £E

Wild Duck Creek (Heathcote) www.wildduckcreekestate.com
This small winery, established and run by David Anderson, is best known for the cult wine Duck Muck, made in minute quantities. Also made are a range of several other relatively small-volume cuvées from both Anderson's own vineyards in the Heathcote region and other sites of which he has a specialised knowledge. Duck Muck Shiraz is made from the most extreme selection of late-harvested fruit vinified in open fermenters and hand-plunged. There is little or no addition of sulphur. It is aged in 100% new oak, a mixture of French and American. The much more affordable Springflat Shiraz is aged in 60% new oak but follows a similar approach to vinification. It typically shows impressive fruit richness and character in a well-defined structure and deserves to be drunk with 5–10 years' age. Other wines include Alan's Cabernets and a more modest but characterful Yellow Hammer Hill Shiraz/Malbec. Sparkling Shiraz is also made.
Recommended Reds:
Shiraz Reserve ★★★★ £G Shiraz Springflat ★★★ £F
Shiraz/Malbec Yellow Hammer Hill ★★ £D

❁ **Yarra Yering (Yarra Valley)** www.yarrayering.com
At times considered eccentric by some of his neighbours, the late Bailey Carrodus produced a remarkable array of very good to exceptional wines even if on occasion the results have been variable. The estate is now owned by the investors behind Kaesler

Wines in the Barossa Valley who intend to carry on in the same vein as Carrodus. Many of the vines are relatively venerable, particularly for the Yarra, with some plantings now well over 30 years old. Dry White No.1 is a Sauvignon Blanc/Sémillon blend but it is the reds, vinified in small open fermenters, that have long attracted a cult following. Dry Red No.1 is a blend of mainly Cabernet Sauvignon with Merlot, Cabernet Franc and Malbec. With Dry Red No.2 he takes up the Shiraz baton, arguably with even more success. Mainly Shiraz with a little Viognier, this is a wine of terrific fruit richness and depth. Also extremely impressive is the Underhill Shiraz but all of the reds are very fine, concentrated and show real finesse. The Pinot Noir is made in a rich, powerful, extracted style, while the few bottles of Carrodus Merlot made caused a sensation with an audacious cellar-door price tag from the very first vintage. A Carrodus Viognier is similarly priced for those with deep pockets and the Carrodus Cabernet Merlot even more so. New and more reasonably priced are Dry Red No.3, based on Touriga Nacional with a hatful of other Portuguese varieties. Also made is a small amount of an impressive fortified port-style wine, Potsorts and a further red blend Agincourt, a touch more upfront than the other reds.

Recommended Reds:
Carrodus Merlot ★★★★★ £G
Dry Red No.1 ★★★★★ £F
Dry Red No.2 ★★★★★ £F
Shiraz Underhill ★★★★☆ £F
Pinot Noir ★★★★☆ £F
Recommended Whites:
Chardonnay ★★★★☆ £F

Yering Station/ Yarrabank (Yarra Valley) *www.yering.com*
Yering Station was the name of a historic property in the Yarra Valley established in the first half of the 19th century. Today part of the original estate has been revived complete with a major new winemaking complex. The winemaking team is led by Willy Lunn, furnished by investment and direction from the Rathbone family (also owners of MOUNT LANGI GHIRAN, XANADU and PARKER COONAWARRA ESTATE). Relatively new is Pinot Noir ED Rosé which is typical of the well-priced estate range insofar as it is stylish, with pristine fruit, but has the structure to pair with food. Reserves show added class, depth and expression and are made only in the best years. The Reserve Cabernet Sauvignon in particular needs time, as much as 8–10 years. In common with other Yarra producers, Yering Station has started to produce single vineyard wines aimed at showcasing *terroir* over technique. These include Chardonnays, Pinot Noirs and a Shiraz Viognier. Willow Lake Old Vine Chardonnay is an early picked, pared back, flinty style of Chardonnay which really is in a Chablis mold. Little Yering is a second label from generally more widely sourced fruit. Yarrabank is Yering Station's joint venture with Champagne house DEVAUX. The vintage dated Yarrabank Brut Cuvée, which spends 3 years on its lees, is one of Australia's finest sparkling wines. Made from 50 percent each of Pinot Noir and Chardonnay and, with no malolactic fermentation (the house style), it is intense and finely honed, and shows considerable complexity with age.

Yarrabank
Recommended Whites:
Yarrabank Brut Cuvée ★★★★ £D
Yering Station
Recommended Reds:
Shiraz/Viognier Reserve ★★★★ £F

Shiraz ★★ £C
Cabernet Sauvignon Reserve ★★★★ £F
Cabernet Sauvignon ★★ £C
Pinot Noir Reserve ★★★☆ £F
Pinot Noir ★★ £C
Recommended Whites:
Chardonnay Reserve ★★★★ £F
Chardonnay ★★★ £C
Chardonnay Willow Lake Old Vine ★★★☆ £E
Recommended Rosés: Pinot Noir ED ★★ £C
Little Yering
Recommended Reds: Cabernet Shiraz ★★☆ £B
Pinot Noir ★☆ £B
Recommended Whites:
Chardonnay ★☆ £B

Yeringberg (Yarra Valley) *www.yeringberg.com*
Guill de Pury replanted just 2ha of the slopes made famous by his grandfather in the late 19th century. The original Yeringberg vineyard was just one of many to go in to terminal decline due a combination of phylloxera and the economic consequences of the First World War. The wines are gentle and pure but with an underlying strength and intensity that comes from an artisanal approach to winemaking. Modern technological adjustments may be common elsewhere in Australia but here you are more likely to see the true character of the vintage. Yet only occasionally do the reds want for more body or ripeness. Both the whites are subtle and restrained but possess real elegance and flair. They are ageworthy too. The Dry Red is a blend of Cabernet Sauvignon, Merlot, Cabernet Franc and Malbec. Developing richness and a savoury complexity with age, it also acquires a level of elegance and finesse seen in few other Australian reds.

Recommended Reds:
Yeringberg Dry Red ★★★★☆ £F
Pinot Noir ★★★☆ £F
Recommended Whites:
Marsanne/Roussanne ★★★★ £F
Chardonnay ★★★★ £F

Other wines of note

Apsley Gorge Vineyard (Tasmania)
Recommended Reds:
Pinot Noir ★★★ £D
Buckshot Vineyard (Heathcote)
Recommended Reds:
Shiraz ★★★ £E
Craig Avon Vineyard (Mornington Peninsula)
Recommended Whites:
Chardonnay ★★★☆ £D
Blue Pyrenees (Pyrenees)
Recommended Reds:
Shiraz Richardson Series ★★★★ £E   Shiraz ★★ £B
Cabernet Sauvignon Richardson Series ★★★★ £E
Cabernet Sauvignon ★★ £B
Recommended Whites: Chardonnay ★★ £B
Midnight Cuvée Blanc De Blancs ★★★ £C
Brown Brothers (King Valley)
Recommended Whites: Patricia Sparkling ★★★ £E
Noble Riesling Patricia ★★★ £F

Wine behind the label

Victoria & Tasmania

Orange Muscat & Flora ★ £C
Liqueur Muscat ★★ £C   Very Old Tokay ★★ £C
Bulong Estate (Yarra Valley)
Recommended Whites: Sauvignon Blanc ★★ £C
Pinot Gris ★★ £C   Chardonnay ★★★ £D
Recommended Reds: Pinot Noir ★★ £D
Chateau Leamon (Bendigo)
Recommended Reds:
Shiraz Reserve ★★★ £E
Circe (Mornington Peninsula)
Recommended Reds:
Pinot Noir ★★★★ £D
Clyde Park (Geelong)
Recommended Reds:
Shiraz Geelong ★★★ £E
Craigow (Tasmania)
Recommended Whites:
Riesling ★★★ £D
Curlewis (Geelong)
Recommended Reds:
Pinot Noir Geelong ★★★ £E
Downing Estate (Heathcote)
Recommended Reds: Shiraz ★★★☆ £E
Cabernet Sauvignon ★★★ £E
Merlot ★★★ £E
Eastern Peake (Ballarat)
Recommended Reds:
Pinot Noir ★★☆ £F
Eppalock Ridge (Heathcote)
Recommended Reds:
Shiraz ★★★☆ £D
Farr Rising (Geelong)
Recommended Reds:
Pinot Noir Geelong ★★★ £E
Recommended Whites:
Chardonnay ★★★ £E
Freycinet (Tasmania)
Recommended Reds:
Pinot Noir ★★★ £F
Recommended Whites: Chardonnay ★★★ £D
Riesling ★★★ £C
Gembrook Hill (Yarra Valley)
Recommended Whites: Sauvignon Blanc ★★★ £D
Chardonnay ★★★ £E
Recommended Reds: Pinot Noir ★★★ £E
Glaetzer-Dixon (Tasmania)
Recommended Whites: Riesling Berblanc ★★★ £C
Recommended Reds: Shiraz Mon Père ★★ £F
Granite Hills (Macedon Ranges)
Recommended Whites: Riesling ★★★☆ £C
Recommended Reds: Shiraz ★★★ £E
Greenstone Vineyard (Heathcote)
Recommended Reds: Shiraz ★★★☆ £D
Sangiovese ★★★☆ £D
Grey Sands (Tasmania)
Recommended Whites:
Pinot Gris Glengarry ★★★ £B
Hoddles Creek (Yarra Valley)
Recommended Whites:
Pinot Blanc ★★ £D

Hood/Wellington (Tasmania)
Recommended Reds:
Pinot Noir Frogmore ★★★ £E
Recommended Whites:
Chardonnay Wellington ★★★☆ £C
Riesling Wellington ★★ £C
Jones Road (Mornington Peninsula)
Recommended Whites: Chardonnay The Nepean ★★★☆ £C
Pinot Gris ★★★ £B
Recommended Reds: Pinot Noir The Nepean ★★★ £E
Pinot Noir ★★★ £D
Karina Vineyard (Mornington Peninsula)
Recommended Whites: Chardonnay ★★★ £D
Riesling ★★ £C
Nicholson River Winery (Gippsland)
Recommended Whites: Chardonnay ★★★ £F
Recommended Reds: Pinot Noir ★★ £F
Occams Razor (Heathcote)
Shiraz ★★☆ £F
Ocean Eight (Mornington Peninsula)
Recommended Whites:
Chardonnay Verve ★★★☆ £E
Recommended Reds:
Pinot Noir Aylwood ★★★★ £F
Pinot Noir ★★★☆ £E
O'Shea & Murphy (Macedon Ranges)
Recommended Reds:
Roseberry Hill (Cab Sauv/Cab Franc/Merlot) ★★☆ £D
Oakridge Estate (Yarra Valley)
Recommended Reds: Shiraz ★★ £E
Recommended Whites: Chardonnay ★★ £E
Chardonnay 864 ★★★☆ £F
Paradise IV (Geelong)
Recommended Reds:
Shiraz Dardel ★★★★ £E
Passing Clouds (Bendigo)
Recommended Reds:
Angel Blend (Cabernet Sauvignon) ★★★ £C
Pfeifer (Rutherglen)
Recommended Whites: Rutherglen Muscat ★☆ £D
Riesling Carlyle ★★ £D
Plunkett/ Plunkett Fowles
Recommended Reds:
Shiraz Strathbogie Ranges Reserve ★★ £E
Recommended Whites: Chardonnay Stone Dwellers ★★★ £D
Riesling Stone Dwellers ★★ £C
Riesling Ladies Who Shoot Their Lunch ★★★☆ £E
Dominique Portet
Recommended Reds:
Shiraz André Heathcote/Yarra Valley ★★★ £G
Cabernet Sauvignon Yarra Valley ★★★ £E
Pressing Matters (Tasmania)
Recommended Whites:
Riesling R9 ★★★ £D
Provenance (Geelong)
Recommended Whites: Pinot Gris ★★★ £D
Recommended Reds: Shiraz ★★★★ £D
Pinot Noir ★★★★ £D
Red Edge (Heathcote)
Recommended Reds: Shiraz ★★★★ £E
Shiraz Jackson's Vineyard ★★★☆ £C

Cabernet Sauvignon ★★★ £E
Red Hill Estate (Mornington Peninsula)
Recommended Whites: Chardonnay Estate ★★☆ £C
Pinot Grigio Estate ★★☆ £B
Recommended Reds: Pinot Noir Classic Release ★★ £C
Cabernet Sauvignon Briars ★★☆ £C
Redbank (Pyrenees)
Recommended Reds: Shiraz The Anvil ★★★ £E
Recommended Whites: Pinot Gris Sunday Morning ★★☆ £C
Redesdale Estate (Heathcote)
Recommended Reds:
Shiraz Estate Grown ★★★☆ £D
Sanguine Estate (Heathcote)
Recommended Reds: Shiraz ★★★ £D
Tempranillo ★★★ £E
Savaterre (Beechworth)
Recommended Whites:
Chardonnay ★★★★☆ £F
Shelmerdine (Yarra Valley & Heathcote)
Recommended Whites: Viognier Heathcote ★★☆ £D
Sauvignon Blanc Yarra Valley ★★☆ £D
Chardonnay Yarra Valley ★★★☆ £C
Recommended Reds: Pinot Noir Yarra Valley ★★☆ £C
Shiraz Merindoc Vineyard Heathcote ★★★★ £E
Shiraz Heathcote ★★★☆ £D
Cabernet Sauvignon Heathcote ★★★ £C
Spear Gully (Yarra Valley/Heathcote/Mclaren Vale)
Recommended Reds:
Shiraz ★★★ £C
Springvale (Tasmania)
Recommended Whites: Chardonnay ★★★ £C
Recommended Reds: Pinot Noir ★★★ £E
Stoney Rise (Tasmania)
Recommended Reds: Pinot Noir Tamar Valley ★★☆ £D
Pinot Noir Holyman ★★★★ £E
Symphonia (King Valley)
Recommended Whites:
Pinot Grigio King Valley ★★★ £C
Recommended Reds:
Las Triadas Winemakers Reserve (Tempranillo) ★★★☆ £C
Saperavi King Valley ★★★☆ £D
Syrahmi (Heathcote)
Recommended Reds:
Shiraz Climat ★★★ £F
Tellurian (Heathcote)
Recommended Reds:
Shiraz ★★★☆ £E Shiraz Pastiche ★★★ £D
The Wanderer (Yarra Valley)
Recommended Reds:
Pinot Noir ★★★★ £F Shiraz ★★ £F
Thousand Candles (Yarra Valley)
Recommended Reds:
Thousand Candles Red ★★★★☆ £F
Wedgetail Estate (Yarra Valley)
Recommended Whites: Chardonnay ★★★☆ £E
Recommended Reds: Pinot Noir ★★★ £E
Yabby Lake (Mornington Peninsula)
Recommended Whites:
Chardonnay ★★★☆ £E
Recommended Reds:
Pinot Noir Block 2 ★★★★ £F

Pinot Noir ★★★☆ £E
Pinot Noir Red Claw ★★ £D

Work in progress!!

Producers under consideration for the next edition
Heathcote Estate (Heathcote)
Jamsheed (Yarra Valley)
Montalto Vineyards (Mornington Peninsula)
Prince Albert (Geelong)
Scorpo (Mornington Peninsula)
Domaines Tatiarra (Heathcote)
Tayloroo (Heathcote)

Author's choice

Diverse first-rate Victorian Shiraz
Armstrong Vineyards   Armstrong
Best's   Shiraz Bin O Great Western
Castagna   Syrah Genesis
Craiglee   Shiraz
Dalwhinnie   Shiraz Moonambel
Hanging Rock   Shiraz Heathcote
Giaconda   Shiraz Warner Vineyard
Jasper Hill   Shiraz Georgia's Paddock
Mitchelton   Shiraz Print
Mount Langhi Ghiran   Shiraz
Paringa Estate   Shiraz Reserve
Seppelt Great Western   Show Sparkling Shiraz
Tahbilk   Shiraz 1860 Vines
Yarra Yering   Shiraz Underhill
Yering Station   Shiraz/Viognier Reserve

Victorian classics
Reds:
Morris   Old Premium Liqueur Tawny
Mount Mary   Quintet
Stanton & Killeen   Vintage Fortified
Yarra Yering   Dry Red No. 1
Yeringberg   Dry Red
Whites:
Campbells   Rutherglen Tokay Rare Isabella
Chambers Rosewood   Rutherglen Grand Muscat
Chambers Rosewood   Rutherglen Grand Topaque Muscadelle
Morris   Old Premium Liqueur Muscat
Stanton & Killeen   Rutherglen Grand Muscat

Top Victorian/Tasmanian Pinot Noir
Bass Phillip   Pinot Noir Reserve
Bindi   Pinot Noir Original Vineyard Macedon Ranges
By Farr   Pinot Noir Sangreal Geelong
Curly Flat   Pinot Noir Macedon Ranges
Diamond Valley   Pinot Noir Estate
Giaconda   Pinot Noir
Kooyong   Pinot Noir Haven Mornington Peninsula
Mac Forbes   Pinot Noir Coldstream Yarra Valley
Moorooduc   Pinot Noir The Moorooduc Mornington Peninsula
Paringa Estate   Pinot Noir Reserve Mornington Peninsula
Stefano Lubiana   Pinot Noir Tasmania
Main Ridge   Pinot Noir Half Acre
Pipers Brook   Pinot Noir Reserve Tasmania

Victoria & Tasmania

Australia

Ten By Tractor Pinot Noir Wallis Mornington Peninsula

Whites with personality
Brown Brothers Patricia (Sparkling)
By Farr Viognier Geelong
Crawford River Riesling Reserve
Curly Flat Chardonnay
Dalwhinnie Chardonnay Moonambel
Delatite Gewürztrminer Deadman's Hill
Giaconda Nantua Les Deux
Hoddles Creek Estate Pinot Blanc
House Of Arras EJ Carr Late Disgorged (Sparkling)
Jasper Hill Riesling Georgia's Paddock
Kooyong Chardonnay Farrago
Kooyong Pinot Gris Buerrot
Métier Chardonnay Schoolhouse Vineyard
Mitchelton Marsanne/Roussanne/Viognier Airstrip
Mount Langi Ghiran Riesling Langi
Pipers Brook Riesling Estate
Savaterre Chardonnay
Symphonia Pinot Gris King Valley
Taltarni Clover Hill (Sparkling)
Ten By Tractor Chardonnay Wallis Mornington Peninsula
Yeringberg Marsanne/Roussanne

Undervalued wines
Reds:
Balgownie Shiraz Bendigo
Best's Shiraz Bin 1 Great Western
Cobawridge Lagrein Macedon Ranges
Mount Langhi Ghiran Shiraz/Grenache/Cabernet Billi Billi Creek
Red Edge Shiraz Jackson's Vineyard
Symphonia Las Triadas Winemakers Reserve
Whites:
R L Buller & Son Rutherglen Tokay Premium Fine Old
Delatite Riesling
Mitchelton Riesling Blackwood Park
Tahbilk Marsanne

New South Wales not only makes a sizeable contribution to Australia's production of bulk wine but 160 km north-west of its largest city, Sydney, has a wine region of magnetic tourist attraction in the Hunter Valley. Thanks to the Great Dividing Range much potential remains and new regions will continue to make an impact if developed with quality as the foremost consideration.

Hunter Valley

New South Wales' most traditional region is not, regrettably, the state's most suited region to viticulture. The **Lower Hunter Valley** is peppered with estates lying just west of the Brokenback Range but, despite regular cloud cover, conditions are very hot and the greatest part of its rainfall usually comes as the growing season reaches its climax. Great vintages are the exception rather than the norm yet some marvellous ageworthy Shiraz and Sémillon are produced. Many Hunter-based producers now source fruit from Mudgee, Cowra or further south in the Central Ranges as well as producing wines from South Australia yet several of the greatest wines are purely Hunter in origin. Other than the big names of Brokenwood and Rosemount new operations are emerging, not least the very small production of Keith Tulloch, Andrew Thomas and Pepper Tree.

Central Ranges & Southern New South Wales

Mudgee and the other regions which run down the western side of the Great Dividing Range are better protected from cyclonic deluges, making them both cooler and drier. Much of the grape production from Mudgee and **Cowra** has been dominated by the big producers and the harvest has been Hunter-bound, but many of the big players have pulled out of Mudgee and the vineyard area has contracted accordingly. Mudgee produces intensely flavoured well structured Cabernet Sauvignon, Shiraz, Chardonnay and Sémillon, though few producers other than Huntington Estate and Montrose give the region the recognition it deserves. However, there are some interesting wines made from Italian varietals so, like other regions, Mudgee is re-inventing itself. Cowra Chardonnay has a well-established distinctive, lush, full style of its own. Gaining increasing significance are **Orange**, **Hilltops** and, from close to the border with Victoria, the chilly, elevated **Tumbarumba** region. The latter is too remote to be other than a growing region but Orange and Hilltops have a growing number of boutique producers, some of whose wines are primarily sold via the cellar door. Similarly cool and elevated, with the associated risk of frost damage, are the vineyards of the **Canberra District** lying to the north of the country's capital (but still in New SouthWales itself). Despite the difficult, marginal conditions, the best reds are without question lifted and spicy cool climate styles of Shiraz, especially from the (unofficial) Murrumbateman region. The best whites are Riesling, Chardonnay and Viognier.

Big Rivers

Big Rivers suggests a lot of water and the vast vineyards of this zone are dependent on irrigation. The zone incorporates the commercially important bulk-producing regions of **Riverina** and, shared with Victoria on the Murray River, **Murray Darling** and **Swan Hill**. Not generally associated with fine quality, Riverina is the source of De Bortoli's superb Noble One from botrytis enriched Sémillon grapes as well as other good, reasonably priced examples.

Queensland

Producing wine in Queensland is fraught with difficulties. Nonetheless wine is produced from **South Burnett**, around Kingaroy, and in the **Granite Belt** around Stanthorpe, in the Great Dividing Range, where it is cooler and elevated. The coastal hinterland around Mount Tamborine, behind the famous Gold Coast, has also attracted new wineries. Despite sometimes difficult vintage conditions good Shiraz, Cabernet Sauvignon and Merlot have been produced while whites show greatest promise when produced from Chardonnay, Sémillon or Verdelho.

New South Wales vintages

The generalised Vintage charts cover some of the most ageworthy styles and will prove most useful when taken together with comments on style and ageing within individual producer entries. Many wines can be drunk young but an increasing number will not be at their best for at least 5 years. Hunter Valley Sémillon can take two decades in its stride while top Hunter or Mudgee Shiraz and Cabernet have similar ageing potential. Both the vintage ratings and when to drink assessments apply to the top rated examples (3-star or higher).

Recent vintages

2016 Rain in December and January meant the Hunter looked like it was in for a difficult year again after '15. Lady luck came to the rescue and the harvest was in general conducted in dry and warm weather. Some care should be taken with Semillon but the reds look to be very good. Mudgee had a rainy January but thereafter fine weather throughout the vintage. Late season growing conditions were fine in the Central Ranges and Canberra, although the quality will not quite be on a par with 2015.

2015 This was a challenging year in both the Hunter Valley and Mudgee with heavy rainfall up to and around harvest. Some reasonable wines have been made but it will be necessary to be very selective. It was a different story elsewhere in the Central State regions and Canberra district. A warm dry summer was followed by balmy weather up to harvest and an absence of rainfall. Somr very good wines have been made.

2014 A hot, dry summer following a warmer than average winer and spring in the southern half of the State, allowed fully ripe fruit to occur during the harvest despite heavy rains in March which helped to even out the development of the fruit, resulting in a crop of quality and quantity. In the Hunter Valley, rains came in November, but was followed by unbroken sunshine right up to harvest time, allowing the producers to harvest in relaxed conditions. The result is a vintage of exceptional quality with the top reds certain candidates for long cellaring.

2013 Hot dry weather alternated with heavy rainfalls and those producers who managed their vineyards well were rewarded with an outstanding crop and with the exception of Orange, will be producing some outstanding wines, particularly with Sémillon and Shiraz.

2012 Heavy rains in january and February put paid to most of the crop in the Hunter Valley. Sémillon came out best, but there was a huge crop of somewhat dilute wine, whilst the small crop of reds were prone to splitting and rot. Other regions in the State fared a little better. A reduced size of the crop and careful picking has led to some fine wines being made but there is little of it.

2011 There were exceptional growing conditions in the Hunter Valley which has led to an exceptional vintage with all varietals faring extremely well. Elsewhere, persistent rain led to a late harvest with considerable loss of crop although that which was made is of good quality if a little higher in acids.

2010 Yields were down with an early harvest all round owing to a combination of frost, drought. When the rain came, it affected the

New South Wales & Queensland

Australia

harvest of reds in particular so, when fruit was not picked before the rain, selection was key to quality. Expect fair to good reds; whites on the other hand, especially Sémillon, also Chardonnay, were top notch. **2009** Some excellent results across the state, especially in cooler climate regions Canberra District and Orange, also Mudgee. In the Hunter, mid-February rains adversely affected the Hunter Shiraz harvest, but earlier picked Sémillon was very good. **2008** Heavy rain in January and February inhibited quantity and quality. Fortunately, harvesting the Sémillon coincided with a short dry spell and both the

Sémillon and Chardonnay grapes fared better than was first thought. In Queensland, The Granite Belt enjoyed ideal growing conditions to produce one of the best vintages in years. **2007** here echoes much of the gloom to be had in the rest of the country and was similarly hit with drought, heat and much reduced yields. Cooler, higher parts are generally promising for quality though. **2006** looks to be an excellent vintage in the Hunter following a very hot summer. Quantities are down with very good Sémillon and Verdelho and Shiraz approaching 98 or 03 in quality. Mudgee and Orange had early harvests. .

1 South Burnett
2 Granite Belt
3 Hastings River
4 Hunter
5 Broke Fordwich
6 Mudgee
7 Orange
8 Cowra
9 Hilltops
10 Gundagai
11 Tumbarumba
12 Canberra District
13 Southern Highlands
14 Shoalhaven Coast

A-Z of producers by region

New South Wales vintage chart

	Hunter Valley Shiraz	Central Ranges Shiraz	Hunter Valley Sémillon
2016	★★★★ A	★★★★ A	★★★☆ A
2015	★★☆ A	★★★★☆ A	★★★ A
2014	★★★★★ A	★★★★☆ A	★★★★☆ A
2013	★★★★☆ A	★★★★☆ A	★★★★☆ A
2012	★★/★★★ A	★★★☆ B	★★/★★★ B
2011	★★★★☆ B	★★/★★★ B	★★★★ A
2010	★★/★★★ B	★★/★★★★ B	★★★★☆ A
2009	★★★ C	★★★★☆ B	★★★★ B
2008	★★★ C	★★★☆ C	★★★★ B
2007	★★★★ B	★★★★☆ B	★★★★ B
2006	★★★★☆ C	★★★★ C	★★★★☆ C
2005	★★★★ C	★★★★ C	★★★★☆ C
2004	★★/★★★★★ C	★★★★ C	★★★ D
2003	★★★★★ C	★★★☆ D	★★★★★ C
2002	★★★☆ C	★★★★☆ C	★★★★ C
2001	★★★☆ D	★★☆ D	★★★☆ D
2000	★★★★☆ D	★★☆ D	★★★★☆ C

A-Z of producers

Allandale (Hunter Valley) *www.allandalewinery.com.au*
Established in 1978, this is still a relatively small Hunter Valley operation with a reputation for consistently full-flavoured, complex Chardonnay. Archetypal very ripe, oak-influenced Shiraz Viognier and classic Hunter-grown Verdelho and Sémillon are also produced. Bill Sneddon's winemaking has given the wines their individual stamp and impressive flavour intensity: traditional in the best sense, without compromise to the particular winemaking trend of the day. In addition to the fruit from 7ha of Allandale vineyards, grapes are bought in from other Hunter growers and increasingly diverse sources including Mudgee, Hilltops and McLaren Vale. Orange Pinot Noir, Mudgee Sangiovese and Mudgee Shiraz are all now produced, along with a Methode Champenoise William and Anna, and a late-harvest Sémillon/Sauvignon Blanc.

Recommended Reds:
Shiraz Viognier Matthew ★★★ £C
Cabernet Sauvignon Hilltops ★★ £C
Recommended Whites:
Chardonnay ★★★ £C Sémillon ★★ £C Verdelho ★★ £C

Barwang *www.mcwilliamswinesgroup.com/barwang*
Established in 1969 by farmer and RAAF fighter pilot Peter Robinson near Young, Barwang was at the vanguard of Hilltops' twentieth century wine renaissance. Cuttings were procured from MCWILLIAMS who themselves acquired the then 13 ha vineyard in 1989. Since then, investment has seen the area under vine increase to 100 ha, over half of which is planted to lead varieties Cabernet Sauvignon (30 hectares) and Shiraz (30 hectares). A huge 100 million litre dam has been built and, though grapes are crushed at Barwang, the wines (Flagship, Regional and Café Series) are made at McWilliams' state-of-the-art winery at Yenda, near Griffith. The exceptionally good value Regional series includes a Hilltops Cabernet Sauvignon and Shiraz, both benchmark examples of Hilltops' mid-weight elegant style. Even more exciting are Barwang's taut, finely framed Chardonnays, which are sourced from the more elevated, cooler climes of Tumburumba. The flagship Barwang 842 Tumbarumba Chardonnay is particularly impressive, its steely backbone reflecting Tumbarumba's highest vineyard, planted at an altitude of 842 metres. An aromatic, intensely fruity but well defined Pinot Gris also benefits from the Tumbarumba's hallmark bright acidity. (SA)
Recommended Reds:
Shiraz Hilltops ★★☆ £C Cabernet Sauvignon Hilltops ★★☆ £C
Recommended Whites:
Chardonnnay 842Tumburumba ★★★☆ £E
ChardonnnayTumburumba ★★☆ £C PinotGrisTumburumba ★★ £C

Bloodwood Estate (Orange) *www.bloodwood.biz*
This 8 ha vineyard was the first to be established in the Orange district in 1983. Stephen and Rhonda Doyle produce excellent fruit and turn it into expressive, elegant wines (around 5,000 cases per year). Both reds and whites are soft, supple and appealing with good regional fruit character but also manage to be not in the least bit 'made' or over-manipulated. Whites include bright, ripe, limey and gently mineral Riesling and a refined, well-balanced Chardonnay rich in stone fruits and melon and with good depth and structure. Reds are led by intense, flavoursome Shiraz with more than a hint of earth, pepper and eucalyptus and a black-fruited, spicy, cedary/minty Cabernet Sauvignon. Aromatic strawberryish rosé, BigMen in Tights, is from mostly Malbec grapes. Also made but not tasted are Merlot Maurice (a Bordeaux blend), Schubert (Chardonnay), and an occasional very late-harvested Noble Riesling.
Recommended Reds:
Shiraz ★★★ £D Cabernet Sauvignon ★★ £D
Recommended Whites:
Chardonnay ★★★ £D Riesling ★★ £C
Recommended Rosés:
Big Men in Tights ★★ £C

❀ **Brokenwood (Hunter Valley)** *www.brokenwood.com.au*
A benchmark Lower Hunter winery, Brokenwood was established in 1970 by a number of partners including former lawyer and wine writer James Halliday. Production has grown to a not inconsiderable 100,000 cases a year, partly owing to the introduction of wines from relatively new vineyards in Beechworth (Indigo) and Orange

New South Wales & Queensland

(Forest Edge) and, in line with the "make great wine and have fun motto," there is no end of experiment with new varieties, single vineyard parcels, clones even. However, across the board quality remains uniformly high. Winemaker Iain Riggs is responsible for the direction of the widely sourced Brokenwood wines, PJ Charteris his right hand man. The Shiraz has deservedly earned the greatest renown. The Graveyard (Hunter) wines are immensely rich and impressive. Though it retains the Hunter's medium bodied profile, it has remarkable depth, intensity and length, becoming very complex with the 7 or 8 years' age it needs to show at its best. It is among Australia's elite in stunning years like 2003 and 2006. HBA is an impressively deep fruited, super-structured best barrel blend of both vineyards, but wants for a bit of soul in comparison. Less is more. Another Hunter example, the Mistress Block aged in American oak, is more forward in style but has real panache. The Sémillon whites are classic expressions of the grape: low in alcohol, slow to develop,becoming immensely honeyed and very intense as they peak with 8–10 years. The "basic" Sémillon represents terrific value for money (especially if you have the patience to give it five years in bottle), while single vineyard wines (Oakey Creek, Belford, Brycefield and Maxwell) warrant a visit to the cellar door. Flagship ILR Sémillon, with classic length, depth and structure, is only released after 5 years' ageing. Premium Chardonnays are now sourced from the Indigo vineyard in Beechworth and Sauvignon Blanc Forest Edge Vineyard in Orange, the former, supple, muscular even, the latter flinty, with savoury, leesy complexity and bright acidity. The Indigo vineyard is also the source of Pinot Noir, Viognier, Roussanne, Nebbiolo, Sangiovese and a Pinot Gris, all work in progress. Relatively inexpensive Cricket Pitch reds and whites are crafted to be immediately appealing and drinkable. In the Cricket Pitch red, Cabernet Sauvignon and Merlot are the major varieties. Cricket Pitch white is a grassy, citrusy Sauvignon Blanc/Sémillon blend with a hint of barrel-fermentation. The range is completed by two sweeties under the Umpire's Vineyard label and a fortified non-vintage wine, but you'll have to go to the cellar door to get them.

Recommended Reds:
Shiraz HBA ★★★★ £H   Shiraz Graveyard Vineyard ★★★★★ £G
Shiraz Mistress Block ★★★☆ £E   Shiraz ★★★ £D
Cricket Pitch Red ★★ £C
Recommended Whites:
Sémillon ILR Reserve ★★★★☆ £E   Sémillon Maxwell ★★★☆ £E
Sémillon ★★★ £C   Chardonnay Indigo ★★★☆ £E
Chardonnay ★★ £C   Sauvignon Blanc Forest Edge ★★★ £E
Cricket Pitch White ★★ £B

Capercaillie (Hunter Valley) *www.capercailliewine.com.au*
The late Alasdair Sutherland, a Scot, was a highly respected winemaker; his death in 2007 followed by the departure of winemaker Daniel Binet sees this small, family owned winery at a crossroads. Fruit is bought in from both from the Hunter Valley and further afield for a diverse range of wines of good flavour intensity. The whites, at least the Hunter Valley Chardonnay and Sémillon, are if anything more impressive than the reds, with classic Hunter flavours as well as structure and depth. Intense, very berryish Ceilidh Shiraz is the best of the reds, combining Hunter Valley and McLaren Vale fruit. The Clan (Cabernet Sauvignon with Merlot and Cabernet Franc from Barossa) is characterful. The Ghillie Shiraz is made from a special parcel of Hunter Valley fruit in the best vintages. Gewürztraminer (including a dessert style), red Chambourcin and a sparkling red are also made.

Recommended Reds:
Shiraz Ceilidh ★★★ £D   The Clan ★★ £D
Recommended Whites:
Chardonnay ★★★ £D   Sémillon ★★ £C   Gewürztraminer ★☆ £C

Chalkers Crossing (Hilltops) *www.chalkerscrossing.com.au*
Since 2012 this winery has been owned by a Chinese company who have continued the business with the same personnel. Original owner Ted Ambler began planting in the Hilltops region in 1997 and now supplements 10 ha with grapes from the cooler Tumbarumba region. The first wines were made in 2000 but have already a deserved following thanks to the skills of French-born winemaker Celine Rousseau. The style of some of the varietals has varied from year to year yet quality is consistently high. Sémillon for instance has been 100% barrel-fermented since 08 but vinified in stainless steel in earlier vintages. Sauvignon with good weight and structure is also made in stainless steel with a touch of barrel-fermentation. Better still is Chardonnay, barrel-fermented and aged in 40% new oak but restrained and pure, with good weight, breadth and mouthfeel. Both Shiraz and Cabernet Sauvignon are very good too with excellent fruit expression. They are full, soft and concentrated but with an underlying tautness and plenty of extract. An aromatic, bright cherry fruited Cabernet deserves 10 years; Shiraz can be drunk sooner. A cherryish, strawberryish Pinot Noir has some style too, if modest depth, perhaps due to young vines. Prices are very reasonable.

Recommended Reds:
Shiraz Hilltops ★★★ £C   Cabernet Sauvignon Hilltops ★★★ £C
Pinot Noir Tumbarumba ★★ £C
Recommended Whites:
Chardonnay Tumbarumba ★★★ £C
Sémillon Hilltops ★★ £C
Sauvignon Blanc Tumbarumba ★★ £B
Riesling Hilltops ★ £B

✿ Clonakilla (Canberra District) *www.clonakilla.com.au*
Tim Kirk is realising the potential first developed by his father Dr John Kirk, an Australian research scientist of Irish descent. The vineyard is gradually being expanded from the current 6 ha and Kirk is trialling five new Viognier clones which, no doubt find their way into the early bottled Viognier Nouveau label. Clonakilla's top red, Canberra District Shiraz Viognier, includes around 7% Viognier and is now one of the best in the country, distinguished particularly by its individual expression of an Australian Shiraz-based blend. The pepper, spice, floral and berry amalgam is distinctive, elegant and supported by a depth, weight and structure that deserves at least 5 years' ageing and has the pedigree to develop a further five plus. Viognier is very good too, complex with delightful may blossom and ripe peach aromas - it is tighter, with better structure than most Austalian examples, avoiding the excessive ripeness or alcohol of some. Made as they are on a similarly small scale, these really are wines to contrast with examples from good growers of Côte-Rôtie or Condrieu. A Hilltops Shiraz, while much cheaper than the Canberra District version, is quite different: more one dimensional without the same depth, expression or sheer style, but it is still one of the Hilltops' best Shiraz. The mid priced, O'Riada Shiraz made from bought in fruit, may lack the lift and finesse of the estate Canberra District wine, but it is well concentrated with savoury layers. Shiraz from the Murrumbateman vineyard (not tasted) is now being bottle separately and is labelled Syrah. Riesling, Sémillon/Sauvignon Blanc and Cabernet Sauvignon/Cabernet Franc/Merlot are also produced.

Recommended Reds:
Shiraz/Viognier Canberra District ★★★★★ £F
Shiraz Hilltops ★★★ £D Shiraz O'Riada Canberra District ★★★☆ £F
Recommended Whites:
Viognier ★★★★ £F Riesling ★★★ £F

Collector (Canberra District) *www.collectorwines.com.au*
In 2000 HARDYS invested in the Canberra District, establishing the Kamberra wine company. When they pulled out in 2007, Kamberra's talented winemaker, Alex McKay, decided to stay and establish his own label. McKay started out making just two wines, both Shiraz, the region's stand out variety. Drawing on his experience at Hardys when he worked with some 24 growers, McKay has cherry-picked his fruit, especially for the flagship Reserve Shiraz. It comes from the renowned Kyeema Vineyard in Murrumbateman (which belongs to Capital Wines) and features among the region's oldest vines. Planted on well-drained weathered ironstone soils with granite on an elevated saddle between two valleys, its well ventilated site produces a particularly finely structured, aromatic wine. Marked Tree Shiraz is typically made with younger vine material from a select number of vineyards on granite and shale soils. Both wines are fermented naturally, with some whole bunches, before being aged for about a year in French oak (around 40% new for the Reserve, 25% for Marked Tree). With the emphasis on elegance, both are dominated by well-defined, bright red fruits with spice and pepper, supported by ripe but present tannins. In 2010, McKay made his first white Rhône blend, focused on Marsanne (not tasted). (SA)
Recommended Reds:
Shiraz Reserve ★★★★ £E Shiraz MarkedTree ★★★ £D

☸ De Bortoli (Riverina) *www.debortoli.com.au*
De Bortoli's Riverina operation is a vast winery based in the Riverina near Griffith. Output is around 4.5 million cases a year and almost all is accounted for by bulk-market labels. The majority of the fine-wine output is accounted for at the Yarra Valley winery (see DE BORTOLI Victoria). Riverina budget labels include Vat numbered Deen De Bortoli wines (including good value Botrytis Sémillon Vat 5), the Willowglen and Sacred Hill ranges as well as others only likely to be encountered locally. The greatest interest from a quality point of view is the botrytis-influenced Sémillon Noble One and the fortified Black Noble. The latter is produced in a similar fashion to the liqueur Tokays of Rutherglen from a *solera* which is based on Sémillon. A brilliant wine, combining power and elegance, its rich, complex character, filled with finest dates and fruit peel, is superbly balanced. Noble One is a long-established great Australian sweet wine only surpassed by the country's best fortified wines. Now bottled under screwcap, it is rich, complex, refined and beautifully balanced and provides a good alternative to top Sauternes. Stylistic changes over the last decade have resulted in a more elegant but no less intense style. These include earlier picking, tighter grain French oak and less new oak; in fact a component of the blend is now sees no oak at all. It can similarly benefit from long cellaring, needing at least 5 years to fully reveal its remarkable complex, honeyed character; good vintages show well for 20-30 years. Also fine is Old Boys '21 Years' (Shiraz/Grenache derived) which is powerful and concentrated with an intriguing aged, nutty complexity yet full of life and vitality.
Recommended Whites:
Noble One ★★★★☆ £F Black Noble ★★★★☆ £F
Old Boys 21 Years ★★★★ £D Deen Botrytis SemillonVat 5 ★★★ £C
Show Muscat ★★ £D

Glenguin (Hunter Valley) *www.glenguinestate.com.au*
Robin Tedder produces two ranges, the estate-based Glenguin wines from 19 ha of vineyards at Wollombi in the Lower Hunter Valley and Maestro-labelled wines from as far afield as the Adelaide Hills. All the wines show real intensity and ripeness. Premium Aristea Shiraz is sweet-fruited and oak-infused, complex and savoury with age, and there's lots of Hunter character and expression in Schoolhouse Block and lighter Stonybroke versions. Affordable Old Broke Block Sémillon and River Terrace The estate also produces Tannat which goes into a single varietal wine and a Shiraz blend. Better to try the Sticky Botrytis Sémillon which has fine fruit and a spiced honey, preserved citrus and marmalade character, if not the complexity of a great sweet wine.
Recommended Reds:
Shiraz Aristea ★★★★ £E Shiraz Schoolhouse Block ★★★☆ £C
Shiraz Stonybroke ★★★ £D
Recommended Whites:
Botrytis SémillonThe Sticky ★★☆ £E Sémillon Old Broke Block ★★☆ £C

Helm (Canberra District) *www.helmwines.com.au*
Husband and wife team Ken (winemaker and former insect ecologist) and Judith (who focuses on the vines) established the winery in 1973, one of the earliest in the region's modern era. Riesling courses through Ken Helm's blood and he is proud of the fact that he is the fourth generation descendant of German "vinedressers" who established vineyards near Albury and Rutherglen in 1860s. The Helms regularly visit the Mosel and Rhine valley and, in 2000, Ken Helm instigated the Canberra International Riesling Tasting. Helm currently makes three Rieslings, two in Australia's classic bone dry style (the Classic Dry and Premium Riesling) and an off-dry style (Half-Dry), not tasted. The dry Rieslings are among Australia's best. The steely, single vineyard Premium Riesling from ironstone soils, first made in 2005, shows a terrific concentration of minerals and Classic Dry also impresses with its line and length. From 2013, Helm has outsourced fruit in the Orange Central Ranges and Tumbarumba to produce additional Rieslings to take up the extra capacity in the winery. Though consistently ripe, which cannot be taken for granted in these parts, the single vineyard Premium Cabernet Sauvignon's admirably concentrated yet well defined cool climate fruit is somewhat dominated by American (Missouri) oak. A pity. Helm also makes a Cabernet/Shiraz and an (entry level) Cabernet Sauvignon (not tasted). (SA)
Recommended Reds:
Cabernet Sauvignon Premium ★★☆ £F
Recommended Whites:
Riesling Premium ★★★★ £E Riesling Classic Dry ★★★☆ £D

Huntington Estate (Mudgee) *www.huntingtonestate.com.au*
Tim Stevens purchased this operation in 2006 from the Roberts family and has maintained style and quality. Production remains relatively small at around 20,000 cases a year and is spread across a wide range of wines, some of which are only available through mail order and at the cellar door. Cabernet Sauvignon, Shiraz and Cabernet Merlot have long been Mudgee classics. Special Reserves of Cabernet Sauvignon and Shiraz are quite marked by their full, American-oak component and sinewy Mudgee tannins but the quality of the dark but bright and juicy fruit can easily absorb the wood given time, something many Australian wines fail to achieve. Stevens recommends they should ideally be drunk at 10-15 years of age. A number of new wines are being produced under the new regime. These include a Pinot Noir/Merlot Dry Rosé, a Sémillon/

New South Wales & Queensland

Chardonnay, a straight Merlot and a Carbonic Maceration Grenache Shiraz, along with three economically priced offerings, a dry and sweet white under the Four Seasons label. There is also a rich, barrel-fermented Chardonnay. The wines still represent particularly good value for money and are difficult to find outside of Australia.

Recommended Reds:
Cabernet Sauvignon Special Reserve ★★★★ £E
Cabernet Sauvignon ★★★☆ £C
Cabernet Sauvignon Merlot ★★★ £C
Shiraz Special Reserve ★★★★ £E   Shiraz ★★★☆ £C
Recommended Whites:
Chardonnay Barrel Fermented ★★ £C

Lake's Folly (Hunter Valley) *www.lakesfolly.com.au*
This top-quality Lower Hunter producer, originally established in 1963 by Sydney surgeon Max Lake was sold to Peter Fogarty in 2000, who also owns MILLBROOK WINERY and DEEP WOODS Estate, both in Western Australia. Rodney Kempe has taken on the winemaking reins, and has recently added two premium wines to the two wines regularly produced from 12 ha of mature vineyards which translates to around 4,500 cases per year. The Chardonnay in particular was an early benchmark among Australian whites. During the early to mid-1990s the wines were still good but didn't reach the levels of old. However, they are now on top form. The red Cabernet blend (older vintages are labelled Cabernets or simply Cabernet) is mostly Cabernet Sauvignon with some Shiraz, Merlot and Petit Verdot. It is restrained and well-structured with blackcurrant and blackberry fruit but none of the overripeness seen in some Hunter reds. The Chardonnay is rich, opulent and buttery with very well-judged oak adding a subtle, spicy, nutty character; acidity to balance means it will keep for up to a decade from a top year, the Cabernet blend often longer. The two new wines are Hill Block Chardonnay, made from cuttings from the original 1969 Chardonnay vines, planted in 2003 and 3 Estates Red, blended from Cabernet from the Hunter Valley and Margaret River and Shiraz from Perth Hills. Only 175 cases of the 2013 Chardonnay and 280 cases of the 3 Estates Red were made. We haven't tasted these yet and in view of the tiny quantities available, we are unlikely to, but they have been very well rated.
Recommended Reds:
Cabernet Blend ★★★★☆ £F
Recommended Whites:
Chardonnay ★★★★☆ £F

Lark Hill (Canberra District) *www.larkhillwinery.com*
Established in 1978 by Dr David and Sue Carpenter, the vineyard is easily the region's highest at 860m, which explains why Pinot Noir and Riesling (including a tightly focused but layered Auslese) shine. Shiraz (co-fermented with a dash of Viognier) is sourced from the Murrambateman sub-region which, further to the west and, at much lower altitude, is warmer. Since the Carpenter's son Chris joined the winemaking team, Lark Hill has consolidated its reputation for Pinot Noir and Riesling while pursuing new directions. Lark Hill has the distinction of being the region's only certified biodynamic producer (certified in 2008) and its Grüner Veltliner pioneer. Though only planted in 2005 on shale slopes, this Austrian variety shows great potential, with good typicity and plenty of texture and interest thanks to a natural ferment (partly in barrel) and lees aging. The Carpenters have planted more. Throughout the range, hands off winemaking aims to maximise vineyard expression. The wines are complex yet unaffected, with lovely balance and texture. Sparkling wines, a Sangiovese, Chardonnay, Viognier and

Sauvignon Blanc are also made as well as Exaltation, a Super Tuscan inspired blend of Cabernet Sauvignon, Merlot, Sangiovese and Shiraz. (SA)
Recommended Reds:
Shiraz ★★★☆ £E   Pinot Noir ★★★ £E
Recommended Whites:
Riesling Auslese ★★★☆ £F   Riesling Mayfield Vineyard ★★★ £E
Grüner Veltliner ★★ £E

McWilliam's Mount Pleasant *www.mountpleasantwines.com.au*
Though a sixth generation family business, Hunter Valley based McWilliams is a large operation. It produces volume Hanwood Estate wines at the Hanwood winery in the Riverina and including increasingly good wines from Barwang in southern New South Wales, all well made, but its Hunter Valley portfolio is the jewel in the crown. Until recently, the Mount Pleasant label was reserved exclusively for these Hunter Valley wines. It seems a shame that the label is is now being applied more widely, now encompassing, for example an Adelaide Hills Sauvignon Blanc and Coonawarra Cabernet Sauvignon. From the Hunter Valley, Lovedale (single vineyard) and Elizabeth Semillons,only released with 4–5 years' bottle-age (though Elizabeth is now also being released as a young wine), start out slowly but have marvellous toasty, citrus and herb intensity that continues to build in the bottle over many years. The characteristic intense toastiness is not due to oak but the inherent character that develops when these Hunter Semillons are built to last. Shiraz too is deep and individual. The particular fusion of oak, savoury characters, earth, leather, black cherry and licorice give an indication of the complexity but there are other nuances too here that you just won't get anywhere else. Old Paddock & Old Hill comes from two very old estate vineyards and is particularly long-lived. Getting hold of these wines can be a problem unless you happen to live in Australia yet perhaps the most remarkable thing is the very reasonable pricing. If you buy the Sémillon relatively young, put it away somewhere out of reach for a decade or more.
Recommended Reds:
Shiraz Maurice O'Shea ★★★★ £F
Shiraz Old Paddock & Old Hill ★★★★ £D
Shiraz Rosehill ★★ £E   Shiraz Philip ★★ £C
Cabernet Sauvignon Jack ★★☆ £C
Recommended Whites:
Sémillon Lovedale ★★★★☆ £E
Sémillon Elizabeth Cellar Aged ★★★★ £D
Sauvignon Blanc Florence ★ £C

Mayfield Vineyard (Orange) *www.mayfieldvineyard.com*
At 850-930m above sea level, Mayfield Vineyard occupies one of the highest sites in Orange and, it follows, Australia. It was planted in 1998 by Richard Thomas, a business man, who now lives on the 100 hectare estate, of which around 32 hectares are under vine. An extensive range of estate grown wines, first produced in 2004, is contract made. The best wines are bottled under the Mayfield Vineyard label, while Icely Road is the junior label. Unsurprisingly give the vineyard's elevation, Mayfield's strength is its white wines, especially its floral but focused Riesling and a Sauvignon Blanc which leans more towards the Loire than New Zealand. Reds are more challenging and, though well-defined with good varietal typicity, lack concentration. This might be expected to improve in time with vine age but, meantime, the Pinot Noir is somewhat overpriced. A Mayfield sparkling wine (50% Chardonnay and 50% Pinot Noir is also made but has not been tasted. (SA)

Recommended Reds:
Cabernet Sauvignon Mayfield Vineyard ★★☆ £D
Pinot Noir Mayfield Vineyard ★★ £E
Recommended Whites:
Riesling Mayfield Vineyard ★★★☆ £D
Riesling Icely Road ★★★ £C
Chardonnnay Mayfield Vineyard ★★ £D
Chardonnnay Icely Road ★☆ £C
Sauvignon Blanc Icely Road ★★☆ £C

Meerea Park (Hunter Valley) *www.meereapark.com.au*
Rhys Eather, one of two brothers who own this Pokolbin-based winery, makes around 10,000 cases per year. The first vintage was 1991 and the wines are all made from bought-in fruit. Ripe, complex Chardonnay is barrel-fermented with natural yeasts and sourced from old Pokolbin vines while a fresh Verdelho with preserved citrus fruit is a good example of theis variety in the Hunter. Sémillon, like the Verdelho, is unoaked in the classic Hunter Valley style and Eather makes two, the denser, spicier Terracotta from red dirt and the more lifted and lemony Alexander Munro from the region's classic Sémillon alluvial soils. Both will benefit from 4 or 5 years' cellaring. Of the reds the Cabernet/Merlot is aged in French oak and is in a leaner style, almost leafy. The Aunts Shiraz is characterful and intense but Alexander Munro has greater depth and style with powerful spice, pepper and smoky black fruit; Hell Hole sits somewhere in between. (SA)
Recommended Reds:
Shiraz Alexander Munro ★★★★☆ £F
Shiraz Hell Hole ★★★★ £F
Shiraz The Aunts ★★★☆ £D
Recommended Whites:
Sémillon Alexander Munro ★★★★ £E
Sémillon Terracotta ★★★☆ £D
Chardonnay Alexander Munro ★★★☆ £D
Verdelho ★★☆ £B

Printhie Estate (Orange) *www.printhiewines.com.au*
Jim and Ruth Swift established Printhie in 1996, planting 12 hectares of vines. Then the aim was simply to grow grapes however, when their sons Ed and Dave returned to the fold in the early 2000s, the family made a strategic shift into wine production. In 2001, the vineyard was expanded to 33 hectares and, by 2004, when the new plantings had come onstream, the Swifts had built their own winery. Printhie's range comprises the Swift Family Heritage label (estate grown reds), MCC or Mount Canobolas Connection (the middle tier) and the entry level Mountain wines. From top to bottom the wines are well made with good concentration, balance and structure. The secret to this consistency lies in the sourcing. Grapes for the red wines and Viognier come from the estate vineyards which, at 630m, are among the region's lowest. Apart from a rather stemmy Pinot Noir, Mountain and MCC reds share a sweet core of ripe but juicy fruit and smooth tannins with a good lick of oak. Swift Family Heritage Cabernet Sauvignon is a more serious proposition, though it retains an exuberantly fruity quality. Sauvignon Blanc, Pinot Gris, Chardonnay and Riesling come from higher sites rising to a little over 1000m for the finely crafted, zesty MCC Chardonnay. A bright fruited Sauvignon shows an abundance of passion fruit cut with lemony acidity and attractive grassy notes. Made in a more oxidative style, a weighty Pinot Gris and Viognier are focused more on mouthfeel than fruit. Since 2012 they have added a "Super Duper" Chardonnay and Syrah made from best selected fruit among their

vineyard holdings but these have not yet been tasted. (SA)
Recommended Reds:
Cabernet Sauvignon Swift Family Heritage ★★★ £E
Cabernet Sauvignon Mountain ★★☆ £C
Shiraz Viognier MCC ★★☆ £E   Shiraz Mountain ★★ £C
Pinot Noir MCC ★★ £D   Merlot Mountain ★☆ £D
Recommended Whites:
Chardonnnay MCC ★★★☆ £E   Chardonnnay Mountain ★★☆ £C
Riesling MCC ★★☆ £C   Sauvignon Blanc Mountain ★★☆ £C
Pinot Gris Mountain ★★☆ £C

Rosemount Estate (Hunter Valley) *www.rosemountestates.com*
The already substantial Rosemount enterprises (also see ROSEMOUNT MCLAREN VALE) merged with the huge SOUTHCORP operation (now known as Treasury Wine Estates) in 2001. By mid-2003 there had been a significant fall-out which included the departure of veteran winemaker Philip Shaw who for so long maintained generally high standards throughout the extensive portfolio. The premium red Mountain Blue Shiraz/Cabernet Sauvignon (typically 85/15) from Mudgee is dense, concentrated and aged in American oak. The white equivalent is the intense, complex Roxburgh Chardonnay, a distinctive full-bodied Australian example of the variety, if the most Burgundian in style of the Rosemount Chardonnays. Least of the premium Chardonnays, the Show Reserve falls a long way short of its form of a decade or more ago. Usually much better is the Show Reserve Sémillon with more classic Hunter expression but requiring at least 3 or 4 years' ageing. Hill of Gold varietals from Mudgee show good fruit intensity and texture, particularly in good Chardonnay and ripe, black-fruited Shiraz. Lower-priced Diamond varietal and dual varietal labels can offer decent everyday drinking if not a great deal of excitement.
Recommended Reds:
Shiraz/Cabernet Sauvignon Blue Mountain ★★★★ £E
Shiraz Hill of Gold ★★ £C   Cabernet Sauvignon Hill of Gold ★★ £C
Recommended Whites:
Chardonnay Roxburgh ★★★★ £E   Chardonnay Hill of Gold ★★ £D
Chardonnay Show Reserve ★★ £C   Sémillon Show Reserve ★★ £D

✿ Philip Shaw (Orange) *www.philipshaw.com.au*
Philip Shaw, once ROSEMOUNT's almost legendary winemaker, has long owned and developed a vineyard of his own. He purchased the 47 ha Koomooloo vineyard on the slopes of Mount Canobolas back in 1988 but only released the first wines under his own label with the 2004 vintage, having sold off the grapes or made wines for others including CUMULUS in the interim. The cool climate vineyards, on red loam soils over a limestone base rise to over 900m and all qualify as Orange GI (which stipulates a minimum of 600m elevation). Working with Jo Perry there are already some impressive releases. Premium The Number Series wines are given a number but these are mostly of personal significance and are not lot or vineyard numbers. Exciting whites include a pungent nettly, herbaceous Sauvignon Blanc No. 19 with both cooler and riper fruit characters, and a striking, aromatic Chardonnay with good purity. Reds are subject to a long post-fermentation maceration and, with vine age, the tannins have become more refined. An elegant, intense and individual No. 17 (60/20/20 Merlot/Cabernet Franc/Cabernet Sauvignon) is aged in 100% new French *barriques*. Classy, Rhône-like No. 89 Syrah (here 89 denotes the year the vines were planted) instead sees both French (two-thirds) and American oak of which only a portion is new. Subsequent additions to the range include the deeply concentrated yet polished No. 5 Cabernet Sauvignon, a

Australia

finely crafted, bright Pinot Noir No. 8 and a dry, savoury rosé called Pink Billy. A second tier "The Character" range features leesy but taut unoaked Pinot Gris, The Gardener, Chardonnay, The Architect, The Dreamer Viognier, The Conductor Merlot, The Wire Walker Pinot Noir and the floral and peppery The Idiot Shiraz.

Recommended Reds:
Cabernet Sauvignon No 5 ★★★★☆ £F
Shiraz No 89 ★★★★ £E   Shiraz The Idiot ★★★ £C
Pinot Noir No 8 ★★★★ £E
Merlot/Cabernet/Cabernet Franc No 17 ★★★☆ £C
Recommended Whites:
Chardonnay No 11 ★★★★ £E   Chardonnay The Architect ★★★ £C
Sauvignon Blanc No 19 ★★★ £D
Recommended Rosés:
Rosé Pink Billy Saignee ★★ £C

Sirromet (Granite Belt) *www.sirromet.com*
Crossword addicts will immediately recognise that Sirromet is T E Morris backwards, but there is nothing backward about this state of the art winery, which has grown at a furious pace over the last few years to become what is probably the largest in Queensland. Sirromet vineyards are mostly located in the Granite Belt in south Queensland at between 600 and 1500 metres above sea level and are producing not only cool climate wines but other varieties which might be considered as being better served at lower altitudes. Since our last edition, the winery has completely re-branded all its labels - has dropped some varietals and planted new ones and has also considerably increased prices. Without a comprehensive tasting of the wines, we must consider this only as work in progress until we get a chance to make a thorough review. (NB)

Thomas Wines (Hunter Valley) *www.thomaswines.com.au*
Andrew Thomas represents a new generation of Hunter Valley producer specialising in Sémillon and Shiraz. His range of individual vineyard wines made from purchased fruit aims to capture the specific traits of some of the region's best *terroir* while simultaneously introducing subtle tweaks, which lend his wines a certain contemporary appeal. Take Thomas' Semillons, a variety about which this former Tyrrell's winemaker is passionate. Thomas picks at different levels of ripeness and uses light solids to build up texture and enhance complexity. His classic dry Semillons may be a touch gentler on the attack, but they are terrifically concentrated, long and pure. The flagship Braemore from very deep low yielding alluvial sandy soils, produces particularly structured, ageworthy wines. The fruit for OC Sémillon from alluvial flats tends to get a little riper so, though lemony and mouthwatering, it is relatively forward. Thomas also produces an off dry Sémillon, Six Degrees, aimed at winning new fans for the variety. With its fresh acidity, it is hard to believe it has around 40g/l of residual sugar though it is less citrus focused and rounder in mouthfeel. As for Shiraz, Thomas is keen to restore the Hunter's reputation for medium bodied wines of class and distinction. There is not a hint of sweaty saddle here. Though characterful, the wines are bright, with excellent fruit purity. DJV (déjà vu) Shiraz is co-fermented with a small amount of Trebbiano and shows an edge of dried herbs to its sour plum and cherry fruit. The floral, elegantly structured Sweetwater Shiraz hails from a single vineyard at the northern end of the Lower Hunter with patches of limestone. Motel Block Shiraz, a new *cuvée* from a shy bearing vineyard is darker with spicy liquorice and firm tannins. Kiss Shiraz, from another low cropping vineyard situated diagonally opposite BROKENWOOD's Graveyard vineyard, is tightly structured with great

fruit intensity. The wines, including the cheaper Two of a Kind range, are made in Polkobin at the James Winery. Total annual production is around 4000 cases. (SA)

Recommended Reds:
Shiraz Kiss ★★★★ £F   Shiraz Motel Block ★★★★ £F
Shiraz Sweetwater ★★★☆ £E   Shiraz DJV ★★☆ £E
Recommended Whites:
Sémillon Braemore ★★★★☆ £D   Sémillon OC ★★★☆ £C
Sémillon Six Degrees ★☆ £C

Tower Estate (Hunter Valley) *www.towerestatewines.com.au*
Tower Estate, a hospitality complex and winery, was directed by the vastly experienced 'Australian wine personality' Len Evans up until his loss in 2006. A wide range of wines are made by Samantha Connew (ex-WIRRA WIRRA), each in a 1,000-case lot. Those from the Hunter Valley are Chardonnay, Sémillon, Verdelho and Shiraz. Only Chardonnay and Sémillon have been tasted but both show impressive texture, depth and excellent structure that suggests good cellaring potential, particularly for the more austere but intense Sémillon with classic herbal, floral and citrusy fruit. Other wines are likely to be worth a try and include Macedon Ranges Malbec from Victoria, Tasmanian Pinot Noir, Sangiovese and Merlot from Orange, Sauvignon and Chardonnay from the Adelaide Hills, Barossa Shiraz, Coonawarra Cabernet Sauvignon and a Clare Valley Riesling. They are most likely to be encountered in good restaurants both in Australia and internationally.
Recommended Whites:
Chardonnay ★★★☆ £D   Sémillon ★★☆ £C

❀ **Keith Tulloch (Hunter Valley)** *www.keithtullochwine.com.au*
An experienced Hunter Valley winemaker with stints at LINDEMANS and Rothbury Estate under his belt, Keith Tulloch now makes wine under his own name. Production is very small with only a few hundred cases of each wine in the first vintages but the wines are undoubtedly a fine distillation of Tulloch's experience. They seem handmade in the best sense, very Hunter Valley with super Hunter fruit and intensity, excellent weight, texture and length of flavour. Above all, they are classy and complex. Unquestionably they will age impressively too (though a touch of barrel ferment makes the Sémillon broachable relatively early, though it will benefit from ageing); certainly they get better every time you taste them. The stylish fruit in the Forres Blend is predominantly Cabernet Sauvignon but also from Merlot and Petit Verdot. The excellent Shiraz is now joined by a Shiraz Viognier. While not cheap the wines are very well-priced; the splendid Chardonnay and Sémillon are great value for money. Perdiem is for emerging varieties/wine styles and differs from year to year. An exotic, very richly botrytised sweet Sémillon is also ade.
Recommended Reds:
Shiraz Kester ★★★★ £E   Forres Blend ★★★★ £D
Recommended Whites:
Sémillon Braemore ★★★★☆ £D

❀ **Tyrrell's (Hunter Valley)** *www.tyrrells.com.au*
This family-owned and run winery dates back to 1858 and makes an extensive range of wines, around half a million cases even after the recent sale of the Long Flat brand. The top wines are the Winemakers Selection (Vat numbered) series. The bold, powerful and complex Vat 47 has been one of Australia's great Chardonnays for 3 decades. Rich and very concentrated, it has always shown refinement and balance; it ages well too. Vat 1 Sémillon of great

structure and nuance and only released with several years' age (currently 1997) is one of the finest examples in the region. As for reds, in common with other leading Hunter Shiraz, more recent vintages show brighter fruit while retaining the region's classic medium bodied profile. A switch to largely French oak and large format barrels is paying dividends. Of the Winemakers Selection reds, the Vat 9 Shiraz has an extra dimension while Vat 8 Shiraz (from the Hunter) shows more overt (French) oak and less regional nuance. Savoury and soft, Vat 6 Pinot Noir work less well, especially given the leaps and bounds made with this variety in cooler climes. The impressive expanded single vineyard range, which includes Sémillon (Stevens, Belford, HVD), Chardonnay (HVD, Belford) and Shiraz (Stevens, Old Patch 1867, 4 Acres), showcases Tyrrell's prime old vine sites, for Sémillon in particular, lifting the different soil types off the page. The well-priced Rufus Stone reds come from vineyards in Heathcote and McLaren Vale; the Shiraz shows good depth of flavour and ages well. At the level of Brokenback Shiraz, Moon Mountain Chardonnay, Fordwich Verdelho and Brookdale Sémillon (all Hunter sourced) the wines can be full-flavoured though on occasion want for better balance (and less oak). The unwooded Lost Block Sémillon by contrast is more classic as is new release Johnno's Sémillon which is basket pressed and made the old fashioned way, with a warmer ferment and some solids. It shows classic lime and lemongrass and, though tightknit, has a talcy texture and incipient toast in its youth. Of the relatively inexpensive Old Winery wines, which are sourced from both from the Hunter and southern states, the Shiraz has decent, smoky, dark berry fruit, while the Sémillon has good intensity and length and is better with a little age. Moore's Creek is a new label for basic Shiraz, Cabernet, Chardonnay and Sémillon/Sauvignon Blanc, as is Midnight Leap label.

Recommended Reds:
Shiraz Four Acres ★★★★☆ £E
Shiraz Old Patch 1867 ★★★★☆ £E
Shiraz Vat 9 ★★★★ £E Shiraz Vat 8 ★★★ £E
Shiraz Stevens ★★★ £C
Shiraz Rufus Stone Heathcote ★★☆ £C
Shiraz Brokenback ★★ £C Shiraz Old Winery ★ £B
Recommended Whites:
Chardonnay Vat 47 ★★★★ £E
Chardonnay Moon Mountain ★ £C
Chardonnay Shee-Oak ★ £C Sémillon Vat 1 ★★★★ £E
Sémillon Belford ★★★★ £E Sémillon Stevens ★★★ £D
Sémillon Jonno's ★★ £E Sémillon Lost Block ★★ £C

Other wines of note

Albert River Wines (Queensland)
Recommended Whites: Chardonnay Unwooded ★ £B
Recommended Reds: Cabernet/Shiraz/Merlot ★★ £C
Merlot ★★ £C
Allanmere (Hunter)
Recommended Reds: Shiraz ★★ £C
Cabernet Sauvignon ★★ £C
Recommended Whites: Chardonnay Durham ★★ £C
Verdelho ★ £B
Beelgaara (Riverina)
Recommended Whites:
Botrytis Sémillon Promenade Winemakers Selection ★★★ £C
Berton Vineyards (Riverina)
Recommended Reds:
Shiraz Bonsai Eden Valley ★★★ £E

Bidgeebong (Gundagai)
Recommended Whites:
Chardonnay Triangle Tumbarumba ★★ £B
Bimbadgen (Hunter)
Recommended Reds: Shiraz ★ £B
Shiraz Signature ★★ £C
Recommended Whites: Chardonnay ★★ £B
Botrytis Sémillon Myall Road ★★ £C
Briar Ridge (Gundagai)
Recommended Whites:
Sémillon Dairy Hill ★★★ £D
Brindabella Hills (Canberra District)
Recommended Whites: Riesling ★★ £C
Recommended Reds: Shiraz ★★★☆ £E
Capital Wines (Canberra District)
Recommended Reds:
Merlot The Backbencher ★★ £C
Chateau Pato (Hunter Valley)
Recommended Reds:
Shiraz Old Pokolbin ★★★☆ £C
Shiraz DJP ★★★★ £D
Cockfighter's Ghost (Hunter Valley)
Recommended Reds:
Pinot Noir Reserve Tasmania ★★☆ £E
Shiraz McLaren Vale ★★☆ £C
The Legend South Australia ★☆ £C
Cumulus (Orange)
Recommended Whites:
Pinot Grigio Rolling (Sparkling) ★ £B
Sauvignon Blanc/Sémillon Rolling ★ £B
Chardonnay Rolling Unoaked ★ £C
Chardonnay Climbing ★★ £C
Chardonnay Cumulus ★★☆ £C
Recommended Reds: Shiraz Rolling ★ £B
Shiraz Climbing ★☆ £C
Cabernet Sauvignon Climbing ★ £C
Cabernet/Merlot Rolling ★ £B
Merlot Climbing ★ £C
Cuttaway Hill (Southern Highlands)
Recommended Whites:
Sémillon/Sauvignon Blanc ★☆ £C
Chardonnay ★★ £C
Recommended Reds:
Merlot ★★☆ £C Cabernet Sauvignon ★★☆ £C
Delinquente (Riverland)
Recommended Whites:
Screaming Betty (Vermentino) ★★★ £C
Recommended Reds:
Bullet Dodger (Montepulciano) ★★★ £C
Di Lusso (Mudgee)
Recommended Reds:
Barbera ★★ £C
Eden Road (Canberra District)
Recommended Reds: Shiraz Hilltops ★★★★ £E
Pinot Noir The Long Road ★★★☆ £D
Shiraz The Long Road ★★★☆ £D
Recommended Whites:
Chardonnay The Long Road ★★★☆ £D
Riesling The Long Road ★★★ £D
Pinot Gris The Long Road ★★☆ £D

New South Wales & Queensland

Australia

Freeman (Hilltops)
Recommended Reds:
Rondinella Corvina Secco ★★ £D
Hope Estate (Hunter)
Recommended Whites: Verdelho ★ £B
Chardonnay ★ £C
Sémillon ★ £B
Recommended Reds: Merlot ★ £C
Shiraz ★ £C
Lerida Estate (Canberra District)
Recommended Whites:
Chardonnay ★★ £E
Lindemans
Recommended Whites:
Sémillon Classic Release ★★★ £D
Logan (Central Ranges/Orange)
Recommended Whites: Sauvignon Blanc ★★ £C
Pinot Gris Weemala ★★ £B
Gewürztraminer Weemala ★☆ £B
Recommended Reds:
Shiraz Apple Tree Flat ★★☆ £B
Lowe Wines (Mudgee)
Recommended Whites: Riesling ★★★ £C
Riesling Late Harvest ★★★ £C
Recommended Reds:
Shiraz Thistle Hill (Preservative Free) ★★ £C
Shiraz ★★ £D
Zinfandel Reserve ★★★ £D
Margan Family (Hunter)
Recommended Whites: Verdelho ★ £B
Sémillon ★★ £B
Recommended Reds:
Shiraz ★★ £C   Cabernet Sauvignon ★★ £C
Mayfield Estate (Orange)
Recommended Whites:
Riesling Single Vineyard ★★★ £C
Riesling Icely Road ★★★ £C
Sauvignon Blanc Icely Road ★★★ £C
Montrose (Mudgee)
Recommended Reds:
Shiraz Black Label ★★★ £D
Mount Majura (Canberra District)
Recommended Whites:
Riesling ★★★ £C
Recommended Reds:
Tempranillo Shiraz Graciano ★★☆ £D
Tempranillo ★★ £E
Mount View (Hunter)
Recommended Whites:
Sémillon ★★★ £C
Sémillon Reserve ★★★ £C
Pepper Tree (Hunter)
Sémillon Alluvius ★★★★ £E
Recommended Reds:
Shiraz Conquurs ★★★ £D
Phat Wine Co. (Hunter)
Recommended Whites:
Sémillon Hart & Hunter ★★ £C
Poole's Rock (Hunter)
Recommended Whites:
Chardonnay ★★★ £E

Recommended Reds:
Shiraz ★★★☆ £F
Reynolds (Orange)
Recommended Whites:
Chardonnay Orange Reserve ★★ £B
Recommended Reds:
Merlot Orange Marble Man ★★ £C
Cabernet Sauvignon Orange The Jezebal ★★ £C
Ross Hill (Orange)
Recommended Whites:
Chardonnay Pinnacle ★★★☆ £E
Recommended Reds: Shiraz Pinnacle ★★★ £E
Skimstone (Mudgee)
Recommended Reds:
Sangiovese ★★☆ £D
Tamborine Estate (Queensland)
Recommended Whites: Verdelho ★ £B
Recommended Reds: Premium Shiraz/Cabernet ★★ £C
Premium Cabernet Franc ★★ £C
Reserve Black Shiraz ★★ £F
Tatler (Hunter)
Recommended Whites:
Sémillon ★★★ £C
Tempus Two (Hunter)
Recommended Whites:
Verdelho Hunter Valley ★ £B
Chardonnay 'Copper' ★★☆ £B
Pinot Gris 'Pewter' ★★☆ £C
Recommended Reds: Tempranillo ★☆ £B
Cabernet/Merlot 'Copper' ★★ £B
Sangiovese 'Pewter' ★★★ £C
Audrey Wilkinson (Hunter Valley)
Recommended Reds: Shiraz 'The Lake' ★★★★ £F
Shiraz Audley Series ★★☆ £B
Recommended Whites:
Semillon Winemakers Selection ★★★ £C
Semillon Audley Series ★★☆ £B
Windowrie (Cowra)
Recommended Reds: Shiraz Estate ★★ £D
Recommended Whites:
Chardonnay Estate ★★ £D
Word Of Mouth (Orange)
Recommended Whites: Pinot Grigio ★★ £D
Pinot Gris Pinnacle ★★☆ £D
Sauvignon Blanc ★★ £D
Viognier ★★ £C   Riesling ★★ £D
Recommended Reds:
Pinot Noir ★★☆ £D
Yarraman Estate (Hunter)
Recommended Reds:
Chambourcin Black Cypress ★★ £B

Work in progress!!

Producers under consideration for the next edition
Robert Channon (Granite Belt, Queensland)
Faisan (Orange)
Mistletoe (Hunter Valley)
Ravensworth (Canberra District)

Author's choice

Classic Hunter/Mudgee Reds
Brokenwood   Shiraz Graveyard Vineyard
Brokenwood   Shiraz Mistress Block
Huntington Estate   Cabernet Sauvignon Special Reserve
Huntington Estate   Shiraz Special Reserve
Mcwilliam's Mount Pleasant   Shiraz Maurice O'shea
Mcwilliam's Mount Pleasant   Shiraz Old Hill & Old Paddock
Montrose   Shiraz Black Label
Tyrrell's   Shiraz Vat 9
Tyrrell's   Shiraz 4 Acres

Definitive Hunter/Mudgee Whites
Brokenwood   Sémillon Hunter Valley
Brokenwood   Sémillon Ilr Reserve
Mcwilliam's Mount Pleasant   Chardonnay Maurice O'shea
Mcwilliam's Mount Pleasant   Sémillon Lovedale
Meerea Park   Sémillon Hunter Valley Alexander Munro
Mount View   Sémillon Hunter Valley Reserve
Pepper Tree   Sémillon Hunter Valley Alluvius
Pepper Tree   Sémillon Hunter Valley Alluvius
Andrew Thomas   Sémillon Braemore Hunter Valley
Keith Tulloch   Sémillon Hunter Valley
Tyrrell's   Chardonnay Vat 47
Tyrrell's   Sémillon Vat 1

Other Wines Not To Be Missed
Reds:
Clonakilla   Shiraz Canberra District
Collector   Shiraz Reserve Canberra District
Chalkers Crossing   Cabernet Sauvignon Hilltops
Lowe   Zinfandel Reserve
Meerea Park   Shiraz Alexander Munro
Mount Majura   Tempranillo Shiraz Graciano Canberra District
Philip Shaw   Pinot Noir No. 8
Philip Shaw   Cabernet Sauvignon No. 5
Whites:
Brokenwood   Chardonnay Forest Edge Orange
Clonakilla   Viognier Canberra District
De Bortoli   Botrytis Sémillon Noble One
Helm   Riesling Premium Canberra District
Meerea Park   Viognier

Western Australia

Australia's biggest state is virtually all desert but it does have a cool coastal skirt that runs south from the state capital, Perth, and around the southwestern corner to parts kept cool and damp under the influence of the Southern Ocean. WA contributes only a tiny amount to Australia's total wine production (3 per cent) but by our reckoning accounts for an unequal share of its premium wine. That said some have dropped the quality baton in the race for bigger volumes and healthier profits so care is needed among some of the better known names.

Greater Perth

The **Swan District** (Swan Valley) is the historic heart of Western Australian viticulture. It is extremely hot and dry so unsurprisingly, its trump card is world class fortified liqueur styles of Muscat, Verdelho, Shiraz and Pedro Ximinez, but with varieties such as Verdelho, Chenin Blanc, Chardonnay and Sémillon some surprisingly good whites have been produced too. Serious Verdelhos from the likes of Talijancich and John Kosovich are dry and ageworthy. Houghton dominates production and its ageworthy, bigvolume 'White Burgundy' (now HWB) is the most famous and remarkable wine of the region. Reds, including Shiraz and Cabernet Sauvignon, can be characterful and well-made even if the best wines are likely to include a component from Great Southern or increasingly, Margaret River. A number of small, essentially boutique wineries are scattered over the **Perth Hills** where despite hot, dry summers prospects for balanced whites are improved by vineyard elevation

South-West Australia

Nearly all of Western Australia's premium wines come from this zone and its two most important regions, Margaret River and Great Southern.

Margaret River

The **Margaret River** juts into the Indian Ocean but despite problems of wind and the ravenous local wildlife, especially the birds, its 'founding doctors' (establishing Vasse Felix, MossWood and Cullen in the late 60s and early 70s) were soon followed by Leeuwin Estate, CapeMentelle and others. Wines of remarkably rich, pure, deeply textured fruit from Cabernet Sauvignon and Chardonnay have been produced in the decades since and the region continues to grow apace. The central part of the region, especially Wilyabrup (which has a preponderance of well drained ironstone gravel soils), produces particularly powerful, structured reds; its fruit is highly sought after as a blending component by others. To the north, around Yallingup is slightly cooler but, with similar soils, produces robust reds. To the south, between Margaret River township and Karridale it is significantly cooler; whites are a real strength, reds more sinewy. Sauvignon Blanc and Sémillon (especially combined) and Shiraz are made to a high standard too, the former ranging from quaffers to serious oaked examples. To the north and east of Margaret River, **Geographe** incorporates a large swathe of countryside, stretching from the coast inland. Capel Vale, located on the coastal strip, is the leading winery but up-and-coming inland valleys are also being developed like the Ferguson Valley.

Great Southern

Great Southern, as its name suggests, is an especially large region. **Frankland River** is currently the most planted of five sub-regions, and often excels with Riesling, Chardonnay, Shiraz, Cabernet Sauvignon and Cabernet Franc. Producers include the likes of Alkoomi and Frankland Estate but grapes are also sourced by others based outside the region such as Houghton. **Mount Barker's** potential has long been highlighted by Plantagenet, but others too make fine Shiraz as well as excellent Riesling and Chardonnay. **Porongurup** lies east of Mount Barker while **Albany** and **Denmark**, which can be wetter, reach down to the coast - scattered vineyards can provide marvellous fruit.

Other regions of the SW Australia zone

Between Great Southern and Margaret River even more far-flung vineyards are appearing in the gaps between extensive tracts of forest in three emerging areas, **Blackwood Valley**, **Manjimup** and **Pemberton**. The latter, the most exposed to the Southern Ocean, has already achieved wider recognition thanks to Picardy and Salitage. Smokier Pinot Noir it is surely not possible to find, the distinctive wines being influenced by the effects of the controlled burning of forest fires. Sauvignon Blanc, Chardonnay, Shiraz and the Bordeaux varieties are also successful.

Western Australia vintages

2016 This has turned out to be a trying year in the Margaret River. After a fine summer there were consistent wet periods throughout January, February and March with disease a problem. It will be necessary to purchase selectively, and some fine wines will emerge. Conditions throughout the growing season in the Great Southern regions varied although some more restrained but good reds will emerge as well as fine Riesling.

2015 This was a promising vintage for the Margaret River although yields were down with a poor fruit set after flowering. Late harvest growing conditions were good right up to harvesting. Early ripening whites are good and although reds were effected by rain a longer hang time suggests good potential in many wines. Similar early season growing conditions were seen in the Great Southern but across the growing season conditions were more variable.

2014 Once again, ideal growing conditions have occurred in Margaret River, producing in particular, outstanding Cabernets, but other varietals have done almost as well. In the rest of the region whites have generally fared better than reds but once again it is a vintage in which the utmost confidence can be placed.

2013 Storms in October and November seriously affected flowering and yields are well down this year. Hot and dry weather prevailed in January through March in the Margaret Valley but rains later in March affected the reds. Great Southern, with a similar wether pattern have also produced much better whites than reds.

2012 Another good vintage - a hot dry summer followed a mild winter and spring rains to produce wine of excellent quality. Cabernet and Chardonnay excelled in Margaret River and Great Southern also produced some outstanding wines.

2011 An excellent vintage - Margaret River had a hot, dry summer with the harvest completed early, resulting in excellent Cabernet, with Chardonnay only less so. Great Southern suffered rains in January that led to a little mildew and rot, but dry weather in February and March has led to excellent quality wines being produced in all varietals.

2010 Perfect ripening conditions made for a stellar vintage for reds and whites in Margaret River and Geographe. Further south, white/early ripening varieties also fared very well. Otherwise, weather conditions were less stable with significant rainfall in Great Southern, also SwanValley, which affected later ripening reds. **2009** Margaret River experienced another excellent vintage. Further south, rain during harvest failed to stop play and quality is generally high. **2008** January was warm to hot, but thereafter, temperate

conditions allowed all varieties to walk to ripeness, resulting in very good to outstanding reds and whites, with excellent varietal definition and balance. Classic. **2007** was a vintage that was very hot, very dry and very early. The lack of water and reduced yields weren't disimilar to that felt in the eastern states but without some of the additional blows felt there. **2006** though it was at times very hot, very dry and consequently very early, the region's maritime influence provided respite and temperatures during harvest were generally significantly lower than those in the eastern states. A very successful vintage marked by powerful reds and forward, generously fruited whites. **2005** outstanding with even ripening and good harvest conditions - a good follow-up to the successful **2004** vintage.

A-Z of producers by region

Swan District
Houghton	903
John Kosovitch	904
Talijancich	908

Margaret River
Arlewood	898
Cape Mentelle	899
Cloudburst	900
Cullen	900
Depp Woods	900
Evans & Tate	900
Fire Gully	907
Fraser Gallop	902
Gralyn	902
Higher Plane	903
Juniper	904
Leeuwin Estate	904
McHenry Hohnen Vintners	905
Moss Wood	905
Peccavi	906
Pierro	906
Stella Bella	907
Suckfizzle	907
Umamu	908
Vasse Felix	908
Voyager Estate	909
Woodlands	909
Woodside Valley Estate	909
Woody Nook	910
Xanadu	910

Geographe
Capel Vale	899
Hackersley	902
Willow Bridge	909

Frankland River
Alkoomi	898
Ferngrove Vineyards	901
Frankland Estate	901

Mount Barker
Gilberts	902
Plantagenet	907

Denmark
Harewood Estate	902
Howard Park	903
Rickety Gate	907

Manjimup/Pemberton
Batista	898
Bellarmine	898
Forest Hill	901
Lillian	904
Picardy	906
Salitage	907

Porongurup
Castle Rock Estate	899

Perth
Larry Cherubino	899
Marchand & Burch	904
Millbrook	905

1 Swan District
2 Perth Hills
3 Peel
4 Geographe
5 Margaret River
6 Blackwood Valley
7 Manjimup
8 Pemberton
9 Great Southern
10 Frankland River
11 Mount Barker
12 Porongurup
13 Denmark
14 Albany

Western Australia

Australia

Western Australia vintage chart

	Margaret River Cabernet	Great Southern Shiraz	Margaret River Chardonnay
2016	★★★☆ A	★★★★ A	★★★☆ A
2015	★★★★ A	★★★☆ A	★★★★ A
2014	★★★★★ A	★★★★☆ A	★★★★☆ A
2013	★★★★☆ A	★★★★☆ A	★★★★☆ B
2012	★★/★★★ B	★★★☆ B	★★/★★★ B
2011	★★★★☆ A	★★/★★★ B	★★★★ B
2010	★★/★★★ B	★★/★★★★ B	★★★★☆ B
2009	★★★ B	★★★★☆ B	★★★★ B
2008	★★★ B	★★★☆ B	★★★★ C
2007	★★★★ C	★★★★☆ C	★★★★ C
2006	★★★★☆ B	★★★★ C	★★★★☆ C
2005	★★★★ C	★★★★ C	★★★★☆ C
2004	★★/★★★★ C	★★★★ C	★★★ D
2003	★★★★★ C	★★★☆ D	★★★★★ D
2002	★★★☆ C	★★★★☆ C	★★★★ D
2001	★★★☆ D	★★☆ D	★★★☆ D
2000	★★★★☆ D	★★☆ D	★★★★☆ D

A-Z of producers

Alkoomi (Frankland River) www.alkoomiwines.com.au
This winery in remote Frankland River has now grown to a substantial size (around 80,000 cases) but fruit comes entirely from 82 ha of estate vineyards. Black labels denote the top tier wines. Reds include varietal Cabernet Sauvignon, in a refined rather than weighty style, and a Shiraz/Viognier with a more floral component than some but a spicy berry fruit intensity. Jarrah, a premium version of Shiraz from the oldest vines, can have real weight and savoury depth. Equally impressive is another premium red, Blackbutt, a blend of Cabernet Sauvignon, Cabernet Franc, Malbec and Merlot which is structured and intense; it needs 4 or 5 years' ageing. The top white , Wandoo, is unusual in being 100% Sémillon and is partially oak fermented. Others include a fresh and zesty Sauvignon Blanc (sometimes blended with Sémillon), tight and well-structured Chardonnay and a characteristically fine and complex Great Southern Riesling that becomes toasty with age. Fruit-driven basics appear under the White Label range: Shiraz, Cabernet/Merlot, Sauvignon Blanc and unwooded Chardonnay.

Recommended Reds:
Blackbutt Frankland River ★★★☆ £E
Jarrah Shiraz Frankland River ★★★ £D
Cabernet Sauvignon Frankland River ★★ £C
Shiraz/Viognier Frankland River ★★ £C

Recommended Whites:
Wandoo Sémillon Frankland River ★★★ £D
Riesling Frankland River ★★★ £C
Chardonnay Frankland River ★★ £C
Sauvignon Blanc Frankland River ★☆ £B

Arlewood (Margaret River) www.arlewood.com.au
This small Margaret River operation started out making wines from 15 ha of estate vineyards in Wilyabrup. Then, wines were made under contract by Juniper Estate with additional help from Ian Bell

(ex MOSS WOOD). In 2008, following the sale of the vineyard to Vasse Felix and the acquisition of the former Hesperos vineyard, the business transferred lock, stock and barrel to Witchcliffe, 10km south of Margaret River. Here, the wines are now made in-house by Bill Crappsley, who is also a partner. Whites have good breadth and flavour but could still use a little more definition. Sémillon is partly barrique-fermented and aged in both new and used French oak. Chardonnay, which spends a year in barriques (50% new) is full and intense if missing the refinement for a higher rating. A small amount of a Reserve is also made. Reds show good depth and intensity but should be given 5-6 years' age. The Cabernet Sauvignon Reserve which spends 2 years in oak then a further 2 years in bottle before release is the top red. It should be drunk with 10 years' age. New but not tasted is flagship red La Bratta, a Merlot dominated red with Malbec and Cabernet Sauvignon.

Recommended Reds:
Cabernet Sauvignon ★★★★ £F   Shiraz ★★★ £C
Cabernet Sauvignon/Merlot ★★★ £C

Recommended Whites:
Chardonnay ★★★ £E   Sémillon ★★☆ £D
Sauvignon Blanc/Sémillon ★★ £C

Batista (Manjimup)
Bob Peruche inherited his parent's farm perched high on a ridge in Middlesex, Manjimup, overlooking the Warren Valley. Though his father had grown vines, Peruche grubbed them up. In 1988, just five years later, Peruche was approached by PICARDY's Bill Pannell for advice about planting on virgin soil nearby. So it was that Peruche came to plant Smithbrook Estate's vineyard, a joint venture between Pannell and investors in Burgundy's Pousse d'Or. Inevitably, Peruche was introduced to the great Pinot Noirs of Burgundy and himself became smitten by what he calls Pinot Noir's "smell of chook sheds and cow yards," planting his own vines in 1993. Bucking prevailing trends, Peruche predominantly planted the local upright and droopy clones of Pinot Noir (as well as some Bernard/Dijon clones). Describing himself as "just a farmer," the winery, which is housed in a barn, is as unfancy as Peruche's approach to winemaking – "I pick it, I crush it, I ferment it, settle it, taste for tannin and filter." His sensual Pinot Noirs have no shortage of texture or complexity. The Selection, two barrels of the best bottles, combines terrific concentration with graceful balance, length and layer. Both it and the regular cuvée benefit from two to three years in bottle and, in top vintages, can build in complexity for a decade or more. Peruche also grows Merlot, Shiraz, Cabernet Franc and Cabernet Sauvignon. (SA)

Recommended Reds:
Pinot Noir Selection ★★★★☆ £F   Pinot Noir ★★★★ £E

Bellarmine (Pemberton) www.bellarmine.com.au
The 20 ha Bellarmine vineyard was planted in 2000 by German doctor, Dr Willi Schumacher and his wife Gudrun Schumacher. The Schumachers remain resident in Bremerhavn, Germany, leaving winemaking and the overall management of the winery in the capable hands of Dr Di Miller, who has made the wines since the first vintage in 2004. Miller, a former veterinarian, only started making wines in 1999 but it would seem both she and the vineyard are precocious since Bellarmine's Rieslings are, without question, Pemberton's best and among Western Australia's best. They may be overseas, but the Schumacher's influence is readily apparent in the style of Rieslings produced. Bellarmine are at the vanguard of Australia's niche sweet Riesling movement and, in addition to a searingly fresh, classic Australian bone dry Riesling (labelled Dry), the

range features a superbly balanced, deliciously fruity and aromatic Kabinett style (simply labelled Riesling) and a very tight, pure and focused honey-tinged Auslese, each mineral to the core. Evidently the region's gravel laterite soils combined with an elevated site (at 220m) located only 50km from the chilly Great Southern Ocean, suit the variety well. Though the (very reasonably priced) Rieslings are the out and out stars, the Sauvignon Blanc shows good regional typicity (steely grapefruit), while the elegant Chardonnay will appeal to Riesling lovers with its citric backbone, delicately fleshed out with stone fruits and savoury lees. Aside from the meaty, peppery Shiraz, a Petit Verdot and Pinot Noir are a little one dimensional as yet - sappy with a sweet core of fruit. No doubt greater depth and layer will come with vine age. (SA)

Recommended Reds:

Shiraz ★★ £D Petit Verdot ★☆ £D Pinot Noir ★ £D

Recommended Whites:

Riesling ★★★★ £D Riesling Auslese ★★★★ £D
Riesling Dry ★★★☆ £D Chardonnay ★★ £D
Sauvignon Blanc ★★ £C

❀ **Cape Mentelle (Margaret River)** *www.capementelle.com.au*
Cape Mentelle has a lower profile than sister winery CLOUDY BAY inNew Zealand but has a similar reputation for quality thanks to the effortsof founder David Hohnen, who ran operations until 2003 when he was succeeded by the widely respected Dr Tony Jordan, who himself moved on in 2008. A young winemaking team headed by Rob Mann, Jack Mann's grandson, has continued to win plaudits for the wines, made from some of the region's oldest vines. Partially oaked, the Sémillon/Sauvignon Blanc is brights, zesty and long with subtle oak influence; tight on release it benefits from a year in bottle. A single-vineyard selection, Wallcliffe, is from the same grapes (but with more Sauvignon) but, barrel-fermented with natural yeasts vinified in French oak shows much greater complexity, texture and structure. Chardonnay is powerful and complex, in recent years, leaner with more finesse. Among the reds Cabernet/Merlot from Trinders Vineyard has good depth, breadth and intensity allied to a very ripe dark berry fruit character in warm vintages. Better still is a Cabernet Sauvignon deserving of at least 6–7 years' age. Intense and concentrated with well-judged oak, the wine shows an impressive purity of dark berry fruit complexity and length of flavour. Again, under Mann, the style shows greater lift and finesse. Dark fruits and black pepper characterise the Shiraz, which gets limited new oak, predominantly French. One of Margaret River's best examples of the variety, it has the extra depth of fruit and gravitas to its tannin structure that derives from old vine fruit. A rare Australia example of Zinfandel is a classic of the variety: full, brambly and with not inconsiderable alcohol. Available locally are Georgiana, an unoaked blend from a mix of Chardonnay, Sauvignon Blanc, Chenin and Sémillon, and Marmaduke, from mostly Shiraz, Mourvèdre and Grenache. Both are intended for fruity, early drinking.

Recommended Reds:

Cabernet Sauvignon★★★★☆ £E
Cabernet/Merlot Trinders★★★ £D
Shiraz★★★☆ £D Zinfandel★★★☆ £D

Recommended Whites:

Chardonnay ★★★★ £D Wallcliffe ★★★☆ £E
Sémillon/Sauvignon Blanc ★★★ £C

Capel Vale (Geographe) *www.capelvale.com*
An extensive range of reds and whites is produced at this winery to the north of the Margaret River at Geographe. Production is entirely

from 220 ha of estate vineyards but sources include the company's sizeable holdings in Margaret River, Mount Barker and Pemberton as well as Geographe. The top Single Vineyard and Regional label wines can be very good and for the most part not excessively priced for the quality. Particularly good are two wines from Whispering Hill (Mount Barker), a taut Riesling intense, deep and very well structured, not overly subtle or refined but with super toast, smoke and lime flavour and character while the Shiraz is deep fruited but earthy and peppery too. Though not tasted, the Margaret River single vineyard Cabernet Sauvignon, The Scholar, has received rave reviews of which Pratten is very proud. Pungent, mineral Pemberton Sauvignon Blanc and Riesling show fine regional typicity. Of the regular Capel Vale Debut range wines, the Verdelho is very well crafted.

Recommended Reds:

Shiraz Whispering Hill Mount Barker ★★★★ £F

Recommended Whites:

Riesling Whispering Hill ★★★ £E
Sauvignon Blanc Sémillon Pemberton ★★ £B
Verdelho ★★ £B

Recommended Rosés:

Sparkling Cuvée Rosé ★★ £E

Castle Rock Estate (Porongurup) *www.castlerockestate.com.au*
Angelo and Wendy Diletti acquired Castle Rock Estate in 1981, planting their first vines in 1983. Then aged six, their son Robert Diletti helped plant the cool, elevated vineyard on the northeast face of the Porongurup mountain range. Originally, the wines were made at ALKOOMI where, following his graduation from winemaking at Charles Sturt University, Robert was Assistant Winemaker from 1999 to 2000. Since then, Castle Rock wines have been made on site by Robert and Castle Rock's reputation has soared. Dry Riesling is the forte, while Pinot Noir shows great potential. Meticulous attention to detail in the vineyard and minimal intervention at the gravity-fed winery ensure that both varieties reflect their cool climate origins. The classic, dry Riesling is scintillatingly mineral, with great concentration, line and length. It rewards keeping at least two years in bottle and will continue to build in complexity for another decade. New is A & W Riesling (not tasted) an off-dry style, while Turret is a floral, late harvest Riesling made in a relatively approachable style. The Pinot Noir is precise and intense with an excellent purity of pretty red fruits. Chardonnay, Cabernet Sauvignon/Merlot, Liqueur Muscat and a sparkling Pinot Noir, Della, are also made. (SA)

Recommended Reds:

Pinot Noir ★★★ £D

Recommended Whites:

Riesling ★★★★ £D Riesling Turret ★★☆ £C

Larry Cherubino (Great Southern) *www.larrycherubino.com*
Larry Cherubino honed his technical winemaking skills at HARDYS (Tintara) in South Australia before joining its famous Western Australian sister brand HOUGHTON as Chief Winemaker in 1998 at the tender age of 28. Under his tenure, Houghton's medal tally leapt, as did the quality of the red wines in particular. Cherubino left in 2003 to take up various consultancy roles at home and abroad but, since 2005, the apple of his eye has been his own label which he established with his partner Edwina Egerton-Warburton. Warburton's parents own the 85 ha Acacia vineyard in Frankland River from which Cherubino sources fruit. However, Cherubino sources fruit widely using the intimate knowledge of Western

Western Australia

Australia's vineyards that he acquired while at Houghton to great effect: the range is elegant and accomplished from top to bottom. Good value too. The stylishly packaged "entry level" Ad Hoc label puts the fun into sophisticated, while the weightier single site The Yard and flagship Cherubino labels highlight regional strengths. Rieslings are a stand out, not least because they reveal Cherubino's dexterity as a winemaker. For the Ad Hoc Wallflower Riesling, Cherubino does not want an austere wine to put off consumers. Taking a leaf out of German winemakers' books, he uses no sulphur at the press and an element of press juice to soften the wine's texture. On the other hand, though judicious lees stirring lends texture, linear, bone dry and mineral, Cherubino Porongurup Riesling is a terrific expression of this particularly cool Great Southern sub-region. Cherubino also makes An Ad Hoc Pinot Noir and sparkling wine and Cabernet Sauvignons under his Cherubino and The Yard labels (not tasted). (SA)

Recommended Reds:
Shiraz Cherubino Frankland River ★★★☆ £F

Recommended Whites:
Riesling Cherubino Porongurup ★★★★ £D
Riesling Cherubino great Southern ★★★★ £D
Riesling The Yard Whispering Hill Vineyard ★★★☆ £C
Sauvignon Blanc Cherubino Pemberton ★★★ £D
Chardonnay Ad Hoc Hen & Chicken ★★★ £C
Riesling Ad Hoc The Wallflower ★★☆ £C
Sémillon/Sauvignon Ad Hoc Strawman ★★ £C

>> Cloudburst (Margaret River) www.cloudburstwine.com
The Berliner family make three quite extraordinary wines at this Margaret River property. By Australian standards the wines are not bargains, however by contrast with some premium wines from California and elsewhere they are not excessive. The vineyards are all dry-farmed, resulting in deep rooting vines and viticulture is biodynamic. With naturally low vine vigour through close planting the vineyards produce low yields of intensely flavoured grapes. Perhaps the most intriguing of the trio is the Malbec. There are few examples in Australia and one would have to argue this is the best. It has a tremendous spicy, tobacco quality with structured but very supple tannins and great intensity and balance. For all the quality of the Malbec, the Cabernet Sauvignon and Chardonnay have just a touch more depth and dimension. The Cabernet Sauvignon is one of the great examples from the Margaret River. There is a balance of dark berry fruits, blackcurrants, and a cedar quality, all of which are balanced by sturdy but very well rounded tannins. It's also worth noting that while alcohol levels are generally going higher and higher in Australia both these reds tend to weigh in at just over 13%. That fresh edge certainly adds to their appeal. Finally, while one wouldn't say it's a spectacular value the Chardonnay is the best value of these three. Initially restrained and elegant there is an intense citrus quality with very well judged oak. (DM)

Recommended Reds:
Cabernet Sauvignon Cloudburst ★★★★★ £H
Malbec Cloudburst ★★★★☆ £H

Recommended Whites:
Chardonnay Cloudburst ★★★★★ £G

✿ Cullen (Margaret River) www.cullenwines.com.au
The Cullen's Margaret River winery has a long tradition of excellence and now produces around 20,000 cases per year from 28ha of well-established estate vineyards (certified organic). Made by Vanya Cullen, the wines are marked by their finesse, superior structure and complexity, putting Cullen in a different class to most of its neighbours. Certified biodynamic since 2004. With effect from the 2006 vintage, the Chardonnay has been named Kevin John after Vanya Cullen's late father. Now widely recognised as among Australia's best, utilising natural yeasts and whole-bunch pressing, it is a magnificently crafted white full of intense, pure citrus fruit and has unmistakable class and great length. With effect from the 2007 vintage, Cullen make two single vineyard Sémillon Sauvignon blends from Cullen Vineyard and Mangan Vineyard. Because production is now focused on biodynamic wine, Cullen have dropped the Ellen Bussell range, fruit for which was sourced from a vineyard 8km south. Instead, Margaret River Red and Margaret River White are made from Cullen or Mangan vineyard fruit which does not make the cut for the flagship wine. The Cabernet Sauvignon/Merlot, usually around two-thirds Cabernet Sauvignon with up to 10% of Cabernet Franc, is now named in honour of Di Cullen who did so much to establish the Cullen reputation. Of top Bordeaux classed growth quality it sets the standard for the Margaret River. Its superb fruit is highlighted by outstanding breadth, depth and structure. It always deserves at least 5 years' ageing. A powerful, somewhat backward new red blend, Mangan, is named for a vineyard owned by Vanya's brother Rick and his wife and is very good. Unusually it comes from Malbec, Petit Verdot and Merlot.

Recommended Reds:
Cabernet Sauvignon/Merlot Diana Madeline ★★★★★ £F
Mangan ★★★ £E   Margaret River Red ★★ £D

Recommended Whites:
Chardonnay Kevin John ★★★★★ £F
Sauvignon Blanc/Sémillon Cullen Vineyard ★★★★ £D
Sauvignon Blanc/Sémillon Mangan Vineyard ★★★☆ £D
Margaret River White ★☆ £D

>> Deep Woods (Margaret River) www.deepwoods.com.au
This winery located in the northern stretches of the Margaret River is under the same ownership as MILLBROOK (Perth Hills), Smithbrook (Pemberton) and LAKES FOLLY (Hunter Valley). It is most notable for the quality of its Cabernet Sauvignon and Bordeaux based reds. As well as the two Grand Selection Cabernets and the attractively priced Cabernet Merlot reviewed below the winery also makes a well-regarded Cabernet Sauvignon Reserve. Other wines to consider are Chardonnay and Nebbiolo Reserves as well as Sauvignon Blanc, Verdelho and Shiraz. There is also an easy drinking trio of red, white and rosé, Ebony, Ivory and Harmony. The Cabernet Merlot is a great buy, with a tiny proportion of Malbec adding to the blend. Crucially for quality all vineyard parcels are vinified separately and the wine offers a very approachable combination of red and black fruits, a subtle hint of cedar and restrained oak. The two top reds are of a different order, very dense, concentrated and intense. The richly textured Yallingup comes from two sites and is aged for 16 months in small oak, the Wilyabrup comes from a 40 year old single vineyard block and aged for a little less with elegant red fruits and tremendous intensity. Both will develop in bottle for a decade and more. (DM)

Recommended Reds:
Cabernet Sauvignon Wilyabrup Grand Selection ★★★★★ £F
Cabernet Sauvignon Yallingup Grand Selection ★★★★★ £F
Cabernet Sauvignon Merlot ★★★ £C

Evans & Tate (Margaret River) www.evansandtate.com.au
This is now a very substantial operation with most of its

development in the Margaret River, though it was the original producer of quality Shiraz in the very hot Swan Valley. Now purchased by McWilliams the quality of the wines continues to be very good. Of an extensive Margaret River collection, Chardonnay is much improved. Sauvignon Blanc has both grassy and riper notes but can be a bit lean, while Cabernet/Merlot is very flavoursome with very ripe berryish fruit and Shiraz is similarly very ripe with a spicy intensity. The best wines come from the 26 ha Redbrook vineyard in the Wilyabrup Valley sub-region. Chardonnay is crafted using an array of Burgundian techniques but is surprisingly restrained, recalling the quality of mid-90s Margaret River efforts. Shiraz is spicy and intense, one of the best of this variety in the region. Redbrook Cabernet Sauvignon is also impressive and ageworthy.

Recommended Reds:
Cabernet Sauvignon Redbrook ★★★★ £E
Shiraz Redbrook ★★★ £E
Recommended Whites:
Chardonnay Redbrook ★★★ £E Chardonnay Margaret River ★★★ £C
Sauvignon Blanc Margaret River ★★ £C

Ferngrove (Frankland River) *www.ferngrove.com.au*
Murray Burton relinquished his family's beef and dairy farming heritage to switch to grape growing and wine production. This is now a thriving, expanding operation with extensive vineyards. The range has recently been re-structured and, for Frankland River labelled wines, from top to bottom, comprises flagship The Stirlings, the Orchid range, Frankland River and impressive entry level Symbols labels. Leaping Lizard wines include more widely sourced fruit and sport a generic Western Australia label; given the minsicule difference in price point, the Symbols wines are much the better buy, showing greater concentration and character. If there's good value for money in the home grown regular varietals and dual-variety blends, the superior Orchid bottling combine concentration and style. Quite striking is Orchid King Malbec, dark and glossy compared with the more structured, herbal Orchid Majestic Cabernet. Orchid Dragon Shiraz is rich with dense layers. The Stirlings, a blend of finest grapes (latterly Shiraz and Cabernet) is not made every year; is deep and structured it rewards at least 5 years in bottle. Orchid whites are bright fruited with ample concentration. Cossack Riesling, which historically comes from the best five blocks, can age very well if changes in tack (e.g. experimentation with solids) have affected its tight linear style in some vintages. Though flavoursome with ripe stone fruits, Diamond Chardonnay is well structured with good balancing acidity and well integrated oak.

Ferngrove Vineyards
Recommended Reds:
The Stirlings ★★☆ £C Shiraz Orchid Dragon ★★★ £C
Shiraz ★★ £B Shiraz/Viognier Symbols ★★ £B
Malbec Orchid King ★★★ £C Merlot ★ £B
Cabernet Sauvignon Orchid Majestic ★★★ £C
Cabernet/ Merlot Symbols ★★☆ £B
Recommended Whites:
Sémillon/Sauvignon Blanc Symbols ★★ £B
Sauvignon Blanc ★ £B Riesling Orchid Cossack ★★★☆ £B
Chardonnay Orchid Diamond ★★☆ £B Chardonnay ★ £B
Leaping Lizard
Recommended Reds:
Cabernet/Merlot ★★ £B
Recommended Whites:
Sémillon/Sauvignon Blanc ★★ £B

Forest Hill (Denmark) *www.foresthillwines.com.au*
The Great Southern region's first experimental vines - two hectares of Riesling and Cabernet Sauvignon - were planted at Forest Hill's Mount Barker vineyard in 1965. Originally, the fruit was processed by Houghton and, from 1989, at Vasse Felix following the property's acquisition by the Holmes a Court family. In 1996, Perth broker Tim Lyons bought a share in the vineyard and purchased it outright in 1998. Lyons' substantial investment, notably a state-of-the-art winery, cellar door facility/restaurant, has put Forest Hill firmly on the map, as has his talented winemaking team. Michael Ng is now the head winemaker, following on from Larry Cherubino and Clémence Haselgrove. The flagship Block Series is concentrated, yet poised, while the naturally fermented Block 1 Riesling from the original dry grown vines is striking in its chiselled minerality. Block 5 Cabernet Sauvignon goes from strength to strength. The Estate range is also elegant and well made. (Highbury Fields Great Southern Range not tasted). (SA)
Block Series
Recommended Reds:
Shiraz Block 9 ★★★★ £E Cabernet Sauvignon Block 5 ★★★★ £E
Recommended Whites:
Riesling Block 1 ★★★★ £D Chardonnay Block 8 ★★★☆ £D
Estate Range
Recommended Reds:
Shiraz ★★★ £B Cabernet Sauvignon ★★★ £B
Recommended Whites:
Chardonnay ★★★£B Riesling ★★☆ £B

Frankland Estate (Frankland River) *www.franklandestate.com.au*
The vineyards of Frankland Estate, established in 1988, are but a small part of a large Merino sheep farming property located in Frankland River sub-region on the western side of Great Southern. Production has increased to 15,000 cases a year and quality is very good, especially for the Rieslings; among the region's best . Great store is placed on managing the vineyards, including consultancy from expert Richard Smart. The flagship red is Olmo's Reward, a blend of mostly Merlot and Cabernet Franc (but also a little Malbec, Cabernet Sauvignon and Petit Verdot). It is sleek and stylish with ripe, dark, spicy fruit, supple and velvety tannin and good length. While tempting when young, it is best with 10 years' age. The estate-sourced Isolation Ridge wines (certified Western Australia organic with effect from the 2010 vintage), comprising Chardonnay, Riesling, Cabernet Sauvignon and Shiraz, are also impressive. The Riesling stands out with its tight, apple and mineral fruit and has the structure for real ageing. Shiraz is full of black pepper and attractive, brambly fruit, the Cabernet marked by an intense, small berry fruit character. There are now two single vineyard Rieslings, the linear Netley Road and the more forward/generous Poison Hill from white clay soils. The Rocky Gully label includes up-front flavoursome Riesling, cool supple Shiraz/Viognier, and Cabernets - all made from contract-grown fruit. Experimentation with longer ferments in *foudre* has resulted in a kabinett style Riesling Smith Cullam (not tasted), which is made from select low yielding vines within the Isolation Ridge vineyard. This has now been joined by a Smith Cullam Shiraz Cabernet.
Frankland Estate
Recommended Reds:
Olmo's Reward ★★★★ £D Shiraz Isolation Ridge ★★★ £C
Cabernet Sauvignon Isolation Ridge ★★ £C
Recommended Whites:
Riesling Isolation Ridge ★★★★ £C

Western Australia

Riesling Netley Road ★★★★ £C
Riesling Poison Hill ★★★★ £C Chardonnay Isolation Ridge ★★ £C
Rocky Gully
Recommended Reds:
Shiraz/Viognier ★★ £C
Recommended Whites:
Riesling Frankland River ★ £B

Fraser Gallop (Margaret River) *www.frasergallopestate.com.au*
Conceived in 1998, Fraser Gallop Estate is a relatively new name in
Margaret River but founder Nigel Gallop, a businessman, has made
astute choices in terms of lead varieties, site and winemaker (Clive
Otto, ex-VASSE FELIX). The dry-farmed vineyard on Wilyabrup's
renowned gravelly loams is planted to17 acres of Cabernet
Sauvignon (the Houghton clone), one acre of Merlot, one acre of
Petit Verdot, one acre of Cabernet Franc and one acre of Malbec, 18
acres of Chardonnay (Gin Gin clone) and seven acres of Sémillon.
As of 2008, the wines have been made on site at the no expense
spared, gravity-fed winery. Critical acclaim has been swift, especially
for the finely wrought, perfumed reds (Cabernet Sauvignon and
Cabernet Merlot) and restrained Chardonnay. The estate's Sémillon
is blended with Sauvignon Blanc sourced from Karridale, which is
cooler. The partially barrel fermented Sémillon Sauvignon Blanc is
well made if, perhaps, a little too correct. More exciting is Parterre,
an ambitious (oak and steel) barrel fermented and aged Sémillon
Sauvignon Blanc which tips its cap at Bordeaux (Otto has worked
vintage at Domaine de CHEVALIER). First produced in 2009, natural
yeasts and lees ageing bring greater complexity. With more vine
age, the whole range looks set to move up another gear. Now a
Parterre Cabernet Sauvignon with the addition of small amounts
of Merlot, Petit Verdot and Malbec has joined the rank of premium
wine from this estate. (SA)
Recommended Reds:
Cabernet Sauvignon ★★★☆ £E Cabernet Merlot ★★★ £D
Recommended Whites:
Sémillon/Sauvignon Blanc Parterre ★★★☆ £E
Sémillon/Sauvignon Blanc ★★ £C Chardonnay ★★★☆ £E

Gilberts (Mount Barker) *www.gilbertwines.com.au*
Traditionally a stone-fruit farmer, Jim Gilbert planted vines in 1985
and the benefit of nearly 30 years' maturity certainly shows. The
wines are made at the nearby PLANTAGENET winery as there are
no winemaking facilities on the estate. The range is fairly small (by
WA standards!). Riesling has nice flowery fruit with good length
and acidity, if a little lean. Chardonnay sees 8 months in French oak
and has good richness and nicely integrated wood that allows the
citrus flavours to come through. The 3 Devils Shiraz, from 16- and
17 - year-old vines, has good spiciness and soft tannins. The Reserve
Shiraz, from 29-year-old vines, sees 20 months in oak (30% new)
and is a different proposition. With big, tarry but not jammy Shiraz
fruit and spice and pepper on the palate, it is a wine of finesse
and complexity. A new, 3 Lads range has just started with a 2012
Cabernet Sauvignon, but this has not been tasted.
Recommended Reds:
Shiraz Reserve ★★★★ £D Shiraz 3 Devils ★★ £C
Recommended Whites:
Chardonnay ★★★ £D Riesling ★★ £C

Gralyn Estate (Margaret River) *www.gralyn.com.au*
Boutique winery in the Margaret River area with a reputation in
inverse proportion to its size – 2,500 cases cover 15 different wines

so quantities are generally tiny.Whites include an oaked naturally
fermented Chardonnay, elegant with good length. There's also a
fairly intense medium-sweet Late Harvest Riesling (15% Sémillon)
with a backbone of acidity. Reds are better. The stars include Reserve
Shiraz which has real elegance and a lot of finesse with sweet oak
(100% new, mostly French) on the finish. Cabernet Shiraz is two-
thirds Cabernet Sauvignon, one-third Shiraz – a deep and unctuous
wine with a good balance between fruit and acidity. The depth of
the Shiraz is perfectly matched by the red berry fruit of the Cabernet
on the mid-palate. Cabernet Sauvignon is a pure varietal matured
for 20 months in new, predominantly French oak and shows the
full intensity of the 30-year-old vines with smooth and intense
ripe berry flavours and great depth and complexity on the finish.
It is approachable relatively young but will age well. Fortified and
dessert wines are less exciting.
Recommended Reds:
Cabernet Sauvignon ★★★★★ £G Shiraz Reserve ★★★★ £G
Recommended Whites:
Chardonnay ★★ £F Riesling Late Harvest ★★ £D

Hackersley (Geographe) *www.hackersley.com.au*
Jeff Ovens' dream vineyard in the Ferguson Valley came into
existence in 1998 and has gone from strength to strength ever
since. The bulk of the fruit from 9 ha is sold under contract but the
best is kept for 6 varietals produced under the Hackersley label.
Whites show good intensity of fruit – gooseberry in the Sauvignon
(if subdued by some residual sweetness), delicate perfumed rosé
petal in an extremely well-balanced Sémillon, and good pungency
in Verdelho. This has a slightly peppermint taste together with a
touch of saltiness and good persistence, making it an ideal partner
for seafood (especially the great WA seafood). The reds show a great
deal of finesse, particularly the Merlot, which is smooth, rich and
deeply flavoured with red berry fruits. Cabernet Sauvignon is a little
more one-dimensional, but Shiraz has nice tar on the palate and
delivers full ripeness and freshness without being jammy. Given the
youthfulness of the vines, this is a remarkable achievement. This
winery is definitely going places. (NB)
Recommended Reds:
Merlot★★★★ £E Shiraz★★★ £C Cabernet Sauvignon★ £C
Recommended Whites:
Verdelho ★★★ £C Sémillon ★★ £C Sauvignon Blanc ★ £C

✿ **Harewood Estate (Denmark)** *www.harewoodestate.com.au*
James Kellie has set the Great Southern alight like no one else since
his first vintage in 04. Previously the fruit here was sold to the likes
of HOWARD PARK where Kellie formerly worked. There is excellent
quality across the range and that particularly remarkable quality/
price ratio (especially in Chardonnay and Cabernet Sauvignon)
that WA can do like nowhere else on the planet. The fruit comes
from estate vineyards (Chardonnay) or is contract grown. The
Cabernet Sauvignon has the class and purity of good Bordeaux
and a certain oomph besides, easily out doing comparably priced
wines for quality. Arguably even better, Shiraz from Mt Barker and
Frankland River shows a fine minerality running through its lush
pure fruited style. Judicious use of oak for the Sauvignon/Sémillon
Reserve makes for a food friendly wine, with an attractive sweet
herbaceousness. Riesling from different sub-regions depending on
vintage is fine, fresh and floral, its bright citrus acidity sometimes
balanced by a deft touch of residual sugar. A significant proportion
of the fruit is currently sold off.

Recommended Reds:
Cabernet Sauvignon Estate Reserve ★★★★ £D
Shiraz Estate ★★★★ £D
Shiraz/Cabernet Great Southern ★★★★ £C
Recommended Whites:
Chardonnay Estate ★★★☆ £D
Sauvignon Blanc/Sémillon Estate Reserve ★★★ £D
Sauvignon Blanc/Sémillon Estate ★★☆ £C Riesling Denmark ★★ £C

Higher Plane (Margaret River) *www.higherplanewines.com.au*
A small (7 ha), very promising new vineyard established in 1997 and, in 2006, acquired by the owners of JUNIPER ESTATE; Mark Messenger makes the wines of both. While Juniper Estate is located in Wilyabrup, Higher Plane is in southern Margaret River. Planting is relatively dense by Australian standards and the low yields are reflected in the wines. Early releases are very good, particularly the classic Margaret River styles. Chardonnay Reserve has excellent fruit and real verve, while the Cabernet Sauvignon is intense and concentrated with a Bordeaux-like complexity. The top red Bordeaux styled blend The Messenger adds a further dimension. Other reds include a varietal Merlot which is a touch more herbaceous yet with ripe tannins. (DM)
Recommended Reds:
The Messenger ★★★★☆ £F
Cabernet Sauvignon ★★★★ £E
Cabernet Merlot ★★★ £C
Merlot ★★★ £D
Recommended Whites:
Chardonnay Reserve ★★★★ £E
Chardonnay Forest Grove ★★★ £C

Houghton (Swan District) *www.houghton-wines.com.au*
One of the region's biggest operations though, in tune with the times, it is slimming down. Nonetheless, the range is considerable, with fruit sourced throughout the vinegrowing areas of the state. The flagship is the remarkable Jack Mann red, a dense, powerful and sometimes oaky Cabernet Sauvignon, latterly sourced just from Frankland River. It demands 5 or 6 years' ageing to even hint of its best. Regional wines, labelled Houghton Wisdom or Crofters from Frankland River, Pemberton and Margaret River are also impressive. A well structured premium Gladstones version of Margaret River Cabernet Sauvignon is also produced but difficult to find outside of Australia. The more basic Classic range is one of the most successful and impressive of Australia's many volume brands. White Classic is of variable composition but generally includes Chenin Blanc, Muscadelle and Verdelho, it is almost unique among such wines in that it will age well. In addition to a persistent and intense, ripe fruit character it has depth and structure.
Recommended Reds:
Jack Mann Cabernet Sauvignon ★★★★☆ £G
Gladstones Cabernet ★★★★ £F
Shiraz Crofters Frankland River ★★★ £D
Cabernet Sauvignon Wisdom Margaret River ★★ £D
Recommended Whites:
Chardonnay Crofters Pemberton and Margaret River ★★ £C
Sauvignon Blanc Pemberton ★★ £C White Classic ★★ £B

❀ Howard Park (Denmark) *www.burchfamilywines.com.au*
Barely more than a decade ago, this substantial operation with wineries in Denmark in the Great Southern and at Margaret River was a small, high quality label with just a Riesling and Cabernet-

based red produced in small quantities by John Wade while he was winemaker at PLANTAGENET. There are now over 100 ha of estate vineyards including 63.6 ha in Margaret River (the Leston vineyard) and, as of 2004, their very own Great Southern vineyard (the Scotsdale vineyard) in the Porongurups range foothills. At 200 to 380m above sea level, the grandstand parcel is one of the highest vineyards in Western Australia and, farmed organically from the off, promises to yield some exciting fruit. Riesling from elevated parcels found its way into the 2009 vintage for the first time. The two labels are Howard Park and Madfish. The top wines are labelled simply Howard Park. Riesling is a superb, complex, structured and very ageworthy example of the variety, one of the best produced in Western Australia. It has recently been joined by, the Reserve from Gibraltar Rock's biodynamic vineyard in the Porongurups, which Howard Park are now leasing. Abercrombie, The Cabernet Sauvignon is sourced from Margaret River, Pemberton and Denmark. Dense, powerful and profound it remains one of Australia's great reds and is enjoying a welcome return to form. In particular from the 2008 vintage, a vibrating sorting table and small batch fermenters purchased for MARCHAND & BURCH, the Burch's joint venture project with Burgundy's Pascal Marchand, has resulted in more refined tannins and greater lift/perfume. Chardonnay is in a restrained, tight and very structured style, though influenced by the Marchand & Burch project, the use of more solids brings more texture and complexity. Backward when young it will evolve well with age. A Sauvignon Blanc is tight and grassy. Also under the Howard Park range are impressive region-specific Shiraz and Cabernet Sauvignon. The Scotsdale pair are produced from Great Southern while the Leston wines are from Margaret River. The Madfish label offers wines with immediate fruit character and appeal from widely sourced grapes. They are generally well-priced and drink well on release. Though still fruit focused compared with the Howard Park wines, two new, higher Madfish tiers, Sideways, reflecting fruit sourced from Margaret River and Grandstand, reflecting fruit sourced from Great Southern, show greater concentration and structure and are well worth seeking out. There are some Madfish sparkling wines, too.
Howard Park
Recommended Reds:
Cabernet Sauvignon Abercromie ★★★★☆ £F
Cabernet Sauvignon Scotsdale ★★★ £D
Cabernet Sauvignon Leston ★★★ £D Shiraz Scotsdale ★★★ £D
Shiraz Leston ★★★ £D
Recommended Whites:
Riesling Porongurup ★★★★☆ £D Riesling ★★★★ £D
Chardonnay ★★★☆ £D Sauvignon Blanc ★★☆ £C
Madfish
Recommended Reds:
Cabernet Sauvignon Merlot Sideways ★★ £C
Cabernet Sauvignon/Merlot ★ £B Pinot Noir Grandstand ★★ £C
Pinot Noir ★ £B Shiraz Grandstand ★★ £C
Recommended Whites:
Chardonnay Sideways ★★☆ £C Chardonnay Unwooded ★ £B
Sauvignon Blanc/Sémillon Sideways ★★☆ £C
Sauvignon Blanc/Sémillon ★★ £B
Sauvignon Blanc Grandstand ★★ £C
Riesling Grandstand ★★☆ £C Riesling ★★ £B
Riesling Late Harvest ★ £B

Wine behind the label

Western Australia

>> Juniper (Margaret River) www.juniperestate.com.au

Juniper is under the same ownership as the HIGHER PLANE winery. It has recently been renamed Juniper, Margaret River. Located in the centre of the region close to the coast, near neighbours are CULLEN and VASSE FELIX. The vineyard is planted on gravelly loam soils over clay subsoil. Drland viticulture is practiced and the vineyard is naturally low yielding, less than 3 tons per acre, pruning and harvesting are by hand. The wines are divided into two distinct labels. Crossings are generally very good value wines produced from both estate and other sites. Tempranillo and a white Fiano are also made and labelled Small Batch. Both are again well priced (£C). Crossing Semillon Sauvignon Blanc is an attractive forward fruit style with 10% barrel-fermentation adding to the wines texture. Crossing Chardonnay with attractive apple and citrus notes is partly vinified in stainless steel and the balancing half in small oak. Ageing is on lees. The Estate Chardonnay offers a further dimension. Fermentation is in barrel with native yeasts and 50% new barrels are used providing a wine with restrained citrus and vanilla and a round creamy texture. The Crossing reds are again approachable and forward. The Estate wines offer more depth with a firmer structure. Shiraz is particularly well priced. Compelling, spicy dark fruit aromas are underpinned by 18 months in oak hogsheads. The Cabernet Sauvignon is 100% varietal with impressive structure. After 18 months in barriques the balackcurrant, plum and cedar aromas are nicely underpinned by a hint of oak vanilla. An Estate Malbec and Aquitaine Rouge (Cabernet Sauvignon, Merlot and Malbec) are also made. (DM)

Recommended Reds:

Cabernet Sauvignon Estate ★★★★ £F

Shiraz Estate ★★★★ £D

Cabernet Merlot Crossing ★★☆ £C

Shiraz Crossing ★★☆ £C

Recommended Whites:

Chardonnay Estate ★★★☆ £D

Chardonnay Crossing ★★☆ £C

Semillon Sauvignon Blanc Crossing ★★☆ £C

John Kosovich (Swan Valley) www.johnkosovichwines.com.au

The third oldest winery in the Swan Valley, John Kosovich Wines was established in 1922 and known as Westfield Wines until 2003. The atmospheric cellar, dug by hand in 1922, is one of only two original underground cellars in the Swan Valley today. Though the winery forged its reputation on fortified wines, among the country's best, it has also developed its table wine capability. In the 1980s, the family acquired a 15 acre vineyard in Pemberton in the cooler South West which is planted to Chardonnay, Verdelho, Shiraz, Cabernet Sauvignon, Merlot, Malbec and Pinot Noir. The Verdelho is as good as any you will find in the state, a dry, serious wine which develops complexity with a few years under its belt. The Pemberton Chardonnay is elegant and refined with judicious use of oak. John Kosovitch also make a Liqueur Shiraz and Vintage Port (not tasted). (SA)

Recommended Whites:

Muscat Rare ★★★★☆ £H Verdelho Liqueur ★★★★ £G

Chardonnay Pemberton ★★☆ £D Verdelho ★★☆ £C

Leeuwin Estate (Margaret River) www.leeuwinestate.com.au

One of the very best properties in southerly Margaret River, Leeuwin Estate has been producing excellent Chardonnay under the Art Series label for 3 decades now. Production is sizeable at more than 60,000 cases a year but still small by comparison to some Margaret River operations. The Art Series wines are the pinnacle.

The Sauvignon Blanc is a very stylish example with an impressive mineral structure. Though it does not compare with the best of Great Southern, the Riesling shows good intensity with mineral, lime and a toasty persistence with 4 or 5 years' age. Chardonnay is extraordinarily rich and and powerful, yet balanced, intense and complex; a long-lived Australian classic. The fruit and texture are such that the oak is seamlessly integrated with 3 or 4 years' cellaring. Art Series reds include Shiraz and a fine Cabernet Sauvignon which shows a complex fusion of cooler and riper fruit with excellent structure and length. In recent vintages, both show a little more flesh to their sinewy southern bones. A second tier of wines, the Prelude Vineyards label, includes a Classic Dry White, based on Sauvignon Blanc, and a Chardonnay with good richness and structure but which evolves much faster than the Art Series wine. Prelude Cabernet/Merlot has good weight and texture. Siblings, a third label, is for everyday Sauvignon/Sémillon (though it is labelled Prelude in the UK) and Shiraz. Sparkling wine from Great Southern Pinot Noir and Chardonnay was first produced from the 1998 vintage.

Recommended Reds:

Cabernet Sauvignon Art Series ★★★★ £E

Cabernet/Merlot Prelude Vineyards ★★★ £D

Shiraz Art Series ★★★ £D

Recommended Whites:

Chardonnay Art Series ★★★★★ £F

Chardonnay Prelude Vineyards ★★★ £D

Riesling Art Series ★★★ £C

Sauvignon Blanc Art Series ★★★ £D

Sauvignon Blanc/Sémillon Siblings ★☆ £C

Lillian (Pemberton)

John Brocksopp established Lillian Wines in Pemberton in 1993. The former Leeuwin Estate viticulturist rents a pocket-sized winery across the road from Leeuwin to whom he still consults. Unsurprisingly, Brocksopp makes a stunning Chardonnay, silkier than the Leeuwin style since, as he points out, Pemberton produces more structured wines than Margaret River, so it is important to flesh them out. Similarly, Pinot Noir, another Pemberton strength, is plush but well structured with a fine spine of tannin. Both Burgundian varieties are sourced from his neighbour's vineyard, Lefroy Brook, home to Pemberton's oldest vines (planted in 1982). As for his own vineyard, Brocksopp's varietal selection for his coarse sandy soils with a silt and gravel topsoil was less conventional. He planted Viognier in 1992 (head-grafting Mataro which he could not get ripe every year), Marsanne in 1993 and Roussanne in 1998/99. All three tasted from barrel (Brocksopp believes in giving wine air) show excellent varietal typicity, with plenty of texture and layer too. The Marsanne is particularly good, authentically nutty. Brocksopp first worked with the variety in his youth and tells me that it was one of the best wines he made for Seppelt in Rutherglen. The Lillian line up used to include a Shiraz Mataro but, for the Rhône varieties, Brocksopp is now squarely focused on the whites. (SA)

Recommended Reds:

Pinot Noir ★★★☆ £D

Recommended Whites:

Chardonnay ★★★★ £D Marsanne/Roussanne ★★★ £D

Marsanne ★★★ £D Viognier ★★★ £D

Marchand & Burch (Perth) www.burchfamilywines.com.au

Pascal Marchand, winemaker at Domaine COMTE ARMAND and Domaine De La VOUGERAIE, met Jeff and Amy Burch of HOWARD

PARK in Burgundy where the couple own a house. Passionate Pinot Noir fans, the three instantly connected and, in 2006, started to make wine together under their own eponymous label, both in Burgundy and Western Australia. Marchand believes there is no reason why, given Western Australia's climate, it cannot make world class Pinot Noir. The cultural exchange has proved invaluable. Howard Park's viticulturists David Botting and David Burch have utilised time spent in Burgundy to full advantage at the Scotsdale Vineyard in Mount Barker which the Burches acquired in 2004 and developed from scratch. Organic and biodynamic practices have been implemented, new Burgundy clones and *sélection massale* cuttings have been planted at high density. Meantime, the grapes are sourced from select vineyards in Great Southern and Margaret River. Working with small batches in both vineyard and winery and with less intervention (wild yeasts, longer ferments) has resulted in nuanced, textured wines, less fruit-focused than the Howard Park or Madfish range. Unsurprisingly, the Burgundian varieties stand out. The Chardonnay is intense, subtly flavoured and fresh, while the Pinot Noirs, now single vineyard sourced, show lift, spice and a fine edge of tannin. Though it is early days, by comparison, the Shiraz lacks a bit of conviction. A name to watch. (SA)

Recommended Reds:
Pinot Noir Gibraltar Rock ★★★★ £E
Pinot Noir Mount Barrow ★★★☆ £E   Shiraz ★★★ £E
Recommended Whites:
Chardonnay ★★★☆ £E

McHenry Hohnen Vintners (Margaret River) *www.mchv.com.au*
This new operation looks like being something special with the much experienced David Hohnen (founder of CAPE MENTELLE) and his daughter Freya and her partner Ryan Walsh working with his brother-in law Murray McHenry. A new winery was completed just in time for the 2007 vintage at the Rocky Road vineyard south of Margaret River. Between them, the families own four prime vineyards in Margaret River. In the vineyard, "great grand pa farming," entails working within the cycle of nature rather than resorting to chemical intervention. Hohnen's Tamworth and bush pigs do the work of rotary hoes, Wiltshire sheep get rid of Cape Weed and enhance soil quality by spreading nitrogen-fixing clover. In the winery, the policy of minimal intervention continues with natural ferments and judicious use of oak. At Cape Mentelle, Hohnen pioneered Shiraz and Zinfandel and here, works with not only the usual Bordeaux varieties and Shiraz and Zinfandel but also Grenache, Tempranillo, Marsanne and Roussanne, amongst others. The more Mediterranean grapes can be found in flavoursome 3 Amigos red (Shiraz, Grenache, Mourvèdre) and white (Marsanne, Chardonnay, Roussanne), both aged in old oak which lends a savoury note. In time, the Chardonnay will be replaced by Viognier. Chardonnay with real dimension and line comes from the Calgardup block and, since 2007, McHenry Hohnen have released a more generous yet well defined Chardonnay from the Rocky Road vineyard. A zippy Sauvignon Blanc/Sémillon (made with bought in fruit) has classic Margaret River style. An expressive Shiraz has good intensity and well priced but more exciting is Tiger Country, a red which adds Graciano, Petit Verdot and Cabernet Sauvignon to Tempranillo. Aged in used *barriques*, it is supple and fleshy with floral, peppery and berry characters but also has plenty of extract and ripe tannin and is worth keeping at least 6 years to see how it develops. Rocky Road Zinfandel is lush and concentrated, with bright raspberry fruit, while The Rolling Stone, an intense, perfumed blend of Malbec, Cabernet Sauvignon, Merlot and Petit Verdot,

shows more backbone. A well made Cabernet Sauvignon/Merlot is made from bought in fruit.
Recommended Reds:
Tiger Country ★★★☆ £D   The Rolling Stone ★★★☆ £D
Shiraz Margaret River ★★★☆ £D   Zinfandel Rocky Road ★★★ £D
3 Amigos Red ★★★ £C
Recommended Whites:
Chardonnay Rocky Road ★★★★ £D
Chardonnay Calgardup Brook ★★★★ £D
Sauvignon Blanc/SemillonRocky Road ★★★ £C
3 Amigos White ★★ £C

>> Millbrook Winery (Perth Hills) *www.millbrookwinery.com.au*
This is one of the leading wineries in the Perth Hills, located a short distance to the south of the city of Perth and is a part of the Fogarty wine group, which also owns DEEP WOODS (Margaret River), SMITHBROOK (Pemberton) and the iconic LAKES FOLLY (Hunter Valley). Not only are some excellent wines made but some great values as well. Although there are just 8 ha under vine this is one of the most significant operations in this small region. As well as estate fruit, grapes are also sourced from other Perth Hills growers and further afield from Geographe, Great Southern and Margaret River. A diverse range of wines is made in the modern small batch winemaking facility. As well as the wines reviewed below, reds also emerge from Tempranillo, Sangiovese, Pinot Noir and Petit Verdot, with additional whites made from Vermentino, Riesling and Arneis. A small range of fruit driven wines are also released under the Barking Owl label. Sauvignon Blanc and lightly peachy Perth Hills Viognier are both in a crisp fresh style. The Estate Viognier is a more serious prospect. Low yielding vines, hand picking followed by whole bunch pressing and a natural fermentation in small barrels without clarification. The texture of the wine further enriched by ageing on fine lees for eight months. The stylish Limited Release Chardonnay is similarly barrel-fermented with stirred lees in the classic white Burgundy manner offering subtle and restrained hints of melon and citrus with restrained oak. The GSM has a significant proportion of Grenache (over 50%) and offers rich and concentrated red and black fruits. The structured Shiraz Viognier gets a hint of spiciness from the white grape, the wine is hand plunged during fermentation and ageing is for 20 months in French puncheons, less than a third are new. Estate Cabernets combines Cabernet Sauvignon, Petit Verdot and Merlot with a little Shiraz. It's rich and black fruited with well-judged oak. (DM)
Recommended Reds:
Cabernets Estate ★★★★ £D
Shiraz Viognier Estate ★★★★ £D
Grenache Shiraz Mouvedre Geographe ★★★☆ £C
Recommended Whites:
Chardonnay Limited Release Margaret River ★★★★ £E
Viognier Estate ★★★★ £D
Sauvignon Blanc Margaret River ★★☆ £C
Viognier Perth Hills ★★☆ £C

⚫ Moss Wood (Margaret River) *www.mosswood.com.au*
The Mugfords have owned this very fine, small 12 ha Margaret River estate (founded by Bill Pannell of PICARDY in 1969) since 1984. Prior to that, Keith Mugford had been making the wines, making his first vintage at Moss Wood in 1979. The Cabernet Sauvignon is one of the very finest in the region – complex, powerful and structured, even dense and extracted, in contrast to other more fruit driven examples from the region. Rich blackberry and cassis emerge as

Western Australia

the wine becomes increasingly harmonious with age. For reds, Pinot Noir is also a speciality and it is one of Margaret River's better attempts at this grape, which prefers a cooler climate. Sémillon has always been remarkable here and a benchmark for the region. The wine is unwooded and shows restrained fruit in its youth. It will be all the better for 5 years' ageing. Moss Wood Margaret River Chardonnay is in a full, opulent style with smoky, spicy new oak evident in its youth. In order to expand their business but retain the core quality of the Moss Wood wines, the Mugfords purchased the 6-ha Ribbon Vale vineyard and winery in 2000, adding a further 5,000 cases to production. Vinification takes place at Moss Wood. The range has been reduced to just three wines; while Merlot stands out, a very good Sémillon has now been incorporated into the Sémillon/Sauvignon Blanc blend. A third Cabernet-based wine is the bright and lifted Amy's, originally sourced entirely from (and named for) the GLENMORE Vineyard of former winemaker Ian Bell but now based more on the Montgomery brothers vineyard and blended with Petit Verdot, Malbec and Merlot. In 2008, Moss Wood released a new Pinot Noir from Mornington Peninsula. Fruit is sourced from a contract vineyard which is supervised by Moss Wood and the wine is made in Mornington Peninsula. It is several notches up on Moss Wood's Margaret River Pinot Noir, with greater freshness, spice and a fine spine of tannin.

Recommended Reds:
Cabernet Sauvignon Margaret River ★★★★★ £F
Cabernet Sauvignon/Merlot Ribbon Vale Vineyard ★★★ £D
Moss Wood Amy's ★★★★ £D
Pinot Noir Mornington Peninsula ★★★ £D
Pinot Noir Margaret River ★★ £D
Merlot Ribbon Vale Vineyard ★★★ £C

Recommended Whites:
Sémillon Margaret River ★★★★ £C
Sémillon/Sauvignon Blanc Ribbon Vale Vineyard ★★★ £C

>> Peccavi (Margaret River) www.peccavi-wines.com
A small number (fewer than 3,000 cases) of excellent wines are made at this 16 ha property just outside Yallingup in the northerly stretches of the Margaret River. Jeremy Muller had been scouring the globe for an ideal location to carry out his dream of making wine before settling in the Margaret River. The Peccavi label is for the top wines, No Regrets for well priced more approachable examples coming from a mix of home and other vineyards. The vines are planted in loamy soils with a granite bedrock that encourages deep rooting in search of nutrients, the local climate moderated by ocean breezes. Sauvignon Blanc blended with Semillon is a combination that has proved very successful in the Margaret River as have the Bordeaux red varieties. The No Regrets example is fresh, vibrant and full of zesty citrus character. Chardonnay is altogether more complex. There is a fine balance of ripe tropical aromas, white fruits and citrus with well-judged oak. Again the No Regrets Cabernet Merlot is full of approachable berry fruit with lots of style. The Shiraz and Cabernet Sauvignon Peccavi reds are very well crafted with depth and structure. The Shiraz is elegant, refined and marked by intense black fruits, liquorice and black pepper. The Cabernet is no less polished with restrained blackcurrant aromas, cedar and a vibrant fresh edge. The top two reds will evolve well for up to a decade. (DM)

Recommended Reds:
Cabernet Sauvignon Peccavi ★★★★☆ £E
Shiraz Peccavi ★★★★☆ £E
Cabernet Merlot No Regrets ★★★☆ £C

Recommended Whites:
Chardonnay ★★★★ £E
Sauvignon Blanc Semillon No Regrets ★★★ £C

Picardy (Pemberton) www.picardy.com.au
Picardy is arguably Pemberton's top producer, if less well-known than the pioneering SALITAGE. It is a measure of its success that several top Western Australian wines made by producers based in other regions are sourced partly or wholly from Pemberton fruit. Bill Pannell established MOSS WOOD but diverted his attention to Picardy in 1993. The Burgundy varieties and Shiraz are all successful. Cabernet Sauvignon, Merlot and Cabernet Franc are also planted although the results are not quite as good. Merlot/Cabernet is a roughly equal blend of the three varieties. A reserve Bordeaux blend, Merlimont, is made in outstanding years from around 40% Merlot, 30% Cabernet Sauvignon and 30% Cabernet Franc. Chardonnay has excellent structure and texture revealing fine fruit and complexity with a little age. Since 2008, a food-friendly textured and complex lees-aged Sauvignon Blanc-led white has been made from estate fruit. Latterly it has featured an element of (old) barrel fermented fruit and the Sémillon portion has increased, both features of which differentiate it from the region's more typically earlier picked, leaner styles of Sauvignon. Pinot Noir, meticulously sourced from a mix of Western Australia's "droopy" and "upright" clones plus the latest Burgundy clones (114, 115 and 777), is full of dark, berry-fruit aromas which support the judicious oak treatment. In Tête de Cuvée a portion of the Pinot Noir vineyard is cropped even more rigorously and picked earlier in an attempt to produce a more structured and ageworthy, more Burgundian Pinot Noir. It shows great intensity of flavour and builds in the mouth. Shiraz shows a real intensity of spice, pepper and berry fruits.

Recommended Reds:
Pinot Noir Tête de Cuvée ★★★★ £F   Pinot Noir ★★★ £E
Shiraz ★★★ £D   Merlot/Cabernet ★★ £D

Recommended Whites:
Chardonnay ★★★ £E   Sauvignon Blanc Sémillon ★★★ £C

Pierro (Margaret River) www.pierro.com.au
Pierro produces one of the finest, most complex Chardonnays in Western Australia. The wine possesses excellent fruit as well as a remarkable array of secondary flavours. Citrus, mineral, grilled nuts and oatmeal predominate and there is great breadth and intensity on the palate. LTC is a fine, youthfully grassy, melony Sémillon/Sauvignon Blanc with a little touch of Chardonnay (LTC). It shows real intensity and weight and a much better structure than many examples of this blend. While his flagship Chardonnay is relatively opulent for the region when it comes to reds, Peterkin's aim is to avoid the "head and shoulders" upfront profile commonly associated with New World wines in favour of wines of length and backbone. The initial impact is not so dramatic, but the flavour profile builds in the mouth and the wines benefit from a few years in bottle. Of two reds, a berryish, slightly earthy Cabernet Sauvignon/Merlot LTC (= a little touch of Cabernet Franc) has good style and breadth but lacks the concentration of the best Margaret River examples. A reserve example, however, released a year in arrear should show more grip. Pinot Noir has good flavour intensity if at the ripe end of the spectrum. Mike Peterkin also makes the wines of the 9 ha Fire Gully vineyard, also in Wilyabrup, which he acquired in 1998. Whites, including a bright and tight, citrus-driven Chardonnay and fresh and fruity Sémillon/Sauvignon and Sémillon have the edge over the reds, a Cabernet/Merlot and a Shiraz.

Wine behind the label

Pierro
Recommended Reds:
Cabernet Sauvignon/Merlot ★★★ £F   Pinot Noir ★★ £E
Recommended Whites:
Chardonnay ★★★★☆ £F   Sémillon/Sauvignon Blanc LTC ★★★ £C
Fire Gully
Recommended Reds:
Shiraz /Viognier ★☆ £D   Cabernet/Merlot ★ £D
Recommended Whites:
Chardonnay ★★☆ £D   Sémillon/Sauvignon Blanc ★★ £D

Plantagenet (Mount Barker)   *www.plantagenetwines.com*
Plantagenet, home of Great Southern's first winery, has remained a leading light in the region and benefits from some of the oldest vineyards in Mount Barker. Production is now around 100,000 cases a year yet a high standard and remarkable consistency have been maintained by winemaker Gavin Berry. John Durham, formerly of CAPE MENTELLE headed the winemaking team since 2007 and under his lead, the Cabernet Sauvignon is looking particulary polished. Now, since 2012, local girl Cath Oates heads the winemaking team and who, with head viticulturist Jordan Ellis have crafted a new Plantagenet range called Juxtapose of less run-of-the-mill wines which currently comprise of an Off dry Riesling, an Oaked sauvignon Blanc, a Pinot Noir and a Syrah. The winery is also an important source of contract winemaking facilities for many small estates in the region. Wines under the Plantagenet label (sourced only from estate vineyards) include an expressive and undervalued Chardonnay. Great value too is the perfumed, limey and mineral well-structured Riesling, among the finest in the region, particularly with 5 years' age. New in 2008 is Ringbark Riesling (not tasted), a cordon cut dessert wine which hails from the 38 year old Wyjup vineyard. A distinctive Cabernet Sauvignon shows good richness and, while it may not have the power found in the best from the Margaret River, it does has a certain elegance and finesse. Shiraz, on the other hand, provides ample demonstration of why Great Southern trumps Margaret River for this variety. It is impressive, with smoky, minerally, white pepper and dark fruits character – as much Northern Rhône as Western Australia. It ages well too, becoming savoury, gamey even. Omrah is the second label and there is excellent intensity to an impressive Unoaked Chardonnay and good fruit in a Sauvignon Blanc which should be drunk young. Omrah reds include Shiraz, Cabernet/Merlot and Pinot Noir. Hazard Hill red and white are sold locally while fruit is widely sourced for similarly good value exported Hellfire Bay Chardonnay and Shiraz/Grenache.

Plantagenet
Recommended Reds:
Shiraz Mount Barker ★★★★ £E
Cabernet Sauvignon Mount Barker ★★★ £D
Recommended Whites:
Chardonnay Mount Barker ★★★ £C   Riesling Mount Barker ★★★ £C
Omrah
Recommended Reds:
Pinot Noir Great Southern ★★★ £C   Shiraz ★★ £B
Cabernet/Merlot ★ £B
Recommended Whites:
Chardonnay Unoaked ★★ £B   Sauvignon Blanc ★ £B

Rickety Gate (Denmark)   *www.ricketygate.com.au*
Russell Hubbard's passion for wine culminated in the planting of a vineyard in one of the most favourable locations in the southern part of Western Australia in 2000. Renowned consultant winemaker John Wade employs his trademark policies including hand-picking of the grapes, gravity-fed transfers, hand plunging, low yields, many rackings and minimum filtration. The only limitation on quality in the short term is the youthfulness of the vines. A floral Riesling is dry and minerally with excellent length and will flesh out well in time. The elegant Late Harvest version has subtle hints of grapefruit and lemon but, while the sweetness is tempered by the fine streak of acidity, it is a wine for fairly immediate consumption. Unwooded Chardonnay is fresh and fragrant with good weight. The Classic Red blend (Cabernet Sauvignon/Merlot/Cabernet Franc) has good fruit and is smooth but not overly complex. The wine shows quite a marked black fruits character. Three successive vintages of Merlot, confirm the deep and unctuous quality of the fruit and show increasing complexity. In due course this will be a terrific wine. Also made are two reds sourced from Frankland River: a Shiraz intended for a sparkling Shiraz, and a blend of Cabernet Sauvignon,Merlot and Cabernet Franc which displays a stylish finesse, soft tannins and more complexity. A range of reserve wines have been created since 2006 but these have not yet been tasted. (NB)
Recommended Reds:
Merlot ★★★ £C   Shiraz ★★ £C   Classic Red ★★ £B
Recommended Whites:
Riesling ★★★ £C   Riesling Late Harvest ★★ £C
Chardonnay Unoaked ★★ £B

Salitage (Pemberton)   *www.salitage.com.au*
Established in 1988, Salitage is an acronym formed from the names of the four children of John and Jenny Horgan. Prior to venturing into the relative wilderness of Pemberton, John had co-founded LEEUWIN ESTATE with his brother Denis. The 25 ha have been planted to Bordeaux varieties together with Pinot Noir and Chardonnay. The wines, made by Patrick Coutts, are intense and flavoursome with good ageing potential in both red and white. There is generally good balance and decent flavour complexity in Chardonnay and Pinot Noir, if not the refinement and nuance possible from other regions. The latter is typical of Pemberton with smoky cherry/strawberry fruit and a spicy herbal undertone. To fully appreciate the style drink it with 6-8 years' age from a good vintage. A more everyday range of varietals, as well as a Chardonnay/Verdelho blend, is produced under the Treehouse label including a smoky, plummy Pinot with enough substance to make it interesting.

Recommended Reds:
Pinot Noir ★★★☆ £F   Pinot Noir Treehouse ★★☆ £C
Recommended Whites:
Chardonnay Pemberton ★★★☆ £E   Chardonnay Unwooded ★★ £C

Suckfizzle/Stella Bella (Margaret River)   *www.stellabella.com.au*
Owned by dynamic duo Janice McDonald and Stuart Pym, Stella Bella's innovative and consistently well made portfolio has three labels: Skuttlebutt for quaffing, the premium Stella Bella range and Suckfizzle for its flagship red and white Bordeaux blends. The latter are sourced from a single vineyard in Augusta; at the southernmost tip of Margaret River, it is a particularly cool, gravelly site and the wines are ageworthy. With 6 vineyards, mostly on ironstone gravel, with some sand and loam, the portfolio includes an unusually wide spread of varieties. The wines were initially made by McDonald who took charge of winemaking at Deep Woods Estate in Margaret River in July 2010, leaving Pym, her partner, to head up winemaking at Stella Bella. Stella Bella whites have intense, ripe fruit flavours and

Western Australia

reasonable combined with good structure. A rich but well balanced Chardonnay develops complexity and interest with age and, in a good vintage, will cruise along for several years. The Sauvignon and Sémillon/Sauvignon blend show good drive, texture and interest thanks to a judicious element of barrel ferment. A flute bottle highlights the aromatic quality of the relatively new Viognier, which has attractive cedary oak. Stella Bella Pink Muscat with 2% Traminer is a frivolous yet classy rendition of this sweet, slightly sparkling style, with turkish delight and gingery, juicy grape and lychee fruit.There is good style to Shiraz with a definite Margaret River accent, proper regional panache to the Cabernet Sauvignon and plenty of character in a Sangiovese/Cabernet Sauvignon blend that successfully marries riper notes with a more leafy aspect. Tempranillo is promising too. The excellent Suckfizzle Sauvignon Blanc/Sémillon has a barrel-fermented and lees-stirred component in contrast with the herbal, fruit accented Stella Bella version. Flinty and steely like a Pessac Leognan (Pym visited Domaine Chevalier in 1995 and has applied the principles to his fruit), but with a sweeter Margaret River sweet herbal top note and vibrant lemon zest, it develops delicious lanolin notes with age. The cool, cedary Suckfizzle Cabernet Sauvignon is a notch or two up from the Stella Bella reds. It has intense savoury fruit and excellent dimension and depth with ripe tannins, deserving of 5-10 years' age.

Suckfizzle Augusta
Recommended Reds:
Cabernet Sauvignon ★★★★ £E
Recommended Whites:
Sauvignon Blanc/Sémillon ★★★☆ £E

Stella Bella
Recommended Reds:
Cabernet Sauvignon ★★★ £D   Sangiovese Cabernet ★★★ £D
Tempranillo ★★ £D
Recommended Whites:
Chardonnay ★★★ £D   Sauvignon Blanc ★★☆ £C
Sémillon/Sauvignon Blanc ★★☆ £C   Viognier ★★ £D
Recommended Rosés:
Stella Bella Pink Muscat ★★ £D

Talijancich (Swan Valley) *www.taliwine.com.au*
The Talijancich family have been foremost in the Swan Valley since the 1930s. The deteriorating health of their aged soils prompted them to convert the vineyard to biodynamic cultivation – the first in Western Australia to attain biodynamic certification. Their modest production has returned to its focus on fortified wines. Heading the list the Julian James' range which includes a 1961 Solera Reserve Muscat (from Muscat Blanc à Petits Grains), Pedro Ximenez and White Liqueur. The Reserve Muscat is a very smooth liqueur wine with intense flavours of toffee and caramel and a good streak of acidity. The White Liqueur made from Pedro Ximenez, Verdelho and Muscadelle could easily pass for an old Malaga. A straight Pedro Ximenez is liquorous and raisiny with nutty aromas and a smooth nutty flavour on the palate. Also made is a liqueur Shiraz' a 38 year old barrel sample (a blending component) showed super-concentrated flavours of chocolate, macaroons, spice box and coffee. As for table wines, Talijancich no longer makes a Viognier orTempranillo, but has stuck with Shiraz, Chenin Blanc, Graciano and Verdelho for table wines. Verdelho tends to be made in an off-dry, easy-drinking style in Western Australia, but not so at Talijancich. The Verdelho, which sees extended lees maturation is one of the region's most serious and shows weighty but well balanced, juicy

tropical fruit. The museum release Reserve Verdelho from top years sees at least six years bottle age and is edged with savoury white porcini and toast like a Hunter Valley Sémillon, though it retains a vibrant core of salty desert limes and juicy green mango. Shiraz is fairly tarry with biggish fruit, but not a great deal of complexity. New is Graciano from young vines, a big wine that takes no prisoners. It is quite mouth-puckering in the Durif/Petit Sirah vein but likely to add more complexity with greater vine age. (NB)
Recommended Reds:
Liqueur Shiraz ★★★★ £D   Shiraz ★★ £C   Graciano ★★ £C
Recommended Whites:
Pedro Ximenes Julian James ★★★★★ £G
Reserve Muscat Julian James ★★★★ £F
White Liqueurr Julian James ★★★ £E   Verdelho Reserve ★★★★ £D
Verdelho ★☆ £B

>> Umamu (Margaret River) *www.umamuestate.com*
This excellent small Margaret River property produces a range of first class reds and whites. One of the more interesting aspects of the estate is that a number of the wines are released with significant bottle age. The fruit is all sourced from the East West facing estate vineyard which was planted in 1978. 10 km to the east of the Margaret River it provides grapes of increasing old vine complexity. Everything is done as naturally as possible to achieve the best results in the wines. Sauvignon Semillon is richly textured with a honeyed waxy texture emerging with age. to balance the citrus fruit.   The varieties are vinified separately and a portion is barrel fermented. Sauvignon Blanc is fresh and zesty with expressive complex citrus rather than raw green fruits and an edgy minerality. Chardonnay comes from close to 40 year old vineyards and has a restrained Burgundy quality with barrel fermentation in new and used oak. Sparkling Chardonnay is in a real Blanc de Blancs style with a rich citus and bready quality from four and a half years on lees. The range of whites is completed by a cane cut Sauvignon Blanc. Rich, sweet and honeyed but with zesty fresh balance it weighs in at just around 10 % alcohol. Cabernet Merlot also has a little Cabernet Franc including and is supple and rounded with a fine balance of black fruits, plum and creamy oak. It gets 10 months in wood. Shiraz also impresses, with black fruits spices and a hint of pepper and well judged oak in which the fermentation is completed. The Cabernet Franc is a really stylish example, one of the very finest. Supple, structured with 10 months in wood which you barely consider. A mix of red and black berry and cherry fruit are apparent with great length and intensity. Cabernet Sauvignon is among the leading examples from the region. There is an elegant and restrained cedar quality that many of Umamu's near neighbours fail to achieve. It comes from vines planted in 1982 and is aged for 18 months in 50% new French oak which is seamlessly handled. (DM)
Recommended Reds:
Cabernet Sauvignon ★★★★☆ £F
Cabernet Franc ★★★★ £E   Shiraz ★★★☆ £D
Cabernet Merlot ★★★☆ £E
Recommended Whites:
Sparkling Chardonnay ★★★★ £F
Chardonnay ★★★★ £E
Sauvignon Blanc ★★★★ £D
Sauvignon Blanc Semillon ★★★ £C
Sauvignon Blanc Cane Cut ★★★☆ £D

Vasse Felix (Margaret River) *www.vassefelix.com.au*
Vasse Felix is now a sizeable Margaret River operation, producing

some 150,000 cases a year. There is a large range but its reputation has been maintained over a long period by the top reds and, with the talented Virginia Willcock at the helm, the whites have moved up a notch, showing better fruit intensity and balance. The Cabernet/Merlot (supplemented by a small dose of Malbec) shows good plum and bright berry fruit while the Cabernet Sauvignon (also with a little Malbec) is denser and better structured. Shiraz is more subtle than many but has good intensity in the best years. The Heytesbury red is a blend of Cabernet Sauvignon, Petit Verdot and Malbec. Rich and concentrated, it has an additional dimension over the other reds. Fine oak is very well integrated, with the cassis and dark chocolate fruit emerging after 4 or 5 years' ageing. Chardonnay is the leading white, with ripe, full fruit and restrained oak in the regular example but more oak, power and complexity in the Heytesbury version, these days looking sleek too. The bright and zesty estate Sémillon Sauvignon Blanc also sees judicious element of barrel-fermentation which brings a touch more weight, though there is no shortage of line. Classic Dry White Sémillon/Sauvignon Blanc) and Classic Dry Red (Shiraz/Cabernet Sauvignon) offer wines at a price/quality ratio which is hard to beat – all are sourced throughout Western Australia and are not available outside Australia.

Recommended Reds:
Heytesbury ★★★★ £F   Cabernet Sauvignon ★★★★ £D
Cabernet/Merlot ★★★ £C   Shiraz ★★★ £D
Recommended Whites:
Chardonnay Heytesbury ★★★★ £E   Chardonnay ★★ £C
Sauvignon Blanc/Sémillon ★☆ £B

Voyager Estate (Margaret River)   *www.voyagerestate.com.au*
A medium-sized Margaret River producer that has become something of a tourist magnet thanks to its fine rose garden, cellar door and restaurant. The ability to select from an extensive vineyard resource which is meticulously maintained by general manager Steve James places the winery in an enviable position. The wines are rich and powerful and, during the much respected Cliff Royale's tenure, attained that extra degree of finesse that put Voyager in the premier league in quality if not yet price point. Voyager Estate's Chardonnay and Cabernet Sauvignon represent very good value for money. In 2009, Travis Lemm, Royale's assistant winemaker took over the day-to-day winemaking under the watchful eye of James. It is to be hoped that this provides continuity going forward though the use of American oak and pulling back on the acid of the Sauvignon Blanc/Sémillon takes away a bit of the edge and structure which marked the style under Royale. The flagship white is a finely crafted Chardonnay which, these days, includes fruit sourced from Burgundy clones. With excellent structure and length, it will age for several years in a good vintage. Other whites should be drunk fairly young. Reds need a minimum of 5-6 years' age. The premium Tom Price red and white are only made in exceptional years and show great concentration of fruit amply buttressed by new French oak. They are wines for the long haul, especially the Cabernet.

Recommended Reds:
Cabernet Sauvignon/Merlot Tom Price ★★★★☆ £F
Cabernet Sauvignon/Merlot ★★★★ £E
Cabernet Sauvignon/Merlot Girt by Sea ★★★ £C   Shiraz ★★★★ £D
Recommended Whites:
Chardonnay ★★★★ £E Sémillon Sauvignon Blanc Tom Price ★★★ £C
Sauvignon Blanc/Sémillon ★★ £C   Chenin Blanc ★ £C

Willow Bridge Estate (Geographe)   *www.willowbridge.com.au*
This large estate in the Ferguson Valley has already planted more

than 60 ha of vineyards. High summer temperatures are moderated both by elevation (280m) and its proximity to the coast (some 25km away). The strengths seem to lie with blends of Sémillon and Sauvignon Blanc, Sauvignon Blanc and varietal Shiraz. The top Shiraz, Black Dog, is subject to an extended maceration on the skins before 18 months in mostly French oak and reveals intense black plum and licorice fruit on an expansive palate. A Shiraz Viognier is a good medium bodied example of the genre with spice and lift. A basic Dragonfly range includes decent Sauvignon Blanc/Sémillon and Shiraz.

Recommended Reds:
Shiraz Black Dog ★★★ £E   Shiraz/Viognier Gravel Pit ★★ £C
Shiraz Dragonfly ★ £B
Recommended Whites:
Sauvignon Blanc/Sémillon Dragonfly ★ £B

✿ **Woodlands (Margaret River)**   *www.woodlandswines.com.au*
In a remarkably short period of time, Woodlands has firmly established itself in the uppermost echelon of Margaret River Cabernet producers, alongside CULLEN and MOSS WOOD. The secret to its success? Like Cullen and Moss Wood, the 11ha vineyard is based in Wilyabrup which, with its high gravel content, is regarded as the Pauillac of Margaret River. What's more, David and Heather Watson planted the vineyard in 1973, so the vines are among Margaret River's oldest. Though David's early Cabernets bagged trophies on the show circuit, production under the Woodlands' name all but ground to a halt in 1992. Most of the fruit was sold to third parties until 2002, when David's son Stuart took charge of winemaking. Father and son's love of Bordeaux influences the beautifully structured, textured style with, as Stuart puts it, "concentration without sweetness…I like savoury." Each year the flagship Cabernet Sauvignon, a wine of immense concentration, structure and balance, is named after a different family member or friend. The more approachable, lifted and fleshy Reserve Margaret Cabernet blend contains a significant proportion of Malbec as well as Merlot. Also deeply impressive, it will reward ageing for at least a decade. In 2007, a terrific vintage, both reds are a tour de force. In 2005, another great vintage, Woodlands produced a sensual single varietal Cabernet Franc and built-to-last Malbec. They also make tiny quantities of Pinot Noir (not tasted). Though not on par with the reds, an unoaked Chardonnay and oaked Chardonnay (Chloe) show a delicate touch. (SA)

Recommended Reds:
Cabernet Sauvignon Margaret River ★★★★★ £G
Cabernet Merlot Malbec Reserve Margaret River ★★★★ £E
Cabernet Merlot Margaret River ★★★★ £D
Recommended Whites:
Chardonnay Chloe Reserve Margaret River ★★★ £F
Chardonnay Margaret River ★★★ £D

✿ **Woodside Valley Estate**   *www.woodsidevalleyestate.com.au*
The Gunyulgup Valley near Yallingup is at the northern end of the Margaret River region. Here an exceptional new project is unfolding. Contrary to the accepted wisdom, the vines have been planted on south-facing slopes rather than the usual north-facing slopes. Production is currently around 1,000 cases, with 5,000 the eventual aim. Four varietals are made by Kevin McKay, each named for members of a French expedition that mapped Western Australia in 1801–03: Le Bas Chardonnay, Bissy Merlot, Bonnefoy Shiraz and Baudin Cabernet Sauvignon. The wines are distinguished by their elegance and purity and a beautifully delineated fruit expression,

Australia

though Merlot and Chardonnay want for more depth (perhaps due to the relatively young vine age). As good as they are, prices are high.

Recommended Reds:
Cabernet Sauvignon The Baudin ★★★★ £F
Shiraz The Bonnefoy ★★★★ £F Merlot The Bissy ★★★ £F
Recommended Whites:
Chardonnay Le Bas ★★★ £E

>> Woody Nook (Margaret River) *www.woodynook.com.au*
Woody Nook is located in the northern stretches of the Margaret River at Wilyabrup. Established in 1982 by Jeff and Wyn Gallagher, it is now owned by Peter and Jane Bailey and the Gallagher's son Neil has stayed on to look after viticulture and winemaking. A small and interestingly diverse range is made offering good quality and value. The original 1982 vineyard blocks are dry farmed and picking is by hand. More recently planted blocks in 2006 require irrigation and are machine harvested. Semillon Sauvignon has proved a very successful combination in the Margaret River. 'Kelly's Farewell' is an attractive, fresh green-fruited style with restrained tropical aromas and cool fermented. Grassy Sauvignon Blanc is a touch more serious and is similarly vinified. Elegant, lightly oaked Chardonnay is fermented first in stainless steel and then transferred to new and used French oak where it spends eight months with regularly stirred lees. Tempranillo is a relatively rare example it resembles a good modern styled Rioja with vibrant dark cherry fruits and gains a little structure from spending 19 months in barrique. Cabernet Merlot is elegant and cedary with cassis and plum fruits with a supple rounded structure after again 19 months in small wood. Shiraz is dark and spicy with a hint of oak in the background. Richly textured there is a complexity gained from the original un-irrigated blocks from which it's sourced. It spends 18 to 24 months in American oak after vinification. The top wine here is the 'Gallagher's Choice' Cabernet Sauvignon, a supple and refined example of the Margaret River style. Rich and concentrated, with complex dark cassis fruits there is an undertone of mint and cedar. It will evolve well for at least a decade. (DM)

Recommended Reds:
'Gallagher's Choice' Cabernet Sauvignon ★★★★ £E
Shiraz ★★★☆ £D
Cabernet Merlot ★★★ £C
'Killdog Creek' Tempranillo ★★☆ £C
Recommended Whites:
Chardonnay ★★★ £C
Sauvignon Blanc ★★☆ £C
'Kelly's Farewell' Semillon Sauvignon Blanc ★★ £B

Xanadu (Margaret River) *www.xanaduwines.com*
There has already been a radical improvement here since becoming part of the Rathbone group in 2005 (other wineries are the first rate YERING STATION, PARKER COONAWARRA ESTATE and MOUNT LANGI GHIRAN). Founded by Dr John Lagan in 1977, Xanadu was one of the pioneers of the Margaret River but much work was required here by Darren Rathbone and his team to bring it up to the standard of the family's other wineries. Many of the wines produced from the 85ha of vineyard were already established but lacked the vibrancy and structure possible from such a location. A good deal of wine was declassified. Going forward, yields have been reduced and other improvements made. The Margaret River Reserve Chardonnay for instance, is now hand picked and bunch-pressed, barrel-fermented then aged in 50% new oak. Only ambient yeasts are used. It is an

exceptionally concentrated yet focussed wine with a veneer of vanillin oak, which has ample time in which to integrate.

Recommended Reds:
Cabernet Sauvignon Limited Release Margaret River ★★★★ £F
Cabernet Sauvignon Margaret River ★★★☆ £C
Shiraz Margaret River ★★★☆ £C
Recommended Whites:
Chardonnay Reserve Margaret River ★★★★ £E
Chardonnay Margaret River ★★★ £C
Sémillon ★★ £C Sémillon/Sauvignon Blanc Cane Cut ★★ £C

Other wines of note

Amelia Park (Margaret River)
Recommended Reds:
Reserve Shiraz Frankland River ★★★★ £D
Brookland Valley (Margaret River)
Recommended Whites: Sauvignon Blanc Estate ★ £C
Sémillon/Sauvignon Blanc Estate ★★ £C
Sémillon/Sauvignon Blancverse 1 ★ £B
Chardonnay Estate ★★ £C
Chardonnay Reserve Estate ★★★★ £E
Recommended Reds:
Cabernet Sauvignon/Merlot Estate ★★ £C
Cabernet/Merlotverse 1 ★ £B Shirazverse 1 ★ £B
Broomstick Estate (Margaret River)
Recommended Reds:
Shiraz ★★☆ £C
Castelli (Great Southern)
Recommended Whites:
Riesling ★★★ £D
Recommended Reds:
Shiraz ★★★ £D Cabernet Sauvignon ★★★ £E
Carter (Margaret River)
Recommended Whites:
Chardonnay ★★★ £D
Clairault (Margaret River)
Recommended Whites: Chardonnay ★ £B
Sémillon/Sauvignon Blanc ★★ £B Sauvignon Blanc ★★ £B
Recommended Reds: Cabernet Sauvignon ★★ £C
Cabernet Sauvignon Estate ★★★☆ £E
Paul Conti (Swan District)
Recommended Whites:
Chardonnay Tuarts ★★ £B
Recommended Reds:
Shiraz Mariginiup ★★★ £D
Devil's Lair (Margaret River)
Recommended Whites:
Chardonnay ★★★ £D
Recommended Reds:
Margaret River ★★★ £E
Domaine Naturaliste (Margaret River)
Recommended Whites: Purus Chardonnay ★★★★ £E
Artus Chardonnay ★★★★ £E
Sauvage Sauvillon-Semillon ★★★☆ £D
Dukes (Great Southern)
Recommended Whites: Riesling ★★★ £C
Riesling Magpie Hill ★★★ £D
Evoi Wines (Margaret River)
Recommended Whites:
Chardonnay Reserve ★★★★ £E

Wine behind the label

Western Australia

Australia

Fermoy Estate (Margaret River)
Recommended Whites: Sauvignon Blanc ★★ £B
Sémillon ★★ £B Sémillon Reserve ★★★ £C
Chardonnay ★★ £C
Recommended Reds: Shiraz ★★ £C
Nebbiolo ★★ £D
Merlot ★★ £C
Cabernet Sauvignon Reserve ★★★☆ £E
Glenmore (Margaret River)
Recommended Reds:
Cabernet Sauvignon ★★★★ £D
Hamelin Bay (Margaret River)
Recommended Whites:
Sémillon/Sauvignon Blanc ★★★ £C
Sauvignon Blanc ★★★ £C
Jingalla (Great Southern)
Recommended Whites:
Sauvignon Blanc/Verdelho ★ £C
Riesling ★★★ £C
L. A. S. Vino (Margaret River)
Recommended Reds:
Portuguese Pirate (Tourigo Nacional, Tinto Cão, Souzão) ★★★☆ £F
Recommended Whites:
Chardonnay ★★★ £F
CBDB (Chenin Blanc, Viognier, Chardonnay) ★★★ £F
La Violetta (Great Southern)
Recommended Reds: Shiraz La Ciornia ★★★★ £F
Shiraz Up Shiraz ★★★ £E
Lilac Hill Estate (Swan Valley)
Recommended Reds:
Fine Old Tawny La Ciornia ★★★ £E
Lost Lake (Pemberton)
Recommended Whites:
Chardonnay ★★★ £C
Recommended Reds:
Pinot Noir ★ £C Shiraz ★★ £C
Marriwood Park (Margaret River)
Recommended Whites:
Chenin Blanc Reserve ★★★ £D
Chenin Blanc Grandis Brut Reserve ★★☆ £D
Merops (Margaret River)
Recommended Reds: Ornatus ★★★☆ £D
Shiraz ★★★ £D
Mount Trio (Great Southern)
Recommended Whites:
Sauvignon Blanc ★★ £B
Recommended Reds:
Cabernet/Merlot ★★ £B
Myattsfield Vineyards (Perth Hills)
Recommended Reds:
Shiraz Mourvèdre Viognier ★★ £C
Kenneth Green Vintage Fortified ★★ £D
Old Kent River (Great Southern)
Recommended Reds: Pinot Noir ★★ £B
Shiraz ★★★ £C
Pemberley (Pemberton)
Recommended Whites:
Sauvignon Blanc/Sémillon Cable Beach Sunset ★ £B
Sauvignon Blanc ★★☆ £C

Peos (Manjimup)
Recommended Whites:
Chardonnay Aces ★★☆ £D
Recommended Reds: Shiraz Four Aces ★★★ £E
Cabernet Sauvignon ★★★☆ £C
Pepperilly (Geographe)
Recommended Reds:
Grenache ★★ £D
Plan B (Frankland River)
Recommended Reds:
Tempranillo Viognier ★★★ £C
Rosabrook Estate (Margaret River)
Recommended Reds:
Cabernet/Merlot ★★☆ £C
Sandleford (Margaret River)
Recommended Reds:
Cabernet Sauvignon ★★★☆ £D
Sinclair (Manjimup)
Recommended Whites:
Sauvignon Blanc Swallow Hill ★★☆ £B
Recommended Reds:
Cabernet Sauvignon Shiraz Jeremy Simon ★★ £C
Smithbrook (Manjimup)
Recommended Whites:
Sauvignon Blanc ★★☆ £C
Sauvignon Blanc/ Sémillon The Vilgarn ★★☆ £C
Recommended Reds:
Merlot ★★★ £C
Swings & Roundabouts
Recommended Whites:
Sémillon/Sauvignon Blanc ★★ £B
Chardonnay ★★★ £C
Recommended Reds: Shiraz Margaret River ★★ £B
Laneway Shiraz (Shiraz/Viognier) ★★ £C
Laneway Tempranillo ★★ £C
Vinaceous/Reverend V (Margaret River)
Recommended Reds:
Reverend V Cabernet Sauvignon ★★★ £C
Vinaceous Cabernet Sauvignon Raconteur ★★☆ £C
Vinaceous Malbec Voodoo Moon ★★☆ £C
Recommended Whites:
Reverend V Riesling ★★★ £C
Vinaceous Sauvignon Blanc Divine Light ★★ £B
Vinaceous Vermentino Impavido Western Australia ★★ £B
Watershed (Margaret River)
Recommended Whites:
Sauvignon Blanc ★★ £B
Recommended Reds:
Cabernet/Merlot ★★★ £C Shiraz ★★★ £C
We're Wines (Margaret River)
Recommended Reds:
Shiraz ★★☆ £C
West Cape Howe (Denmark)
Recommended Whites: Chardonnay ★★★ £C
Sauvignon Blanc ★★ £B
Riesling ★★★ £C
Recommended Reds:
Shiraz ★★★ £C
Cabernet Sauvignon ★★★ £C

Western Australia

Wignalls (Great Southern)
Recommended Whites:
Chardonnay ★★ £C
Recommended Reds: Shiraz ★★★ £C
Pinot Noir ★ £E
Willespie (Margaret River)
Recommended Whites: Riesling ★★ £C
Sémillon Old School Barrel-Fermented ★★☆ £D
Wise Wine (Margaret River)
Recommended Whites: Riesling ★★ £C
Riesling Eagle Bay Pemberton ★★★ £D
Zarephath (Great Southern)
Recommended Whites:
Riesling ★★★★ £D

Work in progress!!

Producers under consideration for the next edition
Burnside Organic Farm
Flametree Estate
Clownfish (Margaret River)
Herriot Wines (Manjimup)
Tintagel Wines (Margaret River)

Author's choice

Top Margaret River reds
Cape Mentelle   Cabernet Sauvignon
Cullen   Cabernet Sauvignon/Merlot Diana Madeline
Cullen   Mangan
Fraser Gallop   Cabernet Sauvignon Margaret River
Glenmore   Cabernet Sauvignon Margaret River
Howard Park   Cabernet Sauvignon Leston
Leeuwin Estate   Cabernet Sauvignon Art Series
Moss Wood   Cabernet Sauvignon Margaret River
Pierro   Cabernet Sauvignon/Merlot
Xanadu   Lagan Estate Reserve
Vasse Felix   Cabernet Sauvignon
Vasse Felix   Heytesbury
Voyager Estate   Cabernet Sauvignon/Merlot
Woodlands   Cabernet Sauvignon
Woodlands   Cabernet Sauvignon/Merlot Malbec Reserve
Xanadu   Cabernet Sauvignon/Merlot Limited Release

Distinguished WA whites
Bellarmine   Riesling Auslese Frankland River
Bellarmine   Riesling Frankland River
Castle Rock   Riesling Porongurup
Cape Mentelle   Chardonnay Margaret River
Cullen   Chardonnay Kevin John Margaret River
Cullen   Sauvignon Blanc/Sémillon Cullen Estate Margaret River
Dukes   Riesling Magpie Hill Porongurup
Evoi Wines   Chardonnay Reserve Margaret River
Forest Hill   Riesling Block 1 Mount Barker
Frankland Estate   Riesling Isolation Ridge Frankland River
Frankland Estate   Riesling Cooladerah Frankland River
Howard Park   Riesling Great Southern
Larry Cherubino   Riesling The Yard Mount Barker
Larry Cherubino   Riesling Cherubino Porongurup
Leeuwin Estate   Chardonnay Arts Series
Lillian   Chardonnay Pemberton

Lillian   Marsanne/Roussanne Pemberton
Marchand & Burch   Chardonnay Great Southern
Mchenry Hohnen   Chardonnay Calgardup Brook Margaret River
Pierro   Chardonnay Margaret River
Stella Bella   Sauvignon Blanc/Sémillon Suckfizzle Margaret River
Talijancic   Verdelho James Talijancich Reserve Swan District
Vasse Felix   Chardonnay Heytesbury Margaret River
Voyager Estate   Chardonnay Margaret River

Great Southern red stars
Alkoomi   Shiraz Frankland River Jarrah
Batista   Pinot Noir Manjimup
Batista   Pinot Noir Selection Manjimup
Castle Rock   Pinot Noir Porongurup
Ferngrove Vineyards   Cabernet/Shiraz The Stirlings Frankland River
Forest Hill   Cabernet Sauvignon Block 9 Mount Barker
Forest Hill   Shiraz Block 5 Mount Barker
Frankland Estate   Olmo's Reward Frankland River
Houghton   Jack Mann Frankland River
Howard Park   Cabernet Sauvignon/Merlot Scotsdale Great Southern
La Violetta   Shiraz La Ciornia Great Southern
Picardy   Pinot Noir Pemberton
Plantagenet   Shiraz Mount Barker

Excellent value for money wines
Reds:
Cape Mentelle   Cabernet/Merlot Trinders
Clairault   Cabernet Sauvignon Estate Margaret River
Cullen   Margaret River Red Margaret River
Ferngrove Vineyards   Cabernet/Merlot Symbols Great Southern
Harewood Estate   Shiraz/Cabernet Great Southern
Madfish   Cabernet Sauvignon Golden Turtle Margaret River
Mchenry Hohnen Vintners   Three Amigos Margaret River
Moss Wood   Amy's Margaret River
Rosabrook Estate   Cabernet/Merlot Margaret River

Whites:
Alkoomi   Riesling Frankland River
Capel Vale   Verdelho
Harewood Estate   Chardonnay Denmark
Houghton's   HWB
John Kosovich   Verdelo Swan Valley
Larry Cherubino   Riesling Ad Hoc Wallflower Great Southern
Larry Cherubino   Chardonnay Hens & Chickens Margaret River
Picardy   Sauvignon Blanc Pemberton
Pierro   Sémillon/Sauvignon Blanc Ltc Margaret River
Plantagenet Omrah   Riesling
Stella Bella   Chardonnay Margaret River
Vasse Felix   Sémillon/Sauvignon Blanc Margaret River
Willow Bridge Estate   Sémillon/Sauvignon Blanc Dragonfly Geographe

New Zealand's wine profile, with an image first centred on intense, vibrant, fruit-driven whites for immediate consumption is now in a state of perpetual evolution. It's true many winemakers have fashioned wines based on a dogma of technological expertise but the influence of the European quality revival, that is, one underpinned by better health in the vineyard, is also apparent. Slowly too, the best sites are being unearthed even if more time is still needed to emulate many of the premium old world areas where they've had centuries to define and redefine the grape and site match. The direction for New Zealand provided by well-educated, widely travelled, outward-looking winemakers is now being given increased focus as new talent, be it home-grown or imported, is attracted to what is seen as an increasingly glamourous vocation in a beautiful setting. The result is not only wines of better structure and increased longevity but also of greater individuality and flair.

Changing colours

Despite rapid expansion over the last two decades, New Zealand's output (white dominated) is still small in the global context. With a generally cool climate the question of which grape varieties to plant and where became more important than in warmer, easier climes. Thirty years ago Müller-Thurgau dominated the vineyard area; 10 years later Sauvignon Blanc took on a significance way beyond the area planted to it; and in the last couple of decades Chardonnay has been the vine planted in greatest numbers, with Pinot Noir coming up on the rails. Along the way Cabernet Sauvignon has found its place (in Hawkes Bay and on Waiheke Island) and Merlot has been more than a mere flirtation. Gradually the industry has moved southwards through Gisborne and Hawkes Bay before confirming Marlborough as its leading region. There is increasing regional or even site-specific identification for many quality wines with less cross-regional blending than previously.

The regions
Auckland

New Zealand's first vineyard was planted in the far north of New Zealand in the the Bay of Islands but its early history was centred around Auckland, the country's largest city. Despite the city's often warm, humid conditions, some favourable mesoclimates are to be found in **Kumeu** and **Huapai** (to the west), where producers have been successful with Chardonnay as well as Merlot and Cabernet Sauvignon. Other vineyard pockets on the fringes of a sea of suburbia include **Matakana**, Cleveden and Mangere but it is offshore in the Hauraki Gulf on **Waiheke Island**, where conditions are generally warmer and drier, that Merlot and Cabernet have been most successful, a fact highlighted and confirmed in many vintages since Stonyridge's first in 1987. There are now more than 30 wineries on the island.

Gisborne

In the eastern central part of the North Island are its two most productive regions. Gisborne often struggles with rain and humidity during the growing season yet with the right dedication can also show that good quality fruit is not the sole preserve of the more illustrious Hawkes Bay.

Hawkes Bay

Here it is drier in what has become the country's leading area for blends based on the classic Bordeaux varieties. Malbec, Merlot and Cabernet Franc as well as Cabernet Sauvignon make an important contribution to the region's reds. The number of fine, fully ripe examples and the number of premium reds continues to increase. The best have an intense berryish fruit, balanced oak, good acidity and ripe tannins. The **Gimblett Gravels**, free draining gravels centred on an old river bed, are being promoted by a consortium of producers as a geographically-defined 'appellation'. Many leading producers now also make some stylish but ripe Syrah, while Zinfandel is also gaining a foothold. Whites are led by Chardonnay but there's also good Gewürztraminer.

Martinborough/Wairarapa

A long way south of Hawkes Bay is the **Wairarapa** region, lying within the political region anchored by the country's capital, Wellington. The most prized viticultural land, the terraces around the small town of **Martinborough**, is extremely limited, but other favoured pockets of viticulture could yet emerge from a region that benefits, like other protected eastern regions, from a relatively low autumnal rainfall. The best early examples of New Zealand Pinot Noir came from here though they remain relatively few in number. Some potential has also been realised for Chardonnay, Riesling and, lately, Pinot Gris.

Marlborough & Nelson

Marlborough at the north-eastern tip of the South Island is New Zealand's most important viticultural area. Like Hawkes Bay it is favoured both climatically, often with fine weather late into the growing season, and geologically, thanks to mostly free-draining soils. Yet most of the major decisions about where and what to plant were made on a purely commercial basis. That is, where the land was cheapest and the grape most prolific. Montana's (now Brancott Estate) development of Marlborough in the 1970s was intended as a cheap source of Müller-Thurgau but some Sauvignon was planted as well and it has never looked back. The vineyard area continues to swallow up increasing amounts of its two main valleys, the Wairau and the Awatere, and even some hillside slopes. The most important grapes are Sauvignon Blanc, source of many of the country's top examples, Chardonnay and Pinot Noir. The range and intensity of flavour can be most impressive where yields are restricted, while the best producers also draw out increased depth and structure. Of growing importance is Pinot Gris, while Riesling, both in dry and sweeter styles, has been successful. **Nelson**, slightly cooler and wetter than Marlborough, perseveres with a similar grape mix but site selection is more critical as is the dedication required from top producers such as Neudorf.

Waipara/Canterbury

The vineyards of **Canterbury** lie to the west of Christchurch, the South Island's largest city, and are well-protected from the worst weather from the west by the Southern Alps. The most promising sub-region, **Waipara**, though usually afforded long fine autumns, requires further protection from north-westerly winds in the form of windbreaks. Although the soils are calcareous and well drained, there seems only just sufficient heat to fully ripen Pinot Noir, Chardonnay and Riesling – the most successful varieties in the region as a whole. Pegasus Bay is Waipara's leading wine producer. In the very south of Canterbury is emerging the country's newest wine region, the **Waitaki Valley**, a source of Pinot Noir from limestone slopes south of the Waitaki River.

Central Otago

In **Central Otago** conditions are like nowhere else in the country. There is even a continental-type climate influence with long hot

Wine behind the label

New Zealand

days and cool nights during the growing season. Interestingly the rock types are much older geologically and hillsides are favoured in order to limit frost damage. Pinot Noir is emerging as the most important variety, though the potential for fine Riesling, Chardonnay, Pinot Gris and Gewürztraminer is already proven too. After a slow start new vineyards and wineries have taken root at

an ever increasing pace since the mid-90s. Foreign investment, celebrity ownership (such as actor Sam Neill's Two Paddocks) and high prices for Pinot are all part of the mix but the hype is already backed by some serious quality. How much more is to come with still greater identification of the top sites and from more mature vineyards?

1 Northland
2 Matakana
3 Kumeu/Huapai
4 Waiheke Island
5 Waikato
6 Bay of Plenty
7 Gisborne
8 Hawke's Bay
9 Martinborough/Wairarapa
10 Nelson
11 Marlborough
12 Waipara
13 Canterbury
14 Waitaki
15 Central Otago

A-Z of producers by region

New Zealand vintages

Only in the last few years have New Zealand whites begun to show a greater propensity for ageing. Improved, more natural wine-making techniques mean better structured examples, particularly Chardonnay, actually improve with 2-3 years' age and the very best will keep for longer. While most Marlborough Sauvignon still need to be consumed within the first year after the vintage a few will develop not unlike a top Sancerre or Pouilly-Fumé.

Reds too have a growing reputation for keeping thanks to improved viticultural and winemaking practices. The best Cabernet Sauvignon and Merlot-based reds show an increasing propensity to age. Top examples, coming in the main from Waiheke or Hawkes Bay, now usually need at least 5 years' ageing but can keep for 10 from an excellent vintage. Shiraz and Pinot Noir are also ageworthy. For most good examples, 3-6 years' age is likely to be the window of optimum drinking but it is very producer dependent - some of the bigger, more extracted styles might need 5 years or more.

Recent vintages

2016 Growers are pleased this year to see an increase in the harvest size after the good but lower yielding 2015. Although the yield didn't match 2014 quite, quality across all the regions was good to very good.

2015 The yield this year was a touch down on 2014 but some good wines have been made. The main problem in both the North and South Islands was spring frost. Growing season conditions though were very propitious, so quality was good in Hawkes Bay, Marlborough and Central Otago.

2014 The run of good vintages continued with one of the hottest and driest growing seasons on record. A large crop did not detract from the quality of the fruit harvested and in all regions, producers reported record conditions for making top quality wines.

2013 Perfect weather with rain, heat and warmth occurring just at the right time for ideal growing conditions has led to this vintage as being the best for many a year. Whites display great balance between fruit and acidity whilst reds are concentrated and complex.

2012 A cool growing season and a frantic harvest has led to lower yields but what has been produced is of excellent quality. Both in Marlborough and Central Otago, the Pinot Noirs showed deep colours and concentrated fruit.

2011 Fortunately the Christchurch earthquake did not affect the wine growing districts too much but wet weather in the North Island caused some rot and a subsequent diminution in quality. In the South Island, earlier ripening crops has led to more austere wines, showing minerality and structure without being overblown.

2010 has been a very successful vintage and yields were sufficient to cover demand in the marketplace. Quality was up on a fine 2009. There were excellent growing conditions across the country. Marlborough basked in an Indian summer, Central Otago had lower than normal yields but the fruit had great intensity, while in Hawkes Bay excellent reds and whites emerged.

2009 saw some excellent wines made after propitious weather conditions in March and April. A good yield across the regions was achieved with Hawkes Bay enjoying an increase of 20% over a challenging previous vintage.

2008 A bumper harvest, although quality was variable. A fine, dry summer was spoilt in some areas with late rains, Gisborne and Marlborough faring the worst. However, quality was above average in Auckland, Nelson, Wairarapa and Central Otago.

2007 After excellent conditions in the late summer and early autumn New Zealand winemakers were full of optimism for 07. Yet another a record crop but once again resulting from an ever expanding vineyard area coming into production rather than from abundant yields. In fact yields were down with Martinborough particularly hard hit.

2006 After a warm summer both Marlborough (where yields were slightly down) and Hawkes Bay experienced a precocious harvest and good quality. A fine year for Marlborough but Hawkes Bay was troubled by rain and damp conditions in late March prior to picking for reds. Martinborough also had some rain but quality is high while Central Otago weathered a sustained burst of heat.

2005 Characterised by a very cool early summer and wet March in both Marlborough and Hawkes Bay but fine, dry conditions in April ensured good quality from the healthiest vineyards.

2004 Most producers were happy with quality despite significant late summer rain. Some fine Hawkes Bay Cabernet, Merlot and Syrah

New Zealand

has now been released. A record harvest at the time, it was more than twice that of 2003. In a reversal of fortunes from 03 Central Otago suffered frost and a drop in both quality and quantity in 04. **Older vintages** should only be considered from a top producer. 2003 was a vintage decimated by frost (worst felt in Hawkes Bay). 2002, 2000 and 1998 can provide some excellent drinking in Hawkes Bay Cabernet-based reds. For aged Pinot Noir consider 2002 or 1998 from Martinborough or any of 2003, 02, 01, 2000 or 1998 from Central Otago.

New Zealand vintage chart

	Hawkes Bay Top reds	Martinborough Pinot Noir	Central Otago Pinot Noir
2016	★★★★☆ A	★★★★☆ A	★★★★☆ A
2015	★★★★☆ A	★★★★☆ A	★★★★☆ A
2014	★★★★★ A	★★★★☆ A	★★★★☆ A
2013	★★★★☆ A	★★★★☆ B	★★★★☆ A
2012	★★/★★★ A	★★★☆ B	★★/★★★ B
2011	★★★★☆ B	★★/★★★ B	★★★★ B
2010	★★/★★★ B	★★/★★★★ B	★★★★☆ B
2009	★★★ B	★★★★☆ C	★★★★ C
2008	★★★ B	★★★☆ C	★★★★ C
2007	★★★★ C	★★★★☆ C	★★★★ C
2006	★★★★☆ C	★★★★ C	★★★★☆ C
2005	★★★★ C	★★★★ D	★★★★☆ C
2004	★★/★★★★ D	★★★★ D	★★★ D
2003	★★★★★ C	★★★☆ D	★★★★★ D
2002	★★★☆ D	★★★★☆ D	★★★★ D
2001	★★★☆ D		★★★☆ D
2000	★★★★☆ D		★★★★☆ D

A-Z of producers

Alpha Domus (Hawkes Bay) *www.alphadomus.co.nz*
Alpha Domus was established in 1991 and has only been making wines since 1995, yet it has produced some of the best reds from Hawkes Bay in recent top vintages. Grapes are sourced exclusively from vineyards planted to Sauvignon Blanc, Sémillon and Chardonnay, plus Merlot, Cabernet Sauvignon, Cabernet Franc and some Malbec. The Navigator, based on Merlot but complemented by the Cabernets and Malbec, is ripe and composed with good concentration – as, too, is a regular Merlot/Cabernet Sauvignon. AD is the premium label. The Aviator (Cabernet Sauvignon with some Merlot, Malbec and Cabernet Franc) is very impressive in its ripeness, intensity and concentration and better balanced than previously. AD Chardonnay is slightly over-worked but richly textured, while an unoaked Chardonnay is tangy and peachy if wanting for more expression. Sémillon appears in a regular, very ripe style, more complex AD version as well as rich botrytised AD Noble Selection.
Recommended Reds:
AD The Aviator ★★★★ £E The Navigator ★★★ £D
Merlot/Cabernet Sauvignon ★★ £C
Recommended Whites:
Chardonnay AD ★★★ £C Chardonnay Unoaked ★★ £B
Sémillon AD ★★★ £C Sémillon ★★ £B Sauvignon Blanc ★ £B

Amisfield (Central Otago) *www.amisfield.co.nz*
At Amisfield there is now ample evidence of the dividend of

investment combined with expertise. The American ownership has enlisted the services of Jeff Sinnott who is now into his stride crafting whites of similar precision and structure that established ISABEL ESTATE as one of Marlborough leading wineries. Since 2006 fruit from over 80 ha of vineyard now receives the best possible handling at a new winery facility at Lowburn. Dry Riesling is a fine Central Otago example with plenty of life and elegance while the Pinot Gris is fruit centred but nicely detailed with good breadth. Pinot Noir comes from the foot of the Pisa range and is lush and expressive with a profile closest to Volnay in Burgundian terms. Also made are Sauvignon Blanc and Lowburn Terrace Riesling, a lighter style, with lower alcohol. There is more to consider - look out especially for a new Waitaki sourced Pinot Noir. Visitors to region can (and should) take advantage of Amisfield's Bistro. Under the same ownership are the Lake Hayes wines.
Recommended Reds:
Pinot Noir Central Otago ★★★☆ £D
Recommended Whites:
Pinot Gris ★★★ £D Riesling ★★★ £C

Ata Rangi (Martinborough) *www.atarangi.co.nz*
From an original 5 ha site, brother and sister Clive and Alison Paton and their partners have built an enviable reputation. Their vineyards are sited mostly on the Martinborough Terrace, either owned (this includes the recent acquisition of the Walnut Ridge vineyard) or subject to long-term contracts with neighbouring families. Yields are low, the vine age now averages over 25 years and the quality of the fruit shows in the wines. Clive Paton and Oliver Masters have forged New Zealand's most consistently fine Pinot Noir over the past decade or so. The wine has a depth and structure that requires a little patience but brings a richness and complexity with 3–5 years' age. A second Pinot, Crimson, comes from younger vines. Project Crimson supports the replanting of native Rata and Pohutukawa trees. The quality of the spicy, cedary, berryish Célèbre (Syrah/ Merlot/Cabernets) is more vintage dependent but usually offers good depth and richness in a cool style. Craighall, the premium Chardonnay, is produced from a 2.8 ha vineyard adjacent to the winery; a second, Petrie, comes from a 4.5 ha vineyard at East Taratahi to the north of Martinborough. Pinot Gris with intense quince-like fruit is one of the most promising Antipodean examples. Some Sauvignon is made along with a botrytised Riesling, Kahu (when conditions permit), and a varietal Syrah.
Recommended Reds:
Pinot Noir Martinborough ★★★★ £E
Pinot Noir Crimson ★★★☆ £C Célèbre ★★★☆ £D
Recommended Whites:
Chardonnay Craighall ★★★ £E Chardonnay Petrie ★★ £C
Pinot Gris Lismore ★★ £C

Bald Hills (Central Otago) *www.baldhills.co.nz*
Here is another rising star to add to the lexicon of Central Otago Pinot Noir. From a prime Bannockburn location the 7.5 ha of vineyard is planted at low densities but yields are kept relatively low. The first vines were planted only in 1997 and like many in the region, are only now beginning to give an indication of their full potential. The Hunts have also had the services of winemaker Pete Bartle who employs a cold maceration for a week on some whole bunches, adding to the Pinot's fine aromatic profile. Also made are a second Pinot Noir 3 Acres, Pinot Gris (Pigeon Rocks) and a slightly off-dry Riesling (Last Light).

Recommended Reds:
Pinot Noir Single Vineyard ★★★☆ £E

Borthwick (Wairarapa) *www.borthwick.co.nz*
Widely experienced Roseworthy graduate Paddy Borthwick has pioneered viticulture in the Dakins Road area since the company was established in 1996. His 27 ha of vineyards are planted on free-draining river terraces, like those to the south in Martinborough, and he has similarly placed his faith in Pinot Noir. Though the vines are still very young, the wine already shows impressive ripeness, breadth and complexity. Riesling is promising too: intense and pungent if not yet with the structure to stand long ageing. Sauvignon Blanc, with more than a hint of the tropical fruits trait the region can provide, is similarly intense but should be drunk young. Other wines, all estate-sourced, include varietal Chardonnay and Pinot Gris.
Recommended Reds:
Pinot Noir ★★★ £C
Recommended Whites:
Sauvignon Blanc ★★ £C Riesling ★★ £B

Brancott Estate (Marlborough) *www.brancottestate.com*
Brancott Estate (formerly Montana) is New Zealand's largest producer, responsible for a considerable amount of the country's total output. Lion Brewing has now acquired the Corbans and Lindauer brands, which were originally owned by Pernod Ricard. The Brancott Estate volume comes from its Marlborough brands, which include consistently drinkable Chardonnay, Sauvignon Gris and Sauvignon Blanc with good varietal character. There are no silly prices here and the Letter series wines can add more sophistication, structure and concentration. Also made is a 'T' Pinot Noir, which shows promise but doesn't yet rival Marlborough's best. In addition to the more than 1,400ha of Marlborough vineyards including the Brancott Estate, there is also 300ha in the Awatere Valley. From these sites Awatere Terroir Series Sauvignon Blanc and Pinot Noir are also now released. The pinnacle Sauvignon Blanc released by the winery is the Brancott Estate Chosen Rows. In collaboration with DEUTZ (Champagne house), some of New Zealand's best sparkling wines have also been made in Marlborough. A small range of well-established Stoneleigh varietals are also made under the Pernod Ricard umbrella as are the wines at Church Road in Hawkes Bay.
Brancott Estate Winery
Recommended Reds:
Pinot Noir ★ £B
Recommended Whites:
Sauvignon Blanc 'B' ★★ £C Sauvignon Blanc ★ £B
Sauvignon Gris 'R' ★★ £C Chardonnay ★ £B
Deutz Marlborough
Recommended Whites:
Deutz Marlborough Blanc de Blancs Vintage ★★★ £D
Deutz Marlborough Cuvée Non-Vintage ★★★ £D

Cable Bay (Waiheke Island) *www.cablebayvineyards.co.nz*
Neil Culley (ex-BABICH) founded this winery in 1996, with the first vineyards planted on Waiheke Island in 1998. However the initial releases were only in 2002. The company has more than 20 ha on Waiheke, spread over several different vineyard sites, making it one of the island's most important producers. Chardonnay already shows breadth, intensity and class. The red Five Hills (Merlot, Malbec and Cabernet Sauvignon) show good style too if lacking a little depth and concentration due to the young vines. More recently

Viognier and Pinot Gris have also been planted. But this is only half the story as Cable Bay also sources grapes from its own vineyards in Marlborough. Again the wines show promise with good fruit intensity, decent structure and a lightness of touch that others miss. Sauvignon is good and velvety Pinot Noir now from Central Otago has good weight and complexity. All are certain to be wines to follow.
Recommended Reds:
Pinot Noir Central Otago ★★★ £D   Five Hills Waiheke ★★ £D
Recommended Whites:
Sauvignon Blanc Marlborough ★★★ £C
Chardonnay Waiheke ★★★ £C

Carrick (Central Otago) *www.carrick.co.nz*
Steve Davies, Carrick's winemaker, seems to be getting into his stride with the latest releases from the Cairnmuir terraces in the Bannockburn district of Central Otago. The main focus in the estate vineyards is Pinot Noir. The wine has real depth, concentration and spicy, plummy fruit complexity and it is now amongst the best of the region if missing the extra class of Felton Road or Mount Edward. Chardonnay is also one of the region's best – intense and stylish with depth and breadth, even a hint of minerality, and the structure to improve for at least 2–3 years. Sauvignon (a small part made in used oak) is cool and zesty. The spice, melon and pear fruit intensity still wants for better definition but shows promise. Other wines include Riesling, a more richly oaked Chardonnay EBM, a more everyday version of Pinot Noir (Unravelled) and now a Rosé. A new Pinot Noir has been produced from 2005 from the single Excelsior Vineyard.
Recommended Reds:
Pinot Noir Bannockburn ★★★ £D
Recommended Whites:
Chardonnay Bannockburn ★★★ £D
Sauvignon Blanc ★★ £C   Pinot Gris ★★ £C

Church Road (Hawkes Bay) *www.churchroad.co.nz*
Compared with BRANCOTT's vast Marlborough vineyard estates, the Church Road winery in Hawkes Bay is a (relatively) small separate entity. Red wines have been developed under guidance from Bordeaux *négociant* Cordier. A regular Merlot/Cabernet Sauvignon/Malbec is soundly made but usually wants for a little more richness and ripeness, while a Reserve Cabernet Sauvignon/Merlot blend shows good extract and becomes increasingly Bordeaux-like with 5 years' age. An extensive range of varietals are also now released under the Church Road McDonald Series banner. Church Road's winemaker, Chris Scott, also fashions Brancott's flagship red, Tom, named after Tom McDonald, the pioneer of Cabernet in Hawkes Bay. Made from Cabernet Sauvignon and Merlot, this complex, cedary red is more Bordeaux than Hawkes Bay and has excellent dimension and depth but requires patience. A Tom Chardonnay and Syrah are also made.
Tom
Recommended Reds:
Tom ★★★★ £F
Church Road
Recommended Reds:
Cabernet Sauvignon/Merlot Grand Reserve ★★★☆ £E
Merlot/Cabernet Sauvignon/Malbec ★★ £C
Recommended Whites:
Chardonnay Grand Reserve ★★★☆ £E
Chardonnay ★★☆ £C

New Zealand

Churton (Marlborough) *www.churtonwines.co.nz*
The Weavers produce Sauvignon Blanc and Pinot Noir as well as Petit Manseng and Viognier. They have a total of 25 ha of vines on an elevated hillside site with farming being moved fully to organic practices. Sam's CV features several leading Marlborough wineries including ISABEL. The Sauvignon has good concentration and shows good underlying structure and fruit expression. The Pinot Noir is cool and more Burgundian than most with cherry and raspberry fruit and a certain elegance. Both offer decent value at present but promise to deliver still more with future vintages.
Recommended Reds:
Pinot Noir ★★★ £C
Recommended Whites:
Sauvignon Blanc ★★☆ £C

Cloudy Bay (Marlborough) *www.cloudybay.co.nz*
Established in 1985 by David Hohnen of CAPE MENTELLE (Western Australia), Cloudy Bay is probably New Zealand's best-known winery internationally and produces its most famous Sauvignon Blanc. The pair of Cape Mentelle and Cloudy Bay come under the umbrella of French luxury goods giant LVMH. Despite substantial volumes and changing vineyard sources – there are now 140 ha of vineyards supplemented by bought-in grapes – the Sauvignon remains one of Marlborough's best, thanks largely to the efforts of Kevin Judd, the original winemaker. The stylish aromas and range of fruit flavours (nettles, blackcurrant leaf and tropical notes) are complemented by a structure that provides an uncharacteristic ability (in the region) to age for at least a year or two, often much longer. Te Koko is a barrel fermented and aged version; the oak gives complexity yet the nettly fruit is not overwhelmed and it shows considerable style and finesse. It's very good with two or three years' age but likely to prove even more age worthy. Chardonnay has long been made to a high standard though can be a bit overdone in flavour and structure, lacking expression and finesse, while Pinot Noir shows an upfront fruity intensity if not yet the texture or dimension of the best New Zealand examples. A Central Otago example, Te Wahi may show greater potential in future. Another highly acclaimed wine is Pelorus, both a creamy, soft fruit-centred and bread dough example with lots of immediate appeal and a rich meaty vintage-dated version. A rosé has also been added. Late Harvest and dry Riesling, Pinot Gris and Gewürztraminer are also made.
Recommended Reds:
Pinot Noir ★★☆ £D
Recommended Whites:
Sauvignon Blanc Te Koko ★★★ £D   Sauvignon Blanc ★★★ £C
Chardonnay ★★★ £D   Pelorus Vintage ★★★ £E
Pelorus Non-Vintage ★★☆ £D

❀ Craggy Range (Hawkes Bay) *www.craggyrange.com*
This winery is named for the Craggy Range in Hawkes Bay's Tukituki Valley, a stunning new winery complex has been built to process grapes from a patchwork of outstanding vineyard sites split between Hawkes Bay, Martinborough and Marlborough. Direction comes from viticultural expert Steve Smith, who established a reputation while providing high-quality fruit for VILLA MARIA. From the outset all varietals were concentrated and well structured with an extra intensity and definition not seen in most New Zealand wines. These include Marlborough Sauvignon Blanc Avery Vineyard. An expanding range of Martinborough varietals include Te Muna Riesling, Sauvignon Blanc, with an infusion of tropical fruits, and Pinot Noir from young vines which shows good potential. A series

of 'Prestige' wines includes: Les Beaux Cailloux, a Gimblett Gravels Chardonnay; The Quarry, also from Gimblett Gravels, mostly Cabernet Sauvignon with some Merlot and a little Cabernet Franc; Sophia, Merlot-based but complemented by Cabernet Franc and Malbec; and Syrah, Le Sol. All show great promise.
Recommended Reds:
Le Sol ★★★★ £F   Pinot Noir Te Muna Road ★★★ £E
Sophia ★★★ £E   The Quarry ★★★ £E
Recommended Whites:
Les Beaux Cailloux ★★★☆ £E
Chardonnay Gimblett Gravels ★★★ £D
Sauvignon Blanc Avery Vineyard ★★★ £C
Sauvignon Blanc Te Muna ★★★ £C
Riesling Te Muna ★★★ £C

The Crossings Estate (Marlborough) *www.thecrossings.co.nz*
The Crossings represents a substantial investment in Marlborough with vineyards spread across three estates, all in the Awatere Valley. The wines are made by George Elworthy solely from grapes sourced from these vineyards. The focus is on Sauvignon, which does particularly well in the Awatere Valley as has long been illustrated by VAVASOUR. The regular Sauvignon has excellent structure with classic Awatere style, showing subtle mineral, citrus and passionfruit aroma and flavour – intense and long, it also promises to be ageworthy. A Reserve version is partly fermented and aged in barrel, adding a little more breadth and texture. It can be slightly less expressive than the regular version but nonetheless pungent and minerally with 3 years' age. In addition Chardonnay and Riesling and a Pinot Rosé are produced but have not yet been tasted.
Recommended Reds:
Pinot Noir ★★★ £D
Recommended Whites:
Sauvignon Blanc Reserve ★★★☆ £D   Sauvignon Blanc ★★★ £C

❀ Dog Point Vineyard (Marlborough) *www.dogpoint.co.nz*
Of Marlborough's new names this is arguably the hottest. Both the owners have had a long relationship with CLOUDY BAY – James Healy on the winemaking side, Ivan Sutherland as a viticulturalist. They have only recently launched their own label and then only from a portion of their vineyards as the intention is to remain a small, hands-on operation. The wines are less 'made' than many in the region and only indigenous yeasts are used. Section 94 Sauvignon Blanc has attracted the most interest. It comes from a specific plot, is vinified and aged in used French oak with extended lees contact and has atypical density and extract. It is well balanced, with more structure and richness than other Marlborough examples in this style. A regular Sauvignon vinified in stainless steel is also made. Full but well structured, it exudes exuberant red capiscum and tropical fruit. There's also an impressive Chardonnay that spends 18 months in French oak. It is concentrated and powerful yet restrained with an intense grapefruit and mealy complexity. Pinot Noir is also made but hasn't been tasted.
Recommended Whites:
Sauvignon Blanc Section 94 ★★★☆ £D   Sauvignon Blanc ★★★ £C
Chardonnay ★★★ £D

❀ Dry River (Martinborough) *www.dryriver.co.nz*
This small estate acquired an enviable cult following due to the unstinting devotion of Dr Neil McCallum to producing the highest quality fruit from prime Martinborough vineyards. Though now under new (American) ownership (the same as for TE AWA FARM),

the same direction is being maintained. Dry River has arguably the best record in the country of producing high-quality ageworthy reds and whites. Yet despite its wide acclaim and the evident complexity, depth and richness of texture in the wines – including some of the very best Gewürztraminer and Riesling in the country – relatively few other producers seem to have been inspired to reach the same levels. The Gewürztraminer has been produced from two different blocks since 2000 and each is bottled separately whenever possible; in Estate and Lovat versions. Previously leased, the Arapoff vineyard was renamed Lovat after its purchase and wines from this vineyard are now labelled accordingly. To date the wines have been mostly sold in New Zealand through an exclusive mailing list but a little is exported. Don't hesitate to try these wines if the opportunity arises.

Recommended Reds:
Pinot Noir ★★★★ £F   Syrah Lovat Vineyard ★★★☆ £F
Recommended Whites:
Gewürztraminer Estate ★★★★ £E
Gewürztraminer Lovat Vineyard ★★★★ £E
Pinot Gris ★★★ £E   Chardonnay ★★★ £E

Escarpment (Wairarapa) www.escarpment.co.nz
This 24 ha property is the new project (established 1999) of Larry McKenna, who both through the success of MARTINBOROUGH VINEYARD and as prime mover and consultant, is at least partly responsible for sizeable tracts of New Zealand countryside being turned into Pinot Noir territory. The bulk of Escarpment is planted to it; the balance coming from Chardonnay, Pinot Gris, Riesling and Pinot Blanc. The Te Muna district with deep, free draining gravels (some 5km from Martinborough proper) is becoming increasingly planted up - the Escarpment vines at higher than typical densities. The McKenna style has always been for richly textured, well-structured Pinot Noir capable of long ageing. Since 2003 the Te Muna grapes have come on-stream and the resulting wine is sturdy, powerful and oaky - needing some time to show its full potential. A number of premium Pinot Noir examples are also available, Kupe (£F) is the priciest, as well as well priced Pinot Noir and Pinot Gris under The Edge brand.

Recommended Reds:
Pinot Noir ★★★☆ £E
Recommended Whites:
Chardonnay ★★★ £D   Pinot Gris ★★★ £C   Pinot Blanc ★★★ £C

Esk Valley (Hawkes Bay) www.eskvalley.co.nz
Esk Valley wines are made by Gordon Russell and are deserving of a separate entry (also see VILLA MARIA). The outstanding wine is The Terraces, a blend of Malbec, Merlot and Cabernet Franc. Made only in top vintages, it is a rich, intense and powerful Hawkes Bay red and the group's finest wine (recent vintages are 2009, 06, 04, 02, and 2000). Esk Valley Reserve Merlot/Cabernet Sauvignon/Malbec can also be very good if slightly more variable in quality, while a regular version is increasingly composed and characterful if not at the same level. Whites are good too, particularly the somewhat Meursault-like Reserve Chardonnay. Other varietals have modest structures but are attractive, ripe and fruit-accented, including a very ripe, exotic Riesling. The Terraces will cost an arm and a leg due to high demand but otherwise these wines are reasonable value for money.

Recommended Reds:
The Terraces ★★★★☆ £G
Merlot/Cabernet/Malbec Gimblett Gravels Reserve ★★★☆ £E
Merlot/Cabernet Sauvignon /Malbec ★★☆ £C

Recommended Whites:
Chardonnay Reserve ★★★ £D   Chardonnay ★★☆ £C
Riesling ★★ £B   Chenin Blanc ★★ £B   Pinot Gris ★★ £B

Felton Road (Central Otago) www.feltonroad.com
Every now and then a very talented winemaker comes to the fore with unprecedented results in a given region. Blair Walter is one such. Yet with Pinot-mad Englishman Nigel Greening taking over Stewart Elm's inspired creation in 2000 and Gareth King in the vineyard, this is very much a team effort. The estate comprises 14 ha (The Elms) with an additional 7.6 ha at Cornish Point, which protrudes into Lake Dunstan. The latter is highly promising despite still relatively young vines. Felton Road Pinots show a richness and complexity that most other New Zealand examples have only hinted at – a quality of fruit effortlessly expressed. While there are a number of other promising efforts in Central Otago, the single-vineyard Block 3 and Block 5 in particular have set the standard for the region. Calvert (from a 4.6 ha site) is a newly added example. Riesling (both a dry and medium-dry style) and Chardonnay too are very good. Chardonnay includes a rare and excellent unoaked Elms version, a fuller barrel-fermented (Central Otago) example and a stylish, lightly mineral Block 2. Demand has pushed prices up, particularly for the Pinots, but whites remain affordable. Single-vineyard Block 1 Riesling is made in a rich medium-dry Spätlese style. New Vin Gris from both Felton Road and Cornish Point Vineyard show not even a hint of colour from Pinot Noir grapes and offer good structure and flavour if not finesse.

Felton Road
Recommended Reds:
Pinot Noir Block 3 ★★★★☆ £F
Pinot Noir Block 5 ★★★★☆ £F
Pinot Noir ★★★☆ £D
Recommended Whites:
Chardonnay Block 2 ★★★★ £E
Chardonnay Central Otago ★★★☆ £D
Chardonnay Elms ★★★ £C
Riesling Dry ★★★☆ £C
Riesling ★★★ £C   Vin Gris ★★ £C
Cornish Point Vineyard
Recommended Reds:
Pinot Noir ★★★☆ £D
Recommended Whites:
Vin Gris ★★ £C

Forrest Estate (Marlborough) www.forrest.co.nz
Forrest Estate is relatively small Marlborough winery achieving good consistency. The wines may not be stunning but they have intense fruit with good varietal character and decent structure. They are not heavy or over-manipulated but show classic Marlborough fruit and vigour. There is an encouraging correlation between price and quality and these wines make a good solid bet especially if drunk young. John Forrest Collection bottlings, available locally, add a small premium. Newton Forrest Estate is a collaboration with Bob Newton producing Hawkes Bay reds from a vineyard in Gimblett Gravels. A Cabernet/Merlot/Malbec is something of a fruit bomb but has good ripeness and fine tannins. New Syrah shows more promise with similar fruit richness but more personality. Wine is also being produced from Central Otago and the new Waitaki region.

Forrest Estate
Recommended Reds:
Pinot Noir Waitaki John Forrest Collection ★★★★ £F

New Zealand

Pinot Noir ★★ £C
Recommended Whites:
Chardonnay John Forrest Collection ★★★ £D
Sauvignon Blanc ★★ £B
Riesling Dry ★★ £B
Newton Forrest Estate
Recommended Reds:
Cabernet/Merlot/Malbec Cornerstone ★★ £E

❀ **Fromm (Marlborough)** *www.frommwineries.com*
Fromm is not one winery but two. One is in Malans in Switzerland, the other in Marlborough. Marlborough's Fromm Vineyard is planted almost exclusively to red grapes with a strong leaning towards Pinot Noir (as are the Swiss vineyards). Grapes are also sourced from other growers, which provides more Pinot Noir as well as other grapes, including Chardonnay and Riesling for the white wines. A separate bottling of Pinot Noir is produced from the gently undulating 15 ha Clayvin Vineyard,. This complex, deep, classy and beautifully crafted Pinot is the equivalent of a fine premier cru red Burgundy and one of New Zealand's very finest. The wines are made by George (Georg) Fromm and Hätsch Kalberer and the philosophy is one of low yields, fully ripe grapes and minimal intervention in the winemaking to give as natural an expression of the wines as possible. All show good character, flavour intensity and structure but the range of wines produced from year to year varies. Only those recently tasted have been rated but Syrah is also impressive. Malbec, small quantities of Gewürztramier and Sauvignon Blanc are also made.

La Strada
Recommended Reds:
Pinot Noir Fromm Vineyard ★★★☆ £D   Pinot Noir ★★★ £D
Recommended Whites:
Chardonnay ★★☆ £C   Riesling ★★☆ £C
Clayvin Vineyard
Recommended Reds:
Pinot Noir Clayvin Vineyard ★★★★ £E
Recommended Whites:
Chardonnay Clayvin Vineyard ★★★☆ £E

>> **Giesen Wines (Marlborough)** *www.giesenwines.com*
The Giesen family are now firmly established in Marlborough although the head office remains in their original Christchurch base. An extensive range of wines is now made and includes a number of varietal wines under the Estate label, which also includes Chardonnay, Pinot Gris, Riesling, Merlot and a fresh sparkler Giesen Classic Cuvée. Sauvignon Blanc is a key wine here. The Estate is fresh and zesty, with marked green fruit and gooseberry notes coming from a whole spectrum of sites across the Wairau and Awatere Valleys. An organic Sauvignon Blanc is also made. The top two Sauvignon Blanc's are impressive. The intensely crisp, zesty and mineral Brothers Sauvignon comes from five separate vineyards across the Wairau and Awatere Valleys. The wines are vinified separately by lot and cool fermented. Impressively complex and concentrated is the August 1888, which is barrel-fermented in varied sizes of vessel from 225 to 1,000 litres and then aged for close to a year on fine lees. The top white is the very classy Chardonnay Fuder from the Clayvin Vineyard, one of a number in their Single Vineyard Series. The site is organically farmed with close spaced vines and a number of different rootstocks established. Fermentation is in new 1000 litre German Fuders and ageing is for 11 months on fine lees. It is onw of the country's best examples. Pinot Noir comes in a

number of guises, including an example from the Clayvin Vineyard. The Estate Pinot is soft, bright and forward. The Clayvin Vineyard example is much more intense, complex and concentrated. It gets a cold soak followed by fermentation with hand plunging and a small proportion of whole bunches. Ageing is in just over half new 300 litre barrels. A number of other single vineyard Pinots are also made. The priciest of the reds is the Brothers Syrah, which again comes from the Clayvin Vineyard. Intense black fruits and spicy black pepper aromas mark the wine. There are a number of clones and a period of cold maceration as well as a proportion of whole bunch fruit used. Wisely new oak is not overdone and around three quarters of the small oak barrels are used. Also made under the Brothers banner are Chardonnay, Gewurztraminer and Pinot Noir. (DM)
Recommended Reds:
Syrah The Brothers ★★★★☆ £F
Pinot Noir Clayvin Vineyard ★★★★ £E
Pinot Noir Estate Marlborough ★☆ £B
Recommended Whites:
Chardonnay Fuder Clayvin Vineyard ★★★★☆ £E
Sauvignon Blanc The August 1888 ★★★★ £E
Sauvignon Blanc The Brothers ★★★ £C
Sauvignon Blanc Estate Marlborough ★☆ £B

>> **Goldwater (Marlborough)** *www.goldieestate.co.nz*
Kim Goldwater originally established the Goldwater winery name on Waiheke Island. He continues to operate there under the GOLDIE ESTATE umbrella. Now owned by the Foley Family Wines group, the Goldwater operation is based in the Wairau Valley in Marlborough producing well-priced wines from both estate and other vineyards from the region. These include under the Goldwater label, Pinot Noir, Sauvignon Blanc, Pinot Gris and Chardonnay (not tasted). There is also a crisp and fresh styled second label Sauvignon Blanc, Boatshed Bay also from vineyards in the Awatere and Wairau Valleys. All the fruit for both brands is farmed sustainably. Harvesting is done in the early morning to preserve aromatic fruit flavours and vinification carried out in a very much a non-oxidative regime. The Sauvignon Blanc is from the Wairau Valley and is in an opulent style with intense citrus and peach fruit aromas, quite distinct from other more green-fruited wines from the region. Pinot Noir is in a bright red berry fruited style and great value. Oak is restrained with a mix of old and new barrels and kept to nine months. The range is completed by the zesty, fresh Pinot Gris which has a fine combination of green and peach fruits. (DM)
Recommended Reds:
Pinot Noir ★★★ £D
Recommended Whites:
Sauvignon Blanc Wairau Valley ★★★ £C
Pinot Gris Wairau Valley ★★☆ £C
Boatshed Bay
Sauvignon Blanc ★★ £B

>> **Greenhough (Nelson)** *www.greenhough.co.nz*
From humble beginnings in 1997 Greenhough has become a first class boutique operation. Despite a relatively low profile it brings a little more glamour to the relatively unsung Nelson region, now dwarfed in viticultural terms by Marlborough to the east. Owner and winemaker Andrew Greenhough makes all the wines to a high standard but like that other regional star NEUDORF has really excelled with Pinot Noir. A regular Nelson version always has good intensity and expression but can on occasion struggle for full

ripeness. That from the Hope Vineyard shows added concentration, ripeness, depth and an expansive palate with a structure that only opens out fully with 4-5 years' age. Chardonnay also excels from the Hope Vineyard with impressive texture and a finely detailed complexity with 3-4 years' age. Riesling is fine too with impressive length and good ageing potential. A lightly floral, slightly exotic scented Sauvignon is well crafted with a certain restraint and structure that contrasts with the vitality and exuberance of Marlborough's best examples. A Pinot Blanc from the Hope Vineyard is also now made.

Recommended Reds:
Pinot Noir Hope Vineyard ★★★☆ £E   Pinot Noir Nelson ★★★ £C
Recommended Whites:
Chardonnay Hope Vineyard ★★★☆ £D
Riesling Dry ★★★ £C   Sauvignon Blanc Nelson ★★★ £C

>> Greystone Wines (Waipara Valley) *www.greystonewines.co.nz*
This small and high quality winery produces some of the best Pinot Noir from the Waipara Valley, with the wines through the small range being well priced. The Thomas family also make wines at a separate operation, Muddy Waters, including Pinotage, which is very rare in New Zealand. At Greystone as well as the wines covered below Chardonnay, Riesling, Gewürztraminer and a couple of pricier single vineyard Pinot Noirs are also made. The property was established in 2000 and 13 blocks planted by 2004 on a mix of limestone and clay. The first wines from the home vineyards emerged in 2008. Sauvignon Blanc is in a fuller style than many New Zealand examples. It is not only barrel-fermented but a small proportion goes through the malolactic fermentation adding significant weight and texture to restrained citrus and green fruit flavours. The Sand Dollar Pinot Gris is a bone-dry example of the variety. Cool fermented to lift the fruit and then stirred on lees to enrich it. The Pinot Noir is undoubtedly a great value example of the variety. Elegant and medium bodied with impressive depth and intensity. A small proportion is whole bunch fermented and ageing in oak is kept below a year for balance. (DM)
Recommended Reds:
Pinot Noir Waipara Valley ★★★★ £D
Recommended Whites:
Pinot Gris Sand Dollar ★★★ £C
Sauvignon Blanc Waipara Valley ★★★ £C

Grove Mill (Marlborough) *www.grovemill.co.nz*
Now owned by Fp;ey Family Wines, Grove Mill has grown rapidly since being established in 1988. While many of the grapes are supplied under contract, a series of vineyards have been either leased or bought outright to increase the amount under the winery's direct control. Since the first vintage the wines have delivered consistently ripe fruit and are characterised by their almost overwhelming fruit intensity and concentration and continue to do so. In the Sauvignon this is slightly at the expense of greater expression and complexity. A partially *barrique*-fermented and oak-aged Chardonnay, like several of the better examples in the region, can be a touch overdone, not lacking for weight or structure but somewhat dominated by secondary, winemaking-given characters (including the oak) at the expense of a clearer expression of the fruit. A Pinot Gris displays less varietal expression than some but nonetheless shows good richness and balanced acidity, while Pinot Noir is fresh and berry fruited. A second Sauvignon Blanc is made under the Frog Haven label.

Recommended Reds:
Pinot Noir ★★★ £C
Recommended Whites:
Sauvignon Blanc ★★★ £C   Riesling ★★ £B
Chardonnay ★★ £C   Pinot Gris ★★ £B

Hans Herzog (Marlborough) *www.herzog.co.nz*
The wines from the Herzog winery are now labelled Hans Herzog in Australasia and simply Hans in other markets as a result of action by a Californian winery. As immigrants from Switzerland Hans and Therese Herzog are new on the Marlborough scene but have already made considerable impact with tiny quantities of handmade reds. With considerable winemaking experience to draw upon, the philosophy is for unfined, unfiltered wines from low yielding, hand picked grapes coming entirely from their own modest biodynamically run 11 ha vineyard. Spirit of Marlborough is a Bordeaux-style red from Merlot, Cabernet Sauvignon, Cabernet Franc and Malbec roughly two-thirds Merlot. There is a cool component to the fruit and tannins again in but with time this contributes to a stylish, nuanced flavour complexity. Much fuss has been made about an unusual Montepulciano (which includes 15% Cabernet Franc). Ripe and characterful, this shows plenty of Montepulciano flesh and depth as well as good intensity, concentration and length given the relative immaturity of the vines. The wine will unquestionably benefit from 3 or 4 years patience. Young vines also limit the potential of a Pinot Noir yet it already shows a seductive immediacy on the palate. Small amounts of Chardonnay, Pinot Gris and even Viognier, with something of a cult following, are also made. The Viognier is very ripe and exotic, Pinot Gris intense and concentrated. The winery restaurant is establishing a similarly enviable reputation.
Recommended Reds:
Spirit of Marlborough ★★★☆ £E   Montepulciano ★★★☆ £E
Pinot Noir Marlborough ★★★☆ £E
Recommended Whites:
Viognier Marlborough ★★★ £E   Pinot Gris Marlborough ★★☆ £E

Huia (Marlborough) *www.huia.net.nz*
Claire and Mike Allan produce a range of attractive and well-made wines with good varietal expression. The majority of the grapes are currently estate-grown from organically farmed vineyards. There are decent examples of Pinot Gris, Gewürztraminer, Riesling and Sauvignon for drinking young. All have decent intensity and fruit expression without being heavy or over-made. Chardonnay is hand picked and whole-bunch-pressed and although in a slightly exaggerated, oaky style, has good fruit, breadth and length. Pinot Noir with intense berry/cherry fruit show promise while the full, biscuity sparkling wine made with slightly more Chardonnay than Pinot Noir and Pinot Meunier shouldn't be ignored.
Recommended Reds:
Pinot Noir ★★ £D
Recommended Whites:
Marlborough Brut ★★★ £E   Chardonnay ★★★ £C
Sauvignon Blanc ★★ £C   Riesling ★★ £C
Gewürztraminer ★★ £C   Pinot Gris ★★ £C

Hunter's (Marlborough) *www.hunters.co.nz*
Jane Hunter remains one of the best-known personalities in the New Zealand wine industry, having produced some of Marlborough's best wines for two decades. The wines, show a harmony, a charm and a gentler character when compared with

New Zealand

some of Marlborough's brasher efforts. Sauvignon Blanc in two versions has always been the focus of production. If the regular unoaked version doesn't show quite the structure or intensity of some of the newer top examples, there is a very fine ripe fruit depth, good concentration and the wine is consistently long and stylish. The Kaho Roa version has always shown a rare deft touch when integrating a gentle oak structure and creaminess with a, ripe tropical fruit intensity. The perfumed raspberry and cherry Pinot Noir is also a good expression of its fruit if missing the intensity or concentration of others. The sparkling wine is also most attractive: well structured, not hugely complex but with a, fresh and ripe fruit intensity to it. A little Merlot and Cabernet Sauvignon is also made along with an unusual Breidecker (a Muller-Thurgau and Chancellor or Seibel crossing).

Recommended Reds:
Pinot Noir ★★★ £D
Recommended Whites:
Miru Miru Brut Vintage ★★★ £C Sauvignon Blanc Kaho Roa ★★★ £C
Sauvignon Blanc ★★★ £C Chardonnay ★★★ £C
Riesling ★★ £C Gewürztraminer ★★ £C

Isabel Estate (Marlborough) *www.isabelestate.com*
The finest privately owned estate in Marlborough produces five outstanding varietals from its own well-established vineyards. For many years the grapes had been sold to others before production under the Isabel label commenced in 1994; almost immediately it became the source of, arguably, New Zealand's finest (certainly in the top three or four) Sauvignon Blancs. If less established than CLOUDY BAY it has been more consistent over recent vintages. Early vintages showed unprecendented structure and concentration but more recently there has been greater expression and refinement including a hint of mineral and smokiness. It can be drunk young or with a little age. The wines come only from estate vineyards planted at around twice the average density, accounting at least in part for the extra intensity and concentration. Pinot Noir usually impresses with vivid plum, cherry and raspberry flavours and a savoury complexity, with a promising texture and breadth. Chardonnay has been exciting but not consistently so: at its best it is intense without becoming syrupy and has good dimension and depth. A bright, crunchy Riesling shows typical Isabel fruit intensity including limey, citrus and stone fruit flavours. The Pinot Gris, with an attractive pear and quince fruit, is one of the better New Zealand examples. Noble Sauvage, a botrytised Sauvignon Blanc, is made when conditions are particularly beneficial.

Recommended Reds:
Pinot Noir ★★★☆ £D
Recommended Whites:
Chardonnay ★★★☆ £D Sauvignon Blanc ★★★☆ £C
Riesling Dry ★★★ £C Pinot Gris ★★★ £C

⬤ Kumeu River (Kumeu, Auckland) *www.kumeuriver.co.nz*
Michael Brajkovich is one of New Zealand's most important winemakers. Although the family vineyards are in the now less than fashionable Kumeu district, west of Auckland, his intelligent, non-conformist approach showed it was possible to make better wines by rejecting some of the rigid, purely technical doctrines of winemaking that dominated styles in the late 20th century. Instead he adapted to a New Zealand context the best from established wine cultures and has made arguably the country's best Chardonnay for well more than a decade. The use of indigenous yeasts, hand picking grapes and then whole-bunch pressing have

now been adopted by others. Both the Kumeu River Chardonnay and Maté's Vineyard (an original vineyard replanted in 1990) are barrel-fermented and aged, and put through full malolactic fermentation. The resulting wines are richly textured, concentrated and complex with well-integrated oak characters and are also atypically ageworthy for New Zealand Chardonnay; they are usually best with 3–5 years' age but often keep for longer. Maté's version with fabulous fruit has the richness and texture of grand cru Burgundy if not the nuance. Melba is a ripe, characterful blend of Merlot, Malbec and Cabernet Franc. In recent vintages both Pinot Noir and a rich Pinot Gris with intense pear, quince and melon fruit have been made. 2004 was the first vintage of a stylish, richly textured and well-structured Sauvignon from Marlborough. Two further single vineyard Chardonnays, Hunting Hill and Coddington are also now made. Both are a little cheaper (£E) than Maté's Vineyard. The inexpensive second label is now known as Kumeu River Village. All the wines are now bottled under Stelvin caps.

Recommended Whites:
Chardonnay Maté's Vineyard ★★★★☆ £F
Chardonnay Hunting Hill Vineyard ★★★★☆ £F
Chardonnay ★★★★ £D Sauvignon Blanc Marlborough ★★★ £C
Pinot Gris ★★★ £C

>> Mahana Estates (Nelson) *www.mahana.nz*
A small range of wines is made at this Nelson winery under two separate labels. Mahana Clays and Gravels (not tasted) and Mahana. Under the Mahana label in addition to the Pinot Noir and Riesling the winery makes Pinot Gris, which is fermented relatively warm in older barriques on solid lees for weight and texture, a Pinot Noir rosé and a Method Traditionelle Brut sparkling white. The wines are all made from estate-grown fruit, organically farmed and vinified in a state of the art gravity flow winery facility. The vineyards are all dry farmed, with a south west facing exposition and naturally low yielding. The dark, spicy and supple Pint Noir comes from clay gravel soils and is vinified with a proportion of whole clusters and vatted for up to a month. The malolactic fermentation follows with ageing in one-fifth new wood before bottling without fining or filtration. The intense a floral scented Riesling gets additional weight and palate texture from a small proportion of barrel fermentation in old wood and ageing on fine lees. It is bottled unfined. A similar vinification regime is used for the Sauvignon Blanc with 20% barrel fermentation in old barrels. A floral, green fruits character, is underpinned by a subtle minerality. (DM)

Recommended Reds:
Pinot Noir Mahana ★★★☆ £D
Recommended Whites:
Riesling Mahana ★★★ £C
Sauvignon Blanc Mahana ★★☆ £C

Margrain Vineyard *www.margrainvineyard.co.nz*
From modest beginnings in 1992, this Martinborough husband-and-wife operation now makes a fine small range from vineyards either owned or leased. Much of the land includes vines over 20 years old. Part is on the original Martinborough terrace (including what used to be the Chifney vineyard) as well as a part on terraces to the south of Martinborough. The wines are made by the Australian-trained Strat Canning and include decent examples of ripe-fruited Sauvignon Blanc, Riesling, Pinot Gris and Gewürztraminer, the last with a rosewater intensity in a medium-dry style. Better, though, is a very ripe yet almost Meursault-like Chardonnay with good purity, breadth and concentration. Pinot Noir is subject to a lengthy pre

fermentation maceration and the Home Block has a smoky plum and cherry/berry fruit intensity with a forest-floor aspect. It is full and quite fleshy, with good weight, breadth and a supple structure. A second label Pinot Noir Rivers Edge is also now made. Some Chenin Blanc and a traditional method sparkler La Michelle are also made.

Recommended Reds:

Pinot Noir Home Block ★★★ £E

Recommended Whites:

Chardonnay ★★★ £C Sauvignon Blanc ★★ £C
Gewürztraminer ★★ £C
Pinot Gris ★★ £C

Martinborough Vineyard *www.martinborough-vineyard.co.nz*
Martinborough Vineyard built an international reputation following the recruitment of Larry McKenna as full-time winemaker. From his first vintage in 1986 he set about making Pinot Noir and Chardonnay from fully ripe grapes of the highest possible quality. His success brought acclaim for the region as a whole; its free-draining soil and particularly dry mesoclimate had been recommended in a scientific study and this originally led to the company's establishment by Duncan Milne. Despite a tendency to over-extraction in the Reserve in the mid-1990s, the underlying fruit quality of the Pinot Noir has generally been very good, developing impressive texture and a stylish complexity with 3–4 years' age or more. Larry McKenna left to develop his own project in 1999 (ESCARPMENT). Current releases now come from winemaker Paul Mason, who has worked in Europe as well as New Zealand. The wines show a gentler touch than of old with the usual flavour complexity. The Pinot Noir has a real *sauvage* fruit character, impressive length and a refined structure. A second Pinot, Te Téra is also very impressive. An occasionally released reserve, Marie Zelie is very pricy (£H). Also showing increasing refinement, Chardonnay was previously bold, oaky and structured with intense, ripe peachy/melony fruit and depth but improving for at least 3 or 4 years. Riesling is full and intensely flavoured but better structured than many New Zealand examples. Riesling is also late-picked and partially botrytised for a richer, off-dry style called Manu. Pinot Gris, unusual in being partly barrel-fermented, and Sauvignon Blanc (Pirinoa Block) are also made and a separate estate Burnt Spur was established in 2003 and from which Pinot Noir, Pinot Gris and Sauvignon Blanc are grown and the wines offer decent value.

Recommended Reds:

Pinot Noir Home Block ★★★★ £E
Pinot Noir Te Téra ★★ £C

Recommended Whites:

Chardonnay Home Block ★★★ £D
Riesling Jackson Block ★★ £C

Matakana Estate (Matakana) *www.greenpointwines.com.au*
Conditions on the Matakana peninsula can be similar to those on Waiheke Island. On the 34 ha of granulated clays of Matakana Estate, a classy, individual premium red, Moko, is fashioned from varying percentages of Merlot, Cabernet Franc, Cabernet Sauvignon and Malbec. Whatever the blend, the wine is only made when the fruit is of a sufficient standard. Recent vintages are excellent. Also very good is a ripe pear- and quince-laden Pinot Gris of good purity and intensity. Goldridge Estate wines are sourced both from estate vineyards in Marlborough and contract growers in Hawkes Bay.

Recommended Reds:

Moko ★★★☆ £D Syrah ★★★ £C

Recommended Whites:

Pinot Gris ★★★ £C

⚫ Millton (Gisborne) *www.millton.co.nz*
The Miltons are leading New Zealand proponents of biodynamics and run the leading winery in the Gisborne region, where most of the vineyards are in the hands of the big producers. Endeavouring to produce 'natural' wines, the Milltons have succeeded admirably in making whites of good fruit richness and intensity. The warm but humid Gisborne autumns favour the development of botrytis and the wines are often characterised by the extra intensity and flavours this brings. From around 20 ha there has been real success with three varieties in particular: Chenin Blanc, Riesling and Chardonnay. Chenin Blanc has been the country's best since the late 80s and the Riesling has rarely been surpassed, but there is a purity and intensity to the fruit in all three wines. More recently, a Viognier and a Gewürztraminer have been made. Late-harvested 'Special Bunch Selection' Viognier is also produced as is some red, including Syrah and Pinot Noir. A red blend, Cosmo red as well a Chenin and a Chardonnay are made under the very affordable (£B) Crazy by Nature label. A number of further premium releases also emerge from the Clos de Ste. Anne Estate which has been developed from the original Naboth's Vineyard, where Chardonnay and Pinot Noir were initially planted in 1980. Pinot Noir is elegant and restrained but with a well rounded supple structure. Chardonnay is very edgy and mineral, showing great depth and intensity. Syrah is planted on the higher plateau of the site but in a hot site facing north and protected from maritime breezes so ripens well. Chenin Blanc by contrast comes from lower lying vines, it is full and concentrated but with good acidity. Finally Viognier is richly textured, with a subtle floral component. It is grown in a warm site protected by woodland. (DM)

Clos de Ste. Anne

Recommended Reds:

Clos de Ste. Ann Syrah The Crucible ★★★★☆ £F
Clos de Ste. Anne Pinot Noir Naboth's Vineyard ★★★★ £E

Recommended Whites:

Clos de Ste. Ann Chenin Blanc La Bas ★★★★☆ £F
Clos de Ste. Anne Chardonnay Naboth's Vineyard ★★★★☆ £F
Clos de Ste. Anne Viognier Le Arbres ★★★★ £E

Millton

Recommended Reds:

Pinot Noir La Cote ★★★☆ £D

Recommended Whites:

Viognier Clos Samuel SBS ★★★★ £F
Viognier Riverpoint ★★★ £C
Chenin Blanc Te Arai Vineyard ★★★☆ £D
Chardonnay Opou Vineyard ★★★☆ £D
Riesling Opou Vineyard ★★★ £D
Gewürztraminer Riverpoint ★★★ £C

Mt Difficulty (Central Otago) *www.mtdifficulty.co.nz*
One of the most promising of a new wave of wineries in Central Otago, originally established in 1992 and now made in a modern winemaking facility by Matt Dicey. The four partners, including Matt's father, Robin Dicey, own some 32 ha of vineyard with further vines leased. This gives scope for small amounts of single-vineyard interpretations as well as blended examples. Pinot Noir is the star wine with the estate version from Bannockburn fruit continues to improve, adding more weight and density than previously seen. The widely sourced Roaring Meg is relatively simple and in a fruit driven style. Several single vineyard examples are also now made of a number of varieties. Small volume Chardonnay and Sauvignon Blanc are stylish with better structure than previously. Pinot Gris is a lively,

New Zealand

fruit-driven example; a Mansons Farm version is late-harvested. Riesling is made in different versions, varying both in origin and the degree of sweetness.

Recommended Reds:
Pinot Noir ★★★☆ £E
Recommended Whites:
Chardonnay ★★★☆ £D
Pinot Gris ★★★ £C
Sauvignon Blanc ★★☆ £C

❀ Mount Edward (Central Otago) *www.mountedward.co.nz*
This small Central Otago winery was the creation of regional pioneer Alan Brady who founded the nearby Gibbston Valley. The project is now run by winemaker Duncan Forsyth and proprietor John Buchanan. As well as some top-flight Pinot Noir small quantities of Riesling, Pinot Blanc, Pinot Gris, Chardonnay and Gruner Veltliner have also been made. Sourced from quite well established vines the Pinot has a very attractive ripe yet sappy quality that adds richness with a little age. Successive vintages show increasing weight and depth. A number of single vineyard examples have also been released in recent vintages. Quantities are likely to remain small but these are some of the finest examples of Central Otago Pinot Noir.

Recommended Reds:
Pinot Noir Morrison ★★★★☆ £F
Pinot Noir ★★★★ £E

Mountford (Mountford, Canterbury)
Mountford's owners are among those who have put their faith in Waipara's limestone-rich soils. They are aided in their quest to make one of New Zealand's best Pinot Noirs by employing specialist vineyard and winemaking expertise. Viticultural improvements to 5 ha of vineyards have enabled an extra class and complexity in the Pinot Noir. Chardonnay is also made in a full-bodied, concentrated, oak-influenced style. Both wines suggest that the winery has got it right although others in Waipara are still struggling for both ripeness and structure.

Recommended Reds:
Pinot Noir ★★★ £E
Recommended Whites:
Chardonnay ★★★ £D

Mud House (Marlborough) *www.mudhouse.co.nz*
If not one of the out and out stars of the region, Mudhouse has established a consistent and reasonably priced range of varietals since the first vintage in 1996. Grapes are sourced both from estate vineyards in Marlborough, the Waipara Valley and Central Otago as well as from other growers. Winemaking consultancy has come from roving winemaker Matt Thomson and wineries are now in operation not only in Marlborough but also in Waipara. Whites are attractive with reasonable structure and good depth and intensity. However Pinot Noir comes across as the real focal point, with a lovely black cherry and savoury intensity in the Central Otago Estate example. There are also now a number of Single Vineyard releases from Estate sites. Mud House has now been purchased by Accolade Wines so there may well be changes afoot.

Recommended Reds:
Pinot Noir Central Otago Estate ★★★ £D
Pinot Noir ★★ £C
Recommended Whites:
Sauvignon Blanc Marlborough Estate ★★ £C

Murdoch James Estate (Martinborough) *www.murdochjames.co.nz*
Pinot Noir and Syrah are the main thrust of production at this expanding organic estate in Martinborough. Pinot, especially in the top Fraser Estate and Blue Rock bottlings, is ripe, rich and fleshy with something of a Pommard-like strength. A tendency to slightly overripe fruit and the use of 100% French oak give the wines a distinctive stamp but they are nonetheless very good. Syrah is in the same mould with lots of extract; it needs a little more refinement but is promising too. A Cabernet Franc comes from the Blue Rock Vineyard as well. Sauvignon Blanc is a good Martinborough example and Riesling and Pinot Gris are also made.

Recommended Reds:
Pinot Noir Blue Rock ★★★ £D
Pinot Noir Fraser ★★★ £D
Pinot Noir Martinborough ★★☆ £C
Syrah Blue Rock ★★☆ £D
Recommended Whites:
Chardonnay Blue Rock ★★☆ £C
Sauvignon Blanc Blue Rock ★★ £C

Neudorf (Nelson) *www.neudorf.co.nz*
Neudorf stood for fine quality in the Nelson region when neighbouring Marlborough was a fraction of the size it is now. Yet while Marlborough has expanded rapidly wine quality in Nelson has been advanced by Neudorf and just a few others dedicated to maximising the quality of the fruit in their vineyards. Moderately high densities and relatively low yields play a part in producing wines with good concentration but which aren't overworked in the winery. There is a fine Sauvignon Blanc from local Moutere fruit. A rich, complex Moutere Chardonnay has been successful too and is a good deal better than most Marlborough examples. Sometimes showing a botrytis influence, it is deep, powerful and if not subtle can be impressively complex with a little age. A second Chardonnay is more widely sourced, while a perfumed Moutere Riesling with floral and mineral aromas has been consistently good. Pure, silky Pinot Noir has become a Neudorf speciality, the fine Moutere example surpassed by a Moutere Home Vineyard version. A little Pinot Gris has also been made along with a well priced additional Pinot Noir Tom's Block.

Recommended Reds:
Pinot Noir Moutere ★★★★ £E
Recommended Whites:
Chardonnay Moutere ★★★★ £E
Chardonnay Nelson ★★☆ £C
Riesling Dry Moutere ★★★☆ £C
Riesling Moutere ★★★ £C
Pinot Gris Moutere ★★★ £C
Sauvignon Blanc Nelson ★★☆ £C

Obsidian (Waiheke Island) *www.obsidian.co.nz*
This small Waiheke operation produces an increasingly good estate red for which it deserves to be better known. The Obsidian red, now from over 20-year-old vines, is Cabernet Sauvignon/Merlot - based but includes significant percentages of Malbec and Cabernet Franc. It is very individual and stylish with good depth and reveals oak spice, chocolate, coffee, even a mineral quality in its complex aromas and flavours. An Obsidian Cabernet Sauvignon/Merlot red is blended also with a touch of Petit Verdot, Cabernet Franc and Malbec and is cool, supple and stylish for a second wine. A rosé also comes from Merlot grapes. A second premium Bordeaux styled blend The Mayor comes from Cabernet Franc, Petit Verdot

and Malbec, while Syrah (including a Reserve), Montepulciano, Tempranillo, Chardonnay, Pinot Gris and Viognier are also made.
Recommended Reds:
Obsidian Red ★★★★ £E
Obsidian Cabernet/Merlot ★★★ £C

Palliser Estate (Martinborough) *www.palliser.co.nz*
Palliser was one of the early quality leaders in Martinborough with a deserved reputation for Sauvignon Blanc and promise with Pinot Noir. As volumes increased during the 90s quality levelled off while others forged ahead. Nonetheless the wines are consistent and Palliser continues to offer reasonably priced interpretations of varietals from the district. The estate Pinot Noir continues to be produced in small quantities and draws in part on 25-year-old vines. It is complex and stylish with good length if missing the extra concentration and dimension of the region's best. A very special release, Great Dogs (which has not yet been tasted) is also now made. It is seriously expensive (£G), certainly in a New Zealand context. Pencarrow is a second label and includes soundly made Sauvignon and Pinot Noir.
Recommended Reds:
Pinot Noir ★★★ £D
Pinot Noir Pencarrow ★☆ £C
Recommended Whites:
Chardonnay ★★☆ £C
Sauvignon Blanc ★★ £C
Sauvignon Blanc Pencarrow ★☆ £B
Riesling ★★ £C
Pinot Gris ★★ £C

❂ Pegasus Bay (Waipara Valley) *www.pegasusbay.com*
Pegasus Bay is Waipara's and Canterbury's leading winery. This is very much a family operation and one of Ivan Donaldson's sons, Matthew, has established a very successful winemaking duo with his wife Lynette Hudson. Both are trained winemakers. Matthew's reds include an increasingly good plummy, fleshy Pinot Noir capable of a little age. Prima Donna is a superior selection made only in the best vintages. A Cabernet/ Merlot is also produced though this is more variable in quality. Maestro is another special selection. The whites, made by Lynette, are arguably more consistent and include good richly textured examples of Chardonnay and Sauvignon/Sémillon as well as a fruit-rich Riesling, especially good in a late harvested, botrytis-affected version, Aria.
Recommended Reds:
Pinot Noir ★★★★ £E
Recommended Whites:
Chardonnay ★★★★ £E
Riesling Aria ★★★☆ £C
Riesling ★★★ £C
Sauvignon Blanc/Sémillon ★★★ £C

❂ Pisa Range (Central Otago) *www.pisarangeestate.co.nz*
Warwick and Jenny Hawker have the kind of focus that a region as exciting as Central Otago deserves. They make Riesling and of course Pinot Noir. Having planted on virgin wine territory in 1995, they produced their first vintage in 2000. The wine sees 12 months in French oak (one-third new). It is a deep, complex example with good breadth and length as well as a touch of class. This is a fine example of Pinot, deserving 5–6 years' age. Although it is already one of the region's best, expect more as the vines take on more age. A Riesling is also made as well as a second tier Pinot Noir Run 245.

Recommended Reds:
Pinot Noir Black Poplar Block ★★★★ £E

Redmetal Vineyards (Hawkes Bay) *www.redmetalvineyards.co.nz*
This small 7 ha estate is property of Grant Edmonds, a winemaker at SILENI and once head winemaker for the VILLA MARIA group. Redmetal refers to the local name for the often reddish, coloured river gravels on which many of the region's leading vineyards lie. Two-thirds of the vineyard is planted to Merlot, the rest mostly to Cabernet Franc with only a little Cabernet Sauvignon. The main focus is the Basket Press Merlot/Cabernet Franc red, a ripe and structured wine usually better with 3–5 years' age. Quality is maintained by the production of a more accessible Merlot/Cabernet Franc blend. Also made but only in exceptional vintages, is The Merlot, the most recent release 2007 from the Erinview Vineyard. A selection of the very best fruit, it is intense and richly berryish and the classic scent of very fine Merlot as well as a slightly overripe plum/prune component as well as an impressive structure and good ageing potential. A Syrah, a Chardonnay and some rosé are also made.
Recommended Reds:
The Merlot ★★★★ £F
Merlot/Cabernet Franc Basket Press ★★★ £D
Merlot/Cabernet Franc ★☆ £C

>> Domaine Rewa (Central Otago) *www.domainerewa.com*
Very fine, elegant Burgundian style Pinot Noir is made at this small biodynamically farmed winery as well Chardonnay and Riesling, with Pinot Gris also planted. The first vintage here was only in 2011 although the vines were first planted in 1997, adding a little complexity in the wine. Less than 1,000 cases are made a year. The small 5.5 ha vineyard is nestled into the foothills of the regions Pisa Range. The Riesling (not tasted) is off dry in style. The Chardonnay is barrel-fermented with restrained use of oak and offers fine white fruits, intense citrus notes and a buttery undercurrent. Pinot Noir is very much in a dark red-fruited style with hints of cherry and plum. The wine is fully de-stemmed and then ageing is in one-third new wood for just over eight months for balance. Finely structured with fresh edgy acidity and supply polished tannins the wine should evolve nicely for at six to seven years. (DM)
Recommended Reds:
Pinot Noir Central Otago ★★★★ £E
Chardonnay Central Otago ★★★★ £E

>> Rippon Vineyard (Central Otago) *www.rippon.co.nz*
The first vinifera vines were planted here as long ago as 1975 and the winery is one of the regional benchmarks for top Pinot Noir and Riesling. The vineyards, which are farmed biodynamically, are on the shores of Lake Wanaka with a spectacular backdrop, in the northerly stretches of the region. The climate of the area with warm summers and low annual rainfall coupled with a wide diurnal variation in daily temperature during the growing season provides excellent growing conditions for winegrowing. The body of Lake Wanaka also helps in guarding against frost. As well as the wines included below there are young vine examples, of both Pinot Noir and Riesling, Gamay and Osteiner which comes from Riesling and Sylvaner. The roundly textured Sauvignon Blanc gets a proportion of the fruit barrel-fermented as well as then short ageing on fine lees. It offers restrained green fruit and citrus with a mineral edge. Gewürztraminer is richly textured and finely structured with lees enrichment and restrained spicy, varietal aromas. Riesling gains from

significant vine age. The wine displays an intense, floral, citrus fruit quality and is nicely underpinned by a real mineral character from the schist soils. Pinot Noir is very fine, the age of the vines clearly showing through in the complexity of the wines with a rich, gamey quality and intense dark fruits. Both Emma's Block and Tinkers Field offer a touch more intensity and depth. (DM)

Recommended Reds:
Pinot Noir Emma's Block Mature Vine ★★★★☆ £F
Pinot Noir Tinker's Field Mature Vine ★★★★☆ £F
Pinot Noir Rippon Mature Vine ★★★★ £E

Recommended Whites:
Riesling Mature Vine ★★★☆ £D
Gewürztraminer ★★★ £C
Sauvignon Blanc ★★★ £C

>> Rockburn (Central Otago) www.rockburn.co.nz
Small winery producing generally well priced examples from the region. It started life in 1991 as a hobby for owner Richard Bunton. There are now two separate vineyard sites with a state of the art winery facility. An unusual trick is to play loud rock music to the fermenting wines. As well as those wines reviewed here a Fumé Blanc, Stolen Kiss Rosé Pinot Noir and two further wines under the Devils Staircase label are also made. A much pricier Rockburn Pinot Noir, Eleven Barrels (£F) is also available. Pinot Gris is in a zesty, peachy style, fermented cool with some lees enrichment and just a small touch of residual sugar. Chardonnay is similarly crisp and fresh, with minimal oak influence only a small proportion goes through barrel fermentation and then the wine enjoys a full malolactic, adding weight and texture. Riesling retains its aromatic qualities with a cool ferment and is in an off-dry style. Sauvignon Blanc is green fruited but offers weight and a rounded texture being part barrel-fermented and part stainless steel fermented. The well-priced regular Pinot Noir is in a dark cherry fruited style with nicely judged oak, being aged for 10 months and a 5 to 7 day cold soak adding to the wines approachable fruit character. (DM)

Recommended Reds:
Pinot Noir ★★★☆ £D

Recommended Whites:
Pinot Gris ★★★ £C
Chardonnay ★★☆ £D
Riesling ★★☆ £C Sauvignon Blanc ★★☆ £C

Saint Clair (Marlborough) www.saintclair.co.nz
Saint Clair, founded in 1994, has taken full advantage of the considerable involvement of Matt Thomson (also at the laudable LAKE CHALICE and DELTA) who works with Hamish Clark and two other winemakers. Now a sizeable operation (150,000 - 200,000 cases) Saint Clair does an admirable job of sustaining quality with increased volumes. There is solid quality in a regular Marlborough range of Premium labeled varietals, particularly whites including Sauvignon, Riesling and Chardonnay that reveal good fruit intensity and adequate structure. Better are the Reserves that include a dense, textured mineral-imbued Wairau Reserve Sauvignon - although there is some lees contact for this wine generally Matt doesn't generally favour lees or oak-influenced Sauvignon, preferring to show off the pristine fruit quality possible in Marlborough. Small site-specific batches are bottled under the Pioneer Block label; there are 10 different Sauvignons alone but each shows a slightly different fruit spectrum and structure. Other excellent (and reasonably priced) Reserves include an Omaka Chardonnay with a semblance to a fine Saint-Aubin. For Pinot Noir

there's a decent Bourgogne Rouge equivalent in the fruit-driven Marlborough example but there's much more excitement at the Reserve level. Both Omaka bottling and Doctor's Creek come from partly clayey soils and see a proportion of new oak, slightly more in the slightly denser, riper (cherry, plum) and classy Omaka. Doctor's Creek is slightly cooler (more floral and redcurrant) but is elegant too. A Merlot Reserve is a rare fine example for Marlborough; it has lush cedary berry, plummy fruit within a fine frame. Other Reserves (not tasted) include Gewürztraminer (Godfrey's Creek), Riesling (Godfrey's Creek) and Pinot Gris (Godfrey's Creek). It is likely that all should be a fair bet based on the consistency and quality achieved here. Only a basic Vicar's Choice range is generally more ordinary if reasonable quaffing wine.

Recommended Reds:
Pinot Noir Omaka Reserve ★★★★ £E
Pinot Noir Doctor's Creek Reserve ★★★☆ £D
Pinot Noir Premium Marlborough ★★☆ £C
Merlot Rapaura Reserve ★★★☆ £C

Recommended Whites:
Chardonnay Omaka Reserve ★★★☆ £D
Chardonnay Premium Marlborough ★★☆ £C
Sauvignon Blanc Wairau Reserve ★★★☆ £D
Sauvignon Blanc Pioneer Block 1 ★★★ £C
Sauvignon Blanc Pioneer Block 2 ★★★ £C
Sauvignon Blanc Pioneer Block 7 ★★★ £C
Viognier Hawkes Bay ★★☆ £C
Gruner Veltliner Premium Marlborough ★★☆ £C
Riesling Premium Marlborough ★★ £B

✿ Schubert (Martinborough) www.schubert.co.nz
Schubert is the most exciting new name to emerge from Martinborough/Wairarapa in recent years. Germans Kai Schubert (trained at Geisenheim) and Marion Deimling made a start here in 1998 and now have around 14 ha of vineyards. Most are located at on terraces in East Taratahi (near Gladstone) but the balance is from Martinborough terraces. The quality of the reds is very impressive given the youth of the vines. Hand picked grapes are completely de-stemmed and the artisanal nature of the winemaking includes open fermenters, a pre-fermentation maceration, around 3 weeks in total on skins and ageing in French oak (50% or more new). Most striking is the quality of tannins. Of the very good Pinot Noirs, an estate version surpasses Marion's Vineyard (which comes from different clones), showing more density, class and a cooler fruit spectrum. A third, Block B comes from Dijon Clones. Other reds include a Bordeaux-styled blend Con Brio, which is very berryish and succulent with a cool streak. There are also tiny amounts of a deep, concentrated Syrah with super fruit, almost like a cross between Wairarapa and the northern Rhône. A perfumed, ripe-fruited white, Tribianco, is an unusual blend of Chardonnay, Pinot Grigio and Müller-Thurgau. A sweet white, Dolce, is also made from the latter variety. A stonefruit and tropical Sauvignon Blanc is also made as well as a rosé Pinot Noir.

Recommended Reds:
Pinot Noir Wairarapa ★★★★☆ £E
Pinot Noir Marion's Vineyard ★★★★ £E
Syrah Wairarapa ★★★★ £E
Con Brio Wairarapa ★★★ £D

Recommended Whites:
Sauvignon Blanc Wairarapa ★★☆ £C
Tribianco ★★☆ £C

New Zealand

Seresin (Marlborough) *www.seresin.co.nz*
Unquestionably style and image play a bigger part than usual in the projection of this rather sophisticated Marlborough winery established by film producer Michael Seresin in 1992. Consistent and fruit-intense wines are made among the regular varietals. There is more depth and complexity in Reserve Chardonnay and plenty of intensity and extract in the Leah Pinot Noir and there are additional Home and Rachel. Newish vineyards (Tatou Block and Raupo Creek) add substantially to the existing Seresin Estate block of 45 ha now certified organic and biodynamic. A Pinot Noir is also produced from each. Small amounts of a Malbec and 'Cabernets' (Cabernet Sauvignon /Cabernet Franc) have also previously been made. Marama Sauvignon is a 100% *barrique*-fermented and aged Sauvignon. A Reserve bottling is also now released. It has good potential in terms of texture, breadth and length with a marked leesy character. Olive oil production is also taken seriously too.

Recommended Reds:
Pinot Noir Leah ★★★☆ £E
Recommended Whites:
Chardonnay Reserve ★★★☆ £D
Chardonnay ★★★ £C
Pinot Gris ★★★ £C
Sauvignon Blanc ★★★ £C
Riesling ★★☆ £C

>> Sileni Estates (Hawkes Bay) *www.sileni.co.nz*
Based in Hawkes Bay, Sileni also have vineyard holdings in Marlborough from which a fairly extensive range of wines is made. A number of varieties are planted in Hawkes Bay, whereas just Sauvignon Blanc comes from Marlborough. The project was established in 1997 by entrepreneur Graeme Avery and his friend Grant Edmonds who is in charge of winemaking. The Cellar Selection wines offer great value and are fruit forward and approachable for early drinking. The Estate Selection wines have more depth and intensity. The Circle has lightly tropical, citrus fruit and is hand harvested. It has around 20% fermented in barrel and the wine then spends four months on lees to enrich it. The Lodge is sourced from separate Hawkes Bay sub regions adding to the wines complexity. Whole bunch pressing is followed by fermentation and then ageing on fine lees for ten months providing a rich texture, well judged oak and hints of citrus and white fruits. Estate Selection Straits Sauvignon Blanc offers a combination of grassy, gooseberry fruit with riper tropical notes as well. The fruit is sourced from a number of sites and after a cool fermentation with wine spends a short time on lees. Sileni are unusual in cultivating Pinot Noir at Hawkes Bay. The Plateau comes from cooler elevated river terraces and is marked by dark cherry fruit with good intensity. Vinification is in a mix of open and closed fermenters and then the malolactic fermentation occurs in small oak, a quarter new and then ageing for nine months. A number of other wines are also made under the Estate Selection label along with a handful of premium Exceptional Vintage releases. (DM)

Recommended Reds:
Estate Selection Plateau Pinot Noir ★★★ £D
Cellar Selection Pinot Noir ★☆ £B
Cellar Selection Merlot ★☆ £B
Recommended Whites:
Estate Selection Straits Sauvignon Blanc Marlborough ★★★ £C
Cellar Selection Sauvignon Blanc Marlborough ★★ £B
Estate Selection Chardonnay The Lodge ★★★ £C
Estate Selection Sémillon The Circle ★★★ £C

Cellar Selection Pinot Gris ★★ £B

Spy Valley (Marlborough) *www.spyvalleywine.co.nz*
This is a large Marlborough operation complete with winery, which stands out for the style of wines it produces at reasonably affordable prices. All the varietals show a fresh, exuberant character with good purity and intensity. This direct, expressive character contrasts with too many similarly priced Marlborough examples that suffer from being overly made, relying too much on yeasts, enzymes, sugar or oak. Nor are there any weak wines amongst those tasted below. The concentrated, stylish Gewürztraminer has to be the best ever produced in the region. The range also includes Chardonnay, Merlot, Syrah, Rosé, Echelon Méthode Traditionelle sparkler and a number of late harvested whites. A number of wines are also now made under the Envoy label from single estate vineyards.

Recommended Reds:
Pinot Noir ★★ £C
Recommended Whites:
Gewürztraminer★★★ £B
Riesling ★★ £B
Sauvignon Blanc ★★ £B
Pinot Gris ★★ £B

Staete Landt (Marlborough) *www.staetelandt.co.nz*
Staete Landt was the first European name given to New Zealand by passing explorer Abel Tasman (in 1642). 354 years later two more Dutch travellers chose it for their 21 ha of Marlborough vineyard. An emphasis on vineyard health and the highest quality fruit is already apparent in the wines, all of which show an intensity and breadth, which set them apart from standard Marlborough examples. The whites are well structured and concentrated. A small portion of the Sauvignon is barrel-fermented and aged but this is not in the least intrusive, while a complex Chardonnay shows a hint of minerality. Alsace-like Pinot Gris is ripe and pure and not heavy. The cool-fruited Pinot Noir has herbal and wild red fruits as well as a touch of forest floor but should develop a fine silky texture with a little age. Viognier, Syrah and Riesling in dry and Auslese styles are also released.

Recommended Reds:
Pinot Noir Marlborough ★★☆ £D
Recommended Whites:
Sauvignon Blanc Marlborough ★★★☆ £C
Chardonnay Marlborough ★★★ £C
Pinot Gris Marlborough ★★★ £C

❀ Stonecroft (Hawkes Bay) *www.stonecroft.co.nz*
Stonecroft, the project of the former owner soil scientist Dr Alan Limmer, earned a reputation for rich, characterful examples of Syrah and Gewürztraminer that helped to broaden interest among New Zealand producers in varieties other than the mainstream Chardonnay, Sauvignon Blanc, etc. All the Stonecroft wines, from approximately 10 ha of sheltered and particularly warm vineyards, are bold and richly textured, with concentrated fruit. Syrah, Gewürztraminer and Chardonnay are now the focus of production. The latter is bold and powerful, with a depth and substance missing from most New Zealand Chardonnay if not yet showing the refinement or elegance that should be possible here. Syrah Reserve, with a refined mineral, blackcurrant, plum character and a hint of white pepper, is the real star. Structured but with the rich fruit on the finish that is common to all these wines, it is best drunk with 5 years' age or more. A second string Syrah Serine is also now

New Zealand

made. Ruhanui is a varying blend of Cabernet Sauvignon and Merlot. It shows ripe, stylish fruit and ages impressively. From the same varieties a cheaper blend, Crofters, is also made. Zinfandel was added in 1999. Stonecroft's Sauvignon is good if unusually spicy and tropical.

Recommended Reds:
Syrah Reserve ★★★★ £E
Ruhanui ★★ £D
Recommended Whites:
Chardonnay Old Vine ★★★ £C
Gewürztraminer ★★★ £C
Sauvignon Blanc ★★ £C

❂ Stonyridge (Waiheke Island) www.stonyridge.co.nz

Stephen White's small north-facing vineyard is managed along organic lines and produces what is deservedly the most famous wine from Waiheke Island. The stated aim is to produce the best Bordeaux-style red in the world. Nonetheless it is very much a lifestyle-oriented project with the pleasures of sun and sea woven into its otherwise serious pursuit. Made since 1987, Larose Cabernets is a blend of predominantly Cabernet Sauvignon with lesser amounts of Merlot, Cabernet Franc, Malbec and Petit Verdot. Aided by naturally low fertility, the fruit quality owes much to meticulous vineyard care, resulting in yields typically around 25 hl/ha. The grapes are then transformed into a rich but harmonious blend of new oak and intense berry fruit with impressive ripeness, depth and balance. The fruit intensity holds up well with age though there is perhaps not quite the mellowed evolution in the structure that would be seen in a northern hemisphere red of similar quality. Optimum drinking therefore is probably between 3 and 6 years of age, though they will keep for much longer. As well as Larose, a Syrah/Mourvèdre/Grenache blend Pilgrim, a Malbec Luna Negra as well as a second wine, Airfield are also made. .

Recommended Reds:
Larose Cabernets ★★★★ £F

>> Te Kairanga (Martinborough) www.tkwine.co.nz

Originally established in 1984, this property is now a part of the Foley Wine Estates group of premium New Zealand wineries and under the same ownership as neighbouring MARTINBOROGH VINEYARDS. Other properties in the group are GOLDWATER ESTATE, VAVASOUR and GROVE MILL in Marlborough. Pinot Noir is the main focus although Chardonnay, Riesling, Sauvignon Blanc and Pinot are also made. The vines are planted in free draining stony river terraces with naturally low yields and farmed sustainably. The region is in fact cooler than Central Otago but this is complemented by a dry growing season with cool nights promoting a fresh edge in the resulting wines. The fruit is all estate grown and there are now 105 ha spread across four vineyard sites. The Home and Mcleod vineyards are planted on the Martinborough Terrace, the latter producing only high quality Pinot Noir. Spring Rock has a north-south orientation with hillside vines planted at an altitude of 100 metres or so. The Rua Vineyard is higher, 180 metres, and provides intense late ripened fruit. In the winery small fermenters are used and a gravity system installed. There is a fine, zesty floral scented and citrus flavoured Riesling with good weight and texture. As well as the TK Chardonnay (not yet tasted) the John Martin example is very stylish and intense. White fruits and citrus are balanced by subtle use of oak. Of the three Pint Noirs, the TK Pinot is bright and forward with attractive berry fruit. The Runholder is firmer and more structured. The supple and richly textured John Martin is in a darker

fruit style and sourced from the wineries best-sited plots. The TK Pinot Gris and Sauvignon Blanc (not tasted) are likely to be worth looking at. (DM)

Recommended Reds:
Pinot Noir John Martin ★★★★ £E
Pinot Noir Runholder ★★★☆ £D
Pinot Noir ★★★ £C
Recommended Whites:
Chardonnay John Martin ★★★★ £E
Riesling ★★★ £C

❂ Te Mata (Hawkes Bay) www.temata.co.nz

John Buck revived Te Mata in late 1978 (vines were first planted here in 1892) and almost immediately established it as, arguably, New Zealand's finest. Despite greatly increased competition Te Mata is still a leading light. There has always been a coherence to the estate's direction that has proved an inspiration to other would-be New Zealand winemakers. Production has reached 25,000 cases but the range has not expanded greatly and the quality and image of the wines has been at least maintained. The wines, made by Peter Cowley since 1994, impress for their style, harmony and elegance yet rarely lack for fruit or intensity. One wine, Coleraine, symbolises the estate; its ability to age with some grace and an appreciable mellowing of its structure is almost unique in the country. There can be a trace of greenness in cooler years but with 5 years' age or more it is usually distinguished by soft, caressing blackcurrant, cherry and berry fruit and a long richly textured finish. Both Coleraine and the more variable Awatea are labelled as Cabernet/Merlot but include Cabernet Franc as well as Cabernet Sauvignon in the blend. Syrah with a stylish, cool pepper, raspberry and black fruit intensity is another star as is the *barrique*-fermented and aged Elston Chardonnay, long one of New Zealand's best. Barrel-fermented Cape Crest Sauvignon Blanc, quite Bordeaux-like in style, is a rare fine Hawkes Bay example. A number of other estate wines are more affordable but less exciting. The Merlot/Cabernets needs a bit more oomph though the Syrah is promising. Also made is a Viognier Zara as well as a Gamay Noir.

Recommended Reds:
Cabernet/Merlot Coleraine ★★★★ £F
Cabernet/Merlot Awatea ★★★ £D
Syrah Bullnose ★★★☆ £E
Syrah Estate ★★ £C
Merlot/Cabernets Estate ★☆ £C
Recommended Whites:
Chardonnay Elston ★★★☆ £E
Chardonnay Estate ★★ £C
Sauvignon Blanc Cape Crest ★★★ £D
Sauvignon Blanc ★☆ £C

>> Te Whare Ra (Marlborough) www.twrwines.co.nz

This small 11 ha certified organic property is producing striking Pinot Noir and a number of whites. Their vineyard is in fact one of the oldest in Marlborough, planted in 1979 in loam over clay soils. It is naturally low yielding, both organic and biodynamic practices followed and everything done by hand. In the winery everything is done with minimal intervention and by small batch. The striking Pinot Noir offers great value. After a cold soak for around a week vinification is in small open fermenters with hand plunging. Ageing is then in small French oak for 11 months, around a third new. Vine age adds to complexity and there is a mix of both red and darker plum fruits. A second pricier single vineyard example SV 5182 is

also made as well as a Syrah. A range of whites is made including stylish, elegant and restrained Sauvignon Blanc with the bulk of the fruit coming from the Awatere Valley with warmer days and cooler nights. Mainly vinified in stainless steel a small proportion, up to one-tenth, is barrel fermented adding extra depth and structure. Again a single vineyard label is also made. There two single vineyard Rieslings from the 5182 site, M and D, not surprisingly Medium and Dry. Riesling D is gently whole bunch pressed and fermented cool. From old vines the wine offers very impressive depth and concentration with a zesty fresh edge. Gewürztraminer SV again comes from the 1979 established vineyard, the wine undoubtedly gaining from the vines age with complex, ripe lychee and citrus fruits after vinification solely in stainless steel. The single vineyard Toru (meaning three in Maori) is a blend of Gewürztraminer, Riesling and Pinot Gris offering an array of aromatic, spicy citrus flavours. Chardonnay and Pinot Gris varietals are also made. (DM)

Recommended Reds:
Pinot Noir Marlborough ★★★★ £D
Recommended Whites:
Riesling D Marlborough ★★★ £C
Gewürztraminer Marlborough ★★★ £C
Sauvignon Blanc Marlborough ★★★ £C
Toru Marlborough ★★★ £C

>> Terra Sancta Estate (Central Otago) www.terrasancta.co.nz
Former New Zealand financier Mark Weldon and his wife Sarah Eliott purchased Olssens in 2011, renaming it Terra Sancta Estate. Like Mt DIFFICULTY and FELTON ROAD, Terra Sancta is located in the superior Bannockburn sub-region of Central Otago, which found itself at the heart of a gold rush in the 19th century. All fruit is estate-grown and more than half is planted to Pinot Noir. This is subject to a lengthy cold pre-fermentation maceration, which no doubt contributes to the depth and expansive quality of the wines, particularly in the fine Jackson's Block example. Two further Single Block examples are also made, Slapjack and Shingle Beach. The lime, citrus and floral aromas of the Riesling show something of a regional style if missing the extra definition to be really fine. Other Estate whites include Lola's Block Pinot Gris and a further Riesling, Miro's Block. Chardonnay is barrel-fermented, rich and full-bodied. An Estate rosé comes from Pinot Noir, while under an additional label Mysterious Diggings, Pinot Noir, Pinot Gris, Gewürztraminer and a Dessert Riesling are made.

Recommended Reds:
Pinot Noir Jackson's Block ★★★☆ £E
Pinot Noir Estate ★★★ £D
Recommended Whites:
Chardonnay Estate Riverblock ★★★ £D
Riesling Estate Slapjack Block ★★☆ £C

◉ TerraVin (Marlborough) www.terravin.co.nz
It was Mike Eaton who bought and established the Clayvin vineyard in1989 (see FROMM) and now he has repeated the trick with a new hillside estate purchased in 1998. All 9.5 ha, not all of it in production yet but planted mostly to Pinot Noir, are on free-draining soils and densely planted (in a New Zealand context) to a variety of different clones. The wines are made by the widely travelled Mike Weersing (ex-NEUDORF), who has a promising venture at Waikari in North Canterbury (PYRAMID VALLEY). A lot of effort goes into fruit selection with amazing results for such young vines – just 15 years old. The very reasonably priced Terravin bottling has real style and impressive texture, while the Eaton Family Vineyard is a

step up with more weight and fruit intensity, easily absorbing a sizeable proportion of new oak ageing. More depth and complexity will come with greater vine age. There is a Sauvignon Blanc of reasonable structure and classic nettle, ripe gooseberry and red capsicum fruit. The range also includes a red blend J (£F) and a barrel fermented Sauvignon Te Ahu (£D).

Recommended Reds:
Pinot Noir Eaton Family Vineyard ★★★★☆ £F
Pinot Noir TerraVin Hillside Reserve ★★★★☆ £E
Pinot Noir TerraVin ★★★★ £D
Recommended Whites:
Sauvignon Blanc ★★★ £D

Trinity Hill (Hawkes Bay) www.trinityhill.com
John Hancock is one of the industry stalwarts in the modern era of New Zealand winemaking, who first helped establish Morton Estate as a quality leader in the 80s before moving on to form Trinity Hill in the 90s. He has always produced ripe, concentrated, fruit-driven wines – powerful and full, and sometimes oaky in the past. Although the winemaking is now more sophisticated, it comes across as Californian rather than European in style. Trinity Hill wines ooze fruit and have great intensity and are usually well balanced, though they can taste a little 'made', especially at lower levels. Despite the fruit richness, some of the wines can be a bit one-dimensional. Elegance, subtlety and class don't feature highly either but the wines have deserved wide appeal and success. Gimblett Gravels The Gimblett (a Bordeaux styled blend of Merlot, the Cabernets, Petit Verdot and Malbec) is concentrated and cedary with cassis and berry fruit. Also made under the Gimblett Gravels banner is a stylish Syrah as well as a Viognier and an Arneis. Super-premium Homage Syrah includes a touch of Viognier and is powerful and concentrated with fine minerality and depth. Trinity partners the Wilsons are owners of the London restaurants Bleeding Heart and The Sign of the Don.

Recommended Reds:
Homage Syrah ★★★★ £F
Syrah Gimblett Gravels ★★★ £D
The Gimblett Gimblett Gravels ★★★ £D
The Trinity Merlot/Cabernet Franc/Cabernet Sauvignon ★★ £C
Pinot Noir Hawkes Bay ★★☆ £C
Recommended Whites:
Chardonnay Hawkes Bay ★★☆ £C
Sauvignon Blanc Hawkes Bay ★★ £B

Two Paddocks (Central Otago) www.twopaddocks.com
Actor Sam Neill (Jurassic Park – as well as more demanding roles) is a celebrity wine producer in a fashionable wine region. But don't let that put you off as beneath the lightly irreverent façade there is serious intent here – and very good Pinot Noir. The wines are currently made by Dean Shaw at the Central Otago Wine Company, in which Neill is a partner. First Paddock is from the Gibbston Valley while Last Chance Pinot Noir is from the 3 ha Alex Paddocks site in the Earnscleugh Valley. Another site here, Redbank, will provide a third example. Grapes are hand-picked, with an emphasis on low yields and sustainable viticulture. Around 20% new French oak is used. Last Chance has more depth and class, First Paddock is more floral and fruit-intense. Accessible now, both should keep for 5 years. Picnic is a second label for Pinot Noir, Riesling and more but these have not been tasted.

Recommended Reds:
Pinot Noir First Paddock ★★★ £D
Pinot Noir Last Chance ★★★ £D

New Zealand

❀ Unison (Hawkes Bay) *www.unisonvineyard.co.nz*
Unison has been dedicated to the production of a top-quality blended red in the Gimblett Gravels of Hawkes Bay since 1993. Two versions are produced, Unison and Unison Selection, based on a 6 ha high-density, low-yielding vineyard (down to 1kg per vine) planted to Merlot, Syrah and Cabernet Sauvignon. The composition of the wines varies according to the success of each variety in a given year. Unison has a moderately long maceration time (typically 16–18 days) and spends a year in oak but only a third of it in *barriques*. Though there is not always a significant step up in quality, the Selection is based on the very best fruit and undergoes a longer maceration (3 weeks) and spends 12 months exclusively in *barriques* (new and second use) before further ageing in large oak. Though occasionally struggling for ripeness, both add more breadth, depth and complexity over some of the more overtly fruit driven Hawkes Bay reds. The Selection is a super wine, very full, intense and complex but deserving of another 3-5 years' age. New Syrah is dense and compact yet wonderfully expressive with black fruits, mineral and licorice; another great wine from the country's most under-rated producer. A Merlot Reserve as well as whites, Chardonnay, Sauvignon Blanc and Pinot Gris are also made.

Recommended Reds:
Unison Selection Gimblett Gravels ★★★★☆ £E
Unison Gimblett Gravels ★★★☆ £D
Syrah Hawkes Bay ★★★★ £E

Vavasour (Marlborough) *www.vavasour.com*
Vavasour's vineyards are a little south and east in the Awatere Valley, where there has recently been extensive planting by other producers and where it is claimed to be drier without the high water table common to much of the plantings in the Wairau Valley. There are two ranges of wines from 30 ha of estate vineyards as well as grapes bought in under contract. Excellent Sauvignon shows a minerally, ripe fruit intensity and structure and depth matched by few other Marlborough examples. Tight but creamy Chardonnay and a relatively light but fresh, aromatic Riesling are also impressive. Pinot Noir, sourced from still relatively young Awatere vines and Wairau fruit has made real progress with impressive depth and weight. Dashwood varietals are by no means a poor second (as is too often the case with a second label) and include an excellent zingy, nettly Sauvignon Blanc and an attractive gently oaked Chardonnay, a honeyed Pinot Gris as well as a fine Pinot Noir

Vavasour
Recommended Reds:
Pinot Noir Awatere Valley ★★★☆ £D
Recommended Whites:
Chardonnay Awatere Valley ★★★ £D
Sauvignon Blanc Awatere Valley ★★★ £C
Riesling Awatere Valley ★★★ £C
Pinot Gris Awatere Valley ★★★ £C
Dashwood
Recommended Reds:
Pinot Noir ★★ £C
Recommended Whites:
Chardonnay ★★ £C   Sauvignon Blanc ★★ £B
Pinot Gris ★★ £B

❀ Villa Maria (Auckland & Marlborough) *www.villamaria.co.nz*
The formidable Villa Maria group, with impressive wineries in both Auckland and Marlborough, also includes the independently run Hawkes Bay estates of ESK VALLEY and Vidal Estate. Most enviable

is the company's record of combining quality, quantity and consistency. Current winemaking direction comes from Alastair Maling MW. Most impressive are the Reserve-level and new single vineyard wines. Reserve Chardonnay can impress for its fruit intensity and improves with a little age while the Reserve Sauvignon Blancs have been among Marlborough's best in a succession of good vintages. New single-vineyard Sauvignon promise even more, both Southern Clays and Taylor's Pass (in the Awatere Valley) are impressively structured with a minerally intensity. Single vineyard Chardonnay from Taylors Pass is richly textured (and superb value). Single-vineyard Pinot Gris are also very good, including a floral and classy Seddon Vineyard example (also Awatere but on the southern side). Reserve Riesling is rich, ripe and intense and a Noble Late Harvest example is also made. There is considerable ambition too with Pinot Noir, as seen in the Reserve and contrasting new Seddon Vineyard and Taylor's Pass releases. All are deeply coloured, intense and concentrated but the single vineyard examples are more individual, expansive and Burgundian. Fine Reserve reds (based on Merlot and Cabernet Sauvignon) from Hawkes Bay have been made for more than a decade both from Villa Maria and Vidal Estate and show lots of ripe plum, berry and blackcurrant fruit intensity. The top Vidal wines take the Legacy label and include a Chardonnay as well as a Gimblett Gravels Cabernet Sauvignon/Merlot and a Gimblett Gravels Syrah. The third tier to the Villa Maria range, the Cellar Selection varietals and dual-variety reds and whites, can provide good varietal fruit but the whites need to be drunk young. Even the least expensive Private Bin whites can be very drinkable. All the wines are now bottled under Stelvin caps. Also see ESK VALLEY.

Villa Maria
Recommended Reds:
Merlot Reserve Gimblett Gravels ★★★★ £E
Cabernet Sauvignon/Merlot Reserve ★★★★ £D
Merlot/Cabernet Sauvignon Cellar Selection ★★☆ £C
Pinot Noir Taylor's Pass Vineyard ★★★☆ £E
Pinot Noir Seddon Vineyard ★★★☆ £E
Pinot Noir Reserve ★★★ £D
Pinot Noir Cellar Selection ★★ £B
Recommended Whites:
Chardonnay Taylor's Pass ★★★☆ £D
Chardonnay Reserve Marlborough ★★★ £C
Chardonnay Cellar Selection ★★ £B
Sauvignon Blanc Taylor's Pass Vineyard ★★★☆ £C
Sauvignon Blanc Southern Clays Vineyard ★★★ £C
Sauvignon Blanc Reserve Wairau River ★★★ £C
Sauvignon Blanc Reserve Clifford Bay ★★★ £C
Sauvignon Blanc Cellar Selection ★★ £B
Pinot Gris Seddon Vineyard ★★★☆ £C
Riesling Reserve ★★☆ £C
Riesling Cellar Selection ★★ £B
Vidal
Recommended Reds:
Merlot/Cabernet Sauvignon Reserve Gimblett Gravels ★★★ £D
Syrah Reserve Gimblett Gravels ★★★ £D
Recommended Whites:
Chardonnay Legacy Series ★★★★ £F
Chardonnay Reserve ★★★☆ £D

Other wines of note

Please Note That 'Cabernets' indicates that both Cabernet Sauvignon and Cabernet Franc are Included In a blend.

.

Auckland
Foxes Island
Recommended Whites:
Sauvignon Blanc Estate Sur Lie Aged Marlborough ★★★☆ £C
Riesling Dry Estate Marlborough ★★★ £C
Recommended Reds:
Pinot Noir Estate Marlborough ★★★☆ £D
Pinot Noir Fox Marlborough ★★★ £C
Karaka Point (South Auckland)
Recommended Reds: Syrah ★★ £C
Nobilo
Recommended Whites:
Sauvignon Blanc Icon Series ★★☆ £C
Providence (Matakana)
Recommended Reds: Cabernet/Merlot ★★★ £F
Michelle Richardson
Recommended Whites: Chardonnay Central Otago ★★★ £D
Sauvignon Blanc Marlborough ★★★ £C
Recommended Reds: Pinot Noir Central Otago ★★★ £E

Waiheke Island, Auckland
Te Motu
Recommended Reds: Cabernet/Merlot ★★★☆ £E
Goldie Estate
Recommended Reds:
Cabernet Sauvigon Merlot Franc Estate Reserve ★★★☆ £E
Merlot Cabernet Sauvigon ★★ £C
Recommended Whites: Chardonnay Estate Reserve ★★★ £D
Chardonnay Estate ★★ £C   Sauvignon Blanc Estate ★★ £C
The Hay Paddock
Recommended Reds: Syrah ★★★★ £F
Syrah Harvest Reserve ★★★ £D
Man O' War
Recommended Reds: Syrah Dreadnought ★★★★ £F
Ironclad ★★★★ £F   Cabernet/Merlot ★★★☆ £E
Recommended Whites: Chardonnay Valhalla ★★★☆ £E
Passage Rock
Recommended Reds: Syrah ★★★☆ £D
Gisborne
Bushmere Estate
Recommended Whites: Gewürztraminer ★★ £C
Vinoptima (Nick Nobilo)
Recommended Whites: Gewürztraminer Ormond ★★★☆ £D

Hawkes Bay
Babich
Recommended Reds: Syrah Winemaker's Reserve ★★ £C
Pinotage Winemaker's Reserve ★★ £C
Cabernet Sauvignon The Patriarch ★★★☆ £E
Cabernet Merlot Gimblett Gravels ★★ £B
Pinot Noir Winemaker's Reserve Marlborough ★★ £C
Recommended Whites:
Chardonnay Irongate ★★★ £C   Chardonnay Gimblett Gravels ★ £B
Sauvignon Blanc Winemaker's Reserve Marlborough ★★ £C
Bridge Pa
Recommended Reds: Syrah Hawkes Bay ★★★☆ £C

Syrah Louiis Hawkes Bay ★★★ £C
Cypress Wines
Recommended Reds: The Terraces Syrah Hawkes Bay ★★★☆ £D
Elephant Hill
Recommended Reds: Syrah Hawkes Bay ★★★☆ £D
Hatton Estate
Recommended Reds:
Tahi Gimblett Gravels (Cabernets/Merlot) ★★★ £E
Syrah Gimblett Gravels ★★★ £D
Matariki
Recommended Whites: Sauvignon Blanc Hawkes Bay ★★ £B
Recommended Reds:
Quintology Gimblett Gravels ★★★☆ £D
Syrah Gimblett Gravels Reserve ★★★ £C
Cabernet Sauvignon Gimblett Gravels Reserve ★★★ £D
Rod McDonald Wines
Recommended Reds: Syrah Trademark ★★★★ £F
Syrah Te Awanga Estate ★★★ £D
Mission Estate
Recommended Reds: Syrah Jewelstone ★★★ £D
Cabernet Merlot Jewelstone ★★★ £D
Morton Estate
Recommended Whites: Chardonnay Black Label ★★★ £C
Chardonnay Coniglio ★★★ £E
Sauvignon Blanc Stone Creek Marlborough ★ £B
Recommended Reds: Merlot/Cabernet Black Label ★★★ £D
Ngatarawa
Recommended Reds:
Merlot/Cabernet Sauvignon Alwyn Reserve ★★★ £D
Recommended Whites: Chardonnay Alwyn Reserve ★★ £D
Riesling Noble Harvest Alwyn Reserve ★★★ £E
Pask Winery
Recommended Reds: Cabernet/Merlot ★★ £C
Merlot Reserve ★★★ £D   Cabernet Sauvignon Reserve ★★★ £D
Declaration Reserve (Cab Sauv/Malbec/Merlot) ★★★☆ £E
Sacred Hill
Recommended Whites: Sauvignon Blanc Halo ★★☆ £C
Southbank Estate
Recommended Whites: Chardonnay The Terraces ★★ £B
Sauvignon Blanc The Terraces Marlborough ★☆ £B
Recommended Reds:
Merlot/Cabernet The Terraces ★★☆ £B
Syrah The Terraces ★★ £C   Pinot Noir The Terraces ★ £C
Squawking Magpie
Recommended Reds:
Cabernet/Merlot Gimblett Gravels (Cab Sauv/Merlot/Malbec) ★★★ £D
Syrah The Stoned Crow ★★☆ £D
Recommended Whites: Chardonnay the Chatterer ★★★ £C
Te Awa Winery
Recommended Reds:
Boundary Gimblett Gravels (Merlot/Cabernets) ★★★ £D
Syrah Gimblett Gravels ★★★ £C

Martinborough/Wairarapa
Alana Estate
Recommended Reds:
Pinot Noir Martinborough ★★★ £D
Ashwell
Recommended Reds:
Pinot Noir Martinborough ★★☆ £D

New Zealand

Cottier Estate
Recommended Whites: Sauvignon Blanc ★★☆ £B
Chardonnay Emily ★★★ £B
Recommended Reds: Pinot Noir ★★★ £C
The Elder
Recommended Reds: Pinot Noir Martinborough ★★★★ £E
Gem
Recommended Reds: Pinot Noir Martinborough ★★★☆ £D
Gladstone
Recommended Whites: Sauvignon Blanc ★★ £B   Riesling ★ £B
Pinot Gris ★★ £C
Recommended Reds: Pinot Noir ★★☆ £D
Pinot Noir Jealous Sisters ★★☆ £C
Julicher Estate
Recommended Reds: Pinot Noir Martinborough ★★★ £D
Recommended Whites: Sauvignon Blanc Martinborough ★★ £B
Matahiwi
Recommended Whites: Sauvignon Blanc Wairarapa ★★ £B
Recommended Reds: Pinot Noir Holly ★★★ £C
Pinot Noir Wairarapa ★★ £B
Merlot Hawkes Bay ★★ £C
Nga Waka
Recommended Whites: Sauvignon Blanc ★ £B   Riesling ★ £B
Chardonnay ★★ £C   Chardonnay Home Block ★★☆ £D
Recommended Reds: Pinot Noir ★★ £D
Porters
Recommended Reds: Pinot Noir ★★☆ £C
Te Hera
Recommended Reds: Pinot Noirte Muna Road ★★★ £C
Vynfields
Recommended Reds: Pinot Noir Reserve ★★★★ £E
Pinot Noir ★★★☆ £D
Recommended Whites: Dry Riesling ★★★ £C
Classic Riesling ★★★ £C

Marlborough
Astrolabe
Recommended Whites: Sauvignon Blanc ★★★ £C
Chardonnay Unoaked ★★☆ £C
Riesling Single Vineyard ★★☆ £C
Pinot Gris ★★★ £C
Recommended Reds: Pinot Noir Marlborough ★★★☆ £D
Auntsfield
Recommended Whites: Sauvignon Blanc Long Cow ★★ £C
Awatere River Wine Company
Recommended Whites:
Sauvignon Blanc (by Louis Vavasour) ★★★ £C
Pinot Gris (by Louis Vavasour) ★★☆ £C
Blind River Estate
Recommended Whites: Sauvignon Blanc Marlborough ★★★☆ £C
Clifford Bay Estate
Recommended Whites: Sauvignon Blanc Marlborough ★★ £B
Clos Henri (Henri Bourgeois)
Recommended Whites: Sauvignon Blanc Marlborough ★★★☆ £C
Sauvignon Blanc Bel Echo Marlborough ★★★ £C
Recommended Reds: Pinot Noir Marlborough ★★★★ £D
Pinot Noir Bel Echo Marlborough ★★★ £C
Corofin
Recommended Reds:
Pinot Noir Settlement Vineyard East Slope Marlborough ★★★★☆ £E

Kim Crawford
Recommended Whites:
Sauvignon Blanc 'SP' Spitfire Marlborough ★★☆ £B
Sauvignon Blanc Marlborough ★★ £B
Chardonnay 'SP' Wild Grace Hawkes Bay ★★ £C
Riesling Marlborough Dry ★★ £B   Pinot Gris Marlborough ★★ £B
Recommended Reds:
Pinot Noir 'SP' Rise and Shine Central Otago ★★☆ £C
Pinot Noir Marlborough ★☆ £C   Merlot Hawkes Bay ★★ £B
Delta Vineyard
Recommended Whites: Sauvignon Blanc Marlborough ★★☆ £C
Recommended Reds: Pinot Noir Hatter's Hill ★★★☆ £D
Pinot Noir Marlborough ★★☆ £C
Fairhall Downs
Recommended Whites: Chardonnay ★★★ £C
Sauvignon Blanc ★★☆ £B   Pinot Gris ★★ £C
Recommended Reds: Pinot Noir ★★★ £D
Framingham Wines
Recommended Whites: Sauvignon Blanc ★★☆ £C
Gewürztraminer ★★☆ £C   Riesling Classic ★★ £C
Recommended Reds: Pinot Noir ★★★ £D
Montepulciano ★★★ £D
Jackson Estate
Recommended Reds:
Pinot Noir Vintage Widow Marlborough ★★★ £D
Recommended Whites:
Sauvignon Blanc Estate Marlborough ★★☆ £C
Sauvignon Blanc Stich Marlborough ★★☆ £C
Lake Chalice
Recommended Whites: Sauvignon Blanc Marlborough ★★★ £C
Recommended Reds: Pinot Noir Marlborough ★★★☆ £D
Lawson's Dry Hills
Recommended Whites: Sauvignon Blanc ★★☆ £C
Chardonnay ★★ £C   Gewürztraminer ★★ £C
Riesling ★★ £C
Little Beauty
Recommended Whites:
Pinot Gris Black Edition Marlborough ★★★☆ £D
Pinot Gris Limited Edition Marlborough ★★★ £C
Sauvignon Blanc Black Edition Marlborough ★★☆ £B
Sauvignon Blanc Limited Edition Marlborough ★★☆ £C
Gewurztraminer Limited Edition Marlborough ★★☆ £C
Riesling Limited Edition Marlborough ★★ £B
Recommended Reds:
Pinot Noir Black Edition Marlborough ★★★☆ £D
Pinot Noir Liimited Edition Marlborough ★★☆ £C
Marisco Vineyards
Recommended Whites: The Ned Pinot Gris ★★★ £C
The Ned Sauvignon Blanc ★★★ £C
Recommended Reds: King's Wrath Pinot Noir ★★★ £C
The Ned Pinot Noir ★★★ £C
Maven Wines
Recommended Whites: Sauvignon Blanc ★★☆ £B
Chardonnay Marlborough ★★☆ £C
Chardonnay Reserve Marlborough ★★★☆ £D
Pinot Gris ★★☆ £B
Recommended Reds: Pinot Noir Marlborough ★★★ £D
Mount Riley
Recommended Whites: Sauvignon Blanc Estate ★☆ £B
Sauvignon Blanc Seventeen Valley ★★★ £B
Chardonnay Seventeen Valley ★★★ £C

Recommended Reds: Pinot Noir Estate ★☆ £C
Pinot Noir Seventeen Valley ★★★ £C

Nautilus
Recommended Reds: Pinot Noir Marlborough ★★★ £D
Recommended Whites: Chardonnay Marlborough ★★☆ £C
Sauvignon Blanc Marlborough ★★ £B

Ohau Wines
Recommended Whites:
Sauvignon Blanc Ohau Gravels Marlborough ★★★ £C
Sauvignon Blanc Woven Stone Marlborough ★★ £B
Pinot Gris Ohau Gravels Marlborough ★★☆ £C
Pinot Gris Woven Stone Marlborough ★★ £B

Allan Scott
Recommended Whites: Chardonnay Marlborough ★★ £B
Riesling Marlborough ★★ £B
Sauvignon Blanc Marlborough ★★ £B
Methode Traditionelle Blanc de Blancs Brut Non-Vintage ★★ £C
Recommended Reds: Pinot Noir Generations ★★★ £D
Pinot Noir Marlborough ★★ £C

Stoneburn
Recommended Whites: Sauvignon Blanc Marlborough ★★☆ £B
Chardonnay Marlborough ★★☆ £B

Tohu
Recommended Reds:
Pinot Noir Rore Reserve Marlborough ★★★★ £E
Recommended Whites:
Sauvignon Blanc Awatere Single Vineyard Marlborough ★★★☆ £C

Two Rivers
Recommended Reds: Altitude Pinot Noir Marlborough ★★★☆ £D
Tributary Pinot Noir Marlborough ★★★ £D
Recommended Whites:
Chardonnay Clos des Pierres Marlborough ★★★ £D
Sauvignon Blanc Convergence Marlborough ★★★ £C
Riesling Juliet Marlborough ★★☆ £C

Wairau River
Recommended Reds: Pinot Noir Reserve ★★★ £D

Whitehaven
Recommended Whites: Sauvignon Blanc ★★ £C
Recommended Reds: Pinot Noir ★★ £D

Wither Hills
Recommended Whites: Sauvignon Blanc ★★ £B
Chardonnay ★★ £C
Recommended Reds: Pinot Noir ★★☆ £C

Nelson
Kahurangi Estate
Recommended Whites: Sauvignon Blanc Estate ★★☆ £B
Riesling Estate Dry ★★ £B   Riesling Estate ★★☆ £B

Seifried Estate
Recommended Whites:
Riesling Winemaker's Collection Sweet Agnes ★★★☆ £D
Gewürztraminer Dry Winemaker's Collection ★★★ £C
Sauvignon Blanc ★★ £B   Riesling ★★ £B
Recommended Reds:
Pinot Noir Winemaker's Collection ★★★ £D

Te Mania
Recommended Whites: Sauvignon Blanc ★★☆ £B
Chardonnay Reserve ★★☆ £C
Recommended Reds:
Pinot Noir ★★☆ £C

Waipara/Canterbury
Sherwood Estate Wines
Recommended Whites: Sauvignon Blanc Marlborough ★★☆ £C
Riesling Waipara ★★☆ £B
Recommended Reds: Pinot Noir Estate Waipara ★★☆ £C

Terrace Edge
Recommended Reds: Pinot Noir ★★ £D

Torlesse
Recommended Reds: Pinot Noir Omihi Road Reserve ★★★ £D
Recommended Whites: Sauvignon Blanc Omihi Road ★★ £C

Waipara Hills
Recommended Reds: Pinot Noir Waipara Valley ★★★ £C
Recommended Whites: Riesling Dry Waipara Valley ★★★ £C
Sauvignon Blanc Marlborough ★★☆ £C

Waipara West
Recommended Reds: Pinot Noir Waipara ★★☆ £C
Recommended Whites:
Sauvignon Blanc Waipara ★★☆ £C   Riesling Waipara ★★☆ £C

Charles Wiffen
Recommended Whites: Chardonnay Marlborough ★★ £C
Riesling Marlborough ★☆ £B
Sauvignon Blanc Marlborough ★☆ £B

Central Otago
Aitken's Folly
Recommended Reds: Pinot Noir Riverbank Road ★★★☆ £D
Recommended Whites: Chardonnay ★★★ £C

Akarua
Recommended Reds: Pinot Noir ★★★☆ £E
Pinot Noir Rua ★★★ £D
Recommended Whites: Chardonnay ★★★ £C
Pinot Gris ★★☆ £C

Akitu
Recommended Reds: Pinot Noir A1 Akitu ★★★☆ £E

Ceres
Recommended Reds: Pinot Noir Composition ★★★ £E

Gibbston Valley
Recommended Whites: Chardonnay China Terrace ★★★☆ £D
Recommended Reds: Pinot Noir Reserve ★★★★ £F
Pinot Noir Central Otago ★★★☆ £D

Hawksburn Terrace
Recommended Reds: Pinot Noir ★★★☆ £D

Judge Rock
Recommended Reds: Pinot Noir ★★★☆ £E

Kawarau Estate
Recommended Reds: Pinot Noir Reserve ★★ £D
Pinot Noir ★☆ £C

Lowburn Ferry
Recommended Reds: Pinot Noir Home Block ★★★☆ £E

Misha's Vineyard
Recommended Reds: Pinot Noir High Note ★★★☆ £E

Mount Maude
Recommended Reds: Pinot Noir ★★★☆ £D

Mount Michael
Recommended Reds: Pinot Noir Bessies Block ★★★☆ £E
Pinot Noir ★★★ £D

Nevis Bluff
Recommended Reds: Pinot Noir ★★★ £E

Peregrine
Recommended Whites: Riesling ★★☆ £C
Pinot Gris ★★☆ £C

New Zealand

Recommended Reds:
Pinot Noir ★★★ £D

Quartz Reef
Recommended Reds:
Pinot Noir ★★★☆ £D
Recommended Whites:
Methode Traditionnelle Brut Non-Vintage (Pinot Noir/Chardonnay) ★★★ £C

Shaky Bridge
Recommended Reds:
Pinot Noir ★★☆ £D

Valli
Recommended Reds:
Pinot Noir Gibbston Vineyard ★★★★ £E

Wild Earth
Recommended Reds:
Pinot Noir Central Otago ★★★☆ £D

Wooing Tree
Recommended Reds:
Pinot Noir ★★★ £D

Work in progress!!

Producers under consideration for the next edition
Bell Hill (Waikari, Canterbury)
Kathy Lynskey (Marlborough)
Muddy Water (Waipara, Canterbury)
Pyramid Valley (Waikari, Canterbury)
Stonecutter Vineyard (Martinborough)

Author's choice

Arresting Sauvignon Blanc
Cloudy Bay   Sauvignon Blanc Marlborough
Craggy Range   Sauvignon Blanc Marlborough Old Renwick
Dog Point   Sauvignon Blanc Marlborough Section 94
Hunter's   Sauvignon Blanc Marlborough Winemaker's Selection
Isabel Estate   Sauvignon Blanc Marlborough
Neudorf   Sauvignon Blanc Marlborough
Palliser Estate   Sauvignon Blanc Martinborough
Staete Landt   Sauvignon Blanc Marlborough
Vavasour   Sauvignon Blanc Marlborough Single Vineyard
Villa Maria   Sauvignon Blanc Marlborough Taylor's Pass

Most Convincing Chardonnay
Ata Rangi   Chardonnay Martinborough Craighall
Carrick   Chardonnay Central Otago
Craggy Range   Les Beaux Cailloux Chardonnay Gimblett Gravels
Esk Valley   Chardonnay Hawkes Bay Reserve
Felton Road   Chardonnay Central Otago Barrel-Fermented
Kumeu River   Chardonnay Kumeu
Matua Valley   Chardonnay Gisborne Judd Estate
Millton   Chardonnay Gisborne Opou Vineyard
Pegasus Bay   Chardonnay Waipara
Te Mata   Chardonnay Hawkes Bay Elston
Vavasour   Chardonnay Marlborough Awatere Valley
Villa Maria   Chardonnay Marlborough Fletcher Vineyard

Other diverse high quality whites
Ata Rangi   Pinot Gris Martinborough Lismore
Cloudy Bay   Pelorus Vintage

Deutz   Marlborough Cuvée Non-Vintage
Dry River   Pinot Gris Martinborough
Felton Road   Riesling Central Otago Dry
Millton   Chenin Blanc Gisborne Te Arai Vineyard
Seifried   GewüRztraminer Nelson Winemakers Collection Dry
Stonecroft   GewüRztraminer Hawkes Bay

Top Cabernet or Merlot based reds
Alpha Domus   AD The Aviator Hawkes Bay
Craggy Range   The Quarry Gimblett Gravels
Esk Valley   The Terraces Hawkes Bay
Matakana Estate   Moko Matakana
Matariki   Quintology Gimblett Gravels
Obsidian   Obsidian Waiheke Island
Red Metal   The Merlot Hawkes Bay
Stonyridge   Larose Cabernets Waiheke Island
Te Mata   Coleraine Hawkes Bay
Te Motu Vineyard   Cabernet Sauvignon/Merlot Waiheke Island
Unison   Selection Gimblett Gravels

Leading Pinot Noir
Ata Rangi   Pinot Noir Martinborough
Bald Hills   Pinot Noir Central Otago
Carrick   Pinot Noir Central Otago
Felton Road   Pinot Noir Central Otago Block 3
Fromm   La Strada Pinot Noir Marlborough Fromm Vineyard
Greenhough   Pinot Noir Hope Vineyard
Martinborough Vineyard   Pinot Noir Martinborough
Mount Difficulty   Pinot Noir Central Otago
Mount Edward   Pinot Noir Central Otago
Mountford   Pinot Noir Waipara
Murdoch James Estate   Pinot Noir Martinborough Fraser
Neudorf   Pinot Noir Moutere
Olssens   Pinot Noir Central Otago Jackson Barry
Pisa Range   Pinot Noir Central Otago Black Poplar Block
Schubert   Pinot Noir Wairarapa
Terravin   Pinot Noir Marlborough Hillside Selection
Two Paddocks   Pinot Noir Central Otago Last Chance
Villa Maria   Pinot Noir Marlborough Seddon Vineyard

And Promising Syrah
Babich   Syrah Hawkes Bay Winemakers Reserve
Craggy Range   Syrah Gimblett Gravels Block 14
Dry River   Syrah Martinborough
Murdoch James Estate   Syrah Martinborough
Newton Forrest Estate   Syrah Cornerstone
Schubert   Syrah
Stonecroft   Syrah Hawkes Bay
Te Mata   Syrah Hawkes Bay Bullnose
Trinity Hill   Syrah Hawkes Bay
Unison   Syrah Hawkes Bay

Dramatic and positive change in South Africa has seen increased involvement in the wine industry by all ethnic groups and much work and research have gone into improving the quality of the nation's vineyards. There is no doubting that wine quality at the upper end of the market here is good and improving. An increasing number of dynamic and truly exciting new producers are continuing to emerge. A number of reds of true world class are also being made, some at world class prices too. However South Africa still wants for more wines of such indisputable style and complexity. There has been a recent trend towards micro-production garage-style wines but it remains to be seen how many of these will stand the test of time.

The Regions

Quality wine production in South Africa is centred around **Stellenbosch** WO. The region is one of the most attractive to visit anywhere in the world, with towering mountains rising seemingly out of the ocean. Stellenbosch itself is not only home to some of the largest wine companies in the country but also to some of its most impressive. There is a wide variation of mesoclimates within the WO with maritime breezes and the Simonsberg and Helderberg mountains playing a role in tempering conditions. In the coolest areas Sauvignon Blanc and Chardonnay (including some impressive barrel-fermented examples) are both successful, as is the occasional Riesling. Chenin Blanc tends to be much in the local style with some residual sugar. Stellenbosch reds are among the best in the country. Pinotage can be particularly striking in the warm vineyards to the north-east of Stellenbosch. Decent Bordeaux-style reds abound and a number of wineries are producing excellent results with Shiraz. Merlot can be good but also a touch vegetal. Although the wines are less rustic than of old and with much of the virus infection once prevalent now removed, a marked minty note found in a number of reds can be overpowering.

To the north of Stellenbosch is the second-largest region, **Paarl**. The area is warm and reds including some very successful Shiraz and Merlot are produced. There are also a number of cooler mesoclimates where the odd decent Sauvignon Blanc and Sémillon are made, as well as Chardonnay and some fine Pinot Noir. White Rhône varieties are also increasingly widely planted. To the immediate east is Franschhoek. The valley here gets cooler as you move east and up to higher altitudes. Again, very good Shiraz and Cabernet Sauvignon are produced as well as earlier-ripening whites and Pinot Noir. To the east of Stellenbosch is the cool Durbanville region and newly established Philadelphia. Then south of Cape Town Constantia is home to a small number of good producers. The climate is cool and moderated by both Indian and Atlantic Ocean breezes and whites are more successful than the reds. Some way to the east of Stellenbosch are the regions of Worcester and Robertson. The latter has some potential for good whites grown in limestone soils.

The vast, semi-desert and arid expanse of the Klein Karoo, several hundred kilometres inland, sees the production of some reasonable fortified styles but is too hot to produce fine table wines. Swartland just to the north-west of Paarl appears to have real potential. Hillside vineyards planted on well-drained granite soils are the source of good Pinotage, Shiraz and Merlot. The high diurnal variation of mountainous vineyards of Tulbagh to the east of Swartland would suggest excellent potential. Great wines are emerging. To the south-east of Cape Town is the district of Overberg which includes Elgin and on the coast immediately south Walker Bay is a source of great Pinot Noir and Chardonnay. Elim and Cape Agulhas to the east is centred around South Africa's southernmost tip and provides great scope for cool grape growing. Swellendam, some distance to the east of the Cape also appears to have much potential.

A-Z of producers by region

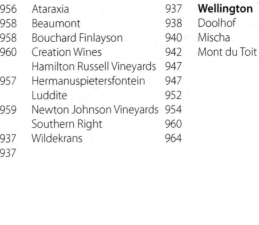

Wine behind the label

South Africa

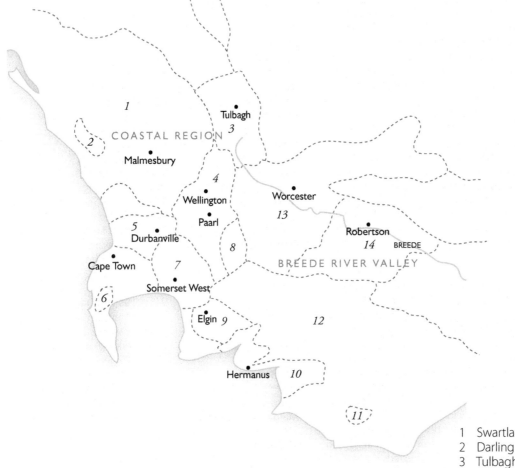

1 Swartland
2 Darling
3 Tulbagh
4 Paarl
5 Durbanville
6 Constantia
7 Stellenbosch
8 Franschhoek
9 Elgin
10 Walker Bay
11 Elim
12 Overberg
13 Worcester
14 Robertson

South Africa vintages

The top Cape reds will develop and keep well, the best for up to a decade. The majority should be approached sooner. Whites generally need drinking soon after release, although the odd barrel-fermented Chardonnay and some other richer whites will develop in the short term. 2016 has produced low yields but warm weather during the growing season will see some fine wines produced. 2015 enjoyed good weather throughout the growing season with good wines produced 2014 was promising for early ripening whites, Chardonnay, Chenin Blanc and Sauvignon Blanc. Later ripening red varieties are more variable but overall yields were good. 2013 was genrally successful with very occasional wet weather during harvest. Good early ripening whites and fine reds, albeit a little more elegant than riper years. 2012 was a good year with cool late season growing conditions and good fruit harvested relatively late. The harvest in 2011 was earlier than usual with ripe reds and whites showing more overt tropical flavours than green notes. Yields were generally good. 2010 produced good flavoursome whites and well-ripened and characterful reds. The only real downside is a crop somewhat down on 2009. 2008 is good for both reds and whites and reds which have lower than normal recent alcohol levels. An early heatwave in 2007 did not aid early-ripening varieties but was good for reds including Cabernet and Syrah. 2006 reds were harvested at excellent phenolic ripeness. 2005 was sound if variable. 2004 was good for reds but there was also uneven ripening. 2003 looks to be a very good year for the Cape and earlier years to consider for premium reds are 2002, 2001, 2000, 1998 and 1997

A-Z of producers

>> 4 G Wines (Cape Town) *www.4g-wines.com*

The G red sets new standards for the price of super premium reds from the Cape winelands. It is around three times the price of any local competition and is placed firmly at competing with the most expensive from the Napa Valley. Some commentators are proclaiming it as potentially the SCREAMING EAGLE of South Africa. There have only been a handful of vintages so far, so its still a case of waiting and seeing. Certainly the two examples tasted for this update show a progression in quality and also refinement. It is clearly potentially a super five star wine but then so it should be. Until recently the winemaking team comprised Giorgio Dalle Cia, the late Denis Dubourdieu and Mia Fischer. It remains to be seen what the loss of the Dubourdieu input will be. The G is very much a hand made wine, output is tiny, just 4,488 bottles for the 2013 Waldweben. The wine is havested by the berry with a selection from an array of vineyards. Vinification follows artisan methods using a combination of wood and stainless steel and then ageing in small French oak for 18 months. The Waldweben (each vintage has a separate name and label design) has an intensity a fresh balance absent in the previous L'Aube de La Vigne. The blend is made up of Petit Verdot, Syrah, and Cabernet Sauvignon. There is also a secondary label Echo of G which is a touch more approachable and affordable. (DM)

Recommended Reds:
G Red Coastal Region ★★★★★ £H
Echo of G Coastal Region ★★★★☆ £G

Alheit (Walker Bay) *www.alheitvineyards.co.za*

Husband and wife winemaking team Chris and Suzaan Alheit produce a stunning Chenin Blanc dominated white, Cartology, of remarkable dimension from highly selected sites across the Cape.

They refer to their work as 99% vineyard and 1% cellar. To this they have now added two single vineyard Chenins both of which are grown at altitude and dry farmed. Magnetic North comes from bush vines just to the north-west of Clanwilliam, while the Radio Lazarus comes from old vines in Stellenbosch. One of the keys to maintaining the quality of their work is farming the vineyards they work with themselves. Cartology comes from a number of sites and includes a small proportion of old Sémillon from Franschhoek. The Chenin Blanc is grown at Skurfberg close to the Magnetic North site, Kasteelberg and Perdeberg in Swartland and the Hemelrand mountain farm on the Hemel & Aarde Ridge at Walker Bay. The sites are all planted to dry farmed old bush vines. Traditionally vinified the wine offers an exceptional intensity of citrus, white fruits and a light honeyed quality all underpinned by a subtle minerality. Expect a richer complexity to develop with age. Undoubtedly the two single vineyard wines will be well worth trying as well. (DM)

Recommended Whites:
Cartology Western Cape ★★★★☆ £E

❀ Anwilka (Stellenbosch) *www.kleinconstantia.com*

There is no doubt, Anwilka has emerged as one of the Cape's very greatest reds and a wine of indisputable world-class. The vineyard is a joint venture between Bruno Prats, who formerly owned the great Saint-Estèphe Second Growth COS D'ESTOURNEL, Hubert de Boüard de Laforest, the co-proprietor of Château ANGÉLUS and Lowell Jooste, whose family own KLEIN CONSTANTIA. The wine is a blend of Cabernet Sauvignon and Syrah and comes from the firms wholly owned vineyard in Helderberg. The vineyard was originally planted in 1998 and benefits from cooling ocean breezes barely four miles away coming from False Bay The soils are sparse and provide low vigour in the vines and have good drainage, reducing the need for irrigation. Vigorous pruning and green harvesting are practised and the wine comes from the best plots only. Winemaking is very much on Bordeaux lines resulting in a wine of supple tannins and impressive depth and intensity. Wisely the new wood is not overdone and the wine spends just 9 months in oak. (DM)

Recommended Reds:
Anwilka Red Stellenbosch ★★★★☆ £F

❀ Ashbourne (Walker Bay)

This is Anthony HAMILTON-RUSSELL's flagship Pinotage and offering a good deal more in depth and intensity than his nevertheless very good bottling of the variety under the label of his SOUTHERN RIGHT property. His Bastenburg vineyard was planted in 1996 in clay-rich, shale derived soils. The variety is early ripening and the cooler environment of Walker Bay provides a style of less overt alcohol. His aim here is to produce a Pinotage that stands comparison with other great reds and the wine is undoubtedly very impressive. Real intensity as well as elegance are married to a firm structure and seamlessly integrated tannins. Very different from many examples of the grape with a hint of spice and cedar and just a subtle bright dark berry component. Expect the wine to develop well for a decade. (DM)

Recommended Reds:
Ashbourne Walker Bay ★★★★☆ £F

Ataraxia (Walker Bay) *www.ataraxiawines.co.za*

Although a relatively new name in the Hemel en Aarde Valley with a maiden vintage in 2005 Ataraxia Mountain Vineyards is located just to the north east of HAMILTON RUSSELL and BOUCHARD FINLAYSON, it has emerged as one of the benchmarks for the

South Africa

area. In particular for a very stylish and so far a very well-priced Burgundian styled Chardonnay. The home vineyards are planted at altitude on the slopes of the Babylonstoren. Kevin Grant was the winemaker for Hamilton Russell and is following a similar style for his own Chardonnay. Fruit is sourced from a number of sites throughout the Cape and the wines currently take the Western Cape denomination, although the intention is to produce from the home *terroir* in time. The Chardonnay comes from a number of cool sites in Elgin and Hemel en Aarde. The wine has a very subtle tropical fruit intensity and an excellent underlying structure from part new oak barrel-fermentation. The Sauvignon Blanc is a clean, fresh and zesty style with no recourse to wood. The Serenity red is an undisclosed blend with a rich and supple black fruits quality and mineral edge that should ensure it works very well with food. (DM)

Recommended Reds:
Serenity Western Cape ★★★☆ £D
Recommended Whites:
Chardonnay Western Cape ★★★★ £D
Sauvignon Blanc ★★★☆ £C

Backsberg (Paarl) www.backsberg.co.za

This sizeable Paarl winery has always produced solid wines however they have moved onto a new plain in recent vintages under owner Michael Back and winemaker Alicia Rechner who also has five vintages in Europe and Australia to aid her repertoire. There are 110 ha under vine on the slopes of the Simonsberg Mountains between Stellenbosch and Paarl. Four main ranges of wines are produced. As well as the good value Premium range wines and pricier Black Label wines profiled here Backsberg also make a number of Kosher wines, fortifieds and from the best plots a Family Reserve Red and White. The Premium range includes good dark, spicy Merlot, fresh crisp Sauvignon Blanc and appley Chenin Blanc. Other wines also produced are Chardonnay, Cabernet, Pinotage, a red blend and a rosé. Quite a bit more serious are the Black Label wines. These include a fine green-fruited John Martin Reserve Sauvignon with some mineral and citrus hints which gets a touch of barrel-fermentation and will stand a little age. Pumphouse Shiraz is in a dark, spicy vibrant style with ageing in both French and American oak, just 15% new to emphasise the fruit. The Klein Babylonstoren is a blend of 50/50 Cabernet Sauvignon and Merlot with nicely perfumed, cassis scented tones. It gets 16 months in oak. Richer and fuller is the Family Reserve Red which is dominated by Cabernet, with the balance Merlot. Dense and structured it will develop in bottle for up to a decade. This like the Family Reserve White, a blend of Chardonnay, Roussanne and Viognier comprise the wineries top two wines. (DM)

Recommended Reds:
Family Reserve Red Paarl ★★★☆ £E
Pumphouse Shiraz Paarl ★★★ £C
Klein Babylonstoren Paarl ★★★ £C   Merlot Paarl ★☆ £C
Recommended Whites:
John Martin Reserve Sauvignon Blanc Paarl ★★☆ £C
Sauvignon Blanc Paarl ★☆ £B   Chenin Blanc Paarl ★☆ £B

AA Badenhorst (Swartland) www.aabadenhorst.com

This is a tremendously exciting small winery based in Swartland halfway between Wellington and Malmesbury producing great red and white. As well as the two premium labels covered here the winery also produces a well-priced second label red and white both called Secateurs. The Badenhorst cousins have restored a run-down cellar on their farm which was used originally as a winery

in the 1930s. No doubt a key element in the quality of the wines is the holding of old bush vines including Chenin Blanc, Cinsault and some Grenache that is close to 60 years. These are planted in a range of soils with elements of clay, granite and shale providing a well-drained *terroir*. There is no crushing or de-stemming for either the reds or the whites. The dark-fruited pepper spiced Badenhorst red, a blend of Shiraz, Cinsault, Mourvèdre and Grenache can get up to 4 months post fermentation maceration and ageing is in 500 litre used casks. The intense citrus, mineral scented white is a blend of Chenin Blanc (which it is felt is the most important variety), Roussanne, Grenache Blanc, Viognier, Verdelho, Chardonnay and a tiny amount of Sauvignon Blanc. Varieties that ripen at similar times are fermented together, others separately and then blended back after 13 months in used barrels. The output of the white is about half the red, just 500 cases or so but both are worth seeking out. Occasionally released as well is the Funky White made from a wide range of varieties and aged in a form of *solera* with up to five vintages. (DM)

Recommended Reds:
AA Badenhorst Red Coastal Region ★★★★ £E
Secateurs Coastal Region ★★★ £C
Recommended Whites:
AA Badenhorst White Coastal Region ★★★★ £E
AA Badenhorst NV Funky White Coastal Region ★★★☆ £E
Secateurs Coastal Region ★★★☆ £C

Beaumont (Walker Bay) www.beaumont.co.za

Based in the Bot River Valley, the Beaumont family farm is halfway between the coastal village of Hermanus and the higher altitude vineyards of Elgin. Good reds are fashioned here as well as some of the better Chenin Blancs in the Cape. In addition to the wines covered here Goutte d'Or (Sémillon/Sauvignon Blanc), the premium Vitruvian red blend and Mouvèdre along with a port should be well worth seeking out. The regular Chenin Blanc is cool-fermented and has a small portion fermented in barrel. Drink it young and fresh. The Hope Marguerite is altogether firmer and more structured with dried apricot and citrus fruit and an underlying mineral character. From the oldest vines, naturally low-yielding, this sees 14 months in oak on lees. Pinotage provides another example of the potential here for this variety. Fresh and berry-fruited with good structure and acidity it avoids much of the overpoweringly acetone character found in other examples. Ageing is in a mix of mainly French and American oak, around a quarter new. The Ariane is an elegant berry-laden, lightly plummy and minty Bordeaux styled blend of Merlot, Cabernet Sauvignon and Cabernet Franc aged in French oak, 25% new. Also among the reds and offering real depth and character is the darkly spicy blackberry and herb-spiced Shiraz Mourvèdre. (DM)

Recommended Reds:
Shiraz Mourvèdre Walker Bay ★★★☆ £D
Ariane Stellenbosch ★★★ £C   Pinotage Walker Bay ★★★ £C
Recommended Whites:
Hope Marguerite Walker Bay ★★☆ £C
Chenin Blanc Walker Bay ★★ £B

Beyerskloof (Stellenbosch) www.beyerskloof.co.za

Beyers Truter, runs this property in a partnership which includes UK based wine merchant Simon Halliday. Here he makes stylish and vibrant Pinotage in a light and elegant style and a dense and burly premium red, the Field Blend which combines Cabernet Sauvignon with Merlot. This is in a rich chocolatey style with abundant evidence of new oak. It will be better with five years' cellaring. Newly

Wine behind the label

added are a fruity rosé and a well-priced red blend, Synergy. This comprises Merlot, Pinotage and Cabernet Sauvignon and is sourced from a number of sites around Stellenbosch. It is ripe, plummy and forward with a spicy hint of oak and can be enjoyed with a couple of years' ageing. A Brut Pinotage Rosé sparkler has also been added along with Lagare Cape, a fortified style from Touriga Nacional and Pinotage and a white Chenin/Pinotage. The range also includes two further premium reds. Diesel Pinotage and Faith a blend of Cabernet Sauvignon, Pinotage and Merlot. (DM)

Recommended Reds:
Field Blend Stellenbosch ★★★★ £E Synergy Stellenbosch ★★ £C
Pinotage Reserve Stellenbosch ★★ £B
Pinotage Stellenbosch ★☆ £B

Bilton (Stellenbosch) *www.biltonwines.com*
Big, full-blown reds are made here with no shortage of new oak being used. The original Helderberg property dates back to 1726 although Bilton as a modern wine producer was much more recently established with the maiden vintage of 1998 providing just 100 cases. The potential though is much greater than that, the estate vineyards cover some 80 ha and as well as the Bordeaux varieties, Mourvèdre and Viognier are also planned. The 100% varietal Cabernet Sauvignon is the firmest and most structured of this trio. As with all the reds here a 48 hour cold-soak is employed to lift the wines fruit and ageing is in French oak for 17 months. Merlot is plusher, rounder with dark, spicy plummy fruit and hints of dark cherries. Supple blackberry scented Shiraz is ripe and very full, although the youthfully toasted oak seems better harnessed here than with the Bordeaux styles. All the wines will benefit from 3 or 4 years' age. A new flagship Bordeaux blend "Sir Percy" has recently been added, along with the a premium Viognier and The Bilton a super premium red with a price tag to match the worlds most expensive. (DM)

Recommended Reds:
Cabernet Sauvignon Stellenbosch ★★★ £D
Shiraz Stellenbosch ★★★ £C Merlot Stellenbosch ★★★ £C

Bizoe Wines (Stellenbosch) *www.bizoe.co.za*
Small winery based at Somerset West producing one white and one red in a handcrafted artisan style. At present the focus is on a single white and a single red although a straw wine Bizoe Tiny was released with the 2010 vintage in very small quantities. It will only be made in exceptional years. The richly textured Henrietta white blend comes from the Franschhoek Valley and the fruit is harvested in the early morning to preserve as much primary aroma as possible before pressing and then natural barrel fermentation and ageing in barrel for 7 months or so on lees. The wine offers an impressive array of citrus, lightly tropical fruits as well as a restrained creamy, toasty character. The Estalet Shiraz comes from fruit sourced in the Breedekloof Valley , to the east of Paarl and offers a combination of rich sweet dark berry fruit and a nice balancing black pepper spiciness. After a two week vatting the wine is aged for around 16 months in a combination of new and used French oak. Expect both wines to be attractive on release. (DM)

Recommended Reds:
Estalet Shiraz ★★★☆ £D
Recommended Whites:
Henrietta Sémillon/Sauvignon Blanc ★★★★ £D

Black Pearl (Paarl) *www.blackpearlwines.com*
The Nash family have planted just 7.5 ha of their sizeable

Rhenosterkop farm on the western slope of Paarl Mountain to Shiraz and Cabernet Sauvignon. 2001 was their first vintage. Output is small and two reds are currently released by winemaker Mary-Lou Nash as well as a white Chenin Blanc from fruit sourced from 20 to 40 year old vines grown on the Paarl/Swartland border. Their vineyards are cultivated as naturally as possible and no pesticides or herbicides are used. The same approach is carried through to the cellar where minimal is the keyword and SO2 additions are kept very low. The wines are vinified in small open fermenters and then gently basket-pressed before ageing in small oak. The richly textured dark berry fruited Mischief Maker is a blend of Shiraz and a small proportion of Mourvèdre. The Oro is a blend dominated by Cabernet Sauvignon with a little Shiraz. Full of ripe dark berry fruit, the wine is finely structured and balanced after 12 months maturation in French oak. (DM)

Recommended Reds:
Mischief Maker Paarl ★★★☆ £D Black Pearl Oro Paarl ★★★☆ £D
Recommended Whites:
Chenin Blanc Paarl ★★☆ £C

Bon Cap (Robertson) *www.boncaporganic.co.za*
Michelle and Roelf du Preez make a well-crafted range of organic reds at their small Robertson farm and have recently added Viognier. The family has in fact been farming in the Robertson region for seven generations but winemaking is much more recent. Production is by no means small and 52 ha are now under vine. Fruit that is not considered up to scratch is sold off in bulk. The vineyards are farmed organically because Roelf du Preez believes this provides a better balance in the wines. The minimalist approach is carried over to the vinification and ageing, with no fining and absolute minimal sulphur additions. The resulting wines have good depth and real varietal purity and offer great value for money. There are two pricipal ranges. The Bon Cap wines are the top organic labels while the Ruins are more approachable and immediately fruit driven. There is also an export Green House label. The white Ruins wines are cool fermented to emphasise their fruit and bottled as soon as possible. These should be enjoyed as close to the vintage as possible. The Ruins Pinotage is aged in tank, while the Bon Cap reds all see some oak for up to 10 months. Mainly French barrels are used with a fifth being American oak. (DM)

Recommended Reds:
Cape Blend Robertson ★★★ £C
Cabernet Sauvignon Robertson ★★☆ £C
Syrah Robertson ★★☆ £C Pinotage Robertson ★★☆ £B
Pinotage Green House Robertson ★★☆ £B
Pinotage The Ruins ★☆ £B
Recommended Whites:
Sauvignon Blanc The Ruins ★☆ £B
Chardonnay/Viognier The Ruins ★☆ £B

❀ Boekenhoutskloof (Franschhoek) *www.boekenhoutskloof.co.za*
This farm is located on the higher and cooler slopes of Franschhoek and is producing some of the most stylish wines in the Cape. Syrah is intense, refined and full of black, spicy fruit. It displays the weight and texture of good Hermitage. The Cabernet Sauvignon is in a dense and cedary style with supple, velvety tannin. It will benefit from at least four or five years' ageing. There is also pure and subtly oaked Sémillon and a Noble-Late Harvest white. The Sémillon is structured and worth cellaring and is of a different order to most South African examples. A full, brambly and spicy Rhône-style blend, the Chocolate Block, is sourced from Franschhoek fruit

and comprises Syrah, Grenache and some very old-vine Cinsault. A further red Wolftrap is also Syrah based. In addition to the Boekenhoutskloof wines there is also a range of attractively fruity and characterful varietal wines under the Porcupine Ridge label, which are sourced from Coastal Region fruit. A super premium Swartland Syrah is also now made at PORSELEINBERG. (DM)

Boekenhoutskloof
Recommended Reds:
Cabernet Sauvignon Estate Franschhoek ★★★★☆ £F
Shiraz Estate Franschhoek ★★★★ £E
Recommended Whites:
Sémillon Estate Franschhoek ★★★☆ £E
Porcupine Ridge
Recommended Reds:
Cabernet Sauvignon Porcupine Ridge ★☆ £B
Syrah Porcupine Ridge ★☆ £B
Recommended Whites:
Sauvignon Blanc Porcupine Ridge ★ £B

Boplaas (Calitzdorp) www.boplaas.co.za
The Nel family origins stretch back over 100 years at this traditional late harvest and fortified wine specialist. Based in the Klein Karoo some way north of Mossel Bay, the warm climate here supports the production of rich, characterful Port styles. As well as these an extensive range of well-priced everyday reds and whites are produced, although most of these have not been tasted for this year's edition. The fortifieds though are the key. A Cape Ruby and Late Bottled Vintage are also produced as well as a richly unctuous berry laden Tawny and a very impressive Cape Vintage Reserve, very much a benchmark here and dominated by the oldest Touriga vines on the property. It will develop much complexity with a decade or more in your cellar. (DM)
Recommended Reds:
Cape Vintage Reserve Calitzdorp ★★★☆ £E
Cape Tawny Calitzdorp ★★☆ £C

Bouchard Finlayson (Walker Bay) www.bouchardfinlayson.co.za
Peter Finlayson was originally the winemaker at neighbouring HAMILTON RUSSELL before establishing his own operation in partnership with Paul Bouchard of the Bouchard family, former owners of BOUCHARD PÈRE ET FILS. There are 19 ha of vineyard on a property of 125 hectares, dominated by Pinot Noir. The style differs from Hamilton Russell: the wine is denser, more extracted thanks to a period of post-fermentation maceration that makes it darker and showing firmer tannins. It will develop nicely with two or three years. A barrel selection Tête de Cuvée is also produced. There are three Chardonnays, Sans Barrique - unwooded, Kaaimansgat from the Overberg WO and the opulent, homegrown Missionvale bottling. There is also a clean, zesty Sauvignon Blanc as well as a fresh and crisp clean-fruited blend of Viognier, Sauvignon Blanc, Chardonnay, Pinot Blanc and Weisser Riesling labelled Blanc de Mer. Chardonnay will stand a little ageing; Sauvignon should be drunk young. The most recent addition is Hannibal, an unusual red blend of Sangiovese, Nebbiolo, Mourvèdre, Barbera, Shiraz and Pinot Noir. It offers a nice blend of dark-cherry fruit and typically zesty acidity and a firm tannic edge. (DM)
Recommended Reds:
Pinot Noir Galpin Peak Walker Bay ★★★☆ £E
Hannibal Walker Bay ★★★☆ £E
Recommended Whites:
Chardonnay Missionvale Walker Bay ★★★☆ £E

Chardonnay Kaaimansgat Overberg ★★★ £D
Chardonnay Sans Barrique Overberg ★★☆ £C
Sauvignon Blanc Walker Bay ★★☆ £C
Blanc de Mer Western Cape ★★ £C

>> Capaia (Philadelphia) www.capaia.eu
The von Essen family acquired this 140 hectare estate in 1997 and now have some 58 hectares under vine. Count Stefan von Niepperg, the owner of CH. CANON LA GAFFALIÈRE and other properties, has been consulting here since 2005 and has recently become part owner of this estate. Located on clay-schist slopes in the Philadelphia area, 30km north of Cape Town and 10km from the Atlantic Ocean, it produces three different cuvées. The Sauvignon Blanc is aromatic and zingy and a perfect foil for Asian cuisine, the Cabernet/Merlot blend (44% Cabernet Sauvignon, 37% Merlot and 19% Cabernet Franc) matured for 12 months in 2nd and 3rd year French oak, displays fresh berry fruit with soft tannins and balanced acidity, whilst the Capaia One (78% Cabernet Sauvignon, 9% Shiraz, 7% Merlot, 6% Cabernet Franc) spends 12 months in 60% new French oak barriques, full and round on the palate with some spiciness and complexity. Will cellar easily for a decade. (NB)
Recommended Reds:
Capaia One Coastal Region ★★★★ £D
Cabernet/Merlot Tygerberg ★★★ £C
Recommended Whites:
Sauvignon Blanc Tygerberg ★★★ £B

Cape Chamonix (Franschhoek) www.chamonix.co.za
This property, full name the Cape Chamonix Wine Farm is owned by Chris Hellinger and was purchased in 1990. Since then the neighbouring Uitkyk farm has been added to the holding and Cape Chamonix is located on the eastern mountain slopes of the Franschhoek appellation. A good range of reds and whites are made here and they offer very decent value for money. As well as the wines covered below there is a red Chamonix Rouge, a Bordeaux blend, a white Chamonix Blanc blending Sauvignon, Chenin Blanc and Chardonnay as well as a varietal Sauvignon Blanc. The Sauvignon Blanc Reserve is fuller and richer, more of a Graves style being blended with Sémillon and is cold settled on the skins and then barrel-fermented and aged for just under a year. Both the Chardonnays are quite elegant and restrained in style, the Reserve coming from a single plot, it is a touch richer and more opulent. Both are barrel-fermented and aged on fine lees, the Reserve for up to 14 months. The Greywacke Pinotage is named after the sandstone soils in which the vines are planted. It has both elegance and impressive, almost bitter dark berry fruit intensity, fairly rare in the variety, perhaps helped by the inclusion of a little Pinot Noir and a proportion of dried grapes. Troika is a blend of Cabernet Franc, Cabernet Sauvignon and Merlot. The wine is aged 18 months in almost all new French oak with the malolactic fermentation occurring naturally. The Pinot Noir Reserve is very Burgundian in style as is the approach to vinification. The fruit is stemmed not crushed and the result is a deep fruited red with hints of red cherry and strawberry. Around 15 months in Allier French oak barrels provides balance and an approachable structure. (DM)
Recommended Reds:
Pinot Noir Reserve Franschhoek ★★★★ £E
Troika Franschhoek ★★★☆ £D
Pinotage Greywacke Franschhoek ★★★☆ £D
Recommended Whites:
Chardonnay Reserve Franschhoek ★★★☆ £D

Chardonnay Franschhoek ★★★☆ £C
Sauvignon Blanc Reserve Franschhoek ★★★ £C

Cape Point (Cape Point) *www.cpv.co.za*
Cape Point Vineyards is among South Africa's best white wine producers with vineyards located to the south of Cape Town overlooking the Atlantic on the Cape Point Peninsula. Sauvignon Blanc is the main focus but a Chardonnay is also made as well as approachable and forward fresh and grassy Sauvignon Blanc and spicy, berry fruited Shiraz/Cabernet Sauvignon under the Stonehaven label. The creamy and subtly citrus infused Chardonnay is whole bunch pressed and then barrel fermented and aged on lees for approaching a year with around a third going through the malolactic. The Sauvignon Blanc's are both blended with a smattering of Sémillon which adds depth. The green and citrus fruited Sauvignon gets just a small proportion barrel fermented and the wine is aged on lees for up to 7 months. The more rounded Reserve offers more intensity and concentration and a marginally higher proportion of Sémillon. The top wine, Isliedh is also dominated by Sauvignon Blanc but there is a significant proportion of Sémillon, generally approaching a quarter and the wine is richly textured as well as offering a real underlying mineral intensity. It comes from a windswept plot which produces miserly yields and the wine offers restrained oak tones from fermentation in a mix of new and used barrels gently supporting the wines fruit. Its worth noting if visiting that there is a restaurant with stunning views across the vineyards towards the ocean. (DM)
Recommended Reds:
Stonehaven Shiraz/Cabernet Sauvignon Western Cape ★★ £B
Recommended Whites:
Isliedh ★★★★ £E
Sauvignon Blanc Reserve ★★★★ £D
Sauvignon Blanc ★★★☆ £C   Chardonnay ★★★☆ £D
Stonehaven Sauvignon Blanc Western Cape ★★☆ £B

❀ **Cederberg (Cederberg)** *www.cederbergwine.com*
Located in the Cederberg mountains, as its own ward in the Olifants region, Cederbergs vineyards are the highest in the Western Cape at an altitude of some 1,000 metres above sea level. A cool continental climate provides warm summers and cool nights with a significant drop in night time temperature. The result is full blown reds as well as grassy, herb-scented whites from Sauvignon Blanc and Chenin Blanc. The whites are cool fermented styles full of zesty fruit and bracing, nicely balanced acidity. The Chenin benefitting from the added depth provided by older vines. Reds include an elegant structured berry-scented Cabernet Sauvignon as well as a dark, spicy and characterful Shiraz. The flagship red, Five Generations is dense, structured and ageworthy, it comes from a single over 15 year old block of vineyards. The wine will benefit from at least five years cellaring. There is also a richly concentrated white version made from Chenin Blanc. With an output of less than 3,000 bottles on release, these are inevitably pretty scarce. Additionally made is a sweet white Bukettraube and a vibrant, ripe and approachable red blend of Merlot and Shiraz. David Nieuwoudt has another brand Ghost Corner, with grapes sourced from Elim providing three well made crisp, fresh and mineral scented whites; a Sauvignon Blanc, a Sémillon and The Bowline which is a blend of the two. New wines also available under the Ghost Corner banner are a Wild Ferment Sauvignon Blanc, and a Pinot Noir. (DM)
Recommended Reds:
V Generations Cederberg ★★★★ £E

Shiraz Cederberg ★★★ £C
Cabernet Sauvignon Cederberg ★★★ £C
Merlot Shiraz Cederberg ★★★ £C
Cederberger Cederberg ★★☆ £C
Recommended Whites:
V Generations Chenin Blanc Cederberg ★★★★ £D
The Bowline Ghost Corner Elim ★★★☆ £C
Sauvignon Blanc Ghost Corner Elim ★★★ £C
Sémillon Ghost Corner Elim ★★★ £C
Sauvignon Blanc Cederberg ★★☆ £C
Chenin Blanc Cederberg ★★ £B
Bukketraube Cederberg ★★ £B
Recommended Rosés:
Sustainable Rosé Cederberg ★★ £B

Cloof Estate (Darling) *www.cloof.co.za*
The vineyards here are located 70km to the north of Cape Town. The warm Darling climate is moderated by south-easterly breezes. Most of the vineyard consists of naturally low-yielding dryland (non-irrigated) bush vines cultivated on decomposed granite soils which provides grapes of impressive flavour intensity. A good flavourful, easy drinking and fruit-forward range are produced under the Daisy, Ruby and Rosy Darling labels. The Cellar Blend is a ripe and spicy blend of Cabernet Sauvignon, Pinotage and Shiraz, mostly coming from press wine. Of the top reds the dark, spicy and brambly Pinotage comes from vineyards planted in 1976 and 1987. It gets a cold soak and is aged in 50% new wood. The impressive Lynchpin comes from a blend of Merlot and Cabernet Franc and is cellared for 18 months in mainly new French oak. The dark, peppery and spice laden Crucible Shiraz, similarly cropped at tiny yields, is the best wine here. It is dark, brooding and impressively structured with the new oak (100%) very well integrated. This has been joined by a more approachable bottling, Very Sexy which is rich and sumptuous certainly. A number of new labels have been added; among the reds are Duckitt Merlot/Cabernet Sauvignon, Happy Dragon Pinotage/Shiraz, The Dark Side Cabernet/Shiraz and Inkspot which is dominated by Pinotage. Of the whites the is a Very Vivacious Viognier and a Summertime Sauvignon Blanc. (DM)
Recommended Reds:
Cloof Crucible Shiraz Darling ★★★★☆ £F
Cloof Lynchpin Darling ★★★☆ £D
Cloof Very Sexy Shiraz Darling ★★★ £C
Cloof Pinotage Darling ★★★ £C
Cloof Cellar Blend Darling ★★ £B

Clos Malverne (Stellenbosch) *www.closmalverne.co.za*
Medium-sized producer with wines released under both the Clos Malverne and a number of other export market labels. As well as the wines rated here Sauvignon Blanc, including a sparkling version, Chardonnay and a Merlot are also produced. There are 29ha under vine and output is around 25,000 cases a year. The reds are vinified in open top fermenters and basket presses are used to maintain the quality of the fruit. Pinotage is the main focus here and accounts for close to half the output either as a varietal or as part of a blend. The regular Le Café bottling is bright and berry laden with a good spicy lightly acetone character and a hint of oak. The Reserve is fuller and richer with dark plummy fruit and is aged in a mix of French and American oak. The Cabernet Shiraz is soft, supple and fruit driven with a hint of spice and mint. The Cabernet Sauvignon/Merlot is firmer and offers greater depth and persistence. It is aged in oak for 12 months. The top label Auret is an unusual blend of

South Africa

Cabernet Sauvignon and Pinotage. Ripe and opulent with loads of dark, mulberry and chocolatey fruit the wine is aged for 12 months in a mix of both French and American oak. The wines all get a light filtration prior to bottling. The top reds will develop well for 4 to 5 years. (DM)

Recommended Reds:
Auret Stellenbosch ★★★ £D
Pinotage Reserve Stellenbosch ★★★ £D
Cabernet Sauvignon/Merlot Stellenbosch ★★ £C
Pinotage Le Cafe Stellenbosch ★★ £B
Cabernet Shiraz Stellenbosch ★☆ £B

Paul Cluver (Elgin) www.cluver.com

Pioneering wine farm in rhe cooler vineyards of Elgin. The Cluver family have been established here for well over a decade, producing piercingly varietal wines of good intensity and depth. Much of this is to do with the estate vineyards being planted at an altitude of 400 to 500m on the Elgin plateau. As a consequence they benefit from cooler summer evenings as well as from sea breezes due to the close proximity of the ocean. To the immediate north, the mountains complete an ideal viticultural environment. Pinot Noir is now the only red made here. There is a good ripe and full berry scented Estate example and a much pricier Seven Flags label. The whites are particularly striking here. Sauvignon is fresh and grassy with mineral hints and less overtly tropical than many others. It should be drunk young and fresh. Riesling is very impressive, with a lively citrus and toasty character. Gewürztraminer offers an aromatic, spicy intensity. Chardonnay is particularly stylish with impressive depth and concentration together with a subtle barrel-fermentation character and a rich leesy texture. Marked by tight citrus and melon notes, it's cool origins show through. There is a stunning late harvest Riesling with both intensity and a mineral balanced edge. A spatlese style, Close Encounter is also made. In general, drink the wines young, although, with the exception of the Sauvignon Blanc, they will develop nicely over the short term, the Estate Pinot Noir for four or five years. (DM)

Recommended Reds:
Pinot Noir Seven Flags Elgin ★★★★ £E
Pinot Noir Elgin ★★★ £C

Recommended Whites:
Riesling Noble Late Harvest Elgin ★★★★ £E
Chardonnay Elgin ★★★ £C
Gewürztraminer Elgin ★★☆ £C
Riesling Elgin ★★☆ £B
Riesling Close Encounter Elgin ★★☆ £B
Sauvignon Blanc Elgin ★★☆ £B

✿ Creation Wines (Walker Bay) www.creationwines.com

This Walker Bay based winery is a further indication of the potential in this small region to the east of Cape Town along the coast. It was originally established by Swiss Jean-Claude Martin and his wife Carolyn Finlayson who comes from the family who founded GLEN CARLOU. They established 22 ha of vineyard on the Hemel-en-Aarde Ridge in 2002 and have been joined in the venture in 2013 by Jonathan Drake. A small modern state of the art winery has been built right in the centre of the vineyards to optimise the handling of their fruit. Sustainable viticulture is practiced and the winery is a member of the Biodiversity & Wine Initiative. The climate of the area is very benign with warm rather than hot summers and although rainfall is low, the clay and shale soils have good moisture retaining properties. Sauvignon Blanc is crisp and fresh with subtle tropical

notes underpinned by a fine mineral quality. Blended with Sémillon it has more depth and structure. Viognier is ripe and full with a creamy, peachy character. Chardonnay is subtle and restrained with a somewhat Burgundian character. A fine Art of Chardonnay adds a further dimension. Among the reds the Bordeaux blend is ripe and full with concentrated black fruits, the Merlot a touch firmer and more structured but with classic varietal berry and plum fruit and a Reserve with more depth. The Syrah Grenache is very much Syrah driven with spice and black pepper notes apparent, a full-bodied, ripe berry fruited quality confirming the warmth of Grenache. The varietal Syrah has a firmer edge to its tannins. A number of fine Pinot Noirs are made, the Reserve more concentrated and with more dark fruit character, The Art of Pinot Noir now one of the regional benchmarks. (DM)

Recommended Reds:
The Art of Pinot Noir Walker Bay ★★★★☆ £E
Pinot Noir Reserve Walker Bay ★★★★ £E
Pinot Noir Walker Bay ★★★☆ £D
Merlot Reserve Walker Bay ★★★☆ £E
Merlot Walker Bay ★★★☆ £D
Syrah Walker Bay ★★★☆ £D
Merlot Reserve Walker Bay ★★★☆ £E
Merlot Walker Bay ★★★☆ £D
Syrah Grenache Walker Bay ★★★☆ £C
Merlot Cabernet Savignon Petit Verdot Walker Bay ★★★ £C

Recommended Whites:
The Art of Chardonnay Walker Bay ★★★★ £E
Chardonnay Walker Bay ★★★ £C
Sauvignon Blanc Sémillon Walker Bay ★★★ £C
Sauvignon Blanc Walker Bay ★★☆ £C
Viognier Walker Bay ★★★ £C

Jean Daneel (Franschhoek)

Jean and René Daneel's small Franschhoek property is the source of some of the better red Bordeaux styles and Chenin Blancs from not just the Franschhoek Valley but the whole of the Cape. Daneel himself has a pedigree second to none as the former winemaker at both BUITENVERWACHTING and MORGENHOF. The wines are all marked by their subtlety and elegance rather than the rich and often extracted style found in many of his neighbours wines. He makes some brilliant examples of Chenin Blanc. In the Initial bottling Chenin is blended with Sauvignon Blanc; both lightly peachy and honeyed, it also offers a hint of grassiness and green nettle freshness from the Sauvignon. Much bigger, richer and fuller is the Signature Chenin Blanc. Fully varietal it is barrel-fermented and aged on fine lees for 7 months. While finely structured there is a lovely rich honeyed component in the background that should develop well with a year or two of ageing. Bordeaux styled reds are equally impressive with subtlety and restraint again the key to the style. The Initial bottling is lightly leafy and minty, 22 months ageing in oak lending structure and depth. The Signature, while again subtle and youthfully backward, having been aged in 100% new wood shows greater weight, flesh and mid palate dimension. It is likely to develop very well over the medium term. (DM)

Recommended Reds:
Signature Cabernet/Sauvignon/Merlot Franschhoek ★★★☆ £E
Initial Cabernet Sauvignon/Merlot Franschhoek ★★★ £C

Recommended Whites:
Signature Chenin Blanc Franschhoek ★★★ £C
Initial Chenin Blanc/Sauvignon Blanc Franschhoek ★★☆ £B

De Toren (Stellenbosch) *www.de-toren.com*
Located in the Polkadraai Hills sub-region of Stellenbosch, De Toren makes just 3,000 cases of one of the more striking Bordeaux red blends in the region. The Five is named for the grape varieties which make up the blend: Cabernet Sauvignon, Malbec, Merlot, Cabernet Franc and Petit Verdot. It is a finely structured, dense and concentrated wine with just a slight minty undertone to its plummy, cedary fruit. Aged in a combination of new and one-year-old oak, both French and American, the wine is comfortably capable of developing well in bottle for 10 years or more. A well-priced second label, Z, is a softer and more approachable alternative to the *grand vin* and aged in older oak. Drink it soon after release. (DM)
Recommended Reds:
Fusion V Coastal Region ★★★☆ £E
Z Coastal Region ★★★ £C

❀ **De Trafford (Stellenbosch)** *www.detrafford.co.za*
Now firmly established as one of the Cape's finest producers, David Trafford produces just 3,500 cases a year from his vineyards which are located at an altitude of nearly 400 metres between the Stellenbosch and Helderberg mountains. The first vines were planted in 1983 but commercial quantities were only undertaken with the 1991 vintage. Cabernet Sauvignon, Merlot and Chenin Blanc are also sourced from other Stellenbosch and Helderberg vineyards. In addition to the wines rated below a Pinot Noir, a Cabernet Franc and Plan B, a second Bordeaux red blend, are also made. Among the reds the elegant, dark fruited Elevation 393 is blended from Cabernet Sauvignon, Merlot and Syrah from the family's Mont Fleur close planted vineyard. The richly textured and impressively concentrated 393 Syrah (now renamed to reflect its European style) with dark, spicy blackberry fruit is amongst the best in the region. The second Syrah (also renamed dropping the name Shiraz), Blueprint is softer and more approachable. The Cabernet Sauvignon and Merlot also impress. All the reds are vinified with natural yeasts and are aged in mainly French oak with malolactic in barrel. Of the whites there is a very fine Straw Wine a Vin de Paille, made from old Chenin Blanc grapes concentrated on drying mats and a rarity outside France. The dry Chenin Blanc has a depth and intensity rarely found in Cape examples of the variety. Some very low yielding old vine fruit is used and the wine is barrel-fermented with natural yeasts and kept on fine lees in around 20% new French oak. The reds will benefit from four to five years patience and keep well for a decade or longer. A new partnership project SIJNN WINES with vineyards planted 230 km east of Cape Town was harvested for the first time with the 2007 vintage and is planted to a range of southern European and Mediterranean varieties. (DM)
Recommended Reds:
Elevation 393 Stellenbosch ★★★★☆ £F
Syrah 393 Stellenbosch ★★★★☆ £F
Cabernet Sauvignon Stellenbosch ★★★★ £F
Blueprint Syrah Stellenbosch ★★★☆ £D
Merlot Stellenbosch ★★★☆ £D
Recommended Whites:
Straw Wine Stellenbosch ★★★★★ £F
Chenin Blanc Blanc Stellenbosch ★★★☆ £C

Doolhof (Wellington) *www.doolhof.com*
This is one of the newer names in the Wellington appellation in the north of the Paarl district. There has been a farm on the site for three centuries although the current wine estate was only founded in 1993. Historic buildings have been restored and there is a deluxe guest house with six luxury bedrooms. The farm covers a substantial area 380 ha of which just 40 ha are currently planted to vines so there are a wide variety of soils, microclimates and *terroirs*. Most varieties planted are red along with Sauvignon Blanc and Chardonnay. Sustainable farming is the bedrock here and the estate is now a part of the Biodiversity in Wine Initiative. There is a fairly extensive range offered and the wines are generally great value across the board. There is a straightforward fruit driven series, the Cape Range including red, white and rosé the most striking is a Bordeaux style blend of Cabernet Sauvignon and Merlot, Cape Boar. The main focus though is on the Signatures Range which is mainly varietal bottles with a Renaissance red which is Cabernet/ Merlot. A fine tobacco-scented Malbec and finely structured Petit Verdot stand out among the reds. Chardonnay Unwooded is floral and fruit driven, Sauvignon Blanc quite restrained and mineral and barrel-fermented Chardonnay richer and fuller. Among the Legends of the Labyrinth range there are fruit driven Dark Lady Pinotage, Lady in Red an approachable Bordeaux style and the top red of the winery, the impressively structured and intense dark-fruited red The Minotaur. This is a complex blend of Merlot, Malbec, Cabernet Sauvignon, Shiraz, Pinotage and Petit Verdot. (DM)
Recommended Reds:
The Minotaur Wellington ★★★☆ £E
Malbec Wellington ★★★☆ £D Pinotage Wellington ★★★ £C
The Lady in Red Wellington ★★☆ £C
Dark Lady Wellington ★★☆ £C Shiraz Wellington ★★☆ £C
Renaissance Wellington ★★ £C
Merlot Wellington ★★ £C Cape Boar Red Wellington ★☆ £B
Recommended Whites:
Chardonnay Wellington ★★☆ £C
Chardonnay Unwooded Wellington ★★ £B
Sauvignon Blanc Wellington ★☆ £B

Dornier Wines (Stellenbosch) *www.dornierwines.co.za*
This newly established and impressive Stellenbosch winery produces a small range from mainly the Bordeaux varieties along with a little Shiraz, Pinotage and Chenin Blanc. The Donatus Red blends Cabernet Sauvignon, Merlot, Shiraz and Cabernet Franc. The vineyards plots are vinified separately and the fermenting juice macerated on skins for up to three weeks. Shiraz is aged in American oak, the other varieties in French oak. It is supple, round and fleshy with a fine and elegant cedary as well as berry-fruit character. The spicy, plummy dark-fruited Merlot is similarly macerated on skins for up to three weeks and solely aged in French oak. This has now been joined by a lightly cedary, elegant Cabernet as well as a Pinotage and a Cabernet Merlot blend. The Donatus White blend is an unusual combination of Chenin Blanc, Sémillon and a touch of Sauvignon Blanc which adds a fresh and grassy component. Cool fermented after a little skin contact the wine is aged for 6 months in small oak. The Chenin Blanc comes from dry farmed bush vines in Swartland. The range is completed by the Cocoa Hill wines which are soft, forward and approachable and also include a Sauvignon Blanc. The top reds will stand a little age, the Donatus White should be enjoyed soon after release. (DM)
Recommended Reds:
Donatus Red Stellenbosch ★★★☆ £E
Merlot Stellenbosch ★★★ £C
Pinotage Stellenbosch ★★★ £C
Cabernet Merlot Stellenbosch ★★☆ £C
Cabernet Sauvignon Stellenbosch ★★☆ £C
Cocoa Hill Red Western Cape ★☆ £B

South Africa

Recommended Whites:
Donatus White Stellenbosch ★★★ £C
Chenin Blanc Swartland ★★☆ £B
Cocoa Hill Chenin Blanc Stellenbosch ★☆ £B
Recommended Rosés:
Cocoa Hill Rosé Stellenbosch ★★ £B

Neil Ellis (Stellenbosch) *www.neilellis.com*

This operation was established by the two partners in 1993 when winemaker Neil Ellis joined Hans Peter Schroder at his Jonkershoek Valley property just outside Stellenbosch. The wines have become increasingly rich and refined over the intervening period. Fruit has always been sourced from other growers, which the partners feel gives them the best balance of grape variety and growing conditions. The Jonkershoek Valley is a primary source for the reds, while Groenekloof has emerged as an excellent source for grassy, piercing Sauvignon Blanc from vineyards grown at nearly 400 metres on the west coast as well as elegant Syrah. Similarly cool Elgin provides an elegant, citrus scented, barrel-fermented Chardonnay, restrained in both its Burgundian style as well as its alcohol level and a Sauvignon Blanc. Other good examples under the Premium label are ripe, blackberry-fruited Stellenbosch Shiraz, minty, smoky Cabernet Sauvignon and a lighter, more earthy and mineral Cabernet Merlot. All three will benefit from three or four years cellaring. The top wines rated here are the two Vineyard Selection reds. A limited release Sauvignon Blanc is also produced and this comes from Jonkershoek and gets a touch of barrel-fermentation. A Pinotage has also been added from granite soils in Stellenbosch as well as a Grenache from Piekenierskloof. Syrah is rich, sweet-fruited with a leathery, smoky tar-like quality in the background. The Cabernet is firm and structured with restrained dark-berry and cassis fruit and needs a year or two longer in bottle than the Syrah, give it at least five or six years ageing and your patience will be well rewarded. (DM)
Recommended Reds:
Cabernet Sauvignon Vineyard Selection Jonkershoek Valley ★★★☆ £D
Syrah Vineyard Selection Jonkershoek Valley ★★★☆ £D
Cabernet Sauvignon Stellenbosch ★★★ £C
Shiraz Groenekloof ★★★ £C
Cabernet Merlot Stellenbosch ★★☆ £C
Recommended Whites:
Chardonnay Elgin ★★★ £C
Sauvignon Blanc Groenekloof ★★☆ £C

✿ Ernie Els (Stellenbosch) *www.ernieelswines.com*

This joint venture between Jean Engelbrecht of RUST EN VREDE and his friend, the celebrated golfer Ernie Els, produces a small range of wines, the top three reds are particularly striking. As well as these there are a number of varietal wines and a fruit driven Big Easy red and white. The small volume Ernie Els Signature label red is one of the most expensive wines yet to have emerged from the Cape. The reds here are in quite marked contrast to those at Rust en Vrede. The vineyards are at a higher altitude and a tighter, firmer character is apparent. All five Bordeaux red varieties are planted and the Ernie Els Proprietor's Blend bottling shows more depth and complexity than most from the region with a dark, peppery edge from a small proportion of Shiraz. The Ernie Els Signature red is richer, fuller and more intense, offering very good length and persistence of dark, blackberry, minty fruit. Winemaker Louis Strydom also vinifies an excellent, elegant Rhône style Syrah, Ernie Els Proprietor's Syrah. As well as the association with Rust en Vrede, Els and Engelbrecht also make some very well-priced wines under the GUARDIAN PEAK label. (DM)
Recommended Reds:
Ernie Els Signature Stellenbosch ★★★★☆ £G
Ernie Els Proprietor's Syrah Stellenbosch ★★★★☆ £F
Ernie Els Proprietor's Blend Stellenbosch ★★★★ £F

Fairview Estate (Paarl) *www.fairview.co.za*

Charles Back makes an extensive range at his Paarl farm, with much of the focus centred on Rhône styles. The humorously-named red and white Goats do Roam are well-crafted, fruit forward Rhône blends. These have been supplemented by Goat Roti, which despite its name actually blends Shiraz with Grenache, Carignan and Viognier. There is also a Goats in Villages Viognier white and a Goats in Villages red from Shiraz and Pinotage as well as the Goatfather, which is variable blend of mainly Rhône and Italian red varieties. As well as these a small range of varietal wines labelled La Capra have also been introduced. Of more significance are the Cyril Back Shiraz and Primo Pinotage. The latter is produced from low-yielding old bush vines and avoids some of the more excessive bubble-gum, acetate aromas that the variety can display. A Beacon Block Shiraz is also now produced from younger vines, as is a Eenzaamheid Shiraz, aged in a combination of French and American oak. New is a fine Grenache from old bush vines at Piekenierskloof and Caldera combines Shiraz, Grenache and Mourvèdre. A further label Jakkalsfontein from old bush vines has also been added. Among the regular Fairview labels is a honeyed, peachy Viognier and a Chardonnay which shows subtle oak with lightly tropical and citrus qualities. Fine crisp and fresh Chenin Blanc and Sauvignon Blanc come from the Darling WO. Very stylish is Nurok, a lightly peachy, honeyed and minerally blend of Viognier, Chenin Blanc, Grenache Blanc and Roussanne. Drink the whites young; the reds are very approachable early but will stand limited ageing, the top Shiraz bottlings will improve for five years and longer. Charles Back also owns the SPICE ROUTE COMPANY in Swartland. (DM)
Recommended Reds:
Shiraz Cyril Back Paarl ★★★☆ £D
Shiraz Eenzaamheid Paarl ★★★☆ £D
Pinotage Primo Paarl ★★★ £D Shiraz Beacon Paarl ★★★ £C
Caldera Paarl ★★★ £C Goat Roti Coastal Region ★★☆ £C
Grenache Piekenierskloof ★★☆ £B
Shiraz Coastal Region ★★ £B Pinotage Coastal Region ★★ £B
Recommended Whites:
Nurok Paarl ★★★☆ £C Viognier Paarl ★★☆ £B
Chenin Blanc Darling ★★☆ £B
Chardonnay Coastal Region ★★ £B
Sauvignon Blanc Darling ★★ £B

Ken Forrester (Stellenbosch) *www.kenforresterwines.com*

Top South African restaurateur Ken Forrester's winery homestead dates back to 1689. The wines though are thoroughly modern in style, albeit from some of the older vines in the region. The Rhône varieties, over 50 year old Grenache and 30 year old Syrah, together with some old Chenin Blanc are the key to the quality and interest here. There are three well-priced easy drinking wines Petit Chenin, Petit Cabernet Sauvignon/Merlot and Petit Pinotage. All are typically fruit foward and uncomplicated in style and should be drunk young. A juicy fleshy Merlot Reserve Pat's Garden is vinified to emphasise its fruit. Sauvignon Blanc is grassy and fresh, gaining some weight from 8 weeks on lees. The Old Vine Reserve Chenin Blanc is richer and fuller in style. Barrel-fermented in second and third fill oak and

left on lees for up to 12 months, it gains additional complexity from a hint of botrytised fruit. The Renegade Grenache/Shiraz is also very impressive. The old vine Grenache component adds complexity to the dark, spicy fruit which precedes a characterful herb-scented finish. Aged mostly in used French oak, just 5% is aged instead in new American wood. There are several Icon labelled wines. The FMC Chenin Blanc is from old hand-picked bush vines, including some botrytis affected fruit, and is fermented with natural yeasts in 400 litre French oak. Some late harvested Chenin is also blended in and the wine has a little residual sugar, somewhat in the style of a *demi-sec* Vouvray. It is rich, full and impressively concentrated. The late harvest T Noble is full of rich botrytis character, concentrated and peachy, coming from fruit yielding just 3 tonnes per ha and is similarly barrel-fermented in 400 litre French oak where it spends 18 months. The Gypsy is a blend of old Grenache and slightly younger Shiraz. The Grenache yields just 3 tonnes to the ha the Shiraz around double that. Aged in new oak for 20 months it is smoky, vanilla scented and full of rich, dark-berry fruit. Recently added also is a sparkling Traditional Method from Chenin Blanc. Old vines and low yields lift the fruit quality giving a zesty style with 14 months on lees in bottle. The most recent project is a joint venture in California with Jesse Katz making a 100% Cabernet Sauvignon The Bridge from the Farrow Ranch in the Alexander Valley. Stylish and supple, it offers better value than many of their near California neighbours. (DM)

Recommended Reds:

The Bridge Cabernet Sauvignon Stellenbosch ★★★★ £F

The Gypsy Stellenbosch ★★★★ £E

Renegade Grenache Shiraz Stellenbosch ★★★ £C

Merlot Reserve Pat's Garden Stellenbosch ★★☆ £C

Recommended Whites:

T Noble Late-Harvest Stellenbosch ★★★★ £E

FMC Chenin Blanc Stellenbosch ★★★☆ £D

Old Vine Reserve Chenin Blanc Stellenbosch ★★★ £C

Sparklehorse (MCC) Stellenbosch ★★☆ £C

Sauvignon Blanc Reserve Stellenbosch ★★☆ £B

The Foundry (Stellenbosch) *www.thefoundry.co.za*

This small boutique sized operation with an output of barely 1,000 cases a year was only founded in 2000. Yet in a short space of time they have established a formidable reputation for some of the best Syrah to emerge from the Cape. It is a partnership between James Reid and MEERLUST winemaker Chris Williams, with the wine vinified at Meerlust. Fruit for the Syrah is sourced from right across the Cape vineyards. The team work very closely with their growers and have built up long term contracts even including specific rows. The vines are mature and low-yielding and the fruit is always harvested at physiological ripeness. Malolactic is in barrel after a relatively short vatting to avoid over-extraction. Maturation is then in a mix of 225 and 300 litre barrels but only 10% new so that the quality of the fruit is emphasized. The wine is dark, blackberry-scented, spicy and penetratingly pure, and likely to develop very well for up to a decade. An unusual second wine is also produced. Double Barrel is a blend of Tinta Barocca and Cabernet Sauvignon. There's also a fine peachy, honeyed Viognier and Grenache Blanc and Roussanne have also now been released. (DM)

Recommended Reds:

Syrah Coastal Region ★★★★ £E

Recommended Whites:

Viognier Coastal Region ★★★☆ £D

Fryers Cove (Bamboes Bay) *www.fryerscove.co.za*

Located a considerable distance to the north of Cape Town (around 250 kilometres), the key to quality here in Bamboes Bay is the proximity of the Atlantic Ocean and the influence of a combination of cooling marine breezes and sea fogs drifting a short distance inland. To some small degree this is not dissimilar to the sea fogs that enable successful viticulture in California. The climate just a few kilometres inland in the Olifants River region is strikingly different, very hot and producing large volume wines of moderate quality. There are 6 ha of vineyards at Fryers Cove and they are planted very close to the sea. Sauvignon Blanc is the key variety with 4 ha cultivated while there is a single hectare each of Pinot Noir and Merlot. The sandy soils have proved very propitious with limestone and sea shells in the lower layers. The Pinot Noir is quite Burgundian in character with rich red berry fruit and an underlying gamey and mineral quality. Vinification is modern with a 24 hour cold soak, malolactic in barrel and ageing in new, 1 and 2 year old oak. The estate Sauvignon Blanc is fresh and herbaceous but with a fine mineral quality also. It is fermented cool but not excessively so and is stirred on lees. A further dimension is added from a small proportion of the must being fermented in small oak. A second Sauvignon Blanc is also produced from vineyards nearby, a little further inland and a Merlot from estate fruit. (DM)

Recommended Reds:

Pinot Noir Bamboes Bay ★★★ £D

Recommended Whites:

Sauvignon Blanc Bamboes Bay ★★★ £C

Glen Carlou (Paarl) *www.glencarlou.co.za*

This Swiss owned operation produces particularly impressive Chardonnay, quite different from and more stylish than most examples from the Cape. The property consists of over 100 ha of vineyards in the foothills of the Simonsberg Mountains. There are no overtly rich or tropical notes in either Chardonnay. They are tight, minerally and restrained, impressively concentrated, with citrus, cheesy lees notes and toasty oak all entering the equation. The top label Quartz Stone is structured with great intensity and capable of at least three or four years' bottle-development. The Pinot Noir, Cabernet Sauvignon and Grand Classique Bordeaux blend are good and ripe but just lack the flair of the Chardonnay. Syrah as well as Zinfandel are also now produced and the dark, spicy Syrah is particularly striking. A further premium prestige wine is also produced, the Gravel Quarry Cabernet Sauvignon. It is 100% varietal with ageing in all new French oak. A soft approachable red Tortoise Hill (mainly Cabernet Sauvignon) and grassy Tortoise Hill white (dominated by Chenin Blanc) complete the line-up. (DM)

Recommended Reds:

Gravel Quarry Cabernet Sauvignon Paarl ★★★★ £F

Syrah Paarl ★★★☆ £D   Grand Classique Paarl ★★★ £D

Cabernet Sauvignon Paarl ★★★ £D

Pinot Noir Paarl ★★☆ £C   Tortoise Hill Paarl ★☆ £B

Recommended Whites:

Quartz Stone Chardonnay Paarl ★★★★ £E

Chardonnay Paarl ★★★☆ £C   Tortoise Hill Paarl ★☆ £B

Glenelly Estate (Stellenbosch) *www.glenellyestate.com*

The estate owner, May de Lencquesaing, will be familiar to many readers as the former famed proprietor of the Pauillac property Château PICHON-LONGUEVILLE-LALANDE. It is interesting that she has challenged herself in the southern hemisphere with a less traditional project. The wines though are very much made in

South Africa *(sidebar)*

a restrained and elegant style. While the Bordeaux red varieties are important here, Chardonnay and Shiraz are also cultivated, vinified and blended. The estate is located on the southern slopes of the Simonsberg Mountain with 60 ha planted and a gravity fed winery constructed. The approach to vinification is minimalist using natural yeasts and a scarcity of additions. Winemaker Luke O'Cuinneagain is working with consultant Adi Badenhorst (AA BADENHORST) in producing wines with real character. The Glass Collection range offers approachable fruit qualities as well as some depth at good values. Both Grand Vin wines are full of character. Creamy, citrus infused Chardonnay is whole bunch pressed and then vinified and aged in barrel, a proportion new, the barrels being 500 litres for balance of flavour. The Red is an interesting blend of Shiraz, Cabernet Sauvignon, Merlot and a very small proportion of Petit Verdot. After a traditional vatting the wine goes through the malolactic fermentation in barrel with a total of 18 months ageing. The Lady May is a clear step up as the fagship wine here, full of elegant as well as black fruited and cedary complexity. The wine is a combination of mainly Cabernet Sauvignon but around a tenth of Petit Verdot is included. The wine spends 24 months in barrel, which is well integrated and is likely to offer further development with four or five years in bottle. (DM)

Recommended Reds:
Lady May Stellenbosch ★★★★ £E
Grand Vin de Glenelly Red Stellenbosch ★★★ £D
Glass Collection Syrah Stellenbosch ★★☆ £C
Glass Merlot Stellenbosch ★★☆ £C
Glass Cabernet Sauvignon Stellenbosch ★★☆ £C
Recommended Whites:
Grand Vin de Glenelly Chardonnay Stellenbosch ★★★ £D
Glass Chardonnay Stellenbosch ★★☆ £C

>> Ernst Gouws & Co (Stellenbosch) *www.glenellyestate.com*
The Gouws family have been involved in winegrowing in the Cape for many generations. They make a small range of very well priced wines, the best of which have real character and quality. Both the Chenin Blanc and Sauvignon Blanc are in a zesty, fresh style and un-wooded. The Sauvignon Blanc is particularly impressive, with a combination of green fruits and a ripe, tropical undercurrent. Chardonnay is full and richly textured. It is barrel fermented and aged but in second fill wood. Nineteen Fifty Two was first released with the 2015 vintage to celebrate Ernst Gouws 60th birthday. It is the flagship white blending Semillon and Sauvignon Blanc from Franschhoek, the grapes vinified separately and aged on fine lees in French barrels for seven months. It offers impressive intensity with green fruits, citrus and a rich underlying creamy texture. Pinot Noir comes from a combination of Elgin and Stellenbosch sources while the other reds are all Stellenbosch and like the Merlot is lighter in style than the three stand out reds. Shiraz and Pinotage are both notably good values. Shiraz is full of black, spicy fruit and a supple structure supported by 12 months in French oak. Pinotage is full of blackberry and blueberry fruits and classic varietal character without an excess of acetate. It is matured in second fill barrels to balance the black fruits. Most expensive of the wines is the Family Reserve 100% Cabernet Sauvignon. Blackcurrant, plum and cherry fruit is underpinned with a hint of cedar, it will continue to evolve with three or four years in bottle. (DM)

Recommended Reds:
Family Reserve Cabernet Sauvignon Stellenbosch ★★★ £D
Pinotage Stellenbosch ★★★ £C   Shiraz Stellenbosch ★★★ £C
Merlot Stellenbosch ★★ £C

Pinot Noir Stellenbosch ★☆ £C
Recommended Whites:
Nineteen Fifty Two Franschhoek ★★★ £C
Chardonnay Stellenbosch ★★☆ £C
Sauvignon Blanc Stellenbosch ★★☆ £B
Chenin Blanc Stellenbosch ★★ £B

Graceland (Stellenbosch) *www.gracelandvineyards.com*
The McNaughtons acquired the Graceland winefarm in 1990 and have set about making a small range of well made reds marked by their elegant fruit and supple structure rather than some of the rich extracted styles of a number of their neighbours. There are just 4ha of Cabernet Sauvignon, 3.5ha of Shiraz and a mere 2.5ha of Merlot. The Bordeaux varieties appear to work best here. The Shiraz is good although the wine shows a touch of green pepper along with a spicy cocoa note from ageing in 40% new American oak. Merlot is dark, plummy and supple with good weight and a soft and supple texture. It gets 25% new French oak. Firmer, more structured and with greater depth the Cabernet Sauvignon has a rich almost chocolatey character and gets 30% ageing in new oak. Top of the tree is the Three Graces a blend of roughly half Cabernet Sauvignon and the balance equal proportions of Shiraz and Merlot. The varieties are matured separately for 14 months and then blended together and aged for a further 6 months to fully integrate the three components. Rich and cedary with a darkly spicy undercurrent this will improve in bottle for 4 or 5 years at least. The wines are fined but bottled unfiltered. (DM)

Recommended Reds:
The Three Graces Stellenbosch ★★★☆ £E
Cabernet Sauvignon Stellenbosch ★★★ £C
Merlot Stellenbosch ★★☆ £C   Shiraz Stellenbosch ★★☆ £C

>> Grande Provence (Franschhoek) *www.grandeprovence.co.za*
This old wine estate was originally established in 1694. It has been owned since 2004 by a consortium of Dutch and Belgian investors. Today as well as the wine estate there is a restaurant and wine tasting area and visitors can stay in the winelands at the estate cottage La Provençale or the luxurious Owners Cottage. Two ranges of wines are made here. Angels Tears are softy, fruity and approachable, while the Grande Provence wines are a clear step up, although offering good value. The Cabernet vines are grown in protected south westerley facing sandstone soils resulting in an elegant, minty style with supple tannins and 15 months barrel ageing adding structure. The Chenin Blanc Viognier is a fresh and zesty white with a hint of opulence in its fruit. The varieties are picked in the cool of the morning and separately. Chardonnay comes from the cooler Robertsvlei Valley sector of the Franschhoek region. Barrel fermentation is followed by ageing for 11 months, producing a wine with subtle citrus fruit and creamy oak. Sauvignon Blanc is in a fresh, green fruited style and sourced from a number of Durbanville sites where the vineyards are moderated by Atlantic sea breezes. A wooded Sauvignon Blanc is also made from Durbanville fruit. Other wines that readers should be aware of are premium Grande Provence Red and White, a Franschhoek Pinot Noir, Shiraz sourced from Stellenbosch, a rose from Merlot and Cabernet, a Méthode Cap Classique and Ampora, a Chenin Blanc fermented on skins and aged in clay amphorae. (DM)

Recommended Reds:
Cabernet Sauvignon Franschhoek ★★☆ £C
Recommended Whites:
Chardonnay Franschhoek ★★★ £C

Sauvignon Blanc Coastal Region/Durbanville ★★☆ £B
Chenin Blanc Viognier Franschhoek ★★☆ £B

Grangehurst (Stellenbosch) *www.grangehurst.co.za*
Jeremy Walker produces a small handcrafted range of red wines from his 15 ha of vineyards. They are stylish, concentrated and among the better examples produced in the Cape. The Pinotage is impressively ripe and full-bodied with plenty of spicy, dark berry fruit. Nikela is an unusual blend which, as well as those usual suspects Cabernet Sauvignon and Merlot, contains a sizeable dollop of Pinotage. Good and reasonably concentrated it has a vibrant dark-berry fruit character with a hint of menthol in the background. The top wine is the Cabernet Sauvignon/Merlot which is structured and in need of three or four years' cellaring and this has been joined by a Cabernet Sauvignon Reserve and Grangehurst a true Bordeaux blend of Cabernet Sauvignon, Merlot and Petit Verdot. A Shiraz/Cabernet Sauvignon is also new to the range. (DM)

Recommended Reds:
Cabernet Sauvignon/Merlot Stellenbosch ★★★☆ £E
Nikela Stellenbosch ★★★ £D   Pinotage Stellenbosch ★★☆ £C

Guardian Peak (Stellenbosch) *www.guardianpeak.com*
This small range of good value reds is produced by the same team of golfer Ernie Els and Jean Engelbrecht who are partners in ERNIE ELS. Very good results are produced from the Bordeaux and Rhône varieties with sound varietal Merlot and Shiraz as well as a straightforward blend, Frontier, which combines Cabernet Sauvignon with both Shiraz and Merlot. Of the top wines SMG, a blend of Shiraz, Mourvèdre and Grenache, is a clear step up from the other three bottlings. Shiraz very much drives the fruit in the wine although there is an interesting minerality as well as black pepper character to it. The Malbec Tannat is in a rich opulent style, more so than you would expect from a Madiran in France. The Lapa Cabernet Sauvignon is rich, cedary and opulent. (DM)

Recommended Reds:
Lapa Cabernet Sauvignon Stellenbosch ★★★☆ £E
SMG Western Cape ★★★ £D
Malbec Tannat Western Cape ★★★ £D
Shiraz Western Cape ★★☆ £C   Merlot Western Cape ★★ £C
Frontier Western Cape ★★ £B

❀ Hamilton Russell (Walker Bay) *www.hamiltonrussellvineyards.co.za*
Hamilton Russell is the original and remains among the most impressive producers of both Pinot Noir and Chardonnay in the cool and visually stunning Walker Bay. The wines have much improved over the last decade or so, with better clones planted and a concerted effort to isolate the very best aspects of the vineyards for each variety. No artificial fertilisers are used in the stony, clay soils and cover crops are planted to optimise fruit ripening. Chardonnay is refined but has attractive, lightly tropical notes and real intensity with a pure, almost European mineral undercurrent. Pinot Noir is rich and full of dark berry fruit, with just a hint of hung meat. Chardonnay, like Pinot Noir is consistently on the cusp of four stars. A second property, SOUTHERN RIGHT, is for Sauvignon and Pinotage, with wines showing impressive potential. Anthony Hamilton-Russell is also producing world class Pinotage from his ASHBOURNE vineyard. (DM)

Recommended Reds:
Pinot Noir Walker Bay ★★★★ £E
Recommended Whites:
Chardonnay Walker Bay ★★★★ £E

Hartenberg (Stellenbosch) *www.hartenbergestate.com*
A fairly sizeable range of wine is made at this estate to the north of Stellenbosch in a freely draining valley, which enjoys a range of soil types and mesoclimates. As well as the 99 ha vineyard area a further 80 ha is being maintained as wetlands and the property is a part of the South African Biodiversity and Wine Initiative. Consistent efforts are being made to reduce the influence of chemicals and this is helped by the development of three separate weather stations in the vineyard. Spraying is now half what it was five years ago. Among the wines there are two main ranges, Premium and the Super Premium individually named wines. A further wine, which is labelled Gravel Hill and labelled Ultra Premium is a Shiraz which has achieved impressive results and prices at the CWG Auctions. Among the Premium bottlings the tar and spicy Shiraz and vibrant Pinotage stand out. The Eleanor Chardonnay is a subtle restrained, almost Burgundian style with rich, citrus and oak tones, it is barrel-fermented and aged for over a year in new French oak. The Mackenzie is a Cabernet Sauvignon/Merlot blend from a single parcel and gets the benefit again of all new French wood for close to 20 months. Most striking though is the splendidly rich, dark and spicy Stork Shiraz. Once again it is a special vineyard selection. (DM)

Recommended Reds:
The Stork Stellenbosch ★★★★ £E
The Mackenzie Stellenbosch ★★★☆ £E
Shiraz Stellenbosch ★★★ £C
Cabernet Sauvignon Stellenbosch ★★☆ £C
Cabernet Sauvignon Shiraz Stellenbosch ★★ £B
Merlot Stellenbosch ★★ £B
Recommended Whites:
The Eleanor Stellenbosch ★★★☆ £D
Chardonnay Stellenbosch ★★☆ £C   Riesling Stellenbosch ★★ £B

Hermanuspietersfontein (Walker Bay) *www.hpf1855.co.za*
A good range of both reds and whites are made here along with a rosé. The Sauvignon Nr 5 is among the better Sauvignon examples in the Cape. The wine farm is named for the original village name for Hermanus which was founded in 1855. A wide range of grapes are planted and it is not surprising that Sauvignon has the largest holding, just over 27 ha of the 61 ha or so that are now under vine. Cooling Atlantic breezes moderate the climate here and the granite and gravel soils provide an elegant minerality in the wines. As well as the Nr 5 white there are a number of approachable, easy drinking styles. Bloos is a rosé made from the Bordeaux varieties, Nr 7 is a crisp and fresh styled Sauvignon Blanc and 1855 Postmeester is a fruit driven red, again from the Bordeaux varieties. The finely structured, elegant and cedary Die Arnoldus is the leading red, blended from the five red Bordeaux varieties. It is traditionally vinified with malolactic in tank and spends over two years in small new oak. Die Martha is a black, pepper-spiced Rhône style blend dominated by Shiraz with some Mourvèdre and Viognier. Kleinbot is a blend of the Bordeaux varieties aged in larger *foudres* to emphasise its fruit while Swartskaap is a characterful herb-scented Cabernet Franc. The Nr 5 varietal Sauvignon Blanc gains depth and structure from a warmish fermentation and ageing in new and used larger oak for around 10 months. (DM)

Recommended Reds:
Die Arnoldus Sundays Glen ★★★☆ £E
Die Martha Sundays Glen ★★★☆ £E
Swartskop Walker Bay ★★★ £D
Kleinboet Sundays Glen ★★★ £C

South Africa

Recommended Whites:
Nr 5 Sundays Glen ★★★ £D   Nr 7 Sundays Glen ★★ £C
Nr 3 Sundays Glen ★★ £C

Hughes Family Wines (Swartland) www.nativo.co.za

The Hughes are one of an increasing new breed of producers from the Swartland WO to the north of Cape Town producing characterful, artisan styled wines. Like a number of their neighbours they are a member of the "Swartland Independent" initiative. Members have to focus on a number of key elements to improve quality. These include avoiding various additives, using natural yeasts and minimising the use of new wood. From 27 ha of their own organically farmed and certified vineyards they produce just one white and one red. The Nativo Red is an earthy, rounded, characterful and dark fruited combination dominated by Shiraz with Grenache, Mourvèdre, Pinotage and Tempranillo all included. The malolactic fermentation is in barrel and a minimum of new wood is used. The white is a combination of Viognier and Chenin Blanc with hints of white fruits and an underlying citrus quality. Viognier is barrel fermented in used oak and the Chenin component tank fermented. Ageing is for around 9 months before bottling. The white will stand a further couple of years cellaring, while the red is likely to improve for up to five years from the vintage. (DM)

Recommended Reds:
Nativo Red Swartland ★★★ £C
Recommended Whites:
Nativo White Swartland ★★★ £C

>> Highlands Road (Elgin) www.highlandsroadestate.co.za/

A small range of well-crafted reds and particularly whites are made at this small Elgin property established in 2004. Sine Cera is their most striking wine, a characterful Graves styled blend of Semillon and Sauvignon Blanc. There is minimal intervention in the vinification and the wine offers an attractive mix of green fruits and citrus with an impressive flint and mineral depth and intensity. A varietal Sauvignon Blanc also impresses, which is fresh, crisp and floral. Chardonnay is in a restrained and elegant style with hints of melon and citrus. A very limited amount of Reserve Sauvignon is made as well as a couple of late harvested whites. Pinot Noir is in a lighter style, while a Shiraz/Mourvèdre shows impressive substance. The latter variety one wouldn't automatically associate with Elgin but the wine is nicely ripened with spicy black fruits, a hint of pepper and restrained oak. The variety no doubt cultivated in the warmest plots. (DM)

Recommended Reds:
Shiraz/Mourvèdre Elgin ★★★ £C   Pinot Noir Elgin ★★☆ £C
Recommended Whites:
Sine Cera Elgin ★★★☆ £C   Chardonnay Elgin ★★★ £D
Sauvignon Blanc Elgin ★★★ £C

Ingwe Wine Estate (Paarl) www.ingwewines.co.za

Bordelais' Alain Moueix from the famous French dynasty who are so important on the Right Bank of Bordeaux, purchased this property in 1997. He has 29 ha planted close to Somerset West overlooking the Atlantic Ocean. Not surprisingly the Bordeaux varieties both red and white dominate the plantings and the resulting wines seem to offer as much of the character of Bordeaux as they do the Cape. The top wine is a barrel selection offering just a touch more depth and intensity than the equally dense and subtly cedary Ingwe red, both are a blend of Merlot and Cabernet Sauvignon. The Amehlo red is altogether softer, and more approachable. Bordeaux red varieties are used here as well as around 10 % of Shiraz which just gives a black fruit lift to the style. The Amehlo white is a Graves lookalike blending Sauvignon Blanc and around two-thirds Sémillon. This is a subtle and restrained style which gets a little extra depth from five months on lees. (DM)

Recommended Reds:
Ingwe Barrique-Selection Stellenbosch ★★★☆ £E
Ingwe Stellenbosch ★★★ £D   Amehlo Stellenbosch ★★☆ £C
Recommended Whites:
Amehlo Stellenbosch ★★☆ £C

Iona (Elgin) www.iona.co.za

Sauvignon Blanc is one of the key wines here although Andrew Gunn has also added a very good, subtle and restrained Chardonnay which is more Burgundian than Cape in style and is full of lightly barrel-fermented nutty character and understated melon and citrus fruit. He also produces an a fine, and concentrated red berry scented Pinot Noir Limited along with a stylish Syrah dominated red blend One Man Band. The vineyards are in distinctly cool Elgin which is particularly suitable for varietally pure and intense Sauvignon Blanc and a limited amount of a botrytised sweet example of the variety, Noble Iona is occasionally produced. They are planted above 420 metres on a high plateau and the first vines established in 1998. The fruit is sourced from two different sites adding to the wines complexity. Like most Cape Sauvignon Blanc this should be enjoyed young and fresh, Chardonnay will add more with a little age. (DM)

Recommended Reds:
One Man Band Elgin ★★★★ £E
Pinot Noir Limited Release Elgin ★★★☆ £D
Recommended Whites:
Chardonnay Elgin ★★★☆ £D
Sauvignon Blanc Elgin ★★★ £C

Jordan (Stellenbosch) www.jordanwines.com

The Jordans have been making top quality wines here for over a decade. Their vineyards are planted at an altitude ranging from 160 to over 410 metres above sea level and get the cooling benefit of breezes and early morning fog from both the Indian and Atlantic Oceans. In the winery operations are all handled by gravity. While the regular Chardonnay is largely barrel-fermented and aged on fine lees, a tank fermented portion gives the wine a lifted fruit character. The impressive Nine Yards bottling is a clear step up with richly textured fruit and real concentration. Sourced from higher altitude vineyards this wine is aged sur-lie for around 14 months. The regular Cabernet Sauvignon is tight and quite lean in its youth with a very pronounced minty character. The Cobblers Hill red, a Bordeaux blend of Cabernet Sauvignon and Merlot is the top red here. A similar cool climate mintiness runs through the wine but there is a greater underlying richness and some toasty, dark berry fruit character as well. The Jordans also produce a crisp and grassy varietal Sauvignon Blanc and a barrel-fermented example, Chenin Blanc as well as Merlot and a vibrant, concentrated Syrah, The Prospector. Well-priced wines are also made under the Bradgate and Chameleon labels. The wines are released under the "Jardin" label in the USA. (DM)

Recommended Reds:
Cobblers Hill Stellenbosch ★★★☆ £E
Cabernet Sauvignon Stellenbosch ★★☆ £C
The Prospector Stellenbosch ★★★ £C
Recommended Whites:
Chardonnay Nine Yards Stellenbosch ★★★☆ £E

Chardonnay Stellenbosch ★★☆ £C
Sauvignon Blanc Stellenbosch ★★ £C

Kaapzicht (Stellenbosch) *www.kaapzicht.co.za*
The magnificently sited vineyards here look west towards Table Mountain. Most of the 135 ha of vines are planted on north-facing slopes and Chenin Blanc is gradually being replanted and replaced with top red varieties. In addition, much care is lavished on some old bush vine plantings of Pinotage. A comprehensive range is currently offered including Chenin Blanc, Sauvignon Blanc and the Combination which blends the two. The most important wines are the reds. As well as the richly textured Steytler Vision and the minty Cabernet Sauvignon some excellent Pinotage is produced, the Steytler among the best in the region. Of the lighter reds are a fruit driven Classic red and a more serious Estate red which blends Cabernet Sauvignon, Cinsault and Shiraz. There are also good estate bottlings of Merlot and Shiraz and the forward Bin 3 which blends Merlot with Cabernet and Pinotage. (DM)
Recommended Reds:
Vision Steytler Stellenbosch ★★★☆ £E
Pinotage Steytler Stellenbosch ★★★☆ £D
Pinotage Stellenbosch ★★★ £C
Cabernet Sauvignon Stellenbosch ★★☆ £C

Kanonkop (Stellenbosch) *www.kanonkop.co.za*
Among the best Pinotage producers in South Africa. An extensive holding of old bush vines is a major contributing factor. The wines are always powerful and chunky with firm but not aggressive tannins. Very good Cabernet Sauvignon is also produced here; the Paul Sauer label is blended with Cabernet Franc and Merlot and has an extra dimension. Both wines are rich, cedary and ageworthy with a refinement of fruit rarely encountered in the Cape. Kadette is a cheerful soft and plummy blend of Pinotage, Cabernet Sauvignon and Merlot. (DM)
Recommended Reds:
Paul Sauer Stellenbosch ★★★★ £F
Cabernet Sauvignon Stellenbosch ★★★☆ £E
Pinotage Stellenbosch ★★★☆ £D
Kadette Pinotage Stellenbosch ★☆ £C

Katbakkies (Stellenbosch)
Andries van der Walt is an architect by profession and makes a small amount of wine from a range of Stellenbosch grape sources. Although output is very minimal, around 500 cases or so a year, the wines offer real character and class. As well as the those profiled and rated below, a regular Syrah and a Viognier are also produced. The Chenin Blanc offers lovely varietal purity with lightly grassy, peachy and citrus scented fruit and just a hint of background minerality. The reds though are the stand out wines. Very good modern cedar and cassis scented Cabernet Sauvignon is finely structured and offers elegance and refinement as well as depth. The almost fiery and alcoholic Syrah Reserve, nevertheless possesses real breadth and an impressive grip. In no way is the wine overblown or jammy. Its certainly worth noting that all the wines offer very good value, particularly if you are travelling in the Cape winelands. (DM)
Recommended Reds:
Syrah Reserve Stellenbosch ★★★☆ £D
Cabernet Sauvignon Stellenbosch ★★★ £C
Recommended Whites:
Chenin Blanc Stellenbosch ★★☆ £B

>> Richard Kershaw (Elgin) *www.kleinood.com*
Owner and winemaker Richard Kershaw produces some very impressive Chardonnay and Syrah. He is a rarity; a Master of Wine and a winemaker. The property is very young, established only in 2012. Richard was previously group winemaker for MULDERBOSCH and KANU. Although at a close proximity to the Ocean his vineyards are at a reasonable altitude and the wide diurnal variation in temperature provides wines with a really fresh edge. A range of clones is cultivated and the varieties site specific. The Clonal Selection Chardonnay comes from vineyards planted to low yielding Dijon clones. The result is a subtly barrel-fermented wine with a restrained mineral, citrus and white fruits quality. The Clonal Selection Syrah is very much in the elegant style of the variety but offering real depth and intensity. Not dissimilar to a fine Côte Rôtie, it is a style marked by restrained black fruits and pepper and underpinned by supple, polished tannins. The wine is vinified by gravity without any pumping and is bottled free of additives. (DM)
Recommended Reds:
Syrah Elgin ★★★★☆ £E
Recommended Whites:
Chardonnay Elgin ★★★★☆ £E

Klein Constantia (Constantia) *www.kleinconstantia.com*
This is one of the benchmark properties on the narrow Cape Peninsula which is home to the Constantia WO. The property is sizeable with a classic Cape Dutch homestead and consists of 146 ha of which 75 ha are planted to vines. The origins of the farm go back to 1685 when vines were planted at Constantia by the first Dutch Governor, Simon Van der Stel. The vineyards were the source in the 18th and 19th centuries of the Cape's most famous and historically renowned wine, Vin de Constance. The property had fallen into disrepair before the Jooste family acquired it in the early 1980s and they have re-established this famous sweet white, an unctuously rich honeyed Muscat underpinned by fine citrus scents and fresh acidity. An extensive small range of wines are made from vineyards planted at 90 to 300 metres above sea level. The lower and warmer north facing slopes are suitable for red varieties, the cooler and higher south facing plots are planted to white grapes. The Cabernet has a hint of Loire like leafiness which can also be found to a lesser extent in the richer Marlbrook red Bordeaux blend of Cabernet Sauvignon, Merlot and Cabernet Franc. It is the whites that dominate output though and there is a Mme. Marlbrook white to compliment the red. The most striking of the whites is the Perdeblokke Sauvignon Blanc which comes from a particularly low vigour site of excellent potential. There is a real mineral quality to the wine and unlike most Cape examples this will age well for close to a decade. Riesling and Sauvignon Blanc are both attractively fresh and approachable with fine varietal qualities. Well priced KC wines are also produced along with a sparkler Cap Classique. (DM)
Recommended Reds:
Marlbrook Constantia ★★★ £D
Cabernet Sauvignon Constantia ★★☆ £D
Recommended Whites:
Vin de Constance Constantia ★★★★☆ £F
Perdeblokke Sauvignon Blanc Constantia ★★★ £D
Sauvignon Blanc Constantia ★★☆ £C
Riesling Constantia ★★☆ £C

Kleinood (Stellenbosch) *www.kleinood.com*
This is a property focussing on Syrah and Viognier. The farm is small with just 12 ha currently under vine. The approach in both

the vineyards and winery is minimalist and sustainable farming practiced with must pomaces being spread back across the vineyards as mulch. The dark fruited, subtly black pepper spiced Syrah is the key wine on the farm and in the style of Côte Rôtie, a small proportion of Viognier is included. Vinification is in stainless steel with a two week vatting period and then the wine aged in oak of which only a small proportion is new. The wine is marked by restrained peach and citrus aromas and the balance of flavour and acidity is ensured with a number of picking dates depending on the plot. Fermentation is in a proportion of used oak and followed by ageing on fine lees adding to the wines texture. A premium Syrah, John Spicer, also now comes from a single plot and a fresh rosé Syrah is also made. (DM)

Recommended Reds:
Tamboerskloof Syrah ★★★☆ £D

Recommended Whites:
Tamboerskloof Viognier ★★★ £C

Recommended Rosés:
Tamboerskloof Syrah ★★★☆ £C

Kleine Zalze (Stellenbosch) www.kleinezalze.com
This substantial estate has been making impressive strides in quality in recent vintages, producing wines of character and value at all levels. There are a number of ranges. The Zalze label wines are the most approachable while the Cellar Selection offers a little more depth. The Vineyard Selection wines are a significant step up in quality, coming from select sites and parcels. The flagship range, the Family Reserve labels are sourced from the firms best single vineyards. Two additional ranges are also made Cleefs Classic and Reserve Collections. The estate has been making wines on a significant basis since 1996 when the property was purchased by Kobus Basson. Since then there has been an ongoing process of investment in both vineyard and cellar, isolating the best soils and sites as well as installing the best vinification equipment. There are currently 120 ha under vine on the estate and other fruit is also sourced from their other farms and from other sites. Among the Zalze wines the Rhône styled reds and Chenin Blanc stand out, in particular the vibrant berry fruited Shiraz Mourvèdre Viognier blend. The Cellar Selection whites are fresh, fruit driven styles, with additional complexity and texture imparted from four months on lees. The reds are given additional structure from around 14 months in used oak but maintain a forward fruit character. The Vineyard Selection whites are richer, fuller styles both being barrel fermented. There is a marked old vine complexity to the Chenin from Stellenbosch fruit, the Chardonnay is both fresh and with some toasty character from a portion of new wood. The Vineyard Selection Cabernet Sauvignon offers dark currant fruit and minty undertones, 22 months in barrel adding structure. Both the Rhône style Vineyard Selection reds impress. Shiraz is very much the dominant variety in the blended example and Viognier plays a minor role in the style of a Côte-Rôtie. The dark, spicy black peppered varietal Shiraz completing the malolactic fermentation in barrel. The Family Reserve whites are not only full of depth and fruit intesnsity, they both offer good value. The rich citrus infused Chenin Blanc offering a mineral intensity and a round, rich texture from 12 months in barrel on lees. The Sauvignon Blanc gaining weight and a rich texture after 14 months on lees in tank. The reds are pricier but good, in a full, rich opulent and dark fruited style after ageing in new French oak. They will make good cellaring propositions. The Klein Zalze estate also offers visitors a lodge to stay amongst the vineyards and a restaurant "Terroir". (DM)

Recommended Reds:
Family Reserve Shiraz Stellenbosch ★★★★ £E
Family Reserve Cabernet Sauvignon Stellenbosch ★★★☆ £E
Family Reserve Pinotage Stellenbosch ★★★☆ £E
Vineyard Selection Shiraz Stellenbosch ★★★ £C
Vineyard Selection Shiraz Mourvèdre Viognier Stellenbosch ★★★ £C
Vineyard Selection Cabernet Sauvignon Stellenbosch ★★☆ £C
Cellar Selection Cabernet Sauvignon Stellenbosch ★★ £B
Cellar Selection Pinotage Stellenbosch ★★ £B
Cellar Selection Merlot Stellenbosch ★☆ £B
Zalze Shiraz Mourvèdre Viognier Stellenbosch ★☆ £A
Zalze Shiraz Grenache Viognier Stellenbosch ★ £A

Recommended Whites:
Family Reserve Chenin Blanc Stellenbosch ★★★☆ £C
Family Reserve Sauvignon Blanc Stellenbosch ★★★ £C
Vineyard Selection Chardonnay ★★☆ £C
Vineyard Selection Chenin Blanc ★★☆ £C
Cellar Selection Chenin Blanc Bush Vines Stellenbosch ★★ £B
Cellar Selection Sauvignon Blanc Stellenbosch ★☆ £B
Cellar Selection Chardonnay Stellenbosch ★☆ £B
Zalze Chenin Blanc Bush Vines Stellenbosch ★☆ £A

La Motte (Franschhoek) www.la-motte.com
This is one of the longest established wine farms in the sheltered vineyards of the Franschhoek valley. Indeed a number of the buildings are historic and date back to the 18th Century. The fruit for the wines comes from both the La Motte estates as well as from a number of other sources, including the new La Motte Nabot farm in Walker Bay which is farmed organically and provides Sauvignon Blanc for the Pierneef premium label of the variety. The regular wines are nicely crafted and the licoricy, spicy Shiraz is the stand out wine and has been for some time here. The Rhône is also key in the two other top labelled Pierneef reds. There is a more southern Rhône styled Pierneef Shiraz/Grenache and an excellent Cotie-Rotie lookalike, Shiraz Viognier with impressive intensity and a spicy undertone from the Viognier. The Shiraz for this comes from a range of sites and the Viognier from Wellington. (DM)

Recommended Reds:
Pierneef Shiraz Viognier Western Cape ★★★☆ £E
Shiraz Franschhoek ★★★ £D
Millenium Franschhoek ★★☆ £C
Cabernet Sauvignon Franschhoek ★★ £D

Recommended Whites:
Chardonnay Franschhoek ★★ £C
Sauvignon Blanc Franschhoek ★★ £C

Lammershoek (Malmesbury) www.lammershoek.co.za
The origins of this Malmesbury wine farm date back to 1718. Since the Kretzels acquired the farm in 1995 impressive Rhône style wines have been produced. The vineyards are on the border of the Paarl and Swartland regions and located some 50km north of Cape Town. The vines are naturally low yielding, planted on relatively porous sandstone, granite and clay soils. This allied to long sunny days and cool nights ensures both rich fruit flavours and fresh acidity in the grapes. Chenin Blanc comes from over 40 year old dryland bush vines and is barrel-fermented in used oak at cool temperatures and offers opulent, citrus as well as green fruits and notes of quince with a fine mineral undercurrent. The Roulette red and white also both offer excellent value for money. The white is dominated by old-vine Chenin Blanc but also some Chardonnay to fill out the mid-palate and a little Viognier for fragrance. It is aged on lees for 8 months.

The Roulette red is a very characterful blend of Shiraz, Grenache, Carignan with a touch of Viognier. The wine gets a cold soak and is aged in used French and American oak for 14 months. The dark, spicy and ripely black pepper scented Syrah is similarly aged in a mix of French and American oak although 60% is new. The reds will drink very well young although the Syrah is likely to add further complexity for five years or more. As well as the wines covered here also look out for an intensely sweet Lammershoek Straw wine as well as a range of unusual experimental wines under the Cellar Foot label. Easy drinking red and white are also produced under the LAM label (DM)

Recommended Reds:
Syrah Swartland ★★★☆ £D   Roulette Swartland ★★★ £C
Recommended Whites:
Roulette Swartland ★★☆ £C
Chenin Blanc Barrique Swartland ★★ £C

Landau du Val (Franschhoek)
This small Franschhoek property originally known as La Brie was originally built in 1689. Purchased by ex industrialist Basil Landau in 1988 the farm and vineyards have had substantial investment to bring the estate back to prime condition. A rarity in the Cape is the substantial holding of 90 to 100 year old Sémillon bush vines. Tiny yields of 2 to 3 tons to the ha mean they produce one of the best examples of the variety not only from South Africa but from the new world and a rival to some of the great examples from South Australia and the Hunter Valley in New South Wales. Very rich, full and heady in style, the wine offers aromas of tropical and citrus fruits with a really complex nutty undercurrent. Matured in French oak for 6 months expect the wine to develop well for at least 6 or 7 years. (DM)

Recommended Whites:
Sémillon Franschhoek ★★★☆ £D

La Petite Ferme (Franschhoek) www.lapetiteferme.co.za
This small Franschhoek winery enjoys an excellent aspect for its west facing vineyards planted on steep slopes, 400 metres above sea level in a combination of gravel and other dry soils. Supplementary irrigation is used to optimise ripening and ensure small and flavourful berries but this is kept to a minimum. For the Sauvignon Blanc, a proportion of the canopy is kept in direct shade in order to ensure a balance of crisp grassy flavours in the wine and as a result despite the warm climate of the area the alcohol in the wine is kept in check. As well as the crisp and fresh Blanc Fumé covered here the winery also produces small volumes of a range of other wines, including Chardonnay and a full and quite fat Viognier along with a number of white blends. Among the reds there is a fine plummy, lightly minty and quite ripe Merlot which is aged in second fill American oak barrels and a dark-fruited, spicy Shiraz with underlying hints of licorice and cinnamon which is also aged in used American oak to emphasise the wine's fruit and lend structure. The top red is a new Bordeaux style blend, Verdict, with classic hints of cedar, mint as well as ripe dark berry fruit. There is also an easy drinking very approachable red blend Maison Rouge which combines Cabernet Sauvignon, Shiraz and Malbec. If you are travelling in the area there is a very good and spectacularly situated restaurant along with a number of luxury guest houses. The wines all offer great value (DM)

Recommended Reds:
Verdict Franschhoek ★★★ £C   Shiraz Franschhoek ★★☆ £B
Merlot Franschhoek ★★ £B
Maison Rouge Franschhoek ★☆ £B

Recommended Whites:
Blanc Fumé Franschhoek ★★ £B
Viognier Franschhoek ★☆ £B

Le Riche (Stellenbosch) www.leriche.co.za
A small range of fine wines is made by the Le Riche family at their Stellenbosch property with vineyards on the slopes of the Helderberg Mountain. Cabernet Sauvignon is very much the predominant variety however a well priced Chardonnay is also made along with Richesse a red made from Cabernet Sauvignon with Merlot, Petit Verdot and a smattering of Malbec. The small winery has been constructed with artisan winemaking at its heart. The fermentation tankss are all concrete and output is kept down to less than 50,000 bottles annually, the Reserve Cabernet barely more than 5,000 bottles. Etienne Le Riche is also one of the founders of the Cape Winemakers Guild and and each year he releases a Le Riche CWG Auction Reserve which will invariably be ★★★★ plus. Across the range grapes are selected from a range of top growers throughout Stellenbosch and vineyards planted in a combination of granite and sandy gravels. The Cabernet Sauvignon is a more approachable berry fruited and cedary style with well rounded supple tannins. It goes through a five day fermentation followed by the malolactic fermentation in tank and ageing for 20 months in small oak, just 20% new for balance. The Reserve is altogether more serious it is a special selection from both vineyard and cellar. After the primary fermentation the wine spends a further two weeks on skins to polymerise the tannins and then ageing in barrel follows for a couple of years in around two-thirds new wood. (DM)

Recommended Reds:
Cabernet Sauvignon Reserve Stellenbosch ★★★★ £E
Cabernet Sauvignon Stellenbosch ★★★ £C

Leopard Frog (Stellenbosch) www.leopard-frog.com
A number of big, structured and concentrated reds are made by Canadian David John Bate at this small Stellenbosch winery. At present only a handful of barrels are produced here each year and a number of releases are one-off. Over two-thirds is released under the Proprietor's Limited Release label, which includes the Bordeaux blend Tantra and Kiss & Tell, coming from an *assemblage* of Shiraz, Merlot, Malbec and Mourvèdre. Other red releases include The Tribe a blend of Pinotage, Pinot Noir and Cinsault as well as Tao from Zinfandel, Sangiovese and Barbera. Two Limited Release whites are made; Spellbinding is from Chenin Blanc while Singularity is a Viognier made solely from free run juice. From the 2011 comes a brut sparkler from Pinotage, Titillation. A very small amount of a top red is also released under the Private Release Series label. Midnight Masai is a varietal Shiraz which, in contrast to the other two reds which see 18 months in oak, gets no less than 60 months with the malolactic in barrel and the wine is a rich and rounded example with sumptuous albeit quite evolved fruit. Following on from the 2002 release of Midnight Maasai, there was a one off release of a Cabernet Franc, Aphrodite Africa and from the 2010 vintage a Pinot Noir Woman in Chains which is released in 2016. These wines feature prominent labels created by some of the countries foremost artists. (DM)

Recommended Reds:
Midnight Maasai Private Release Stellenbosch ★★★☆ £F
Tantra Proprietor's Limited Release Stellenbosch ★★★ £E
Kiss & Tell Proprietor's Limited Release Stellenbosch ★★★ £E

South Africa

Luddite (Walker Bay) www.luddite.co.za
Niels and Penny Verburg have now established their own 6 ha property on the eastern slopes of the Houw Hoek Mountains, close to the small town of Bot River. Richly textured and impressive Syrah is made here as well as a Chenin Blanc and two blends. The Luddite Shiraz is an opulent red full of dark, black pepper fruit and smoky underlying vanilla oak, it is an excellent example of small boutique scale winemaking, offering a wine of real character and individuality. Despite high alcohol levels approaching 14% and higher the wine retains an excellent balance and firm structure. The Saboteur red is blended from a combination of Shiraz, Mourvèdre and Cabenet Sauvignon. Intense black fruits, pepper and spice are all apparent in a vibrant, approachable style. A Luddite Chenin Blanc and a Saboteur white from Chenin Blanc, Viognier, Sauvignon Blanc and Chardonnay are also made. (DM)
Recommended Reds:
Shiraz Coastal Region ★★★★ £E
Saboteur Coastal Region ★★★☆ £C

Lynx Winery (Franschhoek) www.lynxwines.co.za
A small range of wines are made at this Franschhoek winery, all from estate grown fruit. Although the three reds here are stand out wines a low volume red the Lynx a special barrel selection is now the most expensive wine in the range, £F. Merlot, a Cabernet Franc, a Grenache and SMV a Rhône blend are also produced along with a Blanc de Noir, a Rosado and a Vino Tinto red blend. Close to 100 tonnes of fruit are produced on the estate but only around a third are selected for the Lynx labels. The reds are all given a 5 to 6 day cold soak and then the *cuvaison* lasts for up to three weeks. Bottling is carried out with just a coarse filtration. These are supple and approachable berry-laden reds, the Shiraz just offering the most intense fruit character with an attractive dark and spicy quality. Xanache is a Bordeaux blend of Merlot and the two Cabernets. (DM)
Recommended Reds:
Shiraz Franschhoek ★★★ £D
Cabernet Sauvignon Franschhoek ★★★ £D
Xanache Franschhoek ★★★ £C

Catherine Marshall Wines (Elgin) www.cmwines.co.za
Small bespoke wine producer established in 1997 and now based in Elgin. They source fruit from a number of different sites and appellations. The Syrah/Mouvèdre/Grenache is one of the mainstays of the range, it is a fine dark and spicy example coming from vineyards in southern Paarl and Malmesbury. Also made is the Myriad a fortified Pinot and Merlot blend as well as Amatra which comes from Merlot. Cool fermented Sauvignon Blanc is typically zesty and grassy with a hint of tropical fruit. It gains added weight from 4 months on fine lees. Drink young and fresh. The Pinot Noir is one of the better examples in the Cape and is sourced from Elgin fruit. The wine gets a cold soak and the majority is whole berry fermented, providing a ripe gamey and dark-berry fruited character. It has now been joined by a second Pinot, Black Label Reserve. Expect the reds to develop with a little age. (DM)
Recommended Reds:
Pinot Noir Elgin ★★★ £D
Syrah/Mourvèdre/Grenache Coastal Region ★★★ £D
Recommended Whites:
Sauvignon Blanc Elgin ★★☆ £C

Meerlust (Stellenbosch) www.meerlust.co.za
Historic old wine farm first established in 1693 and located just to the south of Stellenbosch in a relatively cool mesoclimate. Reds, produced from the Bordeaux varieties, and intense citrus-infused and very subtly toasty Chardonnay are among the very best of their kind in the Cape. Vineyard holdings are not small: there is a total of 110 ha under vine. Merlot is very good, as is Cabernet Sauvignon and the Cabernet/Merlot/Cabernet Franc Rubicon blend is rich, concentrated and marked by cedar and exotic dark fruits, with not a hint of the baked and jammy flavours often found among its peers. Pinot Noir is good – ripe enough and oaky but it just fails to reach quite the same heights. (DM)
Recommended Reds:
Rubicon Stellenbosch ★★★★ £F
Cabernet Sauvignon Stellenbosch ★★★☆ £E
Merlot Stellenbosch ★★★☆ £E
Pinot Noir Reserve Stellenbosch ★★☆ £E
Recommended Whites:
Chardonnay Stellenbosch ★★★★ £E

Meinert (Stellenbosch) www.meinertwines.com
Martin Meinert was the winemaker at VERGELEGEN before André van Rensburg. He established his own label in 1997 in the Devon Valley and produces a small range from the red Bordeaux varieties and a Pinotage, Printers Ink as well as a white Sauvignon Blanc, La Barry. A Cabernet Sauvignon is also made which includes a little Merlot and Cabernet Franc. The Merlot, aged in older wood, is reasonably rich, concentrated and plummy with firm tannins providing the structure for ageing over five years or so. The Devon Crest Merlot/Cabernet Sauvignon and Franc is tight and backward in its youth, quite a lean style that needs cellaring to put on weight but should become increasingly refined and harmonious with age. Meinert also produces a premium red blend, Synchronicity a rich and stylish combination of mainly Cabernet Sauvignon, with the balance comprising Merlot, Pinotage and Cabernet Franc. (DM)
Recommended Reds:
Synchronicity Devon Valley ★★★☆ £D
Devon Crest Devon Valley ★★★ £D   Merlot Devon Valley ★★☆ £C

Nico van der Merwe (Stellenbosch)
Nico van der Merwe has made at SAXENBURG and CHÂTEAU CAPION in France's Languedoc region. Under his own label he produces a very fine blend of Shiraz and Cabernet Sauvignon as well as now, several other reds, a white and well priced wines labelled Robert Alexander. In the Mas Nicolas the Shiraz component is sourced from well over 40-year-old vines grown in granite soils, the Cabernet from somewhat younger vines. The vineyards are carefully managed with summer pruning to keep yields low and irrigation is avoided. Nico also plans to include fruit in the future from his own vineyards towards Walker Bay. Vinification is modern with both hand-plunging and pumping over the cap during fermentation and the wine is kept on its skins for a further two weeks. Malolactic is in barrel and 50 per cent new oak used for ageing. The result is a dense, classically minty style of Cape red but with real depth and concentration. The wine will drink well young but can evolve over a decade or more. (DM)
Recommended Reds:
Mas Nicolas Stellenbosch ★★★★ £E

Mischa (Wellington) www.mischaestate.com
Based at Wellington to the north of Paarl, the Barns have been successful nurserymen for a number of decades. Their own fruit prior to 1996 was sold to the local co-op. However since then they

have been crafting their own wines both from the home Mischa farm and their neighbouring Eventide property. The Eventide labels are the lighter and more accessible of the wines. The Shiraz moderately dark and spicy, the Cabernet minty and a touch leafy. Both wines are aged for 12 months in oak, all American oak for the Shiraz. The Mischa Cabernet Sauvignon is denser and fuller than the Eventide bottling. Ripe and a touch minty, the wines offer a reasonable depth of dark and plummy fruit. The best red is the Mischa Shiraz, made in a full-bodied, supple style with sufficiently firm tannin and dark spicy fruit that will evolve well over 5 years or so. Both Mischa reds are aged in top quality tight-grained French oak. A Merlot and most recently a Roussanne are also produced under the Mischa label and Sauvignon Blanc and Viognier under the Eventide label. (DM)

Recommended Reds:
Mischa Shiraz Wellington ★★★ £D
Mischa Cabernet Sauvignon Wellington ★★☆ £D
Eventide Shiraz Wellington ★★ £C
Eventide Cabernet Sauvignon Wellington ★ £C

Mont du Toit (Wellington) *www.montdutoit.co.za*
Stephan du Toit's property provides some of the most striking reds outside the established Cape regions. His vineyards are at the foot of the Hawequa mountain bordering Paarl and he has 26ha planted on weathered granite slopes with a north to north-eastern aspect. Intervention is minimal and the winery is purely gravity fed. The Mont du Toit is effectively the second wine, a blend likely to be similar to the unspecified *grand vin* of Cabernet Sauvignon, Merlot, Shiraz and Cabernet Franc. Ageing for both is in small French oak for 23 months - a selection of the best fruit going into the richly opulent dark-berryfruited Le Sommet which is only released in the best years. A third more approachable red, Hawequas, ensures the fruit integrity and quality of the top wines. It spends 16 months in barrel and although more obviously fruit-driven, it nevertheless possesses a finely crafted structure. A range of cultivars are also now released under the Les Côteaux label and Stephan du Toit works with his employees on their own label wines, the Blouvlei range from which a Cabernet Sauvignon/Merlot blend, a Sauvignon Blanc and a rosé are made. (DM)

Recommended Reds:
Mont du Toit Le Sommet Wellington ★★★★ £F
Mont du Toit Wellington ★★★ £D
Mont du Toit Hawequas Wellington ★★☆ £C

Moreson (Franschhoek) *www.moreson.co.za*
This winery, nestled into the slopes of the spectacularly sited Franschhoek Valley, makes a small range of well crafted and very good value reds and whites. As well as the Moreson label a range of straightforward easy drinking wines are made under the Miss Molly brand. The Moreson whites are sourced only from Franschhoek vineyards while the reds are also sourced from Stellenbosch and Paarl. The wines are characterised their elegant style and a real purity of fruit. The Premium Chardonnay is one of the better value examples of the variety. Subtle oak and a pure citrus and lightly mineral character define the wine. Pinotage is ripe and smoky with well judged oak and a lightly porty character. The Magia red is a Bordeaux based blend with dense, very ripe fruit which spends 18 months in oak. This will stand a little age but the other wines should be drunk young. Cap Classique sparklers, Cabernet Franc, Mata Mata a further red blend and Knoputibak a white blend are also released under the Moreson label. (DM)

Recommended Reds:
Magia Coastal Region ★★★ £E
The Widow Maker Pinotage Coastal Region ★★☆ £C
Recommended Whites:
Mercator Premium Chardonnay Franschhoek ★★★ £C

Morgenhof (Stellenbosch) *www.morgenhof.com*
Medium-sized, French-owned estate producing a small range including sparkling and fortified wines. Chardonnay is in an oaky style with marked buttery malolactic character, Sauvignon Blanc is typically zesty and fresh, and there is a good, weighty, lightly tropical scented barrel-fermented Chenin Blanc. Reds include Merlot, as well as an impressive estate Red which was previously labelled as Première Selection. This latter wine is a blend of Cabernet Sauvignon, Merlot and Cabernet Franc. It is sweet and offers good depth and a rich cedary character. Both will stand a little age. Recently added are the red and white Fantail wines which offer attractive forward fruit and excellent value. (DM)

Recommended Reds:
Estate Red Stellenbosch ★★★☆ £E
Estate Merlot Stellenbosch ★★★ £C
Fantail Pinotage Stellenbosch ★☆ £B
Recommended Whites:
Chardonnay Stellenbosch ★★☆ C
Chenin Blanc Stellenbosch ★★☆ £C
Fantail Sauvignon Blanc/Chenin Blanc Stellenbosch ★☆ £B

Morgenster (Stellenbosch) *www.morgenster.co.za*
Located in the foothills of the Helderberg and Hottentots Holland Mountains which provide a natural amphitheatre for the vineyards, the climate at this 40ha property benefits further from cooling breezes drifting inland from False Bay. The Bordeaux varieties Merlot, Cabernets Sauvignon and Franc as well as a plot of Petit Verdot are planted in well drained shale soils. The vineyard has a number of aspects facing north, north-west and north-east. Three wines are now produced. The top label Morgenster is like both the wines here dominated by Merlot, with 25% of Cabernet Franc also. Sourced from the steepest slopes on the property, the wine is full, fleshy with dark-plummy fruit and a lightly cedary edge with very good intensity and a firm mineral structure. The second label Lourens River Valley is a good deal more than a Bordeaux second wine and is impressively dense and concentrated, a blend of Merlot and both Cabernets. Two impressive new reds have also been added. Nabucco is a rich and intense Nebbiolo with softer tannins than might be expected from northwest Italy and Tosca is a dark cherry scented blend of Sangiovese, Merlot and Cabernet Sauvignon. The Morgenster will continue to develop well with six or seven years ageing. The property is also an excellent source of fine olive oil. (DM)

Recommended Reds:
Morgenster Stellenbosch ★★★☆ £F
Morgenster Nabucco Stellenbosch ★★★☆ £F
Morgenster Tosca Stellenbosch ★★★ £E
Morgenster Lourens River Valley Stellenbosch ★★★ £D

Mulderbosch (Stellenbosch) *www.mulderbosch.co.za*
Mulderbosch was acquired in 2011 by US investment group Terroir Capital. The acquisition did not include its sister winery Kanu Holdings. Mulderbosch is famed for one of their piercing varietal Sauvignon Blancs. This is surprising because the mesoclimate of the vineyard here is reasonably hot. The key is tightly controlled yields and harvesting ripe but not over ripe grapes. Subtly oaked

South Africa

Chardonnay, now in Barrel Fermented and regular bottlings, and a Barrel Fermented Sauvignon Blanc are also very good. The regular Sauvignon, is cool-fermented in tank and kept for a short time on fine lees. A Chenin Blanc, Steen-op-Hout, sees a touch of oak and there is a lightly leafy peppery red blend, Faithful Hound, comprising the Bordeaux varieties Merlot, Cabernets Sauvignon and Franc and a touch of Malbec. (DM)

Recommended Reds:
Faithful Hound Stellenbosch ★★☆ £D
Recommended Whites:
Chardonnay Barrel Fermented Stellenbosch ★★★ £D
Sauvignon Blanc Barrel Fermented Stellenbosch ★★★ £C
Sauvignon Blanc Stellenbosch ★★★ £C

❂ **Mullineux & Leeu (Swartland)** *www.mlfwines.com/*
This winery is now established as one of the benchmarks in the small Swartland region where a host of characterful artisan styled reds and whites have emerged in recent vintages. They take a minimalist approach in both vineyard and cellar. Aside from the use of minimal sulphur levels for stability, the use or addition of any yeasts, acids or enzymes is avoided and the wines are bottled unfined and unfiltered. In the cellar excessive use of new oak is avoided and They work with a small number of growers following sustainable farming practices and vineyards are planted in a mix of shale, granite, gravel and iron based soils providing a base for a potentially complex array of flavours in the wines. The Kloof Street labelled wines are forward fresh and approachable. The Chenin Blanc is vinified in a combination of stainless steel and wood. The fresh and dark fruited red is sourced from a number of parcels and is a Rhône styled blend of Mourvèdre, Cinsault, Syrah, Carignan and Grenache. The Mullineux labelled wines are a step up in quality and offer more complexity. The White Swartland is dominated by old Chenin Blanc and has a number of other varieties included in small proportions in its blend. The wine is intense and characterful with restrained citrus hints and an underlying mineral quality. The Straw Wine offers a rich and profound expression of sweet Chenin Blanc. There is a luscious concentration of nutty, honeyed peachy flavours with hints of dried fruits and a finely balanced fresh edge. Syrah is in a dark and rich fruited style but with a black peppered, mineral edge. Premium Terroir examples are also made. (DM)

Recommended Reds:
Mullineux Syrah Swartland ★★★★ £E
Mullineux Kloof Street Rouge Swartland ★★★ £C
Recommended Whites:
Mullineux Straw Wine Chenin Blanc Swartland ★★★★☆ £E
Mullineux White Swartland ★★★☆ £D
Mullineux Kloof Street Chenin Blanc Swartland ★★★ £C

Muratie (Stellenbosch) *www.muratie.co.za*
The land at this wine estate was first farmed in the late 1600s and was purchased in 1763 by Martin Melck, an ancestor of the Melck family, the current owners. There is quite an extensive range and as well as the wines profiled here a sparkler, three fortifieds and a small fruit driven range, Melck's are produced and bottled under screwcap. Under the Muratie Premium Range Pinot Noir, Cabernet Sauvignon and Merlot are also made. The 45 ha of vineyards are in the foothills of the Simonsberg and are dry-farmed with irrigation taking place after the harvest. The estate is also a member of the Bio Diversity in Wine Initiative and no pesticides are used. The Premium Isabella Chardonnay like all the wines is hand harvested and whole bunch pressed. A full bodied style with ripe fruit it is

part barrel-fermented and part in stainless steel. Part of the wine goes through malolactic to provide a fresh edge and ageing is for seven months before blending and bottling. The Laurens Campher white is a characterful blend of Chenin Blanc, Verdehlo, Viognier and Sauvignon Blanc with rich, lightly honeted tropical fruit and a green and fresh undercurrent. The Ansela Van de Caab is a cedary Bordeaux style blend of Cabernet Sauvignon, Merlot, Cabernet Franc and just a little Shiraz. All the varieties are aged separately for 12 months and then blended before ageing for a further 6 months. The wine is bottled unfiltered. The other top red is the Ronnie Melck Family Selection Shiraz a rich and concentrated traditionally styled almost earthy red with a real note of the Northern Rhône about it. The wine comes from a near 40 year old vineyard. Vinification is in open fermenters and then a hint of the modern with malolactic in 100% new oak and then 16 months ageing. Better with four or five years cellaring. A second dark, spicy approachable Shiraz is labelled just Ronnie Melck. (DM)

Recommended Reds:
Shiraz Ronnie Melck Family Selection Stellenbosch ★★★☆ £E
Ansela Van de Caab Stellenbosch ★★★☆ £D
Shiraz Ronnie Melck Stellenbosch ★★☆ £C
Recommended Whites:
Isabella Chardonnay Stellenbosch ★★★ £C
Laurens Campher Stellenbosch ★★★ £C

Newton Johnson Vineyards *www.newtonjohnson.com*
Small family owned winery in the burgeoning quality conscious Walker Bay area. The winery was founded in 1997 and their base in the Upper Hemel-en-Aarde Valley is ideal for cultivating both Chardonnay and Pinot Noir as well as the Rhône varieties in warmer micro sites. Key to quality are the maritime winds which moderate the local climate. The family now have 140 ha of which 18 ha is planted vines with both north and south facing sites. Planted in a mix of quartz and clay soils the vines are free of the leaf roll virus that has afflicted so many Cape vineyards. This is as a result of a sustainable, natural approach to vineyard farming. The final component in ensuring wine quality is a four storey, gravity fed winemaking facility. Sauvignon Blanc has a touch of Sémillon which is barrel-fermented and aged on lees, not dissimilar to the Cloudy Bay approach. Chardonnay is subtle, elegant and with a creamy character from a combination of barrel-fermentation, malolactic fermentation and ageing on lees. Full Stop Rock ia a recently added Rhône blend which includes Syrah, Grenache and Mouvèdre and there is a new Grenache blend from the 2010 vintage which has great potential. Of the Pinot Noirs, the regular bottling is clearly more fruit driven, the Domaine bottling complex, gamey and with real concentration. A Domaine Chardonnay is also made. (DM)

Recommended Reds:
Pinot Noir Domaine Upper Hemel-en-Aarde ★★★★ £E
Pinot Noir Elgin ★★★☆ £D   Full Stop Rock Walker Bay ★★★☆ £D
Recommended Whites:
Chardonnay Overberg ★★★☆ £D
Sauvignon Blanc Walker Bay & Elgin ★★★ £D

Nitida Cellars (Durbanville) *www.nitida.co.za*
From their Durbanville property, the Vellers make a well-made small range of well-priced reds and whites from just 12 ha of vines planted in well drained Clovelly Hutton soils. While not in the upper echelon in the Cape the wines are among the areas best values. A bright, forward vibrant fruit quality marks the reds and the whites are clean and fresh with some zesty fruit, particularly

the grassy cool-fermented Sauvignon Blanc. Sémillon is rounder, fatter and more honeyed. An excellent Late Harvest Modjadji is made and there is a further dry blended white from the two main white grapes, Coronata. Of the reds the Cabernet Sauvignon is in a lighter style than the other reds with a hint of black fruit and a minty, leafy undercurrent. Pinotage is full throttle, ripe and marked by dark jammy fruit and a hint of acetate. It can be a touch raw and alcoholic. Shiraz is nicely smoky and spicy with attractive upfront dark berry fruit. Calligraphy is a blend of Merlot, Cabernet Franc and Cabernet Sauvignon and offers a touch more structure and grip than the varietal wines. Dark fruit is nicely meshed with a hint of cedar and well chiselled soft supple tannins. Ageing is in a small proportion of new oak. The reds will stand a little age, three or four years for the Calligraphy. (DM)

Recommended Reds:
Calligraphy Durbanville ★★☆ £C   Shiraz Durbanville ★★☆ £C
Cabernet Sauvignon Durbanville ★★ £B
Pinotage Durbanville ★★ £B
Recommended Whites:
Modjadji Durbanville ★★★ £C
Sauvignon Blanc Durbanville ★★ £B   Sémillon Durbanville ★★ £B

Oak Valley (Elgin) www.oakvalley.co.za
This winery has vineyards planted in the high altitude vineyards of Elgin between Cape Town and Walker Bay. As well as wines the property produces fresh cut flowers, farms naturally reared beef and has 350 ha of apple and pear trees planted. The vineyards date back to 1985 although their first wine was a Sauvignon Blanc from the 2003 vintage. Five wines are now produced from 48 ha. As well as the Sauvignon Blanc there is a minerally intense Chardonnay, a fine gamey, berry-scented Pinot Noir, a red blend the Oak Valley Blend and a Sauvignon/Sémillon blend. The vineyards are planted on south-west facing slopes on gravelly top soils which are underpinned by clay and the altitude varies from 300 to 500 metres above sea level. Savignon Blanc is excellent value, fresh and crisp with some underlying tropical fruit beneath its green fruit character. It gets a period of skin contact and is then very cool-fermented and left on lees for a couple of months. Chardonnay is barrel-fermented in 40% new wood and the malolactic fermentation adds a rich creamy texture, although the wine has a fine edgy mineral character. The Oak Valley Blend is in a structured and restrained style given the aspect and relatively cool climate of the vineyards. It blends Merlot with Cabernet Franc and Cabernet Sauvignon. A fine Pinot Noir is quite Burgundian in style, a cold soak is avoided and the oak is reined in. The wine getting just around 9 months in barrel. (DM)

Recommended Reds:
Pinot Noir Elgin ★★★ £E   The Oak Valley Blend Elgin ★★★ £D
Recommended Whites:
Chardonnay Elgin ★★★☆ £D   Sauvignon Blanc Elgin ★★☆ £C

● Oldenburg Vineyards www.oldenburgvineyards.com
This fine Stellenbosch property winery was established in its current form in 2003 and at present produces three excellent reds along with Chardonnay and Chenin Blanc. The 30 ha of sustainably farmed vineyards are at some altitude, around 300 to 450 metres above sea level moderating the climate and providing a fresh edge in the wines and they also enjoy a significant advantage in sunlight hours compared to some of the lower lying sites. The Rondekop hill where the vineyards are sited provides a wide range of microclimates and soils and a number of Rhône varieties besides Syrah have also been planted. Near neighbours include THELEMA and TOKARA. The fruit

is all hand harvested and the grapes cooled on arrival at the winery. The wines are made at the GLENELLY estate, which is owned by the former proprietor at PICHON-LONGUEVILLE LA COMTESSE, Mme. May de Lencquesaing. Winemaker Luke O'Cuinneagain has previous experience at SCREAMING EAGLE, Château FIEUZAL, Château ANGELUS and at RUSTENBERG. Gravity plays a key part in minimising handling of must and wine. The complex and subtly leafy Cabernet Franc is given a three-day cold soak, as are all three wines, and it is aged for 15 months in French oak which is wisely reined to just 20% new barrels for harmony. The Cabernet Sauvignon has a touch more structure and requires a year or two extra in your cellar. Vinification is similar and the wine sees more new oak (50%). The dark-berried, spicy Syrah shows classic white pepper undertones and possesses a complex mineral quality. Four or five years will add a further dimension. The Chenin Blanc includes a little Chardonnay adding to the wine's mid palate texture and both whites are barrel-fermented and aged in slightly larger 300 litre barrels. (DM)

Recommended Reds:
Syrah Stellenbosch ★★★★ £E
Cabernet Sauvignon Stellenbosch ★★★★ £E
Cabernet Franc Stellenbosch ★★★★ £E
Recommended Whites:
Chenin Blanc Stellenbosch ★★★☆ £D
Chardonnay Stellenbosch ★★★☆ £D

>> Painted Wolf (Swartland) www.paintedwolfwines.com
This project led by Jeremy and Emma Borg with a number of friends and vineyard suppliers involved produces a small range of low volume artisan style wines offering excellent character and quality from a number of sources including Stellenbosch, Paarl and Swartland. Importantly a proportion of the revenue of the project goes to conservation and the name comes from the endangered African Wild Dog. A range of varieties is vinified although the bulk of the wines come from Rhône grapes as well as Chenin Blanc. There are three main ranges, the Den, Peloton and "Our Pack". The red and white Den both offer brilliant value and are in a vbrant fruit driven style. The red and white Peloton labels both offer a little more depth and structure. The Blanc, which is whole-bunch pressed and barrel-fermented on lees is a blend of bush vine Chenin Blanc, Viognier and Roussanne from vineyards in Swartland and Malmesbury. The Rouge again comes from Paarl and Swartland (organic) and combines a spicy black-fruited mix of Shiraz, Pinotage, Mourvèdre and Grenache. As well as the "Our Pack" current range a number wines have also been released under "Black Pack" label. Shiraz, the most recent vintage being the 2010, was sourced from Swartland, Paarl and Stellenbosch. Syrah enthusiasts should also be aware of the Swartland Syrah. The peachy and lightly citrus infused Penny Viognier is solely from Swartland vines and gains a light, weight and texture from barrel fermentation in 500 litre oak. Paarl Roussanne offers intense citrus and white fruits, it is vinified on stirred Chenin lees and the malolactic fermentation blocked for freshness. The bright berry fruited Lycaon Grenache is blended with just 5% Shiraz and shows undercurrents of herb and black pepper spices. Guillermo Pinotage from organic Swartland fruit is impressively stylish with richly flavoured black fruits and exotic spices. After the primary fermentation the wine goes through the malolactic and is then aged in small oak. The top wine is the densely black-fruited Pictus (2011 III is the latest release) with depth and impressive structure. It is classic blend of Shiraz, Mourvèdre and Grenache from Swartland fruit. Small batch winemaking is followed by ageing for 18 months. Around two-thirds new wood is seamlessly handled.

South Africa

(DM)

Recommended Reds:
Pictus Swartland ★★★☆ £D
Our Pack Guillermo Pinotage Swartland ★★★☆ £D
Our Pack Lycaon Grenache Swartland ★★★ £D
Black Pack Shiraz Coastal Region ★★★ £C
Peloton Rouge Coastal Region ★★★ £C
The Den Pinotage Coastal Region ★★☆ £B
Recommended Whites:
Our Pack Roussanne Paarl ★★★ £C
Our Pack Penny Viognier Swartland ★★☆ £C
Peloton Blanc Coastal Region ★★★ £C
The Den Chenin Blanc Coastal Region ★★☆ £B

Porseleinberg (Swartland) www.porseleinberg.com
Marc Kent is also known for his BOEKENHOUTSKLOOF and
PORCUPINE RIDGE labels. Here he makes just one Syrah, which is
one of South Africa's very best, with viticulturalist and winemaker
Callie Loew who established his reputation at the highly respected
Tulbagh Mountain Vineyards (now FABLE). The first release was in
2010 and an extensive selection is made before the rest of the fruit
goes to Boekenhoutskloof. The vineyards which are organically
farmed are planted in slate mountainside soils at high density and
to a combination of bush and trellised vines. Winemaking is strictly
artisan with the fruit whole bunch pressed before fermentation and
then ageing in a mix cone shaped concrete eggs and 2,500 litre
foudres for a minimum of 16 months. More northern Rhône than
new world, the wine offers a really impressive depth and intensity
of dark spicy black fruits and a mineral backbone. Unfortunately the
wine is inevitably somewhat scarce. (DM)
Recommended Reds:
Porseleinberg Red Swartland ★★★★☆ £F

Quoin Rock (Stellenbosch) www.quoinrock.com
This recently established Stellenbosch property is owned by
Scotsman Dave King. There are 60 ha of vineyards now planted,
including Chardonnay and Sauvignon Blanc at Agulhas the
southernmost tip of Africa. Around 5,000 cases are produced a year
under the Quoin Rock label, the bulk of the 180 ton annual grape
crush is sold off. Vineyard practices are as natural as possible and
no herbicides/pesticides are used. The cool climate character of
the whites clearly comes across, tight and almost minerally. The
Sauvignon Blanc possesses none of the overt raw blackcurrant and
tropical notes found elsewhere. Chardonnay is subtle and quite
restrained with well-judged oak. The Oculus is Sauvignon Blanc
barrel-fermented and is arguably the most structured of the whites
with piercing intensity and should develop well for two or three
years. A Cape Agulhas barrel-fermented example Nicobar is also
now being made and there is a Vine Dried sweet Sauvignon from
the Simonsberg. The Merlot while impressively dark, spicy and
plummy can show a lot of new oak young. The Simonsberg Syrah
is dense and smoky with an attractive black pepper compoment.
Expect both reds to benefit with four or five years ageing. (DM)
Recommended Reds:
Syrah Stellenbosch ★★★ £C
Merlot Western Cape ★★☆ £C
Recommended Whites:
Chardonnay Cape Agulhas ★★★ £D
Oculus Stellenbosch ★★☆ £C
Sauvignon Blanc Cape Agulhas ★★☆ £C
Glenrose Sauvignon Blanc/Viognier Simonsberg ★☆ £B

✿ Raats (Stellenbosch) www.raats.co.za
This small estate which focusses on Chenin Blanc and Cabernet
Franc is run by Bruwer Raats and his wife Janice. Chenin Blanc is the
most important variety here and considerable effort has gone into
sourcing older low-yielding vineyards on the most propritious soils.
On average the vines are over 25 years old and found at an altitude
of over 250 metres, helping to promote natural acidity in the wines.
The Original Chenin Blanc is the most approachable. It is harvested
in different pickings from a range of soil types and is cool fermented
in stainless steel. Greengage and ripe tropical notes are evident
along with a fine mineral undercurrent. The Stellenbosch Chenin
is richer and fuller coming from older vines, over 40 years and gets
a proportion of the wine vinified and aged in oak. That mineral
undercurrent is again present here. The Cabernet Franc is in a rich
and ripe style with evident black fruits, it comes from unirrigated
bush vines grown on decomposed granite. Ageing is for 14 months
in one-third new French oak and the wine is bottled unfined and
unfiltered. A more approachable Cabernet Franc, Dolomite is
also made as well as a red blend Jasper, comprising a majority of
Cabernet Franc with Petit Verdot, Cabernet Sauvignon and Malbec.
Produced in very small volume is the super premium red Mvemve
Raats de Compostella, a blend of the Cabernets, Petit Verdot, Malbec
and Merlot. It is a wine of really impressive dimension. (DM)
Recommended Reds:
Mvemve Raats de Compostella ★★★★★ £F
Cabernet Franc Stellenbosch ★★★★ £E
Red Jasper Stellenbosch ★★★☆ £C
Dolomite Cabernet Franc Stellenbosch ★★★ £C
Recommended Whites:
Old Vine Chenin Blanc Stellenbosch ★★★☆ £C
Original Chenin Blanc Coastal Region ★★☆ £B

Rall Wines (Stellenbosch) www.rallwines.co.za
This small winery was only recently established with the first wines
released from the 2008. Donovan Rall draws on the vineyards and
small growers of Swartland and Stellenbosch in the production of
just one red and one white produced from old vines. The wines are
vinified naturally and by individual vineyard parcels. The majority of
the fruit comes from Swartland and a total of 10 separate vineyard
sites are sources. The white comes from grapes grown generally
in decomposed granite, the red from schist soils. The hands of
approach is continued in the winery with minimal SO2, natural
yeasts and avoiding any further additions or nutrients. The resulting
wines are characterful and intense with impressive depth. The
dark fruited, restrained, fresh and elegant red is a blend of Syrah
and Grenache and solely from Swartland vineyards. The wine is
lent structure but not aroma or aggressive tannin from 22 months
in neutral oak. The white is a blend of Chenin blanc, Verdelho,
Chardonnay and Viognier and as well as Swartland, Stellenbosch is
also a source. A lengthy barrel fermentation in older oak is followed
by 10 months on fine lees which are regularly stirred. Both wines are
subtle but approachable and will stand a little cellaring. (DM)
Recommended Reds:
Rall Red Swartland ★★★★ £D
Recommended Whites:
Rall White Western Cape ★★★★ £D

Remhoogte (Stellenbosch) www.remhoogte.co.za
This 60 ha property is owned by Murray Boustred in partnership
with French wine consultant Michel Rolland, who became
involved with the 2002 vintage. There are 35 ha under vine and

plantings include Cabernet Sauvignon, Pinotage, Merlot, Syrah and Chenin Blanc planted on the stony slopes of the Simonsberg. The environment means naturally low-yielding fruit is obtained. Vinification has the Rolland stamp on it with regular *pigéage*, malolactic in barrel and ageing of between 14 and 22 months in barrel. The French influence shows through in the style of the wines which are certainly ripe and supple but also have a cedary, dry spicy character as well. The Estate Wine is dominated by Merlot with Cabernet Sauvignon and around 10% Pinotage. It offers more dark plum fruit and a firmer edge to its tannins. There is also a soft, forward red, Aigle Noir as well as crisp Chenin Blanc, No 6, a Cabernet Sauvignon and a Syrah, Valentino. The main wine in the range is now the Merlot Reserve. (DM)

Recommended Reds:
Estate Wine Stellenbosch ★★★ £D

Ridgeback (Paarl) *www.ridgebackwines.co.za*
Recently established Paarl based winery producing some very impressive reds, particularly a smoky, dense and opulent Shiraz, the most exciting wine profiled here. As well as the reds, Viognier, Sauvignon Blanc and Dry White and Dry Red are also made. The latter two wines take the Vansha label, as does a new Rhône style red SGMV. Merlot is dense and fleshy with a marked dark plum fruit character and noticeable smoky oak. Cabernet Sauvignon is characteristically minty and lightly cedary with some rich cassis and chocolatey notes. The Cabernet Franc/Merlot is the lightest of the four reds offering a mix of dark plum, subtle minerality and a leafiness from the Cabernet Franc. Rich toasty oak is a characteristic running through the wines with abundant fruit. The pHs in the wines run at up to 3.8 in a very European, minimal interference manner. With their vibrant upfront character all will drink well young. (DM)

Recommended Reds:
Shiraz Paarl ★★★☆ £D   Cabernet Sauvignon Paarl ★★★☆ £D
Cabernet Franc/Merlot Paarl ★★★ £C   Merlot Paarl ★★★ £C

Rijk's (Tulbagh) *www.rijks.co.za*
A sizeable little range of red and white wines are made at this fine Tulbagh based wine farm. Output is by no means considerable at around 15,000 cases a year and there is a positively artisan feel to the wine. All offer not only good quality but excellent value as well. The vineyards were planted on virgin wine territory in Tulbagh and the family have a farm covering a total of 136 ha of land. The vineyard area now covers a total of just under 28 ha, with the best and most propitious sites for viticulture identified and then organised by blocks for planting. No single block is larger than a single hectare, which aids the management of the vines' development during the growing season. Of the whites, which are all picked at night to retain fresh flavour, both the Private Cellar Chardonnay and Chenin Blanc are barrel-fermented and aged and there are marginally pricier Reserve examples. The Fascination is a blend of Sémillon and Sauvignon Blanc, the Sémillon component vinified and raised in barrel. Of the reds the varietal Reserve Pinotage and Estate Syrah stand out and compare favourably with the ripe largely Rhône styled blend The Master, the top red, a blend of Syrah, Mourvèdre, Pinotage, Carignan, Trincadeira and Viognier. Private Cellar Pinotage and Shiraz are also made and there are some more approachable wines labelled Rijk's Touch of Oak and include a Chenin, a Pinotage and a Shiraz. (DM)

Recommended Reds:
Estate The Master Tulbagh ★★★☆ £E

Syrah Estate Tulbagh ★★★☆ £E
Pinotage Reserve Tulbagh ★★★☆ £E
Recommended Whites:
Fascination Tulbagh ★★☆ £C
Chardonnay Tulbagh ★★☆ £C
Chenin Blanc Tulbagh ★★ £C

Rudera (Paarl) *www.rudera.co.za*
This winery produced its first wines with the 2000 vintage and continues to offer excellent quality. The property has been relocated to the d'Olyfboom Family Estate on the eastern slopes of Paarl Rock Mountain. Chenin Blanc is a particular focus here as well as Cabernet Sauvignon and Syrah. The Chenin Blanc Tradisie is produced in a lush, rich almost tropical style although an increasing mineral quality is becoming apparent. It is matured in barrel on its fine lees. A second Chenin, the unusual Robusto, is not dissimilar in style to a good Vouvray or Montlouis *demi-sec* although riper and more opulent with less minerality and less residual sugar. The Late Harvest bottling offers a rich concentrated peachy character and despite missing the structure and grip found in the best Loire examples, it is very impressive nonetheless. The Platinum white is again Chenin and sourced from cool climate Elgin fruit. It is elegant, mineral and finely structured. The Syrah is the lightest of the three reds with soft upfront berry fruit and just a hint of spice. More serious are the Cabernet Sauvignon and the newly added cedary Platinum Red, also a varietal Cabernet from Stellenbosch fruit. Both are subtle and have intensely cedary fruit. Expect them to develop well for 5 or 6 years. (DM)

Recommended Reds:
Platinum Red Stellenbosch ★★★☆ £E
Cabernet Sauvignon Stellenbosch ★★★☆ £E
Syrah Stellenbosch ★★★ £D
Recommended Whites:
Chenin Blanc Noble Late Harvest Stellenbosch ★★★ £E
Platinum White Elgin ★★★ £C
Chenin Blanc Robusto Stellenbosch ★★★ £C
Chenin Blanc Tradisie Stellenbosch ★★ £C

Rupert & Rothschild *www.rupert-rothschildvignerons.com*
This is a partnership between the Rupert family who also own the Cape farms LA MOTTE and L'Ormarins and Baron Benjamin de Rothschild who is one of the family partners in LAFITE-ROTHSCHILD and also owns Château CLARKE in Listrac-Medoc. Consultancy comes from Michel Rolland. The intended style here – successfully achieved – is one of elegance and restraint as opposed to some of the more opulent examples of some of their neighbours. The red Classique is a blend of Cabernet Sauvignon, Merlot and unusually a little Pinotage. It is more obviously fruit-driven than the sturdier and more backward Baron Edmond which blends purely Cabernet Sauvignon and Merlot (the proportion is roughly 2:1). Both wines get just under 20 months maturation in French oak, new in the case of the Baron Edmond. The restrained melon and lightly citrus aromas of the Baroness Nadine Chardonnay are achieved through just 20 per cent new oak and 20 per cent of the wine going through malolactic fermentation. Unlike many South African examples of the grape the Baroness Nadine will benefit from three or four years' age. Both reds will develop well in the medium term, the Baron Edmond for up to a decade. (DM)

Recommended Reds:
Baron Edmond Coastal Region ★★★☆ £E
Classique Coastal Region ★★☆ £C

South Africa

Recommended Whites:
Baroness Nadine Coastal Region ★★★ £D

● Rustenberg (Stellenbosch) *www.rustenberg.co.za*
Considerable investment has been put into this farm in recent years and the winery is now gravity-fed, with some good results. There are a range of attractive, varietal as well as blended wines released as the winery's Regional Range. These include crisp, ripe Sauvignon Blanc, an unwooded Chardonnay, a well crafted Roussanne as well as a Schoongezicht white from an interesting combination of Sémillon, Viognier and Roussanne and a red blend RM Nicholson comprising Cabernet Sauvignon, Shiraz, Cabernet Franc, Merlot and Malbec. Of real substance are the Flagship and Site Specific wines. Two Chardonnays are produced with intense citrus notes and well-judged oak, as well as the Rustenberg John X Merriman and Peter Barlow reds. The former, a Bordeaux blend with a sizeable proportion of both Cabernet Sauvignon and Merlot, shows sweet berry fruit and spicy oak. Peter Barlow is a more structured and ageworthy varietal Cabernet Sauvignon. Syrah, Merlot and a Straw Wine are also included in the range. The Brampton range has recently been sold to the DGB Group. (DM)

Recommended Reds:
Cabernet Sauvignon Peter Barlow Stellenbosch ★★★★☆ £F
John X Merriman Stellenbosch ★★★★ £E
RM Nicholson Stellenbosch ★★★ £C

Recommended Whites:
Chardonnay Five Soldiers Stellenbosch ★★★★ £E
Chardonnay Stellenbosch ★★★☆ £D
Roussanne Stellenbosch ★★★ £D
Unwooded Chardonnay Stellenbosch ★★☆ £C
Sauvignon Blanc Stellenbosch ★★☆ £C
Schoongezicht Stellenbosch ★★ £B

● Rust En Vrede (Stellenbosch) *www.rustenvrede.com*
Jean Engelbrecht now has increasing premium interests in the Cape winelands having taken over this historic farm in 1978. He has established a partnership with golfing superstar Ernie Els at ERNIE ELS and at GUARDIAN PEAK. Ernie Els winemaker, Coenie Snyman is in charge of vinification here also. Rust en Vrede itself was established in 1694 and is one of the very oldest wine farms. The vineyards located to the south of Stellenbosch have a spectacular backdrop looking across to the Helderberg mountains. This is a red only property producing Shiraz, Merlot, Cabernet Sauvignon, an Estate blend of Cabernet Sauvignon, Shiraz and Merlot, a new and entirely more opulent Syrah label and one of the Capes most expensive new reds the rich and concentrated 1694, a blend of Syrah and Cabernet. All the wines are more opulent than many others from the Cape. Some of the overtly minty character found elsewhere is absent here. While the Cabernet Sauvignon, Merlot and Shiraz varietal bottlings are impressively dense and concentrated, the Estate Red, along with the new labelled Syrah and 1694 are a clear step up. While all the wines will all evolve nicely in the medium term, the top three will continue to add complexity with up to 10 years' ageing. (DM)

Recommended Reds:
1694 Stellenbosch ★★★★★ £H
Syrah Stellenbosch ★★★★☆ £G
Estate Red Stellenbosch ★★★★ £F
Shiraz Stellenbosch ★★★☆ £E
Cabernet Sauvignon Stellenbosch ★★★ £D
Merlot Stellenbosch ★★★ £D

● Sadie Family Wines (Swartland)
Eben Sadie, the original winemaker at SPICE ROUTE, formed his own small Sadie Family winery in the late 1990s. The very fine red, Columella, is a blend of Syrah with Mourvèdre, Grenache, Cinsaut and Carignan. It is a wine of remarkable dark, spicy complexity; rich, almost exotic, with a supple texture and great intensity. Inevitably it is made from very low yields, from leased vineyard parcels around Swartland, half of which are populated with old bush vines. Eben controls all the viticultural aspects. There is no irrigation and he prefers to control vine growth through crop thinning. The must gets a cold soak prior to fermentation and maceration often lasts longer than five weeks. The wine is basket-pressed and aged in old wooden casks and concrete for close to two years and fining and filtration are avoided. While almost immediately approachable, Columella will develop very well for a decade or more. The white Palladius, a blend of a number of varieties was first made with the 2002 vintage. It is piercingly intense, with a lovely minerality. He is also involved in a new project in Priorat in Spain, TERROIR AL LIMIT. Sadie also purchased the Sequillo Cellars, Swartland based project from ANURA in 2006. They are producing a supple, rounded fleshy fruit-driven Southern Rhône styled red from a blend of Syrah, Cinsault and Tinta Barocca. A similar approach is taken to the Sadie wines - a cold soak, natural fermentation and an absence of fining or filtration. A year or two will bring greater harmony. A series of 8 old vine selections has also been made in small quantities including T Voetpad, a blend of Sémillon, Chenin Blanc, Palomino and Muscat. Sequillo now has its own winery and vineyards and is also a source of a newly added white crafted from a blend of Chenin Blanc, Clairette, Viognier, Verdelho and Palomino. (DM)

Sadie Family
Recommended Reds:
Columella Swartland ★★★★★ £G
Recommended Whites:
Palladius Swartland ★★★★☆ £F T Voetpad Swartland ★★★★ £E
Sequillo Cellars
Recommended Reds:
Sequillo Red Swartland ★★★☆ £E

Saxenburg (Stellenbosch) *www.saxenburg.co.za*
The Swiss owners of this farm also own CHÂTEAU CAPION in France's Languedoc region. There are over 90 ha of vineyards here supplemented by bought-in fruit. The Guinea Fowl and Grand Vin red and white provide decent fruit-driven reds and whites but it is the Private Collection Label that particularly stands out. A Cap Classique sparkler, a Chardonnay and a Sauvignon Blanc can be impressive, with good varietal fruit and stylishly handled oak in the Chardonnay. The Private Collection reds comprise a warm and plummy Merlot with rich vanilla oak; a tightly structured Cabernet Sauvignon marked by notes of cassis and cedar; and impressive Shiraz full of dark black fruit and Rhône-like licorice and black pepper. Shiraz Select Special Reserve is richer and fuller with very fine, ripe and supple tannins, long and harmonious. It is also now very pricy. Both Shirazes stand out among South African reds. (DM)

Recommended Reds:
Shiraz Select Special Reserve Stellenbosch ★★★★ £G
Cabernet Sauvignon Private Collection Stellenbosch ★★★ £D
Shiraz Private Collection Stellenbosch ★★★ £D
Merlot Private Collection Stellenbosch ★★☆ £C
Shiraz Private Collection Stellenbosch ★★☆ £C

Recommended Whites:
Chardonnay Private Collection Stellenbosch ★★☆ £C

Sauvignon Blanc Private Collection Stellenbosch ★★☆ £C

Scali (Voor-Paadeberg) *www.scaliwines.wordpress.com*
This recently established small property to the north of Paarl is producing some ripe, smoky and very attractive Pinotage and Shiraz. The De Waal family are fifth generation *vignerons*, their property planted on finely drained shale soils. Everything is done as naturally as possible. The fruit is all hand-harvested and sorted prior to vinification. Fermentation is traditional in open top vats and the cap is gently basket-pressed before barrel ageing. Roughly 50% new oak is employed which is well-integrated and a little American as well as French is used in the case of the ripe, smoky, blackberry-scented Pinotage. The Shiraz is just a touch firmer and will require 2 or 3 years' patience. In line with the approach to quality here, the wines are both bottled unfiltered. Look out also for a number of whites including Chenin Blanc, Chardonnay, Roussanne, Viognier and Sauvignon Blanc. (DM)

Recommended Reds:
Scali Shiraz Voor-Paardeberg ★★★ £C
Scali Pinotage Voor-Paardeberg ★★★ £C

◉ Signal Hill Winery (Cape Town)
This is the only Cape Town city winery, taking the concept of the warehouse winery a step further. However the quality of the wines is very good indeed, this is no gimmicky operation. The overriding focus here is sweet wine, probably the best collection in South Africa. The Vin de L'Empereur is a rich Muscat d'Alexandre, with a smoky, peachy almost honeyed character. It is the most approachable of the sweet offerings. The wine perhaps needs just a touch more structure and acidity. A second Muscat is also made a Creme de Tete which is quite a bit pricier as well as a Straw Wine, from dried grapes and an intensely sweet *moelleux* style of enormous richness, Eszencia. Some very fine red is also produced. Petit Verdot is structured and smoky with not only real persistence and breadth but refinement too. The extraordinary, dark pepper-scented black fruit infused Syrah Clos d'Orange comes from the only vineyard in Cape Town, it is richly textured with dusty fine tannins and very impressive intensity. It is only available in tiny quantities. Jean-Vincent Ridon also has a small property in France's Agly Valley in the Roussillon. (DM)

Recommended Reds:
Syrah Clos d'Orange Western Cape ★★★★★ £G
Petit Verdot Western Cape ★★★ £D
Recommended Whites:
Eszencia Western Cape ★★★★★ £H
Straw Wine Western Cape ★★★★ £E
Vin de L'Empereur Western Cape ★★★ £C

Sijnn (Malgas) *www.sijnn.co.za*
A relatively new project for the DE TRAFFORD family producing very fine red and white wines some considerable distance from Cape Town, 230 kms in fact to its east, close to the remote Swellendam WO, in the Malgas Wine Ward. It is an isolated area, certainly from a viticultural point of view and identified as a potential site for its complex stony soils and close coastal influence which on the immediate evidence can provide wines of tremendous character and complexity. The site, originally a grain and ostrich farm was acquired in 2004. The climate is warm but distinctly maritime and moderated by sea breezes. At presesent a fascinating mix of European varieties have been planted, focussing on the Rhône Valley and Portugal. The first wines were vinified from the 2007

vintage and in the De Trafford winery where for the time being this will continue. The Sijnn Red is a beguiling, smoky, mineral scented red blended from Shiraz, Mourvèdre, Touriga Nacional and Trincadeira, on the palate really seeming like a mix of the Rhône and the Douro. Varietal examples of both a Shiraz and a Touriga are also impressive. The white focuses not only on Chenin Blanc but also Viognier offering rich fruit, structure and perfume. The reds spend a relatively short time on skins, up to 9 days, and are then aged in barrel for around 22 months. The white gets a very short time pre-fermentation on skins and is then barrel-fermented and aged for 10 months. A Cabernet Sauvigon is also made as well as a more approachable red blend Low Profile and a deep coloured rosé Saignée which combines Mourvèdre with Trincadeira and Shiraz. (DM)

Recommended Reds:
Sijnn Red Swellendam ★★★★ £E
Sijnn Shiraz Swellendam ★★★★ £D
Sijnn Touriga Nacional Swellendam ★★★☆ £D
Recommended Whites:
Sijnn White Swellendam ★★★☆ £D

Solms-Delta (Franschhoek) *www.solms-delta.co.za*
The origins of this wine estate go back to 1690 although the excellent range of wine now being created is far more recent with the custodianship of the property being assumed in 2002 by neuroscientist Mark Solms. His vision has gone much further than re-establishing the vineyards and cellars of the estate and he wanted to address the pressing social and economic problems facing South Africa today. Solms and his partner Richard Aster each control one-third of the estate while the remaining one-third is owned by the Wijn de Caab trust which benefits the estate's historically disadvantaged residents and employees. The property is located in Franschhoek and enjoys a warm, dry and windy Mediterranean climate. Because of this Rhône varieties were planted and blended with tried and tested old Cape varietals. Mark Solms and winemaker Hilko Hegewisch introduced dessication - a largely forgotten, ancient Mediterranean vineyard practice. The result is two ranges of wines that deliver a unique style. The Solms-Delta range consists entirely of Rhône varietals: Hiervandaan is a red blend of Shiraz, Mourvèdre, Grenache, Carignan and Viognier; Amalie is a white blend of Viognier and Grenache Blanc; Lekkerwijn is a free-run rosé blended from Shiraz, Mourvèdre, Viognier and Grenache. Africana, a 100% Shiraz and Koloni, a dry oak aged Muscat, are made entirely from dessicated grapes. They are impressively intense and concentrated wines with a fascinating bittersweet, mineral character. From similarly dessicated fruit the Gemoedsrus is an unusual fortified red, not dissimilar to a young vintage Port but with a bitter dark cherry edge and more obviously vibrant fruit. The Solms-Astor range are more immediately approachable styles and offer great value. These wines are made from undessicated grapes and are marked by their fruit. Langarm is a red blend of Pinotage, Touriga Nacional, Tannat, Grenache, Cabernet Sauvignon and Primitivo; Vastrap is a white blend of Chenin Blanc, Clairette, and Sémillon. Completing the range is the unusual Cape Jazz, a pétillant red Shiraz "Lambrusco" style. (DM)

Recommended Reds:
Africana Franschhoek ★★★★ £E
Gemoedsrus Western Cape ★★★☆ £E
Hiervandaan Western Cape ★★★☆ £C
Langarm Western Cape ★★☆ £C
Cape Jazz Shiraz Western Cape ★☆ £B

Wine behind the label

South Africa

Recommended Whites:
Amalie Coastal Region ★★★☆ £C
Koloni Western Cape ★★★ £C   Vastrap Western Cape ★★☆ £B
Recommended Rosés:
Lekkerwijn Coastal Region ★★ £B

Southern Right (Walker Bay)
Anthony HAMILTON-RUSSELL established Southern Right in 1994 with the main aim of producing top flight Walker Bay Pinotage in an approachable style and at a good price as well as fresh mineral Sauvignon Blanc. Fruit is grown on a 440 ha property and benefits from the cooling maritime influence in the Hemel-en-Aarde Valley, just inland of Hermanus. If you're visiting in late Autumn you may get a glimpse of the whales featured on the label here. The Pinotage is ripe and spicy with supple tannins and is more restrained than many other Cape examples. In part this is down to the cooler climate and with the grape being early ripening, it has no problem achieving excellent phenolic maturity here. Sauvignon is fresh and zesty with a mineral structure and impressive depth and intensity. Anthony also produces a world-class Pinotage under his ASHBOURNE label which is well worth adding to your cellar for a classically styled and structured example of the variety. (DM)
Recommended Reds:
Pinotage Western Cape ★★★ £C
Recommended Whites:
Sauvignon Blanc Western Cape ★★☆ £C

❀ Spice Route Company (Swartland) www.spiceroutewines.co.za
Now wholly owned by Charles Back of FAIRVIEW, this warm-climate Swartland property has been good to sometimes very good in recent vintages. There are approachable bright fruit driven examples of Grenache, Pinotage as well as Mourvèdre. Along with sound, fruity and slightly mineral and citrus scented Sauvignon Blanc, whites also include Chenin Blanc and a really intense Flagship Sauvignon Blanc, The Amos Block. Among the other reds, Chakalaka is a diverse and interesting blend of Syrah, Mourvèdre, Petite Sirah, Carignan, Grenache and Tannat. Vinified in open fermenters and aged in a mix of French and American oak, there are spicy red and black fruits and well balanced but restrained oak. The round and supple Terra de Bon Syrah is one of four single vineyard wines under the same label icluding a Mourvedre, a Carignan and a Semillon from Darling. The Terra de Bon Syrah is full of dark blackberry and spice; it is aged for a total of 21 months in French oak, one third new, with the malolactic fermenation completed in barrel. The top wine is one of South Africa's best reds. The dense and concentrated Malabar is a splendid blend of mainly Shiraz with Mourvèdre, Pinotage, Grenache (from near 60 year old vines), Petite Sirah and Viognier. Needless to say it is bottled unfiltered. All the top reds will develop well in the medium term, the Malabar for up to a decade. (DM)
Recommended Reds:
Malabor Swartland ★★★★☆ £F   Chakalaka Swartland ★★★☆ £D
Terra de Bron Swartland ★★★☆ £D
Pinotage Swartland ★★★ £C   Mourvèdre Swartland ★★★ £C
Grenache Swartland ★★★ £C
Recommended Whites:
Sauvignon Blanc The Amos Block Western Cape ★★★☆ £C
Sauvignon Blanc Western Cape ★★ £B
Chenin Blanc Western Cape ★★ £B

Springfield (Robertson) www.springfieldestate.com
The best property in the warm Robertson area is producing decent fresh, grassy Sauvignon Blanc Life from Stone and some good to very good Chardonnay with close-to-organic practices. Cabernet Sauvignon has become much more impressive in recent vintages. A Méthode Anciènne Cabernet has now been added which is fermented from wild yeasts and goes through malolactic in barrel. It is bottled without filtration. There is an impressive Bordeaux blend too, The Work of Time which is again bottled without filtration. Chardonnay is tight and citrusy with well-judged oak and a rich, buttery component provided by malolactic fermentation. Of additional weight and substance is the very good special bottling of Chardonnay Méthode Anciènne, produced only in the best years. Wild yeasts are again used to vinify both Chardonnays and filtration is avoided. (DM)
Recommended Reds:
Cabernet Sauvignon Méthode Anciènne Robertson ★★★☆ £E
The Work of Time Robertson ★★★ £D
Cabernet Sauvignon Whole Berry Robertson ★★★ £C
Recommended Whites:
Chardonnay Méthode Anciènne Robertson ★★★☆ £D
Chardonnay Wild Yeast Robertson ★★★ £C
Sauvignon Blanc Life from Stone Robertson ★★☆ £C

Stark Condé (Stellenbosch) www.stark-conde.co.za
Family-run boutique operation with an output of just a few thousand cases a year. Quality is good and some striking Cabernet Sauvignon as well as Syrah is produced here from family owned vineyards in the Jonkershoek Valley. The top wines are the impressive Cabernet and Syrah Three Pines, from a single, high elevation block on the property. The Cabernet is very much in a minty, berry and lightly cassis-scented style with just the merest hint of cedar. Supple and nicely rounded tannins should ensure further development with three or four years in bottle. The Syrah is elegant and spicy with a subtle licoricey component and impressive depth. The Stark-Condé wines are a touch lighter but both offer attractive fruit with impressive depth and have a supple and approachable structure. Cabernet is marked by minty, eucalyptus characters, Syrah is spicy and offers black pepper notes as well as elegant dark fruit. A Stark-Condé Merlot is also produced and the wines are all bottled unfined and unfiltered. A new label Pepin-Condé is also offered with a Sauvignon Blanc and Cabernet Sauvignon both of which are very well priced along with a somewhat pricier Pinot Noir. (DM)
Recommended Reds:
Cabernet Sauvignon Three Pines Stellenbosch ★★★☆ £E
Syrah Three Pines Stellenbosch ★★★☆ £E
Stark-Condé Cabernet Sauvignon Stellenbosch ★★★ £C
Stark-Condé Syrah Stellenbosch ★★★ £C

Steenberg (Constantia) www.steenbergfarm.com
This is the oldest wine farm in the Cape. A fine range of piercingly pure whites and improving reds are now being produced since the establishment of the cellar here in 1996. In part this is down to the low vigour of the farm's soils and the influence of the cool maritime breezes moderating the Cape peninsula. Soft and forward reds and whites from a range of sources and a couple of Cap Classique sparklers are also made. The core of the farm's output though are the wines from their Constantia vineyards. Sauvignon Blanc comes from a Loire clone and is fresh, grassy and pure. The Sauvignon Blanc Magna Carta comes from a selectionof the best vines; similarly cool-fermented, it has a more structured mineral core. The excellent Sémillon comes from some of the lowest yielding vines at Steenberg, just 4 tonnes per ha is obtained. Initially cool-fermented,

the juice is then racked to barrels and malolactic fermentation is blocked to ensure a fresh, richly citrus style. The plummy, fleshy Merlot has a pronounced minty undercurrent and is aged in oak with malolactic in barrel. Denser and more characterful is the spicy berry laden Shiraz. For this wine too the malolactic is in barrel with maturation in new oak. The top red is the dark, berry scented Catharina, a blend of Merlot, Shiraz, Cabernet Sauvignon and Cabernet Franc as well as a tiny proportion of Nebbiolo (now also produced as a varietal). A blend of Sauvignon Blanc and Sémillon, Magna Carta has also been added to the range. (DM)

Recommended Reds:
Catharina Constantia ★★★☆ £E
Shiraz Constantia ★★★ £D   Merlot Constantia ★★★ £D

Recommended Whites:
Sauvignon Blanc Magna Carta Constantia ★★★☆ £E
Sémillon Constantia ★★★ £C
Sauvignon Blanc Constantia ★★☆ £C

Stellekaya (Stellenbosch) *www.stellekaya.com*

Founded in 1999 the Stellekaya cellar itself was established in 2002 in KWVs old brandy cellar in Stellenbosch. Production is very much small scale with a maximum output for any wine of less than 2,000 cases a year. The 24-ha estate is planted to a mix of Cabernet Sauvignon, Merlot, Pinotage and Sangiovese with relatively high density planting of around 2,500 vines per ha. The vineyards located between Stellenbosch and Somerset West are unirrigated and benefit from moderating breezes off False Bay. Winemaker Ntsiki Biyela and consultant Mark Carmichael-Green weave a level of elegance and red berry fruit purity into their wines which is so often absent in other Cape efforts. The Cape Cross red is a vibrant blend of Merlot and Pinotage with a small percentage of Cabernet Sauvignon. Hercules has a Tuscan feel to it blending Sangiovese with Merlot and Cabernet Sauvignon. The Cabernet Sauvignon itself is 100% varietal while the top red, Orion is a special barrel-selection Bordeaux blend that is based on Cabernet Sauvignon but with some Merlot and Cabernet Franc. Vinification is very modern with a short cold-soak, malolactic fermentation in barrel and around 22 months ageing in French oak. The wines will all develop nicely over the medium term. (DM)

Recommended Reds:
Orion Stellenbosch ★★★☆ £E
Cabernet Sauvignon Stellenbosch ★★★ £D
Hercules Stellenbosch ★★★ £C   Cape Cross Stellenbosch ★★☆ £C

Stellenzicht (Stellenbosch) *www.stellenzicht.co.za*

A quite extensive range is produced at this Stellenbosch farm by winemaker Guy Webber, who took over from André van Rensburg after he moved to VERGELEGEN. A regular range of varietals under the Hill & Dale label offers decent value and both red and white varietals appear under the Golden Triangle label. Sauvignon Blanc is fresh and zesty and there is some nutty, toasty Chardonnay. The Pinotage is ripe and brambly, with a hint of that acetate character frequent in the variety, while the Cabernet is dark and minty. Best of the whites is a restrained, well-crafted Sémillon Reserve. The flagship Syrah is very classy stuff: structured and impressive with well-judged oak, it will develop well with three or four years' ageing. A premium blend Rhapsody blends Pinotage and Shiraz. (DM)

Recommended Reds:
Syrah Stellenbosch ★★★☆ £E   Rhapsody Stellenbosch ★★☆ £D
Golden Triangle Pinotage Stellenbosch ★★ £B
Golden Triangle Cabernet Sauvignon Stellenbosch ★☆ £B

Recommended Whites:
Sémillon Reserve Stellenbosch ★★★ £C
Golden Triangle Chardonnay Stellenbosch ★☆ £B
Golden Triangle Sauvignon Blanc Stellenbosch ★☆ £B

Sterhuis (Stellenbosch) *www.sterhuis.co.za*

The Kruger family established their small wine farm in 1980 and now produce some of the most striking whites to emerge from Stellenbosch. The wines are produced in small lots ranging from 200 to just over 1,000 cases. The reds are also well crafted but not at quite the same level. The best among them is the classy Astra Red a selection of ten of the best barrels and generally a blend of Cabernet Sauvignon and Merlot. The wine offers good depth and a firm structure, a hint of cedar and mint and is released with a little bottle age. Sauvignon Blanc is in a fresh, grassy style from vines planted at an altitude of 400 to 450 metres. Additional depth is provided by a small barrel-fermented portion of the fruit. The Blanc de Blancs sparkler is one of the better examples from the Cape. It's a zero *dosage* example, barrel fermented with six months on lees in cask followed by 26 months on its yeast in bottle providing a fine, biscuity and intense style. Chardonnay is in a classic Burgundy style with 100% new barrel fermentation, lees stirring and then barrel ageing a further 10 months. The Astra White is the leading wine here. It is a blend of roughly equal parts Sauvignon Blanc, Chenin Blanc and Chardonnay which are barrel fermented (not in new oak to preserve the character of the fruit) and aged. Like the red this is released with a little bottle age. Other whites that will be worth considering are a Viognier, a varietal Chenin Blanc and an unwooded Chardonnay. (DM)

Recommended Reds:
Astra Red Stellenbosch ★★★☆ £D

Recommended Whites:
Astra White Stellenbosch ★★★★ £E
Chardonnay Stellenbosch ★★★☆ £D
Blanc de Blancs Brut Vintage Methode Cap Classique ★★★ £C
Sauvignon Blanc Stellenbosch ★★☆ £C

Thelema (Stellenbosch) *www.thelema.co.za*

Gyles Webb is generally accepted as one of the best viticulturalists and winemakers in the Cape. The family's vineyard and winery are located at altitude on the slopes of the Simonsberg and this contributes to the quality of the fruit. The vineyards are well managed and controlled yields are nevertheless reasonably productive. There's good Chardonnay and Cabernet Sauvignon as well as steely, minerally Riesling. Merlot can be less impressive but is reasonably concentrated and ripely plummy. Sauvignon is piercing and full of lightly tropical, green fruits. A cooler, more minerally example is also now offered from Webb's new Elgin vineyards and Riesling and Chardonnay now emanate from here as well. Reserves of Merlot and Cabernet Sauvignon, the latter now labelled 'The Mint' are a step up from the regular examples. Other wines under the Thelema Stellenbosch banner include a Bordeaux blend Rabelais, a reserve Chardonnay, Ed's Reserve and a late harvest Muscat and Riesling. As well as the Sauvignon Sutherland label from Elgin an extensive range is also now offered including a Riesling, a Viognier/Roussanne blend a Chardonnay and among reds a Syrah, a Pinot Noir and a Cabernet Sauvignon/Petit Verdot. (DM)

Recommended Reds:
Cabernet Sauvignon The Mint Stellenbosch ★★★★ £E
Merlot Reserve Stellenbosch ★★★☆ £E
Cabernet Sauvignon Stellenbosch ★★★ £D

South Africa

Merlot Stellenbosch ★★☆ £C
Recommended Whites:
Chardonnay Stellenbosch ★★★ £C
Sauvignon Blanc Sutherland Elgin ★★☆ £C
Sauvignon Blanc Stellenbosch ★★☆ £C
Riesling Stellenbosch ★★ £B

Tokara (Stellenbosch) *www.tokara.com*
An impressive Stellenbosch operation with vineyards originally planted in 1994. Sitting on the summit of the Helshootge Pass there are some of the most spectacular vineyard views in the Cape overlooking Stellenbosch and across to Table Mountain in the distance. Winemaker Miles Mossop has the most sophisticated state of the art equipment to work with in the cellars. There are well-priced Tokara wines as well as premium label Tokara Reserve bottlings. The Tokara reds are both oak-aged; a mix of new and used French oak. Fruit comes from both estate vineyards and bought-in sources. Chenin comes from over 30 year old unirrigated bush vines and like the Chardonnay is barrel-fermented and kept on lees with batonnage and neither wine goes through malolactic fermentation. Tokara Reserve wines are a clear step up in both quality and price. The Walker Bay Sauvignon Blanc shows its cooler climate origins; attractively nettly with raw gooseberry aromas the wine is cool-fermented at around 15C and aged on lees for 3 months. A similarly priced example is also made from Elgin fruit. The Chardonnay Reserve, like the two Directors Reserve Stellenbosch wines comes solely from home vineyards. More elegant and structured than the Zondenaam it gets around a third new oak and 30% goes through malolactic. The characterful Tokara Directors Reserve White is a blend of Sauvignon Blanc and Sémillon, barrel-fermented and impressively structured with subtle green and citrus fruits and an impressive piercing spiciness across the palate from a mix of new and used French oak. The ageworthy Tokara Directors Reserve red is a Bordeaux style blend of Cabernet Sauvignon, Petit Verdot, Merlot and Malbec. Fermentation is in both stainless steel and wooden vats and malolactic is in barrel. Around four-fifths new wood is used to age the wine for just under two years. (DM)
Recommended Reds:
Tokara Directors Reserve Red Stellenbosch ★★★☆ £E
Tokara Shiraz Stellenbosch ★★☆ £C
Tokara Cabernet Sauvignon Stellenbosch ★★ £C
Recommended Whites:
Tokara Directors Reserve Stellenbosch ★★★☆ £D
Tokara Reserve Chardonnay Stellenbosch ★★★ £C
Tokara Reserve Sauvignon Blanc Walker Bay ★★★ £C
Tokara Chardonnay Stellenbosch ★★ £B
Tokara Chenin Blanc Stellenbosch ★★ £B

Uva Mira (Stellenbosch) *www.uvamira.co.za*
This relatively understated winery makes some of the best wine not only in Stellenbosch but in the Cape. The winery itself is spectacularly situated with panoramic views from its Helderberg Mountain site. The vineyards themselves range from 420 to 620 metres above sea level and this helps define the quality and character of the wines. The approach to vinification is very much old world. Fruit is hand harvested, vinification is in small lots, wild yeast ferments are preferred and there is minimal intervention throughout the winemaking and cellaring stages. In addition to the wines profiled here there is a premium Syrah which is aged in French oak for 18 months and a couple of marginally lower priced wines under the Cellar Selection label, a red dominated by Merlot and a white

Sauvignon Blanc. The Single Vineyard Chardonnay is one of the Cape benchmarks. It comes from the highest slopes on the Helderberg and from vines grown on decomposed granite and shale soils. Rich, creamy and impressively structured it offers an intensity and depth rarely encountered on the Côte d'Or. The red Single Vineyard Selection *cuvée* is a very richly textured but elegant cedary mixed blend of Cabernet Sauvignon, Merlot, Shiraz and Cabernet Franc, one of the Cape's great reds. (DM)
Recommended Reds:
Vineyard Selection Stellenbosch ★★★★☆ £F
Recommended Whites:
Chardonnay Single Vineyard Selection Stellenbosch ★★★★ £E

Veenwouden (Paarl) *www.veenwouden.com*
The Van der Walt family are continuing to craft a fine range of reds as well as Chardonnay at this Paarl farm. The reputation of the property is based on two wines, both of which have their roots in Bordeaux. Merlot Reserve in particular has been outstanding among Cape examples: supple and rich with a real mineral hint of its *terroir*. The Classic, a typical Bordeaux red, is also impressive. It blends Cabernet Sauvignon and Merlot with a little Cabernet Franc and Malbec. A Syrah is also now released under the Veenwouden label. There is a good value Chardonnay Reserve and a much pricier Premium Collection. A Cuvée Brut Reserve sparkler is also made and the winery are also producing two further expensive reds. The Renevatio is a Shiraz, Cabernet, Merlot blend while the more expensive (£G) Hugh Masekela Collection is a selection of Merlot and Cabernet Sauvignon. (DM)
Recommended Reds:
Merlot Paarl ★★★☆ £E   Classic Paarl ★★★ £E

✿ **Vergelegen (Stellenbosch)** *www.vergelegen.co.za*
This historic wine farm dates back to 1700 and is located on hillside vineyards south of Stellenbosch. The winery was designed by French architects but it more closely resembles a new-wave Napa Valley operation than anything else. Gravity plays an important role in cellar-handling operations. André van Rensburg took on the winemaking mantle here after Martin MEINERT moved on to produce his own label. Varietal Sauvignon Blanc and Chardonnay are both impressive, particularly the Reserves, which have real structure and grip. Premium label Shiraz and Cabernet Merlot are good while the Reserve reds are a step up. Merlot is ripe and vibrant and contains a little of both Cabernets. Cabernet Sauvignon has a hint of Merlot and Cabernet Franc, while the Vergelegen Red is one of the better reds yet from the Cape. Shiraz has now been added to the range and is impressively refined and stylish. A white Bordeaux style blend, Vergelegen White promises much while a super premium red Vergelegen V now takes South African wines to both new heights of quality and price. (DM)
Recommended Reds:
Vergelegen V Stellenbosch ★★★★★ £G
Vergelegen GVB Stellenbosch ★★★★ £F
Cabernet Sauvignon Reserve Stellenbosch ★★★☆ £E
Shiraz Reserve Stellenbosch ★★★☆ £E
Merlot Reserve Stellenbosch ★★☆ £C
Recommended Whites:
Vergelegen GVB Stellenbosch ★★★★ £F
Chardonnay Reserve Stellenbosch ★★★☆ £E
Sauvignon Blanc Reserve Stellenbosch ★★★☆ £E
Premium Chardonnay Stellenbosch ★★☆ £C
Premium Sauvignon Blanc Stellenbosch ★★☆ £C

❀ Vilafonte (Paarl) www.vilafonte.co.za

This is the first American/South African joint venture partnership between Californians Zelma Long, former ground-breaking winemaker at SIMI, viticulturalist Phil Freese and Mike Ratcliffe MD of WARWICK ESTATE in Stellenbosch. The focus here is very much on producing a luxury wine brand, of which there are few in the Cape, targetting the US market specifically. Just two wines are produced and this will remain the case. The wines are produced in a full and ripe style with alcohol levels approaching 15 degrees but with an impressive refinement and elegance as well. The estate totals 40 ha on the slopes of the Simonsberg mountain planted in gravelly-clay soils with a north-westerly exposure. The vines are all Bordeaux varieties in very close spaced vineyards (for South Africa) with over 5,000 vines per hectare. Series M is essentially a Right Bank style, comprising Merlot, Malbec and Cabernet Sauvignon, rich and fleshy with concentrated black fruits and finely structured backbone. Series C is very much Bordeaux Left Bank, firm and structured for long ageing it is mostly Cabernet Sauvignon with Cabernet Franc and some Merlot adding a little flesh. Winemaking is "micro-managed" in the words of the winery, extreme care in sorting and indigenous yeasts are used to encourage a sense of place. Certainly the wines have real potential and as yet are reasonably priced in the context of other luxury wine brands from elsewhere. (DM)

Recommended Reds:

Series C Paarl ★★★★☆ £F   Series M Paarl ★★★★☆ £F

Villiera (Stellenbosch) www.villiera.co.za

This fairly sizeable wine farm produces an extensive range of wines, characterised by their good value, from around 300 ha. The vineyards started life largely planted to white varieties although this has gradually changed and reds now account for 40% of the holding. Organic methods have been increasingly employed and insecticides have been avoided for close to a decade. A range of varietal based wines are produced including, Shiraz, Cabernet Sauvignon, Pinotage, Sauvignon Blanc and Chenin Blanc. All are well priced andl look out too for simple fruit driven blends Down to Earth red, white and rosé. Cap Classique sparkling wine is also a notable item here. Non-vintaged white and rosé are both produced and there is a varietal Chardonnay Brut Natural. The prestige *cuvée* is the Monro Brut which blends Pinot Noir with Chardonnay. Only the best quality juice is used and the primary fermentation of the Chardonnay component takes place in used small oak. Among the other top wines, the Monro red is a cedary, black-fruited Bordeaux style blend of Merlot and Cabernet Sauvignon, the top examples of Chenin Blanc and Sauvignon Blanc from the farms vineyards see the richly textured Chenin barrel matured on lees for four five months, while the Sauvignon coming from old bush vines has a varietally intense grassy, herbaceous quality. Late harvest whites are also produced from botrytis affected Riesling and Chenin Blanc, the latter labelled Inspiration and there is a port styled fortified red, Fired Earth. The Grier family have also invested in a new domaine in southern France's Côtes du Roussillon region, Domaine GRIER. The potential of that area is tremendous. (DM)

Recommended Reds:

Monro Red Stellenbosch ★★★ £C

Recommended Whites:

Monro Brut Stellenbosch ★★★ £D
Chenin Blanc Traditional Barrel-Fermented Stellenbosch ★★☆ £B
Sauvignon Blanc Traditional Bush Vine Paarl ★★☆ £B

Vriesenhof (Stellenbosch) www.vriesenhof.co.za

Former Springbok rugby player Jan Coetzee makes two separate ranges of wines at his Stellenbosch farm in the Paradyskloof valley nestled between Stellenbosch and the Helderberg mountains. The Paradyskloof labelled wines are simple straightfoward fruit driven styles and include Chardonnay, Pinotage, Cabernet Sauvignon and a Grenache/Malbec/Shiraz blend. From the Vriesenhof vineyards come Pinot Noir, Kallista - a blend of Merlot as well as both Cabernets – Pinotage, Grenache and Cabernet Sauvignon. The Chardonnay is a full and fairly traditional example with reasonable depth and intensity, ripe tropical fruit and lashings of oak. The Kallista is subtle and cedary with spicy oak and piercing red berry fruit and offers real depth. Pinot Noir is very much in a full gamey style. The Kallista in particular, will stand 4 or 5 years' ageing adding further complexity. (DM)

Recommended Reds:

Vriesenhof Kallista Stellenbosch ★★★ £D
Vriesenhof Pinot Noir Stellenbosch ★★☆ £D

Recommended Whites:

Vriesenhof Chardonnay Stellenbosch ★★☆ £C

Warwick Estate (Stellenbosch) www.warwickwine.co.za

The Bordeaux red varieties are the most significant plantings on this medium sized property neighbouring KANONKOP, where Norma Ratcliffe was the first lady winemaker and her first wine Trilogy was released in 1986. Like its neighbour Warwick Estate also has old Pinotage bush vines and these produce one of the better examples of the variety, brambly and concentrated. Some of the harvest is regularly sold off and the balance results in some very good Cabernet Franc as well as the stylish, structured Trilogy blend, produced from Cabernet Sauvignon, Cabernet Franc and Merlot. Three Cape Ladies which comprises Cabernet Sauvignon, Merlot and some Pinotage can be enjoyed with just a little age, while the First Lady Cabernet Sauvignon is supple and approachable. Two further premium reds are made. The Blue Lady is another Cabernet Sauvignon, barrel-aged in 50% new wood for over two years and there is a Syrah, Black Lady. Of the whites there are two Chardonnay releases; the leesy, concentrated White Lady and the unoaked First Lady. The zesty, gooseberry-laden Sauvignon Blanc, Professor Black also offers lots of character and varietal purity. Managing Director Mike Ratcliffe is a partner in the newly established luxury red producer, VILAFONTÉ. (DM)

Recommended Reds:

Trilogy Stellenbosch ★★★★ £E
Cabernet Franc Stellenbosch ★★★★ £E
Three Cape Ladies Stellenbosch ★★★☆ £C
Pinotage Old Bush Vines Stellenbosch ★★★ £C
The First Lady Cabernet Sauvignon Stellenbosch ★★☆ £C

Recommended Whites:

Chardonnay White Lady Stellenbosch ★★★☆ £D
Sauvignon Blanc Professor Black Stellenbosch ★★☆ £C

Waterford Estate (Stellenbosch) www.waterfordestate.co.za

Kevin Arnold used to be the wine maker at RUST-EN-VREDE but is now in partnership with Jeremy Ord in this winery nestled into the base of the Helderberg Mountains above Stellenbosch. They produce two ranges. There are some well made easy drinking reds and whites released under the Pecan Stream label, while the Waterford Estate wines are a significant step up, particularly the reds which really stand out here. The Waterford Estate Sauvignon is a subtle, restrained and lightly grassy, mineral cool-fermented

example. A further Waterford Sauvignon is made which comes from Elgin fruit. The lightly smoky, toasty citrusy Chardonnay is barrel-fermented in small French oak (30% new) where it spends just 6 months on the lees with *bâtonnage*. The Cabernet Sauvignon is deeply-coloured, earthy, cedary and characterful, with good grip and impressive structure. It is blended with 5% each of Cabernet Franc, Merlot and Malbec and aged for 18 months in 40% new wood. The Kevin Arnold Shiraz which is dark, spicy and similarly structured has real depth and style. It includes 6% Mourvèdre and aged in French oak. Both the top reds will improve for six years or more. There is also a pricey new flagship red, The Jem, which blends the Bordeaux varieties with a little Shiraz, Mourvèdre, Sangiovese and Barbera. (DM)

Recommended Reds:
Waterford Kevin Arnold Shiraz Stellenbosch ★★★☆ £E
Waterford Estate Cabernet Sauvignon Stellenbosch ★★★☆ £D
Pecan Stream Pebble Hill Stellenbosch ★★ £B

Recommended Whites:
Waterford Estate Chardonnay Stellenbosch ★★★ £D
Waterford Estate Sauvignon Blanc Stellenbosch ★★☆ £C
Pecan Stream Sauvignon Blanc Stellenbosch ★☆ £B
Pecan Stream Chenin Blanc Stellenbosch ★☆ £B

Welgemeend (Paarl)
A Paarl property which is now owned by eight shareholders. The main focus here is a finely crafted and elegant Estate Reserve red made from a Right Bank blend of Merlot, Cabernet Sauvignon and Cabernet Franc. Two further Bordeaux reds are also produced. Soopjeshoogte blends the same varieties as the Estate Reserve in a lighter style, while Douelle comprises Cabernet Sauvignon, Malbec, Cabernet Franc and a little Merlot and is leafier in style. Amadé by contrast is a Rhône-dominated blend of Shiraz, Grenache and Pinotage, a mix of black pepper and tarry, dark berry fruit. The wines will all benefit from three or four years' patience, particularly the Estate Reserve. There a couple of fresh and crisp whites and the range is completed with a rosé in dry Loire style from Cabernet Franc . (DM)

Recommended Reds:
Estate Reserve Paarl ★★★ £C   Douelle Paarl ★★☆ £C
Amadé Paarl ★★☆ £B   Soopjeshoogte Paarl ★★ £B

Recommended Whites:
Sauvignon Blanc Paarl ★★ £B   Chenin Blanc Paarl ★☆ £B

Recommended Rosés:
Private Cellar Rosé ★☆ £B

Wildekrans (Walker Bay) www.wildekranswines.co.za
This property is located further inland than most of the Walker Bay estates. As a result, striking, elegant Pinotage as well as the Bordeaux varieties are successfully made here. Some refreshing straightforward, fruit-driven whites offer excellent value: Sauvignon Blanc and Chenin Blanc are both sound as is a blend of the two with Chardonnay, Caresse Marine, which offers upfront, lightly tropical, citrusy and herby flavours. Reserve bottlings of Sémillon and Chardonnay are both vinified in oak. There is a good minty, lightly cedary Cabernet Franc/Merlot as well as varietal examples of Cabernet Sauvignon and Shiraz. Other wines include a Bordeaux red blend, Warrant and a Cap Classique sparkler. The Pinotages are particularly good. Marked by intense berry fruit, they are subtler than most examples of the variety and show less of the aggressive acetone notes found elsewhere. The Barrel Select Osiris will develop well in the short to medium term. Barrel Select Osiris wines are also

made from Chenin Blanc, Sauvignon Blanc and Shiraz. (DM)

Recommended Reds:
Pinotage Barrel Select Osiris Bot River ★★★ £C
Pinotage Bot River ★★ £B   Cabernet Franc/Merlot Bot River ★★ £B

Recommended Whites:
Caresse Marine Bot River ★☆ £B   Chenin Blanc Bot River ★☆ £B

Winery of Good Hope www.thewineryofgoodhope.com
This impressive Stellenbosch based operation headed up by Alex Dale makes four distinctive ranges of wines with an increasing move towards natural farming and winemaking and less use of new oak. The Winery of Good Hope labels are bright, attractive wines offering good value and drinkability. There are two Vinum Africa wines which are sourced solely from Stellenbosch fruit. Chenin Blanc comes from old bush vines grown on the slopes of the Helderberg mountains. Lightly tropical and citrus scented it is nicely underpinned by fresh acidity. It also typically has a good deal less residual sugar than many other Cape examples. Cabernet Sauvignon comes from Helderberg and benefiting from cooling maritime breezes. Subtle, minty and lightly cedary, it gets 14 months in oak (mainly French) and a portion goes through malolactic in barrel. Under the premium Radford Dale label The Black Rock red is sourced from the Pederburg-Swartland appellation. It is a classic Midi blend with 35 plus year old Carignan adding a really spicy dark-fruited complexity. Almost all is aged in French oak and a third is new with the wine kept on lees in barrel. The Radford Dale Chardonnay comes from Helderberg vineyards. It is subtle, lightly leesy with subtle citrus notes and less of the overt tropical flavours found in other examples from the region. Fermentation is coolish at 18C and the malolactic is blocked to retain freshness. The rich, characterful Renaissance Chenin Blanc is whole-bunch pressed and barrel fermented. The Radford Dale Syrah comes from both the Helderberg and Devon Valley sites. Elegant, ripe dark fruit, pepper and spice notes are apparent and the wine has a supple yet firm structure. New oak is used and like the élévage in the other wines micro-oxygenation is employed to avoid bruising the wine. A second Syrah, Nudity is aged without the addition of sulpur and kept on its lees with the malolactic in barrel. Frankenstein Pinotage comes from 40 year old bush vines planted in marly soils at the foot of the Helderberg. Full of characterful dark fruits the more acetate like aromas often found in the variety are avoided and ageing is in used barrels to enhance that fruit. Pinot Noir, fresh, aromatic and full of red fruits comes from three separate vineyards in cool Elgin. The Gravity, as one would expect from the name, is handled almost exclusively by gravity even pressing. A blend of Cabernet Sauvignon, Merlot and Shiraz this is one of the most expressive reds from the Cape. Ageing is in both *barriques* and *demi-muids*. Land of Hope is a project that the winery is involved in. It is a trust that aims to put back the returns from wine sales into the formerly disadvantaged employees of the winery and ensure their children's future education. Impressive Chenin Blanc, Bordeaux blends and Pinot Noir are all being made. A small range of fresh easy drinking wines with moderate alcohol, less than 12%, are also made under the Radford Dale Thirst label. (DM)

Recommended Reds:
Radford Dale Gravity Stellenbosch ★★★★ £E
Radford Dale Nudity Stellenbosch ★★★★ £D
Radford Dale Frankenstein Pinotage ★★★☆ £D
Radford Dale Freedom Pinot Noir Elgin ★★★☆ £D
Radford Dale Syrah Stellenbosch ★★★☆ £D
Black Rock Red Blend Swartland ★★★☆ £D
Land of Hope Reserve Cabernet Sauvignon Stellenbosch ★★★☆ £D

Vinum Cabernet Sauvignon Stellenbosch ★★☆ £C
Radford Dale Thirst Cinsault Stellenbosch ★★ £B
Radford Dale Thirst Gamay Coastal Region ★☆ £B
Recommended Whites:
Radford Dale Renaissance Chenin Blanc Stellenbosch ★★★☆ £D
Radford Dale Chardonnay Stellenbosch ★★★ £D
Land of Hope Reserve Chenin Blanc Stellenbosch ★★★ £C
Land of Hope Chardonnay Stellenbosch ★★☆ £C
Vinum Chenin Blanc Stellenbosch ★★☆ £B
Radford Dale Thirst Clairette Chenin Blanc Verdelho Stellenbosch ★☆ £B

Other wines of note

Aaldering
Recommended Reds: Pinotage Devon Valley ★★★☆ £D
Shiraz Devon Valley ★★★☆ £D
Cabernet Sauvignon/Merlot Devon Valley ★★★ £D
Recommended Whites: Chardonnay Devon Valley ★★★☆ £D
Adoro
Recommended Reds: Adoro Red Western Cape ★★★ £D
Recommended Whites: Naudé White Western Cape ★★★ £D
Allée Bleue
Recommended Reds: L'Amour Toujours Western Cape ★★☆ £D
Pinotage Western Cape ★★ £C
Recommended Whites: Sauvignon Blanc Stellenbosch ★★ £B
Alto
Recommended Reds: Cabernet Sauvignon Paarl ★★☆ £D
Shiraz Paarl ★★☆ £D
Annandale
Recommended Reds: Cabernet Sauvignon Stellenbosch ★★☆ £D
Anura
Recommended Reds: Syrah/Mourvèdre Reserve Paarl ★★★ £C
Pinotage Paarl ★★☆ £C
Asara
Recommended Reds: Bell Tower Estate Red Stellenbosch ★★★☆ £E
Ashanti
Recommended Reds: Cabernet Sauvignon Paarl ★★ £C
Pinotage Paarl ★★ £B
Bartinney
Recommended Reds: Cabernet Sauvignon Stellenbosch ★★★☆ £D
Recommended Whites:
Sauvignon Blanc Stellenbosch ★★★ £C
Graham Beck
Recommended Whites:
Bowed Head Chenin Blanc Coastal Region ★★★ £C
Game Reserve Chenin Blanc Coastal Region ★★☆ £C
Blanc de Blancs Vintage Robertson ★★☆ £C
Pheasant's Run Sauvignon Blanc Robertson ★★☆ £C
Recommended Reds:
Coffeestone Cabernet Stellenbosch ★★☆ £C
Bellingham
Recommended Reds: Cabernet Franc Spitz Coastal Region ★★ £C
Pinotage Spitz Coastal Region ★★ £C
The Berrio
Recommended Reds: Cabernet Sauvignon Elim ★★★ £D
Recommended Whites: The Weather Girl Elim ★★★ £C
Sauvignon Blanc Elim ★★☆ £C
Blackwater
Recommended Whites:
Underdog Chenin Blanc Stellenbosch ★★★ £C

BLANKbottle
Recommended Reds: My Koffer Swartland ★★★★ £E
Sigh of Relief Stellenbosch ★★★★ £E
Familiemoord ★★★★ £E
My Koffer ★★★☆ £D
Second Eulogy Botrivier ★★★☆ £D
Recommended Whites: Limbic Western Cape ★★★★ £D
Im Hinterhofkabuff Elgin ★★★☆ £D
Dok Elgin ★★★☆ £D
Boschendal
Recommended Reds: Shiraz Paarl ★★ £C
Recommended Whites: Chardonnay Reserve Paarl ★★ £B
Bon Courage
Recommended Reds: Inkará Shiraz Robertson ★★★ £D
Recommended Whites:
Jacques Bruère Blancs de Blancs Robertson ★★★ £D
Jacques Bruère Brut Reserve Robertson ★★★ £D
Chardonnay Prestige Cuvée Robertson ★★☆ £C
Recommended Rosés:
Jacques Bruère Blancs de Blancs Robertson ★★★ £D
Boschrivier
Recommended Reds: Shiraz Western Cape ★★★ £C
Bosman
Recommended Whites: Adama White Western Cape ★★★ £C
Recommended Reds: Adama Red Wellington ★★★ £C
Botanica
Recommended Reds:
The Mary Delaney Collection Pinot Noir Elgin ★★★ £D
Recommended Whites:
The Mary Delaney Collection Chenin Blanc Elgin ★★★ £C
Brampton
Recommended Reds: OVR Coastal Region ★★☆ £B
Shiraz Coastal Region ★★ £B
Cabernet Sauvignon Coastal Region ★★ £B
Recommended Whites: Unoaked Chardonnay Coastal Region ★★ £B
Sauvignon Blanc Coastal Region ★★ £B
Viognier Coastal Region ★★ £B
Recommended Rosés: Brampton Coastal Region ★☆ £B
Buitenverwachting
Recommended Reds: Christine Constantia ★★★☆ £D
Recommended Whites: Chardonnay Constantia ★★★ £C
Sauvignon Blanc Constantia ★★☆ £C
Cape Legends
Recommended Whites: Pongrácz Non Vintage Stellenbosch ★★ £D
Constantia Uitsig
Recommended Whites: Chardonnay Reserve Constantia ★★★ £D
Sémillon Reserve Constantia ★★☆ £C
Sauvignon Blanc/Sémillon Constantia ★★ £C
Crystallum
Recommended Reds: Pinot Noir Mabalel Overberg ★★★★ £E
Pinot Noir Cuvee Cinema Hemel-en-Aarde ★★★★ £E
Pinot Noir Peter Max Western Cape ★★★☆ £D
Recommended Whites:
Chardonnay Clay Shales Overberg ★★★☆ £D
Chardonnay The Agnes Western Cape ★★★☆ £D
Dalla Cia
Recommended Reds: Giorgio Stellenbosch ★★★★ £E
Recommended Whites: Sauvignon Blanc Stellenbosch ★★☆ £B
Darling Cellars
Recommended Reds: Kroon Onyx Darling ★★☆ £C
Cabernet Sauvignon Onyx Darling ★★ £C

South Africa

Shiraz Onyx Darling ★★☆ £C

Delaire Graff Estate
Recommended Reds: Botmaskop Stellenbosch ★★★ £C
Recommended Whites: Chardonnay Stellenbosch ★★★☆ £C

Delheim
Recommended Reds: Shiraz Vera Cruz Estate Stellenbosch ★★☆ £C
Cabernet Sauvignon Shiraz Stellenbosch ★☆ £B
Recommended Whites: Chardonnay Sur Lie Stellenbosch ★★★ £D

De Morgenzon
Recommended Reds: DMZ Syrah Stellenbosch ★★☆ £C
DMZ Concerto Stellenbosch ★★☆ £C
Recommended Whites: Chenin Blanc Reserve ★★★☆ £D
Maestro White Stellenbosch ★★★☆ £D
DMZ Chenin Blanc Stellenbosch ★★☆ £C
DMZ Chardonnay Stellenbosch ★★ £B
DMZ Sauvignon Blanc Stellenbosch ★☆ £B

De Waal
Recommended Reds: Pinotage Top of the Hill Stellenbosch ★★★ £D

De Wetshof
Recommended Whites: Chardonnay Bateleur Robertson ★★★ £D
Chardonnay d'Honneur Robertson ★★☆ £C
Chardonnay Bon Vallon Robertson ★★ £B
Sauvignon Blanc Robertson ★☆ £B

Diemersdal
Recommended Whites:
8 Rows Sauvignon Blanc Durbanville ★★★☆ £D
Chardonnay Reserve Durbanville ★★★ £D

Diemersfonteine
Recommended Reds:
Cabernet Sauvignon Carpe Diem Wellington ★★★ £D
Pinotage Carpe Diem Wellington ★★☆ £D
Pinotage Coffee Wellington ★★ £C
Recommended Whites:
Chenin Blanc Carpe Diem Wellington ★★★ £D
Viognier Carpe Diem Wellington ★★★ £D

Eagles' Nest
Recommended Reds: Eagles' Nest Shiraz Constantia ★★★☆ £C
Eagles' Nest Merlot Constantia ★★★ £C
Recommended Whites: Eagles' Nest Viognier Constantia ★☆ £C

Edgebaston
Recommended Reds: The Berry Box Stellenbosch ★★☆ £C
GS Cabernet Sauvignon Stellenbosch ★★★★ £F
Shiraz Stellenbosch ★★★☆ £D
Cabernet Sauvignon Stellenbosch ★★★☆ £D
David Finlayson Pinot Noir Coastal Region ★★★ £C
The Pepper Pot Stellenbosch ★★★ £C
Recommended Whites: Chardonnay Stellenbosch ★★★ £D
Sauvignon Blanc Stellenbosch ★★ £C

Eikendal
Recommended Reds: Classique Stellenbosch ★★★ £D
Cabernet Sauvignon Stellenbosch ★★☆ £C
Recommended Whites: Chardonnay Stellenbosch ★★☆ £C
Sauvignon Blanc Stellenbosch ★★ £B

Escapade Winery
Recommended Whites: Escapades Sémillon Stellenbosch ★★ £C
Escapades Sauvignon Blanc Stellenbosch ★★★ £D
Escapades Sémillon Sauvignon Blanc Coastal Region ★★☆ £C
Recommended Reds: Escapades Pinotage Stellenbosch ★★★ £D
Recommended Rosés: Escapades Pinotage Coastal Region ★★ £C

Fable Mountain Vineyards
Recommended Reds: Syrah Tulbagh ★★★★☆ £E

Night Sky Coastal Region (Shiraz/Grenache/Mourvèdre) ★★★★ £D
Recommended Whites:
Jackal Bird Western Cape ★★★☆ £D

Flagstone
Recommended Reds:
Time Manor Place Pinotage Breedekloof ★★★☆ £E
Writers Block Pinotage Western Cape ★★★ £D
Music Room Cabernet Sauvignon Stellenbosch ★★★☆ £D
Dark Horse Shiraz Stellenbosch ★★★☆ £D
Longitude Red Western Cape ★★★ £C
Dragon Tree Cabernet Shiraz Pinotage Western Cape ★★★ £C
Recommended Whites:
Free Run Reserve Sauvignon Blanc Elgin ★★★☆ £C
Treaty Tree Reserve Sauvignon Sémillon Cape South Coast ★★★☆ £C

The Goose
Recommended Reds:
The Goose Expression Upper-Langkloof ★★★ £D
Recommended Whites:
The Goose Sauvignon Blanc Upper-Langkloof ★★★ £C

Groot Constantia
Recommended Reds: Gouverneurs Reserve Constantia ★★★ £D
Recommended Whites: Chardonnay Reserve Constantia ★★★ £D
Sauvignon Blanc Constantia ★★ £C

Groote Post
Recommended Whites: Chardonnay Stellenbosch ★★☆ £B
Recommended Reds: Merlot Stellenbosch ★★☆ £C

Haskell Vineyards
Recommended Whites: Anvil Chardonnay Stellenbosch ★★★★ £E

Haute Cabrière Estate
Recommended Whites:
Pierre Jourdan Blanc de Blancs NV Franschhoek ★★☆ £C

Hidden Valley
Recommended Reds: Cabernet Sauvignon Stellenbosch ★★★ £C
Pinotage Stellenbosch ★★★ £C

Jacobsdal
Recommended Reds: Pinotage Stellenbosch ★★ £B

Joostenberg
Recommended Reds: Shiraz/Viognier Paarl ★★★ £C
Recommended Whites: Chenin Blanc Paarl ★☆ £B

Joubert Tradouw
Recommended Whites: Chardonnay Klein Karoo ★★☆ £C

Journey's End
Recommended Reds:
Cape Doctor Cabernet Sauvignon Stellenbosch ★★★☆ £E
Shiraz Stellenbosch ★★☆ £C   Merlot Stellenbosch ★★ £C
Pastors Blend Stellenbosch ★☆ £B
Recommended Whites:
Single Vineyard Chardonnay Stellenbosch ★★★ £C
Haystack Chardonnay Stellenbosch ★★ £B
Weather Station Sauvignon Blanc Stellenbosch ★★ £B

Keermont Vineyards
Recommended Reds: Keermont Syrah Stellenbosch ★★★★ £E
Keermont Red Stellenbosch ★★★ £D
Recommended Whites: Terrasse White Stellenbosch ★★★★ £D

KWV
Recommended Whites: Mentors Chardonnay Elgin ★★☆ £D
Mentors Grenache Blanc Western Cape ★★☆ £D

Ladera
Recommended Reds: Syrah Western Cape ★★☆ £D

Laibach
Recommended Reds: Cabernet/Merlot Stellenbosch ★★ £C

Recommended Whites: Chardonnay Stellenbosch ★★ £C
L'Avenir
Recommended Reds: Single Block Pinotage Stellenbosch ★★★☆ £E
Pinotage Stellenbosch ★★ £C
Recommended Whites:
Single Block Chenin Blanc Stellenbosch ★★★ £D
La Vierge
Recommended Whites: Original Sin Walker Bay ★★☆ £C
Le Bonheur
Recommended Reds: Cabernet Sauvignon Stellenbosch ★★ £C
Lomond
Recommended Whites:
Sauvignon Blanc Sugarbush Vineyard Cape Agulhas ★★☆ £C
Sauvignon Blanc Cape Agulhas ★★ £C
Louisvale
Recommended Whites: Chardonnay Stellenbosch ★★★ £C
Chavant Chardonnay Stellenbosch ★★☆ £C
Lourensford
Recommended Whites:
Chardonnay Winemaker's Selection Stellenbosch ★★☆ £C
Markview
Recommended Reds: Capensis Stellenbosch ★★★ £D
Cabernet Sauvignon Stellenbosch ★★★ £D
Merlot Stellenbosch ★★☆ £C
Recommended Whites: Chardonnay Stellenbosch ★★☆ £C
Matzikama
Recommended Reds: Shiraz Vredendal ★★☆ £B
Mellasat Vineyards
Recommended Whites: Chardonnay Paarl ★★☆ £C
Miles Mossop
Recommended Reds: Max Stellenbosch ★★★★ £E
Recommended Whites: Kika Stellenbosch ★★★★ £D
JH Meyer
Recommended Reds: Signature Pino Noir Elgin ★★★★☆ £E
Recommended Whites: Ivory White Swartland ★★★ £C
Nederburg
Recommended Whites:
Edelkeur Noble Late Harvest Auction Reserve Paarl ★★★ £E
Neethlingshof
Recommended Reds: The Caracal Stellenbosch ★★★ £C
Recommended Whites: Noble Late Harvest Stellenbosch ★★☆ £C
Opstal
Recommended Whites:
Carl Everson Chenin Blanc Slanghoek ★★★☆ £C
Overgaauw
Recommended Reds: Tria Corda Stellenbosch ★★★ £E
Quando Vineyards
Recommended Reds: Pinot Noir Robertson ★★★ £C
Recommended Whites: Sauvignon Blanc Robertson ★★☆ £C
Reyneke
Recommended Reds: Syrah Stellenbosch ★★★☆ £D
Cornerstone Red Stellenbosch ★★★☆ £D
Recommended Whites: Reserve White Stellenbosch ★★★★ £E
Chenin Blanc Stellenbosch ★★★ £C
Rickety Bridge
Recommended Reds: The Foundation Stone Western Cape ★★ £C
Anthonij Rupert Wines
Recommended Reds: Optima Western Cape ★★★ £D
Basson Pinotage Swartland ★★★ £D
Recommended Whites:
Van Lill & Visser Chenin Blanc Citrusdal Mountain ★★☆ £C

Sanctum
Recommended Reds: Shiraz Sanctum Western Cape ★★★★ £E
Saronsberg
Recommended Reds: Full Circle Tulbagh ★★★★ £E
Shiraz Tulbagh ★★★☆ £E   Provenance Shiraz Tulbagh ★★☆ £C
Savage Wines
Recommended Reds: Savage Red Western Cape ★★★☆ £D
Recommended Whites: Savage White Western Cape ★★★☆ £D
Julien Schaal
Recommended Reds: Syrah Elgin ★★★☆ £D
Recommended Whites: Chardonnay Elgin ★★★☆ £D
Shannon Vineyards
Recommended Reds: Syrah Elgin ★★★☆ £D
Recommended Whites: Chardonnay Elgin ★★★☆ £D
Simonsig
Recommended Reds: Pinotage Redhill Stellenbosch ★★★☆ £E
Tiara Red Stellenbosch ★★★☆ £E
Merindol Syrah Stellenbosch ★★★☆ £E
The SMV (Shiraz Mourvèdre Viognier) ★★★ £D
Labyrinth Cabernet Sauvignon Stellenbosch ★★★ £C
Recommended Whites:
Chenin Blanc Avec Chêne Stellenbosch ★★★ £D
Sunbird Sauvignon Blanc Stellenbosch ★★ £B
Siyabonga
Recommended Reds: Pinotage Wellington ★★★ £C
Spier
Recommended Reds: 21 Gables Pinotage Western Cape ★★★ £D
Creative Block 5 Coastal Region ★★★ £D
Creative Block 3 Western Cape ★★★ £D
Recommended Whites:
21 Gables Chenin Blanc Western Cape ★★★ £D
Creative Block 2 Western Cape ★★★ £C
Signature Chenin Blanc Western Cape ★★ £C
Spioenkop
Recommended Reds: 1900 Pinotage Elgin ★★★☆ £D
Recommended Whites: Riesling Elgin ★★★ £C
Sauvignon Blanc Elgin ★★★ £C
1900 Sauvignon Blanc Elgin ★★☆ £B
1900 Chenin Blanc Elgin ★★☆ £B
Stonewall
Recommended Reds: Cabernet Sauvignon Stellenbosch ★★☆ £C
Pinotage Stellenbosch ★★ £C
Recommended Whites: Sauvignon Blanc Stellenbosch ★★ £B
Thorne & Daughters
Recommended Whites: Tin Soldier Western Cape ★★★☆ £D
Rocking Horse Western Cape ★★★☆ £D
Vondeling
Recommended Reds: Shiraz Erica Paarl ★★☆ £C
Cabernet Sauvignon Voor Paardeberg ★★ £C
Petit Rouge Western Cape ★★ £B
Recommended Whites: Barbiana Paarl ★★★ £C
Chardonnay Paarl ★★☆ £C   Sauvignon Blanc Western Cape ★★ £B
Yardstick Wines
Recommended Reds: Pinot Noir Western Cape ★★★ £C
Marvelous Red Western Cape ★★★ £C
Marvelous Blue Western Cape ★★ £B
Recommended Whites: Chardonnay Western Cape ★★☆ £C
Marvelous Yellow Western Cape ★★☆ £B
Zevenwacht
Recommended Reds: Z Collection CMC Stellenbosch ★★★ £D
Z Collection SGM Stellenbosch ★★★ £D

South Africa

Recommended Whites:

Chardonnay Stellenbosch ★★☆ £C

360 Sauvignon Blanc Stellenbosch ★★ £C

Work in progress!!

Producers under consideration for the next edition

Beau Constantia (Constantia)

David & Nadia (Swartland)

Domaine des Dieux (Walker Bay)

Teddy Hall (Stellenbosch)

Hogan Wines (Swartland)

Intellego (Swartland)

Tim Martin Wines (Swartland)

Carsten Migliarina (Stellenbosch)

Meerhof Family Vineyards (Swartland)

Restless River (Walker Bay)

Rudi Schultz (Stellenbosch)

Storm (Walker Bay)

Vins d'Orrance (Stellenbosch)

Author's choice

A selection of emerging Cape new red classics

Anwilka   Anwilka Red Stellenbosch

Ashbourne   Ashbourne Pinotage Walker Bay

Beyerskloof   Field Blend Stellenbosch

Boekenhoutskloof   Cabernet Sauvignon Estate Franschhoek

Cederberg   V Generations Cederberg

Cloof   Cloof Crucible Shiraz Darling

De Trafford   Syrah 393 Stellenbosch Stellenbosch

Ernie Els   Signature Red Stellenbosch

Hamilton Russell Vineyards   Pinot Noir Walker Bay

De Trafford   Syrah 393 Stellenbosch Stellenbosch

Glenelly   Lady May Stellenbosch

Le Riche   Cabernet Sauvignon Reserve Stellenbosch

Nico Van Der Merwe   Mas Nicolas Stellenbosch

Oldenberg Vineyards   Syrah Stellenbosch

Porseleinberg   Porseleinberg Red Swartland

Raats   Mvemve Raats de Compostella

Rustenberg   Cabernet Sauvignon Peter Barlow Stellenbosch

Rust-en-Vrede   1694 Stellenbosch

Sadie Family Wines   Columella Swartland

Saxenburg   Shiraz Select Stellenbosch

Spice Route Company   Malabor Swartland

Thelema   Cabernet Sauvignon The Mint Stellenbosch

Uva Mira   Vineyard Selection Stellenbosch

Vergelegen   Vergelegen V Stellenbosch

Vilafonte   Series M Paarl

A selection of fine whites

Alheit   Cartology Western Cape

Ataraxia   Chardonnay Western Cape

Bizoe Wines   Henrietta Semillon/Sauvignon Blanc

Cape Point Vineyards   Isliedh Cape Point

De Trafford   Straw Wine Stellenbosch

Ken Forrester   T Noble Late-Harvest Stellenbosch

The Foundry   Viognier Coastal Region

Glen Carlou   Quartz Stone Chardonnay Paarl

Ghost Corner   The Bowline Ghost Corner Elim

Hartenberg   The Eleanor Stellenbosch

Hermanuspietersfontein   Die Bartho Walker Bay

Klein Constantia   Vin de Constance Constantia

Landau du Val   Semillon Franschhoek

Meerlust   Chardonnay Stellenbosch

Mullineux   Mullineux Straw Wine Chenin Blanc Swartland

Rustenberg   Chardonnay Five Soldiers Stellenbosch

Signal Hill   Eszencia Western Cape

Springfield   Chardonnay Méthode Anciènne Robertson

Sterhuis   Astra White Stellenbosch

Some finer values
Reds:

Backsberg   Klein Babylonstoren Paarl

Beaumont   Pinotage Walker Bay

Bon Cap   Cape Blend Robertson

Doolhof   Malbec Wellington

Fairview   Shiraz Beacon Paarl

Jordan   The Prospector Stellenbosch

Kanonkop   Pinotage Stellenbosch

Kleinood   Tamboerskloof Syrah

Lammershoek   Syrah Swartland

Catherine Marshall Wines   S/M/G Coastal Region

Newton Johnson Vineyards   Full Stop Rock Walker Bay

Rall Wines   Rall Red Swartland

Saxenburg   Pinotage Private Collection Stellenbosch

Scali   Scali Shiraz Voor-Paardeberg

Sijnn   Shiraz Swellendam

Solms-Delta   Hiervandaan Western Cape

Southern Right   Pinotage Western Cape

Stellekaya   Hercules Stellenbosch

Villiera   Monro Red Stellenbosch

Warwick Estate   Pinotage Old Bush Vines Stellenbosch

Waterford Estate   Cabernet Sauvignon Stellenbosch

Winery of Good Hope   Black Rock Red Blend Swartland

Whites:

AA Badenhorst   Secateurs Coastal Region

Black Pearl   Chenin Blanc Paarl

Bouchard Finlayson   Chardonnay Kaaimansgat Overberg

Cape Chamonix   Sauvignon Blanc Reserve Franschhoek

Paul Cluver   Riesling Close Encounter Elgin

Creation Wines   Viognier Walker Bay

Dornier   Donatus White Stellenbosch

Fryers Cove   Sauvignon Blanc Bamboes Bay

Hughes Family   Nativo White Swartland

Iona   Sauvignon Blanc Elgin

Kleine Zalze   Family Reserve Chenin Blanc Stellenbosch

Muratie   Laurens Campher Stellenbosch

Quoin Rock   Chardonnay Cape Agulhas

Tokara   Reserve Sauvignon Blanc Walker Bay

Vergelegen   Sauvignon Blanc Stellenbosch

Readers will find below a glossary of grape varieties and a general glossary of wine terms. We hope the two glossaries will be easy to cross reference throughout the guide and be a valuable learning aid as well.

Grapes

Agiorgitiko Greek for St George and a characterful variety widely planted on the Peloponnese. The only grape variety used for Nemea which can be long-lived.

Aglianico Late ripening, southern Italy red grape of real importance and considerable potential. Ageworthy with a noble structure, its smoky, minerally, berry-fruited character gains greater complexity and refined texture with keeping. The best wines come from Campania (Taurasi and various IGTs) and to some extent Basilicata (Aglianico del Vulture) and Puglia but don't expect greatness from the increasing amounts of inexpensive Aglianico now appearing from the same regions.

Airén A white grape that dominates plantings in Spain's central region La Mancha, producing a veritable sea of generally unexciting dull wines. At its best it can be lightly fruity and moderately attractive.

Albana White variety responsible for mostly nondescript Albana di Romagna DOCG. Much better as a sweet wine produced from dried grapes in passito versions.

Albarín A relatively rare white grape grown in northern Asturias in Spain and also planted in the Tierra de León DO as well as being included in Vinos de la Tierra whites from Castilla y León. Yields need to be controlled and the wine is often quite alcoholic with a light herbaceous character. At its best contributes to wines of real character.

Albariño Top quality white grape mainly found in Galicia in north-west Spain. It has often been compared to Viognier. It shares some of that varieties perfume and it's similarly best to focus on buying from good producers. Yields need to be kept low for the best results. Wines vary from light fresh and for youthful drinking to more serious barrel-fermented and aged examples, although these are much rarer. Most are aged on their fine lees for a few months. The same variety, Alvarinho is cultivated across the border in Portugal and is a major component of Vinho Verde and other good crisp northern Portuguese whites. A handful of examples are appearing elsewhere including California.

Albillo Emerging good quality white grape when handled correctly with restricted yields. Found mainly in west central Spain in the Vinos de Madrid DO with other wines taking the Vinos de la Tierra Castilla y León classification. Also planted in Ribera del Duero and the Canary Islands.

Aleatico Italian variety found in Puglia, Lazio and southern Tuscany usually vinified as a perfumed sweet red.

Alfrocheiro Preto Portuguese variety most likely to be encountered in Dão but planted in Bairrada and further south. Best used to add colour and complexity to a blend but has also recently been produced varietally.

Alicante Bouschet Characterful red-fleshed *teinturier* crossing (that claims Grenache as a parent) once heavily planted in southern France. Though more often used as a blending grape decent varietal examples are made in Portugal's Alentejo, Central Italy (especially Tuscany or Emilia) and California. It goes by the name of Garnacha Tintorera in Spain. See Garnacha Tintorera.

Aligoté Decent examples of Aligoté can be found the length and breadth of Burgundy but relatively few have the verve and subtle spice (without green or hard edges) that make it interesting.

Altesse see Roussette

Alvarinho see Albariño

Ansonica see Inzolia

Aragonês see Tempranillo

Antão Vaz White portuguese variety increasingly used in the Alentejo, both varietally and in blends.

Arinto One of Portugal's few native white grapes of substantially proven quality. Its good acidity and citrusy fruit form the basis of many of the better whites in southern Portugal.

Arneis Piedmont's leading white grape for dry whites is starting to make an impression in California and Australia. Light, dry but rather enticing perfumed examples generally need to be drunk very young; lightly oaked versions will keep a little longer but aren't necessarily superior.

Assyrtiko/Asyrtiko Greek white grape of good acidity and fruit with the potential for wines of good structure and minerality. Of Santorini orgins but increasingly widely planted.

Auxerrois A white variety of significant importance in Alsace where it is often blended with Pinot Blanc as well as being used in Crémant d'Alsace. Also cultivated in Germany, Luxembourg and England where it is both oak aged and incorporated in some sparkling wine blends.

Bacchus Not a noble variety as perhaps the name deserves but a German crossing bred for high sugar levels. Some of the best examples of herbal and exotic whites are produced by English wine growers but only when the grapes are fully ripe.

Baga The grape of Portugal's Bairrada region. Potentially a bruiser but when fully ripe from modest yielding vines it produces wines of great character if not seductive charm. Its distinctive earth, coffee, plum and berry fruit character is allied to depth and richness with age. In decline in the neighbouring Dão region where it is less suited.

Barbera Marvellous Piedmont grape which comes in any number of styles and quality levels. The greatest acclaim comes for rich, modern oaked-aged versions but some unoaked versions can also be stunning. There are many good examples as both Barbera d'Alba and Barbera d'Asti and occasionally convincing versions from Emilia. Simple, supple, fruity, quaffing Barbera can be good too. Once important in California, this is where the next best examples can be found; Australia also makes adequate versions while potential also exists in Argentina.

Bastardo A name that can rarely be used to describe the contents of a bottle if speaking varietally as this Portuguese grape is usually found only as minor component in a blend in Dão or for Port. One and the same as Trousseau in France's Jura.

Bical One of the best native Portuguese varieties for dry whites though that's not saying much. Good body, aroma and acidity are possible if rarely achieved. Luis Pato's single vineyard Vinha Formal seems likely to realise the limits of what is possible. Also made sparkling.

Blaufränkisch Important red variety in Austria's Burgenland where it is often blended with other varieties to moderate its relatively high acidity and tannin. Of minor importance in Washington State and Germany where it is known as Lemberger. One and the same as Hungary's Kékfrankos.

Boal Madeira's Boal or Bual is one of the noble varieties giving dark coloured wines of spicy dried fruits intensity. The resulting style is typically sweeter than Verdelho but less rich if more refined than Malvasia. It is also grown in north-west Spain and northern Portugal. See Doña Blanca.

Grapes

Bobal Widely planted red variety in central Spain capable of producing concentrated smoky, black-fruited reds. Some powerful reds, rich in fruit and extract, from unirrigated, low-yielding old vine fruit are starting to emerge, in particular from Manchuela.

Bonarda In Italy what is called Bonarda is most important in Oltrepò Pavese and Colli Piacentini (as Croatina). In the latter, it can be blend with Barbera for a characterful red, Gutturnio. Argentina's Bonarda is not related but from old vines complex, aromatic, supple reds can be produced. This same variety is referred to as Charbono in California.

Bourboulenc White grape widely planted throughout southern France. It is late ripening and retains very good acidity. If vinified correctly it is a very valueable blending component. If picked insufficiently ripe it is lean, dilute and tart.

Brachetto Unusual Piedmontese variety that has obtained DOCG status in Brachetto d'Acqui. Often it is medium-dry and either frizzante or fully sparkling but with a wonderful, grapey perfume and flavour if drunk young and fresh from a producer like Braida.

Brancellao Variety grown in Ribeira Sacra in Spain, providing lightly coloured wine. It is always a part of a blend for which it can provide additional backbone.

Bual see Boal.

Cabernet Franc Parent variety of the more famous Cabernet Sauvignon it is more successful in cooler soils. Only in the Anjou and Touraine in the Loire Valley does it thrive as a varietal as despite its importance on Bordeaux's Right Bank it is almost invariably blended with Merlot and some Cabernet Sauvignon. Its importance as a component in Bordeaux style blends both at home and around the world is undeniable. Though it can emulate the flavours of its off-spring, it can miss its extra richness and depth and also show more of a raspberry-like fruit and a more leafy, herbal or even floral, component. Cabernet Sauvignon Grown almost everywhere, a grape of forceful and easily recognisable personality, it is much more fussy in showing at its best. Though capable of great richness, depth and structure, a lack of full ripeness in both fruit and tannin tends to detract from so many examples. A long growing season and well-drained soils are two prerequisites to producing the greatest elegance and classic telltale blackcurrant but also black cherry or blackberry flavours that mesh so well with new French oak. Though Cabernet Sauvignon dominates blends, the majority of top examples many do include a percentage of complementary varietals such as Merlot or Cabernet Franc which complement it in both flavour and structure. Many countries have identified at least one region where it really excels with the greatest riches from the Médoc, Napa Valley, Tuscany, Coonawarra and Margaret River. A significant number of world class examples have also come from Washington State, New Zealand, Chile, Argentina as well as a few from Spain and South Africa.

Caiño Blanco Very rare Spanish white grape which can a be component in blends from Rias Baixas.

Caiño Tinto Rare red variety cultivated in Ribeiro (where it may be referred to as Caiño Longo) and Rias Baixas producing wines with marked acidity and a typically nervy character from these cooler climes.

Caiño Tinto see Caiño Tinto.

Callet Good quality red grape native to Mallorca.

Canaiolo Chiefly Tuscan variety and used to complement Sangiovese but discarded by many in favour of Merlot or Cabernet Sauvignon for their Chianti Classico. A mini revival is underway as some producers seek to produce reds of more individual character.

Cannonau Sardinian version of Grenache, for long produced as an inexpensive quaffing red, Cannonau di Sardegna. Several committed growers are now realizing its true potential, sometimes as IGT reds. Rare good fortified versions are also made from late-harvested or dried grapes.

Carignan This variety, particularly in the Midi was long seen as no more than a bulk workhorse variety. However the movement in both the Midi and in Spain as Cariñena (occasionally Mazuelo), mainly in Montsant and Priorat to recover old vine plantings and restrict yields for quality has the shown the potentially excellent quality that can be achieved from the grape. Fully ripened and from old vines the wines are intense mineral and richly sicy and full of striking dark fruit. As well as Languedoc and Spain, the variety can be found in Provence and the southern Rhône, as Carignano in Sardinia and as Carignane in California. It is also planted in Australia.

Carignan Blanc This is a very rare white variety. It is a mutation of Carignan Gris which is itself mutated from the red Carignan. Some very good wines are being produced in both Languedoc and Roussillon which include the variety to a greater or lesser degree. In Spain it is known as Cariñena Blanca and there are very isolated plantings in Empordà.

Carignan Gris see Carignan Blanc.

Carignane see Carignan.

Carignano see Carignan.

Cariñena see Carignan.

Cariñena Blanca see Carignan.

Carmenère Old Bordeaux variety of increasing importance in Chile where much of it continues to be sold as Merlot. As they are often planted in a field blend together the disparity in ripening times further compromises the quality of fruit from high-yielding vines. Once isolated and made from well-established low-yielding vines it has excellent potential with a characterful wild berry and spice character. Also thought to be confused with other grapes in regions where plantings were established from Bordeaux cuttings in the 19th century.

Casavecchia Obscure grape variety very recently revived by Pepe Mancini (Terre del Principe) in Campania in Southern Italy. Castelão Portuguese grape also still widely known as Periquita, extensively grown in the southern regions but most successful in the Palmela DOC in the Terras do Sado region.

Cayetana White grape grown in southern Spain in the Extremadura, Montilla-Morilles and Jerez where it is generally distilled for use in brandy. At best it makes lightly fruity, herb scented wines.

Cencibel see Tempranillo.

Cesanese d'Affile Another potential Italian star grape and one that Lazio looks like making it own after years of making decent but slightly boring reds from both Cabernets and Merlot. A recent proliferation of examples, some under relatively obscure DOCs already provide sufficient evidence of its class, texture and spicy red fruits complexity. It is considered superior to that called simply Cesanese (or Cesanese Comune).

Charbono see Bonarda.

Chardonnay Ironically the only significant wine regions where this grape is not grown are found in France. The great white grape of Burgundy has a great affinity for oak and can produce whites of marvellous texture, depth and richness but will also render a wonderful expression of its origins where yields are low. Some of the top mineral-imbued examples of Chablis are aged only in large used oak while others see no oak whatsoever. High quality grapes allied to winemaking sophistication is essential – too many

examples, wherever they are made, show a clumsy winemaking fingerprint (excessive leesy, skin contact or oak flavours) or inferior fruit (under-ripe, over-ripe) or are simply unclean, acidified or lacking balance. Outstanding examples are produced from California to the Antipodes (the latter including some of the best values) and beyond. Chardonnay also forms a part of almost all top quality sparkling wines, especially Champagne. When varietal and sparkling it is known as Blanc de Blancs. Rich botrytised versions are unusual but have been made to a high standard in the Mâconnais, Austria and New Zealand.

Chasselas Relatively neutral white grape also known as Fendant in Switzerland where it assumes greater importance and produces whites of higher quality than anywhere else in the world. The best examples reflect something of the specific terroirs with good structure and minerality in Dézaley and Calamin. From the opposite, southern shore of Lac Léman in Savoie come the best French examples (including Crépy). Rare decent examples are also made in the Loire (Pouilly-sur-Loire) and Alsace.

Chenin Blanc High quality white grape of Touraine and Anjou in the Loire Valley. Outstanding long-lived wines ranging from dry to sweet are made and owe much to the grape's high acidity. Apple and citrus flavours within a firm, demanding texture are usually complemented by floral, honey and mineral characters with quince, peach even apricot in sweeter styles. Despite there being more extensive plantings in California and South Africa, good examples from outside the Loire remain few. Washington State and New Zealand also provide one or two. Also an important base for some good quality sparkling wines.

Ciliegiolo Difficult central Italian variety, not least, to pronounce. One of several natives (also see Colorino, Canaiolo) being revived by committed growers seeking more authentic Tuscan reds than those that rely in part or whole on foreign varieties. One or two varietal examples from old vine fruit show a captivating wild cherry character.

Cinsaut/Cinsault Characterful Rhône variety where taken seriously. Can add perfume and complexity both to southern Rhône blends and wines from the Languedoc and Corsica, especially when yields are low.

Coda di Volpe Ancient Campanian variety mentioned by Pliny the Elder in Naturalis Historia. Often forming part of a blend it has also been produced varietally but as yet without any great distinction.

Colorino Deep coloured red grape of Central Italy and Tuscany, once used to beef up Chianti made by the governo technique. Mostly used along with Canaiolo to complement Sangiovese but very occasionally contributes significantly to reds of tremendous character, depth and richness, from isolated locations where the vines are of high quality.

Cortese Piedmont grape of moderate quality best known for the mostly undistinguished Gavi. A handful of producers have improved both concentration and character of their wines through lower yields; the subtle use of oak can also help. Other examples such as those from the Monferrato hills can be attractively fruity if rarely showing much depth or refinement.

Corvina Leading red variety in Italy's Veneto for Valpolicella, Amarone and Recioto della Valpolicella. Though only giving moderate colour and tannin its thickish skins help it to resist rot during the drying process or appassimento. The related Corvinone can bring more colour, concentration and structure to a blend.

Crespiello A native red variety of Aragón only recovered very recently. Produces impressive, characterful results through the work of the Bioenos laboratory. The variety produces wines with good natural balance but is difficult to cultivate. The original name of the variety is Vivadillo of Almonacid and is also known as Vidadillo.

Dolcetto Piedmont grape capable of wonderful fruit intensity yet lively acidity and moderate tannin. Most of the best examples with a mineral or herbal streak to black cherry or black plum fruit, are unoaked and mean't to be drunk with between one and three years' age but there are ageworthy exceptions, especially those from old low-yielding vines whether in the Dogliani or Alba zones. Known as Ormeasco in Liguria.

Doña Blanca Good quality white grape largely found in north-western Spain and Portugal where it is known as Dona Branco. It is thick skinned so responds well in the maritime climate of Galicia but needs at best absolutely minimal skin contact before fermentation. Good wines are produced in Monterrei, Valdeorras and Bierzo. In Portugal on the island of Madeira it is known as Boal. See Boal.

Dona Branco see Doña Blanca.

Dornfelder German red grape bred to produce good colour and retain good acidity. It responds reasonably well to ageing in oak and produces good concentrations of sugar during ripening in marginal climates.

Durif Red grape variety found in the USA, particularly in California, southern France, Australia and Israel. The wines are dark, inky and potentially quite tannic with hints of pepper and spice. See Petite Sirah

Encruzado Portuguese variety starting to show considerable quality in the Dão region. Subtly oaked it can show good depth, a gentle texture and a refined, perfumed, slightly exotic fruit character.

Erbaluce Little seen Piedmont white of pronounced acidity but with attractive fruit when fully ripe and dry as Erbaluce di Caluso. Caluso Passito, from dried grapes is potentially better quality while a little sparkling wine is also made.

Espadeiro A red grape of Portuguese origin, found in small holdings in Galicia, particularly Valdeorras and Rias Baixas. It offers soft berry flavoured wines, generally as a part of a blend.

Falanghina Another potential star grape from southern Italy set to rival Fiano and Greco. Though still not widely seen the number of good examples, showing impressive texture and flavour with a couple of years' age, is on the increase.

Favorita see Vermentino.

Ferrón Red variety found in the Ribeiro DO in Spain's Galicia region where it can be a minor component in blends.

Fiano Perfumed and flavoursome white grape from Campania from which increasing amounts of spicy, dry whites with fullish peachy, slightly nutty fruit are made. Late-harvested versions and those from botrytis affected grapes have also been successfully made.

Fogoneu is a red grape planted in the Balearic Islands. It can be found in wines from the Mallorca and Formentera VTs and in Plà i Llevant.

Folle Blanche is a white grape originating from the south west of France and found in the Loire Valley where it is used to make the somewhat tart wines of Gros Plant du Nantais, the name of which is a synonym. There a small plantings in the Chacoli area.

Frappato Fragrant red Sicilian variety that character to Cerasuolo di Vittoria reds.

Freisa Characterful, perfumed Piedmont grape often made frizzante (lightly sparkling), sometimes with a little residual sugar. A handful of dry versions are excellent where its predisposition to astringency on the finish has been mastered.

Friulano Now officially Friulano (formerly Tocai Friulano), found in North-East Italy, this grape produces refined dry whites with herb (jasmine), citrus and nectarine character. It is difficult to believe but

Grapes

it is said to be related to the poor quality Sauvignonasse (Sauvignon Vert) variety still widely grown in Chile and for long passed off as Sauvignon Blanc.

Furmint Top quality Hungarian grape giving its greatest expression as the basis of the sweet wines of the Tokaj region thanks to its high acidity, susceptibility to noble rot and refined flavours. Also occasionally made in good dry versions and used by some producers in Austria's Burgenland for sweet Ausbruch wines.

Gaglioppo Late-ripening southern Italian red variety of chief importance in Calabria. The colour can develop quite quickly and the tannin and alcohol levels can be high. From moderate yields, wines can show impressive depth and develop a rich, chocolaty, savoury complexity.

Gamay The grape of the Beaujolais region and well-suited to its granitic soils. Examples range from the dilute and insipid to the impressively deep and fruity. Most but not all of it is produced by semi- carbonic maceration producing a supple texture but partly compromising its cherry fruit perfume and flavour. Plantings extend into the Mâconnais to the north where it performs poorly; mercifully, some at least, is being replaced by Chardonnay. The only really significant other area where the true Gamay grape is planted is in Touraine in the Loire Valley where some fresh and attractive examples are made.

Garganega The 'good' grape of Soave capable of producing intense, sleek whites when yields are low. Even more impressive when made from late-harvested or dried grapes (for Recioto di Soave).

Garnacha/Garnacha Tinta see Grenache.

Garnacha Blanca see Grenache Blanc.

Garnacha Gris see Grenache Gris.

Garnacha Tintorera Increasingly important red grape grown in central and south-eastern Spain achieving real quality in Alicante and in particular in the Almansa DO. The variety is a *teinturier* (red fleshed) and goes by the name of Alicante Bouschet in France and California. See Alicante Bouschet.

Gewürztraminer / Traminer Both of these names are used to describe a remarkably aromatic distinctive grape variety that has produced good examples from around the world. This versatile grapy white is redolent in scents from the floral and musky to rose petal, lychee and spices. Styles range from the light and fresh to rich, oily textured wines and from dry to off-dry through late-harvested to sweet, botrytised wines. Weaker efforts lack definition and a certain coarseness, particularly on the finish, is only avoided in top quality examples. The greatest range of styles and highest quality comes from Alsace which is followed by Italy's Alto Adige and Germany. Though fewer in number the best new world examples arguably come from New Zealand but there is good quality too in Australia, California, Oregon and Canada and in Chile's Casablanca Valley.

Godello Good quality white grape grown in Galicia in north-west Spain, particularly in the Valdeorras and Monterrei DOs. There are also a handful of plots in nearby Bierzo in Castilla y León. The wines produced have good body and fresh acidity with hints of citrus, floral aromas and an underlying minerality in the best examples. Good barrel-fermented as well as tank vinified wines are made.

Grauburgunder see Pinot Gris

Graciano Good quality red grape found mainly in Rioja where it is generally blended with Tempranillo and sometimes Garnacha as well. It is naturally low yielding and adds both structure and depth. An increasing number of very impressive wines, either varietal examples, or wines dominated by Graciano are also being produced.

Grechetto White variety of greatest significance in Umbria where it is used as a component in Orvieto and Colli Martani but also leading whites such as Cervaro della Sala.

Greco Greco or more specifically Greco di Tufo (to distinguish it from other similar names) does come originally from Greece and does well on the volcanic soils in Campania's Avellino hills in southern Italy. At its best it is attractively scented with citrus, peachy fruit and a firm texture and slightly nutty finish.

Grenache Leading grape variety in the southern Rhône where it forms the backbone wines from the leading appellations, including Châteauneuf-du-Pape and Gigondas. Quality and style vary enormously but is capable of great longevity when produced from low-yielding fruit. Grenache also forms a component of many of Languedoc-Roussillon's reds including Banyuls and Collioure near the border with Spain. In Spain too, as Garnacha, the variety can produce exceptional reds, in particular in Priorat, Montsant and in the Gredos Mountains in Toledo. Other good examples also come from Emporda and Navarra and the grape is a constituent of Rioja. In Sardinia, it goes under the name of Cannonau. In Australia some of the best vines were uprooted before its quality potential was reassessed. It is now part of, often high quality, fashionable blends that usually include Shiraz and Mourvèdre with a similar situation in California. The grape is also grown successfully in Argentina, Chile, Uruguay and South Africa.

Grenache Blanc Previously undistinguished grape. When it is restricted in yield it can provide characterful wines with nutty, herb-spiced, citrusy hints and certainly weight from its naturally high potential alcohol. Works well in blends with Roussanne as well as other varieties throughout the southern Rhône and particularly the Roussillon and is occasionally vinified as a varietal. It is also significant in Spain, as Garnacha Blanca, in regions to the south of the Pyrenees. Priorat, Terra Alta and Alella in Cataluña are all sources and the grape can also be found in Navarra and Aragon. It is permitted in Rioja but rarely used.

Grenache Gris A pink tinged mutation of the Grenache family found in small quantities in Languedoc-Roussillon and in Empordà on the north-east Mediterrannean coast where it is known as Garnacha Gris.

Gros Manseng Important grape of South-West France, particularly for the production of the dry wines of Jurançon with an exotic fruit character. Also used for the sweet wines, often together with the related but finer Petit Manseng. In the basque Country in Spain it is known as Izkiriot Handi.

Grüner Veltliner From terraces above the Danube in the Wachau region in Lower Austria, this relatively unknown grape can produce remarkably good full-bodied whites. Neighbouring regions of Kremstal, Kamptal and Traisental can also produce peppery, citrus, yellow plum flavoured wines that become gently honeyed and increasingly complex with age. Its tendency to high alcohol needs to be balanced by good acidity and fruit richness. More everyday examples can be dilute and lack charm. Its cultivation is increasing with vines grown in the Czech Republic and Slovakia and there are small parcels in Hungary. The grape is now being grown in a number of US regions; Oregon, New York, Napa Valley and the Santa Ynez Valley are also sources. Grüner has also been planted in isolated locations in both Australia and New Zealand.

Hárslevelü Complementary variety to Furmint in the production of Tokaji when it adds aroma. Also makes spicy, perfumed dry whites in other parts of Hungary. Inzolia Increasingly important white variety in Sicily for fresh dry whites with good perfume and flavour; also a component of some of the best Marsala. As a minor variety in Tuscany it is known as Ansonica.

Hondarribí Beltza Red grape variety grown in the three Txakoli appellations in Spain's Basque country (Pais Vasco). Marked by its fresh acidity and red fruit and leafy notes it can be very good and striking.

Hondarrabí Zuri is the white grape native to the Txakoli DOs. This is more commonly encountered than the Hondarribí Beltza and the wines can be good to very good with citrus, apple scents, herbs and a floral component all showing themselves.

Incrocio Manzoni see Manzoni Bianco.

Inzolia Decent quality white grape grown in Sicily and used in the production of Marsala. Can also be found in Tuscany where it is called Ansonica.

Izkiriot Handi is a white grape of French origins. Tiny amounts are planted in the Bizkaiko Txakolina DO in Spain's Basque Country. It is much better known in its native Jurançon in south western France where it produces characterful aromatic whites as Gros Manseng.

Jaen Important component in red Dão blends and capable of good fruit intensity if relatively modest structure. Its smoky, spicy, berryish fruit has occasionally been fully expressed in one or two varietal examples. The variety is like the Spanish Mencia, which is almost certainly the same, characterised by its vibrant, at best complex dark, spicy berry fruit, fresh acidity and relatively soft supple tannin structure.

Juan García red grape found in Zamora in Spain and an authorised variety in the recently established Arribes DO. The best examples are ripe and forward, offering a supple, soft structure with attractive cherry flavours and a little depth.

Kékfrankos see Blaufränkisch

Kerner K is also for Kerner, a productive German crossing (Trollinger x Riesling) of potentially good quality. Though in decline it is still Germany's fourth most planted white variety. Mostly confined to Rheinhessen and Pfalz but also Württemberg and Mosel, often used in large volume, branded whites. Occasionally made varietally - unusually good expressions of the variety come from the Abbazia di Novacella in the south Tyrol (see North-East Italy).

Lacrima Black grape found only in Italy's Marche region. Almost extinct in the 1970s, it potential loss some would argue was not worth shedding a tear over. Now considerably revived, typical examples Lacrima di Morro d'Alba reds are rose and tea scented without much substance yet can reveal hard, green tannins. A mere handful of producers do far better with a persuasive, lushly textured red that goes superbly with white meats. Not to be confused with Campania's DOC Lacryma Christi del Vesuvio which is based on Piedirosso.

Lado A white grape variety which is a minor component in the white wines of Ribeiro in Galicia in northern Spain. It adds aromatic complexity and refreshing acidity

Lagrein Grape found in Trentino-Alto Adige (North-East Italy) and fast becoming the most important red variety in the region. Both supple, fruity everyday reds and deep coloured, concentrated, often oak-aged, reds full of bramble, dark plum and cherry fruit, are being made in increasing numbers. It has the fruit intensity of other native North-East reds but more moderate tannin and acidity levels that suggest it has potential elsewhere too.

Lambrusco The grape behind one of Italy's most discredited wine styles. Real Lambrusco, red and sparkling but dry, refreshing and a good food match too will usually come from one of the best, localised sub-varieties such as Grasparossa, Salamino or Sorbara.

Lemberger see Blaufränkisch

Listán Blanca Lightly herb scented white grape grown in the Canary Islands.

Listán Negra Red grape, native to the Canary Islands making fresh, fruit-driven wines that should be drunk young.

Loureiro Along with Alvarinho and Trajadura one of the principal grapes of Vinho Verde. Like Alvarinho of sufficient quality to be produced varietally for fine, scented dry whites.

Magliocco Potentially high quality grape variety 'rescued' by Librandi in Calabria in southern Italy. Appears to be capable of producing deeply coloured, distinctive full-bodied and ageworthy reds.

Macabeo/Viura One of northern Spains most important white grape varieties. As Viura it is widely planted in Rioja and it is found in north-west Spain as well. As well as in Rioja it has significant plantings in Cataluña and in particular in Penedés in the production of Cava. Also goes by the pseudonyms Macabeu and Subirat. It is extensively planted in the Languedoc and in the Roussillon where it is respectively known under the pseudonyms Maccabéo or Maccabeu

Macabeu see Macabeo/Viura

Maccabéo see Macabeo/Viura

Maccabeu see Macabeo/Viura

Madeleine Angevine An attractively flowery, lightly aromatic grape with a diverse parentage that grows well in cool regions. It produces good crisp dry wines with plenty of acidity and is well suited to the English climate.

Malbec Essentially another of Bordeaux's rejects, the peppery, blackfruited Malbec has found favour as the major constituent of Cahors in South-West France but has become even more strongly associated with Argentina. The latter examples tend to be softer and more approachable though can want for structure but there is high quality from both sources. Good quality is also obtained from a limited amount of old vine plantings in South Australia while it is on the increase in Chile and performs well in New Zealand. It is of minor importance in the Loire Valley where it is known as Cot

Malvar The main native white grape of the Madrid region which adds dimension to wines blended with Airén. Also produces reasonable, albeit quite simple fruit driven wines when bottled as a varietal.

Malvasia This name covers a great many closely related varieties from Italy, Spain and Portugal. In North-East Italy Malvasia Istriana can be a characterful dry white. In Tuscany dried Malvasia grapes bring more quality when added to Trebbiano for Vin Santo while in Lazio Malvasia can rescue the whites of the Colli Albani, such as Frascati, from blandness. In the south it turns sweet when made from passito grapes on the volcanic island of Lipari. In Spain it can add substance to some white Rioja and can be found in both the Canary and Balearic Islands while in Portugal's Douro Malvasia grapes could end up in White Port or as a dry white. As Malvasia Fina one or two good varietal white Dão are made while on Madeira it is the grape responsible for the richest, sweetish style of Madeira, Malmsey.

Malvasia Nera A black version of Malvasia of considerable importance in Puglia but also found elsewhere in Italy, mostly in the south but also in Tuscany. Aromatic, its distinctive black plum fruit adds character to reds usually based on either Negroamaro, Primitivo or Sangiovese.

Mandó A rare and experimental red grape planted in Valencia. It would appear to have some potential, producing small clusters and being naturally low yielding.

Manto Negro Red grape, indigenous to the Balearics and widely planted in the Binissalem DO. Works well in blends with both Callet and Cabernet Sauvignon.

Grapes

Grape Glossary

Mantonico Grape found in Southern Italy usually made into light but elegant sweet whites but also made in a dry, oaked version by Librandi in Calabria.

Manzoni Bianco One of six different grapes of the Manzoni family originating in the Veneto in northern Italy and also just known as Incrocio Manzoni. It is a cross of Pinot Bianco and Riesling and is mainly found in the Veneto but there are isolated plantings elsewhere including Penedés.

Marsanne At its best this is an intensely flavoured white with succulent peach and apricot fruit and often a tell-tale honeysuckle character. It is particularly important in northern Rhône whites, sometimes in partnership with Roussanne. It is also produced in Hermitage as Vin de Paille. It crops up again in blends in Côtes du Rhône whites (but not white Châteauneuf-du-Pape), Languedoc-Roussillon and even in Provence. It is grown too in Switzerland's Valais (as Ermitage) and makes a rare appearance (or two) in Italy. Its use in California is likely to increase while the best examples in Australia come from the Goulburn Valley in Victoria.

Marselan Newly created red grape which is a cross between Cabernet Sauvignon and Grenache. Found mainly in the Languedoc, there are also plantings in Spain.

Mataro see Mourvèdre

Maturana Tinta A rare red grape from Rioja. Experimental winemaking is producing characterful results.

Mavrodaphne Greek grape responsible for the bold, sweet reds of Pátras but also used as a blending component in dry reds.

Mazuelo refer to Cariñena.

Melon de Bourgogne The grape responsible for the many bland dry whites of Muscadet. The best examples however can be both refreshing and flavoursome, usually owed, at least in part, to ageing *sur lie*. Also grown in Oregon, Washington State and Ontario.

Mencía An important red variety in north-west Spain and in particular Bierzo where some exceptional dark-fruited, very mineral wines are being produced, marked more by their acidity than their tannin. Also planted in the nearby Galician DOs of Valdeorras and Ribeira Sacra. DNA fingerprinting has also established that it is the same variety as the Portuguese Jaen which is found in Dão

Merlot There are very few significant wine producing countries where there isn't at least some Merlot, even Switzerland and Canada have plenty of it. Its home though is in Bordeaux and it can range from a few per cent to almost varietal (as in Château Pétrus). Much Merlot is lean, weedy and under-ripe. In fact few Merlot-dominated wines in fact come close to those of Bordeaux's Right Bank. Although good ripe, lush reds have been produced from Australia, New Zealand, Chile, Argentina, South Africa, California, Washington State, Italy and Spain, very few of these combine that richness with the classic berry plumminess and fruitcake, spice, fig or clove character that make it so enticing. Tuscany and California do it most often but in Chile (where it is mixed up with Carmenère) and elsewhere, great examples are the exception.

Merseguera is a white grape found on Spain's south eastern Mediterranean coast and a significant element of white blends in the Valencia DO.

Monastrell see Mourvèdre

Mondeuse Characterful French grape from Savoie. High in acidity but capable of intense beetroot, plum and cherry flavours and an attractive floral scent. . It is often blended with Pinot Noir, Gamay and Poulsard. Though a localised variety, one producer (Cottanera) has planted it at altitude in Sicily. It may be one and the same as Fruili's Refosco. Also cultivated in Argentina, Australia and California.

Monica Sardinian variety that has been in decline - mostly transformed into simple fruity everyday reds.

Montepulciano Gutsy spicy red variety that dominates the adriatic seaboard in central Italy. Most examples are fruit rich (distinctive red and black cherry) with good extract and colour but verge on the rustic without competent vinification. Both the Abruzzo and Marche regions increasingly provide top quality versions which reveal impressive breadth, refinement and complexity. NOT to be confused with Vino Nobile di Montepulciano from the Tuscan hill top town of the same name which is based primarily on Sangiovese (Prugnolo Gentile).

Moravia Dulce is a relatively rare red grape found in Spain's Manchuela DO and across La Mancha. At its best providing aromatic character in blends with Garnacha it has a tendency to yield heavily.

Moravia Agria is a native red variety of La Mancha, which can blend successfully with Garnacha and differs from Moravia Dulce, being higher in natural acidity.

Moscatel Muscat from Spain or Portugal. Mostly of the Muscat of Alexandria form, styles range from dry and aromatic to sweet, often fortified (as with Moscatel de Setúbal). Moscatel de Grano Menudo is the superior Muscat Blanc à Petit Grains form. Also see Muscat

Moscato see Muscat

Moschofilero Decent Greek pink-hued grape variety used increasingly in dry white blends. Muscat like it adds spice and aroma.

Mourvèdre High quality grape found in southern France at the very limits of ripening. It is most important incarnation is as powerful, tannic and ageworthy Bandol but some in Châteauneuf-du-Pape use it for blending as do producers in the Languedoc-Roussillon. In Spain (as Monastrell) it has been rather neglected in terms of producing high quality but an increasing number of producers in Jumilla and elsewhere are starting to realize its potential there. In Australia and California it is sometimes called Mataro but in both places it can also excel both varietally and in blends.

Müller Thurgau Although it once formed the major part of white wine production in New Zealand and still yields generously for basic plonk in Germany, this German crossing of has few admirers. It lacks the structure and class of one of its parents (Riesling) but still makes attractive wine in good hands - selected producers in the Alto Adige (North-East Italy) take it as seriously as any.

Muscadelle Relatively unsung grape of Bordeaux where it is used sparingly in sweet wines (including Sauternes) and in some of the lesser dry whites. Its true potential however, where it can achieve extraordinary complexity (as Topaque, formerly Tokay), is seen in Victoria, Australia - mostly in and around Rutherglen in the North-East of the state.

Muscadet see Melon de Bourgogne

Muscat There is a whole family of Muscat grapes and it comes in many guises however there three principal grapes: Muscat Blanc à Petits Grains, Muscat of Alexandria and Muscat Ottonel. It can be dry, medium-dry or sweet – whether from dried grapes or fortified or a combination of the two. It is also made sparkling. What all the best examples have in common is the intense, heady grapiness – that taste of the grape itself. Only occasionally is it a wine for ageing. Alsace makes it both dry and intensely sweet, in southern France there are the Vins Doux Naturel of Beaumes de Venises and Rivesaltes (amongst others). In Spain Moscatel can be found in the south and south-east and on the Canary Islands while Portugal has the sweet fortified Moscatel de Setúbal. In Italy there's Asti or the better Moscato d'Asti and there's also yellow and pink forms of it (Moscato Giallo and Moscato Rosa) in the North-East – usually made off-dry or medium-sweet. Off-shore from Sicily the

grapes Zibibbo are dried for raisiny, apricotty Passito di Pantelleria. In Germany (called Muskateller) it ranges from dry to sweet and Austria's best examples are also sweet. Gelber Muskateller is for the yellow/gold-skinned variant, Roter Muskateller for the red-skinned version. In Greece, Samos Muscat is produced. In North-East Victoria the intense raisiny Rutherglen Muscat is produced while in the US dry, medium-dry and sweet examples are produced by a few (but including Black Muscat and Orange Muscat). From South Africa comes the famed rich, sweet Vin de Constance. In fact there is seemingly no end to it.

Muskateller see Muscat

Nebbiolo The classic variety of Piedmont that remains almost exclusively the source of high quality examples of the grape. Capable of exquisite aroma and flavour its youthful austerity and tannin, while less formidable than in the past, can still present a challenge to some palates. Its dark raspberry, cherry or blackberry fruit, herb and floral aromas take on increasing complexity with age and the best examples give a wonderful expression of their *terroir*. Oak needs to be used with care in order not to overwhelm its unique perfumes and flavour. Lighter, fragrant but fruity examples of the grape can be a bit hit and miss, often being produced from less good sites. The only source of Nebbiolo-based wines in any significant quantity outside Piedmont is as Valtellina Superiore in Lombardy where it is called Chiavennasca. There are a handful of examples to be found in California (where it has enjoyed some success on the Central Coast) and Australia.

Negramoll Red grape grown in the Canaries.

Négrette Grape of South-West France of greatest importance in Côtes du Frontonnais where it forms the major part of the blend. It gives supple, perfumed berryish wines with a slightly wild edge.

Negroamaro For long the basis of many of the often rustic, raisiny reds from Puglia's Salento peninsula in southern Italy including Salice Salentino. Its dark, bitter flavours are not to everyone's taste but are sometimes toned down by other varieties such as Malvasia Nera. Subject to better winemaking it has recently shown much greater potential including some exciting varietal examples.

Nerello Mascalese Once seen only as a high-yielding blending variety, it is now emerging both as a complementary grape to the increasingly highly-regarded Nero d'Avola as well as a top quality varietal in its own right. From its origins on volcanic soils around the slopes of Mount Etna, it can show impressive class, complexity and texture. It also often blended with the related Nerello Cappuccio.

Nero d'Avola Widely planted in Sicily and currently seen as the island's best native red variety. It produces rich, intense, deep-coloured reds with a peppery black-fruited character and adding more depth and complexity with age. Is said to be related to Syrah.

Neuburger Unsung Austrian grape that is a crossing of Weissburgunder (Pinot Blanc) and Silvaner. Can form an important component of both sweet (often high quality) and dry wines in Burgenland.

Nielluccio Leading black grape on the island of Corsica shown to be identical to Sangiovese though seems a more rugged variety from tasting evidence. Often blended with Sciacarello.

Ortega White grape cross-bred from Müller-Thurgau and Siegerrebe. It has a floral, peachy quality and is favoured in cool climate viticulture for its early ripening qualities with good sugar levels. Although vineyard holdings are decreasing in Germany it is being newly planted in England.

Pallagrello Bianco Interesting white variety grown in Campania giving wines of good structure and depth. Now considered to be distinct from Coda di Volpe with which it was previously considered

one and the same. Currently made by just two producers of note: Vestini Campagnano and Terre del Principe.

Pallagrello Nero Like Casavecchia a previously obscure grape variety very recently revived by Pepe Mancini (Terre del Principe) in Campania in Southern Italy.

Palomino (Fino) The humble grape that dominates the chalky soils of Jerez is responsible for the diverse, often extraordinary wines that result from the elaboration of Sherry. When vinified as a dry white it is quite ordinary.

Parraleta A native red grape of Somontano in northern Spain.

Parellada is a white grape cultivated at higher altitudes in Cataluña. As a dry wine it provides crisp fresh examples that should not be cellared. It is also one of the traditional grapes in Cava sparkling wines.

Pecorino Here not referring to Italian ewes milk cheeses but an Italian grape variety planted in Abruzzo where whites of good structure have recently emerged.

Pedro Ximenez this grape is commonly found in the DOs of Málaga and Montilla-Morilles as well as in Jerez where some excellent fortified and very sweet wines are produced. At its richest it often makes an excellent accompaniment for vanilla ice cream, rather than to drink on its own.

Petit Manseng Quality grape producing sometimes exquisite dry and sweet wines of Jurançon in South-West France. Increasingly used by growers in the Languedoc for its exotic, floral and spice character that is supported by good acidity. Also gaining a foothold in California and Virginia in the USA with small holdings in Australia.

Petit Verdot Sometimes an important minor component in Bordeaux, especially the Médoc but increasingly too in similar blends made in many other regions where Cabernet Sauvignon is successful. Late ripening, as a variety it can show more than hint of violet in aroma as well as intense blackberry fruit and pencil shavings. There are also a small number of single variety examples showing real potential in places like the upper reaches of the Sierras de Málaga in southern Spain, the Napa Valley and elsewhere. Planted as well in South America in Chile and Argentina as well as in Australia.

Petite Arvine Of greatest significance in Switzerland's Valais, fine if demanding minerally whites are produced in a range of styles from dry to sweet. Also produced in Italy's Valle d'Aosta.

Petite Sirah The name given to Durif in California which produces powerful, robust tannic varietal wines with dense spicy, brambly fruit. Also used to add complexity to some leading examples of Zinfandel.

Phoenix A white German variety created at the Geiweilerhof Institute. It is a cross of Bacchus and a hybrid variety and bred to increase flavour quality and provide better disease resistance. Mainly grown in Germany there are small plantings in England and Wales.

Picapoll see Picpoul Blanc

Picolit White grape in Friuli (North-East Italy) from which are produced stylish, moderately sweet whites with dried peach, pear and floral characters. Its individuality and elegance are often dismissed by those expecting something richer and more powerful.

Picpoul Blanc White grape found in the Languedoc where it is the constituent of the Picpoul de Pinet AC and in Cataluña, particularly the small DO of Pla de Bages, where it is generally part of a blend but varietal examples are made. It is also one of the permitted grape varieties in Châteauneuf-du-Pape along with its Picpoul Noir counterpart.

Picpoul Noir see Picpoul Blanc

Piedirosso A grape variety probably used by the Romans and

Grapes

undergoing something of a revival in Campania's current rebirth. It has good acidity and a dark wild fruit character but is mostly used in blends, often complementing Aglianico.

Pigato For wines from Pigato, visit Liguria in North-East Italy. Sold under the Riviera di Ligure di Ponente DOC, the best show a terse minerality and contrast with Vermentino from the region.

Pignolo Previously obscure Friulian variety capable of showing an impressive black-fruited richness and the vibrant acidity typical of reds from native varieties in North-East Italy.

Pinot Bianco see Pinot Blanc

Pinot Blanc Variety most associated with Alsace and Italy's Alto Adige and Friuli. In Alsace old low yielding vines give it good character though is often blended with the delightfully scented Auxerrois which can make the better wine. It is also the basis of most Crémant d'Alsace. The Italians take it as seriously as anyone and produce some fine (both oaked and unoaked) whites with a cream and walnuts character. German examples can show good intensity but can be spoilt by a lack of balance or too much oak. Decent examples have also been produced in California, Oregon and Canada and the variety is also found in Austria and Hungary.

Pinot Grigio see Pinot Gris

Pinot Gris Excellent white grape, in fact a mutant of Pinot Noir. It is most associated with Alsace where it produces distinctively flavoured whites of intense spice, pear and quince flavours. Late-harvested it takes on an almost exotic, honeyed richness and nobly-rotted Sélection des Grains Nobles can be superb. In Germany as Grauburgunder or Ruländer good examples are made in warmer regions. Beyond simple Italian Pinot Grigio, there are some fine concentrated, delicately creamy examples from Friuli and Alto Adige. Oregon has made something of a speciality of it to complement its Pinot Noir while despite its proven potential in New Zealand it has only recently captured the imagination of a wider number of wine producers. Good examples are also made in California, Victoria and Canada.

Pinot Meunier Very important component in most Champagne blends if rarely used for anything else. Early ripening and as a wine, early developing, it complements both Chardonnay and Pinot Noir. While ignored by many New World producers of premium sparkling wines, some do have significant plantings of the variety.

Pinot Noir Success with Pinot Noir beyond Burgundy has been slow coming but there are now many regions in the world at least emulating the fabulous flavour complexity if not the structure and supreme texture of the top Burgundies. Flavours include cherry, raspberry, strawberry but can also include sappy, undergrowth characters or become more gamey in response to both origin and wine making. The expressions of *terroir* and differing winemaking interpretations in Burgundy are almost endless. Outside of Burgundy those regions or countries emerging with the greatest potential for Pinot Noir are New Zealand, California, Oregon, Tasmania but also cool parts of Victoria, South Australia and Western Australia. Success in Italy, Germany, Austria, Spain, Chile and South Africa is more limited yet further potential exists. Pinot Noir is also very important as a component of most of the world's best sparkling wines.

Pinotage Characterful yet tainted South African variety due to its tendency to produce unattractive paint-like aromas (isoamyl acetate). A crossing of Cinsaut and Pinot Noir, from old bush vines in particular it can produce deep, concentrated reds with spicy, plum and berry fruit flavours uncompromised by any volatile esters. The occasional adequate example is also produced in New Zealand.

Plantafina is a white grape found in the Valencia DO in Spain.

Poulsard Variety of France's Jura giving relatively light coloured reds

and rosés. Most wines are for everyday drinking being soft and fruity yet with an acid sinew. Can also form a part of Vin de Paille with Savagnin and Chardonnay.

Prensal/ Prensal Blanc An indigenous Mallorcan white grape. It contributes lightly floral, herb scented aromas, mainly in blends although occasionally as a varietal.

Prieto Picudo Characterful red grape from the north-west of Spain. It is a hardy variety and will grow successfully in cool conditions. Some very good examples have emerged from the recently created DO of Tierra de León.

Primitivo DNA fingerprinted as one and the same as Zinfandel, though debate continues about where in Europe they originated from. As Primitivo it is increasingly important in southern Italy, particularly in Puglia where old alberello-trained vines produce robust, characterful reds with moderate ageing potential.

Prosecco The grape with the potential for a delightful undemanding sparkling wine of the same name from Italy's Veneto. Pretention or overelaboration as well as anything more than a smidgen of residual sugar can distort its exuberant, direct freshness.

Refosco (dal Peduncolo Rosso) Somewhat derided grape but the 'red-stemmed' version has the potential for quality. Only occasionally encountered outside its native Friuli in North-East Italy, poorer examples are characterised by harsh tannins and high acidity but more care in the vineyard is resulting in high quality fruit with a brambly character. Produced both as part of a blend and varietally, good examples are on the increase. It may be related to Mondeuse.

Ribolla Ribolla Gialla, as it is often called, produces characterful herbscented dry whites in its native Friuli in North-East Italy.

Rieslaner High quality late-ripening crossing of Riesling and Silvaner. Tiny amounts of outstanding sweet wines can be produced in Germany's Pfalz, Baden and Franken regions when the grapes are fully ripe.

Riesling This outstanding white grape has an almost infinite number of expressions. Styles vary from bone dry to intensely sweet, from low alcohol to powerful and full-bodied. Its impressive range of flavours including apple, citrus, peach and apricot, are complemented by a minerality that subtle differences of place or *terroir* bring. It is nearly almost made varietally and aged in stainless steel or large old wood. Obtaining full ripeness and the right balance between sugar and acidity is crucial to quality. The most delicate, exquisite Riesling comes from Germany though there are many different expressions there while Alsace provides the fullest, most powerful examples. Austria's Wachau is closer to this style than Germany but with purity and minerality of its own. Australia also produces high quality Riesling, showing different expressions from Western Australia to the Clare, Eden Valley and Tasmania. The considerable potential for Riesling in New Zealand has yet to be fully realised. Good examples also come from the US; as much in Washington State and the Fingers Lakes region of New York State as California or Oregon. Some examples of Canadian Icewine are based on Riesling. A small number of decent wines have also emerged from Spain, South Africa and Chile.

Rondo Hybrid grape variety that has enjoyed some success in England. It originates in Germany where it is planted in the Rheinhessen region and can be found as far north as Denmark. The key to success is early ripening with good colour and sugar concentration. Generally at its best in blends with other varieties.

Rossese Mostly confined to basic rendings of the Ligurian DOC Rossese di Dolceaqua (Giuncheo's oak-aged version is good) but can form a part of other decent reds from the region.

Roussette Fine white grape found in Savoie in eastern France where

it is also known as Altesse. The best wines with good structure and weight have a mineral, herb and citrus intensity as well as more exotic nuances when produced from low yielding vines on the best steep slopes.

Roussanne High quality white grape that is difficult to grow. Roussanne's impressive texture and depth can be seen in wines from both the northern and southern Rhône, sometimes on its own but other times complementing Marsanne. It is also favoured by some of the leading quality producers in Languedoc-Roussillon and Provence, if mostly in blends. Also the grape used for fine perfumed Chignin-Bergeron whites in Savoie. Outside France, California, Washington State and Australia have a few high quality whites based, at least partly, on Roussanne.

Rufete One of the red grapes native to the small Arribes DO on the Portuguese/Spanish border that makes attractive fruit driven berry and herb spiced wines.

Rülander see Pinot Gris

Sagrantino Central Italian variety localized at Montefalco in Umbria. Potentially rich in extract, tannin and with high acidity its true potential as an outstanding dry red has long been realized by Caprai. Recently a wave of promising new examples thanks to better viticulture and winemaking. Rarer are good sweet passito versions, from dried grapes.

Samling 88 see Scheurebe.

Samsó A synonym used in Cataluña for the Cariñena red grape. There is some confusion regarding this because this is also a synonym used for the French Cinsault variety. The grape is additionally referred to by the producer Torres as a recovered native variety of Cataluña and is listed as a separate component of their Conca de Barbarà Gran Muralles red blend that also includes Cariñena. See also Cariñena.

Sangiovese The leading variety in Italy and the grape that dominates production in Tuscany. All the classic Tuscan appellations are based on it and the improvement in quality is on-going as the revolution in winemaking is being followed by one in the vineyard. Styles range from the light and fruity to oaky, powerful and tannic but the best are pure, refined and individual. It is made to a very high standard both varietally and in blends with Cabernet Sauvignon and Merlot yet some of the most distinctive expressions include a small percentage of minor native varieties such as Canaiolo or Colorino. The most important area for its production outside Tuscany is Romagna but it also plays an important role in Umbria. Good examples have been produced in California – both varietally or in blends with Cabernet or other varieties. One or two adequate examples are also made in Australia, Washington State, Argentina, Chile and South Africa.

St-Laurent Pinot Noir like Austrian grape held in high regard locally. Only the very best examples, however show a texture and complexity that suggests top Pinot Noir or Burgundy. It has recently been reintroduced to Luxembourg.

Saperavi Highly regarded grape of Georgia (on the Black Sea). Top modern examples of the varieties remain rare but one or two hints at enormous potential. It is hoped that this might yet spur its revival. Also small plantings in the King Valley in Victoria, Australia have been turned into a good varietal version by Symphonia.

Sauvignon Blanc Aromatic white grape capable of a wide range of expression and quality. The most structured and ageworthy examples come from France whether the classic mineral-laced wines of Sancerre and Pouilly-Fumé (now richer and riper than previously) or the more oak influenced, peachy examples from Bordeaux (some blended with Sémillon) that will age for more than a decade. The most overt fruit expression is seen in examples from Marlborough in New Zealand but most of these need to be drunk within a year of the vintage. Bright gooseberryish Sauvignon for immediate drinking is also made in Chile's Casablanca Valley and good vibrant, nettly Sauvignon Blanc from South Africa is on the increase. Some of the best Australian examples of Sauvignon Blanc have very ripe gooseberry fruit with a hint of tropical flavours; it is also sometimes blended with Sémillon. California offers both fresh, more herbaceous examples and riper, melon and fig versions capable of some age. North-East Italy provides high quality Sauvignon with good structure but more restraint. Reasonable examples come from northern Spain and Austria too though the latter are usually best when unoaked. Sauvignon Blanc is also important in combination with Sémillon for Bordeaux's sweet wines.

Savagnin A grape best known for the production of Vin Jaune, the speciality of the Jura region. It can also form a part of some of the best dry whites of the region but impresses too when produced varietally. A naturally firm structure can be enhanced by the intelligent use of oak cradling, with intense citrus and mineral fruit that becomes more nutty with age.

Scheurebe German crossing that can produce intensely flavoured whites from Spätlese levels and higher. Balance and ripeness are essential to rich and succulent wines with a piercing blackcurrant, grapefruit or peach character. Known as Samling 88 in Austria.

Schiava One and the same as Vernatsch and Trollinger (in Germany's Württemberg). Good light, attractive reds as Alto Adige DOC varietals or under the subzone of Santa Maddalena.

Schioppettino Native of Italy's Friuli, this obscure grape with high acidity but a spicy, wild berry fruit intensity, has recently been treated seriously by one or two dedicated producers.

Schönburger A white variety with a pink tinged skin producing attractive, fruity wines from early riepening grapes. As a result it is popular in cool climates and can be found in England, Western Oregon, the western stretches of Washington State as well as British Columbia and its native Germany.

Sémillon Almost all great Sémillon comes from either of two sources: France or Australia. In Bordeaux Sémillon is made both dry, in usually oak-aged blends with Sauvignon Blanc (as it is in Bergerac), or sweet where it is typically the dominant component in all its great sweet wines. Botrytis enrichment is the key to the power, flavour richness and complexity of the best long-lived Sauternes and Barsac. Lesser appellations can also make attractive sweet wines and some good examples come from neighbouring Monbazillac. The classic Australian Sémillon comes from the Hunter Valley. Though increasing rare, unoaked wines become remarkably toasty and honeyed with a decades' age or more. Oaked-aged examples are made to give more immediate pleasure; those from the Margaret River are usually combined with Sauvignon Blanc. Just a few rich, sweet Australian examples are also made. New Zealand and South Africa have had some success with dry examples of the grape. Elsewhere there are small plantings in Washington State, where some icewine is made, California, Chile and Argentina.

Sercial One of Madeira's noble varieties that translates into the driest palest style. Its usually high voltage acidity can prove too much for some palates but the wines can be superb (and very ageworthy) when the balance is right. There are also plantings on the Portuguese mainland where the variety is referred to as Esgana or Esgana Cão.

Seyval Blanc Decent quality hybrid grape that manages to get ripe in the coolest of winemaking countries. Can show good weight and an attractively herbal, appley, citrusy freshness. The best examples

Grapes

come from England, Canada and the eastern US.

Shiraz Australian name for the French grape Syrah but also favoured by some South African producers. Australia produces a galaxy of styles from the powerful, American-oaked blockbuster to more elegant, more Rhône like expressions aged in French oak. Every region produces a different stamp whether Hunter Valley, Clare, Barossa, Eden Valley, McLaren Vale, Grampians, Heathcote, Great Southern or one of many other exciting areas to which is added the interpretation and quality achieved by individual producers. Sparkling Shiraz is an Australian speciality and not as frightening as it sounds though a tannic finish can mar some flavousome examples. South Africa also has an increasing number of high quality examples. Also see Syrah.

Siegerrebe German white variety which ripens early and produces good sugar concentrations and as a result is popular in England, Washington State and the Okanagan Valley in British Columbia. Wines tend to have a marked aromatic character.

Silvaner/Sylvaner The majority of good Silvaner comes from Germany's Franken region while that given the French spelling, Sylvaner, comes from Alsace. A relatively neutral grape it can take on real richness and and a smoky, spicy flavour in the latter (especially when produced from old vines) while the German examples can show more of a minerally, nuanced subtlety – an intriguing earthy, appley character. Occasional good examples are produced in most other German regions but also in Italy's Alto Adige and (as Johannisberg) in Switzerland's Valais and occasionally in Australia.

Sousón is a minor red variety and a native of Spain's Galician wine regions of Rias Baixas and Ribeiro.

Spanish Torrontés see Torrontés.

Spätburgunder see Pinot Noir.

Subirat refer to Macabeo.

Sumoll Relatively rare red grape, grown in northern Spain's Conca de Barberá DO and in other areas near Barcelona, including Penedès. It contributes quality to red blends and is also found in rosados.

Sylvaner see Silvaner.

Syrah The home of Syrah is in the northern Rhône where a range of appellations give the most classic expression to one of the most exciting red grapes in the world. Those showing the most aromatic, smoky, white pepper and herbs expression come from Côte Rôtie (where they often include a little Viognier); broader, more powerful, minerally versions come from the hill of Hermitage. Many good examples also come from the surrounding appellations of Crozes-Hermitage, Cornas and Saint-Joseph. Syrah is also made varietally in the southern Rhône but more often is used to complement Grenache. As well as being important in Provence many of the best wines from the Languedoc-Roussillon are either based on it or include a significant percentage. Some very good varietal Syrah also comes from Italy where it is also added in small amounts to an increasing number of reds. Spain and Portugal also have good quality interpretations of the grape but Australia apart (also see Shiraz) the best Syrah outside of France comes from the US, primarily California but also Washington State and increasingly Oregon. A few good examples of Syrah also come from South Africa, New Zealand, Chile and Argentina.

Susumaniello This is another yet another exciting grape being revived in southern Italy, in this instance in Puglia. The quality of the reds based on it (from Tenute Rubino and others) suggest more examples will follow.

Tannat Vine from France's basque country, most important in Madiran where its powerful tannins need to be softened. Also an important component in other reds from this south-west corner of

France – such as Irouléguy. Widely grown too in Uruguay but its few decent quality examples have yet to show real consistency. There are small amounts also to be found on California's Central Coast, Argentina and Australia

Teroldego Extremely localised red grape grown on the gravelly soils of the Campo Rotaliano in Italy's Trentino region. From low yields it produces an impressive smoky, minerally black-fruited red capable of long ageing. Seems certain to have potential elsewhere.

Tempranillo Spain's leading red grape and a first class one though that has not always been apparent going by the quality from the most famous appellation based on it – Rioja. The grapes need to be concentrated and retain acidity, something more often achieved in Ribera del Duero (as Tinto Fino or Tinta del País) where the best powerful blackberry and black plum reds are among Spain's very best. Tempranillo is also important in many other regions including Toro (as Tinta de Toro) Central Spain (as Cencibel) and Costers del Segre (as Ull de Llebre) –– both varietally or as blends. Tempranillo Peludom is a strain of the variety, naturally low-yielding and of high quality. As Tinta Roriz it is extremely important both in the production of Port but also as a component in Douro reds where its splendid aromatic complexity is sometimes fully realised. It is also important both varietally and in blends in several other Portuguese regions where there has recently been a massive increase in planting. In Alentejo in southern Portugal (as Aragonês) it is usually combined with Trincadeira and can develop into deep, savoury reds with age. The variety can also be found in the Roussillon as Ull de Llebre and has potential in Australia, California's Central Coast, Chile, Argentina and the Umpqua Valley in Oregon.

Tempranillo Blanco White grape, a natural mutation of Tempranillo and found in Rioja. It produces wines with good depth and potentially rich extract. Tricky to grow and very sensitive to powdery mildew.

Tempranillo Peludom see Tempranillo.

Timorasso Little known variety transformed into varietal examples of good body and exotic fruit character by a growing band of producers in Piedmont's Colli Tortonesi. Made both oaked and unoaked.

Tinta Amarela Another of the more significant and interesting varieties of the Douro. Though productive it can be difficult to maximise its quality and is consequently disliked by some growers. Also appears in some blends from the Dão and Alentejo.

Tinta Barroca Important component of much Port and red Douro blends giving good colour, perfume and a certain earthiness usually from cooler slopes (in order to prevent raisining). Also one of the leading grapes for fortified styles (and some gutsy table wines) in South Africa.

Tinta de Toro see Tempranillo.

Tinta del País see Tempranillo.

Tinta Negra Mole All but the best Madeira tends to be based on this one, prolific grape variety. Only those Madeira that state one of the noble varieties on the label now come from them. Good Madeira however can be produced from Tinta Negra Mole if yields are kept down and high standards are maintained.

Tinta Roriz/Aragonês see Tempranillo

Tinto Cão Little planted yet one of the important quality grapes of the Douro (one of the five most recommended) undergoing a small revival due to its perceived quality. Low-yielding and difficult to manage successfully it is prized for its ability to age and the greater class that comes with it.

Tinto Fino see Tempranillo

Tocai Friulano see Friulano.

Wine behind the label

Grapes

Grape Glossary

Torrontés Argentine white grape which is grown using the same name in Spain mainly in the Ribeiro region as well as in the Canaries, Montilla-Morilles and Madrid. DNA testing in fact suggests there is no similarity between the two grapes and this is shown in their flavour profiles. In Ribeiro the Torrontés is regarded for the acidity it brings to a blend rather than its flavour. Torrontés in Argentina by contrast is both floral and richly aromatic and grown at altitude retains a naturally fresh acidity. Small plantings can also be found in Chile.

Touriga Franca The backbone of much Port and usually blended with Tinta Roriz and Touriga Nacional amongst others. Also important in table wines from the Douro. It has even been made varietally but a profusion of such examples seems unlikely as it usually lacks the definition and distinction of Touriga Nacional and the potential stylish complexity of Tinta Roriz. If sourced from old vines, however, it can show great class and complexity. Previously known as Touriga Francesa.

Touriga Francesca see Touriga Franca.

Touriga Nacional The most fashionable grape in Portugal's Douro. Increasingly made varietally both in the Douro and most other Portuguese regions. An integral part of most Port blends but often in much smaller percentages than is generally perceived. It is characterised by its deep colour, floral even violet aromas and dark damson plum, mulberry or blackberry fruit and a dash of pepper. Though capable of producing deep, fleshy varietal reds it is usually better complemented by Tinta Roriz, Touriga Franca and other grapes (as it is when made as port).

Treixadura A white grape of significant importance in Ribeiro in north-west Spain. It has crisp apple, citrus and mineral scented aromas and blends well with Albariño. It can also be found in blends in Rias Baixas and Ribeira Sacra.

Trepat Red grape, a native of Cataluña and found in the DOs of Costers del Segre and Conca de Barberá. Generally makes crisp, light rosés and is important in the production of rosado Cavas.

Trincadeira Important southern Portuguese grape. It doesn't like rain and needs to be fully ripe – its spicy, blackberry character forms a vital part of most Alentejo red blends.

Triomphe Hybrid red grape which was first created in Alsace and originally known as Triomphe d'Alsace. It is not eligible to be cultivated there because of its hybrid parentage. It is planted in England, although not widely but has proved to successful in red blends adding colour in particular.

Trousseau Important variety in the Jura, particularly Arbois for red wines. Produced both varietally and in blends it is often firm and structured with a tendency to being too tough but the best examples need to be kept.

Uva di Troia Potentially high quality variety of Puglia, particularly around Castel del Monte. Its intriguing complexity and ageing potential together with the current revival in Puglian viticulture should ensure it becomes better known.

Verdejo Spanish variety of greatest importance in the continental climate of Castilla y León and in particular Rueda where attractive herbal scented whites are produced. The best examples have decent structure and some ability to age, notably barrel fermented examples. More than holds its own against Sauvignon and Viura and also found in Toro and Cigales.

Verdelho Another of the noble varieties of Madeira that arguably produces the best style of all. A lightly honeyed and preserved citrus character togther with its vibrancy, refinement and general versatility secure its appeal. Known in the Douro as Gouveio, a component of Niepoort's fine dry white Redoma. There are significant plantings in Australia for often very attractive relatively inexpensive dry whites. It is also cultivated in Galicia in Spain where is is known as Verdello.

Verdello see Verdelho.

Verdicchio Leading variety in Italy's Marche region on the Adriatic coast. Made both oaked and unoaked (but usually better without) it can produce flavoursome versatile whites of good body, texture and acidity. Although they can last remarkably well only rarely do they add a great deal more complexity.

Verdil A white grape found on the south eastern Mediterranean Spanish coast in Valencia and Alicante.

Vermentino Lemony, herb-scented Italian variety that shows at its best on the Tuscan coast and in the north of Sardinia. The best are extremely stylish and a delight to drink young if only rarely showing more depth or weight. The Piemonte grown Favorita is a relative. Outside Italy there are plantings in Languedoc-Roussillon, in Patrimonio in Corsica and in the small appellation of Bellet in the hills behind Nice

Vernaccia Refers to any number of different unrelated grapes in Italy. The Vernaccia of San Gimignano is dry, with some character and style in the best examples.

Verduzzo Verduzzo Friulano, widely grown in North-East Italy, can be made into a refined sweet wine when late-harvested or from dried grapes. One small zone, Ramandolo, has recently been granted DOCG status.

Vespaiolo Named for the vespe (wasps) drawn to its sweet grapes in the autumn, this white grape is responsible for the late-harvested and passito style sweet whites of one famous producer (Maculan) in Italy's Veneto. It also produces attractive dry whites.

Vidadillo see Crespiello.

Vijariego A native Spanish white grape grown in the east of Andalucia mainly in the eastern provinces of Granada and Almeria as well as in the Canaries. Shows lots of citrus and herb-spiced character in its best renditions.

Viognier There is no other Viognier quite like the best Condrieu (in the northern Rhône). From this small appellation the wine is opulent, lush and superbly aromatic – rich in apricot and peach with floral, blossom, honeysuckle and spice. Most are dry and best drunk young though a few age quite well, especially when they have acquired an enhanced structure from delicate oak treatment. One or two examples are made from late-harvested grapes. Viognier has become increasingly important in the southern Rhône, Languedoc-Roussillon and Provence, sometimes made varietally but as often injecting some perfume and fruit into a blend. There's a little in Italy, Austria and Greece. In California, Virginia and Australia there are a fair number of good examples but only handful of these have the concentration and balance to suffice as a substitute for Condrieu. There are also significant plantings in Chile and Argentina and also now a few in Uruguay.

Viura see Macabeo.

Weissburgunder see Pinot Blanc.

Welschriesling White grape with a poor reputation due to the nasty whites produced from it in central and eastern Europe. However in Austria's Burgenland it is an important component in many of the best sweet whites. Known as Riesling Italico in North-East Italy.

Xarel.lo Important white Spanish variety and one of the three traditional grapes used to make Cava and only cultivated in Cataluña. Produces wines with a marked floral character.

Xynomavro The 'acid black' Greek grape important in the production of Naoussa and Goumenissa and for dark, slightly rasping if soft centred reds in northern Greece generally.

1

Glossary

Zibibbo A form of Muscat of Alexandria grown on the windswept volcanic isle of Pantelleria between the coasts of Sicily and Tunisia for the increasingly popular Moscato di Pantelleria and Passito di Pantelleria sweet wines - the best have a rich apricotty succulence. Also see Muscat

Zinfandel The grape California made its own. From a rich resource of old free-standing vines, rich, powerful and concentrated wines are produced – most typically full of peppery, blackberry fruit and sometimes a riper raisiny, pruny character. Great examples come from Dry Creek, Russian River, Sonoma Valley, even Napa but also the Sierra Foothills and the Central Coast. It also grown successfully in Arizona and Washington State and there's also a little Zinfandel in New Zealand, Australia, Chile and South Africa. Also see Primitivo.

Zweigelt Austrian grape produced from a crossing of St. Laurent and Blaufränkisch. Widely planted, most examples are rather ordinary but as well as one or two decent varietal examples, it also contributes to some leading blended Austrian reds.

Glossary

A

AC see Appellation Controlée.

Acetic Acid One of the volatile acids in wine which when found in relatively high levels and exposed to air may react with bacteria and cause off odours before converting the wine to vinegar.

Acetobacter The bacteria that causes the conversion of wine to vinegar.

Acidification The addition of acid to grape must or wine where a wine has naturally low acidity and where the local regulations permit. Tartaric acid is most commonly used.

Acidity Gives wine its freshness. The three main wine acids are tartaric, malic and lactic. The first two are naturally present, the third created through the malolactic fermentation.

Albariza Soil which comprises chalk, limestone, clay and sand. It is encountered in Jerez y Manzanilla and in Montilla-Moriles and one of the benefits is its potential in aiding photosynthesis by reflecting sunlight back to the vines.

Alberello Free standing bush vines, common in southern Italy

Alleinbesitz German for sole ownership of a vineyard site, equivalent of (Burgundian) *monopole*.

Aldehyde An organic compound formed in wine by the oxidation of alcohol.

Allier One of the French forests where oak is sourced for barrel making.

Ampelography The science of identifying grape varieties. Traditionally done by observing grape leaves and clusters it is much aided now by DNA fingerprinting.

Anthocyanins Are polyphenols found in and just under grape skins that give grapes and wines their colour and add to flavour.

Appellation Strictly speaking means a French Appellation Controlée region. Also used to make reference genetically to a quality wine region.

Appellation Controlée or Appellation d'Origine Controlée The top quality category for French wine. Denominación de Origen is Spain's similar, main classification. There are specific rules and regulations relating to origin, permitted grape varieties, viticulture and wine characteristics.

Aspect The topography of a vineyard or one or more of its plots/parcels. This includes its altitude as well as its direction and angle of slope.

Assemblage French term referring to the blend of a wine just prior to bottling. This will be from both components of the same grape variety and the blend of varieties if a number of grapes are included. Wines can often be vinified by variety, vineyard site or plot and then the components cellared in different ageing vessels. All may play a part in the blend of the final wine.

Autolysis The process in sparkling winemaking where dead yeast cells or lees add increased flavour and texture to wine aged in bottle, usually under a crown cap. The longer the wine is in contact with the yeast deposit the more striking and complex the character becomes. In general wines spending less than 18 months on yeast will have minimal or no autolytic character, the wines will be much more marked by varietal and fruit flavours. Many top sparkling wines, including Cavas, may spend many years on their yeast deposit.

B

Bâtonnage The stirring of a wines fine lees after primary fermentation which results in greater flavour and a richer texture. This is now a popular process with top quality barrel fermented white wines. As well as the addition of flavour the process guards against reduced hydrogen sulphide aromas which can be difficult to remove. The limited controlled oxidation the wine receives achieves this.

Barrique A universally popular and widely used oak barrel typically of 225 litre capacity. A range of other smaller barrel sizes are now used by winemakers, in general the larger the vessel the less overt oak influence is desired in the wines flavour if the barrels are new.

Bentonite see Fining.

Biodynamic A specific method of organic farming. Proponents believe that the holistic relationship between soils, plants and animals provides a self-sustaining system that promotes sustainable viticulture and improves the quality and resulting flavour of the wines produced. Natural treatments are used to protect the vineyard and applications carried out in line with lunar and planetary activity. Like other forms of organic farming natural treatments are prepared for use in the vineyard. This was a fairly controversial science until quite recently with many sceptics but the quality of wines being produced along these lines across the globe suggests biodynamic farming has much going for it.

Blanc de Blancs A sparkling wine made solely from white grape varieties.

Blanc de Noirs A sparkling wine made solely from red grapes.

Bocksbeutel Squat, flattened flask-shaped bottle used in Germany's Franken region.

Botte/Botti Large wooden vessels used for ageing wines in Italy. There will be no oak influence on flavour and the containers are often of substantial size. Foudres in France provide similar conditions.

Botrytis Botrytis or Botrytis Cinerea is a fungal infection of the vine which is particularly harmful to red grapes. In certain unique conditions though it provides for the development of Noble Rot in areas such as Sauternes, the Mosel and the Loire Valleys Côteaux du Layon. In late warm harvests with early morning humidity and sunny days the grapes will dehydrate concentrating their sugar and flavour. Wines produced from such grapes have a uniquely intense, peachy character.

Botrytised A term referring to wine made from grapes effected by "Noble Rot".

Bottle Shock A term for the temporarily muted state a wine goes into shortly after it is bottled.

Brettanomyces A spoilage yeast in wines causing off odours somewhat farmyard like. Often referred to just as Brett.

Brut Nature see Dosage.

C

Canopy refers to the vine canopy which is made up during the growing cycle of the plants shoots and leaves.

Canopy Management A series of techniques for managing the vineyard and improving quality and sometimes yield as well as protecting against disease. This is achieved by controlling the canopy's growth and ensuring a good flow of light and air to reach the grape bunches. A number of trellising systems have been developed over the past two decades which aid fruit ripening.

Carbonic maceration A winemaking process where whole grapes in bunches are fermented within the grape skins themselves under anaerobic conditions in an environment rich in carbon dioxide. Generally carried out in fairly small containers the bunches at the bottom will split and ferment conventionally. There are variations on the process where wines can be either fermented entirely or partly by this process. Red wines vinified with whole bunches will often produce a partial effect of carbonic maceration. Wines produced by carbonic maceration will have lower levels of tannin and be more obviously fruity. A bubble gum type of aroma tends to indicate carbonic maceration. A downside can also be slightly green aromas from the presence of the stalks if the stems are not fully ripe.

Canteiro Term that refers to the supports given to casks of Madeira where they are stored to be heated solely by natural means (without recourse to estufagem) - refers to this system of ageing generally.

Cépage A term in French for a grape variety but used elsewhere.

Cépage ameliorateurs This means an improving variety. The term has been widely used in Languedoc-Roussillon where there have been increasing amounts of Syrah, Grenache and Mourvèdre planted in addition to the widely distributed Carignan. Becoming less important as sophisticated wine growing develops in these regions.

Champagne method The process used to make sparkling wines in Champagne. A secondary fermentation takes place in bottle with the wine left on its yeast lees. Virtually all the world's finest sparkling wine comes from this method including Cava.

Chaptalization Process whereby sugar can be added to grape must or fruit after fermentation has commenced. While the basic objective is to raise the resulting wines alcoholic strength, many winemakers believe, if added later in fermentation it will extend it and add further complexity.

Clarification Refers to a number of cellar processes used to remove suspended solids and prevent cloudiness. Both fining and filtration may be used to create stable wines.

Climat Essentially Burgundian term referring to any specific vineyard or identifiable part of it.

Clonal Selection see Clones.

Clones Vines reproduced from the cuttings of original plants. The result tends to produce consistency of yield and flavour characteristics, often in different *terroirs*. Counter arguments suggest lower flavour complexity is achieved this way with wines having less of a sense of "place". Other vine growers prefer to plant new vineyards with a range of original cuttings. See Mass Selection.

Cold maceration is a process before fermentation where crushed red grapes can be kept with the grape juice or must at cool temperatures. This extracts both primary, fruit derived flavours and colour and enables the resulting wine to have less tannin if this is desired in the style.

Cold soaking Another more throwaway slang term for Cold maceration.

Cold stabilization Not strictly a stabilization process because this is undertaken with white wines in particular to precipitate out tartaric acid that may form harmless crystals resembling glass shards if stored in very cold conditions. The wine temperature is reduced below freezing and the tartrates precipitate out.

Cork taint Wine spoilage problem where chlorine reacts with cork causing off-aromas and bitter flavours that ruin wine. Although cork taint remains a problem in spoilt wine with alternative closures increasingly used, quality control appears to be much improved, at least in our experience with the many wine samples we receive. See also TCA.

Commerciante Italian Broker or Merchant

Côtes/Coster A term referring to an individual vineyard slope in France/Spain. It can also be used to refer to the vineyard slopes of an area or region, for example Costers del Segre or in southern France, Côtes du Rhône.

Coulure A viticultural hazard that occurs after flowering where the grapes fail to develop fully because of cold and often wet weather. One of the benefits can be a reduction in yield and intensity of flavour in the harvested fruit.

Criança Refer to Crianza.

Crianza An ageing classification. A red wine must be aged for a minimum of two years with 6 months in oak. For whites and rosés the minimum is one year.

Crush The process after harvest where the grapes are generally crushed and possibly de-stemmed as well, enabling the pulp to macerate with the juice. Some whites are immediately pressed and some red grapes destined for red wines commence fermentation in whole bunches and may be trodden by foot. Crush also refers to the grape harvest.

Cru Classé (CC) Classification of Bordeaux wines. Those from the Médoc (from 1er to 5ème Cru Classé/ first to fifth growth) and Barsac/Sauternes (1er or 2ème Cru Classé/ first and second growths) are covered by a famous classification of 1855. Graves (1959) and Saint-Émilion (Grand Cru Classé or Premier Grand Cru Classé) are also classified, the latter is now subject to revision every ten years (the last in 1996 because of recent legal disputes).

Cryo-extraction The process concentrating grape must by freezing it. See Must concentration.

Cuvaison Term referring to the period that the solids, mainly grape skins are kept mixed in solution with the grape juice. This can include a period of pre-fermentation maceration, sometimes referred to as a cold soak, or cold maceration, the primary fermentation and any further period of post fermentation maceration. The latter is increasingly popular with winemakers in achieving suppler tannins and a finer structure and balance in the resulting wines. See also Maceration.

Cuve French term for a wine vat or tank. Can be used for fermentation or storage/ageing and is made from wood, stainless steel or concrete.

D

DAC Austria's new regulatory system (Districtus Austriae Controllatus in full) providing official certified origins for Austrian wine. Weinviertel was the first region to use it, in 2003. Others now include Mittelburgenland and Traisental.

Débourbage A French term referring to the period where solid matter from crushed or pressed grape bunches is left to settle. With richer barrel fermented whites, particularly Chardonnay, a certain level of retained solid matter may be desirable to provide a richer texture in the resulting wine. For more aromatic varieties, Riesling for example it is best for the juice to be fully settled.

Dégorgement or disgorging The removal of a sparkling wine from

Wine behind the label

Glossary

its yeast sediment in bottle after its second fermentation.

Demi-muid A wooden barrel of, generally 600 litre capacity. Although sometimes used to refer to smaller sizes they are always considerably larger than a barrique. (also see Tonneaux).

Demi-sec Term for moderate to medium sweet wine, the term Semi-dulce means the same.

Denominación de Origen see DO.

Denominación de Origen Calificada see DO.

De-stemmed Reference to the process where the majority of red and white wines are made from fruit that is crushed and destemmed prior to vinification. The occasional white will also be whole bunch pressed prior to fermentation while whole bunch fermentations are often seen in red winemaking, particularly Pinot Noir. Wines made by carbonic maceration are also vinified with whole bunches. The key to reds made without destemming is that the stems as well as the grapes themselves should be fully physiologically ripe, avoiding potential green flavours in the wine.

DO Full name Denominación de Origen is Spain's main classification for quality wine produced in a specific region or appellation. Two regions, Rioja and Priorat are afforded a higher classification, DOCa (Denominación de Origen Calificada). Spain is also unusual in possessing a number of single estate DOs or DOPs (Vinos de Pago), perhaps the most famous being the Marques de Grinon's Pagos de Familia wines produced under the Dominio de Valdepusa DO.

DOC The Italian Denominazione di Origine Controllata is the main category for that country's protection of wine names and styles. Regulations cover origin, grape varieties and both the type and length of ageing permitted. Many have been revised or at least modified in response to progress to higher quality but there is much debate as to how best protect tradition while accomodating those committed to higher quality. There are well over 300 and many of these include sub-categories. While some DOCs boast numerous quality wines, others fail to deliver even a single premium wine. Also see DOCG. In Portugal Denominação de Origem Controlada is the highest regulated category recently extended to include broad regional areas (with sub-zones) to make for easier identification as Portuguese wines increase in popularity.

DOCG The top level of Italian wine appellations, Denominazione di Origine Controllata e Garantita includes a guarantee of origin and stipulates grape varieties but like the French AC it does not ensure top quality.

Dolç Term referring to a sweet or late harvest wine.

DOP see DO.

Dosage The process during the making of Champagne or Traditional method sparkling wines. After the lees from the secondary fermentation have been disgorged a bottle will be topped up with liqueur d'expédition. This is generally a blend of base wine, sometimes a touch of cognac and sucrose which will determine the style of the wine and the level of residual sugar after final bottling.

Dulce A sweet or late harvest style of wine.

E

Einzellage Individual vineyard site usually preceded by a village name on a label. While providing better definition of a wines origins than a grosslage name there is no classification system that differentiates the best sites from inferior ones. However a classification system is currently being promoted (see Grosses Gewächs).

Élévage French term which refers to all the wine handling and cellar processes from fermentation to bottling.

En Rama Refers to new Fino and Manzanilla styles of sherry which are bottled straight from cask without clarification, filtration and other processes.

En Vaso Term for bush-trained vines. In many cases these will be of considerable age and adding to a wines quality.

Enology The American English spelling of oenology.

Enologist The American English spelling of oenologist.

Esters are compounds formed during fermentation and then ageing which add to aroma.

Ethanol is ethyl alcohol, the primary alcohol in wine.

Erste Lage The term used in the Mosel for the first-rate vineyard sites that equate to Grosses Gewächs.

Erstes Gewächs The top tier of the VDP sponsored classification system of top vineyard sites as used in the Rheingau (also see Grosses Gewächs)

Estufagem The process of heating wine (in hot stores or estufa) in the production of Madeira, simulating the sea voyages across the tropics that gave rise to the style.

Extract All the compounds in wine such as tannins. Does not include water, sugar, alcohol, or acidity. Prolonging the contact with the skins during cuvaison will increase the level of extract.

Extraction Process where tannins, colour and other matter is extracted during Maceration. (also see Cuvaison).

F

Federspiel Austrian wine term used in the Wachau region to denote a particular level of ripeness in dry Riesling and Grüner Veltliner styles. Between the basic Steinfeder and riper top quality Smaragd levels.

Fermentation is the conversion with yeast of the sugar in grape juice to roughly equal proportions of alcohol and carbon dioxide.

Field blend Refers to wine produced from a mix of different varieties interplanted in a vineyard. Field blends generally come from very old vineyards and are increasingly rare.

Filtration The filtering of grape juice or wine to remove solid matter. Many fine wines are now bottled unfiltered with solid matter left to settle naturally in tank, cask or barrel.

Fining The clarification process to remove the smallest (soluble) microscopic particles in grape juice or wine. Fining agents such as bentonite and egg whites are added which attach themselves to and hence remove the particles. Excess use, particularly with grape juice will be detrimental to flavour.

Flor The film forming yeast produced during the making of Fino and Manzanilla styles of sherry in Jerez and similar wines in Montilla-Moriles. Not all wines will sustain this yeast film and it is susceptible to high alcohol. It produces a unique salty quality in the wines flavour.

Fortification is the process of adding grape spirit to wine either during or after fermentation resulting in higher alcohol and if added during fermentation higher residual sugar because the fermentation is arrested. Fortified wines include, Sherry, as well some Montilla-Moriles and Málaga whites.

Foudre French term for a large wooden vessel ranging in size from 20 to 120 hectolitres used to store and age wine.

Fudre is the German term for a foudre.

G

GI Geographical Indications is the slowly evolving Australian delimitation of its wine regions and is split into four levels. The broadest is the political boundary of 'state' (for example, South Australia), followed by 'zones' (Mount Lofty Ranges) which split the state into smaller parts and give some coherency to a group of often already well-established 'regions' (Adelaide Hills, Clare Valley). More definition within both established or new regions is made

982

possible by the granting of subregions (Lenswood and Piccadilly in the Adelaide Hills).

Gelatine is a fining agent used particularly in the removal of excessive tannins. Refer to fining.

Gran Reserva An ageing classification. In Spain Gran Reserva reds must spend a total of 5 years ageing with a minimum of 18 months in oak and 36 months in bottle. Whites and rosés must be aged for 4 years in total with a minimum of 6 months in oak.

Grand cru French wine classification. In Burgundy and Alsace this refers to specific vineyard sites. In Champagne to villages with vineyards of the best potential. For Bordeaux see Cru Classé.

Green harvesting Process in which the greener less mature grape bunches will be removed in a vineyard in order to aid ripening and improve concentration and flavour with a reduction in yield. The process should be carried out before veraison (when the berries change colour). May be used in areas which achieve naturally high yields and in regions where maximum yields are set down in regulations.

Grosses Gewächs German system of classification being promoted by the VDP, a consortium of leading estates. The term Grosses Gewächs is used in regions other than the Mosel (see Erste Lage) and Rheingau (see Erstes Gewächs).

Grosslage Broad grouping of vineyards in Germany, often permits the inclusion of grapes from inferior plots in a blend.

Guyot French vine training system developed in the second half of the 19th century. Cane pruning is employed with either one or two replacement canes trained along wires and the new seasons shoots vertically positioned above on a second wire. The system works well in naturally low yielding sites.

Gyropalette see Riddling.

H

Hybrid Vine variety produced by crossing two different vine species. It should not be confused with a Crossing which is produced from two varieties of the same species. Hybrids of Vinifera formed with the more hardy American vine species are generally held in low regard but a few such as Seyval Blanc can yield good quality wine without any trace of a so-called 'foxy' quality.(also see Crossing, Vinifera)

Hydrogen sulphide Produced when hydrogen combines with sulphur dioxide creating off flavours that smell of rotten eggs. It is produced when the wine is in a reduced state.

I

IGP is the abbreviation for the new French and Spanish country wine classifications (Indication Géographique Protégée in France and Indicación Geográfica Protegida in Spain). The former classifications were Vin de Pays (VdP) and Vinos de la Tierra (VdT). At present many wines are on the market with the old classification on their labels, particularly in Spain.

IGT Indicazione Geografica Tipica is the Italian equivalent of the French Indication Géographique Protégée

Inox French term to describe stainless steel tanks. Winemakers refer to vinifying and ageing in inox.

Irrigation Widely practiced in areas of the new world during the vine growth cycle where there is often insufficient water available to sustain the vine in good health. It is also permitted in a select number of regions in southern Europe. Spanish quality wine has certainly benefitted from this in the warmer, more arid areas. Drip irrigation is generally considered the best system with controlled deficit supply of just sufficient water to sustain vine growth and minimise stress. Some vine stress particularly in the ripening process is beneficial and will increase flavour intensity in grapes.

J

Joven is a Spanish term for a young wine which is generally fruit-riven without recourse to barrel or cask ageing.

L

Lactic acid This is created from malic acid during the malolactic fermentation.

Late disgorged Refers to sparkling wine that has spent an extended period on its yeast lees after the secondary fermentation before disgorging.

Lees The sediment including dead yeast cells left after a wine has completed fermentation. In general red wines vinified in vats and tanks will be racked off the lees and then racked one or more times for clarity. A number of reds though will be aged on their lees and a technique, micro-oxygenation, minimises the need for racking and protects the wine from reduced aromas which the lees naturally produce. Good quality white wines will generally spend a period of time on the fine lees, a finer sediment left after racking, even those aged for just a short period in tank. This increases flavour intensity and enriches the wines texture. Barrel-fermented whites will not only remain on their fine lees in cask these will also be stirred. See also Bâtonnage.

Lieu-dit A specific vineyard (or climat) which has no official classification but identified on a label when that site has been bottled separately from other village-level wine. Regularly found on Alsace and Burgundy labels.

Liqueur de tirage French term describing the mixture of sugar and yeast that is used to instigate the secondary bottle fermentation in traditional method sparkling wines.

Liqueur d'expedition see Dosage.

Llicorella A term for the soil found in the Priorat DOCa which it is believed contributes substantially to the intensely mineral aromas found in the wines. It is volcanic black slate based and also serves the purpose of reflecting sunlight and storing and radiating heat back to the to the vines. Black slate soils are also found in the vineyards of the Roussillon.

M

Maceration Refers to the period where crushed grape must as well as pressed whole bunches remain in solution with the solid matter from the grapes. The maceration process extracts colour, tannin and flavour as well as an array of other compounds in tiny amounts. The approach to macerating the wine will determine its character and style. There may be a period of cold maceration which will extract colour and more primary, fruity flavours. The fermentation on the wine skins will provide additional flavour, colour and tannin. In general the cooler the fermentation the softer and more approachable the wine will be. Warmer ferments are likely to provide wines with a firmer structure and more tannin. Continuing to keep the new wine for a short period on its solid matter helps polymerise the tannins and achieve a softer,better balance. The cap of grape skins formed during fermentation needs to be kept in solution with the fermenting must and various methods are used which also aid extraction. These include hand plunging (*pigéage*) and pumping the fermenting must over the cap (*remontage*). Some skin contact prior to fermentation is also practiced by a number of producers of white wines (see Macération Pelliculaire). See also Cuvaison.

Macération carbonique is the French spelling of Carbonic Maceration. See Carbonic Maceration.

Macération pelliculaire French expression meaning skin contact. In effect it refers to the period of just a few hours where white wine must is macerated with its skins prior to fermentation. Sémillon and

Sauvignon Blanc in Bordeaux and Chenin Blanc in the Loire as well as more aromatic varieties like Muscat have all successfully been vinified using this technique. Excessive skin contact will result in coarseness and very early oxidation.

Malic acid is one of the three main acids with a strong taste in wine reminiscent of green apple. The wine can be softened by converting the malic acid or a part of it through the malolactic fermentation.

Malolactic fermentation Or MLF is a chemical process after the primary fermentation has been completed where the relatively harsh malic acid naturally present in wine is converted to softer, lactic acid. All reds are put through MLF, sometimes in larger tanks or vats and increasingly in new wood during the ageing process providing a softer, rounder texture. This has had proponents and critics over recent years. More aromatic whites like Riesling will have the process blocked. This avoids the more creamy flavour and richer texture that comes from the process but retains acidity and emphasises varietal fruit character. Top whites, particularly Chardonnay grown in cooler areas with marked acidity, benefit from the process having greater weight and depth and show a creamier texture. It may often be blocked with warmer grown Chardonnay to preserve acidity.

Mass Selection see Sélection Massale.

Mercaptans result from the reaction of alcohol and hydrogen sulphide and produce faulty wines smelling of onions, burnt rubber and garlic.

Meritage Term used in the United States to describe a Bordeaux style blend either red or white. Becoming increasingly rare.

Mesoclimate/Microclimate Refers to the very local climate of a small area often just a single vineyard and contributes to the character of wines produced. Many observers also refer to the term microclimate when characterising those same areas and wines. Some viticulturalists have maintained that this is incorrect and that microclimate refers more specifically to the environment around the vine canopy. However readers will find wide reference to microclimate elsewhere which will inevitably be concerning vineyards and sites.

Méthode Traditionelle see Traditional Method.

Metodo Classico see Traditional Method.

Micro-oxygenation Process whereby small amounts of oxygen are pumped into wine ageing in barrel or vat. Developed in Madiran with the objective of rounding the often substantial tannins found in the regions wines. In addition the process also reduces the need for wine handling, particularly racking in the first year of ageing. Reds can also more safely be left on their lees because the risk of reduction is countered.

Millerandage Irregular fruit development after flowering caused by cool weather. Yield is reduced because some berries are smaller. Quality though is likely to improve. This characteristic of smaller and larger berries in the same grape bunch is often referred to as hen and chicken.

Must The juice from crushed and/or pressed grapes prior to fermentation. As well as juice, must contains all the skins, pulp and solid matter.

Must concentration Process of removing water from grape juice with the objective of increasing the concentration of the other components. A number of techniques are used including freeze concentration. To some degree this is reproducing natural conditions found in Icewines (Eisweins in Germany), where the fruit is naturally frozen in the vineyard. Refer to Cryo-extraction).

N

Négociant French term for a wine merchant. They may buy grapes as well as finished wine and also have their own vineyards and properties. While there has been a trend in Burgundy and other areas to more wines being Domaine bottled an increasing number of small producers are also now acting as négociants as well.

Négociant-manipulant In Champagne, a merchant who also makes wine. Includes all the great Champagne houses.

Noble Rot see Botrytis.

O

Oenologist A winemaker.

Oenologue French term for an enologist.

Oenology The study of wine.

Organic An increasing number of winegrowers around the world are now producing wines without recourse to chemical treatments in the vineyard and with very selective chemical additives during vinification and ageing. See also Biodynamic.

Oxidation is the exposure of must or wine to air. In general oxidation should be avoided however a limited amount of controlled oxidation during the ageing of wine prior to bottling can be beneficial. It is likely to add further complexity in particular in fortified wines. Oxidation of grape juice can also add complexity in some barrel fermented white wines. Reduction is the opposite of oxidation. See also Reduction.

P

Passerillage Grapes that are late-harvested and have dried and become partially raisined concentrating their sugar but are not effected by noble rot.

Passito Italian for wine made from dried grapes.

Phenols The compounds naturally present in grapes, in the skin, stem and pips. Tannin, flavour and anthocyanins, which produce colour, are all extracted during vinification through both maceration and the temperature of fermentation. See also Cuvaison, Extraction and Maceration.

Photosynthesis is the vinegrowing process where sunlight is harnessed by chlorophyll in the vine leaves to then convert into sucrose.

Phylloxera An aphid and the most significant pest for grapevines. Native to North America it became infested in many of the worlds vineyards in the 19th century. Certain soils such as sand are resistant to the aphid but in the vast majority of instances the only protection is to graft the vinifera vine onto an American vine rootstock which has good resistance.

Pigéage is the punching down of the cap of grape skins and pulp formed during fermentation to submerge it. This can be done by hand, using special machines or even by foot. This helps extraction and guards against oxidation. It is a more gentle process than pumping over. See Roto-fermenter.

Propagation Meaning reproduction. In viticultural terms this most commonly refers to vegetative propagation using cuttings taken from other vines.

Pumping over see Remontage.

Punching down see to Pigéage.

Pyrazines Term referring to a group of aromatic compounds found in grapes in varying degrees. These include green bell pepper aromas in Cabernet Sauvignon and the grassy tones often found in Sauvignon Blanc. An excess of green aromas in wine can indicate an excessively vigorous vine canopy that has impeded full grape ripening.

Q

Quinta Portuguese term which refers to either a wine estate or a single vineyard.

R

Racking is the process where wine is transferred from one barrel or vat to another. The benefits are twofold, wine is removed from precipitated solids and is also gently aerated. Traditionally pumps were used but increasingly winery operations are carried out by gravity.

Rancio Maderised character with burnt, toffee like aromas produced in the development of aged fortified wines through a combination of controlled oxidation and exposure to heat. The wines are often exposed to direct sunlight as well. Banyuls, Maury and Rivesaltes in the Roussillon as well as the fortified Muscats and Tokays of Rutherglen all show classic rancio character.

Reduction is a term referring to wines that are heavily reduced and can develop foul smelling sulphides. A balanced cellar regime with sufficient aeration of the wine and lees if the wine is being aged this way should prevent this. In chemical terms if something is being oxidised it is not being reduced and vice-versa.

Reductive Refers to wines that are in a reduced state.

Ried Term used in Austria to denote a specific vineyard site.

Remontage is a French term for the extraction process during maceration of pumping the juice over the cap of grape skins. Generally considered a less gentle method than punching down.

Reserva is an ageing classification. For red Reservas there is a minimum period of three years ageing and at least one year in oak. For both whites and rosés the periods are 2 years ageing and 6 months in barrel.

Residual Sugar There is always a small portion of unfermentable sugar in wine even those that are technically classified as dry. It is commonplace in some whites particularly straightforward fruit driven styles to purposely leave a hint of residual sugar. More serious wines from cooler regions like Alsace and the Mosel may well be completed with some sugar left naturally. Late harvested wines are deliberately left on the vine to accumulate sufficient sugar to ensure considerable sweetness after vinification. See also Botrytis.

Riddling is the process during the making of Traditional method sparkling wines where the yeast deposit after the secondary fermentation is moved to the neck of the bottle by twisting and tilting. Can be done by hand or automated with gyropalettes which is popular with larger producers.

Ripasso Term registered by Valpolicella producer Masi. Used to refer to an enrichment of the already the fermented wine by passing it over the skins of Amarone, adding alcohol, texture and character. Variations exist – see Introduction to North-East, Central & Southern Italy.

Roble The Spanish for oak. It has recently become commonplace in describing wines aged for a short period in oak barrels.

Rootstock The plant formed from the root system of the vine to which the scion (fruiting part) is grafted. Most vinifera vines (the european species to which most quality grape varieties belong) are grafted on to rootstocks of American vines (or hybrids of them) due to its resistance to phylloxera. As well as guarding against phylloxera a rootstock can benefit growth being adaptable to certain soils and resistant to other vine maladies.

Roseworthy Famous winemaking college in South Australia whose graduates have had an impact both in Australasia and around the globe.

Roto-fermenter A piece of winemaking equipment that automatically mixes the grape skins and pulp during fermentation and maceration. It is a horizontal spinning tank.

S

Saignée Running off some free run juice prior to fermentation in order to increase the ratio of skins and solids in the must and therefore flavour and tannin. Regularly practiced in the production of top quality Pinot Noir.

Screw cap An alternative closure to a cork that neutralises the risk of TCA cork taint. See Stelvin Cap.

Sélection Massale Mass Selection – the propagation of new plants from existing vines selected for their quality and performance, particularly in a specific vineyard rather than the use of a single clone. Easier to use effectively in older vineyards and labour intensive.

Sin crianza Term referring to a young wine bottled without ageing. Refer to Crianza.

Smaragd The top level of ripeness in Austria's Wachau region, named for a little green lizard. Includes nearly all the most structured and ageworthy examples of Riesling and Grüner Veltliner.

Solera A system of fractional blending used in Jerez in the production of sherry to provide consistency and enrichment. It has long been established in Jerez in the ageing of Sherry. It is also practiced in Montilla-Moriles and used to some extent in other fortified production such as at Rutherglen or Madeira. The name is derived from the bottom rung of a series of barrels containing the oldest wine. Only a small part of the wine is drawn from this bottom level at one time. Successive levels are then replenished by younger wines from the level above.

Semi-dulce A Spanish term for a moderate to medium sweet wine. Refer to Demi-sec.

Stabilization is a reference to a range of wine making processes that remove particles which may undergo further chemical reactions in bottle. These include fining, filtration, the addition of sulphur dioxide. Refer to Cold Stabilization.

Steinfeder Austrian term used in the Wachau region referring to lowest of 3 levels of ripeness. Federspiel and, especially, Smaragd levels encompass wines of higher quality and longevity.

Steirische Klassik An increasingly widely adopted designation used for white wines in Austria's Südsteiermark. Typically (if not always) made in stainless steel, the wines show no discernable oak character.

Stelvin cap A screw cap closure that also has a plastic neutral liner inside the cap. See Screw Cap

Sulphur dioxide The all purpose wine anti septic. Sulphur dioxide, SO2 is added to wine to prevent oxidation and the development of bacteria.

Süssreserve German term for unfermented grape juice used to add sweetness to wines as a means of improving the balance between sweetness and acidity. Less satisfactory than balance that is achieved naturally.

T

TBA Short for Trockenbeerenauslese - the richest, sweetest level of QmP wines in Germany, determined by a minimum must weight (or sugar level in the grapes). Of similar style and sweetness in Austrian examples. Many are prohibitively expensive (and only sold at auction) due to both demand and a labour intensive production. Also see Germany (Making sense of German wine styles).

TCA Chemical compound, its full name is 2,4,6-trichloroanisole, responsible for most of the off flavours in wine caused by contaminated corks. Chlorine reacts with the cork to produce the contamination and the aroma can be picked up in minute quantities. Although quality control has much improved in recent years cork taint remains a significant problem in spoilt wine and alternative methods of closure are on the increase. The chemical or variants of it can also be found elsewhere and has been a cause of

Glossary

contamination in some wine cellars.

Terra Rossa Reddish coloured loam over a limestone base, most famously associated with Coonawarra in South Australia but also found in other wine regions.

Terroir Concept used by French winegrowers and referred to by others around the globe that considers all the natural and environmental characteristics that may influence a vine growing site, such as soil, aspect, climate and so on. Also refers to the character in a wine that is derived from its origins rather than the grape variety.

Tonneaux A bordeaux barrel size of 900 litres but can often be used to refer to considerably smaller vessels. What is referred to in Italy as tonneaux can vary from double-sized barriques to that of demi-muid.

Traditional method The classic method of Champagne production (see Champagne method) as it is referred to in other regions for sparkling wines made in this way. Known as méthode traditionelle or méthode classique in other parts of France, as metodo classico in Italy.

Triage French term which refers to the sorting and selection of grapes prior to fermentation. Top quality wines will be subjected to a very rigorous triage.

Tris Multiple passages through a vineyard to selectively pick late harvested or botrytis effected grapes. In order to produce great wines it may be necessary to make many such passes. In Bordeaux Tri also refers to the sorting of grapes generally after harvest. This selection process is vital in all wineries to ensure top quality wines.

U

Unfiltered See filtration.

Unirrigated See Irrigation.

V

Varietal is a wine made from one grape variety.

Vatting Term referring to the time that grape must and then wine spends in contact with the skins during fermentation and maceration. See also Cuvaison.

VDP Verband Deutsches Prädikatsweinguter - a consortium of Germany's leading estates (currently with 200 members) founded in 1910. To qualify estates must have vineyards of recognised quality and achieve higher standards than that required by German wine law. The VDP is also behind a three tier classification model for German wines (see Grosses Gewächs). Members use the VDP 'eagle' on their capsules or labels.

Vendange vert See Green Harvesting.

Veraison The point in the vines growth cycle where the grapes change colour, the sugar flux to the grape bunches takes place and the fruit ripens.

Versteigerungswein Auction wines, specifically those set aside by German producers for sale at the annual VDP auction.

Vignaiolo Italian term for a vine-grower.

Vignoble A vineyard or close grouping of vineyards.

Vin Doux Naturels French term for fortified wines. These are sweet, achieved by adding fortifying spirit part way through fermentation in much the same way as is practiced in producing Port.

Vin de France The category that covers the production of table wine in France. The odd top class wine is released under the classification to give wine makers more freedom of choice.

Vin de Paille French term meaning 'Straw Wine' which comes from dried grapes. Wines are made with varying levels of residual sugar. Traditionally the fruit was laid out on straw mats although grapes are now generally hung and then dried. The wines are a feature in the Jura there has been a small revival in the Rhône.

Vin de Pays Former French category of regional identification for wines that fall outside either the boundaries or regulations of an AC. Now superceded by IGP. See IGP

Vin Jaune Jura wine made from Savagnin grapes aged in old casks under a voile (a film of yeast not unlike Flor that covers Fino sherry) that results in a distinctive oxidised nutty character.

Vinegar is a very sour tasting liquid with high acid levels created from wine and other alcoholic liquids where the ethanol has oxidised.

Vinifera is the vine species, Vitis Vinifera, which accounts for the vast majority of wine producing grape varieties.

Vino de Mesa (V d M) is the classification for Spanish table wines. As elsewhere some impressive wines are made as V d M.

Vinos de la Tierra (VT) is the classification for regional Spanish wines which has been partly superceded by new regulations. See IGP.

Vinos de Licor are traditional sweet wines.

Voile The thin yeast film that develops on Vin Jaune, the speciality of the Jura, is not dissimilar to the Flor that grows on dry Fino and Manzanilla sherries. The powerful tangy wines take on a nutty, oxidised complexity with age.

Volatile Acids These are the acids in wine which are unstable and can evaporate at low temperature and include acetic and carbonic acids. Wines may be referred to as having volatile acidity and have off aromas similar to similar to nail varnish. See also Acetic Acid.

W

Warehouse Winery This refers specifically to non-estate based wine operations - often located outside the region or regions where the grapes are grown. In some instances the wines are made at another winery and the premises are simply used to age or store the wines.

Winzergenossenschaft German for co-operative.

Y

Yield is the measurement of the crop produced from a vineyard or specified plot of vines. Traditionally this is measured in hectolitres produced per hectare. In simple terms the lower the yield the higher the quality of the wine produced. The vine should not overproduce because it will be difficult to achieve physiological ripeness in the fruit. A number of additional factors should also be considered. A vine needs to be balanced to provide optimum quality grapes with intense flavour. If the yield is reduced too far then the vine's balance and equilibrium will be disturbed and quality will suffer. Many quality conscious vinegrowers now measure yield per vine as a better judge of potential quality rather than per hectare because of the variable conditions within a vineyard and the density of planting. Older vines are naturally less productive and when their crop is reduced the resulting grapes can be of exceptional quality. In all cases the yield of a vine should be sufficiently restricted in order to achieve complete physiological ripeness.

This producer index of **Full Winery profiles** is ordered according to the name by which an estate is most commonly referred. There is priority to surnames but otherwise they appear as they written. 'Domaine' is ignored but 'Chateau', 'Castello', 'Quinta' etc are respected as is the definite article when implicitly part of the name(eg Il Poggione appears under 'I'. The only exception is in Bordeaux where 'Chateau' is also ignored and the name of the chateau or estate takes precedent.

Index of profiles

Wine behind the label

Wine behind the label

Index of profiles

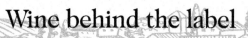

Index of profiles

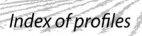

Wine behind the label

Index of profiles

Wine behind the label

Index of profiles

Wine behind the label

999

CPSIA information can be obtained
at www.ICGtesting.com
Printed in the USA
BVOW07*0357291217
503854BV00009B/92/P

9 781910 891131